RAVELING WITH YOUR PET

THE AAA PETBOOK®

The AAA guide to more than 13,000
pet-friendly, AAA-RATED® hotels
and campgrounds across the
United States and Canada

12th Edition

AAA PUBLISHING

AAA wishes to acknowledge the following for their assistance:
Dogpark.com®
Veterinary Emergency & Critical Care Society

Cover Photos

Front: Editors' Pick - Yukon Jack at Otter Cliff, Mount Desert Island, Maine (Acadia National Park)
Submitted by owner Lisa Bourque
Back: 1st place Photo Contest Winner: Belle, Ortiz and Rosie visiting Cape Cod Canal, Mass.
Submitted by owner Wendy Russell
Spine: 2nd place Photo Contest Winner: Jack visiting Monument Valley, Utah
Submitted by owners Susan and Howard Schwartz

Published by AAA Publishing
1000 AAA Drive, Heathrow, Florida 32746

Twelfth Edition Copyright © 2010 AAA Publishing. All rights reserved.
ISBN: 978-1-59508-372-2 Stock Number 552210
Printed in the USA by Dickinson Press, Inc.

ABOUT THIS BOOK

Welcome to the 12th edition of ***Traveling With Your Pet: The AAA PetBook***®. *Traveling With Your Pet* is a must for the traveler who's also an animal lover. This comprehensive book provides all the information you need to know about taking a four-legged friend on the road. Will Spot be a good car passenger? Is it safe to take Snowball on a plane? What are the important rules of pet etiquette? Is pet insurance a good idea? *Traveling With Your Pet* answers all of these questions and more. Here are just some of the features covered:

- Dog parks where you and your furry friends can play, exercise or just relax.

- An extensive listing of emergency animal clinics compiled by the Veterinary Emergency & Critical Care Society. Names, addresses and phone numbers provide valuable information for unexpected or emergency situations, both en route and at your destination.

- A roundup of pet-friendly attractions.

- National public lands in the United States and Canada that allow pets, along with recreation information.

- Border crossing procedures and tips for travelers — both entering Canada from the United States and vice versa.

- Policies pertaining to service animals.

Traveling With Your Pet lists more than 13,000 AAA-RATED® hotels and campgrounds. And the listings show AAA's trustworthy diamond ratings, the traveler's assurance of quality. Other handy features include:

- Informative highway directions.

- Specific information about lodgings' pet policies: deposits and fees (rounded to the nearest dollar), housekeeping service, designated rooms and other stipulations relating to travelers with pets.

- Additional details about the lodgings themselves, including icons for amenities, recreation, dining and accessibility.

- Icons designating AAA's member discount programs.

- Listings for AAA's highest rated campgrounds, including rate and pet policy information and service/amenity icons.

All of this valuable information is packaged in a contemporary, easy-to-read format, making *Traveling With Your Pet: The AAA PetBook*® as indispensable an on-the-road companion as Spot's water dish or Snowball's litter box. Don't leave home without it, and remember: It always pays to *Travel With Someone You Trust*®.

Have some great pictures from traveling with your pet? The AAA PetBook Photo Contest, sponsored by AAA and Best Western®, gives you a chance at winning some great prizes and seeing your pet's photo on a cover of *Traveling With Your Pet: The AAA PetBook*®. Check out more information about the contest winners on the next page and see some adorable photos of traveling pets in the middle section of this guide. For details on how to enter the annual Photo Contest and to obtain an entry form, please visit www.AAA.com/Petbook.

Picture Your Pet as the Next AAA PetBook® Cover Model!

For a chance to see your pet in an upcoming edition of **Traveling With Your Pet: The AAA PetBook®**, enter the AAA PetBook Photo Contest Sponsored by Best Western, open yearly from May 1 to Nov. 30. Visit **AAA.com/PetBook** for an entry form, prize listing, complete contest rules and photos of winners and runners up.

Editors' Pick – Yukon Jack

Every so often, we get a photo contest entry that's so compelling our editors simply beg us to place it on the front cover. This year, for the first time ever, we've awarded this honor to Yukon Jack, an experienced traveler and people magnet from Colorado.

Shown here at Acadia National Park, Yukon enjoyed a sunset windjammer trip in Frenchman Bay where he visited with fellow passengers over a bite of cheese (no wine, thanks). Afterward, Yukon was treated to his own lobster tail and side of shrimp on the pier—a memorable meal for a dog who can't get fresh seafood most of the year.

As a Rocky Mountain dog, Yukon is also a huge fan of Telluride, Colo., where several hotels hold open their doors to his kind. He loves getting a doggie massage in the pet-friendly town and riding one of the many "dog gondolas" that connect the mountain village and town.

1st place winner – Belle, Ortiz and Rosie

This cheery trio stole our hearts, receiving first place fame on the back cover. Rosie (far right) is the mother of Belle and Ortiz. While visiting downtown Kennebunk, ME., the dogs were served dog-friendly cake and ice cream by a local pet store. These adorable faces live in the southern New England area.

2nd place winner – Jack Schwartz

Jack, a huggable labradoodle from Northern California, is pictured on the book's spine in a photo taken while visiting Monument Valley in Utah. Jack is a great traveling companion and makes friends with just about everyone. Their mutual love of swimming in remote lakes and rivers often leads Jack's family to fun places to take a dip during their travels.

Turn to Page 353 to view a sampling of more highlights from the photo contest.

TABLE OF CONTENTS

AAA PetBook® Photo Contest

Traveling With Pets

Pet-Friendly Places

Pet-Friendly Lodgings

U.S. Lodgings

Canadian Lodgings

Pet-Friendly Campgrounds

Many people view their pets as full-fledged members of the family. Spot and Snowball often have their own beds, premium-quality foods, a basketful of toys and a special place in their humans' heart.

Until it's time to go on vacation, that is. Then the family dog or cat is consigned to "watching the fort" at home while everyone else experiences the joy of traveling. Many animal lovers hesitate to take their pet with them because they don't think they'll be able to find accommodations that accept four-legged guests. Others aren't sure how — or if — their furry friends will adapt.

The truth is, including a pet in the family vacation is fairly easy, so long as you plan ahead. Most pets respond well to travel, a fact that isn't lost on the tourism industry. More than 13,000 AAA-RATED® hotels and campgrounds from coast to coast are pet-friendly, and airline bookings for pet passengers are on the rise. Great companions at home, pets are earning their stripes on the road, too.

So if you've been longing to hit the trail with a canine or feline companion, read the tips on the following pages. You may find that a getaway can be far more enjoyable with than without your pet.

Should Your Pet Travel?

Before you make reservations, determine if your pet is able to travel. Most animals can and do make the most of the experience, but a small percentage simply are not cut out for traveling. Illness, physical condition and temperament are important factors, as is your pet's ability to adjust to such stresses as changes to his environment and routine. When in doubt, check with your veterinarian. If you feel your pet isn't up to the trip, it's better for everyone if he stays home.

🐾 **Rule 1: Pets who are very young, very old, pregnant, sick, injured, prone to biting or excessive vocalizing, or who cannot follow basic obedience commands should not travel.**

Even if Spot and Snowball are seasoned travelers, take into account the type of vacation and activities you have planned. No pet is going to be happy (or safe) cooped up in a car or hotel room. Likewise, the family dog may love camping and hiking, but the family cat may not. Putting a little thought toward your animal's needs and safety will pay off in a more enjoyable vacation for everyone.

🐾 **Rule 2: If your pet can't actively participate in the trip, she should stay home.**

Most of the information in this book pertains to cats and dogs. If you own a bird, hamster, pig, ferret, lizard or other exotic creature, remember that unusual animals are not always accepted as readily as more conventional pets. Always specify the type of pet you have when making arrangements.

Also check states' animal policies. **Hawaii** imposes a 5-days-or-less quarantine for all imported dogs, cats and other carnivores to prevent the importation of rabies. Guide dogs and service dogs are exempt from the quarantine provided they have: a standard health certificate issued within 30 days prior to arrival; a current rabies vaccination with documentation of the product name, lot number and lot expiration date; a successful result of an OIE-FAVN rabies blood test conducted after 1 year of age; and an electronic identification microchip implanted and operational. Upon arrival, guide dogs and service dogs still must be examined for external parasites. For additional details, obtain the Hawaii Rabies Quarantine Information Brochure from the Hawaii Department of Agriculture, Animal Quarantine Station, 99-951 Halawa Valley St., Aiea, HI 96701-5602; phone (808) 483-7151, e-mail rabiesfree@hawaii.gov. The Web site address is www.hawaii.gov/hdoa/ai/aqs/info.

North Carolina has stringent restrictions regarding pets in lodgings. Make certain you understand an accommodation's specific policies before making reservations.

🐾 **Rule 3: Be specific when making travel plans that include your pet. Nobody wants unpleasant surprises on vacation.**

If Spot and Snowball stay behind, leave them in good hands while you're gone. **Family, friends and neighbors** make good sitters (provided they're willing), especially if they know your pet and can care for him in your home. Provide detailed instructions for feeding, exercise and medication, as well as phone numbers for your destination, your veterinarian and your local animal emergency clinic.

Professional pet sitters offer a range of services, from feeding and walking your pet daily to full-time house sitting while you are gone. Interview several candidates, and always check credentials and references. For additional information, contact the National Association of Professional Pet Sitters or Pet Sitters International. *(See sidebars on p. 8 and p. 9.)*

Kennels board many animals simultaneously and generally are run by professionals who will provide food and exercise according to your instructions. Pets usually are kept in a run (dogs) or cage (cats and small dogs) and may not get the same level of human interaction as at home. **Veterinary clinics** also board pets and may be the best choice if yours is sick, injured or needs special medical care. For further information on how to select a kennel, contact the Pet Care Services Association.

Veterinarians, fellow pet owners and professional associations are a good source of referrals for sitters and kennels.

🐾 **Rule 4: Never leave your pet with someone you don't trust.**

Travelers Who Have Disabilities

Individuals with disabilities who own service animals to assist them with everyday activities undoubtedly face challenges, but traveling should not be one of them. Service animals (the accepted term for animals trained to help people with disabilities) are not pets and thus are not subject to many of the laws or policies pertaining to pets.

The Americans With Disabilities Act (ADA) defines a service animal as "any guide dog, signal dog or other animal individually trained to provide assistance to an individual with a disability." ADA regulations stipulate that public accommodations are required to modify policies, practices and procedures to permit the use of a service animal by an individual with a disability.

The purpose of these regulations is to provide equal access opportunities for people with disabilities and to ensure that they are not separated from their service animals. A tow truck operator, for example, must allow a service animal to ride in the truck with her owner rather than in the towed vehicle.

Public accommodations may charge a fee or deposit to an individual who has a disability — provided that fee or deposit is required of all customers — but no fees or deposits may be charged for the service animal, even those normally charged for pets.

The handler/owner is responsible for the animal's care and behavior; if the dog creates an altercation or poses a direct threat, the handler may be required to remove it from the premises and pay for any resulting damages.

CHOOSING A PET SITTER

Before hiring a pet sitter, ask:
- Is he or she insured (for commercial liability) and bonded?
- What is included in the fee?
- Does the sitter require that your pet have a current vaccination?
- What kind of animals does the sitter typically care for?
- How will a medical, weather or home emergency be handled?
- Does he or she fully understand your pet's medical or dietary needs?
- How much time will be spent with your pet?

The pet sitter should:
- Have a polished, professional attitude.
- Provide references.
- Have a standard contract outlining terms of service.
- Have experience in caring for animals.
- Insist on current vaccinations.
- Ask about your pet's health, temperament, schedule and needs.
- Visit and interact with your pet before you leave.
- Devote time and attention to your pet.
- Be affiliated with pet care organizations.

Be sure you:
- Explain your pet's personality — favorite toys, good and bad habits, hiding spots, general health, etc.
- Leave care instructions, keys, food and water dishes, extra supplies (food, medication, etc.), and phone numbers for your veterinarian and an emergency contact.
- Bring pets inside before leaving.

CHOOSING A KENNEL

Before reserving a kennel, ask:
- What is included in the fee?
- Are current vaccinations required?
- What kind of animals do they board?
- How will a medical or weather emergency be handled?
- Will your pet be kept in a cage or run?
- Will your pet receive daily exercise?
- Does the kennel fully understand your pet's medical or dietary needs?
- How and how often will staff interact with your pet?

The kennel should:
- Require proof of current vaccinations.
- Be clean, well-ventilated and offer adequate protection from the elements.
- Have separate areas for dogs, cats and other animals, with secure fencing and caging.
- Clean and disinfect facilities daily.
- Give your pet his regular food on his regular schedule.
- Provide soft bedding in runs/cages.
- Understand your pet's medical needs.
- Provide or obtain veterinary care if necessary.
- Offer sufficient supervision.
- Have a friendly, animal-loving staff.

Be sure you:
- Notify staff of behavior quirks (dislike of other animals, children, etc.).
- Provide food and medication.
- Leave a familiar object with your pet.
- Leave phone numbers for your veterinarian and an emergency contact.
- Spend time with your pet before boarding him.

The **Delta Society,** an organization devoted to companion and service animals, has information about laws that affect people and service animals in public accommodations. Phone (425) 679-5500 for a catalog, or visit www.deltasociety.org.

Preparing Your Pet for Travel

Happily, many vacations can be planned to include fun activities for pets. Trips to parks, nature trails, the ocean or lakes offer exposure to the world beyond the window or fence at home, as well as the chance to explore new sights and sounds. Even the streets of an unfamiliar city can provide a smorgasbord of discoveries for your animal friend to enjoy.

Once you decide Spot and Snowball are ready to hit the road, plan accordingly:

❧ **Get a clean bill of health from the veterinarian.** Update your pet's vaccinations, check his general physical condition and obtain a health certificate showing proof of up-to-date inoculations, particularly rabies, distemper and kennel cough. Such documentation will be necessary if you cross state or country lines, and also may come in handy in the unlikely event your pet gets lost and must be retrieved from the local shelter. Don't forget to ask the doctor about potential health risks at your destination (Lyme disease, heartworm infection) and the necessary preventive measures.

If your pet is taking prescribed medicine, pack a sufficient supply plus a few days' extra. Also take the prescription in case you need a refill. Be prepared for emergencies by getting the names and numbers of clinics or doctors at your destination from your veterinarian or the American Animal Hospital Association. **Hint:** Obtain these references before you leave and keep them handy throughout the trip.

Make sure your pet is in good physical shape overall, especially if you are planning an active vacation. If your animal is primarily sedentary or overweight, he may not be up to lengthy hikes through the woods.

Note: Some owners believe a sedated animal will travel more easily than one that is fully aware, but this is rarely the case. In fact, tranquilizing an animal can make travel much more stressful. Always consult a veterinarian about what is best for your pet, and administer sedatives only under the doctor's direction. In addition, never give an animal medication that is specifically prescribed for humans. The dosage may be too high for an animal's much smaller body mass, or may cause dangerous side effects.

❧ **Acclimate your pet to car travel.** Even if you're flying, your pet will have to ride in the car to get to the airport or terminal, and you don't want any unpleasant surprises before departure.

CONTACT INFORMATION

The following organizations offer information, tips, brochures and other travel materials designed to help you and your pet enjoy a happy and safe vacation.

American Animal Hospital Association
12575 W. Bayaud Ave., Lakewood, CO 80228
(303) 986-2800 — www.healthypet.com

American Society for the Prevention of Cruelty to Animals
424 E. 92nd St., New York, NY 10128-6804
(212) 876-7700 — www.aspca.org

American Veterinary Medical Association
1931 N. Meacham Rd., Suite 100
Schaumburg, IL 60173
(800) 248-2862 — www.avma.org

Dogpark.com®
820 Fifth Ave., Suite B, San Rafael, CA 94901
www.dogpark.com

The Humane Society of the United States
2100 L St. N.W., Washington, DC 20037
(202) 452-1100 — www.hsus.org

National Association of Professional Pet Sitters
15000 Commerce Pkwy., Suite C
Mt. Laurel, NJ 08054
(856) 439-0324 — www.petsitters.org

Pet Care Services Association
2760 N. Academy Blvd., Suite 120
Colorado Springs, CO 80917
(877) 570-7788 — www.petcareservices.org

PetGroomer.com
P.O. Box 2489
Yelm, WA 98597
(360) 446-5348 — www.petgroomer.com

Pet Sitters International
201 E. King St., King, NC 27021
(336) 983-9222 — www.petsit.com

USDA-APHIS
USDA-APHIS-Animal Care
4700 River Rd., Unit 84
Riverdale, MD 20737-1234
(301) 734-7833
www.aphis.usda.gov/animal_welfare/index.shtml

Some animals are used to riding in the car and even enjoy it. But most associate the inside of the carrier or the car with one thing only: the annual visit to the V-E-T. Considering that these visits usually end with a jab from a sharp needle, it's no wonder that some pets forget their training and act up in the car. If this is your situation, you will have to re-train your animal to view a drive as a reward, not a punishment.

Begin by allowing your pet to become used to the car without actually going anywhere. Then take short trips to places that are fun for animals, such as the park or the drive-through window at a fast-food restaurant. (Keep those indulgent snacks to a minimum!) Be sure to praise her for good behavior with words, petting and healthy treats. It shouldn't take long before you and your furry friend are enjoying leisurely drives without incident. *(See Traveling by Car, p. 12.)*

❧ **Brush up on behavior.** Will Snowball make a good travel companion? Or will he be an absolute terror on the road? Don't wait until the vacation is already under way to find out; review general behavioral guidelines with respect to your animal, keeping in mind that the unfamiliarity of travel situations may test the temperament of even the most well-behaved pet.

It's a good idea to socialize Spot by exposing her to other people and animals (especially if she normally stays inside). You're likely to encounter both on your trip, and it is important that she learns to behave properly in the company of strangers. Make her introduction to the outside world gradual, such as a walk in a new neighborhood or taking her along while you run errands. Exposure to new situations will help reduce fear of the unknown and result in more socially acceptable behavior.

Is your pet housebroken? How is he around children? Does he obey vocal commands? Be honest about your animal's ability to cope in unfamiliar surroundings. Depending on the length and nature of the trip and your pet's level of command response, an obedience refresher course might be a good idea.

❧ **Learn about your destination.** Check into quarantines or other restrictions well in advance, and make follow-up calls as your departure date approaches. Find out what types of documentation will be required — not just en route, but on the way home as well.

Be aware of potential safety or health risks where you're going, and plan accordingly. For example, the southeastern United States — particularly Florida — is home to alligators and heartworm-carrying mosquitoes, and many mountainous and wooded areas may harbor ticks that transmit Lyme disease.

Confirm all travel plans within a few days of your departure, especially with lodgings and airlines; their policies may have changed after you made the reservations. If you plan to visit state parks or attractions that accept pets on the premises, obtain their animal regulations in advance.

WHAT TO TAKE

❑ Carrier or crate. *(See Selecting a Carrier or Crate, p. 11, for specifications.)*

❑ Nylon or leather collar or harness, license tag, ID tag(s) and leash. All should be sturdy and should fit your pet properly.

❑ Food and water dishes.

❑ Can opener and spoon (for canned food).

❑ An ample supply of food, plus a few days' extra.

❑ Bottled water from home. (Many animals are finicky about their drinking water.)

❑ Cooler with ice.

❑ Healthy treats.

❑ Medications, if necessary.

❑ Health certificate and other required documents.

❑ A blanket or other bedding. (If your pet is used to sleeping on the furniture, bring an old blanket or sheet to place on top of the hotel's bedding.)

❑ Litter supplies (for cats or other small animals), a scooper and plastic bags (for dogs).

❑ Favorite toys.

❑ Carpet deodorizer.

❑ Chewing preventative.

❑ A recent photograph and a written description including name, breed, gender, height, weight, coloring and distinctive markings.

❑ Grooming supplies:
comb/brush
nail clippers
shampoo
cloth and paper towels
cotton balls/tissues

❑ First-aid kit:
gauze, bandages and adhesive tape
hydrogen peroxide
rubbing alcohol
ointment
muzzle
scissors
tweezers (for removing ticks, burrs, splinters, etc.)
local emergency phone numbers
first-aid guide (such as *Pet First Aid: Cats & Dogs*, published by The Humane Society of the United States and the American Red Cross)

❧ **Determine the best mode of transportation.** Most people traveling with pets drive. Many airlines do accept animals in the passenger cabin or cargo hold, and as more people choose to fly with their pet airlines are becoming more pet-conscious. Restrictions vary as to the type and number of pets an airline will carry, however, so inquire about animal shipping and welfare policies before making reservations. If your pet must travel in the cargo hold, heed the cautionary advice in the Traveling by Air section. *(See p. 13.)*

Flying is really the only major option to car travel. Amtrak, as well as Greyhound and other interstate bus lines, do not accept pets. **Note:** Seeing-eye dogs and other service animals are exempt from the regulations prohibiting pets on Amtrak and interstate bus lines. Local rail and bus companies may allow pets in small carriers, but this is an exception rather than a rule.

The only cruise ship that currently permits pets is the Cunard Line's *Queen Mary 2* (on transatlantic crossings only); kennels are provided, but animals are accepted on a very limited basis. Some small charter and sightseeing boat companies permit pets onboard, however.

A word of advice: Never try to sneak your pet onto any mode of public transportation where she is not permitted. You may face legal action or fines, and the animal may be confiscated if discovered.

❧ **Pack as carefully for your pet as you do for yourself.** *(See What To Take, p. 10.)* Make sure she has a collar with a license tag and ID tag(s) listing her name and yours, along with your address and phone number. As an added precaution, some owners outfit their dog with a second tag listing the name and number of a contact person at home. Popular backup identification methods are to have your animal tattooed with an ID number (usually a social security number) or to implant a microchip under her skin.

If your pet requires medication, make sure that is specified on his tag. This helps others understand your animal's needs and also may prevent people from keeping a found pet or from stealing one to sell.

Note: Choke chains, collars that tighten when they are pulled, may be useful during training sessions, but they do not make good full-time collars. If the chain catches on something, your pet could choke herself trying to pull free. For regular wear, use a harness or a conventional collar made of nylon or leather.

Selecting a Carrier or Crate

This is one of the most important steps in ensuring your pet's safety when traveling. A good-quality carrier not only contains your pet during transit, it also gives him a safe, reassuring place to stay when confinement is necessary at your destination. Acclimate the animal before the trip so he views the crate as a cozy den, not a place of exile.

If you plan to travel by car, a carrier will confine your pet en route, and also may come in handy if Spot or Snowball must stay in the room unsupervised. A secured crate will prevent your pet from escaping from the room when the cleaning staff arrives, or at night if camping in the open. *(See At Your Destination, p. 16.)*

Some airlines allow small pets to travel in the passenger cabin as carry-on luggage. There are no laws dictating the type of carrier to use, but remember that it must be small enough to fit under a standard airplane seat and should not exceed 45 linear inches (length + width + height), or roughly **22 by 14 by 9 inches.** If your pet will be flying in the cargo hold, you must use a carrier that meets U.S. Department of Agriculture Animal and Plant Health Inspection Service (USDA-APHIS) specifications. *(See Traveling by Air, p. 13.)*

Crates are available at pet supply stores; some airlines also sell carriers. Soft-sided travel bags are handy for flyers with small pets. Before you make the investment, make sure your carrier is airline-approved.

Even if you never take to the skies, these common-sense guidelines provide a good rule of thumb in selecting a crate for other uses. USDA-APHIS rules stipulate the following:

❧ The crate must be enclosed, but with ventilation openings occupying at least 14 percent of total wall space, at least one-third of which must be located on the top half of the kennel. A three-quarter-inch lip or rim must surround the exterior to prevent air holes from being blocked.

❧ The crate must open easily, but must be sufficiently strong to hold up during normal cargo transit procedures (loading, unloading, etc.).

❧ The floor must be solid and leakproof, and must be covered with an absorbent lining or material (such as an old towel or litter).

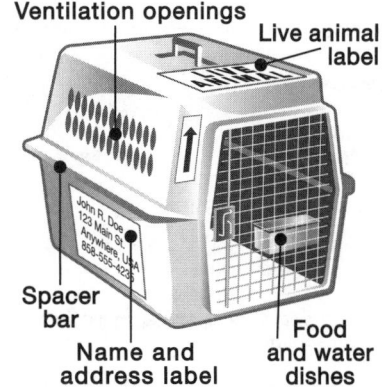

Ventilation openings

Live animal label

Spacer bar

Name and address label

Food and water dishes

HEATSTROKE
AND
HYPOTHERMIA

The best way to treat heatstroke or hypothermia is to prevent it. Do not leave pets unattended in a car, even if only for a few minutes. Also heed airlines' restrictions on pet travel, and carefully investigate animal welfare policies to make certain the airline has safeguards to protect your pet from both conditions.

Other preventive measures are to avoid strenuous exercise — including such activities as hiking and "fetch" — when the sun is strongest (10 a.m.-2 p.m.), and to provide your pet access to clean, fresh drinking water at all times.

Following are the warning signs and basic first aid for heatstroke and hypothermia. Always be alert to your pet's physical condition and watch for symptoms — immediate attention to the situation may mean the difference between life and death. If your pet is struck with either disorder, take him to an animal hospital or veterinarian as fast as safely possible.

HEATSTROKE

Symptoms
- rapid, shallow breathing
- excessive salivation
- heavy panting
- hot to the touch
- glazed eyes
- unsteadiness, dizziness
- deep red or purple tongue or gums
- vomiting
- body temperature of 104 F or higher

First Aid
- place pet in the shade
- quickly dampen with cool water, especially on the head and neck
- give small amounts of water

HYPOTHERMIA

Symptoms
- shivering
- weakness
- lethargy
- cold to the touch
- body temperature of 95 F or lower

First Aid
- place in a warm area
- wrap in towels or a blanket
- quickly warm by gently massaging the head, chest and extremities

❧ The crate must be just large enough to allow the animal to turn freely while standing, and to have a full range of normal movement while standing or lying down.

❧ The crate must offer exterior grips or handles so that handlers do not have to place their hands or fingers inside.

❧ Food and water dishes must be securely attached and accessible without opening the kennel.

❧ If the carrier has wheels, they must be removed or immobilized prior to loading.

❧ One-inch lettering stating "Live Animals" must be placed visibly on the exterior, and must be accompanied by directional arrows showing the crate's proper orientation. It also is a good idea to label the crate with your name, home address and home phone number, as well as an address and phone number where you can be reached during the trip. **Hint:** Use an adhesive label or an indelible marker and write directly on the crate, as paper may be ripped off accidentally in transit.

❧ Attach a list of care instructions (feeding, watering, etc.) for a 24-hour period to the exterior of the carrier. This will help airport workers care for your pet if he is sent to the wrong destination.

❧ If you are traveling with multiple pets, note that crates may contain only one animal whose weight exceeds 20 pounds. Smaller animals may travel together under the following guidelines: one species to a crate, except compatible dogs and cats of similar size; two puppies or kittens under 6 months of age; 15 guinea pigs or rabbits; 50 hamsters. **Note:** These are federal limits; airlines may impose more stringent regulations.

Traveling by Car

The first step in ensuring your pet's well-being during a vacation is to train her to ride in the car. For safety reasons, pets should be confined to the back seat, either in a carrier or a harness attached to the car's seat belt. This keeps the animal from interfering with or distracting the driver, and also may save her life in the event of an accident. And a restrained animal will not be able to break free and run away the second the car door is opened.

To help prevent car sickness, feed your pet a light meal four to six hours before departing. Do not give an animal food or water in a moving vehicle.

Never allow your pet to ride in the bed of a pickup truck. It's illegal in some states; he also can jump out or be thrown, endangering himself and others on the road. Harnessing or leashing him to the truck bed is not advisable either: If he tries to jump out, he could be dragged along the road or the restraint could become a noose.

Avoid placing animals in campers or trailers as well. **If your pet cannot ride in the car with you, leave him at home.**

Don't let your dog stick her head out the window, no matter how enjoyable it seems. Road debris and other flying objects can injure delicate eyes and ears, and the animal is at greater risk for severe injury if the vehicle should stop suddenly or be struck. If it is hot outside, run the air conditioner instead of opening the windows, and be sure that the air flow is reaching your pet.

AAA recommends that drivers stop every two hours to stretch their legs and take a quick break from driving. Your pet will appreciate the same break. Plan to visit a rest stop every four hours or so to let him have a drink and a chance to answer the call of nature. (Cat owners should bring along a litter box; dog owners should clean up afterward.)

Be sure your pet is leashed before opening the car door. This is not merely a courtesy to fellow travelers; it will prevent her from unexpectedly breaking free and running away. Keep in mind that even the most obedient pet may become disoriented during travel or in strange places and set off for home. **Hint:** If your pet is not used to traveling, use a harness instead of a collar; it is more difficult for an animal to wriggle out of a harness.

NEVER leave an animal in a parked car, even if the windows are partially open. Even on pleasant days the temperature inside a car can soar to well over 100 degrees in less than 10 minutes, placing your pet at risk for heatstroke and possibly death. On very cold days, hypothermia is a risk. Also, animals left unattended in parked cars frequently are stolen.

Traveling by Air

(Service animals are normally exempt from most of the regulations and fees specified in this section. Check policies with the airline when making reservations.)

Opinion is divided as to whether air travel is truly safe for pets. Statistically, it is less dangerous than being a passenger in a car, but some experts warn of potentially deadly conditions for animals. The truth lies somewhere in between: Most pets arrive at their destination in fine condition, but death or injury is always a possibility. Before you decide to fly, know the risk factors and the necessary precautions to keep your pet safe.

❧ **Determine whether your pet is fit to fly.** The Animal Welfare Act (AWA), administered by USDA-APHIS, specifies that dogs and cats must be at least 8 weeks old and weaned at least 5 days before air travel. Animals that are very young, very old, pregnant, ill or injured should not fly at all. Cats, snub-nosed dogs (pugs, boxers, etc.) and long-nosed dogs (shelties, collies, etc.) are prone to severe respiratory difficulties in an airplane's poorly ventilated cargo hold and should travel only in the passenger cabin (if size allows) with their owner. Some airlines will not accept snub-nosed breeds if the temperature exceeds 70 degrees anywhere in the routing.

❧ **Decide where your pet will fly.** Most animals fly in the hold as checked baggage when traveling with their owners, or as cargo when they are unaccompanied. The AWA was enacted to ensure animals traveling in this manner are treated humanely and are not subjected to dangerous or life-threatening conditions. For specific requirements pertaining to your animal, check with the airline in advance, as policies vary. Some airlines will not ship dogs as checked baggage, and others will only accept dogs shipped as cargo from "known shippers"; i.e., commercial shippers or licensed pet breeders. Except for service animals, Southwest accepts no pets in the cabin or cargo compartment.

Items classified as "dangerous goods" (dry ice or toxic chemicals, for example) must be transported in a different part of the hold from where live animals are carried. Some planes are designed to have separate hold areas, but so-called "people mover" airlines that are primarily interested in getting human passengers from one point to another as quickly as possible may not give priority to

---

Airline Contact Information

Following is a list of the major North American airlines and their toll-free reservation numbers.

Web site addresses include information about flying with animals. **Hint:** Look under links for baggage, cargo or special travel needs, or do a site search for "pets."

Air Canada . . . . (888) 247-2262
www.aircanada.com

Alaska Airlines . . . . (800) 252-7522
www.alaskaair.com

American Airlines . . . . (800) 433-7300
www.aa.com

Continental Airlines . . . . (800) 523-3273
www.continental.com

Delta Airlines . . . . (800) 221-1212
Northwest Airlines . . . . (800) 225-2525
www.delta.com

Southwest Airlines . . . . (800) 435-9792
www.southwest.com

United Airlines . . . . (800) 864-8331
www.united.com

US Airways . . . . (800) 428-4322
www.usairways.com

this feature. Check your airline's specific baggage policies so you know exactly where in the hold your pet will be traveling.

Small pets may be taken into the passenger cabin with you as carry-on luggage on most airlines. This places the animal's welfare squarely in your hands but is feasible only if he is very well-behaved and fits comfortably in a container that meets standard carry-on regulations. *(See Selecting a Carrier or Crate, p. 11.) Keep in mind that the carrier — with the animal inside — must be kept under the seat in front of you throughout the flight. Most airlines charge a fee (anywhere from $50-$100 each way) for carry-on pets.* **Note:** AWA regulations do not apply to animals traveling in the cabin.

❧ **Do your homework.** Investigate the airline's animal transport and welfare policies, especially if you are flying with a small or commuter airline. All airlines are subject to basic AWA regulations, but specific standards of care vary greatly from one company to another. Do your research well in advance and confirm the information 24-48 hours before departing.

The more information an airline provides, the better care your pet is likely to receive. Beware of companies that have vague animal welfare guidelines, or none at all. All

---

PET INSURANCE

Just like their owners, pets can experience major medical problems at some point in their lifetime — even those that live indoors. And if illness strikes while you're on the road, it may be necessary to obtain care quickly. As a result, more and more people who travel with their devoted companion are considering pet health insurance.

Insurance plans run the gamut from basic coverage and routine care for illness and injury to comprehensive health maintenance, vaccinations and exams. Annual premiums range from less than $100 to more than $350, depending on the type of pet and plan. When choosing your plan, consider the following:

- What are the enrollment guidelines (age, breed, specific restrictions, etc.)?

- Which expenses are covered and which are excluded?

- What is the plan's policy concerning existing health problems?

- Does the plan allow you to use your own veterinarian?

- How are veterinary fees paid?

- Is a multiple pet discount offered?

---

major airlines provide information about pet transport on their Web sites. Also talk to fellow travelers and pet owners about their experiences. Finally, keep in mind that airlines are not required to transport live animals and can refuse to carry them for any reason.

❧ **Protect your investment.** Most people think of their pets as part of the family, but the legal system assigns them the same value as a piece of luggage. Inquire about insurance — an airline that won't insure animals in its care may not be the right one for your pet. (Always read the fine print before purchasing any insurance policy.) Also ask if the airline's workers are trained to handle animals. Few are, but it doesn't hurt to check. Remember, it's up to you to choose an airline that values pets and will treat yours with care.

❧ **Understand the potential hazards.** Because a plane's cargo hold is neither cooled nor heated until take-off, the most dangerous time for your pet is that spent on the ground in this unventilated compartment. In summer the space absorbs heat while the plane sits on the tarmac; the reverse is true in winter, when it is no warmer inside the hold than outside. Both instances expose pets to the possibility of serious injury or death from heatstroke or hypothermia. **Note:** The latter also may be a concern during flight if the hold's heater is disabled or turned off, allowing the temperature to drop to near-freezing levels.

To minimize these risks, USDA-APHIS rules prohibit animals from being kept in the hold or on the tarmac for more than 45 minutes when temperatures are above 85 F or below 45 F. Some airlines impose even tighter temperature restrictions and may not permit animals to fly on planes going to cities where the ground temperatures may exceed these limits. (Exceptions may be made for animals whose veterinarians certify they are acclimated to colder temperatures, but never warmer.)

❧ **Make stress-free travel arrangements.** Once you decide to fly, reserve space for Spot or Snowball when you arrange your own tickets, preferably well in advance of your travel date. Airlines accept only a limited number of animals per flight — usually two to four in the passenger cabin and one pet per passenger — on a first-come, first-served basis. More animals are generally allowed in the cargo hold.

Prepare to pay a fee each way; the cost is often greater for large animals traveling on a flight without their owner. (Unfortunately, pets are not eligible for frequent flyer miles.) Always reconfirm your reservations and flight information 24-48 hours before departure.

If your pet will be flying in the hold, travel on the same plane and reserve a nonstop flight. This not only reduces the danger of heatstroke or hypothermia during layovers, it also eliminates the possibility that she will be placed on the wrong connecting flight. In summer, fly during the early morning or late evening when temperatures are cooler. Because of large crowds and the chance of heavy air traffic causing delays, avoid holiday travel whenever possible.

Additional precautions may be necessary when traveling outside the United States and Canada. Other countries may impose lengthy quarantines, and airline workers outside North America may not be bound by animal welfare laws. *(See International Travel, p. 18.)*

☙ **Play an active role in your pet's well-being.** Flying safely with your pet requires careful planning and attention to his welfare. See the veterinarian within 10 days of departure for a health certificate (required by most airlines) and a pre-flight check-up.

Address any concerns you have about your pet traveling by air, especially if you are considering tranquilization. Sedation usually is not recommended for cats and dogs, regardless of whether they fly in the cabin or in the hold. Exposure to increased altitude pressure can create respiratory and cardiovascular problems; animals with short, wide heads are particularly susceptible to disorientation and possible injury. Sedation should never be administered without your veterinarian's approval.

Obtain an airline-approved carrier and acclimate your pet to its presence by leaving it open with a familiar object inside. A sturdy, well-ventilated crate adds an additional measure of protection.

Because animals are classified as luggage, they may be loaded on the plane via conveyor belt. If the crate falls off the belt, your pet could be injured or released. Ask that she be hand-carried on and off the plane, and that you be permitted to watch both procedures. Also ask about "counter-to-counter" shipping, in which the animal is loaded immediately before departure and unloaded immediately after arrival. There usually is an additional fee for this service.

Make sure you will have access to your pet if there is a lengthy layover or delay. Think twice about flying on an airline that won't allow you to check on your animal under such circumstances.

☙ **Prepare for the flight.** Keep in mind that traveling with an animal will require additional pre-flight time and preparation on your part. Exercise your pet before the flight, and arrive at least two but not more than four hours before departure. If he is traveling as carry-on luggage, check-in is normally at the passenger terminal; if he is traveling as checked baggage or as cargo in the cargo hold, proceed to the airline's cargo terminal, which is often in a different location. Find this out when making reservations and again when confirming flight information.

Make sure your animal's crate is properly labeled and secured, but do not lock it in case airline personnel have to provide emergency care. Include an ice pack for extra comfort on a hot day or a hot water bottle on a cold day. **Hint:** Wrap in a towel to prevent leaking.

Do not feed your pet less than four hours before departure, but provide water up until boarding. **Hint:** Freeze water in the bowl so that it melts throughout the trip, providing a constant drinking source.

Spot or Snowball should wear a sturdy collar (breakaway collars are recommended for cats) and two identification tags marked with your name, home address and phone number, and travel address and phone number. It's also a good idea to clip your pet's nails before departure so they won't accidentally get caught on any part of the carrier.

Note: You may be required to take your pet out of the carrier as you pass through security on your way to the gate. Make sure the animal is wearing a collar and leash or harness.

Attach food and water dishes inside the carrier so that airline workers can reach them without opening the door. If the trip will take longer than 12 hours, also attach a plastic bag with at least one meal's worth of dry food. Animals under 16 weeks of age must be fed every 12 hours, adult animals every 24 hours. Water must be provided at least every 12 hours, regardless of the animal's age.

Allow your pet to answer the call of nature before boarding, but do not take her out of the carrier while in the terminal. As a courtesy, wait until you are outside and away from fellow travelers. Keep her leash with you — do not leave it inside or attached to the kennel.

If your pet is traveling as carry-on luggage, let the passenger sitting next to you know. Someone with allergies may want to change seats.

Perhaps the most important precaution is to alert the flight crew and the captain that your pet is aboard. The pilot must activate the heater for the cargo hold; make sure this is done once you are in the air. If there are layovers or delays, ask the flight crew to be sure your pet has adequate shelter and/or ventilation; better yet, ask them to allow you to check in person.

If you have arranged to watch your pet being unloaded, ask a flight attendant to call the baggage handlers and let them know you are on the way. Above all, do not hesitate to voice any concerns you have for your pet's welfare — it is your responsibility to do so.

☙ **Be prepared for emergencies.** In the unlikely event your pet gets lost en route, contact the airline, local humane shelters, animal control agencies or USDA-APHIS. Many airlines can trace a pet that was transferred to the wrong flight. If your pet is injured in transit, proceed to the nearest animal hospital; register any complaints with USDA-APHIS. **Hint:** Carry a list of emergency contact numbers and a current photograph of your pet in your wallet or purse, just in case.

At Your Destination

How well you and your companion behave on the road directly affects the way future furry travelers will be treated. Always clean up after your pet and keep him under your control. This is not only a courtesy to fellow human travelers; it's the surest way to enjoy a safe and happy vacation.

Inquire about pet policies before making lodging reservations. Properties may impose restrictions on the type or size of pet allowed, or they may designate only certain rooms, such as smoking rooms, for travelers with animals. If you have a dog, get a room on the first floor with direct access outside, preferably near a walking area; keep her leashed on any excursion.

Lodgings may have supervision policies requiring that pets be crated when unattended or that they may not be left alone at all. Allow your pet only in designated exercise or animal-approved areas; never take him into such off-limits places as the lobby, pool area, patio or restaurant. Prepare to receive limited housekeeping service, or none at all.

Expect to pay some type of additional charge, which may be per room or per pet and may include any of the following: refundable deposit, non-refundable deposit, daily fee, weekly fee.

If staying with friends or relatives, make certain your pet is a welcome guest. Know and respect their "house rules," especially if they have small children or pets of their own.

Once in the room, check for such hazards as chemically treated toilet water, hiding spaces and electrical cords before freeing your pet. Give her time to adjust to her new surroundings under your supervision.

Above all, practice good "petiquette":

🐾 Try not to leave your pet alone, but if you must, crate or otherwise confine her.

🐾 Crate at night as well.

🐾 To keep your pet and the housekeeper from having an unexpected encounter, leave the "Do Not Disturb" sign on the door when you go out without him.

🐾 Barking dogs make poor hotel neighbors — keep your pet quiet.

🐾 Don't allow your pet on the furniture. If she insists on sleeping on the bed, bring a bedspread or sheet from home and place that on top of the hotel bedding.

🐾 Clean up after your pet immediately — inside the room and out — and leave no trace of him behind when checking out.

🐾 Dispose of litter and other "accidents" properly — check with housekeeping.

🐾 Notify the management immediately if something is damaged, and be ready to pay for repairs.

🐾 Add a little extra to the housekeeping tip.

🐾 When you take your pet out of the room, keep her leashed, especially in wilderness areas and around small children. No matter how obedient she is at home, new stimuli and distractions may cause her to forget or ignore vocal commands. Know and obey animal policies at parks, beaches and other public areas. Check before arriving to make certain animals still are welcome, even if you've been there before — the rules may have changed.

🐾 Look for outdoor cafes when selecting restaurants. For health reasons, pets are not permitted inside eating establishments, but many restaurants allow animals to sit quietly with their owners at outdoor tables. Drive-through restaurants are another alternative.

In Case of Emergency

Be prepared for any turn of events by knowing how to get to the nearest animal hospital. (See Emergency Animal Clinics, p. 53.) Also have the name and number of a local animal shelter and a local veterinarian handy — ask your veterinarian for a recommendation. Take first-aid supplies with you and know how to use them. An animal in pain may become aggressive, so exercise caution at all times.

Emergency evacuation shelters do not accept pets, and domesticated animals do not fare well if left to weather an emergency on their own, especially when far from home. Avert a potential tragedy by planning in advance where you will go with your pet in case of evacuation. Use the listings in this book to find other lodgings willing to take you and your pet. Above all, don't wait for disaster to strike. Leave as soon as the evacuation order is announced, and take your animal with you.

The Great Outdoors

Travelers planning an active or camping vacation should make some additional preparations. Check in advance to be sure your pet is permitted at campgrounds, parks, beaches, trails and anywhere else you will be visiting. If there are restrictions — and there usually are — follow them. Remember that pets other than service animals usually are not allowed in public buildings.

Note: It is not advisable to take animals other than dogs into wilderness areas. For example, bringing a pet is not recommended at some national parks in Alaska. Also keep in mind that rural areas often have few veterinarians and even fewer boarding kennels.

Use common sense. Clean up after your pet, do not allow excessive vocalizing and keep her under your control. If the property requires your pet to be leashed or crated at all times, do so. Few parks or natural areas will allow a pet to be unattended, even when chained — the risk of disagreeable encounters with other travelers or wildlife is too great. The National Park Service may confiscate pets that harm wildlife or other visitors.

If camping, crate your pet at night to protect him from the elements and predators. (Chaining confines the animal but won't keep him from becoming a midnight snack.)

When hiking, stick to the trail and keep your pet on a short leash. It is all too easy for an unleashed pet to wander off and get lost or fall prey to a larger animal. Keep an eye out for such wildlife as alligators, bears, big cats, porcupines and skunks, and avoid other dogs and small children. Be aware of indigenous poisonous plants, such as English ivy and oleander, or those causing physical injury, such as cactus, poison ivy or stinging nettle. Your veterinarian or local poison control center should be able to give you a full list of hazardous flora.

Before setting out on the trail, make sure both of you are in good physical shape. An animal that rarely exercises at home will not suddenly be ready for a 10-mile trek across uneven terrain. Plan a hike well within the limits of your pet's endurance, and don't push — remember, if Spot gets too tired to make it back on her own, you'll have to carry her.

Carry basic first-aid supplies, including a first-aid guide. *(See What to Take, p. 10.)* Also carry fresh drinking water for both of you — "found" water may contain harmful germs or toxins. Drink often, not just when thirst strikes, and have your pet do the same. Watch for signs of dehydration, leg or foot injuries, heat exhaustion or heatstroke. Stop immediately and return home or to camp if any of these occur.

Note: Dogs can carry their own backpacks (check your local pet store for specially designed packs), but should never carry more than one-third of their body weight. Train the dog to accept the pack beforehand, and only use it with a strong, healthy animal in excellent physical condition.

No matter where or how you spend your vacation, visit the veterinarian when you return home to check for injuries, parasites and general health.

Note: Most campgrounds accept pets. The AAA CampBook guides are an excellent source for obtaining detailed information regarding pet policies, restrictions and extra charges for campgrounds in the United States and Canada. AAA members may obtain complimentary copies of the CampBook guides at their local AAA club.

Traveling Between the United States and Canada

Traveling across the international border with your pet — either from the United States into Canada or from Canada into the United States — should prove largely hassle-free, although some basic regulations need to be kept in mind. All U.S. and Canadian citizens traveling between the United States and Canada are required to show a passport or other accepted secure document. For additional information about secure documents visit travel.state.gov or phone (877) 487-2778.

U.S. Customs grants returning U.S. citizens who stay in Canada more than 48 hours an individual $800 duty-free exemption (if not used within the prior 30 days). Any amount over the $800 exemption is subject to duty.

The exemption is based on fair retail value and applies to goods acquired for personal or household use or as gifts but not intended for sale. All items for which the exemption is claimed must accompany you upon return.

A 5 percent goods and services tax (GST) is levied on most items sold and most services rendered in Canada. A 13 percent harmonized sales tax (HST), which includes the GST, is charged on goods and services in New Brunswick, Nova Scotia and Newfoundland and Labrador, and also is expected to be adopted by Ontario and British Columbia beginning in July 2010.

U.S. citizens taking pet cats and dogs 3 months of age and older into Canada must carry a rabies vaccination certificate signed by a licensed veterinarian that describes the animal, provides proof of rabies vaccination and includes documentation of the product name, lot number and lot expiration date. Collar tags are not sufficient proof of immunization. The certificate also is needed to bring a pet dog back into the United States; make sure the vaccination doesn't expire while you're in Canada. **Note:** Pit bulls are not permitted to be taken into Ontario.

Service animals are exempt from import restrictions. Also exempt are puppies and kittens under 3 months old; obtain a certificate of health from your veterinarian indicating that the animal is too young to vaccinate. **Note:** For details on pet imports, contact the Canadian Embassy; 501 Pennsylvania Ave. N.W., Washington, DC 20001; phone (202) 682-1740. The Web site address is www.canadianembassy.org.

The Canadian Food Inspection Agency (CFIA) provides additional pet information; phone (800) 442-2342 or visit the Web site at www.inspection.gc.ca. If you need assistance while in Canada, contact the U.S. Embassy, P.O. Box 866/ Station B, Ottawa, ON, Canada K1P 5T1; phone (613) 688-5335.

Canadian Customs allows Canadian citizens to bring back from the United States, duty and tax free, goods valued up to $400 any number of times per year, provided the visit is 48 hours or more. A $50 exemption, excluding alcoholic beverages and tobacco products, may be claimed if the visit is 24 hours or more and no other exemption is being used. If returning from a visit of 7 days or more (not counting the day of departure from Canada), the exemption goes up to $750.

Canadian travelers may take pet cats and dogs into the United States with no restrictions, but U.S. Customs requires that dogs have proof of rabies vaccination no less than 30 days before arrival. For additional information on U.S. regulations, contact the USDA-APHIS National Center for Import and Export, (301) 734-8364.

International Travel

If you plan to travel abroad with Spot or Snowball, prepare for a lengthy flight and at least a short quarantine period. Be aware that airline and animal workers in other countries may not be bound by the same animal welfare laws that exist in the United States and Canada. Contact the embassy or consulate at your destination for information about documentation and quarantine requirements, animal control laws and animal welfare regulations.

As with any trip, have your pet checked by your regular veterinarian within 10 days of departure to obtain a health certificate showing proof of rabies and other inoculations. If you are traveling with an animal other than a domesticated dog or cat, check with USDA-APHIS for restrictions or additional documentation required.

The booklet "Pets and Wildlife: Licensing and Health Requirements" has general information about traveling abroad with animals; write U.S. Customs & Border Protection, 1300 Pennsylvania Ave. N.W., Washington, DC 20229, or visit www.customs.gov.

Note: Island nations such as Australia and the United Kingdom, which are rabies-free, have adopted the Pet Travel Scheme (PETS) to allow entry for dogs and cats from the U.S. and Canada without the usual 6-month quarantine. Pets must be tested and vaccinated for rabies at least 6 months prior to travel, be implanted with microchip identification and receive a certificate of treatment from an official government veterinarian. For information, visit the U.K. Web site for the Department for Environment, Food and Rural Affairs (DEFRA) at www.defra.gov.uk. Hawaii, which has a standard 120-day quarantine for all imported animals except guide dogs, has adopted a similar expedited program of 5 days or less; a pet must have been vaccinated at least *twice* for rabies in its lifetime.

Loss Prevention Tips

Searching the woods or an unfamiliar town for a missing pet is easily prevented by following these helpful tips:

❧ Have your pet wear a sturdy nylon or leather collar with current ID and rabies tags firmly attached. Be sure the ID tag includes the phone number of an emergency contact. Consider having your pet implanted with microchip identification; it's a simple procedure similar to a vaccination.

❧ Keep your pet on a leash or harness. Even trained animals can become agitated or disoriented in unfamiliar surroundings and fail to obey vocal commands.

❧ Attach the leash or harness while your pet is still inside the closed car or crate.

❧ Do not leave your pet unattended at any time, anywhere. A stolen pet is extremely difficult to recover.

❧ Escape-proof your hotel room by crating your pet and asking hotel management to make certain no one enters your room while you are gone. (Inform the property that you're traveling with an animal when making reservations.)

❧ Take along a recent picture and a detailed written description of your pet.

If your pet gets lost these steps will improve your chances of recovery:

❧ If your pet is lost in transit, contact the airline immediately. Ask to trace the animal via the airline's automated baggage tracking system.

❧ Contact local police, animal control, animal shelters, humane organizations and veterinary clinics with a description and a recent photograph. Stay in contact until your pet is found, and provide your home and destination phone numbers.

❧ Post signs and place an ad in the local newspaper so that anyone who comes across your pet knows she is lost and how to reach you.

The Last Word

You are ultimately responsible for your pet's welfare and behavior while traveling. Since animals cannot speak for themselves, it is up to you to focus on your pet's well-being every step of the way. It also is important to make sure he conducts himself properly so that other pets will be welcome visitors in the future. Following the common-sense information in this book will help ensure that both you and your animal companion have a safe and happy trip.

Pet-Friendly
Places

in the United States and Canada

Dog Parks
Attractions
National Public Lands
Emergency Animal Clinics

DOG PARKS

A dog park is a place where people and their dogs can play together. These places offer dogs an area to play, exercise and socialize with other dogs while their owners enjoy the park-like setting. Dog park size and features vary greatly from location to location, from several hundred square feet in urban areas to several hundred acres in the suburbs and rural locations. Dog owners should remember to always keep their animal leashed until they reach the dog park entrance, to maintain voice control of their animal at all times, to bring their own supply of bags for picking up after their pet (and to be diligent in doing so), and to always have fresh water available for their dog. Please observe all dog park rules.

This list of dog parks in the United States and Canada is provided by Dogpark.com®. Dogpark.com is all about dogs — all breeds, all mixes of breeds, and all shapes, sizes and dispositions. It provides articles and information about dogs and their care, health and play. Online, visit www.dogpark.com.

The dog parks listed here welcome people who travel with their dogs; private parks or parks requiring local residency are not included. **Note:** Fence types and heights vary, and some areas have no fencing at all, requiring that the dog be under firm voice control.

United States

ARIZONA

Lewis Kingman Park - Kingman
parks.cityofkingman.gov
2201 E. Andy Devine Ave.
Daily 6 a.m.-10 p.m.
Fenced, 9 acres, double-gated entry, trees, shade, benches, shelter, picnic area and grills, multi-purpose field, separate areas for large and small dogs, water, disposal bags, parking, lights, restrooms, access for the disabled.

Quail Run Park - Mesa
mesaaz.gov/parksrec
4155 E. Virginia, in Quail Run Park north of McDowell Road and off Greenfield
Daily sunrise-10 p.m.; closed Thursdays for maintenance
More than 3 acres, completely fenced, park benches, separate areas for active and timid dogs, water fountains for people and dogs, parking, disposal bags, trash cans.

Echo Mountain Off Leash Area - Phoenix
phoenix.gov, (602) 262-6696
2302 E. Grovers Ave. (located in Grovers Basin on 20th Street at Cave Creek Road)
Daily 6:30 a.m.-10 p.m.
Fenced, 2.5 acres with grass surface, disposal bags, trash cans, separate areas for large and small dogs; bring your own water.

PETsMART Dog Park at Washington Park - Phoenix
phoenix.gov, (602) 262-6971
21st Avenue north of Mayland, between Bethany Home and Glendale roads
Daily 6:30 a.m.-10 p.m.
Fenced, 2.65 acres with grass surface, double-gated entries, benches, water fountain, two dog-watering stations, disposal bags, trash cans, separate areas for large and small dogs. Access for the disabled.

RJ Dog Park at Pecos Park - Phoenix
phoenix.gov, (602) 262-6111
48th Street and Pecos Parkway (enter from 48th Street via Chandler Boulevard)
Daily 6 a.m.-11 p.m.
Fenced, 2 acres with grass surface, double-gated entry, benches, water fountain, separate areas for large and small dogs. Access for the disabled.

Rose Mofford Sports Complex - Phoenix
phoenix.gov, (602) 262-8011
9833 N. 25th Ave. (north of Dunlap)
Daily 6:30 a.m.-10 p.m.
Fenced, 2.65 acres with grass surface, double-gated entries, benches, trees, water fountain, disposal bags, trash cans, separate areas for large and small dogs. Access for the disabled.

Steele Indian School Park - Phoenix
phoenix.gov
West side of 7th Street, just north of Indian School Road
Daily 6 a.m.-10 p.m.
Fenced, 1.83 acres with granite surface, double-gated entries, disposal bags, trash cans, separate areas for large and small dogs. Access for the disabled.

Chaparral Park - Scottsdale
scottsdaleaz.gov
5401 N. Hayden Rd. at McDonald Drive
Daily 5:30 a.m.-10 p.m., May-Oct.; 6 a.m.-10 p.m., rest of year. Closed for maintenance Tues. and Fri. 8-noon and in wet conditions. Phone (480) 312-9663 for status.
Fenced, 4 acres, benches, shade, restroom, water, separate areas for large and small dogs.

Horizon Park - Scottsdale
scottsdaleaz.gov
15444 N. 100th St. at Thompson Peak Parkway (east of SR 101 off Frank Lloyd Wright Boulevard)
Daily dawn-dusk.
Fenced, lighted, benches, some shade, tables, disposal bags, trash cans, parking, phones, restrooms; bring your own water.

Vista del Camino Park - Scottsdale
scottsdaleaz.gov
7700 E. Pierce St. (take Pierce Street heading west from Hayden Road)
Daily 5:30 a.m.-10 p.m.
Fenced, ½ acre, lighted, grass turf, benches, restrooms nearby, water fountains for dogs and people, mutt mitt stations.

Creamery Park - Tempe
tempe.gov, (480) 350-5200
8th Street and Una Avenue (just south of University Drive near Rural Road)
Daily 6 a.m.-10 p.m.
Fenced, lighted, benches, disposal bags, trash cans, parking, water.

Jaycee Park - Tempe
tempe.gov, (480) 350-5200
5th Street and Hardy Drive
Daily 6 a.m.-10 p.m.
Fenced, lighted, trees, benches, disposal bags, trash cans, parking, water. Access for the disabled.

Mitchell Park - Tempe
tempe.gov, (480) 350-5200
Mitchell Drive and 9th Street
Daily 6 a.m.-10 p.m.; closed Mondays for maintenance
Fenced, lighted, trees, benches, disposal bags, trash cans, parking, water. Access for the disabled.

Papago Park - Tempe
tempe.gov, (480) 350-5200
Curry Road and College Avenue
Daily 6 a.m.-10 p.m.
Fenced, lighted, trees, disposal bags, trash cans, parking, water.

Tempe Sports Complex - Tempe
tempe.gov, (480) 350-5200
Warner Road and Hardy Drive
Daily 6 a.m.-10 p.m.
Fenced, lighted, trees, disposal bags, trash cans, parking, water.

Christopher Columbus Park - Tucson
tucsonaz.gov, (520) 791-4873
4600 N. Silverbell Rd.
Daily dawn to 2-3 hours after dusk.
Fenced, ⅓ acre, water fountain for dogs, scrambling area, shaded area with ramada, scooper dispenser.

Gene C. Reid Park - Miko's Corner Playground - Tucson
tucsonaz.gov, (520) 837-8071
Country Club Road and 22nd Street (use Picnic Place or Concert Place entrances off Country Club Road)
Daily 7 a.m.-10 p.m.
Fenced, lighted, three double-entry gates, large turf areas, divided 2-acre site for large and small dogs, dog-friendly potable water fountains, scooper dispenser, ramada with tables. Named after Miko, a Tucson police dog that lost its life in the line of duty.

Jacobs Park - Tucson
tucsonaz.gov, (520) 791-4873
3300 N. Fairview Ave. on the west side of Jacobs Park
Daily 6 a.m.-10:30 p.m.
Fenced, turf area, walkway, picnic table, double-entry gate.

Palo Verde Park - Tucson
tucsonaz.gov, (520) 791-5930
300 S. Mann Ave. (south of Broadway Boulevard, west of Kolb Road)
Daily 6 a.m.-10:30 p.m.
Fenced, separate areas for large and small dogs, both with separate double-entry gates; entire facility lighted; DG/pea gravel surface, no turf; picnic tables; trash cans; water fountains for dogs on each side; scooper dispensers.

Sixth Avenue Dog Park - Tucson
tucsonaz.gov, (520) 791-4873
2075 N. Sixth Ave. (east side of Sixth Avenue across from Northwest Center and Mansfield Park)
Daily 6 a.m.-10:30 p.m.
Fenced, ramada, tables, wash area, double-entry gate.

Udall Park - Tucson
tucsonaz.gov, (520) 791-5930
7290 E. Tanque Verde Rd.
Daily 6 a.m.-10 p.m.
Fenced, 1 acre, trash cans, seating, water for dogs.

CALIFORNIA

Calabasas Bark Park - Calabasas
cityofcalabasas.com
4232 Las Virgenes Rd. (approximately 2 miles west of US 101 on the south side)
Daily 5 a.m.-9 p.m.
Fenced, lighted, trees, benches, scoops, trash cans, paved parking, water fountain for dogs, separate areas for large and small dogs.

Canine Corral - Carmichael
carmichaelpark.com
5750 Grant Ave. at Fair Oaks Blvd.
Daily sunrise-10 p.m.
Fenced, 1 acre, double-gated entry, trees, benches, shade, small dog area, disposal bags, trash cans, water, parking, lights. Access for the disabled.

Costa Mesa Bark Park - Costa Mesa
cmbarkpark.org, (949) 733-4101 or (714) 754-5041
Arlington Drive and Newport Boulevard (across from the Orange County Fairgrounds Equestrian Center)
Wed.-Mon. dawn-9 p.m.
Fenced, 2.1 acres, night lights dusk-9 p.m., grass turf, trees, benches, tables, disposal bags, trash cans, parking, restrooms, water fountains, water for dogs, separate small dog area. Access for the disabled.

Jacinto Creek Park - Dog Park - Elk Grove
cityofsacramento.org
8600 W. Stockton Blvd.
Daily 5 a.m.-10 p.m.
Fenced, 2 acres, double-gated entry, water fountain for dogs, turf and decomposed granite areas, trees, obstacle course for dogs, benches.

Ernie Smith Dog Park - El Verano
sonoma-county.org
18776 Gilman Dr.
Daily dawn-dusk.
Fenced, ½ acre, double-gated entry, water fountain for dogs, picnic tables, disposal bags, trash can, free parking.

Elizabeth Anne Perrone Dog Park - Glen Ellen
sonoma-county.org
13630 Sonoma Hwy. in Sonoma Valley Regional Park (SR 12 between Arnold Drive and Madrone Road)
Daily dawn-dusk. Parking fee $5 or annual park pass.
Fenced, 1 acre, double-gated entry, covered gazebo, shade trees, water fountain for dogs, disposal bags, trash can.

Huntington Dog Beach - Huntington Beach
dogbeach.org
Pacific Coast Highway between 21st and Seapoint streets
Daily 5 a.m.-10 p.m.; parking lot closes at 10 p.m.
Unfenced, benches and tables on the bluffs above the beach, disposal bags, trash cans, metered parking, restrooms. Dogs may be off leash anywhere on the beach while under an owner's supervision. Access for the disabled to the sand.

Laguna Niguel Pooch Park - Laguna Niguel
ci.laguna-niguel.ca.us
31461 Golden Lantern near Chapparosa Park
Tues.-Thurs. and Sat. 7 a.m.-dusk, Sun. 8 a.m.-dusk, Mon. and Fri. noon-dusk.
Fenced, 1 acre, wood chip ground cover, picnic tables, shelters, disposal bag dispenser, parking, restroom, water faucet with hose, separate fenced area for small dogs. Access for the disabled.

Long Beach Recreation Dog Park - Long Beach
recreationdogpark.org
5201 E. 7th St. at Park Avenue
Daily 6 a.m.-10 p.m.; closed Mondays until noon for
maintenance
Fenced, 2 acres, lighted, trees, crushed-granite surface,
benches, tables, disposal bags, trash cans, parking, water,
separate fenced area for small dogs. Access for the disabled.

Mill Valley Dog Park - Mill Valley
millvalleydogpark.org
Camino Alto and Sycamore Ave.
Daily dawn-dusk
Partially fenced, 3 acres, trees, shade, disposal bags, trash
cans, water. The park fronts Richardson Bay and is fenced on
the land sides only. Parking is available about 350 feet from
the park; dogs must be leashed from the parking areas to the
park. Access for the disabled.

Morgan Hill Dog Park - Morgan Hill
morganhilldog.org
Edmundson Avenue and Monterey Road (entrance is shared
with Centennial Recreation Center)Daily sunrise-sunset; closed
Wednesday morning for maintenance
Fenced, between 2 and 3 acres, separate small dog area,
natural grass, trees, tables, parking, water, double-gated entry,
bulletin board, disposal bags, trash cans.

Palm Springs Dog Park - Palm Springs
palmspringsca.gov
3200 E. Tahquitz Canyon Way, behind City Hall
Daily dawn-10 p.m.
Fenced, lighted, double-gated entry, trees, benches, tables,
shelter, disposal bags, trash cans, parking, phones, dual-level
water fountains, separate areas for large and small dogs,
antique fire hydrants, unusual iron fence created by sculptor
Phill Evans. Access for the disabled.

Alice's Dog Park - Pasadena
pasadenapooch.org
3026 E. Orange Grove (located within Vina Vieja Park, east of
Sierra Madre Boulevard)
Daily dawn-dusk
Fenced, 2.5 acres for large dogs, 1 acre for small dogs,
double-gated entry, trees, benches, water, shelter, disposal
bags, trash cans, parking. Access for the disabled.

Redondo Beach Dog Park - Redondo Beach
rbdogpark.com
Southeast corner of 190th Street and Flagler Lane
Daily dawn-dusk; closed Wed. dawn-noon for maintenance.
Fenced, trees, benches, disposal bags, trash cans, parking,
phones, water, separate fenced area for small dogs. Access
for the disabled.

Bannon Creek Park - Sacramento
cityofsacramento.org
2780 Azevedo Dr. (near West El Camino Avenue)
Daily 5 a.m.-10 p.m.
Fenced, .6 acres, double-gated entry, benches, disposal bag
dispensers, water fountain/faucet for dogs.

Glenbrook Dog Park - Sacramento
cityofsacramento.org
8500 La Riviera Dr. in Glenbrook Park, behind the little league
fields
Daily 5 a.m.-10 p.m.
Fenced, 1 acre, double-gated entry, water fountain for dogs,
shade, trees, seating, picnic tables.

Granite Dog Park - Sacramento
cityofsacramento.org
Ramona Avenue off Power Inn Road in Granite Regional Park
Daily 5 a.m.-10 p.m.
Fenced, 2 acres, double-gated entry, bench, disposal bags,
trash cans, water spigot for dogs. Access for the disabled.

Jacinto Creek Park Dog Park - Sacramento
cityofsacramento.org
8600 W. Stockton Blvd., South Sacramento
Daily 5 a.m.-10 p.m.
Fenced, 2 acres, double-gated entry, drinking fountain for
dogs, turf and decomposed granite areas, trees, obstacle
course for dogs, benches.

North Natomas Regional Park Dog Park - Sacramento
cityofsacramento.org
2501 New Market Dr.
Daily dawn-dusk
Fenced, 2.5 acres, separate small dog area, grass and
crushed granite surface, benches, trash cans, water.

Partner Park - Sacramento
cityofsacramento.org
5699 South Land Park Dr. at Fruitridge Road (behind the
Belle Cooledge Community Center)
Daily 5 a.m.-10 p.m.
Fenced, 2 acres, lighted, double-gated entry, landscaped with
turf and mature trees, bench, disposal bags, trash cans, water
spigot for dogs. Access for the disabled.

Regency Community Park - Dog Park - Sacramento
cityofsacramento.org
5500 Honor Pkwy. in North Natomas
Daily 5 a.m.-10 p.m.
Fenced, 2 acres, double-gated entry, water fountain for dogs,
turf and decomposed granite areas, trees, benches.

Sutters Landing Dog Park - Sacramento
cityofsacramento.org
20 28th St. (cross street is B Street)
Daily dawn-dusk
Fenced, 2.5 acres, separate small dog area, trash cans,
water.

Tanzanite Community Park - Sacramento
cityofsacramento.org
2220 Tanzanite Way in Tanzanite Community Park
Daily 5 a.m.-10 p.m.
Fenced, 2 acres, double-gated entry, landscaped with turf and
native grass, trees, benches, disposal bags, trash cans, water
fountain for dogs.

Balboa Park - San Diego
sandiego.gov
Daily 24 hours.
Unfenced, large field.
Two off-leash areas:
(1) Nate's Point at El Prado, on the southwest side of Cabrillo
Bridge
(2) Morley Field, northwest of the tennis courts

Cadman Community Park - San Diego
sandiego.gov
4280 Avati Dr.
Daily 7-9:30 a.m. and 5-7:30 p.m., in summer; 7:30-10 a.m.
and 4:30-7 p.m., rest of year.
Unfenced.

Capehart Park (Pacific Beach) - San Diego
sandiego.gov
Soledad Mountain Road and Feldspar Street
Daily 24 hours.
Fenced, 1 acre, picnic tables, benches, parking, separate
grass-turf areas for large and small dogs, areas to provide
water to dogs, water fountain.

Dog Beach - San Diego
sandiego.gov
Voltaire Street in Ocean Beach (enter the parking lot at the
west end of Voltaire Street)
Daily 24 hours.
Unfenced, disposal bags, trash cans, water, restrooms nearby.
Access for the disabled.

Doyle Community Park - San Diego
sandiego.gov
8175 Regents Rd. (behind the Doyle Recreation Center)
Daily 24 hours.
Fenced, no lights, separate grass-turf areas for large and small dogs.

Fiesta Island - San Diego
sandiego.gov
Part of Mission Bay Park
Daily 6 a.m.-10 p.m.
This island allows dogs anywhere outside the fenced areas.

Grape Street Park - San Diego
sandiego.gov
Grape Street and Granada Avenue
Mon.-Fri. 7:30 a.m.-9 p.m., Sat.-Sun. and holidays 9-9.
Unfenced, 5 acres, lighted, trees, benches, tables, trash cans, parking, restrooms, water.

Kearny Mesa Community Park - San Diego
sandiego.gov
3170 Armstrong St.
Daily 6:30 a.m.-10 p.m.
Unfenced, 1 acre, lights, water.

San Dimas Dog Park - San Dimas
sandimasdogpark.org
301 Horsethief Canyon Rd. (cross streets are Sycamore and San Dimas Canyon Road)
Daily dawn-dusk (closed alternating Wednesdays from noon-2 for maintenance)
Fenced, 1 acre, double-gated entry, trees, grass, benches, shelter, tables, separate small dog area, disposal bags, trash cans, water, parking. Access for the disabled.

San Francisco
San Francisco regularly reviews its off-leash ("dog play area") policies. Refer to sfgov.org for the most recent information on dog parks.

Alta Plaza Park - San Francisco
sfgov.org
Clay Street between Scott and Steiner streets on the second terrace of the park
Daily 6 a.m.-10 p.m.
Unfenced, ½ acre; dogs must be under firm voice control.

Bernal Heights - San Francisco
sfgov.org
Bernal Heights Boulevard at the top of the hill
Daily 6 a.m.-10 p.m.
Unfenced; dogs must be under firm voice control.

Buena Vista Park - San Francisco
sfgov.org
Buena Vista West Avenue at Central Avenue
Daily 6 a.m.-10 p.m.
Unfenced; dogs must be under firm voice control.

Corona Heights - San Francisco
sfgov.org
Roosevelt Way and Museum Way in the field next to the Randall Museum
Daily 6 a.m.-10 p.m.
Fenced.

Dolores Park - San Francisco
sfgov.org
Between Church and Dolores streets, south of the tennis courts and soccer field
Daily 6 a.m.-10 p.m.
Unfenced; dogs must be under firm voice control.

Douglass Park - San Francisco
sfgov.org
27th and Douglass streets, upper field
Daily 6 a.m.-10 p.m.
Unfenced; dogs must be under firm voice control.

Eureka Valley Recreation Center - San Francisco
sfgov.org
Collingwood Street, adjacent to the tennis courts and east of the baseball diamond
Daily 6 a.m.-10 p.m.
Fenced.

Golden Gate Park - San Francisco
sfgov.org
Four off-leash areas:
(1) Southeast section bounded by Lincoln Way, King Drive and 5th and 7th avenues
(2) Northeast section at Stanyan and Grove streets
(3) South-central area bounded by King Drive, Middle Drive and 34th and 38th avenues
(4) Fenced dog-training area near 38th Avenue and Fulton Street

Lafayette Park - San Francisco
sfgov.org
Near Sacramento Street between Octavia and Gough streets
Daily 6 a.m.-10 p.m.
Unfenced; dogs must be under firm voice control.

Lake Merced - San Francisco
sfgov.org
Lake Merced Boulevard and Middlefield Drive, northern lake area
Daily 6 a.m.-10 p.m.
Unfenced; dogs must be under firm voice control.

McKinley Square - San Francisco
sfgov.org
San Bruno Avenue and 20th Street, on the west slope
Daily 6 a.m.-10 p.m.
Unfenced; dogs must be under firm voice control.

McLaren Park - San Francisco
sfgov.org
Daily 6 a.m.-10 p.m.
Two off-leash areas:
(1) Top of hill at Shelly Drive and Mansell Street
(2) South entrance at 1600 block of Geneva Avenue, exclusive of natural area (the open area fenced on roadway)

Mountain Lake Park - San Francisco
sfgov.org
North of Lake Street at 8th Avenue, east end of the park
Daily 6 a.m.-10 p.m.
Unfenced; dogs must be under firm voice control.

Potrero Hill Mini Park - San Francisco
sfgov.org
22nd Street between Arkansas and Connecticut streets
Daily 6 a.m.-10 p.m.
Unfenced; dogs must be under firm voice control.

St. Mary's Recreation Center - San Francisco
sfgov.org
Justin and Benton streets, lower terrace of the park
Daily 6 a.m.-10 p.m.
Fenced.

Stern Grove - San Francisco
sfgov.org
Wawona Street between 21st and 23rd avenues, north side
Daily 6 a.m.-10 p.m.
Unfenced; dogs must be under firm voice control.

Upper Noe Recreation Center - San Francisco
sfgov.org
30th Street between Church and Sanchez streets, behind and along the baseball field
Daily 6 a.m.-10 p.m.
Fenced.

Field of Dogs - San Rafael
fieldofdogs.org
3540 Civic Center Dr. (near the intersection of US 101 and North San Pedro Road)
Daily dawn-dusk.
Fenced, double-gated entry, trees, benches, tables, shelter, disposal bags, trash cans, parking, water. Access for the disabled.

DeTurk Roundbarn Park - Santa Rosa
ci.santa-rosa.ca.us
819 Donahue St. (between West 8th and 9th streets)
Daily dawn-dusk.
Fenced, water (small neighborhood park).

Doyle Park Dog Park - Santa Rosa
ci.santa-rosa.ca.us
700 Hoen Ave. in Doyle Park (go west on Sonoma Avenue, turn left on Hoen Avenue and then turn right into the parking lot; the fenced dog park is behind the stadium)
Daily dawn-dusk.
Fenced, bench, disposal bags, water, separate areas for large and small dogs.

Galvin Dog Park - Santa Rosa
ci.santa-rosa.ca.us
3330 Yulupa Ave. in Don Galvin Park (next to Bennet Valley Golf Course)
Daily dawn-dusk.
Fenced, ½ acre, double-gated entry, trees, trash cans, parking, water, picnic tables, restrooms. Access for the disabled.

Northwest Community Dog Park - Santa Rosa
ci.santa-rosa.ca.us
2620 W. Steele Ln. in Northwest Community Park (go west on Gurneville Road, turn right on Marlow Road and then turn right at the first traffic light into the park's parking lot; walk east along the path to the dog park on the left)
Daily dawn-dusk.
Fenced, ½ acre, benches, disposal bags, trash cans, restrooms nearby, water, separate area for small dogs.

Rincon Valley Dog Park - Santa Rosa
ci.santa-rosa.ca.us
5108 Badger Rd. in Rincon Valley Community Park
Daily dawn-dusk.
Fenced, ½ acre, trees, benches, tables, disposal bags, trash cans, parking, phones, restrooms, water, separate fenced areas for large and small dogs (area for large dogs closed during the winter), fenced pond area for dogs (open year-round). Monitors are present during peak hours to enforce rules. Access for the disabled.

Off-leash, unfenced, under voice control areas:

700 Doyle Park Drive - Santa Rosa
ci.santa-rosa.ca.us
700 Doyle Park Dr. (go west on Sonoma Avenue, turn left on Hoen Avenue and then turn right into the parking lot; the unfenced, off-leash area is to the right of the fenced dog park)
Daily 6-8 a.m.

Franklin Park - Santa Rosa
ci.santa-rosa.ca.us
2095 Franklin Ave.
Daily 6-8 a.m.

Southwest Community - Santa Rosa
ci.santa-rosa.ca.us
1698 Hearn Ave.
Daily 6-8 a.m.

Youth Community - Santa Rosa
ci.santa-rosa.ca.us
1725 Fulton Rd.
Daily 6-8 a.m.

Remington Dog Park - Sausalito
sausalitodogpark.org
Ebbtide Avenue at Bridgeway Boulevard
Mon.-Fri. 7-7, Sat.-Sun. 8-7
Fenced, lighted, safety-gated entry, picnic tables, benches, tents for shelter, scoops and scooper cleaning station, trash cans, parking, water, tennis balls and racquets provided.

Animal Care Center Dog Park - Sebastopol
sonoma-county.org
500 Ragle Rd.
Daily dawn-dusk. Parking fee $5 or annual park pass.
Fenced, ½ acre, double-gated entry, disposal bags, trash can, water fountain for dogs.

Arbor Dog Park - Seal Beach
arbordogpark.com
4665 Lampson Ave., between Valley View Street and Los Alamitos Boulevard off Lampson Avenue
Daily dawn-dusk; closed Thursday 8 a.m.-noon for maintenance. Non-resident user license available for a $12 annual fee; see Web site
Fenced, 2.2 acres, double-gated entry, trees, benches, disposal bags, trash cans, water, parking. Access for the disabled.

Sierra Madre Dog Park - Sierra Madre
cityofsierramadre.com
611 E. Sierra Madre Blvd. in Sierra Vista Park, south of the tennis courts
Daily 6 a.m.-10 p.m. Permit required; daily permit $5. Daily and annual permits are available at City Hall; the Sierra Madre Police Department, 242 W. Sierra Madre Blvd.; or the Sierra Madre Community Recreation Center, 611 E. Sierra Madre Blvd.
Fenced, lighted, double-gated entry, trees, benches, disposal bags, trash cans, parking, phones, restrooms, water, separate fenced areas for large/active dogs and "special needs" dogs. Access for the disabled.

Baldy View Dog Park - Upland
baldyviewdogpark.com
11th Street between Mountain Avenue and San Antonio Avenue
Daily dawn-dusk.
Fenced, 1.3 acres, double-gated entry and exit, grass turf, shade trees, benches, free parking, separate areas for large and small dogs, water stations for dogs.

Heather Farms Dog Park - Walnut Creek
wcdog.org
550 N. San Carlos Dr. in Heather Farms Park
Mon.-Fri. sunrise-sunset, Sat.-Sun. and holidays 8 a.m.-sunset
Fenced, double-gated entry, separate areas for large and small dogs, grass, trees, benches, tables, disposal bags, water, trash cans, parking. Access for the disabled.

COLORADO

Grandview Off-Leash Dog Park - Aurora
auroragov.org
17900 E. Quincy Ave. (just east of Pitkin Street, adjacent to Quincy Reservoir on the lake's west side)
Daily dawn-dusk.
Fenced, trash cans, parking, water.

East Boulder Community - Boulder City
bouldercolorado.gov
5660 Sioux Dr.
Daily dawn-dusk.
Fenced, disposal bags, trash cans, parking, water, fenced-off swimming area. Access for the disabled.

Foothills Community Park - Boulder City
bouldercolorado.gov
Locust Avenue and Lee Hill Road, west of Broadway Street
Daily dawn-dusk.
Fenced, 2 acres, separate areas for large and small dogs, disposal bags, trash cans, parking, water. Access for the disabled.

Howard H. Hueston Park - Boulder City
bouldercolorado.gov
34th Street near O'Neal Parkway
Daily dawn-dusk.
Unfenced, trees, benches, tables, trash cans, parking. Dogs must be under voice control and kept in sight at all times. Access for the disabled.

Valmont Dog Park - Boulder City
bouldercolorado.gov
Valmont and Airport roads
Daily dawn-dusk.
Fenced, 3 acres, disposal bags, trash cans, parking, water (available seasonally). Access for the disabled.

Carter Park Dog Park - Breckenridge
townofbreckenridge.com
South end of High Street
Daily dawn-dusk
Fenced, almost 1 acre, grass, trees, benches, tables, disposal bags, trash cans, water, parking. Access for the disabled.

Palmer Park - Colorado Springs
springsgov.com
Maizeland Road and Academy Boulevard
Daily 5 a.m.-11 p.m., May-Oct.; 5 a.m.-9 p.m., rest of year.
Fenced, benches, tables, disposal bags, trash cans, parking, restrooms, water. Access for the disabled.

Rampart Dog Park - Colorado Springs
springsgov.com
8270 Lexington Dr. (from the intersection of Lexington Drive and North Union Boulevard, go north on Lexington, then turn left into the park entrance)
Daily 5 a.m.-11 p.m., May-Oct.; 5 a.m.-9 p.m., rest of year.
Fenced, trees, benches, disposal bags, trash cans, parking, water. Access for the disabled.

Barnum Park - Denver
denvergov.org
Hooker Street and West 5th Avenue
Daily dawn-dusk.
Natural barriers (turf with split-rail fencing to delineate boundaries), 3 acres, trees, disposal bags, trash cans, parking, restroom, bulletin board.

Berkeley Park - Denver
denvergov.org
Sheridan Boulevard and West 46th Avenue, west of the lake
Daily dawn-dusk.
Fenced, 2 acres, turf, double-gate entry, trees, disposal bags, trash cans, parking, bulletin board.

Fuller Park - Denver
denvergov.org
Franklin Street and East 29th Avenue, northwest section (enter from 29th Avenue)
Daily dawn-dusk.
Fenced, 1 acre, turf, double-gate entry, disposal bags, trash cans, bulletin board, on-street neighborhood parking only.

Green Valley Ranch East Park - Denver
denvergov.org
Jebel Street and East 45th Avenue, southwest section (dog park accessible from parking lot)
Daily dawn-dusk.
Natural barriers (native vegetation and split-rail fencing to delineate boundaries), 2 acres, disposal bags, trash cans, parking.

Kennedy Park - Denver
denvergov.org
Hampden Avenue and South Dayton Street, southwest section
Daily dawn-dusk.
Natural barriers (native vegetation and split-rail fencing to delineate boundaries), 3 acres, disposal bags, trash cans, bulletin board, very limited parking (complex parking lot not open to dog park visitors).

City Bark at City Park - Pueblo
pueblo.us
800 Goodnight Ave.
Daily 6 a.m.-10 p.m.
Fenced, 2.3 acres, double-gated entry, trees, benches, shade, tables, disposal bags, trash cans, water, parking. Access for the disabled.

Westminster Dog Park - Westminster
ci.westminster.co.us
105th Avenue and Simms Street
Daily sunrise-sunset
Partially fenced, 420-acre open space, trees, benches, shelter, shade, disposal bags, trash cans, water, parking. Access for the disabled.

CONNECTICUT

Southbury Dog Park - Southbury
southbury-ct.org
Roxbury Road (Route 67), adjacent to Red Sable Horse Farm
Daily sunrise-sunset
Fenced, double-gated entry, benches, tables, separate small dog area, disposal bags, trash cans, water, parking, onsite stream accessed by a new staircase.

DELAWARE

Levels Road Park - Middletown
Levels Road (Route 15), located within Levels Road Park
Daily 6 a.m.-dusk
Fenced, 5-acre large dog area, 3-acre small dog area, double-gated entry, trees, benches, shade, grass, disposal bags, trash cans, water, parking.

Rockford Park Off-Leash Area - Wilmington
destateparks.com/park
Park Drive and Red Oak Road
Daily 8 a.m.-dusk
Unfenced, more than 5 acres, trees, benches, shade, disposal bags, trash cans, water.

FLORIDA

Canine Cove at South County Regional Park - Boca Raton
pbcgov.com
12551 Glades Rd., west of Boca Raton in South County Regional Park
Daily dawn-dusk; closed Wednesday noon-3 for maintenance
Fenced, 4 acres, paved pathways, shaded sitting areas, disposal bag dispensers and receptacles, trash cans, restrooms and parking nearby, gazebos, separate areas for large and small dogs, canine drinking stations, dog wash area.

Happy Tails Canine Park - Bradenton
mymanatee.org
51st Street West at G.T. Bray Park, about halfway between Manatee Avenue and Cortez Road
Daily dawn-dusk
Eight-foot fence, 3 acres, trees, benches, tables, disposal bags, trash cans, parking, restrooms nearby, water.

Dr. Paul's Memorial Dog Park - Coral Springs
toppetcare.com/petutopiawelcome.html
Sportsplex Drive in the Sportsplex Regional Park Complex (park off Sportsplex Drive at the west pedestrian entrance)
Daily 7:30 a.m.-9:30 p.m.
Enclosed, lighted, trees, shaded area, paved running path, picnic table, gazebo, disposal bag dispensers, trash cans, indoor restroom, separate areas for large and small dogs, water fountains for dogs and people, dog shower, dog statues, weatherproof dog agility equipment.

The Dog Park in Lake Ida Park - Delray Beach
pbcgov.com
2929 Lake Ida Rd. (take the Atlantic Avenue West exit off I-95, proceed west to Congress Avenue, go north on Congress for 1 mile, turn right onto Lake Ida Road and proceed east under I-95; park entrance is on the left)
Daily dawn-dusk; closed Thurs. noon-3 for maintenance.
Fenced, 2.5 acres, partial paved pathway, eight shaded sitting areas, disposal bag dispensers and receptacles, restrooms and parking nearby, separate fenced areas for large and small dogs, two canine drinking stations, dog washing area, information kiosk.

Pooch Pines Dog Park at Okeeheelee Park - Delray Beach
pbcgov.com
7715 Forest Hill Blvd. (off I-95 exit Forest Hill Boulevard, west to the main Okeeheelee Park entrance on the north side of the road; follow the park road to the Pooch Pines sign, turn right and continue to the top of the hill)
Daily dawn-dusk; closed Wed. noon-3 for maintenance.
Fenced, 5 acres, paved pathways, shaded sitting areas, disposal bag dispensers and receptacles, trash cans, restrooms and parking nearby, separate areas for large and small dogs, canine drinking stations, dog washing area.

Bark Park at Snyder Park - Fort Lauderdale
ci.fort-lauderdale.fl.us
3299 S.W. 4th Ave.
Daily 7 a.m.-dusk; closed Thursday 8-11 a.m. for maintenance. Closed Jan. 1 and Dec. 25.
Entry fee varies; canine beach $7.
Fenced, two open-air pavilions, benches, disposal bags, trash cans, parking, restrooms, water, separate area for small dogs, two hose stations, water fountains, agility equipment, small nature area with more than 20 labeled native trees, canine swimming in East Lake, canine beach (hours vary). Access for the disabled. **Note:** Dogs must remain in the car until arrival at Bark Park and are not permitted in the remainder of Snyder Park.

Millennium Dog Park - Ocala
millenniumdogpark.com
2399 S.E. 32nd Ave.
Tues.-Wed. and Sat.-Sun. 8 a.m.-7 p.m., in summer; 8-6 in winter
Fenced, 4.5 acres, double-gated entry, grass, trees, benches, shelter, shade, small dog area, disposal bags, trash cans, water, parking. Access for the disabled.

Dog Leg Park at Buffalo Creek - Palmetto
mymanatee.org
7550 69th St. E.
Daily dawn-dusk
Fenced, 3 acres, trees, separate small dog area, disposal bags, doggie drinking fountains, shelter.

Paw Park of Historic Sanford - Sanford
pawparksanford.org
427 French Ave. (US 17/92) in Sanford's Historic District, 20 minutes north of downtown Orlando. From I-4, take the SR 46 exit (exit 101C, Sanford/Mount Dora), proceed east on SR 46 approximately 4 miles to French Avenue, turn right (southbound) and get into the left thru-lane; the Paw Park is on the left just past the Burger King
Daily 7:30 a.m.-8 p.m.
Fenced, double-gated entry, shaded with mature oak trees, historic lighting, paved walkway, benches, tables, disposal bag dispensers, parking, self-watering bowls, water misting station, dog showers, separate area for small dogs, community bulletin board. Access for the disabled.

Davis Islands Dog Park - Tampa
tampagov.net
1002 Severn St.
Daily dawn-dusk
Fenced, with two areas at the south end of the island: a 1-acre dry area and a 1.5-acre beach with more than 200 feet of waterfront. Both areas have double-gated entries, disposal bags, trash cans and water. Designated off-leash area on the beach.

Gadsden Park - Tampa
tampagov.net
6901 S. MacDill Ave., southwest corner of the grounds
Daily dawn-dusk
Fenced, 1 acre, double-gated entry, water, disposal bags, trash cans, benches, tables, shade trees.

Giddens Park - Tampa
tampagov.net
5202 N. 12th St.
Daily dawn-dusk
Fenced, 1 acre, double-gated entry, drinking fountains for dogs and people, disposal bags, trash cans, benches, tables, shade trees.

James Urbanski Dog Park at Al Lopez Park - Tampa
tampagov.net
4810 N. Himes Ave.
Daily dawn-dusk
Fenced, separate area for small dogs, double-gated entry, disposal bags, trash cans, benches, tables, shade trees.

Palma Ceia Park - Tampa
tampagov.net
2200 Marti St.
Mon.-Fri. 8 a.m.-dusk or 7:15 p.m. (whichever is earlier), Sat.-Sun. 9 a.m.-dusk or 7:15 p.m. (whichever is earlier).
Fenced, ¾ acre, double-gated entry, disposal bags, trash cans, benches, tables, shade trees.

Picnic Island Park - Tampa
tampagov.net
7409 Picnic Island Blvd.
Daily dawn-dusk
Fenced, double-gated entry, disposal bags, trash cans, benches, tables, shade trees. Designated off-leash area on beach.

Rowlett Park - Tampa
tampagov.net
2401 E. Yukon St.
Daily dawn-dusk
Fenced, 1.75 acre, double-gated entry, disposal bags, trash cans, benches, tables, shade trees, separate areas for large and small dogs, agility equipment.

North Lake Community Park Dog Park - Umatilla
lakecountyfl.gov
40730 Roger Giles Rd. within North Lake Community Park
Daily 6:30 a.m.-9 p.m.
Fenced, double-gated entry, trees, benches, shelter, shade, disposal bags, grass, trash cans, water, parking, lights. Access for the disabled.

Brohard Beach & Paw Park - Venice
venicegov.com
1600 Harbor Dr. S.
Daily 7 a.m.-dusk
Six-foot fence, trees, benches, tables, shelter, disposal bags, trash cans, parking, water, dog shower, separate area for small dogs, community bulletin board. Dog Beach is accessed by a boardwalk from Paw Park. Dogs are permitted in a restricted area along Brohard Beach as indicated by beach signs. Access for the disabled.

Woodmere Park & Woodmere Paw Park - Venice
scgov.net
3951 Woodmere Park Blvd. (2 blocks north of US 41 on Jacaranda Boulevard)
Daily dawn-dusk.
Fenced, 2.5 acres, double-gated entry, trees, benches, tables, disposal bags, trash cans, parking, restrooms, water, double-gated section for small dogs near the front gate, dog shower, community bulletin board.

IDAHO

Moscow Dog Park - Moscow
dogparkfriends.org
2019 White Ave. (adjacent to the Humane Society of the Palouse)
Daily dawn-dusk
Fenced, 1 acre, grass, two double-gated entries, trees, shade, benches, disposal bags, trash cans, water, parking, large tire structures for dogs to climb on or run through. Access for the disabled.

Nampa Dog Park - Nampa
nampaparks.org
East Amity Avenue and 2nd Street South, near the Kings Road overpass
Daily half an hour before sunrise to half an hour after sunset
Fenced, 6 acres, grass, double-gated entry, trees, benches, walking trails, shelter, shade, tables, separate small dog area, disposal bags, trash cans, water, parking. Access for the disabled.

IOWA

Rita's Ranch Off Leash Dog Park - Iowa City
jcdogpac.org
Scott Boulevard between E. Court and Muscatine Avenue
Daily dawn-dusk
Day pass $5, yearly tag $25 ($5 discount for neutered dogs)
Fenced, approximately 3 acres, double-gated entry, disposal bags, trash cans, parking.

Thornberry Off Leash Dog Park - Iowa City
jcdogpak.org
End of Foster Road; closest cross street is Canton Street
Daily dawn-dusk
Day pass $5, yearly tag $25 ($5 discount for neutered dogs)
Fenced, 10 acres, four separately fenced areas (all dogs, small dogs, training area and a pond for dog swimming and wading), grass, trees, disposal bags, trash cans, asphalt walking path, parking. Water is trucked in except during winter; bring your own container. Access for the disabled.

Lewis and Clark Dog Park - Sioux City
sola-sc.org
5100 Correctionville Rd.
Daily 7 a.m.-dusk
Fenced, 4 acres for larger dogs, 1 acre for small dogs, double-gated entry, trees, grass, benches, trash cans, water, parking, disposal bags. Access for the disabled.

ILLINOIS

Rover's Run Dog Park - Homewood
hfparks.com, (708) 957-0300
Near 191st Street and Center Avenue in Apollo Park
Daily dawn-dusk.
Annual membership fee $25 (non-residents); $15 (residents). A list of current vaccinations is required.
Fenced, 3 acres, double-gated entry, separate training area and entrance, benches, covered picnic tables, free parking, walking path, water fountain for dogs and people.

Bradley Dog Park - Peoria
peoriaparks.org
1314 N. Park Rd. (cross street Farmington Road)
Daily dawn-dusk
Fenced, 5 acres, double-gated entry, trees, benches, shade, tables, separate small dog area, disposal bags, trash cans, water, parking, grass and wood mulch. Access for the disabled.

East Side Sports Complex Dog Park - St. Charles
st-charlesparks.org
3565 Legacy Blvd. (east of Kirk Road and about 1 mile south of Rt. 64)
Daily 9 a.m.-dusk (weather permitting)
Fenced, just under 1 acre, separate small dog area, interactive play equipment, water.

West Side Community Park Dog Park - St. Charles
st-charlesparks.org
Corner of Campton Hills and Peck Road
Daily 9 a.m.-dusk, March-November (weather permitting)
Fenced, three-quarters of an acre, double-gated entry, trees, benches, disposal bags, trash cans, parking, water.

KANSAS

El Dorado Dog Park - El Dorado
visiteldoradoks.com
400 East Locust
Daily dawn-dusk
Fenced, one-half acre, double-gated entry, trees, grass, benches, water, disposal bags, trash cans, parking. Access for the disabled.

KENTUCKY

Kenton County Kentucky Paw Park - Covington
kentonpawpark.com
3950 Madison Pike (Rt. 17) at Pioneer Park
Daily sunrise-sunset
Fenced, double-gated entry, trees, grass, benches, tables, separate areas for large and small dogs, disposal bags. Beautiful creekside setting with additional area for agility (not always available).

Judy Rains Memorial Dog Park - Richmond
parks.richmond.ky.us
299 Lake Reba Dr.
Daily 8 a.m.-dusk
Fenced, half an acre, double-gated entry, trees, grass, benches, tables, separate small dog area, disposal bags, trash cans, water, parking, lights.

MARYLAND

Rebel's Dog Park - Fallston
HarfordShelter.org
2208 Connolly Rd. (at the junction with Rt. 152)
Mon.-Fri. 8-6, Sat. 8-5, Sun. 8-4
Fenced, double-gated entry, benches, shade, separate small
dog area, disposal bags, trash cans, water, parking.

MASSACHUSETTS

The South Boston Bark Park - Boston
sbbarkpark.org
Columbia Road and Day Boulevard
Daily dawn-8 p.m.
Fenced, 3,000 square feet, double-gated entry, trees, benches,
separate small dog area, trash cans, water, pea stone with
cement walkways, street parking. Access for the disabled.

French Park Dog Park - Egremont
FrenchParkDogPark.com
Baldwin Hill Road (North/South) and Prospect Lake Road
Daily dawn-dusk
Fenced, approximately 1 acre, double-gated entry, trees,
grass, benches, disposal bags, trash cans, parking.

Pilgrim Bark Park - Provincetown
provincetowndogpark.com
Shank Painter Road at Rt. 6. Do not park on Shank Painter
Road; park on the east side of Rt. 6.
Daily dawn-dusk
Fenced, nearly 1 acre, separate small dog area, disposal
bags, trash cans. Many features, like the custom benches and
welcome sign, have been made by local artists.

MICHIGAN

Pet Supplies "Plus" Dog Park at Hillcrest Park - Grand Rapids
grdogpark.com
1415 Lyon St. N.E. and Benjamin Street N.E. at Hillcrest Park
Daily dawn-dusk
Fenced, 1 acre, double-gated entry, separate small dog area,
shade, water, disposal bags. Street parking is available, or
park at Fuller Park and walk to Hillcrest.

Orion Oaks Bark Park - Lake Orion
oakgov.com
South of Clarkston Road on Joslyn Road (park at the north
Joslyn Road entrance and follow the signs)
Daily half-hour before dawn to half-hour after dusk, or as
posted.
A park pass is required; a daily pass is available at the Lake
Orion Township office (open Mon.-Fri.) on Joslyn Road south
of the park; or at the Independence Oaks County Park (open
daily) on Sashabaw Road, 2.5 miles north of I-75.
Day pass per private vehicle $12 (non-resident); $7 (resident);
$4 (ages 63+). Annual pass per private vehicle $46
(non-resident); $30 (resident); $28 (ages 63+).
Fenced, 7 acres, trees, benches, tables, disposal bags, trash
cans, parking, portable toilet, water. A portion of Lake Sixteen
is reserved for canine swimming. Access for the disabled.

Soldan Dog Park at Hawk Island County Park - Lansing
lansingdogparks.com
1601 E. Cavanaugh Rd., just north of Hawk Island County
Park; the dog park main entrance is through the park. The
dog park also can be accessed from the west off the River
Trail in Scott Woods; drive to the very north end of the Hawk
Island parking area, then walk a short distance (with your dog
or dogs on-leash) past the Hawk Island Maintenance Building
to the main dog park entrance.
Daily 6 a.m. to half an hour after sunset, May 15-Aug. 15;
daily 7 a.m. to half an hour after sunset, Aug. 16-Sept. 14;
daily 8 a.m. to half an hour after sunset, rest of year.
Parking fee Tues.-Sun. $2 for residents, $4 for non-residents
Fenced, 17 acres, double-gated entry, diverse natural area
with trails, a large pond and an open field, disposal bags,
parking, dog and human drinking fountains. Access for the
disabled.

Lyon Oaks Bark Park - Lyon Township
oakgov.com
Pontiac Trail between Wixom and Old Plank roads
Daily half-hour before dawn to half-hour after dusk, or as
posted.
A park pass is required and is available at the park.
Day pass per private vehicle $12 (non-resident); $7 (resident);
$4 (ages 63+). Annual pass per private vehicle $46
(non-resident); $30 (resident); $28 (ages 63+).
Fenced, 13 acres of open fields, benches, tables, disposal
bags, trash cans, parking, restrooms, water pump.

MINNESOTA

Note: In the greater Minneapolis area there are multiple
off-leash sites within a 15-minute drive of downtown
Minneapolis/St. Paul. There are additional sites in rural/
suburban areas of the seven-county metropolitan area. Some
parks require a permit for use. Please read descriptions
carefully.

Alimagnet Dog Park - Burnsville (south metro suburb)
alimagnetdogpark.org
1200 Alimagnet Pkwy. (from central St. Paul, go south on
I-35E to the CR 42 exit, east to CR 11, then north on CR 11
to Alimagnet Parkway and turn right; the dog park is on the
right)
Daily 5 a.m.-10 p.m. Permit required; for more information visit
the Web site or phone the Recreation Department at (952)
895-4500.
Fenced, 7 acres, double-gated entry, wooded areas, open
fields, mowed prairie-grass trail, benches, tables, disposal
bags, trash cans, parking, phones, restrooms, water, pond.

Coates/Dakota County (south metro rural)
co.dakota.mn.us
Blaine Avenue south of CR 46 (160th Street East) in the
center of Dakota County near Coates
Daily 5 a.m.-10 p.m. Permit required.
Fenced, 16 acres of wooded and open spaces with a walking
trail loop, tables, disposal bag dispensers, trash cans, parking,
portable toilets, no surface water; bring your own water.

Elm Creek Park Reserve - Dayton (northwest metro rural)
threeriversparkdistrict.org
13080 Territorial Rd.
Daily 5 a.m.-dusk. Permit required; day permits are available
at the site. Annual special-use permits may be obtained by
phoning Park Guest Services at (763) 559-9000.
Fenced, 30 acres with a mowed trail, trees, tables, trash cans,
parking, restrooms.

Battle Creek Off-Leash Site - Maplewood (east central metro)
co.ramsey.mn.us
Lower Afton and McKnight roads
Daily dawn-dusk. No permit required.
Partially fenced, 12 acres, tables, trash cans, parking.

Franklin Terrace - Minneapolis
minneapolisparks.org
Franklin Terrace and 30th Avenue South
Daily 6 a.m.-10 p.m. Permit required.
Fully fenced, 1.6 acres, double-gated entry at the east and west ends of the site, bench, disposal bag dispensers, on-street parking.

Lake of the Isles Park - Minneapolis
minneapolisparks.org
Lake of the Isles Parkway and West 28th Street
Daily 6 a.m.-10 p.m. Permit required.
Fully fenced, 3.6 acres, double-gated entry at the northern end of the site, lighted at the southern end, benches, disposal bag dispensers.

Loring Park - Minneapolis
minneapolisparks.org
Maple Street and Harmon Place
Daily 6 a.m.-10 p.m. Permit required.
Fenced, ¼ acre, disposal bag dispensers, limestone boulders for climbing and sitting, crushed limestone surface.

Minnehaha Park - Minneapolis
minneapolisparks.org
Minnehaha Avenue and East 54th Street
Daily 6 a.m.-10 p.m. Permit required.
Partially fenced, 4.2 acres along the Mississippi River (where dogs can swim), disposal bag dispensers, lighted parking area (parking permit required), portable toilet in parking area.

St. Anthony Parkway - Minneapolis
minneapolisparks.org
St. Anthony Parkway off Central Avenue
Daily 6 a.m.-10 p.m. Permit required.
Fully fenced, 2 acres, double-gated entry at the east and west ends of the park, bench, disposal bag dispensers, parking.

Egan Park's Off-Leash Area - Plymouth
ci.plymouth.mn.us
CR 47 in northwest Plymouth, about 2 blocks west of Dunkirk Lane on the south side of CR 47
Daily dawn-dusk. No permit required.
Unfenced, 10 acres, trash cans; bring your own water and disposal bags.

Cleary Lake Regional Park - Prior Lake (south metro rural)
threeriversparkdistrict.org
18106 Texas Ave.
Daily 5 a.m.-dusk. Permit required; day permits are available at the site. Annual special-use permits may be obtained by phoning Park Guest Services at (763) 559-9000.
Fenced, 35 acres, tables, trash cans, parking, restrooms, pond. Trails are mowed in summer, packed in winter.

Crow-Hassan Park Reserve - Rogers (northwest metro rural)
threeriversparkdistrict.org
Sylvan Lake Road west of Rogers (from I-94, take the Rogers exit and go south through town to the T intersection, turn right on CR 116 and proceed to CR 203, turn left and follow CR 203 to the park entrance)
Daily 5 a.m.-dusk. Permit required; day permits are available at the site. Annual special-use permits may be obtained by phoning Park Guest Services at (763) 559-9000.
Fenced, 30 acres with a mowed trail, trees, tables, trash cans, parking, restrooms.

Woodview Dog Park - Roseville (central)
co.ramsey.mn.us
Larpenteur Avenue, just east of Dale Street (access gate to main off-leash area is about 100 yards down the bike trail)
Daily dawn-dusk. No permit required.
Partially fenced (along bike trail only), 3 acres, trees, tables, disposal bags, trash cans, parking, water, separate fenced area for small dogs. Access for the disabled.

Arlington-Arkwright (ArlArk) Dog Park - St. Paul
stpaul.gov
Arkwright Street at Arlington Avenue (from I-35E, take the Maryland Avenue exit east to Arkwright Street, then go north; the park is on the right)
Daily dawn-dusk. No permit required.
Fenced, 4.5 acres with trails and woods, tables, disposal bags, trash cans, parking. Park users sometimes leave gates open; keep your dog under voice control to prevent escapes.

Rice Creek Off-Leash Site - Shoreview (northeast metro)
co.ramsey.mn.us
Lexington Avenue, just south of CR J
Daily dawn-dusk. No permit required.
Unfenced, 12 acres of flat prairie vegetation, tables, trash cans, parking, small pond.

Otter Lake Dog Park - White Bear Township (northeast suburban)
co.ramsey.mn.us
Otter Lake Road (take I-35E to the CR J exit, then CR J east to Otter Lake Road, following it south to the dog park; the entrance is next to the boat launch)
Daily dawn-dusk. No permit required.
Partially fenced, 10 acres of rolling hills with wooded and open prairie vegetation, separate 1-acre fenced area for small dogs. The park is fenced adjacent to Otter Lake Road and along most of the south boundary, bounded on the east by a large wetland and on the north by Otter Lake.

NEBRASKA

Omaha Dog Park/Hefflinger Dog Park - Omaha
omahadogpark.org
11111 W. Maple Rd. (Old Maple Road and N. 112th Avenue)
Daily dawn-dusk
Fenced, 7.5 acres, double-gated entry, separate small dog area, trees, benches, shade, tables, disposal bags, trash cans, parking. Water is available Memorial Day through Labor Day. The off-leash area is inside the dog park gates; a leash is required in all other areas.

Scottsbluff Dog Park - Scottsbluff
scottsbluff.org
1600 S. Beltline Hwy. West (within Riverside Park and behind the zoo)
Daily dawn-dusk
Fenced, double-gated entry, disposal bags, swimming areas, water, parking. Access for the disabled. The main section is 1.5 acres, the second section is three-quarters of an acre; the surface is kennel rock, mulch and natural turf (near the river).

NEVADA

All Clark County/Las Vegas dog park areas include water, seating and waste receptacles.

Desert Breeze Park Dog Park - Clark County/Las Vegas (NW)
accessclarkcounty.com
8425 W. Spring Mountain Rd. at Durango Drive
Mon.-Fri. 7 a.m.-8 p.m., Sat. 9-4
Three runs, trees.

Desert Inn Dog Park - Clark County/Las Vegas (SE)
accessclarkcounty.com
3570 Vista del Monte Dr. (near Lamb Boulevard and Boulder Highway)
Daily 6 a.m.-11 p.m.

Dog Fancier's Park - Clark County/Las Vegas (SE)
accessclarkcounty.com, (702) 455-8200
5800 E. Flamingo Rd. at Jimmy Durante Boulevard
Daily 6 a.m.-11 p.m. Since this 12-acre park also is used for dog shows and training, phone ahead to confirm schedule.

Molasky Park Dog Park - Clark County/Las Vegas (SE)
accessclarkcounty.com
1065 E. Twain Ave. (west of Maryland Parkway; dog run is south of Twain Avenue)
Daily 6 a.m.-11 p.m.
Ten acres.

Shadow Rock Dog Park - Clark County/Las Vegas (NE)
accessclarkcounty.com
2650 Los Feliz St. at Lake Mead Boulevard (east of Hollywood Boulevard; dog run is east of the park area)
Daily 6 a.m.-11 p.m.
Tree, two shade shelters.

Silverado Ranch Park Dog Park - Clark County/Las Vegas (SE)
accessclarkcounty.com
9855 S. Gillespie St.
Daily 6 a.m.-11 p.m.
Two runs, one for dogs under 30 pounds and another for dogs over 29 pounds; lights.

Sunset Park - Clark County/Las Vegas (SE)
accessclarkcounty.com
2601 E. Sunset Rd. (closest parking is off Eastern Avenue between Sunset and Warm Springs roads)
Daily 6 a.m.-11 p.m.
Two runs for large and small dogs.

NEW HAMPSHIRE

Derry Dog Park - Derry
derry.nh.us
45 Fordway St.
Daily dawn-dusk.
Fenced, ½ acre, double-gated entry, gazebo, picnic tables, separate area for small dogs, bone-shaped dog pool (open in summer only). Tunnel, seesaw, tire jump and other agility items are provided. Children under 9 are not permitted. Rules are posted on fence inside and out. Parking is free but somewhat limited after 25 vehicles.

Dog Park at South Mill Pond - Portsmouth
seacoastdogs.org
South Mill Pond at Junkins Avenue and South Street
Daily dawn-dusk
Fenced, double-gated entry, separate large and small dog areas, stone and grass surface, benches, shelter, tables, disposal bags, trash cans, water, parking.

NEW MEXICO

Santa Fe Village Dog Park - Albuquerque
cabq.gov
5700 Bogart St. N.W.
Daily 6 a.m.-10 p.m.
Fenced, double-gated entry, trees, benches, shade, disposal bags, trash cans, water. Access for the disabled.

NEW YORK

Barkyard-LaSalle Off-Leash Dog Park - Buffalo
thebarkyard.org
101-397 Dar Dr.
Daily dawn-dusk. Small dog hours: Tues. 4-6, Sun. 1-3
Fenced, 1.6 acres, double-gated entry, benches, trash cans. Access for the disabled.

Wegmans Good Dog Park - Liverpool
onondagacountyparks.com
2500 Cold Springs, Onondaga Lake Park
Daily sunrise-sunset
Fenced, 1 acre, double-gated entry, playground quality pea gravel and grass, trees, separate small dog area, agility equipment, benches, water, disposal bags, trash cans, parking.

New York City (Manhattan and boroughs)
urbanhound.com
nycgovparks.org

Canine Court, Van Cortlandt Park - Bronx
West 252nd Street and Broadway (enter on the path on 252nd and follow it about 100 feet to the left)
Daily dawn-dusk.
Fenced with two large runs: a basic dog run and a canine agility playground with teeter-totter, hurdles, ladder, three chutes and a hanging tire.

Ewen Park ("John's Run") - Bronx (Riverdale)
Riverdale to Johnson avenues, south of West 232nd Street and down the steps in the clearing on the right
Daily dawn-dusk.
Unfenced, plastic lawn furniture, scenic views.

Seton Park - Bronx (Riverdale)
West 235th Street and Independence Avenue (west of Independence on 235th Street, near the Spuyten Duyvil Library)
Daily dawn-dusk.

Prospect Park - Brooklyn
fidobrooklyn.org
Grand Army Plaza and Flatbush; off-leash areas may be accessed from all park entrances
Daily 9 p.m.-1 a.m. and 5-9 a.m. At all other times dogs must be on a leash; minimum fine for non-compliance $100. Off-leash areas are the Long Meadow, Nethermead and Peninsula open meadows. Ball fields are off-limits to dogs at all times. **Note:** Use of the park is at the owner's risk. Dogs may be off-leash with appropriate supervision in the three large meadows at the hours specified above; please observe all off-leash rules. Rules are posted online and at park entrances. Dogs must be on a leash at all other places and times.

Owl's Head Park - Brooklyn (Bay Ridge)
68th Street and Shore Road
Tree, grass surface, disposal bags.

Hillside Park - Brooklyn Heights
Columbia Heights and Middagh Street
Daily 24 hours.
Fenced.

Palmetto Playground - Brooklyn Heights
Columbia Place and State Street (in the corner by the Brooklyn-Queens Expressway)
Daily 24 hours.
Benches, one park light, water.

Tompkins Square Park - Manhattan (East Village)
East 9th Street at Avenue B
Daily 6 a.m.-midnight.
Benches, picnic tables, water, a canine memorial.

Madison Square Park - Manhattan (Gramercy/Flatiron/ Union Square)
East 24th Street at Fifth Avenue
Daily 6 a.m.-midnight.
Trees, benches, disposal bags, water.

Thomas Jefferson Park - Manhattan (Harlem)
East 112th Street at First Avenue
Daily 24 hours.
Benches, wood chip surface.

J. Hood Wright Park - Manhattan (Inwood/Ft. George/ Washington Heights)
West 173rd Street between Fort Washington Avenue and Haven Avenue

Fishbridge Park - Manhattan (Lower East Side)
Dover Street at Pearl Street, just south of the Brooklyn Bridge
Daily dawn-dusk.
Benches, water hose, wading pool (open in summer only), lockbox for toys, lockbox with newspapers for picking up after your dog.

Peter Detmold Park - Manhattan (Midtown East)
East 49th Street at FDR Drive (behind Beekman Place)
Daily dawn-9 p.m., June-Sept.; dawn-8 p.m., Mar.-May and Oct.-Nov.; dawn-7 p.m., rest of year.
Trees, benches, historical lamps, disposal bags.

Carl Schurz Park - Manhattan (Upper East Side)
East 86th Street at East End Avenue
Daily dawn-1 a.m.
Benches, scoops, pea gravel surface. A second run for small dogs (past the main run, toward the East River) has a scenic view of the river and the 59th Street Bridge.

Riverside Park at 72nd Street - Manhattan (Upper West Side/Morningside Heights)
West 72nd Street
Daily 6 a.m.-1 a.m.
Bench, hanging flowerpots, disposal bags, scoopers.

Riverside Park at 87th Street - Manhattan (Upper West Side/Morningside Heights)
West 87th Street
Daily dawn-dusk.
Separate areas for large and small dogs, water fountain and hose.

Riverside Park at 105th Street - Manhattan (Upper West Side/Morningside Heights)
riversidedog.org
West 105th Street, Riverside Park Central Promenade
Daily dawn-dusk.
Trees, crushed granite surface, benches, disposal bag dispensers, water fountain, water faucet for dogs, separate area for small dogs.

Theodore Roosevelt Park - Manhattan (Upper West Side/Morningside Heights)
West 81st Street at Columbus Avenue
Daily 8 a.m.-10 p.m.
Shade trees, benches, dog water faucet, separate run for small dogs.

Washington Square Park - Manhattan (West Village)
West 4th Street at Thompson Street
Daily 6 a.m.-midnight.
Trees, pea gravel surface, benches, scoopers, water hose, water bowls.

Freeway Dog Park - Queens (Rockaway Beach)
arfarfrockaway.org
Rockaway Freeway between Beach 83rd and Beach 81st streets
Daily 8 a.m.-9 p.m.
Fenced, double-gated entry, trees, separate small dog area, benches, disposal bags. Access for the disabled.

Doughboy Plaza - Queens (Woodside)
Woodside Avenue from 54th to 56th streets (also south of Woodside at 56th Street) at Windmuller Park
Daily dawn-dusk.
Fenced, trash can.

Peekskill Dog Park - Peekskill
peekskilldogpark.com
1795 Main St.
Daily dawn-dusk
Fenced, double-gated entry, trees, benches, shade, tables, separate small dog area, disposal bags, trash cans, parking.

NORTH CAROLINA

Poston Dog Park - Gastonia
Co.gaston.nc.us
1101 Lowell Spencer Mountain Rd.
Daily 7 a.m.-dusk
Fenced, 5 acres, double-gated entry, separate small dog area, trees, benches, grass, disposal bags, trash cans, water, parking.

Southwest Park Dog Park - Greensboro
southwestpark.info
6309 Southwest Park Dr.
Wed.-Sun. 8 a.m.-dusk; closed Jan. 1, Thanksgiving and Dec. 24-25.
Fenced, 2.5 acres, double-gated entry, trees, separate small dog area, water.

Down East Dog Park - New Bern
newbern-nc.org
303 Glenburnie Dr. in Glenburnie Park
Daily dawn-dusk.
Annual fee $35 for the first dog, $20 for each additional dog. Weekly pass $5. Proof of current rabies vaccination is required. Phone (252) 639-7588 for more information.
Fenced. The main 1-acre area is for large dogs over 25 pounds, but dogs of any size may use it; a separate area is set aside for puppies and small dogs.

OHIO

Park 4 Paws - Avon Lake
avonlake.org
33401 Weber Rd. at Weiss Field
Daily 7 a.m.-9 p.m.
Fenced, double-gated entry, trees, benches, shade, separate small dog area, disposal bags, trash cans, water, parking. Access for the disabled.

Armleder Park Dog Park - Cincinnati
greatparks.org/dogpark.htm
5057 Wooster Pl.
Daily dawn-dusk (check Web site for dog park opening status)
Fenced, trees, shelter, parking, separate large and small dog areas, canine showers and drinking fountains, paved walking trail.

Mt. Airy Dog Park - Cincinnati
cincinnati-oh.gov
Westwood Northern Boulevard in Mt. Airy Forest's Highpoint Picnic Area, between Montana Avenue and North Bend Road
Daily dawn-dusk.
Fenced, 2 acres, trees, benches, tables, shelter, trash cans, parking, restrooms, water. Access for the disabled.

Big Walnut Dog Park - Columbus
bigwalnutdogpark.com
5000 E. Livingston Ave. in Big Walnut Park (across from Walnut Ridge High School)
Daily 7 a.m.-11 p.m.
Fenced, 3 acres, two double-gated entries, swimming pond, shade trees, picnic tables, paved parking.

Pooch Playground - Gahanna
poochplayground.com
940 Pizzurro Pkwy. From I-270 South, take exit 37 to
Hamilton Road. Turn right (south) onto Hamilton and
immediately get in the left lane to turn left into Pizzurro Park.
Daily dawn-dusk
Fenced, 4 acres, double-gated entry, trees, benches, separate
agility area, disposal bags, trash cans, water (spring through
fall), parking. Access for the disabled. There are trees along
the perimeter and in the small dog area. Dogs may swim in
the creek outside the fenced enclosure.

Mentor Dog Park - Mentor
cityofmentor.com
6645 Hopkins Rd.
Daily dawn-dusk
Fenced, approximately three-quarters of an acre, double-gated
entry, benches, shelter, shade, tables, separate small dog
area, disposal bags, trash cans, water, parking. Access for the
disabled.

OKLAHOMA

Joe Station Bark Park - Tulsa
cityoftulsa.org
2279 Charles Page Blvd.
Daily 5 a.m.-11 p.m., in summer; 5 a.m.-9 p.m., in winter.
Closed Wed. until noon for maintenance
Fenced, separate small dog area, water, shade, parking,
lights. Located at a former baseball field and named for one
of the trolley stops along the historic Interurban Line that once
connected Tulsa and Sand Springs.

OREGON

Awbrey Reservoir - Bend
DogPAC.org
N.W. 10th and Trenton
Daily dawn-dusk
Unfenced 5-acre area with access to trails, parking.

Big Sky - Bend
DogPAC.org
21690 Neff Rd.
Daily dawn-dusk
5 fenced acres, 6 unfenced acres.

Deschutes River Trail - Bend
DogPAC.org
Meadow Camp downstream to Sunrise Village
Daily dawn-dusk
Year-round off-leash section starts a quarter of a mile
downstream from the parking area. From Meadow Camp
upstream to Benham Falls, a leash is required May 15-Sept.
15.

Gooddog! Offleash Area - Bend
DogPAC.org
Century Drive, west of Entrada Lodge
Daily dawn-dusk
Unfenced, several miles of trails with river access.

Hollinshead Dog Park - Bend
DogPAC.org
1235 N.E. Jones Rd.
Daily dawn-dusk
Unfenced, 3 acres.

Overturf Butte Reservoir - Bend
DogPAC.org
Skyliner Summit Loop
Daily dawn-dusk
4 partially fenced acres.

Pine Nursery - Bend
DogPAC.org
Deschutes Market Road and Yeoman Road (entrance on
Yeoman Road)
Daily dawn-dusk
18 fenced acres with an open area

Ponderosa Dog Park - Bend
DogPAC.org
225 S.E. 15th St., south of Bear Creek Road
Daily dawn-dusk
4 fenced acres.

Riverbend Beach - Bend
DogPAC.org
799 N.W. Columbia St.
Daily dawn-dusk
Fenced, double-gated entry, benches, disposal bags, trash
cans, water, swimming access.

Alton Baker Park - Eugene
eugene-or.gov
South of Leo Harris Parkway (park in the lot south of Autzen
Stadium and cross the pedestrian bridge to the dog park)
Daily 6 a.m.-11 p.m.
Fenced, benches, tables, simple shelters for protection from
sun and rain, disposal bag receptacles, water.

Amazon Park - Eugene
eugene-or.gov
East of 29th Street and Amazon Parkway
Daily 6 a.m.-11 p.m.
Fenced, benches, tables, simple shelters for protection from
sun and rain, disposal bag receptacles, water, parking nearby.

Candlelight Park - Eugene
eugene-or.gov
Royal Avenue and Throne Drive
Daily 6 a.m.-11 p.m.
Fenced, benches, tables, disposal bag receptacles.

Wayne Morse Family Farm - Eugene
eugene-or.gov
Crest Drive and Lincoln Street (park in the main parking area
at 595 Crest Dr. and take the trail east)
Daily 6 a.m.-11 p.m.
Fenced, benches, tables, simple shelters for protection from
sun and rain, disposal bag receptacles, water.

Brentwood Park - Portland
portlandonline.com
Southeast 60th Avenue and Duke Street
Daily 5 a.m.-midnight.
Fenced.

Chimney Park - Portland
portlandonline.com
9360 N. Columbia Blvd.
Daily 5 a.m.-midnight.
Fenced, 6 acres of off-leash meadow and trails. Dogs should
be under excellent voice command.

Delta Park - Portland
portlandonline.com
North Denver Avenue and Martin Luther King Jr. Boulevard
(off I-5 exit 307 across from the East Delta Sports Complex)
Daily 6 a.m.-midnight, May-Oct. (open during dry season
only).
Fenced, 5 acres of off-leash field, trees, benches; bring your
own water. Dogs are not allowed on the sports fields.

Gabriel Park - Portland
portlandonline.com
Southwest 45th Avenue and Vermont Street
Daily 5 a.m.-midnight, May-Oct. (open during dry season only).
Fenced, off-leash area, trees, picnic tables, water. Dogs must remain leashed when not in the off-leash area.

Normandale Park - Portland
portlandonline.com
Northeast 57th Avenue and Halsey Street
Daily 5 a.m.-midnight.
Fenced.

PENNSYLVANIA

Canine Meadows Off-Leash Dog Area - York
ycwebserver.york-county.org
400 Mundis Race Rd.
Daily 8 a.m.-dusk. Area is closed during wet conditions; phone (717) 840-7440 for information.
Fenced, 13.5 acres, double-gated entry, three separate dog areas, information kiosk, disposal bags, water, trash cans, parking.

TEXAS

White Rock Lake Dog Park - Dallas
whiterockdogpark.com
8000 Mockingbird Point within White Rock Lake Park
Daily 5 a.m.-midnight (weather permitting); closed for maintenance second and fourth Mon. of the month.
Fenced, 2.5 acres, trees, benches, disposal bags, trash cans, parking, restrooms, water fountains, separate fenced areas for large and small dogs, fenced swimming area for dogs in White Rock Lake.

Independence Dog Park - Pearland
pearlandparks.com
3919 Liberty Dr.
Daily 6 a.m.-10 p.m.
Fenced, separate small dog area, agility equipment, covered picnic area, disposal bags, water.

Southdown Dog Park - Pearland
pearlandparks.com
2150 Countryplace Pkwy., within Southdown Park near the Westside Event Center
Daily 6 a.m.-10 p.m.
Fenced, separate small dog area, agility equipment, shade, disposal bags, water.

Jack Carter Park - Plano
plano.gov
Pleasant Valley Drive and Spring Creek Parkway (½ block north of the intersection on Pleasant Valley Drive)
Daily dawn-dusk (weather permitting); closed for maintenance first and third Tues. of the month.
Fenced, 2 acres, double-gated entry, benches, disposal bags, trash cans, parking, water fountains for dogs and people.

Round Rock Dog Depot - Round Rock
roundrocktexas.gov
800 Deerfoot Dr.
Daily 6 a.m.-8 p.m., Apr. 1-Oct. 1; daily 6-6, rest of year
Fenced, approximately 2 acres, grass, agility equipment, double-gated entry, disposal bags, has a train depot theme with a windmill and a water tower that acts as a mister for hot dogs in summer.

VERMONT

Watson Dog Park - Hartford
watsondogpark.org
Maple Street/Rt. 14 North, between Rt. 5 North and Christian Street
Daily dawn-9 p.m., May-Oct.; check Web site for winter hours.
Fenced, 1 acre, double-gated entry, trees, benches, separate small dog area, disposal bags, water, parking. Access for the disabled.

VIRGINIA

Note: Disposal bag receptacles are provided at Alexandria parks; patrons must provide their own bags.

Ben Brenman Park - Alexandria
alexandriava.gov
Cameron Station along Backlick Creek
Daily 6 a.m.-10 p.m.
Fenced, disposal bag receptacles, trash cans, parking.

Dog Park - Alexandria
alexandriava.gov
5000 block of Duke Street east of the Charles E. Beatley Jr. Library
Daily 6 a.m.-10 p.m.
Fenced, disposal bag receptacles, trash cans, parking.

Dog Run at Carlyle - Alexandria
alexandriava.gov
450 Andrews Ln.
Daily 6 a.m.-10 p.m.
Fenced, disposal bag receptacles, trash cans, parking.

Montgomery Park - Alexandria
alexandriava.gov
Fairfax and 1st streets
Daily 6 a.m.-10 p.m.
Fenced, disposal bag receptacles, trash cans, parking.

Simpson Stadium Park - Alexandria
alexandriava.gov
Monroe Avenue
Daily 6 a.m.-10 p.m.
Fenced, disposal bag receptacles, trash cans, parking, water fountains for dogs.

Off-leash, unfenced, under voice control areas:

Braddock Road - Alexandria
alexandriava.gov
Southeast corner of Braddock Road and Commonwealth Avenue
Daily 6 a.m.-10 p.m.
Unfenced.

Chambliss Street - Alexandria
alexandriava.gov
Chambliss Street at Grigsby Avenue, south of the tennis courts
Daily 6 a.m.-10 p.m.
Unfenced; area is marked by traffic barriers.

Chinquapin Park - Alexandria
alexandriava.gov
King Street at the east end of the loop road
Daily 6 a.m.-10 p.m.
Unfenced; area is marked by traffic barriers.

Edison Street - Alexandria
alexandriava.gov
Edison Street, west of the cul-de-sac between the bike trail and Berkey Photo Processing
Daily 6 a.m.-10 p.m.
Unfenced; area is marked by traffic barriers.

Ft. Williams - Alexandria
alexandriava.gov
Ft. Williams and New Ft. Williams Parkway
Daily 6 a.m.-10 p.m.
Unfenced; area is marked by traffic barriers.

Founders Park - Alexandria
alexandriava.gov
Oronoco Street and Union Street, northeast corner
Daily 6 a.m.-10 p.m.
Unfenced; 100-by-100-foot area is marked by traffic barriers.

Hooff's Run - Alexandria
alexandriava.gov
East of Commonwealth Avenue between Oak and Chapman
streets
Daily 6 a.m.-10 p.m.
Unfenced; area is marked by traffic barriers.

Monticello Park - Alexandria
alexandriava.gov
Beverly Drive, east of the entrance
Daily 6 a.m.-10 p.m.
Unfenced; 50-by-200-foot area is marked by traffic barriers.

North Fort Ward Park - Alexandria
alexandriava.gov
Braddock Road, east side of entrance
Daily 6 a.m.-10 p.m.
Unfenced; 100-by-100-foot area is marked by traffic barriers.

Tarleton Park - Alexandria
alexandriava.gov
Mill Run west of Gordon Street
Daily 6 a.m.-10 p.m.
Unfenced.

Timberbranch Parkway - Alexandria
alexandriava.gov
Median to Timberbranch Parkway between Braddock Road
and Oakley Place
Daily 6 a.m.-10 p.m.
Unfenced; area is marked by traffic barriers.

Windmill Hill Park - Alexandria
alexandriava.gov
Gibbon and Union streets
Daily 6 a.m.-10 p.m.
Unfenced.

W&OD Railroad - Alexandria
alexandriava.gov
Raymond Avenue (200 feet of the W&OD Railroad
right-of-way south of Raymond)
Daily 6 a.m.-10 p.m.
Unfenced; area is marked by traffic barriers.

Benjamin Banneker Park - Arlington County
arlingtondogs.org
1600 block of North Sycamore Street (take I-66 west to
Sycamore Street/exit 69, turn left on Sycamore and proceed
past the East Falls Church Metro Station, turn right onto North
16th Street and take the first right, which dead-ends at the
dog exercise area)
Daily dawn to half-hour after dusk.
Fully fenced, 11 acres, picnic table, benches, water.

Fort Barnard Park - Arlington County
arlingtondogs.org
South Pollard Street and South Walter Reed Drive (from Rte.
50, take Glebe Road south, turn right on South Walter Reed
Drive and proceed to Pollard Street; the park is on the right)
Daily dawn to half-hour after dusk.
Fully fenced, picnic table, benches, water.

Glencarlyn Park - Arlington County
arlingtondogs.org
301 S. Harrison St. (from Rte. 50, head west to Carlin Springs
Road, exit right and then turn left at the stop sign, pass under
Rte. 50 and follow Carlin Springs to 4th Street, turn left on 4th
Street and proceed 5 blocks until the road ends at the
Glencarlyn Park sign, following the park road until it ends;
park and walk over a small bridge and stream to the exercise
area)
Daily dawn to half-hour after dusk.
Unfenced area near a creek and woods, picnic table,
benches.

Shirlington Park - Arlington County
arlingtondogs.org
2601 S. Arlington Mill Dr., bordering South Four Mile Run
between Shirlington Road and South Walter Reed Drive along
the bicycle path between a storage facility and the water, near
but not in Jennie Dean Park (from South Four Mile Run, turn
south onto Nelson and park behind the storage facility; there
are no signs indicating the dog park)
Daily dawn to half-hour after dusk.
Partially fenced, picnic table, benches, water.

Towers Park - Arlington County
arlingtondogs.org
801 S. Scott St., behind the tennis courts
Daily dawn to half-hour after dusk.
Fully fenced, 3.5 acres, separate small dog area, parking.

The Hanover Dog Park - Ashland
co.hanover.va.us
13017 Taylor Complex Ln.
Mon.-Tues. and Thurs.-Fri. 9-4:30, Wed. 9-6, Sat. 10-3:30
Fenced, grass, dog agility equipment, water, disposal bags,
benches, parking.

Red Wing Park - Virginia Beach
vbgov.com
1398 General Booth Blvd.
Daily 7:30 a.m.-dusk.
Annual fee for first-time visitors $10; owners must register at
the park office, show proof of pet's rabies shot and vaccines,
and obtain a city dog license.
Fenced, benches, disposal bags, parking, restrooms, water.
Access for the disabled.

Woodstock Community Park - Virginia Beach
vbgov.com
5709 Providence Rd.
Daily 7:30 a.m.-dusk.
Annual fee for first-time visitors $10; owners must register at
the park office, show proof of pet's rabies shot and vaccines,
and obtain a city dog license.
Fenced, benches, disposal bags, restrooms, parking. Access
for the disabled.

WASHINGTON

Cedar River Dog Park - Renton
rentonoffleash.org
1156 S. 3rd St., adjacent to Cedar River Trail
Daily dawn-dusk
Fenced, 3.5 acres with 8,000 square feet reserved for
small/shy dogs, short grass, mulch, gravel, water, benches,
trees, shelter, tables, parking.

I-5 Colonnade Park - Seattle
coladog.org
Lakeview Boulevard and Franklin Avenue East in the Eastlake
neighborhood beneath I-5, south of East Howe Street
Daily 6 a.m.-11 p.m.
Fenced, 1.2 acres, double-gated entry, water fountain for
dogs; the I-5 freeway deck provides shelter from the elements.

I-90 "Blue Dog Pond" - Seattle
coladog.org
Martin Luther King Jr. Way and South Massachusetts Street, on the northwest corner
Daily 6 a.m.-11 p.m.
Fenced, 1 acre, parking, water fountain for dogs, Blue Dog sculpture. No off-leash areas in I-90 Lid Park, just east of Blue Dog Pond.

Dr. Jose Rizal Park - Seattle
coladog.org
1008 12th Ave. S. on North Beacon Hill; off-leash area is in the lower portion of the park
Daily 6 a.m.-11 p.m.
Fenced, 4 acres, double-gated entry, parking, water fountain for dogs, scenic view of downtown.

Genesee Park - Seattle
coladog.org
46th Avenue South and South Genesee Street
Daily 6 a.m.-11 p.m.
Fenced, 3 acres, double-gated entry, parking, water fountain for dogs.

Golden Gardens Park - Seattle
coladog.org
8498 Seaview Pl. N.W. in Ballard
Daily 6 a.m.-11 p.m.
Fenced, 1 acre, lighted, parking, water fountain for dogs. The off-leash area is in the upper (eastern) portion of the park; dogs are not allowed on the lower beach area.

Magnuson Park - Seattle
coladog.org
6500 Sandpoint Way N.E. (enter the park at 74th Street and drive to the end of the road)
Daily 6 a.m.-11 p.m.
Fenced, 9 acres, double-gated entry, shelter, parking, separate area for small/shy dogs, water fountain for dogs, beach access.

Northacres Park - Seattle
coladog.org
North 130th Street, west of I-5; off-leash area is in the northeast corner of the park at 12530 Third Ave. N.E., north of the ball field. Parking is available on the west side of the park along 1st Street Northeast and on the south side along North 125th Street
Daily 6 a.m.-11 p.m.
Fenced, double-gated entry, parking, water fountain for dogs.

Plymouth Pillars Park - Seattle
coladog.org
Boren Avenue and Pike Street on Capitol Hill above I-5
Daily 6 a.m.-11 p.m.
Fenced, 9,800 square feet, double-gated entry, water fountain for dogs, scenic view of downtown Seattle.

Regrade Park - Seattle
coladog.org
3rd Avenue and Bell Street, downtown
Fenced, 13,000 square feet, double-gated entry, water fountain for dogs.

Westcrest Park - Seattle
coladog.org
8806 8th Ave. S.W. in West Seattle
Daily 6 a.m.-11 p.m.
Fenced, 5 acres, parking, water fountain for dogs. The off-leash area is along the east side of the reservoir.

Woodland Park - Seattle
coladog.org
West Green Lake Way North, west of the tennis courts
Daily 6 a.m.-11 p.m.
Fenced, 1 acre, double-gated entry, parking, water fountain for dogs.

SCRAPS Off-Leash Park - Spokane
spokanecounty.org
26715 E. Spokane Bridge Rd. in Gateway Park
Daily dawn-dusk
Fenced, 3.5 acres, grass and wooded walking area, double-gated entry, parking, water fountain for dogs (not available in winter), restrooms, disposal bags, trash cans. Access for the disabled.

Walla Walla Dog Park - Walla Walla
wallawalladogpark.com
Myra Road and Dalles-Military Road
Daily dawn-dusk
Fenced, 2.25 acres, double-gated entry, separate small dog area, trees, trash cans, benches, shelter, disposal bags, grass, information kiosk. Parking is available on Dalles-Military Road or down the hill within Ft. Walla Walla Park.

Canada

ALBERTA

91 Street Right of Way - Edmonton
edmonton.ca, (780) 496-1475
Berm east of 91 Street from 10 Avenue north to Whitemud
Freeway and east to 76 Street
Unfenced.

Buena Vista Great Meadow - Edmonton
edmonton.ca, (780) 496-1475
North of Laurier Park and Buena Vista Drive and south of
Melton Ravine in the vicinity of 88 Avenue
Unfenced; area does not include the pedestrian bridge access
trail, Yorath property or the trail north to McKenzie Ravine.
This is a hot-air balloon site, so please leash your dog during
balloon launches.

Hermitage Park North - Edmonton
edmonton.ca, (780) 496-1475
129 Avenue to 137 Avenue; also 22 Street along the riverbank
where signs designate an off-leash area.
Unfenced. This is a multiuse area in the valley north of the
park's fishing pond and picnic area.

Jackie Parker Park - Edmonton
edmonton.ca, (780) 496-1475
Whitemud Freeway and 50th Street
Unfenced. Includes the area south of the 44 Avenue entrance;
dogs are not allowed on the golf course.

Keehewin Blackmud - Edmonton
edmonton.ca, (780) 496-1475
Pipeline corridor, 104 Street and 20 Avenue to the south end
of 109 Street (excludes Bearspaw Drive West and Blackmud
Creek and Ravine)
Unfenced.

Kennedale - Edmonton
edmonton.ca, (780) 496-1475
Ravine west of the 40 Street loop, west to 47 Street and the
top of the bank
Unfenced.

Lauderdale - Edmonton
edmonton.ca, (780) 496-1475
South end of Grand Trunk Park, from 127 to 129 Avenue and
113A to 109 Street
Unfenced.

Mill Creek Ravine - Edmonton
edmonton.ca, (780) 496-1475
68 Avenue and 93 Street, accessible from the west or north
sides of Argyll Park
Unfenced. A granular trail along the bottom of the ravine leads
to the Whyte (82) Avenue overpass.

Terwillegar Park - Edmonton
edmonton.ca, (780) 496-1475
Rabbit Hill Road
Unfenced. This is a multiuse area.

MANITOBA

Bourkevale Park - Winnipeg
winnipeg.ca
100 Ferry Rd., south of the dike along the riverbank
Daily 6 a.m.-10 p.m.
Unfenced, trash cans, parking; bring your own disposal bags.

Juba Park & Pioneer Avenue - Winnipeg
winnipeg.ca
Pioneer Avenue, all vacant land west of the walkway to Juba
Park
Daily 6 a.m.-10 p.m.
Unfenced, trash cans, parking; bring your own disposal bags.

Kil-Cona Park - Winnipeg
winnipeg.ca
Lagimodiere Boulevard in the area north of the west parking
lot
Daily 6 a.m.-10 p.m.
Unfenced, trash cans, parking; bring your own disposal bags.

King's Park - Winnipeg
winnipeg.ca
King's Drive, south end of the park, south of the lake
Daily 6 a.m.-10 p.m.
Unfenced, trash cans, parking; bring your own disposal bags.

Little Mountain Park - Winnipeg
winnipeg.ca
West side of the park adjacent to Klimpike Road entrance
Daily 6 a.m.-10 p.m.
Unfenced, trash cans, parking; bring your own disposal bags.

Maple Grove Park - Winnipeg
winnipeg.ca
Frobisher Road, north area of the park
Daily 6 a.m.-10 p.m.
Unfenced, trash cans, parking; bring your own disposal bags.

St. Boniface Industrial Park - Winnipeg
winnipeg.ca
Area surrounding retention pond, bordered by Mazenod Road,
Camiel Sys Street and Beghin Street
Daily 6 a.m.-10 p.m.
Unfenced, trash cans, parking; bring your own disposal bags.

Westview Park - Winnipeg
winnipeg.ca
Midland Street; entire park is an off-leash area
Daily 6 a.m.-10 p.m.
Unfenced, trash cans, parking; bring your own disposal bags.

Woodsworth Park - Winnipeg
winnipeg.ca
Northeast of King Edward Avenue and Park Lane
Daily 6 a.m.-10 p.m.
Unfenced, trash cans, parking; bring your own disposal bags.

United States

CALIFORNIA

 Disneyland® Resort

(714) 781-4565, 1313 S. Harbor Blvd. via I-5 Disneyland Drive and Disney Way exits, Anaheim
Disneyland® Resort consists of two family-oriented theme parks — Disneyland® and Disney's California Adventure® — and the shops, restaurants and entertainment of Downtown Disney® District. Indoor kennel facilities. Both theme parks are open daily with extended hours during the summer, on some holidays and on weekends. Admission to either park $72; $70 (ages 60+); $62 (ages 3-9). Parking fee. disneyland.disney.go.com

 SeaWorld San Diego

(800) 257-4268, 500 SeaWorld Dr., San Diego
SeaWorld San Diego offers animal shows, rides and exhibits featuring marine creatures from around the world, including killer whales, sharks, penguins and sea lions. In May 2010 the park unveils "Blue Horizons," a spectacular new show featuring dolphins, pilot whales and a colorful array of exotic birds along with aerialists and divers. Pet facility provided for a nominal charge on a first-come, first-serve basis. Park open daily at 9 or 10, mid-June through Labor Day; at 10, rest of year. Closing times vary. Hours are extended during summer and holiday periods; phone ahead. Admission $69; $59 (ages 3-9). Parking fee. www.seaworldsandiego.com

Universal Studios Hollywood

(800) 864-8377, off Hollywood Freeway (US 101) at Lankershim Boulevard, Universal City
In addition to thrill rides and attractions, Universal Studios gives visitors a behind-the-scenes look at the workings of a major film and TV studio. Complimentary kennel service. Park open daily 9-9, in summer; hours vary rest of year. Box office closes nightly at 5, in summer; at 4, rest of year. Admission $69; $59 (under 48 inches tall). Parking fee. www.universalstudioshollywood.com

DISTRICT OF COLUMBIA

Washington Monument

(202) 426-6841, 15th Street and Constitution Avenue N.W., Washington, D.C.
This instantly recognizable 555-foot marble obelisk commemorates our nation's first president and is surrounded by expansive grounds. Pets on leash. Daily 9-4:45; closed Dec. 25. Free. www.nps.gov/wamo

FLORIDA

Busch Gardens Tampa Bay

(866) 353-8622 or (888) 800-5447, 3000 E. Busch Blvd., Tampa
This family entertainment park combines world-class thrill rides, live entertainment and one of North America's largest zoos, providing an adventure for the entire family. Indoor kennel facilities. Generally open daily at 9 or 10; closing times vary. Phone ahead to confirm hours. Admission $74.95; $64.95 (ages 3-9). Parking fee. www.buschgardens.com

SeaWorld Orlando

(407) 351-3600 or (800) 327-2424, 7007 SeaWorld Dr. at I-4 and SR 528 (Beachline Expressway), Orlando
This marine life adventure park presents crowd-pleasing animal shows starring a family of performing killer whales. SeaWorld also features numerous attractions and rides, including a flying coaster, Manta, which opened in May 2009, a penguin encounter area and simulated helicopter rides. Air-conditioned kennels. Park open daily at 9; closing times vary. Phone ahead to confirm hours. Admission $79.95; $74.95 (ages 3-9). Parking fee. www.seaworldorlando.com

Universal Orlando® Resort

(407) 363-8000, off I-4 exit 75A (eastbound) or 74B (westbound) following signs, Orlando
At Universal Orlando you can "ride the movies" at the Universal Studios® theme park, cavort with superheroes and cartoon characters at Universal's Islands of Adventure® theme park, or visit the specialty shops, themed restaurants and entertainment venues at Universal CityWalk®. Air-conditioned kennels. Theme parks open daily at 9; closing times vary by season. Phone ahead to confirm hours. CityWalk open daily 11 a.m.-2 a.m. One-day admission to either theme park $79; $69 (ages 3-9). Individual CityWalk venue charges vary. Parking fee. www.universalorlando.com

Walt Disney World® Resort

(407) 824-4321 or (407) 934-7639, theme parks accessible from US 192, Osceola Parkway and several I-4 exits, Lake Buena Vista
Walt Disney World has — count 'em — four theme parks: Magic Kingdom® Park, Epcot®, Disney's Animal Kingdom® Theme Park and Disney's Hollywood Studios™ plus shopping, dining and entertainment at the Downtown Disney® area. Air-conditioned kennels. Theme parks generally open daily at 9; closing times vary. One-day, one-park admission $79; $68 (ages 3-9). Parking fee. www.DisneyWorld.com

GEORGIA

Six Flags Over Georgia

(770) 739-3400, 275 Riverside Pkwy. SW (off I-20), Austell
Six Flags offers rides, attractions, live shows and a July 4 fireworks display. Kennel facilities. Park open daily; hours and closing times vary. Admission $44.99; $29.99 (under 48 inches tall); free (ages 0-2). Parking fee. www.sixflags.com

ILLINOIS

 Six Flags Great America

(847) 249-1776, One Great America Parkway, Gurnee
Six Flags Great America offers 13 coasters, a 20-acre water park, shows, parades, rides and attractions for the whole family. Kennel facilities available. Park open late Apr. to late Oct.; phone ahead or visit the Web site to confirm hours and days. Admission $54.99; $34.99 (under 48 inches tall); free (ages 0-2). Parking fee. www.sixflags.com

IOWA

 Pella Historical Village

(641) 628-2409 or (641) 628-4311, 507 Franklin St., Pella
A country store, log cabin, grist mill, windmill, smithy and other buildings (including Wyatt Earp's boyhood home) are reminders of this town's Dutch Heritage. Pets on leash (grounds only). Mon.-Sat. 9-5, Mar.-Dec. Admission $8; $2 (ages 5-18).

MASSACHUSETTS

 Bunker Hill Monument

(617) 242-5641, in Monument Square on Breed's Hill, Charlestown
Part of Boston National Historical Park, this 221-foot-tall granite obelisk commemorates the site of the Battle of Bunker Hill, which occurred on June 17, 1775. Pets on leash (grounds only); must pick up after pet. Visitor lodge and exhibits daily 9-5. Free.
www.nps.gov/bost/Bunker_Hill/htm

MISSISSIPPI

 Vicksburg National Military Park

(601) 636-0583, entered via I-20 exit 4B, then .2 miles west on Clay St. (US 80)
More than 1,260 memorials, monuments, statues, tablets, bronze portraits and markers honor the Union and Confederate troops who engaged in the siege of Vicksburg in 1863. Pets on leash. Grounds open daily dawn-dusk. Visitor center daily 8-5. Admission $8 per private vehicle. www.nps.gov/vick

MISSOURI

 The Gateway Arch

(877) 982-1410, Memorial Drive and Market Street, St. Louis
This curved, stainless steel monument soars 630 feet high and symbolizes the gateway to the West. A tram ride takes visitors to an observation deck. Pets on leash (grounds only). Tram ticket center open daily 8 a.m.-10 p.m., Memorial Day-Labor Day; 9-6, rest of year. Closed Jan. 1, Thanksgiving and Dec. 25. Tram ride $10; $5 (ages 3-15). www.gatewayarch.com

NORTH CAROLINA

 Carowinds Theme Park

(704) 588-2600 or (803) 548-5300, 10 miles south on I-77 to exit 90, Charlotte
Depicting the past and present of the Carolinas, the themed areas at this park offer roller coasters, water rides, children's play areas and other family entertainment. Air-conditioned kennels. Park open daily at 10, early June to mid-Aug.; Sat.-Sun. at 10, mid-Mar. to early June and mid-Aug. to early Oct. Closing times vary; phone ahead to confirm hours. Admission $48.99; $21.99 (ages 3-6, ages 62+ and under 48 inches tall). Parking fee. www.carowinds.com

OHIO

 Kings Island

(513) 754-5700, Kings Island Drive (off I-71 exits 24 and 25), Kings Mills
Kings Island is a family entertainment park featuring 15 hair-raising roller coasters; Boomerang Bay, a 15-acre water park; costumed Peanuts cartoon characters; and a variety of live shows. Kennel facilities (fee). Park open daily at 10, May 22-Aug. 30; some Fri., Sat. and Sun., mid-Apr. to mid-May and early Sept.-Nov. 1 (opening times vary). Phone ahead to confirm hours. Admission $48.99; $31.99 (ages 3-6, ages 62+ and under 48 inches tall). Prices may vary. Parking fee. www.visitkingsisland.com

PENNSYLVANIA

 Hersheypark

(800) 437-7439, 100 W. Hersheypark Dr. (just off SR 743 and US 422), Hershey
Hersheypark has more than 65 rides and attractions — including 11 roller coasters — plus live entertainment. Visitors can enjoy a marine mammal show, song and dance reviews and concerts highlighting big-name performers. Zooamerica North American Wildlife Park covers 11 acres. Kennel facilities. Park open daily at 10, Memorial Day-Labor Day; Fri.-Sun. at 10, May 1-Sun. before Memorial Day weekend; Sat.-Sun. at 10, day after Labor Day-late Sept. Closing times vary; phone ahead to confirm hours. Admission (Memorial Day weekend-late Sept.) $51.95; $30.95 (ages 3-8 and 55-69); $20.95 (ages 70+). Admission (early May-late May) $43.95; $24.95 (ages 3-8 and 55-69); $17.95 (ages 70+). Parking fee. www.hersheypark.com

TEXAS

 SeaWorld San Antonio

(800) 700-7786, 10500 SeaWorld Dr. (off SR 151 at the junction of Westover Hills Boulevard and Ellison Drive), San Antonio
A 250-acre marine life adventure park, SeaWorld San Antonio entertains and educates with shark exhibits, a penguin habitat, the "Believe" show starring world-famous killer whale Shamu, and a high-energy whale and dolphin show. Such thrill rides as Journey to Atlantis, the Steel Eel and Great White coasters, and the Rio Loco and Texas Splashdown water rides add to the excitement. Outdoor kennel facilities (owner must provide food). Park open daily at 10, early Mar.-late Nov.; closing times vary. Phone ahead to confirm hours. Admission $56.99; $48.99 (ages 3-9). Prices may vary. Parking fee. www.seaworld.com

Six Flags Over Texas

(817) 530-6000, 2201 Road to Six Flags (at the junction of I-30 and SR 360 exit 30), Arlington

Themed areas, each featuring thrill rides, food and entertainment, depict Texas under six different flags: Spain, France, Mexico, the Republic of Texas, the Confederate States of America and the United States. Air-conditioned kennels (fee). Park open daily, mid-May to late Aug.; Sat.-Sun. and some Fri., Feb. 28-May 10, Sept. 5-Nov. 1 and day after Thanksgiving-Dec. 31. Schedule varies; phone ahead. Admission $49.99; $31 (under 48 inches tall); free (ages 0-2). Prices may vary. Parking fee. www.sixflags.com

VIRGINIA

 Busch Gardens Williamsburg

(800) 343-7946, 3 miles east on US 60 or off I-64 exit 243A, Williamsburg

This European-themed adventure park offers something for the entire family, from thrill rides to entertaining shows to villages representing England, Germany, France and other nations. Kennel facilities (England parking lot); fee $10 per pet per day. Park open daily at 10, Mar.-May and closing times vary. Phone ahead to confirm schedule. Admission $61.95; $51.95 (ages 3-9). Parking fee. www.buschgardens.com/va

ONTARIO

 Upper Canada Village

(613) 543-4328 or (800) 437-2233, 7 miles (11 kilometers) east on CR 2 off Hwy. 401, Morrisburg

Upper Canada Village re-creates life during the 1860s through a working community of artisans and costumed interpreters who perform chores typical of the era. Pets on leash (grounds only). Daily 9:30-5, late May-early Oct. Village admission $19.95; $18.95 (ages 65+); $11.95 (ages 5-18); $3.95 (ages 2-4). www.uppercanadavillage.com

 Kings Dominion

(804) 876-5000, 16000 Theme Park Way (on SR 30 ½ mile east off I-95 exit 98), Doswell

This 400-acre park features a water park, thrill rides, children's play areas, costumed characters, live shows and specialty shopping. Kennel facilities (fee); water provided, but not food. Park open daily, Memorial Day-Labor Day; Fri.-Sun., late Mar.-day before Memorial Day and first Fri. after Labor Day-late Oct. Hours vary seasonally; phone ahead. Admission $55.99; $31.99 (ages 62+ and under 48 inches tall); free (ages 0-2). Parking fee. www.kingsdominion.com

WASHINGTON

 Hovander Homestead

(360) 384-3444, 1 mile south via Hovander Road, Ferndale

This restored house, dating from 1903 and furnished with antiques, is within a large park encompassing gardens, picnic sites and a children's farm area. Pets on leash (grounds only). Grounds open daily 8 a.m.-dusk. The Hovander House is open to the public Thurs.-Sun. noon-4:30, June 1-Labor Day; Sat.-Sun. noon-4:30, in May. House $1; 50 cents (ages 5-12). www.co.whatcom.wa.us/parks/hovander/hovander.jsp

Canada

 Canada's Wonderland

(905) 832-7000 or (905) 832-8131, off Hwy. 400 (Rutherford Road exit northbound or Major MacKenzie Drive E. exit southbound) at 9580 Jane St., Vaughan

Thrill rides at this theme park include the hair-raising Behemoth rollercoaster and the Backlot Stunt Coaster, while Nickelodeon Central and Hanna-Barbera Land will entertain little ones. Air-conditioned kennels (fee). Park open daily, mid-May to early October; phone ahead to confirm opening and closing times. Phone ahead or check the Web site to confirm admission rates for grounds and rides. Parking fee. www.canadaswonderland.com

NATIONAL PUBLIC LANDS

The National Public Lands listed below permit pets on a leash. Keep in mind that animals may be prohibited from entering public buildings and even some areas outdoors, particularly those that are ecologically sensitive. Where swimming is permitted, there are usually no lifeguards on duty; people and pets swim at their own risk. Specific pet policies vary from park to park and are subject to change. Always check in advance regarding any applicable regulations and to confirm that pets are still permitted where you are going.

Be aware of dangers to your pet in natural areas, including snakes, ticks and fast-moving currents in rivers and streams. An unleashed dog may chase after a wild animal and become separated from its owner, increasing the risk of loss or injury. Never leave your pet unattended. Keep him leashed or crated at all times. Follow park guidelines faithfully, and monitor your pet's behavior; the National Park Service may confiscate pets that harm wildlife or other visitors. *For additional information on outdoor vacations, see The Great Outdoors, p. 16.*

United States

ALABAMA

Conecuh National Forest
On the Alabama-Florida border.
(334) 222-2555
🚲 🔺 🥾 ⛱ 🏊

Eufaula National Wildlife Refuge
On the Chattahoochee River.
(334) 687-4065
🏠

Horseshoe Bend National Military Park
12 mi. north of Dadeville on SR 49.
(256) 234-7111
🥾 ⛱ 🏠

Talladega National Forest
In central Alabama.
(256) 362-2909
🔺 🥾 ⛱ 🏊

Tuskegee National Forest
Northeast of Tuskegee.
(334) 727-2652
🔺 🥾 ⛱

William B. Bankhead National Forest
In northwestern Alabama.
(205) 489-5111
🚲 🔺 🥾 ⛱ 🏊 🏠

Wheeler National Wildlife Refuge
Between Decatur and Huntsville.
(256) 350-6639
🚲 🥾 ⛱ 🏠

ALASKA

Chugach National Forest
Along the Gulf of Alaska from Cape Suckling to Seward.
(907) 743-9500
🔺 🥾 ⛱ 🏠

Denali National Park and Preserve
In south-central Alaska.
(907) 683-2294
🔺 🥾 ⛱ 🏠 🍴

Glacier Bay National Park and Preserve
North of Cross Sound to the Canadian border.
(907) 697-2230
🔺 🥾 🏠

Kenai Fjords National Park
Southeastern side of the Kenai Peninsula.
(907) 224-7500 or (907) 224-2132
🔺 🥾 ⛱ 🏠

Lake Clark National Park and Preserve
In southern Alaska.
(907) 644-3626
🔺 🏠

Tongass National Forest
In southeastern Alaska.
(907) 225-3101 or (907) 228-6220
🔺 🥾 ⛱ 🏠

Wrangell-St. Elias National Park and Preserve
In southeastern Alaska, northwest of Tongass National Forest.
(907) 822-5234
🔺 🥾 ⛱ 🏠

ARIZONA

Apache-Sitgreaves National Forests
In east-central Arizona.
(928) 333-4301
🚲 🔺 🥾 ⛱ 🏠 🍴

Bill Williams River National Wildlife Refuge
Off SR 95 near Parker.
(928) 667-4144
🥾 ⛱ 🏠

Buenos Aires National Wildlife Refuge
North of Sasabe on SR 286.
(520) 823-4251
🔺 🥾 ⛱ 🏠

Coconino National Forest
In north-central Arizona.
(928) 527-3600
🚲 🔺 🥾 ⛱ 🏊 🏠

🚲 Bicycling Trails   🔺 Camping   🥾 Hiking Trails   ⛱ Picnic Facilities
🏊 Swimming   🏠 Visitor Center   🍴 Food Service

Coronado National Forest
In southeastern Arizona and southwestern New Mexico.
(520) 388-8300

Glen Canyon National Recreation Area
In northern Arizona and Southern Utah.
(928) 608-6200 or (928) 608-6404

Grand Canyon National Park
In northwestern Arizona.
(928) 638-7888

Kaibab National Forest
In north-central Arizona.
(928) 635-8200

Lake Mead National Recreation Area
In northwestern Arizona and southeastern Nevada.
(702) 293-8990

Petrified Forest National Park
In east-central Arizona, east of Holbrook.
(928) 524-6228

Prescott National Forest
In central Arizona.
(928) 443-8000

Saguaro National Park
Two districts, 15 mi. east and west of Tucson.
(520) 733-5153 or (520) 733-5158

Tonto National Forest
In central Arizona.
(602) 225-5200

ARKANSAS
Buffalo National River
In northwestern Arkansas.
(870) 741-5443 or (870) 439-2502

Felsenthal National Wildlife Refuge
7 mi. west of Crossett on US 82.
(870) 364-3167

Hot Springs National Park
In western Arkansas.
(501) 620-6701 or TDD (501) 624-2308

Ouachita National Forest
In west-central Arkansas and southeastern Oklahoma.
(501) 321-5202

Ozark-St. Francis National Forests
In northwestern and east-central Arkansas.
(479) 964-7200

Pea Ridge National Military Park
Northeast of Rogers in northwest Arkansas.
(479) 451-8122

CALIFORNIA
Angeles National Forest
In southern California.
(626) 574-5200

Cleveland National Forest
In southwestern California.
(858) 673-6180

Death Valley National Park
Along the Nevada border in east-central California.
(760) 786-2331 for recorded information

Eldorado National Forest
In central California.
(530) 644-6048

Golden Gate National Recreation Area
North of the Golden Gate Bridge and in northern and western San Francisco.
(415) 561-4700

Inyo National Forest
In east-central California.
(760) 873-2400

Joshua Tree National Park
East of Desert Hot Springs.
(760) 367-5500

Klamath National Forest
In northern California.
(530) 842-6131

Lassen National Forest
In northeastern California.
(530) 257-2151

Lassen Volcanic National Park
In northeastern California.
(530) 595-4444

Los Padres National Forest
In southern California.
(805) 968-6640

Mendocino National Forest
In northwestern California.
(530) 934-2350 or (530) 934-3316, or TDD (530) 934-7724
🚲 ⛺ 🥾 🌳 🏊 🏛

Modoc National Forest
In northeastern California.
(530) 233-5811
🚲 ⛺ 🥾 🌳 🏊 🏛

Mojave National Preserve
Between I-15 and I-40 in southeastern California.
(760) 252-6100
⛺ 🥾 🌳 🏛 🍴

Plumas National Forest
In northern California.
(530) 283-2050
🚲 ⛺ 🥾 🌳 🏊 🏛 🍴

Point Reyes National Seashore
Along the California coast just north of San Francisco.
(415) 464-5100
🚲 ⛺ 🥾 🌳 🏛 🍴

Redwood National and State Parks
On the northern California coast.
(707) 464-6101
🚲 ⛺ 🥾 🌳 🏊 🏛

San Bernardino National Forest
In southern California.
(909) 382-2600
🚲 ⛺ 🥾 🌳 🏊 🏛 🍴

Santa Monica Mountains National Recreation Area
West from Griffith Park in Los Angeles past the Ventura County line.
(805) 370-2301
🚲 ⛺ 🥾 🌳 🏛 🍴

Sequoia and Kings Canyon National Parks
In east-central California.
(559) 565-3341
⛺ 🥾 🌳 🏛 🍴

Sequoia National Forest
In south-central California.
(559) 784-1500
🚲 ⛺ 🥾 🌳 🏊

Shasta-Trinity National Forests
In northern California.
(530) 226-2500
🚲 ⛺ 🥾 🌳 🏊 🏛 🍴

Sierra National Forest
In central California.
(559) 297-0706
🚲 ⛺ 🥾 🌳 🏊 🍴

Six Rivers National Forest
In northwestern California.
(707) 442-1721
🚲 ⛺ 🥾 🌳 🏊 🏛 🍴

Smith River National Recreation Area
Within Six Rivers National Forest in northwestern California.
(707) 457-3131
🚲 ⛺ 🥾 🌳 🏊 🏛

Stanislaus National Forest
In central California.
(209) 532-3671
🚲 ⛺ 🥾 🌳 🏊 🍴

Tahoe National Forest
In north-central California.
(530) 265-4531
🚲 ⛺ 🥾 🌳 🏊 🏛 🍴

Whiskeytown-Shasta-Trinity National Recreation Area
North and west of Redding.
(530) 246-1225 in Whiskeytown, (530) 275-1589 in Shasta or (530) 623-2121 in Trinity
🚲 ⛺ 🥾 🌳 🏊 🏛

Yosemite National Park
In central California.
(209) 372-0200
🚲 ⛺ 🥾 🌳 🏊 🏛 🍴

COLORADO

Arapaho and Roosevelt National Forests and Pawnee National Grassland
In north-central Colorado.
(970) 295-6700
🚲 ⛺ 🥾 🌳 🏛 🍴

Arapaho National Recreation Area
In north-central Colorado.
(970) 887-4100
🚲 ⛺ 🥾 🌳 🏊 🏛

Black Canyon of the Gunnison National Park
In western Colorado.
(970) 641-2337
🚲 ⛺ 🥾 🌳 🏛

Curecanti National Recreation Area
In south-central Colorado between Gunnison and Montrose, paralleling US 50.
(970) 641-2337
🚲 ⛺ 🥾 🌳 🏊 🏛 🍴

Grand Mesa-Uncompahgre-Gunnison National Forests
In west-central Colorado.
(970) 874-6600
🚲 ⛺ 🥾 🌳 🏛

Great Sand Dunes National Park and Preserve
Northeast of Alamosa.
(719) 378-6300
⛺ 🥾 🌳 🏊 🏛

🚲 Bicycling Trails   ⛺ Camping   🥾 Hiking Trails   🌳 Picnic Facilities
🏊 Swimming   🏛 Visitor Center   🍴 Food Service

Mesa Verde National Park
In southwestern Colorado.
(970) 529-4465
[A] [⚡] [⛏] [⛺] [♨]

Pike and San Isabel National Forest
In south-central Colorado.
(719) 553-1400
[♿] [A] [⚡] [⛏] [⛺]

Rio Grande National Forest
In south-central Colorado.
(719) 852-5941
[♿] [A] [⚡] [⛏] [⛺]

Rocky Mountain National Park
In north-central Colorado.
(970) 586-1206
[A] [⚡] [⛏] [⛺]

Routt National Forest
In northwestern Colorado.
(970) 870-2299
[♿] [A] [⚡] [⛏] [⛺]

San Juan National Forest
In southwestern Colorado.
(970) 247-4874
[♿] [A] [⚡] [⛏] [♨] [⛺]

White River National Forest
In west-central Colorado.
(970) 945-2521
[♿] [A] [⚡] [⛏] [♨] [⛺]

DELAWARE
Bombay Hook National Wildlife Refuge
South of Smyrna.
(302) 653-9345
[♿] [⚡] [⛏] [⛺]

Prime Hook National Wildlife Refuge
North of Milton via SR 1.
(302) 684-8419
[⚡] [⛏] [⛺]

FLORIDA
Apalachicola National Forest
In northwestern Florida.
(850) 926-3561
[♿] [A] [⚡] [⛏] [♨]

Biscayne National Park
In southeast Florida.
(305) 230-7275
[A] [⛏] [♨] [⛺] [♨]

J.N. "Ding" Darling National Wildlife Refuge
1 Wildlife Dr. in Sanibel.
(239) 472-1100
[♿] [⚡⛺]

Ocala National Forest
In north-central Florida.
(352) 236-0288
[♿] [A] [⚡] [⛏] [♨] [⛺] [♨]

Osceola National Forest
Near the Georgia border.
(386) 752-2577 or (386) 752-0147
[♿] [A] [⚡] [⛏] [♨] [⛺]

GEORGIA
Chattahoochee and Oconee National Forests
In central and northern Georgia.
(770) 297-3000
[♿] [A] [⚡] [⛏] [♨] [⛺] [♨]

Chattahoochee River National Recreation Area
North of Atlanta.
(678) 538-1200
[♿] [⚡] [⛏] [♨] [⛺]

Chickamauga and Chattanooga National Military Park
On the Georgia-Tennessee border.
(706) 866-9241 or (423) 752-5213, ext 123
[♿] [⚡] [⛏] [⛺]

Kennesaw Mountain National Battlefield Park
Northwest of Marietta.
(770) 427-4686
[⚡] [⛏] [⛺]

IDAHO
Boise National Forest
In southwestern Idaho.
(208) 373-4007
[♿] [A] [⚡] [⛏] [♨] [⛺] [♨]

Caribou-Targhee National Forest
In southeastern Idaho.
(208) 524-7500
[A] [⚡] [⛏] [♨] [⛺]

Clearwater National Forest
In northeastern Idaho.
(208) 476-8267
[A] [⚡] [⛏] [♨] [⛺] [♨]

Hells Canyon National Recreation Area
In western Idaho and northeastern Oregon.
(509) 758-0616
[♿] [A] [⚡] [⛏] [♨] [⛺]

Idaho Panhandle National Forests
In northern and northwestern Idaho.
(208) 765-7223
[♿] [A] [⚡] [⛏] [♨]

Nez Perce National Forest
In northwestern Idaho.
(208) 983-1950
[♿] [A] [⚡] [⛏] [♨] [⛺] [♨]

Payette National Forest
In west-central Idaho.
(208) 634-0700
[♿] [A] [⚡] [⛏] [♨] [⛺] [♨]

Salmon-Challis National Forest
In east-central Idaho.
(208) 756-5100
[A] [⚡] [⛏] [♨] [⛺]

Sawtooth National Forest
In south-central Idaho.
(208) 737-3200 or (800) 260-5970
🚴 ⛺ 🥾 🏕 🏊 🛖 🍴

Sawtooth National Recreation Area
In south-central Idaho.
(208) 727-5013 or (800) 260-5970
🚴 ⛺ 🥾 🏕 🏊 🛖 🍴

ILLINOIS

Chautauqua National Wildlife Refuge
Near Havana.
(309) 535-2290
🚴 🥾 🏕

Shawnee National Forest
In southern Illinois.
(618) 253-7114 or (800) 699-6637
⛺ 🥾 🏕 🏊 🛖

INDIANA

George Rogers Clark National Historical Park
Off US 50 and US 41 near Vincennes.
(812) 882-1776
🥾 🏕 🛖

Hoosier National Forest
In southern Indiana.
(812) 275-5987
🚴 ⛺ 🥾 🏕 🏊

Indiana Dunes National Lakeshore
On the southern shore of Lake Michigan.
(219) 926-7561, ext. 225
🚴 ⛺ 🥾 🏕 🏊 🛖

Muscatatuck National Wildlife Refuge
East of jct. I-65 and US 50 near Seymour.
(812) 522-4352
🚴 🥾 🛖

KANSAS

Kirwin National Wildlife Refuge
702 E. Xavier Rd.
(785) 543-6673
🚴 🥾 🛖

KENTUCKY

Big South Fork National River and Recreation Area
In southeastern Kentucky and northeastern Tennessee.
(423) 286-7275 or (606) 376-5073
🚴 ⛺ 🥾 🏕 🏊 🛖

Cumberland Gap National Historical Park
At the borders of Kentucky, Tennessee and Virginia.
(606) 248-2817
🚴 ⛺ 🥾 🏕 🛖

Daniel Boone National Forest
Five districts in eastern and southeastern Kentucky.
(859) 745-3100
🚴 ⛺ 🥾 🏕 🏊 🛖

Land Between the Lakes National Recreation Area
In western Kentucky and Tennessee.
(270) 924-2000 or (800) 525-7077
🚴 ⛺ 🥾 🏕 🏊 🛖

Mammoth Cave National Park
In south-central Kentucky 10 mi. west of Cave City.
(270) 758-2180
🚴 ⛺ 🥾 🏕 🛖 🍴

LOUISIANA

Bayou Sauvage National Wildlife Refuge
Within the New Orleans city limits.
(985) 882-2000
🚴 🥾 🏕

Kisatchie National Forest
In central and northern Louisiana.
(318) 473-7160
🚴 ⛺ 🥾 🏕 🏊 🛖

MAINE

Acadia National Park
Along the Atlantic coast southeast of Bangor.
(207) 288-3338
🚴 ⛺ 🥾 🏕 🏊 🛖 🍴

Moosehorn National Wildlife Refuge
Near Baring and Dennysville.
(207) 454-7161
🚴 🥾

MARYLAND

Assateague Island National Seashore
In southeastern Maryland south of Ocean City.
(410) 641-1441 or (410) 641-3030
🚴 ⛺ 🥾 🏕 🏊 🛖

Chesapeake and Ohio Canal National Historical Park
From Georgetown to Cumberland.
(301) 739-4200
🚴 ⛺ 🥾 🏕 🛖 🍴

MASSACHUSETTS

Cape Cod National Seashore
Occupies 40 miles along the shoreline.
(508) 255-3421
🚴 🥾 🏕 🏊 🛖

MICHIGAN

Hiawatha National Forest
In Michigan's Upper Peninsula.
(906) 786-4062
🚴 ⛺ 🥾 🏕 🏊 🛖 🍴

🚴 Bicycling Trails   ⛺ Camping   🥾 Hiking Trails   🏕 Picnic Facilities
🏊 Swimming   🛖 Visitor Center   🍴 Food Service

Huron-Manistee National Forests
In the northern part of the Lower Peninsula.
(231) 775-2421 or (800) 821-6263
🚵 ⛺ 🥾 🏕 ⚱ 🛏 🍽

Ottawa National Forest
In Michigan's Upper Peninsula.
(906) 932-1330 or (800) 562-1201
🚵 ⛺ 🥾 🏕 ⚱ 🛏 🍽

Pictured Rocks National Lakeshore
Along Lake Superior in Michigan's Upper Peninsula.
906-387-3700 or (906) 387-2607
⛺ 🥾 🏕 ⚱ 🛏

Sleeping Bear Dunes National Lakeshore
Along Lake Michigan in the northwestern part of the Lower
Peninsula.
(231) 326-5134
⛺ 🥾 🏕 ⚱ 🛏 🍽

MINNESOTA
Chippewa National Forest
In north-central Minnesota.
(218) 335-8600
🚵 ⛺ 🥾 🏕 ⚱ 🛏 🍽

Minnesota Valley National Wildlife Refuge
3815 E. American Blvd, Bloomington
(952) 854-5900
🚵 🥾 🛏

Superior National Forest
In northeastern Minnesota.
(218) 626-4300
🚵 ⛺ 🥾 🏕 ⚱ 🛏 🍽

MISSISSIPPI
Bienville National Forest
In central Mississippi.
(601) 469-3811
⛺ 🥾 🏕 ⚱ 🛏

Gulf Islands National Seashore
Along the Gulf of Mexico in southern Mississippi.
(228) 875-9057
🚵 ⛺ 🥾 🏕 🛏

MISSOURI
Mark Twain National Forest (Big Bay)
1 mi. southeast of Shell Knob on SR 39, then 3 mi.
southeast on CR YY.
(573) 364-4621
🚵 🏕 ⚱

Mark Twain National Forest (Council Bluff)
13 mi. s. of Potosi on CR P, 4 mi. w. on CR C , then 8
mi. s. on CR DD.
(573) 364-4621
🚵 ⛺ 🥾 🏕 ⚱

Mark Twain National Forest (Crane Lake)
12 mi. south of Ironton off SR 49 and CR E.
(573) 364-4621
🚵 🥾 🏕 ⚱

Mark Twain National Forest (Fourche Lake)
18 mi. west of Doniphan on SR 160.
(573) 364-4621
🥾 🏕 ⚱

Mark Twain National Forest (Noblett Lake)
8 mi. west of Willow Springs on SR 76, then 1.5 mi. south
on SR 181, 3 mi. southeast on CR AP and 1 mi.
southwest on FR 857.
(573) 364-4621
🚵 🥾 🏕

Mark Twain National Forest (Pinewoods Lake)
2 mi. west of Ellsinore on SR 60.
(573) 364-4621
🚵 🥾 🏕 ⚱

Mark Twain National Forest (Red Bluff)
1 mi. east of Davisville on CR V, then 1 mi. north on FR
2011.
(573) 364-4621
⛺ 🥾 🏕 ⚱

Ozark National Scenic Riverways
In southeastern Missouri.
(573) 323-4236
⛺ 🥾 🏕 ⚱ 🛏 🍽

MONTANA
Beaverhead-Deerlodge National Forest
In southwestern Montana.
(406) 683-3900
🚵 ⛺ 🥾 🏕 ⚱ 🍽

Bighorn Canyon National Recreation Area
In southern Montana and northern Wyoming.
(406) 666-2412
⛺ 🥾 🏕 ⚱ 🛏 🍽

Bitterroot National Forest
In western Montana.
(406) 363-7100
🚵 ⛺ 🥾 🏕 ⚱ 🛏

Custer National Forest
In southeastern Montana.
(406) 657-6200
🚵 ⛺ 🥾 🏕 ⚱

Flathead National Forest
In northwestern Montana.
(406) 758-5204
🚵 ⛺ 🥾 🏕 ⚱ 🛏

Gallatin National Forest
In south-central Montana.
(406) 522-2520
🚵 ⛺ 🥾 🏕 ⚱ 🛏

Glacier National Park
In northwestern Montana.
(406) 888-7800
🚵 ⛺ 🥾 🏕 ⚱ 🛏 🍽

Helena National Forest
In west-central Montana.
(406) 449-5201
🚵 ⛺ 🥾 🏕 ⚱ 🛏

Kootenai National Forest
In northwestern Montana.
(406) 293-6211
🚲 🔺 🥾 🏕 ⚓ 🏛 🍴

Lewis and Clark National Forest
In central Montana.
(406) 791-7700
🚲 🔺 🥾 🏕 🏛

NEBRASKA
Fort Niobrara National Wildlife Refuge
East of Valentine on SR 12.
(402) 376-3789
🥾 🏕

Nebraska National Forest
In central and northwestern Nebraska.
(308) 432-0300 or TDD (308) 432-0304
🚲 🔺 🥾 🏕

Oglala National Grassland
In northwestern Nebraska, 6 mi. north of Crawford via SR 2.
(308) 432-0300
🔺 🥾 🏕

NEVADA
Great Basin National Park
In central Nevada, 5 mi. west of Baker near the Nevada-Utah border.
(775) 234-7331
🔺 🥾 🏕 🏛 🍴

Humboldt-Toiyabe National Forest
In central, western, northern and southern Nevada and eastern California.
(775) 331-6444
🚲 🔺 🥾 🏕 🍴

Lake Mead National Recreation Area
In southeastern Nevada and northwestern Arizona.
(702) 293-8990
🚲 🔺 🥾 🏕 🏛 🏛 🍴

NEW HAMPSHIRE
White Mountain National Forest
In northern New Hampshire.
(603) 528-8721
🚲 🔺 🥾 🏕 🏛 🏛

NEW JERSEY
Edwin B. Forsythe National Wildlife Refuge
US 9 and Great Creek Road near Oceanville
(609) 652-1665
🥾 🏕 🏛

Gateway National Recreation Area (Sandy Hook Unit)
In northeastern New Jersey.
(732) 872-5970
🚲 🥾 🏕 🏛 🏛 🍴

Morristown National Historical Park
Four units in Morristown and southwest.
(973) 539-2016
🥾 🏛

NEW MEXICO
Carson National Forest
In north-central New Mexico.
(575) 758-6200
🚲 🔺 🥾 🏕 🏛 🍴

Chaco Culture National Historical Park
In northwestern New Mexico.
(505) 786-7014
🚲 🔺 🥾 🏕 🏛

Cibola National Forest
In central New Mexico.
(505) 346-3900
🚲 🔺 🥾 🏕 🏛 🏛

Gila National Forest
In southwestern New Mexico.
(575) 388-8201
🚲 🔺 🥾 🏕 🏛

Lincoln National Forest
In south-central New Mexico.
(575) 434-7200
🚲 🔺 🥾 🏕 🍴

Santa Fe National Forest
In north-central New Mexico between the Jemez Mountains and the Sangre de Cristo Mountains.
(505) 438-7840
🚲 🔺 🥾 🏕 🏛 🍴

NEW YORK
Finger Lakes National Forest
In south-central New York on a ridge between Seneca and Cayuga lakes, via I-90, I-81 and SR 17.
(607) 546-4470
🚲 🔺 🥾 🏕 🏛

Fire Island National Seashore
In southeastern New York on Fire Island, off the south shore of Long Island.
(631) 687-4750
🔺 🥾 🏕 🏛 🏛 🍴

Gateway National Recreation Area (Jamaica Bay Unit)
In Brooklyn and Queens boroughs in New York City.
(718) 338-3799
🚲 🔺 🥾 🏕 🏛 🏛 🍴

Gateway National Recreation Area (Staten Island Unit)
On Staten Island borough in New York City.
(718) 354-4500
🚲 🔺 🥾 🏕 🏛 🏛 🍴

🚲 Bicycling Trails   🔺 Camping   🥾 Hiking Trails   🏕 Picnic Facilities
🏛 Swimming   🏛 Visitor Center   🍴 Food Service

Saratoga National Historical Park
8 miles south of Schuylerville on US 4.
(518) 664-9821, ext. 224
🚶 👫 ⛲ 🏕

NORTH CAROLINA
Cape Hatteras National Seashore
In eastern North Carolina along the Outer Banks.
(252) 473-2111
🚶 ⛺ 👫 ⛲ 🛶 🏕 🍴

Croatan National Forest
In southeastern North Carolina.
(252) 638-5628
🚶 ⛺ 👫 ⛲ 🛶

Great Smoky Mountains National Park
In western North Carolina and eastern Tennessee.
(865) 436-1200
🚶 ⛺ 👫 ⛲ 🏕

Nantahala National Forest
At North Carolina's southwestern tip.
(828) 257-4200 or (828) 524-6441
🚶 ⛺ 👫 ⛲ 🛶

Pisgah National Forest
In western North Carolina.
(828) 257-4200
🚶 ⛺ 👫 ⛲ 🛶 🏕

Pisgah National Forest (Lake Powhatan)
7 mi. southwest of Asheville on SR 191 and FR 3807.
(828) 257-4200
🚶 ⛺ 👫 ⛲ 🛶

Pisgah National Forest (Rocky Bluff)
3 mi. south of Hot Springs on SR 209.
(828) 257-4200
⛺ 👫 ⛲

Uwharrie National Forest
In central North Carolina.
(910) 576-6391
🚶 ⛺ 👫 ⛲ 🛶 🏕

NORTH DAKOTA
Little Missouri National Grassland
Between the Missouri River and South Dakota.
(701) 227-7800
🚶 ⛺ 👫 ⛲

Sheyenne National Grassland
Along the Sheyenne River south of Fargo.
(701) 683-4342
⛺ 👫 ⛲

Theodore Roosevelt National Park (North Unit)
In western North Dakota.
(701) 842-2333
⛺ 👫 ⛲ 🏕

Theodore Roosevelt National Park (South Unit)
In western North Dakota.
(701) 623-4466
⛺ 👫 ⛲ 🏕 🍴

OHIO
Cuyahoga Valley National Park
In northeastern Ohio.
(216) 524-1497
🚶 👫 ⛲ 🏕 🍴

Hopewell Culture National Historical Park
About 3 mi. north of Chillicothe on SR 104.
(740) 774-1126
🚶 👫 ⛲ 🏕

Wayne National Forest
In southeast Ohio.
(740) 753-0101
🚶 ⛺ 👫 ⛲ 🛶 🏕

OKLAHOMA
Chickasaw National Recreation Area
In south-central Oklahoma.
(580) 622-3165
🚶 ⛺ 👫 ⛲ 🛶 🏕

Ouachita National Forest
In southeastern Oklahoma and west-central Arkansas.
(501) 321-5202
🚶 ⛺ 👫 ⛲ 🛶 🏕 🍴

Salt Plains National Wildlife Refuge
Off SR 38, 2 mi. south of jct. SRs 11 and 38 at Cherokee.
(580) 626-4794
⛺ 👫 🏕

OREGON
Crater Lake National Park
On the crest of the Cascade Range off SR 62.
(541) 594-3100
⛺ 👫 ⛲ 🏕 🍴

Deschutes National Forest
In central Oregon 6 mi. south of Bend via US 97.
(541) 383-5300
🚶 ⛺ 👫 ⛲ 🛶 🏕 🍴

Fremont-Winema National Forests
In south-central Oregon.
(541) 947-2151
🚶 ⛺ 👫 ⛲ 🛶 🏕

Hells Canyon National Recreation Area
In northeastern Oregon and western Idaho.
(541) 426-5546
🚶 ⛺ 👫 ⛲ 🏕

Malheur National Forest
In eastern Oregon.
(541) 575-3000
🚶 ⛺ 👫 ⛲ 🛶 🍴

Mount Hood National Forest
In northwestern Oregon.
(888) 622-4822
🚲 ⛺ 🥾 🏕 ⛲ 👥 🍴

Ochoco National Forest
In central Oregon off US 26.
(541) 416-6500
🚲 ⛺ 🥾 🏕 ⛲

Oregon Dunes National Recreation Area
Between North Bend and Florence.
(541) 271-6000
🚲 ⛺ 🥾 🏕 ⛲ 👥

Rogue River-Siskiyou National Forest
In southwestern Oregon off I-5 from Medford.
(541) 858-2200
🚲 ⛺ 🥾 🏕 ⛲ 👥 🍴

Siuslaw National Forest
In western Oregon.
(541) 750-7000
🚲 ⛺ 🥾 🏕 ⛲ 👥 🍴

Umatilla National Forest
In northeastern Oregon.
(541) 278-3716
🚲 ⛺ 🥾 🏕 ⛲ 👥

Umpqua National Forest
In southwestern Oregon 33 mi. east of Roseburg on SR 138.
(541) 672-6601
🚲 ⛺ 🥾 🏕 ⛲ 👥 🍴

Wallowa-Whitman National Forest
In northeastern Oregon.
(541) 523-6391
🚲 ⛺ 🥾 🏕 ⛲ 👥 🍴

Willamette National Forest
In western Oregon.
(541) 225-6300
🚲 ⛺ 🥾 🏕 ⛲ 👥 🍴

PENNSYLVANIA
Allegheny National Forest
In northwestern Pennsylvania.
(814) 723-5150 or TDD (814) 726-2710
🚲 ⛺ 🥾 🏕 ⛲ 👥 🍴

Delaware Water Gap National Recreation Area
In eastern Pennsylvania and northwestern New Jersey.
(570) 426-2457
🚲 ⛺ 🥾 🏕 ⛲ 👥

Gettysburg National Military Park
Surrounding the town of Gettysburg at SR 134.
(717) 334-1124
🚲 🥾 ⛲ 👥 🍴

John Heinz National Wildlife Refuge at Tinicum
I-95S exit 14 near Philadelphia
(215) 365-3118
🚲 🥾 👥

Valley Forge National Historical Park
1400 N. Outer Line Dr.
(610) 783-1077
🚲 🥾 ⛲ 👥 🍴

SOUTH CAROLINA
Congaree National Park
Southeast of Hopkins.
(803) 776-4396
⛺ 🥾 ⛲ 👥

Francis Marion National Forest
On the Coastal Plain north of Charleston.
(803) 561-4000
🚲 ⛺ 🥾 ⛲ 👥

Kings Mountain National Military Park
South of Kings Mountain, N.C., off I-85.
(864) 936-7921
⛺ 🥾 👥

Sumter National Forest
In western South Carolina.
(803) 561-4000
🚲 ⛺ 🥾 ⛲ 🍴

SOUTH DAKOTA
Badlands National Park
In southwestern South Dakota.
(605) 433-5361, ext. 100
⛺ 🥾 ⛲ 👥 🍴

Black Hills National Forest
In southwestern South Dakota.
(605) 673-9200 or TDD (605) 673-4954
🚲 ⛺ 🥾 🏕 ⛲ 👥 🍴

Custer National Forest
In northwestern South Dakota and southeastern Montana.
(605) 797-4432
🚲 ⛺ 🥾 ⛲

Wind Cave National Park
In southwestern South Dakota.
(605) 745-4600
⛺ 🥾 ⛲ 👥

TENNESSEE
Big South Fork National River and Recreation Area
In northeastern Tennessee and southeastern Kentucky.
(423) 286-7275
🚲 ⛺ 🥾 🏕 ⛲ 👥

Cherokee National Forest
In eastern Tennessee.
(423) 476-9700
🚲 ⛺ 🥾 🏕 ⛲ 👥

🚲 Bicycling Trails   ⛺ Camping   🥾 Hiking Trails   🏕 Picnic Facilities
⛲ Swimming   👥 Visitor Center   🍴 Food Service

Chickamauga and Chattanooga National Military Park
On the Georgia-Tennessee border.
(706) 866-9241
⬥ 🚶 ⛱ 🏕

Great Smoky Mountains National Park
In eastern Tennessee and western North Carolina.
(865) 436-1200
⬥ ⛺ 🚶 ⛱ 🏕

Land Between the Lakes National Recreation Area
In western Kentucky and Tennessee.
(270) 924-2000 or (800) 525-7077
⬥ ⛺ 🚶 ⛱ ⚓ 🏕

TEXAS
Amistad National Recreation Area
Northwest of Del Rio via US 90.
(830) 775-7491
⛺ 🚶 ⛱ ⚓ 🏕

Angelina National Forest
In east Texas.
(936) 897-1068
⛺ 🚶 ⛱ ⚓

Big Bend National Park
In southwest Texas.
(432) 477-2251 or (432) 477-1188
⛺ 🚶 ⛱ 🏕 🍴

Davy Crockett National Forest
In east Texas.
(936) 655-2299
⛺ 🚶 ⛱ ⚓ 🍴

Guadalupe Mountains National Park
110 mi. east of El Paso on US 62/180.
(915) 828-3251
⛺ 🚶 ⛱ 🏕

Lake Meredith National Recreation Area
45 mi. northeast of Amarillo and 9 mi. west of Borger via SR 136.
(806) 857-3151
⛺ ⛱ ⚓ 🏕🍴

Padre Island National Seashore
On Padre Island near Corpus Christi.
(361) 949-8173
⬥ ⛺ 🚶 ⛱ ⚓ 🏕 🍴

Sabine National Forest
In east Texas.
(409) 625-1940
⛺ 🚶 ⛱ ⚓

Sam Houston National Forest
40 mi. north of Houston in east Texas.
(936) 344-6205 or (888) 361-6908
⬥ ⛺ 🚶 ⛱ ⚓ 🏕 🍴

UTAH
Ashley National Forest
In northeastern Utah.
(435) 789-1181
⬥ ⛺ 🚶 ⛱ ⚓ 🏕 🍴

Canyonlands National Park
In southeastern Utah.
(435) 719-2100
⛺ 🚶 ⛱ 🏕

Capitol Reef National Park
10 mi. east of Torrey on SR 24.
(435) 425-3791, ext. 111
⛺ 🚶 ⛱ 🏕

Dixie National Forest
In southwestern Utah.
(435) 865-3700
⬥ ⛺ 🚶 ⛱ ⚓ 🏕 🍴

Fishlake National Forest
In south-central Utah.
(435) 896-9233
⬥ ⛺ 🚶 ⛱ ⚓ 🏕 🍴

Flaming Gorge National Recreation Area
In northeastern Utah.
(435) 784-3445
⬥ ⛺ 🚶 ⛱ ⚓ 🏕 🍴

Glen Canyon National Recreation Area
In south-central Utah.
(928) 608-6200
⛺ 🚶 ⛱ ⚓ 🏕 🍴

Manti-La Sal National Forest
In southeastern Utah.
(435) 637-2817
⬥ ⛺ 🚶 ⛱ ⚓ 🏕

Uinta-Wasatch-Cache National Forest
In north-central, central and northeastern Utah.
(801) 236-3400 or (801) 466-6411
⬥ ⛺ 🚶 ⛱ ⚓ 🏕 🍴

Zion National Park
In southwestern Utah.
(435) 772-3256
⬥ ⛺ 🚶 ⛱ 🏕 🍴

VERMONT
Green Mountain National Forest
In south-central Vermont.
(802) 747-6700
⛺ 🚶 ⛱ ⚓🏕

Marsh-Billings-Rockefeller National Historical Park
Off SR 12 near Woodstock.
(802) 457-3368, ext. 22
🚶🏕

VIRGINIA
George Washington and Jefferson National Forests
In western Virginia and the eastern edge of West Virginia.
(540) 265-5100 or (888) 265-0019
⬥ ⛺ 🚶 ⛱ ⚓

Mount Rogers National Recreation Area
In southwestern Virginia.
(276) 783-5196 or (800) 628-7202
⬥ ⛺ 🚶 ⛱ ⚓ 🏕

Shenandoah National Park
In northwestern Virginia.
(540) 999-3500
🅰 🏃 🌲 🏠 🍽

WASHINGTON
Colville National Forest
In northeastern Washington.
(509) 684-7000
🚲 🅰 🏃 🌲 🏊

Gifford Pinchot National Forest
In southwestern Washington.
(360) 891-5001 or (360) 891-5002
🚲 🅰 🏃 🌲 🏊 🏠

Lake Chelan National Recreation Area
In north-central Washington.
(509) 682-2549
🅰 🏃 🌲 🏠 🍽

Lake Roosevelt National Recreation Area
In northeastern Washington.
(509) 633-9441
🚲 🅰 🏃 🌲 🏊 🏠 🍽

Mount Baker-Snoqualmie National Forest
2 mi. east of Glacier on SR 542.
(425) 783-6000 or (800) 627-0062, ext. 0
🚲 🅰 🏃 🌲 🏊 🏠 🍽

Okanogan National Forest
In north-central Washington.
(509) 996-4000
🚲 🅰 🏃 🌲 🏊 🏠

Olympic National Forest
In northwestern Washington.
(360) 956-2400
🚲 🅰 🏃 🌲 🏊 🏠 🍽

Ross Lake National Recreation Area
Between the north and south sections of North Cascades
National Park.
(360) 854-7200
🅰 🏃 🌲 🏊 🏠

WEST VIRGINIA
Monongahela National Forest
In eastern West Virginia.
(304) 636-1800
🚲 🅰 🏃 🌲 🏊 🏠 🍽

New River Gorge National River
Between Fayetteville and Hinton.
(304) 465-0508
🚲 🅰 🏃 🌲 🏠

Spruce Knob-Seneca Rocks National Recreation Area
In east-central West Virginia.
(304) 257-4488
🚲 🅰 🏃 🌲 🏠

WISCONSIN
Apostle Islands National Lakeshore
Off northern Wisconsin's Bayfield Peninsula in Lake
Superior.
(715) 779-3397
🅰 🏃 🌲 🏊 🏠

Chequamegon-Nicolet National Forest
In north-central and northeastern Wisconsin.
(715) 762-2461 (Chequamegon) or (715) 362-1300
(Nicolet)
🚲 🅰 🏃 🌲 🏊

St. Croix National Scenic Riverway
Running 252 mi. from Cable to Prescott.
(715) 483-2274
🅰 🏃 🌲 🏠

WYOMING
Bighorn Canyon National Recreation Area
In southern Montana and northern Wyoming.
(307) 548-2251
🅰 🏃 🌲 🏊 🏠

Bighorn National Forest
In north-central Wyoming.
(307) 674-2600
🚲 🅰 🏃 🌲 🏠 🍽

Devils Tower National Monument
Between Sundance and Hulett.
(307) 467-5283
🅰 🏃 🌲 🏠

Flaming Gorge National Recreation Area
On the Wyoming-Utah border.
(435) 784-3445
🚲 🅰 🏃 🌲 🏊 🏠 🍽

Fossil Butte National Monument
14 mi. west of Kemmerer on US 30.
(307) 877-4455
🏃 🌲 🏠

Grand Teton National Park
In northwestern Wyoming.
(307) 739-3300
🚲 🅰 🏃 🌲 🏊 🏠 🍽

Medicine Bow National Forest
In southeastern Wyoming.
(307) 745-2300
🚲 🅰 🏃 🌲 🏠

Shoshone National Forest
In northwestern Wyoming.
(307) 527-6241
🚲 🅰 🏃 🌲 🏠 🍽

Yellowstone National Park
In northwestern Wyoming.
(307) 344-7311
🅰 🏃 🌲 🏊 🏠 🍽

🚲 Bicycling Trails   🅰 Camping   🏃 Hiking Trails   🌲 Picnic Facilities
🏊 Swimming   🏠 Visitor Center   🍽 Food Service

Canada

ALBERTA

Banff National Park of Canada
In southwestern Alberta, west of Calgary.
(403) 762-1550

Elk Island National Park of Canada
In central Alberta, east of Edmonton.
(780) 992-2950

Jasper National Park of Canada
In west-central Alberta along the British Columbia border.
(780) 852-6176

Waterton Lakes National Park of Canada
In Alberta's southwestern corner.
(403) 859-2224

BRITISH COLUMBIA

Gulf Islands National Park Reserve of Canada
Off the southeast coast of Vancouver Island.
(250) 654-4000

Glacier National Park of Canada
In southeastern British Columbia.
(250) 837-7500

Kootenay National Park of Canada
In southeastern British Columbia.
(250) 347-9505 or (888) 773-8888

Mount Revelstoke National Park of Canada
In southeastern British Columbia.
(250) 837-7500

Pacific Rim National Park Reserve of Canada
On the southwestern coast of Vancouver Island.
(250) 726-3500

Yoho National Park of Canada
On the British Columbia-Alberta border.
(250) 343-6783

MANITOBA

Riding Mountain National Park of Canada
In southwestern Manitoba.
(204) 848-7275

NEW BRUNSWICK

Fundy National Park of Canada
On Hwy. 114, 130 km. southwest of Moncton.
(506) 887-6000

Kouchibouguac National Park of Canada
On Hwy. 134, north of Moncton.
(506) 876-2443 or TDD (506) 876-4205

NEWFOUNDLAND

Gros Morne National Park of Canada
On Newfoundland's western coast.
(709) 458-2417 or TDD (709) 772-4564

Terra Nova National Park of Canada
In eastern Newfoundland.
(709) 533-2801

NORTHWEST TERRITORIES

Nahanni National Park Reserve of Canada
145 km. west of Fort Simpson in southwestern Northwest Territories.
(867) 695-3151

Wood Buffalo National Park of Canada
On the Northwest Territories-Alberta border.
(867) 872-7960

NOVA SCOTIA

Cape Breton Highlands National Park of Canada
5 km. northeast of Chéticamp on Cabot Tr.
(902) 224-2306 or (888) 773-8888

Kejimkujik National Park and National Historic Site of Canada
In southwestern Nova Scotia off Hwy. 8 at Maitland Bridge.
(902) 682-2772

ONTARIO

Bruce Peninsula National Park of Canada
In southwestern Ontario.
(519) 596-2233

Georgian Bay Islands National Park
Along the southeastern portion of Georgian Bay.
(705) 526-9804

Point Pelee National Park of Canada
South of Leamington.
(519) 322-2365 or (888) 773-8888
🚲 𝕸 ⛱ ⚓ 🏠 🍽

Pukaskwa National Park of Canada
On the north shore of Lake Superior.
(807) 229-0801, ext. 242
⛺ 𝕸 ⛱ ⚓ 🏠

St. Lawrence Islands National Park of Canada
In the St. Lawrence River between Kingston and
Brockville.
(613) 923-5261
⛺ 𝕸 ⛱ ⚓ 🏠

PRINCE EDWARD ISLAND
**Port La Joye-Fort Amherst National Historic Site of
Canada**
West of Charlottetown on Hwy. 1.
(902) 566-7626
𝕸 ⛱ 🏠 🍽

Prince Edward Island National Park of Canada
Along the island's northern shore.
(902) 672-6350 or TTY (902) 566-7061
🚲 ⛺ 𝕸 ⛱ ⚓ 🏠 🍽

QUEBEC
Forillon National Park of Canada
20 km. northeast of Gaspé via Hwy. 132.
(418) 368-5505 or (888) 773-8888

🚲 ⛺ 𝕸 ⛱ ⚓ 🏠 🍽

La Mauricie National Park of Canada
North of Trois-Rivières via Hwy. 55.
(819) 538-3232 or (888) 773-8888
🚲 ⛺ 𝕸 ⛱ ⚓ 🏠 🍽

SASKATCHEWAN
Grasslands National Park of Canada
Between Val Marie and Killdeer in southern
Saskatchewan.
(306) 298-2257
⛺ 𝕸 🏠

Prince Albert National Park of Canada
In central Saskatchewan.
(306) 663-4522
🚲 ⛺ 𝕸 ⛱ ⚓ 🏠 🍽

YUKON TERRITORY
Kluane National Park of Canada
West of Haines Junction.
(867) 634-7250
🚲 ⛺ 𝕸 ⛱ ⚓ 🏠 🍽

This list of emergency animal clinics in the United States and Canada is provided by the Veterinary Emergency & Critical Care Society (VECCS) as a service to the community for information purposes only. This is not to be construed as a certification or an endorsement of any clinic listed. For further information, contact the society at (210) 698-5575 or online at www.veccs.org. Note: Hours frequently change, and not all clinics are open 24 hours or in the evening. In addition, not all facilities listed here are emergency clinics. In non-emergency situations, it's best to call first.

If you are traveling to an area not covered in this list, be prepared for an emergency by asking your regular veterinarian to recommend a clinic or veterinarian at your destination. The American Animal Hospital Association also can recommend veterinary clinics that meet the association's high standards for veterinary care. For additional information contact the association at (303) 986-2800.

United States

ALABAMA

Auburn University Small Animal Teaching Hospital
Hoerlein Hall, 1185 Wire Rd., Auburn
(334) 844-4690

Emergency & Specialty Animal Medical Center
2864 Acton Rd., Birmingham
(205) 967-7389

Southern Regional Veterinary Emergency Services
301 Westgate Pkwy., Dothan
(334) 699-7787

Animal Emergency Clinic of North Alabama
2112 Memorial Pkwy. S.W., Huntsville
(256) 533-7600

Animal Emergency & Referral Center of Mobile
2573 Government Blvd., Mobile
(251) 706-0890

ALASKA

Pet Emergency Treatment, Inc.
2320 E. Dowling Rd., Anchorage
(907) 274-5636

After Hours Veterinary Emergency Clinic
8 Bonnie Ave., Fairbanks
(907) 479-2700

ARIZONA

First Regional Animal Hospital
1233 W. Warner Rd., Chandler
(480) 732-0018

Emergency Animal Clinic, PLC
86 W. Juniper, Gilbert
(480) 497-0222

1st Emergency Pet Care
1423 S. Higley Rd. #102, Mesa
(480) 924-1123

VCA Mesa Animal Hospital
858 N. Country Club, Mesa
(480) 833-7330

Emergency Animal Clinic, PLC
9875 W. Peoria Ave., Peoria
(623) 974-1520

Emergency Animal Clinic, PLC
2260 W. Glendale Ave., Phoenix
(602) 995-3757

North Valley Regional Animal Hospital
520 W. Union Hills Dr. #105, Phoenix
(623) 516-8571

Sonora Veterinary Specialists
4015 E. Cactus Rd., Phoenix
(602) 765-3700

Emergency Animal Clinic, PLC
14202 N. Scottsdale Rd., Suite 163, Scottsdale
(480) 949-8001

Paradise Valley Emergency Animal Clinic
6969 E. Shea Blvd., #225, Scottsdale
(480) 991-1848

Ina Road Animal Hospital
7320 N. La Cholla, Suite 114, Tucson
(520) 544-7700

Pima Pet Clinic - Animal Emergency Service
4832 E. Speedway Blvd., Tucson
(520) 327-5624

Southern Arizona Veterinary Specialty and Emergency Center
141 E. Fort Lowell, Tucson
(520) 888-3177, ext. 1

Southern Arizona Veterinary Specialty and Emergency Center
7474 E. Broadway Blvd., Tucson
(520) 888-3177, ext. 2

Valley Animal Hospital
4984 E. 22nd St., Tucson
(520) 748-0331

Veterinary Specialty Center of Tucson
4909 N. La Canada Dr., Tucson
(520) 795-9955

ARKANSAS

Ft. Smith Animal Emergency Clinic
4301 Regions Park Dr., Suite 3, Fort Smith
(479) 649-3100

After Hours Animal Hospital
290 Smokey Ln., North Little Rock
(501) 955-0911

Animal Emergency & Specialty Clinic
8735 Sheltie Dr., Suite G, North Little Rock
(501) 224-3784

Animal Emergency Clinic of Northwest Arkansas
1110 Mathias Dr., Suite E, Springdale
(479) 927-0007

CALIFORNIA

East Bay Veterinary Emergency
1312 Sunset Dr., Antioch
(925) 754-5001

Central Coast Pet Emergency Clinic
1558 W. Branch St., Arroyo Grande
(805) 489-6573

Atascadero Pet Hospital and Emergency Center
9575 El Camino Real, Atascadero
(805) 466-3880

Animal Emergency & Urgent Care
4300 Easton Dr., Suite 1, Bakersfield
(661) 322-6019

Pet Emergency Treatment Service
1048 University Ave., Berkeley
(510) 548-6684

United Emergency Animal Clinic
905 Dell Ave., Campbell
(408) 371-6252

**Pacific Veterinary Specialists and
Emergency Critical Care Center**
1980 41st Ave., Capitola
(831) 476-0667

North Valley Emergency Veterinary Clinic
2500 Zanella Way, Chico
(530) 899-1720

Contra Costa Veterinary Emergency Center
1410 Monument Blvd., Suite 108, Concord
(925) 798-2900

VCA Acacia Animal Hospital
939 W. 6th St., Corona
(951) 371-1002

Advanced Critical Care
9599 Jefferson Blvd., Culver City
(310) 558-6100

**UC Davis Veterinary Medical Teaching Hospital
Small Animal Clinic**
One Shields Ave., Davis
(530) 752-1393

Tri-Valley Animal Emergency Center
7111 Amador Plaza Rd., Dublin
(925) 771-5630

Vetcare Emergency & Specialty Care Center
7660 Amador Valley Blvd., Dublin
(925) 556-1234

Emergency Pet Clinic of San Gabriel Valley
3254 Santa Anita Ave., El Monte
(626) 579-4550

North Coast Veterinary and Emergency
414 Encinitas Blvd., Encinitas
(760) 632-1072

Animal Urgent Care
2430 S. Escondido Blvd., Suite A, Escondido
(760) 738-9600

Animal Emergency Center
3954 A Jacobs Ave., Eureka
(707) 443-2776

Solano-Napa Pet Emergency Clinic
4437 Central Pl., Fairfield
(707) 864-1444

VCA All-Care Animal Referral Center
18440 Amistad St., Suite E, Fountain Valley
(714) 963-0909

Ohlone Veterinary Emergency Clinic
1618 Washington Blvd., Fremont
(510) 657-6620

Central California Veterinary Specialty Center
6606 N. Blackstone Ave., Fresno
(559) 451-0800

Fresno Pet Emergency (Pet ER)
7375 N. Palm Bluffs Ave., Fresno
(559) 437-3766

Veterinary Emergency Service, Inc.
1639 N. Fresno St., Fresno
(559) 486-0520

Orange County Emergency Pet Clinic
12750 Garden Grove Blvd., Garden Grove
(714) 537-3032

Animal Emergency Clinic
12022 La Crosse Ave., Grand Terrace
(909) 825-9350

Irvine Regional Animal Emergency Hospital
1371 Reynolds Ave., Irvine
(949) 833-9020

North Orange County Emergency Pet Clinic
1474 S. Harbor Blvd., La Habra
(714) 441-2925

Pet Emergency and Specialty Center
5232 Jackson Dr. #105, La Mesa
(619) 462-4800

Animal Emergency Clinic
1055 W. Avenue M, Suite 101, Lancaster
(661) 723-3959

Animal Specialty Group
4641 Colorado Blvd., Los Angeles
(818) 244-7977

Animal Surgical and Emergency Center (ASEC)
1535 S. Sepulveda Blvd., Los Angeles
(310) 473-5906

Eagle Rock Emergency Pet Clinic
4254 Eagle Rock Blvd., Los Angeles
(323) 254-7382

VCA West Los Angeles Animal Hospital
1818 S. Sepulveda Blvd., Los Angeles
(310) 473-2951

Animal Urgent Care
2805 Hillcrest, Mission Viejo
(949) 364-6228

Portola Plaza Veterinary Hospital
27752 Santa Margarita Pkwy., Mission Viejo
(949) 859-2101

Modesto Veterinary Emergency Clinic
1800 Prescott Rd., Modesto
(209) 527-8844

Monterey Peninsula Veterinary Emergency & Specialty Center
20 Lower Ragsdale, Suite 150, Monterey
(831) 373-7374

All Creatures Emergency Center
22722 Lyons Ave., #5, Newhall
(661) 291-1121

Central Orange County Emergency Animal Clinic
3720 Campus Dr., Suite D, Newport Beach
(949) 261-7979

Crossroads Animal Emergency and Referral Clinic
11057 E. Rosecrans Ave., Norwalk
(562) 863-2522

Orange Veterinary Hospital
1100 W. Chapman Ave., Orange
(714) 997-8200

South Peninsula Veterinary Emergency Clinic
3045 Middlefield Rd., Palo Alto
(650) 494-1461

Animal Emergency Clinic of Pasadena
2121 E. Foothill Blvd., Pasadena
(626) 564-0704

Animal Emergency Clinic of San Diego
12775 Poway Rd., Poway
(858) 748-7387

Animal Care Center of Sonoma County
6470 Redwood Dr., Rohnert Park
(707) 584-4343

Atlantic St. Veterinary Hospital Pet Emergency Center
1100 Atlantic St., Roseville
(916) 783-4655

El Camino Veterinary Hospital
4000 El Camino Ave., Sacramento
(916) 488-6878

Mueller Pet Medical Center
6420 Freeport Blvd., Sacramento
(916) 428-9202

Northern California Veterinary Specialists
7425 Greenhaven Dr., Sacramento
(916) 231-0696

VCA Sacramento Veterinary Referral Center
9801 Old Winery Pl., Sacramento
(916) 362-3111

Animal E.R. of San Diego
5610 Kearny Mesa Rd., Suite A, San Diego
(858) 569-0600

VCA Emergency Animal Hospital and Referral Center
2317 Hotel Cir. S., San Diego
(619) 299-2400

Veterinary Specialty Hospital
10435 Sorrento Valley Rd., San Diego
(858) 875-7500

All Animals Emergency Hospital
1333 Ninth Ave., San Francisco
(415) 566-0531

Pets Unlimited
2343 Fillmore St., San Francisco
(415) 563-6700

San Francisco Veterinary Specialists
600 Alabama St., San Francisco
(415) 401-9200

Emergency Animal Clinic of South San Jose
5440 Thornwood Dr., Suite E, San Jose
(408) 578-5622

Bay Area Veterinary Emergency Clinic
14790 Washington Ave., San Leandro
(510) 352-6080

California Veterinary Specialists
100 N. Rancho Santa Fe Rd., San Marcos
(760) 734-4433

North Peninsula Veterinary Emergency Clinic, Inc.
227 N. Amphlett Blvd., San Mateo
(650) 348-2575

The Pet Emergency and Specialty Center of Marin
901 E. Francisco Blvd., Suite C, San Rafael
(415) 456-7372

California Animal Referral & Emergency Hospital
301 E. Haley St., Santa Barbara
(805) 899-2273

Santa Cruz Veterinary Hospital
2585 Soquel Dr., Santa Cruz
(831) 475-5400

Westside Animal Emergency Hospital
1304 Wilshire Blvd., Santa Monica
(310) 451-8962

Emergency Animal Hospital of Santa Rosa
1946 Santa Rosa Ave., Santa Rosa
(707) 544-1647

PetCare Veterinary Hospital
1370 Fulton Rd., Santa Rosa
(707) 579-5900

Beverly Oaks Animal Hospital and Emergency Animal Clinic
14302 Ventura Blvd., Sherman Oaks
(818) 788-7860

TLC Pet Medical Centers-South Pasadena
1412 Huntington Dr., South Pasadena
(626) 441-8555

Associated Veterinary Emergency Services
3008 E. Hammer Ln. #115, Stockton
(209) 952-8387

Animal Emergency Centre
11730 Ventura Blvd., Studio City
(818) 760-3882

Emergency Pet Clinic of Temecula
27443 Jefferson Ave., Temecula
(951) 695-5044

Pet Emergency Clinic, Inc.
2967 N. Moorpark Rd., Thousand Oaks
(805) 492-2436

Animal Emergency Referral Center
3511 Pacific Coast Hwy., Suite A, Torrance
(310) 325-3000

Emergency Pet Clinic of South Bay
2325 Torrance Blvd., Torrance
(310) 320-8300

Monte Vista Small Animal Hospital
901 E. Monte Vista Ave., Turlock
(209) 634-0023

Advanced Critical Care & Internal Medicine
3021 Edinger Ave., Tustin
(949) 654-8950

Inland Valley Emergency Pet Clinic
10 W. 7th St., Upland
(909) 931-7871

Pet Emergency Clinic, Inc.
2301 S. Victoria Ave., Ventura
(805) 642-8562

Veterinary Medical and Surgical Group
2199 Sperry Ave., Ventura
(805) 339-2290

Animal Emergency Clinic
12180 Ridgecrest Rd., Suite 122, Victorville
(760) 962-1122

Tulare-Kings Veterinary Emergency Service
4240 W. Mineral King Ave., Visalia
(559) 739-7054

TLC Pet Medical Centers-West Hollywood
8725 Santa Monica Blvd., West Hollywood
(310) 859-4852

COLORADO

Animal Urgent Care
7851 Indiana St., Arvada
(303) 420-7387

Aurora Veterinary Emergency Center
18511 E. Hampden Ave., Suite 212, Aurora
(303) 699-1665

Valley Emergency Pet Care
180 Fiou Ln., Suite 101, Basalt
(970) 927-5066

Alpenglow Veterinary Specialty & Emergency Center
3640 Walnut St., Boulder
(303) 443-4569

Boulder Emergency Pet Clinic
1658 30th St., Boulder
(303) 440-7722

VCA Douglas County Animal Hospital
531 Jerry St., Castle Rock
(303) 688-2480

Animal Emergency Care Centers
3775 Airport Rd., Colorado Springs
(719) 578-9300

Animal Emergency Care Centers
5520 N. Nevada Ave., Colorado Springs
(719) 260-7141

VCA Alameda East Veterinary Hospital
9770 E. Alameda Ave., Denver
(303) 366-2639

Central Veterinary Emergency Services
3550 S. Jason St., Englewood
(303) 874-7387

Pet Emergency Clinic
3629 23rd Ave., Evans
(970) 339-8700

Fort Collins Veterinary Emergency Hospital
816 S. Lemay Ave., Fort Collins
(970) 484-8080

James L. Voss Veterinary Teaching Hospital Colorado State University
300 W. Drake Rd., Fort Collins
(970) 221-4535

Grand Valley Veterinary Emergency Center
1660 North Ave., Grand Junction
(970) 255-1911

Animal Hospital Specialty Center
5640 County Line Pl., Suite 1, Highland Ranch
(303) 740-9595

Animal Critical Care & Emergency Services, Inc.
1597 Wadsworth Blvd., Lakewood
(303) 239-1200

Animal E.R.
221 W. County Line Rd., Littleton
(720) 283-9348

Columbine Animal Hospital & Emergency Clinic
5546 W. Canyon Tr., Littleton
(303) 979-4040

Aspen Meadow Veterinary Specialists
104 S. Main St., Longmont
(303) 678-8844

VCA Vet Specialists of Northern Colorado
201 W. 67th Ct., Loveland
(970) 278-0668

Animal Emergency & Specialty Center
17701 Cottonwood Dr., Parker
(720) 842-5050

Northside Emergency Pet Clinic
945 W. 124th Ave., Westminster
(303) 252-7722

Wheat Ridge Animal Hospital / Wheat Ridge Veterinary Specialists
3695 Kipling St., Wheat Ridge
(303) 424-3325

CONNECTICUT

Farmington Valley Veterinary Emergency Hospital
9 Avonwood Rd., Avon
(860) 674-1886

East of the River Veterinary Emergency Clinic
222 Boston Turnpike, Bolton
(860) 646-6134

VCA Cheshire Veterinary Hospital
1572 South Main St., Cheshire
(203) 271-1577

Veterinary Emergency Treatment Services (VETS)
8 Enterprise Ln., Montville
(860) 444-8870

New Haven Central Hospital for Veterinary Medicine, Inc.
843 State St., New Haven
(203) 865-0878

VCA Veterinary Referral & Emergency Center
123 W. Cedar St., Norwalk
(203) 854-9960

Animal Emergency Hospital of Central Connecticut
588 Cromwell Ave., Rocky Hill
(860) 563-4447

V-E-T-S (Veterinary Emergency Treatment Services)
8 Enterprise Ln., Oakdale

Connecticut Veterinary Center
470 Oakwood Ave., West Hartford
(860) 233-8564

DELAWARE

VCA Newark Animal Hospital
1360 Marrows Rd., Newark
(302) 737-8100

Veterinary Emergency Center of Delaware
1212 E. Newport Pike, Wilmington
(302) 691-3647

Wincrest Animal Emergency Hospital
3705 Lancaster Pike, Wilmington
(302) 998-2995

DISTRICT OF COLUMBIA

Friendship Hospital for Animals
4105 Brandywine St., Washington
(202) 363-7300

FLORIDA

Boca Veterinary Emergency Center
6900 Congress Ave., Boca Raton
(561) 443-3699

Animal Emergency and Referral Center
2246 N. Congress Ave., Boynton Beach
(561) 752-3232

Animal Emergency Clinic of Brandon
693 W. Lumsden Rd., Brandon
(813) 684-3013

Veterinary Emergency Clinic of Central Florida, Inc.
195 Concord Dr., Casselberry
(407) 644-4449

Animal Emergency and Critical Care Services of S. Florida
9410 Stirling Rd., Cooper City
(954) 432-5611

Coral Springs Animal Hospital & Emergency Service
2160 N. University Dr., Coral Springs
(954) 753-1800

Florida Veterinary Referral Center & 24 Hour Emergency & Critical Care
9220 Estero Park Commons Blvd., Suite 7, Estero
(239) 992-8878

Animal Emergency Trauma Center
2200 W. Oakland Park Blvd., Fort Lauderdale
(954) 731-4228

Pet Emergency Center
921 E. Cypress Creek Rd., Fort Lauderdale
(954) 772-0420

Emergency Veterinary Clinic, Inc.
2045 Collier Ave., Fort Myers
(239) 939-5542

Animal Emergency and Referral Center
3984 S. US 1, Fort Pierce
(772) 466-3441

Affiliated Pet Emergency Services
7314 W. University Ave., Gainesville
(352) 373-4444

Hollywood Animal Hospital
2864 Hollywood Blvd., Hollywood
(954) 920-3556

Animal ER
3444 Southside Blvd., Suite 101, Jacksonville
(904) 642-4357

Emergency Pet Care, LLC
14185 Beach Blvd., Suite 7, Jacksonville
(904) 223-8000

Emergency Pet Care of Jupiter
300 S. Central Blvd., Jupiter
(561) 746-0555

Tampa Bay Veterinary Emergency Service
1501-A Belcher Rd., Suite 1A, Largo
(727) 531-5752

Veterinary Emergency Clinic of Central Florida-Lake County Facility
33040 Professional Dr., Leesburg
(352) 728-4450

Animal Emergency and Critical Care Center of Brevard
2281 W. Eau Gallie Blvd., Melbourne
(321) 725-5365

AEC-Animal Emergency Clinic South
8429 S.W. 132nd St., Miami
(305) 251-2096

Doral Centre Animal Clinic
9589 N.W. 41st St., Miami
(305) 598-1234

Knowles Snapper Creek Emergency Clinic
9933 Sunset Dr., Miami
(305) 279-2323

Miami Pet Emergency
11774 S.W. 88th St., Miami
(305) 273-8100

Miami Veterinary Specialists
8601 Sunset Dr., Miami
(305) 665-2820

The Pet Emergency Room
6394 S. Dixie Hwy., Miami
(305) 666-4142

VCA Cabrera Animal Hospital
6390 S.W. 8th St., Miami
(305) 261-2374

Emergency Pet Hospital of Collier County
6530 Dudley Dr., Naples
(239) 263-8010

Animal ER of SW Florida
15201 N. Cleveland Ave. #1400, North Fort Myers
(239) 995-7755

Ocala Animal Emergency Hospital
1815 N.E. Jacksonville Rd., Ocala
(352) 840-0044

Clay-Duval Pet Emergency Clinic
275 Corporate Way, Suite 200, Orange Park
(904) 264-8281

Veterinary Emergency Clinic of Central Florida, South Facility
2080 Principal Row, Orlando
(407) 438-4449

Pet Emergency and Critical Care Clinic
3816 Northlake Blvd., Palm Beach Gardens
(561) 691-9999

A.A. Animal ER Center, LLC
36401 US 19N, Palm Harbor
(727) 787-5402

Animal Emergency of Countryside, Inc.
30610 US 19N, Palm Harbor
(727) 786-5755

St. Francis Emergency Animal Hospital
6602 Pines Blvd., Pembroke Pines
(954) 962-0300

Veterinary Emergency Referral Center
4800 N. Davis Hwy., Pensacola
(850) 477-3914

The Veterinary Emergency Clinic
17829 Murdock Cir., Port Charlotte
(941) 255-5222

Animal Specialty and Emergency Hospital
5775 Schenck Ave., Rockledge
(321) 752-7600

Sarasota Veterinary Emergency Hospital
7515-7517 S. Tamiami Tr., Sarasota
(941) 923-7260

Animal Emergency Clinic of St. Petersburg
3165 22nd Ave. N., St. Petersburg
(727) 323-1311

Noahs Animal Hospital and 24 Hour Emergency
2050 62nd Ave. N., St. Petersburg
(727) 522-6640

Pet Emergency of Martin County
2239 S. Kanner Hwy., Stuart
(772) 781-3302

FVS (Florida Veterinary Specialists)
3000 Busch Lake Blvd., Tampa
(813) 933-8944

Tampa Bay Veterinary Emergency Service
238 E. Bearss Ave., Tampa
(813) 265-4043

Animal E.R.
8237 Cooper Creek Blvd., University Park
(941) 355-2884

Palm Beach Veterinary Specialists
3092 Forest Hill Blvd., West Palm Beach
(561) 434-5700

GEORGIA

All Pets Emergency and Referral Center, P.C.
6460 Hwy. 9N, Alpharetta
(678) 366-2125

University of Georgia - Vet Teaching Hospital
College of Veterinary Medicine, Athens
(706) 542-3221

East Metro Animal Emergency Clinic
6225 Hwy. 278 N.W., Covington
(678) 212-0300

All Species Animal Hospital
4075 Pleasant Hill Rd., Duluth
(678) 475-1262

Southern Crescent Animal Emergency Clinic
1270 Hwy. 54 E., Fayetteville
(770) 460-8166

An-Emerg Animal Emergency Center
275 #3 Pearl Nix Pkwy., Gainesville
(770) 534-2911

VCA Animal Emergency Center of Gwinnett
1956 Lawrenceville-Suwanee Rd., Lawrenceville
(770) 277-3220

Cobb Emergency Veterinary Clinic
630 Cobb Pkwy. N., Suite C, Marietta
(770) 424-9157

Animal Emergency Center of North Fulton
900 Mansell Rd., Suite 19, Roswell
(770) 594-2266

Animal Emergency Center of Sandy Springs
228 Sandy Springs Pl. N.E., Sandy Springs
(404) 252-7881

Georgia Veterinary Specialists and Emergency Care
455 Abernathy Rd. N.E., Sandy Springs
(404) 459-0903

Savannah Veterinary Emergency Clinic
317 Eisenhower Dr., Savannah
(912) 355-6113

DeKalb-Gwinnet Animal Emergency Clinic
6430 Lawrenceville Hwy., Tucker
(770) 491-0661

Cherokee Emergency Veterinary Clinic
7800 Hwy. 92, Woodstock
(770) 924-3720

IDAHO
Mountain View Animal Hospital
3435 N. Cole Rd., Boise
(208) 375-0251

WestVet Animal Emergency & Specialty Center
5019 N. Sawyer Ave., Garden City
(208) 375-1600

Idaho Falls Veterinary Emergency Clinic
3120 S. Woodruff, Idaho Falls
(208) 552-0662

All Valley Animal Care Center
2326 E. Cinema Dr., Meridian
(208) 888-0818

WestVet Animal Emergency
3085 E. Magic View Dr., Ste. 110, Meridian
(208) 288-0400

North Idaho Pet Emergency
2700 E. Seltice Way #12, Post Falls
(208) 777-2707

ILLINOIS
Animal E.R. of Arlington Heights
1195 E. Palatine Rd., Arlington Heights
(847) 394-6049

VCA Aurora Animal Hospital
2600 W. Galena Blvd., Aurora
(630) 896-8541

Animal Emergency Clinic of McLean County
2505 E. Oakland Ave., Bloomington
(309) 665-5020

Veterinary Specialty Center
1515 Busch Pkwy., Buffalo Grove
(847) 459-7535

Animal Emergency Clinic of Champaign County
1713 S. State St. #4, Champaign
(217) 359-1977

Chicago Veterinary Emergency Services
3123 N. Clybourne Ave., Chicago
(773) 281-7110

Animal Emergency Center
2005 Mall St., Collinsville
(618) 346-1898

Emergency Veterinary Care South, Assoc.
13715 S. Cicero Ave., Crestwood
(708) 388-3771

Animal Emergency of McHenry County
1095 Pingree Rd., Suite 120, Crystal Lake
(815) 479-9119

Arboretum View Animal Hospital
2551 Warrenville Rd., Downers Grove
(630) 963-0424

Dundee Animal Hospital
199 Penny Ave., Dundee
(847) 428-6114

Midwest Animal Emergency Hospital
7510 W. North Ave., Elmwood Park
(708) 453-4755

VCA Franklin Park Animal Hospital
9846 W. Grand Ave., Franklin Park
(847) 455-4922

Hawthorne Animal Hospital
#5 Cougar Dr., Glen Carbon
(618) 288-3971

Animal Emergency & Treatment Center
1810 E. Belvidere Rd., Grayslake
(847) 548-5300

Emergency Veterinary Services
820 Ogden Ave., Lisle
(630) 960-2900

Animal Emergency of Mokena
19110 S. 88th Ave., Mokena
(708) 326-4800

Animal Emergency and Referral Center
1810 Skokie Blvd., Northbrook
(847) 564-5775

Tri-County Animal Emergency Clinic
1800 N. Sterling Ave., Peoria
(309) 672-1565

Animal Emergency Clinic of Rockford
4236 Maray Dr., Rockford
(815) 229-7791

Animal 911
3735 W. Dempster St., Skokie
(847) 673-9110

Animal Emergency Clinic of Springfield
1333 W. Wabash Ave., Springfield
(217) 698-0870

Emergency Veterinary Services of St. Charles
530 Dunham Rd., St. Charles
(630) 584-7447

ASPCA Animal Poison Control Center
1717 South Philo Rd., Urbana
(217) 337-5030

University of Illinois College of Veterinary Medicine
1008 W. Hazelwood Dr., Urbana
(217) 333-5300

INDIANA
VCA Northwood Animal Hospital
3255 N. SR 9, Anderson
(765) 649-5218

St. Francis Family Pet Health Care
822 W. Plymouth St., Breman
(574) 546-9005

Veterinary Emergency Specialty Hospital
5818 Maplecrest Rd., Fort Wayne
(219) 426-1062

Airport Animal Emergi-Center
5235 W. Washington St., Indianapolis
(317) 248-0832

VCA Indiana Veterinary Specialty & Emergency Center
8250 Bash St., Indianapolis
(317) 849-4925

Indianapolis Veterinary Emergency Center
5425 Victory Dr., Indianapolis
(317) 782-4484

Noahs Animal Hospital, P.C.
5510 Millersville Rd., Indianapolis
(317) 253-1327

Animal Emergency Clinic of Tippecanoe County
1343 Sagamore Pkwy. N., Lafayette
(765) 449-2001

Calumet Emergency Veterinary Clinic
150 W. Lincoln Hwy., Schererville
(219) 865-0970

North Central Veterinary Emergency Center
1645 S. US 421, Westville
(219) 785-7300

IOWA

Iowa State University Veterinary Clinical Sciences Teaching Hospital
1600 S. 16th St., Ames
(515) 294-4900

Animal Emergency Center of the Quad Cities
1510 State St., Bettendorf
(563) 344-9599

Eastern Iowa Veterinary Specialty Center
755 Capital Dr. S.W., Cedar Rapids
(319) 841-5161

Iowa Veterinary Specialties
6110 Creston Ave., Des Moines
(515) 280-3051

KANSAS

Kansas State University Vet. Med. Teaching Hospital
1800 Denison Ave., Manhattan
(785) 532-4100

Mission MedVet
5914 Johnson Dr., Mission
(913) 722-5566

Veterinary Specialty & Emergency Center
11950 W. 110th St., Overland Park
(913) 642-9563

Central Kansas Veterinary Center
515 W. Blanchard Ave., South Hutchinson
(620) 663-8387

Animal Emergency Treatment Center
839 S.W. Fairlawn Rd., Topeka
(785) 272-2926

Veterinary Emergency and Specialty Hospital of Wichita
727 S. Washington, Wichita
(316) 262-5321

KENTUCKY

AA Small Animal Emergency Service
150 Dennis Dr., Lexington
(859) 276-2505

Jefferson Animal Hospital and Regional Emergency Center
4504 Outer Loop, Louisville
(502) 966-4104

Louisville Veterinary Specialty and Emergency Services
13160 Magisterial Dr., Louisville
(502) 244-3036

Greater Cincinnati Veterinary Specialists & Emergency Services
11 Beacon Dr., Wilder
(859) 572-0560

LOUISIANA

Baton Rouge Pet Emergency Hospital
1514 Cottondale Dr., Baton Rouge
(225) 925-5566

The Veterinary Emergency and Critical Care Hospital
2611 Florida St., Mandeville
(985) 626-4862

Southeast Veterinary Emergency and Critical Care
3409 Division St., Metairie
(504) 219-0444

MAINE

Eastern Maine Emergency Veterinary Clinic
15 Dirigo Dr., Brewer
(207) 989-6267

Animal Emergency Clinic of Mid-Maine
37 Strawberry Ave., Lewiston
(207) 777-1110

Animal Emergency Clinic
739 Warren Ave., Portland
(207) 878-3121

Maine Veterinary Referral Center
1500 Technology Way, Enterprise Business Park, Scarborough
(207) 885-1290

MARYLAND

Anne Arundel Veterinary Emergency Clinic
808 Bestgate Rd., Annapolis
(410) 224-0331

Falls Road Animal Hospital
6314 Falls Rd., Baltimore
(410) 825-9100

Animal Emergency Hospital
807B Belair Rd., Bel Air
(410) 420-7297

Harford Emergency Veterinary Services
526 Underwood Ln., Bel Air
(410) 420-8000

Emergency Veterinary Clinic, Inc.
32 Mellor Ave., Catonsville
(410) 788-7040

Emergency Animal Hospital of Ellicott City
10270 Baltimore National Pike (SR 40W), Ellicott City
(410) 750-1177

Frederick Emergency Animal Hospital
434 Prospect Blvd., Frederick
(301) 662-6622

VCA Veterinary Referral Associates
500 Perry Pkwy., Gaithersburg
(301) 340-3224

Mountain View Animal Emergency
17747 Virginia Ave., Hagerstown
(301) 733-7339

Metropolitan Emergency Animal Clinic
12106 Nebel St., Rockville
(301) 770-5225

Pets ER
329 Tilghman Rd., Suite 100, Salisbury
(410) 543-8400

PET ER
1209 Cromwell Bridge Rd., Towson
(410) 252-8387

VCA Southern Maryland Veterinary Referral Center
3485 Rockefeller Ct., Waldorf
(301) 638-0988

Central Carroll Animal Emergency
1030 Baltimore Blvd., Suite 180, Westminster
(410) 871-2000

MASSACHUSETTS
Animal Emergency Care
164 Great Rd., Acton
(978) 263-1742

MSPCA Angell Animal Medical Center
350 S. Huntington Ave., Boston
(617) 522-7282

Cape Cod Veterinary Specialists
11 Bourne Bridge Approach, Buzzards Bay
(508) 759-5125

Wignall Animal Hospital
1837 Bridge St., Dracut
(978) 454-8272

Fall River Animal Hospital
33 18th St., Fall River
(508) 675-6374

Essex County Veterinary Emergency Hospital
247 Chickering Rd., North Andover
(978) 725-5544

Tufts University Cummings School of Veterinary Medicine
200 Westboro Rd., North Grafton
(508) 839-5395

Animal ER
1634 West Housatonic St., Pittsfield
(413) 997-3425

Veterinary Emergency & Specialty Hospital
141 Greenfield Rd., South Deerfield
(413) 665-4911

Cape Animal Referral and Emergency Center
79 Theophilus Smith Rd., South Dennis
(508) 398-7575

VCA South Shore Animal Hospital
595 Columbian St., South Weymouth
(781) 337-6622

VCA Boston Road Animal Hospital
1235 Boston Rd., Springfield
(413) 783-1203

TUFTS Veterinary Emergency Treatment and Specialties
525 South St., Walpole
(508) 668-5454

Vetcision
293 Second Ave., Waltham
(781) 810-1010

Veterinary Emergency & Specialty Center of New England
180 Bear Hill Rd., Waltham
(781) 684-8387

New England Animal Medical Center
595 W. Center St., West Bridgewater
(508) 580-2515

Massachusetts Veterinary Referral Hospital
20 Cabot Rd., Woburn
(781) 932-5802

Woburn Animal Hospital
373 Russell St., Woburn
(781) 933-0170

MICHIGAN
Animal Emergency Clinic
4126 Packard Rd., Ann Arbor
(734) 971-8774

Ann Arbor Animal Hospital
2150 W. Liberty, Ann Arbor
(734) 662-4474

Michigan Veterinary Specialists
3412 E. Walton Blvd., Auburn Hills
(248) 371-3713

Oakland Veterinary Emergency & Critical Care
1400 Telegraph Rd., Bloomfield Hills
(248) 334-6877

Animal Emergency Hospital of Macomb
43731 N. Gratiot Ave., Clinton Township
(586) 307-3730

Michigan State University Veterinary Teaching Hospital
Michigan State University, Wilson Rd., East Lansing
(517) 353-5420

Animal Emergency Hospital
1007 S. Ballenger Hwy., Flint
(810) 238 7557

Animal Emergency Hospital
3260 Plainfield Ave. N.E., Grand Rapids
(616) 361-9911

Southwest Michigan Animal Emergency Hospital
3301 S. Burdick, Kalamazoo
(269) 381-5228

Lansing Veterinary Urgent Care
3276 E. Jolly Rd., Lansing
(517) 393-9200

Veterinary Emergency Service-East
28223 John R Rd., Madison Heights
(248) 547-4677

Veterinary Care Specialists
205 Rowe Rd., Milford
(248) 684-0468

Animal Emergency Center
24360 Novi Rd., Novi
(248) 348-1788

Veterinary Emergency Service-West
40850 Ann Arbor Rd., Plymouth
(734) 207-8500

Great Lakes Pet Emergencies
1221 Tittabawassee Rd., Saginaw
(989) 752-1960

Michigan Veterinary Specialists
29080 Inkster Rd., Southfield
(248) 354-6660

Affiliated Veterinary Emergency Service
14085 Northline Rd., Southgate
(734) 284-1700

MINNESOTA
South Metro Animal Emergency Care
14690 Pennock Ave., Apple Valley
(952) 953-3737

Midwest Veterinary Specialty Group
11850 Aberdeen St., N.E., Blaine
(763) 754-5000

Affiliated Emergency Veterinary Hospital
1615 Coon Rapids Blvd., Coon Rapids
(763) 754-9434

Affiliated Emergency Veterinary Service
2314 W. Michigan St., Duluth
(218) 302-8000

Affiliated Emergency Veterinary Service
7717 Flying Cloud Dr., Eden Prairie
(952) 942-8272

Affiliated Emergency Veterinary Service
4708 Hwy. 55, Golden Valley
(763) 529-6560

Animal Emergency Clinic
7166 10th St. N., Oakdale
(651) 501-3766

Affiliated Emergency Veterinary Service
121 23rd Ave. S.W., Rochester
(507) 424-3976

Affiliated Emergency Veterinary Service
4180 Thielman Ln., St. Cloud
(320) 258-3481

Animal Emergency Clinic
301 University Ave., St. Paul
(651) 293-1800

University of Minnesota, College of Veterinary Medicine
1365 Gortner Ave., St. Paul
(612) 626-8387

MISSOURI
Animal Emergency Clinic
12501 Natural Bridge Rd., Bridgeton
(314) 739-1500

University of Missouri-Columbia Veterinary Med. Teaching Hospital
900 E. Campus Dr., Columbia
(573) 882-4589

Animal Emergency Center
8141 N. Oak Traffic Way, Kansas City
(816) 455-5430

Animal Emergency & Referral Hospital
3495 N.E. Ralph Powell Rd., Lee's Summit
(816) 554-4990

Animal Emergency Clinic
334 Fort Zumwalt Sq., O'Fallon
(636) 240-5496

Emergency Veterinary Clinic of Southwest Missouri
400 S. Glenstone Ave., Springfield
(417) 890-1600

Animal Emergency Clinic
9937 Big Bend Blvd., St. Louis
(314) 822-7600

MONTANA
Western Montana Small Animal Emergency Clinic
1914 S. Reserve St., Missoula
(406) 829-9300

NEBRASKA
Veterinary Emergency Services of Lincoln
3700 S. 9th St., Lincoln
(402) 489-6800

Animal Emergency Clinic
9664 Mockingbird Dr., Omaha
(402) 339-6232

NEVADA
Animal Emergency Center of Las Vegas
3340 E. Patrick Ln., Las Vegas
(702) 457-8050

Las Vegas Animal Emergency Hospital
5231 W. Charleston Blvd., Las Vegas
(702) 822-1045

Warm Springs Veterinary Emergency Clinic
2500 W. Warm Springs Rd., Las Vegas
(702) 614-5454

Animal Emergency Center
6425 S. Virginia St., Reno
(775) 851-3600

NEW HAMPSHIRE
Capital Area Veterinary Emergency Service
22 Bridge St., Concord
(603) 227-1199

Veterinary Emergency Center of Manchester
55 Carl Dr., Manchester
(603) 666-6677

Winnipesaukee Veterinary Emergency Center
8 Maple St., Suite 2, Meredith
(603) 279-1117

Animal Medical Center of New England
168 Main Dunstable Rd., Nashua
(603) 821-7222

The Veterinary Emergency, Critical Care & Cancer Treatment Center of NH
15 Piscataqua Dr., Portsmouth
(603) 431-3600

NEW JERSEY
NorthStar VETS
34 Trenton Lakewood Rd., Clarksburg
(609) 259-8300

Animal Emergency Referral Associates
1237 Broomfield Ave., Fairfield
(973) 226-3282

Central Jersey Veterinary Emergency Services
643 Lincoln Hwy., Iselin
(732) 283-3535

Jersey Shore Veterinary Emergency Service
1000 Rt. 70, Lakewood
(732) 363-3200

Red Bank Veterinary Hospital Linwood
535 Maple Ave., Linwood
(609) 926-5300

North Jersey Veterinary Emergency Services
724 Ridge Rd., Lyndhurst
(201) 438-7122

Animal Emergency Service of South Jersey
220 Moorestown-Mount Laurel Rd., Mount Laurel
(856) 727-1332

Newton Veterinary Hospital
116 Hampton House Rd., Newton
(973) 383-4321

Oradell Animal Hospital
580 Winters Ave., Paramus
(201) 262-0010

Alliance Emergency Veterinary Clinic
540 Rt. 10W, Randolph
(973) 328-2844

Animerge
21 Rt. 206S, Raritan
(908) 707-9077

Garden State Veterinary Specialists
1 Pine St., Tinton Falls
(732) 922-0011

Red Bank Veterinary Hospital
197 Hance Ave., Tinton Falls
(732) 747-3636

Regional Veterinary Emergency Service
4250 Rt. 42, Turnersville
(856) 728-1400

NEW MEXICO
Staley's Veterinary Medical Clinic
1407 Indian Wells Rd., Alamogordo
(575) 437-3063

Albuquerque Animal Emergency Clinic
4000 Montgomery Blvd. N.E., Albuquerque
(505) 884-3433

VCA Vet Care Animal Hospital & Referral Center
9901 Montgomery Blvd. N.E., Albuquerque
(505) 292-5353

Emergency Veterinary Clinic of Santa Fe
2001 Vivigen Way, Santa Fe
(505) 984-0625

NEW YORK
Greater Buffalo Veterinary Emergency Services
4949 Main St., Amherst
(716) 839-4043

Veterinary Emergency & Critical Care Center
2115 Downer Street Rd., Baldwinsville
(315) 638-3500

Katonah Bedford Veterinary Center
546 N. Bedford Rd., Bedford Hills
(914) 241-7700

Atlantic Coast Veterinary Specialists
3250 Veterans Memorial Hwy., Bohemia
(631) 285-7780

Veterinary Emergency and Referral Group
318 Warren St., Brooklyn
(718) 522-9400

Animal Emergency Service
6230-C Jericho Tpke., Commack
(631) 462-6044

Veterinary Medical Center of Central New York
5841 Bridge St., Suite 200, East Syracuse
(315) 446-7933

New York Veterinary Specialty and Emergency Center
2233 Broadhollow Rd., Farmingdale
(631) 694-3400

Natural Vet for Pets
585 Warburton Ave., Hastings-on-Hudson
(914) 478-4100

Animal Emergency Clinic of the Hudson Valley
1112 Morton Blvd., Kingston
(845) 336-0713

Capital District Animal Emergency Clinic
222 Troy-Schenectady Rd., Latham
(518) 785-1094

Orange County Animal Emergency Service
517 Rt. 211E, Middletown
(845) 692-0260

The Veterinary Referral Center of Ultravet Diagnostics
220 E. Jericho Tpke., Mineola
(516) 294-6680

Fifth Avenue Veterinary Specialists
1 West 15th St., New York
(212) 924-3311

Manhattan Veterinary Group
240 E. 80th St., New York
(212) 988-1000

NYC Veterinary Specialists and Cancer Treatment Center
410 W. 55th St., New York
(212) 767-0099

Orchard Park Veterinary Medical Center
3930 N. Buffalo Rd., Orchard Park
(716) 662-6660

Long Island Veterinary Specialists & Animal Emergency & Critical Care Center
163 S. Service Rd., Plainview
(516) 501-1700

Animal Emergency Clinic of the Hudson Valley
84 Patrick Ln., Poughkeepsie
(845) 471-8242

East End Veterinary Emergency Center
67 Commerce Dr., Riverhead
(631) 369-4513

Animal Hospital of Pittsford
2816 Monroe Ave., Rochester
(585) 271-7700

Veterinary Specialists of Rochester and Animal Emergency Service
825 White Spruce Blvd., Rochester
(585) 424-1277 or (585) 424-1260

Animal Emergency Service
280-L Middle Country Rd., Selden
(631) 698-2225

Valley Cottage Animal Hospital
202 Rt. 303, Valley Cottage
(845) 268-9263

Central Veterinary Associates
73 West Merrick Rd., Valley Stream
(516) 825-3066

Nassau Animal Emergency Group
740 Old Country Rd., Westbury
(516) 333-6262

The Center for Specialized Veterinary Care
609-5 Cantiague Rock Rd., Westbury
(516) 420-0000

The Veterinary Emergency Group
193 Tarrytown Rd., White Plains
(914) 949-8779

Animal Specialty Center
9 Odell Plaza, Yonkers
(914) 457-4000

NORTH CAROLINA
Regional Emergency Animal Care Hospital
677 Brevard Rd., Asheville
(828) 665-4399

Animal Emergency Clinic of the High Country
1126 Blowing Rock Rd., Suite A, Boone
(828) 268-2833

Animal Emergency Clinic of Cary
220 High House Rd., Cary
(919) 462-8989

Veterinary Specialty Hospital of the Carolinas
6405 Tryon Rd., Cary
(919) 233-4911

Animal Medical Hospital
3832 Monroe Rd., Charlotte
(704) 334-4684

Carolina Veterinary Specialists-Animal Emergency and Trauma Center
2225 Township Rd., Charlotte
(704) 504-9608

Triangle Veterinary Emergency Clinic
3319 Chapel Hill Blvd., Durham
(919) 489-0615

After Hours Veterinary Emergency Clinic
5505 W. Friendly Ave., Greensboro
(336) 851-1990

Carolina Veterinary Specialists-Animal Emergency and Trauma Center
501 Nicholas Rd., Greensboro
(336) 632-0605

Happy Trails Veterinary Emergency Clinic
2936 Battleground Ave., Greensboro
(336) 288-2688

After Hours Emergency Veterinary Clinic
126 Hwy. 321 S.W., Hickory
(828) 328-2660

Carolina Veterinary Specialists-Animal Emergency and Trauma Center
12117 Statesville Rd., Huntersville
(704) 949-1100

Cabarrus Emergency Veterinary Clinic
1317 S. Cannon Blvd., Kannapolis
(704) 932-1182

Emergency Veterinary Clinic, PA
2440 Plantation Center Dr., Matthews
(704) 844-6440

After Hours Small Animal Emergency Clinic
409 Vick Ave., Raleigh
(919) 781-5145

Quail Corners Animal Hospital & 24 Hour Emergency Care
1613 E. Millbrook Rd., Raleigh
(919) 876-0739

Thomasville Veterinary Hospital
303 National Hwy., Thomasville
(336) 475-9119

Small Animal Emergency Services
5091 US Hwy. 1, Vass
(910) 944-0405

Eastern Carolina Veterinary Emergency Treatment Service
4909-D Expressway Dr., Wilson
(252) 265-9920

Animal Emergency Services of Forsyth County
7781 North Point Blvd., Winston-Salem
(336) 377-2866

Carolina Veterinary Specialists-Animal Emergency and Trauma Center
1600 Hanes Mall Blvd., Winston-Salem
(336) 896-0902

NORTH DAKOTA
Red River Animal Emergency Clinic
1401 Oak Manor Ave. S., #2, Fargo
(701) 478-9299

OHIO
Akron Veterinary Referral & Emergency Center
1321 Centerview Cir., Akron
(330) 665-4996

Metropolitan Veterinary Hospital
1053 S. Cleveland-Massillon Rd., Akron
(330) 666-2976

Great Lakes Veterinary Specialists
5035 Richmond Rd., Bedford Heights
(216) 831-6789

Animal Emergency Clinic West
5320 W. 140th St., Brook Park
(216) 362-6001

Stark County Veterinary Emergency Clinic, LLC
2705 Fulton Dr. N.W., Canton
(330) 452-5116

Dayton Care Center
6405 Clyo Rd., Centerville
(937) 428-0911

Cincinnati Animal Referral and Emergency Center
6995 E. Kemper Rd., Cincinnati
(513) 530-0911

Capital Veterinary Referral & Emergency Clinic
5230 Renner Rd., Columbus
(614) 870-0480

Ohio State University Veterinary Teaching Hospital
601 Vernon L. Tharp St., Columbus
(614) 292-3551

Dayton Emergency Veterinary Clinic
2714 Springboro W., Dayton
(937) 293-2714

After Hours Animal Emergency Clinic, Inc.
2680 W. Liberty St., Girard
(330) 530-8387

Animal Emergency Center, Inc.
5152 Grove Ave., Lorain
(440) 240-1400

Aaron Animal Clinic and Emergency Hospital
7640 Broadview Rd., Parma
(216) 901-9980

Animal Emergency & Critical Care Center of Toledo, Inc.
2785 W. Central Ave., Toledo
(419) 473-0328

Green Animal Medical Center
1620 Corporate Woods Cir., Uniontown
(330) 896-4040

MedVet Associates, Ltd.
300 E. Wilson Bridge Rd., Worthington
(614) 846-5800

OKLAHOMA
Animal Emergency Center
931 S.W. 74th, Oklahoma City
(405) 631-7828

Neel Veterinary Hospital
2700 N. MacArthur, Oklahoma City
(405) 947-8387

Veterinary Emergency and Critical Care Hospital
1800 W. Memorial Rd., Oklahoma City
(405) 749-6989

Animal Emergency Center, Inc.
7220 E. 41st St., Tulsa
(918) 665-0508

OREGON
Animal Emergency Center of Central Oregon
1245 S.E. 3rd St., Suite C3, Bend
(541) 385-9110

VCA Northwest Veterinary Specialists
16756 S.E. 82nd Dr., Clackamas
(503) 656-3999

Animal Emergency and Critical Care Center
1562 S.W. 3rd St., Corvallis
(541) 753-5750

Southern Oregon Veterinary Specialty Center
3265 Biddle Rd., Medford
(541) 282-7999

Dove Lewis Emergency Animal Hospital
1945 N.W. Pettygrove, Portland
(503) 228-7281

VCA Southeast Portland Animal Hospital
13830 S.E. Stark St., Portland
(503) 255-8139

Salem Veterinary Emergency Clinic
3215 Market St. N.E., Salem
(503) 588-8082

Emergency Veterinary Hospital
103 W. Q St., Springfield
(541) 746-0112

Emergency Veterinary Clinic of Tualatin
19314 S.W. Mohave Ct., Tualatin
(503) 691-7922

PENNSYLVANIA
Northwest Pennsylvania Pet Emergency Center
429 W. 38th St., Erie
(814) 866-5920

Center for Animal Referral and Emergency Services
2010 Cabot Blvd. W., Suite D, Langhorne
(215) 750-2774

Veterinary Specialty & Emergency Center
1900 W. Old Lincoln Hwy., Langhorne
(215) 750-7884

Gwynedd Veterinary Hospital and Emergency Service
1615 W. Point Pike, Lansdale
(215) 699-9294

Allegheny Veterinary Emergency Trauma & Specialty
4224 Northern Pike, Monroeville
(412) 373-4200

Emergency Service, Veterinary Hospital of the University of Pennsylvania
3900 Delancey St., Philadelphia
(215) 898-4685

VCA Castle Shannon Animal Hospital Service
3610 Library Rd., Pittsburgh
(412) 885-2500

Veterinary Emergency Clinic
807 Camp Horn Rd., Pittsburgh
(412) 366-3400

Animal Emergency Clinic of Wyoming Valley
755 S. Township Blvd., Pittston
(570) 655-3600

Hickory Veterinary Hospital
2303 Hickory Rd., Plymouth Meeting
(610) 828-3054

Metropolitan Emergency Service
2626 Van Buren Ave., Norristown
(610) 666-0914

Creature Comforts Veterinary Service
Old Route 115, Saylorsburg
(570) 992-0400

Central Pennsylvania Veterinary Emergency Treatment Services
1522 Martin St., State College
(814) 237-4670

Bucks County Veterinary Emergency Trauma Service
978 Easton Rd., Warrington
(215) 918-2200

Animal Emergency Center
395 Susquehanna Tr., Watsontown
(570) 742-7400

Valley Central Emergency Veterinary Hospital
210 Fullerton Ave., Whitehall
(610) 435-5588

Animal Emergency & Referral Center of York
1640 S. Queen St., York
(717) 767-5355

RHODE ISLAND
Ocean State Veterinary Specialists
1480 S. County Tr., East Greenwich
(401) 886-6787

SOUTH CAROLINA
South Carolina Veterinary Emergency Care
3924 Fernandina Rd., Columbia
(803) 798-3837

Palmetto Regional Emergency Hospital for Animals
921 Spears Creek Ct., Elgin
(803) 865-1418

Animal Emergency Clinic
393 Woods Lake Rd., Greenville
(864) 232-1878

Veterinary Emergency Care
930 Pine Hollow Rd., Suite B, Mt. Pleasant
(843) 216-7554

Animal Emergency Hospital of the Strand
303 Hwy. 15, Suite 1, Myrtle Beach
(843) 445-9797

Veterinary Emergency Care
3163 W. Montague Ave., North Charleston
(843) 744-3372

Spartanburg Veterinary Emergency Clinic
1291 Asheville Hwy., Spartanburg
(864) 591-1923

SOUTH DAKOTA
Veterinary Emergency Hospital
3508 S. Minnesota Ave., Suite 104, Sioux Falls
(605) 977-6200

TENNESSEE
Midland Pet Emergency Center, Inc.
235 Calderwood St., Alcoa
(865) 982-1007

Airport Pet Emergency Clinic
2436 Hwy. 75, Blountville
(423) 279-0574

BluePearl Veterinary Partners
1668 Mallory Ln., Brentwood
(615) 333-1212

Regional Institute for Veterinary Emergencies & Referral
2132 Amnicola Hwy., Chattanooga
(423) 698-4612

Animal Emergency Clinic of Maury County, LLC
1900B Shady Brook St., Columbia
(931) 380-1929

PetMed Emergency Center, LLC
830 N. Germantown Pkwy., Suite 105, Cordova
(901) 624-9002

Jackson Pet Emergency Clinic
2815-D N. Highland, Jackson
(731) 660-4343

Knoxville Pet Emergency Clinic
1819 Ailor Ave., Knoxville
(865) 637-0114

University of Tennessee Veterinary Teaching Hospital
2407 River Dr., Knoxville
(865) 974-8387

Animal Medical Center
234 River Rock Blvd., Murfreesboro
(615) 867-7575

Nashville Pet Emergency Clinic
2000 12th Ave. S., Nashville
(615) 383-2600

TEXAS

I-20 Animal Medical Center
5820 W. I-20, Arlington
(817) 478-9238

AM/PM Animal Hospital
2239 S. Lamar Blvd., Austin
(512) 448-2676

Austin Vet Care
4106 N. Lamar, Austin
(512) 459-4336

Emergency Animal Hospital of Northwest Austin
12034 Research Blvd., Suite 8, Austin
(512) 331-6121

Emergency Animal Hospital of Northwest Austin - South Branch
4434 Frontier Tr., Austin
(512) 899-0955

White Angel Animal Hospital
1901 RR 620 N., Austin
(512) 266-7838

Southeast Texas Animal Emergency Clinic
3420 W. Cardinal Dr., Beaumont
(409) 842-3239

Burleson Animal Emergency Hospital
805-B N.E. Alsbury Blvd., Burleson
(817) 447-9194

North Texas Emergency Pet Clinic
1712 W. Frankford Rd., Suite 108, Carrollton
(972) 323-1310

Heritage Veterinary Hospital
3930 Glade Road, Suite 120, Colleyville
(817) 358-0404

Emergency Animal Clinic
12101 Greenville Ave., Suite 118, Dallas
(972) 994-9110

The E-Clinic, Inc.
3337 Fitzhugh Ave., Dallas
(214) 520-8388

Grayson County Animal Emergency Clinic
3301 Woodlawn Blvd., Denison
(903) 337-0898

Denton County Animal Emergency Room
4145 S. I-35E, Suite 101, Denton
(940) 271-1200

El Paso Animal Emergency Center
1220 Airway Blvd., El Paso
(915) 545-1148

Airport Frwy. Animal Emergency Clinic
411 N. Main St., Euless
(817) 571-2088

DFW North Emergency Veterinary Clinic
2311 Cross Timbers, Suite 319, Flower Mound
(469) 464-2964

Metro West Emergency Veterinary Center
3201 Hulen St., Fort Worth
(817) 731-3734

Animal Emergency Hospital of North Texas
2700 W. SR 114, Grapevine
(817) 410-2273

Animal Emergency Center of West Houston
4823 Hwy. 6N, Houston
(832) 593-8387

Animal Emergency Clinic
1111 West Loop S. #200, Houston
(713) 693-1100

Animal Emergency Clinic SH 249
19311 SH 249, Houston
(281) 890-8875

VCA Animal Emergency Hospital Southeast
10331 Gulf Frwy., Houston
(713) 941-8460

Veterinary Emergency Referral Group, Inc.
8921 Katy Frwy., Houston
(713) 932-9589

Animal Emergency Clinic Northeast
9817 Old 1960 Rd., Humble-Westfield Road, Humble
(281) 446-4900

VCA Metroplex Animal Hospital & Pet Lodge
700 W. Airport Frwy., Irving
(972) 438-7113

After Hours Veterinary Services
2501 South W.S. Young, Killeen
(254) 628-5017

VCA Animal Emergency Hospital Southeast-Calder Rd.
1108 Gulf Frwy. S., Suite 280, League City
(281) 332-1678

Lake Ray Hubbard Emergency Pet Care Center
4651 N. Beltline Rd., Mesquite
(972) 226-3377

Angel of Mercy Animal Critical Care, Inc.
8734 Grissom Rd., San Antonio
(210) 684-2105

Animal Emergency Room
4315 Fredericksburg Rd., Suite 2, San Antonio
(210) 737-7380

Emergency Pet Clinic, Inc.
8503 Broadway #105, San Antonio
(210) 822-2873

I-10 Pet Emergency
10822 Fredericksburg Rd., San Antonio
(210) 691-0900

Northeast Emergency Animal Clinic
8365 Perrin Beitel, San Antonio
(210) 650-3141

Veterinary Referral and Emergency Center of South Texas
503 E. Sonterra Blvd., San Antonio
(210) 858-0200

Sugar Land Veterinary Specialty and Emergency Center
1515 Lake Pointe Pkwy., Sugar Land
(281) 491-7800

VCA Southwest Freeway Animal Hospital & Emergency Center
15575 Southwest Frwy., Sugar Land
(281) 491-8387

Animal Emergency & Urgent Care Center of The Woodlands
27870 I-45 N, The Woodlands
(281) 367-5444

Texas Animal Medical Center
4900 Steinbeck Bend, Waco
(254) 753-0901

UTAH
Central Valley Veterinary Hospital
55 E. Miller Ave., Salt Lake City
(801) 487-1325

Pet E.R. - The Pet Emergency Room
6360 S. Highland Dr., Salt Lake City
(801) 278-0505

Animal Emergency Center
2465 N. Main St., Sunset
(801) 776-8118

VERMONT
Burlington Emergency & Veterinary Specialists
200 Commerce St., Williston
(802) 863-2387

VIRGINIA
Alexandria Veterinary Emergency Service
2660 Duke St., Alexandria
(703) 823-3601

Veterinary Emergency Treatment Services, Inc.
370 Greenbrier Dr., Suite A-2, Charlottesville
(434) 973-3519

Greenbrier Veterinary Emergency Center
1100 Eden Way N., Suite 101B, Chesapeake
(757) 366-9000

SouthPaws Veterinary Specialists & Emergency Center
8500 Arlington Blvd., Fairfax
(703) 752-9100

Fredericksburg Regional Veterinary Emergency Center
2301 ½ Jefferson Davis Highway, Fredericksburg
(540) 372-3470

Animal Emergency Critical Care Associates
165 Fort Evans Rd. N.E., Leesburg
(703) 777-5755

Animal Emergency & Critical Care of Lynchburg
3432 Odd Fellows Rd., Lynchburg
(434) 846-1504

Veterinary Referral & Critical Care (VRCC)
1596 Hockett Rd., Manakin Sabot
(804) 784-8722

Prince William Emergency Veterinary Clinic
8610 Centreville Rd., Manassas
(703) 361-8287

Veterinary Emergency Center South
2460 Colony Crossing Pl., Midlothian
(804) 744-9800

Blue Ridge Veterinary Associates
120 E. Cornwell Ln., Purcellville
(540) 338-7387

Veterinary Emergency Center, Inc.
3312 W. Cary St., Richmond
(804) 353-9000

Emergency Veterinary Services of Roanoke
4902 Frontage Rd. N.W., Roanoke
(540) 563-8575

Regional Veterinary Referral Center
6651 Backlick Rd., Springfield
(703) 451-8900

The Hope Center for Advanced Veterinary Medicine
140 Park St. S.E., Vienna
(703) 281-5121

Beach Veterinary Emergency Center
1124 Lynnhaven Pkwy., Virginia Beach
(757) 468-4900

Tidewater Animal Emergency & Referral Center
364 S. Independence Blvd., Virginia Beach
(757) 499-5463

Valley Emergency Veterinary Clinic
164-4 Garber Ln., Winchester
(540) 662-7811

Woodbridge Animal Hospital
2703 Caton Hill Rd., Woodbridge
(703) 897-5665

Peninsula Emergency Veterinary Clinic
1120 George Washington Memorial Hwy., Yorktown
(757) 874-8115

WASHINGTON

After Hours Animal Emergency Clinic
718 Auburn Way N., Auburn
(253) 939-6272

Animal Emergency Care
317 Telegraph Rd., Bellingham
(360) 758-2200

Animal Emergency Clinic of Everett
3625 Rucker Ave., Everett
(425) 258-4466

VCA Alpine Animal Hospital
888 N.W. Sammamish Rd., Issaquah
(425) 392-8888

Animal Emergency Service, East
636 7th Ave., Kirkland
(425) 827-8727

Seattle Veterinary Specialists
11814 115th Ave. N.E., Suite 102, Kirkland
(425) 823-9111

VCA Veterinary Specialty Center of Seattle
20115 44th Ave. W., Lynnwood
(425) 697-6106

Pet Emergency Center
14434 Avon Allen Rd., Mount Vernon
(360) 848-5911

Mid-Columbia Pet Emergency Services
8913 Sandifur Pkwy., Pasco
(509) 547-3577

Animal Emergency & Trauma Center
320 Lindvig Way, Poulsbo
(360) 697-7771

VCA Central Kitsap Animal Hospital
10310 Central Valley Rd. N.E., Poulsbo
(360) 692-6162

Washington State University
Veterinary Teaching Hospital, 100 Grimes Way, Pullman
(509) 335-0711

Animal Critical Care & Emergency Services (ACCES)
11536 Lake City Way, N.E., Seattle
(206) 364-1660

Emerald City Emergency Clinic
4102 Stone Way N., Seattle
(206) 634-9000

VCA Five Corners Veterinary Hospital
15707 1st Ave. S., Seattle
(206) 243-2982

**PSCVM Small Animal Emergency
and Critical Care Center**
11308 92nd St. S.E., Snohomish
(360) 568-9111

Pet Emergency Clinic
21 E. Mission Ave., Spokane
(509) 326-6670

The Animal Emergency Clinic
5608 S. Durango St., Tacoma
(253) 474-0791

Columbia River Veterinary Specialists
6818 N.E. 4th Plain Blvd., Suite C, Vancouver
(360) 694-3007

St. Francis 24 Hr. Animal Hospital
12010 N.E. 65th St., Vancouver
(360) 253-5446

Yakima Pet Emergency Service
510 W. Chestnut Ave., Yakima
(509) 452-4138

WEST VIRGINIA

Kanawha Valley Animal Emergency Clinic
5304 MacCorkle Ave. S.W., Charleston
(304) 768-2911

Animal Urgent Care, Inc.
4201 Wood St., Wheeling
(304) 233-0002

WISCONSIN

Fox Valley Animal Referral Center
4706 New Horizons Blvd., Appleton
(920) 993-9193

Animal Emergency Center & Specialty Services
2100 W. Silver Spring Dr., Glendale
(414) 540-6710

Green Bay Animal Emergency Center
933 Anderson Dr., Suite F, Green Bay
(920) 494-9400

Animal Emergency Center, South
4607 S. 108th St., Greenfield
(414) 427-1731

Emergency Clinic for Animals
229 W. Beltline Hwy., Madison
(608) 274-7772

University of Wisconsin Veterinary Teaching Hospital
2015 Linden Dr., Madison
(608) 263-7600

Veterinary Emergency Service
4902 E. Broadway, Madison
(608) 222-2455

Veterinary Emergency Service
1612 N. High Point Rd., Suite 100, Middleton
(608) 831-1101

Emergency Vets of Central Wisconsin, LLC
1420 Kronenwetter Dr., Mosinee
(715) 693-6934

Lakeshore Veterinary Specialists and Emergency Hospital
207 W. Seven Hills Rd., Port Washington
(262) 268-7800

The Animal ER of Kenosha & Racine
4333 S. Green Bay Rd., Racine
(262) 553-9223

Wisconsin Veterinary Referral Center
360 Bluemound Rd., Waukesha
(262) 542-3241

Canada

ALBERTA

Calgary Animal Referral and Emergency Centre
7140 12th St. S.E., Calgary
(403) 520-8387

Calgary North Veterinary Hospital and Emergency Service
4204 4th St. N.W., Calgary
(403) 277-0135

Animal Emergency Hospital South, Ltd.
3823 99th St., Edmonton
(780) 436-5880

Edmonton Veterinarians Emergency Clinic
11104 102nd Ave., Edmonton
(780) 433-9505

BRITISH COLUMBIA

Central Animal Emergency Clinic
812 Roderick Ave., Coquitlam
(604) 931-1911

Animal Emergency Clinic of the Fraser Valley
#306-6325 204th St., Langley
(604) 514-1711

Mainland Animal Emergency Clinic
15338 Fraser Hwy., Surrey
(604) 588-4000

Canada West Veterinary Specialists & Critical Care Hospital
1988 Kootenay St., Vancouver
(604) 473-4882

Vancouver Animal Emergency Clinic, Ltd.
1590 W. 4th St., Vancouver
(604) 734-5104

Central Victoria Veterinary Hospital
760 Roderick St., Victoria
(250) 475-2495

MANITOBA

Winnipeg Animal Emergency Hospital
400 Pembina Hwy., Winnipeg
(204) 452-9427

NOVA SCOTIA

Metro Animal Emergency Clinic
201 Brownlow Ave., Unit 32, Dartmouth
(902) 468-0674

ONTARIO

Huronia Veterinary Emergency Clinic
115 Bell Farm Rd., Barrie
(705) 722-0377

Emergency Veterinary Clinic
#1 Wexford Rd., Brampton
(905) 495-9907

North Town Veterinary Hospital
496 Main St. N., Brampton
(905) 451-2000

Burgess Veterinary Emergency Clinic
775 Woodview Rd., Burlington
(905) 637-8111

Halton-Wentworth Emergency Vet Clinic
505 King St. W., Hamilton
(905) 529-1004

Veterinary Emergency Clinic
41 Adelaide St. N., #43, London
(519) 432-7341

Veterinary Emergency Clinic of York Region
1210 Journey's End Cir., New Market
(905) 953-5351

Mississauga-Oakville Veterinary Emergency Hospital & Referral Group
2285 Bristol Cir., Oakville
(905) 829-9444

Alta Vista Animal Hospital
2616 Bank St., Ottawa
(613) 731-9911

Vaughan-Richmond Hill Veterinary Emergency Clinic
10303 Yonge St., Richmond Hill
(905) 884-1832

Niagara Veterinary Emergency Clinic
3300 Merrittville Hwy., Unit 1A, Thorold
(905) 641-3185

Veterinary Emergency Clinic & Referral Center
920 Yonge St. #117, Toronto
(416) 920-2002

Animal Emergency Clinic
1910 Dundas St. E., Unit 122, Whitby
(905) 576-3031

QUEBEC

DMV Veterinary Centre
2300 54e, Lachine
(514) 633-8888

University of Montreal/Companion Animal Clinic
1525 rue des Veterinaires, St-Hyacinthe
(450) 778-8111

Pet-Friendly Lodgings

How to Use the Listings

U.S. Lodgings

Canadian Lodgings

Campground Listings

Some 13,000 AAA-RATED® hotels and campgrounds across North America accept traveling pets. This guide provides listings for those lodgings in the United States and Canada that roll out the welcome mat for pets as well as the people who love them.

For the purpose of this book, "pets" are domestic cats or dogs. If you are planning to travel with any other kind of animal — particularly such exotic pets as birds or reptiles — check with the property before making definite plans. Expect to keep nontraditional pets crated at all times.

Note: Always inform the management that you are traveling with an animal; you may be fined if you do not declare your pet. Many properties require guests with pets to sign a waiver or release form and to pay for the room with a credit card. Of course, whether you pay in cash or by credit card, you will be held liable for any damages caused by your pet, even if the property does not charge a deposit or pet fee. It is not a good idea to leave your pet unattended in the room, but if you must, crate him and notify management. When in public areas, keep your pet leashed and do not allow him to disturb other guests.

About the Listings

Geographic listings are used for accuracy and consistency; lodgings are listed under the city or town in which they physically are located — or in some cases under the nearest recognized city or town. For a complete list of all cities within a state or province, see the comprehensive City Index at the beginning of the corresponding section.

U.S. properties are shown first, followed by Canadian properties. Most listings are alphabetically organized by state or province, city and establishment name. Reflecting contemporary travel patterns, properties in some cities or towns may instead be listed within destination cities or areas. Such "vicinity cities" and their listings will be shown alphabetically in the destination city or area, and the vicinity city also will appear in alphabetical order in the City Index, along with the page number on which the listings begin.

Each listing provides the following information (see sample listing, next page):

❶ Symbol denoting Official Appointment (OA) properties. The OA program permits properties to display and advertise the 🅰🅰🅰 or 🅒🅐🅐 logo. OAs have a special interest in serving AAA/CAA members. Ask if they offer special member amenities such as free breakfast, early check-in/late check-out, free room upgrade, free local phone calls, etc.

❷ Diamond Rating

❸ Property name

❹ Lodging classification
(see next page for descriptions)

❺ Special amenities offered. These properties provide an additional benefit to pets, such as treats, toys or gifts, pet sitting and/or walking, a pet menu, food/water dishes, pet sheets or pillows, pet beds or other extras.

❻ Telephone number

❼ Two-person (2P) rate year-round, and cancellation notice validity period (if more than 48 hours). Rates listed are daily. **Note:** Most properties accept any or all of the major credit cards, including American Express, MasterCard and VISA. If a property accepts only cash, the phrase "(no credit cards)" follows the rates. "Call for rates" indicates rates were not available at time of printing. Please contact property for current rate information.

❽ Physical address and/or highway location, if available

❾ Exterior or interior corridors

❿ Pet policies. If the phrase "pets accepted" appears, the property does accept pets but specific information was unavailable at press time. Otherwise, pet-specific policies are denoted as follows:

Size. "Very small" denotes pets weighing up to 10 pounds; "small," up to 25 pounds; "medium," up to 50 pounds; and "large," up to 100 pounds. If no size is specified, the property accepts pets of all sizes.

Species. "Other" indicates the property accepts animals other than dogs and cats. Always call ahead and specify the type of pet you plan to bring.

Deposits and fees. Includes the dollar amount, the type of charge (refundable deposit or nonrefundable fee), the frequency of the charge and whether the charge is per pet or per room.

Designated rooms. Guests with pets are placed in certain rooms, often smoking rooms or those on the ground floor.

Housekeeping service. The phrase "service with restrictions" denotes properties that require the pet to be crated, removed or attended by the owner during housekeeping service.

Supervision. The pet is required to be supervised at all times.

Crate. The pet must be crated when the owner is not present.

⓫ Member values, services and facilities:

🅴🅲🅾 Indicates lodgings that have been certified by well-established government and/or private eco-certification organizations. For more information about these organizations and their programs, visit AAA.com/eco.

🆂🅰🆅🅴 Discounted standard room rate or lowest public rate available at time of booking for dates of stay

🅰🆂🅺 May offer discount

⊠ Designated non-smoking rooms

🅰🅼 Accessible features
(call property for available services and amenities)

🔲 Refrigerator

🔲 Coffee maker

🍴 Restaurant on premises

🏊 Pool

🎣 Recreational activities

🅺 No air conditioning

🆇 No TV

🆉 No telephones

> Please note: Some in-room amenities represented by the icons in the listings may be available only in selected rooms, and may incur an extra fee. Please inquire when making your reservations.

It is important to remember that animal policies do change; always confirm policies, restrictions and fees with the lodging when making reservations and again 1-2 days before departure.

Listing information is subject to change. All listing information was accurate at press time. However, lodging rates and policies change and the publisher cannot be held liable for changes occurring after publication. AAA cannot guarantee the safety of guests or their pets at any facility.

AAA Diamond Ratings

Before a property is listed by AAA, it must satisfy a set of minimum standards regarding basic lodging needs as identified by AAA members. If a property meets those requirements (determined during an unannounced evaluation by a AAA inspector), it is assigned a Diamond Rating.

Once an establishment becomes AAA Approved, it is then assigned a rating of one to five Diamonds, indicating the extensiveness of its facilities, amenities and services, from basic to moderate to luxury. The Diamond Ratings guide members in selecting establishments appropriately matched to their needs and expectations.

◈ These establishments typically appeal to the budget-minded traveler. They provide essential, no-frills accommodations and basic comfort and hospitality.

◈◈ These establishments appeal to family travelers seeking affordable yet more than the basic accommodations. Facilities, décor and amenities are modestly enhanced.

◈◈◈ These establishments offer a distinguished style. Properties are multifaceted, with marked upgrades in physical attributes, amenities and guest comforts.

◈◈◈◈ These establishments are refined and stylish. Physical attributes are upscale. The fundamental hallmarks at this level include an extensive array of amenities combined with a high degree of hospitality, service, and attention to detail.

◈◈◈◈◈ These establishments reflect the characteristics of the ultimate in luxury and sophistication. Physical attributes are extraordinary in every manner. Service is meticulous, exceeding guest expectations and maintaining impeccable standards of excellence. Extensive personalized services and amenities provide first-class comfort.

Lodging Classifications

🅱🅱 **Bed & Breakfast:** Typically smaller scale properties emphasizing a high degree of personal touches that provide guests an "at home" feeling. Guest units tend to be individually decorated. Rooms may not include some modern amenities such as televisions and telephones, and may have a shared bathroom. Usually owner-operated with a common room or parlor separate from the innkeeper's living quarters, where guests and operators can interact during evening and breakfast hours. Evening office closures are normal. A continental or full, hot breakfast is served and is included in the room rate.

🅲🅰 **Cabin/Cottage:** Vacation-oriented, small-scale, freestanding houses or cabins. Units vary in design and décor and often contain one or more bedrooms, living

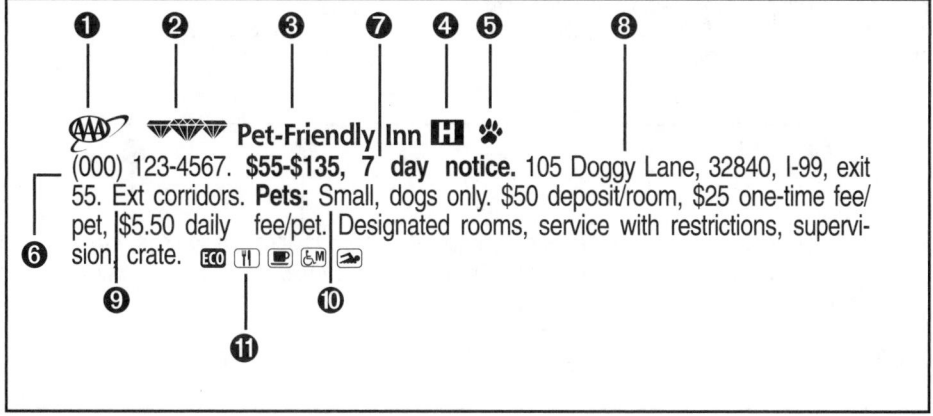

room, kitchen, dining area and bathroom. Studio-type models combine the sleeping and living areas into one room. Typically, basic cleaning supplies, kitchen utensils, and complete bed and bath linens are supplied. The guest registration area may be located off-site.

CO Condominium: Vacation-oriented—commonly for extended-stay purposes—apartment-style accommodations of varying design or décor. Routinely available for rent through a management company, units often contain one or more bedrooms, a living room, full kitchen, and an eating area. Studio-type models combine the sleeping and living areas into one room. As a rule, basic cleaning supplies, kitchen utensils, and complete bed and bath linens are supplied. The guest registration area may be located off site.

CI Country Inn: Although similar in definition to a bed and breakfast, country inns are usually larger in scale with spacious public areas and offer a dining facility that serves at least breakfast and dinner.

H Hotel: Commonly, a multistory establishment with interior room entrances offering a variety of guest unit styles. The magnitude of the public areas is determined by the overall theme, location and service level, but may include a variety of facilities such as a restaurant, shops, fitness center, spa, business center, and/or meeting rooms.

M Motel: Commonly, a one- or two-story establishment with exterior room entrances and drive up parking. Typically, guest units have one bedroom with a bathroom of similar décor and design. Public areas and facilities are often limited in size and/or availability.

RA Ranch: Typically a working ranch with an obvious rustic, Western theme featuring equestrian-related activities and a variety of guest unit styles.

VH Vacation Rental House: Vacation-oriented—commonly for extended-stay purposes—typically larger scale, freestanding, and of varying design or décor. Routinely available for rent through a management company, houses often contain two or more bedrooms, a living room, full kitchen, dining room, and multiple bathrooms. As a rule, basic cleaning supplies, kitchen utensils, and complete bed and bath linens are supplied. The guest registration area may be located off site.

Campground Listings

Geographic listings are used for accuracy and consistency. Campgrounds are listed under the city or town in which they physically are located — or in some cases under the nearest recognized city or town. Not all listings include physical addresses. U.S. campgrounds are listed first, followed by Canadian campgrounds. Listings are alphabetically organized by state or province, city and campground name.

Note: Call first before taking your pet on a camping trip, as campground policies regarding pets may change, including any possible fees that may be assessed.

Each listing provides the following information (see sample listing):

❶ Location

❷ Campground name

❸ Symbol denoting Official Appointment (OA) campgrounds. The OA program permits privately operated campgrounds to display and advertise the AAA or CAA logo. OAs have a special interest in serving AAA/CAA members.

❹ Telephone number

❺ Fee range for a specified number of persons, including the fee for an extra person (XP) staying at the campground.

❻ Most campgrounds accept any or all of the major credit cards, including American Express, MasterCard and Visa. If a campground accepts only cash, the phrase "(no credit cards)" appears.

❼ Physical address and/or highway location and mailing address (if available).

❽ Member values, services and facilities:

   🅂 10% senior discount for members over 59

   🅰 No Tents

   🅿 Pool

   🅇 Recreational activities

   ♿ Accessible features
      (call property for available
      services and amenities)

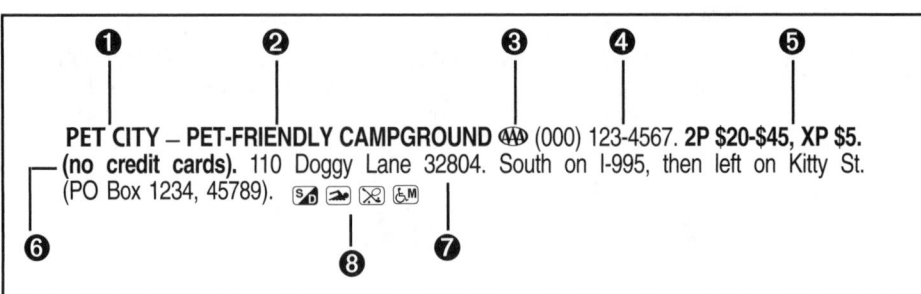

United States Lodgings

ALABAMA

ABBEVILLE

◢◣◢ ▼▼ Best Western-Abbeville Inn M
(334) 585-5060. $59-$89. 1237 US Hwy 431 36310. Jct SR 27. Ext corridors. Pets: Other species. $8 daily fee/pet. Service with restrictions, crate.
[SAVE] [X] [▯] [▭] [≈]

ALBERTVILLE

▼▼ Jameson Inn H
(256) 891-2600. $78-$85. 315 Martling Rd 35950. On US 431, just e of SR 75. Ext corridors. Pets: Accepted. [ASK] [X] [▯] [▭] [≈]

▼▼ Microtel Inn & Suites H
(256) 894-4000. Call for rates. 220 Hwy 75 N 35950. Jct US 431 and SR 75, just ne. Int corridors. Pets: Accepted. [X] [▯] [▭] [≈]

ALEXANDER CITY

◢◣◢ ▼▼ Comfort Inn H
(256) 234-5900. $80-$110. 2945 US Hwy 280 35010. US 280, just ne of jct SR 22. Int corridors. Pets: Other species. $15 daily fee/room. Designated rooms, service with restrictions, crate. [SAVE] [X] [▯] [▭] [≈]

▼▼ Jameson Inn H
(256) 234-7099. $78-$85. 4335 US Hwy 280 35010. US 280, just s of jct SR 22; just w of jct SR 63. Ext corridors. Pets: Other species. $15 daily fee/pet. No service, supervision. [ASK] [X] [▯] [▭] [≈]

ANDALUSIA

▼▼ Days Inn & Suites M
(334) 427-0050. $70-$82. 1604 Dr. MLK Jr Expwy 36420. On US 84 Bypass. Ext corridors. Pets: Accepted. [ASK] [X] [▯] [▭] [≈]

◢◣◢ ▼▼ Econo Lodge M
(334) 222-7511. Call for rates. 1421 Dr. MLK Jr Expwy 36420. On US 84 Bypass. Ext corridors. Pets: Small, dogs only. $10 daily fee/pet. Service with restrictions, supervision. [SAVE] [X] [▯] [▭] [ⵎ] [≈]

ANNISTON

▼▼ Long Leaf Lodge at McClellan M
(256) 820-9494. Call for rates. 74 Exchange Ave 36205. I-20, exit 185, 10 mi n on SR 21, then 1.5 mi e into McClellan-Baltzell Gate. Ext corridors. Pets: Accepted. [X] [▯] [▭] [≈]

▼▼▼ The Victoria, a Country Inn CI
(256) 236-0503. $90. 1600 Quintard Ave 36201. I-20, exit 185, 4 mi n on SR 21/US 431. Ext/int corridors. Pets: Large, other species. $25 one-time fee/room. Designated rooms. [X] [▯] [▭] [≈]

ARAB

▼▼ Jameson Inn H
(256) 586-5777. $78-$85. 706 N Brindlee Mountain Pkwy 35016. On US 231, 0.5 mi n of jct SR 69. Ext corridors. Pets: Accepted.
[ASK] [X] [▯] [▭] [≈]

ATHENS

◢◣◢ ▼▼ Best Western Athens Inn H
(256) 233-4030. $65-$90. 1329 Hwy 72 35611. I-65, exit 351, just w. Ext corridors. Pets: Medium. $20 daily fee/pet. Service with restrictions, supervision. [SAVE] [X] [▯] [▭] [≈]

▼▼ Comfort Inn H
(256) 232-2704. Call for rates. 1218 Kelli Dr 35613. I-65, exit 351, just e on US 72, then just s. Ext corridors. Pets: Accepted.
[X] [▯] [▭] [≈]

▼▼ Sleep Inn Athens H
(256) 232-4700. Call for rates. 1115 Audubon Ln 35611. I-65, exit 351, just nw. Int corridors. Pets: Accepted. [X] [▯] [▭] [≈]

ATTALLA

▼▼ Days Inn Attalla H
(256) 538-7861. Call for rates. 801 Cleveland Ave 35954. I-59, exit 183 northbound, just e; exit southbound, through first set of lights, then just e. Ext corridors. Pets: Other species. $15 daily fee/pet. Service with restrictions, supervision. [X] [▯] [▭] [≈]

AUBURN

◢◣◢ ▼▼▼ The Crenshaw Guest House BB
(334) 821-1131. Call for rates. 371 N College St 36830. Just w of downtown. Ext/int corridors. Pets: Accepted. [SAVE] [X] [▯] [▭]

◢◣◢ ▼▼▼ The Hotel at Auburn University & Dixon Conference Center H ✿
(334) 821-8200. $99-$199. 241 S College St 36830. Just e of downtown. Int corridors. Pets: $250 deposit/room. Supervision.
[SAVE] [X] [⚹] [▯] [▭] [ⵎ] [≈]

▼▼ Jameson Inn M
(334) 502-5020. $83-$90. 1212 Mall Pkwy 36831. Adjacent to Colonial Mall. Ext corridors. Pets: Accepted. [ASK] [X] [▯] [▭] [≈]

◢◣◢ ▼▼▼ Lexington Hotel University Convention Center H
(334) 821-7001. $100-$260. 1577 S College St 36830. I-85, exit 51, 1.4 mi w on US 29/SR 147. Ext corridors. Pets: Medium. $25 one-time fee/ room. Service with restrictions. [SAVE] [X] [▯] [▭] [≈]

◢◣◢ ▼▼▼ Microtel Inn & Suites H
(334) 826-1444. $56-$199, 14 day notice. 2174 S College St 36832. I-85, exit 51, just w. Int corridors. Pets: Small, dogs only. $10 daily fee/ pet. Service with restrictions, supervision. [SAVE] [X] [▯] [▭]

BIRMINGHAM METROPOLITAN AREA

BESSEMER

Best Western Hotel & Suites 🄷 ✿

(205) 481-1950. **$95-$160, 7 day notice.** 5041 Academy Ln 35022. I-20/59, exit 108, just sw. Int corridors. **Pets:** Other species. $15 daily fee/pet. Designated rooms, service with restrictions, supervision.

SAVE ✕ 🛏 💻 ➜

Jameson Inn 🄷

(205) 428-3194. **$88-$95.** 5021 Academy Ln 35022. I-20/59, exit 108, just sw. Ext corridors. **Pets:** Accepted. ASK ✕ 🛏 💻 ➜

Sleep Inn 🄷 ✿

(205) 424-0000. **$70-$200.** 1259 Greenmor Dr 35022. I-459, exit 6, just s, then just w. Int corridors. **Pets:** Small, other species. $20 daily fee/pet. Designated rooms, service with restrictions, supervision.

✕ 🛏 💻 ➜

BIRMINGHAM

Best Western Mountain Brook Ⓜ

(205) 991-9977. **$89.** 4627 Hwy 280 E 35242. I-459, exit 19 (US 280), 1.4 mi e. Ext corridors. **Pets:** Cats only. $10 one-time fee/pet. Service with restrictions, supervision. SAVE ✕ 🛏 💻 ➜ ✕

Days Inn 🄷

(205) 324-4510. **$65-$150.** 905 11th Ct W 35204. I-20/59, exit 123, just sw. Ext/int corridors. **Pets:** $10 daily fee/pet. Service with restrictions, supervision. ASK ✕ 🛏 💻 ➜

Drury Inn & Suites-Birmingham Southeast 🄷

(205) 967-2450. **$90-$199.** 3510 Grandview Pkwy 35243. I-459, exit 19 (US 280), just e; in Grandview. Int corridors. **Pets:** Other species. No service, supervision. ASK ✕ 🛏 💻 ➜

Homestead Studio Suites-Birmingham Perimeter Park South 🄷

(205) 967-3800. **$58-$110.** 12 Perimeter Park S 35243. I-459, exit 19 (US 280), 0.5 mi e, then just s. Ext corridors. **Pets:** Other species. $25 daily fee/room. Designated rooms, service with restrictions, crate.

ASK ✕ 🛏

La Quinta Inn & Suites Birmingham 🄷 ✿

(205) 995-9990. **$49-$119.** 513 Cahaba Park Cir 35242. I-459, exit 19 (US 280), 1.2 mi e. Int corridors. **Pets:** Medium, other species. Service with restrictions, supervision. ASK ✕ 🛏 💻

Residence Inn By Marriott 🄷

(205) 991-8686. **$170-$208.** 3 Greenhill Pkwy 35242. I-459, exit 19 (US 280), 2 mi e. Ext corridors. **Pets:** Accepted.

SAVE ✕ 🛏 💻 ➜ ✕

Sheraton Birmingham Hotel 🄷

(205) 324-5000. **$109-$289.** 2101 Richard Arrington Jr Blvd N 35203. I-20/59, exit 22nd St. Int corridors. **Pets:** Accepted.

SAVE ✕ 💻 🍽 ➜ ✕

CALERA

Holiday Inn Express 🄷

(205) 668-3641. **Call for rates.** 357 Hwy 304 35040. I-65, exit 231, just se. Ext corridors. **Pets:** Accepted. ✕ 🛏 💻 ➜

FULTONDALE

Holiday Inn Express Fultondale 🄷

(205) 439-6300. **Call for rates.** 1733 Fulton Rd 35068. I-65, exit 267, just e. Int corridors. **Pets:** Small. $40 one-time fee/pet. Designated rooms, service with restrictions, supervision. ✕ 🛏 💻 ➜

GARDENDALE

Microtel Inn & Suites-Birmingham North-Gardendale 🄷

(205) 631-6320. **Call for rates.** 850 Odum Rd 35071. I-65, exit 271, just e, then just s. Int corridors. **Pets:** Accepted. ✕ 🛏 💻 ➜

HOMEWOOD

aloft Birmingham Soho Square 🄷 ✿

(205) 874-8055. **Call for rates.** 1903 29th Ave S 35209. I-59, exit 126A, 3.5 mi s on US 31, then just w. Int corridors. **Pets:** Medium, dogs only. Service with restrictions, supervision.

SAVE ✕ 🛏Ⓜ 🛏 💻 🍽 ➜

Best Western Carlton Suites 🄷

(205) 940-9990. **$85-$95.** 140 State Farm Pkwy 35209. I-65, exit 255, just w to Wildwood Pkwy, then just n. Int corridors. **Pets:** Small, dogs only. $10 daily fee/pet. No service, supervision. SAVE ✕ 🛏 💻 ➜

Drury Inn & Suites-Birmingham Southwest 🄷

(205) 940-9500. **$105-$189.** 160 State Farm Pkwy 35209. I-65, exit 255, 0.5 mi on northwest frontage road. Int corridors. **Pets:** Other species. No service, supervision. ASK ✕ 🛏 💻 ➜

La Quinta Inn & Suites Birmingham (Homewood) 🄷 ✿

(205) 290-0150. **$72-$139.** 60 State Farm Pkwy 35209. I-65, exit 255, 0.9 mi on northwest frontage road. Int corridors. **Pets:** Medium, other species. Service with restrictions, supervision. ASK ✕ 🛏 💻 ➜

Residence Inn by Marriott 🄷

(205) 943-0044. **$188-$230.** 50 State Farm Pkwy 35209. I-65, exit 255, 1 mi on northwest frontage road. Int corridors. **Pets:** Accepted.

SAVE ✕ 🛏 💻 ➜ ✕

Super 8 🄷

(205) 945-9888. **$47-$70, 7 day notice.** 140 Vulcan Rd 35209. I-65, exit 256 northbound; exit 256A southbound, just nw. Int corridors. **Pets:** Small, other species. $5 daily fee/pet. Service with restrictions.

ASK ✕ 🛏 💻

TownePlace Suites by Marriott 🄷

(205) 943-0114. **$152-$186.** 500 Wildwood Cir 35209. I-65, exit 255, 0.6 mi w, then just n. Int corridors. **Pets:** $100 one-time fee/room. Service with restrictions. SAVE ✕ 🛏Ⓜ 🛏 💻 ➜

HOOVER

Days Inn at the Galleria 🄷

(205) 985-7500. **$74-$140.** 1800 Riverchase Dr 35244. I-459, exit 13, 0.5 mi s on US 31, then 0.4 mi w on SR 150. Ext corridors. **Pets:** Small. $25 daily fee/pet. Service with restrictions. SAVE ✕ 🛏 💻 ➜

Homewood Suites by Hilton 🄷

(205) 995-9823. **$159-$169.** 215 Inverness Center Dr 35242. I-459, exit 19 (US 280), 1.8 mi e, then just s. Int corridors. **Pets:** Accepted.

✕ 🛏 💻 ➜ ✕

Residence Inn by Marriott Birmingham/Hoover 🄷

(205) 733-1655. **$130-$158.** 2725 John Hawkins Pkwy 35244. I-459, exit 13A, 0.5 mi se to SR 150, then 1.5 mi s. Int corridors. **Pets:** Small, other species. $100 one-time fee/room. Service with restrictions.

✕ 🛏Ⓜ 🛏 💻 ➜

IRONDALE

Quality Inn Birmingham East 🄷

(205) 956-4100. **Call for rates.** 3910 Kilgore Memorial Dr 35210. I-20, exit 133, just e. Ext corridors. **Pets:** Small. $20 daily fee/pet. Service with restrictions. ✕ 🛏 💻 ➜

LEEDS

△△△△ ▼▼▼▼ **Best Western Bass Hotel & Suites** ⊞
(205) 640-5300. **$85-$250, 3 day notice.** 1949 Village Dr 35094. I-20, exit 144A westbound; 144B eastbound, just ne. Int corridors. **Pets:** Very small. $10 daily fee/pet. Service with restrictions, supervision.
SAVE ✕ 🖥 💻 ➰

△△△ ▼▼▼▼ **Days Inn of Leeds** Ⓜ
(205) 699-9833. **$69-$180.** 1838 Ashville Rd 35094. I-20, exit 144A eastbound; exit 144B westbound, just s. Ext corridors. **Pets:** Other species. $10 daily fee/pet. Service with restrictions. SAVE ✕ 🖥 💻 ➰

ONEONTA

△△△ ▼▼▼ **Best Western Colonial Inn** ⊞
(205) 274-2200. **$73-$139.** 293 Valley Rd 35121. On SR 75, 0.5 mi n of jct US 231. Ext corridors. **Pets:** Accepted. SAVE ✕ 🖥 💻 ➰

PELHAM

△△△ ▼▼ **Quality Inn** ⊞
(205) 444-9200. **Call for rates.** 110 Cahaba Valley Pkwy 35124. I-65, exit 246, just nw. Ext corridors. **Pets:** Small. $25 daily fee/room. Designated rooms, service with restrictions, supervision.
SAVE ✕ 🖥 💻 ➰

TRUSSVILLE

▼▼ **Jameson Inn** ⊞
(205) 661-9323. **$93-$100.** 4730 Norrell Dr 35173. I-59, exit 141, just e on Chalkville Rd, then just n. Ext corridors. **Pets:** Accepted.
ASK ✕ 🖥 💻 ➰

END METROPOLITAN AREA

CHILDERSBURG

▼▼ **Key West Inn Childersburg** Ⓜ
(256) 378-0337. **$64.** 32210 US Hwy 280 35044. Just s of jct CR 235. Ext corridors. **Pets:** Accepted. ASK ✕ 🖥 💻 ➰

CLANTON

△△△ ▼▼▼ **Best Western Inn** ⊞
(205) 280-1006. **$65-$100.** 801 Bradberry Ln 35046. I-65, exit 205, 0.5 mi e. Ext corridors. **Pets:** Small. $10 daily fee/pet. Service with restrictions, supervision. SAVE ✕ 🖥 💻 ➰

▼▼ **GuestHouse International Inn** Ⓜ
(205) 280-0306. **$59-$73.** 946 Lake Mitchell Rd 35045. I-65, exit 208, just w. Ext corridors. **Pets:** Other species. $6 one-time fee/pet. Service with restrictions, supervision. ASK ✕ 🖥 💻 ➰

CULLMAN

△△△ ▼▼▼ **Best Western Fairwinds Inn** ⊞ ❀
(256) 737-5009. **$72-$90.** 1917 Commerce Ave NW 35055. I-65, exit 310, just e. Ext corridors. **Pets:** Medium, other species. $25 daily fee/pet. Designated rooms, service with restrictions. SAVE ✕ 🖥 💻 ➰

▼▼ **Days Inn** ⊞
(256) 739-3800. **$75-$95.** 1841 4th St SW 35055. I-65, exit 308, just e. Ext corridors. **Pets:** Accepted. ASK ✕ 🖥 💻 ➰

△△△ ▼▼▼ **Econo Lodge** Ⓜ ❀
(256) 734-2691. **Call for rates.** 1655 CR 437 35055. I-65, exit 304, just e. Ext corridors. **Pets:** Small, dogs only. $10 daily fee/pet. Service with restrictions, supervision. SAVE ✕ 🖥 💻

▼▼ **Quality Inn** ⊞
(256) 734-1240. **Call for rates.** 5917 Alabama Hwy 157 NW 35058. I-65, exit 310, just e. Ext corridors. **Pets:** Small. $20 one-time fee/room. Designated rooms, service with restrictions, supervision.
✕ 🖥 💻 ➰

DAPHNE

▼▼▼▼ **Homewood Suites by Hilton Mobile East Bay/Daphne** ⊞
(251) 621-0100. **$144-$179.** 29474 N Main St 36526. I-10, 35A eastbound; 35 westbound, just s. Int corridors. **Pets:** Accepted.
✕ 🔐 🖥 💻 ➰

DECATUR

△△△ ▼▼▼ **Best Western River City Hotel** ⊞
(256) 301-1388. **$63-$105.** 1305 Front Ave 35603. I-65, exit 334, 8 mi n. Int corridors. **Pets:** Medium. $25 one-time fee/pet. Service with restrictions, supervision. SAVE ✕ 🔐 🖥 💻 ➰

△△△ ▼▼ **Comfort Inn & Suites** ⊞
(256) 355-1999. **$68-$86.** 2212 Danville Rd SW 35601. SR 67, jct Beltline Rd SW. Int corridors. **Pets:** Other species. $15 daily fee/room.
SAVE ✕ 🖥 💻 ➰

▼▼▼ **Holiday Inn Hotel & Suites** ⊞
(256) 355-3150. **$94.** 1101 6th Ave NE 35601. Just w of jct US 31, 72A and SR 20. Ext/int corridors. **Pets:** Medium. $15 one-time fee/room. Designated rooms, service with restrictions, crate.
ASK ✕ 🖥 💻 🍴 ➰ ✕

▼▼ **Jameson Inn** ⊞
(256) 355-2229. **$73-$78.** 2120 Jameson Pl SW 35603. SR 67, 1.6 mi s of jct US 72A; 3.9 mi n of jct US 31. Ext corridors. **Pets:** Accepted.
ASK ✕ 🖥 💻 ➰

▼▼ **La Quinta Inn** Ⓜ ❀
(256) 355-9977. **$50-$100.** 918 Beltline Rd SW 35601. Jct US 31 and SR 67, 1.6 mi w. Int corridors. **Pets:** Medium, other species. Service with restrictions, supervision. ASK ✕ 🖥 💻 ➰

▼▼ **Microtel Inn & Suites** ⊞
(256) 301-9995. **$59-$79, 14 day notice.** 2226 Beltline Rd SW 35601. On SR 67, 4 mi w of jct US 31. Int corridors. **Pets:** Medium. $75 one-time fee/pet. Service with restrictions, supervision.
ASK ✕ 🔐 🖥 💻 ➰

DEMOPOLIS

△△△ ▼▼▼▼ **Best Western Two Rivers Hotel & Suites** ⊞ ❀
(334) 289-2611. **$110-$120.** 662 US Hwy 80 W 36732. Jct US 43, 0.8 mi w. Int corridors. **Pets:** Medium. $25 deposit/pet. Service with restrictions, supervision. SAVE ✕ 🖥 💻 ➰

DOTHAN

△△△ ▼▼ **Americas Best Value Inn & Suites** Ⓜ
(334) 793-5200. **$45-$99.** 2901 Ross Clark Cir 36301. 0.8 mi s of jct US 84; west end of town. Ext corridors. **Pets:** Accepted.
SAVE ✕ 🖥 💻 ➰

▼▼ **Days Inn** Ⓜ
(334) 671-3700. **$45-$65.** 3071 Ross Clark Cir 36301. Just s of jct US 84; west end of town. Ext corridors. **Pets:** Accepted. ASK ✕ 🔐 💻

▼▼ **Howard Johnson Inn** Ⓜ
(334) 792-3339. **Call for rates.** 2244 Ross Clark Cir 36301. 1.4 mi s of jct SR 52; west end of town. Ext corridors. **Pets:** Dogs only. $15 daily fee/pet. Supervision. ✕ 🖥 💻 ➰

▼▼ **Knights Inn Dothan** Ⓜ
(334) 793-2550. **$48-$52.** 2841 Ross Clark Cir 36301. 0.9 mi s of jct US 84; west end of town. Ext corridors. **Pets:** Accepted. ASK ✕ 🖥 ➰

▼▼▼▼ La Quinta Inn & Suites-Dothan 🅷 🐾
(334) 793-9090. **$69-$139.** 3593 Ross Clark Cir 36303. Just w of jct US 231; northwest part of town. Int corridors. **Pets:** Medium, other species. Service with restrictions, supervision. (ASK) ⊠ ⚙ⓜ ⛬ 🖙 🏊

▼ Motel 6 #1233 🅼
(334) 793-6013. **$33-$45.** 2907 Ross Clark Cir 36301. 0.8 mi s of jct US 84; west end of town. Ext corridors. **Pets:** Other species. Service with restrictions, supervision. ⊠ ⛬ 🖙

▼▼ Westgate Inn 🅼
(334) 794-6601. **$41-$65.** 3053 Ross Clark Cir 36301. Just s of jct US 84; west end of town. Ext corridors. **Pets:** Accepted.
(ASK) ⊠ ⚙ⓜ 🖙 🍴 🏊

ENTERPRISE
▼▼ Comfort Inn 🅼
(334) 393-2304. **Call for rates.** 615 Boll Weevil Cir 36330. On US 84 Bypass. Ext corridors. **Pets:** Accepted. ⊠ ⛬ 🖙 🏊

EUFAULA
▼▼▼ Eufaula Comfort Suites 🅷
(334) 616-0114. **$80-$90.** 12 Paul Lee Pkwy 36027. 1.7 mi s on US 431 from jct US 82 E, then just e. Int corridors. **Pets:** Accepted.
(ASK) ⊠ ⚙ⓜ ⛬ 🖙 🏊 ⊠

▼▼ Jameson Inn 🅼
(334) 687-7747. **$83-$90.** 136 Towne Center Blvd 36027. On US 431, 1 mi s of US 82 E. Ext corridors. **Pets:** Accepted.
(ASK) ⊠ ⛬ 🖙 🏊

EVERGREEN
▲▲▲⁷ ▼▼▼ Comfort Inn 🅼
(251) 578-4701. **Call for rates.** 1571 Ted Bates Rd 36401. I-65, exit 96, just w. Ext corridors. **Pets:** Other species. $15 one-time fee/pet. Designated rooms, service with restrictions. (SAVE) ⛬ 🖙 🏊

▼▼ Days Inn of Evergreen 🅼
(251) 578-2100. **$70-$95.** 215 Hwy 83 36401. I-65, exit 96, just w. Ext corridors. **Pets:** Accepted. (ASK) ⊠ ⛬ 🖙

FAIRHOPE
▼▼ Key West Inn 🅼
(251) 990-7373. **$59-$109.** 231 S Greeno Rd 36532. On US 98, 1.9 mi s of jct SR 104. Ext corridors. **Pets:** Medium. $15 daily fee/pet. Designated rooms, service with restrictions, supervision.
(ASK) ⊠ ⛬ 🖙 🏊

FLORENCE
▼▼ Jameson Inn 🅷
(256) 764-5326. **$88-$95.** 115 Ana Dr 35630. On US 43/72, just nw of jct SR 133 (Cox Creek Pkwy). Ext corridors. **Pets:** Accepted.
(ASK) ⊠ ⛬ 🖙 🏊

▼▼▼ ▼▼▼ Marriott Shoals Hotel and Spa 🅷
(256) 246-3600. **$164-$185.** 800 Cox Creek Pkwy S 35630. From jct US 43/72 and SR 133 (Cox Creek Pkwy), 1.5 mi s; at Wilson Dam. Int corridors. **Pets:** Other species. $75 one-time fee/pet. Service with restrictions, crate. ⊠ ⚙ⓜ ⛬ 🖙 🍴 🏊 ⊠

FOLEY
▲▲▲⁷ ▼▼▼ Econo Lodge & Suites 🅷
(251) 943-9100. **$70-$190.** 2682 S McKenzie St 36535. On SR 59, 1.9 mi s of jct US 98. Ext corridors. **Pets:** Small, other species. $20 one-time fee/pet. Service with restrictions, crate. (SAVE) ⊠ ⚙ⓜ ⛬ 🖙 🏊

▲▲▲⁷ ▼▼▼ Key West Inn 🅼
(251) 943-1241. **$69-$139.** 2520 S McKenzie St 36535. On SR 59, 1.8 mi s of jct US 98. Ext corridors. **Pets:** Medium. $20 daily fee/pet. Designated rooms, service with restrictions, supervision.
(SAVE) ⊠ ⛬ 🖙 🏊

GADSDEN
▼▼ Gadsden Inn & Suites 🅷
(256) 543-7240. **$59-$159.** 200 Albert Rains Blvd 35901. Jct US 411 and 431/278; enter on 2nd St off US 431. Ext corridors. **Pets:** Small. $25 one-time fee/pet. Service with restrictions, crate. ⊠ ⛬ 🖙 🏊

GENEVA
▼▼ Briarwood Inn of Geneva 🅼
(334) 684-7715. **$69-$102.** 1503 W Magnolia Ave 36340. On SR 52, 0.3 mi w of jct SR 196. Ext corridors. **Pets:** Accepted.
(ASK) ⊠ ⛬ 🖙 🏊

GREENVILLE
▲▲▲⁷ ▼▼▼ Days Inn 🅼
(334) 382-3118. **$65-$95, 7 day notice.** 946 Fort Dale Rd 36037. I-65, exit 130, just s on SR 185. Ext corridors. **Pets:** Accepted.
(SAVE) ⊠ ⛬ 🖙 🏊

▼▼ Jameson Inn 🅼
(334) 382-6300. **$78-$85.** 71 Jameson Ln 36037. I-65, exit 130, just n on SR 185, then just w on Cahaba Rd. Ext corridors. **Pets:** Accepted.
(ASK) ⊠ ⛬ 🖙 🏊

GULF SHORES
▼▼ La Quinta Inn 🅷 🐾
(251) 967-3500. **$50-$160.** 213 W Fort Morgan Rd 36542. On SR 180, just w of jct SR 59. Int corridors. **Pets:** Medium, other species. Service with restrictions, supervision. (ASK) ⊠ ⚙ⓜ ⛬ 🖙 🏊 ⊠

GUNTERSVILLE
▼ Super 8-Guntersville 🅼
(256) 582-8444. **Call for rates.** 14341 Hwy 431 S 35976. Jct SR 69, 2 mi s. Ext corridors. **Pets:** Accepted. ⊠ ⛬ 🖙

HAMILTON
▼▼ Days Inn 🅷
(205) 921-1790. **$59-$89.** 1849 Military St S 35570. US 78, exit 14, 1 mi n, then 1 mi w on US 43. Ext corridors. **Pets:** Other species. $10 daily fee/pet. Service with restrictions, supervision. (ASK) ⊠ ⛬ 🖙 🏊

HUNTSVILLE
▲▲▲⁷ ▼▼▼ America's Best Inn 🅼
(256) 539-9671. **$64-$74.** 1304 N Memorial Pkwy 35801. I-565, exit 19B, 0.5 mi n on US 231/431, exit Cook Ave. Ext corridors. **Pets:** Accepted.
(SAVE) ⊠ ⛬ 🖙 🏊

◆▼ Extended StayAmerica Huntsville-U.S. Space and Rocket Center 🅷
(256) 830-9110. **$70-$98.** 4751 Governors House Dr 35805. I-565, exit 17A, just s, then 0.5 mi w. Ext corridors. **Pets:** Other species. $25 daily fee/room. Designated rooms, service with restrictions, crate.
(ASK) ⊠ ⚙ⓜ ⛬ 🖙

▼▼▼ Holiday Inn Express Hotel & Suites 🅷
(256) 721-1000. **$90-$135.** 3808 University Dr 35816. I-565, exit 17A, just e. Int corridors. **Pets:** Small. $50 one-time fee/room. Service with restrictions, supervision. (ASK) ⊠ ⛬ 🖙 🏊

▼▼▼ Holiday Inn Huntsville Downtown 🅷
(256) 533-1400. **Call for rates.** 401 Williams Ave SW 35801. Just w of Church St; downtown. Int corridors. **Pets:** Small, other species. $30 one-time fee/pet. Service with restrictions, supervision.
⊠ ⛬ 🖙 🍴 🏊

▼▼▼ La Quinta Inn & Suites Huntsville 🅷 🐾
(256) 830-8999. **$59-$129.** 4890 University Dr NW 35816. I-565, exit 14B, 2.6 mi n on Research Park Blvd, then 1 mi e on US 72. Int corridors. **Pets:** Medium, other species. Service with restrictions, supervision.
(ASK) ⊠ ⛬ 🖙 🏊

▼▼▼ **La Quinta Inn Huntsville (Research Park)** 🏨 ❖
(256) 830-2070. **$45-$109.** 4870 University Dr NW 35816-1847. I-565, exit 14B, 2.6 mi n on Research Park Blvd, then 1 mi e on US 72. Ext corridors. **Pets:** Medium, other species. Service with restrictions, supervision. ⟨ASK⟩ ⟨✕⟩ 🛏 💻 ⟨🐾⟩

▼▼▼ **La Quinta Inn Huntsville (Space Center)** 🏨 ❖
(256) 533-0756. **$42-$109.** 3141 University Dr NW 35816. I-565, exit 17A, 1.1 mi n on SR 53 (Jordan Ln), then 0.6 mi e on US 72. Ext corridors. **Pets:** Medium, other species. Service with restrictions, supervision. ⟨ASK⟩ ⟨✕⟩ 🛏 💻 ⟨🐾⟩

▼▼ **Microtel Inn & Suites** 🏨
(256) 859-6655. **$50-$99.** 1820 Chase Creek Row 35811. Jct US 72 and Shields Rd, just n, then just w. Int corridors. **Pets:** Other species. $25 deposit/room, $10 one-time fee/pet. Designated rooms, service with restrictions. ⟨ASK⟩ ⟨✕⟩ ⟨&M⟩ 🛏 💻 ⟨🐾⟩

▼▼▼ **TownePlace Suites by Marriott** 🏨
(256) 971-5277. **$107-$131.** 1125 McMurtrie Dr 35806. I-565, exit 14B, 2.6 mi n on Research Park Blvd, 0.8 mi w on US 72, then just s. Int corridors. **Pets:** Medium, other species. $100 one-time fee/room. Service with restrictions, crate. ⟨✕⟩ ⟨&M⟩ 🛏 💻 ⟨🐾⟩

⟨AAA⟩ ▼▼▼▼ **The Westin Huntsville** 🏨 ❖
(256) 428-2000. **Call for rates.** 6800 Governors West NW 35806. I-565, exit 14A, 0.5 mi n on SR 255 (Research Park Blvd), just w on Old Madison Pike, then 0.5 mi n. Int corridors. **Pets:** Large, dogs only. Crate. ⟨SAVE⟩ ⟨✕⟩ ⟨&M⟩ 🛏 💻 ⟨🍴⟩ ⟨🐾⟩ ⟨✕⟩

JACKSON

⟨AAA⟩ ▼▼▼ **Econo Lodge** Ⓜ
(251) 246-4111. **$70-$83.** 3680 N College Ave 36545. I-65, exit 19, on US 43. Ext corridors. **Pets:** Other species. Service with restrictions, crate. ⟨SAVE⟩ ⟨✕⟩ 🛏 💻

JASPER

▼▼ **Jameson Inn** 🏨
(205) 387-7710. **$83-$90.** 1100 Hwy 78/118 E 35501. SR 118, 1.8 mi w of jct SR 69. Ext corridors. **Pets:** Accepted. ⟨ASK⟩ ⟨✕⟩ ⟨&M⟩ 🛏 💻 ⟨🐾⟩

MILLBROOK

▼▼ **Key West Inn** Ⓜ
(334) 309-2004. **$69-$89.** 2275 Cobbs Ford Rd 36054. I-65, exit 179, just w. Ext corridors. **Pets:** Medium. $7 daily fee/pet. Designated rooms, service with restrictions, supervision. ⟨ASK⟩ ⟨✕⟩ 🛏 💻 ⟨🐾⟩

MOBILE

⟨AAA⟩ ▼▼▼▼ **The Battle House, a Renaissance Hotel** 🏨
(251) 338-2000. **$179-$219.** 26 N Royal St 36602. I-10, exit 26B (Water St) eastbound, w on Government St, then just n. Int corridors. **Pets:** $50 one-time fee/room. Service with restrictions, crate. ⟨SAVE⟩ ⟨✕⟩ ⟨&M⟩ 🛏 💻 ⟨🍴⟩ ⟨🐾⟩ ⟨✕⟩

⟨AAA⟩ ▼▼ **Best Western Battleship Inn** Ⓜ
(251) 432-2703. **$89.** 2701 Battleship Pkwy 36602. I-10, exit 27, just e. Ext corridors. **Pets:** Accepted. ⟨SAVE⟩ ⟨✕⟩ 🛏 💻 ⟨🍴⟩ ⟨🐾⟩

▼▼▼▼ **Drury Inn-Mobile** Ⓜ
(251) 344-7700. **$90-$144.** 824 W I-65 Service Rd S 36609. I-65, exit 3 (Airport Blvd), just w, then just s on service road. Int corridors. **Pets:** Other species. No service, supervision. ⟨ASK⟩ ⟨✕⟩ 🛏 💻 ⟨🐾⟩

▼▼ **Extended StayAmerica Mobile-Spring Hill** 🏨
(251) 344-2514. **$59-$79.** 508 Spring Hill Plaza Ct 36608. I-65, exit 5A, just w, then just n. Ext corridors. **Pets:** Other species. $25 daily fee/room. Designated rooms, service with restrictions. ⟨ASK⟩ ⟨✕⟩ 🛏 💻

▼▼ **La Quinta Inn Mobile** Ⓜ ❖
(251) 343-4051. **$59-$129.** 816 W I-65 Service Rd S 36609. I-65, exit 3 (Airport Blvd), just w, then just s. Ext/int corridors. **Pets:** Medium, other species. Service with restrictions, supervision. ⟨ASK⟩ ⟨✕⟩ 🛏 💻 ⟨🐾⟩

⟨AAA⟩ ▼▼ **Olsson Motel** Ⓜ
(251) 661-5331. **$45-$85, 10 day notice.** 4137 Government Blvd 36693. I-65, exit 1, 2 mi w on US 90; I-10, exit 15B, 4 mi e on US 90. Ext corridors. **Pets:** Accepted. ⟨SAVE⟩ ⟨✕⟩ 🛏

▼▼▼▼ **Residence Inn by Marriott Mobile** 🏨
(251) 304-0570. **$139-$169.** 950 W I-65 Service Rd S 36609. I-65, exit 3 (Airport Blvd), just w, then 0.4 mi s. Int corridors. **Pets:** Accepted. ⟨✕⟩ ⟨&M⟩ 🛏 💻 ⟨🐾⟩ ⟨✕⟩

▼▼▼ **TownePlace Suites by Marriott** 🏨
(251) 345-9588. **$148-$180.** 1075 Montlimar Dr 36609. I-65, exit 3 (Airport Blvd), 0.5 mi w, then 0.5 mi s. Int corridors. **Pets:** Large, other species. $75 one-time fee/room. Service with restrictions, crate. ⟨✕⟩ 🛏 💻 ⟨🐾⟩

MONROEVILLE

▼▼ **Americas Best Value Inn** Ⓜ
(251) 743-3154. **$50-$200.** 50 Hwy 21 S 36460. On SR 21, just s of jct US 84. Ext corridors. **Pets:** Medium. $15 daily fee/pet. No service, supervision. ⟨ASK⟩ ⟨✕⟩ 🛏

⟨AAA⟩ ◆ ▼▼▼ **Best Western of Monroeville** Ⓜ
(251) 575-9999. **$69-$99.** 4419 S Alabama Ave 36460. On SR 21, 0.5 mi n of jct US 84. Ext corridors. **Pets:** Accepted. ⟨SAVE⟩ ⟨✕⟩ 🛏 💻 ⟨🐾⟩

▼▼ **Days Inn of Monroeville** Ⓜ
(251) 743-3297. **Call for rates.** 4389 S Alabama Ave 36460. On SR 21, 0.5 mi n of jct US 84. Ext corridors. **Pets:** Accepted. ⟨✕⟩ 🛏 💻 ⟨🐾⟩

⟨AAA⟩ ▼▼▼ **Holiday Inn Express** 🏨
(251) 743-3333. **$110-$165.** 120 Hwy 21 S 36460. On SR 21, just s of jct US 84. Int corridors. **Pets:** Small. $20 daily fee/pet. Designated rooms, no service, supervision. ⟨SAVE⟩ ⟨✕⟩ ⟨&M⟩ 🛏 💻 ⟨🐾⟩

MONTGOMERY

▼▼ **America's Best Inn-Montgomery** 🏨
(334) 270-9199. **$63.** 5135 Carmichael Rd 36106. I-85, exit 6, just s on Eastern Blvd, then just w. Int corridors. **Pets:** Service with restrictions, supervision. ⟨ASK⟩ ⟨✕⟩ 🛏 💻 ⟨🐾⟩

▼▼ **Baymont Inn & Suites** Ⓜ
(334) 272-0370. **$59-$99.** 5837 Monticello Dr 36117. I-85, exit 6, just n, then just e. Ext corridors. **Pets:** $10 daily fee/pet. Service with restrictions, supervision. ⟨ASK⟩ ⟨✕⟩ 🛏 💻 ⟨🐾⟩

⟨AAA⟩ ▼▼▼ **Days Inn Midtown** Ⓜ
(334) 269-9611. **$59-$64.** 2625 Zelda Rd 36107. I-85, exit 3, just s on Ann St. Ext corridors. **Pets:** Large, other species. $10 daily fee/pet. Service with restrictions, supervision. ⟨SAVE⟩ ⟨✕⟩ 🛏 💻 ⟨🐾⟩

▼▼▼▼ **Drury Inn & Suites-Montgomery** 🏨
(334) 273-1101. **$90-$189.** 1124 Eastern Blvd 36117. I-85, exit 6, just n. Int corridors. **Pets:** Other species. No service, supervision. ⟨ASK⟩ ⟨✕⟩ ⟨&M⟩ 🛏 💻 ⟨🐾⟩

▼▼ **Econo Lodge** Ⓜ
(334) 284-3400. **Call for rates.** 4135 Troy Hwy 36116. On US 82/231, 0.7 mi e of jct South and East blvds. Ext corridors. **Pets:** Accepted. ⟨✕⟩ 🛏 💻 ⟨🐾⟩

⟨AAA⟩ ▼▼▼▼ **Embassy Suites Montgomery Conference Center** 🏨 ❖
(334) 269-5055. **$99-$179.** 300 Tallapoosa St 36104. Between Molton and Commerce sts; in historic downtown. Int corridors. **Pets:** Medium, other species. $40 one-time fee/room. Service with restrictions. ⟨SAVE⟩ ⟨✕⟩ ⟨&M⟩ 🛏 💻 ⟨🍴⟩ ⟨🐾⟩

▼▼ **Extended StayAmerica Montgomery-Eastern Blvd** 🏨
(334) 279-1204. **$55-$95.** 2491 Eastern Blvd 36117. I-85, exit 6, 1.3 mi s on US 231. Ext corridors. **Pets:** Other species. $25 daily fee/room. Designated rooms, service with restrictions, crate. ⟨ASK⟩ ⟨✕⟩ 🛏 💻

▼▼▼▼ **La Quinta Inn & Suites** 🅷 ❀
(334) 277-6000. **$49-$109.** 5225 Carmichael Rd 36106. I-85, exit 6, just s on Eastern Blvd, then just w. Int corridors. **Pets:** Medium, other species. Service with restrictions, supervision. (ASK) ✕ ⓜ 🖥 🖨 ➹

▼▼ **La Quinta Inn Montgomery** 🅼 ❀
(334) 271-1620. **$42-$109.** 1280 East Blvd 36117-2231. I-85, exit 6, just s. Ext corridors. **Pets:** Medium, other species. Service with restrictions, supervision. (ASK) ✕ 🖥 🖨 ➹

▼ **Motel 6 #4263** 🅼
(334) 280-1866. **$46-$60.** 7760 Slade Plaza Blvd 36105. I-65, exit 164, just s. Int corridors. **Pets:** Other species. Service with restrictions, supervision. (ASK) ✕ 🖥 ➹

▼▼ **Quality Inn & Suites-Convention Center** 🅷
(334) 288-2800. **$54-$69.** 2705 E South Blvd 36116. I-85, exit 6, 3.7 mi s on East Blvd. Ext corridors. **Pets:** Accepted. ✕ 🖥 🖨 ➹

◈◈◈ ▼▼◈ **Red Roof Inn Montgomery** 🅷
(334) 270-0007. **$64-$79, 30 day notice.** 5601 Carmichael Rd 36117. I-85, exit 6, just s on Eastern Blvd, then just e. Ext/int corridors. **Pets:** Large. Service with restrictions, crate. (SAVE) ✕ 🖥 ➹

▼▼◈ **Residence Inn by Marriott** 🅷
(334) 270-3300. **$143-$175.** 1200 Hilmar Ct 36117. I-85, exit 6, just s on Eastern Blvd, then just e. Ext/int corridors. **Pets:** Accepted. ✕ 🖥 🖨 ➹ ✕

▼▼◈ **Sleep Inn & Suites** 🅷
(334) 387-1004. **Call for rates.** 5005 Carmichael Rd 36106. I-85, exit 6, just s. Int corridors. **Pets:** Medium. $10 daily fee/pet. Designated rooms, service with restrictions, supervision. ✕ 🖥 🖨 ➹

▼▼◈ **StudioPLUS Montgomery-Carmichael Rd** 🅷
(334) 273-0075. **$65-$105.** 5115 Carmichael Rd 36106. I-85, exit 6, just s, then just w. Int corridors. **Pets:** Other species. $25 daily fee/room. Designated rooms, service with restrictions, crate. (ASK) ✕ 🖥 🖨 ➹

▼▼◈ **TownePlace Suites by Marriott** 🅷
(334) 396-5505. **$107-$131.** 5047 Townplace Dr 36106. I-85, exit 6, just s on Eastern Blvd, then just w on Carmichael Rd. Int corridors. **Pets:** Accepted. ✕ ⓜ 🖥 🖨 ➹

OXFORD

▼▼◈ **Baymont Inn Anniston/Oxford** 🅷
(256) 835-1492. **Call for rates.** 1600 Hwy 21 S 36203. I-20, exit 185, just s. Ext corridors. **Pets:** Accepted. ✕ 🖥 🖨 ➹

▼▼◈ **Hampton Inn & Suites** 🅷
(256) 831-8958. **$79-$139.** 210 Colonial Dr 36203. I-20, exit 188, just n, then w. Int corridors. **Pets:** Accepted. ✕ 🖥 🖨 ➹ ✕

▼▼◈ **Holiday Inn Express & Suites Anniston/Oxford** 🅷 ❀
(256) 835-8768. **$89-$109.** 160 Colonial Dr 36203. I-20, exit 188, just n, then w. Int corridors. **Pets:** Other species. $25 daily fee/room. Service with restrictions, supervision. (ASK) ✕ ⓜ 🖥 🖨 ➹ ✕

▼▼ **Jameson Inn Oxford** 🅼
(256) 835-2170. **$88-$95.** 161 Colonial Dr 36203. I-20, exit 188, just n, then w. Ext corridors. **Pets:** Accepted. (ASK) ✕ 🖥 🖨 ➹

OZARK

◈◈◈ ▼▼◈ **All American Ozark Inn** 🅼
(334) 774-5166. **$40-$45.** 2064 Hwy 231 S 36360. 1 mi s of jct SR 249. Ext corridors. **Pets:** Accepted. (SAVE) ✕ 🖥 🖨 ➹

▼▼◈ **Jameson Inn** 🅼
(334) 774-0233. **$78-$81.** 1360 S US Hwy 231 36360. 0.3 mi s of jct SR 249. Ext corridors. **Pets:** Small, other species. $15 daily fee/pet. Service with restrictions, supervision. (ASK) ✕ ⓜ 🖥 🖨 ➹

PRATTVILLE

▼▼ **Jameson Inn** 🅷
(334) 361-6463. **$78-$85.** 104 Jameson Ct 36067. I-65, exit 179, 1 mi w. Ext corridors. **Pets:** Accepted. (ASK) ✕ 🖥 🖨 ➹

▼▼▼▼ **La Quinta Inn & Suites** 🅷 ❀
(334) 358-5454. **$79-$139.** 261 Interstate Commercial Park Loop 36066. I-65, exit 181, just w. Int corridors. **Pets:** Medium, other species. Service with restrictions, supervision. (ASK) ✕ 🖥 🖨 ➹

PRICEVILLE

▼▼ **Comfort Inn** 🅷
(256) 355-1037. **Call for rates.** 3239 Point Mallard Pkwy 35601. I-65, exit 334, just w. Int corridors. **Pets:** Medium, other species. $10 daily fee/pet. Designated rooms, service with restrictions, supervision. ✕ 🖥 🖨 ➹

▼▼ **Super 8 Decatur/Priceville** 🅼
(256) 355-2525. **$49-$99.** 70 Marco Dr 35603. I-65, exit 334, just e. Ext corridors. **Pets:** Accepted. (ASK) ✕ 🖥 🖨 ➹

SARALAND

◈◈◈ ▼▼◈ **Microtel Inn & Suites** 🅷
(251) 675-5045. **$69-$129, 30 day notice.** 1124 Shelton Beach Rd 36571. I-65, exit 13, just e, then just n. Int corridors. **Pets:** Medium. $25 one-time fee/room. Service with restrictions, crate. (SAVE) ✕ ⓜ 🖥 🖨

SCOTTSBORO

▼▼ **Jameson Inn** 🅷
(256) 574-6666. **$88-$95.** 208 Micah Way 35768. On US 72, just s of jct SR 35. Ext corridors. **Pets:** Small, other species. $15 daily fee/pet. No service, supervision. (ASK) ✕ 🖥 🖨 ➹

SELMA

▼▼ **Jameson Inn** 🅼
(334) 874-8600. **$78-$85.** 2420 Broad St 36701. On SR 22, just n of jct US 80. Ext corridors. **Pets:** Accepted. (ASK) ✕ 🖥 🖨 ➹

▼▼ **Ramada Inn Selma** 🅷
(334) 872-0461. **$65-$100, 3 day notice.** 1710 W Highland Ave 36701. On US 80. Ext corridors. **Pets:** Accepted. (ASK) ✕ 🖥 🖨 🍴 ➹

STEVENSON

▼ **Budget Host Inn** 🅼
(256) 437-2215. **$45-$65.** 42973 US Hwy 72 35772. On US 72, just s of CR 85. Ext corridors. **Pets:** Very small, dogs only. $10 daily fee/pet. Designated rooms, service with restrictions, supervision. (ASK) ✕ 🖥 🖨

SYLACAUGA

▼▼ **Jameson Inn** 🅷
(256) 245-4141. **$78-$85.** 89 Gene Stewart Blvd 35151. Off US 280, just s. Ext corridors. **Pets:** Very small. $15 daily fee/pet. No service, crate. (ASK) ✕ 🖥 🖨 ➹

TROY

▼▼ **Holiday Inn Express** 🅷
(334) 670-0012. **$77-$89.** Hwy 231 at US 29 36081. On US 231, just n of jct US 29. Ext corridors. **Pets:** Accepted. (ASK) ✕ 🖥 🖨

▼▼ **Holiday Inn of Troy** 🅷
(334) 566-1150. **Call for rates.** Hwy 231 at US 29 36081. On US 231, just n of jct US 29. Ext corridors. **Pets:** Accepted. ✕ 🖥 🖨 🍴 ➹

TUSCALOOSA

◈◈◈ ▼▼ **Americas Best Value Inn** 🅷
(205) 556-7950. **$59-$145, 3 day notice.** 3501 McFarland Blvd 35405. I-59/20, exit 73, just ne on US 82. Ext corridors. **Pets:** Medium. $10 daily fee/pet. Designated rooms, service with restrictions, supervision. (SAVE) ✕ 🖥 🖨 ➹

AAA ▼▼ Comfort Inn **H**

(205) 556-3232. **$81.** 4700 Doris Pate Dr 35405. I-59/20, exit 76, just n. Int corridors. **Pets:** Medium, other species. $25 one-time fee/room. Designated rooms, service with restrictions, supervision.

[SAVE] [X] [H] [P] [~]

▼▼ Jameson Inn **H**

(205) 345-5018. **$88-$95.** 5021 Oscar Baxter Dr 35403. I-59/20, exit 71A, just s. Ext corridors. **Pets:** Accepted. [ASK] [X] [H] [P] [~]

▼▼ La Quinta Inn Tuscaloosa **M** ❀

(205) 349-3270. **$52-$139.** 4122 McFarland Blvd E 35405. I-59/20, exit 73, just sw on US 82. Ext corridors. **Pets:** Medium, other species. Service with restrictions, supervision. [ASK] [X] [H] [P] [~]

AAA ▼ Masters Inn **M**

(205) 556-2010. **$45-$150, 3 day notice.** 3600 McFarland Blvd 35405. I-59/20, exit 73, just nw on US 82. Ext corridors. **Pets:** Small. $10 one-time fee/pet. Service with restrictions, supervision. [SAVE] [X] [H] [~]

VANCE

▼▼▼ Graystone Inn & Suites **H**

(205) 556-3606. **$85-$150.** 11170 Will Walker Rd/Daimler Benz Blvd 35490. I-59/20, exit 89 southbound, just s; exit northbound, 0.8 mi n on Mercedes Dr, 0.3 mi w, then just s. Int corridors. **Pets:** Accepted.

[ASK] [X] [&M] [H] [P]

ALASKA

CITY INDEX

ANCHORAGE

 Clarion Suites Downtown 🅷 ❀
(907) 222-5005. **$89-$232, 3 day notice.** 1110 W 8th Ave 99501. Corner of L St and W 8th Ave. Int corridors. **Pets:** Large, dogs only. $150 one-time fee/pet. Service with restrictions, supervision.

Comfort Inn Ship Creek 🅷 ❀
(907) 277-6887. **Call for rates.** 111 W Ship Creek Ave 99501. At 3rd and E sts, 0.3 mi n on E St, across the railway, then just e; downtown. Int corridors. **Pets:** Other species. $15 daily fee/pet. Designated rooms, service with restrictions, supervision.

Hilton Anchorage 🅷
(907) 272-7411. **$99-$309.** 500 W 3rd Ave 99501. At E St; downtown. Int corridors. **Pets:** Accepted.

Microtel Inn & Suites 🅼
(907) 245-5002. **$75-$170.** 5205 Northwood Dr 99517. Jct International Airport Rd, just n. Int corridors. **Pets:** Accepted.

Millennium Alaskan Hotel Anchorage 🅷
(907) 243-2300. **$149-$300.** 4800 Spenard Rd 99517. Jct International Airport Rd, just n. Int corridors. **Pets:** Accepted.

Motel 6–4216 🅼
(907) 677-8000. **$65-$150.** 5000 a St 99503. Jct C St, just e on International Airport Rd, then just n. Int corridors. **Pets:** Other species. Service with restrictions, supervision.

Ramada Anchorage Downtown 🅼
(907) 272-7561. **$89-$339.** 115 E 3rd Ave 99501. Jct Barrow St; downtown. Ext/int corridors. **Pets:** Accepted.

Residence Inn by Marriott 🅷
(907) 563-9844. **$169-$295.** 1025 E 35th Ave 99508. Corner of SR 1 (Seward Hwy) and 36th Ave. Int corridors. **Pets:** Accepted.

Sheraton Anchorage Hotel & SPA 🅷
(907) 276-8700. **$149-$369.** 401 E 6th Ave 99501. 6th Ave and Denali St. Int corridors. **Pets:** Accepted.

CANTWELL

Backwoods Lodge 🅼 ❀
(907) 768-2232. **$90-$170, 10 day notice.** Denali Hwy MM 133.8 99729. Parks Hwy, (Milepost 210), just e. Ext corridors. **Pets:** Medium. Service with restrictions, supervision.

EAGLE RIVER

 Eagle River Microtel Inn & Suites 🅷
(907) 622-6000. **$120-$180, 7 day notice.** 13049 Old Glenn Hwy 99577. Jct Glenn Hwy (SR 1), exit Eagle River, 1.7 mi e. Int corridors. **Pets:** Accepted.

Eagle River Motel 🅼
(907) 694-5000. **Call for rates.** 11111 Old Eagle River Rd 99577. Glenn Hwy (SR 1), exit Eagle River, just e, just s on Monte Rd, then just w. Ext corridors. **Pets:** Accepted.

FAIRBANKS

Comfort Inn-Chena River 🅷
(907) 479-8080. **Call for rates.** 1908 Chena Landings Loop 99701. Airport Way, just n on Peger Rd, then just e on Phillips Field Rd, follow signs in wooded area south of road. Int corridors. **Pets:** Large. $10 one-time fee/pet. Designated rooms, service with restrictions, crate.

Extended Stay Deluxe Fairbanks-Old Airport Way 🅷
(907) 457-2288. **$89-$144.** 4580 Old Airport Rd 99709. Near jct Parks Hwy and Airport Rd. Int corridors. **Pets:** Other species. $25 daily fee/room. Designated rooms, service with restrictions, crate.

Pike's Waterfront Lodge 🅷
(907) 456-4500. **$89-$450.** 1850 Hoselton Rd 99709. Jct Airport Way and Hoselton rds. Ext/int corridors. **Pets:** Accepted.

Super 8 🅼
(907) 451-8888. **Call for rates.** 1909 Airport Way 99701. Airport Way at Wilbur St. Int corridors. **Pets:** Medium. $20 daily fee/pet. Service with restrictions, crate.

HAINES

Captain's Choice Inc Motel 🅼
(907) 766-3111. **$129-$192.** 108 2nd Ave N 99827. Jct 2nd Ave and Dalton St. Ext corridors. **Pets:** Other species. $25 one-time fee/room. Service with restrictions, supervision.

HOMER

Best Western Bidarka Inn 🅷
(907) 235-8148. **$89-$199.** 575 Sterling Hwy 99603. Just n of Pioneer Ave on Sterling Hwy (SR 1). Int corridors. **Pets:** Large, other species. $15 daily fee/pet. Designated rooms, service with restrictions, supervision.

JUNEAU

Extended Stay Deluxe Juneau 🅷
(907) 790-6435. **$114-$154.** 1800 Shell Simmons Dr 99801. At Juneau International Airport. Int corridors. **Pets:** Other species. $25 daily fee/room. Designated rooms, service with restrictions, crate.

Westmark Baranof 🅷
(907) 586-2660. **$149-$279.** 127 N Franklin St 99801. At 2nd and Franklin sts; downtown. Int corridors. **Pets:** Accepted.

KETCHIKAN

Best Western Landing 🅷
(907) 225-5166. **$142-$235.** 3434 Tongass Ave 99901. Across from the Alaska Marine Hwy ferry terminal. Ext/int corridors. **Pets:** Accepted.

Cape Fox Lodge 🅷
(907) 225-8001. **$110-$210.** 800 Venetia Way 99901. Above Creek St (tramway from Creek St). Ext/int corridors. **Pets:** $30 daily fee/room. Designated rooms, service with restrictions, supervision.

KODIAK

Best Western Kodiak Inn H
(907) 486-5712. **$100-$260.** 236 W Rezanof Dr 99615. 0.3 mi w of ferry terminal; center. Ext/int corridors. **Pets:** Medium. $50 deposit/room, $25 one-time fee/pet. Designated rooms, service with restrictions, crate.

SAVE ✕ 🔥M 🛇 📺 ❖ 🅰

Comfort Inn Kodiak H
(907) 487-2700. **$99-$225, 3 day notice.** 1395 Airport Way 99615. Adjacent to Kodiak Airport. Int corridors. **Pets:** Medium, dogs only. $15 daily fee/pet. Designated rooms, service with restrictions, supervision.

ASK ✕ 🔥M 🛇 📺 ❖ 🅰

SEWARD

Hotel Seward H 🐾
(907) 224-8001. **$79-$359, 3 day notice.** 221 Fifth Ave 99664. Just n of Alaska SeaLife Center; downtown. Int corridors. **Pets:** Medium, dogs only. $25 daily fee/pet. Designated rooms, supervision.

SAVE ✕ 🔥M 🛇 📺 ❖ 🅰

SITKA

Shee Atika Totem Square Inn H
(907) 747-3693. **$89-$179.** 201 Katlian St 99835. Center; in Totem Square Complex, near Municipal Office. Int corridors. **Pets:** Small, other species. $50 deposit/pet, $10 daily fee/pet. Service with restrictions, crate.

SAVE ✕ 🔥M 🛇 📺 ❖ 🅰

Super 8-Sitka H
(907) 747-8804. **$89-$185.** 404 Sawmill Creek Rd 99835. Just e from corner of Lake St and Halibut Point/Sawmill Creek rds; center. Int corridors. **Pets:** Medium. $10 daily fee/pet. Designated rooms, service with restrictions, supervision. ASK ✕ 🔥M 🛇 📺

SKAGWAY

Westmark Inn Skagway M
(907) 983-6000. **$135-$145.** 3rd & Spring St 99840. Downtown. Ext/int corridors. **Pets:** Accepted. SAVE ✕ 🛇 📺 ❖ 🅰

TOK

Cleft of the Rock Bed & Breakfast CA
(907) 883-4219. **$95-$160, 3 day notice.** 0.5 Sundog Tr 99780. Jct SR 1 and 2 (Alaskan Hwy), 2.5 mi w on SR 2 (Alaskan Hwy) to Sundog Tr, then 0.5 mi n. Ext/int corridors. **Pets:** $15 daily fee/pet. Designated rooms, crate. SAVE ✕ 🛇 📺 ✂ 🅰

Westmark Inn Tok M
(907) 883-5174. **Call for rates.** Jct Alaska & Glenn Hwys 99780. On SR 1; jct SR 2 (Alaskan Hwy). Ext corridors. **Pets:** Large. Designated rooms, supervision. SAVE ✕ 📺 ❖

TRAPPER CREEK

Gate Creek Cabins CA
(907) 733-1393. **$120-$520, 10 day notice.** Mile 10.5 Petersville Rd 99683. From MM 114 (Parks Hwy), 10.5 mi w at Petersville Rd. Ext corridors. **Pets:** Accepted. ASK ✕ 🛇 📺 ✂ 🅰 🛢

Trapper Creek Inn & RV Park M
(907) 733-2302. **$99-$139, 7 day notice.** Mile 114.6 Parks Hwy 99683. George Parks Hwy (SR 3), Milepost 114. Ext corridors. **Pets:** $50 deposit/pet. Designated rooms, service with restrictions, supervision.

ASK ✕ 🛇 📺 ❖ 🅰 🛢

VALDEZ

Best Western Valdez Harbor Inn H
(907) 835-3434. **$150-$200.** 100 N Harbor Dr 99686. Just s at Meals Ave. Int corridors. **Pets:** Medium. $50 deposit/pet, $10 daily fee/pet. Designated rooms, service with restrictions, supervision.

SAVE ✕ 🔥M 🛇 📺 ❖ 🅰

WASILLA

Best Western Lake Lucille Inn H
(907) 373-1776. **$99-$200.** 1300 W Lake Lucille Dr 99654. SR 3 (George Parks Hwy), just w on Hallea Ln; center. Int corridors. **Pets:** Large. $20 daily fee/room. Service with restrictions.

SAVE ✕ 🔥M 🛇 📺 ✂ 🅰

ARIZONA

AJO

▼ La Siesta Motel M
(520) 387-6569. **$50-$60.** 2561 N Ajo-Gila Bend Hwy 85321. On SR 85, 1.8 mi n of town plaza. Ext corridors. **Pets:** Accepted.

AMADO

▼▼▼▼ Amado Territory Inn BB
(520) 398-8684. **$105-$165, 7 day notice.** 3001 E Frontage Rd 85645. I-19, exit 48, just e, then just s. Int corridors. **Pets:** Accepted.

ANTHEM

⚫ ▼▼▼▼ Hampton Inn at Anthem H
(623) 465-7979. **$59-$199.** 42415 N 41st Dr 85086. I-17, exit 229 (Anthem Way), just w. Int corridors. **Pets:** Small. $50 one-time fee/room. Designated rooms, service with restrictions, supervision.

BENSON

⚫ ▼▼▼ Best Western-Quail Hollow Inn H ✿
(520) 586-3646. **$72-$150.** 699 N Ocotillo Rd 85602. I-10, exit 304 (Ocotillo Rd), just s. Ext corridors. **Pets:** $10 one-time fee/pet. Designated rooms, service with restrictions, supervision.

▼▼▼ Super 8 M
(520) 586-1530. **Call for rates.** 855 N Ocotillo Rd 85602. I-10, exit 304 (Ocotillo Rd), just n. Ext corridors. **Pets:** Other species. $10 one-time fee/room. Service with restrictions, supervision.

BISBEE

⚫ ▼▼▼ Americas Best Value Inn & Suites M
(520) 432-2293. **$69-$325.** 1372 Hwy 92 85603. 0.8 mi w of jct Naco Hwy; sw of downtown. Ext corridors. **Pets:** Medium, dogs only. $10 daily fee/pet. Designated rooms, service with restrictions, supervision.

▼▼▼▼ Audrey's Inn CO
(520) 227-6120. **$105-$125.** 20 Brewery Ave 85603. Just ne of Main St; in historic district. Int corridors. **Pets:** $75 deposit/pet. Designated rooms, no service.

⚫ ▼▼▼ San Jose Lodge M
(520) 432-5761. **$69-$145.** 1002 Naco Hwy 85603. SR 92 W, 1.5 mi s. Ext corridors. **Pets:** Other species. $10 daily fee/pet. Designated rooms, service with restrictions, supervision.

BULLHEAD CITY

⚫ ▼▼▼ Best Western Bullhead City Inn H
(928) 754-3000. **$65-$99.** 1126 Hwy 95 86429. 1.8 mi s of Laughlin Bridge. Ext corridors. **Pets:** Medium. $20 one-time fee/pet. Service with restrictions, supervision.

⚫ ▼ Lake Mohave Resort Motel M
(928) 754-3245. **$90-$125, 3 day notice.** 2690 E Katherine Spur Rd 86429. Jct SR 95, 1.5 mi e on SR 68, 1 mi n, then 5.4 mi e; at Katherine Landing; in Lake Mead National Recreation area. Ext corridors. **Pets:** Large. $50 deposit/pet, $10 daily fee/pet. Service with restrictions, supervision.

⚫ ▼ Lodge on The River M
(928) 758-8080. **$45-$82, 7 day notice.** 1717 Hwy 95 86442. 3.8 mi s of Laughlin Bridge. Ext corridors. **Pets:** Medium, other species. $100 deposit/room, $10 daily fee/pet. Service with restrictions, crate.

⚫ ▼ Travelers Inn of B.H.C AZ M
(928) 763-1002. **$75-$85, 3 day notice.** 1616 Hwy 95 86442. Jct SR 68, 3.2 mi s on SR 95. Int corridors. **Pets:** Accepted.

CAMERON

⚫ ▼▼ Cameron Trading Post Motel, Restaurant & Gift Shop M
(928) 679-2231. **$59-$109.** US 89 86020. 1 mi from east gate turn off. Ext corridors. **Pets:** Accepted.

CAMP VERDE

⚫ ▼▼ Comfort Inn-Camp Verde H ✿
(928) 567-9000. **$85-$100.** 340 N Goswick Way 86322. I-17, exit 287, just e, then just s. Int corridors. **Pets:** Other species. $15 one-time fee/room. Service with restrictions, supervision.

⚫ ▼ Days Inn & Suites of Camp Verde H
(928) 567-3700. **$50-$126.** 1640 W Hwy 260 86322. I-17, exit 287, just e, then just n. Int corridors. **Pets:** Medium, other species. $10 daily fee/pet. Designated rooms, service with restrictions, crate.

⚫ ▼▼▼ The Lodge At Cliff Castle Casino H
(928) 567-6611. **$89-$209.** 333 Middle Verde Rd 86322. I-17, exit 289, 0.4 mi se. Ext corridors. **Pets:** Medium. $20 daily fee/pet. No service, supervision.

▼ Super 8-Camp Verde M
(928) 567-2622. **$54-$149.** 1550 W Hwy 260 86322. I-17, exit 287, just e. Int corridors. **Pets:** Accepted.

CASA GRANDE

▼▼▼ Francisco Grande Hotel & Golf Resort H
(520) 836-6444. **$79-$219.** 2684 W Gila Bend Hwy (SR 84) 85293. I-8, exit 172 (Thornton Rd), 3.5 mi n, then 4.2 mi w. Ext corridors. **Pets:** Accepted.

♨♨♨ Holiday Inn Hotel H

(520) 426-3500. **$69-$169.** 777 N Pinal Ave 85122. I-10, exit 194 (SR 287), 3.9 mi w. Int corridors. **Pets:** Accepted.

SAVE X 🖧 🖪 💻 🍴 🏊

♨♨ Super 8 H

(520) 836-8800. **$60-$110.** 2066 E Florence Blvd 85222. I-10, exit 194 (SR 287), 0.6 mi w. Int corridors. **Pets:** Other species. $10 daily fee/pet. Service with restrictions, supervision. SAVE X 🖧 🖪 💻 🏊

CHINLE

♨ Thunderbird Lodge M

(928) 674-5841. **$65-$125.** Indian Rt 7 86503. US 191, 3.5 mi e; just e of visitor center. Ext corridors. **Pets:** Accepted. X 🖧 🍴

COTTONWOOD

♨♨♨ Best Western Cottonwood Inn H

(928) 634-5575. **$105, 7 day notice.** 993 S Main St 86326. On SR 89A, at SR 260. Ext corridors. **Pets:** Very small, dogs only. $10 daily fee/pet. Designated rooms, supervision. SAVE X 🖧 🖪 💻 🏊

♨♨ Little Daisy Motel M

(928) 634-7865. **$56-$140.** 34 S Main St 86326. On SR 89A, just n. Ext corridors. **Pets:** Dogs only. $10 daily fee/room. Service with restrictions, crate. SAVE X 🖧

♨♨♨ Motel 6 M

(928) 634-3678. **$60-$129.** 1089 Hwy 260 86326. On SR 260, just e of jct SR 89A. Ext corridors. **Pets:** Other species. Service with restrictions, supervision. SAVE X 🖧 🏊

♨♨ Pines Motel, Inc M

(928) 634-9975. **$59-$129.** 920 S Camino Real 86326. Jct SR 260, just nw on SR 89A, then just s. Ext corridors. **Pets:** Other species. $10 daily fee/room. Service with restrictions, supervision. SAVE X 🖧 💻 🏊

♨♨ The View Motel M

(928) 634-7581. **$59-$129.** 818 S Main St 86326. On SR 89A, 0.4 mi nw of jct SR 260. Ext corridors. **Pets:** Dogs only. $10 daily fee/pet. Service with restrictions, supervision. SAVE X 🖧 🏊

DOUGLAS

♨ Motel 6 #305 M

(520) 364-2457. **$45-$61.** 111 16th St (SR 80) 85607. 1.2 mi e of jct SR 191. Ext corridors. **Pets:** Other species. Service with restrictions, supervision. X 🖧 🏊

EAGAR

♨♨♨ Best Western Sunrise Inn M

(928) 333-2540. **$100-$130.** 128 N Main St 85925. Jct SR 260, just n; jct US 60, 1.5 mi s. Ext corridors. **Pets:** Other species. $10 one-time fee/room. Service with restrictions, supervision. SAVE X 🖧 💻

EHRENBERG

♨♨♨ Best Western Desert Oasis H

(928) 923-9711. **$79-$89.** S Frontage Rd 85334. I-10, exit 1, just s; 0.5 mi e of Colorado River. Int corridors. **Pets:** Accepted.

SAVE X 🖧 💻 🏊

ELOY

♨ Motel 6–1263 M

(520) 836-3323. **$45-$55.** 4965 S Sunland Gin Rd 85231. I-10, exit 200, just w. Ext corridors. **Pets:** Other species. Service with restrictions, supervision. X 🖧 🏊

FLAGSTAFF

♨♨♨ Best Western Pony Soldier Inn and Suites H

(928) 526-2388. **$65-$150.** 3030 E Route 66 86004. I-40, exit 201, just n, then 1 mi w. Int corridors. **Pets:** Other species. $15 one-time fee/room. Designated rooms, service with restrictions, supervision.

SAVE X 🖧 💻 🏊

♨♨♨ Comfort Inn I-17/I-40 H

(928) 774-2225. **$79-$149.** 2355 S Beulah Blvd 86001. I-40, exit 195, just n to Forest Meadows St, then 1 blk w. Int corridors. **Pets:** Accepted.

SAVE X 🖧 💻 🏊

♨♨♨ Days Inn & Suites H

(928) 527-1477. **$59-$189.** 3601 E Lockett Rd 86004. I-40, exit 201, just n, 0.5 mi w on I-40 business loop, then just n. Ext corridors. **Pets:** Other species. $20 one-time fee/room. Service with restrictions, supervision.

SAVE X 🖧 💻 🏊

♨♨♨ Days Inn Route 66 M ❀

(928) 774-5221. **$46-$130, 7 day notice.** 1000 W Route 66 86001. I-40, exit 195, 1.5 mi n on Milton Rd, then just w. Ext corridors. **Pets:** Other species. $10 daily fee/pet. Service with restrictions, supervision. SAVE X 🖧 💻 🏊

♨♨♨ Drury Inn & Suites H

(928) 773-4900. **$100-$234.** 300 S Milton Rd 86001. I-40, exit 195, 1.8 mi n on SR 89A (Milton Rd). Int corridors. **Pets:** Other species. No service, supervision. ECO ASK X 🖧 🖪 💻 🏊

♨♨♨ Econo Lodge-University M

(928) 774-7326. **$44-$99.** 914 S Milton Rd 86001. I-40, exit 195, 1.2 mi n. Ext corridors. **Pets:** Other species. $10 daily fee/pet. Designated rooms, service with restrictions, supervision. SAVE X 🖧 🏊

♨♨♨ Howard Johnson Inn-Lucky Lane M ❀

(928) 779-5121. **$54-$129.** 2520 E Lucky Ln 86004. I-40, exit 198 (Butler Ave), just n, then just e. Ext corridors. **Pets:** Medium. $15 daily fee/pet. Designated rooms, service with restrictions, supervision.

SAVE X 🖧 💻 🏊

♨♨♨♨ La Quinta Inn & Suites H ❀

(928) 556-8666. **$49-$159.** 2015 S Beulah Blvd 86001. I-40, exit 195, just n to Forest Meadow St, then just w. Int corridors. **Pets:** Medium, other species. Service with restrictions, supervision.

ASK X 🖧 💻 🏊

♨ Motel 6-Flagstaff West #1000 M

(928) 779-3757. **$45-$59.** 2745 S Woodlands Village Blvd 86001. I-40, exit 195, just n to Forest Meadows St, w to Beulah Blvd, just s, then just w. Ext corridors. **Pets:** Other species. Service with restrictions, supervision. X 🖧 🖪 🏊

♨♨♨ Quality Inn I-40/I-17 H

(928) 774-8771. **$54-$124.** 2000 S Milton Rd 86001. I-40, exit 195, just n to Forest Meadows St, then right. Int corridors. **Pets:** Other species. $10 daily fee/room. Service with restrictions, supervision. SAVE X 💻 🏊

♨♨ Ramada Inn H

(928) 779-3614. **$45-$120.** 2350 E Lucky Ln 86004. I-40, exit 198 (Butler Ave), just n, then just e. Ext corridors. **Pets:** Medium. $10 daily fee/pet. Service with restrictions, supervision. ASK X 🖧 🖪 💻

♨♨♨♨ Residence Inn by Marriott Flagstaff H ❀

(928) 526-5555. **$159-$189.** 3440 N Country Club Dr 86004. I-40, exit 201, 0.5 mi s. Ext/int corridors. **Pets:** Other species. $100 one-time fee/room. Service with restrictions, supervision. X 🖧 🖪 💻 🏊 X

♨♨ Rodeway Inn-Near NAU M

(928) 774-8820. **$39-$189.** 121 S Milton Rd 86001. I-40, exit 195, 2.5 mi n. Ext corridors. **Pets:** Accepted. SAVE X 🖧 💻

♨♨ Sleep Inn M

(928) 556-3000. **Call for rates.** 2765 S Woodlands Village Blvd 86001. I-40, exit 195, just n to Forest Meadows St, w to Beulah Rd, just s, then just w. Int corridors. **Pets:** Accepted. X 🖧 🖪 💻

♨♨ Super 8–Flagstaff Mall M

(928) 526-0818. **$50-$120.** 3725 Kasper Ave 86004. I-40, exit 201, just n, 0.5 mi w on I-40 business loop, then just n. Int corridors. **Pets:** Other species. $15 daily fee/pet. Designated rooms, service with restrictions, supervision. ASK X 🖧 💻

AAA **WWW** Super 8-Lucky Lane **M** 🐾
(928) 773-4888. **$49-$125.** 2540 E Lucky Ln 86004. I-40, exit 198 (Butler Ave), just n, then just e. Ext corridors. **Pets:** Medium. $15 daily fee/pet. Designated rooms, service with restrictions, supervision.
[SAVE] [X] 🔒 💻 ➔

AAA **WW** Travel Inn **M**
(928) 774-3381. **$39-$119, 3 day notice.** 801 W Route 66 86001. I-40, exit 195, 1.2 mi n on Milton Rd, then just w. Ext corridors. **Pets:** Other species. $10 daily fee/room. No service, supervision. [SAVE] [X] 🔒

FLORENCE
WWW Rancho Sonora Inn **M**
(520) 868-8000. **$79-$225, 3 day notice.** 9198 N Hwy 79 85232. On SR 79, 5 mi s of SR 287. Ext corridors. **Pets:** Accepted.
[ASK] [X] 🔒 💻 ➔

FOREST LAKES
AAA **WW** Forest Lakes Lodge **M**
(928) 535-4727. **$54-$84.** 876 AZ Hwy 260 85931. On SR 260; between MM 288 and 289. Ext corridors. **Pets:** Small, dogs only. $30 one-time fee/room. Supervision. [SAVE] [X] 🔒 [A/C]

GILA BEND
WW America's Choice Inn & Suites **M**
(928) 683-6311. **$65.** 2888 Butterfield Tr 85337. I-8, exit 119, just nw. Int corridors. **Pets:** Accepted. [ASK] [X] 🔒 ➔

AAA **WWW** Best Western Space Age Lodge **M**
(928) 683-2273. **$85-$125.** 401 E Pima St 85337. Business Loop I-8; center. Ext corridors. **Pets:** Designated rooms, service with restrictions.
[SAVE] [X] 🔒 💻 🍴 ➔

GLOBE
WW Quality Inn **M**
(928) 425-7575. **$99-$180.** 1515 South St 85501. On US 60, 1 mi e of town. Ext corridors. **Pets:** Medium. $10 one-time fee/pet. No service, supervision. [ASK] [X] 🔒 💻 ➔

GRAND CANYON NATIONAL PARK AREA

GRAND CANYON NATIONAL PARK (SOUTH RIM)
AAA **WWWW** Canyon Plaza Resort Grand Canyon **H** 🐾
(928) 638-2673. **$83-$268.** 116 Hwy 64 86023. On SR 64; 2 mi s of South Rim entrance. Ext/int corridors. **Pets:** Medium, other species. $50 one-time fee/pet. Designated rooms, service with restrictions, crate.
[SAVE] [X] 🔒 💻 🍴 ➔

AAA **WWWW** The Grand Hotel **H**
(928) 638-3333. **$119-$259, 3 day notice.** Hwy 64 86023. On SR 64; 2 mi s of South Rim entrance. Int corridors. **Pets:** Accepted.
[SAVE] [X] [&M] 🔒 💻 🍴 ➔ [X]

AAA **WWW** Red Feather Lodge **H**
(928) 638-2414. **$69-$182.** Hwy 64 86023. On SR 64; 2 mi s of South Rim entrance. Ext/int corridors. **Pets:** Other species. $50 deposit/pet, $10 daily fee/pet. Designated rooms, service with restrictions, supervision.
[SAVE] [X] [&M] 🔒 💻 🍴 ➔

END AREA

HEBER
AAA **WW** Best Western Sawmill Inn **M**
(928) 535-5053. **$69-$84.** 1877 Hwy 260 85928. 0.5 mi e of center. Ext corridors. **Pets:** Accepted. [SAVE] [X] 🔒 💻

HOLBROOK
AAA **WW** America's Best Inn **M**
(928) 524-2654. **$41-$56.** 2211 E Navajo Blvd 86025. I-40, exit 289, 1 mi w. Ext corridors. **Pets:** Other species. $5 daily fee/pet. Designated rooms, service with restrictions, supervision. [SAVE] [X] 🔒 💻

AAA **WWW** Best Western Adobe Inn **M**
(928) 524-3948. **$60-$110.** 615 W Hopi Dr 86025. I-40, exit 285, 1 mi e on US 180 (Hopi Dr). Ext corridors. **Pets:** $25 one-time fee/room. Service with restrictions, supervision. [SAVE] [X] 🔒 💻 ➔

AAA **WWW** Best Western Arizonian Inn **H**
(928) 524-2611. **$105-$127.** 2508 Navajo Blvd 86025. I-40, exit 289, 0.5 mi w. Ext corridors. **Pets:** Other species. $75 deposit/pet. Designated rooms, service with restrictions, supervision. [SAVE] [X] 🔒 💻 ➔

AAA **WWW** Comfort Inn **H**
(928) 524-6131. **$69-$99.** 2602 E Navajo Blvd 86025. I-40, exit 289, just w. Ext corridors. **Pets:** Accepted. [SAVE] [X] 🔒 💻 ➔

JEROME
WWW Connor Hotel of Jerome **H**
(928) 634-5006. **$90-$165, 3 day notice.** 164 Main St 86331. Center. Int corridors. **Pets:** Accepted. [ASK] [X] 🔒 💻

KAYENTA
WWW Hampton Inn of Kayenta **H**
(928) 697-3170. **Call for rates.** Hwy 160 86033. Just w. Int corridors. **Pets:** Accepted. [X] [&M] 💻 🍴 ➔

KINGMAN
AAA **WWW** Americas Best Value Inn **M**
(928) 753-6262. **$40-$60.** 3100 E Andy Devine Ave 86401. I-40, exit 53, on I-40 business loop, then 0.3 mi w. Ext corridors. **Pets:** Small, other species. $10 daily fee/room. Designated rooms, service with restrictions, supervision. [SAVE] [X] 🔒 💻

AAA **WWWW** Best Western a Wayfarer's Inn & Suites **H**
(928) 753-6271. **$93-$120.** 2815 E Andy Devine Ave 86401. I-40, exit 53, 0.5 mi w on Route 66. Ext corridors. **Pets:** Medium. $8 one-time fee/pet. Service with restrictions, supervision. [SAVE] [X] 🔒 💻 ➔

WW Comfort Inn **M**
(928) 718-1717. **$80-$109.** 3129 E Andy Devine Ave 86401. I-40, exit 53, just w on Route 66. Int corridors. **Pets:** Medium, dogs only. $20 one-time fee/room. Designated rooms, service with restrictions, supervision.
[ASK] [X] 🔒 💻 ➔

Days Inn West M

(928) 753-7500. **$50-$120.** 3023 E Andy Devine Ave 86401. I-40, exit 53, just w on Route 66. Ext corridors. **Pets:** Other species. $10 daily fee/room. Service with restrictions, crate.

Motel 6–1114 M

(928) 753-9222. **$39-$52.** 424 W Beale St 86401. I-40, exit 48, just se on Business Loop I-40/US 93. Ext corridors. **Pets:** Other species. Service with restrictions, supervision.

Motel 6 E–1366 M

(928) 757-7151. **$55-$65.** 3351 E Andy Devine Ave 86401. I-40, exit 53, just e on Route 66. Ext corridors. **Pets:** Other species. Service with restrictions, supervision.

Super 8 H

(928) 757-4808. **$50-$100.** 3401 E Andy Devine Ave 86401. I-40, exit 53, just e on Route 66. Int corridors. **Pets:** Accepted.

KOHLS RANCH

Kohl's Ranch Lodge CO

(928) 478-4211. **Call for rates.** 202 S Kohl's Ranch Lodge Rd 85541. From SR 87, 16.6 mi e on US 260, MM 238-239. Ext/int corridors. **Pets:** Accepted.

LAKE HAVASU CITY

Days Inn Lake Havasu M ❁

(928) 855-7841. **Call for rates.** 1700 McCulloch Blvd N 86403. Just ne of Lake Havasu Ave; center. Ext corridors. **Pets:** Other species. $25 one-time fee/room. Service with restrictions.

Hampton Inn Lake Havasu H

(928) 855-4071. **$98-$190.** 245 London Bridge Rd 86403. 0.5 mi n of London Bridge. Ext/int corridors. **Pets:** Accepted.

Island Inn Hotel H

(928) 680-0606. **$60-$250, 3 day notice.** 1300 W McCulloch Blvd 86403. 0.7 mi w of London Bridge/SR 95. Int corridors. **Pets:** Medium, other species. $10 one-time fee/pet. Service with restrictions, supervision.

Island Suites H

(928) 855-7333. **Call for rates.** 236 S Lake Havasu Ave 86403. Just s of jct McCulloch Blvd. Int corridors. **Pets:** Accepted.

Lake Havasu City Super 8 M

(928) 855-8844. **$55-$175.** 305 London Bridge Rd 86403. Just w of SR 95, exit Palo Verde; 0.5 mi n of London Bridge. Int corridors. **Pets:** Accepted.

Lake Place Inn M

(928) 855-2146. **$55-$250, 3 day notice.** 31 Wing's Loop 86403. 1 mi e of SR 95 via Swanson Ave; downtown. Ext corridors. **Pets:** Medium, other species. $10 one-time fee/pet. Service with restrictions, supervision.

Motel 6 Lakeside M

(928) 855-3200. **Call for rates.** 111 London Bridge Rd 86403. 0.3 mi n of London Bridge. Int corridors. **Pets:** Other species. Service with restrictions, supervision.

Quality Inn & Suites M

(928) 855-1111. **$70-$150.** 271 S Lake Havasu Ave 86403. SR 95, just e on Swanson Ave, then just s. Ext corridors. **Pets:** Large, other species. $50 deposit/room, $20 one-time fee/room. Designated rooms, service with restrictions.

Travelodge-Lake Havasu City M

(928) 680-9202. **$50-$300, 3 day notice.** 480 London Bridge Rd 86403. 1 mi n of London Bridge. Int corridors. **Pets:** Large, other species. $50 deposit/pet, $10 daily fee/pet. Designated rooms, service with restrictions, supervision.

MUNDS PARK

Motel In The Pines M

(928) 286-9699. **$39-$89.** 80 W Pinewood Rd 86017. I-17, exit 322, just e. Ext corridors. **Pets:** Other species. $10 daily fee/pet. Service with restrictions, supervision.

NOGALES

Candlewood Suites H

(520) 281-1111. **$79-$135.** 875 N Frank Reed Rd 85621. I-19, exit 4, just w to Frank Reed Rd, then just nw. Int corridors. **Pets:** Accepted.

Holiday Inn Express H

(520) 281-0123. **Call for rates.** 850 W Shell Rd 85621. I-19, exit 4, just w to Frank Reed Rd, then just nw. Int corridors. **Pets:** Accepted.

Motel 6 Nogales #71 M

(520) 281-2951. **$45-$55.** 141 W Mariposa Rd 85621. I-19, exit 4, 0.9 mi e. Ext corridors. **Pets:** Other species. Service with restrictions, supervision.

PAGE

Americas Best Value Inn M

(928) 645-2858. **$49-$120.** 75 S 7th Ave 86040. 1 mi e of US 89 via Loop 89; just n of Lake Powell Blvd. Ext corridors. **Pets:** Accepted.

Best Western Arizona Inn H

(928) 645-2466. **$66-$101.** 716 Rimview Dr 86040. 0.7 mi e of US 89 via Loop 89. Int corridors. **Pets:** Accepted.

Lake Powell Days Inn & Suites H

(928) 645-2800. **$69-$189.** 961 N Hwy 89 86040. On US 89, just s. Int corridors. **Pets:** $10 daily fee/pet. Service with restrictions, supervision.

Lake Powell Resort and Marina H

(928) 645-2433. **Call for rates.** 100 Lakeshore Dr 86040. 4 mi n of Glen Canyon Dam via US 89. Int corridors. **Pets:** Accepted.

Motel 6-Page/Lake Powell #4013 H

(928) 645-5888. **$39-$83, 3 day notice.** 637 S Lake Powell Blvd 86040. On Loop 89, just e of US 89. Int corridors. **Pets:** Other species. Service with restrictions, supervision.

Quality Inn Lake Powell H

(928) 645-8851. **$55-$97.** 287 N Lake Powell Blvd 86040. 0.8 mi e of US 89/Loop 89. Int corridors. **Pets:** Medium. $20 daily fee/pet. Designated rooms, no service, supervision.

Super 8 Gateway to Lake Powell H

(928) 645-5858. **$59-$119, 3 day notice.** 649 S Lake Powell Blvd 86040. On Loop 89, just e of US 89. Int corridors. **Pets:** Small, dogs only. $10 daily fee/pet. Designated rooms, service with restrictions, supervision.

PARKER

Best Western Parker Inn M

(928) 669-6060. **$80-$104.** 1012 Geronimo Ave 85344. SR 95, just e. Int corridors. **Pets:** Small, other species. Service with restrictions, supervision.

PAYSON

Americas Best Value Inn M

(928) 474-2283. **$50-$121.** 811 S Beeline Hwy 85541. SR 87, 0.7 mi s of SR 260. Ext/int corridors. **Pets:** Small, dogs only. $15 daily fee/pet. Designated rooms, service with restrictions, supervision.

Best Western Payson Inn 🅷 ❖

(928) 474-3241. **Call for rates.** 801 N Beeline Hwy 85541. SR 87, 0.6 mi n of SR 260. Ext corridors. **Pets:** Other species. $25 daily fee/room. Service with restrictions, supervision. (SAVE) ⊠ 🖪 💻 ➦

PHOENIX METROPOLITAN AREA

APACHE JUNCTION

Apache Junction Super 8 🅷 ❖

(480) 288-8888. **$99-$119.** 251 E 29th Ave 85119. US 60, exit 196 (Idaho Rd/SR 88 E), just n. Ext/int corridors. **Pets:** Large. $100 deposit/ room, $25 daily fee/pet. Designated rooms, service with restrictions, crate. (SAVE) ⊠ 🖪 💻 ➦

BUCKEYE

Days Inn-Buckeye 🅷

(623) 386-5400. **$70-$140.** 25205 W Yuma Rd 85326. I-10, exit 114 (Miller Rd), just sw. Ext corridors. **Pets:** Accepted. (ASK) ⊠ 🖪 💻 ➦

CAREFREE

The Boulders Resort 🅷

(480) 488-9009. **$99-$699.** 34631 N Tom Darlington Dr 85377. Scottsdale Rd, 11 mi n of Bell Rd. Ext corridors. **Pets:** Medium. $100 one-time fee/ room. Service with restrictions, supervision. (SAVE) ⊠ 🖪 💻 🍴 ➦ ⊠

Carefree Resort & Villas 🅷

(480) 488-5300. **$79-$870, 3 day notice.** 37220 Mule Train Rd 85377. SR 101, exit 36 (Pima Rd), 12.2 mi n to Cave Creek Rd, 1 mi w, then 0.4 mi n. Ext/int corridors. **Pets:** Accepted. (ASK) ⊠ 🖪 💻 🍴 ➦ ⊠

CHANDLER

Chandler Super 8 🅷

(480) 961-3888. **Call for rates.** 7171 W Chandler Blvd 85226. I-10, exit 160 (Chandler Blvd), just e. Int corridors. **Pets:** Accepted. (SAVE) ⊠ 🖪 💻 ➦

Comfort Inn 🅷

(480) 705-8882. **$70-$120.** 255 N Kyrene Rd 85226. I-10, exit 160 (Chandler Blvd), 1.5 mi e, then just n. Int corridors. **Pets:** Accepted. (SAVE) ⊠ 🌜ᴹ 🖪 💻 ➦

Crowne Plaza San Marcos Golf Resort 🅷

(480) 812-0900. **$79-$299.** 1 San Marcos Pl 85225. Jct Chandler Blvd, just s on Arizona Ave, just w on Buffalo St; in historic downtown. Ext corridors. **Pets:** Small, dogs only. $50 one-time fee/room. Designated rooms, service with restrictions, supervision. (SAVE) ⊠ 🖪 💻 🍴 ➦ ⊠

Hawthorn Suites Chandler 🅷 ❖

(480) 705-8881. **$79-$199.** 5858 W Chandler Blvd 85226. I-10, exit 160 (Chandler Blvd), 1.5 mi e. Int corridors. **Pets:** Small, dogs only. $15 daily fee/pet. Service with restrictions, supervision. (SAVE) ⊠ 🖪 💻 ➦

Homewood Suites by Hilton 🅷

(480) 753-6200. **$149-$239.** 7373 W Detroit St 85226. I-10, exit 160 (Chandler Blvd), 0.4 mi e, n on 54th St, then just w. Int corridors. **Pets:** Medium. $100 one-time fee/room. Service with restrictions. ⊠ 🌜ᴹ 🖪 💻 ➦

Red Roof Inn-Chandler 🅷

(480) 857-4969. **Call for rates.** 7400 W Boston St 85226. I-10, exit 160 (Chandler Blvd), just e, then s on Southgate Dr. Int corridors. **Pets:** Large. Service with restrictions, crate. (SAVE) ⊠ 🌜ᴹ 🖪 💻 ➦

Residence Inn-Chandler Fashion Center 🅷

(480) 782-1551. **$109-$169.** 200 N Federal St 85226. I-10, exit 160 (Chandler Blvd), 4.2 mi e, just n on N Metro Blvd, then just e. Int corridors. **Pets:** Accepted. ⊠ 🌜ᴹ 🖪 💻 ➦ ⊠

Sheraton Wild Horse Pass Resort & Spa 🅷

(602) 225-0100. **$119-$810, 3 day notice.** 5594 W Wild Horse Pass Blvd 85226. I-10, exit 162, 2.4 mi w. Int corridors. **Pets:** Accepted. (SAVE) ⊠ 🖪 💻 🍴 ➦ ⊠

Windmill Suites of Chandler 🅷 ❖

(480) 812-9600. **$85-$169.** 3535 W Chandler Blvd 85226. I-10, exit 160 (Chandler Blvd), 4 mi e. Int corridors. **Pets:** Other species. Designated rooms, service with restrictions, supervision. (SAVE) ⊠ 🖪 💻 ➦ ⊠

FOUNTAIN HILLS

Comfort Inn 🅷

(480) 837-5343. **$60-$140.** 17105 E Shea Blvd 85268. 0.5 mi w of SR 87 (Beeline Hwy). Int corridors. **Pets:** Accepted. (SAVE) ⊠ 🖪 💻 ➦

Holiday Inn Hotel & Suites-Fountain Hills/Mayo Clinic 🅷

(480) 837-6565. **$49-$159.** 12800 N Saguaro Blvd 85268. Jct Shea Blvd, 2.2 mi n; center. Int corridors. **Pets:** Accepted. (ASK) ⊠ 🖪 💻 🍴 ➦ ⊠

GLENDALE

Comfort Suites Glendale 🅷 ❖

(623) 271-9005. **$69-$169.** 9824 W Camelback Rd 85305. Loop 101, exit 5 (Camelback Rd), just w to 99th St, then just n. Int corridors. **Pets:** Medium, other species. $25 one-time fee/room. Service with restrictions, supervision. (SAVE) ⊠ 🌜ᴹ 🖪 💻 ➦

Residence Inn by Marriott Glendale 🅷

(623) 772-8900. **$129-$229.** 7350 W Zanjero Blvd 85305. Loop 101, exit 7 (Glendale Ave), then e. Int corridors. **Pets:** Medium. $100 one-time fee/room. Service with restrictions. ⊠ 🌜ᴹ 🖪 💻 ➦ ⊠

Staybridge Suites 🅷

(623) 842-0000. **$149-$229.** 9340 W Cabela Dr 85305. Loop 101, exit 7 (Glendale Ave), e on Zanjero, then left. Int corridors. **Pets:** Accepted. (ASK) ⊠ 🖪 💻 ➦

GOODYEAR

Best Western Phoenix Goodyear Inn 🅷

(623) 932-3210. **$69-$149.** 55 N Litchfield Rd 85338. I-10, exit 128, 0.8 mi s. Ext/int corridors. **Pets:** Large, other species. $15 daily fee/room. (SAVE) ⊠ 🖪 💻 🍴 ➦

Comfort Suites Goodyear 🅷 ❖

(623) 266-2884. **$70-$130.** 15575 W Roosevelt St 85338. I-10, exit 126, just s on Estrella Pkwy, then just w. Int corridors. **Pets:** Medium. $25 one-time fee/pet. Designated rooms, service with restrictions, supervision. (SAVE) ⊠ 🌜ᴹ 🖪 💻 ➦

Hampton Inn & Suites 🅷

(623) 536-1313. **$109-$249.** 2000 N Litchfield Rd 85395. I-10, exit 128, 0.5 mi n. Int corridors. **Pets:** Accepted. ⊠ 🌜ᴹ 🖪 💻 ➦ ⊠

Holiday Inn Express 🅷

(623) 535-1313. **$109-$199.** 1313 N Litchfield Rd 85395. I-10, exit 128, just n. Int corridors. **Pets:** Accepted. (ASK) ⊠ 🖪 💻 ➦ ⊠

Holiday Inn Hotel & Suites 🅷

(623) 547-1313. **$109-$209.** 1188 N Dysart Rd 85395. I-10, exit 129 (Dysart Rd), just n. Int corridors. **Pets:** $35 one-time fee/room. Service with restrictions, crate. (ASK) ⊠ 🖪 💻 ➦

▼▼ Quality Inn & Suites Goodyear �H ❀
(623) 932-9191. **$59-$149.** 950 N Dysart Rd 85338. I-10, exit 129 (Dysart Rd), just s. Ext corridors. **Pets:** Medium, other species. $50 deposit/pet, $15 daily fee/pet. Service with restrictions, supervision.
(A$K) ⊠ 🛏 💻 ⊃

▼▼▼ Residence Inn by Marriott �H
(623) 866-1313. **$139-$209.** 2020 N Litchfield Rd 85395. I-10, exit 128, 0.6 mi n. Int corridors. **Pets:** Other species. $100 one-time fee/room.
⊠ 🛏 💻 ⊃

LITCHFIELD PARK

◈◈◈ ▼▼▼ ▼▼▼ The Wigwam Golf Resort & Spa �H
(623) 935-3811. **$99-$629, 3 day notice.** 300 Wigwam Blvd 85340. I-10, exit 128 (Litchfield Rd), 2.4 mi n, then 0.4 mi e. Ext corridors. **Pets:** Large. $15 deposit/room. Designated rooms, service with restrictions. (SAVE) ⊠ 🛏 💻 ⊃ ⊠

MESA

◈◈◈ ▼▼▼ Arizona Golf Resort & Conference Center �H ❀
(480) 832-3202. **$76-$225.** 425 S Power Rd 85206. 1.3 mi n of US 60 (Superstition Frwy), exit 188 (Power Rd); southeast corner of Broadway and Power rds; entrance on Broadway Rd. Ext corridors. **Pets:** Designated rooms, service with restrictions, supervision.
(SAVE) ⊠ 🛏 💻 🍴 ⊃ ⊠

◈◈◈ ▼▼▼ Best Western Mesa Inn �H
(480) 964-8000. **$66-$140.** 1625 E Main St 85203. 2 mi n of US 60 (Superstition Frwy), exit Stapley Dr, 0.5 mi e. Ext corridors.
Pets: Accepted. (SAVE) ⊠ 🛏 💻 ⊃

◈◈◈ ▼▼▼ Best Western Mezona Inn �H ❀
(480) 834-9233. **$89-$179.** 250 W Main St 85201. Just e of Country Club Dr; downtown. Ext corridors. **Pets:** $20 one-time fee/room. Designated rooms, service with restrictions, crate. (SAVE) ⊠ 🛏 💻 ⊃

◈◈◈ ▼▼▼ Best Western Superstition Springs Inn �H
(480) 641-1164. **$84-$150.** 1342 S Power Rd 85206. Just n of US 60 (Superstition Frwy), exit 188 (Power Rd); northwest corner of Power Rd and Hampton Ave. Ext corridors. **Pets:** Small, other species. $10 daily fee/pet. Designated rooms, service with restrictions, supervision.
(SAVE) ⊠ 🛏 💻 ⊃

▼▼ Days Hotel �H
(480) 844-8900. **$62-$180.** 333 W Juanita 85210. US 60 (Superstition Frwy), exit 179 (Country Club Dr), just s, then just e. Int corridors. **Pets:** Other species. $5 daily fee/pet. Service with restrictions, supervision. (A$K) ⊠ 🛏 💻 ⊃

◈◈◈ ▼▼▼ Days Inn & Suites Mesa �H
(480) 969-3600. **$70-$130.** 1750 E Main St 85203. US 60, exit 182 (Gilbert Rd), 2.1 mi n, then 0.3 mi w. Ext corridors. **Pets:** Accepted.
(SAVE) ⊠ 🛏 💻 ⊃

▼▼ Days Inn-East Mesa �H
(480) 981-8111. **$49-$119.** 5531 E Main St 85205. 0.4 mi e of Higley Rd. Ext corridors. **Pets:** Small, dogs only. $10 daily fee/pet. Designated rooms, service with restrictions, crate. (A$K) ⊠ 🛏 💻 ⊃

▼▼ Extended StayAmerica-Phoenix/Mesa �H
(480) 632-0201. **$64-$89.** 455 W Baseline Rd 85210. US 60 (Superstition Frwy), exit 179 (Country Club Dr), 0.4 mi s on SR 87, then just w. Int corridors. **Pets:** Other species. $25 daily fee/room. Designated rooms, service with restrictions, crate. (A$K) ⊠ 🛏 💻

◈◈◈ ▼▼▼ Hilton Phoenix East/Mesa �H ❀
(480) 833-5555. **$159-$279.** 1011 W Holmes Ave 85210. US 60 (Superstition Frwy), exit 178 (Alma School Rd), just n, then just e. Int corridors. **Pets:** Medium. $75 one-time fee/room. Service with restrictions.
(SAVE) ⊠ 🛏 💻 🍴 ⊃ ⊠

▼▼ Holiday Inn Hotel & Suites �H
(480) 964-7000. **$89-$169.** 1600 S Country Club Dr 85210. US 60 (Superstition Frwy), exit 179 (Country Club Dr), just s. Ext/int corridors.
Pets: Accepted. (A$K) ⊠ 🛏 💻 🍴 ⊃

▼▼ Homestead Studio Suites Hotel Phoenix-Mesa �H
(480) 752-2266. **$59-$84.** 1920 W Isabella 85202. Just s of US 60 (Superstition Frwy), exit 177 (Dobson Rd). Ext corridors. **Pets:** Other species. $25 daily fee/room. Designated rooms, service with restrictions, crate. (A$K) ⊠ 🛏 💻

▼▼ La Quinta Inn & Suites Phoenix (Mesa East) �H ❀
(480) 654-1970. **$59-$179.** 6530 E Superstition Springs Blvd 85206. US 60 (Superstition Frwy), exit 187 (Superstition Springs Blvd) eastbound, just se; exit 188 (Power Rd) westbound, just sw. Int corridors. **Pets:** Medium, other species. Service with restrictions, supervision.
(A$K) ⊠ ♿ 🛏 💻 ⊃

▼▼ La Quinta Inn & Suites Phoenix (Mesa West) �H ❀
(480) 844-8747. **$49-$169.** 902 W Grove Ave 85210. US 60 (Superstition Frwy), exit 178 (Alma School Rd), just n, then just e. Int corridors. **Pets:** Medium, other species. Service with restrictions, supervision.
(A$K) ⊠ 🛏 💻 ⊃

▼ Motel 6-Mesa South #1030 🅜
(480) 834-0066. **$45-$65.** 1511 S Country Club Dr 85210. US 60 (Superstition Frwy), exit 179 (Country Club Dr), northeast corner. Ext corridors. **Pets:** Other species. Service with restrictions, supervision.
⊠ ♿ 🛏 ⊃

◈◈◈ ▼▼ Quality Inn & Suites Mesa/Phoenix �H
(480) 964-2897. **$35-$170.** 1410 S Country Club Dr 85210. US 60, exit 179 (Country Club Dr), just n. Ext corridors. **Pets:** Medium, other species. $10 daily fee/pet. Designated rooms, service with restrictions, supervision.
(SAVE) ⊠ 🛏 💻 ⊃

▼▼▼ Residence Inn by Marriott Phoenix Mesa �H
(480) 610-0100. **$124-$224.** 941 W Grove Ave 85210. US 60 (Superstition Frwy), exit 178 (Alma School Rd), just n, then just e. Int corridors. **Pets:** Accepted. ⊠ ♿ 🛏 💻 ⊃ ⊠

▼▼ Sleep Inn of Mesa �H
(480) 807-7760. **$70-$129.** 6347 E Southern Ave 85206. US 60 (Superstition Frwy), exit 188 (Power Rd), 0.8 mi n, then 0.4 mi w to mall entrance. Int corridors. **Pets:** Large. $15 daily fee/pet. Service with restrictions, supervision. (A$K) ⊠ 🛏 💻 ⊃

◈◈◈ ▼▼ Super 8-Mesa/Gilbert Rd �H
(480) 545-0888. **Call for rates.** 1550 S Gilbert Rd 85204. US 60 (Superstition Frwy), exit 182 (Gilbert Rd), 1 blk n. Int corridors. **Pets:** Accepted.
(SAVE) ⊠ 🛏 💻 ⊃

▼▼ Travelodge Suites Mesa �H ❀
(480) 832-5961. **$40-$150.** 4244 E Main St 85205. US 60 (Superstition Frwy), exit 185 (Greenfield Rd), 2 mi n, then just w. Ext corridors. **Pets:** $10 daily fee/pet. Service with restrictions, supervision.
(A$K) ⊠ 🛏 💻 ⊃

◈◈◈ ▼▼▼ Windemere Hotel and Conference Center �H
(480) 985-3600. **$59-$229.** 5750 E Main St 85205. 0.6 mi e of Higley Rd. Ext corridors. **Pets:** Medium. $25 one-time fee/pet. Service with restrictions, supervision. (SAVE) ⊠ 🛏 💻 ⊃

PARADISE VALLEY

▼▼▼ Hermosa Inn �H
(602) 955-8614. **$159-$569, 7 day notice.** 5532 N Palo Cristi Rd 85253. 1 mi s of Lincoln Dr; corner of Stanford Dr. Ext corridors.
Pets: Accepted. (A$K) ⊠ 🛏 💻 🍴 ⊃ ⊠

▼▼ ▼▼ **InterContinental Montelucia Resort &**
Spa 🅷 ❅

(480) 627-3200. **Call for rates.** 4949 E Lincoln Dr 85253. Southeast corner of Lincoln Dr and Tatum Blvd, enter from Lincoln Dr. Ext/int corridors. **Pets:** Medium, other species. $100 one-time fee/room. Service with restrictions, crate.

🆇 ☎ 💻 🍴 ➿ 🆇

Ⓐ ▼▼ ▼▼ **Sanctuary on Camelback**
Mountain 🅷 ❅

(480) 948-2100. **$235-$725, 7 day notice.** 5700 E McDonald Dr 85253. Loop 101, exit McDonald Dr, 3.9 mi w; 1.8 mi w of jct Scottsdale Rd. Ext corridors. **Pets:** Medium. $100 one-time fee/room. Service with restrictions, supervision. 🆂🅰🆅🅴 🆇 💻 🍴 ➿ 🆇

PEORIA

▼▼ ▼▼ **Comfort Suites by Choice Hotels/Sports**
Complex 🅷 ❅

(623) 334-3993. **$79-$199.** 8473 W Paradise Ln 85382. Loop 101, exit 14 (Bell Rd), just e to 83rd Ave, just s, then just w. Int corridors. **Pets:** Medium, other species. $25 one-time fee/room. Service with restrictions. 🅰🆂🅺 🆇 ☎ 💻 ➿

▼▼ ▼▼ **Extended StayAmerica Phoenix-Peoria** 🅷

(623) 487-0020. **$69-$99.** 7345 W Bell Rd 85382. Loop 101, exit 14 (Bell Rd), 1.2 mi e. Int corridors. **Pets:** Other species. $25 daily fee/room. Designated rooms, service with restrictions, crate. 🅰🆂🅺 🆇 ☎ 💻

▼▼ ▼▼ **Holiday Inn Express Hotel & Suites** 🅷

(623) 853-1313. **$79-$209.** 16771 N 84th Ave 85382. Loop 101, exit 14 (Bell Rd), just w, then just s. Int corridors. **Pets:** Accepted.

🅰🆂🅺 🆇 🅼 ☎ 💻 ➿

▼▼ ▼▼ **La Quinta Inn & Suites Phoenix**
(West/Peoria) 🅷 ❅

(623) 487-1900. **$59-$229.** 16321 N 83rd Ave 85382. Loop 101, exit 14 (Bell Rd), just e, then just s. Int corridors. **Pets:** Medium, other species. Service with restrictions, supervision. 🅰🆂🅺 🆇 ☎ 💻 ➿

▼▼ ▼▼ **Residence Inn by Marriott** 🅷

(623) 979-2074. **$139-$259.** 8435 W Paradise Ln 85382. Loop 101, exit 14 (Bell Rd), just e, just s on 83rd Ave, then just w. Int corridors. **Pets:** Accepted. 🆇 ☎ 💻 ➿ 🆇

PHOENIX

Ⓐ ▼▼ ▼▼ **Arizona Biltmore, The Waldorf Astoria**
Collection 🅷 ❅

(602) 955-6600. **$129-$760.** 2400 E Missouri Ave 85016. Jct Camelback Rd, 0.5 mi n on 24th St, then 0.4 mi e. Ext/int corridors. **Pets:** Medium, other species. $50 deposit/pet, $50 one-time fee/pet. Designated rooms.

🆂🅰🆅🅴 🆇 💻 🍴 ➿ 🆇

Ⓐ ▼▼ ▼▼ **The Bell Hotel An Independent Magnuson**
Hotel 🅷

(602) 993-8300. **$45-$179.** 17211 N Black Canyon Hwy 85023. I-17, exit 212, just n of Bell Rd on frontage road. Ext corridors. **Pets:** Accepted.

🆂🅰🆅🅴 🆇 ☎ 💻 ➿

Ⓐ ▼▼ ▼▼ **Best Western Airport Inn** 🅷

(602) 273-7251. **$80-$139.** 2425 S 24th St 85034. I-10, exit 150B (24th St) westbound, just s; exit 151 (University Dr) eastbound, just n to I-10 westbound, 1 mi w to exit 150B (24th St), then just s. Ext/int corridors.

Pets: Accepted. 🆂🅰🆅🅴 🆇 ☎ 💻 ➿ 🆇

Ⓐ ▼▼ ▼▼ **Best Western InnSuites Phoenix Biltmore**
Hotel & Suites 🅷

(602) 997-6285. **$79-$199.** 1615 E Northern Ave 85020. SR 51, exit 7, 0.6 mi w. Ext corridors. **Pets:** Accepted. 🆂🅰🆅🅴 🆇 ☎ 💻 ➿

Ⓐ ▼▼ ▼▼ **Best Western Metrocenter Inn** 🅷

(602) 864-6233. **$69-$139.** 8101 N Black Canyon Hwy 85021. I-17, exit 206 (Northern Ave), just e, then just n; on east side of freeway. Ext corridors. **Pets:** Accepted. 🆂🅰🆅🅴 🆇 ☎ 💻 ➿

▼▼ ▼▼ **Candlewood Suites** 🅷

(602) 861-4900. **$79-$159.** 11411 N Black Canyon Hwy 85029. I-17, exit 208 (Peoria Ave), just e, then 0.4 mi n. Int corridors. **Pets:** Other species. $75 one-time fee/room. Service with restrictions, supervision.

🅰🆂🅺 🆇 ☎ 💻 ➿

▼▼ ▼▼ **Clarion Hotel @ Phoenix Tech Center** 🅷

(480) 893-3900. **$69-$159.** 5121 E La Puenta Ave 85044. I-10, exit 157 (Elliot Rd), just w, just n on 51st St, then just e. Ext corridors. **Pets:** Other species. $25 one-time fee/room. Service with restrictions, crate.

🅰🆂🅺 🆇 ☎ 💻 ➿

Ⓐ ▼▼ ▼▼ **Comfort Inn I-10 West/Central** 🅷

(602) 415-1623. **$60-$120.** 1344 N 27th Ave 85009. I-10, exit 27th Ave eastbound, just n; exit 141 (35th Ave) westbound, just n, 1 mi e on McDowell Rd, then s. Int corridors. **Pets:** Accepted.

🆂🅰🆅🅴 🆇 ☎ 💻 ➿

Ⓐ ▼▼ ▼▼ **Comfort Inn Phoenix** 🅷

(602) 242-8011. **$49-$109.** 5050 N Black Canyon Hwy 85017. I-17, exit 203 (Camelback Rd), just w, then just n; on west side of freeway. Ext corridors. **Pets:** Accepted. 🆂🅰🆅🅴 🆇 ☎ 💻 ➿

Ⓐ ▼▼ ▼▼ **Comfort Inn-Phoenix North** 🅷

(602) 978-2222. **$40-$90.** 2641 W Union Hills Dr 85027. I-17, exit 214A (Union Hills Dr), just w. Int corridors. **Pets:** Medium. $10 daily fee/pet. Service with restrictions, supervision. 🆂🅰🆅🅴 🆇 ☎ 💻 🍴 ➿

▼▼ ▼▼ **Comfort Suites by Choice Hotels** 🅷

(602) 861-3900. **$86-$126.** 10210 N 26th Dr 85021. I-17, exit 208 (Peoria Ave), just e, just s on 25th Ave, then 0.3 mi w on W Beryl Ave. Int corridors. **Pets:** Large, other species. $25 one-time fee/room. Service with restrictions, crate. 🅰🆂🅺 🆇 🅼 ☎ 💻 ➿

▼▼ ▼▼ **Crossland Economy Studios-Phoenix West** 🅷

(602) 272-8571. **$54-$74.** 4861 W McDowell Rd 85035. I-10, exit 139 (51st Ave), just n, then just e. Ext corridors. **Pets:** Other species. $25 daily fee/room. Designated rooms, service with restrictions, crate.

🅰🆂🅺 🆇 ☎ 💻

Ⓐ ▼▼ ▼▼ **Crowne Plaza Phoenix** 🅷

(602) 943-2341. **$55-$179.** 2532 W Peoria Ave 85029. I-17, exit 208 (Peoria Ave), just e, then just n on 25th Ave. Int corridors.

Pets: Accepted. 🆂🅰🆅🅴 🆇 🅼 ☎ 💻 🍴 ➿

▼▼ ▼▼ **Crowne Plaza Phoenix Airport** 🅷

(602) 273-7778. **$79-$209.** 4300 E Washington St 85034. Loop 202, exit 2 (44th St), 0.7 mi s. Int corridors. **Pets:** Medium, other species. $50 one-time fee/room. Service with restrictions, supervision.

🅰🆂🅺 🆇 ☎ 💻 🍴 ➿

▼▼ ▼▼ **Days Inn Phoenix I-17 & Thomas** 🅷

(602) 257-0801. **$60-$160.** 2420 W Thomas Rd 85015. I-17, exit 201 (Thomas Rd), just e. Int corridors. **Pets:** Medium. $25 one-time fee/pet. Designated rooms, service with restrictions, supervision.

🅰🆂🅺 🆇 ☎ 💻 ➿

Ⓐ ▼▼ ▼▼ **Embassy Suites Phoenix Airport at 24th**
St 🅷 ❅

(602) 957-1910. **$89-$289.** 2333 E Thomas Rd 85016. SR 51, exit 2 (44th St), just e. Ext corridors. **Pets:** $20 daily fee/pet. Designated rooms, service with restrictions. 🆂🅰🆅🅴 🆇 ☎ 💻 🍴 ➿

▼▼ ▼▼ **Embassy Suites Phoenix Airport at 44th St** 🅷

(602) 244-8800. **$89-$299.** 1515 N 44th St 85008. Loop 202, exit 2 (44th St), 0.3 mi n. Ext corridors. **Pets:** Accepted. 🆇 ☎ 💻 🍴 ➿

▼▼ ▼▼ **Embassy Suites Phoenix-Biltmore** 🅷

(602) 955-3992. **$99-$409.** 2630 E Camelback Rd 85016. Just n of Camelback Rd, on 26th St. Int corridors. **Pets:** Accepted.

🆇 ☎ 💻 🍴 ➿

Embassy Suites Phoenix North
(602) 375-1777. **$69-$299.** 2577 W Greenway Rd 85023. I-17, exit 211, just e. Ext corridors. **Pets:** $50 one-time fee/room. Service with restrictions, crate.

Extended StayAmerica Phoenix/Airport/E Oak St
(602) 225-2998. **$65-$90.** 4357 E Oak St 85008. Loop 202, exit 2 (44th St), 1 mi n. Ext corridors. **Pets:** Other species. $25 daily fee/room. Designated rooms, service with restrictions, crate.

Extended StayAmerica-Phoenix-Chandler
(480) 785-0464. **$69-$89.** 14245 S 50th St 85044. I-10, exit 159, just w on Ray Rd, just s, then just e. Int corridors. **Pets:** Other species. $25 daily fee/room. Designated rooms, service with restrictions, crate.

Extended StayAmerica Phoenix-Chandler-E Chandler Blvd
(480) 753-6700. **$69-$84.** 5035 E Chandler Blvd 85048. I-10, exit 160 (Chandler Blvd), just w. Ext corridors. **Pets:** Other species. $25 daily fee/room. Designated rooms, service with restrictions, crate.

Extended StayAmerica Phoenix-Deer Valley
(623) 879-6609. **$64-$94.** 20827 N 27th Ave 85027. I-10, exit 215 (Rose Garden Ln), just w; exit 215B southbound, just w, then 0.4 mi s. Int corridors. **Pets:** Other species. $25 daily fee/room. Designated rooms, service with restrictions, crate.

Extended StayAmerica Phoenix-Metro Center
(602) 870-2999. **$59-$89.** 11211 N Black Canyon Hwy 85029. I-17, exit 208 (Peoria Ave), just e, then 0.3 mi n; on east side of freeway. Ext corridors. **Pets:** Other species. $25 daily fee/room. Designated rooms, service with restrictions, crate.

Extended Stay Deluxe Phoenix-Biltmore
(602) 265-6800. **$65-$115.** 5235 N 16th St 85016. Jct SR 51, just w on Camelback Rd, then just n. Int corridors. **Pets:** Other species. $25 daily fee/room. Designated rooms, service with restrictions, crate.

Extended Stay Deluxe (Phoenix/Midtown)
(602) 279-9000. **$70-$110.** 217 W Osborn Rd 85013. Just w of Central Ave; between Indian School and Thomas rds. Int corridors. **Pets:** Other species. $25 daily fee/room. Designated rooms, service with restrictions, crate.

Four Points by Sheraton Phoenix North
(602) 997-5900. **$54-$239.** 10220 N Metro Pkwy E 85051. I-17, exit 208 (Peoria Ave), 0.3 mi w to 28th Dr, just s, then just e. Int corridors. **Pets:** Medium. $15 daily fee/pet. Service with restrictions, crate.

Hilton Garden Inn Phoenix Airport North
(602) 306-2323. **$169-$289.** 3838 E Van Buren St 85008. Loop 202, exit 2 (40th St), 0.5 mi s, then just w. Int corridors. **Pets:** Accepted.

Hilton Phoenix Airport
(480) 894-1600. **$125-$329.** 2435 S 47th St 85034. I-10, exit 151 (University Dr), 2 mi n, then just w. Int corridors. **Pets:** Accepted.

Hilton Suites-Phoenix
(602) 222-1111. **$89-$314.** 10 E Thomas Rd 85012. Just e of Central Ave; in Phoenix Plaza. Int corridors. **Pets:** Medium. $25 one-time fee/room. Designated rooms, service with restrictions, supervision.

Holiday Inn Phoenix West
(602) 484-9009. **$69-$149.** 1500 N 51st Ave 85043. I-10, exit 139 (51st Ave), just n. Int corridors. **Pets:** Accepted.

Homestead Studio Suites Hotel-Phoenix North/Metro Center
(602) 944-7828. **$56-$79.** 2102 W Dunlap Ave 85021. I-17, exit 207 (Dunlap Ave), 0.7 mi e. Ext corridors. **Pets:** Other species. $25 daily fee/room. Designated rooms, service with restrictions, crate.

Homewood Suites by Hilton
(602) 508-0937. **$229-$269.** 2001 E Highland Ave 85016. Just e of 20th St. Int corridors. **Pets:** Accepted.

Homewood Suites Hotel
(602) 674-8900. **$79-$149.** 2536 Beryl Ave 85021. I-17, exit 208 (Peoria Ave), just e, just s on 25th Ave, then just w. Int corridors. **Pets:** Medium. $49 one-time fee/pet. Service with restrictions, crate.

Homewood Suites Phoenix North/Happy Valley
(623) 580-1800. **$149-$199.** 2470 W Charlotte Dr 85085. I-17, exit 217 (Pinnacle Peak Rd), 0.6 mi n on Hwy Frontage Rd. Int corridors. **Pets:** Other species. $50 one-time fee/room. Service with restrictions, crate.

La Quinta Inn & Suites Phoenix (Chandler)
(480) 961-7700. **$45-$169.** 15241 S 50th St 85044. I-10, exit 160 (Chandler Blvd), just w, then just n. Int corridors. **Pets:** Medium, other species. Service with restrictions, supervision.

La Quinta Inn & Suites Phoenix I-10 West
(602) 595-7601. **$79-$259.** 4929 W McDowell Rd 85035. I-10, exit 139 (51st Ave), just n, then just e. Int corridors. **Pets:** Medium, other species. Service with restrictions, supervision.

La Quinta Inn Phoenix Airport North
(602) 956-6500. **$60-$165.** 4727 E Thomas Rd 85018. Just w of 48th St. Ext/int corridors. **Pets:** Medium, other species. Service with restrictions, supervision.

La Quinta Inn Phoenix (North)
(602) 993-0800. **$45-$139.** 2510 W Greenway Rd 85023. I-17, exit 211, just e. Ext corridors. **Pets:** Medium, other species. Service with restrictions, supervision.

La Quinta Inn Phoenix (Thomas Road)
(602) 258-6271. **$45-$129.** 2725 N Black Canyon Hwy 85009. I-17, exit 201 (Thomas Rd), just e, then just s; on east side of freeway. Ext corridors. **Pets:** Medium, other species. Service with restrictions, supervision.

Lexington Hotel Central Phoenix
(602) 252-2100. **$100-$339, 3 day notice.** 1100 N Central Ave 85004. Just s of McDowell Rd. Int corridors. **Pets:** Accepted.

MainStay Suites by Choice Hotels
(602) 395-0900. **Call for rates.** 9455 N Black Canyon Hwy 85021. I-17, exit 207 (Dunlap Ave), just e, then 0.4 mi n. Int corridors. **Pets:** Accepted.

Motel 6 Phoenix East #18
(602) 267-8555. **$55-$65.** 5315 E Van Buren St 85008. Loop 202 E, exit 4 (52nd St/Van Buren St), just s, then just e. Ext corridors. **Pets:** Other species. Service with restrictions, supervision.

Motel 6 Phoenix-North #344
(602) 993-2353. **$49-$61.** 2330 W Bell Rd 85023. I-17, exit 212, just e. Ext corridors. **Pets:** Other species. Service with restrictions, supervision.

Motel 6 Phoenix West #696
(602) 272-0220. **$51-$61.** 1530 N 52nd Dr 85043. I-10, exit 139 (51st Ave), just n to McDowell Rd, just w, then just s. Ext corridors. **Pets:** Other species. Service with restrictions, supervision.

Pointe Hilton Squaw Peak Resort H
(602) 997-2626. **$99-$309.** 7677 N 16th St 85020. SR 51, exit Glendale Ave, 0.4 mi w, then 0.6 mi n. Ext corridors. **Pets:** Accepted.
SAVE ✕ 🔒 💻 ❘❘ 🏊 ✕

Pointe Hilton Tapatio Cliffs Resort H 🐾
(602) 866-7500. **$89-$259.** 11111 N 7th St 85020. I-17, exit 207 (Dunlap Ave), 3 mi e, then 2 mi n. Ext corridors. **Pets:** Large. $75 one-time fee/room. Service with restrictions, supervision.
SAVE ✕ 🔥M 🔒 💻 ❘❘ 🏊 ✕

Radisson Hotel Phoenix Airport North H
(602) 220-4400. **$59-$169.** 427 N 44th St 85008. Loop 202, exit 2 (44th St), 0.5 mi s. Int corridors. **Pets:** Accepted.
ASK ✕ 🔥M 🔒 💻 ❘❘ 🏊

Red Roof Inn H
(602) 233-8004. **$67-$87.** 5215 W Willetta 85043. I-10, exit 139 (51st Ave), just n, just e on McDowell Rd, then just s. Int corridors.
Pets: Large. Service with restrictions, crate. SAVE ✕ 🔥M 🔒 🏊

Residence Inn by Marriott Phoenix H
(602) 864-1900. **$109-$169.** 8242 N Black Canyon Hwy 85051. I-17, exit 207 (Dunlap Ave), just w, then 0.8 mi s. Ext/int corridors. **Pets:** Accepted.
SAVE ✕ 🔥M 🔒 💻 🏊 ✕

Residence Inn by Marriott Phoenix Airport H 🐾
(602) 273-9220. **$149-$279.** 801 N 44th St 85008. Loop 202, exit 2 (44th St), just s. Int corridors. **Pets:** Other species. $25 one-time fee/room. Service with restrictions. ✕ 🔥M 🔒 💻 🏊 ✕

Residence Inn by Marriott Phoenix North/Happy Valley H 🐾
(623) 580-8833. **$119-$209.** 2035 W Whispering Wind Dr 85085. I-17, exit 128 (Happy Valley Rd), 0.4 mi e to 23rd Ave, just s, then just e. Int corridors. **Pets:** Large, other species. $100 one-time fee/room. Service with restrictions, supervision. ✕ 🔒 💻 🏊 ✕

The Ritz-Carlton, Phoenix H 🐾
(602) 468-0700. **Call for rates.** 2401 E Camelback Rd 85016. Southeast corner of Camelback Rd and 24th St. Int corridors. **Pets:** Small, dogs only. $250 deposit/room. Designated rooms, service with restrictions, supervision. ✕ 🔒 💻 ❘❘ 🏊 ✕

Royal Palms Resort and Spa H
(602) 840-3610. **$139-$599, 7 day notice.** 5200 E Camelback Rd 85018. Just e of 52nd St. Ext/int corridors. **Pets:** Accepted.
SAVE ✕ 🔒 💻 ❘❘ 🏊 ✕

Sheraton Crescent Hotel H
(602) 943-8200. **$79-$329.** 2620 W Dunlap Ave 85021. I-17, exit 207 (Dunlap Ave), just e. Int corridors. **Pets:** Accepted.
SAVE ✕ 🔥M 🔒 💻 ❘❘ 🏊 ✕

Sheraton Phoenix Downtown Hotel H 🐾
(602) 262-2500. **$99-$579.** 340 N 3rd St 85004. I-10, exit 145A (7th St), 0.5 mi s to Fillmore St, just w, then just s. Int corridors. **Pets:** Medium, dogs only. $200 deposit/room. Service with restrictions.
SAVE ✕ 🔥M 🔒 💻 ❘❘ 🏊 ✕

Sleep Inn Phoenix North H
(602) 504-1200. **$49-$160.** 18235 N 27th Ave 85053. I-17, exit 214A (Union Hills Dr), just w, then just s. Int corridors. **Pets:** Small. $50 deposit/room, $15 daily fee/pet. Designated rooms, crate.
SAVE ✕ 🔒 💻 🏊

Sleep Inn Sky Harbor Airport H
(480) 967-7100. **$52-$160.** 2621 S 47th Pl 85034. I-10, exit 151 (University Dr), 2 mi n, then just w. Int corridors. **Pets:** Accepted.
SAVE ✕ 🔒 💻 🏊

Studio 6 Phoenix-Deer Valley #6030 H
(602) 843-1151. **$61-$71.** 18405 N 27th Ave 85053. I-17, exit 214A (Union Hills Dr), just w, then just s. Ext corridors. **Pets:** Other species. $10 daily fee/room. Service with restrictions, supervision. ✕ 🔒 💻

Super 8-Phoenix West H
(602) 415-0888. **$60-$90.** 1242 N 53rd Ave 85043. I-10, exit 139 (51st Ave), just s to Latham Rd, then just w. Int corridors. **Pets:** Accepted.
ASK ✕ 🔒 💻

TownePlace Suites by Marriott H
(602) 943-9510. **$110-$120.** 9425 N Black Canyon Frwy 85021. I-17, exit 207 (Dunlap Ave), just e, then 0.3 mi n. Int corridors. **Pets:** Medium. $75 one-time fee/pet. Service with restrictions, supervision.
✕ 🔒 💻 🏊

SCOTTSDALE

Best Western Sundial H
(480) 994-4170. **$80-$400.** 7320 E Camelback Rd 85251. Just e of Scottsdale Rd. Ext corridors. **Pets:** Other species. $25 daily fee/pet. Service with restrictions, supervision. SAVE ✕ 🔥M 🔒 💻 🏊

Camelback Inn, a JW Marriott Resort & Spa H
(480) 948-1700. **$199-$499, 3 day notice.** 5402 E Lincoln Dr 85253. 0.5 mi e of Tatum Blvd; on north side of Lincoln Dr. Ext corridors. **Pets:** Small. $250 deposit/pet. Service with restrictions.
SAVE ✕ 🔥M 🔒 💻 🏊 ✕

The Canyon Suites at The Phoenician H 🐾
(480) 423-2880. **$575-$3000, 7 day notice.** 6000 E Camelback Rd 85251. 0.5 mi w of 64th St; in The Phoenician. Int corridors. **Pets:** Very small, dogs only. $150 one-time fee/room. Supervision.
SAVE ✕ 🔥M ❘❘ 💻 🏊 ✕

Chaparral Suites Resort H
(480) 949-1414. **$99-$279.** 5001 N Scottsdale Rd 85250. At Chaparral Rd. Ext corridors. **Pets:** Medium, dogs only. $25 one-time fee/pet. Service with restrictions, supervision. SAVE ✕ 🔥M 🔒 💻 ❘❘ 🏊 ✕

Clarion Hotel Scottsdale H
(480) 945-4392. **$59-$229.** 5101 N Scottsdale Rd 85250. Just n of Chaparral Rd. Ext corridors. **Pets:** Accepted.
SAVE ✕ 🔥M 🔒 💻 ❘❘ 🏊

Comfort Inn of Scottsdale H 🐾
(480) 596-6559. **$59-$139.** 7350 E Gold Dust Ave 85258. Just e of Scottsdale Rd; just s of Shea Blvd; on north side of Gold Dust Ave. Int corridors. **Pets:** Other species. $15 daily fee/room. Designated rooms, service with restrictions, crate. SAVE ✕ 🔒 💻 🏊

Comfort Suites by Choice Hotels-Old Town H
(480) 946-1111. **Call for rates.** 3275 N Drinkwater Blvd 85251. N of Thomas Rd; just e of Scottsdale Rd. Int corridors. **Pets:** $25 one-time fee/pet. Service with restrictions, supervision. ✕ 🔥M 🔒 💻

Country Inn & Suites By Carlson H
(480) 314-1200. **$99-$134, 3 day notice.** 10801 N 89th Pl 85260. SR 101, exit 41, just e on Shea Blvd, then just n. Int corridors.
Pets: Medium. $50 one-time fee/room. Designated rooms, service with restrictions, supervision. ASK ✕ 🔒 💻 🏊

Days Inn Scottsdale Fashion Square M 🐾
(480) 947-5411. **$60-$170.** 4710 N Scottsdale Rd 85251. Just n of Camelback Rd. Ext corridors. **Pets:** Medium. $25 one-time fee/room. Designated rooms, service with restrictions, crate. SAVE ✕ 🔒 💻 🏊

Doubletree Paradise Valley Resort H
(480) 947-5400. **$89-$269.** 5401 N Scottsdale Rd 85250. Just n of Chaparral Rd; on east side of Scottsdale Rd. Ext corridors. **Pets:** Accepted.
SAVE ✕ 🔒 💻 ❘❘ 🏊 ✕

▼▼ Extended StayAmerica-Phoenix-Scottsdale 🅗
(480) 607-3767. **$69-$114.** 15501 N Scottsdale Rd 85254. SR 101, exit Frank Lloyd Wright Blvd, 2 mi w, 0.5 mi s on Scottsdale Rd, then just e on Tierra Buena Ln. Ext corridors. **Pets:** Other species. $25 daily fee/room. Designated rooms, service with restrictions, crate.
(A$K) ⊠ 🖥 🖵

▼▼ Extended Stay Deluxe Phoenix-Scottsdale 🅗
(480) 483-1333. **$79-$134.** 10660 N 69th St 85254. Jct Scottsdale Rd, just w on Shea Blvd, then just n. Int corridors. **Pets:** Other species. $25 daily fee/room. Designated rooms, service with restrictions, crate.
(A$K) ⊠ 🖥 🖵

◈◈◈ ▼▼▼ Fairmont Scottsdale 🅗 🐾
(480) 585-4848. **$129-$1179, 7 day notice.** 7575 E Princess Dr 85255. SR 101, exit 34 (Scottsdale Rd), 0.8 mi s, then just e; 0.6 mi n of Bell Rd. Ext/int corridors. **Pets:** Small. $25 one-time fee/pet. Designated rooms, service with restrictions.
(SAVE) ⊠ ☾ᴹ 🖥 🖵 🍽 ⚓ ⊠

◈◈◈ ▼▼▼▼ FireSky Resort & Spa, a Kimpton Hotel 🅗
(480) 945-7666. **$115-$469, 3 day notice.** 4925 N Scottsdale Rd 85251. Southeast corner of Scottsdale and Chaparral rds. Int corridors. **Pets:** Accepted. (SAVE) ⊠ ☾ᴹ 🖥 🖵 🍽 ⚓ ⊠

◈◈◈ ▼▼▼▼▼ Four Seasons Resort Scottsdale at Troon North 🅗
(480) 515-5700. **$195-$645, 7 day notice.** 10600 E Crescent Moon Dr 85262. SR 101, exit 36 (Pima Rd), 4.7 mi n, 2 mi e on Happy Valley Rd, then 1.5 mi n on Alma School Rd. Ext corridors. **Pets:** Accepted.
(SAVE) ⊠ ☾ᴹ 🖥 🖵 🍽 ⚓ ⊠

◈◈◈ ▼▼▼▼ Gainey Suites Hotel 🅗
(480) 922-6969. **$119-$289.** 7300 E Gainey Suites Dr 85258. Just e of Scottsdale Rd. Int corridors. **Pets:** Small, dogs only. $100 deposit/room. Service with restrictions, crate. (SAVE) ⊠ 🖥 🖵 ⚓ ⊠

◈◈◈ ▼▼▼▼ Hampton Inn Scottsdale 🅗
(480) 443-3233. **$59-$199.** 10101 N Scottsdale Rd 85253. Just s of Shea Blvd. Int corridors. **Pets:** Other species. Designated rooms, service with restrictions, supervision. (SAVE) ⊠ ☾ᴹ 🖥 🖵 ⚓

◈◈◈ ▼▼▼ ▼▼▼ Hilton Scottsdale Resort & Villas 🅗
(480) 948-7750. **$119-$329.** 6333 N Scottsdale Rd 85250. SR 101, exit 45, 2.1 mi w on McDonald Dr, then 0.3 mi n. Int corridors.
Pets: Accepted. (SAVE) ⊠ ☾ᴹ 🖥 🖥 🖵 🍽 ⚓ ⊠

▼▼ Homestead Studio Suites Hotel-Phoenix-Scottsdale Ⓜ
(480) 994-0297. **$64-$99.** 3560 N Marshall Way 85251. Just w of Scottsdale Rd on Goldwater, just s. Ext corridors. **Pets:** Other species. $25 daily fee/room. Designated rooms, service with restrictions, crate.
(A$K) ⊠ ☾ᴹ 🖥 🖵

◈◈◈ ▼▼▼▼ Hotel Indigo Scottsdale 🅗
(480) 941-9400. **$79-$179.** 4415 N Civic Center Plaza 85251. Scottsdale Rd, just e on Camelback Rd, just s on 75th St. Ext/int corridors.
Pets: Accepted. (SAVE) ⊠ ☾ᴹ 🖥 🖵 🍽 ⚓

◈◈◈ ▼▼▼▼ Hotel Valley Ho 🅗
(480) 248-2000. **$99-$359.** 6850 E Main St 85251. 0.4 mi w of Scottsdale Rd, just s of Indian School Rd; on north side of Main St. Ext/int corridors. **Pets:** Accepted. (SAVE) ⊠ 🖥 🖵 🍽 ⚓ ⊠

◈◈◈ ▼▼▼ ▼▼▼ Hyatt Regency Scottsdale Resort & Spa at Gainey Ranch 🅗 🐾
(480) 444-1234. **$129-$605, 3 day notice.** 7500 E Doubletree Ranch Rd 85258. SR 101, exit 43, 2.6 mi w on Via de Ventura. Ext/int corridors. **Pets:** Medium, other species. $50 one-time fee/room. Designated rooms.
(SAVE) ⊠ 🖥 🖵 🍽 ⚓ ⊠

◈◈◈ ▼▼▼▼ Hyatt Summerfield Suites Scottsdale/Old Town 🅗
(480) 946-7700. **$69-$499.** 4245 N Drinkwater Blvd 85251. 0.3 mi e of Scottsdale Rd. Ext corridors. **Pets:** Accepted.
(SAVE) ⊠ ☾ᴹ 🖥 🖵 ⚓ ⊠

◈◈◈ ▼▼▼▼ The Inn at Pima, a Condominium Suite Hotel 🅒🅞 🐾
(480) 948-3800. **$59-$338.** 7330 N Pima Rd 85258. 0.4 mi n of Indian Bend Rd; on west side of Pima Rd. Ext/int corridors. **Pets:** Medium. $10 daily fee/room. Designated rooms, service with restrictions, supervision.
(SAVE) ⊠ 🖥 🖵 ⚓ ⊠

▼▼▼▼ La Quinta Inn & Suites Phoenix (Scottsdale) 🅗 🐾
(480) 614-5300. **$49-$179.** 8888 E Shea Blvd 85260. SR 101, exit Shea Blvd, northeast corner. Int corridors. **Pets:** Medium, other species. Service with restrictions, supervision. (A$K) ⊠ ☾ᴹ 🖥 🖵 ⚓

◈◈◈ ▼▼▼▼ Millennium Resort Scottsdale McCormick Ranch 🅗
(480) 948-5050. **$59-$339, 3 day notice.** 7401 N Scottsdale Rd 85253. 0.8 mi n of Indian Bend Rd. Int corridors. **Pets:** Accepted.
(SAVE) ⊠ 🖥 🖵 🍽 ⚓ ⊠

▼▼ Motel 6 Scottsdale #29 Ⓜ
(480) 946-2280. **$55-$91.** 6848 E Camelback Rd 85251. Just w of Scottsdale Rd. Ext corridors. **Pets:** Other species. Service with restrictions, supervision. ⊠ 🍽 ⚓

◈◈◈ ▼▼▼▼ The Phoenician 🅗 🐾
(480) 941-8200. **$189-$759, 7 day notice.** 6000 E Camelback Rd 85251. 0.5 mi w of 64th St. Ext/int corridors. **Pets:** Medium. $150 one-time fee/room. Designated rooms. (SAVE) ⊠ 🖥 🖵 🍽 ⚓ ⊠

◈◈◈ ▼▼▼ ▼▼▼ Radisson Fort McDowell Resort & Casino 🅗 🐾
(480) 789-5300. **$79-$499.** 10438 N Fort McDowell Rd 85264. Jct Shea Blvd, 1.6 mi ne on SR 87. Int corridors. **Pets:** Medium, dogs only. $10 daily fee/pet. Service with restrictions, supervision.
(SAVE) ⊠ ☾ᴹ 🖥 🖵 🍽 ⚓ ⊠

◈◈◈ ▼▼▼▼ Residence Inn by Marriott, Scottsdale/ Paradise Valley 🅗
(480) 948-8666. **$129-$289.** 6040 N Scottsdale Rd 85253. Just n of McDonald Dr. Ext/int corridors. **Pets:** Other species. $100 one-time fee/room. (SAVE) ⊠ ☾ᴹ 🖥 🖵 ⚓ ⊠

▼▼▼▼ Residence Inn Scottsdale North 🅗 🐾
(480) 563-4120. **$129-$299.** 17011 N Scottsdale Rd 85255. SR 101, exit 34 (Scottsdale Rd), 1.1 mi s, at northeast corner of Frank Lloyd Wright Blvd and Scottsdale Rd. Int corridors. **Pets:** Medium, other species. $100 one-time fee/room. Service with restrictions, crate.
⊠ 🖥 🖵 ⚓ ⊠

◈◈◈ ▼▼▼▼ Scottsdale Cottonwoods Resort 🅗
(480) 991-1414. **$89-$319.** 6160 N Scottsdale Rd 85253. Just n of McDonald Dr. Ext corridors. **Pets:** Accepted.
(SAVE) ⊠ ☾ᴹ 🖥 🖵 🍽 ⚓ ⊠

◈◈◈ ▼▼▼ ▼▼▼ Scottsdale Marriott at McDowell Mountains 🅗
(480) 502-3836. **$119-$279.** 16770 N Perimeter Dr 85260. SR 101, exit 36 (Princess Dr), just w to N Perimeter Dr, then 0.6 mi s. Int corridors.
Pets: Accepted. (SAVE) ⊠ ☾ᴹ 🖥 🖵 🍽 ⚓ ⊠

◈◈◈ ▼▼▼ ▼▼▼ Scottsdale Resort & Conference Center 🅗
(480) 991-9000. **$79-$359.** 7700 E McCormick Pkwy 85258. Just w of Hayden Rd; 0.7 mi e of Scottsdale Rd. Ext/int corridors. **Pets:** Large, other species. $150 deposit/room. Designated rooms, service with restrictions, crate. (SAVE) ⊠ 🖥 🖵 🍽 ⚓ ⊠

🛰 💎💎💎 Scottsdale Thunderbird Suites 🅷

(480) 951-4000. **$50-$249.** 7515 E Butherus Dr 85260. 0.8 mi n of Thunderbird Rd; 0.5 mi e of Scottsdale Rd. Ext corridors. **Pets:** Dogs only. $10 daily fee/pet. Service with restrictions, crate.

[SAVE] [✕] [🔒] [▦] [🍴] [🏊]

🛰 💎💎 Sleep Inn North Scottsdale/Phoenix 🅷 🐾

(480) 998-9211. **$59-$159.** 16630 N Scottsdale Rd 85254. Just s of Bell Rd. Int corridors. **Pets:** Other species. $20 daily fee/room. Service with restrictions. [SAVE] [✕] [🔒M] [🔒] [▦] [🏊]

💎💎💎 SpringHill Suites by Marriott-Scottsdale North 🅷 🐾

(480) 922-8700. **$129-$269.** 17020 N Scottsdale Rd 85255. Just n of Frank Lloyd Wright Blvd. Int corridors. **Pets:** Medium. $50 one-time fee/room. [✕] [🔒M] [🔒] [▦] [🏊]

💎💎 TownePlace Suites Scottsdale by Marriott 🅷

(480) 551-1100. **$129-$229.** 10740 N 90th St 85260. SR 101, exit Shea Blvd, just e to 90th St, then just n. Int corridors. **Pets:** Accepted.

[✕] [🔒M] [🔒] [▦] [🏊]

🛰 💎💎💎💎 The Westin Kierland Resort & Spa 🅷 🐾

(480) 624-1000. **$159-$679, 7 day notice.** 6902 E Greenway Pkwy 85254. 0.5 mi w of Scottsdale Rd. Int corridors. **Pets:** Dogs only. Service with restrictions, supervision. [SAVE] [✕] [▦] [🍴] [🏊] [✕]

🛰 💎💎💎💎 W Scottsdale 🅷

(480) 970-2100. **$159-$749.** 7277 E Camelback Rd 85252. Just e of Scottsdale Rd. Int corridors. **Pets:** Accepted.

[SAVE] [✕] [🔒] [▦] [🍴] [🏊]

🛰 💎💎💎 Xona Resort Suites 🅷

(480) 585-1234. **$69-$359.** 7677 E Princess Blvd 85255. SR 101, exit 34 (Scottsdale Rd), 0.8 mi s, then just e. Ext corridors. **Pets:** Accepted.

[SAVE] [✕] [🔒] [🔒] [▦] [🍴] [🏊] [✕]

SURPRISE

💎💎💎 Comfort Inn & Suites of Surprise 🅷

(623) 544-6874. **$62-$161.** 13337 W Grand Ave 85374. Jct Bell Rd, 0.4 mi se. Int corridors. **Pets:** Accepted. [ASK] [✕] [🔒M] [🔒] [▦] [🏊]

🛰 💎💎 Days Inn & Suites 🅷

(623) 933-4000. **$49-$250.** 12477 W Bell Rd 85374. US 60 (Grand Ave), 1.1 mi e, then just s on Greasewood St. Int corridors. **Pets:** Very small. $20 daily fee/pet. Designated rooms, service with restrictions, supervision. [SAVE] [✕] [🔒M] [🔒] [▦] [🏊]

🛰 💎💎 Hampton Inn & Suites Surprise 🅷 🐾

(623) 537-9122. **$89-$199.** 14783 W Grand Ave 85374. Jct Bell Rd, 2 mi nw. Int corridors. **Pets:** Large, other species. Designated rooms, service with restrictions, supervision. [SAVE] [✕] [🔒M] [🔒] [▦] [🏊]

💎💎 Quality Inn & Suites 🅷

(623) 583-3500. **$62-$153.** 16741 N Greasewood St 85374. US 60 (Grand Ave), 1.1 mi e on Bell Rd, then just s. Int corridors. **Pets:** Very small. $20 daily fee/pet. Designated rooms, service with restrictions, supervision. [ASK] [✕] [🔒] [▦] [🏊]

🛰 💎💎 Windmill Suites in Surprise 🅷 🐾

(623) 583-0133. **$79-$179.** 12545 W Bell Rd 85374. US 60 (Grand Ave), 1 mi e. Int corridors. **Pets:** Medium, other species. Designated rooms, service with restrictions, supervision. [SAVE] [✕] [🔒] [▦] [🏊] [✕]

TEMPE

🛰 💎💎💎 aloft Tempe 🅷 🐾

(480) 621-3300. **$109-$229.** 951 E Playa Del Norte Dr 85281. SR 202 Loop (Red Mountain Frwy), exit 7 (Rural Rd), just s on Scottsdale Rd, then just e. Int corridors. **Pets:** Medium, dogs only. Service with restrictions, supervision. [SAVE] [✕] [🔒M] [🔒] [▦] [🏊]

🛰 💎💎💎 Best Western Inn of Tempe 🅷

(480) 784-2233. **$59-$149.** 670 N Scottsdale Rd 85281. SR 202 Loop (Red Mountain Frwy), exit 7 (Rural Rd S), just s. Int corridors. **Pets:** Small, other species. $20 one-time fee/room. Service with restrictions. [SAVE] [✕] [🔒] [▦]

🛰 💎💎💎 Best Western Tempe by the Mall 🅷 🐾

(480) 820-7500. **$69-$139, 3 day notice.** 5300 S Priest Dr 85283. I-10, exit 155 (Baseline Rd), 0.4 mi e, then just s. Int corridors. **Pets:** Small, other species. $25 one-time fee/pet. Designated rooms, service with restrictions, supervision. [SAVE] [✕] [🔒] [▦] [🏊]

💎💎 Country Inn & Suites By Carlson 🅷

(480) 345-8585. **$65-$150.** 1660 W Elliot Rd 85284. I-10, exit 157, just e. Ext corridors. **Pets:** Accepted. [ASK] [✕] [🔒] [▦] [🏊]

💎💎 Country Inn & Suites By Carlson, Phoenix Airport at Tempe 🅷 🐾

(480) 858-9898. **$79-$209.** 808 N Scottsdale Rd 85281. SR 202 Loop (Red Mountain Frwy), exit 7 (Rural Rd S), just n. Int corridors. **Pets:** Other species. $50 one-time fee/room. Crate.

[ASK] [✕] [🔒M] [🔒] [▦] [🏊]

💎💎 Hampton Inn & Suites 🅷 🐾

(480) 675-9799. **$79-$209.** 1429 N Scottsdale Rd 85281. SR 202 Loop (Red Mountain Frwy), exit 7 (Rural Rd S), 0.5 mi n. Ext corridors. **Pets:** Other species. Service with restrictions, supervision.

[✕] [🔒] [▦] [🏊] [✕]

💎💎 Homestead Studio Suites Hotel-Phoenix/Airport/Tempe 🅷

(480) 557-8880. **$56-$89.** 2165 W 15th St 85281. I-10, exit 153 (Broadway Rd), 0.3 mi ne, just nw on S 52nd St, then just w. Int corridors. **Pets:** Other species. $25 daily fee/room. Designated rooms, service with restrictions, crate. [ASK] [✕] [🔒] [▦] [🏊]

🛰 💎💎💎 Hotel Tempe/Phoenix Airport InnSuites Hotel & Suites 🅷 🐾

(480) 897-7900. **$69-$159.** 1651 W Baseline Rd 85283. I-10, exit 155 (Baseline Rd), just e. Ext corridors. **Pets:** Small. $25 one-time fee/pet. Designated rooms, service with restrictions, crate.

[SAVE] [✕] [🔒] [▦] [🍴] [🏊] [✕]

💎💎💎 La Quinta Inn Phoenix (Sky Harbor South) 🅷 🐾

(480) 967-4465. **$79-$169.** 911 S 48th St 85281. I-10, exit 153 (Broadway Rd) eastbound; exit 153A (University Dr) westbound, 0.8 mi n; on south side of University Dr; east side of SR 143 (Hohokam Expwy). Ext/int corridors. **Pets:** Medium, other species. Service with restrictions, supervision. [ASK] [✕] [🔒] [▦] [🏊]

🛰 💎💎💎 Quality Suites near Old Town Scottsdale 🅷

(480) 947-3711. **$65-$89, 3 day notice.** 1635 N Scottsdale Rd 85281. SR 202 Loop (Red Mountain Frwy), exit 7, 0.6 mi n. Ext corridors. **Pets:** Medium, other species. $10 daily fee/room. Supervision.

[SAVE] [✕] [🔒] [▦] [🏊] [✕]

💎💎 Ramada Inn–Arizona Mills Mall 🅷

(480) 413-1188. **$54-$149.** 1701 W Baseline Rd 85283. I-10, exit 155 (Baseline Rd), just e. Ext corridors. **Pets:** Medium. $15 daily fee/pet. Designated rooms, service with restrictions. [ASK] [✕] [🔒] [▦] [🏊]

💎💎 Ramada Limited Tempe-University Ⓜ

(480) 736-1700. **$79-$189.** 1915 E Apache Blvd 85281. US 60 (Superstition Frwy), exit 175, 1.9 mi n on McClintock Dr, then 0.3 mi e. Ext corridors. **Pets:** Medium. $50 deposit/pet, $15 one-time fee/pet. Service with restrictions, supervision. [ASK] [✕] [🔒] [▦] [🏊]

🛰 💎💎 Red Roof Inn Phoenix Airport 🅷

(480) 449-3205. **$59-$90.** 2135 W 15th St 85281. I-10, exit 153 (Broadway Rd), just nw on S 52nd St, then just w. Int corridors. **Pets:** Large. Service with restrictions, crate. [SAVE] [✕] [🔒] [🏊]

▼▼▼▼ Residence Inn by Marriott 🅗 ❀
(480) 756-2122. **$149-$259.** 5075 S Priest Dr 85282. I-10, exit 155
(Baseline Rd), 0.4 mi e, then just n. Ext/int corridors. **Pets:** Other species.
$100 one-time fee/room. Service with restrictions.
⊠ 🔒 🖵 🌄 ⊠

▲▲▲▼ ▼▼▼▼ Sheraton Phoenix Airport
Hotel-Tempe 🅗 ❀
(480) 967-6600. **$69-$369.** 1600 S 52nd St 85281. I-10, exit 153B
(Broadway Rd) westbound; exit 153A (48th St) eastbound, 0.3 mi ne. Int
corridors. **Pets:** Medium, dogs only. $75 one-time fee/room. Service with
restrictions, crate. ⊠ ⊠ 🔒 🖵 🍴 🌄 ⊠

▼▼ Studio 6 Extended Stay #6031 🅜
(602) 414-4470. **$53-$63.** 4909 S Wendler Dr 85282. I-10, exit 155
(Baseline Rd), just w, then 0.4 mi n. Ext corridors. **Pets:** Other species.
$10 daily fee/room. Service with restrictions, supervision.
⊠ 🔒 🖵 🌄

▲▲▲▼ ▼▼▼ Super 8 Tempe/ASU 🅜
(480) 967-8891. **$49-$129.** 1020 E Apache Blvd 85281. Just e of Rural
Rd. Ext corridors. **Pets:** Small, dogs only. $75 deposit/pet, $10 daily fee/
pet. Designated rooms, service with restrictions, supervision.
⊠ ⊠ 🔒 🖵 🌄

▲▲▲ ▼▼▼▼ Tempe Mission Palms Hotel 🅗
(480) 894-1400. **$109-$319, 3 day notice.** 60 E 5th St 85281. Jct University Dr, just n on Mill Ave, then just e; downtown. Int corridors.
Pets: Medium. $25 one-time fee/pet. Service with restrictions, supervision.
⊠ ⊠ 🔒 🖵 🍴 🌄 ⊠

TOLLESON
▲▲▲▼ ▼▼▼ Premier Inns 🅗
(623) 533-4660. **$52-$70.** 8399 W Lynwood St 85353. I-10, exit 135
(83rd Ave), just n, then just w. Ext corridors. **Pets:** Accepted.
⊠ ⊠ 🔒 🌄

YOUNGTOWN
▲▲▲▼ ▼▼▼▼ Best Western Inn & Suites of Sun City 🅗
(623) 933-8211. **$60-$160.** 11201 Grand Ave 85363. On US 60, just se
of 113th Ave. Ext/int corridors. **Pets:** Accepted. ⊠ ⊠ 🔒 🖵 🌄

END METROPOLITAN AREA

PINETOP-LAKESIDE
▲▲▲▼ ▼▼▼ Best Western Inn of Pinetop 🅜
(928) 367-6667. **$79-$119.** 404 E White Mountain Blvd 85935. On SR
260. Ext corridors. **Pets:** Other species. $10 daily fee/pet. Designated
rooms, service with restrictions, supervision. ⊠ ⊠ 🔒 🖵

▲▲▲▼ ▼▼▼▼ Hon-Dah Resort Casino & Conference
Center 🅗 ❀
(928) 369-0299. **$109-$200.** 777 Hwy 260 85935. Jct SR 260 and 73;
east end of town. Int corridors. **Pets:** Large, other species. $50 one-time
fee/room. Service with restrictions, supervision.
⊠ ⊠ 🅛 🔒 🖵 🍴 🌄 ⊠

▼▼ Lazy Oaks Resort 🅒🅐
(928) 368-6203. **$79-$329, 30 day notice.** 1075 Larson Rd 85929. Off
SR 260, 0.8 mi s on Rainbow Lake Dr, then 0.6 mi w; west end of town.
Ext corridors. **Pets:** Other species. No service, crate.
🔒 🖵 ⊠ 🎾 🗲

▲▲▲▼ ▼▼ Mountain Hacienda Lodge 🅜
(928) 367-4146. **$49-$89.** 1023 E White Mountain Blvd 85935. On SR
260; east end of town. Ext corridors. **Pets:** Medium, dogs only. $10 daily
fee/pet. Designated rooms, service with restrictions, supervision.
⊠ ⊠ 🔒 🖵

▼▼▼▼ Northwoods Resort 🅒🅐
(928) 367-2966. **Call for rates.** 165 E White Mountain Blvd 85935. On
SR 260, MM 352. Ext corridors. **Pets:** Accepted.
⊠ 🔒 🖵 ⊠ 🎾 🗲

▲▲▲▼ ▼▼▼ Super 8 🅗
(928) 367-3161. **$54-$139.** 1202 E White Mountain Blvd 85935. On SR
260; east end of town. Int corridors. **Pets:** Accepted.
⊠ ⊠ 🔒 🖵 🌄

▼▼ TimberLodge Inn 🅜
(928) 367-4463. **$45-$99.** 1078 E White Mountain Blvd 85935. On SR
260; east end of town. Ext corridors. **Pets:** Medium, other species. $10
daily fee/pet. Designated rooms, service with restrictions, supervision.
🅐🅢🅚 ⊠ 🔒 🖵 🎾

▲▲▲▼ ▼▼▼ Woodland Inn & Suites 🅜
(928) 367-3636. **$74-$169, 3 day notice.** 458 E White Mountain Blvd
85935. On SR 260; east end of town. Ext corridors. **Pets:** Medium. $10
daily fee/pet. Service with restrictions, supervision. ⊠ ⊠ 🔒 🖵

PRESCOTT
▲▲▲▼ ▼▼▼ Americas Best Value Inn 🅜 ❀
(928) 776-1282. **$60-$120.** 1105 E Sheldon St 86301. 0.4 mi e of jct SR
89. Int corridors. **Pets:** Dogs only. $25 one-time fee/room. Service with
restrictions, supervision. ⊠ ⊠ 🔒 🖵 🌄

▲▲▲▼ ▼▼▼▼ Best Western Prescottonian Motel 🅜
(928) 445-3096. **$79-$139.** 1317 E Gurley St 86301. On SR 89, just s of
jct SR 69. Ext corridors. **Pets:** Medium. $10 daily fee/pet. Designated
rooms, service with restrictions, supervision.
⊠ ⊠ 🔒 🖵 🌄

▲▲▲▼ ▼▼▼ Comfort Inn of Prescott 🅜
(928) 778-5770. **$70-$109.** 1290 White Spar Rd 86303. On SR 89, 1.5
mi s of town center. Ext corridors. **Pets:** Medium, dogs only. $20 daily
fee/pet. Designated rooms, service with restrictions, supervision.
⊠ ⊠ 🔒 🖵

▼▼ Motel 6 #0166 🅜
(928) 776-0160. **$45-$57.** 1111 E Sheldon St 86301. 0.4 mi e of jct SR
89; center. Ext corridors. **Pets:** Other species. Service with restrictions,
supervision. ⊠ 🔒 🌄

▼▼ Prescott Cabin Rentals- Lynx Creek Farm 🅗
(928) 778-9573. **$99-$219, 31 day notice.** 5555 Onyx Dr 86303. Jct SR
89, 5 mi e on SR 69, 0.4 mi s on dirt/gravel road. Ext corridors.
Pets: Accepted. ⊠ 🔒 🖵 ⊠

▲▲▲▼ ▼▼▼▼ Residence Inn by Marriott 🅗
(928) 775-2232. **$159-$189.** 3599 Lee Cir 86301. Jct SR 69, just n on
Lee Blvd, then just e. Int corridors. **Pets:** Accepted.
⊠ ⊠ 🅛 🔒 🖵 🌄 ⊠

▲▲▲▼ ▼▼▼▼ SpringHill Suites by Marriott 🅗
(928) 776-0998. **$139-$149.** 200 E Sheldon St 86301. On SR 89; at
Marina St. Int corridors. **Pets:** Accepted. ⊠ ⊠ 🅛 🔒 🖵 🌄

▲▲▲▼ ▼▼▼▼ Wyndham Garden Hotel Prescott 🅗 ❀
(928) 777-0770. **Call for rates.** 4499 Hwy 69 86301. On SR 69, 3.6 mi
e of jct SR 89. Int corridors. **Pets:** Other species. $25 one-time fee/room.
Service with restrictions, supervision.
⊠ ⊠ 🔒 🖵 🍴 🌄 ⊠

PRESCOTT VALLEY

AAA ▼▼▼ **Americas Best Value Inn H**
(928) 772-2200. **$65-$155.** 8383 E Hwy 69 86314. On SR 69, just w of N Navajo Dr. Int corridors. **Pets:** Large. $6 daily fee/pet. Designated rooms, service with restrictions, supervision. SAVE ✕ 🖶 💻 ⊇

AAA ▼▼▼▼ **Comfort Suites Prescott Valley H** ❀
(928) 771-2100. **$80-$126.** 2601 N Crownpointe Dr 86314. Just w on SR 69, then n on Market St. Int corridors. **Pets:** Medium, dogs only. $25 one-time fee/room. Designated rooms, service with restrictions, supervision. SAVE ✕ 🔆M 🖶 💻 ⊇

AAA ▼▼▼ **Days Inn/Prescott Valley H**
(928) 772-8600. **$79-$129.** 7875 E Hwy 69 86314. On SR 69; corner of Windsong Rd. Ext corridors. **Pets:** Other species. $50 deposit/room. Service with restrictions. SAVE ✕ 🖶 💻 ⊇

QUARTZSITE

▼ **Super 8-Quartzsite M** ❀
(928) 927-8080. **$135-$165, 14 day notice.** 2050 W Dome Rock Rd 85359. I-10, exit 17, just s to Frontage Rd, then 0.6 mi w. Int corridors. **Pets:** Other species. $10 daily fee/pet. Service with restrictions, supervision. ASK ✕ 🖶 💻

RIO RICO

AAA ▼▼▼▼ **Esplendor Resort at Rio Rico H** ❀
(520) 281-1901. **$134-$249.** 1069 Camino Caralampi 85648. I-19, exit 17 (Rio Rico Dr), just w to Camino Caralampi, then just s. Ext corridors. **Pets:** $25 one-time fee/room. Service with restrictions.
SAVE ✕ 🔆M 🖶 💻 ¶¶ ⊇ ✕

SAFFORD

AAA ▼▼▼ **Best Western Desert Inn M**
(928) 428-0521. **Call for rates.** 1391 W Thatcher Blvd 85546. US 191, 1 mi w on US 70. Ext corridors. **Pets:** Accepted. SAVE ✕ 🖶 💻 ⊇

▼▼▼ **Days Inn M**
(928) 428-5000. **Call for rates.** 520 E Hwy 70 85546. US 191, 0.5 mi e. Ext corridors. **Pets:** Small. $20 daily fee/room. Service with restrictions, crate. ✕ 🔆M 🖶 💻 ⊇

ST. JOHNS

▼▼ **Days Inn M**
(928) 337-4422. **Call for rates.** 125 E Commercial St 85936. On US 191/SR 61; center. Ext corridors. **Pets:** Accepted. ✕ 🖶 💻

ST. MICHAELS

AAA ▼▼▼ **Navajoland Inn & Suites H**
(928) 871-5690. **$70-$90, 14 day notice.** 392 W Hwy 264 86511. From jct SR 12, 1.5 mi w. Ext corridors. **Pets:** $20 daily fee/pet. Service with restrictions, crate. SAVE ✕ 🖶 💻 ¶¶ ⊇ ✕

SEDONA

AAA ▼▼▼▼ **Amara Hotel, Restaurant & Spa H**
(928) 282-4828. **$155-$295, 3 day notice.** 100 Amara Ln 86336. Jct SR 179, 0.4 mi ne; center. Int corridors. **Pets:** Dogs only. $75 one-time fee/room. Designated rooms, service with restrictions, supervision.
SAVE ✕ 🖶 💻 ¶¶ ⊇ ✕

AAA ▼▼▼ **Best Western Inn of Sedona H** ❀
(928) 282-3072. **$125-$195.** 1200 W Hwy 89A 86336. Jct SR 179, 1.2 mi w. Ext corridors. **Pets:** Medium, other species. $20 one-time fee/room. Designated rooms, service with restrictions, supervision.
SAVE ✕ 🖶 💻 ⊇

AAA ▼▼▼▼ **Casa Sedona Bed and Breakfast Inn BB**
(928) 282-2938. **$159-$319, 7 day notice.** 55 Hozoni Dr 86336. Jct SR 179, 3 mi w on SR 89A, then 3 blks nw via Tortilla, Southwest and Hozoni drs. Ext/int corridors. **Pets:** Accepted. SAVE ✕ 🖶 ✕

AAA ▼▼▼ **Desert Quail Inn H**
(928) 284-1433. **$69-$189.** 6626 Hwy 179 86351. Jct Bell Rock Blvd, 0.9 mi s. Ext corridors. **Pets:** Accepted. SAVE ✕ 🖶 💻 ⊇

AAA ▼▼▼▼ **El Portal Sedona Luxury Inn H** ❀
(928) 203-9405. **$199-$399.** 95 Portal Ln 86336. Jct SR 89A, just s on SR 179, then just w. Ext/int corridors. **Pets:** Other species. Designated rooms, service with restrictions, supervision. SAVE ✕ 🖶

AAA ▼▼▼▼ **Hilton Sedona Resort & Spa H** ❀
(928) 284-4040. **$159-$369.** 90 Ridge Trail Dr 86351. Jct SR 89A, 7.3 mi s on SR 179. Int corridors. **Pets:** Medium, other species. $75 one-time fee/room. Designated rooms, service with restrictions, supervision.
SAVE ✕ 🖶 💻 ¶¶ ⊇ ✕

▼▼▼ **King's Ransom Sedona Hotel H** ❀
(928) 282-7151. **$99-$225.** 771 SR 179 86336. 0.7 mi s of jct SR 89A. Ext/int corridors. **Pets:** Medium. $15 daily fee/room. Designated rooms, service with restrictions, supervision.
ASK ✕ 🖶 💻 ¶¶ ⊇ ✕

AAA ▼▼▼▼ **Kokopelli Suites H** ❀
(928) 204-1146. **$139-$239, 3 day notice.** 3119 W Hwy 89A 86336. Jct SR 179, 3 mi w. Ext corridors. **Pets:** Medium, dogs only. $50 one-time fee/room. Designated rooms, service with restrictions, crate.
SAVE ✕ 🖶 💻 ⊇

AAA ▼▼▼▼ **La Quinta Inn Sedona H** ❀
(928) 284-0711. **$69-$199.** 6176 Hwy 179 86351. Jct Bell Rock Blvd, just s. Int corridors. **Pets:** Medium, other species. Service with restrictions, supervision. SAVE ✕ 🔆M 🖶 💻 ⊇

AAA ▼▼▼▼ **L'Auberge de Sedona Inn and Spa H** ❀
(928) 282-1661. **$229-$425, 7 day notice.** 301 L'Auberge Ln 86336. Jct SR 179, just n on SR 89A, then ne; down the hill. Ext/int corridors. **Pets:** Dogs only. $50 daily fee/room. Service with restrictions, supervision.
SAVE ✕ 🖶 💻 ¶¶ ⊇ ✕

AAA ▼▼▼▼ **The Lodge at Sedona BB** ❀
(928) 204-1942. **$189-$339, 14 day notice.** 125 Kallof Pl 86336. Jct SR 179, 1.8 mi w on SR 89A, then just s. Ext/int corridors. **Pets:** Medium, dogs only. $35 daily fee/pet. Designated rooms, service with restrictions, supervision. SAVE ✕ ✕ ✉

▼▼▼ **Los Abrigados Resort & Spa CO** ❀
(928) 282-1777. **$110-$425, 3 day notice.** 160 Portal Ln 86336. Jct SR 89A, just s on SR 179, just w. Ext corridors. **Pets:** Medium, other species. $20 daily fee/pet. Service with restrictions.
ASK ✕ 🖶 💻 ¶¶ ⊇ ✕

AAA ▼▼▼ **Matterhorn Inn M** ❀
(928) 282-7176. **$89-$179.** 230 Apple Ave 86336. Jct SR 179, just ne on SR 89A; uptown. Ext corridors. **Pets:** Large, other species. $10 daily fee/pet. Designated rooms, service with restrictions.
SAVE ✕ 🖶 💻 ⊇

AAA ▼▼▼ **Sedona Real Inn & Suites H** ❀
(928) 282-1414. **$95-$340.** 95 Arroyo Pinon Dr 86336. Jct SR 179, 3.4 mi w on SR 89A, just sw. Ext corridors. **Pets:** Medium, other species. $30 one-time fee/pet. Designated rooms, service with restrictions, supervision. SAVE ✕ 🖶 💻 ⊇

AAA ▼▼▼▼ **Sedona Rouge Hotel & Spa H** ❀
(928) 203-4111. **$209-$279, 3 day notice.** 2250 W Hwy 89A 86336. Jct SR 179, 2 mi w. Ext/int corridors. **Pets:** Medium, dogs only. $100 deposit/pet, $50 one-time fee/pet. Designated rooms.
SAVE ✕ 🖶 💻 ¶¶ ⊇ ✕

▼▼ **Sedona Super 8 H** ❀
(928) 282-1533. **$80-$130.** 2545 W Hwy 89A 86336. Jct SR 179, 2.4 mi w. Int corridors. **Pets:** Medium. $25 one-time fee/pet. Designated rooms, service with restrictions, supervision. ASK ✕ 🖶 💻 ⊇

▼▼▼ Sky Ranch Lodge M
(928) 282-6400. **$80-$250.** Airport Rd 86336. Jct SR 179, 1 mi w on SR 89A, then 1 mi s. Ext corridors. **Pets:** Large, other species. $10 daily fee/pet. Service with restrictions, supervision. 🅇 🅱 🅿 🏊

▼▼▼▼ Southwest Inn at Sedona H ❀
(928) 282-3344. **Call for rates.** 3250 W Hwy 89A 86336. Jct SR 179, 3.5 mi w. Ext corridors. **Pets:** Medium, dogs only. $30 one-time fee/room. Designated rooms, service with restrictions. 🅇 🅱 🅿 🏊

▼▼ The Views Inn Sedona H
(928) 284-2487. **$69-$129.** 65 E Cortez Dr 86351. Jct Bell Rock Blvd, 0.9 mi s on SR 179, just e. Ext corridors. **Pets:** Accepted.
ASK 🅇 🅱 🅿 🏊

◆◆ ▼ Village Lodge M
(928) 284-3626. **$49-$59, 3 day notice.** 105 Bell Rock Plaza 86351. Jct SR 179, just w. Ext/int corridors. **Pets:** Small, dogs only. $10 one-time fee/pet. Designated rooms, supervision. SAVE 🅇 🅱 🅿

SELIGMAN

◆◆ ▼ Canyon Lodge M
(928) 422-3255. **Call for rates.** 114 E Chino Ave 86337. I-40, exit 121, 1 mi n, then 0.7 mi e on Route 66. Ext corridors. **Pets:** Small. $10 one-time fee/pet. Service with restrictions, supervision. SAVE 🅇 🅔 🅱 🅿

◆◆ ▼ Deluxe Inn Motel M
(928) 422-3244. **$42-$52.** 22296 Old Hwy 66 86337. I-40, exit 121 eastbound, 1 mi n, then 0.7 mi e on Route 66; exit 123 westbound, just ne on I-40 business loop, then 2.4 mi w. Ext corridors. **Pets:** Other species. $10 one-time fee/room. Designated rooms, service with restrictions, supervision. SAVE 🅇 🅱

SHOW LOW

◆◆ ▼▼ Best Western Paint Pony Lodge M
(928) 537-5773. **$75-$200.** 581 W Deuce of Clubs Ave 85901. On US 60 and SR 260. Ext corridors. **Pets:** Other species. $10 daily fee/pet. Designated rooms, service with restrictions, supervision.
SAVE 🅇 🅱 🅿

▼▼ Days Inn M
(928) 537-4356. **$69-$95, 3 day notice.** 480 W Deuce of Clubs Ave 85901. On US 60 and SR 260. Ext/int corridors. **Pets:** Medium. $10 one-time fee/room. Service with restrictions, supervision.
ASK 🅇 🅱 🅿 🍽 🏊

◆◆ ▼ Kiva Motel M
(928) 537-4542. **$58-$68, 3 day notice.** 261 E Deuce of Clubs Ave 85901. On US 60 and SR 260; center. Ext corridors. **Pets:** Small, dogs only. $5 daily fee/pet. Service with restrictions, supervision.
SAVE 🅇 🅱 🅿

◆◆ ▼▼ Sleep Inn H
(928) 532-7323. **$75-$100.** 1751 W Deuce of Clubs Ave 85901. 2 mi w of jct SR 260 and US 60, south side. Int corridors. **Pets:** Other species. $15 daily fee/room. Service with restrictions, supervision.
SAVE 🅇 🅔 🅱 🅿 🏊

SIERRA VISTA

◆◆ ▼▼ Americas Best Value Inn M ❀
(520) 459-5380. **Call for rates.** 100 Fab Ave 85635. Jct Business SR 90 and Fry Blvd, then just e of main gate to Fort Huachuca. Ext corridors. **Pets:** Dogs only. $20 one-time fee/room. No service, supervision.
SAVE 🅇 🅱 🅿 🏊

◆◆ ▼▼ Best Western Mission Inn H
(520) 458-8500. **$80-$93.** 3460 E Fry Blvd 85635. Just w of jct SR 90/92. Ext corridors. **Pets:** $10 daily fee/pet. Service with restrictions, supervision. SAVE 🅇 🅔 🅱 🅿 🏊

▼▼ Candlewood Suites H
(520) 439-8200. **$119-$152.** 1904 S Hwy 92 85635. Jct SR 90 and 92, 1.4 mi s. Int corridors. **Pets:** Other species. $75 one-time fee/pet. Service with restrictions, supervision. ASK 🅇 🅱 🅿

▼▼▼ Holiday Inn Express H
(520) 439-8800. **$108-$119.** 1902 S Hwy 92 85635. Jct SR 90/92, 1.4 mi s. Int corridors. **Pets:** Accepted. ASK 🅇 🅱 🅿 🏊

◆◆ ▼▼ Quality Inn H
(520) 458-7900. **$81-$91.** 1631 S Hwy 92 85635. On SR 92, 1 mi s of jct SR 90. Int corridors. **Pets:** Large. $10 daily fee/pet. Designated rooms, service with restrictions, crate. SAVE 🅇 🅱 🅿 🏊 🅧

▼▼▼ TownePlace Suites by Marriott H
(520) 515-9900. **$125-$153.** 3399 Rodeo Dr 85635. Jct SR 90, 1.5 mi s on SR 92, just w on Avenida Cochise, just s on Oakmont, then just e. Int corridors. **Pets:** Other species. $100 one-time fee/room.
🅇 🅱 🅿 🏊

SNOWFLAKE

▼▼ Comfort Inn H
(928) 536-3888. **$54-$89.** 2055 S Main St 85937. SR 77, just s of town. Int corridors. **Pets:** Other species. $15 one-time fee/pet. Service with restrictions, supervision. ASK 🅇 🅱 🅿 🏊

TAYLOR

◆◆ ▼▼ Rodeway Inn–Silver Creek Inn M
(928) 536-2600. **$63-$80.** 825 N Main St 85939. On SR 77. Ext corridors. **Pets:** $100 deposit/room, $25 daily fee/room. Service with restrictions, supervision. SAVE 🅇 🅱 🅿

TOMBSTONE

◆◆ ▼▼ Best Western Lookout Lodge H ❀
(520) 457-2223. **$100-$113.** 781 N Hwy 80 85638. On SR 80, 1 mi n. Ext corridors. **Pets:** Large. $20 daily fee/pet. Designated rooms, service with restrictions, crate. SAVE 🅇 🅱 🅿 🍽 🏊

TUBAC

◆◆ ▼▼▼ Tubac Golf Resort and Spa H ❀
(520) 398-2211. **$129-$289, 7 day notice.** 1 Otero Rd 85646. I-19, exit 40 (Chavez Siding Rd), on east side, then 2 mi s. Ext corridors. **Pets:** Medium. $25 one-time fee/pet. Designated rooms, no service, crate.
SAVE 🅇 🅱 🅿 🍽 🏊 🅧

TUBA CITY

◆◆ ▼▼ Quality Inn Navajo Nation H
(928) 283-4545. **$75-$128.** 10 N Main St 86045. 1 mi n of US 160. Int corridors. **Pets:** Accepted. SAVE 🅇 🅱 🅿 🍽

TUCSON METROPOLITAN AREA

CATALINA

◆◆ ▼▼ Best Western Catalina Inn H
(520) 818-9500. **$86-$120.** 15691 N Oracle Rd 85739. 4.6 mi n of Tangerine Rd. Ext/int corridors. **Pets:** Small, dogs only. $100 deposit/pet, $10 daily fee/pet. Service with restrictions, supervision.
SAVE 🅇 🅱 🅿 🏊

GREEN VALLEY

◆◆ ▼▼▼ Comfort Inn H
(520) 399-3736. **$70-$120.** 90 W Esperanza Blvd 85614. I-19, exit 65, just w. Int corridors. **Pets:** Medium. $15 daily fee/pet. Designated rooms, service with restrictions, supervision. SAVE 🅇 🅱 🅿 🏊

ⓐⓐⓐ ▼▼▼ **Holiday Inn Express** 🄷
(520) 625-0900. **Call for rates.** 19200 S I-19 Frontage Rd 85614. I-19, exit 69 (Duval Mine Rd), west side of interstate, then just s. Int corridors. **Pets:** Accepted. ⓢⓐⓥⓔ ☒ 🛆 🖵 🏊

▼▼ 🔷 **Quality Inn Green Valley** 🄷
(520) 625-2250. **$65-$159.** 111 S La Canada Dr 85614. I-19, exit 65, just w, then just s. Int corridors. **Pets:** Small. $10 daily fee/pet. Designated rooms, service with restrictions, supervision.
ⓐⓢⓚ ☒ 🛆 🖵 🍴 🏊

MARANA
▼▼ 🔷 **Days Inn & Suites-Tucson/Marana** 🄷
(520) 744-6677. **Call for rates.** 8370 N Cracker Barrel Rd 85743. I-10, exit 246 (Cortaro Rd), just w. Int corridors. **Pets:** Accepted.
☒ 🛆 🖵 🏊

▼▼▼▼ **La Quinta Inn & Suites** 🄷 🐾
(520) 572-4235. **$49-$259.** 6020 W Hospitality Rd 85743. I-10, exit 246 (Cortaro Rd), just w, then just n. Int corridors. **Pets:** Medium, other species. Service with restrictions, supervision.
ⓐⓢⓚ ☒ 🔬M 🛆 🖵 🏊

ⓐⓐⓐ ▼▼▼ **Red Roof Inn Tucson North** 🄷
(520) 744-8199. **$62-$118.** 4940 W Ina Rd 85743. I-10, exit 248 (Ina Rd), just w. Int corridors. **Pets:** Large. Service with restrictions, crate.
ⓢⓐⓥⓔ ☒ 🛆 🖵 🏊

▼▼▼ **Super 8** 🄷
(520) 572-0300. **$50-$100.** 8351 N Cracker Barrel Rd 85743. I-10, exit 246 (Cortaro Rd), just w. Int corridors. **Pets:** Accepted.
ⓐⓢⓚ ☒ 🛆 🖵 🏊

ORO VALLEY
ⓐⓐⓐ ▼▼▼▼ **Hilton Tucson El Conquistador Golf & Tennis Resort** 🄷
(520) 544-5000. **$149-$309.** 10000 N Oracle Rd 85704. I-10, exit 248 (Ina Rd), jct Ina Rd, 4.4 mi n. Ext/int corridors. **Pets:** Accepted.
ⓢⓐⓥⓔ ☒ 🔬M 🛆 🖵 🍴 🏊 ☒

TUCSON
ⓐⓐⓐ ▼▼▼ **Americas Best Value Inn-Tucson** 🄷 🐾
(520) 884-5800. **$44-$160.** 810 E Benson Hwy 85713. I-10, exit 262, just s. Ext corridors. **Pets:** Other species. $25 deposit/room. Service with restrictions, crate. ⓢⓐⓥⓔ ☒ 🛆 🖵

ⓐⓐⓐ ▼▼▼ **Best Western InnSuites Tucson Foothills Hotel & Suites** 🄷
(520) 297-8111. **$79-$149.** 6201 N Oracle Rd 85704. I-10, exit 250 (Orange Grove Rd), 4 mi e, then just s. Ext corridors. **Pets:** Medium. $50 one-time fee/room. Designated rooms, service with restrictions, supervision. ⓢⓐⓥⓔ ☒ 🛆 🖵 🏊 ☒

ⓐⓐⓐ ▼▼▼ **Comfort Suites** 🄷
(520) 295-4400. **$79-$189.** 6935 S Tucson Blvd 85756. Just n of Tucson International Airport. Int corridors. **Pets:** Medium. $10 daily fee/pet. Service with restrictions, crate. ⓢⓐⓥⓔ ☒ 🛆 🖵 🏊

▼▼ 🔷 **Comfort Suites at Sabino Canyon** 🄷
(520) 298-2300. **$65-$149.** 7007 E Tanque Verde Rd 85715. Jct Grand Rd, 0.4 mi ne. Ext corridors. **Pets:** Accepted. ⓐⓢⓚ ☒ 🛆 🖵 🏊

▼▼ 🔷 **Comfort Suites at Tucson Mall** 🄷
(520) 888-6676. **$99-$199.** 515 W Auto Mall Dr 85705. I-10, exit 254 (Prince Rd), 1.9 mi n, then 1.2 mi n. Int corridors. **Pets:** Accepted.
ⓐⓢⓚ ☒ 🛆 🖵 🏊 ☒

▼▼ **Crossland Economy Studios-Tucson-Butterfield Dr** 🄷
(520) 745-3612. **$54-$74.** 4800 S Butterfield Dr 85714. I-10, exit 264B eastbound, just n to Irvington, just e to Hotel Dr, then just n; exit 264 westbound, just n. Ext corridors. **Pets:** Other species. $25 daily fee/room. Designated rooms, service with restrictions, crate. ⓐⓢⓚ ☒ 🛆 🖵

ⓐⓐⓐ ▼▼▼▼ **Doubletree Hotel at Reid Park** 🄷 🐾
(520) 881-4200. **$79-$289.** 445 S Alvernon Way 85711. I-10, exit 259 (22nd St), 4 mi e, then just n. Ext/int corridors. **Pets:** Medium. $50 one-time fee/pet. Designated rooms, service with restrictions, supervision.
ⓢⓐⓥⓔ ☒ 🛆 🖵 🍴 🏊 ☒

ⓐⓐⓐ ▼▼ **Econo Lodge** Ⓜ
(520) 622-6714. **$39-$179.** 1136 N Stone Ave 85705. I-10, exit 257 (Speedway Blvd) eastbound, just e, then just n. Ext corridors.
Pets: Accepted. ⓢⓐⓥⓔ ☒ 🛆 🖵

▼▼ **Extended StayAmerica-Tucson-Grant Rd** 🄷
(520) 795-9510. **$59-$104.** 5050 E Grant Rd 85712. 0.5 mi e of Swan Rd. Ext corridors. **Pets:** Other species. $25 daily fee/room. Designated rooms, service with restrictions, crate. ⓐⓢⓚ ☒ 🛆 🖵

ⓐⓐⓐ ▼▼▼ **Hampton Inn North** 🄷
(520) 206-0602. **$85-$194.** 1375 W Grant Rd 85745. I-10, exit 256 (Grant Rd), just w. Int corridors. **Pets:** Designated rooms, service with restrictions, supervision. ⓢⓐⓥⓔ ☒ 🔬M 🛆 🖵

ⓐⓐⓐ ▼▼▼ **Hilton-Tucson East** 🄷 🐾
(520) 721-5600. **$119-$238.** 7600 E Broadway Blvd 85710. 0.5 mi e of Kolb Rd. Int corridors. **Pets:** Large, other species. $75 one-time fee/room. Service with restrictions, crate. ⓢⓐⓥⓔ ☒ 🔬M 🛆 🖵 🍴 🏊 ☒

ⓐⓐⓐ ▼▼▼ **Holiday Inn Express Hotel & Suites Tucson Airport** 🄷
(520) 889-6600. **$99-$189.** 2548 E Medina Rd 85706. 0.5 mi n of Tucson International Airport entrance. Int corridors. **Pets:** Accepted.
ⓢⓐⓥⓔ ☒ 🔬M 🛆 🖵

ⓐⓐⓐ ▼▼▼ **The Hotel Arizona** 🄷
(520) 624-8711. **$67-$139.** 181 W Broadway Blvd 85701. I-10, exit 258 (Broadway Blvd/Congress St), just e. Int corridors. **Pets:** Other species. $50 one-time fee/room. Service with restrictions.
ⓢⓐⓥⓔ ☒ 🛆 🖵 🍴 🏊

ⓐⓐⓐ ▼▼▼ **Hotel Tucson City Center InnSuites Conference Suite Resort** 🄷 🐾
(520) 622-3000. **$69-$299.** 475 N Granada Ave 85701. I-10, exit 258 (Broadway Blvd/Congress St), just e, then 0.4 mi n. Ext/int corridors. **Pets:** Medium. $50 one-time fee/pet. Designated rooms, service with restrictions, supervision. ⓢⓐⓥⓔ ☒ 🛆 🖵 🍴 🏊 ☒

▼▼▼ **La Posada Lodge & Casitas** 🄷
(520) 887-4800. **$105-$172.** 5900 N Oracle Rd 85704. 0.5 mi s of Orange Grove Rd. Ext corridors. **Pets:** Accepted.
ⓐⓢⓚ ☒ 🛆 🖵 🍴 🏊

▼▼▼ **La Quinta Inn & Suites Tucson Airport** 🄷 🐾
(520) 573-3333. **$45-$179.** 7001 S Tucson Blvd 85706. Just n of Tucson International Airport. Int corridors. **Pets:** Medium, other species. Service with restrictions, supervision. ⓐⓢⓚ ☒ 🔬M 🛆 🖵 🏊

ⓐⓐⓐ ▼▼▼ **La Quinta Inn Downtown** 🄷 🐾
(520) 624-4455. **$59-$169.** 750 W Starr Pass Blvd 85713. I-10, exit 259 (Starr Pass Blvd), just w. Int corridors. **Pets:** Medium, other species. Service with restrictions, supervision. ⓢⓐⓥⓔ ☒ 🛆 🖵 🏊

▼▼▼ **La Quinta Inn Tucson (East)** 🄷 🐾
(520) 747-1414. **$49-$139.** 6404 E Broadway Blvd 85710. Just e of Wilmot Rd. Ext corridors. **Pets:** Medium, other species. Service with restrictions, supervision. ⓐⓢⓚ ☒ 🛆 🖵 🏊

ⓐⓐⓐ ▼▼▼▼ **The Lodge At Ventana Canyon** 🄷 🐾
(520) 577-1400. **$99-$799, 21 day notice.** 6200 N Clubhouse Ln 85750. I-10, exit 256 (Grant Rd), 8.6 mi e, 0.6 mi e on Tanque Verde Rd, 2 mi n on Sabino Canyon Rd, then 3.2 mi n on Kolb Rd. Ext/int corridors. **Pets:** Medium. $50 one-time fee/room. Service with restrictions, supervision. ⓢⓐⓥⓔ ☒ 🛆 🖵 🍴 🏊 ☒

Lodge on the Desert H
(520) 320-2000. **$99-$379, 3 day notice.** 306 N Alvernon Way 85711. I-10, exit 258 (Broadway Blvd/Congress St), 4 mi e, then just n. Ext corridors. **Pets:** Accepted.

Loews Ventana Canyon Resort H ❋
(520) 299-2020. **$149-$449, 7 day notice.** 7000 N Resort Dr 85750. I-10, exit 256 (Grant Rd), 8.6 mi e, 0.6 mi ne on Tanque Verde Rd, 2 mi n on Sabino Canyon Rd, then 3.5 mi n on Kolb Rd. Ext/int corridors. **Pets:** Other species. $25 one-time fee/room.

Motel 6 Tucson-Congress Street #50 M
(520) 628-1339. **$41-$71.** 960 S Freeway 85745. I-10, exit 258 (Broadway Blvd/Congress St), 0.7 mi s; on west side of interstate. Ext corridors. **Pets:** Other species. Service with restrictions, supervision.

Motel 6 Tucson North #1127 H
(520) 744-9300. **$49-$69.** 4630 W Ina Rd 85741. I-10, exit 248 (Ina Rd), just e to Camino de Oeste, then just n. Int corridors. **Pets:** Other species. Service with restrictions, supervision.

Omni Tucson National Resort H ❋
(520) 297-2271. **$149-$459, 3 day notice.** 2727 W Club Dr 85742. I-10, exit 246 (Cortaro Rd), 3.5 mi e, then n on Shannon Rd. Ext corridors. **Pets:** Medium. $50 one-time fee/room. Designated rooms, service with restrictions, supervision.

Quality Inn at Tucson Airport H
(520) 294-2500. **$64-$129.** 2803 E Valencia Rd 85706. 1 mi ne of Tucson International Airport; just e of Tucson Blvd. Ext/int corridors. **Pets:** Large. $10 daily fee/pet. Service with restrictions, supervision.

Radisson Suites Tucson H ❋
(520) 721-7100. **$109-$269.** 6555 E Speedway Blvd 85710. Just e of Wilmot Rd. Ext corridors. **Pets:** Other species. $25 deposit/pet. Designated rooms, service with restrictions, crate.

Ramada Inn & Suites Foothills Resort H
(520) 886-9595. **$65-$210.** 6944 E Tanque Verde Rd 85715. Jct Campbell Ave, 5.5 mi e on Grant Rd, then just ne. Ext corridors. **Pets:** Accepted.

Randolph Park Hotel and Suites H
(520) 795-0330. **$70-$165, 3 day notice.** 102 N Alvernon Way 85711. Jct Campbell Ave, 2.2 mi e on Broadway Blvd, then just n. Ext/int corridors. **Pets:** $25 one-time fee/room. Designated rooms, service with restrictions, supervision.

Red Roof Inn-Tucson South H
(520) 571-1400. **$55-$118.** 3704 E Irvington Rd 85714. I-10, exit 264 westbound; exit 264B eastbound. Ext corridors. **Pets:** Large. Service with restrictions, crate.

Residence Inn by Marriott H ❋
(520) 721-0991. **$169-$229.** 6477 E Speedway Blvd 85710. Just e of Wilmot Rd. Ext corridors. **Pets:** $100 one-time fee/room.

Residence Inn by Marriott Williams Centre H
(520) 790-6100. **$159-$219.** 5400 E Williams Cir 85711. Jct Campbell Ave, 3.8 mi e on Broadway Blvd, then just s and just e on Williams Blvd. Int corridors. **Pets:** Accepted.

Residence Inn Tucson Airport H
(520) 294-5522. **$149-$259.** 2660 E Medina Rd 85706. 0.5 mi n of airport entrance on Tucson Blvd, just e. Int corridors. **Pets:** Medium, other species. $100 one-time fee/room. Service with restrictions, crate.

Riverpark Inn H ❋
(520) 239-2300. **$89-$299.** 350 S Freeway 85745. I-10, exit 258 (Broadway Blvd/Congress St), just w, then 0.4 mi s. Ext/int corridors. **Pets:** Other species. $35 one-time fee/pet. Designated rooms, service with restrictions, crate.

Rodeway Inn-University of AZ M
(520) 622-6446. **$45-$129.** 1248 N Stone Ave 85705. I-10, exit 257 (Speedway Blvd) eastbound, just e, then just n. Ext corridors. **Pets:** Small. $10 daily fee/room. Service with restrictions, crate.

Studio 6 Extended Stay #6002 M
(520) 746-0030. **$53-$63.** 4950 S Outlet Center Dr 85706. I-10, exit 264A eastbound; exit 264B westbound, just s, then just nw on Julian Dr. Ext corridors. **Pets:** Other species. $10 daily fee/room. Service with restrictions, supervision.

TownePlace Suites by Marriott H
(520) 292-9697. **$109-$149.** 405 W Rudasill Rd 85704. Jct Orange Grove Rd, 0.5 mi s on Oracle Rd, then just e. Int corridors. **Pets:** Other species. $75 one-time fee/pet. Service with restrictions, crate.

The Westin La Paloma Resort & Spa H ❋
(520) 742-6000. **$129-$539, 7 day notice.** 3800 E Sunrise Dr 85718. SR 77 (Oracle Rd), 4.6 mi e on Ina Rd via Skyline and Sunrise drs, then just s on Via Palomita. Ext corridors. **Pets:** Medium, dogs only. Service with restrictions.

Westward Look Resort H
(520) 297-1151. **$149-$449, 7 day notice.** 245 E Ina Rd 85704. I-10, exit 248 (Ina Rd), 6 mi e, then just n on Westward Look Dr. Ext corridors. **Pets:** Medium. $75 one-time fee/room. Designated rooms, service with restrictions.

Windmill Suites at St. Philip's Plaza H ❋
(520) 577-0007. **$99-$199.** 4250 N Campbell Ave 85718. I-10, exit 254 (Prince Rd), 4 mi e, then 1 mi n. Int corridors. **Pets:** Other species. Designated rooms, service with restrictions.

END METROPOLITAN AREA

WELLTON

Microtel Inn & Suites at Coyote Wash H
(928) 785-3777. **Call for rates.** 28784 Commerce Way 85356. I-8, exit 30, just s. Int corridors. **Pets:** Medium. Designated rooms, service with restrictions, supervision.

WICKENBURG

Best Western Rancho Grande H ❋
(928) 684-5445. **$65-$110.** 293 E Wickenburg Way 85390. On US 60; center. Ext corridors. **Pets:** $8 daily fee/room. Designated rooms, service with restrictions, crate.

Super 8 Wickenburg M
(928) 684-0808. **$65-$90.** 1021 N Tegner St 85390. 1 mi n of US 60 and 93. Ext/int corridors. **Pets:** $10 daily fee/pet. Designated rooms, service with restrictions, supervision.

Wickenburg Inn H
(928) 684-5461. **$69-$95, 5 day notice.** 850 E Wickenburg Way 85390. 1.3 mi se on US 60. Int corridors. **Pets:** Small. $6 daily fee/pet. Service with restrictions, supervision. [SAVE] [X] [fork] [tv] [swim]

WILLCOX

Best Western Plaza Inn H ✿
(520) 384-3556. **$72-$90.** 1100 W Rex Allen Dr 85643. I-10, exit 340, just s. Ext corridors. **Pets:** Other species. $15 one-time fee/pet. Service with restrictions, supervision. [SAVE] [X] [fork] [tv] [fork] [swim]

Days Inn M
(520) 384-4222. **$60-$80.** 724 N Bisbee Ave 85643. I-10, exit 340, just s. Ext corridors. **Pets:** Medium. $5 daily fee/pet. Service with restrictions, supervision. [SAVE] [X] [fork] [tv] [swim]

Holiday Inn Express & Suites Willcox H
(520) 384-3333. **Call for rates.** 1251 N Virginia Ave 85643. I-10, exit 340, just n. Int corridors. **Pets:** Medium. $20 daily fee/pet. Designated rooms, no service, supervision. [X] [&M] [fork] [tv] [swim]

Motel 6 Willcox #410 M
(520) 384-2201. **$41-$53.** 921 N Bisbee Ave 85643. I-10, exit 340, just s. Ext corridors. **Pets:** Other species. Service with restrictions, supervision. [X] [fork] [swim]

Super 8 H
(520) 384-0888. **$60-$85.** 1500 W Ft. Grant Rd 85643. I-10, exit 340, just n. Int corridors. **Pets:** Small. $6 daily fee/pet. Designated rooms, no service, supervision. [ASK] [X] [&M] [fork] [tv] [swim]

WILLIAMS

Americas Best Value Inn of Williams M
(928) 635-2202. **$39-$84.** 1001 W Route 66 86046. I-40, exit 161, 0.9 mi e. Ext/int corridors. **Pets:** Medium. $8 daily fee/pet. No service, supervision. [SAVE] [X] [fork] [swim]

Best Western Inn of Williams H
(928) 635-4400. **$159-$209.** 2600 W Route 66 86046. I-40, exit 161, just e. Int corridors. **Pets:** Accepted. [SAVE] [X] [fork] [tv] [fork] [swim]

Days Inn M
(928) 635-4051. **$59-$175.** 2488 W Route 66 86046. I-40, exit 161, just e. Int corridors. **Pets:** Small. Service with restrictions, supervision. [SAVE] [X] [fork] [tv] [swim]

El Rancho Motel M
(928) 635-2552. **$38-$88.** 617 E Route 66 86046. I-40, exit 163, 0.6 mi s, then just e. Ext corridors. **Pets:** $5 one-time fee/pet. Designated rooms, service with restrictions, supervision. [SAVE] [X] [fork] [tv] [swim]

Holiday Inn Williams H
(928) 635-4114. **$95-$170.** 950 N Grand Canyon Blvd 86046. I-40, exit 163, just s. Int corridors. **Pets:** Accepted. [X] [&M] [fork] [tv] [fork] [swim]

Motel 6–4010 M
(928) 635-9000. **$44-$90.** 831 W Route 66 86046. I-40, exit 161, 1 mi e. Int corridors. **Pets:** Other species. Service with restrictions, supervision. [ASK] [X] [fork] [swim]

Quality Inn Mountain Ranch Resort H
(928) 635-2693. **$79-$169.** 6701 E Mountain Ranch Rd 86046. I-40, exit 171 (Deer Farm Rd), just s. Ext corridors. **Pets:** Medium. $45 one-time fee/room. Service with restrictions, supervision. [SAVE] [X] [fork] [tv] [fork] [swim] [X]

Travelodge Williams M
(928) 635-2651. **$40-$150.** 430 E Route 66 86046. I-40, exit 163, 0.5 mi s, then just e. Ext corridors. **Pets:** Dogs only. $8 deposit/pet. No service, supervision. [SAVE] [X] [fork] [tv] [swim]

WINDOW ROCK

Quality Inn Navajo Nation Capital H
(928) 871-4108. **$66-$101.** 48 W Hwy 264 86515. Center. Ext corridors. **Pets:** $50 deposit/pet. Service with restrictions, supervision. [SAVE] [X] [fork] [tv] [fork]

WINSLOW

Econo Lodge at I-40 M
(928) 289-4687. **$85-$115.** 1706 N Park Dr 86047. I-40, exit 253, just s. Ext corridors. **Pets:** Medium, other species. $5 one-time fee/room. Service with restrictions, crate. [SAVE] [X] [fork] [tv] [swim]

La Posada Hotel H
(928) 289-4366. **$99-$169, 7 day notice.** 303 E 2nd St 86047. I-40, exit 253, 1 mi s to Route 66 (2nd St), then just e; in historic downtown. Int corridors. **Pets:** Other species. $10 one-time fee/room. Service with restrictions, supervision. [X] [&M] [fork] [fork] [X]

YUMA

Best Western Coronado Motor Hotel M
(928) 783-4453. **$89-$149.** 233 4th Ave 85364. I-8, exit 172 (4th Ave) eastbound, 0.5 mi s; exit 1 (Harold C. Giss Pkwy) westbound, 1 mi w. Ext corridors. **Pets:** Accepted. [SAVE] [X] [fork] [tv] [fork] [swim]

Best Western InnSuites Yuma Mall Hotel & Suites H
(928) 783-8341. **$71-$149.** 1450 Castle Dome Ave 85365. I-8, exit 2 (16th St/US 95), just e to Yuma Palms Pkwy, just n, then just w. Ext corridors. **Pets:** Accepted. [SAVE] [X] [fork] [tv] [fork] [swim] [X]

Candlewood Suites H
(928) 726-2800. **$90-$189.** 2036 S Ave 3 E 85365. I-8, exit 3, just n, then just w on Frontage Rd. Int corridors. **Pets:** Accepted. [ASK] [X] [&M] [fork] [tv]

Clarion Suites H
(928) 726-4830. **$102-$129.** 2600 S 4th Ave 85364. I-8, exit 2 (16th St/US 95) eastbound, 1 mi w, then 1.3 mi s; exit 3 (SR 280) westbound, 0.5 mi s, then 2 mi w. Ext corridors. **Pets:** Accepted. [ASK] [X] [fork] [tv] [swim] [X]

Comfort Inn H
(928) 782-1200. **$89-$134.** 1691 S Riley Ave 85365. I-8, exit 2 (16th St/US 95), just w. Int corridors. **Pets:** Medium. $15 daily fee/room. Designated rooms, service with restrictions, supervision. [ASK] [X] [&M] [fork] [tv] [swim]

Holiday Inn H
(928) 782-9300. **$129-$189.** 1901 E 18th St 85365. I-8, exit 2 (16th St/US 95), 0.4 mi e on 16th St, just s on Pacific Ave, then just w. Int corridors. **Pets:** Medium, other species. $15 daily fee/pet. Service with restrictions, supervision. [ASK] [X] [&M] [fork] [tv] [swim]

Holiday Inn Express H ✿
(928) 317-1400. **$99-$199.** 2044 S Ave 3 E 85365. I-8, exit 3, just n, then just w on Frontage Rd. Int corridors. **Pets:** Medium. $15 daily fee/pet. Designated rooms, service with restrictions, supervision. [ASK] [X] [&M] [fork] [tv]

Homewood Suites by Hilton H
(928) 782-4100. **$159-$199.** 1955 E 16th St 85365. I-8, exit 2 (16th St/US 95), 0.4 mi e. Int corridors. **Pets:** Accepted. [X] [&M] [fork] [tv] [swim] [X]

Howard Johnson Inn H
(928) 344-1420. **$59-$99.** 3181 S 4th Ave 85364. I-8, exit 3E (SR 280 S), 1 mi s to 32nd St, then 2 mi w. Ext corridors. **Pets:** Accepted. [SAVE] [X] [fork] [tv] [swim]

Microtel Inn & Suites H
(928) 345-1777. **$57-$140.** 11274 S Fortuna Rd 85367. I-8, exit 12 (Fortuna Rd), just s, then w on frontage road. Int corridors. **Pets:** Accepted. [ASK] [X] [fork] [tv] [swim]

▼▼ Oak Tree Inn H 🐾

(928) 539-9000. **$69-$99.** 1731 Sunridge Dr 85364. I-8, exit 2 (16th St/US 95), just e, then just s. Int corridors. **Pets:** Service with restrictions, supervision. ASK ⊠ 🛏 🖥 🏊

AAA ▼▼ Quality Inn Airport H

(928) 726-4721. **$79-$109.** 711 E 32nd St 85365. I-8, exit 3E (SR 280), 1.2 mi s, then 1.9 mi w. Ext corridors. **Pets:** $25 one-time fee/room. Service with restrictions, crate. SAVE ⊠ 🛏 🖥 🍴 🏊

▼▼▼ Radisson Hotel Yuma H

(928) 783-8000. **$99-$199.** 1501 S Redondo Center Dr 85365. I-8, exit 2 (16th St/US 95), just w, then just n. Int corridors. **Pets:** Accepted.
ASK ⊠ 🛏 🖥 🍴 🏊

AAA ▼▼ Shilo Inn Hotel & Suites-Yuma H 🐾

(928) 782-9511. **$145-$250.** 1550 S Castle Dome Ave 85365. I-8, exit 2 (16th St/US 95), just e to Yuma Palms Pkwy, just n, then just w. Int corridors. **Pets:** Dogs only. $25 one-time fee/room. Designated rooms, service with restrictions, supervision. SAVE ⊠ ♿M 🛏 🖥 🍴 🏊 ⊠

▼▼▼ TownePlace Suites by Marriott H

(928) 783-6900. **$134-$164.** 1726 S Sunridge Dr 85365. I-8, exit 2 (16th St/US 95), just e to Sunridge Dr, then just s. Int corridors.
Pets: Accepted. ⊠ ♿M 🛏 🖥 🏊

AAA ▼▼ Yuma Cabana Motel M

(928) 783-8311. **$46-$130, 3 day notice.** 2151 S 4th Ave 85364. I-8, exit 2 (16th St/US 95), 1 mi w, then 0.5 mi s. Int corridors. **Pets:** Dogs only. $6 daily fee/pet. Service with restrictions, supervision.
SAVE ⊠ 🛏 🏊

▼▼ Yuma Super 8 H

(928) 782-2000. **$89-$149, 7 day notice.** 1688 S Riley Ave 85365. I-8, exit 2 (16th St/US 95), just w. Int corridors. **Pets:** Medium. $15 daily fee/room. Service with restrictions, supervision.
ASK ⊠ ♿M 🛏 🖥 🏊

ARKANSAS

ALMA

▼▼▼ **Comfort Inn & Suites** 🅷 ❀
(479) 632-4141. **$59-$95.** 439 Hwy 71 N 72921. I-40, exit 13, just n. Ext/int corridors. **Pets:** Small. $25 one-time fee/room. Designated rooms, service with restrictions, supervision. (A$K) (X) 🛡 💻

ARKADELPHIA

🔺🔺🔺 ▼▼▼ **Best Western-Continental Inn** 🅷
(870) 246-5592. **$65-$99.** 136 Valley St 71923. I-30, exit 78, just e. Ext corridors. **Pets:** Large. $12 daily fee/pet. Service with restrictions, crate. (SAVE) (X) 🛡 💻 ⇆

BATESVILLE

▼▼ **Ramada Inn of Batesville** 🅷 ❀
(870) 698-1800. **$85-$165.** 1325 N St. Louis St 72501. 1 mi n on US 167. Ext corridors. **Pets:** Small. $20 one-time fee/pet. Service with restrictions, crate. (A$K) (X) 🛡 💻 (¶) ⇆

▼ **Super 8-Batesville** Ⓜ
(870) 793-5888. **$59-$75.** 1287 N St. Louis St 72501. 1 mi n on US 167. Int corridors. **Pets:** Dogs only. $25 one-time fee/room. No service, supervision. (A$K) (X) 🛡 💻

BENTON

🔺🔺🔺 ▼▼▼ **Best Western Inn Benton** 🅷
(501) 778-9695. **$65-$70.** 17036 I-30 72019. I-30, exit 117, just w. Ext corridors. **Pets:** Medium. $10 daily fee/pet. Service with restrictions. (SAVE) (X) 🛡 💻 ⇆

BENTONVILLE

▼▼▼▼ **Clarion Hotel & Convention Center** 🅷 ❀
(479) 464-4600. **$84-$119.** 211 SE Walton Blvd 72712. I-540, exit 85, 1.2 mi w. Ext/int corridors. **Pets:** Other species. Service with restrictions, crate. (A$K) (X) (♿M) 🛡 💻 (¶) ⇆

🔺🔺🔺 ▼▼▼ **Comfort Suites Bentonville/Rogers** 🅷
(479) 254-9099. **Call for rates.** 2011 SE Walton Blvd 72712. I-540, exit 85, just w. Int corridors. **Pets:** Accepted. (SAVE) (X) 🛡 💻 ⇆

▼▼▼ **La Quinta Inn & Suites** 🅷 ❀
(479) 271-7555. **$55-$139.** 1001 SE Walton Blvd 72712. I-540, exit 85, 0.7 mi w. Int corridors. **Pets:** Medium, other species. Service with restrictions, supervision. (A$K) (X) (♿M) 🛡 💻 ⇆

▼▼ **Microtel Inn & Suites Bentonville** 🅷
(479) 271-6699. **$55-$65.** 911 SE Walton Blvd 72712. I-540, exit 85, 0.8 mi w. Int corridors. **Pets:** Accepted. (X) 🛡 💻

▼▼ **Sleep Inn** 🅷
(479) 464-4400. **$69-$89, 4 day notice.** 215 SE Walton Blvd 72712. I-540, exit 85, 1.2 mi w. Int corridors. **Pets:** Accepted. (A$K) (X) 💻 ⇆

▼▼▼▼ **TownePlace Suites by Marriott Bentonville/Rogers** 🅷
(479) 621-0202. **$121-$147.** 3100 SE 14th St 72712. I-540, exit 86, just e. Int corridors. **Pets:** Accepted. (X) (♿M) 🛡 💻 ⇆

▼▼▼ **Wingate by Wyndham** 🅷
(479) 418-5400. **Call for rates.** 7400 SW Old Farm Blvd 72712. 7.4 mi w of jct Walton and SW Regional Airport blvds. Int corridors. **Pets:** Small. $75 one-time fee/room. Service with restrictions, supervision. (X) (♿M) 🛡 💻 ⇆

BLYTHEVILLE

▼▼ **Hampton Inn** 🅷
(870) 763-5220. **Call for rates.** 301 N Frontage Rd 72315. I-55, exit 67, just nw. Ext corridors. **Pets:** Small. $10 one-time fee/pet. No service, crate. (X) 🛡 💻 (¶) ⇆

▼▼▼ **Holiday Inn** 🅷
(870) 763-5800. **$90-$104.** 1121 E Main St 72315. I-55, exit 67, just w. Ext/int corridors. **Pets:** Accepted. (A$K) (X) 🛡 💻 (¶) ⇆

▼▼ **Quality Inn** 🅷
(870) 763-7081. **$72-$78.** 1520 E Main St 72315. I-55, exit 67, just w. Ext corridors. **Pets:** Accepted. (A$K) (X) 🛡 💻 (¶) ⇆

BRYANT

▼▼ **Americas Best Value Inn** Ⓜ
(501) 653-7800. **$55-$90.** 407 W Commerce St 72022. I-30, exit 123, just sw. Ext corridors. **Pets:** Medium, dogs only. $10 daily fee/pet. Designated rooms, service with restrictions, supervision. (A$K) (X) 🛡 💻

▼▼ **Super 8** Ⓜ
(501) 847-7888. **$50-$75.** 201 Dell Dr 72022. I-30, exit 123, just e. Ext corridors. **Pets:** Dogs only. $10 one-time fee/pet. Designated rooms, service with restrictions, supervision. (A$K) (X) 🛡 💻

🔺🔺🔺 ▼▼▼ **Vista Inn & Suites** 🅷
(501) 847-7120. **$65-$96, 7 day notice.** 210 Office Park Dr 72022. I-30, exit 123, just w. Ext corridors. **Pets:** Small. $15 daily fee/pet. Service with restrictions, crate. (SAVE) (X) 🛡 💻 ⇆

CAMDEN

▼▼ **Comfort Inn** 🅷
(870) 836-9000. **Call for rates.** 1 Ridgecrest Dr 71701. Just w of jct US 79 and 278. Int corridors. **Pets:** Accepted. (X) (♿M) 🛡 💻 ⇆ (X̄)

▼▼ **Holiday Inn Express** 🅷
(870) 836-8100. **Call for rates.** 1450 US Hwy 278 W 71701. 1 mi w of jct US 79 and 278. Int corridors. **Pets:** Accepted. (X) (♿M) 🛡 💻 ⇆

CLARKSVILLE

🔺🔺🔺 ▼▼▼ **Best Western Sherwood Inn** 🅷
(479) 754-7900. **$53-$79.** 1207 S Rogers Ave 72830. I-40, exit 58, just n. Ext corridors. **Pets:** Service with restrictions, supervision. (SAVE) (X) 🛡 💻 ⇆

CONWAY

🔺🔺🔺 ▼▼▼ **Best Western Conway** 🅷 ❀
(501) 329-9855. **$70-$75.** 816 E Oak St 72032. I-40, exit 127, just n. Ext corridors. **Pets:** Medium, other species. Service with restrictions, supervision. (SAVE) (X) 🛡 💻 ⇆

▼▼▼ Candlewood Suites ⊞ ❀
(501) 329-8551. **$89-$149.** 2360 Sanders St 72033. I-40, exit 125, just se. Int corridors. **Pets:** Medium, other species. $75 one-time fee/room. Service with restrictions, supervision. ⒜ⓈⓀ ⊠ 🛏 🖵

◈◈ ▼▼▼ Quality Inn ⊞
(501) 329-0300. **Call for rates.** 150 Hwy 65 N 72033. I-40, exit 125, just n. Ext corridors. **Pets:** Accepted. ⓈⒶⓋⒺ ⊠ 🛏 🖵 ⇌

EL DORADO

▼▼▼▼ La Quinta Inn El Dorado ⊞ ❀
(870) 863-6677. **$55-$100.** 2303 Junction City Rd 71730. Just e of jct US 167 and 82B. Ext/int corridors. **Pets:** Medium, other species. Service with restrictions, supervision. ⒜ⓈⓀ ⊠ 🛏 🖵 ⇌

EUREKA SPRINGS

◈◈ ▼▼▼▼ 1886 Crescent Hotel & Spa ⊞
(479) 253-9766. **$169-$219, 3 day notice.** 75 Prospect Ave 72632. 1.3 mi n of jct SR 23 on US 62B Historic Loop. Int corridors. **Pets:** Medium. $25 daily fee/pet. ⓈⒶⓋⒺ ⊠ 🛏 🖵 ⑪ ⇌ ⊠

◈◈ ▼▼▼ 1905 Basin Park Hotel ⊞
(479) 253-7837. **$89-$149, 3 day notice.** 12 Spring St 72632. 0.7 mi n of jct US 62 via SR 23 N; downtown. Int corridors. **Pets:** Medium. $25 daily fee/pet. ⓈⒶⓋⒺ ⊠ 🛏 🖵 ⑪

▼▼▼▼ Arsenic & Old Lace B&B ⒝⒝ ❀
(479) 253-5454. **$139-$279, 15 day notice.** 60 Hillside Ave 72632. 1.2 mi n on SR 23, just sw; downtown. Ext/int corridors. **Pets:** Medium, dogs only. $30 one-time fee/room. Designated rooms, service with restrictions, crate. ⒜ⓈⓀ ⊠

▼▼▼ Bavarian Inn ⊞
(479) 253-8128. **$68-$130, 3 day notice.** 325 W Van Buren St 72632. 1 mi w of jct US 62 and SR 23. Ext corridors. **Pets:** Accepted.
⊠ 🛏 🖵 ⇌

◈◈ ▼▼▼ Best Western-Eureka Inn ⊞
(479) 253-9551. **$60-$120.** 101 E Van Buren St 72632. Just w of jct US 62 and SR 23 N. Ext/int corridors. **Pets:** Small, dogs only. $10 daily fee/pet. Designated rooms, service with restrictions, crate.
ⓈⒶⓋⒺ ⊠ 🛏 🖵 ⑪ ⇌ ⊠

◈◈ ▼▼▼ Best Western Inn of the Ozarks ⊞ ❀
(479) 253-9768. **$60-$200, 3 day notice.** 207 W Van Buren St 72632. 0.5 mi w of jct US 62 and SR 23. Ext corridors. **Pets:** Medium, dogs only. $10 daily fee/pet. Service with restrictions, supervision.
ⓈⒶⓋⒺ ⊠ 🛏 🖵 ⑪ ⇌ ⊠

▼▼▼ Brackenridge Lodge Ⓜ
(479) 253-6803. **$42-$149, 7 day notice.** 352 W Van Buren St 72632. 1 mi w of jct US 62 and SR 23. Ext corridors. **Pets:** Very small, dogs only. $25 deposit/room. Designated rooms, service with restrictions, supervision. ⒜ⓈⓀ ⊠ 🛏 🖵 ⇌ ⓩ

◈◈ ▼▼▼ Colonial Inn ⊞ ❀
(479) 253-7300. **$48-$150, 3 day notice.** 154 Huntsville Rd 72632. Just s of jct US 62 and SR 23. Ext/int corridors. **Pets:** Small. $10 daily fee/room. Service with restrictions, crate. ⓈⒶⓋⒺ ⊠ 🛏 🖵 ⇌

▼▼▼ Days Inn Ⓜ ❀
(479) 253-8863. **$54-$179, 3 day notice.** 120 W Van Buren St 72632. Just w of jct US 62 and SR 23. Ext corridors. **Pets:** Dogs only. $15 daily fee/room. Service with restrictions, supervision. ⒜ⓈⓀ ⊠ 🛏 🖵 ⇌

FAYETTEVILLE

◈◈ ▼▼▼ Best Western Windsor Suites ⊞
(479) 587-1400. **$72-$81.** 1122 S Futrall Dr 72701. I-540, exit 62, just se. Ext corridors. **Pets:** Medium, other species. $10 one-time fee/room. Designated rooms, service with restrictions. ⓈⒶⓋⒺ ⊠ 🛏 🖵 ⇌

▼▼▼ Sleep Inn by Choice Hotels ⊞
(479) 587-8700. **$60-$100.** 728 Millsap Rd 72703. I-540, exit 67, 1.6 mi e, then just s on US 71B. Int corridors. **Pets:** Other species. $25 one-time fee/room. Service with restrictions. ⒜ⓈⓀ ⊠ 🛏 🖵

FORDYCE

▼▼▼ Days Inn ⊞
(870) 352-2400. **$72-$105.** 2500 W 4th St 71742. US 79/167, 1 mi w. Ext/int corridors. **Pets:** Small. $10 daily fee/pet. Designated rooms, service with restrictions, supervision. ⊠ 🛏 🖵 ⇌

FORREST CITY

◈◈ ▼▼▼ Best Western Colony Inn ⊞
(870) 633-0870. **Call for rates.** 2333 N Washington St 72335. I-40, exit 241A, just s. Ext corridors. **Pets:** Accepted. ⓈⒶⓋⒺ ⊠ 🛏 🖵 ⇌

▼▼▼ Holiday Inn ⊞
(870) 633-6300. **$70-$100.** 200 Holiday Dr 72335. I-40, exit 241B, just n. Ext corridors. **Pets:** Small, other species. $15 one-time fee/room. Service with restrictions, supervision. ⒜ⓈⓀ ⊠ 🛏 🖵 ⑪ ⇌

FORT SMITH

▼▼▼ Aspen Hotel & Suites ⊞
(479) 452-9000. **Call for rates.** 2900 S 68th St 72903. I-540, exit 8B (Rogers Ave), just e. Int corridors. **Pets:** Accepted. ⊠ 🛏 🖵 ⇌

▼▼▼ Baymont Inn & Suites Fort Smith ⊞
(479) 484-5770. **Call for rates.** 2123 Burnham Rd 72903. I-540, exit 8A (Rogers Ave), just w. Int corridors. **Pets:** Accepted. ⊠ 🛏 🖵 ⇌

▼▼▼ Comfort Inn ⊞
(479) 484-0227. **$80-$110.** 2120 Burnham Rd 72903. I-540, exit 8A (Rogers Ave), just w. Int corridors. **Pets:** Accepted.
⒜ⓈⓀ ⊠ 🛏 🖵 ⇌ ⊠

◈◈ ▼▼▼ Courtyard by Marriott Downtown Fort Smith ⊞ ❀
(479) 783-2100. **$125-$153.** 900 Rogers Ave 72901. Just s of US 64 (Garrison Ave); downtown. Int corridors. **Pets:** Medium, other species. $75 one-time fee/room. Service with restrictions, crate.
ⓈⒶⓋⒺ ⊠ Ⓜ 🛏 🖵 ⑪ ⇌ ⊠

◈◈ ▼▼▼ GuestHouse Inn ⊞
(479) 646-5100. **$59-$72.** 3600 Grinnell Ave 72908. I-540, exit 12, 0.5 mi se. Int corridors. **Pets:** Very small, dogs only. $20 daily fee/pet. Service with restrictions, supervision. ⓈⒶⓋⒺ ⊠ 🛏 🖵 ⇌

◈◈ ▼▼▼▼ Holiday Inn City Center Fort Smith ⊞
(479) 783-1000. **Call for rates.** 700 Rogers Ave 72901. Just s of US 64 (Garrison Ave); downtown. Int corridors. **Pets:** Accepted.
ⓈⒶⓋⒺ ⊠ Ⓜ 🛏 🖵 ⑪ ⇌ ⊠

▼▼▼ Holiday Inn Express ⊞
(479) 452-7500. **Call for rates.** 6813 Phoenix Ave 72903. I-540, exit 8A (Rogers Ave), 0.6 mi e, then 0.5 mi s. Int corridors. **Pets:** Other species. $25 daily fee/pet. Designated rooms, service with restrictions, supervision.
⊠ 🛏 🖵 ⇌

▼▼▼ Residence Inn by Marriott ⊞
(479) 478-8300. **$116-$142.** 3005 S 74th St 72903. I-540, exit 8A (Rogers Ave), 0.8 mi e. Int corridors. **Pets:** Medium, other species. $75 one-time fee/room. Service with restrictions. ⊠ 🛏 🖵 ⇌ ⊠

GENTRY

▼▼▼▼ Apple Crest Inn Bed & Breakfast ⒝⒝
(479) 736-8201. **$89-$180, 14 day notice.** 12758 S Hwy 59 72734. On SR 59, 1 mi s. Int corridors. **Pets:** Accepted. ⒜ⓈⓀ ⊠

HARRISON

▼▼▼▼ Holiday Inn Express Hotel & Suites ⊞
(870) 741-3636. **$89-$125.** 117 Hwy 43 E 72601. Just e of jct US 62/65/412 and SR 43. Int corridors. **Pets:** Small. $25 daily fee/pet. Service with restrictions, supervision. ⒜ⓈⓀ ⊠ 🛏 🖵 ⇌ ⊠

▼▼▼ **Quality Inn** �H

(870) 741-7676. **Call for rates.** 1210 Hwy 62/65 N 72601. 1 mi n on US 62/65/412. Ext/int corridors. **Pets:** Small. $25 daily fee/pet. Service with restrictions, supervision. ⊠ 📧 🖵 ⋙

HOPE

🔷 ▼▼▼ **Best Western of Hope** �H

(870) 777-9222. **$86-$105.** 1800 Holiday Dr 71801. I-30, exit 30, just nw. Ext corridors. **Pets:** Other species. $10 daily fee/room. Service with restrictions, crate. SAVE ⊠ 📧 🖵 ⋙

HOT SPRINGS

▼▼▼ **Clarion Resort** �H

(501) 525-1391. **$85-$165.** 4813 Central Ave 71913. 5.5 mi s of jct US 270 and SR 7. Int corridors. **Pets:** Medium. $10 daily fee/room, $35 one-time fee/room. Designated rooms, service with restrictions, supervision.

ASK ⊠ 📧 🖵 🍴 ⋙ ⊠

🔷 ▼▼▼ **Embassy Suites Hot Springs-Hotel & Spa** �H ❀

(501) 624-9200. **$109-$259.** 400 Convention Blvd 71901. Just w of jct US 70. Int corridors. **Pets:** Large, other species. $35 daily fee/room. Service with restrictions, supervision.

SAVE ⊠ ⅃M 📧 🖵 🍴 ⋙ ⊠

🔷 ▼▼▼ **Staybridge Suites** �H

(501) 525-6500. **$89-$199.** 103 Lookout Cir 71913. 3.5 mi s of jct US 270 and SR 7. Int corridors. **Pets:** Medium, other species. $75 one-time fee/room. Supervision. SAVE ⊠ ⅃M 📧 🖵 ⋙

JONESBORO

▼▼ **Comfort Inn & Suites** �H

(870) 972-9000. **$65-$78.** 2911 Gilmore Dr 72401. US 63, exit Stadium Blvd/Caraway Rd, just n. Int corridors. **Pets:** Other species. $10 daily fee/room. Service with restrictions. ASK ⊠ 📧 🖵 ⋙

▼▼▼ **Holiday Inn of Jonesboro** �H 🐾

(870) 935-2030. **$72-$99.** 3006 S Caraway Dr 72401. US 63, exit Stadium Blvd/Caraway Rd, just n. Ext/int corridors. **Pets:** Medium. $15 daily fee/room. Service with restrictions, supervision.

ASK ⊠ 📧 🖵 🍴 ⋙ ⊠

LITTLE ROCK

▼▼ **Airport Travelodge** �H

(501) 490-2200. **$60-$69.** 7615 Fluid Dr 72206. I-440, exit 5, just n. Ext corridors. **Pets:** Other species. $10 daily fee/pet. No service, crate.

ASK ⊠ 📧 🖵

🔷 ▼▼▼ **Best Western Luxury Inn & Suites** �H

(501) 562-4448. **$80-$90.** 8219 I-30 72209. I-30, exit 133, just se on E Service Rd. Ext corridors. **Pets:** Accepted. SAVE ⊠ 📧 🖵 ⋙

🔷 ▼▼▼ **Comfort Inn & Suites, Downtown Little Rock @ The Clinton Library** �H

(501) 687-7700. **$79-$119.** 707 I-30 72202. I-30, exit 140A, just e. Int corridors. **Pets:** Medium. $25 one-time fee/room. Designated rooms, service with restrictions, supervision. SAVE ⊠ ⅃M 📧 🖵 ⋙

🔷 ▼▼▼ **Embassy Suites Hotel Little Rock** �H

(501) 312-9000. **$119-$219.** 11301 Financial Centre Pkwy 72211. Jct I-430 and 630, just w. Int corridors. **Pets:** Accepted.

SAVE ⊠ ⅃M 📧 🖵 🍴 ⋙ ⊠

🔷 ▼▼▼ **Hilton Little Rock Metro Center** �H ❀

(501) 664-5020. **$99-$199.** 925 S University Ave 72204. I-630, exit 5 (University Ave), just s. Int corridors. **Pets:** Medium. $75 one-time fee/room. Service with restrictions. SAVE ⊠ ⅃M 📧 🖵 🍴 ⋙

▼▼▼ **Holiday Inn Express Airport** �H

(501) 490-4000. **Call for rates.** 3121 Bankhead Dr 72206. I-440, exit 3, just s. Ext/int corridors. **Pets:** $25 one-time fee/room. Designated rooms, service with restrictions, supervision. ⊠ 📧 🖵 ⋙

▼▼▼ **Residence Inn by Marriott** �H

(501) 312-0200. **$130-$158.** 1401 S Shackleford Rd 72211. I-430, exit 5, just n. Int corridors. **Pets:** Medium, other species. $100 one-time fee/room. Service with restrictions. ⊠ 📧 🖵 ⋙ ⊠

LONOKE

🔷 ▼▼▼ **Days Inn** �H

(501) 676-5138. **$60-$75.** 105 Dee Dee Ln 72086. I-40, exit 175, just n. Ext corridors. **Pets:** Small. $10 one-time fee/pet. Designated rooms, service with restrictions, supervision. SAVE ⊠ 📧 🖵 ⋙

🔷 ▼▼▼ **Holiday Inn Express Hotel & Suites** �H

(501) 676-7800. **$104-$151.** 104 Dee Dee Ln 72086. I-40, exit 175, just n. Int corridors. **Pets:** Small, other species. $25 one-time fee/room. Designated rooms, service with restrictions, supervision.

SAVE ⊠ ⅃M 📧 🖵 ⋙

🔷 ▼▼▼ **Super 8** �H

(501) 676-8880. **$70-$80.** 102 Dee Dee Ln 72086. I-40, exit 175, just n. Int corridors. **Pets:** Medium. $10 daily fee/pet. Designated rooms, service with restrictions, supervision. SAVE ⊠ 📧 🖵 ⋙

MARION

🔷 ▼▼▼ **Best Western-Regency Motor Inn** �H

(870) 739-3278. **$60-$66.** 3635 I-55 72364. I-55, exit 10, just nw. Ext corridors. **Pets:** Accepted. SAVE ⊠ 📧 🖵 ⋙

MCGEHEE

🔷 ▼▼▼ **Best Western McGehee** 🅜

(870) 222-3564. **$71-$74.** 1202 Hwy 65 N 71654. Center. Ext corridors. **Pets:** Very small, dogs only. $5 daily fee/pet. Designated rooms, service with restrictions, supervision. SAVE ⊠ 📧 🖵 ⋙

MOUNTAIN HOME

🔷 ▼▼ **Comfort Inn** �H ❀

(870) 424-9000. **$70-$165.** 1031 Highland Cir 72653. 1.5 mi e on US 62B. Ext/int corridors. **Pets:** Small, dogs only. $25 one-time fee/room. Service with restrictions, supervision. SAVE ⊠ ⅃M 📧 🖵 ⋙

▼▼ **Days Inn** �H

(870) 425-1010. **$69-$77.** 1746 E Hwy 62B 72653. On US 62B, 2.3 mi e. Int corridors. **Pets:** Medium, other species. $8 one-time fee/pet. Service with restrictions, supervision. ASK ⊠ ⅃M 📧 🖵 ⋙

▼▼▼ **Holiday Inn Express** �H

(870) 425-6200. **$95-$115.** 1005 Coley Dr 72653. 1.4 mi e on US 62B. Int corridors. **Pets:** Accepted. ASK ⊠ ⅃M 📧 🖵 ⋙

▼ **Super 8-Mountain Home** 🅜

(870) 424-5600. **$65.** 865 Hwy 62 E 72653. On US 62B, 1.3 mi e. Int corridors. **Pets:** Small. $7 daily fee/pet. No service, supervision.

ASK ⊠ 📧 🖵

🔷 ▼▼▼ **Teal Point Resort** 🅒🅐

(870) 492-5145. **$75-$419, 45 day notice.** 715 Teal Point Rd 72653-7151. 7 mi e on US 62, 0.6 mi n on CR 406, follow signs. Ext corridors. **Pets:** $7 daily fee/pet. Designated rooms, service with restrictions, supervision. SAVE 📧 ⋙ ⊠ ▣

MOUNTAIN VIEW

🔷 ▼▼▼ **Best Western Fiddlers Inn** 🅜

(870) 269-2828. **$60-$111, 7 day notice.** 601 Sylomore Ave 72560. 1 mi n on SR 5, 9 and 14. Ext corridors. **Pets:** Small, dogs only. $10 daily fee/pet. Service with restrictions, crate. SAVE ⊠ 📧 🖵 ⋙

NORTH LITTLE ROCK

▼▼ **Comfort Inn** �H

(501) 955-9453. **Call for rates.** 5710 Pritchard Dr 72117. I-40, exit 157, just s. Int corridors. **Pets:** Accepted. ⊠ 📧 🖵 ⋙

▼▼▼ **Holiday Inn-North** H
(501) 758-1851. **$90-$99.** 120 W Pershing Blvd 72114. I-40, exit 152 westbound; exit 153A eastbound. Int corridors. **Pets:** Medium, other species. $30 one-time fee/room. Service with restrictions, supervision.
ASK ✕ 🛏 💻 🍴 ⟿

▼▼ **La Quinta Inn** H ❁
(501) 758-8888. **$55-$79.** 4100 E McCain Blvd 72117. Jct US 67/167, exit 1A northbound; exit 1 southbound. Ext corridors. **Pets:** Medium, other species. Service with restrictions, supervision. ASK ✕ 🛏 💻 ⟿

▼◆ **La Quinta Inn & Suites** H ❁
(501) 945-0808. **$69-$95.** 4311 Warden Rd 72116. US 67/167, exit 1B northbound; exit 1 southbound. Int corridors. **Pets:** Medium, other species. Service with restrictions, supervision. ASK ✕ 🛏 💻 ⟿

♦♦♦ ▼▼ **Red Roof Inn** H
(501) 945-0080. **$68-$85.** 5711 Pritchard Dr 72117. I-40, exit 157, just s. Int corridors. **Pets:** Large. Service with restrictions, crate.
SAVE ✕ ⟿

▼▼▼ **Residence Inn by Marriott-North** H
(501) 945-7777. **$135-$165.** 4110 Healthcare Dr 72117. I-40, exit 156. Int corridors. **Pets:** Accepted. ✕ 🛏 💻 ⟿ ✕

PINE BLUFF

♦♦♦ ▼▼▼ **Best Western Presidential Hotel** H
(870) 535-6300. **$70-$140.** 3104 Market St 71601. I-530, exit 46, just n. Int corridors. **Pets:** Accepted. SAVE ✕ 🛏 💻 ⟿

▼▼ **Days Inn & Suites** H
(870) 534-1800. **$64-$69.** 406 N Blake St 71601. Just n of jct US 65B and 79B. Ext corridors. **Pets:** Accepted. ASK ✕ 🛏 💻 ⟿

▼▼▼ **Holiday Inn Express Hotel & Suites** H
(870) 879-3800. **$94-$104.** 3620 Camden Rd 71603. I-530, exit 39, just sw. Int corridors. **Pets:** Small. $15 daily fee/pet. Service with restrictions, supervision. ASK ✕ �&M 🛏 💻 ⟿

POCAHONTAS

▼▼ **Days Inn & Suites** H
(870) 892-9500. **Call for rates.** 2805 Hwy 67 S 72455. 1.7 mi s. Int corridors. **Pets:** $25 deposit/room, $10 daily fee/pet. Service with restrictions, supervision. ✕ 🛏 💻 ⟿ ✕

ROGERS

♦♦♦ ▼▼▼ **aloft Rogers-Bentonville** H ❁
(479) 268-6799. **Call for rates.** 1103 S 52nd St 72758. I-540, exit 83, just nw. Int corridors. **Pets:** Medium. Designated rooms, service with restrictions, supervision. SAVE ✕ 🛏 💻 ⟿

▼▼ **Candlewood Suites** H ❁
(479) 636-2783. **$103-$132.** 4601 W Rozell St 72757. I-540, exit 85, 0.5 mi n on 46th St. Int corridors. **Pets:** Medium. $75 one-time fee/room. Service with restrictions, supervision. ASK ✕ 🛏 💻

♦♦♦ ▼▼▼ **Embassy Suites Northwest Arkansas** H ❁
(479) 254-8400. **$109-$259.** 3303 Pinnacle Hills Pkwy 72758. I-540, exit 83, just w, then 0.6 mi s. Int corridors. **Pets:** Medium, other species. $50 one-time fee/pet. Service with restrictions, crate.
SAVE ✕ �&M 🛏 💻 🍴 ⟿ ✕

◆ ▼▼ **Microtel Inn & Suites** H
(479) 636-5551. **$49-$89.** 909 S 8th St 72756. 0.5 mi s of jct Walnut St. Int corridors. **Pets:** Accepted. ASK ✕ 💻

▼▼▼ **Residence Inn by Marriott** H
(479) 636-5900. **$139-$169.** 4611 W Locust St 72756. I-540, exit 85, 0.4 mi n on 46th St. Int corridors. **Pets:** Medium. $75 one-time fee/room. Service with restrictions, crate. ✕ ⦵M 🛏 💻 ⟿ ✕

RUSSELLVILLE

▼▼ **Holiday Inn** H
(479) 968-4300. **$75-$79.** 2407 N Arkansas Ave 72801. I-40, exit 81, just s. Ext corridors. **Pets:** Accepted. ASK ✕ 🛏 💻 🍴 ⟿

▼▼ **Quality Inn** H
(479) 967-7500. **$65-$90.** 3019 E Parkway Dr 72802. I-40, exit 84, just s. Ext corridors. **Pets:** Accepted. ASK ✕ 🛏 💻 ⟿

SILOAM SPRINGS

▼▼ **Super 8** M
(479) 524-8898. **$63-$80.** 1800 Hwy 412 W 72761. Center. Ext corridors. **Pets:** Very small, dogs only. $25 daily fee/room. Service with restrictions, supervision. ASK ✕ 🛏 💻 ⟿

SPRINGDALE

♦♦♦ ▼▼▼ **Hampton Inn & Suites** H ❁
(479) 756-3500. **$79-$149.** 1500 S 48th St 72762. I-540, exit 72, just e. Int corridors. **Pets:** Service with restrictions, supervision.
SAVE ✕ ⦵M 🛏 💻 ⟿

▼◆▼ **Holiday Inn Northwest AR Hotel & Convention Center** H ❁
(479) 751-8300. **$89-$159.** 1500 S 48th St 72762. I-540, exit 72, just e. Int corridors. **Pets:** Medium, other species. $35 one-time fee/room. No service, supervision. ASK ✕ 🛏 💻 🍴 ⟿ ✕

▼▼▼ **La Quinta Inn & Suites** H ❁
(479) 751-2626. **Call for rates.** 1300 N 48th St 72764. I-540, exit 72, just e. Int corridors. **Pets:** Medium, other species. Service with restrictions, supervision. ✕ ⦵M 🛏 💻 ⟿ ✕

▼▼▼ **Residence Inn by Marriott** H
(479) 872-9100. **$125-$153.** 1740 S 48th St 72762. I-540, exit 72, just e to 48th St, then just s. Int corridors. **Pets:** Other species. $75 one-time fee/room. ✕ 🛏 💻 ⟿ ✕

STAR CITY

▼▼ **Star City Inn & Suites** H
(870) 628-6883. **$57-$95.** 1308 N Lincoln St 71667. Just n on US 425. Int corridors. **Pets:** Accepted. ASK ✕ 🛏 💻 ⟿

STUTTGART

♦♦♦ ▼▼ **Days Inn & Suites** H
(870) 673-3616. **$77-$150.** 708 W Michigan St 72160. Just w on US 63/79. Ext corridors. **Pets:** Medium. $10 daily fee/pet. Designated rooms, service with restrictions, supervision. SAVE ✕ 🛏 💻 ⟿

TEXARKANA

♦♦♦ ▼▼▼ **Clarion Hotel La Crosse** H
(870) 774-3521. **$109.** 5100 N State Line Ave 71854. I-30, exit 223B, just n. Int corridors. **Pets:** Small. $50 one-time fee/pet. Service with restrictions, supervision. SAVE ✕ 🛏 💻 🍴 ⟿ ✕

▼▼ **La Quinta Inn & Suites** H ❁
(870) 773-1000. **$79-$99.** 5102 N State Line Ave 71854. I-30, exit 223B, just n. Int corridors. **Pets:** Medium, other species. Service with restrictions, supervision. ASK ✕ 🛏 💻 ⟿

TRUMANN

▼▼ **Days Inn & Suites** H
(870) 483-8383. **Call for rates.** 400 Commerce Dr 72472. US 63, exit 29, just e. Ext/int corridors. **Pets:** Accepted. ✕ 🛏 💻 ⟿

VAN BUREN

♦♦♦ ▼▼ **Best Western Van Buren Inn** H
(479) 474-8100. **$75-$83.** 1903 N 6th St 72956. I-40, exit 5, just n. Ext corridors. **Pets:** Other species. $25 daily fee/pet. Service with restrictions.
SAVE ✕ 💻 ⟿

◆◆◆ Sleep Inn & Suites 🅷 ❀
(479) 262-6776. **$67-$77.** 1633 N 12th Ct 72956. 0.6 mi e of jct SR 59. Int corridors. **Pets:** Medium, other species. $15 daily fee/room.
(ASK) (✕) (&M) (🖹) (💻) (⤴)

WEST MEMPHIS

🅐🅐🅐 ◆◆ Best Western West Memphis Inn 🅷 ❀
(870) 735-7185. **$75-$105, 7 day notice.** 3401 Service Loop Rd 72301. I-55, exit 4, just nw. Int corridors. **Pets:** Small. Designated rooms, service with restrictions, supervision. (SAVE) (✕) (🖹) (💻) (⤴)

CALIFORNIA

CITY INDEX

ALTURAS

Best Western Trailside Inn

(530) 233-4111. **$90-$105.** 343 N Main St 96101. Just s of jct US 395/SR 299 and Main St; jct W 4th St; center. Ext corridors. **Pets:** Medium, dogs only. $10 one-time fee/pet. Designated rooms, service with restrictions, supervision.

Rim Rock Motel

(530) 233-5455. **$58-$75.** 22760 US 395 96101. Jct SR 299 and US 395, 0.7 mi ne on US 395. Ext corridors. **Pets:** Accepted.

ANAHEIM

Anabella Hotel

(714) 905-1050. **$109-$369, 3 day notice.** 1030 W Katella Ave 92802. I-5, exit 109 (Katella Ave/Disney Way) northbound; exit 109A (Katella Ave/Orangewood Ave) southbound, 1.2 mi w. Ext corridors. **Pets:** Medium, dogs only. $100 one-time fee/pet. Designated rooms, service with restrictions, crate.

Anaheim Plaza Hotel & Suites

(714) 772-5900. **$89-$218.** 1700 S Harbor Blvd 92802. I-5, exit 110 (Harbor Blvd/Ball Rd) northbound; exit 110A (Harbor Blvd) southbound, 0.6 mi s. Ext corridors. **Pets:** Medium. $10 daily fee/pet. Designated rooms, service with restrictions, supervision.

Clarion Hotel Anaheim Resort

(714) 750-3131. **$69-$239.** 616 Convention Way 92802. I-5, exit 109 (Katella Ave/Disney Way) northbound; exit 109A (Katella Ave/Orangewood Ave) southbound, 0.8 mi w to Harbor Blvd, just s, then just w. Int corridors. **Pets:** Medium. $25 deposit/pet, $10 daily fee/pet. Designated rooms, service with restrictions.

Embassy Suites Hotel Anaheim-North

(714) 632-1221. **$119-$249.** 3100 E Frontera St 92806. SR 91, exit 31 (Kramer Blvd/Glasset St) eastbound; exit 32 westbound just s, then just e. Int corridors. **Pets:** Medium, other species. $35 daily fee/pet. Designated rooms, service with restrictions.

Extended StayAmerica-Orange County-Anaheim Convention Center

(714) 502-9988. **$70-$100.** 1742 S Clementine St 92802. I-5, exit 109 (Katella Ave/Disney Way) northbound; exit 109A (Katella Ave/Orangewood Ave) southbound, just w, then just n. Int corridors. **Pets:** Other species. $25 daily fee/room. Designated rooms, service with restrictions, crate.

Hilton Anaheim

(714) 750-4321. **$99-$399.** 777 Convention Way 92802. I-5, exit 109 (Katella Ave/Disney Way) northbound; exit 109A (Katella Ave/Orangewood Ave) southbound, 0.8 mi w on Katella Ave, just s on Harbor Blvd, then just w. Int corridors. **Pets:** Medium. $75 one-time fee/room. Designated rooms, service with restrictions, supervision.

Hotel Menage

(714) 758-0900. **$129-$299.** 1221 S Harbor Blvd 92805. I-5, exit 110 (Harbor Blvd/Ball Rd) northbound; exit 110A (Harbor Blvd) southbound, just n. Ext corridors. **Pets:** Accepted.

La Quinta Inn & Suites

(714) 635-5000. **$59-$169.** 1752 S Clementine St 92802. I-5, exit 109 (Katella Ave/Disney Way) northbound; exit 109A (Katella Ave/Orangewood Ave) southbound, just w, then just n. Int corridors. **Pets:** Medium, other species. Service with restrictions, supervision.

Motel 6 Anaheim-Maingate #1066

(714) 520-9696. **$55-$85.** 100 W Disney Way 92802. I-5, exit 109 (Katella Ave/Disney Way) northbound; exit 109B (Disney Way/Anaheim Blvd) southbound, just w, just n on Anaheim Blvd, then just w. Ext corridors. **Pets:** Other species. Service with restrictions, supervision.

Red Lion Hotel Anaheim

(714) 750-2801. **$99-$250, 3 day notice.** 1850 S Harbor Blvd 92802. I-5, exit 109 (Katella Ave/Disney Way) northbound; exit 109A (Katella Ave/Orangewood Ave) southbound, 0.8 mi w, then just s. Int corridors. **Pets:** Other species. $20 one-time fee/room. Service with restrictions, supervision.

Residence Inn by Marriott Anaheim Maingate

(714) 533-3555. **$188-$230.** 1700 S Clementine St 92802. I-5, exit 109 (Katella Ave/Disney Way) northbound; exit 109A (Katella Ave/Orangewood Ave) southbound, just w on Katella Ave, then just n. Ext corridors. **Pets:** Accepted.

Sheraton Anaheim Hotel

(714) 778-1700. **$135-$275.** 900 S Disneyland Dr 92802. I-5, exit 110 (Harbor Blvd/Ball Rd) northbound; exit 110A (Harbor Blvd) southbound, just n, just w on Ball Rd, then just n. Int corridors. **Pets:** Large. $25 one-time fee/room. Service with restrictions.

Sheraton Park Hotel at the Anaheim Resort

(714) 750-1811. **$99-$284, 3 day notice.** 1855 S Harbor Blvd 92802. I-5, exit 109 (Katella Ave/Disney Way) northbound; exit 109A (Katella Ave/Orangewood Ave) southbound, 0.8 mi w, then just s. Int corridors. **Pets:** Medium, dogs only. Designated rooms, service with restrictions, supervision.

Staybridge Suites -Anaheim Resort

(714) 748-7700. **$95-$139.** 1855 S Manchester Ave 92802. I-5, exit 109 (Katella Ave/Disney Way) northbound; exit 109A (Katella Ave/Orangewood Ave) southbound, just w on Katella Ave, then 0.3 mi s; adjacent to west side of freeway. Int corridors. **Pets:** Accepted.

TownePlace Suites By Marriott

(714) 939-9700. **$116-$142.** 1730 S State College Blvd 92806. I-5, exit 109 (Katella Ave/Disney Way) northbound; exit 109A (Katella Ave/Orangewood Ave) southbound, 0.7 mi e, then just n. Int corridors. **Pets:** Accepted.

ANAHEIM HILLS

Best Western Anaheim Hills

(714) 779-0252. **$80.** 5710 E La Palma Ave 92807. SR 91, exit 36 (SR 90 W/Imperial Hwy), 0.3 mi n. Ext/int corridors. **Pets:** Medium. $15 daily fee/pet. Designated rooms, service with restrictions, supervision.

ANDERSON

Best Western Anderson Inn

(530) 365-2753. **$70-$100.** 2688 Gateway Dr 96007. I-5, exit 668 (Central Anderson) eastbound; exit Lassen Park westbound, just e. Ext corridors. **Pets:** Medium. $15 daily fee/pet. Service with restrictions, supervision.

Gaia Hotel Shasta, Woodside Grill Restaurant and Lotus Spa

(530) 365-7077. **Call for rates.** 4125 Riverside Pl 96007. I-5, exit 670 (Riverside Ave), just e. Ext corridors. **Pets:** Other species. $25 one-time fee/room. Designated rooms, service with restrictions.

ANGELS CAMP

Angels Inn Motel

(209) 736-4242. **$69-$189.** 600 N Main St 95221. On SR 49; north end of town. Ext corridors. **Pets:** Accepted.

Best Western Cedar Inn & Suites

(209) 736-4000. **$79-$199.** 444 S Main St 95222. On SR 49; center. Ext/int corridors. **Pets:** Accepted.

Gold Country Inn

(209) 736-4611. **$60-$190.** 720 S Main St 95222. 1 mi s of jct SR 49 and 4. Ext corridors. **Pets:** Other species. $10 daily fee/pet. Service with restrictions, supervision.

AAA **W** **Jumping Frog Motel** **M**

(209) 736-2191. **$60-$150, 3 day notice.** 330 Murphys Grade Rd 95222. Just e of jct SR 49; center. Ext corridors. **Pets:** Accepted.

SAVE ✕ 🐾 💻

APTOS

WW **Bayview Hotel** **CI**

(831) 688-8654. **$89-$269, 10 day notice.** 8041 Soquel Dr 95003. SR 1, exit State Park Dr E, 0.8 mi s. Int corridors. **Pets:** Accepted.

ASK ✕ 🍴

ARCATA

AAA **W** **Arcata Super 8** **H**

(707) 822-8888. **Call for rates.** 4887 Valley West Blvd 95521. US 101, exit Giuntoli Ln/Janes Rd, just e, then just s. Int corridors.
Pets: Accepted. SAVE ✕ 🐾 💻

AAA **WW** **Best Western Arcata Inn** **M** 🐾

(707) 826-0313. **$79-$169.** 4827 Valley West Blvd 95521. US 101, exit Giuntoli Ln/Janes Rd, just e, then just s. Ext corridors. **Pets:** Dogs only. $20 one-time fee/room. Designated rooms, service with restrictions, supervision. SAVE ✕ 🐾 💻 🏊

AAA **WW** **Comfort Inn** **M**

(707) 826-2827. **Call for rates.** 4701 Valley West Blvd 95521. US 101, exit Giuntoli Ln/Janes Rd, just e, then just s. Ext corridors.
Pets: Accepted. SAVE ✕ 🐾 🐾 💻 🏊

AAA **WW** **Days Inn** **H**

(707) 822-4861. **Call for rates.** 4975 Valley West Blvd 95521. US 101, exit Giuntoli Ln/Janes Rd, just e, then s. Int corridors. **Pets:** Accepted.

SAVE ✕ 💻 🍴 🏊

ARNOLD

AAA **WW** **Arnold Meadowmont Lodge** **M**

(209) 795-1394. **$59-$125.** 2011 Hwy 4 95223. On SR 4; west end of town. Ext corridors. **Pets:** Dogs only. $15 daily fee/pet. Designated rooms, service with restrictions, supervision. SAVE ✕ 🐾 🐾 💻 AC

ARROYO GRANDE

AAA **WW** **Premier Inns** **M**

(805) 481-4774. **$35-$120.** 555 Camino Mercado 93420. US 101, exit 188 (Oak Park Rd), just e, then 0.3 mi s. Ext corridors. **Pets:** Accepted.

SAVE ✕ 🐾 🏊

AUBURN

AAA **WWW** **Best Western Golden Key** **H** 🐾

(530) 885-8611. **$85-$160.** 13450 Lincoln Way 95603. I-80, exit 121 (Foresthill-Auburn Ravine rds), just e, then n. Ext corridors. **Pets:** $15 one-time fee/pet. Designated rooms, service with restrictions, crate.

SAVE ✕ 🐾 🐾 🏊

AAA **W** **Foothills Motel** **M**

(530) 885-8444. **$65-$98.** 13431 Bowman Rd 95603. I-80, exit 121 (Foresthill-Auburn Ravine rds), just w, then just n. Ext corridors.
Pets: Dogs only. $50 deposit/room, $10 daily fee/pet. Designated rooms, service with restrictions, supervision. SAVE ✕ 🐾 🐾 🏊

WWW **Holiday Inn-Auburn** **H**

(530) 887-8787. **$119-$169.** 120 Grass Valley Hwy 95603. I-80, exit SR 49, just nw. Int corridors. **Pets:** Small, dogs only. $20 one-time fee/pet. Designated rooms, service with restrictions, supervision.

ECO ASK ✕ 🐾 🐾 💻 🍴 🏊

W **Motel 6 #4152** **M**

(530) 888-7829. **Call for rates.** 1819 Auburn Ravine Rd 95603. I-80, exit 121 (Foresthill-Auburn Ravine rds), just w. Int corridors. **Pets:** Other species. Service with restrictions, supervision. ✕ 🐾 🐾 🏊

AAA **WW** **Quality Inn** **M**

(530) 885-7025. **$90-$125.** 13490 Lincoln Way 95603. I-80, exit 121 (Foresthill-Auburn Ravine rds), just e, then just n. Ext/int corridors.
Pets: Small, dogs only. $15 daily fee/pet. Designated rooms, service with restrictions, supervision. SAVE ✕ 🐾 🐾 💻 🏊

AVILA BEACH

WWW **Avila Village Inn** **H**

(805) 627-1810. **$119-$399.** 6655 Bay Laurel Dr 93424. US 101, exit 195 (Avila Beach Dr), 1.2 mi w to San Luis Bay Dr, just n, then just w. Int corridors. **Pets:** Medium. $25 daily fee/room. Designated rooms, service with restrictions, supervision. ASK ✕ 🐾 🐾 💻

BAKERSFIELD

WWW **Bakersfield Red Lion Hotel** **H**

(661) 327-0681. **$99-$139.** 2400 Camino Del Rio Ct 93308. SR 99, exit 26 (SR 58 W/Rosedale Hwy), just w, then just s. Ext/int corridors.
Pets: Other species. $20 one-time fee/room. Service with restrictions, supervision. ASK ✕ 🐾 🐾 💻 🍴 🏊

AAA **WWW** **Best Western Crystal Palace Inn & Suites** **H**

(661) 327-9651. **$73-$86.** 2620 Buck Owens Blvd 93308. SR 99, exit 26B (Buck Owens Blvd) northbound, just s; exit 26 (SR 58 W/SR 178 E) southbound, just e, then just n. Int corridors. **Pets:** Accepted.

SAVE ✕ 🐾 🐾 💻 🍴 🏊

AAA **WWW** **Best Western Heritage Inn** **M**

(661) 764-6268. **$90-$120.** 253 Trask St 93314. I-5, exit 253 (Stockdale Hwy), just e. Ext corridors. **Pets:** Accepted.

SAVE ✕ 🐾 🐾 💻 🏊

AAA **WWW** **Best Western Hill House** **H** 🐾

(661) 327-4064. **$79-$139.** 700 Truxton Ave 93301. SR 99, exit 25 (California Ave), 1.2 mi e, 0.4 mi n on Chester Ave, then 0.4 mi e. Int corridors. **Pets:** Medium. $10 daily fee/pet. Service with restrictions, supervision. SAVE ✕ 🐾 🐾 💻 🍴 🏊

AAA **WWW** **California Best Inn** **M**

(661) 834-3377. **$55-$65.** 1030 Wible Rd 93304. SR 99, exit 23 (Ming Ave), just e, then 0.7 mi n. Ext corridors. **Pets:** Medium. $10 daily fee/pet. Service with restrictions, supervision. SAVE ✕ 🐾 🐾 💻 🏊

WWW **Doubletree Hotel Bakersfield** **H**

(661) 323-7111. **$85-$199.** 3100 Camino Del Rio Ct 93308. SR 99, exit 26 (SR 58 W/Rosedale Hwy), just w, then just s. Int corridors.
Pets: Other species. $50 one-time fee/room. Service with restrictions, supervision. ECO ✕ 🐾 🐾 💻 🍴 🏊

WW **Extended StayAmerica-Bakersfield-California Avenue** **H**

(661) 322-6888. **$50-$65.** 3318 California Ave 93304. SR 99, exit 25 (California Ave), on east side of freeway, just n. Int corridors. **Pets:** Other species. $25 daily fee/room. Designated rooms, service with restrictions, crate. ASK ✕ 🐾 🐾 💻

WWW **Extended Stay Deluxe Bakersfield-Chester Lane** **H**

(661) 328-8181. **$80-$100.** 3600 Chester Ln 93309. SR 99, exit 25 (California Ave), just w to Real Rd, just s, then just w. Int corridors.
Pets: Other species. $25 daily fee/room. Designated rooms, service with restrictions, crate. ASK ✕ 🐾 🐾 💻

AAA **WWW** **Garden Suites Inn** **H**

(661) 833-6066. **$55-$60.** 2310 Wible Rd 93304. SR 99, exit Ming Ave, just e. Int corridors. **Pets:** Medium. $10 one-time fee/room. Supervision.

SAVE ✕ 🐾 🐾 💻

AAA **WWW** **Howard Johnson Inn** **H**

(661) 396-1425. **$64.** 2700 White Ln 93304. SR 99, exit 21 (White Ln), just e. Ext corridors. **Pets:** Other species. $5 daily fee/pet. Service with restrictions, supervision. SAVE ✕ 🐾 🐾 💻 🏊

⏚ ▼▼▼▼ La Quinta Inn & Suites 🅷 🐾

(661) 393-7775. **$79-$160.** 8858 Spectrum Park Way 93308. SR 99, exit 30 (SR 65) northbound, just e to Merle Haggard Dr, just n to Spectrum Park Way, then just w; exit 31 (7th Standard Rd) southbound, just e, then just s. Int corridors. **Pets:** Medium, other species. Service with restrictions, supervision. (SAVE) ⊠ 🗡ᴹ 🛢 💻 🏊

▼▼▼▼ La Quinta Inn Bakersfield 🅼 🐾

(661) 325-7400. **$49-$119.** 3232 Riverside Dr 93308. SR 99, exit 26B (SR 58 W/Rosedale Hwy) southbound, just e, then just n; exit 26B (Buck Owens Blvd) northbound, just s. Ext corridors. **Pets:** Medium, other species. Service with restrictions, supervision. (ASK) ⊠ 🗡ᴹ 🛢 💻 🏊

⏚ ▼▼▼ Ramada Limited-Central 🅼 🐾

(661) 831-1922. **$59-$199.** 830 Wible Rd 93304. SR 99, exit 23 (Ming Ave), just e, then 0.8 mi n. Ext corridors. **Pets:** Medium. $10 daily fee/pet. Service with restrictions, supervision. (SAVE) ⊠ 🛢 💻 🏊

▼▼▼▼ Residence Inn by Marriott 🅷

(661) 321-9800. **$152-$186.** 4241 Chester Ln 93309. SR 99, exit 25 (California Ave), 0.5 mi w, then just n. Ext corridors. **Pets:** Accepted. ⊠ 🛢 💻 🏊 ⊠

⏚ ▼▼ Rodeway Inn 🅼

(661) 764-5221. **$65-$75.** 200 Trask St 93314. I-5, exit 253 (Stockdale Hwy), just e. Ext corridors. **Pets:** Accepted. (SAVE) ⊠ 🛢 💻 🏊

⏚ ▼▼ Sleep Inn 🅷

(661) 399-2100. **$69-$169.** 6257 Knudson Dr 93308. SR 99, exit 28 (Olive Dr), just w, then just n. Int corridors. **Pets:** $10 daily fee/pet. Service with restrictions, crate. (SAVE) ⊠ 🗡ᴹ 🛢 💻

⏚ ▼▼ Super 8 🅼

(661) 833-1000. **$55-$85.** 3620 Wible Rd 93309. SR 99, exit 21 (White Ln), just w, then 0.3 mi n. Ext corridors. **Pets:** Small, other species. $5 daily fee/pet. Service with restrictions, supervision. (SAVE) ⊠ 🛢 💻 🏊

⏚ ▼▼ Super 8 Bakersfield 🅼

(661) 322-1012. **$65-$85.** 901 Real Rd 93309. SR 99, exit 25 (California Ave), just w, then just s. Ext corridors. **Pets:** Small. $25 daily fee/pet. Designated rooms, service, supervision. (SAVE) ⊠ 🛢 💻 🏊

⏚ ▼▼ Travelodge of Bakersfield 🅼

(661) 325-0772. **$57-$69.** 1011 Oak St 93304. SR 99, exit 25 (California Ave), just e, then just s. Ext/int corridors. **Pets:** Other species. $10 one-time fee/pet. Designated rooms. (ASK) ⊠ 🛢 💻 🏊

⏚ ▼▼ Vagabond Inn South 🅼

(661) 831-9200. **$45-$65.** 6501 Colony St 93307. SR 99, exit 20 (Panama Ln), just e, then just s. Ext corridors. **Pets:** Accepted. (ASK) ⊠ 🛢 💻 🏊

BANNING

⏚ ▼▼▼ Banning Travelodge 🅼

(951) 849-1000. **$66-$299.** 1700 W Ramsey St 92220. I-10, exit 99 (22nd St), just n, then 0.5 mi e. Ext corridors. **Pets:** Dogs only. $10 daily fee/pet. Designated rooms, service with restrictions, supervision. (SAVE) ⊠ 🛢 💻 🏊

⏚ ▼▼ Days Inn 🅼

(951) 849-0092. **$65-$200.** 2320 W Ramsey St 92220. I-10, exit 99 (22nd St), just n, then just w. Ext corridors. **Pets:** Medium. $10 daily fee/pet. Service with restrictions, supervision. (SAVE) ⊠ 🛢 💻

▼▼▼▼ Hampton Inn & Suites 🅷

(951) 922-1000. **$89-$149.** 6071 Joshua Palmer Way 92220. I-10, exit 96 (Highland Springs Ave), just n, then just e. Int corridors. **Pets:** Medium. $25 one-time fee/pet. Service with restrictions, supervision. ⊠ 🛢 💻 🏊

⏚ ▼▼ Super 8 🅼

(951) 849-8888. **$60-$300.** 1690 W Ramsey St 92220. I-10, exit 99 (22nd St), just n, then 0.4 mi e. Int corridors. **Pets:** Dogs only. $10 daily fee/pet. Designated rooms, service with restrictions, supervision. (SAVE) ⊠ 🛢 💻

BARSTOW

▼▼ Barstow-Super 8 🅼

(760) 256-8443. **$72-$77.** 170 Coolwater Ln 92311. I-15, exit 184B (E Main St) northbound; exit 184 (E Main St/I-40 E/Needles) southbound, 0.3 mi w, then just s; I-40 westbound, exit 1 (E Main St), 0.7 mi w, then just s. Ext corridors. **Pets:** Other species. $10 daily fee/pet. Service with restrictions, supervision. (ASK) ⊠ 🛢 💻 🏊

⏚ ▼▼▼ Best Western Desert Villa Inn 🅼

(760) 256-1781. **$73-$130.** 1984 E Main St 92311. I-15, exit 184B (E Main St) northbound; exit 184 (E Main St/I-40/Needles) southbound, 0.5 mi e; I-40, exit 1 (E Main St) westbound, just w. Ext corridors. **Pets:** Other species. $15 daily fee/pet. Service with restrictions, supervision. (SAVE) ⊠ 🗡ᴹ 🛢 💻 🏊

▼▼▼ Comfort Suites 🅷

(760) 253-3600. **$89-$199.** 2571 Fisher Blvd 92311. I-15, exit 178 (Lenwood Rd), just ne; n of Barstow Outlets. Int corridors. **Pets:** Medium. $25 one-time fee/room. Service with restrictions, supervision. (ASK) ⊠ 🗡ᴹ 🛢 💻 🏊

⏚ ▼▼▼ Days Inn South at Lenwood 🅼

(760) 253-2121. **$70-$90.** 2551 Commerce Pkwy 92311. I-15, exit 178 (Lenwood Rd), just w; 8 mi s of town. Ext corridors. **Pets:** Accepted. (SAVE) ⊠ 🛢 💻 🏊

▼▼▼ Hampton Inn & Suites 🅷

(760) 253-2600. **$99-$209.** 2710 Lenwood Rd 92311. I-15, exit 178 (Lenwood Rd), just e, then 0.4 mi s. Int corridors. **Pets:** Accepted. ⊠ 🗡ᴹ 🛢 💻 🏊

▼▼▼ Holiday Inn Express, Barstow-Historic Route 66 🅷

(760) 256-1300. **$84-$129.** 1861 W Main St 92311. I-15, exit 181 (L St), 0.5 mi n, then just e. Int corridors. **Pets:** Other species. $25 one-time fee/room. No service, supervision. (ASK) ⊠ 🛢 💻 🏊

▼▼▼ Holiday Inn Express Hotel & Suites 🅷

(760) 253-9200. **$155-$202.** 2700 Lenwood Rd 92311. I-15, exit 178 (Lenwood Rd), just e, then 0.5 mi s. Int corridors. **Pets:** Accepted. (ASK) ⊠ 🗡ᴹ 🛢 💻 🏊 ⊠

▼▼ Motel 6 Barstow #1355 🅼

(760) 256-1752. **$45-$55.** 150 N Yucca Ave 92311. I-15, exit 184B (E Main St) northbound; exit 184 (E Main St/I-40 E/Needles) southbound, 0.5 mi w, then just n; I-40, exit 1 (E Main St) westbound, 1 mi w, then just n. Ext corridors. **Pets:** Other species. Service with restrictions, supervision. ⊠ 🏊

▼▼ Quality Inn 🅼 🐾

(760) 256-6891. **$75-$129.** 1520 E Main St 92311. I-15, exit 184B (E Main St) northbound; exit 184 (E Main St/I-40 E/Needles) southbound, 0.3 mi w; I-40, exit 1 (E Main St) westbound, 0.8 mi w. Ext corridors. **Pets:** Small, dogs only. $10 one-time fee/room. Designated rooms, service with restrictions. (ASK) ⊠ 🛢 💻 🍴 🏊

⏚ ▼▼▼ Ramada Inn 🅷

(760) 256-5673. **$95-$120.** 1511 E Main St 92311. I-15, exit 184B (E Main St) northbound; exit 184 (E Main St/I-40 E/Needles) southbound, 0.3 mi w; I-40, exit 1 (E Main St) westbound, 0.8 mi w. Int corridors. **Pets:** Medium. $20 one-time fee/room. Service with restrictions, supervision. (SAVE) ⊠ 🛢 💻 🍴 🏊

⏚ ▼▼▼ Rodeway Inn 🅼

(760) 256-7581. **$43-$80.** 1261 E Main St 92311. I-15, exit 184B (E Main St) northbound; exit 184 (E Main St/I-40 E/Needles) southbound, 0.8 mi w; I-40, exit 1 (E Main St) westbound, 1.3 mi w. Ext corridors. **Pets:** Medium, dogs only. $10 daily fee/room, $25 one-time fee/room. Designated rooms, service with restrictions, supervision. (SAVE) ⊠ 🛢 💻 🏊

AAA ▼ Stardust Inn M
(760) 256-7116. **$40-$60.** 901 E Main St 92311. I-15, exit 183 (Barstow Rd), 0.8 mi n, then 0.4 mi e. Ext corridors. **Pets:** Small, dogs only. $5 daily fee/pet. Designated rooms, service with restrictions, crate.
[SAVE] [X] [▮] [▰]

AAA ▼ Travelodge M
(760) 256-8931. **$55-$85.** 1630 E Main St 92311. I-15, exit 184B (E Main St) northbound; exit 184 (E Main St/I-40 E/Needles) southbound, just e; I-40 westbound, exit 1 (E Main St), just w. Ext corridors. **Pets:** $8 daily fee/pet. Service with restrictions, supervision. [SAVE] [X] [▮] [▰]

BASS LAKE

▼▼ The Pines Resort Chalets CA
(559) 642-3121. **$119-$369, 7 day notice.** 54432 Rd 432 93604. 6 mi e of SR 41, exit CR 222, e on CR 274, then s on CR 434. Ext corridors. **Pets:** Accepted. [ASK] [X] [▮] [▰] [▯] [▰] [X]

BEAUMONT

AAA ▼ Americas Best Value Inn M
(951) 845-2185. **$70-$199.** 625 E 5th St 92223. I-10, exit 94 (SR 79/Beaumont Ave), just n. Ext corridors. **Pets:** Large. $5 daily fee/pet. Service with restrictions, supervision. [SAVE] [X] [▮] [▰]

AAA ▼▼ Best Western El Rancho Motor Inn M ❖
(951) 845-2176. **$90-$107.** 480 E 5th St 92223. I-10, exit 94 (SR 79/Beaumont Ave), just n, then just e. Ext corridors. **Pets:** Medium. $25 daily fee/pet. Designated rooms, service with restrictions, supervision.
[SAVE] [X] [▮] [▰] [▯] [▰]

AAA ▼ Rodeway Inn M
(951) 845-1436. **$66-$299.** 1265 E 6th St 92223. I-10, exit 94 (SR 79/Beaumont Ave), just n, 0.3 mi w. Ext corridors. **Pets:** Medium, dogs only. $10 daily fee/pet. Service with restrictions, supervision.
[SAVE] [X] [▮] [▰] [▰]

BENICIA

AAA ▼▼ Best Western Heritage Inn H ❖
(707) 746-0401. **$120-$150.** 1955 E 2nd St 94510. I-780, exit Central Benicia/E 2nd St, just e. Int corridors. **Pets:** Medium. $25 one-time fee/pet. Service with restrictions, supervision. [SAVE] [X] [▮] [▰] [▰]

BEN LOMOND

AAA ▼▼ Quality Inn & Suites Santa Cruz Mountains M
(831) 336-2292. **$70-$260, 7 day notice.** 9733 Hwy 9 95005. SR 9, 0.3 mi n; on San Lorenzo River. Ext corridors. **Pets:** Accepted.
[SAVE] [X] [▮] [▰] [▰]

BERKELEY

AAA ▼ Best Value Golden Bear Inn M
(510) 525-6770. **$80-$160.** 1620 San Pablo Ave 94702. I-80, exit 12 (Gilman St), 0.5 mi e, then just s. Ext corridors. **Pets:** Accepted.
[SAVE] [X] [▮] [▰] [▯]

AAA ▼▼▼ Claremont Resort and Spa H
(510) 843-3000. **$169-$389.** 41 Tunnel Rd 94705. SR 13 and 24 eastbound, exit SR 24 (Claremont Ave), 1 mi n; I-80, exit 11 (University Ave E), just e, then 1.5 mi s on San Pablo Ave, 2.6 mi e on Ashby Ave, then just e; in Berkeley Hills. Int corridors. **Pets:** Accepted.
[SAVE] [X] [▮] [▰] [▰] [X]

AAA ▼▼▼ Doubletree Hotel and Executive Meeting Center Berkeley Marina H
(510) 548-7920. **$119-$229.** 200 Marina Blvd 94710. I-80, exit 11 (University Ave), 0.5 mi w; on Berkeley Marina. Int corridors. **Pets:** Accepted.
[ECO] [SAVE] [X] [▮] [▰] [▰] [X]

AAA ▼▼▼ Hotel Durant, a Joie de Vivre hotel H ❖
(510) 845-8981. **$135-$445.** 2600 Durant Ave 94704. I-80, exit 11 (University Ave), 2 mi e to Oxford St, 0.3 mi s, then 0.5 mi e; jct Bowditch St. Int corridors. **Pets:** Medium. Service with restrictions, supervision.
[ECO] [SAVE] [X] [▰] [▰]

BIG BEAR LAKE

▼▼ Bear Manor Cabins CA
(909) 866-6800. **Call for rates.** 40393 Big Bear Blvd 92315. SR 18, 0.8 mi w of village. Ext corridors. **Pets:** Small, dogs only. $150 deposit/room. Designated rooms, no service, supervision. [X] [▮] [▰] [X]

AAA ▼▼▼ Best Western Big Bear Chateau H
(909) 866-6666. **$139-$399.** 42200 Moonridge Rd 92315. SR 18, 1.5 mi e of Pine Knot Ave, 0.5 mi s. Int corridors. **Pets:** Accepted.
[SAVE] [X] [▮] [▰] [▯] [▰] [X] [X]

AAA ▼▼ Cozy Hollow Lodge CA
(909) 866-9694. **$59-$299, 15 day notice.** 40409 Big Bear Blvd 92315. SR 18, 0.8 mi w. Ext corridors. **Pets:** Medium, dogs only. $100 deposit/room, $10 daily fee/room, $25 one-time fee/room. Designated rooms, no service, supervision. [SAVE] [X] [▮] [▰] [X]

▼▼ Eagle's Nest Bed & Breakfast BB ❖
(909) 866-6465. **$120-$185, 5 day notice.** 41675 Big Bear Blvd 92315. SR 18, 1 mi e of Pine Knot Ave. Ext/int corridors. **Pets:** Other species. $10 daily fee/pet. Designated rooms, service with restrictions, crate.
[ASK] [X] [▮] [▰]

AAA ▼▼▼ Golden Bear Cottages CA ❖
(909) 866-2010. **$99-$799, 90 day notice.** 39367 Big Bear Blvd 92315. SR 18, 2 mi w of village. Ext corridors. **Pets:** Large, other species. $10 one-time fee/pet. Designated rooms, service with restrictions, crate.
[SAVE] [X] [▮] [▰] [▰] [X] [X]

AAA ▼▼▼ Grey Squirrel Resort CA
(909) 866-4335. **$94, 14 day notice.** 39372 Big Bear Blvd 92315. SR 18, 2.5 mi w of village. Ext corridors. **Pets:** Other species. $10 daily fee/pet. Designated rooms, no service, crate.
[SAVE] [X] [▮] [▰] [▰] [X] [X]

▼▼ Pine Knot Guest Ranch CA ❖
(909) 866-6500. **$99-$199.** 908 Pine Knot Ave 92315. Just s of SR 18 and downtown area. Ext corridors. **Pets:** Other species. $10 daily fee/pet. Service with restrictions. [ASK] [X] [▮] [▰]

▼▼ Sleepy Forest Cottages CA
(909) 866-7444. **$99-$299, 15 day notice.** 426 Eureka Dr 92315. SR 18, 0.7 mi e of Pine Knot Ave, then just n. Ext corridors. **Pets:** Dogs only. $25 daily fee/room. Designated rooms, service with restrictions, supervision. [ASK] [X] [▮] [▰] [X]

AAA ▼▼ Timber Haven Lodge CA ❖
(909) 866-7207. **$109-$320, 7 day notice.** 877 Tulip Ln 92315. SR 18, 1.8 mi w of Pine Knot Ave, 0.4 mi s. Ext corridors. **Pets:** Medium, dogs only. $20 daily fee/pet. Designated rooms, service with restrictions, supervision. [SAVE] [X] [▮] [▰] [X] [X]

BIG PINE

▼▼ Big Pine Motel M
(760) 938-2282. **Call for rates.** 370 S Main St 93513. On US 395. Ext corridors. **Pets:** Accepted. [X] [▮] [▰]

AAA ▼▼ Bristlecone Motel M ❖
(760) 938-2067. **$55-$80.** 101 N Main St 93513. On US 395. Ext corridors. **Pets:** Other species. Service with restrictions, supervision.
[SAVE] [X] [▮] [▰]

BISHOP

AAA ▼▼▼ Americas Best Value Inn M
(760) 873-4912. **$80-$200.** 192 Short St 93514. US 395 to Short St, just e. Ext corridors. **Pets:** $10 daily fee/pet. Designated rooms, service with restrictions, supervision. [SAVE] [X] [▮] [▰] [▰]

AAA ▼▼▼ Best Western Bishop Holiday Spa Lodge M ❖
(760) 873-3543. **$90-$300.** 1025 N Main St 93514. On US 395. Ext corridors. **Pets:** Other species. $15 daily fee/room. Designated rooms, service with restrictions, supervision. [SAVE] [X] [▮] [▰] [▰] [▰]

AAA ▼▼▼ Comfort Inn M
(760) 873-4284. **$77-$129.** 805 N Main St 93514. On US 395. Ext corridors. **Pets:** Accepted. SAVE ✕ ⬛M 🛏 💻 ⊃

AAA ▼▼▼ Holiday Inn Express Hotel & Suites H
(760) 872-2423. **$109-$279.** 636 N Main St 93514. On US 395. Int corridors. **Pets:** Medium, dogs only. $25 daily fee/pet. Designated rooms, service with restrictions, supervision.
SAVE ✕ ⬛M 🛏 💻 ⊃ ✕

▼▼▼ La Quinta Inn-Bishop H 🐾
(760) 873-6380. **$70-$280.** 651 N Main St 93514. On US 395. Int corridors. **Pets:** Medium, other species. Service with restrictions, supervision.
ASK ✕ ⬛M 🛏 💻

▼▼ Motel 6–#4094 M
(760) 873-8426. **$65-$180.** 1005 N Main St 93514. On US 395. Ext corridors. **Pets:** Other species. Service with restrictions, supervision.
ASK ✕ ⬛M 🛏 ⊃

AAA ▼▼▼ Ramada Limited M 🐾
(760) 872-1771. **$80-$165.** 155 E Elm St 93514. On US 395, just e. Ext corridors. **Pets:** Medium. $15 daily fee/pet. Designated rooms, service with restrictions, supervision. SAVE ✕ ⬛M 🛏 💻 ⊃

▼▼ Super 8 M
(760) 872-1386. **Call for rates.** 535 S Main St 93514. On US 395. Ext corridors. **Pets:** Accepted. ✕ 🛏 💻 ⊃

▼▼ Thunderbird Motel M
(760) 873-4215. **Call for rates.** 190 W Pine St 93514. Just w of US 395. Ext corridors. **Pets:** Accepted. ✕ 🛏 💻

AAA ▼▼▼ Vagabond Inn M 🐾
(760) 873-6351. **$80-$195.** 1030 N Main St 93514. On US 395. Ext corridors. **Pets:** Medium. $15 daily fee/pet. Designated rooms, no service, supervision. SAVE ✕ ⬛M 🛏 💻 ⊃

BLYTHE

AAA ▼▼ Best Western Sahara Motel M 🐾
(760) 922-7105. **$99-$169.** 825 W Hobsonway 92225. I-10, exit 239 (Lovekin Blvd), just n, then just w. Ext corridors. **Pets:** Small. $10 one-time fee/room. Service with restrictions, supervision.
SAVE ✕ 🛏 💻 ⊃

AAA ▼▼ Days Inn M
(760) 922-5101. **$69-$179.** 9274 E Hobsonway 92225. I-10, exit 239 (Intake Blvd), just n, then just w. Ext corridors. **Pets:** Accepted.
SAVE ✕ 🛏 💻 ⊃

▼▼ Regency Inn & Suites M
(760) 922-4146. **$65-$169.** 903 W Hobsonway 92225. I-10, exit 239 (Lovekin Blvd), just n, then just w. Ext corridors. **Pets:** Small. $10 daily fee/pet. Service with restrictions, supervision. ASK ✕ 🛏 💻 ⊃

AAA ▼▼ Super 8 M
(760) 922-8881. **$70-$140.** 550 W Donlon St 92225. I-10, exit 239 (Lovekin Blvd), just e. Int corridors. **Pets:** Medium, other species. $10 daily fee/pet. Service with restrictions, supervision.
SAVE ✕ 🛏 💻 ⊃

BORREGO SPRINGS

AAA ▼▼▼ Borrego Springs Resort Hotel H
(760) 767-5700. **$89-$175.** 1112 Tilting T Dr 92004. SR 22, 1.5 mi s on Borrego Valley Rd, just w. Int corridors. **Pets:** Small, dogs only. $20 daily fee/pet. Designated rooms, service with restrictions, crate.
SAVE ✕ 🛏 💻 🍴 ✕

▼▼ Palm Canyon Resort M
(760) 767-5341. **Call for rates.** 221 Palm Canyon Dr 92004. 1.5 mi w on CR S-22. Ext corridors. **Pets:** Accepted. ✕ 🛏 💻 🍴 ⊃

BRAWLEY

AAA ▼▼▼ Best Western Main Street Inn M
(760) 351-9800. **$110-$140.** 1562 E Main St 92227. On SR 78. Int corridors. **Pets:** Accepted. SAVE ✕ 🛏 💻 ⊃

BREA

AAA ▼▼▼ Chase Suite Hotels M
(714) 579-3200. **$129-$299.** 3100 E Imperial Hwy 92821. SR 57, exit 9 (SR 90), 1.5 mi e on Imperial Hwy. Ext corridors. **Pets:** Accepted.
SAVE ✕ 🛏 💻 ⊃

▼▼ Homestead Studio Suites Hotel-Orange County-Brea M
(714) 528-2500. **$65.** 3050 E Imperial Hwy 92821. SR 57, exit 9 (SR 90), 1.4 mi e on Imperial Hwy. Ext corridors. **Pets:** Other species. $25 daily fee/room. Designated rooms, service with restrictions, crate.
ASK ✕ 🛏 💻

BRIDGEPORT

AAA ▼▼▼ Redwood Motel M 🐾
(760) 932-7060. **$59-$250.** 425 Main St 93517. On US 395; on north side of town. Ext corridors. **Pets:** Large. $10 daily fee/pet. Designated rooms, service with restrictions, supervision. SAVE ✕ 🛏 💻

AAA ▼▼ Ruby Inn M
(760) 932-7241. **$125-$200.** 333 Main St 93517. On US 395; center. Ext corridors. **Pets:** Medium, dogs only. Service with restrictions, supervision.
SAVE ✕ 💻

AAA ▼▼ Silver Maple Inn M
(760) 932-7383. **$80-$140.** 310 Main St 93517. On US 395; center. Ext corridors. **Pets:** Other species. Supervision. SAVE ✕ 🛏 💻 📷

AAA ▼▼ Walker River Lodge M
(760) 932-7021. **$85-$220.** 100 Main St 93517. On US 395; at south end of town. Ext corridors. **Pets:** Other species. Supervision.
SAVE ✕ 🛏 💻 ⊃

BUELLTON

▼▼ Quality Inn Solvang/Buellton M
(805) 688-0022. **$69-$149.** 630 Ave of the Flags 93427. US 101, exit 140B (Ave of the Flags) southbound, just s; exit 140A (SR 246) northbound, just w, then just n. Ext/int corridors. **Pets:** Large, other species. $25 one-time fee/room. Designated rooms, service with restrictions.
ASK ✕ 🛏 💻

AAA ▼▼▼ Santa Ynez Valley Marriott H 🐾
(805) 688-1000. **$155-$189.** 555 McMurray Rd 93427. US 101, exit 140A (SR 246), just e, then just n. Int corridors. **Pets:** Other species. $75 one-time fee/room. Designated rooms, service with restrictions.
SAVE ✕ 🛏 💻 🍴 ⊃ ✕

BUENA PARK

AAA ▼▼ Red Roof Inn M
(714) 670-9000. **$50-$100.** 7121 Beach Blvd 90620. SR 91, exit 23B (Beach Blvd/SR 39), just n. Ext corridors. **Pets:** Large. Service with restrictions, crate. SAVE ✕ 🛏 ⊃

BURNEY

AAA ▼▼ Charm Motel M
(530) 335-3300. **$69-$99, 3 day notice.** 37363 Main St 96013. 0.5 mi ne on SR 299; jct Roff Way. Ext corridors. **Pets:** Accepted.
SAVE ✕ 🛏 💻

AAA ▼▼▼ Green Gables Motel M
(530) 335-3300. **$69-$129, 3 day notice.** 37385 Main St 96013. 0.5 mi ne on SR 299; jct Roff Way and SR 299. Ext corridors. **Pets:** Accepted.
SAVE ✕ 🛏 💻 ⊃

BUTTONWILLOW

▼▼ Super 8 **M**

(661) 764-5117. **$40-$70.** 20681 Tracy Ave 93206. I-5, exit 257 (SR 58), just e, then just n. Ext corridors. **Pets:** Accepted.

ASK ⊠ ᗠᴹ 🖥 💻 ⇰

CALEXICO

ⒶⒶⒶ ▼▼▼ Best Western John Jay Inn **M**

(760) 768-0442. **$89-$99.** 2421 Scaroni Rd 92231. I-8, exit 118A (SR 111 S), 5.5 mi s, just w on W Cole Rd, then just n. Int corridors.
Pets: Accepted. SAVE ⊠ ᗠᴹ 🖥 💻 ⇰

CALIMESA

ⒶⒶⒶ ▼▼▼ Calimesa Inn Motel **M**

(909) 795-2536. **$60-$150.** 1205 Calimesa Blvd 92320. I-10, exit 88 (Calimesa Blvd), just ne. Ext corridors. **Pets:** Small. $10 daily fee/room. Designated rooms, service with restrictions, crate. SAVE ⊠ 🖥 ⇰

CAMBRIA

▼▼▼ Blue Dolphin Inn **H** 🐾

(805) 927-3300. **$129-$349.** 6470 Moonstone Beach Dr 93428. SR 1, exit Moonstone Beach Dr, 0.7 mi n. Int corridors. **Pets:** $25 daily fee/pet. Designated rooms, service with restrictions, supervision.

ASK ⊠ 🖥 💻 🐾

▼▼▼ Cambria Shores Inn **M** 🐾

(805) 927-8644. **$150-$350, 7 day notice.** 6276 Moonstone Beach Dr 93428. SR 1, exit Moonstone Beach Dr, just w, then 0.8 mi s. Ext corridors. **Pets:** Dogs only. $15 daily fee/pet. Supervision. ⊠ 🖥 💻

▼▼▼ Creekside Inn **M** 🐾

(805) 927-4021. **$79-$159.** 2618 Main St 93428. SR 1 to Main St, 2 mi e. Ext corridors. **Pets:** Other species. Designated rooms, service with restrictions, supervision. ASK ⊠ 🖥 💻 🐾

ⒶⒶⒶ ▼▼▼ Mariners Inn by the Sea **M**

(805) 927-4624. **$89-$595, 3 day notice.** 6180 Moonstone Beach Dr 93428. SR 1, exit Moonstone Beach Dr, just w, then 1 mi s. Ext corridors. **Pets:** Accepted. SAVE ⊠ 🖥 🐾

▼▼▼ Sand Pebbles Inn **H** 🐾

(805) 927-5600. **$109-$299.** 6252 Moonstone Beach Dr 93428. SR 1, exit Moonstone Beach Dr, just w, then 0.9 mi s. Int corridors. **Pets:** $25 daily fee/pet. Designated rooms, service with restrictions, supervision.

ASK ⊠ 🖥 💻 🐾

▼▼▼ Sea Otter Inn **M**

(805) 927-5888. **$99-$299, 3 day notice.** 6656 Moonstone Beach Dr 93428. SR 1, exit Moonstone Beach Dr, just w, then 0.5 mi s. Ext corridors. **Pets:** Accepted. ASK ⊠ 🖥 💻 ⇰ 🐾

CAMPBELL

ⒶⒶⒶ ▼▼▼ Larkspur Landing Campbell **H**

(408) 364-1514. **$99-$199.** 550 W Hamilton Ave 95008. SR 17, exit Hamilton Ave, 1 mi w. Int corridors. **Pets:** Accepted.

SAVE ⊠ ᗠᴹ 🖥 💻

▼▼▼ Residence Inn by Marriott-San Jose **H**

(408) 559-1551. **$197-$241.** 2761 S Bascom Ave 95008. SR 17, exit Camden Ave E, just n. Ext corridors. **Pets:** Accepted.

⊠ ᗠᴹ 🖥 💻 ⇰

▼▼▼ TownePlace Suites by Marriott-San Jose/Campbell **H**

(408) 370-4510. **$170-$208.** 700 E Campbell Ave 95008. SR 17, exit Hamilton Ave E, 0.3 mi to Bascom Ave, 0.3 mi s, then 0.3 mi w. Int corridors. **Pets:** Other species. $75 one-time fee/room. Service with restrictions, supervision. ⊠ ᗠᴹ 🖥 💻

CAPITOLA

ⒶⒶⒶ ▼▼▼ Capitola Inn **M**

(831) 462-3004. **$65-$280.** 822 Bay Ave 95010. SR 1, exit Bay Ave, just w. Ext/int corridors. **Pets:** Accepted. SAVE ⊠ 🖥 💻 ⇰

CARLSBAD

ⒶⒶⒶ ▼▼▼▼ Four Seasons Resort Aviara **H**

(760) 603-6800. **$395-$4800, 3 day notice.** 7100 Four Seasons Point 92009. I-5, exit 45 (Poinsettia Ln/Aviara Pkwy), 1 mi e on Poinsettia Ln, then 1 mi s on Aviara Pkwy. Int corridors. **Pets:** Accepted.

SAVE ⊠ 💻 🍴 ⇰ 🐾

▼▼▼ Homewood Suites by Hilton Carlsbad-North San Diego County **H**

(760) 431-2266. **$169-$189.** 2223 Palomar Airport Rd 92011. I-5, exit 47 (Palomar Airport Rd), 3.1 mi e. Int corridors. **Pets:** Accepted.

⊠ ᗠᴹ 🖥 💻 ⇰ 🐾

▼▼▼ La Quinta Inn Carlsbad **M** 🐾

(760) 438-2828. **$79-$199.** 760 Macadamia Dr 92009. I-5, exit 45 (Poinsettia Ln/Aviara Pkwy), just w to Ave Encinas, just n, then just e. Ext corridors. **Pets:** Medium, other species. Service with restrictions, supervision. ASK ⊠ 🖥 💻 ⇰

▼▼▼ Quality Inn & Suites North Legoland Area **H** 🐾

(760) 931-1185. **$79-$179.** 751 Raintree Dr 92011. I-5, exit 45 (Poinsettia Ln), just w to Ave Encinas, then just n. Ext corridors. **Pets:** Large. $10 daily fee/pet. Designated rooms, service with restrictions, supervision.

ASK ⊠ 🖥 💻 ⇰

ⒶⒶⒶ ▼▼▼ Ramada Inn & Suites **M**

(760) 438-2285. **$79-$309.** 751 Macadamia Dr 92011. I-5, exit 45 (Poinsettia Ln), just w to Ave Encinas, then 0.3 mi n. Ext corridors.
Pets: Accepted. SAVE ⊠ 🖥 💻 ⇰

▼▼▼ West Inn & Suites **H** 🐾

(760) 448-4500. **$169-$399, 3 day notice.** 4970 Avenida Encinas 92008. I-5, exit 48 (Cannon Rd), just w, then just n. Int corridors. **Pets:** $75 one-time fee/room. Service with restrictions, supervision. ASK ⊠ ᗠᴹ 🖥 💻 🍴 ⇰

CARPINTERIA

ⒶⒶⒶ ▼▼▼ Holiday Inn Express Hotel & Suites **H**

(805) 566-9499. **$109-$239.** 5606 Carpinteria Ave 93013. US 101, exit 86A (Casitas Pass Rd), just s, then just e. Int corridors. **Pets:** Large. $10 daily fee/room. Designated rooms, service with restrictions, supervision.

SAVE ⊠ ᗠᴹ 🖥 💻 ⇰

CASSEL

ⒶⒶⒶ ▼▼▼ Burney Mountain Guest Ranch **H**

(530) 335-4087. **Call for rates.** 22800 Hat Creek Powerhouse #2 96016. Jct SR 89 and 299, 2.7 mi ne on SR 299, 0.3 mi se on Hat Creek Powerhouse to jct with Guest Ranch Rd; up unmaintained Guest Ranch Rd, 0.9 mi se. Ext corridors. **Pets:** Accepted.

SAVE ⊠ 🖥 ⇰ 🐾 🌀

CASTAIC

ⒶⒶⒶ ▼▼▼ Rodeway Inn **M** 🐾

(661) 295-1100. **$60-$100.** 31558 Castaic Rd 91384. I-5, exit 175A (Parker Rd) northbound, just e on Ridge Route Rd, then just n; exit 176 (Lake Hughes Rd/Castaic) southbound, just s on The Old Rd, just e on Sloan Canyon Rd, then 0.4 mi s. Ext corridors. **Pets:** Small. $10 daily fee/pet. Designated rooms, service with restrictions, supervision.

SAVE ⊠ 🖥 💻 ⇰

CASTRO VALLEY

▼▼▼ Quality Inn **H**

(510) 538-9501. **$90-$250.** 2532 Castro Valley Blvd 94546. I-580, exit Castro Valley Blvd, 0.3 mi n. Int corridors. **Pets:** Small, dogs only. $10 daily fee/pet. Designated rooms, service with restrictions, supervision.

ASK ⊠ ᗠᴹ 🖥 💻 ⇰

CATHEDRAL CITY

▼▼▼ Doral Desert Princess Resort, Palm Springs **H**

(760) 322-7000. **$99-$359, 3 day notice.** 67-967 Vista Chino 92234. I-10, exit 126 (Date Palm Dr), 0.5 mi s, then 1 mi w. Int corridors.
Pets: Accepted. ASK ⊠ 🖥 💻 🍴 ⇰ 🐾

Quality Inn & Suites Date Palm M
(760) 324-5939. **$64-$199.** 69-151 E Palm Canyon Dr 92234. I-10, exit 126 (Date Palm Dr), 5 mi s, then just e. Ext corridors. **Pets:** Accepted.

CAYUCOS

Cayucos Beach Inn M
(805) 995-2828. **$85-$215, 3 day notice.** 333 S Ocean Ave 93430. On SR 1 business route. Ext corridors. **Pets:** Other species. $10 daily fee/room. Service with restrictions, supervision.

Cypress Tree Motel M
(805) 995-3917. **$50-$117.** 125 S Ocean Ave 93430. On SR 1 business route. Ext corridors. **Pets:** Other species. $10 one-time fee/room. Service with restrictions.

Estero Bay Motel M
(805) 995-3614. **$60-$160, 3 day notice.** 25 S Ocean Ave 93430. On SR 1 business route. Ext corridors. **Pets:** Medium, dogs only. $15 daily fee/pet. Designated rooms, no service, supervision.

Shoreline Inn...On The Beach M
(805) 995-3681. **$105-$225.** 1 N Ocean Ave 93430. On SR 1 business route. Ext corridors. **Pets:** Accepted.

Vagabond Inn M
(805) 995-2133. **Call for rates.** 501 S Ocean Ave 93430. On SR 1 business route. Ext corridors. **Pets:** Accepted.

CEDARVILLE

Sunrise Motel M
(530) 279-2161. **$65-$75, 7 day notice.** 62271 Hwy 299 W 96104. Jct SR 299 and CR 1, 0.6 mi w on CR 1. Ext corridors. **Pets:** Small. $10 one-time fee/pet. Designated rooms, service with restrictions, supervision.

CHESTER

Best Western Rose Quartz Inn H
(530) 258-2002. **$105-$135.** 306 Main St 96020. On SR 36; center. Int corridors. **Pets:** Accepted.

CHICO

Best Western Heritage Inn-Chico H
(530) 894-8600. **$95-$120.** 25 Heritage Ln 95926. Just e of SR 99, via Cohasset Rd. Int corridors. **Pets:** Accepted.

Heritage Inn Express M
(530) 343-4527. **$89-$109.** 725 Broadway 95928. SR 99, exit 385 (SR 32), 1.1 mi w; jct W 8th St; downtown. Ext corridors. **Pets:** Accepted.

Holiday Inn of Chico H
(530) 345-2491. **$79-$299.** 685 Manzanita Ct 95926. SR 99, exit 387A (Mangrove Ave/Cohasset Rd), follow Mangrove Ave, just sw. Int corridors. **Pets:** Accepted.

Music Express Inn Bed & Breakfast BB
(530) 345-8376. **$86-$135, 3 day notice.** 1145 El Monte Ave 95928. SR 99, exit 385 (SR 32), 1 mi e to El Monte Ave, then just n. Ext/int corridors. **Pets:** Dogs only. $20 one-time fee/room. Service with restrictions, supervision.

Oxford Suites H
(530) 899-9090. **$119-$169.** 2035 Business Ln 95928. SR 99, exit 384 (E 20th St), just e, then just s. Int corridors. **Pets:** Accepted.

Residence Inn H
(530) 894-5500. **$121-$147.** 2485 Carmichael Dr 95928. SR 99, exit Skyway/Park Ave, (exit 383), just w, then just n. Int corridors. **Pets:** Accepted.

Super 8 H
(530) 345-2533. **$60-$200.** 655 Manzanita Ct 95926. SR 99, exit 387A (Mangrove Ave/Cohasset Rd), follow Mangrove Ave, then just se. Int corridors. **Pets:** Medium. $10 daily fee/pet. Service with restrictions, supervision.

CHOWCHILLA

Days Inn M
(559) 665-4821. **$59-$89.** 220 E Robertson Blvd 93610. SR 99, exit Robertson Blvd W. Ext corridors. **Pets:** Large, other species. $10 daily fee/pet. Service with restrictions, crate.

Holiday Inn Express & Suites Gateway to Yosemite H
(559) 665-3300. **$79-$169.** 309 Prosperity Blvd 93610. SR 99, exit Robertson Blvd, just w. Int corridors. **Pets:** Large, other species. $25 daily fee/pet. Service with restrictions, supervision.

CLIO

Molly's Bed & Breakfast BB
(530) 836-4436. **Call for rates.** 276 Lower Main St 96106. Just n of SR 89; center. Int corridors. **Pets:** $15 daily fee/pet. Designated rooms, service with restrictions, supervision.

COALINGA

Best Western Big Country Inn M
(559) 935-0866. **Call for rates.** 25020 W Dorris Ave 93210. I-5, exit SR 198/Hanford-Lemoore, just w. Ext corridors. **Pets:** Medium. $20 daily fee/pet. Designated rooms, service with restrictions, supervision.

The Inn at Harris Ranch H
(559) 935-0717. **$149-$350.** 24505 W Dorris Ave 93210. I-5, exit SR 198/Hanford-Lemoore, just e. Ext/int corridors. **Pets:** Accepted.

COLUMBIA

Columbia Gem Motel M
(209) 532-4508. **$89-$149.** 22131 Parrotts Ferry Rd 95370. 3 mi n of Sonora; 1 mi from Columbia State Historic Park. Ext corridors. **Pets:** Dogs only. Service with restrictions, supervision.

CONCORD

Best Western Heritage Inn H
(925) 686-4466. **$70-$80.** 4600 Clayton Rd 94521. 3 mi e at Wharton Way. Ext corridors. **Pets:** Accepted.

Concord Inn & Suites H
(925) 827-8998. **Call for rates.** 1370 Monument Blvd 94520. I-680, exit Monument Blvd, 0.5 mi e. Int corridors. **Pets:** Accepted.

Crowne Plaza Hotel Concord/Walnut Creek H
(925) 825-7700. **$99-$153.** 45 John Glenn Dr 94520. I-680, exit Concord Ave, just e. Int corridors. **Pets:** Accepted.

Holiday Inn Concord H
(925) 687-5500. **Call for rates.** 1050 Burnett Ave 94520. I-680, exit E Concord Ave, just e. Ext/int corridors. **Pets:** Accepted.

Premier Inns H
(925) 674-0888. **$52-$72.** 1581 Concord Ave 94520. SR 242, exit Clayton Rd northbound; exit Concord Ave southbound, just e. Ext corridors. **Pets:** Accepted.

CORNING

Best Western Inn Corning 🅼 ❖

(530) 824-2468. **$90-$140.** 2165 Solano St 96021. I-5, exit 631 (Central Corning), just e. Ext corridors. **Pets:** Medium. $10 daily fee/pet. Service with restrictions, supervision. (SAVE) ⊠ ⑤ⓜ 🖥 🖵 🏊

Holiday Inn Express Hotel & Suites 🅷 ❖

(530) 824-6400. **$85-$105.** 3350 Sunrise Way 96021. I-5, exit 630 (South Ave), just s. Int corridors. **Pets:** Large, other species. $10 daily fee/pet. Designated rooms, service with restrictions.
(SAVE) ⊠ 🖥 🖵 🏊 ⊠

Ramada Inn & Suites 🅷 ❖

(530) 824-8300. **$99-$129.** 2645 Barham Ave 96021. I-5, exit 628 (Liberal Ave/SR 99), just w, then just s. Int corridors. **Pets:** $10 daily fee/pet. Designated rooms, service with restrictions. (SAVE) ⊠ 🖥 🖵 🏊

CORONA

Ayres Suites Corona West 🅷

(951) 738-9113. **$99-$169.** 1900 Frontage Rd 92882. SR 91, exit 48 (Maple St/W 6th St) eastbound; exit 48 (Maple St) westbound, just s. Ext/int corridors. **Pets:** Accepted. ⊠ 🖥 🖵 🏊

Hotel Paseo 🅼

(951) 371-7185. **$89-$150.** 1805 W 6th St 92882. SR 91, exit 48 (Maple St/W 6th St) eastbound; exit 48 (Maple St) westbound, just s. Ext corridors. **Pets:** Accepted. (ASK) ⊠ 🖥 🖵 🏊

Residence Inn by Marriott Corona 🅷 ❖

(951) 371-0107. **$153-$187.** 1015 Montecito Dr 92879. I-15, exit 95 (Magnolia Ave), just e, just n on El Camino, just w on Carly Way, then just n. Int corridors. **Pets:** Medium. $75 one-time fee/pet. Service with restrictions. ⊠ ⑤ⓜ 🖥 🏊 ⊠

COSTA MESA

Hilton Orange County/Costa Mesa 🅷

(714) 540-7000. **$149-$359.** 3050 Bristol St 92626. I-405, exit 9B (Bristol St), just s. Int corridors. **Pets:** Accepted.
(ECO) ⊠ ⑤ⓜ 🖥 🖵 🍽 🏊 ⊠

The Hotel Hanford 🅷 ❖

(714) 557-3000. **$89-$149.** 3131 S Bristol St 92626. I-405, exit 9B (Bristol St), just s. Int corridors. **Pets:** $50 daily fee/room. Service with restrictions, supervision. (SAVE) ⊠ 🖥 🖵 🍽 🏊

La Quinta Inn Costa Mesa (John Wayne/Orange Co. Airport) 🅼 ❖

(714) 957-5841. **$79-$179.** 1515 S Coast Dr 92626. I-405, exit 11B (Harbor Blvd), just n, then just w. Ext corridors. **Pets:** Medium, other species. Service with restrictions, supervision. (ASK) ⊠ 🖥 🖵 🏊

Ramada Inn & Suites 🅷

(949) 645-2221. **$85-$195.** 1680 Superior Ave 92627. Just w of SR 55 (Newport Blvd) at 17th St. Ext corridors. **Pets:** Medium. $150 deposit/room, $5 daily fee/room. Designated rooms, service with restrictions, supervision. (SAVE) ⊠ ⑤ⓜ 🖥 🖵 🍽 🏊

Residence Inn by Marriott 🅷

(714) 241-8800. **$161-$197.** 881 W Baker St 92626. SR 73, exit 17B (Bear St); SR 55, exit 5B (Baker St). Ext corridors. **Pets:** Accepted.
⊠ 🖥 🖵 🏊 ⊠

Travelodge-Orange County Airport 🅼

(714) 557-8700. **$75-$125.** 1400 Bristol St 92626. Adjacent to SR 73, just w of Red Hill Ave. Ext corridors. **Pets:** Accepted.
(SAVE) ⊠ 🖥 🖵 🏊

Vagabond Inn 🅼 ❖

(714) 557-8360. **$65-$119.** 3205 Harbor Blvd 92626. I-405, exit 11 (Harbor Blvd), just s; entrance from Gisler Ave, just w of Harbor. Ext corridors. **Pets:** Small, other species. $10 daily fee/pet. Designated rooms, service with restrictions, crate. (SAVE) ⊠ 🖥 🖵 🏊

The Westin South Coast Plaza Hotel 🅷

(714) 540-2500. **$149-$375.** 686 Anton Blvd 92626. I-405, exit 9B (Bristol St), just n, then just e. Int corridors. **Pets:** Accepted.
(SAVE) ⊠ ⑤ⓜ 🖥 🍽 🏊 ⊠

Wyndham Orange County Airport 🅷

(714) 751-5100. **$89-$179.** 3350 Ave of the Arts 92626. I-405, exit 9B (Bristol St), n to Anton Blvd, just e, then just n. Int corridors.
Pets: Accepted. (SAVE) ⊠ 🖥 🖵 🏊

CRESCENT CITY

Americas Best Value Inn 🅼

(707) 464-4141. **$50-$125.** 440 Hwy 101 N 95531. Center. Ext corridors. **Pets:** Medium, dogs only. $10 daily fee/pet. Designated rooms, service with restrictions, supervision. (SAVE) ⊠ 🖥 🖵 🅰🅲

Hiouchi Motel 🅼 ❖

(707) 458-3041. **$65-$81.** 2097 Hwy 199 95531. On US 199, 5.5 mi e of jct US 101. Ext corridors. **Pets:** Other species. Service with restrictions, supervision. (SAVE) ⊠ 🖥 🅰🅲 ☎

Pacific Inn 🅼

(707) 464-9553. **$59-$109.** 220 M St 95531. On US 101; between 2nd and 3rd sts; center. Ext corridors. **Pets:** Accepted.
(SAVE) ⊠ 🖥 🖵 🅰🅲

Quality Inn & Suites 🅷

(707) 464-3885. **Call for rates.** 100 Walton St 95531. Just w of US 101. Ext corridors. **Pets:** Accepted. (SAVE) ⊠ 🖥 🖵

Super 8 🅼 ❖

(707) 464-4111. **$55-$150.** 685 Hwy 101 S/Redwood Hwy 95531. On US 101. Ext corridors. **Pets:** Small, dogs only. $12 daily fee/pet. Designated rooms, service with restrictions, supervision. (SAVE) ⊠ 🖥 🖵 🅰🅲

CUPERTINO

Cypress Hotel 🅷 ❖

(408) 253-8900. **$99-$299.** 10050 S De Anza Blvd 95014. I-280, exit De Anza Blvd, 0.7 mi s. Int corridors. **Pets:** Other species.
(ECO) (SAVE) ⊠ ⑤ⓜ 🖥 🍽 🏊

DANA POINT

Doubletree Guest Suites Doheny Beach 🅷 ❖

(949) 661-1100. **$149-$289.** 34402 Pacific Coast Hwy 92629. I-5, exit 79 (Beach Cities Dr) northbound; exit 79 (Pacific Coast Hwy) southbound, 0.6 mi w, U-turn at Doheny Park Dr, then 0.8 mi s. Int corridors. **Pets:** Medium. $30 daily fee/pet. Service with restrictions, supervision.
(ECO) ⊠ 🖥 🖵 🍽 🏊 ⊠

Holiday Inn Express Hotel & Suites 🅷

(949) 248-1000. **$119-$399.** 34280 Pacific Coast Hwy 92629. I-5, exit 79 (Pacific Coast Hwy) southbound; exit 79 (Beach Cities Dr) northbound, 0.6 mi w, then 0.5 mi n. Ext/int corridors. **Pets:** Accepted.
(ASK) ⊠ ⑤ⓜ 🖥 🖵 🏊

The Ritz-Carlton, Laguna Niguel 🅷 ❖

(949) 240-2000. **$425-$595, 3 day notice.** One Ritz-Carlton Dr 92629. I-5, exit 79 (Pacific Coast Hwy) northbound, 3 mi n; exit 86 (Crown Valley Pkwy) southbound, 3 mi w, 1 mi s on Pacific Coast Hwy, then just w. Int corridors. **Pets:** $50 daily fee/room, $150 one-time fee/room. Designated rooms, service with restrictions. (SAVE) ⊠ ⑤ⓜ 🖥 🍽 🏊 ⊠

St. Regis Resort, Monarch Beach 🅷

(949) 234-3200. **$345-$6000, 7 day notice.** One Monarch Beach Resort 92629. I-5, exit 79 (Pacific Coast Hwy) northbound, 3 mi n; exit 86 (Crown Valley Pkwy) southbound, 3 mi w, 1 mi s on Pacific Coast Hwy, then 0.5 mi e on Niguel Rd. Int corridors. **Pets:** Accepted.
(SAVE) ⊠ ⑤ⓜ 🍽 🏊 ⊠

DAVIS

La Quinta Inn & Suites H ❀
(530) 758-2600. **Call for rates.** 1771 Research Park Dr 95616. I-80, exit 72A (Richards Blvd) westbound, just se, then just n; exit 72 (Richards Blvd) eastbound. Int corridors. **Pets:** Medium, other species. Service with restrictions, supervision. SAVE ✕ 🔥 🛢 💻 🏊

University Park Inn & Suites H
(530) 756-0910. **$80-$159.** 1111 Richards Blvd 95616. I-80, exit 72B (Richards Blvd) westbound; exit 72 (Richards Blvd) eastbound, just nw. Ext corridors. **Pets:** Small, other species. $10 daily fee/pet. Designated rooms, service with restrictions, supervision.
SAVE ✕ 🔥 🛢 💻 🏊

DEATH VALLEY NATIONAL PARK

Stovepipe Wells Village M
(760) 786-2387. **$104-$124.** SR 190 92328. On SR 190; 24 mi nw of visitor center. Ext corridors. **Pets:** $20 deposit/room. Service with restrictions. ✕ 🔥 🛢 🍴 🏊 ☎

DELANO

Rodeway Inn M
(661) 725-1022. **$69-$89.** 2211 Girard St 93215. SR 99, exit 58 (County Line Rd), just e, then just s. Ext corridors. **Pets:** Accepted.
ASK ✕ 🛢 💻 🏊

DESERT HOT SPRINGS

Desert Hot Springs Spa Hotel H
(760) 329-6000. **$49-$119, 3 day notice.** 10-805 Palm Dr 92240. I-10, exit 123 (Gene Autry Tr/Palm Dr), 6.7 mi n. Ext corridors. **Pets:** Accepted.
ASK ✕ 🛢 💻 🍴 ⊠

DINUBA

Reedley Country Inn BB
(559) 638-2585. **$85-$95, 3 day notice.** 43137 Rd 52 93618. SR 99, exit 121 (Manning Ave), 10 mi e, then 1 mi s. Ext/int corridors.
Pets: Accepted. ✕

DIXON

Best Western Inn Dixon H
(707) 678-1400. **$89.** 1345 Commercial Way 95620. I-80, exit 64 (Pitt School Rd), just se. Ext/int corridors. **Pets:** $15 daily fee/room. Designated rooms, service with restrictions, crate.
SAVE ✕ 🔥 🛢 💻 🏊 ⊠

Red Roof Inn M
(707) 693-0606. **$59-$129.** 1480 Ary Ln 95620. I-80, exit 64 (Pitt School Rd), just s, then just w. Int corridors. **Pets:** Large. Service with restrictions, crate. SAVE ✕ 🔥 🛢 💻 🏊

Super 8 ❀
(707) 678-3399. **$55-$115.** 2500 Plaza Ct 95620. I-80, exit West a St, follow signs for West a St, just n on Gateway Dr. Int corridors.
Pets: Accepted. ASK ✕ 🛢 💻 🏊

DORRIS

Golden Eagle Motel M
(530) 397-3114. **$39-$99.** 100 N Main St 96023. US 97; center. Ext corridors. **Pets:** $6 daily fee/pet. Designated rooms, service with restrictions, supervision. SAVE ✕ 🛢

DOWNIEVILLE

Riverside Inn M
(530) 289-1000. **$80-$104, 3 day notice.** 206 Commercial St (SR 49) 95936. SR 49; center. Ext corridors. **Pets:** Other species. $10 daily fee/pet. Service with restrictions, supervision. SAVE ✕ 🛢 💻 🐾 ☎

DUBLIN

La Quinta Inn & Suites Dublin–Pleasanton H ❀
(925) 828-9393. **$60-$190.** 6275 Dublin Blvd 94568. I-580, exit Hopyard/Dougherty Rd, just n. Int corridors. **Pets:** Medium, other species. Service with restrictions, supervision. ASK ✕ 🔥 🛢 💻

DUNNIGAN

Motel 6 Dunnigan M
(530) 724-3471. **Call for rates.** 3930 County Rd 89 95937. I-5, exit 556 (Dunnigan), just ne. Ext corridors. **Pets:** Other species. Service with restrictions, supervision. SAVE ✕ 🔥 🛢 💻 🏊

DUNSMUIR

Caboose Motel-Railroad Park Resort M ❀
(530) 235-4440. **$90-$130, 3 day notice.** 100 Railroad Park Rd 96025. I-5, exit 728 (Railroad Park Rd), just nw. Ext corridors. **Pets:** Medium, dogs only. $15 daily fee/pet. Service with restrictions, supervision.
SAVE ✕ 🛢 💻 🍴 🏊

EAST PALO ALTO

Four Seasons Hotel Silicon Valley at East Palo Alto H
(650) 566-1200. **$295-$415.** 2050 University Ave 94303. US 101, exit University Ave. Int corridors. **Pets:** Accepted.
✕ 🔥 💻 🍴 🏊 ⊠

EL CENTRO

Barbara Worth Golf Resort H
(760) 356-2806. **Call for rates.** 2050 Country Club Dr 92250. I-8, exit 120 (Bowker Rd), 2 mi n, 3 mi e on CR S-80; then 0.4 mi s. Ext/int corridors. **Pets:** Accepted. ✕ 🛢 💻 🍴 🏊 ⊠

Comfort Inn & Suites M
(760) 335-3502. **$79-$129.** 2354 S 4th St 92243. I-8, exit 115 (4th St/SR 86), just s. Int corridors. **Pets:** Small. $25 one-time fee/room. Service with restrictions, supervision. SAVE ✕ 🛢 💻 🏊 ⊠

Rodeway Inn & Suites M
(760) 352-6620. **$49-$69.** 455 W Wake Ave 92243. I-8, exit 115 (4th St/SR 86), just s, then just w. Ext corridors. **Pets:** Small. $5 daily fee/pet. Service with restrictions, supervision. SAVE ✕ 🛢 💻 🏊

Vacation Inn & Suites M 🐾
(760) 352-9700. **$60-$95.** 2015 Cottonwood Cir 92243. I-8, exit 114 (Imperial Ave), just n, then just w on Octotillo Dr, then just s. Ext corridors. **Pets:** Medium, dogs only. Designated rooms, supervision.
ASK ✕ 🛢 💻 🍴 🏊

ELK GROVE

Extended StayAmerica-Sacramento-Elk Grove H
(916) 683-3753. **$80-$95.** 2201 Longport St 95758. I-5, exit Laguna Blvd, 0.5 mi e, just s on Harbour Point Dr, then just w. Int corridors. **Pets:** Other species. $25 daily fee/room. Designated rooms, service with restrictions, crate. ASK ✕ 🔥 🛢 💻

EL PORTAL

Yosemite View Lodge H
(209) 379-2681. **$95-$729, 14 day notice.** 11136 Hwy 140 95318. Just w of Yosemite National Park West Gate. Ext corridors. **Pets:** $10 daily fee/pet. Service with restrictions, supervision.
SAVE ✕ 🔥 🛢 💻 🍴 🏊 ⊠

EMERYVILLE

Woodfin Hotel San Francisco Bay Bridge H
(510) 601-5880. **$139-$239.** 5800 Shellmound St 94608. I-80, exit Powell St. Int corridors. **Pets:** Small, other species. $250 deposit/room, $10 daily fee/pet. Designated rooms, service with restrictions.
SAVE ✕ 🔥 🛢 💻 🍴 🏊

ENCINITAS

Best Western Encinitas Inn & Suites at Moonlight Beach M 🐾
(760) 942-7455. **$105-$221.** 85 Encinitas Blvd 92024. I-5, exit 41B (Encinitas Blvd), just w. Ext corridors. **Pets:** $55 one-time fee/room. Designated rooms, service with restrictions, supervision.
SAVE ✕ 🛢 💻 🍴 🏊

Econo Lodge Encinitas M
(760) 436-4999. **$69-$139.** 410 N Coast Hwy 101 92024. I-5, exit 41B (Encinitas Blvd), 0.6 mi w, then 0.6 mi n. Int corridors. **Pets:** Small. $15 daily fee/pet. Designated rooms, service with restrictions, crate.

Howard Johnson-Encinitas M
(760) 944-3800. **$63-$135.** 607 Leucadia Blvd 92024. I-5, exit 43 (Leucadia Blvd), east side. Ext corridors. **Pets:** Accepted.

Quality Inn & Suites North Coast M
(760) 944-0301. **$69-$159.** 186 N Coast Hwy 92024. I-5, exit 41B (Encinitas Blvd), 0.6 mi w, then just n. Ext corridors. **Pets:** Medium, other species. $15 one-time fee/pet. Designated rooms, service with restrictions, supervision.

ESCONDIDO

Best Western Escondido H
(760) 740-1700. **$99-$189, 3 day notice.** 1700 Seven Oaks Rd 92026. I-15, exit 33 (El Norte Pkwy), just e. Int corridors. **Pets:** Small, other species. $25 one-time fee/pet. Service with restrictions, supervision.

Comfort Inn Escondido H
(760) 489-1010. **$79-$149.** 1290 W Valley Pkwy 92029. I-15, exit 31 (Valley Pkwy), just w. Int corridors. **Pets:** Accepted.

Rodeway Inn M
(760) 746-0441. **$59-$109.** 250 W El Norte Pkwy 92026. I-15, exit 33 (El Norte Pkwy), 1 mi e. Ext corridors. **Pets:** Medium, dogs only. $25 daily fee/pet. Service with restrictions, supervision.

EUREKA

Best Western Bayshore Inn H
(707) 268-8005. **$80-$250.** 3500 Broadway 95503. US 101; south end of town. Ext corridors. **Pets:** Accepted.

Carter House Inns CI
(707) 444-8062. **$155-$612, 3 day notice.** 301 L St 95501. Just w of US 101 S. Int corridors. **Pets:** Large. $50 one-time fee/room. Designated rooms, service with restrictions, supervision.

Eureka Town House Motel M
(707) 443-4536. **$55-$150.** 933 4th St 95501. On US 101 southbound; corner of K St. Ext corridors. **Pets:** Medium, dogs only. $10 daily fee/pet. Designated rooms, service with restrictions, supervision.

Quality Inn Eureka M
(707) 443-1601. **$78-$250.** 1209 4th St 95501. On US 101 southbound; between M and N sts. Ext corridors. **Pets:** Accepted.

Red Lion Hotel Eureka H
(707) 445-0844. **$100-$250.** 1929 4th St 95501. On US 101 southbound; between T and V sts. Int corridors. **Pets:** Other species. $20 one-time fee/room. Service with restrictions, supervision.

Scottfeild Executive Hotels H
(707) 443-2206. **$99-$259, 3 day notice.** 270 5th St 95501. On US 101 northbound; corner of D St. Int corridors. **Pets:** Accepted.

FAIRFIELD

Cordelia Inn & Suites M
(707) 864-2426. **$45-$100.** 4625 Central Way 94534. I-80, exit Suisun Valley Rd, just e. Ext corridors. **Pets:** Accepted.

Days Inn M
(707) 864-1728. **Call for rates.** 4376 Central Pl 94534. I-80, exit Suisun Valley Rd, just e. Ext corridors. **Pets:** Accepted.

Extended StayAmerica-Fairfield-Napa Valley H
(707) 438-0932. **$90-$105.** 1019 Oliver Rd 94534. I-80, exit Texas St, just w. Int corridors. **Pets:** Other species. $25 daily fee/room. Designated rooms, service with restrictions, crate.

Homewood Suites Fairfield-Napa Valley Area H
(707) 863-0300. **$119-$149.** 4755 Business Center Dr 94534. I-80, exit Green Valley Rd/Suisun Valley Rd, n on Green Valley Rd, then just e. Int corridors. **Pets:** Medium. $100 one-time fee/room. Service with restrictions, crate.

Staybridge Suites Fairfield-Napa Valley Area H
(707) 863-0900. **$109-$144.** 4775 Business Center Dr 94534. I-80, exit Green Valley Rd/Suisun Valley Rd, n on Green Valley Rd, then just e. Int corridors. **Pets:** Medium. $50 one-time fee/pet.

FALL RIVER MILLS

Hi-Mont Motel M 🐾
(530) 336-5541. **$69-$99, 3 day notice.** 43021 Bridge St 96028. 0.4 mi sw on SR 299; jct SR 299 E and Bridge St; across from Fort Crook Museum. Ext corridors. **Pets:** $10 daily fee/pet. Service with restrictions, supervision.

FERNDALE

Shaw House Inn Bed & Breakfast BB
(707) 786-9958. **$125-$275, 15 day notice.** 703 Main St 95536. Center. Ext/int corridors. **Pets:** Accepted.

FILLMORE

Best Western La Posada Motel M
(805) 524-0440. **$89-$120, 3 day notice.** 827 Ventura Ave 93015. On SR 126. Ext corridors. **Pets:** Small. $10 daily fee/pet, $15 one-time fee/pet. Supervision.

FIREBAUGH

Best Western Apricot Inn M
(559) 659-1444. **$89-$95.** 46290 W Panoche Rd 93622. I-5, exit W Panoche Rd, just w. Ext corridors. **Pets:** Medium. $25 one-time fee/room. Service with restrictions, supervision.

FISH CAMP

The Cottages at Tenaya Lodge H 🐾
(559) 683-6555. **$129-$389, 7 day notice.** 1122 Hwy 41 93623. 2 mi from Yosemite National Park South Gate. Ext corridors. **Pets:** Dogs only. $75 one-time fee/room. Designated rooms, service with restrictions, supervision.

The Narrow Gauge Inn H 🐾
(559) 683-7720. **$79-$250, 4 day notice.** 48571 Hwy 41 93623. 4 mi from Yosemite National Park South Gate. Ext corridors. **Pets:** Medium. $25 one-time fee/pet. Designated rooms, service with restrictions, supervision.

Tenaya Lodge at Yosemite H 🐾
(559) 683-6555. **$129-$389, 7 day notice.** 1122 Hwy 41 93623. 2 mi from Yosemite National Park South Gate. Int corridors. **Pets:** Dogs only. $75 one-time fee/room. Designated rooms, service with restrictions, supervision.

FOLSOM

Lake Natoma Inn H
(916) 351-1500. **$89-$169.** 702 Gold Lake Dr 95630. US 50, exit Folsom Blvd, 3 mi n, 0.5 mi e on Riley St; behind The Lakes Specialty Shopping Center. Int corridors. **Pets:** Medium. $15 daily fee/pet, $45 one-time fee/room. Designated rooms, service with restrictions, supervision.

Larkspur Landing Folsom H
(916) 355-1616. **$89-$169.** 121 Iron Point Rd 95630. US 50, exit Folsom Blvd, 0.5 mi n to Iron Point Rd, then 0.3 mi e. Int corridors.
Pets: Accepted.

Residence Inn by Marriott H
(916) 983-7289. **$153-$187.** 2555 Iron Point Rd 95630. US 50, exit Bidwell St, just n, then just w. Int corridors. **Pets:** Other species. $100 onetime fee/room. Service with restrictions, crate.

FORTUNA

Best Western Country Inn M
(707) 725-6822. **$79-$210.** 2025 Riverwalk Dr 95540. US 101, exit 687 (Kenmar Rd), just w. Ext corridors. **Pets:** Small, dogs only. $20 one-time fee/pet. Designated rooms, service with restrictions, supervision.

Fortuna Super 8 M
(707) 725-2888. **$70-$200.** 1805 Alamar Way 95540. US 101, exit 687 (Kenmar Rd), 0.3 mi w on Riverwalk Dr. Ext corridors. **Pets:** Accepted.

Holiday Inn Express H
(707) 725-5500. **$90-$140.** 1859 Alamar Way 95540. US 101, exit 687 (Kenmar Rd), 0.3 mi w on Riverwalk Dr to Alamar Way. Ext corridors. **Pets:** $20 daily fee/room. Service with restrictions, supervision.

FOUNTAIN VALLEY

Residence Inn by Marriott H
(714) 965-8000. **$188-$230.** 9930 Slater Ave 92708. I-405, exit 14 (Brookhurst St), just n, then just w. Ext corridors. **Pets:** Medium, other species. $100 one-time fee/room. Service with restrictions.

FREMONT

Best Western Garden Court Inn H
(510) 792-4300. **$80-$180.** 5400 Mowry Ave 94538. I-880, exit Mowry Ave, just e. Int corridors. **Pets:** Large. $15 daily fee/pet. Designated rooms, service with restrictions, supervision.

Extended StayAmerica-Fremont-Newark H
(510) 794-8040. **$85-$100.** 5355 Farwell Pl 94536. I-880, exit Mowry Ave, just e. Int corridors. **Pets:** Other species. $25 daily fee/room. Designated rooms, service with restrictions, crate.

Fremont Marriott H
(510) 413-3700. **$152-$186.** 46100 Landing Pkwy 94538. I-880, exit Fremont Blvd/Cushing Pkwy, then w. Int corridors. **Pets:** Large. $100 onetime fee/room. Service with restrictions.

La Quinta Inn & Suites Fremont H
(510) 445-0808. **$49-$139.** 46200 Landing Pkwy 94538. I-880, exit Fremont Blvd/Cushing Pkwy, just w. Int corridors. **Pets:** Medium, other species. Service with restrictions, supervision.

Residence Inn by Marriott H
(510) 794-5900. **$143-$175.** 5400 Farwell Pl 94536. I-880, exit Mowry Ave, just e. Ext corridors. **Pets:** Accepted.

FRESNO

Ambassador Inn & Suites M
(559) 442-1082. **$55-$80.** 1804 W Olive Ave 93728. SR 99, exit Olive Ave, just w. Ext corridors. **Pets:** Accepted.

Crossland Economy Studios Fresno-West H
(559) 277-8700. **$55-$70.** 3460 W Shaw Ave 93711. SR 99, exit Shaw Ave, 1.8 mi e. Ext corridors. **Pets:** Other species. $25 daily fee/room. Designated rooms, service with restrictions, crate.

Days Inn-Parkway M
(559) 268-6211. **Call for rates.** 1101 N Parkway Dr 93728. SR 99, exit Olive Ave, just w. Ext corridors. **Pets:** Accepted.

Extended StayAmerica Fresno-North H
(559) 438-7105. **$97-$112.** 7135 N Fresno St 93720. SR 41, exit Herndon Ave, just e, then just n. Ext corridors. **Pets:** Other species. $25 daily fee/room. Designated rooms, service with restrictions, crate.

La Quinta Inn & Suites H
(559) 449-0928. **$99-$229.** 330 E Fir Ave 93720. SR 41, exit Herndon Ave, just e. Int corridors. **Pets:** Medium, other species. Service with restrictions, supervision.

La Quinta Inn Fresno/Yosemite H
(559) 442-1110. **$49-$139.** 2926 Tulare St 93721. SR 99, exit Fresno St, 1 mi e to R St, then s, then just e. Ext/int corridors. **Pets:** Medium, other species. Service with restrictions, supervision.

Motel 6 M
(559) 276-1910. **$50-$80, 14 day notice.** 5021 N Barcus Ave 93722. SR 99, exit Shaw Ave, just e. Ext corridors. **Pets:** Other species. Service with restrictions, supervision.

Quality Inn-Fresno M
(559) 275-2727. **$79.** 4278 W Ashlan Ave 93722. SR 99, exit Ashlan Ave, just w. Ext corridors. **Pets:** Accepted.

Residence Inn by Marriott H
(559) 222-8900. **$167-$204.** 5322 N Diana St 93710. SR 41, exit Shaw Ave, 0.3 mi w, n on Blackstone Ave, then e on Barstow Ave. Int corridors. **Pets:** Accepted.

Rodeway Inn H
(559) 431-3557. **$60-$150.** 6730 N Blackstone Ave 93710. SR 41, exit Herndon Ave, then w. Ext corridors. **Pets:** Small. $10 daily fee/pet. Designated rooms, service with restrictions, supervision.

Super 8-Parkway M
(559) 268-0741. **$57-$89.** 1087 N Parkway Dr 93728. SR 99, exit Olive Ave, just w. Ext corridors. **Pets:** $10 daily fee/pet. Service with restrictions, supervision.

TownePlace Suites by Marriott H
(559) 435-4600. **$131-$160.** 7127 N Fresno St 93720. SR 41, exit Herndon Ave E. Int corridors. **Pets:** Medium. $100 one-time fee/room. Service with restrictions, crate.

University Inn H
(559) 294-0224. **$59-$99.** 2655 E Shaw Ave 93710. SR 168, exit Shaw Ave, just w. Ext corridors. **Pets:** Accepted.

Valley Inn M
(559) 233-3913. **$45-$65.** 933 N Parkway Dr 93728. SR 99, exit Olive Ave, then w. Ext corridors. **Pets:** Small, dogs only. $5 daily fee/room. Designated rooms, service with restrictions, supervision.

FULLERTON

Fullerton Marriott Hotel at California State Univ H
(714) 738-7800. **$152-$186.** 2701 E Nutwood Ave 92835. SR 57, exit 7 (Nutwood Ave) northbound; exit 7 (Nutwood Ave/Chapman Ave) southbound, just w. Int corridors. **Pets:** Medium. $100 deposit/room, $35 daily fee/room. Designated rooms, service with restrictions, supervision.

GARBERVILLE

AAA **▼▼▼** **Benbow Inn** 🅷 🐾
(707) 923-2124. **$125-$695, 5 day notice.** 445 Lake Benbow Dr 95542. US 101, exit Benbow, just w; 2 mi s of downtown. Int corridors. **Pets:** Other species. $30 daily fee/pet. Designated rooms, service with restrictions, crate. (SAVE) ✕ 🔲 🔳 🍴 ⚓ ✕

AAA **▼▼▼** **Best Western Humboldt House Inn** 🅼
(707) 923-2771. **$131-$155.** 701 Redwood Dr 95542. US 101, exit Garberville, just e. Ext corridors. **Pets:** Small, dogs only. $10 one-time fee/pet. Designated rooms, service with restrictions, supervision.
(SAVE) ✕ 🔲 🔳 ⚓

GARDEN GROVE

AAA **▼▼▼** **Anaheim Marriott Suites** 🅷
(714) 750-1000. **$278-$340.** 12015 Harbor Blvd 92840. I-5, exit 107B (Chapman Ave) northbound, 1.5 mi w on Chapman Ave, then just s; exit 107C (State College/The City Dr) southbound, just s on State College Blvd, 1.5 mi w on Chapman Ave, then just s. Int corridors. **Pets:** Medium, other species. $35 daily fee/pet. Designated rooms, service with restrictions, crate. (SAVE) ✕ 🔲🅼 🔲 🔳 🍴 ⚓ ✕

▼▼▼ **Candlewood Suites Anaheim-South** 🅷
(714) 539-4200. **$90-$140.** 12901 Garden Grove Blvd 92843. SR 22, exit 13 (Haster St) westbound; exit 13 (Fairview St) eastbound, just n, then just w. Int corridors. **Pets:** Medium. $75 one-time fee/room. Service with restrictions, supervision. (ASK) ✕ 🔲🅼 🔲 🔳

▼▼▼ **Residence Inn Anaheim Resort Area** 🅷
(714) 591-4000. **$188-$230.** 11931 Harbor Blvd 92840. I-5, exit 107B (Chapman Ave) northbound, 1.5 mi w, then just n; exit 107C (State College/The City Dr) southbound, just s on State College Blvd, 1.5 mi w on Chapman Ave, then just n. Int corridors. **Pets:** Small. $75 one-time fee/pet. Service with restrictions, supervision.
✕ 🔲🅼 🔲 🔳 ⚓ ✕

AAA **▼▼▼** **Sheraton Garden Grove Anaheim South** 🅷
(714) 703-8400. **$119-$189.** 12221 Harbor Blvd 92840. I-5, exit 110 (Harbor Blvd/Ball Rd), 2.2 mi s. Int corridors. **Pets:** Accepted.
(SAVE) ✕ 🔲 🔳 🍴 ⚓

GILROY

AAA **▼▼▼** **Best Western Forest Park Inn** 🅷
(408) 848-5144. **$89-$239.** 375 Leavesley Rd 95020. US 101, exit Leavesley Rd, just w. Int corridors. **Pets:** Small. $30 daily fee/pet. Designated rooms, service with restrictions, supervision.
(SAVE) ✕ 🔲🅼 🔲 🔳 ⚓ ✕

AAA **▼▼▼** **Quality Inn & Suites** 🅷
(408) 847-5500. **$69-$249.** 8430 Murray Ave 95020. US 101, exit Leavesley Rd, just w. Ext corridors. **Pets:** Accepted.
(SAVE) ✕ 🔲 🔳 ⚓

AAA **▼▼▼** **Super 8** 🅷
(408) 848-4108. **$69-$159.** 8435 San Ysidro Ave 95020. US 101, exit Leavesley Rd, just e. Int corridors. **Pets:** Accepted.
(ASK) ✕ 🔲 🔳 ⚓

GLENNVILLE

▼▼ **The Bunkhouse Motel** 🅼
(661) 536-9100. **$65-$75.** 12044 Hwy 155 S 93226. On SR 155 at Granite Rd. Ext corridors. **Pets:** Accepted. (ASK) ✕ 🔲 🔳 🍴

GRAEAGLE

▼▼▼ **Chalet View Lodge** 🅷
(530) 832-5528. **$89-$315, 7 day notice.** 72056 Hwy 70 96103. Jct SR 70 and 89, 5.7 mi e on SR 70. Ext corridors. **Pets:** Accepted.
(ASK) ✕ 🔲 🔳 🍴 ⚓ ✕

GRASS VALLEY

AAA **▼▼▼** **Best Western Gold Country Inn** 🅼
(530) 273-1393. **$90-$126.** 972 Sutton Way 95945. SR 20 and 49, exit 183 (Brunswick Rd), just e; midway between Grass Valley and Nevada City. Ext corridors. **Pets:** Accepted. (SAVE) ✕ 🔲🅼 🔲 🔳 ⚓

AAA **▼▼** **Golden Chain Resort Motel** 🅼
(530) 273-7279. **$55-$99.** 13413 State Hwy 49 95949. On SR 49, 2.5 mi s. Ext corridors. **Pets:** Medium. $10 one-time fee/pet. Service with restrictions, supervision. (SAVE) ✕ 🔲🅼 🔲 🔳 ⚓

▼▼▼ **Grass Valley Courtyard Suites** 🅷
(530) 272-7696. **$145-$350, 3 day notice.** 210 N Auburn St 95945. SR 49, exit 182B (E Main St/Grass Valley) southbound, just w to S Auburn St, then just n; exit 182A (SR 174/Colfax/Central Grass Valley) northbound, just n on S Auburn St; jct Richardson St. Ext corridors. **Pets:** Accepted. (ASK) ✕ 🔲🅼 🔲 🔳 ⚓ ✕

GROVELAND

AAA **▼▼▼** **Groveland Hotel at Yosemite National Park** 🅲🅸 🐾
(209) 962-4000. **$145-$285.** 18767 Main St 95321. Center. Int corridors. **Pets:** $20 daily fee/pet. Service with restrictions, crate.
(SAVE) ✕ 🔳 🍴

HANFORD

▼▼ **Irwin Street Inn** 🅱🅱
(559) 583-8000. **$72-$135.** 522 N Irwin St 93230. Downtown. Ext corridors. **Pets:** Accepted. (ASK) ✕ 🔲 🔳 🍴

AAA **▼▼▼** **Sequoia Inn** 🅷
(559) 582-0338. **$79.** 1655 Mall Dr 93230. SR 198, exit 12th Ave, then n. Int corridors. **Pets:** Other species. $100 deposit/room. Service with restrictions, crate. (SAVE) ✕ 🔲 🔳 ⚓ ✕

HAYWARD

▼▼▼ **Comfort Inn** 🅷
(510) 538-4466. **$69-$170.** 24997 Mission Blvd 94544. 1.8 mi e of I-880, exit SR 92 (Jackson St), 0.5 mi s on SR 238 (Mission Blvd). Ext corridors. **Pets:** Small. $100 deposit/room, $15 daily fee/pet. Designated rooms, service with restrictions, supervision. (ASK) ✕ 🔲 🔳

▼▼▼ **La Quinta Inn & Suites Hayward/Oakland Airport** 🅷 🐾
(510) 732-6300. **$79-$169.** 20777 Hesperian Blvd 94541. I-880, exit a St, 0.5 mi w. Int corridors. **Pets:** Medium, other species. Service with restrictions, supervision. (ASK) ✕ 🔲 🔳 ⚓

HEMET

AAA **▼▼▼** **Best Western Inn of Hemet** 🅼
(951) 925-6605. **$89-$109.** 2625 W Florida Ave 92545. 2.4 mi w of SR 79 N (San Jacinto St) on SR 74/79. Ext corridors. **Pets:** Accepted.
(SAVE) ✕ 🔲 🔳 ⚓

AAA **▼▼▼** **Quality Inn** 🅼
(951) 766-1902. **$89-$149.** 1201 W Florida Ave 92543. 1.5 mi w of SR 79 N (San Jacinto St) on SR 74/79. Ext corridors. **Pets:** Small, dogs only. $20 daily fee/pet. Designated rooms, service with restrictions, supervision. (SAVE) ✕ 🔲🅼 🔲 🔳 ⚓

HESPERIA

▼▼ **Econo Lodge** 🅼 🐾
(760) 949-1515. **$54-$79.** 11976 Mariposa Rd 92345. I-15, exit 147 (Bear Valley Rd), just e, then just s. Ext corridors. **Pets:** Small, dogs only. $10 daily fee/pet. Service with restrictions, supervision. (ASK) ✕ 🔲 🔳

AAA **▼▼▼▼** **Holiday Inn Express Hotel & Suites** 🅷
(760) 244-7674. **$65-$99.** 9750 Key Pointe Dr 92345. I-15, exit 143 (Hesperia/Main St), just w on Main St, then just n. Int corridors. **Pets:** Medium, other species. $25 one-time fee/pet. Service with restrictions, supervision. (SAVE) ✕ 🔲 🔳 ⚓

AAA **▼▼▼** **La Quinta Inn & Suites Victorville** 🅷 🐾
(760) 949-9900. **$70-$140.** 12000 Mariposa Rd 92345. I-15, exit 147 (Bear Valley Rd), just e, then just s. Int corridors. **Pets:** Medium, other species. Service with restrictions, supervision.
(SAVE) ✕ 🔲🅼 🔲 🔳 ⚓ ✕

HOLLISTER

⚛️ ◈◈ Best Western San Benito Inn H

(831) 637-9248. **$100-$180.** 660 San Felipe Rd 95023. 1.5 mi n on SR 25 and 156. Ext corridors. **Pets:** Accepted. 📳 ✖️ 📇 📠 ➿

HUNTINGTON BEACH

◈◈ Extended StayAmerica-Orange County/Huntington Beach H

(714) 799-4887. **$80-$100.** 5050 Skylab W Cir 92647. I-405, exit 21 (SR 22/Valley View Blvd) northbound, 1.8 mi s; exit 18 (Bolsa Ave) southbound, 2 mi s. Int corridors. **Pets:** Other species. $25 daily fee/room. Designated rooms, service with restrictions, crate.

📳 ✖️ 📶 📇 📠

⚛️ ◈◈◈ Hilton Waterfront Beach Resort H 🐾

(714) 845-8000. **$189-$659.** 21100 Pacific Coast Hwy 92648. I-405, exit 16 (Beach Blvd), 6 mi s, then just w. Int corridors. **Pets:** Medium. $75 daily fee/pet. Designated rooms, service with restrictions, crate.

📳 ✖️ 📶 📇 📠 🍴 ➿ ✖️

IDYLLWILD

◈◈ Fireside Inn CA 🐾

(951) 659-2966. **$65-$130, 10 day notice.** 54540 N Circle Dr 92549. From SR 243 and town center, 0.3 mi ne. Ext corridors. **Pets:** Medium, dogs only. $10 daily fee/room. Service with restrictions, supervision.

📳 ✖️ 📇 📠 ✖️

◈◈ Quiet Creek Inn M 🐾

(951) 659-6110. **$117-$160, 14 day notice.** 26345 Delano Dr 92549. From SR 243, 0.8 mi sw of town center, 0.4 mi w on Toll Gate Rd, then just n. Ext corridors. **Pets:** Other species. $35 one-time fee/room. Supervision. 📳 ✖️ 📇 📠 ✖️

◈◈ Woodland Park Manor M 🐾

(951) 659-2657. **$95-$195, 10 day notice.** 55350 S Circle Dr 92549. From SR 243 and town center, 1.5 mi ne. Ext corridors. **Pets:** Designated rooms, supervision. ✖️ 📇 📠 ➿ ✖️ ✖️

INDEPENDENCE

◈ Independence Courthouse Motel M

(760) 878-2732. **Call for rates.** 157 N Edwards 93526. On US 395. Ext corridors. **Pets:** Accepted. ✖️ 📇 📠

INDIAN WELLS

⚛️ ◈◈◈ Hyatt Grand Champions Resort H 🐾

(760) 341-1000. **$89-$499, 7 day notice.** 44-600 Indian Wells Ln 92210. I-10, exit 136 (Cook St), 4.4 mi s, 1.5 mi e on SR 111, then just n. Ext/int corridors. **Pets:** Medium. $100 one-time fee/room. Designated rooms, service with restrictions, crate.

📳 ✖️ 📶 📇 📠 🍴 ➿ ✖️

⚛️ ◈◈◈ Miramonte Resort and Spa H

(760) 341-2200. **$139-$499, 3 day notice.** 45-000 Indian Wells Ln 92210. I-10, exit 136 (Cook St), 4.4 mi s, 1.5 mi e, then just s. Ext/int corridors. **Pets:** Medium, dogs only. $50 one-time fee/room. Designated rooms, service with restrictions, supervision.

📳 ✖️ 📇 📠 🍴 ➿ ✖️

INDIO

⚛️ ◈◈ Best Western Date Tree Hotel M 🐾

(760) 347-3421. **$79-$350.** 81-909 Indio Blvd 92201. I-10, exit 139 (Jefferson St/Indio Blvd) westbound, 2 mi se; eastbound, south across freeway, then 2.8 mi e. Int corridors. **Pets:** Other species. $10 daily fee/pet. Service with restrictions, crate. 📳 ✖️ 📇 📠 ➿

⚛️ ◈◈ Indian Palms Country Club & Resort H 🐾

(760) 775-4444. **$84-$209.** 48-630 Monroe St 92201. I-10, exit 142 (Monroe St), 2 mi s. Ext corridors. **Pets:** Medium, dogs only. $15 daily fee/room. Service with restrictions, crate.

📳 ✖️ 📇 📠 🍴 ➿ ✖️

◈◈ Quality Inn M

(760) 347-4044. **$69-$99.** 43-505 Monroe St 92201. I-10, exit 142 (Monroe St), 0.5 mi s. Int corridors. **Pets:** Accepted. 📳 ✖️ 📇 📠 ➿

IRVINE

◈◈◈ Embassy Suites Hotel-Orange County Airport H

(949) 553-8332. **$119-$279.** 2120 Main St 92614. I-405, exit 8 (MacArthur Blvd/John Wayne Airport), just n, then 0.5 mi e. Int corridors. **Pets:** Medium. $100 one-time fee/room. Service with restrictions, supervision. 🌿 ✖️ 📶 📇 📠 🍴 ➿ ✖️

⚛️ ◈◈◈ Hilton Irvine/Orange County Airport H

(949) 833-9999. **$119-$249.** 18800 MacArthur Blvd 92612. I-405, exit 8 (MacArthur Blvd/John Wayne Airport), 0.5 mi s. Int corridors. **Pets:** Accepted. 📳 ✖️ 📶 📇 📠 🍴 ➿

◈◈ La Quinta Inn Irvine Spectrum (Old Historic Site) M 🐾

(949) 551-0909. **$49-$139.** 14972 Sand Canyon Ave 92618. I-5, exit 96 (Sand Canyon Ave) northbound; exit 96A (Sand Canyon Ave) southbound, just w. Ext/int corridors. **Pets:** Medium, other species. Service with restrictions, supervision. 📳 ✖️ 📇 📠 ➿

◈◈ Residence Inn by Marriott Irvine John Wayne Airport H

(949) 261-2020. **$170-$208.** 2855 Main St 92614. I-405, exit 7 (Jamboree Blvd), just n, then just e. Int corridors. **Pets:** Large, other species. $100 one-time fee/room. Service with restrictions.

✖️ 📶 📇 📠 ➿ ✖️

◈◈ Residence Inn by Marriott-Irvine Spectrum H 🐾

(949) 380-3000. **$206-$252.** 10 Morgan 92618. I-5, exit 94 (Alton Pkwy); 94B (Alton Pkwy) northbound, 2 mi e. Ext corridors. **Pets:** $100 one-time fee/room. Supervision. ✖️ 📶 📇 📠 ➿ ✖️

JACKSON

⚛️ ◈◈ Best Western Amador Inn H

(209) 223-0211. **$70-$150.** 200 S Hwy 49 95642. On SR 49. Int corridors. **Pets:** Medium, other species. $15 daily fee/pet. Service with restrictions, supervision. 📳 ✖️ 📇 📠 ➿

◈◈ The Jackson Lodge M

(209) 223-0486. **$65-$145.** 850 N Hwy 49 95642. On SR 49 and 88, 0.5 mi w. Ext corridors. **Pets:** Large. $15 daily fee/pet. Designated rooms, service with restrictions, supervision. 📳 ✖️ 📇 📠 ➿

JAMESTOWN

⚛️ ◈◈◈ 1859 Historic National Hotel, a Country Inn CI 🐾

(209) 984-3446. **$140-$160, 3 day notice.** 18183 Main St 95327. Downtown. Int corridors. **Pets:** Medium, other species. $25 daily fee/pet. Service with restrictions, supervision. 📳 ✖️ 🍴 🪑 ✖️

◈◈ Country Inn Sonora M

(209) 984-0315. **$59-$289.** 18730 Hwy 108 95327. SR 108 and 49, 1 mi e of town. Ext corridors. **Pets:** Medium. $10 daily fee/pet. Designated rooms, service with restrictions, crate. 📳 ✖️ 📇 📠 ➿

⚛️ ◈ Jamestown Railtown Motel M

(209) 984-3332. **$40-$80, 3 day notice.** 10301 Willow St 95327. Center. Ext corridors. **Pets:** Medium, dogs only. $10 daily fee/pet. Service with restrictions. 📳 ✖️ 📇 ➿

◈◈◈ Victorian Gold Bed & Breakfast BB 🐾

(209) 984-3429. **$110-$185, 5 day notice.** 10382 Willow St 95327. Center. Int corridors. **Pets:** Small, dogs only. $15 daily fee/room. Designated rooms, service with restrictions, supervision. 📳 ✖️ 📇 ✖️

JUNE LAKE

Double Eagle Resort/Spa 🄲🄰

(760) 648-7004. **$169-$400, 30 day notice.** 5587 Hwy 158 93529. On SR 158; 3 mi w of village. Ext corridors. **Pets:** Other species. $50 one-time fee/pet. Designated rooms, service with restrictions, supervision.

[SAVE] [X] [&M] [🛏] [💻] [¶] [🖘] [X] [AC]

June Lake Villager 🄼

(760) 648-7712. **$65-$95.** 2640 Hwy 158 Dr 93529. On SR 158; center of village. Ext corridors. **Pets:** Accepted. [ASK] [X] [🛏] [💻] [AC] [☎]

KERNVILLE

Barewood Inn & Suites 🄼

(760) 376-1910. **$75-$195.** 7013 Wofford Blvd 93285. In Wofford Heights. Ext corridors. **Pets:** Dogs only. $50 deposit/room. Designated rooms, service with restrictions, supervision. [ASK] [X] [🛏] [💻]

River View Lodge 🄼

(760) 376-6019. **Call for rates.** 2 Sirretta St 93238. On Kernville Rd; at the bridge. Ext corridors. **Pets:** Accepted. [X] [🛏]

KETTLEMAN CITY

Best Western Kettleman Inn & Suites 🄼

(559) 386-0804. **$79-$165.** 33410 Powers Dr 93239. E of and adjacent to I-5, exit SR 41 N, 0.3 mi to Bernard, then 0.3 mi n. Ext corridors. **Pets:** Accepted. [SAVE] [X] [🛏] [💻] [🖘]

Super 8 🄼

(559) 386-9530. **$59-$119.** 33415 Powers Dr 93239. E of and adjacent to I-5, exit SR 41 N, 0.3 mi to Bernard, then 0.3 mi n. Ext corridors. **Pets:** Accepted. [SAVE] [X] [🛏] [💻] [🖘]

KLAMATH

Motel Trees 🄼 🐾

(707) 482-3152. **$70-$149.** 15495 Hwy 101 N 95548. On US 101, 4.5 mi n. Ext corridors. **Pets:** Other species. $10 daily fee/pet. Designated rooms, supervision. [SAVE] [X] [🛏] [💻] [¶] [AC]

LAGUNA BEACH

Aliso Creek Inn 🄷

(949) 499-2271. **$139-$402.** 31106 S Coast Hwy 92651. SR 133, 3 mi s on SR 1, then 0.3 mi e. Ext corridors. **Pets:** Accepted.

[SAVE] [X] [🛏] [💻] [¶] [🖘] [X] [AC]

Art Hotel-Laguna Beach 🄼

(949) 494-6464. **$89-$159, 3 day notice.** 1404 N Coast Hwy 92651. SR 133, 1.1 mi n on SR 1. Ext corridors. **Pets:** Designated rooms.

[ASK] [X] [🛏] [💻] [🖘]

Best Western Laguna Brisas Spa Hotel 🄷

(949) 497-7272. **$99-$499, 3 day notice.** 1600 S Coast Hwy 92651. SR 133, 1 mi s on SR 1. Ext/int corridors. **Pets:** Accepted.

[SAVE] [X] [🛏] [💻] [🖘]

The Carriage House-Bed & Breakfast 🄱🄱

(949) 494-8945. **$160-$225.** 1322 Catalina St 92651. SR 133, 1 mi s on S Coast Hwy to Cress St, then just e. Ext corridors. **Pets:** Accepted.

[X] [🛏] [AC] [☎]

Casa Laguna Inn and Spa 🄱🄱 ❀

(949) 494-2996. **$150-$650, 5 day notice.** 2510 S Coast Hwy 92651. SR 133, 1.3 mi s on SR 1. Ext corridors. **Pets:** Medium, dogs only. $25 daily fee/pet. Service with restrictions, supervision. [X] [🛏] [💻] [🖘]

Montage Laguna Beach 🄷 ❀

(949) 715-6000. **$450-$1095, 7 day notice.** 30801 S Coast Hwy 92651. SR 133, 3 mi s. Ext/int corridors. **Pets:** Small, dogs only. $100 one-time fee/room. Designated rooms. [SAVE] [X] [¶] [🖘] [X]

Surf & Sand Resort 🄷

(949) 497-4477. **$435-$695, 3 day notice.** 1555 S Coast Hwy 92651. SR 133, 1 mi s. Ext corridors. **Pets:** Accepted.

[SAVE] [X] [&M] [💻] [¶] [🖘] [X]

LAGUNA HILLS

Holiday Inn Laguna Hills 🄷

(949) 586-5000. **$134-$234.** 25205 La Paz Rd 92653. I-5, exit 89 (La Paz Rd), just w. Int corridors. **Pets:** Accepted.

[ASK] [X] [&M] [🛏] [💻] [¶] [🖘]

LAKE ARROWHEAD

Arrowhead Saddleback Inn 🄲🄸

(909) 336-3571. **$137-$648, 7 day notice.** 300 S SR 173 92352. On SR 173, jct SR 189; across from entrance to Lake Arrowhead Village. Ext/int corridors. **Pets:** Other species. $8 daily fee/pet. Designated rooms, service with restrictions, crate. [SAVE] [X] [🛏] [💻] [¶]

Arrowhead Tree Top Lodge 🄼

(909) 337-2311. **$69-$217, 7 day notice.** 27992 Rainbow Dr 92352. 0.3 mi s of Lake Arrowhead Village on SR 173. Ext corridors. **Pets:** Other species. $8 daily fee/pet. Service with restrictions, crate.

[SAVE] [X] [🛏] [💻] [🖘] [AC] [☎]

Bracken Fern Manor 🄱🄱

(909) 337-8557. **$90-$270, 7 day notice.** 815 Arrowhead Villas Rd 92352. 0.8 mi n of SR 18, 0.4 mi e of jct SR 173. Int corridors. **Pets:** Accepted. [ASK] [X] [🛏] [AC] [☎]

Lake Arrowhead Resort and Spa 🄷

(909) 336-1511. **$169-$449, 3 day notice.** 27984 Hwy 189 92352. Just w of SR 173; in Lake Arrowhead Village. Int corridors. **Pets:** Small, other species. $20 daily fee/pet. Designated rooms, service with restrictions, supervision. [ASK] [X] [&M] [🛏] [💻] [¶] [🖘] [X]

LAKE FOREST

Quality Inn & Suites 🄼

(949) 458-1900. **$89-$200.** 23702 Rockfield Blvd 92630. I-5, exit 92A (Lake Forest Dr) northbound; exit 92 (Bake Pkwy/Lake Forest Dr) southbound, 0.5 mi e on Lake Forest Dr, then just s. Int corridors. **Pets:** Large. $25 daily fee/pet. Designated rooms, service with restrictions, supervision.

[SAVE] [X] [🛏] [💻] [¶] [🖘]

Staybridge Suites Irvine East/Lake Forest 🄷

(949) 462-9500. **$139-$399.** 2 Orchard 92630. I-5, exit 92B (Bake Pkwy) northbound; exit 92 (Bake Pkwy/Lake Forest Dr) southbound, 4.7 mi e, then just s on Rancho Pkwy S. Int corridors. **Pets:** Other species. $75 one-time fee/room. Designated rooms, service with restrictions.

[ASK] [X] [&M] [🛏] [💻] [🖘] [X]

LAKE TAHOE AREA

SOUTH LAKE TAHOE

Alpenrose Inn 🄼

(530) 544-2985. **$49-$165, 7 day notice.** 4074 Pine Blvd 96150. W of US 50 via Park Ave, then just n; 3 blks from casino area. Ext corridors. **Pets:** Accepted. [SAVE] [X] [🛏] [💻]

Ambassador Motor Lodge 🄼

(530) 544-6461. **$30-$199, 3 day notice.** 4130 Manzanita Ave 96150. Just w of US 50 off Stateline Ave. Ext corridors. **Pets:** Accepted.

[SAVE] [X] [🛏] [💻] [🖘] [AC]

Best Western Timber Cove Lodge 🄷

(530) 541-6722. **$137-$220, 3 day notice.** 3411 Lake Tahoe Blvd 96150. 1.5 mi w of casino area; 0.5 mi w of Ski Run Blvd. Ext corridors. **Pets:** Medium, other species. $100 deposit/room, $25 daily fee/room. Designated rooms, service with restrictions, supervision.

[SAVE] [X] [&M] [🛏] [💻] [¶] [🖘] [X]

▓▓ ▼▼▼ Big Pines Mountain House of Tahoe Ⓜ ❖
(530) 541-5155. **$75-$209.** 4083 Cedar Ave 96150. US 50, exit Friday Ave, toward the lake; near casino area. Ext corridors. **Pets:** Other species. $15 daily fee/pet. Service with restrictions, crate.
[SAVE] [✕] [♿M] [🛏] [💻] [🐾]

▓▓ ▼▼▼▼ Fireside Lodge–An All Inclusive Premier Bed & Breakfast 🅱🅱 ❖
(530) 544-5515. **$99-$199, 7 day notice.** 515 Emerald Bay Rd 96150. 1 mi n of jct US 50 and SR 89. Ext corridors. **Pets:** Other species. $100 deposit/room, $20 daily fee/pet. [SAVE] [✕] [🛏] [💻] [✕] [🄰🄲]

▼▼▼ Highland Inn Ⓜ
(530) 544-3862. **$69-$299, 3 day notice.** 3979 Lake Tahoe Blvd 96150. US 50, just sw of casino area; near Heavenly Village. Ext corridors. **Pets:** Accepted. [ASK] [✕] [🛏] [🍴]

▼▼▼ Pistantes Coyote Den Ⓜ
(530) 541-2282. **$55-$375, 4 day notice.** 1211 Emerald Bay Rd 96150. US 50, 0.5 mi n of airport. Ext corridors. **Pets:** Large, dogs only. $10 one-time fee/pet. Designated rooms, service with restrictions, supervision.
[ASK] [✕] [🛏] [🄰🄲]

▓▓ ▼▼▼ Tahoe Keys Resort 🄲🄾 ❖
(530) 544-5397. **$112-$1300.** 599 Tahoe Keys Blvd 96150. US 50, 1 mi n. Ext corridors. **Pets:** Dogs only. $100 deposit/pet, $25 one-time fee/pet. Designated rooms, service with restrictions, supervision.
[SAVE] [✕] [🛏] [💻] [🐾] [✕] [🄰🄲]

▓▓ ▼▼ Tahoe Valley Lodge Ⓜ
(530) 541-0353. **$125-$495, 7 day notice.** 2241 Lake Tahoe Blvd 96150. 0.5 mi e of jct US 50 and SR 89. Ext corridors. **Pets:** Accepted.
[SAVE] [✕] [🛏] [💻] [🐾]

TAHOE CITY

▓▓ ▼▼ Lake of the Sky Motor Inn Ⓜ
(530) 583-3305. **$59-$199, 3 day notice.** 955 N Lake Blvd 96145. 1 mi e of jct SR 89. Ext corridors. **Pets:** Large. $15 daily fee/pet. Designated rooms, service with restrictions, supervision.
[SAVE] [✕] [♿M] [🛏] [🐾] [🄰🄲]

▓▓ ▼▼▼ Mother Nature's Inn Ⓜ ❖
(530) 581-4278. **$59-$159, 7 day notice.** 551 N Lake Blvd 96145. SR 28, 0.5 mi e of jct SR 89; behind Mother Nature's Store. Int corridors. **Pets:** $15 daily fee/pet. Designated rooms, service with restrictions, supervision. [SAVE] [✕] [🛏] [💻]

TAHOE VISTA

▼▼ Holiday House Ⓜ ❖
(530) 546-2369. **$125-$225.** 7276 N Lake Blvd 96148. SR 28, 1 mi w of SR 267. Ext corridors. **Pets:** Other species. $30 one-time fee/pet. Supervision. [✕] [♿M] [🛏] [💻] [🄰🄲]

▼▼ Knights Inn Cedar Glen Lodge Ⓜ ❖
(530) 546-4281. **$64-$119.** 6589 N Lake Blvd 96148. SR 28, 1.5 mi w of SR 267. Ext corridors. **Pets:** $30 daily fee/room. Designated rooms, service with restrictions, supervision. [ASK] [✕] [♿M] [🛏] [💻] [🐾] [🄰🄲]

TRUCKEE

▓▓ ▼▼▼ Best Western Larkspur Hotel Truckee ⛤
(530) 587-4525. **$129-$179.** 11331 Brockway Rd 96161. I-80, exit 188 westbound; exit 188B (SR 267) eastbound, 1.5 mi se. Int corridors.
Pets: Accepted. [SAVE] [✕] [🛏] [💻] [🐾] [✕]

▼▼◆▼ The Cedar House Sport Hotel ⛤ ❖
(530) 582-5655. **$170-$320, 3 day notice.** 10918 Brockway Rd 96161. I-80, exit 188 (SR 267) westbound; exit 188B (SR 267) eastbound, 1.5 mi s, then 0.8 mi nw. Int corridors. **Pets:** Medium, dogs only. $50 one-time fee/room. Designated rooms, service with restrictions, supervision.
[ASK] [✕] [🛏] [💻]

END AREA

LANCASTER

▼▼▼ Antelope Valley Inn Ⓜ
(661) 948-4651. **Call for rates.** 44055 N Sierra Hwy 93534. SR 14, exit 42 (Ave K), 2.3 mi e. Ext/int corridors. **Pets:** Accepted.
[✕] [🛏] [💻] [🍴] [🐾]

▓▓ ▼▼▼▼ Holiday Inn Express ⛤
(661) 951-8848. **$129-$199.** 43719 17th St W 93534. SR 14, exit 42 (Ave K), just e, then just n. Int corridors. **Pets:** Dogs only. $100 deposit/room, $10 daily fee/pet. Designated rooms, service with restrictions, supervision. [SAVE] [✕] [♿M] [🛏] [💻] [🐾]

▓▓ ▼▼ Inn of Lancaster Ⓜ ❖
(661) 945-8771. **$80-$100.** 44131 Sierra Hwy 93534. SR 14, exit 42 (Ave K), 2 mi e, then just n. Ext corridors. **Pets:** Medium. $35 deposit/pet. Supervision. [SAVE] [✕] [🛏] [💻] [🐾] [✕]

▼▼▼ Oxford Inn & Suites Ⓜ ❖
(661) 949-3423. **$119-$159.** 1651 W Ave K 93534. SR 14, exit 42 (Ave K), just w. Int corridors. **Pets:** Dogs only. $50 one-time fee/pet. Designated rooms, service with restrictions, crate.
[ASK] [✕] [♿M] [🛏] [💻] [🐾]

LA PALMA

▼▼▼ La Quinta Inn & Suites Orange County (Buena Park) ⛤ ❖
(714) 670-1400. **$59-$139.** 3 Center Pointe Dr 90623. SR 91, exit 21 (Orangethorpe Ave/Valley View St) eastbound; exit 22 (Orangethorpe Ave/Valley View St) westbound, just n. Int corridors. **Pets:** Medium, other species. Service with restrictions, supervision. [ASK] [✕] [🛏] [💻] [🐾]

LATHROP

▼▼ Days Inn ⛤
(209) 982-1959. **$80-$90.** 14750 S Harlan Rd 95330. I-5, exit Lathrop Rd, just e. Int corridors. **Pets:** Medium, other species. $10 daily fee/pet. Service with restrictions, crate. [ASK] [✕] [♿M] [🛏] [💻] [🐾]

LEBEC

▓▓ ▼▼▼ Best Rest Inn Ⓜ
(661) 248-2700. **$79-$109.** 51541 N Peace Valley Rd 93243. I-5, exit 205 (Frazier Park), just w. Int corridors. **Pets:** Accepted.
[SAVE] [✕] [♿M] [🛏] [💻] [🐾]

▓▓ ▼▼▼ Ramada Limited Grapevine Ⓜ
(661) 248-1530. **$69-$99.** 9000 Country Side Ct 93243. I-5, exit 215 (Grapevine Rd), just w. Ext corridors. **Pets:** Accepted.
[SAVE] [✕] [🛏] [💻] [🐾]

LEE VINING

▓▓ ▼▼▼ Lake View Lodge Ⓜ
(760) 647-6543. **$59-$159.** 51285 Hwy 395 93541. US 395; in town. Ext corridors. **Pets:** Accepted. [SAVE] [✕] [🛏] [💻]

AAA ▼▼▼ Murphey's Motel M
(760) 647-6316. **$58-$113.** 51493 Hwy 395 93541. US 395; in town. Ext corridors. **Pets:** Medium. $5 one-time fee/pet. Service with restrictions, supervision. (SAVE) (✕) (🛌) (🎴)

LEMOORE

AAA ▼▼▼ Days Inn Lemoore M
(559) 924-1261. **$115-$185, 3 day notice.** 877 E "D" St 93245. SR 198, exit Houston St, 0.8 mi nw. Ext corridors. **Pets:** Accepted.
(SAVE) (✕) (🛌M) (🎴) (💻) (🏊)

LINDSAY

AAA ▼▼▼ Super 8 M
(559) 562-5188. **$85-$99.** 390 N Hwy 65 93247. SR 65. Ext corridors. **Pets:** Medium, dogs only. $10 daily fee/room. Service with restrictions, supervision. (SAVE) (✕) (🛌) (💻) (🏊)

LIVERMORE

▼▼ La Quinta Inn H ❀
(925) 373-9600. **$69-$179.** 7700 Southfront Rd 94551. I-580, exit Greenville Rd, just s. Int corridors. **Pets:** Medium, other species. Service with restrictions, supervision. (ASK) (✕) (🛌M) (🛌) (💻) (🏊) (✕)

▼▼▼▼ Residence Inn by Marriott H
(925) 373-1800. **$161-$197.** 1000 Airway Blvd 94551. I-580, exit Airway Blvd/Collier Canyon Rd, just n. Ext corridors. **Pets:** Accepted.
(✕) (🛌) (💻) (🏊) (✕)

LODI

AAA ▼▼▼ El Rancho Motel M 🐾
(209) 368-0651. **$60-$65.** 603 N Cherokee Ln 95240. SR 99, exit Turner Rd, just s. Ext corridors. **Pets:** Small. $10 one-time fee/pet. Service with restrictions, supervision. (SAVE) (✕) (🛌M) (🛌) (🏊)

AAA ▼▼▼ Microtel Inn & Suites H
(209) 367-9700. **$69-$99.** 6428 W Banner St 95242. I-5, exit SR 12, just e. Int corridors. **Pets:** Accepted. (SAVE) (✕) (🛌M) (🛌) (💻) (🏊)

▼▼▼▼ Wine & Roses Hotel and Restaurant CI
(209) 334-6988. **$169-$495.** 2505 W Turner Rd 95242. I-5, exit Turner Rd, 5 mi e; SR 99, exit Turner Rd, 2 mi w. Int corridors. **Pets:** Medium. $45 daily fee/room. Designated rooms, service with restrictions, crate. (ASK) (✕) (🛌M) (🛌) (💻) (🍴) (🏊)

LOMA LINDA

AAA ▼▼ Loma Linda Inn M
(909) 583-2500. **$75-$85, 10 day notice.** 24532 University Ave 92354. I-10, exit 74 (Anderson St/Tippecanoe Ave), 1 mi s, just w on Stewart, just s on Campus, then just w. Ext corridors. **Pets:** Medium, other species. $35 one-time fee/room. Service with restrictions, supervision. (SAVE) (✕) (🛌M) (🛌) (💻)

LOMPOC

AAA ▼▼▼ Americas Best Value Inn M
(805) 735-3737. **$60-$130.** 1200 N H St 93436. SR 1, 1.3 mi n of Ocean Ave. Ext corridors. **Pets:** $25 one-time fee/pet. Service with restrictions, crate. (SAVE) (✕) (🛌M) (🛌) (💻) (🎴)

▼▼▼▼ Days Inn M
(805) 735-7744. **$99-$199.** 1122 N H St 93436. SR 1, 1.2 mi n of Ocean Ave. Ext/int corridors. **Pets:** $25 one-time fee/room. Service with restrictions, supervision. (ASK) (✕) (🛌) (💻) (🏊)

▼▼ O'Cairns Inn M
(805) 735-6444. **$69-$119.** 1020 E Ocean Ave 93436. SR 1, 1.5 mi w of H St. Ext corridors. **Pets:** Medium, other species. $25 one-time fee/room. Designated rooms, service with restrictions. (ASK) (✕) (🛌) (💻)

AAA ▼▼▼ Quality Inn & Executive Suites H
(805) 735-8555. **$99-$199.** 1621 N H St 93436. SR 1, 1.8 mi n of Ocean Ave. Int corridors. **Pets:** Medium, dogs only. $25 one-time fee/pet. Designated rooms, service with restrictions, supervision.
(SAVE) (✕) (🛌) (💻) (🏊)

▼▼ White Oaks Hotel M
(805) 733-5000. **$80-$199.** 3955 Apollo Way 93436. SR 1, exit 211 (Constellation Blvd), just e; 3.5 mi n of Ocean Ave. Ext/int corridors. **Pets:** Accepted. (ASK) (✕) (🛌) (💻) (🏊) (✕) (🏍)

LONE PINE

AAA ▼▼▼▼ Best Western Frontier Motel M
(760) 876-5571. **$89-$134.** 1008 S Main St 93545. US 395; south end of town. Ext corridors. **Pets:** Other species. Supervision.
(SAVE) (✕) (🛌M) (🛌) (💻) (🏊)

AAA ▼▼▼▼ Comfort Inn H
(760) 876-8700. **$65-$200.** 1920 S Main St 93545. US 395, 1.5 mi s of town. Int corridors. **Pets:** Accepted. (SAVE) (✕) (🛌) (💻) (🏊)

AAA ▼▼▼▼ Dow Villa Motel M
(760) 876-5521. **$74-$147.** 310 S Main St 93545. US 395; center of town. Ext corridors. **Pets:** Medium, other species. $50 deposit/room. Designated rooms, service with restrictions, supervision.
(SAVE) (✕) (🛌M) (🛌) (💻) (🏊)

AAA ▼▼ Timberline Motel M
(760) 876-4555. **$45-$99.** 215 E Post St 93545. US 395, just e. Ext corridors. **Pets:** Small, dogs only. $10 daily fee/pet. Designated rooms, service with restrictions, supervision. (SAVE) (✕) (🛌) (💻) (🎴)

AAA ▼▼▼ Trails Motel M
(760) 876-5555. **$49-$125, 3 day notice.** 633 S Main St 93545. US 395; center of town. Ext corridors. **Pets:** Very small, dogs only. $10 daily fee/pet. Designated rooms, service with restrictions, supervision.
(SAVE) (✕) (🛌) (💻) (🏊)

LOS ALAMITOS

▼▼▼▼ Residence Inn by Marriott-Cypress/Los Alamitos H
(714) 484-5700. **$143-$175.** 4931 Katella Ave 90720. I-605, exit 1D (Katella Ave) southbound; exit 1B (Katella Ave/Willow St) northbound, 1.9 mi e. Int corridors. **Pets:** Accepted. (✕) (🛌) (💻) (🏊) (✕)

LOS ALTOS

▼▼▼▼ Residence Inn-Palo Alto/Los Altos H
(650) 559-7890. **$251-$307.** 4460 El Camino Real 94022. US 101, exit San Antonio Rd, 2 mi w to SR 82, then just n. Int corridors. **Pets:** Accepted. (✕) (🛌M) (💻) (🏊) (✕)

LOS ANGELES METROPOLITAN AREA

ALHAMBRA

AAA ▼▼▼ Super 8 M
(323) 225-2310. **$69-$85.** 5350 Huntington Dr 90032. I-10, exit 22 (Fremont Ave), 2.5 mi n, then 0.5 mi w. Ext corridors. **Pets:** Accepted.
(SAVE) (✕) (🛌M) (🛌) (💻)

ARCADIA

▼▼ Extended StayAmerica-Los Angeles-Arcadia H
(626) 446-6422. **$90-$110.** 401 E Santa Clara St 91006. I-210, exit 33 (Huntington Dr), just w to 5th, just n, then just w. Int corridors. **Pets:** Other species. $25 daily fee/room. Designated rooms, service with restrictions, crate. (ASK) (✕) (🛌M) (🛌) (💻)

▼▼▼ **Residence Inn by Marriott** H

(626) 446-6500. **$199-$309.** 321 E Huntington Dr 91006. I-210, exit 33 (Huntington Dr), 0.5 mi w, then just n on Gateway Dr. Ext corridors. **Pets:** Accepted. ⬛ ⊠ ⬛ ⬛ ⬛ ⊠

BEVERLY HILLS

▼▼▼ **Avalon Hotel** H

(310) 277-5221. **Call for rates.** 9400 W Olympic Blvd 90212. I-10, exit 6 (Robertson Blvd), 1.7 mi n, then 0.8 mi w. Ext/int corridors. **Pets:** Accepted. ⬛ ⊠ ⬛ ⬛ ⬛

🅰🅰🅰 ▼▼▼▼ **The Beverly Hills Hotel and Bungalows** H ❀

(310) 276-2251. **$480-$8625.** 9641 Sunset Blvd 90210. I-405, exit 57 (Sunset Blvd), 3.7 mi e. Int corridors. **Pets:** Small. $200 one-time fee/room. Designated rooms, service with restrictions.
⬛ ⊠ ⬛ ⬛ ⬛ ⊠

▼▼▼▼ **The Beverly Hilton** H

(310) 274-7777. **$275-$450.** 9876 Wilshire Blvd 90210. I-405, exit 55 (Wilshire Blvd), 2.2 mi e. Int corridors. **Pets:** Accepted.
⬛ ⊠ ⬛ ⬛ ⬛ ⊠

▼▼▼ ▼▼▼ **Beverly Wilshire a Four Seasons Hotel** H

(310) 275-5200. **Call for rates.** 9500 Wilshire Blvd 90212. I-405, exit 55 (Wilshire Blvd), 4.5 mi e. Int corridors. **Pets:** Accepted.
⊠ ⬛ ⬛ ⬛ ⊠

▼▼▼ ▼▼▼ **Montage Beverly Hills** H ❀

(310) 860-7800. **$595-$7500.** 225 N Canon Dr 90210. I-405, exit 55A (Santa Monica Blvd), 3.4 mi e, then 0.4 mi s. Int corridors. **Pets:** Other species. $30 daily fee/room. Service with restrictions.
⬛ ⊠ ⬛ ⬛ ⬛ ⊠

🅰🅰🅰 ▼▼▼▼ **The Peninsula Beverly Hills** H ❀

(310) 551-2888. **$495-$6000.** 9882 S Santa Monica Blvd 90212. I-405, exit 55A (Santa Monica Blvd), 2.2 mi e at Wilshire Blvd. Int corridors. **Pets:** Other species. $55 daily fee/pet.
⬛ ⊠ ⬛ ⬛ ⬛ ⊠

🅰🅰🅰 ▼▼▼ ▼▼▼ **Raffles L'Ermitage Beverly Hills** H ❀

(310) 278-3344. **$383-$1350.** 9291 Burton Way 90210. I-10, exit 6 (Robertson Blvd), 3.1 mi n, then just w. Int corridors. **Pets:** Medium. $150 one-time fee/pet. Service with restrictions, supervision.
⬛ ⊠ ⬛ ⬛ ⬛ ⊠

🅰🅰🅰 ▼▼▼ ▼▼▼ **SLS Hotel at Beverly Hills** H

(310) 247-0400. **$329-$599.** 465 S La Cienega Blvd 90048. I-10, exit 7A (La Cienega Blvd), 2.5 mi n. Ext corridors. **Pets:** Accepted.
⬛ ⊠ ⬛ ⬛ ⊠

BURBANK

🅰🅰🅰 ▼▼▼▼ **Burbank Airport Marriott Hotel & Convention Center** H ❀

(818) 843-6000. **$197-$241.** 2500 Hollywood Way 91505. I-5, exit 149 (Hollywood Way), 1 mi s. Int corridors. **Pets:** Small. $75 one-time fee/pet. Service with restrictions, supervision.
⬛ ⬛ ⊠ ⬛ ⬛ ⬛

▼▼ **Extended StayAmerica-Los Angeles-Burbank Airport** H

(818) 567-0952. **$90-$110.** 2200 Empire Ave 91504. I-5, exit 146B (Burbank Blvd), just w, then 0.7 mi n on Victory Pl. Int corridors. **Pets:** Other species. $25 daily fee/room. Designated rooms, service with restrictions, crate. ⬛ ⊠ ⬛ ⬛

🅰🅰🅰 ▼▼▼ **Hotel Amarano Burbank** H

(818) 842-8887. **$330-$585.** 322 N Pass Ave 91505. SR 134, exit 2 (Hollywood Way) westbound, just w on Alameda Ave, then 0.5 mi n; exit 2 (Pass Ave) eastbound, 0.5 mi n. Ext corridors. **Pets:** Accepted.
⬛ ⊠ ⬛ ⬛ ⬛ ⬛ ⊠

▼▼▼ **Residence Inn by Marriott Burbank Downtown** H

(818) 260-8787. **$249-$309.** 321 S First St 91502. I-5, exit 146A (Olive Ave) northbound, just e on Angeleno Ave, then just s; exit 146A (Verdugo Ave) southbound, just s on Front St, just e on Verdugo Ave, then just n. Int corridors. **Pets:** Other species. $100 one-time fee/room. Service with restrictions, crate. ⊠ ⬛ ⬛ ⬛ ⊠

🅰🅰🅰 ▼▼▼ **Safari Inn, a Coast Hotel** M

(818) 845-8586. **$129-$299.** 1911 W Olive Ave 91506. I-5, exit 146A (Olive Ave), 1.3 mi sw. Ext corridors. **Pets:** Accepted.
⬛ ⊠ ⬛ ⬛ ⬛ ⊠

CARSON

▼▼▼ **Extended StayAmerica-Los Angeles/Carson** H

(310) 323-2080. **$70-$90.** 401 E Albertoni St 90746. SR 91, exit 7B (Avalon Blvd) just s, then just w. Int corridors. **Pets:** Other species. $25 daily fee/room. Designated rooms, service with restrictions, crate.
⬛ ⊠ ⬛ ⬛ ⬛

CERRITOS

🅰🅰🅰 ▼▼▼ **Sheraton Cerritos Hotel at Towne Center** H ❀

(562) 809-1500. **$119-$219.** 12725 Center Court Dr 90703. SR 91, exit 19B (Artesia/Bloomfield Dr), just s to Town Center Dr, just e, then just s. Int corridors. **Pets:** Medium. $50 deposit/room. Service with supervision. ⬛ ⊠ ⬛ ⬛ ⊠

CHATSWORTH

🅰🅰🅰 ▼▼▼ **Ramada Inn** H ❀

(818) 998-5289. **$89-$120.** 21340 Devonshire St 91311. SR 118, exit 35 (De Soto Ave), 1.5 mi, then 0.5 mi w. Int corridors. **Pets:** Small. $10 daily fee/pet. Designated rooms, service with restrictions, supervision.
⬛ ⊠ ⬛ ⬛ ⬛ ⊠

CHINO

▼▼ **Extended StayAmerica Los Angeles-Chino Valley** H

(909) 597-8675. **$80-$100.** 4325 Corporate Center Ave 91710. SR 71, exit Chino Hills Pkwy, just e to Ramona Ave, just n, then just w. Int corridors. **Pets:** Other species. $25 daily fee/room. Designated rooms, service with restrictions, crate. ⬛ ⊠ ⬛ ⬛ ⬛

CLAREMONT

▼▼▼ **Hotel Claremont & Tennis Club** M ❀

(909) 621-4831. **$89-$109.** 840 S Indian Hill Blvd 91711. I-10, exit 47 (Indian Hill Blvd), just s; enter on Auto Center Dr. Ext corridors. **Pets:** Large, other species. Service with restrictions, crate.
⬛ ⊠ ⬛ ⬛ ⬛ ⊠ ⊠

COMMERCE

▼▼▼ **Doubletree Los Angeles/Commerce** H ❀

(323) 887-8100. **$99-$219.** 5757 Telegraph Rd 90040. I-5, exit 128B (Washington Blvd), just e, then just s. Int corridors. **Pets:** Medium. $25 daily fee/pet. Service with restrictions, supervision.
⊠ ⬛ ⬛ ⬛ ⬛ ⊠

▼▼ **Ramada Commerce** H

(562) 806-4777. **$69-$119.** 7272 E Gage Ave 90040. I-5, exit 126B (Slauson Ave), just e, then just s. Int corridors. **Pets:** Medium. $30 one-time fee/pet. Designated rooms, service with restrictions, supervision.
⬛ ⊠ ⬛ ⬛ ⬛

CULVER CITY

🅰🅰🅰 ▼▼▼ **Four Points by Sheraton la Westside** H

(310) 641-7740. **$99-$160 (no credit cards), 3 day notice.** 5990 Green Valley Cir 90230. I-405, exit 49 (Howard Hughes Pkwy), just n, then just e. Int corridors. **Pets:** Accepted. ⬛ ⊠ ⬛ ⬛ ⬛ ⊠

▼▼▼ **Radisson Hotel-LA Westside** H ❀

(310) 649-1776. **$89-$229.** 6161 W Centinela Ave 90230. I-405, exit 50 (Jefferson Blvd), just s, then just nw. Int corridors. **Pets:** Medium, other species. $50 one-time fee/room. Designated rooms, service with restrictions, supervision. ⬛ ⊠ ⬛ ⬛ ⬛ ⬛ ⊠

DIAMOND BAR

▼▼▼▼ Ayres Suites Diamond Bar H
(909) 860-6290. **$109-$159.** 21951 Golden Springs Dr 91765. SR 57/60, exit 24B (Grand Ave), just s, then 0.5 mi w. Int corridors. **Pets:** Dogs only. $45 one-time fee/pet. Service with restrictions, supervision.

EL SEGUNDO

▼▼▼ Embassy Suites-LAX South H
(310) 640-3600. **$119-$291.** 1440 E Imperial Ave 90245. I-405, exit 45B (Imperial Hwy), 1.6 mi w. Int corridors. **Pets:** Small, other species. $35 daily fee/pet. Service with restrictions, supervision.

▼▼ Homestead Studio Suites Hotel-Los Angeles-LAX Airport-El Segundo M
(310) 607-4000. **$85-$105.** 1910 E Mariposa Ave 90245. I-105, exit 1B (Sepulveda Blvd), 1 mi s. Ext corridors. **Pets:** Other species. $25 daily fee/room. Designated rooms, service with restrictions, crate.

⚫ ▼▼▼ Hyatt Summerfield Suites Los Angeles LAX/El Segundo H
(310) 725-0100. **$99-$499.** 810 S Douglas St 90245. I-405, exit 43 (Rosecrans Ave), 0.5 mi e, then just n. Ext/int corridors. **Pets:** Medium. $10 daily fee/room, $100 one-time fee/pet. Designated rooms, service with restrictions.

▼▼▼ Residence Inn by Marriott-LAX/El Segundo H
(310) 333-0888. **$206-$252.** 2135 E El Segundo Blvd 90245. I-405, exit 44 (El Segundo Blvd), 1.4 mi w. Int corridors. **Pets:** Accepted.

GLENDALE

⚫ ▼▼▼▼ Hilton Los Angeles North/Glendale & Executive Meeting Center H 🐾
(818) 956-5466. **$169-$349.** 100 W Glenoaks Blvd 91202. SR 134, exit 7B (Brand Blvd), just n, then just w. Int corridors. **Pets:** Small. $75 one-time fee/room. Designated rooms, service with restrictions, supervision.

▼▼▼ Homestead Studio Suites Hotel-Los Angeles-Glendale H
(818) 956-6665. **$95-$115.** 1377 W Glenoaks Blvd 91201. I-5, exit 145A (Western Ave), 0.4 mi e, then 0.6 mi s. Int corridors. **Pets:** Other species. $25 daily fee/room. Designated rooms, service with restrictions, crate.

▼▼ Los Angeles Days Inn-Glendale H
(818) 956-0202. **$94-$149, 7 day notice.** 450 W Pioneer Dr 91203. SR 134, exit 7A (Pacific Ave), just s, then just e. Int corridors. **Pets:** Small. $50 deposit/room. Designated rooms, service with restrictions, supervision.

▼▼▼ Vagabond Inn Glendale M
(818) 240-1700. **$76-$94.** 120 W Colorado St 91204. SR 134, exit 7B (Brand Blvd), 1 mi s, then just w. Ext corridors. **Pets:** $10 daily fee/pet. Designated rooms, service with restrictions, supervision.

HAWTHORNE

▼▼ TownePlace Suites by Marriott M
(310) 725-9696. **$125-$153.** 14400 Aviation Blvd 90250. I-405, exit 43 (Rosecrans Ave), 0.4 mi w. Int corridors. **Pets:** Other species. $100 one-time fee/room. Service with restrictions, supervision.

HOLLYWOOD

⚫ ▼▼▼ Best Western Hollywood Hills Hotel M
(323) 464-5181. **$119-$249.** 6141 Franklin Ave 90028. US 101, exit Gower St, just n, then just e. Ext/int corridors. **Pets:** Very small. $75 daily fee/pet. Service with restrictions, supervision.

⚫ ▼▼▼ Hollywood Hotel Near Universal Studios–A Ramada Hotel H
(323) 315-1800. **$90-$189.** 1160 N Vermont Ave 90029. US 101, exit 6A (Vermont Ave), 0.5 mi n. Int corridors. **Pets:** Small. $50 daily fee/pet. Service with restrictions, supervision.

⚫ ▼▼▼ Motel 6 Hollywood M
(323) 464-6006. **$70-$150.** 1738 N Whitley Ave 90028. US 101, exit 9C southbound, just s, just w, then just s. Int corridors. **Pets:** Other species. Service with restrictions, supervision.

HUNTINGTON PARK

▼▼ Rodeway Inn Near la Live M
(323) 589-5971. **$60-$140.** 6340 Santa Fe Ave 90255. I-710, exit 17B (Atlantic Blvd), southbound (Bandini Blvd W), 1.1 mi sw, 2.6 mi on Slauson Ave, then 0.4 mi s. Ext/int corridors. **Pets:** Accepted.

INDUSTRY

▼▼▼ Pacific Palms Resort H
(626) 810-4455. **Call for rates.** One Industry Hills Pkwy 91744. SR 60, exit 18 (Azusa Ave), 1.3 mi n, 0.5 mi w. Int corridors. **Pets:** Accepted.

LA MIRADA

▼▼ Extended StayAmerica-Los Angeles-La Mirada H
(714) 670-8579. **$79-$95.** 14775 Firestone Blvd 90638. I-5, exit 118 (Valley View Ave), just n, then 0.7 mi e. Int corridors. **Pets:** Other species. $25 daily fee/room. Designated rooms, service with restrictions, crate.

▼▼ Residence Inn by Marriott H
(714) 523-2800. **$152-$186.** 14419 Firestone Blvd 90638. I-5, exit 118 (Valley View Ave), just n, then 0.5 mi e. Ext corridors. **Pets:** Accepted.

LONG BEACH

⚫ ▼▼ Colonial Pool and Spa Motel M
(562) 591-8327. **$60-$80.** 802 E Pacific Coast Hwy 90806. I-710, exit 2 (SR 1/Pacific Coast Hwy), 1.8 mi e. Ext corridors. **Pets:** Accepted.

▼▼ Extended StayAmerica-Los Angeles-Long Beach H
(562) 989-4601. **$80-$100.** 4105 E Willow St 90815. I-405, exit 27 (Lakewood Blvd), 0.3 mi sw. Int corridors. **Pets:** Other species. $25 daily fee/room. Designated rooms, service with restrictions, crate.

⚫ ▼▼▼ GuestHouse Hotel Long Beach M
(562) 597-1341. **$109-$169.** 5325 E Pacific Coast Hwy 90804. I-405, exit 23 (SR 22/Long Beach) northbound, 2 mi nw; exit 27 (Lakewood Blvd) southbound, 2 mi se on SR 1. Ext corridors. **Pets:** Medium. $10 daily fee/pet. Designated rooms, crate.

▼▼▼ Hilton Long Beach H 🐾
(562) 983-3400. **$149-$377.** 701 W Ocean Blvd 90831. I-710, exit Downtown/Broadway, just e to Daisy Ave, just s to Ocean Blvd, then just w. Int corridors. **Pets:** Large, other species. $75 deposit/room. Service with restrictions, crate.

⚫ ▼▼▼ Hotel Maya, a Joie de Vivre hotel H
(562) 435-7676. **$139-$269.** 700 Queensway Dr 90802. I-710, exit 14 (Harbor Scenic Dr/Queen Mary), 1 mi s. Ext corridors. **Pets:** Accepted.

▼▼▼ Renaissance Long Beach Hotel H
(562) 437-5900. **$170-$208.** 111 E Ocean Blvd 90802. I-710, exit Downtown/Broadway, 0.8 mi e to Long Beach Blvd, just s, then just w. Int corridors. **Pets:** $75 one-time fee/room. Service with restrictions, supervision.

Residence Inn by Marriott Long Beach 🅷

(562) 595-0909. **$143-$175.** 4111 E Willow St 90815. I-405, exit 27 (Lakewood Blvd), just s, then just w. Ext corridors. **Pets:** Small, other species. $100 one-time fee/room. Service with restrictions, crate.

Residence Inn Long Beach Downtown South Waterfront 🅷 🐾

(562) 495-0700. **$143-$175.** 600 Queensway Dr 90802. I-720, exit 14 (Harbor Scenic Dr/Queen Mary), 1.3 mi s. Int corridors. **Pets:** Other species. $100 one-time fee/room. Service with restrictions, crate.

The Westin Long Beach 🅷 🐾

(562) 436-3000. **$149-$399.** 333 E Ocean Blvd 90802. I-710, exit Downtown/Broadway, 0.8 mi e to Long Beach Blvd, then just s. Int corridors. **Pets:** Small, other species. No service, supervision.

LOS ANGELES

Beverly Laurel Motor Hotel 🅼

(323) 651-2441. **$114-$155.** 8018 Beverly Blvd 90048. I-10, exit 7B (Fairfax Ave), 2.8 mi n, then just w. Ext corridors. **Pets:** $25 daily fee/pet. Service with restrictions, supervision.

Extended StayAmerica-Los Angeles/LAX Airport 🅷

(310) 568-9337. **$115-$135.** 6531 S Sepulveda Blvd 90045. I-405, exit 49 (Howard Hughes Pkwy), 0.9 mi w, then just n. Int corridors. **Pets:** Other species. $25 daily fee/room. Designated rooms, service with restrictions, crate.

Four Seasons Hotel Los Angeles at Beverly Hills 🅷 🐾

(310) 273-2222. **$495-$6950.** 300 S Doheny Dr 90048. I-10, exit 6 (Robertson Blvd), 3 mi n to Burton Way, then w. Int corridors. **Pets:** Very small. Service with restrictions, supervision.

Hotel Palomar la Westwood 🅷

(310) 475-8711. **Call for rates.** 10740 Wilshire Blvd 90024. I-405, exit 55B (Wilshire Blvd), 1 mi w; in Westwood. Int corridors. **Pets:** Accepted.

Hyatt Regency Century Plaza 🅷 🐾

(310) 228-1234. **$179-$499.** 2025 Avenue of the Stars 90067. I-10, exit 6 (Robertson Blvd), 2.7 mi n to Olympic Blvd, 1.9 mi w, then just n. Int corridors. **Pets:** Small, dogs only. $35 daily fee/pet. Designated rooms, service with restrictions, supervision.

InterContinental Los Angeles Century City

(310) 284-6500. **$209-$399.** 2151 Avenue of the Stars 90067. I-10, exit 6 (Robertson Blvd), 2.7 mi n to Olympic Blvd, 1.9 mi w, then just n. Int corridors. **Pets:** Accepted.

La Quinta Inn & Suites-LAX 🅷 🐾

(310) 645-2200. **$65-$199.** 5249 W Century Blvd 90045. I-405, exit 46 (Century Blvd), just w. Int corridors. **Pets:** Medium, other species. Service with restrictions, supervision.

Los Angeles Airport Hilton & Towers 🅷 🐾

(310) 410-4000. **$129-$249.** 5711 W Century Blvd 90045. I-405, exit 46 (Century Blvd), 0.8 mi w. Int corridors. **Pets:** Medium, other species. $50 one-time fee/pet. Designated rooms, service with restrictions, crate.

Luxe Hotel Sunset Boulevard 🅷

(310) 476-6571. **$209-$490.** 11461 Sunset Blvd 90049. I-405, exit 57 (Sunset Blvd), just w. Int corridors. **Pets:** Accepted.

The Orlando 🅷

(323) 658-6600. **$229-$329.** 8384 W 3rd St 90048. I-10, exit 7A (La Cienega Blvd), 2.3 mi n, then just e. Int corridors. **Pets:** Small, dogs only. $50 daily fee/pet. Designated rooms, service with restrictions, supervision.

Radisson Hotel at Los Angeles Airport 🅷

(310) 670-9000. **$89-$269.** 6225 W Century Blvd at Sepulveda Blvd 90045. I-405, exit 46 (Century Blvd), 1.6 mi w. Int corridors.
Pets: Accepted.

Residence Inn by Marriott-Beverly Hills 🅷 🐾

(310) 223-4100. **$239-$249.** 1177 S Beverly Dr 90035. I-10, exit 6 (Robertson Blvd), 1.6 mi n to Pico Blvd, then 0.6 mi w. Int corridors. **Pets:** $10 daily fee/pet, $100 one-time fee/room. Service with restrictions.

Sheraton Gateway Hotel, Los Angeles Airport 🅷 🐾

(310) 642-1111. **$119-$249.** 6101 W Century Blvd 90045. I-405, exit 46 (Century Blvd), 1.3 mi w. Int corridors. **Pets:** Medium, dogs only. $25 daily fee/room. Service with restrictions, supervision.

Sheraton Los Angeles Downtown 🅷 🐾

(213) 488-3500. **$109-$284.** 711 S Hope St 90017. SR 110, exit 6th St southbound, just e, then just s. Int corridors. **Pets:** Medium, other species. Designated rooms, service with restrictions, supervision.

Sofitel Los Angeles 🅷 🐾

(310) 278-5444. **$235-$2000, 3 day notice.** 8555 Beverly Blvd 90048. I-10, exit 7A (La Cienega Blvd), 2.5 mi n. Int corridors. **Pets:** Small, dogs only. Designated rooms, service with restrictions, supervision.

The Tower–Beverly Hills 🅷

(310) 277-2800. **$169-$499.** 1224 S Beverwil Dr 90035. I-10, exit 6 (Robertson Blvd), 1.8 mi n, then 0.7 mi e. Int corridors. **Pets:** Accepted.

Travelodge Hotel at Lax 🅷

(310) 649-4000. **$65-$110.** 5547 W Century Blvd 90045. I-405, exit 46 (Century Blvd), 0.5 mi w. Ext/int corridors. **Pets:** Accepted.

Vagabond Inn Los Angeles-USC 🅼

(213) 746-1531. **$84-$149.** 3101 S Figueroa St 90007. SR 110, exit Adams Blvd, 0.5 mi s. Ext corridors. **Pets:** Accepted.

The Westin Bonaventure Hotel & Suites 🅷

(213) 624-1000. **$109-$2459.** 404 S Figueroa St 90071. SR 110, exit 6th St, just n on Figueroa St, then e on 4th St, then s on Flower St. Int corridors. **Pets:** Accepted.

The Westin Hotel-Los Angeles Airport 🅷

(310) 216-5858. **$87-$231, 3 day notice.** 5400 W Century Blvd 90045. I-405, exit 46 (Century Blvd), just w. Int corridors. **Pets:** Accepted.

MANHATTAN BEACH

The Belamar, a Larkspur Collection Hotel 🅷

(310) 750-0300. **$139-$499.** 3501 S Sepulveda Blvd 90266. I-405, exit 43 (Rosecrans Ave), 1.5 mi w, then just s. Int corridors. **Pets:** Accepted.

Residence Inn by Marriott 🅷

(310) 421-3100. **$169-$179.** 1700 N Sepulveda Blvd 90266. I-405, exit 43B (Rosecrans Ave), 1.5 mi w, then 1 mi s on SR 1. Ext corridors.
Pets: Accepted.

MARINA DEL REY

The Ritz-Carlton, Marina del Rey H ❖

(310) 823-1700. **Call for rates.** 4375 Admiralty Way 90292. SR 90 (Marina Frwy), just s on Lincoln Blvd (SR 1), just w on Bali Way. Int corridors. **Pets:** Medium. $125 one-time fee/pet. Designated rooms, service with restrictions, supervision. SAVE ✕ ⛖M ▦ ▭ ⅋ ⚓ ✕

MONROVIA

Homestead Studio Suites Hotel-Los Angeles-Monrovia H

(626) 256-6999. **$95-$115.** 930 S Fifth Ave 91016. I-210, exit 33 (Huntington Dr), just w, then just n. Int corridors. **Pets:** Other species. $25 daily fee/room. Designated rooms, service with restrictions, crate. ASK ✕ ▦ ▭

NORTHRIDGE

Extended StayAmerica-Los Angeles/Northridge H

(818) 734-1787. **$102-$125.** 19325 Londelius St 91324. SR 118, exit 37 (Tampa Ave), 3 mi s. Int corridors. **Pets:** Other species. $25 daily fee/room. Designated rooms, service with restrictions, crate. ASK ✕ ⛖M ▦ ▭

PASADENA

Quality Inn Pasadena M

(626) 796-9291. **$83-$99.** 3321 E Colorado Blvd 91107. I-210, exit 29B (Madre St), just s, then 0.3 mi e. Ext corridors. **Pets:** $20 daily fee/pet. Service with restrictions, supervision. ASK ✕ ▦ ▭ ⚓ ✕

Sheraton Pasadena Hotel H

(626) 449-4000. **$139-$379.** 303 E Cordova St 91101. I-210, exit 26B (Lake Ave), 0.7 mi s, then just w. Int corridors. **Pets:** Accepted. SAVE ✕ ⛖M ▦ ▭ ⅋ ⚓

Vagabond Inn Executive M

(626) 449-3170. **$90-$130.** 1203 E Colorado Blvd 91106. I-210, exit 27A (Hill Ave), just s, then just w. Ext/int corridors. **Pets:** Accepted. SAVE ✕ ⛖M ▦ ▭

The Westin-Pasadena H

(626) 792-2727. **$155-$399.** 191 N Los Robles Ave 91101. I-210, exit Los Robles Ave, just s; in Plaza Las Fuentes. Int corridors. **Pets:** Accepted. SAVE ✕ ⛖M ▦ ▭ ⅋ ⚓ ✕

Westway Inn M

(626) 304-9678. **$59-$280, 30 day notice.** 1599 E Colorado Blvd 91106. I-210, exit 27B (Allen Ave) westbound; exit 27 (Hill Ave) eastbound, 0.8 mi s. Ext corridors. **Pets:** Medium, dogs only. $10 daily fee/pet. Designated rooms, service with restrictions, supervision. SAVE ✕ ▦ ▭ ⚓

POMONA

Sheraton Fairplex H

(909) 622-2220. **$119-$249.** 601 W McKinley Ave 91768. I-10, exit 45A (White Ave) eastbound, 0.5 mi n, then just w; exit 43 (Fairplex Dr) westbound, 1 mi n, then 0.7 mi e. Int corridors. **Pets:** Accepted. SAVE ✕ ⛖M ▦ ▭ ⅋ ⚓ ✕

Shilo Inn Suites Hotel–Pomona Hilltop H ❖

(909) 598-7666. **$179-$233.** 3101 Temple Ave 91768. SR 57, exit 20 (Temple Ave), just w. Int corridors. **Pets:** Dogs only. $25 one-time fee/room. Designated rooms, service with restrictions, supervision. SAVE ✕ ▦ ▭ ⅋ ⚓ ✕

SAN PEDRO

Doubletree Hotel San Pedro H

(310) 514-3344. **$119-$289.** 2800 Via Cabrillo Marina 90731. I-110, exit Gaffey St, 1.5 mi s, then 0.5 mi w on 22nd St. Int corridors. **Pets:** Small. $50 one-time fee/room. Service with restrictions, supervision. SAVE ✕ ▦ ▭ ⅋ ⚓ ✕

Vagabond Inn San Pedro M

(310) 831-8911. **$74-$109.** 215 S Gaffey St 90731. I-110, exit Gaffey St, just s of terminus. Ext corridors. **Pets:** Medium. $25 one-time fee/pet. Designated rooms, service with restrictions, supervision. SAVE ✕ ▦ ▭ ⚓

SANTA CLARITA

Best Western Valencia Inn M

(661) 255-0555. **$90-$120.** 27413 Wayne Mills Pl 91355. I-5, exit 170 (Magic Mountain Pkwy), just e. Ext corridors. **Pets:** Accepted. SAVE ✕ ▦ ▭ ⚓

Comfort Suites H ❖

(661) 254-7700. **$86-$120.** 25380 The Old Rd 91381. I-5, exit 167 (Lyons Ave), just w. Int corridors. **Pets:** Medium. $5 daily fee/room, $25 one-time fee/pet. Service with restrictions, supervision. SAVE ✕ ⛖M ▦ ▭ ⚓

Extended StayAmerica Los Angeles-Valencia H

(661) 255-1044. **$85-$100.** 24940 W Pico Canyon Rd 91381. I-5, exit 167 (Lyons Ave), just w. Int corridors. **Pets:** Other species. $25 daily fee/room. Designated rooms, service with restrictions, crate. ASK ✕ ▦ ▭

La Quinta Inn & Suites Stevenson Ranch H ❖

(661) 286-1111. **$89-$149.** 25201 The Old Rd 91381. I-5, exit 167 (Lyons Ave), just w to Chiquella Ln, just s, then just sw. Int corridors. **Pets:** Medium, other species. Service with restrictions, supervision. ASK ✕ ▦ ▭ ⚓

Residence Inn by Marriott H

(661) 290-2800. **$169-$179.** 25320 The Old Rd 91381. I-5, exit 167 (Lyons Ave), just w. Int corridors. **Pets:** Accepted. ✕ ⛖M ▦ ▭ ⚓ ✕

SANTA MONICA

The Fairmont Miramar Hotel & Bungalows H

(310) 576-7777. **$279-$1287.** 101 Wilshire Blvd 90401. I-10, exit 1B (Lincoln Blvd), 0.6 mi n, then 0.6 mi w. Ext/int corridors. **Pets:** Accepted. SAVE ✕ ⛖M ⅋ ⚓ ✕

The Georgian H ❖

(310) 395-9945. **$252-$528.** 1415 Ocean Ave 90401. I-10, exit 1B (Lincoln Blvd), just n, then 0.5 mi w on Broadway. Int corridors. **Pets:** Small. $100 one-time fee/pet. Service with restrictions, supervision. ASK ✕

Le Merigot–A JW Marriott Beach Hotel & Spa H ❖

(310) 395-9700. **$329-$402.** 1740 Ocean Ave 90401. I-10, exit 1B (Lincoln Blvd), 0.3 mi s, 0.6 mi w on Pico Blvd, then just n. Int corridors. **Pets:** $150 deposit/pet, $100 one-time fee/pet. Service with restrictions. SAVE ✕ ⛖M ▭ ⅋ ⚓ ✕

Loews Santa Monica Beach Hotel H ❖

(310) 458-6700. **$299-$2600.** 1700 Ocean Ave 90401. I-10, exit 1B (Lincoln Blvd), 0.3 mi s, 0.6 mi w on Pico Blvd, then just n. Int corridors. **Pets:** Other species. $25 one-time fee/room. Service with restrictions. SAVE ✕ ⛖M ▭ ⅋ ⚓ ✕

Sheraton Delfina Santa Monica H ❖

(310) 399-9344. **$229-$399.** 530 Pico Blvd 90405. I-10, exit 1B (Lincoln Blvd), just s. Int corridors. **Pets:** Medium, dogs only. $70 one-time fee/pet. Supervision. SAVE ✕ ▦ ▭ ⅋ ⚓

Travelodge-Santa Monica/Pico Blvd M

(310) 450-5766. **$109-$199.** 3102 Pico Blvd 90405. I-10, exit 2 (Centinela Ave), just n, then just w. Ext corridors. **Pets:** Small. Designated rooms, service with restrictions, supervision. SAVE ✕ ▦ ▭

▼▼▼ Viceroy Santa Monica **H**

(310) 260-7500. **Call for rates.** 1819 Ocean Ave 90401. I-10, exit 1B (Lincoln Blvd), 0.3 mi s, 0.6 mi w on Pico Blvd, then just n. Int corridors. **Pets:** Accepted. ⊠ ⌖M ⑂ ⊴

SEAL BEACH

⚏⚏ ▼▼▼ The Pacific Inn **H**

(562) 493-7501. **$119-$189.** 600 Marina Dr 90740. SR 1 (Pacific Coast Hwy), just s. Ext/int corridors. **Pets:** Large, other species. $50 one-time fee/room. Designated rooms, service with restrictions, supervision.

SAVE ⊠ 🖥 🖵 ⊴ ⊠

SHERMAN OAKS

⚏⚏ ▼▼▼ Best Western Carriage Inn **M**

(818) 787-2300. **$139-$209.** 5525 Sepulveda Blvd 91411. I-405, exit 64 (Burbank Blvd), just e, then just s. Ext/int corridors. **Pets:** Medium. $50 deposit/room. Designated rooms, service with restrictions, supervision.

SAVE ⊠ ⌖M 🖥 🖵 ⑂ ⊴

SOUTH EL MONTE

▼▼ Rodeway Inn South El Monte **M**

(626) 579-4490. **$55-$90.** 1228 N Durfee Ave 91733. SR 60, exit 11 (Peck Rd), just s, then just e. Ext corridors. **Pets:** Accepted.

ASK ⊠ 🖥 ⊴

STUDIO CITY

⚏⚏ ▼▼▼ Sportsmen's Lodge Hotel **H**

(818) 769-4700. **$127-$181.** 12825 Ventura Blvd 91604. US 101, exit 15 (Coldwater Canyon Ave), 0.8 mi s, then just e. Int corridors. **Pets:** Accepted. SAVE ⊠ ⌖M 🖥 🖵 ⑂ ⊴

TARZANA

⚏⚏ ▼▼ St. George Inn & Suites **M**

(818) 345-0000. **$80-$110.** 19454 Ventura Blvd 91356. US 101, exit 24 (Tampa Ave), just s, then just w. Ext corridors. **Pets:** Accepted.

SAVE ⊠ 🖥 🖵 ⊴

TORRANCE

▼▼ Extended StayAmerica-Los Angeles-Torrance **H**

(310) 540-5442. **$65-$90.** 3525 Torrance Blvd 90503. I-405, exit 42A (Hawthorne Blvd), 3.5 mi s, then 0.4 mi e. Int corridors. **Pets:** Other species. $25 daily fee/room. Designated rooms, service with restrictions, crate. ASK ⊠ ⌖M 🖥 🖵

▼▼ Extended StayAmerica-Los Angeles/Torrance Harbor Gateway **H**

(310) 328-6000. **$85-$105.** 19200 Harborgate Way 90501. I-405, exit 38A (Normandie Ave), just s, then just w via 190th St. Int corridors. **Pets:** Other species. $25 daily fee/room. Designated rooms, service with restrictions, crate. ASK ⊠ ⌖M 🖥 🖵

▼▼▼ Holiday Inn Torrance **H**

(310) 781-9100. **$99-$199.** 19800 S Vermont Ave 90502. I-110, exit 9 (190th St), just e, then 0.4 mi n. Int corridors. **Pets:** Other species. $75 deposit/room. Service with restrictions, crate.

ASK ⊠ ⌖M 🖥 🖵 ⑂ ⊴ ⊠

▼▼▼ Homestead Studio Suites Hotel-Los Angeles-Torrance **H**

(310) 543-0048. **$75-$110.** 3995 Carson St 90503. I-405, exit 42A (Hawthorne Blvd), 3.6 mi s; I-110, exit 7B (Carson St), 4.5 mi w. Int corridors. **Pets:** Other species. $25 daily fee/room. Designated rooms, service with restrictions, crate. ASK ⊠ ⌖M 🖥 🖵

⚏⚏ ▼▼ Ramada Inn **M**

(310) 325-0660. **$109-$119.** 2880 Pacific Coast Hwy 90505. I-405, exit 39 (Crenshaw Blvd), 5 mi s, then just w. Ext corridors. **Pets:** Accepted.

SAVE ⊠ 🖥 🖵 ⊴

▼▼▼ Residence Inn by Marriott **H**

(310) 543-4566. **$143-$175.** 3701 Torrance Blvd 90503. I-405, exit 42A (Hawthorne Blvd), 3.2 mi s, then just e. Ext corridors. **Pets:** Other species. $100 one-time fee/room. Service with restrictions, supervision.

⊠ 🖥 🖵 ⊴ ⊠

▼▼▼ Staybridge Suites **M**

(310) 371-8525. **$150-$200.** 19901 Prairie Ave 90503. I-405, exit 39 (Crenshaw Blvd), just s to 190th St, 1 mi w, then just s. Ext/int corridors. **Pets:** Medium. $75 one-time fee/room. Service with restrictions, crate.

ASK ⊠ 🖥 🖵 ⊴

UNIVERSAL CITY

⚏⚏ ▼▼▼ Sheraton Universal Hotel, at Universal Studios **H** 🐾

(818) 980-1212. **$169-$449.** 333 Universal Hollywood Dr 91608. US 101, exit 12A (Lankershim Blvd), just n, then just e. Int corridors. **Pets:** Dogs only. $200 one-time fee/room. Service with restrictions, supervision.

SAVE ⊠ 🖥 🖵 ⑂ ⊴

WALNUT

▼▼▼ Quality Inn & Suites **H**

(909) 594-9999. **$70-$110.** 1170 Fairway Dr 91789. SR 60, exit 21 (Fairway Dr), 0.3 mi s. Int corridors. **Pets:** Accepted.

ASK ⊠ ⌖M 🖥 🖵 ⊴ ⊠

WEST HOLLYWOOD

⚏⚏ ▼▼▼ The Grafton on Sunset **H** 🐾

(323) 654-4600. **$185-$335.** 8462 Sunset Blvd 90069. I-10, exit 7A (La Cienega Blvd), 4.4 mi n, then just e. Int corridors. **Pets:** Medium, other species. $100 one-time fee/room. Service with restrictions.

SAVE ⊠ ⑂ ⊴

▼▼▼ Le Montrose Suite Hotel **H**

(310) 855-1115. **Call for rates.** 900 Hammond St at Cynthia St 90069. I-10, exit 7A (La Cienega Blvd), 2.6 mi n to San Vicente Blvd, 1.3 mi nw, then just w on Cynthia St. Int corridors. **Pets:** Accepted.

⊠ 🖥 🖵 ⑂ ⊴ ⊠

▼▼▼ Le Parc Suite Hotel **H** 🐾

(310) 855-8888. **$229-$399.** 733 N West Knoll Dr 90069. I-10, exit 7A (La Cienega Blvd), 3.5 mi n, just w on Melrose Ave, then just n. Int corridors. **Pets:** Medium. $75 one-time fee/room. Service with restrictions.

ASK ⊠ 🖥 🖵 ⑂ ⊴ ⊠

⚏⚏ ▼▼▼ The London West Hollywood **H**

(310) 854-1111. **$189-$379.** 1020 N San Vicente Blvd 90069. I-10, exit 7A (La Cienega Blvd), 2.6 mi n, then 1.5 mi nw. Int corridors. **Pets:** Accepted. SAVE ⊠ 🖵 ⑂ ⊴

WHITTIER

▼▼ Vagabond Inn **M**

(562) 698-9701. **$70-$120.** 14125 E Whittier Blvd 90605. I-605, exit 15 (Whittier Blvd), 3.5 mi e. Ext corridors. **Pets:** Large, other species. $15 daily fee/pet. Designated rooms, service with restrictions, supervision.

⊠ 🖥 🖵 ⊴

WOODLAND HILLS

▼▼ Extended StayAmerica-Los Angeles-Woodland Hills **H**

(818) 710-1170. **$87-$110.** 20205 Ventura Blvd 91364. US 101, exit 25 (Winnetka Ave), just s, then just w. Int corridors. **Pets:** Other species. $25 daily fee/room. Designated rooms, service with restrictions, crate.

ASK ⊠ 🖥 🖵

AAA ▼▼▼ **Warner Center Marriott Hotel** 🅗
(818) 887-4800. **$206-$252.** 21850 Oxnard St 91367. US 101, exit 27A
(Topanga Canyon Blvd N), 0.6 mi n, then just e. Int corridors.
Pets: Accepted. (SAVE) ⊠ ⚹M 🛇 💻 🍽 ⇌ ⊠

END METROPOLITAN AREA

LOS BANOS

AAA ▼ **Americas Best Value Inn** Ⓜ
(209) 826-5002. **$62-$77.** 330 W Pacheco Blvd 93635. On SR 152; center. Ext corridors. **Pets:** Medium, dogs only. $10 daily fee/pet. Designated rooms, service with restrictions, supervision. (SAVE) ⊠ 🛇 💻 ⇌

AAA ▼▼ **Best Western Executive Inn** 🅗
(209) 827-0954. **$70-$99.** 301 W Pacheco Blvd 93635. On SR 152; center. Int corridors. **Pets:** Medium, dogs only. $20 daily fee/pet. Service with restrictions, supervision. (SAVE) ⊠ ⚹M 🛇 💻 ⇌ ⊠

▼▼ **Los Banos Motel** Ⓜ
(209) 826-2700. **$55-$75, 7 day notice.** 2509 E Pacheco Blvd 93635. East end of town. Ext corridors. **Pets:** Small, dogs only. $10 daily fee/pet. Service with restrictions, supervision. (ASK) ⊠ ⚹M 🛇 💻

AAA ▼▼▼ **Vagabond Inn Executive** 🅗
(209) 827-4677. **$75-$115.** 20 W Pacheco Blvd 93635. On SR 152; center. Int corridors. **Pets:** Medium. $10 daily fee/pet. Designated rooms, service with restrictions, supervision. (SAVE) ⊠ 🛇 💻 ⇌

LOS GATOS

AAA ▼▼▼ **Los Gatos Lodge** 🅗
(408) 354-3300. **$99-$179.** 50 Los Gatos/Saratoga Rd 95032. SR 17, exit E Los Gatos, just e. Ext/int corridors. **Pets:** Accepted.
(SAVE) ⊠ ⚹M 🛇 💻 🍽 ⇌

AAA ▼▼▼ **Toll House, a Larkspur Collection Hotel** 🅗
(408) 395-7070. **$109-$329.** 140 S Santa Cruz Ave 95030. SR 17, exit SR 9, 0.5 mi w. Int corridors. **Pets:** Accepted.
(SAVE) ⊠ 🛇 💻 🍽 ⊠

MADERA

AAA ▼▼▼ **Madera Valley Inn** 🅗
(559) 664-0100. **$59-$169.** 317 North G St 93637. SR 99, exit Central Madera, just e. Int corridors. **Pets:** Accepted.
(SAVE) ⊠ 🛇 💻 🍽 ⇌

▼▼ **Super 8** Ⓜ
(559) 661-1131. **$60-$70.** 1855 W Cleveland Ave 93637. SR 99, exit Cleveland Ave, just w. Ext corridors. **Pets:** Accepted.
(ASK) ⊠ 🛇 💻 ⇌

MAMMOTH LAKES

▼▼ **Econo Lodge Wildwood Inn** Ⓜ
(760) 934-6855. **$99-$239, 3 day notice.** 3626 Main St 93546. On SR 203, 0.7 mi w of Old Mammoth Rd. Ext corridors. **Pets:** Accepted.
(ASK) ⊠ 🛇 💻 ⇌ 🄰🄲

▼▼ **Mammoth Mountain Inn** 🅗
(760) 934-2581. **Call for rates.** 1 Minaret Rd 93546. 5 mi w of town on SR 203. Int corridors. **Pets:** Accepted.
⊠ 🛇 💻 🍽 ⇌ ⊠ 🄰🄲

▼▼ **Mammoth Ski & Racquet Club** 🄲🄾
(760) 934-7368. **$110-$485, 30 day notice.** 248 Mammoth Slopes Dr 93546. From Old Mammoth Rd, 1 mi w on SR 203, just n; Canyon Blvd, 0.8 mi w, then just s. Int corridors. **Pets:** Dogs only. $25 daily fee/room. Designated rooms, service with restrictions, crate.
(ASK) ⊠ 🛇 💻 ⇌ ⊠ 🄰🄲

AAA ▼▼▼ **Shilo Inn Suites-Mammoth Lakes** 🅗 ❀
(760) 934-4500. **$110-$280.** 2963 Main St 93546. On SR 203, just e of Old Mammoth Rd. Int corridors. **Pets:** Dogs only. $25 one-time fee/room. Designated rooms, service with restrictions, supervision.
(SAVE) ⊠ 🛇 💻 ⇌ ⊠

AAA ▼▼▼ **Sierra Lodge** 🅗
(760) 934-8881. **$69-$199.** 3540 Main St 93546. On SR 203, 0.6 mi w of Old Mammoth Rd. Int corridors. **Pets:** Other species. $10 daily fee/pet. Designated rooms, service with restrictions. (SAVE) ⊠ 🛇 💻 🄰🄲

▼▼ **Sierra Nevada Rodeway Inn** 🅗
(760) 934-2515. **$109-$239, 7 day notice.** 164 Old Mammoth Rd 93546. Just s of SR 203. Ext/int corridors. **Pets:** Accepted.
(ASK) ⊠ 🛇 💻 ⇌ 🄰🄲

AAA ▼▼▼◆ **The Westin Monache Resort** 🅗 ❀
(760) 934-0400. **$149-$529, 7 day notice.** 50 Hillside Dr 93546. SR 203, 1 mi w to Minaret Rd, 0.3 mi n to Forest Tr, just w, then just nw. Int corridors. **Pets:** Medium, dogs only. Designated rooms, service with restrictions, supervision. (SAVE) ⊠ ⚹M 🛇 💻 🍽 ⇌

MANTECA

AAA ▼▼▼ **Best Western Executive Inn & Suites** 🅗
(209) 825-1415. **$69-$169.** 1415 E Yosemite Ave 95336. Jct SR 99 and 120, exit E Yosemite Ave. Ext corridors. **Pets:** Other species. $30 one-time fee/room. Service with restrictions, supervision.
(SAVE) ⊠ ⚹M 🛇 💻 ⇌

MARIPOSA

AAA ▼▼▼ **Americas Best Value Inn–Mariposa Lodge** 🅗
(209) 966-3607. **$59-$139.** 5052 Hwy 140 95338. Center. Ext corridors. **Pets:** Medium. $10 daily fee/pet. No service, supervision.
(SAVE) ⊠ 🛇 💻 ⇌

AAA ▼▼ **Best Western Yosemite Way Station Motel** 🅗
(209) 966-7545. **$69-$189.** 4999 Hwy 140 95338. SR 140 at SR 49 S. Ext corridors. **Pets:** Medium. $10 daily fee/pet. Designated rooms, service with restrictions, supervision. (SAVE) ⊠ ⚹M 💻 ⇌

AAA ▼▼▼ **Comfort Inn Yosemite Valley Gateway** 🅗
(209) 966-4344. **$79-$129.** 4994 Bullion St 95338. Jct SR 140 and 49 S, just e. Ext corridors. **Pets:** Small, other species. $15 daily fee/pet. Service with restrictions, supervision. (SAVE) ⊠ ⚹M 💻 ⇌

AAA ▼▼▼ **Miners Inn** 🅗
(209) 742-7777. **$63-$179.** 5181 Hwy 49 N 95338. On SR 49, n at SR 140. Ext/int corridors. **Pets:** Accepted. (SAVE) ⊠ 🛇 💻 🍽 ⇌

MARYSVILLE

AAA ▼▼▼ **Baymont Inn & Suites** 🅗
(530) 742-2700. **$89-$199.** 1111 N Beale Rd 95901. SR 70, exit 20A (Feather River Blvd/Yuba College) northbound; exit 20B southbound, just w. Int corridors. **Pets:** Other species. $50 deposit/room, $10 daily fee/pet. Service with restrictions, crate. (SAVE) ⊠ 🛇 💻 ⇌

AAA ▼▼▼ **Comfort Suites** 🅗
(530) 742-9200. **$80-$124.** 1034 N Beale Rd 95901. SR 70, exit 20A (Feather River Blvd/Yuba College) northbound, just nw; exit 20B southbound, just e. Int corridors. **Pets:** Medium. $100 deposit/room, $10 daily fee/pet. Designated rooms, service with restrictions, crate.
(SAVE) ⊠ 🛇 💻 ⇌

MCCLOUD

▼▼ ◆◆ McCloud Dance Country RV Resort 🄲🄰
(530) 964-2252. **Call for rates.** 480 Hwy 89 96057. Jct SR 89 and Squaw Valley Rd, just s; behind big red barn. Ext corridors. **Pets:** Accepted. ⊠ 🛏 ▣ 🆓

▼◆◆▼ McCloud Mercantile Hotel 🄷
(530) 964-2330. **$129-$250, 10 day notice.** 241 Main St 96057. Jct SR 89 and W Minnesota Ave, 0.3 mi se on w Minnesota Ave to Main St, then just n. Int corridors. **Pets:** Accepted. A$K ⊠ 🍽

MERCED

▲▲▲ ▼◆◆ Merced-Yosemite Travelodge 🄼
(209) 722-6224. **$65-$95.** 1260 Yosemite Pkwy 95340. SR 99, exit SR 140, just e. Ext corridors. **Pets:** Dogs only. $15 deposit/pet. Service with restrictions, supervision. SAVE ⊠ ⬥M 🛏 ▣ 🆓

▼◆◆▼ Ramada Inn 🄷
(209) 723-3121. **$72-$126.** 2010 E Childs Ave 95340. SR 99, exit E Childs Ave, just e. Ext/int corridors. **Pets:** Accepted.
A$K ⊠ 🛏 ▣ 🆓

MILPITAS

▲▲▲ ▼◆◆▼ Best Western Brookside Inn 🄷
(408) 263-5566. **$79-$129.** 400 Valley Way 95035. I-880, exit Calaveras Blvd (SR 237), just e. Ext/int corridors. **Pets:** Small. $15 daily fee/pet. Service with restrictions, crate. SAVE ⊠ 🛏 ▣ 🆓 🆇

▲▲▲ ▼◆◆▼ Beverly Heritage Hotel 🄷
(408) 943-9080. **$79-$209.** 1820 Barber Ln 95035. Northwest quadrant of I-880 and Montague Expwy. Int corridors. **Pets:** Accepted.
SAVE ⊠ ⬥M 🛏 ▣ 🍽 🆓 🆇

▼◆◆▼ Embassy Suites Milpitas/Silicon Valley 🄷
(408) 942-0400. **$109-$259.** 901 E Calaveras Blvd 95035. I-680, exit Calaveras Blvd (SR 237), just w. Int corridors. **Pets:** Accepted.
ECO ⊠ ⬥M 🛏 ▣ 🍽 🆓

▼◆◆ Extended StayAmerica-San Jose/Milpitas 🄷
(408) 941-9977. **$82-$97.** 1000 Hillview Ct 95035. I-680, exit Calaveras Blvd W (SR 237), just n. Int corridors. **Pets:** Other species. $25 daily fee/room. Designated rooms, service with restrictions, crate.
A$K ⊠ ⬥M ▣

**▼◆◆ Homestead Studio Suites Hotel-San
      Jose-Milpitas** 🄷
(408) 433-9700. **$105-$120.** 330 Cypress Dr 95035. SR 237, exit McCarthy S. Ext/int corridors. **Pets:** Other species. $25 daily fee/room. Designated rooms, service with restrictions, crate. A$K ⊠ 🛏 ▣

▲▲▲ ▼◆◆▼ Larkspur Landing Milpitas/San Jose 🄷
(408) 719-1212. **$89-$229.** 40 Ranch Dr 95035. SR 237, exit McCarthy, just n. Int corridors. **Pets:** Accepted. SAVE ⊠ ⬥M ▣

▲▲▲ ▼◆◆ Milpitas Travelodge 🄼
(408) 263-0500. **$69-$189, 3 day notice.** 378 W Calaveras Blvd 95035. I-880, exit Calaveras Blvd E (SR 237), just e. Ext corridors.
Pets: Accepted. SAVE ⊠ 🛏 ▣ 🆓

▼◆◆▼ Residence Inn by Marriott 🄷
(408) 941-9222. **$134-$164.** 1501 California Cir 95035. I-880, exit Dixon Landing Rd E, just s. Int corridors. **Pets:** Other species. $100 one-time fee/room. Service with restrictions, crate. ⊠ ⬥M 🛏 ▣ 🆓 🆇

▲▲▲ ▼◆◆▼ Sheraton San Jose Hotel 🄷
(408) 943-0600. **$89-$309.** 1801 Barber Ln 95035. 4 mi n of San Jose International Airport; 0.3 mi nw of I-880 and Montague Expwy. Ext/int corridors. **Pets:** Accepted. SAVE ⊠ ⬥M 🛏 ▣ 🍽 🆓 🆇

▼◆◆▼ TownePlace Suites by Marriott 🄷
(408) 719-1959. **$134-$164.** 1428 Falcon Dr 95035. I-680, exit Montague Expwy, just w, then just n. Int corridors. **Pets:** Accepted.
⊠ ⬥M ▣ 🆓

MIRANDA

▲▲▲ ▼◆◆▼ Miranda Gardens Resort 🄲🄰
(707) 943-3011. **$105-$265, 7 day notice.** 6766 Ave of the Giants 95553. US 101, exit 650, just e on French Rd, 0.3 mi s on Maple Hills Rd, then 1.5 mi e. Ext corridors. **Pets:** Accepted.
SAVE ⊠ 🛏 ▣ 🆓 🄰🄲 🆓

MI-WUK VILLAGE

▲▲▲ ▼◆◆▼ Christmas Tree Inn 🄷
(209) 586-1005. **$89-$129, 3 day notice.** 24685 Hwy 108 95346. On SR 108, 15 mi e of Sonora. Ext corridors. **Pets:** Small, dogs only. $20 one-time fee/pet. Designated rooms, service with restrictions, supervision.
SAVE ⊠ 🛏 ▣ 🆓

MODESTO

▲▲▲ ▼◆◆▼ Best Western Town House Lodge 🄷
(209) 524-7261. **$71-$86.** 909 16th St 95354. SR 99, exit Central Modesto, 1 mi e, at I St. Ext corridors. **Pets:** Medium. $25 one-time fee/pet. Service with restrictions, supervision. SAVE ⊠ ⬥M 🛏 ▣ 🆓

▲▲▲ ▼◆◆▼ Clarion Hotel 🄷
(209) 521-1612. **$69-$239.** 1612 Sisk Rd 95350. SR 99, exit Briggsmore Ave, just e. Int corridors. **Pets:** Medium, other species. $50 one-time fee/room. Designated rooms, service with restrictions, supervision.
SAVE ⊠ ⬥M 🛏 ▣ 🍽 🆓 🆇

▲▲▲ ▼◆◆ Days Inn 🄷
(209) 527-1010. **$69-$109.** 1312 McHenry Ave 95350. SR 99, exit Briggsmore Ave, 2.3 mi e, then 0.5 mi s. Ext/int corridors. **Pets:** $20 daily fee/pet. Designated rooms, service with restrictions, crate.
SAVE ⊠ ⬥M 🛏 ▣ 🆓

▲▲▲ ▼◆◆▼ Doubletree Modesto 🄷
(209) 526-6000. **$79-$209.** 1150 9th St 95354. SR 99, exit Central Modesto northbound; exit Maze Blvd southbound, just e. Int corridors.
Pets: Small, dogs only. Service with restrictions, supervision.
ECO SAVE ⊠ ⬥M 🛏 ▣ 🍽 🆓

▲▲▲ ▼◆◆▼ Howard Johnson Express Inn 🄼
(209) 537-4821. **$55-$75.** 1672 Herndon Rd 95307. SR 99, exit Hatch Rd E, then s. Ext corridors. **Pets:** Very small, other species. $50 deposit/pet. Service with restrictions, crate. SAVE ⊠ 🛏 ▣ 🆓

▲▲▲ ▼◆◆ Microtel Inn & Suites 🄷
(209) 538-6466. **$60-$99.** 1760 Herndon Rd 95307. SR 99, exit Hatch Rd E, just s. Int corridors. **Pets:** Very small, other species. $50 deposit/pet. Designated rooms, service with restrictions, crate.
SAVE ⊠ ⬥M 🛏 ▣ 🆓

▲▲▲ ▼◆◆ Ramada Inn 🄷
(209) 521-9000. **$72-$89.** 2001 W Orangeburg Ave 95350. SR 99, exit Briggsmore Ave, just s. Ext corridors. **Pets:** Accepted.
SAVE ⊠ ⬥M 🛏 ▣ 🆓

▲▲▲ ▼◆◆ Super 8 🄷
(209) 543-9000. **$79-$139.** 4100 Salida Blvd 95358. SR 99, exit Pelandale Ave, just w. Ext corridors. **Pets:** Large, other species. $25 one-time fee/room. Designated rooms, service with restrictions.
SAVE ⊠ 🛏 ▣ 🆓 🆇

MOJAVE

▲▲▲ ▼◆◆ Americas Best Value Inn 🄼
(661) 824-9317. **$60-$65.** 16352 Sierra Hwy 93501. On SR 14 and 58. Ext corridors. **Pets:** Accepted. SAVE ⊠ 🛏 ▣ 🆓

▲▲▲ ▼◆◆ Best Western Desert Winds 🄼
(661) 824-3601. **$89-$112.** 16200 Sierra Hwy 93501. On SR 14 and 58. Ext corridors. **Pets:** Medium. $10 one-time fee/pet. Designated rooms, service with restrictions, supervision. SAVE ⊠ 🛏 ▣ 🆓

▼◆◆▼ Days Inn-Mojave 🄼
(661) 824-2421. **$70-$200.** 16100 Sierra Hwy 93501. On SR 14. Ext corridors. **Pets:** Accepted. A$K ⊠ 🛏 ▣ 🆓

Desert Inn M

(661) 824-2518. **$45-$65.** 1954 Hwy 58 93501. Just e of SR 14. Ext corridors. **Pets:** Medium. Service with restrictions, crate.

Econo Lodge M

(661) 824-2463. **$49-$62.** 2145 Hwy 58 93501. Just e of SR 14. Ext corridors. **Pets:** Medium. $5 daily fee/pet. Service with restrictions, super-vision.

MONTEREY PENINSULA AREA

CARMEL-BY-THE-SEA

Briarwood Inn BB

(831) 626-9056. **$99-$249, 7 day notice.** San Carlos St 93923. 3 blks n of Ocean Ave; jct 4th Ave. Ext corridors. **Pets:** Medium, dogs only. $25 daily fee/room. Designated rooms, service with restrictions, supervision.

Carmel Country Inn BB

(831) 625-3263. **$275-$425, 7 day notice.** Dolores St & 3rd Ave 93921. 4 blks n of Ocean Ave. Ext corridors. **Pets:** Other species. $20 daily fee/pet. Service with restrictions, supervision.

Carmel Fireplace Inn Bed & Breakfast BB

(831) 624-4862. **$99-$249, 7 day notice.** San Carlos St & 4th Ave 93921. 3 blks n of Ocean Ave. Ext corridors. **Pets:** Medium, dogs only. $25 daily fee/room. Designated rooms, service with restrictions, supervision.

Carmel Lodge H

(831) 624-1255. **$119-$309.** San Carlos St & 5th Ave 93921. 2 blks n of Ocean Ave. Ext/int corridors. **Pets:** Accepted.

Carmel Mission Inn H

(831) 624-1841. **$99-$529.** 3665 Rio Rd 93923. 1 mi s on SR 1. Ext/int corridors. **Pets:** Medium. $35 one-time fee/room. Designated rooms, service with restrictions.

Carmel Resort Inn M

(831) 624-3113. **$109-$450, 3 day notice.** Carpenter St & 1st Ave 93923. SR 1, exit Carpenter St, 0.5 mi w. Ext corridors. **Pets:** Other species. $20 daily fee/pet. Service with restrictions, supervision.

Carmel River Inn M

(831) 624-1575. **$99-$369, 3 day notice.** Hwy One 93922. 1 mi s on SR 1; n of Carmel River Bridge at Oliver Rd. Ext corridors. **Pets:** $20 daily fee/pet. Service with restrictions, supervision.

Coachman's Inn H

(831) 624-6421. **$145-$435, 3 day notice.** San Carlos St at 7th Ave 93921. Just s of Ocean Ave on San Carlos St; between 7th and 8th aves. Ext corridors. **Pets:** Dogs only. $25 daily fee/pet. Designated rooms, service with restrictions, supervision.

Cypress Inn H

(831) 624-3871. **Call for rates.** Lincoln & 7th Ave 93922. Just s off Ocean Ave. Ext/int corridors. **Pets:** $30 daily fee/pet. Supervision.

Hofsas House H

(831) 624-2745. **$90-$400, 3 day notice.** San Carlos St 93921. 3 blks n off Ocean Ave; between 3rd and 4th aves. Ext corridors. **Pets:** Dogs only. $25 daily fee/pet. Designated rooms, service with restrictions, supervision.

Horizon Inn & Ocean View Lodge H

(831) 624-5327. **$129-$390, 3 day notice.** 3rd Ave & Junipero Ave 93921. 4 blks n off Ocean Ave. Ext corridors. **Pets:** Medium, dogs only. $20 daily fee/pet. Designated rooms, service with restrictions, supervision.

Svendsgaard's H

(831) 624-1511. **$159-$259, 7 day notice.** 4th Ave & San Carlos 93921. 3 blks n off Ocean Ave. Ext corridors. **Pets:** Other species. $25 one-time fee/pet. Designated rooms, service with restrictions, supervision.

Tradewinds Carmel H

(831) 624-2776. **$225-$550, 3 day notice.** Mission St and 3rd Ave 93921. 4 blks n off Ocean Ave. Ext corridors. **Pets:** Medium. $25 daily fee/pet. Designated rooms, service with restrictions, supervision.

CARMEL VALLEY

Los Laureles Lodge H

(831) 659-2233. **$125-$650, 3 day notice.** 313 W Carmel Valley Rd 93924. 10.5 mi e of SR 1. Ext corridors. **Pets:** Accepted.

MONTEREY

Bay Park Hotel H

(831) 649-1020. **$99-$350.** 1425 Munras Ave 93940. SR 1, exit Soledad Dr/Munras Ave, just w. Int corridors. **Pets:** Other species. $20 daily fee/pet. Designated rooms, service with restrictions, supervision.

Best Western Beach Resort Monterey H

(831) 394-3321. **$100-$526.** 2600 Sand Dunes Dr 93940. SR 1, exit Del Rey Oaks, just w. Ext corridors. **Pets:** Accepted.

Best Western Victorian Inn H

(831) 373-8000. **$109-$700.** 487 Foam St 93940. SR 1, exit Monterey, 3.4 mi w. Ext/int corridors. **Pets:** Other species. $30 daily fee/room. Designated rooms.

Casa Munras, a Larkspur Collection Hotel H

(831) 375-2411. **$119-$349, 3 day notice.** 700 Munras Ave 93940. SR 1, exit Soledad Dr/Munras Ave, 0.8 mi w. Ext/int corridors. **Pets:** Accepted.

El Adobe Inn M

(831) 372-5409. **$49-$199, 3 day notice.** 936 Munras Ave 93940. SR 1, exit Soledad Dr/Munras Ave, 0.6 mi w. Ext corridors. **Pets:** Accepted.

Hyatt Regency Monterey Resort & Spa on Del Monte Golf Course H

(831) 372-1234. **$99-$439, 3 day notice.** 1 Old Golf Course Rd 93940. SR 1, exit Aguajito Rd northbound; exit Monterey southbound, just e. Int corridors. **Pets:** $75 one-time fee/room. Designated rooms, service with restrictions, supervision.

La Quinta Inn H

(831) 373-7100. **$79-$179.** 2401 Del Monte Ave 93940. SR 1, exit Del Rey Oaks, just e. Int corridors. **Pets:** Medium, other species. Service with restrictions, supervision.

Mariposa Inn & Suites H

(831) 649-1414. **$149-$419, 3 day notice.** 1386 Munras Ave 93940. SR 1, exit Soledad Dr/Munras Ave, just w. Ext/int corridors. **Pets:** Dogs only. $40 daily fee/pet. Service with restrictions, supervision.

Monterey Bay Lodge H
(831) 372-8057. **$79-$349.** 55 Camino Aguajito 93940. SR 1, exit Aguajito Rd, just w. Ext corridors. **Pets:** Medium, dogs only. $15 daily fee/pet. Designated rooms, service with restrictions.

Monterey Bay Travelodge H
(831) 373-3381. **$169, 14 day notice.** 2030 N Fremont St 93940. Jct SR 1 and Fremont St, at SR 68. Ext/int corridors. **Pets:** Medium. $20 daily fee/room. Designated rooms, service with restrictions, supervision.

Monterey Fireside Lodge M
(831) 373-4172. **$69-$599, 3 day notice.** 1131 10th St 93940. SR 1, exit Aguajito Rd or Monterey, just w. Ext corridors. **Pets:** Other species. $20 daily fee/pet. Designated rooms, no service, supervision.

PACIFIC GROVE

Bide-A-Wee Inn & Cottages M
(831) 372-2330. **$69-$399, 3 day notice.** 221 Asilomar Ave 93950. 1 mi n of SR 68. Ext corridors. **Pets:** Medium. $15 daily fee/pet. Designated rooms, service with restrictions, supervision.

Deer Haven Inn & Suites H
(831) 373-7784. **$99-$209, 3 day notice.** 740 Crocker Ave 93950. Just e of SR 68 via Sinex Ave. Ext corridors. **Pets:** Accepted.

Lighthouse Lodge and Suites M
(831) 655-2111. **Call for rates.** 1150 Lighthouse Ave 93950. 0.5 mi w of Seventeen Mile Dr. Ext corridors. **Pets:** $25 daily fee/pet. Designated rooms, service with restrictions.

Pacific Gardens Inn H
(831) 646-9414. **$90-$203, 7 day notice.** 701 Asilomar Blvd 93950. Just n of SR 68; across conference grounds. Ext corridors. **Pets:** Accepted.

Sea Breeze Inn and Cottages H
(831) 372-7771. **$79-$499.** 1100 Lighthouse Ave 93950. Just w of Seventeen Mile Dr; jct Lighthouse Ave and Grove Acre. Ext/int corridors. **Pets:** Other species. $25 one-time fee/pet. Designated rooms, service with restrictions, supervision.

Sea Breeze Lodge M
(831) 372-3431. **$79-$499.** 1101 Lighthouse Ave 93950. Just w of Seventeen Mile Dr. Ext corridors. **Pets:** Other species. $25 one-time fee/pet. Designated rooms, service with restrictions, supervision.

PEBBLE BEACH

The Lodge at Pebble Beach H
(831) 624-3811. **$695-$3475, 14 day notice.** 1700 Seventeen Mile Dr 93953. Off SR 1. Ext/int corridors. **Pets:** Medium, dogs only. Crate.

SEASIDE

Econo Lodge Bay Breeze M
(831) 899-7111. **$49-$90.** 2049 Fremont Blvd 93955. SR 1, exit Sand City/Seaside, just e. Ext/int corridors. **Pets:** Small. $20 daily fee/pet. Designated rooms, service with restrictions, supervision.

Thunderbird Motel M
(831) 394-6797. **$39-$199, 3 day notice.** 1933 Fremont Blvd 93955. SR 1 business route, 0.3 mi n. Ext corridors. **Pets:** Medium. $50 deposit/pet. Service with restrictions, supervision.

END AREA

MORENO VALLEY

Comfort Inn M
(951) 242-0699. **$69-$89.** 23330 Sunnymead Blvd 92553. SR 60, exit 62 (Perris Blvd) westbound, just s, then 1.3 mi w; eastbound, 1 mi w. Ext/int corridors. **Pets:** Medium, other species. $50 deposit/pet, $10 daily fee/pet. Service with restrictions, crate.

MORGAN HILL

Extended StayAmerica-San Jose-Morgan Hill H
(408) 779-9660. **$75-$90.** 605 Jarvis Dr 95037. US 101, exit Cochrane W, s on Sutter Blvd, then just e. Int corridors. **Pets:** Other species. $25 daily fee/room. Designated rooms, service with restrictions, crate.

Residence Inn by Marriott H
(408) 782-8311. **$165-$170.** 18620 Madrone Pkwy 95037. US 101, exit Cochrane W, just n. Int corridors. **Pets:** Accepted.

MORRO BAY

Best Western El Rancho M
(805) 772-2212. **$95-$195, 3 day notice.** 2460 Main St 93442. SR 1, exit SR 41, 0.5 mi n. Ext corridors. **Pets:** Accepted.

Days Inn M
(805) 772-2711. **$69-$179, 3 day notice.** 1095 Main St 93442. SR 1, exit Morro Bay Blvd, 0.7 mi w, then just n. Ext corridors. **Pets:** Accepted.

Econo Lodge M
(805) 772-5609. **$49-$215, 3 day notice.** 1100 Main St 93442. SR 1, exit Morro Bay Blvd, 0.7 mi w, then just n. Ext corridors. **Pets:** Small. $15 daily fee/pet. No service, supervision.

Rodeway Inn–Morro Bay M
(805) 772-7503. **$43-$150, 3 day notice.** 540 Main St 93442. SR 1, exit Morro Bay Blvd, 0.7 mi w, then 0.4 mi s. Ext corridors. **Pets:** Large, other species. $30 one-time fee/pet. Service with restrictions, supervision.

Sea Pines Golf Resort M
(805) 528-5252. **$99-$219.** 1945 Solano St 93402. SR 1, exit Los Osos/Baywood Park, 4 mi s on S Bay Blvd, 1.6 mi w on Los Osos Valley Rd, 0.3 mi n on Pecho Rd, then just w on Skyline Dr. Ext corridors. **Pets:** Accepted.

MOUNTAIN VIEW

Homestead Studio Suites Hotel-San Jose, Mountain View H
(650) 962-1500. **$102-$117.** 190 E El Camino Real 94040. SR 82, just w of SR 85. Ext corridors. **Pets:** Other species. $25 daily fee/room. Designated rooms, service with restrictions, crate.

MOUNT SHASTA

A-1 Choice Inn M
(530) 926-4811. **$69-$149, 3 day notice.** 1340 S Mount Shasta Blvd 96067. I-5, exit 737 (Mount Shasta City), 0.9 mi n. Ext corridors. **Pets:** Very small, dogs only. $10 daily fee/pet. Designated rooms, service with restrictions, supervision.

Best Western Tree House Motor Inn Ⓗ
(530) 926-3101. **$124-$219.** 111 Morgan Way 96067. I-5, exit 738 (Central Mount Shasta), just e. Ext/int corridors. **Pets:** Large, other species. $15 daily fee/pet. Service with restrictions, supervision.

Cold Creek Inn Ⓜ ☙
(530) 926-9851. **$69-$129, 3 day notice.** 724 N Mount Shasta Blvd 96067. I-5, exit 738 (Central Mount Shasta), 0.5 mi ne on W Lake St, then 0.4 mi nw. Ext corridors. **Pets:** Other species. $10 daily fee/pet. Service with restrictions, supervision.

Mt Shasta Ranch Bed & Breakfast ⒷⒷ
(530) 926-3870. **$80-$150, 3 day notice.** 1008 W a Barr Rd 96067. I-5, exit 738 (Central Mount Shasta), 0.4 mi w, then 0.8 mi s; jct W Ream Ave. Ext/int corridors. **Pets:** Other species. $10 one-time fee/pet. Supervision.

Swiss Holiday Lodge Ⓜ
(530) 926-3446. **$65-$180.** 2400 S Mount Shasta Blvd 96067. I-5, exit 736 (McCloud/SR 89), just ne on SR 89, then just nw. Ext corridors. **Pets:** Small. $10 daily fee/pet. Service with restrictions, supervision.

MYERS FLAT

Myers Inn ⒷⒷ ☙
(707) 943-3259. **$185-$250, 14 day notice.** 12913 Ave of the Giants 95554. US 101, exit Myers Flat, just w. Int corridors. **Pets:** Medium, dogs only. $25 daily fee/room. Service with restrictions, supervision.

NEEDLES

Americas Best Value Inn Ⓜ ☙
(760) 326-4501. **$36-$77, 3 day notice.** 1102 E Broadway 92363. I-40, exit 144 (US 95/E Broadway), just sw. Ext corridors. **Pets:** Other species. $10 one-time fee/room. Supervision.

Best Western Colorado River Inn Ⓜ ☙
(760) 326-4552. **$79-$129.** 2371 W Broadway 92363. I-40, exit 141 (W Broadway/River Rd), 0.3 mi e; on Business Loop I-40. Ext corridors. **Pets:** Other species. $15 daily fee/room. Service with restrictions, crate.

Best Western Royal Inn Ⓜ
(760) 326-5660. **Call for rates.** 1111 Pashard St 92363. I-40, exit 141 (W Broadway/River Rd). Ext corridors. **Pets:** Other species. $15 daily fee/room. Designated rooms, service with restrictions, supervision.

Travelers Inn Ⓜ
(760) 326-4900. **$40-$50.** 1195 3rd St Hill 92363. I-40, exit 142 (J St), just e, then just n. Ext corridors. **Pets:** Accepted.

NEWARK

Chase Suite Hotel Ⓗ
(510) 795-1200. **$119-$129.** 39150 Cedar Blvd 94560. I-880, exit Mowry Ave, just w, then 0.3 mi s. Ext corridors. **Pets:** Accepted.

Hilton Newark/Fremont Ⓗ ☙
(510) 490-8390. **$79-$239.** 39900 Balentine Dr 94560. I-880, exit Stevenson Blvd, just w. Int corridors. **Pets:** Other species. $75 one-time fee/room. Designated rooms, service with restrictions, supervision.

Homewood Suites by Hilton Ⓗ
(510) 791-7700. **$129-$199.** 39270 Cedar Blvd 94560. I-880, exit Mowry Ave, w to Cedar Blvd, then 0.3 mi s. Int corridors. **Pets:** Medium, other species. $10 daily fee/room, $50 one-time fee/room. Service with restrictions, crate.

Residence Inn by Marriott Newark/Silicon Valley Ⓗ
(510) 739-6000. **$125-$153.** 35466 Dumbarton Ct 94560. SR 84, exit Newark Blvd, just s. Int corridors. **Pets:** Other species. $100 one-time fee/room.

NEWPORT BEACH

The Balboa Bay Club & Resort Ⓗ ☙
(949) 645-5000. **$239-$559.** 1221 W Coast Hwy 92663. SR 73, exit 15 (Jamboree Rd), 3.5 mi s, then just w. Int corridors. **Pets:** Small, dogs only. $25 deposit/room. Service with restrictions, supervision.

Best Western Newport Beach Inn Ⓜ
(949) 642-8252. **$80-$290.** 6208 W Coast Hwy 92663. SR 55, 1 mi nw on SR 1. Int corridors. **Pets:** Small. $50 one-time fee/room. Designated rooms, service with restrictions, supervision.

Extended StayAmerica-Orange County/John Wayne Airport Ⓗ
(949) 851-1711. **$80-$100.** 4881 Birch St 92660. I-405, exit 8 (MacArthur Blvd), 0.8 mi s, then just e. Int corridors. **Pets:** Other species. $25 daily fee/room. Designated rooms, service with restrictions, crate.

Fairmont Newport Beach Ⓗ
(949) 476-2001. **Call for rates.** 4500 MacArthur Blvd 92660. I-405, exit 8 (MacArthur Blvd), 1 mi s. Int corridors. **Pets:** Accepted.

Island Hotel Newport Beach Ⓗ ☙
(949) 759-0808. **$420-$5000.** 690 Newport Center Dr 92660. SR 73, exit 14 (MacArthur Blvd) northbound, 3 mi s to San Joaquin Hills Rd, then 0.5 mi w; exit 15 (Jamboree Rd) southbound, 2.5 mi s to San Joaquin Hills Rd, then 0.5 mi e. Int corridors. **Pets:** Medium. $100 deposit/room. Service with restrictions, supervision.

NIPOMO

Kaleidoscope Inn & Gardens B&B ⒷⒷ
(805) 929-5444. **$125-$160, 7 day notice.** 130 E Dana St 93444. US 101, exit 179 (Tefft St), 0.7 mi e, just s on Thompson Rd, then just e. Ext/int corridors. **Pets:** Other species. Designated rooms, service with restrictions, supervision.

NOVATO

Inn Marin Ⓗ ☙
(415) 883-5952. **$129-$329.** 250 Entrada Dr 94949. US 101, exit Ignacio Blvd, just w, then just n on Enfrente Rd. Ext corridors. **Pets:** Other species. $20 daily fee/pet. Service with restrictions, supervision.

Novato Days Inn Ⓗ
(415) 897-7111. **$73-$200.** 8141 Redwood Blvd 94945. US 101, exit San Marin Dr, 1 mi n. Ext corridors. **Pets:** Small, dogs only. $10 daily fee/pet. Designated rooms, service with restrictions, supervision.

Travelodge Ⓜ
(415) 892-7500. **$69-$89.** 7600 Redwood Blvd 94945. US 101, exit Atherton Ave/San Marin Dr, just sw. Ext corridors. **Pets:** Small, dogs only. $10 daily fee/pet. Designated rooms, service with restrictions, supervision.

OAKDALE

Holiday Motel Ⓜ
(209) 847-7023. **$49-$99, 3 day notice.** 950 East F St 95361. 1 mi e on SR 108 and 120. Ext corridors. **Pets:** Accepted.

OAKHURST

Americas Best Value Inn Yosemite Ⓗ
(559) 658-5500. **$59-$259.** 48800 Royal Oaks Dr 93644. SR 41, just s of SR 49. Int corridors. **Pets:** Small. $10 daily fee/pet. Designated rooms, no service, supervision.

Best Western Yosemite Gateway Inn H
(559) 683-2378. **$70-$168.** 40530 Hwy 41 93644. SR 49, 0.8 mi n. Ext corridors. **Pets:** Accepted.

Château du Sureau CI
(559) 683-6860. **$385-$585, 14 day notice.** 48688 Victoria Ln 93644. Just w of jct SR 41 and 49. Int corridors. **Pets:** Very small, dogs only. $75 one-time fee/pet. Designated rooms, service with restrictions, supervision.

Comfort Inn Yosemite Area H
(559) 683-8282. **$60-$190.** 40489 Hwy 41 93644. SR 49, 0.5 mi n. Ext corridors. **Pets:** Other species. $20 daily fee/room. Designated rooms, service with restrictions, supervision.

Oakhurst Lodge M
(559) 683-4417. **Call for rates.** 40302 Hwy 41 93644. Jct SR 41 and CR 426, just n. Ext corridors. **Pets:** Accepted.

Shilo Inn Suites-Oakhurst H
(559) 683-3555. **$70-$230.** 40644 Hwy 41 93644. SR 49, 0.8 mi n. Int corridors. **Pets:** Dogs only. $25 one-time fee/room. Designated rooms, service with restrictions, supervision.

OAKLAND

Hilton Oakland Airport H
(510) 635-5000. **$119-$229.** 1 Hegenberger Rd 94621. I-880, exit Hegenberger Rd, 1 mi w; 1.3 mi e of Metropolitan Oakland International Airport. Int corridors. **Pets:** Accepted.

Homewood Suites H
(510) 663-2700. **$139-$199.** 1103 Embarcadero 94606. I-880, exit 16th Ave/Embarcadero southbound; exit 5th Ave/Embarcadero northbound, just w. Int corridors. **Pets:** Accepted.

La Quinta Inn Oakland Airport Coliseum H
(510) 632-8900. **$70-$140.** 8465 Enterprise Way 94621. I-880, exit Hegenberger Rd, just e. Int corridors. **Pets:** Medium, other species. Service with restrictions, supervision.

Quality Inn H
(510) 562-4888. **$59-$139.** 8471 Enterprise Way 94621. I-880, exit Hegenberger Rd, just e. Ext corridors. **Pets:** Small. $100 deposit/room, $10 daily fee/pet. Service with restrictions, supervision.

Waterfront Hotel, a Joie de Vivre hotel H
(510) 836-3800. **$105-$349.** Ten Washington St 94607. I-880, exit Broadway, 0.5 mi w. Int corridors. **Pets:** Accepted.

OCEANO

Oceano Inn M
(805) 473-0032. **$69-$219, 3 day notice.** 1252 Pacific Blvd 93445. On SR 1. Ext corridors. **Pets:** Small, dogs only. $15 daily fee/pet. Service with restrictions, supervision.

OCEANSIDE

Best Western Marty's Valley Inn M
(760) 757-7700. **$69-$129.** 3240 Mission Ave 92058. I-5, exit 53 (Mission Ave), 2 mi e. Ext/int corridors. **Pets:** Accepted.

Extended StayAmerica-San Diego/Oceanside H
(760) 439-1499. **$100-$135.** 3190 Vista Way 92056. I-5, exit 51B (SR 78 E) 1.5 mi e to El Camino Real, just n, then just e. Int corridors. **Pets:** Other species. $25 daily fee/room. Designated rooms, service with restrictions, crate.

La Quinta Inn H
(760) 450-0730. **$69-$435.** 937 N Coast Hwy 92054. I-5, exit 54 (Coast Hwy), just w. Int corridors. **Pets:** Medium, other species. Service with restrictions, supervision.

Motel 6 #4208 M
(760) 721-1543. **$70-$110, 7 day notice.** 909 N Coast Hwy 92054. I-5, exit 54B (Coast Hwy), just w. Int corridors. **Pets:** Other species. Service with restrictions, supervision.

Residence Inn by Marriott San Diego/Oceanside H
(760) 722-9600. **$189-$209.** 3603 Ocean Ranch Blvd 92056. I-5, exit 52 (Oceanside Blvd), 3.3 mi e, then 0.5 mi n. Int corridors. **Pets:** $100 one-time fee/room. Service with restrictions, crate.

OJAI

Best Western Casa Ojai M
(805) 646-8175. **$89-$160.** 1302 E Ojai Ave 93023. 0.8 mi e on SR 150. Ext corridors. **Pets:** Large. $25 daily fee/pet. Designated rooms, service with restrictions, supervision.

Blue Iguana Inn M
(805) 646-5277. **$119-$269, 7 day notice.** 11794 N Ventura Ave 93023. 2.5 mi w of town on SR 33. Ext corridors. **Pets:** Large, dogs only. $100 deposit/pet, $20 daily fee/pet. Service with restrictions, supervision.

Oakridge Inn M
(805) 649-4018. **$65-$140, 3 day notice.** 780 N Ventura Ave 93022. 4 mi s on SR 33; 2 mi e of Lake Casitas; in Oak View. Ext corridors. **Pets:** Medium. $15 daily fee/pet. Service with restrictions, supervision.

Ojai Valley Inn & Spa H
(805) 646-1111. **$400-$3000, 3 day notice.** 905 Country Club Rd 93023. 1 mi w on SR 150, 0.3 mi s. Ext/int corridors. **Pets:** Dogs only. $50 one-time fee/pet. Service with restrictions.

ONTARIO

Ayres Boutique Suites Ontario Airport H
(909) 937-9700. **$89-$169.** 204 N Vineyard Ave 91764. I-10, exit 54 (Vineyard Ave), 0.3 mi s. Int corridors. **Pets:** Accepted.

Best Western InnSuites Hotel & Suites Ontario/LA H
(909) 466-9600. **$79-$119.** 3400 Shelby St 91764. I-10, exit 56 (Haven Ave), just n to Inland Empire Blvd, just w, then just se. Ext corridors. **Pets:** Accepted.

Doubletree Hotel Ontario H
(909) 937-0900. **$89-$199.** 222 N Vineyard Ave 91764. I-10, exit 54 (Vineyard Ave), 0.4 mi s. Int corridors. **Pets:** Accepted.

Extended StayAmerica-Los Angeles-Ontario Airport H
(909) 944-8900. **$75-$100.** 3990 E Inland Empire Blvd 91764. I-10, exit 56 (Haven Ave), just n, then 0.5 mi e. Int corridors. **Pets:** Other species. $25 daily fee/room. Designated rooms, service with restrictions, crate.

Hilton Ontario Airport H
(909) 980-0400. **$79-$259.** 700 N Haven Ave 91764. I-10, exit 56 (Haven Ave), just n. Int corridors. **Pets:** Accepted.

Hotel Indigo-Ontario Rancho Cucamonga H
(909) 948-7000. **$99-$149.** 3333 Shelby St 91764. I-10, exit 56 (Haven Ave), just n to Inland Empire Blvd, just w, then just s. Int corridors. **Pets:** Accepted.

▼▼▼ La Quinta Inn & Suites Ontario (Airport) 🅷 ❖

(909) 476-1112. **$79-$199.** 3555 Inland Empire Blvd 91764. I-10, exit 56 (Haven Ave), just n, then just e. Int corridors. **Pets:** Medium, other species. Service with restrictions, supervision.

[ASK] [✕] [&M] [🛏] [💻] [🏊] [✕]

🔷🔷 ▼▼▼ Quality Inn Ontario Airport 🅼

(909) 937-2999. **$79-$119.** 514 N Vineyard Ave 91764. I-10, exit 54 (Vineyard Ave), just s. Ext corridors. **Pets:** Medium, other species. $20 daily fee/pet. Designated rooms, service with restrictions, supervision.

[SAVE] [✕] [🛏] [🏊]

▼▼▼ Residence Inn by Marriott 🅷

(909) 937-6788. **$134-$164.** 2025 Convention Center Way 91764. I-10, exit 54 (Vineyard Ave), just s, then 1 blk e. Ext corridors. **Pets:** Accepted.

[✕] [&M] [🛏] [💻] [🏊] [✕]

🔷🔷 ▼▼▼ Sheraton Ontario Airport Hotel 🅷 🐾

(909) 937-8000. **$89-$259.** 429 N Vineyard Ave 91764. I-10, exit 54 (Vineyard Ave), just s. Int corridors. **Pets:** Small. Service with restrictions, crate. [SAVE] [✕] [🛏] [💻] [🍴] [🏊]

ORANGE

▼▼▼ Doubletree Hotel Anaheim/Orange County 🅷

(714) 634-4500. **$109-$199.** 100 The City Dr 92868. I-5, exit 107B (Chapman Ave) northbound, just w; exit 107C (State College/The City Dr) southbound, just s on State College Blvd, then just w. Int corridors. **Pets:** Medium. $75 one-time fee/pet. Designated rooms, service with restrictions, crate. [✕] [&M] [🛏] [💻] [🍴] [🏊] [✕]

▼▼▼ Hilton Suites Anaheim/Orange 🅷

(714) 938-1111. **$119-$219.** 400 N State College Blvd 92868. I-5, exit 107C (State College Blvd/The City Dr), just n. Int corridors. **Pets:** Accepted. [✕] [🛏] [💻] [🍴] [🏊] [✕]

ORICK

🔷 ▼▼▼ Elk Meadow Cabins 🅲🅰

(707) 488-2222. **$200-$300, 14 day notice.** 7 Valley Green Camp Rd 95555. US 101, milepost 124. Ext corridors. **Pets:** Medium. $15 daily fee/pet. No service, supervision. [SAVE] [✕] [🛏] [💻] [✕] [Ⓜ]

ORLAND

🔷 ▼▼▼ Orland Inn 🅼 ❖

(530) 865-7632. **$65-$75.** 1052 South St 95963. I-5, exit 618 (CR 16/South St), just ne; in Stony Creek Shopping Center. Ext corridors. **Pets:** Large, other species. $5 daily fee/pet. Service with restrictions, crate. [SAVE] [✕] [&M] [🛏] [💻]

OROVILLE

🔷 ▼▼▼ Americas Best Value Inn & Suites 🅼

(530) 533-7070. **$60-$165.** 580 Oro Dam Blvd 95965. SR 70, exit SR 162 (Oroville Dam Blvd), 0.3 mi e. Ext corridors. **Pets:** Medium, other species. $10 daily fee/pet. Designated rooms, service with restrictions, supervision. [SAVE] [✕] [&M] [🛏] [🏊]

🔷 ▼▼▼ Days Inn-Oroville 🅼

(530) 533-3297. **$75-$149.** 1745 Feather River Blvd 95965. SR 70, exit E Montgomery St, just e to Feather River Blvd, then 0.5 mi s. Ext corridors. **Pets:** Accepted. [SAVE] [✕] [🛏] [💻] [🏊]

OXNARD

🔷 ▼▼▼ Best Western Oxnard Inn 🅼

(805) 483-9581. **$90-$100.** 1156 S Oxnard Blvd 93030. US 101, exit 61 (Rose Ave) northbound, 3 mi s, then 1 mi se; exit 62B (Oxnard Blvd) southbound, 3.5 mi s. Ext corridors. **Pets:** Small, other species. $40 one-time fee/pet. Service with restrictions, supervision.

[SAVE] [✕] [&M] [🛏] [💻] [🏊]

🔷 ▼▼▼ Comfort Inn-Oxnard/Camarillo 🅼

(805) 201-6000. **$90-$180.** 1001 E Channel Islands Blvd 93033. US 101, exit 61 (Rose Ave), 3.5 mi s, then 1.5 mi w. Ext corridors. **Pets:** Accepted. [SAVE] [✕] [🛏] [💻] [🏊] [✕]

▼▼▼ Residence Inn At River Ridge 🅷

(805) 278-2200. **$149-$159.** 2101 W Vineyard Ave 93036. US 101, exit 62A (Vineyard Ave), 1.8 mi w. Ext corridors. **Pets:** Accepted.

[✕] [&M] [🛏] [💻] [🏊] [✕]

🔷 ▼▼▼ Vagabond Inn Oxnard 🅼

(805) 983-0251. **$66-$80.** 1245 N Oxnard Blvd 93030. US 101, exit 62A (Vineyard Ave) northbound; exit 62B (Oxnard Blvd) southbound, 1.5 mi s. Ext corridors. **Pets:** Accepted. [SAVE] [✕] [&M] [🛏] [💻] [🏊]

PALMDALE

▼▼▼ Residence Inn by Marriott 🅷

(661) 947-4204. **$153-$187.** 514 W Ave P 93551. SR 14, exit Rancho Vista, just e. Int corridors. **Pets:** Small. $100 one-time fee/room. Service with restrictions. [✕] [&M] [🛏] [💻] [🏊] [✕]

▼▼▼ Super 8 🅼

(661) 273-8000. **Call for rates.** 200 W Palmdale Blvd 93551. SR 14, exit 35 (Palmdale Blvd), just e. Int corridors. **Pets:** Other species. $20 daily fee/pet. Service with restrictions, supervision. [✕] [🛏] [🏊]

PALM DESERT

🔷 ▼▼▼ Best Western Palm Desert Resort 🅼

(760) 340-4441. **$79-$299.** 74-695 Hwy 111 92260. I-10, exit 134 (Cook St), 4.4 mi s, then 0.3 mi w. Ext corridors. **Pets:** Other species. $10 daily fee/room. Service with restrictions, supervision.

[SAVE] [✕] [&M] [🛏] [💻] [🏊] [✕]

🔷 ▼▼▼ Comfort Suites 🅼

(760) 360-3337. **$79-$199.** 39-585 Washington St 92211. I-10, exit 137 (Washington St), just n. Int corridors. **Pets:** Other species. $20 daily fee/room. Service with restrictions, supervision.

[ECO] [SAVE] [✕] [&M] [🛏] [💻] [🏊] [✕]

🔷 ▼▼▼ The Inn at Deep Canyon 🅼

(760) 346-8061. **$47-$127, 3 day notice.** 74-470 Abronia Tr 92260. I-10, exit 134 (Cook St), 4.4 mi s to SR 111, 0.5 mi w, then just s on Deep Canyon Rd. Ext corridors. **Pets:** Large, other species. $10 daily fee/pet. Designated rooms, service with restrictions.

[SAVE] [✕] [&M] [🛏] [💻] [🏊] [✕]

▼▼▼ Residence Inn by Marriott 🅷

(760) 776-0050. **$99-$169.** 38-305 Cook St 92211. I-10, exit 134 (Cook St), 0.8 mi s. Ext corridors. **Pets:** Accepted. [✕] [🛏] [💻] [🏊] [✕]

PALM SPRINGS

▼▼▼ A Place In The Sun 🅼 ❖

(760) 325-0254. **$99-$379, 7 day notice.** 754 San Lorenzo Rd 92264. Just e of Palm Canyon Dr via Mesquite Ave and Random Rd. Ext corridors. **Pets:** $15 daily fee/pet. [✕] [🛏] [💻] [🏊]

▼▼▼ Casa Cody Country Inn 🅼

(760) 320-9346. **$89-$639, 3 day notice.** 175 S Cahuilla Rd 92262. SR 111, just w of Palm Canyon Dr on Tahquitz Canyon Way, then just s. Ext corridors. **Pets:** Accepted. [✕] [🛏] [💻] [🏊] [✕]

▼▼▼ Hilton Palm Springs 🅷 ❖

(760) 320-6868. **$165-$325.** 400 E Tahquitz Canyon Way 92262. Just e of Indian Canyon Dr. Int corridors. **Pets:** Medium. $75 one-time fee/room. Designated rooms, service with restrictions, crate.

[✕] [🛏] [💻] [🍴] [🏊] [✕]

▼▼▼ Holiday Inn Palm Springs-City Center 🅷

(760) 323-1711. **$79-$299.** 1800 E Palm Canyon Dr 92264. 2 mi se of Tahquitz Canyon Way. Ext/int corridors. **Pets:** Accepted.

[ASK] [✕] [🛏] [💻] [🍴] [🏊]

▼▼▼ Hotel California 🅼 ❖

(760) 322-8855. **$99-$250, 3 day notice.** 424 E Palm Canyon Dr 92264. 1.5 mi s of Tahquitz Canyon Way. Ext corridors. **Pets:** Small, dogs only. $100 deposit/room, $25 daily fee/room. Designated rooms, service with restrictions, supervision. [ASK] [✕] [🛏] [💻] [🏊]

▼▼▼▼ Hotel Zoso H

(760) 325-9676. **$99-$349, 3 day notice.** 150 S Indian Canyon Dr 92262. Just s of Tahquitz Canyon Way. Int corridors. **Pets:** Accepted.

[ASK] [X] [B] [P] [¶] [≈]

▼▼▼ Quality Inn Palm Springs M

(760) 323-2775. **$59-$149.** 1269 E Palm Canyon Dr 92264. 2.3 mi se of Tahquitz Canyon Way. Ext corridors. **Pets:** Accepted.

[ASK] [X] [B] [P] [≈]

▼▼ Ramada Palm Springs M

(760) 320-0555. **$59-$229, 3 day notice.** 2000 N Palm Canyon Dr 92262. 1.5 mi n of Tahquitz Canyon Way. Ext/int corridors. **Pets:** Small, dogs only. $25 daily fee/pet. Service with restrictions, supervision.

[ASK] [X] [B] [P] [≈]

◇◇◇ ▼▼▼▼ Shilo Inn Suites–Palm Springs M ❀

(760) 320-7676. **$115-$255.** 1875 N Palm Canyon Dr 92262. 1.5 mi n of Tahquitz Canyon Way. Ext corridors. **Pets:** Dogs only. $25 one-time fee/room. Designated rooms, service with restrictions, supervision.

[SAVE] [X] [B] [P] [≈] [X]

PALO ALTO

◇◇◇ ▼▼▼▼ Crowne Plaza Cabana Hotel H

(650) 857-0787. **$179-$305.** 4290 El Camino Real 94306. US 101, exit San Antonio Rd, 0.4 mi n. Ext/int corridors. **Pets:** Small. $50 one-time fee/room. Designated rooms, service with restrictions, supervision.

[ECO] [SAVE] [X] [&M] [B] [P] [¶] [≈]

◇◇◇ ▼▼▼▼ Days Inn Stanford M

(650) 493-4222. **$55-$195.** 4238 El Camino Real 94306. US 101, exit San Antonio Rd, 2 mi w to SR 82, then 1 mi n. Ext corridors.

Pets: Accepted. [SAVE] [X] [&M] [B] [P]

◇◇◇ ▼▼▼▼ Sheraton Palo Alto Hotel H

(650) 328-2800. **$129-$429, 3 day notice.** 625 El Camino Real 94301. US 101, exit Embarcadero, 1.8 mi w, then just n on SR 82. Int corridors. **Pets:** Service with restrictions, supervision.

[SAVE] [X] [&M] [B] [P] [¶] [≈]

◇◇◇ ▼▼▼▼ The Westin Palo Alto H

(650) 321-4422. **$159-$529, 3 day notice.** 675 El Camino Real 94301. US 101, exit 402 (Embarcadero), 1.8 mi w, then just n on SR 82. Int corridors. **Pets:** Service with restrictions, supervision.

[SAVE] [X] [&M] [B] [P] [¶] [≈] [X]

PARADISE

◇◇◇ ▼▼▼ Comfort Inn H

(530) 876-0191. **$85-$165.** 5475 Clark Rd 95969. SR 191, 0.5 mi s of Pearson Rd. Int corridors. **Pets:** Dogs only. $100 deposit/room, $10 daily fee/pet. Designated rooms, service with restrictions, supervision.

[SAVE] [X] [&M] [B] [P] [≈]

◇◇◇ ▼ Lantern Inn M

(530) 877-5553. **$55-$82.** 5799 Wildwood Ln 95969. Just n of jct Pearson Rd and Skyway, then 1 blk w off Skyway. Ext corridors. **Pets:** $10 daily fee/pet. Service with restrictions, supervision.

[SAVE] [X] [B] [P] [≈]

◇◇◇ ▼ Paradise Inn M

(530) 877-2127. **$58-$65.** 5423 Skyway 95969. Jct Pearson Rd, 1.5 mi w. Ext corridors. **Pets:** $10 daily fee/pet. [SAVE] [X] [B] [P] [≈]

◇◇◇ ▼▼▼ Ponderosa Gardens Motel M ❀

(530) 872-9094. **$119-$159.** 7010 Skyway 95969. 2 blks e; center. Ext corridors. **Pets:** Other species. $10 daily fee/pet. Designated rooms, service with restrictions, supervision. [SAVE] [X] [&M] [B] [P] [≈]

PASO ROBLES

◇◇◇ ▼▼▼▼ Hampton Inn & Suites H

(805) 226-9988. **Call for rates.** 212 Alexa Ct 93446. US 101, exit 228 (SR 46 W), just sw. Int corridors. **Pets:** Accepted.

[SAVE] [X] [&M] [B] [P] [≈]

▼▼▼▼ La Quinta Inn & Suites H ❀

(805) 239-3004. **$99-$189.** 2615 Buena Vista Dr 93446. US 101, exit 234 northbound; exit 231B (SR 46 E) southbound, 0.3 mi e, then just n. Int corridors. **Pets:** Medium, other species. Service with restrictions, supervision. [ASK] [X] [B] [P] [≈]

PATTERSON

◇◇◇ ▼▼▼▼ Best Western Villa Del Lago Inn H

(209) 892-5300. **$79-$134.** 2959 Speno Dr 95363. I-5, exit Sperry Rd, just e. Int corridors. **Pets:** Other species. $15 one-time fee/room. Service with restrictions, supervision. [SAVE] [X] [B] [P] [¶] [≈] [X]

PHELAN

◇◇◇ ▼▼▼ Best Western Cajon Pass M

(760) 249-6777. **$70-$90.** 8317 Hwy 138 92371. I-15, exit 131 (SR 138/ Palmdale), just w. Ext corridors. **Pets:** Accepted.

[SAVE] [X] [B] [P] [≈]

PISMO BEACH

▼▼▼ Cliffs Resort H

(805) 773-5000. **Call for rates.** 2757 Shell Beach Rd 93449. US 101, exit 193 (Spyglass Dr) northbound; exit 193 (Shell Beach Rd) southbound, just w, then just n. Int corridors. **Pets:** Accepted.

[X] [B] [P] [¶] [≈] [X]

▼▼▼ Cottage Inn by the Sea M ❀

(805) 773-4617. **$109-$399.** 2351 Price St 93449. US 101, exit 191B (Shell Beach Rd) northbound, just w, 0.5 mi s; exit 191B (Price St) southbound, just w, then just s. Ext corridors. **Pets:** Medium, other species. $20 daily fee/room. Designated rooms, service with restrictions, supervision. [ASK] [X] [&M] [B] [P] [≈] [K]

◇◇◇ ▼▼▼ ▼▼▼ Dolphin Bay Resort & Spa CO ❀

(805) 773-4300. **$325-$1200.** 2727 Shell Beach Rd 93449. US 101, exit 193 (Spyglass Dr) northbound; exit 193 (Shell Beach Rd) southbound, just w, then just n; in Shell Beach area. Ext corridors. **Pets:** Medium, dogs only. $65 daily fee/room. Designated rooms, service with restrictions. [SAVE] [X] [B] [P] [¶] [≈] [X] [K]

◇◇◇ ▼▼▼▼ Oxford Suites H ❀

(805) 773-3773. **$99-$229.** 651 Five Cities Dr 93449. US 101, exit 189 (4th St), just w, then just s. Ext corridors. **Pets:** Medium. $10 daily fee/pet. Designated rooms, service with restrictions, supervision. [SAVE] [X] [B] [P] [≈] [X]

▼▼▼ Sandcastle Inn M ❀

(805) 773-2422. **$125-$499.** 100 Stimson Ave 93449. US 101, exit 190 (Price St) northbound, 0.3 mi s, then just w; exit 190B (Hinds Ave) southbound, just w, then just s. Ext/int corridors. **Pets:** Dogs only. $20 daily fee/room. Designated rooms, service with restrictions, supervision. [ASK] [X] [&M] [B] [P]

◇◇◇ ▼▼▼ SeaCrest Resort M ❀

(805) 773-4608. **$89-$399.** 2241 Price St 93449. US 101, exit 191B (Shell Beach Rd) northbound, just w, then 0.5 mi s; exit 191B (Price St) southbound, just w, then just s. Ext/int corridors. **Pets:** Small, dogs only. $20 daily fee/pet. Designated rooms, service with restrictions, supervision. [SAVE] [X] [B] [P] [≈] [K]

▼▼ Sea Gypsy Motel CO

(805) 773-1801. **$55-$250.** 1020 Cypress St 93449. US 101, exit 191A (Wadsworth Ave) northbound, 0.3 mi w to Cypress St, then just s; exit 191A (SR 1) southbound, just w on Wadsworth Ave, then just s. Ext/int corridors. **Pets:** Other species. $15 daily fee/pet. Service with restrictions, supervision. [X] [B] [P] [≈]

▼▼ Shell Beach Inn M

(805) 773-4373. **$65-$225.** 653 Shell Beach Rd 93449. US 101, exit 191B (Shell Beach Rd) northbound, just w, then 1.2 mi s; exit 191B (Price St) southbound, just w, then 1 mi n. Ext corridors. **Pets:** Accepted.

[ASK] [X] [B] [P] [≈] [K]

▼▼▼▼ Spyglass Inn H

(805) 773-4855. **$109-$399.** 2705 Spyglass Dr 93449. US 101, exit 193 (Spyglass Dr) northbound; exit 193 (Shell Beach Rd) southbound, just w, then just n. Ext corridors. **Pets:** Dogs only. $20 daily fee/pet. Designated rooms, service with restrictions, supervision.

ASK ✕ &M ▤ � ¶1 ⇌ ✗

PLACENTIA

▼▼▼ Residence Inn by Marriott H ❖

(714) 996-0555. **$152-$186.** 700 W Kimberly Ave 92870. SR 57, exit 6 (Orangethorpe Ave) southbound; exit 6A (Orangethorpe Ave) northbound, just w, just n on Placentia Ave, then just e. Ext corridors. **Pets:** Other species. $100 one-time fee/pet. Service with restrictions, crate.

✕ ▤ ▤ ⇌ ✗

PLACERVILLE

▲▲▲ ▼▼▼▼ Best Western Placerville Inn H

(530) 622-9100. **$89-$299.** 6850 Green Leaf Dr 95667. US 50, exit 44A (Missouri Flat Rd S), just e. Int corridors. **Pets:** Large, other species. $25 daily fee/pet. Designated rooms, service with restrictions, supervision.

SAVE ✕ &M ▤ ▤ ⇌

▲▲▲ ▼ Mother Lode Motel M

(530) 622-0895. **$48-$78, 7 day notice.** 1940 Broadway 95667. US 50, exit 49 (Point View Dr), just e. Ext corridors. **Pets:** Accepted.

SAVE ✕ ▤ ▤ ⇌

PLEASANT HILL

▼▼ Extended StayAmerica-Pleasant Hill-Buskirk Ave H

(925) 945-6788. **$112-$127.** 3220 Buskirk Ave 94523. I-680, exit Treat Blvd/Geary Rd E, just n. Int corridors. **Pets:** Other species. $25 daily fee/room. Designated rooms, service with restrictions, crate.

ASK ✕ ▤ ▤

▲▲▲ ▼▼▼▼ Hyatt Summerfield Suites Pleasant Hill H ❖

(925) 934-3343. **$99-$299.** 2611 Contra Costa Blvd 94523. I-680, exit Contra Costa Blvd, then w. Int corridors. **Pets:** Large. $250 one-time fee/ room. Service with restrictions, crate.

SAVE ✕ &M ▤ ▤ ⇌ ✗

▼▼▼ Residence Inn by Marriott-Pleasant Hill H

(925) 689-1010. **$179-$219.** 700 Ellinwood Way 94523. I-680, exit Willow Pass Rd W to S Contra Costa Blvd, e on Ellinwood Dr, then n. Ext/int corridors. **Pets:** Accepted. ✕ &M ▤ ⇌ ✗

PLEASANTON

▲▲▲ ▼▼▼ Best Western Pleasanton Inn H

(925) 463-1300. **$69-$109, 7 day notice.** 5375 Owens Ct 94588. I-580, exit Hopyard Rd, just s. Ext corridors. **Pets:** Large, other species. $35 daily fee/pet. Designated rooms, service with restrictions.

SAVE ✕ ▤ ▤ ⇌

▼▼ Extended Stay Deluxe Pleasanton-Chabot Dr H

(925) 730-0000. **$100-$115.** 4555 Chabot Dr 94588. I-580, exit Hopyard Rd, 1 mi s, e on Stoneridge Dr, then s. Int corridors. **Pets:** Other species. $25 daily fee/room. Service with restrictions, crate.

ASK ✕ ⇌

▼▼▼▼ Hilton Pleasanton at the Club H ❖

(925) 463-8000. **$72-$204.** 7050 Johnson Dr 94588. In southeast quadrant of jct I-580 and 680. Int corridors. **Pets:** Medium. $75 one-time fee/ room. Service with restrictions, crate.

✕ &M ▤ ▤ ¶1 ⇌ ✗

▲▲▲ ▼▼▼▼ Hyatt Summerfield Suites Pleasanton H

(925) 730-0070. **$89-$299.** 4545 Chabot Dr 94588. I-580, exit Hopyard Rd, 1 mi s, e on Stoneridge Dr, then s. Ext corridors. **Pets:** Accepted.

SAVE ✕ &M ▤ ⇌ ✗

▲▲▲ ▼▼▼▼ Larkspur Landing Pleasanton H

(925) 463-1212. **$149-$179.** 5535 Johnson Ave 94588. I-580, exit Hopyard Rd S, w on Owen. Int corridors. **Pets:** Accepted. SAVE ✕ &M ▤

▼▼▼▼ Residence Inn by Marriott H ❖

(925) 227-0500. **$143-$175.** 11920 Dublin Canyon Rd 94588. I-580, exit Foothill Blvd S, then w. Int corridors. **Pets:** Other species. $100 one-time fee/room. Service with restrictions, supervision. ✕ &M ▤ ⇌ ✗

▲▲▲ ▼▼▼▼ Sheraton Pleasanton Hotel H

(925) 463-3330. **$89-$229.** 5990 Stoneridge Mall Rd 94588. Jct I-580 and 680, 0.5 mi sw; I-580, exit Foothill Rd, 0.3 mi s, then 0.3 mi e on Canyon Way. Int corridors. **Pets:** Accepted.

SAVE ✕ &M ▤ ▤ ¶1 ⇌

PORTOLA

▼ Sleepy Pines Motel M

(530) 832-4291. **Call for rates.** 74631 Hwy 70 96122. 1 mi w of center. Ext corridors. **Pets:** Accepted. ✕ ▤ ▤

RAMONA

▲▲▲ ▼▼▼ Ramona Valley Inn M

(760) 789-6433. **$75-$125.** 416 Main St 92065. On SR 78, 0.5 mi e of jct SR 67. Ext corridors. **Pets:** Very small, dogs only. $100 one-time fee/ room. Designated rooms, service with restrictions, supervision.

SAVE ✕ ▤ ⇌

RANCHO CORDOVA

▲▲▲ ▼▼▼ Comfort Inn & Suites H

(916) 351-1213. **$70-$160.** 12249 Folsom Blvd 95742. US 50, exit Hazel Ave, just s, then just w. Ext corridors. **Pets:** Medium, other species. $20 daily fee/pet. Designated rooms, supervision.

SAVE ✕ &M ▤ ▤ ⇌ ✗

▼▼ Extended StayAmerica-Sacramento-White Rock Rd H

(916) 635-2363. **$65-$80.** 10721 White Rock Rd 95670. US 50, exit Zinfandel Dr, just s. Ext corridors. **Pets:** Other species. $25 daily fee/room. Designated rooms, service with restrictions, crate. ASK ✕ ▤ ▤

▼▼▼ Hawthorn Suites H

(916) 351-9192. **$119.** 12180 Tributary Point Dr 95670. US 50, exit Hazel Ave, just n. Int corridors. **Pets:** Medium. $50 one-time fee/room. Service with restrictions, supervision. ASK ✕ &M ▤ ▤ ⇌

▲▲▲ ▼▼▼▼ Holiday Inn Rancho Cordova H

(916) 635-4040. **$109-$159.** 11269 Point East Dr 95742. US 50, exit Sunrise Blvd S, e on Folsom Blvd, then just n. Int corridors. **Pets:** Large. $25 one-time fee/pet. Designated rooms, service with restrictions, supervision. ECO SAVE ✕ &M ▤ ▤ ¶1 ⇌ ✗

▼▼▼▼ La Quinta Inn & Suites Rancho Cordova/Sacramento H ❖

(916) 638-1111. **$59-$129.** 11131 Folsom Blvd 95670. US 50, exit Sunrise Blvd, just s, then just w. Int corridors. **Pets:** Medium, other species. Service with restrictions, supervision. ASK ✕ &M ▤ ▤ ⇌

▲▲▲ ▼▼▼ Red Roof Inn-Rancho Cordova-Sacramento East M

(916) 638-2500. **$55-$80.** 10800 Olson Dr 95670. US 50, exit Zinfandel Dr, just n. Ext corridors. **Pets:** Large. Service with restrictions, crate.

SAVE ✕ &M ▤ ⇌

▼▼▼▼ Residence Inn by Marriott H

(916) 851-1550. **$126-$154.** 2779 Prospect Park Dr 95670. US 50, exit Zinfandel Dr, just s to White Rock Rd, just e, then just n; at jct Gold Center Dr. Int corridors. **Pets:** Accepted. ✕ &M ▤ ⇌ ✗

▼▼▼▼ Vagabond Inn Executive-Rancho Cordova H

(916) 631-7500. **$62-$90.** 10713 White Rock Rd 95670. US 50, exit Zinfandel Dr, just s. Ext/int corridors. **Pets:** Dogs only. Designated rooms, service with restrictions, supervision. ASK ✕ &M ▤ ▤ ⇌

RANCHO CUCAMONGA

aloft Ontario-Rancho Cucamonga H ❀
(909) 484-2018. **$69-$299, 7 day notice.** 10480 4th St 91730. I-10, exit 59 (Haven Ave), 0.3 m n, then just w. Int corridors. **Pets:** Small, dogs only. Service with restrictions, supervision.
[SAVE] ⊠ &M 🔒 💻 🍴 ➦

Homewood Suites H
(909) 481-6480. **$149-$219.** 11433 Mission Vista Dr 91730. I-15, exit 110 (4th St), just w to Richmond Pl, just n, then just w. Int corridors. **Pets:** Accepted. ⊠ &M 🔒 💻 ➦ ⊠

TownePlace Suites by Marriott H
(909) 466-1100. **$99-$129.** 9625 Milliken Ave 91730. I-10, exit 57 (Milliken Ave), 0.6 mi n. Int corridors. **Pets:** Accepted.
[SAVE] ⊠ &M 🔒 💻 ➦

RANCHO MIRAGE

The Westin Mission Hills Resort & Spa H ❀
(760) 328-5955. **$95-$550, 7 day notice.** 71-333 Dinah Shore Dr 92270. I-10, exit 130 (Ramon Rd), 0.3 mi w, 1 mi s on Bob Hope Dr, then 0.6 mi w. Ext corridors. **Pets:** Small, dogs only. Service with restrictions, supervision. [SAVE] ⊠ 🔒 💻 🍴 ➦ ⊠

RED BLUFF

Best Western Antelope Inn H
(530) 527-8882. **$86-$100.** 203 Antelope Blvd 96080. I-5, exit 649 (SR 36), just e. Int corridors. **Pets:** Other species. $10 daily fee/pet. Designated rooms, service with restrictions, supervision.
[SAVE] ⊠ 🔒 💻 ➦

Comfort Inn H
(530) 529-7060. **Call for rates.** 90 Sale Ln 96080. I-5, exit 649, Central Red Bluff/Antelope Blvd (SR 36), 0.3 mi e. Int corridors. **Pets:** Dogs only. $15 daily fee/pet. Designated rooms, service with restrictions, supervision.
[SAVE] ⊠ &M 🔒 💻 ➦

Sportsman Lodge M
(530) 527-2888. **$55-$150, 3 day notice.** 768 Antelope Blvd 96080. I-5, exit 649 (SR 36), 1.5 mi e. Ext corridors. **Pets:** Medium. $7 daily fee/pet. Service with restrictions, supervision. [SAVE] ⊠ 🔒 💻 ➦

Super 8 Red Bluff M
(530) 529-2028. **$55-$150.** 30 Gilmore Rd 96080. I-5, exit 649 (SR 36), just w, then just s. Ext corridors. **Pets:** Accepted.
[SAVE] ⊠ &M 🔒 💻 ➦

REDCREST

Redcrest Resort CA ❀
(707) 722-4208. **$60-$205, 14 day notice.** 26459 Ave of the Giants 95569. US 101, exit Redcrest southbound; exit Redcrest/Holmes northbound, just e, then just n. Ext corridors. **Pets:** $8 daily fee/pet. Designated rooms, no service, supervision.
[SAVE] ⊠ 🔒 💻 ⊠ 🎾 📼

REDDING

Baymont Inn & Suites Redding H
(530) 722-9100. **$99-$199.** 2600 Larkspur Ln 96002. I-5, exit 677 (Cypress Ave), just e, then just s. Int corridors. **Pets:** Accepted.
[SAVE] ⊠ &M 🔒 💻 ➦

Best Western Twin View Inn & Suites H
(530) 241-5500. **$99-$199.** 1080 Twin View Blvd 96003. I-5, exit 681 (Twin View Blvd), just w. Int corridors. **Pets:** Accepted.
[SAVE] ⊠ &M 🔒 💻 ➦

Comfort Inn H
(530) 221-4472. **$89-$112.** 850 Mistletoe Ln 96002. I-5, exit 677 (Cypress Ave), 0.8 mi n on Hilltop Dr, then just e. Int corridors. **Pets:** Accepted. [SAVE] ⊠ 🔒 💻 ➦

La Quinta Inn Redding H ❀
(530) 221-8200. **$49-$129.** 2180 Hilltop Dr 96002. I-5, exit 677 (Cypress Ave), just e, then just n. Int corridors. **Pets:** Medium, other species. Service with restrictions, supervision. [A$K] ⊠ 🔒 💻 ➦

Oxford Suites H
(530) 221-0100. **$105-$159.** 1967 Hilltop Dr 96002. I-5, exit 677 (Cypress Ave), just e, then just n. Ext/int corridors. **Pets:** Accepted.
[A$K] ⊠ 🔒 💻 ➦

Quality Inn M
(530) 221-6530. **Call for rates.** 2059 Hilltop Dr 96002. I-5, exit 677 (Cypress Ave), just e, then 0.3 mi n. Ext corridors. **Pets:** $15 one-time fee/room. Service with restrictions, supervision. [SAVE] ⊠ 🔒 💻 ➦

Redding Travelodge H
(530) 243-5291. **$68-$135.** 540 N Market St 96003. I-5, exit 680 (Lake Blvd) northbound, 0.5 mi w to Market St, then 0.5 mi s; exit Market St southbound, 2 mi s. Ext corridors. **Pets:** Other species. $8 daily fee/pet. Designated rooms, service with restrictions, supervision.
[SAVE] ⊠ 🔒 💻 ➦

Red Lion Hotel Redding H
(530) 221-8700. **$109-$189.** 1830 Hilltop Dr 96002. I-5, exit SR 44 (Hilltop Dr) southbound, just e, then just s; exit 677 (Cypress Ave) northbound, just e, then 0.6 mi n. Int corridors. **Pets:** Other species. $20 one-time fee/room. Service with restrictions, supervision.
[A$K] ⊠ &M 🔒 💻 🍴 ➦

REDLANDS

Dynasty Suites-Redlands M ❀
(909) 793-6648. **$89-$159, 3 day notice.** 1235 W Colton Ave 92374. I-10, exit 77C (Tennessee St) eastbound; exit 77B (Tennessee St) westbound, just s, then just w. Ext corridors. **Pets:** Small. $15 daily fee/pet. Designated rooms, service with restrictions, supervision.
[SAVE] ⊠ 🔒 💻 ➦ ⊠

Howard Johnson Inn M
(909) 793-2001. **$49-$189.** 1120 W Colton Ave 92374. I-10, exit 77C (Tennessee St) eastbound; exit 77B (Tennessee St) westbound, just s, then just e. Ext corridors. **Pets:** Accepted. [SAVE] ⊠ 🔒 💻 ➦

REDWAY

Dean Creek Resort M
(707) 923-2555. **$80-$140.** 4112 Redwood Dr 95560. US 101, exit Redwood Dr northbound; exit Redway/Shelter Cove southbound, just w. Ext corridors. **Pets:** Accepted. [SAVE] ⊠ 🔒 💻 ➦ ⊠

REDWOOD CITY

Sofitel San Francisco Bay H
(650) 598-9000. **$111-$380.** 223 Twin Dolphin Dr 94065. US 101, exit Marine Pkwy E, 0.5 mi s. Int corridors. **Pets:** Accepted.
[SAVE] ⊠ &M 🍴 ➦

TownePlace Suites by Marriott H
(650) 593-4100. **$179-$219.** 1000 Twin Dolphin Dr 94065. US 101, exit Redwood Shores Pkwy, 0.3 mi e, then just s. Int corridors. **Pets:** $75 one-time fee/room. Service with restrictions. ⊠ &M 🔒 💻

REEDLEY

Edgewater Inn M
(559) 637-7777. **$75-$79.** 1977 W Manning Ave 93654. 12 mi e of SR 99 via Manning Ave. Ext corridors. **Pets:** $8 daily fee/pet. Service with restrictions, supervision. [SAVE] ⊠ 🔒 💻 ➦

RIALTO

Empire Inn & Suites M
(909) 877-0690. **$73-$110, 3 day notice.** 475 W Valley Blvd 92376. I-10, exit 68 (Riverside Ave), just n, then 0.5 mi w. Ext corridors. **Pets:** Medium. $15 daily fee/pet. Service with restrictions, supervision.
[SAVE] ⊠ 🔒 💻 🍴 ➦

RIDGECREST

Best Western China Lake Inn M
(760) 371-2300. **$91-$140.** 400 S China Lake Blvd 93555. On US 395 business route. Ext corridors. **Pets:** Small. $25 daily fee/pet. Service with restrictions, supervision. [SAVE] [X] [&M] [⊟] [▣] [≈]

Carriage Inn M
(760) 446-7910. **$109-$169.** 901 N China Lake Blvd 93555. On SR 178 and US 395 business route. Ext corridors. **Pets:** Small. $75 one-time fee/pet. Service with restrictions, supervision.
[SAVE] [X] [&M] [⊟] [▣] [¶¶] [≈] [⊠]

Comfort Inn M
(760) 375-9731. **$89-$145.** 507 S China Lake Blvd 93555. On US 395 business route. Ext corridors. **Pets:** Small. $25 daily fee/pet. Designated rooms, service with restrictions, supervision. [SAVE] [X] [⊟] [▣] [≈]

Econo Lodge Inn & Suites M
(760) 446-2551. **$82-$108.** 201 Inyokern Rd 93555. On SR 178 and US 395 business route, just w of China Lake Blvd. Ext corridors. **Pets:** Small, dogs only. $10 one-time fee/pet. Service with restrictions, supervision.
[SAVE] [X] [⊟] [▣] [≈]

Heritage Inn & Suites H
(760) 446-7951. **$80-$95.** 1050 N Norma 93555. On US 395 business route, just w. Int corridors. **Pets:** Other species. $100 deposit/room. Service with restrictions, crate. [SAVE] [X] [&M] [⊟] [▣] [¶¶] [≈]

Rodeway Inn M 🐾
(760) 384-3575. **Call for rates.** 131 W Upjohn Ave 93555. On US 395 business route, just w. Ext corridors. **Pets:** Medium. $10 daily fee/pet. Designated rooms, service with restrictions, supervision. [X] [⊟] [▣]

Vagabond Inn M
(760) 375-2220. **$65-$89.** 426 China Lake Blvd 93555. On US 395 business route. Ext corridors. **Pets:** Small. $10 daily fee/pet. Service with restrictions, supervision. [SAVE] [X] [&M] [⊟] [▣]

RIO DELL

Humboldt Gables Motel M
(707) 764-5609. **$55-$135.** 40 W Davis St 95562. US 101, exit Wildwood Ave, 0.5 mi w. Ext corridors. **Pets:** Small, dogs only. $20 daily fee/room. Supervision. [SAVE] [X] [⊟] [▣] [⊠]

RIPON

La Quinta Inn & Suites H 🐾
(209) 599-8999. **$74-$156.** 1524 Colony Rd 95366. SR 99, exit Jack Tone Rd, just e. Int corridors. **Pets:** Medium, other species. Service with restrictions, supervision. [SAVE] [X] [&M] [⊟] [▣] [≈]

RIVERSIDE

Comfort Inn University M
(951) 683-6000. **$69-$99.** 1590 University Ave 92507. I-215 and SR 60, exit 32 (University Ave), 0.5 mi w. Ext corridors. **Pets:** Small, dogs only. $25 one-time fee/room. Service with restrictions, crate.
[A$K] [X] [⊟] [▣] [≈]

Rodeway Inn Riverside M
(951) 359-0770. **$59-$109.** 10518 Magnolia Ave 92505. SR 91, exit 56 (Tyler St), 0.5 mi nw, then 0.3 mi sw. Ext corridors. **Pets:** Medium, other species. $20 daily fee/pet. Designated rooms, service with restrictions, supervision. [SAVE] [X] [⊟] [▣] [≈]

ROCKLIN

Heritage Inn Express, Rocklin H 🐾
(916) 632-3366. **$69-$99, 3 day notice.** 4480 Rocklin Rd 95677. I-80, exit Rocklin Rd, just w, then just s. Int corridors. **Pets:** Small. $25 one-time fee/room. Service with restrictions, supervision.
[SAVE] [X] [⊟] [▣] [≈]

Howard Johnson O'Cairns Inn & Suites H
(916) 624-4500. **$79-$99.** 4420 Rocklin Rd 95677. I-80, exit Rocklin Rd, just w, then just s. Int corridors. **Pets:** Accepted.
[SAVE] [X] [&M] [⊟] [▣] [≈]

Staybridge Suites H 🐾
(916) 781-7500. **$89-$169.** 6664 Lonetree Blvd 95765. SR 65, exit Blue Oaks Blvd, just e, just n to Redwood Dr, then just w; behind Blue Oaks Town Center Shopping Center. Int corridors. **Pets:** Medium. $65 one-time fee/pet. Designated rooms, service with restrictions, supervision.
[A$K] [X] [&M] [⊟] [▣] [≈]

ROSEVILLE

Best Western Roseville Inn H 🐾
(916) 782-4434. **$71-$78.** 220 Harding Blvd 95678. I-80, exit 103 westbound; exit 103B eastbound, just w, then just n. Ext corridors. **Pets:** $10 daily fee/pet. Designated rooms, service with restrictions, supervision.
[SAVE] [X] [&M] [⊟] [▣] [≈]

Extended StayAmerica-Sacramento-Roseville H
(916) 781-9001. **$80-$95.** 1000 Lead Hill Blvd 95678. I-80, exit 103 westbound; exit 103B eastbound, just w, then 0.6 mi n on Harding Blvd. Int corridors. **Pets:** Other species. $25 daily fee/room. Designated rooms, service with restrictions, crate. [A$K] [X] [⊟] [▣]

Heritage Inn Express H
(916) 782-4466. **Call for rates.** 204 Harding Blvd 95678. I-80, exit Douglas Blvd, just w, then just n. Ext corridors. **Pets:** Other species. $10 daily fee/room. Designated rooms, service with restrictions, crate.
[SAVE] [X] [⊟] [▣] [¶¶] [≈]

Homewood Suites by Hilton H 🐾
(916) 783-7455. **$159-$209.** 401 Creekside Ridge Ct 95678. I-80, exit SR 65, 1 mi w to Galleria Blvd, 0.5 mi s to Antelope Creek Rd, then just e to Creekside Ridge Ct. Int corridors. **Pets:** Medium. $75 one-time fee/room. Service with restrictions, crate. [X] [&M] [⊟] [▣] [≈] [⊠]

Larkspur Landing Roseville H
(916) 773-1717. **$89-$169.** 1931 Taylor Rd 95661. I-80, exit 105A (Atlantic St/Eureka Rd), just e on Eureka Rd, then 0.4 mi n. Int corridors. **Pets:** Accepted. [SAVE] [X] [&M] [⊟] [▣]

Orchid Suites Roseville H 🐾
(916) 784-2222. **$100-$180.** 130 N Sunrise Ave 95661. I-80, exit Douglas Blvd, just e, then 0.3 mi n. Ext/int corridors. **Pets:** Small. $20 daily fee/pet. Designated rooms, service with restrictions, supervision.
[SAVE] [X] [&M] [⊟] [▣] [≈]

Residence Inn by Marriott H
(916) 772-5500. **$152-$186.** 1930 Taylor Rd 95661. I-80, exit 105A (Atlantic St/Eureka Rd), just n. Int corridors. **Pets:** Accepted.
[X] [&M] [⊟] [▣] [≈] [⊠]

TownePlace Suites by Marriott Roseville H 🐾
(916) 782-2232. **$125-$153.** 10569 Fairway Dr 95678. SR 65, exit Blue Oaks Blvd, just e. Int corridors. **Pets:** Large, other species. $100 one-time fee/room. Service with restrictions, crate. [X] [&M] [⊟] [▣] [≈] [⊠]

SACRAMENTO

Best Western Expo Inn H
(916) 922-9833. **$80-$140.** 1413 Howe Ave 95825. US 50, exit Howe Ave, 2.5 mi n; I-80 business route, exit Howe Ave, then 2 mi s; just n of jct Hurley and Howe Ave. Int corridors. **Pets:** Other species. $25 one-time fee/room. [SAVE] [X] [&M] [⊟] [▣] [≈]

Best Western Sandman Motel H
(916) 443-6515. **$89-$130, 3 day notice.** 236 Jibboom St 95814. I-5, exit Richards Blvd, just w. Ext corridors. **Pets:** Accepted.
[SAVE] [X] [&M] [⊟] [▣] [¶¶] [≈]

The Citizen, a Joie de Vivre hotel H 🐾
(916) 447-2700. **$149-$299.** 926 J St 95814. I-5, exit J St (Old Sacramento), 0.6 mi e; jct 10th St; downtown. Int corridors. **Pets:** Medium. Service with restrictions, crate. [SAVE] [X] [&M] [▣] [¶¶]

AAA ♦♦ Clarion Hotel Mansion Inn 🅷 ❀

(916) 444-8000. **$99-$139.** 700 16th St 95814. At 16th and H sts; downtown. Int corridors. **Pets:** Medium. $50 one-time fee/room. Designated rooms, service with restrictions, supervision.

[ECO] [SAVE] [✕] [🅱] [🖥] [🍴] [≈]

AAA ♦♦♦ Doubletree Hotel 🅷

(916) 929-8855. **$119-$209.** 2001 Point West Way 95815. Business Rt I-80, exit via Arden Way, then just e. Int corridors. **Pets:** Medium. $50 one-time fee/room. Service with restrictions, supervision.

[SAVE] [✕] [🅱] [🖥] [🍴] [≈]

AAA ♦ Econo Lodge Ⓜ

(916) 443-6631. **$59-$129.** 711 16th St 95814. Business Rt I-80, exit 15th St eastbound; exit 16th St westbound; I-5, exit J St (Old Sacramento); jct H and 16th sts; downtown. Ext corridors. **Pets:** $6 daily fee/pet. Designated rooms, service with restrictions. [SAVE] [✕] [🅱]

♦♦ Extended StayAmerica-Sacramento-Arden Way 🅷

(916) 921-9942. **$65-$80.** 2100 Harvard St 95815. I-80 business route, exit Arden Way, just w. Ext corridors. **Pets:** Other species. $25 daily fee/room. Designated rooms, service with restrictions, crate.

[ASK] [✕] [🅱] [🖥]

AAA ♦♦♦ Hawthorn Suites 🅷

(916) 441-1200. **$99-$199.** 321 Bercut Dr 95814. I-5, exit Richards Blvd, just e. Int corridors. **Pets:** $50 one-time fee/room. Service with restrictions, supervision. [SAVE] [✕] [🅱] [🖥] [≈] [✕]

AAA ♦♦♦ Hilton Sacramento Arden West 🅷

(916) 922-4700. **$99-$259.** 2200 Harvard St 95815. Business Rt I-80, exit Arden Way, just w, then just n. Int corridors. **Pets:** Large. $75 one-time fee/room. Designated rooms, service with restrictions.

[SAVE] [✕] [🅱] [🖥] [🍴] [≈]

AAA ♦♦♦ Holiday Inn Express Sacramento Convention Center 🅷 ❀

(916) 444-4436. **$89-$199.** 728 16th St 95814. Jct H and 16th sts; downtown. Int corridors. **Pets:** Medium. $50 one-time fee/room. Designated rooms, service with restrictions, supervision.

[ECO] [SAVE] [✕] [🅱] [🖥]

♦♦ Homestead Studio Suites Hotel-Sacramento-S. Natomas 🅷

(916) 564-7500. **$80-$95.** 2810 Gateway Oaks Dr 95833. I-5, exit El Camino Ave, just w, then 0.4 mi n; I-80, exit W El Camino Ave, 1.5 mi e, then 0.4 mi n. Ext corridors. **Pets:** Other species. $25 daily fee/room. Designated rooms, service with restrictions, crate.

[ASK] [✕] [🅱] [🖥]

♦♦♦ La Quinta Inn Sacramento (Downtown) 🅷 ❀

(916) 448-8100. **$49-$129.** 200 Jibboom St 95814. I-5, exit Richards Blvd, just w. Ext corridors. **Pets:** Medium, other species. Service with restrictions, supervision. [ASK] [✕] [🅱] [🖥] [≈]

♦♦♦ La Quinta Inn Sacramento (North) 🅷 ❀

(916) 348-0900. **$49-$119.** 4604 Madison Ave 95841. I-80, exit Madison Ave, 0.3 mi e. Ext corridors. **Pets:** Medium, other species. Service with restrictions, supervision. [ASK] [✕] [🅱] [🖥] [≈]

AAA ♦♦♦ Larkspur Landing Sacramento 🅷

(916) 646-1212. **$99-$179, 7 day notice.** 555 Howe Ave 95825. US 50, exit Howe Ave, 1.5 mi n. Int corridors. **Pets:** Accepted.

[SAVE] [✕] [🅱] [🖥] [✕]

AAA ♦♦♦ Lions Gate Hotel 🅷 ❀

(916) 643-6222. **$79-$109.** 3410 Westover St 95652. I-80, exit Watt Ave, 1.3 mi n to Palm St, just w, then just s on Arnold Ave. Ext/int corridors. **Pets:** Medium. $25 daily fee/pet. Service with restrictions, supervision. [SAVE] [✕] [🅱] [🖥] [🍴]

AAA ♦♦♦ Quality Inn Natomas 🅷

(916) 927-7117. **$55-$75.** 3796 Northgate Blvd 95834. I-80, exit Northgate Blvd, just s. Ext corridors. **Pets:** Small, other species. $25 one-time fee/room. Designated rooms, supervision. [SAVE] [✕] [🅱] [🖥] [≈]

AAA ♦♦♦ Radisson Hotel 🅷

(916) 922-2020. **$89-$209.** 500 Leisure Ln 95815. Business Rt I-80, exit Cal Expo/Exposition Blvd), 0.4 mi w on Exposition Blvd; SR 160, exit Exposition Blvd; just sw. Ext corridors. **Pets:** Dogs only. $50 one-time fee/room. Service with restrictions, supervision.

[SAVE] [✕] [🅱] [🖥] [🍴] [≈] [✕]

AAA ♦♦♦ Ramada Limited-Discovery Park 🅷

(916) 442-6971. **$69-$150.** 350 Bercut Dr 95814. I-5, exit Richards Blvd, just e, then just n. Ext corridors. **Pets:** Accepted.

[SAVE] [✕] [🅱] [🖥]

AAA ♦♦♦ Red Lion Hotel at Arden Village 🅷

(916) 922-8041. **$119-$149.** 1401 Arden Way 95815. I-80 business route, exit Arden Way. Ext/int corridors. **Pets:** Other species. $20 one-time fee/room. Service with restrictions, supervision.

[SAVE] [✕] [🅱] [🖥] [🍴] [≈]

♦♦♦ Residence Inn by Marriott- Cal Expo 🅷

(916) 920-9111. **$112-$136.** 1530 Howe Ave 95825. US 50, exit Howe Ave, 2.5 mi n; Business Rt I-80 (Capitol City Frwy), 1 mi e on Arden Way, then just s. Ext corridors. **Pets:** Accepted.

[ECO] [✕] [🅱] [🖥] [≈] [✕]

♦♦♦ Residence Inn by Marriott-Sacramento Airport Natomas 🅷

(916) 649-1300. **$143-$175.** 2410 W El Camino Ave 95833. I-5, exit El Camino Ave, just w; I-80, exit W El Camino Ave, 1.5 mi e; jct Gateway Oak Dr. Ext corridors. **Pets:** Accepted.

[SAVE] [✕] [🅱] [🖥] [≈] [✕]

♦♦♦ Residence Inn by Marriott- Sacramento at Capitol Park 🅷

(916) 443-0500. **$179-$219.** 1121 15th St 95814. Jct 15th and L sts; just e of state capitol; downtown. Int corridors. **Pets:** Accepted.

[✕] [🅱] [🖥] [≈]

AAA ♦♦♦♦ Sheraton Grand Sacramento Hotel 🅷 ❀

(916) 447-1700. **$139-$375.** 1230 J St 95814. I-5, exit J St (Old Sacramento), 1 mi e; at jct 12th St; downtown. Int corridors. **Pets:** Medium, other species. $100 deposit/room. Service with restrictions, crate.

[ECO] [SAVE] [✕] [🅱] [🍴] [≈]

♦♦♦ Staybridge Suites Sacramento 🅷 ❀

(916) 575-7907. **Call for rates.** 140 Promenade Cir 95834. I-80, exit Truxel Rd, just nw, n on Gateway Park Blvd, e on N Freeway Blvd, then just s. Int corridors. **Pets:** Other species. $25 one-time fee/room. Service with restrictions, crate. [✕] [🅱] [🖥] [≈]

AAA ♦♦♦ TownePlace Suites by Marriott Sacramento Cal Expo 🅷

(916) 920-5400. **$107-$131.** 1784 Tribute Rd 95815. Business Rt I-80, exit Cal Expo westbound, just w; exit Exposition Blvd eastbound, just w. Int corridors. **Pets:** Medium, other species. $100 one-time fee/room. Service with restrictions. [SAVE] [✕] [🅱] [🖥] [≈]

♦♦♦ Vagabond Executive Inn Old Town 🅷

(916) 446-1481. **$99-$169.** 909 3rd St 95814. I-5, exit J St (Old Sacramento); 8 blks w of state capitol; jct J and 3rd sts; downtown. Ext corridors. **Pets:** Medium. $10 daily fee/pet. Service with restrictions, supervision. [ASK] [✕] [🅱] [🖥] [≈]

SALIDA

AAA ♦♦♦ La Quinta Inn & Suites 🅷 ❀

(209) 579-8723. **$74-$174.** 4909 Sisk Rd 95368. SR 99, exit SR 219, just e. Int corridors. **Pets:** Medium, other species. Service with restrictions, supervision. [SAVE] [✕] [🅱] [🖥] [≈]

SALINAS

AAA ♦♦♦ Econo Lodge Ⓜ

(831) 422-5111. **$49-$199.** 180 S Sanborn Rd 93905. US 101, exit Sanborn Rd or Fairview Ave, just e. Ext corridors. **Pets:** Accepted.

[SAVE] [✕] [🅱]

▼▼◆◆ **Residence Inn by Marriott-Salinas** �H
(831) 775-0410. **$190-$200.** 17215 El Rancho Way 93907. US 101, exit Laurel Dr, just w. Int corridors. **Pets:** Accepted. 🗙 🔧M 🈁 🈯 🐾 🗙

▼▼ ▼▼ **Super 8 Motel** 🄼
(831) 758-4693. **$59-$229.** 131 Kern St 93905. US 101, exit Market St, just e. Ext corridors. **Pets:** Accepted. 🄰$🄺 🗙 🔧M 🈁 🈯 🐾

SAN ANDREAS

▼▼▼▼ **The Robins Nest** 🅱🅱 🐾
(209) 754-1076. **$100-$175, 7 day notice.** 247 W St. Charles St 95249. SR 49; north end of town. Int corridors. **Pets:** Designated rooms, service with restrictions, crate. 🄰$🄺 🗙 🔧 🈁 🈯

SAN BERNARDINO

◆◆◆ ▼▼ ▼▼ **Best Western Hospitality Lane** 🄼
(909) 381-1681. **$89-$110.** 294 E Hospitality Ln 92408. I-10, exit 73 (Waterman Ave) westbound; exit 73B (Waterman Ave) eastbound, just nw. Ext corridors. **Pets:** Medium, dogs only. $10 daily fee/pet. Service with restrictions, supervision. 🅂🄰🅅🄴 🗙 🈁 🈯 🐾

▼▼▼▼▼▼ **Hilton-San Bernardino** 🄷
(909) 889-0133. **$89-$169.** 285 E Hospitality Ln 92408. I-10, exit 73 (Waterman Ave) westbound; exit 73B (Waterman Ave) eastbound, just n, then just w. Int corridors. **Pets:** Accepted. 🗙 🔧M 🈁 🈯 🍴 🐾

▼▼◆◆ **La Quinta Inn San Bernardino** 🄼 🐾
(909) 888-7571. **$49-$119.** 205 E Hospitality Ln 92408. I-10, exit 73 (Waterman Ave) westbound; 73B (Waterman Ave N) eastbound, just n, then 0.3 mi w. Ext corridors. **Pets:** Medium, other species. Service with restrictions, supervision. 🄰$🄺 🗙 🈁 🈯 🐾

◆◆◆ ▼▼◆◆ **Quality Inn** 🄼
(909) 888-4827. **$79-$119.** 1750 S Waterman Ave 92408. I-10, exit 73 (Waterman Ave), 0.5 mi n. Ext corridors. **Pets:** Accepted. 🅂🄰🅅🄴 🗙 🈁 🈯 🐾

▼▼▼▼ **Residence Inn San Bernardino** 🄷 🐾
(909) 382-4564. **$171-$209.** 1040 E Harriman Pl 92408. I-10, exit 74 (Tippecanoe Ave) eastbound; exit 74 (Anderson St/Tippecanoe Ave) westbound, just n, then just w. Int corridors. **Pets:** Large, other species. $100 one-time fee/room. Service with restrictions, crate. 🗙 🈁 🈯 🐾 🗙

SAN CLEMENTE

◆◆◆ ▼▼◆◆ **Best Western Casablanca Inn** 🄷
(949) 361-1644. **$89-$199.** 1601 N El Camino Real 92672. I-5, exit 76 (Avenida Pico), 0.8 mi sw, then just s. Ext corridors. **Pets:** $25 daily fee/room. Designated rooms, service with restrictions, supervision. 🅂🄰🅅🄴 🗙 🈁 🈯 🐾

▼▼▼▼ **Holiday Inn-San Clemente Resort** 🄷
(949) 361-3000. **$119-$250.** 111 S Avenida de la Estrella 92672. I-5, exit 75 (Avenida Palizada) southbound; exit 75 (Avenida Presidio) northbound, just s, then just w. Int corridors. **Pets:** Accepted. 🄰$🄺 🗙 🔧M 🈁 🈯 🍴 🐾

SAN DIEGO METROPOLITAN AREA

CHULA VISTA

▼▼▼▼ **La Quinta Inn San Diego (Chula Vista)** 🄼 🐾
(619) 691-1211. **$59-$169.** 150 Bonita Rd 91910. I-805, exit 7C (E St/Bonita Rd), just w. Ext corridors. **Pets:** Medium, other species. Service with restrictions, supervision. 🄰$🄺 🗙 🈁 🈯 🐾

CORONADO

▼▼▼▼ **Crown City Inn** 🄼 🐾
(619) 435-3116. **$100-$300.** 520 Orange Ave 92118. I-5, exit 14A (Coronado Bridge), 1.5 mi w, then just s. Ext corridors. **Pets:** Other species. $8 daily fee/pet. Designated rooms, service with restrictions, supervision. 🗙 🔧M 🈁 🈯 🍴 🐾

◆◆◆ ▼▼ ▼▼ **Loews Coronado Bay** 🄷 🐾
(619) 424-4000. **$179-$399, 3 day notice.** 4000 Coronado Bay Rd 92118. I-5, exit 14A (Coronado Bridge), 1.7 mi w to Orange Ave, 1 mi sw to Silver Strand Blvd, then 4.5 mi s to Coronado Cays. Ext/int corridors. **Pets:** Large, other species. $25 one-time fee/room. 🅂🄰🅅🄴 🗙 🈁 🈯 🍴 🐾 🗙

DEL MAR

◆◆◆ ▼▼▼▼ **Best Western Stratford Inn** 🄼
(858) 755-1501. **$99-$299, 3 day notice.** 710 Camino Del Mar 92014. I-5, exit 34 (Del Mar Heights Rd), 1 mi w, then 0.3 mi n. Int corridors. **Pets:** Other species. $50 one-time fee/room. Designated rooms, service with restrictions, supervision. 🅂🄰🅅🄴 🗙 🔧M 🈁 🈯 🐾

◆◆◆ ▼▼▼▼ **Doubletree Hotel Del Mar** 🄷 🐾
(858) 481-5900. **$125-$225.** 11915 El Camino Real 92130. I-5, exit 33 (Carmel Valley Rd), 0.3 mi e. Int corridors. **Pets:** Dogs only. $50 one-time fee/room. Designated rooms, service with restrictions, supervision. 🄴🄲🄾 🅂🄰🅅🄴 🗙 🈁 🈯 🍴 🐾

▼▼▼▼ **Hilton San Diego Del Mar** 🄷 🐾
(858) 792-5200. **$119-$209.** 15575 Jimmy Durante Blvd 92014. I-5, exit 36 (Via de la Valle), just w. Int corridors. **Pets:** Medium. $50 one-time fee/room. Service with restrictions. 🗙 🈁 🈯 🍴 🐾

EL CAJON

◆◆◆ ▼▼▼▼ **Best Western Courtesy Inn** 🄼 🐾
(619) 440-7378. **$88-$140, 7 day notice.** 1355 E Main St 92021. I-8, exit 19 (2nd St), 0.5 mi s, then just e. Ext corridors. **Pets:** Small. $20 daily fee/pet. Designated rooms, service with restrictions, supervision. 🅂🄰🅅🄴 🗙 🈁 🈯 🐾

▼▼▼▼ **Quality Inn & Suites San Diego East County** 🄷 🐾
(619) 588-8808. **$69-$129.** 1250 El Cajon Blvd 92020. I-8, exit 14C (Severin Dr) westbound, 1 mi e on Murray Rd; exit 15 (El Cajon Blvd) eastbound, 0.5 mi w. Ext corridors. **Pets:** Medium. $10 daily fee/pet. Service with restrictions, supervision. 🄰$🄺 🗙 🈁 🈯 🐾

LA JOLLA

▼▼▼▼ **Hilton La Jolla/Torrey Pines** 🄷 🐾
(858) 558-1500. **$249-$429.** 10950 N Torrey Pines Rd 92037. I-5, exit 29 (Genesee Ave), 0.8 mi w, then just n. Int corridors. **Pets:** $75 one-time fee/room. Service with restrictions. 🄴🄲🄾 🗙 🔧M 🈁 🈯 🐾 🗙

▼▼▼▼ **Hotel La Jolla At The Shores** 🄷 🐾
(858) 459-0261. **$159-$399.** 7955 La Jolla Shores Dr 92037. I-5, exit 28 (La Jolla Village Dr) southbound, 1 mi w to Torrey Pines Rd, 1.7 mi sw, then just n; exit 26A (La Jolla Pkwy) northbound, 1.5 mi n to Torrey Pines Rd, just w, then just n. Ext corridors. **Pets:** Medium, dogs only. $75 one-time fee/room. Designated rooms, service with restrictions. 🄰$🄺 🗙 🈁 🈯 🍴 🐾 🗙

◆◆◆ ▼▼ ▼▼ **La Jolla Cove Suites** 🄷
(858) 459-2621. **$149-$615, 3 day notice.** 1155 Coast Blvd 92037. I-5, exit 28 (La Jolla Village Dr), 1 mi w to Torrey Pines Rd, 2.5 mi to Prospect St, 0.5 mi s to Girard Ave, then just w. Ext corridors. **Pets:** Small. $25 daily fee/pet. Designated rooms, service with restrictions, supervision. 🅂🄰🅅🄴 🗙 🈁 🈯 🐾 🗙

▼▼▼▼ **Residence Inn by Marriott La Jolla** 🄷
(858) 587-1770. **$169-$189.** 8901 Gilman Dr 92037. I-5, exit 27 (Gilman Dr), 1.5 mi nw. Ext corridors. **Pets:** Other species. $100 one-time fee/room. Service with restrictions. 🗙 🔧M 🈁 🈯 🐾 🗙

▼▼▼ San Diego Marriott La Jolla **H** ❖
(858) 587-1414. **$161-$197.** 4240 La Jolla Village Dr 92037. I-5, exit 28
(La Jolla Village Dr), 0.5 mi e. Int corridors. **Pets:** Small. $100 one-time
fee/room. Service with restrictions, supervision.
⊠ 🄼 🚪 ▦ ▥ ⅋

▲▲▲ ▼▼▼ Sheraton La Jolla Hotel **H**
(858) 453-5500. **$109-$295.** 3299 Holiday Ct 92037. I-5, exit 28 (La Jolla
Village Dr), just w to Villa La Jolla Dr, then just s at top of hill. Int corridors. **Pets:** Medium, dogs only. $40 one-time fee/room. Service with
restrictions, supervision. ⌂ⅆ ⊠ 🄼 🚪 ▦ ▥ ⅋ ⅋

NATIONAL CITY

▲▲▲ ▼▼▼ Best Western Marina Gateway **H**
(619) 259-2800. **Call for rates.** 800 Bay Marina Dr 91950. I-5, exit 10
(Bay Marina Dr), just w. Int corridors. **Pets:** Small. $150 deposit/room,
$25 daily fee/pet. Designated rooms, service with restrictions, supervision.
⌂ⅆ ⊠ 🚪 ▥ ⅋

▲▲▲ Comfort Inn San Diego South Bay **M**
(619) 424-2400. **$79-$169.** 1645 E Plaza Blvd 91950. I-805, exit 10
(Plaza Blvd), just w. Int corridors. **Pets:** Accepted.
⌂⟨⟩ ⊠ 🄼 🚪 ▥ ⅋

POWAY

▲▲▲ ▼▼▼ Best Western Country Inn **M** ❖
(858) 748-6320. **$70-$200.** 13845 Poway Rd 92064. I-15, exit 18 (Poway
Rd), 4 mi e. Ext corridors. **Pets:** $30 one-time fee/room. Service with
restrictions, supervision. ⌂ⅆ ⊠ 🚪 ▥ ⅋

▼▼▼ Ramada Hotel **H**
(858) 748-7311. **$79-$209.** 12448 Poway Rd 92064. I-15, exit 18 (Poway
Rd), 3 mi e. Ext corridors. **Pets:** Accepted. ⌂⟨⟩ ⊠ 🚪 ▥ ⅋

RANCHO BERNARDO

▼▼▼▼ La Quinta Inn Scrupps Poway **H** ❖
(858) 484-8800. **$59-$169.** 10185 Paseo Montril 92129. I-15, exit 18
(Rancho Penasquitos Blvd), just w. Ext corridors. **Pets:** Medium, other
species. Service with restrictions, supervision. ⌂⟨⟩ ⊠ 🚪 ▥ ⅋

▲▲▲ ▼▼▼ Radisson Suite Hotel **H**
(858) 451-6600. **$130-$190.** 11520 W Bernardo Ct 92127. I-15, exit 24
(Rancho Bernardo Rd), just w, then 0.5 mi s. Ext corridors. **Pets:** Small,
dogs only. $25 one-time fee/room. Designated rooms, service with restric-
tions, crate. ⌂ⅆ ⊠ 🚪 ▥ ⅋

SAN DIEGO

▲▲▲ ▼▼▼ Best Western Lamplighter Inn & Suites **M**
(619) 582-3088. **$95-$130.** 6474 El Cajon Blvd 92115. I-8, exit 11 (70th
St), 0.5 mi s, then 1 mi w. Ext corridors. **Pets:** Medium, dogs only. $15
daily fee/pet. Service with restrictions, supervision.
⌂ⅆ ⊠ 🚪 ▥

▲▲▲ ▼▼▼ Best Western Mission Bay Inn **M** ❖
(619) 275-5700. **$89-$169.** 4540 Mission Bay Dr 92109. I-5, exit 22
(Clairemont Dr/Mission Bay Dr), just e. Ext corridors. **Pets:** Small, dogs
only. $15 daily fee/pet. Designated rooms, service with restrictions, super-
vision. ⌂ⅆ ⊠ 🚪 ▥ ⅋

▼▼▼ Comfort Inn Mission Bay SeaWorld Area **M**
(858) 274-7888. **$79-$169.** 2575 Clairemont Dr 92109. I-5, exit 23A
(Grand/Garnet aves) northbound, 0.5 mi n; exit 23 (Balboa Ave) southbound, 0.3 mi s. Int corridors. **Pets:** Medium. $25 daily fee/pet. Desig-
nated rooms, service with restrictions, supervision.
⌂⟨⟩ ⊠ 🚪 ▥ ⅋

▼▼▼ Doubletree Hotel San Diego-Mission Valley **H**
(619) 297-5466. **$119-$274.** 7450 Hazard Center Dr 92108. SR 163, exit
4 (Friars Rd), 0.3 mi e to Frazee Rd, then just s. Int corridors.
Pets: Accepted. 🄴🄲🄾 ⊠ 🄼 🚪 ▦ ▥ ⅋ ⅋

▼▼▼ Extended StayAmerica-San Diego/Hotel Circle **H**
(619) 296-5570. **$85-$120.** 2087 Hotel Cir S 92108. I-8, exit 4A (Hotel
Cir), south side. Int corridors. **Pets:** Other species. $25 daily fee/room.
Designated rooms, service with restrictions, crate.
⌂⟨⟩ ⊠ 🄼 🚪 ▥

▼▼ Extended StayAmerica–San Diego/Mission Valley
Stadium **H**
(858) 292-8927. **$90-$125.** 3860 Murphy Canyon Dr 92123. I-15, exit 8
(Aero Dr), just w, then 1 mi n. Int corridors. **Pets:** Other species. $25
daily fee/room. Designated rooms, service with restrictions, crate.
⌂⟨⟩ ⊠ 🄼 🚪 ▥

▲▲▲ ▼▼▼▼ Four Points by Sheraton San Diego **H**
(858) 277-8888. **$89-$179, 3 day notice.** 8110 Aero Dr 92123. SR 163,
exit 7B (Balboa Ave E) southbound, 1 mi se via Kearny Villa Rd; exit 10
(Kearny Villa Rd) northbound, 0.8 mi ne. Int corridors. **Pets:** Medium.
$100 deposit/room, $25 one-time fee/room. Designated rooms, service
with restrictions, supervision. ⌂ⅆ ⊠ 🄼 🚪 ▥ ▦ ⅋ ⅋

▲▲▲ ▼▼▼▼ The Grand Del Mar **H** ❖
(858) 314-2000. **$355-$535, 7 day notice.** 5300 Grand Del Mar Ct
92130. I-5, exit 33 (Carmel Valley Rd), 1.9 mi e, 0.8 mi s, then just e. Int
corridors. **Pets:** Small, dogs only. $100 one-time fee/room. Designated
rooms, service with restrictions, supervision.
⌂ⅆ ⊠ 🚪 ▥ ▦ ⅋ ⅋

▼▼▼ Hawthorn Suites **M**
(619) 299-3501. **$109-$249.** 1335 Hotel Cir S 92108. I-8, exit 4A (Hotel
Cir), south side. Ext/int corridors. **Pets:** Other species. $75 one-time fee/
room. Service with restrictions, crate. ⌂⟨⟩ ⊠ 🚪 ▥ ⅋

▲▲▲ ▼▼▼ Heritage Inn San Diego–SeaWorld **M**
(619) 223-9500. **$55-$175.** 3333 Channel Way 92110. I-5/8, exit 20
(Rosecrans St), 0.5 mi s, 1 mi nw on Sports Arena Blvd, then just e. Ext
corridors. **Pets:** Accepted. ⌂ⅆ ⊠ 🄼 🚪 ▥ ⅋

▼▼▼ Hilton San Diego Gaslamp Quarter **H**
(619) 231-4040. **$229-$399.** 401 K St 92101. I-5, exit 7B (J St) northbound, 0.8 mi w to 4th Ave, then just s; exit 17 (Front St) southbound,
0.5 mi e to 4th Ave, then 1 mi s; in Historic Gaslamp Quarter. Int corridors. **Pets:** Accepted. ⊠ 🄼 ▥ ▦ ⅋

▼▼▼ Hilton San Diego Mission Valley **H**
(619) 543-9000. **$113-$193.** 901 Camino del Rio S 92108. I-8, exit 5
(Mission Center Rd), just s. Int corridors. **Pets:** Accepted.
🄴🄲🄾 ⊠ 🚪 ▥ ▦ ⅋

▲▲▲ ▼▼▼ Holiday Inn on the Bay **H**
(619) 232-3861. **$129-$239.** 1355 N Harbor Dr at Ash St 92101. I-5, exit
17 (Hawthorn St) northbound, 0.4 mi w, then 0.4 mi s; exit 17 (Front St)
southbound, 0.5 mi s to Ash St, then just w. Int corridors. **Pets:** Accepted.
⌂ⅆ ⊠ 🚪 ▥ ▦ ⅋

▼▼ Homestead Studio Suites Hotel-San Diego/Sorrento
Mesa **M**
(858) 623-0100. **$90-$135.** 9880 Pacific Heights Blvd 92121. I-805, exit
27 (Mira Mesa Blvd), 1 mi e. Ext corridors. **Pets:** Other species. $25 daily
fee/room. Designated rooms, service with restrictions, crate.
⌂⟨⟩ ⊠ 🚪

▲▲▲ ▼▼▼ Kona Kai Resort Spa & Marina **H**
(619) 221-8000. **$139-$229.** 1551 Shelter Island Dr 92106. I-5, exit 20
(Rosecrans St) southbound, 3 mi sw; exit 17 (Hawthorn St) northbound, 3
mi nw on Harbor Dr to Scott Rd, then 0.5 mi w. Ext/int corridors.
Pets: Small. $75 one-time fee/room. Service with restrictions, supervision.
⌂ⅆ ⊠ 🚪 ▥ ▦ ⅋ ⅋

▼▼▼ La Quinta Inn Mission Valley **M** ❖
(619) 295-6886. **$79-$229.** 641 Camino Del Rio S 92108. I-8, exit 5
(Mission Center Rd), just s, then just w. Ext corridors. **Pets:** Medium,
other species. Service with restrictions, supervision.
⌂⟨⟩ ⊠ 🄼 🚪 ▥ ⅋

▽▽▽▽ La Quinta Inn Old Town/Airport M ❖
(619) 291-9100. **$89-$249.** 2380 Moore St 92110. I-5, exit 19 (Old Town Ave), just n via Frontage Rd on west side of freeway. Ext/int corridors. **Pets:** Medium, other species. Service with restrictions, supervision.
[ASK] [✕] [&M] [🛏] [💻] [🏊]

▲▲▲ ▽▽▽▽ ▽▽▽▽ Manchester Grand Hyatt San Diego H ❖
(619) 232-1234. **$159-$499, 7 day notice.** One Market Pl 92101. I-5, exit 17 (Front St), 1.3 mi s, then just w. Int corridors. **Pets:** Medium, dogs only. $30 daily fee/pet. Designated rooms, service with restrictions, supervision. [SAVE] [✕] [&M] [🛏] [💻] [🍽] [🏊] [✕]

▲▲▲ ▽▽ ▽▽ Marina Inn & Suites M
(619) 232-7551. **$99-$399.** 1943 Pacific Hwy 92101. I-5, exit 17 (Front St) southbound, just s to Cedar St, 0.3 mi n, then just n; exit 17 (Hawthorn St) northbound, 0.4 mi w, then just s. Ext corridors. **Pets:** Other species. $50 deposit/room. Service with restrictions, crate.
[SAVE] [✕] [🛏] [💻]

▽▽ Mission Valley Resort H
(619) 298-8281. **$79-$179.** 875 Hotel Cir S 92108. I-8, exit 4A (Hotel Cir), south side. Ext corridors. **Pets:** Other species. $75 one-time fee/room. Service with restrictions, supervision.
[ASK] [✕] [🛏] [💻] [🍽] [🏊] [✕]

▲▲▲ ▽▽ Mission Valley Travelodge M
(619) 297-2271. **$99-$139.** 1201 Hotel Cir S 92108. I-8, exit 4A (Hotel Cir), south side. Ext corridors. **Pets:** Accepted. [SAVE] [✕] [🛏] [💻]

▲▲▲ ▽▽ Ocean Villa Inn M ❖
(619) 224-3481. **$99-$399.** 5142 W Point Loma Blvd 92107. I-8, exit Sunset Cliff Blvd, 1.5 mi sw. Ext corridors. **Pets:** Dogs only. $25 one-time fee/pet. Designated rooms, service with restrictions, supervision.
[SAVE] [✕] [🛏] [💻] [🏊]

▲▲▲ ▽▽ Old Town Inn M
(619) 260-8024. **$74-$199.** 4444 Pacific Hwy 92110. I-5, exit 21 (Sea-World Dr), just w, then 1 mi s. Ext corridors. **Pets:** Medium. $15 daily fee/pet. Service with restrictions, supervision. [SAVE] [✕] [🛏] [💻] [🏊]

▽▽▽ Omni San Diego Hotel H ❖
(619) 231-6664. **$199-$389.** 675 L St 92101. I-5, exit 17 (Front St/Civic Center), 0.3 mi s, 0.3 mi e on a St, 0.6 mi s on 6th Ave, then just e; connected via skybridge to Petco Park. Int corridors. **Pets:** Medium, dogs only. $50 one-time fee/room. Service with restrictions, crate.
[ASK] [✕] [&M] [💻] [🍽] [🏊] [✕]

▲▲▲ ▽▽ Pacific Inn Hotel & Suites M
(619) 232-6391. **$59-$289.** 1655 Pacific Hwy 92101. I-5, exit 17 (Front St) southbound, just s to Cedar St, 0.5 mi w, then just n; exit 17 (Hawthorn St) northbound, 0.6 mi w, then just s. Ext corridors. **Pets:** Accepted.
[SAVE] [✕] [🛏] [💻] [🏊]

▲▲▲ ▽▽ Pacific Shores Inn M
(858) 483-6300. **$109-$269, 3 day notice.** 4802 Mission Blvd 92109. I-5, exit 23 (Garnet Ave), 2.5 mi w, then 0.3 mi n. Ext corridors. **Pets:** Medium, dogs only. $35 one-time fee/room. Service with restrictions, crate. [SAVE] [✕] [🛏] [💻] [🏊]

▲▲▲ ▽▽▽ Point Loma Inn & Suites M
(619) 222-4704. **$39-$129.** 2933 Fenelon St 92106. I-8, exit Nimitz Blvd, 2 mi s, then 0.4 mi sw; in Point Loma area. Ext corridors. **Pets:** Other species. $20 daily fee/pet. Service with restrictions, crate.
[SAVE] [✕] [🛏] [💻]

▲▲▲ ▽▽▽▽ Porto Vista Hotel & Suites H
(619) 544-0164. **$95-$199.** 1835 Columbia St 92101. I-5, exit 17 (Front St) southbound, just w on Cedar St, then just n on State St; exit 17 (Hawthorn St) northbound, just e, then just s. Ext/int corridors. **Pets:** Accepted. [SAVE] [✕] [🛏] [💻] [🍽]

▲▲▲ ▽▽▽▽ Premier Inns Mission Valley/Hotel Circle M
(619) 291-8252. **$50-$109.** 2484 Hotel Circle Pl 92108. I-8, exit 3 (Taylor St), just n. Ext corridors. **Pets:** Accepted. [SAVE] [✕] [🛏] [💻] [🏊]

▽▽▽▽ Residence Inn by Marriott-San Diego Central H
(858) 278-2100. **$199-$249.** 5400 Kearny Mesa Rd 92111. SR 163, exit 8 (Clairemont Mesa Blvd). Ext corridors. **Pets:** Medium, other species. $75 one-time fee/room. Service with restrictions.
[✕] [🛏] [💻] [🏊]

▽▽▽▽ Residence Inn by Marriott San Diego Downtown H
(619) 338-8200. **$199-$229.** 1747 Pacific Hwy 92101. I-5, exit 17 (Front St) southbound, just s to Grape St, 0.3 mi w, then just n; exit 17 (Hawthorn St) northbound, 0.4 mi w, then just s. Int corridors. **Pets:** Medium, other species. $75 one-time fee/pet. Service with restrictions.
[✕] [&M] [🛏] [💻] [🏊]

▽▽▽▽ Residence Inn San Diego/Mission Valley/SeaWorld Area H
(619) 881-3600. **$215-$263.** 1865 Hotel Cir S 92108. I-8, exit 4A (Hotel Cir), south side. Int corridors. **Pets:** Accepted.
[✕] [&M] [🛏] [💻] [🏊] [✕]

▽▽▽▽ Residence Inn San Diego Ranch Bernardo/Scripps Poway H ❖
(858) 635-5724. **$219-$229.** 12011 Scripps Highland Dr 92131. I-805, exit 17 (Mercy Rd/Scripps Poway Pkwy), just e, then just n. Int corridors. **Pets:** Large, other species. $75 one-time fee/room. Service with restrictions, supervision. [✕] [&M] [🛏] [💻] [🏊] [✕]

▽▽▽▽ Residence Inn San Diego-Sorrento Mesa H
(858) 552-9100. **$179-$199.** 5995 Pacific Mesa Ct 92121. I-805, exit 27 (Mira Mesa Blvd), 1.5 mi e. Int corridors. **Pets:** Other species. $100 one-time fee/room. [ECO] [✕] [🛏] [💻] [🏊] [✕]

▲▲▲ ▽▽▽▽ ▽▽▽▽ San Diego Marriott Hotel & Marina H
(619) 234-1500. **$302-$369.** 333 W Harbor Dr 92101. I-5, exit 17 (Front St), 1.3 mi s, then just w. Int corridors. **Pets:** Accepted.
[SAVE] [✕] [🛏] [💻] [🍽] [🏊] [✕]

▽▽▽▽ San Diego Marriott Mission Valley H
(619) 692-3800. **$134-$164.** 8757 Rio San Diego Dr 92108. I-8, exit 6A (Qualcomm Way), just n. Int corridors. **Pets:** Large, dogs only. $75 one-time fee/room. Designated rooms, service with restrictions, supervision.
[✕] [&M] [🛏] [💻] [🍽] [🏊] [✕]

▲▲▲ ▽▽▽▽ ▽▽▽▽ Sheraton San Diego Hotel and Marina H ❖
(619) 291-2900. **$139-$369.** 1380 Harbor Island Dr 92101. I-5, exit 17 (Hawthorn St) northbound, just e to Harbor Dr, 1.5 mi w, then just s; exit 18A (Kettern/Hancock) southbound, just s to Laurel St, just w to Harbor Dr, 1.5 mi w, then just s. Ext/int corridors. **Pets:** Medium. Designated rooms, service with restrictions, supervision.
[SAVE] [✕] [💻] [🍽] [🏊] [✕]

▽▽▽▽ Sheraton San Diego, Mission Valley H
(619) 260-0111. **$129-$249, 3 day notice.** 1433 Camino del Rio S 92108. I-8, exit 5 (Mission Center Rd), south side. Int corridors.
Pets: Accepted. [ASK] [✕] [&M] [💻] [🍽] [🏊]

▲▲▲ ▽▽▽▽ Sheraton Suites San Diego at Symphony Hall H
(619) 696-9800. **$145-$399.** 701 a St/7th Ave 92101. I-5, exit 17 (Front St), 0.5 mi s. Int corridors. **Pets:** Accepted.
[SAVE] [✕] [&M] [💻] [🍽] [🏊] [✕]

▲▲▲ ▽▽▽▽ The Sofia Hotel H ❖
(619) 234-9200. **$109-$209.** 150 W Broadway 92101. I-5, exit 17 (Front St), 1 mi s. Int corridors. **Pets:** $50 one-time fee/room. Designated rooms, service with restrictions, supervision. [SAVE] [✕] [&M] [🛏] [💻] [🍽]

▽▽▽▽ Sommerset Suites Hotel H
(619) 692-5200. **$129-$309.** 606 Washington St 92103. SR 163, exit 2B (Washington St), just w. Ext/int corridors. **Pets:** Small, other species. $50 one-time fee/pet. [ASK] [✕] [🛏] [💻] [🏊]

▼▼▼ Staybridge Suites by Holiday Inn-Sorrento Mesa **H**
(858) 453-5343. **$129-$169.** 6639 Mira Mesa Blvd 92121. I-805, exit 27 (Mira Mesa Blvd), 2.3 mi e. Int corridors. **Pets:** Accepted.
ASK ✕ ﾐM 🛏 🖥 ➤

▼▼▼ Staybridge Suites Carmel Mountain **H**
(858) 487-0900. **$99-$199.** 11855 Ave of Industry 92128. I-15, exit 21 (Carmel Mountain Rd), 1 mi ne to second Rancho Carmel Dr, just w to Innovation Dr, just n, then just e. Int corridors. **Pets:** Accepted.
ASK ✕ ﾐM 🛏 🖥 ➤

🅐🅐 ▼▼▼▼ The US Grant **H**
(619) 232-3121. **$199-$569.** 326 Broadway 92101. I-5, exit 17 (Front St) southbound, 0.9 mi s to Broadway, just e; exit 16B (6th Ave) northbound, 0.6 mi s, just w. Int corridors. **Pets:** Accepted.
SAVE ✕ ﾐM 🖥 🍴 ✕

▼▼ ▼▼ Vagabond Inn-Point Loma **M**
(619) 224-3371. **$69-$329.** 1325 Scott St 92106. I-8, exit Nimitz Blvd, 2 mi s to Rosecrans St, just w to Jarvis St, then just s; in Point Loma area. Ext corridors. **Pets:** Accepted. ASK ✕ 🛏 🖥 ➤

🅐🅐 ▼▼ ▼▼ Vagabond Inn SeaWorld **M**
(619) 297-1691. **$49-$289.** 625 Hotel Cir S 92108. I-8, exit 4A (Hotel Cir), south side. Ext corridors. **Pets:** Large, other species. $20 daily fee/pet. Designated rooms, service with restrictions, supervision.
SAVE ✕ 🛏 🖥 ➤

🅐🅐 ▼▼▼ The Westin Gaslamp Quarter **H**
(619) 239-2200. **$189-$449.** 910 Broadway Cir 92101. I-5, exit 17 (Front St) southbound, 0.9 mi s to Broadway, just e, then just s; exit 16B (6th Ave) northbound, 0.6 mi s, just w, then just s. Int corridors.
Pets: Accepted. SAVE ✕ ﾐM 🛏 🖥 🍴 ➤ ✕

🅐🅐 ▼▼▼ ▼▼ The Westin San Diego **H** 🐾
(619) 239-4500. **$169-$289.** 400 W Broadway 92101. Between Columbia and State sts. Int corridors. **Pets:** Medium, dogs only. Service with restrictions, supervision. SAVE ✕ ﾐM 🖥 🍴 ➤ ✕

🅐🅐 ▼▼▼ ▼▼ Woodfin Suite Hotel **H** 🐾
(858) 597-0500. **$109-$399.** 10044 Pacific Mesa Blvd 92121. I-805, exit 27 (Mira Mesa Blvd), 1.1 mi e, then just n. Int corridors. **Pets:** Other species. $10 daily fee/pet. Service with restrictions.
SAVE ✕ ﾐM 🛏 🖥 🍴 ➤

END METROPOLITAN AREA

SAN FRANCISCO METROPOLITAN AREA

BELMONT

🅐🅐 ▼▼▼▼ Hyatt Summerfield Suites-Belmont/Redwood Shores **H**
(650) 591-8600. **$89-$249.** 400 Concourse Dr 94002. US 101, exit Ralston Ave/Belmont, just e, then 0.3 mi n on Island Pkwy. Ext corridors. **Pets:** Medium, other species. $100 one-time fee/room. Service with restrictions, crate. SAVE ✕ ﾐM 🖥 ➤ ✕

BRISBANE

▼▼▼ Homewood Suites By Hilton **H**
(650) 589-1600. **$149-$189.** 2000 Shoreline Ct 94005. US 101, exit Sierra Point Pkwy, just e. Int corridors. **Pets:** Accepted.
✕ ﾐM 🛏 🖥 ➤

BURLINGAME

▼▼▼ Crowne Plaza **H**
(650) 342-9200. **$99-$209.** 1177 Airport Blvd 94010. US 101, exit Broadway-Burlingame or Old Bayshore Hwy, just e. Int corridors.
Pets: Accepted. ASK ✕ ﾐM 🛏 🖥 🍴 ➤

🅐🅐 ▼▼▼▼ Doubletree Hotel-San Francisco Airport **H**
(650) 344-5500. **$99-$209.** 835 Airport Blvd 94010. US 101, exit Broadway-Burlingame or Anza Blvd, just e. Int corridors. **Pets:** Accepted.
ECO SAVE ✕ ﾐM 🛏 🖥 🍴

▼▼▼ Embassy Suites-San Francisco Airport-Burlingame **H**
(650) 342-4600. **$159-$299.** 150 Anza Blvd 94010. US 101, exit Broadway-Burlingame, just e. Int corridors. **Pets:** Accepted.
ECO ✕ ﾐM 🛏 🖥 🍴 ➤ ✕

🅐🅐 ▼▼▼ ▼▼ Hilton San Francisco Airport **H** 🐾
(650) 340-8500. **$119-$369.** 600 Airport Blvd 94010. US 101, exit Broadway-Burlingame or Anza Blvd, 0.3 mi e. Int corridors.
Pets: Medium. $75 one-time fee/room. Designated rooms, service with restrictions. SAVE ✕ ﾐM 🛏 🖥 🍴 ➤

🅐🅐 ▼▼▼ Red Roof Inn **M**
(650) 342-7772. **$60-$140.** 777 Airport Blvd 94010. US 101, exit Broadway-Burlingame or E Anza Blvd; just s of airport. Ext corridors.
Pets: Large. Service with restrictions, crate. SAVE ✕ ﾐM 🛏 ➤

▼▼▼ San Francisco Airport Marriott **H**
(650) 692-9100. **$179-$219.** 1800 Old Bayshore Hwy 94010. US 101, exit Millbrae Ave, just e. Int corridors. **Pets:** Other species. $75 one-time fee/room. ✕ ﾐM 🛏 🖥 🍴 ➤ ✕

CORTE MADERA

🅐🅐 ▼▼▼ Marin Suites Hotel **H**
(415) 924-3608. **$159-$209.** 45 Tamal Vista Blvd 94925. US 101, exit Tamalpais Rd/Paradise Dr. Ext corridors. **Pets:** Accepted.
SAVE ✕ ﾐM 🛏 🖥 ➤ ✕ 🐾

HALF MOON BAY

🅐🅐 ▼▼▼ Comfort Inn Half Moon Bay **H** 🐾
(650) 712-1999. **$89-$209.** 2930 N Cabrillo Hwy 94019. On SR 1, 2 mi n of jct SR 92 and 1. Ext corridors. **Pets:** Medium. $10 daily fee/pet. Designated rooms, service with restrictions, supervision.
SAVE ✕ ﾐM 🛏 🖥

▼▼ ▼▼ Harbor View Inn **M**
(650) 726-2329. **$69-$275.** 51 Ave Alhambra 94018. SR 1, exit Capistrano Ave, just e; 4 mi n of jct SR 92. Ext corridors. **Pets:** Small, dogs only. $10 daily fee/pet. Designated rooms, service with restrictions, supervision. ASK ✕ ﾐM 🛏 🐾

🅐🅐 ▼▼▼ Holiday Inn Express **H**
(650) 726-3400. **$98-$169.** 230 S Cabrillo Hwy 94019. On SR 1, just s of SR 92. Ext corridors. **Pets:** Large, other species. $15 daily fee/pet. Service with restrictions, supervision. SAVE ✕ ﾐM 🛏 🖥

▼▼▼ Landis Shores Oceanfront Inn **BB** 🐾
(650) 726-6642. **$225-$395, 7 day notice.** 211 Mirada Rd 94019. 3 mi n of jct SR 92 and 1, exit SR 1 W at Medio Ave, just n. Int corridors. **Pets:** Medium, dogs only. $30 daily fee/pet. Designated rooms, service with restrictions, supervision. ✕ ﾐM 🛏 ✕ 🐾

▼▼▼▼▼ The Ritz-Carlton, Half Moon Bay 🅷
(650) 712-7000. **$249-$2900.** 1 Miramontes Point Rd 94019. 3 mi s of jct
SR 92 and 1; w of SR 1 at Miramontes Point Rd. Ext/int corridors.
Pets: Accepted. (ASK) 🔀 🚭ᴹ 🖥 🔲 ⊟ ⁞¶ ⊷ 🔀

MILLBRAE

▼▼▼ Clarion Hotel-San Francisco Airport 🅷
(650) 692-6363. **$75-$85.** 401 E Millbrae Ave 94030. US 101, exit Millbrae Ave, just e. Int corridors. **Pets:** Accepted.
(ASK) 🔀 🚭ᴹ 🖥 🔲 ⁞¶ ⊷

𝔸𝔸𝔸 ▼▼▼ The Westin San Francisco Airport 🅷
(650) 692-3500. **$109-$349.** 1 Old Bayshore Hwy 94030. Just e of US
101, exit Millbrae Ave. Int corridors. **Pets:** Accepted.
(ECO) (SAVE) 🔀 🚭ᴹ 🔲 ⁞¶ ⊷ 🔀

MILL VALLEY

𝔸𝔸𝔸 ▼▼▼ Acqua Hotel, a Joie de Vivre hotel 🅷 🐾
(415) 380-0400. **$189-$279.** 555 Redwood Hwy 94941. US 101, exit
Seminary Dr. Ext/int corridors. **Pets:** Other species. Designated rooms,
service with restrictions. (SAVE) 🔀 🚭ᴹ 🖥

PACIFICA

▼▼ Pacifica Motor Inn 🅼
(650) 359-7700. **Call for rates.** 200 Rockaway Beach Ave 94044. Just w
on SR 1. Ext corridors. **Pets:** Accepted. 🔀 🚭ᴹ 🖥

SAN BRUNO

𝔸𝔸𝔸 ▼▼▼ Staybridge Suites 🅷
(650) 588-0770. **$104-$199.** 1350 Huntington Ave 94066. I-380, exit El
Camino Real N, e on Sneath Ln. Ext corridors. **Pets:** Other species. $50
one-time fee/room. (SAVE) 🔀 🚭ᴹ 🖥 🔲 ⊷ 🔀

SAN FRANCISCO

𝔸𝔸𝔸 ▼▼▼ Argonaut Hotel 🅷 🐾
(415) 563-0800. **$209-$429, 3 day notice.** 495 Jefferson St 94109.
Fisherman's Wharf; adjacent to The Cannery. Int corridors. **Pets:** Small.
$250 deposit/room. Service with restrictions, supervision.
(ECO) (SAVE) 🔀 🚭ᴹ 🔲 ⁞¶

𝔸𝔸𝔸 ▼▼▼ Beresford Arms Hotel 🅷 🐾
(415) 673-2600. **$99-$259.** 701 Post St 94109. 3 blks w of Union Square
at Jones St. Int corridors. **Pets:** $25 one-time fee/pet. Designated rooms,
service with restrictions, supervision. (SAVE) 🔀 🚭ᴹ 🖥 🔲 ⁞🐾

𝔸𝔸𝔸 ▼▼▼ Beresford Hotel 🅷 🐾
(415) 673-9900. **$89-$159.** 635 Sutter St 94102. 1 blk nw of Union
Square at Mason St. Int corridors. **Pets:** $25 one-time fee/pet. Designated
rooms, service with restrictions, supervision. (SAVE) 🔀 🚭ᴹ ⁞¶ ⁞🐾

𝔸𝔸𝔸 ▼▼▼ Best Western Americania 🅷
(415) 626-0200. **$119-$209.** 121 7th St 94103. Just s of Market St;
between Minna and Natoma sts. Ext corridors. **Pets:** Accepted.
(SAVE) 🔀 🚭ᴹ 🔲 ⁞¶ ⊷ ⁞🐾

𝔸𝔸𝔸 ▼▼▼ Best Western Tuscan Inn at Fisherman's
Wharf 🅷 🐾
(415) 561-1100. **$189-$279.** 425 Northpoint St 94133. Just s of Fisherman's Wharf at Mason St. Int corridors. **Pets:** Other species. Service with
restrictions, crate. (ECO) (SAVE) 🔀 🚭ᴹ 🔲 ⁞¶

▼▼▼ Campton Place, a Taj Hotel 🅷 🐾
(415) 781-5555. **$275-$675.** 340 Stockton St 94108. Just n of Union
Square; jct Sutter St. Int corridors. **Pets:** Large, other species. $100 one-
time fee/room. Service with restrictions, crate. (ASK) 🔀 🚭ᴹ ⁞¶

𝔸𝔸𝔸 ▼▼▼▼ The Fairmont San Francisco 🅷 🐾
(415) 772-5000. **$199-$999.** 950 Mason St (atop Nob Hill) 94108. Atop
Nob Hill at California St. Int corridors. **Pets:** Small, dogs only. $25 daily
fee/room. Service with restrictions, supervision. (SAVE) 🔀 🚭ᴹ ⁞¶

▼▼▼ ▼▼▼ Four Seasons Hotel San Francisco 🅷 🐾
(415) 633-3000. **$395-$550.** 757 Market St 94103. Between 3rd and 4th
sts. Int corridors. **Pets:** Small, other species. Service with restrictions,
crate. 🔀 🚭ᴹ 🖥 🔲 ⁞¶ ⊷ 🔀

𝔸𝔸𝔸 ▼▼▼ Galleria Park Hotel, a Joie de Vivre
hotel 🅷 🐾
(415) 781-3060. **$169-$649.** 191 Sutter St 94104. 2 blks ne of Union
Square; between Kearny and Trinity sts. Int corridors. **Pets:** No service,
supervision. (ECO) (SAVE) 🔀 🚭ᴹ 🔲

𝔸𝔸𝔸 ▼▼▼ Good Hotel, a Joie de Vivre hotel 🅷
(415) 621-7001. **Call for rates.** 112 7th St 94103. Just s of Market St; at
Mission St. Int corridors. **Pets:** Accepted. (SAVE) 🔀 🚭ᴹ 🔲 ⁞¶

𝔸𝔸𝔸 ▼▼▼ Harbor Court Hotel 🅷 🐾
(415) 882-1300. **$209-$359.** 165 Steuart St 94105. On Embarcadero;
between Howard and Mission sts. Int corridors. **Pets:** Other species.
Service with restrictions, crate. (ECO) (SAVE) 🔀 🚭ᴹ ⁞¶

▼▼▼ ▼▼▼ Hilton San Francisco 🅷
(415) 771-1400. **$149-$389.** 333 O'Farrell St 94102. Just w of Union
Square at Mason St. Int corridors. **Pets:** Accepted.
(ECO) 🔀 🚭ᴹ 🖥 🔲 ⁞¶ ⊷ 🔀

𝔸𝔸𝔸 ▼▼▼ Hilton San Francisco Financial District 🅷
(415) 433-6600. **$149-$359.** 750 Kearny St 94108. Between Clay and
Washington sts. Int corridors. **Pets:** Accepted.
(SAVE) 🔀 🚭ᴹ 🖥 🔲 ⁞¶ 🔀

𝔸𝔸𝔸 ▼▼▼ Holiday Inn Civic Center 🅷
(415) 626-6103. **$99-$389.** 50 8th St 94103. 2 blks from Civic Audito-
rium; just s of Market St and BART Station. Int corridors. **Pets:** Accepted.
(SAVE) 🔀 🚭ᴹ 🖥 ⁞¶ ⊷

𝔸𝔸𝔸 ▼▼▼ Holiday Inn Golden Gateway 🅷
(415) 441-4000. **Call for rates.** 1500 Van Ness Ave 94109. US 101 (Van
Ness Ave) at Pine St. Int corridors. **Pets:** Small. $75 one-time fee/room.
Service with restrictions. (SAVE) 🔀 🚭ᴹ 🖥 🔲 ⁞¶ ⊷

𝔸𝔸𝔸 ▼▼▼ Hotel Abri 🅷
(415) 392-8800. **$159-$269.** 127 Ellis St 94102. Just w of Union Square
at Mason St. Int corridors. **Pets:** Medium. Service with restrictions, crate.
(ECO) (SAVE) 🔀 🚭ᴹ 🔲 ⁞¶

𝔸𝔸𝔸 ▼▼▼ Hotel Carlton, a Joie de Vivre hotel 🅷
(415) 673-0242. **$89-$249.** 1075 Sutter St 94109. 0.5 mi w of Union
Square; between Hyde and Larkin sts. Int corridors. **Pets:** Accepted.
(ECO) (SAVE) 🔀 🚭ᴹ 🖥 🔲 ⁞¶ ⁞🐾

𝔸𝔸𝔸 ▼▼▼ Hotel Diva 🅷
(415) 885-0200. **$129-$369.** 440 Geary St 94102. Just w of Union
Square. Int corridors. **Pets:** Accepted. (SAVE) 🔀 🖥 🔲 ⁞¶

𝔸𝔸𝔸 ▼▼▼ Hotel Frank 🅷 🐾
(415) 986-2000. **$149-$399.** 386 Geary St 94102. Just w of Union
Square at Mason St. Int corridors. **Pets:** Medium, dogs only. $25 one-
time fee/pet. Service with restrictions, supervision. (SAVE) 🔀 🚭ᴹ 🔲

𝔸𝔸𝔸 ▼▼▼ Hotel Kabuki, a Joie de Vivre hotel 🅷
(415) 922-3200. **$99-$299.** 1625 Post St 94115. Jct Laguna St; in Japan
Center. Int corridors. **Pets:** Accepted. (SAVE) 🔀 🚭ᴹ 🔲 ⁞¶

𝔸𝔸𝔸 ▼▼ Hotel Metropolis 🅷
(415) 775-4600. **$89-$269.** 25 Mason St 94102. Jct Market St. Int corridors. **Pets:** Accepted. (SAVE) 🔀 🚭ᴹ 🔲 ⁞¶ ⁞🐾

𝔸𝔸𝔸 ▼▼▼ Hotel Monaco 🅷
(415) 292-0100. **$179-$329.** 501 Geary St 94102. Just w of Union
Square at Taylor St. Int corridors. **Pets:** Accepted.
(ECO) (SAVE) 🔀 🚭ᴹ ⁞¶ 🔀

Hotel Nikko San Francisco H
(415) 394-1111. **Call for rates.** 222 Mason St 94102. At O'Farrell St. Int corridors. **Pets:** Accepted. ☒☒☒☒☒☒☒☒☒

Hotel Palomar H
(415) 348-1111. **$209-$369.** 12 Fourth St 94103. At Market St. Int corridors. **Pets:** Accepted. ☒☒☒☒☒

Hotel Rex, a Joie de Vivre hotel H
(415) 433-4434. **$189-$409.** 562 Sutter St 94102. Just nw of Union Square; between Mason and Powell sts. Int corridors. **Pets:** Accepted.
☒☒☒☒☒

Hotel Triton H ❀
(415) 394-0500. **$129-$369.** 342 Grant Ave 94108. Near Union Square at Bush St. Int corridors. **Pets:** Other species. Designated rooms, service with restrictions. ☒☒☒☒☒

Hotel Union Square H
(415) 397-3000. **$129-$369.** 114 Powell St 94102. At Ellis St; just n of cable car turnaround. Int corridors. **Pets:** Accepted.
☒☒☒☒☒

Hotel Vertigo H
(415) 885-6800. **$119-$349.** 940 Sutter St 94109. Between Leavenworth and Hyde sts. Int corridors. **Pets:** Medium, dogs only. $25 one-time fee/room. Service with restrictions, supervision. ☒☒☒☒

Hotel Vitale, a Joie de Vivre hotel H
(415) 278-3700. **$399-$799.** 8 Mission St 94105. At Embarcadero. Int corridors. **Pets:** Accepted. ☒☒☒☒☒☒

InterContinental San Francisco H
(415) 616-6500. **$159-$589.** 888 Howard St 94103. Between 4th and 5th sts; in the SoMa District. Int corridors. **Pets:** Accepted.
☒☒☒☒☒☒

JW Marriott San Francisco H
(415) 771-8600. **$224-$274.** 500 Post St 94102. Just w of Union Square at Mason St. Int corridors. **Pets:** Accepted. ☒☒☒☒☒

Kensington Park Hotel H
(415) 788-6400. **$129-$369.** 450 Post St 94102. Just w of Union Square. Int corridors. **Pets:** Accepted. ☒☒☒☒☒☒☒

Larkspur Hotel Union Square H
(415) 421-2865. **$129-$199.** 524 Sutter St 94102. Union Square at Powell St. Int corridors. **Pets:** Accepted. ☒☒☒☒☒

Laurel Inn, a Joie de Vivre hotel H ❀
(415) 567-8467. **$149-$249.** 444 Presidio Ave 94115. 1 mi w of US 101 (Van Ness Ave); 1 mi e of Park Presidio Blvd (SR 1) at California St. Int corridors. **Pets:** Other species. Service with restrictions, supervision.
☒☒☒☒☒☒

Le Meridien San Francisco H
(415) 296-2900. **$159-$399.** 333 Battery St 94111. At Clay St; in financial district. Int corridors. **Pets:** Accepted. ☒☒☒☒

Mandarin Oriental, San Francisco H
(415) 276-9888. **$345-$4200.** 222 Sansome St 94104. Between Pine and California sts; in financial district. Int corridors. **Pets:** Accepted.
☒☒☒☒☒☒

Omni San Francisco Hotel H ❀
(415) 677-9494. **$159-$699.** 500 California St 94104. At Montgomery St; in financial district. Int corridors. **Pets:** Small. $50 one-time fee/pet. Designated rooms, service with restrictions, supervision.
☒☒☒☒

The Opal San Francisco H
(415) 673-4711. **$129-$269.** 1050 Van Ness Ave 94109. On US 101 (Van Ness Ave); between Geary and Myrtle sts. Int corridors.
Pets: Accepted. ☒☒☒☒

Palace Hotel H
(415) 512-1111. **$149-$489.** 2 New Montgomery St 94105. Just e of Union Square at Market St. Int corridors. **Pets:** Accepted.
☒☒☒☒☒☒

Parc 55 Hotel San Francisco H
(415) 392-8000. **$159-$329, 3 day notice.** 55 Cyril Magnin St 94102. Corner of Cyril Magnin and Eddy sts; 3 blks sw of Union Square. Int corridors. **Pets:** Small, dogs only. $40 one-time fee/room.
☒☒☒☒☒

The Powell Hotel H
(415) 398-3200. **$139-$155.** 28 Cyril Magnin St 94102. At Powell cable car turnaround. Int corridors. **Pets:** Accepted.
☒☒☒☒☒☒

The Prescott Hotel H
(415) 563-0303. **$149-$399.** 545 Post St 94102. Just w of Union Square. Int corridors. **Pets:** Accepted. ☒☒☒☒

The Ritz-Carlton, San Francisco H
(415) 296-7465. **Call for rates.** 600 Stockton St 94108. Just n of Union Square at California St. Int corridors. **Pets:** Accepted.
☒☒☒☒☒☒

St. Regis Hotel San Francisco H
(415) 284-4000. **$329-$799.** 125 3rd St 94103. At Mission St. Int corridors. **Pets:** Accepted. ☒☒☒☒☒

San Francisco Marriott Fisherman's Wharf H
(415) 775-7555. **$199-$249.** 1250 Columbus Ave 94133. Just s of Fisherman's Wharf at Bay St. Int corridors. **Pets:** Accepted.
☒☒☒☒

Serrano Hotel H
(415) 885-2500. **$159-$359.** 405 Taylor St 94102. Just w of Union Square at O'Farrell St. Int corridors. **Pets:** Accepted.
☒☒☒☒☒☒

Sheraton Fisherman's Wharf H ❀
(415) 362-5500. **$129-$419.** 2500 Mason St 94133. Just se of Fisherman's Wharf at Beach St. Int corridors. **Pets:** Medium, other species. Designated rooms, service with restrictions, supervision.
☒☒☒☒☒☒☒

Sir Francis Drake Hotel H ❀
(415) 392-7755. **$139-$439.** 450 Powell St 94102. Just n of Union Square at Sutter St. Int corridors. **Pets:** Large, other species. Designated rooms, service with restrictions. ☒☒☒☒☒☒

The Stanford Court, a Renaissance Hotel H
(415) 989-3500. **$179-$219.** 905 California St 94108. Atop Nob Hill; corner of California and Powell sts. Int corridors. **Pets:** Small, dogs only. $25 one-time fee/pet. Service with restrictions, supervision.
☒☒☒☒☒☒

Travelodge at the Presidio M
(415) 931-8581. **$79-$189.** 2755 Lombard St 94123. Between Lyon and Baker sts. Ext corridors. **Pets:** Medium, other species. $20 daily fee/pet. Service with restrictions, supervision. ☒☒☒☒

Travelodge By The Bay M ❀
(415) 673-0691. **$59-$359.** 1450 Lombard St 94123. On US 101 (Lombard St). Ext/int corridors. **Pets:** Large, dogs only. $20 daily fee/pet. Designated rooms, service with restrictions, crate. ☒☒☒☒☒

△△△ ▽▽▽▽ Villa Florence, a Larkspur Collection Hotel **H**
(415) 397-7700. **$169-$269.** 225 Powell St 94107. Just s of Union Square; between O'Farrell and Geary sts. Int corridors. **Pets:** Accepted.
🔲 🆂🅰🆅🅴 ⊠ ᴛᴍ 🔲 💻 ⑪

△△△ ▽▽▽▽ The Westin St. Francis **H**
(415) 397-7000. **$129-$489.** 335 Powell St 94102. On Union Square. Int corridors. **Pets:** Accepted. 🆂🅰🆅🅴 ⊠ ᴛᴍ 🔲 💻 ⑪ ⊠

△△△ ▽▽▽▽ Westin San Francisco Market Street **H**
(415) 974-6400. **Call for rates.** 50 3rd St 94103. Just n of Moscone Convention Center; between Jessie and Stevenson sts. Int corridors. **Pets:** Accepted. 🆂🅰🆅🅴 ⊠ ᴛᴍ 💻 ⑪

△△△ ▽▽▽▽ W San Francisco **H** ❀
(415) 777-5300. **$209-$2000.** 181 3rd St 94103. At Howard St. Int corridors. **Pets:** Medium. $100 one-time fee/room. Service with restrictions, supervision. 🔲 🆂🅰🆅🅴 ⊠ ᴛᴍ 🔲 💻 ⑪ 🌊 ⊠

SAN MATEO
▽▽▽▽ Comfort Inn **H**
(650) 344-6376. **$79-$119.** 350 N Bayshore Blvd 94401. US 101, exit Dore Ave northbound; exit 3rd Ave E southbound, re-enter US 101, then exit Dore Ave. Ext/int corridors. **Pets:** Small. $35 one-time fee/pet. Service with restrictions, supervision. 🅰🆂🅺 ⊠ ᴛᴍ 🔲 💻

▽▽▽▽ Residence Inn by Marriott **H**
(650) 574-4700. **$197-$241.** 2000 Winward Way 94404. 0.8 mi se from jct US 101 and SR 92; exit SR 92 via Edgewater Blvd. Ext corridors. **Pets:** Accepted. ⊠ ᴛᴍ 🔲 💻 🌊 ⊠

SAN RAFAEL
▽▽▽▽ Gerstle Park Inn **BB**
(415) 721-7611. **$189-$275, 3 day notice.** 34 Grove St 94901. US 101, exit Central San Rafael, 0.5 mi w on 4th St, 0.5 mi s on D St, then just w on San Rafael Ave. Ext/int corridors. **Pets:** Dogs only. $10 daily fee/pet. Designated rooms, service with restrictions, supervision. ⊠ ᴛᴍ

SOUTH SAN FRANCISCO
▽▽▽▽ Embassy Suites San Francisco Airport-South San Francisco **H**
(650) 589-3400. **$140-$300.** 250 Gateway Blvd 94080. US 101, exit 425A (Grand Ave), just e. Int corridors. **Pets:** Accepted.
🔲 ⊠ ᴛᴍ 🔲 💻 ⑪ 🌊

△△△ ▽▽▽ Howard Johnson Express Inn **M**
(650) 589-9055. **$39-$189.** 222 S Airport Blvd 94080. US 101, exit S Airport Blvd, just e. Ext corridors. **Pets:** Accepted.
🆂🅰🆅🅴 ⊠ ᴛᴍ 🔲 💻

▽▽▽▽ La Quinta Inn San Francisco (Airport) **H** ❀
(650) 583-2223. **$49-$139.** 20 Airport Blvd 94080. US 101, exit S Airport Blvd, just w. Int corridors. **Pets:** Medium, other species. Service with restrictions, supervision. 🅰🆂🅺 ⊠ ᴛᴍ 🔲 💻

△△△ ▽▽▽▽ Larkspur Landing South San Francisco **H**
(650) 827-1515. **$99-$219.** 690 Gateway Blvd 94080. US 101 S, exit 425A (Grand Ave), 0.4 mi n on Gateway Blvd; US 101 N, exit 425B (Oyster Point Blvd e), 0.5 mi e, 0.5 mi s on Gateway Blvd, then U-turn. Int corridors. **Pets:** Accepted. 🆂🅰🆅🅴 ⊠ ᴛᴍ 🔲 💻

▽▽▽▽ Residence Inn by Marriott at Oyster Point **H**
(650) 837-9000. **$152-$186.** 1350 Veterans Blvd 94080. US 101, 425B, just ne. Int corridors. **Pets:** $100 one-time fee/room. Service with restrictions, supervision. ⊠ ᴛᴍ 🔲 💻 🌊 ⊠

TIBURON
△△△ ▽▽▽▽ The Lodge at Tiburon, a Larkspur Collection Hotel **H**
(415) 435-3133. **$149-$469.** 1651 Tiburon Blvd 94920. US 101, exit Tiburon-Belvedere, 4 mi e; in village; 1 blk from bay. Ext corridors. **Pets:** Accepted. 🆂🅰🆅🅴 ⊠ ᴛᴍ 🔲 💻 ⑪ 🌊

END METROPOLITAN AREA

SANGER
△△△ ▽▽▽▽ Blossom Trail Bed & Breakfast **BB**
(559) 875-6036. **$119-$169, 7 day notice.** 3700 S Newmark Ave 93657. SR 180, 3.5 mi s on Reed Ave, 5 mi w on Goodfellow to Newmark, then just n. Ext/int corridors. **Pets:** $35 daily fee/room. Designated rooms, supervision. 🆂🅰🆅🅴 ⊠ ᴛᴍ 🔲 💻 🆆

SAN JOSE
▽▽▽▽ Crowne Plaza San Jose–Downtown **H**
(408) 998-0400. **$79-$249.** 282 Almaden Blvd 95113. I-280, exit Almaden-Vine, 6 blks n. Int corridors. **Pets:** Medium, other species. $50 one-time fee/pet. Designated rooms, service with restrictions, supervision.
🅰🆂🅺 ⊠ ᴛᴍ 🔲 💻 ⑪

△△△ ▽▽▽ Days Inn Airport **H**
(408) 437-9100. **$89-$99.** 1280 N 4th St 95112. US 101, exit N 1st St, 0.5 mi s to Rosemary St, then just e. Ext corridors. **Pets:** Small. $20 daily fee/room. Designated rooms, service with restrictions, supervision.
🆂🅰🆅🅴 ⊠ 🔲 💻

△△△ ▽▽▽ ▽▽▽ Doubletree Hotel San Jose **H**
(408) 453-4000. **$89-$289.** 2050 Gateway Pl 95110. 0.3 mi e of Norman Y. Mineta San Jose International Airport via Airport Blvd; w of US 101, exit N 1st St; US 101 northbound, exit Brokaw Rd. Int corridors. **Pets:** Accepted. 🔲 🆂🅰🆅🅴 ⊠ ᴛᴍ 🔲 💻 ⑪ 🌊

▽▽▽▽ Extended Stay Deluxe-San Jose-Downtown **H**
(408) 453-3000. **$110-$130.** 55 E Brokaw Rd 95112. US 101, exit 1st St/Brokaw Rd, just e. Int corridors. **Pets:** Other species. $25 daily fee/room. Designated rooms, service with restrictions, crate.
🅰🆂🅺 ⊠ 💻 🌊

▽▽▽ Extended Stay Deluxe San Jose–South–Edenvale **H**
(408) 229-9188. **$95-$110.** 6189 San Ignacio Ave 95119. US 101, exit Bernal Rd E, just n. Int corridors. **Pets:** Other species. $25 daily fee/room. Designated rooms, service with restrictions, crate.
🅰🆂🅺 ⊠ ᴛᴍ 🔲 💻 🌊

▽▽▽▽ Fairfield Inn & Suites **H**
(408) 453-3133. **$143-$175.** 1755 N 1st St 95112. US 101, exit N 1st St, just w. Int corridors. **Pets:** Medium. $50 one-time fee/room. Designated rooms, service with restrictions, crate. ⊠ ᴛᴍ 🔲 💻

△△△ ▽▽▽▽ The Fairmont San Jose **H** ❀
(408) 998-1900. **$149-$369.** 170 S Market St 95113. At Fairmont Plaza. Int corridors. **Pets:** Dogs only. $75 one-time fee/room. Service with restrictions, supervision. 🔲 🆂🅰🆅🅴 ⊠ ᴛᴍ 💻 ⑪ 🌊 ⊠

△△△ ▽▽▽▽ Hilton San Jose **H**
(408) 287-2100. **$109-$349.** 300 Almaden Blvd 95110. SR 87, exit Santa Clara St E, 0.4 mi s; at W San Carlos St. Int corridors. **Pets:** Accepted.
🆂🅰🆅🅴 ⊠ ᴛᴍ 🔲 💻 ⑪ 🌊

△△△ ▽▽▽▽ Holiday Inn San Jose **H**
(408) 793-3300. **$79-$209.** 1740 N 1st St 95112. W of US 101, exit N 1st St; 0.5 mi e of Norman Y. Mineta San Jose International Airport via Airport Pkwy. Int corridors. **Pets:** Accepted.
🆂🅰🆅🅴 ⊠ ᴛᴍ 🔲 💻 ⑪ 🌊 ⊠

▼▼ Homestead Studio Suites Hotel-San Jose-Downtown 🅷

(408) 573-0648. **$100-$115.** 1560 N 1st St 95112. 1 mi e of Norman Y. Mineta San Jose International Airport; US 101, exit N 1st St, then s. Int corridors. **Pets:** Other species. $25 daily fee/room. Designated rooms, service with restrictions, crate. 🅰🆂🅺 ⊠ 💻

▼▼◆▼ Homewood Suites by Hilton 🅷

(408) 428-9900. **$99-$209.** 10 W Trimble Rd 95131. US 101, exit Trimble Rd, 1.3 mi e; 2 mi e of Norman Y. Mineta San Jose International Airport. Ext/int corridors. **Pets:** Accepted. ⊠ 🅖🅜 🛏 💻 🏊 🗙

🆔 ▼▼◆▼◆▼ Hotel De Anza 🅷

(408) 286-1000. **$129-$399.** 233 W Santa Clara St 95113. SR 87, exit Santa Clara St, just e. Int corridors. **Pets:** Small. $50 one-time fee/room. Designated rooms, service with restrictions, crate.

[SAVE] ⊠ 🅖🅜 🛏 💻 🍽

🆔 ▼▼◆▼ Howard Johnson Inn 🅼

(408) 280-5300. **$79-$225, 14 day notice.** 1215 S 1st St 95110. Jct I-280 and SR 82, 0.8 mi s. Ext corridors. **Pets:** Accepted.

[SAVE] ⊠ 🛏 💻

▼▼◆▼ La Quinta Inn San Jose Airport 🅷 ❀

(408) 435-8800. **$79-$139, 7 day notice.** 2585 Seaboard Ave 95131. US 101, exit Trimble Rd E; 1 mi ne of Norman Y. Mineta San Jose International Airport. Int corridors. **Pets:** Medium, other species. Service with restrictions, supervision. 🅰🆂🅺 ⊠ 🛏 💻 🏊

▼▼◆▼ Residence Inn by Marriott 🅷 ❀

(408) 226-7676. **$170-$208.** 6111 San Ignacio Ave 95119. US 101, exit Bernal Rd, then e. Int corridors. **Pets:** Medium. $100 one-time fee/room. Service with restrictions, supervision. ⊠ 🅖🅜 🛏 💻 🏊 🗙

▼▼◆▼◆▼ Staybridge Suites San Jose 🅷

(408) 436-1600. **$95-$195.** 1602 Crane Ct 95112. US 101, exit 1st St/Brokaw Rd, 0.4 mi e to Bering S, then 0.5 mi. Ext corridors. **Pets:** Accepted. 🅰🆂🅺 ⊠ 🛏 💻 🏊

▼▼◆▼ TownePlace Suites by Marriott San Jose/Cupertino 🅷

(408) 984-5903. **$179-$219.** 440 Saratoga Ave 95129. I-280, exit Saratoga Ave, just n. Int corridors. **Pets:** Accepted. ⊠ 🅖🅜 🛏 💻 🏊

SAN JUAN BAUTISTA

🆔 ◆▼ San Juan Inn 🅼

(831) 623-4380. **$69-$99.** 410 The Alameda 95045. Jct SR 156. Ext corridors. **Pets:** Accepted. [SAVE] ⊠ 🛏 💻 🏊

SAN JUAN CAPISTRANO

🆔 ▼▼◆▼ Best Western Capistrano Inn 🅼

(949) 493-5661. **$79-$149.** 27174 Ortega Hwy 92675-2702. I-5, exit 82 (SR 74/Ortega Hwy), just e. Ext corridors. **Pets:** Other species. $25 one-time fee/room. Service with restrictions. [SAVE] ⊠ 🛏 💻 🏊

SAN LUIS OBISPO

🆔 ▼▼◆▼ Best Western Royal Oak Hotel 🅼 ❀

(805) 544-4410. **Call for rates.** 214 Madonna Rd 93405. US 101, exit 201 (Madonna Rd), just s. Ext/int corridors. **Pets:** Large. $300 deposit/room, $15 one-time fee/pet. Service with restrictions, supervision.

[SAVE] ⊠ 🅖🅜 🛏 💻 🏊

🆔 ▼▼◆▼ Days Inn-San Luis Obispo 🅼 ❀

(805) 549-9911. **$69-$219.** 2050 Garfield St 93401. US 101, exit 204 (Monterey St), just sw. Ext corridors. **Pets:** Medium, dogs only. $50 deposit/pet, $15 daily fee/pet. Designated rooms, service with restrictions, supervision. [SAVE] ⊠ 🅖🅜 🛏 💻 🏊

▼▼ Heritage Inn Bed & Breakfast 🅱🅱

(805) 544-7440. **$85-$165, 7 day notice.** 978 Olive St 93405. US 101, exit 203B (SR 1/Morro Bay) northbound, just w on Santa Rosa St, then just s; exit 203A (Santa Rosa St) southbound, just ne. Int corridors. **Pets:** Accepted. ⊠ 🅺 🅿 🐾

🆔 ▼▼◆▼ Ramada Inn Olive Tree 🅼

(805) 544-2800. **$79-$399.** 1000 Olive St 93405. US 101, exit 203B (Morro Bay) northbound, just w on Santa Rosa St, then just s; exit 203A (Santa Rosa St) southbound, just ne. Ext corridors. **Pets:** Accepted.

[SAVE] ⊠ 🅖🅜 🛏 💻 🏊

🆔 ▼▼◆▼ Sands Inn & Suites 🅼

(805) 544-0500. **$79-$249.** 1930 Monterey St 93401. US 101, exit 204 (Monterey St), just sw. Ext corridors. **Pets:** $25 one-time fee/pet. Service with restrictions, supervision. [SAVE] ⊠ 🛏 💻 🏊 🗙

🆔 ▼▼◆▼ Super 8 🅼

(805) 544-6888. **$49-$299.** 1951 Monterey St 93401. US 101, exit 204 (Monterey St), just e. Ext corridors. **Pets:** Accepted.

[SAVE] ⊠ 🛏 💻

SAN MARCOS

▼▼◆▼ Lake San Marcos Resort 🅷

(760) 744-0120. **$59-$469.** 1025 La Bonita Dr 92078. SR 78, exit Rancho Santa Fe Rd, 2 mi s, then 0.5 mi e via Lake San Marcos and San Marino drs; at Lake San Marcos. Ext/int corridors. **Pets:** Dogs only. $75 one-time fee/pet. Service with restrictions.

🅰🆂🅺 ⊠ 🛏 💻 🍽 🏊 🗙

SAN RAMON

▼▼◆▼ Homestead Studio Suites Hotel-San Ramon-Bishop Ranch 🅷

(925) 277-0833. **$80-$95.** 18000 San Ramon Valley Blvd 94583. I-680, exit Bollinger Canyon Rd E, just n. Ext corridors. **Pets:** Other species. $25 daily fee/room. Designated rooms, service with restrictions, crate.

🅰🆂🅺 ⊠ 🛏 💻

▼▼◆▼◆▼ Residence Inn by Marriott 🅷

(925) 277-9292. **$152-$186.** 1071 Market Pl 94583. I-680, exit Bollinger Canyon Rd E, 0.5 mi e. Ext corridors. **Pets:** $100 one-time fee/room. Service with restrictions, supervision. ⊠ 🅖🅜 🛏 💻 🏊 🗙

▼▼◆▼◆▼ San Ramon Marriott at Bishop Ranch 🅷

(925) 867-9200. **$152-$186.** 2600 Bishop Dr 94583. I-680, exit Bollinger Canyon Rd E, n on Sunset, then just w. Int corridors. **Pets:** Accepted.

[ECO] ⊠ 🅖🅜 🛏 💻 🍽 🏊

SAN SIMEON

🆔 ▼▼◆▼ Best Western Cavalier Oceanfront Resort 🅷

(805) 927-4688. **$99-$319.** 9415 Hearst Dr 93452. SR 1, exit Pico W, just s; exit Vista del Mar W, just n. Ext corridors. **Pets:** Supervision.

[SAVE] ⊠ 🅖🅜 🛏 💻 🍽 🏊 🗙 🅺

🆔 ▼▼◆▼ Courtesy Inn 🅼

(805) 927-4691. **$69-$109, 7 day notice.** 9450 Castillo Dr 93452. East side of SR 1. Ext corridors. **Pets:** Dogs only. $20 daily fee/pet. Designated rooms, service with restrictions, supervision.

[SAVE] ⊠ 🛏 💻 🏊

🆔 ▼▼◆▼ San Simeon Lodge 🅷 ❀

(805) 927-4601. **$50-$220, 3 day notice.** 9520 Castillo Dr 93452. On SR 1. Ext corridors. **Pets:** Medium. $10 daily fee/pet. Service with restrictions, supervision. [SAVE] ⊠ 🛏 💻 🍽 🏊 🅺

🆔 ▼▼◆▼ Silver Surf Motel 🅼 ❀

(805) 927-4661. **$59-$189.** 9390 Castillo Dr 93452. Just e of SR 1. Ext corridors. **Pets:** $10 daily fee/pet. Designated rooms, service with restrictions, supervision. [SAVE] ⊠ 🛏 💻 🏊 🅺

SANTA ANA

▼▼◆▼ La Quinta Inn & Suites Santa Ana 🅼 ❀

(714) 540-1111. **$49-$119.** 2721 Hotel Terrace Dr 92705. SR 55, exit 8 (Dyer Rd) northbound; exit 8B (Dyer Rd W) southbound, just w, then just s. Ext corridors. **Pets:** Medium, other species. Service with restrictions, supervision. 🅰🆂🅺 ⊠ 🛏 💻 🏊

▼▼ Red Roof Inn M
(714) 542-0311. **$67-$70.** 2600 N Main St 92701. I-5, exit 105B (Main St), 0.3 mi n. Ext/int corridors. **Pets:** Large. Service with restrictions, crate. ASK ⊠ 🗋 🖥

SANTA BARBARA

〰 ▼▼▼ Best Western South Coast Inn M
(805) 967-3200. **$135-$250.** 5620 Calle Real 93117. 7 mi nw of town center via US 101, exit 104 (Patterson Rd), just e, then 0.7 mi n. Ext corridors. **Pets:** Accepted. SAVE ⊠ 🗋 🖥 ➔

▼▼ Blue Sands Motel M
(805) 965-1624. **$85-$275, 3 day notice.** 421 S Milpas St 93103. US 101, exit 96A (Milpas St), 0.3 mi s. Ext corridors. **Pets:** Dogs only. $10 daily fee/pet. Service with restrictions. ⊠ 🗋 🖥 ➔ 🐾

▼▼ Extended StayAmerica Santa Barbara-Calle Real H
(805) 692-1882. **$115-$155.** 4870 Calle Real 93111. US 101, exit Turnpike Rd, just e, then just n. Int corridors. **Pets:** Other species. $25 daily fee/room. Designated rooms, service with restrictions, crate.
ASK ⊠ 🗋 🖥

〰 ▼▼▼ Fess Parker's Doubletree Resort H 🐾
(805) 564-4333. **$205-$559.** 633 E Cabrillo Blvd 93103. US 101, exit 96A (Milpas St), just s, then just w. Ext/int corridors. **Pets:** Other species. $25 daily fee/room. Designated rooms, service with restrictions, supervision. ECO SAVE ⊠ 🗋 🖥 ➔ 🐾

〰 ▼▼▼ Four Seasons Biltmore Santa Barbara H 🐾
(805) 969-2261. **Call for rates.** 1260 Channel Dr 93108. US 101, exit 94A (Olive Mill Rd), 0.3 mi s; in Montecito. Ext corridors. **Pets:** Small, other species. Designated rooms, service with restrictions.
SAVE ⊠ 🗋 🖥 🐾 ➔ 🐾

〰 ▼▼▼ Harbor House Inn M
(805) 962-9745. **$129-$349.** 104 Bath St 93101. US 101, exit 94B (Cabrillo Blvd) (left hand exit), 3 mi n, then just e; exit 97 (Castillo St) southbound, 0.4 mi w, just s on Cabrillo Blvd, then just e. Ext corridors. **Pets:** Dogs only. $15 daily fee/pet. Designated rooms, service with restrictions, supervision. SAVE ⊠ 🗋 🖥 🐾

〰 ▼▼▼ Hotel MarMonte H
(805) 963-0744. **$159-$304, 3 day notice.** 1111 E Cabrillo Blvd 93103. US 101, exit 96A (Milpas St), 0.3 mi s, then just e. Int corridors. **Pets:** Dogs only. $75 one-time fee/pet. Designated rooms, service with restrictions, supervision. SAVE ⊠ 🗋 🖥 🐾 ➔ 🐾

▼▼▼ Marina Beach Motel M
(805) 963-9311. **$99-$324.** 21 Bath St 93101. US 101, exit 96B (Garden St), 0.3 mi w to Cabrillo Blvd, 0.4 mi n to Bath St, then just e. Ext corridors. **Pets:** Small. $15 daily fee/pet. Designated rooms, service with restrictions, supervision. ⊠ 🗋 🖥

▼▼▼ Pacifica Suites H
(805) 683-6722. **$179-$389.** 5490 Hollister Ave 93111. US 101, exit 104A (Patterson Ave), 0.5 mi w, then 0.5 mi n. Ext/int corridors. **Pets:** Medium, dogs only. $20 daily fee/pet. Designated rooms, service with restrictions, supervision. ASK ⊠ 🗋 🖥 ➔

▼▼▼ The Parkside Inn M
(805) 963-0744. **$79-$189, 3 day notice.** 424 Por La Mar 93103. US 101, exit 96A (Milpas St), 0.3 mi s, just e on Cabrillo Blvd, then just n. Int corridors. **Pets:** Dogs only. $75 one-time fee/pet. Service with restrictions, supervision. ASK ⊠ 🗋 🖥 ➔ 🐾

SANTA CATALINA ISLAND

〰 ▼▼▼ Catalina Canyon Resort & Spa M
(310) 510-0325. **$109-$329, 3 day notice.** 888 Country Club Dr 90704. In Avalon; 0.5 mi from harbor via Sumner Ave. Ext corridors. **Pets:** $50 one-time fee/pet. Service with restrictions, supervision.
SAVE ⊠ 🗋 🖥 🐾 ➔ 🐾

SANTA CLARA

〰 ▼▼▼ Biltmore Hotel & Suites/Silicon Valley H
(408) 988-8411. **$89-$259.** 2151 Laurelwood Rd 95054. US 101, exit Montague Expwy, just e; 1 mi s of Great America Pkwy. Ext/int corridors. **Pets:** Dogs only. $50 one-time fee/room. Designated rooms, service with restrictions, crate. SAVE ⊠ 🗋 🖥 🐾 ➔

〰 ▼▼▼ Hilton Santa Clara Hotel H
(408) 330-0001. **$99-$359.** 4949 Great America Pkwy 95054. US 101, exit Great America Pkwy, 0.5 mi n. Int corridors. **Pets:** Dogs only. $100 deposit/pet. Designated rooms, service with restrictions, supervision.
ECO SAVE ⊠ 🗋 🖥 🐾 ➔

〰 ▼▼▼ Quality Inn & Suites M
(408) 241-3010. **$75-$145.** 2930 El Camino Real 95051. SR 82, 0.5 mi w of San Tomas Expwy; US 101, exit S Bowers Ave. Ext corridors. **Pets:** Small. $20 daily fee/pet. Designated rooms, service with restrictions, supervision. SAVE ⊠ 🗋 🖥 ➔

▼▼▼ Santa Clara Marriott Hotel H
(408) 988-1500. **$179-$219.** 2700 Mission College Blvd 95054. 0.5 mi e off US 101, exit Great America Pkwy; 0.8 mi s of Great America Theme Park. Int corridors. **Pets:** Accepted. ⊠ 🐾 🗋 🖥 🐾 ➔ 🐾

〰 ▼▼ The Vagabond Inn M
(408) 241-0771. **$69-$199.** 3580 El Camino Real 95051. On SR 82, southeast corner of Lawrence Expwy Cloverleaf. Ext corridors. **Pets:** $20 daily fee/pet. Designated rooms, service with restrictions, supervision.
SAVE ⊠ 🗋 🖥 ➔

SANTA CRUZ

▼▼ GuestHouse International Pacific Inn H
(831) 425-3722. **$70-$220.** 330 Ocean St 95060. 1 mi from jct SR 1 and 17. Int corridors. **Pets:** Accepted. ⊠ 🗋 🖥 ➔

▼▼ Hilton Santa Cruz/Scotts Valley H 🐾
(831) 440-1000. **$169-$409.** 6001 La Madrona Dr 95060. SR 17, exit Mt. Hermon Rd. Int corridors. **Pets:** Dogs only. $50 one-time fee/room. Designated rooms, service with restrictions, supervision.
⊠ 🐾 🗋 🖥 🐾 ➔

〰 ▼▼▼ The Inn at Pasatiempo H
(831) 423-5000. **$99-$305.** 555 Hwy 17 95060. 0.8 mi n of jct SR 1 and 17; exit SR 17, exit Pasatiempo Dr. Ext corridors. **Pets:** Small, dogs only. $25 daily fee/pet. Designated rooms, service with restrictions, supervision.
SAVE ⊠ 🗋 🖥 🐾 ➔ 🐾

〰 ▼▼▼ Santa Cruz Beach Inn H
(831) 458-9660. **$80-$400, 3 day notice.** 600 Riverside Ave 95060. 4 blks from beach. Ext corridors. **Pets:** Dogs only. $15 daily fee/pet. Service with restrictions, supervision. SAVE ⊠ 🗋 🖥 ➔ 🐾

SANTA MARIA

〰 ▼▼▼ Best Western Big America M 🐾
(805) 922-5200. **$125-$189.** 1725 N Broadway 93454. US 101, exit 173 (SR 135/S Broadway), 0.5 mi s. Ext corridors. **Pets:** Other species. Service with restrictions, supervision. SAVE ⊠ 🗋 🖥 ➔

▼▼▼ Historic Santa Maria Inn H 🐾
(805) 928-7777. **$114-$169.** 801 S Broadway 93454. US 101, exit 171 (Main St), 1 mi w, then 0.5 mi s. Ext corridors. **Pets:** Small, dogs only. $50 one-time fee/room. Designated rooms, service with restrictions, supervision. ASK ⊠ 🗋 🖥 🐾 ➔ 🐾

〰 ▼▼▼ Holiday Inn Hotel & Suites H
(805) 928-6000. **$135-$229.** 2100 N Broadway 93454. US 101, exit 173 (SR 135/S Broadway), just s. Int corridors. **Pets:** Accepted.
SAVE ⊠ 🐾 🗋 🖥 🐾 ➔

〰 ▼▼▼ Quality Inn & Suites M
(805) 922-5891. **$96-$106.** 210 S Nicholson Ave 93454. US 101, exit 171 (Main St), just e, then just s. Int corridors. **Pets:** Medium, dogs only. $25 one-time fee/pet. Service with restrictions, supervision.
SAVE ⊠ 🗋 🖥 ➔

SANTA NELLA

Best Western Andersen's Inn H
(209) 826-5534. **$89-$109.** 12367 Hwy 33 S 95322. I-5, exit 407 (SR 33), just e. Ext corridors. **Pets:** Accepted. SAVE [icons]

Holiday Inn Express H 🐾
(209) 826-8282. **$69-$99.** 28976 Plaza Dr 95322. I-5, exit 407 (SR 33), just e. Ext corridors. **Pets:** Other species. $12 one-time fee/pet. Designated rooms, supervision. SAVE [icons]

Motel 6 of Santa Nella H
(209) 827-8700. **$45-$99.** 28821 W Gonzaga Rd 95322. 2.5 mi w of I-5; SR 152, exit Gonzaga Rd, just s. Ext corridors. **Pets:** Other species. Service with restrictions, supervision. SAVE [icons]

Ramada Mission de Oro M
(209) 826-4444. **Call for rates.** 13070 State Hwy 33 95322. I-5, exit 407 (SR 33), just w. Ext/int corridors. **Pets:** Accepted.
[icons]

SANTA PAULA

Glen Tavern Inn H
(805) 933-5550. **$79-$89.** 134 N Mill St 93060. SR 126, exit 12 (10th St) northbound, 0.5 mi w, just s on Santa Barbara St, then just e. Int corridors. **Pets:** Medium. $10 one-time fee/pet. Designated rooms, service with restrictions, crate. SAVE [icons]

SCOTTS VALLEY

Best Western Inn Scotts Valley H
(831) 438-6666. **$89-$155.** 6020 Scotts Valley Dr 95066. SR 17, exit Granite Creek, just w. Ext corridors. **Pets:** Accepted.
SAVE [icons]

SELMA

Holiday Inn-Swan Court H
(559) 891-8000. **$96-$135.** 2950 Pea Soup Anderson Blvd 93662. SR 99, exit Floral Ave, just w. Int corridors. **Pets:** Accepted.
SAVE [icons]

Super 8 Selma/Fresno Area H
(559) 896-2800. **$70-$110.** 3142 S Highland Ave 93662. SR 99, exit Floral Ave. Int corridors. **Pets:** Accepted. SAVE [icons]

SHASTA LAKE

Bridge Bay Resort M
(530) 275-3021. **$85-$190, 3 day notice.** 10300 Bridge Bay Rd 96003. I-5, exit 690, just w. Ext corridors. **Pets:** Accepted.
SAVE [icons]

Fawndale Lodge & RV Resort M
(530) 275-8000. **$63-$115.** 15215 Fawndale Rd 96003. I-5, exit 689, exit Fawndale Rd; just e; 10 mi n of Redding; 1 mi s of Shasta Lake. Ext corridors. **Pets:** Accepted. SAVE [icons]

SIERRA CITY

Herrington's Sierra Pines M
(530) 862-1151. **$79-$140, 10 day notice.** 104 Main St 96125. 0.5 mi w on SR 49; 12 mi n of Downieville; center. Ext corridors. **Pets:** Other species. Supervision. SAVE [icons]

SIMI VALLEY

Extended StayAmerica-Los Angeles-Simi Valley H
(805) 584-8880. **$80-$100.** 2498 Stearns St 93063. SR 118, exit 28 (Stearns St), just s. Int corridors. **Pets:** Other species. $25 daily fee/room. Designated rooms, service with restrictions, crate. ASK [icons]

SMITH RIVER

Ship Ashore Resort M
(707) 487-3141. **$54-$105.** 12370 Hwy 101 N 95567. On US 101, 3.7 mi s of Oregon border. Ext corridors. **Pets:** Very small. Service with restrictions, supervision. [icons]

SOLEDAD

Valley Harvest Inn H
(831) 678-3833. **$89-$189.** 1155 Front St 93960. US 101, exit Soledad, just e. Ext/int corridors. **Pets:** Accepted. SAVE [icons]

SOLVANG

Meadowlark Inn M 🐾
(805) 688-4631. **Call for rates.** 2644 Mission Dr 93463. On SR 246, 1.6 mi e. Ext corridors. **Pets:** Dogs only. $100 deposit/pet, $25 daily fee/pet. Designated rooms, service with restrictions, supervision.
[icons]

Royal Copenhagen Inn M
(805) 688-5561. **$85-$275, 3 day notice.** 1579 Mission Dr 93463. On SR 246. Ext/int corridors. **Pets:** Large, other species. $20 daily fee/pet. Designated rooms, service with restrictions, supervision.
SAVE [icons]

Wine Valley Inn & Cottages H 🐾
(805) 688-2111. **$119-$459, 30 day notice.** 1564 Copenhagen Dr 93463. SR 246, just s on 5th St. Ext/int corridors. **Pets:** Other species. $25 daily fee/pet. Service with restrictions, supervision.
SAVE [icons]

SONORA

Aladdin Motor Inn H 🐾
(209) 533-4971. **$79-$87.** 14260 Mono Way (Hwy 108) 95370. On SR 108, 3.5 mi e. Ext/int corridors. **Pets:** Medium, other species. $15 one-time fee/room. Designated rooms, service with restrictions, supervision.
SAVE [icons]

Best Western Sonora Oaks H 🐾
(209) 533-4400. **$119-$139.** 19551 Hess Ave 95370. 3.5 mi e on SR 108. Ext/int corridors. **Pets:** Medium, dogs only. $25 daily fee/room. Designated rooms, service with restrictions, supervision.
SAVE [icons]

Inns of California-Sonora H 🐾
(209) 532-3633. **$90-$180.** 350 S Washington St 95370. 3 blks e of jct SR 49 and 108; downtown. Ext corridors. **Pets:** $100 deposit/room, $25 one-time fee/room. Designated rooms, service with restrictions, supervision. SAVE [icons]

Union Hill Inn BB
(209) 533-1494. **$150-$195, 3 day notice.** 21645 Parrotts Ferry Rd 95370. Jct SR 49 and Parrotts Ferry Rd; 3 mi n of downtown. Ext corridors. **Pets:** Accepted. ASK [icons]

STOCKTON

Clarion Inn & Suites H 🐾
(209) 931-3131. **$79.** 4219 E Waterloo Rd 95215. East of SR 99; jct SR 88. Int corridors. **Pets:** Small, dogs only. $25 daily fee/room. Designated rooms, service with restrictions, supervision.
SAVE [icons]

Comfort Inn H 🐾
(209) 478-4300. **$66-$77.** 2654 W March Ln 95207. I-5, exit March Ln, just e. Ext corridors. **Pets:** $20 one-time fee/room. Service with restrictions, crate. SAVE [icons]

Extended StayAmerica-Stockton-March Lane H
(209) 472-7588. **$85-$100.** 2844 W March Ln 95219. I-5, exit March Ln, just w. Int corridors. **Pets:** Other species. $25 daily fee/room. Designated rooms, service with restrictions, crate. ASK [icons]

Hilton Stockton H
(209) 957-9090. **$99-$189.** 2323 Grand Canal Blvd 95207. I-5, exit March Ln, 0.4 mi e. Int corridors. **Pets:** Accepted.
SAVE [icons]

WWW Howard Johnson Express Inn-Marina H
(209) 948-6151. **$65-$99.** 33 N Center St 95202. 1 blk n; w off El
Dorado St via Weber; SR 99, exit Wilson Way southbound; exit northbound, w via Mariposa Rd to Charter Way; I-5, exit downtown. Ext corridors. **Pets:** Small. $10 daily fee/pet. Designated rooms, no service,
supervision. (ASK) (X) (&M) 🛏 💻 🏊

WWW La Quinta Inn Stockton H ❀
(209) 952-7800. **$49-$119.** 2710 W March Ln 95219-6571. I-5, exit
March Ln, just w. Ext corridors. **Pets:** Medium, other species. Service with
restrictions, supervision. (ASK) (X) (&M) 🛏 💻 🏊

AAA WWWW Lexington Plaza Waterfront Hotel H
(209) 944-1140. **Call for rates.** 110 W Fremont St 95202. I-5, exit Fremont St, 0.5 mi e. Int corridors. **Pets:** Accepted.
(ECO) (SAVE) (X) (&M) 🛏 💻 🍴 🏊

WWWW Ramada Plaza Stockton H
(209) 474-3301. **Call for rates.** 111 E March Ln 95207. I-5, exit March
Ln, 2.5 mi e; corner of El Dorado St. Int corridors. **Pets:** Medium, other
species. $25 one-time fee/pet. Service with restrictions, supervision.
(X) (&M) 🛏 💻 🍴 🏊

AAA WWWW Residence Inn by Marriott H
(209) 472-9800. **$152-$186.** 3240 W March Ln 95219. I-5, exit March Ln,
0.5 mi w. Int corridors. **Pets:** Accepted.
(SAVE) (X) (&M) 🛏 💻 🏊 (X)

SUNNYVALE

AAA WWWW Larkspur Landing Sunnyvale H
(408) 733-1212. **$89-$269.** 748 N Mathilda Ave 94085. US 101, exit
Mathilda Ave, just s. Int corridors. **Pets:** Accepted. (SAVE) (X) (&M) 💻

AAA WWWW Maple Tree Inn H
(408) 720-9700. **$109-$169.** 711 E El Camino Real 94087. On SR 82;
between Fair Oaks and Wolfe Rd; 2.5 mi w of US 101. Int corridors.
Pets: Accepted. (SAVE) (X) (&M) 🛏 💻 🏊

WWW Quality Inn-Sunnyvale H
(408) 744-1100. **Call for rates.** 1280 Persian Dr 94089. US 101, exit
Lawrence Expwy N, 1 mi n to Persian Dr, then 0.3 mi w. Int corridors.
Pets: Accepted. (X) (&M) 🛏 💻 🏊

AAA WWW Ramada Inn-Silicon Valley H
(408) 245-5330. **$99-$159.** 1217 Wildwood Ave 94089. US 101, exit
Lawrence Expwy N, just n. Ext corridors. **Pets:** Small. $200 deposit/room,
$15 daily fee/room. Service with restrictions, supervision.
(SAVE) (X) (&M) 🛏 💻 🍴 🏊

WWWW Residence Inn by Marriott H
(408) 720-1000. **$224-$274.** 750 Lakeway Dr 94085. US 101, exit
Lawrence Expwy S, e on Oakmead. Ext corridors. **Pets:** Accepted.
(X) (&M) 🛏 💻 🏊 (X)

WWWW Residence Inn by Marriott H ❀
(408) 720-8893. **$224-$274.** 1080 Stewart Dr 94085. US 101, exit
Lawrence Expwy S, w on Duane Ave W. Ext corridors. **Pets:** Other species. $100 one-time fee/room. Service with restrictions.
(X) (&M) 🛏 💻 🏊 (X)

AAA WWWW Staybridge Suites H
(408) 745-1515. **$102-$180.** 900 Hamlin Ct 94089. SR 237, exit Mathilda
Ave S, w on Ross Dr. Ext corridors. **Pets:** Accepted.
(SAVE) (X) (&M) 🛏 💻 🏊 (X)

**WWWW TownePlace Suites by Marriott Sunnyvale/Mountain
View** H
(408) 733-4200. **$189-$199.** 606 S Bernardo Ave 94087. SR 85, exit SR
82, 0.5 mi s. Int corridors. **Pets:** Accepted. (X) (&M) 💻

AAA WWW Vagabond Inn M
(408) 734-4607. **$59-$259.** 816 Ahwanee Ave 94086. US 101, exit
Mathilda Ave S, then s. Ext corridors. **Pets:** Other species. $10 daily fee/
pet. Service with restrictions, supervision. (SAVE) (X) (&M) 🛏 💻 🏊

SUSANVILLE

WWW America's Best Inn M
(530) 257-4522. **$45-$95.** 2705 Main St 96130. From jct SR 36 and 139,
0.7 mi se on SR 36. Ext corridors. **Pets:** Accepted. (X) 🛏

AAA WWW WWWW River Inn Motel M
(530) 257-6051. **$45-$75.** 1710 Main St 96130. From jct SR 36 and 139,
just se on SR 36. Ext corridors. **Pets:** Accepted. (SAVE) (X) 🛏 🍴

WWWW The Roseberry House Bed & Breakfast BB
(530) 257-5675. **$110-$135, 5 day notice.** 609 North St 96130. From jct
SR 36 and 139, 0.7 mi nw to N Lassen St, then just ne. Int corridors.
Pets: Other species. $10 daily fee/pet. No service, supervision. (X) (📠)

AAA WWW WWWW Super 8 M ❀
(530) 257-2782. **$65-$75.** 2975 Johnstonville Rd 96130. From jct SR 36
and 139, 0.9 mi se on SR 139. Ext corridors. **Pets:** Medium, other species. $10 daily fee/pet. Designated rooms, service with restrictions, super-
vision. (SAVE) (X) 🛏 💻 🏊

TEHACHAPI

AAA WWW Best Western Mountain Inn M
(661) 822-5591. **$80-$93.** 418 W Tehachapi Blvd 93561. SR 58, exit 148
(SR 202), 1 mi s, then e. Ext corridors. **Pets:** Accepted.
(SAVE) (X) 🛏 💻 🏊

WWW La Quinta Inn & Suites M ❀
(661) 823-8000. **$69-$149.** 500 Steuber Rd 93561. SR 58, exit 151
(Monolith/Tehachapi Blvd), just s. Int corridors. **Pets:** Medium, other species. Service with restrictions, supervision. (ASK) (X) 🛏 💻 🏊

TEMECULA

WWW Extended StayAmerica-Temecula-Wine Country M
(951) 587-8881. **$75-$100.** 27622 Jefferson Ave 92590. I-15, exit 61 (SR
79 N), just w on Winchester Rd, then 0.4 mi s. Int corridors. **Pets:** Other
species. $25 daily fee/room. Designated rooms, service with restrictions,
crate. (ASK) (X) 🛏 💻

AAA WWWW La Quinta Inn & Suites Temecula H ❀
(951) 296-1003. **$89-$149.** 27330 Jefferson Ave 92590. I-15, exit 61 (SR
79 N), just w on Winchester Rd, then just n; on east side of Rancho
Temecula Plaza. Int corridors. **Pets:** Medium, other species. Service with
restrictions, supervision. (SAVE) (X) 🛏 💻 🏊

WWW Quality Inn Temecula Wine Country M
(951) 296-3788. **$69-$199.** 27338 Jefferson Ave 92590. I-15, exit 61 (SR
79 N), just w, then just n; on east side of Rancho Temecula Plaza. Ext
corridors. **Pets:** Dogs only. $20 daily fee/pet. Designated rooms, service
with restrictions. (ASK) (X) 🛏 💻

AAA WWWW Temecula Creek Inn H
(951) 694-1000. **$119-$249, 3 day notice.** 44501 Rainbow Canyon Rd
92592. I-15, exit 58 (SR 79 S), 0.8 mi e to Pechanga Pkwy, then 0.3 mi
se. Ext corridors. **Pets:** Accepted. (SAVE) (X) 🛏 💻 🍴 🏊 (X)

THOUSAND OAKS

WWW La Quinta Inn & Suites M ❀
(805) 499-5910. **$59-$139.** 1320 Newbury Rd 91320. US 101, exit 46
(Ventu Park Rd), just se. Ext corridors. **Pets:** Medium, other species.
Service with restrictions, supervision. (ASK) (X) (&M) 🛏 💻 🏊

WWW Motel 6 #1360 Thousand Oaks M
(805) 499-0711. **$55-$65.** 1516 Newbury Rd 91320. US 101, exit 46
(Ventu Park Rd), just w, then just n. Ext corridors. **Pets:** Other species.
Service with restrictions, supervision. (X) 🏊

AAA WWW Premier Inns M
(805) 499-0755. **$54.** 2434 W Hillcrest Dr 91320. US 101, exit 47B (Bor-
chard Rd), just e, then just n. Ext corridors. **Pets:** Accepted.
(SAVE) (X) 🛏 🏊

▼▼▼ Quality Inn & Suites [M]
(805) 495-7011. **$79-$129, 3 day notice.** 12 Conejo Blvd 91360. US 101, exit 44 (Moorpark Rd), just n to Thousand Oaks Blvd, then just w. Ext/int corridors. **Pets:** Accepted. [ASK] [X] [⊟] [▦] ❀

▼▼▼ TownePlace Suites by Marriott [H] 🐾
(805) 499-3111. **$148-$180.** 1712 Newbury Rd 91320. US 101, exit 46 (Ventu Park Rd), just w, then just n. Int corridors. **Pets:** Other species. $75 one-time fee/room. Service with restrictions. [X] [⊟] [▦] [🏊]

THOUSAND PALMS
▼▼ Red Roof Inn [M]
(760) 343-1381. **Call for rates.** 72-215 Varner Rd 92276. I-10, exit 130 (Ramon Rd), just n, then just w. Ext corridors. **Pets:** Large. Service with restrictions, crate. [X] [⊟] [▦] [🏊]

THREE RIVERS
AAA▷ ▼▼▼ Americas Best Value Inn–Lazy J Ranch [M]
(559) 561-4449. **$100-$115, 3 day notice.** 39625 Sierra Dr 93271. SR 198, 3 mi sw of town center. Ext corridors. **Pets:** Other species. $10 one-time fee/pet. Service with restrictions, supervision.

[SAVE] [X] [⊟] [▦] [🏊] [X]

AAA▷ ▼▼▼ Buckeye Tree Lodge [M]
(559) 561-5900. **$78-$143, 7 day notice.** 46000 Sierra Dr 93271. SR 198, 6 mi ne of town center; 0.5 mi sw of entrance to Sequoia National Park. Ext corridors. **Pets:** Other species. $10 daily fee/pet. Service with restrictions, supervision. [SAVE] [X] [⊟] [▦] [🏊]

AAA▷ ▼▼▼ Comfort Inn & Suites [M]
(559) 561-9000. **$70-$180.** 40820 Sierra Dr 93271. SR 198, 1.5 mi sw of town center. Ext/int corridors. **Pets:** Small. $35 one-time fee/pet. Designated rooms, service with restrictions, supervision.

[SAVE] [X] [⅏] [⊟] [▦] [🏊] [X]

▼▼▼ Gateway Lodge [M]
(559) 561-4133. **$79-$179, 3 day notice.** 45978 Sierra Dr 93271. SR 198, 6 mi ne of town center; 0.5 mi sw of entrance to Sequoia National Park. Ext corridors. **Pets:** Other species. $15 one-time fee/pet. Service with restrictions. [ASK] [X] [⊟] [▦] [🍴] [Z]

▼▼▼ Sequoia River Dance Bed & Breakfast [BB]
(559) 561-4411. **$95-$135, 10 day notice.** 40534 Cherokee Oaks Dr 93271. SR 198, 2 mi sw of town center, then 0.3 mi e. Int corridors. **Pets:** Other species. $10 daily fee/pet. Supervision. [ASK] [X] [W] [Z]

AAA▷ ▼▼▼ Sequoia Village Inn [CA]
(559) 561-3652. **$77-$305, 7 day notice.** 45971 Sierra Dr 93271. SR 198, 6 mi ne of town center; 0.5 mi sw of entrance to Sequoia National Park. Ext corridors. **Pets:** Other species. $10 daily fee/pet. Service with restrictions, supervision. [SAVE] [X] [⊟] [▦] [🏊] [Z]

AAA▷ ▼▼▼ Western Holiday Lodge Three Rivers [M]
(559) 561-4119. **$59-$199.** 40105 Sierra Dr 93271. SR 198, 2 mi sw of town center. Ext corridors. **Pets:** $15 daily fee/pet. Designated rooms, service with restrictions, supervision. [SAVE] [X] [⊟] [▦] [🏊] [X]

TRACY
AAA▷ ▼▼▼ Best Western Luxury Inn [H]
(209) 832-0271. **$79-$90.** 811 W Clover Rd 95376. I-205, exit Central Tracy, just s, then just w. Int corridors. **Pets:** Medium, other species. $10 daily fee/pet. Service with restrictions, supervision.

[SAVE] [X] [⅏] [⊟] [▦] [🏊]

AAA▷ ▼▼▼ Quality Inn-Tracy [H]
(209) 835-1335. **$60-$76.** 3511 N Tracy Blvd 95376. I-205, exit Central Tracy/Tracy Blvd, just s. Ext/int corridors. **Pets:** Medium. $15 daily fee/room. Service with restrictions, supervision.

[SAVE] [X] [⅏] [⊟] [▦] [🏊]

TRINIDAD
AAA▷ ▼ Bishop Pine Lodge [CA]
(707) 677-3314. **Call for rates.** 1481 Patrick's Point Dr 95570. US 101, exit Seawood Dr, just w, then 0.8 mi s. Ext corridors. **Pets:** Accepted.
[SAVE] [X] [⊟] [▦] [🐾]

AAA▷ ▼▼▼ Emerald Forest of Trinidad [CA]
(707) 677-3554. **$120-$185, 5 day notice.** 753 Patrick's Point Dr 95570. US 101, exit Trinidad, just w on Main St, then 0.7 mi n. Ext corridors. **Pets:** Accepted. [SAVE] [X] [⊟] [▦] [X] [🐾] [Z]

AAA▷ ▼▼▼ Trinidad Inn [CA] ❀
(707) 677-3349. **$110-$180.** 1170 Patrick's Point Dr 95570. US 101, exit Trinidad, just w on Main St, then 1.3 mi n. Ext corridors. **Pets:** Dogs only. $10 daily fee/pet. Supervision. [SAVE] [X] [⊟] [▦]

TULARE
AAA▷ ▼▼▼ Best Western Town & Country Lodge [M]
(559) 688-7537. **$85-$200.** 1051 N Blackstone St 93274. SR 99, exit 88 (Prosperity Ave/Blackstone St), just w. Int corridors. **Pets:** Medium. $20 one-time fee/room. Service with restrictions, supervision.

[SAVE] [X] [⊟] [▦] [🏊]

▼▼▼ Charter Inn & Suites [H] 🐾
(559) 685-9500. **$89-$199.** 1016 E Prosperity Ave 93274. SR 99, exit 88 (Prosperity Ave/Blackstone St), just e. Int corridors. **Pets:** Large. $100 deposit/room, $10 daily fee/pet. [ASK] [X] [⅏] [⊟] [▦] [🏊]

▼▼ La Quinta Inn & Suites [H] ❀
(559) 685-8900. **$99-$179.** 1500 Cherry Ct 93274. SR 99, exit 88 (Prosperity Ave/Blackstone St), just w. Int corridors. **Pets:** Medium, other species. Service with restrictions, supervision. [ASK] [X] [⊟] [▦] [🏊]

AAA▷ ▼▼▼ Quality Inn [M]
(559) 686-3432. **$70-$190.** 1010 E Prosperity Ave 93274. SR 99, exit 88 (Prosperity Ave/Blackstone St), just e. Int corridors. **Pets:** Small, dogs only. $15 daily fee/pet. Service with restrictions, supervision.
[SAVE] [X] [⊟] [▦] [🏊] [X]

TURLOCK
AAA▷ ▼▼▼▼ Best Western Orchard Inn [H]
(209) 667-2827. **$79-$99, 14 day notice.** 5025 N Golden State Blvd 95382. SR 99, exit Taylor Rd, just e. Ext corridors. **Pets:** Other species. $25 one-time fee/room. Service with restrictions.
[SAVE] [X] [⅏] [⊟] [▦] [🏊]

AAA▷ ▼▼ Travelodge [H]
(209) 668-3400. **$59-$109.** 201 W Glenwood Ave 95380. SR 99, exit Lander W. Ext corridors. **Pets:** $10 daily fee/pet. Service with restrictions, supervision. [SAVE] [X] [⅏] [⊟] [▦] [🏊]

TWAIN HARTE
AAA▷ ▼▼▼▼ McCaffrey House Bed & Breakfast Inn [BB]
(209) 586-0757. **$139-$169, 7 day notice.** 23251 Hwy 108 95383. 0.5 mi on SR 108; just beyond 4000' elevation marker. Int corridors. **Pets:** Other species. $25 daily fee/pet. Designated rooms, service with restrictions, supervision. [SAVE] [X]

TWENTYNINE PALMS
AAA▷ ▼▼▼ Roughley Manor [BB]
(760) 367-3238. **$135-$160, 3 day notice.** 74744 Joe Davis Rd 92277. SR 62, 0.7 mi n on Utah Tr, 0.4 mi e on Joe Davis Rd, then just n. Ext/int corridors. **Pets:** Designated rooms, service with restrictions, supervision. [SAVE] [X] [⊟] [▦] [🏊] [Z]

▼▼ Sunnyvale Garden Suites Hotel [CO]
(760) 361-3939. **$120.** 73843 Sunnyvale Dr 92277. SR 62, 0.7 mi n on Adobe Rd, just e on S Slope, just n on Ocotillo, then just e. Ext corridors. **Pets:** Accepted. [ASK] [X] [⊟] [▦] [X]

UNION CITY

▼▼ ▼▼ **Extended StayAmerica-Union City-Dyer St** 🅷
(510) 441-9616. **$82-$97.** 31950 Dyer St 94587. I-880, exit Alvarado-Niles Rd, just w, then just n; in Union Landing Shopping Center. Int corridors. **Pets:** Other species. $25 daily fee/room. Designated rooms, service with restrictions, crate. (A$K) ⊠ 🛆 📶 🖵 ⊠

VACAVILLE

🔷🔷🔷 ▼▼▼ **Best Western Heritage Inn** 🅼
(707) 448-8453. **$85-$115.** 1420 E Monte Vista Ave 95688. I-80, exit Monte Vista Ave, just nw. Ext corridors. **Pets:** Accepted.
(SAVE) ⊠ 🛆 📶 🖵 ⊠

▼▼ ▼▼ **Extended StayAmerica-Sacramento-Vacaville** 🅷
(707) 469-1371. **$70-$85.** 799 Orange Dr 95687. I-80, exit Leisure Town Rd, just s; just e of I-505 interchange. Int corridors. **Pets:** Other species. $25 daily fee/room. Designated rooms, service with restrictions, crate.
(A$K) ⊠ 🛆 📶 🖵

▼▼▼▼ **Residence Inn by Marriott** 🅷
(707) 469-0300. **$179-$189.** 360 Orange Dr 95687. I-80, exit Orange Dr eastbound, 0.5 mi ne; exit Monte Vista westbound, freeway overpass to E Nut Tree Pkwy, then just ne. Int corridors. **Pets:** Accepted.
⊠ 🛆 📶 🖵 ⊠ ⊠

VALLEJO

🔷🔷🔷 ▼▼▼ **Best Western Inn & Suites at Discovery Kingdom** 🅷
(707) 554-9655. **$69-$129.** 1596 Fairgrounds Dr 94589. I-80, exit SR 37 (Marine World Pkwy) N, 0.3 mi w. Int corridors. **Pets:** Accepted.
(SAVE) ⊠ 🛆 📶 🖵 ⊠

▼▼▼ **Courtyard by Marriott** 🅷
(707) 644-1200. **$119-$169.** 1000 Fairgrounds Dr 94589. I-80, exit SR 37 (Marine World Pkwy), 0.3 mi n. Int corridors. **Pets:** Accepted.
⊠ 🛆 📶 🖵 🍴 ⊠

🔷🔷 ▼▼ **Ramada Inn** 🅷
(707) 643-2700. **$62-$159.** 1000 Admiral Callaghan Ln 94591. I-80, exit Columbus Pkwy, 0.5 mi w. Ext corridors. **Pets:** Medium, other species. $25 one-time fee/room. Designated rooms, service with restrictions, supervision. (A$K) ⊠ 🛆 📶 🖵 ⊠

VENTURA

▼▼▼ **Crowne Plaza Ventura Beach Resort** 🅷
(805) 648-2100. **$89-$199.** 450 E Harbor Blvd 93001. US 101, exit 70A (California St) northbound, just s; exit 71 (Main St) southbound, 0.5 mi e to California St, then just s. Int corridors. **Pets:** Accepted.
(A$K) ⊠ 📶 🖵 🍴 ⊠

🔷🔷🔷 ▼▼▼ **Four Points by Sheraton Ventura Harbortown** 🅷
(805) 658-1212. **$115-$350, 3 day notice.** 1050 Schooner Dr 93001. US 101, exit 68 (Seaward Ave), just w, then 1.5 mi s on Harbor Blvd; at Ventura Harbor. Ext corridors. **Pets:** Other species. $75 one-time fee/room. Designated rooms, service with restrictions, supervision.
(SAVE) ⊠ 📶 🖵 🍴 ⊠ ⊠

▼▼▼ **La Quinta Inn Ventura** 🅼 🐾
(805) 658-6200. **$49-$139.** 5818 Valentine Rd 93003. US 101, exit 64 (Victoria Ave), just s, then just n. Ext/int corridors. **Pets:** Medium, other species. Service with restrictions, supervision.
(A$K) ⊠ 🛆 📶 🖵 ⊠

▼▼▼ **Marriott Ventura Beach Hotel** 🅷 🐾
(805) 643-6000. **$169-$219.** 2055 E Harbor Blvd 93001. US 101, exit 68 (Seaward Ave), just w, then 0.5 mi n. Int corridors. **Pets:** $75 one-time fee/room. Service with restrictions, supervision.
(ECO) ⊠ 🛆 📶 🖵 🍴 ⊠

▼▼ ▼▼ **Vagabond Inn Ventura** 🅼
(805) 648-5371. **$79-$249.** 756 E Thompson Blvd 93001. US 101, exit 70A (California St) northbound, just n, then just e; exit 70A (Ventura Ave) southbound, 0.6 mi e. Ext corridors. **Pets:** Accepted.
(A$K) ⊠ 📶 🖵 🍴 ⊠

VICTORVILLE

▼▼▼ **Comfort Suites** 🅷
(760) 245-6777. **$79-$139.** 12281 Mariposa Rd 92392. I-15, exit 147 (Bear Valley Rd), just e, then just n. Int corridors. **Pets:** Other species. $15 one-time fee/pet. Designated rooms, service with restrictions.
(A$K) ⊠ 🛆 📶 🖵 ⊠

▼▼▼ **Hawthorn Suites** 🅷 🐾
(760) 949-4700. **$70-$130.** 11750 Dunia Rd 92392. I-15, exit 147 (Bear Valley Rd), just w, just s on Amargosa Rd, then 0.3 mi w. Int corridors. **Pets:** Other species. $5 daily fee/room. Service with restrictions, supervision. (A$K) ⊠ 🛆 📶 🖵 ⊠ ⊠

🔷🔷🔷 ▼▼▼ **Hotel Extended Studio** 🅷
(760) 843-3800. **$99-$159.** 14786 Monarch Blvd 92395. I-15, exit 147 (Bear Valley Rd), just e to Mariposa Rd, just n, then just e. Int corridors. **Pets:** Accepted. (SAVE) ⊠ 📶 🖵 ⊠ ⊠

▼▼▼ **Quality Inn & Suites Green Tree** 🅷
(760) 245-3461. **$69-$129.** 14173 Green Tree Blvd 92392. I-15, exit 150 (SR 18/ W Palmdale Rd), just e. Ext corridors. **Pets:** Accepted.
(A$K) ⊠ 📶 🖵 ⊠

🔷🔷🔷 ▼▼▼ **Travelodge Victorville** 🅼
(760) 241-7200. **$59-$89.** 12175 Mariposa Rd 92395. I-15, exit 147 (Bear Valley Rd), just e, then just n. Ext corridors. **Pets:** Medium, dogs only. $10 one-time fee/room. No service, supervision. (SAVE) ⊠ 📶 🖵 ⊠

VISALIA

▼▼▼ **Ben Maddox House** 🅱🅱
(559) 739-0721. **$140-$185, 7 day notice.** 601 N Encina St 93291. SR 198, exit 107A (Central Visalia/SR 63 N), 0.4 mi n to Murray St, just w, then just n. Ext/int corridors. **Pets:** Accepted.
(A$K) ⊠ 📶 🖵 ⊠ ⊠

🔷🔷🔷 ▼▼▼ **Holiday Inn Hotel & Conference Center** 🅷
(559) 651-5000. **$110-$149.** 9000 W Airport Dr 93277. SR 198, exit 102 (Plaza Dr), then just s. Int corridors. **Pets:** Accepted.
(SAVE) ⊠ 🛆 📶 🖵 🍴 ⊠

🔷🔷🔷 ▼▼▼ **Lamp Liter Inn** 🅼
(559) 732-4511. **$79-$139.** 3300 W Mineral King Ave 93291. SR 198, exit 105B (SR 63 S/Mooney Blvd) westbound, 0.5 mi w; exit eastbound, just n, then 0.5 mi w. Ext corridors. **Pets:** Accepted.
(SAVE) ⊠ 📶 🖵 🍴 ⊠

▼▼▼ **La Quinta Inn & Suites** 🅷 🐾
(559) 739-9800. **$79-$154.** 5438 W Cypress Ave 93277. SR 198, exit 104 (Akers St), just s, then just w. Int corridors. **Pets:** Medium, other species. Service with restrictions, supervision. (A$K) ⊠ 📶 🖵 ⊠

▼▼ ▼▼ **Rodeway Inn** 🅼
(559) 732-4561. **Call for rates.** 623 W Main St 93291. SR 198, exit 105B (SR 63 S/Mooney Blvd), just n, then 0.9 mi e. Ext corridors. **Pets:** Accepted. ⊠ 🖵 ⊠ ⊠

VISTA

🔷🔷🔷 ▼▼▼ **Americas Best Value Inn & Suites** 🅷
(760) 726-2900. **$59-$189.** 330 Mar Vista Dr 92083. SR 78, exit Mar Vista Dr, just e. Ext corridors. **Pets:** Small, dogs only. $10 daily fee/pet. Designated rooms, service with restrictions, supervision.
(SAVE) ⊠ 📶 🖵 ⊠ ⊠

▼▼▼ **La Quinta Inn San Diego (Vista)** 🅼 🐾
(760) 727-8180. **$48-$159.** 630 Sycamore Ave 92083. SR 78, exit Sycamore Ave, just sw. Ext/int corridors. **Pets:** Medium, other species. Service with restrictions, supervision. (A$K) ⊠ 📶 🖵 ⊠

WALNUT CREEK

🔷🔷🔷 ▼▼▼ **Holiday Inn Express Walnut Creek** 🅷
(925) 932-3332. **$79-$169.** 2730 N Main St 94597. I-680, exit N Main St, just n. Int corridors. **Pets:** Dogs only. $25 one-time fee/room. Service with restrictions, supervision. (SAVE) ⊠ 🛆 📶 🖵 ⊠

WATSONVILLE

Best Western Rose Garden Inn H
(831) 724-3367. **$90-$200.** 740 Freedom Blvd 95076. On SR 152. Ext corridors. **Pets:** Large. $20 daily fee/pet. Designated rooms, service with restrictions, supervision. [SAVE] [X] [B] [C] [≈]

Comfort Inn Watsonville H
(831) 728-2300. **$70-$259.** 112 Airport Blvd 95019. SR 1, exit Airport Blvd, 1 mi e. Int corridors. **Pets:** Medium. $15 daily fee/pet. Designated rooms, service with restrictions, supervision. [SAVE] [X] [B] [C]

Red Roof Inn H
(831) 740-4520. **Call for rates.** 1620 W Beach St 95076. SR 1, exit Riverside Dr (SR 129), just w. Int corridors. **Pets:** Large. Service with restrictions, crate. [SAVE] [X] [&M] [B] [C] [≈]

WEAVERVILLE

49er Gold Country Inn M
(530) 623-4937. **$50-$120, 3 day notice.** 718 Main St (Hwy 299) 96093. Jct SR 3 and 299, just se on SR 299. Ext corridors.
Pets: Accepted. [SAVE] [X] [B] [C] [≈]

Motel Trinity M
(530) 623-2129. **$70-$95, 3 day notice.** 1270 Main St 96093. Jct SR 3 and 299, 0.7 mi se on SR 299. Ext corridors. **Pets:** Dogs only. $5 daily fee/room. Service with restrictions, supervision. [SAVE] [X] [B] [C] [≈]

Red Hill Motel CA
(530) 623-4331. **$42-$90, 7 day notice.** Red Hill Rd 96093. Jct SR 3 and 299, just nw on SR 299, then just n. Ext corridors. **Pets:** $5 one-time fee/pet. Service with restrictions, supervision. [X] [B] [C]

Weaverville Victorian Inn M
(530) 623-4432. **$79-$169.** 2051 Main St 96093. Jct SR 3 and 299, 1.5 mi se on SR 299. Ext corridors. **Pets:** Accepted.
[ASK] [X] [B] [C] [Y] [≈]

WEED

Comfort Inn H
(530) 938-1982. **$79-$159.** 1844 Shastina Dr 96094. I-5, exit 745 (S Weed Blvd), just e, then just n. Int corridors. **Pets:** Dogs only. $10 daily fee/pet. Designated rooms, service with restrictions, supervision.
[SAVE] [X] [B] [C]

Quality Inn & Suites H 🐾
(530) 938-1308. **Call for rates.** 1830 Black Butte Dr 96094. I-5, exit 745 (S Weed Blvd), just ne. Int corridors. **Pets:** Large, other species. $15 daily fee/pet. Designated rooms, service with restrictions, supervision.
[SAVE] [X] [B] [C]

Sis-Q-Inn Motel M
(530) 938-4194. **$65-$150.** 1825 Shastina Dr 96094. I-5, exit 745 (S Weed Blvd), just e, then just n. Int corridors. **Pets:** Small. $10 daily fee/pet. Service with restrictions, supervision. [SAVE] [X] [B]

WESTLAKE VILLAGE

Four Seasons Hotel Westlake Village H
(818) 575-3000. **$235-$4500.** Two Dole Dr 91362. US 101, exit Lindero Canyon Rd, just e, then just n on Via Colinas. Int corridors.
Pets: Accepted. [SAVE] [X] [&M] [B] [C] [Y] [≈]

Residence Inn by Marriott H 🐾
(818) 707-4411. **$143-$175.** 30950 Russell Ranch Rd 91362. US 10, exit 39 (Lindero Canyon Rd), just e, then just s. Int corridors. **Pets:** Other species. $100 one-time fee/room. [X] [B] [C] [≈] [X]

WESTLEY

Econo Lodge M
(209) 894-3900. **$55-$95, 3 day notice.** 7100 McCracken Rd 95387. I-5, exit Westley, just e. Ext corridors. **Pets:** $10 daily fee/pet. No service, supervision. [SAVE] [X] [B] [C] [≈]

Holiday Inn Express H 🐾
(209) 894-8940. **$74-$119.** 4525 Howard Rd 95387. I-5, exit Westley, just e. Int corridors. **Pets:** Large, other species. $25 one-time fee/room. Designated rooms, service with restrictions, supervision.
[SAVE] [X] [B] [C] [≈]

WESTMORLAND

Americas Best Value Inn M
(760) 351-7100. **Call for rates.** 351 W Main St 92281. On SR 86. Int corridors. **Pets:** Accepted. [X] [B] [C] [≈]

WEST SACRAMENTO

Extended StayAmerica-Sacramento-West Sacramento H
(916) 371-1270. **$80-$95.** 795 Stillwater Rd 95605. I-80, exit Reed Ave, just n, just w, then just s. Int corridors. **Pets:** Other species. $25 daily fee/room. Designated rooms, service with restrictions, crate.
[ASK] [X] [B] [C]

Ramada Inn & Plaza Harbor Conference Center H
(916) 371-2100. **$79-$109.** 1250 Halyard Dr 95691. I-80 business route (Capital City Frwy), exit Harbour Blvd, just s. Ext/int corridors.
Pets: Medium. $20 one-time fee/pet. Service with restrictions, supervision.
[SAVE] [X] [&M] [B] [C] [Y] [≈] [X]

Rodeway Inn Capitol M
(916) 371-6983. **$55-$99.** 817 W Capitol Ave 95691. Business Rt I-80 (Capital City Frwy), exit Jefferson Blvd, 0.3 mi n, then just e. Ext corridors. **Pets:** Small, dogs only. $10 one-time fee/pet. Service with restrictions, supervision. [SAVE] [X] [B] [C]

WILLIAMS

Granzella's Inn M
(530) 473-3310. **$95-$135.** 391 6th St 95987. I-5, exit 577 (Williams), 0.5 mi w, then just n. Int corridors. **Pets:** Other species. $20 daily fee/room. Service with restrictions, supervision.
[SAVE] [X] [&M] [B] [C] [Y] [≈]

Quality Inn M
(530) 473-2381. **$79-$149.** 400 C St 95987. I-5, exit 577 (Williams), just w on E St (SR 20 business route), just n on 4th St; at 76 gas station, then just e. Ext corridors. **Pets:** $10 daily fee/pet. Service with restrictions, supervision. [SAVE] [X] [&M] [B] [C] [≈]

Ramada H
(530) 473-5120. **Call for rates.** 374 Ruggieri Way 95987. I-5, exit 577 (Williams), just e. Int corridors. **Pets:** $10 one-time fee/pet. Service with restrictions, supervision. [SAVE] [X] [&M] [B] [C]

Stage Stop Inn M
(530) 473-2281. **$45-$55.** 330 7th St 95987. I-5, exit 577 (Williams), just w on E St (SR 20 business route), then just n. Ext corridors.
Pets: Accepted. [SAVE] [X] [B] [C] [≈]

Traveler's Inn M
(530) 473-5387. **$38-$60.** 215 7th St 95987. I-5, exit 577 (Williams), just w on E St (SR 20 business route), then 0.3 mi n. Ext corridors.
Pets: Accepted. [SAVE] [X] [B] [C]

WILLOW CREEK

Bigfoot Motel M
(530) 629-2142. **$75-$160, 5 day notice.** 39039 Hwy 299 95573. On SR 299; just e of SR 96; center. Ext corridors. **Pets:** Accepted.
[SAVE] [X] [B] [≈]

WILLOWS

Baymont Inns & Suites Willows H
(530) 934-9700. **$65-$99.** 199 N Humboldt Ave 95988. I-5, exit 603 (SR 162 Willows/Oroville), just e, then s. Int corridors. **Pets:** Accepted.
[SAVE] [X] [B] [C] [≈]

AAA' ▼▼ Days Inn M
(530) 934-4444. **$60-$150.** 475 N Humboldt Ave 95988. I-5, exit 603 (SR 162 Willows/Oroville), just e, then just n. Ext corridors. **Pets:** Accepted.
[SAVE] [X] [&M] [▯] [▯] [≈]

AAA' ▼▼ Economy Inn M
(530) 934-4224. **$55-$80, 3 day notice.** 435 N Tehama St 95988. I-5, exit 603 (SR 162 Willows/Oroville), 1 mi e, then just n. Ext corridors. **Pets:** Small. $7 daily fee/pet. Designated rooms, service with restrictions, supervision. [SAVE] [X] [▯]

AAA' ▼▼▼ Holiday Inn Express Willows H
(530) 934-8900. **$99-$139.** 545 N Humboldt Ave 95988. I-5, exit 603 (Willows/Oroville SR 162), just e, then just n. Int corridors.
Pets: Accepted. [SAVE] [X] [&M] [▯] [▯] [≈]

AAA' ▼▼ Motel 6 #4273 M
(530) 934-7026. **$49-$99.** 452 N Humboldt Ave 95988. I-5, exit 603 (SR 162 Willows/Oroville), just e, then just n. Ext corridors. **Pets:** Other species. Service with restrictions, supervision. [SAVE] [X] [▯] [≈]

AAA' ▼▼ Super 8 of Willows H
(530) 934-2871. **$54-$148.** 457 Humboldt Ave 95988. I-5, exit 603 (SR 162/Willows/Oroville), just e, then just n. Int corridors. **Pets:** Accepted.
[SAVE] [X] [▯] [≈]

WINE COUNTRY AREA

ALBION

▼▼▼ Fensalden Inn BB
(707) 937-4042. **$139-$253, 7 day notice.** 33810 Navarro Ridge Rd 95410. 1.5 mi s on SR 1, 0.5 mi e. Ext/int corridors. **Pets:** Dogs only. $50 one-time fee/room. Designated rooms, supervision.
[ASK] [X] [▯] [▯] [K] [W] [Z]

CALISTOGA

AAA' ▼▼▼ Brannan Cottage Inn BB ❀
(707) 942-4200. **$165-$255.** 109 Wapoo Ave 94515. At Lincoln Ave. Ext corridors. **Pets:** Other species. $100 deposit/room, $25 daily fee/room. Designated rooms, service with restrictions, crate. [SAVE] [X] [▯] [Z]

AAA' ▼▼▼▼ Chelsea Garden Inn BB ❀
(707) 942-0948. **$155-$305, 14 day notice.** 1443 Second St 94515. Just n of Lincoln Ave. Ext/int corridors. **Pets:** Other species. $25 daily fee/pet. Designated rooms, crate. [SAVE] [X] [&M] [▯] [▯] [≈] [Z]

▼▼▼▼ Garnett Creek Inn BB
(707) 942-9797. **$108-$325, 7 day notice.** 1139 Lincoln Ave 94515. On SR 29. Int corridors. **Pets:** Accepted. [ASK] [X] [&M] [▯]

CLOVERDALE

AAA' ▼▼▼ Old Crocker Inn BB
(707) 894-4000. **$130-$245, 8 day notice.** 1126 Old Crocker Inn Rd 95425. US 101, exit Citrus Fair Dr, just e, 0.5 mi n on Asti Rd, 0.8 mi e on Crocker Rd 3.8 mi s on River Rd, 1.1 mi e on Asti Ridge Rd, then just n. Ext corridors. **Pets:** Dogs only. Designated rooms, service with restrictions, supervision. [SAVE] [X] [≈] [Z]

FORT BRAGG

▼▼ Anchor Lodge M
(707) 964-0569. **$45-$100.** 32260 N Harbor Dr 95437. SR 1, exit N Harbor Dr, 1.5 mi e; at Silver's at the Wharf. Ext/int corridors.
Pets: Accepted. [ASK] [X] [▯] [▯] [K]

AAA' ▼▼▼ Beachcomber Motel M ❀
(707) 964-2402. **$119-$269, 3 day notice.** 1111 N Main St 95437. 1 mi n on SR 1. Ext corridors. **Pets:** Other species. $20 daily fee/pet. Designated rooms, supervision. [SAVE] [X] [▯] [▯] [K]

AAA' ▼▼▼ Beach House Inn M ❀
(707) 961-1700. **$69-$250.** 100 Pudding Creek Rd 95437. 0.7 mi n on SR 1. Int corridors. **Pets:** Dogs only. $20 daily fee/pet. Service with restrictions, supervision. [SAVE] [X] [▯] [▯] [K]

▼▼ Coast Inn and Spa M
(707) 964-2852. **$65-$279.** 18661 N Hwy 1 95437. 0.3 mi s of SR 20. Ext corridors. **Pets:** Accepted. [ASK] [X] [▯] [▯] [K]

AAA' ▼▼▼ Emerald Dolphin Inn & Mini Golf H ❀
(707) 964-6699. **$63-$200, 7 day notice.** 1211 S Main St 95437. On SR 1. Ext corridors. **Pets:** Dogs only. $10 daily fee/room. Designated rooms, service with restrictions, supervision.
[SAVE] [X] [&M] [▯] [▯] [X] [K]

AAA' ▼▼▼ Quality Inn & Suites/Tradewinds H
(707) 964-4761. **$72-$199, 3 day notice.** 400 S Main St 95437. 6 blks s on SR 1. Ext corridors. **Pets:** Accepted.
[SAVE] [X] [&M] [▯] [▯] [TT] [≈] [K]

AAA' ▼▼▼ Seabird Lodge M ❀
(707) 964-4731. **$75-$140.** 191 South St 95437. 0.8 mi n of Noyo River Bridge; 1 blk e off SR 1. Ext corridors. **Pets:** Other species. $10 daily fee/room. Designated rooms, service with restrictions, supervision.
[SAVE] [X] [▯] [▯] [≈] [K]

▼▼▼ Super 8 M
(707) 964-4003. **$56-$140.** 888 S Main St 95437. 0.5 mi s on SR 1; north end of Noyo River Bridge. Ext corridors. **Pets:** Accepted.
[ASK] [X] [&M] [▯] [▯]

AAA' ▼▼▼ Surf Motel and Gardens M ❀
(707) 964-5361. **$54-$259, 3 day notice.** 1220 S Main St 95437. 1 mi s on SR 1; s of Noyo River Bridge; 0.3 mi n of jct SR 20. Ext corridors. **Pets:** Dogs only. $10 daily fee/pet. Designated rooms, service with restrictions, supervision. [SAVE] [X] [▯] [▯] [K]

GUALALA

AAA' ▼▼▼ Gualala Country Inn M
(707) 884-4343. **$95-$190, 3 day notice.** 47955 Center St 95445. South end of town on east side of SR 1. Ext/int corridors. **Pets:** Other species. $10 one-time fee/pet. Service with restrictions, supervision.
[SAVE] [X] [▯] [▯] [K]

AAA' ▼▼▼ North Coast Country Inn BB
(707) 884-4537. **$164-$245, 3 day notice.** 34591 S SR 1 95445. On SR 1, 4.5 mi n. Ext corridors. **Pets:** Accepted.
[SAVE] [X] [▯] [▯] [K] [W] [Z]

AAA' ▼▼▼ Surf Motel M ❀
(707) 884-3571. **$79-$199, 3 day notice.** 39170 S SR 1 95445. Center. Ext/int corridors. **Pets:** Other species. $15 daily fee/pet. Service with restrictions, supervision. [SAVE] [X] [▯] [▯] [K]

GUERNEVILLE

▼▼▼▼ Applewood Inn & Restaurant CI
(707) 869-9093. **$195-$345, 14 day notice.** 13555 SR 116 95446. 0.5 mi s of River Rd. Ext corridors. **Pets:** Accepted. [X] [TT] [≈]

AAA' ▼▼▼ Ferngrove Cottages CA ❀
(707) 869-8105. **$89-$269, 3 day notice.** 16650 SR 116 95446. Just w of downtown. Ext corridors. **Pets:** Large, other species. $25 daily fee/pet. Designated rooms, service with restrictions, supervision.
[SAVE] [X] [▯] [▯] [≈] [K] [Z]

HEALDSBURG

Americas Best Value Inn & Suites Ⓜ
(707) 433-5548. **$79-$249.** 74 Healdsburg Ave 95448. US 101, exit Central Healdsburg, just se. Ext corridors. **Pets:** Small. $25 daily fee/pet. Service with restrictions, supervision.

Bella Villa Messina BB
(707) 433-6655. **$220-$390, 7 day notice.** 316 Burgundy Rd 95448. US 101, exit Dry Creek Rd, just e to Grove St, 0.5 mi n to Chiquita Rd, then 0.5 mi w. Int corridors. **Pets:** Accepted.

Best Western Dry Creek Inn Ⓗ
(707) 433-0300. **$89-$299.** 198 Dry Creek Rd 95448. US 101, exit Dry Creek Rd, just se. Ext corridors. **Pets:** $30 daily fee/pet. Designated rooms, service with restrictions, supervision.

Hotel Healdsburg Ⓗ
(707) 431-2800. **Call for rates.** 25 Matheson St 95448. On the Plaza. Int corridors. **Pets:** Accepted.

JENNER

Jenner Inn & Cottages CI
(707) 865-2377. **Call for rates.** 10400 Hwy 1 95450. On SR 1 at SR 116. Ext corridors. **Pets:** Dogs only. $35 one-time fee/pet. Service with restrictions.

KENWOOD

Birmingham Bed and Breakfast BB
(707) 833-6996. **$160-$295, 14 day notice.** 8790 Hwy 12 95452. SR 12, just n of town. Int corridors. **Pets:** Dogs only. $10 daily fee/pet. Designated rooms, no service, supervision.

LAKEPORT

Rainbow Lodge Ⓜ
(707) 263-4309. **$39-$129.** 2569 Lakeshore Blvd 95453. SR 29, exit 103 (11th St), 8 mi e, just n on Main St, just w on Clearlake Ave, 0.4 mi n on N High St, then 0.6 mi n. Ext corridors. **Pets:** Accepted.

LEGGETT

Redwoods River Resort CA
(707) 925-6249. **$75-$165, 7 day notice.** 75000 Hwy 101 95585. 6.5 mi n of jct SR 1. Ext corridors. **Pets:** Accepted.

LITTLE RIVER

Auberge Mendocino-Rachel's Inn BB
(707) 937-0088. **$189-$355, 21 day notice.** 8200 N SR 1 95456. On SR 1, 0.3 mi n of Van Damme State Park entrance. Ext/int corridors. **Pets:** Medium, dogs only. $100 deposit/room, $35 one-time fee/pet. Designated rooms, service with restrictions, supervision.

The Inn at Schoolhouse Creek BB
(707) 937-5525. **$175-$399, 14 day notice.** 7051 N SR 1 95456. On SR 1, 0.8 mi s of Van Damme State Park entrance. Ext corridors. **Pets:** Other species. $50 one-time fee/room. Service with restrictions.

Little River Inn CI
(707) 937-5942. **$130-$365, 5 day notice.** 7901 N SR 1 95456. On SR 1, just s of Van Damme State Park entrance. Ext/int corridors. **Pets:** Accepted.

Stevenswood Spa Resort CI
(707) 937-2810. **$159-$965.** 8211 N Hwy 1 95456. On SR 1, 0.4 mi n of Van Damme State Park entrance. Int corridors. **Pets:** Other species. $50 one-time fee/pet. Service with restrictions.

MENDOCINO

Abigail's Bed & Breakfast BB
(707) 937-0934. **$99-$319, 14 day notice.** 951 Ukiah St 95460. Just e of Lansing St; center. Ext/int corridors. **Pets:** Accepted.

Agate Cove Inn CA
(707) 937-0551. **$159-$339, 14 day notice.** 11201 N Lansing St 95460. Just w on Little Lake Rd from jct SR 1, then 0.6 mi n. Ext corridors. **Pets:** Other species. $20 one-time fee/room. Designated rooms, supervision.

Blackberry Inn Ⓜ
(707) 937-5281. **$100-$255, 14 day notice.** 44951 Larkin Rd 95460. 0.5 mi n on SR 1, then just e. Ext corridors. **Pets:** Other species. $10 daily fee/pet. Designated rooms, service with restrictions, supervision.

Hill House Inn Ⓗ
(707) 937-0554. **Call for rates.** 10701 Pallette Dr 95460. Just w on Little Lake St from jct SR 1, just n on Lansing St. Ext corridors. **Pets:** Large. $25 one-time fee/room. Service with restrictions, supervision.

MacCallum House Inn CI
(707) 937-0289. **$175-$475, 7 day notice.** 45020 Albion St 95460. Just w of Lansing St; center. Ext/int corridors. **Pets:** $40 daily fee/pet. Designated rooms, supervision.

Mendocino Hotel & Garden Suites Ⓗ
(707) 937-0511. **$129-$345, 5 day notice.** 45080 Main St 95460. 0.4 mi w on Main St from jct SR 1. Ext/int corridors. **Pets:** Medium. $25 one-time fee/room. Designated rooms, service with restrictions, supervision.

Mendocino Seaside Cottage BB
(707) 485-0239. **$187-$299, 7 day notice.** 10940 Lansing St 95460. Just w on Little Lake Rd from jct SR 1, then 0.3 mi n. Ext/int corridors. **Pets:** Accepted.

Stanford Inn by the Sea & Spa CI
(707) 937-5615. **$195-$475, 7 day notice.** 44850 Comptche-Ukiah Rd 95460. SR 1, exit Comptche-Ukiah Rd, just e. Ext corridors. **Pets:** Other species. $45 one-time fee/pet. Supervision.

NAPA

The Chablis Inn Ⓜ
(707) 257-1944. **$89-$250, 3 day notice.** 3360 Solano Ave 94558. Just w off SR 29 via Redwood Rd, then just s. Ext corridors. **Pets:** Dogs only. $20 daily fee/pet. Service with restrictions, supervision.

Embassy Suites Napa Valley Ⓗ
(707) 253-9540. **$159-$349.** 1075 California Blvd 94559. SR 29, exit 1st St E. Ext/int corridors. **Pets:** Medium. $75 one-time fee/room. Designated rooms, service with restrictions, crate.

The Meritage Resort and Spa Ⓗ
(707) 251-1900. **$159-$409.** 875 Bordeaux Way 94558. 0.5 mi n of jct SR 29/SR 121; SR 121 N, follow Downtown Napa/Lake Berryessa, w on Napa Valley Corporate Way, then just s. Int corridors. **Pets:** $50 one-time fee/pet. Service with restrictions.

The Napa Inn BB
(707) 257-1444. **$125-$295, 10 day notice.** 1137 Warren St 94559. SR 29, exit 1st St, 0.5 mi w, then 0.3 mi n. Int corridors. **Pets:** $20 daily fee/room. Designated rooms, service with restrictions, crate.

▼▼▼ Napa River Inn H ❀
(707) 251-8500. $219-$599. 500 Main St 94559. Downtown. Int corridors. Pets: $25 daily fee/pet. Service with restrictions, supervision.
A$K ⊠ ᴸM ⊟ ⊑

♨ ▼ Napa Valley Redwood Inn M ❀
(707) 257-6111. $67-$150, 3 day notice. 3380 Solano Ave 94558. Just w off SR 29 via Redwood Rd, just s. Ext corridors. Pets: Other species. $10 daily fee/pet. Service with restrictions, supervision.
SAVE ⊠ ᴸM ⊟ ⊸

NICE

♨ ▼▼▼ Featherbed Railroad Co. BB
(707) 274-8378. Call for rates. 2870 Lakeshore Blvd 95464. 0.5 mi s of SR 20. Ext corridors. Pets: Accepted.
SAVE ⊠ ⊟ ⊑ ⊸ ⊗ ☏

▼▼▼ Gingerbread Cottages B&B CA ❀
(707) 274-0200. $125-$195, 7 day notice. 4057 E Hwy 20 95464. On SR 20, south of town. Ext corridors. Pets: Small, dogs only. $25 daily fee/pet. Service with restrictions, supervision.
A$K ⊠ ⊟ ⊑ ⊸ ⊗

OCCIDENTAL

♨ ▼▼▼ Inn at Occidental BB
(707) 874-1047. $209-$359, 10 day notice. 3657 Church St 95465. Town center. Int corridors. Pets: Medium, dogs only. $35 daily fee/room. Designated rooms, service with restrictions, supervision.
SAVE ⊠ ᴸM ⊟ ᴾ

♨ ▼▼ Occidental Lodge M
(707) 874-3623. $94-$145. 3610 Bohemian Hwy 95465. In the village. Ext corridors. Pets: Medium. $10 one-time fee/pet. Service with restrictions, supervision. SAVE ⊠ ᴸM ⊟ ⊑ ⊸

PETALUMA

♨ ▼▼▼ Best Western Petaluma Inn H
(707) 763-0994. $89-$169. 200 S McDowell Blvd 94954. US 101, exit Washington St, 1 blk e. Ext corridors. Pets: Other species. $20 one-time fee/pet. Designated rooms, service with restrictions, supervision.
SAVE ⊠ ᴸM ⊟ ⊑ ⊸

♨ ▼▼▼ Quality Inn-Petaluma H
(707) 664-1155. $90-$219. 5100 Montero Way 94954. US 101, exit Old Redwood Hwy-Penngrove northbound; exit Petaluma Blvd N-Penngrove southbound (east side). Ext/int corridors. Pets: Other species. $15 daily fee/room. Service with restrictions, supervision.
SAVE ⊠ ᴸM ⊟ ⊑ ⊸ ⊗

♨ ▼▼ Sheraton Sonoma
County-Petaluma H ❀
(707) 283-2888. $109-$269. 745 Baywood Dr 94954. US 101, exit SR 116 (Lakeville Hwy), just se. Int corridors. Pets: Medium, dogs only. Designated rooms, service with restrictions, supervision.
SAVE ⊠ ᴸM ⊟ ⊑ �"| ⊸ ⊗

ROHNERT PARK

♨ ▼▼▼ Best Western Inn H ❀
(707) 584-7435. $95-$135. 6500 Redwood Dr 94928. US 101, exit Rohnert Park Expwy, just w. Ext corridors. Pets: Medium. $25 one-time fee/room. Designated rooms, service with restrictions, supervision.
SAVE ⊠ ᴸM ⊟ ⊑ ⊸

♨ ▼▼▼ Doubletree Hotel Sonoma Wine
Country H
(707) 584-5466. $129-$239. One DoubleTree Dr 94928. US 101, exit Golf Course Dr; 3 mi s of Santa Rosa. Int corridors. Pets: Medium, dogs only. $35 daily fee/pet. Designated rooms, service with restrictions, supervision. ECO SAVE ⊠ ᴸM ⊟ ⊑ "| ⊸ ⊗

ST. HELENA

♨ ▼▼▼ El Bonita Motel H
(707) 963-3216. $99-$290, 3 day notice. 195 Main St 94574. 0.8 mi s on SR 29. Ext corridors. Pets: Large, other species. $15 daily fee/pet. Service with restrictions. SAVE ⊠ ᴸM ⊟ ⊑ ⊸

♨ ▼▼▼ Harvest Inn H ❀
(707) 963-9463. $219-$899, 14 day notice. One Main St 94574. 1.5 mi s on SR 29. Ext corridors. Pets: Dogs only. $75 one-time fee/room. Designated rooms, service with restrictions, supervision.
SAVE ⊠ ᴸM ⊟ ⊑ ⊸ ⊗

SANTA ROSA

♨ ▼▼▼ Americas Best Value Inn M
(707) 523-3480. $70-$179. 1800 Santa Rosa Ave 95407. US 101, exit Baker Ave northbound; exit Corby Ave southbound. Ext corridors.
Pets: Accepted. SAVE ⊠ ᴸM

♨ ▼▼▼ Best Western Garden Inn H ❀
(707) 546-4031. $88-$123. 1500 Santa Rosa Ave 95404. US 101, exit Baker Ave northbound; exit Corby Ave southbound. Ext corridors.
Pets: Dogs only. $15 daily fee/pet. Designated rooms, no service, supervision. SAVE ⊠ ᴸM ⊟ ⊑ "| ⊸

♨ ▼▼ Comfort Inn M
(707) 542-5544. Call for rates. 2632 Cleveland Ave 95403. US 101, exit Steele Ln, 1 mi n. Int corridors. Pets: Large. $25 deposit/pet. Service with restrictions, supervision. ⊠ ᴸM ⊟ ⊑ ⊸

▼▼ Extended StayAmerica-Santa Rosa-North H
(707) 541-0959. $95-$110. 100 Fountain Grove Pkwy 95403. US 101, exit Mendocino Ave/Old Redwood Hwy northbound, 0.3 mi e; exit Hopper Ave southbound, 0.6 mi e. Int corridors. Pets: Other species. $25 daily fee/room. Designated rooms, service with restrictions, crate.
A$K ⊠ ᴸM ⊟ ⊑

▼▼ Extended StayAmerica-Santa Rosa-South H
(707) 546-4808. $75-$90. 2600 Corby Ave 95407. US 101, exit Hearn Ave/Yolanda Ave northbound; exit Hearn Ave southbound. Ext corridors.
Pets: Other species. $25 daily fee/room. Designated rooms, service with restrictions, crate. A$K ⊠ ᴸM ⊟ ⊑

♨ ▼▼▼ Flamingo Conference Resort and Spa H
(707) 545-8530. $99-$359. 2777 4th St 95405. Off SR 12; at Farmers Ln. Int corridors. Pets: Other species. $50 one-time fee/room. Designated rooms, service with restrictions, supervision.
SAVE ⊠ ᴸM ⊟ ⊑ "| ⊸ ⊗

▼▼▼ Fountaingrove Inn, Hotel & Conference Center H
(707) 578-6101. $119-$299. 101 Fountaingrove Pkwy 95403. 2.5 mi n on US 101, exit Mendocino Ave/Old Redwood Hwy, just e. Int corridors.
Pets: Small, dogs only. $25 daily fee/pet. Designated rooms, service with restrictions, supervision. A$K ⊠ ᴸM ⊟ ⊑ "| ⊸

♨ ▼▼▼ Hillside Inn Motel M
(707) 546-9353. $84-$99, 3 day notice. 2901 4th St 95409. US 101, 2.5 mi e on SR 12; at Farmers Ln and 4th St. Ext corridors.
Pets: Accepted. SAVE ⊠ ⊑ "| ⊸

♨ ▼▼▼ Hilton Sonoma Wine Country H
(707) 523-7555. $149-$309. 3555 Round Barn Blvd 95403. US 101, exit Mendocino Ave/Old Redwood Hwy; just ne at top of hill. Int corridors.
Pets: Medium. $50 one-time fee/room. Designated rooms, service with restrictions, supervision. ECO SAVE ⊠ ᴸM ⊟ ⊑ "| ⊸

♨ ▼▼▼ Holiday Inn Express H
(707) 545-9000. $112-$299. 870 Hopper Ave 95403. US 101, exit Mendocino Ave/Old Redwood Hwy northbound, just w; exit Hopper Ave southbound. Ext corridors. Pets: Dogs only. $20 one-time fee/room. Designated rooms, service with restrictions, supervision.
SAVE ⊠ ᴸM ⊟ ⊑ ⊸

▼▼ Quality Inn & Suites Santa Rosa H
(707) 521-2100. Call for rates. 3000 Santa Rosa Ave 95407. US 101, exit Todd Rd, 1.2 mi n. Int corridors. Pets: Small. $15 daily fee/pet. Service with restrictions, supervision. ⊠ ᴸM ⊟ ⊑

◬ ▼▼ Sandman Inn 🅷 ❀
(707) 544-8570. **$89-$125.** 3421 Cleveland Ave 95403. US 101, exit W
Mendocino Ave/Old Redwood Hwy. Ext corridors. **Pets:** Dogs only. $25
one-time fee/pet. Service with restrictions, supervision.
[SAVE] [✕] [&M] [🛏] [🖵] [⇌]

▼▼ Santa Rosa Downtown Travelodge 🅼
(707) 544-4141. **$70-$170.** 635 Healdsburg Ave 95401. US 101, exit
College Ave, 0.3 mi e, then just s; at Mendocino Ave. Ext corridors.
Pets: Accepted. [ASK] [✕] [🛏] [🖵] [⇌]

◬ ▼▼▼ Travelodge 🅼
(707) 542-3472. **$65-$180.** 1815 Santa Rosa Ave 95407. US 101, exit
Baker Ave northbound; exit Corby Ave southbound. Ext corridors.
Pets: $15 daily fee/pet. Service with restrictions, supervision.
[SAVE] [✕] [&M] [🛏] [🖵] [⇌]

SONOMA

◬ ▼▼▼ Best Western Sonoma Valley Inn 🅷
(707) 938-9200. **Call for rates.** 550 2nd St W 95476. 1 blk w of town
plaza. Ext corridors. **Pets:** Small. $35 daily fee/pet. Designated rooms,
service with restrictions, supervision.
[SAVE] [✕] [&M] [🛏] [🖵] [⇌] [✕]

◬ ▼▼▼ ▼▼ The Fairmont Sonoma Mission Inn &
Spa 🅷
(707) 938-9000. **Call for rates.** 100 Boyes Blvd 95476. 2.5 mi n on SR
12. Ext/int corridors. **Pets:** Accepted.
[SAVE] [✕] [&M] [🖵] [🍴] [⇌] [✕]

◬ ▼▼▼ ▼▼ The Lodge at Sonoma, a Renaissance
Resort & Spa 🅷
(707) 935-6600. **$259-$339, 7 day notice.** 1325 Broadway 95476. On
SR 12, 1 mi s of Sonoma Plaza. Ext/int corridors. **Pets:** Accepted.
[SAVE] [✕] [&M] [🛏] [🖵] [🍴] [⇌] [✕]

UKIAH

◬ ▼▼▼ Best Western Orchard Inn 🅷
(707) 462-1514. **$109.** 555 S Orchard Ave 95482. US 101, exit Gobbi St,
0.5 mi w. Int corridors. **Pets:** Medium. $25 daily fee/pet. Designated
rooms, service with restrictions. [SAVE] [✕] [&M] [🛏] [🖵] [⇌]

▼▼▼ Comfort Inn & Suites 🅷
(707) 462-3442. **$70-$110.** 1220 Airport Park Blvd 95482. US 101, exit
Talmage Rd, just w, then just s. Int corridors. **Pets:** Medium, dogs only.
$20 daily fee/pet. Designated rooms, service with restrictions, supervision.
[ASK] [✕] [&M] [🛏] [🖵] [⇌]

◬ ▼▼▼ Days Inn 🅼
(707) 462-7584. **$69-$199, 7 day notice.** 950 N State St 95482. US
101, exit N State St, 0.5 mi s. Ext corridors. **Pets:** Medium. $10 daily
fee/pet. Designated rooms, service with restrictions, supervision.
[SAVE] [✕] [🛏] [🖵] [⇌]

▼▼ Discovery Inn 🅷
(707) 462-8873. **$89-$129.** 1340 N State St 95482. US 101, exit N State
St, just sw. Ext corridors. **Pets:** Medium. $25 one-time fee/pet. Desig-
nated rooms, service with restrictions, supervision.
[ASK] [✕] [&M] [🛏] [🖵] [⇌]

◬ ▼▼▼ Quality Inn 🅼
(707) 462-2906. **$79-$139.** 1050 S State St 95482. US 101, exit Talmage
Rd, 0.4 mi w, then just n. Ext corridors. **Pets:** Dogs only. $10 daily fee/
pet. Service with restrictions, supervision. [SAVE] [✕] [🛏] [🖵] [⇌]

◬ ▼▼▼ Super 8 Ukiah 🅼 ❀
(707) 468-8181. **$49-$119.** 693 S Orchard Ave 95482. US 101, exit
Gobbi St W, just nw. Ext corridors. **Pets:** Other species. $10 daily fee/pet.
Supervision. [SAVE] [✕] [🛏] [🖵] [🍴] [⇌]

UPPER LAKE

◬ ▼▼▼ Super 8 🅼
(707) 275-0888. **$59-$169, 3 day notice.** 450 E Hwy 20 95485. Jct SR
29, 0.5 mi e. Ext corridors. **Pets:** Accepted. [SAVE] [✕] [🛏] [🖵] [⇌]

▼▼▼ Tallman Hotel 🅷 ❀
(707) 275-2244. **Call for rates.** 9550 Main St 95485. Just n of SR 20;
downtown. Ext/int corridors. **Pets:** Small. $150 deposit/room, $30 daily
fee/room. Designated rooms, service with restrictions, supervision.
[✕] [🛏] [🖵] [🍴] [⇌]

WILLITS

◬ ▼▼▼ Baechtel Creek Inn & Spa, an Ascend
Collection hotel 🅷 ❀
(707) 459-9063. **$90-$160.** 101 Gregory Ln 95490. US 101, just w. Ext
corridors. **Pets:** Small, dogs only. $20 daily fee/pet. Designated rooms,
service with restrictions, supervision. [SAVE] [✕] [🛏] [🖵] [⇌]

WINDSOR

▼▼▼ Hampton Inn & Suites-Windsor/Sonoma Wine
Country 🅷
(707) 837-9355. **$119-$249.** 8937 Brooks Rd S 95492. US 101, exit
Central Windsor, just n. Int corridors. **Pets:** Small. Service with restrictions, supervision. [✕] [&M] [🛏] [🖵] [⇌]

YOUNTVILLE

◬ ▼▼▼ ▼▼ Vintage Inn 🅷
(707) 944-1112. **$225-$700, 7 day notice.** 6541 Washington St 94599.
SR 29, exit Yountville; center. Ext corridors. **Pets:** Accepted.
[SAVE] [✕] [&M] [🛏] [🖵] [⇌] [✕]

End Area

WOODLAND

◬ ▼▼ Days Inn 🅷
(530) 666-3800. **$75-$109.** 1524 E Main St 95776. I-5, exit 537 (Main St)
northbound; exit SR 113 (Davis) southbound, just w. Int corridors.
Pets: Small. $10 one-time fee/pet. Service with restrictions, supervision.
[SAVE] [✕] [&M] [🛏] [🖵] [⇌]

YERMO

◬ ▼▼▼ Oak Tree Inn 🅷
(760) 254-1148. **Call for rates.** 35450 Yermo Rd 92398. I-15, exit 191
(Ghost Town Rd), just e, then just s. Int corridors. **Pets:** Accepted.
[SAVE] [✕] [🛏] [🖵] [🍴] [⇌]

YOSEMITE NATIONAL PARK

▼▼ The Redwoods In Yosemite 🆅🅷
(209) 375-6666. **$175-$880, 30 day notice.** 8038 Chilnualna Falls Rd
95389. 6 mi inside southern entrance via SR 41 and Chilnualna Falls Rd.
Ext corridors. **Pets:** $10 daily fee/pet. Designated rooms, no service,
supervision. [ASK] [✕] [🛏] [🖵]

YREKA

◬ ▼▼▼ Baymont Inn & Suites 🅷
(530) 841-1300. **$69-$140.** 148 Moonlit Oaks Ave 96097. I-5, exit 773,
just w. Int corridors. **Pets:** Medium. $10 one-time fee/room. Designated
rooms, service with restrictions, supervision.
[SAVE] [✕] [🛏] [🖵] [⇌] [✕]

Best Western Miner's Inn M ❖

(530) 842-4355. **$85-$160.** 122 E Miner St 96097. I-5, exit 776 southbound, just w to N Main St, then just s; exit 775 northbound, just w to N Main St, then just n. Ext corridors. **Pets:** Medium. $10 daily fee/pet. Designated rooms, service with restrictions, supervision.

(SAVE) ⊠ 🖥 💻 🏊 ⊠

Comfort Inn H

(530) 842-1612. **Call for rates.** 1804-B Fort Jones Rd 96097. I-5, exit 773, just w. Int corridors. **Pets:** Accepted. ⊠ 🖥 💻 🏊

Econo Lodge Inn & Suites M

(530) 842-4404. **Call for rates.** 526 S Main St 96097. I-5, exit 775, just w to Main St, then just s. Ext corridors. **Pets:** Small. $20 deposit/pet, $10 daily fee/pet. Service with restrictions, supervision.

(SAVE) ⊠ 🖥 💻 🏊

Mountain View Inn/Motel M

(530) 842-1940. **$48-$68.** 801 N Main St 96097. I-5, exit 776, just w. Ext corridors. **Pets:** Very small. $6 daily fee/pet. Service with restrictions, supervision. (SAVE) ⊠ 🖥 💻

Rodeway Inn M ❖

(530) 842-4412. **$48.** 1235 S Main St 96097. I-5, exit 775 southbound, just w to Main St, then 0.9 mi s; exit 773 northbound, just w to Main St, then 1.1 mi n. Ext corridors. **Pets:** $25 deposit/pet, $7 one-time fee/pet. Service with restrictions, supervision. (SAVE) ⊠ 🖥 💻 🏊

Super 8-Yreka M

(530) 842-5781. **$55-$95.** 136 Montague Rd 96097. I-5, exit 776, just w. Ext corridors. **Pets:** $10 daily fee/pet. Service with restrictions, supervision. (SAVE) ⊠ 🖥 💻 🏊

YUBA CITY

Econo Lodge Inn & Suites M

(530) 674-1592. **$50-$60.** 730 Palora Ave 95991. 0.5 mi s of jct SR 99 and 20, just e on Bridge St, then just n. Int corridors. **Pets:** Accepted.

(SAVE) ⊠ 🖥 💻 🏊

Quality Inn & Suites H

(530) 674-0201. **Call for rates.** 4228 S Hwy 99 95991. On SR 99, 4.5 mi s of SR 20. Ext corridors. **Pets:** Accepted.

⊠ 🖥 💻 🍴 🏊

YUCCA VALLEY

Super 8 M

(760) 228-1773. **$69-$129.** 57096 Twentynine Palms Hwy 92284. On SR 62, 0.3 mi w of jct SR 247. Int corridors. **Pets:** Accepted.

(ASK) ⊠ 🖥 💻 🏊

COLORADO

ALAMOSA

Best Western Alamosa Inn H ❀
(719) 589-2567. **$79-$109.** 2005 W Main St 81101. 1 mi w on US 160. Ext corridors. **Pets:** Medium, dogs only. $10 daily fee/pet. Designated rooms, service with restrictions, supervision. SAVE ✕ ⦿ 🖵 ⊇

Comfort Inn of Alamosa H
(719) 587-9000. **Call for rates.** 6301 Rd 107 S 81101. 2.3 mi w on US 160. Int corridors. **Pets:** Medium, dogs only. $20 one-time fee/pet. Designated rooms, service with restrictions, supervision. ✕ ⦿ 🖵 ⊇

Holiday Inn Express H
(719) 589-4026. **$106-$150.** 3418 Mariposa St 81101. 1.8 mi w on US 160. Int corridors. **Pets:** Small. $50 daily fee/pet, $50 one-time fee/pet. Designated rooms, service with restrictions, supervision.
✕ ⦿ 🖵 ⊇ ✕

ASPEN

Aspen Meadows Resort, a Dolce Resort H
(970) 925-4240. **$125-$600,** 30 day notice. 845 Meadows Rd 81611. 3 blks n of SR 82 via 7th Ave, then just w. Ext/int corridors. **Pets:** $100 one-time fee/room. Designated rooms, service with restrictions.
SAVE ✕ ⦿ 🖵 ⑪ ⊇ ✕ ⒜

Aspen Mountain Lodge H
(970) 925-7650. **$116-$435,** 7 day notice. 311 W Main St 81611. Just w on SR 82; between 2nd and 3rd sts. Int corridors. **Pets:** Dogs only. $20 daily fee/pet. ASK ✕ 🖵 ⊇

Hotel Jerome H ❀
(970) 920-1000. **$180-$1850,** 30 day notice. 330 E Main St 81611. On SR 82; downtown. Int corridors. **Pets:** Dogs only. $75 one-time fee/room. Service with restrictions. SAVE ✕ ⑪ ⊇ ✕

Hotel Lenado H ❀
(970) 925-6246. **$125-$645,** 30 day notice. 200 S Aspen St 81611. Just s of SR 82 via Aspen St; jct Hopkins St. Ext/int corridors. **Pets:** Designated rooms. ASK ✕ ⦿

Limelight Lodge H ❀
(970) 925-3025. **$129-$750,** 14 day notice. 355 S Monarch St 81611. Just s of SR 82; at Monarch and Cooper sts. Int corridors. **Pets:** Other species. $25 daily fee/pet. Designated rooms, service with restrictions, crate. SAVE ✕ ⦿ 🖵 ⊇

The Little Nell H ❀
(970) 920-4600. **$250-$5900,** 30 day notice. 675 E Durant Ave 81611. Beside the gondola at base of Aspen Mountain. Int corridors. **Pets:** Other species. $25 daily fee/room, $125 one-time fee/room. Crate.
SAVE ✕ ⦿ 🖵 ⑪ ⊇ ✕

Molly Gibson Lodge H ❀
(970) 925-3434. **Call for rates.** 101 W Main St 81611. Just w on SR 82. Ext/int corridors. **Pets:** Dogs only. $20 daily fee/pet. Service with restrictions, supervision. ✕ ⦿ 🖵 ⊇

Mountain House Lodge H ❀
(970) 920-2550. **$79-$229,** 30 day notice. 905 E Hopkins St 81611. Just e of SR 82. Int corridors. **Pets:** Other species. $20 daily fee/pet. Designated rooms. SAVE ✕ ⦿ 🖵 ⒜

St. Regis Aspen Resort H
(970) 920-3300. **$165-$1840,** 21 day notice. 315 E Dean St 81611. SR 82, s on Monarch St, then just e. Int corridors. **Pets:** Accepted.
SAVE ✕ ⑪ ⊇ ✕

Sky Hotel H ❀
(970) 925-6760. **$185-$679,** 30 day notice. 709 E Durant Ave 81611. At base of Aspen Mountain. Ext/int corridors. **Pets:** Other species. Service with restrictions, supervision. SAVE ✕ ⦿ 🖵 ⑪ ⊇ ✕

AVON

Comfort Inn-Vail/Beaver Creek H
(970) 949-5511. **$130-$250.** 161 W Beaver Creek Blvd 81620. I-70, exit 167, just s on Avon Rd, then just w. Int corridors. **Pets:** Medium. $50 one-time fee/room. Service with restrictions, supervision.
SAVE ✕ ⦿ 🖵 ⊇

The Westin Riverfront Resort & Spa, Avon H ❀
(970) 790-6000. **$129-$559,** 30 day notice. 126 Riverfront Ln 81620. I-70, exit 167, 0.5 mi s on Avon Rd, then just w; jct Avon Rd at Riverfront Village. Int corridors. **Pets:** Dogs only. Service with restrictions, supervision. ECO SAVE ✕ ⦿ 🖵 ⑪ ⊇ ✕

BAYFIELD

Wilderness Trails Ranch CA
(970) 247-0722. **$1450-$2250,** 120 day notice. 23486 CR 501 81122. US 160, 23 mi n of town; on east side of Vallecito Reservoir. Ext corridors. **Pets:** Dogs only. $100 deposit/pet. No service, supervision.
SAVE ✕ ⦿ 🖵 ⑪ ⊇ ✕ ⒲ ⓔ

BEAVER CREEK

The Ritz-Carlton, Bachelor Gulch H
(970) 748-6200. **$273-$1295,** 30 day notice. 130 Daybreak Ridge 81620. I-70, exit 167, s on Avon and Village rds (beyond gatehouse), w on Prater Rd, follow signs to Bachelor Gulch Village. Int corridors.
Pets: Accepted. SAVE ✕ ⓜ ⦿ 🖵 ⑪ ⊇ ✕

BOULDER

▲▲ **▼▼▼▼** Best Western Boulder Inn 🅷
(303) 449-3800. **$110-$150.** 770 28th St 80303. US 36 (28th St) at Baseline Rd. Int corridors. **Pets:** Accepted.
[SAVE] [X] [📠] [💻] [≈] [X]

▲▲ **▼▼▼** Boulder Outlook Hotel & Suites 🅷
(303) 443-3322. **Call for rates.** 800 28th St 80303. US 36 (28th St), exit Baseline Rd via Frontage Rd. Ext/int corridors. **Pets:** Accepted.
[SAVE] [X] [📠] [💻] [🍴] [≈] [X]

▲▲ **▼▼▼** Boulder Twin Lakes Inn 🅷 🐾
(303) 530-2939. **$69-$130, 3 day notice.** 6485 Twin Lakes Rd 80301. Jct US 36 (28th St) and SR 119, 5 mi n, 1 mi ne on SR 119, 1.3 mi e on Jay Rd, 0.3 mi n on 63rd St, then just e. Int corridors. **Pets:** Large, other species. $10 daily fee/pet. Designated rooms.
[SAVE] [X] [📠] [💻] [X]

▲▲ **▼▼▼** Boulder University Inn 🅼 🐾
(303) 417-1700. **$60-$119.** 1632 Broadway 80302. US 36 (28th St), exit Baseline Rd, 0.3 mi s, then 3 mi nw. Ext corridors. **Pets:** Medium, other species. $100 deposit/room, $15 daily fee/room. Designated rooms, service with restrictions, supervision. [SAVE] [X] [📠] [💻] [≈]

▲▲ **▼▼** Foot of The Mountain Motel 🅼 🐾
(303) 442-5688. **$75-$90.** 200 Arapahoe Ave 80302. 1.8 mi w of US 36 (28th St). Ext corridors. **Pets:** Large. $50 deposit/room, $5 daily fee/pet. Designated rooms, service with restrictions, supervision.
[SAVE] [X] [📠] [💻] [X]

▼▼ **▼▼** Holiday Inn Express 🅷
(303) 442-6600. **$114-$199.** 4777 N Broadway 80304. 3 mi n of Pearl Street Pedestrian Mall; jct US 36 (28th St), 0.3 mi s. Int corridors.
Pets: Accepted. [ASK] [X] [📠] [💻] [≈]

▼▼ **▼▼** Homewood Suites by Hilton 🅷 🐾
(303) 499-9922. **$119-$219.** 4950 Baseline Rd 80303. 1.2 mi e of US 36 (28th St); jct SR 157 (Foothills Pkwy), just w; entry off Baseline Rd. Ext/int corridors. **Pets:** Other species. $50 one-time fee/room. Service with restrictions, crate. [X] [📠] [💻] [≈] [X]

▲▲ **▼▼▼▼** Quality Inn & Suites Boulder
　　　　　Creek 🅷 🐾
(303) 449-7550. **$99-$150.** 2020 Arapahoe Ave 80302. US 36 (28th St), 0.5 mi w. Ext/int corridors. **Pets:** Large, other species. $100 deposit/room, $15 daily fee/room. Designated rooms, service with restrictions, supervision. [SAVE] [X] [📠] [💻] [≈] [X]

▼▼ **▼▼** Residence Inn by Marriott 🅷
(303) 449-5545. **$170-$208.** 3030 Center Green Dr 80301. 0.5 mi e of US 36 (28th St), e on Valmont Rd; from Foothills Pkwy, just w on Valmont Rd. Ext corridors. **Pets:** Accepted. [ECO] [X] [📠] [💻] [≈] [X]

BRECKENRIDGE

▼▼▼ Great Divide Lodge 🅷
(970) 547-5550. **Call for rates.** 550 Village Rd 80424. Jct Main St, just w on S Park Ave, then just sw. Int corridors. **Pets:** Accepted.
[ECO] [X] [☾M] [📠] [💻] [≈] [X] [X]

BROOMFIELD

▲▲ **▼▼▼** aloft Broomfield Denver 🅷 🐾
(303) 635-2000. **$89-$199.** 8300 Arista Pl 80021. US 36 (Boulder Tpke), exit US 287/CR 121, 0.6 mi s, then 0.4 mi w on Uptown Ave. Int corridors. **Pets:** Medium. Designated rooms, service with restrictions.
[SAVE] [X] [📠] [💻] [≈] [X]

▼▼▼ **▼▼▼** Omni Interlocken Resort 🅷 🐾
(303) 438-6600. **$119-$389.** 500 Interlocken Blvd 80021. US 36 (Boulder Tpke), exit Interlocken Loop, 0.4 mi s, then 0.4 mi e. Int corridors. **Pets:** Medium, dogs only. $50 one-time fee/room. Service with restrictions. [ASK] [X] [☾M] [📠] [💻] [🍴] [≈] [X]

▼▼ **▼▼** TownePlace Suites by Marriott
　　　　　Boulder/Broomfield 🅷
(303) 466-2200. **$179-$199.** 480 Flatiron Blvd 80021. US 36 (Boulder Tpke), exit Interlocken Loop, 0.4 mi s, just w on Interlocken Blvd, then just s. Int corridors. **Pets:** Accepted. [X] [☾M] [📠] [💻] [≈]

BURLINGTON

▲▲ **▼** Chaparral Motor Inn 🅼
(719) 346-5361. **$49-$65.** 405 S Lincoln St 80807. I-70, exit 437, just n on jct US 385. Ext corridors. **Pets:** Medium. $7 daily fee/pet. Designated rooms, service with restrictions, supervision. [SAVE] [X] [📠] [💻] [≈]

▼▼ **▼▼** Comfort Inn Burlington 🅷
(719) 346-7676. **$70-$120.** 282 S Lincoln St 80807. I-70, exit 437, just n on US 385. Int corridors. **Pets:** Medium. $50 deposit/room, $15 daily fee/room. Designated rooms, service with restrictions, supervision.
[ASK] [X] [📠] [💻] [≈]

CANON CITY

▼▼▼ Comfort Inn 🅷
(719) 276-6900. **Call for rates.** 311 Royal Gorge Blvd 81212. On US 50; just w of downtown. Int corridors. **Pets:** Accepted.
[X] [📠] [💻] [≈]

▼▼ **▼▼** Holiday Inn Express 🅷
(719) 275-2400. **$85-$130.** 110 Latigo Ln 81212. 2.5 mi e of SR 115 on US 50. Int corridors. **Pets:** Medium. $15 daily fee/pet. Designated rooms, service with restrictions, supervision. [ASK] [X] [📠] [💻] [≈]

CARBONDALE

▲▲ **▼▼▼▼** Comfort Inn & Suites 🅷 🐾
(970) 963-8880. **$102-$240.** 920 Cowen Dr 81623. Jct of SR 82 and 133, just s. Int corridors. **Pets:** $15 daily fee/pet. Service with restrictions, supervision. [SAVE] [X] [📠] [💻] [≈] [X]

▲▲ **▼▼▼** Days Inn 🅷
(970) 963-9111. **$90-$190, 3 day notice.** 950 Cowen Dr 81623. Jct SR 82 and 133. Int corridors. **Pets:** Other species. $10 daily fee/pet. Designated rooms, service with restrictions, supervision.
[SAVE] [X] [📠] [≈] [X]

CASTLE ROCK

▲▲ **▼▼** **▼▼** Best Western Inn & Suites of Castle
　　　　　Rock 🅷 🐾
(303) 814-8800. **$90-$150.** 595 Genoa Way 80109. I-25, exit 184 (Meadows Pkwy), just w to Castleton Way, just s, then e. Int corridors.
Pets: Medium. $15 daily fee/pet. Designated rooms, service with restrictions, supervision. [SAVE] [X] [📠] [💻] [≈]

▼▼▼ Hampton Inn 🅷
(303) 660-9800. **$89-$119.** 4830 Castleton Way 80109. I-25, exit 184 (Meadows Pkwy), sw to N Castleton Rd, just s, then e. Int corridors.
Pets: Medium, other species. $5 daily fee/room, $25 one-time fee/room. Designated rooms. [X] [☾M] [📠] [💻] [≈]

▼▼▼ Holiday Inn Express 🅷
(303) 660-9733. **Call for rates.** 884 Park St 80109. I-25, exit 182, just w. Int corridors. **Pets:** Accepted. [X] [📠] [💻] [≈]

CEDAREDGE

▼▼ **▼▼** Howard Johnson Express Inn 🅼
(970) 856-7824. **$79-$99.** 530 S Grand Mesa Dr 81413. Just s on SR 65. Int corridors. **Pets:** Large. $10 daily fee/pet. Designated rooms, service with restrictions, supervision. [ASK] [X] [📠] [💻] [≈]

CIMARRON

▼▼ **▼▼** The Inn at Arrowhead 🅱🅱
(970) 862-8206. **$135-$175, 14 day notice.** 21401 Alpine Plateau Rd 81220. 11 mi e on US 50, then 5.1 mi s, follow signs. Int corridors.
Pets: Accepted. [ASK] [X] [🍴] [X] [W] [🐕]

COLORADO SPRINGS METROPOLITAN AREA

CHIPITA PARK

▼▼▼▼ Chipita Lodge B&B [BB] ❀

(719) 684-8454. **$100-$175, 7 day notice.** 9090 Chipita Park Rd 80809. Jct US 24, just s on Fountain Blvd (Pine Peak Hwy), then 1.5 mi w; right at fork. Ext/int corridors. **Pets:** Large, dogs only. $25 one-time fee/room. Designated rooms, no service, crate. [ASK] [✕] [🛏] [💻] [⚠]

COLORADO SPRINGS

◈◈▼ ▼▼▼▼ Antlers Hilton Colorado Springs [H] ❀

(719) 473-5600. **$99-$239.** 4 S Cascade Ave 80903. I-25, exit 142 (Bijou St), just e, then just s; downtown. Int corridors. **Pets:** Medium, other species. $75 one-time fee/room. Designated rooms.

[SAVE] [✕] [♿M] [🛏] [💻] [🍴] [🐾] [✕]

◈◈◈ ▼▼▼ Apollo Park Executive Suites [CO] ❀

(719) 634-0286. **$49-$105, 3 day notice.** 805 S Circle Dr, 2-B 80910. I-25, exit 138, 2.5 mi e. Int corridors. **Pets:** Medium. $10 daily fee/pet. Designated rooms, service with restrictions, supervision.

[SAVE] [✕] [🛏] [💻] [🐾]

◈◈◈ ▼▼▼ Best Western Executive Inn & Suites [H]

(719) 576-2371. **$59-$120.** 1440 Harrison Rd 80905. I-25, exit 138, just w; on northwest corner of interchange; entrance through restaurant. Int corridors. **Pets:** Other species. $20 one-time fee/room. Designated rooms, crate. [SAVE] [✕] [♿M] [🛏] [💻] [🐾]

◈◈◈ ▼▼▼▼ Best Western The Academy Hotel [H]

(719) 598-5770. **$69-$119.** 8110 N Academy Blvd 80920. I-25, exit 150, just s. Int corridors. **Pets:** Medium. $10 daily fee/pet. Designated rooms, service with restrictions. [SAVE] [✕] [♿M] [🛏] [💻] [🍴] [🐾] [✕]

◈◈◈ ▼▼▼▼ The Broadmoor [H] ❀

(719) 634-7711. **$300-$7500, 7 day notice.** 1 Lake Ave 80906. I-25, exit 138, 3 mi w on Circle Dr (which becomes Lake Ave). Ext/int corridors. **Pets:** $35 daily fee/pet. Service with restrictions, crate.

[SAVE] [✕] [♿M] [🛏] [💻] [🍴] [🐾] [✕]

◈◈◈ ▼▼▼▼ Cheyenne Mountain Resort [H] ❀

(719) 538-4000. **$99-$299.** 3225 Broadmoor Valley Rd 80906. I-25, exit 138, 1.4 mi w to SR 115, 0.5 mi s, just w on Cheyenne Mountain Dr, then just s. Ext/int corridors. **Pets:** Medium, dogs only. $35 one-time fee/pet. Designated rooms, service with restrictions, supervision.

[SAVE] [✕] [♿M] [🛏] [💻] [🍴] [🐾] [✕]

◈◈◈ ▼▼▼ Comfort Inn Airport [H]

(719) 380-9000. **$70-$129.** 2115 Aerotech Dr 80916. I-25, exit 139, 4.2 mi e on US 24 Bypass, 0.4 mi s on Powers Blvd, just w on Astrozon Blvd, then just n. Int corridors. **Pets:** Accepted. [SAVE] [✕] [🛏] [💻] [🐾]

◈◈◈ ▼▼▼ Comfort Inn South [H]

(719) 579-6900. **$99-$139.** 1410 Harrison Rd 80905. I-25, exit 138, just w to Rand Rd, then ne. Int corridors. **Pets:** $25 one-time fee/pet. Designated rooms. [SAVE] [✕] [🛏] [💻] [🐾]

◈◈◈ ▼▼▼ Crowne Plaza Colorado Springs [H]

(719) 576-5900. **$79-$299.** 2886 S Circle Dr 80906. I-25, exit 138, just e. Int corridors. **Pets:** Accepted. [SAVE] [✕] [🛏] [💻] [🍴] [🐾] [✕]

◈◈◈ ▼▼▼ Doubletree Hotel Colorado Springs, World Arena [H]

(719) 576-8900. **$89-$189.** 1775 E Cheyenne Mountain Blvd 80906. I-25, exit 138, just w. Int corridors. **Pets:** Accepted.

[SAVE] [✕] [♿M] [🛏] [💻] [🍴] [🐾] [✕]

▼▼▼▼ Drury Inn-Pikes Peak [H]

(719) 598-2500. **$65-$139.** 8155 N Academy Blvd 80920. I-25, exit 150, just s, then e. Int corridors. **Pets:** Other species. No service, supervision.

[ASK] [✕] [🛏] [💻] [🐾]

◈◈◈ ▼▼▼▼ Fairfield Inn & Suites Colorado Springs North/Air Force Academy [H]

(719) 488-4644. **$99-$109.** 15275 W Struthers Rd 80921. I-25, exit 158, just e on Baptist Rd, then just s. Int corridors. **Pets:** Medium, dogs only. $50 one-time fee/room. Service with restrictions, supervision.

[SAVE] [✕] [♿M] [🛏] [💻] [🐾] [✕]

▼▼▼▼ Fairfield Inn by Marriott-South [H]

(719) 576-1717. **$119-$139.** 2725 Geyser Dr 80906. I-25, exit 138, just w to E Cheyenne Mountain Blvd, then just s. Int corridors. **Pets:** Medium. $75 one-time fee/room. Designated rooms, service with restrictions, crate.

[✕] [♿M] [🛏] [💻] [🐾]

◈◈◈ ▼▼▼ Garden of the Gods Motel [M]

(719) 636-5271. **$44-$125.** 2922 W Colorado Ave 80904. I-25, exit 141, 2.5 mi nw on US 24, just n on 31st St, then e. Ext/int corridors. **Pets:** Dogs only. $15 one-time fee/pet. Service with restrictions, crate.

[SAVE] [✕] [🛏] [🐾]

◈◈◈ ▼▼▼▼ Holiday Inn Express Air Force Academy [H] ❀

(719) 592-9800. **$79-$209.** 7110 Commerce Center Dr 80919. I-25, exit 149 (Woodman Rd), just w, then just n. Int corridors. **Pets:** Large, dogs only. $25 daily fee/pet. Designated rooms, service with restrictions, crate.

[SAVE] [✕] [♿M] [🛏] [💻] [🐾] [✕]

▼▼▼▼ Homewood Suites by Hilton Colorado Springs Airport [H]

(719) 574-2701. **$95-$129.** 2875 Zeppelin Rd 80916. I-25, exit 139, 4 mi e on US 24 Bypass, 1.1 mi s on Powers Blvd, then just e. Int corridors. **Pets:** Medium. $50 one-time fee/pet. Service with restrictions, supervision.

[✕] [🛏] [💻] [🐾] [✕]

▼▼▼▼ Homewood Suites by Hilton Colorado Springs-North [H]

(719) 265-6600. **$89-$299.** 9130 Explorer Dr 80920. I-25, exit 151 (Briargate Pkwy), 0.8 mi e; across from Focus on the Family. Int corridors. **Pets:** $25 one-time fee/pet. Supervision. [✕] [♿M] [🛏] [💻] [🐾]

◈◈◈ ▼▼▼ Hyatt Summerfield Suites Colorado Springs [H]

(719) 268-9990. **$109-$399.** 5805 Delmonico Dr 80919. I-25, exit 148 (Rockrimmon Blvd), just nw on Rockrimmon Blvd, then ne; entry around the bank. Int corridors. **Pets:** Other species. $20 daily fee/room, $150 one-time fee/room. Service with restrictions.

[SAVE] [✕] [🛏] [💻] [🐾] [✕]

▼▼▼▼ La Quinta Inn & Suites Colorado Springs (South/Airport) [H] ❀

(719) 527-4788. **$62-$199.** 2750 Geyser Dr 80906. I-25, exit 138, just w to Cheyenne Mountain Blvd, then just s. Int corridors. **Pets:** Medium, other species. Service with restrictions, supervision.

[✕] [♿M] [🛏] [💻] [🐾]

▼▼▼ La Quinta Inn Colorado Springs (Garden of the Gods) [H] ❀

(719) 528-5060. **$29-$109.** 4385 Sinton Rd 80907. I-25, exit 146 (Garden of the Gods Rd), just e. Ext/int corridors. **Pets:** Medium, other species. Service with restrictions, supervision. [ASK] [✕] [🛏] [💻] [🐾]

◈◈◈ ▼▼▼ Microtel Inn & Suites [H]

(719) 598-7500. **$59-$120.** 7265 Commerce Center Dr 80919. I-25, exit 149 (Woodman Rd), just w, then n. Int corridors. **Pets:** Other species. $20 one-time fee/room. Designated rooms, crate.

[SAVE] [✕] [🛏] [💻] [🐾]

Radisson Hotel Colorado Springs Airport

(719) 597-7000. **$119-$185.** 1645 N Newport Rd 80916. I-25, exit 139, 4.5 mi e on US 24 Bypass. Int corridors. **Pets:** Medium, other species. $100 deposit/room, $25 one-time fee/pet. Crate.

Rainbow Lodge and Inn

(719) 632-4551. **$52-$195, 3 day notice.** 3709 W Colorado Ave 80904. I-25, exit 141, 2.5 mi w on US 24, just n on 31st St, then 0.7 mi w. Ext corridors. **Pets:** Accepted.

Residence Inn by Marriott-Central

(719) 574-0370. **$129-$169.** 3880 N Academy Blvd 80917. I-25, exit 146, 4.5 mi e on Garden of the Gods Rd/Austin Bluffs Pkwy, then 0.3 mi s. Ext corridors. **Pets:** Accepted.

Residence Inn by Marriott Colorado Springs North at Interquest Pkwy

(719) 388-9300. **$109-$119.** 9805 Federal Dr 80921. I-25, exit 153, just e, then s. Int corridors. **Pets:** Medium. $75 one-time fee/pet. Service with restrictions, supervision.

Residence Inn by Marriott-Colorado Springs South

(719) 576-0101. **$139-$169.** 2765 Geyser Dr 80906. I-25, exit 138, just w to E Cheyenne Mountain Blvd, then just s. Int corridors. **Pets:** Accepted.

Sleep Inn

(719) 260-6969. **$50-$120.** 1075 Kelly Johnson Blvd 80920. I-25, exit 150, just s on Academy Blvd to Kelly Johnson Blvd, then w. Int corridors. **Pets:** Small. $10 daily fee/pet. Designated rooms, service with restrictions, supervision.

Staybridge Suites-Air Force Academy

(719) 590-7829. **$89-$199.** 7130 Commerce Center Dr 80919. I-25, exit 149 (Woodmen Rd), just w, then n. Int corridors. **Pets:** Other species. $150 one-time fee/room. Service with restrictions, supervision.

TownePlace Suites by Marriott-Colorado Springs

(719) 594-4447. **$99-$109.** 4760 Centennial Blvd 80919. I-25, exit 146 (Garden of the Gods Rd), 1 mi w on, just n on Centennial Blvd, then first left. Int corridors. **Pets:** Other species. $100 one-time fee/room. Service with restrictions.

TownePlace Suites Colorado Springs South

(719) 638-0800. **$89-$109.** 1530 N Newport Rd 80916. I-25, exit 139, 5 mi e on US 24 Bypass, then just n. Int corridors. **Pets:** Accepted.

Travel Inn

(719) 636-3986. **Call for rates.** 512 S Nevada Ave 80903. I-25, exit 141, 0.7 mi e to Nevada Ave, then just s. Ext/int corridors. **Pets:** Accepted.

Travelodge

(719) 632-4600. **$50-$95.** 2625 Ore Mill Rd 80904. I-25, exit 141, 2.3 mi nw on US 24; entry via 26th St. Int corridors. **Pets:** Other species. $10 one-time fee/room. Service with restrictions, supervision.

MANITOU SPRINGS

El Colorado Lodge

(719) 685-5485. **$56-$136, 7 day notice.** 23 Manitou Ave 80829. I-25, exit 141, 4 mi w on US 24, then just ne on US 24 business route. Ext corridors. **Pets:** Accepted.

Park Row Lodge

(719) 685-5216. **$49-$79.** 54 Manitou Ave 80829. I-25, exit 141, 4 mi w on US 24, then just ne on US 24 business route. Ext corridors. **Pets:** Medium, dogs only. $10 one-time fee/room. Designated rooms, service with restrictions, supervision.

Red Wing Motel

(719) 685-5656. **$40-$119.** 56 El Paso Blvd 80829. I-25, exit 141, 4 mi w on US 24, just ne on US 24 business route/Manitou Ave, then just w on Beckers Ln. Ext corridors. **Pets:** Other species. $10 one-time fee/room. Designated rooms.

END METROPOLITAN AREA

CORTEZ

Baymont Inn & Suites

(970) 565-3400. **Call for rates.** 2321 E Main St 81321. 1.3 mi e on US 160. Ext/int corridors. **Pets:** Other species. $10 one-time fee/room. Designated rooms, service with restrictions, supervision.

Best Western Turquoise Inn & Suites

(970) 565-3778. **$79-$195.** 535 E Main St 81321. On US 160. Ext corridors. **Pets:** $15 one-time fee/room. Service with restrictions.

Budget Host Inn

(970) 565-3738. **$42-$108.** 2040 E Main St 81321. 1.3 mi e on US 160, w of jct SR 145. Ext corridors. **Pets:** Medium, dogs only. $10 daily fee/ pet. Designated rooms, service with restrictions, supervision.

Econo Lodge

(970) 565-3474. **$69-$139.** 2020 E Main St 81321. 1.3 mi e on US 160. Ext corridors. **Pets:** Accepted.

Holiday Inn Express

(970) 565-6000. **$119-$179.** 2121 E Main St 81321. 1.3 mi e on US 160. Int corridors. **Pets:** Accepted.

Rodeway Inn

(970) 565-3761. **$49-$104.** 1120 E Main St 81321. 0.3 mi e on US 160. Ext/int corridors. **Pets:** Accepted.

Tomahawk Lodge

(970) 565-8521. **$49-$99.** 728 S Broadway 81321. 1 mi w on US 160. Ext corridors. **Pets:** Dogs only. $25 deposit/pet. Designated rooms, service with restrictions, supervision.

CRAIG

Best Western Deer Park Inn & Suites

(970) 824-9282. **$89-$199.** 262 Commerce St (Hwy 13) 81625. Jct US 40, 0.3 mi s on SR 13. Int corridors. **Pets:** $100 deposit/room, $10 one-time fee/room. Service with restrictions, supervision.

Holiday Inn & Suites

(970) 824-4000. **$99-$179.** 300 S Hwy 13 81625. Jct US 40, 0.3 mi s. Int corridors. **Pets:** Accepted.

CRESTED BUTTE

Old Town Inn

(970) 349-6184. **$89-$149, 14 day notice.** 708 6th St 81224. On SR 135, just s of Elk Ave. Int corridors. **Pets:** Accepted.

▼▼▼ WestWall Lodge **CO**
(970) 349-1280. **$159-$2300, 3 day notice.** 14 Hunter Hill Rd 81225. 2.2 mi n, then just e; in Mt. Crested Butte. Int corridors. **Pets:** Accepted.
(ASK) ⊠ 🛏 🖥 🏊 ⊠ ⚿

CRIPPLE CREEK

△△△ ▼▼▼ Gold King Mountain Inn of Cripple Creek **H**
(719) 689-2600. **$69-$149.** 601 E Galena Ave 80813. 0.3 mi e off SR 67; entrance 50 yards below sign. Int corridors. **Pets:** Accepted.
(SAVE) ⊠ 🔊 🛏 🖥 🏊 ⊠

DELTA

△△△ ▼▼ Best Western Sundance **H**
(970) 874-9781. **$65-$116.** 903 Main St 81416. 0.5 mi s on US 50. Ext corridors. **Pets:** Accepted. (SAVE) ⊠ 🛏 🖥 🍴 🏊

▼▼▼ Comfort Inn **H**
(970) 874-1000. **Call for rates.** 180 Gunnison River Dr 81416. Just n, then just w of jct US 50 and 92. Int corridors. **Pets:** $10 daily fee/pet. Designated rooms, service with restrictions. ⊠ 🛏 🖥

▼▼ Riverwood Inn **M**
(970) 874-5787. **Call for rates.** 677 US 50 81416. 0.5 mi n. Int corridors. **Pets:** Accepted. ⊠ 🛏 🖥

DENVER METROPOLITAN AREA

AURORA

△△△ ▼▼▼▼ aloft Denver International Airport **H** 🐾
(303) 371-9500. **$69-$189.** 16470 E 40th Cir 80011. I-25, exit 196 (Dry Creek Rd), just n, 0.7 mi s, then just s. Int corridors. **Pets:** Medium, dogs only. Service with restrictions, crate. (SAVE) ⊠ 🛏 🖥 🍴 🏊

△△△ ▼▼▼ Best Western Gateway Inn & Suites **H**
(720) 748-4800. **$79-$150.** 800 S Abilene St 80012. I-225, exit 7 (Mississippi Ave), just e, then 0.3 mi n. Int corridors. **Pets:** Medium. $15 daily fee/room. Service with restrictions, crate.
(SAVE) ⊠ 🔊 🛏 🖥 🏊 ⊠

▼▼ Comfort Inn Denver Southeast **H**
(303) 755-8000. **$70-$120.** 14071 E Iliff Ave 80014. I-225, exit 5 (E Iliff Ave), just e. Int corridors. **Pets:** Accepted. (ASK) ⊠ 🔊 🛏 🖥

△△△ ▼▼▼ Comfort Inn DIA Airport **H**
(303) 367-5000. **$79-$129.** 16921 E 32nd Ave 80011. I-70, exit 285, just s on Airport Blvd; on southeast corner. Int corridors. **Pets:** Small, other species. $10 daily fee/pet. Designated rooms, service with restrictions.
(SAVE) ⊠ 🛏 🖥

▼▼ Crestwood Suites Extended Stay Hotels **H**
(303) 481-0379. **$60-$70.** 14090 E Evans Ave 80014. I-225, exit 5 (E Iliff Ave), e to Blackhawk St, then 0.4 mi nw. Int corridors. **Pets:** Accepted.
(ASK) ⊠ 🛏 🖥

▼▼ Crystal Inn DIA **H**
(303) 340-3800. **Call for rates.** 3300 N Ouray St 80011. I-70, exit 285, just s on Airport Blvd, then w on 32nd Ave. Int corridors. **Pets:** Accepted.
⊠ 🔊 🛏 🖥 🏊

▼▼ Extended Stay Deluxe Denver-Aurora **H**
(303) 400-5300. **$67-$77.** 14095 E Evans Ave 80014. I-225, exit 5 (E Iliff Ave), just e to Blackhawk St, then 0.4 mi nw. Int corridors. **Pets:** Other species. $25 daily fee/room. Designated rooms, service with restrictions, crate. (ASK) ⊠ 🔊 🛏 🖥 🏊

▼▼ La Quinta Inn Denver (Aurora) **M** 🐾
(303) 337-0206. **$39-$109.** 1011 S Abilene St 80012. I-225, exit 7 (Mississippi Ave), just e, then n. Ext corridors. **Pets:** Medium, other species. Service with restrictions, supervision. ⊠ 🔊 🛏 🖥 🏊

△△△ ▼▼▼ Sleep Inn Denver International Airport **H**
(303) 373-1616. **$59-$169.** 15900 E 40th Ave 80011. I-70, exit 283 (Chambers Rd); from airport, Pena Blvd S to 40th Ave W. Int corridors. **Pets:** Other species. $25 deposit/room, $10 daily fee/room. Service with restrictions. (SAVE) ⊠ 🔊 🛏 🖥 🏊

CENTENNIAL

△△△ ▼▼▼ Candlewood Suites **H**
(303) 792-5393. **$49-$139.** 6780 S Galena St 80112. I-25, exit 197 (Arapahoe Rd), 0.7 mi e, then just s. Int corridors. **Pets:** Small. $75 one-time fee/room. Service with restrictions. (SAVE) ⊠ 🛏 🖥

▼▼ Days Inn Denver Tech Center **H**
(303) 768-9400. **$59-$89.** 9719 E Geddes Ave 80112. I-25, exit 196 (Dry Creek Rd), just e to S Clinton St, just n, then just e. Int corridors.
Pets: Accepted. (ASK) ⊠ 🔊 🛏 🖥

△△△ ▼▼▼ Embassy Suites Denver Tech Center **H**
(303) 792-0433. **$99-$229.** 10250 E Costilla Ave 80112. I-25, exit 197 (Arapahoe Rd), 1 mi e, 0.3 mi s on Havana St, then w. Int corridors.
Pets: Accepted. (SAVE) ⊠ 🔊 🛏 🖥 🍴 🏊

▼▼▼ Staybridge Suites Denver Tech Center **H**
(303) 858-9990. **$85-$105.** 7150 S Clinton St 80112. I-25, exit 197 (Arapahoe Rd), just e to S Clinton St, then just s. Int corridors.
Pets: Accepted. (ASK) ⊠ 🔊 🛏 🖥 🏊

DENVER

△△△ ▼▼▼ Brown Palace Hotel and Spa **H**
(303) 297-3111. **$139-$569.** 321 17th St 80202. I-25, exit 210 (E Colfax Ave) to Lincoln St, just n, just w on 18th St, then s. Int corridors.
Pets: Accepted. (SAVE) ⊠ 🛏 🖥 🍴

△△△ ▼▼▼ Comfort Inn Central **H** 🐾
(303) 297-1717. **$89-$98.** 401 E 58th Ave 80216. I-25, exit 215, just e, then n on Logan St; connected to Denver Merchandise Mart. Int corridors. **Pets:** Large, other species. $10 daily fee/pet. Designated rooms, service with restrictions, crate. (SAVE) ⊠ 🔊 🛏 🖥 🏊

▼▼▼ Comfort Inn Downtown Denver **H**
(303) 296-0400. **$59-$249.** 401 17th St 80202. I-25, exit 210 (E Colfax Ave) to Lincoln St, just n, just w on 18th St, then s; opposite Brown Palace Hotel and Spa. Int corridors. **Pets:** Accepted. (ASK) ⊠ 🛏 🖥

▼▼▼ Courtyard by Marriott **H**
(303) 333-3303. **$98-$120.** 7415 E 41st Ave 80216. I-70, exit 278, s on Quebec St, exit Smith Rd, then e to Frontage Rd; I-270, exit 4. Int corridors. **Pets:** Accepted. (ECO) ⊠ 🛏 🖥 🍴 🏊

△△△ ▼▼▼ Crowne Plaza Denver International
Airport **H** 🐾
(303) 371-9494. **$89-$169.** 15500 E 40th Ave 80239. I-70, exit 283 (Chambers Rd), just n, then just e. Int corridors. **Pets:** Large. $30 one-time fee/room. Designated rooms, service with restrictions, supervision.
(SAVE) ⊠ 🔊 🛏 🖥 🍴 🏊

▼▼▼ Doubletree Hotel Denver **H** 🐾
(303) 321-3333. **$99-$249.** 3203 Quebec St 80207. I-70, exit 278, 0.5 mi s; I-270, exit 4. Int corridors. **Pets:** Small, other species. $75 one-time fee/room. Service with restrictions, supervision. ⊠ 🛏 🖥 🏊 ⊠

▼▼▼ Drury Inn-Denver East **H**
(303) 373-1983. **$95-$134.** 4380 Peoria St 80239. I-70, exit 281 eastbound; exit 282 westbound, just n. Int corridors. **Pets:** Other species. No service, supervision. (ASK) ⊠ 🛏 🖥 🏊

ⒶⒶⒶ ▼▼▼ Embassy Suites Denver-Aurora 🅷 🐾
(303) 375-0400. **$99-$209.** 4444 N Havana St 80239. I-70, exit 280, just n. Int corridors. **Pets:** Large. $50 deposit/room. Service with restrictions.
[SAVE] [✕] [♿M] [🛏] [💻] [🍴] [🚭]

▼▼▼ Embassy Suites Denver Southeast 🅷
(303) 696-6644. **$99-$319.** 7525 E Hampden Ave 80231. I-25, exit 201, 1 mi e. Int corridors. **Pets:** Accepted. [✕] [🛏] [💻] [🍴] [🏊]

▼▼▼ Hampton Inn & Suites Denver Tech Center 🅷 🐾
(303) 804-9900. **$69-$189.** 5001 S Ulster St 80237. I-25, exit 199, e to Ulster St, then just n. Int corridors. **Pets:** Medium. Designated rooms, service with restrictions, supervision. [✕] [♿M] [🛏] [💻] [🏊]

ⒶⒶⒶ ▼▼▼ Hampton Inn DIA 🅷
(303) 371-0200. **$120-$160.** 6290 Tower Rd 80249. I-70, exit 286 (Tower Rd), 3.5 mi n. Int corridors. **Pets:** Small. $50 deposit/room. Designated rooms, service with restrictions, crate. [SAVE] [✕] [♿M] [💻] [🏊]

ⒶⒶⒶ ▼▼▼ Holiday Chalet a Victorian Bed & Breakfast 🅱🅱 🐾
(303) 437-8245. **$94-$160.** 1820 E Colfax Ave 80218. I-25, exit 210 (Colfax Ave), 2.3 mi e on US 40. Int corridors. **Pets:** Other species. $5 daily fee/room. Crate. [SAVE] [✕] [🛏] [💻]

▼▼ Holiday Inn-Denver Central 🅷
(303) 371-0200. **$114-$123.** 4849 Bannock St 80216. I-25, exit 215 northbound; exit 214B southbound, just w to Broadway, then 1.2 mi s. Ext/int corridors. **Pets:** Accepted. [ASK] [✕] [♿M] [🛏] [💻] [🍴] [🏊]

ⒶⒶⒶ ▼▼▼ Hotel Monaco Denver 🅷
(303) 296-1717. **$159-$379.** 1717 Champa St 80202. I-25, exit 210A (W Colfax Ave), 1 mi e to Kalamath St, 0.7 mi ne, just nw on 18th St, then just sw. Int corridors. **Pets:** Accepted. [SAVE] [✕] [♿M] [🍴] [🚭]

ⒶⒶⒶ ▼▼▼ Hotel Teatro 🅷 🐾
(303) 228-1100. **$189-$1500.** 1100 14th St 80202. I-25, exit 212 (Speer Blvd), just ne on Lawrence St, then e to 14th St; exit Auraria Pkwy northbound. Int corridors. **Pets:** Dogs only. [SAVE] [✕] [🛏] [💻] [🍴] [🚭]

▼▼ Hotel VQ 🅷
(303) 433-8331. **$49-$169.** 1975 Mile High Stadium Cir 80204. I-25, exit 210B, just w. Int corridors. **Pets:** Accepted.
[ASK] [✕] [🛏] [💻] [🍴] [🏊]

ⒶⒶⒶ ▼▼▼ Hyatt Regency Denver Tech Center 🅷
(303) 779-1234. **$79-$369.** 7800 E Tufts Ave 80237. I-225, exit 2 (Tamarac St), just s to Tufts Ave; I-25, exit 199 (Belleview Ave), e to S Ulster St, then 0.5 mi n. Int corridors. **Pets:** Accepted.
[SAVE] [✕] [♿M] [🛏] [💻] [🍴] [🏊] [🚭]

ⒶⒶⒶ ▼▼▼ The Inn at Cherry Creek 🅷
(303) 350-4440. **$189-$345.** 233 Clayton St 80206. Between 2nd and 3rd aves; in Cherry Creek Village. Int corridors. **Pets:** Medium.
[SAVE] [✕] [🛏] [💻] [🍴]

ⒶⒶⒶ ▼▼▼ JW Marriott Denver At Cherry Creek 🅷 🐾
(303) 316-2700. **$269-$329.** 150 Clayton Ln 80206. I-25, exit 205 (University Blvd), 2.4 mi n to 1st Ave, just e, then just n. Int corridors. **Pets:** Dogs only. Designated rooms, service with restrictions, supervision.
[SAVE] [✕] [♿M] [💻] [🍴] [🚭]

▼▼▼ La Quinta Inn & Suites Denver (Airport/DIA) 🅷 🐾
(303) 371-0888. **$59-$139.** 6801 Tower Rd 80249. I-70, exit 286 (Tower Rd), 4.2 mi n; 0.8 mi s of Pena Blvd. Int corridors. **Pets:** Medium, other species. Service with restrictions, supervision.
[ASK] [✕] [♿M] [🛏] [💻] [🏊]

▼▼ La Quinta Inn Denver (Cherry Creek) 🅷 🐾
(303) 758-8886. **$49-$129.** 1975 S Colorado Blvd 80222. I-25, exit 204, just s. Ext corridors. **Pets:** Medium, other species. Service with restrictions, supervision. [ASK] [✕] [🛏] [💻] [🏊]

▼▼ Microtel Inn D.I.A 🅷
(303) 371-8300. **Call for rates.** 18600 E 63rd Ave 80249. I-70, exit 286 (Tower Rd), 3.6 mi n. Int corridors. **Pets:** Accepted. [✕] [♿M] [🛏]

▼▼ The Oxford Hotel 🅷
(303) 628-5400. **$130-$220.** 1600 17th St 80202. Corner of 17th and Wazee sts. Int corridors. **Pets:** Accepted. [ASK] [✕] [🍴] [🚭]

ⒶⒶⒶ ▼▼▼ Quality Inn Denver East 🅷
(303) 371-5640. **$60-$140.** 3975 Peoria Way 80239. I-70, exit 281 eastbound; exit 282 westbound, just s. Ext corridors. **Pets:** $10 one-time fee/pet. Service with restrictions, crate. [SAVE] [✕] [🛏] [💻] [🏊]

▼▼▼ Radisson Hotel Denver Stapleton Plaza 🅷
(303) 321-3500. **$129-$199.** 3333 Quebec St 80207. I-70, exit 278, 0.3 mi s; I-270, exit 4. Int corridors. **Pets:** Accepted.
[ASK] [✕] [♿M] [💻] [🍴] [🏊] [🚭]

▼▼▼ Red Lion Denver Central 🅷
(303) 321-6666. **$69-$219.** 4040 Quebec St 80216. I-70, exit 278, s on Quebec St, exit Smith Rd, then e to Frontage Rd; I-270, exit 4. Int corridors. **Pets:** Other species. $20 one-time fee/room. Service with restrictions, supervision. [ASK] [✕] [🛏] [💻] [🏊]

ⒶⒶⒶ ▼▼▼ Renaissance Denver Hotel 🅷
(303) 399-7500. **$152-$186.** 3801 Quebec St 80207. I-70, exit 278, just s via Smith Rd exit. Int corridors. **Pets:** Accepted.
[SAVE] [✕] [💻] [🍴] [🏊]

▼▼▼ Residence Inn by Marriott Denver City Center 🅷
(303) 296-3444. **$251-$307.** 1725 Champa St 80202. I-25, exit 212A (Speer Blvd S), 1.3 mi s to Stout St, 0.6 mi e, just n on 18th St, then just s. Int corridors. **Pets:** Accepted. [✕] [🛏] [💻]

▼▼▼ Residence Inn by Marriott Denver Downtown 🅷
(303) 458-5318. **$197-$241.** 2777 Zuni St 80211. I-25, exit 212B, just w, then just n. Ext corridors. **Pets:** Accepted. [✕] [🛏] [💻] [🏊]

▼▼ ▼▼ The Ritz-Carlton, Denver 🅷
(303) 312-3800. **$179-$379.** 1881 Curtis St 80202. I-25, exit 212C (20th St), 1 mi se, just sw on Arapahoe St, then just se on 17th St; jct 18th and Curtis sts. Int corridors. **Pets:** Accepted.
[ASK] [✕] [♿M] [🛏] [💻] [🍴] [🏊] [🚭]

ⒶⒶⒶ ▼▼▼ Sheraton Denver Downtown Hotel 🅷 🐾
(303) 893-3333. **$99-$329.** 1550 Court Pl 80202. I-25, exit 210A (W Colfax Ave), 1.2 mi e, then just ne. Int corridors. **Pets:** Medium, dogs only. Service with restrictions, supervision.
[SAVE] [✕] [♿M] [🛏] [💻] [🍴] [🏊]

▼▼▼ Timbers Hotel 🅷 🐾
(303) 373-1444. **Call for rates.** 4411 Peoria St 80239. I-70, exit 281, just n. Int corridors. **Pets:** Dogs only. $50 one-time fee/room. Designated rooms, service with restrictions, supervision. [✕] [♿M] [🛏] [💻] [🍴]

▼▼ TownePlace Suites by Marriott-Denver Southeast 🅷
(303) 759-9393. **$143-$175.** 3699 S Monaco Pkwy 80237. I-25, exit 201, just e to Monaco Pkwy, then s. Int corridors. **Pets:** $100 one-time fee/room. Service with restrictions. [✕] [🛏] [💻] [🏊]

▼▼ TownePlace Suites by Marriott Downtown Denver 🅷
(303) 722-2322. **$199-$219.** 685 Speer Blvd 80204-4513. I-25, exit 212A (Speer Blvd), 2.2 mi s, stay in right lane, just past second Bannock St, exit towards Broadway, then right on Acoma St. Int corridors.
Pets: Accepted. [✕] [♿M] [🛏] [💻]

(AAA) ▼▼▼▼ **Warwick Denver Hotel** **H**
(303) 861-2000. **$109-$499.** 1776 Grant St 80203. I-25, exit 210 a (E Colfax Ave), 1.7 mi to Logan St, just n to 18th St, then just w. Int corridors. **Pets:** Accepted. [SAVE] [X] [B] [🖵] [🍴] [🐾]

(AAA) ▼▼▼ ▼▼▼ **The Westin Tabor Center Denver** **H** ✿
(303) 572-9100. **$169-$499.** 1672 Lawrence St 80202. I-25, exit 212B (Speer Blvd) southbound, 1 mi s to Lawrence St, then e; exit 212A (Speer Blvd) northbound. Int corridors. **Pets:** Medium, dogs only. $200 deposit/pet. [SAVE] [X] [&M] [B] [🖵] [🍴] [🐾] [X]

ENGLEWOOD
(AAA) ▼▼▼ ▼▼▼ **Comfort Suites Denver Tech Center** **H**
(303) 858-0700. **$70-$160.** 7374 S Clinton St 80112. I-25, exit 196 (Dry Creek Rd), just e, then n. Int corridors. **Pets:** Accepted.
[SAVE] [X] [&M] [B] [🖵] [🐾]

▼▼▼ **Drury Inn & Suites-Denver Near the Tech Center** **H**
(303) 694-3400. **$90-$159.** 9445 E Dry Creek Rd 80112. I-25, exit 196 (Dry Creek Rd), just w, on northwest corner. Int corridors. **Pets:** Other species. No service, supervision. [ASK] [X] [B] [🖵] [🐾]

▼▼ **Extended Stay Deluxe-Denver Tech Center South** **H**
(303) 858-0292. **$57-$67.** 9604 E Easter Ave 80112. I-25, exit 197 (Arapahoe Rd), just e to Clinton St, 0.5 mi s, then just e. Int corridors. **Pets:** Other species. $25 daily fee/room. Designated rooms, service with restrictions, crate. [X] [B] [🖵] [🐾]

▼▼▼ **Holiday Inn Express Hotel & Suites** **H**
(303) 662-0777. **$71-$117.** 7380 S Clinton St 80112. I-25, exit 196 (Dry Creek Rd), e to S Clinton St, then just n. Int corridors. **Pets:** Small. $50 one-time fee/room. Service with restrictions, crate.
[ASK] [X] [B] [🖵] [🐾]

▼▼▼ **Homewood Suites by Hilton–DTC/Inverness** **H**
(303) 706-0102. **$79-$189.** 199 Inverness Dr W 80112. I-25, exit 195 (County Line Rd), 0.3 mi ne to traffic light, then just n. Int corridors. **Pets:** Medium. $100 one-time fee/pet. Designated rooms, service with restrictions, crate. [X] [B] [🖵] [🐾] [X]

▼▼▼ **Residence Inn by Marriott-Denver Tech Center** **H**
(303) 740-7177. **$166-$202.** 6565 S Yosemite St 80111. I-25, exit 197 (Arapahoe Rd), just w, then n. Ext corridors. **Pets:** Accepted.
[X] [B] [🖵] [🐾] [X]

▼▼▼ **Residence Inn Park Meadows** **H**
(720) 895-0200. **$169-$179.** 8322 S Valley Hwy 80112. I-25, exit 195 (County Line Rd), just e to S Valley Hwy, then just s. Int corridors. **Pets:** Accepted. [X] [&M] [B] [🖵] [🐾] [X]

▼▼▼ **TownePlace Suites Denver Tech Center** **H**
(720) 875-1113. **$152-$186.** 7877 S Chester St 80112. I-25, exit 196 (Dry Creek Rd), just w to Chester St, then 0.3 mi s. Int corridors. **Pets:** Accepted. [X] [&M] [B] [🖵] [🐾]

GLENDALE
▼▼ **Crossland Studios-Denver/Cherry Creek** **H**
(303) 333-2545. **$55-$65.** 4850 Leetsdale Dr 80246. I-25, exit 204, 1.2 mi n, just e on Alameda, then 0.3 mi se. Ext corridors. **Pets:** Other species. $25 daily fee/room. Designated rooms, service with restrictions, crate. [ASK] [X] [🖵]

(AAA) ▼▼▼ ▼▼▼ **Loews Denver Hotel** **H** ✿
(303) 782-9300. **$89-$279.** 4150 E Mississippi Ave 80246. I-25, exit 204, 0.8 mi n on Colorado Blvd, then just e. Int corridors. **Pets:** Other species. $25 one-time fee/room. Designated rooms.
[SAVE] [X] [&M] [B] [🖵] [🍴]

▼▼▼ **Staybridge Suites Denver/Cherry Creek** **H**
(303) 321-5757. **$89-$149.** 4220 E Virginia Ave 80246. I-25, exit 204, 1.5 mi n on Colorado Blvd to Virginia Ave, then just e. Int corridors. **Pets:** Accepted. [ASK] [X] [&M] [B] [🖵] [X]

GOLDEN
(AAA) ▼▼▼▼ **The Golden Hotel, an Ascend Collection hotel** **H** ✿
(303) 279-0100. **$149-$189.** 800 11th St 80401. At 11th St and Washington Ave; downtown. Int corridors. **Pets:** Medium. $100 deposit/room, $15 daily fee/room. Designated rooms, service with restrictions, supervision.
[SAVE] [X] [B] [🖵]

▼▼ **La Quinta Inn Denver (Golden)** **H** 🐾
(303) 279-5565. **$52-$129.** 3301 Youngfield Service Rd 80401. I-70, exit 264 (32nd Ave) westbound, just w, then n; exit eastbound, just e, n on 32nd, then just e. Ext corridors. **Pets:** Medium, other species. Service with restrictions, supervision. [ASK] [X] [B] [🖵] [🐾]

▼▼▼ **Residence Inn by Marriott Denver West/Golden** **H**
(303) 271-0909. **$150-$160.** 14600 W 6th Ave Frontage Rd 80401. US 6, exit Indiana Ave, just s to frontage road, then just e. Int corridors. **Pets:** Accepted. [X] [&M] [B] [🖵] [🐾] [X]

(AAA) ▼▼▼▼ **Table Mountain Inn** **H** 🐾
(303) 277-9898. **$111-$209.** 1310 Washington Ave 80401. US 6, exit 19th St, 0.5 mi n to Washington Ave, 0.5 mi w; downtown, just s of arch. Int corridors. **Pets:** Other species. $10 daily fee/room. Designated rooms, service with restrictions, supervision. [SAVE] [X] [&M] [B] [🖵] [🍴]

GREENWOOD VILLAGE
▼▼▼ **Hampton Inn Denver Southeast** **H**
(303) 792-9999. **Call for rates.** 9231 E Arapahoe Rd 80112. I-25, exit 197 (Arapahoe Rd), just e. Int corridors. **Pets:** Accepted.
[X] [&M] [B] [🖵] [🐾]

▼▼ **Homestead Studio Suites Hotel-Denver/Tech Center South-Greenwood** **H**
(303) 858-1669. **$65-$75.** 9253 E Costilla Ave 80112. I-25, exit 197 (Arapahoe Rd), just e, just se on Clinton St to Costilla St, then w. Int corridors. **Pets:** Other species. $25 daily fee/room. Designated rooms, service with restrictions, crate. [ASK] [X] [&M] [B] [🖵]

(AAA) ▼▼▼ ▼▼▼ **Hyatt Summerfield Suites Denver Tech Center** **H**
(303) 706-1945. **$89-$309.** 9280 E Costilla Ave 80112. I-25, exit 197 (Arapahoe Rd), e to Clinton St, then just s. Int corridors. **Pets:** Accepted. [SAVE] [X] [&M] [B] [🖵] [🐾]

▼▼▼ **La Quinta Inn & Suites Denver Tech Center** **H** ✿
(303) 649-9969. **$49-$129.** 7077 S Clinton St 80112. I-25, exit 197 (Arapahoe Rd), e to Clinton St, then 0.5 mi s. Int corridors. **Pets:** Medium, other species. Service with restrictions, supervision.
[ASK] [X] [&M] [B] [🖵] [🐾]

(AAA) ▼▼▼ ▼▼▼ **Sheraton Denver Tech Center Hotel** **H**
(303) 799-6200. **Call for rates.** 7007 S Clinton St 80112. I-25, exit 197 (Arapahoe Rd), just e, then s. Int corridors. **Pets:** Accepted.
[SAVE] [X] [&M] [B] [🖵] [🍴] [🐾]

HIGHLANDS RANCH
▼▼▼ **Residence Inn by Marriott Denver Highlands Ranch** **H**
(303) 683-5500. **$143-$175.** 93 Centennial Blvd 80129. SR 470, exit Broadway, just s, then w. Int corridors. **Pets:** Large, other species. $100 one-time fee/room. Service with restrictions, supervision.
[X] [&M] [B] [🖵] [🐾] [X]

LAKEWOOD
(AAA) ▼▼▼ ▼▼ **Best Western-Denver Southwest** **H**
(303) 989-5500. **$90-$120.** 3440 S Vance St 80227. Just ne of jct US 285 (Hampden Ave) and S Wadsworth Blvd, e on Girton Dr, then just s. Int corridors. **Pets:** Designated rooms, service with restrictions, supervision. [SAVE] [X] [B] [🖵] [🐾]

▼▼ Comfort Suites–Lakewood/Golden ⛽

(303) 231-9929. **$89-$129.** 11909 W 6th Ave 80401. US 6, exit Simms St/Union Blvd, westbound travelers must turn right at traffic light, but do not use right turn lane, follow signs to frontage road. Int corridors.
Pets: Accepted. (ASK) ⊠ 🖬 🛇 🛋 🐾

◉ ▼▼ Holiday Inn Lakewood ⛽

(303) 980-9200. **$79-$129.** 7390 W Hampden Ave 80227. US 285 (W Hampden Ave), exit Wadsworth Blvd, just e on Jefferson Ave, then n on Vance. Int corridors. **Pets:** Accepted.
(SAVE) ⊠ 🖬 🛇 🍴 🛋 🐾

▼▼ Lakewood Comfort Suites ⛽

(303) 988-8600. **$90-$100.** 7260 W Jefferson Ave 80235. Just se of US 285 (W Hampden Ave) and Wadsworth Blvd, then e. Int corridors. **Pets:** Medium, dogs only. $15 daily fee/pet. Designated rooms, service with restrictions, supervision. (ASK) ⊠ 🖬 🛇 🛋

▼▼▼ Residence Inn by Marriott Denver SW/Lakewood ⛽

(303) 985-7676. **$130-$140.** 7050 W Hampden Ave 80227. Just se of jct US 285 (W Hampden Ave) and Wadsworth Blvd, e on Jefferson Ave, then n on frontage road. Int corridors. **Pets:** Other species. $100 one-time fee/room. Service with restrictions, supervision.
⊠ 🛇🅼 🖬 🛇 🛋 🐾

◉ ▼▼ Sheraton-Denver West Hotel ⛽

(303) 987-2000. **Call for rates.** 360 Union Blvd 80228. US 6, exit Simms St/Union Blvd, just s on Union Blvd; 3 mi e of jct I-70, exit 261. Int corridors. **Pets:** Accepted. (SAVE) ⊠ 🖬 🛇 🍴 🛋 🐾

▼▼ TownePlace Suites by Marriott-Denver West/Federal Center ⛽ 🐾

(303) 232-7790. **$116-$142.** 800 Tabor St 80401. US 6, exit Simms St/Union Blvd, just n to 8th St, then w. Int corridors. **Pets:** Other species. $100 one-time fee/room. Service with restrictions.
⊠ 🛇🅼 🖬 🛇 🛋

LITTLETON

◉ ▼▼▼ Holiday Inn Express Hotel & Suites ⛽

(720) 981-1000. **$119-$139.** 12683 W Indore Pl 80127. I-70 to SR 470 and Ken Caryl Ave; I-25 to SR 470 and Ken Caryl Ave, to Shaffer Ave, just n, then w. Int corridors. **Pets:** Accepted.
(SAVE) ⊠ 🛇🅼 🖬 🛇 🛋

▼▼▼ Homewood Suites by Hilton-Denver Littleton ⛽

(720) 981-4763. **$69-$129.** 7630 Shaffer Pkwy 80127. SR 470, exit Ken Caryl Ave, just e, then just s. Int corridors. **Pets:** Other species. $50 one-time fee/room. Designated rooms, service with restrictions, crate.
⊠ 🛇🅼 🖬 🛇 🛋 🛇

LONE TREE

▼▼▼ Staybridge Suites Denver South-Lone Tree ⛽

(303) 649-1010. **$69-$159.** 7820 Park Meadows Dr 80124. I-25, exit 195 (County Line Rd), w to Acres Green, s to E Park Meadows Dr, then just w; SR 470, exit Quebec St, just s, then just e. Int corridors.
Pets: Accepted. (ASK) ⊠ 🛇🅼 🖬 🛇 🛋 🛇

THORNTON

▼▼ Sleep Inn North Denver ⛽

(303) 280-9818. **$64-$159.** 12101 Grant St 80241. I-25, exit 223, e to Grant St, then n. Int corridors. **Pets:** Medium, other species. $10 daily fee/pet. Service with restrictions, crate. (ASK) ⊠ 🛇🅼 🖬 🛇 🛋

WESTMINSTER

◉ ▼▼ Comfort Inn Northwest ⛽

(303) 428-3333. **$65-$150.** 8500 Turnpike Dr 80031. US 36 (Boulder Tpke), exit Sheridan Ave, just s, left on Turnpike Dr at 87th Ave, then 0.4 mi. Int corridors. **Pets:** Other species. $10 daily fee/pet. Designated rooms, service with restrictions. (SAVE) ⊠ 🛇🅼 🖬 🛇 🛋

▼▼ Denver North-Westminster-Super 8 ⛽

(303) 451-7200. **Call for rates.** 12055 Melody Dr 80234. I-25, exit 223, just w. Int corridors. **Pets:** Accepted. ⊠ 🛇

◉ ▼▼ Doubletree Hotel Denver North ⛽ 🐾

(303) 427-4000. **$89-$189.** 8773 Yates Dr 80031. US 36 (Boulder Tpke), exit Sheridan Ave, n to 92nd Ave, e to Yates Dr, then 0.5 mi s. Int corridors. **Pets:** Medium. $25 one-time fee/room. Service with restrictions, supervision. (SAVE) ⊠ 🖬 🛇 🍴 🛋

▼▼ La Quinta Inn Denver (Westminster Mall) ⛽ 🐾

(303) 425-9099. **$45-$109.** 8701 Turnpike Dr 80031. US 36 (Boulder Tpke), exit Sheridan Ave, just s, then left on Turnpike Dr at 87th Ave. Ext/int corridors. **Pets:** Medium, other species. Service with restrictions, supervision. (ASK) ⊠ 🛇🅼 🖬 🛇 🛋

▼▼ Residence Inn by Marriott ⛽

(303) 427-9500. **$117-$143.** 5010 W 88th Pl 80031. US 36 (Boulder Tpke), exit Sheridan Ave, n to 92nd Ave, e to Yates Dr, then s. Int corridors. **Pets:** Accepted. ⊠ 🛇🅼 🖬 🛇 🛋

◉ ▼▼▼ The Westin Westminster ⛽ 🐾

(303) 410-5000. **$119-$329.** 10600 Westminster Blvd 80020. US 36 (Boulder Tpke), exit 104th Ave, just n. Int corridors. **Pets:** Medium, dogs only. Service with restrictions, supervision.
(SAVE) ⊠ 🛇🅼 🖬 🛇 🍴 🛋 🛇

WHEAT RIDGE

▼▼▼ Holiday Inn Express Hotel & Suites ⛽

(303) 424-8300. **$111-$130.** 10101 W 48th Ave 80033. I-70, exit 267, just sw. Int corridors. **Pets:** Accepted. (ASK) ⊠ 🖬 🛋 🛋

END METROPOLITAN AREA

DILLON

◉ ▼▼ Best Western Ptarmigan Lodge ⛽

(970) 468-2341. **$76-$260, 3 day notice.** 652 Lake Dillon Dr 80435. I-70, exit 205, 1.3 mi se on US 6, then 0.3 mi s. Ext/int corridors. **Pets:** $15 one-time fee/pet. Designated rooms, service with restrictions, supervision. (SAVE) ⊠ 🖬 🛋 🛇 🅰🅲

DURANGO

◉ ▼▼▼ Apple Orchard Inn 🅱🅱 🐾

(970) 247-0751. **$90-$250, 21 day notice.** 7758 CR 203 81301. 8.5 mi n on US 550, just w at Trimble Ln, then 1.3 mi n. Ext/int corridors. **Pets:** Dogs only. $20 daily fee/pet. Designated rooms, service with restrictions, supervision. (SAVE) ⊠ 🖬 🛋 🅰🅲

▼▼ Caboose Motel Ⓜ

(970) 247-1191. **$58-$190.** 3363 Main Ave 81301. On US 550, 2.5 mi n. Ext corridors. **Pets:** Medium, dogs only. $10 daily fee/pet. Designated rooms, service with restrictions, supervision. (ASK) ⊠ 🖬 🛋

▼▼▼ **Doubletree Hotel** H
(970) 259-6580. **$89-$229.** 501 Camino Del Rio 81301. Jct US 160 and 550. Int corridors. **Pets:** Accepted. ⊠ 🛅 💻 🍽 🐾 ⊠

▼▼ **Holiday Inn** H
(970) 247-5393. **$109-$179.** 800 Camino Del Rio 81301. On US 550, just n of jct US 160. Ext corridors. **Pets:** Accepted.
ASK ⊠ 💻 🍽 🐾 ⊠

▼◆▼ **Leland House Bed & Breakfast Suites** BB 🐾
(970) 385-1920. **$119-$369, 14 day notice.** 721 E 2nd Ave 81301. Just e of Main Ave via 7th St, then just n. Ext/int corridors. **Pets:** $20 daily fee/pet. Designated rooms, supervision. ASK ⊠ 🛅 💻

▼▼ **Quality Inn** M
(970) 259-5373. **$70-$180.** 2930 N Main Ave 81301. On US 550, 2 mi n. Ext corridors. **Pets:** Medium, other species. $15 daily fee/pet. Designated rooms, service with restrictions, supervision. ASK ⊠ 💻 🐾

▼▼▼ **Residence Inn by Marriott** H
(970) 259-6200. **$139-$214.** 21691 Hwy 160 W 81301. On US 160, just w. Int corridors. **Pets:** Large, other species. $75 one-time fee/room. Service with restrictions, crate. ⊠ 🕯M 🛅 💻 🐾 ⊠

▼▼▼ **The Rochester Hotel** BB 🐾
(970) 385-1920. **$119-$369, 14 day notice.** 726 E 2nd Ave 81301. Just e of Main Ave via 7th St, then just n. Int corridors. **Pets:** $20 daily fee/pet. Designated rooms, supervision. ASK ⊠ 🛅 💻

▼ **Siesta Motel** M
(970) 247-0741. **$58-$145.** 3475 N Main Ave 81301. On US 550, 2.6 mi n. Ext corridors. **Pets:** Accepted. ASK ⊠ 🛅 💻

EAGLE

▲▲▲ ▼▼▼ **Best Western Eagle Lodge & Suites** H
(970) 328-6316. **Call for rates.** 200 Loren Ln 81631. I-70, exit 147, just s. Int corridors. **Pets:** Dogs only. $50 deposit/pet, $10 daily fee/pet. Designated rooms, service with restrictions, supervision.
SAVE ⊠ 🛅 💻 🐾 ⊠

EDWARDS

▼▼▼ **Inn & Suites at Riverwalk** H
(970) 926-0606. **$100-$800, 14 day notice.** 27 Main St 81632. I-70, exit 163, 0.3 mi s. Int corridors. **Pets:** Large, other species. $5 daily fee/pet, $25 one-time fee/pet. Designated rooms, service with restrictions, crate.
ASK ⊠ 🛅 💻 🍽 🐾

ESTES PARK

▲▲▲ ▼▼◆ **Castle Mountain Lodge** CA 🐾
(970) 586-3664. **$70-$575, 30 day notice.** 1520 Fall River Rd 80517. 1 mi w on US 34. Ext corridors. **Pets:** Dogs only. $15 daily fee/pet. Designated rooms, service with restrictions, supervision.
SAVE ⊠ 🛅 💻 ⊠ 🎿 ☎

▼◆▼ **Holiday Inn Rocky Mountain Park** H 🐾
(970) 586-2332. **Call for rates.** 101 S St Vrain Ave 80517. 0.5 mi se; on SR 7 at US 36, in Holiday Inn Rocky Mountain Park. Int corridors. **Pets:** Other species. $30 one-time fee/room. Designated rooms, service with restrictions, supervision. ⊠ 🕯M 🛅 💻 🍽 🐾 ⊠

▼▼ **McGregor Mountain Lodge** CA
(970) 586-3457. **$65-$395, 30 day notice.** 2815 Fall River Rd 80517. 3.5 mi w on US 34. Ext corridors. **Pets:** Dogs only. $25 daily fee/pet. Designated rooms, service with restrictions, supervision.
⊠ 🛅 💻 ⊠ 🎿 ☎

▼◆▼ **Mountain Shadows Resort** CA 🐾
(970) 577-0397. **$144-$174, 30 day notice.** 871 Riverside Dr 80517. 1.8 mi sw on US 36, just s on Mary's Lake Rd to Riverside Dr, then just e. Ext corridors. **Pets:** $10 daily fee/pet. Service with restrictions, supervision. ASK ⊠ 🛅 💻 🎿 ☎

▲▲▲ ▼◆▼ **Silver Moon Inn** M
(970) 586-6006. **$80-$280.** 175 Spruce Dr 80517. Just w on US 34, then just ne. Ext corridors. **Pets:** Designated rooms, supervision.
SAVE ⊠ 🛅 💻 🐾 ⊠

▼▼ **Tyrol Mountain Inn** M
(970) 586-3382. **$69-$179.** 1240 Big Thompson Ave 80517. 1.3 mi e on US 34. Ext corridors. **Pets:** Large, dogs only. $10 daily fee/pet. Designated rooms, service with restrictions, supervision.
ASK ⊠ 🛅 💻 🐾

EVANS

▼▼ **Select Stay** H
(970) 356-2180. **Call for rates.** 3025 8th Ave 80620. Just sw of jct US 34 and 85 Bypass. Int corridors. **Pets:** Accepted.
⊠ 🕯M 🛅 💻 🐾

EVERGREEN

▼▼▼ **Quality Suites at Evergreen Parkway** H 🐾
(303) 526-2000. **$109-$149, 3 day notice.** 29300 US Hwy 40 80439. I-70, exit 252 (Evergreen Pkwy) westbound, on west side of El Rancho Restaurant; exit 251 eastbound. Int corridors. **Pets:** Large. $10 daily fee/pet. Designated rooms, service with restrictions, crate.
ASK ⊠ 🕯M 🛅 💻 🐾 ⊠

FIRESTONE

▲▲▲ ▼▼▼ **Comfort Suites** H
(720) 864-2970. **$100-$190.** 11292 Business Park Cir 80504. I-25, exit 240, just e on Firestone Blvd, just n on Frontage Rd, then just e. Int corridors. **Pets:** Accepted. SAVE ⊠ 🛅 💻 🐾

FORT COLLINS

▲▲▲ ▼▼▼ **AmericInn Lodge & Suites of Fort Collins South** H 🐾
(970) 226-1232. **$69-$169.** 7645 Westgate Dr 80528. I-25, exit 262, just se off SR 392. Int corridors. **Pets:** Dogs only. $15 daily fee/room. Designated rooms, service with restrictions. SAVE ⊠ 🕯M 🛅 💻 🐾

▲▲▲ ▼▼▼ **Best Western Kiva Inn** H
(970) 484-2444. **$70-$150.** 1638 E Mulberry St (Hwy 14) 80524. I-25, exit 269B, 1.5 mi w on SR 14. Ext/int corridors. **Pets:** Other species. $10 daily fee/pet. Designated rooms, service with restrictions, supervision.
SAVE ⊠ 🛅 💻 🐾 ⊠

▲▲▲ ▼▼▼ **Best Western University Inn** M
(970) 484-1984. **$69-$159.** 914 S College Ave 80524. I-25, exit 268, 4 mi w to College Ave, then just n on US 287. Ext/int corridors. **Pets:** Other species. $15 daily fee/pet. Designated rooms, service with restrictions, supervision. SAVE ⊠ 🛅 💻 🐾 ⊠

▼▼ **Comfort Suites by Choice Hotels** H
(970) 206-4597. **Call for rates.** 1415 Oakridge Dr 80525. I-25, exit 265, 3.3 mi w to McMurray Ave, just s, then w. Int corridors. **Pets:** Accepted.
⊠ 🛅 💻 🐾

▼▼▼ **Hampton Inn** H
(970) 229-5927. **Call for rates.** 1620 Oakridge Dr 80525. I-25, exit 265 (Harmony Rd), 3.3 mi w, s on McMurray Ave to Oakridge Dr, then just e. Int corridors. **Pets:** Accepted. ⊠ 🕯M 🛅 💻

▲▲▲ ▼▼▼ **Hilton Ft Collins** H
(970) 482-2626. **$109-$189.** 425 W Prospect Rd 80526. I-25, exit 268, 4.3 mi w. Int corridors. **Pets:** Accepted.
SAVE ⊠ 🛅 💻 🍽 🐾 ⊠

▼▼▼ **Homewood Suites by Hilton Fort Collins** H 🐾
(970) 225-2400. **$89-$119.** 1521 Oakridge Dr 80525. I-25, exit 265 (Harmony Rd), 3 mi w, just s on McMurray, then just w. Int corridors. **Pets:** Medium. $75 one-time fee/room. Service with restrictions, supervision. ⊠ 🛅 💻 🐾 ⊠

La Quinta Inn 🏨 ❀

(970) 493-7800. **$55-$159.** 3709 E Mulberry St 80524. I-25, exit 269B, just w, then just sw on frontage road. Int corridors. **Pets:** Medium, other species. Service with restrictions, supervision.

🗝 ✖ 🛏 💻 🏊 🗶

Quality Inn & Suites 🏨

(970) 282-9047. **$79-$209.** 4001 S Mason St 80525. I-25, exit 265 (Harmony Rd), 4.6 mi w to Mason St, then 0.5 mi n. Int corridors. **Pets:** Accepted. ASK ✖ 🔥M 🛏 💻 🏊

Sleep Inn 🏨

(970) 484-5515. **$55-$80.** 3808 E Mulberry St 80524-8536. I-25, exit 269B, just nw. Int corridors. **Pets:** Accepted. ASK ✖ 🛏 💻

Super 8 🏨

(970) 493-7701. **$52-$150, 14 day notice.** 409 Centro Way 80524. I-25, exit 269B, just w. Int corridors. **Pets:** Other species. $10 daily fee/pet. Service with restrictions, supervision. ASK ✖ 🛏 💻 🗶

FORT MORGAN

Best Western Park Terrace Inn 🏨 ❀

(970) 867-8256. **$75-$89.** 725 Main St 80701. I-76, exit 80, 0.5 mi s. Ext corridors. **Pets:** Large. $10 one-time fee/room. Designated rooms, service with restrictions, crate. 🗝 ✖ 🛏 💻 🍽 🏊

Central Motel 🅼

(970) 867-2401. **$52-$69.** 201 W Platte Ave 80701. I-76, exit 80, 0.6 mi s, then w on US 34. Ext corridors. **Pets:** Other species. $10 one-time fee/room. Service with restrictions, supervision. 🗝 ✖ 🛏 💻

Rodeway Inn 🅼 ❀

(970) 867-9481. **$79-$169.** 1409 Barlow Rd 80701. I-76, exit 82 (Barlow Rd), just n. Ext/int corridors. **Pets:** $10 daily fee/room. Designated rooms, service with restrictions, supervision. ASK ✖ 🛏 💻 🍽

FRISCO

Best Western Lake Dillon Lodge 🏨

(970) 668-5094. **$84-$209.** 1202 N Summit Blvd 80443. I-70, exit 203, just s. Int corridors. **Pets:** Other species. $20 one-time fee/room. Designated rooms, service with restrictions, supervision.

🗝 ✖ 🛏 💻 🏊 🗶

Hotel Frisco 🏨 ❀

(970) 668-5009. **$59-$319, 14 day notice.** 308 Main 80443. I-70, exit 201, 0.7 mi e; center. Ext/int corridors. **Pets:** Other species. $10 daily fee/pet. No service. ASK ✖ 🛏 💻 🅰𝒞

New Summit Inn 🏨

(970) 668-3220. **$49-$159, 15 day notice.** 1205 N Summit Blvd 80443. I-70, exit 203, just s, then just e. Int corridors. **Pets:** Accepted.

🗝 ✖ 🛏 💻

Ramada Limited Frisco 🏨 ❀

(970) 668-8783. **Call for rates.** 990 Lakepoint Dr 80443. I-70, exit 203, just s. Int corridors. **Pets:** Other species. $10 daily fee/room. Designated rooms, service with restrictions, supervision. 🗝 ✖ 🔥M 🛏 💻

Snowshoe Motel 🅼

(970) 668-3444. **$49-$140.** 521 Main St 80443. I-70, exit 203 westbound, 1 mi s to Main St, then just w; exit 201 eastbound, 0.8 mi e. Ext corridors. **Pets:** Medium. $10 one-time fee/pet. Designated rooms, service with restrictions, supervision. 🗝 ✖ 🛏 💻 🅰𝒞

FRUITA

Balanced Rock Motel 🅼

(970) 858-7333. **$55-$65, 3 day notice.** 126 S Coulson 81521. I-70, exit 19, just n to Aspen Ave, then just w. Ext corridors. **Pets:** Accepted.

ASK ✖ 🛏

Comfort Inn 🏨 ❀

(970) 858-1333. **$55-$199.** 400 Jurassic Ave 81521. I-70, exit 19, 0.3 mi s; just e of Dinosaur Journey Museum. Int corridors. **Pets:** Other species. Designated rooms, service with restrictions, supervision.

🗝 ✖ 🛏 💻

La Quinta Inn & Suites 🏨 ❀

(970) 858-8850. **$79-$249.** 570 Raptor Rd 81521. I-70, exit 19, 0.3 mi s; next to Dinosaur Journey Museum. Int corridors. **Pets:** Medium, other species. Service with restrictions, supervision. 🗝 ✖ 🛏 💻 🏊

Super 8 🅼

(970) 858-0808. **$55-$89.** 399 Jurassic Ave 81521. I-70, exit 19, 0.3 mi s; just e of Dinosaur Journey Museum. Int corridors. **Pets:** Accepted.

🗝 ✖ 🛏 💻 🏊

GLENWOOD SPRINGS

AmericInn Lodge & Suites of Glenwood Springs 🏨

(970) 928-8188. **$99-$235.** 52000 Two Rivers Plaza Rd 81601. I-70, exit 116, just w on US 6 and 24. Int corridors. **Pets:** Accepted.

ASK ✖ 🛏 💻 🏊 🗶

Hotel Colorado 🏨

(970) 945-6511. **Call for rates.** 526 Pine St 81601. I-70, exit 116, just ne. Int corridors. **Pets:** Accepted. 🗝 ✖ 🛏 💻 🍽 🗶 🅰𝒞

Hotel Denver 🏨

(970) 945-6565. **Call for rates.** 402 7th St 81601. I-70, exit 116; across from historic train station; in town center. Int corridors. **Pets:** Accepted.

✖ 🛏 💻 🍽

Quality Inn & Suites 🏨

(970) 945-5995. **$89-$189.** 2650 Gilstrap 81601. I-70, exit 114, just s, then w. Int corridors. **Pets:** Accepted. ASK ✖ 🛏 💻 🏊

Ramada Inn & Suites 🏨

(970) 945-2500. **$85-$143.** 124 W 6th St 81601. I-70, exit 116, just w. Ext/int corridors. **Pets:** $15 daily fee/room. Service with restrictions, supervision. ASK ✖ 🛏 💻 🍽 🏊

GRAND JUNCTION

Americas Best Value Inn 🅼

(970) 245-1410. **$66-$120.** 754 Horizon Dr 81506. I-70, exit 31, 0.3 mi n. Ext corridors. **Pets:** Other species. $10 daily fee/pet. Service with restrictions, supervision. 🗝 ✖ 🛏 💻 🏊

Best Western Sandman Motel 🏨 ❀

(970) 243-4150. **$55-$120.** 708 Horizon Dr 81506. I-70, exit 31, 0.3 mi s. Ext corridors. **Pets:** Small, dogs only. $25 one-time fee/pet. Designated rooms, service with restrictions, supervision. 🗝 ✖ 🛏 💻 🏊

Clarion Inn 🏨

(970) 243-6790. **$89-$139.** 755 Horizon Dr 81506. I-70, exit 31, just n. Ext/int corridors. **Pets:** Other species. Designated rooms, service with restrictions, supervision. 🗝 ✖ 🛏 💻 🍽 🏊

Hawthorn Suites 🏨

(970) 242-2525. **$99-$159.** 225 Main St 81501. At 2nd and Main sts; downtown. Int corridors. **Pets:** Accepted. ASK ✖ 🛏 💻 🏊

La Quinta Inn & Suites 🏨 ❀

(970) 241-2929. **$69-$149.** 2761 Crossroads Blvd 81506. I-70, exit 31, n to Crossroads Blvd, then just w. Int corridors. **Pets:** Medium, other species. Service with restrictions, supervision. ASK ✖ 🛏 💻 🏊

Quality Inn of Grand Junction 🏨

(970) 245-7200. **$70-$120.** 733 Horizon Dr 81506. I-70, exit 31, just s. Int corridors. **Pets:** $10 daily fee/room. Designated rooms, service with restrictions, supervision. 🗝 ✖ 🛏 💻 🍽 🏊

▼▼▼ **Residence Inn by Marriott** 🅷 ❀
(970) 263-4004. **$134-$184.** 767 Horizon Dr 81506. I-70, exit 31, 0.3 mi n. Int corridors. **Pets:** Other species. $100 one-time fee/room. Service with restrictions. ☒ 🛏 💻 ⛱ ☒

ⒶⒶⒶ ▼▼ **Super 8** Ⓜ
(970) 248-8080. **$69-$97.** 728 Horizon Dr 81506. I-70, exit 31, just s. Int corridors. **Pets:** Accepted. 🆂🅰🆅🅴 ☒ 🛏 💻

GRAND LAKE
ⒶⒶⒶ ▼▼ **Spirit Lake Lodge** Ⓜ
(970) 627-3344. **$55-$200, 7 day notice.** 829 Grand Ave 80447. US 34, just e; downtown. Ext corridors. **Pets:** $15 daily fee/pet. Designated rooms, no service, supervision. 🆂🅰🆅🅴 ☒ 🛏 💻

GREELEY
ⒶⒶⒶ ▼▼ **Comfort Inn-Greeley** 🅷 ❀
(970) 330-6380. **$81-$109.** 2467 W 29th St 80631. US 34 Bypass, exit 23rd Ave, just sw. Int corridors. **Pets:** Other species. $15 daily fee/pet. Service with restrictions, supervision. 🆂🅰🆅🅴 ☒ 🛏 💻 ⛱

▼▼ **Country Inn & Suites By Carlson** 🅷 ❀
(970) 330-3404. **$95-$140.** 2501 W 29th St 80631. US 34 Bypass, exit 23rd Ave, just s, then w. Int corridors. **Pets:** Medium. $20 daily fee/pet. Service with restrictions, supervision. 🅰🆂🅺 ☒ 🅶🅼 🛏 💻 ⛱

GUNNISON
ⒶⒶⒶ ▼ **ABC Motel** Ⓜ
(970) 641-2400. **$56-$99.** 212 E Tomichi Ave 81230. On US 50; near Western State College. Ext corridors. **Pets:** Accepted. 🆂🅰🆅🅴 ☒ 🛏

ⒶⒶⒶ ▼▼ **Affordable Inns at Tomichi Village** Ⓜ
(970) 641-1131. **$50-$99.** 41883 Hwy 50 E 81230. On US 50, 2 mi e. Ext corridors. **Pets:** Dogs only. Designated rooms, service with restrictions, supervision. 🆂🅰🆅🅴 ☒ 🛏 💻 ⛱

▼▼ **Alpine Inn** Ⓜ
(970) 641-2804. **$56-$180.** 1011 W Rio Grande 81230. Jct US 50 and SR 135, 1.1 mi w. Int corridors. **Pets:** Accepted.
🅰🆂🅺 ☒ 🛏 💻 ⛱

ⒶⒶⒶ ▼ **Gunnison Inn** Ⓜ
(970) 641-0700. **$55-$85.** 412 E Tomichi Ave 81230. On US 50; near Western State College. Ext corridors. **Pets:** Accepted. 🆂🅰🆅🅴 ☒ 🛏

▼▼ **Rodeway Inn** Ⓜ
(970) 641-0500. **Call for rates.** 37760 W Hwy 50 81230. US 50, 2.3 mi w. Ext corridors. **Pets:** Accepted. ☒ 🛏 💻

▼▼ **Super 8** Ⓜ ❀
(970) 641-3068. **$60-$125.** 411 E Tomichi Ave 81230. On US 50; near Western State College. Int corridors. **Pets:** Dogs only. $15 daily fee/pet. Designated rooms, no service, supervision. 🅰🆂🅺 ☒ 🛏 💻

ⒶⒶⒶ ▼▼ **Water Wheel Inn** 🅷 ❀
(970) 641-1650. **$69-$109.** 37478 W Hwy 50 81230. On US 50, 2.5 mi w. Ext/int corridors. **Pets:** $5 daily fee/pet. Designated rooms, service with restrictions, supervision. 🆂🅰🆅🅴 ☒ 🛏 💻 ☒

HOT SULPHUR SPRINGS
ⒶⒶⒶ ▼ **Canyon Motel** Ⓜ ❀
(970) 725-3395. **$49-$139.** 221 Byers Ave 80451. On US 40. Ext corridors. **Pets:** Other species. $10 daily fee/room. Designated rooms, no service, supervision. 🆂🅰🆅🅴 ☒ 🛏 💻 🅺

JULESBURG
ⒶⒶⒶ ▼ **Budget Host Platte Valley Inn** 🅷
(970) 474-3336. **$53-$65.** 15225 Hwy 385 80737. I-76, exit 180, just n. Ext corridors. **Pets:** Dogs only. $7 daily fee/pet. Designated rooms, service with restrictions, supervision. 🆂🅰🆅🅴 ☒ 🛏 💻 🍴 ⛱

KEYSTONE
ⒶⒶⒶ ▼▼▼ **The Inn at Keystone** 🅷 ❀
(970) 496-4825. **$109-$325, 21 day notice.** 23044 Hwy 6 80435. I-70, exit 205, 6.5 mi e on US 6; at Keystone Ski area. Int corridors. **Pets:** Other species. $25 daily fee/room. Service with restrictions.
🆂🅰🆅🅴 ☒ 🛏 💻 🍴 ☒ 🅰🅲

LA JUNTA
▼▼▼ **Holiday Inn Express** Ⓜ
(719) 384-2900. **$99-$109.** 27994 US Hwy 50 Frontage Rd 81050. On US 50, 0.8 mi w. Int corridors. **Pets:** $20 daily fee/room. Service with restrictions, supervision. 🅰🆂🅺 ☒ 🛏 💻 ⛱

LAKE GEORGE
ⒶⒶⒶ ▼▼▼ **Mule Creek Outfitters/M Lazy C Ranch** 🆁🅰
(719) 748-3398. **$75-$110, 30 day notice.** 801 CR 453 80827. 5 mi w on US 24, 0.8 mi n on dirt road. Ext corridors. **Pets:** Dogs only. $5 daily fee/pet. Designated rooms, service with restrictions, supervision.
🆂🅰🆅🅴 ☒ 🛏 💻 ☒ 🅰🅲 🅿🆅 🅕

LAMAR
ⒶⒶⒶ ▼ **Blue Spruce Motel** Ⓜ ❀
(719) 336-7454. **$55-$85.** 1801 S Main St 81052. 1.3 mi s on US 287 and 385. Ext corridors. **Pets:** Other species. $7 daily fee/pet. Designated rooms, service with restrictions, crate. 🆂🅰🆅🅴 ☒ 🛏 💻 ⛱

ⒶⒶⒶ ▼ **Chek Inn** Ⓜ
(719) 336-4331. **$50-$75.** 1210 S Main St 81052. 1 mi s on US 287 and 385. Ext corridors. **Pets:** Other species. $10 daily fee/pet. Designated rooms, service with restrictions, crate. 🆂🅰🆅🅴 ☒ 🛏 💻 ⛱

LAS ANIMAS
ⒶⒶⒶ ▼▼▼ **Best Western Bent's Fort Inn** Ⓜ
(719) 456-0011. **$64-$82, 3 day notice.** 10950 E US 50 81054. On US 50, 1.5 mi e on frontage road. Int corridors. **Pets:** Other species. $15 daily fee/pet. Service with restrictions, crate.
🆂🅰🆅🅴 ☒ 🛏 💻 🍴 ⛱

LEADVILLE
ⒶⒶⒶ ▼▼ **Alps Motel** Ⓜ
(719) 486-1223. **$60-$85, 5 day notice.** 207 Elm St 80461. Just s on US 24. Int corridors. **Pets:** Accepted. 🆂🅰🆅🅴 ☒ 🛏 💻 🅺

LIMON
▼▼ **Quality Inn & Suites** 🅷
(719) 775-0277. **Call for rates.** 925 T Ave 80828. I-70, exit 359, just s. Int corridors. **Pets:** Accepted. ☒ 🛏 💻

ⒶⒶⒶ ▼ **Safari Motel** Ⓜ
(719) 775-2363. **$45-$110.** 637 Main St 80828. I-70, exit 361, 0.8 mi w. Ext corridors. **Pets:** Other species. $5 daily fee/pet. Service with restrictions, supervision. 🆂🅰🆅🅴 ☒ 🛏 💻 ⛱

LONGMONT
ⒶⒶⒶ ▼▼ **Hawthorn Suites** 🅷
(303) 774-7100. **$89-$189.** 2000 Sunset Way 80501. Jct US 287, 1.3 mi w on Ken Pratt Blvd (SR 119), just n on Sunset St, then just w on Korte Pkwy. Int corridors. **Pets:** Medium, other species. $75 deposit/pet. Service with restrictions, supervision. 🆂🅰🆅🅴 ☒ 🅶🅼 🛏 💻 ☒

ⒶⒶⒶ ▼▼▼ **Holiday Inn Express & Suites** 🅷
(303) 684-0404. **$122-$139.** 1335 Dry Creek Dr 80503. Jct Main St and Ken Pratt Blvd (SR 119), 2.2 mi w, just n, then just ne. Int corridors. **Pets:** Accepted. 🆂🅰🆅🅴 ☒ 🛏 💻 ⛱

ⒶⒶⒶ ▼▼▼ **Radisson Hotel & Conference Center Longmont-Boulder** 🅷
(303) 776-2000. **$79-$159.** 1900 Ken Pratt Blvd 80501. Jct US 287, 1.3 mi sw on Ken Pratt Blvd (SR 119). Int corridors. **Pets:** Large. $100 deposit/room. Service with restrictions, supervision.
🆂🅰🆅🅴 ☒ 🛏 💻 🍴 ⛱ ☒

Residence Inn by Marriott Boulder/Longmont 🏨

(303) 702-9933. **$160-$180.** 1450 Dry Creek Dr 80503. Jct Main St and Ken Pratt Blvd (SR 119), 2.2 mi w, just n, then just ne; jct Hoover Rd and SR 119. Int corridors. **Pets:** Accepted. 🗙 ⬛ 🛗 📶 📱 🛏 🗙

Super 8 Twin Peaks, Longmont 🏨

(303) 772-8106. **$59-$169.** 2446 N Main St 80501. I-25, exit 240, 6.9 mi w to US 287, then 3.5 mi n at jct SR 66. Int corridors. **Pets:** Medium. $25 daily fee/pet. Designated rooms, service with restrictions, supervision. 🆂🅰🆅🅴 🗙 🛗 📱

LOUISVILLE

Comfort Inn in Boulder County 🏨 🐾

(303) 604-0181. **$60-$130.** 1196 Dillon Rd 80027. US 36 (Boulder Tpke), exit Superior (SR 170), just n on McCaslin Blvd, then just w. Int corridors. **Pets:** Medium, dogs only. $15 daily fee/pet. Designated rooms, supervision. 🆂🅰🆅🅴 🗙 ⬛ 🛗 📱

La Quinta Inn & Suites Denver (Louisville/Boulder) 🏨 🐾

(303) 664-0100. **$49-$129.** 902 Dillon Rd 80027. US 36 (Boulder Tpke), exit Superior (SR 170), just n on McCaslin Blvd, then e. Int corridors. **Pets:** Medium, other species. Service with restrictions, supervision. 🅰🆂🅺 🗙 ⬛ 🛗 📱 🛏

Quality Inn & Suites 🏨

(303) 327-1215. **Call for rates.** 960 W Dillon Rd 80027. US 36 (Boulder Tpke), exit Superior (SR 170), just n on McCaslin Blvd to Dillon Rd, then just e. Int corridors. **Pets:** Accepted. 🗙 🛗 📱 🛏

Residence Inn by Marriott-Boulder/Louisville 🏨 🐾

(303) 665-2661. **$140-$160.** 845 Coal Creek Cir 80027. US 36 (Boulder Tpke), exit Superior (SR 170), n on McCaslin Blvd to Dillon Rd, then 0.6 mi e. Int corridors. **Pets:** Other species. $100 one-time fee/room. Service with restrictions. 🗙 ⬛ 🛗 📱 🛏 🗙

LOVELAND

Best Western Crossroads Inn & Conference Center 🏨 🐾

(970) 667-7810. **$79-$159.** 5542 E US Hwy 34 80537. I-25, exit 257B, just w. Ext/int corridors. **Pets:** Large, other species. $15 daily fee/pet. Service with restrictions, crate. 🆂🅰🆅🅴 🗙 🛗 📱 🍽 🛏

Embassy Suites Loveland 🏨 🐾

(970) 593-6200. **$99-$179.** 4705 Clydesdale Pkwy 80538. I-25, exit 259, just e, then just n. Int corridors. **Pets:** Medium. $25 one-time fee/room. Designated rooms, service with restrictions, supervision. 🆂🅰🆅🅴 🗙 🛗 📱 🍽 🛏 🗙

La Quinta Inn & Suites 🏨 🐾

(970) 622-8600. **Call for rates.** 1450 Cascade Ave 80538. I-25, exit 257B, 7.3 mi w. Int corridors. **Pets:** Medium, other species. Service with restrictions, supervision. 🗙 🛗 📱 🛏

Residence Inn By Marriott Loveland 🏨

(970) 622-7000. **$169-$189.** 5450 McWhinney Blvd 80538. I-25, exit 257B, 0.5 mi w to Outlet Mall entry, just n, then just e. Int corridors. **Pets:** Accepted. 🗙 🛗 📱 🛏 🗙

MESA VERDE NATIONAL PARK

Far View Lodge 🅼

(970) 529-4421. **$99-$149, 3 day notice.** 1 Navajo Hill, MM 15 81330. 14 mi from park gate. Ext corridors. **Pets:** Medium, dogs only. $50 one-time fee/room. Designated rooms, no service, supervision. 🆂🅰🆅🅴 🗙 🛗 📱 🍽 🎦

MONTE VISTA

Best Western Movie Manor 🏨

(719) 852-5921. **$80-$140.** 2830 W Hwy 160 81144. On US 160, 2 mi w. Ext corridors. **Pets:** Accepted. 🆂🅰🆅🅴 🗙 📱

MONTROSE

Best Western Red Arrow 🏨 🐾

(970) 249-9641. **$69-$129.** 1702 E Main St 81401. 1 mi e on US 50. Ext/int corridors. **Pets:** Other species. $10 one-time fee/pet. Service with restrictions, supervision. 🆂🅰🆅🅴 🗙 🛗 📱 🛏 🗙

Days Inn 🅼

(970) 249-4507. **$49-$120.** 1417 E Main St 81401. East end of town. Ext corridors. **Pets:** Accepted. 🅰🆂🅺 🗙 🛗 📱 🛏

Hampton Inn 🏨

(970) 252-3300. **Call for rates.** 1980 N Townsend Ave 81401. On US 550, just n of jct US 50. Int corridors. **Pets:** Accepted. 🗙 📱 🛏 🗙

Holiday Inn Express Hotel & Suites 🏨

(970) 240-1800. **$119-$149.** 1391 S Townsend Ave 81401. 1 mi s on US 550, e on Niagara Ave. Int corridors. **Pets:** Accepted. 🆂🅰🆅🅴 🗙 ⬛ 🛗 📱

Quality Inn & Suites 🏨

(970) 249-1011. **$99-$149.** 2751 Commercial Way 81401. 2 mi s on US 550, w on O'Delle. Int corridors. **Pets:** Accepted. 🅰🆂🅺 🗙 🛗 📱 🛏

Rodeway Inn 🅼

(970) 249-9294. **$50-$100.** 1705 E Main St 81401. 1 mi e on US 50. Int corridors. **Pets:** Small. $10 daily fee/pet. Service with restrictions, supervision. 🆂🅰🆅🅴 🗙 🛗 📱

Uncompahgre Bed & Breakfast 🅱🅱

(970) 240-4000. **$90-$150.** 21049 Uncompahgre Rd 81401. 8 mi s on US 550. Int corridors. **Pets:** Dogs only. Designated rooms, service with restrictions, supervision. 🅰🆂🅺 🗙 🛗 🅩

Western Motel 🅼

(970) 249-3481. **$50-$150.** 1200 E Main St 81401. 0.8 mi e on US 50. Ext corridors. **Pets:** Accepted. 🅰🆂🅺 🗙 🛗 🛏

NEW CASTLE

Rodeway Inn 🅼

(970) 984-2363. **Call for rates.** 781 Burning Mountain Ave 81647. I-70, exit 105, just n, then w. Int corridors. **Pets:** Cats only. $10 daily fee/pet. Supervision. 🆂🅰🆅🅴 🗙 🛗 📱 🛏

OURAY

Best Western Twin Peaks Lodge & Hot Springs 🏨

(970) 325-4427. **$99-$250.** 125 3rd Ave 81427. Just s on US 550, then just w. Ext corridors. **Pets:** Accepted. 🆂🅰🆅🅴 🗙 🛗 📱 🍽 🛏

Comfort Inn 🅼

(970) 325-7203. **$69-$189.** 191 5th Ave 81427. Just w of US 550 via 5th Ave. Ext corridors. **Pets:** Dogs only. $15 daily fee/pet. Designated rooms, service with restrictions, supervision. 🅰🆂🅺 🗙 ⬛ 🛗 📱

Ouray Riverside Inn & Cabins 🅼

(970) 325-4061. **$60-$210, 3 day notice.** 1804 N Main St 81427. 1 mi n on US 550. Ext corridors. **Pets:** Accepted. 🆂🅰🆅🅴 🗙 🛗 📱

Ouray Victorian Inn 🅼 🐾

(970) 325-7222. **$68-$199.** 50 3rd Ave 81427-1812. Just w of US 550 via 3rd Ave. Ext corridors. **Pets:** Dogs only. $10 daily fee/room. Designated rooms, service with restrictions, supervision. 🆂🅰🆅🅴 🗙 🛗 📱 🎦

River's Edge Motel 🅼 🐾

(970) 325-4621. **$59-$249.** 110 7th Ave 81427. Just w US 550 via 7th Ave. Ext corridors. **Pets:** Dogs only. $10 daily fee/pet. Service with restrictions, supervision. 🆂🅰🆅🅴 🗙 🛗 📱 🎦

PAGOSA SPRINGS

Alpine Inn of Pagosa Springs M
(970) 731-4005. **$55-$109.** 8 Solomon Dr 81147. 2.5 mi w on US 160.
Ext/int corridors. **Pets:** Accepted. SAVE X 🐾 🖨 💻

Fireside Inn Cabins CA ❧
(970) 264-9204. **$105-$189, 30 day notice.** 1600 E Hwy 160 81147.
1.3 mi e on US 160. Ext corridors. **Pets:** Dogs only. $9 daily fee/pet.
Service with restrictions, crate. X 🖨 💻 X 🐾

High Country Lodge M
(970) 264-4181. **$110.** 3821 E Hwy 160 81147. On US 160, 3 mi e. Ext
corridors. **Pets:** Accepted. ASK X 🖨 💻 🍴 🐾

Pagosa Lodge M
(970) 731-4141. **Call for rates.** 3505 W Hwy 160 81147. 3.5 mi w on
US 160. Int corridors. **Pets:** Accepted. X 🖨 💻 🐾 🐾

Pagosa Springs Inn & Suites M
(970) 731-3400. **$65-$179.** 519 Village Dr 81147. 3.8 mi w on US 160.
Int corridors. **Pets:** Medium. $10 daily fee/pet. Designated rooms, service
with restrictions, supervision. ASK X 🖨 💻 🐾

PARKER

Holiday Inn H
(303) 248-2147. **$106-$123.** 19308 Cottonwood Dr 80138. E-470 toll
road, exit 5 (Parker Rd/SR 83) eastbound, straight at light, follow signs to
Cottonwood Dr; exit westbound, just s to Crown Crest, follow signs to
Cottonwood Dr. Int corridors. **Pets:** Accepted.
ASK X 🖨 💻 🍴 🐾

Super 8-Parker H
(720) 851-2644. **$89-$99.** 6230 E Pine Ln 80138. E-470 toll road, exit 5
(Parker Rd/SR 83), 0.4 mi se, then just e. Int corridors. **Pets:** Other species. $25 one-time fee/pet. Designated rooms, service with restrictions,
crate. ASK X 🖨 💻

PLACERVILLE

The Blue Jay Lodge & Cafe M
(970) 728-0830. **$110-$215.** 22332 Hwy 145 81430. Just n on SR 145.
Int corridors. **Pets:** Accepted. SAVE X 🖨 💻 🍴 🐾

PUEBLO

Best Western Eagle Ridge Inn & Suites H
(719) 543-4644. **$80-$150.** 4727 N Elizabeth St 81008. I-25, exit 102,
just w, then just n. Int corridors. **Pets:** Large, other species. $15 daily
fee/pet. Service with restrictions, supervision.
SAVE X 🖨 💻 🐾 🐾

Holiday Inn Hotel & Suites H ❧
(719) 542-8888. **$79-$159.** 4530 Dillon Dr 81008. I-25, exit 102, just e,
then just s. Int corridors. **Pets:** Medium, other species. $20 one-time fee/
pet. Designated rooms, service with restrictions, supervision.
ASK X 🐾M 🖨 💻 🍴 🐾

La Quinta Inn & Suites Pueblo H ❧
(719) 542-3500. **$69-$149.** 4801 N Elizabeth St 81008. I-25, exit 102,
just nw. Int corridors. **Pets:** Medium, other species. Service with restrictions, supervision. ASK X 🖨 💻 🐾

Microtel Inn & Suites H
(719) 242-2020. **Call for rates.** 3343 Gateway Dr 81004. I-25, exit 94,
just w, then just s. Int corridors. **Pets:** Accepted. X 🐾M 🖨 💻

The Ramada of Pueblo H
(719) 544-4700. **$69-$119.** 4703 N Freeway 81008. I-25, exit 102, just w.
Ext corridors. **Pets:** Other species. $15 one-time fee/room. Service with
restrictions. ASK X 🖨 💻 🐾

RIDGWAY

Ridgway-Ouray Lodge & Suites H
(970) 626-5444. **$75-$110.** 373 Palomino Tr 81432. E at jct US 550 and
SR 62, just s. Int corridors. **Pets:** Large. $15 daily fee/pet. Service with
restrictions, supervision. ASK X 🖨 💻 🐾 X

RIFLE

Hampton Inn & Suites Rifle H ❧
(970) 625-1500. **$129-$149.** 499 Airport Rd 81650. I-70, exit 90, just s,
then just e. Int corridors. **Pets:** Small. $25 one-time fee/room. Service
with restrictions, supervision. SAVE X 🖨 💻 🐾

La Quinta Inn & Suites H ❧
(970) 625-2676. **$99-$169.** 600 Wapiti Ct 81650. I-70, exit 90, just s,
then just e. Int corridors. **Pets:** Medium, other species. Service with
restrictions, supervision. SAVE X 🖨 💻 🐾

Rusty Cannon Motel M
(970) 625-4004. **$82-$112.** 701 Taughenbaugh Blvd 81650. I-70, exit 90,
just s. Ext corridors. **Pets:** Dogs only. $25 one-time fee/room. Designated
rooms, service with restrictions, supervision. SAVE X 🖨 💻 🐾

SALIDA

Aspen Leaf Lodge M
(719) 539-6733. **$49-$109.** 7350 W Hwy 50 81201. Just w of Hot
Springs Pool. Ext corridors. **Pets:** Medium, other species. $5 daily fee/pet.
Service with restrictions, supervision. SAVE X 🖨

Chalets at Tudor Rose VH ❧
(719) 539-2002. **$200, 30 day notice.** 6720 CR 104 81201. Just e on
US 50, s on CR 104, 0.5 mi up the hill, follow signs. Ext corridors.
Pets: Dogs only. $25 deposit/pet, $10 daily fee/pet. Designated rooms, no
service, crate. X 🐾M 🖨 💻 🐾

Gateway Inn & Suites H
(719) 539-2895. **$39-$179.** 1310 E Hwy 50 81201. On US 50, just e;
between Blake and Palmer sts. Ext corridors. **Pets:** Medium, dogs only.
$10 one-time fee/pet. Designated rooms, service with restrictions, supervi-
sion. ASK X 🖨 💻

Great Western Colorado Lodge H
(719) 539-2514. **$39-$82.** 352 W Rainbow Blvd 81201. On US 50. Ext
corridors. **Pets:** Very small. $10 daily fee/pet. Designated rooms, service
with restrictions, supervision. SAVE X 🖨 💻

Silver Ridge Lodge M ❧
(719) 539-2553. **$59-$159.** 545 W Rainbow Blvd 81201. On US 50, just
w of Chamber of Commerce. Ext corridors. **Pets:** Medium, dogs only. $10
daily fee/pet. Designated rooms, service with restrictions, supervision.
SAVE X 🖨 💻 🐾

Super 8 M
(719) 539-6689. **$69-$149.** 525 W Rainbow Blvd 81201. On US 50. Ext
corridors. **Pets:** Medium. Service with restrictions, supervision.
ASK X 🖨 💻 🐾

Travelodge M
(719) 539-2528. **Call for rates.** 7310 Hwy 50 81201. On US 50 W, just
w of Hot Springs Pool. Ext corridors. **Pets:** Accepted.
X 🖨 💻 🐾

Woodland Motel M ❧
(719) 539-4980. **$50-$155.** 903 W 1st St 81201. 0.5 mi w on 1st St (SR
291); center of historic downtown. Ext corridors. **Pets:** Other species.
SAVE X 🖨 💻

SILVERTHORNE

Quality Inn & Suites H ❧
(970) 513-1222. **$79-$229.** 530 Silverthorne Ln 80498. I-70, exit 205, just
n on SR 9, just e on Rainbow Dr, then just e on Tanglewood Ln. Int corridors. **Pets:** Large. $10 daily fee/pet. Designated rooms, service with
restrictions. ASK X 🐾M 🖨 💻 🐾

SILVERTON

Silverton's Inn of the Rockies at the Historic Alma House BB
(970) 387-5336. **$99-$149, 7 day notice.** 220 E 10th St 81433. On 10th St, just se of Greene St (Main St). Int corridors. **Pets:** Accepted.
SAVE ⊠ 🐾 🖉

Villa Dallavalle Inn BB
(970) 387-5555. **$89-$125.** 1257 Blair St 81433. Corner of 13th and Blair sts. Int corridors. **Pets:** Medium, dogs only. $15 one-time fee/pet. Service with restrictions, supervision. ASK ⊠ 🖵 🐾

The Wyman Hotel & Inn BB
(970) 387-5372. **Call for rates.** 1371 Greene St 81433. Corner of Greene (Main St) and 14th sts. Int corridors. **Pets:** Accepted.
⊠ 🛗 🐾

SOUTH FORK

Ute Bluff Lodge & Cabins M
(719) 873-5595. **$49-$208, 14 day notice.** 27680 W Hwy 160 81154. 2.5 mi e of jct US 160 and SR 149. Ext corridors. **Pets:** Medium, dogs only. $5 daily fee/pet. Designated rooms, service with restrictions, supervision. ASK ⊠ 🛗 🖵 🐾

STEAMBOAT SPRINGS

Comfort Inn H
(970) 879-6669. **$75-$495.** 1055 Walton Creek Rd 80487. 2.8 mi e on US 40. Int corridors. **Pets:** Dogs only. $20 daily fee/pet. Designated rooms, service with restrictions, supervision.
ASK ⊠ 🐾 🛗 🖵 🏊

Fairfield Inn & Suites by Marriott H 🐾
(970) 870-9000. **$89-$159.** 3200 S Lincoln Ave 80487. 3 mi e on US 40. Int corridors. **Pets:** $25 one-time fee/pet. Designated rooms, service with restrictions, crate. SAVE ⊠ 🐾 🛗 🖵 🏊

Holiday Inn Steamboat Springs H
(970) 879-2250. **$119-$239, 3 day notice.** 3190 S Lincoln Ave 80487. 3 mi e on US 40. Int corridors. **Pets:** Accepted.
SAVE ⊠ 🐾 🛗 🖵 🍴 🏊 🐾

Nordic Lodge M
(970) 879-0531. **Call for rates.** 1036 Lincoln Ave 80477. Between 10th and 11th sts; downtown. Ext corridors. **Pets:** $10 daily fee/room. Service with restrictions, supervision. ⊠ 🛗 🏊

Rabbit Ears Motel M
(970) 879-1150. **$89-$189, 3 day notice.** 201 Lincoln Ave 80477. Just e on US 40. Ext corridors. **Pets:** $15 one-time fee/room. Service with restrictions, supervision. SAVE ⊠ 🛗 🖵

Sheraton Steamboat Resort H 🐾
(970) 879-2220. **$119-$519, 30 day notice.** 2200 Village Inn Ct 80487. 2.3 mi e on US 40, 1 mi n on Mt Werner Rd; at ski area. Int corridors. **Pets:** Large, dogs only. $35 one-time fee/room. Designated rooms, service with restrictions, supervision. SAVE ⊠ 🛗 🖵 🍴 🏊 🐾

Steamboat Hotel H
(970) 879-5230. **$59-$115.** 3195 S Lincoln Ave 80487. 3 mi e on US 40. Int corridors. **Pets:** Medium, dogs only. $15 daily fee/pet. Designated rooms, service with restrictions, supervision.
ASK ⊠ 🛗 🖵 🏊 🐾

STERLING

Best Western Sundowner M
(970) 522-6265. **$79-$120.** 125 Overland Trail St 80751. I-76, exit 125, just w. Ext/int corridors. **Pets:** Other species. $12 daily fee/room. Designated rooms, service with restrictions, supervision.
SAVE ⊠ 🛗 🖵 🐾

Ramada Inn H
(970) 522-2625. **$77-$120.** 22140 E Hwy 6 80751. I-76, exit 125, 0.5 mi e on US 6. Ext/int corridors. **Pets:** Other species. $25 deposit/room. Designated rooms, service with restrictions, supervision.
ASK ⊠ 🛗 🖵 🍴 🏊 🐾

STRATTON

Best Western Golden Prairie Inn H
(719) 348-5311. **$89-$119.** 700 Colorado Ave 80836. I-70, exit 419, just n. Ext corridors. **Pets:** Accepted. SAVE ⊠ 🛗 🖵 🍴 🏊

TELLURIDE

Fairmont Heritage Place Franz Klammer Lodge CO
(970) 728-3318. **$250-$2200, 45 day notice.** 567 Mountain Village Blvd 81435. 2.3 mi e; in Mountain Village. Int corridors. **Pets:** Accepted.
⊠ 🛗 🖵 🏊 🐾 🖉

Hotel Columbia H 🐾
(970) 728-0660. **$215-$1555, 30 day notice.** 301 W San Juan Ave 81435. Corner of Aspen St and San Juan Ave. Int corridors. **Pets:** Dogs only. $20 daily fee/room. Designated rooms, service with restrictions.
SAVE ⊠ 🛗 🍴

The Hotel Telluride H 🐾
(970) 369-1188. **$129-$499.** 199 N Cornet St 81435. Just s of roundabout, then just e. Int corridors. **Pets:** Other species. $100 one-time fee/room. Service with restrictions, crate. ASK ⊠ 🐾 🛗 🖵 🐾

Ice House Lodge & Condominiums H
(970) 728-6300. **$185-$550, 45 day notice.** 310 S Fir St 81435. Just s of SR 145 (Colorado Ave). Int corridors. **Pets:** Accepted.
SAVE ⊠ 🛗 🐾 🐾 🖉

The Peaks Resort & Golden Door Spa H
(970) 728-6800. **$99-$599, 7 day notice.** 136 Country Club Dr 81435. 2.5 mi e; in Mountain Village. Int corridors. **Pets:** Accepted.
SAVE ⊠ 🛗 🍴 🐾 🐾 🖉

TRINIDAD

Best Western Trinidad Inn M
(719) 846-2215. **$59-$109.** 900 W Adams St 81082. I-25, exit 13A northbound; exit Cross Bridge southbound, just ne. Ext corridors. **Pets:** Accepted. SAVE ⊠ 🛗 🖵 🐾

Budget Host Derrick Motel M
(719) 846-3307. **$79-$99.** 10301 Santa Fe Trail Dr 81082. I-25, exit 11, 0.5 mi ne. Ext corridors. **Pets:** Medium. $10 daily fee/pet. Supervision.
ASK ⊠ 🛗 🖵

Holiday Inn Hotel & Suites H
(719) 845-8400. **$79-$159.** 3130 Santa Fe Trail Dr 81082. I-25, exit 11, just e, then 1.2 mi n. Int corridors. **Pets:** Medium, other species. $20 one-time fee/room. Designated rooms, service with restrictions, supervision. ASK ⊠ 🐾 🛗 🖵 🍴 🐾

Super 8 M
(719) 846-8280. **Call for rates.** 1924 Freedom Rd 81082. I-25, exit 15, just ne. Int corridors. **Pets:** Accepted. ⊠ 🛗 🖵

VAIL

The Arrabelle at Vail Square, a RockResort H
(970) 754-7777. **$165-$1275.** 675 Lionshead Pl 81657. I-70, exit 176, just w on S Frontage Rd, then just e on W Lionshead Cir. Int corridors.
Pets: Accepted. ⊠ 🛗 🖵 🍴 🐾 🐾

Evergreen Lodge at Vail H
(970) 476-7810. **$119-$430, 30 day notice.** 250 S Frontage Rd W 81657. I-70, exit 176, just w. Int corridors. **Pets:** Medium. $40 daily fee/pet. Designated rooms, service with restrictions, crate.
ASK ⊠ 🛗 🖵 🍴 🐾 🐾 🖉

Holiday Inn Apex Vail 🅷
(970) 476-2739. **$99-$249.** 2211 N Frontage Rd 81657. I-70, exit 173, just e. Int corridors. **Pets:** Accepted.
ASK ✕ ᴹ 🛏 💻 🍽 ≈ ✕

The Lodge at Vail, a RockResort & Spa 🅷 🐾
(970) 476-5011. **$149-$866, 45 day notice.** 174 E Gore Creek Dr 81657. I-70, exit 176, s on Vail Rd to center of village. Ext/int corridors. **Pets:** Dogs only. $50 daily fee/pet. Designated rooms, service with restrictions, crate. SAVE ✕ 🛏 💻 🍽 ≈ ✕

WALSENBURG

Best Western Rambler 🅷
(719) 738-1121. **$70-$112.** 457 US Hwy 85-87 81089. I-25, exit 52, just w. Ext/int corridors. **Pets:** Medium, other species. $10 daily fee/pet. Designated rooms, service with restrictions, supervision.
SAVE ✕ 🛏 💻 ≈

WELLINGTON

Days Inn Wellington 🅷
(970) 568-0444. **Call for rates.** 7860 6th St 80549. I-25, exit 278, just w, then just s. Int corridors. **Pets:** Accepted. ✕ 🛏 💻 ≈

WINDSOR

Super 8 Motel 🅷
(970) 686-5996. **$65-$125.** 1265 Main St 80550. I-25, exit 262, 3.8 mi e; in shopping/restaurant complex. Int corridors. **Pets:** Other species. $15 one-time fee/pet. Service with restrictions, crate.
ASK ✕ ᴹ 🛏 💻

WINTER PARK

Best Western Alpenglo Lodge 🅷 🐾
(970) 726-8088. **$78-$165.** 78665 US Hwy 40 80482. On US 40; center. Int corridors. **Pets:** Large, other species. $10 daily fee/pet. Designated rooms, supervision. SAVE ✕ ᴹ 🛏 💻

YAMPA

Oak Tree Inn 🅷
(970) 638-1000. **$85-$125.** 98 Moffat Ave 80483. Just off SR 131. Int corridors. **Pets:** Accepted. ASK ✕ 🛏 💻

CONNECTICUT

CITY INDEX

BETHEL

◆◆◆ Microtel Inn & Suites 🅷

(203) 748-8318. **$79-$99.** 80 Benedict Rd 06801. I-84, exit 8, 1 mi e on US 6. Int corridors. **Pets:** $100 deposit/pet, $11 daily fee/pet. Service with restrictions, supervision. (ASK) (X) 🛄 💻

BRANFORD

◉◉◉ ◆◆◆ Baymont Inn & Suites 🅷

(203) 488-4991. **$59-$179.** 3 Business Park Dr 06405. I-95, exit 56, just n. Int corridors. **Pets:** Medium. $20 daily fee/pet. Service with restrictions, supervision. (SAVE) (X) 🛄 💻 🐾 (X)

BRIDGEPORT

◆◆◆◆ Bridgeport Holiday Inn & Convention Center 🅷

(203) 334-1234. **$119-$159.** 1070 Main St 06604. SR 8, exit 2 north-bound, 0.7 mi se; exit southbound, just s, then just e. Int corridors. **Pets:** Medium. $15 daily fee/room. Service with restrictions, supervision.

(ASK) (X) (♿M) 🛄 💻 (¶) 🐾

BROOKFIELD

◆◆◆ The Newbury Inn 🅼

(203) 775-0220. **$89-$99.** 1030 Federal Rd 06804. Jct SR 25, 0.9 mi nw. Ext/int corridors. **Pets:** Accepted. (ASK) (X) 🛄 💻

DANBURY

◆◆◆◆ Danbury Plaza Hotel & Conference Center 🅷 🐾

(203) 794-0600. **$89-$149.** 18 Old Ridgebury Rd 06810. I-84, exit 2 east-bound; exit 2A westbound. Int corridors. **Pets:** Medium, dogs only. Desig-nated rooms, service with restrictions. (ASK) (X) 🛄 💻 (¶) 🐾

◆◆◆ Ethan Allen Hotel 🅷 🐾

(203) 744-1776. **$95-$144.** 21 Lake Ave Ext 06811. I-84, exit 4, 0.3 mi w on US 6 and 202. Int corridors. **Pets:** $15 daily fee/room. Designated rooms, service with restrictions, crate. (ASK) (X) 🛄 💻 (¶) 🐾

◆◆◆ Holiday Inn 🅷

(203) 792-4000. **$89-$159.** 80 Newtown Rd 06810. I-84, exit 8 (Newtown Rd), 0.5 mi s on US 6 W. Int corridors. **Pets:** Large, other species. $15 daily fee/pet. Designated rooms, service with restrictions, supervision.

(ASK) (X) 🛄 💻 (¶) 🐾

◉◉◉ ◆◆◆ Maron Hotel & Suites 🅷

(203) 791-2200. **$89-$189.** 42 Lake Ave Extension 06811. I-84, exit 4, 0.5 mi w on US 6 and 202. Int corridors. **Pets:** Other species. $25 daily fee/room. Designated rooms, service with restrictions.

(SAVE) (X) (♿M) 🛄 💻 (¶)

◆◆◆ Residence Inn Danbury 🅷 🐾

(203) 797-1256. **$161-$197.** 22 Segar St 06810. I-84, exit 4 eastbound, just n; exit westbound, just e on Lake Ave Extension, then just s. Int corri-dors. **Pets:** Medium. $75 one-time fee/room. Service with restrictions, supervision. (X) 🛄 💻 🐾

DAYVILLE

◆◆◆ Comfort Inn & Suites 🅷 🐾

(860) 779-3200. **$110-$130.** 16 Tracy Rd 06241. I-395, exit 94, just w. Int corridors. **Pets:** Medium. $15 daily fee/pet. Designated rooms, service with restrictions, supervision. (ASK) (X) (♿M) 🛄 💻 🐾

EAST HAVEN

◉◉◉ ◆◆◆ Quality Inn 🅷

(203) 469-5321. **$69-$180.** 30 Frontage Rd 06512. I-95, exit 51 east-bound, 0.5 mi e; exit westbound, 0.8 mi w on N Frontage Rd to over-pass, then 0.8 mi e. Ext/int corridors. **Pets:** $15 daily fee/room. Designated rooms, service with restrictions, crate.

(SAVE) (X) 🛄 💻 🐾

FAIRFIELD

◉◉◉ ◆◆◆ Best Western Black Rock Inn 🅷

(203) 659-2200. **$99-$209.** 100 Kings Hwy Cutoff 06824. I-95, exit 24, just sw. Int corridors. **Pets:** Accepted. (SAVE) (X) (♿M) 🛄 💻

GREENWICH

◆◆◆ The Stanton House Inn 🅱🅱

(203) 869-2110. **$159-$239, 7 day notice.** 76 Maple Ave 06830. Just n of US 1; center. Ext/int corridors. **Pets:** Accepted. (X) 🛄 🐾

HAMDEN

◆◆◆ Clarion Hotel & Suites Hamden-New Haven 🅼

(203) 288-3831. **$129-$139.** 2260 Whitney Ave 06518. Just n off SR 15, exit 61. Int corridors. **Pets:** Small. $50 deposit/room. Designated rooms, service with restrictions, crate. (ASK) (X) (♿M) 🛄 💻 🐾

HARTFORD METROPOLITAN AREA

AVON

◆◆◆ Avon Old Farms Hotel 🅷

(860) 677-1651. **$109-$229.** 279 Avon Mountain Rd 06001. Jct US 44 and SR 10. Ext/int corridors. **Pets:** Accepted.

(ASK) (X) 🛄 💻 (¶) 🐾 (X)

◆◆◆ Residence Inn by Marriott Hartford-Avon 🅷

(860) 678-1666. **$170-$208.** 55 Simsbury Rd (SR 202 & SR 10) 06001. Jct US 44, just n. Int corridors. **Pets:** Accepted.

(X) (♿M) 🛄 💻 🐾 (X)

CROMWELL

◇◇◇ ▼▼▼ Comfort Inn H

(860) 635-4100. **$69-$160.** 111 Berlin Rd 06416. I-91, exit 21, just e on SR 372. Int corridors. **Pets:** Accepted. (SAVE) ⊠ 🛏 💻

EAST HARTFORD

▼▼▼▼ Holiday Inn H

(860) 528-9611. **$90-$169.** 363 Roberts St 06108. I-84, exit 58, just w. Int corridors. **Pets:** Accepted. (ASK) ⊠ 🛏 💻 🍴 ⇌

◇◇◇ ▼▼▼▼ Sheraton Hartford Hotel H

(860) 528-9703. **$89-$229.** 100 E River Dr 06108. I-84, exit 53 eastbound, just s; exit 54 westbound to exit 3 (Darlin St), just n. Int corridors. **Pets:** Accepted. (SAVE) ⊠ 🛁M 🛏 💻 🍴 ⇌

EAST WINDSOR

◇◇◇ ▼▼▼▼ Clarion Inn & Suites H

(860) 623-9411. **$73-$86.** 161 Bridge St 06088. I-91, exit 45, just w. Int corridors. **Pets:** Medium. $30 one-time fee/room. Service with restrictions, supervision. (SAVE) ⊠ 🛁M 🛏 💻 🍴 ⇌

◇◇◇ ▼▼▼▼ Holiday Inn Express East Windsor–Airport H ☼

(860) 627-6585. **$70-$110.** 260 Main St (US 5) 06088. I-91, exit 44, just s. Int corridors. **Pets:** Medium. $40 one-time fee/pet. Service with restrictions, crate. (SAVE) ⊠ 🛏 💻

ENFIELD

▼▼ Red Roof Inn # 7105 M

(860) 741-2571. **$56-$109.** 5 Hazard Ave 06082. I-91, exit 47E. Ext corridors. **Pets:** Large. Service with restrictions, crate. (ASK) ⊠ 🛁M 🛏

FARMINGTON

◇◇◇ ▼▼▼ Centennial Inn Suites CO

(860) 677-4647. **$121-$181.** 5 Spring Ln 06032. US 6, 0.3 mi e of jct SR 177. Ext/int corridors. **Pets:** Other species. $15 daily fee/pet. Designated rooms, service with restrictions. (SAVE) ⊠ 🛁M 🛏 💻 ⇌

◇◇ ▼▼ Extended StayAmerica Deluxe Hartford-Farmington H

(860) 676-2790. **$89-$129.** 1 Batterson Park Rd 06032. I-84, exit 37, just ne. Int corridors. **Pets:** Other species. $25 daily fee/room. Designated rooms, service with restrictions, crate. (ASK) ⊠ 🛁M 🛏 💻

▼▼▼▼ The Farmington Inn H

(860) 269-3401. **$109-$179.** 827 Farmington Ave 06032. I-84, exit 39, 1.8 mi w on SR 4. Int corridors. **Pets:** Accepted. (ASK) ⊠ 🛏 💻

▼▼▼▼ Homewood Suites by Hilton H

(860) 321-0000. **$109-$169.** 2 Farm Glen Blvd 06032. I-84, exit 39, 0.6 mi e on SR 4. Int corridors. **Pets:** Accepted. ⊠ 🛁M 🛏 💻 ⇌

GLASTONBURY

◇◇◇ ▼▼▼▼ Homewood Suites by Hilton Hartford South-Glastonbury H

(860) 652-8111. **$110-$209.** 65 Glastonbury Blvd 06033. SR 3, exit Main St, just se. Int corridors. **Pets:** Accepted. (SAVE) ⊠ 🛁M 🛏 💻 ⇌

HARTFORD

▼▼▼▼ Crowne Plaza Hartford Downtown H

(860) 549-2400. **$99-$199.** 50 Morgan St 06120. I-91, exit 32B; I-84, exit 50 eastbound; exit 52 westbound. Int corridors. **Pets:** Accepted. (ASK) ⊠ 🛁M 🛏 💻 🍴 ⇌

◇◇◇ ▼▼▼▼ The Hilton Hartford Hotel H

(860) 728-5151. **$109-$259.** 315 Trumbull St 06103. Downtown. Int corridors. **Pets:** Accepted. (SAVE) ⊠ 🛁M 🛏 💻 🍴 ⇌ ✕

◇◇◇ ▼▼▼▼ Holiday Inn Express Downtown Hartford H ☼

(860) 246-9900. **$99-$189.** 440 Asylum St 06103. I-84, exit 48, just se via Spring St. Int corridors. **Pets:** Large, other species. $50 one-time fee/room. Service with restrictions. (SAVE) ⊠ 🛏 💻

▼▼▼▼ Holiday Inn Express Hotel & Suites Hartford H

(860) 525-1000. **$100-$145.** 185 Brainard Rd 06114. I-91, exit 27, just e, then just s. Int corridors. **Pets:** Accepted. (ASK) ⊠ 🛏 💻 ⇌

▼▼▼▼ Homewood Suites by Hilton Hartford Downtown H ☼

(860) 524-0223. **$139-$219.** 338 Asylum St 06103. Between Ann and High sts; downtown. Int corridors. **Pets:** Medium. $50 one-time fee/pet. Service with restrictions. ⊠ 🛁M 🛏 💻

▼▼▼▼ Residence Inn by Marriott Downtown Hartford H ☼

(860) 524-5550. **$220-$268.** 942 Main St 06103. I-91, exit 29A northbound; exit 31 southbound. Int corridors. **Pets:** $100 one-time fee/room. ⊠ 🛏 💻

MANCHESTER

▼▼ Extended StayAmerica Hartford-Manchester H

(860) 643-5140. **$79-$129.** 340 Tolland Tpke 06040. I-84, exit 63, 0.3 mi se on SR 30, then just sw. Int corridors. **Pets:** Other species. $25 daily fee/room. Designated rooms, service with restrictions, crate. (ASK) ⊠ 🛁M 🛏 💻

▼▼▼▼ Residence Inn Hartford/Manchester H ☼

(860) 432-4242. **$152-$186.** 201 Hale Rd 06042. I-84, exit 63, 0.5 mi nw, then 0.6 mi sw. Int corridors. **Pets:** Other species. $75 one-time fee/room. Service with restrictions, crate. ⊠ 🛁M 🛏 💻 ⇌ ✕

NEW BRITAIN

▼▼▼▼ La Quinta Inn & Suites New Britain/South Hartford H ☼

(860) 348-1463. **$59-$109.** 65 Columbus Blvd 06051. SR 9, exit 26 northbound; exit 27 southbound, then just nw. Int corridors. **Pets:** Medium, other species. Service with restrictions, supervision. (ASK) ⊠ 🛁M 🛏 💻

ROCKY HILL

▼▼▼▼ Residence Inn by Marriott Hartford-Rocky Hill H

(860) 257-7500. **$180-$190.** 680 Cromwell Ave 06067. I-91, exit 23, 0.4 mi w on West St, then just n. Int corridors. **Pets:** Accepted. ⊠ 🛁M 🛏 💻 ⇌ ✕

SIMSBURY

▼▼▼▼ Simsbury 1820 House CI

(860) 658-7658. **$129-$229.** 731 Hopmeadow St 06070. US 202/SR 10, 2 mi n of jct SR 185; center. Ext/int corridors. **Pets:** Accepted. (ASK) ⊠ 🛏 💻

SOUTHINGTON

▼▼▼▼ Residence Inn Southington H

(860) 621-4440. **$152-$186.** 778 West St 06489. I-84, exit 31, just s. Int corridors. **Pets:** Medium, other species. $100 one-time fee/room. Designated rooms, crate. ⊠ 🛁M 🛏 💻 ⇌ ✕

WINDSOR

◇◇◇ ▼▼▼▼ Hyatt Summerfield Suites Hartford North/Windsor H

(860) 298-8000. **$99-$399.** 200 Corporate Dr 06095. I-91, exit 38 northbound; exit 38B southbound. Int corridors. **Pets:** Medium. $200 one-time fee/room. Designated rooms, service with restrictions, crate. (SAVE) ⊠ 🛁M 🛏 💻 ⇌ ✕

▼▼▼▼ The Residence Inn by Marriott
Hartford-Windsor **H**
(860) 688-7474. **$152-$186.** 100 Dunfey Ln 06095. I-91, exit 37, just w on SR 305 to Dunfey Ln, then 0.3 mi n. Ext corridors. **Pets:** Other species. $100 one-time fee/room. Service with restrictions.

WINDSOR LOCKS

▼▼▼ Candlewood Suites **H**
(860) 623-2000. **$79-$149.** 149 Ella T Grasso Tpke 06096. I-91, exit 40, 2.5 mi w on SR 20, then 0.6 mi n on SR 75. Int corridors. **Pets:** Medium. $75 one-time fee/pet. Service with restrictions, crate.

▼▼▼▼ Homewood Suites by Hilton **H**
(860) 627-8463. **$109-$179.** 65 Ella T Grasso Tpke 06096. I-91, exit 40, 2.5 mi w on SR 20, then just n on SR 75. Ext/int corridors.
Pets: Accepted.

▼▼ La Quinta Inn Hartford-Airport **H** ❀
(860) 623-3336. **$65-$129.** 64 Ella T Grasso Tpke 06096. I-91, exit 40, 2.5 mi w on SR 20, then just n on SR 75. Int corridors. **Pets:** Medium, other species. Service with restrictions, supervision.

▼▼ Ramada Inn Bradley International Airport **H**
(860) 623-9494. **$89-$99.** 5 Ella T Grasso Tpke 06096. I-91, exit 40, 2.5 mi w on SR 20, then just n on SR 75. Int corridors. **Pets:** Accepted.

▲▲▲ ▼▼▼▼ Sheraton Hotel At Bradley International
Airport **H**
(860) 627-5311. **$109-$299, 3 day notice.** 1 Bradley International Airport 06096. At Bradley International Airport terminal. Int corridors.
Pets: Accepted.

END METROPOLITAN AREA

IVORYTON

▼▼▼ The Copper Beech Inn **CI**
(860) 767-0330. **$225-$400, 14 day notice.** 46 Main St 06442. SR 9, exit 3, 1.7 mi w. Int corridors. **Pets:** Accepted.

LAKEVILLE

▲▲▲ ▼▼▼▼ Interlaken Inn Resort and Conference
Center **H** ❀
(860) 435-9878. **$169-$259, 7 day notice.** 74 Interlaken Rd 06039. On SR 112, 0.5 mi w of jct SR 41. Ext/int corridors. **Pets:** Dogs only. $15 daily fee/pet. Designated rooms, service with restrictions, supervision.

LEDYARD

▼▼▼ Almost In Mystic/Mares Inn **BB**
(860) 572-7556. **$125-$225, 14 day notice.** 333 Colonel Ledyard Hwy 06339. I-95, exit 89, 1 mi ne to Gold Star Hwy, 0.6 mi w, then 0.7 mi n. Int corridors. **Pets:** Designated rooms, no service.

LITCHFIELD

▲▲▲ ▼▼▼ Litchfield Inn **CI** ❀
(860) 567-4503. **$200-$336, 3 day notice.** 432 Bantam Rd 06759. 1.5 mi w on US 202. Int corridors. **Pets:** Dogs only. Designated rooms, service with restrictions, supervision.

MERIDEN

▼▼▼ Extended StayAmerica Hartford-Meriden **H**
(203) 630-1927. **$74-$129.** 366 Bee St 06450. I-91, exit 17 northbound, just e on E Main St, then 0.7 mi n; exit 19 southbound, 0.5 mi w on Baldwin Ave, then 0.6 mi s. Int corridors. **Pets:** Other species. $25 daily fee/room. Designated rooms, service with restrictions, crate.

▼▼▼ Residence Inn Meriden **H**
(203) 634-7770. **$134-$164.** 390 Bee St 06450. I-91, exit 16 northbound, just e on E Main St, then 0.7 mi n; exit 19 southbound, 0.5 mi w on Baldwin Ave, then 0.5 mi s. Ext/int corridors. **Pets:** $100 one-time fee/room. Service with restrictions, supervision.

MILFORD

▼▼▼▼ Residence Inn Milford **H**
(203) 283-2100. **$159-$174.** 62 Rowe Ave 06460. I-95, exit 35, just nw. Int corridors. **Pets:** Accepted.

MORRIS

▼▼▼▼ Winvian **H**
(860) 567-9600. **$750-$2300, 60 day notice.** 155 Alain White Rd 06763. Jct SR 109, 1 mi n. Ext/int corridors. **Pets:** Dogs only. Designated rooms, service with restrictions.

MYSTIC

▲▲▲ ▼▼▼▼ Comfort Inn of Mystic **H**
(860) 572-8531. **$71-$180.** 48 Whitehall Ave 06355. I-95, exit 90, just n on SR 27. Int corridors. **Pets:** Medium, other species. $100 deposit/room, $25 one-time fee/pet. Service with restrictions, crate.

▲▲▲ ▼▼▼▼ Hilton Mystic **H**
(860) 572-0731. **$209-$259.** 20 Coogan Blvd 06355. I-95, exit 90, 0.5 mi s, then e. Int corridors. **Pets:** Medium, dogs only. $75 one-time fee/pet. Service with restrictions, supervision.

▲▲▲ ▼▼▼▼ Inn at Mystic **M** ❀
(860) 536-9604. **$95-$315.** 3 Williams Ave 06355. On US 1 at SR 27. Ext/int corridors. **Pets:** Other species. $15 deposit/pet, $15 daily fee/pet. Designated rooms, service with restrictions, supervision.

▼▼▼▼ Residence Inn Mystic Groton **H**
(860) 536-5150. **$149-$199.** 40 Whitehall Ave 06355. I-95, exit 90, just n on SR 27. Int corridors. **Pets:** Other species. $100 one-time fee/room. Designated rooms, service with restrictions, crate.

NEW HAVEN

▼▼▼ La Quinta Inn & Suites **H** ❀
(203) 562-1111. **$99-$199.** 400 Sargent Dr 06511. I-95, exit 46. Int corridors. **Pets:** Medium, other species. Service with restrictions, supervision.

▼▼▼▼ Omni New Haven Hotel at Yale **H**
(203) 772-6664. **$159-$289.** 155 Temple St 06510. Center of downtown. Int corridors. **Pets:** Accepted.

▼▼▼▼ Premiere Hotel & Suites **H**
(203) 777-5337. **$149-$239.** 3 Long Wharf Dr 06511. I-95, exit 46, 0.6 mi nw. Ext corridors. **Pets:** Medium. $75 one-time fee/room. Service with restrictions, crate.

NEW LONDON

▼▼▼ Red Roof Inn #7145 **M**
(860) 444-0001. **$55-$100.** 707 Colman St 06320. I-95, exit 82A northbound, 0.4 mi e, then just n; exit 83 southbound, 0.6 mi s. Ext corridors. **Pets:** Large. Service with restrictions, crate.

NEW MILFORD

▼▼▼ The Homestead Inn **BB**
(860) 354-4080. **$105-$220.** 5 Elm St 06776. Just e of village green off Main St; center. Ext/int corridors. **Pets:** Other species. $10 one-time fee/room. Designated rooms, service with restrictions, supervision.

NIANTIC

▼ Motel 6–1063 **M**
(860) 739-6991. **$55-$65.** 269 Flanders Rd 06357. I-95, exit 74, just s. Ext corridors. **Pets:** Other species. Service with restrictions, supervision.
⊠ 🛄 🖎

NORTH STONINGTON

▼▼▼ The Inn at Lower Farm B & B **BB**
(860) 535-9075. **$105-$185, 7 day notice.** 119 Mystic Rd 06359. I-95, exit 90, 1.5 mi n on SR 27, 1.4 mi e on SR 184, then 3.4 mi n on SR 201. Int corridors. **Pets:** Medium. $10 daily fee/pet. Designated rooms, service with restrictions, supervision. ⊠ Ⓦ ☎

NORWALK

⨁ ▼▼▼ Four Points by Sheraton Norwalk **H** ❀
(203) 849-9828. **Call for rates.** 426 Main Ave 06851. I-95, exit 15, 3.5 mi n via US 7, just e, then 0.7 mi s. Int corridors. **Pets:** Medium, dogs only. $25 one-time fee/pet. Service with restrictions, supervision.
SAVE ⊠ ᏪM 🛄 🖭

▼▼ Homestead Studio Suites-Norwalk-Stamford **H**
(203) 847-6888. **$105-$149.** 400 Main Ave 06851. I-95, exit 15, 3.5 mi n via US 7, just e, then 1 mi s. Int corridors. **Pets:** Other species. $25 daily fee/room. Designated rooms, service with restrictions, crate.
ASK ⊠ 🛄 🖭

OLD SAYBROOK

▼ Days Inn **M**
(860) 388-3453. **Call for rates.** 1430 Boston Post Rd 06475. I-95, exit 66, 0.3 mi s on SR 166, then 0.5 mi e on US 1 N. Ext corridors.
Pets: Accepted. ⊠ 🛄 🖭

▼ Liberty Inn **M**
(860) 388-1777. **$58-$130.** 55 Spring Brook Rd 06475. I-95, exit 68 southbound; exit 67 northbound, 0.9 mi n on US 1, then w. Ext corridors. **Pets:** Medium, dogs only. $15 one-time fee/pet. Designated rooms, service with restrictions, supervision. ASK ⊠ 🛄 🖭

⨁ ▼▼▼ Saybrook Point Inn & Spa **H**
(860) 395-2000. **$199-$899, 3 day notice.** 2 Bridge St 06475. On SR 154, 2.2 mi s of jct US 1; at Saybrook Point. Int corridors.
Pets: Accepted. SAVE ⊠ ᏪM 🛄 🖭 ⑪ 🖎 ⊠

PLAINFIELD

▼▼ Quality Inn **H**
(860) 564-4021. **$66-$100.** 55 Lathrop Rd 06374. I-395, exit 87, just se. Int corridors. **Pets:** Accepted. ASK ⊠ 🛄 🖭 🖎

RIVERTON

▼▼ Old Riverton Inn **CI**
(860) 379-8678. **$99-$225, 10 day notice.** 436 E River Rd (SR 20) 06065. Center. Int corridors. **Pets:** Accepted. ⊠ 🛄 ⑪

SHELTON

▼▼ Homestead Studio Suites-Shelton-Fairfield County **H**
(203) 926-6868. **$105-$149.** 945 Bridgeport Ave 06484. SR 8, exit 11, 0.5 mi w. Int corridors. **Pets:** Other species. $25 daily fee/room. Designated rooms, service with restrictions, crate. ASK ⊠ ᏪM 🛄 🖭

▼▼▼ Residence Inn Shelton Fairfield County **H**
(203) 926-9000. **$152-$186.** 1001 Bridgeport Ave 06484. SR 8, exit 11, 0.3 mi w. Ext corridors. **Pets:** Accepted. ⊠ ᏪM 🛄 🖭 🖎 ⊠

SOUTHBURY

▼▼▼ Cornucopia at Oldfield Bed and Breakfast **BB**
(203) 267-6772. **$150-$250, 14 day notice.** 782 Main St N 06488. I-84, exit 15, 1.1 mi n. Int corridors. **Pets:** Small, dogs only. Designated rooms, service with restrictions, supervision. ASK ⊠ 🖎 ☎

⨁ ▼▼▼ Crowne Plaza Southbury **H**
(203) 598-7600. **$109-$159.** 1284 Strongtown Rd 06488. I-84, exit 16, just n on SR 188. Int corridors. **Pets:** Accepted.
SAVE ⊠ ᏪM 🛄 🖭 ⑪ 🖎 ⊠

▼▼▼ Heritage Hotel **H**
(203) 264-8200. **$99-$179.** 522 Heritage Rd 06488. I-84, exit 15, 0.4 mi n on SR 67, then 1 mi w. Int corridors. **Pets:** Accepted.
ASK ⊠ ᏪM 🛄 🖭 ⑪ 🖎 ⊠

STAMFORD

⨁ ▼▼▼ Amsterdam Hotel–Greenwich/Stamford **H**
(203) 327-4300. **$90-$170.** 19 Clarks Hill Ave 06902. I-95, exit 8 northbound, just n on Atlantic St, 0.6 mi ne on Tresser Blvd, then just s; exit southbound, just nw on Elm St, ne on Main St, then just s. Int corridors. **Pets:** $20 daily fee/pet. Designated rooms, service with restrictions, supervision. SAVE ⊠ ᏪM 🛄 🖭

⨁ ▼▼▼ Hilton Stamford Hotel & Executive Meeting Center **H** ❀
(203) 967-2222. **$89-$289.** 1 First Stamford Pl 06902. I-95, exit 7 northbound, just s on Greenwich Ave, then just w; exit 6 southbound, just s on West Ave, 0.3 mi w on Baxter Ave, just n on Fairfield Ave, then just e. Int corridors. **Pets:** Large. $75 one-time fee/room. Designated rooms, service with restrictions, supervision. SAVE ⊠ 🛄 🖭 ⑪ 🖎 ⊠

⨁ ▼▼▼ Holiday Inn Stamford Downtown **H**
(203) 358-8400. **$99-$259.** 700 E Main St 06901. I-95, exit 8 southbound, just n on Elm; exit northbound, n on Atlantic St, 0.3 mi e on Tresser Blvd, then just n on Elm; downtown. Int corridors. **Pets:** Accepted.
SAVE ⊠ 🛄 🖭 ⑪ 🖎

▼▼▼ La Quinta Inn & Suites Stamford **H** ❀
(203) 357-7100. **$79-$199.** 135 Harvard Ave 06902. I-95, exit 6 northbound, just s; exit southbound, just w on Grenhart Rd, then just s. Int corridors. **Pets:** Medium, other species. Service with restrictions, supervision. ASK ⊠ ᏪM 🛄 🖭 ⑪ 🖎

⨁ ▼▼▼ Stamford Marriott Hotel & Spa **H**
(203) 357-9555. **$209-$239.** 243 Tresser Blvd 06901. I-95, exit 8, just n under viaduct, then n. Int corridors. **Pets:** Dogs only. $49 one-time fee/pet. Designated rooms, service with restrictions, supervision.
SAVE ⊠ ᏪM 🛄 🖭 ⑪ 🖎 ⊠

⨁ ▼▼▼ Stamford Plaza Hotel and Conference Center **H**
(203) 359-1300. **$119-$349.** 2701 Summer St 06905. I-95, exit 8 northbound, 1.7 mi w on Atlantic and Bedford sts; exit 7 southbound, n on Atlantic and Bedford sts. Int corridors. **Pets:** Small. $39 one-time fee/pet. Designated rooms, service with restrictions, supervision.
SAVE ⊠ 🛄 🖭 ⑪ 🖎 ⊠

STONINGTON

⨁ ▼▼▼ Another Second Penny Inn **BB**
(860) 535-1710. **$99-$215, 7 day notice.** 870 Pequot Tr 06378. I-95, exit 91, 0.8 mi s on SR 234. Int corridors. **Pets:** Medium, other species. $25 one-time fee/pet. Designated rooms, supervision. SAVE ⊠ 🛄

STRATFORD

▼▼▼ Homewood Suites by Hilton **H** ❀
(203) 377-3322. **$119-$189.** 6905 Main St 06614. SR 15, exit 53, just n. Int corridors. **Pets:** Medium, other species. $25 daily fee/pet. Service with restrictions, supervision. ⊠ ᏪM 🛄 🖭 🖎

WALLINGFORD

▼▼▼ Homewood Suites by Hilton New Haven/Wallingford **H**
(203) 284-2600. **$89-$189.** 90 Miles Dr 06492. I-91, exit 15, nw on SR 68, then just s. Int corridors. **Pets:** Other species. $100 one-time fee/room. Service with restrictions. ⊠ ᏪM 🛄 🖭 🖎 ⊠

WATERFORD

Oakdell Motel M

(860) 442-9446. **$60-$150.** 983 Hartford Tpke 06385. I-95, exit 82, 2 mi n on SR 85. Ext/int corridors. **Pets:** Large, dogs only.

[SAVE] [X] [☐] [≈]

Rodeway Inn at Crossroad M

(860) 442-7227. **$60-$150.** 211 Parkway N 06385. I-95, exit 81 northbound, just nw; exit southbound, 0.6 mi w. Ext corridors. **Pets:** Other species. $30 daily fee/pet. [ASK] [X] [☐] [≈]

WOODSTOCK

Inn At Woodstock Hill CI

(860) 928-0528. **$135-$250, 3 day notice.** 94 Plaine Hill Rd 06281. 0.8 mi n on SR 169. Int corridors. **Pets:** Other species. $15 one-time fee/pet. Designated rooms. [X] [☐] [▭] [¶]

DELAWARE

DEWEY BEACH

▼▼▼▼ Bellbuoy Motel 𝗠
(302) 227-6000. **$55-$375, 3 day notice.** 21 Van Dyke St 19971. SR 1, on oceanside. Ext corridors. **Pets:** Accepted. ⊠ 🛢 🕿

◈◈◈ ▼▼▼ Sea-Esta Motel I 𝗠
(302) 227-7666. **$49-$199.** 2306 Coastal Hwy 19971. SR 1 at Houston St. Ext corridors. **Pets:** Other species. $8 daily fee/pet. Service with restrictions, crate. 🆂🅰🆅🅴 ⊠ 🛢 🖵

◈◈◈ ▼▼▼ Sea-Esta Motel III 𝗠
(302) 227-4343. **$55-$229.** 1409 Coastal Hwy 19971. Jct SR 1 and Rodney St. Ext corridors. **Pets:** Other species. $8 daily fee/pet. Service with restrictions, crate. 🆂🅰🆅🅴 ⊠ 🛢 🖵

DOVER

▼▼▼ Comfort Inn-Dover 𝗠
(302) 674-3300. **$79-$119.** 222 S DuPont Hwy 19901. SR 1, exit 95, 2 mi n on US 113, then 0.3 mi n on US 13. Ext corridors. **Pets:** Medium, other species. $35 one-time fee/room. Service with restrictions.
🅰🆂🅺 ⊠ 🛢 🖵 ⇆

▼▼▼▼ Hampton Inn-Dover 🄷
(302) 736-3500. **$89-$169.** 1568 N DuPont Hwy 19901. SR 1, exit 104, 1 mi s. Int corridors. **Pets:** Accepted. ⊠ ♿ 🛢 🖵 ⇆

▼▼▼▼ Holiday Inn Express Hotel & Suites Dover 🄷 🐾
(302) 678-0600. **$79-$199.** 1780 N DuPont Hwy 19901. SR 1, exit 104, just s on US 13. Int corridors. **Pets:** $10 daily fee/pet. Service with restrictions, crate. 🅰🆂🅺 ⊠ ♿ 🛢 🖵 ⇆

◈◈◈ ▼▼▼▼ Sheraton Dover Hotel 🄷
(302) 678-8500. **Call for rates.** 1570 N DuPont Hwy 19901. SR 1, exit 104, 1 mi s on US 13. Int corridors. **Pets:** Accepted.
🆂🅰🆅🅴 ⊠ 🖵 🍴 ⇆

GEORGETOWN

◈◈◈ ▼▼▼ Comfort Inn & Suites-Georgetown 🄷
(302) 854-9400. **$70-$300.** 20530 DuPont Blvd 19947. On US 113, 0.5 mi n of jct SR 404. Int corridors. **Pets:** Other species. $15 daily fee/pet. Designated rooms, service with restrictions, supervision.
🆂🅰🆅🅴 ⊠ 🛢 🖵 ⇆

HARRINGTON

▼▼▼ AmericInn Lodge & Suites of Harrington 🄷
(302) 398-3900. **$89-$169.** 1259 Corn Crib Rd 19952. On US 13, 0.6 mi s of jct SR 14. Int corridors. **Pets:** Dogs only. $20 daily fee/room. Service with restrictions, crate. 🅰🆂🅺 ⊠ ♿ 🛢 🖵 ⇆

LEWES

◈◈◈ ▼▼▼▼ The Inn at Canal Square 🄷
(302) 644-3377. **$105-$310, 7 day notice.** 122 Market St 19958. On the canal. Int corridors. **Pets:** Medium, dogs only. Designated rooms, service with restrictions, supervision. 🆂🅰🆅🅴 ⊠ 🛢 🖵 ⊠

▼▼▼ Sleep Inn & Suites 🄷 🐾
(302) 645-6464. **$59-$279.** 18451 Coastal Hwy 19958. On SR 1, 1.5 mi s. Int corridors. **Pets:** Medium, other species. $25 daily fee/pet. Service with restrictions, supervision. 🅰🆂🅺 ⊠ 🛢 🖵 ⇆

LONG NECK

◈◈◈ ▼▼▼ Sea-Esta II 𝗠
(302) 945-5900. **$45-$149.** 100 Rudder Rd 19966. On SR 23, 1.1 mi s of jct SR 24, 5 and 23. Ext corridors. **Pets:** Other species. $8 daily fee/pet. Service with restrictions, crate. 🆂🅰🆅🅴 ⊠ 🛢 🖵 ⇆

MIDDLETOWN

▼▼▼▼ Hampton Inn Middletown 🄷
(302) 378-5656. **$109-$169.** 117 Sandhill Dr 19709. SR 1, exit 136, 2.8 mi w on SR 299, then just n on SR 15. Int corridors. **Pets:** Accepted.
⊠ ♿ 🛢 🖵 ⇆

MILLSBORO

▼▼▼ Atlantic Inn-Millsboro 𝗠 🌼
(302) 934-6711. **Call for rates.** 28534 DuPont Blvd 19966. US 113, just s of SR 24. Ext corridors. **Pets:** Dogs only. $25 one-time fee/room. Designated rooms, service with restrictions, supervision. ⊠ 🛢 ⇆

NEWARK

◈◈◈ ▼▼▼ Days Inn Wilmington/Newark 𝗠
(302) 368-2400. **$59-$299.** 900 Churchmans Rd 19713. I-95, exit 4B, 0.3 mi n on SR 7, exit 166, then 0.3 mi w on SR 58 (Churchmans Rd). Ext corridors. **Pets:** $10 daily fee/pet. No service, supervision.
🆂🅰🆅🅴 ⊠ 🛢 🖵 ⇆

◈◈◈ ▼▼▼▼ Hilton Wilmington/Christiana 🄷 🐾
(302) 454-1500. **$144-$299.** 100 Continental Dr 19713. I-95, exit 4B, 0.3 mi n on SR 7, exit 166, then 0.4 mi w on SR 58 (Churchmans Rd). Int corridors. **Pets:** Medium. $49 one-time fee/room. Designated rooms, service with restrictions, supervision.
🄴🄲🄾 🆂🅰🆅🅴 ⊠ 🛢 🖵 🍴 ⇆ ⊠

▼▼▼ Homestead Studio Suites Hotel-Newark/Christiana 🄷
(302) 283-0800. **$89-$149.** 333 Continental Dr 19713. I-95, exit 4B, 0.3 mi n on SR 7, exit 166, then 0.4 mi w on SR 58 (Churchmans Rd). Int corridors. **Pets:** Other species. $25 daily fee/room. Designated rooms, service with restrictions, crate. 🅰🆂🅺 ⊠ ♿ 🛢 🖵

▼▼▼▼ Homewood Suites by Hilton Newark/Wilmington South 🄷
(302) 453-9700. **$99-$399.** 640 S College Ave 19713. I-95, exit 1B southbound; exit 1 northbound, 0.8 mi n on SR 896. Int corridors.
Pets: Accepted. ⊠ ♿ 🛢 🖵 ⇆

◈◈◈ ▼▼▼ Howard Johnson Inn & Suites–Newark/Wilmington 🄷
(302) 368-8521. **$59-$299.** 1119 S College Ave 19713. I-95, exit 1B southbound; exit 1 northbound, 0.3 mi n on SR 896. Int corridors. **Pets:** $10 daily fee/pet. No service, supervision.
🆂🅰🆅🅴 ⊠ 🛢 🖵 ⇆

▼▼▼ Red Roof Inn-Wilmington 𝗠
(302) 292-2870. **$54-$130.** 415 Stanton Christiana Rd 19713. I-95, exit 4B, 0.5 mi n on SR 7. Ext corridors. **Pets:** Large. Service with restrictions, crate. 🅰🆂🅺 ⊠ ♿ 🛢

▼▼▼▼ Residence Inn by Marriott 🄷
(302) 453-9200. **$152-$186.** 240 Chapman Rd 19702. I-95, exit 3 southbound; exit 3A northbound, 0.3 mi e on SR 273 E, then 0.5 mi s. Ext corridors. **Pets:** Accepted. ⊠ 🛢 🖵 ⇆ ⊠

▼▼▼ Staybridge Suites-Newark/Wilmington ⊞

(302) 366-8097. **$109-$289.** 270 Chapman Rd 19702. I-95, exit 3 southbound; exit 3A northbound, 0.3 mi e on SR 273 E, then just n. Int corridors. **Pets:** Large. $75 one-time fee/pet. Service with restrictions, crate.

(ASK) (✕) (🛁ᴹ) (📶) (💷) (🏊)

ⒶⒶⒹ ▼▼▼ TownePlace Suites by

Marriott-Wilmington/Newark ⊞ 🐾

(302) 369-6212. **$134-$164.** 410 Eagle Run Rd 19702. I-95, exit 3 southbound; exit 3A northbound, just e. Int corridors. **Pets:** Small, other species. $100 one-time fee/pet. Designated rooms.

(SAVE) (✕) (🛁ᴹ) (📶) (💷) (🏊)

NEW CASTLE

▼▼▼ Clarion Hotel–The Belle ⊞

(302) 428-1000. **$99-$189.** 1612 N DuPont Hwy 19720. Jct I-295, just n on SR 13. Int corridors. **Pets:** Medium. $10 daily fee/room. Designated rooms, service with restrictions, supervision.

(ECO) (ASK) (✕) (🛁ᴹ) (📶) (💷) (🍴) (🏊)

ⒶⒶⒹ ▼▼ Quality Inn & Suites Ⓜ

(302) 328-6666. **$80-$130.** 147 N DuPont Hwy 19720. I-95, exit 5A, 0.8 mi s on SR 141, exit 1B, then 0.5 mi s on US 13, 40 and 301; I-295, exit New Castle Airport/US 13 S, 1.8 mi s on US 13, 40 and 301. Ext/int corridors. **Pets:** Other species. $10 daily fee/room. Designated rooms, service with restrictions, crate. (ECO) (SAVE) (✕) (🛁ᴹ) (📶) (💷) (🏊)

▼▼ Super 8 Ⓜ

(302) 322-9480. **$65-$85.** 215 S DuPont Hwy 19720. I-95, exit 3A, 4.3 mi e on SR 273, then 0.8 mi s on US 13. Int corridors. **Pets:** Medium, other species. $10 daily fee/pet. Designated rooms, service with restrictions, supervision. (ASK) (✕) (📶) (💷)

REHOBOTH BEACH

▼▼ AmericInn Lodge & Suites of Rehoboth

Beach ⊞ 🐾

(302) 226-0700. **$69-$249, 3 day notice.** 36012 Airport Rd 19971. Just w of SR 1; just w on Miller Rd, then just s. Int corridors. **Pets:** Dogs only. $20 daily fee/pet. Designated rooms, service with restrictions, crate.

(ASK) (✕) (🛁ᴹ) (📶) (💷) (🏊)

▼▼ The Atlantis Inn Ⓜ

(302) 227-9446. **$69-$299, 7 day notice.** 154 Rehoboth Ave 19971. At Rehoboth Ave and 2nd St; downtown. Ext corridors. **Pets:** Accepted.

(ECO) (ASK) (✕) (📶) (💷) (🏊)

▼▼▼ The Breakers Hotel & Suites Ⓜ

(302) 227-6688. **$60-$230, 3 day notice.** 105 2nd St 19971. Just n of Rehoboth Ave. Ext corridors. **Pets:** Dogs only. $30 daily fee/pet. Designated rooms, service with restrictions. (ASK) (✕) (📶) (💷) (🏊)

ⒶⒶⒹ ▼▼ Sea-Esta IV Ⓜ

(302) 227-5882. **$47-$189.** 20902 Coastal Hwy 19971. 1 mi s of jct SR 24. Ext corridors. **Pets:** Other species. $8 daily fee/pet. Service with restrictions, crate. (SAVE) (✕) (📶) (💷) (🏊)

SEAFORD

▼▼▼ Comfort Suites ⊞

(302) 628-5400. **Call for rates.** 23420 Sussex Hwy 19973. On US 13, just n jct SR 20. Int corridors. **Pets:** Medium, other species. $25 daily fee/room. Service with restrictions, crate. (✕) (🛁ᴹ) (📶) (💷) (🏊)

▼▼▼ Holiday Inn Express-Seaford ⊞

(302) 629-2000. **Call for rates.** 210 N Dual Hwy 19973. On US 13, just s of SR 20 W. Int corridors. **Pets:** Accepted. (✕) (🛁ᴹ) (📶) (💷) (🏊)

WILMINGTON

ⒶⒶⒹ ▼▼▼ Best Western Brandywine Valley Inn ⊞

(302) 656-9436. **$99-$119.** 1807 Concord Pike 19803. I-95, exit 8, 1 mi n on US 202. Ext corridors. **Pets:** Other species. $25 one-time fee/room. Service with restrictions, supervision. (SAVE) (✕) (📶) (💷) (🏊)

ⒶⒶⒹ ▼▼ Days Inn Wilmington Ⓜ

(302) 478-0300. **$64-$79.** 5209 Concord Pike 19803. I-95, exit 8, 4 mi n on US 202; jct SR 92 (Naamans Rd). Ext corridors. **Pets:** Small. $15 daily fee/pet. Designated rooms, service with restrictions, crate.

(SAVE) (✕) (📶) (💷)

ⒶⒶⒹ ▼▼▼ ▼▼ Hotel du Pont ⊞

(302) 594-3100. **$139-$499.** 1007 Market St 19801. I-95, exit 7, 0.5 mi se; downtown at 11th St. Int corridors. **Pets:** Accepted.

(SAVE) (✕) (📶) (💷) (🍴) (✕)

ⒶⒶⒹ ▼▼▼ Quality Inn & Suites ⊞ 🐾

(302) 478-2222. **$72-$108, 3 day notice.** 4000 Concord Pike 19803. I-95, exit 8, 3 mi n on US 202. Ext corridors. **Pets:** Medium, other species. Designated rooms, service with restrictions, supervision.

(SAVE) (✕) (📶) (💷) (🏊)

ⒶⒶⒹ ▼▼▼ Sheraton Suites Wilmington ⊞

(302) 654-8300. **$109-$319.** 422 Delaware Ave 19801. I-95, exit 7 northbound; exit 7A southbound, 0.3 mi e; downtown. Int corridors.

Pets: Accepted. (SAVE) (✕) (🛁ᴹ) (📶) (💷) (🍴) (🏊)

DISTRICT OF COLUMBIA

DISTRICT OF COLUMBIA METROPOLITAN AREA

WASHINGTON

▼▼▼▼ Capital Hilton 🅷
(202) 393-1000. **$129-$549.** 1001 16th St NW 20036. 16th and K sts NW. Int corridors. **Pets:** Accepted. ⊠ 📧 💻 🍴 ⊠

ⒶⒶ ▼▼▼▼ Capitol Hill Suites 🅷 ✿
(202) 543-6000. **$139-$799.** 200 C St SE 20003. 2 blks from Capitol grounds; at 2nd and C sts SE. Int corridors. **Pets:** Small. $75 one-time fee/room. Designated rooms, service with restrictions, supervision.
[SAVE] ⊠ 📧 💻

▼▼▼▼ Doubletree Guest Suites, Washington DC 🅷
(202) 785-2000. **$119-$329.** 801 New Hampshire Ave NW 20037. Just sw at Washington Circle. Int corridors. **Pets:** Accepted.
⊠ 🚹 📧 💻 ⇌

ⒶⒶ ▼▼▼▼ The Fairfax at Embassy Row, Washington, D.C.–The Luxury Collection 🅷
(202) 293-2100. **$179-$699.** 2100 Massachusetts Ave NW 20008. Just w of Dupont Circle; at 21st St. Int corridors. **Pets:** Accepted.
[SAVE] ⊠ 💻 🍴

ⒶⒶ ▼▼▼▼ The Fairmont Washington, D.C. 🅷
(202) 429-2400. **Call for rates.** 2401 M St NW 20037. 24th and M sts NW. Int corridors. **Pets:** Accepted. [SAVE] ⊠ 🚹 💻 🍴 ⇌ ⊠

ⒶⒶ ▼▼▼▼ Four Seasons Hotel Washington D.C. 🅷
(202) 342-0444. **$595-$1995, 30 day notice.** 2800 Pennsylvania Ave NW 20007. In Georgetown. Int corridors. **Pets:** Accepted.
[SAVE] ⊠ 🚹 📧 💻 🍴 ⊠

▼▼▼▼ Hamilton Crowne Plaza Hotel Washington DC 🅷
(202) 682-0111. **$79-$489.** 1001 14th St NW 20005. 14th and K sts NW. Int corridors. **Pets:** Large, other species. $250 deposit/room. Service with restrictions, crate. [ASK] ⊠ 🚹 📧 💻 🍴

▼▼▼▼ The Hay-Adams 🅷
(202) 638-6600. **$900-$1100.** 800 16th St NW 20006. 16th and H sts NW; just n of the White House. Int corridors. **Pets:** Accepted.
[ECO] ⊠ 📧 🍴

▼▼▼▼ Hilton Washington 🅷
(202) 483-3000. **$199-$499.** 1919 Connecticut Ave NW 20009. Just n of Dupont Circle at T St NW. Int corridors. **Pets:** Accepted.
⊠ 📧 💻 🍴 ⇌

ⒶⒶ ▼▼▼▼ The Hotel George 🅷
(202) 347-4200. **Call for rates.** 15 E St NW 20001. On Capitol Hill, just n of Capitol grounds. Int corridors. **Pets:** Accepted.
[SAVE] ⊠ 🚹 📧 🍴

ⒶⒶ ▼▼▼▼ Hotel Helix-A Kimpton Hotel 🅷
(202) 462-9001. **$139-$549 (no credit cards).** 1430 Rhode Island Ave NW 20005. Just e of Scott Circle. Int corridors. **Pets:** Accepted.
[SAVE] ⊠ 📧 🍴

ⒶⒶ ▼▼▼▼ Hotel Madera 🅷
(202) 296-7600. **Call for rates.** 1310 New Hampshire Ave NW 20036. Between 20th and N sts NW. Int corridors. **Pets:** Accepted.
[SAVE] ⊠ 📧 🍴

ⒶⒶ ▼▼▼▼ Hotel Monaco Washington DC 🅷 ✿
(202) 628-7177. **Call for rates.** 700 F St NW 20004. Between 7th and 8th sts NW. Int corridors. **Pets:** Other species. [SAVE] ⊠ 🍴

ⒶⒶ ▼▼▼▼ Hotel Palomar-A Kimpton Hotel 🅷 ✿
(202) 448-1800. **$159-$429.** 2121 P St NW 20037. Between 21st and 22nd sts NW; just w of Dupont Circle. Int corridors. **Pets:** Other species. Service with restrictions. [SAVE] ⊠ 📧 🍴 ⇌

ⒶⒶ ▼▼▼▼ Hotel Rouge-A Kimpton Hotel 🅷
(202) 232-8000. **$139-$409.** 1315 16th St NW 20036. Just n of Scott Circle. Int corridors. **Pets:** Other species. [SAVE] ⊠ 📧 🍴

▼▼▼▼ L'Enfant Plaza Hotel 🅷
(202) 484-1000. **$119-$579.** 480 L'Enfant Plaza SW 20024. I-395, exit L'Enfant Plaza/12th St. Int corridors. **Pets:** Accepted.
[ASK] ⊠ 🚹 📧 💻 🍴 🏊 ⊠

ⒶⒶ ▼▼▼▼ The Liaison Capitol Hill, An Affinia Hotel 🅷
(202) 638-1616. **$119-$799.** 415 New Jersey Ave NW 20001. On Capitol Hill. Int corridors. **Pets:** Accepted. [SAVE] ⊠ 🚹 📧 💻 🍴 ⇌

ⒶⒶ ▼▼▼▼ The Madison, a Loews Hotel 🅷
(202) 862-1600. **$189-$459.** 1177 15th St NW 20005. 15th and M sts NW. Int corridors. **Pets:** Accepted. [SAVE] ⊠ 💻 🍴 ⊠

▼▼▼▼ Mandarin Oriental, Washington D.C. 🅷 ✿
(202) 554-8588. **$495-$8000.** 1330 Maryland Ave SW 20024. Jct Independence Ave SW, just s on 12th St SW. Int corridors. **Pets:** Medium, dogs only. $50 daily fee/room, $50 one-time fee/room. Designated rooms, service with restrictions, supervision.
[ASK] ⊠ 🚹 🍴 ⇌ ⊠

ⒶⒶ ▼▼▼▼ The Mayflower-A Renaissance Hotel 🅷
(202) 347-3000. **$359-$419.** 1127 Connecticut Ave NW 20036. Just n of K St NW; in business district. Int corridors. **Pets:** Accepted.
[SAVE] ⊠ 🚹 💻 🍴

▼▼▼▼ The Melrose Hotel, Washington DC 🅷
(202) 955-6400. **$189-$449.** 2430 Pennsylvania Ave NW 20037. Between 24th and 25th sts NW. Int corridors. **Pets:** Other species. $100 one-time fee/room. Service with restrictions, crate. [ASK] ⊠ 📧 💻 🍴

ⒶⒶ ▼▼▼▼ Omni Shoreham Hotel 🅷
(202) 234-0700. **Call for rates.** 2500 Calvert St NW 20008. Just w of Connecticut Ave. Int corridors. **Pets:** Small. $50 one-time fee/pet. Service with restrictions, supervision. [SAVE] ⊠ 📧 💻 🍴 ⇌ ⊠

ⒶⒶ ▼▼▼▼ Park Hyatt Washington 🅷 ✿
(202) 789-1234. **$249-$577, 3 day notice.** 1201 24th St NW 20037. 24th and M sts NW. Int corridors. **Pets:** Dogs only. $150 one-time fee/room. [SAVE] ⊠ 🚹 💻 🍴 ⇌

▼▼▼ The Quincy 🅷
(202) 223-4320. **$99-$339.** 1823 L St NW 20036. Between 18th and 19th sts NW. Int corridors. **Pets:** Accepted. [ASK] ⊠ 📧 💻 🍴

ⒶⒶ ▼▼▼ Red Roof Inn Downtown Washington, D.C. 🅷
(202) 289-5959. **Call for rates.** 500 H St NW 20001. At 5th and H sts NW; in Chinatown. Int corridors. **Pets:** Large. Service with restrictions, crate. [SAVE] ⊠ 📧 💻

▼▼▼▼ Residence Inn by Marriott Capitol 🅷
(202) 484-8280. **$289-$359.** 333 E St SW 20024. Between 3rd and 4th sts SW. Int corridors. **Pets:** Other species. $10 daily fee/pet, $200 one-time fee/room. Service with restrictions. ⊠ 🚹 📧 💻 ⇌

WWW Residence Inn by Marriott-Dupont Circle H
(202) 466-6800. **$299-$369.** 2120 P St NW 20037. Between 21st and
22nd sts NW; just w of Dupont Circle. Int corridors. **Pets:** Medium. $10
daily fee/pet, $100 one-time fee/pet. [X] [&M] [] []

**WWW Residence Inn by Marriott-Washington DC-Vermont
Ave** H ❀
(202) 898-1100. **$279-$349.** 1199 Vermont Ave NW 20005. Jct 14th St
and Vermont Ave NW, at Thomas Circle. Int corridors. **Pets:** Medium. $10
daily fee/room, $100 one-time fee/room. Designated rooms, service with
restrictions, crate. [ECO] [X] [&M] [] []

WWWW The Ritz-Carlton, Georgetown H
(202) 912-4100. **Call for rates.** 3100 South St NW 20007. Just s of jct
M St and Wisconsin Ave; in Georgetown. Int corridors. **Pets:** Accepted.
[X] [&M] [] [¶] [X]

WWWWW The Ritz-Carlton, Washington, D.C. H
(202) 835-0500. **Call for rates.** 1150 22nd St NW 20037. At 22nd and
M sts NW. Int corridors. **Pets:** Accepted. [X] [&M] [¶] [≈] [X]

AAA WWWW St. Regis, Washington, D.C. H ❀
(202) 638-2626. **$395-$875.** 923 16th St NW 20006. 16th and K sts; just
n of the White House. Int corridors. **Pets:** Small, dogs only. $25 daily
fee/pet, $100 one-time fee/pet. [SAVE] [X] [¶]

WWWW Sofitel Washington DC Lafayette Square H
(202) 730-8800. **Call for rates.** 806 15th St NW 20005. Jct 15th and H
sts NW. Int corridors. **Pets:** Accepted. [X] [&M] [¶]

AAA WWWW Topaz Hotel-A Kimpton Hotel H
(202) 393-3000. **Call for rates.** 1733 N St NW 20036. Just e of Connecticut Ave. Int corridors. **Pets:** Accepted. [SAVE] [X] [¶]

**AAA WWWW Washington Marriott Wardman Park
Hotel** H
(202) 328-2000. **$279-$329.** 2660 Woodley Rd NW 20008. Just w of
Connecticut Ave; at Woodley Park/Zoo Metro Station. Int corridors.
Pets: Medium. $50 one-time fee/pet. No service, supervision.
[SAVE] [X] [&M] [] [] [¶] [≈] [X]

AAA WWWW Washington Suites Georgetown H
(202) 333-8060. **$169-$424.** 2500 Pennsylvania Ave NW 20037. Jct 25th
St NW and Pennsylvania Ave; 2 blks from Foggy Bottom Metro Station.
Int corridors. **Pets:** Small, other species. $20 daily fee/pet. Designated
rooms, service with restrictions. [SAVE] [X] [&M] [] []

AAA WWWW The Westin Grand, Washington, D.C. H
(202) 429-0100. **Call for rates.** 2350 M St NW 20037. 24th and M sts
NW. Int corridors. **Pets:** Accepted. [SAVE] [X] [] [¶] [≈]

**AAA WWWW The Westin Washington DC City Center
Hotel** H ❀
(202) 429-1700. **$120-$500.** 1400 M St NW 20005. Just w of Thomas
Circle. Int corridors. **Pets:** Medium, dogs only. Service with restrictions,
supervision. [SAVE] [X] [] [¶]

AAA WWWW The Willard InterContinental H
(202) 628-9100. **$279-$799.** 1401 Pennsylvania Ave NW 20004. Just e
of the White House. Int corridors. **Pets:** Accepted.
[SAVE] [X] [&M] [] [¶] [X]

END METROPOLITAN AREA

FLORIDA

ALACHUA

Econo Lodge H
(386) 462-2414. **Call for rates.** 15920 NW Hwy 441 32615. I-75, exit 399, just e. Ext corridors. **Pets:** Large, dogs only. $10 daily fee/pet. Designated rooms, service with restrictions, supervision.
[SAVE] [X] [♿] [▢] [🐾]

Quality Inn Alachua H
(386) 462-2244. **Call for rates.** 15960 NW Hwy 441 32615. I-75, exit 399, just e. Ext corridors. **Pets:** Accepted. [SAVE] [X] [♿] [▢] [🐾]

APALACHICOLA

Coombs House Inn BB
(850) 653-9199. **$119-$269, 7 day notice.** 80 Sixth St (Hwy 98) 32320. Corner of US 98 and 6th St; center. Int corridors. **Pets:** Accepted.
[SAVE] [X] [♿] [▢]

Gibson Inn CI ❀
(850) 653-2191. **$115-$260, 14 day notice.** 51 Ave C 32320. On US 98 at west end of bridge. Int corridors. **Pets:** Other species. $25 daily fee/pet. Designated rooms, service with restrictions, supervision.
[SAVE] [X] [🍴]

Water Street Hotel & Marina CO
(850) 653-3700. **$129-$325, 7 day notice.** 329 Water St 32320. Jct Ave I and Water St. Ext corridors. **Pets:** $20 daily fee/pet. Service with restrictions. [SAVE] [X] [♿] [▢] [🐾] [X]

ARCADIA

Knights Inn of Arcadia M
(863) 494-4884. **$49-$129.** 504 S Brevard Ave 34266. 0.6 mi s of SR 70; on US 17. Ext corridors. **Pets:** $25 daily fee/pet. Service with restrictions, supervision. [SAVE] [X] [♿] [▢] [🐾]

AVON PARK

Econo Lodge M
(863) 453-2000. **$60-$105.** 2511 US Hwy 27 S 33825. 2.5 mi s of jct SR 17 and 64 (W Main St). Ext corridors. **Pets:** Other species. $10 daily fee/room. Designated rooms, service with restrictions, crate.
[SAVE] [X] [🐾]

Reeds Motel & Oasis Banquet Hall M
(863) 453-3194. **$69-$199, 3 day notice.** 102 US Hwy 27 S 33825. Just n of SR 64 (W Main St). Ext corridors. **Pets:** Accepted.
[SAVE] [X] [♿] [▢] [🐾]

BARTOW

The Stanford Inn BB
(863) 533-2393. **$140-$205, 7 day notice.** 555 E Stanford St 33830. Main St, s on S Broadway to E Stanford St; downtown. Ext/int corridors. **Pets:** Small. $200 deposit/pet. Designated rooms, service with restrictions.
[ASK] [X] [♿] [▢] [🐾]

BOCA RATON

Boca Raton Bridge Hotel H
(561) 368-9500. **$89-$409.** 999 E Camino Real 33432. Just w of SR A1A, 1 mi s of jct SR 798 (Palmetto Park Rd). Int corridors.
Pets: Accepted. [SAVE] [X] [♿] [▢] [🍴] [🐾] [X]

Boca Raton Resort and Club H
(561) 447-3000. **$169-$529, 7 day notice.** 501 E Camino Real 33432. I-95, exit 44 (Palmetto Park Rd), 1.9 mi e to Federal Hwy, s to Camino Real, then 0.5 mi e. Ext/int corridors. **Pets:** Accepted.
[ECO] [SAVE] [X] [♿] [♿] [▢] [🍴] [🐾] [X]

Fairfield Inn & Suites by Marriott H
(561) 417-8585. **$89-$169.** 3400 Airport Rd 33431. I-95, exit 45 (SR 808/Glades Rd), just e, then 1.1 mi n. Int corridors. **Pets:** Accepted.
[ECO] [X] [♿] [♿] [▢] [🐾]

AAA ▼▼ Hilton Suites Boca Raton **H** ❀
(561) 483-3600. **$89-$329.** 7920 Glades Rd 33434. Florida Tpke, exit 75 (SR 808/Glades Rd); in Arvida Parkway Center. Int corridors. **Pets:** Medium. $75 one-time fee/room. Service with restrictions, supervision. **ECO** **SAVE** ⊠ 🛏 📺 ⊠

▼▼ Homestead Studio Suites Hotel-Boca
Raton/Commerce **M**
(561) 994-2599. **$69-$109.** 501 NW 77th St 33487. I-95, exit 50, just s on Congress Ave to NW 6th Ave. Ext corridors. **Pets:** Other species. $25 daily fee/room. Designated rooms, service with restrictions, crate.
ASK ⊠ 🛏 📺

AAA ▼▼▼ Residence Inn by Marriott-Boca Raton **H**
(561) 994-3222. **$119-$259.** 525 NW 77th St 33487. I-95, exit 50, w on Congress Ave to NW 6th Ave, then to NW 77th St. Ext corridors.
Pets: Accepted. **SAVE** ⊠ 🛏 📺 ⊅ ⊠

AAA ▼▼▼ TownePlace Suites by Marriott **H**
(561) 994-7232. **$199-$319.** 5110 NW 8th Ave 33487. I-95, exit 48B (Yamato Rd), just w; in Arvida Corporate Park. Int corridors.
Pets: Accepted. **SAVE** ⊠ ⤓M 🛏 📺

AAA ▼▼▼ Wyndham Garden Hotel **H**
(561) 368-5200. **$75-$309.** 1950 Glades Rd 33431. I-95, exit 45 (SR 808/Glades Rd), just w. Ext/int corridors. **Pets:** Accepted.
SAVE ⊠ ⤓M 🛏 📺 🍽 ⊅ ⊠

BONITA SPRINGS

▼▼▼ AmericInn Hotel & Suites of Bonita Springs **H**
(239) 495-9255. **$69-$179.** 28600 Trails Edge Blvd 34134. On US 41 (Tamiami Tr), 0.7 mi s of jct CR 865 (Bonita Beach Rd SE), just w; in Woods Edge. Int corridors. **Pets:** Small, other species. $15 daily fee/pet. Designated rooms, service with restrictions, supervision.
ASK ⊠ ⤓M 🛏 📺 ⊅

AAA ▼▼▼ Holiday Inn Express Hotel & Suites **H**
(239) 948-0699. **$72-$135.** 27891 Crown Lake Blvd 34135. I-75, exit 116, 3.4 mi w on CR 865 (Bonita Beach Rd SE), then just n. Int corridors.
Pets: Accepted. **SAVE** ⊠ ⤓M 🛏 📺 ⊅

AAA ▼▼▼▼ Hyatt Regency Coconut Point Resort &
Spa **H** ❀
(239) 444-1234. **$129-$569, 3 day notice.** 5001 Coconut Rd 34134. I-75, exit 123, 1.9 mi w on CR 850 (Corkscrew Rd), 2.3 mi s on US 41 (Tamiami Tr), then 1.5 mi w. Int corridors. **Pets:** Medium, dogs only. $50 daily fee/room, $100 one-time fee/room. Designated rooms, service with restrictions. **ECO** **SAVE** ⊠ 🛏 📺 🍽 ⊅ ⊠

AAA ▼▼▼▼ Inn at the Springs **H**
(239) 949-5913. **$79-$249, 3 day notice.** 8901 Highland Woods Blvd 34135. I-75, exit 116, 3.5 mi w on CR 865 (Bonita Beach Rd SE), 1.4 mi n on US 41 (Tamiami Tr), then e. Int corridors. **Pets:** Accepted.
ECO **SAVE** ⊠ ⤓M 🛏 📺 ⊅

BRADENTON

AAA ▼▼▼ Howard Johnson Express Inn **M**
(941) 756-8399. **Call for rates.** 6511 14th St W 34207. On US 41, 1.5 mi s of jct SR 70. Ext corridors. **Pets:** Accepted.
SAVE ⊠ 🛏 📺 ⊅

AAA ▼▼▼ Quality Inn North **M**
(941) 758-7199. **$60-$180.** 6727 14th St W 34207. On US 41, 2 mi s of jct SR 70. Ext corridors. **Pets:** Small, dogs only. $10 daily fee/pet. Service with restrictions, supervision. **SAVE** ⊠ 🛏 📺 ⊅

AAA ▼▼▼ Super 8-Bradenton **M**
(941) 756-6656. **$50-$120.** 6516 14 St W 34207. On US 41, 1.5 mi s of jct SR 70. Ext corridors. **Pets:** Small, dogs only. $10 daily fee/pet. Service with restrictions, supervision. **SAVE** ⊠ 🛏 ⊅

BRADENTON BEACH

AAA ▼▼▼▼ Tortuga Inn Beach Resort **CO**
(941) 778-6611. **$120-$375, 14 day notice.** 1325 Gulf Dr N 34217. On Sarasota Bay and Anna Maria Island; on SR 789, 0.3 mi n of jct SR 684. Ext corridors. **Pets:** Small. $25 one-time/pet. Designated rooms, service with restrictions, supervision. **SAVE** ⊠ 🛏 📺

AAA ▼▼▼▼ Tradewinds Resort **CA**
(941) 779-0010. **$130-$335, 14 day notice.** 1603 Gulf Dr N 34217. On Sarasota Bay and Anna Maria Island; on SR 789, 0.5 mi n of jct SR 684. Ext corridors. **Pets:** Small. $25 one-time fee/pet. Designated rooms, service with restrictions, supervision. **SAVE** ⊠ 🛏 📺

BROOKSVILLE

AAA ▼▼ Days Inn **M** ❀
(352) 796-9486. **$59-$89.** 6320 Windmere Rd 34602. I-75, exit 301, just e on US 98/SR 50. Ext corridors. **Pets:** Other species. $15 one-time fee/pet. Service with restrictions, crate. **SAVE** ⊠ ⤓M 🛏 📺 ⊅

▼▼ Microtel Inn & Suites **H**
(352) 796-9025. **$65-$85.** 6298 Nature Coast Blvd 34602. Just w on SR 50, then just s. Int corridors. **Pets:** Accepted.
ASK ⊠ ⤓M 🛏 📺 ⊅

▼▼ Quality Inn & Suites **M**
(352) 796-9481. **$52-$129.** 30307 Cortez Blvd 34602. I-75, exit 301, just w on US 98/SR 50. Ext corridors. **Pets:** Accepted.
ASK ⊠ ⤓M 🛏 📺 🍽 ⊅

CAPE CANAVERAL

▼▼▼ Residence Inn by Marriott Cape Canaveral/Cocoa
Beach **H**
(321) 323-1100. **$152-$186.** 8959 Astronaut Blvd 32920. On SR A1A, 0.3 mi s of jct SR 528. Int corridors. **Pets:** Large, other species. $75 one-time fee/room. Service with restrictions, crate. **ECO** ⊠ 🛏 📺 ⊅ ⊠

CAPE CORAL

▼▼ Dockside Inn **M**
(239) 542-0061. **Call for rates.** 3817 Del Prado Blvd S 33904. 1.2 mi n of jct Cape Coral Pkwy. Ext corridors. **Pets:** Accepted.
⊠ 🛏 ⊅ ⊠

▼▼▼ Holiday Inn Express Cape Coral **H**
(239) 542-2121. **$90-$179.** 1538 Cape Coral Pkwy E 33904. Jct Del Prado Blvd. Int corridors. **Pets:** Medium, other species. $15 daily fee/room. Designated rooms, service with restrictions.
ASK ⊠ ⤓M 🛏 📺 ⊅

CARRABELLE

▼▼ The Moorings At Carrabelle **H** ❀
(850) 697-2800. **$70-$150.** 1000 Hwy 98 32322. On US 98, just e of bridge. Ext corridors. **Pets:** Other species. $50 deposit/room, $10 daily fee/pet. Service with restrictions. **ASK** ⊠ 🛏 ⊅ ⊠

CEDAR KEY

AAA ▼▼▼ Cedar Key Bed and Breakfast **BB**
(352) 543-9000. **$99-$225, 7 day notice.** 810 3rd St 32625. 0.3 mi n of SR 24. Ext/int corridors. **Pets:** Accepted. **SAVE** ⊠ 🛏 📺 ⓩ

AAA ▼▼▼ Park Place Motel & Condominiums **M**
(352) 543-5737. **$65-$120.** 211 2nd St 32625. At a St. Ext corridors.
Pets: Accepted. **SAVE** ⊠ 🛏 📺

▼▼▼▼ Seahorse Landing Condominiums **CO**
(352) 543-5860. **$160-$175, 3 day notice.** 4050 G St 32625. Just w on 6th St. Ext corridors. **Pets:** Medium, dogs only. $15 daily fee/room. Designated rooms, no service, supervision. **ECO** 🛏 📺 ⊅ ⊠

CHIEFLAND

AAA ▼▼ Best Western Suwannee Valley Inn **H**
(352) 493-0663. **$85-$100.** 1125 N Young Blvd 32626. On US 19/98, just n of jct US 129. Ext corridors. **Pets:** Small. $15 daily fee/pet. Designated rooms, service with restrictions, supervision. **SAVE** ⊠ 🛏 📺 ⊅

▼▼ Holiday Inn Express 🅷

(352) 493-9400. **Call for rates.** 809 NW 21st Ave 32626. US 19/98, 1.5 mi n of jct US 129. Ext corridors. **Pets:** Accepted.
⊠ 🔊 🏠 💻 ≈

CHIPLEY
▼▼ Super 8 Ⓜ

(850) 638-8530. **Call for rates.** 1150 Motel Dr 32428. I-10, exit 120, just n. Ext corridors. **Pets:** Accepted. ⊠ 🏠 💻

COCOA
🔷 ▼▼ Econo Lodge-Space Center 🅷

(321) 632-4561. **Call for rates.** 3220 N Cocoa Blvd 32926. US 1, just n of jct SR 528. Ext corridors. **Pets:** Medium. $15 one-time fee/room. Designated rooms, service with restrictions, crate. [SAVE] ⊠ 🏠 💻 ≈

COCOA BEACH
🔷 ▼▼ Best Western Ocean Beach Hotel & Suites 🅷

(321) 783-7621. **$89-$159.** 5600 N Atlantic Ave 32931. SR A1A, 0.8 mi n of jct SR 520. Ext/int corridors. **Pets:** Large. $25 one-time fee/room. Designated rooms, service with restrictions, supervision.

[SAVE] ⊠ 🏠 💻 ≈

🔷 ▼▼▼ Four Points by Sheraton Cocoa Beach 🅷

(321) 783-8717. **Call for rates.** 4001 N Atlantic Ave 32931. SR A1A, just s of jct SR 520. Int corridors. **Pets:** Accepted.
[ECO] [SAVE] ⊠ 🏠 💻 🍽 ≈ ⊠

▼▼ Holiday Inn Cocoa Beach Oceanfront Resort 🅷

(321) 783-2271. **$79-$189.** 1300 N Atlantic Ave 32931. SR A1A, 1.8 mi s of jct SR 520. Ext corridors. **Pets:** Accepted.
[ECO] [ASK] ⊠ 🏠 💻 🍽 ≈ ⊠

🔷 ▼▼ La Quinta Inn Cocoa Beach 🅷 ❀

(321) 783-2252. **$60-$180.** 1275 N Atlantic Ave 32931. On SR A1A, 1.7 mi s. Ext corridors. **Pets:** Medium, other species. Service with restrictions, supervision. [SAVE] ⊠ 🏠 💻 🍽 ≈

▼▼ Quality Suites Cocoa Beach 🅷

(321) 783-6868. **$79-$149.** 3655 N Atlantic Ave 32931. SR A1A, 0.3 mi s of jct SR 520. Int corridors. **Pets:** Accepted. [ECO] ⊠ 🔊 🏠 💻

▼ Surf Studio Beach Resort Ⓜ

(321) 783-7100. **$100-$215, 7 day notice.** 1801 S Atlantic Ave 32931. SR A1A northbound, 5 mi s of jct SR 520 at Francis St; 1.3 mi n of Patrick AFB. Ext corridors. **Pets:** Medium. $20 daily fee/pet. Service with restrictions, supervision. ⊠ 🏠 💻 ≈

CRESCENT BEACH
🔷 ▼▼ Beacher's Lodge Oceanfront Suites 🆑

(904) 471-8849. **$89-$225, 3 day notice.** 6970 A1A S 32080. Just s of jct SR 206. Ext corridors. **Pets:** Medium, other species. $50 one-time fee/pet. Designated rooms, service with restrictions, crate.

[SAVE] ⊠ 🏠 💻 ≈

CRESTVIEW
▼▼ Jameson Inn 🅷

(850) 683-1778. **$93-$100.** 151 Cracker Barrel Dr 32536. I-10, exit 56, just s. Int corridors. **Pets:** Small, other species. $15 daily fee. Designated rooms, service with restrictions, supervision.

[ASK] ⊠ 🏠 💻 ≈

🔷 ▼▼▼ Super 8 Ⓜ

(850) 682-9649. **$53-$78.** 3925 S Ferdon Blvd 32539. I-10, exit 56, 0.3 mi s. Ext corridors. **Pets:** Other species. $5 daily fee/pet. Designated rooms, service with restrictions, supervision. [SAVE] ⊠ 🏠 💻

CRYSTAL RIVER
🔷 ▼▼▼ Best Western Crystal River Resort 🅷

(352) 795-3171. **$120-$160.** 614 NW Hwy 19 34428. On US 19/98, 0.8 mi n of jct SR 44. Ext corridors. **Pets:** Other species. $3 daily fee/pet. Service with restrictions, supervision. [SAVE] ⊠ 🏠 💻 ≈ ⊠

🔷 ▼▼▼ Days Inn 🅷

(352) 795-2111. **$65-$140.** 2380 NW Hwy 19 34428. US 19, 2.2 mi n of jct SR 44. Ext corridors. **Pets:** $15 daily fee/pet. Designated rooms, service with restrictions, supervision. [SAVE] ⊠ 🏠 💻 🍽

CUTLER BAY
▼▼ La Quinta Inn & Suites 🅷 ❀

(305) 278-0001. **$59-$149.** 10821 Caribbean Blvd 33189. Florida Tpke, exit 12 (US 1), northwest corner. Int corridors. **Pets:** Medium, other species. Service with restrictions, supervision.

[ASK] ⊠ 🔊 🏠 💻 ≈

DAYTONA BEACH
🔷 ▼▼ Days Inn Speedway Ⓜ

(386) 255-0541. **$45-$349.** 2900 W International Speedway Blvd 32124. I-95, exit 261B southbound; exit 261 northbound, just w on US 92. Ext corridors. **Pets:** Accepted. [SAVE] ⊠ 🏠 💻 🍽 ≈

▼▼ Extended Stay Deluxe Daytona Beach-International Speedway 🅷

(386) 257-4311. **$69-$109.** 255 Bill France Blvd 32114. I-95, exit 261, 2.5 mi e, then just n. Int corridors. **Pets:** Other species. $25 daily fee/room. Designated rooms, service with restrictions, crate.

[ASK] ⊠ 🔊 🏠 💻 ≈

▼▼▼ Homewood Suites by Hilton Daytona Speedway/Airport 🅷

(386) 258-2828. **$149-$159.** 165 Bill France Blvd 32114. I-95, exit 261, 2.5 mi e, then just n. Int corridors. **Pets:** Accepted.

⊠ 🔊 🏠 💻 ≈ ⊠

🔷 ▼▼▼ Plaza Ocean Club Hotel 🅷

(386) 239-9800. **$89-$499, 3 day notice.** 640 N Atlantic Ave 32118. On SR A1A, 1 mi n of jct SR 90. Int corridors. **Pets:** Small. $50 deposit/room, $20 daily fee/pet. Designated rooms, service with restrictions.

[SAVE] ⊠ 🔊 🏠 💻 🍽 ≈

▼▼ Ramada Inn Speedway 🅷

(386) 255-2422. **$89, 30 day notice.** 1798 W International Speedway Blvd 32114. I-95, exit 261A southbound; exit 261 northbound, 2 mi e on US 92. Ext corridors. **Pets:** Medium. $25 one-time fee/room. Service with restrictions, crate. [ASK] ⊠ 🏠 💻 ≈

🔷 ▼▼▼ Residence Inn by Marriott 🅷

(386) 252-3949. **$179-$209.** 1725 Richard Petty Blvd 32114. I-95, exit 261, 2.6 mi e, then just s. Int corridors. **Pets:** Accepted.
[ECO] [SAVE] ⊠ 🔊 🏠 💻 ≈ ⊠

▼ Scottish Inns Ⓜ

(386) 258-5742. **$39-$250, 15 day notice.** 1515 S Ridgewood Ave 32114. I-95, exit 260A, 2.5 mi on SR 400, then just n on US 1 (Ridgewood Ave). Ext corridors. **Pets:** Very small, dogs only. $8 daily fee/pet. Designated rooms, service with restrictions, supervision.

[ASK] ⊠ 🏠 ≈

DAYTONA BEACH SHORES
🔷 ▼▼ Atlantic Ocean Palm Inn Ⓜ

(386) 761-8450. **$59-$139, 30 day notice.** 3247 S Atlantic Ave 32118. On SR A1A, 5 mi s of jct US 92. Ext corridors. **Pets:** Small, dogs only. $15 daily fee/pet. Designated rooms, service with restrictions, supervision.

[SAVE] ⊠ 🏠 ≈

🔷 ▼▼ ▼▼ The Shores Resort & Spa 🅷

(386) 767-7350. **$99-$499, 3 day notice.** 2637 S Atlantic Ave 32118. On SR A1A, 3.2 mi s of jct US 92. Int corridors. **Pets:** Accepted.
[ECO] [SAVE] ⊠ 🔊 🏠 💻 🍽 ≈ ⊠

DE FUNIAK SPRINGS
🔷 ▼▼▼ Best Western Crossroads Inn 🅷

(850) 892-5111. **$80-$90.** 2343 Freeport Rd 32435. I-10, exit 85, just s. Ext/int corridors. **Pets:** Medium. $20 one-time fee/room. Designated rooms, service with restrictions, supervision.

[SAVE] ⊠ 🏠 💻 🍽 ≈

DELAND

🐾 ♦♦♦ University Inn 🅼

(386) 734-5711. **$79-$199.** 644 N Woodland Blvd 32720. US 17, 0.9 mi n of jct SR 44. **Pets:** Medium. $10 daily fee/pet. Designated rooms, service with restrictions, supervision. 〔SAVE〕 ⊠ 🔋 💷 🐾

DELRAY BEACH

🐾 ♦♦♦♦ Colony Hotel & Cabana Club 🅷

(561) 276-4123. **$99-$329, 3 day notice.** 525 E Atlantic Ave 33483. On SR 806 (Atlantic Ave) at US 1 northbound; center. Int corridors. **Pets:** Other species. $25 daily fee/pet. 〔ECO〕〔SAVE〕 ⊠ 🐾

♦♦♦♦ Residence Inn Delray Beach 🅷

(561) 276-7441. **$159-$329.** 1111 E Atlantic Ave 33483. I-95, exit 52 (SR 806/Atlantic Ave), 1.7 mi e. Int corridors. **Pets:** Accepted.
〔ECO〕 ⊠ 🔋 🔋 💷 🐾

DELTONA

🐾 ♦♦♦ Best Western Deltona Inn 🅷

(386) 860-3000. **$80-$300.** 481 Deltona Blvd 32725. I-4, exit 108, just ne. Ext corridors. **Pets:** Medium. $10 daily fee/pet. Designated rooms, service with restrictions, supervision. 〔SAVE〕 ⊠ 🔋 💷 🍴 🐾

DESTIN

♦♦ Beachside Inn 🅷 ♣

(850) 650-9099. **$79-$199.** 2931 Scenic Hwy 98 32541. 1 mi s of US 98. Ext corridors. **Pets:** Other species. $25 one-time fee/pet. Designated rooms, service with restrictions. 〔ASK〕 ⊠ 🔋 💷 🍴 🐾

♦♦♦♦ Residence Inn Sandestin at Grand Boulevard 🅷

(850) 650-7811. **$189-$279.** 300 Grand Blvd 32550. 6 mi w on US 98 from jct US 331. Int corridors. **Pets:** Accepted.
⊠ 🔋 🔋 💷 🐾 ⊠

🐾 ♦♦♦♦ Sandestin Golf and Beach Resort 🆑 ♣

(850) 267-8000. **$89-$1349.** 9300 Emerald Coast Pkwy W 32550. On US 98, 10 mi e; through main bayside gate, check in at Grand Sandestin. Ext/int corridors. **Pets:** Other species. $150 one-time fee/room.
〔SAVE〕 ⊠ 🔋 💷 🍴 🐾 ⊠

♦♦ Sleep Inn 🅷 ♣

(850) 654-7022. **Call for rates.** 10775 Emerald Coast Pkwy 32541. 7.5 mi e of Mid Bay Bridge. Int corridors. **Pets:** Small. $25 one-time fee/pet. Service with restrictions, crate. ⊠ 🔋 💷 🐾

ELKTON

🐾 ♦♦♦ Quality Inn St. Augustine 🅷

(904) 829-3435. **$62-$70.** 2625 SR 207 32033. I-95, exit 311, just w. Ext corridors. **Pets:** Accepted. 〔SAVE〕 ⊠ 🔋 💷 🐾

ELLENTON

🐾 ♦♦♦ Sleep Inn & Suites Riverfront 🅷 ♣

(941) 721-4933. **Call for rates.** 5605 18th St E 34222. I-75, exit 224, just n on US 301, just e on 19th St E, then 0.3 mi sw. Int corridors. **Pets:** Large. $20 daily fee/room. Designated rooms, service with restrictions, supervision. 〔SAVE〕 ⊠ 🔋 🔋 💷 🐾

FLAGLER BEACH

🐾 ♦♦ Topaz Motel 🅷

(386) 439-3301. **$70-$185, 14 day notice.** 1224 S Oceanshore Blvd 32136. On SR A1A, 0.5 mi s of SR 100. Ext/int corridors.
Pets: Accepted. 〔SAVE〕 ⊠ 🔋 💷 🍴 🐾

FLORAL CITY

♦♦ Moonrise Resort 🆑

(352) 726-2553. **$85-$1800 (no credit cards), 14 day notice.** 8801 E Moonrise Ln, Lot 18 34436. Just e on CR 48, then 1.5 mi n on Old Floral City Rd. Ext corridors. **Pets:** Dogs only. $20 daily fee/pet. No service.
🔋 ⊠ ⒵

THE FLORIDA KEYS AREA

ISLAMORADA

♦♦♦♦ The Islander Resort 🅼

(305) 664-2031. **$159-$460, 3 day notice.** 82100 Overseas Hwy 33036. US 1 at MM 82.1. Ext corridors. **Pets:** Accepted.
〔ASK〕 🔋 💷 🍴 🐾 ⊠

🐾 ♦♦♦ Sands of Islamorada 🅼 ♣

(305) 664-2791. **$120-$350, 3 day notice.** 80051 Overseas Hwy 33036. US 1 at MM 80. Ext corridors. **Pets:** Large, other species. $20 daily fee/pet. Service with restrictions, supervision. 〔SAVE〕 ⊠ 🔋 💷 🐾 ⊠

KEY LARGO

🐾 ♦♦♦♦ Key Largo Grande Hilton 🅷 ♣

(305) 852-5553. **$129-$399.** 97000 S Overseas Hwy 33037. US 1 at MM 97; Bayside. Ext corridors. **Pets:** Medium, dogs only. $50 one-time fee/room. Service with restrictions, supervision.
〔SAVE〕 ⊠ 🔋 💷 🍴 🐾 ⊠

♦♦♦♦ Tarpon Flats Inn & Marina 🅱🅱

(305) 453-1313. **$189-$229, 30 day notice.** 29 Shoreland Dr 33037. US 1 at MM 103.5, 0.3 mi e on Transylvania, then s on Oceanview to Shoreland Dr. Ext corridors. **Pets:** Accepted. 〔ASK〕 ⊠ 🔋 💷 🐾 ⊠

KEY WEST

♦♦♦ Ambrosia Key West 🅱🅱

(305) 296-9838. **$219-$639, 30 day notice.** 622 Fleming St 33040. Just n of Simonton St; in Old Town. Ext corridors. **Pets:** Accepted.
⊠ 🔋 💷 🐾

♦♦♦ Banana Bay Resort & Marina-Key West 🅼

(305) 296-6925. **Call for rates.** 2319 N Roosevelt Blvd 33040. On US 1, 1 mi s of entrance to island. Ext corridors. **Pets:** Accepted.
〔ECO〕 ⊠ 🔋 💷 🐾 ⊠

🐾 ♦♦♦ ♦♦♦ Casa Marina Resort, The Waldorf Astoria Collection 🅷

(305) 296-3535. **$129-$499, 7 day notice.** 1500 Reynolds St 33040-6552. 4 mi s on Flagler (CR 5A) from jct SR A1A. Ext/int corridors.
Pets: Accepted. 〔ECO〕〔SAVE〕 ⊠ 🔋 💷 🍴 🐾 ⊠

🐾 ♦♦♦♦ Chelsea House Pool & Gardens 🅱🅱 ♣

(305) 296-2211. **$119-$389, 7 day notice.** 709 Truman Ave 33040. Corner of Elizabeth St and Truman Ave. Ext/int corridors. **Pets:** Large, other species. $20 daily fee/room. Designated rooms, service with restrictions, crate. 〔SAVE〕 ⊠ 🔋 💷 🐾

🐾 ♦♦♦ Courtney's Place Historic Cottages & Inn 🆑

(305) 294-3480. **$109-$349, 21 day notice.** 720 Whitmarsh Ln 33040. Just e of jct Petronia and Simonton sts; in Old Town. Ext corridors.
Pets: Accepted. 〔SAVE〕 ⊠ 🔋 💷 🐾

🐾 ♦♦♦ Curry Mansion Inn 🅱🅱

(305) 294-5349. **$195-$365, 14 day notice.** 511 Caroline St 33040-6604. Just n of jct Duval St; in Old Town. Ext/int corridors.
Pets: Accepted. 〔SAVE〕 ⊠ 🔋 🐾

▲▲▲ ▼▼▼ **Cypress House Bed & Breakfast** BB
(305) 294-6969. **$159-$550, 30 day notice.** 601 Caroline St 33040. Jct Simonton St; in Old Town. Ext/int corridors. **Pets:** Dogs only. Service with restrictions, supervision. ⬛ ⬛ ⬛ ⬛ ⬛ ⬛

▼▼▼ **Frances Street Bottle Inn** BB 🐾
(305) 294-8530. **Call for rates.** 535 Frances St 33040. US 1/Roosevelt Blvd, w on White St, then just s on Southard St; corner of Frances and Southard sts; in Old Town. Ext/int corridors. **Pets:** Medium, other species. $50 one-time fee/room. Designated rooms, service with restrictions.
⬛ ⬛ ⬛ ⬛

▲▲▲ ▼▼▼ ▼▼▼ **Hyatt Key West Resort & Spa** H
(305) 809-1234. **$255-$655, 7 day notice.** 601 Front St 33040. Simonton and Front sts; just n of Mallory Square; in Old Town. Ext corridors. **Pets:** Accepted. ⬛ ⬛ ⬛ ⬛ ⬛ ⬛ ⬛ ⬛

▲▲▲ ▼▼▼ ▼▼▼ **The Palms Hotel** BB 🐾
(305) 294-3146. **$120-$420, 7 day notice.** 820 White St 33040. Just w of Truman Ave. Ext corridors. **Pets:** Large. Designated rooms, service with restrictions, supervision. ⬛ ⬛ ⬛ ⬛ ⬛

▲▲▲ ▼▼▼ ▼▼▼ **The Reach Resort, The Waldorf Astoria Collection** H 🐾
(305) 296-5000. **$129-$499, 7 day notice.** 1435 Simonton St 33040. Just s of jct Truman Ave and Simonton St. Ext corridors. **Pets:** Small, dogs only. $125 one-time fee/room. Service with restrictions, supervision.
⬛ ⬛ ⬛ ⬛ ⬛ ⬛ ⬛ ⬛

▲▲▲ ▼▼▼ ▼▼▼ **Sheraton Suites-Key West** H
(305) 292-9800. **Call for rates.** 2001 S Roosevelt Blvd 33040. Jct US 1 and SR A1A, 3 mi s. Ext/int corridors. **Pets:** Medium, other species. Service with restrictions, supervision.
⬛ ⬛ ⬛ ⬛ ⬛ ⬛ ⬛ ⬛

▲▲▲ ▼▼▼ ▼▼▼ **The Westin Key West Resort & Marina** H
(305) 294-4000. **$206-$2003, 7 day notice.** 245 Front St 33040. Adjacent to Mallory Square; in Old Town. Ext/int corridors. **Pets:** Accepted.
⬛ ⬛ ⬛ ⬛ ⬛ ⬛ ⬛ ⬛

MARATHON

▲▲▲ ▼▼▼ **Hawks Cay Resort** H
(305) 743-7000. **$95-$575, 7 day notice.** MM 61 33050. On Duck Key; 0.5 mi s of US 1. Ext/int corridors. **Pets:** Accepted.
⬛ ⬛ ⬛ ⬛ ⬛ ⬛ ⬛

END AREA

FORT LAUDERDALE METROPOLITAN AREA

CORAL SPRINGS

▼▼▼ **La Quinta Inn Coral Springs North** H 🐾
(954) 753-9000. **$59-$159.** 3701 University Dr 33065. SR 817, just n of jct SR 834 (Sample Rd). Int corridors. **Pets:** Medium, other species. Service with restrictions, supervision. ⬛ ⬛ ⬛ ⬛ ⬛ ⬛

▼▼▼ **La Quinta Inn South** H 🐾
(954) 344-2200. **$65-$169.** 3100 N University Dr 33065. SR 817, just s of jct SR 834 (Sample Rd). Int corridors. **Pets:** Medium, other species. Service with restrictions, supervision. ⬛ ⬛ ⬛ ⬛ ⬛

▼▼▼ **Studio 6 #6027** M
(954) 796-0011. **$65-$79.** 5645 University Dr 33067. SR 869 (Sawgrass Expwy), exit 12 (University Dr), just s. Ext corridors. **Pets:** Other species. $10 daily fee/room. Service with restrictions, supervision. ⬛ ⬛ ⬛

DANIA BEACH

▲▲▲ ▼▼▼ ▼▼▼ **Sheraton Fort Lauderdale Airport & Cruise Port Hotel** H
(954) 920-3500. **Call for rates.** 1825 Griffin Rd 33004. I-95, exit 23, just e. Int corridors. **Pets:** Accepted.
⬛ ⬛ ⬛ ⬛ ⬛ ⬛ ⬛ ⬛

DAVIE

▼▼▼ **Homestead Studio Suites Hotel-Fort Lauderdale-Plantation** M
(954) 476-1211. **$74-$114.** 7550 SR 84 E 33317. I-595, exit 5, 0.3 mi. Ext corridors. **Pets:** Other species. $25 daily fee/room. Designated rooms, service with restrictions, crate. ⬛ ⬛ ⬛ ⬛ ⬛

DEERFIELD BEACH

▲▲▲ ▼▼▼ ▼▼▼ **Comfort Inn-Oceanside** H 🐾
(954) 428-0650. **$60-$425.** 50 S Ocean Dr 33441. SR A1A, jct SR 810 (Hillsboro Blvd). Int corridors. **Pets:** Large, other species. $25 daily fee/pet. Designated rooms, service with restrictions, supervision.
⬛ ⬛ ⬛ ⬛ ⬛ ⬛

▲▲▲ ▼▼▼ **Comfort Suites** H
(954) 570-8887. **$69-$189.** 1040 E Newport Center Dr 33442. I-95, exit 41, jct SW 10th St to SW 12th Ave, then s; in Newport Center Complex. Ext corridors. **Pets:** Accepted. ⬛ ⬛ ⬛ ⬛

▲▲▲ ▼▼▼ ▼▼▼ **Embassy Suites-Deerfield Beach Resort & Spa** H
(954) 426-0478. **$120-$410.** 950 Ocean Dr (SR A1A) 33441. SR A1A, 0.5 mi s of jct SR 810 (Hillsboro Blvd). Int corridors. **Pets:** Accepted.
⬛ ⬛ ⬛ ⬛ ⬛ ⬛ ⬛

▼▼▼ **Extended StayAmerica-Fort Lauderdale-Deerfield Beach** H
(954) 428-5997. **$59-$99.** 1200 FAU Research Park Blvd 33441. I-95, exit 41, just e to FAU Research Park Rd, then just s. Int corridors. **Pets:** Other species. $25 fee/room. Designated rooms, service with restrictions, crate. ⬛ ⬛ ⬛ ⬛ ⬛

▲▲▲ ▼▼▼ ▼▼▼ **Hilton Deerfield Beach/Boca Raton** H
(954) 427-7700. **$209-$349.** 100 Fairway Dr 33441. I-95, exit 42A southbound, just e on SR 810 (Hillsboro Blvd); exit 37A northbound. Int corridors. **Pets:** Accepted. ⬛ ⬛ ⬛ ⬛ ⬛ ⬛ ⬛

▼▼▼ ▼▼▼ **La Quinta Inn & Suites** H 🐾
(954) 428-0661. **$59-$169.** 100 SW 12th Ave 33442. I-95, exit 42B, just w on SR 810 (Hillsboro Blvd), then just s. Int corridors. **Pets:** Medium, other species. Service with restrictions, supervision.
⬛ ⬛ ⬛ ⬛ ⬛ ⬛

▼▼▼ **La Quinta Inn Ft. Lauderdale (Deerfield Beach)** H 🐾
(954) 421-1004. **$59-$159.** 351 W Hillsboro Blvd 33441-1801. I-95, exit 42A, 0.3 mi e on SR 810. Ext/int corridors. **Pets:** Medium, other species. Service with restrictions, supervision. ⬛ ⬛ ⬛ ⬛ ⬛ ⬛

FORT LAUDERDALE

▼▼ Angela's Beach Resort Ⓜ
(954) 563-7926. **Call for rates.** 3016 Windamar St 33304. On SR A1A, 6 blks s of SR 838 (Sunrise Blvd); west corner of Breakers Ave and Windamar St. Ext corridors. **Pets:** Accepted. ⊠ 🛏 💻 🌊

Ⓐ **▼▼▼▼ Bahia Mar Beach Resort & Yachting Center** Ⓗ
(954) 764-2233. **$99-$369.** 801 Seabreeze Blvd 33316. SR A1A, 0.5 mi s of Las Olas Blvd. Int corridors. **Pets:** Small, dogs only. $75 one-time fee/pet. Service with restrictions, crate.
ⒺⒸⓄ SAVE ⊠ 🛏 💻 🍴 🌊 ⊠

Ⓐ **▼▼▼▼ Candlewood Suites Fort Lauderdale Air/Seaport** Ⓗ
(954) 522-8822. **$139-$269, 3 day notice.** 1120 W State Rd 84 33315. I-95, exit 25. Int corridors. **Pets:** Accepted. SAVE ⊠ 🛏M 🛏 💻

▼▼ Crossland Studios-Fort Lauderdale/Commercial Blvd Ⓜ
(954) 484-5115. **$44-$89.** 3031 W Commercial Blvd 33309. I-95, exit 32 (SR 870/Commercial Blvd), 2 mi w; Florida Tpke, exit 62, 1.5 mi e. Ext corridors. **Pets:** Other species. $25 daily fee/room. Designated rooms, service with restrictions, crate. ASK ⊠ 🛏 💻

▼▼▼ Embassy Suites-Fort Lauderdale-17th Street Ⓗ
(954) 527-2700. **$120-$390.** 1100 SE 17th St 33316. On SR A1A, just e of jct US 1 (Federal Hwy). Int corridors. **Pets:** Accepted.
ⒺⒸⓄ ⊠ 🛏 💻 🍴 🌊 ⊠

Ⓐ **▼▼ Extended StayAmerica-Fort Lauderdale-Convention Center-Marina** Ⓗ
(954) 761-9055. **$84-$149.** 1450 SE 17th St Cswy 33316. 1 mi e of US 1 (Federal Hwy) on SR A1A. Int corridors. **Pets:** Other species. $25 daily fee/room. Designated rooms, service with restrictions, crate.
ASK ⊠ 🛏 💻

▼▼ Extended StayAmerica-Fort Lauderdale-Cypress Creek-Andrews Ave Ⓜ
(954) 776-9447. **$59-$99.** 5851 N Andrews Ave Ext 33309. I-95, exit 33 (Cypress Creek), just w, 0.3 mi s on N Andrews Ave, then left. Ext corridors. **Pets:** Other species. $25 daily fee/room. Designated rooms, service with restrictions, crate. ASK ⊠ 🛏 💻

▼▼ Extended Stay Deluxe–Fort Lauderdale/Cypress Creek-NW 6th Way Ⓗ
(954) 772-3155. **$69-$109.** 6001 NW 6th Way 33309. I-95, exit 33 (Cypress Creek), 0.4 mi w, then just s. Int corridors. **Pets:** Other species. $25 daily fee/room. Designated rooms, service with restrictions, crate.
ASK ⊠ 🛏M 🛏 💻 🌊

▼▼▼ Hampton Inn Fort Lauderdale Airport North Ⓗ
(954) 524-9900. **Call for rates.** 2301 SW 12th Ave 33315. I-95, exit 25 (SR 84), 0.7 mi e to SW 12th Ave, then just n. Int corridors.
Pets: Accepted. ⒺⒸⓄ ⊠ 🛏M 🛏 💻 🌊

Ⓐ **▼▼▼▼ Hilton Fort Lauderdale Marina** Ⓗ
(954) 463-4000. **$99-$529.** 1881 SE 17th St Cswy 33316. SR A1A, 1 mi e of jct US 1 (Federal Hwy). Ext/int corridors. **Pets:** Accepted.
ⒺⒸⓄ SAVE ⊠ 🛏 💻 🍴 🌊 ⊠

▼▼▼▼ Il Lugano Suite Hotel Ⓗ 🐾
(954) 564-4400. **$159-$999, 3 day notice.** 3333 NE 32nd Ave 33308. 1.4 mi s of Commercial Blvd on N Ocean Dr (SR A1A), right on NE 34th St; on Intracoastal Waterway. Int corridors. **Pets:** Medium, dogs only. $100 one-time fee/room. Service with restrictions, supervision.
ASK ⊠ 🛏M 🛏 💻 🍴 🌊 ⊠

▼▼▼▼ La Quinta Inn Fort Lauderdale (Cypress Creek/I-95) Ⓗ 🐾
(954) 491-7666. **$69-$159.** 999 W Cypress Creek Rd 33309. I-95, exit 33 (Cypress Creek Rd), 0.7 mi w. Int corridors. **Pets:** Medium, other species. Service with restrictions, supervision. ASK ⊠ 🛏 💻 🌊

▼▼▼▼ La Quinta Inn-Fort Lauderdale NE Ⓗ 🐾
(954) 491-2500. **$59-$149.** 5727 N Federal Hwy 33308. 0.5 mi n on US 1 (Federal Hwy) from SR 870 (Commercial Blvd). Ext/int corridors. **Pets:** Medium, other species. Service with restrictions, supervision.
ASK ⊠ 🛏M 🛏 💻 🌊

▼ Motel 6–Ft Lauderdale #55 Ⓗ
(954) 760-7999. **$59-$79.** 1801 SR 84 33315. I-95, exit 25 (SR 84 E), just e, then U-turn at light. Int corridors. **Pets:** Other species. Service with restrictions, supervision. ⊠ 🌊

Ⓐ **▼▼▼▼ Renaissance Fort Lauderdale Hotel** Ⓗ
(954) 626-1700. **$149-$259.** 1617 SE 17th St Cswy 33316. SR A1A, just e of US 1 (Federal Hwy). Int corridors. **Pets:** Accepted.
ⒺⒸⓄ SAVE ⊠ 🛏M 🛏 💻 🍴 🌊

Ⓐ **▼▼▼▼▼ The Ritz-Carlton–Fort Lauderdale** Ⓗ 🐾
(954) 465-2300. **$159-$5000, 7 day notice.** 1 N Ft Lauderdale Beach Blvd 33304. On SR A1A, 1 mi s of SR 838 (Sunrise Blvd). Int corridors. **Pets:** Small, dogs only. $250 one-time fee/pet. Service with restrictions, supervision. SAVE ⊠ 🛏M 🛏 💻 🍴 🌊 ⊠

Ⓐ **▼▼▼ Rodeway Inn & Suites Airport/Cruise Port** Ⓗ
(954) 792-8181. **$79-$129.** 2440 W State Road 84 33312. I-95, exit 25 (SR 84), just w; on south side of road. Ext/int corridors. **Pets:** Accepted.
SAVE ⊠ 🛏 💻 🍴 🌊

Ⓐ **▼▼▼▼ Sheraton Suites Cypress Creek** Ⓗ
(954) 772-5400. **$99-$599.** 555 NW 62nd St 33309. I-95, exit 33B northbound, then w; exit 33 southbound, then w on SR 811 (Cypress Creek Rd). Int corridors. **Pets:** Accepted.
ⒺⒸⓄ SAVE ⊠ 🛏 💻 🍴 🌊 ⊠

Ⓐ **▼▼▼▼ TownePlace Suites by Marriott** Ⓗ
(954) 484-2214. **$199-$299.** 3100 Prospect Rd 33309. I-95, exit 33, 2.7 mi w, then 0.5 mi s on NW 31st St. Int corridors. **Pets:** Accepted.
SAVE ⊠ 🛏 💻 🌊

Ⓐ **▼▼▼▼ The Westin Beach Resort, Fort Lauderdale** Ⓗ
(954) 467-1111. **$159-$1100, 3 day notice.** 321 N Ft. Lauderdale Beach Blvd, A1A 33304. I-95, exit 29, on SR A1A (N Ft. Lauderdale Beach Blvd), 0.8 mi s of Sunrise Blvd. Int corridors. **Pets:** Accepted.
SAVE ⊠ 🛏 💻 🍴 🌊 ⊠

Ⓐ **▼▼▼▼ Westin, Fort Lauderdale** Ⓗ
(954) 772-1331. **$69-$499.** 400 Corporate Dr 33334-3642. I-95, exit 33A (Cypress Creek Blvd), then e; in Radice Corporate Park. Int corridors.
Pets: Accepted. SAVE ⊠ 🛏 💻 🍴 🌊 ⊠

HOLLYWOOD

Ⓐ **▼▼ Comfort Inn-Airport/Cruise Port South** Ⓗ
(954) 922-1600. **$64-$275.** 2520 Stirling Rd 33020. I-95, exit 22, just e; 2 mi s of airport. Ext corridors. **Pets:** Small. $25 one-time fee/room. Designated rooms, service with restrictions, crate.
SAVE ⊠ 🛏M 🛏 💻 🌊

▼▼▼ Days Inn Fort Lauderdale/Hollywood Airport South Ⓗ
(954) 923-7300. **$89-$299.** 2601 N 29th Ave 33020. I-95, exit 21, just nw on SR 822 (Sheridan St). Int corridors. **Pets:** Other species. $10 one-time fee/pet. Designated rooms, service with restrictions, supervision.
ASK ⊠ 🛏 💻 🌊

▼▼▼ La Quinta Inn & Suites Ft. Lauderdale (Airport) Ⓗ 🐾
(954) 922-2295. **$69-$189.** 2620 N 26th Ave 33020. I-95, exit 21, just e to Oakwood, then just left. Int corridors. **Pets:** Medium, other species. Service with restrictions, supervision. ASK ⊠ 🛏M 🛏 💻 🌊

(AAA) ▼▼ Quality Inn & Suites Hollywood Blvd M

(954) 981-1800. **$89-$179.** 4900 Hollywood Blvd 33021. I-95, exit 20, 1.6 mi w; Florida Tpke, exit 49, 1.3 mi e. Ext corridors. **Pets:** Accepted.

[SAVE] [X] [🛏] [💻] [🏊]

(AAA) ▼▼ ▼▼ Seminole Hard Rock Hotel & Casino Hollywood H ❀

(954) 327-7625. **$299-$399.** 1 Seminole Way 33314. I-95, exit 22, 2.9 mi w, then just n on SR 7/US 441; Florida Tpke, exit 53, 0.5 mi e, then 0.8 mi s. Int corridors. **Pets:** Medium. $100 one-time fee/room. Designated rooms, service with restrictions, crate.

[ECO] [SAVE] [X] [&M] [🛏] [💻] [🍴] [🏊] [X]

LAUDERDALE-BY-THE-SEA

▼▼ ▼▼ Buena Vista Hotel & Beach Club H

(954) 489-9870. **$99-$279, 30 day notice.** 4225 El Mar Dr 33308. Just s of SR 870 (Commercial Blvd). Ext/int corridors. **Pets:** Accepted.

[ASK] [X] [🛏] [💻] [X]

▼▼ ▼▼ Courtyard Villa On The Ocean M

(954) 776-1164. **$125-$359, 30 day notice.** 4312 El Mar Dr 33308. SR 870 (Commercial Blvd), just s. Ext corridors. **Pets:** Accepted.

[ASK] [X] [🛏] [💻] [X]

MIRAMAR

▼▼ ▼▼ Residence Inn by Marriott Fort Lauderdale SW/Miramar H

(954) 450-2717. **$170-$230.** 14700 Hotel Rd 33027. I-75, exit 7A (Miramar Pkwy), just e to SW 145th Ave, then n. Int corridors. **Pets:** Large. $100 one-time fee/room. Service with restrictions, supervision.

[ECO] [X] [&M] [🛏] [💻] [🏊]

PLANTATION

▼▼ Extended StayAmerica-Fort Lauderdale/Plantation H

(954) 382-8888. **$79-$119.** 7755 SW 6th St 33324. Just w of SR 817 (University Dr). Int corridors. **Pets:** Other species. $25 daily fee/room. Designated rooms, service with restrictions, crate.

[ASK] [X] [🛏] [💻] [🏊]

▼▼ ▼▼ Holiday Inn Express Hotel & Suites Plantation H

(954) 472-5600. **Call for rates.** 1701 N University Dr 33322. SR 817 (University Dr), just s of jct SR 838 (Sunrise Blvd). Int corridors. **Pets:** Accepted. [X] [🛏] [💻] [🏊]

▼▼ ▼▼ La Quinta Inn H ❀

(954) 473-8257. **$65-$169.** 7901 SW 6th St 33324. 0.3 mi w of SR 817 (University Dr); 0.5 mi sw of jct SR 842 (Broward Blvd). Int corridors. **Pets:** Medium, other species. Service with restrictions, supervision.

[ASK] [X] [🛏] [💻] [🏊]

▼▼ ▼▼ La Quinta Inn & Suites Ft. Lauderdale (Plantation) H ❀

(954) 476-6047. **$65-$159.** 8101 Peters Rd 33324. I-595, exit 5 (SR 817 N/University Dr), just n, then just w; in Crossroad Office Park. Int corridors. **Pets:** Medium, other species. Service with restrictions, supervision.

[ASK] [X] [&M] [🛏] [💻] [🏊]

(AAA) ▼▼ ▼▼ Quality Inn Sawgrass Conference Center H

(954) 556-8200. **$59-$399, 7 day notice.** 1711 N University Dr 33322. On SR 817 (University Dr), just s of Sunrise Blvd (SR 838). Ext corridors. **Pets:** Medium. $25 one-time fee/room. Designated rooms, service with restrictions. [SAVE] [X] [🛏] [💻] [🍴] [🏊]

▼▼ ▼▼ Residence Inn by Marriott–Ft Lauderdale Plantation H

(954) 723-0300. **$169-$239.** 130 N University Dr 33324. I-95, exit 27 (Broward Blvd), 5.2 mi e, then just n. Int corridors. **Pets:** Accepted.

[ECO] [X] [&M] [🛏] [💻] [🏊] [X]

(AAA) ▼▼ ▼▼ Sheraton Suites-Plantation H

(954) 424-3300. **Call for rates.** 311 N University Dr 33324. I-595, exit 5 (SR 817/University Dr), 0.7 mi n; 0.3 mi n of jct Broward Blvd (SR 842); at Fashion Mall. Int corridors. **Pets:** Accepted.

[ECO] [SAVE] [X] [🛏] [💻] [🍴] [🏊] [X]

▼▼ ▼▼ Staybridge Suites Ft Lauderdale-Plantation H

(954) 577-9696. **Call for rates.** 410 N Pine Island Rd 33324. I-595, exit 4 (Pine Island Rd), 1.7 mi n. Int corridors. **Pets:** Accepted.

[X] [&M] [🛏] [💻] [🏊]

POMPANO BEACH

▼▼ ▼▼ Extended Stay Deluxe–Cypress Creek Park North H

(954) 783-1050. **$74-$114.** 1401 SW 15th St 33069. I-95, exit 33B (Cypress Creek Rd) to Andrews Ave, just s, then left on McNab St. Int corridors. **Pets:** Other species. $25 daily fee/room. Designated rooms, service with restrictions, crate. [ASK] [X] [🛏] [💻] [🏊]

(AAA) ▼▼ ▼▼ The Ocean Sands Resort and Spa H ❀

(954) 590-1000. **$119-$529.** 1350 N Ocean Blvd 33062. On SR A1A, 1.4 mi n of SR 814 (Atlantic Blvd). Ext/int corridors. **Pets:** Medium. $75 one-time fee/room. Service with restrictions, supervision.

[SAVE] [X] [&M] [🛏] [💻] [🍴] [🏊] [X]

SUNRISE

▼▼ ▼▼ La Quinta Inn & Suites Sunrise H ❀

(954) 845-9929. **$65-$159.** 13600 NW 2nd St 33325. SW 136th Ave, 0.3 mi n of jct I-595, exit 1A and SR 84; 0.5 mi e of jct I-75 and SR 869 (Sawgrass Expwy). Int corridors. **Pets:** Medium, other species. Service with restrictions, supervision. [ASK] [X] [🛏] [💻] [🏊]

▼▼ ▼▼ La Quinta Inn-Sawgrass Mills Outlet Mall H ❀

(954) 846-1200. **$59-$159.** 13651 NW 2nd St 33325. SW 136th Ave, 0.3 mi n of jct I-595, exit 1A and SR 84; 0.5 mi e of jct I-75 and SR 869 (Sawgrass Expwy). Int corridors. **Pets:** Medium, other species. Service with restrictions, supervision. [ASK] [X] [🛏] [💻] [🏊]

TAMARAC

▼▼ ▼▼ Homestead Studio Suites Hotel-Ft Lauderdale-Tamarac M

(954) 733-6644. **$49-$94.** 3873 W Commercial Blvd 33309. SR 870 (Commercial Blvd), 0.7 mi e of Florida Tpke, exit 62; just e of jct US 441 and SR 7. Ext corridors. **Pets:** Other species. $25 daily fee/room. Designated rooms, service with restrictions, crate. [ASK] [X] [🛏] [💻]

▼▼ ▼▼ La Quinta Inn & Suites H ❀

(954) 484-6909. **$59-$169.** 5070 N SR 7 33319. SR 7 and US 441, just n of jct SR 870 (Commercial Blvd); 0.5 mi e of Florida Tpke, exit 62, then n. Int corridors. **Pets:** Medium, other species. Service with restrictions, supervision. [ASK] [X] [🛏] [💻] [🏊]

WESTON

(AAA) ▼▼ ▼▼ Hawthorn Suites Weston H

(954) 659-1555. **$100-$300.** 2201 N Commerce Pkwy 33326. I-75, exit 15, 0.5 mi w on Arvida Pkwy to Weston Rd, n to N Commerce Pkwy, then just e. Int corridors. **Pets:** Small. $10 daily fee/room. Service with restrictions, crate. [SAVE] [X] [&M] [🛏] [💻] [🏊]

(AAA) ▼▼ ▼▼ Hyatt Regency Bonaventure Conference Center and Spa H

(954) 616-1234. **$99-$499.** 250 Racquet Club Rd 33326. I-75, exit 21 (Indian Trace) southbound, 1.6 mi e on SR 84 to E Mall Dr, then just s; exit northbound, U-turn to SR 84, 1.6 mi to E Mall Dr, then just s. Ext corridors. **Pets:** Accepted. [ECO] [SAVE] [X] [🛏] [💻] [🍴] [🏊] [X]

▼▼ ▼▼ Residence Inn by Marriott Weston H

(954) 659-8585. **$279-$309.** 2605 Weston Rd 33331. I-75, exit 15 to Weston Rd, just s. Int corridors. **Pets:** Other species. $100 one-time fee/room. Service with restrictions, crate. [X] [&M] [🛏] [💻] [🏊] [X]

▼▼▼▼ TownePlace Suites by Marriott Weston ⛫
(954) 659-2234. **$219-$259.** 1545 Three Village Rd 33326. I-75, exit 15,
1 mi e on Arvida Pkwy to Bonaventure Blvd, n to Three Village Rd, then
w. Int corridors. **Pets:** Accepted. ☒ ⛬Ⓜ ▯ ▭ ⌕

END METROPOLITAN AREA

FORT MYERS

Ⓐ ▼▼ Best Western Airport Inn ⛫ ❀
(239) 561-7000. **$79-$160.** 8955 Daniels Pkwy 33912. I-75, exit 131, 0.6
mi w on CR 879 (Daniels Pkwy). Int corridors. **Pets:** Medium. $15 daily
fee/pet. Designated rooms, service with restrictions, supervision.
☒▣ ☒ ▯ ▭ ⌕ ☒

Ⓐ ▼▼▼ Best Western Coral Bridge Inn &
Suites ⛫
(239) 454-6363. **$85-$131.** 9200 College Pkwy 33919. 1.3 mi w of US
41 at McGregor Blvd; in Southpointe Commons. Int corridors.
Pets: Accepted. ☒▣ ☒ ⛬Ⓜ ▯ ▭ ⌕ ☒

Ⓐ ▼▼▼▼ Candlewood Suites ⛫
(239) 344-4400. **$69-$119.** 3626 Colonial Ct 33913. I-75, exit 136, just e
on SR 884 (Colonial Blvd), then just s; in Colonial Plaza. Int corridors.
Pets: Accepted. ☒▣ ☒ ⛬Ⓜ ▯ ▭

▼▼ Comfort Suites Airport/University Ⓜ
(239) 768-0005. **$59-$129.** 13651 Indian Paint Ln 33912. I-75, exit 131,
just w on CR 879 (Daniels Pkwy). Int corridors. **Pets:** Small. $10 daily
fee/pet. Service with restrictions, supervision. ☒ ▯ ▭ ⌕

Ⓐ ▼▼▼ Country Inn & Suites By Carlson,
Sanibel-Gateway ⛫
(239) 454-9292. **$89-$249.** 13901 Shell Point Plaza 33908. Just w of jct
McGregor Blvd. Int corridors. **Pets:** Accepted.
Ⓔ ☒▣ ☒ ⛬Ⓜ ▯ ▭ ⌕

▼▼▼▼ Holiday Inn Downtown Historic District ⛫
(239) 332-3232. **$50-$200.** 2431 Cleveland Ave 33901. On US 41, just s
of jct Edison Ave. Int corridors. **Pets:** Accepted.
Ⓐ☒Ⓚ ☒ ⛬Ⓜ ▯ ▭ ⑪ ⌕

▼▼▼▼ Homewood Suites by Hilton Fort Myers
Airport/FGCU ⛫
(239) 210-7300. **$129-$199.** 16450 Corporate Commerce Way 33913.
I-75, exit 128 (Alico Rd), just e. Int corridors. **Pets:** Large, other species.
$75 one-time fee/room. ☒ ⛬Ⓜ ▯ ▭ ⌕

▼▼▼▼ Homewood Suites by Hilton-Ft. Myers ⛫
(239) 275-6000. **$119-$219.** 5255 Big Pine Way 33907. Just e of jct US
41; just n of jct Daniels Pkwy; in Bell Tower Shops. Int corridors.
Pets: Large. $75 one-time fee/room. Designated rooms, service with
restrictions, supervision. ☒ ⛬Ⓜ ▯ ▭ ⌕

▼▼▼▼ Hotel Indigo-Ft. Myers-River District ⛫ 🐾
(239) 337-3446. **$139.** 1520 Broadway 33901. Just w of jct Broadway;
downtown. Int corridors. **Pets:** Medium. $75 one-time fee/room. Desig-
nated rooms, service with restrictions, crate.
Ⓐ☒Ⓚ ☒ ▯ ▭ ⑪ ⌕

▼▼▼▼ La Quinta Inn & Suites ⛫ ❀
(239) 466-1200. **$69-$184.** 20091 Summerlin Rd SW 33908. Jct John
Morris Rd. Ext corridors. **Pets:** Medium, other species. Service with
restrictions, supervision. Ⓐ☒Ⓚ ☒ ⛬Ⓜ ▯ ▭ ⌕

Ⓐ ▼▼▼▼ La Quinta Inn & Suites-Airport ⛫ ❀
(239) 466-0012. **$69-$179.** 9521 Marketplace Rd 33912. I-75, exit 131,
0.4 mi w on CR 879 (Daniels Pkwy), then just n on Danport Blvd. Int
corridors. **Pets:** Medium, other species. Service with restrictions, supervision. Ⓔ ☒▣ ☒ ⛬Ⓜ ▯ ▭ ⌕

▼▼▼ La Quinta Inn Fort Myers Ⓜ ❀
(239) 275-3300. **$59-$154.** 4850 S Cleveland Ave 33907-1320. On US
41, just s of jct N Airport Rd. Ext corridors. **Pets:** Medium, other species.
Service with restrictions, supervision. Ⓐ☒Ⓚ ☒ ⛬Ⓜ ▯ ▭ ⌕

▼▼▼▼ Residence Inn by Marriott ⛫ 🐾
(239) 936-0110. **$159-$259.** 2960 Colonial Blvd 33912. I-75, exit 136, 3.5
mi w on SR 884. Int corridors. **Pets:** Other species. $100 one-time fee/
room. Ⓔ ☒ ⛬Ⓜ ▯ ▭ ⌕ ☒

▼▼▼ The Springs Resort Ⓜ
(239) 267-7900. **$79-$129, 7 day notice.** 18051 S Tamiami Tr 33908.
On US 41 at Constitution Blvd. Ext corridors. **Pets:** Medium. $15 daily
fee/pet. Supervision. Ⓐ☒Ⓚ ☒ ▯ ▭ ⑪ ⌕

▼▼▼ Suburban Extended Stay Hotel ⛫
(239) 938-0100. **$55-$130.** 10150 Metro Pkwy 33912. I-75, exit 136, 3.4
mi w on SR 884 (Colonial Blvd); just s on SR 739. Int corridors.
Pets: Medium. $15 daily fee/pet. Designated rooms, service with restric-
tions, supervision. Ⓔ ☒ ⛬Ⓜ ▯ ▭ ⌕

▼▼▼ Wynstar Inn & Suites ⛫
(239) 791-5000. **$69-$259.** 10150 Daniels Pkwy 33913. I-75, exit 131,
just e on CR 879 (Daniels Pkwy). Int corridors. **Pets:** Small, dogs only.
$15 daily fee/pet. Service with restrictions, supervision.
Ⓐ☒Ⓚ ☒ ⛬Ⓜ ▯ ▭ ⌕

FORT MYERS BEACH

Ⓐ ▼▼▼▼ Best Western Beach Resort ⛫
(239) 463-6000. **$189-$309, 7 day notice.** 684 Estero Blvd 33931. 0.4
mi n of Matanzas Pass Bridge (SR 865). Ext corridors. **Pets:** Accepted.
☒▣ ☒ ⛬Ⓜ ▯ ▭ ⌕

Ⓐ ▼▼▼▼ Casa Playa All Suite Resort Ⓒ 🐾
(239) 765-0510. **$109-$199, 14 day notice.** 510 Estero Blvd 33931. 0.5
mi n of Matanzas Pass Bridge (SR 865) via 5th St. Ext corridors.
Pets: Medium. $25 daily fee/pet. Service with restrictions, supervision.
☒▣ ☒ ▯ ▭ ⌕

Ⓐ ▼▼▼ Lighthouse Resort Inn & Suites ⛫
(239) 463-9392. **$72-$325, 3 day notice.** 1051 5th St 33931. Jct Matanzas Pass Bridge (SR 865). Ext corridors. **Pets:** Small. $25 daily fee/pet.
Service with restrictions, supervision. ☒▣ ☒ ▯ ▭ ⑪ ⌕

Ⓐ ▼▼▼ Matanzas Inn Ⓜ
(239) 463-9258. **$69-$199, 30 day notice.** 414 Crescent St 33931. Just
e of Matanzas Pass Bridge (SR 865), then just n. Ext corridors.
Pets: Accepted. ☒▣ ☒ ▯ ▭ ⑪ ⌕ ☒

FORT PIERCE

Ⓐ ▼▼ Dockside Inn & Resort ⛫
(772) 468-3555. **$79-$155.** 1160 Seaway Dr 34949. SR A1A southbound,
2 mi e of jct US 1. Ext corridors. **Pets:** Medium, other species. $50 one-
time fee/pet. Designated rooms, service with restrictions, crate.
☒▣ ☒ ▯ ▭ ⌕ ☒

▼▼▼▼ Fairfield Inn & Suites by Marriott Ft. Pierce ⛫
(772) 462-2900. **$119-$159.** 6502 Metal Dr 34945. I-95, exit 129
(Okeechobee Rd), 0.6 mi w; Florida Tpke, exit 152, 0.3 mi e. Int corridors. **Pets:** Accepted. Ⓔ ☒ ⛬Ⓜ ▯ ▭ ⌕

▼▼ Fountain Resort Ⓜ
(772) 466-7041. **Call for rates.** 4889 N US 1 34946. I-95, exit 138
(Indrio Rd), 5.5 mi e, then just n. Ext corridors. **Pets:** Accepted.
☒ ▯ ▭ ⌕

▼▼ ▼▼ **Holiday Inn Express Fort Pierce** 🅷
(772) 464-5000. **Call for rates.** 7151 Okeechobee Rd 34945. I-95, exit 129, 0.7 mi w on SR 70; Florida Tpke, exit 152. Ext corridors.
Pets: Accepted. ☒ ㋲ 🔲 💻

▼▼ **Motel 6-Fort Pierce #1207** Ⓜ
(772) 461-9937. **$41-$55.** 2500 Peters Rd 34945. I-95, exit 129, just w, then n. Ext corridors. **Pets:** Other species. Service with restrictions, supervision. ☒ 🔲 ⌲

🔺🔺 ▼▼ ▼▼ **Royal Inn Beach Hotel Hutchinson Island** Ⓜ ❀
(772) 672-8888. **$89-$259.** 222 Hernando St 34949. 2.5 mi e on SR A1A southbound to Hernando St, then just s. Ext corridors. **Pets:** $25 daily fee/room. 〔SAVE〕 ☒ 🔲 💻

▼▼ ▼▼ **The Sandhurst Hotel & Suites** 🅷
(772) 595-0711. **$99-$199.** 1230 Seaway Dr 34949. Jct US 1 and SR A1A southbound, 2 mi e. Int corridors. **Pets:** Accepted.
〔ASK〕 ☒ 🔲 💻 ⌲ ☒

GAINESVILLE

🔺🔺 ▼▼ ▼▼ ▼▼ **Best Western Gateway Grand** 🅷 ❀
(352) 331-3336. **$129-$229.** 4200 NW 97th Blvd 32606. I-75, exit 390, just n of SR 222, then just w. Int corridors. **Pets:** Large, other species. $25 daily fee/room. Designated rooms, service with restrictions.
〔ECO〕〔SAVE〕 ☒ ㋲ 🔲 🍴 ⌲ ☒

🔺🔺 ▼▼ ▼▼ **Comfort Inn** 🅷
(352) 373-6500. **$68-$144, 7 day notice.** 2435 SW 13th St 32608. I-75, exit 382, 2 mi ne on SR 331, then 1 mi n on US 441. Ext corridors. **Pets:** Medium. $10 daily fee/pet. Service with restrictions, supervision.
〔SAVE〕 ☒ 🔲 💻 ⌲

▼▼ ▼▼ **Comfort Inn West** 🅷 ❀
(352) 264-1771. **$89-$199.** 3440 SW 40th Blvd 32608. I-75, exit 384, just e, then just n. Int corridors. **Pets:** Other species. $10 daily fee/pet. Service with restrictions, supervision. ☒ ㋲ 🔲 💻

▼▼ ▼▼ **Extended StayAmerica Gainesville-I-75** 🅷
(352) 375-0073. **$49-$109.** 3600 SW 42nd St 32608. I-75, exit 384, just e. Ext corridors. **Pets:** Other species. $25 daily fee/room. Designated rooms, service with restrictions, crate. 〔ASK〕 ☒ 🔲 💻

🔺🔺 ▼▼ ▼▼ ▼▼ **Hilton University of Florida Conference Center Gainesville** 🅷
(352) 371-3600. **$119-$329.** 1714 SW 34th St 32607. I-75, exit 384, 0.9 mi e on SR 24, then 0.7 mi n on SR 121; in University of Florida. Int corridors. **Pets:** Medium. $50 one-time fee/room. Designated rooms, service with restrictions, supervision.
〔ECO〕〔SAVE〕 ☒ ㋲ 🔲 💻 🍴 ⌲ ☒

🔺🔺 ▼▼ ▼▼ **Holiday Inn Express** 🅷
(352) 376-0004. **$108-$113.** 3905 SW 43rd St 32608. I-75, exit 384, just w; behind Cracker Barrel. Int corridors. **Pets:** Medium. $15 one-time fee/room. Designated rooms, service with restrictions, supervision.
〔SAVE〕 ☒ ㋲ 🔲 💻 ⌲

▼▼ ▼▼ ▼▼ **Homewood Suites** 🅷
(352) 335-3133. **$139-$239.** 3333 SW 42nd St 32608. I-75, exit 384, just e. Int corridors. **Pets:** Other species. $65 one-time fee/room. Service with restrictions. 〔ECO〕 ☒ ㋲ 🔲 💻 ⌲ ☒

🔺🔺🔺 ▼▼ ▼▼ ▼▼ **Red Roof Inn-Gainesville** 🅷
(352) 336-3311. **$55-$140.** 3500 SW 42nd St 32608. I-75, exit 384, just e. Int corridors. **Pets:** Large. Service with restrictions, crate.
〔SAVE〕 ☒ ㋲ 🔲 💻

HERNANDO

▼▼ ▼▼ **Citrus Hills Lodge** 🅷
(352) 527-0015. **$95-$115.** 350 E Norvell Bryant Hwy 34442. CR 486 at Citrus Hills Blvd, 3.3 mi w of US 41. Int corridors. **Pets:** Accepted.
〔ASK〕 ☒ ㋲ 🔲 💻 ⌲

INDIALANTIC

🔺🔺🔺 ▼▼ ▼▼ ▼▼ **DoubleTree Guest Suites Melbourne Beach Oceanfront** 🅷 ❀
(321) 723-4222. **$150-$229.** 1665 N SR A1A 32903. On SR A1A, 1.5 mi n of jct US 192. Ext corridors. **Pets:** Medium. $75 one-time fee/pet. Designated rooms, service with restrictions, supervision.
〔ECO〕〔SAVE〕 ☒ 🔲 💻 🍴 ⌲

▼▼ ▼▼ **Oceanfront Cottages** 🅒🅐
(321) 725-8474. **$125-$175, 60 day notice.** 612 Wavecrest Ave 32903. Just s of east end of US 192. Ext corridors. **Pets:** Small. $25 one-time fee/room. Service with restrictions, crate. ☒ 🔲 💻

INDIAN HARBOUR BEACH

▼▼ ▼▼ **Lexington Hotel on the Island** 🅷
(321) 773-0325. **$89-$139.** 1894 S Patrick Dr 32937. I-95, exit 183 (SR 518), 8 mi e on Eau Gallie Blvd, then 1 mi n on SR 513. Ext/int corridors. **Pets:** Accepted. 〔ASK〕 ☒ 🔲 💻 ⌲

INGLIS

🔺🔺🔺 ▼▼ ▼▼ ▼▼ **Pine Lodge Bed & Breakfast** 🅱🅱
(352) 447-7463. **$68-$150, 7 day notice.** 649 Hwy 40 W 34449. 1.5 mi w of US 19. Ext/int corridors. **Pets:** Small. $25 one-time fee/room. Designated rooms, service with restrictions, supervision.
〔ECO〕〔SAVE〕 ☒ 🔲 💻 ⌲ ✉

INVERNESS

▼▼ ▼▼ ▼▼ **Van der Valk Inverness** 🆅🅷
(352) 637-1140. **$111-$286, 60 day notice.** 4543 E Windmill Dr 34453. 2.7 mi n on US 41. Ext corridors. **Pets:** Accepted.
〔ASK〕 ☒ 🔲 💻 🍴 ⌲

JACKSONVILLE METROPOLITAN AREA

BALDWIN

🔺🔺🔺 ▼▼ ▼▼ **Best Western Baldwin Inn** Ⓜ
(904) 266-9759. **$64-$75.** 1088 US 301 S 32234. I-10, exit 343, just s. Ext corridors. **Pets:** Large, other species. $10 daily fee/pet. Designated rooms, service with restrictions, supervision. 〔SAVE〕 ☒ 🔲 💻 ⌲

FERNANDINA BEACH

🔺🔺🔺 ▼▼ ▼▼ ▼▼ **Amelia Island Plantation-Inn & Conference Center** 🅷
(904) 261-6161. **$219-$429, 7 day notice.** 6800 First Coast Hwy 32034. In Fernandina Beach; SR A1A, 6.5 mi s of the bridge. Ext corridors.
Pets: Accepted. 〔ECO〕〔SAVE〕 ☒ 💻 🍴 ⌲ ☒

🔺🔺🔺 ▼▼ ▼▼ **Days Inn & Suites** 🅷
(904) 277-2300. **$70-$180.** 2707 Sadler Rd 32034. In Fernandina Beach; I-95, exit 373, 12.3 mi e, then 1.2 mi. Ext corridors. **Pets:** Medium. $25 daily fee/room. Designated rooms, service with restrictions, supervision.
〔SAVE〕 ☒ 🔲 💻 ⌲

▼▼ ▼▼ **Hampton Inn Amelia Island** 🅷
(904) 321-1111. **Call for rates.** 2549 Sadler Rd 32034. In Fernandina Beach; just w of jct SR A1A and Sadler Rd. Int corridors. **Pets:** Accepted. ☒ ㋲ 🔲 💻 ⌲

JACKSONVILLE

Best Western Hotel JTB/Southpoint 🅷
(904) 281-0900. **$79-$169.** 4660 Salisbury Rd 32256. I-95, exit 344 (SR 202), just ne, then just s. Int corridors. **Pets:** Accepted.

Best Western Jacksonville Airport 🅷
(904) 741-4980. **$89-$149.** 1170 Airport Entrance Rd 32218. I-95, exit 363B, just w, then just s on Duval Rd. Ext corridors. **Pets:** Medium. $25 daily fee/pet. Service with restrictions, supervision.

Candlewood Suites 🅷
(904) 296-7785. **Call for rates.** 4990 Belfort Rd 32256. I-95, exit 344 (SR 202), ne to Belfort Rd, then just s. Int corridors. **Pets:** Medium, other species. $75 one-time fee/room. Service with restrictions, crate.

Extended StayAmerica-Jacksonville-Butler Blvd 🅷
(904) 296-0181. **$64-$89.** 6961 Lenoir Ave 32216. I-95, exit 344 (SR 202), just sw, then 0.3 mi n. Int corridors. **Pets:** Other species. $25 daily fee/room. Designated rooms, service with restrictions, crate.

Extended Stay Deluxe-Jacksonville-Butler Blvd 🅷
(904) 332-6512. **$69-$94.** 4699 Lenoir Ave S 32216. I-95, exit 344 (SR 202), just sw, then just n. Int corridors. **Pets:** Other species. $25 daily fee/room. Designated rooms, service with restrictions, crate.

Extended Stay Deluxe (Jacksonville/Deerwood Park) 🅷
(904) 620-9008. **$69-$94.** 8801 Perimeter Park Blvd 32216. I-95, exit 344 (SR 202), 2.5 mi e on J Turner Butler Blvd to Southside Blvd, then just n on west side of road. Int corridors. **Pets:** Other species. $25 daily fee/room. Designated rooms, service with restrictions, crate.

Holiday Inn Airport 🅷
(904) 741-4404. **$120-$180.** 14670 Duval Rd 32218. I-95, exit 363, just w. Ext/int corridors. **Pets:** Medium. $75 one-time fee/room. Service with restrictions, crate.

Holiday Inn Express & Suites Jacksonville 🅷
(904) 696-3333. **$100-$150.** 10148 New Berlin Rd 32226. I-95, exit 362A southbound, 4.9 mi s on SR 9A to Heckscher Dr, then just w; exit 358A northbound, 5.8 mi ne on Heckscher Dr; 0.6 mi from Jaxport Terminal. Int corridors. **Pets:** Accepted.

Homestead Jacksonville-Southside-St. Johns Towne Center Ⓜ
(904) 642-9911. **$57-$82.** 10020 Skinner Lake Dr 32246. I-95, exit 344 (SR 202), 3.5 mi e on J Turner Butler Blvd to Gate Pkwy, then just w. Ext corridors. **Pets:** Other species. $25 daily fee/room. Designated rooms, service with restrictions, crate.

Homewood Suites by Hilton Jacksonville South/Town Center 🅷
(904) 641-7988. **$179-$209.** 10434 Midtown Pkwy 32246. I-95, exit 344 (SR 202), 4 mi e on J Turner Butler Blvd to Gate Pkwy, 0.3 mi n to Town Center Pkwy, 0.5 mi e to Midtown Pkwy, then 0.3 mi s. Int corridors. **Pets:** Accepted.

Howard Johnson Inn & Suites Ⓜ
(904) 281-0198. **$50-$130.** 4300 Salisbury Rd N 32256. I-95, exit 344 (SR 202), just nw to Salisbury Rd, then just n. Ext corridors. **Pets:** Accepted.

Hyatt Regency Jacksonville Riverfront 🅷
(904) 588-1234. **$89-$399.** 225 Coast Line Dr E 32202. Downtown; just e of The Landing. Int corridors. **Pets:** Accepted.

Jameson Inn 🅷
(904) 296-0968. **$93-$100.** 7030 Bonneval Rd 32216. I-95, exit 344 (SR 202), just w. Int corridors. **Pets:** Accepted.

La Quinta Inn & Suites 🅷 🐾
(904) 268-9999. **$55-$90.** 3199 Hartley Rd 32257. I-295, exit 5A northbound; exit 5 southbound at SR 13, just n and e. Int corridors. **Pets:** Medium, other species. Service with restrictions, supervision.

La Quinta Inn & Suites Jacksonville (Butler Blvd) 🅷 🐾
(904) 296-0703. **$69-$144.** 4686 Lenoir Ave S 32216. I-95, exit 344 (SR 202), just sw, then just nw. Int corridors. **Pets:** Medium, other species. Service with restrictions, supervision.

La Quinta Inn Jacksonville (Airport/Cruise Port) 🅷 🐾
(904) 751-6960. **$49-$94.** 812 Dunn Ave 32218. I-95, exit 360, southwest corner. Ext corridors. **Pets:** Medium, other species. Service with restrictions, supervision.

La Quinta Inn Jacksonville (Orange Park) 🅷 🐾
(904) 778-9539. **$49-$94.** 8555 Blanding Blvd 32244-5797. I-295, exit 12, just s on SR 21. Ext corridors. **Pets:** Medium, other species. Service with restrictions, supervision.

Microtel Inn & Suites Butler Blvd/Southpoint 🅷
(904) 281-2244. **$49-$79.** 4940 Mustang Rd 32216. I-95, exit 344 (SR 202), just sw, then just nw. Int corridors. **Pets:** Accepted.

Omni Jacksonville Hotel 🅷
(904) 355-6664. **$139-$349, 5 day notice.** 245 Water St 32202. Corner of Pearl and Water sts; on north side of St. Johns River; downtown; adjacent to The Landing. Int corridors. **Pets:** Accepted.

Ramada Conference Center Mandarin 🅷 🐾
(904) 268-8080. **$89-$129.** 3130 Hartley Rd 32257. I-295, exit 5A northbound; exit 5 southbound, just n on SR 13. Ext corridors. **Pets:** Other species. $30 one-time fee/pet. Designated rooms, service with restrictions, crate.

Residence Inn by Marriott Butler Blvd 🅷
(904) 996-8900. **$179-$219.** 10551 Deerwood Park Blvd 32256. I-95, exit 344 (SR 202), 3.5 mi e on J Turner Butler Blvd to Gate Pkwy, just s, then just w. Int corridors. **Pets:** Accepted.

Residence Inn by Marriott Jacksonville Baymeadows 🅷
(904) 733-8088. **$125-$153.** 8365 Dix Ellis Tr 32256. I-95, exit 341 (SR 152), just w to Freedom Commerce Pkwy, then just s. Ext corridors. **Pets:** Accepted.

Sheraton Jacksonville Hotel 🅷 🐾
(904) 564-4772. **$99-$320, 3 day notice.** 10605 Deerwood Park Blvd 32256. I-95, exit 344 (SR 202), 3.5 mi e on J Turner Butler Blvd to Gate Parkway exit, then just s and w. Int corridors. **Pets:** Large. Service with restrictions, supervision.

TownePlace Suites Jacksonville Butler Blvd 🅷
(904) 296-1661. **$134-$164.** 4801 Lenoir Ave 32216. I-95, exit 344 (J Turner Butler Blvd), just w, then just n. Int corridors. **Pets:** Accepted.

JACKSONVILLE BEACH

Holiday Inn Express 🅷 🐾
(904) 435-3000. **$119-$149.** 1101 Beach Blvd 32250. 0.5 mi w of 3rd St. Int corridors. **Pets:** Medium. $39 daily fee/pet. Designated rooms, service with restrictions, supervision.

Quality Suites Oceanfront 🅷 🐾
(904) 435-3535. **$130-$290.** 11 1st St N 32250. Just n of Beach Blvd (US 90). Int corridors. **Pets:** Medium. $39 daily fee/pet. Designated rooms, service with restrictions, supervision.

ORANGE PARK

▼▼ Comfort Inn 🅗
(904) 644-4444. **$65-$149.** 341 Park Ave 32073. I-295, exit 10 (US 17), just s. Ext corridors. **Pets:** Medium. $30 one-time fee/pet. Service with restrictions, supervision. 🗙 🛑 🖵 🔁

▼▼ Howard Johnson Inn 🅗
(904) 264-9513. **$59-$79.** 150 Park Ave 32073. I-295, exit 10 (US 17), just s. Ext corridors. **Pets:** Accepted. (ASK) 🗙 🛑 🖵 🍽 🔁

PONTE VEDRA BEACH

▼▼▼▼ Sawgrass Golf Resort & Spa, a Marriott Resort 🅗
(904) 285-7777. **$199-$249.** 1000 PGA Tour Blvd 32082. 2.5 mi s of J Turner Butler Blvd. Ext/int corridors. **Pets:** Accepted.
(ECO) 🗙 🛑 🖵 🍽 🔁 🗙

YULEE

▼▼ America's Best Value Inn 🅗
(904) 225-6200. **$60-$80.** 852380 US Hwy 17 N 32097. I-95, exit 380 (US 17), just w. Ext corridors. **Pets:** Accepted. 🗙 🛑 🔁

▼▼ Comfort Inn 🅗
(904) 225-2600. **$65-$150.** 76043 Sidney Pl 32097. I-95, exit 373, just e on SR 200/A1A. Int corridors. **Pets:** Accepted. 🗙 🛑 🖵 🔁

END METROPOLITAN AREA

JUPITER

▼▼▼▼ Fairfield Inn & Suites by Marriott 🅗 🐾
(561) 748-5252. **$119-$229.** 6748 W Indiantown Rd 33458. I-95, exit 87A, 0.8 mi e on SR 706 (Indiantown Rd). Int corridors. **Pets:** Medium, other species. Service with restrictions, crate. (ECO) 🗙 🛑 🖵 🔁

LAKE CITY

(AAA) ▼▼▼ Best Western Lake City Inn 🅗
(386) 752-3801. **$63-$86.** 3598 W Hwy 90 32055. I-75, exit 427, just w. Ext corridors. **Pets:** Small, other species. $10 one-time fee/room. Designated rooms, service with restrictions, supervision.
(SAVE) 🗙 🛑 🖵 🔁

(AAA) ▼▼ Days Inn I-10 🅗
(386) 758-4224. **$59-$99.** 3430 N Hwy 441 32055. I-10, exit 303, just s. Ext corridors. **Pets:** Other species. $10 daily fee/pet. Service with restrictions, crate. (SAVE) 🗙 🛑 🖵 🔁

(AAA) ▼▼ Driftwood Inn 🅜
(386) 755-3545. **$42-$70.** 2764 W Hwy 90 32055. I-75, exit 427, 0.7 mi e. Ext corridors. **Pets:** Accepted. (SAVE) 🗙 🛑

▼▼ Red Roof Inn 🅗
(386) 752-6693. **Call for rates.** 414 SW Florida Gateway Dr 32024. I-75, exit 427, just w, then 0.4 mi s. Ext corridors. **Pets:** Large. Service with restrictions, crate. 🗙 🛑 🔁

(AAA) ▼▼ Rodeway Inn 🅜
(386) 755-5203. **Call for rates.** 205 SW Commerce Dr 32025. I-75, exit 427, just e. Ext corridors. **Pets:** Medium. $7 daily fee/pet. Designated rooms, service with restrictions, supervision. (SAVE) 🗙 🛑 🖵

LAKE HELEN

▼▼▼▼ The Ann Stevens House 🅑🅑
(386) 228-0310. **Call for rates.** 201 E Kicklighter Rd 32744. I-4, exit 116, 1 mi e on Main St, 0.5 mi s on CR 4139, turn left on Ohio St, right on Pleasant Rd, then right. Ext/int corridors. **Pets:** Accepted. 🗙

LAKELAND

▼▼▼ Crestwood Suites Lakeland 🅗
(863) 904-2050. **$85-$115.** 4360 Lakeland Park Dr 33809. I-4, exit 33, just s. Int corridors. **Pets:** Accepted. (ASK) 🗙 🛑 🖵 🔁

▼▼ Howard Johnson Inn Executive Center 🅗
(863) 688-7972. **$49-$125.** 939 W Robson St 33805. I-4, exit 32, just s. Ext corridors. **Pets:** Accepted. (ASK) 🗙 🛑 🖵 🍽 🔁

(AAA) ▼▼▼ Imperial Swan Hotel & Suites 🅗
(863) 647-3000. **$102-$495, 3 day notice.** 4141 S Florida Ave 33813. SR 37, 3.5 mi s of US 98 business route. Int corridors. **Pets:** Medium. $75 one-time fee/pet. Service with restrictions, crate.
(SAVE) 🗙 🅜 🛑 🖵 🍽 🔁

▼▼ Jameson Inn 🅗
(863) 858-9070. **$78-$85.** 4375 Lakeland Park Dr 33809. I-4, exit 33, just nw. Int corridors. **Pets:** Medium. $15 daily fee/room. Designated rooms, service with restrictions. (ASK) 🗙 🅜 🛑 🖵 🔁

▼▼▼ Lakeland Residence Inn by Marriott 🅗
(863) 680-2323. **$148-$180.** 3701 Harden Blvd 33803. I-4, exit 27 (Polk Pkwy), go s on SR 570 (toll road) to exit 5, then just n. Int corridors. **Pets:** Accepted. 🗙 🛑 🖵 🔁 🗙

▼▼ La Quinta Inn & Suites Lakeland 🅗 🐾
(863) 859-2866. **$65-$120.** 1024 Crevasse St 33809. I-4, exit 32, just n on US 98. Int corridors. **Pets:** Medium, other species. Service with restrictions, supervision. (ASK) 🗙 🅜 🛑 🖵 🔁

▼▼ La Quinta Inn East 🅗 🐾
(863) 815-0606. **$59-$104.** 4315 Lakeland Park Dr 33809. I-4, exit 33; jct SR 33, just nw. Int corridors. **Pets:** Medium, other species. Service with restrictions, supervision. (ASK) 🗙 🅜 🛑 🖵 🔁

▼▼ Ramada Inn 🅗
(863) 284-5760. **$59-$279, 7 day notice.** 4620 Socrum Loop Rd 33809. I-4, exit 33, just s. Int corridors. **Pets:** Small. $50 one-time fee/room. Designated rooms, service with restrictions, supervision.
(ASK) 🗙 🛑 🖵 🔁

LAKE WORTH

(AAA) ▼▼▼ ▼▼▼ Sabal Palm House B & B Inn 🅑🅑
(561) 582-1090. **$125-$275, 14 day notice.** 109 N Golfview Rd 33460. Just n of SR 802; west side of Intracoastal Bridge. Ext/int corridors. **Pets:** Accepted. (SAVE) 🗙 🖵

LANTANA

▼▼ Motel 6 Lantana #688 🅜
(561) 585-5833. **$49-$69.** 1310 W Lantana Rd 33462. I-95, exit 61 (SR 812), just e, then s. Ext corridors. **Pets:** Other species. Service with restrictions, supervision. 🗙 🔁

(AAA) ▼▼▼ Super 8 Lantana 🅜
(561) 585-3970. **$59-$139.** 1255 Hypoluxo Rd 33462. I-95, exit 60 (Hypoluxo Rd), just e on north side. Ext corridors. **Pets:** Accepted. (SAVE) 🗙 🛑 🖵 🔁

LIVE OAK

(AAA) ▼▼▼ Best Western Suwannee River Inn 🅗
(386) 362-6000. **$46-$146.** 6819 US 129 N 32060. I-10, exit 283, 0.3 mi s. Ext corridors. **Pets:** Accepted. (SAVE) 🗙 🛑 🖵 🔁

(AAA) ▼▼▼ Econo Lodge 🅗
(386) 362-7459. **Call for rates.** 6811 N US 129 & I-10 32060. I-10, exit 283, just s. Ext corridors. **Pets:** Other species. $10 one-time fee/room. Service with restrictions, supervision. (SAVE) 🗙 🛑 🖵 🔁

LONGBOAT KEY

▼▼◆ Sandpiper Inn 🅜
(941) 383-2552. **$139-$249, 30 day notice.** 5451 Gulf of Mexico Dr 34228. On SR 789, 5 mi se of jct SR 684 (Cortez Rd). Ext corridors. **Pets:** Small. $100 deposit/pet. No service, supervision.

(ASK) ✕ 🖪 ➥

LYNN HAVEN

▼▼▼◆ Wingate Inn 🅗
(850) 248-8080. **$95-$150.** 2610 Lynn Haven Pkwy 32444. Jct 23rd St (Panama City), 2.3 mi n on SR 77. Int corridors. **Pets:** Accepted.

(ASK) ✕ �ᴹ 🖪 🖳 ➤ ✕

MACCLENNY

⏺ ▼▼◆ Econo Lodge 🅜
(904) 259-3000. **$55-$65.** 151 Woodland Rd 32063. I-10, exit 335, just s of jct SR 121. Ext corridors. **Pets:** Medium. $10 one-time fee/room. Service with restrictions, supervision. (SAVE) ✕ 🖪 🖳 ➤

MANALAPAN

⏺ ▼▼▼▼◆ The Ritz-Carlton, Palm Beach 🅗 ❀
(561) 533-6000. **$199-$749, 15 day notice.** 100 S Ocean Blvd 33462. On SR A1A; 9 mi s of Palm Beach. Int corridors. **Pets:** Large, other species. $50 one-time fee/pet. Service with restrictions, supervision.

(ECO) (SAVE) ✕ 🖪 (Ⅱ) ➤ ✕

MARIANNA

▼▼◆ Americas Best Value Inn 🅗
(850) 526-5666. **$59-$99.** 2086 Hwy 71 S 32448. I-10, exit 142, 0.3 mi s. Ext corridors. **Pets:** Accepted. (ASK) ✕ 🖪 🖳 ➤

▼▼ Microtel Inn & Suites 🅗
(850) 526-5005. **Call for rates.** 4959 White Tail Dr 32448. I-10, exit 142, just n. Int corridors. **Pets:** Accepted. ✕ ⬛ᴹ 🖪 🖳 ➤

▼▼ Quality Inn 🅗
(850) 526-5600. **Call for rates.** 2175 Hwy 71 S 32448. I-10, exit 142, just n. Ext corridors. **Pets:** Accepted. ✕ 🖪 🖳 ➤

MELBOURNE

▼▼▼ Candlewood Suites Hotel 🅗 ❀
(321) 821-9009. **Call for rates.** 2930 Pineda Cswy 32940. I-95, exit 191, 4.5 mi e, then just n. Int corridors. **Pets:** Small. $75 one-time fee/pet. Service with restrictions, supervision. ✕ 🖪 🖳

▼▼▼▼ Crane Creek Inn Waterfront Bed & Breakfast 🆎
(321) 768-6416. **Call for rates.** 907 E Melbourne Ave 32901. Jct US 192, just s on Babcock, 0.9 mi e. Ext/int corridors. **Pets:** Accepted.

✕ 🖪 🖳 ➤ ✕

⏺ ▼▼▼▼ Hilton Melbourne Beach
        Oceanfront 🅗 ❀
(321) 777-5000. **$129-$249.** 3003 N SR A1A 32903. 3 mi n of jct US 192. Int corridors. **Pets:** Medium. $75 one-time fee/pet. Service with restrictions, crate. (ECO) (SAVE) ✕ 🖪 🖳 (Ⅱ) ➤

▼▼▼ Hilton Melbourne Rialto Place 🅗
(321) 768-0200. **$99-$229.** 200 Rialto Pl 32901. 1 mi w of US 1, 0.8 mi n of US 192 via Airport Blvd. Int corridors. **Pets:** Accepted.

✕ ⬛ᴹ 🖪 🖳 (Ⅱ) ➤ ✕

▼▼▼ La Quinta Inn & Suites Melbourne 🅗 ❀
(321) 242-9400. **$59-$159.** 7200 George T Edwards Dr 32940. I-95, exit 191 (CR 509), just w. Int corridors. **Pets:** Medium, other species. Service with restrictions, supervision. (ASK) ✕ 🖪 🖳 ➤

⏺ ▼▼▼▼ Residence Inn by Marriott Melbourne 🅗
(321) 723-5740. **$112-$136.** 1430 S Babcock St 32901. Jct US 192. Int corridors. **Pets:** Large, other species. $100 one-time fee/room. Service with restrictions, supervision. (SAVE) ✕ ⬛ᴹ 🖪 🖳 ➤

MIAMI-MIAMI BEACH METROPOLITAN AREA

AVENTURA

⏺ ▼▼▼ ▼▼▼ The Fairmont Turnberry Isle Resort &
            Club 🅗 ❀
(305) 932-6200. **$179-$5800, 3 day notice.** 19999 W Country Club Dr 33180. 0.5 mi w of SR A1A via SR 856; from US 1 at NE 199th St and Biscayne Blvd. Ext/int corridors. **Pets:** Small. $25 one-time fee/pet. Service with restrictions, supervision.

(ECO) (SAVE) ✕ ⬛ᴹ 🖪 🖳 (Ⅱ) ➤ ✕

⏺ ▼▼▼ Residence Inn by Marriott-Aventura
        Mall 🅗 ❀
(786) 528-1001. **$279-$429.** 19900 W Country Club Dr 33180. 0.5 mi w of SR A1A via SR 856; from US 1 at NE 199th St and Biscayne Blvd. Int corridors. **Pets:** Medium. $100 one-time fee/room. Service with restrictions, supervision. (ECO) (SAVE) ✕ ⬛ᴹ 🖪 🖳 ➤

COCONUT GROVE

⏺ ▼▼▼ ▼▼▼ Mayfair Hotel & Spa 🅗 ❀
(305) 441-0000. **$139-$339.** 3000 Florida Ave 33133. At Florida Ave and Virginia St; center. Ext/int corridors. **Pets:** Medium, other species. $30 one-time fee/pet. Service with restrictions, crate.

(SAVE) ✕ 🖳 (Ⅱ) ➤

▼▼▼ Residence Inn by Marriott Miami Coconut
      Grove 🅗
(305) 285-9303. **$149-$279.** 2835 Tigertail Ave 33133. S Bayshore Dr, w on SW 27th Ave/Cornelia Dr, then s. Ext corridors. **Pets:** Other species. $100 one-time fee/pet. ✕ 🖪 🖳 ➤

CORAL GABLES

⏺ ▼▼▼ ▼▼▼ The Biltmore Hotel Coral Gables 🅗
(305) 445-1926. **$169-$399.** 1200 Anastasia Ave 33134. 1 mi w of Le Jeune Rd. Int corridors. **Pets:** Accepted. (SAVE) ✕ 🖪 (Ⅱ) ➤ ✕

◆◆ Extended StayAmerica-Miami-Coral Gables 🅗
(305) 443-7444. **$89-$129.** 3640 Coral Way/SW 22nd St 33145. Just e of Douglas Rd. Int corridors. **Pets:** Other species. $25 daily fee/room. Designated rooms, service with restrictions, crate.

(ASK) ✕ ⬛ᴹ 🖪 🖳

⏺ ▼▼▼ ▼▼▼ The Westin Colonnade Coral
            Gables 🅗
(305) 441-2600. **$109-$559.** 180 Aragon Ave 33134. At Aragon Ave and Ponce de Leon Blvd; downtown. Int corridors. **Pets:** Accepted.

(ECO) (SAVE) ✕ 🖪 🖳 (Ⅱ) ➤ ✕

CUTLER RIDGE

⏺ ▼▼▼▼ Best Western Floridian Hotel 🅗
(305) 253-9960. **Call for rates.** 10775 Caribbean Blvd 33189. Florida Tpke, exit 12 (US 1), then w. Ext corridors. **Pets:** Accepted.

(SAVE) ✕ 🖪 🖳 ➤

FLORIDA CITY

⏺ ▼▼▼ Coral Roc Motel 🅜
(305) 246-2888. **$39-$159.** 1100 N Krome Ave 33034. On SR 997; just w of US 1; 0.5 mi s of Homestead. Ext corridors. **Pets:** Small, dogs only. $50 deposit/pet. Service with restrictions, supervision.

(SAVE) ✕ 🖪 ➤

Travelodge M
(305) 248-9777. **$55-$199.** 409 SE 1st Ave 33034. On US 1, just s of Florida Tpke terminus. Ext corridors. **Pets:** Medium, other species. $10 daily fee/pet. Service with restrictions, supervision.

HOMESTEAD

Everglades Motel M
(305) 247-4117. **$39-$129.** 605 S Krome Ave 33030. Just w of US 1; between Lucy and 6th sts; on SR 997, 0.5 mi s of center of town. Ext corridors. **Pets:** $25 one-time fee/room. Service with restrictions, supervision.

KEY BISCAYNE

The Ritz-Carlton, Key Biscayne H
(305) 365-4500. **$189-$529, 3 day notice.** 455 Grand Bay Dr 33149. Crandon Blvd, just e. Int corridors. **Pets:** Accepted.

MIAMI

Candlewood Suites Miami Airport West H
(305) 591-9099. **$109.** 8855 NW 27th St 33172. SR 826 (Palmetto Expwy), 0.8 mi w on nw 36th St, 0.4 mi s. Int corridors. **Pets:** Accepted.

Doubletree Miami Mart Airport Hotel H
(305) 261-3800. **$99-$279.** 711 NW 72nd Ave 33126. At Milam Dairy Rd off SR 836 (Dolphin Expwy). Int corridors. **Pets:** Accepted.

Epic Hotel H
(305) 424-5226. **$149-$839, 3 day notice.** 270 Biscayne Boulevard Way 33131. Just e of US 1 (SE 2nd Ave). Int corridors. **Pets:** Other species. Service with restrictions, crate.

Extended StayAmerica-Miami-Brickell-Port of Miami H
(305) 856-3700. **$89-$129.** 298 SW 15th Rd 33129. I-95, exit 1B (SW 7th St) to SW 8th St, then e, s on SW 2nd Ave, then w. Int corridors. **Pets:** Other species. $25 daily fee/room. Designated rooms, service with restrictions, crate.

Extended Stay Deluxe-Miami Airport-Doral H
(305) 716-9005. **$74-$114.** 7750 NW 25th St 33122. From SR 836 (Dolphin Expwy), exit NW 25th St, then w; turn into The Shoppes at MICC Center. Int corridors. **Pets:** Other species. $25 daily fee/room. Designated rooms, service with restrictions, crate.

Four Seasons Hotel Miami H
(305) 358-3535. **$475-$600.** 1435 Brickell Ave 33131. Jct 14th Terr on US 1. Int corridors. **Pets:** Small. Service with restrictions, supervision.

Hilton Miami Airport H
(305) 262-1000. **$99-$329.** 5101 Blue Lagoon Dr 33126. Se of jct SR 836 (Dolphin Expwy), exit Red Rd, 0.7 mi e. Int corridors.
Pets: Accepted.

Homestead Studio Suites Hotel-Miami/Airport at Doral H
(305) 436-1811. **$64-$104.** 8720 NW 33rd St 33172. SR 826 (Palmetto Expwy), 0.8 mi w on NW 36th St, just s. Ext corridors. **Pets:** Other species. $25 daily fee/room. Designated rooms, service with restrictions, crate.

Homestead Studio Suites Hotel–Miami Airport–Blue Lagoon M
(305) 260-0085. **$64-$104.** 6605 NW 7th St 33126. SR 836 (Dolphin Expwy), exit Milam Dairy Rd S, 0.3 mi e; in Blue Lagoon Office Park. Ext corridors. **Pets:** Other species. $25 daily fee/room. Designated rooms, service with restrictions, crate.

Hotel Indigo Miami-Dadeland H
(305) 595-6000. **$113-$170.** 7600 N Kendall Dr 33156. SR 826 (Palmetto Expwy), exit SW 88th St (N Kendall Dr), 0.6 mi w. Int corridors. **Pets:** Medium, other species. $20 daily fee/pet. Supervision.

Hyatt Summerfield Suites Miami Airport H
(305) 269-1922. **$109-$399.** 5710 Blue Lagoon Dr 33126. Se of jct SR 836 (Dolphin Expwy), exit Red Rd, just w. Int corridors. **Pets:** $150 one-time fee/room. Service with restrictions, crate.

La Quinta Inn & Suites Miami (Airport West) H
(305) 436-0830. **$79-$189.** 8730 NW 27th St 33172. SR 836 (Dolphin Expwy), just n on 87th NW Ave. Int corridors. **Pets:** Medium, other species. Service with restrictions, supervision.

La Quinta Inn Miami (Airport North) M
(305) 599-9902. **$59-$159.** 7401 NW 36th St 33166. Just e of jct SR 826 (Palmetto Expwy). Ext/int corridors. **Pets:** Medium, other species. Service with restrictions, supervision.

Mandarin Oriental, Miami H
(305) 913-8288. **$435-$775.** 500 Brickell Key Dr 33131. US 1 (Brickell Ave), just e on SE 8th St (Brickell Key Dr). Int corridors. **Pets:** Small. $100 deposit/room, $100 one-time fee/room. Supervision.

Quality Inn-South at The Falls M
(305) 251-2000. **$83-$200.** 14501 S Dixie Hwy (US 1) 33176. US 1 at SW 145th St. Ext corridors. **Pets:** Medium, other species. $10 daily fee/room. Service with restrictions.

Residence Inn by Marriott H
(305) 591-2211. **$209-$309.** 1212 NW 82nd Ave 33126. SR 836 (Dolphin Expwy), exit 87th Ave NW, just n to NW 82nd Ave; then e. Ext corridors. **Pets:** Accepted.

Sofitel Miami H
(305) 264-4888. **$125-$540.** 5800 Blue Lagoon Dr 33126. Just sw of jct SR 836 (Dolphin Expwy), exit Red Rd. Int corridors. **Pets:** Accepted.

Staybridge Suites Miami/Doral Area H
(305) 500-9100. **Call for rates.** 3265 NW 87th Ave 33172. 0.4 mi s of jct NW 36th St. Int corridors. **Pets:** Accepted.

TownePlace Suites by Marriott H
(305) 718-4144. **$139-$199.** 10505 NW 36th St 33178. Florida Tpke, exit 29, 1.2 mi e to 107th Ave, then just s. Int corridors. **Pets:** Other species. $100 one-time fee/room. Service with restrictions.

MIAMI BEACH

The Claridge Hotel H
(305) 604-8485. **$99-$499, 3 day notice.** 3500 Collins Ave 33140. Corner of Collins Ave and 35th St. Int corridors. **Pets:** Medium. $75 one-time fee/room. Service with restrictions, supervision.

Eden Roc, a Renaissance Beach Resort & Spa H
(305) 531-0000. **$269-$429, 3 day notice.** 4525 Collins Ave 33140. SR A1A (Collins Ave), just n of 41st St. Int corridors. **Pets:** Accepted.

Fontainebleau Miami Beach H
(305) 538-2000. **$269-$1349, 3 day notice.** 4441 Collins Ave 33140. On SR A1A. Int corridors. **Pets:** Medium. $75 one-time fee/pet. Designated rooms, service with restrictions, supervision.

△△△ ▽▽ Greenview Hotel H
(305) 531-6588. **$70-$159, 3 day notice.** 1671 Washington Ave 33139. From SR A1A (Collins Ave), just e on Lincoln Rd, then just n. Int corridors. **Pets:** Accepted. [SAVE]

▽▽▽ Hotel Ocean H
(305) 672-2579. **$139-$749, 3 day notice.** 1230 Ocean Dr 33139. E of jct SR A1A (Collins Ave) and 12th St. Int corridors. **Pets:** $49 daily fee/room. Service with restrictions, crate. [ASK] [X] [🔒] [🍴]

△△△ ▽▽▽▽ Hotel Victor H
(305) 428-1234. **$229-$799, 3 day notice.** 1144 Ocean Dr 33139. Corner of Ocean Dr and 11th St. Int corridors. **Pets:** Accepted.
[SAVE] [X] [🔒] [🍴] [🏊]

▽▽ The Kent Hotel H
(305) 604-5068. **$69-$450, 3 day notice.** 1131 Collins Ave 33139. On SR A1A, jct Collins Ave and 11th St. Int corridors. **Pets:** Accepted.
[ASK] [X] [🔒]

△△△ ▽▽▽▽ Loews Miami Beach Hotel H
(305) 604-1601. **$249-$599, 3 day notice.** 1601 Collins Ave 33139. On SR A1A, jct Collins and 16th aves. Int corridors. **Pets:** Accepted.
[SAVE] [X] [🔒] [🍴] [🏊] [🗙]

△△△ ▽▽▽▽ Marriott South Beach H
(305) 536-7700. **$249-$389, 3 day notice.** 161 Ocean Dr 33139. Just e of SR A1A (Collins Ave); just s of 2nd St. Int corridors. **Pets:** Accepted.
[SAVE] [X] [🔒] [🍴] [🏊] [🗙]

▽▽▽ ▽▽ The Ritz-Carlton, South Beach H
(786) 276-4000. **Call for rates.** 1 Lincoln Rd 33139. Jct SR A1A. Int corridors. **Pets:** Small, other species. $250 one-time fee/room. Supervision. [ECO] [X] [🔒] [🍴] [🏊] [🗙]

△△△ ▽▽▽▽ The Setai H
(305) 520-6000. **$550-$1400.** 2001 Collins Ave 33139. On SR A1A (Collins Ave); at 20th St. Int corridors. **Pets:** Accepted.
[ECO] [SAVE] [X] [🔒] [🍴] [🏊] [🗙]

MIAMI LAKES

▽▽ La Quinta Inn & Suites H ☆
(305) 821-8274. **$65-$169.** 7925 NW 154th St 33016. Jct SR 826 (Palmetto Expwy), just w. Int corridors. **Pets:** Medium, other species. Service with restrictions, supervision. [ASK] [X] [🔒] [🏊]

△△△ ▽▽▽▽ TownePlace Suites by Marriott H
(305) 512-9191. **$139-$199.** 8079 NW 154th St 33016. SR 826 (Palmetto Expwy), exit 154th St, 0.4 mi w. Int corridors. **Pets:** Medium. $100 one-time fee/room. Service with restrictions.
[SAVE] [X] [🏊] [🔒] [🏊]

MIAMI SPRINGS

▽▽ Homestead Studio Suites Hotel-Miami/Airport/Miami Springs H
(305) 870-0448. **$79-$119.** 101 Fairway Dr 33166. I-95 to SR 112 W, exit NW 36th St, then w, right on Palmetto Dr, then w; between Le Jeune Rd and SR 826 (Palmetto Expwy); behind Clarion Hotel. Int corridors. **Pets:** Other species. $25 daily fee/room. Designated rooms, service with restrictions, crate. [ASK] [X] [🔒] [🏊]

▽▽▽ La Quinta Inn &Suites H ☆
(305) 871-1777. **$59-$169.** 3501 NW Le Jeune Rd 33142. SR 953 (Le Jeune Rd) at jct SR 112. Int corridors. **Pets:** Medium, other species. Service with restrictions, supervision. [ASK] [X] [🔒] [🏊]

△△△ ▽▽▽ Red Roof Inn Miami Airport H
(305) 871-4221. **$69-$269.** 3401 NW Le Jeune Rd 33142. On SR 953 (Le Jeune Rd) at SR 112; 0.5 mi n of airport entrance. Int corridors. **Pets:** Large. Service with restrictions, crate. [SAVE] [X] [🔒] [🏊]

SUNNY ISLES BEACH

△△△ ▽▽▽▽▽ Acqualina Resort and Spa on the Beach H ☆
(305) 918-8000. **$375-$2850, 30 day notice.** 17875 Collins Ave 33160. On SR A1A (Collins Ave); corner of 178th St; just s of William Lehman Cswy. Int corridors. **Pets:** Small. $100 one-time fee/room. Designated rooms. [SAVE] [X] [🏊] [🔒] [🍴] [🏊] [🗙]

△△△ ▽▽▽ ▽▽ Le Meridien Sunny Isles Beach H
(305) 503-6000. **$159-$2000, 3 day notice.** 18683 Collins Ave 33160. From north, just s from William Lehman Cswy, U-turn at 186th St, then just n; from south, SR 826, 1.3 mi n. Int corridors. **Pets:** Accepted.
[SAVE] [X] [🔒] [🏊] [🍴] [🏊] [🗙]

△△△ ▽▽▽ Newport Beachside Hotel & Resort H ☆
(305) 949-1300. **$99-$299, 3 day notice.** 16701 Collins Ave 33160. SR A1A, jct SR 826 and Sunny Isles Blvd. Int corridors. **Pets:** Small. $50 one-time fee/pet. Service with restrictions, supervision.
[SAVE] [X] [🔒] [🏊] [🍴] [🏊] [🗙]

END METROPOLITAN AREA

MIDWAY

△△△ ▽▽▽ ▽▽ Best Western Panhandle Capital Inn & Suites H
(850) 514-2222. **$75-$160.** 85 River Park Dr 32343. I-10, exit 192, just s. Int corridors. **Pets:** Accepted. [SAVE] [X] [🔒] [🏊] [🏊]

MILTON

△△△ ▽▽ Comfort Inn H
(850) 623-1511. **Call for rates.** 8936 Hwy 87 S 32583. I-10, exit 31, just s. Int corridors. **Pets:** Small, other species. $20 daily fee/pet. Designated rooms, service with restrictions, crate. [SAVE] [X] [🏊] [🔒] [🏊]

△△△ ▽▽▽ Red Roof Inn & Suites H
(850) 995-6100. **$65-$95.** 2672 Avalon Blvd 32583. I-10, exit 22, just s. Int corridors. **Pets:** Large. Service with restrictions, crate.
[SAVE] [X] [🏊] [🔒] [🏊]

NAPLES

△△△ ▽▽▽▽ Hawthorn Suites Hotel of Naples H
(239) 593-1300. **$109-$279.** 3557 Pine Ridge Rd 34109. I-75, exit 107, 0.5 mi w on CR 896. Int corridors. **Pets:** Accepted.
[ECO] [SAVE] [X] [🏊] [🔒] [🏊] [🗙]

△△△ ▽▽▽ ▽▽ Hilton Naples H ☆
(239) 430-4900. **$234-$354.** 5111 Tamiami Tr N 34103. Just s of jct CR 896 (Pine Ridge Rd). Int corridors. **Pets:** Medium. $75 deposit/room, $200 one-time fee/room. Designated rooms, service with restrictions, supervision. [ECO] [SAVE] [X] [🏊] [🔒] [🏊] [🍴] [🏊] [🗙]

▽▽▽▽ La Quinta Inn & Suites H ☆
(239) 793-4646. **$69-$184.** 1555 5th Ave S 34102. Just w of jct SR 84 (Davis Blvd) and US 41. Int corridors. **Pets:** Medium, other species. Service with restrictions, supervision. [ASK] [X] [🔒] [🏊] [🏊]

▽▽ La Quinta Inn & Suites Naples East H ☆
(239) 352-8400. **$59-$154.** 185 Bedzel Cir 34104. I-75, exit 101, just w on SR 84 (Davis Blvd). Int corridors. **Pets:** Medium, other species. Service with restrictions, supervision. [ASK] [X] [🔒] [🏊] [🏊]

△△△ ▽▽ ▽▽ Ramada Inn of Naples M ☆
(239) 263-3434. **$79-$179.** 1100 Tamiami Tr N 34102. On US 41 (Tamiami Tr); jct 13th Ave n. Ext corridors. **Pets:** Medium, other species. $25 daily fee/room. Designated rooms, service with restrictions.
[ECO] [SAVE] [X] [🔒] [🏊] [🍴] [🏊]

Red Roof Inn 🏨
(239) 774-3117. **$65-$170.** 1925 Davis Blvd 34104. Just e of jct US 41 (Tamiami Tr). Ext corridors. **Pets:** Large. Service with restrictions, crate.

Residence Inn by Marriott, Naples 🏨 🐾
(239) 659-1300. **$209-$345.** 4075 Tamiami Tr N 34103. I-75, exit 107, 3.8 mi w on CR 896 (Pine Ridge Rd), then 1 mi s on US 41. Int corridors. **Pets:** Large, other species. $75 one-time fee/room. Service with restrictions, crate.

The Ritz-Carlton Golf Resort 🏨 🐾
(239) 593-2000. **$189-$649, 7 day notice.** 2600 Tiburon Dr 34109. I-75, exit 111, 1.6 mi w on CR 846 (Immokalee Rd), 1.3 mi s on CR 31 (Airport-Pulling Rd), then just e. Int corridors. **Pets:** Small. $150 one-time fee/room. Designated rooms, service with restrictions, supervision.

Staybridge Suites by Holiday Inn 🏨
(239) 643-8002. **Call for rates.** 4805 Tamiami Tr N 34103. I-75, exit 107, 3.8 mi w on CR 896 (Pine Ridge Rd), then 0.9 mi s on US 41. Int corridors. **Pets:** Accepted.

NEW SMYRNA BEACH

Buena Vista Inn Ⓜ
(386) 428-5565. **$75-$130, 14 day notice.** 500 N Causeway 32169. 2 mi e on SR 44 Business Rt; at west end North Causeway Bridge. Ext corridors. **Pets:** Accepted.

Longboard Inn BB
(386) 428-3499. **$115-$160, 14 day notice.** 312 Washington St 32168. 0.3 mi w of jct N Riverside Dr. Ext corridors. **Pets:** Other species. $10 daily fee/room. Designated rooms.

Night Swan Intracoastal Bed & Breakfast BB 🐾
(386) 423-4940. **$120-$220, 3 day notice.** 512 S Riverside Dr 32168. Just s of SR 44 Intracoastal Waterway bridge; west side of Intracoastal Waterway. Ext/int corridors. **Pets:** Medium, other species. Designated rooms.

NORTH FORT MYERS

Best Western Fort Myers Waterfront 🏨
(239) 997-5511. **$80-$200.** 13021 N Cleveland Ave 33903. On US 41, 0.6 mi s of SR 78A (Pondella Rd), jct N Bay Dr and Caloosahatchee Bridge. Ext corridors. **Pets:** Small, dogs only. $25 daily fee/room. Designated rooms, service with restrictions.

OCALA

Budget Host Inn Ⓜ
(352) 732-6940. **$40-$95.** 4013 NW Bonnie Heath Blvd 34482. I-75, exit 354, 0.3 mi n on US 27. Ext corridors. **Pets:** Medium, other species. $10 daily fee/pet. Service with restrictions, supervision.

Days Inn 🏨
(352) 629-7041. **$60-$110, 3 day notice.** 3811 NW Bonnie Heath Blvd 34482. I-75, exit 354, just n on US 27. Ext/int corridors. **Pets:** Medium. $5 daily fee/pet. Service with restrictions, supervision.

Hilton Ocala 🏨
(352) 854-1400. **$119-$229.** 3600 SW 36th Ave 34474. I-75, exit 350, 0.3 mi e on SR 200. Int corridors. **Pets:** Accepted.

La Quinta Inn & Suites Ocala 🏨 🐾
(352) 861-1137. **$65-$130.** 3530 SW 36th Ave 34474. I-75, exit 350, just e on SR 200. Int corridors. **Pets:** Medium, other species. Service with restrictions, supervision.

Quality Inn Ocala Hotel and Conference Center 🏨
(352) 629-0381. **Call for rates.** 3621 W Silver Springs Blvd 34475. I-75, exit 352, just e on SR 40. Ext corridors. **Pets:** Accepted.

Ramada Inn & Conference Center 🏨
(352) 732-3131. **$56-$104.** 3810 NW Bonnie Heath Blvd 34482. I-75, exit 354, just w. Ext corridors. **Pets:** Accepted.

Red Roof Inn & Suites 🏨
(352) 732-4590. **$60-$150.** 120 NW 40th Ave 34482. I-75, exit 352, just w. Int corridors. **Pets:** Large. Service with restrictions, crate.

Residence Inn by Marriott Ocala 🏨 🐾
(352) 547-1600. **$119-$179.** 3610 SW 38th Ave 34474. I-75, exit 350, just w on SR 200, then n. Int corridors. **Pets:** Large, other species. $75 one-time fee/room. Service with restrictions.

Travelodge Ocala 🏨
(352) 629-8850. **$69-$129.** 4040 W Silver Springs Blvd 34482. I-75, exit 352, just w on SR 40. Ext corridors. **Pets:** Medium. $5 daily fee/pet. Service with restrictions, supervision.

OLD TOWN

Suwannee Gables Motel Ⓜ
(352) 542-7752. **$98-$210, 3 day notice.** 27659 SE Hwy 19, Alt 27 32680. US 19, 98 and 27A; 2 mi s of jct SR 349. Ext corridors. **Pets:** Accepted.

ORANGE CITY

Alling House Bed and Breakfast BB
(386) 775-7648. **$95-$145, 7 day notice.** 215 E French Ave 32763. I-4, exit 114, 3 mi nw on SR 472, 2.3 mi s on US 17-92, then just e. Ext corridors. **Pets:** Other species. $10 daily fee/room. Designated rooms, crate.

Comfort Inn 🏨
(386) 775-7444. **Call for rates.** 445 S Volusia Ave 32763. I-4, exit 114, 2.8 mi w on SR 472, then 2 mi s on US 17-92. Ext corridors. **Pets:** Accepted.

ORLANDO METROPOLITAN AREA

ALTAMONTE SPRINGS

Candlewood Suites 🏨
(407) 767-5757. **$59-$109.** 644 Raymond Ave 32701. I-4, exit 92, just w to Douglas Ave, 0.8 mi n to Central Pkwy, then just e. Int corridors. **Pets:** Accepted.

Clarion-Orlando North 🏨
(407) 862-4455. **$79-$149.** 230 W SR 436 32714. I-4, exit 92, just sw. Ext/int corridors. **Pets:** Accepted.

Days Inn & Suites 🏨
(407) 788-1411. **$69-$120.** 150 S Westmonte Dr 32714. I-4, exit 92, 0.3 mi w on SR 436, then just s. Ext corridors. **Pets:** Accepted.

Embassy Suites Orlando North 🏨 🐾
(407) 834-2400. **$109-$249.** 225 Shorecrest Dr 32701. I-4, exit 92, 0.3 mi e on SR 436, then just n on North Lake Blvd. Int corridors. **Pets:** Medium. $20 daily fee/pet. Designated rooms, service with restrictions, crate.

▼▼ Homestead Studio Suites Hotel-Orlando/Altamonte Springs H

(407) 332-9300. $55-$100. 302 North Lake Blvd 32701. I-4, exit 92, just e, then 0.3 mi s. Int corridors. Pets: Other species. $25 daily fee/room. Designated rooms, service with restrictions, crate.

ASK ✕ &M 🖥 🖵

▼▼▼ Residence Inn by Marriott H ❖

(407) 788-7991. $197-$241. 270 Douglas Ave 32714. I-4, exit 92, just w on SR 436, then just n. Ext corridors. Pets: Medium. $75 one-time fee/room. Service with restrictions, crate. ✕ &M 🖥 🖵 ⊰ ✕

CHAMPIONSGATE

◍ ▼▼▼ ▼▼▼ Omni Orlando Resort at ChampionsGate H

(407) 390-6664. $129-$389, 3 day notice. 1500 Masters Blvd 33896. I-4, exit 58, 0.3 mi w. Int corridors. Pets: Small, dogs only. $50 one-time fee/room. Designated rooms, service with restrictions, crate.

ECO SAVE ✕ &M 🖥 🖵 ¶ ⊰ ✕

CLERMONT

◍ ▼▼▼ Fairfield Inn & Suites Clermont H ❖

(352) 394-6585. $84-$102. 1750 Hunt Trace Blvd 34711. Jct US 27 and SR 50, 0.5 mi e on SR 50, just n. Int corridors. Pets: Medium, other species. $75 one-time fee/pet. Designated rooms, service with restrictions, crate. ECO SAVE ✕ 🖥 🖵 ⊰

DAVENPORT

▼▼▼ Calabay Parc-The Florida Store VH

(407) 846-1722. Call for rates. 325 Calabay Parc Blvd 33897. Jct US 192 and 27, 4 mi s. Ext corridors. Pets: Accepted. ✕ 🖥 🖵 ⊰

▼▼▼ Hampton Inn Orlando-South of Walt Disney World Resorts H

(863) 420-9898. $89-$99. 44117 Hwy 27 33897. I-4, exit 55, just nw. Int corridors. Pets: $25 daily fee/room. Designated rooms, service with restrictions, crate. ✕ &M 🖥 🖵 ⊰

▼▼▼ Holiday Inn Express & Suites Orlando South-Davenport H

(863) 420-6611. Call for rates. 44019 US Hwy 27 33897. I-4, exit 55, just n. Int corridors. Pets: Accepted. ✕ &M 🖥 🖵 ⊰

▼▼▼ Southern Dunes-The Florida Store VH

(407) 846-1722. Call for rates. 2684 Hemingway Dr 34741. I-4, exit 68, 3.5 mi s on SR 535, then 3.8 mi e on US 192. Ext corridors. Pets: Accepted. ✕ 🖥 🖵 ¶ ⊰ ✕

KISSIMMEE

◍ ▼▼ Baymont Inn Kissimmee H

(407) 994-1900. $39-$129, 3 day notice. 4156 W Vine St 34741. I-4, exit 64A, 6 mi e. Ext corridors. Pets: Accepted.

SAVE ✕ 🖥 🖵 ⊰

◍ ▼▼▼ Champions World Resort H ❖

(407) 396-4500. $29-$69. 8660 W Irlo Bronson Memorial Hwy 34747. I-4, exit 64B, 5.6 mi w on US 192. Ext corridors. Pets: Medium. $35 one-time fee/room. Designated rooms, service with restrictions, crate.

SAVE ✕ 🖥 🖵 ¶ ⊰ ✕

◍ ▼▼▼ Clarion Resort & Water Park-Conference Center H

(407) 846-2221. $60-$150, 3 day notice. 2261 E Irlo Bronson Memorial Hwy 34744. Florida Tpke, exit 244, then just w. Ext corridors. Pets: Accepted. SAVE ✕ 🖥 🖵 ¶ ⊰ ✕

▼▼▼ Indian Creek-The Florida Store VH

(352) 243-2853. Call for rates. 8009 Bow Creek Rd 34746. I-4, exit 64B, 3.2 mi on US 192 to Formosa Gardens Blvd, then 1.2 mi s. Ext corridors. Pets: Accepted. ✕ 🖥 🖵 ⊰

◍ ▼▼ Masters Inn-Main Gate H

(407) 396-7743. $45-$150, 3 day notice. 2945 Entry Point Blvd 34747. I-4, exit 64, 2.5 mi w on US 192; 1 mi w of Disney World main gate. Ext corridors. Pets: Accepted. SAVE ✕ 🖥 🖵 ⊰

▼▼ Motel 6-#0436 H

(407) 396-6422. $35-$51. 7455 W Irlo Bronson Memorial Hwy 34747. I-4, exit 64B, 1.3 mi w on US 192. Int corridors. Pets: Other species. Service with restrictions, supervision. ✕ ⊰

▼▼ Motel 6-#0464 M

(407) 396-6333. $29-$55. 5731 W Hwy 192 34746. I-4, exit 64A, 2 mi e. Ext corridors. Pets: Other species. Service with restrictions, supervision. ✕ &M ⊰

◍ ▼▼▼ Palms Hotel and Villas CO

(407) 396-2229. $89-$139. 3100 Parkway Blvd 34747. I-4, exit 64A, 0.3 mi e on US 192, then 0.5 mi n. Ext/int corridors. Pets: Medium, dogs only. $100 one-time fee/room. Designated rooms, service with restrictions, supervision. SAVE ✕ 🖥 🖵 ⊰ ✕

◍ ▼▼▼ Seralago Hotel & Suites Main Gate East H

(407) 396-4488. $45-$89. 5678 W Irlo Bronson Memorial Hwy 34746. I-4, exit 64A; between MM 9 and 10. Ext corridors. Pets: Medium, other species. $40 one-time fee/room. Designated rooms, service with restrictions. SAVE ✕ &M 🖥 🖵 ¶ ⊰ ✕

▼▼▼ Venetian Bay–Ventura Resort Rentals CO

(407) 273-8770. $79-$500, 15 day notice. 4008 San Gallo Dr 34747. SR 417, exit 11, 3 mi s on Orange Blossom Tr, then 2 mi w on West Carroll. Ext corridors. Pets: Small. $100 deposit/pet, $100 one-time fee/pet. Service with restrictions, supervision. ASK 🖥 🖵 ⊰

◍ ▼▼ Westgate Inn & Suites M

(863) 424-2621. $39-$129. 9200 W Irlo Bronson Memorial Hwy 34714. Jct US 27 and 192, 0.3 mi e. Ext corridors. Pets: Accepted.

SAVE ✕ 🖥 🖵 ⊰ ✕

LADY LAKE

◍ ▼▼▼ Comfort Suites in the Villages H

(352) 259-6578. Call for rates. 1202 Avenida Central N 32159. Just n on US 441. Int corridors. Pets: Medium, other species. $35 one-time fee/pet. Service with restrictions. SAVE ✕ 🖥 🖵 ⊰

◍ ▼▼▼ Holiday Inn Express Hotel & Suites H

(352) 750-3888. Call for rates. 1205 Avenida Central N 32159. Just n on US 441. Int corridors. Pets: Medium, other species. $35 one-time fee/pet. Service with restrictions. SAVE ✕ 🖥 🖵 ⊰

▼▼ Microtel Inn & Suites H

(352) 259-0184. $51-$300. 850 US 27/441 32159. 1 mi s. Int corridors. Pets: Accepted. ASK ✕ 🖥 🖵 ⊰

◍ ▼▼▼ TownePlace Suites by Marriott at the Villages H

(352) 753-8686. $119-$134. 1141 Alonzo Ave 32159. US 441/27 to Main St. Int corridors. Pets: Accepted. SAVE ✕ &M 🖥 🖵 ⊰

LAKE BUENA VISTA

◍ ▼▼▼ Comfort Inn Lake Buena Vista H

(407) 996-7300. $59-$129. 8442 Palm Pkwy 32836. I-4, exit 68, 0.6 mi n on SR 535, then 0.5 mi e. Ext corridors. Pets: Accepted.

SAVE ✕ &M 🖥 🖵 ¶ ⊰

▼▼▼ Holiday Inn Express Lake Buena Vista H

(407) 239-8400. $89. 8686 Palm Pkwy 32836. I-4, exit 68, 0.5 mi n on SR 535, then 0.3 mi e. Int corridors. Pets: Medium, other species. $50 one-time fee/pet. Service with restrictions, supervision. ECO ASK ✕ 🖥 🖵 ⊰ ✕

Orlando Vista Hotel

(407) 239-4646. **$59-$119.** 12490 Apopka-Vineland Rd 32836. I-4, exit 68, 0.4 mi n on SR 535. Int corridors. **Pets:** Medium. $50 one-time fee/room. Designated rooms, service with restrictions, crate.

Residence Inn Orlando Lake Buena Vista

(407) 465-0075. **$139-$219, 3 day notice.** 11450 Marbella Palms Ct 32836. I-4, exit 68, 0.4 mi n on SR 535, then 0.5 mi e on Palm Pkwy. Int corridors. **Pets:** Accepted.

Sheraton Safari Hotel & Suites

(407) 239-0444. **$89-$219.** 12205 Apopka-Vineland Rd 32836. I-4, exit 68, 0.5 mi n on SR 535. Ext/int corridors. **Pets:** Large, dogs only. Service with restrictions, supervision.

LAKE MARY

Candlewood Suites Lake Mary-Heathrow

(407) 585-3000. **Call for rates.** 1130 Greenwood Blvd 32746. I-4, exit 98, just e to Lake Emma Rd, 0.5 mi s to Greenwood Blvd, then 0.6 mi w. Int corridors. **Pets:** Accepted.

Extended StayAmerica-Lake Mary-Heathrow

(407) 833-0011. **$55-$95.** 1036 Greenwood Blvd 32746. I-4, exit 98, just e to Lake Emma Rd, then 0.5 mi. Int corridors. **Pets:** Other species. $25 daily fee/room. Designated rooms, service with restrictions, crate.

Homestead Studio Suites-Orlando/Lake Mary–Heathrow

(407) 829-2332. **$65-$105.** 1040 Greenwood Blvd 32746. I-4, exit 98, 0.5 mi s on Lake Emma Rd; in Commerce Park. Int corridors. **Pets:** Other species. $25 daily fee/room. Designated rooms, service with restrictions, crate.

LEESBURG

Leesburg Super 8

(352) 787-6363. **$50-$175, 3 day notice.** 1392 North Blvd W 34748. Jct US 27 and 441. Int corridors. **Pets:** Small. $10 daily fee/pet. Service with restrictions, supervision.

MAITLAND

Extended Stay Deluxe-Orlando-Maitland-Pembrook Dr

(407) 475-1675. **$65-$100.** 1776 Pembrook Dr 32810. I-4, exit 90B, 0.5 mi w. Int corridors. **Pets:** Other species. $25 daily fee/room. Designated rooms, service with restrictions, crate.

Homewood Suites by Hilton Orlando North

(407) 875-8777. **$139-$169.** 290 Southhall Ln 32751. I-4, exit 90, just w, then just s on Lake Destiny. Int corridors. **Pets:** Accepted.

Sheraton Orlando North

(407) 660-9000. **Call for rates.** 600 N Lake Destiny Dr 32751. I-4, exit 90B, just w. Int corridors. **Pets:** Medium, dogs only. Service with restrictions.

MOUNT DORA

Heron Cay Lakeview Bed & Breakfast

(352) 383-4050. **$155-$295, 15 day notice.** 495 Old Hwy 441 32757. On CR 441 (Old US 441), 0.3 mi w. Int corridors. **Pets:** Other species. $25 daily fee/room. Designated rooms, service with restrictions, supervision.

OCOEE

Best Western Turnpike West-Orlando

(407) 656-5050. **$79-$89.** 10945 W Colonial Dr 34761. I-4, exit 84, 10 mi w on SR 50; 0.5 mi e of Florida Tpke, exit 267B. Ext corridors. **Pets:** Accepted.

Red Roof Inn Orlando West

(407) 347-0140. **Call for rates.** 11241 W Colonial Dr 34761. I-4, exit 84, 10 mi w on SR 50; 0.6 mi e of Florida Tpke, exit 267. Int corridors. **Pets:** Large. Service with restrictions, crate.

ORLANDO

AmeriSuites Orlando Airport/Northeast

(407) 240-3939. **$79-$199.** 7500 Augusta National Dr 32822. SR 528 (Beachline Expwy), exit 11, 0.5 mi n on SR 436, just e on TG Lee Blvd, then just s. Int corridors. **Pets:** Accepted.

Baymont Inn & Suites Florida Mall

(407) 851-8200. **$80-$159.** 8820 S Orange Blossom Tr 32809. Florida Tpke, exit 254, just n. Int corridors. **Pets:** Accepted.

Best Western Orlando Gateway

(407) 351-5009. **Call for rates.** 7299 Universal Blvd 32819. I-4, exit 75A, just e of International Dr. Int corridors. **Pets:** Accepted.

Best Western Orlando West

(407) 841-8600. **$69-$125, 14 day notice.** 2014 W Colonial Dr 32804. I-4, exit 84, 1.5 mi w on SR 50; 0.4 mi e of SR 423. Int corridors. **Pets:** Small, dogs only. $50 deposit/room, $7 daily fee/pet. Service with restrictions, supervision.

Comfort Suites Downtown

(407) 228-4007. **$89-$159.** 2416 N Orange Ave 32804. I-4, exit 85, just e on Princeton, then just n. Int corridors. **Pets:** Small, other species. $30 daily fee/pet. Designated rooms, service with restrictions.

Comfort Suites Orlando

(407) 351-5050. **$79-$149.** 9350 Turkey Lake Rd 32819. I-4, exit 74A, just w on SR 482 (Sand Lake Rd), then 1.5 mi s. Ext corridors. **Pets:** Medium. $49 one-time fee/room. Designated rooms, service with restrictions, supervision.

Country Inn & Suites By Carlson, Orlando International Airport

(407) 856-8896. **Call for rates.** 5440 Forbes Pl 32812. SR 528 (Beachline Expwy), exit 11, 0.6 mi n on SR 436, then just w. Int corridors. **Pets:** Medium. $75 one-time fee/room. Designated rooms, service with restrictions, crate.

Courtyard by Marriott Orlando International Airport

(407) 240-7200. **$139-$199.** 7155 N Frontage Rd 32812. SR 436, 0.3 mi n of SR 528 (Beachline Expwy). Int corridors. **Pets:** Accepted.

Extended StayAmerica/Orlando Convention Center/Westwood Blvd

(407) 352-3454. **$53-$100.** 6451 Westwood Blvd 32821. I-4, exit 72, just e on SR 528 (Beachline Expwy) to exit 1 (International Dr), just s, then just w. Int corridors. **Pets:** Other species. $25 daily fee/room. Designated rooms, service with restrictions, crate.

Extended StayAmerica-Orlando Universal Studios

(407) 351-1788. **$60-$100.** 5620 Major Blvd 32819. I-4, exit 75B, just n, then just e. Int corridors. **Pets:** Other species. $25 daily fee/room. Designated rooms, service with restrictions, crate.

Extended Stay Deluxe Orlando Convention Center/Pointe Orlando

(407) 903-1500. **$65-$150.** 8750 Universal Blvd 32819. I-4, exit 74A, 0.5 mi e on SR 482 (Sand Lake Rd), then 0.7 mi s. Int corridors. **Pets:** Other species. $25 daily fee/room. Service with restrictions, crate.

Extended Stay Deluxe/Orlando Convention Center/ Westwood Blvd. H
(407) 351-1982. **$75-$165.** 6443 Westwood Blvd 32821. I-4, exit 72, just e on SR 528 (Beachline Expwy) to exit 1 (International Dr), just s, then just w. Int corridors. **Pets:** Other species. $25 daily fee/room. Designated rooms, service with restrictions, crate. (ASK) (X) (■) (■) (≈)

Extended Stay Deluxe Orlando-Universal Studios H
(407) 370-4428. **$75-$110.** 5610 Vineland Rd 32819. I-4, exit 75B, just n, then e. Int corridors. **Pets:** Other species. $25 daily fee/room. Designated rooms, service with restrictions, crate. (ASK) (X) (&M) (■) (■) (≈)

Floridays Resort Orlando CO
(407) 238-7700. **$150-$450.** 12550 Floridays Resort Dr 32821. I-4, exit 72, just e on SR 528 (Beachline Expwy), exit 1, then 3 mi s. Ext corridors. **Pets:** Medium. $100 one-time fee/room. Service with restrictions, supervision. (ECO) (SAVE) (X) (&M) (■) (■) (¶) (≈) (✕)

The Grand Bohemian Hotel H
(407) 313-9000, **3 day notice.** 325 S Orange Ave 32801. Corner of Jackson St. Int corridors. **Pets:** Accepted.
(ECO) (SAVE) (X) (&M) (■) (¶) (≈) (✕)

Hard Rock Hotel at Universal Orlando® H ☀
(407) 503-2000. **$234-$514, 5 day notice.** 5800 Universal Blvd 32819. I-4, exit 75A, 1 mi n, follow signs. Int corridors. **Pets:** Other species. $25 one-time fee/room. Designated rooms, service with restrictions, supervision. (ECO) (SAVE) (X) (&M) (■) (■) (¶) (≈) (✕)

Hawthorn Suites Orlando Airport H
(407) 438-2121. **$95-$250.** 7450 Augusta National Dr 32822. SR 528 (Beachline Expwy), exit 11, 0.5 mi n on SR 436, just e, then just s. Int corridors. **Pets:** Accepted. (ECO) (SAVE) (X) (&M) (■) (■) (≈) (✕)

Holiday Inn Express Orlando International Airport H
(407) 581-7900. **$99-$149.** 7900 Conway Rd 32812. SR 528 (Beachline Expwy), exit 9, just n. Int corridors. **Pets:** Accepted.
(ASK) (X) (&M) (■) (■) (≈)

Holiday Inn-International Drive Resort H
(407) 351-3500. **$79-$169.** 6515 International Dr 32819. I-4, exit 74A, just e on SR 482 (Sand Lake Rd), then 0.5 mi n. Ext/int corridors.
Pets: Accepted. (ECO) (ASK) (X) (&M) (■) (■) (¶) (≈) (✕)

Howard Johnson Inn H
(407) 851-1050. **$139-$749.** 9393 S Orange Blossom Tr 32837. Florida Tpke, exit 254, just s. Ext corridors. **Pets:** Other species. $15 one-time fee/room. Designated rooms, service with restrictions, crate.
(SAVE) (X) (■) (■)

International Plaza Resort & Spa H ☀
(407) 352-1100. **$89-$239, 3 day notice.** 10100 International Dr 32821. I-4, exit 72, just s on International Dr; SR 528 (Beachline Expwy), exit 1, just e. Ext/int corridors. **Pets:** Small. $100 one-time fee/pet. Designated rooms, service with restrictions.
(ECO) (SAVE) (X) (&M) (■) (¶) (≈) (✕)

La Quinta Inn & Suites Orlando (Convention Center) H ☀
(407) 345-1365. **$69-$159.** 8504 Universal Blvd 32819. I-4, exit 74A, 0.5 mi e on SR 482 (Sand Lake Rd), then 0.5 mi s. Int corridors. **Pets:** Medium, other species. Service with restrictions, supervision.
(ASK) (X) (&M) (■) (■) (≈)

La Quinta Inn & Suites Orlando (U.C.F.) H ☀
(407) 737-6075. **$59-$139.** 11805 Research Pkwy 32826. Just se of jct University Blvd and SR 434 (Alafaya Tr). Int corridors. **Pets:** Medium, other species. Service with restrictions, supervision.
(ASK) (X) (&M) (■) (■) (≈)

La Quinta Inn International Dr North H ☀
(407) 351-4100. **$49-$129.** 5825 International Dr 32819. I-4, exit 75A, just w. Int corridors. **Pets:** Medium, other species. Service with restrictions, supervision. (ASK) (X) (■) (■) (≈)

La Quinta Inn Orlando (Airport West) H ☀
(407) 857-9215. **$59-$139.** 7931 Daetwyler Dr 32812. SR 528 (Beachline Expwy), exit 9 (Tradeport), via McCoy Rd. Ext corridors. **Pets:** Medium, other species. Service with restrictions, supervision. (ASK) (■) (≈)

La Quinta Inn Orlando South H ☀
(407) 240-0500. **$59-$139.** 2051 Consulate Dr 32837. From SR 528 (Beachline Expwy), exit 4, just se; Florida Tpke, exit 254, s on US 441, then right. Int corridors. **Pets:** Medium, other species. Service with restrictions, supervision. (ASK) (X) (■) (■) (≈)

Loews Portofino Bay Hotel at Universal Orlando® H ☀
(407) 503-1000. **$274-$554, 5 day notice.** 5601 Universal Blvd 32819. I-4, exit 74B westbound; exit 75A eastbound, 1 mi n, follow signs. Int corridors. **Pets:** Other species. $25 one-time fee/room. Designated rooms, service with restrictions, supervision.
(ECO) (SAVE) (X) (&M) (■) (■) (¶) (≈) (✕)

Loews Royal Pacific Resort at Universal Orlando® H ☀
(407) 503-3000. **$219-$469, 5 day notice.** 6300 Hollywood Way 32819. I-4, exit 74B, just n. Int corridors. **Pets:** Other species. $25 one-time fee/room. Designated rooms, service with restrictions.
(ECO) (SAVE) (X) (&M) (■) (■) (¶) (≈) (✕)

Motel 6 Orlando-International Drive #1079 H
(407) 351-6500. **$35-$55.** 5909 American Way 32819. I-4, exit 75A, just w of SR 435, then just n. Int corridors. **Pets:** Other species. Service with restrictions, supervision. (X) (≈)

Quality Inn & Suites H
(407) 996-4600. **$55-$140.** 8700 S Orange Blossom Tr 32809. On US 17-92 and 441, 0.5 mi n of SR 528 and Florida Tpke, exit 254. Ext corridors. **Pets:** Small. $20 one-time fee/pet. Designated rooms, service with restrictions, crate. (SAVE) (X) (■) (■) (≈)

Quality Inn International H
(407) 996-1600. **$49-$79.** 7600 International Dr 32819. I-4, exit 74A, just e on SR 482 (Sand Lake Rd), then just n. Ext corridors. **Pets:** Accepted.
(X) (&M) (■) (■) (¶) (≈)

Quality Inn Plaza H ☀
(407) 996-8585. **$60-$130.** 9000 International Dr 32819. I-4, exit 74A, just e on SR 482 (Sand Lake Rd), then 1 mi s. Ext corridors. **Pets:** $10 daily fee/pet. Designated rooms, service with restrictions, crate.
(X) (&M) (■) (■) (¶) (≈) (✕)

Red Roof Inn Convention Center H
(407) 352-1507. **$50-$126, 3 day notice.** 9922 Hawaiian Ct 32819. I-4, exit 72, 0.9 mi e on SR 528 (Beachline Expwy) to exit 1, then just n. Ext corridors. **Pets:** Large. Service with restrictions, crate.
(SAVE) (X) (&M) (■) (≈)

Residence Inn by Marriott Orlando Convention Center H
(407) 226-0288. **$139-$199.** 8800 Universal Blvd 32819. I-4, exit 74A, 0.5 mi e on SR 482 (Sand Lake Rd), then 0.8 mi s. Int corridors.
Pets: Accepted. (SAVE) (X) (&M) (■) (■) (≈) (✕)

Residence Inn by Marriott Orlando International Airport H
(407) 856-2444. **$159-$199.** 7024 Augusta National Dr 32822. SR 528 (Beach Line Expwy), exit 11, 1 mi n; 1 mi e of Orlando International Airport. Int corridors. **Pets:** Accepted. (SAVE) (X) (&M) (■) (■) (≈) (✕)

Ⓐ ▼▼▼ **Residence Inn by Marriott-Orlando International Dr** 🅷

(407) 345-0117. **$259-$309.** 7975 Canada Ave 32819. I-4, exit 74A, just e on SR 482 (Sand Lake Rd). Ext corridors. **Pets:** Other species. $75 one-time fee/room. Service with restrictions.

ⓈⒶⓋⒺ ⊠ 🛏 🖵 ⇌ ⊠

Ⓐ ▼▼▼ **Residence Inn SeaWorld International Center** 🅷

(407) 313-3600. **$339-$369.** 11000 Westwood Blvd 32821. I-4, exit 72. Int corridors. **Pets:** Medium, other species. $75 one-time fee/room. Service with restrictions, crate. ⓈⒶⓋⒺ ⊠ ⓛⓜ 🛏 🖵 🍴 ⇌ ⊠

▼▼ **Rodeway Inn International** 🅷

(407) 996-4444. **$46-$90.** 6327 International Dr 32819. I-4, exit 75A, just e on SR 482 (Sand Lake Rd), then 0.7 mi n. Ext/int corridors. **Pets:** Accepted. ⓛⓜ 🛏 🖵 🍴 ⇌

Ⓐ ▼▼▼ **Sheraton Orlando Downtown Hotel** 🅷

(407) 425-4455. **$99-$299.** 60 S Ivanhoe Blvd 32804. I-4, exit Ivanhoe Blvd. Int corridors. **Pets:** Accepted.

ⒺⒸⓄ ⓈⒶⓋⒺ ⊠ 🛏 🖵 🍴 ⇌ ⊠

Ⓐ ▼▼▼ **Sheraton Suites Orlando Airport** 🅷

(407) 240-5555. **$89-$279.** 7550 Augusta National Dr 32822. 2 mi n of airport terminal via SR 436 and TG Lee Blvd. Int corridors. **Pets:** Accepted. ⒺⒸⓄ ⓈⒶⓋⒺ ⊠ ⓛⓜ 🛏 🖵 🍴 ⇌

▼▼▼ **TownePlace Suites by Marriott Orlando East/UCF** 🅷

(407) 243-6100. **$161-$197.** 11801 High Tech Ave 32817. 2.2 mi e of SR 417 on University Blvd. Int corridors. **Pets:** Medium, other species. $25 daily fee/room. Service with restrictions, supervision. ⊠ 🛏 🖵 ⇌

▼▼▼ **Ventura Cove-Ventura Country Club-Ventura Resort Rentals** 🆅🅷

(407) 273-8770. **$79-$500, 15 day notice.** 3763 Ventura Club 32822. 0.6 mi e of SR 436. Ext corridors. **Pets:** Small. $100 deposit/pet, $100 one-time fee/pet. Designated rooms, service with restrictions, supervision.

ⒶⓈ🅚 🛏 🖵 ⇌ ⊠

Ⓐ ▼▼▼ **Wyndham Orlando Resort** 🅷 🐾

(407) 351-2420. **$83-$194, 3 day notice.** 8001 International Dr 32819. I-4, exit 74A, just e at SR 482 (Sand Lake Rd). Ext/int corridors. **Pets:** Medium, other species. $50 one-time fee/room. Service with restrictions, supervision. ⓈⒶⓋⒺ ⊠ 🛏 🖵 🍴 ⇌ ⊠

ST. CLOUD

Ⓐ ▼▼ **Budget Inn of St Cloud** 🅼

(407) 892-2858. **$35-$90, 3 day notice.** 602 13th St 34769. On US 192, 0.5 mi e of The Water Tower, 2 mi w of jct CR 15. Ext corridors. **Pets:** Very small, dogs only. $10 daily fee/pet. Service with restrictions, supervision. ⓈⒶⓋⒺ ⊠ 🛏

END METROPOLITAN AREA

ORMOND BEACH

▼▼ **Jameson Inn** 🅷

(386) 672-3675. **$83-$90.** 175 Interchange Blvd 32174. I-95, exit 268, just w, then just s. Int corridors. **Pets:** Other species. $15 daily fee/room. Designated rooms, service with restrictions, supervision.

ⒶⓈ🅚 ⊠ 🛏 ⇌

PALATKA

▼▼ **Sleep Inn & Suites** 🅷

(386) 325-8889. **$80-$150.** 3805 Reid St 32177. 2 mi n on SR 100, jct SR 19. Int corridors. **Pets:** Small, other species. $100 deposit/room, $20 daily fee/pet. Designated rooms, service with restrictions, crate.

⊠ 🛏 🖵 ⇌

PALM BAY

▼▼▼ **Jameson Inn** 🅷

(321) 725-2952. **$78-$85.** 890 Palm Bay Rd 32905. I-95, exit 176. Int corridors. **Pets:** Small, dogs only. $15 daily fee/room. Service with restrictions, supervision. ⒶⓈ🅚 ⊠ ⓛⓜ 🛏 🖵 ⇌

PALM BEACH

Ⓐ ▼▼▼ ▼▼▼ **The Brazilian Court** 🅷

(561) 655-7740. **$249-$2999, 3 day notice.** 301 Australian Ave 33480. From Royal Palm Way (SR 704), s on Cocoanut Row, 2 blks to Australian Ave, then just e; corner of Hibiscus and Australian aves. Int corridors. **Pets:** Accepted. ⓈⒶⓋⒺ ⊠ 🛏 🍴 ⇌ ⊠

Ⓐ ▼▼▼ ▼▼▼ **The Four Seasons Resort, Palm Beach** 🅷 🐾

(561) 582-2800. **$195-$779, 14 day notice.** 2800 S Ocean Blvd 33480. SR A1A, 0.3 mi n of jct SR 802. Int corridors. **Pets:** Small, other species. ⒺⒸⓄ ⓈⒶⓋⒺ ⊠ ⓛⓜ 🛏 🖵 🍴 ⇌ ⊠

PALM BEACH GARDENS

Ⓐ ▼▼▼ **Homewood Suites by Hilton Palm Beach Gardens** 🅷

(561) 622-7799. **$155-$189.** 4700 Donald Ross Rd 33418. I-95, exit 83 (Donald Ross Rd), 1.1 mi e. Int corridors. **Pets:** Small, other species. $75 one-time fee/room. Service with restrictions, supervision.

ⓈⒶⓋⒺ ⊠ ⓛⓜ 🛏 🖵 ⇌ ⊠

Ⓐ ▼▼▼ ▼▼▼ **PGA National Resort & Spa** 🅷

(561) 627-2000. **$109-$369, 3 day notice.** 400 Ave of the Champions 33418. I-95, exit 79AB, 2 mi w; Florida Tpke, exit 109, just w. Int corridors. **Pets:** Accepted. ⒺⒸⓄ ⓈⒶⓋⒺ ⊠ 🛏 🖵 🍴 ⇌ ⊠

▼▼▼ **Windsor Gardens Hotel & Conference Center** 🅷

(561) 844-8448. **Call for rates.** 11360 US Hwy 1 33408. Just s of jct PGA Blvd (SR 786). Int corridors. **Pets:** Accepted.

ⒺⒸⓄ ⊠ 🛏 🖵 🍴 ⇌

PALM BEACH SHORES

▼▼▼ **Hilton Singer Island Oceanfront Resort** 🅷

(561) 848-3888. **$139-$359.** 3700 N Ocean Dr 33404. On Singer Island; 1.8 mi n, e on SR A1A from jct US 1. Int corridors. **Pets:** Accepted.

ⒺⒸⓄ ⊠ ⓛⓜ 🛏 🖵 🍴 ⇌ ⊠

Ⓐ ▼▼▼ **SeaSpray Inn Beach Resort** 🅷

(561) 844-0233. **$90-$185, 14 day notice.** 123 S Ocean Ave 33404. On Singer Island; 0.5 mi s of SR A1A. Int corridors. **Pets:** Accepted.

ⓈⒶⓋⒺ ⊠ 🛏 🖵 🍴 ⇌

PALM COAST

Ⓐ ▼▼▼ **Best Western Palm Coast** 🅷

(386) 446-4457. **$74-$260.** 5 Kingswood Dr 32137. I-95, exit 289, 0.5 mi se via Old Kings Rd; in Kingswood Center. Ext corridors. **Pets:** Accepted.

ⓈⒶⓋⒺ ⊠ 🛏 ⇌

▼▼▼ **Fairfield Inn & Suites** 🅷 🐾

(386) 445-3450. **$89-$109.** 400 Old Kings Rd N 32137. I-95, exit 289, 0.3 mi e, then 0.3 mi s. Int corridors. **Pets:** Large, other species. $50 one-time fee/room. Designated rooms, service with restrictions, crate.

⊠ ⓛⓜ 🛏 🖵 ⇌

▼▼ **Microtel Inn & Suites** 🅷

(386) 445-8976. **$60-$170.** 16 Kingswood Dr 32137. I-95, exit 289, 0.5 mi se via Old Kings Rd. Int corridors. **Pets:** Small, dogs only. $15 daily fee/pet. Designated rooms, service with restrictions, supervision.

ⒶⓈ🅚 ⊠ ⓛⓜ 🛏 🖵 ⇌

◇ **▽▽▽▽** **Palm Coast Villas** Ⓜ ❀
(386) 445-3525. **$69-$79, 7 day notice.** 5454 N Oceanshore Blvd
32137. I-95, exit 289, 2.8 mi e to SR A1A, then 1.8 mi n. Ext corridors.
Pets: $5 daily fee/pet. Designated rooms, service with restrictions, super-
vision. 🅂🄰🅅🄴 ⊠ 🛏 💻 ⩘

PANAMA CITY

◇ **▽▽▽▽** **Comfort Inn & Conference Center** Ⓗ
(850) 769-6969. **$79-$159, 3 day notice.** 1013 E 23rd St 32405. SR
368, just w of jct US 231. Ext corridors. **Pets:** Other species. $50 deposit/
room, $10 one-time fee/pet. Designated rooms, service with restrictions,
supervision. 🅂🄰🅅🄴 ⊠ 🛏 💻 ⩘

▽▽▽ **Super 8** Ⓜ
(850) 784-1988. **$49-$129.** 207 Hwy 231 N 32405. Just n of jct US 98.
Ext/int corridors. **Pets:** Small, dogs only. $15 daily fee/pet. Service with
restrictions, crate. 🄰🅂🄺 ⊠ 🛏 💻 ⩘

PANAMA CITY BEACH

◇ **▽▽▽▽** **La Quinta Inn & Suites Panama City**
Beach Ⓗ ❀
(850) 234-3133. **$69-$194.** 7115 Coastal Palms Blvd 32408. 2 mi s of
US 98. Int corridors. **Pets:** Medium, other species. Service with restrictions, supervision. 🄴🄲🄾 🅂🄰🅅🄴 ⊠ 🛢🄼 🛏 💻 ⩘

PENSACOLA

▽▽▽ **La Quinta Inn Pensacola** Ⓗ ❀
(850) 474-0411. **$59-$149.** 7750 N Davis Hwy 32514-7557. I-10, exit 13,
just n. Ext corridors. **Pets:** Medium, other species. Service with restrictions, supervision. 🄰🅂🄺 ⊠ 🛏 💻 ⩘

◇ **▽▽▽** **Red Roof Inn** Ⓜ
(850) 476-7960. **Call for rates.** 7340 Plantation Rd 32504. I-10, exit 13,
just s. Ext corridors. **Pets:** Large. Service with restrictions, crate.
🅂🄰🅅🄴 ⊠ 🛏

▽▽▽▽ **Residence Inn By Marriott** Ⓗ
(850) 479-1000. **$161-$197.** 7230 Plantation Rd 32504. I-10, exit 13, just
s, then 0.3 mi w. Ext corridors. **Pets:** Small. $100 one-time fee/room.
Service with restrictions. ⊠ 🛢🄼 🛏 💻 ⩘ 🄍

▽▽▽▽ **TownPlace Suites by Marriott–Pensacola** Ⓗ ❀
(850) 484-7022. **$94-$114.** 481 Creighton Rd 32504. I-10, exit 13, 0.3 mi
s, then just w. Int corridors. **Pets:** $100 one-time fee/room. Designated
rooms, service with restrictions, supervision. 🄴🄲🄾 ⊠ 🛏 💻 ⩘

PERRY

◇ **▽▽▽** **Best Budget Inn** Ⓜ ❀
(850) 584-6231. **$56-$62.** 2220 US 19 S 32348. US 19 and 98, 0.4 mi s
of jct US 221. Ext corridors. **Pets:** Medium. $10 daily fee/pet. Designated
rooms, service with restrictions. 🅂🄰🅅🄴 ⊠ 🛏 💻 ⩘

PORT CHARLOTTE

▽▽▽ **Country Inn & Suites By Carlson** Ⓗ
(941) 235-1035. **$82-$160.** 24244 Corporate Ct 33954. I-75, exit 170, just
w on Kings Hwy (CR 769). Int corridors. **Pets:** Accepted.
🄰🅂🄺 ⊠ 🛢🄼 🛏 💻 ⩘

◇ **▽▽** **Days Inn of Port Charlotte** Ⓗ
(941) 627-8900. **$59-$139.** 1941 Tamiami Tr 33948. On US 41, 2.3 mi s
of jct Toledo Blade Blvd (CR 779). Ext corridors. **Pets:** Accepted.
🄰🅂🄺 ⊠ 🛏 💻 🍴 ⩘

PORT ST. JOE

◇ **▽▽▽▽** **MainStay Suites** Ⓗ
(850) 229-6246. **$85-$170.** 3951 E Hwy 98 32456. 3 mi e of center. Int
corridors. **Pets:** Small. $25 daily fee/room. Supervision.
🄴🄲🄾 🅂🄰🅅🄴 ⊠ 🛢🄼 🛏 💻 ⩘

PORT ST. LUCIE

▽▽▽ **Holiday Inn-Port St Lucie** Ⓗ
(772) 337-2200. **Call for rates.** 10120 S Federal Hwy, Rt 1 34952. US
1, 0.5 mi n of jct SR 716 (Port St Lucie Blvd). Int corridors.
Pets: Accepted. 🄴🄲🄾 ⊠ 🛏 💻 🍴 ⩘

▽▽ **MainStay Suites at PGA Village** Ⓗ
(772) 460-8882. **$70-$170.** 8501 Champions Way 34986. I-95, exit 121,
just w. Int corridors. **Pets:** Accepted. ⊠ 🛏 💻 ⩘

PUNTA GORDA

◇ **▽▽▽▽** **Best Western Waterfront** Ⓗ
(941) 639-1165. **$69-$169.** 300 Retta Esplanade 33950. Jct US 41
southbound, just s of jct US 41 northbound. Int corridors. **Pets:** Accepted.
🅂🄰🅅🄴 🛏 💻 🍴 ⩘ 🄍

◇ **▽▽▽▽** **Wyvern Hotel** Ⓗ
(941) 639-7700. **$119-$279.** 101 E Retta Esplanade 33950. Jct US 41
northbound; just e of jct US 41 southbound. Int corridors. **Pets:** Accepted.
🅂🄰🅅🄴 ⊠ 🛏 💻 🍴 ⩘

QUINCY

▽▽▽ **Allison House Inn** 🄱🄱
(850) 875-2511. **$85-$175, 21 day notice.** 215 N Madison St 32351.
Just e of town center; in historic district. Int corridors. **Pets:** Small, dogs
only. Designated rooms, service with restrictions, supervision. 🄰🅂🄺 ⊠

RIVER RANCH

▽▽▽ **Westgate River Ranch Resort** Ⓜ
(863) 892-1321. **$71-$170.** 3200 River Ranch Rd 33867. I-4, exit 55,
24.8 mi s on US 27, then 25.5 mi e on SR 60; Florida Tpke, exit 193
(Yeehaw Jct), 21.2 mi w. Ext corridors. **Pets:** Accepted.
⊠ 🛏 💻 🍴 ⩘ 🄍

▽▽▽ **Westgate River Ranch Resort Cabins** 🄲🄾
(863) 692-1321. **$80-$199, 7 day notice.** 3200 River Ranch Blvd
33867. I-4, exit 55, 24.8 mi s on US 27, then 25.5 mi e on SR 60;
Florida Tpke, exit 193 (Yeehaw Junction), 21.2 mi w. Ext corridors.
Pets: Accepted. 🄰🅂🄺 ⊠ 🛏 💻 🍴 ⩘ 🄍

ST. AUGUSTINE

◇ **▽▽▽** **Alhambra Inn & Suites** Ⓗ
(904) 824-2883. **$69-$79.** 2700 N Ponce de Leon Blvd 32084. On US 1,
jct SR 16. Ext corridors. **Pets:** Small, dogs only. $25 one-time fee/room.
Designated rooms, service with restrictions, supervision.
🅂🄰🅅🄴 ⊠ 🛢🄼 🛏 💻 🍴 ⩘

▽▽▽▽ **Bayfront Marin House Bed & Breakfast Inn** 🄱🄱
(904) 824-4301. **$119-$279, 8 day notice.** 142 Avenida Menendez
32084. 1 blk s of Bridge of Lions. Ext corridors. **Pets:** Other species. $25
daily fee/pet. Designated rooms, service with restrictions. 🄰🅂🄺 ⊠

▽▽▽▽ **Bayfront Westcott House** 🄱🄱
(904) 825-4602. **$119-$379, 7 day notice.** 146 Avenida Menendez
32084-5049. 1 blk s of Bridge of Lions. Ext/int corridors. **Pets:** Accepted.
🄰🅂🄺 ⊠

◇ **▽▽▽** **Best Western St. Augustine I-95** Ⓗ
(904) 829-1999. **$69-$139.** 2445 SR 16 32092. I-95, exit 318, just w. Ext
corridors. **Pets:** Medium, other species. $10 daily fee/room. Designated
rooms, service with restrictions, crate. 🅂🄰🅅🄴 ⊠ 💻 ⩘

◇ **▽▽▽▽** **Casablanca Inn on the Bay** 🄱🄱
(904) 829-0928. **$99-$379, 7 day notice.** 24 Avenida Menendez 32084.
US 1 business route and SR A1A, then just n. Ext corridors.
Pets: Accepted. 🅂🄰🅅🄴 ⊠ 🛏

▽▽▽ **Casa De Solana Bed & Breakfast Inn** 🄱🄱
(904) 824-3555. **Call for rates.** 21 Aviles St 32084. Aviles St at Cadiz
St; in historic district. Int corridors. **Pets:** Accepted. ⊠ 🛏 🆉

△△△ ▼▼▼ ▼▼▼ **Casa Monica Hotel** 🅷 ❖
(904) 827-1888. **$189-$379, 3 day notice.** 95 Cordova St 32084. Downtown; across from Lightner Museum and Flagler College. Int corridors. **Pets:** Small, dogs only. $150 one-time fee/pet. Designated rooms, service with restrictions, crate. 🅴🅲🅾 🆂🅰🆅🅴 ✖ 🔌 💻 🍴 ➿ ✖

▼▼ **Castle Garden Bed & Breakfast** 🅱🅱
(904) 829-3839. **$99-$229, 7 day notice.** 15 Shenandoah St 32084. From jct US 1, 0.5 mi e on W Castillo Dr, then just e crossing jct of A1A. Int corridors. **Pets:** Accepted. 🅰🆂🅺 ✖ ⊘

△△△ ▼ **The Cozy Inn** 🅼 ❖
(904) 824-2449. **$49-$209, 30 day notice.** 202 San Marco Ave 32084. 0.3 mi s of jct SR 16. Ext corridors. **Pets:** Medium. $20 one-time fee/room. Service with restrictions. 🆂🅰🆅🅴 ✖ 🔌 💻

▼ **The Inn At Camachee Harbor** 🅷 ❖
(904) 825-0003. **$139-$199, 7 day notice.** 201 Yacht Club Dr 32084. On Intracoastal Waterway at west side of Usine Bridge; 1 mi e of jct N SR A1A and San Marco Blvd. Ext/int corridors. **Pets:** Medium, other species. $15 daily fee/pet. Designated rooms, service with restrictions, crate. 🅰🆂🅺 ✖ 🔌 💻

▼▼▼ **La Quinta Inn & Suites** 🅷 ❖
(904) 209-2580. **$69-$209.** 250 Prime Outlet Blvd 32084. I-95, exit 318 (SR 16), just e, then n. Int corridors. **Pets:** Medium, other species. Service with restrictions, supervision. 🅰🆂🅺 ✖ 🔌 💻 ➿

△△△ ▼▼ **Rodeway Inn** 🅷
(904) 829-6581. **$52-$99.** 2800 N Ponce de Leon Blvd 32084. US 1 at SR 16; in historic district. Ext corridors. **Pets:** Medium, other species. $10 daily fee/pet. Designated rooms, service with restrictions, supervision. 🆂🅰🆅🅴 ✖ 🔌 💻 ➿

▼▼ **St. Francis Inn** 🅱🅱
(904) 824-6068. **Call for rates.** 279 St George St 32084. Just s; in historic district. Ext/int corridors. **Pets:** Accepted. ✖ 🔌 💻 ➿

ST. AUGUSTINE BEACH

△△△ ▼▼▼ **Comfort Inn at St. Augustine Beach** 🅷
(904) 471-1474. **$65-$160.** 901 A1A Beach Blvd 32080. On Business Rt SR A1A, 1.6 mi s of jct SR 312 and A1A. Ext corridors. **Pets:** Other species. $10 one-time fee/pet. Service with restrictions. 🆂🅰🆅🅴 ✖ 🔌 💻 ➿

△△△ ▼▼▼ **Holiday Inn-St Augustine Beach** 🅷 ❖
(904) 471-2555. **$109-$189.** 860 A1A Beach Blvd 32080. On Business Rt SR A1A, 1.8 mi s of jct SR 312 and A1A. Int corridors. **Pets:** Medium, other species. $20 daily fee/pet. Designated rooms, no service, supervision. 🅴🅲🅾 🆂🅰🆅🅴 ✖ 🅼 🔌 💻 🍴 ➿

△△△ ▼▼▼ **House of Sea and Sun** 🅱🅱
(904) 461-1716. **$99-$225, 7 day notice.** 2 B St 32080. Jct SR 312 and A1A, 1 mi e, s on A1A Beach Blvd. Ext/int corridors. **Pets:** Accepted. 🆂🅰🆅🅴 ✖

▼▼ **St. Augustine Island Inn** 🅷
(904) 471-1440. **$59-$249, 7 day notice.** 894 A1A Beach Blvd 32080. On Business Rt SR A1A, 2 mi s of jct SR 312 and A1A. Int corridors. **Pets:** Medium. $20 one-time fee/pet. Service with restrictions, supervision. 🅰🆂🅺 ✖ 🔌 💻 ➿

ST. PETERSBURG-CLEARWATER AND BEACHES METROPOLITAN AREA

CLEARWATER

△△△ ▼▼▼ **Best Western Clearwater Grand Hotel & Suites** 🅷
(727) 799-1181. **$79-$99.** 20967 US 19 N 33765. On US 19, just n of jct SR 60. Ext/int corridors. **Pets:** Accepted. 🆂🅰🆅🅴 ✖ 🅼 🔌 💻 🍴 ➿ ✖

▼▼▼ **Candlewood Suites Clearwater-St Petersburg** 🅷
(727) 573-3344. **Call for rates.** 13231 49th St N 33762. I-275, exit 31 southbound, 3 mi w on SR 688, then just s; exit 30 northbound, 1.4 mi w on SR 686, 1.6 mi w on SR 688 (Ulmerton Rd), then just s. Int corridors. **Pets:** Accepted. ✖ 🅼 🔌 💻 ➿

△△△ ▼▼▼ **Days Inn Clearwater/St. Petersburg Airport** 🅷
(727) 573-3334. **$59-$109.** 3910 Ulmerton Rd 33762. I-275, exit 31 southbound, 2 mi w on SR 688; exit 30 northbound, 1.4 mi w on SR 686, 0.7 mi w. Int corridors. **Pets:** Small, other species. $25 one-time fee/room. Designated rooms, service with restrictions. 🆂🅰🆅🅴 ✖ 🅼 🔌 💻 ➿

▼▼ **Extended StayAmerica-St. Petersburg-Clearwater** 🅷
(727) 561-9032. **$49-$84.** 3089 Executive Dr 33762. I-275, exit 31 southbound; exit 30 northbound, 1.8 mi w on SR 699, just n on 34th St N, then 0.3 mi ne. Int corridors. **Pets:** Other species. $25 daily fee/room. Designated rooms, service with restrictions, crate. 🅰🆂🅺 ✖ 🅼 🔌 💻

▼▼ **Homestead Studio Suites Hotel-St Petersburg-Clearwater** 🅼
(727) 572-4800. **$59-$84.** 2311 Ulmerton Rd 33762. I-275, exit 31 southbound, 1.3 mi w on SR 688; exit 30 northbound, 1.4 mi w on SR 686; 0.6 mi on SR 688. Ext corridors. **Pets:** Other species. $25 daily fee/room. Designated rooms, service with restrictions, crate. 🅰🆂🅺 ✖ 🅼 🔌 💻 ➿

▼▼ **Homewood Suites by Hilton** 🅷
(727) 573-1500. **$159-$169.** 2233 Ulmerton Rd 33762. I-275, exit 31 southbound, 1.3 mi w on SR 688 (Ulmerton Rd); exit 30 northbound, 1.4 mi w on SR 686, 0.6 mi e on SR 688. Int corridors. **Pets:** Accepted. ✖ 🅼 🔌 💻 ➿

▼▼ **Howard Johnson Inn & Suites** 🅼
(727) 796-0135. **$60-$130.** 27988 US Hwy 19 N 33761. On US 19, 0.6 mi n of jct SR 580. Ext corridors. **Pets:** Medium, other species. $50 deposit/room, $10 daily fee/pet. Designated rooms, service with restrictions. 🅰🆂🅺 ✖ 🔌 💻 ➿

▼▼ **La Quinta Inn Tampa Bay (Clearwater Airport)** 🅷 ❖
(727) 572-7222. **$49-$94.** 3301 Ulmerton Rd 33762. I-275, exit 31 southbound; exit 30 northbound, 1.7 mi w on SR 688; in The Centres Office Park. Int corridors. **Pets:** Medium, other species. Service with restrictions, supervision. 🅰🆂🅺 ✖ 🔌 💻 ➿ ✖

△△△ ▼▼▼ **Residence Inn by Marriott Clearwater Downtown** 🅷
(727) 562-5400. **$139-$229.** 940 Court St 33756. On SR 60 at jct S Prospect Ave. Int corridors. **Pets:** Other species. $100 one-time fee/room. Designated rooms, service with restrictions, supervision. 🆂🅰🆅🅴 ✖ 🅼 🔌 💻 ➿

△△△ ▼▼▼ **Residence Inn by Marriott St. Petersburg/Clearwater** 🅷 ❖
(727) 573-4444. **$199-$229.** 5050 Ulmerton Rd 33760. I-275, exit 31 southbound, 3.1 mi w on SR 688; exit 30 northbound, 1.4 mi w on SR 686, then 1.7 mi w on SR 688. Ext corridors. **Pets:** Medium. $100 one-time fee/room. Service with restrictions, supervision. 🆂🅰🆅🅴 ✖ 🔌 💻 ➿ ✖

AAA ▼▼◆◆ Super 8 Clearwater/St. Petersburg Airport/ Tampa Bay H

(727) 572-8881. **$40-$200.** 13260 34th St N 33762. I-275, exit 31 southbound; 1.8 mi w on SR 688 (Ulmerton Rd), then just s; exit 30 northbound, 1.4 mi w on SR 686. Int corridors. **Pets:** Large. $10 daily fee/pet. Designated rooms, service with restrictions, supervision.

SAVE ⊠ 🖥 💻 🏊

▼▼◆◆ TownePlace Suites by Marriott St. Petersburg/Clearwater H

(727) 299-9229. **$139-$189.** 13200 49th St N 33762. I-275, exit 31 southbound; exit 30 northbound, 3 mi w on SR 688, then just s; in Turtle Creek. Int corridors. **Pets:** Accepted. ⊠ &M 🖥 💻 🏊

INDIAN ROCKS BEACH

▼▼◆ Sea Star Motel & Apartments M ✿

(727) 596-2525. **$75-$130, 30 day notice.** 1805 Gulf Blvd 33785. On SR 699, 1.2 mi n of jct SR 688 (Walsingham Rd). Ext corridors. **Pets:** Other species. $10 daily fee/pet. No service.

⊠ 🖥 💻 ⊠ ✂

INDIAN SHORES

AAA ▼▼◆◆ Sea Club Resort Condominiums CO

(727) 596-2046. **$80-$157 (no credit cards), 45 day notice.** 19725 Gulf Blvd 33785. On SR 699, 1.1 mi n of jct CR 694. Ext corridors. **Pets:** Accepted. SAVE ⊠ 🖥 🏊 ⊠

LARGO

AAA ▼▼◆◆ Hampton Inn & Suites H

(727) 585-1000. **Call for rates.** 100 E Bay Dr 33770. On SR 686, 3.4 mi w of jct US 19; at jct Alt US 19. Int corridors. **Pets:** Accepted.

ECO SAVE ⊠ &M 🖥 💻 🏊

MADEIRA BEACH

AAA ▼▼◆◆ Snug Harbor Inn Waterfront Bed & Breakfast M ✿

(727) 395-9256. **$75-$140, 21 day notice.** 13655 Gulf Blvd 33708. On SR 699, 0.9 mi s of jct Tom Stuart Cswy. Ext corridors. **Pets:** Other species. Service with restrictions. SAVE ⊠ 🖥 💻 🏊 ⊠

NEW PORT RICHEY

AAA ▼▼◆ River Side Inn M

(727) 845-4990. **$50-$100.** 7631 US 19 34652. On US 19, 0.8 mi n of jct Main St. Ext corridors. **Pets:** Medium. $6 daily fee/room. Designated rooms, no service, supervision. SAVE ⊠ 🖥 💻 🏊

OLDSMAR

AAA ▼▼◆◆ Residence Inn Tampa/Oldsmar H

(813) 818-9400. **$189-$259.** 4012 Tampa Rd 34677. On SR 580; jct St. Pete Dr. Int corridors. **Pets:** Medium, other species. $100 one-time fee/room. Designated rooms, service with restrictions.

SAVE ⊠ &M 🖥 💻 ⊠

PALM HARBOR

AAA ▼▼◆◆ Innisbrook Resort & Golf Club CO

(727) 942-2000. **$109-$509, 3 day notice.** 36750 US Hwy 19 N 34684. On US 19, 2.8 mi s of jct SR 582; at jct Olde Post Rd, follow signs. Int corridors. **Pets:** Accepted. SAVE ⊠ 🖥 💻 ❌ 🏊 ⊠

▼▼◆ Knights Inn-Clearwater/Palm Harbor M

(727) 789-2002. **$45-$85.** 34106 US 19 N 34684. On US 19, 1.8 mi n of CR 752 (Tampa Rd). Ext corridors. **Pets:** Other species. $10 daily fee/room. Designated rooms, service with restrictions.

A$K ⊠ &M 🖥 💻 🏊

PINELLAS PARK

▼▼◆◆ La Quinta Inn Tampa (Pinellas Park/Clearwater) H ✿

(727) 545-5611. **$59-$114.** 7500 US Hwy 19 N 33781. I-275, exit 28, 1.4 mi s on Gandy Blvd (SR 694), then just n. Ext/int corridors. **Pets:** Medium, other species. Service with restrictions, supervision.

A$K ⊠ &M 🖥 💻 🏊

PORT RICHEY

▼▼◆ Comfort Inn M

(727) 863-3336. **Call for rates.** 11810 US 19 34668. On US 19, just s of jct SR 52. Ext corridors. **Pets:** Accepted. ⊠ 🖥 💻 🏊

ST. PETE BEACH

AAA ▼◆ Bay Palms Waterfront Resort M ✿

(727) 360-7642. **$49-$189, 14 day notice.** 4237 Gulf Blvd 33706. On SR 699, 0.6 mi n of Pinellas Bayway. Ext corridors. **Pets:** Large, other species. $50 deposit/room, $10 daily fee/pet.

ECO SAVE ⊠ 🖥 🏊 ⊠

AAA ▼▼◆ Bayview Plaza Waterfront Resort M ✿

(727) 367-2791. **$55-$229, 14 day notice.** 4321 Gulf Blvd 33706. On SR 699; 0.6 mi n of Pinellas Bayway. Ext/int corridors. **Pets:** Large, other species. $50 deposit/room, $10 daily fee/pet. ECO SAVE ⊠ 🖥

AAA ▼▼◆◆ Beach House Suites By The Don Cesar H

(727) 363-0001. **$169-$524, 3 day notice.** 3860 Gulf Blvd 33706. On SR 699, 0.4 mi n of jct Pinellas Bayway. Ext corridors. **Pets:** Accepted.

SAVE ⊠ 🖥 💻 🏊 ⊠

AAA ▼▼◆ ▼◆ Don CeSar Beach Resort, a Loews Hotel H

(727) 360-1881. **$159-$689, 3 day notice.** 3400 Gulf Blvd 33706. On SR 699, jct Pinellas Bayway. Int corridors. **Pets:** Accepted.

ECO SAVE ⊠ &M 🖥 💻 ❌ 🏊 ⊠

ST. PETERSBURG

AAA ▼▼◆◆ Best Western Gateway Inn H

(727) 525-1800. **$100.** 6638 4th St N 33702. I-275, exit 26, 1.7 mi e on 54th Ave N (CR 202), then 0.8 mi n. Int corridors. **Pets:** Accepted.

SAVE ⊠ &M 🖥 💻

▼▼◆◆ La Quinta Inn Tampa Bay Area (St. Petersburg) M ✿

(727) 527-8421. **$59-$114.** 4999 34th St N 33714. I-275, exit 26 southbound; exit 26B northbound, just w on 54th Ave N, then just s on US 19. Ext corridors. **Pets:** Medium, other species. Service with restrictions, supervision. A$K ⊠ &M 🖥 💻 🏊

▼▼◆◆ Mansion House B & B BB ✿

(727) 821-9391. **$159-$260, 7 day notice.** 105 5th Ave NE 33701. 0.5 mi n at 1st St N. Ext/int corridors. **Pets:** Very small, dogs only. $25 daily fee/room. Designated rooms, crate. A$K ⊠ 🖥 🏊

AAA ▼▼◆ Ramada Inn Mirage M ✿

(727) 525-1181. **$60-$70.** 5005 34th St N 33714. I-275, exit 26 southbound; exit 26B northbound, 0.8 mi w on 54th Ave N, then 0.3 mi s on US 19. Ext corridors. **Pets:** Medium. $25 one-time fee/pet. Designated rooms, service with restrictions, supervision.

SAVE 🖥 💻 ❌ 🏊

TREASURE ISLAND

AAA ▼▼◆◆ Residence Inn St. Petersburg/Treasure Island H

(727) 367-2761. **$219-$299.** 11908 Gulf Blvd 33706. On SR 699, 0.7 mi n of jct Treasure Island Cswy. Ext/int corridors. **Pets:** Accepted.

SAVE ⊠ &M 🖥 💻 🏊

END METROPOLITAN AREA

SANTA ROSA BEACH

▼▼▼▼ A Highlands House Bed & Breakfast Inn **BB**
(850) 267-0110. **Call for rates.** 4193 W Scenic CR 30A 32459. US 98, 2 mi s on CR 393, just e. Int corridors. **Pets:** Accepted. ⊠ 🎵 🐾

SARASOTA

▼▼ Comfort Inn, Sarasota I-75 **H**
(941) 921-7750. **$80-$180.** 5778 Clark Rd 34233. I-75, exit 205, just w on SR 72. Int corridors. **Pets:** $10 daily fee/room. Designated rooms, service with restrictions, supervision. **ECO** ⊠ ৬M 🔋 🖥 🏊

♨♨♨ ▼▼▼▼ Holiday Inn Express-Siesta Key/Sarasota **H**
(941) 924-4900. **Call for rates.** 6600 S Tamiami Tr 34231. On US 41, just s of jct SR 72 (Clark Rd/Stickney Point Rd). Ext corridors. **Pets:** Medium, dogs only. $150 deposit/room, $50 one-time fee/pet. Designated rooms, service with restrictions, supervision.
SAVE ⊠ ৬M 🔋 🖥 🏊

▼▼▼ Homewood Suites by Hilton **H**
(941) 365-7300. **$149-$169.** 3470 Fruitville Rd 34237. I-75, exit 210, 3.2 mi w on SR 780 (Fruitville Rd). Int corridors. **Pets:** Accepted.
ECO ⊠ ৬M 🔋 🖥 🏊 🐾

▼▼▼ Hotel Indigo **H**
(941) 487-3800. **$95-$274.** 1223 Boulevard of the Arts 34236. Jct US 41 (N Tamiami Tr). Int corridors. **Pets:** Accepted.
ASK ⊠ ৬M 🔋 🖥 🍴

♨♨♨ ▼▼▼▼ Hyatt Regency Sarasota **H**
(941) 953-1234. **$99-$369, 3 day notice.** 1000 Boulevard of the Arts 34236. Just w of jct US 41 (Tamiami Tr). Int corridors. **Pets:** Medium. $150 one-time fee/room. Designated rooms, service with restrictions, supervision. **ECO** **SAVE** ⊠ ৬M 🔋 🖥 🍴 🏊 🐾

▼▼▼ La Quinta Inn & Suites Sarasota Airport **H** 🐾
(941) 366-5128. **$69-$184.** 1803 N Tamiami Tr 34234. On US 41, 1 mi n of jct SR 780 (Fruitville Rd). Int corridors. **Pets:** Medium, other species. Service with restrictions, supervision. **ASK** ⊠ ৬M 🔋 🖥 🏊

▼▼▼ Residence Inn Sarasota **H** 🐾
(941) 358-1468. **$149-$239.** 1040 University Pkwy 34234. Just e of jct US 41 (Tamiami Tr). Int corridors. **Pets:** Other species. $75 one-time fee/pet. Service with restrictions, crate.
ECO ⊠ ৬M 🔋 🖥 🏊 🐾

♨♨♨ ▼▼▼▼ The Ritz-Carlton, Sarasota **H**
(941) 309-2000. **$179-$494.** 1111 Ritz-Carlton Dr 34236. On US 41, jct John Ringling Blvd. Int corridors. **Pets:** Small, dogs only. $125 one-time fee/room. Designated rooms, service with restrictions, crate.
ECO **SAVE** ⊠ ৬M 🔋 🖥 🍴 🏊 🐾

SEBRING

♨♨♨ ▼▼▼▼ Four Points by Sheraton Sebring Chateau Elan **H**
(863) 655-7200. **Call for rates.** 150 Midway Dr 33870. US 27, 2.2 mi e on US 98; at entrance to Sebring International Raceway. Int corridors.
Pets: Accepted. **ECO** **SAVE** ⊠ 🔋 🖥 🍴 🏊 🐾

♨♨♨ ▼▼▼▼ Inn On The Lakes **H**
(863) 471-9400. **$69-$219, 3 day notice.** 3100 Golfview Rd 33875. On US 27, 1.5 mi n of jct SR 17. Ext/int corridors. **Pets:** $40 one-time fee/room. Designated rooms, service with restrictions.
SAVE ⊠ 🔋 🖥 🍴 🏊

♨♨♨ ▼ Kenilworth Lodge **H**
(863) 385-0111. **$75-$205, 3 day notice.** 1610 Lakeview Dr 33870. On US 27, 1 mi e on SR 17. Ext/int corridors. **Pets:** Other species. $15 daily fee/pet. Designated rooms, service with restrictions, supervision.
SAVE ⊠ 🔋 🖥 🏊 🐾

♨♨♨ ▼▼▼▼ Residence Inn by Marriott–Sebring **H** 🐾
(863) 314-9100. **$159-$227.** 3221 Tubbs Rd 33875. On US 27, 1 mi n of jct SR 17. Int corridors. **Pets:** Other species. $15 daily fee/room. Designated rooms, service with restrictions, crate.
SAVE ⊠ 🔋 🖥 🏊 🐾

SIESTA KEY

♨♨♨ ▼▼▼▼ Tropical Breeze Resort & Spa of Siesta Key **CO** 🐾
(941) 349-1125. **$89-$359, 14 day notice.** 153 Avenida Messina 34242. Jct Ocean Blvd; in Siesta Village. Ext corridors. **Pets:** Dogs only. $10 daily fee/room. Service with restrictions. **SAVE** ⊠ 🔋 🖥 🏊 🐾

♨♨♨ ▼▼▼ Tropical Breeze Vacations **M**
(941) 349-1125. **$99-$369.** 153 Avenida Messina 34242. Jct Ocean Blvd; in Siesta Village. Ext corridors. **Pets:** Accepted.
SAVE ⊠ 🔋 🖥 🏊 🐾

SPRING HILL

♨♨♨ ▼▼▼ Quality Inn Weeki Wachee **M**
(352) 596-2007. **$89-$149.** 6172 Commercial Way 34606. On US 19, jct SR 50 (Cortez Blvd). Ext corridors. **Pets:** Other species. $15 daily fee/pet. Service with restrictions, supervision.
SAVE ⊠ 🔋 🖥 🍴 🏊 🐾

STARKE

♨♨♨ ▼▼▼ Best Western Starke **H**
(904) 964-6744. **$75-$130.** 1290 N Temple Ave 32091. 1 mi n on US 301 from jct SR 100. Ext corridors. **Pets:** Small. $10 daily fee/pet. Designated rooms, service with restrictions, supervision.
SAVE ⊠ 🔋 🖥 🏊

STEINHATCHEE

▼▼▼ Steinhatchee Landing Resort **VH** 🐾
(352) 498-3513. **$140-$649, 14 day notice.** SR 51 32359. SR 51, 8 mi w of jct US 19/98. Ext corridors. **Pets:** Medium, dogs only. $100 deposit/room. Designated rooms, service with restrictions, supervision.
ASK ⊠ 🔋 🖥 🏊 🐾

STUART

♨♨♨ ▼▼▼ Monterey Inn & Marina **M**
(772) 283-3500. **$79-$129.** 300 SW Monterey Rd 34994. Jct SR 76 and CR 714, just w. Ext corridors. **Pets:** Accepted. **SAVE** ⊠ 🔋

♨♨♨ ▼▼▼ Pirate's Cove Resort & Marina **H**
(772) 287-2500. **$150-$225.** 4307 SE Bayview St 34997. 0.3 mi e of SR A1A. Ext corridors. **Pets:** Accepted. **SAVE** ⊠ 🔋 🖥 🍴 🏊 🐾

TALLAHASSEE

♨♨♨ ▼▼▼ Best Western Pride Inn & Suites **H**
(850) 656-6312. **$70-$190.** 2016 Apalachee Pkwy 32301. 1 mi se of US 27. Ext corridors. **Pets:** Other species. $10 daily fee/pet. Service with restrictions, crate. **SAVE** ⊠ 🔋 🖥 🏊

♨♨♨ ▼▼▼ Best Western Seminole Inn **M**
(850) 656-2938. **$70-$180, 3 day notice.** 6737 Mahan Dr 32308. I-10, exit 209A, just w on US 90. Ext corridors. **Pets:** Accepted.
SAVE ⊠ 🔋 🖥 🏊

♨♨♨ ▼▼▼ Days Inn University Center **H**
(850) 222-3219. **$50-$190.** 1350 W Tennessee St 32304. 1.6 mi w of US 27. Int corridors. **Pets:** Accepted. **SAVE** ⊠ 🔋 🖥 🏊

♨♨♨ ▼▼▼ Econo Lodge **M**
(850) 385-6155. **$40-$129.** 2681 N Monroe St 32303. I-10, exit 199, 0.5 mi s. Ext corridors. **Pets:** Large, other species. $15 one-time fee/room. Service with restrictions, supervision. **SAVE** ⊠ 🔋 🖥

AAA ▼▼ Four Points by Sheraton Tallahassee North H
(850) 671-2020. **$85-$225.** 1978 Village Green Way 32308. I-10, exit 203, southeast corner. Int corridors. **Pets:** Accepted.
ECO SAVE X &M ▯ 🖵 ∼

▼▼▼▼ Holiday Inn Capital East H
(850) 877-3171. **$89-$161.** 1355 Apalachee Pkwy 32301. 1.3 mi se on US 27. Int corridors. **Pets:** Accepted. ASK X ▯ 🖵 ❯ ∼

▼▼▼▼ Homewood Suites by Hilton H
(850) 402-9400. **$149-$159.** 2987 Apalachee Pkwy 32301. US 27, 3.5 mi s. Int corridors. **Pets:** Accepted. ECO X ▯ 🖵 ∼ X

▼▼▼▼ La Quinta Inn Tallahassee (North) H ❀
(850) 385-7172. **$49-$119.** 2905 N Monroe St 32303-3636. I-10, exit 199, just s on US 27. Ext corridors. **Pets:** Medium, other species. Service with restrictions, supervision. ASK X ▯ 🖵 ∼

▼▼▼▼ La Quinta Inn Tallahassee (South) H ❀
(850) 878-5099. **$49-$119.** 2850 Apalachee Pkwy 32301-3608. 3 mi se on US 27. Ext corridors. **Pets:** Medium, other species. Service with restrictions, supervision. ASK X &M ▯ 🖵 ∼

▼ Motel 6 #1073 H
(850) 877-6171. **$35-$48.** 1027 Apalachee Pkwy 32301. 1 mi se on US 27. Ext corridors. **Pets:** Other species. Service with restrictions, supervision. X ▯ ∼

▼ Motel 6 #1191 H
(850) 386-7878. **$33-$45.** 2738 N Monroe St 32303. I-10, exit 199, just s on US 27. Ext corridors. **Pets:** Other species. Service with restrictions, supervision. X ▯ ∼

▼ Motel 6 #420 M
(850) 668-2600. **$39-$51.** 1481 Timberlane Rd 32308. I-10, exit 203, just n, then w. Ext corridors. **Pets:** Other species. Service with restrictions, supervision. X ∼

▼▼ Ramada Conference Center H
(850) 386-1027. **$59-$189, 3 day notice.** 2900 N Monroe St 32303. I-10, exit 199, just s. Ext/int corridors. **Pets:** Accepted.
ASK X ▯ 🖵 ❯ ∼

▼▼ Red Roof Inn M
(850) 385-7884. **$40-$65.** 2930 Hospitality St 32303. I-10, exit 199, just sw off US 27. Ext corridors. **Pets:** Large. Service with restrictions, crate.
ASK X &M ▯

AAA ▼▼▼▼ Residence Inn by Marriott Tallahassee Universities at the Capitol H ❀
(850) 329-9080. **$189-$219.** 600 W Gaines St 32304. 0.5 mi w of S Monroe St; downtown. Int corridors. **Pets:** Medium, other species. $100 one-time fee/room. SAVE X &M ▯ 🖵 ❯ ∼

▼▼▼▼ Residence Inn Capital Circle/I-10 H
(850) 422-0093. **$144-$194.** 1880 Raymond Diehl Rd 32308. I-10, exit 203, just s. Int corridors. **Pets:** Accepted. ECO X &M ▯ 🖵 ∼

▼▼▼▼ Staybridge Suites Tallahassee H
(850) 219-7000. **Call for rates.** 1600 Summit Lake Dr 32317. I-10, exit 209B, just n. Int corridors. **Pets:** Accepted. ECO X ▯ 🖵 ∼

▼▼▼▼ StudioPLUS-Tallahassee-Killearn H
(850) 383-1700. **$64-$94.** 1950 Raymond Diehl Rd 32308. I-10, exit 203, 2.4 mi s, then just n. Int corridors. **Pets:** Other species. $25 daily fee/ room. Designated rooms, service with restrictions, crate.
X &M ▯ 🖵 ∼

AAA ▼ Super 8 H
(850) 386-8286. **$45-$150.** 2801 N Monroe St 32303. I-10, exit 199, just s. Ext corridors. **Pets:** $10 daily fee/room. Service with restrictions, supervision. SAVE X ▯ 🖵 ∼

▼▼▼▼ TownePlace Suites Tallahassee H
(850) 219-0122. **$139-$179.** 1876 Capital Cir NE 32308. 3.3 mi e on US 90, 1 mi n on US 319. Int corridors. **Pets:** Other species. $100 one-time fee/room. Designated rooms, service with restrictions, supervision.
ECO X &M ▯ 🖵 ∼

TAMPA METROPOLITAN AREA

BRANDON

▼▼ Homestead Studio Suites Hotel-Tampa/Brandon M
(813) 643-5900. **$59-$94.** 330 Grand Regency Blvd 33510. I-75, exit 257, just e on SR 60, then 0.4 mi n; in Regency Corporate Park. Ext corridors. **Pets:** Other species. $25 daily fee/room. Designated rooms, service with restrictions, crate. ASK X &M ▯ 🖵

▼▼▼▼ La Quinta Inn & Suites Tampa Bay (Brandon) H ❀
(813) 643-0574. **$59-$114.** 310 Grand Regency Blvd 33510. I-75, exit 257, just e on SR 60, then 0.5 mi n; in Regency Corporate Office. Int corridors. **Pets:** Medium, other species. Service with restrictions, supervision. ASK X &M ▯ 🖵 ∼

LUTZ

AAA ▼▼▼▼ Residence Inn by Marriott Tampa/Suncoast/Northpointe H ❀
(813) 792-8400. **$149-$189.** 2101 NorthPointe Pkwy 33558. Just s of jct SR 54; Suncoast Pkwy, exit 19, just e; in NorthPointe at Suncoast Crossings. Int corridors. **Pets:** $100 one-time fee/room. Service with restrictions, crate. ECO SAVE X &M ▯ 🖵 ∼

PLANT CITY

AAA ▼▼▼▼ Comfort Inn of Plant City H
(813) 707-6000. **$69-$249.** 2003 S Frontage Rd 33566. I-4, exit 22, just ne on Park Rd. Int corridors. **Pets:** Medium. $20 daily fee/pet. Service with restrictions, crate. SAVE X &M ▯ 🖵 ∼

▼▼▼▼ Red Rose Inn & Suites M
(813) 752-3141. **Call for rates.** 2011 N Wheeler St 33563. I-4, exit 21, 0.4 mi se; at jct SR 39. Ext corridors. **Pets:** Accepted.
X &M ▯ 🖵 ❯ ∼

RUSKIN

▼▼▼▼ Southern Comfort Bed & Breakfast BB ❀
(813) 645-6361. **$75-$195, 30 day notice.** 2409 Ravine Dr W 33570. Jct US 41, 1.1 mi sw on 1st St, just w on 24th Ave SW, then just s. Ext/ int corridors. **Pets:** Medium. $10 daily fee/pet. Designated rooms, crate.
ASK X ▯ 🖵 ∼ X ✆

SEFFNER

AAA ▼▼▼▼ Country Inn & Suites By Carlson, Tampa East H
(813) 675-8600. **$89-$199.** 11551 Discovery Ln 33584. I-4, exit 10, just n on CR 579. Int corridors. **Pets:** Small, other species. $25 daily fee/pet. Designated rooms, service with restrictions, crate.
SAVE X &M ▯ 🖵 ∼

TAMPA

▼▼▼▼ Baymont Inn & Suites Ⓜ

(813) 622-8557. **$79-$169.** 10007 Princess Palm Ave 33619. I-75, exit 260 southbound; exit 260B northbound, 0.5 mi w on SR 574 (Dr. Martin Luther King Jr Blvd), just s on Falkenburg Rd, then just w; in Sabal Corporate Park. Int corridors. **Pets:** Accepted. 🅰🆂🅺 ⊠ 🛋 📶 💻 ⇌

⨁ ▼▼▼ Best Western Brandon Hotel & Conference Center Ⓜ

(813) 621-5555. **$63-$83.** 9331 Adamo Dr 33619. I-75, exit 257, 1.2 mi w on SR 60. Ext corridors. **Pets:** Accepted.

ⓈⒶⓋⒺ ⊠ 🛋 💻 🍽 ⇌

⨁ ▼▼▼▼ Best Western Tampa Airport Inn and Suites ⒣ ❀

(813) 490-9090. **$75-$100.** 3826 W Waters Ave 33614. Just w of jct US 92 (Dale Mabry Hwy). Int corridors. **Pets:** Medium. $20 daily fee/pet. Service with restrictions, crate. ⓈⒶⓋⒺ ⊠ 🛋 📶 💻 ⇌ ⊠

⨁ ▼▼▼▼ Chase Suite Hotel Ⓜ

(813) 281-5677. **$149-$399.** 3075 N Rocky Point Dr 33607. I-275, exit 39 southbound; exit 39B northbound, 3 mi w on SR 60, then just n; in Rocky Point Harbour. Ext corridors. **Pets:** Small, other species. $20 daily fee/pet. Designated rooms, service with restrictions.

ⓈⒶⓋⒺ ⊠ 🛋 📶 💻 ⇌ ⊠

▼▼▼ Comfort Inn Hotel & Suites Tampa Stadium/Airport Ⓜ

(813) 877-6061. **$69-$89.** 4732 N Dale Mabry Hwy 33614. I-275, exit 41B, 2 mi n. Ext corridors. **Pets:** Accepted.

⊠ 📶 🛋 💻 ⇌ ⊠

▼▼▼ Extended StayAmerica-Tampa Airport-West Shore ⒣

(813) 873-2850. **$59-$94.** 4312 W Spruce St 33607. I-275, exit 40B, 0.6 mi n on Lois Ave, then just w. Int corridors. **Pets:** Other species. $25 daily fee/room. Designated rooms, service with restrictions, crate.

🅰🆂🅺 ⊠ 📶 🛋 💻 ⇌

▼▼▼▼ Extended Stay Deluxe Tampa–Airport ⒣

(813) 886-5253. **$69-$104.** 4811 Memorial Hwy 33634. Veteran's Expwy, exit 3, just sw on CR 576. Int corridors. **Pets:** Other species. $25 daily fee/room. Designated rooms, service with restrictions, crate.

🅰🆂🅺 ⊠ 📶 🛋 💻 ⇌

▼▼ Extended Stay Deluxe-Tampa-Airport-N West Shore Blvd ⒣

(813) 637-8990. **$69-$104.** 1805 N Westshore Blvd 33607. I-275, exit 40A southbound, 0.5 mi nw; exit 39A northbound, 1 mi e on Kennedy Blvd, then 1.3 mi nw. Int corridors. **Pets:** Other species. $25 daily fee/room. Designated rooms, service with restrictions, crate.

🅰🆂🅺 ⊠ 📶 🛋 💻 ⇌

⨁ ▼▼▼ ▼▼▼ Grand Hyatt Tampa Bay ⒣

(813) 874-1234. **$109-$399.** 2900 Bayport Dr 33607. SR 60, east end of Courtney Campbell Cswy. Ext/int corridors. **Pets:** Medium. $75 one-time fee/pet. Designated rooms, service with restrictions, supervision.

ⒺⒸⓄ ⓈⒶⓋⒺ ⊠ 📶 🛋 💻 🍽 ⇌ ⊠

▼▼▼ Hampton Inn Veterans Expressway ⒣

(813) 901-5900. **$99-$179.** 5628 W Waters Ave 33634. SR 589 (Veteran's Expwy), exit 6A, just e on CR 584. Int corridors. **Pets:** Medium, other species. $10 daily fee/room. Designated rooms, service with restrictions, supervision. ⊠ 📶 🛋 💻 ⇌

⨁ ▼▼▼ ▼▼ Hilton Tampa Airport Westshore ⒣ ❀

(813) 877-6688. **$149-$349.** 2225 N Lois Ave 33607. I-275, exit 40B, 0.8 mi n. Int corridors. **Pets:** Small, dogs only. $75 one-time fee/room. Designated rooms, service with restrictions, supervision.

ⒺⒸⓄ ⓈⒶⓋⒺ ⊠ 📶 🛋 💻 🍽 ⇌ ⊠

⨁ ▼▼▼ ▼▼ Holiday Inn Express Hotel & Suites ⒣

(813) 910-7171. **$129.** 8310 Galbraith Rd 33647. I-75, exit 270, 0.3 mi n on CR 581 (Bruce B Downs Blvd), just w on Highwoods Preserve Pkwy, then just n; in Highwoods Preserve. Int corridors. **Pets:** Accepted.

ⒺⒸⓄ ⓈⒶⓋⒺ ⊠ 📶 🛋 💻 ⇌

▼▼▼▼ Holiday Inn Express Hotel & Suites Tampa-USF-Busch Gardens ⒣

(813) 936-8200. **$89-$126.** 2807 E Busch Blvd 33612. I-75, exit 50, 1.8 mi e on Busch Blvd (SR 580), jct N 30th St. Int corridors.
Pets: Accepted. ⒺⒸⓄ 🅰🆂🅺 ⊠ 📶 🛋 💻 ⇌

▼▼ Homestead Studio Suites Hotel-Tampa/North Airport Ⓜ

(813) 243-1913. **$54-$89.** 5401 Beaumont Ctr Blvd E 33634. SR 589 (Veterans Expwy), exit 4, just w on SR 580. Ext/int corridors. **Pets:** Other species. $25 daily fee/room. Designated rooms, service with restrictions, crate. 🅰🆂🅺 ⊠ 📶 🛋 💻

▼▼▼▼ Homewood Suites Brandon/Tampa ⒣

(813) 685-7099. **$129-$229.** 10240 Palm River Rd 33619. I-75, exit 257, 0.4 mi w on SR 60, just s on S Falkenburg Rd, then 0.3 mi e. Int corridors. **Pets:** Accepted. ⒺⒸⓄ ⊠ 📶 🛋 💻 ⇌ ⊠

▼▼▼ Homewood Suites by Hilton Tampa Airport/Westshore ⒣

(813) 282-1950. **$139-$169.** 5325 Avion Park Dr 33607. I-275, exit 40A southbound, 0.7 mi on Westshore Blvd; exit 39A northbound, 1 mi e on Kennedy Blvd (SR 60), 1.2 mi n on Westshore Blvd, just w on Spruce St, then just s on O'Brien St; in Avion Park Westshore. Int corridors.
Pets: Accepted. ⒺⒸⓄ ⊠ 📶 🛋 💻 ⇌ ⊠

▼▼ Howard Johnson Plaza Downtown Tampa ⒣

(813) 223-1351. **$99-$169, 7 day notice.** 111 W Fortune St 33602. I-275, exit 44, just s on Ashley Dr. Int corridors. **Pets:** Other species. $75 one-time fee/room. Service with restrictions.

🅰🆂🅺 ⊠ 📶 🛋 💻 🍽 ⇌

▼▼ La Quinta Inn & Suites Tampa Bay (Airport) Ⓜ 🐾

(813) 287-0440. **$59-$154.** 4730 W Spruce St 33607-1497. I-275, exit 40A, 0.7 mi on Westshore Blvd; exit 39A northbound, 1 mi e on Kennedy Blvd, 1.2 mi n on Westshore Blvd, then just w. Ext/int corridors. **Pets:** Medium, other species. Service with restrictions, supervision.

🅰🆂🅺 ⊠ 📶 🛋 💻 ⇌

▼▼▼▼ La Quinta Inn & Suites Tampa Bay (U.S.F./Near Busch Gardens) ⒣ 🐾

(813) 910-7500. **$75-$130.** 3701 E Fowler Ave 33612. I-275, exit 51, 2.2 mi e on SR 582. Int corridors. **Pets:** Medium, other species. Service with restrictions, supervision. 🅰🆂🅺 ⊠ 📶 🛋 💻 ⇌

▼▼ La Quinta Inn Tampa East Fairgrounds ⒣ 🐾

(813) 626-0885. **$55-$120.** 4811 US 301 N 33610. I-4, exit 6 westbound; exit 6A eastbound, just se. Int corridors. **Pets:** Medium, other species. Service with restrictions, supervision. 🅰🆂🅺 ⊠ 📶 🛋 💻 ⇌

▼▼▼▼ La Quinta Inn Tampa South ⒣ 🐾

(813) 835-6262. **$99-$159.** 4620 W Gandy Blvd 33611. Just e of jct S Westshore Blvd. Int corridors. **Pets:** Medium, other species. Service with restrictions, supervision. 🅰🆂🅺 ⊠ 📶 🛋 💻 ⇌

▼▼▼▼ La Quinta Inn West Tampa-Brandon ⒣ 🐾

(813) 684-4007. **$65-$130.** 602 S Falkenburg Rd 33619. I-75, exit 257, just w on SR 60, then just n. Int corridors. **Pets:** Medium, other species. Service with restrictions, supervision. 🅰🆂🅺 ⊠ 📶 🛋 💻 ⇌

▼▼▼▼ Mainsail Suites Hotel & Conference Center ⒣

(813) 243-2600. **$99-$249.** 5108 Eisenhower Blvd 33634. SR 589 (Veteran's Expwy), exit 4, just w on SR 580; main entrance on Hillsborough Ave. Ext corridors. **Pets:** $150 one-time fee/room. Service with restrictions, crate. 🅰🆂🅺 ⊠ 📶 🛋 💻 🍽 ⇌ ⊠

⨁ ▼▼▼▼ Quorum Hotel-Tampa ⒣

(813) 289-8200. **$99-$239.** 700 N Westshore Blvd 33609. I-275, exit 40A southbound, just nw on CR 587; exit 39A northbound, 1 mi n on Kennedy Blvd, then 0.9 mi nw on Westshore Blvd (CR 587); jct W Cypress St. Int corridors. **Pets:** Medium. $30 one-time fee/room. Service with restrictions, crate. ⒺⒸⓄ ⓈⒶⓋⒺ ⊠ 💻 🍽 ⇌ ⊠

▼▼▼ **Red Roof Inn-Brandon** Ⓗ
(813) 681-8484. **$50-$100.** 10121 Horace Ave 33619. I-75, exit 257, just w on SR 60 (Adamo Dr), just n on Falkenburg Rd, then just e. Ext corridors. **Pets:** Large. Service with restrictions, crate.
Ⓐ$Ⓚ ⊠ ⓖM 🛏 💻 ⤳

🄐🄐🄐 ▼▼▼ **Red Roof Inn-Fairgrounds** Ⓜ
(813) 623-5245. **$61-$300.** 5001 N US 301 33610. I-4, exit 7 westbound; exit 7A eastbound, just se. Ext corridors. **Pets:** Large. Service with restrictions, crate. Ⓢ🄰🄵🄴 ⊠ 🛏

▼▼◆▼ **Residence Inn by Marriott Sabal Park** Ⓗ ❖
(813) 627-8855. **$144-$194.** 9719 Princess Palm Ave 33619. I-75, exit 260 southbound; exit 260B northbound, just w on SR 574 (Dr. Martin Luther King Jr Blvd), just s on Falkenburg Rd, then 0.4 mi w; in Sabal Corporate Center. Int corridors. **Pets:** Other species. $25 one-time fee/room. Service with restrictions. ⊠ ⓖM 🛏 💻 ⤳ ⊠

▼▼◆▼ **Residence Inn by Marriott Tampa Downtown** Ⓗ
(813) 221-4224. **$169-$239.** 101 E Tyler St 33602. I-275, exit 44, 0.5 mi se on W Ashley and Tampa sts; exit 45A southbound, 1.5 mi se on W Ashley St. Int corridors. **Pets:** Other species. $100 one-time fee/room. Service with restrictions. ⊠ ⓖM 🛏 💻 ⤳ ⊠

▼▼▼ **Residence Inn by Marriott Tampa Westshore/Airport** Ⓗ
(813) 877-7988. **$179-$239.** 4312 Boy Scout Blvd 33607. I-275, exit 40A southbound, 0.7 mi on Westshore Blvd; exit 39A northbound, 1 mi e on Kennedy Blvd (SR 60), 1.2 mi n on Westshore Blvd, 0.5 mi e. Int corridors. **Pets:** Accepted. ⊠ ⓖM 🛏 💻 ⤳

🄐🄐🄐 ▼▼◆▼ **Seminole Hard Rock Hotel and Casino Tampa** Ⓗ
(813) 627-7625. **$229-$409.** 5223 N Orient Rd 33610. I-4, exit 6, just w. Int corridors. **Pets:** Accepted. Ⓢ🄰🄵🄴 ⊠ ⓖM 🛏 💻 🍴 ⤳ ⊠

🄐🄐🄐 ▼▼◆▼ **Sheraton Suites Tampa Airport** Ⓗ
(813) 873-8675. **$99-$405.** 4400 W Cypress St 33607. I-275, exit 40A southbound, just nw on CR 587; exit 39A northbound, just nw on Westshore Blvd (CR 587), then just e. Int corridors. **Pets:** Accepted.
Ⓔ🄲🄾 Ⓢ🄰🄵🄴 ⊠ 🛏 💻 🍴 ⤳

🄐🄐🄐 ▼▼◆▼ **Sheraton Tampa Riverwalk** Ⓗ
(813) 223-2222. **$109-$339, 24 day notice.** 200 N Ashley Dr 33602. I-275, exit 44, 0.8 mi s. Int corridors. **Pets:** Accepted.
Ⓢ🄰🄵🄴 ⊠ ⓖM 🛏 💻 🍴 ⤳

▼▼◆▼ **Staybridge Suites Tampa-Sabal Park** Ⓗ ❖
(813) 227-4000. **$84-$119.** 3624 N Falkenburg Rd 33619. I-75, exit 260 southbound; exit 260B northbound, just w on SR 574 (Dr. Martin Luther King Blvd), then just s. Int corridors. **Pets:** Medium, other species. $75 one-time fee/pet. Service with restrictions, crate.
Ⓐ$Ⓚ ⊠ ⓖM 🛏 💻 ⤳

▼▼◆▼ **TownePlace Suites by Marriott Tampa Westshore** Ⓗ
(813) 282-1081. **$129-$149.** 5302 Avion Park Dr 33607. I-275, exit 40A southbound, 0.7 mi n on Westshore Blvd; exit 39A northbound, 1 mi e on Kennedy Blvd (SR 60), 1.2 mi n on Westshore Blvd, just w on Spruce St, then just s on O'Brien St; in Avion Park Westshore. Int corridors.
Pets: Accepted. Ⓔ🄲🄾 ⊠ ⓖM 🛏 💻 ⤳

🄐🄐🄐 ▼▼◆▼ ▼▼◆▼ **The Westin Tampa Bay** Ⓗ ❖
(813) 281-0000. **$109-$339.** 7627 Courtney Campbell Cswy 33607. At east end of Courtney Campbell Cswy (SR 60). Int corridors.
Pets: Medium, dogs only. Service with restrictions, supervision.
Ⓢ🄰🄵🄴 ⊠ ⓖM 🛏 💻 🍴 ⤳ ⊠

🄐🄐🄐 ▼▼◆▼ **The Westin Tampa Harbour Island** Ⓗ
(813) 229-5000. **$109-$439.** 725 S Harbour Island Blvd 33602. I-275, exit 44 eastbound, 2 mi s on Tampa St, follow signs to Convention Center and Harbour Island; exit 45A westbound. Int corridors. **Pets:** Accepted.
Ⓔ🄲🄾 Ⓢ🄰🄵🄴 ⊠ ⓖM 🛏 💻 🍴 ⤳ ⊠

TEMPLE TERRACE
▼▼ **Extended Stay America-Tampa North-USF Attractions** Ⓗ
(813) 989-2264. **$59-$94.** 12242 Morris Bridge Rd 33637. I-75, exit 266, just w on Fletcher Ave (CR 582A). Int corridors. **Pets:** Other species. $25 daily fee/room. Designated rooms, service with restrictions, crate.
Ⓐ$Ⓚ ⊠ ⓖM 🛏 💻

▼▼▼ **La Quinta Inn & Suites** Ⓗ ❖
(813) 972-9800. **$69-$139.** 13294 Telecom Dr 33637. I-75, exit 266, 1.4 mi w on Fletcher Ave (CR 582A), just s; in Rivers Edge at Telecom Park. Int corridors. **Pets:** Medium, other species. Service with restrictions, supervision. Ⓔ🄲🄾 Ⓐ$Ⓚ ⊠ ⓖM 🛏 💻 ⤳

▼▼◆▼ **Residence Inn by Marriott Tampa North** Ⓗ
(813) 972-4400. **$144-$189.** 13420 N Telecom Dr 33637. I-75, exit 266, 1.1 mi w on Fletcher Ave (CR 582A), then just s; in Telecom Tampa Park. Int corridors. **Pets:** Accepted. ⊠ ⓖM 🛏 💻 ⤳ ⊠

▼▼▼ **TownePlace Suites Tampa North/I-75 Fletcher** Ⓗ
(813) 975-9777. **$139-$169.** 6800 Woodstork Rd 33637. I-75, exit 266, 1.1 mi w on Fletcher Ave, then just s; in Telecom Tampa. Int corridors.
Pets: $100 one-time fee/room. Service with restrictions, crate.
⊠ 🛏 💻 ⤳

WESLEY CHAPEL
🄐🄐🄐 ▼▼◆▼ **Holiday Inn Express** Ⓗ
(813) 907-1379. **Call for rates.** 27615 SR 54 W 33543. I-75, exit 279, just w. Int corridors. **Pets:** Accepted. Ⓢ🄰🄵🄴 ⊠ ⓖM 🛏 💻 ⤳

END METROPOLITAN AREA

TITUSVILLE
🄐🄐🄐 ▼▼ **Best Western Space Shuttle Inn Kennedy Space Center** Ⓗ
(321) 269-9100. **$60-$160.** 3455 Cheney Hwy 32780. I-95, exit 215 (SR 50), just e. Ext corridors. **Pets:** Other species. $10 daily fee/pet. Designated rooms, service with restrictions.
Ⓢ🄰🄵🄴 ⊠ 🛏 💻 🍴 ⤳ ⊠

🄐🄐🄐 ▼▼▼ **Comfort Inn Titusville** Ⓗ
(321) 269-7110. **$80-$100.** 3655 Cheney Hwy 32780. I-95, exit 215 (SR 50), just w. Ext corridors. **Pets:** Accepted. Ⓢ🄰🄵🄴 ⊠ 🛏 💻 ⤳

🄐🄐🄐 ▼▼▼ **Days Inn Titusville** Ⓗ
(321) 269-4480. **$59-$189, 14 day notice.** 3755 Cheney Hwy 32780. I-95, exit 215 (SR 50). Ext corridors. **Pets:** Medium, dogs only. $15 daily fee/pet. Designated rooms, service with restrictions, supervision.
Ⓢ🄰🄵🄴 ⊠ 🛏 💻 🍴 ⤳

🄐🄐🄐 ▼▼◆▼ **Fairfield Inn & Suites by Marriott** Ⓗ ❖
(321) 385-1818. **$129-$149.** 4735 Helen Hauser Blvd 32780. I-95, exit 215 (SR 50), just w. Int corridors. **Pets:** Small. $75 one-time fee/room. Designated rooms, service with restrictions, supervision.
Ⓢ🄰🄵🄴 ⊠ ⓖM 🛏 💻 ⤳

▼▼▼ **Ramada Inn & Suites-Kennedy Space Center** Ⓗ
(321) 269-5510. **$59-$89.** 3500 Cheney Hwy 32780. I-95, exit 215 (SR 50), just e. Int corridors. **Pets:** Accepted.
Ⓐ$Ⓚ ⊠ 🛏 💻 🍴 ⤳ ⊠

VENICE
▼▼◆▼ **Holiday Inn Express Hotel & Suites** Ⓗ
(941) 584-6800. **Call for rates.** 380 Commercial Ct 34292. I-75, exit 193, just w on Jacaranda Blvd (CR 765), then just n. Int corridors.
Pets: Other species. $30 one-time fee/room. Service with restrictions, crate. ⊠ ⓖM 🛏 💻 ⤳

◆◆◆◆ Horse and Chaise Inn a Bed & Breakfast BB

(941) 488-2702. **$115-$189, 7 day notice.** 317 Ponce de Leon 34285. Just s of jct Venice Ave on Nassau St, just sw; downtown. Ext/int corridors. **Pets:** Medium. $10 daily fee/room. Designated rooms, supervision.

⊠ 🛢 🗗

VERO BEACH

🜨 ◆◆◆◆ The Vero Beach Hotel & Spa H

(772) 231-5666. **$179-$1009, 14 day notice.** 3500 Ocean Dr 32963. Just n of SR 60. Ext/int corridors. **Pets:** Accepted.

SAVE ⊠ �&M 🛢 ⟨1⟩ ⇆

WEST MELBOURNE

◆◆ Extended Stay Deluxe Melbourne-Airport H

(321) 733-6050. **$59-$79.** 1701 Evans Rd 32904. I-95, exit 180 (US 192), 3 mi e, then 0.3 mi n. Int corridors. **Pets:** Other species. $25 daily fee/room. Designated rooms, service with restrictions, crate.

ASK ⊠ 🛢 🖵 ⇆

🜨 ◆◆◆ Fairfield Inn & Suites by Marriott H

(321) 722-2220. **$109-$149.** 4355 W New Haven Ave 32904. I-95, exit 180 (US 192), just e. Int corridors. **Pets:** Small, dogs only. $50 one-time fee/room. Designated rooms, service with restrictions, crate.

SAVE ⊠ �&M 🛢 🖵 ⇆

WEST PALM BEACH

🜨 ◆◆◆ Comfort Inn & Conference Center H

(561) 689-6100. **$79-$109.** 1901 Palm Beach Lakes Blvd 33409. I-95, exit 71 (Palm Beach Lakes Blvd), just w. Int corridors. **Pets:** Medium. $10 daily fee/room. Designated rooms, service with restrictions, supervision.

SAVE ⊠ 🛢 🖵 ⟨1⟩ ⇆

◆◆ Extended Stay Deluxe-West Palm Beach-Northpoint Corporate Park H

(561) 683-5332. **$79-$119.** 700 Northpoint Pkwy 33407. I-95, exit 74 (45th St), just w, then n. Int corridors. **Pets:** Other species. $25 daily fee/room. Designated rooms, service with restrictions, crate.

ASK ⊠ 🛢 🖵 ⇆

◆◆◆◆ Hibiscus House Bed & Breakfast BB

(561) 863-5633. **$89-$210, 14 day notice.** 501 30th St 33407. 1.2 mi n on Flagler Dr from jct Palm Beach Lakes Blvd, 0.3 mi w. Int corridors. **Pets:** Other species. ASK ⊠ 🛢 ⇆

🜨 ◆◆◆◆ Hilton Palm Beach Airport H

(561) 684-9400. **$109-$249.** 150 Australian Ave 33406. I-95, exit 68 (Southern Blvd), 0.3 mi w; at Australian Ave and Southern Blvd. Int corridors. **Pets:** Accepted. ECO SAVE ⊠ 🛢 🖵 ⟨1⟩ ⇆ ⊠

🜨 ◆◆ Red Roof Inn-West Palm Beach M

(561) 697-7710. **$80-$110.** 2421 Metrocentre Blvd E 33407. I-95, exit 74 (45th St), just w on CR 702; in Metrocentre Corporate Park. Ext/int corridors. **Pets:** Large. Service with restrictions, crate.

SAVE ⊠ �&M 🛢 ⇆

◆◆◆◆ Residence Inn by Marriott West Palm Beach H

(561) 687-4747. **$149-$259.** 2461 Metrocentre Blvd 33407. I-95, exit 74, just w on 45th St; in Metrocentre Corporate Park. Int corridors. **Pets:** Accepted. ⊠ �&M 🛢 🖵 ⇆ ⊠

WINTER HAVEN

🜨 ◆◆◆ Best Western Admiral's Inn and Conference Center H

(863) 324-5950. **$89-$326.** 5665 Cypress Gardens Blvd 33884. SR 540, 3 mi e of jct US 17; 3.9 mi w of jct US 27. Ext/int corridors. **Pets:** Accepted. SAVE ⊠ 🛢 🖵 ⟨1⟩ ⇆

GEORGIA

ADAIRSVILLE

AAA ▼▼▼ Quality Inn **M**

(770) 773-2886. **$61-$100.** 107 Princeton Blvd 30103. I-75, exit 306, just w. Ext corridors. **Pets:** Medium. $10 daily fee/pet. Service with restrictions, supervision. SAVE ✕ 🔊 🛏 💻 ≈

▼▼▼ Ramada Limited **M**

(770) 769-9726. **Call for rates.** 500 Georgia North Cir 30103. I-75, exit 306, 0.3 mi w. Ext corridors. **Pets:** Accepted. ✕ 🔊 🛏 💻 ≈

ADEL

▼▼▼ Hampton Inn **H**

(229) 896-3099. **$70-$95.** 1500 W 4th St 31620. I-75, exit 39, just w. Int corridors. **Pets:** Medium. Designated rooms, service with restrictions. ✕ 🔊 🛏 💻 ≈

▼▼ Super 8 I-75 **M**

(229) 896-2244. **$45-$69.** 1103 W 4th St 31620. I-75, exit 39, just e. Ext corridors. **Pets:** Medium. $11 one-time fee/pet. Service with restrictions, crate. ASK ✕ 🛏 💻 ≈

ALBANY

AAA ▼▼▼ Best Western Albany Mall Inn & Suites **H**

(229) 446-2001. **$63-$116.** 2729 Pointe North Blvd 31721. Just se of jct Dawson Rd and US 82 W. Int corridors. **Pets:** Accepted. SAVE ✕ 🔊 🛏 💻 ≈

▼▼ Jameson Inn **H**

(229) 435-3737. **$78-$85.** 2720 Dawson Rd 31707. 0.5 mi s of jct US 82 and SR 520. Ext corridors. **Pets:** Accepted. ASK ✕ 🛏 💻 ≈

▼▼ Quality Inn-Merry Acres **M**

(229) 435-7721. **Call for rates.** 1500 Dawson Rd 31707. 3.3 mi w. Ext corridors. **Pets:** Medium, dogs only. $10 daily fee/room. Designated rooms, service with restrictions, crate. ✕ 🛏 💻 ≈

▼▼▼ Wingate By Wyndham **H**

(229) 883-9800. **Call for rates.** 2735 Dawson Rd 31707. Jct US 82 and SR 520, 0.4 mi s. Int corridors. **Pets:** Accepted. ✕ 🔊 🛏 💻 ≈

ALMA

▼▼ Days Inn **M**

(912) 632-7000. **Call for rates.** 930 S Pierce St 31510. Jct SR 32/US 1, 0.4 mi s on US 1. Ext corridors. **Pets:** Accepted. ✕ 🛏 💻 ≈

AMERICUS

▼▼▼ 1906 Pathway Inn Bed & Breakfast **BB**

(229) 928-2078. **$99-$145, 3 day notice.** 501 S Lee St 31709. 0.5 mi s of US 280 on SR 377. Int corridors. **Pets:** Accepted. ASK ✕

▼▼▼ Holiday Inn Express **H**

(229) 928-5400. **Call for rates.** 1611 E Lomar St 31709. On US 280, just w of jct US 27. Ext corridors. **Pets:** Accepted. ✕ 🛏 💻 ≈

▼▼ Quality Inn **H**

(229) 924-4431. **$63.** 1205 Martin Luther King Jr Blvd 31709. On US 19 S, 1 mi w of downtown. Ext corridors. **Pets:** Small. $10 daily fee/pet. Designated rooms, service with restrictions, supervision. ✕ 🛏 💻 🍴 ≈

ASHBURN

AAA ▼▼▼ Best Western Ashburn Inn **H**

(229) 567-0080. **$69-$79.** 820 Shoney's Dr 31714. I-75, exit 82, just w. Ext corridors. **Pets:** Small. $10 daily fee/pet. Designated rooms, service with restrictions, supervision. SAVE ✕ 🛏 💻 ≈

AAA ▼▼▼ Days Inn **H**

(229) 567-3346. **$59-$69.** 823 E Washington Ave 31714. I-75, exit 82, just w on SR 112. Ext corridors. **Pets:** Small. $10 daily fee/pet. Designated rooms, service with restrictions, supervision. SAVE ✕ 🛏 ≈

▼▼ Super 8 **H**

(229) 567-4688. **$45-$65.** 749 E Washington Ave 31714. I-75, exit 82, just w. Ext corridors. **Pets:** Medium. $10 daily fee/pet. Supervision. ASK ✕ 🛏 💻

ATHENS

AAA ▼▼▼ Best Western-Colonial Inn **M**

(706) 546-7311. **$70-$90.** 170 N Milledge Ave 30601. Jct US 78 business route (Broad St), 0.5 mi w on SR 15. Ext corridors. **Pets:** Accepted. SAVE ✕ 🛏 💻 ≈

AAA ▼▼▼ Comfort Suites Downtown Athens **H**

(706) 995-4000. **$89-$149.** 255 North Ave 30601. SR 10 Loop, exit 11B (Dougherty St/North Ave); 1 mi n of downtown. Int corridors. **Pets:** Small. $25 daily fee/pet. Service with restrictions, supervision. SAVE ✕ 🛏 💻 ≈

(AAA) ▼▼▼ **Microtel Inn** 🅷
(706) 548-5676. **$54-$130.** 1050 Ultimate Dr 30605. Jct US 78 business route (Broad St) and SR 10 Loop, 1.4 mi e. Int corridors. **Pets:** Medium, dogs only. $25 one-time fee/room. Service with restrictions, supervision.
SAVE ☒ 🅕ᴹ 🔋 🖥

ATLANTA METROPOLITAN AREA

ACWORTH

(AAA) ▼▼▼ **America's Best Inn** 🅜
(770) 974-5400. **$45-$50, 7 day notice.** 5320 Cherokee St 30101. I-75, exit 278, just w. Ext corridors. **Pets:** $5 daily fee/pet. Service with restrictions, supervision. SAVE ☒ 🔋 🖥 ⊃

(AAA) ▼▼▼ **Best Western Acworth Inn** 🅜
(770) 974-0116. **$65-$85.** 5155 Cowan Rd 30101. I-75, exit 277, just w. Ext corridors. **Pets:** Other species. $10 daily fee/pet. Service with restrictions, supervision. SAVE ☒ 🔋 🖥 ⊃

▼▼ **Econo Lodge** 🅜
(770) 974-1922. **Call for rates.** 4980 Cowan Rd 30101. I-75, exit 277, just w. Ext corridors. **Pets:** Accepted. ☒ 🔋 🖥 ⊃

▼▼▼ **La Quinta Inn Acworth** 🅷 🐾
(770) 975-9920. **$69-$129.** 184 N Point Way 30102. I-75, exit 277, just e. Ext/int corridors. **Pets:** Medium, other species. Service with restrictions, supervision. ASK ☒ 🅕ᴹ 🔋 🖥 ⊃

▼▼ **Motel 6** 🅜
(770) 974-1700. **Call for rates.** 5035 Cowan Rd 30101. I-75, exit 277, just w. Ext corridors. **Pets:** Other species. Service with restrictions, supervision. ☒ 🔋 🖥 ⊃

▼▼ **Super 8** 🅜
(770) 966-9700. **$60-$80.** 4970 Cowan Rd 30101. I-75, exit 277, just w. Ext corridors. **Pets:** Medium. $10 daily fee/pet. Service with restrictions, supervision. ASK ☒ 🔋 🖥 ⊃

ALPHARETTA

▼▼▼ **Embassy Suites Hotel Alpharetta** 🅷 🐾
(678) 566-8800. **$109-$229.** 5955 North Point Pkwy 30022. SR 400, just e to North Point Pkwy, then just n. Int corridors. **Pets:** Small, dogs only. $25 daily fee/pet. Designated rooms, service with restrictions, supervision.
☒ 🅕ᴹ 🔋 🖥 🍴 ⊃

▼▼ **Extended StayAmerica Atlanta-Alpharetta-Rock Mill** 🅷
(770) 475-2676. **$54-$69.** 1950 Rock Mill Rd 30022. SR 400, exit 9, just e. Int corridors. **Pets:** Other species. $25 daily fee/room. Designated rooms, service with restrictions, crate. ASK ☒ 🅕ᴹ 🔋 🖥

▼▼▼ **Extended Stay Deluxe Atlanta-Alpharetta-Northpoint** 🅷
(770) 569-1730. **$59-$84.** 3329 Old Milton Pkwy 30005. SR 400, exit 10, just e. Int corridors. **Pets:** Other species. $25 daily fee/room. Designated rooms, service with restrictions, crate. ASK ☒ 🅕ᴹ 🔋 🖥 ⊃

▼▼▼ **Homewood Suites** 🅷
(770) 998-1622. **$159-$204.** 10775 Davis Dr 30004. SR 400, exit 8, northwest corner. Int corridors. **Pets:** Accepted. ☒ 🅕ᴹ 🔋 🖥 ⊃

▼▼▼ **La Quinta Inn & Suites Atlanta (Alpharetta)** 🅷 🐾
(770) 754-7800. **$69-$139.** 1350 North Point Dr 30022. SR 400, exit 9, 0.5 mi e. Int corridors. **Pets:** Medium, other species. Service with restrictions, supervision. ASK ☒ 🅕ᴹ 🔋 🖥 ⊃

(AAA) ▼▼▼▼ **Residence Inn Atlanta Alpharetta North Point Mall** 🅷
(770) 587-1151. **$184-$224.** 1325 North Point Dr 30022. SR 400, exit 9, just e to North Point Dr, then just s. Int corridors. **Pets:** Accepted.
SAVE ☒ 🅕ᴹ 🔋 🖥 ⊃ ☒

(AAA) ▼▼▼▼ **Residence Inn by Marriott** 🅷
(770) 664-0664. **$170-$208.** 5465 Windward Pkwy W 30004. SR 400, exit 11, 0.4 mi w. Ext/int corridors. **Pets:** Medium, other species. $100 one-time fee/room. Service with restrictions.
SAVE ☒ 🅕ᴹ 🔋 🖥 ⊃ ☒

▼▼▼ **Staybridge Suites** 🅷
(770) 569-7200. **$89-$162.** 3980 North Point Pkwy 30005. SR 400, exit 10, 0.5 mi e. Int corridors. **Pets:** Accepted.
ASK ☒ 🅕ᴹ 🔋 🖥 ⊃ ☒

▼▼▼ **StudioPLUS-Atlanta-Alpharetta-Northpoint** 🅷
(770) 475-7871. **$56-$81.** 3331 Old Milton Pkwy 30005. SR 400, exit 10, just e. Int corridors. **Pets:** Other species. $25 daily fee/room. Designated rooms, service with restrictions, crate. ASK ☒ 🅕ᴹ 🔋 🖥 ⊃

▼▼▼ **TownePlace Suites by Marriott** 🅷
(770) 664-1300. **$130-$158.** 7925 S Westside Pkwy 30004. SR 400, exit 9, 0.3 mi w. Int corridors. **Pets:** Accepted. ☒ 🔋 🖥 ⊃

▼▼▼ **Wingate Inn** 🅷
(770) 649-0955. **Call for rates.** 1005 Kingswood Pl 30004. SR 400, exit 8, 0.7 mi w. Int corridors. **Pets:** Medium. Service with restrictions, supervision. ☒ 🅕ᴹ 🔋 🖥

ATLANTA

▼▼▼ **Artmore Hotel** 🅷
(404) 876-6100. **Call for rates.** 1302 W Peachtree St 30309. I-75/85, exit 250 (14th St), just e, then just n on W Peachtree St to 16th St. Int corridors. **Pets:** Accepted. ☒ 🔋 🖥

▼▼ **Beverly Hills Inn** 🅱🅱
(404) 233-8520. **$129-$249, 3 day notice.** 65 Sheridan Dr NE 30305. Jct Piedmont and Peachtree rds, 1.1 mi s on Peachtree Rd to Sheridan Dr, then just e. Int corridors. **Pets:** Other species. $50 one-time fee/room. Service with restrictions, crate. ASK ☒ 🔋 🖥

▼▼▼ **Crowne Plaza Atlanta Perimeter NW** 🅷
(770) 955-1700. **$72-$189.** 6345 Powers Ferry Rd NW 30339. I-285, exit 22, just s. Int corridors. **Pets:** Accepted.
ASK ☒ 🅕ᴹ 🔋 🖥 🍴 ⊃

▼▼▼ **Extended StayAmerica Atlanta-Clairmont** 🅷
(404) 679-4333. **$59-$89.** 3115 Clairmont Rd 30329. I-85, exit 91, 0.6 mi w. Int corridors. **Pets:** Other species. $25 daily fee/room. Designated rooms, service with restrictions, crate. ASK ☒ 🅕ᴹ 🔋 🖥

▼▼▼ **Extended StayAmerica Atlanta-Perimeter** 🅷
(770) 396-5600. **$59-$79.** 905 S Crestline Pkwy 30328. I-285, exit 28 westbound, 0.7 mi n; exit 26 eastbound, 0.5 mi n to Hammond Dr, 0.5 mi e, then 0.3 mi n. Int corridors. **Pets:** Other species. $25 daily fee/room. Designated rooms, service with restrictions, crate.
ASK ☒ 🅕ᴹ 🔋 🖥

▼▼▼ **Extended Stay Deluxe Atlanta-Lenox** 🅷
(404) 237-9100. **$74-$94.** 3967 Peachtree Rd 30319. I-85, exit 89, 2.8 mi w. Int corridors. **Pets:** Other species. $25 daily fee/room. Designated rooms, service with restrictions, crate. ASK ☒ 🅕ᴹ 🔋 🖥 ⊃

▼▼▼ **Extended Stay Deluxe (Atlanta/Marietta/Powers Ferry Rd)** 🅷
(770) 933-8010. **$59-$74.** 2010 Powers Ferry Rd 30339. I-75, exit 260 (Windy Hill Rd), 0.5 mi e, then just s. Int corridors. **Pets:** Other species. $25 daily fee/room. Designated rooms, service with restrictions, crate.
ASK ☒ 🅕ᴹ 🔋 🖥 ⊃

▼▼▼▼ Extended Stay Deluxe (Atlanta/Marietta/Windy Hill/Int. N Pkwy) 🅗

(770) 226-0242. **$74-$99.** 2225 Interstate North Pkwy 30339. I-75, exit 260 (Windy Hill Rd), just e to Interstate North Pkwy, then just s. Int corridors. **Pets:** Other species. $25 daily fee/room. Designated rooms, service with restrictions, crate. [ASK] [X] [✆M] [🛏] [🖥] [🏊]

▼▼▼▼ Extended Stay Deluxe Atlanta-Perimeter 🅗

(770) 379-0111. **$69-$94.** 6330 Peachtree-Dunwoody Rd NE 30328. I-285, exit 28 westbound, 0.7 mi n; exit 26 eastbound, 0.5 mi n to Hammond Dr, 0.5 mi e, then 0.3 mi n. Int corridors. **Pets:** Other species. $25 daily fee/room. Designated rooms, service with restrictions, crate. [ASK] [X] [✆M] [🛏] [🖥] [🏊]

▼▼▼▼ Extended Stay Deluxe Atlanta-Vinings 🅗

(770) 436-1511. **$64-$99.** 2474 Cumberland Pkwy SE 30339. I-285, exit 18, just e. Int corridors. **Pets:** Other species. $25 daily fee/room. Designated rooms, service with restrictions, crate. [ASK] [X] [✆M] [🛏] [🖥]

🆔🆔🆔 ▼▼▼▼ Four Seasons Hotel Atlanta 🅗 🐾

(404) 881-9898. **$395-$4500.** 75 14th St 30309. I-75/85, exit 250 (14th St), 0.3 mi e. Int corridors. **Pets:** Small. Service with restrictions. [ASK] [X] [✆M] [🍴] [🏊] [✕]

▼▼▼▼ The Glenn Hotel 🅗

(404) 521-2250. **Call for rates.** 110 Marietta St NW 30303. I-75/85, exit 248C northbound, 0.8 mi w, then just n; exit 249A southbound, just s to Baker St, just w, then just n. Int corridors. **Pets:** Accepted. [X] [✆M] [🛏] [🖥] [🍴]

🆔🆔🆔 ▼▼▼▼ Grand Hyatt Atlanta 🅗 🐾

(404) 237-1234. **$139-$409.** 3300 Peachtree Rd NE 30305. Corner of Peachtree and Piedmont rds. Int corridors. **Pets:** Small. $100 one-time fee/room. Service with restrictions. [SAVE] [X] [✆M] [🛏] [🖥] [🍴] [🏊] [✕]

🆔🆔🆔 ▼▼▼▼ Hawthorn Suites-Atlanta NW 🅗

(770) 952-9595. **$129-$149.** 1500 Parkwood Cir 30339. I-75, exit 260 (Windy Hill Rd), 0.5 mi e, then 0.3 mi s on Powers Ferry Rd. Ext corridors. **Pets:** Accepted. [SAVE] [X] [🛏] [🖥] [🏊] [✕]

▼▼▼▼ Hilton Atlanta 🅗

(404) 659-2000. **$204-$379.** 255 Courtland St NE 30303. I-75/85, exit 249A southbound; exit 248C northbound, just w to Piedmont Ave, just n to Baker St, then just w. Int corridors. **Pets:** Accepted. [X] [🖥] [🍴] [🏊] [✕]

▼▼▼▼ Hilton Suites Atlanta Perimeter 🅗

(770) 668-0808. **$129-$299.** 6120 Peachtree-Dunwoody Rd 30328. I-285, exit 28 westbound, 0.4 mi n; exit 26 eastbound, 0.5 mi n to Hammond Dr, 0.5 mi e to Peachtree-Dunwoody Rd, then just n. Int corridors. **Pets:** Accepted. [X] [✆M] [🛏] [🖥] [🍴] [🏊]

▼▼▼ Holiday Inn Atlanta Perimeter 🅗

(770) 457-6363. **$69-$109.** 4386 Chamblee-Dunwoody Rd 30341. I-285, exit 30 eastbound, just s; exit westbound, follow access road 1.3 mi to Chamblee-Dunwoody Rd, then just s. Int corridors. **Pets:** Accepted. [ASK] [X] [✆M] [🛏] [🖥] [🍴] [🏊]

▼▼ Homestead Studio Suites Hotel-Atlanta/Perimeter 🅗

(770) 522-0025. **$64-$89.** 1050 Hammond Dr 30328. I-285, exit 26 eastbound, 0.5 mi n to Hammond Dr, then 0.5 mi e; exit 28 westbound, just n to Hammond Dr, then just w. Ext corridors. **Pets:** Other species. $25 daily fee/room. Designated rooms, service with restrictions, crate. [ASK] [X] [✆M] [🛏] [🖥]

▼▼▼▼ Homewood Suites-Atlanta Buckhead 🅗

(404) 365-0001. **$159-$179.** 3566 Piedmont Rd 30305. SR 400, exit 2, just s to Piedmont Rd, then 1 mi w. Int corridors. **Pets:** Accepted. [X] [✆M] [🛏] [🖥] [🏊]

▼▼▼▼ Homewood Suites-Cumberland 🅗

(770) 988-9449. **$149-$169.** 3200 Cobb Pkwy SW 30339. I-285, exit 19 eastbound; exit 20 westbound, 0.7 mi se on US 41 (Cobb Pkwy). Ext/int corridors. **Pets:** Accepted. [X] [✆M] [🛏] [🖥] [🏊] [✕]

▼▼▼▼ Hotel Indigo Atlanta Midtown 🅗 🐾

(404) 874-9200. **$99-$189.** 683 Peachtree St NE 30308. I-75/85, exit 249D, 0.5 mi e to Peachtree St, then just n. Int corridors. **Pets:** Other species. Designated rooms. [ASK] [X] [✆M] [🛏] [🖥] [🍴]

🆔🆔🆔 ▼▼▼▼ Inn at the Peachtrees 🅗

(404) 577-6970. **$79-$119, 7 day notice.** 330 W Peachtree St 30308. I-75/85, exit 249D northbound, 0.4 mi w to Peachtree St, then 0.3 mi n; exit 249C southbound, just s to Peachtree Pl, then just e. Ext/int corridors. **Pets:** Accepted. [SAVE] [X] [🛏] [🖥]

🆔🆔🆔 ▼▼▼▼ InterContinental Buckhead Atlanta 🅗

(404) 946-9000. **$161-$359.** 3315 Peachtree Rd NE 30326. Jct Piedmont and Peachtree rds NE, just e. Int corridors. **Pets:** Accepted. [SAVE] [X] [✆M] [🖥] [🍴] [🏊] [✕]

▼▼▼▼ La Quinta Inn & Suites Atlanta (Paces Ferry/Vinings) 🅗 🐾

(770) 801-9002. **$75-$145.** 2415 Paces Ferry Rd SE 30339. I-285, exit 18, just w. Int corridors. **Pets:** Medium, other species. Service with restrictions, supervision. [ASK] [X] [✆M] [🛏] [🖥] [🏊]

▼▼▼▼ La Quinta Inn & Suites Atlanta (Perimeter/Medical Center) 🅗 🐾

(770) 350-6177. **$75-$145.** 6260 Peachtree-Dunwoody 30328. I-285, exit 28 westbound, 0.7 mi n; exit 26 eastbound, 0.5 mi n to Hammond Dr, 0.7 mi e, then 0.5 mi n. Int corridors. **Pets:** Medium, other species. Service with restrictions, supervision. [ASK] [X] [✆M] [🛏] [🖥] [🏊]

▼▼▼▼ La Quinta Inn-Buckhead 🅗 🐾

(404) 321-0999. **$62-$129.** 2535 Chantilly Dr NE 30324. I-85, exit 88 southbound; exit 86 northbound, 2 mi on Buford Hwy to Lenox Rd, then just e under highway. Int corridors. **Pets:** Medium, other species. Service with restrictions, supervision. [ASK] [X] [🛏]

▼▼▼ Motel 6 Atlanta Downtown 🅗

(404) 659-4545. **Call for rates.** 311 Courtland St NE 30303. I-75/85, exit 249A southbound; exit 249B northbound. Ext/int corridors. **Pets:** Other species. Service with restrictions, supervision. [X] [✆M] [🛏]

🆔🆔🆔 ▼▼▼▼ Omni Hotel at CNN Center 🅗

(404) 659-0000. **$159-$389, 3 day notice.** 100 CNN Center 30303. I-75/85, exit 248C northbound, 0.4 mi w; exit 249C southbound to International Blvd, then 0.5 mi w. Int corridors. **Pets:** Accepted. [SAVE] [X] [🖥] [🍴] [🏊] [✕]

🆔🆔🆔 ▼▼▼ Red Roof Inn-Druid Hills 🅜

(404) 321-1653. **Call for rates.** 1960 N Druid Hills Rd 30329. I-85, exit 89, just w. Ext corridors. **Pets:** Large. Service with restrictions, crate. [SAVE] [X] [🛏]

▼▼▼▼ Residence Inn Atlanta Midtown at 17th Street 🅗

(404) 745-1000. **$170-$208.** 1365 Peachtree St 30309. I-75/85, exit 250 (14th St), 0.5 mi e to Peachtree St, then 0.3 mi n. Int corridors. **Pets:** Accepted. [X] [✆M] [🛏] [🖥]

🆔🆔🆔 ▼▼▼▼ Residence Inn-Buckhead/Lenox 🅗 🐾

(404) 467-1660. **$206-$252.** 2220 Lake Blvd 30319. I-85, exit 89, 1.6 mi w on N Druid Hills (which becomes E Roxboro), then just n on Lenox Park Blvd. Int corridors. **Pets:** Medium, other species. $100 one-time fee/room. [SAVE] [X] [✆M] [🛏] [🖥] [✕]

🆔🆔🆔 ▼▼▼▼ Residence Inn by Marriott-Atlanta/Buckhead 🅗

(404) 239-0677. **$197-$241.** 2960 Piedmont Rd NE 30305. Jct Piedmont and Pharr rds, just s. Ext corridors. **Pets:** Accepted. [SAVE] [X] [🛏] [🖥] [🏊] [✕]

▼▼▼▼ Residence Inn by Marriott-Atlanta Downtown 🅗

(404) 522-0950. **$179-$219.** 134 Peachtree St NW 30303. I-75/85, exit 248C northbound, 0.4 mi w, then just s; exit 249A southbound to International Blvd, just w, then just s. Int corridors. **Pets:** Accepted. [X] [🛏] [🖥]

Residence Inn by Marriott Atlanta Dunwoody 🅷
(770) 455-4446. **$134-$164.** 1901 Savoy Dr 30341. I-285, exit 30, just e. Ext corridors. **Pets:** Accepted.

Residence Inn by Marriott Midtown 🅷
(404) 872-8885. **$157-$191.** 1041 W Peachtree St 30309. I-75/85, exit 250 (10th St), just e to W Peachtree St, then just n; corner of 11th St. Int corridors. **Pets:** Other species. $100 one-time fee/room. Service with restrictions.

Residence Inn by Marriott-Perimeter Center 🅷
(404) 252-5066. **$206-$252.** 6096 Barfield Rd 30328. I-285, exit 26 eastbound, 0.5 mi n on Glenridge to Hammond Dr, then 0.3 mi e to Barfield Rd; exit 28 westbound (Peachtree-Dunwoody Rd), 0.5 mi n to Hammond Dr, then just w. Ext corridors. **Pets:** Accepted.

The Ritz-Carlton, Buckhead 🅷 🐾
(404) 237-2700. **$309-$479.** 3434 Peachtree Rd NE 30326. I-85, exit 86, 1.8 mi n on Cheshire Bridge-Lenox Rd. Int corridors. **Pets:** Small. $250 one-time fee/room. Service with restrictions, crate.

Sheraton Atlanta Hotel 🅷 🐾
(404) 659-6500. **$119-$389, 3 day notice.** 165 Courtland St NE 30303. I-75/85, exit 249A southbound; exit 248C northbound, just w. Int corridors. **Pets:** Medium. Designated rooms, service with restrictions.

Sheraton Suites Galleria 🅷
(770) 955-3900. **$79-$309.** 2844 Cobb Pkwy SE 30339. I-285, exit 20 westbound; exit 19 eastbound, just s on US 41 (Cobb Pkwy). Int corridors. **Pets:** Accepted.

Staybridge Suites 🅷
(404) 842-0800. **$99-$144.** 540 Pharr Rd 30305. Jct Pharr and Piedmont rds, just w. Int corridors. **Pets:** Accepted.

Staybridge Suites-Atlanta-Mt. Vernon 🅷
(404) 250-0110. **$90-$150.** 760 Mt Vernon Hwy NE 30328. I-285, exit 25, 0.8 mi n on Roswell Rd, then 1 mi e. Ext/int corridors. **Pets:** Accepted.

Staybridge Suites Atlanta Perimeter 🅷
(678) 320-0111. **$100-$180.** 4601 Ridgeview Rd 30338. I-285, exit 29 (Ashford-Dunwoody Rd), 0.5 mi n, 0.5 mi w on Perimeter Center W to Crowne Pointe Dr, then just n. Int corridors. **Pets:** Accepted.

Super 8 🅼
(404) 873-5731. **$69-$109.** 1641 Peachtree St NE 30309. I-75/85, exit 250 (14th St), 0.3 mi e to Peachtree St, then 1 mi n. Ext/int corridors. **Pets:** Medium. $10 daily fee/pet. Service with restrictions, supervision.

TownePlace Suites Atlanta Buckhead 🅷
(404) 949-4820. **$170-$208.** 820 Sidney Marcus Blvd 30324. I-85, exit 86 northbound, 1.9 mi n to Sidney Marcus Blvd, then just w; exit 88 southbound, just w to Sidney Marcus Blvd, then just w. Int corridors. **Pets:** Accepted.

University Inn at Emory 🅼
(404) 634-7327. **$96-$175.** 1767 N Decatur Rd 30307. I-85, exit 91, 3.8 mi s on Clairmont Rd to N Decatur Rd, then 0.8 mi w. Ext corridors. **Pets:** Large, other species. $25 daily fee/room. Service with restrictions.

W Atlanta Buckhead 🅷
(678) 500-3100. **$99-$559.** 3377 Peachtree Rd NE 30326. Jct Piedmont and Peachtree rds, 0.3 mi e. Int corridors. **Pets:** Accepted.

W Atlanta Midtown 🅷
(404) 892-6000. **$179-$539.** 188 14th St NE 30361. I-75/85, exit 250 (14th St), 0.5 mi. Int corridors. **Pets:** Accepted.

W Atlanta Perimeter 🅷 🐾
(770) 396-6800. **$119-$429.** 111 Perimeter Center W 30346. I-285 E, exit 29 (Ashford-Dunwoody Rd), 0.5 mi n. Int corridors. **Pets:** Medium, other species. $25 daily fee/pet, $100 one-time fee/pet. Designated rooms, service with restrictions, supervision.

The Westin Atlanta North 🅷
(770) 395-3900. **$109-$329.** 7 Concourse Pkwy 30328. I-285, exit 28 westbound; exit 26 eastbound, 0.5 mi n to Hammond Dr, then 0.4 mi e. Int corridors. **Pets:** Accepted.

The Westin Buckhead Atlanta 🅷
(404) 365-0065. **$139-$409.** 3391 Peachtree Rd NE 30326. Adjacent to Lenox Square Mall. Int corridors. **Pets:** Accepted.

The Westin Peachtree Plaza 🅷
(404) 659-1400. **Call for rates.** 210 Peachtree St 30303. I-75/85, exit 248C northbound, 0.4 mi w; exit 249C southbound, 0.5 mi s. Int corridors. **Pets:** Accepted.

AUSTELL

Baymont Inn-Six Flags 🅷
(770) 944-2110. **$59-$209.** 7377 Six Flags Dr 30168. I-20, exit 46 eastbound; exit 46B westbound, just n. Ext/int corridors. **Pets:** Accepted.

Quality Inn & Suites of Six Flags 🅼
(770) 941-1499. **$59-$68.** 1100 N Blairs Bridge Rd 30168. I-20, exit 44, just n, then just e. Ext corridors. **Pets:** Small, other species. $15 daily fee/pet. Service with restrictions, supervision.

COLLEGE PARK

Country Inn & Suites By Carlson, Atlanta Airport South 🅷
(770) 991-1099. **Call for rates.** 1808 Phoenix Blvd 30349. I-285, exit 60 (Riverdale Rd N), just s, then 0.5 mi w. Int corridors. **Pets:** Accepted.

Econo Lodge 🅼
(404) 768-1241. **Call for rates.** 4874 Old National Hwy 30337. I-285, exit 62, just n. Ext corridors. **Pets:** $15 one-time fee/pet. Service with restrictions, supervision.

Embassy Suites Hotel at Atlanta Airport 🅷
(404) 767-1988. **$109-$209.** 4700 Southport Rd 30337. I-85, exit 71, 0.3 mi w on Riverdale Rd. Int corridors. **Pets:** Accepted.

Holiday Inn Express-Atlanta Airport 🅷
(404) 761-6500. **$79-$159.** 4601 Best Rd 30337. I-85, exit 71, northwest corner. Int corridors. **Pets:** Accepted.

La Quinta Inn & Suites Atlanta Airport 🅷 🐾
(770) 996-0000. **$79-$179.** 4820 Massachusetts Blvd 30337. I-85, exit 71, just e to Airport Rd, then just s. Int corridors. **Pets:** Medium, other species. Service with restrictions, supervision.

Microtel Inn-Atlanta Airport 🅷
(770) 994-3003. **$46.** 4839 Massachusetts Blvd 30337. I-85, exit 71, just e to Airport Rd, then just s; I-285, exit 60 (Riverdale Rd N), 1 mi to Sullivan Rd, then just s. Int corridors. **Pets:** Accepted.

AAA ▼▼▼ **Sheraton Gateway Hotel, Atlanta Airport** H ☞

(770) 997-1100. **$79-$269, 3 day notice.** 1900 Sullivan Rd 30337. I-85, exit 71, just e to Airport Rd, then just s. Int corridors. **Pets:** Medium, other species. $100 deposit/room. Service with restrictions, crate.

SAVE X ⊟ ▣ ¶ ⇌

AAA ▼▼▼ ▼▼▼ **The Westin Hotel-Atlanta Airport** H ☞

(404) 762-7676. **Call for rates.** 4736 Best Rd 30337. I-85, exit 71, just w, se on access road to Best Rd, then just s. Int corridors. **Pets:** Small. $100 one-time fee/room. Service with restrictions, crate.

SAVE X ⅛M ▣ ¶ ⇌ X

DECATUR

▼▼ ▼ **America's Best Inn & Suites** M

(404) 286-2500. **$60.** 4095 Covington Hwy 30032. I-285, exit 43, just w. Ext corridors. **Pets:** $10 daily fee/pet. Service with restrictions, crate.

ASK ⅛M ⇌

▼▼ ▼ **Holiday Inn** H

(404) 371-0204. **$119-$149.** 130 Clairmont Ave 30030. Downtown. Int corridors. **Pets:** Accepted. ASK X ⊟ ▣ ¶ ⇌

DORAVILLE

▼▼ ▼ **Holiday Inn Northeast/Doraville** H

(770) 455-3700. **$79-$90.** 2001 Clearview Ave 30340. I-285, exit 32, southeast corner. Int corridors. **Pets:** Accepted.

ASK X ⅛M ⊟ ▣ ¶ ⇌

AAA ▼ ▼ **Super 8 Atlanta NE** M

(770) 458-2671. **$46-$65.** 2822 Chamblee Tucker Rd 30341. I-85, exit 94, just w. Ext corridors. **Pets:** Small. Service with restrictions, supervision. SAVE X ⊟

DOUGLASVILLE

AAA ▼▼▼ **Best Western Garden Inn & Suites** H ☞

(770) 489-4863. **$67-$76.** 8304 Cherokee Blvd 30134. I-20, exit 37, just n to Cherokee Blvd, then just e. Int corridors. **Pets:** Medium. $20 daily fee/pet. Service with restrictions, supervision.

SAVE X ⅛M ⊟ ⇌

▼▼ ▼ **Days Inn** M

(770) 949-1499. **Call for rates.** 5489 Westmoreland Plaza 30134. I-20, exit 37, just n. Ext corridors. **Pets:** Medium. $20 daily fee/pet. Service with restrictions, supervision. X ⊟ ▣ ⇌

▼▼▼ ▼ **La Quinta Inn & Suites** H ☞

(770) 577-3838. **$69-$129.** 1000 Linnenkohl Dr 30134. I-20, exit 34, just n. Int corridors. **Pets:** Medium, other species. Service with restrictions, supervision. ASK X ⅛M ⊟ ▣ ⇌

DULUTH

▼▼ ▼ **Candlewood Suites-Atlanta** H

(678) 380-0414. **$53-$93.** 3665 Shackleford Rd 30096. I-85, exit 104, just e to Shackleford Rd, then just s. Int corridors. **Pets:** Accepted.

ASK X ⅛M ⊟ ▣

▼▼ ▼ **Days Inn Gwinnett Place** H

(770) 476-8700. **$55-$60.** 1920 Pleasant Hill Rd 30096. I-85, exit 104; northwest corner. Int corridors. **Pets:** Accepted. ASK X ▣

▼▼▼ ▼ **Extended Stay Deluxe Atlanta-Gwinnett Place** H

(770) 623-6800. **$64-$84.** 3390 Venture Pkwy NW 30096. I-85, exit 104, just w to Venture Pkwy, then just n. Int corridors. **Pets:** Other species. $25 daily fee/room. Designated rooms, service with restrictions, crate.

ASK X ⅛M ⊟ ▣ ⇌

▼▼▼ ▼ **Holiday Inn Express** H ☞

(770) 935-7171. **$79-$99.** 3670 Shackleford Rd 30096. I-85, exit 104, just e to Shackleford Rd, then just s. Int corridors. **Pets:** Large. $50 one-time fee/pet. Designated rooms, service with restrictions, supervision.

ASK X ⅛M ⊟ ▣ ⇌

▼▼ ▼ **Holiday Inn-Gwinnett Center** H

(770) 476-2022. **$71-$169.** 6310 Sugarloaf Pkwy 30097. I-85, exit 108, just w. Int corridors. **Pets:** Accepted.

ASK X ⅛M ⊟ ▣ ¶ ⇌

AAA ▼▼▼ **La Quinta Inn Duluth** H ☞

(678) 957-0500. **$59-$139.** 2370 Stephen Center Dr 30096. I-85, exit 107, just w. Int corridors. **Pets:** Medium, other species. Service with restrictions, supervision. SAVE X ⅛M ⊟ ▣ ⇌

▼▼▼ ▼ **Quality Inn–Gwinnett Mall** M

(770) 623-9300. **$60-$90.** 3500 Venture Pkwy 30096. I-85, exit 104, just w to Venture Pkwy, then just n. Ext/int corridors. **Pets:** Other species. $10 daily fee/pet. Service with restrictions, supervision.

X ⅛M ⊟ ▣ ⇌

▼▼ ▼ **Residence Inn-Atlanta Gwinnett** H

(770) 921-2202. **$117-$143.** 1760 Pineland Rd 30096. I-85, exit 104, just e to Shackleford Rd, just s to Pineland Rd, then just e. Int corridors. **Pets:** Accepted. X ⅛M ⊟ ▣ ⇌ X

▼▼ ▼ **Studio 6 #6023** M

(770) 931-3113. **$51-$57.** 3525 Breckinridge Blvd 30096. I-85, exit 104, just e to Breckinridge Blvd, then just n. Ext corridors. **Pets:** Other species. $10 daily fee/room. Service with restrictions, supervision.

X ⅛M ▣

EAST POINT

▼▼ ▼ **Comfort Inn & Suites Atlanta Airport Camp Creek** H

(404) 762-5566. **Call for rates.** 3601 N Desert Dr 30344. I-285, exit 2, just e. Int corridors. **Pets:** Accepted. X ⅛M ⊟ ▣ ⇌

▼▼▼ ▼ **Crowne Plaza Hotel and Resort Atlanta Airport** H

(404) 768-6660. **Call for rates.** 1325 Virginia Ave 30344. I-85, exit 73 southbound; exit 73B northbound, just w. Int corridors. **Pets:** Accepted. X ⅛M ▣ ¶ ⇌

▼▼▼ ▼ **Drury Inn & Suites-Atlanta Airport** H

(404) 761-4900. **$90-$179.** 1270 Virginia Ave 30344. I-85, exit 73 southbound; exit 73A northbound, just e. Int corridors. **Pets:** Other species. No service, supervision. ASK X ⅛M ⊟ ⇌

AAA ▼▼▼ **Ramada Atlanta Airport Conference Center** H

(404) 762-8411. **$89-$109.** 1380 Virginia Ave 30344. I-85, exit 73 southbound; exit 73B northbound, just w. Ext/int corridors. **Pets:** Accepted.

SAVE X ⅛M ⊟ ▣ ¶ ⇌

▼▼ ▼ **Red Roof Inn-Atlanta Airport North** H

(404) 209-1800. **$69-$91.** 1200 Virginia Ave 30344. I-85, exit 73 southbound; exit 73A northbound, just e. Int corridors. **Pets:** Large. Service with restrictions, crate. ASK X ⅛M ⊟ ⇌

FOREST PARK

▼▼ ▼ **Days Inn-Airport East** M

(404) 768-6400. **$53-$95, 14 day notice.** 5116 Hwy 85 30297. I-75, exit 237A southbound; exit 237 northbound, 0.5 mi w. Ext corridors. **Pets:** Small, other species. $25 deposit/pet, $25 daily fee/pet. Service with restrictions, supervision. ASK X ⊟ ⇌

▼▼ ▼ **Econo Lodge** M ☞

(404) 363-6429. **$45.** 5060 Frontage Rd 30297. I-75, exit 237, just e to Frontage Rd, then just s. Ext corridors. **Pets:** Other species. $15 daily fee/pet. Service with restrictions, crate. X ⊟

▼▼ ▼ **Super 8** M

(404) 363-8811. **$49-$149.** 410 Old Dixie Way 30297. I-75, exit 235, just e. Ext corridors. **Pets:** Medium, other species. $7 daily fee/pet. Service with restrictions, supervision. ASK X ⊟ ▣ ⇌

HAPEVILLE

Hilton Atlanta Airport H
(404) 767-9000. **$119-$249.** 1031 Virginia Ave 30354. I-85, exit 73 southbound; exit 73A northbound, just e. Int corridors. **Pets:** Accepted.

Residence Inn Atlanta Airport H
(404) 761-0511. **$179-$219.** 3401 International Blvd 30354. I-85, exit 73 southbound; exit 73A northbound, 0.5 mi e to International Blvd, then just n. Ext/int corridors. **Pets:** Accepted.

JONESBORO

Clarion Hotel Atlanta Airport South H
(770) 968-4300. **Call for rates.** 6288 Old Dixie Hwy 30236. I-75, exit 235, just w. Int corridors. **Pets:** Medium. $50 deposit/pet, $50 daily fee/pet. Designated rooms, service with restrictions, supervision.

KENNESAW

Best Western Kennesaw Inn H
(770) 424-7666. **$80-$86.** 3375 Busbee Dr 30144. I-75, exit 271, just e. Ext corridors. **Pets:** Large. $10 daily fee/pet. Service with restrictions, crate.

Days Inn M
(770) 419-1576. **$55-$79, 7 day notice.** 760 Cobb Place Blvd 30144. I-75, exit 269, just w. Ext corridors. **Pets:** Medium. $15 daily fee/pet. Service with restrictions, supervision.

Extended StayAmerica Atlanta Kennesaw H
(770) 422-1403. **$57-$81.** 3000 George Busbee Pkwy 30144. I-75, exit 269, just e to George Busbee Pkwy, then 0.8 mi n. Int corridors. **Pets:** Other species. $25 daily fee/room. Designated rooms, service with restrictions, crate.

Green Roof Inn & Suites M
(770) 529-3370. **$45-$120.** 3027 Cobb Pkwy NW 30152. I-75, exit 271, 2.5 mi w, then 2.2 mi n on US 41. Ext corridors. **Pets:** Accepted.

Hilton Garden Inn-Atlanta NW/Kennesaw Town Center H
(678) 322-1140. **$99-$189.** 895 Cobb Place Blvd 30144. I-75, exit 269, just w to Cobb Place Blvd, then just n. Int corridors. **Pets:** Accepted.

La Quinta Inn H
(770) 426-0045. **$69-$119.** 2625 George Busbee Pkwy 30144. I-75, exit 269, just e to George Busbee Pkwy, then just n. Int corridors. **Pets:** Medium, other species. Service with restrictions, supervision.

Quality Inn M
(770) 419-1530. **$60-$90.** 750 Cobb Place Blvd 30144. I-75, exit 269, just w. Ext corridors. **Pets:** Medium. $15 daily fee/pet. Service with restrictions, supervision.

Red Roof Inn-Town Center Mall M
(770) 429-0323. **$50-$100, 14 day notice.** 520 Roberts Ct NW 30144. I-75, exit 269, just e. Ext corridors. **Pets:** Large. Service with restrictions, crate.

Residence Inn by Marriott Town Center H
(770) 218-1018. **$170-$208.** 3443 Busbee Dr 30144. I-75, exit 271, just e. Int corridors. **Pets:** Accepted.

StudioPLUS Atlanta-Kennesaw H
(770) 425-6101. **$57-$81.** 3316 Busbee Dr 30144. I-75, exit 271, just e to Busbee Dr, then just s. Int corridors. **Pets:** Other species. $25 daily fee/room. Designated rooms, service with restrictions, crate.

Travelodge M
(770) 590-0519. **$45-$79.** 1460 George Busbee Pkwy 30144. I-75, exit 273, just e. Ext corridors. **Pets:** Medium, other species. $15 daily fee/pet. Designated rooms, service with restrictions, supervision.

LAWRENCEVILLE

Best Western Lawrenceville Inn H
(770) 513-0028. **$55-$65.** 571 Budford Dr 30045. Jct SR 316 and 20/124, 0.5 mi s. Int corridors. **Pets:** Accepted.

Days Inn M
(770) 995-7782. **$70-$121.** 731 Duluth Hwy 30045. Jct SR 316, just e on SR 120. Ext corridors. **Pets:** $20 one-time fee/pet. Service with restrictions, supervision.

Extended StayAmerica Atlanta-Lawrenceville M
(770) 962-5660. **$44-$74.** 474 W Pike St 30045. SR 316, exit SR 120, 0.8 mi s. Ext corridors. **Pets:** Other species. $25 daily fee/room. Designated rooms, service with restrictions, crate.

Hampton Inn H
(770) 338-9600. **$89-$159.** 1135 Lakes Pkwy 30043. SR 316, exit Riverside Pkwy, just n. Int corridors. **Pets:** Accepted.

LITHONIA

Red Roof Inn H
(770) 322-1400. **$70-$90.** 5400 Fairington Rd 30038. I-20, exit 71, just s to Fairington Rd, then just ne. Int corridors. **Pets:** Large. Service with restrictions, crate.

MARIETTA

Americas Best Value Inn H
(770) 952-0052. **$50-$100.** 1940 Leland Dr 30067. I-75, exit 260, just e, then 0.3 mi n. Ext/int corridors. **Pets:** Small. $5 daily fee/pet. No service, crate.

Comfort Inn-Marietta H
(770) 952-3000. **$56-$81.** 2100 Northwest Pkwy 30067. I-75, exit 261, 0.3 mi w to Franklin Rd, then just s. Ext corridors. **Pets:** Medium. $25 one-time fee/room. Service with restrictions, supervision.

Crowne Plaza Atlanta-Marietta H
(770) 428-4400. **Call for rates.** 1775 Parkway Pl NW 30067. I-75, exit 263, just w. Int corridors. **Pets:** Accepted.

Drury Inn & Suites-Atlanta Northwest H
(770) 612-0900. **$70-$149.** 1170 Powers Ferry Pl 30067. I-75, exit 261, just e. Int corridors. **Pets:** Other species. No service, supervision.

Extended StayAmerica Atlanta-Marietta Windy Hill H
(770) 690-9477. **$47-$67.** 1967 Leland Dr 30067. I-75, exit 260, just e to Leland Dr, then just n. Int corridors. **Pets:** Other species. $25 daily fee/room. Designated rooms, service with restrictions, crate.

Hilton Atlanta/Marietta Hotel & Conference Center H
(770) 427-2500. **$89-$169.** 500 Powder Springs St 30064. I-75, exit 263, 3.5 mi w to Powder Springs St, then just w. Int corridors. **Pets:** Medium. $75 one-time fee/room. Designated rooms, service with restrictions, crate.

Homestead Studio Suites Hotel-Atlanta-Marietta-Powers Ferry Rd H
(770) 303-0043. **$49-$69.** 2239 Powers Ferry Rd 30067. I-285, exit 22, just n. Int corridors. **Pets:** Other species. $25 daily fee/room. Designated rooms, service with restrictions, crate.

▼▼ ▼▼ **Hometown Inn Atlanta-Marietta-Canton Rd** Ⓜ
(770) 499-9550. **$30-$50.** 1051 Canton Rd 30066. I-75, exit 267A northbound, 1.8 mi w. Ext corridors. **Pets:** Accepted. (ASK) ⊠ 🖬 💻

ⒶⒶⒶ ▼▼▼▼ **Hyatt Regency Suites Atlanta NW** Ⓗ ❀
(770) 956-1234. **$79-$329, 3 day notice.** 2999 Windy Hill Rd 30067. I-75, exit 260, 0.5 mi e at Powers Ferry Rd. Int corridors. **Pets:** Small, other species. $50 one-time fee/room. Service with restrictions, supervision. (SAVE) ⊠ 🖬 💻 ¶ ⇆

▼▼▼ ▼ **La Quinta Inn** Ⓗ ❀
(770) 951-0026. **$42-$109.** 2170 Delk Rd 30067-8761. I-75, exit 261, 0.3 mi w. Ext/int corridors. **Pets:** Medium, other species. Service with restrictions, supervision. (ASK) ⊠ 🖬 💻 ⇆

ⒶⒶⒶ ▼▼ **Masters Inn Marietta** Ⓜ
(770) 951-2005. **$45-$52.** 2682 Windy Hill Rd 30067. I-75, exit 260, just w to Circle 75 Pkwy, then just s. Ext corridors. **Pets:** Small, other species. $10 one-time fee/pet. Designated rooms, service with restrictions, crate. (SAVE) ⊠

MORROW

ⒶⒶⒶ ▼▼▼ **Best Western Southlake Inn** Ⓜ
(770) 961-6300. **$65-$89.** 6437 Jonesboro Rd 30260. I-75, exit 233, just e. Ext corridors. **Pets:** Accepted. (SAVE) ⊠ 🖬 💻 ⇆

▼▼▼▼ **Drury Inn & Suites-Atlanta South** Ⓗ
(770) 960-0500. **$75-$159.** 6520 S Lee St 30260. I-75, exit 233, just e. Int corridors. **Pets:** Other species. No service, supervision.
(ASK) ⊠ 🖬 🖬 💻 ⇆

▼▼▼▼ **Extended StayAmerica-Atlanta-Morrow** Ⓗ
(770) 472-0727. **$65-$95.** 2265 Mt. Zion Pkwy 30260. I-75, exit 231, just w, then just s. Int corridors. **Pets:** Other species. $25 daily fee/room. Designated rooms, service with restrictions, crate. (ASK) ⊠ 🖬 💻

ⒶⒶⒶ ▼▼▼ **Red Roof Inn-South** Ⓜ
(770) 968-1483. **$50-$90, 14 day notice.** 1348 Southlake Plaza Dr 30260. I-75, exit 233, just e to Southlake Plaza Dr, then just n. Ext corridors. **Pets:** Large. Service with restrictions, crate. (SAVE) ⊠ 🖬 🖬

ⒶⒶⒶ ▼▼▼ **Sleep Inn** Ⓗ
(770) 472-9800. **$45-$129.** 2185 Mt. Zion Pkwy 30260. I-75, exit 231, just w to Mt. Zion Pkwy, then just s. Int corridors. **Pets:** Medium, dogs only. $10 daily fee/pet. Designated rooms, service with restrictions, supervision. (SAVE) ⊠ 🖬 🖬 💻 ⇆

NORCROSS

▼▼▼ **America's Best Inn** Ⓗ
(770) 449-7322. **$59-$79.** 6045 Oakbrook Pkwy 30093. I-85, exit 99, just e to Live Oak Pkwy, 1 mi n, then w. Ext/int corridors. **Pets:** Accepted.
(ASK) ⊠ 🖬 💻

▼▼▼▼ **Comfort Inn & Suites** Ⓗ
(770) 263-8883. **$69-$99.** 5200 Peachtree Industrial Blvd 30071. I-285, exit 31B, 5.5 mi n; I-85, exit 99, 4 mi w to Peachtree Industrial Blvd, then 1.5 mi n. Int corridors. **Pets:** $25 daily fee/pet. Service with restrictions, crate. ⊠ 🖬 🖬 💻 ⇆

▼▼ ▼▼ **Days Inn & Suites** Ⓗ
(770) 416-9021. **Call for rates.** 5385 Peachtree Industrial Blvd 30092. I-285, exit 31B, 5.5 mi n; I-85, exit 99, 4 mi w to Peachtree Industrial Blvd, then 1.5 mi n. Int corridors. **Pets:** Accepted.
⊠ 🖬 🖬 💻 ⇆

ⒶⒶⒶ ▼▼▼ **Days Inn Atlanta NE** Ⓜ
(770) 368-0218. **$50-$100.** 5990 Western Hills Dr 30071. I-85, exit 99, 0.8 mi w to Norcross Tucker Rd to Western Hills Dr, then just n. Ext corridors. **Pets:** Accepted. (SAVE) ⊠ 🖬 💻 ⇆

▼▼▼▼ **Drury Inn & Suites-Atlanta Northeast** Ⓗ
(770) 729-0060. **$75-$149.** 5655 Jimmy Carter Blvd 30071. I-85, exit 99, just w. Int corridors. **Pets:** Other species. No service, supervision.
(ASK) ⊠ 🖬 🖬 💻 ⇆

▼▼ ▼▼ **Extended StayAmerica Atlanta-Jimmy Carter Blvd.** Ⓜ
(770) 446-9245. **$54-$74.** 6295 Jimmy Carter Blvd 30071. I-85, exit 99, 2.5 mi w. Ext corridors. **Pets:** Other species. $25 daily fee/room. Designated rooms, service with restrictions, crate. (ASK) ⊠ 🖬 🖬 💻

▼▼ ▼▼ **Extended StayAmerica Atlanta-Norcross** Ⓗ
(770) 729-8100. **$54-$74.** 200 Lawrenceville St 30071. Downtown; behind post office. Ext corridors. **Pets:** Other species. $25 daily fee/room. Designated rooms, service with restrictions, crate. (ASK) ⊠ 🖬 💻

▼▼ ▼▼ **GuestHouse Inn & Suites** Ⓜ
(770) 564-0492. **$49-$89, 7 day notice.** 2050 Willowtrail Pkwy 30093. I-85, exit 101, just e. Ext corridors. **Pets:** Accepted.
(ASK) ⊠ 🖬 💻 ⇆

▼▼ ▼▼ **Hilton Atlanta Northeast** Ⓗ
(770) 447-4747. **$99-$199.** 5993 Peachtree Industrial Blvd 30092. I-285, exit 31B, 4.5 mi ne. Int corridors. **Pets:** Accepted.
⊠ 🖬 💻 ¶ ⇆

▼▼ ▼▼ **Holiday Inn-Peachtree Corners** Ⓗ
(770) 448-4400. **$72-$89.** 6050 Peachtree Industrial Blvd NW 30071. I-285, exit 31B, 4.5 mi ne; I-85, exit 99, 4 mi w to Peachtree Industrial Blvd, 0.4 mi n, then just w on Holcomb Bridge Rd. Int corridors.
Pets: Accepted. (ASK) ⊠ 🖬 🖬 💻 ⇆

▼▼ ▼▼ **Homestead Studio Suites Hotel-Atlanta/Peachtree Corners** Ⓜ
(770) 449-9966. **$51-$66.** 7049 Jimmy Carter Blvd 30092. I-85, exit 99, 4 mi n; I-285, exit 31B, 4 mi n. Ext corridors. **Pets:** Other species. $25 daily fee/room. Designated rooms, service with restrictions, crate.
(ASK) ⊠ 🖬 💻

▼▼▼▼ **Homewood Suites by Hilton** Ⓗ
(770) 448-4663. **$129-$159.** 450 Technology Pkwy 30092. I-85, exit 99, 4 mi w to Peachtree Industrial Blvd, 0.4 mi n, w on Holcomb Bridge Rd, then 2 blks n on Peachtree Pkwy; I-285, exit 31B, 5 mi n on SR 141. Ext/int corridors. **Pets:** Accepted. ⊠ 🖬 🖬 💻 ⇆ ⊠

▼▼▼▼ **Horizon Inn & Suites** Ⓗ
(770) 448-8686. **Call for rates.** 6187 Dawson Blvd 30093. I-85, exit 99, just e to McDonough Dr, then just s. Ext corridors. **Pets:** Accepted.
⊠ 🖬 💻 ⇆

▼▼▼▼ **Howard Johnson** Ⓗ
(678) 736-6610. **$40-$50.** 5375 Peachtree Industrial Blvd 30092. I-285, exit 31B, 5.5 mi n; I-85, exit 99, 4 mi w to Peachtree Industrial Blvd, then 1.5 mi n. Ext/int corridors. **Pets:** Medium. $10 daily fee/pet. Service with restrictions, supervision. (ASK) ⊠ 🖬 💻 ⇆

ⒶⒶⒶ ▼▼▼▼ **La Quinta Inn** Ⓗ ❀
(770) 368-9400. **$59-$119.** 5945 Oakbrook Pkwy 30093. I-85, exit 99, 0.5 mi e to Live Oak Pkwy, then 0.8 mi w. Int corridors. **Pets:** Medium, other species. Service with restrictions, supervision. (SAVE) ⊠ 🖬 💻 ⇆

▼▼▼▼ **Red Roof Inn & Suites** Ⓗ
(770) 446-2882. **Call for rates.** 5395 Peachtree Industrial Blvd 30092. I-285, exit 31B, 5.5 mi n; I-85, exit 99, 4 mi w to Peachtree Industrial Blvd, then 1.5 mi n. Int corridors. **Pets:** Large. Service with restrictions, crate. ⊠ 🖬 💻 ⇆

▼▼ ▼▼ **Red Roof Inn-Indian Trail** Ⓜ
(770) 448-8944. **Call for rates.** 5171 Brook Hollow Pkwy 30071. I-85, exit 101, just w to Brook Hollow Pkwy, then just s. Ext corridors.
Pets: Large. Service with restrictions, crate. ⊠

▼▼ ▼▼ **StudioPlus-Atlanta Peachtree Corners** Ⓗ
(770) 582-9984. **$54-$69.** 7065 Jimmy Carter Blvd 30092. I-85, exit 99, 4 mi n; I-285, exit 31B, 4 mi n. Int corridors. **Pets:** Other species. $25 daily fee/room. Designated rooms, service with restrictions, crate.
(ASK) ⊠ 🖬 🖬 💻 ⇆

ROSWELL

▼▼ Brookwood Inn 🅷

(770) 587-5161. **Call for rates.** 9995 Old Dogwood Rd 30076. SR 400, exit 7B, just w to Old Dogwood Rd, then just n. Ext corridors. **Pets:** Other species. $10 daily fee/pet. Designated rooms, service with restrictions, crate. ⊠ 🛢 💻 ➔

▼▼▼ La Quinta Inn & Suites 🅷 ❀

(770) 552-0200. **$42-$109.** 575 Old Holcomb Bridge Rd 30076. SR 400, exit 7B, just w. Int corridors. **Pets:** Medium, other species. Service with restrictions, supervision. 🅰🆂🅺 ⊠ 🅼 🛢 💻 ➔

▼▼ Studio 6 #6025 🅼

(770) 992-9449. **$49-$57.** 9955 Old Dogwood Rd 30076. SR 400, exit 7B, just w. Ext corridors. **Pets:** Other species. $10 daily fee/room. Service with restrictions, supervision. 🅼 🛢 💻

SMYRNA

▼▼ Baymont Inn & Suites 🅷

(404) 794-1600. **$59-$79.** 5130 S Cobb Dr 30082. I-285, exit 15, 0.3 mi w. Int corridors. **Pets:** Accepted. ⊠ 🅼 🛢 💻 ➔ ⊠

🆎 ▼▼▼ Holiday Inn Express Atlanta / Smyrna Cobb Galleria Center 🅷

(770) 435-4990. **$59-$75, 3 day notice.** 2855 Springhill Pkwy 30080. I-285, exit 20 westbound; exit 19 eastbound, just n on US 41 (Cobb Pkwy), then just w on Spring Rd. Int corridors. **Pets:** Accepted.
🆂🅰🆅🅴 ⊠ 🅼 🛢 💻 ➔ ⊠

▼▼ Homestead Studio Suites Hotel-Atlanta/Cumberland Mall 🅼

(770) 432-4000. **$54-$84.** 3103 Sports Ave 30080. I-285, exit 20 westbound; exit 19 eastbound, just n to Spring Rd, then 0.3 mi w. Ext corridors. **Pets:** Other species. $25 daily fee/room. Designated rooms, service with restrictions, crate. 🅰🆂🅺 ⊠ 🅼 🛢 💻

🆎 ▼▼▼ Red Roof Inn-North 🅼

(770) 952-6966. **$45-$90, 14 day notice.** 2200 Corporate Plaza 30080. I-75, exit 260, just w to Corporate Plaza, then just s. Ext corridors. **Pets:** Large. Service with restrictions, crate. 🆂🅰🆅🅴 ⊠ 🅼 🛢

🆎 ▼▼▼▼ Residence Inn-Atlanta Cumberland 🅷

(770) 433-8877. **$170-$208.** 2771 Cumberland Blvd 30080. I-285, exit 20 westbound; exit 19 eastbound, just n to Spring Rd, 0.3 mi w to Cumberland Blvd, then just n. Ext corridors. **Pets:** Accepted.
🆂🅰🆅🅴 ⊠ 🅼 🛢 💻 ➔ ⊠

SNELLVILLE

▼▼ Crestwood Suites 🅷

(770) 982-5250. **Call for rates.** 1784 Presidential Cir 30078. Jct Ronald Reagan Pkwy and SR 124, just w. Int corridors. **Pets:** Accepted.
⊠ 🛢 💻

🆎 ▼▼▼▼ La Quinta Inn & Suites 🅷 ❀

(770) 736-4723. **$74-$120.** 2971 Main St W 30078. Jct US 78 and SR 124, 0.9 mi w. Int corridors. **Pets:** Medium, other species. Service with restrictions, supervision. 🆂🅰🆅🅴 ⊠ 🅼 🛢 💻 ➔

STONE MOUNTAIN

🆎 ▼▼ ◆ Best Western Stone Mountain 🅼

(770) 465-1022. **$80-$120.** 1595 E Park Place Blvd 30087. US 78, exit E Park Place Blvd, just n. Ext corridors. **Pets:** Medium. $25 daily fee/pet. Designated rooms, service with restrictions, supervision.
🆂🅰🆅🅴 ⊠ 🛢 💻

SUWANEE

🆎 ▼▼ Best Western Gwinnett Inn 🅷 ❀

(770) 271-5559. **$80-$90, 7 day notice.** 77 Gwinco Blvd 30024. I-85, exit 111, just e to Gwinco Blvd, then just s. Int corridors. **Pets:** $15 daily fee/pet. Service with restrictions, supervision.
🆂🅰🆅🅴 ⊠ 🅼 🛢 💻 ➔

🆎 ▼▼ Comfort Inn 🅼

(770) 945-1608. **Call for rates.** 2945 Lawrenceville Suwanee Rd 30024. I-85, exit 111, just e. Ext corridors. **Pets:** Other species. $25 one-time fee/room. Service with restrictions. 🆂🅰🆅🅴 ⊠ 🛢 💻 ➔

TUCKER

🆎 ▼▼▼ Atlanta Northlake TownePlace Suites 🅷

(770) 938-0408. **$139-$169.** 3300 Northlake Pkwy 30345. I-285, exit 36 southbound, just w; exit 37 northbound, just w to Parklake Dr, 0.5 mi n, then just w. Int corridors. **Pets:** Accepted.
🅴🅲🅾 🆂🅰🆅🅴 ⊠ 🅼 🛢 💻 ➔

🆎 ▼▼▼ DoubleTree Hotel Atlanta NE 🅷

(770) 938-1026. **$79-$179.** 4156 Lavista Rd 30084. I-285, exit 37, just w. Int corridors. **Pets:** Accepted. 🆂🅰🆅🅴 ⊠ 🅼 💻 🍽 ➔

🆎 ▼▼ Econo Lodge 🅼

(770) 939-8440. **$50-$70.** 1820 Mountain Industrial Blvd 30084. US 78, exit 4, just n. **Pets:** Small. $10 daily fee/pet. Designated rooms, service with restrictions, supervision. 🆂🅰🆅🅴 ⊠ 🛢 💻

🆎 ▼▼ Masters Inn Tucker 🅼

(770) 938-3552. **$42-$75.** 1435 Montreal Rd 30084. I-285, exit 38, just w. Ext corridors. **Pets:** Accepted. 🆂🅰🆅🅴 ⊠ 🛢 ➔

▼▼ Motel 6 #2007 🅼

(770) 496-1311. **$41-$51.** 2810 Lawrenceville Hwy 30084. I-285, exit 38, just w. Ext corridors. **Pets:** Other species. Service with restrictions, supervision. ⊠

🆎 ▼▼ Quality Inn Atlanta/Northlake 🅼

(770) 491-7444. **$75-$99.** 2155 Ranchwood Dr 30345. I-285, exit 37, 0.4 mi w, then just n. Ext/int corridors. **Pets:** Small. $15 daily fee/pet. Designated rooms, service with restrictions. 🆂🅰🆅🅴 ⊠ 🅼 🛢 💻 ➔

UNION CITY

▼▼ Days Inn 🅼

(770) 306-6067. **$45-$85.** 6840 Shannon Pkwy S 30291. I-85, exit 64, 0.3 mi w to Shannon Pkwy, then just s. Ext corridors. **Pets:** Medium, dogs only. $10 daily fee/pet. Supervision. 🅰🆂🅺 ⊠ 🛢 💻 ➔

🆎 ▼▼ Microtel Inn & Suites 🅷

(770) 306-3800. **$50-$70.** 6690 Shannon Pkwy 30291. I-85, exit 64, 0.3 mi w to Shannon Pkwy, then just n. Int corridors. **Pets:** Small. $15 daily fee/pet. Service with restrictions, supervision. 🆂🅰🆅🅴 ⊠ 🅼 🛢 💻

END METROPOLITAN AREA

AUGUSTA

▼▼▼▼ Candlewood Suites Augusta 🅷 ❀

(706) 733-3300. **Call for rates.** 1080 Claussen Rd 30907. I-20, exit 200 (River Watch Pkwy), just nw, then just sw. Int corridors. **Pets:** Medium. $75 one-time fee/room. Service with restrictions, crate.
⊠ 🅼 🛢 💻

▼▼▼ DoubleTree Hotel Augusta 🅷

(706) 855-8100. **$79-$159.** 2651 Perimeter Pkwy 30909. I-520, exit 1C (Wheeler Rd), just w to Perimeter Pkwy, then just n. Int corridors.
Pets: Accepted. ⊠ 🅼 🛢 💻 🍽 ➔ ⊠

▼▼▼▼ **Hilton Garden Inn Augusta** H
(706) 739-9990. **$129-$229.** 1065 Stevens Creek Rd 30907. I-20, exit 199 (Washington Rd), just w on Washington Rd, then just ne. Int corridors. **Pets:** Accepted. ⊠ ⓂⓂ 🛏 💻 ⑪ ⌷

▼▼▼▼ **Holiday Inn Gordon Highway at Bobby Jones** M
(706) 737-2300. **Call for rates.** 2155 Gordon Hwy 30909. I-520, exit 3A (US 78), just w. Ext corridors. **Pets:** Accepted. ⊠ 🛏 💻 ⑪ ⌷

▼▼▼▼ **Jameson Suites** H
(706) 733-4656. **$100-$125.** 1062 Clausen Rd 30907. I-20, exit 200 (River Watch Pkwy), just nw, then just sw. Int corridors. **Pets:** Accepted. ASK ⊠ ⓂⓂ 🛏 💻 ⌷

▼▼ **La Quinta Inn Augusta** M 🐾
(706) 733-2660. **$49-$89.** 3020 Washington Rd 30907. I-20, exit 199 (Washington Rd), just w. Ext/int corridors. **Pets:** Medium, other species. Service with restrictions, supervision. ASK ⊠ ⓂⓂ 🛏 💻 ⌷

▲▲▲ ▼▼▼▼ **Marriott Augusta Hotel & Suites** H
(706) 722-8900. **$170-$208.** 2 10th St 30901. I-20, exit 200 (River Watch Pkwy), 5.4 mi se, then just n; downtown. Int corridors. **Pets:** Medium. $25 one-time fee/pet. Designated rooms, service with restrictions, crate. SAVE ⊠ ⓂⓂ 🛏 💻 ⑪ ⌷ ⌷

▲▲▲ ▼▼▼▼ **The Partridge Inn** H
(706) 737-8888. **$119-$249.** 2110 Walton Way 30904. 1.3 mi w off 15th St. Int corridors. **Pets:** Accepted. SAVE ⊠ 🛏 💻 ⑪ ⌷

▲▲▲ ▼▼ **Quality Inn Medical Center** M
(706) 722-2224. **$60-$70.** 1455 Walton Way 30901. I-20, exit 199 (Washington Rd), 4.5 mi e on SR 28, then just sw on 15th St. Ext corridors. **Pets:** Accepted. SAVE ⊠ 🛏 💻 ⌷

▼▼▼▼ **Staybridge Suites** H
(706) 733-0000. **$89-$109.** 2540 Center West Pkwy 30909. I-20, exit 199 (Washington Rd), just e, then just n. Int corridors. **Pets:** Accepted. ASK ⊠ ⓂⓂ 🛏 💻

BAINBRIDGE

▼▼ **Jameson Inn** H
(229) 243-7000. **$88-$93.** 1403 Tallahassee Hwy 39819. Just s of US 84 Bypass on US 27. Ext corridors. **Pets:** Accepted. ASK ⊠ 🛏 💻 ⌷

BARNESVILLE

▼▼ **Lamar Inn & Suites** H
(770) 358-0967. **$145-$250.** 648 Hwy 341 S 30204. Jct US 341 and 41, 2.3 mi s. Int corridors. **Pets:** Accepted. ASK ⊠ 🛏 💻

BLUE RIDGE

▲▲▲ ▼▼▼ **Douglas Inn & Suites** M
(706) 258-3600. **$45-$69.** 1192 Windy Ridge Rd 30513. Just off SR 515 and US 76; behind Wendy's. Ext corridors. **Pets:** Accepted. SAVE ⊠ ⓂⓂ 🛏 💻 ⌷

BRASELTON

▲▲▲ ▼▼▼ **Best Western Braselton Inn** H
(706) 654-3081. **$89-$165, 3 day notice.** 303 Zion Church Rd 30517. I-85, exit 129, 0.3 mi n. Ext corridors. **Pets:** Small, other species. $15 daily fee/pet. Designated rooms, service with restrictions. SAVE ⊠ 🛏 💻 ⌷

BREMEN

▼▼ **Days Inn** M
(770) 537-4646. **$65, 14 day notice.** 35 Price Creek Rd 30110. I-75, exit 11, just n. Ext corridors. **Pets:** Accepted. ASK ⊠ 🛏 💻 ⌷

▲▲▲ ▼▼▼ **Holiday Inn Express Hotel & Suites** H
(770) 537-3770. **$79-$89.** 125 US Hwy 27 Bypass 30110. I-20, exit 11, just n. Int corridors. **Pets:** Small. $35 one-time fee/room. Designated rooms, service with restrictions, supervision. SAVE ⊠ ⓂⓂ 🛏 💻 ⌷

▲▲▲ ▼▼▼ **Microtel Inn & Suites** H
(770) 537-8000. **$60-$85.** 104 Price Creek Rd 30110. I-20, exit 11, just n. Int corridors. **Pets:** Accepted. SAVE ⊠ ⓂⓂ 🛏 💻 ⌷

BRUNSWICK

▲▲▲ ▼▼▼ **Best Western Brunswick Inn** H 🐾
(912) 264-0144. **$75-$168.** 5323 New Jesup Hwy 31523. I-95, exit 36B (New Jesup Hwy/US 25), just nw. Ext corridors. **Pets:** Small, other species. Service with restrictions, supervision. SAVE ⊠ 🛏 💻 ⑪ ⌷

▲▲▲ ▼▼▼ **Hampton Inn Brunswick** H 🐾
(912) 261-0002. **Call for rates.** 230 Warren Mason Blvd 31520. I-95, exit 36A (New Jesup Hwy/US 25), just se, then just sw on Tourist Dr. Ext/int corridors. **Pets:** Medium. Designated rooms, service with restrictions, supervision. SAVE ⊠ 🛏 💻 ⌷

▼▼▼▼ **Jameson Inn Brunswick** H
(912) 267-0800. **$78-$85.** 661 Scranton Rd 31520. I-95, exit 38 (Golden Isles Pkwy), 1.6 mi se, then just sw. Ext corridors. **Pets:** Accepted. ASK ⊠ 🛏 💻 ⌷

▼▼▼▼ **La Quinta Inn & Suites Brunswick** H 🐾
(912) 265-7725. **$55-$104.** 165 Warren Mason Blvd 31520. I-95, exit 36A (New Jesup Hwy/US 25), just se, then sw on Tourist Dr. Int corridors. **Pets:** Medium, other species. Service with restrictions, supervision. ASK ⊠ 🛏 💻 ⌷

▲▲▲ ▼▼ **Super 8** H
(912) 264-8800. **$45-$125.** 5280 New Jesup Hwy 31523. I-95, exit 36B (New Jesup Hwy/US 25), just nw. Int corridors. **Pets:** $10 daily fee/pet. Service with restrictions, supervision. SAVE ⊠ 🛏 💻

BYRON

▲▲▲ ▼▼▼ **Best Western Inn & Suites** H 🐾
(478) 956-3056. **$63-$69.** 101 Dunbar Rd 31008. I-75, exit 149 (SR 49), just ne. Ext corridors. **Pets:** Large. $10 daily fee/pet. Service with restrictions, crate. SAVE ⊠ 🛏 💻 ⌷

▼▼▼ **Quality Inn** H
(478) 956-1600. **Call for rates.** 115 Chapman Rd 31008. I-75, exit 149 (SR 49), just sw, then n. Ext corridors. **Pets:** Accepted. ⊠ 🛏 💻 ⌷

CAIRO

▲▲▲ ▼▼▼ **Best Western Executive Inn** H
(229) 377-8000. **$70-$80.** 2800 Hwy 84 E 31728. 2 mi e. Ext corridors. **Pets:** Accepted. SAVE ⊠ 🛏 💻 ⑪ ⌷

CALHOUN

▼▼▼ **Comfort Inn** M
(706) 629-8271. **Call for rates.** 742 Hwy 53 SE 30701. I-75, exit 312, just w. Ext corridors. **Pets:** Large. $10 deposit/pet. Service with restrictions, supervision. ⊠ 🛏 💻 ⑪ ⌷

▼▼▼ **Country Inn & Suites By Carlson** H
(706) 625-6500. **$80-$149, 3 day notice.** 1033 Fairmount Hwy 30701. I-75, exit 312, just e. Int corridors. **Pets:** Other species. Service with restrictions, supervision. ASK ⊠ ⓂⓂ 🛏 💻 ⌷

▲▲▲ ▼▼▼ **Days Inn** M
(706) 629-9501. **$55-$75.** 915 Hwy 53 E SE 30701. I-75, exit 312, just e. Ext corridors. **Pets:** Accepted. SAVE ⊠ ⓂⓂ 🛏 💻 ⑪ ⌷

▼▼▼ **Jameson Inn** M
(706) 629-8133. **$83-$90.** 189 Jameson St 30701. I-75, exit 312, just w. Ext corridors. **Pets:** Medium, other species. $15 daily fee/room. Service with restrictions, supervision. ASK ⊠ 🛏 💻 ⌷

▼▼ **Ramada Limited** M
(706) 629-9207. **$55-$100.** 1204 Red Bud Rd NE 30701. I-75, exit 315, just w. Ext corridors. **Pets:** Small. $10 daily fee/pet. Designated rooms, service with restrictions, supervision. ASK ⊠ 🛏 💻 ⌷

▼▼▼ Smith Motel **M**

(706) 629-8427. **$30-$33.** 1437 US Hwy 41 N 30701. I-75, exit 318, just w. Ext corridors. **Pets:** $10 daily fee/pet. Service with restrictions.
[ASK] [✕] [🛗]

CARROLLTON
▼▼▼ Jameson Inn **M**

(770) 834-2600. **$78-$85.** 700 S Park St 30117. On US 27, just s of downtown. Ext corridors. **Pets:** Accepted. [ASK] [✕] [&M] [🛗] [🖵] [≈]

CARTERSVILLE
(AAA) ▼▼▼ Best Western Garden Inn & Suites **M**

(770) 386-1569. **$58-$88.** 5663 Hwy 20 NE 30121. I-75, exit 290, 0.3 mi e. Ext corridors. **Pets:** Medium. $10 daily fee/pet. Designated rooms, service with restrictions, supervision. [SAVE] [✕] [&M] [🛗] [🖵] [≈]

▼▼▼ Country Inn & Suites By Carlson **H**

(770) 386-5888. **$80-$149.** 43 SR 20 Spur 30121. I-75, exit 290, 0.3 mi se. Int corridors. **Pets:** Accepted. [ASK] [✕] [&M] [🛗] [🖵] [≈]

(AAA) ▼▼▼ Days Inn **M**

(770) 382-1824. **$55-$60.** 5618 Hwy 20 SE 30120. I-75, exit 290, just w. Ext corridors. **Pets:** Other species. $10 daily fee/pet. Designated rooms, service with restrictions, supervision. [SAVE] [✕] [🛗] [🖵] [≈]

▼▼▼▼ Holiday Inn **H**

(770) 386-0830. **$99.** 2336 Hwy 411 30120. I-75, exit 293, southwest corner. Int corridors. **Pets:** Small, other species. $10 daily fee/pet. Service with restrictions, supervision. [ASK] [✕] [&M] [🛗] [🖵] [¶¶] [≈]

▼▼▼ Howard Johnson Express **M**

(770) 386-0700. **Call for rates.** 25 Carson Loop NW 30121. I-75, exit 296, just w. Ext corridors. **Pets:** Accepted. [✕] [🛗] [🖵] [¶¶] [≈]

(AAA) ▼▼▼ Knights Inn **M**

(770) 386-7263. **$55-$75.** 420 E Church St 30121. I-75, exit 288, 1.5 mi w. Ext corridors. **Pets:** Medium. $10 daily fee/pet. Designated rooms, service with restrictions, supervision. [SAVE] [✕] [🛗] [🖵] [≈]

▼▼▼ Motel 6–4046 **M**

(770) 386-1449. **Call for rates.** 5657 Hwy 20 NE 30121. I-75, exit 290, 0.3 mi e. Ext corridors. **Pets:** Other species. Service with restrictions, supervision. [✕] [🛗] [🖵] [≈]

▼▼▼ Quality Inn **M**

(770) 386-0510. **$65-$90.** 235 Dixie Ave 30120. I-75, exit 288, 2.5 mi w. Ext corridors. **Pets:** Accepted. [✕] [🖵] [¶¶] [≈]

(AAA) ▼▼▼ Red Roof Inn **M**

(770) 387-1800. **$43-$66.** 28 SR 20 Spur 30121. I-75, exit 290, 0.3 mi se. Ext corridors. **Pets:** Large. Service with restrictions, crate. [SAVE] [✕] [🛗] [🖵] [≈]

▼▼▼ Sleep Inn **H**

(770) 386-9259. **$80-$130.** 11 Kent Dr 30121. I-75, exit 296, just e. Int corridors. **Pets:** Accepted. [✕] [&M] [🛗] [🖵] [≈]

(AAA) ▼▼▼ Super 8 **M**

(770) 382-8881. **$48-$65.** 41 SR 20 Spur SE 30121. I-75, exit 290, 0.3 mi e. Int corridors. **Pets:** $5 daily fee/pet. Service with restrictions, supervision. [SAVE] [✕] [🛗] [≈]

CEDARTOWN
▼▼▼ Country Hearth Inn **H**

(770) 749-9951. **$49-$89.** 925 N Main St 30125. 1.5 mi n on US 27. Int corridors. **Pets:** Medium. $10 one-time fee/room. Service with restrictions, crate. [✕] [&M] [🛗] [🖵]

CHATSWORTH
(AAA) ▼▼▼ Best Western Fairwinds Inn & Suites **M**

(706) 695-1411. **$65-$79.** 613 S 3rd Ave 30705. On US 411/SR 76, 0.3 mi s. Ext corridors. **Pets:** Accepted. [SAVE] [✕] [&M] [🛗] [🖵] [≈]

▼▼▼ Key West Inn **M**

(706) 517-1155. **Call for rates.** 501 GI Maddox Pkwy 30705. Jct SR 76 and US 411. Ext corridors. **Pets:** Accepted. [✕] [🛗] [🖵]

CLAYTON
▼▼▼ Americas Best Value Inn **H**

(706) 782-4702. **$45-$95.** 698 Hwy 441 S 30525. 0.8 mi s. Int corridors. **Pets:** Accepted. [ASK] [✕] [🛗] [🖵]

▼▼▼ Days Inn **M**

(706) 782-4258. **$46-$100.** 54 Hwy 441 30525. Center. Ext corridors. **Pets:** Very small, dogs only. $10 daily fee/pet. Designated rooms, service with restrictions, supervision. [ASK] [✕] [🛗] [🖵] [¶¶] [≈]

(AAA) ▼▼▼ Regal Inn **M**

(706) 782-4269. **$37-$95.** 707 Hwy 441 S 30525. 0.8 mi s. Ext corridors. **Pets:** Small, dogs only. $7 daily fee/pet. Designated rooms, service with restrictions, supervision. [SAVE] [✕] [🛗] [🖵]

COLQUITT
▼▼▼ Tarrer Inn **CI**

(229) 758-2888. **$99-$149, 7 day notice.** 155 S Cuthbert St 39837. Corner of SR 91 and 27; center of town square. Int corridors. **Pets:** Accepted. [ASK] [✕] [&M] [🖵] [¶¶]

COLUMBUS
▼▼▼ Extended StayAmerica-Columbus-Airport **M**

(706) 653-0131. **$65-$85.** 5020 Armour Rd 31904. I-185, exit 8, 1.5 mi e, then 0.5 mi n. Ext corridors. **Pets:** Other species. $25 daily fee/room. Designated rooms, service with restrictions, crate. [ASK] [✕] [🛗] [🖵]

▼▼▼ Extended StayAmerica-Columbus-Bradley Park **H**

(706) 653-9938. **$66-$96.** 1721 Rollins Way 31904. I-185, exit 10 (US 80 and SR 22), 1.5 mi w on US 80, exit 3A, just s to Whittlesey Rd, 0.3 mi e to Rollins Way, then just n. Int corridors. **Pets:** Other species. $25 daily fee/room. Designated rooms, service with restrictions, crate. [ASK] [✕] [🛗] [🖵]

▼▼▼ Howard Johnson Express Inn & Suites **M**

(706) 322-6641. **$65-$99.** 1011 Veterans Pkwy 31901. I-185, exit 7 southbound; exit 7A northbound, 1.2 mi w to Veterans Pkwy, then 3.2 mi s. Ext corridors. **Pets:** Other species. $15 one-time fee/room. Service with restrictions. [ASK] [✕] [🛗] [🖵] [¶¶] [≈]

(AAA) ▼▼▼▼ Hyatt Place Columbus-North **H**

(706) 507-5000. **$109-$149.** 2974 Northlake Pkwy 31909. US 80 and SR 22, exit Veterans Pkwy, 0.6 mi n, then just e. Int corridors. **Pets:** Small. $100 one-time fee/room. Service with restrictions. [SAVE] [✕] [&M] [🛗] [🖵]

▼▼▼ La Quinta Inn Columbus Midtown **M** ✿

(706) 568-1740. **$59-$139.** 3201 Macon Rd, Suite 200 31906-1717. I-185, exit 6, just w. Ext/int corridors. **Pets:** Medium, other species. Service with restrictions, supervision. [ASK] [✕] [🛗] [🖵] [≈]

▼▼▼ La Quinta Inn Columbus State University **H** ✿

(706) 323-4344. **$69-$149.** 2919 Warm Springs Rd 31909. I-185, exit 7 southbound; exit 7A northbound, just e. Int corridors. **Pets:** Medium, other species. Service with restrictions, supervision. [ASK] [✕] [&M] [🛗] [🖵] [≈]

▼▼▼ Motel 6 #58 **M**

(706) 687-7214. **$49-$59.** 3050 Victory Dr 31903. I-185, exit 1B, 3 mi w. Ext corridors. **Pets:** Other species. Service with restrictions, supervision. [✕] [🛗] [≈]

▼▼▼▼ Rothschild-Pound House Inn **CI**

(706) 322-4075. **Call for rates.** 201 7th St 31901. Jct US 27 (Veterans Pkwy/7th St), just w; downtown. Ext/int corridors. **Pets:** Accepted. [✕] [🛗] [🖵] [¶¶] [✎]

COMMERCE

Best Western Commerce Inn 🅷
(706) 335-3640. **$55-$160.** 157 Eisenhower Dr 30529. I-85, exit 149, just ne. Int corridors. **Pets:** Medium. $10 one-time fee/room. Designated rooms, service with restrictions, supervision.
[SAVE] [X] [&M] [🛏] [💻] [🏊]

Comfort Suites Commerce 🅷
(706) 336-0000. **$90-$249, 3 day notice.** 30490 Hwy 441 S 30529. I-85, exit 149, just ne. Int corridors. **Pets:** Small. $25 one-time fee/room. Service with restrictions, crate. [X] [&M] [🛏] [💻] [🏊]

Howard Johnson Inn & Suites Ⓜ
(706) 335-5581. **$53-$140.** 148 Eisenhower Dr 30529. I-85, exit 149, just ne. Ext corridors. **Pets:** Accepted. [ASK] [X] [🛏] [💻] [🏊]

Quality Inn Ⓜ
(706) 335-9001. **$60-$200.** 165 Eisenhower Dr 30529. I-85, exit 149, just ne. Ext corridors. **Pets:** Medium, other species. $10 daily fee/pet. Service with restrictions, supervision. [X] [🛏] [💻] [🏊]

Super 8 Ⓜ
(706) 336-8008. **$49-$140.** 152 Eisenhower Dr 30529. I-85, exit 149, just ne. Ext corridors. **Pets:** Accepted. [ASK] [X] [💻]

CONYERS

Comfort Inn 🅷
(770) 760-0300. **$77-$129.** 1363 Klondike Rd 30094. I-20, exit 80, just s. Int corridors. **Pets:** Accepted. [X] [&M] [🛏] [💻] [🏊]

Country Inn & Suites By Carlson 🅷 ❀
(770) 785-2400. **$90-$120.** 1312 Old Covington Hwy SE 30013. I-20, exit 82, just n. Int corridors. **Pets:** Small. $45 one-time fee/room. Designated rooms, service with restrictions, supervision.
[SAVE] [X] [&M] [🛏] [💻] [🏊]

Hampton Inn 🅷
(770) 483-8838. **Call for rates.** 1340 Dogwood Dr 30013. I-20, exit 82, just n, then just e. Int corridors. **Pets:** Accepted.
[X] [&M] [🛏] [💻] [🏊]

Jameson Inn Ⓜ
(770) 760-1230. **$88-$95.** 1164 Dogwood Dr 30012. I-20, exit 82, just n, then just w. Ext corridors. **Pets:** Accepted. [ASK] [X] [🛏] [💻] [🏊]

La Quinta Inn & Suites Atlanta (Conyers) 🅷 ❀
(770) 918-0092. **$69-$139.** 1184 Dogwood Dr 30012. I-20, exit 82, just n, then just w. Int corridors. **Pets:** Medium, other species. Service with restrictions, supervision. [ASK] [X] [&M] [🛏] [💻] [🏊]

Ramada Inn & Conference Center Ⓜ
(770) 483-5200. **Call for rates.** 1351 Dogwood Dr 30012. I-20, exit 80, just n, then 0.4 mi w. Ext corridors. **Pets:** Accepted.
[X] [&M] [🛏] [💻] [🏊]

CORDELE

Best Western Colonial Inn 🅷
(229) 273-5420. **$62-$69.** 1706 E 16th Ave (US 280) 31015. I-75, exit 101 (US 280), just w. Ext/int corridors. **Pets:** Accepted.
[SAVE] [X] [🛏] [💻] [🏊]

Lake Blackshear Resort & Golf Club 🅷
(229) 276-1004. **$99-$199, 7 day notice.** 2459-H US 280 W 31015. I-75, exit 101 (US 280), 10 mi w. Ext/int corridors. **Pets:** $50 one-time fee/room. Service with restrictions, supervision.
[SAVE] [X] [&M] [🛏] [💻] [🍴] [🏊] [X]

Ramada Inn 🅷 ❀
(229) 273-5000. **$69-$79.** 2016 E 16th Ave (US 280) 31015. I-75, exit 101 (US 280), just e. Ext corridors. **Pets:** Medium. $10 daily fee/pet. Service with restrictions, supervision. [SAVE] [X] [🛏] [💻] [🏊]

Travelodge Ⓜ
(229) 273-2456. **$45-$60.** 1618 16th Ave E (US 280) 31015. I-75, exit 101 (US 280), just w. Ext corridors. **Pets:** Other species.
[SAVE] [X] [🛏] [💻]

CORNELIA

Comfort Inn 🅷
(706) 778-9573. **$60-$100.** 2965 J Warren Rd 30531. Jct SR 365 and US 441 business route, just w. Int corridors. **Pets:** Medium. $25 daily fee/pet. Service with restrictions, crate. [X] [&M] [🛏] [💻] [🏊]

COVINGTON

Baymont Inn & Suites Ⓜ
(770) 787-4900. **$70-$150.** 10111 Alcovy Rd 30014. I-20, exit 92, just n. Ext corridors. **Pets:** Small. $15 daily fee/pet. Service with restrictions, supervision. [SAVE] [X] [&M] [🛏] [💻] [🏊]

Quality Inn Ⓜ
(770) 784-1849. **$53-$150.** 10225 Hwy 142 N 30014. I-20, exit 93, just s. Ext corridors. **Pets:** Small, other species. $25 daily fee/pet. Service with restrictions, crate. [X] [&M] [🛏] [💻] [🏊]

Super 8-Covington Ⓜ
(770) 786-5800. **$55-$150, 3 day notice.** 10130 Alcovy Rd 30014. I-20, exit 92, just n. Ext corridors. **Pets:** Accepted. [ASK] [X] [🛏] [💻]

DAHLONEGA

Econo Lodge Ⓜ
(706) 864-6191. **$60-$150.** 619 N Grove St 30533. 0.5 mi n on US 19 business route. Ext corridors. **Pets:** Small, dogs only. $10 daily fee/pet. Designated rooms, service with restrictions, supervision.
[SAVE] [X] [🛏] [💻] [🏊]

Super 8 Ⓜ
(706) 864-4343. **$79-$199, 7 day notice.** 20 Mountain Dr 30533. 0.5 mi s on US 19 and SR 60. Ext corridors. **Pets:** Accepted.
[ASK] [X] [🛏] [💻] [🏊]

DALLAS

Days Inn Ⓜ
(770) 505-4567. **Call for rates.** 1007 Old Harris Rd 30132. Jct Business Rt SR 6 (Atlanta Hwy). Ext corridors. **Pets:** Accepted.
[X] [&M] [🛏] [💻]

DALTON

America's Best Inn Ⓜ
(706) 226-1100. **$44-$69.** 1529 W Walnut Ave 30720. I-75, exit 333, just e. Ext corridors. **Pets:** Other species. $10 daily fee/pet. Designated rooms, service with restrictions, supervision. [SAVE] [X] [🛏] [💻] [🏊]

Best Western Inn of Dalton Ⓜ
(706) 226-5022. **$59-$64.** 2106 Chattanooga Rd 30720. I-75, exit 336, just w. Ext corridors. **Pets:** Small, dogs only. $5 one-time fee/pet. Service with restrictions, supervision. [SAVE] [X] [&M] [🛏] [💻] [🏊]

Comfort Inn & Suites 🅷
(706) 259-2583. **$89-$149.** 905 Westbridge Rd 30720. I-75, exit 333, just w to Westbridge Rd, then just s. Int corridors. **Pets:** Medium. $15 daily fee/pet. Designated rooms, service with restrictions, supervision.
[X] [&M] [🛏] [💻] [🏊]

Econo Lodge Ⓜ
(706) 278-4300. **Call for rates.** 2007 Tampico Way 30720. I-75, exit 336, just e. Int corridors. **Pets:** Accepted. [X] [🛏] [🏊]

Jameson Inn Ⓜ
(706) 281-1880. **$73-$78.** 790 College Dr 30720. I-75, exit 333, just w, then 0.3 mi n. Ext corridors. **Pets:** Accepted. [ASK] [X] [🛏] [💻] [🏊]

La Quinta Inn & Suites 🅷 ❀
(706) 272-9099. **$40-$134.** 715 College Dr 30720. I-75, exit 333, just w to Holiday Dr, then 0.5 mi n. Int corridors. **Pets:** Medium, other species. Service with restrictions, supervision. [ASK] [X] [&M] [🛏] [💻] [🏊]

DARIEN

AAA **▼▼▼** Comfort Inn **H**
(912) 437-4200. **Call for rates.** 703 Frontage Rd 31305. I-95, exit 49 (SR 251), just nw. Int corridors. **Pets:** Accepted.
[SAVE] [X] [🛏] [💻] [≈]

▼▼▼ Quality Inn **H**
(912) 437-5373. **Call for rates.** 101 GA Hwy 251 31305. I-95, exit 49 (SR 251), just w. Int corridors. **Pets:** $10 one-time fee/room. Service with restrictions, supervision. [X] [🛏] [💻] [≈]

DAWSONVILLE

AAA **▼▼▼** Best Western Dawson Village Inn **H**
(706) 216-4410. **$70-$90, 7 day notice.** 76 N Georgia Ave 30534. Jct SR 400/53, 0.5 mi s. Int corridors. **Pets:** Small, dogs only. $20 daily fee/pet. Designated rooms, service with restrictions, supervision.
[SAVE] [X] [🛏] [💻] [≈]

▼▼▼ Comfort Inn **H**
(706) 216-1900. **$68-$135.** 127 Beartooth Pkwy 30534. Jct SR 400/53, 0.5 mi s. Int corridors. **Pets:** Other species. $15 daily fee/pet. Service with restrictions. [X] [🛏M] [🛏] [💻] [≈]

▼▼▼ Super 8 **H**
(706) 216-6801. **$50-$100, 6 day notice.** 205 N 400 Center Ln 30534. Jct SR 400/53, just n. Int corridors. **Pets:** Accepted.
[ASK] [X] [🛏M] [🛏] [💻] [≈]

DILLARD

AAA **▼▼▼** Dillard House **M** ✣
(706) 746-5348. **$59-$149, 3 day notice.** 768 Franklin St 30537. US 441, just e via Old Dillard Rd. Ext corridors. **Pets:** Medium. Service with restrictions, supervision. [SAVE] [X] [🛏] [💻] [🍴] [≈] [X]

▼▼▼ Knights Inn **M** ✣
(706) 746-5321. **$60-$140.** 3 Best Inn Way 30537. Center. Ext corridors. **Pets:** Very small, dogs only. $10 daily fee/pet. Service with restrictions, supervision. [ASK] [X] [🛏] [💻] [≈]

AAA **▼▼▼** Mountain Valley Inn **M**
(706) 746-5373. **$35-$110.** 13 Royalty Ln 30537. Just n of town center. Ext corridors. **Pets:** Medium. $8 daily fee/pet. Designated rooms, service with restrictions, supervision. [SAVE] [X] [🛏] [💻] [≈]

DOUGLAS

▼▼ Jameson Inn **M**
(912) 384-9432. **Call for rates.** 1628 S Peterson Ave 31535. Jct US 221/441/SR 31 and SR 206/353, just s. Ext corridors. **Pets:** Accepted.
[X] [🛏] [💻] [≈]

DUBLIN

▼▼ Comfort Inn **H**
(478) 274-8000. **$55-$70.** 2110 Hwy 441 S 31021. I-16, exit 51 (US 441), 0.6 mi n. Ext corridors. **Pets:** Medium. $10 daily fee/pet. Service with restrictions, supervision. [X] [🛏M] [🛏] [💻] [≈]

▼▼ Jameson Inn **H**
(478) 275-3008. **$78-$85.** 100 PM Watson Dr 31021. I-16, exit 51 (US 441), just n. Ext corridors. **Pets:** Medium, other species. $15 daily fee/pet. Service with restrictions, crate. [ASK] [X] [🛏] [💻] [≈]

▼▼▼ La Quinta Inn & Suites **H** ✣
(478) 272-3110. **$79-$239.** 101 Travel Center Blvd 31021. I-16, exit 51 (US 441), just s. Int corridors. **Pets:** Medium, other species. Service with restrictions, supervision. [ASK] [X] [🛏] [💻] [≈]

▼▼ Travelodge Suites and Conference Center **H**
(478) 275-2650. **$50-$60, 3 day notice.** 2121 Hwy 441 S 31021. I-16, exit 51 (US 441), 0.5 mi n. Ext corridors. **Pets:** Accepted.
[ASK] [X] [🛏] [💻] [≈]

EAST ELLIJAY

AAA **▼▼▼** Best Western Mountain View Inn **H**
(706) 515-1500. **$60-$140.** 43 Coosawattee Dr 30539. 0.8 mi s on SR 515. Int corridors. **Pets:** Small, dogs only. $10 daily fee/pet. Designated rooms, service with restrictions, crate. [SAVE] [X] [🛏M] [🛏] [💻] [≈]

AAA **▼▼▼** Stratford Motor Inn **M**
(706) 276-1080. **$60-$100.** 79 Maddox Cir 30540. Jct Maddox Cir and SR 515; behind Waffle King. Ext corridors. **Pets:** Other species. $10 daily fee/pet. Service with restrictions, supervision. [SAVE] [X] [🛏] [≈]

EATONTON

▼▼▼ The Lodge on Lake Oconee **H**
(706) 485-7785. **Call for rates.** 930 Lake Oconee Pkwy 31024. I-20, exit 130 (SR 44), 12.3 mi s. Int corridors. **Pets:** Accepted.
[X] [🛏] [💻] [≈] [X]

FITZGERALD

▼▼▼ Country Hearth Inn **H**
(229) 409-9911. **$50-$90.** 125 Stuart Way 31750. Just n of US 319/107, just e. Int corridors. **Pets:** Accepted. [ASK] [X] [🛏] [💻]

▼▼ Western Motel **H**
(229) 424-9500. **Call for rates.** 111 Bull Run Rd 31750. Just n of US 319/107, on US 129. Ext corridors. **Pets:** Accepted. [X] [🛏] [💻] [≈]

FORSYTH

AAA **▼▼▼** Best Western Hilltop Inn **M**
(478) 994-9260. **$60-$90.** 951 Hwy 42 N 31029. I-75, exit 188 (SR 42), just ne via Frontage Rd. Ext corridors. **Pets:** Accepted.
[SAVE] [X] [🛏] [💻] [≈]

AAA **▼▼▼** Comfort Inn **H**
(478) 994-3400. **$70-$100.** 333 Harold G Clark Pkwy 31029. I-75, exit 185 (SR 18), just w. Ext corridors. **Pets:** Accepted.
[SAVE] [X] [🛏] [💻] [≈]

AAA **▼▼▼** Econo Lodge **M** ✣
(478) 994-5603. **Call for rates.** 320 Cabiness Rd 31029. I-75, exit 187 (SR 83), just ne. Int corridors. **Pets:** Medium. $10 daily fee/pet. No service, supervision. [SAVE] [X] [🛏] [💻] [≈]

▼▼▼ Holiday Inn Express **H** ✣
(478) 994-9697. **$94-$165.** 520 Holiday Cir 31029. I-75, exit 186 (Juliette Rd), just w, then just s on Aaron St. Int corridors. **Pets:** Small, other species. $10 daily fee/room. Service with restrictions, supervision.
[ASK] [X] [🛏M] [🛏] [💻]

▼▼▼ Holiday Inn Forsyth **H**
(478) 994-5691. **Call for rates.** 480 Holiday Cir 31029. I-75, exit 186 (Juliette Rd), just w, then just s on Aaron St. Ext corridors.
Pets: Accepted. [X] [🛏] [💻] [🍴] [≈]

AAA **▼▼▼** Super 8 **H**
(478) 994-5101. **$58-$100.** 436 Tift College Dr 31029. I-75, exit 186 (Juliette Rd), just w. Ext/int corridors. **Pets:** Small, dogs only. $15 daily fee/pet. Designated rooms, service with restrictions, supervision.
[SAVE] [X] [🛏] [💻] [≈]

GAINESVILLE

▼▼▼ Country Hearth Inn & Suites **M**
(770) 287-3205. **$55-$60.** 766 Jesse Jewell Pkwy 30501. I-985, exit 20, 1.9 mi w to Jesse Jewell Pkwy, then just s. Ext corridors. **Pets:** Accepted.
[ASK] [X] [🛏] [💻]

▼▼ Days Inn **M**
(770) 535-8100. **Call for rates.** 520 Queen City Pkwy SW 30501. I-985, exit 20, 1.8 mi nw on SR 60/Queen City Pkwy. Ext corridors.
Pets: Accepted. [X] [🛏] [💻] [≈]

GARDEN CITY

▼▼▼ Baymont Inn & Suites H

(912) 964-8669. **$60-$120.** 357 Main St 31408. I-95, exit 109 (SR 21), 6.5 mi se to Spur SR 21 (Brampton Rd), 0.3 mi n to Coastal Hwy/Main St, then just se. Int corridors. **Pets:** Small. $50 one-time fee/pet. Service with restrictions, crate. ASK ⊠ 🛈 🖵 ⤰

GLENNVILLE

◈◈◈ ▼ Cheeri-O Inn M

(912) 654-2176. **$45-$50.** 820 S Downing Musgrove St 30427. 0.8 mi s on US 25 and 301. Ext corridors. **Pets:** Medium. $7 daily fee/pet. Designated rooms, service with restrictions, supervision. SAVE ⊠ 🛈 🖵

GOLDEN ISLES AREA

JEKYLL ISLAND

◈◈◈ ▼▼▼ Quality Inn & Suites H ❀

(912) 635-2202. **$70-$200.** 700 N Beachview Dr 31527. Jct Ben Fortson Pkwy (SR 520)/Beachview Dr, 1.5 mi n. Ext corridors. **Pets:** Medium. $10 daily fee/pet. Service with restrictions, supervision.

SAVE ⊠ 🛈 🖵 ⤰

◈◈◈ ▼▼▼▼ Villas by the Sea CO

(912) 635-2521. **$128-$369, 7 day notice.** 1175 N Beachview Dr 31527. Jct Ben Fortson Pkwy (SR 520)/Beachview Dr, 4 mi n. Ext corridors. **Pets:** Accepted. SAVE ⊠ 🕭 🛈 🖵 🍴 ⤰ ⊠

END AREA

GREENSBORO

▼▼▼▼▼ The Ritz-Carlton Lodge, Reynolds
Plantation H

(706) 467-0600. **$199-$559.** One Lk Oconee Tr 30642. I-20, exit 130, 7.2 mi sw on SR 44 (Old Eatonton Rd), 1.5 mi e on Linger Longer Rd, then 2 mi ne. Ext/int corridors. **Pets:** Accepted.

ASK ⊠ 🕭 🛈 🖵 🍴 ⤰ ⊠

GROVETOWN

▼▼ Super 8-Augusta H

(706) 396-1600. **$80-$425.** 456 Park West Dr 30813. I-20, exit 194 (SR 383), just s, then w. Int corridors. **Pets:** Accepted.

ASK ⊠ 🛈 🖵 ⤰

HAMPTON

▼▼▼ Country Hearth Inn H

(770) 707-1477. **$62-$65, 7 day notice.** 1078 Bear Creek Blvd 30228. 1 mi w of center of town; at US 41 and 19. Int corridors. **Pets:** Accepted.

ASK ⊠ 🕭 🛈 🖵

HARTWELL

◈◈◈ ▼▼▼ Best Western Lake Hartwell Inn &
Suites H

(706) 376-4700. **$63-$120.** 1357 E Franklin St 30643. I-85, exit 177, 2 mi on US 29 E. Int corridors. **Pets:** Small, other species. $20 one-time fee/pet. Service with restrictions, crate. SAVE ⊠ 🛈 🖵 ⤰

HAWKINSVILLE

◈◈◈ ▼▼▼ Budget Inn M

(478) 783-2002. **Call for rates.** 509 Broad St 31036. Downtown. Ext corridors. **Pets:** Very small, dogs only. $10 daily fee/pet. No service.

SAVE ⊠ 🛈 🖵 ⤰

HELEN

▼▼ The Helendorf River Inn & Conference Center M

(706) 878-2271. **$34-$159, 10 day notice.** 33 Munich Strasse 30545. SR 17 and 75; center. Ext corridors. **Pets:** Other species. $10 daily fee/pet. Designated rooms, service with restrictions, supervision.

⊠ 🛈 🖵 ⤰

▼▼ Kountry Peddler Tanglewood Resort Cabins CA

(706) 878-3286. **$89-$179, 14 day notice.** 3387 Hwy 356 30571. 1 mi n on SR 75, then 3 mi ne. Ext corridors. **Pets:** Accepted. ⊠ 🛈 🖵

◈◈◈ ▼▼ Quality Inn & Suites M

(706) 878-2268. **$60-$250.** 15 Yonah St 30545. Just w of Mack St. Ext corridors. **Pets:** Accepted. SAVE ⊠ 🛈 🖵 ⤰

◈◈◈ ▼ ◈ Riverbend Motel & Cabins M

(706) 878-2155. **$45-$139, 3 day notice.** 134 River St 30545. Just w off Main St. Ext corridors. **Pets:** Accepted. SAVE ⊠ 🛈 🖵

HIAWASSEE

▼▼ ▼ Enota B & B, Cabins & Conference Lodge CA

(706) 896-9966. **$80-$165.** 1000 Hwy 180 30546. E on US 76 to SR 75/17, 6 mi s to SR 180, then 3 mi w. Ext corridors. **Pets:** Accepted.

⊠ 🛈 🖵 ⊠ ✍

▼▼▼ Ramada at Lake Chatuge Lodge H

(706) 896-5253. **$69-$209.** 653 US Hwy 76 30546. 1 mi w. Int corridors. **Pets:** Small. $25 deposit/room. Designated rooms, service with restrictions. ASK ⊠ 🕭 🛈 🖵

HIRAM

▼▼▼ Country Inn & Suites By Carlson H

(770) 222-0456. **$75-$120.** 70 Enterprise Path 30134. Jct SR 92/6 and US 278, 0.3 mi w. Int corridors. **Pets:** Medium. $15 daily fee/pet. Service with restrictions, crate. ASK ⊠ 🛈 🖵 ⤰

HOGANSVILLE

▼▼ Key West Inn & Suites M

(706) 637-9395. **$60-$120.** 1888 E Main St 30230. I-85, exit 28, just w. Ext corridors. **Pets:** Small, dogs only. $10 daily fee/pet. Designated rooms, service with restrictions, supervision. ASK ⊠ 🛈 🖵 ⤰

JASPER

▼▼ Microtel Inn & Suites H

(706) 299-5500. **$64-$129.** 171 H Mullins Ct 30143. Jct SR 515/53, 0.9 mi n. Int corridors. **Pets:** Accepted. ASK ⊠ 🕭 🛈 🖵

▼▼ ▼ Super 8 M

(706) 253-3297. **Call for rates.** 100 Whitfield Dr 30143. Jct SR 515/53; in Lawsons Crossing. Ext corridors. **Pets:** Accepted.

⊠ 🕭 🛈 🖵 ⤰

JESUP

▼▼ Jameson Inn of Jesup H

(912) 427-6800. **$73-$78.** 205 N Hwy 301 31545. Jct US 341, just n. Ext corridors. **Pets:** Other species. $15 daily fee/room. Service with restrictions, supervision. ASK ⊠ 🛈 🖵 ⤰

KINGSLAND

▼▼ Econo Lodge M

(912) 673-7336. **Call for rates.** 1135 E King Ave 31548. I-95, exit 3 (SR 40), just nw. Ext corridors. **Pets:** Medium. $5 daily fee/pet. Designated rooms, service with restrictions, supervision. ⊠ 🕭 🛈 🖵 ⤰

▼▼ Jameson Inn M

(912) 729-9600. **$78-$85.** 105 May Creek Blvd 31548. I-95, exit 3 (SR 40), just w, then s at Boone Ave. Ext corridors. **Pets:** Accepted.

ASK ⊠ 🕭 🛈 🖵 ⤰

▼▼▼ **La Quinta Inn & Suites** 🅷 ✼
(912) 882-8010. **$69-$139.** 104 May Creek Dr 31548. I-95, exit 3 (SR 40), just sw. Int corridors. **Pets:** Medium, other species. Service with restrictions, supervision. (A$K) ⊠ 🖲 🍴 💻 ⤳

🆑 ▼▼ **Microtel Inn & Suites** 🅷
(912) 729-1555. **$49-$79.** 1325 E King Ave 31548. I-95, exit 3 (SR 40), just ne. Int corridors. **Pets:** Small. $10 daily fee/pet. Service with restrictions, supervision. (SAVE) ⊠ 🍴 💻 ⤳

🆑 ▼▼ **Red Roof Kingsland** 🅷
(912) 729-1130. **$50-$75.** 1363 Hwy 40 E 31548. I-95, exit 3 (SR 40), just se. Ext corridors. **Pets:** Large. Service with restrictions, crate.
(SAVE) ⊠ 🖲 🍴 💻 ⤳

▼ **Super 8** 🅼
(912) 729-6888. **$50-$100.** 120 Robert L Edenfield Dr 31548. I-95, exit 3 (SR 40), just se. Int corridors. **Pets:** Other species. $10 daily fee/pet. Service with restrictions. (A$K) ⊠ 🍴 💻

LA FAYETTE
▼▼ **Days Inn** 🅼
(706) 639-9362. **$50-$65.** 2209 N Main St 30728. 2.5 mi n on US 27. Ext corridors. **Pets:** Medium. $10 daily fee/pet. Service with restrictions, supervision. (A$K) ⊠ 🍴 💻 ⤳

▼▼ **Key West Inn** 🅼
(706) 638-8200. **Call for rates.** 2221 N Main St 30728. 2.5 mi n on US 27. Ext corridors. **Pets:** Medium, dogs only. $15 daily fee/pet. Designated rooms, service with restrictions, supervision. ⊠ 🖲 🍴 ⤳

LAGRANGE
🆑 ▼▼ **Days Inn-LaGrange/Callaway Gardens** 🅼
(706) 882-8881. **$60.** 2606 Whitesville Rd 30240. I-85, exit 13, just e. Ext corridors. **Pets:** Medium. $15 daily fee/pet. Service with restrictions, supervision. (SAVE) ⊠ 🍴 💻 ⤳

▼▼ **Jameson Inn** 🅼
(706) 882-8700. **$78-$85.** 110 Jameson Dr 30240. I-85, exit 18 (Lafayette Pkwy), 0.3 mi w. Ext corridors. **Pets:** Accepted.
(A$K) ⊠ 🖲 🍴 💻 ⤳

▼▼ **Red Roof Inn LaGrange** 🅼
(706) 882-9540. **Call for rates.** 1601 Lafayette Pkwy 30241. I-85, exit 18 (Lafayette Pkwy), just e. Ext corridors. **Pets:** Large. Service with restrictions, crate. ⊠ 🍴 💻 ⤳

LAKE PARK
🆑 ▼▼ **Days Inn** 🅷
(229) 559-0229. **$59-$89.** 4913 Timber Dr 31636. I-75, exit 5, just nw. Ext corridors. **Pets:** Accepted. (SAVE) ⊠ 🍴 💻 ⤳

🆑 ▼▼ **Super 8** 🅷
(229) 559-8111. **$55-$75.** 4907 Timber Dr 31636. I-75, exit 5, just w, then n. Ext corridors. **Pets:** Very small, other species. $10 daily fee/pet. Service with restrictions, supervision. (SAVE) ⊠ 🍴

LAVONIA
🆑 ▼▼ **Best Western Regency Inn & Suites** 🅼
(706) 356-4000. **$69-$99.** 13705 Jones St 30553. I-85, exit 173, just e. Ext corridors. **Pets:** Accepted. (SAVE) ⊠ 🍴 💻 ⤳

▼▼▼ **Holiday Inn Express & Suites** 🅷
(706) 356-2100. **Call for rates.** 110 Owens Dr 30553. I-85, exit 173, just w on SR 17. Int corridors. **Pets:** Small. $30 one-time fee/room. Service with restrictions, supervision. ⊠ 🖲 🍴 💻 ⤳

▼▼ **Super 8-Lavonia** 🅼
(706) 356-8848. **Call for rates.** 14227 Jones St 30553. I-85, exit 173, just w. Ext corridors. **Pets:** Accepted. ⊠ 🖲 🍴 💻 ⤳

LOCUST GROVE
🆑 ▼▼▼ **La Quinta Inn & Suites** 🅷 ✼
(678) 583-8088. **$59-$139.** 4832 Bill Gardner Pkwy 30248. I-75, exit 212, just e. Int corridors. **Pets:** Medium, other species. Service with restrictions, supervision. (SAVE) ⊠ 🖲 🍴 💻 ⤳

🆑 ▼▼ **Red Roof Inn** 🅷
(678) 583-0004. **$53-$109.** 4840 Bill Gardner Pkwy 30248. I-75, exit 212, just e. Int corridors. **Pets:** Large. Service with restrictions, crate.
(SAVE) ⊠ 🖲 🍴 💻

MACON
🆑 ▼▼▼ **Best Western Inn & Suites of Macon** 🅼 ✼
(478) 781-5300. **$70-$80.** 4681 Chambers Rd 31206. I-475, exit 3 (Eisenhower Pkwy/US 80), just ne, then just se. Ext corridors. **Pets:** Medium. $10 daily fee/room. Designated rooms, service with restrictions, supervision. (SAVE) ⊠ 🍴 💻 ⤳

🆑 ▼▼▼ **Best Western Riverside Inn** 🅷
(478) 743-6311. **$60-$70.** 2400 Riverside Dr 31204. I-75, exit 167 (Riverside Dr), just w, then 0.4 mi se. Int corridors. **Pets:** Medium. $10 daily fee/pet. Designated rooms, supervision. (SAVE) ⊠ 🍴 💻 ⤳

▼▼ **Extended Stay Deluxe Macon-North** 🅷
(478) 474-2805. **$65-$80.** 3980 Riverside Dr 31210. I-75, exit 169 (Arkwright Rd), just sw, then 0.4 mi nw. Int corridors. **Pets:** Other species. $25 daily fee/room. Designated rooms, service with restrictions, crate.
(A$K) ⊠ 🍴 ⤳

▼▼▼ **La Quinta Inn & Suites Macon** 🅷 ✼
(478) 475-0206. **$79-$159.** 3944 River Place Dr 31210. I-75, exit 169 (Arkwright Rd), just n, then e. Int corridors. **Pets:** Medium, other species. Service with restrictions, supervision. (A$K) ⊠ 🖲 🍴 💻 ⤳

▼▼▼ **Ramada Inn Macon West** 🅼
(478) 788-0120. **$72.** 4755 Chambers Rd 31206-5364. I-475, exit 3 (Eisenhower Pkwy/US 80), just e. Ext corridors. **Pets:** Large. $25 one-time fee/room. Designated rooms, service with restrictions, supervision.
(A$K) ⊠ 🍴 💻 ⤳

🆑 ▼▼ **Rodeway Inn** 🅼 ✼
(478) 781-4343. **Call for rates.** 4999 Eisenhower Pkwy 31206. I-475, exit 3 (Eisenhower Pkwy/US 80), just ne. Ext corridors. **Pets:** Medium. $5 daily fee/pet. Designated rooms, service with restrictions, crate.
(SAVE) ⊠ 🍴 💻 ⤳

🆑 ▼▼▼ **Sleep Inn I-475** 🅷
(478) 476-8111. **Call for rates.** 140 Plantation Inn Dr 31210. I-475, exit 9 (Zebulon Rd), just e to Peake Rd, then just s. Int corridors.
Pets: Accepted. (SAVE) ⊠ 🖲 🍴 💻 ⤳

MCDONOUGH
🆑 ▼▼▼ **Comfort Inn/McDonough** 🅼 ✼
(770) 954-9110. **Call for rates.** 80 Hwy 81 W 30253. I-75, exit 218, just nw. Ext corridors. **Pets:** Medium. $10 daily fee/pet. Service with restrictions, crate. (SAVE) ⊠ 🍴 ⤳

🆑 ▼▼▼ **Country Inn & Suites By Carlson** 🅷 ✼
(770) 957-0082. **$89-$190.** 115 E Greenwood Rd 30253. I-75, exit 216, just w. Int corridors. **Pets:** Small, other species. $10 daily fee/pet. Service with restrictions, crate. (SAVE) ⊠ 🖲 🍴 💻 ⤳

🆑 ▼▼▼ **Days Inn** 🅼
(770) 957-5261. **$59-$120.** 744 Hwy 155 S 30253. I-75, exit 216, just e. Ext corridors. **Pets:** $7 daily fee/pet. Service with restrictions, supervision.
(SAVE) ⊠ 🍴 💻 ⤳

🆑 ▼ **Econo Lodge** 🅼 ✼
(770) 957-2651. **$38-$110.** 1279 Hwy 20 W 30253. I-75, exit 218, just w. Ext corridors. **Pets:** Small. $10 daily fee/pet. Designated rooms.
(SAVE) ⊠ 🍴 💻

◇◇ ▼▼▼ Quality Inn & Suites Conference Center M
(770) 957-5291. **$69-$199.** 930 Hwy 155 S 30253. I-75, exit 216, just w. Ext corridors. **Pets:** $10 daily fee/room. Service with restrictions, supervision. SAVE ☒ ⎙M ⊟ ⊒ ⊺⊺ ⊇

MILLEDGEVILLE

▼▼▼▼ Holiday Inn Express Hotel & Suites H
(478) 454-9000. **Call for rates.** 1839 N Columbia St 31061. US 441, 2 mi n of downtown. Int corridors. **Pets:** Accepted.
☒ ⎙M ⊟ ⊒ ⊇

NEWNAN

◇◇ ▼▼▼ Best Western-Shenandoah Inn M
(770) 304-9700. **$54-$99.** 620 Hwy 34 E 30265. I-85, exit 47, just w. Ext corridors. **Pets:** Medium, other species. $10 daily fee/room. Service with restrictions, supervision. SAVE ☒ ⎙M ⊟ ⊒ ⊇

▼▼ ▼▼ Howard Johnson Inn M
(770) 683-1499. **$50-$75.** 1310 Hwy 29 S 30263. I-85, exit 41, just w. Ext corridors. **Pets:** Small. $15 daily fee/pet. Designated rooms, service with restrictions, supervision. ASK ☒ ⊟ ⊒ ⊇

▼▼▼▼ La Quinta Inn & Suites H ❖
(770) 502-8430. **$60-$110.** 600 Bullsboro Rd 30265. I-85, exit 47, 0.3 mi w. Int corridors. **Pets:** Medium, other species. Service with restrictions, supervision. ASK ☒ ⎙M ⊟ ⊒

OAKWOOD

▼▼▼▼ Country Inn & Suites By Carlson H
(770) 535-8080. **Call for rates.** 4535 Oakwood Rd 30566. I-985, exit 16, just sw. Int corridors. **Pets:** Accepted. ☒ ⊟ ⊒ ⊇

▼▼ ▼▼ Jameson Inn M
(770) 533-9400. **$60-$70.** 3780 Merchants Way 30566. I-985, exit 16, 0.4 mi w. Ext corridors. **Pets:** Very small. $15 daily fee/pet. Designated rooms, service with restrictions, supervision.
ASK ☒ ⎙M ⊟ ⊒ ⊇

PEACHTREE CITY

◇◇ ▼▼ ▼▼ Best Western Inn & Suites M
(770) 632-9700. **$72-$120.** 976 Crosstown Dr 30269. Jct SR 74 and 54, 2.1 mi s on SR 74. Ext corridors. **Pets:** $25 daily fee/pet. Service with restrictions, crate. SAVE ☒ ⎙M ⊟ ⊒ ⊇

PERRY

◇◇ ▼▼▼▼ Henderson Village G
(478) 988-8696. **$159-$297, 3 day notice.** 125 S Langston Cir 31069. I-75, exit 127 (SR 26), 1.3 mi w. Ext/int corridors. **Pets:** Accepted.
SAVE ☒ ⊟ ⊒ ⊺⊺ ⊇ ☒

▼▼▼▼ Holiday Inn H ❖
(478) 987-3313. **$75-$85.** 200 Valley Dr 31069. I-75, exit 136 (Sam Nunn Blvd), just w, then s. Ext corridors. **Pets:** Small. $10 daily fee/room, $35 one-time fee/room. Designated rooms, service with restrictions, supervision. ASK ☒ ⊟ ⊒ ⊺⊺ ⊇ ☒

▼▼▼▼ Jameson Inn-Perry M
(478) 987-5060. **Call for rates.** 200 Market Place Dr 31069. I-75, exit 136 (Sam Nunn Blvd), just e, then s. Ext corridors. **Pets:** Accepted.
☒ ⊟ ⊒ ⊇

▼▼▼▼ New Perry Hotel H
(478) 987-1000. **$59-$125.** 800 Main St 31069. I-75, exit 136 (Sam Nunn Blvd) southbound, 1.2 mi se on US 341, then just w; exit 135 (US 41) northbound, 1.5 mi ne, then just s. Ext/int corridors. **Pets:** Accepted.
ASK ☒ ⊟ ⊒ ⊺⊺ ⊇

◇◇ ▼▼ ▼▼ Rodeway Inn M
(478) 987-1345. **Call for rates.** 1504 Sam Nunn Blvd 31069. I-75, exit 136 (Sam Nunn Blvd), just w. Ext corridors. **Pets:** Accepted.
SAVE ☒ ⊟ ⊒

◇◇ ▼▼ ▼▼ Super 8 H
(478) 987-0999. **$45-$111, 3 day notice.** 102 Plaza Dr 31069. I-75, exit 136 (Sam Nunn Blvd), just e. Ext corridors. **Pets:** Accepted.
SAVE ☒ ⊟ ⊒ ⊇

PINE MOUNTAIN

◇◇ ▼▼▼▼ Mountain Creek Inn at Callaway Gardens M
(706) 663-2281. **$119-$239, 7 day notice.** 17800 Hwy 27 31822. Jct SR 354, 1.5 mi s on US 27/SR 1; in Callaway Gardens. Ext corridors.
Pets: Accepted. SAVE ☒ ⎙M ⊟ ⊒ ⊺⊺ ⊇ ☒

▼▼ White Columns Motel M ❖
(706) 663-2312. **$59-$80, 3 day notice.** 524 S Main Ave 31822. Jct SR 354, just n on US 27/SR 1. Ext corridors. **Pets:** Medium. $10 daily fee/pet. Designated rooms, service with restrictions, supervision.
ASK ☒ ⊟

POOLER

◇◇ ▼▼▼▼ Best Western Bradbury Suites H
(912) 330-0330. **$79-$189.** 155 Bourne Ave 31322. I-95, exit 102 (US 80), just e. Int corridors. **Pets:** Accepted.
SAVE ☒ ⎙M ⊟ ⊒ ⊇ ☒

◇◇ ▼▼▼▼ Holiday Inn Hotel & Suites–Savannah/Pooler H
(912) 330-5100. **$79-$109.** 103 San Dr 31322. I-95, exit 102 (US 80), just w. Int corridors. **Pets:** Accepted.
SAVE ☒ ⎙M ⊟ ⊒ ⊺⊺ ⊇

▼▼ ▼▼ Jameson Inn H
(912) 748-0017. **$93-$100.** 125 Bourne Ave 31322. I-95, exit 102 (US 80), just e. Int corridors. **Pets:** Other species. $15 daily fee/room. Service with restrictions, supervision. ASK ☒ ⊟ ⊒ ⊇

◇◇ ▼▼▼▼ La Quinta Inn & Suites H ❖
(912) 748-3771. **$69-$129.** 414 Gray St 31322. I-95, exit 102 (US 80), just w. Int corridors. **Pets:** Medium, other species. Service with restrictions, supervision. SAVE ☒ ⊟ ⊒ ⊇

◇◇ ▼▼ ▼▼ Travelodge Suites H ❖
(912) 748-6363. **$59-$149.** 130 Continental Blvd 31322. I-95, exit 102 (US 80), just e. Int corridors. **Pets:** Other species. $10 daily fee/pet. Service with restrictions, supervision. SAVE ☒ ⊟ ⊒ ⊇

PORT WENTWORTH

▼▼▼▼ Comfort Suites Savannah North H
(912) 965-1445. **$70-$100.** 115 Travelers Way 31407. I-95, exit 109 (SR 21), just nw. Int corridors. **Pets:** Small. $20 one-time fee/pet. Service with restrictions. ☒ ⎙M ⊟ ⊒ ⊇

◇◇ ▼▼ ▼▼ Sleep Inn-Savannah North H
(912) 966-9800. **Call for rates.** 7206 Hwy 21 31407. I-95, exit 109 (SR 21), just n. Int corridors. **Pets:** Medium. $25 daily fee/pet. Designated rooms, service with restrictions, crate. SAVE ☒ ⊟ ⊒ ⊇

◇◇ ▼▼ ▼▼ Wingate by Wyndham H
(912) 964-0840. **$69-$129.** 115 O' Leary Rd 31407. I-95, exit 109 (SR 21), just e, then just n. Int corridors. **Pets:** Small. $20 daily fee/pet. Service with restrictions, supervision. SAVE ☒ ⎙M ⊟ ⊒

RICHMOND HILL

◇◇ ▼▼▼▼ Best Western Richmond Hill Inn H ❖
(912) 756-7070. **$70-$150.** 4564 Hwy 17 31324. I-95, exit 87 (Ocean Hwy/US 17), just w. Int corridors. **Pets:** Large, other species. $10 daily fee/pet. Service with restrictions. SAVE ☒ ⊟ ⊒ ⊇

▼▼▼▼ Comfort Suites H ❖
(912) 756-6668. **$80-$180.** 4601 Hwy 17 31324. I-95, exit 87 (Ocean Hwy/US 17), 0.4 mi sw. Int corridors. **Pets:** Large, other species. $10 daily fee/pet. Designated rooms, service with restrictions, supervision.
☒ ⊟ ⊒ ⊇ ☒

RINGGOLD

◇◇◇◇ ▼▼▼▼ Baymont Inn & Suites 🅷
(706) 935-4000. **$79-$119.** 177 Frontage Rd 30736. I-75, exit 348, just w. Int corridors. **Pets:** Small. $10 daily fee/pet. Designated rooms, service with restrictions, supervision. [SAVE] [✕] [♿M] 🖥 🖥 🏊

◇◇◇ ▼▼▼ Hometown Inn 🅷 ❀
(706) 937-7070. **$60-$75.** 22 Gateway Business Park Dr 30736. I-75, exit 350, just e. Int corridors. **Pets:** Small. $10 one-time fee/pet. Service with restrictions, supervision. [SAVE] [✕] [♿M] 🖥 🖥 🏊

▼▼▼ Super 8 🅼
(706) 965-7080. **Call for rates.** 5400 Alabama Hwy 30736. I-75, exit 348, just e. Ext corridors. **Pets:** Accepted. [✕] [♿M] 🖥 🖥 🏊

ROCKMART

▼▼▼ Days Inn 🅼
(770) 684-9955. **$50-$54.** 105 GTM Pkwy 30165. Jct US 278 and SR 101, just n. Ext corridors. **Pets:** Accepted. [ASK] [✕] [♿M] 🖥 🖥

ROME

▼▼▼▼ Jameson Inn 🅷
(706) 291-7797. **$93-$100.** 40 Grace Dr 30161. On US 411, 2.2 mi e. Int corridors. **Pets:** Accepted. [ASK] [✕] [♿M] 🖥 🖥 🏊

SANDERSVILLE

▼▼▼ Days Inn Sandersville 🅼
(478) 553-0393. **Call for rates.** 128 Commerce St 31082. On SR 15 at jct SR 24/88, just s. Ext corridors. **Pets:** Accepted.
[✕] [♿M] 🖥 🖥 🏊

SAVANNAH

◇◇◇ ▼▼▼▼ Best Western Promenade Hotel in the Historic District 🅷
(912) 233-0020. **Call for rates.** 412 W Bay St 31401. I-16, exit 167 (Montgomery St), just ne. Ext corridors. **Pets:** Medium, dogs only. $75 one-time fee/room. No service, supervision. [SAVE] [✕] 🖥 🖥

▼▼▼▼ Catherine Ward House Inn 🆎
(912) 234-8564. **$369, 3 day notice.** 118 E Waldburg St 31401. Between Drayton and Abercorn sts. Ext/int corridors. **Pets:** Dogs only. $25 one-time fee/room. Designated rooms, service with restrictions.
[ASK] [✕] 🖥 🖼

▼▼▼▼ Clarion Inn & Suites 🅷
(912) 920-3200. **$70-$140.** 16 Gateway Blvd E 31419. I-95, exit 94 (SR 204/Abercorn St), just e. Int corridors. **Pets:** Accepted.
[✕] [♿M] 🖥 🖥 🏊

▼▼▼▼ Comfort Suites Historic District 🅷
(912) 629-2001. **$99-$289.** 630 W Bay St 31401. I-16, exit 167 (Montgomery St), 0.9 mi n to Bay St, then just w. Int corridors. **Pets:** Small. $50 one-time fee/pet. Designated rooms, service with restrictions, supervision. [✕] [♿M] 🖥 🖥 🏊

▼▼▼ Comfort Suites Savannah Airport 🅷
(912) 721-9100. **$59-$89.** 1 Yvette Johnson Hagins Dr 31408. I-95, exit 104, 0.4 mi e. Int corridors. **Pets:** Accepted. [✕] [♿M] 🖥 🖥 🏊

▼▼▼ Extended StayAmerica Savannah-Midtown 🅷
(912) 692-0076. **$69-$99.** 5511 Abercorn St 31405. Jct SR 21 and 204 (Abercorn St), just s. Int corridors. **Pets:** Other species. $25 daily fee/room. Designated rooms, service with restrictions, crate.
[ASK] [✕] 🖥 🖥

◇◇◇ ▼▼▼▼ Foley House Inn 🆎
(912) 232-6622. **$199-$399, 10 day notice.** 14 W Hull St on Chippewa Square 31401. Between Bull and Whitaker sts; in historic district. Ext/int corridors. **Pets:** Other species. $50 one-time fee/pet. Designated rooms, service with restrictions, crate. [SAVE] [✕]

▼▼▼ The Forsyth Park Inn 🆎
(912) 233-6800. **$185-$295, 14 day notice.** 102 W Hall St 31401. Between Whitaker and Howard sts; on Forsyth Park. Int corridors. **Pets:** Accepted. [ASK] [✕] 🖥

◇◇◇ ▼▼▼▼ Hamilton-Turner Inn 🆎
(912) 233-1833. **$189-$369, 10 day notice.** 330 Abercorn St 31401. Between E Charlton and E Harris sts; overlooking Lafayette Square; in historic district. Ext/int corridors. **Pets:** Small, other species. $50 one-time fee/room. Designated rooms, service with restrictions, supervision.
[SAVE] [✕]

◇◇◇ ▼▼▼▼ Hilton Savannah DeSoto 🅷
(912) 232-9000. **$159-$269.** 15 E Liberty St 31401. Between Bull and Drayton sts; in historic district. Int corridors. **Pets:** Accepted.
[SAVE] [✕] 🖥 🖥 🍽 🏊

▼▼▼▼ Homewood Suites by Hilton 🅷 ❀
(912) 353-8500. **$129-$199.** 5820 White Bluff Rd 31405. Jct SR 21 and 204 (Abercorn St), 0.5 mi s. Ext/int corridors. **Pets:** Other species. $75 one-time fee/room. Service with restrictions, crate.
[✕] 🖥 🏊 🖥

▼▼▼ Joan's on Jones B & B 🆎 ❀
(912) 234-3863. **$160-$185 (no credit cards), 7 day notice.** 17 W Jones St 31401. Between Whitaker and Bull sts. Ext corridors. **Pets:** Dogs only. $50 one-time fee/room. [✕] 🖥 🖥

▼▼▼ La Quinta Inn & Suites 🅷 ❀
(912) 927-7660. **$49-$119.** 8484 Abercorn St 31406. 2.4 mi s of jct SR 21 and 204 (Abercorn St). Int corridors. **Pets:** Medium, other species. Service with restrictions, supervision. [ASK] [✕] 🖥 🖥 🏊

▼▼▼ La Quinta Inn Savannah (I-95) 🅷 ❀
(912) 925-9505. **$49-$99.** 6 Gateway Blvd S 31419. I-95, exit 94 (SR 204/Abercorn St), just e, then s. Ext corridors. **Pets:** Medium, other species. Service with restrictions, supervision. [ASK] [✕] [♿M] 🖥 🖥

◇◇◇ ▼▼▼▼ The Mansion on Forsyth Park 🅷
(912) 238-5158. **$179-$509, 3 day notice.** 700 Drayton St 31401. Between E Hall and E Gwinnett sts; on Forsyth Park. Int corridors. **Pets:** Accepted. [ECO] [SAVE] [✕] 🖥 🖥 🍽 🏊

◇◇◇ ▼▼▼▼ Olde Harbour Inn 🆎 ❀
(912) 234-4100. **$199-$309, 7 day notice.** 508 E Factors Walk 31401. Lincoln St ramp off E Bay St; in historic riverfront district. Ext corridors. **Pets:** Medium. $35 one-time fee/room. Designated rooms, service with restrictions, crate. [SAVE] [✕] 🖥 🖥

◇◇◇ ▼▼▼ Red Roof Inn Midtown 🅷
(912) 355-4100. **$65-$120.** 201 Stephenson Ave 31405. 1.1 mi s of jct SR 21 and 204 (Abercorn St), just e. Ext corridors. **Pets:** Large. Service with restrictions, crate. [SAVE] [✕] 🖥 🖥 🏊

▼▼▼▼ Residence Inn by Marriott Savannah 🅷
(912) 356-3266. **$154-$174.** 5710 White Bluff Rd 31405. Jct SR 21, 0.5 mi s. Int corridors. **Pets:** Small. $100 one-time fee/room. Service with restrictions, supervision. [✕] 🖥 🖥 🏊 [✕]

◇◇◇ ▼▼▼▼ Staybridge Suites Savannah Historic District 🅷
(912) 721-9000. **$109-$199.** 301 E Bay St 31401. Corner of Lincoln St; in historic district. Int corridors. **Pets:** Medium. $75 one-time fee/room. Designated rooms, no service, crate. [SAVE] [✕] [♿M] 🖥 🖥

▼▼▼ The Thunderbird Inn 🅼 ❀
(912) 232-2661. **Call for rates.** 611 W Oglethorpe Ave 31401. Just w of Martin Luther King Jr Blvd. Ext corridors. **Pets:** Medium. $50 one-time fee/room. Service with restrictions, crate. [✕] 🖥 🖥

▼▼▼ TownePlace Suites Savannah Airport 🅷 ❀
(912) 629-7775. **$112-$136.** 4 Jay R Turner Dr 31408. I-95, exit 104, just e. Int corridors. **Pets:** Other species. $25 daily fee/pet. No service.
[✕] [♿M] 🖥 🖥

▼▼▼▼ TownePlace Suites Savannah Midtown 🅗
(912) 920-9080. **$169-$179.** 11309 Abercorn St 31419. Jct SR 21 and 204 (Abercorn St), 4.6 mi s. Int corridors. **Pets:** Accepted.
🗙 🛢 🖵 ≋

🔷 ▼▼▼▼ The Westin Savannah Harbor Golf Resort and Spa 🅗
(912) 201-2000. **$189-$449, 3 day notice.** 1 Resort Dr 31421. On Hutchinson Island; 1 mi se of first exit after Eugene Talmadge Memorial Bridge and US 17. Int corridors. **Pets:** Accepted.
SAVE 🗙 ᵫM 🛢 🖵 🍴 ≋ 🗙

STATESBORO

🔷 ▼▼▼ Best Western University Inn Ⓜ
(912) 681-7900. **$55-$62.** 1 Jameson Ave 30458. Jct US 25/301 and SR 67, 0.9 mi s on US 25/301. Ext corridors. **Pets:** Accepted.
SAVE 🗙 🛢 🖵 ≋

▼▼ La Quinta Inn Statesboro 🅗 🐾
(912) 871-2525. **$59-$119.** 225 Lanier Dr 30458. Jct US 301 Bypass and SR 67, 1.2 mi w on US 301, just n of Georgia Southern University. Int corridors. **Pets:** Medium, other species. Service with restrictions, supervision. ASK 🗙 ᵫM 🛢 🖵 ≋

🔷 ▼▼▼ Quality Inn & Suites 🅗
(912) 489-3995. **$64-$140.** 230 S Main St 30458. On US 301/25, 0.8 mi s of center; near downtown. Ext corridors. **Pets:** Medium, dogs only. $15 one-time fee/pet. Designated rooms, service with restrictions, crate.
SAVE 🗙 🛢 🖵 🍴 ≋

🔷 ▼▼▼▼ Statesboro Inn & Restaurant 🅒
(912) 489-8628. **Call for rates.** 106 S Main St 30458. US 301/25, just s of town center; downtown. Int corridors. **Pets:** Accepted.
SAVE 🗙 🛢 🖵 🍴

▼▼ Trellis Garden Inn 🅗
(912) 489-8781. **$75-$105.** 107 S Main St (US 301/25) 30458. On US 301/25, just s of center; downtown. Ext corridors. **Pets:** Large. Designated rooms, service with restrictions, supervision. ASK 🗙 🛢 ≋

STOCKBRIDGE

🔷 ▼▼▼▼ Baymont Inn & Suites Ⓜ
(770) 507-6500. **$59-$99.** 100 N Park Ct 30281. I-75, exit 224, just e, then just n on Rock Quarry Rd. Int corridors. **Pets:** Medium. $10 daily fee/pet. Service with restrictions, supervision. SAVE 🗙 🛢 🖵 ≋

🔷 ▼▼▼▼ La Quinta Inn & Suites 🅗 🐾
(770) 506-9991. **$74-$134.** 3581 Cameron Pkwy 30281. I-75, exit 228, just e on SR 138, then just n; I-675, exit 1, just w on SR 138, then just n. Int corridors. **Pets:** Medium, other species. Service with restrictions, supervision. SAVE 🗙 ᵫM 🛢 🖵 ≋ 🗙

▼▼▼ Microtel Inn & Suites 🅗
(678) 782-6100. **$65-$150, 21 day notice.** 195 Country Club Dr 30281. I-75, exit 224, just e, then just se. Int corridors. **Pets:** Small, other species. $10 deposit/pet. Designated rooms, no service, supervision.
ASK 🗙 ᵫM 🛢 🖵 ≋

▼▼▼ Sleep Inn & Suites 🅗
(770) 474-3870. **$60-$129.** 7423 Davidson Cir W 30281. I-675, exit 1, just e, then just s; I-75, exit 228, 1 mi e on SR 138, then just s. Int corridors. **Pets:** Small. $10 daily fee/pet. Service with restrictions, supervision.
🗙 ᵫM 🛢 🖵 ≋

🔷 ▼▼▼ Super 8 Atlanta South Ⓜ
(770) 474-5758. **$59-$79.** 1451 Hudson Bridge Rd 30281. I-75, exit 224, just w. Ext corridors. **Pets:** Accepted. SAVE 🗙 🛢 🖵 ≋

SWAINSBORO

🔷 ▼▼▼ Best Western Bradford Inn Ⓜ
(478) 237-2400. **$48-$65.** 688 S Main St 30401. I-16, exit 90 (US 1), 12.4 mi n. Ext corridors. **Pets:** Medium. $15 daily fee/pet. Supervision.
SAVE 🗙 🛢 🖵 ≋

THOMASTON

▼▼ Jameson Inn Ⓜ
(706) 648-2232. **$73-$80.** 1010 Hwy 19 N 30286. Jct SR 74, 2.3 mi n. Ext corridors. **Pets:** Accepted. ASK 🗙 ᵫM 🛢 🖵 ≋

THOMASVILLE

▼▼ Comfort Inn Ⓜ
(229) 228-5555. **$55-$85.** 14866 US 19 S 31759. Jct SR 300/US 19/84 and SR 122. Ext corridors. **Pets:** Large. $35 deposit/pet. Service with restrictions. 🗙 🛢 🖵 ≋

▼▼ Jameson Inn Ⓜ
(229) 227-9500. **$78-$81.** 1470 Remington Ave 31792. US 19, just w on CR 122. Ext corridors. **Pets:** Accepted. ASK 🗙 ᵫM 🛢 🖵 ≋

🔷 ▼▼▼ Quality Inn & Suites Ⓜ
(229) 225-2134. **$59.** 15138 US Hwy 19 S 31757. 0.3 mi s of US 319. Ext corridors. **Pets:** Medium. $10 daily fee/pet. Designated rooms, service with restrictions, supervision. SAVE 🗙 ᵫM 🛢 🖵 🍴 ≋

THOMSON

🔷 ▼▼▼▼ Best Western White Columns Inn Ⓜ
(706) 595-8000. **$82-$92.** 1890 Washington Rd 30824. I-20, exit 172 (US 78), just s. Ext corridors. **Pets:** $10 daily fee/pet, $10 one-time fee/pet. Designated rooms, no service. SAVE 🗙 🛢 🖵 🍴 ≋ 🗙

TIFTON

▼▼▼ Days Inn & Suites 🅗
(229) 382-8505. **$69-$119.** 1199 Hwy 82 W 31793. I-75, exit 62, just w. Int corridors. **Pets:** Accepted. ASK 🗙 🛢 🖵 ≋

▼▼▼ Hampton Inn 🅗
(229) 382-8800. **$90-$110.** 720 Hwy 319 S 31794. I-75, exit 62, just e. Ext corridors. **Pets:** Medium, other species. Supervision.
🗙 🛢 🖵 ≋

🔷 ▼▼▼ Holiday Inn 🅗
(229) 382-6687. **$69-$79.** 1208 Hwy 82 W 31793. I-75, exit 62; jct US 82 and 319. Ext corridors. **Pets:** No service, crate.
SAVE 🗙 🛢 🖵 🍴 ≋

▼▼▼ Ramada Limited and Conference Center 🅗
(229) 382-8500. **$64-$119.** 1211 Hwy 82 W 31793. I-75, exit 62, just w. Ext corridors. **Pets:** Other species. $10 daily fee/pet. Service with restrictions. ASK 🗙 🛢 🖵 ≋

TRENTON

▼▼▼ Days Inn Ⓜ
(706) 657-2550. **$57-$70.** 95 Killian Ave 30752. I-59, exit 11, just e. Ext corridors. **Pets:** Accepted. ASK 🗙 ᵫM 🛢 🖵 ≋

VALDOSTA

🔷 ▼▼▼ Best Western King of the Road 🅗
(229) 244-7600. **$69-$89, 7 day notice.** 1403 N St Augustine Rd 31602. I-75, exit 18, just w off of SR 94. Ext corridors. **Pets:** Accepted.
SAVE 🗙 🛢 🖵 ≋

🔷 ▼▼▼ Comfort Inn Conference Center 🅗
(229) 242-1212. **$81-$136.** 2101 W Hill Ave 31602. I-75, exit 16, just w. Ext/int corridors. **Pets:** Small, other species. Designated rooms, service with restrictions, supervision. SAVE 🗙 🛢 🖵 🍴 ≋ 🗙

▼▼▼ Days Inn I-75 North 🅗
(229) 244-4460. **$59-$79.** 4598 N Valdosta Rd 31602. I-75, exit 22, just w. Ext corridors. **Pets:** Accepted. ASK 🗙 🛢 🖵 ≋

🔷 ▼▼▼ Econo Lodge 🅗
(229) 671-1511. **Call for rates.** 3022 James Rd 31602. I-75, exit 18, just w. Int corridors. **Pets:** Large. $25 one-time fee/room. Designated rooms, service with restrictions, supervision. SAVE 🗙 ᵫM 🛢 🖵 ≋

Hawthorn Suites Valdosta �H

(229) 241-9221. **$109-$199.** 4025 Northlake Dr 31602. I-75, exit 22, just e on N Valdosta Rd, then just n. Int corridors. **Pets:** Other species. $50 one-time fee/room. Service with restrictions. [ASK] [✕] [♿M] [📧] [💻]

 La Quinta Inn & Suites Valdosta �H 🐾

(229) 247-7755. **$80-$150.** 1800 Clubhouse Dr 31601. I-75, exit 18, 0.3 mi e, then just s off SR 94. Int corridors. **Pets:** Medium, other species. Service with restrictions, supervision. [SAVE] [✕] [📧] [💻] [🏊]

Quality Inn North

(229) 244-8510. **Call for rates.** 1209 N St Augustine Rd 31601. I-75, exit 18, 0.3 mi e on SR 94. Ext corridors. **Pets:** Very small, other species. $10 daily fee/pet. Service with restrictions, supervision.

[SAVE] [✕] [♿M] [📧] [💻] [🏊]

Quality Inn South �H 🐾

(229) 244-4520. **Call for rates.** 1902 W Hill Ave 31601. I-75, exit 16, just e on US 84. Ext corridors. **Pets:** Medium, other species. $8 daily fee/pet. Service with restrictions, crate. [✕] [📧] [💻] [🏊]

Wingate by Wyndham Valdosta �H 🐾

(229) 242-1225. **$122-$170, 3 day notice.** 2010 W Hill Ave 31601. I-75, exit 16, just e. Int corridors. **Pets:** Medium, other species. $50 one-time fee/room. Designated rooms, service with restrictions, supervision.

[ASK] [✕] [♿M] [📧] [💻] [🏊] [✕]

VILLA RICA

Days Inn �H

(770) 459-8888. **$50-$115.** 195 Hwy 61 Connector 30180. I-20, exit 24, just n. Int corridors. **Pets:** Medium, dogs only. $10 daily fee/pet. Designated rooms, service with restrictions, supervision.

[ASK] [✕] [📧] [💻] [🏊]

Super 8 M

(770) 459-8000. **$49-$130, 7 day notice.** 128 Hwy 61 Connector 30180. I-20, exit 24, just n. Ext corridors. **Pets:** Accepted.

[ASK] [✕] [📧] [💻] [🏊]

WARM SPRINGS

Best Western White House Inn �H

(706) 655-2750. **$79-$99.** 2526 White House Pkwy 31830. Jct US 27 and 41, 0.5 mi s. Ext/int corridors. **Pets:** Accepted.

[SAVE] [✕] [📧] [💻] [🏊]

WARNER ROBINS

Best Western Peach Inn �H

(478) 953-3800. **$51-$69.** 2739 Watson Blvd 31093. I-75, exit 146 (SR 247C), 4.1 mi e. Ext corridors. **Pets:** Medium, other species. $10 daily fee/pet. Designated rooms, service with restrictions.

[SAVE] [✕] [📧] [💻] [🏊]

Colony Inn M

(478) 923-8871. **Call for rates.** 2024 Watson Blvd 31093. I-75, exit 146 (SR 247C), 5.6 mi e. Ext corridors. **Pets:** Accepted. [✕] [📧] [💻] [🏊]

Comfort Inn & Suites �H

(478) 922-7555. **$77-$99.** 95 S Hwy 247 31088. Jct SR 247C and US 129/SR 247, 1.6 mi s on US 129/SR 247. Ext/int corridors. **Pets:** Small, other species. $10 daily fee/room. Designated rooms, service with restrictions, crate. [✕] [📧] [💻] [🏊]

Jameson Inn-Warner Robins �H

(478) 953-5522. **$78-$85.** 2731 Watson Blvd 31093. I-75, exit 146 (SR 247C), 4.1 mi e. Ext corridors. **Pets:** Small, other species. $15 daily fee/room. Designated rooms, service with restrictions, crate.

[✕] [📧] [💻] [🏊]

 La Quinta Inn & Suites �H 🐾

(478) 333-3444. **$69-$139.** 109 Willie Lee Pkwy 31088. I-75, exit 146 (SR 247C), 2.8 mi e. Int corridors. **Pets:** Medium, other species. Service with restrictions, supervision. [SAVE] [✕] [♿M] [📧] [💻] [🏊]

WAYCROSS

Jameson Inn M

(912) 283-3800. **$73-$78.** 950 City Blvd 31501. Between US 1 and 82, east of city. Ext corridors. **Pets:** Accepted.

[ASK] [✕] [♿M] [📧] [💻] [🏊]

WAYNESBORO

Jameson Inn M

(706) 437-0500. **$78-$85.** 1436 N Liberty St 30830. 0.9 mi n of downtown center on US 25. Ext corridors. **Pets:** Accepted.

[ASK] [✕] [📧] [💻] [🏊]

WINDER

Best Western Winder Hotel �H

(770) 868-5303. **$80-$146.** 177 W Athens St 30680. Jct Broad St, 0.8 mi n; downtown. Int corridors. **Pets:** Medium. $25 daily fee/pet. Service with restrictions, supervision. [SAVE] [✕] [♿M] [📧] [💻] [🏊]

Jameson Inn M

(770) 867-1880. **$83-$90.** 9 Stafford St 30680. Jct SR 81, 11, 53 and 8; center. Ext corridors. **Pets:** Accepted. [ASK] [✕] [📧] [💻] [🏊]

YOUNG HARRIS

Brasstown Valley Resort �H

(706) 379-9900. **$129-$239, 7 day notice.** 6321 US Hwy 76 30582. US 76 and US 76/SR 515. Int corridors. **Pets:** Accepted.

[ECO] [SAVE] [✕] [📧] [💻] [🍴] [🏊] [✕]

HAWAII

HONOLULU

◆◆◆◇ ▼▼▼ ▼▼▼ The Kahala Hotel & Resort �**H** ❀
(808) 739-8888. **$395-$1095, 3 day notice.** 5000 Kahala Ave 96816. E of Diamond Head at end of Kahala Ave. Int corridors. **Pets:** Small, dogs only. $150 one-time fee/room. Service with restrictions, supervision.
[ECO] [SAVE] [✕] [&M] [🔒] [💻] [¶¶] [🏊] [✕]

KAANAPALI

◆◆◆◇ ▼▼▼ ▼▼▼ The Westin Maui Resort & Spa �**H**
(808) 667-2525. **$285-$505, 3 day notice.** 2365 Kaanapali Pkwy 96761. Off SR 30, via Kaanapali Pkwy; in Kaanapali Beach resort area. Int corridors. **Pets:** Accepted. [SAVE] [✕] [&M] [🔒] [💻] [¶¶] [🏊] [✕]

KAUPULEHU

▼▼▼ ▼▼▼ Four Seasons Resort Hualalai at Historic Ka'upulehu �**H**
(808) 325-8000. **$725-$1155, 21 day notice.** 72-100 Ka'upulehu Dr 96740. Off SR 19, 6 mi n of Kona International Airport. Ext corridors.
Pets: Accepted. [✕] [&M] [🔒] [💻] [¶¶] [🏊] [✕]

KOHALA COAST

◆◆◆◇ ▼▼▼ ▼▼▼ The Fairmont Orchid, Hawaii �**H** ❀
(808) 885-2000. **$459-$6999, 14 day notice.** 1 N Kaniku Dr 96743. On SR 19, 20 mi n of Kona International Airport, 2 mi w; in Mauna Lani resort area. Int corridors. **Pets:** Small. $25 daily fee/room. Designated rooms, supervision. [SAVE] [✕] [&M] [🔒] [💻] [¶¶] [🏊] [✕]

LANAI CITY

▼▼▼ ▼▼▼ Four Seasons Resort Lana'i at Manele Bay �**H**
(808) 565-2000. **$345-$7400, 21 day notice.** 1 Manele Bay Rd 96763. From airport, 4 mi e on Kaumalapau Hwy to Lana'i City, 7 mi s on SR 440. Ext corridors. **Pets:** Accepted. [✕] [&M] [🔒] [💻] [¶¶] [🏊] [✕]

▼▼▼ ▼▼▼ Four Seasons Resort Lana'i, The Lodge at Koele �**H**
(808) 565-4000. **$345-$1700, 21 day notice.** One Keomoku Hwy 96763. From airport, 4 mi e on Kaumalapau Hwy to Lana'i City, 2 mi n on SR 440, follow signs. Int corridors. **Pets:** Accepted.
[✕] [&M] [🔒] [💻] [¶¶] [🏊] [✕]

WAILEA

◆◆◆◇ ▼▼▼ ▼▼▼ Four Seasons Resort Maui at Wailea �**H**
(808) 874-8000. **$445-$1275, 21 day notice.** 3900 Wailea Alanui Dr 96753. From end of SR 31, 0.5 mi s. Int corridors. **Pets:** Accepted.
[SAVE] [✕] [&M] [🔒] [💻] [¶¶] [🏊] [✕]

IDAHO

AHSAHKA

The High Country Inn BB ❖
(208) 476-7570. **$85-$125, 7 day notice.** 70 High Country Ln 83520. 0.5 mi w to Dworshak Visitors Center Rd, 2 mi n, then just w. Ext/int corridors. **Pets:** Other species. $25 one-time fee/room. Designated rooms, crate.

BLACKFOOT

Best Western Blackfoot Inn H
(208) 785-4144. **$81-$117.** 750 Jensen Grove Dr 83221. I-15, exit 93, just e on Bergener, then 0.4 mi n on Parkway Dr. Int corridors. **Pets:** Other species. Service with restrictions, supervision.

Super 8 H
(208) 785-9333. **$59-$110.** 1279 Parkway Dr 83221. I-15, exit 93, just e; shared driveway with McDonald's. Int corridors. **Pets:** Other species. $10 one-time fee/room. Service with restrictions.

BLISS

Amber Inn Motel H
(208) 352-4441. **$40-$60.** 17286 US Hwy 30 83314. I-84, exit 141, just s. Int corridors. **Pets:** Accepted.

BOISE

Best Western Airport Inn H
(208) 384-5000. **$70-$100.** 2660 Airport Way 83705. I-84, exit 53 (Vista Ave), just s. Ext corridors. **Pets:** Accepted.

Best Western Vista Inn at the Airport H
(208) 336-8100. **$79-$95.** 2645 Airport Way 83705. I-84, exit 53 (Vista Ave), just s. Ext/int corridors. **Pets:** Medium, dogs only. $95 daily fee/room. Designated rooms, service with restrictions, supervision.

Doubletree Club Hotel H
(208) 345-2002. **$57-$159.** 475 W Parkcenter Blvd 83706. I-84, exit 54 (Broadway), 2 mi n, then 0.3 mi e on Beacon St and Parkcenter Blvd. Int corridors. **Pets:** Accepted.

Fairfield Inn by Marriott H ❖
(208) 331-5656. **$98-$120.** 3300 S Shoshone St 83705. I-84, exit 53 (Vista Ave), just n to Elder St, then just w. Int corridors. **Pets:** Other species. $20 daily fee/pet. Designated rooms, service with restrictions, supervision.

Hampton Inn H
(208) 331-5600. **$79-$129.** 3270 S Shoshone St 83705. I-84, exit 53 (Vista Ave), just n to Elder St, then just w. Int corridors. **Pets:** Small, other species. Designated rooms, service with restrictions, supervision.

Holiday Inn Boise Airport H ❖
(208) 343-4900. **$69-$119.** 3300 Vista Ave 83705. I-84, exit 53 (Vista Ave), just n. Int corridors. **Pets:** $25 one-time fee/room. Designated rooms, service with restrictions, supervision.

Holiday Inn Express H
(208) 388-0800. **Call for rates.** 2613 S Vista Ave 83705. I-84, exit 53 (Vista Ave), 0.5 mi n. Int corridors. **Pets:** Accepted.

Modern Hotel and Bar H ❖
(208) 424-8244. **Call for rates.** 1314 W Grove St 83702. Jct 14th St; downtown. Ext/int corridors. **Pets:** Dogs only. $20 one-time fee/pet. Designated rooms, service with restrictions, supervision.

Oxford Suites H
(208) 322-8000. **$99-$169.** 1426 S Entertainment Ave 83709. I-84, exit 50A westbound; exit 50B eastbound, just s to Spectrum St, just w, then just n. Int corridors. **Pets:** Medium. $25 one-time fee/pet. Designated rooms, service with restrictions, crate.

Red Lion Hotel Boise Downtowner H
(208) 344-7691. **$69-$135.** 1800 Fairview Ave 83702. I-184, exit 3 (Fairview Ave), 1 mi n. Int corridors. **Pets:** Other species. $20 one-time fee/room. Service with restrictions, supervision.

Residence Inn by Marriott-Boise Central H
(208) 344-1200. **$149-$159.** 1401 S Lusk Ave 83706. I-84, exit 53 (Vista Ave), 2.4 mi n, just w on Ann Morrison, then just s on Lois Ave. Ext corridors. **Pets:** Other species. $75 one-time fee/room. Service with restrictions, crate.

Residence Inn by Marriott-Boise West H
(208) 385-9000. **$107-$131.** 7303 W Denton St 83704. I-84, exit 50A westbound; exit 50B eastbound, 2 mi n on Cole Rd, then just w. Int corridors. **Pets:** Medium. $100 one-time fee/room. Designated rooms, service with restrictions, supervision.

Safari Inn Downtown H
(208) 344-6556. **$79-$99.** 1070 Grove St 83702. At 11th and Grove sts; center. Int corridors. **Pets:** $10 one-time fee/room. Designated rooms, service with restrictions, supervision.

Shilo Inn Suites-Boise Airport H ❖
(208) 343-7662. **$80-$170.** 4111 Broadway Ave 83705. I-84, exit 54 (Broadway Ave), just sw. Int corridors. **Pets:** Dogs only. $25 one-time fee/room. Designated rooms, service with restrictions, supervision.

SpringHill Suites by Marriott Boise H
(208) 939-8266. **$104-$127.** 6325 N Cloverdale Rd 83713. I-84, exit 46 (Eagle Rd), 4.3 mi n to Chinden, 0.9 mi e, then just s. Int corridors. **Pets:** Medium. $50 one-time fee/room. Service with restrictions, supervision.

SpringHill Suites by Marriott-Boise ParkCenter H
(208) 342-1044. **$125-$153.** 424 E Parkcenter Blvd 83706. I-84, exit 54 (Broadway Ave), 2.3 mi n, then just e on Beacon and Parkcenter blvds. Int corridors. **Pets:** Large. $50 one-time fee/room. Designated rooms, service with restrictions, supervision.

BONNERS FERRY

♨ ▼▼▼▼ Best Western Kootenai River Inn Casino & Spa �H ❀

(208) 267-8511. **$130-$155.** 7169 Plaza St 83805. On US 95; city center. Int corridors. **Pets:** Medium. $25 daily fee/pet. Service with restrictions, supervision. SAVE ⊠ 🗎 🖃 ¶ ➣ ⊠

BURLEY

♨ ▼▼▼ Best Western Burley Inn & Convention Center �H

(208) 678-3501. **$66-$90.** 800 N Overland Ave 83318. I-84, exit 208, just s. Ext/int corridors. **Pets:** Accepted. SAVE ⊠ 🗎 🖃 ¶ ➣ ⊠

♨ ▼▼ Budget Motel 🅼 ❀

(208) 678-2200. **$56-$73.** 900 N Overland Ave 83318. I-84, exit 208, just s. Ext corridors. **Pets:** $8 daily fee/pet. Designated rooms, service with restrictions, supervision. SAVE ⊠ ᴹ 🗎 ➣

♨ ▼▼ Super 8–Burley �H ❀

(208) 678-7000. **Call for rates.** 336 S 600 W 83318. I-84, exit 208, just n. Int corridors. **Pets:** $10 daily fee/room. Designated rooms, service with restrictions, supervision. SAVE ⊠ ᴹ 🗎 ➣

CALDWELL

♨ ▼▼▼ Best Western Caldwell Inn & Suites 🅼 ❀

(208) 454-7225. **$72-$159.** 908 Specht Ave 83605. I-84, exit 29, just s. Int corridors. **Pets:** Other species. $5 one-time fee/pet. Service with restrictions, supervision. SAVE ⊠ 🗎 🖃 ➣

▼▼ La Quinta Inn Caldwell �H ❀

(208) 454-2222. **Call for rates.** 901 Specht Ave 83605. I-84, exit 29, just s. Int corridors. **Pets:** Medium, other species. Service with restrictions, supervision. ⊠ 🗎 🖃 ➣

COEUR D'ALENE

♨ ▼▼▼▼ Best Western Coeur d'Alene Inn & Conference Center �H ❀

(208) 765-3200. **$100-$180.** W 506 Appleway Ave 83814. I-90, exit 12, just nw. Int corridors. **Pets:** Large, dogs only. $25 daily fee/room. Service with restrictions, supervision. SAVE ⊠ ᴹ 🗎 🖃 ¶ ➣

▼▼▼▼ The Coeur d'Alene Resort �H

(208) 765-4000. **$119-$485, 7 day notice.** 115 S 2nd St 83814. I-90, exit 11 (Northwest Blvd), 2 mi s. Ext/int corridors. **Pets:** Dogs only. $75 one-time fee/pet. Service with restrictions, crate. ASK ⊠ 🖃 ¶ ➣ ⊠

♨ ▼▼▼▼ Comfort Inn Coeur D'Alene �H

(208) 664-1649. **Call for rates.** 2303 N 4th St 83814. I-90, exit 13, just n. Int corridors. **Pets:** Accepted. SAVE ⊠ 🗎 🖃 ➣

▼▼ Days Inn-Coeur d'Alene �H

(208) 667-8668. **Call for rates.** 2200 Northwest Blvd 83814. I-90, exit 11 (Northwest Blvd), just se. Int corridors. **Pets:** Accepted. ⊠ ᴹ 🗎 🖃

▼▼ Guest House Inn & Suites �H

(208) 765-3011. **$45-$99.** 330 W Appleway Ave 83814. I-90, exit 12, just n, then just e. Int corridors. **Pets:** Accepted. ASK ⊠ 🗎 🖃

▼▼▼ Holiday Inn Express Hotel & Suites Coeur d'Alene �H

(208) 667-3100. **Call for rates.** 2300 W Seltice Way 83814. I-90, exit 11 (Northwest Blvd), just s. Int corridors. **Pets:** Accepted. ⊠ 🗎 🖃 ➣

♨ ▼▼▼▼ La Quinta Inn & Suites Coeur D'Alene (East) �H ❀

(208) 667-6777. **$69-$159.** 2209 E Sherman Ave 83814. I-90, exit 15 (Sherman Ave), just s. Int corridors. **Pets:** Medium, other species. Service with restrictions, supervision. SAVE ⊠ ᴹ 🗎 🖃 ➣

▼▼▼▼ La Quinta Inn Coeur D'Alene (Appleway) �H ❀

(208) 765-5500. **$69-$159.** 280 W Appleway Ave 83814. I-90, exit 12, just ne. Int corridors. **Pets:** Medium, other species. Service with restrictions, supervision. ASK ⊠ ᴹ 🗎 🖃 ➣ ⊠

▼▼▼▼ The Roosevelt Inn, Inc 🅱🅱

(208) 765-5200. **$89-$319, 14 day notice.** 105 Wallace Ave 83814. I-90, exit 13, 2 mi s, then just w; downtown. Int corridors. **Pets:** Accepted. ASK ⊠ ⊠ 🅿 🗹

♨ ▼▼▼▼ Shilo Inn Suites–Coeur d'Alene �H ❀

(208) 664-2300. **$90-$180.** 702 W Appleway Ave 83814. I-90, exit 12, just n, then just w. Int corridors. **Pets:** Dogs only. $25 one-time fee/room. Designated rooms, service with restrictions, supervision. SAVE ⊠ ᴹ 🗎 🖃 ➣ ⊠

GRANGEVILLE

♨ ▼▼▼ Gateway Inn–Grangeville 🅼

(208) 983-2500. **$62-$99.** 700 W Main St 83530. Jct SR 13 and US 95. Ext corridors. **Pets:** $10 daily fee/room. Designated rooms, service with restrictions, supervision. SAVE ⊠ 🗎 🖃 ➣

HAGERMAN

♨ ▼▼▼ Hagerman Valley Inn 🅼

(208) 837-6196. **$63-$108.** 661 Frog's Landing 83332. South end of town on US 30. Ext/int corridors. **Pets:** $7 daily fee/pet. Designated rooms, service with restrictions, supervision. SAVE ⊠ 🗎 🖃

HAILEY

▼▼ Airport Inn 🅼

(208) 788-2477. **$80-$150.** 820 4th Ave S 83333. Just n of SR 75 at 4th Ave; near airport. Ext corridors. **Pets:** Accepted. ⊠ 🗎 🖃

♨ ▼▼▼ AmericInn Lodge & Suites of Hailey �H

(208) 788-7950. **$89-$209.** 51 Cobblestone Ln 83333. Just n on SR 75, then just e. Int corridors. **Pets:** Dogs only. $15 one-time fee/room. Designated rooms, service with restrictions, supervision. SAVE ⊠ ᴹ 🗎 🖃 ➣ ⊠

▼▼▼ Wood River Inn �H

(208) 578-0600. **$106-$164.** 603 N Main St 83333. Just n of downtown on SR 75. Int corridors. **Pets:** Large, other species. $25 one-time fee/room. Designated rooms, service with restrictions, supervision. ASK ⊠ ᴹ 🗎 🖃 ➣ ⊠

HAYDEN

▼▼▼ Holiday Inn Express Hotel & Suites �H

(208) 772-7900. **$90-$370.** 151 W Orchard Ave 83835. I-90, exit 12, 3.5 mi n. Int corridors. **Pets:** Accepted. ASK ⊠ ᴹ 🗎 🖃 ⊠

IDAHO FALLS

♨ ▼▼▼ Best Western Driftwood Inn �H ❀

(208) 523-2242. **$79-$139.** 575 River Pkwy 83402. I-15, exit 118 (Broadway), 0.5 mi e, then 0.3 mi n. Ext corridors. **Pets:** Other species. $12 daily fee/room. Supervision. SAVE ⊠ 🗎 🖃 ➣ ⊠

▼▼ Candlewood Suites �H ❀

(208) 525-9800. **$69-$139.** 665 Pancheri Dr 83402. I-15, exit 118 (Broadway), 1 mi e (cross bridge), 0.5 mi s on S Capital Ave. Int corridors. **Pets:** Other species. $25 one-time fee/room. ASK ⊠ ᴹ 🗎 🖃

▼▼▼ GuestHouse Inn & Suites �H

(208) 523-6260. **$59-$119.** 850 Lindsay Blvd 83402. I-15, exit 119, just e. Ext/int corridors. **Pets:** Accepted. ASK ⊠ 🗎 🖃 ¶ ➣ ⊠

Le Ritz Hotel & Suites 🅷 ❀

(208) 528-0880. **$89-$129.** 720 Lindsay Blvd 83402. I-15, exit 118 (Broadway), 0.5 mi e, then just n. Int corridors. **Pets:** $10 daily fee/room. Designated rooms, service with restrictions. ⟨SAVE⟩ ⊠ 🖬 💻 🐾

Red Lion Hotel on the Falls 🅷

(208) 523-8000. **Call for rates.** 475 River Pkwy 83402. I-15, exit 118 (Broadway), 0.5 mi e, then just n. Ext/int corridors. **Pets:** Other species. $20 one-time fee/room. Service with restrictions, supervision.

⊠ 🖬 💻 🍴 🐾 ⊠

JACKSON HOLE AREA (NEARBY WYOMING)

DRIGGS

Teton Valley Cabins 🅲🅰 ❀

(208) 354-8153. **$79-$109, 7 day notice.** 388 Ski Hill Rd 83422. 0.8 mi e on Little Ave from SR 33 E. Ext corridors. **Pets:** $15 daily fee/room. Service with restrictions, crate. ⟨ASK⟩ ⊠ 🖬 💻 ⊠ 🐾

END AREA

JEROME

Best Western Sawtooth Inn & Suites 🅷 ❀

(208) 324-9200. **$85-$100.** 2653 S Lincoln Ave 83338. I-84, exit 168, just n on SR 79. Int corridors. **Pets:** Other species. Designated rooms, service with restrictions. ⟨SAVE⟩ ⊠ 🖬 💻 🐾

KELLOGG

Kellogg Inn 🅷 ❀

(208) 783-1234. **$75-$114.** 601 Bunker Ave 83837. I-90, exit 49, 0.5 mi se. Int corridors. **Pets:** Other species. $15 deposit/room, $5 one-time fee/room. Service with restrictions, supervision.

⟨SAVE⟩ ⊠ ⟨&M⟩ 🖬 💻 🐾

Morning Star Lodge Ⓜ ❀

(208) 783-0202. **$143-$590.** 602 Bunker Ave 83837. I-90, exit 49, 0.5 mi se. Int corridors. **Pets:** $30 one-time fee/room. Designated rooms, service with restrictions, crate. ⟨ASK⟩ ⊠ 🖬 💻 🍴 ⊠

Silverhorn Motor Inn 🅷 ❀

(208) 783-1151. **$69-$92.** 699 W Cameron Ave 83837. I-90, exit 49, just ne. Int corridors. **Pets:** Other species. Supervision. ⊠ 🖬 🍴

KETCHUM

Best Western Tyrolean Lodge 🅷

(208) 726-3344. **$79-$149.** 260 Cottonwood St 83340. South end of town; just w of SR 75 (Main St) on Rivers St, then just s on 3rd Ave. Int corridors. **Pets:** Accepted. ⟨SAVE⟩ ⊠ 🖬 💻 🐾 ⊠

Tamarack Lodge Ⓜ

(208) 726-3344. **$89-$164, 3 day notice.** 291 Walnut Ave N 83340. Just ne on Sun Valley Rd from jct SR 75 (Main St); downtown. Ext/int corridors. **Pets:** Other species. $25 one-time fee/room. Service with restrictions, supervision. ⟨ASK⟩ ⊠ 🖬 💻 🐾

KOOSKIA

River Dance Lodge 🅲🅰

(208) 926-4300. **$129-$239, 45 day notice.** 7743 Hwy 12 83539. On US 12, 16 mi e. Ext corridors. **Pets:** $15 daily fee/pet. Designated rooms, service with restrictions, crate.

⟨ASK⟩ ⊠ 🖬 💻 🍴 ⊠ 🐾 🐾 🐾

LEWISTON

Comfort Inn 🅷

(208) 798-8090. **$69-$109.** 2128 8th Ave 83501. 1.2 mi s on US 12 from jct US 95, just s on 21st St. Int corridors. **Pets:** Accepted.

⟨ASK⟩ ⊠ ⟨&M⟩ 🖬 💻 🐾

Shilo Inn Suites Hotel-Idaho Falls 🅷 ❀

(208) 523-0088. **$95-$185.** 780 Lindsay Blvd 83402. I-15, exit 119, just se. Int corridors. **Pets:** Dogs only. $25 one-time fee/room. Designated rooms, service with restrictions, supervision.

⟨SAVE⟩ ⊠ 🖬 💻 🍴 🐾 ⊠

Holiday Inn Express 🅷

(208) 750-1600. **$79-$199.** 2425 Nez Perce Dr 83501. 1.2 mi s on US 12 from jct US 95, 1.2 mi s on 21st St, then just e. Int corridors. **Pets:** Accepted. ⟨SAVE⟩ ⊠ ⟨&M⟩ 🖬 💻 🐾 ⊠

Super 8 🅷

(208) 743-8808. **$53-$71.** 3120 North & South Hwy 83501. Just e on US 12 from jct US 95. Int corridors. **Pets:** $10 daily fee/pet. Service with restrictions. ⟨ASK⟩ ⊠ ⟨&M⟩ 🖬 💻

LOWER STANLEY

Salmon River Cabins & Motel 🅲🅰

(208) 774-3566. **$70-$135, 7 day notice.** 55 Lower Stanley (US Hwy 75) 83278. 1 mi n on US 75 from jct SR 21. Ext corridors. **Pets:** $10 daily fee/pet. Service with restrictions, supervision.

⟨SAVE⟩ ⊠ 🖬 💻 🐾

MCCALL

Best Western McCall Lodge 🅷

(208) 634-2230. **$110-$120.** 211 S 3rd St 83638. On SR 55; south end of town. Int corridors. **Pets:** Accepted.

⟨SAVE⟩ ⊠ ⟨&M⟩ 🖬 💻 🐾 ⊠

Super 8-McCall Ⓜ ❀

(208) 634-4637. **$89-$109.** 303 S 3rd St 83638. On SR 55; south end of town. Int corridors. **Pets:** Other species. $10 daily fee/pet. Service with restrictions, supervision. ⟨SAVE⟩ ⊠ ⟨&M⟩ 🖬 💻

Western Mountain Lodge 🅷

(208) 634-6300. **$94-$160.** 415 N 3rd St 83638. SR 55, just s of jct Lake St. Int corridors. **Pets:** Accepted. ⟨SAVE⟩ ⊠ ⟨&M⟩ 🖬 💻 🐾

MERIDIAN

Candlewood Suites Boise-Meridian 🅷

(208) 888-5121. **$65-$129.** 1855 S Silverstone Way 83642. I-84, exit 46 (Eagle Rd), 0.6 mi s, just e on Overland, then just s. Int corridors. **Pets:** Accepted. ⟨ASK⟩ ⊠ ⟨&M⟩ 🖬 💻

Comfort Suites-Meridian 🅷

(208) 288-2060. **$60-$80.** 2610 E Freeway Dr 83642. I-84, exit 46 (Eagle Rd), just n to St Lukes Rd, then just w to Allen St, follow signs. Int corridors. **Pets:** Dogs only. $25 one-time fee/room. Service with restrictions, supervision. ⟨SAVE⟩ ⊠ ⟨&M⟩ 🖬 💻 🐾

Holiday Inn Express Hotel & Suites 🅷

(208) 288-2100. **$109-$159.** 800 S Allen St 83642. I-84, exit 46 (Eagle Rd), northwest corner. Int corridors. **Pets:** Accepted.

⟨SAVE⟩ ⊠ ⟨&M⟩ 🖬 💻 🐾

▼▼▼ TownPlace Suites by Marriott ℍ
(208) 884-8550. **$79-$84.** 1415 S Eagle Rd 83642. I-84, exit 46 (Eagle Rd), just s. Int corridors. **Pets:** Small, other species. $75 one-time fee/room. Service with restrictions. ⊠ 🛄 💻 🏊

MONTPELIER

𝔸𝔸𝔸 ▼▼▼ Clover Creek Inn ℍ
(208) 847-1782. **$75-$105.** 243 N 4th St 83254. Just n on US 30 from jct US 89 S. Ext corridors. **Pets:** Other species. $25 daily fee/pet. Designated rooms, service with restrictions, supervision. SAVE ⊠ 🛄 💻

MOSCOW

𝔸𝔸𝔸 ▼▼▼▼ Best Western University Inn ℍ
(208) 882-0550. **$109-$199.** 1516 Pullman Rd 83843. Jct US 95, 1 mi w on SR 8. Int corridors. **Pets:** Small, other species. $25 daily fee/room. Designated rooms, service with restrictions, crate.
SAVE ⊠ 🛄 🛗 💻 🍴 🏊 ⊠

▼▼▼ La Quinta Inn ℍ 🐾
(208) 882-5365. **$69-$169.** 185 Warbonnet Dr 83843. 1.6 mi w on SR 8 from jct US 93, just n. Int corridors. **Pets:** Medium, other species. Service with restrictions, supervision. ASK ⊠ 🛄 💻 🏊

▼▼▼ Super 8 ℍ
(208) 883-1503. **Call for rates.** 175 Peterson Dr 83843. Jct US 95, 0.8 mi w on SR 8, just n. Int corridors. **Pets:** $10 daily fee/pet. Supervision. ⊠ 🛄 💻

MOUNTAIN HOME

𝔸𝔸𝔸 ▼▼▼ Best Western Foothills Motor Inn ℍ
(208) 587-8477. **$70-$100.** 1080 Hwy 20 83647. I-84, exit 95, just n. Ext corridors. **Pets:** Medium. $10 daily fee/pet. Designated rooms, service with restrictions, supervision. SAVE ⊠ 🛗 🛄 💻 🏊

▼▼▼ Sleep Inn ℍ
(208) 587-9743. **$70-$95.** 1180 Hwy 20 83647. I-84, exit 95, just n. Int corridors. **Pets:** Medium. $10 daily fee/pet. Designated rooms, service with restrictions, supervision. ASK ⊠ 🛄 💻

NAMPA

𝔸𝔸𝔸 ▼▼▼▼ Shilo Inn Suites Hotel-Nampa ℍ 🐾
(208) 465-3250. **$85-$165.** 1401 Shilo Rd 83687. I-84, exit 36, just nw. Int corridors. **Pets:** Dogs only. $25 one-time fee/room. Designated rooms, service with restrictions, supervision.
SAVE ⊠ 🛄 💻 🍴 🏊 ⊠

OROFINO

𝔸𝔸𝔸 ▼▼▼ Best Western Lodge at River's Edge ℍ
(208) 476-9999. **$84-$124.** 615 Main St 83544. Downtown. Int corridors. **Pets:** Accepted. SAVE ⊠ 🛄 💻 🍴 🏊 ⊠

𝔸𝔸𝔸 ▼▼▼ Konkolville Motel Ⓜ
(208) 476-5584. **$60-$90.** 2000 Konkolville Rd 83544. 2.7 mi e on Michigan Ave. Ext corridors. **Pets:** Other species. $15 daily fee/pet. Designated rooms, service with restrictions, supervision.
SAVE ⊠ 🛗 🛄 💻 🏊

POCATELLO

𝔸𝔸𝔸 ▼▼▼▼ Best Western CottonTree Inn ℍ 🐾
(208) 237-7650. **$76-$119.** 1415 Bench Rd 83201. I-15, exit 71, just e. Int corridors. **Pets:** Other species. Service with restrictions.
SAVE ⊠ 🛄 💻 🏊

▼▼▼▼ Holiday Inn-Pocatello ℍ
(208) 237-1400. **$85-$99.** 1399 Bench Rd 83201. I-15, exit 71, just e. Ext/int corridors. **Pets:** Medium. $10 daily fee/room. Designated rooms, service with restrictions, supervision.
ASK ⊠ 🛄 💻 🍴 🏊 ⊠

𝔸𝔸𝔸 ▼▼▼ Pocatello Super 8 ℍ 🐾
(208) 234-0888. **$65-$100.** 1330 Bench Rd 83201. I-15, exit 71, just e. Int corridors. **Pets:** Other species. $15 one-time fee/room. Designated rooms, service with restrictions, supervision. SAVE ⊠ 🛄 💻

𝔸𝔸𝔸 ▼▼▼ Red Lion Hotel Pocatello ℍ
(208) 233-2200. **$75-$130.** 1555 Pocatello Creek Rd 83201. I-15, exit 71, just e. Int corridors. **Pets:** Other species. $20 one-time fee/room. Service with restrictions, supervision. SAVE ⊠ 🛄 💻 🍴 🏊

▼ Thunderbird Motel Ⓜ
(208) 232-6330. **$40-$69.** 1415 S 5th Ave 83201. I-15, exit 67, 1.3 mi n; just s of Idaho State University. Ext corridors. **Pets:** Accepted.
ASK ⊠ 🛄 🏊

▼▼▼ TownePlace Suites by Marriott ℍ
(208) 478-7000. **$98-$120.** 2376 Via Caporatti Dr 83201. I-15, exit 69 (Clark St), just e. Int corridors. **Pets:** Medium, other species. $100 one-time fee/room. Service with restrictions, supervision.
⊠ 🛗 🛄 💻 🏊

PONDERAY

𝔸𝔸𝔸 ▼▼▼ Howard Johnson Sandpoint/Ponderay ℍ
(208) 263-5383. **$50-$120.** 477255 Hwy 95 N 83852. 1.2 mi n on US 95 from jct SR 200. Int corridors. **Pets:** Other species. Service with restrictions, supervision. SAVE ⊠ 🛗 🛄 💻

▼▼▼ Super 8 Ⓜ
(208) 263-2210. **Call for rates.** 476841 Hwy 95 N 83852. 0.7 mi n on US 95 from jct SR 200. Int corridors. **Pets:** Accepted. ⊠ 🛗 🛄

POST FALLS

𝔸𝔸𝔸 ▼▼▼ Howard Johnson Express ℍ
(208) 773-4541. **$59-$200.** 3647 W 5th Ave 83854. I-90, exit 2, just ne. Int corridors. **Pets:** Other species. $10 daily fee/pet. Service with restrictions, supervision. SAVE ⊠ 🛗 🛄 💻 🏊

𝔸𝔸𝔸 ▼▼▼▼ Red Lion Templin's Hotel on the River–Post Falls ℍ
(208) 773-1611. **$89-$199.** 414 E First Ave 83854. I-90, exit 5 eastbound, just s to First Ave; exit 6 westbound, 0.7 mi w on Seltice Way to Spokane St, 0.5 mi s, then just e. Int corridors. **Pets:** Other species. $20 one-time fee/room. Service with restrictions, supervision.
SAVE ⊠ 🛗 🛄 💻 🍴 ⊠

▼▼ Sleep Inn ℍ 🐾
(208) 777-9394. **$59-$139, 7 day notice.** 157 S Pleasant View Rd 83854. I-90, exit 2, just s. Int corridors. **Pets:** Dogs only. $15 one-time fee/room. Designated rooms, service with restrictions, supervision.
ASK ⊠ 🛗 🛄 💻

PRIEST RIVER

▼▼ Eagle's Nest Motel Ⓜ
(208) 448-2000. **$55-$100.** 1007 Albeni Hwy 83856. US 2, 0.5 mi w. Ext corridors. **Pets:** Accepted. ⊠ 🛗 🛄 💻

REXBURG

𝔸𝔸𝔸 ▼▼▼ AmericInn Lodge & Suites of Rexburg ℍ 🐾
(208) 356-5333. **$80-$210.** 1098 Golden Beauty Dr 83440. US 20, exit 332 (S Rexburg). Int corridors. **Pets:** Other species. $100 deposit/room, $20 one-time fee/room. Designated rooms, service with restrictions, crate.
SAVE ⊠ 🛄 💻 🏊 ⊠

𝔸𝔸𝔸 ▼▼▼ Best Western Mountain View Inn ℍ
(208) 356-4646. **$80-$115, 7 day notice.** 450 W 4th St S 83440. US 20, exit 332 (S Rexburg), 1 mi e. Int corridors. **Pets:** Small. $10 daily fee/pet. Designated rooms, service with restrictions, supervision.
SAVE ⊠ 🛄 💻 🏊

𝔸𝔸𝔸 ▼▼▼ Comfort Inn ℍ
(208) 359-1311. **$79-$129.** 885 W Main St 83440. US 20, exit 333 (Salmon), just e. Int corridors. **Pets:** Other species. Service with restrictions, supervision. SAVE ⊠ 🛄 💻 🏊

RIGBY

▼▼▼▼ **Blue Heron Inn** 🅱🅱 ❖

(208) 745-9922. **$129-$229, 7 day notice.** 4175 E Menan Lorenzo Hwy 83442. 18 mi n on US 20 from jct I-15, just e. Ext/int corridors. **Pets:** $10 one-time fee/room. Designated rooms, service with restrictions, crate.

(ASK) ⊠ (&M) (⊠) (☎)

RIGGINS

🅰🅰 ▼▼▼▼ **Best Western Salmon Rapids Lodge** 🅷 ❖

(208) 628-2743. **$90-$197.** 1010 S Main St 83549. Just e of US 95; downtown. Int corridors. **Pets:** Other species. $15 daily fee/pet. Designated rooms, service with restrictions, supervision.

(SAVE) ⊠ (&M) 🖥 💻 ⊠

▼▼▼ **Pinehurst Resort Cabins** 🅲🅰

(208) 628-3323. **$65-$95.** 5604 Hwy 95 83654. On US 95, 13 mi s. Ext corridors. **Pets:** Accepted. (ASK) ⊠ 🖥 💻 📶 (☎)

SAGLE

▼▼▼ **Bottle Bay Resort & Marina** 🅲🅰

(208) 263-5916. **$129-$239.** 115 Resort Rd 83860. 8.3 mi e on Bottle Bay Rd from US 95. Ext corridors. **Pets:** $10 daily fee/pet. No service, supervision. 🖥 💻 🍴 ⊠ 📶 (☎)

SALMON

▼▼ **Stagecoach Inn** Ⓜ

(208) 756-2919. **Call for rates.** 201 Riverfront Dr (US 93 N) 83467. Just n on US 93 from jct SR 28. Int corridors. **Pets:** Accepted.

⊠ 🖥 💻 ➔

SANDPOINT

🅰🅰 ▼▼▼▼ **Best Western Edgewater Resort** 🅷

(208) 263-3194. **$139-$259.** 56 Bridge St 83864. Just e of US 95 N; downtown. Int corridors. **Pets:** Other species. $10 daily fee/pet. Service with restrictions, supervision. (SAVE) ⊠ 🖥 💻 🍴 ➔ ⊠

▼▼▼▼ **La Quinta Inn Sandpoint** 🅷 ❖

(208) 263-9581. **$79-$229.** 415 Cedar St 83864. Jct US 2 and 95; downtown. Ext/int corridors. **Pets:** Medium, other species. Service with restrictions, supervision. (ASK) ⊠ (&M) 🖥 💻 🍴 ➔

▼▼▼ **Quality Inn Sandpoint** 🅷

(208) 263-2111. **$89-$149.** 807 N 5th Ave 83864. US 2 and 95, just s of jct SR 200. Int corridors. **Pets:** Other species. $10 daily fee/pet. Service with restrictions, supervision. (ASK) ⊠ 🖥 💻 🍴 ➔

TWIN FALLS

🅰🅰 ▼▼▼▼ **Best Western Twin Falls Hotel** 🅷

(208) 736-8000. **$89-$129.** 1377 Blue Lakes Blvd N 83301. I-84, exit 173, 3.9 mi s on US 93. Int corridors. **Pets:** Medium. $20 one-time fee/room. Designated rooms, service with restrictions, supervision.

(SAVE) ⊠ (&M) 🖥 💻 ➔ ⊠

▼▼ **Comfort Inn** 🅷 ❖

(208) 734-7494. **$79-$140.** 1910 Fillmore St 83301. I-84, exit 173, 3.5 mi s on US 93. Int corridors. **Pets:** Other species. $20 daily fee/pet. Designated rooms, service with restrictions, supervision.

(ASK) ⊠ 🖥 💻 ➔

▼▼ **Days Inn** 🅷

(208) 324-6400. **$74-$94.** 1200 Centennial Spur 83338. I-84, exit 173, just n on US 93. Int corridors. **Pets:** Other species. $15 daily fee/pet. Service with restrictions. (ASK) ⊠ 🖥 💻

🅰🅰 ▼▼▼▼ **Red Lion Hotel Canyon Springs** 🅷

(208) 734-5000. **$90-$169.** 1357 Blue Lakes Blvd N 83301. I-84, exit 173, 4 mi s on US 93. Int corridors. **Pets:** Other species. $20 one-time fee/room. Service with restrictions, supervision.

(SAVE) ⊠ (&M) 🖥 💻 🍴 ➔

🅰🅰 ▼▼▼▼ **Shilo Inn Suites Hotel-Twin Falls** 🅷 ❖

(208) 733-7545. **$90-$195.** 1586 Blue Lakes Blvd N 83301. I-84, exit 173, 3.7 mi s on US 93. Int corridors. **Pets:** Dogs only. $25 one-time fee/room. Designated rooms, service with restrictions, supervision.

(SAVE) ⊠ (&M) 🖥 💻 ➔ ⊠

▼▼ **Twin Falls Super 8** Ⓜ

(208) 734-5801. **Call for rates.** 1260 Blue Lakes Blvd N 83301. I-84, exit 173, 4.1 mi s on US 93. Int corridors. **Pets:** Accepted.

⊠ 🖥 💻

🅰🅰 ▼▼▼▼ **Wingate by Wyndham** 🅷

(208) 644-1200. **$110-$120.** 379 Crossroads Point Blvd 83338. I-84, exit 173, 0.5 mi n. Int corridors. **Pets:** Accepted.

(SAVE) ⊠ (&M) 🖥 💻

WALLACE

🅰🅰 ▼▼▼ **Stardust Motel** Ⓜ

(208) 752-1213. **$46-$130.** 410 Pine St 83873. I-90, exit 61 (Business Rt 90), 0.7 mi e; downtown. Ext corridors. **Pets:** Other species. $20 daily fee/room. Service with restrictions, supervision. (SAVE) ⊠ 🖥 💻

🅰🅰 ▼▼▼ **The Wallace Inn** 🅷

(208) 752-1252. **$72-$124, 3 day notice.** 100 Front St 83873. I-90, exit 61 (Business Rt 90), just se. Int corridors. **Pets:** Other species. $20 one-time fee/pet. Service with restrictions, supervision.

(SAVE) ⊠ (&M) 🖥 💻 🍴 ➔ ⊠

WHITE BIRD

▼▼ **Hells Canyon Jet Boat Trips & Lodging** Ⓜ ❖

(208) 839-2255. **$70-$80, 7 day notice.** 3252 Waterfront Dr 83554. 1 mi s of White Bird on US 95. Ext corridors. **Pets:** $15 daily fee/pet. Service with restrictions. ⊠ 🖥 💻 ⊠ (☎)

WORLEY

▼▼▼ **Coeur d'Alene Casino Resort Hotel** 🅷

(208) 686-0248. **Call for rates.** 27068 S Hwy 95 83876. On US 95, 3 mi n. Int corridors. **Pets:** Accepted. ⊠ 🖥 💻 🍴 ➔ ⊠

ILLINOIS

ALTON

▼▼ Comfort Inn H
(618) 465-9999. **Call for rates.** 11 Crossroads Ct 62002. Off SR 3, jct SR 140. Int corridors. **Pets:** Accepted. ⊠ 🅜 🛏 💻 🏊

▼ Super 8 H
(618) 465-8885. **$70-$75.** 1800 Homer Adams Pkwy 62002. On SR 111, 1.8 mi e of jct US 67. Int corridors. **Pets:** Accepted.

ASK ⊠ 🅜 🛏 💻

ANNAWAN

◈◈◈ ▼▼▼ Best Western Annawan Inn H
(309) 935-6565. **$80-$110, 7 day notice.** 315 N Canal St 61234. I-80, exit 33, just s. Int corridors. **Pets:** Small. $75 deposit/pet, $25 daily fee/pet. Designated rooms, service with restrictions, supervision.

SAVE ⊠ 🅜 🛏 💻

ARCOLA

▼▼ Comfort Inn H
(217) 268-4000. **Call for rates.** 610 E Springfield Rd 61910. I-57, exit 203 (SR 133), just w. Int corridors. **Pets:** Medium. $7 one-time fee/pet. Service with restrictions, crate. ⊠ 🛏 💻 🏊

BELLEVILLE

◈◈◈ ▼▼ The Shrine Hotel H
(618) 397-1162. **$70-$85.** 451 S Demazenod Dr 62223. I-255, exit 17A, 1 mi e on SR 15; in Shrine of Our Lady of the Snows Complex. Int corridors. **Pets:** Medium. Designated rooms, service with restrictions, crate.

SAVE ⊠ 🛏 💻 🍴 ⊗

BLOOMINGTON

▼▼▼ Doubletree Hotel Bloomington H
(309) 664-6446. **$89-$189.** 10 Brickyard Dr 61701. I-55 business route (Veterans Pkwy), just n of US 150. Int corridors. **Pets:** Accepted.

⊠ 🛏 💻 🍴 🏊 ⊗

▼▼ Eastland Suites Hotel & Conference Center H
(309) 662-0000. **$99-$169.** 1801 Eastland Dr 61704. Jct I-55 business route (Veterans Pkwy) and SR 9, just s to Eastland Dr, then just e. Ext/int corridors. **Pets:** Accepted. ASK ⊠ 🛏 💻 🏊

▼▼ La Quinta Inn H 🐾
(309) 828-6000. **Call for rates.** 505 Brock Dr 61701. I-55/74, exit 160 (SR 9), just e. Int corridors. **Pets:** Medium, other species. Service with restrictions, supervision. ⊠ 🛏 💻

▼▼ Ramada Limited Inn & Suites Bloomington/Normal-West H
(309) 828-0900. **$69-$129.** 919 Maple Hill Rd 61705. I-55/74, exit 160 (SR 9), 0.3 mi w to Wylie Dr, just n, then just e. Int corridors. **Pets:** Accepted. ASK ⊠ 🛏 💻 🏊

CARBONDALE

▼▼▼ Hampton Inn H
(618) 549-6900. **$99-$159.** 2175 Reed Station Pkwy 62901. I-57, exit 54B, 11.7 mi w on SR 13. Int corridors. **Pets:** Small. Service with restrictions, supervision. ⊠ 🅜 🛏 💻 🏊

▼▼▼ Holiday Inn Hotel and Conference Center H
(618) 549-2600. **$109-$129.** 2300 Reed Station Pkwy 62901. I-57, exit 54B, 12 mi w on SR 13. Int corridors. **Pets:** Accepted.

ASK ⊠ 🅜 🛏 💻 🍴 🏊

▼ Super 8 H
(618) 457-8822. **Call for rates.** 1180 E Main St 62901. I-57, exit 54B, 13.9 mi w on SR 13. Int corridors. **Pets:** Service with restrictions, supervision. ⊠ 🛏 💻

CARLINVILLE

◈◈◈ ▼▼ Best Western Carlinville Inn H
(217) 324-2100. **$75-$95.** 19067 W Frontage Rd 62626. I-55, exit 60 (SR 108), just w. Int corridors. **Pets:** Medium. $15 daily fee/room. Designated rooms, service with restrictions, supervision.

SAVE ⊠ 🛏 💻 🍴 🏊

CHAMPAIGN

◈◈◈ ▼▼▼ Baymont Inn & Suites H
(217) 356-8900. **$79-$199.** 302 W Anthony Dr 61822. I-74, exit 182 (Neil St), just nw. Int corridors. **Pets:** Medium, other species. $10 daily fee/pet. Designated rooms, service with restrictions, crate. SAVE ⊠ 🛏 💻

▼▼▼ Drury Inn & Suites-Champaign H
(217) 398-0030. **$90-$209.** 905 W Anthony Dr 61821. I-74, exit 181 (Prospect Ave), just n. Int corridors. **Pets:** Other species. No service, supervision. ASK ⊠ 🅜 🛏 💻 🏊 ⊗

▼▼ Extended StayAmerica-Champaign-Urbana H
(217) 351-8899. **$52-$62.** 610 W Marketview Dr 61822. I-74, exit 181 (Prospect Ave), just n, then just e. Int corridors. **Pets:** Other species. $25 daily fee/room. Designated rooms, service with restrictions, crate.

ASK ⊠ 🛏 💻

◇◇◇ Hawthorn Suites Champaign ⊞

(217) 398-3400. **Call for rates.** 101 Trade Centre Dr 61820. I-74, exit 182 (Neil St), 2.5 mi s. Int corridors. **Pets:** Large. $25 one-time fee/room. Designated rooms, service with restrictions, crate.

[SAVE] [X] [&M] [🛏] [📺] [⊃]

◇◇ La Quinta Inn Champaign ⊞ ❀

(217) 356-4000. **$49-$89.** 1900 Center Dr 61820. I-74, exit 182B (Neil St), just n. Int corridors. **Pets:** Medium, other species. Service with restrictions, supervision. [ASK] [X] [&M] [🛏] [📺] [⊃]

CHESTER

◇◇◇ Best Western Reids' Inn ⊞

(618) 826-3034. **$80-$129.** 2150 State St 62233. SR 150, 1 mi e of SR 3. Int corridors. **Pets:** Small, other species. $25 deposit/pet, $5 daily fee/pet. Designated rooms, supervision. [SAVE] [X] [&M] [🛏] [📺] [⊃]

CHICAGO METROPOLITAN AREA

ALGONQUIN

◇◇◇ Holiday Inn Express Hotel & Suites ⊞

(847) 458-6000. **$69-$169.** 2595 Bunker Hill Rd 60102. I-90, exit Randall Rd N, 6.1 mi n to Bunker Hill Rd, then just w. Int corridors.
Pets: Accepted. [ASK] [X] [&M] [🛏] [📺] [⊃] [X]

ALSIP

◇◇ Baymont Inn-Midway South ⊞

(708) 597-3900. **$70-$75.** 12801 S Cicero Ave 60803. I-294, exit SR 50 (Cicero Ave S). Int corridors. **Pets:** Other species. $50 deposit/room, $10 one-time fee/room. Service with restrictions, crate. [ASK] [X] [🛏] [📺]

ANTIOCH

◇◇ Comfort Inn & Suites by Choice Hotels ⊞

(847) 395-3606. **$80-$200.** 350 Rt 173 60002. SR 173, 0.5 mi w of jct SR 83. Int corridors. **Pets:** Medium. $15 daily fee/pet. Designated rooms, service with restrictions, supervision. [SAVE] [X] [🛏] [📺] [⊃]

ARLINGTON HEIGHTS

◇◇ Jameson Suites ⊞

(847) 956-1400. **$80-$85.** 2111 S Arlington Heights Rd 60005. I-90, exit Arlington Heights Rd, 0.6 mi n. Int corridors. **Pets:** Medium, other species. $15 daily fee/room. Service with restrictions.

[ASK] [X] [🛏] [📺] [X]

◇◇ La Quinta Inn Chicago (Arlington Heights) ⊞ ❀

(847) 253-8777. **$55-$89.** 1415 W Dundee Rd 60004. SR 53, exit Dundee Rd, just e. Int corridors. **Pets:** Medium, other species. Service with restrictions, supervision. [ASK] [X] [🛏] [📺] [⊃]

◇ Motel 6-1048 ⊞

(847) 806-1230. **$45-$59.** 441 W Algonquin Rd 60005. I-90, exit Arlington Heights Rd, 0.5 mi n, then 0.5 mi w. Int corridors. **Pets:** Other species. Service with restrictions, supervision. [X] [&M] [🛏]

◇◇ Red Roof Inn #7102 Ⓜ

(847) 228-6650. **$42-$80.** 22 W Algonquin Rd 60005. I-90, exit Arlington Heights Rd, 0.5 mi n, then just w. Ext corridors. **Pets:** Large. Service with restrictions, crate. [SAVE] [X]

AURORA

◇◇◇ Staybridge Suites Aurora/Naperville ⊞ ❀

(630) 978-2222. **Call for rates.** 4320 Meridian Pkwy. I-88, exit SR 59, 2 mi s to Meridian Pkwy, then just w. Int corridors. **Pets:** Other species. $75 one-time fee/room. Service with restrictions, crate.

[X] [&M] [🛏] [📺] [⊃] [X]

BANNOCKBURN

◇◇◇ La Quinta Inn & Suites Deerfield ⊞ ❀

(847) 317-7300. **$65-$99.** 2000 S Lakeside Dr 60015. I-94, exit Half Day Rd (SR 22), just e to Lakeside Dr, then just s. Int corridors.
Pets: Medium, other species. Service with restrictions, supervision.

[ASK] [X] [&M] [🛏] [📺] [⊃] [X]

BEDFORD PARK

◇◇ Extended StayAmerica Chicago-Midway ⊞

(708) 496-8211. **$65-$110.** 7524 State Rd 60638. Jct SR 50, just w. Int corridors. **Pets:** Other species. $25 daily fee/room. Designated rooms, service with restrictions, crate. [ASK] [X] [&M] [🛏] [📺]

◇◇◇ Residence Inn Midway Airport ⊞

(708) 458-7790. **$189-$219.** 6638 S Cicero Ave 60638. I-55, exit 286 (Cicero Ave). Int corridors. **Pets:** Accepted. [X] [&M] [🛏] [📺] [⊃]

BLOOMINGDALE

◇◇◇ Hilton Chicago Indian Lakes Resort ⊞

(630) 529-0200. **$99-$249.** 250 W Schick Rd 60108. I-355, exit Lake St (US 20), 2.5 mi w, just s on Bloomingdale Rd, then 0.6 mi w. Int corridors. **Pets:** Medium. $75 one-time fee/room. Service with restrictions, supervision. [X] [📺] [🍴] [⊃] [X]

◇◇◇ Residence Inn by Marriott ⊞

(630) 893-9200. **$140-$155.** 295 Knollwood Dr 60108. I-355, exit Army Trail Rd, 4 mi w, then just n. Int corridors. **Pets:** Medium, other species. $100 one-time fee/room. Service with restrictions, crate.

[X] [&M] [🛏] [📺] [⊃] [X]

BOLINGBROOK

◇◇◇ AmericInn Lodge & Suites of Bolingbrook ⊞ ❀

(630) 378-5300. **$89-$119.** 175 W Remington Blvd 60440. I-55, exit 267, just n on SR 53. Int corridors. **Pets:** Medium, dogs only. $25 one-time fee/room. Service with restrictions, supervision.

[SAVE] [X] [&M] [🛏] [📺] [⊃]

◇◇ La Quinta Inn & Suites Chicago-Bolingbrook ⊞ ❀

(630) 226-0000. **$69-$125.** 225 W South Frontage Rd 60440. I-55, exit 267, 0.5 mi sw. Int corridors. **Pets:** Medium, other species. Service with restrictions, supervision. [ASK] [X] [🛏] [📺] [⊃]

BRIDGEVIEW

◇◇ Days Inn Bridgeview ⊞

(708) 430-1818. **Call for rates.** 9625 S 76th Ave 60455. I-294, exit 95th St, just s. Int corridors. **Pets:** Accepted. [X] [🛏] [📺]

BUFFALO GROVE

◇◇ Extended StayAmerica-Chicago-Buffalo Grove-Deerfield ⊞

(847) 215-0641. **$50-$95.** 1525 Busch Pkwy 60089. I-94, exit W Lake Cook Rd, 2 mi w to Milwaukee Ave (US 45/SR 21), then 1.3 mi n. Int corridors. **Pets:** Other species. $25 daily fee/room. Designated rooms, service with restrictions, crate. [ASK] [X] [🛏] [📺]

BURR RIDGE

◇◇ Extended StayAmerica Chicago-Burr Ridge ⊞

(630) 323-6630. **$50-$80.** 15 W 122nd S Frontage Rd 60527. I-55, exit 276A (County Line Rd), just sw. Int corridors. **Pets:** Other species. $25 daily fee/room. Designated rooms, service with restrictions, crate.

[ASK] [X] [🛏] [📺]

CHICAGO

◇◇◇ Affinia Chicago Hotel ⊞

(312) 787-6000. **$129-$499.** 166 E Superior St 60611. Just e of Michigan Ave. Int corridors. **Pets:** Accepted. [SAVE] [X] [🛏] [📺] [🍴] [X]

Allegro Chicago, a Kimpton Hotel 🅷
(312) 236-0123. **Call for rates.** 171 W Randolph St 60601. Jct La Salle St; in theater district. Int corridors. **Pets:** Accepted.

Amalfi Hotel Chicago 🅷 ☼
(312) 395-9000. **$139-$649.** 20 W Kinzie St 60654. Between State and Dearborn sts. Int corridors. **Pets:** Large, other species. Designated rooms.

Avenue Crowne Plaza Chicago Downtown 🅷
(312) 787-2900. **Call for rates.** 160 E Huron St 60611. Just e of N Michigan Ave. Int corridors. **Pets:** Accepted.

Carlton Inn Midway Ⓜ ☼
(773) 582-0900. **$99-$159.** 4944 S Archer Ave 60632. I-55, exit 287 (Pulaski), 1.8 mi s to Archer Ave, then just e. Ext corridors. **Pets:** Medium, other species. $50 deposit/pet, $5 daily fee/pet. Designated rooms, service with restrictions, crate.

Conrad Chicago 🅷
(312) 645-1500. **Call for rates.** 521 N Rush St 60611. Jct Grand Ave. Int corridors. **Pets:** Accepted.

Crowne Plaza Chicago Metro 🅷 ☼
(312) 829-5000. **$89-$299.** 733 W Madison St 60661. I-90/94, exit 51D (Madison St); jct Halsted St. Int corridors. **Pets:** Small, other species. $50 one-time fee/room. Service with restrictions, supervision.

Dana Hotel & Spa 🅷
(312) 202-6000. **Call for rates.** 660 N State St 60611. Between Huron and Erie sts. Int corridors. **Pets:** Accepted.

The Drake Hotel, Chicago 🅷
(312) 787-2200. **$149-$429.** 140 E Walton Pl 60611-1501. Jct N Michigan Ave and Lake Shore Dr. Int corridors. **Pets:** Accepted.

Fairmont Chicago, Millennium Park 🅷
(312) 565-8000. **$139-$494.** 200 N Columbus Dr 60601. Jct Michigan Ave and Wacker Dr, just e. Int corridors. **Pets:** Accepted.

Four Seasons Hotel Chicago 🅷 ☼
(312) 280-8800. **$385-$505.** 120 E Delaware Pl 60611. Jct Michigan Ave; just nw of John Hancock building. Int corridors. **Pets:** Very small. Designated rooms, service with restrictions, supervision.

Hard Rock Hotel Chicago-A Preferred Hotel 🅷 ☼
(312) 345-1000. **$139-$559.** 230 N Michigan Ave 60601. Between Lake St and Wacker Dr. Int corridors. **Pets:** Medium. $25 daily fee/pet. Service with restrictions.

Hilton Chicago 🅷 ☼
(312) 922-4400. **$179-$534.** 720 S Michigan Ave 60605. I-290 (Congress Pkwy), exit Michigan Ave, just s. Int corridors. **Pets:** Medium, other species. $75 one-time fee/pet. Designated rooms, service with restrictions, supervision.

Hilton Chicago O'Hare Airport 🅷
(773) 686-8000. **$189-$438.** O'Hare Int'l Airport 60666. Opposite and connected to terminal buildings at Chicago O'Hare International Airport, accessed via I-190. Int corridors. **Pets:** Accepted.

Hilton Suites Chicago/Magnificent Mile 🅷
(312) 664-1100. **$149-$369.** 198 E Delaware Pl 60611. Just e of Michigan Ave. Int corridors. **Pets:** Accepted.

Holiday Inn Chicago O'Hare 🅷
(773) 693-5800. **$69-$179.** 5615 N Cumberland Ave 60631. I-90, exit 79B (N Cumberland Ave S), just s. Int corridors. **Pets:** Accepted.

Hotel Burnham Chicago 🅷 ☼
(312) 782-1111. **Call for rates.** One W Washington St 60602. Jct State St. Int corridors. **Pets:** Other species.

Hotel Indigo Chicago Downtown Gold Coast 🅷
(312) 787-4980. **$119-$329.** 1244 N Dearborn St 60610. Just n of Division St. Int corridors. **Pets:** Accepted.

Hotel Monaco Chicago 🅷
(312) 960-8500. **$119-$599.** 225 N Wabash Ave 60601. Jct Wacker Dr. Int corridors. **Pets:** Accepted.

Hotel Sax Chicago 🅷
(312) 245-0333. **$169-$569.** 333 N Dearborn St 60654. Between Dearborn and State sts. Int corridors. **Pets:** Accepted.

InterContinental Chicago 🅷
(312) 944-4100. **Call for rates.** 505 N Michigan Ave 60611. Just n of Chicago River; between E Grand Ave and E Illinois St. Int corridors. **Pets:** $50 deposit/room, $50 one-time fee/room. Service with restrictions, supervision.

The James 🅷
(312) 337-1000. **$169-$599.** 55 E Ontario St 60611. Just w of N Michigan Ave. Int corridors. **Pets:** Accepted.

Omni Chicago Hotel 🅷
(312) 944-6664. **$309-$579.** 676 N Michigan Ave 60611. Jct Huron St. Int corridors. **Pets:** Accepted.

Palmer House–A Hilton Hotel 🅷 ☼
(312) 726-7500. **$174-$534.** 17 E Monroe St 60603. Between State St and Wabash Ave. Int corridors. **Pets:** Large, other species. $75 one-time fee/pet. Service with restrictions, supervision.

Park Hyatt Chicago 🅷
(312) 335-1234. **$337-$517, 3 day notice.** 800 N Michigan Ave 60611. Jct Chicago Ave at Water Tower Square. Int corridors. **Pets:** Accepted.

The Peninsula Chicago 🅷
(312) 337-2888. **$385-$675.** 108 E Superior St 60611. Jct Michigan Ave. Int corridors. **Pets:** Accepted.

Renaissance Chicago Hotel 🅷 ☼
(312) 372-7200. **$169-$289.** 1 W Wacker Dr 60601. Jct State St. Int corridors. **Pets:** Small. $45 one-time fee/pet. Service with restrictions, supervision.

Residence Inn by Marriott Chicago Downtown/ Magnificent Mile 🅷 ☼
(312) 943-9800. **$169-$249.** 201 E Walton Pl 60611. Just e of Michigan Ave at Mies van der Rohe. Int corridors. **Pets:** Other species. $100 one-time fee/room.

Residence Inn by Marriott River North 🅷 ☼
(312) 494-9301. **$169-$239.** 410 N Dearborn St 60610. Between W Kinzie and W Hubbard sts. Int corridors. **Pets:** Medium, other species. $100 one-time fee/room. Designated rooms, service with restrictions.

The Ritz-Carlton Chicago (A Four Seasons Hotel) H
(312) 266-1000. **$295-$465.** 160 E Pearson St 60611. Jct N Michigan Ave. Int corridors. **Pets:** Accepted.

Sheraton Chicago Hotel & Towers H
(312) 464-1000. **$119-$549.** 301 E North Water St 60611. Columbus Dr at Chicago River; just e of Michigan Ave. Int corridors. **Pets:** Accepted.

Sofitel Chicago Water Tower H 🐾
(312) 324-4000. **Call for rates.** 20 E Chestnut St 60611. Jct Wabash Ave and Chestnut St, 1/2 blk w of Rush St. Int corridors. **Pets:** Medium, dogs only. $200 deposit/room. Service with restrictions, supervision.

The Sutton Place Hotel H
(312) 266-2100. **$170-$590.** 21 E Bellevue Pl 60611. Jct Rush St. Int corridors. **Pets:** Accepted.

Swissotel Chicago H
(312) 565-0565. **$159-$399.** 323 E Wacker Dr 60601. Just e of Michigan Ave. Int corridors. **Pets:** Accepted.

Trump International Hotel & Tower H
(312) 588-8000. **$575-$2000.** 401 N Wabash Ave 60611. Between Hubbard and Kinzie sts; just s of Kinzie St. Int corridors. **Pets:** Accepted.

W Chicago-City Center H
(312) 332-1200. **$169-$599.** 172 W Adams St 60603-3604. Between La Salle and Wells sts. Int corridors. **Pets:** Accepted.

W Chicago Lakeshore H
(312) 943-9200. **$149-$599.** 644 N Lakeshore Dr 60611. Jct Ontario St. Int corridors. **Pets:** Accepted.

The Westin Chicago River North H 🐾
(312) 744-1900. **$149-$599.** 320 N Dearborn St 60654. Just n of Chicago River; between Dearborn and Clark sts. Int corridors. **Pets:** Medium, dogs only. Service with restrictions, supervision.

The Westin Michigan Avenue Chicago H
(312) 943-7200. **$169-$579, 3 day notice.** 909 N Michigan Ave 60611. Across from John Hancock Center. Int corridors. **Pets:** Accepted.

CRESTWOOD

Hampton Inn-Chicago/Crestwood H
(708) 597-3330. **$99-$179.** 13330 S Cicero Ave 60445. On SR 50 and 83, 0.8 mi s of jct I-294. Int corridors. **Pets:** Medium. Service with restrictions, supervision.

CRYSTAL LAKE

Comfort Inn by Choice Hotels H
(815) 444-0040. **$79-$109.** 595 Tracy Tr 60014. Jct US 14 and SR 31, 0.4 mi w, then just s on Pingree Rd. Int corridors. **Pets:** Accepted.

Holiday Inn Chicago-Crystal Lake H
(815) 477-7000. **$89-$159.** 800 S SR 31 60014. At Three Oaks Rd, 0.3 mi s of jct US 14. Int corridors. **Pets:** Small, dogs only. $20 daily fee/pet. Designated rooms, service with restrictions, crate.

Super 8 H
(815) 788-8888. **Call for rates.** 577 Crystal Point Dr 60014. On US 14, 1 mi w of jct SR 31. Int corridors. **Pets:** Accepted.

DARIEN

Extended StayAmerica Chicago-Darien H
(630) 985-4708. **$50-$80.** 2345 Sokol Ct 60561. I-55, exit 271A, 0.5 mi s to Westgate Rd, then 0.5 mi ne via frontage road. Int corridors. **Pets:** Other species. $25 daily fee/room. Designated rooms, service with restrictions, crate.

DEERFIELD

Chicago Marriott Suites Deerfield H
(847) 405-9666. **$209-$229.** 2 Parkway North 60015. I-94, exit Deerfield Rd northbound, just w; exit Lake Cook Rd southbound, 0.3 mi e to Saunders Rd, then 0.5 mi n. Int corridors. **Pets:** Medium. $75 one-time fee/room. Service with restrictions, crate.

Red Roof Inn #188 M
(847) 205-1755. **$66-$78.** 340 S Waukegan Rd 60015. I-94, exit SR 43 (Waukegan Rd). Ext corridors. **Pets:** Large. Service with restrictions, crate.

Residence Inn by Marriott Chicago/Deerfield H
(847) 940-4644. **$159-$169.** 530 Lake Cook Rd 60015. I-94, exit Lake Cook Rd, 1.8 mi e, then 3 blks n on Corporate 500 Dr access road. Ext corridors. **Pets:** Accepted.

DES PLAINES

Comfort Inn O'Hare H
(847) 635-1300. **$70-$359.** 2175 E Touhy Ave 60018. I-294, exit Touhy Ave westbound, just w; exit Golf Rd (SR 58) eastbound, 0.3 mi w to River Rd, then 5.5 mi s. Int corridors. **Pets:** Small. $20 daily fee/pet. Designated rooms, service with restrictions, supervision.

Extended StayAmerica-Chicago-O'Hare H
(847) 294-9693. **$50-$85.** 1201 E Touhy Ave 60018. At SR 72 (Higgins Rd), 0.6 mi, w of US 12/45 (Mannheim Rd). Int corridors. **Pets:** Other species. $25 daily fee/room. Designated rooms, service with restrictions, crate.

Extended Stay Deluxe Chicago-O'Hare H
(847) 768-0395. **$55-$90.** 1207 E Touhy Ave 60018. At SR 72 (Higgins Rd), 0.6 mi w of US 12/45 (Mannheim Rd). Int corridors. **Pets:** Other species. $25 daily fee/room. Designated rooms, service with restrictions, crate.

Hilton Garden Inn Chicago-O'Hare Airport H
(847) 296-8900. **$89-$229.** 2930 S River Rd 60018. I-294, exit Touhy Ave westbound, just s on River Rd, then 0.3 mi s; exit Golf Rd (SR 58) eastbound, 0.3 mi w to River Rd, then 6 mi s. Int corridors. **Pets:** Medium. $50 one-time fee/room. Designated rooms, service with restrictions, supervision.

DOWNERS GROVE

Red Roof Inn M
(630) 963-4205. **$59-$94.** 1113 Butterfield Rd 60515. I-355, exit Butterfield Rd (SR 56), on frontage road; I-88, exit Highland Ave N, just w. Ext corridors. **Pets:** Large. Service with restrictions, crate.

ELGIN

Quality Inn-Elgin H
(847) 608-7300. **$80-$120.** 500 Tollgate Rd 60123. I-90, exit SR 31 N, just n. Int corridors. **Pets:** Accepted.

ELK GROVE VILLAGE

Baymont Inn & Suites H
(847) 803-9400. **Call for rates.** 2881 Touhy Ave 60007. Jct SR 72 (Higgins Rd) and 83 (Busse Rd), 1.5 mi e on SR 72 (Higgins Rd). Int corridors. **Pets:** Accepted.

Days Inn Schaumburg/Elk Grove H
(847) 895-2085. **$49-$79.** 1000 W Devon Ave 60007. I-290, exit Thorndale Ave, 0.5 mi w to Rohlwing Rd, 0.3 mi n to Devon Ave, then 0.3 mi e. Int corridors. **Pets:** Accepted.

La Quinta Inn Chicago/O'Hare H ❀
(847) 439-6767. **$55-$119.** 1900 E Oakton St 60007. Jct SR 72 (Higgins Rd) and 83 (Busse Rd). Int corridors. **Pets:** Medium, other species. Service with restrictions, supervision.

Quality Inn & Suites O'Hare/Elk Grove H ❀
(847) 593-8600. **$70-$190.** 100 Busse Rd 60007. Just n of jct SR 72 (Higgins Rd). Int corridors. **Pets:** Medium. $30 one-time fee/pet. Designated rooms, service with restrictions, supervision.

Sheraton Suites Chicago Elk Grove H
(847) 290-1600. **$69-$179.** 121 Northwest Point Blvd 60007. I-90, exit Arlington Heights Rd, just s; in Northwest Point Corporate Park. Int corridors. **Pets:** Accepted.

Super 8 O'Hare H
(847) 827-3133. **$59-$89.** 2951 Touhy Ave 60007. Jct SR 72 (Higgins Rd) and 83 (Busse Rd), 1.5 mi e on SR 72 (Higgins Rd). Int corridors. **Pets:** Accepted.

ELMHURST

Extended StayAmerica Chicago-Elmhurst-O'Hare H
(630) 530-4353. **$50-$85.** 550 W Grand Ave 60126. Jct US 20 (Lake St), 0.4 mi ne; adjacent to I-290 overpass. Int corridors. **Pets:** Other species. $25 daily fee/room. Designated rooms, service with restrictions, crate.

EVANSTON

Hotel Orrington H ❀
(847) 866-8700. **$119-$339.** 1710 Orrington Ave 60201. Jct Church St. Int corridors. **Pets:** Medium, other species. $50 one-time fee/room. Designated rooms, service with restrictions, supervision.

GLEN ELLYN

Crowne Plaza Glen Ellyn-Lombard H
(630) 629-6000. **$100-$200.** 1250 Roosevelt Rd 60137. I-355, exit Roosevelt Rd, 0.8 mi e on SR 38. Int corridors. **Pets:** Accepted.

GLENVIEW

Staybridge Suites H
(847) 657-0002. **$89-$169.** 2600 Lehigh Ave 60026. I-294, exit Willow Rd, 2.4 mi e. Int corridors. **Pets:** Accepted.

Wyndham Glenview Suites H
(847) 803-9800. **$98-$233.** 1400 N Milwaukee Ave 60025. I-294, exit Willow Rd, 0.3 mi w to Sanders Rd, 1.3 mi s to Milwaukee Ave (SR 21), then 1 mi s. Int corridors. **Pets:** Accepted.

GURNEE

Best Western Gurnee Hotel & Suites H
(847) 782-0890. **Call for rates.** 5430 Grand Ave 60031. I-94, exit Grand Ave (SR 132 E), 0.5 mi e. Int corridors. **Pets:** Small, dogs only. $50 one-time fee/room. Service with restrictions, supervision.

Comfort Inn by Choice Hotels H
(847) 855-8866. **Call for rates.** 6080 Gurnee Mills Cir E 60031. I-94, exit Grand Ave (SR 132 W), just nw. Int corridors. **Pets:** Medium. $50 one-time fee/room. Service with restrictions, supervision.

Country Inn & Suites By Carlson H
(847) 625-9700. **Call for rates.** 5420 Grand Ave 60031. I-94, exit Grand Ave (SR 132 E), 0.5 mi e. Int corridors. **Pets:** Accepted.

La Quinta Inn & Suites Chicago–Gurnee H ❀
(847) 662-7600. **$62-$129.** 5688 Northridge Dr 60031. I-94, exit Grand Ave (SR 132 E), just e via service road. Int corridors. **Pets:** Medium, other species. Service with restrictions, supervision.

HANOVER PARK

Extended StayAmerica-Chicago-Hanover Park H
(630) 893-4823. **$50-$80.** 1075 Lake St 60133. On US 20; between Gary Ave and Elgin-O'Hare Expwy. Int corridors. **Pets:** Other species. $25 daily fee/room. Designated rooms, service with restrictions, crate.

HILLSIDE

Best Western Chicago Hillside H
(708) 544-9300. **$99-$149.** 4400 Frontage Rd 60162. I-290, exit 14B eastbound, follow to US 12/45 (Mannheim Rd), just nw via frontage road; exit 17 westbound to US 12/45 (Mannheim Rd), just nw via frontage road. Int corridors. **Pets:** Medium. $50 one-time fee/room. Designated rooms, service with restrictions, supervision.

HOFFMAN ESTATES

La Quinta Inn Chicago (Hoffman Estates) H ❀
(847) 882-3312. **$49-$89.** 2280 Barrington Rd 60169. I-90, exit Barrington Rd westbound, 0.3 mi s; exit SR 59 eastbound, 0.5 mi n to SR 72 (Higgins Rd), 2 mi e to Barrington Rd, then just n. Int corridors. **Pets:** Medium, other species. Service with restrictions, supervision.

Red Roof Inn #10199 M
(847) 885-7877. **$50-$90.** 2500 Hassell Rd 60169. I-90, exit Barrington Rd westbound, 0.3 mi s; exit SR 59 eastbound, 0.5 mi n to SR 72 (Higgins Rd), 2 mi e to Barrington Rd, then just n. Ext corridors. **Pets:** Large. Service with restrictions, crate.

ITASCA

Extended StayAmerica-Chicago-Itasca H
(630) 250-1111. **$45-$75.** 1181 Rohlwing Rd 60143. I-290, exit Thorndale Ave, 0.5 mi w. Int corridors. **Pets:** Other species. $25 daily fee/room. Designated rooms, service with restrictions, crate.

The Westin Chicago Northwest H
(630) 773-4000. **$99-$349.** 400 Park Blvd 60143. I-290, exit Thorndale Ave, just e. Int corridors. **Pets:** Accepted.

JOLIET

Comfort Inn by Choice Hotels North H
(815) 436-5141. **$70-$75.** 3235 Norman Ave 60435. I-55, exit 257, just e. Int corridors. **Pets:** Accepted.

Comfort Inn by Choice Hotels-South H
(815) 744-1770. **$69-$139.** 135 S Larkin Ave 60436. I-80, exit 130B, 0.5 mi n. Int corridors. **Pets:** Accepted.

Fairfield Inn by Marriott-South H
(815) 741-3499. **$89-$109.** 1501 Riverboat Center Dr 60431. I-80, exit 127, just n. Int corridors. **Pets:** Other species. $25 one-time fee/room. Designated rooms, service with restrictions.

Red Roof Inn #7071 M
(815) 741-2304. **Call for rates.** 1750 McDonough St 60436. I-80, exit 130B, just off Larkin Ave. Ext corridors. **Pets:** Large. Service with restrictions, crate.

(AAA) ▼▼▼▼ **TownePlace Suites by Marriott Joliet** [H]
(815) 741-2400. **$109-$119.** 1515 Riverboat Center Dr 60431. I-80, exit 127, just n. Int corridors. **Pets:** Other species. $100 one-time fee/room. Service with restrictions. [SAVE] [X] [&M] [🛏] [💻] [≈]

LANSING

▼▼ **Extended StayAmerica-Chicago-Lansing** [H]
(708) 895-6402. **$50-$85.** 2520 173rd St 60438. I-80/94, exit 161 (Torrence Ave), just n. Int corridors. **Pets:** Other species. $25 daily fee/room. Designated rooms, service with restrictions, crate.

[ASK] [X] [&M] [🛏] [💻]

LIBERTYVILLE

▼▼ **Candlewood Suites Chicago-Libertyville** [H]
(847) 247-9900. **Call for rates.** 1100 N US 45 60048. I-94, exit SR 137 (Buckley Rd), 5.6 mi w to US 45, then 1.4 mi s. Int corridors.
Pets: Accepted. [X] [&M] [🛏] [💻]

▼▼▼ **Holiday Inn Express Hotel & Suites** [H]
(847) 549-7878. **$89-$139.** 77 Buckley Rd 60048. I-94, exit SR 137 (Buckley Rd), 2.3 mi w. Int corridors. **Pets:** Small, dogs only. $50 one-time fee/room. Service with restrictions, supervision.

[ASK] [X] [🛏] [💻] [≈]

LINCOLNSHIRE

▼▼▼▼ **Homewood Suites by Hilton Chicago-Lincolnshire** [H]
(847) 945-9300. **$89-$169.** 10 Westminster Way 60069. I-94, exit Half Day Rd, just w. Int corridors. **Pets:** Accepted. [X] [🛏] [💻] [≈]

▼▼▼ **Staybridge Suites Lincolnshire** [H]
(847) 821-0002. **Call for rates.** 100 Barclay Blvd 60069. I-94, exit Half Day Rd, 2.2 mi w to Barclay Blvd, then just s; just w of jct US 45 and SR 21; in Lincolnshire Corporate Center. Int corridors. **Pets:** $50 one-time fee/room. Service with restrictions. [X] [&M] [🛏] [💻] [≈]

LISLE

▼▼ **Extended StayAmerica-Chicago-Lisle** [H]
(630) 434-7710. **$50-$80.** 445 Warrenville Rd 60532. I-355, exit Ogden Ave E. Int corridors. **Pets:** Other species. $25 daily fee/room. Designated rooms, service with restrictions, crate. [ASK] [X] [🛏] [💻]

LOMBARD

(AAA) ▼▼▼▼ **Embassy Suites Hotel Chicago-Lombard/Oak Brook** [H] 🐾
(630) 969-7500. **$99-$209.** 707 E Butterfield Rd 60148. I-88, exit Highland Ave, just n to Butterfield Rd (SR 56), then 0.5 mi e. Int corridors. **Pets:** Large, other species. $50 daily fee/room. Service with restrictions, crate. [SAVE] [X] [&M] [🛏] [💻] [🍴] [≈] [X]

▼▼▼ **Extended Stay Deluxe-Chicago-Lombard-Oak Brook** [H]
(630) 424-1000. **$55-$90.** 260 E 22nd St 60148. I-88, exit Highland Ave, 0.8 mi n to 22nd St, then just e. Int corridors. **Pets:** Other species. $25 daily fee/room. Designated rooms, service with restrictions, crate.

[ASK] [X] [&M] [🛏] [💻] [X]

▼▼ **Homestead Studio Suites Hotel-Chicago/Lombard-Oak Brook** [H]
(630) 928-0202. **$50-$80.** 2701 Technology Dr 60148. I-88, exit Highland Ave, just n, 0.6 mi e on Butterfield Rd (SR 56), then just s. Int corridors. **Pets:** Other species. $25 daily fee/room. Designated rooms, service with restrictions, crate. [ASK] [X] [&M] [🛏] [💻]

▼▼▼ **Residence Inn by Marriott Chicago Lombard** [H]
(630) 629-7800. **$119-$129.** 2001 S Highland Ave 60148. I-88, exit Highland Ave, 0.8 mi n. Ext corridors. **Pets:** Medium. $75 one-time fee/room. Service with restrictions, supervision. [X] [🛏] [💻] [≈] [X]

▼▼▼ **TownePlace Suites by Marriott Chicago Lombard** [H]
(630) 932-4400. **$99-$119.** 455 E 22nd St 60148. I-88, exit Highland, 0.8 mi, then 0.3 mi. Int corridors. **Pets:** Accepted. [X] [&M] [🛏] [💻] [≈]

(AAA) ▼▼▼▼ **The Westin Lombard Yorktown Center** [H] 🐾
(630) 719-8000. **$129-$309.** 70 Yorktown Center 60148. Jct Highland Ave and Butterfield Rd (SR 56), just e. Int corridors. **Pets:** Service with restrictions, supervision. [SAVE] [X] [&M] [🛏] [💻] [🍴] [≈] [X]

MATTESON

(AAA) ▼▼▼ **Holiday Inn Chicago-Matteson** [H]
(708) 747-3500. **Call for rates.** 500 Holiday Plaza Dr 60443. I-57, exit 340A, just e. Int corridors. **Pets:** Medium. $15 daily fee/room. Service with restrictions, crate. [SAVE] [X] [🛏] [💻] [🍴] [≈] [X]

▼▼ **La Quinta Inn Chicago-Matteson** [H] 🐾
(708) 503-0999. **$59-$109.** 5210 W Southwick Dr 60443. I-57, exit 340A, 0.3 mi e on US 30, then 0.3 mi s on Cicero Ave (SR 50). Int corridors. **Pets:** Medium, other species. Service with restrictions, supervision. [ASK] [X] [🛏] [💻]

METTAWA

▼▼▼ **Residence Inn by Marriott Chicago Lake Forest-Mettawa** [H]
(847) 615-2701. **$80-$190.** 26325 N Riverwoods Blvd 60045. I-94, exit SR 60 (Town Line Rd). Int corridors. **Pets:** Accepted.
[X] [&M] [🛏] [💻] [≈] [X]

MUNDELEIN

▼▼▼ **Doubletree Libertyville Mundelein** [H]
(847) 949-5100. **$89-$159.** 510 E Illinois Rt 83 60060. Jct US 45. Int corridors. **Pets:** Accepted. [ASK] [X] [🛏] [💻] [🍴] [≈]

NAPERVILLE

▼ **Baymont Inn & Suites** [H]
(630) 357-0022. **Call for rates.** 1585 Naperville/Wheaton Rd 60563. I-88, exit Naperville Rd, 0.5 mi s. Int corridors. **Pets:** Accepted. [X] [🛏] [💻]

(AAA) ▼▼▼ **Best Western Naperville Inn** [H]
(630) 505-0200. **$76-$90.** 1617 Naperville Rd 60563. I-88, exit Naperville Rd, just e on Diehl Rd to Naperville Rd, then just s. Ext/int corridors. **Pets:** Medium. $10 daily fee/pet. Designated rooms, service with restrictions, supervision. [SAVE] [X] [🛏] [💻]

▼▼ **Homestead Studio Suites Hotel-Chicago-Naperville** [H]
(630) 577-0200. **$50-$80.** 1827 Centre Point Cir 60563. I-88, exit Naperville Rd, just s to Diehl Rd, 0.8 mi w, then just n. Int corridors. **Pets:** Other species. $25 daily fee/room. Designated rooms, service with restrictions, crate. [ASK] [X] [&M] [🛏] [💻]

(AAA) ▼▼▼▼ **Hotel Arista** [H]
(630) 579-4100. **$139-$499.** 2139 CityGate Ln 60563. I-88, exit SR 59, just n. Int corridors. **Pets:** Accepted. [SAVE] [X] [&M] [💻] [🍴] [X]

(AAA) ▼▼ **Red Roof Inn #195** [M]
(630) 369-2500. **$55-$90.** 1698 W Diehl Rd 60563. I-88, exit SR 59, just s. Ext corridors. **Pets:** Large. Service with restrictions, crate.
[SAVE] [X] [🛏]

▼▼▼ **TownePlace Suites by Marriott Naperville** [H]
(630) 548-0881. **$120-$130.** 1843 W Diehl Rd 60563. I-88, exit SR 59, just s to Diehl Rd, then just w. Int corridors. **Pets:** Other species. $100 one-time fee/room. Service with restrictions. [X] [🛏] [💻] [≈] [X]

NORTHBROOK

(AAA) ▼▼▼▼ **Hilton Chicago/Northbrook** [H]
(847) 480-7500. **$99-$269.** 2855 N Milwaukee Ave 60062. On SR 21, s of jct US 45 and Willow Rd. Int corridors. **Pets:** Medium. $75 one-time fee/room. Designated rooms, service with restrictions.
[SAVE] [X] [🛏] [💻] [🍴] [≈] [X]

AAA ▼▼▼▼ **Renaissance Chicago North Shore Hotel** H

(847) 498-6500. **$188-$230.** 933 Skokie Blvd 60062. I-94, exit Dundee Rd W northbound; exit SR 43 (Waukegan Rd) southbound, 0.5 mi s to SR 68, then 1.5 mi e. Int corridors. **Pets:** Other species. $75 one-time fee/room. Service with restrictions, supervision.

SAVE ✕ 🖥 💻 🍴 🏊 ✕

AAA ▼▼▼▼ **Sheraton Chicago Northbrook Hotel** H 🐾

(847) 480-1900. **$89-$189.** 1110 Willow Rd 60062. 2 mi w of jct I-94; 3.2 mi e of jct I-294. Int corridors. **Pets:** Medium, dogs only. Service with restrictions, supervision. SAVE ✕ 🖥 🖥 💻 🍴 🏊

OAK BROOK

▼▼▼ **Residence Inn by Marriott Chicago/Oak Brook** H

(630) 571-1200. **$140-$160.** 790 Jorie Blvd 60523. I-88, exit Midwest Rd eastbound, just n to 22nd St (Cermak Rd), 1.7 mi e to Jorie Blvd, then just sw; exit 22nd St (Cermak Rd) westbound, 0.4 mi e to Jorie Blvd. Int corridors. **Pets:** Accepted. ✕ 🖥 🖥 💻 🏊 ✕

OAKBROOK TERRACE

▼▼▼ **La Quinta Inn Chicago (Oak Brook)** H 🐾

(630) 495-4600. **$59-$89.** 1 S 666 Midwest Rd 60181. I-88, exit Midwest Rd eastbound, just n then just n of 22nd St (Cermak Rd); exit 22nd St (Cermak Rd) westbound, 1.1 mi w to Midwest Rd, then just n. Int corridors. **Pets:** Medium, other species. Service with restrictions, supervision.

ASK ✕ 🖥 💻 🏊

▼▼▼ **Staybridge Suites Chicago-Oakbrook Terrace** H

(630) 953-9393. **Call for rates.** 200 Royce Blvd 60181. I-88, exit Midwest Rd eastbound (Cermak Rd), 0.4 mi w to Butterfield Rd (SR 56), just n, then just n on Renaissance Blvd; exit 22nd St (Cermak) westbound, 2.5 mi w on 22nd St to SR 56, just n, then just n on Renaissance Blvd. Int corridors. **Pets:** Medium. $75 one-time fee/room. Service with restrictions. ✕ 🖥 🖥 💻

PALATINE

▼▼▼ **Holiday Inn Express Palatine/Arlington Heights** H 🐾

(847) 934-4900. **Call for rates.** 1550 E Dundee Rd 60074. SR 53, exit Dundee Rd (SR 68), just w. Int corridors. **Pets:** Large. $50 one-time fee/room. Designated rooms, service with restrictions, crate.

✕ 🖥 🖥 💻 🏊 ✕

AAA ▼▼▼ **Hotel Indigo Chicago-Schaumburg North** H 🐾

(847) 359-6900. **$79-$159.** 920 US 14 (Northwest Hwy) 60074. SR 53, exit Northwest Hwy (US 14), just w. Int corridors. **Pets:** Large. $25 daily fee/room. Service with restrictions, supervision.

SAVE ✕ 🖥 🖥 💻 🍴 🏊

PROSPECT HEIGHTS

▼▼ **Super 8-Prospect Heights** H

(847) 459-0545. **Call for rates.** 540 N Milwaukee Ave 60070. Jct SR 21 and US 45. Int corridors. **Pets:** Other species. $25 daily fee/room. Service with restrictions, crate. ✕ 🖥 💻

RICHMOND

▼▼ **Super 8 Richmond/Geneva Lakes** H

(815) 678-4711. **$55-$149.** 11200 N Rt 12 60071. 0.5 mi n of jct SR 173. Int corridors. **Pets:** Accepted. ASK ✕ 🖥 💻 🏊

ROMEOVILLE

▼▼ **Extended Stay America Chicago–Romeoville/Bollingbrook** H

(630) 226-8966. **$55-$85.** 1225 Lakeview Dr 60446. I-55, exit 263, just n. Int corridors. **Pets:** Other species. $25 daily fee/room. Designated rooms, service with restrictions, crate. ASK ✕ 🖥 💻

ROSEMONT

AAA ▼▼▼▼ **aloft Chicago O'Hare** H

(847) 671-4444. **Call for rates.** 9700 Balmoral Ave 60018. I-190, exit 1B, just s. Int corridors. **Pets:** Accepted. SAVE ✕ 🖥 🖥 💻 🏊

AAA ▼▼▼▼ **Crowne Plaza Chicago O'Hare Hotel & Conference Center** H 🐾

(847) 671-6350. **$89-$249.** 5440 N River Rd 60018. I-190, exit 1B (River Rd), just s. Int corridors. **Pets:** Medium. $50 one-time fee/room. Service with restrictions, supervision. SAVE ✕ 🖥 🖥 💻 🍴 🏊

AAA ▼▼▼▼ **Doubletree Hotel Chicago O'Hare Airport-Rosemont** H

(847) 292-9100. **$99-$229.** 5460 N River Rd 60018. I-190, exit 1B (River Rd), just s. Int corridors. **Pets:** Medium. $75 deposit/room, $25 one-time fee/room. Service with restrictions, crate.

SAVE ✕ 🖥 💻 🍴 🏊 ✕

AAA ▼▼▼▼ **Embassy Suites Hotel O'Hare Rosemont** H

(847) 678-4000. **$119-$249.** 5500 N River Rd 60018. I-190, exit 1B (River Rd), just s. Int corridors. **Pets:** Medium. $75 deposit/room, $25 one-time fee/room. Service with restrictions, crate.

SAVE ✕ 🖥 💻 🍴 🏊

▼▼▼▼ **Residence Inn by Marriott Chicago-O'Hare** H

(847) 375-9000. **$179-$219.** 7101 Chestnut St 60018. Jct US 12, 45 and Touhy Ave. Int corridors. **Pets:** Accepted. ✕ 🖥 💻 🏊 ✕

AAA ▼▼▼▼ **Sheraton Gateway Suites O'Hare** H

(847) 699-6300. **Call for rates.** 6501 N Mannheim Rd 60018. On US 12 and 45, at SR 72 (Higgins Rd). Int corridors. **Pets:** Accepted.

SAVE ✕ 🖥 💻 🍴 🏊 ✕

AAA ▼▼▼▼ **The Westin O'Hare** H

(847) 698-6000. **$99-$319.** 6100 N River Rd 60018. I-190, exit 1B (River Rd), just n. Int corridors. **Pets:** Accepted.

SAVE ✕ 🖥 💻 🍴 🏊 ✕

ST. CHARLES

AAA ▼▼▼ **Best Western Inn of St. Charles** H 🐾

(630) 584-4550. **$70-$120.** 1635 E Main St 60174. On SR 64, 0.5 mi e of SR 25. Ext/int corridors. **Pets:** Dogs only. $10 daily fee/pet. Designated rooms, service with restrictions, supervision. SAVE ✕ 🖥 💻 🏊

▼▼▼ **Courtyard by Marriott Chicago-St Charles** H

(630) 377-6370. **$134-$164.** 700 Courtyard Dr 60174. Jct SR 59 and 64, 3.4 mi w on SR 64, just n on Kirk Rd, then just w on Foxfield. Int corridors. **Pets:** Medium, dogs only. $75 one-time fee/pet. Service with restrictions. ✕ 🖥 💻 🍴 🏊 ✕

AAA ▼▼ **Holiday Inn Express** H 🐾

(630) 584-5300. **$85-$125.** 1600 E Main St 60174. On SR 64, 0.5 mi e of SR 25. Int corridors. **Pets:** Medium, dogs only. $50 one-time fee/room. Designated rooms, service with restrictions, supervision.

SAVE ✕ 🖥 💻 🏊

AAA ▼▼ **Super 8-St. Charles** H

(630) 377-8388. **$70-$80.** 1520 E Main St 60174. On SR 64, 1 mi e. Int corridors. **Pets:** Small. $15 daily fee/pet. Service with restrictions, supervision. SAVE ✕ 🖥 💻

SCHAUMBURG

▼▼ **Extended StayAmerica Chicago-Schaumburg-Convention Center** H

(847) 882-7011. **$45-$90.** 2000 N Roselle Rd 60195. I-90, exit Roselle Rd, just sw. Int corridors. **Pets:** Other species. $25 daily fee/room. Designated rooms, service with restrictions, crate. ASK ✕ 🖥 💻

▼▼ **Extended StayAmerica-Chicago-Woodfield** 🅷
(847) 517-7255. **$50-$90.** 1200 American Ln 60173. I-290, exit SR 72
(Higgins Rd), 0.5 mi w to Meacham Rd, 0.5 mi n to American Ln, then
just w. Int corridors. **Pets:** Other species. $25 daily fee/room. Designated
rooms, service with restrictions, crate. 🅰🆂🅺 ⊠ 📷 💻

▼▼ **Homestead Studio Suites**
        Chicago-Schaumburg-Convention Center 🅷
(847) 882-6900. **$45-$80.** 51 E State Pkwy 60173. I-90, exit Roselle Rd,
0.8 mi s, then just e. Int corridors. **Pets:** Other species. $25 daily fee/
room. Designated rooms, service with restrictions, crate.
🅰🆂🅺 ⊠ 🅖🅜 📷 💻

▼▼▼ **Homewood Suites by Hilton-Schaumburg** 🅷
(847) 605-0400. **$89-$149.** 815 E American Ln 60173. I-290, exit SR 72
(Higgins Rd), 1.5 mi w, then 0.4 mi n on Plum Grove Rd. Ext/int corridors. **Pets:** Accepted. ⊠ 🅖🅜 📷 💻 🔁 ⊠

🔺🔺🔺 ▼▼▼ **Hyatt Summerfield Suites**
        Chicago/Schaumburg 🅷
(847) 706-9007. **$109-$399.** 1251 E American Ln 60173. I-290, exit SR
72 (Higgins Rd), 0.5 mi w to Meacham Rd, 0.5 mi n to American Ln,
then just w. Int corridors. **Pets:** Small. $75 one-time fee/room. Service
with restrictions, crate. 🆂🅰🆅🅴 ⊠ 🅖🅜 📷 💻 🔁 ⊠

▼▼ **La Quinta Inn (Schaumburg)** 🅷 🐾
(847) 517-8484. **$49-$89.** 1730 E Higgins Rd 60173. I-290, exit SR 72
(Higgins Rd), just w. Int corridors. **Pets:** Medium, other species. Service
with restrictions, supervision. 🅰🆂🅺 ⊠ 📷 💻 🔁

▼▼ **Quality Inn** 🅷
(847) 517-7737. **$75-$90.** 600 N Martingale Rd 60173. I-290, exit SR 72
(Higgins Rd), just w, then just n. Int corridors. **Pets:** Accepted.
🅰🆂🅺 ⊠ 📷 💻 🔁

▼▼▼ **Residence Inn by**
        Marriott-Chicago/Schaumburg 🅷 🐾
(847) 517-9200. **$160-$180.** 1610 McConnor Pkwy 60173. I-290, exit 1A
(Woodfield Rd/Golf Rd) northbound, follow signs just n to Golf Rd, just w
to McConnor Pkwy, then 0.8 mi n; exit 1B (Woodfield/Golf rds) southbound. Int corridors. **Pets:** $100 one-time fee/room. Service with restric-
tions, supervision. ⊠ 🅖🅜 📷 💻 🔁 ⊠

▼▼▼ **Staybridge Suites Chicago/Schaumburg** 🅷
(847) 619-6677. **$99-$179.** 901 E Woodfield Office Ct 60173. I-290, exit
SR 72 (Higgins Rd), 1.5 mi w, then 0.3 mi n on Plum Grove Rd. Ext/int
corridors. **Pets:** Accepted. 🅰🆂🅺 ⊠ 📷 💻 🔁 ⊠

SCHILLER PARK
🔺🔺🔺 ▼▼▼ **Comfort Suites by Choice Hotels at**
        O'Hare 🅷
(847) 233-9000. **$79-$99.** 4200 N River Rd 60176. Jct SR 19 (Irving
Park Rd) and Des Plaines St/River Rd, just n. Int corridors. **Pets:** Other
species. $50 one-time fee/pet. Service with restrictions, crate.
🆂🅰🆅🅴 ⊠ 🅖🅜 📷 💻 🍴

🔺🔺🔺 ▼▼▼ **Four Points by Sheraton Chicago O'Hare**
        Airport 🅷
(847) 671-6000. **$79-$249.** 10249 W Irving Park Rd 60176. Jct US 12,
45 and SR 19 (Irving Park Rd). Int corridors. **Pets:** Medium, other species. $100 deposit/room. Service with restrictions, crate.
🆂🅰🆅🅴 ⊠ 🅖🅜 📷 💻 🍴 🔁 ⊠

SKOKIE
🔺🔺🔺 ▼▼▼ **Comfort Inn Northshore-Skokie** 🅷
(847) 679-4200. **$89-$99.** 9333 Skokie Blvd 60077. I-94, exit 35 (Old
Orchard Rd), 0.4 mi w to Skokie Blvd (US 41), then 0.3 mi s. Int corridors. **Pets:** Small. $15 daily fee/pet. Service with restrictions, supervision.
🆂🅰🆅🅴 ⊠ 📷 💻 🔁

▼▼▼ **Extended StayAmerica-Chicago-Skokie** 🅷
(847) 663-9031. **$65-$110.** 5211 Old Orchard Rd 60077. I-94, exit 35
(Old Orchard Rd). Int corridors. **Pets:** Other species. $25 daily fee/room.
Designated rooms, service with restrictions, crate. 🅰🆂🅺 ⊠ 📷 💻

▼▼▼▼ **Holiday Inn Chicago North Shore** 🅷
(847) 679-8900. **$99-$189.** 5300 W Touhy Ave 60077. I-94, exit 39A, 0.5
mi w. Int corridors. **Pets:** Accepted. 🅰🆂🅺 ⊠ 📷 💻 🍴 🔁

TINLEY PARK
▼▼ **La Quinta Inn & Suites Chicago-Tinley Park** 🅷 🐾
(708) 633-1200. **$69-$129.** 7255 W 183rd St 60477. I-80, exit 148B, 0.5
mi n to 183rd St, then just w to North Creek Business Center. Int corridors. **Pets:** Medium, other species. Service with restrictions, supervision.
🅰🆂🅺 ⊠ 🅖🅜 📷 💻 🔁

VERNON HILLS
▼▼ **Extended StayAmerica-Chicago-Vernon Hills-Lake**
        Forest 🅷
(847) 821-7101. **$55-$90.** 215 N Milwaukee Ave 60061. I-94, exit SR 60
(Town Line Rd), 2.1 mi w to SR 21 (Milwaukee Ave), then 0.3 mi s; in
The Marketplace At Vernon Hills. Int corridors. **Pets:** Other species. $25
daily fee/room. Designated rooms, service with restrictions, crate.
🅰🆂🅺 ⊠ 🅖🅜 📷 💻

▼▼ **Holiday Inn Express** 🅷
(847) 367-8031. **Call for rates.** 975 Lakeview Pkwy 60061. Jct SR 21
(Milwaukee Ave), 0.7 mi w on SR 60 (Town Line Rd) to Lakeview Pkwy,
then just n. Int corridors. **Pets:** Accepted. ⊠ 🅖🅜 📷 💻 🔁 ⊠

▼▼ **Homestead Studio Suites Hotel-Chicago/Vernon**
        Hills-Lincolnshire 🅷
(847) 955-1111. **$50-$90.** 675 Woodlands Pkwy 60061. I-94, exit SR 60
(Town Line Rd), 2.1 mi w to SR 21 (Milwaukee Ave), 1.9 mi s to Woodlands Pkwy, then just w. Int corridors. **Pets:** Other species. $25 daily fee/
room. Designated rooms, service with restrictions, crate.
🅰🆂🅺 ⊠ 📷 💻

▼▼▼ **Hotel Indigo Chicago/Vernon Hills** 🅷
(847) 918-1400. **Call for rates.** 450 N Milwaukee Ave 60061. I-94, exit
SR 60 (Town Line Rd), 2.1 mi w to SR 21 (Milwaukee Ave), then 0.3 mi
s. Int corridors. **Pets:** Accepted. ⊠ 🅖🅜 📷 💻 🍴 🔁

WARRENVILLE
▼▼▼ **Residence Inn by Marriott Chicago**
        Naperville/Warrenville 🅷
(630) 393-3444. **$160-$180.** 28500 Bella Vista Pkwy 60555. I-88, exit
Winfield Rd, just n to Ferry Rd, then just e. Int corridors. **Pets:** Accepted.
⊠ 🅖🅜 📷 💻 🔁 ⊠

WAUKEGAN
🔺🔺🔺 ▼▼▼ **America's Best Value Inn & Suites** 🅷
(847) 244-6100. **$60-$160.** 411 S Green Bay Rd 60085. I-94, exit SR
120 (Belvidere Rd) eastbound, 2.3 mi e to Green Bay Rd, then just n.
Ext/int corridors. **Pets:** Accepted. 🆂🅰🆅🅴 ⊠ 📷 💻 🔁

▼▼ **Candlewood Suites Chicago/Waukegan** 🅷 🐾
(847) 578-5250. **$149-$189.** 1151 S Waukegan Rd 60085. I-94, exit SR
137 (Buckley Rd), 0.5 mi e to SR 43 (Waukegan Rd), then 1.9 mi n. Int
corridors. **Pets:** $75 one-time fee/room. Service with restrictions, crate.
🅰🆂🅺 ⊠ 📷 💻

🔺🔺🔺 ▼▼▼ **Comfort Inn by Choice Hotels** 🅷 🐾
(847) 623-1400. **$69-$125.** 3031 Belvidere Rd 60085. I-94, exit SR 120
(Belvidere Rd), 2.3 mi e. Int corridors. **Pets:** Other species. $25 one-time
fee/pet. Designated rooms, crate. 🆂🅰🆅🅴 ⊠ 📷 💻

▼▼ **Crossland Studios-Chicago-Waukegan** Ⓜ
(847) 688-0402. **$37-$70.** 1177 S Northpoint Blvd 60085. At US 41;
between US 41 and SR 43. Ext corridors. **Pets:** Other species. $25 daily
fee/room. Designated rooms, service with restrictions, crate.
🅰🆂🅺 ⊠ 📷 💻

▼▼▼ **Residence Inn by Marriott-Waukegan/Gurnee** 🅷
(847) 689-9240. **$139-$169.** 1440 S White Oak Dr 60085. I-94, exit SR
137 (Buckley Rd), 0.5 mi e to SR 43 (Waukegan Rd), 1.5 mi n to Lakeside Dr, then just e. Int corridors. **Pets:** Accepted.
🄴🄲🄾 ⊠ 🅖🅜 📷 💻 🔁 ⊠

WEST DUNDEE

▼▼ TownePlace Suites by Marriott-Chicago/Elgin H ✿
(847) 608-6320. **$80-$98.** 2185 Marriott Dr 60118. I-90, exit SR 31, 0.4 mi n to Marriott Dr, then just e. Int corridors. **Pets:** Other species. $75 one-time fee/room. Service with restrictions. ECO 🗙 🖪 🖵 ⌦

WESTMONT

AAA ▼▼▼ ClubHouse Inn & Suites H
(630) 920-2200. **Call for rates.** 630 Pasquinelli Dr 60559. Just off US 34 (Ogden Ave), 0.3 mi nw of jct SR 83. Int corridors. **Pets:** Small. $10 daily fee/pet. Service with restrictions, supervision.
SAVE 🗙 🖪 🖵 ⌦ 🗙

▼▼ Homestead Studio Suites Hotel-Chicago/Westmont-Oak Brook H
(630) 323-9292. **$55-$85.** 855 Pasquinelli Dr 60559. SR 83, exit US 34 (Ogden Ave), just w to Pasquinelli Dr, then 0.5 mi n. Int corridors. **Pets:** Other species. $25 daily fee/room. Designated rooms, service with restrictions, crate. ASK 🗙 ♿ 🖪 🖵

WHEELING

AAA ▼▼▼ The Westin Chicago North Shore H
(847) 777-6500. **Call for rates.** 601 N Milwaukee Ave 60090. Jct Lake Cook Rd, just s. Int corridors. **Pets:** Accepted.
SAVE 🗙 ♿ 🖪 🖵 🍴 ⌦ 🗙

WILLOWBROOK

AAA ▼ Red Roof Inn #7167 M
(630) 323-8811. **$54-$77.** 7535 Kingery Hwy 60527. I-55, exit 274, 0.5 mi n on SR 83. Ext corridors. **Pets:** Large. Service with restrictions, crate.
SAVE 🗙 🖪

WOODSTOCK

▼ Super 8 H
(815) 337-8808. **$50-$112.** 1220 Davis Rd 60098. On SR 47, s of jct US 14. Int corridors. **Pets:** Accepted. ASK 🗙 🖪 🖵

END METROPOLITAN AREA

COLLINSVILLE

▼▼ Drury Inn-St. Louis/Collinsville H
(618) 345-7700. **$85-$159.** 602 N Bluff Rd 62234. I-55/70, exit 11 (SR 157), just n. Int corridors. **Pets:** Other species. No service, supervision.
ASK 🗙 ♿ 🖪 🖵 ⌦

DANVILLE

AAA ▼▼ Best Western Regency Inn H
(217) 446-2111. **$55-$150.** 360 East Gate Dr 61834. I-74, exit 220 (Lynch Dr), just n. Ext/int corridors. **Pets:** Small, dogs only. $10 daily fee/pet. Designated rooms, service with restrictions, supervision.
SAVE 🗙 🖪 🖵 ⌦

▼▼ Comfort Inn by Choice Hotels H
(217) 443-8004. **$52-$120.** 383 Lynch Dr 61834. I-74, exit 220 (Lynch Dr), just n. Int corridors. **Pets:** Accepted. ASK 🗙 🖪 🖵 ⌦

▼▼ Sleep Inn & Suites H
(217) 442-6600. **Call for rates.** 361 Lynch Dr 61834. I-74, exit 220 (Lynch Dr), just n. Int corridors. **Pets:** Other species. $15 daily fee/pet. Service with restrictions, supervision. 🗙 🖪 🖵 ⌦

▼▼ Super 8 H
(217) 443-4499. **$59-$99.** 377 Lynch Dr 61834. I-74, exit 220 (Lynch Dr), just n. Int corridors. **Pets:** Accepted. ASK 🗙 🖪 🖵

DECATUR

▼▼▼ Decatur Conference Center & Hotel H
(217) 422-8800. **$99, 3 day notice.** 4191 W Hwy 36 62522. I-72, exit 133A (US 36), 1 mi e. Int corridors. **Pets:** Medium, other species. $50 one-time fee/room. Service with restrictions, crate.
ASK 🗙 ♿ 🖪 🖵 🍴 ⌦ 🗙

▼▼▼ Holiday Inn Express Hotel & Suites H
(217) 875-5500. **$104-$121, 7 day notice.** 5170 Wingate Dr 62526. I-72, exit 141 (US 51 N), 0.5 mi n, then just e. Int corridors. **Pets:** Other species. $10 daily fee/room. Service with restrictions, crate.
ASK 🗙 ♿ 🖪 🖵 ⌦ 🗙

▼▼ Sleep Inn H
(217) 872-7700. **Call for rates.** 3920 E Hospitality Ln 62521. I-72, exit 144 (SR 48), just s to Brush College Rd, then just e. Int corridors.
Pets: Accepted. 🗙 🖪 🖵 ⌦

DEKALB

AAA ▼▼ Best Western DeKalb Inn & Suites H
(815) 758-8661. **$89-$129.** 1212 W Lincoln Hwy 60115. I-88, exit Annie Glidden Rd, 2 mi n to W Lincoln Hwy (SR 38), then just w. Ext/int corridors. **Pets:** Dogs only. $50 deposit/room, $10 daily fee/room. Designated rooms, service with restrictions, supervision. SAVE 🗙 🖪 🖵 ⌦

DIXON

AAA ▼▼ Comfort Inn by Choice Hotels H
(815) 284-0500. **$86-$110.** 136 Plaza Dr 61021. I-88, exit SR 26, just n, then just e. Int corridors. **Pets:** Medium, other species. $100 deposit/room, $15 daily fee/pet. Service with restrictions, supervision.
SAVE 🗙 🖪 🖵 ⌦

AAA ▼▼▼ Quality Inn & Suites by Choice Hotels H
(815) 288-2001. **$95-$120.** 154 Plaza Dr 61021. I-88, exit SR 26, just n, then just e. Int corridors. **Pets:** Medium, other species. $100 deposit/room, $15 daily fee/pet. Service with restrictions, supervision.
SAVE 🗙 🖪 🖵 ⌦ 🗙

EAST MOLINE

▼▼ Comfort Inn & Suites H
(309) 792-4660. **Call for rates.** 2209 John Deere Expy 61244. I-74, exit 4B (John Deere Rd), 5 mi e; I-80, exit 4A, 6 mi w on SR 5. Int corridors.
Pets: Accepted. 🗙 ♿ 🖪 🖵 ⌦

▼ Super 8-East Moline H
(309) 796-1999. **$54-$60, 4 day notice.** 2201 John Deere Rd 61244. I-74, exit 4B (John Deere Rd), 5.5 mi e on SR 5. Int corridors.
Pets: Accepted. ASK 🗙 🖪 🖵

EAST PEORIA

▼▼ Super 8 H
(309) 698-8889. **$57-$97.** 725 Taylor St 61611. I-74, exit 96, just e. Int corridors. **Pets:** Accepted. ASK 🗙 🖪 🖵

EFFINGHAM

AAA ▼▼ Best Western Raintree Inn H
(217) 342-4121. **$60-$75.** 1811 W Fayette Ave 62401. I-57/70, exit 159, just n. Ext/int corridors. **Pets:** Other species. Service with restrictions.
SAVE 🗙 🖵 ⌦

▼▼ Comfort Inn H
(217) 347-5050. **$60-$80.** 1304 W Evergreen Dr 62401. I-57/70, exit 160 (SR 32/33), just e, then just n. Int corridors. **Pets:** Other species. $10 one-time fee/pet. Designated rooms, service with restrictions, supervision.
ASK 🗙 ♿ 🖪 🖵 ⌦ 🗙

▼▼▼▼ Comfort Suites **H**

(217) 342-3151. **$64-$99.** 1310 W Fayette Ave 62401. I-57/70, exit 159, 0.4 mi e. Int corridors. **Pets:** Accepted. [ASK] [X] [&M] [📶] [💻] [🏊]

AAA ▼▼▼ Days Inn **H**

(217) 347-7131. **$44-$79.** 1205 N Keller Dr 62401. I-57/70, exit 160 (SR 32/33), just n. Int corridors. **Pets:** Other species. $10 daily fee/pet. Service with restrictions, supervision. [SAVE] [X] [📶] [💻]

AAA ▼▼▼ Econo Lodge **M**

(217) 342-9271. **Call for rates.** 1412 W Fayette Ave 62401. I-57/70, exit 159, just e. Ext corridors. **Pets:** Accepted. [SAVE] [X] [📶] [💻] [🏊]

▼▼▼▼ Fairfield Inn & Suites **H**

(217) 540-5454. **$85-$99.** 1111 Henrietta St 62401. I-57/70, exit 160 (SR 32/33), just se. Int corridors. **Pets:** $15 one-time fee/pet. Service with restrictions, supervision. [X] [&M] [📶] [💻] [🏊]

▼▼▼▼ Holiday Inn Express **H**

(217) 540-1111. **Call for rates.** 1103 Ave of Mid-America 62401. I-57/70, exit 160 (SR 32/33), just n. Int corridors. **Pets:** Accepted. [X] [&M] [📶] [💻] [🏊]

AAA ▼▼▼ Rodeway Inn **M**

(217) 347-7515. **Call for rates.** 1205A N Keller Dr 62401. I-57/70, exit 160 (SR 32/33), just n. Ext corridors. **Pets:** Other species. $10 daily fee/pet. Service with restrictions, supervision. [SAVE] [X] [📶] [💻] [🏊] [X]

▼▼▼▼ Super 8-Effingham **M**

(217) 342-6888. **Call for rates.** 1400 Thelma Keller Ave 62401. I-57/70, exit 160 (SR 32/33), 0.5 mi n. Int corridors. **Pets:** Other species. Service with restrictions, supervision. [X] [📶] [💻]

FAIRFIELD

▼ Briarwood Inn **M**

(618) 842-3667. **Call for rates.** 116 N Market Ave 62837. West end of town. Int corridors. **Pets:** Accepted. [X] [&M] [📶] [💻] [🏊]

FAIRVIEW HEIGHTS

▼▼▼▼ Comfort Suites **H**

(618) 394-0202. **$89-$99.** 137 Ludwig Dr 62208. I-64, exit 12 (SR 159), just n to Ludwig Dr, then 0.4 mi w. Int corridors. **Pets:** Small, other species. $10 daily fee/pet. Service with restrictions, crate. [ASK] [X] [&M] [📶] [💻] [🏊]

▼▼▼▼ Drury Inn & Suites-Fairview Heights **H**

(618) 398-8530. **$85-$164.** 12 Ludwig Dr 62208. I-64, exit 12 (SR 159). Int corridors. **Pets:** Other species. No service, supervision. [ASK] [X] [📶] [💻] [X]

AAA ▼▼▼ Ramada Inn Fairview Heights **H** 🐾

(618) 632-4747. **$67-$81.** 6900 N Illinois St 62208. I-64, exit 12 (SR 159), just n. Int corridors. **Pets:** $25 one-time fee/room. Service with restrictions, crate. [SAVE] [X] [📶] [💻] [🍴] [🏊]

FLORA

AAA ▼▼▼ Best Western Lorson Inn **H**

(618) 662-3054. **$70-$90.** 201 Hagen Dr 62839. Jct US 45 and 50. Int corridors. **Pets:** Small. $12 one-time fee/pet. Service with restrictions, supervision. [SAVE] [X] [&M] [📶] [💻] [X]

FREEPORT

AAA ▼▼▼▼ Baymont Inn & Suites-Freeport **H**

(815) 599-8510. **$79-$150.** 1060 Riverside Dr 61032. Jct US 20 Bypass and SR 26, just s. Int corridors. **Pets:** Other species. $25 one-time fee/room. Service with restrictions, crate. [SAVE] [X] [📶] [💻] [🏊]

AAA ▼▼▼▼ Hampton Inn **H**

(815) 232-7100. **$79-$92.** 109 S Galena Ave 61032. Jct Main St; downtown. Int corridors. **Pets:** Medium, dogs only. Designated rooms, service with restrictions, crate. [SAVE] [X] [&M] [📶] [💻] [🏊]

GALENA

AAA ▼▼▼▼ Eagle Ridge Resort & Spa **H**

(815) 777-5000. **$159-$209, 7 day notice.** 444 Eagle Ridge Dr 61036. US 20, 6 mi e to E Glen Hollow Rd, 4.5 mi n. Ext/int corridors. **Pets:** Medium, dogs only. $75 one-time fee/pet. Designated rooms, service with restrictions, crate. [SAVE] [X] [📶] [💻] [🍴] [🏊] [X]

GALESBURG

AAA ▼▼▼▼ Best Western Prairie Inn **H**

(309) 343-7151. **$75-$110.** 300 S Soangetaha Rd 61401. I-74, exit 48 (Main St), just e, then just s. Int corridors. **Pets:** Accepted. [SAVE] [X] [📶] [💻] [🍴] [🏊] [X]

▼▼▼ Comfort Inn by Choice Hotels **H**

(309) 344-5445. **$68-$120.** 907 W Carl Sandburg Dr 61401. US 34, exit US 150 E. Int corridors. **Pets:** Other species. $20 one-time fee/room. Service with restrictions, crate. [ASK] [X] [&M] [📶] [💻]

▼▼▼ Holiday Inn Express **H** 🐾

(309) 343-7100. **$84-$149.** 2285 Washington St 61401. I-74, exit 48A (US 150), just w to Michigan Ave, just s to Washington St, then just e. Int corridors. **Pets:** Other species. $25 one-time fee/room. Service with restrictions, supervision. [ASK] [X] [&M] [📶] [💻] [🏊] [X]

GALVA

AAA ▼▼▼▼ Galva Inn & Suites **H**

(309) 932-2841. **Call for rates.** 301 Commercial St 61434. Jct US 34 and SR 17, just ne; downtown. Int corridors. **Pets:** Accepted. [SAVE] [X] [📶] [💻]

GILMAN

AAA ▼▼▼ Super 8 **H**

(815) 265-7000. **$63-$85.** 1301 S Crescent St 60938. I-57, exit 283, 0.3 mi e. Int corridors. **Pets:** Small. $25 deposit/pet, $10 daily fee/pet. Service with restrictions, supervision. [SAVE] [X] [📶] [💻]

GRAYVILLE

▼▼▼ Super 8 **H**

(618) 375-7288. **$63-$75.** 2060 CR 2450 N 62844. I-64, exit 130 (SR 1), just n. Int corridors. **Pets:** Other species. $15 one-time fee/room. Service with restrictions, crate. [ASK] [X] [&M] [📶] [💻]

▼▼▼ Windsor Oaks Inn **H**

(618) 375-7930. **Call for rates.** 2200 S Court St 62844. I-64, exit 130 (SR 1), just n. Int corridors. **Pets:** Accepted. [X] [📶] [💻] [🍴] [🏊]

GREENVILLE

▼▼▼▼ Sleep Inn and Suites **H** 🐾

(618) 664-9700. **$70-$160.** 2265 SR 127 62246. I-70, exit 45, just s. Int corridors. **Pets:** Medium. $25 daily fee/pet. Designated rooms, service with restrictions, supervision. [ASK] [X] [&M] [📶] [💻] [🏊]

▼▼▼ Super 8-Greenville **H**

(618) 664-0800. **$56-$66.** 1700 SR 127 S 62246. I-70, exit 45, just n. Int corridors. **Pets:** $10 daily fee/pet. Service with restrictions, supervision. [ASK] [X] [📶] [💻]

JACKSONVILLE

AAA ▼▼ Starlite Motel **M**

(217) 245-7184. **$40-$65.** 1910 W Morton Ave 62650. I-72, exit 64, 2.3 mi n on SR 267 (Main St) to SR 104 (Morton Ave), then 1.8 mi w. Ext corridors. **Pets:** Small. $5 daily fee/pet. Service with restrictions. [SAVE] [X] [📶] [💻]

▼▼▼ Super 8 **H**

(217) 479-0303. **$45-$90.** 1003 W Morton Ave 62650. I-72, exit 64, 2.3 mi n on SR 267 (Main St) to SR 104 (Morton Ave), then 0.8 mi w. Int corridors. **Pets:** Other species. $10 daily fee/pet. Service with restrictions. [ASK] [X] [📶] [💻]

KEWANEE

▼▼▼ **AmericInn Lodge & Suites of Kewanee** H
(309) 856-7200. **$85-$142.** 925 S Tenney St 61443. On SR 78, 1.9 mi s of jct US 34. Int corridors. **Pets:** Accepted.
A$K ⊠ ᴍ 🛏 💻 🏊

LINCOLN

ⱮⱯ▼ ▼▼▼ **Best Western Lincoln Inn** H
(217) 732-9641. **$75-$100.** 1750 5th St 62656. I-55, exit 126 (US 121), 1.6 mi s to Lincoln Pkwy, then 0.5 mi w. Int corridors. **Pets:** Accepted.
SAVE ⊠ 🛏 💻

ⱮⱯⱯ ▼▼▼ **Hampton Inn–Lincoln** H
(217) 732-6729. **$82-$94.** 1019 N Heitman Dr 62656. I-55, exit 126 (US 121), just e. Int corridors. **Pets:** Medium. $50 deposit/room. Service with restrictions, supervision. SAVE ⊠ ᴍ 🛏 💻 🏊

▼▼▼ **Holiday Inn Express** H
(217) 735-5800. **$89.** 130 Olson Dr 62656. I-55, exit 126 (US 121), just e to Heitman Dr, just w to Olson Dr, then just n. Int corridors.
Pets: Medium. Designated rooms, service with restrictions, supervision.
A$K ⊠ 🛏 💻 🏊

LITCHFIELD

ⱮⱯⱯ ▼▼▼ **Hampton Inn** H
(217) 324-4441. **$79-$144.** 11 Thunderbird Cir 62056. I-55, exit 52 (SR 16), on Corvette Dr, then just e. Int corridors. **Pets:** Medium. $50 deposit/room. Service with restrictions, supervision.
SAVE ⊠ ᴍ 🛏 💻 🏊

▼▼▼ **Holiday Inn Express** H
(217) 324-4556. **$89-$139.** 1405 W Hudson Dr 62056. I-55, exit 52 (SR 16), just e to Ohren Ln, just s to W Hudson Dr, then just w. Int corridors.
Pets: Other species. Designated rooms, service with restrictions, supervision. A$K ⊠ 🛏 💻 🏊

LOVES PARK

▼▼▼ **Holiday Inn Express Hotel & Suites Rockford North** H
(815) 654-4100. **$100-$160.** 7552 Park Pl 61111. I-39/90, exit E Riverside Blvd, just nw. Int corridors. **Pets:** Accepted.
A$K ⊠ ᴍ 🛏 💻 🏊 ⊠

▼▼▼ **Quality Inn & Suites Rockford/Loves Park** H
(815) 282-9300. **$70-$200.** 4313 Bell School Rd 61111. I-39/90, exit E Riverside Blvd, just nw. Int corridors. **Pets:** Accepted.
A$K ⊠ ᴍ 🛏 💻 🏊

MACOMB

▼ **Super 8** H ❀
(309) 836-8888. **$59-$125.** 313 University Dr 61455. 1.1 mi n on US 67 to University Dr, 0.5 mi w. Int corridors. **Pets:** Other species. $10 one-time fee/pet. Service with restrictions, supervision. A$K ⊠ 🛏 💻

MANTENO

▼▼▼ **Country Inn & Suites By Carlson** H
(815) 468-2600. **$79-$199.** 380 S Cypress St 60950. I-57, exit 322, just se via frontage road. Int corridors. **Pets:** Medium, other species. $150 deposit/room, $15 daily fee/pet. Service with restrictions, supervision.
A$K ⊠ ᴍ 🛏 💻 🏊

MARION

▼▼ **Drury Inn-Marion** H
(618) 997-9600. **$95-$159.** 2706 W DeYoung St 62959. I-57, exit 54B (SR 13), 0.5 mi w. Int corridors. **Pets:** Other species. No service, supervision. A$K ⊠ ᴍ 🛏 💻 🏊

▼ **Super 8** H
(618) 993-5577. **Call for rates.** 2601 W DeYoung St 62959. I-57, exit 54B (SR 13), just w. Int corridors. **Pets:** Accepted. ⊠ 🛏 💻

MATTOON

▼▼ **Baymont Inn & Suites** H
(217) 234-2355. **Call for rates.** 206 McFall Rd 61938. I-57, exit 190B, just w. Int corridors. **Pets:** Accepted. ⊠ 🛏 💻 🏊

▼▼▼ **Holiday Inn Express Hotel & Suites** H
(217) 235-2060. **$99-$159.** 121 Swords Dr 61938. I-57, exit 190B, just w. Int corridors. **Pets:** $25 one-time fee/room. Designated rooms, service with restrictions, crate. A$K ⊠ ᴍ 🛏 💻 🏊

▼▼ **Super 8** M
(217) 235-8888. **$59-$79.** 205 McFall Rd 61938. I-57, exit 190B, just w. Int corridors. **Pets:** Small, other species. $10 daily fee/room. Designated rooms, service with restrictions, supervision. A$K ⊠ 🛏 💻

MONMOUTH

▼▼ **AmericInn Lodge & Suites of Monmouth** H ❀
(309) 734-9958. **$90-$170.** 1 AmericInn Way 61462. Jct US 34 and N Main St, just s; 18 mi w of jct I-74 and US 34. Int corridors. **Pets:** Small, dogs only. $75 one-time fee/room. Designated rooms, service with restrictions, supervision. A$K ⊠ ᴍ 🛏 💻 🏊 ⊠

MONTICELLO

ⱮⱯⱯ ▼▼▼ **Best Western Monticello Gateway Inn** H
(217) 762-9436. **$74-$175.** 805 Iron Horse Pl 61856. I-72, exit 166, just s. Ext/int corridors. **Pets:** Other species. $10 daily fee/pet. Service with restrictions, supervision. SAVE ⊠ 🛏 💻 🏊

MORRIS

▼▼ **Comfort Inn by Choice Hotels** H
(815) 942-1433. **Call for rates.** 70 Gore Rd 60450. I-80, exit 112 (SR 47), 0.3 mi nw. Int corridors. **Pets:** Large, other species. $25 one-time fee/room. Service with restrictions, crate. ⊠ 🛏 💻 🏊

▼▼ **Quality Inn** H
(815) 942-6600. **Call for rates.** 200 Gore Rd 60450. I-80, exit 112 (SR 47), 0.3 mi nw. Int corridors. **Pets:** Accepted. ⊠ 🛏 💻 🏊 ⊠

MORTON

ⱮⱯⱯ ▼▼▼ **Baymont Inn & Suites** H
(309) 266-8888. **$75-$120.** 210 E Ashland St 61550. I-74, exit 102, 0.4 mi ne. Int corridors. **Pets:** Accepted. SAVE ⊠ 🛏 💻 🏊

ⱮⱯⱯ ▼▼▼ **Best Western Ashland House Inn & Conference Center** H
(309) 263-5116. **$80-$110.** 201 E Ashland St 61550. I-74, exit 102, 0.3 mi ne. Int corridors. **Pets:** Small, dogs only. $15 one-time fee/room. Designated rooms, service with restrictions, supervision.
SAVE ⊠ 🛏 💻 🍴 🏊

▼▼ **Quality Inn by Choice Hotels** H
(309) 266-8310. **$65-$80.** 115 E Ashland St 61550. I-74, exit 102B, just w. Ext/int corridors. **Pets:** Accepted. A$K ⊠ 🛏 💻

MOUNT VERNON

▼▼▼ **Holiday Inn** H
(618) 244-7100. **$70-$142.** 222 Potomac Blvd 62864. I-57/64, exit 95 (SR 15), just w to Potomac Blvd, then just n. Int corridors. **Pets:** Medium, other species. $20 one-time fee/pet. Designated rooms, service with restrictions, crate. A$K ⊠ ᴍ 🛏 💻 🍴 🏊 ⊠

NASHVILLE

ⱮⱯⱯ ▼▼▼ **Best Western U.S. Inn** H
(618) 478-5341. **$65-$85.** 11640 SR 127 62263. I-64, exit 50 (SR 127), 0.3 mi s. Int corridors. **Pets:** Small. $10 daily fee/pet. Designated rooms, service with restrictions, supervision. SAVE ⊠ ᴍ 🛏 💻 🏊

NORMAL

ⱮⱯⱯ ▼▼▼ **Best Western University Inn** H
(309) 454-4070. **$80-$130.** 6 Traders Cir 61761. I-55, exit 165A (US 51), just s, then return on frontage road. Int corridors. **Pets:** Accepted.
SAVE ⊠ 🛏 💻 🏊

Comfort Suites by Choice Hotels Bloomington/Normal 🅷

(309) 452-8588. **$80-$130.** 310 B Greenbriar Dr 61761. I-55, exit 167, follow I-55 business route (Veterans Pkwy), 1.3 mi s; jct Fort Jesse Rd. Int corridors. **Pets:** Small. $20 daily fee/room. Service with restrictions, crate. [ASK] [X] [&M] [🏠] [💻] [🏊]

Holiday Inn Express Hotel & Suites Bloomington/Normal 🅷

(309) 862-1600. **$79-$119.** 1715 Parkway Plaza Dr 61761. I-55, exit 167, follow I-55 business route (Veterans Pkwy), 1.7 mi s to Parkway Plaza Dr, then just e. Int corridors. **Pets:** Accepted. [ASK] [X] [🏠] [💻] [🏊] [X]

O'FALLON

Candlewood Suites 🅷

(618) 622-9555. **$84-$139.** 1332 Park Plaza Dr 62269. I-64, exit 14 (US 50), just s on Lincoln Hwy, 0.5 mi w on Hartman Ln, then just n on 2nd entrance to Park Plaza Dr. Int corridors. **Pets:** Accepted.

[ASK] [X] [&M] [🏠] [💻]

Days Inn O'Fallon 🅷

(618) 628-9700. **$50-$69.** 1320 Park Plaza Dr 62269. I-64, exit 14 (US 50), just s, 0.3 mi e, then just n. Int corridors. **Pets:** Medium. $10 daily fee/pet. Designated rooms, service with restrictions, supervision.

[ASK] [X] [🏠] [💻] [🏊]

Drury Inn & Suites-O'Fallon 🅷

(618) 624-2211. **$90-$184.** 1118 Central Park Dr 62269. I-64, exit 16, just s. Int corridors. **Pets:** Other species. No service, supervision.

[ASK] [X] [&M] [🏠] [💻] [🏊] [X]

Extended StayAmerica-St. Louis-O'Fallon 🅷

(618) 624-1757. **$79-$89.** 154 Regency Park Dr 62269. I-64, exit 14 (US 50), just w to Regency Park Dr, then 0.4 mi s. Int corridors. **Pets:** Other species. $25 daily fee/room. Designated rooms, service with restrictions, crate. [ASK] [X] [&M] [🏠] [💻]

Settle Inn & Suites 🅷 ❀

(618) 624-6060. **$69-$149.** 1100 Eastgate Dr 62269. I-64, exit 19B (SR 158), 0.5 mi n, then just sw. Int corridors. **Pets:** Large, other species. $50 deposit/pet. Service with restrictions. [SAVE] [X] [🏠] [💻] [🏊]

OGLESBY

Holiday Inn Express 🅷

(815) 883-3535. **Call for rates.** 900 Holiday St 61348. I-39, exit 54, just e. Int corridors. **Pets:** Accepted. [X] [🏠] [💻] [🏊]

OTTAWA

Hampton Inn-Starved Rock Area 🅷

(815) 434-6040. **Call for rates.** 4115 Holiday Ln 61350. I-80, exit 90 (SR 23), just n. Int corridors. **Pets:** Accepted. [X] [&M] [🏠] [🏊]

Holiday Inn Express 🅷

(815) 433-0029. **$114-$164.** 120 W Stevenson Rd 61350. I-80, exit 90 (SR 23), just n. Int corridors. **Pets:** Other species. Designated rooms, service with restrictions, supervision. [ASK] [X] [🏠] [💻] [🏊]

PEORIA

Baymont Inn & Suites 🅷

(309) 686-7600. **Call for rates.** 2002 W War Memorial Dr 61614. I-74, exit 89 (US 150/War Memorial Dr); just n; entrance through Northwoods Mall. Ext/int corridors. **Pets:** Accepted. [SAVE] [X] [🏠] [💻] [🏊]

Candlewood Suites Peoria at Grand Prairie 🅷

(309) 691-1690. **Call for rates.** 5300 W Landens Way 61615. SR 6, exit 2 (US 150/War Memorial Dr), follow US 150 NW to Summershade Cir, then just w. Int corridors. **Pets:** Accepted. [X] [&M] [🏠] [💻]

Comfort Suites by Choice Hotels 🅷

(309) 688-3800. **Call for rates.** 1812 W War Memorial Dr 61614. I-74, exit 89 (US 150/War Memorial Dr), just e, then just s. Int corridors. **Pets:** Medium, dogs only. $25 one-time fee/pet. Service with restrictions, crate. [X] [🏠] [💻] [🏊]

Country Inn & Suites By Carlson, Peoria-North 🅷 ❀

(309) 589-0044. **Call for rates.** 5309 W Landens Way 61615. SR 6, exit 2 (US 150/War Memorial Dr), just n. Int corridors. **Pets:** $75 one-time fee/room. Service with restrictions, supervision.

[X] [&M] [🏠] [💻] [🏊] [X]

Red Roof Inn #0057 Ⓜ

(309) 685-3911. **$45-$80.** 1822 W War Memorial Dr 61614. I-74, exit 89 (US 150/War Memorial Dr), just e. Ext corridors. **Pets:** Large. Service with restrictions, crate. [ASK] [X] [🏠]

Residence Inn by Marriott 🅷

(309) 681-9000. **$150-$170.** 2000 W War Memorial Dr 61614. I-74, exit 89 (US 150/War Memorial Dr), just w; entrance through Northwoods Mall. Int corridors. **Pets:** Accepted. [X] [🏠] [💻] [🏊] [X]

Super 8 🅷

(309) 688-8074. **Call for rates.** 1816 W War Memorial Dr 61614. I-74, exit 89 (US 150/War Memorial Dr), just e. Int corridors. **Pets:** Accepted. [X] [🏠] [💻]

Wingate by Wyndham Peoria 🅷 ❀

(309) 589-0033. **$129-$139.** 7708 N Rt 91 61615. SR 6, exit 2, just w on US 150 (War Memorial Dr), then 0.3 mi n. Int corridors. **Pets:** Other species. $75 one-time fee/room. Service with restrictions, crate. [ASK] [X] [&M] [🏠] [💻] [🏊] [X]

PERU

La Quinta Inn Peru 🅷 ❀

(815) 224-9000. **$79-$119.** 4389 Venture Dr 61354. I-80, exit 75 (SR 251), 0.4 mi s to 38th St, just w to Venture Dr, then 0.4 mi nw. Int corridors. **Pets:** Medium, other species. Service with restrictions, supervision. [ASK] [X] [🏠] [💻] [🏊]

QUAD CITIES AREA

MOLINE

Comfort Inn by Choice Hotels 🅷

(309) 762-7000. **$69-$89.** 2600 52nd Ave 61265. I-280/74, exit 18A eastbound; exit 5B westbound, just s on US 6 and 150, then 0.5 mi nw on 27th St. Int corridors. **Pets:** Accepted. [ASK] [X] [🏠] [💻] [🏊]

Days Inn & Suites 🅷

(309) 762-8300. **$65-$75.** 6910 27th St 61265. I-280/74, exit 18A eastbound; exit 5B westbound, just s on US 6 and 150, then just nw. Int corridors. **Pets:** Small. $25 one-time fee/room. Service with restrictions, crate.

[ASK] [X] [🏠] [💻]

Fairfield Inn by Marriott 🅷

(309) 762-9083. **$75-$95.** 2705 48th Ave 61265. I-280/74, exit 5B westbound; exit 18A eastbound, just s on US 6 to traffic light, then 1 mi nw on 27th St. Int corridors. **Pets:** Accepted. [X] [&M] [🏠] [💻] [🏊] [X]

La Quinta Inn Moline 🅷 ❀

(309) 762-9008. **$49-$89.** 5450 27th St 61265. I-280/74, exit 18A eastbound; exit 5B westbound, just s on US 6 and 150 to traffic light, then just nw. Int corridors. **Pets:** Medium, other species. Service with restrictions, supervision. [ASK] [X] [🏠] [💻] [🏊]

▼▼ **Ramada Airport Conference Center** 🅷

(309) 762-8811. **$76-$81.** 6902 27th St 61265. I-280/74, exit 18A eastbound; exit 5B westbound, just s on US 6 and 150, then just nw. Int corridors. **Pets:** Small. $25 one-time fee/room. Service with restrictions, crate.

(ASK) ⊠ 🛡 🖵 🍴 ⊅ ⊠

▼ **Super 8** 🅷

(309) 797-5580. **Call for rates.** 2501 52nd Ave 61265. I-280/74, exit 18A eastbound; exit 5B westbound, just s on US 6 and 150, then 1 mi nw on 27th St. Int corridors. **Pets:** Accepted. ⊠ 🛡 🖵

ROCK ISLAND

🅐🅐🅐 ▼▼▼ **Holiday Inn Rock Island Hotel & Conference Center** 🅷

(309) 794-1212. **$109-$139, 30 day notice.** 226 17th St 61201. Just e of Centennial Bridge; at 3rd Ave and 17th St; downtown. Int corridors. **Pets:** Accepted. (SAVE) ⊠ 🛡 🖵 🍴 ⊅ ⊠

END AREA

QUINCY

▼▼ **Comfort Inn by Choice Hotels** 🅷

(217) 228-2700. **Call for rates.** 4122 Broadway 62305. I-172, exit 14 (SR 104), 1.3 mi w. Int corridors. **Pets:** Other species. $10 daily fee/pet. Designated rooms, service with restrictions, supervision.

⊠ 🛡 🖵 ⊅

▼▼▼ **Country Inn & Suites By Carlson** 🅷

(217) 222-8949. **$95-$500.** 110 N 54th St 62305. I-172, exit 14 (SR 104), just w. Int corridors. **Pets:** Medium. $25 daily fee/pet. Designated rooms, service with restrictions, supervision. (ASK) ⊠ 🛡 🖵 ⊅ ⊠

▼▼ **Super 8** 🅷

(217) 228-8808. **Call for rates.** 224 N 36th St 62301. I-172, exit 14 (SR 104), 1.8 mi w, then just s. Int corridors. **Pets:** Small, other species. $15 one-time fee/pet. Designated rooms, service with restrictions, supervision.

⊠ (&M) 🛡 🖵

RANTOUL

🅐🅐🅐 ▼▼ **Best Western Heritage Inn** 🅼

(217) 892-9292. **$57-$61.** 420 S Murray Rd 61866. I-57, exit 250 (US 136), 0.5 mi e, then just s. Ext corridors. **Pets:** Small. $8 daily fee/pet. Service with restrictions, supervision. (SAVE) ⊠ 🛡 🖵 ⊅

▼▼ **Super 8** 🅷

(217) 893-8888. **$65-$160.** 207 S Murray Rd 61866. I-57, exit 250 (US 136), just e. Int corridors. **Pets:** Small, dogs only. $10 daily fee/pet. Designated rooms, service with restrictions, supervision. (ASK) ⊠ 🛡 🖵

ROBINSON

🅐🅐🅐 ▼▼ **Best Western Robinson Inn** 🅷

(618) 544-8448. **$67-$78.** 1500 W Main St 62454. 1.2 mi w on SR 33. Int corridors. **Pets:** Medium, other species. $5 daily fee/room. Service with restrictions, crate. (SAVE) ⊠ 🛡 🖵

ROCHELLE

▼▼ **Baymont Inn & Suites** 🅷

(815) 562-9530. **$79-$159.** 567 E Hwy 38 61068. I-39, exit 99 (SR 38), 1 mi w. Int corridors. **Pets:** Large, other species. $10 daily fee/pet. Service with restrictions, supervision. (ASK) ⊠ 🛡 🖵 ⊅

🅐🅐🅐 ▼▼▼ **Comfort Inn & Suites by Choice Hotels** 🅷 ❁

(815) 562-5551. **$79-$189.** 1133 N 7th St 61068. I-39, exit 99 (SR 38), 2.5 mi w; jct SR 38 and 251; downtown. Int corridors. **Pets:** Medium, other species. $25 daily fee/pet. Service with restrictions, supervision.

(SAVE) ⊠ 🛡 🖵 ⊅ ⊠

ROCKFORD

▼▼ **Baymont Inn & Suites Rockford** 🅷 ❁

(815) 229-8200. **$69-$150.** 662 N Lyford Rd 61107. I-90, exit US 20 business route, just e, then just n. Int corridors. **Pets:** Other species. $20 one-time fee/room. Designated rooms, no service, supervision.

(ASK) ⊠ 🛡 🖵 ⊅ ⊠

▼▼ **Candlewood Suites** 🅷 ❁

(815) 229-9300. **$89-$139.** 7555 Walton St 61108. I-90, exit US 20 business route, 0.3 mi e to Bell School Rd, just s to Walton St, then just e. Int corridors. **Pets:** Medium, other species. $25 one-time fee/pet. Designated rooms, service with restrictions. (ASK) ⊠ 🛡 🖵

▼▼ **Comfort Inn by Choice Hotels** 🅷

(815) 398-7061. **Call for rates.** 7392 Argus Dr 61107. I-90, exit US 20 business route, just w to Bell School Rd, then just n. Int corridors. **Pets:** Large, other species. $25 one-time fee/room. Service with restrictions, crate. ⊠ 🛡 🖵 ⊅

▼▼ **Days Inn Rockford** 🅷

(815) 332-4915. **$49-$119.** 220 S Lyford Rd 61108. I-90, exit US 20 business route, just e, then just s. Int corridors. **Pets:** Accepted.

(ASK) ⊠ 🛡 🖵

▼▼ **Extended StayAmerica-Rockford East** 🅷

(815) 226-8969. **$45-$75.** 653 Clark Dr 61107. I-90, exit US 20 business route, just w. Int corridors. **Pets:** Other species. $25 daily fee/room. Designated rooms, service with restrictions, crate. (ASK) ⊠ 🛡 🖵

▼▼ **Quality Suites** 🅷

(815) 227-1300. **$70.** 7401 Walton St 61108. I-90, exit US 20 business route, just w to Bell School Rd, then just s. Int corridors. **Pets:** Small, other species. $25 daily fee/room. Designated rooms, service with restrictions, crate. (ASK) ⊠ 🛡 🖵 ⊅ ⊠

🅐🅐🅐 ▼ **Red Roof Inn #7035** 🅼

(815) 398-9750. **$55-$90.** 7434 E State St 61108. I-90, exit US 20 business route, just w. Ext corridors. **Pets:** Large. Service with restrictions, crate. (SAVE) ⊠

▼▼▼ **Residence Inn by Marriott** 🅷

(815) 227-0013. **$120-$140.** 7542 Colosseum Dr 61107. I-90, exit US 20 business route, just w. Int corridors. **Pets:** Large. $100 one-time fee/room. Service with restrictions, crate. ⊠ 🛡 🖵 ⊅ ⊠

▼▼ **StudioPLUS Deluxe Studios Rockfort-East** 🅷

(815) 397-8316. **$50-$80.** 747 N Bell School Rd 61107. I-90, exit US 20 business route, just w to Bell School Rd, then 0.3 mi n. Int corridors. **Pets:** Other species. $25 daily fee/room. Designated rooms, service with restrictions, crate. (ASK) ⊠ 🛡 🖵

SALEM

▼ **Super 8** 🅷

(618) 548-5882. **$64-$76.** 118 Woods Ln 62881. I-57, exit 116 (US 50), just w. Ext/int corridors. **Pets:** Large. Designated rooms, service with restrictions, supervision. (ASK) ⊠ (&M) 🛡 🖵

SOUTH BELOIT

🅐🅐🅐 ▼▼▼ **Best Western Legacy Inn & Suites** 🅷

(815) 389-4211. **$89-$150.** 5910 Technology Dr 61080. I-90/39, exit 1, just sw. Int corridors. **Pets:** Medium. $25 daily fee/pet. Service with restrictions, supervision. (SAVE) ⊠ 🛡 🖵 ⊅ ⊠

SOUTH JACKSONVILLE

Comfort Inn by Choice Hotels-South Jacksonville H

(217) 245-8372. **$69-$99, 3 day notice.** 200 Comfort Dr 62650. I-72, exit 64, just n. Int corridors. **Pets:** Accepted. [SAVE] [X] [♿] [🖥] [≈]

Econo Lodge Inn & Suites by Choice Hotels H

(217) 245-9575. **Call for rates.** 1914 Southbrooke Rd 62650. I-72, exit 64, just n. Int corridors. **Pets:** Accepted. [X] [♿] [🖥] [🖥]

Holiday Inn Express & Suites Jacksonville H 🐾

(217) 245-6500. **$94-$99.** 2501 Holliday Ln 62650. I-72, exit 64, just n. Int corridors. **Pets:** Medium. $10 daily fee/pet. Service with restrictions, crate. [ASK] [X] [♿] [🖥] [🖥] [≈]

SPRINGFIELD

Baymont Inn & Suites Springfield H

(217) 529-6655. **$59-$99.** 5871 S 6th St Frontage Road 62703. I-55, exit 90 (Toronto Rd), just e to 6th St, then just n. Int corridors. **Pets:** Medium. $10 daily fee/pet. Designated rooms, service with restrictions, supervision. [SAVE] [X] [♿] [🖥] [🖥] [≈]

Best Western Clearlake Plaza H

(217) 525-7420. **$89-$150.** 3440 E Clearlake Ave 62702. I-55, exit 98B, just w. Int corridors. **Pets:** $35 one-time fee/pet. Service with restrictions, supervision. [SAVE] [X] [♿] [🖥] [🖥] [≈]

Drury Inn & Suites-Springfield H

(217) 529-3900. **$85-$159.** 3180 S Dirksen Pkwy 62703. I-55, exit 94 (Stevenson Dr), just w to Dirksen Pkwy, then just n. Int corridors. **Pets:** Other species. No service, supervision.
[ASK] [X] [♿] [🖥] [🖥] [≈]

Hilton Springfield H 🐾

(217) 789-1530. **$99-$224.** 700 E Adams St 62701. At 7th St; just e of Old State Capitol; downtown. Int corridors. **Pets:** Small, dogs only. $75 one-time fee/pet. Designated rooms, service with restrictions, supervision.
[X] [🖥] [🖥] [🍴] [≈]

Holiday Inn Express Hotel & Suites H

(217) 529-7771. **$89-$111.** 3050 S Dirksen Pkwy 62703. I-55, exit 94 (Stevenson Dr), just w to S Dirksen Pkwy, then 0.4 mi n. Int corridors. **Pets:** Medium, other species. $25 one-time fee/room. Service with restrictions, supervision. [SAVE] [X] [♿] [🖥] [🖥] [≈]

Mansion View Inn & Suites H

(217) 544-7411. **$89.** 529 S 4th St 62701. I-55, exit 92 (6th St), 3.9 mi n to Edwards St, then just w, follow signs. Ext/int corridors. **Pets:** Small. $25 one-time fee/room. Designated rooms, service with restrictions, crate. [SAVE] [X] [🖥] [🖥]

Microtel Inn & Suites H

(217) 753-2636. **$69-$99.** 2636 Sunrise Dr 62703. I-55, exit 94 (Stevenson Dr), just w to Dirksen Pkwy, then 0.4 mi n. Int corridors. **Pets:** Small, dogs only. $5 daily fee/pet. Service with restrictions, crate.
[ASK] [X] [♿] [🖥] [🖥] [≈]

Pear Tree Inn by Drury-Springfield H

(217) 529-9100. **$50-$109.** 3190 S Dirksen Pkwy 62703. I-55, exit 94 (Stevenson Dr), just w. Int corridors. **Pets:** Other species. No service, supervision. [ASK] [X] [🖥]

Red Roof Inn #10040 M

(217) 753-4302. **$47-$90.** 3200 Singer Ave 62703. I-55, exit 96B, just w. Ext corridors. **Pets:** Large. Service with restrictions, crate. [ASK] [X]

Sleep Inn by Choice Hotels H

(217) 787-6200. **Call for rates.** 3470 Freedom Dr 62704. I-72, exit 93 (Veterans Pkwy), 0.7 mi n to Lindbergh Blvd, just w to Freedom Dr, then just s. Int corridors. **Pets:** Accepted. [X] [🖥] [🖥]

Staybridge Suites Springfield South H

(217) 793-6700. **$134-$194.** 4231 Schooner Dr 62711. I-72, exit 93 (Veterans Pkwy), 0.4 mi se. Int corridors. **Pets:** Accepted.
[ASK] [X] [♿] [🖥] [🖥] [≈] [X]

STAUNTON

Staunton Super 8 H

(618) 635-5353. **$54.** 1527 Herman Rd 62088. I-55, exit 41, 0.5 mi w. Int corridors. **Pets:** Medium. $10 one-time fee/room. Designated rooms, service with restrictions, supervision. [ASK] [X] [🖥] [🖥]

STOCKTON

Country Inn & Suites By Carlson H

(815) 947-6060. **$90-$142.** 200 Dillon Ave 61085. On US 20, just e of SR 78. Int corridors. **Pets:** Large. $20 daily fee/pet. Designated rooms, service with restrictions, crate. [ASK] [X] [♿] [🖥] [🖥] [≈]

SYCAMORE

Americas Best Value Inn & Suites H

(815) 899-6500. **$89-$129.** 1860 Dekalb Ave 60178. On SR 23, 0.9 mi s of Peace Rd. Int corridors. **Pets:** Medium. $10 daily fee/pet. Service with restrictions, supervision. [ASK] [X] [♿] [🖥] [🖥]

TROY

Super 8 H

(618) 667-8888. **$60-$90, 3 day notice.** 910 Edwardsville Rd 62294. I-55/70, exit 18, just w. Int corridors. **Pets:** Medium. $10 daily fee/room. Service with restrictions, supervision. [SAVE] [X] [🖥] [🖥] [≈]

TUSCOLA

Baymont Inn & Suites H

(217) 253-3500. **$79-$112.** 1006 Southline Rd 61953. I-57, exit 212 (US 36), 0.3 mi w. Int corridors. **Pets:** Small. $10 daily fee/room. Service with restrictions, supervision. [ASK] [X] [♿] [🖥] [🖥] [≈]

Holiday Inn Express H

(217) 253-6363. **$99-$125.** 1201 Tuscola Blvd 61953. I-57, exit 212 (US 36), 0.3 mi w to Progress Blvd, just s to Tuscola Blvd, then 0.4 mi se. Int corridors. **Pets:** Accepted. [ASK] [X] [♿] [🖥] [🖥]

Super 8-Tuscola H

(217) 253-5488. **$53-$70.** 1007 E Southline Rd 61953. I-57, exit 212 (US 36), 0.4 mi w. Int corridors. **Pets:** Other species. $10 daily fee/pet. Designated rooms, service with restrictions, supervision. [ASK] [X] [🖥] [🖥]

URBANA

Ramada-Urbana/Champaign H 🐾

(217) 328-4400. **$75-$135.** 902 W Killarney St 61801. I-74, exit 183 (Lincoln Ave), just s to Killarney St, then just w. Int corridors. **Pets:** $10 one-time fee/room. Service with restrictions. [SAVE] [X] [🖥] [🖥] [≈]

Sleep Inn H

(217) 367-6000. **Call for rates.** 1908 N Lincoln Ave 61801. I-74, exit 183 (Lincoln Ave), 0.5 mi s. Int corridors. **Pets:** Accepted.
[SAVE] [X] [🖥] [🖥] [≈]

VANDALIA

Days Inn-Vandalia M

(618) 283-4400. **$67-$85.** 1920 Kennedy Blvd 62471. I-70, exit 63 (US 51), 0.6 mi n. Ext corridors. **Pets:** Other species. $10 deposit/room. Service with restrictions, supervision. [SAVE] [X] [🖥] [🖥] [≈]

Holiday Inn Express Hotel & Suites H

(618) 283-0010. **Call for rates.** 21 Mattes Ave 62471. I-70, exit 61, just s. Int corridors. **Pets:** Accepted. [X] [♿] [🖥] [🖥] [≈]

Jay's Inn M

(618) 283-1200. **$56-$65.** 720 Gochenour St 62471. I-70, exit 63 (US 51), just s. Ext corridors. **Pets:** Other species. Service with restrictions. [SAVE] [X] [🖥] [🖥]

◆◆ Ramada Vandalia [H]

(618) 283-1400. **$60-$100.** 2707 Veterans Ave 62471. I-70, exit 61, just s. Int corridors. **Pets:** Other species. $10 one-time fee/pet. No service, crate. (ASK) (X) ⬛ 🖥 ⬱

WASHINGTON
◆ Super 8 [H]

(309) 444-8881. **$46-$62, 10 day notice.** 1884 Washington Rd 61571. On Business Rt US 24, 1.5 mi w. Int corridors. **Pets:** Medium, other species. $8 one-time fee/pet. Service with restrictions. (ASK) (X) ⬛ 🖥

WATSEKA
(AAA) ◆◆ Super 8 [H]

(815) 432-6000. **$63-$85.** 710 W Walnut St 60970. On US 24; center of downtown. Int corridors. **Pets:** Small. $25 deposit/pet, $10 daily fee/pet. Service with restrictions, supervision. (SAVE) (X) ⬛ 🖥

WENONA
◆◆ Super 8 [H] ❀

(815) 853-4371. **$64-$69.** 5 Cavalry Dr 61377. I-39, exit 35. Int corridors. **Pets:** Large. $5 daily fee/pet. Designated rooms, service with restrictions, supervision. (ASK) (X) ⬛ 🖥

INDIANA

ANGOLA

▽▽▽▽ Ramada Inn 🅗
(260) 665-9471. **$75-$155.** 3855 N SR 127 46703. I-69, exit 154, just e, then 0.4 mi s. Int corridors. **Pets:** Other species. $25 one-time fee/room. Service with restrictions, supervision.

Ⓐ🆂🅺 ✕ 🛢 💻 🍴 ⊁ ⊠

AUBURN

🔺🔺🔺 ▽▽▽▽ The Auburn Inn 🅗
(260) 925-6363. **$80-$130.** 225 Touring Dr 46706. I-69, exit 129 (SR 8), just e, then just s. Int corridors. **Pets:** Other species. $50 deposit/room, $20 one-time fee/room. Designated rooms, service with restrictions, supervision. Ⓢ🅰🆅🅴 ✕ 🛢 💻 ⊁

▽▽▽ Holiday Inn Express 🅗
(260) 925-1900. **Call for rates.** 404 Touring Dr 46706. I-69, exit 129 (SR 8), just e, then just s. Int corridors. **Pets:** Accepted.

✕ 🄼 🛢 💻 ⊁

▽▽ La Quinta Inn Auburn 🅗 🌼
(260) 920-1900. **Call for rates.** 306 Touring Dr 46706. I-69, exit 129 (SR 8), 0.5 mi e. Int corridors. **Pets:** Medium, other species. Service with restrictions, supervision. ✕ 🛢 💻 ⊁

▽▽▽ Super 8-Auburn 🅗
(260) 927-8800. **Call for rates.** 503 Ley Dr 46706. I-69, exit 129 (SR 8), just e, then just s. Int corridors. **Pets:** Accepted. ✕ 🛢 💻

BEDFORD

🔺🔺🔺 ▽▽▽▽ Bedford Comfort Inn 🅗
(812) 279-8111. **$70-$99.** 911 Constitution Ave 47421. Jct SR 37 and 58, just s on SR 37. Int corridors. **Pets:** Medium. $25 one-time fee/pet. Designated rooms, service with restrictions, supervision.

Ⓢ🅰🆅🅴 ✕ 🄼 🛢 💻 🍴 ⊁

▽▽▽ Bedford Super 8 🅗
(812) 275-8881. **$65-$145.** 501 Bell Back Rd 47421. Jct SR 37 and 58, just e on SR 58. Int corridors. **Pets:** $10 daily fee/pet.

Ⓐ🆂🅺 ✕ 🛢 💻 ⊁ ⊠

🔺🔺🔺 ▽▽▽▽ Holiday Inn Express 🅗
(812) 279-1206. **$85-$121.** 2800 Express Ln 47421. On US 50/SR 37, 1.4 mi s of jct SR 450. Int corridors. **Pets:** Accepted.

Ⓢ🅰🆅🅴 ✕ 🛢 💻 ⊁

BERNE

▽▽ Black Bear Inn & Suites 🅗
(260) 589-8955. **$68-$73.** 1335 US 27 N 46711. On US 27, 1 mi n. Int corridors. **Pets:** Small. $5 daily fee/pet. Designated rooms, service with restrictions, crate. Ⓐ🆂🅺 ✕ 🛢 💻 ⊁

BLOOMINGTON

▽▽▽▽ Comfort Inn Bloomington 🅗
(812) 650-0010. **$89-$209.** 1700 N Kinser Pike 47404. On SR 45 and 45 Bypass, 1 mi e of jct SR 37. Int corridors. **Pets:** Accepted.

Ⓐ🆂🅺 ✕ 💻 ⊁

▽▽▽▽ Crowne Plaza 🅗
(812) 334-3252. **$109-$159.** 1710 N Kinser Pike 47404. On SR 45 and 46 Bypass, 1 mi e of jct SR 37. Int corridors. **Pets:** Small. $75 one-time fee/room. Designated rooms, service with restrictions, supervision. Ⓐ🆂🅺 ✕ 🄼 💻 🍴 ⊁

▽▽▽▽ Fairfield Inn by Marriott 🅗
(812) 331-1122. **$116-$142.** 120 Fairfield Dr 47404. Just e from SR 37 at 3rd St. Int corridors. **Pets:** Small, dogs only. $75 one-time fee/room.

✕ 🄼 🛢 💻 ⊁

▽▽▽ Hampton Inn 🅗
(812) 334-2100. **$99-$449.** 2100 N Walnut St 47404. 1 mi e of jct SR 37 on SR 45/46 Bypass, then just s on College Ave/Walnut St. Int corridors. **Pets:** Accepted. ✕ 🛢 💻 ⊁

▽▽▽ TownePlace Suites By Marriott 🅗
(812) 334-1234. **$116-$142.** 105 S Franklin Rd 47404. Just e from SR 37 at 3rd St, then 0.3 mi n. Int corridors. **Pets:** Accepted.

✕ 🛢 💻 ⊁

BREMEN

▽▽▽▽ Scottish Bed and Breakfast 🅑🅑 🌼
(574) 220-6672. **$99-$139, 14 day notice.** 2180 Miami Tr 46506. Jct SR 331, 2 mi w on SR 106, just s. Int corridors. **Pets:** Dogs only. $25 one-time fee/room. Designated rooms, service with restrictions, supervision. Ⓐ🆂🅺 ✕ 🛢 ⊁ ⊘

CENTERVILLE

▽▽▽▽ Historic Lantz House Inn 🅑🅑
(765) 855-2936. **Call for rates.** 214 W Main St 47330. I-70, exit 145, 3 mi s to US 40 (W Main St), then just w. Ext/int corridors. **Pets:** Accepted.

✕ 🛢 💻 🆆 ⊘

CHESTERTON

▽▽▽▽ Gray Goose Inn 🅑🅑 🌼
(219) 926-5781. **$110-$195, 10 day notice.** 350 Indian Boundary Rd 46304. I-94, exit 26A, 0.6 mi s, then just w. Int corridors. **Pets:** $25 one-time fee/pet. Service with restrictions, supervision. Ⓐ🆂🅺 ✕

CINCINNATI METROPOLITAN AREA (NEARBY OHIO)

LAWRENCEBURG

ⒶⒶⒶ ▼▼▼ Comfort Inn & Suites 🅷
(812) 539-3600. **$80-$170.** 1610 Flossie Dr 47025. I-275, exit 16, 0.3 mi e. Int corridors. **Pets:** Small. $20 daily fee/pet. Designated rooms, service with restrictions, crate. 🆂🅰🆅🅴 ☒ ⓖⓜ 🎁 💻 ⇴

▼▼ Quality Inn & Suites 🅷
(812) 539-4770. **$80-$90.** 1000 E Eads Pkwy 47025. I-275, exit 16, 0.5 mi w on US 50. Int corridors. **Pets:** Accepted. 🅰🆂🅺 ☒ 🎁 💻 ⇴

END METROPOLITAN AREA

CLARKSVILLE

ⒶⒶⒶ ▼▼▼ Best Western Green Tree Inn Ⓜ
(812) 288-9281. **$80-$100.** 1425 Broadway St 47129. I-65, exit 4, just w. Ext corridors. **Pets:** Medium, dogs only. Service with restrictions, crate. 🆂🅰🆅🅴 ☒ 🎁 💻 ⇴

CLOVERDALE

▼▼ Super 8 Cloverdale/Greencastle 🅷 🐾
(765) 795-7373. **$56-$150.** 1020 N Main St 46120. I-70, exit 41, just s on US 231. Int corridors. **Pets:** Dogs only. Service with restrictions. 🅰🆂🅺 ☒ ⓖⓜ 🎁 💻 ⇴

COLUMBIA CITY

▼▼ Quality Inn 🅷
(260) 248-4551. **Call for rates.** 701 W Connexion Way 46725. 1 mi w of SR 9, just off US 30. Int corridors. **Pets:** Medium. $10 daily fee/pet. Service with restrictions, supervision. ☒ ⓖⓜ 🎁 💻 ⇴

COLUMBUS

▼▼▼ Columbus Holiday Inn and Conference Center 🅷
(812) 372-1541. **Call for rates.** 2480 Jonathan Moore Pike 47201. I-65, exit 68, just e on SR 46. Ext/int corridors. **Pets:** Other species. $25 one-time fee/room. Designated rooms, service with restrictions, supervision. ☒ ⓖⓜ 🎁 💻 🍽 ⇴ ☒

▼▼ Hotel Indigo 🅷
(812) 375-9100. **$99-$189.** 400 Brown St 47201. Jct 4th St. Int corridors. **Pets:** Accepted. 🅰🆂🅺 ☒ ⓖⓜ 🎁 💻 🍽 ⇴

CRAWFORDSVILLE

ⒶⒶⒶ ▼▼▼ Comfort Inn 🅷
(765) 361-0665. **$69-$159.** 2991 N Gandhi Dr 47933. I-74, exit 34, just s on US 231. Int corridors. **Pets:** Accepted. 🆂🅰🆅🅴 ☒ 🎁 💻 ⇴

▼▼ Quality Inn Crawfordsville 🅷
(765) 362-8700. **$69-$125.** 2500 N Lafayette Rd 47933. I-74, exit 34, 0.3 mi s on US 231. Ext corridors. **Pets:** Small, other species. $15 daily fee/room. Designated rooms, service with restrictions, supervision. 🅰🆂🅺 ☒ ⓖⓜ 🎁 💻 🍽 ⇴

DALE

ⒶⒶⒶ ▼▼▼ Best Western Lincolnland Inn 🅷
(812) 937-7000. **$80-$200.** 1339 N Washington St 47523. I-64, exit 57 (US 231), just s. Int corridors. **Pets:** Medium. $10 daily fee/pet. Designated rooms, service with restrictions, supervision. 🆂🅰🆅🅴 ☒ ⓖⓜ 🎁 💻 ⇴

DECATUR

▼▼ Americas Best Value Inn Ⓜ
(260) 728-2196. **$55-$79.** 1033 N 13th St 46733. On US 27 and 33, 0.5 mi n of jct US 224. Ext/int corridors. **Pets:** Dogs only. $5 daily fee/pet. Service with restrictions, crate. 🅰🆂🅺 ☒ 🎁 💻 ⇴

▼▼ Baymont Inn & Suites 🅷
(260) 728-4600. **$69-$89.** 1201 S 13th St 46733. On US 27 and 33, 1 mi s of jct US 224. Int corridors. **Pets:** Accepted. ☒ ⓖⓜ 🎁 💻 ⇴

▼▼ Quality Inn 🅷
(260) 724-8888. **$75-$95, 7 day notice.** 1302 S 13th St 46733. 1 mi s on US 27 and 33. Int corridors. **Pets:** Accepted. 🅰🆂🅺 ☒ ⓖⓜ 🎁 💻 ⇴

ELKHART

▼▼▼ Candlewood Suites 🅷
(574) 262-8600. **$80-$225.** 300 Northpointe Blvd 46514. I-80/90, exit 92, just n on SR 19, then just w. Int corridors. **Pets:** Accepted. 🅰🆂🅺 ☒ ⓖⓜ 🎁 💻

▼▼▼ Jameson Inn Elkhart 🅷
(574) 264-7222. **$80-$85.** 3010 Brittany Ct 46514. I-80/90, exit 92, 0.3 mi s on SR 19. Int corridors. **Pets:** Other species. $15 daily fee/pet. Service with restrictions. 🅰🆂🅺 ☒ ⓖⓜ 🎁 💻 ⇴

EVANSVILLE

ⒶⒶⒶ ▼▼▼▼ Baymont Inn & Suites Evansville East 🅷
(812) 477-2677. **$79.** 8005 E Division St 47715. I-164, exit 7B (SR 66/Lloyd Expwy), 0.5 mi w to Cross Pointe Blvd, just n to Division St, then 0.5 mi e. Int corridors. **Pets:** Medium. $10 daily fee/pet. Designated rooms, service with restrictions, crate. 🆂🅰🆅🅴 ☒ ⓖⓜ 🎁 💻 ⇴

ⒶⒶⒶ ▼▼▼ Best Western Gateway Inn & Suites 🅷
(812) 868-8000. **$60-$130.** 324 Rusher Creek Rd 47725. I-64, exit 25A (US 41), 0.5 mi s, then just w. Int corridors. **Pets:** Accepted. 🆂🅰🆅🅴 ☒ ⓖⓜ 🎁 💻 ⇴

ⒶⒶⒶ ▼▼▼ Casino Aztar Hotel 🅷
(812) 433-4000. **$109-$159.** 421 NW Riverside Dr 47708. SR 62 (Lloyd Expwy), just s on Fulton. Int corridors. **Pets:** Small, dogs only. $250 deposit/room. Designated rooms, service with restrictions. 🆂🅰🆅🅴 ☒ ⓖⓜ 🎁 💻 🍽

▼▼ Comfort Inn East 🅷
(812) 476-3600. **$74-$89.** 8331 E Walnut St 47715. I-164, exit 7B (SR 66/Lloyd Expwy), 0.5 mi w to Eagle Crest Blvd, just s to Fuquay St, just s to Walnut St, then 0.4 mi e. Int corridors. **Pets:** Small, other species. $10 one-time fee/room. Designated rooms, service with restrictions. 🅰🆂🅺 ☒ ⓖⓜ 🎁 💻 ⇴

▼▼ Comfort Inn North 🅷
(812) 867-1600. **Call for rates.** 19622 Elpers Rd 47725. I-64, exit 25A (US 41), 0.5 mi s, then just w. Int corridors. **Pets:** Accepted. ☒ 🎁 💻 ⇴

▼▼▼ Drury Inn & Suites-Evansville East 🅷
(812) 471-3400. **$90-$169.** 100 Cross Pointe Blvd 47715. I-164, exit 7B (SR 66/Lloyd Expwy), 0.5 mi w. Int corridors. **Pets:** Other species. No service, supervision. 🅰🆂🅺 ☒ ⓖⓜ 🎁 💻 ⇴ ☒

▼▼▼ Drury Inn & Suites-Evansville North 🅷
(812) 423-5818. **$85-$154.** 3901 US 41 N 47711. On US 41, 2.5 mi n of jct SR 62 and 66 (Lloyd Expwy), 3.3 mi sw of Evansville Regional Airport entrance. Int corridors. **Pets:** Other species. No service, supervision. 🅰🆂🅺 ☒ 🎁 💻 ⇴

ⒶⒶⒶ ▼▼▼ Holiday Inn Express–Evansville West 🅷 ❀

(812) 421-9773. **$89-$199.** 5737 Pearl Dr 47712. Jct US 41 and SR 62, 5.7 mi w on SR 62, then just s on Boehne Camp Rd. Int corridors. **Pets:** Medium, other species. $15 one-time fee/room. Service with restrictions, crate. SAVE ⊠ ⓜ 🛏 💻 🛶

▼▼ HomeLife Studios & Suites 🅼

(812) 475-1700. **Call for rates.** 100 S Green River Rd 47715. I-164, exit 7B (SR 66/Lloyd Expwy), 2 mi w to Green River Rd, then just s. Ext corridors. **Pets:** Accepted. ⊠ 🛏 💻 🛶

▼▼▼ Jameson Inn Evansville 🅷

(812) 476-9626. **$80-$85.** 1101 N Green River Rd 47715. I-164, exit 9 (SR 62 E/Morgan Ave), 1.5 mi w on SR 62, then just s. Int corridors. **Pets:** Accepted. ASK ⊠ ⓜ 🛏 💻 🛶

▼▼▼ La Quinta Inn & Suites 🅷 🐾

(812) 471-3414. **Call for rates.** 8015 E Division St 47715. I-164, exit 7B (SR 66/ Lloyd Expwy), 0.5 mi w to Cross Pointe Blvd, just n, then 0.5 mi e. Int corridors. **Pets:** Medium, other species. Service with restrictions, supervision. ⊠ 🛏 💻 🛶

▼▼▼ Residence Inn by Marriott Evansville East 🅷

(812) 471-7191. **$139-$149.** 8283 E Walnut St 47715. I-164, exit 7B (SR 66/Lloyd Expwy), 0.5 mi w to Eagle Crest Blvd, 0.3 mi se to Fuquay St, then 0.3 mi e. Int corridors. **Pets:** Other species. $100 one-time fee/room. Service with restrictions, crate. ⊠ ⓜ 🛏 💻 🛶 ⊠

▼▼ Studio Plus Evansville East 🅷

(812) 479-0103. **$62-$72.** 301 Eagle Crest Dr 47715. I-164, exit 7B (SR 66/Lloyd Expwy), 0.5 mi w to Eagle Crest Blvd, 0.5 mi s, then just e. Int corridors. **Pets:** Other species. $25 daily fee/room. Designated rooms, service with restrictions, crate. ASK ⊠ 🛏 🛶

FERDINAND

▼▼▼ Comfort Inn 🅷

(812) 367-1122. **Call for rates.** 440 S Main St 47532. I-64, exit 63. Int corridors. **Pets:** Medium. $10 daily fee/pet. Designated rooms, service with restrictions, supervision. ⊠ ⓜ 🛏 💻 🛶

FORT WAYNE

▼▼ Baymont Inn Fort Wayne 🅷

(260) 489-2220. **$60-$89.** 1005 W Washington Center Rd 46825. I-69, exit 111B, just n on SR 3, then 0.4 mi e. Int corridors. **Pets:** Other species. $100 deposit/room. Service with restrictions, crate.

ASK ⊠ 🛏 💻

ⒶⒶⒶ ▼▼▼ Best Western Luxbury Inn Fort Wayne 🅷

(260) 436-0242. **$80-$90.** 5501 Coventry Ln 46804. I-69, exit 102. Int corridors. **Pets:** Medium. $10 daily fee/pet. Designated rooms, service with restrictions, supervision. SAVE ⊠ 🛏 💻 🛶

▼▼▼ Candlewood Suites 🅷

(260) 484-1400. **$94-$149.** 5250 Distribution Dr 46809. I-69, exit 111A, just e. Int corridors. **Pets:** Accepted. ASK ⊠ ⓜ 🛏 💻 🛶

▼▼▼ Don Hall's Guesthouse 🅷

(260) 489-2524. **$89-$99, 3 day notice.** 1313 W Washington Center Rd 46825. I-69, exit 111B, just n on SR 3, then 0.3 mi e. Ext/int corridors. **Pets:** Medium, dogs only. $10 daily fee/pet. Service with restrictions, crate. ASK ⊠ 🛏 💻 🍴 🛶 ⊠

▼▼▼ Extended StayAmerica-Fort Wayne-South 🅷

(260) 432-1916. **$54-$64.** 8309 W Jefferson Blvd 46804. I-69, exit 102, 0.4 mi e on US 24, then 0.6 mi s. Int corridors. **Pets:** Other species. $25 daily fee/room. Designated rooms, service with restrictions, crate.

ASK ⊠ 🛏 💻

ⒶⒶⒶ ▼▼▼ Hilton Fort Wayne at Grand Wayne Convention Center 🅷 ❀

(260) 420-1100. **$99-$189.** 1020 S Calhoun St 46802. Jct Jefferson Blvd; center. Int corridors. **Pets:** Large. $50 one-time fee/pet. Service with restrictions, crate. SAVE ⊠ ⓜ 🛏 💻 🍴 🛶

ⒶⒶⒶ ▼▼▼ Quality Inn 🅷

(260) 489-5554. **$74-$99.** 1734 W Washington Center Rd 46818. I-69, exit 111B, just n on SR 3. Int corridors. **Pets:** Accepted.

SAVE ⊠ 🛏 💻 🛶

▼▼▼▼ Residence Inn by Marriott Fort Wayne 🅷

(260) 484-4700. **$161-$197.** 4919 Lima Rd 46808. I-69, exit 111A, 0.4 mi s on US 27. Ext corridors. **Pets:** Other species. $100 one-time fee/room. Service with restrictions. ⊠ 🛏 💻 🛶 ⊠

▼▼▼▼ Residence Inn Southwest 🅷

(260) 432-8000. **$116-$142.** 7811 W Jefferson Blvd 46804. I-69, exit 102, 0.5 mi e. Int corridors. **Pets:** Accepted. ⊠ 🛏 💻 🛶 ⊠

▼▼▼▼ Staybridge Suites 🅷

(260) 432-2427. **Call for rates.** 5925 Ellison Rd 46804. I-69, exit 102, just w. Int corridors. **Pets:** Accepted. ⊠ ⓜ 🛏 💻 🛶 ⊠

FRENCH LICK

▼▼▼▼ Comfort Suites 🅷

(812) 936-5300. **$100-$160.** 9530 W SR 56 47432. Jct SR 145, 1.2 mi sw. Int corridors. **Pets:** Accepted. ASK ⊠ ⓜ 🛏 💻 🛶

ⒶⒶⒶ ▼▼▼▼ French Lick Resort 🅷

(812) 936-9300. **$139-$299, 3 day notice.** 8670 W SR 56 47432. Jct SR 145. Int corridors. **Pets:** Dogs only. $50 one-time fee/room. Designated rooms, service with restrictions, crate. SAVE ⊠ ⓜ 🛏 💻 🍴 🛶 ⊠

GAS CITY

ⒶⒶⒶ ▼▼▼ Best Western Gas City 🅼

(765) 998-2331. **$79-$85.** 4936 Kaybee Dr 46933. I-69, exit 59, just e. Int corridors. **Pets:** $20 one-time fee/pet. Designated rooms, service with restrictions, supervision. SAVE ⊠ ⓜ 🛏 💻 🛶

GOSHEN

ⒶⒶⒶ ▼▼▼ Best Western Inn 🅼 ❀

(574) 533-0408. **$96.** 900 Lincolnway E 46526. 1 mi se on US 33. Ext corridors. **Pets:** Service with restrictions, crate. SAVE ⊠ 🛏 💻

GREENCASTLE

▼▼ College Inn 🅼

(765) 653-4167. **$35-$75, 7 day notice.** 315 Bloomington St 46135. I-70, exit 41, 8 mi n on US 231. Ext corridors. **Pets:** Accepted.

ASK ⊠ 🛏

GREENSBURG

ⒶⒶⒶ ▼▼▼ Hampton Inn & Suites 🅷 ❀

(812) 663-5000. **$74-$169.** 2075 N Michigan Ave 47240. I-74, exit 132, just se. Int corridors. **Pets:** Medium, other species. Service with restrictions, supervision. SAVE ⊠ ⓜ 🛏 💻 🛶

▼▼▼ Holiday Inn Express 🅷

(812) 663-5500. **$89-$159.** 915 Ann Blvd 47240. I-74, exit 134A, 1.4 mi s on SR 3. Int corridors. **Pets:** Other species. $25 deposit/pet. Service with restrictions, supervision. ASK ⊠ 🛏 💻 🛶

HAMMOND

ⒶⒶⒶ ▼▼▼ Best Western Northwest Indiana Inn 🅷

(219) 844-2140. **$100-$130.** 3830 179th St 46323. I-80/94, exit 5, 0.6 mi s on Cline Ave (SR 912), then 0.6 mi n on frontage road (179th St). Int corridors. **Pets:** Medium, other species. $45 deposit/room, $10 daily fee/pet. Designated rooms, service with restrictions, supervision.

SAVE ⊠ 🛏 💻 🍴 🛶

▼▼▼▼ Residence Inn by Marriott Chicago Southeast 🅷 ❀

(219) 844-8440. **$159-$179.** 7740 Corinne Dr 46323. I-80/94, exit 3 (Kennedy Ave S), just s. Int corridors. **Pets:** Medium, other species. $100 one-time fee/room. Service with restrictions, crate.

⊠ ⓜ 🛏 💻 🛶 ⊠

HOWE

▼▼▼▼ Holiday Inn Express-Howe/Sturgis **H**

(260) 562-3660. **$99-$159.** 0045 W 750 N 46746. I-80/90, exit 121 (US 66). Int corridors. **Pets:** Other species. $35 one-time fee/room. Service with restrictions. (A$K) ⊠ (&M) 🔒 🖵 ⇒

HUNTINGTON

▼▼ Super 8 **H**

(260) 358-8888. **$59-$100.** 2801 Guilford St 46750. From US 24, just n. Int corridors. **Pets:** Accepted. (A$K) ⊠ 🔒 🖵 ⇒

INDIANAPOLIS METROPOLITAN AREA

BROWNSBURG

▼▼▼▼ Holiday Inn Express Brownsburg **H** 🐾

(317) 852-5353. **$99-$159.** 31 Maplehurst Dr 46112. I-74, exit 66, just n on SR 267. Int corridors. **Pets:** Other species. $25 one-time fee/room. Service with restrictions, crate. (A$K) ⊠ 🔒 🖵 ⇒

CARMEL

▼▼▼▼ Jameson Inn Carmel **H**

(317) 816-1616. **$90-$95.** 10201 N Meridian St 46290. I-465, exit 31, 0.3 mi n on US 31. Int corridors. **Pets:** Accepted.

(A$K) ⊠ (&M) 🔒 🖵 ⇒ ⊠

▼▼▼▼ Residence Inn by Marriott Indianapolis/Carmel **H**

(317) 846-2000. **$134-$164.** 11895 N Meridian St 46032. I-465, exit 31, 2 mi n on US 31, just e on 116th St, then just n on Pennsylvania Rd. Int corridors. **Pets:** Accepted. ⊠ (&M) 🔒 🖵 ⇒ ⊠

EDINBURGH

(AAA) ▼▼▼ Best Western Horizon Inn **H**

(812) 526-9883. **$76-$130, 14 day notice.** 11780 N US 31 46124. I-65, exit 76B, just n. Int corridors. **Pets:** Accepted. (SAVE) ⊠ 🔒 🖵 ⇒

FISHERS

(AAA) ▼▼▼▼ Comfort Suites **H**

(317) 578-1200. **$75-$190, 3 day notice.** 9760 Crosspoint Blvd 46256. I-69, exit 3, just w on 96th St, then just n. Int corridors. **Pets:** Large. $10 daily fee/pet. Service with restrictions, supervision.

(SAVE) ⊠ 🔒 🖵 ⇒

▼▼▼▼ Hotel Indigo **H** 🐾

(317) 558-4100. **$94-$199.** 9791 North by Northeast Blvd 46037. I-69, exit 3, just ne. Int corridors. **Pets:** Other species. $20 one-time fee/room. Service with restrictions, crate. (A$K) ⊠ (&M) 🔒 🖵 🍴 ⇒ ⊠

▼▼▼▼ Residence Inn by Marriott Indianapolis/Fishers **H**

(317) 842-1111. **$139-$169.** 9765 Crosspoint Blvd 46256. I-69, exit 3, just nw. Int corridors. **Pets:** Accepted. ⊠ (&M) 🔒 🖵 ⇒ ⊠

▼▼▼▼ Staybridge Suites Indianapolis-Fishers **H**

(317) 577-9500. **$99-$189.** 9780 Crosspoint Blvd 46256. I-69, exit 3, just nw. Int corridors. **Pets:** Accepted. (A$K) ⊠ (&M) 🔒 🖵 ⇒ ⊠

GREENFIELD

(AAA) ▼▼▼ Comfort Inn-Greenfield/Indianapolis **H**

(317) 467-9999. **$70-$159.** 178 E Martindale Dr 46140. I-70, exit 104, 0.4 mi s on State St. Int corridors. **Pets:** Accepted.

(SAVE) ⊠ 🔒 🖵 ⇒

(AAA) ▼▼▼ Quality Inn Greenfield **H** 🐾

(317) 462-7112. **$60-$150.** 2270 N State St 46140. I-70, exit 104, just s. Int corridors. **Pets:** Large. $25 daily fee/pet. Designated rooms, service with restrictions, supervision. (SAVE) ⊠ 🔒 🖵 ⇒

GREENWOOD

(AAA) ▼▼▼ Red Roof Inn **M**

(317) 887-1515. **Call for rates.** 110 Sheek Rd 46143. I-65, exit 99, just w. Ext corridors. **Pets:** Large. Service with restrictions, crate.

(SAVE) ⊠ 🔒 ⇒

INDIANAPOLIS

(AAA) ▼▼▼ Baymont Inn & Suites **H**

(317) 322-2000. **$89-$159, 3 day notice.** 1540 Brookville Crossing Way 46239. I-465, exit 47, 0.3 mi e. Int corridors. **Pets:** Service with restrictions, supervision. (SAVE) ⊠ (&M) 🔒 🖵 ⇒

(AAA) ▼▼▼▼ Best Western Airport Suites **H**

(317) 246-1505. **$80-$90, 30 day notice.** 55 S High School Rd 46241. I-465, exit 13B, just w. Int corridors. **Pets:** Accepted. (SAVE) ⊠ 🔒 🖵

(AAA) ▼▼▼▼ Best Western Castleton Inn **H**

(317) 842-9190. **$59-$199.** 8300 Craig St 46250. I-69, exit 1, 0.5 mi w. Int corridors. **Pets:** Medium. $25 one-time fee/pet. Service with restrictions, crate. (SAVE) ⊠ 🔒 🖵 ⇒

▼▼ Candlewood Suites **H** 🐾

(317) 595-9292. **$80-$159.** 8111 Bash St 46250. I-69, exit 1, just w. Int corridors. **Pets:** Large, other species. $25 one-time fee/room.

(A$K) ⊠ 🔒 🖵 ⇒ ⊠

▼▼▼▼ Candlewood Suites Indianapolis NW **H**

(317) 298-8000. **Call for rates.** 7455 Woodland Dr 46278. I-465, exit 21 (73rd St), just n. Int corridors. **Pets:** Large, other species. $25 one-time fee/room. Service with restrictions, crate. ⊠ (&M) 🔒 🖵 ⇒

▼▼▼▼ Clarion Hotel & Conference Center **H**

(317) 299-8400. **$52-$224.** 2930 Waterfront Parkway Dr W 46214. I-465, exit 16A, 0.3 mi se, then 0.8 mi w on US 136. Int corridors. **Pets:** Medium, other species. $50 deposit/room, $25 one-time fee/room. Designated rooms, service with restrictions, crate.

(A$K) ⊠ 🔒 🖵 🍴 ⇒

▼▼▼▼ Conrad Indianapolis **H**

(317) 713-5000. **Call for rates.** 50 W Washington St 46204. Jct Illinois St. Int corridors. **Pets:** Accepted. ⊠ (&M) 🔒 🖵 🍴 ⇒ ⊠

▼▼▼▼ Drury Inn & Suites Indianapolis Northeast **H**

(317) 849-8900. **$90-$239.** 8180 N Shadeland Ave 46250. I-69, exit 1, just e. Int corridors. **Pets:** Other species. No service, supervision.

(A$K) ⊠ (&M) 🔒 🖵 ⇒

▼▼▼ Drury Inn-Indianapolis **H**

(317) 876-9777. **$75-$174.** 9320 N Michigan Rd 46268. I-465, exit 27, just s. Int corridors. **Pets:** Other species. No service, supervision.

(A$K) ⊠ 🔒 🖵 ⇒

▼▼ Extended StayAmerica Indianapolis-Castleton **H**

(317) 596-1288. **$49-$59.** 7940 N Shadeland Ave 46250. I-69, exit 1, 0.5 mi s. Int corridors. **Pets:** Other species. $25 daily fee/room. Designated rooms, service with restrictions, crate. (A$K) ⊠ 🔒 🖵

▼▼ Extended StayAmerica-Indianapolis North **H**

(317) 843-1181. **$47-$52.** 9750 Lakeshore Dr 46280. I-465, exit 33, 0.4 mi n on Keystone Dr, 0.6 mi e on 96th St, then just n on Bauer Dr. Int corridors. **Pets:** Other species. $25 daily fee/room. Designated rooms, service with restrictions, crate. (A$K) ⊠ 🔒 🖵 ⇒

▼▼ Extended StayAmerica-Indianapolis-Northwest-College Park **H**

(317) 872-3090. **$44-$54.** 9030 Wesleyan Rd 46268. I-465, exit 27, just s to Depauw Blvd, just e, then just s. Int corridors. **Pets:** Other species. $25 daily fee/room. Designated rooms, service with restrictions, crate.

(A$K) ⊠ 🔒 🖵

Hilton Indianapolis 🏨 ❀
(317) 972-0600. **$119-$359.** 120 W Market St 46204. Jct Illinois St. Int corridors. **Pets:** Other species. $75 one-time fee/room. Service with restrictions, crate. SAVE ✕ ⬤M 🛏 💻 🍽 ➷ ✕

Hilton Indianapolis North Hotel 🏨
(317) 849-6668. **$109-$249.** 8181 N Shadeland Ave 46250. I-69, exit 1, just e. Int corridors. **Pets:** Accepted. ✕ 🛏 💻 🍽 ➷

Homestead Studio Suites Hotel-Indianapolis/Northwest 🏨
(317) 334-7829. **$49-$59.** 8520 Northwest Blvd 46278. I-465, exit 23, just e. Int corridors. **Pets:** Other species. $25 daily fee/room. Designated rooms, service with restrictions, crate. ASK ✕ ⬤M 🛏 💻 ➷

Indianapolis Marriott East 🏨
(317) 352-1231. **$152-$186.** 7202 E 21st St 46219. I-70, exit 89, 0.3 mi se; 0.5 mi w of jct I-465. Int corridors. **Pets:** Medium. $75 one-time fee/room. Designated rooms, service with restrictions, crate.
SAVE ✕ ⬤M 🛏 💻 🍽 ➷

Jameson Inn Indianapolis Castleton 🏨
(317) 849-8555. **$80-$85.** 8380 Kelly Ln 46250. I-465, exit 35 (Allisonville Rd), just s. Int corridors. **Pets:** Medium. $15 daily fee/room. Service with restrictions. ASK ✕ ⬤M 🛏 💻 ➷

Jameson Inn of Indianapolis South 🏨
(317) 784-7006. **$80-$85.** 4402 E Creekview Dr 46237. I-65, exit 103, just w. Int corridors. **Pets:** Accepted. ASK ✕ 🛏 💻 ➷

La Quinta Inn & Suites Indianapolis-Airport 🏨 ❀
(317) 244-8100. **$49-$89.** 2650 Executive Dr 46241. I-465, exit 11A southbound; exit 11B northbound, 0.3 mi e. Int corridors. **Pets:** Medium, other species. Service with restrictions, supervision.
ASK ✕ ⬤M 🛏 💻

La Quinta Inn Indianapolis Airport 🏨 ❀
(317) 247-4281. **$49-$89.** 5316 W Southern Ave 46241-5510. I-465, exit 11A, 0.5 mi e on Sam Jones Expwy to Lynhurst Dr. Int corridors. **Pets:** Medium, other species. Service with restrictions, supervision.
ASK ✕ 🛏 💻 ➷

La Quinta Inn Indianapolis (East) 🏨 ❀
(317) 359-1021. **$59-$129.** 7304 E 21st St 46219. I-70, exit 89, just s, then just e; 0.5 mi w of jct I-465. Int corridors. **Pets:** Medium, other species. Service with restrictions, supervision. ASK ✕ 🛏 💻 ➷

Omni Severin Hotel 🏨 ❀
(317) 634-6664. **Call for rates.** 40 W Jackson Pl 46225. Opposite Union Station. Int corridors. **Pets:** Small, dogs only. $50 one-time fee/room. Service with restrictions, supervision. SAVE ✕ ⬤M 🛏 💻 🍽 ➷

Quality Inn & Suites Airport 🏨
(317) 381-1000. **$70-$100.** 2631 S Lynhurst Dr 46241. I-465, exit 11A, 0.5 mi e on Sam Jones Expwy to Lynhurst Dr. Int corridors. **Pets:** Other species. $10 daily fee/pet. Designated rooms, service with restrictions.
ASK ✕ 🛏 💻 ➷

Quality Inn Downtown South 🏨
(317) 788-4774. **$70-$199.** 4502 S Harding St 46217. I-465, exit 4, just n. Int corridors. **Pets:** Accepted. SAVE ✕ 💻

Ramada Limited 🏨
(317) 297-1848. **$79-$199, 30 day notice.** 3851 Shore Dr 46254. I-465, exit 17, just w on 38th St, then just n. Ext corridors. **Pets:** Accepted.
ASK ✕ 🛏 💻 ➷

Residence Inn by Marriott Indianapolis Airport 🏨
(317) 244-1500. **$125-$153.** 5224 W Southern Ave 46241. I-465, exit 11A, 0.5 mi e on Sam Jones Expwy, exit Lynhurst Dr. Int corridors.
Pets: Accepted. ✕ ⬤M 🛏 💻 ➷ ✕

Residence Inn by Marriott Indianapolis Downtown on the Canal 🏨
(317) 822-0840. **$161-$197.** 350 W New York St 46202. Jct Senate Ave. Int corridors. **Pets:** Accepted. ✕ ⬤M 🛏 💻 ➷

Residence Inn by Marriott Northwest-Indianapolis 🏨
(317) 275-6000. **$125-$153.** 6220 Digital Way 46278. I-465, exit 21, just w. Int corridors. **Pets:** Small. $100 one-time fee/room. Service with restrictions, supervision. ✕ ⬤M 🛏 💻 ➷ ✕

Sheraton Indianapolis City Centre 🏨 ❀
(317) 635-2000. **Call for rates.** 31 W Ohio St 46204. Jct Meridian St; just n of Monument Cir. Int corridors. **Pets:** Small, dogs only. Service with restrictions, supervision. SAVE ✕ ⬤M 🛏 💻 🍽 ➷

Sheraton Indianapolis Hotel & Suites 🏨
(317) 846-2700. **$115-$269.** 8787 Keystone Crossing 46240. I-465, exit 33, 0.5 mi s on SR 431, just e on 86th St, then just n. Int corridors.
Pets: Accepted. SAVE ✕ ⬤M 🛏 💻 ➷

Staybridge Suites City Centre 🏨
(317) 536-7500. **$100-$199.** 535 S West St 46225. Just s of South St. Int corridors. **Pets:** Accepted. ASK ✕ ⬤M 🛏 💻 ➷

Suburban Extended Stay Hotel 🏨
(317) 598-1914. **$59-$99.** 8055 Bash St 46250. I-69, exit 1, just w. Int corridors. **Pets:** Accepted. ASK ✕ ⬤M 🛏 💻 ➷

TownePlace Suites by Marriott Keystone 🏨
(317) 255-3700. **$99-$109.** 8468 Union Chapel Rd 46240. I-465, exit 33, 0.5 mi s on SR 431, just e on 86th St, then just s. Int corridors.
Pets: Accepted. ✕ 🛏 💻 ➷

TownePlace Suites by Marriott Park 100 🏨 ❀
(317) 290-8900. **$107-$131.** 5802 W 71st St 46278. I-465, exit 21, 0.3 mi e. Int corridors. **Pets:** Large, other species. $50 one-time fee/room. Service with restrictions, crate. ✕ 🛏 💻 ➷

The Westin Indianapolis 🏨 ❀
(317) 262-8100. **$149-$359.** 50 S Capitol Ave 46204. Jct Washington and Maryland sts. Int corridors. **Pets:** Medium, dogs only. Service with restrictions, supervision. SAVE ✕ ⬤M 💻 🍽 ➷ ✕

Wingate Inn-Airport 🏨
(317) 243-8310. **$79-$109.** 5797 Rockville Rd 46224. I-465, exit 13A, just e. Int corridors. **Pets:** $25 one-time fee/room. Service with restrictions.
ASK ✕ ⬤M 🛏 💻 ➷

LEBANON

Comfort Inn 🏨
(765) 482-4800. **Call for rates.** 210 N Sam Ralston Rd 46052. I-65, exit 140. Int corridors. **Pets:** Accepted. SAVE ✕ 🛏 💻 ➷

Holiday Inn Express 🏨
(765) 483-4100. **$99-$159.** 335 N Mt Zion Rd 46052. I-65, exit 140, just w. Int corridors. **Pets:** Medium. $10 daily fee/pet. Designated rooms, service with restrictions, supervision. ASK ✕ ⬤M 🛏 💻 ➷

Super 8 🏨
(765) 482-9999. **Call for rates.** 405 N Mt Zion Rd 46052. I-65, exit 140, just w. Int corridors. **Pets:** Accepted. ✕ 🛏 💻 ➷

MARTINSVILLE

Best Western Martinsville Inn 🏨
(765) 342-1842. **$80-$149.** 50 Bill's Blvd 46151. SR 37 to Ohio St, just w. Int corridors. **Pets:** $10 daily fee/pet. Service with restrictions, supervision. SAVE ✕ ⬤M 🛏 💻

NOBLESVILLE

▼▼ Quality Inn & Suites H ❀

(317) 770-6772. **$63-$130.** 16025 Prosperity Dr 46060. I-69, exit 5, 4 mi n on SR 37. Int corridors. **Pets:** Other species. $10 daily fee/pet. Designated rooms, service with restrictions, supervision.

ASK ✕ 🛅 🖵 ⊅

PLAINFIELD

▼▼▼ Staybridge Suites Indianapolis Airport H ❀

(317) 839-2700. **$124-$179.** 6295 Cambridge Way 46168. I-70, exit 66, 0.4 mi n on SR 267, just e on Hadley Rd, then just s. Int corridors. **Pets:** Other species. Service with restrictions, crate.

ASK ✕ 🕭 🛅 🖵 ⊅

END METROPOLITAN AREA

JASPER

▼▼ Days Inn Jasper H

(812) 482-6000. **$70-$90.** 272 Brucke Strasse 47546. Jct SR 164, just w. Ext/int corridors. **Pets:** Accepted. ASK ✕ 🛅 🖵 🍴 ⊅ ✕

JEFFERSONVILLE

▼▼▼ Comfort Suites Louisville North H

(812) 282-2100. **Call for rates.** 360 Eastern Blvd 47130. I-65, exit 2 (Eastern Blvd), just e. Int corridors. **Pets:** Accepted. ✕ 🕭 🛅 🖵

AAA ▼▼▼ Sheraton Louisville Riverside Hotel H

(812) 284-6711. **$87-$208.** 700 W Riverside Dr 47130. I-65, exit 0, just w. Int corridors. **Pets:** Accepted. SAVE ✕ 🛅 🖵 🍴 ⊅

▼▼ TownePlace Suites by Marriott H

(812) 280-8200. **$95-$116.** 703 N Shore Dr 47130. I-65, exit 0, just w. Int corridors. **Pets:** Other species. $100 one-time fee/room. Service with restrictions. ✕ 🛅 🖵 ⊅

KENDALLVILLE

AAA ▼▼▼ Holiday Inn Express Kendallville H

(260) 343-0000. **$65-$155.** 1917 Dowling St 46755. I-69, exit 134, 9.3 mi e on US 6. Int corridors. **Pets:** Medium. $10 daily fee/pet. Designated rooms, service with restrictions, supervision.

SAVE ✕ 🕭 🛅 🖵 ⊅ ✕

KOKOMO

▼▼ Comfort Inn by Choice Hotels H

(765) 452-5050. **$54-$99.** 522 Essex Dr 46901. Jct US 35, 0.3 mi n on US 31. Int corridors. **Pets:** Other species. $15 one-time fee/room. Service with restrictions. ASK ✕ 🛅 🖵 ⊅

▼▼ Days Inn & Suites M

(765) 453-7100. **$56-$80.** 264 S 00 EW 46902. US 31, 2.8 mi s of jct US 35. Ext corridors. **Pets:** $10 one-time fee/room. Service with restrictions, supervision. ASK ✕ 🛅 🖵 🍴 ⊅

▼▼▼ Hampton Inn & Suites H

(765) 455-2900. **$79-$139.** 2920 S Reed Rd (US Hwy 31) 46902. US 31, 2 mi s of jct US 35. Int corridors. **Pets:** Large, other species. Designated rooms, service with restrictions, crate.

✕ 🕭 🛅 🖵 ⊅ ✕

LAFAYETTE

AAA ▼▼▼ Best Western Lafayette Executive Plaza & Conference Center H

(765) 447-0575. **$90-$300, 30 day notice.** 4343 SR 26 E 47905. I-65, exit 172, just w. Int corridors. **Pets:** Small. $25 daily fee/room. Designated rooms, service with restrictions, supervision.

SAVE ✕ 🕭 🛅 🖵 🍴 ⊅ ✕

▼▼▼ Comfort Inn H

(765) 447-3434. **$80-$160.** 4701 Meijer Ct 47905. I-65, exit 172, just e on SR 26. Int corridors. **Pets:** Small, other species. $25 one-time fee/pet. Designated rooms, service with restrictions, supervision.

ASK ✕ 🛅 🖵 ⊅

▼▼▼ Days Inn & Suites H

(765) 446-8558. **$80-$90, 7 day notice.** 151 Frontage Rd 47905. I-65, exit 172, just e. Int corridors. **Pets:** Accepted. ASK ✕ 🛅 🖵

▼▼▼ Homewood Suites by Hilton H ❀

(765) 448-9700. **$104-$329.** 3939 SR 26 E 47905. I-65, exit 172, 0.8 mi w. Ext/int corridors. **Pets:** Medium. $250 deposit/room, $10 daily fee/pet, $50 one-time fee/pet. Service with restrictions, crate.

✕ 🛅 🖵 ⊅ ✕

AAA ▼▼▼ Lafayette Inn & Suites H

(765) 449-4808. **$90-$99.** 201 Frontage Rd 47905. I-65, exit 172, just e on SR 26, then just n. Int corridors. **Pets:** Small, dogs only. $15 one-time fee/pet. Designated rooms, no service, supervision. SAVE ✕ 🛅 🖵

▼▼▼ Loeb House Inn BB

(765) 420-7737. **$109-$189, 5 day notice.** 708 Cincinnati St 47901. SR 38, 0.4 mi n on 9th St, then just w. Int corridors. **Pets:** Medium. Service with restrictions. ASK ✕

▼▼▼ Motel 6 M

(765) 447-7566. **$50-$119.** 139 Frontage Rd 47905. I-65, exit 172. Ext corridors. **Pets:** Other species. Service with restrictions, supervision.

ASK ✕ 🛅

▼▼▼ Quality Inn & Suites H

(765) 447-9460. **$64-$129.** 4221 SR 26 E 47905. I-65, exit 172, 0.3 mi w. Int corridors. **Pets:** Other species. $10 daily fee/pet.

ASK ✕ 🛅 🖵 ⊅

▼▼▼ Red Roof Inn-Lafayette #7062 M

(765) 448-4671. **Call for rates.** 4201 SR 26 E 47905. I-65, exit 172, 0.3 mi w. Ext corridors. **Pets:** Large. Service with restrictions, crate. ✕ 🛅

▼▼▼ TownePlace Suites by Marriott H

(765) 446-8668. **$98-$120.** 163 Frontage Rd 47905. I-65, exit 172, just e. Int corridors. **Pets:** Accepted. ✕ 🛅 🖵 ⊅

LA PORTE

AAA ▼▼▼ Best Western La Porte Hotel and Conference Center H

(219) 362-4585. **$109-$149.** 444 Pine Lake Ave 46350. 1.5 mi n on US 35. Int corridors. **Pets:** Accepted. SAVE ✕ 🛅 🖵 🍴 ⊅ ✕

LOGANSPORT

▼▼ Ramada H

(574) 753-6351. **Call for rates.** 3550 E Market St 46947-0813. 2.5 mi e on Business Rt US 24. Int corridors. **Pets:** Accepted.

✕ 🛅 🖵 🍴 ⊅

MARION

▼▼▼ Comfort Suites-Marion 🅗

(765) 651-1006. **$85-$125.** 1345 N Baldwin Ave 46952. 1.5 mi n of jct SR 9 and 18. Int corridors. **Pets:** Other species. $10 one-time fee/room. Service with restrictions. [ASK] [X] 🛏 📺 🏊 [X]

MERRILLVILLE

▼▼ Candlewood Suites 🅗 🐾

(219) 791-9100. **$99-$114.** 8339 Ohio St 46410. I-65, exit 253, 0.3 mi e, just s on Mississippi St, 0.4 mi w on 83rd Ave, then just s. Int corridors. **Pets:** Medium. $75 one-time fee/pet. Service with restrictions, supervision. [ASK] [X] 🛏 📺

▼▼ Extended StayAmerica-Merrillville-US Rte 30 🅗

(219) 769-4740. **$50-$80.** 1355 E 83rd Ave 46410. I-65, exit 253, 0.3 mi e on US 30, just s on Mississippi St, then 0.4 mi w. Int corridors. **Pets:** Other species. $25 daily fee/room. Designated rooms, service with restrictions, crate. [ASK] [X] 🛏 📺

▼▼▼ Residence Inn by Marriott Merrillville 🅗 🐾

(219) 791-9000. **$144-$176.** 8018 Delaware Pl 46410. I-65, exit 253, 0.3 mi nw. Int corridors. **Pets:** Medium, other species. $100 one-time fee/room. Service with restrictions, crate. [X] [♿M] 🛏 📺 🏊 [X]

🆀 ▼ Super 8 🅗

(219) 736-8383. **$45-$80.** 8300 Louisiana St 46410. I-65, exit 253, 0.3 mi e, just s on Mississippi St, then just w on 83rd Ave. Int corridors. **Pets:** Medium, other species. $25 deposit/pet, $5 daily fee/pet. Designated rooms, service with restrictions, supervision.
[SAVE] [X] [♿M] 🛏 📺

MISHAWAKA

▼▼▼ Residence Inn by Marriott South Bend/Mishawaka 🅗

(574) 271-9283. **$149-$159.** 231 Park Pl 46545. I-80/90, exit 83, just n on SR 331 to SR 23, 1.6 mi sw, then 1.3 mi s on Main St. Int corridors. **Pets:** Accepted. [X] [♿M] 🛏 📺 🏊 [X]

MONTGOMERY

▼▼ Gasthof Amish Village Inn 🅗

(812) 486-2600. **Call for rates.** 6747 E Gasthof Village Rd 47558. US 50, 0.8 mi n on First St. Int corridors. **Pets:** Accepted.
[X] 🛏 📺 🍽 🏊 [X]

MOUNT VERNON

▼▼ Four Seasons Motel Ⓜ

(812) 838-4821. **$56-$100.** 70 Hwy 62 W 47620. 1.8 mi w. Ext corridors. **Pets:** Medium. $25 one-time fee/pet. Service with restrictions, supervision. [ASK] [X] 🛏 📺 🏊

MUNCIE

▼▼▼ Comfort Inn & Suites 🅗

(765) 587-0294. **$70-$159.** 3400 N Marleon Dr 47304. I-69, exit 41, 6.3 mi e on SR 332, then just n. Int corridors. **Pets:** Accepted.
[ASK] [X] [♿M] 🛏 📺 🏊

▼▼ Days Inn Muncie 🅗

(765) 288-2311. **Call for rates.** 3509 N Everbrook Ln 47304. I-69, exit 41, 6.3 mi e on SR 332, then just n. Int corridors. **Pets:** Large. $10 one-time fee/pet. Service with restrictions, supervision. [X] 🛏 📺

▼▼ Super 8 🅗

(765) 286-4333. **$45-$95, 3 day notice.** 3601 W Fox Ridge Ln 47304. I-69, exit 41, 6.3 mi e on SR 332. Int corridors. **Pets:** Medium, dogs only. $10 one-time fee/pet. Service with restrictions, supervision.
[ASK] [X] 🛏 📺

NORTH VERNON

▼▼ Comfort Inn 🅗

(812) 352-9999. **$80-$110.** 150 FDR Dr 47265. Jct US 50, 0.6 mi n on SR 7. Int corridors. **Pets:** Accepted. [ASK] [X] 🛏 📺 🏊

PERU

🆀 ▼▼▼ Best Western Circus City Inn 🅗

(765) 473-8800. **$87-$97, 3 day notice.** 2642 Business Rt US 31 S 46970. Just e of jct US 31. Int corridors. **Pets:** Large. $10 daily fee/pet. Designated rooms, supervision. [SAVE] [X] 🛏 📺 🏊

PLYMOUTH

▼▼ Super 8 🅗

(574) 936-8856. **$55-$135.** 2160 N Oak Rd 46563. US 30, just s. Int corridors. **Pets:** Accepted. [ASK] [X] 🛏 📺 🏊

PORTAGE

▼▼ Comfort Inn 🅗

(219) 763-7177. **$69-$179.** 2300 Willow Creek Rd 46368. I-80/90, exit 23; I-94, exit 19, 1.5 mi s on CR 249. Int corridors. **Pets:** Accepted.
[ASK] [X] 🛏 📺

▼▼ Super 8 Portage 🅗

(219) 762-8857. **Call for rates.** 6118 Melton Rd 46368. I-94, exit 19, just s on CR 249, then just w on US 20; I-80, exit 23, 1.2 mi n on CR 249, then just w on US 20. Int corridors. **Pets:** Accepted. [X] 🛏 📺

PRINCETON

▼▼▼ Fairfield Inn by Marriott 🅗

(812) 385-4300. **$80-$98.** 2828 Dixon St 47670. Jct US 41 and SR 64, 0.3 mi w. Int corridors. **Pets:** Medium. $25 one-time fee/pet. Service with restrictions, crate. [X] [♿M] 🛏 📺 🏊

RICHMOND

▼▼ Days Inn Ⓜ

(765) 966-4900. **$45-$70.** 5775 National Rd E 47374. I-70, exit 156A, just s. Ext corridors. **Pets:** Small. $10 daily fee/pet. Designated rooms, service with restrictions, supervision. [ASK] [X] 🛏 📺

▼▼▼ Holiday Inn-Richmond 🅗 🐾

(765) 966-7511. **$89-$325.** 5501 National Rd E 47374. I-70, exit 156A, 0.3 mi w. Int corridors. **Pets:** $25 one-time fee/room. Supervision.
[ASK] [X] [♿M] 🛏 📺 🍽 🏊 [X]

🆀 ▼▼ Knights Inn Ⓜ

(765) 966-1505. **$55-$89.** 3020 E Main St 47374. I-70, exit 156A, 2 mi w. Ext corridors. **Pets:** Small. $8 daily fee/pet. Service with restrictions, supervision. [SAVE] [X] 🛏 📺

ROCKVILLE

🆀 ▼ Parke Bridge Motel Ⓜ

(765) 569-3525. **$35-$150, 3 day notice.** 304 E Ohio St 47872. On US 36, 0.5 mi e of jct US 41, just e of center. Ext corridors. **Pets:** Accepted.
[SAVE] [X] 📺

RUSHVILLE

▼▼ Comfort Inn 🅗

(765) 932-2999. **$79-$129.** 320 Conrad Harcourt Way 46173. Just e of SR 3. Int corridors. **Pets:** Accepted. [ASK] [X] 🛏 📺

SCOTTSBURG

▼▼▼ Hampton Inn & Suites 🅗

(812) 752-1999. **Call for rates.** 1535 W McClain Ave 47170. I-65, exit 29, just w. Int corridors. **Pets:** Accepted. [X] 🛏 📺 🏊 [X]

🆀 ▼▼▼ Mariann Travel Inn Ⓜ 🐾

(812) 752-3396. **$59-$69.** I-65 & SR 56 47170. I-65, exit 29A, just e. Ext corridors. **Pets:** Dogs only. $15 one-time fee/pet. Designated rooms, service with restrictions, supervision. [SAVE] [X] 🛏 🍽 🏊 [X]

SELLERSBURG

▼▼ Home Lodge 🅗

(812) 246-6332. **$69.** 363 Triangle Dr 47172. I-65, exit 9, just e. Int corridors. **Pets:** Other species. $25 one-time fee/room. Service with restrictions, supervision. [ASK] [X] 🛏 📺

▼▼▼ **Ramada** 🅷
(812) 246-3131. **$79.** 360 Triangle Dr 47172. I-65, exit 9, just e. Int corridors. **Pets:** Small, other species. $25 one-time fee/room. Designated rooms, service with restrictions, supervision. (ASK) ⊠ 📠 💻 🏊

SEYMOUR

▼ **Motel 6 Seymour #4153** 🅷
(812) 524-7443. **Call for rates.** 365 Tanger Blvd 47274. I-65, exit 50A. Int corridors. **Pets:** Other species. Service with restrictions, supervision. ⊠ 📠 💻 🏊

▼▼ **Seymour Quality Inn** 🅷
(812) 522-6767. **$60.** 2025 E Tipton St 47274. I-65, exit 50B, 0.5 mi w on US 50. Ext corridors. **Pets:** Other species. (ASK) ⊠ 📠 💻 🏊

SOUTH BEND

▼▼▼ **Comfort Suites South Bend** 🅷 🐾
(574) 272-1500. **$90-$120.** 52939 SR 933 N 46637. I-80/90, exit 77, just e to Business Rt US 31/SR 933, then 1 mi n. Int corridors. **Pets:** Other species. $10 daily fee/pet. Service with restrictions, crate. (ASK) ⊠ 📠 💻 🏊 ⊠

🅐🅐🅐 ▼▼▼ ▼▼▼ **Cushing Manor Inn** 🅑🅑
(574) 288-1990. **$95-$165, 14 day notice.** 508 W Washington St 46601. 0.4 mi w of jct SR 933 and Business Rt US 31. Int corridors. **Pets:** Accepted. (SAVE) ⊠

▼▼▼ **The English Rose Bed & Breakfast Guest House** 🅑🅑
(574) 288-1990. **$95-$165, 14 day notice.** 116 S Taylor St 46601. Business Rt US 31, 0.3 mi w on Washington St to Taylor St, then just s. Int corridors. **Pets:** Accepted. (ASK) ⊠ ☎

▼▼▼ **Oliver Inn Bed & Breakfast** 🅑🅑
(574) 232-4545. **$135-$339, 14 day notice.** 630 W Washington St 46601. 0.3 mi w of SR 933 and Business Rt US 31. Int corridors. **Pets:** $10 one-time fee/room. Designated rooms, service with restrictions, supervision. (ASK) ⊠ 📠 💻

🅐🅐🅐 ▼▼▼ **Sleep Inn** 🅷 🐾
(574) 232-3200. **$69-$280.** 4134 Lincolnway W 46628. I-80/90, exit 72, 1.5 mi s on US 31 to South Bend Regional Airport exit, then 2 mi e. Int corridors. **Pets:** Large. $10 daily fee/pet. Service with restrictions, crate. (SAVE) ⊠ 📠 💻 🏊

🅐🅐🅐 ▼▼▼ **Suburban Extended Stay Hotel** 🅷
(574) 968-4737. **$72-$81.** 52825 SR 933 N 46637. I-80/90, exit 77, just e to Business Rt US 31/SR 933, then 1 mi n. Int corridors. **Pets:** Accepted. (SAVE) ⊠ 🔵M 📠 💻 🏊

🅐🅐🅐 ▼▼▼ **Super 8–South Bend** 🅷
(574) 243-0200. **$79-$249, 30 day notice.** 4124 Ameritech Dr 46628. I-80/90, exit 72, 0.7 mi n on US 31, just e on Cleveland Rd, then just s. Int corridors. **Pets:** Medium. $10 daily fee/pet. Designated rooms, service with restrictions, supervision. (SAVE) ⊠ 📠 💻 🏊

▼▼▼ **Waterford Estates Lodge** 🅷
(574) 272-5220. **Call for rates.** 52890 SR 933 N 46637. I-80/90, exit 77, 1 mi n. Int corridors. **Pets:** Accepted. ⊠ 🔵M 📠 💻 🍴 🏊

TAYLORSVILLE

▼ **Red Roof Inn** 🅼
(812) 526-9747. **Call for rates.** 10330 US 31 47280. I-65, exit 76A, just s. Ext corridors. **Pets:** Large. Service with restrictions, crate. ⊠ 📠 💻 🏊

TELL CITY

▼▼▼ **Holiday Inn Express** 🅷
(812) 547-0800. **Call for rates.** 310 Orchard Hill Dr 47586. Just off SR 66, 1.7 mi se of jct SR 37. Int corridors. **Pets:** Accepted. ⊠ 🔵M 📠 💻 🏊

▼▼ **Ramada Limited** 🅷
(812) 547-3234. **$69-$99.** 235 Orchard Hill Dr 47586. Just off SR 66, 1.7 mi se of jct SR 37. Int corridors. **Pets:** Small, other species. $10 daily fee/pet. Designated rooms, service with restrictions, supervision. (ASK) ⊠ 📠 💻 🏊

TERRE HAUTE

▼▼▼ **Candlewood Suites** 🅷
(812) 234-3400. **Call for rates.** 721 Wabash Ave 47807. I-70, exit 7, 2.2 mi n, 0.4 mi e, then just s. Int corridors. **Pets:** Accepted. ⊠ 🔵M 📠 💻

▼▼▼ **Drury Inn-Terre Haute** 🅷
(812) 238-1206. **$85-$164.** 3040 Hwy 41 S 47802. I-70, exit 7 (US 41/150), just n. Int corridors. **Pets:** Other species. No service, supervision. (ASK) ⊠ 🔵M 📠 💻 🏊 ⊠

▼▼▼ **Holiday Inn** 🅷 🐾
(812) 232-6081. **$89-$109.** 3300 US 41 S 47802. I-70, exit 7 (US 41/150), just s. Int corridors. **Pets:** $30 one-time fee/room. Service with restrictions, supervision. (ASK) ⊠ 📠 💻 🍴 🏊 ⊠

▼▼ **Pear Tree Inn by Drury-Terre Haute** 🅷
(812) 234-4268. **$65-$119.** 3050 US 41 S 47802. I-70, exit 7 (US 41/150), just n. Int corridors. **Pets:** Other species. No service, supervision. (ASK) ⊠ 💻

▼ **Super 8-Terre Haute** 🅷 🐾
(812) 232-4890. **$45-$125.** 3089 S 1st St 47802. I-70, exit 7 (US 41/150), just nw. Int corridors. **Pets:** Large. $10 one-time fee/room. Designated rooms, service with restrictions, supervision. (ASK) ⊠ 📠

VALPARAISO

▼▼▼ **Courtyard by Marriott Valparaiso** 🅷
(219) 465-1700. **$109-$119.** 2301 E Morthland Dr 46383. On US 30, just w of jct SR 49. Int corridors. **Pets:** Accepted. ⊠ 📠 💻 🏊

WARREN

▼▼ **Comfort Inn Warren** 🅷
(260) 375-4800. **$50-$70.** 7275 S 75 E 46792. I-69, exit 78, just n on SR 5. Int corridors. **Pets:** Accepted. (ASK) ⊠ 🔵M 📠 💻 🏊 ⊠

WARSAW

▼▼▼ **Comfort Inn & Suites-Warsaw** 🅷
(574) 269-6655. **$69-$199.** 3328 E Center St 46580. 3.2 mi e of SR 15 on US 30. Int corridors. **Pets:** Medium. $10 daily fee/room. Service with restrictions, crate. ⊠ 📠 💻 🏊

▼▼▼ **Ramada Plaza of Warsaw** 🅷 🐾
(574) 269-2323. **$99-$110.** 2519 E Center St 46580. 2.8 mi e of SR 15 on US 30, just s. Int corridors. **Pets:** Medium. Service with restrictions, crate. (ASK) ⊠ 📠 💻 🍴 🏊 ⊠

WASHINGTON

▼▼▼ **Baymont Inn & Suites Washington** 🅷
(812) 254-7000. **$84-$120.** 7 Cumberland Dr 47501. Just ne of jct US 50 and SR 257. Int corridors. **Pets:** Accepted. (ASK) ⊠ 📠 💻 🏊

▼▼▼ **Holiday Inn Express** 🅷
(812) 254-6666. **Call for rates.** 1808 E National Hwy 47501. On US 50 business route, 0.4 mi e of SR 257. Int corridors. **Pets:** Accepted. ⊠ 📠 💻 🏊

WEST BADEN SPRINGS

🅐🅐🅐 ▼▼▼ ▼▼▼ **West Baden Springs Hotel** 🅷
(812) 936-1902. **$180-$325.** 8538 W Baden Ave 47469. On SR 56. Int corridors. **Pets:** Accepted. (SAVE) ⊠ 🔵M 📠 💻 🍴 🏊 ⊠

IOWA

ADAIR

▼ Adair Budget Inn Ⓜ

(641) 742-5553. **$33-$54.** 100 S 5th St 50002. I-80, exit 76, just n. Ext corridors. **Pets:** Large, other species. $20 deposit/room. Designated rooms, service with restrictions, supervision. (ASK) ⊠ 🖬

ALBIA

▼ Indian Hills Inn Ⓗ

(641) 932-7181. **$62-$129.** 100 Hwy 34 E 52531. Just e of jct US 34 and SR 5. Ext/int corridors. **Pets:** $10 daily fee/pet. Designated rooms, service with restrictions, crate. ⊠ 🖬 🔳 🍽 ➰

ALGONA

▼▼ AmericInn Lodge & Suites of Algona Ⓗ

(515) 295-3333. **$85-$129.** 600 Hwy 18 W 50511. Just w of jct US 169/18. Int corridors. **Pets:** Accepted. ⊠ 🔂 🖬 🔳 ➰ ⊠

ALTOONA

▼▼ Settle Inn & Suites-Altoona Ⓗ

(515) 967-7888. **$79-$99.** 2101 Adventureland Dr 50009. I-80, exit 142A, just se. Int corridors. **Pets:** Medium, dogs only. $15 daily fee/pet. Designated rooms, service with restrictions, supervision.

(ASK) ⊠ 🖬 🔳 ➰

AMES

🔷 ▼▼▼ Best Western University Park Inn & Suites Ⓗ

(515) 296-2500. **$90-$140.** 2500 University Blvd 50010. I-35, exit 111B, 3.5 mi w on US 30, exit 146 (Elwood Dr), then just s. Int corridors. **Pets:** $5 one-time fee/pet. Service with restrictions, supervision.

(SAVE) ⊠ 🖬 🔳 ➰

🔷 ▼▼ Comfort Inn-Ames Ⓗ 🐾

(515) 232-0689. **$70-$135.** 1605 S Dayton Pl 50010. I-35, exit 111B, just w on US 30, exit 150. Int corridors. **Pets:** $10 daily fee/pet. Designated rooms, supervision. (SAVE) ⊠ 🖬 🔳 ➰

▼▼▼ Gateway Hotel & Conference Center Ⓗ

(515) 292-8600. **$69-$149.** 2100 Green Hills Dr 50014. I-35, exit 111B, 3.5 mi w on US 30, exit 146 (Elwood Dr). Int corridors. **Pets:** Other species. Designated rooms, service with restrictions, crate.

(ASK) ⊠ 🔂 🖬 🔳 🍽 ➰ ⊠

🔷 ▼▼▼ GrandStay Residential Suites Ⓗ

(515) 232-8363. **$77-$87.** 1606 S Kellogg Ave 50010. I-35, exit 111B, 1 mi w, then just nw on Duff Ave to Kellogg Ave. Int corridors. **Pets:** Accepted. (SAVE) ⊠ 🔂 🖬 🔳 ➰ ⊠

▼▼▼ Holiday Inn Ames Conference Center-ISU Ⓗ

(515) 268-8808. **$79-$199.** 2609 University Blvd 50010. I-35, exit 111B, 3.5 mi w on US 30, exit 146 (Elwood Dr), then just s. Int corridors. **Pets:** Accepted. (ASK) ⊠ 🔂 🖬 🔳 🍽 ➰

▼▼ Microtel Inn & Suites Ⓗ 🐾

(515) 233-4444. **$49-$149.** 2216 SE 16th St 50010. I-35, exit 111B, just w on US 30, exit 150. Int corridors. **Pets:** Large. $10 daily fee/room. Designated rooms, service with restrictions, crate. (ASK) ⊠ 🔂 🖬 🔳

▼▼ Quality Inn & Suites Starlite Village Conference Center Ⓗ

(515) 232-9260. **$90-$120, 3 day notice.** 2601 E 13th St 50010. I-35, exit 113 (13th St), 0.5 mi w. Int corridors. **Pets:** Medium. $10 one-time fee/room. Service with restrictions, supervision.

(ASK) ⊠ 🔂 🖬 🔳 🍽 ➰

ANAMOSA

▼▼ AmericInn Lodge & Suites Ⓗ

(319) 462-4119. **$85-$160.** 101 Harley Ave 52205. US 151, exit 54, just nw. Int corridors. **Pets:** Small, dogs only. $50 deposit/room, $10 daily fee/pet. Designated rooms, service with restrictions, crate.

⊠ 🖬 🔳 ➰

▼▼ Super 8-Anamosa Ⓗ

(319) 462-3888. **$55-$100.** 100 Grant Wood Dr 52205. US 151, exit 54, just e on SR 64. Int corridors. **Pets:** Medium. $10 daily fee/pet. Designated rooms, service with restrictions, supervision. (ASK) ⊠ 🖬 🔳

ANKENY

🔷 ▼▼▼ Comfort Inn Ⓗ

(515) 963-1100. **$79-$159.** 2602 SE Creekview Dr 50021. I-35, exit 90, just ne. Int corridors. **Pets:** Small, dogs only. $25 daily fee/pet. Designated rooms, service with restrictions, supervision.

(SAVE) ⊠ 🖬 🔳 ➰

ARNOLDS PARK

🔷 ▼▼▼ Bridges Bay Resort 🔲

(712) 332-2202. **Call for rates.** 630 Linden Dr 51331. Just e of US 71. Int corridors. **Pets:** Other species. Service with restrictions, crate.

(SAVE) ⊠ 🖬 🔳 ➰ ⊠

▼▼ Fillenwarth Beach Ⓜ

(712) 332-5646. **$70-$912 (no credit cards), 60 day notice.** 87 Lake Shore Dr 51331. Just w of US 71; on West Lake Okoboji. Ext corridors. **Pets:** Other species. Designated rooms. ⊠ 🖬 🔳 ➰ ⊠

ATLANTIC

▼▼ Americas Best Value Inn 🅷 ❀
(712) 243-4067. **$55-$90.** 64968 Boston Rd 50022. I-80, exit 60 (US 71), 0.5 mi s. Int corridors. **Pets:** Large, other species. $8 daily fee/pet. Designated rooms, service with restrictions, supervision.
[ASK] [✕] 🛢 🖵 🏊

▼▼ Super 8 🅷
(712) 243-4723. **$60-$99.** 1902 E 7th St 50022. I-80, exit 60 (US 71), 6 mi s, then 2 mi w; east side of town. Int corridors. **Pets:** Accepted.
[ASK] [✕] [&M] 🛢 🖵 🏊

BURLINGTON

◬ ▼▼▼ Comfort Suites Hotel & Conference Center 🅷
(319) 753-1300. **$92-$112.** 1780 Stonegate Center Dr 52601. On US 61, 2 mi s of US 34. Int corridors. **Pets:** Large. $15 daily fee/pet. Designated rooms, service with restrictions, crate.
[SAVE] [✕] [&M] 🛢 🖵 🍴 🏊 [✕]

◬ ▼▼ Quality Inn 🅷
(319) 753-0000. **Call for rates.** 3051 Kirkwood Ave 52601. Jct US 61 and 34, just n. Int corridors. **Pets:** Medium. $10 daily fee/pet. Service with restrictions, supervision. [SAVE] [✕] 🛢 🖵 🏊

▼▼ Super 8 🅷
(319) 752-9806. **$45-$85.** 3001 Kirkwood St 52601. Jct US 61 and 34, just n. Int corridors. **Pets:** Accepted. [ASK] [✕] 🛢 🖵

CARTER LAKE

◬ ▼▼▼ Holiday Inn Express & Suites-Omaha Airport 🅷
(402) 505-4900. **$79-$159.** 2510 Abbott Plaza 51510. I-480 W, exit 4 to 10th St, 2 mi n, follow Eppley Airfield signs. Int corridors. **Pets:** Medium, other species. $100 deposit/room, $10 daily fee/room. Designated rooms, service with restrictions, crate. [SAVE] [✕] [&M] 🛢 🖵 🏊

◬ ▼▼▼ La Quinta Inn & Suites 🅷 ❀
(712) 347-6595. **Call for rates.** 1201 Ave H 51510. I-480 W, exit 4 to 10th St, 2 mi n, follow Eppley Airfield signs. Int corridors. **Pets:** Medium, other species. Service with restrictions, supervision.
[SAVE] [✕] [&M] 🛢 🖵 🏊

▼▼ Super 8 🅷
(712) 347-5588. **$77-$154.** 3000 Airport Dr 51510. I-480 W, exit 4 to 10th St, 2.3 mi n, follow Eppley Airfield signs. Int corridors. **Pets:** $10 one-time fee/room. Service with restrictions, supervision.
[ASK] [✕] 🛢 🖵

CEDAR FALLS

▼▼▼ Comfort Suites 🅷
(319) 273-9999. **$99-$122.** 7402 Nordic Dr 50613. US 20, exit 225, just nw. Int corridors. **Pets:** Accepted. [ASK] [✕] [&M] 🛢 🖵 🏊

▼▼ Days Inn 🅷
(319) 266-1222. **$59-$89.** 5826 University Ave, Suite 2 50613. 0.7 mi e of jct SR 58. Int corridors. **Pets:** Accepted. [ASK] [✕] 🛢 🖵

◬ ▼▼ University Inn 🅷 ❀
(319) 277-1412. **$50-$112.** 4711 University Ave 50613. 1.6 mi e of jct SR 58. Ext/int corridors. **Pets:** Dogs only. $30 deposit/pet. Designated rooms, service with restrictions, crate. [SAVE] [✕] 🛢 🖵

CEDAR RAPIDS

▼▼ AmericInn Lodge & Suites of Cedar Rapids 🅷
(319) 632-1800. **$90-$185.** 8910 6th St SW 52404. I-380, exit 13, just nw. Int corridors. **Pets:** Other species. $50 deposit/room, $12 daily fee/pet. Designated rooms, service with restrictions, supervision.
[ASK] [✕] [&M] 🛢 🖵 🏊 [✕]

◬ ▼▼▼ Baymont Inn & Suites 🅷
(319) 378-8000. **$85-$125.** 1220 Park Pl NE 52402. I-380, exit 24A (SR 100/Collins Rd), 0.9 mi e, then just n. Int corridors. **Pets:** Small. $15 daily fee/pet. Designated rooms, service with restrictions, supervision.
[SAVE] [✕] [&M] 🛢 🖵

◬ ▼▼▼ Best Western Cooper's Mill Hotel & Restaurant 🅷
(319) 366-5323. **$85-$110.** 100 F Ave NW 52405. I-380, exit 19C northbound, take right at end of exit, make immediate U-turn and go under I-380; exit 20A southbound, cross river, right on 1st St NW. Int corridors. **Pets:** Medium. $10 daily fee/pet. Crate.
[SAVE] [✕] 🛢 🖵 🍴 🏊 [✕]

◬ ▼▼▼▼ Best Western Longbranch Hotel & Convention Center 🅷
(319) 377-6386. **$120-$130.** 90 Twixt Town Rd NE 52402. I-380, exit 24A (SR 100/Collins Rd), 2.5 mi e, then just n. Int corridors. **Pets:** Medium, other species. $10 daily fee/pet. Designated rooms, service with restrictions, supervision. [SAVE] [✕] 🛢 🖵 🍴 🏊 [✕]

▼▼▼ Clarion Hotel & Convention Center 🅷
(319) 366-8671. **$86-$170.** 525 33rd Ave SW 52404. I-380, exit 17 (33rd Ave SW), just w. Int corridors. **Pets:** Accepted.
[ASK] [✕] 🛢 🖵 🍴 🏊 [✕]

▼▼ Collins Inn & Suites 🅷
(319) 378-8888. **$76-$126.** 2025 Werner Ave NE 52402. I-380, exit 24A (SR 100/Collins Rd), just se. Int corridors. **Pets:** Small. $10 daily fee/pet. Service with restrictions, supervision. [ASK] [✕] 🛢 🖵 🏊

▼▼ Comfort Inn by Choice Hotels North 🅷
(319) 393-8247. **$65-$90.** 5055 Rockwell Dr NE 52402. I-380, exit 24A (SR 100/Collins Rd), 1 mi e. Int corridors. **Pets:** Accepted.
[ASK] [✕] 🛢 🖵

▼▼ Comfort Inn by Choice Hotels South 🅷
(319) 363-7934. **$50-$90.** 390 33rd Ave SW 52404. I-380, exit 17 (33rd Ave SW), just w. Int corridors. **Pets:** Medium. $15 one-time fee/room. Designated rooms, service with restrictions, crate. [ASK] [✕] 🛢 🖵

◬ ▼▼ Country Inn & Suites By Carlson, Cedar Rapids Airport 🅷
(319) 363-3789. **$99-$149.** 9100 Atlantic Dr SW 52404. I-380, exit 13, just w. Int corridors. **Pets:** Medium. $20 one-time fee/pet. Designated rooms, service with restrictions, supervision.
[SAVE] [✕] [&M] 🛢 🖵 🏊

▼▼▼ Hawthorn Suites 🅷
(319) 294-8700. **Call for rates.** 4444 Czech Ln NE 52402. I-380, exit 24A (SR 100/Collins Rd), just s. Int corridors. **Pets:** Accepted.
[✕] [&M] 🛢 🖵 🏊

▼▼ Howard Johnson Ⓜ
(319) 366-2475. **Call for rates.** 616 33rd Ave SW 52404. I-380, exit 17 (33rd Ave SW), 0.3 mi w. Int corridors. **Pets:** Other species. $25 deposit/room. Service with restrictions. [✕] 🛢 🖵

▼▼▼ Mainstay Suites 🅷
(319) 363-7829. **$70-$99.** 5145 Rockwell Dr NE 52402. I-380, exit 24A (SR 100/Collins Rd), 1 mi e, then just n. Int corridors. **Pets:** Accepted.
[ASK] [✕] [&M] 🛢 🖵 🏊 [✕]

▼▼ Quality Inn of Cedar Rapids 🅷
(319) 393-8800. **$70-$199.** 4747 1st Ave SE 52402. I-380, exit 24A (SR 100/Collins Rd), 2.5 mi e, then 1st Ave SE. Int corridors. **Pets:** Accepted.
[ASK] [✕] [&M] 🛢 🖵 🏊

▼▼▼▼ Red Roof Inn Cedar Rapids 🅷
(319) 364-2000. **$45-$90.** 3243 Southridge Dr SW 52404. I-380, exit 17 (33rd Ave SW), just nw. Ext/int corridors. **Pets:** Large. Service with restrictions, crate. [ASK] [✕] [&M] 🛢 🖵 🏊

▼▼▼ **Residence Inn by Marriott** 🏨 🐾
(319) 395-0111. **$160-$165.** 1900 Dodge Rd NE 52402. I-380, exit 24A (SR 100/Collins Rd), just e. Int corridors. **Pets:** Other species. $84 one-time fee/room. Crate. 🖂 ⊹M 🔋 💻 🛥 🖂

▼ 💎 **Super 8** 🏨
(319) 362-6002. **$59-$74, 3 day notice.** 720 33rd Ave SW 52404. I-380, exit 17 (33rd Ave SW), 0.4 mi w. Int corridors. **Pets:** Accepted.
ASK 🖂 🔋 💻

▼ 💎 **Super 8** 🏨
(319) 363-1755. **Call for rates.** 400 33rd Ave SW 52404. I-380, exit 17 (33rd Ave SW), just w. Int corridors. **Pets:** Accepted. 🖂 🔋 💻

CHARLES CITY
▼▼ 💎 **Sleep Inn & Suites** 🏨
(641) 257-6700. **Call for rates.** 1416 S Grand Ave 50616. US 218/18, exit 218, 0.7 mi n on US 218 business route; south side of town. Int corridors. **Pets:** Accepted. 🖂 ♿M 🔋 💻 🛥

▼ ▼ **Super 8–Charles City** 🏨
(641) 228-2888. **$55-$99.** 1411 S Grand Ave 50616. US 218/18, exit 218, 0.8 mi n on US 218 business route; south side of town. Int corridors. **Pets:** Accepted. ASK 🖂 ♿M 🔋 💻

CHEROKEE
💎💎 ▼ 💎 **Best Western La Grande Hacienda** 🏨
(712) 225-5701. **$85-$95.** 1401 N 2nd St 51012. Just s of jct SR 3 and US 59 (N 2nd St). Int corridors. **Pets:** Medium. $25 daily fee/pet. Service with restrictions, supervision. SAVE 🖂 ♿M 💻 🍴 🛥

CLARINDA
▼▼ 💎 **Clarinda Super 8** 🏨
(712) 542-6333. **$55-$88.** 1203 S 12th St 51632. Jct US 71 and SR 2, just e. Int corridors. **Pets:** Service with restrictions, supervision.
ASK 🖂 ♿M 🔋 💻 🛥

CLEAR LAKE
▼▼ 💎 **AmericInn Lodge & Suites of Clear Lake** 🏨
(641) 357-8954. **$91-$111.** 1406 N 25th St 50428. I-35, exit 194 (US 18), just nw. Int corridors. **Pets:** Other species. Designated rooms, service with restrictions, supervision. ASK 🖂 🔋 💻 🛥

💎💎 ▼ ▼ **Best Western Holiday Lodge** 🏨
(641) 357-5253. **$89-$119.** 2023 7th Ave N 50428. I-35, exit 194 (US 18), 0.3 mi w. Ext/int corridors. **Pets:** Other species. $10 one-time fee/room. Service with restrictions, supervision.
SAVE 🖂 ♿M 🔋 💻 🍴 🛥 🖂

💎💎 ▼ ▼ **Budget Inn** Ⓜ
(641) 357-8700. **$40-$90.** 1306 N 25th St 50428. I-35, exit 194 (US 18), just nw. Int corridors. **Pets:** Accepted. SAVE 🖂 🔋 🛥

▼ 💎 **Lake Country Inn** Ⓜ
(641) 357-2184. **$49-$69.** 518 US 18 50428. I-35, exit 194 (US 18), 1.9 mi w. Ext corridors. **Pets:** Other species. $5 daily fee/pet. Designated rooms, service with restrictions, supervision. 🖂 🔋

▼ ▼ **Microtel Inn** 🏨
(641) 357-0966. **$67-$100.** 1305 N 25th St 50428. I-35, exit 194 (US 18), just nw. Int corridors. **Pets:** Accepted. ASK 🖂 ♿M 🔋 💻

▼ ▼ **Super 8** 🏨
(641) 357-7521. **Call for rates.** 2809 4th Ave S 50428. I-35, exit 193, just se. Int corridors. **Pets:** Accepted. 🖂 🔋 💻

CLINTON
💎💎 ▼▼ 💎 **Best Western-Frontier** 🏨
(563) 242-7112. **$80-$130.** 2300 Lincoln Way 52732. On US 30, just e of jct US 30 and 67. Int corridors. **Pets:** Small, other species. $10 daily fee/pet. Service with restrictions, crate.
SAVE 🖂 🔋 💻 🍴 🛥 🖂

💎💎 ▼ 💎 **Country Inn & Suites By Carlson** 🏨
(563) 244-9922. **$89-$119.** 2224 Lincoln Way 52732. On US 30, just e of jct US 30 and 67. Int corridors. **Pets:** $10 daily fee/pet. Service with restrictions, supervision. SAVE 🖂 ♿M 🔋 💻 🛥

▼▼ 💎 **Oak Tree Inn** 🏨
(563) 243-1000. **Call for rates.** 2300 Valley West Ct 52732. Just n of jct US 30 and 67; west side of town. Int corridors. **Pets:** Accepted.
🖂 ♿M 🔋 💻

▼▼ 💎 **Super 8-Clinton** 🏨
(563) 242-8870. **$50-$70.** 1711 Lincoln Way 52732. On US 30, 0.7 mi e of jct US 67. Int corridors. **Pets:** Other species. $10 one-time fee/pet. Service with restrictions, supervision. ASK 🖂 🔋 💻

CLIVE
💎💎 ▼ 💎 **Best Western Des Moines West** 🏨
(515) 221-2345. **$80-$100.** 1450 NW 118th St 50325. I-80/35, exit 124 (University Ave), just nw. Int corridors. **Pets:** Accepted.
SAVE 🖂 ♿M 🔋 💻

💎💎 ▼ 💎 **Chase Suites Hotel by Woodfin** 🏨 🐾
(515) 223-7700. **$94-$139.** 11428 Forest Ave 50325. I-80/35, exit 124 (University Ave), just ne. Ext corridors. **Pets:** Other species. $10 one-time fee/pet. Service with restrictions, crate.
SAVE 🖂 ♿M 🔋 🔋 💻 🛥 🖂

▼ ▼ **La Quinta Inn & Suites West Des Moines-Clive** 🏨 🐾
(515) 221-9200. **$49-$89.** 1390 NW 118th St 50325. I-80/35, exit 124 (University Ave). Int corridors. **Pets:** Medium, other species. Service with restrictions, supervision. ASK 🖂 ♿M 🔋 💻 🛥

COLFAX
💎💎 ▼ ▼ **Comfort Inn** 🏨
(515) 674-4455. **$67-$120.** 1402 N Walnut St 50054. I-80, exit 155 (SR 117), just ne. Int corridors. **Pets:** Other species. $13 daily fee/room. Service with restrictions, crate. SAVE 🖂 ♿M 🔋 💻

💎💎 ▼ ▼ **Microtel Inn & Suites** 🏨
(515) 674-0600. **Call for rates.** 11000 Federal Ave 50054. I-80, exit 155 (SR 117). Int corridors. **Pets:** Other species. $10 one-time fee/room. No service. SAVE 🖂 ♿M 🔋 💻

CORALVILLE
💎💎 ▼ 💎 **Baymont Inn & Suites** 🏨
(319) 337-9797. **$85-$159.** 200 6th St 52241. I-80, exit 242, just s on 1st Ave, then just w. Int corridors. **Pets:** $50 deposit/room, $10 daily fee/room. Service with restrictions. SAVE 🖂 🔋 💻 🛥

💎💎 ▼ ▼ **Best Western-Canterbury Inn & Suites** 🏨
(319) 351-0400. **$69-$159.** 704 1st Ave 52241. I-80, exit 242, just s. Int corridors. **Pets:** Medium, dogs only. $10 daily fee/pet. Designated rooms, service with restrictions. SAVE 🖂 🔋 💻 🍴 🛥 🖂

▼ ▼ **Comfort Inn by Choice Hotels** 🏨
(319) 351-8144. **$63-$160.** 209 W 9th St 52241. I-80, exit 242, just s. Int corridors. **Pets:** Accepted. ASK 🖂 ♿M 🔋 💻 🛥

💎💎 ▼▼ ▼ **Days Inn** Ⓜ
(319) 354-4400. **$63-$140.** 205 2nd St 52241. I-80, exit 242, 1 mi s to 2nd St, then just w. Ext corridors. **Pets:** Accepted. SAVE 🖂 🔋 💻

💎💎 ▼▼ ▼ **Holiday Inn** 🏨
(319) 351-5049. **$89-$269.** 1220 1st Ave 52241. I-80, exit 242, just n. Int corridors. **Pets:** Other species. $20 one-time fee/room. Designated rooms, service with restrictions, crate. SAVE 🖂 ♿M 🔋 💻 🍴 🛥

▼ ▼ **Super 8** 🏨
(319) 337-8388. **$60-$130.** 611 1st Ave 52241. I-80, exit 242, 0.4 mi s. Int corridors. **Pets:** Accepted. ASK 🖂 ♿M 🔋 💻

COUNCIL BLUFFS

◆◆◆ ▼▼▼ **Best Western Crossroads of the Bluffs** 🅷
(712) 322-3150. **$89-$129.** 2216 27th Ave 51501. I-29/80, exit 1B (24th St), just ne. Int corridors. **Pets:** Accepted. [SAVE] ✕ 🛅 🖃 ⇌

▼▼ **Days Inn** 🅷
(712) 366-9699. **Call for rates.** 3208 S 7th St 51501. I-29/80, exit 3 (US 92), just sw. Int corridors. **Pets:** Accepted. ✕ 🛅 🖃

◆◆◆ ▼▼▼ **Days Inn** 🅷
(712) 323-2200. **$50-$110.** 3619 9th Ave 51501. I-29, exit 53A (9th Ave). Int corridors. **Pets:** $10 daily fee/pet. Service with restrictions, supervision. [SAVE] ✕ 🛅 🖃

▼ **Super 8** 🅷
(712) 322-2888. **$69-$95.** 2712 S 24th St 51501. I-29/80, exit 1B (24th St), just nw. Int corridors. **Pets:** Service with restrictions, supervision. [ASK] ✕

◆◆◆ ▼▼▼ **Western Inn** 🅷
(712) 322-4499. **$59-$109.** 1842 Madison Ave 51503. I-80, exit 5 (Madison Ave), just s. Int corridors. **Pets:** Small. $10 one-time fee/pet. Service with restrictions, crate. [SAVE] ✕ ⇌

CRESCO

◆◆◆ ▼ **Cresco Motel** Ⓜ
(563) 547-2240. **$53-$81.** 620 2nd Ave SE (SR 9) SE 52136. On SR 9; east side of town. Ext corridors. **Pets:** Dogs only. Designated rooms, supervision. [SAVE] ✕ 🛅 🖃

CRESTON

▼▼ **Super 8-Creston** 🅷
(641) 782-6541. **$55-$75.** 804 W Taylor St 50801. Jct US 34 and SR 25, on US 34. Int corridors. **Pets:** Accepted. [ASK] ✕ 🛅 🖃

DENISON

▼▼ **Denison Super 8** 🅷
(712) 263-5081. **$69-$149.** 502 Boyer Valley Rd 51442. Jct US 30/59 and SR 141, 0.3 mi sw. Int corridors. **Pets:** Large. $6 one-time fee/pet. Service with restrictions, crate. [ASK] ✕ 🛅 🖃

DES MOINES

◆◆◆ ▼▼▼ **Best Western Des Moines Airport Hotel** 🅷 ❀
(515) 287-6464. **$85-$109.** 1810 Army Post Rd 50315. Across from airport. Int corridors. **Pets:** Large, other species. $25 one-time fee/pet. Designated rooms, service with restrictions, crate.
[SAVE] ✕ 🛅 🖃 🍴 ⇌

▼▼ **Comfort Inn by Choice Hotels** 🅷 ❀
(515) 287-3434. **$80-$116.** 5231 Fleur Dr 50321. Opposite the airport. Int corridors. **Pets:** Other species. $10 daily fee/pet.
[ASK] ✕ 🛅 🖃 ⇌

◆◆◆ ▼▼▼ **Des Moines Marriott Downtown** 🅷
(515) 245-5500. **$161-$197.** 700 Grand Ave 50309. Downtown. Int corridors. **Pets:** Other species. $75 one-time fee/room. Service with restrictions, supervision. [SAVE] ✕ 🛅 🖃 🍴 ⇌

◆◆◆ ▼▼▼ **Econo Lodge** 🅷
(515) 278-8858. **Call for rates.** 4755 Merle Hay Rd 50322. I-80/35, exit 131 (Merle Hay Rd), just s. Int corridors. **Pets:** $10 daily fee/pet. Service with restrictions, supervision. [SAVE] ✕ 🛅 🖃

▼▼ **Motel 6-30** Ⓜ
(515) 287-6364. **$39-$49.** 4817 Fleur Dr 50321. Opposite the airport. Ext corridors. **Pets:** Other species. Service with restrictions, supervision. ✕

▼▼▼ **Quality Inn & Suites Event Center** 🅷
(515) 282-5251. **$81-$150.** 929 3rd St 50309. I-235, exit 3rd St; downtown. Int corridors. **Pets:** Accepted. [ASK] ✕ 🛅 🖃 🍴 ⇌

◆◆◆ ▼▼▼ **Red Roof Inn & Suites** 🅷
(515) 266-6800. **Call for rates.** 4950 NE 14th St 50313. I-80, exit 136 (US 69). Int corridors. **Pets:** Large. Service with restrictions, crate.
[SAVE] ✕ 🛅 🖃

DE SOTO

▼ **Edgetowner Motel** Ⓜ ❀
(515) 834-2641. **$49.** 804 Guthrie St 50069. I-80, exit 110, just s. Ext corridors. **Pets:** Dogs only. Designated rooms, service with restrictions.
[ASK] ✕ 🛅

DUBUQUE

◆◆◆ ▼▼▼ **Best Western Midway Hotel** 🅷
(563) 557-8000. **$90-$190.** 3100 Dodge St 52003. US 20, 2.3 mi w of jct US 52/61/151 and Mississippi Bridge. Int corridors. **Pets:** Small. $10 daily fee/pet. Designated rooms, service with restrictions, supervision.
[SAVE] ✕ 🛅 🖃 🍴 ⇌ 🐾

▼▼ **Comfort Inn by Choice Hotels** 🅷
(563) 556-3006. **$65-$110.** 4055 McDonald Dr 52002. US 20, 3.8 mi w of jct US 52/61/151 and Mississippi Bridge. Int corridors. **Pets:** Accepted. [ASK] ✕ 🛅 🖃 ⇌

◆◆◆ ▼▼▼ **Days Inn** 🅷
(563) 583-3297. **$60-$90.** 1111 Dodge St 52003. US 20, 0.8 mi w of jct US 52/61/151 and Mississippi Bridge, exit Hill/Bryant. Ext corridors. **Pets:** Other species. $10 one-time fee/pet. Designated rooms, service with restrictions. [SAVE] ✕ 🛅 🖃 ⇌

◆◆◆ ▼▼▼ **Holiday Inn Dubuque/Galena** 🅷
(563) 556-2000. **$85-$117.** 450 Main St 52001. At Main and 4th sts; downtown. Int corridors. **Pets:** $25 one-time fee/room. Service with restrictions. [SAVE] ✕ 🛅 🖃 🍴 ⇌ 🐾

▼▼▼ **MainStay Suites** 🅷
(563) 557-7829. **$70-$110.** 1275 Associates Dr 52002. Just n of jct US 20 and NW Arterial Rd; west side of town. Int corridors. **Pets:** Small, other species. $20 one-time fee/room. Service with restrictions, crate.
[ASK] ✕ 🛅 🖃

DYERSVILLE

▼▼ **Comfort Inn** 🅷
(563) 875-7700. **$79-$180.** 527 16th Ave SE 52040. US 20, exit 294 (SR 136), just nw. Int corridors. **Pets:** Small. $13 daily fee/pet. Designated rooms, service with restrictions, supervision. [ASK] ✕ 🛅 🖃 ⇌

▼▼ **Super 8** 🅷
(563) 875-8885. **$50-$99.** 925 15th Ave SE 52040. US 20, exit 294 (SR 136), just n. Int corridors. **Pets:** Medium. $10 daily fee/pet. Service with restrictions, supervision. [ASK] ✕ 🛅 🖃

ELK HORN

◆◆◆ ▼▼▼ **AmericInn Lodge & Suites of Elkhorn** 🅷
(712) 764-4000. **$85-$155.** 4037 Main St 51531. I-80, exit 54 (SR 173), 6.4 mi n. Int corridors. **Pets:** $10 daily fee/room. Designated rooms, service with restrictions, supervision. [SAVE] ✕ 🛅 🖃 ⇌

EMMETSBURG

▼▼ **Super 8** 🅷
(712) 852-2667. **Call for rates.** 3501 Main St 50536. Jct US 18 and SR 4, 0.8 mi w. Int corridors. **Pets:** Accepted. ✕ 🛅 🖃

ESTHERVILLE

◆◆◆ ▼▼▼ **Sleep Inn & Suites** 🅷
(712) 362-5522. **$72-$140.** 2008 Central Ave 51334. Jct SR 4 and 9, 1 mi e. Int corridors. **Pets:** Other species. $20 one-time fee/pet. Service with restrictions, supervision. [SAVE] ✕ 🛅 🖃 ⇌

▼▼ **Super 8** 🅷
(712) 362-2400. **$50-$70.** 1919 Central Ave 51334. Jct SR 4 and 9, 1 mi e. Int corridors. **Pets:** Small, dogs only. Supervision. [ASK] ✕ 🛅 🖃

EVANSDALE

▼▼ Days Inn ☐

(319) 235-1111. **$79-$110.** 450 Evansdale Dr 50707. I-380/20, exit 68, just n. Int corridors. **Pets:** Accepted. (A$K) ⊠ 🖼 🖬 💻 ⌕

FAIRFIELD

(AAA) ▼▼▼ Best Western Fairfield Inn ☐

(641) 472-2200. **$84-$124.** 2200 W Burlington Ave 52556. On US 34, 1 mi w of jct SR 1. Int corridors. **Pets:** Accepted.
(SAVE) ⊠ 🖬 💻 ⑪ ⌕

(AAA) ▼▼▼ Super 8 ☐

(641) 469-2000. **$73-$125.** 3001 W Burlington Ave 52556. On US 34, 1.5 mi w of jct SR 1. Int corridors. **Pets:** Medium. $50 deposit/room, $5 daily fee/pet. No service, supervision. (SAVE) ⊠ 🖬 💻 ⌕

FORT DODGE

(AAA) ▼▼▼ AmericInn Lodge & Suites of Fort Dodge ☐

(515) 576-2100. **$110-$200.** 100 Kenyon Rd W 50501. 3 mi n of jct US 20 and 169. Int corridors. **Pets:** Accepted.
(SAVE) ⊠ 🖬 🖼 💻 ⌕

(AAA) ▼▼▼ Comfort Inn ☐

(515) 573-5000. **$90-$150.** 2938 5th Ave S 50501. US 20, exit 124 (Coalville), 3.5 mi n on CR P59, then 1.3 mi w on 5th Ave and Business Rt US 20. Int corridors. **Pets:** Accepted. (SAVE) ⊠ 🖼 🖬 💻 ⌕

▼▼ Fort Dodge Inn ☐

(515) 576-8000. **$64-$74, 7 day notice.** 3040 5th Ave S 50501. US 20, exit 124 (Coalville), 3.5 mi n on CR P59, then 1.2 mi w on Business Rt US 20. Int corridors. **Pets:** Small. $25 daily fee/pet. Designated rooms, service with restrictions, supervision. (A$K) ⊠ 🖬 💻

FORT MADISON

(AAA) ▼▼▼ Comfort Inn & Suites ☐

(319) 372-6800. **$90-$110.** 6169 Reve Ct 52627. Just e of jct US 61 and SR 2, on US 61. Int corridors. **Pets:** Accepted.
(SAVE) ⊠ 🖬 💻 ⌕ ⊠

▼ Knights Inn ☒

(319) 372-7740. **$65-$105, 7 day notice.** 3440 Ave L 52627. 2.1 mi e of jct US 61 and SR 2. Ext corridors. **Pets:** Medium. $10 daily fee/pet. Designated rooms, service with restrictions, supervision.
(A$K) ⊠ 🖬 💻

▼▼ Super 8-Ft Madison ☐

(319) 372-8500. **$50-$69.** 5107 Ave O 52627. 1 mi e of jct US 61 and SR 2. Int corridors. **Pets:** Other species. $10 daily fee/pet. Service with restrictions, supervision. (A$K) ⊠ 🖬 💻

GRIMES

▼▼ AmericInn Lodge & Suites of Grimes ☐ ❀

(515) 986-9900. **Call for rates.** 251 Gateway Cir 50111. Just sw of jct US 44 and SR 141. Int corridors. **Pets:** Medium. $10 daily fee/pet. Designated rooms, service with restrictions, supervision.
⊠ 🖼 🖬 💻 ⌕ ⊠

GRINNELL

▼▼▼ Comfort Inn & Suites ☐

(641) 236-5236. **Call for rates.** 1630 West St S 50112. I-80, exit 182, 0.7 mi n. Int corridors. **Pets:** Accepted. ⊠ 🖼 🖬 💻 ⌕ ⊠

HAMPTON

(AAA) ▼▼▼ AmericInn Lodge & Suites of Hampton ☐

(641) 456-5559. **$80-$160.** 702 Central Ave W 50441. On SR 3 (Central Ave W), 0.7 mi w of jct US 65 and SR 3. Int corridors. **Pets:** Accepted.
(SAVE) ⊠ 🖬 💻 ⌕ ⊠

IDA GROVE

▼ Delux Motel ☒

(712) 364-3317. **$50-$60.** 5981 US Hwy 175 51445. Jct US 59 S and 175. Ext/int corridors. **Pets:** $10 daily fee/pet. Designated rooms, service with restrictions, supervision. ⊠ 🖬

▼▼ Super 8 ☐

(712) 364-3988. **$60-$93.** 90 E Hwy 175 51445. Just n of SR 175. Int corridors. **Pets:** Other species. $10 one-time fee/room. Designated rooms, service with restrictions. (A$K) ⊠ 🖼 🖬 💻

INDEPENDENCE

▼▼ Super 8 ☐

(319) 334-7041. **$66-$125.** 2000 1st St W 50644. US 20, exit 252, 1.4 mi n. Int corridors. **Pets:** Small, dogs only. $25 daily fee/pet. Service with restrictions, crate. (A$K) ⊠ 🖼 🖬 💻

IOWA CITY

(AAA) ▼▼▼ Alexis Park Inn & Suites ☐

(319) 337-8665. **$68-$220, 3 day notice.** 1165 S Riverside Dr 52246. I-80, exit 239 (US 218), 5 mi s, 2 mi e on US 6, then just s. Ext corridors. **Pets:** $10 daily fee/pet. Designated rooms, service with restrictions, crate. (SAVE) ⊠ 🖬 💻 ⌕

(AAA) ▼▼▼▼ hotelVetro conference center ☐

(319) 337-4961. **$159-$309.** 201 S Linn St 52240. I-80, exit 244, s on Dubuque St, e on Washington St, then s. Int corridors. **Pets:** Medium, dogs only. $50 one-time fee/pet. Service with restrictions, supervision.
(SAVE) ⊠ 🖬 💻 ⌕

(AAA) ▼▼▼▼ Sheraton Iowa City Hotel ☐ ❀

(319) 337-4058. **$99-$399.** 210 S Dubuque St 52240. Jct Dubuque and Burlington sts (SR 1); downtown. Int corridors. **Pets:** Medium, dogs only. Service with restrictions, supervision.
(SAVE) ⊠ 🖼 🖬 💻 ⑪ ⌕ ⊠

IOWA FALLS

▼▼ Iowa Falls Super 8 ☐

(641) 648-4618. **Call for rates.** 839 S Oak St 50126. Jct US 65 and Washington Ave, 1 mi s; US 20, exit 168, 3.8 mi n. Int corridors. **Pets:** Accepted. ⊠ 🖬 💻 ⌕

JOHNSTON

▼▼▼ TownePlace Suites by Marriott Des Moines/Urbandale ☐

(515) 727-4066. **$98-$120.** 8800 Northpark Dr 50131. I-35/80, exit 129 (86th St), just nw. Int corridors. **Pets:** Other species. $100 one-time fee/room. Service with restrictions. ⊠ 🖬 💻 ⌕

KEOKUK

▼▼▼ Holiday Inn Express ☐

(319) 524-8000. **$80-$89.** 325 Main St 52632. 4th and Main sts; downtown. Int corridors. **Pets:** Medium, dogs only. $15 daily fee/pet. Designated rooms, service with restrictions, crate.
⊠ 🖼 🖬 💻 ⌕ ⊠

▼▼ Super 8-Keokuk ☐

(319) 524-3888. **$50-$79.** 3511 Main St 52632. On Business Rt US 61/218, 2 mi n of jct US 136. Int corridors. **Pets:** Other species. $10 daily fee/room. Service with restrictions, supervision. (A$K) ⊠ 🖼 🖬 💻

LE CLAIRE

▼▼▼ Comfort Inn & Suites-Riverview ☐ ❀

(563) 289-4747. **$99-$130.** 902 Mississippi View Ct 52753. I-80, exit 306 (US 67), 0.5 mi n to Eagle Ridge Rd, then just sw. Int corridors. **Pets:** Medium. $10 daily fee/pet. Service with restrictions, crate.
(A$K) ⊠ 🖼 🖬 💻 ⌕

▼▼▼ Holiday Inn Express ☐

(563) 289-9978. **$109-$219.** 1201 Canal Shore Dr 52753. I-80, exit 306 (US 67), just n. Int corridors. **Pets:** Medium, other species. $25 one-time fee/room. Designated rooms, service with restrictions, supervision.
(A$K) ⊠ 🖬 💻

▼▼ ▼▼ Super 8 of LeClaire 🅷 ❀
(563) 289-5888. **$75-$170.** 1552 Welcome Center Dr 52753. I-80, exit 306 (US 67), 0.5 mi n to Eagle Ridge Rd, then just sw to Mississippi View Ct. Int corridors. **Pets:** Medium. $10 daily fee/pet. Service with restrictions, crate. (A$K) ⊠ ⬥M 🔲 💻

LE MARS
▼▼ Americas Best Value Inn 🅷
(712) 546-8800. **Call for rates.** 1201 Hawkeye Ave SW 51031. US 75, exit 116, 1.6 mi ne. Int corridors. **Pets:** $10 daily fee/pet. Service with restrictions, supervision. ⊠ ⬥M 🔲 💻 ⌇

MANCHESTER
(AAA) ▼▼ Super 8 🅷
(563) 927-2533. **$60-$70.** 1020 W Main St 52057. Jct US 20 and SR 13, exit 275, 1.3 mi n, then 0.3 mi e. Int corridors. **Pets:** Other species. $10 daily fee/room. Designated rooms, service with restrictions.
(SAVE) ⊠ ⬥M 🔲 💻

MARION
▼▼ Microtel Inn & Suites 🅷
(319) 373-7400. **$55-$85.** 5500 Dyer Ave 52302. Jct US 151 and SR 13. Int corridors. **Pets:** Small. $50 deposit/room. Service with restrictions, supervision. (A$K) ⊠ ⬥M 🔲 💻

MARQUETTE
▼▼ The Frontier Motel Ⓜ
(563) 873-3497. **$67-$115.** 101 S 1st St 52158. Just s of jct US 18 and SR 76; between Mississippi River Bridge and casino. Ext corridors. **Pets:** Accepted. (A$K) ⊠ 🔲 💻 ⌇

MARSHALLTOWN
(AAA) ▼▼▼ Best Western Regency Inn 🅷 ❀
(641) 752-6321. **$81-$90.** 3303 S Center St 50158. Jct US 30 and SR 14. Int corridors. **Pets:** Other species. $10 daily fee/room. Service with restrictions, supervision. (SAVE) ⊠ ⬥M 🔲 💻 🍽 ⌇

▼▼ Comfort Inn 🅷
(641) 752-6000. **$77-$110.** 2613 S Center St 50158. 0.5 mi n of jct US 30 and SR 14. Int corridors. **Pets:** $10 daily fee/room. Service with restrictions, supervision. (A$K) ⊠ 🔲 💻 ⌇

▼▼ Super 8 🅷 ❀
(641) 753-3333. **$53-$72.** 3315 S Center St 50158. Just n of jct US 30 and SR 14. Int corridors. **Pets:** Other species. $10 daily fee/room. Service with restrictions, supervision. (A$K) ⊠ 🔲 💻

MASON CITY
▼▼ Days Inn Mason City 🅷
(641) 424-0210. **Call for rates.** 2301 4th St SW 50401. I-35, exit 194 (SR 122), 6 mi e. Int corridors. **Pets:** Accepted. ⊠ 🔲 💻

(AAA) ▼▼▼ Holiday Inn 🅷
(641) 423-1640. **$89-$169.** 2101 4th St SW (Hwy 122) 50401. I-35, exit 194 (SR 122), 6 mi e. Ext/int corridors. **Pets:** $15 one-time fee/room. Service with restrictions, crate. (SAVE) ⊠ ⬥M 🔲 💻 🍽 ⌇ ⊠

▼▼▼ Mason City Super 8 🅷
(641) 423-8855. **$65-$85.** 3010 4th St SW 50401. I-35, exit 194 (SR 122), 5.3 mi e. Int corridors. **Pets:** $10 daily fee/room. Service with restrictions, supervision. (A$K) ⊠ ⬥M 🔲 💻

MISSOURI VALLEY
(AAA) ▼▼▼ Oak Tree Inn 🅷
(712) 642-3000. **$63-$84.** 128 S Willow Rd 51555. I-29, exit 75, 0.4 mi ne. Int corridors. **Pets:** Accepted. (SAVE) ⊠ ⬥M 🔲 💻

MONTICELLO
▼▼ The Blue Inn 🅷
(319) 465-6116. **$35-$129.** 250 N Main St 52310. On Business Rt US 151; north end of town. Int corridors. **Pets:** Accepted.
(A$K) ⊠ 🔲 💻 ⌇

MOUNT PLEASANT
▼▼ Super 8 🅷 ❀
(319) 385-8888. **$55-$80.** 1000 N Grand Ave 52641. US 218/27, exit 45, 0.6 mi s. Int corridors. **Pets:** Other species. $10 daily fee/pet. Service with restrictions, supervision. (A$K) ⊠ 🔲 💻

MOUNT VERNON
▼▼ Sleep Inn & Suites 🅷
(319) 895-0055. **Call for rates.** 310 Virgil Ave 52314. Jct US 30 and SR 1, just se. Int corridors. **Pets:** Medium. $13 one-time fee/room. Service with restrictions, supervision. ⊠ ⬥M 🔲 💻 ⌇

MUSCATINE
▼▼ AmericInn Lodge & Suites of Muscatine 🅷
(563) 263-0880. **Call for rates.** 3115 Hwy 61 N 52761. Jct US 61 and SR 38, just n. Int corridors. **Pets:** Accepted.
⊠ ⬥M 🔲 💻 ⌇ ⊠

▼ Muscatine Super 8 🅷
(563) 263-9100. **$53-$69.** 2900 N Hwy 61 52761. Jct US 61 and SR 38. Int corridors. **Pets:** Accepted. (A$K) ⊠ 🔲 💻

NEWTON
▼▼ Days Inn of Newton 🅷
(641) 792-2330. **$55-$150.** 1605 W 19th St S 50208. I-80, exit 164 (SR 14), just n. Int corridors. **Pets:** $10 daily fee/room. Service with restrictions, supervision. (A$K) ⊠ 🔲 💻

▼▼▼ Holiday Inn Express 🅷
(641) 792-3333. **Call for rates.** 208 W 4th St N 50208. Downtown. Int corridors. **Pets:** Accepted. ⊠ ⬥M 🔲 💻 ⌇

▼▼ Quality Inn of Newton Iowa 🅷
(641) 792-7722. **$72-$108.** 1700 W 19th St S 50208. I-80, exit 164 (SR 14), just nw. Int corridors. **Pets:** Accepted. (A$K) ⊠ 🔲 💻

NORTH LIBERTY
▼▼▼ Sleep Inn & Suites 🅷
(319) 665-2700. **$70-$169.** 485 Madison Ave N 52317. I-380, exit 4 (North Liberty). Int corridors. **Pets:** Small. $13 daily fee/room. Service with restrictions, supervision. (A$K) ⊠ ⬥M 🔲 💻 ⌇

NORTHWOOD
(AAA) ▼▼▼ Country Inn & Suites By Carlson 🅷
(641) 323-7000. **$120-$130, 14 day notice.** 711 Diamond Jo Ln 50459. I-35, exit 214, just nw. Int corridors. **Pets:** Small. $25 one-time fee/room. Designated rooms, service with restrictions, supervision.
(SAVE) ⊠ ⬥M 🔲 💻 ⌇

OELWEIN
▼▼ Super 8-Oelwein Ⓜ
(319) 283-2888. **$65-$95.** 210 10th St SE 50662. Jct SR 3 and 150, 1 mi s on SR 150; south end of downtown. Int corridors. **Pets:** Small, dogs only. $20 daily fee/pet. Designated rooms, service with restrictions.
(A$K) ⊠ 🔲 💻

OKOBOJI
▼▼ AmericInn Lodge & Suites of Okoboji 🅷
(712) 332-9000. **$79-$269, 7 day notice.** 1005 Brooks Park Dr 51355. Jct US 71 and SR 9, 2.5 mi s on US 71. Int corridors. **Pets:** Medium, dogs only. $25 one-time fee/pet. Service with restrictions, supervision.
⊠ ⬥M 🔲 💻 ⌇

(AAA) ▼▼▼ Arrowwood Resort & Conference Center by ClubHouse 🅷
(712) 332-2161. **Call for rates.** 1405 US 71 S 51355. Jct US 71 and SR 9, 3 mi s. Ext/int corridors. **Pets:** Other species. Service with restrictions, crate. (SAVE) ⊠ ⬥M 🔲 💻 🍽 ⌇ ⊠

OSCEOLA

△△△ ▽▽ ▽▽ Americas Best Value Inn **M**

(641) 342-2123. **$66-$69.** 1520 Jeffreys Dr 50213. I-35, exit 33 (Osceola/US 34), just e. Int corridors. **Pets:** Other species.

[SAVE] [X] [▦]

▽▽ ▽▽ AmericInn Lodge & Suites of Osceola **H**

(641) 342-9400. **$90-$160.** 111 Ariel Cir 50213. I-35, exit 33 (Osceola/US 34), just w. Int corridors. **Pets:** Small, dogs only. $50 deposit/pet, $10 one-time fee/room. Designated rooms, service with restrictions, supervision. [ASK] [X] [&M] [▦] [▦] [≈]

▽▽ ▽▽ Days Inn **H**

(641) 342-6666. **$70-$149.** 710 Warren Ave 50213. I-35, exit 33 (Osceola/US 34), just e. Int corridors. **Pets:** Large. $10 daily fee/pet. No service, supervision. [ASK] [X] [▦] [▦] [≈]

OSKALOOSA

▽▽ ▽▽ Comfort Inn **H**

(641) 676-6000. **$90-$170.** 2401 a Ave W 52577. SR 163, exit 57 (SR 92), just e. Int corridors. **Pets:** Accepted. [ASK] [X] [▦] [▦] [≈]

▽▽ ▽▽ Super 8-Oskaloosa **H**

(641) 673-8481. **$59-$95.** 306 S 17th St 52577. Just s of SR 92 and 23. Int corridors. **Pets:** Accepted. [ASK] [X] [&M] [▦] [▦]

PELLA

▽▽ ▽▽ Super 8 **H**

(641) 628-8181. **$33-$100.** 105 E Oskaloosa St 50219. SR 163, exit 42, 1 mi n, then 0.5 mi e. Int corridors. **Pets:** Other species. $10 daily fee/pet. Service with restrictions, crate. [ASK] [X] [&M] [▦] [▦]

PERCIVAL

▽▽ ▽▽ Americas Best Value Inn & Suites **H**

(712) 382-2100. **$77-$115.** 2113 Sapp Brothers Dr 51648. I-29, exit 10 (SR 2), just w. Int corridors. **Pets:** Accepted. [ASK] [X] [▦] [▦] [≈]

△△△ ▽▽ ▽▽ Nebraska City Super 8 **H**

(712) 382-2828. **$62-$69.** 2103 249th St 51648. I-29, exit 10 (SR 2), just w. Int corridors. **Pets:** Other species. $10 one-time fee/room. Supervision. [SAVE] [X] [&M] [▦] [▦]

PLEASANT HILL

△△△ ▽▽ ▽▽ Sleep Inn & Suites **H**

(515) 299-9922. **$80-$150.** 5850 Morning Star Ct 50327. US 65, exit 79 (SR 163/E University Ave), just e. Int corridors. **Pets:** Other species. $13 daily fee/room. Service with restrictions. [SAVE] [X] [&M] [▦] [▦] [≈]

QUAD CITIES AREA

BETTENDORF

▽▽ ▽▽ ▽▽ The Lodge-Hotel & Conference Center **H**

(563) 359-7141. **$105.** 900 Spruce Hills Dr 52722. I-74, exit 2, just e. Int corridors. **Pets:** Accepted. [ASK] [X] [▦] [▦] [¶¶] [≈] [X]

▽▽ ▽▽ ▽▽ Ramada Inn **H**

(563) 355-7575. **Call for rates.** 3020 Utica Ridge Rd 52722. I-74, exit 2, just e. Int corridors. **Pets:** Accepted. [X] [&M] [▦] [▦] [≈]

DAVENPORT

△△△ ▽▽ ▽▽ ▽▽ Best Western SteepleGate Inn **H**

(563) 386-6900. **$90-$130.** 100 W 76th St 52806. I-80, exit 295A (US 61), 0.5 mi s to 65th St and west frontage road entrance, then just nw. Int corridors. **Pets:** Small, other species. $10 daily fee/pet. Service with restrictions, supervision. [SAVE] [X] [▦] [▦] [¶¶] [≈]

△△△ ▽▽ ▽▽ ▽▽ Clarion Hotel & Conference Center **H**

(563) 391-1230. **$75-$99.** 5202 Brady St 52806. I-80, exit 295A (US 61), 1.6 mi s. Int corridors. **Pets:** Large. $10 daily fee/room. Designated rooms, service with restrictions, crate. [SAVE] [X] [&M] [▦] [▦] [¶¶] [≈] [X]

△△△ ▽▽ ▽▽ Comfort Inn & Suites-Davenport **H**

(563) 324-8300. **$99-$149.** 8300 Northwest Blvd 52806. I-80, exit 292 (Northwest Blvd), just n. Int corridors. **Pets:** Accepted. [SAVE] [X] [&M] [▦] [▦] [≈]

▽▽ ▽▽ Country Inn & Suites By Carlson **H**

(563) 388-6444. **$79-$129.** 140 E 55th St 52806. I-80, exit 295A (US 61), 1.4 mi s. Int corridors. **Pets:** Accepted. [ASK] [X] [&M] [▦] [▦] [≈]

▽▽ ▽▽ Econo Lodge Inn & Suites **H**

(563) 391-8222. **$55-$70.** 7222 Northwest Blvd 52806. I-80, exit 292 (Northwest Blvd), 0.3 mi s. Ext corridors. **Pets:** Accepted. [ASK] [X] [▦] [▦]

▽▽ ▽▽ Fairfield Inn by Marriott **H**

(563) 355-2264. **$90-$100.** 3206 E Kimberly Rd 52807. I-74, exit 2, just w. Int corridors. **Pets:** Other species. $35 one-time fee/room. Service with restrictions, supervision. [X] [&M] [▦] [▦] [≈]

▽▽ ▽▽ Residence Inn by Marriott **H**

(563) 391-8877. **$130-$140.** 120 E 55th St 52806. I-80, exit 295A (US 61), 1.4 mi s. Int corridors. **Pets:** Medium, other species. $75 one-time fee/room. Service with restrictions. [X] [&M] [▦] [▦] [≈] [X]

▽▽ ▽▽ ▽▽ Staybridge Suites **H**

(563) 359-7829. **$99-$189.** 4729 Progress Dr 52807. I-74, exit 1 (53rd St), 0.5 mi e, then 0.4 mi s on CR 216 (Utica Ridge Rd). Int corridors. **Pets:** Medium, other species. $10 daily fee/room. Service with restrictions, crate. [ASK] [X] [&M] [▦] [▦] [≈] [X]

▽▽ ▽▽ Super 8 **H**

(563) 388-9810. **Call for rates.** 410 E 65th St 52807. I-80, exit 295A (US 61), 0.5 mi s, then just e. Int corridors. **Pets:** Accepted. [X] [▦] [▦]

▽▽ ▽▽ Travelodge **H**

(563) 386-6350. **$45-$84.** 6310 N Brady Ave 52806. I-80, exit 295A (US 61), 0.5 mi s; use frontage road on west side. Int corridors. **Pets:** Accepted. [ASK] [X] [▦] [▦]

END AREA

RIVERSIDE

▽▽ ▽▽ ▽▽ Riverside Casino & Golf Resort **H**

(319) 648-1234. **$70-$250.** 3184 Hwy 22 52327. I-218, exit 80, 1.5 mi ne. Int corridors. **Pets:** Medium, dogs only. $30 daily fee/room. Designated rooms, service with restrictions, crate. [ASK] [X] [&M] [▦] [▦] [¶¶] [≈] [X]

SHELDON

▽▽ ▽▽ Super 8 **H**

(712) 324-8400. **Call for rates.** 210 N 2nd Ave 51201. SR 60, exit 34, 2 mi w on US 18, then just n on Business Rt SR 60. Int corridors. **Pets:** Accepted. [X] [&M] [▦] [▦] [≈]

SIBLEY

▼▼ Super 8 H
(712) 754-3603. **Call for rates.** 1108 2nd Ave 51249. SR 60, exit 48, 1 mi w. Int corridors. **Pets:** Accepted. ⊠ 🔊ᴹ 🔋 🖵

SIOUX CENTER

▼▼ Econo Lodge H
(712) 722-4000. **Call for rates.** 86 9th St Cir NE 51250. On US 75, 1 mi n of jct SR 840; north side of town. Ext/int corridors. **Pets:** Accepted. ⊠ 🔊ᴹ 🔋 🖵

SIOUX CITY

▼▼ AmericInn Lodge & Suites of Sioux City H
(712) 255-1800. **$77-$160.** 4230 S Lewis Blvd 51106. I-29, exit 143, just e. Int corridors. **Pets:** Other species. $10 daily fee/room. Designated rooms, service with restrictions, supervision.
ASK ⊠ 🔊ᴹ 🔋 🖵 ⇄ 🗶

▼▼ Comfort Inn by Choice Hotels H
(712) 274-1300. **$59-$80.** 4202 S Lakeport St 51106. I-29, exit 144A, 1 mi e on US 20, then just s. Int corridors. **Pets:** Medium, other species. $25 one-time fee/room. Service with restrictions, supervision.
ASK ⊠ 🔋 🖵 ⇄

▼▼ Holiday Inn Express H
(712) 274-1400. **$72-$149.** 4230 S Lakeport St 51106. I-29, exit 144A, 1 mi e on US 20, then just s. Int corridors. **Pets:** Accepted.
ASK ⊠ 🔊ᴹ 🔋 🖵

🐪 ▼▼ Ramada City Centre H
(712) 277-1550. **$55-$100, 30 day notice.** 130 Nebraska St 51101. I-29, exit 147B (Tyson Event Center), just w on Gordon Dr, then just n. Int corridors. **Pets:** Other species. $10 daily fee/room. Designated rooms, service with restrictions, supervision. SAVE ⊠ 🔋 🖵 ⇄

▼▼ Super 8 H
(712) 274-1520. **$55-$78.** 4307 Stone Ave 51106. I-29, exit 144A northbound, US 75 to exit 4B, 1.5 mi w on Gordon Dr; exit 147B southbound to Gordon Dr, 3 mi e. Int corridors. **Pets:** Small. $10 daily fee/pet. Designated rooms, service with restrictions, supervision. ASK ⊠ 🔋 🖵

SLOAN

▼▼ Winna Vegas Inn H
(712) 428-4280. **Call for rates.** 1862 Hwy 141 51055. I-29, exit 127, just e. Int corridors. **Pets:** Accepted. ⊠ 🔊ᴹ 🔋 🖵

SPIRIT LAKE

▼▼ Ramada H 🐾
(712) 336-3984. **$79-$199, 5 day notice.** 2704 17th St 51360. Jct US 71 and SR 9, just w. Int corridors. **Pets:** Large. $50 deposit/room. Service with restrictions, supervision. ASK ⊠ 🔋 🖵 ⇄

▼▼ Spirit Lake Super 8 H
(712) 336-4901. **Call for rates.** 2203 Circle Dr W 51360. Jct US 71 and SR 9. Int corridors. **Pets:** $10 one-time fee/room. Service with restrictions, supervision. ⊠ 🔊ᴹ 🔋 🖵

SPRINGDALE

🐪 ▼ Econo Lodge M
(319) 627-2171. **$70.** 1943 Garfield Ave 52776. I-80, exit 259, just sw. Ext corridors. **Pets:** Accepted. SAVE ⊠ 🖵

STORY CITY

▼▼▼ Comfort Inn H
(515) 733-6363. **Call for rates.** 425 Timberland Dr 50248. I-35, exit 124, just sw. Int corridors. **Pets:** Large, other species. $13 one-time fee/room. Service with restrictions, supervision. ⊠ 🔊ᴹ 🔋 🖵 ⇄ 🗶

▼▼ Super 8 H
(515) 733-5281. **$51-$66.** 515 Factory Outlet Dr 50248. I-35, exit 124, just sw. Int corridors. **Pets:** Other species. $10 daily fee/pet. Designated rooms, service with restrictions, supervision. ASK ⊠ 🔋 🖵

STUART

▼▼ AmericInn Lodge & Suites of Stuart H
(515) 523-9000. **$70-$99.** 420 SW 8th St 50250. I-80, exit 93, just w. Int corridors. **Pets:** Accepted. ASK ⊠ 🔊ᴹ 🔋 🖵 ⇄ 🗶

▼▼ Super 8 H
(515) 523-2888. **Call for rates.** 203 SE 7th St 50250. I-80, exit 93. Int corridors. **Pets:** Accepted. ⊠ 🔊ᴹ 🔋 🖵 ⇄

TOLEDO

▼▼ Designer Inn & Suites H
(641) 484-5678. **$45-$129.** 403 US 30 W 52342. On US 30, just w of jct US 63 and 30. Int corridors. **Pets:** $7 daily fee/pet. Designated rooms.
ASK ⊠ 🔋 🖵 ⇄

▼▼ Super 8-Toledo H
(641) 484-5888. **$67-$110.** 207 Hwy 30 W 52342. On US 30, just w of jct US 63 and 30. Ext/int corridors. **Pets:** Accepted. ASK ⊠ 🔋 🖵

URBANA

▼▼ Urbana Inn & Suites H
(319) 443-8888. **$59-$71.** 5369 Hutton Dr 52345. I-380, exit 43, just s on east access road. Int corridors. **Pets:** Small. $15 one-time fee/room. Service with restrictions, supervision. ASK ⊠ 🔊ᴹ 🔋 🖵 ⇄ 🗶

URBANDALE

▼▼ Extended StayAmerica H
(515) 276-1929. **$54-$59.** 3940 114th St 50322. I-35/80, exit 126 (Douglas Ave), just e to 114th St, then 0.4 mi nw. Int corridors. **Pets:** Other species. $25 daily fee/room. Designated rooms, service with restrictions, crate. ASK ⊠ 🔊ᴹ 🔋 🖵

🐪 ▼▼▼ Holiday Inn Hotel & Suites Northwest H
(515) 278-4755. **$84-$124.** 4800 Merle Hay Rd 50322. I-35/80, exit 131 (Merle Hay Rd), just s. Int corridors. **Pets:** Accepted.
SAVE ⊠ 🔊ᴹ 🔋 🖵 🍴 ⇄ 🗶

▼▼ Sleep Inn H 🌼
(515) 270-2424. **$59-$109.** 11211 Hickman Rd 50322. I-35/80, exit 125 (Hickman Rd), just ne. Int corridors. **Pets:** Other species. $10 daily fee/pet. Designated rooms, service with restrictions, crate.
ASK ⊠ 🔊ᴹ 🔋 🖵 ⇄ 🗶

WALNUT

▼▼ Super 8 H 🌼
(712) 784-2221. **$50-$100.** 2109 Antique City Dr 51577. I-80, exit 46, just n. Int corridors. **Pets:** Other species. $8 daily fee/pet. Designated rooms, service with restrictions, supervision. ASK ⊠ 🔊ᴹ 🔋 🖵 ⇄

WASHINGTON

▼▼ Super 8-Washington M
(319) 653-6621. **Call for rates.** 119 Westview Dr 52353. 1.5 mi w on SR 1 and 92. Int corridors. **Pets:** Medium, dogs only. $10 one-time fee/pet. Designated rooms, crate. ⊠ 🔋 🖵

WATERLOO

▼▼ Baymont Inn & Suites H
(319) 233-9191. **Call for rates.** 2141 LaPorte Rd 50702. I-380, exit 72 (E San Marnan Dr). Int corridors. **Pets:** Accepted.
⊠ 🔊ᴹ 🔋 🖵 ⇄

▼▼▼ Candlewood Suites H
(319) 235-7000. **Call for rates.** 2056 LaPorte Rd 50702. I-218, exit 72 (E San Marnan Dr), just sw. Int corridors. **Pets:** Accepted.
⊠ 🔊ᴹ 🔋 🖵

▼▼ Comfort Inn by Choice Hotels H
(319) 234-7411. **$70-$90.** 1945 LaPorte Rd 50702. I-380, exit 72 (E San Marnan Dr). Int corridors. **Pets:** Large. Designated rooms, service with restrictions, supervision. ASK ⊠ 🔋 🖵 ⇄

◆◆ Ramada Hotel & Convention Center 🅷

(319) 233-7560. **$88-$165.** 205 W 4th St 50701. 4th and Commercial sts; downtown. Int corridors. **Pets:** Accepted.

(ASK) ✕ 🐾 🔌 💻 🍴 ⊸ ✕

◆◆ Super 8 🅷

(319) 233-1800. **$65-$80.** 1825 LaPorte Rd 50702. I-380, exit 72 (E San Marnan Dr), just nw. Int corridors. **Pets:** Accepted. (ASK) ✕ 🔌 💻

WAVERLY

◆◆ Comfort Inn 🅷

(319) 352-0399. **$80-$169.** 404 29th Ave SW 50677. US 218, exit 198, 0.7 mi n. Int corridors. **Pets:** Medium, dogs only. $10 daily fee/pet. Designated rooms, service with restrictions, supervision.

(ASK) ✕ 🐾 🔌 💻 ⊸ ✕

◆◆ Super 8 Waverly 🅷

(319) 352-0888. **Call for rates.** 301 13th Ave SW 50677. US 218, exit 198, 1.4 mi n. Int corridors. **Pets:** Medium, other species. $10 daily fee/pet. Designated rooms, service with restrictions, supervision.

✕ 🐾 🔌 💻

WEBSTER CITY

◆◆ AmericInn Motel & Suites of Webster City 🅷

(515) 832-3999. **Call for rates.** 411 Closz Dr 50595. Just s of jct US 20 and SR 17. Int corridors. **Pets:** Accepted. ✕ 🐾 🔌 💻 ⊸

◆◆ Super 8 🅷

(515) 832-2000. **$50-$75.** 305 Closz Dr 50595. Just s of jct US 20 and SR 17. Int corridors. **Pets:** Small. $6 daily fee/pet. Designated rooms, service with restrictions, supervision. (ASK) ✕ 🔌 💻 ⊸

WEST BEND

◆◆ Park View Inn & Suites and Conference Center 🅷

(515) 887-3611. **Call for rates.** 13 4th St NE 50597. Jct CR B63, 1 mi n on SR 15, then just w. Int corridors. **Pets:** Small. $15 one-time fee/room. Designated rooms, service with restrictions, supervision. ✕ 🔌 ⊸

WEST BURLINGTON

◆◆ AmericInn Lodge & Suites of Burlington 🅷

(319) 758-9000. **$70-$150.** 628 S Gear Ave 52655. US 34, exit 260 (Gear Ave), just ne. Int corridors. **Pets:** Medium. $10 daily fee/pet. Designated rooms, service with restrictions, supervision.

(ASK) ✕ 🔌 💻 ⊸ ✕

WEST DES MOINES

◆◆ Candlewood Suites-West Des Moines 🅷

(515) 221-0001. **$65-$130.** 7625 Office Plaza Dr N 50266. I-80, exit 121 (Jordan Creek Pkwy), just sw. Int corridors. **Pets:** Accepted.

(ASK) ✕ 🐾 🔌 💻

◆◆◆ Drury Inn & Suites 🅷

(515) 457-9500. **$90-$184.** 5505 Mills Civic Pkwy 50266. I-35, exit 70 (Mills Civic Pkwy), just w. Int corridors. **Pets:** Other species. No service, supervision. (ASK) ✕ 🐾 🔌 💻 ⊸

◆◆ Motel 6–1408 🅷

(515) 267-8885. **$45-$59.** 7655 Office Plaza Dr N 50266. I-80, exit 121 (Jordan Creek Pkwy), just sw. Int corridors. **Pets:** Other species. Service with restrictions, supervision. ✕ 🐾 ⊸

◆◆◆ Residence Inn-Des Moines West 🅷

(515) 267-0338. **$160-$170.** 160 S Jordan Creek Pkwy 50266. I-35, exit 70 (Mills Civic Pkwy), 1.2 mi w to 68th St, then just nw. Int corridors. **Pets:** Medium, other species. $100 one-time fee/room. Service with restrictions, crate. ✕ 🔌 💻 ⊸ ✕

Ⓐ ◆◆◆ Sheraton West Des Moines 🅷 🐾

(515) 223-1800. **$79 (no credit cards), 24 day notice.** 1800 50th St 50266. I-80/35, exit 124 (University Ave), just e. Int corridors. **Pets:** Medium, dogs only. $75 one-time fee/pet. Designated rooms, no service, supervision. (SAVE) ✕ 🐾 🔌 💻 🍴 ⊸

◆◆◆ Staybridge Suites 🅷

(515) 223-0000. **Call for rates.** 6905 Lake Dr 50266. I-80, exit 121 (Jordan Creek Pkwy), just ne. Int corridors. **Pets:** Accepted.

✕ 🐾 🔌 💻 ⊸

◆◆◆ West Des Moines Marriott 🅷

(515) 267-1500. **$143-$175.** 1250 Jordan Creek Pkwy 50266. I-80, exit 121 (Jordan Creek Pkwy), just sw. Int corridors. **Pets:** Large. $75 one-time fee/room. Service with restrictions, supervision.

✕ 🐾 🔌 💻 🍴 ⊸ ✕

WILLIAMS

Ⓐ ◆◆ Best Western Norseman Inn 🅼

(515) 854-2281. **$65-$71.** 3086 220th St 50271. I-35, exit 144, just e. Int corridors. **Pets:** Medium, dogs only. $10 daily fee/pet. Service with restrictions, supervision. (SAVE) ✕ 🔌 💻

WILLIAMSBURG

Ⓐ ◆◆ Best Western Cozy House Suites 🅷

(319) 668-9777. **$99-$159.** 1708 N Highland St 52361. I-80, exit 220, 0.8 mi n. Int corridors. **Pets:** Other species. $16 daily fee/pet. Designated rooms, service with restrictions, supervision. (SAVE) ✕ 🔌 💻 ⊸

Ⓐ ◆◆ Clarion Inn Amana Colonies and Wasserbahn Waterpark Resort 🅷

(319) 668-1175. **$100-$150.** 2211 U Ave 52361. I-80, exit 225 (US 151). Int corridors. **Pets:** Accepted. (SAVE) ✕ 🔌 💻 🍴 ⊸ ✕

Ⓐ ◆◆ Crest Country Inn 🅼

(319) 668-1522. **$60-$85.** 340 W Evans St 52361. I-80, exit 220, just nw. Ext corridors. **Pets:** Accepted. (SAVE) ✕

◆◆ Heritage Inn Hotel & Suites Amana Colonies 🅷

(319) 668-2700. **$77-$160.** 2185 U Ave 52361. I-80, exit 225 (US 151), just n. Int corridors. **Pets:** Accepted. (ASK) ✕ 🔌 💻 ⊸

Ⓐ ◆◆ Super 8 🅷

(319) 668-9718. **$70-$80.** 1708 N Highland St 52361. I-80, exit 220, 0.8 mi n. Ext/int corridors. **Pets:** Other species. $16 daily fee/pet. Designated rooms, service with restrictions, supervision. (SAVE) ✕ 🔌 💻

KANSAS

ABILENE

▲▲▲ ▼▼ Diamond Motel M
(785) 263-2360. **$40-$75.** 1407 NW 3rd St 67410. I-70, exit 275, 1.3 mi s, then 1 mi w. Ext corridors. **Pets:** Small. $7 daily fee/pet. Designated rooms, service with restrictions, crate. [SAVE] ⊠ 🖶

▼▼▼▼ Holiday Inn Express Hotel & Suites H
(785) 263-4049. **$94-$104.** 110 E Lafayette Ave 67410. I-70, exit 275, just n. Int corridors. **Pets:** Accepted.
[ASK] ⊠ 🔚 🖶 🖳 🌊 ⊠

▼▼ Super 8 H 🐾
(785) 263-4545. **$63-$82, 5 day notice.** 2207 N Buckeye 67410. I-70, exit 275, just s. Int corridors. **Pets:** Large. $25 deposit/room, $13 one-time fee/pet. Designated rooms, service with restrictions, supervision.
[ASK] ⊠ 🔚 🖶 🖳

ANDOVER

▲▲▲ ▼▼▼ Andover Express Inn M
(316) 733-8881. **$57-$63.** 222 W US Hwy 54 67002. 2.2 mi e of jct SR 96. Ext corridors. **Pets:** Small, other species. $10 daily fee/pet. Service with restrictions, supervision. [SAVE] ⊠ 🖶 🌊

ATCHISON

▼▼▼ AmericInn Lodge & Suites of Atchison H
(913) 367-4000. **$74-$85.** 500 US 73 66002. Just s at US 59 and 73. Int corridors. **Pets:** Accepted. [ASK] ⊠ 🔚 🖶 🖳 🌊

BAXTER SPRINGS

▼▼ Baxter Inn-4-Less H
(620) 856-2106. **$43-$70.** 2451 Military Ave 66713. On US 69 alternate route, 1 mi s of jct US 166. Int corridors. **Pets:** Small. $20 deposit/pet. Designated rooms, service with restrictions, supervision. [ASK] ⊠ 🖶

BELLEVILLE

▲▲▲ ▼▼▼ Americas Best Value Inn M
(785) 527-2231. **$49-$54.** 1616 Hwy 36 66935. Jct US 81 and 36; northwest corner; just up hill. Ext corridors. **Pets:** Accepted.
[SAVE] ⊠ 🖶 🖳 🌊

▼▼ Super 8 H
(785) 527-2112. **Call for rates.** 1410 28th St 66935. On US 36, 0.5 mi e of jct US 81. Int corridors. **Pets:** Other species. $10 daily fee/pet. Service with restrictions, supervision. ⊠ 🖶 🖳

BELOIT

▼▼ Super 8 H
(785) 738-4300. **$54-$99, 3 day notice.** 3018 W Hwy 24 67420. Just e of jct SR 14. Ext/int corridors. **Pets:** Accepted. [ASK] ⊠ 🔚 🖶 🖳

BURLINGTON

▼▼ Country Haven Inn H
(620) 364-8260. **$65-$75.** 207 Cross St 66839. Just e of US 75; 1 mi n of center. Int corridors. **Pets:** Accepted. [ASK] ⊠ 🔚 🖶 🖳

CHANUTE

▼▼ Chanute Safari Inn M
(620) 431-9460. **$40-$50.** 3428 S Santa Fe 66720. US 169, exit 35th St, 1.5 mi e. Ext corridors. **Pets:** Accepted. [ASK] ⊠ 🖶 🌊

▼▼ Guest House Motor Inn M
(620) 431-0600. **$40-$50.** 1814 S Santa Fe 66720. US 169, exit 35th St, 2.5 mi ne. Ext corridors. **Pets:** Accepted. [ASK] ⊠ 🖶 🌊

CLAY CENTER

▼▼ Cedar Court Motel M
(785) 632-2148. **$49-$75.** 905 Crawford St 67432. On US 24, just e of jct SR 15. Ext corridors. **Pets:** Small, dogs only. $5 daily fee/pet. Designated rooms, service with restrictions, supervision.
[ASK] ⊠ 🔚 🖶 🖳 🍴 🌊

COLBY

▼▼ Comfort Inn H 🐾
(785) 462-3833. **$84-$130.** 2225 S Range Ave 67701. I-70, exit 53 (SR 25), just s. Int corridors. **Pets:** Other species. $5 daily fee/pet. Designated rooms, service with restrictions, supervision.
[ASK] ⊠ 🔚 🖶 🖳 🍴 🌊

▲▲▲ ▼▼▼ Crown Inn M
(785) 462-3943. **$55-$80.** 2320 S Range Ave 67701. I-70, exit 53 (SR 25), just s. Ext corridors. **Pets:** Accepted. [SAVE] ⊠ 🖶 🖳

▲▲▲ ▼▼▼ Days Inn H
(785) 462-8691. **$75-$90.** 1925 S Range Ave 67701. I-70, exit 53 (SR 25), 0.3 mi n. Int corridors. **Pets:** Small. $15 daily fee/pet. Designated rooms, service with restrictions, supervision. [SAVE] ⊠ 🖶 🖳 🌊

▲▲▲ ▼▼▼▼ Holiday Inn Express Hotel & Suites H
(785) 462-8787. **$95-$155.** 645 W Willow St 67701. I-70, exit 53 (SR 25), just ne. Int corridors. **Pets:** Accepted.
[SAVE] ⊠ 🔚 🖶 🖳 🌊 ⊠

▲▲▲ ▼▼ Motel 6 #4245 H
(785) 462-8201. **$40-$70.** 1985 S Range Ave 67701. I-70, exit 53 (SR 25), just n. Ext/int corridors. **Pets:** Other species. Service with restrictions, supervision. [SAVE] ⊠ 🖶

▲▲▲ ▼▼▼ Super 8 H
(785) 462-8248. **$65-$75.** 1040 Zelfer Ave 67701. I-70, exit 53 (SR 25), 0.3 mi n, then just w. Int corridors. **Pets:** Accepted. [SAVE] ⊠ 🖶 🖳

CONCORDIA

▼▼ Super 8-Concordia H
(785) 243-4200. **$60-$65.** 1320 Lincoln St 66901. On US 81, 1 mi s of center. Ext/int corridors. **Pets:** Accepted. [ASK] ⊠ 🖶 🖳

COTTONWOOD FALLS

◆◆◆◆ Grand Central Hotel ⊡

(620) 273-6763. **$160-$190.** 215 Broadway 66845. Just w of US 177; center of downtown. Int corridors. **Pets:** Designated rooms, service with restrictions, supervision. (SAVE) ⊠ ⊡ ⊟

COUNCIL GROVE

◆◆◆ The Cottage House Hotel & Motel ⊞

(620) 767-6828. **$50-$175, 7 day notice.** 25 N Neosho 66846. Just n of Main St; downtown. Ext/int corridors. **Pets:** Other species. $15 daily fee/room. Service with restrictions, crate. (SAVE) ⊠ ⊟ ⊡ ⊠

DODGE CITY

◆◆◆ Best Western Country Inn & Suites ⊞

(620) 225-7378. **$100-$120.** 506 N 14th Ave 67801. Just n of jct US 50 business route (Wyatt Earp Blvd). Ext/int corridors. **Pets:** Dogs only. $25 daily fee/pet. Designated rooms, service with restrictions, crate.

(SAVE) ⊠ ⊠ ⊟ ⊡ ⊇

◆◆◆ Holiday Inn Express ⊞

(620) 227-5000. **Call for rates.** 2320 W Wyatt Earp Blvd 67801. 1.4 mi w on US 50 business route. Int corridors. **Pets:** Accepted.

⊠ ⊟ ⊡ ⊇

◆◆◆ La Quinta Inn & Suites ⊞ ❀

(620) 225-7373. **$89-$139.** 2400 W Wyatt Earp Blvd 67801. 1.4 mi w on US 50 business route. Int corridors. **Pets:** Medium, other species. Service with restrictions, supervision. ⊠ ⊠ ⊟ ⊡ ⊇

◆◆ Super 8 ⊞

(620) 225-3924. **Call for rates.** 1708 W Wyatt Earp Blvd 67801. 1.2 mi w on US 50 business route. Int corridors. **Pets:** Accepted.

⊠ ⊟ ⊡ ⊇

EL DORADO

◆◆◆ Best Western Red Coach Inn ⊞

(316) 321-6900. **$65-$120.** 2525 W Central Ave 67042. I-35, exit 71, 0.5 mi e. Ext corridors. **Pets:** Very small. $15 daily fee/pet. Designated rooms, service with restrictions. (SAVE) ⊠ ⊟ ⊡ ⊇ ⊠

◆◆ Super 8-El Dorado Ⓜ

(316) 321-4888. **$45-$95.** 2530 W Central Ave 67042. I-35, exit 71, 0.5 mi e. Int corridors. **Pets:** Other species. $15 daily fee/pet. Service with restrictions, supervision. (ASK) ⊠ ⊟ ⊡

ELLSWORTH

◆◆◆ Americas Best Value Inn ⊞

(785) 472-3116. **Call for rates.** 1414 Foster Rd 67439. Jct SR 140 and 156. Ext corridors. **Pets:** Accepted. (SAVE) ⊠ ⊠ ⊟ ⊡ ⊇

EMPORIA

◆◆◆ Best Western Hospitality House ⊞

(620) 342-7587. **$70-$90.** 3021 W Hwy 50 66801. I-35, exit 127, just e. Ext/int corridors. **Pets:** Other species. Designated rooms, service with restrictions, crate. (SAVE) ⊠ ⊟ ⊡ ⊟ ⊇

◆◆ Candlewood Suites ⊞ ❀

(620) 343-7756. **$79-$129.** 2602 Candlewood Dr 66801. I-35, exit 128 (Industrial St), just n, then just e. Int corridors. **Pets:** Other species. $75 one-time fee/room. No service. (ASK) ⊠ ⊟ ⊡

◆◆ Comfort Inn ⊞

(620) 342-9700. **Call for rates.** 2836 W 18th Ave 66801. I-35, exit 128 (Industrial St), just nw. Int corridors. **Pets:** Small. $15 daily fee/pet. Service with restrictions, supervision. ⊠ ⊟ ⊡ ⊇

◆◆◆ Super 8 Ⓜ

(620) 342-7567. **Call for rates.** 2913 W Hwy 50 66801. I-35, exit 127, 0.8 mi e. Int corridors. **Pets:** Small. $10 daily fee/pet. Designated rooms, supervision. (SAVE) ⊠ ⊟ ⊡

FORT SCOTT

◆◆ Fort Scott Inn ⊞

(620) 223-0100. **Call for rates.** 101 State St 66701. On US 69 Bypass, exit US 54 southbound; exit 3rd St northbound. Ext/int corridors. **Pets:** Accepted. ⊠ ⊟ ⊟ ⊇ ⊠

GARDEN CITY

◆◆◆ AmericInn Lodge & Suites of Garden City ⊞ ❀

(620) 272-9860. **$89-$165.** 3020 E Kansas Ave 67846. Jct US 50, 83 and SR 156. Int corridors. **Pets:** Other species. $50 deposit/room, $10 daily fee/room. Designated rooms, service with restrictions, supervision. (ASK) ⊠ ⊟ ⊡ ⊇ ⊠

◆◆◆ Best Western Red Baron Hotel ⊞

(620) 275-4164. **$76-$80.** 2205 E Hwy 50 67846. 2.3 mi e on US 50 business route, at US 83 Bypass. Ext corridors. **Pets:** Accepted.

(SAVE) ⊠ ⊟ ⊡ ⊇

◆◆◆ Clarion Inn & Conference Center ⊞ ❀

(620) 275-7471. **$85-$120.** 1911 E Kansas Ave 67846. 0.5 mi w of US 50 and 83 Bypass, on SR 156. Int corridors. **Pets:** Small. $20 one-time fee/pet. Service with restrictions, supervision.

(SAVE) ⊠ ⊟ ⊡ ⊟ ⊇

◆◆◆ Comfort Inn ⊞ ❀

(620) 275-5800. **Call for rates.** 2608 E Kansas Ave 67846. Jct US 50, 83 and SR 156. Int corridors. **Pets:** Other species. $10 daily fee/pet.

(SAVE) ⊠ ⊟ ⊡ ⊇ ⊠

◆◆◆ Holiday Inn Express Hotel & Suites ⊞

(620) 275-5900. **Call for rates.** 2502 E Kansas Ave 67846. Jct US 50, 83 and SR 156. Int corridors. **Pets:** Accepted. ⊠ ⊟ ⊡ ⊇

◆◆◆ Wheat Lands Rodeway Inn ⊞

(620) 276-2387. **$57-$81, 5 day notice.** 1311 E Fulton St 67846. 1 mi e on US 50 business route. Ext corridors. **Pets:** Other species. Service with restrictions, crate. (SAVE) ⊠ ⊟ ⊡ ⊇

GARNETT

◆◆◆ Garnett Inn Suites & RV Park ⊞

(785) 448-6800. **$60-$78.** 109 Prairie Plaza Pkwy 66032. On US 169, 1.6 mi n of jct US 59. Int corridors. **Pets:** Accepted.

(ASK) ⊠ ⊠ ⊟ ⊡

GODDARD

◆◆◆ Express Inn Ⓜ

(316) 794-3366. **$56-$65.** 19941 W Kellogg Dr 67052. Just se of jct US 54/400 and 199th St. Ext corridors. **Pets:** Small, other species. $10 daily fee/pet. Service with restrictions, supervision. (SAVE) ⊠ ⊟

GOODLAND

◆◆◆ Comfort Inn ⊞

(785) 899-7181. **$89-$120.** 2519 Enterprise Rd 67735. I-70, exit 17 (SR 27), just n. Int corridors. **Pets:** Small. $15 one-time fee/pet. Designated rooms, service with restrictions, supervision.

(ASK) ⊠ ⊠ ⊟ ⊡ ⊇

◆◆◆ Holiday Inn Express Hotel & Suites ⊞

(785) 890-9060. **$96-$135.** 2631 Enterprise Rd 67735. I-70, exit 17 (SR 27), just s. Int corridors. **Pets:** Accepted. (SAVE) ⊠ ⊠ ⊟ ⊡ ⊇

◆◆◆ Super 8 ⊞

(785) 890-7566. **$66-$78.** 2520 Commerce Rd 67735. I-70, exit 17 (SR 27), just n. Ext corridors. **Pets:** Accepted. (ASK) ⊠ ⊟ ⊡

GREAT BEND

◆◆◆ Best Western Angus Inn ⊞ ❀

(620) 792-3541. **$68-$78.** 2920 10th St 67530. 0.8 mi w on US 56 and SR 96/156. Ext/int corridors. **Pets:** Other species. $5 daily fee/pet. Designated rooms, service with restrictions, crate.

(SAVE) ⊠ ⊟ ⊡ ⊟ ⊇ ⊠

Highland Hotel & Convention Center H
(620) 792-2431. **$64-$85.** 3017 W 10th St 67530. 1 mi w on US 56 and SR 96/156. Ext/int corridors. **Pets:** Large. $10 daily fee/pet. Designated rooms, service with restrictions, supervision.
[SAVE] [X] [🛏] [🖥] [🍴] [🏊] [⊗]

HAYS

Americas Best Value Inn Vagabond M
(785) 625-2511. **$60-$163.** 2524 Vine St 67601. I-70, exit 159 (US 183), 1 mi s. Ext corridors. **Pets:** Large. $5 daily fee/pet. Designated rooms, supervision. [ASK] [X] [🛏] [🖥] [🍴] [🏊]

Baymont Inn & Suites H
(785) 625-8103. **$69-$74.** 3801 N Vine St 67601. I-70, exit 159 (US 183), just sw. Ext/int corridors. **Pets:** Accepted. [ASK] [X] [🛏] [🖥]

HERINGTON

Herington Inn & Suites H
(785) 258-3300. **$65-$86.** 565 Hwy 77 67449. US 77, just w. Int corridors. **Pets:** Very small, dogs only. $25 one-time fee/pet. Designated rooms, supervision. [ASK] [X] [🛏] [🖥]

HESSTON

AmericInn Lodge & Suites of Hesston H
(620) 327-2053. **$80-$150.** 2 Leonard Ct 67062. I-135, exit 40, just e. Int corridors. **Pets:** Accepted. [ASK] [X] [🛏] [🖥] [🏊]

HILLSBORO

Country Haven Inn H
(620) 947-2929. **$64-$75.** 804 Western Heights 67063. On US 56; center. Int corridors. **Pets:** Small, other species. $25 deposit/room, $25 one-time fee/room. Designated rooms, service with restrictions, supervision.
[ASK] [X] [🛏]

HUTCHINSON

Comfort Inn H
(620) 663-7822. **Call for rates.** 1621 Super Plaza 67501. Just w of jct SR 61 and N 17th Ave. Int corridors. **Pets:** Accepted.
[X] [🛏] [🖥] [🏊]

Days Inn H
(620) 665-3700. **Call for rates.** 1420 N Lorraine St 67501. Just nw of jct SR 61 and N 11th Ave. Int corridors. **Pets:** Dogs only. $12 daily fee/pet. Crate. [X] [🛏] [🖥]

Holiday Inn Express Hotel & Suites H
(620) 669-5200. **$105-$165.** 1601 Super Plaza 67501. Just w of jct SR 61 and N 17th Ave. Int corridors. **Pets:** Accepted.
[ASK] [X] [🛏] [🖥] [🏊]

INDEPENDENCE

Appletree Inn H
(620) 331-5500. **$99-$145.** 201 N 8th St 67301. At 8th and Laurel sts. Ext/int corridors. **Pets:** Accepted. [X] [🛏] [🖥] [🏊]

Microtel Inn & Suites H
(620) 331-0088. **$73-$80, 7 day notice.** 2917 W Main St 67301. 1.2 mi e of jct US 75 and 160. Int corridors. **Pets:** Accepted.
[SAVE] [X] [🛏] [🖥]

Super 8 H
(620) 331-8288. **$61-$76.** 2800 W Main St 67301. 1.3 mi e of jct US 160 and 75. Int corridors. **Pets:** $15 daily fee/pet. No service, supervision.
[ASK] [X] [🛏] [🖥] [🏊]

IOLA

Best Western Inn M
(620) 365-5161. **$62-$69.** 1315 N State St 66749. Jct US 54 and 169, 1.5 mi w on US 54, then 0.8 mi n. Ext corridors. **Pets:** Small, dogs only. $10 daily fee/pet. Designated rooms, service with restrictions, supervision.
[SAVE] [X] [🛏] [🖥] [🍴] [🏊]

Super 8 Iola H
(620) 365-3030. **Call for rates.** 200 Bills Way 66749. Jct US 54 and 169. Int corridors. **Pets:** Very small, dogs only. $15 daily fee/pet. Designated rooms, no service, supervision. [X] [🛏] [🖥] [🏊]

JUNCTION CITY

Best Western J.C. Inn H
(785) 210-1212. **$85-$100.** 604 E Chestnut St 66441. I-70, exit 298, just w. Int corridors. **Pets:** Accepted. [SAVE] [X] [🛏] [🖥] [🏊]

Candlewood Suites H
(785) 238-1454. **$80-$179.** 100 S Hammons Dr 66441. I-70, exit 298, just w. Int corridors. **Pets:** Accepted. [ASK] [X] [🛏] [🖥]

Courtyard by Marriott Junction City H
(785) 210-1500. **$89-$109.** 310 Hammons Dr 66441. I-70, exit 298, just w. Int corridors. **Pets:** Medium. $75 one-time fee/room. Service with restrictions, crate. [X] [🛏] [🖥] [🏊]

Holiday Inn Express H
(785) 762-4200. **$99-$150.** 120 N East St 66441. I-70, exit 298, just nw. Int corridors. **Pets:** Medium. $50 deposit/room, $5 daily fee/pet. No service, crate. [ASK] [X] [🛏] [🖥] [🏊]

KANSAS CITY METROPOLITAN AREA

GARDNER

Super 8 H
(913) 856-8887. **$65-$150.** 2001 E Santa Fe 66030. I-35, exit 210. Int corridors. **Pets:** Other species. $10 daily fee/pet. Service with restrictions, supervision. [ASK] [X] [🛏] [🖥] [🏊]

KANSAS CITY

Best Western Inn and Conference Center H
(913) 677-3060. **$90.** 501 Southwest Blvd 66103. I-35, exit 234 (7th St), 0.4 mi s to Southwest Blvd, then just w. Int corridors. **Pets:** Accepted.
[SAVE] [X] [🛏] [🖥] [🏊]

Candlewood Suites H
(913) 788-9929. **$89-$109.** 10920 Parallel Pkwy 66109. I-435, exit 14B, just w. Int corridors. **Pets:** Medium. $10 daily fee/pet. Service with restrictions, crate. [ASK] [X] [🛏] [🖥]

LENEXA

Extended Stay Deluxe-Kansas City-Lenexa-87th St H
(913) 894-5550. **$55-$120.** 8015 Lenexa Dr 66215. I-35, exit 227 (75th St), 1 mi s on east frontage road. Ext corridors. **Pets:** Other species. $25 daily fee/room. Designated rooms, service with restrictions, crate.
[ASK] [X] [🛏] [🖥]

La Quinta Inn Kansas City (Lenexa) H ❀
(913) 492-5500. **$49-$119.** 9461 Lenexa Dr 66215. I-35, exit 224 (95th St), just ne; entrance left on Monrovia Rd, off 95th St. Int corridors. **Pets:** Medium, other species. Service with restrictions, supervision.
[ASK] [X] [🛏] [🖥]

Super 8-Lenexa H
(913) 888-8899. **$55-$120.** 9601 Westgate Dr 66215. I-35, exit 224 (95th St), just se. Int corridors. **Pets:** $10 daily fee/pet. Service with restrictions, supervision. [ASK] [X] [🛏] [🖥]

MERRIAM

Drury Inn-Merriam/Shawnee Mission Parkway
(913) 236-9200. **$65-$149.** 9009 W Shawnee Mission Pkwy 66202. I-35, exit 228B (Shawnee Mission Pkwy), just se. Int corridors. **Pets:** Other species. No service, supervision.

Homestead Studio Suites Hotel-Kansas City-Shawnee Mission
(913) 236-6006. **$50-$110.** 6451 E Frontage Rd 66202. I-35, exit 228B (Shawnee Mission Pkwy), just se. Ext corridors. **Pets:** Other species. $25 daily fee/room. Designated rooms, service with restrictions, crate.

Quality Inn
(913) 262-4448. **$60-$80.** 6601 E Frontage Rd 66202. I-35, exit 228A, just ne. Ext/int corridors. **Pets:** Small. $10 daily fee/pet. Designated rooms, service with restrictions, crate.

OLATHE

Best Western Olathe Hotel & Suites
(913) 440-9762. **$90-$150.** 1580 S Hamilton Cir 66061. I-35, exit 215 (151st St), just nw. Int corridors. **Pets:** Medium, dogs only. $10 daily fee/room. Service with restrictions, crate.

Candlewood Suites Olathe
(913) 768-8888. **$83-$99.** 15490 S Rogers Rd 66062. I-35, exit 215 (151st St), just sw. Int corridors. **Pets:** Accepted.

Holiday Inn
(913) 829-4000. **$84-$154.** 101 W 151st St 66061. I-35, exit 215 (151st St). Int corridors. **Pets:** Medium, dogs only. $30 one-time fee/room. Service with restrictions, crate.

La Quinta Inn & Suites
(913) 254-0111. **$90-$200 (no credit cards).** 20570 W 151st St 66061. I-35, exit 215 (151st St), just w. Int corridors. **Pets:** Medium, other species. Service with restrictions, supervision.

Microtel Inn Olathe
(913) 397-9455. **Call for rates.** 1501 S Hamilton Cir 66061. I-35, exit 215 (151st St); jct 151st St and CR 7 N, just nw of jct I-35. Int corridors. **Pets:** Accepted.

Sleep Inn
(913) 390-9500. **$85-$105.** 20662 W 151st St 66061. I-35, exit 215 (151st St), 0.4 mi sw, follow signs. Int corridors. **Pets:** Other species. $10 daily fee/pet. Service with restrictions, crate.

OVERLAND PARK

Candlewood Suites
(913) 469-5557. **$59-$99.** 11001 Oakmont St 66210. I-435, exit 82 (Quivira Rd), 0.5 mi s, 0.3 mi w on College Ave, then just n. Int corridors. **Pets:** Medium. $75 daily fee/room. Service with restrictions, supervision.

Chase Suites Convention Center
(913) 491-3333. **$89-$209.** 6300 W 110th St 66211. I-435, exit 79 (Metcalf Ave/US 169), 0.3 mi s on US 169, 0.5 mi e on College Blvd to Lamar Ave, then just n. Ext corridors. **Pets:** Large, other species. $10 daily fee/pet. Designated rooms, service with restrictions, crate.

Comfort Inn & Suites
(913) 648-7858. **Call for rates.** 7200 W 107th St 66212. I-435, exit 79 (Metcalf Ave/US 169), just nw. Int corridors. **Pets:** Accepted.

Drury Inn & Suites-Overland Park
(913) 345-1500. **$85-$199.** 10963 Metcalf Ave 66210. I-435, exit 79 (Metcalf Ave/US 169), just se. Int corridors. **Pets:** Other species. No service, supervision.

Econo Lodge Inn & Suites
(913) 262-9600. **$60-$90.** 7508 Shawnee Mission Pkwy 66202. I-35, exit 228B, 0.5 mi e. Ext corridors. **Pets:** Other species. $10 daily fee/pet. Service with restrictions, supervision.

Extended StayAmerica-Kansas City-Overland Park/Convention Center
(913) 661-9299. **$55-$120.** 10750 Quivira Rd 66210. I-435, exit 82 (Quivira Rd), just sw. Int corridors. **Pets:** Other species. $25 daily fee/room. Designated rooms, service with restrictions, crate.

Extended Stay Deluxe Kansas City-Overland Park-Metcalf
(913) 642-2299. **$65-$140.** 7201 W 106th St 66212. I-435, exit 79 (Metcalf Ave/US 169), just nw. Int corridors. **Pets:** Other species. $25 daily fee/room. Designated rooms, service with restrictions, crate.

Holtze Executive Village
(913) 344-8100. **$79-$219.** 11400 College Blvd 66210. I-435, exit 82 (Quivira Rd), 0.5 mi s, then just e. Ext corridors. **Pets:** Accepted.

La Quinta Inn & Suites
(913) 648-5555. **$59-$129.** 10610 Marty St 66212. I-435, exit 79 (Metcalf Ave/US 169), just nw. Int corridors. **Pets:** Medium, other species. Service with restrictions, supervision.

Pear Tree Inn by Drury-Overland Park
(913) 451-0200. **$60-$124.** 10951 Metcalf Ave 66210. I-435, exit 79 (Metcalf Ave/US 169), just se. Int corridors. **Pets:** Other species. No service, supervision.

Ramada Overland Park-Mission
(913) 262-3010. **$69-$149.** 7240 Shawnee Mission Pkwy 66202. I-35, exit 228B (Shawnee Mission Pkwy), 1 mi e. Ext/int corridors. **Pets:** Accepted.

Red Roof Inn-Overland Park
(913) 341-0100. **$45-$100.** 6800 W 108th St 66211. I-435, exit 79 (Metcalf Ave/US 169), just ne. Ext corridors. **Pets:** Large. Service with restrictions, crate.

Residence Inn by Marriott
(913) 491-4444. **$159-$179.** 12010 Blue Valley Pkwy 66213. I-435, exit 79 (Metcalf Ave/US 169), 1.3 mi s. Int corridors. **Pets:** Accepted.

Sheraton Overland Park Hotel at the Convention Center
(913) 234-2100. **Call for rates.** 6100 College Blvd 66211. I-435, exit 79 (Metcalf Ave/US 169), just s to College Blvd, then 0.6 mi e. Int corridors. **Pets:** Accepted.

Super 8
(913) 341-4440. **$55-$65.** 10750 Barkley St 66211. I-435, exit 79 (Metcalf Ave/US 169), just n to 107th St, then just e. Int corridors. **Pets:** Medium, other species. $10 daily fee/pet. Service with restrictions, supervision.

▼▼▼ Wyndham Garden Hotel-Overland Park H
(913) 383-2550. **Call for rates.** 7000 W 108th St 66211. I-435, exit 79 (Metcalf Ave/US 169), just ne. Int corridors. **Pets:** Accepted.
⊠ ᵭᴍ 🔲 ⫴ ⇝

END METROPOLITAN AREA

LANSING
▼▼ Econo Lodge H
(913) 727-2777. **$50-$70.** 504 N Main 66043. I-70, exit 224 (Leavenworth), 10 mi n on US 73 and SR 7. Int corridors. **Pets:** Accepted.
ASK ⊠ 🔒 🔲

LARNED
ⒶⒶⒶ ▼▼▼ Best Western Townsman Inn H
(620) 285-3114. **$56-$66.** 123 E 14th St 67550. Jct US 56 and SR 156. Ext corridors. **Pets:** Accepted. SAVE ⊠ 🔒 🔲 ⇝

LAWRENCE
ⒶⒶⒶ ▼▼ Best Western Lawrence H
(785) 843-9100. **$90-$120.** 2309 Iowa St 66046. On US 59; jct SR 10. Ext/int corridors. **Pets:** Large, dogs only. $8 daily fee/pet. Designated rooms, service with restrictions, supervision.
SAVE ⊠ ᵭᴍ 🔒 🔲 ⇝

▼▼ Econo Lodge H
(785) 842-7030. **$49-$199.** 2222 W 6th St 66049. I-70, exit 202, 1 mi s. Int corridors. **Pets:** Medium, other species. $10 daily fee/room. Designated rooms, service with restrictions, crate.
ASK ⊠ 🔒 🔲 ⫴ ⇝

ⒶⒶⒶ ▼▼▼ Holiday Inn H
(785) 841-7077. **$99-$119.** 200 McDonald Dr 66044. I-70, exit 202, 0.5 mi s on US 59. Int corridors. **Pets:** Other species. $25 one-time fee/room. Service with restrictions, supervision. SAVE ⊠ 🔲 ⫴ ⇝ ⊠

ⒶⒶⒶ ▼▼▼ Holiday Inn Express Hotel & Suites H
(785) 749-7555. **$89-$174.** 3411 SW Iowa St 66046. I-70, exit 197 (SR 10), 8.4 mi e to US 59, then just n. Int corridors. **Pets:** Accepted.
SAVE ⊠ ᵭᴍ 🔒 🔲 ⇝ ⊠

▼▼ Quality Inn M
(785) 842-5100. **$69-$169.** 801 Iowa St 66049. I-70, exit 202, 1 mi s on US 59. Ext/int corridors. **Pets:** Accepted. ASK ⊠ 🔒 🔲 ⇝

▼▼ Super 8 H
(785) 842-5721. **Call for rates.** 515 McDonald Dr 66049. I-70, exit 202, 0.8 mi s, then just w. Int corridors. **Pets:** Accepted. ⊠ 🔒 🔲

LIBERAL
ⒶⒶⒶ ▼▼ Americas Best Value Inn M
(620) 624-6203. **$54-$64.** 564 E Pancake Blvd 67901. 0.8 w of jct US 54 and 83. Ext corridors. **Pets:** $6 one-time fee/pet. Service with restrictions, supervision. SAVE ⊠ 🔒 🔲

ⒶⒶⒶ ▼▼▼ Liberal Inn H
(620) 624-7254. **$65-$79.** 603 E Pancake Blvd 67901. 0.5 mi w of jct US 54 and 83. Int corridors. **Pets:** Medium. Designated rooms, service with restrictions, crate. SAVE ⊠ 🔒 🔲 ⫴ ⇝

LYONS
▼▼ Celebration Centre Inn & Suites M
(620) 680-6022. **$65-$100.** 1108 E Hwy 56 67554. 2 mi e of jct SR 14 and US 56. Int corridors. **Pets:** Medium. $25 one-time fee/room. Designated rooms, service with restrictions, crate. ASK ⊠ 🔒 🔲

ⒶⒶⒶ ▼▼ Lyons Inn M ❖
(620) 257-5185. **$59-$76.** 817 W Main St 67554. 0.8 mi w on SR 96 and US 56. Int corridors. **Pets:** Very small, dogs only. $10 one-time fee/pet. Designated rooms, service with restrictions, supervision.
SAVE ⊠ 🔒

MANHATTAN
ⒶⒶⒶ ▼▼▼ Best Western Manhattan Inn H
(785) 537-8300. **Call for rates.** 601 E Poyntz Ave 66502. SR 177, 0.4 mi e on US 24 (Frontage Rd). Int corridors. **Pets:** $10 daily fee/pet. Supervision. SAVE ⊠ ᵭᴍ 🔒 🔲 ⇝

ⒶⒶⒶ ▼▼▼ Clarion Hotel H
(785) 539-5311. **$70-$139.** 530 Richards Dr 66502. On SR 18 (Ft. Riley Blvd), 0.3 mi e of jct SR 113. Ext/int corridors. **Pets:** Small, other species. $20 deposit/room. Service with restrictions, supervision.
SAVE ⊠ 🔒 🔲 ⫴ ⇝ ⊠

▼▼▼ Holiday Inn at the Campus H
(785) 539-7531. **$99-$199.** 1641 Anderson Ave 66502. 1 mi n of SR 18 (Ft. Riley Blvd). Int corridors. **Pets:** $75 one-time fee/room.
ASK ⊠ 🔒 🔲 ⫴ ⇝

▼▼ Manhattan Super 8 H
(785) 537-8468. **$65-$125.** 200 Tuttle Creek Blvd 66502. Jct US 24 (Frontage Rd) and SR 177. Int corridors. **Pets:** $25 one-time fee/room. Designated rooms, service with restrictions, supervision.
ASK ⊠ 🔒 🔲

▼ Motel 6–152 M
(785) 537-1022. **$45-$61.** 510 Tuttle Creek Blvd 66502. 0.3 mi ne on US 24 (Frontage Rd) and SR 177. Ext corridors. **Pets:** Other species. Service with restrictions, supervision. ⊠ ᵭᴍ ⇝

▼▼ Quality Inn H
(785) 770-8000. **$70-$170.** 150 E Poyntz Ave 66502. Jct US 24 (Frontage Rd) and SR 177. Int corridors. **Pets:** Accepted.
ASK ⊠ ᵭᴍ 🔒 🔲 ⇝

MARYSVILLE
▼▼ Heritage Inn Express H
(785) 562-5588. **Call for rates.** 1155 Pony Express Hwy 66508. 2 mi e on US 36 (Pony Express Hwy). Int corridors. **Pets:** Other species. $10 one-time fee/room. Designated rooms, service with restrictions, supervision. ⊠ 🔒 🔲

▼▼ Marysville Surf Motel M
(785) 562-2354. **$55-$86, 7 day notice.** 2105 Center St 66508. 1 mi e on US 36 (Pony Express Hwy). Ext/int corridors. **Pets:** Medium. $10 daily fee/pet. Designated rooms, service with restrictions, supervision.
ASK ⊠ 🔒 🔲 ⊠

MCPHERSON
ⒶⒶⒶ ▼▼▼ Americas Best Value Inn H
(620) 241-8881. **$56-$95, 3 day notice.** 2110 E Kansas Ave 67460. I-135, exit 60, just w. Int corridors. **Pets:** Medium. $20 daily fee/pet. Service with restrictions, supervision. SAVE ⊠ ᵭᴍ 🔒 🔲

ⒶⒶⒶ ▼▼▼ Best Western Holiday Manor Motel H
(620) 241-5343. **$75-$95.** 2211 E Kansas Ave 67460. I-135, exit 60, just w. Ext/int corridors. **Pets:** Medium. $10 daily fee/pet. Service with restrictions. SAVE ⊠ 🔒 🔲 ⫴ ⇝

NEWTON

⟨AAA⟩ ▽▽▽ Best Western Red Coach Inn H
(316) 283-9120. **$80-$100.** 1301 E 1st St 67114. I-135, exit 31, just w. Ext/int corridors. **Pets:** Small, dogs only. $15 daily fee/pet. Designated rooms, service with restrictions, supervision.
[SAVE] [X] [🔒] [💻] [🍴] [≈] [X]

OTTAWA

⟨AAA⟩ ▽▽▽ Best Western Ottawa Inn H
(785) 242-2224. **$80-$130.** 212 E 23rd St 66067. I-35, exit 183 (US 59). Ext/int corridors. **Pets:** Accepted. [SAVE] [X] [&M] [🔒] [💻] [≈]

⟨AAA⟩ ▽▽▽ Econo Lodge H
(785) 242-3400. **$55-$70.** 2331 S Cedar Rd 66067. I-35, exit 183 (US 59). Int corridors. **Pets:** Small. $10 daily fee/pet. Service with restrictions, supervision. [SAVE] [X] [🔒] [💻] [≈]

PAOLA

▽▽ Paola Inn and Suites H
(913) 294-3700. **$95-$98.** 1600 E Hedge Lane Ct 66071. US 169, exit 127 (Baptiste Dr), just w. Int corridors. **Pets:** Accepted.
[ASK] [X] [&M] [🔒] [💻] [≈]

PARK CITY

⟨AAA⟩ ▽▽▽ Best Western Hotel & Suites H
(316) 832-9387. **$70-$100.** 915 E 53rd St N 67219. I-135, exit 13, just w. Ext/int corridors. **Pets:** Accepted. [SAVE] [X] [🔒] [💻] [🍴] [≈] [X]

⟨AAA⟩ ▽▽▽ Park City Express Inn & Suites H
(316) 927-3900. **$63-$80.** 792 Beaumont St 67219. I-135, exit 14, just sw. Int corridors. **Pets:** Small, other species. $10 daily fee/pet. Service with restrictions, supervision. [SAVE] [X] [🔒] [≈]

▽▽ Super 8-Wichita North/Park City M
(316) 744-2071. **$45-$70.** 6075 Air Cap Dr 67219. I-135, exit 14, just sw. Int corridors. **Pets:** Accepted. [ASK] [X] [🔒]

PARSONS

⟨AAA⟩ ▽▽▽ Best Western Parsons Inn H
(620) 423-0303. **$70-$125, 3 day notice.** 101 E Main St 67357. 1.5 mi e. Int corridors. **Pets:** $15 daily fee/pet. Service with restrictions, crate.
[SAVE] [X] [🔒] [💻] [≈]

⟨AAA⟩ ▽▽▽ Sleep Inn & Suites H
(620) 421-6126. **$70-$82.** 1807 Harding Dr 67357. Just sw of jct US 59 and 400. Int corridors. **Pets:** Small. $25 one-time fee/room. Service with restrictions, supervision. [SAVE] [X] [&M] [🔒] [💻] [≈]

PHILLIPSBURG

▽▽ Cottonwood Inn M
(785) 543-2125. **$65-$99, 7 day notice.** 1200 State St 67661. 1 mi e on US 36/183. Ext corridors. **Pets:** Accepted. [ASK] [X] [≈]

PITTSBURG

▽▽ Super 8 H
(620) 232-1881. **$53-$69.** 3108 N Broadway Ave 66762. 2.1 mi n on US 69 from jct SR 126. Int corridors. **Pets:** Accepted. [ASK] [X] [🔒] [💻]

PRATT

▽▽▽ Comfort Suites H
(620) 672-9999. **$120-$160.** 704 Allison Ln 67124. Just n of jct US 54 and SR 81. Int corridors. **Pets:** $25 one-time fee/room. Designated rooms, service with restrictions, supervision. [ASK] [X] [🔒] [💻] [≈]

▽▽ Evergreen Inn & RV Park M
(620) 672-6431. **$59-$100.** 20001 W US Hwy 54 67124. 3 mi w. Ext corridors. **Pets:** Medium, dogs only. $5 one-time fee/pet. Service with restrictions, supervision. [ASK] [X] [🔒] [≈]

▽▽ Regency Inn & Suites H
(620) 672-9433. **$78.** 1401 W US Hwy 54 67124. 2 mi w. Int corridors. **Pets:** Medium, other species. Service with restrictions, supervision.
[ASK] [X] [🔒] [💻] [≈]

RUSSELL

▽▽▽ AmericInn Lodge & Suites of Russell H
(785) 483-4200. **$75-$125.** 1430 S Fossil St 67665. I-70, exit 184 (US 281), just n. Int corridors. **Pets:** Accepted.
[ASK] [X] [&M] [🔒] [💻] [≈] [X]

▽▽ Days Inn M
(785) 483-6660. **Call for rates.** 1225 S Fossil St 67665. I-70, exit 184 (US 281), just n. Ext corridors. **Pets:** Accepted. [X] [🔒] [💻] [≈]

SALINA

⟨AAA⟩ ▽▽▽ America's Best Inn H
(785) 825-2500. **$56-$79.** 429 W Diamond Dr 67401. I-70, exit 252, just n. Int corridors. **Pets:** Accepted. [SAVE] [X] [&M] [🔒]

▽▽ Baymont Inn & Suites H
(785) 493-9800. **Call for rates.** 745 W Schilling Rd 67401. I-135, exit 89 (Schilling Rd), just w. Int corridors. **Pets:** Accepted.
[X] [&M] [🔒] [💻] [≈] [X]

⟨AAA⟩ ▽▽▽ Best Western Heart of America Inn H
(785) 827-9315. **$78-$95.** 632 Westport Blvd 67401. I-135, exit 92, just e. Ext/int corridors. **Pets:** Medium, other species. $10 one-time fee/pet. Designated rooms, service with restrictions, supervision. [SAVE] [X] [💻] [≈]

⟨AAA⟩ ▽▽▽ Best Western Mid-America Inn M
(785) 827-0356. **$88-$92, 30 day notice.** 1846 N 9th St 67401. I-70, exit 252, just s. Ext corridors. **Pets:** $50 deposit/pet. Service with restrictions, crate. [SAVE] [X] [&M] [💻] [🍴] [≈]

▽▽ Candlewood Suites H
(785) 823-6939. **$55-$109.** 2650 Planet Ave 67401. I-135, exit 89 (Schilling Rd), just e to S 9th St, 0.5 mi n to Belmont, then just w. Int corridors. **Pets:** Large, other species. $25 one-time fee/room. Service with restrictions, crate. [ASK] [X] [&M] [🔒] [💻]

▽▽ Comfort Inn H
(785) 826-1711. **Call for rates.** 1820 W Crawford St 67401. I-135, exit 92, just e. Int corridors. **Pets:** Small, other species. $20 one-time fee/pet. Service with restrictions, supervision. [X] [&M] [🔒] [💻] [≈]

▽▽ Days Inn H
(785) 823-9791. **$55-$129.** 407 W Diamond Dr 67401. I-70, exit 252, just n. Int corridors. **Pets:** Medium. $25 one-time fee/room. Designated rooms, service with restrictions, supervision. [ASK] [X] [🔒] [💻] [≈]

▽▽▽ Holiday Inn Express Hotel & Suites H
(785) 827-9000. **$85-$149.** 201 E Diamond Dr 67401. I-70, exit 252, just ne. Int corridors. **Pets:** Accepted. [ASK] [X] [&M] [🔒] [💻] [≈]

⟨AAA⟩ ▽▽▽ Quality Inn & Suites H
(785) 825-2111. **Call for rates.** 2110 W Crawford St 67401. I-135, exit 92, just w. Int corridors. **Pets:** Accepted.
[SAVE] [X] [&M] [🔒] [💻] [🍴] [≈] [X]

⟨AAA⟩ ▽▽▽ Super 8 I-70 H
(785) 823-8808. **Call for rates.** 120 E Diamond Dr 67401. I-70, exit 252, just ne. Int corridors. **Pets:** $15 daily fee/pet. No service, supervision. [SAVE] [X] [&M] [🔒] [💻] [≈]

SHARON SPRINGS

▽▽ Oak Tree Inn H
(785) 852-4664. **Call for rates.** 801 N Hwy 27 67758. Jct US 40 and SR 27. Ext/int corridors. **Pets:** Other species. [X] [&M] [🔒] [💻] [🍴]

TOPEKA

ⒶⒶⒶ ▼▼◆ Best Western Topeka Inn & Suites 🅷
(785) 228-2223. **$75-$100.** 700 SW Fairlawn Rd 66606. I-70, exit 357A, just ne. Int corridors. **Pets:** Medium. $10 daily fee/pet, $150 one-time fee/room. Designated rooms, service with restrictions, supervision.
🆂🅰🆅🅴 ⊠ 🅷 🖵 🏊

▼▼◆ Capitol Plaza Hotel 🅷
(785) 431-7200. **$79-$149.** 1717 SW Topeka Blvd 66612. I-70, exit SE 8th Ave, 1.6 mi s; I-470, exit Topeka Blvd, 2.9 mi n. Int corridors. **Pets:** $50 one-time fee/room. Service with restrictions, crate.
🅰🅢🅺 ⊠ 🅼 🅷 🖵 🍴 🏊 ⊠

ⒶⒶⒶ ▼▼▼◆ ClubHouse Inn & Suites 🅷
(785) 273-8888. **Call for rates.** 924 SW Henderson 66615. I-70, exit 356 (Wanamaker Rd), just sw. Int corridors. **Pets:** Accepted.
🆂🅰🆅🅴 ⊠ 🅷 🖵 🏊

▼▼◆ Comfort Inn by Choice Hotels 🅷
(785) 273-5365. **$70-$129.** 1518 SW Wanamaker Rd 66604. I-470, exit 1 (Wanamaker Rd). Int corridors. **Pets:** Accepted.
🅰🅢🅺 ⊠ 🅷 🖵 🏊

▼▼◆ Country Inn & Suites By Carlson, Topeka West 🅷
(785) 478-9800. **$75-$125.** 6020 SW 10th St 66615. I-70, exit 356 (Wanamaker Rd), just sw. Int corridors. **Pets:** Accepted.
🅰🅢🅺 ⊠ 🅼 🅷 🖵 🏊

▼▼◆ Ramada Hotel & Convention Center 🅷
(785) 234-5400. **Call for rates.** 420 SE 6th Ave 66607. I-70, exit 362B, just e. Int corridors. **Pets:** Accepted.
⊠ 🅼 🅷 🖵 🍴 🏊 ⊠

▼▼◆ Residence Inn by Marriott 🅷 🐾
(785) 271-8903. **$89-$109.** 1620 SW Westport Dr 66604. I-470, exit 1 (Wanamaker Rd), just se. Int corridors. **Pets:** Other species. $100 one-time fee/room. Service with restrictions. ⊠ 🅼 🅷 🖵 🏊 ⊠

▼▼◆ The Senate Luxury Suites 🅷
(785) 233-5050. **$80-$120.** 900 SW Tyler St 66612. Just w of state capitol; downtown. Int corridors. **Pets:** Accepted. 🅰🅢🅺 ⊠ 🅷 🖵

▼▼◆ Sleep Inn & Suites 🅷
(785) 228-2500. **$80-$100.** 1024 SW Wanamaker Rd 66604. I-70, exit 356 (Wanamaker Rd), just s. Int corridors. **Pets:** Other species. $10 daily fee/pet. Service with restrictions, supervision.
🅰🅢🅺 ⊠ 🅼 🅷 🖵 🏊

ⒶⒶⒶ ▼▼◆ Super 8 at Forbes Landing 🅷 🐾
(785) 862-2222. **$70-$140.** 5922 S Topeka Blvd 66619. I-470, exit 6, 2.2 mi s. Int corridors. **Pets:** Dogs only. $20 one-time fee/room. Service with restrictions, supervision. 🆂🅰🆅🅴 ⊠ 🅼 🅷 🖵 🏊

ULYSSES

▼▼◆ Single Tree Inn 🅷
(620) 356-1500. **Call for rates.** 2033 W Oklahoma St 67880. 1.5 mi w on US 160. Int corridors. **Pets:** Accepted. ⊠ 🅷 🖵

UNIONTOWN

▼◆ Wyatt Earp Inn & Hotel 🅷
(620) 756-4990. **$65-$200, 30 day notice.** 100 5th St 66779. On SR 3; west side of town. Int corridors. **Pets:** Accepted. 🅰🅢🅺 ⊠ 🅷

WAKEENEY

ⒶⒶⒶ ▼▼▼◆ Best Western Wakeeney Inn & Suites 🅷
(785) 743-2700. **$70-$120.** 525 S 1st St 67672. I-70, exit 127, just n. Int corridors. **Pets:** Other species. $10 daily fee/pet. Designated rooms, service with restrictions, supervision. 🆂🅰🆅🅴 ⊠ 🅼 🅷 🖵 🏊

▼▼◆ Super 8 🅷
(785) 743-6442. **$55-$85.** 709 S 13th St 67672. I-70, exit 128, just n. Int corridors. **Pets:** Accepted. 🅰🅢🅺 ⊠ 🅷 🖵

WAMEGO

ⒶⒶⒶ ▼◆ Simmer Motel 🅜
(785) 456-2304. **$46-$100, 7 day notice.** 1215 Hwy 24 W 66547. Jct SR 99, 0.5 mi w. Ext corridors. **Pets:** Accepted.
🆂🅰🆅🅴 ⊠ 🅷 🖵 🏊

WICHITA

ⒶⒶⒶ ▼▼◆ AmericInn of Wichita 🅷
(316) 529-4848. **$75-$94.** 4848 S Laura 67216. I-135, exit 1 A/B (47th St S), just ne. Int corridors. **Pets:** Other species. $25 one-time fee/room. Service with restrictions, crate. 🆂🅰🆅🅴 ⊠ 🖵 🏊

ⒶⒶⒶ ▼▼◆ Best Western Airport Inn & Conference Center 🅷
(316) 942-5600. **$91-$120.** 6815 W Kellogg St 67209. I-235, exit 7, 0.6 mi w on US 54 (S Frontage Rd). Int corridors. **Pets:** Accepted.
🆂🅰🆅🅴 ⊠ 🅷 🖵 🍴 🏊 ⊠

ⒶⒶⒶ ▼▼◆ Best Western Governors Inn & Suites 🅷
(316) 522-0775. **$79-$89.** 4742 S Emporia 67216. I-135, exit 1 A/B (47th St S), just sw. Int corridors. **Pets:** Small. $10 daily fee/pet. Supervision.
🆂🅰🆅🅴 ⊠ 🅷 🖵 🏊

▼▼◆ Candlewood Suites 🅷
(316) 942-0400. **$69-$129.** 570 S Julia 67209. I-235, exit 7, 0.4 mi nw on Dugan Rd. Int corridors. **Pets:** Accepted. 🅰🅢🅺 ⊠ 🅷 🖵

▼▼◆ Candlewood Suites-Wichita Northeast 🅷
(316) 634-6070. **$81-$82.** 3141 N Webb Rd 67226. SR 96, exit Webb Rd, just nw. Int corridors. **Pets:** Accepted. 🅰🅢🅺 ⊠ 🅼 🅷 🖵

ⒶⒶⒶ ▼▼◆ Comfort Inn 🅷 🐾
(316) 522-1800. **$59-$72, 7 day notice.** 4849 S Laura 67216. I-135, exit 1A/B (47th St S), just e. Int corridors. **Pets:** Other species. $10 daily fee/pet. Service with restrictions, supervision. 🆂🅰🆅🅴 ⊠ 🅷 🖵 🏊

▼▼◆ Comfort Inn by Choice Hotels 🅷
(316) 686-2844. **Call for rates.** 9525 E Corporate Hills Dr 67207. I-35, exit 50, just ne. Int corridors. **Pets:** Accepted. ⊠ 🅷 🖵 🏊

▼▼▼◆ Cresthill Suites Hotel 🅷 🐾
(316) 689-8000. **$108.** 12111 E Central Ave 67206. 1.7 mi e of jct Webb Rd. Int corridors. **Pets:** Medium. $50 one-time fee/pet. Service with restrictions, supervision. 🅰🅢🅺 ⊠ 🅷 🖵 🏊

▼▼▼◆ Hampton Inn by Hilton 🅷
(316) 686-3576. **$89-$149.** 9449 E Corporate Hills Dr 67207. I-35, exit 50, just ne. Int corridors. **Pets:** Accepted. ⊠ 🅼 🅷 🖵 🏊

▼▼▼◆ Hawthorn Suites at Reflection Ridge 🅷
(316) 729-5700. **$109-$139, 3 day notice.** 2405 N Ridge Rd 67205. I-235, exit 10, 1.7 mi w on Zoo Blvd/21st St N, then just n. Int corridors. **Pets:** Medium. $25 daily fee/pet. Designated rooms, service with restrictions, supervision. 🅰🅢🅺 ⊠ 🅷 🖵

▼▼▼◆ Hawthorn Suites Wichita East 🅷
(316) 686-7331. **$80-$116.** 411 S Webb Rd 67207. I-35, exit 50, just ne. Ext corridors. **Pets:** $125 one-time fee/room. Service with restrictions, crate. 🅰🅢🅺 ⊠ 🅷 🖵 🏊 ⊠

ⒶⒶⒶ ▼▼◆ Holiday Inn 🅷
(316) 686-7131. **$72-$101.** 549 S Rock Rd 67207. I-35, exit 50, 0.5 mi w. Ext/int corridors. **Pets:** Small, dogs only. $25 daily fee/room. Designated rooms, service with restrictions, crate.
🆂🅰🆅🅴 ⊠ 🅷 🖵 🍴 🏊 ⊠

▼▼▼◆ Holiday Inn Hotel & Suites Convention Center 🅷
(316) 269-2090. **$79-$109.** 221 E Kellogg St 67211. Just sw of jct US 54/400 and Broadway. Int corridors. **Pets:** Accepted.
🅰🅢🅺 ⊠ 🅼 🅷 🖵 🍴 🏊 ⊠

▼▼▼ Homewood Suites by Hilton@The
Waterfront ❚❚ ❀

(316) 260-8844. **$119-$169.** 1550 N Waterfront Pkwy 67206. Just e of jct 13th and Webb rds. Int corridors. **Pets:** Large. $100 deposit/pet, $50 one-time fee/pet. Designated rooms, service with restrictions.

⊠ ⓜ ❚ ▣ ⌁ ⊠

▼▼▼▼ La Quinta Inn & Suites ❚❚ ❀

(316) 943-2181. **$89-$159.** 5500 W Kellogg Dr 67209. I-235, exit 7, just nw. Int corridors. **Pets:** Medium, other species. Service with restrictions, supervision. (ASK) ⊠ ❚ ▣ ⓣ ⌁

✿✿ ▼▼▼ Quality Suites Airport ❚❚

(316) 945-2600. **$90-$129, 3 day notice.** 658 Westdale Dr 67209. Jct I-235 and US 54. Int corridors. **Pets:** Small. $15 daily fee/pet. Service with restrictions, supervision. (SAVE) ⊠ ❚ ▣ ⌁

▼▼▼▼ Residence Inn by Marriott at Plazzio ❚❚

(316) 682-7300. **$143-$175.** 1212 N Greenwich 67206. SR 96, exit 13th St, 0.5 mi sw. Int corridors. **Pets:** $75 one-time fee/pet. Service with restrictions, crate. ⊠ ⓜ ❚ ▣ ⌁ ⊠

▼▼ Super 8-Wichita/East ❚❚

(316) 686-3888. **$51-$90.** 527 S Webb Rd 67207. I-35, exit 50, just e. Int corridors. **Pets:** Accepted. (ASK) ⊠ ❚ ▣

▼▼ TownePlace Suites by Marriott ❚❚

(316) 631-3773. **$107-$131.** 9444 E 29th St N 67226. SR 96, exit Webb Rd, just sw. Int corridors. **Pets:** Other species. $75 one-time fee/room.

⊠ ⓜ ❚ ▣

▼▼ Wesley Inn ❚❚

(316) 858-3343. **$91.** 3343 E Central Ave 67208. Just e of jct Hillside St. Int corridors. **Pets:** Small. $25 one-time fee/room. Service with restrictions, crate. (ASK) ⊠ ❚ ▣

WINFIELD

▼▼▼▼ Comfort Inn ❚❚

(620) 221-7529. **$90-$99.** 3800 S Pike Rd 67156. On US 77, 1 mi s. Ext/int corridors. **Pets:** Accepted. (ASK) ⊠ ❚ ▣ ⌁

▼▼ Econo Lodge Ⓜ

(620) 221-9050. **$60-$120.** 1710 Main St 67156. 0.5 mi s of jct US 77 and 160. Ext corridors. **Pets:** Small, other species. $10 daily fee/pet. Designated rooms, supervision. (ASK) ⊠ ❚ ▣

KENTUCKY

ASHLAND

🔷 ◈◈◈◈ Best Western River Cities 🅷

(606) 326-0357. **$100-$110.** 31 Russell Plaza Dr 41101. I-64, exit 185, 6 mi nw on US 60, then 3 mi n on US 23. Int corridors. **Pets:** Accepted.
SAVE ✕ &M 🛏 💻 ⌯

◈◈◈◈ Holiday Inn Express Hotel & Suites 🅷 🐾

(606) 929-1720. **$85-$159.** 13131 Slone Ct 41101. I-64, exit 185, just n. Int corridors. **Pets:** $25 daily fee/pet. Designated rooms, service with restrictions, supervision. ASK ✕ &M 🛏 💻 ⌯

◈◈ Quality Inn 🅷

(606) 325-8989. **Call for rates.** 4708 Winchester Ave 41101. I-64, exit 191, 4.8 mi n on US 23. Ext corridors. **Pets:** Large. $15 daily fee/pet. Service with restrictions, crate. ✕ &M 🛏 💻 ⌯

BARDSTOWN

🔷 ◈ Bardstown-Parkview Motel 🅼

(502) 348-5983. **$45-$80.** 418 E Stephen Foster Ave 40004. 0.5 mi e on US 150; e of jct US 62. Ext corridors. **Pets:** Accepted.
SAVE ✕ 🛏 🍴 ⌯

🔷 ◈◈ Best Western General Nelson Inn 🅷

(502) 348-3977. **$69-$139.** 411 W Stephen Foster Ave 40004. 0.5 mi w on US 62. Ext corridors. **Pets:** Small. $15 one-time fee/room. Service with restrictions, crate. SAVE ✕ 🛏 💻 ⌯

◈◈◈ Hampton Inn 🅷

(502) 349-0100. **$99-$109.** 985 Chambers Blvd 40004. Just s of US 245. Int corridors. **Pets:** Accepted. ✕ &M 🛏 💻 ⌯

BENTON

◈◈◈ Comfort Inn & Suites 🅷

(270) 527-5300. **$74-$99.** 173 Carroll Rd 42025. Purchase Pkwy, exit 47. Int corridors. **Pets:** Accepted. ✕ &M 🛏 💻 ⌯

BEREA

🔷 ◈◈◈ Boone Tavern Hotel & Restaurant of Berea College 🅷

(859) 985-3700. **$117-$139.** 100 Main St 40404. I-75, exit 76, 1.5 mi ne on SR 21. Int corridors. **Pets:** Small, dogs only. $50 one-time fee/room. Service with restrictions, supervision. SAVE ✕ 💻 🍴

◈◈◈ Comfort Inn & Suites 🅷

(859) 985-5500. **Call for rates.** 1003 Paint Lick Rd 40403. I-75, exit 76, just w. Int corridors. **Pets:** Accepted. ✕ &M 🛏 💻 ⌯

◈◈◈ Holiday Inn Express Hotel 🅷

(859) 985-1901. **Call for rates.** 365 Peggy Flats Rd 40403. I-75, exit 77, just w. Int corridors. **Pets:** Accepted. ✕ &M 🛏 💻 ⌯

BOWLING GREEN

🔷 ◈◈◈ Candlewood Suites 🅷

(270) 843-5505. **$89-$139.** 540 Wall St 42103. I-65, exit 22 (Scottsville Rd), just n. Int corridors. **Pets:** Accepted. SAVE ✕ &M 🛏 💻 ⌯

🔷 ◈◈◈ Country Hearth Inn 🅷

(270) 783-4443. **$45-$90.** 395 Corvette Dr 42101. I-65, exit 28, just w. Int corridors. **Pets:** Small. $5 daily fee/pet. Service with restrictions, supervision. SAVE ✕ &M 🛏 💻

◈◈◈ Drury Inn-Bowling Green 🅷

(270) 842-7100. **$95-$164.** 3250 Scottsville Rd 42104. I-65, exit 22 (Scottsville Rd), just w. Int corridors. **Pets:** Other species. No service, supervision. ASK ✕ &M 🛏 💻 ⌯

🔷 ◈◈◈ Holiday Inn University Plaza 🅷

(270) 745-0088. **Call for rates.** 1021 Wilkinson Trace 42103. I-65, exit 22 (Scottsville Rd), 2.5 mi w, then just n. Int corridors. **Pets:** Accepted.
SAVE ✕ 🛏 💻 🍴 ⌯

🔷 ◈◈◈ News Inn of Bowling Green 🅼

(270) 781-3460. **$49-$149.** 3160 Scottsville Rd 42104. I-65, exit 22 (Scottsville Rd). Ext corridors. **Pets:** Large. $5 daily fee/pet. Service with restrictions, crate. SAVE ✕ 🛏 💻 ⌯

🔷 ◈◈◈ Red Roof Inn 🅷

(270) 781-6550. **$50-$150.** 3140 Scottsville Rd 42104. I-65, exit 22 (Scottsville Rd), 0.3 mi w. Ext corridors. **Pets:** Large. Service with restrictions, crate. SAVE ✕ 🛏

CALVERT CITY

◈◈◈ Super 8 Calvert City/KY Lake 🅷

(270) 395-5566. **$62-$70.** 86 Campbell Dr 42029. I-24, exit 27 (US 62), just n. Int corridors. **Pets:** Accepted. ASK ✕ &M 🛏 💻 ⌯

CAMPBELLSVILLE

◈◈◈ Holiday Inn Express 🅷

(270) 465-2727. **$80-$91.** 102 Plantation Dr 42718. Jct US 68 and SR 55, 0.5 mi n. Int corridors. **Pets:** Accepted.
ASK ✕ &M 🛏 💻 ⌯

CARROLLTON

🔷 ◈◈◈ Best Western Executive Inn 🅷

(502) 732-8444. **$66-$131.** 10 Slumber Ln 41008. I-71, exit 44, just nw. Int corridors. **Pets:** Accepted. SAVE ✕ &M 🛏 💻 ⌯

◈◈ Super 8 Carrollton 🅷

(502) 732-0252. **Call for rates.** 130 Slumber Ln 41008. I-71, exit 44, just nw. Int corridors. **Pets:** Accepted. ✕ 🛏 💻

CATLETTSBURG

◈◈◈ Ramada Limited Hotel 🅷

(606) 739-5700. **$84-$94.** 6000 Crider Dr 41129. I-64, exit 191, 0.5 mi n on US 23. Int corridors. **Pets:** Accepted. ASK ✕ 🛏 💻 ⌯

CAVE CITY

Best Western Kentucky Inn ⬛
(270) 773-3161. **$50-$110.** 1009 Doyle Ave 42127. I-65, exit 53, just e. Ext corridors. **Pets:** Small, dogs only. $10 daily fee/pet. Designated rooms, service with restrictions, supervision. 🆂🅰🆅🅴 ⊠ 🖥 📱 ➰

Super 8 ⬛
(270) 773-2500. **$49-$99.** 799 Mammoth Cave St 42127. I-65, exit 53, just ne. Ext corridors. **Pets:** Small. $10 daily fee/pet. Service with restrictions, supervision. 🆂🅰🆅🅴 ⊠ 🔶 🖥 📱 ➰

CORBIN

Best Western-Corbin Inn ⬛
(606) 528-2100. **$70-$100.** 2630 Cumberland Falls Hwy 40701. I-75, exit 25. Ext corridors. **Pets:** $15 daily fee/pet. Designated rooms, service with restrictions, supervision. 🆂🅰🆅🅴 ⊠ 🖥 📱 ➰

COVINGTON

Embassy Suites Cincinnati RiverCenter ⬛
(859) 261-8400. **$140-$230.** 10 E RiverCenter Blvd 41011. I-71/75, exit 192, 0.8 mi e on 5th St, then 0.3 mi n on Madison Ave. Int corridors. **Pets:** Small. $25 one-time fee/pet. Service with restrictions, supervision.
🆂🅰🆅🅴 ⊠ 🔶 🖥 📱 🍽 ➰

Extended StayAmerica Cincinnati-Covington ⬛
(859) 581-3000. **$95-$104.** 650 W 3rd St 41011. I-71/75, exit 192, 0.5 mi ne on SR 8. Int corridors. **Pets:** Other species. $25 daily fee/room. Designated rooms, service with restrictions, crate. 🅰🆂🅺 ⊠ 🔶 🖥 📱

DANVILLE

Best Western Danville Inn ⬛
(859) 824-7121. **Call for rates.** 210 Brenda Ave 40422. Just e on US 127 Bypass and 150 (Perryville Rd). Int corridors. **Pets:** Accepted.
🆂🅰🆅🅴 ⊠ 🔶 🖥 📱 ➰

Holiday Inn Express-Danville ⬛
(859) 236-8600. **Call for rates.** 96 Daniel Dr 40422. Just e of US 127 on US 150 Bypass. Int corridors. **Pets:** Other species. $25 one-time fee/pet. Service with restrictions, supervision. ⊠ 🔶 🖥 📱 ➰

DRY RIDGE

Holiday Inn Express ⬛
(859) 824-5025. **$84-$99.** 1050 Fashion Ridge Rd 41035. I-75, exit 159, just nw. Int corridors. **Pets:** Medium. $10 one-time fee/pet. Designated rooms, service with restrictions, supervision. 🅰🆂🅺 ⊠ 🖥 📱

EDDYVILLE

Eddy Creek Marina Resort Ⓜ
(270) 388-2271. **$74-$170, 45 day notice.** 7612 SR 93 S 42038. I-24, exit 45, 4 mi s. Ext corridors. **Pets:** Accepted.
⊠ 🖥 📱 🍽 ➰ 🔲 ☎

ELIZABETHTOWN

Best Western Atrium Gardens ⬛
(270) 769-3030. **$80-$139.** 1043 Executive Dr 42702. I-65, exit 94, just nw. Int corridors. **Pets:** Other species. $25 one-time fee/room. Service with restrictions, crate. 🆂🅰🆅🅴 ⊠ 🖥 📱 ➰

Comfort Inn ⬛
(270) 765-4166. **$80-$130.** 2009 N Mulberry St 42701. I-65, exit 94, just sw. Int corridors. **Pets:** Accepted. ⊠ 🔶 🖥 📱 ➰

Country Hearth Inn & Suites ⬛
(270) 769-2344. **$77-$107.** 1058 N Mulberry St 42701. I-65, exit 94, nw. Ext corridors. **Pets:** Accepted. 🅰🆂🅺 ⊠ 🖥 📱 🍽 ➰

Holiday Inn Express ⬛
(270) 769-1334. **$103-$150.** 107 Buffalo Creek Dr 42701. I-65, exit 94, just w. Int corridors. **Pets:** Small. $50 daily fee/pet. Designated rooms, service with restrictions, crate. 🅰🆂🅺 ⊠ 🔶 🖥 📱 ➰

La Quinta Inn Elizabethtown ⬛ 🐾
(270) 765-4747. **$79-$179.** 210 Commerce Dr 42701. I-65, exit 94, just nw. Int corridors. **Pets:** Medium, other species. Service with restrictions, supervision. 🆂🅰🆅🅴 ⊠ 🔶 🖥 📱 ➰

ERLANGER

Comfort Inn-Cincinnati Airport ⬛
(859) 727-3400. **$72-$110.** 630 Donaldson Rd 41018. I-71/75, exit 184, off SR 236 southbound; exit 184B northbound. Int corridors.
Pets: Accepted. ⊠ 🖥 📱 ➰

Residence Inn by Marriott, Cincinnati Airport ⬛ 🐾
(859) 282-7400. **$180-$200.** 2811 Circleport Dr 41018. I-275, exit 2. Int corridors. **Pets:** Large, other species. $100 one-time fee/room. Service with restrictions. ⊠ 🔶 🖥 📱 ➰ ⊠

FLORENCE

Ashley Quarters ⬛
(859) 525-9997. **$86-$140.** 4880 Houston Rd 41042. I-71/75, exit 182, 0.6 mi w on Turfway and Houston rds. Int corridors. **Pets:** Accepted.
🅰🆂🅺 ⊠ 🖥 📱 ➰

Best Western Inn Florence ⬛
(859) 525-0090. **$55-$100.** 7821 Commerce Dr 41042. I-71/75, exit 181, just ne. Int corridors. **Pets:** Medium, dogs only. $15 daily fee/pet. Service with restrictions, supervision. 🆂🅰🆅🅴 ⊠ 🔶 🖥 📱 ➰

Extended StayAmerica-Cincinnati-Florence ⬛
(859) 282-7829. **$66-$76.** 7350 Turfway Rd 41042. I-71/75, exit 182, just w. Int corridors. **Pets:** Other species. $25 daily fee/room. Designated rooms, service with restrictions, crate. 🅰🆂🅺 ⊠ 🔶 🖥 📱

Florence Super 8 ⬛
(859) 283-1221. **$59-$89.** 7928 Dream St 41042. I-71/75, exit 180, just e on US 42, then just n. Int corridors. **Pets:** Accepted.
🆂🅰🆅🅴 ⊠ 🖥 📱 ➰

Hilton Cincinnati Airport ⬛
(859) 371-4400. **$100-$220.** 7373 Turfway Rd 41042. I-71/75, exit 182, 0.4 mi sw. Int corridors. **Pets:** Accepted.
🆂🅰🆅🅴 ⊠ 🔶 🖥 📱 🍽 ➰

La Quinta Inn & Suites ⬛ 🐾
(859) 282-8212. **$89-$130.** 350 Meijer Dr 41042. I-71/75, exit 182, 0.4 mi sw. Int corridors. **Pets:** Medium, other species. Service with restrictions, supervision. 🅰🆂🅺 ⊠ 🔶 🖥 📱 ➰

Red Roof Inn Ⓜ
(859) 647-2700. **$61-$87.** 7454 Turfway Rd 41042. I-71/75, exit 182, 0.8 mi sw. Int corridors. **Pets:** Large. Service with restrictions, crate.
🆂🅰🆅🅴 ⊠ 🖥

FRANKFORT

Best Western Parkside Inn ⬛
(502) 695-6111. **$74-$345.** 80 Chenault Rd 40601. I-64, exit 58. Ext/int corridors. **Pets:** Accepted. 🆂🅰🆅🅴 ⊠ 🖥 📱 ➰

Capital Plaza Hotel ⬛
(502) 227-5100. **$83-$89.** 405 Wilkinson Blvd 40601. Adjacent to Frankfort Convention Center. Int corridors. **Pets:** Accepted.
🅰🆂🅺 ⊠ 🔶 🖥 📱 ➰

FRANKLIN

Comfort Inn ⬛
(270) 586-6100. **Call for rates.** 3794 Nashville Rd 42134. I-65, exit 2. Ext corridors. **Pets:** Accepted. 🆂🅰🆅🅴 ⊠ 🔶 🖥 📱 ➰

Holiday Inn Express & Suites-Franklin ⬛
(270) 586-7626. **$99.** 85 Neha Dr 42134. I-65, exit 2, just n. Int corridors.
Pets: Accepted. 🅰🆂🅺 ⊠ 🔶 🖥 📱 ➰

GLASGOW

▼▼▼▼ Comfort Inn M
(270) 651-9099. **$60-$110.** 210 Calvary Dr 42141. Cumberland Pkwy, exit 11, just n. Ext corridors. **Pets:** $10 daily fee/pet. Service with restrictions.
❌ 🛇 💻 🌊

GRAND RIVERS

▼▼▼▼ Kentucky Barkley Lakes Inn H
(270) 928-2700. **$47-$130.** 720 Complex Dr 42045. I-24, exit 31 (SR 453), just s. Ext/int corridors. **Pets:** Accepted. ASK ❌ 🛇 💻 🌊

GRAYSON

▼▼▼▼ Quality Inn-Grayson, KY H
(606) 474-7854. **Call for rates.** 205 SR 1947 41143. I-64, exit 172, just n. Ext corridors. **Pets:** Accepted. ❌ 🛇M 🛇 💻 🌊

▼▼▼▼ Super 8 H
(606) 474-8811. **$58-$98.** 125 Super 8 Ln 41143. I-64, exit 172, just s. Int corridors. **Pets:** Small. $10 daily fee/pet. Designated rooms, service with restrictions, supervision. ASK ❌ 🛇M 🛇 💻

HARLAN

▼▼▼▼ Holiday Inn Express Harlan H
(606) 573-3385. **$71-$82.** 2608 S Hwy 421 40831. On US 421, 2.8 mi s. Int corridors. **Pets:** Small. $10 deposit/pet. No service, crate.
ASK ❌ 🛇 💻 🌊

HARRODSBURG

▼▼▼▼ Country Hearth Inn H
(859) 734-2400. **$61-$97.** 105 Commercial Dr 40330. 0.6 mi n on College St. Int corridors. **Pets:** Small. $20 one-time fee/pet. Service with restrictions, supervision. ASK ❌ 🛇 💻

▼▼▼▼ Shaker Village of Pleasant Hill CI
(859) 734-5411. **$79-$170.** 3501 Lexington Rd 40330. On US 68, 7 mi ne. Ext/int corridors. **Pets:** Accepted. ❌ 🛇 💻 🍴

HEBRON

Ⓐ▼▼▼▼ Doubletree Hotel Cincinnati Airport H
(859) 371-6166. **$100-$240.** 2826 Terminal Dr 41048. I-71/75, exit 185 (I-275), 4 mi w, exit 4B (SR 212), then 1.3 mi w. Int corridors.
Pets: Accepted. SAVE ❌ 🛇M 🛇 💻 🍴 🌊

HENDERSON

▼▼▼▼ Ramada Inn H
(270) 826-6600. **Call for rates.** 2044 US 41 N 42420. On US 41, 1 mi n. Int corridors. **Pets:** Accepted. ❌ 🛇 💻 🌊

HOPKINSVILLE

Ⓐ ▼▼▼▼ Holiday Inn H
(270) 886-4413. **$89-$109.** 2910 Ft Campbell Blvd 42240. Pennyrile Pkwy, exit 7A, 0.6 mi n on US 41A. Int corridors. **Pets:** Accepted.
SAVE ❌ 🛇 💻 🍴 🌊 ❌

Ⓐ ▼▼▼▼ Hopkinsville Best Western H ❀
(270) 886-9000. **$80-$90.** 4101 Ft Campbell Blvd 42240. Pennyrile Pkwy, exit 7A, just s on US 41A. Int corridors. **Pets:** Very small, dogs only. $10 daily fee/pet. Service with restrictions, supervision.
SAVE ❌ 💻 🌊

KUTTAWA

▼▼▼▼ Days Inn H ❀
(270) 388-4060. **$60-$140.** 139 Days Inn Dr 42055. I-24, exit 40 (US 62), just s. Ext corridors. **Pets:** Large. $10 one-time fee/room. Service with restrictions, supervision. ASK ❌ 🛇M 🛇 💻 🌊

Ⓐ ▼▼▼▼ Relax Inn M
(270) 388-2285. **$45-$70.** 224 New Circle Dr 42055. I-24, exit 40 (US 62), just e. Ext corridors. **Pets:** Very small, dogs only. $6 one-time fee/room. Designated rooms, service with restrictions, supervision.
SAVE ❌ 🛇

LEBANON

▼▼▼▼ Hampton Inn Lebanon H
(270) 699-4000. **$90-$105.** 1125 Loretto Rd 40033. Jct SR 49 and 84. Int corridors. **Pets:** Small. $25 one-time fee/room. Service with restrictions, supervision. ❌ 🛇M 🛇 💻 🌊

LEITCHFIELD

▼▼▼▼ Hatfield Inn H
(270) 259-0464. **$78-$125.** 769 White St 42754. Western Kentucky Pkwy, exit 107, just nw. Int corridors. **Pets:** Accepted. ASK ❌ 🛇

LEWISPORT

Ⓐ ▼▼▼▼ Best Western Hancock Inn M
(270) 295-3234. **$90-$110.** 9040 US Hwy 60 W 42351. On US 60. Int corridors. **Pets:** Medium. $15 daily fee/pet. Service with restrictions, supervision. SAVE ❌ 🛇 💻 🌊

LEXINGTON

Ⓐ ▼▼▼▼ Best Western Lexington Conference Center H
(859) 263-5241. **$79-$89.** 5532 Athens-Boonesboro Rd 40509. I-75, exit 104, just e. Int corridors. **Pets:** Medium, other species. $25 daily fee/pet. Service with restrictions, supervision. SAVE ❌ 🛇 💻 🌊 ❌

▼▼▼▼ Comfort Suites by Choice Hotels H
(859) 296-4446. **$100-$160.** 3060 Fieldstone Way 40513. Jct New Circle and Harrodsburg rds, just sw. Int corridors. **Pets:** Accepted.
❌ 🛇M 🛇 💻 🌊 ❌

▼▼▼▼ Days Inn-South H
(859) 263-3100. **$45-$65.** 5575 Athens-Boonesboro Rd 40509. I-75, exit 104, just e. Ext corridors. **Pets:** Accepted. ASK ❌ 🛇M 🛇 💻

▼▼▼▼ DoubleTree Guest Suites Lexington H
(859) 268-0060. **$119-$239.** 2601 Richmond Rd 40509. I-75, exit 104, 5.5 mi w. Int corridors. **Pets:** Accepted. ❌ 🛇M 🛇 💻 🍴 🌊

▼▼▼▼ Extended StayAmerica-Lexington-Nicholasville Rd H
(859) 278-9600. **$62-$77.** 2650 Wilhite Dr 40503. Jct US 27 and SR 4. Ext corridors. **Pets:** Other species. $25 daily fee/room. Designated rooms, service with restrictions, crate. ASK ❌ 🛇M 🛇 💻

▼▼▼▼ Extended StayAmerica-Tates Creek H
(859) 271-6160. **$66-$76.** 3575 Tates Creek Rd 40517. New Circle Rd (SR 4), exit 18, 0.4 mi s. Int corridors. **Pets:** Other species. $25 daily fee/room. Designated rooms, service with restrictions, crate.
ASK ❌ 🛇 💻

Ⓐ ▼▼▼▼ Four Points Sheraton Hotel H
(859) 259-1311. **Call for rates.** 1938 Stanton Way 40511. I-75/64, exit 115, just se on SR 922. Int corridors. **Pets:** Accepted.
SAVE ❌ 🛇M 🛇 💻 🍴 🌊

▼▼▼▼ Griffin Gate Marriott Resort H ❀
(859) 231-5100. **$199-$219.** 1800 Newtown Pike 40511. I-75/64, exit 115, 0.5 mi sw. Int corridors. **Pets:** Medium, dogs only. $100 one-time fee/room. Designated rooms, service with restrictions.
❌ 🛇M 🛇 💻 🍴 ❌

▼▼▼▼ Hampton Inn I-75 H
(859) 299-2613. **Call for rates.** 2251 Elkhorn Rd 40505. I-75, exit 110, 0.4 mi nw. Int corridors. **Pets:** Service with restrictions, supervision.
❌ 🛇M 🛇 💻 🌊

Ⓐ ▼▼▼▼ Hilton Suites of Lexington Green H
(859) 271-4000. **$299-$499.** 245 Lexington Green Cir 40503. New Circle Rd (SR 4), exit 19, just s. Int corridors. **Pets:** Medium. $50 one-time fee/room. Designated rooms, service with restrictions, crate.
SAVE ❌ 🛇M 🛇 💻 🍴 🌊

▼▼▼▼ **Holiday Inn Express Hotel & Suites-Lexington** 🅗
(859) 389-6800. **$99-$199.** 1000 Export St 40504. I-75/64, exit 113, 4.5 mi s, then just e. Int corridors. **Pets:** Accepted.
🄰🅂🄺 ⊠ ⛫ 🔲 🆒

⬧⬧ ▼▼▼▼ **Holiday Inn-Lexington North** 🅗
(859) 233-0512. **Call for rates.** 1950 Newtown Pike 40511. I-75/64, exit 115, just s. Ext/int corridors. **Pets:** Accepted.
🆂🄰🆅🄴 ⊠ ⛫ 🔲 🍴 🆒 ⊠

▼▼ **La Quinta Inn & Suites** 🅗 🐾
(859) 543-1877. **$65-$165.** 100 Canebrake Dr 40509. I-75, exit 104, just e. Int corridors. **Pets:** Medium, other species. Service with restrictions, supervision. 🄰🅂🄺 ⊠ ⛫ 🔲 🆒

⬧⬧ ▼▼▼▼ **Lexington Downtown Hotel & Conference Center, a Hilton Affiliate Hotel** 🅗
(859) 231-9000. **$89-$259.** 369 W Vine St 40507. Corner of Vine St and Broadway. Int corridors. **Pets:** Accepted.
🆂🄰🆅🄴 ⊠ ⛫ 🔲 🍴 🆒 ⊠

⬧⬧ ▼▼▼ **Red Roof Inn-North** 🅗
(859) 293-2626. **$50-$149, 14 day notice.** 1980 Haggard Ct 40505. I-75/64, exit 113, 0.3 mi nw. Ext corridors. **Pets:** Large. Service with restrictions, crate. 🆂🄰🆅🄴 ⊠

⬧⬧ ▼▼▼ **Red Roof Inn South** 🅗
(859) 277-9400. **$50-$80, 14 day notice.** 2651 Wilhite Dr 40503. Jct US 27 and SR 4. Ext corridors. **Pets:** Large. Service with restrictions, crate.
🆂🄰🆅🄴 ⊠ ⛫ ⛫

▼▼▼ **Residence Inn by Marriott** 🅗
(859) 231-6191. **$157-$191.** 1080 Newtown Pike 40511. I-75/64, exit 115, 1 mi s on SR 922. Ext corridors. **Pets:** Accepted.
⊠ ⛫ 🔲 🆒 ⊠

▼▼▼▼ **Residence Inn South @ Hamburg** 🅗
(859) 263-9979. **$134-$164.** 2688 Pink Pigeon Pkwy 40509. I-75, exit 108, just se. Int corridors. **Pets:** Large. $75 one-time fee/room. Service with restrictions. ⊠ ⛫ ⛫ 🔲 🍴 🆒 ⊠

▼▼ **Sleep Inn Lexington** 🅗
(859) 543-8400. **$99-$149, 7 day notice.** 1920 Plaudit Pl 40509. I-75, exit 108, just sw. Int corridors. **Pets:** Accepted. ⊠ ⛫ 🔲 🆒

LONDON
▼ **Budget Host Westgate Inn** 🅗 🐾
(606) 878-7330. **$42-$62, 3 day notice.** 254 Russell Dyche Memorial Hwy 40741-9623. I-75, exit 41, just w on SR 80. Ext/int corridors. **Pets:** Small. Designated rooms, service with restrictions, supervision.
🄰🅂🄺 ⊠ ⛫ ⛫ 🆒

▼▼ **Econo Lodge** 🅗
(606) 877-9700. **Call for rates.** 105 Melcon Ln 40741. I-75, exit 41, southeast corner. Int corridors. **Pets:** Accepted. ⊠ ⛫ ⛫ 🔲 🆒

▼▼ **National Heritage Inn & Suites** 🅗
(606) 877-3400. **$50-$80.** 1895 W Hwy 192 40741. I-75, exit 38. Int corridors. **Pets:** Large. $10 daily fee/room. Designated rooms, service with restrictions, supervision. ⊠ ⛫ ⛫ 🔲 🆒

▼▼ **Red Roof Inn** 🅗
(606) 862-8844. **Call for rates.** 110 Melcon Ln 40741. I-75, exit 41, southwest corner. Int corridors. **Pets:** Large. Service with restrictions, crate. ⊠ ⛫ ⛫ 🔲 🆒

LOUISA
▼▼ **Super 8-Louisa** 🅗
(606) 638-7888. **$58-$75.** 191 Falls Creek Dr 41230. Jct US 23 and SR 3. Int corridors. **Pets:** Accepted. 🄰🅂🄺 ⊠ ⛫ ⛫

LOUISVILLE METROPOLITAN AREA

BROOKS
▼▼ **Baymont Inn** 🅗
(502) 957-6900. **$59-$265.** 149 Willabrook Dr 40109. I-65, exit 121, just nw. Int corridors. **Pets:** Accepted. 🄰🅂🄺 ⊠ ⛫ 🔲 🆒

HURSTBOURNE
▼▼▼ **Drury Inn & Suites-Louisville** 🅗
(502) 326-4170. **$85-$174.** 9501 Blairwood Rd 40222. I-64, exit 15. Int corridors. **Pets:** Other species. No service, supervision.
🄰🅂🄺 ⊠ ⛫ ⛫ 🔲 🆒

⬧⬧ ▼▼▼ **Red Roof Inn Louisville–East #034** 🅗
(502) 426-7621. **$50-$80.** 9330 Blairwood Rd 40222. I-64, exit 15, 0.3 mi nw of Hurstbourne Pkwy. Ext corridors. **Pets:** Large. Service with restrictions, crate. 🆂🄰🆅🄴 ⊠ ⛫

JEFFERSONTOWN
⬧⬧ ▼▼▼ **Holiday Inn-Hurstbourne** 🅗 🐾
(502) 426-2600. **Call for rates.** 1325 S Hurstbourne Pkwy 40222. I-64, exit 15, just n. Ext/int corridors. **Pets:** $35 one-time fee/pet. Service with restrictions, supervision. 🆂🄰🆅🄴 ⊠ ⛫ ⛫ 🔲 🍴 🆒 ⊠

▼▼ **Homestead Studio Suites Louisville–Alliant Drive** 🅗
(502) 267-4454. **$71-$81.** 1650 Alliant Ave 40299. I-64, exit 17, just s. Int corridors. **Pets:** Other species. $25 daily fee/room. Designated rooms, service with restrictions, crate. 🄰🅂🄺 ⊠ ⛫ 🅷 ⛫ 🔲 🆒

▼▼ **Jameson Inn Louisville East** 🅗
(502) 267-8100. **Call for rates.** 1301 Kentucky Mills Dr 40299. I-64, exit 17, just s. Ext/int corridors. **Pets:** Accepted.
⊠ ⛫ ⛫ 🔲 🆒 ⊠

▼▼ **La Quinta Inn & Suites** 🅗 🐾
(502) 267-8889. **$50-$350.** 1501 Alliant Ave 40299. I-64, exit 17, just e. Int corridors. **Pets:** Medium, other species. Service with restrictions, supervision. 🄰🅂🄺 ⊠ ⛫ ⛫ 🔲 🆒

▼▼ **Microtel Inn Louisville East** 🅗
(502) 266-6590. **$50-$65.** 1221 Kentucky Mills Dr 40299. I-64, exit 17. Int corridors. **Pets:** Small. $20 one-time fee/pet. Designated rooms, service with restrictions, supervision. 🄰🅂🄺 ⊠ ⛫

LA GRANGE
▼▼▼ **Comfort Suites** 🅗
(502) 225-4125. **$87-$135.** 1500 E Crystal Dr 40031. I-71, exit 22, just e. Int corridors. **Pets:** Accepted. ⊠ ⛫ ⛫ 🔲 🆒

⬧⬧ ▼▼▼ **Holiday Inn Express** 🅗
(502) 222-5678. **Call for rates.** 1001 Paige Pl 40031. I-71, exit 22, just se. Int corridors. **Pets:** Accepted. 🆂🄰🆅🄴 ⊠ ⛫ 🔲 🆒

LOUISVILLE
▼▼▼▼ **21C Museum Hotel** 🅗
(502) 217-6300. **$159-$299.** 700 W Main St 40202. Jct 7th and Main sts. Int corridors. **Pets:** Accepted. ⊠ ⛫ 🔲 🍴 ⊠

▼▼▼ **Aleksander House Bed and Breakfast** 🅱🅱 🐾
(502) 637-4985. **$115-$195, 3 day notice.** 1213 S 1st St 40203. I-65, exit 135 (St Catherine St), just s. Int corridors. **Pets:** $40 one-time fee/pet. 🄰🅂🄺 ⊠ ⛫ ⛫

Best Western Airport East Expo Center [H] ❖

(502) 456-4411. **$69-$175.** 1921 Bishop Ln 40218. I-264, exit 15B westbound, 0.3 mi s; exit 15 eastbound. Int corridors. **Pets:** Other species. $25 one-time fee/pet. Service with restrictions, crate.

Crowne Plaza Louisville [H]

(502) 367-2251. **$99-$189.** 830 Phillips Ln 40209. I-264, exit 11 (Fairgrounds/Expo Center Main Gate). Int corridors. **Pets:** Other species. $250 one-time fee/room. Service with restrictions, supervision.

Fern Valley Hotel & Conference Center [H]

(502) 964-3311. **Call for rates.** 2715 Fern Valley Rd 40213. I-65, exit 128 (Fern Valley Rd), northeast corner. Int corridors. **Pets:** Accepted.

Homewood Suites [H]

(502) 429-9070. **$109-$499.** 9401 Hurstbourne Trace 40222. I-64, exit 15, 2.5 mi n. Int corridors. **Pets:** Large, other species. $100 one-time fee/room. Designated rooms, service with restrictions, crate.

Jameson Inn Airport South [H]

(502) 968-4100. **$93-$100.** 6515 Signature Dr 40213. I-65, exit 128 (Fern Valley Rd), southeast corner. Int corridors. **Pets:** Accepted.

La Quinta Inn & Suites Airport & Expo-Louisville [H] ❖

(502) 368-0007. **$80-$160.** 4125 Preston Hwy 40213. I-65, exit 130, 1 mi n. Int corridors. **Pets:** Medium, other species. Service with restrictions, supervision.

Ramada Limited & Suites [H]

(502) 637-6336. **$60-$100.** 2912 Crittenden Dr 40209. I-264, exit 11 (Fairgrounds/Expo Center Main Gate), 0.6 mi n. Int corridors.
Pets: Accepted.

Red Roof Inn-Airport-Fairgrounds [H]

(502) 968-0151. **Call for rates.** 4704 Preston Hwy 40213. I-65, exit 130, northeast corner. Ext corridors. **Pets:** Large. Service with restrictions, crate.

Red Roof Inn-Southeast-Fairgrounds [H]

(502) 456-2993. **$55-$105, 14 day notice.** 3322 Red Roof Inn Pl 40218. I-264, 15B westbound, 0.3 mi s; exit 15 eastbound. Ext corridors. **Pets:** Large. Service with restrictions, crate.

Residence Inn by Marriott-Louisville Airport [H]

(502) 363-8800. **$139-$500.** 700 Phillips Ln 40209. I-264, exit 11 (Fairgrounds/Expo Center Main Gate), 0.4 mi w. Int corridors. **Pets:** Other species. $100 one-time fee/room. Service with restrictions, crate.

Residence Inn by Marriott Louisville Downtown [H]

(502) 589-8998. **$198-$242.** 333 E Market St 40202. Corner of Preston and E Market. Int corridors. **Pets:** Accepted.

Residence Inn by Marriott-Louisville NE [H]

(502) 412-1311. **$180-$219.** 3500 Springhurst Commons Dr 40241. I-265, exit 32, 0.5 mi w on Westport Rd, then just n. Int corridors. **Pets:** Other species. $100 one-time fee/room. Service with restrictions.

Residence Inn Louisville East [H]

(502) 425-1821. **$125-$153.** 120 N Hurstbourne Pkwy 40222. I-64, exit 15, 1.8 mi n. Ext corridors. **Pets:** Large, other species. $100 one-time fee/room. Service with restrictions.

The Seelbach Hilton Louisville [H]

(502) 585-3200. **$109-$269.** 500 4th St 40202. I-65, exit 136C (Muhammad Ali Blvd), 0.3 mi w, then just s. Int corridors. **Pets:** Accepted.

Sleep Inn Fairgrounds [H]

(502) 368-9597. **Call for rates.** 3330 Preston Hwy 40213. I-264, exit 11 (Fairgrounds/Expo Center Main Gate), 0.5 mi e on Phillips Ln, then just n. Int corridors. **Pets:** Large, other species. $35 one-time fee/pet. Service with restrictions, supervision.

Staybridge Suites by Holiday Inn [H] ❖

(502) 244-9511. **$75-$169.** 11711 Gateworth Way 40299. I-64, exit 17, just n. Int corridors. **Pets:** Medium, dogs only. $150 one-time fee/room. Designated rooms, service with restrictions, crate.

Super 8 [H]

(502) 635-0799. **Call for rates.** 101 Central Ave 40209. I-65, exit 132, just s. Int corridors. **Pets:** Accepted.

SHEPHERDSVILLE

Best Western South [H]

(502) 543-7097. **$77-$89.** 211 S Lakeview Dr 40165. I-65, exit 117 (SR 44 W), just se. Int corridors. **Pets:** Small. Service with restrictions, supervision.

Super 8 [H]

(502) 543-8870. **$46-$225, 14 day notice.** 275 Keystone Crossroads 40165. I-65, exit 117 (SR 44 W), just w. Int corridors. **Pets:** Accepted.

SHIVELY

Holiday Inn Southwest Fair Expo [H]

(502) 448-2020. **$99-$169.** 4110 Dixie Hwy 40216. I-264, exit 8B, just n on US 31 W and 60. Int corridors. **Pets:** Accepted.

END METROPOLITAN AREA

MAYSVILLE

Best Western Maysville Inn [H]

(606) 759-5696. **$65-$70.** 1428 a US 68 41056. Jct US 68 and SR 9 (AA Hwy). Ext corridors. **Pets:** Accepted.

Super 8, Maysville KY [H]

(606) 759-8888. **$54-$113.** 550 Tucker Dr 41056. Just e of US 68. Int corridors. **Pets:** Small. $20 daily fee/pet. Service with restrictions, supervision.

MOREHEAD

Comfort Inn & Suites [H] ❖

(606) 780-7378. **$63-$130.** 2650 Kentucky 801 N 40351. I-64, exit 133, just s. Int corridors. **Pets:** Other species. $10 daily fee/room. Service with restrictions, crate.

Holiday Inn Express of Morehead [H]

(606) 784-5796. **Call for rates.** 110 Toms Dr 40351. I-64, exit 137 (SR 32), just sw. Int corridors. **Pets:** Accepted.

MORTONS GAP

Best Western Pennyrile Inn ⚊
(270) 258-5201. **Call for rates.** White City Rd 42440. Pennyrile Pkwy, exit 37 (US 41). Ext corridors. **Pets:** Accepted. 🅢🅐🅥🅔 ⊠ 🔌 💻 🏊

MOUNT VERNON

Days Inn-Renfro Valley ⚊
(606) 256-3300. **$49-$90.** 1630 Richmond St 40456. I-75, exit 62, just n. Ext corridors. **Pets:** Small. $20 one-time fee/pet. Service with restrictions, supervision. 🅐🅢🅚 ⊠ 🔌 💻

MUNFORDVILLE

Super 8 ⚊
(270) 524-4888. **Call for rates.** 88 Bull Run Rd 42765. I-65, exit 65, 0.5 mi s. Int corridors. **Pets:** Accepted. ⊠ 🔌 💻

MURRAY

Best Western University Inn ⚊
(270) 753-5353. **$60-$90.** 1503 N 12th St 42071. 1.9 mi n on US 641. Ext corridors. **Pets:** Accepted. 🅢🅐🅥🅔 ⊠ 🔌 💻 🏊

Days Inn-Murray, KY ⚊
(270) 753-6706. **$80-$100.** 517 S 12th St 42071. 1 mi s on US 641. Ext corridors. **Pets:** Accepted. 🅐🅢🅚 ⊠ 🔌 💻 🏊

OAK GROVE

Holiday Inn Express ⚊
(270) 439-0022. **Call for rates.** 12759 Ft Campbell Blvd 42262. I-24, exit 86, just s. Int corridors. **Pets:** Small. $10 daily fee/pet. Designated rooms, service with restrictions. ⊠ 🅶🅼 🔌 💻 🏊

Quality Inn @ Ft. Campbell ⚊
(270) 439-3311. **$65-$99.** 201 Auburn St 42262. I-24, exit 86, just s. Ext corridors. **Pets:** Accepted. 🅢🅐🅥🅔 ⊠ 🅶🅼 🔌 💻 🏊

OWENSBORO

Motel 6 #205 ⚊
(270) 686-8606. **$49-$59.** 4585 Frederica St 42301. US 60 Bypass, exit 4 at US 431, just n. Ext corridors. **Pets:** Other species. Service with restrictions, supervision. ⊠ 🅶🅼 🔌 🏊

Super 8-Owensboro ⚊
(270) 685-3388. **$60-$90.** 1027 Goetz Dr 42301. US 60 Bypass, exit 4 at US 431. Int corridors. **Pets:** Small, dogs only. $20 daily fee/pet. Designated rooms, service with restrictions, supervision.
🅐🅢🅚 ⊠ 🅶🅼 🔌 💻

PADUCAH

Americas Best Value Inn ⚊
(270) 575-9605. **$50-$60.** 5125 Old Cairo Rd 42001. I-24, exit 3 (SR 305), just e. Ext corridors. **Pets:** Accepted. 🅢🅐🅥🅔 ⊠ 🔌

Candlewood Suites Paducah ⚊
(270) 442-3969. **Call for rates.** 3940 Coleman Crossing Cir 42001. I-24, exit 4 (US 60), just n. Int corridors. **Pets:** Accepted. ⊠ 🅶🅼 🔌 💻

Days Inn ⚊
(270) 442-7500. **$50-$90.** 3901 Hinkleville Rd 42001. I-24, exit 4 (US 60), just e. Ext corridors. **Pets:** Accepted. 🅐🅢🅚 ⊠ 🔌 💻 🏊

Drury Inn-Paducah ⚊
(270) 443-3313. **$85-$144.** 3975 Hinkleville Rd 42001. I-24, exit 4 (US 60), just n. Int corridors. **Pets:** Other species. No service, supervision.
🅐🅢🅚 ⊠ 🔌 💻 🏊

Drury Suites-Paducah ⚊
(270) 441-0024. **$95-$154.** 2930 James-Sanders Blvd 42001. I-24, exit 4 (US 60), just w. Int corridors. **Pets:** Other species. No service, supervision. 🅐🅢🅚 ⊠ 🅶🅼 🔌 💻 🏊

Holiday Inn Express ⚊
(270) 442-8874. **$94-$129.** 3994 Hinkleville Rd 42001. I-24, exit 4 (US 60), just e. Int corridors. **Pets:** Accepted. 🅐🅢🅚 ⊠ 🔌 💻 🏊

Pear Tree Inn-Paducah ⚊
(270) 444-7200. **$72-$115.** 5006 Hinkleville Rd 42001. I-24, exit 4 (US 60), just w. Int corridors. **Pets:** Other species. No service, supervision.
🅐🅢🅚 ⊠ 🅶🅼 🔌 💻 🏊

Residence Inn by Marriott-Paducah ⚊ 🐾
(270) 444-3966. **$109-$129.** 3900 Coleman Crossing Cir 42001. I-24, exit 4 (US 60), just n. Int corridors. **Pets:** Medium, other species. $75 one-time fee/room. Designated rooms. ⊠ 🅶🅼 🔌 💻 🏊 ⊠

Thrifty Inn ⚊
(270) 444-0157. **$60-$105.** 5002 Hinkleville Rd 42001. I-24, exit 4 (US 60), just w. Ext corridors. **Pets:** Other species. No service, supervision.
🅐🅢🅚 ⊠ 💻 🏊

PRESTONSBURG

Heritage House Hotel ⚊
(606) 886-0001. **$82, 10 day notice.** 1887 N US 23 41653. 2 mi s. Ext corridors. **Pets:** Accepted. 🅐🅢🅚 ⊠ 🅶🅼 🔌 💻 🍽 🏊 ⊠

Super 8 Prestonsburg Ⓜ
(606) 886-3355. **Call for rates.** 550 US 23 S 41653. Jct SR 14 and US 23. Int corridors. **Pets:** Accepted. ⊠ 🔌 💻

RICHMOND

Comfort Suites ⚊
(859) 624-0770. **Call for rates.** 2007 Colby Taylor Dr 40475. I-75, exit 87, just e. Int corridors. **Pets:** Accepted. ⊠ 🅶🅼 🔌 💻

Holiday Inn Express Hotel & Suites ⚊
(859) 624-4055. **Call for rates.** 1990 Colby Taylor Dr 40745. I-75, exit 87, just w. Int corridors. **Pets:** Medium. $25 daily fee/pet. Service with restrictions, supervision. ⊠ 🅶🅼 🔌 💻 🏊

Jameson Inn ⚊
(859) 623-0063. **$83-$90.** 1007 Colby Taylor Dr 40475. I-75, exit 87, just w. Int corridors. **Pets:** Accepted. 🅐🅢🅚 ⊠ 🅶🅼 🔌 💻 🏊

Super 8 ⚊
(859) 624-1550. **$60-$65, 7 day notice.** 107 N Keeneland Dr 40475. I-75, exit 90. Int corridors. **Pets:** Accepted. 🅢🅐🅥🅔 ⊠ 🅶🅼 🔌 💻

SCOTTSVILLE

Executive Inn Ⓜ
(270) 622-7770. **$54-$179.** 57 Burnley Rd 42164. US 31 E, jct SR 231. Ext corridors. **Pets:** Accepted. 🅢🅐🅥🅔 ⊠ 🔌 🏊

SHELBYVILLE

Best Western Shelbyville Lodge ⚊
(502) 633-4400. **$73-$120.** 115 Isaac Shelby Dr 40065. I-64, exit 32, 0.5 mi n on SR 55. Int corridors. **Pets:** Large, other species. $10 daily fee/room. Service with restrictions, supervision. 🅢🅐🅥🅔 ⊠ 🔌 💻 🏊

Country Hearth Inn ⚊
(502) 633-5771. **$55-$90.** 100 Howard Dr 40065. I-64, exit 32, 0.5 mi n on SR 55. Int corridors. **Pets:** Accepted. 🅢🅐🅥🅔 ⊠ 🔌 💻

Ramada ⚊
(502) 633-9933. **$79-$129, 3 day notice.** 251 Breighton Cir 40065. I-64, exit 32, just s. Int corridors. **Pets:** Small. $25 one-time fee/room. Designated rooms, service with restrictions, supervision.
🅐🅢🅚 ⊠ 🔌 💻

SMITHS GROVE

Bryce Inn Ⓜ
(270) 563-5141. **$49-$65.** 592 S Main St 42171. I-65, exit 38, 0.3 mi w. Ext corridors. **Pets:** Small, dogs only. $10 one-time fee/pet. Service with restrictions, supervision. 🅢🅐🅥🅔 ⊠ 🔌 💻 🏊

SPARTA

▼▼▼ Ramada at the Kentucky Speedway **H**

(859) 567-7223. **$79-$129, 3 day notice.** 525 Dale Dr 41086. I-71, exit 57, just w. Int corridors. **Pets:** Medium. $25 one-time fee/room. Designated rooms, service with restrictions, crate.

(ASK) (X) (&M) (🛏) (🖳) (🏊)

VERSAILLES

▼▼▼ 1823 Historic Rose Hill Inn **BB**

(859) 873-5957. **Call for rates.** 233 Rose Hill 40383. Just s on SR 33 (S Main St), then just w. Ext/int corridors. **Pets:** Accepted. (X) (🛏) (🖳)

WEST LIBERTY

▼▼ Days Inn **H**

(606) 743-4206. **Call for rates.** 1613 W Main St 41472. Jct SR 519 and 460, just w. Int corridors. **Pets:** Large, dogs only. $10 one-time fee/room. Service with restrictions, supervision. (X) (&M) (🖳)

WILLIAMSBURG

▼▼▼ Cumberland Inn **H**

(606) 539-4100. **$94.** 649 S 10th St 40769. I-75, exit 11. Int corridors. **Pets:** Small. $15 one-time fee/room. Designated rooms, service with restrictions, supervision. (ASK) (X) (&M) (🛏) (🖳) (🍴) (🏊)

WINCHESTER

◢◣◥◤ ▼▼▼ Best Western-Country Squire **H**

(859) 744-7210. **$59-$99.** 1307 W Lexington Ave 40391. I-64, exit 94 (US 60), 0.9 mi se. Ext corridors. **Pets:** Medium. $20 one-time fee/pet. Service with restrictions, crate. (SAVE) (X) (🛏) (🖳) (🏊)

LOUISIANA

ALEXANDRIA

▼▼▼▼ La Quinta Inn & Suites Alexandria ⓗ ☙
(318) 442-3700. $79-$144. 6116 W Calhoun Dr 71303. I-49, exit 90 (Air Base Rd), just w. Int corridors. **Pets:** Medium, other species. Service with restrictions, supervision. (ASK) (X) (&M) 🛏 📭 🖢

ⒶⒶⒶ ▼▼▼ Ramada ⓗ ☙
(318) 448-1611. $75-$93. 742 MacArthur Dr 71303. 0.4 mi s of jct SR 28 and US 71/165 (MacArthur Dr). Ext corridors. **Pets:** Medium, other species. $10 daily fee/pet. Service with restrictions, crate.
(SAVE) 🛏 📭 🖢

BATON ROUGE

ⒶⒶⒶ ▼▼▼▼ Best Western Richmond Suites Hotel–Baton Rouge ⓗ
(225) 924-6500. $109-$249. 5668 Hilton Ave 70808. I-10, exit 158, just ne. Int corridors. **Pets:** Other species. $75 one-time fee/room. Service with restrictions, crate. (SAVE) (X) 🛏 📭 🖢 (X)

ⒶⒶⒶ ▼▼▼▼ Chase Suites by Woodfin ⓗ
(225) 927-5630. $149-$209. 5522 Corporate Blvd 70808. I-10, exit 158, just n on College Dr, then just e. Ext corridors. **Pets:** Medium, other species. $200 deposit/room, $10 daily fee/pet, $50 one-time fee/room. Designated rooms, service with restrictions. (SAVE) (X) 🛏 📭 🖢 (X)

ⒶⒶⒶ ▼▼▼▼ Crowne Plaza Executive Center ⓗ ☙
(225) 925-2244. $99. 4728 Constitution Ave 70808. I-10, exit 158, just s, then just e. Int corridors. **Pets:** Large, other species. $30 one-time fee/pet. Service with restrictions, supervision.
(SAVE) (X) (&M) 🛏 📭 (¶) 🖢

▼▼▼▼ Drury Inn & Suites Baton Rouge ⓗ
(225) 766-2022. $80-$209. 7939 Essen Park Ave 70809. I-10, exit 160 (Essen Ln), just s. Int corridors. **Pets:** Other species. No service, supervision. (ASK) (X) (&M) 🛏 📭 🖢

ⒶⒶⒶ ▼▼▼▼ Hilton Baton Rouge Capitol Center ⓗ ☙
(225) 344-5866. $139-$249. 201 Lafayette St 70801. I-10, exit 155B (I-110 N), 0.8 mi n to exit 1C (Florida Blvd), 0.5 mi w to Lafayette, then just s. Int corridors. **Pets:** Medium. $75 one-time fee/room. Designated rooms, service with restrictions, supervision.
(SAVE) (X) 🛏 📭 (¶) 🖢

ⒶⒶⒶ ▼▼▼ Holiday Inn-College @ I-10 ⓗ
(225) 448-2030. $89-$109. 4848 Constitution Ave 70808. I-10, exit 158, just s, then just e. Int corridors. **Pets:** Medium. $30 one-time fee/pet. Service with restrictions, crate. (SAVE) (X) 🛏 📭 (¶) 🖢

ⒶⒶⒶ ▼▼▼ La Quinta Inn Baton Rouge-Siegen Lane ⓗ ☙
(225) 291-6600. $79-$124. 10555 Reiger Rd 70809. I-10, exit 163 (Siegen Ln), just n, then just e. Int corridors. **Pets:** Medium, other species. Service with restrictions, supervision. (ASK) (X) 🛏 📭 🖢

ⒶⒶⒶ ▼▼▼ Microtel Inn & Suites Baton Rouge Airport ⓗ
(225) 356-9191. **Call for rates.** 3444 Harding Blvd 70807. I-110, exit 6, just e. Int corridors. **Pets:** Medium. $15 daily fee/pet. Service with restrictions. (SAVE) (X) (&M) 🛏 📭

ⒶⒶⒶ ▼▼▼▼ Radisson Hotel Baton Rouge ⓗ
(225) 236-4000. $129-$409, 3 day notice. 2445 S Acadian Thruway 70808. I-10, exit 157B, just n. Int corridors. **Pets:** Accepted.
(SAVE) (X) 🛏 📭 (¶) 🖢

▼▼▼▼ Residence Inn by Marriott-Baton Rouge-Siegen Lane ⓗ
(225) 293-8700. $143-$175. 10333 N Mall Dr 70809. I-10, exit 163 westbound, just s on Siegen Ln, then just e; exit eastbound, 0.5 mi to S Mall Dr, just e to Andrea (at Lowe's), then just n. Int corridors. **Pets:** Accepted.
(X) (&M) 🛏 📭 🖢 (X)

▼▼▼▼ Residence Inn by Marriott Baton Rouge-Towne Center at Cedar Lodge ⓗ
(225) 925-9100. $152-$186. 7061 Commerce Cir 70809. I-10, exit 158 (College Dr), just n to Corporate Blvd, then 1.8 mi e. Int corridors.
Pets: Accepted. (X) 🛏 📭 🖢 (X)

ⒶⒶⒶ ▼▼▼▼ Sheraton Baton Rouge Convention Center Hotel ⓗ ☙
(225) 242-2600. **Call for rates.** 102 France St 70802. I-110, exit 1A (Government St), 0.8 mi w to St. James, then just s. Int corridors.
Pets: Medium, other species. Service with restrictions, supervision.
(SAVE) (X) 🛏 📭 (¶) 🖢

▼▼▼ TownePlace Suites by Marriott ⓗ
(225) 819-2112. $143-$175. 8735 Summa Ave 70809. I-10, exit 162 (Bluebonnet Blvd), just s to Picardy, just w to Summa Ave, then 0.5 mi nw. Int corridors. **Pets:** Accepted. (X) (&M) 🛏 📭 🖢

BOSSIER CITY

▼▼▼ Hampton Inn ⓗ
(318) 752-1112. **Call for rates.** 1005 Gould Dr 71111. I-20, exit 21, 0.5 mi ne on service road. Int corridors. **Pets:** Accepted.
(X) (&M) 🛏 📭

▼▼▼ Howard Johnson Bossier City ⓗ
(318) 742-6000. $49-$79. 1984 Airline Dr 71112. I-20, exit 22 (Airline Dr), just n. Ext corridors. **Pets:** Accepted. (ASK) (X) 🛏 📭 (¶) 🖢

▼▼▼ La Quinta Inn Bossier City ⓗ ☙
(318) 747-4400. $49-$125. 309 Preston Blvd 71111-4969. I-20, exit 21, just n. Ext corridors. **Pets:** Medium, other species. Service with restrictions, supervision. (ASK) (X) 🛏 📭 🖢

▼▼▼ Microtel Inn & Suites ⓗ
(318) 742-7882. $65-$119. 2713 Village Ln 71112. I-20, exit 22 (Airline Dr), just s, then just w. Int corridors. **Pets:** Accepted.
(ASK) (X) (&M) 🛏 📭

▼▼▼ Quality Inn & Suites ⓗ
(318) 742-7890. $77-$200. 2717 Village Ln 71112. I-20, exit 22 (Airline Dr), just s, then just w. Int corridors. **Pets:** Accepted.
(X) (&M) 🛏 📭 🖢

▼▼▼▼ Residence Inn by Marriott-Shreveport/Bossier City ⓗ
(318) 747-6220. $179-$219. 1001 Gould Dr 71111. I-20, exit 21, just ne. Ext corridors. **Pets:** Accepted. (X) 🛏 📭 🖢 (X)

CONVENT

▼▼▼ Felix Poche Plantation Bed & Breakfast & RV Resort 🅱🅱

(225) 562-7728. **$119-$198, 15 day notice.** 6554 Louisiana Hwy 44 70723. 10.1 mi s of Sunshine Bridge (SR 70); SR 44 and 641. Ext/int corridors. **Pets:** Other species. $25 one-time fee/room. Service with restrictions, supervision. A$K ✕ 🛗 💻 ⌘

DELHI

🆔 ▼▼▼ Best Western Delhi Inn Ⓜ

(318) 878-5126. **$75-$85.** 135 Snider Rd 71232. I-20, exit 153, just s. Ext corridors. **Pets:** Accepted. SAVE ✕ 🛗 💻 ⌘

HAMMOND

🆔 ▼▼ Best Western University Inn Ⓗ

(985) 345-0003. **$72-$77.** 46053 N Puma Dr 70401. I-55, exit 32 (Wardline/University), just e. Ext corridors. **Pets:** Accepted.

SAVE ✕ 🛗 💻 ⌘

🆔 ▼▼▼ Michabelle Inn 🅲

(985) 419-0550. **$75-$125, 4 day notice.** 1106 S Holly St 70403. I-12, exit 40 (US 51), 0.8 mi n, just e on Old Covington Hwy, then n, follow signs. Ext/int corridors. **Pets:** Accepted. SAVE ✕ 🛗 💻 🍴 ⌘

HOUMA

▼▼▼▼ La Quinta Inn & Suites Houma Ⓗ ❀

(985) 879-1646. **$69-$189.** 189 Synergy Center Blvd 70360. US 90, exit 202, 3.4 mi s on Main St to Martin Luther King Jr Blvd, then just w. Int corridors. **Pets:** Medium, other species. Service with restrictions, supervision. A$K ✕ &M 🛗 💻 ⌘

IOWA

▼▼ Howard Johnson Express Inn Ⓗ

(337) 582-2440. **Call for rates.** 107 E Frontage Rd 70647. I-10, exit 43, just n, then just e. Int corridors. **Pets:** Accepted. ✕ 🛗 💻

KINDER

🆔 ▼▼▼ Best Western Inn At Coushatta Ⓗ

(337) 738-4800. **$99-$109.** 12102 US Hwy 165 N 70648. 5 mi n of jct US 190/165. Int corridors. **Pets:** Small, other species. $25 deposit/room. Service with restrictions, supervision. SAVE ✕ 🛗 💻 ⌘

LAFAYETTE

🆔 ▼▼▼▼ Candlewood Suites Ⓗ

(337) 984-6900. **Call for rates.** 2105 Kaliste Saloom Rd 70508. I-10, exit 103A, 3.9 mi s, then 3.6 mi w. Int corridors. **Pets:** $75 one-time fee/pet. Service with restrictions, supervision. SAVE ✕ 🛗 💻

▼▼▼▼ Carriage House Hotel Ⓗ

(337) 769-8400. **Call for rates.** 603 Silverstone Rd 70508. I-10, exit 103A, 3.5 mi s to Pinhook Rd, 1.6 mi sw to Kaliste Saloom Rd, 2 mi w to Camellia Blvd, 0.4 mi n to Silverstone Rd, then just w. Int corridors. **Pets:** Medium, dogs only. $25 daily fee/pet. Designated rooms, service with restrictions, supervision. ✕ 🛗 💻 🍴 ⌘ 🐾

▼▼▼▼ Drury Inn & Suites-Lafayette Ⓗ

(337) 262-0202. **$95-$164.** 120 Alcide Dominique 70506. I-10, exit 101 (SR 182), just s on University Ave, then just w. Int corridors. **Pets:** Other species. No service, supervision. A$K ✕ &M 🛗 💻

🆔 ▼▼▼▼ Hilton Lafayette Ⓗ

(337) 235-6111. **$129-$299.** 1521 W Pinhook Rd 70503. I-10, exit 103A, 3.5 mi s, then 1.3 mi w. Int corridors. **Pets:** Large, other species. $35 one-time fee/room. Designated rooms, service with restrictions, crate. SAVE ✕ 🛗 💻 🍴 ⌘

🆔 ▼▼▼▼ Holiday Inn Lafayette Ⓗ

(337) 233-6815. **$89-$149.** 2032 NE Evangeline Thruway 70501. I-10, exit 103A, just s. Ext/int corridors. **Pets:** Accepted. SAVE ✕ 🛗 💻 🍴 ⌘ 🐾

▼▼▼ Jameson Inn of Lafayette Ⓗ

(337) 291-2916. **$93-$100.** 2200 NE Evangeline Thruway 70501. I-10, exit 103A, just s. Int corridors. **Pets:** Medium. $15 one-time fee/pet. Service with restrictions, supervision. A$K ✕ 🛗 💻 ⌘

▼▼▼▼ La Quinta Inn & Suites Lafayette Oil Center Ⓗ ❀

(337) 291-1088. **$85-$135.** 1015 W Pinhook Rd 70503. I-10, exit 101 (University Ave), 3.5 mi to SR 182 (Pinhook Rd), then 0.5 mi w. Int corridors. **Pets:** Medium, other species. Service with restrictions, supervision. A$K ✕ 🛗 💻

▼▼▼ Pear Tree Inn By Drury Ⓗ

(337) 289-9907. **$80-$124.** 126 Alcide Dominique 70506. I-10, exit 101, just s on University, then just w. Int corridors. **Pets:** Other species. No service, supervision. A$K ✕ 💻 ⌘

▼▼▼ Ramada Inn Ⓗ

(337) 235-0858. **$65-$82.** 120 E Kaliste Saloom Rd 70508. I-10, exit 103A, 3.9 mi s on US 90 to Kaliste Saloom Rd, then 1 mi w. Ext corridors. **Pets:** Accepted. A$K ✕ 🛗 💻 ⌘

▼▼▼ Residence Inn Airport Lafayette Ⓗ

(337) 232-3341. **$152-$186.** 128 James Comeaux Rd 70508. I-10, exit 103A, 3.9 mi s to Kaliste Saloom Rd, then 1 mi w. Int corridors. **Pets:** Medium, other species. $100 one-time fee/room. Service with restrictions, crate. ✕ &M 🛗 💻 ⌘

LAKE CHARLES

🆔 ▼▼▼▼ Best Western Richmond Suites Hotel Ⓗ

(337) 433-5213. **$109-$119.** 2600 Moeling St 70615. I-10, exit 33, just n. Ext/int corridors. **Pets:** Accepted. SAVE ✕ 🛗 💻 ⌘

◆ ▼▼▼ Super 8-Lake Charles Ⓜ ❀

(337) 477-1606. **$79-$150, 7 day notice.** 1350 E Prien Lake Rd 70601. I-210, exit 6B (Enterprise Blvd), just n, then just e. Int corridors. **Pets:** Small. $20 daily fee/pet. Service with restrictions, supervision. A$K ✕ 🛗 💻 ⌘

MANY

🆔 ▼▼▼▼ Cypress Bend Resort Golf, Spa & Conference Center Ⓗ

(318) 590-1500. **$129-$159, 7 day notice.** 2000 Cypress Bend Pkwy 71449. 13 mi w on SR 6, 3 mi s on SR 191, 3 mi w on Cypress Bend Dr, then 1.5 mi w. Int corridors. **Pets:** Other species. $50 one-time fee/room. Service with restrictions. SAVE ✕ &M 🛗 💻 🍴 ⌘ 🐾

MINDEN

🆔 ▼▼▼ Best Western Minden Inn Ⓗ

(318) 377-1001. **$85-$95.** 1411 Sibley Rd 71055. I-20, exit 47, just n. Ext corridors. **Pets:** $15 daily fee/pet. Service with restrictions, supervision. SAVE ✕ 🛗 💻 ⌘

MONROE

▼▼▼ Holiday Inn Hotel & Suites Conference Center Ⓗ

(318) 387-5100. **$80-$109.** 1051 Hwy 165 Bypass 71203. I-20, exit 118B, just ne on US 165 service road. Ext/int corridors. **Pets:** Accepted. A$K ✕ 🛗 💻 🍴 ⌘ 🐾

▼▼▼ La Quinta Inn Monroe Ⓗ ❀

(318) 322-3900. **$52-$94.** 1035 Martin Luther King Dr 71203-5542. I-20, exit 118B, just ne on US 165 service road. Ext corridors. **Pets:** Medium, other species. Service with restrictions, supervision. A$K ✕ 🛗 💻 ⌘

▼▼▼ Residence Inn by Marriott Ⓗ

(318) 387-0210. **$107-$131.** 4960 Millhaven Rd 71203. I-20, exit 120, just n of Pecanland Mall. Int corridors. **Pets:** Other species. $75 one-time fee/room. Service with restrictions, crate. ✕ &M 🛗 💻 ⌘ 🐾

MORGAN CITY

▼▼▼▼ Holiday Inn-Morgan City H

(985) 385-2200. **$92.** 520 Roderick St 70380. 1.5 mi s of jct US 90 and SR 70. Ext corridors. **Pets:** Small, other species. $50 one-time fee/room. Service with restrictions, crate. [ASK] [X] [&M] [B] [B] [T] [≈]

▼▼▼▼ La Quinta Inn & Suites H 🐾

(985) 300-0200. **$85-$99.** 2018 Allison St 70380. US 90, exit Dr Martin Luther King Jr Blvd, just s. Int corridors. **Pets:** Medium, other species. Service with restrictions, supervision. [ASK] [X] [&M] [B] [B] [≈]

NATCHITOCHES

▼▼▼ ▼▼▼▼ Best Western Natchitoches Inn H 🐾

(318) 352-6655. **$86-$169.** 5131 University Pkwy 71457. I-49, exit 138, just e. Int corridors. **Pets:** Other species. $45 one-time fee/pet. No service, supervision. [SAVE] [X] [B] [B] [≈]

NEW ORLEANS METROPOLITAN AREA

COVINGTON

▼▼▼ ▼▼▼▼ Courtyard by Marriott H

(985) 871-0244. **$143-$175.** 101 N Park Blvd 70433. I-12, exit 63B, 0.5 mi n, then just w. Int corridors. **Pets:** Accepted.

[SAVE] [X] [B] [B] [T] [≈]

▼▼▼▼ La Quinta Inn & Suites Covington H 🐾

(985) 871-0356. **$89-$129.** 200 Pinnacle Pkwy 70433. I-12, exit 59, just n, then just e. Int corridors. **Pets:** Medium, other species. Service with restrictions, supervision. [ASK] [X] [&M] [B] [B] [≈]

GRETNA

▼▼▼ La Quinta Inn New Orleans (West Bank) H 🐾

(504) 368-5600. **$65-$125.** 50 Terry Pkwy 70056-2564. S US 90 business route, exit 9A (Terry Pkwy); N US 90 (Westbank Expwy), exit 9 (Terry Pkwy/General DeGaulle). Ext corridors. **Pets:** Medium, other species. Service with restrictions, supervision. [ASK] [X] [B] [B] [≈]

KENNER

▼▼▼ ▼▼▼▼ Hilton New Orleans Airport H

(504) 469-5000. **$129-$229.** 901 Airline Dr 70062. I-10, exit 223A (Williams Blvd), 2 mi s, then 0.8 mi w. Int corridors. **Pets:** Medium. $75 one-time fee/room. Designated rooms, service with restrictions, crate.

[SAVE] [X] [B] [B] [T] [≈]

▼▼▼▼ La Quinta Inn New Orleans (Airport) H 🐾

(504) 466-1401. **$69-$129.** 2610 Williams Blvd 70062. I-10, exit 223A (Williams Blvd), 0.3 mi s. Int corridors. **Pets:** Medium, other species. Service with restrictions, supervision. [ASK] [X] [B] [B] [≈]

▼▼▼ ▼▼▼▼ Lexington Hotel New Orleans Airport H

(504) 464-1644. **$60-$80.** 1021 Airline Dr 70062. US 61, 0.6 mi w from jct SR 49. Ext corridors. **Pets:** Accepted. [SAVE] [X] [B] [B] [T] [≈]

LA PLACE

▼▼▼ ▼▼▼▼ Best Western La Place Inn H

(985) 651-4000. **$100-$110, 3 day notice.** 4289 Main St 70068. I-10, exit 209, just s. Ext corridors. **Pets:** Small. $10 daily fee/pet. Service with restrictions, supervision. [SAVE] [X] [B] [B] [≈]

METAIRIE

▼▼ ▼▼ La Quinta Inn New Orleans (Causeway) H 🐾

(504) 835-8511. **$59-$115.** 3100 I-10 Service Rd 70001-2091. I-10, exit 228 (Causeway Blvd), just s. Ext corridors. **Pets:** Medium, other species. Service with restrictions, supervision. [ASK] [X] [B] [B] [≈]

▼▼▼ La Quinta Inn New Orleans (Veterans) H 🐾

(504) 456-0003. **$59-$105.** 5900 Veterans Memorial Blvd 70003-1738. I-10, exit 225, just n. Ext corridors. **Pets:** Medium, other species. Service with restrictions, supervision. [ASK] [X] [B] [B] [≈]

▼▼▼▼ Residence Inn by Marriott-Metairie H

(504) 832-0888. **$152-$186.** 3 Galleria Blvd 70001. I-10, exit 228 (Causeway Blvd), just se to 36th St, then just e. Int corridors. **Pets:** Accepted. [X] [B] [B] [≈] [X]

▼▼▼ ▼▼▼▼ Sheraton Metairie New Orleans H 🐾

(504) 837-6707. **Call for rates.** 4 Galleria Blvd 70001. I-10, exit 228 (Causeway Blvd), just s to 36th St, just e, then just n. Int corridors. **Pets:** Medium, other species. $50 one-time fee/pet. Supervision. [SAVE] [X] [B] [T]

NEW ORLEANS

▼▼▼ ▼▼▼▼ Best Western St. Christopher Hotel H

(504) 648-0444. **$79-$299, 3 day notice.** 114 Magazine St 70130. Between Canal and Common sts. Int corridors. **Pets:** Accepted. [SAVE] [X] [B]

▼▼▼ ▼▼▼▼ The Bienville House Hotel H 🐾

(504) 529-2345. **$79-$209, 3 day notice.** 320 Decatur St 70130. Between Conti and Bienville sts. Ext/int corridors. **Pets:** Other species. $25 daily fee/pet, $100 one-time fee/pet. Designated rooms, service with restrictions, supervision. [SAVE] [X] [B] [B] [T] [≈]

▼▼▼▼ Clarion Inn & Suites H

(504) 299-9900. **$69-$199, 3 day notice.** 1300 Canal St 70112. Jct Saratoga St. Int corridors. **Pets:** Accepted. [X] [B] [B]

▼▼▼▼ Drury Inn & Suites-New Orleans H

(504) 529-7800. **$80-$279.** 820 Poydras St 70112. Between Baronne and Carondelet sts. Int corridors. **Pets:** Other species. No service, supervision. [ASK] [X] [&M] [B] [B] [≈]

▼▼▼ ▼▼▼▼ Elysian Fields Inn BB

(504) 948-9420. **$109-$269, 15 day notice.** 930 Elysian Fields Ave 70117. I-610, exit 3 (Elysian Fields Ave), 1.2 mi s. Int corridors. **Pets:** Medium. $25 daily fee/pet. Service with restrictions, crate. [SAVE] [X]

▼▼▼ ▼▼▼▼ Hilton New Orleans Riverside H

(504) 561-0500. **$119-$479.** 2 Poydras St 70140. At the Mississippi River. Int corridors. **Pets:** Accepted. [SAVE] [X] [&M] [B] [B] [T] [≈] [X]

▼▼▼ ▼▼▼▼ Hotel Monteleone H 🐾

(504) 523-3341. **$119-$399, 3 day notice.** 214 Royal St 70130. Between Iberville and Bienville sts. Int corridors. **Pets:** Medium. $25 daily fee/room, $100 one-time fee/room. Designated rooms, crate. [SAVE] [X] [B] [B] [T] [≈]

▼▼▼ ▼▼▼▼ The Iberville Suites H

(504) 523-2400. **$89-$449, 3 day notice.** 910 Iberville St 70112. Between Burgundy and Dauphine sts. Int corridors. **Pets:** Accepted. [SAVE] [X] [B] [B]

▼▼▼ ▼▼▼▼ La Quinta Inn & Suites New Orleans–Downtown Flagship H 🐾

(504) 598-9977. **$69-$184.** 301 Camp St 70130. Corner of Gravier and Camp sts. Int corridors. **Pets:** Medium, other species. Service with restrictions, supervision. [ASK] [X] [&M] [B] [B] [≈]

▼▼▼ ▼▼▼▼ Loews New Orleans Hotel H 🐾

(504) 595-3300. **$109-$500, 3 day notice.** 300 Poydras St 70130. Corner of S Peters St. Int corridors. **Pets:** Other species. $25 one-time fee/room. Service with restrictions, supervision. [SAVE] [X] [B] [T] [≈] [X]

Omni Royal Crescent Hotel 🅷
(504) 527-0006. **$99-$289, 3 day notice.** 535 Gravier St 70130. 0.3 mi w of Canal St. Int corridors. **Pets:** Accepted.
[SAVE] [✕] 🛏 💷 🍴 [✕]

Omni Royal Orleans Hotel 🅷 ❀
(504) 529-5333. **$109-$359, 3 day notice.** 621 St. Louis St 70140. At Royal and St. Louis sts. Int corridors. **Pets:** Small, other species. $50 one-time fee/room. Designated rooms, service with restrictions.
[SAVE] [✕] 🛏 💷 🍴 ≈

The Ritz-Carlton New Orleans 🅷 ❀
(504) 524-1331. **$149-$389, 3 day notice.** 921 Canal St 70112. Between Dauphine and Burgundy sts. Int corridors. **Pets:** Medium. $150 one-time fee/pet. Service with restrictions, supervision.
[SAVE] [✕] [♿M] 💷 🍴 [✕]

Royal Sonesta Hotel New Orleans 🅷
(504) 586-0300. **$129-$329, 3 day notice.** 300 Bourbon St 70130. Garage entrance on Conti or Bienville sts. Int corridors. **Pets:** Small. $50 one-time fee/room. Service with restrictions, supervision.
[SAVE] [✕] [♿M] 🛏 💷 🍴 ≈

St. James Hotel 🅷
(504) 304-4000. **Call for rates.** 330 Magazine St 70130. Jct Magazine and Natchez sts. Int corridors. **Pets:** Accepted. [✕] 💷 🍴

The Sheraton New Orleans Hotel 🅷 ❀
(504) 525-2500. **$79-$389, 3 day notice.** 500 Canal St 70130. Between Camp and Magazine sts. Int corridors. **Pets:** Large, dogs only. Service with restrictions, supervision. [SAVE] [✕] [♿M] 💷 🍴 ≈ [✕]

Westin New Orleans Canal Place 🅷 ❀
(504) 566-7006. **Call for rates.** 100 Iberville St 70130. At Canal Place, near Mississippi River. Int corridors. **Pets:** Medium, dogs only. Designated rooms, service with restrictions, supervision.
[SAVE] [✕] 🛏 💷 🍴 ≈

W French Quarter 🅷
(504) 581-1200. **Call for rates.** 316 Chartres St 70130. Between Conti and Bienville sts. Int corridors. **Pets:** Accepted. [SAVE] [✕] 🍴 ≈

Windsor Court Hotel 🅷 ❀
(504) 523-6000. **$199-$650.** 300 Gravier St 70130. Between Magazine and Tchoupitoulas sts. Int corridors. **Pets:** Designated rooms, service with restrictions, crate. [SAVE] [✕] 🛏 🍴 ≈ [✕]

W New Orleans 🅷
(504) 525-9444. **Call for rates.** 333 Poydras St 70130. Jct Poydras and S Peters sts; close to Riverfront area/convention center. Int corridors. **Pets:** Accepted. [SAVE] [✕] [♿M] 🍴 ≈

SLIDELL

La Quinta Inn New Orleans/Slidell 🅷 ❀
(985) 643-9770. **$59-$114.** 794 E I-10 Service Rd 70461. I-10, exit 266 (Gause Blvd), just se. Ext corridors. **Pets:** Medium, other species. Service with restrictions, supervision. [ASK] [✕] 🛏 💷 ≈

END METROPOLITAN AREA

OAKDALE

Best Western Oakdale Inn 🅷
(318) 335-3155. **$89-$110.** 2030 US Hwy 165 S 71463. 1.7 mi s of jct US 165 and SR 10. Int corridors. **Pets:** Accepted.
[SAVE] [✕] 🛏 💷 ≈

PONCHATOULA

Microtel Inn & Suites 🅷
(985) 370-7378. **$80-$129.** 727 W Pine St 70454. I-55, exit 26, just e on SR 22. Int corridors. **Pets:** Accepted. [ASK] [✕] [♿M] 🛏 💷 ≈

ST. FRANCISVILLE

Lake Rosemound Inn Bed & Breakfast BB
(225) 635-3176. **$80-$135, 4 day notice.** 10473 Lindsey Ln 70775. 13 mi n on SR 61, then 3 mi w using Rosemound Loop, Sligo Rd, Lake Rosemound Rd and Lindsey Ln, follow signs. Ext/int corridors. **Pets:** Other species. Designated rooms, no service. [✕] [✕]

SCOTT

Howard Johnson 🅷
(337) 593-0849. **$60-$65.** 103 Harold Gauthe Dr 70583. I-10, exit 97, just s. Int corridors. **Pets:** Medium. $10 daily fee/pet. Service with restrictions, supervision. [ASK] [✕] 🛏 💷 ≈

SHREVEPORT

Candlewood Suites 🅷
(318) 635-8062. **$89.** 5020 Hollywood Ave 71109. I-20, exit 13, 0.4 mi s, then just e. Int corridors. **Pets:** Medium, other species. $25 daily fee/room. Service with restrictions, supervision.
[SAVE] [✕] [♿M] 🛏 💷 ≈

Hilton Shreveport 🅷
(318) 698-0900. **$129-$209.** 104 Market St 71101. Sw corner of N Market and Caddo sts; downtown. Int corridors. **Pets:** Accepted.
[✕] 🛏 💷 🍴

Holiday Inn Shreveport West 🅷
(318) 688-3000. **$92-$104.** 5555 Financial Plaza 71129. I-20, exit 10 (Pines Rd), 1 mi e on frontage road. Int corridors. **Pets:** Accepted.
[ASK] [✕] 🛏 💷 🍴 ≈ [✕]

Homewood Suites–Shreveport 🅷
(318) 549-2000. **$119-$139.** 5485 Financial Plaza 71129. I-20, exit 10 (Pines Rd), 1.2 mi e on frontage road. Int corridors. **Pets:** Medium, other species. $20 daily fee/room. [✕] 🛏 💷 ≈ [✕]

La Quinta Inn & Suites Shreveport 🅷 ❀
(318) 671-1100. **$69-$129.** 6700 Financial Cir 71129. I-20, exit 10 (Pines Rd), 0.5 mi e on frontage road. Int corridors. **Pets:** Medium, other species. Service with restrictions, supervision.
[ASK] [✕] [♿M] 🛏 💷 ≈

Ramada Inn Shreveport 🅷
(318) 631-2000. **Call for rates.** 5101 Westwood Park Dr 71109. I-20, exit 13 (Monkhouse Dr), just ne. Int corridors. **Pets:** Accepted.
[✕] 🛏 💷 ≈

Residence Inn by Marriott 🅷
(318) 635-8000. **$130-$158.** 4910 W Monkhouse Dr 71109. I-20, exit 13, just nw. Int corridors. **Pets:** Medium, other species. $100 one-time fee/room. Service with restrictions. [✕] [♿M] 🛏 💷 ≈ [✕]

SPRINGFIELD

The Villas at Carter Plantation 🅷
(225) 294-7555. **$135-$239.** 23475 Carter Trace 70462. I-12, exit 32, 2.7 mi s on SR 43, 1.1 mi e on SR 42, then 1.5 mi s on Carter Cemetery Rd. Ext corridors. **Pets:** Accepted. [ASK] [✕] 🛏 💷 🍴 ≈

VILLE PLATTE

Best Western Ville Platte 🅷
(337) 360-9961. **$86.** 1919 E Main St (Hwy 167) 70586. Jct SR 1168. Int corridors. **Pets:** Small, dogs only. $5 daily fee/pet. Service with restrictions, supervision. [SAVE] [✕] 🛏 💷 ≈

WEST MONROE

◆◆ Jameson Inn H

(318) 361-0750. **$85-$105.** 213 Constitution Dr 71292. I-20, exit 114 (Thomas Rd), just s to Constitution Dr, then just w. Int corridors. **Pets:** Small. $15 one-time fee/pet. Service with restrictions, supervision.

A$K ⊠ 🔌 💻 ⊇

◆◆ Quality Inn & Suites-West Monroe H

(318) 387-2711. **$74-$87.** 503 Constitution Dr 71292. I-20, exit 114 (Thomas Rd), just s to Constitution Dr, then 0.6 mi w. Int corridors. **Pets:** Accepted. ⊠ &M 🔌 💻 ⊇

WINNFIELD

◆◆ Best Western Winnfield Inn M

(318) 628-3993. **$66-$100.** 700 W Court St 71483. Jct US 84 and 167, just e. Ext corridors. **Pets:** Small. $20 daily fee/pet. Service with restrictions, supervision. SAVE ⊠ 🔌 💻 �11 ⊇

WINNSBORO

◆◆ Best Western Winnsboro M

(318) 435-2000. **$65-$75.** 4198 Front St 71295. Just nw of jct SR 15 and 864. Ext corridors. **Pets:** Very small, dogs only. $10 daily fee/pet. Designated rooms, service with restrictions, supervision.

SAVE ⊠ &M 🔌 💻 ⊇

ZACHARY

◆◆ Best Western Zachary Inn H

(225) 658-2550. **$88-$91.** 4030 Hwy 19 70791. Just s of jct SR 64. Int corridors. **Pets:** Other species. $50 one-time fee/room. Service with restrictions, crate. SAVE ⊠ 🔌 💻 ⊇

MAINE

AUBURN

▼▼ A Fireside Inn & Suites H

(207) 777-1777. $90-$250. 1777 Washington St 04210. I-95, exit 75, 0.5 mi s on US 202, SR 4 and 100. Ext/int corridors. **Pets:** Dogs only. $10 daily fee/pet. Designated rooms, service with restrictions.

ASK ⊠ 🖥 💻 ¶ 🌊

▼▼▼ Residence Inn by Marriott Auburn H

(207) 777-3400. $109-$199. 670 Turner St 04210. I-95, exit 80 south-bound; exit 75 northbound; from SR 100, just w. Int corridors. **Pets:** Medium, other species. $75 one-time fee/room. Service with restrictions, supervision. ⊠ 🖥 💻 🌊 ⊠

▼ Sleepy Time Motel M ❀

(207) 783-1435. $72-$99. 46 Danville Corner Rd 04210. I-95, exit 75, 0.5 mi ne on US 202, then just e. Ext corridors. **Pets:** Medium, other species. $10 daily fee/room. Service with restrictions, supervision.

ASK ⊠ 🖥 💻

AUGUSTA

AAA ▼▼▼ Best Western Senator Inn & Spa H ❀

(207) 622-5804. **Call for rates.** 284 Western Ave 04330. I-95, exit 109 northbound; exit 109A southbound, on US 202, SR 11 and 100. Ext/int corridors. **Pets:** Medium, other species. $50 deposit/room, $10 one-time fee/room. Designated rooms, service with restrictions, supervision.

ECO SAVE ⊠ 🖥 💻 ¶ 🌊 ⊠

▼▼ Comfort Inn H ❀

(207) 623-1000. **Call for rates.** 281 Civic Center Dr 04330. I-95, exit 112B northbound; exit 112 southbound. Int corridors. **Pets:** Large, other species. $100 deposit/room, $10 daily fee/room. Designated rooms, service with restrictions, supervision. ⊠ 🖥 💻 🌊

▼▼ Holiday Inn H ❀

(207) 622-4751. $80-$161. 110 Community Dr 04330. I-95, exit 112A northbound; exit 112 southbound, just s on SR 8, 11 and 27. Int corridors. **Pets:** Large, other species. $100 deposit/room. Service with restrictions, supervision. ASK ⊠ 🖥 💻 ¶ 🌊

BANGOR

▼▼ A Fireside Inn & Suites H

(207) 942-1234. $79-$169, 7 day notice. 570 Main St 04401. I-395, exit 3B. Int corridors. **Pets:** Other species. $10 daily fee/pet. Service with restrictions, supervision. ASK ⊠ 🖥 💻 ¶

AAA ▼▼▼ Best Western White House H ❀

(207) 862-3737. $105-$160. 155 Littlefield Ave 04401. I-95, exit 180 (Coldbrook Rd), 5.5 mi s of downtown. Ext/int corridors. **Pets:** Large, other species. $10 daily fee/pet. Designated rooms, service with restrictions, supervision. SAVE ⊠ 🖥 💻 🌊 ⊠

▼▼ Comfort Inn H

(207) 942-7899. $89-$149. 750 Hogan Rd 04401. I-95, exit 187 (Hogan Rd), 0.5 mi nw. Int corridors. **Pets:** $10 one-time fee/room. Service with restrictions, supervision. ASK ⊠ 🖥 💻

▼▼ Econo Lodge M

(207) 945-0111. $65-$169. 327 Odlin Rd 04401. I-95, exit 182B, just e on US 2 and SR 100. Int corridors. **Pets:** Large, other species. $10 one-time fee/room. Service with restrictions, supervision.

ASK ⊠ 🔥M 🖥 💻 🌊

AAA ▼▼▼▼ Four Points by Sheraton Bangor H

(207) 947-6721. **Call for rates.** 308 Godfrey Blvd 04401. At Bangor International Airport. Int corridors. **Pets:** Accepted.

SAVE ⊠ 🔥M 🖥 💻 ¶ 🌊

▼▼ Holiday Inn-Bangor H

(207) 947-0101. **Call for rates.** 404 Odlin Rd 04401. I-95, exit 182B; jct Odlin Rd and I-395. Int corridors. **Pets:** Accepted.

⊠ 🔥M 🖥 💻 ¶ 🌊

▼▼ Howard Johnson Inn H

(207) 942-5251. $70-$100. 336 Odlin Rd 04401. I-95, exit 182B; jct Odlin Rd and I-395. Int corridors. **Pets:** Accepted.

ASK ⊠ 🖥 💻 ¶ 🌊

▼▼ Ramada H

(207) 947-6961. **Call for rates.** 357 Odlin Rd 04401. I-95, exit 182B; jct Odlin Rd and I-395. Int corridors. **Pets:** Accepted.

⊠ 🖥 💻 ¶ 🌊

▼▼ Riverside Inn H

(207) 973-4100. **Call for rates.** 495 State St 04401. Adjacent to Eastern Maine Medical Center. Int corridors. **Pets:** $5 daily fee/pet. Service with restrictions. ⊠ 🖥 💻

BAR HARBOR

AAA ▼▼▼ Atlantic Eyrie Lodge H

(207) 288-9786. $77-$222, 7 day notice. 6 Norman Rd 04609. 1 mi w on SR 3 to Highbrook Rd. Ext corridors. **Pets:** Large. $35 one-time fee/room. Designated rooms, service with restrictions, supervision.

SAVE ⊠ 🖥 💻 🌊

AAA ▼▼▼ Atlantic Oceanside Hotel & Conference Center H

(207) 288-5801. $109-$209, 14 day notice. 119 Eden St 04609. 1.8 mi w on SR 3. Ext/int corridors. **Pets:** Accepted.

ECO SAVE ⊠ 🖥 💻 🌊 ⊠

▼▼ A Wonder View Inn & Suites H

(207) 288-3358. $69-$259, 3 day notice. 50 Eden St 04609. 0.5 mi w on SR 3. Ext corridors. **Pets:** $20 daily fee/pet. Service with restrictions, supervision. ASK ⊠ 🖥 💻 ¶ 🌊

AAA ▼▼▼ Balance Rock Inn 1903 BB

(207) 288-2610. $155-$625, 14 day notice. 21 Albert Meadow 04609. Just s of Main St; center. Ext/int corridors. **Pets:** Accepted.

SAVE ⊠ 🌊

△△△ ▼▼▼ **Best Western Acadia Park Inn** 🅷
(207) 288-5823. **$79-$165.** 452 State Hwy 3 04609. 4.8 mi w. Ext corridors. **Pets:** Medium. $20 daily fee/pet. Designated rooms, service with restrictions, supervision. (SAVE) ✖ 🛢 💻 ≈

▼▼ **Days Inn** Ⓜ
(207) 288-3321. **Call for rates.** 120 Eden St 04609. 1 mi w on SR 3. Ext corridors. **Pets:** Accepted. ✖ 🛢 💻

▼ **Hutchins Mountain View Cottages** 🆑 ❀
(207) 288-4833. **$66-$98, 14 day notice.** 286 State Rt 3 04609. On SR 3, 4 mi w. Ext corridors. **Pets:** Other species. Service with restrictions.
✖ 🛢 💻 ≈ 🎿 🆉

BATH

△△△ ▼▼▼ **Holiday Inn Bath/Brunswick** 🅷
(207) 443-9741. **$99-$199.** 139 Richardson St 04530. 0.3 mi s on US 1. Int corridors. **Pets:** Other species. Designated rooms, service with restrictions, crate. 🄴🄲🄾 (SAVE) ✖ ⅋Ⓜ 🛢 💻 🍴 ≈

BELFAST

▼▼ **Belfast Harbor Inn** 🅷 ❀
(207) 338-2740. **$64-$159.** 91 Searsport Ave (Rt 1) 04915. On US 1, 1.2 mi n from jct SR 3. Ext/int corridors. **Pets:** Dogs only. $10 daily fee/pet. Designated rooms, service with restrictions, supervision.
(ASK) ✖ 🛢 ≈

▼▼▼ **Comfort Inn Ocean's Edge** 🅷
(207) 338-2090. **$80-$250.** 159 Searsport Ave 04915. On US 1, 2 mi n from jct SR 3. Int corridors. **Pets:** Other species. $10 daily fee/room. Designated rooms, service with restrictions, supervision.
🄴🄲🄾 (ASK) ✖ ⅋Ⓜ 🛢 💻 🍴 ≈ ✖

▼ **Gull Motel** Ⓜ
(207) 338-4030. **$49-$99, 3 day notice.** 196 Searsport Ave 04915. On US 1, 3 mi n from jct SR 3. Ext corridors. **Pets:** Accepted.
(ASK) ✖ 🛢

BETHEL

▼▼▼ **Briar Lea Inn & The Jolly Drayman English Pub** 🄲🄸
(207) 824-4717. **$99-$159, 14 day notice.** 150 Mayville Rd (US 2) 04217. 1 mi n of jct US 2, SR 5 and 26. Int corridors. **Pets:** Accepted.
(ASK) ✖ 🍴

▼▼ **The Inn At the Rostay** Ⓜ
(207) 824-3111. **$68-$140, 14 day notice.** 186 Mayville Rd (US 2) 04217. On US 2, 2 mi e. Ext corridors. **Pets:** Other species. $10 daily fee/pet. Designated rooms, service with restrictions, supervision.
(ASK) ✖ 🛢 ≈

BIDDEFORD

▼▼▼ **Comfort Suites-Biddeford** 🅷 ❀
(207) 294-6464. **$85.** 45 Barra Rd 04005. I-95, exit 32 (SR 111), 0.4 mi ne, then just n. Int corridors. **Pets:** Large, other species. $35 one-time fee/room. Designated rooms, service with restrictions, crate.
(ASK) ✖ ⅋Ⓜ 🛢 💻 ≈

BOOTHBAY

▼▼ **The Boothbay Resort** Ⓜ ❀
(207) 633-3411. **Call for rates.** 301 Adams Pond Rd 04537. US 1, 9 mi s on SR 27, then just w. Ext/int corridors. **Pets:** Dogs only. Designated rooms, service with restrictions, crate. 🄴🄲🄾 ✖ 🛢 💻 ≈ 🆉

▼▼▼ **Kenniston Hill Inn B & B** 🄱🄱 ❀
(207) 633-2159. **$150-$190, 14 day notice.** 988 Wiscasset Rd 04537. US 1 to SR 27, 10 mi s; jct SR 27 S and Country Club Rd. Ext/int corridors. **Pets:** Medium, other species. $45 one-time fee/room. Designated rooms, service with restrictions, supervision. (ASK) ✖ 🆉

△△△ ▼▼ **White Anchor Inn** Ⓜ
(207) 633-3788. **$55-$95.** 609 Wiscasset Rd 04537. US 1 to SR 27, 7.5 mi s. Ext/int corridors. **Pets:** Large, other species. $10 one-time fee/room. Designated rooms, service with restrictions, supervision. (SAVE) ✖ 🛢

BOOTHBAY HARBOR

△△△ ▼▼▼ **Beach Cove Hotel and Resort** Ⓜ ❀
(207) 633-0353. **$69-$135, 14 day notice.** 48 Lakeview Rd 04538. Off SR 27. Ext corridors. **Pets:** Medium. $20 one-time fee/pet. Designated rooms, service with restrictions, supervision. (SAVE) ✖ 🛢 💻 ≈

△△△ ▼▼▼ **Flagship Inn** Ⓜ
(207) 633-5094. **$74-$144, 3 day notice.** 200 Townsend Ave 04538. On SR 27, just n of jct SR 96. Ext corridors. **Pets:** Large, dogs only. Designated rooms, service with restrictions, supervision. (SAVE) ✖ 🛢 ≈

△△△ ▼▼▼▼ **Welch House Inn** 🄱🄱
(207) 633-3431. **Call for rates.** 56 McKown St 04538. Center. Ext/int corridors. **Pets:** Medium, dogs only. $25 one-time fee/room. Designated rooms, service with restrictions, crate. (SAVE) ✖

BRIDGTON

▼▼ **Pleasant Mountain Inn** Ⓜ ❀
(207) 647-4505. **$70-$195, 7 day notice.** 656 N High St 04009. On US 302, 3 mi w of center. Ext corridors. **Pets:** Dogs only. $10 daily fee/pet. Service with restrictions, crate. (ASK) ✖ 🛢 💻 🍴

BRUNSWICK

△△△ ▼▼▼ **Days Inn Brunswick** 🅷
(207) 725-8883. **$65-$200.** 224 Bath Rd 04011. US 1, exit Cooks Corner, left on Bath Rd, then 0.3 mi w. Int corridors. **Pets:** Medium, dogs only. $25 daily fee/pet. Designated rooms, service with restrictions, supervision.
(SAVE) ✖ ⅋Ⓜ 🛢 💻

BRYANT POND

▼ **Mollyockett Motel & Swim Spa** Ⓜ
(207) 674-2345. **$70-$95.** 1132 S Main St 04219. 1.3 mi n on SR 26 from jct SR 219. Ext/int corridors. **Pets:** Dogs only. Supervision.
(ASK) ✖ 🛢 💻 🍴 ≈ ✖

BUCKSPORT

▼ **Bucksport Motor Inn** Ⓜ
(207) 469-3111. **$69-$109.** 70 US Route 1 04416. On US 1; center. Ext corridors. **Pets:** Large, dogs only. $15 one-time fee/room. Designated rooms, service with restrictions, supervision. (ASK) ✖ 🛢 💻

CAMDEN

▼▼▼ **The Camden Riverhouse Hotel & Inns** 🅷 ❀
(207) 236-0500. **$109-$250, 14 day notice.** 11 Tannery Ln 04843. Center. Int corridors. **Pets:** Dogs only. $15 daily fee/pet. Designated rooms, service with restrictions, supervision.
🄴🄲🄾 (ASK) ✖ 🛢 💻 ≈ ✖

▼▼▼ **The Inns at Blackberry Common** 🄱🄱
(207) 236-6060. **$125-$285, 14 day notice.** 82 Elm St 04843. Center. Ext/int corridors. **Pets:** Accepted. 🄴🄲🄾 ✖ 🛢 💻 🆉

△△△ ▼▼▼ **Lord Camden Inn** 🅷 ❀
(207) 236-4325. **$99-$299.** 24 Main St 04843. Center. Int corridors. **Pets:** Dogs only. $25 daily fee/pet. Service with restrictions, supervision.
🄴🄲🄾 (SAVE) ✖ 🛢 💻

CAPE ELIZABETH

△△△ ▼▼▼▼ **Inn by the Sea** 🅷 ❀
(207) 799-3134. **$199-$819, 14 day notice.** 40 Bowery Beach Rd (SR 77) 04107. On SR 77, 7 mi s. Ext/int corridors. **Pets:** Other species. Service with restrictions. 🄴🄲🄾 (SAVE) ✖ ⅋Ⓜ 🛢 💻 ≈ ✖

CARIBOU

AAA **WWWW** **Caribou Inn & Convention Center** **H** ❖
(207) 498-3733. **$98-$146.** 19 Main St 04736. 3 mi s on US 1. Int corridors. **Pets:** Other species. $35 one-time fee/room.

[SAVE] [✕] [🅿] [💻] [🍴] [🏊] [🐾]

WW **Crown Park Inn** **H**
(207) 493-3311. **Call for rates.** 30 Access Hwy 04736. On SR 89, 0.4 mi e of jct US 1. Int corridors. **Pets:** Accepted. [✕] [🅿]

CASTINE

WWW **Pentagoet Inn** **CI**
(207) 326-8616. **$95-$245, 14 day notice.** 26 Main St 04421. Center. Int corridors. **Pets:** Accepted. [✕] [🍴] [🎶] [📺] [☎]

DEDHAM

AAA **WWW** **The Lucerne Inn** **CI**
(207) 843-5123. **$79-$219.** 2517 Main Rd 04429. On US 1A. Int corridors. **Pets:** Medium, dogs only. $25 one-time fee/room. Designated rooms, service with restrictions, supervision.

[SAVE] [✕] [🅿] [💻] [🍴] [🏊]

EAGLE LAKE

WW **Overlook Motel & Lakeside Cabins** **M**
(207) 444-4535. **$76.** 3232 Aroostook Rd 04739. On SR 11; center. Ext/int corridors. **Pets:** Other species. $5 daily fee/pet. Service with restrictions, supervision. [✕] [🅿] [💻] [🐾]

EDGECOMB

WWWW **Sheepscot Harbour Village & Resort** **H**
(207) 882-6343. **Call for rates.** 306 Eddy Rd 04556. 1 mi w on US 1; on east side of Davies Bridge, 1 mi e of Wiscasset. Ext/int corridors. **Pets:** Accepted. [✕] [🅿] [💻] [🏊]

ELLSWORTH

WWW **Acadia Birches Knights Inn** **M**
(207) 667-3621. **$69-$119, 3 day notice.** 19 Thorsen Rd 04605. US 1, 1.5 mi n of SR 3. Ext corridors. **Pets:** Accepted. [ASK] [✕] [🅿] [💻]

AAA **WWW** **Holiday Inn-Acadia Park Hotel** **H**
(207) 667-9341. **$59-$199, 7 day notice.** 215 High St 04605. Jct US 1, 1A and SR 3. Int corridors. **Pets:** Accepted.

[SAVE] [✕] [♿M] [🅿] [💻] [🍴] [🏊] [🐾]

AAA **WWW** **Twilite Motel** **M**
(207) 667-8165. **$54-$120.** 147 Bucksport Rd 04605. Jct US 1A, 1.5 mi w on US 1/SR 3. Ext corridors. **Pets:** Small. $10 daily fee/room. Designated rooms, service with restrictions, supervision. [SAVE] [✕] [🅿] [💻]

FALMOUTH

AAA **WW** **Falmouth Inn** **M**
(207) 781-2120. **$65-$126.** 209 US 1 04105. I-295, exit 10, just e on Buckman Rd, then just s. Ext corridors. **Pets:** Accepted.

[SAVE] [✕] [🅿] [💻]

FARMINGTON

AAA **WWW** **Colonial Valley Motel** **M**
(207) 778-3391. **$44-$76.** 593 Wilton Rd 04938. 2.5 mi w on US 2 and SR 4. Ext corridors. **Pets:** Supervision. [SAVE] [✕] [🅿]

FREEPORT

AAA **WWWW** **Best Western Freeport Inn** **H** ❖
(207) 865-3106. **$80-$200.** 31 US 1 S 04032. I-295, exit 17, 1 mi n. Ext/int corridors. **Pets:** Other species. Designated rooms, service with restrictions. [SAVE] [✕] [🅿] [💻] [🍴] [🏊]

WWWW **Captain Briggs House B & B** **BB**
(207) 865-1868. **$100-$230, 5 day notice.** 8 Maple Ave 04032. Just n of downtown, then just w. Int corridors. **Pets:** Accepted. [ASK] [✕] [☎]

AAA **WWW** **Econo Lodge** **M**
(207) 865-3777. **$59-$169.** 537 US Rt 1 04032. I-295, exit 20, 0.3 mi s. Ext corridors. **Pets:** Other species. $10 daily fee/room. Designated rooms, service with restrictions, supervision. [SAVE] [✕]

WWW **Super 8** **H**
(207) 865-1408. **$49-$149.** 506 US 1 04032. I-295, exit 20, 0.3 mi s. Int corridors. **Pets:** $10 one-time fee/pet. Service with restrictions, supervision. [ASK] [✕] [🅿] [💻]

WWW **White Cedar Inn** **BB** ❖
(207) 865-9099. **$130-$230, 7 day notice.** 178 Main St 04032. I-295, exit 22, 0.5 mi e, then just n on US 1. Ext/int corridors. **Pets:** Dogs only. $25 one-time fee/room. Designated rooms, service with restrictions, supervision. [ECO] [✕] [☎]

GREENVILLE

WWW **Chalet Moosehead Lakefront Motel** **M**
(207) 695-2950. **$73-$145, 7 day notice.** 12 N Birch St 04442. 1.5 mi w on SR 15. Ext corridors. **Pets:** Dogs only. $10 daily fee/pet. Designated rooms, service with restrictions, supervision. [✕] [🅿] [💻] [🐾]

AAA **WWW** **Kineo View Motor Lodge** **M** ❖
(207) 695-4470. **$69-$199.** 50 Overlook Dr 04441. 2.5 mi s on SR 15; gravel access road from highway. Ext corridors. **Pets:** $10 daily fee/room. Designated rooms, no service, supervision. [SAVE] [✕] [🅿] [💻]

HANCOCK

WWW **Le Domaine Inn** **CI**
(207) 422-3395. **Call for rates.** US Rt 1, #1513 04640. On US 1, 9 mi e of Ellsworth; center. Ext corridors. **Pets:** Accepted. [✕] [🍴] [📺]

HOULTON

WWW **Shiretown Inn & Suites** **H**
(207) 532-9421. **$89-$135.** 282 North St 04730. I-95, exit 302, 0.3 mi n on US 1. Ext/int corridors. **Pets:** Accepted. [ASK] [✕] [🅿] [💻] [🏊]

KENNEBUNK

AAA **WWW** **The Lodge at Kennebunk** **M**
(207) 985-9010. **$59-$175, 3 day notice.** 95 Alewive Rd 04043. I-95, exit 25 (Kennebunk), just n on SR 35. Ext corridors. **Pets:** Accepted.

[SAVE] [✕] [🅿] [💻] [🏊] [🐾]

AAA **WWW** **Turnpike Motel** **M**
(207) 985-4404. **$49-$125, 3 day notice.** 77 Old Alewive Rd 04043. I-95, exit 25, just e on SR 35, then just n. Ext/int corridors. **Pets:** Accepted. [SAVE] [✕] [🅿] [💻]

KENNEBUNKPORT

AAA **WWWW** **The Captain Jefferds Inn** **BB**
(207) 967-2311. **Call for rates.** 5 Pearl St 04046. From Dock Square, 0.3 mi s on Ocean Ave, just ne; corner of Pearl and Pleasant sts. Ext/int corridors. **Pets:** Accepted. [SAVE] [✕] [🅿]

AAA **WWWW** **The Colony Hotel** **H** ❖
(207) 967-3331. **$119-$699, 7 day notice.** 140 Ocean Ave 04046. From Dock Square, 1 mi s. Int corridors. **Pets:** Other species. $30 daily fee/pet. [ECO] [SAVE] [✕] [🅿] [🍴] [🏊] [🐾]

WWW **Lodge At Turbat's Creek** **M**
(207) 967-8700. **$69-$179, 14 day notice.** 7 Turbats Creek Rd 04046. From Dock Square, 0.5 mi se on Maine St, 0.6 mi ne on Wildes, then just se. Ext corridors. **Pets:** Other species. $25 one-time fee/room. Designated rooms, supervision. [ASK] [✕] [♿M] [🅿] [🏊]

AAA **WWWW** **The Yachtsman Lodge & Marina** **M** ❖
(207) 967-2511. **$179-$450, 30 day notice.** 57 Ocean Ave 04046. From Dock Square, just s. Ext corridors. **Pets:** Other species. $25 daily fee/pet. Service with restrictions, crate. [SAVE] [✕] [🅿] [💻] [🐾]

KITTERY

AAA **WWWW** The Coachman Inn **H**
(207) 439-4434. **$73-$169.** 380 US Rt 1 03904. I-95, exit 2, 1 mi n. Ext/int corridors. **Pets:** $10 daily fee/pet. Designated rooms, service with restrictions, supervision. **SAVE** **X** **&M** **H** **~**

LINCOLNVILLE

WWW Abbingtons Seaview Motel & Cottages **M**
(207) 236-3471. **$69-$149, 5 day notice.** 4 Seaview Dr 04849. US 1, 1.2 mi s of jct SR 173. Ext corridors. **Pets:** Other species. $15 daily fee/pet. Designated rooms, service with restrictions, supervision. **ASK** **X** **H** **P** **~**

WWW Pine Grove Cottages **CA**
(207) 236-2929. **$85-$195, 7 day notice.** 2076 Atlantic Hwy 04849. US 1, 2 mi s of jct SR 173. Ext corridors. **Pets:** Accepted. **X** **H** **P**

LUBEC

WWW The Eastland Motel **M**
(207) 733-5501. **$68-$78.** 395 County Rd 04652. Jct US 1 and SR 189, 8.4 mi e on SR 189. Ext/int corridors. **Pets:** Accepted. **X** **H**

MACHIAS

AAA **WWW** The Bluebird Motel **M**
(207) 255-3332. **$75-$85, 7 day notice.** 231 Dublin St 04654. On US 1, 1 mi s. Ext corridors. **Pets:** Medium, other species. Service with restrictions, supervision. **SAVE** **X** **&M** **H**

AAA **WWW** Machias Motor Inn **M**
(207) 255-4861. **$70-$119.** 103 Main St 04654. 0.5 mi e on US 1. Ext corridors. **Pets:** Dogs only. $5 daily fee/pet. Designated rooms, supervision. **SAVE** **X** **H** **P**

MEDWAY

WWW Katahdin Shadows Motel **M**
(207) 746-5162. **$59-$79, 5 day notice.** 2166 Medway Rd 04460. I-95, exit 244, 1.5 mi w on SR 157. Ext corridors. **Pets:** Accepted. **X** **H** **~** **~**

MILFORD

WWWW Milford Motel On The River **M**
(207) 827-3200. **$59-$115, 3 day notice.** 174 Main Rd 04461. 0.5 mi n on US 2. Ext/int corridors. **Pets:** Medium, dogs only. Service with restrictions, supervision. **ASK** **X** **H** **P**

MILLINOCKET

WWW Baxter Park Inn **H**
(207) 723-9777. **$69-$119.** 935 Central St 04462. 0.8 mi e on SR 11 and 157. Int corridors. **Pets:** Large, other species. $10 daily fee/pet. Service with restrictions, supervision. **ASK** **X** **H** **P** **~**

NAPLES

WWWW Augustus Bove House **BB**
(207) 693-6365. **$99-$250, 30 day notice.** 11 Sebago Rd 04055. Corner of US 302 and SR 114. Int corridors. **Pets:** Accepted. **ASK** **X** **H** **P**

NEWCASTLE

WWWW Newcastle Inn **BB** **🐾**
(207) 563-5685. **$155-$255, 21 day notice.** 60 River Rd 04553. From jct US 1 and River Rd, 0.5 mi nw. Ext/int corridors. **Pets:** Medium, dogs only. $100 deposit/pet, $25 daily fee/pet. Designated rooms, service with restrictions, crate. **X** **Z**

OGUNQUIT

WW Studio East Motor Inn **M**
(207) 646-7297. **Call for rates.** 267 Main St 03907. On US 1; center. Ext corridors. **Pets:** Accepted. **X** **H** **~**

OLD ORCHARD BEACH

AAA **WWW** Sea View Inn **H**
(207) 934-4180. **$55-$300, 14 day notice.** 65 W Grand Ave (SR 9) 04064. 0.5 mi w on SR 9 (W Grand Ave). Ext corridors. **Pets:** Accepted. **SAVE** **X** **H** **P**

ORONO

WWW Black Bear Inn and Conference Center **H**
(207) 866-7120. **Call for rates.** 4 Godfrey Dr 04473. I-95, exit 193 (Stillwater Ave). Int corridors. **Pets:** Other species. $10 daily fee/pet. Designated rooms, service with restrictions, supervision. **X** **&M** **H** **P**

WWW University Inn Academic Suites **H**
(207) 866-4921. **$69-$119.** 5 College Ave 04473. I-95, exit 191, 1.6 mi n on US 2; 8 mi n of Bangor. Int corridors. **Pets:** Dogs only. Designated rooms, service with restrictions, supervision. **X** **H** **P** **~**

PORTLAND

WWWW Clarion Portland **H**
(207) 774-5611. **$129-$209.** 1230 Congress St 04102. I-295, exit 5, w on SR 22. Int corridors. **Pets:** Accepted. **ASK** **X** **&M** **H** **P** **TI** **~**

AAA **WWWW** Eastland Park Hotel **H** **🐾**
(207) 775-5411. **$71-$207.** 157 High St 04101. At Congress Square; center. Int corridors. **Pets:** Service with restrictions, crate. **SAVE** **X** **H** **P** **TI** **X**

AAA **WWWW** Embassy Suites Hotel **H**
(207) 775-2200. **$109-$249.** 1050 Westbrook St 04102. At Portland International Jetport. Int corridors. **Pets:** $50 one-time fee/pet. Designated rooms, service with restrictions, supervision. **SAVE** **X** **H** **P** **TI** **~** **X**

WWWW Hilton Garden Inn Portland Downtown Waterfront **H**
(207) 780-0780. **$159-$359.** 65 Commercial St 04101. In the Old Port; across from Casco Bay ferry terminal. Int corridors. **Pets:** Accepted. **X** **&M** **H** **P** **TI** **~**

AAA **WWWW** Holiday Inn-West **H**
(207) 774-5601. **$120-$220.** 81 Riverside St 04103. I-95, exit 48. Int corridors. **Pets:** $35 one-time fee/room. Service with restrictions, supervision. **SAVE** **X** **&M** **H** **P** **TI** **~** **X**

WWW Howard Johnson Plaza Hotel **H**
(207) 774-5861. **$80-$225.** 155 Riverside St 04103. I-95, exit 48, jct SR 25. Int corridors. **Pets:** $50 deposit/room. Service with restrictions. **X** **H** **P** **TI** **~**

WWW La Quinta Inn & Suites Portland **H** **🐾**
(207) 871-0611. **$55-$179.** 340 Park Ave 04102. I-295, exit 5A southbound; exit 5 northbound, e on SR 22. Int corridors. **Pets:** Medium, other species. Service with restrictions, supervision. **ASK** **X** **&M** **H** **~**

AAA **WWWW** Portland Harbor Hotel **H**
(207) 775-9090. **$179-$379.** 468 Fore St 04101. In the Old Port. Int corridors. **Pets:** Accepted. **SAVE** **X** **&M** **TI**

WWWW Residence Inn by Marriott Portland Downtown/Waterfront **H**
(207) 761-1660. **$169-$249.** 145 Fore St 04101. In the Old Port; across from Casco Bay ferry terminal. Int corridors. **Pets:** Accepted. **X** **&M** **H** **P** **~**

PRESQUE ISLE

AAA **WWW** Presque Isle Inn & Convention Center **H** **🐾**
(207) 764-3321. **$88-$150.** 116 Main St 04769. 1 mi s on US 1. Int corridors. **Pets:** Other species. $35 one-time fee/room. **SAVE** **X** **H** **P** **TI** **~**

RANGELEY

△△△ ▽▽▽ **Rangeley Saddleback Inn** H
(207) 864-3434. **$85-$250.** 2303 Main St 04970. On SR 4, just s of village. Ext corridors. **Pets:** Accepted. [SAVE] [X] [&M] [fridge] [microwave] [TI] [pool]

ROCKLAND

△△△ ▽▽▽ **Trade Winds Motor Inn** H
(207) 596-6661. **$64-$224.** 2 Park Dr 04841. On US 1; center. Ext/int corridors. **Pets:** Accepted. [SAVE] [X] [fridge] [microwave] [TI] [pool] [X]

ROCKPORT

△△△ ▽▽▽ **The Country Inn At Camden/Rockport** H
(207) 236-2725. **$99-$219.** 8 Country Inn Way 04858. Jct SR 90, 0.9 mi n on US 1. Ext/int corridors. **Pets:** Large. $10 daily fee/pet. Designated rooms, service with restrictions, supervision.
[SAVE] [X] [fridge] [microwave] [pool] [X]

△△△ ▽▽▽ **Glen Cove Inn & Suites** M
(207) 594-4062. **$59-$199.** 866 Commercial St 04856. Jct SR 90, 3 mi s on US 1. Ext corridors. **Pets:** Medium. Designated rooms, service with restrictions, crate. [SAVE] [X] [fridge] [pool]

RUMFORD

△△△ ▽▽▽ **Linnell Motel & RestInn Conference Center** H
(207) 364-4511. **$55-$89.** 986 Prospect Ave 04276. 2 mi w, just off US 2. Ext/int corridors. **Pets:** Accepted. [SAVE] [X] [fridge] [microwave] [X]

SACO

△△△ ▽▽▽▽ **Hampton Inn** H
(207) 282-7222. **$89-$209.** 48 Industrial Park Rd 04072. I-95, exit 36 (I-195), exit 1 (Industrial Park Rd), just ne. Int corridors. **Pets:** Other species. Designated rooms, service with restrictions, supervision.
[SAVE] [X] [&M] [fridge] [microwave] [pool]

△△△ ▽▽▽▽ **Holiday Inn Express Hotel & Suites** H
(207) 286-9600. **$89-$309.** 352 North St (SR 112) 04072. I-95, exit 36 (I-195), exit 1 (Industrial Park Rd), 0.6 mi sw to SR 112, then 0.4 mi nw. Int corridors. **Pets:** Accepted. [SAVE] [X] [&M] [fridge] [microwave]

△△△ ▽▽ **Saco Motel** M
(207) 284-6952. **$50-$90, 3 day notice.** 473 Main St 04072. I-95, exit 36 (I-195), exit 2A (US 1 S), just sw. Ext corridors. **Pets:** Medium, dogs only. $5 daily fee/pet. Service with restrictions, supervision.
[SAVE] [X] [fridge] [pool]

▽▽ **Wagon Wheel Motel** M
(207) 283-3258. **Call for rates.** 726 Portland Rd (US 1) 04072. I-95, exit 36, 1.5 mi se to US 1, then 0.7 mi ne. Ext corridors. **Pets:** Accepted.
[X] [fridge] [microwave] [X]

SANFORD

▽▽ **Super 8** H
(207) 324-8823. **Call for rates.** 1892 Main St (Rt 109) 04073. I-95, exit 19, 7 mi nw. Int corridors. **Pets:** Accepted. [X] [fridge] [microwave]

SCARBOROUGH

△△△ ▽▽▽ **Comfort Inn & Suites Scarborough** H ❖
(207) 883-2700. **$69-$169.** 329 US 1 04074. I-95, exit 42, toward Scarborough, then 0.6 mi n. Int corridors. **Pets:** Medium, dogs only. $25 daily fee/pet. Designated rooms, service with restrictions, crate.
[SAVE] [X] [fridge] [microwave] [pool]

▽▽▽ **Extended StayAmerica Portland-Scarborough** H
(207) 883-0554. **$65-$130.** 2 Ashley Dr 04074. I-95, exit 42, just n. Int corridors. **Pets:** Other species. $25 daily fee/room. Designated rooms, service with restrictions, crate. [ASK] [X] [fridge] [microwave]

△△△ ▽▽▽▽ **Homewood Suites Portland** H
(207) 775-2700. **$99-$229.** 200 Southborough Dr 04074. I-95, exit 45, left on Maine Mall Rd (becomes Payne Rd), then left. Int corridors.
Pets: Accepted. [SAVE] [X] [&M] [fridge] [microwave] [pool] [X]

△△△ ▽▽ **Pride Motel & Cottages** CA ❖
(207) 883-4816. **$65-$215, 7 day notice.** 677 US Rt 1 04074. I-95, exit 36, 0.5 mi e to US 1, then 4.5 mi n. Ext corridors. **Pets:** Large, dogs only. $15 daily fee/room. Service with restrictions, supervision.
[X] [fridge] [microwave] [X] [Z]

▽▽▽▽ **Residence Inn Portland-Scarborough** H ❖
(207) 883-0400. **$139-$219.** 800 Roundwood Dr 04074. I-95, exit 42, 1.5 mi n on Payne Rd. Int corridors. **Pets:** Medium, other species. $50 one-time fee/pet. Service with restrictions, supervision.
[X] [&M] [fridge] [microwave] [X]

▽▽▽▽ **TownePlace Suites Portland/Scarborough** H
(207) 883-6800. **$94-$169.** 700 Roundwood Dr 04074. I-95, exit 42, 1.5 mi n on Payne Rd. Int corridors. **Pets:** Other species. $75 one-time fee/room. Service with restrictions, supervision. [X] [&M] [fridge] [microwave]

SKOWHEGAN

△△△ ▽▽▽ **Belmont Motel** M
(207) 474-8315. **$60-$100.** 273 Madison Ave 04976. 1 mi n on US 201. Ext corridors. **Pets:** Accepted. [SAVE] [X] [&M] [fridge] [microwave]

SOUTHPORT

△△△ ▽▽▽▽ **Ocean Gate Resort** H
(207) 633-3321. **$99-$399, 7 day notice.** 70 Ocean Gate Rd 04576. SR 27, 2.5 mi s of Boothbay Harbor, 0.5 mi s of bridge to Southport Island. Ext corridors. **Pets:** Medium. $25 one-time fee/pet. Designated rooms, service with restrictions, supervision.
[SAVE] [X] [fridge] [microwave] [pool] [X]

SOUTH PORTLAND

△△△ ▽▽▽ **Best Western Merry Manor Inn** H
(207) 774-6151. **$110-$200.** 700 Main St 04106. I-95, exit 45, 1.3 mi e to US 1. Ext/int corridors. **Pets:** Dogs only. Designated rooms, service with restrictions, supervision. [SAVE] [X] [fridge] [microwave] [TI] [pool] [X]

△△△ ▽▽▽ **Comfort Inn** H
(207) 775-0409. **$90-$190.** 90 Maine Mall Rd 04106. I-95, exit 45, 1 mi n. Int corridors. **Pets:** Other species. $25 one-time fee/room. Service with restrictions, supervision. [ECO] [SAVE] [X] [&M] [fridge] [microwave]

△△△ ▽▽▽ **Days Inn Portland-South Portland** H
(207) 772-3450. **$49-$189.** 461 Maine Mall Rd 04106. I-95, exit 45. Int corridors. **Pets:** Medium, dogs only. $10 daily fee/pet. Designated rooms, service with restrictions, supervision. [SAVE] [X] [fridge] [microwave]

▽▽▽ **Hampton Inn Hotel** H
(207) 773-4400. **$89-$259.** 171 Philbrook Ave 04106. I-95, exit 45, just ne. Int corridors. **Pets:** Accepted. [X] [&M] [fridge] [microwave] [X]

▽▽▽ **Holiday Inn Express & Suites** H
(207) 775-3900. **$299.** 303 Sable Oaks Dr 04106. I-95, exit 45, just n on Maine Mall Rd, then just w on Running Hill Rd. Int corridors.
Pets: Accepted. [ASK] [X] [fridge] [microwave] [pool]

▽▽▽ **Howard Johnson Hotel** H
(207) 775-5343. **$84-$189.** 675 Main St 04106. I-95, exit 45, 1.3 mi e to US 1. Int corridors. **Pets:** Accepted. [ASK] [X] [fridge] [microwave]

△△△ ▽▽▽▽ **Portland Marriott at Sable Oaks** H 🐾
(207) 871-8000. **$179-$219.** 200 Sable Oaks Dr 04106. I-95, exit 45, just n on Maine Mall Rd, then just w on Running Hill Rd. Int corridors.
Pets: $35 one-time fee/room. Designated rooms, supervision.
[ECO] [SAVE] [X] [fridge] [microwave] [TI] [X]

△△△ ▽▽▽▽ **Wyndham Portland Airport Hotel** H ❖
(207) 775-6161. **$99-$339.** 363 Maine Mall Rd 04106. I-95, exit 45. Int corridors. **Pets:** Medium, dogs only. Designated rooms, service with restrictions, supervision. [SAVE] [X] [fridge] [microwave] [TI] [pool] [X]

SPRUCE HEAD

▼▼▼ Craignair Inn **CI** ❧

(207) 594-7644. **$88-$162, 14 day notice.** 5 Third St 04859. 2.5 mi w on SR 73, 1.5 mi s on Clark Island Rd; 10 mi s of Rockland. Ext/int corridors. **Pets:** $10 daily fee/room. Designated rooms, service with restrictions, supervision. ⬛ ⊠ ⦿

WATERVILLE

▼▼ Fireside Inn & Suites **H**

(207) 873-3335. **Call for rates.** 356 Main St 04901. I-95, exit 130 (Main St). Int corridors. **Pets:** Accepted. ⊠ ⬛ ⬛ ⦿ ⟶ ⊠

▼▼▼ Holiday Inn **H** ❧

(207) 873-0111. **$99-$219.** 375 Main St 04901. I-95, exit 130 (Main St) on SR 104. Int corridors. **Pets:** Service with restrictions, supervision.

⬛ ⬛ ⊠ ⬛ ⬛ ⦿ ⟶ ⊠

WELLS

▼▼ Wells-Moody Motel **M**

(207) 646-5601. **$49-$149, 10 day notice.** 119 Post Rd (US 1) 04054. I-95, exit 19; jct SR 109/US 1, 3.4 mi s. Ext corridors. **Pets:** Accepted.

⊠ ⬛ ⟶

WEST FORKS

▼▼▼ Inn by the River **CI**

(207) 663-2181. **Call for rates.** 2777 US Rt 201 04985. Center. Int corridors. **Pets:** Accepted. ⬛ ⊠ ⬛ ⦿ ⊠ ⬛ ⬛

WESTPORT

▼▼▼ The Squire Tarbox Inn **CI**

(207) 882-7693. **$115-$199, 14 day notice.** 1181 Main Rd 04578. Jct US 1 and SR 144; in Wiscasset; 8.5 mi s on SR 144, follow signs. Ext/int corridors. **Pets:** Accepted. ⊠ ⦿ ⊠ ⬛ ⬛

WILTON

▼▼▼ Farmington/Wilton Comfort Inn & Suites **H** ❧

(207) 645-5155. **$103-$162.** 1026 US Rt 2 04294. On US 2, just w of jct SR 133. Int corridors. **Pets:** Other species. $35 one-time fee/room. Supervision. ⬛ ⊠ ⬛ ⬛ ⬛ ⟶

YARMOUTH

▲▲▲ ▼▼▼ Down-East Village Motel **M**

(207) 846-5161. **$77-$125.** 705 US Rt 1 04096. I-295, exit 15 northbound; exit 17 southbound. Ext corridors. **Pets:** Other species. $8 daily fee/pet. Service with restrictions, supervision.

⬛ ⊠ ⬛ ⬛ ⦿ ⟶

YORK

▲▲▲ ▼▼▼ Best Western York Inn **M**

(207) 363-8903. **$69-$229.** 2 Brickyard Ln 03909. I-95, exit 4 (York Ogunquit), 1 mi s. Int corridors. **Pets:** Accepted.

⬛ ⊠ ⬛ ⬛ ⬛ ⟶

YORK HARBOR

▼▼▼ Inn At Harmon Park **BB**

(207) 363-2031. **$69-$139 (no credit cards), 7 day notice.** 415 York St 03911. I-95, exit 7, 0.3 mi s on US 1, then 1.5 mi n; to York Village. Int corridors. **Pets:** Supervision. ⬛ ⊠ ⬛ ⬛

MARYLAND

BALTIMORE METROPOLITAN AREA

ABERDEEN

▼▼ Clarion Aberdeen H ❖

(410) 273-6300. **$79-$130.** 980 Hospitality Way 21001. I-95, exit 85, just e on SR 22. Int corridors. **Pets:** Other species. Service with restrictions, crate. [A$K] [✕] [🛏] [▣] [¶] [≈]

◈ ▼▼◈ La Quinta Inn Aberdeen H ✿

(410) 272-6000. **$69-$139.** 793 W Bel Air Ave 21001. I-95, exit 85, just e. Int corridors. **Pets:** Medium, other species. Service with restrictions, supervision. [SAVE] [✕] [🛏] [▣] [¶] [≈]

◈ ▼◈ Red Roof Inn M

(410) 273-7800. **$50-$75.** 988 Hospitality Way 21001. I-95, exit 85, just e on SR 22. Ext corridors. **Pets:** Large. Service with restrictions, crate. [SAVE] [✕] [🛏]

▼▼◈ Residence Inn by Marriott Aberdeen at Ripkin Stadium H ✿

(410) 272-0444. **$179-$189.** 830 Long Dr 21001. I-95, exit 85, 0.5 mi w on SR 22, then 0.5 mi n. Int corridors. **Pets:** Other species. $100 one-time fee/room. [✕] [♿M] [🛏] [▣] [≈]

◈ ▼◈ Super 8 Aberdeen M

(410) 272-5420. **$55-$80.** 1008 Beards Hill Rd 21001. I-95, exit 85, just e on SR 22. Int corridors. **Pets:** Accepted. [SAVE] [✕] [🛏] [▣]

ANNAPOLIS

◈ ▼▼◈ Doubletree Hotel Annapolis H

(410) 224-3150. **$99-$199.** 210 Holiday Ct 21401. 2.3 mi sw on US 50 and 301, exit 22 to Riva Rd, 0.3 mi n. Int corridors. **Pets:** Accepted. [SAVE] [✕] [🛏] [▣] [¶] [≈]

▼▼ Extended StayAmerica-Annapolis/Naval Academy M

(410) 571-9988. **$99-$179.** 1 Womack Dr 21401. 2.3 mi sw on US 50 and 301, exit 22, just s on Admiral Cochrane Dr, then just n on Spruill Rd. Int corridors. **Pets:** Other species. $25 daily fee/room. Designated rooms, service with restrictions, crate. [A$K] [✕] [🛏] [▣]

◈ ▼◈ Homestead Studio Suites Hotel-Annapolis-Naval Academy H

(410) 571-6600. **$109-$189.** 120 Admiral Cochrane Dr 21401. 2.3 mi sw on US 50 and 301, exit 22, just s, then just e. Int corridors. **Pets:** Other species. $25 daily fee/room. Designated rooms, service with restrictions, crate. [A$K] [✕] [♿M] [🛏] [▣]

◈ ▼▼◈ Loews Annapolis Hotel H ✿

(410) 263-7777. **$125-$315.** 126 West St 21401. US 50 and 301, exit 24 eastbound; exit 24A westbound, 1.4 mi s on SR 70, just sw on Calvert St, then just w. Int corridors. **Pets:** $25 one-time fee/room. Supervision. [SAVE] [✕] [🛏] [▣] [¶] [✕]

▼▼ Quality Inn M

(410) 974-4440. **$70-$140.** 1542 Whitehall Rd 21401. 1 mi w of Chesa-peake Bay Bridge, off US 50 and 301, exit 30 eastbound; exit 32 west-bound. Int corridors. **Pets:** Designated rooms, service with restrictions, supervision. [A$K] [✕] [🛏] [▣]

◈ ▼▼◈ Sheraton Annapolis Hotel H ✿

(410) 266-3131. **$99-$349, 3 day notice.** 173 Jennifer Rd 21401. North side of US 50 and 301, exit 23B westbound; exit 23 eastbound. Int corri-dors. **Pets:** Large, other species. $50 one-time fee/room. Service with restrictions, crate. [SAVE] [✕] [♿M] [🛏] [▣] [¶] [≈] [✕]

◈ ▼▼◈ The Westin Annapolis H ✿

(410) 972-4300. **$159-$1599.** 100 Westgate Cir 21401. US 50 and 301, exit 24 eastbound; exit 24A westbound, 0.7 mi s on SR 70, then 0.8 mi e on SR 435; 0.5 mi n of Church Cir. Int corridors. **Pets:** Medium. Service with restrictions, supervision. [SAVE] [✕] [♿M] [🛏] [▣] [¶] [≈] [✕]

BALTIMORE

◈ ▼▼◈ Admiral Fell Inn H ✿

(410) 522-7377. **$149-$269.** 888 S Broadway St 21231. Corner of Broad-way and Thames sts; facing the waterfront. Int corridors. **Pets:** Accepted. [SAVE] [✕] [🛏] [▣] [¶]

◈ ▼◈ Brookshire Suites H

(410) 625-1300. **$129-$249.** 120 E Lombard St 21202. Corner of Calvert and Lombard sts. Int corridors. **Pets:** Medium. Designated rooms, service with restrictions, supervision. [SAVE] [✕] [🛏] [▣]

▼▼ Comfort Inn & Suites Baltimore H

(410) 576-1200. **Call for rates.** 8 E Pleasant St 21202. Just s of US 40 E, off Charles St. Int corridors. **Pets:** Accepted. [✕] [🛏] [▣]

◈ ▼▼▼◈ Hilton Baltimore H ✿

(443) 573-8700. **$149-$409.** 401 W Pratt St 21201. I-95, exit 53, just w of Camden Yards. Int corridors. **Pets:** Large. $75 one-time fee/pet. Super-vision. [SAVE] [✕] [♿M] [🛏] [▣] [¶] [≈] [✕]

▼▼▼ Homewood Suites by Hilton Baltimore Inner Harbor H

(410) 234-0999. **$149-$229.** 625 S President St 21202. Located in Har-bor East section of Inner Harbor. Int corridors. **Pets:** Accepted. [✕] [♿M] [🛏] [▣] [≈] [✕]

◈ ▼▼◈ Pier 5 Hotel H

(410) 539-2000. **$179-$299.** 711 Eastern Ave 21202. On the Inner Har-bor, at Pier 5. Int corridors. **Pets:** Accepted. [SAVE] [✕] [🛏] [▣]

◈ ▼▼▼◈ Radisson Plaza Lord Baltimore H

(410) 539-8400. **$109-$359.** 20 W Baltimore St 21201. At Baltimore and Hanover sts. Int corridors. **Pets:** Medium, dogs only. $10 daily fee/room, $50 one-time fee/room. Designated rooms, service with restrictions, super-vision. [SAVE] [✕] [♿M] [🛏] [▣] [¶]

▼▼▼▼ Residence Inn by Marriott-Baltimore Downtown/Inner Harbor **H**

(410) 962-1220. **$209-$249.** 17 Light St 21202. Jct Redwood and Light sts. Int corridors. **Pets:** Accepted.

AAA ▼▼▼▼ Sheraton Baltimore City Center Hotel **H**

(410) 752-1100. **$100-$380.** 101 W Fayette St 21201. Between Charles and Liberty sts. Int corridors. **Pets:** Accepted.

AAA ▼▼▼▼ Sheraton Inner Harbor Hotel **H** ❖

(410) 962-8300. **$159-$454.** 300 S Charles St 21201. At Conway St. Int corridors. **Pets:** Large, dogs only. Designated rooms, service with restrictions, supervision.

BELCAMP

▼▼ Extended StayAmerica-Baltimore-Bel Air **H**

(410) 273-0194. **$94-$144.** 1361 James Way 21015. I-95, exit 80 (SR 543), just ne. Int corridors. **Pets:** Other species. $25 daily fee/room. Designated rooms, service with restrictions, crate.

COLUMBIA

▼▼ Extended Stay Deluxe Columbia Corporate Park **H**

(410) 872-2994. **$109-$169.** 8890 Stanford Blvd 21045. I-95, exit 41B, 1.3 mi w on SR 175 (Little Patuxent Pkwy), 0.5 mi s on Snowden River Pkwy, just w on McGaw Rd, then 0.3 mi nw. Int corridors. **Pets:** Other species. $25 daily fee/room. Designated rooms, service with restrictions, crate.

▼▼▼ Hilton Columbia **H**

(410) 997-1060. **$114-$259.** 5485 Twin Knolls Rd 21045. Just e on SR 175 (Little Patuxent Pkwy) from jct US 29, just s on Thunder Hill Rd, then 0.3 mi w on Twin Knolls Rd, 5th entrance. Int corridors. **Pets:** Accepted.

▼▼▼▼ Homewood Suites by Hilton Columbia **H**

(410) 872-9200. **$109-$209.** 8320 Benson Dr 21045. I-95, exit 41B, 0.5 mi w on SR 175 (Little Patuxent Pkwy), just nw on SR 108, then just w on Lark Brown Rd. Int corridors. **Pets:** Other species. $75 one-time fee/room. Service with restrictions, crate.

AAA ▼▼▼▼ Sheraton Columbia Town Center Hotel **H**

(410) 730-3900. **Call for rates.** 10207 Wincopin Cir 21044. 1.2 mi w on SR 175 (Little Patuxent Pkwy) from jct US 29, then just s; center. Int corridors. **Pets:** Accepted.

▼▼▼▼ Staybridge Suites Baltimore-Columbia **H**

(410) 964-9494. **$85-$129.** 8844 Columbia 100 Pkwy 21045. I-95, exit 43B, 4 mi w on SR 100, exit 1B, then just e. Int corridors. **Pets:** Medium. $75 one-time fee/room. Service with restrictions, supervision.

▼▼▼▼ StudioPLUS Columbia Gateway Drive **H**

(410) 312-1557. **$89-$149.** 6620 Eli Whitney Dr 21046. I-95, exit 41, 1 mi w on SR 175 (Little Patuxent Pkwy), then just se on Columbia Gateway Dr. Int corridors. **Pets:** Other species. $25 daily fee/room. Designated rooms, service with restrictions, crate.

EDGEWOOD

AAA ▼▼▼ Best Western Invitation Inn **M**

(410) 679-9700. **$75-$130.** 1709 Edgewood Rd 21040. I-95, exit 77A, just e on SR 24. Ext corridors. **Pets:** Other species. $15 daily fee/room. Service with restrictions, crate.

ELLICOTT CITY

▼▼▼▼ Residence Inn by Marriott Columbia **H**

(410) 997-7200. **$179-$199.** 4950 Beaver Run Way 21043. I-95, exit 43B, 4 mi w on SR 100, exit 1B (Executive Park Dr). Int corridors. **Pets:** Accepted.

ESSEX

▼▼ Super 8 Baltimore/Essex **H**

(410) 780-0030. **$82-$128.** 98 Stemmers Run Rd 21221. I-695, exit 36 (SR 702 S) to SR 150 E (Chase exit). Int corridors. **Pets:** Small. $11 daily fee/pet. Designated rooms, service with restrictions, supervision.

GLEN BURNIE

AAA ▼▼▼ Days Inn-Glen Burnie **H**

(410) 761-8300. **$79-$129.** 6600 Ritchie Hwy 21061. I-695, exit 3B eastbound; exit 2 westbound, 0.5 mi s on SR 2. Ext corridors.
Pets: Accepted.

▼▼▼ Extended StayAmerica Baltimore-Glen Burnie **H**

(410) 761-2708. **$109-$169.** 104 Chesapeake Centre Ct 21061. I-695, exit 3B, 0.9 mi s on SR 2, just e on E Ordance Rd, then just s. Int corridors. **Pets:** Other species. $25 daily fee/room. Designated rooms, service with restrictions, crate.

▼▼▼ La Quinta Inn **H** 🐾

(410) 636-4300. **$69-$129.** 6323 Ritchie Hwy 21061. I-695, exit 3A eastbound; exit 2 westbound, jct SR 2. Int corridors. **Pets:** Medium, other species. Service with restrictions, supervision.

HANOVER

▼▼▼ Homewood Suites by Hilton Baltimore/Arundel Mills **H**

(410) 878-7201. **$139-$199.** 7491-B New Ridge Rd 21076. SR 100, exit 10B, 0.3 mi n on SR 713. Int corridors. **Pets:** Accepted.

▼▼▼ Red Roof Inn-BWI Parkway **M**

(410) 712-4070. **$50-$130.** 7306 Parkway Dr S 21076. I-95, exit 43A, 2 mi e on SR 100, exit 8 (Coca-Cola Dr), then 0.5 mi se. Ext corridors. **Pets:** Large. Service with restrictions, crate.

▼▼▼ Residence Inn by Marriott-Arundel Mills/BWI **H** ❖

(410) 799-7332. **$188-$230.** 7035 Arundel Mills Cir 21076. I-95, exit 43A, 3.6 mi e on SR 100, exit 10A (Arundel Mills Blvd). Int corridors. **Pets:** Medium, other species. $100 one-time fee/room. Designated rooms, service with restrictions, crate.

▼▼▼ TownePlace Suites by Marriott Arundel Mills/BWI **H** ❖

(410) 379-9000. **$161-$197.** 7021 Arundel Mills Cir 21076. I-95, exit 43A, 3.6 mi e on SR 100, exit 10A (Arundel Mills Blvd). Int corridors. **Pets:** Medium. $100 one-time fee/room. Service with restrictions, supervision.

HUNT VALLEY

▼▼▼ Baltimore Marriott Hunt Valley **H**

(410) 785-7000. **$149-$159.** 245 Shawan Rd 21031. I-83, exit 20A (Shawan Rd), just e. Int corridors. **Pets:** Accepted.

JESSUP

▼▼▼ Extended StayAmerica-Baltimore-Laurel **H**

(301) 725-3877. **$89-$149.** 8550 Washington Blvd 20794. I-95, exit 38A, 1.4 mi e on SR 32, 0.5 mi n on US 1. Int corridors. **Pets:** Other species. $25 daily fee/room. Designated rooms, service with restrictions, crate.

▼▼▼ La Quinta Inn & Suites-Columbia/Jessup **H** 🐾

(410) 799-1500. **Call for rates.** 7300 Crestmount Rd 20794. I-95, exit 41A, just s of jct US 1 and SR 175. Int corridors. **Pets:** Medium, other species. Service with restrictions, supervision.

▼▼▼ Red Roof Inn-Columbia/Jessup **M**

(410) 796-0380. **$50-$130.** 8000 Washington Blvd 20794. I-95, exit 41A, 0.3 mi s of jct US 1 and SR 175. Ext corridors. **Pets:** Large. Service with restrictions, crate.

LINTHICUM HEIGHTS

◆◆ Candlewood Suites-BWI H
(410) 850-9214. **$99-$149.** 1247 Winterson Rd 21090. I-695, exit 7A, 1 mi s on SR 295, 1.3 mi e on W Nursery Rd, then 0.3 mi w. Int corridors.
Pets: Accepted. [ASK] [✕] [⊟] [⌨]

AAA ◆◆◆ Comfort Inn Airport H
(410) 789-9100. **$74-$124.** 6921 Baltimore Annapolis Blvd 21225. I-695, exit 6A eastbound; exit 5 westbound, at SR 170 and 648. Int corridors.
Pets: Accepted. [SAVE] [✕] [&M] [⊟] [⌨] [↑↓] [🍴] [✕]

◆◆◆ Comfort Suites-BWI Airport H
(410) 691-1000. **$79-$119.** 815 Elkridge Landing Rd 21090. I-695, exit 7A, 1 mi s on SR 295, then 1.3 mi e on W Nursery Rd. Int corridors.
Pets: Accepted. [ASK] [✕] [&M] [⊟] [⌨]

AAA ◆◆◆◆ Four Points by Sheraton BWI Airport H 🐾
(410) 859-3300. **Call for rates.** 7032 Elm Rd 21240. I-195, exit 1A, 0.5 mi n on SR 170, then just e. Int corridors. **Pets:** Medium. $25 one-time fee/pet. Designated rooms, service with restrictions.
[SAVE] [✕] [⊟] [⌨] [🍴] [↑↓]

◆◆◆◆ Hampton Inn BWI Airport H
(410) 850-0600. **Call for rates.** 829 Elkridge Landing Rd 21090. I-695, exit 7A, 1 mi s on SR 295, 1.3 mi e on W Nursery Rd, then just w. Int corridors. **Pets:** Accepted. [✕] [&M] [⊟] [⌨]

◆◆◆◆ Hilton Baltimore BWI Airport H
(410) 694-0808. **$99-$229.** 1739 W Nursery Rd 21090. I-695, exit 7A, 1 mi s on SR 295, then 1.2 mi e. Int corridors. **Pets:** Accepted.
[✕] [&M] [⌨] [🍴] [↑↓] [✕]

◆◆◆◆ Holiday Inn-BWI Airport Conference Center H
(410) 859-8400. **$89-$169.** 890 Elkridge Landing Rd 21090. I-695, exit 7A, 1 mi s on SR 295, 1.3 mi e on W Nursery Rd, then 0.5 mi w. Int corridors. **Pets:** Accepted. [ASK] [✕] [&M] [⊟] [⌨] [🍴] [↑↓] [✕]

◆◆ Homestead Studio Suites Hotel-Baltimore-BWI Airport H
(410) 691-2500. **$89-$159.** 939 International Dr 21090. I-695, exit 7A, 1 mi s on SR 295, then 0.6 mi e on W Nursery Rd. Ext corridors.
Pets: Other species. $25 daily fee/room. Designated rooms, service with restrictions, crate. [ASK] [✕] [⊟] [⌨]

◆◆ La Quinta Inn & Suites BWI Airport H 🐾
(410) 859-2333. **Call for rates.** 1734 W Nursery Rd 21090. SR 295, exit Nursery Rd, 1.2 mi e. Int corridors. **Pets:** Medium, other species. Service with restrictions, supervision. [✕] [⊟] [⌨] [↑↓]

◆ Motel 6 Baltimore-Linthicum Heights #1201 M
(410) 636-9070. **$55-$75.** 5179 Raynor Ave 21090. I-695, exit 8, just e on SR 168. Ext corridors. **Pets:** Other species. Service with restrictions, supervision. [✕] [&M] [↑↓]

◆◆ Red Roof Inn-BWI Airport M
(410) 850-7600. **Call for rates.** 827 Elkridge Landing Rd 21090. I-695, exit 7A, 1 mi s on SR 295, 1.3 mi e on W Nursery Rd, then just w. Ext corridors. **Pets:** Large. Service with restrictions, crate. [✕] [⊟]

◆◆◆ Residence Inn by Marriott-BWI Airport H
(410) 691-0255. **$179-$219.** 1160 Winterson Rd 21090. I-695, exit 7A, 1 mi s on SR 295, 0.7 mi e on W Nursery Rd, then just n. Int corridors.
Pets: Accepted. [✕] [&M] [⊟] [⌨] [↑↓] [✕]

AAA ◆◆◆ Sheraton Baltimore Washington Airport Hotel H
(443) 577-2100. **Call for rates.** 1100 Old Elkridge Landing Rd 21090. I-695, exit 7A, 1 mi s on SR 295, 1.3 mi e on W Nursery Rd, then 0.4 mi w on Winterson Rd. Int corridors. **Pets:** Accepted.
[SAVE] [✕] [⊟] [⌨] [🍴] [↑↓] [✕]

AAA ◆◆◆ Sleep Inn & Suites Airport H
(410) 789-7223. **$69-$119.** 6055 Belle Grove Rd 21225. I-695, exit 6A eastbound; exit 5 westbound, 0.3 mi n to jct SR 170/648. Int corridors.
Pets: Accepted. [SAVE] [✕] [&M] [⊟] [⌨]

◆◆◆ Staybridge Suites BWI H
(410) 850-5666. **$99-$359.** 1301 Winterson Rd 21090. I-695, exit 7A, 1 mi s on SR 295, 1.3 mi e on Nursery Rd, then 0.4 mi w. Int corridors.
Pets: Small. $150 one-time fee/pet. Service with restrictions, supervision.
[ASK] [✕] [&M] [⊟] [⌨] [↑↓]

AAA ◆◆◆ TownePlace Suites by Marriott Baltimore/BWI Airport H 🐾
(410) 694-0060. **$161-$197.** 1171 Winterson Rd 21090. I-695, exit 7A, 1 mi s on SR 295, 0.7 mi e on W Nursery Rd, then just n. Int corridors.
Pets: Other species. $100 one-time fee/room. Service with restrictions, supervision. [ECO] [SAVE] [✕] [&M] [⊟] [⌨] [↑↓]

AAA ◆◆◆ The Westin-Baltimore Washington Airport H
(443) 577-2300. **$119-$319.** 1110 Old Elkridge Landing Rd 21090. I-695, exit 7A, 1 mi s on SR 295, 1.3 mi e on W Nursery Rd, then 0.4 mi w on Winterson Rd. Int corridors. **Pets:** Accepted.
[SAVE] [✕] [&M] [⌨] [🍴] [↑↓]

ROSEDALE

◆◆◆ La Quinta Inn & Suites Baltimore North H 🐾
(410) 574-8100. **Call for rates.** 4 Philadelphia Ct 21237. I-695, exit 34, just n. Int corridors. **Pets:** Medium, other species. Service with restrictions, supervision. [✕] [⊟] [⌨] [↑↓]

SYKESVILLE

◆◆◆ Inn at Norwood BB 🐾
(410) 549-7868. **$135-$225, 7 day notice.** 7514 Norwood Ave 21784. I-70, exit 80 (SR 32), 8 mi n, just w on Main St, then just w on Church St. Int corridors. **Pets:** Dogs only. $20 one-time fee/pet. Designated rooms, no service, crate. [ASK] [✕] [⊟] [⌨] [☎]

TIMONIUM

◆◆ Extended StayAmerica-Baltimore-Timonium H
(410) 628-1088. **$94-$149.** 9704 Beaver Dam Rd 21093. I-83, exit 17, just e, follow signs to Beaver Dam Rd. Int corridors. **Pets:** Other species. $25 daily fee/room. Designated rooms, service with restrictions, crate.
[ASK] [✕] [&M] [⊟] [⌨]

◆◆ Red Roof Inn-Timonium M
(410) 666-0380. **$60-$110.** 111 W Timonium Rd 21093. I-83, exit 16A northbound; exit 16 southbound, just e. Ext corridors. **Pets:** Large. Service with restrictions, crate. [ASK] [✕] [&M] [⊟]

TOWSON

◆◆ Holiday Inn Baltimore-Towson H 🐾
(410) 823-4410. **$89-$149.** 1100 Cromwell Bridge Rd 21286. I-695, exit 29A, just s. Int corridors. **Pets:** Medium, other species. $25 daily fee/room. Designated rooms, service with restrictions.
[ASK] [✕] [⊟] [⌨] [🍴] [↑↓]

AAA ◆◆◆ Sheraton Baltimore North Hotel H 🐾
(410) 321-7400. **Call for rates.** 903 Dulaney Valley Rd 21204. I-695, exit 27A, 0.3 mi s. Int corridors. **Pets:** Medium. Designated rooms, service with restrictions, crate. [SAVE] [✕] [⊟] [⌨] [🍴] [↑↓] [✕]

WESTMINSTER

◆ The Boston Inn M
(410) 848-9095. **$47-$75.** 533 Baltimore Blvd 21157. 0.9 mi se on SR 97/140 from jct SR 27. Ext corridors. **Pets:** Dogs only. Service with restrictions, supervision. [ASK] [✕] [⊟] [⌨] [↑↓]

WHITE MARSH

▼▼▼ Residence Inn by Marriott Baltimore/White Marsh ⊞ ❖

(410) 933-9554. **$152-$186.** 4980 Mercantile Rd 21236. I-95, exit 67B, 0.5 mi w on SR 43 (White Marsh Blvd), just s to Mercantile Rd, then just e. Int corridors. **Pets:** Other species. $75 one-time fee/room. Service with restrictions, crate. ⊠ ⌖M 🛈 💷 ⇝ ⊠

END METROPOLITAN AREA

CAMBRIDGE

▼▼▼ Comfort Inn & Suites Cambridge ⊞

(410) 901-0926. **$90-$170.** 2936 Ocean Gateway 21613. On US 50, 0.8 mi e of jct SR 16. Int corridors. **Pets:** Other species. $25 one-time fee/pet. Service with restrictions. A$K ⊠ ⌖M 🛈 💷 ⇝

(AAA) ▼▼▼▼ Hyatt Regency Chesapeake Bay Golf Resort, Spa and Marina ⊞

(410) 901-1234. **$139-$459, 3 day notice.** 100 Heron Blvd 21613. US 50 E, 1.2 mi e of Frederick C Malkus Jr Bridge. Int corridors.
Pets: Accepted. SAVE ⊠ ⌖M 🛈 💷 ⍨ ⇝ ⊠

CUMBERLAND

▼▼▼ Holiday Inn ⊞

(301) 724-8800. **$99-$149, 3 day notice.** 100 S George St 21502. I-68, exit 43C, just n; downtown. Int corridors. **Pets:** Accepted.
A$K ⊠ 🛈 💷 ⍨ ⇝

DISTRICT OF COLUMBIA METROPOLITAN AREA

BELTSVILLE

(AAA) ▼▼▼▼ Comfort Inn Capital Beltway/I-95 North ⊞

(301) 572-7100. **$85-$129.** 4050 Powder Mill Rd 20705. I-95, exit 29B, just w on SR 212. Int corridors. **Pets:** Accepted.
SAVE ⊠ ⌖M 🛈 💷 ⇝ ⊠

(AAA) ▼▼▼▼ Sheraton Washington North Hotel ⊞ ❖

(301) 937-4422. **$89-$279.** 4095 Powder Mill Rd 20705. I-95, exit 29B, just w on SR 212; 2 mi n of I-495. Int corridors. **Pets:** Medium, dogs only. $50 one-time fee/room. Service with restrictions, supervision.
SAVE ⊠ ⌖M 🛈 💷 ⍨ ⇝

BETHESDA

▼▼▼▼ Residence Inn by Marriott-Bethesda Downtown ⊞

(301) 718-0200. **$249-$309.** 7335 Wisconsin Ave 20814. I-495, exit 34, 2.5 mi s on SR 355; entrance on Waverly St. Int corridors.
Pets: Accepted. ⊠ 🛈 💷 ⇝

BOWIE

(AAA) ▼▼▼▼ Comfort Inn Hotel & Conference Center-Bowie ⊞

(301) 464-0089. **$106-$135.** 4500 NW Crain Hwy 20716. US 50, exit 13A, jct US 50/301 and SR 3. Int corridors. **Pets:** Medium, other species. $15 daily fee/pet. Designated rooms, service with restrictions, crate.
SAVE ⊠ ⌖M 🛈 💷 ⍨ ⇝ ⊠

(AAA) ▼▼▼▼ Hampton Inn-Bowie ⊞

(301) 809-1800. **$109-$179.** 15202 Major Lansdale Blvd 20716. US 50, exit 11, 0.4 mi s on SR 197. Int corridors. **Pets:** Accepted.
SAVE ⊠ ⌖M 🛈 💷 ⇝

CAMP SPRINGS

(AAA) ▼▼▼ Quality Inn Camp Springs/Andrews Air Force Base ⊞ ❖

(301) 420-2800. **$75-$90.** 4783 Allentown Rd 20746. I-95/495, exit 9. Ext/int corridors. **Pets:** Other species. $25 one-time fee/pet. Designated rooms. SAVE ⊠ 🛈 💷

CLINTON

▼▼▼ TownePlace Suites by Marriott Clinton/Andrews AFB ⊞ ❖

(301) 856-2266. **$148-$180.** 7800 Ferry Ave 20735. I-95/495, exit 7A, 2.9 mi s on SR 5, exit Coventry Way E, follow signs to Andrews AFB, 0.5 mi ne on Old Alex Ferry Rd; opposite The Virginia Gate entrance to Andrews AFB. Int corridors. **Pets:** Small. $100 one-time fee/pet. Service with restrictions, supervision. ⊠ ⌖M 🛈 💷 ⇝

COLLEGE PARK

▼▼▼ Super 8-College Park ⊞

(301) 474-0894. **$75-$95.** 9150 Baltimore Ave 20740. I-95/495, exit 25 northbound; exit 25B southbound, 0.9 mi s on US 1. Int corridors.
Pets: Accepted. A$K ⊠ 🛈 💷

GAITHERSBURG

(AAA) ▼▼▼▼ Comfort Inn Shady Grove ⊞ ❖

(301) 330-0023. **$79-$169.** 16216 Frederick Rd 20877. I-270, exit 8, 1 mi e on Shady Grove Rd at SR 355. Int corridors. **Pets:** Large, other species. $15 daily fee/pet. Service with restrictions, crate.
SAVE ⊠ 🛈 💷 ⇝ ⊠

▼▼▼ Extended Stay Deluxe-Washington, DC-Gaithersburg ⊞

(301) 963-3539. **$109-$189.** 201 Professional Dr 20879. I-270, exit 11, 0.4 mi e, then 0.9 mi n on SR 355. Int corridors. **Pets:** Other species. $25 daily fee/room. Designated rooms, service with restrictions, crate.
A$K ⊠ 🛈 💷

(AAA) ▼▼▼▼ Hilton Washington DC North/Gaithersburg ⊞ ❖

(301) 977-8900. **$99-$259.** 620 Perry Pkwy 20877. I-270, exit 11, then e. Int corridors. **Pets:** Medium. $50 one-time fee/room. Designated rooms, service with restrictions, crate. SAVE ⊠ 🛈 💷 ⍨ ⇝ ⊠

(AAA) ▼▼▼▼ Holiday Inn-Gaithersburg ⊞

(301) 948-8900. **$89-$229.** 2 Montgomery Village Ave 20879. I-270, exit 11, 0.3 mi e. Int corridors. **Pets:** Medium, other species. Service with restrictions, crate. SAVE ⊠ ⌖M 🛈 💷 ⍨ ⇝ ⊠

▼▼▼ Homestead Studio Suites Hotel-Washington DC-Gaithersburg-Rockville ⊞

(301) 987-9100. **$99-$189.** 2621 Research Blvd 20850. I-270, exit 8, just w, then just n. Int corridors. **Pets:** Other species. $25 daily fee/room. Designated rooms, service with restrictions, crate. A$K ⊠ ⌖M 🛈 💷

⬨ ▼▼▼ Hyatt Summerfield Suites Gaithersburg Ⓗ
(301) 527-6000. **$99-$219.** 200 Skidmore Blvd 20877. I-370, exit SR 355, just n to Westland Rd. Ext corridors. **Pets:** Medium. $200 one-time fee/room. Designated rooms, service with restrictions, supervision.

[SAVE] [✕] [&M] [🍴] [▣] [🛏] [✕]

▼▼▼ Residence Inn by Marriott-Gaithersburg Ⓗ
(301) 590-3003. **$215-$263.** 9721 Washingtonian Blvd 20878. I-270, exit 9B (I-370/Sam Eig Hwy), just w to Fields Rd, 0.8 mi se, then just ne. Int corridors. **Pets:** Accepted. [✕] [&M] [🍴] [▣] [🛏] [✕]

⬨ ▼▼ TownePlace Suites by
Marriott-Gaithersburg Ⓗ
(301) 590-2300. **$189-$249.** 212 Perry Pkwy 20877. I-270, exit 10 north-bound, just e; exit 11 southbound, just e on SR 124 to SR 355, 0.3 mi s, then 0.5 mi sw. Int corridors. **Pets:** Small, other species. $100 one-time fee/room. Service with restrictions, supervision.

[SAVE] [✕] [&M] [🍴] [▣] [🛏]

GERMANTOWN
▼▼ Extended StayAmerica-Washington,
DC-Germantown Ⓗ
(301) 540-9369. **$84-$144.** 12450 Milestone Center Dr 20876. I-270, exit 16, 0.6 mi e on SR 27 (Father Hurley Blvd), 0.7 mi n on Observation Dr, then just w. Int corridors. **Pets:** Other species. $25 daily fee/room. Designated rooms, service with restrictions, crate. [ASK] [✕] [&M] [🍴] [▣]

GREENBELT
⬨ ▼▼▼ Residence Inn by Marriott-Greenbelt Ⓗ
(301) 982-1600. **$199-$209.** 6320 Golden Triangle Dr 20770. I-95/495, exit 23, 0.5 mi sw of jct SR 201; off SR 193 (Greenbelt Rd), just n on Walker Dr. Int corridors. **Pets:** Accepted.

[SAVE] [✕] [&M] [🍴] [▣] [🛏] [✕]

LAUREL
⬨ ▼▼▼ Holiday Inn Laurel-West Ⓗ
(301) 776-5300. **$89-$169.** 15101 Sweitzer Ln 20707. I-95, exit 33B, just w on SR 198. Ext/int corridors. **Pets:** Accepted.

[SAVE] [✕] [&M] [🍴] [▣] [🍴] [🛏]

⬨ ▼▼▼ Quality Inn & Suites Laurel Ⓗ
(301) 725-8800. **$80-$95, 3 day notice.** 1 2nd St 20707. On US 1, 0.5 mi n of jct SR 198. Ext/int corridors. **Pets:** Small, other species. $35 one-time fee/room. Designated rooms, service with restrictions, supervision.

[SAVE] [✕] [🍴] [▣] [🛏]

NATIONAL HARBOR
⬨ ▼▼▼ aloft Washington National Harbor Ⓗ
(301) 749-9000. **$119-$299.** 156 Waterfront St 20745. I-95/495, exit 2A, 0.5 mi e. Int corridors. **Pets:** Accepted.

[SAVE] [✕] [&M] [🍴] [▣] [🛏] [✕]

▼▼▼ Residence Inn by Marriott National Harbor Ⓗ
(301) 749-4755. **$249-$299.** 192 Waterfront St 20745. I-95/495, exit 2A, 0.5 mi e. Int corridors. **Pets:** Accepted. [✕] [&M] [🍴] [▣] [🛏] [✕]

⬨ ▼▼▼ The Westin National Harbor Ⓗ ❀
(301) 567-3999. **Call for rates.** 171 Waterfront St 20745. I-95/495, exit 2A, just e. Int corridors. **Pets:** Medium, dogs only. No service.

[SAVE] [✕] [&M] [🍴] [▣] [🍴] [🛏] [✕]

ROCKVILLE
⬨ ▼▼▼ Best Western Rockville Hotel & Suites Ⓗ
(301) 424-4940. **$59-$129.** 1251 W Montgomery Ave 20850. I-270, exit 6B, just w on SR 28. Int corridors. **Pets:** Accepted.

[SAVE] [✕] [🍴] [▣] [🍴] [🛏]

⬨ ▼▼▼ Chase Suite Hotel Rockville Ⓗ
(301) 590-9880. **$79-$249.** 1380 Piccard Dr 20850. I-270, exit 8 (Shady Grove Rd), 0.3 mi s; 1 mi w of SR 355 via Redland Rd. Ext corridors. **Pets:** Accepted. [SAVE] [✕] [🍴] [▣] [🍴] [🛏] [✕]

⬨ ▼▼▼ Hilton Rockville Hotel & Executive Meeting
Center Ⓗ ❀
(301) 468-1100. **$99-$309.** 1750 Rockville Pike 20852. SR 355, 2 mi s of jct SR 28. Int corridors. **Pets:** Medium, other species. $75 one-time fee/room. Designated rooms, service with restrictions, crate.

[SAVE] [✕] [🍴] [▣] [🍴] [🛏]

⬨ ▼▼▼ Red Roof Inn-Rockville Ⓜ
(301) 987-0965. **$70-$145.** 16001 Shady Grove Rd 20850. I-270, exit 8 (Shady Grove Rd), 0.5 mi e. Ext corridors. **Pets:** Large. Service with restrictions, crate. [SAVE] [✕] [&M] [🍴]

▼▼ Sleep Inn-Rockville Ⓗ
(301) 948-8000. **$72-$109.** 2 Research Ct 20850. I-270, exit 8 (Shady Grove Rd), just sw. Int corridors. **Pets:** Accepted.

[ASK] [✕] [&M] [🍴] [▣]

SILVER SPRING
⬨ ▼▼▼ Hampton Inn Silver Springs Ⓗ
(301) 588-5887. **Call for rates.** 8728 Colesville Rd 20910. I-495, exit 30B, 1.5 mi s on US 29. Int corridors. **Pets:** Accepted.

[SAVE] [✕] [&M] [🍴] [▣] [🛏] [✕]

⬨ ▼▼▼ Homewood Suites by Hilton Silver
Spring Ⓗ
(301) 565-0005. **$129-$279.** 8728 Colesville Rd 20910. I-495, exit 30B, 1.5 mi s on US 29. Int corridors. **Pets:** Accepted.

[SAVE] [✕] [&M] [🍴] [▣] [🛏] [✕]

▼▼▼ Residence Inn by Marriott Silver Spring Ⓗ
(301) 572-2322. **$179-$209.** 12000 Plum Orchard Dr 20904. I-95, exit 29B, 1.2 mi w on SR 212, then 1 mi n on Cherry Hill Rd. Int corridors. **Pets:** Other species. $100 one-time fee/room. Service with restrictions, supervision. [✕] [&M] [🍴] [▣] [🛏] [✕]

UPPER MARLBORO
⬨ ▼▼ Executive Inn & Suites Ⓜ
(301) 627-3969. **$70-$120.** 2901 Crain Hwy 20774. On US 301, 2.5 mi n of jct SR 4; 7 mi s of jct US 50. Ext corridors. **Pets:** $5 daily fee/pet. Service with restrictions, supervision. [SAVE] [✕] [&M] [🍴] [▣]

END METROPOLITAN AREA

ELKTON
⬨ ▼▼▼ Hawthorn Suites Ⓗ
(410) 620-9494. **Call for rates.** 304 Belle Hill Rd 21921. I-95, exit 109A, just e. Int corridors. **Pets:** Accepted. [SAVE] [✕] [&M] [🍴] [▣] [🛏]

EMMITSBURG
⬨ ▼▼▼ Sleep Inn & Suites in Emmitsburg Ⓗ
(301) 447-0044. **$82-$160.** 501 Silo Hill Pkwy 21727. US 15, exit SR 140, just w, then just n on Silo Hill Pkwy. Int corridors. **Pets:** Other species. $25 daily fee/room. Designated rooms, service with restrictions, crate. [SAVE] [✕] [🍴] [▣] [🛏]

FREDERICK

⬙⬙⬙ Comfort Inn H
(301) 668-7272. **$90-$130.** 7300 Executive Way 21704. I-270, exit 31B, 0.9 mi sw on SR 85. Int corridors. **Pets:** Accepted.
SAVE ✕ &M 🔒 🖥

⬙ Extended StayAmerica-Frederick-Westview Dr M
(301) 668-0808. **$99-$149.** 5240 Westview Dr 21703. I-270, exit 31B, 0.5 mi sw on SR 85, then 0.4 mi n. Int corridors. **Pets:** Other species. $25 daily fee/room. Designated rooms, service with restrictions, crate.
ASK ✕ 🔒 🖥

⬙⬙⬙ Frederick Residence Inn by Marriott H ❀
(301) 360-0010. **$161-$197.** 5230 Westview Dr 21703. I-270, exit 31B, 0.5 mi sw on SR 85, then 0.3 mi n on Crestwood Blvd. Int corridors. **Pets:** Medium. $100 one-time fee/room. Service with restrictions, supervision. ✕ 🔒 🖥 🐾 ⊠

⬙⬙⬙ Hampton Inn H
(301) 698-2500. **$109-$149.** 5311 Buckeystown Pike (SR 85) 21704. I-270, exit 31B, 0.6 mi w. Int corridors. **Pets:** Accepted.
SAVE ✕ 🔒 🖥 ⫴ 🐾

⬙⬙⬙ Holiday Inn & Conference Center H
(301) 694-7500. **$129-$179.** 5400 Holiday Dr 21703. I-270, exit 31A, just se of SR 85. Int corridors. **Pets:** Accepted.
ASK ✕ 🔒 🖥 ⫴ 🐾 ⊠

⬙⬙⬙ Holiday Inn Express-FSK Mall M
(301) 695-2881. **Call for rates.** 5579 Spectrum Dr 21703. I-270, exit 31A, just e on SR 85. Int corridors. **Pets:** Accepted. ✕ 🔒 🖥

⬙⬙⬙ MainStay Suites H
(301) 668-4600. **$90-$110, 7 day notice.** 7310 Executive Way 21704. I-270, exit 31B, 0.7 mi sw on SR 85. Int corridors. **Pets:** Accepted.
SAVE ✕ 🔒 🖥 🐾

⬙⬙⬙ Travelodge Frederick H
(301) 663-0500. **$70-$90.** 200 E Walser Dr 21704. I-70, exit 54, just n. Int corridors. **Pets:** Accepted. SAVE ✕ 🔒 🖥

FROSTBURG

⬙⬙ Days Inn & Suites M
(301) 689-2050. **Call for rates.** 11100 New Georges Creek Rd 21532. I-68, exit 34, 1 mi n on SR 36. Int corridors. **Pets:** Medium. $20 one-time fee/pet. Service with restrictions, supervision. SAVE ✕ 🔒 🖥 ⊠

GRANTSVILLE

⬙⬙⬙ The Stonebow Inn BB ❀
(301) 895-4250. **$160-$200, 7 day notice.** 146 Casselman Rd 21536. I-68, exit 22 westbound, 0.5 mi n on US 219, then 2.1 mi w on US 40; exit 19 eastbound, just n, then 0.9 mi e on US 40; behind Penn Alps Restaurant. Ext/int corridors. **Pets:** Designated rooms, crate.
SAVE ✕ 🔒 🖥 ⊠

GRASONVILLE

⬙⬙ Best Western Kent Narrows Inn M ❀
(410) 827-6767. **$79-$219.** 3101 Main St 21638. US 50 and 301, exit 42; at Kent Narrows Bridge. Ext corridors. **Pets:** Medium, other species. $10 daily fee/pet. Designated rooms, service with restrictions, supervision.
SAVE ✕ 🔒 🖥 ⊠

HAGERSTOWN

⬙⬙⬙ Hagerstown Hotel & Convention Center H
(301) 790-3010. **$55-$95.** 1910 Dual Hwy 21740. I-70, exit 32B, 0.5 mi n. Int corridors. **Pets:** Accepted. ASK ✕ 🔒 🖥 ⫴ 🐾

⬙⬙ Halfway Hagerstown Super 8 M
(301) 582-1992. **$63-$71.** 16805 Blake Rd 21740. I-81, exit 5B, just w. Int corridors. **Pets:** Medium, dogs only. $10 daily fee/pet. Service with restrictions, supervision. ASK ✕ 🔒 🖥

⬙⬙⬙ Sleep Inn & Suites H ❀
(301) 766-9449. **$72-$81.** 18216 Col Henry K Douglas Dr 21740. I-70, exit 29, just s. Int corridors. **Pets:** Other species. $10 daily fee/pet. Designated rooms, service with restrictions, supervision.
SAVE ✕ 🔒 🖥 🐾

INDIAN HEAD

⬙⬙ Super 8 M
(301) 753-8100. **$66-$96.** 4694 Indian Head Hwy 20640. SR 210, 0.6 mi s of jct SR 225. Int corridors. **Pets:** Medium, dogs only. $10 daily fee/pet. Service with restrictions, supervision. SAVE ✕ &M 🔒 🖥

LA VALE

⬙⬙⬙ Best Western Braddock Motor Inn H
(301) 729-3300. **$70-$151.** 1268 National Hwy 21502. On US 40, jct SR 53, adjacent to I-68, exit 39W/40E. Int corridors. **Pets:** Medium, other species. $25 deposit/room, $25 one-time fee/room. Designated rooms, supervision. SAVE ✕ 🔒 🖥 ⫴ 🐾 ⊠

⬙⬙⬙ Red Roof Inn M
(301) 729-6700. **Call for rates.** 12310 Winchester Rd SW 21502. I-68, exit 40, 0.6 mi s. Ext/int corridors. **Pets:** Large. Service with restrictions, crate. SAVE ✕ 🔒

⬙⬙ Super 8 M
(301) 729-6265. **$55-$130.** 1301 National Hwy 21502. I-68, exit 40, 0.4 mi n. Int corridors. **Pets:** Medium, other species. $10 daily fee/pet. Service with restrictions, supervision. SAVE ✕ 🔒 🖥

LEXINGTON PARK

⬙⬙ La Quinta Inn & Suites Lexington Park H 🐾
(301) 862-4100. 22769 Three Notch Rd 20653. 3.2 mi n on SR 235. Int corridors. **Pets:** Medium, other species. Service with restrictions, supervision. ASK ✕ 🔒 🖥 🐾

MCHENRY

⬙⬙⬙ Wisp Resort Hotel & Conference Center H
(301) 387-5581. **$59-$369, 14 day notice.** 290 Marsh Hill Rd 21541. 1 mi s on US 219 from jct SR 42, just w on Sang Run Rd, then 0.3 mi s. Int corridors. **Pets:** Medium, dogs only. $50 one-time fee/room. Designated rooms, service with restrictions, crate.
ASK ✕ 🔒 🖥 ⫴ 🐾 ⊠

NORTH EAST

⬙⬙⬙ Comfort Inn & Suites North East H ❀
(410) 287-7100. **$80-$129.** 1 Center Dr 21901. I-95, exit 100 southbound; exit 100A northbound, just e on SR 272. Int corridors. **Pets:** Small, dogs only. $15 daily fee/pet. Designated rooms, service with restrictions, supervision. SAVE ✕ 🔒 🖥 🐾

OCEAN CITY

⬙⬙⬙ Clarion Resort Fontainebleau Hotel H
(410) 524-3535. **$79-$379, 3 day notice.** 10100 Coastal Hwy 21842. At 101st St. Int corridors. **Pets:** Accepted.
SAVE ✕ 🔒 🖥 ⫴ 🐾 ⊠

⬙⬙⬙ Comfort Suites Ocean City H ❀
(410) 213-7171. **$69-$500.** 12718 Ocean Gateway 21842. US 50; 0.7 mi w of Ocean City Bridge. Int corridors. **Pets:** Other species. $35 daily fee/pet. Designated rooms, supervision. ASK ✕ &M 🔒 🖥 🐾 ⊠

PERRYVILLE

⬙⬙ Ramada Perryville M ❀
(410) 642-2866. **$70-$119.** 61 Heather Ln 21903. I-95, exit 93, just e. Ext corridors. **Pets:** Medium, other species. $20 daily fee/room. Service with restrictions, supervision. SAVE ✕ 🔒 🖥

POCOMOKE CITY

⬙⬙⬙ Holiday Inn Express-Pocomoke H
(410) 957-6444. **Call for rates.** 125 Newtowne Blvd 21851. On SR 756 at US 13, 0.8 mi nw on US 13 from jct US 113. Int corridors. **Pets:** Small. $75 daily fee/pet. Service with restrictions, supervision.
✕ &M 🔒 🖥 🐾

PRINCE FREDERICK

▼▼▼ Super 8-Prince Frederick 🅷

(410) 535-8668. **Call for rates.** 40 Commerce Ln 20678. Off SR 2/4, just s of jct SR 402. Int corridors. **Pets:** Accepted. ⊠ 🛢 💻

ROCK HALL

▼▼▼▼ Inn at Huntingfield Creek 🅱🅱

(410) 639-7779. **$145-$275, 14 day notice.** 4928 Eastern Neck Rd 21661. 1.8 mi s on SR 445 from jct SR 20. Ext/int corridors. **Pets:** $30 daily fee/room. Designated rooms, service with restrictions, crate.

A$K ⊠ 🛢 💻 ⇌ ⊠ 🇿

▼▼ Mariners Motel 🅼 ✿

(410) 639-2291. **Call for rates.** 5681 S Hawthorne Ave 21661. 0.3 mi e of SR 20. Ext corridors. **Pets:** Other species. $10 one-time fee/pet. Service with restrictions, supervision. ⊠ 🛢 💻 ⇌

ST. MICHAELS

▼▼ The Parsonage Inn 🅱🅱

(410) 745-8383. **$110-$215, 10 day notice.** 210 N Talbot St 21663. 0.3 mi w on SR 33. Ext/int corridors. **Pets:** Accepted. ⊠ 🇿

SALISBURY

🔷🔷 ▼▼ 🔷 Best Western Salisbury Plaza 🅼

(410) 546-1300. **$69-$135.** 1735 N Salisbury Blvd 21801. US 13 business route, 0.5 mi s of US 50 Bypass. Ext corridors. **Pets:** Other species. $10 daily fee/room. Service with restrictions, crate.

SAVE ⊠ 🛢 💻 ⇌

🔷🔷 ▼▼ Comfort Inn Salisbury 🅷

(410) 543-4666. **Call for rates.** 2701 N Salisbury Blvd 21801. US 13, 0.5 mi n of jct US 13 business route and Bypass. Int corridors. **Pets:** Other species. No service. SAVE ⊠ 🛢 💻

▼▼ Ramada Inn 🅷

(410) 546-4400. **$99-$250.** 300 S Salisbury Blvd 21801. US 13 business route, 0.4 mi s of jct US 50 business route; downtown. Int corridors. **Pets:** Accepted. A$K ⊠ 🛢 💻 🍽 ⇌

▼▼▼ Residence Inn by Marriott Salisbury 🅷 ✿

(410) 543-0033. **$119-$129.** 140 Centre Rd 21801. Just off US 13 business route at US 50. Int corridors. **Pets:** Other species. $100 one-time fee/room. Service with restrictions, crate. ⊠ 🅜 🛢 💻 ⇌ ⊠

SNOW HILL

🔷🔷 ▼▼▼▼ River House Inn 🅱🅱 ✿

(410) 632-2722. **$95-$300, 7 day notice.** 201 E Market St 21863. 1 mi w on SR 394 from jct SR 113. Ext/int corridors. **Pets:** Dogs only. $10 daily fee/pet. Designated rooms, crate. SAVE ⊠ 🛢 💻 ⇌ 🇿

THURMONT

🔷🔷 ▼▼▼ Cozy Country Inn 🅲🅸 ✿

(301) 271-4301. **$72-$175.** 103 Frederick Rd 21788. US 15, just e to SR 806, 0.4 mi n. Ext corridors. **Pets:** Dogs only. $25 one-time fee/room. Designated rooms, service with restrictions, supervision.

SAVE ⊠ 🛢 💻 🍽

▼▼ Super 8-Thurmont 🅼

(301) 271-7888. **$65-$83.** 300 Tippin Dr 21788. US 15, just w on SR 806. Int corridors. **Pets:** Small, other species. $10 daily fee/pet. Service with restrictions, supervision. A$K ⊠ 🛢 💻

WALDORF

▼▼▼ La Quinta Inn Waldorf 🅷 ✿

(301) 645-0022. **$69-$99.** 11770 Business Park Dr 20601. 1 mi n on US 301 from jct SR 228. Int corridors. **Pets:** Medium, other species. Service with restrictions, supervision. A$K ⊠ 🛢 💻

WILLIAMSPORT

🔷🔷 ▼▼ Red Roof Inn 🅼

(301) 582-3500. **$55-$90.** 310 E Potomac St 21795. I-81, exit 2, 0.3 mi sw on US 11. Ext corridors. **Pets:** Large. Service with restrictions, crate.

SAVE ⊠ 🛢

MASSACHUSETTS

AMHERST

◆ University Lodge Ⓜ
(413) 256-8111. **$59-$159.** 345 N Pleasant St 01002. 0.6 mi n. Ext corridors. **Pets:** Medium. $20 daily fee/pet. Designated rooms, service with restrictions, supervision. [ASK] [✕] [🖬] [▣]

AUBURN

◆◆ Comfort Inn Ⓗ
(508) 832-8300. **$69-$139.** 426 Southbridge St 01501. I-90, exit 10, 1 mi n on SR 12; I-290, exit 9 to SR 12. Int corridors. **Pets:** Large. $20 daily fee/room. Designated rooms, service with restrictions, supervision.
[ASK] [✕] [🖬M] [🖬] [▣]

◆◆ La Quinta Inn Ⓗ 🐾
(508) 832-7000. **$65-$129.** 446 Southbridge St 01501. I-90, exit 10, 1.2 mi n on SR 12. Int corridors. **Pets:** Medium, other species. Service with restrictions, supervision. [ASK] [✕] [🖬] [▣]

BARRE

◆◆◆ Jenkins Inn ⒸⒾ
(978) 355-6444. **$180-$260, 7 day notice.** 7 West St 01005. On SR 122 and 32. Int corridors. **Pets:** Dogs only. $5 daily fee/pet. Service with restrictions, supervision. [✕] [🖬] [▣] [🍴]

BOSTON METROPOLITAN AREA

ANDOVER

◈◈◈ ◆◆◆◆ Homewood Suites by Hilton Ⓗ
(978) 475-6000. **$79-$399.** 4 Riverside Dr 01810. I-93, exit 45, 0.5 mi e. Int corridors. **Pets:** Medium, other species. $75 one-time fee/room. Service with restrictions. [SAVE] [✕] [🖬M] [🖬] [▣] [🢒] [🢒]

◆◆◆◆ La Quinta Inn & Suites Ⓗ 🐾
(978) 685-6200. **$79-$119.** 131 River Rd 01810. I-93, exit 45, just w; I-495, exit 40B, 2 mi n. Int corridors. **Pets:** Medium, other species. Service with restrictions, supervision. [ASK] [✕] [🖬] [▣] [🢒]

◆◆◆◆ Residence Inn by Marriott Boston-Andover Ⓗ
(978) 683-0382. **$139-$159.** 500 Minuteman Rd 01810. I-93, exit 45, 0.3 mi w, then 0.5 mi n. Int corridors. **Pets:** Accepted.
[✕] [🖬M] [🖬] [▣] [🢒] [🢒]

◆◆◆◆ Staybridge Suites Boston/Andover Ⓗ
(978) 686-2000. **$110-$140.** 4 Tech Dr 01810. I-93, exit 45, just sw via Shattuck Rd. Int corridors. **Pets:** Accepted.
[ASK] [✕] [🖬M] [🖬] [▣] [🢒]

◈◈◈ ◆◆◆◆ Wyndham Boston/Andover Hotel Ⓗ
(978) 975-3600. **$109-$199.** 123 Old River Rd 01810. I-93, exit 45, just e on River Rd. Int corridors. **Pets:** Small, dogs only. $50 one-time fee/pet. Service with restrictions, crate. [SAVE] [✕] [🖬] [▣] [🍴] [🢒]

ARLINGTON

◈◈◈ ◆◆◆◆ Homewood Suites by Hilton-Cambridge/Arlington Ⓗ 🐾
(781) 643-7258. **$199-$299.** 1 Massachusetts Ave 02474. On SR 2A, just n of SR 16. Int corridors. **Pets:** Small, other species. $75 one-time fee/room. Service with restrictions. [SAVE] [✕] [🖬M] [🖬] [▣]

BEDFORD

◈◈◈ ◆◆◆◆ Doubletree Hotel Bedford Glen Ⓗ
(781) 275-5500. **$99-$239.** 44 Middlesex Tpke 01730. I-95, exit 32B, 2.5 mi n. Int corridors. **Pets:** Accepted.
[SAVE] [✕] [🖬M] [🖬] [▣] [🍴] [🢒] [🢒]

BILLERICA

◆◆◆◆ Homewood Suites by Hilton Ⓗ
(978) 670-7111. **$109-$199.** 35 Middlesex Tpke 01821. I-95, exit 32B, 2.5 mi n. Int corridors. **Pets:** Accepted. [✕] [🖬M] [🖬] [▣] [🢒]

BOSTON

◈◈◈ ◆◆◆◆ Best Western Roundhouse Suites Ⓗ
(617) 989-1000. **$139-$239.** 891 Massachusetts Ave 02118. I-93, exit 18, just sw; just n of Newmarket Square. Int corridors. **Pets:** Accepted.
[SAVE] [✕] [🖬M] [🖬] [▣]

◈◈◈ ◆◆◆◆ Boston Harbor Hotel Ⓗ
(617) 439-7000. **$285-$645.** 70 Rowes Wharf 02110. At Rowes Wharf. Int corridors. **Pets:** Accepted. [SAVE] [✕] [🍴] [🢒] [🢒]

◈◈◈ ◆◆◆◆ Boston Omni Parker House Hotel Ⓗ
(617) 227-8600. **$159-$599.** 60 School St 02108. Corner of Tremont and School sts; northeast corner of Boston Common. Int corridors.
Pets: Accepted. [SAVE] [✕] [▣] [🍴]

◈◈◈ ◆◆◆◆ The Boston Park Plaza Hotel & Towers Ⓗ
(617) 426-2000. **$129-$369.** 50 Park Plaza at Arlington St 02116. Just s of Boston Common and Public Gardens. Int corridors. **Pets:** Accepted.
[SAVE] [✕] [🖬] [🍴]

◆◆◆◆ Bulfinch Hotel Ⓗ
(617) 624-0202. **$159-$359.** 107 Merrimac St 02114. At Lancaster St. Int corridors. **Pets:** Accepted. [ASK] [✕] [▣] [🍴]

▼▼▼ The Colonnade Hotel Boston H
(617) 424-7000. $189-$429. 120 Huntington Ave 02116. Just s of Copley Square. Int corridors. Pets: Accepted. ASK ⊠ 🖵 ⑪ ⌦

▼▼▼ Comfort Inn Boston H
(617) 287-9200. $99-$179. 900 William T Morrissey Blvd 02122. I-93, exit 13 northbound, 0.5 mi sw; exit 12 southbound, follow signs. Int corridors. Pets: Other species. Service with restrictions, supervision.
ASK ⊠ 🖥 🖵

AAA ▼▼▼ Copley Square Hotel H ❀
(617) 536-9000. $199-$599. 47 Huntington Ave 02116. I-90, exit 22, just n. Int corridors. Pets: Small. $40 one-time fee/pet. Designated rooms, service with restrictions, supervision. SAVE ⊠ ⑪

AAA ▼▼▼ Doubletree Guest
Suites-Boston/Cambridge H
(617) 783-0090. $109-$409. 400 Soldiers Field Rd 02134. I-90, exit 20 westbound; exit 18 eastbound. Int corridors. Pets: Accepted.
SAVE ⊠ 🖥 🖵 ⑪ ⌦

AAA ▼▼ ▼▼ The Eliot Hotel H ❀
(617) 267-1607. $355-$645. 370 Commonwealth Ave 02215. At Massachusetts Ave. Int corridors. Pets: Large. Designated rooms, service with restrictions, crate. SAVE ⊠ ⑪

AAA ▼▼ ▼▼ Fairmont Battery Wharf H ❀
(617) 994-9000. $209-$579. Three Battery Wharf 02109. At Battery Wharf, e of north end. Int corridors. Pets: Small, other species. $25 daily fee/pet. Service with restrictions, supervision. SAVE ⊠ 🖲M 🖵 ⑪

AAA ▼▼ ▼▼ The Fairmont Copley Plaza Boston H
(617) 267-5300. $209-$579. 138 St. James Ave 02116. At Copley Square. Int corridors. Pets: Accepted.
ECO SAVE ⊠ 🖲M 🖥 🖵 ⑪

▼▼ ▼▼ Fifteen Beacon H ❀
(617) 670-1500. $250-$1400. 15 Beacon St 02108. Just e of State House; just ne of Boston Common; center. Int corridors. Pets: Dogs only. $25 one-time fee/room. Designated rooms, service with restrictions, supervision. ASK ⊠ ⑪

AAA ▼▼▼▼ Four Seasons Hotel Boston H
(617) 338-4400. $450-$700. 200 Boylston St 02116. Between Arlington and Charles sts. Int corridors. Pets: Accepted.
SAVE ⊠ 🖲M ⑪ ⌦ ⊠

AAA ▼▼ ▼▼ Hilton Boston Back Bay H ❀
(617) 867-6000. $179-$639. 40 Dalton St 02115. At Dalton and Belvidere sts. Int corridors. Pets: Large. $75 one-time fee/room. Service with restrictions. SAVE ⊠ 🖥 🖵 ⑪ ⌦

AAA ▼▼ ▼▼ Hilton Boston Financial District H
(617) 556-0006. $119-$479. 89 Broad St 02110. Corner of Broad and Franklin sts. Int corridors. Pets: Accepted. SAVE ⊠ 🖲M 🖵 ⑪

AAA ▼▼▼ Hilton Boston Logan Airport H ❀
(617) 568-6700. $169-$639. 1 Hotel Dr 02128. At General Edward Lawrence Logan International Airport. Int corridors. Pets: Large, other species. $25 one-time fee/pet. Service with restrictions, crate.
SAVE ⊠ 🖲M 🖥 🖵 ⑪ ⌦ ⊠

AAA ▼▼▼ Hotel Commonwealth H
(617) 933-5000. $209-$498. 500 Commonwealth Ave 02215. On SR 2; at Beacon St and Brookline Ave. Int corridors. Pets: Accepted.
SAVE ⊠ 🖲M 🖥 ⑪

▼▼ Howard Johnson Hotel Fenway M
(617) 267-8300. $89-$239. 1271 Boylston St 02215. I-90, exit Brookline Ave S, backing onto Fenway Park. Int corridors. Pets: Accepted.
ASK ⊠ 🖥 🖵 ⑪ ⌦

AAA ▼▼ ▼▼ Hyatt Regency Boston H
(617) 912-1234. $159-$599. 1 Ave De Lafayette 02111. Just e of Boston Common at Lafayette Pl. Int corridors. Pets: Medium. Designated rooms, service with restrictions, supervision.
SAVE ⊠ 🖲M 🖵 ⑪ ⌦ ⊠

AAA ▼▼ ▼▼ InterContinental Boston H
(617) 747-1000. $249-$599. 510 Atlantic Ave 02210. I-93, exit 23 southbound; exit 20 northbound; at Pearl St. Int corridors. Pets: Small. $150 one-time fee/room. Designated rooms, service with restrictions, supervision. SAVE ⊠ 🖲M ⑪ ⌦ ⊠

AAA ▼▼ ▼▼ The Langham, Boston H ❀
(617) 451-1900. $195-$535. 250 Franklin St 02110. On Post Office Square; center. Int corridors. Pets: Medium. $100 one-time fee/pet. Service with restrictions, supervision. SAVE ⊠ 🖵 ⑪ ⌦ ⊠

AAA ▼▼ ▼▼ The Lenox Hotel H
(617) 536-5300. $195-$465. 61 Exeter St 02116. I-90, exit 22, just n at Boylston. Int corridors. Pets: Accepted. SAVE ⊠ 🖥 🖵 ⑪

AAA ▼▼ ▼▼ The Liberty Hotel H ❀
(617) 224-4000. $295-$650. 215 Charles St 02114. I-93, exit 26 (Storrow Dr). Int corridors. Pets: Medium, other species. $100 one-time fee/room. Designated rooms, service with restrictions, supervision.
SAVE ⊠ 🖲M ⑪

AAA ▼▼◆▼▼ Mandarin Oriental, Boston H ❀
(617) 535-8888. $345-$995. 776 Boylston St 02199. At Prudential Center. Int corridors. Pets: Medium, other species. SAVE ⊠ 🖲M 🖥 ⑪

AAA ▼▼ ▼▼ The Midtown Hotel H ❀
(617) 262-1000. $99-$309. 220 Huntington Ave 02115. 3 blks sw of Copley Pl; just n of Symphony Hall and Massachusetts Ave. Int corridors. Pets: Medium, other species. $30 one-time fee/pet. Service with restrictions, crate. SAVE ⊠ 🖥 🖵 ⑪ ⌦

AAA ▼▼ ▼▼ Nine Zero Hotel H ❀
(617) 772-5800. $229-$599. 90 Tremont St 02108. Just ne of Boston Common; motor entrance on Bosworth. Int corridors. Pets: Other species. Designated rooms. SAVE ⊠ 🖲M 🖵 ⑪

AAA ▼▼ ▼▼ Onyx Hotel H ❀
(617) 557-9955. $159-$719. 155 Portland St 02114. Just n of corner of Merrimac and Traverse sts; 3 blks s of TD Bank North Garden. Int corridors. Pets: Other species. Designated rooms, service with restrictions, supervision. SAVE ⊠ ⑪

▼▼ ▼▼ Ramada Boston H
(617) 287-9100. $109-$189. 800 William T Morrissey Blvd 02122. I-93, exit 13 northbound, 0.5 mi sw; exit 12 southbound, follow signs. Int corridors. Pets: Other species. Service with restrictions, supervision.
ASK ⊠ 🖥 🖵 ⌦

AAA ▼▼ ▼▼ Residence Inn by Marriott Boston Harbor on
Tudor Wharf H
(617) 242-9000. $229-$349. 34-44 Charles River Ave 02129. Just se of SR 99 at Charlestown Bridge. Int corridors. Pets: Accepted.
SAVE ⊠ 🖲M 🖥 🖵 ⑪ ⌦

▼▼ ▼▼ The Ritz-Carlton, Boston Common H
(617) 574-7100. $395-$795. 10 Avery St 02111. At Washington and Avery sts; 1 blk e of Boston Common. Int corridors. Pets: Accepted.
ASK ⊠ 🖲M 🖵 ⑪ ⌦ ⊠

AAA ▼▼ ▼▼ The Seaport Hotel and Seaport World
Trade Center H
(617) 385-4000. $179-$499. 1 Seaport Ln 02210. MBTA-Silverline, World Trade Center Shop. Int corridors. Pets: Accepted.
SAVE ⊠ 🖲M 🖥 🖵 ⑪ ⌦ ⊠

AAA ▼▼▼ Sheraton Boston H
(617) 236-2000. $169-$599. 39 Dalton St 02199. I-90, exit 22. Int corridors. Pets: Accepted. ECO SAVE ⊠ 🖲M 🖵 ⑪ ⌦ ⊠

Taj Boston H
(617) 536-5700. **Call for rates.** 15 Arlington St 02117. At Arlington and Newbury sts; overlooks the Public Gardens. Int corridors. **Pets:** Accepted.
SAVE ✕ ❙❙ ✕

Westin Boston Waterfront H
(617) 532-4600. **$169-$599.** 425 Summer St 02210. I-93, exit 23, se via Purchase St to Summer St. Int corridors. **Pets:** Accepted.
SAVE ✕ ▣ ❙❙ ➦

The Westin Copley Place Boston H ❀
(617) 262-9600. **$179-$569.** 10 Huntington Ave 02116. I-90, exit 22, at Copley Square. Int corridors. **Pets:** Medium. Designated rooms, service with restrictions, supervision. SAVE ✕ ▣ ❙❙ ➦ ✕

BOXBOROUGH

Holiday Inn Boxborough Woods H
(978) 263-8701. **$99-$169.** 242 Adams Pl 01719. I-495, exit 28, just e on SR 111. Int corridors. **Pets:** $100 deposit/room, $25 one-time fee/room. Service with restrictions, supervision. ASK ✕ ❙ ▣ ❙❙ ➦

BRAINTREE

Candlewood Suites Boston–Braintree H
(781) 849-7450. **$89-$129.** 235 Wood Rd 02184. I-93, exit 6, just n on SR 37, then 0.5 mi w. Int corridors. **Pets:** Accepted. ASK ✕ ❙ ▣

Extended StayAmerica Boston-Braintree H
(781) 356-8333. **$70-$104.** 20 Rockdale St 02184. I-93, exit 6, just se. Int corridors. **Pets:** Other species. $25 daily fee/room. Designated rooms, service with restrictions, crate. ASK ✕ ❙M ❙ ▣

Hampton Inn Braintree H ❀
(781) 380-3300. **$109-$209.** 215 Wood Rd 02184. I-93, exit 6, just n on SR 37, then 0.5 mi w. Int corridors. **Pets:** Medium. Service with restrictions, supervision. SAVE ✕ ❙M ❙ ▣ ➦

Sheraton Braintree Hotel H ❀
(781) 848-0600. **$79-$389.** 37 Forbes Rd 02184. I-93, exit 6, just s on SR 37, then just w. Int corridors. **Pets:** Medium, dogs only. Service with restrictions, crate. ✕ ❙ ▣ ❙❙ ➦

BROOKLINE

Holiday Inn Boston-Brookline H
(617) 277-1200. **$159-$239.** 1200 Beacon St 02446. 1 mi sw of Kenmore Square; at Beacon and St. Paul sts. Int corridors. **Pets:** Small, dogs only. $15 daily fee/pet. Designated rooms, service with restrictions, supervision. ASK ✕ ❙M ❙ ▣ ❙❙ ➦

BURLINGTON

Candlewood Suites Boston-Burlington H ❀
(781) 229-4300. **$59-$90.** 130 Middlesex Tpke 01803. I-95, exit 32B, just n. Int corridors. **Pets:** Medium, other species. $75 one-time fee/room. Service with restrictions, supervision. ASK ✕ ❙M ❙ ▣

Hyatt Summerfield Suites Boston/Burlington H
(781) 270-0800. **$89-$249.** 2 Van de Graaff Dr 01803. I-95, exit 33A, just s on SR 3, then 0.5 mi w on Wayside Rd. Int corridors. **Pets:** Accepted.
SAVE ✕ ❙M ❙ ▣ ➦ ✕

CAMBRIDGE

Best Western Hotel Tria H ❀
(617) 491-8000. **$129-$299.** 220 Alewife Brook Pkwy 02138. Jct SR 2, 16 and US 3; in North Cambridge; I-90 (Massachusetts Tpke), exit Cambridge/Allston to SR 2 W (Fresh Pond Pkwy). Int corridors. **Pets:** Other species. $25 daily fee/room. Service with restrictions, crate.
SAVE ✕ ❙ ▣ ❙❙ ➦

The Charles Hotel, Harvard Square H
(617) 864-1200. **$199-$750.** One Bennett St 02138. Just s of Harvard Square, at Eliot St. Int corridors. **Pets:** Accepted.
SAVE ✕ ❙M ❙ ❙❙ ➦ ✕

Hotel Marlowe H ❀
(617) 868-8000. **$169-$1800.** 25 Edwin H Land Blvd 02141. Just sw of jct SR 28. Int corridors. **Pets:** Other species. Designated rooms.
ECO SAVE ✕ ❙M ❙❙ ✕

Hyatt Regency Cambridge H
(617) 492-1234. **$99-$529.** 575 Memorial Dr 02139. On US 3 and SR 2. Int corridors. **Pets:** Accepted. SAVE ✕ ❙M ❙ ▣ ❙❙ ➦ ✕

The Inn at Harvard H
(617) 491-2222. **$139-$399.** 1201 Massachusetts Ave 02138. Jct Quincy, Bow and Harvard sts. Int corridors. **Pets:** Accepted.
ECO SAVE ✕ ❙M ❙ ❙❙

Le Meridien Cambridge H
(617) 577-0200. **$139-$499, 3 day notice.** 20 Sidney St 02139. On SR 2A, 1 mi n of river. Int corridors. **Pets:** Medium, dogs only. $150 deposit/room. Service with restrictions, supervision. SAVE ✕ ❙M ▣ ❙❙

Residence Inn Boston Cambridge Center H ❀
(617) 349-0700. **$219-$349.** 6 Cambridge Center 02142. Corner of Ames St and Broadway. Int corridors. **Pets:** Medium. $150 one-time fee/room. Service with restrictions. ✕ ❙M ❙ ▣ ➦

Sheraton Commander Hotel H
(617) 547-4800. **$129-$479.** 16 Garden St 02138. Just n of Harvard Square. Int corridors. **Pets:** Accepted. SAVE ✕ ❙ ▣ ❙❙

CONCORD

Best Western at Historic Concord H
(978) 369-6100. **$119-$199.** 740 Elm St 01742. 1.8 mi w, just off SR 2 and 2A. Int corridors. **Pets:** Other species. $10 daily fee/pet. Designated rooms, service with restrictions, supervision. SAVE ✕ ❙ ▣ ➦

The Hawthorne Inn BB
(978) 369-5610. **$145-$325, 14 day notice.** 462 Lexington Rd 01742. 0.8 mi e of town square. Int corridors. **Pets:** Small. $150 deposit/room. Designated rooms. ✕

DANVERS

Comfort Inn North Shore H
(978) 777-1700. **$69-$199.** 50 Dayton St 01923. Just w of US 1; 0.8 mi n of jct SR 114, exit Center St northbound, w under US 1; exit Dayton St southbound. Int corridors. **Pets:** Medium. $10 daily fee/pet, $25 one-time fee/room. Service with restrictions, supervision.
SAVE ✕ ❙M ❙ ▣ ➦

Crown Plaza Boston North Shore and Coco Key Water Resort H
(978) 777-2500. **Call for rates.** 50 Ferncroft Rd 01923. I-95, exit 50, follow signs for US 1 S to Ferncroft Village. Int corridors. **Pets:** Accepted.
SAVE ✕ ❙M ❙ ▣ ❙❙ ➦ ✕

Extended StayAmerica Boston-Danvers H
(978) 762-7414. **$55-$75.** 102 Newbury St 01923. On US 1 southbound. Int corridors. **Pets:** Other species. $25 daily fee/room. Designated rooms, service with restrictions, crate. ASK ✕ ❙M ❙ ▣

Residence Inn Boston-North Shore/Danvers H
(978) 777-7171. **$125-$149.** 51 Newbury St 01923. US 1 N, just s of jct SR 114. Ext corridors. **Pets:** Accepted. ✕ ❙ ▣ ➦ ✕

TownePlace Suites Boston-North Shore/Danvers H
(978) 777-6222. **$104-$124.** 238 Andover St 01923. Southwest corner of jct US 1 and SR 114; SR 114 eastbound, enter just w of US 1 (no westbound entrance); US 1 southbound, enter through shopping center. Int corridors. **Pets:** Accepted. ✕ ❙M ❙ ▣ ➦

DEDHAM

▼▼▼▼ Hilton Boston Dedham ▢ ❀
(781) 329-7900. **$109-$269.** 25 Allied Dr 02026. I-95, exit 14, just e. Int corridors. **Pets:** Medium, other species. $50 one-time fee/room. Service with restrictions, supervision. ⊠ 🛏 🖵 🍴 🏊 ⊠

▼▼▼▼ Residence Inn Boston Dedham ▢
(781) 407-0999. **$159-$189.** 259 Elm St 02026. I-95, exit 15A, just n, then 0.4 mi e. Int corridors. **Pets:** Large. $75 one-time fee/room. Service with restrictions. ⊠ 🛏 🖵 🏊 ⊠

FOXBORO

▼▼▼▼ Foxborough Residence Inn by Marriott ▢
(508) 698-2800. **$165-$169.** 250 Foxborough Blvd 02035. I-95, exit 7A, 0.6 mi s on SR 140, 0.7 mi e, then just n. Int corridors. **Pets:** Accepted.
⊠ ᴹ 🛏 🖵 🏊 ⊠

FRAMINGHAM

ⒶⒶⒶ ▼▼▼ Best Western Framingham ▢
(508) 872-8811. **$90-$130.** 130 Worcester Rd 01702. I-90, exit 13, 0.5 mi s to SR 9; 1 mi w of Speen St; just w of Shopper's World Mall. Int corridors. **Pets:** Medium. Designated rooms, service with restrictions, supervision. ⓈⒶⓋⒺ ⊠ 🛏 🖵 🍴 🏊

ⒶⒶⒶ ▼▼▼ Red Roof Inn #7068 Ⓜ
(508) 872-4499. **$59-$109.** 650 Cochituate Rd 01701. I-90, exit 13, follow SR 30 E. Ext corridors. **Pets:** Large. Service with restrictions, crate.
ⓈⒶⓋⒺ ⊠ 🛏 🖵

ⒶⒶⒶ ▼▼▼▼ Residence Inn Boston/Framingham ▢
(508) 370-0001. **$189-$209.** 400 Staples Dr 01702. SR 9 W to Crossing Blvd, then s. Int corridors. **Pets:** Accepted.
ⓈⒶⓋⒺ ⊠ ᴹ 🛏 🖵 🏊

ⒶⒶⒶ ▼▼▼▼ Sheraton Framingham Hotel & Conference Center ▢ ❀
(508) 879-7200. **$89-$235.** 1657 Worcester Rd 01701. I-90, exit 12, follow signs to SR 9 W. Int corridors. **Pets:** Medium, dogs only. Designated rooms, service with restrictions, supervision.
ⓈⒶⓋⒺ 🛏 🖵 🍴 🏊 ⊠

FRANKLIN

ⒶⒶⒶ ▼▼▼▼ Hawthorn Suites ▢
(508) 553-3500. **$89-$139.** 835 Upper Union St 02038. I-495, exit 16, just s, then 0.3 mi e. Int corridors. **Pets:** Accepted.
ⓈⒶⓋⒺ ⊠ ᴹ 🛏 🖵 ⊠

▼▼▼▼ Residence Inn Boston Franklin ▢ ❀
(508) 541-8188. **$160-$179.** 4 Forge Pkwy 02038. I-495, exit 17, 0.7 mi nw off SR 140 N. Int corridors. **Pets:** Medium, other species. $100 one-time fee/room. Designated rooms, service with restrictions, crate.
⊠ ᴹ 🛏 🖵 🏊 ⊠

GLOUCESTER

▼▼▼ Cape Ann Motor Inn Ⓜ ❀
(978) 281-2900. **$85-$185, 7 day notice.** 33 Rockport Rd 01930. 2 mi n of terminus of SR 128 via SR 127A. Ext corridors. **Pets:** Other species. Service with restrictions, supervision. ⊠ 🛏 🐾

HAVERHILL

ⒶⒶⒶ ▼▼▼▼ Best Western Merrimack Valley ▢
(978) 373-1511. **$74-$189.** 401 Lowell Ave 01832. I-495, exit 49 (SR 110). Int corridors. **Pets:** Other species. $20 daily fee/room. Designated rooms, service with restrictions, supervision. ⓈⒶⓋⒺ ⊠ 🛏 🖵 🏊

ⒶⒶⒶ ▼▼▼ Comfort Suites ▢
(978) 374-7755. **$60-$150.** 106 Bank Rd 01832. I-495, exit 49 (SR 110), 0.5 mi s. Int corridors. **Pets:** $10 daily fee/pet, $25 one-time fee/pet. Designated rooms, service with restrictions, supervision. ⓈⒶⓋⒺ ⊠ 🛏 🖵

LAWRENCE

ⒶⒶⒶ ▼▼▼▼ Holiday Inn Express ▢
(978) 975-4050. **$69-$129, 30 day notice.** 224 Winthrop Ave 01843. I-495, exit 42A, just s on SR 114. Int corridors. **Pets:** Accepted.
ⓈⒶⓋⒺ ⊠ ᴹ 🛏 🖵

LEXINGTON

ⒶⒶⒶ ▼▼▼▼ aloft Lexington ▢ ❀
(781) 761-1700. **$89-$399.** 727 Marrett Rd–A 02173. I-95, exit 30B, just w. Int corridors. **Pets:** Medium, other species. Service with restrictions.
ⓈⒶⓋⒺ ⊠ 🛏 🖵

ⒶⒶⒶ ▼▼▼▼ element Lexington ▢ ❀
(781) 761-1750. **$109-$429.** 727 Marrett Rd 02173. I-95, exit 30B. Int corridors. **Pets:** Medium, other species. Service with restrictions.
ⓈⒶⓋⒺ ⊠ 🛏 🖵 🏊

ⒶⒶⒶ ▼▼▼▼ Quality Inn & Suites ▢
(781) 861-0850. **$63-$90.** 440 Bedford St 02420. I-95, exit 31B, just n on SR 4 and 225, continue n and use jug handle to reverse direction. Ext corridors. **Pets:** Accepted. ⓈⒶⓋⒺ ⊠ ᴹ 🛏 🖵 🏊

LOWELL

▼▼▼▼ Doubletree Riverfront Hotel ▢
(978) 452-1200. **Call for rates.** 50 Warren St 01852. I-495, exit 35C, via Gorham and Church sts, follow signs; 0.5 mi from end of Lowell connector; center. Int corridors. **Pets:** Accepted. ⊠ 🛏 🖵 🍴 🏊 ⊠

MARLBOROUGH

ⒶⒶⒶ ▼▼▼ Best Western Royal Plaza Hotel & Trade Center ▢
(508) 460-0700. **$100-$140.** 181 Boston Post Rd W 01752. I-495, exit 24B, 1 mi w on US 20. Int corridors. **Pets:** Accepted.
ⓈⒶⓋⒺ ⊠ 🖵 🍴 🏊

▼▼▼▼ Courtyard Boston Marlborough ▢
(508) 480-0015. **$170-$208.** 75 Felton St 01752. I-495, exit 24B, just w; just off US 20. Int corridors. **Pets:** Accepted.
⊠ ᴹ 🛏 🖵 🍴 🏊

▼▼▼▼ Embassy Suites Hotel-Boston Marlborough ▢
(508) 485-5900. **$109-$199.** 123 Boston Post Rd W 01752. I-495, exit 24B, 0.5 mi w; just off US 20. Int corridors. **Pets:** Accepted.
⊠ ᴹ 🛏 🖵 🍴 🏊 ⊠

▼▼▼▼ Residence Inn By Marriott Boston Marlborough ▢
(508) 481-1500. **$170-$208.** 112 Donald Lynch Blvd 01752. I-290, exit 25B, 3 mi ne. Int corridors. **Pets:** Accepted.
⊠ ᴹ 🛏 🖵 🏊 ⊠

NATICK

▼▼▼▼ Crowne Plaza Boston-Natick ▢ ❀
(508) 653-8800. **$99-$209.** 1360 Worcester St 01760. I-90, exit 12, 5 mi e; SR 9, 4 mi e of Framingham Center. Int corridors. **Pets:** Medium. $50 one-time fee/pet. Designated rooms, service with restrictions, supervision.
ⒶⓈⓀ ⊠ ᴹ 🛏 🖵 🍴

NEEDHAM

ⒶⒶⒶ ▼▼▼▼ Sheraton Needham Hotel ▢
(781) 444-1110. **$99-$349.** 100 Cabot St 02494. I-95, exit 19A, just e. Int corridors. **Pets:** Accepted. ⓈⒶⓋⒺ ⊠ 🛏 🖵 🍴 🏊

NEWBURYPORT

▼▼▼▼ Garrison Inn ▢ ❀
(978) 499-8500. **$170-$320, 3 day notice.** 11 Brown Square 01950. I-95, exit 57, 2.6 mi e on SR 1A, just n on Green St, just w on Pleasant St, then just s. Int corridors. **Pets:** Other species. $20 daily fee/pet. Supervision. ⊠

NEWTON

Crowne Plaza Boston/Newton H
(617) 969-3010. **$99-$229.** 320 Washington St 02458. I-90, exit 17. Int corridors. **Pets:** Accepted. [SAVE] ⊗ ⊟ ▣ ⑪ ⊷

Hotel Indigo Boston-Newton Riverside H
(617) 969-5300. **$119-$259.** 399 Grove St 02462. I-95, exit 22, just e. Int corridors. **Pets:** Accepted. [SAVE] ⊗ ⊟ ▣ ⑪ ⊷

NORTH CHELMSFORD

Hawthorn Suites by Wyndham H
(978) 256-5151. **$90-$99.** 25 Research Pl 01863. US 3, exit 32, 0.3 mi ne on SR 4. Int corridors. **Pets:** Accepted. [SAVE] ⊗ &M ⊟ ▣

NORWOOD

Hampton Inn H
(781) 769-7000. **$99-$169.** 434 Providence Hwy 02062. I-95, exit 9 northbound, 5.9 mi ne on US 1; exit 11B southbound, 1.3 mi nw on Neponset St, then 0.4 mi n on US 1. Int corridors. **Pets:** Small. $25 one-time fee/room. Service with restrictions, supervision. ⊗ &M ⊟ ▣ ⊷

Residence Inn Boston-Norwood H
(781) 278-9595. **$169-$209.** 275 Norwood Park S 02062. I-95, exit 9 northbound, 3.7 mi n on US 1; exit 11B southbound, 0.5 mi nw on Neponset St, 0.6 mi w on Dean St, then 0.8 mi s on US 1. Int corridors.
Pets: Accepted. [SAVE] ⊗ &M ⊟ ▣ ⊷ ⊠

PEABODY

Homestead Studio Suites Hotel-Boston/Peabody H
(978) 531-6632. **$70-$115.** 200 Jubilee Dr 01960. SR 128, exit 28, just s to Centennial Dr, w to the end, n to Jubilee Dr, then 1.1 mi e. Int corridors. **Pets:** Other species. $25 daily fee/room. Designated rooms, service with restrictions, crate. [ASK] ⊗ ⊟ ▣ ⊷

Homewood Suites by Hilton H
(978) 536-5050. **$89-$209.** 57 Newbury St 01960. On US 1 northbound. Int corridors. **Pets:** Accepted. ⊗ &M ⊟ ▣ ⊷

REVERE

Comfort Inn & Suites Boston Airport H
(781) 485-3600. **$79-$220.** 85 American Legion Hwy 02151. Jct SR 1A and 60, 3 mi n of Boston Logan International Airport. Int corridors.
Pets: Accepted. [ASK] ⊗ ⊟ ▣ ⑪ ⊷

Hampton Inn Boston Logan Airport H
(781) 286-5665. **$80-$330.** 230 Lee Burbank Hwy 02151. On SR 1A, 1.9 mi n of Boston Logan International Airport, then 0.6 mi s of terminus SR 60. Int corridors. **Pets:** Medium, other species. Designated rooms, service with restrictions. ⊗ &M ⊟ ▣ ⑪ ⊷

ROCKPORT

Rockport Inn & Suites H ❖
(978) 546-3300. **$79-$229, 3 day notice.** 183 Main St 01966. On SR 127. Ext corridors. **Pets:** Large. $15 daily fee/pet. Designated rooms, service with restrictions. [SAVE] ⊗ &M ⊟ ▣ ⊷ ⊠

ROWLEY

Country Garden Inn & Spa M
(978) 948-7773. **$89-$329, 10 day notice.** 101 Main St 01969. On SR 1A. Ext corridors. **Pets:** Medium, dogs only. $30 daily fee/pet. Designated rooms, service with restrictions, crate. [SAVE] ⊗ ⊟ ▣ ⊷

SALEM

Hawthorne Hotel H ❖
(978) 744-4080. **$114-$224, 3 day notice.** 18 Washington Square W 01970. On SR 1A. Int corridors. **Pets:** Other species. $100 deposit/room, $10 daily fee/pet. Designated rooms, service with restrictions, supervision. [ASK] ⊗ ⊟ ⑪

The Salem Inn BB
(978) 741-0680. **$119-$350, 7 day notice.** 7 Summer St 01970. On SR 114 at Essex St; SR 128, exit 25A, 3 mi e. Int corridors. **Pets:** Other species. $15 daily fee/pet. Designated rooms, service with restrictions.
[ASK] ⊗ ⊟ ▣

SAUGUS

Red Roof Inn #7305 H
(781) 941-1400. **$85-$110.** 920 Broadway 01906. I-95, exit 44 northbound, 3.2 mi s on US 1; exit Main St/Saugus southbound to U-turn. Int corridors. **Pets:** Large. Service with restrictions, crate.
[SAVE] ⊗ &M ⊟

SOMERVILLE

La Quinta Inn & Suites Boston/Somerville H ❖
(617) 625-5300. **$89-$219.** 23 Cummings St 02143. I-93, exit 29 northbound, just ne on SR 28, then just s on Middlesex Ave; exit 31 southbound, 1 mi e on SR 16, then 0.5 mi s on SR 28 to Middlesex Ave. Int corridors. **Pets:** Medium, other species. Service with restrictions, supervision. [ASK] ⊗ &M ⊟ ▣

TEWKSBURY

Extended StayAmerica Boston-Tewksbury H
(978) 863-9888. **$57-$75.** 1910 Andover St 01876. I-93, exit 43B, just w; I-495, exit 39, just e. Int corridors. **Pets:** Other species. $25 daily fee/room. Designated rooms, service with restrictions, crate.
[ASK] ⊗ ⊟ ▣

Holiday Inn Tewksbury-Andover H
(978) 640-9000. **$89-$179.** 4 Highwood Dr 01876-1138. I-495, exit 39, just w on SR 133. Int corridors. **Pets:** Accepted.
[ASK] ⊗ ⊟ ▣ ⑪ ⊷ ⊠

Residence Inn by Marriott Boston-Tewksbury-Andover H
(978) 640-1003. **$179-$189.** 1775 Andover St 01876. I-495, exit 39, 0.3 mi w on SR 133. Ext corridors. **Pets:** Accepted.
⊗ &M ⊟ ▣ ⊷ ⊠

TownePlace Suites Boston Tewksbury H
(978) 863-9800. **$99-$139.** 20 International Pl 01876. I-495, exit 39, 0.3 mi nw. Int corridors. **Pets:** Accepted. ⊗ &M ⊟ ▣ ⊷

WAKEFIELD

Sheraton Colonial Hotel Boston North & Conference Center H ❖
(781) 245-9300. **$95-$235.** 1 Audubon Rd 01880. I-95, exit 42, just n. Int corridors. **Pets:** Large, other species. Supervision.
[SAVE] ⊗ ⊟ ▣ ⑪ ⊷ ⊠

WALTHAM

Courtyard by Marriott Boston-Waltham H
(781) 419-0900. **$170-$208.** 387 Winter St 02451. I-95, exit 27B northbound; exit 27A southbound, on northeast corner. Int corridors.
Pets: Accepted. ⊗ &M ⊟ ▣ ⑪ ⊷ ⊠

Extended Stay Deluxe Boston-Waltham H
(781) 622-1900. **$79-$99.** 32 4th Ave 02451. I-95, exit 27A, just se. Int corridors. **Pets:** Other species. $25 daily fee/room. Designated rooms, service with restrictions, crate. [ASK] ⊗ &M ⊟ ▣ ⊷

Hilton Garden Inn Boston/Waltham H
(781) 890-0100. **$99-$259.** 420 Totten Pond Rd 02451. I-95, exit 27A, just e. Int corridors. **Pets:** Accepted.
[SAVE] ⊗ &M ⊟ ▣ ⑪ ⊷

Holiday Inn Express Boston/Waltham H
(781) 890-2800. **$84-$158.** 385 Winter St 02451. I-95, exit 27B northbound; exit 27A southbound, just ne. Int corridors. **Pets:** Other species. $50 one-time fee/room. Service with restrictions, crate.
[ASK] ⊗ &M ⊟

◇◇/ ▼▼ ▼▼ The Westin Waltham-Boston 🅷
(781) 290-5600. **$109-$369.** 70 3rd Ave 02451. I-95, exit 27A, just se. Int corridors. **Pets:** Accepted. 🅴🅲🅾 🆂🅰🆅 ⊠ ⟨ℳ ▮ ▯ ⑪ ⨠ 🐾

WESTFORD

▼▼ ▼▼ Residence Inn Boston Westford 🅷 ❀
(978) 392-1407. **$152-$186.** 7 Lan Dr 01886. I-495, exit 32, just s, then 0.5 w on SR 110. Int corridors. **Pets:** Other species. $75 one-time fee/ room. Service with restrictions. ⊠ ⟨ℳ ▮ ▯ ⨠ 🐾

WOBURN

◇◇/ ▼▼ ▼▼ Best Western New Englander 🅷 ❀
(781) 935-8160. **$89-$109.** 1 Rainin Rd 01801. I-93, exit 36, just e. Int corridors. **Pets:** Small. $25 one-time fee/pet. Designated rooms, service with restrictions, supervision. 🆂🅰🆅 ⊠ ⟨ℳ ▮ ▯ ⑪ ⨠

▼▼ ▼▼ Extended Stay Deluxe Boston-Woburn 🅷
(781) 938-3737. **$75-$110.** 831 Main St 01801. I-95, exit 35, just n on SR 38. Int corridors. **Pets:** Other species. $25 daily fee/room. Designated rooms, service with restrictions, crate. 🅰🆂🅺 ⊠ ⟨ℳ ▮ ▯ ⨠

▼▼ ▼▼ Hilton Boston/Woburn 🅷
(781) 932-0999. **$99-$239.** 2 Forbes Rd 01801. I-95, exit 36, 0.5 mi s via Washington St, then just e at Lukoil; jct Cedar St. Int corridors. **Pets:** Accepted. ⊠ ▮ ▯ ⨠ 🐾

◇◇/ ▼▼ ▼▼ Holiday Inn Select 🅷
(781) 935-8760. **$99-$199.** 15 Middlesex Canal Park Rd 01801. I-95, exit 35, s via SR 38. Int corridors. **Pets:** Accepted.
🆂🅰🆅 ⊠ ⟨ℳ ▮ ▯ ⑪ ⨠

◇◇/ ▼▼ ▼▼ Red Roof Inn Woburn #238 🅷
(781) 935-7110. **$59-$130.** 19 Commerce Way 01801. I-95, exit 36, just n, then just w on Mishawum Rd. Int corridors. **Pets:** Large. Service with restrictions, crate. 🆂🅰🆅 ⊠ ⟨ℳ ▮ ▯ ⨠

◇◇/ ▼▼ ▼▼ Residence Inn by
Marriott-Boston/Woburn 🅷
(781) 376-4000. **$199-$219.** 300 Presidential Way 01801. I-93, exit 37C, just nw. Int corridors. **Pets:** Accepted.
🆂🅰🆅 ⊠ ⟨ℳ ▮ ▯ ⨠ 🐾

END METROPOLITAN AREA

BROCKTON

▼▼ ▼▼ Quality Inn 🅷
(508) 588-3333. **$63-$109.** 1005 Belmont St 02301. SR 24, exit 17A, just e on SR 123. Int corridors. **Pets:** Accepted. 🅰🆂🅺 ⊠ ▮ ▯ ⨠

▼▼ ▼▼ Residence Inn Boston Brockton 🅷 ❀
(508) 583-3600. **$139-$159.** 124 Liberty St 02301. SR 24, exit 17B, just w, just s on Pearl St, then 0.3 mi se via Mill St connector. Int corridors. **Pets:** Other species. $100 one-time fee/room. Service with restrictions, supervision. ⊠ ⟨ℳ ▮ ▯ ⨠ 🐾

CAPE COD AREA

BUZZARDS BAY

◇◇/ ▼▼ Bay Motor Inn 🅲🅰
(508) 759-3989. **$62-$139, 7 day notice.** 223 Main St 02532. SR 25, 0.5 mi w of Bourne rotary, exit 3. Ext corridors. **Pets:** $20 daily fee/room. Service with restrictions, supervision. 🆂🅰🆅 ⊠ ▮ ▯ ⨠

EAST FALMOUTH

▼▼ ▼▼ Capewind Waterfront Resort 🅼
(508) 548-3400. **$68-$254, 30 day notice.** 34 Maravista Ext 02536. 2.2 mi e via SR 28, then just s, follow signs. Ext corridors. **Pets:** Accepted.
🅰🆂🅺 ⊠ ▮ ▯ ⨠ 🐾

FALMOUTH

◇◇/ ▼▼ ▼▼ Mariner Motel 🅼
(508) 548-1331. **$69-$189, 14 day notice.** 555 Main St 02540. 0.5 mi e on SR 28. Ext corridors. **Pets:** Accepted. 🆂🅰🆅 ⊠ ▮ ⨠

HYANNIS

▼▼ ▼▼ Cape Cod Harbor House Inn 🅼
(508) 771-1880. **Call for rates.** 119 Ocean St 02601. Opposite ferry docks. Ext corridors. **Pets:** Accepted. ⊠ ▮ ▯

◇◇/ ▼▼ ▼▼ Comfort Inn 🅷
(508) 771-4804. **$89-$210.** 1470 Iyannough Rd 02601. US 6, exit 6, 1.3 mi se on SR 132. Ext/int corridors. **Pets:** Accepted.
🆂🅰🆅 ⊠ ▮ ▯ ⨠ 🐾

ORLEANS

▼▼ ▼▼ Governor Prence Inn 🅼
(508) 255-1216. **$99-$169, 10 day notice.** 66 SR 6A 02653. 0.5 mi w of rotary. Ext corridors. **Pets:** Designated rooms, service with restrictions, supervision. 🅰🆂🅺 ⊠ ▮ ⨠

▼▼ ▼▼ Orleans Inn 🅲🅸
(508) 255-2222. **$250-$450.** 21 SR 6A 02653. On SR 28 and 6A, exit rotary, just w. Int corridors. **Pets:** Dogs only. Service with restrictions.
🅰🆂🅺 ⊠ ▮ ⑪

PROVINCETOWN

▼▼ ▼▼ Bayshore & Chandler 🅲🅾
(508) 487-9133. **$105-$325, 30 day notice.** 493 Commercial St 02657. 0.8 mi e of Town Hall. Ext corridors. **Pets:** Dogs only. $20 daily fee/room. Service with restrictions. ⊠ ▮

▼▼ ▼▼ Surfside Hotel & Suites 🅷 ❀
(508) 487-1726. **$139-$329, 28 day notice.** 542-543 Commercial St 02657. 1 mi e of Town Hall. Ext/int corridors. **Pets:** Large, dogs only. $40 daily fee/pet. Service with restrictions. 🅰🆂🅺 ⊠ ▮ ▯ ⨠

▼▼ ▼▼ White Wind Inn 🅱🅱
(508) 487-1526. **Call for rates.** 174 Commercial St 02657. Just w of Town Hall. Int corridors. **Pets:** Accepted. ⊠ ▮ ▯

SANDWICH

▼▼ Shady Nook Inn & Motel 🅼
(508) 888-0409. **Call for rates.** 14 Old Kings Hwy (SR 6A) 02563. On SR 6A, 1.5 mi w. Ext corridors. **Pets:** Other species. $10 daily fee/pet. Designated rooms, service with restrictions, supervision.
⊠ ▮ ▯ ⨠

SOUTH YARMOUTH

◇◇/ ▼▼ ▼▼ Ambassador Inn & Suites 🅷
(508) 394-4000. **$60-$190.** 1314 Main St 02664. On SR 28, just w of Bass River Bridge. Int corridors. **Pets:** Large. $15 daily fee/pet. Desig- nated rooms, service with restrictions, supervision.
🆂🅰🆅 ⊠ ▮ ▯ ⨠ 🐾

◇ ▽▽◇ Blue Rock Golf Resort **M** ❖

(508) 398-6962. **$95-$215, 10 day notice.** 39 Todd Rd 02664. SR 28, 1 mi ne via N Main St and High Bank Rd, then 0.5 mi nw on Country Club Dr, follow signs. Ext corridors. **Pets:** Other species. $25 daily fee/pet. Designated rooms, service with restrictions, supervision.

[SAVE] [X] 🖥 💻 [Y¶] ◤ [X]

◇ ▽▽◇ Blue Water on The Ocean **H** ❖

(508) 398-2288. **$90-$199, 30 day notice.** 291 S Shore Dr 02664. 1 mi s off SR 28. Ext/int corridors. **Pets:** $25 daily fee/pet. Designated rooms, service with restrictions, supervision. [SAVE] [X] 🖥 💻 [Y¶] ◤

WEST DENNIS

▽▽ ▽▽ Inn at Swan River **M**

(508) 394-5415. **$89-$259, 14 day notice.** 829 Main St 02670. On SR 28, just w of SR 134. Ext corridors. **Pets:** Accepted.

[ASK] [X] 🖥 💻 ◤

END AREA

CHICOPEE

◇ ▽▽▽▽ Quality Inn-Chicopee **H** ❖

(413) 592-6171. **$72-$79.** 463 Memorial Dr 01020. I-90, exit 5, just ne, use jug handle overpass to SR 33 N. Int corridors. **Pets:** $15 one-time fee/room. Service with restrictions, supervision. [SAVE] [X] 🖥 💻 ◤

EAST WAREHAM

◇ ▽▽ Atlantic Motel **M** ❖

(508) 295-0210. **$80-$200, 10 day notice.** 7 Depot St 02538. Between eastbound and westbound lanes of US 6/SR 28; jct SR 25, exit 1. Ext corridors. **Pets:** Medium, dogs only. $20 daily fee/pet. Designated rooms, service with restrictions, supervision. [SAVE] [X] 🖥 ◤

FAIRHAVEN

◇ ▽▽▽▽ Seaport Inn L.L.C **H**

(508) 997-1281. **$89-$159.** 110 Middle St 02719. I-195, exit 15, 1 mi s, then just off US 6. Int corridors. **Pets:** Other species. $25 one-time fee/room. Service with restrictions, crate. [SAVE] [X] 🖥 💻 [Y¶]

FITCHBURG

◇ ▽▽▽▽ Courtyard by Marriott Fitchburg **H**

(978) 342-7100. **$122-$149.** 150 Royal Plaza Dr 01420. SR 2, exit 28, just s on SR 31. Int corridors. **Pets:** Accepted.

[SAVE] [X] [&M] 💻 [Y¶] ◤

GARDNER

▽▽▽▽ Colonial Hotel **H**

(978) 630-2500. **$99-$139.** 625 Betty Spring Rd 01440. SR 2, exit 24 eastbound; exit 24B, 0.9 mi n on SR 140, then 0.5 mi w. Int corridors. **Pets:** Small, other species. $25 one-time fee/room. Designated rooms, service with restrictions, crate. [ASK] [X] 🖥 💻 [Y¶] ◤ [X]

▽▽ Super 8 **M**

(978) 630-2888. **$79-$110.** 22 Pearson Blvd 01440. SR 2, exit 23, just n. Int corridors. **Pets:** Medium. $15 daily fee/pet. Service with restrictions, supervision. [ASK] [X] 🖥 💻

GREAT BARRINGTON

◇ ▽▽ Lantern House Motel **M**

(413) 528-2350. **$55-$189, 21 day notice.** 256 Stockbridge Rd 01230. On US 7, 1.2 mi s of jct SR 183. Ext corridors. **Pets:** Accepted.

[SAVE] [X] 🖥

◇ ▽▽ Monument Mountain Motel **M**

(413) 528-3272. **$59-$199, 14 day notice.** 247 Stockbridge Rd (Rt 7) 01230. On US 7, 1.2 mi s of jct SR 183. Ext corridors. **Pets:** Medium, dogs only. $20 daily fee/pet. Designated rooms, service with restrictions, supervision. [SAVE] [X] 🖥 ◤

GREENFIELD

▽▽▽▽ The Brandt House B&B **BB** ❖

(413) 774-3329. **$95-$295, 30 day notice.** 29 Highland Ave 01301-3605. I-91, exit 26, 1.8 mi e on SR 2A, then se via Crescent St. Int corridors. **Pets:** Dogs only. $25 one-time fee/room. Service with restrictions, supervision. [ASK] [X] 🖥

▽▽ Days Inn **M**

(413) 774-5578. **$79-$180.** 21 Colrain Rd 01301. I-91, exit 26, just n of SR 2 W. Int corridors. **Pets:** Accepted. [ASK] [X] 🖥 💻

HADLEY

▽▽ ▽▽ Howard Johnson Inn **H** ❖

(413) 586-0114. **$79-$209.** 401 Russell St 01035. I-91, exit 19 northbound, 4.3 mi e on SR 9; exit 24 southbound, 10 mi s on SR 116, then just w on SR 9. Int corridors. **Pets:** Other species. $20 daily fee/room. Designated rooms, service with restrictions.

[ASK] [X] [&M] 🖥 💻 ◤

HOLLAND

▽▽▽▽ The Inn at Restful Paws **BB** ❖

(413) 245-7792. **$174, 14 day notice.** 70 Allen Hill Rd 01521. SR 20, 2.1 mi s on E Brimfield Rd, 0.4 mi on Alexander Rd, then 0.7 mi n. Int corridors. **Pets:** Service with restrictions, supervision.

[ASK] [X] 💻 [W] [✆]

HOLYOKE

▽▽▽▽ Homewood Suites by Hilton
Holyoke-Springfield **H**

(413) 532-3100. **$96-$169.** 375 Whitney Ave 01040. I-91, exit 15, just w on Lower Westfield Rd, then 0.4 mi s. Int corridors. **Pets:** Large, other species. $100 one-time fee/room. Service with restrictions.

[X] [&M] 🖥 ◤ [X]

LANESBOROUGH

◇ ▽▽ The Weathervane Motel **M**

(413) 443-3230. **$35-$110, 15 day notice.** 475 S Main St 01237. 1.3 mi s on US 7. Ext corridors. **Pets:** Very small. $10 one-time fee/room. Designated rooms, no service, supervision. [SAVE] [X] 🖥 💻

LENOX

◇ ▽▽▽▽ Blantyre **CI** ❖

(413) 637-3556. **$600-$1850, 30 day notice.** 16 Blantyre Rd 01240. US 20, 1 mi s from jct SR 183. Int corridors. **Pets:** Large, dogs only. $75 daily fee/pet. Designated rooms, service with restrictions, supervision.

[SAVE] [X] 🖥 💻 [Y¶] ◤ [X]

▽▽▽▽ The Kemble Inn **BB**

(413) 637-4113. **$115-$455, 15 day notice.** 2 Kemble St 01240. Jct SR 183 and 7A. Int corridors. **Pets:** $45 daily fee/pet. Designated rooms, supervision. [ASK] [X]

LEOMINSTER

◇ ▽▽▽ Super 8 **M**

(978) 537-2800. **$69-$96.** 482 N Main St 01453. SR 2, exit 31B, just n on SR 12. Int corridors. **Pets:** Accepted. [SAVE] [X] [&M] 🖥 💻

MANSFIELD

▽▽▽▽ Holiday Inn Mansfield **H**

(508) 339-2200. **$99-$159.** 31 Hampshire St 02048. I-95, exit 7A, 0.5 mi s on SR 140, then 1 mi w on Forbes Rd; I-495, exit 12, 2 mi n on SR 140, then w on Forbes Rd. Int corridors. **Pets:** Medium. $15 daily fee/pet. Service with restrictions, supervision.

[ASK] [X] 🖥 💻 [Y¶] ◤ [X]

MARTHA'S VINEYARD AREA

EDGARTOWN

AAA ▼▼▼▼ Colonial Inn of Martha's Vineyard CI
(508) 627-4711. **$95-$425, 14 day notice.** 38 N Water St 02539. Just n from Main St. Int corridors. **Pets:** Dogs only. $35 daily fee/room. Designated rooms, service with restrictions, crate. SAVE ⊠ 🛏 🖵 ⍰

OAK BLUFFS

AAA ▼▼▼▼ The Dockside Inn BB
(508) 693-2966. **$150-$450, 21 day notice.** 9 Circuit Ave Ext 02557. Center. Ext corridors. **Pets:** Accepted. SAVE ⊠ 🛏 🖵

VINEYARD HAVEN

▼▼▼▼ The Doctor's House Bed & Breakfast BB
(508) 696-0859. **$150-$340, 21 day notice.** 60 Mt. Aldworth Rd 02568. 0.4 mi sw to road to Edgartown, 1 blk e. Int corridors. **Pets:** Medium, other species. $25 deposit/room. Service with restrictions, supervision. ⊠ ☎

END AREA

MILFORD

AAA ▼▼▼▼ Holiday Inn Express H
(508) 634-1054. **$79-$159.** 50 Fortune Blvd 01757. I-495, exit 20, just sw on SR 85, then just se. Int corridors. **Pets:** Medium. $25 one-time fee/room. Designated rooms, service with restrictions, supervision.
SAVE ⊠ 🛏M 🛏 🖵 ≋

▼▼▼ La Quinta Inn H ❀
(508) 478-8243. **$75-$139.** 24 Beaver St 01757. I-495, exit 19, just w on SR 109. Int corridors. **Pets:** Medium, other species. Service with restrictions, supervision. ASK ⊠

NORTH ADAMS

AAA ▼▼▼▼ Jae's Inn M
(413) 664-0100. **$95-$160, 3 day notice.** 1111 S State St 01247. 2 mi s on SR 8; center. Int corridors. **Pets:** Large, other species. $20 daily fee/room. Designated rooms, service with restrictions, supervision.
SAVE ⊠ 🛏 ≋ ⊠

NORTHAMPTON

▼▼▼ Clarion Hotel & Conference Center H
(413) 586-1211. **$79-$265.** One Atwood Dr 01060. I-91, exit 18, just s on US 5. Int corridors. **Pets:** Medium. $20 daily fee/room. Designated rooms, service with restrictions, crate. ASK ⊠ 🛏M 🛏 🖵 ⍰ ≋ ⊠

NORTH DARTMOUTH

AAA ▼▼▼ Comfort Inn H
(508) 996-0800. **$89-$149.** 171 Faunce Corner Rd 02747. I-195, exit 12A westbound; exit 12 eastbound, then s. Int corridors. **Pets:** $50 one-time fee/pet. SAVE ⊠ 🛏 🖵 ≋

AAA ▼▼▼ Residence Inn New Bedford Dartmouth H ❀
(508) 984-5858. **$130-$190.** 181 Faunce Corner Rd 02747. I-195, exit 12A westbound; exit 12 eastbound, just s. Int corridors. **Pets:** Medium. $100 one-time fee/pet. Designated rooms, service with restrictions, supervision. SAVE ⊠ 🛏M 🛏 🖵 ≋ ⊠

NORTON

▼▼ ▼▼ Extended StayAmerica-Foxboro-Norton H
(508) 285-7800. **$60-$85.** 280 S Washington St 02766. I-495, exit 9, 0.3 mi se on Bay St, then 0.5 mi nw via Industrial Park Rd. Int corridors. **Pets:** Other species. $25 daily fee/room. Designated rooms, service with restrictions, crate. ASK ⊠ 🛏M 🛏 🖵

ORANGE

AAA ▼▼ Executive Inn M
(978) 544-8864. **$45-$80, 7 day notice.** 110 Daniel Shays Hwy 01364. US 202, exit 16, just n of jct SR 2. Ext/int corridors. **Pets:** Other species. $7 daily fee/pet. Designated rooms, service with restrictions, supervision.
SAVE ⊠ 🛏

PITTSFIELD

AAA ▼▼▼▼ Crowne Plaza Hotel and Resort Pittsfield Berkshires H ❀
(413) 499-2000. **$99-$349.** 1 West St, Berkshire Common 01201. Center. Int corridors. **Pets:** Large, other species. $50 one-time fee/room. Service with restrictions, supervision. SAVE ⊠ 🛏M 🛏 🖵 ⍰ ≋ ⊠

AAA ▼▼▼▼ Patriot Suites Hotel H
(413) 997-3300. **$145-$295, 3 day notice.** 8 Dan Fox Dr 01201. I-90, exit 2, 9 mi nw on US 20, then just w. Int corridors. **Pets:** Small. $75 one-time fee/room. Designated rooms, service with restrictions, supervision. SAVE ⊠ 🛏M 🛏 🖵 ≋

RAYNHAM

AAA ▼▼▼ Quality Inn of Raynham-Taunton M
(508) 824-8647. **$55-$115.** 164 New State Hwy 02767. SR 24, exit 13B, 0.8 mi w on US 44. Ext/int corridors. **Pets:** $10 daily fee/pet. Designated rooms, service with restrictions, crate. SAVE ⊠ 🛏 🖵 ≋

REHOBOTH

▼▼▼ Five Bridge Inn Bed & Breakfast BB ❀
(508) 252-3190. **$98-$145, 3 day notice.** 154 Pine St 02769. 1.6 mi n of US 44; 3.3 mi w of jct SR 118; US 44, n on Blanding, e on Broad, n on Salisbury, then w. Int corridors. **Pets:** Medium. $15 one-time fee/room. Designated rooms, service with restrictions, crate. ASK ⊠ 🛏 🖵 ≋ ⊠

RICHMOND

▼▼▼ The Inn at Richmond BB
(413) 698-2566. **$160-$380, 15 day notice.** 802 State Rd (SR 41) 01254. 2.5 mi s of jct US 20. Ext/int corridors. **Pets:** Accepted. ASK ⊠ 🛏 🖵 ⊠

ROCKLAND

AAA ▼▼▼ Best Western Rockland H ❀
(781) 871-5660. **$109-$169.** 909 Hingham St 02370. SR 3, exit 14, 0.3 mi sw on SR 228. Int corridors. **Pets:** Other species. $20 daily fee/pet. Designated rooms, service with restrictions, crate. SAVE ⊠ 🛏 🖵

SEEKONK

▼▼ Motel 6–1289 M
(508) 336-7800. **$55-$65.** 821 Fall River Ave 02771. I-195, exit 1, just n on SR 114A. Int corridors. **Pets:** Other species. Service with restrictions, supervision. ⊠

▼▼ ▼▼ Ramada Inn-Providence H ❀
(508) 336-7300. **$89-$150.** 940 Fall River Ave 02771. I-195, exit 1, just s. Int corridors. **Pets:** $10 daily fee/pet. Designated rooms, service with restrictions, crate. ASK ⊠ 🛏 🖵 ⍰ ≋ ⊠

SOMERSET

◯◯◯ ▽▽▽ Quality Inn-Fall River/Somerset 🅗 ❀
(508) 678-4545. **$75-$165.** 1878 Wilbur Ave 02725. Jct SR 103 and I-195, exit 4 eastbound; exit 4A westbound. Int corridors. **Pets:** $50 deposit/room. Designated rooms, service with restrictions, supervision.
🆂🅰🆅🅴 ⊠ 🅗 📺 ⊠

SOUTHBOROUGH

◯◯◯ ▽▽▽ Red Roof Inn # 7075 🅜
(508) 481-3904. **$66-$100.** 367 Turnpike Rd 01772. I-495, exit 23A, just e on SR 9. Ext corridors. **Pets:** Large. Service with restrictions, crate.
🆂🅰🆅🅴 ⊠ 🅗

SPRINGFIELD

◯◯◯ ▽▽▽▽ Sheraton Springfield Monarch Place 🅗 ❀
(413) 781-1010. **$99-$229.** 1 Monarch Pl 01144. I-91, 6 northbound; exit 7 southbound, just n; downtown. Int corridors. **Pets:** Medium. $50 deposit/pet. Designated rooms, service with restrictions, supervision.
🆂🅰🆅🅴 ⊠ 🆅🅼 🅗 📺 🍽 ⊠

STURBRIDGE

◯◯◯ ▽▽▽▽ Comfort Inn & Suites Colonial 🅗
(508) 347-3306. **$89-$269.** 215 Charlton Rd 01566. I-90 (Massachusetts Tpke), exit 9, 0.5 mi e; I-84, exit 3A. Ext/int corridors. **Pets:** $15 daily fee/pet. Designated rooms, supervision. 🆂🅰🆅🅴 ⊠ 🆅🅼 🅗 📺 ⊠

◇◇ Days Inn 🅜
(508) 347-3391. **Call for rates.** 66-68 Haynes St (SR 15) 01566. I-84, exit 2, 0.5 mi n, follow signs to SR 131, on I-84 service road. Ext/int corridors. **Pets:** Accepted. ⊠ 🅗 📺 ⊠

▽▽ Publick House Historic Inn & Country Lodge 🅗
(508) 347-3313. **$79-$299.** 295 Main St 01566. I-90 (Massachusetts Tpke), exit 9; I-84, exit 3B, 0.5 mi s of jct US 20. Ext/int corridors. **Pets:** Accepted. 🅰🆂🅺 ⊠ 🅗 📺 🍽 ⊠

◯◯◯ ▽▽◇ Sturbridge Host Hotel and Conference Center on Cedar Lake 🅗
(508) 347-7393. **$115-$199.** 366 Main St 01566. I-90 (Massachusetts Tpke), exit 9, just w on US 20; I-84, exit 3B. Int corridors. **Pets:** $25 daily fee/room. Designated rooms, service with restrictions, supervision.
🆂🅰🆅🅴 ⊠ 🅗 📺 🍽 ⊠

◯◯◯ ▽▽▽ Super 8 🅜
(508) 347-9000. **$59-$169.** 358 Main St 01566. I-90 (Massachusetts Tpke), exit 9; I-84, exit 3B on US 20. Ext corridors. **Pets:** Accepted.
🆂🅰🆅🅴 ⊠ 🅗 📺 ⊠

WESTBOROUGH

▽▽ Extended Stay Deluxe-Boston-Westborough 🅗
(508) 616-9213. **$70-$90.** 180 E Main St 01581. I-495, exit 23B, 1.4 mi w, then just sw on SR 30. Int corridors. **Pets:** Other species. $25 daily fee/room. Designated rooms, service with restrictions, crate.
🅰🆂🅺 ⊠ 🆅🅼 🅗 📺

▽▽▽ Extended Stay Deluxe Boston-Westborough-Computer Dr 🅗
(508) 366-6100. **$70-$90.** 1800 Computer Dr 01581. I-495, exit 23B, just w; north side of SR 9. Int corridors. **Pets:** Other species. $25 daily fee/room. Designated rooms, service with restrictions, crate.
🅰🆂🅺 ⊠ 🆅🅼 🅗 📺 ⊠

▽▽▽ Residence Inn by Marriott Boston/Westborough 🅗
(508) 366-7700. **$152-$186.** 25 Connector Rd 01581. I-495, exit 23B, just w on SR 9, exit Computer and Research drs, then 0.3 mi s. Ext/int corridors. **Pets:** Accepted. ⊠ 🆅🅼 🅗 📺 🍽 ⊠

WESTFIELD

◯◯◯ ◇◇ Econo Lodge & Suites 🅗
(413) 568-2821. **$64-$129.** 2 Southampton Rd 01085. I-90, exit 3, at US 202 and SR 10. Ext/int corridors. **Pets:** Medium, dogs only. $25 one-time fee/pet. Service with restrictions, supervision. 🆂🅰🆅🅴 ⊠ 🅗 📺 ⊠

WESTMINSTER

◯◯◯ ▽▽ Wachusett Village Inn & Conference Center 🅗
(978) 874-2000. **$99-$169.** 9 Village Inn Rd 01473. 0.7 mi w on Village Inn Rd; SR 2, exit 27 westbound, 0.3 mi e; exit 26 eastbound. Ext/int corridors. **Pets:** Medium, other species. $50 one-time fee/room. Designated rooms, service with restrictions, crate.
🆂🅰🆅🅴 ⊠ 🅗 📺 🍽 ⊠

WEST SPRINGFIELD

◯◯◯ ▽▽▽ Candlewood Suites 🅗
(413) 739-1122. **$108-$117.** 572 Riverdale St 01089. I-91, exit 13B, 1.3 mi s. Int corridors. **Pets:** Medium, other species. $25 daily fee/room. Service with restrictions, supervision. 🆂🅰🆅🅴 ⊠ 🆅🅼 🅗 📺 ⊠

▽▽▽ Hampton Inn 🅗
(413) 732-1300. **$109-$179.** 1011 Riverdale St (US 5) 01089. I-91, exit 13B, 0.3 mi s. Int corridors. **Pets:** Accepted.
🅰🆂🅺 ⊠ 🆅🅼 🅗 📺 ⊠

▽▽◇ Residence Inn West Springfield 🅗 ❀
(413) 732-9543. **$150-$190.** 64 Border Way 01089. I-91, exit 13A, on US 5. Int corridors. **Pets:** Other species. $75 one-time fee/room. Service with restrictions, crate. ⊠ 🆅🅼 🅗 📺 🍽 ⊠

WILLIAMSTOWN

▽ Cozy Corner Motel 🅜
(413) 458-8006. **$50-$135, 10 day notice.** 284 Sand Springs Rd (US 7) 01267. On US 7, 1.5 mi n of jct SR 2. Ext corridors. **Pets:** Other species. $10 daily fee/pet. Service with restrictions, crate. ⊠ 🅗

▽▽ Maple Terrace Motel 🅜
(413) 458-9677. **$58-$158, 10 day notice.** 555 Main St 01267. On SR 2, 1 mi e of jct US 7. Ext corridors. **Pets:** Medium, dogs only. $15 one-time fee/room. Designated rooms, service with restrictions, supervision.
⊠ 🅗 🍽

◯◯◯ ◇ The Villager Motel 🅜
(413) 458-4046. **$55-$159, 14 day notice.** 953 Simonds Rd 01267. On US 7, 1.7 mi n of jct SR 2. Ext corridors. **Pets:** Accepted. 🆂🅰🆅🅴 ⊠ 🅗

WORCESTER

◯◯◯ ▽▽◇ Beechwood Hotel 🅗
(508) 754-5789. **$159-$390.** 363 Plantation St 01605. I-290, exit 22 westbound, 0.5 mi w on Lincoln St, then 1.5 mi s; exit 21 eastbound, 1.3 mi s. Int corridors. **Pets:** $50 daily fee/room. Service with restrictions, supervision. 🆂🅰🆅🅴 ⊠ 🆅🅼 🅗 📺 🍽 ⊠

◯◯◯ ▽▽▽▽ Crowne Plaza Hotel 🅗
(508) 791-1600. **$119-$199.** 10 Lincoln Square 01608. I-290, exit 17 eastbound; exit 18 westbound, 0.3 mi s. Int corridors. **Pets:** Accepted.
🆂🅰🆅🅴 ⊠ 🆅🅼 📺 🍽 ⊠

▽▽▽ Residence Inn by Marriott Worcester 🅗
(508) 753-6300. **$164-$179.** 503 Plantation St 01605. I-290, exit 21, 0.5 mi sw. Int corridors. **Pets:** Accepted. ⊠ 🆅🅼 🅗 📺 🍽 ⊠

MICHIGAN

ADRIAN

▼▼▼ Carlton Lodge 🅗
(517) 263-7000. **$91-$101.** 1629 W Maumee St 49221. Jct US 223 and SR 52, 3 mi w on US 223. Int corridors. **Pets:** Accepted.
🅐🆂🅺 ⊠ 🛋 💻 🍴 ⇥

▼▼ Super 8 🅗
(517) 265-8888. **$72-$200.** 1091 W US 223 49221. Jct US 223 and SR 52, just w. Int corridors. **Pets:** Medium, other species. $25 one-time fee/room. Service with restrictions, supervision. 🅐🆂🅺 ⊠ 🛋 💻

ALGONAC

▼▼ Linda's Lighthouse Inn 🅱🅱 ❀
(810) 794-2992. **$95-$135, 14 day notice.** 5965 Pointe Tremble Rd (SR 29) 48001. I-94, exit 243 (23 Mile Rd), 14.3 mi e. Int corridors. **Pets:** Other species. $15 daily fee/pet. Service with restrictions, crate.
⊠ ⊠ 🅦 ✍

ALLEGAN

▼▼▼ Castle In The Country B & B Inn 🅱🅱 ❀
(269) 673-8054. **$115-$245, 7 day notice.** 340 SR 40 S 49010. SR 40 S, 6 mi s. Int corridors. **Pets:** Dogs only. $20 daily fee/pet. Designated rooms, service with restrictions, supervision. ⊠ ⊠ ✍

ALLENDALE

▼▼ Sleep Inn & Suites 🅗 ❀
(616) 892-8000. **$70-$119.** 4869 Becker Dr 49401. I-96, exit 16, 6 mi s, then 2.5 mi e on SR 45. Int corridors. **Pets:** Other species. $10 daily fee/pet. Designated rooms, service with restrictions, crate.
🅐🆂🅺 ⊠ 🅖🅜 🛋 💻 ⇥

ALPENA

⬙⬙ ▼▼▼ Best Western of Alpena 🅜 ❀
(989) 356-9087. **$81-$89.** 1286 Hwy M-32 W 49707. 2.3 mi w of jct US 23. Ext/int corridors. **Pets:** Dogs only. $5 daily fee/pet. Designated rooms, service with restrictions, supervision. 🆂🅰🆅🅴 ⊠ 🛋 💻 ⇥

▼▼▼ Days Inn 🅗
(989) 356-6118. **$80-$120.** 1496 M-32 W 49707. 2.5 mi w of jct US 23. Int corridors. **Pets:** Dogs only. $10 daily fee/room. Service with restrictions, supervision. 🅐🆂🅺 ⊠ 🛋 💻 ⇥ ⊠

▼▼ Holiday Inn 🅗
(989) 356-2151. **$89-$119.** 1000 Hwy 23 N 49707. On US 23, 1 mi n. Int corridors. **Pets:** Medium. Service with restrictions, supervision.
🅐🆂🅺 ⊠ 🛋 💻 🍴 ⇥ ⊠

ANN ARBOR

▼▼▼ Candlewood Suites 🅗
(734) 663-2818. **$69-$129.** 701 Waymarket Way 48103. I-94, exit 175 (Ann Arbor/Saline Rd), just e on Eisenhower Rd. Int corridors.
Pets: Accepted. 🅐🆂🅺 ⊠ 🅖🅜 🛋 💻

▼▼▼ Extended StayAmerica Detroit-Ann Arbor 🅗
(734) 332-1980. **$70-$99.** 1501 Briarwood Circle Dr 48108. I-94, exit 177 (State St), just ne. Int corridors. **Pets:** Other species. $25 daily fee/room. Designated rooms, service with restrictions, crate.
🅐🆂🅺 ⊠ 🅖🅜 🛋 💻

▼▼▼ Extended Stay Deluxe Detroit-Ann Arbor 🅗
(734) 997-7623. **$74-$99.** 3265 Boardwalk St 48108. I-94, exit 177 (State St), just n, then just e on Victors Way. Int corridors. **Pets:** Other species. $25 daily fee/room. Designated rooms, service with restrictions, crate.
🅐🆂🅺 ⊠ 🛋 💻

⬙⬙⬙ ▼▼▼▼ Hampton Inn-North 🅗 ❀
(734) 996-4444. **$89-$269.** 2300 Green Rd 48105. US 23, exit 41 (Plymouth Rd), just nw. Int corridors. **Pets:** Medium, other species. $25 one-time fee/room. Service with restrictions, supervision.
🆂🅰🆅🅴 ⊠ 🅖🅜 🛋 💻 🍴 ⇥

▼▼▼▼ Hawthorn Suites 🅗
(734) 327-0011. **Call for rates.** 3535 Green Ct 48105. US 23, exit 41 (Plymouth Rd), just sw. Int corridors. **Pets:** Other species. $100 one-time fee/room. Service with restrictions, crate. ⊠ 🅖🅜 🛋 💻 ⇥ ⊠

⬙⬙⬙ ▼▼▼ Red Roof Inn #7045 🅜
(734) 996-5800. **$45-$151.** 3621 Plymouth Rd 48105. US 23, exit 41 (Plymouth Rd), just nw. Ext corridors. **Pets:** Large. Service with restrictions, crate. 🆂🅰🆅🅴 ⊠ 🛋

▼▼▼ Residence Inn by Marriott 🅗
(734) 996-5666. **$134-$164.** 800 Victors Way 48108. I-94, exit 177 (State St), just ne. Ext/int corridors. **Pets:** $25 daily fee/room. Service with restrictions. ⊠ 🅖🅜 🛋 💻 ⇥ ⊠

AU GRES

▼▼ Econo Lodge Inn 🅗
(989) 876-4060. **Call for rates.** 510 W US 23 48703. On US 23, just w. Int corridors. **Pets:** Accepted. ⊠ 🛋 💻 ⇥

BAD AXE

▼▼ Econo Lodge Inn & Suites 🅷

(989) 269-3200. **Call for rates.** 898 N Van Dyke Rd 48413. Just s of jct SR 142 and 53 (Van Dyke Rd). Int corridors. **Pets:** Accepted.

❌ 🛏 💻 🏊

BATTLE CREEK

▼▼ ▼▼ Baymont Inn & Suites-Battle Creek 🅷

(269) 979-5400. **$69-$99.** 4725 Beckley Rd 49015. I-94, exit 97 (Capital Ave), just sw. Int corridors. **Pets:** Other species. $10 daily fee/pet. Service with restrictions, supervision. (ASK) ❌ 🛏 💻 🏊

BAY VIEW

▲▲▲ ▼▼ ▼▼ Comfort Inn 🅷 ❖

(231) 347-3220. **$50-$250.** 1314 US 31 N 49770. Jct US 31 and SR 119. Int corridors. **Pets:** Other species. $5 daily fee/pet. Service with restrictions, supervision. (SAVE) ❌ 🛏 💻

BEAR LAKE

▲▲▲ ▼▼ Bella Vista Inn Ⓜ

(231) 864-3000. **$55-$106.** 12273 US 31 49614. On US 31; center. Ext corridors. **Pets:** Dogs only. $12 daily fee/pet. Service with restrictions, supervision. (SAVE) ❌ 🛏 🏊

BEULAH

▲▲▲ ▼▼ ▼▼ Best Western Scenic Hill Resort 🅷

(231) 882-7754. **$65-$250.** 1400 US Hwy 31 49617. 0.8 mi e on US 31. Int corridors. **Pets:** Accepted. (SAVE) ❌ 🛏 💻 🏊 ❌

BIG RAPIDS

▼▼ ▼▼ Holiday Inn Hotel & Conference Center 🅷

(231) 796-4400. **$105-$160.** 1005 Perry St 49307. US 131, exit 139, 1.3 mi e on SR 20. Int corridors. **Pets:** Accepted.

(ASK) ❌ &M 🛏 💻 🍴 🏊 ❌

▲▲▲ ▼▼ ▼▼ Quality Inn & Suites Ⓜ

(231) 592-5150. **$59-$120.** 1705 S State St 49307. US 131, exit 139, 2.1 mi e on SR 20, then 1 mi s. Ext/int corridors. **Pets:** Medium. $10 daily fee/pet. Designated rooms, service with restrictions, supervision.

(SAVE) ❌ 🛏 💻 🏊

BIRCH RUN

▲▲▲ ▼▼ ▼▼ Best Western Birch Run-Frankenmuth 🅷

(989) 624-9395. **$72-$125.** 9087 Birch Run Rd 48415. I-75, exit 136 (Birch Run Rd), just e. Ext/int corridors. **Pets:** Accepted.

(SAVE) ❌ &M 🛏 💻 🍴 🏊 ❌

▼▼ ▼▼ Super 8 🅷

(989) 624-4440. **$50-$150.** 9235 E Birch Run Rd 48415. I-75, exit 136 (Birch Run Rd), just e. Int corridors. **Pets:** Accepted.

(ASK) ❌ 🛏 💻 ❌

BRIDGEPORT

▼▼ ▼▼💎 Baymont Inn & Suites-Frankenmuth/Bridgeport 🅷

(989) 777-3000. **Call for rates.** 6460 Dixie Hwy 48722. I-75, exit 144A. Int corridors. **Pets:** Accepted. ❌ 🛏 💻 🏊

BROOKLYN

▼▼💎 Super 8 Motel 🅷

(517) 592-0888. **$75-$135.** 155 Wamplers Rd 49230. Jct Main St (SR 50) and SR 124; downtown. Int corridors. **Pets:** $10 daily fee/pet. Service with restrictions, supervision. (ASK) ❌ &M 🛏 💻

BYRON CENTER

▲▲▲ ▼▼ ▼▼ ▼▼ Comfort Suites-Grand Rapids South 🅷

(616) 301-2255. **$100-$120.** 7644 Caterpillar Ct SW 49548. US 131, exit 75. Int corridors. **Pets:** Medium. $50 one-time fee/pet. Designated rooms, service with restrictions, supervision.

(SAVE) ❌ &M 🛏 💻 🏊 ❌

CADILLAC

▲▲▲ ▼▼ Econo Lodge 🅷

(231) 775-6700. **$50-$80.** 2501 Sunnyside Dr 49601. Jct SR 55 and 115. Ext/int corridors. **Pets:** Accepted. (SAVE) ❌ 🛏 💻

▲▲▲ ▼▼ ▼▼ McGuires Resort 🅷 ❖

(231) 775-9947. **$79-$109, 7 day notice.** 7880 Mackinaw Tr 49601. US 131, exit 177, 0.7 mi n, then 0.5 mi w. Int corridors. **Pets:** $20 daily fee/room. Service with restrictions, crate.

(SAVE) ❌ 🛏 💻 🍴 🏊 ❌

CALUMET

▼▼ ▼▼ AmericInn Lodge & Suites of Calumet 🅷 ❖

(906) 337-6463. **$95-$146.** 56925 S 6th St 49913. On US 41, just w of Visitors Center. Int corridors. **Pets:** Medium, dogs only. $20 one-time fee/room. Designated rooms, service with restrictions, crate.

(ASK) ❌ 🛏 💻 🏊 ❌

CASCADE

▼▼ ▼▼ Baymont Inn-Grand Rapids Airport 🅷

(616) 956-3300. **Call for rates.** 2873 Kraft Ave SE 49512. I-96, exit 43B, just e. Int corridors. **Pets:** Other species. $10 daily fee/pet. Designated rooms, service with restrictions, supervision. ❌ 🛏 💻

▲▲▲ ▼▼ ▼▼ Best Western Hospitality Hotel & Suites 🅷

(616) 949-8400. **$80-$109.** 5500 28th St SE 49512. I-96, exit 43B, just e on SR 11. Int corridors. **Pets:** Accepted. (SAVE) ❌ 🛏 💻 🏊 ❌

▼▼ ▼▼ Clarion Inn & Suites Grand Rapids Airport 🅷

(616) 956-9304. **$69-$159.** 4981 28th St SE 49512. I-96, exit 43A, 0.5 mi w on SR 11. Int corridors. **Pets:** Large, other species. $10 daily fee/pet. Designated rooms, service with restrictions, crate.

(ASK) ❌ 🛏 💻 🏊

▼▼ ▼▼ Country Inn & Suites By Carlson 🅷 ❖

(616) 977-0909. **$79-$114.** 5399 28th St SE 49512. I-96, exit 43B, just e on SR 11. Int corridors. **Pets:** Other species. Designated rooms, service with restrictions, supervision. (ASK) ❌ &M 🛏 💻 🏊

▼▼ ▼▼💎 Crowne Plaza Grand Rapids 🅷

(616) 957-1770. **$129-$189.** 5700 28th St SE 49546. I-96, exit 43B, 0.3 mi e on SR 11. Int corridors. **Pets:** Medium. $10 daily fee/pet. Service with restrictions. (ASK) ❌ &M 🛏 💻 🍴 🏊 ❌

▼▼ ▼▼ Holiday Inn Express Suites Airport 🅷

(616) 940-8100. **$89-$159.** 5401 28th St SE 49546. I-96, exit 43B, just e on SR 11. Int corridors. **Pets:** Accepted.

(ASK) ❌ &M 🛏 💻 🏊 ❌

▼▼ Red Roof Inn #7011 Ⓜ

(616) 942-0800. **$52-$70.** 5131 E 28th St 49512. I-96, exit 43A, 0.3 mi w on SR 11. Ext corridors. **Pets:** Large. Service with restrictions, crate.

(ASK) ❌

▼▼ Super 8 🅷

(616) 957-3000. **Call for rates.** 4855 28th St SE 49512. I-96, exit 43A, 0.5 mi w on SR 11. Int corridors. **Pets:** Accepted. ❌ 🛏 💻

CHARLEVOIX

▼▼ ▼▼ AmericInn Lodge & Suites of Charlevoix 🅷

(231) 237-0988. **Call for rates.** 11800 US 31 N 49720. On US 31, 2.4 mi n. Int corridors. **Pets:** Accepted. ❌ &M 🛏 💻 🏊

CHARLOTTE

▼▼ ▼▼ Super 8 🅷

(517) 543-8288. **$75-$90.** 828 E Shepherd St 48813. I-69, exit 60 (SR 50), just w. Int corridors. **Pets:** Accepted. (ASK) ❌ 🛏 💻

CHEBOYGAN

Best Western River Terrace Motel M

(231) 627-5688. **$79-$209.** 847 S Main St 49721. 1 mi s on SR 27. Ext/int corridors. **Pets:** Dogs only. $10 daily fee/pet. Service with restrictions, crate. SAVE ⊠ 🛅 💻 ⇌ 🗶

Birch Haus Motel M

(231) 627-5862. **$40-$80.** 1301 Mackinaw Ave 49721. On US 23, 0.8 mi nw. Ext corridors. **Pets:** Small. $5 daily fee/pet. Designated rooms, service with restrictions, supervision. ASK ⊠ 🛅

Continental Inn M

(231) 627-7164. **$39-$99.** 613 N Main St 49721. Jct US 23 and SR 27. Ext corridors. **Pets:** Dogs only. $10 one-time fee/room. Designated rooms, service with restrictions, supervision. ASK ⊠ 🛅 ⇌

CHELSEA

Chelsea Comfort Inn & Village Conference Center H ❀

(734) 433-8000. **$99-$299.** 1645 Commerce Park Dr 48118. I-94, exit 159 (SR 52/Main St), just n. Int corridors. **Pets:** Large. $20 daily fee/room. Service with restrictions, supervision.

ASK ⊠ 🛅 🛅 💻 ⇌

Holiday Inn Express H

(734) 433-1600. **$94-$256.** 1540 Commerce Park Dr 48118. I-94, exit 159 (SR 52/Main St), 0.3 mi n. Int corridors. **Pets:** Medium. $100 deposit/room, $75 one-time fee/room. Designated rooms, service with restrictions, supervision. ASK ⊠ 🛅 🛅 💻 ⇌

CHESANING

 **Colonial Motel** M

(989) 845-3292. **$60-$130, 3 day notice.** 9475 E M-57 48616. On SR 57, 0.5 mi e. Ext corridors. **Pets:** Other species. $10 daily fee/pet. Designated rooms, service with restrictions, supervision. SAVE ⊠ 🛅 💻

CLARE

Days Inn H

(989) 802-0144. **$59-$180.** 10100 S Clare Ave 48617. On Business Rt US 10 and 127, just w of jct US 127 and Old US 27. Int corridors. **Pets:** $15 one-time fee/room. Service with restrictions, supervision.

ASK ⊠ 🛅 🛅 💻 🗶

COLDWATER

Super 8 H

(517) 278-8833. **Call for rates.** 600 Orleans Blvd 49036. I-69, exit 13 (US 12), 0.3 mi w on E Chicago St, just n on N Michigan Ave, then just e. Int corridors. **Pets:** Accepted. ⊠ 🛅 🛅 💻

COMSTOCK PARK

Comfort Suites Grand Rapids North H

(616) 785-7899. **$59-$139.** 350 Dodge St 49321. US 131, exit 91. Int corridors. **Pets:** Accepted. ASK ⊠ 🛅 🛅 💻 ⇌

COOPERSVILLE

Rodeway Inn H

(616) 837-8100. **$69-$149.** 1040 O'Malley Dr 49404. I-96, exit 16, just n. Int corridors. **Pets:** Accepted. ASK ⊠ 🛅 🛅 💻 ⇌

COPPER HARBOR

Lake Fanny Hooe Resort M

(906) 289-4451. **$90-$125, 7 day notice.** 505 2nd St 49918. Just s on Manganese Rd. Ext corridors. **Pets:** Other species. $10 daily fee/pet. Service with restrictions, supervision. ⊠ 🛅 💻 🗶 🐾 🗷

DETROIT METROPOLITAN AREA

ALLEN PARK

Best Western Greenfield Inn H ❀

(313) 271-1600. **$99-$110.** 3000 Enterprise Dr 48101. I-94, exit 206 (Oakwood Blvd), just s, then just w. Int corridors. **Pets:** Medium. $50 deposit/room. Supervision. SAVE ⊠ 🛅 💻 🍴 ⇌ 🗶

AUBURN HILLS

Candlewood Suites H ❀

(248) 373-3342. **$64-$94.** 1650 N Opdyke Rd 48326. I-75, exit 79 (University Dr), just w, then 0.4 mi n. Int corridors. **Pets:** Medium. $75 one-time fee/pet. Designated rooms, supervision. ASK ⊠ 🛅 💻

Extended Stay Deluxe-Detroit Auburn Hills-Featherstone H

(248) 335-5200. **$74-$99.** 2100 Featherstone Rd 48326. I-75, exit 79 (University Dr), just w to Opdyke Rd, s to Featherstone, then just e. Int corridors. **Pets:** Other species. $25 daily fee/room. Designated rooms, service with restrictions, crate. ASK ⊠ 🛅 🛅 💻 ⇌

Hilton Suites Auburn Hills H ❀

(248) 334-2222. **$89-$179.** 2300 Featherstone Rd 48326. I-75, exit 79 (University Dr), just w, 0.5 mi s on Opdyke Rd, then just e. Int corridors. **Pets:** Medium. $50 deposit/pet. Designated rooms, service with restrictions. ⊠ 🛅 🛅 🍴 ⇌ 🗶

Homestead Studio Suites Hotel-Detroit/Auburn Hills H

(248) 340-8888. **$71-$99.** 3315 University Dr 48326. I-75, exit 79 (University Dr), 0.9 mi e. Int corridors. **Pets:** Other species. $25 daily fee/room. Designated rooms, service with restrictions, crate. ASK ⊠ 🛅 💻

Staybridge Suites H

(248) 322-4600. **$89-$189.** 2050 Featherstone Rd 48326. I-75, exit 79 (University Dr), just w, 0.5 mi s on Opdyke Rd, then just e. Int corridors. **Pets:** Accepted. ASK ⊠ 🛅 💻 ⇌

BELLEVILLE

Red Roof Inn Metro Airport #7183 M

(734) 697-2244. **$56-$78, 7 day notice.** 45501 N I-94 Service Dr 48111. I-94, exit 190 (Belleville Rd), just n. Ext corridors. **Pets:** Large. Service with restrictions, crate. SAVE ⊠ 🛅

BIRMINGHAM

Holiday Inn Express–Birmingham H

(248) 642-6200. **Call for rates.** 35270 Woodward Ave 48009. Jct Woodward Ave and Maple Rd; center. Int corridors. **Pets:** Accepted. ⊠ 🛅 💻

The Townsend Hotel H ❀

(248) 642-7900. **$299-$369.** 100 Townsend St 48009. Center. Int corridors. **Pets:** Dogs only. $5 daily fee/room, $150 one-time fee/room. Service with restrictions, supervision. ECO SAVE ⊠ 🛅 🛅 💻 🍴 🗶

CANTON

La Quinta Inn H ❀

(734) 981-1808. **$49-$89.** 41211 Ford Rd 48187. I-275, exit 25 (Ford Rd), just w to jct Haggerty Rd. Int corridors. **Pets:** Medium, other species. Service with restrictions, supervision. ASK ⊠ 🛅 💻

Super 8-Canton H

(734) 722-8880. **$51-$54.** 3933 Lotz Rd 48188. I-275, exit 22 (Michigan Ave), just e on US 12, then just s. Int corridors. **Pets:** $10 daily fee/pet. Service with restrictions, supervision. ASK ⊠ 🛅 💻

DEARBORN

▼▼▼ Extended StayAmerica Detroit Dearborn 🅷
(313) 336-0021. **$81-$109.** 260 Towne Center Dr 48126. SR 39 (Southfield Frwy); between Ford Rd and Michigan Ave exits; just w of jct Service and Hubbard drs. Int corridors. **Pets:** Other species. $25 daily fee/room. Designated rooms, service with restrictions, crate.
(ASK) (✗) 🅓 🅔 🖵

AAA ▼▼▼ Red Roof Inn-Dearborn #7182 Ⓜ
(313) 278-9732. **Call for rates.** 24130 Michigan Ave 48124. Jct US 24 (Telegraph Rd) and 12 (Michigan Ave). Ext corridors. **Pets:** Large. Service with restrictions, crate. (SAVE) (✗) 🅓 🅔

AAA ▼▼▼▼ The Ritz-Carlton, Dearborn 🅷
(313) 441-2000. **$199-$319.** 300 Town Center Dr 48126. SR 39 (Southfield Frwy); between Ford Rd and Michigan Ave exits, on Service Dr. Int corridors. **Pets:** Accepted. (SAVE) (✗) 🅓 🅔 🅨 ➳ (✗)

▼▼ TownePlace Suites 🅷
(313) 271-0200. **$108-$132.** 6141 Mercury Dr 48126. SR 39 (Southfield Frwy), exit 7 (Ford Rd), just e, then 0.8 mi n. Int corridors.
Pets: Accepted. (✗) 🅓 🅔 🅨 ➳

DETROIT

▼▼▼ Doubletree Guest Suites Fort Shelby/Detroit Downtown 🅷
(313) 963-5600. **$99-$229.** 550 W Fort St 48226. Jct Lafayette Blvd. Ext corridors. **Pets:** Accepted. (✗) 🅓 🅔 🅨

▼▼▼ Hilton Garden Inn Detroit/Downtown 🅷
(313) 967-0900. **$109-$379.** 351 Gratiot Ave 48226. Jct Randolph St and Gratiot Ave, just e; in Harmonie Park. Int corridors. **Pets:** Medium. $75 one-time fee/room. Service with restrictions.
(✗) 🅓 🅔 🅨 🅨 ➳

▼▼▼ Holiday Inn Express 🅷
(313) 887-7000. **$89-$189.** 1020 Washington Blvd 48226. Corner of Washington Blvd and Michigan Ave. Int corridors. **Pets:** Small. $25 one-time fee/pet. Service with restrictions, supervision.
(ASK) (✗) 🅓 🅔 🅨 ➳

AAA ▼▼▼▼ MotorCity Casino Hotel 🅷
(313) 237-7711. **$199-$599.** 2901 Grand River Ave 48201. Jct SR 10 (Lodge Frwy). Int corridors. **Pets:** Very small, dogs only. $250 one-time fee/room. Service with restrictions. (SAVE) (✗) 🅓 🅔 🅨 (✗)

▼▼▼▼ Omni Detroit River Place 🅷
(313) 259-9500. **$149-$499.** 1000 River Place Dr 48207. 1.5 mi on E Jefferson Ave, 4 blks s on McDougall. Int corridors. **Pets:** Accepted.
(ASK) (✗) 🅔 🅨

▼▼▼ Residence Inn By Marriott-Dearborn 🅷
(313) 441-1700. **$116-$142.** 5777 Southfield Service Dr 48228. SR 39 (Southfield Frwy), exit Ford Rd, just w. Ext corridors. **Pets:** Accepted.
(✗) 🅓 🅔 ➳ (✗)

AAA ▼▼▼▼ The Westin Book Cadillac Detroit 🅷 🐾
(313) 442-1600. **$179-$399.** 1114 Washington Blvd 48226. Corner of Washington Blvd and Michigan Ave. Int corridors. **Pets:** Medium, dogs only. Service with restrictions, supervision.
(SAVE) (✗) 🅓 🅔 🅨 ➳

FARMINGTON HILLS

▼▼ Candlewood Suites 🅷
(248) 324-0540. **$77-$124.** 37555 Hills Tech Dr 48331. I-696, exit I-96 E/I-275 S/SR 5, just s to SR 5 N, 2 mi n to 12 Mile Rd, 1.3 mi e, then 0.3 mi s on Halsted Rd. Int corridors. **Pets:** Accepted.
(ASK) (✗) 🅓 🅔 🅨

▼▼ Extended StayAmerica Detroit-Farmington Hills 🅷
(248) 473-4000. **$67-$99.** 27775 Stansbury Blvd 48334. I-696, exit 5 (Orchard Lake Rd), just n, just e on 12 Mile Rd, then just s. Int corridors. **Pets:** Other species. $25 daily fee/room. Designated rooms, service with restrictions, crate. (ASK) (✗) 🅓 🅔 🅨

AAA ▼▼▼ Red Roof Inn-Farmington Hills #7038 Ⓜ
(248) 478-8640. **$48-$73.** 24300 Sinacola Ct 48335. I-96/275 and SR 5, exit 165 (Grand River Ave), just w. Ext corridors. **Pets:** Large. Service with restrictions, crate. (SAVE) (✗) 🅓 🅔

LAKE ORION

AAA ▼▼▼ Best Western Palace Inn 🅷
(248) 391-2755. **$79-$99.** 2755 N Lapeer Rd 48360. I-75, exit 81 (Lapeer Rd), 3.3 mi n. Ext/int corridors. **Pets:** Accepted.
(SAVE) (✗) 🅓 🅔 🅨 ➳

LIVONIA

▼▼▼▼ Embassy Suites Hotel 🅷
(734) 462-6000. **$99-$179.** 19525 Victor Pkwy 48152. I-275, exit 169 (7 Mile Rd), just e, then 0.5 mi n. Int corridors. **Pets:** Accepted.
(✗) 🅓 🅔 🅨 ➳

▼▼▼▼ Livonia Marriott 🅷
(734) 462-3100. **$152-$186.** 17100 Laurel Park Dr N 48152. I-275, exit 170 (6 Mile Rd), just w. Int corridors. **Pets:** Accepted.
(ECO) (✗) 🅓 🅔 🅨 ➳

▼▼▼▼ Residence Inn Detroit-Livonia 🅷
(734) 462-4201. **$161-$197.** 17250 Fox Dr 48152. I-275, exit 170 (6 Mile Rd), just w. Int corridors. **Pets:** Accepted. (✗) 🅓 🅔 🅨 ➳ (✗)

▼▼▼ TownePlace Suites by Marriott 🅷
(734) 542-7400. **$99-$121.** 17450 Fox Dr 48152. I-275, exit 170 (6 Mile Rd), just nw. Int corridors. **Pets:** Accepted. (✗) 🅓 🅔 🅨 ➳

MADISON HEIGHTS

▼▼ Motel 6 Madison Heights #1109 Ⓜ
(248) 583-0500. **$36-$46.** 32700 Barrington Rd 48071. I-75, exit 65A (14 Mile Rd), just e. Ext corridors. **Pets:** Other species. Service with restrictions, supervision. (✗) 🅓

AAA ▼▼▼ Red Roof Inn #7084 Ⓜ
(248) 583-4700. **$55-$80.** 32511 Concord Dr 48071. I-75, exit 65A (14 Mile Rd), just e, then just s. Ext corridors. **Pets:** Large. Service with restrictions, crate. (SAVE) (✗) 🅓

▼▼▼ Residence Inn by Marriott-Detroit Troy/Madison Heights 🅷
(248) 583-4322. **$126-$154.** 32650 Stephenson Hwy 48071. I-75, exit 65B (14 Mile Rd), just w, then just s. Ext corridors. **Pets:** Accepted.
(✗) 🅓 🅔 ➳ (✗)

NOVI

▼▼ Extended StayAmerica-Detroit-Novi 🅷
(248) 305-9955. **$71-$99.** 21555 Haggerty Rd 48375. I-275, exit 167 (8 Mile Rd), just w, then 0.5 mi n. Int corridors. **Pets:** Other species. $25 daily fee/room. Designated rooms, service with restrictions, crate.
(ASK) (✗) 🅓 🅔

▼▼▼ Residence Inn by Marriott-Detroit/Novi 🅷
(248) 735-7400. **$134-$164.** 27477 Cabaret Dr 48376. I-96, exit 162 (Novi Rd), just n to 12 Mile Rd, then just w. Int corridors. **Pets:** Accepted.
(✗) 🅓 🅔 🅨 ➳

AAA ▼▼▼ Sheraton-Detroit-Novi 🅷
(248) 349-4000. **$99-$229.** 21111 Haggerty Rd 48375. I-275, exit 167 (8 Mile Rd), just w to Haggerty Rd, then just n. Int corridors.
Pets: Accepted. (ECO) (SAVE) (✗) 🅓 🅔 🅨 🅨 ➳

▼▼▼ Staybridge Suites 🅷
(248) 349-4600. **$90-$199.** 27000 Providence 48374. I-96, exit 160 (Beck Rd), just s to Grand River Ave, then 0.6 mi w. Int corridors. **Pets:** Large. $75 one-time fee/room. Crate. (ASK) (✗) 🅓 🅔 🅨 ➳ (✗)

▼▼ TownePlace Suites 🅷 ❄
(248) 305-5533. **$89-$109.** 42600 11 Mile Rd 48375. I-96, exit 162 (Novi Rd), just s, 0.5 mi e on Crescent Dr, then just s on Town Center Dr. Int corridors. **Pets:** Medium. $100 one-time fee/room. Service with restrictions, crate. 🅴🅲🅾 ⊠ 🅷 🖵 ⊇

PLYMOUTH

🆎 ▼▼▼ Red Roof Inn-Plymouth #7016 🅼
(734) 459-3300. **$55-$110.** 39700 Ann Arbor Rd 48170. I-275, exit 28 (Ann Arbor Rd), just e. Ext corridors. **Pets:** Large. Service with restrictions, crate. 🆂🅰🆅🅴 ⊠ 🅷

PONTIAC

▼▼▼ Residence Inn by Marriott Detroit Pontiac/Auburn Hills 🅷 ❄
(248) 858-8664. **$134-$164.** 3333 Centerpoint Pkwy 48341. I-75, exit 75 (Square Lake Rd), w via Opdyke Rd. Int corridors. **Pets:** Other species. $100 one-time fee/room. Service with restrictions.
⊠ 🅷 🖵 ⊇ ⊠

ROCHESTER HILLS

🆎 ▼▼ Red Roof Inn #7191 🅼
(248) 853-6400. **Call for rates.** 2580 Crooks Rd 48309. Jct Hall Rd (SR 59). Ext corridors. **Pets:** Large. Service with restrictions, crate.
🆂🅰🆅🅴 ⊠ 🅷

ROMULUS

▼▼ Baymont Inn & Suites Detroit-Airport 🅷
(734) 722-6000. **Call for rates.** 9000 Wickham Rd 48174. I-94, exit 198 (Merriman Rd), just n, then just w. Int corridors. **Pets:** Accepted.
⊠ 🅷 🖵

🆎 ▼▼ Best Western Gateway International Hotel 🅷
(734) 728-2800. **$75-$150, 3 day notice.** 9191 Wickham Rd 48174. I-94, exit 198 (Merriman Rd), just n, then just w. Int corridors. **Pets:** Small. $25 one-time fee/room. Designated rooms, service with restrictions, supervision. 🆂🅰🆅🅴 ⊠ 🅷 🖵 🍽 ⊇ ⊠

▼▼ Days Inn 🅷
(734) 946-4300. **$60-$130.** 9501 Middlebelt Rd 48174. I-94, exit 199 (Middlebelt Rd), 0.4 mi s. Int corridors. **Pets:** Small. $20 one-time fee/pet. Designated rooms, service with restrictions, crate.
🅰🆂🅺 ⊠ 🅷 🖵 🍽

▼▼▼ Detroit Metro Airport Marriott 🅷
(734) 729-7555. **$170-$208.** 30559 Flynn Dr 48174. I-94, exit 198 (Merriman Rd), just n, then 0.3 mi e. Int corridors. **Pets:** Accepted.
⊠ 🅼 🅷 🖵 ⊇

▼▼ Extended StayAmerica Detroit-Metro Airport 🅷
(734) 722-7780. **$59-$99.** 30325 Flynn Dr 48174. I-94, exit 198 (Merriman Rd), just n, then 0.4 mi e. Int corridors. **Pets:** Other species. $25 daily fee/room. Designated rooms, service with restrictions, crate.
🅰🆂🅺 ⊠ 🅷 🖵

▼▼ La Quinta Inn Detroit-Metro Airport 🅷 ❄
(734) 641-9006. **$80-$120.** 7680 Merriman Rd 48174. I-94, exit 198 (Merriman Rd), 0.4 mi n. Int corridors. **Pets:** Medium, other species. Service with restrictions, supervision. ⊠ 🅷 🖵

▼▼ Red Roof Inn 🅷
(734) 595-7400. **$60.** 9095 Wickham Rd 48174. I-94, exit 198 (Merriman Rd), just n, then just w. Int corridors. **Pets:** Large. Service with restrictions, crate. 🅰🆂🅺 ⊠ 🅷 🖵

▼▼ Romulus Quality Inn & Suites 🅷
(734) 946-1400. **$60-$70.** 9555 Middlebelt Rd 48174. I-94, exit 199 (Middlebelt Rd), 0.4 mi s. Int corridors. **Pets:** $10 one-time fee/pet. Service with restrictions, supervision. 🅰🆂🅺 ⊠ 🅷 🖵

🆎 ▼▼▼ The Westin Detroit Metropolitan Airport 🅷
(734) 942-6500. **$99-$329.** 2501 Worldgateway Pl 48242. I-94, exit 198 (Merriman Rd); at McNamara Terminal. Int corridors. **Pets:** Accepted.
🆂🅰🆅🅴 ⊠ 🅼 🅷 🖵 🍽 ⊇

ROSEVILLE

🆎 ▼▼ Baymont Inn & Suites Detroit-Roseville 🅷
(586) 296-6910. **$59-$74.** 20675 13 Mile Rd 48066. I-94, exit 232 (Little Mack Ave), just s. Int corridors. **Pets:** Accepted. 🆂🅰🆅🅴 ⊠ 🅷 🖵

🆎 ▼▼▼ Best Western Georgian Inn 🅼
(586) 294-0400. **$74-$189.** 31327 Gratiot Ave 48066. I-94, exit 232 (Little Mack Ave), just s, 0.5 mi n on 13 Mile Rd, then just n. Ext corridors. **Pets:** Dogs only. $8 daily fee/pet. Service with restrictions.
🆂🅰🆅🅴 ⊠ 🅷 🖵 🍽 ⊇

🆎 ▼▼ Red Roof Inn #7012 🅼
(586) 296-0310. **$55-$70.** 31800 Little Mack Ave 48066. I-94, exit 232 (Little Mack Ave), just n. Ext corridors. **Pets:** Large. Service with restrictions, crate. 🆂🅰🆅🅴 ⊠ 🅷

SOUTHFIELD

▼▼ Candlewood Suites 🅷 🐾
(248) 945-0010. **$65-$124.** 1 Corporate Dr 48076. SR 10 (Northwestern Hwy), exit Lahser Rd, just e. Int corridors. **Pets:** Large, other species. $75 one-time fee/room. Service with restrictions, crate.
🅰🆂🅺 ⊠ 🅼 🅷 🖵

▼▼▼ Hampton Inn-Southfield 🅷
(248) 356-5500. **$99-$209.** 27500 Northwestern Service Dr 48034. I-696, exit 9 (Telegraph Rd N), just n to 11 Mile Rd, then 0.5 mi e. Int corridors. **Pets:** Accepted. ⊠ 🅷 🖵 ⊇

🆎 ▼▼ Hawthorn Suites 🅷
(248) 352-8900. **$60-$150.** 26700 Central Park Blvd 48076. I-696, exit 11 (Evergreen Rd), just sw of jct 11 Mile and Evergreen rds. Ext corridors. **Pets:** Accepted. 🆂🅰🆅🅴 ⊠ 🅼 🅷 🖵 ⊇ ⊠

▼▼ Marvin's Garden Inn 🅼
(248) 353-6777. **Call for rates.** 27650 Northwestern Hwy 48034. I-696, exit 9 (Telegraph Rd), just nw. Ext/int corridors. **Pets:** Accepted.
⊠ 🅷 🖵

▼▼ Red Roof Inn-Southfield #7133 🅼
(248) 353-7200. **$39-$109.** 27660 Northwestern Hwy 48034. I-696, exit 9 (Telegraph Rd), just nw. Ext corridors. **Pets:** Large. Service with restrictions, crate. 🅰🆂🅺 ⊠ 🅼 🅷

🆎 ▼▼ ▼▼ The Westin Hotel Southfield-Detroit 🅷
(248) 827-4000. **Call for rates.** 1500 Town Center 48075. SR 10 (Northwestern Hwy), exit 10 (10 Mile Rd/Evergreen Rd), 0.3 mi n. Int corridors. **Pets:** Accepted. 🆂🅰🆅🅴 ⊠ 🅼 🅷 🖵 🍽 ⊇ ⊠

SOUTHGATE

▼▼▼ La Quinta Inn & Suites Detroit-Southgate 🅷 🐾
(734) 374-3000. **$55-$89.** 12888 Reeck Rd 48195. I-75, exit 37 (Northline Rd), just w. Int corridors. **Pets:** Medium, other species. Service with restrictions, supervision. 🅰🆂🅺 ⊠ 🅷 🖵

STERLING HEIGHTS

▼▼ TownePlace Suites 🅷 🐾
(586) 566-0900. **$120-$130.** 14800 Lakeside Cir 48313. 1 mi e of jct SR 53 (Van Dyke Ave) and 59 (Hall Rd). Int corridors. **Pets:** Other species. $75 one-time fee/room. Designated rooms. ⊠ 🅼 🅷 🖵 ⊇

TAYLOR

🆎 ▼▼▼ Red Roof Inn-Taylor #7189 🅼
(734) 374-1150. **$35-$75.** 21230 Eureka Rd 48180. I-75, exit 36 (Eureka Rd), just w. Ext corridors. **Pets:** Large. Service with restrictions, crate.
🆂🅰🆅🅴 ⊠ 🅷

TROY

▼▼▼▼ Drury Inn & Suites-Troy 🅷
(248) 528-3330. **$70-$234.** 575 W Big Beaver Rd 48084. I-75, exit 69 (Big Beaver Rd), just e. Int corridors. **Pets:** Other species. No service, supervision. (ASK) ✕ 🛏 💻 🍴 ➳

▼▼ Holiday Inn-Troy 🅷
(248) 689-7500. **$72-$134.** 2537 Rochester Ct 48083. I-75, exit 67 (Rochester Rd), 0.3 mi sw, then just w. Int corridors. **Pets:** Large, other species. $35 one-time fee/room. Service with restrictions, supervision. (ECO) (ASK) ✕ 🛏 💻 🍴 ➳

▼▼▼▼ The MET Hotel Troy Detroit 🅷
(248) 879-2100. **$89-$209.** 5500 Crooks Rd 48084. I-75, exit 72 (Crooks Rd), just n. Int corridors. **Pets:** Accepted. ✕ 🛗 🛏 💻 🍴 ➳

⏣⏣ ▼▼▼ Red Roof Inn-Troy #7021 Ⓜ
(248) 689-4391. **$53-$63.** 2350 Rochester Ct 48083. I-75, exit 67 (Rochester Rd), 0.3 mi sw. Ext corridors. **Pets:** Large. Service with restrictions, crate. (SAVE) ✕ 🛗 🛏

▼▼▼▼ Residence Inn by Marriott 🅷
(248) 689-6856. **$152-$186.** 2600 Livernois Rd 48083. I-75, exit 69 (Big Beaver Rd), 0.5 mi e to Livernois Rd, then 0.5 mi s. Ext corridors. **Pets:** Accepted. ✕ 🛏 💻 ➳ ✕

UTICA

▼▼▼▼ Comfort Inn 🅷 ❀
(586) 739-7111. **$69-$149.** 11401 Hall Rd 48317. Jct Van Dyke Ave (SR 53). Int corridors. **Pets:** Medium, dogs only. $50 deposit/room. Service with restrictions, crate. (ASK) ✕ 🛏 💻

▼▼▼▼ La Quinta Inn & Suites 🅷 ❀
(586) 731-4700. **$69-$99.** 45311 Park Ave 48315. Jct Van Dyke Ave (SR 53) and Hall Rd (SR 59), just n. Int corridors. **Pets:** Medium, other species. Service with restrictions, supervision. (ASK) ✕ 🛏 💻 ➳

▼▼▼▼ Staybridge Suites-Utica 🅷 ❀
(586) 323-0101. **$129-$189.** 46155 Utica Park Blvd 48315. Jct Van Dyke Ave (SR 53) and Hall Rd (SR 59), just n. Int corridors. **Pets:** Medium, other species. $75 one-time fee/room. No service, supervision. (ASK) ✕ 🛗 🛏 💻 ➳

WARREN

▼▼ ▼▼ Candlewood Suites-Detroit Warren 🅷
(586) 978-1261. **Call for rates.** 7010 Convention Blvd 48092. I-696, exit 23 (Van Dyke Ave), 2.8 mi n. Int corridors. **Pets:** Accepted. ✕ 🛗 🛏 💻

▼▼ ▼▼ Extended Stay Deluxe Detroit-Warren 🅷
(586) 558-5554. **$67-$99.** 30125 N Civic Center Blvd 48093. I-696, exit 23 (Van Dyke Ave), 1.5 mi n, then just e. Int corridors. **Pets:** Other species. $25 daily fee/room. Designated rooms, service with restrictions, crate. (ASK) ✕ 🛗 🛏 💻

▼▼▼▼ Hawthorn Suites 🅷
(586) 558-7870. **Call for rates.** 30180 N Civic Center Blvd 48093. I-696, exit 23 (Van Dyke Ave), 1.8 mi n. Ext/int corridors. **Pets:** Accepted. ✕ 🛗 🛏 💻 ➳

▼▼ ▼▼ La Quinta Inn 🅷 ❀
(586) 574-0550. **$49-$79.** 30900 Van Dyke Ave 48093. I-696, exit 23 (Van Dyke Ave), 1.8 mi n on SR 53. Int corridors. **Pets:** Medium, other species. Service with restrictions, supervision. (ASK) ✕ 🛏 💻

▼▼ ▼▼ Red Roof Inn-Warren #070 Ⓜ
(586) 573-4300. **$54-$74.** 26300 Dequindre Rd 48091. I-696, exit 20 (Dequindre Rd), just ne. Ext corridors. **Pets:** Large. Service with restrictions, crate. (ASK) ✕ 🛗

⏣⏣ ▼▼▼▼ TownePlace Suites by Marriott-Warren 🅷
(586) 264-8800. **$107-$131.** 7601 Chicago Rd 48092. I-696, exit 23 (Van Dyke Ave), 2 mi n. Int corridors. **Pets:** Accepted. (SAVE) ✕ 🛗 🛏 💻 ➳

WATERFORD

▼▼▼▼ Comfort Inn 🅷
(248) 666-8555. **$90-$200.** 7076 Highland Rd 48327. Jct SR 59 (Highland Rd) and Airport Rd, 1 mi w. Int corridors. **Pets:** Accepted. (ASK) ✕ 🛏 💻 ➳

END METROPOLITAN AREA

DEWITT

▼▼ ▼▼ Baymont Inn & Suites De Witt/Lansing North 🅷
(517) 374-0000. **Call for rates.** 1055 Aaron Dr 48820. I-69, exit 87 (Old US 27), just s. Int corridors. **Pets:** Accepted. ✕ 🛗 🛏 💻 ➳

⏣⏣ ▼▼ Sleep Inn 🅷
(517) 669-8823. **$59-$109.** 1101 Commerce Park Dr 48820. I-69, exit 87 (Old US 27), 0.8 mi n. Int corridors. **Pets:** Small, dogs only. $10 daily fee/pet. Service with restrictions, supervision. (SAVE) ✕ 🛏 💻 ➳

DIMONDALE

⏣⏣ ▼▼▼ Comfort Inn & Suites of Lansing 🅷 ❀
(517) 721-0000. **$79-$109.** 9742 Woodlane Dr 48821. I-96, exit 98B (Lansing Rd N), just n. Int corridors. **Pets:** Other species. $30 one-time fee/pet. Designated rooms, service with restrictions. (ECO) (SAVE) ✕ 🛗 🛏 💻 ➳

DOWAGIAC

▼▼ ▼▼ Baymont Inn & Suites of Dowagiac 🅷
(269) 782-4270. **$89-$169.** 29291 Amerihost Dr 49047. 0.4 mi s of jct SR 51 and 62. Int corridors. **Pets:** Medium. $10 one-time fee/room. Designated rooms, service with restrictions, crate. (ASK) ✕ 🛗 🛏 💻 ➳

EAST LANSING

⏣⏣ ▼▼▼▼ Candlewood Suites 🅷 ❀
(517) 351-8181. **$59-$189.** 3545 Forest Rd 48910. I-496, exit 11 (Jolly Rd), just e to Collins Rd, 0.3 mi n, then just e. Int corridors. **Pets:** $75 one-time fee/room. Service with restrictions, crate. (SAVE) ✕ 🛗 🛏 💻 🍴

▼▼ ▼▼ Howard Johnson Inn Ⓜ
(517) 351-5500. **$68-$129.** 1100 Trowbridge Rd 48823. US 127, exit Trowbridge Rd, just e. Ext/int corridors. **Pets:** $25 one-time fee/room. Designated rooms, service with restrictions, crate. (ASK) ✕ 🛏 💻 ➳

▼▼▼▼ Residence Inn by Marriott 🅷
(517) 332-7711. **$125-$153.** 1600 E Grand River Ave 48823. US 127, exit Grand River Ave, 2.6 mi se on SR 43. Ext corridors. **Pets:** Accepted. ✕ 🛏 💻 ➳ ✕

EAST TAWAS

⏣⏣ ▼▼ Tawas Bay Beach Resort 🅷
(989) 362-8601. **$70-$189, 3 day notice.** 300 E Bay St 48730. On US 23 W. Int corridors. **Pets:** Small. $30 one-time fee/room. Designated rooms, service with restrictions, supervision. (SAVE) ✕ 🛏 💻 🍴 ➳ ✕

ESCANABA

Econo Lodge H
(906) 789-1066. **Call for rates.** 921 N Lincoln Rd 49829. 0.5 mi n on US 2/41 and SR 35. Int corridors. **Pets:** Small, other species. $10 daily fee/pet. Supervision. SAVE

Hiawatha Motel M
(906) 786-1341. **$50-$125.** 2400 Ludington St 49829. 0.5 mi w on US 2/41. Ext corridors. **Pets:** Other species. $5 daily fee/room. No service, supervision. SAVE

FENTON

Holiday Inn Express Hotel & Suites H
(810) 714-7171. **$89-$129.** 17800 Silver Pkwy 48430. US 23, exit 78 (Owen Rd), just w, then 0.4 mi n. Int corridors. **Pets:** Small. Service with restrictions, supervision. ASK

FLINT

AmericInn Motel & Suites of Flint H
(810) 232-9000. **$83.** 6075 Hill 23 Dr 48507. US 23, exit 90 (Hill Rd), just w. Int corridors. **Pets:** $25 one-time fee/room. Service with restrictions, supervision. SAVE

Baymont Inn & Suites-Flint H
(810) 732-2300. **Call for rates.** 4160 Pier North Blvd 48504. I-75, exit 122 (Pierson Rd), just w. Int corridors. **Pets:** Accepted.

Holiday Inn Express Flint Campus Area H
(810) 238-7744. **$79-$189.** 1150 Robert T Longway Blvd 48503. I-475, exit 8A (Robert T Longway Blvd), just w. Int corridors. **Pets:** Accepted.
ASK

Residence Inn by Marriott H ✿
(810) 424-7000. **$117-$143.** 2202 W Hill Rd 48507. US 23, exit 90 (Hill Rd), just e. Int corridors. **Pets:** Other species. $100 one-time fee/room. Service with restrictions, supervision.

FOWLERVILLE

Best Western Fowlerville M
(517) 223-9165. **Call for rates.** 950 S Grand Ave 48836. I-96, exit 129 (Fowlerville), just n. Ext corridors. **Pets:** Accepted.
SAVE

FRANKENMUTH

Drury Inn & Suites-Frankenmuth H
(989) 652-2800. **$85-$194.** 260 S Main St 48734. On SR 83; downtown. Int corridors. **Pets:** Other species. No service, supervision.
ASK

Frankenmuth Motel M
(989) 652-6171. **$50-$99.** 1218 Weiss St 48734. Just e of SR 83. Ext corridors. **Pets:** Other species. $10 one-time fee/room. Designated rooms, service with restrictions. ASK

GAYLORD

Alpine Lodge H ✿
(989) 732-2431. **$69-$119, 14 day notice.** 833 W Main St 49735. I-75, exit 282, 0.3 mi e on SR 32. Ext/int corridors. **Pets:** Medium, dogs only. Service with restrictions, supervision.
SAVE

Downtown Motel M
(989) 732-5010. **$46-$80.** 208 S Otsego Ave 49735. I-75, exit 282, 0.5 mi e, then 0.3 mi s on I-75 business loop. Ext corridors. **Pets:** $5 daily fee/pet. Service with restrictions, supervision. SAVE

Quality Inn H ✿
(989) 732-7541. **$50-$110.** 137 West St 49735. I-75, exit 282, 0.3 mi e on SR 32. Int corridors. **Pets:** Other species. $10 daily fee/room. Designated rooms, service with restrictions, supervision.
SAVE

Royal Crest Motel H
(989) 732-6451. **$59-$109, 14 day notice.** 803 S Otsego Ave 49735. I-75, exit 279, 2.3 mi ne on I-75 business loop. Int corridors.
Pets: Accepted. SAVE

GLADSTONE

Shorewood Motel M
(906) 428-9624. **Call for rates.** 1226 N Lakeshore Dr 49837. US 41, exit Kipling northbound; exit business district southbound, 1 mi n. Ext corridors. **Pets:** Accepted.

GRAND MARAIS

Voyageur's Motel M
(906) 494-2389. **$80-$90.** 21914 E Wilson St 49839. 0.5 mi e of SR 77. Ext corridors. **Pets:** Accepted.

GRAND RAPIDS

Homewood Suites by Hilton H
(616) 285-7100. **$79-$159.** 3920 Stahl Dr SE 49546. I-96, exit 43A (28th St SW), 1.5 mi w to E Paris Ave, then just n. Int corridors. **Pets:** Service with restrictions, supervision.

Radisson Hotel Grand Rapids Riverfront H ✿
(616) 363-9001. **$84-$124.** 270 Ann St NW 49504. US 131, exit 88, 1.8 mi n. Int corridors. **Pets:** Other species. $25 one-time fee/room. Supervision. SAVE

GRANDVILLE

Days Inn & Suites H
(616) 531-5263. **$65-$150.** 3825 28th St SW 49418. I-196, exit 70/70A, 0.5 mi e. Int corridors. **Pets:** Small. $10 daily fee/pet. Designated rooms, service with restrictions, supervision. ASK

Residence Inn by Marriott Grand Rapids West H ✿
(616) 538-1100. **$107-$131.** 3451 Rivertown Point Ct SW 49418. I-196, exit 67, 1.7 mi e. Int corridors. **Pets:** Other species. $75 one-time fee/room. Service with restrictions, crate.
ECO

GRAYLING

Ausable Valley Hotel & Conference Center H ✿
(989) 348-7611. **$70-$110.** 2650 S Business Loop 49738. I-75 business loop, 0.8 mi s. Ext/int corridors. **Pets:** Service with restrictions, supervision. ASK

Super 8 H ✿
(989) 348-8888. **Call for rates.** 5828 Nelson a Miles Pkwy 49738. I-75, exit 251, just w. Int corridors. **Pets:** Other species. $50 deposit/room, $7 daily fee/pet. Service with restrictions, supervision.

GREENVILLE

AmericInn Lodge & Suites of Greenville H
(616) 754-4500. **$90-$100.** 2525 W Washington 48838. US 131, exit 101 (SR 57), 13 mi e. Int corridors. **Pets:** $15 daily fee/room. Designated rooms, no service, supervision. ASK

HANCOCK

Best Western Copper Crown Motel H
(906) 482-6111. **$63-$99.** 235 Hancock St 49930. On US 41 S; downtown. Ext/int corridors. **Pets:** Accepted. SAVE

HARRISON

Lakeside Motel & Cottages M ✿
(989) 539-3796. **$62-$99.** 515 E Park St, Business US 127, M-61 48625. US 127, exit US 127 business route/SR 61, 2.2 mi w. Ext corridors.
Pets: Other species. Crate. SAVE

HOLLAND

Microtel Inn & Suites H

(616) 392-3235. **$50-$160.** 643 Hastings Ave 49423. Just w of US 31 and 32nd St. Int corridors. **Pets:** Other species. $10 daily fee/pet. Supervision.

Residence Inn by Marriott H

(616) 393-6900. **$109-$149.** 631 Southpoint Ridge Rd 49423. I-196, exit 49, 0.7 mi n on SR 40. Int corridors. **Pets:** Accepted.

HOUGHTON

Best Western-Franklin Square Inn H

(906) 487-1700. **$80-$110.** 820 Shelden Ave 49931. On US 41; downtown. Int corridors. **Pets:** Other species. $20 daily fee/room. Designated rooms, service with restrictions, supervision.

Country Inn & Suites By Carlson H

(906) 487-6700. **$89-$179.** 919 Razorback Dr 49931. 1.3 mi w on SR 26. Int corridors. **Pets:** Accepted.

HOUGHTON LAKE

Super 8 H

(989) 422-3119. **$59-$109.** 9580 W Lake City Rd 48629. Jct US 127 and SR 55. Int corridors. **Pets:** Medium. $10 daily fee/pet. Service with restrictions, supervision.

HOWELL

Baymont Inn & Suites-Howell H

(517) 546-0712. **Call for rates.** 4120 Lambert Dr 48843. I-96, exit 133 (US 59/Grand River Ave), just n, then 0.5 mi e. Int corridors.
Pets: Accepted.

Best Western Howell M

(517) 548-2900. **$85-$155, 7 day notice.** 1500 Pinckney Rd 48843. I-96, exit 137 (Pinckney Rd), just s on CR D19. Ext corridors.
Pets: Small, dogs only. $15 daily fee/pet. Designated rooms, service with restrictions, supervision.

Holiday Inn Express & Suites H

(517) 548-0100. **Call for rates.** 1397 N Burkhart Rd 48855. I-96, exit 133 (US 59/Grand River Ave), just n, then 0.5 mi e. Int corridors.
Pets: $25 one-time fee/pet. No service, supervision.

HUDSONVILLE

Quality Inn-Hudsonville H

(616) 662-4000. **$75-$85.** 3301 Highland Dr 49426. I-196, exit 62 (32nd Ave), just nw. Int corridors. **Pets:** Accepted.

Super 8 H

(616) 896-6710. **$65.** 3005 Corporate Grove Dr 49426. I-196, exit 62 (32nd Ave), just se. Int corridors. **Pets:** Accepted.

IMLAY CITY

Super 8-Imlay City H

(810) 724-8700. **$59-$99.** 6951 Newark Rd 48444. I-69, exit 168 (SR 53/Van Dyke Rd), just n, then just e. Int corridors. **Pets:** $10 one-time fee/room. Service with restrictions, supervision.

IONIA

Super 8 H

(616) 527-2828. **Call for rates.** 7245 S State Rd 48846. I-96, exit 67 (SR 66). Int corridors. **Pets:** Accepted.

IRON MOUNTAIN

Budget Host Inn M ❀

(906) 774-6797. **$52-$60.** 1663 N Stephenson Ave 49801. 1.5 mi nw on US 2 and 141. Ext corridors. **Pets:** Medium. $5 daily fee/room. Designated rooms, service with restrictions, supervision.

Country Inn & Suites By Carlson H

(906) 774-1900. **Call for rates.** 2005 S Stephenson Ave 49801. Jct SR 141, 0.8 mi w on US 2. Int corridors. **Pets:** Accepted.

IRON RIVER

AmericInn Lodge & Suites of Iron River H

(906) 265-9100. **$84-$136.** 40 E Adams St 49935. On US 2; downtown. Int corridors. **Pets:** Medium, other species. $10 daily fee/room. Designated rooms, service with restrictions, supervision.

IRONWOOD

Americas Best Value Inn H

(906) 932-3395. **$70-$80.** 160 E Cloverland Dr 49938. Jct US 2 and 2 business route. Int corridors. **Pets:** Accepted.

AmericInn of Ironwood H

(906) 932-7200. **$69-$169.** 1117 E Cloverland Dr 49938. 0.8 mi e on US 2. Int corridors. **Pets:** $15 daily fee/room. Service with restrictions.

ISHPEMING

Best Western Country Inn H

(906) 485-6345. **$92-$111, 7 day notice.** 850 US 41 W 49849. US 41, just n of town. Int corridors. **Pets:** Designated rooms, service with restrictions, supervision.

JACKSON

Baymont Inn-Jackson H

(517) 789-6000. **$89-$189, 7 day notice.** 2035 Holiday Inn Dr 49202. I-94, exit 138 (US 127), just nw. Int corridors. **Pets:** Accepted.

Motel 6–1088 M

(517) 789-7186. **$39-$49.** 830 Royal Dr 49202. I-94, exit 138 (US 127), just se. Ext corridors. **Pets:** Other species. Service with restrictions, supervision.

KALAMAZOO

Baymont Inn & Suites H ❀

(269) 372-7999. **$59-$99.** 2203 S 11th St 49009. US 131, exit 36B (Stadium Dr), just w. Int corridors. **Pets:** Other species. $10 daily fee/pet. Supervision.

Best Western Hospitality Inn H ❀

(269) 381-1900. **$72-$140.** 3640 E Cork 49001. I-94, exit 80 (Sprinkle Rd), just nw. Int corridors. **Pets:** Other species. Service with restrictions, supervision.

Best Western Kalamazoo Suites H

(269) 350-5522. **$89-$149.** 2575 S 11th St 49009. US 131, exit 36B (Stadium Dr), just w. Int corridors. **Pets:** Medium, other species. $25 one-time fee/room. Designated rooms, service with restrictions, supervision.

Holiday Inn-West H

(269) 375-6000. **$129-$179.** 2747 S 11th St 49009. US 131, exit 36B (Stadium Dr), just w. Int corridors. **Pets:** Medium, other species. $25 one-time fee/room. Supervision.

Quality Inn H

(269) 381-7000. **Call for rates.** 3820 Sprinkle Rd 49001. I-94, exit 80 (Sprinkle Rd), 0.3 mi s. Int corridors. **Pets:** Medium. $15 one-time fee/room. Service with restrictions, supervision.

Red Roof Inn-West #7025 H

(269) 375-7400. **$50-$85.** 5425 W Michigan Ave 49009. US 131, exit 36B (Stadium Dr), just nw. Ext corridors. **Pets:** Large. Service with restrictions, crate.

Residence Inn by Marriott H
(269) 349-0855. **$116-$142.** 1500 E Kilgore Rd 49001. I-94, exit 78 (Portage Rd), just n, then just w. Int corridors. **Pets:** Accepted.

Staybridge Suites-Kalamazoo H
(269) 372-8000. **$99-$199.** 2001 Seneca Ln 49008. US 131, exit 36A (Stadium Dr), 0.3 mi e. Int corridors. **Pets:** Medium, other species. $25 one-time fee/pet. Service with restrictions, supervision.

Stuart Avenue Inn Bed and Breakfast BB
(269) 342-0230. **$109-$189, 30 day notice.** 229 Stuart Ave 49007. US 131, exit 38A, 3 mi e on W Main St. Int corridors. **Pets:** Accepted.

TownePlace Suites by Marriott Kalamazoo H
(269) 353-1500. **$94-$114.** 5683 S 9th St 49009. I-94, exit 72 (9th St), just s. Int corridors. **Pets:** Accepted.

KENTWOOD

Comfort Inn H
(616) 957-2080. **$66-$140.** 4155 28th St SE 49512. I-96, exit 43A, 1.5 mi w on SR 11. Int corridors. **Pets:** $20 one-time fee/pet. Service with restrictions, supervision.

Extended StayAmerica Grand Rapids-Kentwood H
(616) 977-6750. **$40-$65.** 3747 29th St SE 49512. I-96, exit 43A, 2 mi w on SR 11, then just s. Int corridors. **Pets:** Other species. $25 daily fee/ room. Designated rooms, service with restrictions, crate.

Hilton Grand Rapids Airport H 🐾
(616) 957-0100. **$89-$175.** 4747 28th St SE 49512. I-96, exit 43A, 0.5 mi w on SR 11. Int corridors. **Pets:** Medium, other species. $75 one-time fee/room. Designated rooms, service with restrictions, crate.

Residence Inn by Marriott East H 🐾
(616) 957-8111. **$125-$153.** 2701 E Beltline Ave 49546. Jct SR 11 and E Beltline Ave (SR 37). Ext corridors. **Pets:** Medium, other species. $100 one-time fee/room. Service with restrictions.

Staybridge Suites H
(616) 464-3200. **Call for rates.** 3000 Lake Eastbrook Blvd SE 49512. I-96, exit 43A, 2 mi w on SR 11, then just s. Int corridors. **Pets:** Accepted.

LANSING

Days Inn Lansing Hotel and Conference Center H
(517) 627-8471. **$85-$110, 3 day notice.** 7711 W Saginaw Hwy 48917. I-96, exit 93B (SR 43/Saginaw Hwy), just e. Int corridors. **Pets:** Accepted.

Hampton Inn of Lansing H 🐾
(517) 627-8381. **Call for rates.** 525 N Canal Rd 48917. I-96, exit 93B (SR 43/Saginaw Hwy), just e. Int corridors. **Pets:** Other species. $100 deposit/room. Designated rooms, service with restrictions, crate.

Lexington Lansing Hotel H 🐾
(517) 323-7100. **$150-$300.** 925 S Creyts Rd 48917. I-496, exit 1 (Creyts Rd), just n. Int corridors. **Pets:** Medium. $40 one-time fee/room. Service with restrictions, supervision.

Motel 6 Lansing West #1089 M
(517) 321-1444. **$39-$49.** 7326 W Saginaw Hwy 48917. I-96, exit 93B (SR 43/Saginaw Hwy), just e. Ext corridors. **Pets:** Other species. Service with restrictions, supervision.

Quality Suites Hotel H
(517) 886-0600. **$89-$99.** 901 Delta Commerce Dr 48917. I-96, exit 93B (SR 43/Saginaw Hwy), 0.3 mi e to Bennigan's, then just n. Int corridors. **Pets:** $25 one-time fee/room. Service with restrictions, crate.

Red Roof Inn-West #7020 H
(517) 321-7246. **$44-$65.** 7412 W Saginaw Hwy 48917. I-96, exit 93B (SR 43/Saginaw Hwy), just e. Ext corridors. **Pets:** Large. Service with restrictions, crate.

Residence Inn by Marriott West H
(517) 886-5030. **$115-$125.** 922 Delta Commerce Dr 48917. I-96, exit 93B (SR 43/Saginaw Hwy), 0.4 mi e; behind Bennigan's. Int corridors. **Pets:** Accepted.

LAPEER

Fairfield Inn by Marriott Flint-Lapeer H
(810) 245-7700. **$98-$120.** 927 Demille Rd 48446. I-69, exit 155 (SR 24), 1.2 mi n, then just e. Int corridors. **Pets:** Other species. $15 daily fee/pet, $25 one-time fee/pet. Service with restrictions, supervision.

LUDINGTON

Best Western Splash Park Inn H 🐾
(231) 843-2140. **$52-$154.** 5005 W US 10 49431. Jct US 31, 1 mi w. Int corridors. **Pets:** Dogs only. $15 one-time fee/pet. Designated rooms, service with restrictions, crate.

Holiday Inn Express H
(231) 845-7004. **$89-$249.** 5323 W US 10 49431. Jct US 31, 1.3 mi w. Int corridors. **Pets:** Accepted.

MACKINAW CITY

Aqua Grand Mackinaw M 🐾
(231) 436-8831. **$38-$198, 3 day notice.** 907 S Huron St 49701. 0.8 mi se on US 23. Ext corridors. **Pets:** $100 deposit/room. Designated rooms, supervision.

Baymont Inn & Suites-Mackinaw City H
(231) 436-7737. **$69-$259.** 109 S Nicolet St 49701. I-75, exit 338 southbound, just n. Int corridors. **Pets:** Medium, dogs only. $15 daily fee/pet. Designated rooms, service with restrictions, supervision.

The Beach House CA
(231) 436-5353. **Call for rates.** 11490 W US 23 49701. 1.3 mi s. Ext corridors. **Pets:** Medium, dogs only. $20 one-time fee/room. Service with restrictions, supervision.

Days Inn & Suites "Bridgeview Lodge" M
(231) 436-8961. **$39-$289.** 206 N Nicolet St 49701. I-75, exit 339; at bridge. Ext/int corridors. **Pets:** Small, dogs only. Designated rooms, service with restrictions, supervision.

Days Inn Lakeview M 🐾
(231) 436-5557. **$39-$198, 3 day notice.** 825 S Huron Ave 49701. I-75, exit 337 northbound, 0.5 mi n to US 23, then 0.3 mi e; exit 338 southbound, 0.8 mi se on US 23. Ext corridors. **Pets:** $100 deposit/room. Designated rooms, supervision.

Econo Lodge at the Bridge M
(231) 436-5026. **Call for rates.** 412 N Nicolet St 49701. I-75, exit 339. Ext corridors. **Pets:** Accepted.

Econo Lodge Bayview M
(231) 436-5777. **$38-$178, 3 day notice.** 712 S Huron Ave 49701. I-75, exit 337 northbound, 0.5 mi n to US 23, 0.3 mi e, then just n; exit 338 southbound, 0.8 mi se on US 23, then just n. Ext corridors. **Pets:** Accepted.

◇◇ ▼▼▼ **Holiday Inn Express at the Bridge** 🅷
(231) 436-7100. **$59-$159.** 364 Louvigny 49701. I-75, exit 339. Int corridors. **Pets:** Medium, dogs only. Designated rooms, service with restrictions, supervision. 〔SAVE〕 ⊠ ⅏ 🖬 💻 ⊷ ⊠

◇◇ ▼▼▼ **Super 8-Beachfront** Ⓜ ❀
(231) 436-7111. **$38-$198, 3 day notice.** 519 S Huron Ave 49701. I-75, exit 337 northbound, 0.5 mi n to US 23, 0.3 mi e, then just n; exit 338 southbound, 0.8 mi se on US 23, then just n. Ext corridors. **Pets:** $100 deposit/room. Designated rooms, supervision. 〔SAVE〕 ⊠ 🖬 💻 ⊷

◇◇ ▼▼▼ **Super 8 Bridgeview** 🅷 ❀
(231) 436-5252. **$38-$198, 3 day notice.** 601 N Huron Ave 49701. I-75, exit 339 northbound, just n, then just e. Ext/int corridors. **Pets:** $100 deposit/room. Designated rooms, supervision.
〔SAVE〕 ⊠ 🖬 💻 ⊷ ⊠

MANISTIQUE
▼▼▼ **Comfort Inn** 🅷
(906) 341-6981. **$80-$140.** 617 E Lakeshore Dr 49854. 0.5 mi e on US 2. Int corridors. **Pets:** Other species. $10 daily fee/pet. Service with restrictions, supervision. 〔ASK〕 ⊠ 🖬 💻 ⊠

▼▼ **Econo Lodge Lakeshore** Ⓜ
(906) 341-6014. **$59-$119.** 1101 E Lakeshore Dr 49854. 1.5 mi e on US 2. Ext/int corridors. **Pets:** Accepted. 〔ASK〕 ⊠ 🖬 💻 ⊠

▼▼ **Peninsula Pointe Hotel** 🅷
(906) 341-3777. **$76-$119.** 955 E Lakeshore Dr 49854. 1.4 mi e on US 2. Int corridors. **Pets:** Accepted. 〔ASK〕 ⊠ 🖬 💻

MARQUETTE
◇◇ ▼ **Americas Best Value Inn** 🅷
(906) 249-1712. **$50-$138.** 1010 M-28 E 49855. Jct US 41 S and SR 28 E. Int corridors. **Pets:** Other species. $10 daily fee/room. Designated rooms, service with restrictions, supervision. 〔SAVE〕 ⊠ 🖬 💻 ⊷

◇◇ ▼ **Birchmont Motel** Ⓜ
(906) 228-7538. **$46-$76.** 2090 US 41 S 49855. On US 41 and SR 28, 4.3 mi s. Ext corridors. **Pets:** Other species. $10 daily fee/pet. Designated rooms, service with restrictions, supervision. 〔SAVE〕 ⊠ 🖬 ⊷

▼▼ **Holiday Inn** 🅷
(906) 225-1351. **$99-$149.** 1951 US 41 W 49855. On US 41 and SR 28, 1.8 mi w. Int corridors. **Pets:** Dogs only. $25 daily fee/room. Service with restrictions, supervision. 〔ASK〕 ⊠ ⅏ 🖬 💻 ⑪ ⊷ ⊠

▼▼ **Ramada** 🅷
(906) 228-6000. **$100-$125.** 412 W Washington St 49855. 0.5 mi w on US 42 business route. Int corridors. **Pets:** Dogs only. $25 one-time fee/pet. Service with restrictions, supervision.
〔ASK〕 ⊠ 🖬 💻 ⑪ ⊷ ⊠

MARSHALL
◇◇ ▼ **Arbor Inn of Historic Marshall** Ⓜ
(269) 781-7772. **$45-$69.** 15435 W Michigan Ave 49068. I-69, exit 36 (Michigan Ave), just w. Ext corridors. **Pets:** $5 daily fee/pet. Designated rooms, service with restrictions, crate. 〔SAVE〕 ⊠ 🖬 ⊷

MARYSVILLE
◇◇ ▼▼▼ **Super 8 Motel Port Huron/Marysville** 🅷
(810) 364-7500. **$63-$125.** 1484 Gratiot Blvd 48040. I-94, exit 266 (Gratiot Blvd), 1 mi e, then 0.3 mi s of Port Huron on I-94 business loop. Ext/int corridors. **Pets:** $10 daily fee/room. Designated rooms, service with restrictions. 〔SAVE〕 ⊠ 🖬 💻 ⊷ ⊠

MENOMINEE
▼▼ **Econo Lodge On The Bay** 🅷
(906) 863-4431. **$60-$140.** 2516 10th St 49858. 1 mi n on US 41. Int corridors. **Pets:** Accepted. 〔ASK〕 ⊠ 🖬 💻 ⊠

MIDLAND
◇◇ ▼▼▼ **Best Western Valley Plaza Resort** 🅷
(989) 496-2700. **$90-$130.** 5221 Bay City Rd 48642. US 10, exit Midland/Bay City Rd. Int corridors. **Pets:** Accepted.
〔SAVE〕 ⊠ 🖬 💻 ⑪ ⊷ ⊠

▼▼ **Fairview Inn & Suites** 🅷
(989) 631-0070. **$84-$125.** 2200 W Wackerly St 48640. Jct US 10 and Eastman Rd. Int corridors. **Pets:** Medium. $10 daily fee/room. Service with restrictions, supervision. 〔ASK〕 ⊠ 🖬 💻 ⊷

▼▼ **Midland Resort & Conference Center** 🅷
(989) 631-4220. **Call for rates.** 1500 W Wackerly St 48640. Jct US 10 and Eastman Rd. Ext/int corridors. **Pets:** Medium. $40 one-time fee/room. Designated rooms, service with restrictions, supervision.
⊠ 🖬 💻 ⑪ ⊷ ⊠

▼▼ **Sleep Inn of Midland** 🅷
(989) 837-1010. **$85.** 2100 W Wackerly St 48640. Jct US 10 and Eastman Rd. Int corridors. **Pets:** Other species. $10 daily fee/room. Service with restrictions, supervision. 〔ASK〕 ⊠ ⅏ 🖬 💻 ⊷

MILAN
▼▼ **Sleep Inn & Suites** 🅷
(734) 439-1400. **Call for rates.** 1230 Dexter St 48160. US 23, exit 27 (Carpenter Rd), just w. Int corridors. **Pets:** Accepted.
⊠ ⅏ 🖬 💻 ⊷

MIO
▼ **Mio Motel** Ⓜ
(989) 826-3248. **Call for rates.** 415 N Morenci St 48647. Just n on SR 33 and 72. Ext corridors. **Pets:** Accepted. ⊠ 🖬

MONROE
▼▼▼ **Red Roof Inn** Ⓜ
(734) 289-2330. **Call for rates.** 1900 Welcome Way 48162. I-75, exit 15 (SR 50), just e. Ext corridors. **Pets:** Large. Service with restrictions, crate.
⊠ 🖬 💻

MOUNT PLEASANT
▼▼▼▼ **Comfort Inn & Suites Hotel and Conference Center** 🅷 ❀
(989) 772-4000. **Call for rates.** 2424 S Mission St 48858. 2 mi s on US 127 business route. Int corridors. **Pets:** $25 one-time fee/room. Designated rooms, service with restrictions, crate. ⊠ 🖬 💻 ⊷

▼▼▼ **Fairfield Inn & Suites** 🅷
(989) 775-5000. **$107-$131.** 2525 S University Park Dr 48858. 2 mi s on US 127 business route. Int corridors. **Pets:** Accepted.
⊠ 🖬 💻 ⊷ ⊠

▼▼ **Super 8** 🅷
(989) 773-8888. **Call for rates.** 2323 S Mission St 48858. 1.8 mi s on US 127 business route. Int corridors. **Pets:** Other species. $20 daily fee/room. Service with restrictions, crate. ⊠ ⅏ 🖬 💻

MUNISING
◇◇ ▼ **Alger Falls Motel** Ⓜ
(906) 387-3536. **$45-$115.** E9427 E Hwy M-28 49862. 2 mi e on SR 28 and 94. Ext corridors. **Pets:** Small, dogs only. $5 one-time fee. Designated rooms, service with restrictions, supervision. 〔SAVE〕 ⊠ 🖬

◇◇ ▼ **AmericInn Lodge & Suites of Munising** 🅷
(906) 387-2000. **$70-$170.** E9926 E Hwy M-28 49854. On SR 28, 2.7 mi e. Int corridors. **Pets:** Other species. $10 daily fee/pet. Designated rooms, service with restrictions, supervision.
〔SAVE〕 ⊠ ⅏ 🖬 💻 ⊷ ⊠

◇◇ ▼ **Sunset Motel on the Bay** Ⓜ
(906) 387-4574. **$58-$94.** 1315 Bay St 49862. 1 mi e on E Munising Ave (CR H58). Ext corridors. **Pets:** Medium, dogs only. $10 one-time fee/pet. Designated rooms, service with restrictions, supervision.
〔SAVE〕 ⊠ 🖬 💻 ⊠

△△△ ▽ Terrace Motel M ❀
(906) 387-2735. **$40-$60, 3 day notice.** 420 Prospect St 49862. 0.5 mi e, just off SR 28. Ext corridors. **Pets:** Medium, other species. $5 daily fee/pet. Designated rooms, service with restrictions, supervision.
SAVE ⊠ ⊠ 🐾 ✆

NEW BUFFALO

▽▽▽ Fairfield Inn & Suites H
(269) 586-2222. **$109-$149.** 11400 Holiday Dr 49117. I-94, exit 1 (La Porte Rd). Int corridors. **Pets:** Accepted. ⊠ 🔥ᴹ 🛏 💻 🏊

▽▽▽ Holiday Inn Express Hotel & Suites H
(269) 469-1400. **$79-$299.** 11500 Holiday Dr 49117. I-94, exit 1 (La Porte Rd), just w. Int corridors. **Pets:** Accepted.
ASK ⊠ 🔥ᴹ 🛏 💻 🏊 ✕

NORWAY

▽▽ AmericInn Lodge & Suites of Norway H
(906) 563-7500. **$81-$88.** W 6002 US Hwy 2 49870. 0.7 mi w. Int corridors. **Pets:** Accepted. ASK ⊠ 🛏 💻 🏊 ✕

OKEMOS

▽▽▽ Comfort Inn-E. Lansing/Okemos H
(517) 347-6690. **$67-$157.** 2187 University Park Dr 48864. I-96, exit 110 (Okemos Rd), just n, then just e. Int corridors. **Pets:** Large, dogs only. $25 one-time fee/pet. Service with restrictions, supervision.
ASK ⊠ 🔥ᴹ 🛏 💻

▽▽▽ Holiday Inn Express & Suites H
(517) 349-8700. **$98-$104.** 2209 University Park Dr 48864. I-96, exit 110 (Okemos Rd), just n, then just e. Int corridors. **Pets:** Large, dogs only. $25 one-time fee/pet. Designated rooms, service with restrictions, crate.
ASK ⊠ 🔥ᴹ 🛏 💻 🏊 ✕

▽▽▽ Staybridge Suites–Lansing/Okemos H
(517) 347-3044. **$89-$199.** 3553 Meridian Crossing Dr 48864. I-96, exit 110 (Okemos Rd), just n. Int corridors. **Pets:** Other species. $75 one-time fee/room. Service with restrictions. ASK ⊠ 🔥ᴹ 🛏 💻 🏊

PAW PAW

▽▽ Comfort Inn & Suites H
(269) 655-0303. **Call for rates.** 153 Ampey Rd 49079. I-94, exit 60 (SR 40), just nw. Int corridors. **Pets:** Accepted. ⊠ 🔥ᴹ 🛏 💻 🏊

△△△ ▽▽ Super 8 H
(269) 657-1111. **$55-$169.** 111 Ampey Rd 49074. I-94, exit 60 (SR 40). Int corridors. **Pets:** Accepted. SAVE ⊠ 🔥ᴹ 🛏 💻 🏊

PETOSKEY

△△△ ▽ Days Inn Petoskey M
(231) 348-3900. **Call for rates.** 1420 Spring St 49770. 1.3 mi s. Ext corridors. **Pets:** Accepted. SAVE ⊠ 🛏 💻 🎮

△△△ ▽▽▽ Holiday Inn Express Hotel & Suites H
(231) 487-0991. **Call for rates.** 1751 S US 131 49770. I-75, exit 282, w on SR 32 to US 131 N. Int corridors. **Pets:** Accepted.
SAVE ⊠ 🛏 💻 🏊 ✕

PLAINWELL

△△△ ▽▽▽▽ Comfort Inn H
(269) 685-9891. **$90-$200.** 622 Allegan St 49080. US 131, exit 49A, just e. Int corridors. **Pets:** Medium. $15 daily fee/pet. Designated rooms, service with restrictions, supervision. SAVE ⊠ 🛏 💻 🏊

PORT HURON

△△△ ▽▽ Baymont Inn & Suites H
(810) 364-8000. **$59-$99.** 1611 Range Rd 48074. I-94, exit 269 (Range Rd), just w. Int corridors. **Pets:** $15 daily fee/pet. Designated rooms, service with restrictions, supervision. SAVE ⊠ 🛏 💻 🏊

▽▽ Comfort Inn H
(810) 982-5500. **$80-$150.** 1700 Yeager St 48060. I-94, exit 274 (Water St), just s, then just w. Int corridors. **Pets:** Other species. $7 daily fee/room. Designated rooms, service with restrictions, supervision.
ASK ⊠ 🛏 💻 🏊

PORTLAND

△△△ ▽▽ Best Western American Heritage Inn H
(517) 647-2200. **$69-$149.** 1681 Grand River Ave 48875. I-96, exit 77, just n. Int corridors. **Pets:** Small, dogs only. $10 one-time fee/pet. Service with restrictions, supervision. SAVE ⊠ 🔥ᴹ 🛏 💻 🏊

SAGINAW

▽▽ Americas Best Value Inn Saginaw H
(989) 755-0461. **$59-$129.** 1408 S Outer Dr 48601. I-75, exit 149B (SR 46), just w. Int corridors. **Pets:** Accepted. ASK ⊠ 🛏 💻 🏊 ✕

▽▽ Comfort Suites by Choice Hotels H
(989) 797-8000. **$80-$89.** 5180 Fashion Square Blvd 48603. I-675, exit 6, 0.6 mi w on Tittabawassee Rd. Int corridors. **Pets:** Accepted.
ASK ⊠ 🔥ᴹ 🛏 💻 🏊

▽▽▽ Hampton Inn H
(989) 792-7666. **Call for rates.** 2222 Tittabawassee Rd 48604. Jct I-675. Int corridors. **Pets:** Accepted. ⊠ 🛏 💻 🏊

▽▽▽ Residence Inn by Marriott H ❀
(989) 799-9000. **$149-$159.** 5230 Fashion Square Blvd 48604. I-675, exit 6, 0.8 mi w, then just n. Int corridors. **Pets:** Large, other species. $100 one-time fee/room. Service with restrictions. ⊠ 🛏 💻 🏊 ✕

ST. IGNACE

△△△ ▽▽ Budget Host Inn & Suites H
(906) 643-9666. **$66-$152.** 700 N State St 49781. 1.8 mi n of bridge tollgate on I-75 business route. Ext/int corridors. **Pets:** Other species. $40 deposit/room. Service with restrictions, supervision.
SAVE ⊠ 🛏 🏊 ✕

△△△ ▽▽ Quality Inn Lakefront M
(906) 643-7581. **$48-$174, 3 day notice.** 1021 N State St 49781. 2.3 mi n of bridge tollgate on I-75 business route. Ext corridors. **Pets:** Small, dogs only. $10 one-time fee/room. Designated rooms, service with restrictions, supervision. SAVE ⊠ 🛏 💻 🏊

ST. JOSEPH

▽▽ Silver Beach Hotel H
(269) 983-7341. **$81-$333, 3 day notice.** 100 Main St 49085. I-94, exit 27 eastbound, 5 mi nw to Main St; exit 33 westbound, 4.8 mi w on Business Rt I-94, then nw to Main St. Int corridors. **Pets:** Other species. $35 one-time fee/pet. Designated rooms, service with restrictions, crate.
ASK ⊠ 🛏 💻 🏊 ✕

SAULT STE. MARIE

△△△ ▽ Budget Host Crestview Inn M
(906) 635-5213. **$59-$79.** 1200 Ashmun St 49783. I-75, exit 392, 2.8 mi ne on I-75 business loop. Ext corridors. **Pets:** Other species. $10 one-time fee/pet. Designated rooms, service with restrictions, supervision.
SAVE ⊠ 🛏

△△△ ▽▽ Comfort Inn H
(906) 635-1118. **$70-$200, 30 day notice.** 4404 I-75 Business Spur 49783. I-75, exit 392; at business loop. Int corridors. **Pets:** Dogs only. Service with restrictions, supervision. SAVE ⊠ 🛏 💻 🏊 ✕

△△△ ▽▽ Days Inn H
(906) 635-5200. **$69-$199.** 3651 I-75 Business Spur 49783. I-75, exit 392, 0.8 mi ne on I-75 business loop. Int corridors. **Pets:** Other species. $5 daily fee/room. Designated rooms, service with restrictions, crate.
SAVE ⊠ 🛏 💻 🏊 ✕

△△△ ▽ Park Inn H
(906) 632-6000. **Call for rates.** 3525 I-75 Business Spur 49783. I-75, exit 392, 0.7 mi ne. Int corridors. **Pets:** Accepted.
SAVE ⊠ 🔥ᴹ 🛏 💻 🏊 ✕

▼▼ Quality Inn & Suites 🅷
(906) 635-6918. **$59-$159.** 3290 I-75 Business Loop 49783. I-75, exit 392, 1 mi ne. Int corridors. **Pets:** Accepted.
ASK ⊠ 🔋 💻 🍽 ➳ ⊠

▼ Super 8 🅷
(906) 632-8882. **$55-$70.** 3826 I-75 Business Loop 49783. I-75, exit 392, 0.5 mi ne. Int corridors. **Pets:** Accepted. ASK ⊠ 🔋 💻

SILVER CITY
▼ Mountain View Lodges 🅒🅐
(906) 885-5256. **$165-$265, 30 day notice.** 34042 M-107 49953. Jct SR 64, 0.8 mi w. Ext corridors. **Pets:** Dogs only. $100 one-time fee/pet. Designated rooms, supervision. ⊠ 🔋 💻 🅙

SOUTH HAVEN
AAA ▼▼▼ Comfort Suites 🅷
(269) 639-2014. **$79-$209.** 1755 Phoenix St 49090. I-196, exit 20, 0.5 mi e. Int corridors. **Pets:** Small. $25 daily fee/pet. Service with restrictions, supervision. SAVE ⊠ 🅛🅜 🔋 💻 ➳

SPRING LAKE
▼ Grand Haven Waterfront Holiday Inn 🅷
(616) 846-1000. **Call for rates.** 940 W Savidge St 49456. On SR 104, just e of US 31. Int corridors. **Pets:** Accepted.
⊠ 🔋 💻 🍽 ➳ ⊠

STEVENSVILLE
▼▼ Candlewood Suites 🅷
(269) 428-4400. **$90-$170.** 2567 W Marquette Woods Rd 49127. I-94, exit 23 (Red Arrow Hwy), just w. Int corridors. **Pets:** Medium. $75 one-time fee/pet. Designated rooms, service with restrictions, crate.
ASK ⊠ 🅛🅜 🔋 💻

▼▼ Hampton Inn of St. Joseph I-94 🅷 ❄
(269) 429-2700. **Call for rates.** 5050 Red Arrow Hwy 49127. I-94, exit 23 (Red Arrow Hwy), just se. Int corridors. **Pets:** Service with restrictions.
⊠ 🅛🅜 🔋 💻 ➳

SUTTONS BAY
▼ Red Lion Motor Lodge 🅜
(231) 271-6694. **$59-$195.** 4290 S West Bay Shore Rd 49682. 5 mi s on SR 22. Ext corridors. **Pets:** Other species. $20 one-time fee/room. Service with restrictions, supervision. ⊠ 🔋 💻 🅩

THREE RIVERS
▼▼ Super 8 🅷
(269) 279-8888. **$77-$82.** 711 US 131 49093. Jct US 131 and SR 60 (W Broadway St). Int corridors. **Pets:** Medium, dogs only. $10 daily fee/pet. Designated rooms, service with restrictions, supervision.
ASK ⊠ 🅛🅜 🔋 💻 ➳

TRAVERSE CITY
▼▼ Baymont Inn & Suites-Traverse City 🅷
(231) 933-4454. **$70-$300.** 2326 N US 31 S 49684. 3.5 mi s on SR 37. Int corridors. **Pets:** Accepted. ASK ⊠ 🔋 💻 ➳ ⊠

AAA ▼▼▼ Best Western Four Seasons 🅜 ❄
(231) 946-8424. **$49-$259.** 305 Munson Ave 49686. 2 mi e on US 31. Ext/int corridors. **Pets:** $10 daily fee/room. Service with restrictions, supervision. SAVE ⊠ 🔋 💻 ➳

▼▼ Days Inn & Suites 🅷
(231) 941-0208. **$55-$210.** 420 Munson Ave 49686. 2 mi e on US 31. Int corridors. **Pets:** Accepted. ASK ⊠ 🔋 💻 ➳ ⊠

▼▼ Holiday Inn, West Bay 🅷 ❄
(231) 947-3700. **Call for rates.** 615 E Front St 49686. 0.5 mi e on US 31. Int corridors. **Pets:** Other species. $15 daily fee/pet. Service with restrictions, supervision. ⊠ 🅛🅜 🔋 💻 🍽 ➳ ⊠

▼▼ Park Place Hotel 🅷
(231) 946-5000. **Call for rates.** 300 E State St 49684. Corner of E State and Park sts; downtown. Int corridors. **Pets:** Accepted.
ECO ⊠ 🔋 💻 🍽 ➳ ⊠

AAA ▼▼▼ Quality Inn 🅷 ❄
(231) 929-4423. **$50-$200.** 1492 US 31 N 49686. On US 31, 3.3 mi e. Ext/int corridors. **Pets:** Large, other species. $10 daily fee/room. Designated rooms, service with restrictions, supervision.
SAVE ⊠ 🔋 💻 ➳

AAA ▼▼▼ Traverse Victorian Inn 🅷
(231) 947-5525. **$69-$189.** 461 Munson Ave 49686. 2.4 mi e on US 31. Int corridors. **Pets:** Dogs only. $25 one-time fee/pet. Supervision.
SAVE ⊠ 🔋 💻 ➳

WALKER
▼▼ Baymont Inn & Suites-Grand Rapids North 🅷 ❄
(616) 735-9595. **$69-$129.** 2151 Holton Ct NW 49544. I-96, exit 28 (Walker Ave), just s. Int corridors. **Pets:** Other species. $20 daily fee/room. Service with restrictions, crate. ASK ⊠ 🔋 💻 ➳

▼▼ Quality Inn Grand Rapids North 🅷
(616) 791-8500. **Call for rates.** 2171 Holton Ct 49544. I-96, exit 28 (Walker Ave), just s. Int corridors. **Pets:** Accepted. ⊠ 🔋 💻 ➳

WATERSMEET
▼▼ Dancing Eagles Resort Lac Vieux Desert Casino 🅷
(906) 358-4949. **$45-$90.** N5384 US Hwy 45 49969. 1.8 mi n of US 2. Int corridors. **Pets:** Accepted. ASK ⊠ 🔋 💻 ➳ ⊠

WHITMORE LAKE
AAA ▼▼ Best Western Whitmore Lake 🅜
(734) 449-2058. **$79-$89.** 9897 Main St 48189. US 23, exit 53, just e. Ext corridors. **Pets:** $25 daily fee/pet. Designated rooms, service with restrictions, crate. SAVE ⊠ 🔋 💻 ➳

WYOMING
AAA ▼▼▼ Howard Johnson Plaza Hotel 🅷
(616) 241-6444. **$59-$65.** 255 28th St SW 49548. On SR 11, 0.3 mi e of jct US 131, exit 28th St. Int corridors. **Pets:** Accepted.
SAVE ⊠ 🔋 💻 🍽 ➳ ⊠

▼ Super 8 🅷
(616) 530-8588. **$55-$100.** 727 44th St SW 49509. US 131, exit 79. Int corridors. **Pets:** Accepted. ASK ⊠ 🔋 💻

MINNESOTA

CITY INDEX

AITKIN

Ripple River Motel & RV Park M
(218) 927-3734. **$55-$90.** 701 Minnesota Ave S 56431. US 169, 0.8 mi s of jct SR 210. Ext corridors. **Pets:** Dogs only. $10 daily fee/pet. Designated rooms, service with restrictions, crate.

ALBERT LEA

Albert Lea Countryside Inn Motel M
(507) 373-2446. **$50-$99.** 2102 E Main St 56007. I-35, exit 11, 1.3 mi w on CR 46. Ext/int corridors. **Pets:** Dogs only. $10 daily fee/room. Service with restrictions, supervision.

Comfort Inn H
(507) 377-1100. **Call for rates.** 810 Happy Trails Ln 56007. I-35, exit 11, just se. Int corridors. **Pets:** Other species. $25 one-time fee/pet. Service with restrictions, supervision.

Country Inn & Suites By Carlson H
(507) 373-5513. **$95-$155.** 2214 E Main St 56007. I-35, exit 12 southbound; exit 11 northbound, 1 mi w. Int corridors. **Pets:** Small. $25 one-time fee/room. Designated rooms, service with restrictions, supervision.

ALEXANDRIA

Country Inn & Suites By Carlson H
(320) 763-9900. **$78-$139.** 5304 Hwy 29 S 56308. I-94, exit 103, just sw. Int corridors. **Pets:** Small. $10 one-time fee/room. Designated rooms, service with restrictions, supervision.

Holiday Inn Alexandria H
(320) 763-6577. **$99-$159.** 5637 State Hwy 29 S 56308. I-94, exit 103, just s. Int corridors. **Pets:** Other species. Designated rooms, service with restrictions, supervision.

Super 8 H
(320) 763-6552. **$64-$99, 7 day notice.** 4620 Hwy 29 S 56308. I-94, exit 103, 0.3 mi nw. Int corridors. **Pets:** Accepted.

AUSTIN

Days Inn H
(507) 433-8600. **Call for rates.** 700 16th Ave NW 55912. I-90, exit 178A (4th St NW), just nw. Int corridors. **Pets:** Accepted.

Holiday Inn & Austin Conference Center H
(507) 433-1000. **$89-$109.** 1701 4th St NW 55912. I-90, exit 178A (4th St NW), just nw. Int corridors. **Pets:** Accepted.

BABBITT

Timber Bay Lodge & Houseboats CA
(218) 827-3682. **$165-$798, 60 day notice.** 8347 Timber Bay Rd 55706. 2.8 mi e of jct CR 21 via CR 70 and 623. Ext corridors. **Pets:** Other species. $15 daily fee/pet. No service.

BAUDETTE

AmericInn Lodge & Suites of Baudette H
(218) 634-3200. **Call for rates.** 1179 Main St W 56623. 0.5 mi w on SR 11. Int corridors. **Pets:** Accepted.

BAXTER

Country Inn & Suites By Carlson H
(218) 828-2161. **$89-$139.** 15058 Dellwood Dr N 56425. Jct SR 371 and 210, 1 mi n on SR 371. Int corridors. **Pets:** Dogs only. $10 one-time fee/room. Service with restrictions, supervision.

Holiday Inn Express, Three Bear Waterpark H
(218) 824-3232. **$89-$219.** 15739 Audubon Way 56425. Just se of jct SR 371 and CR 77. Int corridors. **Pets:** Accepted.

BEMIDJI

AmericInn Lodge & Suites of Bemidji H
(218) 751-3000. **$70-$150.** 1200 Paul Bunyan Dr NW 56601. 0.5 mi e of northwest jct US 2, 71 and SR 197. Int corridors. **Pets:** Medium. $30 one-time fee/room. Designated rooms, service with restrictions, supervision.

Best Western Bemidji H
(218) 751-0390. **$75-$135.** 2420 Paul Bunyan Dr 56601. Jct US 71 N and SR 197. Int corridors. **Pets:** Other species. $15 daily fee/room. Service with restrictions, supervision.

Ruttger's Birchmont Lodge CA
(218) 444-3463. **$52-$390, 30 day notice.** 7598 Bemidji Rd NE 56601. Jct SR 197, 3.6 mi n on CR 21 (Bemidji Ave N). Ext/int corridors. **Pets:** Medium. $10 daily fee/pet. Designated rooms, service with restrictions, crate.

BRAINERD

Red Roof Inn H
(218) 829-1441. **Call for rates.** 2115 S 6th St 56401. On SR 371 business route, 1.8 mi s of jct SR 210. Ext/int corridors. **Pets:** Large. Service with restrictions, crate.

BRECKENRIDGE

▼▼ Select Inn of Breckenridge/Wahpeton 🅗

(218) 643-9201. **Call for rates.** 821 Hwy 75 N 56520. Just sw of jct US 75 N and 210. Int corridors. **Pets:** Accepted. ⊠ 🛑 🖵 🔁

CALEDONIA

▼▼ AmericInn of Caledonia 🅗

(507) 725-8000. **$90-$150.** 508 N Kruckow Ave 55921. Jct SR 44 and 76, just sw. Int corridors. **Pets:** $50 deposit/pet. Service with restrictions, supervision. ⊠ 🛑 🖵 🔁

CANNON FALLS

◈ ▼▼◈ Best Western Saratoga Inn 🅗 ❀

(507) 263-7272. **$69-$99.** 31591 64th Ave 55009. Jct SR 19, 1 mi sw on US 52. Int corridors. **Pets:** Small. $15 daily fee/pet. Designated rooms, service with restrictions, supervision. [SAVE] ⊠ 🛑 🖵 🔁

CLOQUET

▼▼◈ AmericInn Lodge & Suites of Cloquet 🅗

(218) 879-1231. **Call for rates.** 111 Big Lake Rd 55720. I-35, exit 237 (SR 33), 2 mi nw. Int corridors. **Pets:** Accepted.
⊠ 🛑 🖵 🔁 ⊠

▼▼ Super 8 🅗 ❀

(218) 879-1250. **$64-$163.** 121 Big Lake Rd 55720. I-35, exit 237 (SR 33), 2 mi nw. Int corridors. **Pets:** Dogs only. $50 deposit/room, $12 daily fee/room. Designated rooms, supervision. [ASK] ⊠ 👤M 🛑 🖵

COOK

▼▼▼▼ Ludlow's Island Resort 🆅🅷 ❀

(218) 666-5407. **$200-$600, 90 day notice.** 8166 Ludlow Dr 55723. US 53, 3.5 mi ne on CR 24, 5.1 mi e on CR 78 and 540. Ext corridors. **Pets:** $30 daily fee/pet. Designated rooms, crate. 🛑 🖵 ⊠

CROOKSTON

▼▼ Northland Inn of Crookston 🅗

(218) 281-5210. **Call for rates.** 2200 University Ave 56716. On US 2 W and 75 N, 1.5 mi n. Int corridors. **Pets:** Medium. $25 one-time fee/pet. Designated rooms, service with restrictions, supervision.
⊠ 🛑 🍴 🔁

CROSSLAKE

◈▼▼◈ Pine Peaks Lodge and Suites 🅗

(218) 692-7829. **Call for rates.** 14047 Swann Dr 56442. Jct CR 66 and Swann Dr. Int corridors. **Pets:** Accepted. ⊠ 🛑 🖵 🍴 🔁 ⊠

DEER RIVER

◈ ▼▼ White Oak Inn & Suites 🅗

(218) 246-9400. **$57-$160.** 201 4th Ave NW 56636. On US 2. Int corridors. **Pets:** Other species. $25 one-time fee/room. Designated rooms, service with restrictions, supervision. [SAVE] ⊠ 🛑 🖵 🔁 ⊠

DEERWOOD

◈ ▼▼◈▼ Country Inn of Deerwood 🅗

(218) 534-3101. **$85-$135.** 23885 Front St 56444. On SR 6 and 210, e of jct CR 12. Int corridors. **Pets:** Medium, other species. $10 daily fee/pet. Service with restrictions, supervision. [SAVE] ⊠ 👤M 🛑 🖵 🔁

DETROIT LAKES

◈ ▼▼ AmericInn Lodge & Suites of Detroit Lakes 🅗

(218) 847-8795. **$75-$190.** 777 Hwy 10 E 56501. 1.4 mi se. Int corridors. **Pets:** $10 daily fee/pet. Service with restrictions, supervision.
[SAVE] ⊠ 👤M 🛑 🖵 🔁 ⊠

◈ ▼▼◈ Best Western Holland House 🅗 ❀

(218) 847-4483. **$89-$229, 3 day notice.** 615 Hwy 10 E 56501. 1.3 mi se. Ext/int corridors. **Pets:** Medium. $15 daily fee/pet. Designated rooms, service with restrictions, supervision. [SAVE] ⊠ 🛑 🖵 🔁

◈ ▼▼ Budget Host Inn 🅜

(218) 847-4454. **$57-$130.** 895 Hwy 10 E 56501. 1.5 mi se. Ext corridors. **Pets:** Accepted. [SAVE] ⊠ 🛑 🖵

◈ ▼▼◈ Country Inn & Suites By Carlson 🅗

(218) 847-2000. **$75-$165.** 1330 Hwy 10 E 56501. Just e of jct US 10 and CR 54 E. Int corridors. **Pets:** $20 one-time fee/room. Service with restrictions, supervision. [SAVE] ⊠ 👤M 🛑 🖵 🔁

DULUTH

◈ ▼▼◈ AmericInn Hotel & Suites of Duluth South 🅗

(218) 624-1026. **$85-$210.** 185 US 2 55810. Jct I-35 and US 2, 0.8 mi n. Int corridors. **Pets:** Accepted. [SAVE] ⊠ 🛑 🖵 🍴 🔁

◈ ▼▼◈ Beacon Pointe Resort 🅒🅞

(218) 724-1100. **$89-$629, 3 day notice.** 2100 Water St 55812. I-35, exit 258 (21st Ave), just e. Int corridors. **Pets:** Dogs only. $15 daily fee/room. Designated rooms, service with restrictions, supervision.
[SAVE] ⊠ 🛑 🖵 🔁 ⊠

◈ ▼▼◈ Best Western Downtown Motel 🅜

(218) 727-6851. **$55-$140.** 131 W 2nd St 55802. 2nd St at 2nd Ave W; center. Ext/int corridors. **Pets:** Accepted. [SAVE] ⊠ 🛑 🖵

◈ ▼▼◈ Country Inn & Suites By Carlson North 🅗

(218) 740-4500. **$109-$229.** 4257 Haines Rd 55811. Just n of US 53. Int corridors. **Pets:** Medium, other species. $10 daily fee/pet. Service with restrictions, crate. [SAVE] ⊠ 🛑 🖵 🔁

◈ ▼▼◈ Country Inn & Suites By Carlson South 🅗

(218) 628-0668. **$85-$170.** 9330 W Skyline Pkwy 55810. I-35, exit 249 (Boundary Ave), just se. Int corridors. **Pets:** Accepted.
[SAVE] ⊠ 🛑 🖵 🔁 ⊠

▼▼ Days Inn-Duluth 🅗

(218) 727-3110. **Call for rates.** 909 Cottonwood Ave 55811. SR 194, just n of jct US 53. Int corridors. **Pets:** $5 daily fee/room. Service with restrictions, supervision. ⊠ 🛑 🖵

◈ ▼▼ Duluth Spirit Mountain Red Roof Inn 🅗

(218) 628-3691. **$59-$299, 3 day notice.** 9315 Westgate Blvd 55810. I-35, exit 249 (Boundary Ave), just sw. Int corridors. **Pets:** Large. Service with restrictions, crate. [SAVE] ⊠ 🛑 🖵 🔁 ⊠

◈ ▼▼ Econo Lodge Airport 🅗

(218) 722-5522. **$76-$199.** 4197 Haines Rd 55811. Just s of US 53. Int corridors. **Pets:** $50 deposit/room, $10 one-time fee/room. Designated rooms, service with restrictions, supervision.
[SAVE] ⊠ 🛑 🖵 🔁 ⊠

◈ ▼▼ Edgewater Resort & Waterpark 🅗 ❀

(218) 728-3601. **$79-$329.** 2400 London Rd 55812. I-35, exit 258 (21st Ave E), just nw. Ext/int corridors. **Pets:** Other species. $20 daily fee/pet. Service with restrictions, supervision.
[SAVE] ⊠ 🛑 🍴 🔁 ⊠

◈ ▼▼◈▼ Fitger's Inn 🅗

(218) 722-8826. **$129-$349.** 600 E Superior St 55802. I-35, exit 256B (Lake Ave), just ne. Int corridors. **Pets:** Large, other species. Designated rooms, service with restrictions, supervision.
[SAVE] ⊠ 🛑 🖵 🍴 ⊠

◈ ▼▼◈▼ The Inn on Lake Superior 🅗

(218) 726-1111. **$109-$329.** 350 Canal Park Dr 55802. In Canal Park area. Int corridors. **Pets:** Accepted. [SAVE] ⊠ 👤M 🛑 🖵 🔁 ⊠

▼▼▼ Radisson Hotel Duluth-Harborview 🅗

(218) 727-8981. **$109-$209.** 505 W Superior St 55802. At 5th Ave W; center. Int corridors. **Pets:** Accepted.
[ASK] ⊠ 🛑 🖵 🍴 🔁 ⊠

AAA WWW Sheraton Duluth Hotel H ✿
(218) 733-5660. **$99-$279.** 301 E Superior St 55802. I-35, exit 256B (Lake Ave), just nw. Int corridors. **Pets:** Medium, dogs only. Designated rooms, service with restrictions, supervision.
SAVE ⊠ &M 🛡 💻 ¶ ⇌

AAA WWW The Suites Hotel at Waterfront Plaza H
(218) 727-4663. **$89-$549.** 325 Lake Ave S 55802. In Canal Park area. Int corridors. **Pets:** Accepted. **SAVE ⊠ &M 🛡 💻 ¶ ⇌ ⊠**

WWW Voyageur Lakewalk Inn M
(218) 722-3911. **$40-$74.** 333 E Superior St 55802. I-35, exit 256 (Superior St), just n at jct 4th Ave E and Superior St. Ext corridors. **Pets:** Dogs only. $15 one-time fee/room. Designated rooms, service with restrictions, crate. **ASK ⊠ 🛡 💻**

ELY

AAA WWWW Grand Ely Lodge Resort and Conference Center H ✿
(218) 365-6565. **$109-$290, 14 day notice.** 400 N Pioneer Rd 55731. SR 169 to Central Ave, just n to Pioneer Rd, then 1 mi n. Ext/int corridors. **Pets:** $15 daily fee/pet. Designated rooms, service with restrictions, supervision. **SAVE ⊠ 🛡 💻 ¶ ⇌ ⊠**

AAA WW Motel Ely-Budget Host M
(218) 365-3237. **$60-$120, 3 day notice.** 1047 E Sheridan St 55731. SR 1 and 169. Ext corridors. **Pets:** $10 one-time fee/pet. Designated rooms, service with restrictions, supervision. **SAVE ⊠ 🛡 💻**

EVELETH

WWW Super 8 H ✿
(218) 744-1661. **$80-$125.** 1080 Industrial Park Dr 55734. On US 53, 0.5 mi n of jct SR 37. Int corridors. **Pets:** Small, dogs only. $10 daily fee/pet. Designated rooms, service with restrictions, supervision.
ASK ⊠ &M 🛡 💻 ⇌ ⊠

FAIRMONT

AAA WWW Comfort Inn H
(507) 238-5444. **$90-$110.** 2225 N State St 56031. I-90, exit 102 (SR 15), just s. Int corridors. **Pets:** Accepted. **SAVE ⊠ 🛡 💻 ⇌**

WWW Holiday Inn H
(507) 238-4771. **$94-$124.** 1201 Torgerson Dr 56031. I-90, exit 102 (SR 15), just s. Int corridors. **Pets:** Accepted.
ASK ⊠ 🛡 💻 ¶ ⇌ ⊠

WWW Super 8 H
(507) 238-9444. **Call for rates.** 1200 Torgerson Dr 56031. I-90, exit 102 (SR 15), just s. Int corridors. **Pets:** Accepted. **⊠ 🛡**

FARIBAULT

WWW AmericInn Motel & Suites of Faribault H
(507) 334-9464. **$83-$185.** 1801 Lavender Dr 55021. I-35, exit 59 (SR 21), 0.3 mi e. Int corridors. **Pets:** Medium, other species. $25 one-time fee/room. Designated rooms, service with restrictions, crate.
ASK ⊠ 🛡 💻 ⇌ ⊠

WWW Days Inn & Suites H
(507) 334-6835. **Call for rates.** 1920 Cardinal Ln 55021. I-35, exit 59 (SR 21), just ne. Int corridors. **Pets:** Accepted. **⊠ &M 🛡 💻 ⇌**

FERGUS FALLS

WWW AmericInn Lodge & Suites of Fergus Falls H ✿
(218) 739-3900. **$80-$150.** 526 Western Ave N 56537. I-94, exit 54 (SR 210), just se. Int corridors. **Pets:** Other species. $50 deposit/room, $10 one-time fee/room. Designated rooms, service with restrictions, crate.
ASK ⊠ &M 🛡 💻 ⇌ ⊠

WWW Comfort Inn H
(218) 736-5787. **$80-$110.** 425 Western Ave 56537. I-94, exit 54 (SR 210), just se. Int corridors. **Pets:** Other species. $50 deposit/room. Designated rooms, service with restrictions, crate.
ASK ⊠ 🛡 💻 ⇌ ⊠

FINLAYSON

WWW Americas Best Value Inn H
(320) 245-5284. **$53-$73.** 60671 State Hwy 23 55735. I-35, exit 195 (SR 23), just ne. Int corridors. **Pets:** Accepted. **ASK ⊠ 🛡**

FOSSTON

WWW Super 8 H
(218) 435-1088. **$59-$125.** 108 S Amber Ave 56542. US 2, 0.5 mi e. Int corridors. **Pets:** Dogs only. $100 deposit/room, $5 one-time fee/room. Service with restrictions, supervision. **ASK ⊠ 🛡**

GARRISON

WWWW Garrison Inn & Suites H
(320) 692-4050. **$75-$149.** 9243 Hwy 169 56540. SR 169, just s of jct SR 18. Int corridors. **Pets:** Accepted. **ASK ⊠ 🛡 💻 ⇌**

GAYLORD

WWW Gold Leaf Inn & Suites M
(507) 237-5860. **$61-$115.** 330 Main Ave E 55334. 1.5 mi e. Int corridors. **Pets:** Small. Designated rooms, service with restrictions, supervision. **⊠ 🛡**

GRAND MARAIS

AAA WWWW Best Western Superior Inn & Suites H ✿
(218) 387-2240. **$99-$329, 3 day notice.** 104 1st Ave E 55604. SR 61, just ne of center. Int corridors. **Pets:** Medium. $15 daily fee/pet. Designated rooms, service with restrictions, supervision. **SAVE ⊠ 🛡 💻**

WWWW Gunflint Lodge VH ✿
(218) 388-2294. **$99-$349, 31 day notice.** 143 S Gunflint Lake 55604. 43 mi n of town; 0.8 mi e of jct CR 12 (Gunflint Tr) and 50. Ext corridors. **Pets:** Other species. $20 daily fee/pet. Service with restrictions, crate.
&M 🛡 💻 ¶ ⊠ 🐾 🍽

WWW Nor'Wester Lodge and Outfitter CA
(218) 388-2252. **Call for rates.** 7778 Gunflint Tr 55604. 30 mi nw on CR 12 (Gunflint Tr) from jct SR 61. Ext corridors. **Pets:** Accepted.
🛡 💻 ⊠ 🐾 📺 🍽

WWW Outpost Motel M
(218) 387-1833. **$49-$115, 7 day notice.** 2935 SR 61 E 55604. SR 61, 9 mi ne. Ext corridors. **Pets:** Other species. $10 daily fee/pet. Supervision. **⊠ 🛡 💻 ⊠ 🐾**

AAA WW Wedgewood Motel M
(218) 387-2944. **$55-$85, 3 day notice.** 1663 E Hwy 61 55604. SR 61, 2.5 mi ne. Ext corridors. **Pets:** Dogs only. $50 daily fee/pet. Designated rooms, service with restrictions, supervision. **SAVE ⊠ 🛡 🐾 🍽**

GRAND RAPIDS

AAA WWW Budget Host Inn M ✿
(218) 326-3457. **$60-$86.** 311 E Hwy 2 55744. Jct US 2 E and 169 N. Ext/int corridors. **Pets:** $50 deposit/pet. Designated rooms, service with restrictions, crate. **SAVE ⊠ 🛡**

WWWW Country Inn & Suites By Carlson H
(218) 327-4960. **$95-$139.** 2601 S Hwy 169 55744. US 2, 2 mi s. Int corridors. **Pets:** Accepted. **ASK ⊠ &M 🛡 💻 ⇌**

AAA WWWW Sawmill Inn H
(218) 326-8501. **$69-$109.** 2301 S Hwy 169 55744. US 2, 2 mi s on US 169. Ext/int corridors. **Pets:** Large, other species. Service with restrictions, supervision. **SAVE ⊠ 🛡 💻 ¶ ⇌ ⊠**

GRANITE FALLS

WWW Granite Falls Super Motel H
(320) 564-4075. **$59-$110.** 845 W SR 212 56241. 0.5 mi w of Jct SR 23. Int corridors. **Pets:** $25 one-time fee/pet. Service with restrictions, supervision. **ASK ⊠ &M 🛡 ⇌**

HINCKLEY

▼▼ ▼▼ Days Inn 🅷
(320) 384-7751. **$60-$130, 5 day notice.** 104 Grindstone Ct 55037. I-35, exit 183 (SR 48), just e. Int corridors. **Pets:** Other species. $10 daily fee/room. Designated rooms, no service, crate. 🄰🅂🄺 ⊠ 🛢 🖵 ➴

HOYT LAKES

▼▼▼▼ Country Inn of Hoyt Lakes 🅷
(218) 225-3555. **$80-$180, 3 day notice.** 99 Kennedy Memorial Dr 55750. On SR 110. Int corridors. **Pets:** Medium, dogs only. $10 daily fee/pet. Designated rooms, service with restrictions, supervision.
🄰🅂🄺 ⊠ 🅓🄼 🛢 🖵 ➴

HUTCHINSON

◈◈◈ ▼▼▼ Best Western Victorian Inn 🅷
(320) 587-6030. **$66-$108.** 1000 Hwy 7 W 55350. SR 15, 1 mi w. Int corridors. **Pets:** $10 daily fee/room. Service with restrictions, supervision.
🅂🄰🅅🄴 ⊠ 🛢 🖵 🍴 ➴

INTERNATIONAL FALLS

◈◈◈ ▼▼▼ Hilltop Motel 🅼
(218) 283-2505. **$49-$84.** 2002 2nd Ave W 56649. US 53, 1 mi s of jct US 53 and SR 11. Ext corridors. **Pets:** Small, dogs only. $10 one-time fee/pet. Service with restrictions, supervision. 🅂🄰🅅🄴 ⊠

▼▼ ▼▼ Holiday Inn 🅷
(218) 283-8000. **Call for rates.** 1500 US 71 W 56649. 1.5 mi w on US 71 and SR 11 W. Int corridors. **Pets:** Accepted.
⊠ 🛢 🖵 🍴 ➴ 🖾

JACKSON

◈◈◈ ▼▼▼▼ AmericInn Lodge & Suites of Jackson 🅷
(507) 847-2444. **$75-$159.** 110 Belmont Ln 56143. I-90, exit 73 (US 71), just sw. Int corridors. **Pets:** Small, dogs only. $50 deposit/room, $10 daily fee/pet. Designated rooms, service with restrictions, crate.
🅂🄰🅅🄴 ⊠ 🅓🄼 🛢 🖵 ➴

▼▼ ▼▼ Econo Lodge 🅷
(507) 847-3110. **Call for rates.** 2007 US 71 N 56143. I-90, exit 73 (US 71), just nw. Ext/int corridors. **Pets:** $10 daily fee/pet. Service with restrictions, supervision. ⊠ 🛢 🖵 🍴 ➴

LAMBERTON

▼▼ Lamberton Motel 🅼
(507) 752-7242. **$48-$55.** 601 1st Ave W 56152. Just s of jct US 14 and Ilex St. Ext corridors. **Pets:** Accepted. 🄰🅂🄺 ⊠ 🛢 🖵

LITCHFIELD

▼▼ ▼▼ ScotWood Motel 🅼
(320) 693-2496. **$50-$100.** 1017 E Frontage Rd 55355. On US 12. Int corridors. **Pets:** Medium. $10 daily fee/room. Service with restrictions, supervision. 🄰🅂🄺 ⊠ 🛢 ➴

LONG PRAIRIE

◈◈◈ ▼▼▼ Budget Host Inn 🅼
(320) 732-6118. **$65-$85.** 417 Lake St 56347. On US 71 and SR 27, just s of jct SR 287. Ext corridors. **Pets:** Medium. $10 daily fee/pet. Service with restrictions, supervision. 🅂🄰🅅🄴 ⊠ 🛢 🖵

LUTSEN

▼▼ ▼▼ Cascade Lodge 🄲🄸 ❀
(218) 387-1112. **$55-$275, 14 day notice.** 3719 W Hwy 61 55612. SR 61, 7 mi ne of jct CR 4 (Caribou Tr). Ext/int corridors. **Pets:** Dogs only. $10 daily fee/pet. Designated rooms, service with restrictions, crate.
🄰🅂🄺 ⊠ 🛢 🖵 🍴 🖾

▼▼ ▼▼ Solbakken Resort 🅼
(218) 663-7566. **$55-$95, 14 day notice.** 4874 W SR 61 55612. SR 61, 1.3 mi n of jct CR 4 (Caribou Tr). Ext corridors. **Pets:** $10 daily fee/pet. Designated rooms, no service, supervision.
🄰🅂🄺 ⊠ 🛢 🖵 🖾 🜨

MADELIA

▼▼▼ ▼▼ AmericInn Lodge & Suites of Madelia 🅷
(507) 642-2004. **$75-$140.** 620 Haynes Ave NE 56062. Just nw of jct SR 60 and CR 3. Int corridors. **Pets:** Medium. $25 daily fee/pet. Designated rooms, service with restrictions, crate.
🄰🅂🄺 ⊠ 🅓🄼 🛢 🖵 ➴ 🖾

MAHNOMEN

◈◈◈ ▼▼▼ Shooting Star Casino Hotel & Events Center 🅷
(218) 935-2701. **$70-$120.** 777 Casino Rd 56557. 1 mi s on SR 59. Int corridors. **Pets:** Accepted. 🅂🄰🅅🄴 ⊠ 🅓🄼 🛢 🍴 ➴ 🖾

MANKATO

▼▼▼ ▼▼ AmericInn Hotel & Conference Center 🅷
(507) 345-8011. **$60-$199.** 240 Stadium Rd 56001. Jct US 14, 2 mi s on SR 22, 0.4 mi w on SR 83, just s on Victory Dr, then 1.5 mi w. Int corridors. **Pets:** Accepted. 🄰🅂🄺 ⊠ 🅓🄼 🛢 🖵 ➴

◈◈◈ ▼▼▼▼ Best Western Hotel & Restaurant 🅷
(507) 625-9333. **$80-$115.** 1111 Range St 56003. 0.6 mi s of jct US 169 and 14. Int corridors. **Pets:** $20 one-time fee/room. Service with restrictions, supervision. 🅂🄰🅅🄴 ⊠ 🛢 🖵 🍴 ➴ 🖾

▼▼ ▼▼ Comfort Inn by Choice Hotels 🅷
(507) 388-5107. **Call for rates.** 131 Apache Pl 56001. Just s of jct US 14 and SR 22 S. Int corridors. **Pets:** $10 daily fee/room. Designated rooms, service with restrictions, supervision. ⊠ 🛢 🖵 ➴

▼▼ ▼▼ Days Inn 🅷 ❀
(507) 387-3332. **Call for rates.** 1285 Range St 56001. 0.3 mi s of jct US 169 and 14. Int corridors. **Pets:** $10 daily fee/pet. Designated rooms, no service, supervision. ⊠ 🛢 🖵 ➴

◈◈◈ ▼▼▼▼ GrandStay Residential Suites Hotel 🅷
(507) 388-8688. **Call for rates.** 1000 Raintree Rd 56001. 0.4 mi se of jct US 14 and CR 3. Int corridors. **Pets:** Small. $10 daily fee/room. Service with restrictions, supervision. 🅂🄰🅅🄴 ⊠ 🛢 🖵 ➴

▼▼▼▼ Holiday Inn Express & Suites Mankato East 🅷
(507) 388-1880. **$109-$159.** 2051 Adams St 56001. SR 22 S to Adams St, then w. Int corridors. **Pets:** Medium. $45 one-time fee/room. Service with restrictions, crate. 🄰🅂🄺 ⊠ 🅓🄼 🛢 🖵 ➴ 🖾

◈◈◈ ▼▼▼▼ Mankato City Center Hotel 🅷
(507) 345-1234. **$90-$120.** 101 E Main St 56001. Main St at Riverfront Dr; downtown. Int corridors. **Pets:** $35 one-time fee/room. Service with restrictions, crate. 🅂🄰🅅🄴 ⊠ 🅓🄼 🛢 🖵 🍴 ➴ 🖾

▼▼▼▼ Microtel Inn & Suites 🅷 ❀
(507) 388-2818. **$59-$92.** 200 St. Andrews Dr 56001. US 14, exit CR 3, 0.4 mi n. Int corridors. **Pets:** Large, other species. $15 one-time fee/room. Service with restrictions, crate. 🄰🅂🄺 ⊠ 🛢 🖵

▼▼ ▼▼ Super 8 🅷
(507) 387-0600. **$68-$98, 3 day notice.** 51578 US Hwy 169 N 56001. Jct US 169 and 14, just n. Int corridors. **Pets:** Dogs only. Service with restrictions, supervision. 🄰🅂🄺 ⊠ 🛢 🖵

MARSHALL

◈◈◈ ▼▼▼ Best Western Marshall Inn 🅷
(507) 532-3221. **$99-$119.** 1500 E College Dr 56258. SR 19, just w of jct SR 23. Int corridors. **Pets:** Other species. $10 daily fee/room. Service with restrictions, crate. 🅂🄰🅅🄴 ⊠ 🛢 🖵 🍴 ➴ 🖾

▼▼ ▼▼ Comfort Inn 🅷 ❀
(507) 532-3070. **$85-$110.** 1511 E College Dr 56258. SR 19, w of jct SR 23. Int corridors. **Pets:** $10 daily fee/pet. Service with restrictions, crate.
🄰🅂🄺 ⊠ 🅓🄼 🛢 🖵 ➴

MCGREGOR

▼▼ ▼▼ Country Meadows Inn 🄷

(218) 768-7378. **$65-$114.** 403 Meadows Dr 55760. Jct SR 65 and 210. Int corridors. **Pets:** Accepted. ⓧ 🛅 🖥 ➣

MILACA

▼▼ ▼▼ Super 8 🄷

(320) 983-2660. **Call for rates.** 215 10th Ave SE 56353. Jct SR 23 and 169. Int corridors. **Pets:** Accepted. ⓧ 🗹ᴹ 🛅 🖥

MINNEAPOLIS-ST. PAUL METROPOLITAN AREA

ANNANDALE

▼▼ ▼▼ AmericInn Lodge & Suites of Annandale 🄷

(320) 274-3006. **$70-$120.** 620 Elm St E 55302. On SR 55. Int corridors. **Pets:** Other species. $50 deposit/room. Designated rooms, service with restrictions, supervision. 🅰🅢🅺 ⓧ 🗹ᴹ 🛅 🖥 ➣

BECKER

◆◆◆ ▼▼▼▼ Sleep Inn & Suites 🄷

(763) 262-7700. **$69-$100.** 14435 Bank St 55308. Just e on US 10. Int corridors. **Pets:** Accepted. 🆂🅰🆅🅴 ⓧ 🛅 🖥 ➣ ⓧ

BLAINE

◆◆◆ ▼▼▼▼ Comfort Suites 🄷

(763) 792-0750. **$79-$109.** 10580 Baltimore St NE 55449. 1.5 mi n of jct SR 65 and US 10 to 107th Ave NE, just e to Baltimore St NE, then just s. Int corridors. **Pets:** Small, dogs only. $25 one-time fee/pet. Designated rooms, service with restrictions, supervision.

🆂🅰🆅🅴 ⓧ 🗹ᴹ 🛅 🖥 ➣

▼▼ ▼▼ Super 8 🄷

(763) 786-8888. **$63-$119.** 9410 Baltimore St NE 55449. Just n of jct US 10 and SR 65 to 93rd Ln (Post Office), just e to Baltimore St NE, then just n. Int corridors. **Pets:** Small, dogs only. $10 daily fee/pet. Designated rooms, service with restrictions, supervision.

🅰🅢🅺 ⓧ 🗹ᴹ 🛅 🖥 ➣

BLOOMINGTON

▼▼ ▼▼ Extended StayAmerica Minneapolis-Bloomington 🄷

(952) 884-1400. **$64-$69.** 7956 Lyndale Ave 55420. I-494, exit 4B (Lyndale Ave), just sw. Int corridors. **Pets:** Other species. $25 daily fee/room. Designated rooms, service with restrictions, crate. 🅰🅢🅺 ⓧ 🛅 🖥

◆◆◆ ▼▼▼▼ Hilton Minneapolis/Bloomington 🄷

(952) 893-9500. **$109-$269.** 3900 American Blvd W 55437. I-494, exit 6B (France Ave). Int corridors. **Pets:** Medium. $75 one-time fee/room. Designated rooms, service with restrictions, supervision.

🆂🅰🆅🅴 ⓧ 🛅 🖥 🍴 ➣

◆◆◆ ▼▼▼▼ Hilton Minneapolis/St. Paul Airport Mall of America 🄷 🐾

(952) 854-2100. **$89-$209.** 3800 American Blvd E 55425. I-494, exit 1B (34th Ave), just se. Int corridors. **Pets:** Medium, dogs only. $75 one-time fee/pet. Service with restrictions, crate.

🆂🅰🆅🅴 ⓧ 🗹ᴹ 🛅 🖥 🍴 ➣

◆◆◆ ▼▼▼▼ Homewood Suites by Hilton 🄷

(952) 854-0900. **$89-$249.** 2261 Killebrew Dr 55425. I-494, exit 2A (24th Ave), 1 mi s, then just w. Int corridors. **Pets:** Accepted.

🆂🅰🆅🅴 ⓧ 🛅 🖥 ➣

▼▼ ▼▼ La Quinta Inn Bloomington West 🄷 🐾

(952) 830-1300. **$62-$105.** 5151 American Blvd W 55437. I-494, exit 6B (France Ave), just se of SR 100, 1 mi w on frontage road. Int corridors. **Pets:** Medium, other species. Service with restrictions, supervision.

🅰🅢🅺 ⓧ 🗹ᴹ 🛅 🖥 🍴 ➣ ⓧ

▼ ▼ La Quinta Inn Minneapolis-Airport (Bloomington) 🄷 🐾

(952) 881-7311. **$59-$89.** 7815 Nicollet Ave S 55420. I-494, exit 4A (Nicollet Ave), just s. Int corridors. **Pets:** Medium, other species. Service with restrictions, supervision. 🅰🅢🅺 ⓧ 🛅 🖥

◆◆◆ ▼▼▼▼ Le Bourget Aero Suites, an Ascend Collection hotel 🄷

(952) 893-9999. **$99-$215.** 7770 Johnson Ave 55435. I-494, exit 6B (France Ave), 0.5 mi nw on frontage road (78th St). Int corridors. **Pets:** Accepted. 🆂🅰🆅🅴 ⓧ 🗹ᴹ 🛅 🖥 🍴 ➣

▼▼▼▼ Park Plaza Hotel Bloomington 🄷

(952) 831-3131. **$79-$189.** 4460 W 78th St Cir 55435. I-494, exit 6B (France Ave), 0.5 mi nw. Int corridors. **Pets:** Accepted.

ⓧ 🛅 🖥 🍴 ➣ ⓧ

◆◆◆ ▼▼▼▼ Ramada Mall of America–Airport 🄷

(952) 854-3411. **$59-$129, 14 day notice.** 2300 E American Blvd 55425-1228. I-494, exit 2A (24th Ave), just s. Int corridors. **Pets:** Accepted. 🆂🅰🆅🅴 ⓧ 🗹ᴹ 🛅 🖥 🍴 ➣ ⓧ

▼▼▼▼ Residence Inn by Marriott 🄷

(952) 876-0900. **$161-$197.** 7850 Bloomington Ave S 55425. I-494, exit 3, on south frontage road; behind Courtyard by Marriott Minneapolis/ Bloomington. Int corridors. **Pets:** Accepted. ⓧ 🛅 🖥 ➣ ⓧ

◆◆◆ ▼▼▼▼ Sheraton Bloomington Hotel Minneapolis South 🄷 🐾

(952) 835-7800. **$99-$269.** 7800 Normandale Blvd 55439. I-494, exit 7A (SR 100). Int corridors. **Pets:** Medium, dogs only. Service with restrictions, supervision. 🆂🅰🆅🅴 ⓧ 🛅 🖥 🍴 ➣ ⓧ

◆◆◆ ▼▼▼▼ Sofitel Minneapolis 🄷 🐾

(952) 835-1900. **$109-$299.** 5601 W 78th St 55439. Just nw of jct I-494 and SR 100, access via SR 100 and Industrial Blvd. Int corridors. **Pets:** Service with restrictions, crate. 🆂🅰🆅🅴 ⓧ 🗹ᴹ 🛅 🖥 🍴

▼▼▼▼ Staybridge Suites 🄷

(952) 831-7900. **$79-$269.** 5150 American Blvd 55437. I-494, exit 6B (France Ave), just se of SR 100, then 1 mi w on frontage road. Int corridors. **Pets:** Accepted. 🅰🅢🅺 ⓧ 🗹ᴹ 🛅 🖥 ➣ ⓧ

◆◆◆ ▼▼▼▼ Super 8 🄷

(952) 888-8800. **$64-$94.** 7800 S 2nd Ave 55420. I-494, exit 4A (Nicollet Ave), just se. Int corridors. **Pets:** Medium, other species. $10 daily fee/pet. Service with restrictions, supervision. 🆂🅰🆅🅴 ⓧ 🛅 🖥 ⓧ

BROOKLYN CENTER

▼▼ ▼▼ Comfort Inn by Choice Hotels 🄷

(763) 560-7464. **$65-$95.** 1600 James Cir N 55430. I-94/694, exit 34 (Shingle Creek Pkwy), just ne. Int corridors. **Pets:** Accepted.

🅰🅢🅺 ⓧ 🗹ᴹ 🛅 🖥

◆◆◆ ▼▼▼▼ Country Inn & Suites By Carlson 🄷

(763) 561-0900. **$81-$129.** 2550 Freeway Blvd 55430. I-94/694, exit 34 (Shingle Creek Pkwy), just nw. Int corridors. **Pets:** Accepted.

🆂🅰🆅🅴 ⓧ 🛅 🖥 ➣

▼▼ ▼▼ Extended StayAmerica-Minneapolis-Brooklyn Center 🄷

(763) 549-5571. **$59-$64.** 2701 Freeway Blvd 55430. I-94/694, exit 34 (Shingle Creek Pkwy), 0.5 mi nw. Int corridors. **Pets:** Other species. $25 daily fee/room. Designated rooms, service with restrictions, crate.

🅰🅢🅺 ⓧ 🛅 🖥

BROOKLYN PARK

▼▼ ▼▼ La Quinta Inn & Suites 🄷 🐾

(763) 971-8000. **$64-$94.** 7011 Northland Cir 55428. I-94/694, exit 30 (Boone Ave), just ne. Int corridors. **Pets:** Medium, other species. Service with restrictions, supervision. 🅰🅢🅺 ⓧ 🗹ᴹ 🛅 🖥 ➣

BURNSVILLE

Americas Best Value Inn M
(952) 894-3400. **$50-$70.** 1101 Burnsville Pkwy 55337. I-35W, exit 2 (Burnsville Pkwy), just sw. Int corridors. **Pets:** Accepted. [SAVE] [X] [I]

Holiday Inn Burnsville/Apple Valley H
(952) 435-2100. **$89-$159.** 14201 Nicollet Ave S 55337. Just n of jct I-35W and CR 42. Int corridors. **Pets:** Small, dogs only. $75 one-time fee/room. Designated rooms, service with restrictions, supervision.
[ASK] [X] [I] [II] [II] [X]

CHANHASSEN

AmericInn of Chanhassen H
(952) 934-3888. **$99-$195.** 570 Pond Promenade 55317. Just se of jct SR 5 and 101 S. Int corridors. **Pets:** Medium. $100 deposit/room, $30 one-time fee/room. Designated rooms, service with restrictions.
[SAVE] [X] [M] [I] [II] [X]

CHASKA

Best Western Chaska River Inn & Suites H
(952) 448-7877. **$80-$130.** 1 Riverbend Pl 55318. Jct US 212, 0.3 mi s on SR 41. Int corridors. **Pets:** Medium. $20 daily fee/pet. Designated rooms, service with restrictions, supervision.
[SAVE] [X] [M] [I] [II] [II] [X]

COON RAPIDS

Country Inn & Suites By Carlson H
(763) 780-3797. **$89-$229, 3 day notice.** 155 Coon Rapids Blvd 55433. US 10, exit Foley Blvd, 0.8 mi s to Coon Rapids Blvd, 0.5 mi e to Springbrook Dr, then just n. Int corridors. **Pets:** Medium, dogs only. $20 daily fee/pet. Designated rooms, service with restrictions, supervision.
[ASK] [X] [I] [II] [II]

Quality Inn Northtown H
(763) 785-4746. **$59-$119.** 9052 University Ave NW 55448. US 10, exit Foley Blvd, 0.6 mi. Int corridors. **Pets:** Other species. $10 daily fee/pet. Designated rooms, service with restrictions, supervision.
[SAVE] [X] [I] [II] [II]

EAGAN

Best Western Dakota Ridge H
(651) 452-0100. **$89-$109.** 3450 Washington Dr 55122. I-35E, exit 97B (Yankee Doodle Rd), just sw. Int corridors. **Pets:** Medium, other species. $15 daily fee/room. Designated rooms, service with restrictions.
[SAVE] [X] [I] [II]

Days Inn H
(651) 681-1770. **$75-$150.** 4510 Erin Dr 55122. Just ne of jct SR 77 and Cliff Rd. Int corridors. **Pets:** Other species. $100 deposit/room, $5 daily fee/pet. Designated rooms, service with restrictions.
[ASK] [X] [M] [I] [II] [II] [X]

Extended StayAmerica Minneapolis-Airport-Eagan H
(651) 681-9991. **$64-$69.** 3384 Norwest Ct 55121. I-35E, exit 97, just nw. Int corridors. **Pets:** Other species. $25 daily fee/room. Designated rooms, service with restrictions, crate. [ASK] [X] [I] [II]

Homestead Studio Suites Hotel-Minneapolis-Airport-Eagan H
(651) 905-1778. **$64-$69.** 3015 Denmark Ave 55121. I-35E, exit 98 (Lone Oak Rd), just se. Int corridors. **Pets:** Other species. $25 daily fee/room. Designated rooms, service with restrictions, crate. [ASK] [X] [I] [II]

Microtel Inn & Suites H
(651) 405-0988. **$59-$89, 7 day notice.** 3000 Denmark Ave 55121. I-35E, exit 98 (Lone Oak Rd), just se. Int corridors. **Pets:** Medium, other species. $15 daily fee/room. Service with restrictions, supervision.
[ASK] [X] [I] [II]

Residence Inn by Marriott-Mpls/St. Paul Airport H
(651) 688-0363. **$143-$175.** 3040 Eagandale Pl 55121. I-35E, exit 98 (Lone Oak Rd), just sw. Ext corridors. **Pets:** Accepted.
[SAVE] [X] [I] [II] [II] [X]

Staybridge Suites H
(651) 994-7810. **Call for rates.** 4675 Rahncliff Rd 55122. I-35E, exit 93 (Cliff Rd), just w, then just s. Int corridors. **Pets:** Accepted.
[X] [I] [II]

TownePlace Suites H
(651) 994-4600. **$125-$153.** 3615 Crestridge Dr 55122. I-35E, exit 97A (Pilot Knob Rd), just se. Int corridors. **Pets:** Large, other species. $75 one-time fee/room. Service with restrictions. [X] [M] [I] [II] [II]

EDEN PRAIRIE

Best Western Eden Prairie Inn H
(952) 829-0888. **$104-$119.** 11500 W 78th St 55344. I-494, exit 11A, just sw. Int corridors. **Pets:** Dogs only. $10 daily fee/pet. Service with restrictions, supervision. [SAVE] [X] [I] [II]

Extended StayAmerica Minneapolis-Eden Prairie H
(952) 941-1113. **$59-$64.** 7550 Office Ridge Cir 55344. I-494, exit 12, just se. Int corridors. **Pets:** Other species. $25 daily fee/room. Designated rooms, service with restrictions, crate. [ASK] [X] [I] [II]

Homestead Studio Suites Hotel-Minneapolis-Eden Prairie H
(952) 942-6818. **$64-$69.** 11905 Technology Dr 55344. Just sw of jct I-494 and US 212 (Flying Cloud Dr). Int corridors. **Pets:** Other species. $25 daily fee/room. Designated rooms, service with restrictions, crate.
[ASK] [X] [M] [I] [II]

Residence Inn by Marriott-Minneapolis SW H
(952) 829-0033. **$154-$169.** 7780 Flying Cloud Dr 55344. I-494, exit 11A, on US 169 S and 212 (Flying Cloud Dr). Int corridors. **Pets:** Accepted.
[X] [I] [II] [II]

EDINA

Residence Inn Minneapolis-Edina H
(952) 893-9300. **$179-$189.** 3400 Edinborough Way 55435. I-494, exit 6B (France Ave), 0.3 mi n to Minnesota Dr, then just e. Int corridors.
Pets: Accepted. [SAVE] [X] [I] [II]

The Westin Edina Galleria H
(952) 567-5000. **$119-$299.** 3201 Galleria 55435. I-494, exit 6B (France Ave), 1.5 mi n, just e at the Galleria. Int corridors. **Pets:** Medium. $50 deposit/room. Designated rooms, service with restrictions, supervision.
[SAVE] [X] [I] [II] [II] [II]

FOREST LAKE

AmericInn Motel of Forest Lake H
(651) 464-1930. **$73-$120.** 1291 W Broadway Ave 55025. I-35, exit 131 (CR 2), just ne. Int corridors. **Pets:** $10 daily fee/pet. Designated rooms, service with restrictions, supervision. [ASK] [X] [I] [II]

HASTINGS

AmericInn Lodge & Suites of Hastings H
(651) 437-8877. **Call for rates.** 2400 Vermillion St 55033. 1.5 mi s on US 61. Int corridors. **Pets:** Accepted. [X] [I] [II] [II]

Country Inn & Suites By Carlson H
(651) 437-8870. **$79-$97.** 300 33rd St 55033. 1.7 mi s on US 61, just e. Int corridors. **Pets:** Accepted. [ASK] [X] [I] [II] [II]

Regency Inn & Suites H
(651) 438-8888. **$55-$150, 14 day notice.** 2450 Vermillion St 55033. 1.5 mi s on US 61. Int corridors. **Pets:** Small. $85 deposit/room, $10 daily fee/pet. Designated rooms, service with restrictions, supervision.
[ASK] [X] [I] [II]

MAPLE GROVE

▼▼ Extended StayAmerica Minneapolis-Maple Grove 🅷
(763) 694-9747. **$59-$64.** 12970 63rd Ave N 55369. I-494, exit 26 (Bass Lake Rd), just ne. Int corridors. **Pets:** Other species. $25 daily fee/room. Designated rooms, service with restrictions, crate.
ASK ☒ ⓛM 🛏 💻

▼▼ Select Inn 🅷 ❄
(763) 493-2277. **$59-$119.** 7285 Forestview Ln N 55369. I-94, exit 28 (CR 61/Hemlock Ln), just se. Int corridors. **Pets:** Other species. $10 daily fee/room. Service with restrictions. ASK ☒ 🛏 💻

▼▼▼ Staybridge Suites Minneapolis-Maple Grove 🅷
(763) 494-8856. **Call for rates.** 7821 Elm Creek Blvd 55369. Just ne of jct I-94/494/694. Int corridors. **Pets:** Medium. $150 one-time fee/room. Service with restrictions, crate. ☒ ⓛM 🛏 💻 ➔ ☒

MAPLEWOOD

◈ ▼▼ Emerald Inn 🅷
(651) 777-8131. **$50-$75.** 2025 E County Rd D 55109. I-694, exit 50 (White Bear Ave), just se. Int corridors. **Pets:** Large. $10 daily fee/pet. Designated rooms, service with restrictions, supervision. SAVE ☒ 🛏

MINNEAPOLIS

◈ ▼▼▼ aloft Minneapolis 🅷 ❄
(612) 455-8400. **Call for rates.** 900 Washington Ave S 55415. Jct 9th Ave. Int corridors. **Pets:** Medium, dogs only. Service with restrictions, supervision. SAVE ☒ ⓛM 🛏 💻 ➔

◈ ▼▼▼ Best Western Normandy Inn 🅷
(612) 370-1400. **$89-$179.** 405 S 8th St 55404. Corner of S 8th St and S 4th Ave. Int corridors. **Pets:** Small, dogs only. $100 deposit/pet. Designated rooms, service with restrictions, supervision.
SAVE ☒ 🛏 💻 ❗ ➔ ☒

◈ ▼▼▼ Days Hotel on University 🅷
(612) 623-3999. **$89-$169.** 2407 University Ave SE 55414. I-35W, exit University Ave, 1 mi se. Int corridors. **Pets:** $20 one-time fee/room. Designated rooms, service with restrictions, supervision. SAVE ☒ 🛏 💻

◈ ▼▼▼▼ Graves 601 Hotel 🅷
(612) 677-1100. **$149-$359.** 601 1st Ave N 55403. Between 6th and 7th sts. Int corridors. **Pets:** Accepted. SAVE ☒ 🛏 ❗ ☒

◈ ▼▼▼▼ Hilton Minneapolis 🅷 ❄
(612) 376-1000. **$99-$299.** 1001 Marquette Ave S 55403. Between S 10th and S 11th sts. Int corridors. **Pets:** Medium, other species. $45 one-time fee/pet. Service with restrictions, crate.
SAVE ☒ ⓛM 🛏 💻 ❗ ➔ ☒

◈ ▼▼▼▼ Hotel Ivy 🅷
(612) 746-4600. **$169-$449.** 201 S 11th St 55404. 2nd Ave and 11th St. Int corridors. **Pets:** Accepted. SAVE ☒ ❗

◈ ▼▼▼▼ The Marquette Hotel 🅷
(612) 333-4545. **$109-$329.** 710 Marquette Ave 55402. Jct Marquette Ave and S 7th St. Int corridors. **Pets:** Accepted.
SAVE ☒ 🛏 💻 ❗

◈ ▼▼▼▼ Radisson Plaza Hotel Minneapolis 🅷
(612) 339-4900. **$89-$399.** 35 S 7th St 55402. Between Nicollet and Hennepin aves. Int corridors. **Pets:** Accepted.
SAVE ☒ ⓛM 🛏 💻 ❗ ☒

◈ ▼▼▼▼ Residence Inn by Marriott Minneapolis Downtown City Center 🅷
(612) 677-1000. **$188-$230.** 45 S 8th St 55402. At 8th St and LaSalle Ave. Int corridors. **Pets:** $100 one-time fee/room. Service with restrictions, crate. SAVE ☒ 🛏 💻

▼▼▼▼ Residence Inn Milwaukee Road Depot 🅷
(612) 340-1300. **$199-$249.** 425 S 2nd St 55401. Jct S 2nd St and 5th Ave S. Int corridors. **Pets:** Accepted. ☒ 🛏 💻

◈ ▼▼▼ Sheraton Minneapolis Midtown Hotel 🅷
(612) 821-7600. **$109-$249.** 2901 Chicago Ave S 55407. At Lake St. Int corridors. **Pets:** Accepted. SAVE ☒ ⓛM 🛏 💻 ❗ ➔

◈ ▼▼▼▼ The Westin Minneapolis 🅷 ❄
(612) 333-4006. **Call for rates.** 88 S 6th St 55402. At Marquette Ave. Int corridors. **Pets:** Medium. Service with restrictions, supervision.
SAVE ☒ 🛏 💻 ❗ ➔ ☒

◈ ▼▼▼▼ W Minneapolis–The Foshay 🅷
(612) 215-3700. **$129-$559.** 821 Marquette Ave 55402. Between 9th and 8th sts. Int corridors. **Pets:** Accepted. SAVE ☒ 🛏 ❗ ☒

MINNETONKA

◈ ▼▼▼▼ Minneapolis Marriott-Southwest 🅷
(952) 935-5500. **$169-$179.** 5801 Opus Pkwy 55343. Just nw of jct US 169 and Cross Town SR 62, exit Bren Rd. Int corridors. **Pets:** Accepted.
SAVE ☒ 🛏 💻 ➔ ☒

◈ ▼▼▼▼ Sheraton Minneapolis West Hotel 🅷 ❄
(952) 593-0000. **$89-$279.** 12201 Ridgedale Dr 55305. I-394, exit 1C (Ridgedale Dr), 0.3 mi s. Int corridors. **Pets:** Large, dogs only. Service with restrictions, supervision. SAVE ☒ 🛏 💻 ❗ ➔

MONTICELLO

◈ ▼▼▼ Best Western Chelsea Inn & Suites 🅷
(763) 271-8880. **$90-$140.** 89 Chelsea Rd 55362. I-94, exit 193, 0.3 mi se. Int corridors. **Pets:** Small, other species. $10 daily fee/pet. Designated rooms, service with restrictions, supervision.
SAVE ☒ 🛏 💻 ➔ ☒

◈ ▼▼▼ Days Inn 🅷
(763) 295-1111. **$59-$79.** 200 E Oakwood Dr 55362. I-94, exit 193, 0.3 mi se. Int corridors. **Pets:** Large, other species. $10 daily fee/pet, $10 one-time fee/pet. Service with restrictions, supervision.
SAVE ☒ 🛏 💻

NORTH BRANCH

◈ ▼▼▼ AmericInn Lodge & Suites of North Branch 🅷
(651) 674-8627. **$79-$180.** 38675 14th Ave 55056. I-35, exit 147 (SR 95), just e, s on Oakview Ave, then w on Oak St. Int corridors.
Pets: Accepted. SAVE ☒ 🛏 💻 ➔ ☒

OAKDALE

▼▼ AmericInn Lodge & Suites of Oakdale 🅷
(651) 730-5700. **$69-$100.** 6630 Hudson Blvd N 55128. I-94, exit 247 (Century Ave), 0.7 mi n on Hudson Blvd (Frontage Rd). Int corridors. **Pets:** Medium, other species. $30 one-time fee/pet. Designated rooms, service with restrictions, supervision. ASK ☒ 🛏 💻 ☒

◈ ▼▼▼ Best Western Regency Plaza Hotel 🅷
(651) 578-8466. **$70-$130.** 970 Helena Ave N 55128. I-694, exit 57, just e, then just s. Int corridors. **Pets:** Medium, other species. $25 one-time fee/room. Service with restrictions, supervision. SAVE ☒ ⓛM 🛏 💻

OAK PARK HEIGHTS

▼▼ AmericInn Lodge & Suites of Oak Park Heights 🅷 ❄
(651) 275-0980. **$60-$180.** 13025 60th St N 55082. SR 36 at Stillwater Blvd, just se. Int corridors. **Pets:** Other species. $15 daily fee/room. Supervision. ASK ☒ 🛏 💻 ➔ ☒

PLYMOUTH

◈ ▼▼▼ Best Western Kelly Inn 🅷
(763) 553-1600. **$90-$120.** 2705 N Annapolis Ln 55441. I-494, exit 22 (SR 55), just e. Int corridors. **Pets:** Large. Designated rooms, service with restrictions, supervision. SAVE ☒ 🛏 💻 ❗ ➔ ☒

▼▼▼ **Comfort Inn** H

(763) 559-1222. **$90-$110.** 3000 Harbor Ln 55447. I-494, exit 22 (SR 55), 0.3 mi nw. Int corridors. **Pets:** Accepted.

ASK ✕ 🛏 🖰 🍴 🏊 🐾

AAA ▼▼▼ **Radisson Hotel & Conference Center Minneapolis** H 🐾

(763) 559-6600. **Call for rates.** 3131 Campus Dr 55441. I-494, exit 22 (SR 55), just e to CR 61 (Northwest Blvd), then 0.8 mi nw. Int corridors. **Pets:** $50 deposit/room. Service with restrictions.

SAVE ✕ 🖰 🍴 🏊 🐾

AAA ▼▼▼ **Red Roof Inn** M

(763) 553-1751. **$50-$65.** 2600 Annapolis Cir N 55441. I-494, exit 22 (SR 55), just se. Ext corridors. **Pets:** Large. Service with restrictions, crate. SAVE ✕ 🛏

▼▼▼ **Residence Inn by Marriott** H 🐾

(763) 577-1600. **$169-$179.** 2750 Annapolis Cir N 55441. I-494, exit 22 (SR 55), just e to CR 61, just nw. Int corridors. **Pets:** Large, other species. $100 one-time fee/room. Service with restrictions, crate.

✕ 🛏 🖰 🏊

RICHFIELD

▼▼▼ **Candlewood Suites** H

(612) 869-7704. **$89-$109.** 351 W 77th St 55423. I-494, exit 4B (Lyndale Ave), just ne. Int corridors. **Pets:** Accepted. ASK ✕ 🖰 🛏 🖰

ROGERS

▼▼ **AmericInn Lodge & Suites of Rogers** H 🐾

(763) 428-4346. **$87-$148.** 21800 Industrial Blvd 55374. I-94, exit 207 (SR 101), just sw. Int corridors. **Pets:** Other species. $10 daily fee/pet. Designated rooms, service with restrictions, supervision.

ASK ✕ 🛏 🖰 🏊

AAA ▼▼▼ **Hampton Inn & Suites** H 🐾

(763) 425-0044. **$89-$189.** 13550 Commerce Blvd 55374. I-94, exit 207 (SR 101), 0.4 mi nw. Int corridors. **Pets:** Medium. Designated rooms, service with restrictions, supervision. SAVE ✕ 🖰 🛏 🖰 🏊

ROSEVILLE

AAA ▼▼ **Days Inn St. Paul NW/Roseville** H

(651) 636-6730. **$69-$119.** 2550 Cleveland Ave N 55113. I-35W, exit 24 (CR C), 0.3 mi se. Int corridors. **Pets:** Small, other species. $15 one-time fee/pet. Designated rooms, service with restrictions, supervision.

SAVE ✕ 🛏 🖰

▼▼▼ **Residence Inn** H

(651) 636-0680. **$169-$184.** 2985 Centre Pointe Dr 55113. I-35W, exit 25A (CR D), just se. Int corridors. **Pets:** Large. $100 one-time fee/room. Service with restrictions. ✕ 🖰 🛏 🖰 🏊 🐾

ST. LOUIS PARK

▼▼▼ **Doubletree Hotel Minneapolis Park Place** H

(952) 542-8600. **$89-$219.** 1500 Park Place Blvd 55416. I-394, exit 5 (Park Place Blvd), just sw. Int corridors. **Pets:** Small. $10 daily fee/pet. Service with restrictions, supervision. ✕ 🛏 🖰 🍴 🏊

▼▼▼ **TownePlace Suites-Minneapolis West** H

(952) 847-6900. **$130-$140.** 1400 Zarthan Ave S 55416. I-394, exit 5 (Park Place Blvd), 0.3 mi w on 16th, then just n. Int corridors. **Pets:** Accepted. ✕ 🛏 🖰 🏊

ST. PAUL

AAA ▼▼ **Best Western Kelly Inn** H

(651) 227-8711. **$79-$199.** 161 St. Anthony Ave 55103. Jct I-35E and 94. Int corridors. **Pets:** Small, other species. Service with restrictions, crate.

SAVE ✕ 🛏 🖰 🍴 🏊

▼▼ **Super 8** H

(651) 771-5566. **$69-$79.** 1739 Old Hudson Rd 55106. I-94, exit 245 (White Bear Ave), just nw. Int corridors. **Pets:** Accepted.

ASK ✕ 🛏 🖰

SHAKOPEE

▼▼▼ **AmericInn Lodge & Suites of Shakopee** H

(952) 445-6775. **$85-$190.** 4100 12th Ave E 55379. Just ne of US 169. Int corridors. **Pets:** Accepted. ASK ✕ 🛏 🖰 🏊 🐾

▼▼ **Canterbury Inn** H

(952) 445-3644. **$89-$139.** 1244 Canterbury Rd 55379. Just nw of US 169. Int corridors. **Pets:** Other species. $10 daily fee/room. Service with restrictions, crate. ASK ✕ 🛏 🖰 🏊

▼▼▼ **Country Inn & Suites By Carlson** H

(952) 445-0200. **$95-$125.** 1204 Ramsey St 55379. Just ne of US 169. Int corridors. **Pets:** Other species. $100 deposit/room, $30 one-time fee/pet. Designated rooms, service with restrictions, crate.

ASK ✕ 🛏 🖰 🏊

▼▼ **Sandalwood Studios & Suites** H

(952) 277-0100. **$39-$109.** 3910 12th Ave E 55379. Just nw of US 169. Int corridors. **Pets:** Small. $10 one-time fee/room. Designated rooms, service with restrictions, supervision. ASK ✕ 🛏

STILLWATER

AAA ▼▼ **Americas Best Value Inn** H

(651) 430-1300. **$50-$120.** 1750 W Frontage Rd 55082. SR 36 at Washington Ave, just ne. Int corridors. **Pets:** Other species. $10 daily fee/room. Service with restrictions, supervision. SAVE ✕ 🖰 🛏 🖰 🏊

▼▼ **Super 8** H

(651) 430-3990. **$56-$99.** 2190 W Frontage Rd 55082. SR 36 at Washington Ave. Int corridors. **Pets:** Accepted. ASK ✕ 🛏 🖰

WACONIA

▼▼ **Americas Best Value Inn Waconia** M

(952) 442-5147. **Call for rates.** 301 E Frontage Rd 55387. On SR 5 at jct CR 10. Int corridors. **Pets:** Medium, other species. $15 one-time fee/pet. Designated rooms, service with restrictions, supervision.

✕ 🛏 🖰

▼▼▼ **AmericInn Lodge & Suites of Waconia** H

(952) 442-8787. **$85-$169.** 550 Cherry Dr 55387. Just nw from jct SR 5. Int corridors. **Pets:** Accepted. ASK ✕ 🛏 🖰 🏊

WHITE BEAR LAKE

▼▼ **AmericInn Lodge & Suites of White Bear Lake** H

(651) 429-7131. **$79-$149.** 4675 White Bear Pkwy 55110. I-35E, exit 117, just ne of jct SR 96. Int corridors. **Pets:** Small, dogs only. $10 one-time fee/pet. Designated rooms, service with restrictions, supervision.

ASK ✕ 🖰 🛏 🖰 🏊 🐾

AAA ▼▼▼ **Best Western White Bear Country Inn** H

(651) 429-5393. **$79-$109.** 4940 N Hwy 61 55110. Jct SR 96, 1 mi n. Int corridors. **Pets:** Other species. $10 daily fee/room. Service with restrictions, supervision. SAVE ✕ 🛏 🖰 🍴 🏊 🐾

WOODBURY

▼▼ **Extended StayAmerica-Minneapolis-Woodbury** H

(651) 501-1085. **$64-$74.** 10020 Hudson Rd 55125. I-94, exit 251, just se. Int corridors. **Pets:** Other species. $25 daily fee/room. Designated rooms, service with restrictions, crate. ASK ✕ 🛏 🖰

▼▼▼ **Holiday Inn Express Hotel & Suites** H 🐾

(651) 702-0200. **$89-$169.** 9840 Norma Ln 55125. I-94, exit 251, just sw. Int corridors. **Pets:** Small, other species. $10 one-time fee/room. Service with restrictions, supervision. ASK ✕ 🛏 🖰 🏊

▼▼ **Red Roof Inn #7063** M

(651) 738-7160. **$50-$70, 7 day notice.** 1806 Wooddale Dr 55125. I-494, exit 59 (Valley Creek Rd), just se. Ext corridors. **Pets:** Large. Service with restrictions, crate. ASK ✕

Sheraton St. Paul Woodbury Hotel 🅷 ☀
(651) 209-3280. **$99-$249.** 676 Bielenberg Dr 55125. I-494, exit 59C
(Tamarack Rd), just ne. Int corridors. **Pets:** Medium, dogs only. Designated rooms, service with restrictions, supervision.

[SAVE] [✕] [♿M] [✆] [💻] [🍴] [🏊]

END METROPOLITAN AREA

MONTEVIDEO

Crossings by GrandStay Inn & Suites 🅷
(320) 269-8000. **$84-$149, 30 day notice.** 1805 E SR 7 56265. On SR
7; east of downtown. Int corridors. **Pets:** Other species. $200 deposit/
room. Designated rooms, service with restrictions, supervision.

[SAVE] [✕] [✆] [💻] [🏊]

MOORHEAD

Super 8 🅷
(218) 233-8880. **$55-$62.** 3621 S 8th St 56560. I-94, exit 1A (US 75),
0.5 mi s. Int corridors. **Pets:** Designated rooms, service with restrictions,
supervision. [SAVE] [✕] [✆] [💻]

Travelodge & Suites 🅷
(218) 233-5333. **$49-$59.** 3027 S Frontage Rd 56560. Just s of US 10
E; east of downtown. Int corridors. **Pets:** Designated rooms, service with
restrictions, supervision. [ASK] [✕] [♿M] [✆] [💻] [🏊]

MOOSE LAKE

AmericInn Lodge & Suites of Moose Lake 🅷
(218) 485-8885. **$70-$175.** 400 Park Place Dr 55767. I-35, exit 214 (SR
73), just sw. Int corridors. **Pets:** Other species. $50 deposit/room, $10
daily fee/room. Designated rooms, service with restrictions, crate.

[ASK] [✕] [✆] [💻] [🏊]

MOUNTAIN IRON

AmericInn of Virginia Lodge & Suites of
Virginia 🅷 ☀
(218) 741-7839. **$100-$180.** 5480 Mountain Iron Dr 55792. US 53, just s
of jct US 169. Int corridors. **Pets:** Small, dogs only. $10 daily fee/pet.
Designated rooms, service with restrictions, supervision.

[✕] [♿M] [✆] [💻] [🏊] [✕]

Holiday Inn Express & Suites 🅷
(218) 741-7411. **Call for rates.** 8570 Rock Ridge Dr 55768. On US 169,
just w of jct US 53. Int corridors. **Pets:** Dogs only. $25 one-time fee/pet.
Service with restrictions, supervision. [✕] [✆] [💻] [🏊]

NEW ULM

Holiday Inn 🅷
(507) 359-2941. **$90-$159.** 2101 S Broadway 56073. SR 15/68, 1.8 mi
se. Int corridors. **Pets:** Accepted. [ASK] [✕] [✆] [💻] [🍴] [🏊] [✕]

Microtel Inn & Suites 🅷
(507) 354-9800. **$57-$115.** 424 20th St S 56073. Just e of jct SR 15/68
and CR 37. Int corridors. **Pets:** Accepted.

[SAVE] [✕] [♿M] [✆] [💻] [🏊]

NORTHFIELD

Super 8 🅷
(507) 663-0371. **Call for rates.** 1420 Riverview Dr 55057. 1.3 mi w of jct
SR 19 and 3. Int corridors. **Pets:** Accepted. [✕] [✆] [💻] [🏊]

ONAMIA

Budget Host Inn & Suites 🅷
(320) 532-3838. **$50-$130.** 40847 US 169 56359. On US 169, 6 mi n.
Int corridors. **Pets:** Accepted. [ASK] [✕] [✆] [💻]

ORR

Gateway Lodge and Suites 🅷
(218) 757-3613. **$85-$230.** 4675 Hwy 53 55771. Just n. Int corridors.
Pets: $20 one-time fee/room. Designated rooms, supervision.

[ASK] [✕] [✆] [💻] [🍴] [🏊] [✕]

North Country Inn 🅷
(218) 757-3778. **$68-$94.** 4483 Hwy 53 55771. 0.3 mi s. Int corridors.
Pets: $10 one-time fee/pet. Service with restrictions, supervision.

[✕] [♿M] [✆]

OTTERTAIL

Thumper Pond Resort 🅷
(218) 367-2000. **$99-$199, 3 day notice.** 300 Thumper Lodge Rd
56571. Jct SR 108 and 78. Int corridors. **Pets:** Medium, dogs only. $15
daily fee/pet. Designated rooms, crate. [SAVE] [✕] [✆] [💻] [🍴] [✕]

OWATONNA

AmericInn of Owatonna 🅷 ☀
(507) 455-1142. **Call for rates.** 245 Florence Ave 55060. I-35, exit 41
(Bridge St), 0.3 mi ne. Int corridors. **Pets:** $10 daily fee/pet. Service with
restrictions, supervision. [✕] [✆] [💻] [🏊] [✕]

Comfort Inn 🅷 ☀
(507) 444-0818. **$90-$170.** 2345 43rd St NW 55060. I-35, exit 45 (Clinton Falls), just sw. Int corridors. **Pets:** $50 deposit/room, $10 daily fee/pet.
Service with restrictions, supervision. [ASK] [✕] [♿M] [✆] [💻] [🏊]

Microtel Inn & Suites 🅷
(507) 446-0228. **Call for rates.** 150 St. John Dr NW 55060. I-35, exit 41
(Bridge St), just nw. Int corridors. **Pets:** Medium, other species. $10 one-
time fee/pet. Service with restrictions, supervision. [✕] [♿M] [✆] [💻]

PARK RAPIDS

C'mon Inn 🅷
(218) 732-1471. **$85-$174.** 1009 1st St E 56470. SR 34, 0.8 mi e of jct
US 71. Int corridors. **Pets:** Accepted. [ASK] [✕] [✆] [💻] [🏊]

PAYNESVILLE

Paynesville Inn & Suites 🅷
(320) 243-4146. **Call for rates.** 700 W Hwy 23 56362. Jct SR 55, 0.3 mi
s. Int corridors. **Pets:** Dogs only. $25 deposit/pet, $10 daily fee/pet. Designated rooms, service with restrictions, supervision. [✕] [✆] [💻] [🏊]

PEQUOT LAKES

AmericInn Lodge & Suites of Pequot Lakes 🅷 ☀
(218) 568-8400. **$75-$219, 7 day notice.** 32912 Paul Bunyan Trail Dr
(SR 371/CR 16) 56472. SR 371, 2 mi n of downtown. Int corridors.
Pets: Large, dogs only. $10 daily fee/pet. Designated rooms, service with
restrictions, supervision. [✕] [✆] [💻] [🏊] [✕]

PERHAM

Crossings by GrandStay Inn & Suites 🅷
(218) 346-2033. **$80-$100.** 231 Market Dr 56573. US 10 W, exit CR
8/SR 78. Int corridors. **Pets:** Accepted. [SAVE] [✕] [✆] [💻] [🏊]

Super 8 🅷
(218) 346-7888. **$66-$83.** 106 Jake St SE 56573. SR 78, just nw of jct
US 10. Int corridors. **Pets:** Accepted. [ASK] [✕] [✆] [💻]

PINE RIVER

▼▼▼ Rodeway Inn Ⓜ

(218) 587-4499. **$60-$90.** 2684 State 371 SW 56474. 1 mi s. Ext corridors. **Pets:** Accepted. (ASK) ✕ 🛏 💻 ⌧

RED WING

ⒶⒶⒶ ▼▼▼ Best Western Rivertown Inn & Suites Ⓗ

(651) 388-1577. **$80-$180.** 752 Withers Harbor Dr 55066. 1.5 mi nw on US 61, at Withers Harbor Dr; opposite side of US 61 from Pottery Mall. Ext/int corridors. **Pets:** Medium. $15 daily fee/pet. Designated rooms, service with restrictions, supervision. (SAVE) ✕ 🔥 🛏 💻 ⌒

▼▼▼ Days Inn Ⓜ

(651) 388-3568. **$54-$131.** 955 E 7th St 55066. US 61/63, 1.7 mi se. Ext corridors. **Pets:** Dogs only. $7 daily fee/pet. Service with restrictions, supervision. (ASK) ✕ 🛏 💻 ⌒

ROCHESTER

▼▼▼ Clarion Inn Ⓗ

(507) 288-1844. **Call for rates.** 1630 S Broadway 55904. 0.5 mi s of jct US 14 and 63 (Broadway). Ext/int corridors. **Pets:** Accepted. ✕ 🛏 💻 🍴 ⌒ ⌧

▼▼▼ Comfort Inn Ⓗ

(507) 289-3344. **$88-$181.** 5708 Bandel Rd NW 55901. US 52, exit 55th St, just n on E Frontage Rd. Int corridors. **Pets:** Medium, dogs only. $35 one-time fee/room. Service with restrictions, supervision. (ASK) ✕ 🔥 🛏 💻 ⌒

▼▼▼ Extended StayAmerica-Rochester North Ⓗ

(507) 289-7444. **$49-$54.** 2814 43rd St NW 55901. Just nw from jct US 52. Int corridors. **Pets:** Other species. $25 daily fee/room. Designated rooms, service with restrictions, crate. (ASK) ✕ 🛏 💻

▼▼▼ Extended StayAmerica-Rochester-South Ⓗ

(507) 536-7444. **$49-$54.** 55 Wood Lake Dr SE 55904. US 63, exit 49th St S, 0.7 mi ne. Int corridors. **Pets:** Other species. $25 daily fee/room. Designated rooms, service with restrictions, crate. (ASK) ✕ 🛏 💻

▼▼▼ GuestHouse International Inn & Suites Ⓗ ❀

(507) 288-9090. **$65.** 435 16th Ave NW 55901. Just se of jct US 14 and 52; exit Civic Center Dr. Int corridors. **Pets:** $15 one-time fee/room. Designated rooms, service with restrictions, supervision.
(ASK) ✕ 🔥 🛏 💻 🍴 ⌒ ⌧

ⒶⒶⒶ ▼▼▼ International Hotel Ⓗ

(507) 328-8000. **$450-$3000.** 20 SW 2nd Ave 55902. Opposite Mayo Clinic and Methodist Hospital; 12th Floor of Kahler Grand Hotel. Int corridors. **Pets:** Accepted. (SAVE) ✕ 🛏 💻 ⌒ ⌧

▼▼▼▼ The Kahler Grand Hotel Ⓗ

(507) 280-6200. **$69-$149.** 20 SW 2nd Ave 55902. Opposite Mayo Clinic and Methodist Hospital. Int corridors. **Pets:** Other species. Service with restrictions, supervision. (ASK) ✕ 🛏 💻 🍴 ⌒ ⌧

▼▼▼ Kahler Inn & Suites Ⓗ

(507) 285-9200. **$89-$159.** 9 NW 3rd Ave 55901. Just n of Mayo Clinic. Int corridors. **Pets:** Accepted. (ASK) ✕ 🛏 💻 🍴 ⌒ ⌧

▼▼▼ Marriott Hotel Ⓗ

(507) 280-6000. **$233-$285.** 101 1st Ave SW 55902. Just e of Mayo Clinic. Int corridors. **Pets:** Other species. $75 one-time fee/room. Designated rooms, service with restrictions, supervision.
✕ 🛏 💻 🍴 ⌒ ⌧

▼▼▼ Microtel Inn & Suites Ⓗ

(507) 286-8780. **Call for rates.** 4210 Hwy 52 N 55901. US 52, exit 58 (41st St NW), just w. Int corridors. **Pets:** Small. $10 daily fee/pet. Designated rooms, service with restrictions. ✕ 🔥 🛏 💻

▼▼▼ Residence Inn by Marriott Ⓗ

(507) 292-1400. **$161-$197.** 441 W Center St 55902. Just n of Mayo Clinic; downtown. Int corridors. **Pets:** Other species. $100 one-time fee/room. Service with restrictions, supervision. ✕ 🔥 🛏 💻

▼▼▼ Sleep Inn & Suites Ⓗ ❀

(507) 536-7000. **$79-$129.** 7320 Airport View Dr SW 55902. On US 63 (Broadway), airport exit. Int corridors. **Pets:** $10 daily fee/room. Designated rooms, service with restrictions, supervision.
(SAVE) ✕ 🔥 🛏 💻 ⌒ ⌧

▼▼▼ Staybridge Suites Ⓗ

(507) 289-6600. **$121-$131.** 1211 2nd St SW 55902. US 52/14, exit 55B (2nd St SW), just e. Int corridors. **Pets:** Accepted.
(ASK) ✕ 🔥 🛏 💻 ⌒

ⒶⒶⒶ ▼▼▼ TownePlace Suites Ⓗ

(507) 281-1200. **$107-$131.** 2829 NW 43rd St 55901. US 52, exit 41st St NW, just w, just n on W Frontage Rd, then just w. Int corridors. **Pets:** $100 one-time fee/room. Service with restrictions, supervision.
(SAVE) ✕ 🔥 🛏 💻 ⌒ ⌧

ROSEAU

ⒶⒶⒶ ▼▼▼ AmericInn Lodge & Suites of Roseau Ⓗ

(218) 463-1045. **$67-$82.** 1110 3rd St NW 56751. 1 mi w on SR 11. Int corridors. **Pets:** Other species. $25 one-time fee/room. No service.
(SAVE) ✕ 🔥 🛏 💻 ⌒ ⌧

▼▼▼ North Country Inn Ⓗ

(218) 463-9444. **$68-$120.** 902 3rd St NW 56751. 0.8 mi w on SR 11. Int corridors. **Pets:** Accepted. (ASK) ✕ 🛏 💻 ⌒

ST. CLOUD

ⒶⒶⒶ ▼▼▼ AmericInn Lodge & Suites of St. Cloud Ⓗ ❀

(320) 253-6337. **$72-$135.** 4385 Clearwater Rd 56301. I-94, exit 171 (CR 75), just ne. Int corridors. **Pets:** Other species. $10 daily fee/pet. Designated rooms, service with restrictions, supervision.
(SAVE) ✕ 🔥 🛏 💻 ⌒

ⒶⒶⒶ ▼▼▼ Best Western Americanna Inn & Conference Center Ⓗ

(320) 252-8700. **$70-$95.** 520 S US Hwy 10 56304. Jct SR 23, 0.3 mi s. Ext/int corridors. **Pets:** Accepted. (SAVE) ✕ 🛏 💻 🍴 ⌒ ⌧

ⒶⒶⒶ ▼▼▼ Best Western Kelly Inn Ⓗ

(320) 253-0606. **$89-$130.** 100 4th Ave S 56301. SR 23 at 4th Ave S; center. Int corridors. **Pets:** $10 daily fee/pet. Designated rooms, service with restrictions, supervision. (SAVE) ✕ 🔥 🛏 💻 🍴 ⌒ ⌧

▼▼▼ Country Inn & Suites By Carlson Ⓗ

(320) 259-8999. **$99-$140.** 235 S Park Ave 56301. Jct SR 15 and 23 W, just w. Int corridors. **Pets:** Small, other species. $15 one-time fee/room. Service with restrictions, supervision. (ASK) ✕ 🔥 🛏 💻 ⌒

ⒶⒶⒶ ▼▼▼ Days Inn Hotel and Waterslide Ⓗ

(320) 253-4444. **$75-$90.** 70 37th Ave S 56301. Jct SR 15 and 23, just e. Int corridors. **Pets:** Other species. $10 daily fee/pet. Designated rooms, service with restrictions, crate. (SAVE) ✕ 🔥 🛏 💻 ⌒

ⒶⒶⒶ ▼▼▼ GrandStay Residential Suites Hotel Ⓗ

(320) 251-5400. **$60-$170.** 213 6th Ave S 56301. SR 23 at 6th Ave S; center. Int corridors. **Pets:** Other species. $10 daily fee/pet. Service with restrictions, crate. (SAVE) ✕ 🛏 💻 ⌒ ⌧

▼▼▼ Holiday Inn Express & Suites Ⓗ ❀

(320) 240-8000. **$99-$189.** 4322 Clearwater Rd 56301. I-94, exit 171 (CR 75), just ne. Int corridors. **Pets:** Other species. Designated rooms, service with restrictions, crate. (ASK) ✕ 🔥 🛏 💻 ⌒

▼▼▼ Holiday Inn Hotel & Suites Ⓗ

(320) 253-9000. **$91-$225.** 75 S 37th Ave 56301. Jct SR 15 and 23. Int corridors. **Pets:** Supervision. (ASK) ✕ 🛏 💻 🍴 ⌒ ⌧

▼▼▼ Quality Inn Ⓗ

(320) 251-1500. **$70-$85.** 4040 2nd St S 56301. Jct SR 15 and 23 W, just w. Int corridors. **Pets:** Medium. $10 daily fee/pet. Designated rooms, service with restrictions, crate. (ASK) ✕ 🔥 🛏 💻 🍴 ⌒ ⌧

▼▼▼▼ **Radisson Suite Hotel-St Cloud** ⬛
(320) 654-1661. **Call for rates.** 404 W St. Germain St 56301. Just n of
SR 23; center. Int corridors. **Pets:** Accepted.
⊠ 🔲 🔲 🔲 🔲 ⊠

▼ **Thrifty Motel** Ⓜ
(320) 253-6320. **$38-$80.** 130 14th Ave NE 56304. Jct US 10 and SR
23, 0.3 mi e. Int corridors. **Pets:** Other species. $5 daily fee/pet. Service
with restrictions, supervision. ⊠ 🔲

SAUK CENTRE

▼▼▼ **AmericInn Lodge & Suites of Sauk Centre** ⬛ ✷
(320) 352-2800. **$74-$149.** 1230 Timberlane Dr 56378. I-94, exit 127, just
ne. Int corridors. **Pets:** Medium, dogs only. $10 one-time fee/pet. Desig-
nated rooms, service with restrictions, supervision.
🅰️$ ⊠ 🔲 🔲 🔲 ⊠

SILVER BAY

▼▼▼▼ **AmericInn Lodge & Suites of Silver Bay** ⬛
(218) 226-4300. **$90-$170.** 150 Mensing Dr 55614. On SR 61, 0.5 mi ne
of jct SR 61 and Outer Dr. Int corridors. **Pets:** Accepted.
⊠ 🔲 🔲 🔲 🔲 ⊠

▲▲▲ ▼▼◆ **Mariner Motel** Ⓜ ✷
(218) 226-4488. **$55-$75, 3 day notice.** 46 Outer Dr 55614. Just w off
SR 61; at traffic signal. Ext corridors. **Pets:** Dogs only. $5 daily fee/pet.
Service with restrictions, supervision. 🆂🅰🆅🅴 ⊠ 🔲 🔲 🔲 ▨

SLEEPY EYE

▼▼▼ **Inn of Seven Gables** ⬛
(507) 794-5390. **$59-$89.** 1100 E Main St 56085. US 14, 0.8 mi e of jct
CR 4 and US 14. Int corridors. **Pets:** Accepted.
🅰️$ ⊠ 🔲 🔲 🔲

SPICER

▼▼▼ **Northern Inn Hotel & Suites** ⬛
(320) 796-2091. **$60-$110.** 154 Lake Ave S 56288. Just e of jct SR 23
and CR 10. Int corridors. **Pets:** $10 one-time fee/pet. Designated rooms,
service with restrictions, crate. ⊠ 🔲 🔲 🔲 🔲

SPRING VALLEY

▼▼▼ **Spring Valley Inn & Suites** ⬛
(507) 346-7788. **$65-$111.** 745 N Broadway 55975. Just w on US 63. Int
corridors. **Pets:** Accepted. 🅰️$ ⊠ 🔲 🔲 🔲

STEWARTVILLE

▲▲▲ ▼▼◆ **Relax Inn** Ⓜ
(507) 533-4747. **$65-$95.** 1700 2nd Ave NW 55976. I-90, exit 209A, 1 mi
s on US 63. Int corridors. **Pets:** Accepted. 🆂🅰🆅🅴 ⊠ 🔲 🔲 🔲

TOFTE

▲▲▲ ▼▼▼ **AmericInn Lodge & Suites of Tofte** ⬛
(218) 663-7899. **$80-$130.** 7231 W SR 61 55615. On SR 61. Int corridors. **Pets:** Other species. $15 daily fee/room. Designated rooms, super-
vision. 🆂🅰🆅🅴 ⊠ 🔲 🔲 🔲 ⊠

▲▲▲ ▼▼◆ **Bluefin Bay on Lake Superior** 🆑 ✷
(218) 663-7296. **$69-$549, 7 day notice.** 7198 W Hwy 61 55615. On
SR 61. Ext corridors. **Pets:** Large. $20 daily fee/room. Designated rooms,
service with restrictions, crate. 🆂🅰🆅🅴 ⊠ 🔲 🔲 🔲 🔲 ⊠

▼▼▼ **Surfside on Lake Superior** 🆑 ✷
(218) 663-6870. **$165-$549, 7 day notice.** 10 Surfside Dr (Hwy 61)
55615. On SR 61. Ext corridors. **Pets:** Large. $20 daily fee/room. Desig-
nated rooms, service with restrictions, crate. ⊠ 🔲 🔲 🔲 ⊠

TWO HARBORS

▼▼▼ **AmericInn Lodge & Suites of Two Harbors** ⬛
(218) 834-3000. **$85-$175.** 1088 SR 61 N 55616. On SR 61, 0.7 mi s.
Int corridors. **Pets:** Accepted. 🅰️$ ⊠ 🔲 🔲 🔲 🔲 ⊠

▼▼▼▼ **Superior Shores Resort** 🆑 ✷
(218) 834-5671. **$49-$479, 14 day notice.** 1521 Superior Shores Dr
55616. On SR 61, 1.5 mi n of center. Ext/int corridors. **Pets:** $15 daily
fee/room. Designated rooms, service with restrictions, supervision.
🅰️$ ⊠ 🔲 🔲 🔲 🔲 ⊠

VERGAS

▼▼▼ **The Log House & Homestead on Spirit Lake** 🅱🅱
(218) 342-2318. **$165-$235, 8 day notice.** 44854 Fredholm Rd 56587.
5 mi sw on CR 4. Ext/int corridors. **Pets:** Accepted.
⊠ 🔲 🔲 ⊠ 🔲 🔲

VIRGINIA

▲▲▲ ▼▼ **Budget Host–Virginia** Ⓜ ✷
(218) 741-6145. **$50-$99.** 1 Midway Dr 55792. US 53, just e on Cuyuna
Dr. Ext/int corridors. **Pets:** Medium, other species. $10 daily fee/pet.
Supervision. 🆂🅰🆅🅴 ⊠ 🔲 🔲

▼ **Lakeshor Motor Inn** Ⓜ
(218) 741-3360. **$40-$104.** 404 6th Ave N 55792. Just n of Chestnut St;
center. Ext corridors. **Pets:** Accepted. 🅰️$ ⊠ 🔲 🔲

WABASHA

▼▼▼ **AmericInn Lodge & Suites of Wabasha** ⬛
(651) 565-5366. **$71-$180.** 150 Commerce Dr 55981. Just ne of jct US
61 and SR 60. Int corridors. **Pets:** Other species. Designated rooms,
service with restrictions, supervision.
🅰️$ ⊠ 🔲 🔲 🔲 🔲 ⊠

WALKER

▼▼▼ **Country Inn & Suites By Carlson** ⬛ ✷
(218) 547-1400. **$76-$225.** 442 Walker Bay Blvd 56484. 1 mi s on SR
371. Int corridors. **Pets:** $25 one-time fee/room. Service with restrictions.
🅰️$ ⊠ 🔲 🔲 🔲 🔲

WARROAD

▼▼ **Can-Am Motel** ⬛
(218) 386-3807. **Call for rates.** 406 Main Ave NE 56763. 0.5 mi w on
SR 11. Int corridors. **Pets:** Accepted. ⊠ 🔲 🔲

▼▼ **The Patch Motel** ⬛
(218) 386-2723. **Call for rates.** 801 State St N 56763. 0.6 mi w on SR
11. Int corridors. **Pets:** Accepted. ⊠ 🔲 🔲 🔲

WILLMAR

▼▼ **AmericInn Motel of Willmar** ⬛
(320) 231-1962. **$80.** 2404 E US 12 56201. 2 mi e. Int corridors.
Pets: Accepted. 🅰️$ ⊠ 🔲 🔲 🔲

▼▼ **Comfort Inn** ⬛
(320) 231-2601. **$70-$200.** 2200 E US 12 56201. 1.8 mi e. Int corridors.
Pets: Other species. $10 daily fee/room. Crate.
🅰️$ ⊠ 🔲 🔲 🔲

▼▼ **Days Inn-Willmar** ⬛
(320) 231-1275. **$60-$80.** 225 28th St SE 56201. 2.3 mi e on US 12. Int
corridors. **Pets:** Other species. $10 daily fee/room. Crate. ⊠ 🔲 🔲

▼▼▼▼ **Holiday Inn & Willmar Conference Center** ⬛
(320) 235-6060. **$95-$150.** 2100 US 12 E 56201. 1.8 mi e. Int corridors.
Pets: Other species. $10 daily fee/room. Crate.
🅰️$ ⊠ 🔲 🔲 🔲 🔲 ⊠

WINONA

▼▼ **Express Suites Riverport Inn** ⬛
(507) 452-0606. **$69-$149.** 900 Bruski Dr 55987. Jct US 14/61 and SR
43, just ne. Int corridors. **Pets:** Accepted. 🅰️$ ⊠ 🔲 🔲 🔲 🔲

▼▼▼ **Holiday Inn Express & Suites** ⬛
(507) 474-1700. **Call for rates.** 1128 Homer Rd 55987. Jct SR 43, just
sw. Int corridors. **Pets:** Accepted. ⊠ 🔲 🔲 🔲 🔲 ⊠

▼▼▼ The Plaza Hotel & Suites 🅷

(507) 453-0303. **$95-$205.** 1025 Hwy 61 E 55987. Jct SR 43, just sw. Int corridors. **Pets:** Other species. $25 daily fee/room. Designated rooms, service with restrictions, supervision.

A$K ⊠ &M 🖥 🖵 ▥ ⩘ ⊠

◈◈◈ ▼▼ Quality Inn 🅷

(507) 454-4390. **$69-$99.** 956 Mankato Ave 55987. Jct US 14/61 and SR 43, just ne. Ext/int corridors. **Pets:** Accepted.

SAVE ⊠ 🖥 🖵 ▥ ⩘ ⊠

WORTHINGTON

◈◈◈ ▼▼ AmericInn Lodge and Suites of Worthington 🅷

(507) 376-4500. **$75-$160.** 1475 Darling Dr 56187. I-90, exit 43 (US 59), just se. Int corridors. **Pets:** Other species. $10 one-time fee/room. Supervision. SAVE ⊠ 🖥 🖵 ⩘ ⊠

MISSISSIPPI

ABERDEEN

⬥⬥ ▼▼ Best Western Aberdeen Inn Ⓜ

(662) 369-4343. **$80-$100, 7 day notice.** 801 E Commerce St 39730. On US 45, just n of jct SR 25 and Tenn-Tom Bridge. Ext corridors. **Pets:** Small, other species. $50 deposit/room, $20 daily fee/pet. Designated rooms, service with restrictions, crate.

[SAVE] [✕] [🛏] [💻] [🍴] [🏊]

AMORY

⬥⬥ ▼▼ Best Western Amory Ⓜ

(662) 256-2120. **$71.** 915 Hwy 278 E 38821. Jct SR 25 (Main St), 0.6 mi e. Ext corridors. **Pets:** Small, dogs only. $5 daily fee/pet. Service with restrictions, supervision. [SAVE] [✕] [🛏] [💻] [🏊]

BATESVILLE

▼▼ Comfort Inn Ⓗ 🐾

(662) 563-1188. **Call for rates.** 290 Power Dr 38606. I-55, exit 243B, just sw on frontage road. Ext corridors. **Pets:** Medium. $15 daily fee/room. Service with restrictions, supervision. [✕] [🛏] [💻] [🏊]

BILOXI

⬥⬥ ▼▼ Edgewater Inn Ⓗ

(228) 388-1100. **Call for rates.** 1936 Beach Blvd 39531. I-110, exit 1B, 3.4 mi w on US 90. Ext corridors. **Pets:** Medium, other species. $50 one-time fee/room. Designated rooms. [SAVE] [✕] [🛏] [💻] [🏊]

⬥⬥ ▼▼ ▼▼ Hard Rock Hotel & Casino Biloxi Ⓗ

(228) 374-7625. **$89-$479.** 777 Beach Blvd 39530. I-110, exit 1A (US 90), just e. Int corridors. **Pets:** Small, other species. $75 one-time fee/room. Service with restrictions, supervision.

[SAVE] [✕] [🔬] [💻] [🍴] [🏊] [✕]

BOONEVILLE

⬥⬥ ▼▼ ▼▼ Best Western College Inn Ⓜ

(662) 728-2244. **$60-$75.** 805 N 2nd St 38829. Jct US 45 and SR 4/30, 1.7 mi e to SR 145, then 1.1 mi s. Ext corridors. **Pets:** $10 daily fee/pet. Service with restrictions, supervision. [SAVE] [✕] [🛏] [💻] [🏊]

▼▼ Super 8 Ⓗ

(662) 720-1688. **$55-$65.** 110 Hospitality Ave 38829. Jct US 45 and SR 4/30, 1.7 mi e to SR 145, then 0.5 mi s. Int corridors. **Pets:** Accepted.

[ASK] [✕] [🛏] [💻] [🏊]

CANTON

⬥⬥ ▼▼ ▼▼ Americas Best Value Inn Ⓗ

(601) 859-2643. **$50-$60.** 119 Soldier Colony Rd 39046. I-55, exit 119, just se. Ext corridors. **Pets:** Small, dogs only. $10 daily fee. Service with restrictions, crate. [SAVE] [✕] [🛏] [💻]

⬥⬥ ▼▼ ▼▼ Best Western-Canton Inn Ⓗ

(601) 859-8600. **$55-$79.** 137 Soldier Colony Rd 39046. I-55, exit 119, just se. Int corridors. **Pets:** Accepted. [SAVE] [✕] [🛏] [💻] [🏊]

⬥⬥ ▼▼ ▼▼ Comfort Inn Ⓗ

(601) 859-7575. **$65-$100, 3 day notice.** 145 Soldier Colony Rd 39046. I-55, exit 119, just se. Int corridors. **Pets:** Large, other species. $25 one-time fee/pet. Service with restrictions, crate. [SAVE] [✕] [🛏] [💻] [🏊]

CLEVELAND

▼▼ Comfort Inn of Cleveland Ⓗ

(662) 846-1525. **Call for rates.** 807 N Davis Ave 38732. 1 mi n of jct US 61 and SR 8. Int corridors. **Pets:** Accepted. [✕] [🛏] [💻] [🏊]

CLINTON

⬥⬥ ▼▼ ▼▼ Best Western Ridgeland Inn Ⓗ

(601) 926-4323. **$75-$85.** 102 Clinton Loop Dr 39056. I-20, exit 36, just s, then just w on Clinton Center Dr. Int corridors. **Pets:** Accepted.

[SAVE] [✕] [🛏] [💻] [🏊]

CORINTH

▼▼ Comfort Inn Ⓗ

(662) 287-4421. **Call for rates.** 2101 Hwy 72 W 38834. Jct US 72 and 45, just e. Ext corridors. **Pets:** Accepted. [✕] [🛏] [💻] [🏊]

FOREST

▼▼ Americas Best Value Inn Ⓗ

(601) 469-2640. **Call for rates.** 1846 Hwy 35 S 39074. I-20, exit 88, just n. Ext corridors. **Pets:** Accepted. [✕] [🛏] [💻] [🏊]

⬥⬥ ▼▼ ▼▼ Econo Lodge Inn & Suites Ⓗ

(601) 469-2100. **Call for rates.** 1250 Hwy 35 S 39074. I-20, exit 88, just n. Ext corridors. **Pets:** Accepted. [SAVE] [✕] [🛏] [💻] [🏊]

GREENVILLE

▼▼ Days Inn Ⓗ

(662) 334-1818. **Call for rates.** 2701 Hwy 82 E 38703. 3 mi e on US 82. Ext corridors. **Pets:** Accepted. [✕] [🛏] [💻] [🏊]

▼▼ Econo Lodge of Greenville Ⓗ

(662) 378-4976. **$60-$90.** 3080 US 82 E 38702. 3 mi e of center. Ext corridors. **Pets:** Accepted. [✕] [🛏] [💻] [🏊]

GREENWOOD

▼▼ Econo Lodge Inn & Suites Ⓗ

(662) 453-5974. **$49-$79.** 401 Hwy 82 W 38930. 0.4 mi w of Main St. Ext corridors. **Pets:** Accepted. [✕] [🛏] [💻] [🏊]

GRENADA

▼▼▼▼ Country Inn & Suites By Carlson Ⓗ

(662) 227-8444. **$78-$130.** 255 SW Frontage Rd 38901. I-55, exit 206, just sw. Int corridors. **Pets:** Medium. $25 one-time fee/room. Service with restrictions, supervision. [ASK] [✕] [🛏] [💻] [🏊]

GULFPORT

▼▼ Americas Best Value Inn Ⓗ

(228) 868-8500. **Call for rates.** 9375 Hwy 49 39503. I-10, exit 34A, just sw. Ext corridors. **Pets:** Other species. $10 daily fee/pet. Designated rooms, service with restrictions, crate. [✕] [🛏] [💻] [🏊]

⬥⬥ ▼▼ ▼▼ Best Western Seaway Inn Ⓗ 🐾

(228) 864-0050. **$59-$139.** 9475 Hwy 49 39503. I-10, exit 34A, just sw. Ext corridors. **Pets:** Medium. $15 daily fee/pet. Designated rooms, service with restrictions, supervision. [SAVE] [✕] [🛏] [💻] [🏊]

▼▼ Motel 6 #416 **M**
(228) 863-1890. **$53-$65.** 9355 US Hwy 49 39503. I-10, exit 34A, just s. Ext corridors. **Pets:** Other species. Service with restrictions, supervision.
⊠ ☂

▼▼ Quality Inn Gulfport **H**
(228) 864-7222. **$69-$119.** 9435 Hwy 49 39503. I-10, exit 34A, 0.6 mi s. Ext corridors. **Pets:** Accepted. ⊠ ▮ ▯

▼▼ Ramada Inn Hotel & Convention Center **H**
(228) 868-8200. **Call for rates.** 9415 Hwy 49 39503. I-10, exit 34A, 0.6 mi s. Ext corridors. **Pets:** Accepted. ⊠ ▮ ▯ ⑪ ☂

▼▼▼ Residence Inn by Marriott Gulfport-Biloxi Airport **H**
(228) 867-1722. **$125-$153.** 14100 Airport Rd 39503. I-10, exit 34A, 0.8 mi s on US 49, then 1.2 mi e. Int corridors. **Pets:** Accepted.
⊠ ♿ ▮ ▯ ☂ ⊠

HATTIESBURG

▼▼▼ Candlewood Suites **H**
(601) 264-9666. **$120.** 9 Gateway Dr 39402. I-59, exit 67B, just nw to Classic Dr, then just sw. Int corridors. **Pets:** Accepted.
A$K ⊠ ♿ ▮ ▯

▼▼ Comfort Inn University **H**
(601) 264-1881. **$90-$120.** 6541 US Hwy 49 39401. I-59, exit 67A, just s. Ext/int corridors. **Pets:** Medium. $25 one-time fee/pet. Designated rooms, service with restrictions, crate. ⊠ ▮ ▯ ☂

▲▲▲ ▼▼ La Quinta Inn **H** ❀
(601) 268-2850. **$62-$107.** 6563 US Hwy 49 39401. I-59, exit 67A, just se. Int corridors. **Pets:** Medium, other species. Service with restrictions, supervision. SAVE ⊠ ▮ ▯ ☂

▲▲▲ ▼▼▼ Ramada Inn on the Hill **H**
(601) 599-2001. **$79-$120.** 6595 Hwy 49 N 39401. I-59, exit 67A, just se. Ext corridors. **Pets:** Accepted. SAVE ⊠ ▮ ▯ ⑪ ☂

HOLLY SPRINGS

▼▼▼▼ Le' Brooks Inn **H**
(662) 252-5444. **$79.** 100 Brooks Rd 38635. US 78, exit 30, just sw. Int corridors. **Pets:** $10 daily fee/pet. Designated rooms, service with restrictions, supervision. A$K ⊠ ▮ ▯ ☂

HORN LAKE

▼▼▼ Drury Inn & Suites-Memphis South **H**
(662) 349-6622. **$95-$174.** 735 Goodman Rd W 38637. I-55, exit 289, just sw. Int corridors. **Pets:** Other species. No service, supervision.
A$K ⊠ ♿ ▮ ▯ ☂

JACKSON

▲▲▲ ▼▼▼ Best Western Executive Inn **H**
(601) 969-6555. **Call for rates.** 725 Larson St 39202. I-55, exit 96B (High St), e to Greymont Ave, then just n. Int corridors. **Pets:** Accepted.
SAVE ⊠ ▮ ▯ ☂

▼▼ Extended StayAmerica Jackson-North **H**
(601) 956-4312. **$60-$95.** 5354 I-55 N 39211. I-55, exit 100, 1 mi n. Ext corridors. **Pets:** Other species. $25 daily fee/room. Designated rooms, service with restrictions, crate. A$K ⊠ ▮ ▯

▲▲▲ ▼▼▼▼ Hilton Jackson **H**
(601) 957-2800. **$99-$189.** 1001 E County Line Rd 39211. I-55, exit 103 (County Line Rd), just e. Int corridors. **Pets:** Accepted.
SAVE ⊠ ▮ ▯ ⑪ ☂

▼▼ Jameson Inn **H**
(601) 206-8923. **$88-$95.** 585 E Beasley Rd 39206. I-55, exit 102, just w. Int corridors. **Pets:** Accepted. A$K ⊠ ♿ ▮ ▯ ☂

▼▼ La Quinta Inn Jackson (North) **H** ❀
(601) 957-1741. **$42-$109.** 616 Briarwood Dr 39211. I-55, exit 102A northbound, just ne on Frontage Rd. Ext corridors. **Pets:** Medium, other species. Service with restrictions, supervision.
A$K ⊠ ♿ ▮ ▯ ☂

▼▼ Red Roof Inn Fairgrounds #131 **M**
(601) 969-5006. **$40-$65, 7 day notice.** 700 Larson St 39202. I-55, exit 96B (High St), e to Greymont Ave, then just ne. Ext corridors. **Pets:** Large. Service with restrictions, crate. A$K ⊠ ▮

▼▼▼ Regency Hotel & Conference Center **H**
(601) 969-2141. **Call for rates.** 400 Greymont Ave 39202. I-55, exit 96B, just w, then just s. Ext/int corridors. **Pets:** Accepted.
⊠ ♿ ▮ ▯ ⑪ ☂

▼▼▼ Residence Inn by Marriott **H**
(601) 355-3599. **$148-$180.** 881 E River Pl 39202. I-55, exit 96C, just e. Ext corridors. **Pets:** Accepted. ⊠ ▮ ▯ ☂ ⊠

KOSCIUSKO

▲▲▲ ▼▼▼ Americas Best Value Inn **M**
(662) 289-6252. **$55-$65.** 1052 Veterans Memorial Dr/Hwy 35 Bypass 39090. Just sw of jct SR 35 and Natchez Trace Pkwy. Ext corridors. **Pets:** Other species. $5 daily fee/pet. Service with restrictions, supervision. SAVE ⊠ ▮ ▯ ☂

LOUISVILLE

▼▼ Quality Inn **M**
(662) 773-9090. **Call for rates.** 201 Hwy 15 N 39339. Jct SR 14, just n on SR 15/25. Ext corridors. **Pets:** Accepted. ⊠ ♿ ▮ ▯ ☂

MACON

▲▲▲ ▼▼▼ Best Western Oak Tree Inn **M**
(662) 726-4334. **$65-$75.** 12710 Hwy 45 39341. Jct SR 14, just s. Ext corridors. **Pets:** Accepted. SAVE ⊠ ♿ ▮ ▯ ☂

MCCOMB

▲▲▲ ▼▼▼ Hawthorn Inn & Suites **H**
(601) 684-8655. **$90.** 2001 Veteran's Blvd 39648. I-55, exit 18, just off interstate. Int corridors. **Pets:** Medium, other species. $50 one-time fee/room. Service with restrictions, crate. SAVE ⊠ ♿ ▮ ▯ ☂

MERIDIAN

▲▲▲ ▼▼▼ Best Western of Meridian **H**
(601) 693-3210. **$71-$74.** 2219 S Frontage Rd 39301. I-20/59, exit 153, just sw. Ext/int corridors. **Pets:** Small. $10 daily fee/pet. Service with restrictions, crate. SAVE ⊠ ▮ ▯ ☂

▼▼▼▼ Drury Inn & Suites **H**
(601) 483-5570. **$95-$189.** 112 Hwy 11 & 80 N 39301. I-20/59, exit 154, jct US 11/80 N. Int corridors. **Pets:** Other species. No service, supervision. A$K ⊠ ♿ ▮ ▯ ☂

▼▼ Econo Lodge **M**
(601) 693-9393. **Call for rates.** 2405 S Frontage Rd 39301. I-20/59, exit 153, 0.5 mi sw. Ext corridors. **Pets:** Accepted. ⊠ ▮ ▯

▼▼▼ Holiday Inn Meridian **H**
(601) 485-5101. **Call for rates.** 111 US 11 & 80 39302. I-20/59, exit 154 westbound, just n to frontage road, then just e; exit 154B eastbound. Ext corridors. **Pets:** Accepted. ⊠ ♿ ▮ ▯ ⑪ ☂

▼▼ Jameson Inn **H**
(601) 483-3315. **$83-$90.** 524 Bonita Lakes Dr 39301. I-20/59, exit 154 southbound; exit 154A northbound, just s. Ext corridors. **Pets:** Accepted.
A$K ⊠ ♿ ▮ ▯ ☂

▼▼ Motel 6 #0424 **M**
(601) 482-1182. **$39-$51.** 2309 S Frontage Rd 39301. I-20/59, exit 153, 0.5 mi sw. Ext corridors. **Pets:** Other species. Service with restrictions, supervision. ⊠ ☂

MOSS POINT

AAA ▼▼▼ **Quality Inn** H

(228) 475-2477. **$60-$90.** 6800 Hwy 63 N 39563. I-10, exit 69, just s. Ext corridors. **Pets:** Small, other species. $10 daily fee/pet. Service with restrictions, crate. SAVE ⊠ 🖪 🖵 ⇴

NATCHEZ

AAA ▼▼▼ **Days Inn of Natchez** H

(601) 445-8291. **$74-$125.** 109 US Hwy 61 S 39120. Just se of jct US 61, 84 and 98. Ext corridors. **Pets:** Small, other species. $10 daily fee/pet. Service with restrictions, supervision. SAVE ⊠ 🖪 🖵 ⇴

AAA ▼▼▼ **Red Carpet Inn** M

(601) 442-3686. **$65-$90.** 271 D'Evereaux Dr 39120. Just n of jct US 61/84. Ext corridors. **Pets:** Small. $10 daily fee/pet. Service with restrictions, supervision. SAVE ⊠ 🖪 🖵

NEWTON

▼▼▼ **Days Inn** M

(601) 683-3361. **Call for rates.** 261 Eastside Dr 39345. I-20, exit 109, just s on SR 15. Ext corridors. **Pets:** Accepted. ⊠ 🖪 🖵 ⇴

OCEAN SPRINGS

▼▼▼ **Quality Inn Ocean Springs** H ❖

(228) 875-7555. **Call for rates.** 7304 Washington Ave 39564. I-10, exit 50, 0.4 mi s on SR 609. Ext corridors. **Pets:** Medium, other species. $20 daily fee/room. Service with restrictions, supervision.

⊠ 🖾 🖪 🖵 ⇴

▼▼▼ **Ramada Limited** H

(228) 872-2323. **$64-$159, 7 day notice.** 8011 Tucker Rd 39532. I-10, exit 50, just n. Ext corridors. **Pets:** Medium, other species. $15 daily fee/pet. Designated rooms, no service, supervision.

ASK ⊠ 🖪 🖵 ⇴

OLIVE BRANCH

▼▼▼ **Candlewood Suites** H

(662) 890-7491. **$79-$82.** 7448 Craft Goodman Rd 38654. US 78, exit 1 westbound, 0.5 mi se; exit 2 eastbound, 1.4 mi ne. Int corridors. **Pets:** Medium. $10 one-time fee/pet. Designated rooms, service with restrictions, supervision. ASK ⊠ 🖾 🖪 ☕

▼▼ **Comfort Inn** H ❖

(662) 895-0456. **$60-$85.** 7049 Enterprise Dr 38654. US 78, exit 2 (SR 302) just w. Int corridors. **Pets:** Medium, other species. $12 daily fee/pet. Designated rooms, service with restrictions. ⊠ 🖪 🖵 ⇴

PASCAGOULA

▼▼ **LaFont Inn** H ❖

(228) 762-7111. **Call for rates.** 2703 Denny Ave 39567. I-10, exit 69, 3.5 mi s on SR 63, then 2 mi w on US 90. Ext corridors. **Pets:** Medium. $30 one-time fee/pet. Service with restrictions.

⊠ 🖪 🖵 🍴 ⇴ 🖾

PEARL

▼▼▼ **Jameson Inn of Pearl** H

(601) 932-6030. **$98-$105.** 434 Riverwind Dr 39208. I-20, exit 48, just nw. Int corridors. **Pets:** Accepted. ASK ⊠ 🖾 🖪 🖵 ⇴

▼▼▼ **La Quinta Inn & Suites Jackson Airport (Pearl)** H ❖

(601) 664-0065. **$67-$94.** 501 S Pearson Rd 39208. I-20, exit 48, just s. Int corridors. **Pets:** Medium, other species. Service with restrictions, supervision. ASK ⊠ 🖪 🖵 ⇴

PHILADELPHIA

▼▼ **Deluxe Inn & Suites** H

(601) 656-0052. **$60-$150.** 1004 Central Dr 39350. Jct SR 15 and 16. Ext corridors. **Pets:** Accepted. ASK ⊠ 🖾 🖪 🖵 ⇴

▼▼▼ **Golden Moon Hotel & Casino** H

(601) 650-1234. **Call for rates.** 13541 Hwy 16 W 39350. From jct SR 15, 2 mi w. Int corridors. **Pets:** Accepted.

⊠ 🖾 🖪 🖵 🍴 ⇴ 🖾

▼▼▼ **Silver Star Hotel & Casino** H

(601) 650-1234. **Call for rates.** 13540 Hwy 16 W 39350. Jct SR 15, 2 mi w. Int corridors. **Pets:** Accepted. ⊠ 🖾 🖪 🖵 🍴 ⇴ 🖾

PICAYUNE

▼▼ **Days Inn** H

(601) 799-1339. **Call for rates.** 450 S Lofton Ave 39466. I-59, exit 4, just nw. Ext corridors. **Pets:** Accepted. ⊠ 🖪 🖵 ⇴

RICHLAND

▼▼▼ **Executive Inn & Suites** H

(601) 664-3456. **$49-$59.** 390 Hwy 49 S 39218. I-20, exit 47, just s. Ext corridors. **Pets:** Small, dogs only. $20 deposit/room. Service with restrictions, supervision. ASK ⊠ 🖪 🖵 ⇴

RIDGELAND

▼▼▼ **Drury Inn & Suites-Jackson, MS** H

(601) 956-6100. **$90-$174.** 610 E County Line Rd 39157. I-55, exit 103 (County Line Rd), just w. Int corridors. **Pets:** Other species. No service, supervision. ASK ⊠ 🖾 🖪 🖵 ⇴

▼▼▼ **Homewood Suites by Hilton** H

(601) 899-8611. **$139-$149.** 853 Centre St 39157. I-55, exit 103 (County Line Rd), just e to Ridgewood Rd, 0.4 mi ne, then just e. Int corridors. **Pets:** Medium, dogs only. Service with restrictions, crate.

⊠ 🖾 🖪 🖵 ⇴

▼▼ **Quality Inn North** H

(601) 956-6203. **$60.** 839 Ridgewood Rd 39157. I-55, exit 103 (County Line Rd), just ne. Ext corridors. **Pets:** Accepted. ⊠ 🖪 🖵 ⇴

▼▼▼ **Residence Inn by Marriott** H ❖

(601) 206-7755. **$134-$164.** 855 Centre St 39157. I-55, exit 103 (County Line Rd), just e to Ridgewood Rd, then just e. Int corridors. **Pets:** Medium, other species. $75 one-time fee/room. Supervision.

⊠ 🖾 🖪 🖵 ⇴ 🖾

RIPLEY

AAA ▼▼▼ **Best Western Ripley** M

(662) 837-0002. **$68-$72.** 922 City Ave S 38663. Jct US 4 and 15, 0.5 mi s. Ext corridors. **Pets:** Small, dogs only. $5 daily fee/room. Designated rooms, service with restrictions, supervision. SAVE ⊠ 🖪 🖵 ⇴

SOUTHAVEN

▼▼ **Magnolia Inn & Suites** H

(662) 280-5555. **$50-$110.** 5069 Pepper Chase Dr 38671. I-55, exit 287, just w. Int corridors. **Pets:** Very small, other species. $12 daily fee/pet. Designated rooms, service with restrictions, crate. ASK ⊠ 🖪

▼▼▼ **Residence Inn Memphis Southaven** H ❖

(662) 996-1500. **$125-$153.** 7165 Sleepy Hollow Dr 38671. I-55, exit 289, just ne. Int corridors. **Pets:** Other species. $100 one-time fee/room. Service with restrictions, supervision. ⊠ 🖾 🖪 🖵 ⇴

STARKVILLE

▼▼▼ **Comfort Suites Starkville** H

(662) 324-9595. **Call for rates.** 801 Russell St 39759. 0.5 mi w of jct US 82 and SR 12. Int corridors. **Pets:** Accepted. ⊠ 🖪 🖵 ⇴

AAA ▼▼▼ **Days Inn & Suites** H

(662) 324-5555. **$99-$175.** 119 Hwy 12 W 39759. SR 12, 1.5 mi w of jct US 82. Ext corridors. **Pets:** Medium. $10 daily fee/pet. Service with restrictions, crate. SAVE ⊠ 🖪 🖵 ⇴

TUNICA

◆◆ Americas Best Value Inn H
(662) 363-0030. **$45-$230.** 4250 Casino Center Dr 38664. Just n of jct US 61; near casinos. Ext/int corridors. **Pets:** Small, other species. $10 daily fee/pet. Designated rooms, service with restrictions, crate.

A$K ⊠ ⊟ ⊑ ➔

◆ Key West Inn Tunica M
(662) 363-0021. **$50-$150.** 11635 Hwy 61 N 38664. US 61, 0.3 mi n of SR 304. Ext corridors. **Pets:** Accepted. A$K ⊠ ⊟ ⊑

TUPELO

◆◆ America's Best Inn M
(662) 842-4403. **Call for rates.** 897 Harmony Ln 38804. US 45, exit Barnes Crossing, 0.5 mi sw, then just e. Ext corridors. **Pets:** Accepted.

⊠ &M ⊟ ⊑ ➔

◆◆ Baymont Inn & Suites H
(662) 844-7660. **Call for rates.** 625 Spicer Dr 38804. On SR 145, 0.4 mi n of McCullough Blvd. Int corridors. **Pets:** Accepted.

⊠ &M ⊟ ⊑ ➔ ⊠

◆◆ Comfort Inn H
(662) 842-5100. **$68-$72.** 1190 N Gloster St 38804. Jct McCullough Blvd and SR 145, 1.3 mi s to McCullough Blvd, w to N Gloster St, then 0.3 mi n. Ext corridors. **Pets:** Small. $25 one-time fee/pet. Service with restrictions, crate. ⊠ ⊟ ⊑

▲▲▲ ◆◆ Days Inn M
(662) 842-0088. **$53-$95.** 1015 N Gloster St 38804. Jct McCullough Blvd and SR 145, 1.3 mi s to McCullough Blvd, w to N Gloster St, then just n. Ext corridors. **Pets:** Accepted. SAVE ⊠ &M ⊟ ⊑

▲▲▲ ◆◆ Super 8 M
(662) 842-0448. **$58-$124.** 3898 McCullough Blvd 38801. US 78, exit 81, just sw. Ext corridors. **Pets:** Medium, dogs only. $10 one-time fee/pet. Service with restrictions, crate. SAVE ⊠ ⊟ ⊑ ➔

VICKSBURG

◆◆◆ Annabelle Bed & Breakfast BB
(601) 638-2000. **Call for rates.** 501 Speed St 39180. I-20, exit 1A, 2.3 mi n on Washington St, then just w. Ext/int corridors. **Pets:** Accepted.

⊠ ⊟ ⊑ ➔

▲▲▲ ◆◆◆ Cedar Grove Mansion CI
(601) 636-1000. **$100-$215, 3 day notice.** 2200 Oak St 39180. I-20, exit 1A, 2.3 mi n on Klein St; to gated entrance. Ext/int corridors. **Pets:** Accepted.

SAVE ⊠ ⊟ ⊑ ⊓ ➔

◆◆◆ Corners Mansion Bed & Breakfast Inn BB
(601) 636-7421. **$125-$210, 3 day notice.** 601 Klein St 39180. I-20, exit 1A, 2.3 mi n on Washington St, then just w. Ext/int corridors.
Pets: Accepted. A$K ⊠ ⊟ ⊑

◆ Jameson Inn H
(601) 619-7799. **$93-$100.** 3975 S Frontage Rd 39180. I-20, exit 4A, on southeast frontage road. Ext corridors. **Pets:** Accepted.

A$K ⊠ &M ⊟ ⊑ ➔

◆ Motel 6 #4189 H
(601) 638-5077. **Call for rates.** 4127 N Frontage Rd 39183. I-20, exit 4B (Clay St), just ne. Int corridors. **Pets:** Other species. Service with restrictions, supervision. ⊠ ➔

◆◆ Quality Inn & Suites M
(601) 636-0804. **$60-$100.** 3332 Clay St 39183. I-20, exit 4B (Clay St), just n. Ext corridors. **Pets:** Other species. $15 one-time fee/room.

⊠ ⊟ ⊑ ➔

◆◆ Travel Inn H
(601) 630-0100. **$45-$100.** 1675 N Frontage Rd 39180. I-20, exit 1C, on northeast frontage road. Ext corridors. **Pets:** Small, dogs only. $10 daily fee/pet. No service, supervision. A$K ⊠ ⊟ ➔

MISSOURI

AVA

◆◆◆ Ava Super 8 H

(417) 683-1343. **$70-$90.** 1711 S Jefferson St 65608. Jct SR 5 S and 76; 1.5 mi s of SR 14. Int corridors. **Pets:** Accepted.

(ASK) (X) (&M) (🖥) (💷)

BETHANY

◆◆◆ ◆◆◆ Comfort Inn Bethany H

(660) 425-8006. **Call for rates.** 496 S 39th St 64424. I-35, exit 92, just nw. Int corridors. **Pets:** Medium. $10 daily fee/pet. Designated rooms, service with restrictions, supervision. (SAVE) (X) (🖥) (💷) (🐾)

◆◆◆ ◆◆◆ Family Budget Inn M

(660) 425-7915. **$45-$54.** 4014 Miller St 64424. I-35, exit 92. Int corridors. **Pets:** Other species. $20 deposit/room, $5 daily fee/pet. Designated rooms, service with restrictions, supervision. (SAVE) (X) (🖥) (🐾)

BOONVILLE

◆◆◆ ◆◆◆ Boonville Comfort Inn H

(660) 882-5317. **$60-$150.** 2427 Mid America Industrial Dr 65233. I-70, exit 101, just sw. Int corridors. **Pets:** Small. $10 daily fee/pet. Designated rooms, service with restrictions, supervision. (SAVE) (X) (🖥) (💷) (🐾)

BRANSON METROPOLITAN AREA

BRANSON

◆◆◆ ◆◆◆◆ Best Western Landing View Inn & Suites H

(417) 334-6464. **$79-$149.** 403 W Main (Hwy 76) 65616. 0.3 mi e from SR 76 (Country Music Blvd) and US 65. Ext corridors. **Pets:** Small, dogs only. $10 daily fee/pet. Designated rooms, service with restrictions, crate. (SAVE) (X) (🖥) (💷) (🐾)

◆◆◆ ◆◆◆◆ Chateau on the Lake Resort & Spa H

(417) 334-1161. **$109-$359, 3 day notice.** 415 N State Hwy 265 65616. Just n of jct SR 165 and 265. Int corridors. **Pets:** Small, dogs only. $25 one-time fee/room. Designated rooms, service with restrictions, crate. (SAVE) (X) (&M) (🖥) (💷) (🍴) (🐾) (X)

◆◆◆ ◆◆◆ Dockers Inn M ❖

(417) 334-3600. **$50-$82.** 3060 Green Mountain Dr 65616. SR 376, 0.7 mi e on SR 76 (Country Music Blvd), just s. Ext corridors. **Pets:** Small, other species. $10 daily fee/pet. Service with restrictions, crate. (SAVE) (X) (💷) (🐾)

◆◆◆ ◆◆◆ Eagle's Lodge H

(417) 336-2666. **$45-$85.** 3221 Shepherd of the Hills Expy 65616. 0.3 mi e of jct SR 76 (Country Music Blvd). Ext corridors. **Pets:** Accepted. (SAVE) (X) (🖥) (💷) (🐾)

◆◆◆ ◆◆◆ Fall Creek Inn & Suites H ❖

(417) 348-1683. **$42-$69.** 995 Hwy 165 65616. Jct SR 76 (Country Music Blvd), 1.5 mi s on SR 165. Ext corridors. **Pets:** Medium, other species. $50 deposit/pet, $10 daily fee/pet. Designated rooms, service with restrictions. (SAVE) (X) (🖥) (💷) (🐾)

◆◆◆ Foxborough Inn & Suites M

(417) 335-4369. **$60-$90.** 235 Expressway Ln 65616. US 65, exit Shepherd of the Hills Expwy, 2.3 mi w, just sw. Ext corridors. **Pets:** Small. $25 one-time fee/room. Service with restrictions, crate. (ASK) (X) (&M) (🖥) (💷) (🐾)

◆◆◆ Golden Arrow Resort M

(417) 338-2245. **$44-$158, 21 day notice.** 2869 Indian Point Rd 65616. Jct SR 76 (Country Music Blvd) and 265, 0.6 mi w, then 2.8 mi s. Ext corridors. **Pets:** Small. $10 daily fee/pet. Designated rooms, no service, crate. (🖥) (💷) (🐾) (X)

◆◆◆ Grand Crowne Resorts CO

(417) 332-8330. **$99-$579, 5 day notice.** 300 Golf View Dr 65616. Jct US 65, 3 mi w on SR 76 (Country Music Blvd), then 1 mi s. Ext corridors. **Pets:** Accepted. (ASK) (X) (&M) (🖥) (💷) (🐾) (X)

◆◆◆ Hampton Inn Branson Hills Pkwy H

(417) 243-7800. **$79-$169.** 200 Payne Stewart Dr 65616. US 65, exit Branson Hills Pkwy, just w, then just n. Int corridors. **Pets:** Medium. $75 one-time fee/room. Service with restrictions, supervision. (X) (&M) (💷) (🐾)

◆◆◆ ◆◆◆◆ Hilton Branson Convention Center H ❖

(417) 336-5400. **$159-$259.** 200 E Main St 65616. Main St; at Branson Landing Shopping Complex. Int corridors. **Pets:** Medium. $75 one-time fee/room. Service with restrictions, supervision. (SAVE) (X) (&M) (🖥) (💷) (🍴) (🐾)

◆◆◆ Hilton Promenade at Branson Landing H ❖

(417) 336-5500. **$129-$324.** 3 Branson Landing 65616. In Branson Landing shopping district. Int corridors. **Pets:** Medium. $75 one-time fee/room. Service with restrictions, supervision. (X) (🖥) (💷) (🍴) (🐾)

◆◆◆ Howard Johnson H

(417) 336-5151. **$72-$92.** 3027-A W Hwy 76 65616. On SR 76 (Country Music Blvd), 3.5 mi w of jct US 65. Ext corridors. **Pets:** Accepted. (ASK) (X) (🖥) (💷) (🐾)

▼▼▼▼ La Quinta Inn Branson (Music City Centre) **H** ❀
(417) 332-1575. **$49-$105.** 1835 W Hwy 76 65616. 1.6 mi w of jct US 65. Ext/int corridors. **Pets:** Medium, other species. Service with restrictions, supervision. [A$K] [✕] [🛏] [💻] [⇌] [✕]

▼ Lazy Valley Resort **M**
(417) 334-2397. **$64-$220, 60 day notice.** 285 River Ln 65616. 1 mi w of US 65 on SR 76 (Country Music Blvd), 2.5 mi s on Fall Creek Rd to River Valley Rd. Ext corridors. **Pets:** Small, dogs only. $10 daily fee/pet. No service, supervision. [✕] [&M] [🛏] [💻] [⇌] [✕] [🐾]

▲▲▷ ▼▼▼ Lilleys' Landing Resort **M** ❀
(417) 334-6380. **$65-$250, 56 day notice.** 367 River Ln 65616. Jct US 65, 1 mi w on SR 76, 2.5 mi s on Fall Creek Rd, follow signs. Ext corridors. **Pets:** Medium, dogs only. $10 daily fee/pet. No service, supervision. [SAVE] [✕] [🛏] [💻] [⇌] [✕]

▼▼ Quality Inn & Suites on the Strip **H**
(417) 334-1194. **Call for rates.** 2834 W Hwy 76 65616. Jct US 65, 2 mi w. Ext corridors. **Pets:** Other species. $10 daily fee/room. Service with restrictions, crate. [✕] [🛏] [💻] [⇌]

▲▲▷ ▼▼▼▼ Radisson Hotel Branson **H**
(417) 335-5767. **$105-$239, 3 day notice.** 120 S Wildwood Dr 65616. Jct US 65, 2 mi w on SR 76 (Country Music Blvd), then just s. Int corridors. **Pets:** Medium. $30 one-time fee/pet. Service with restrictions, crate. [SAVE] [✕] [&M] [🛏] [💻] [¶¶] [⇌] [✕]

▼▼ Ramada Resort & Conference Center **H**
(417) 334-1000. **$59-$109.** 1700 Hwy 76 W 65616. Jct SR 76 (Country Music Blvd) and US 65, 1.5 mi w. Ext corridors. **Pets:** Accepted. [A$K] [✕] [🛏] [💻] [¶¶] [⇌] [✕]

▼▼▼▼ Residence Inn by Marriott **H**
(417) 336-4077. **$89-$139.** 280 Wildwood Dr S 65616. 2 mi w on SR 76 (Country Music Blvd), just s. Int corridors. **Pets:** Other species. $100 one-time fee/room. Service with restrictions, crate. [✕] [&M] [🛏] [💻] [⇌] [✕]

▼ Rock View Resort **M**
(417) 334-4678. **$60-$98, 21 day notice.** 1049 Park View Dr 65672. Jct US 65, 4.4 mi w on SR 165, 0.3 mi s via Dale Dr, then 0.7 mi w. Ext corridors. **Pets:** Medium, dogs only. $8 daily fee/pet. No service, crate. [✕] [🛏] [💻] [⇌] [✕] [🐾]

▲▲▷ ▼▼▼ Scenic Hills Inn **H** ❀
(417) 336-8855. **$40-$120.** 2422 Shepherd of the Hills Expwy 65616. Jct SR 76 (Country Music Blvd), 1.1 mi e. Int corridors. **Pets:** Small. $10 daily fee/room. Designated rooms, service with restrictions, crate. [SAVE] [✕] [🛏] [💻] [⇌]

▲▲▷ ▼▼▼ Stone Castle Hotel & Conference Center **H**
(417) 335-4700. **$69-$119.** 3050 Green Mountain Dr 65616. Jct SR 76 (Country Music Blvd) and US 65, 3 mi w on SR 76, 0.8 mi s. Int corridors. **Pets:** Other species. $12 daily fee/pet. Designated rooms, service with restrictions, supervision. [SAVE] [✕] [🛏] [💻] [⇌]

▼▼ Super 8 Central of Branson **H**
(417) 336-3300. **Call for rates.** 3470 Keeter St 65616. SR 76 (Country Music Blvd), just s; w of Gretna Rd (SR 165). Ext corridors. **Pets:** Accepted. [✕] [&M] [🛏] [💻] [⇌]

▲▲▷ ▼▼▼▼ The Village At Indian Point **CO**
(417) 338-8800. **$100-$270, 31 day notice.** 24 Village Tr 65616. 2.5 mi s of jct SR 76 (Country Music Blvd) on Indian Point Rd. Ext corridors. **Pets:** Medium, dogs only. $10 daily fee/room. Designated rooms, no service, supervision. [SAVE] [✕] [🛏] [💻] [⇌] [✕]

▲▲▷ ▼▼▼▼ Westgate Branson Woods Resort **CO**
(417) 334-2324. **$52-$116.** 2201 Roark Valley Rd 65616. US 65, exit SR 248 (Shepherd of the Hills Expwy), 3.7 mi w, just n. Ext corridors. **Pets:** Accepted. [SAVE] [✕] [🛏] [💻] [¶¶] [⇌] [✕]

HOLLISTER

▲▲▷ ▼▼▼▼ Westgate Branson Lakes at Emerald Pointe **CO**
(417) 334-4944. **$71-$206.** 750 Emerald Pointe Dr 65672. Jct US 65 and SR 265, 1 mi w to Hill Haven Rd, then 2 mi s. Ext corridors. **Pets:** Medium, dogs only. $75 deposit/room, $80 one-time fee/room. Designated rooms, service with restrictions, supervision. [SAVE] [✕] [&M] [🛏] [💻] [⇌] [✕]

END METROPOLITAN AREA

BROOKFIELD

▲▲▷ ▼▼▼ Best Western Brookfield **H**
(660) 258-4900. **$89-$109.** 28622 Hwy 11 64628. US 36, exit Business Rt 36, just se. Int corridors. **Pets:** Accepted. [SAVE] [✕] [&M] [🛏] [💻] [⇌]

CAMERON

▲▲▷ ▼▼▼ Best Western Acorn Inn **M**
(816) 632-2187. **$79-$95.** 2210 E US 36 64429. I-35, exit 54, 0.3 mi e. Ext corridors. **Pets:** Medium, other species. Service with restrictions, supervision. [SAVE] [✕] [🛏] [💻] [⇌]

▼▼▼ Comfort Inn **H**
(816) 632-5655. **Call for rates.** 1803 Comfort Ln 64429. I-35, exit 54, just e. Int corridors. **Pets:** Other species. $10 daily fee/room. Designated rooms, service with restrictions, supervision. [✕] [🛏] [💻] [⇌] [✕]

▲▲▷ ▼▼▼ Econo Lodge **H** ❀
(816) 632-6571. **$60-$75.** 220 E Grand 64429. I-35, exit 54, 0.5 mi w on US 36, then just s on US 69. Ext corridors. **Pets:** Medium. $10 daily fee/pet. Service with restrictions, supervision. [SAVE] [✕] [🛏] [⇌]

▼▼▼ Super 8 **H**
(816) 632-8888. **$62-$78.** 1710 N Walnut St 64429. I-35, exit 54, 0.5 mi w on US 36. Int corridors. **Pets:** Accepted. [A$K] [✕] [🛏] [💻] [⇌]

CANTON

▼▼ Comfort Inn Canton **H**
(573) 288-8800. **Call for rates.** 1701 Oak St 63435. US 61, exit US 61 business route/CR P, just e. Int corridors. **Pets:** Accepted. [✕] [🛏] [💻] [⇌]

CAPE GIRARDEAU

▼▼▼ Drury Lodge-Cape Girardeau **H**
(573) 334-7151. **$80-$130.** 104 S Vantage Dr 63701. I-55, exit 96 (William St), just e. Ext/int corridors. **Pets:** Other species. No service, supervision. [A$K] [✕] [🛏] [💻] [¶¶] [⇌]

▼▼▼ Drury Suites-Cape Girardeau **H**
(573) 339-9500. **$100-$150.** 3303 Campster Dr 63701. I-55, exit 96 (William St), just w. Int corridors. **Pets:** Other species. No service, supervision. [A$K] [✕] [&M] [🛏] [💻] [⇌]

▼▼▼ Hampton Inn-Cape Girardeau **H**
(573) 651-3000. **$108-$133.** 103 Cape W Pkwy 63701. I-55, exit 96 (William St), 0.3 mi sw. Int corridors. **Pets:** Accepted. [✕] [&M] [🛏] [💻]

▼▼ Pear Tree Inn by Drury-Cape Girardeau **H**
(573) 334-3000. **$70-$115.** 3248 William St 63701. I-55, exit 96 (William St), just e. Int corridors. **Pets:** Other species. No service, supervision. [A$K] [✕] [💻] [⇌]

▼▼▼ Victorian Inn & Suites **H**
(573) 651-4486. **Call for rates.** 3265 William St 63701. I-55, exit 96 (William St), just e. Ext/int corridors. **Pets:** Accepted.

CARTHAGE

AAA ▼▼▼ Best Western Precious Moments Hotel **H**
(417) 359-5900. **$72-$130.** 2701 Hazel St 64836. Just e of jct US 71 and SR HH. Int corridors. **Pets:** Accepted. (SAVE) ⓧ 🔒 💻 🏊

AAA ▼▼▼ Econo Lodge **H**
(417) 358-3900. **$54-$64.** 1441 W Central 64836. Just ne of jct US 71 and SR 96. Ext/int corridors. **Pets:** Accepted. (SAVE) ⓧ 🔒 💻 🏊

▼▼ Super 8 **H**
(417) 359-9000. **Call for rates.** 416 W Fir Rd 64836. Just e of jct US 71 and SR HH. Int corridors. **Pets:** Accepted. ⓧ 🔒

CHILLICOTHE

AAA ▼▼▼ Best Western Inn **H**
(660) 646-0572. **$65-$113.** 1020 S Washington St 64601. Jct US 36 and 65 (Washington St). Ext/int corridors. **Pets:** Large. $10 daily fee/pet. Designated rooms, service with restrictions, supervision.
(SAVE) ⓧ 🔒M 🔒 💻 🏊

▼▼ Chillicothe Super 8 **H**
(660) 646-7888. **$55-$78.** 580 Old Hwy 36 E 64601. Jct US 36 and 65 (Washington St), 0.8 mi e. Int corridors. **Pets:** Accepted.
(ASK) ⓧ 🔒 💻

CLINTON

AAA ▼▼▼ Best Western Colonial Motel **M**
(660) 885-2206. **$59-$69.** 106 S Baird St 64735. Jct SR 7 and 13. Ext corridors. **Pets:** Medium, dogs only. $10 daily fee/pet. Designated rooms, service with restrictions. (SAVE) ⓧ 🔒 💻 🏊

COLUMBIA

AAA ▼▼▼ Best Western Columbia Inn **H**
(573) 474-6161. **$69-$105.** 3100 I-70 Dr SE 65201. I-70, exit 128A, just s, then just e. Int corridors. **Pets:** $10 daily fee/room. Service with restrictions. (SAVE) ⓧ 🔒M 🔒 💻 🏊

▼▼ Candlewood Suites **H** 🐾
(573) 817-0525. **$89-$209.** 3100 Wingate Ct 65201. I-70, exit 128A, just s on US 63, just e on I-70 Dr SE, then just s on Keene St. Int corridors. **Pets:** Other species. $25 one-time fee/room. Service with restrictions.
(ASK) ⓧ 🔒M 🔒 💻

▼▼▼ Drury Inn-Columbia **H**
(573) 445-1800. **$85-$179.** 1000 Knipp St 65203. I-70, exit 124 (Stadium Blvd), just s. Int corridors. **Pets:** Other species. No service, supervision.
(ASK) ⓧ 🔒 💻 🏊

▼▼ Extended StayAmerica-Columbia-Stadium Blvd **H**
(573) 445-6800. **$59-$69.** 2000 Business Loop 70 W 65203. I-70, exit 124 (Stadium Blvd), just ne. Int corridors. **Pets:** Other species. $25 daily fee/room. Designated rooms, service with restrictions, crate.
(ASK) ⓧ 🔒 💻

AAA ▼▼▼▼ Holiday Inn Executive Center **H**
(573) 445-8531. **Call for rates.** 2200 I-70 Dr SW 65203. I-70, exit 124 (Stadium Blvd), just w. Int corridors. **Pets:** $25 one-time fee/room. Designated rooms, service with restrictions, supervision.
(SAVE) ⓧ 🔒M 🔒 💻 🍽 🏊 ⓧ

▼▼ Super 8-Clark Lane in Columbia **M**
(573) 474-8488. **$57-$104.** 3216 Clark Ln 65202. I-70, exit 128A, northeast corner. Int corridors. **Pets:** Accepted. (ASK) ⓧ 🔒 💻

CUBA

AAA ▼▼▼ Best Western Cuba Inn **M**
(573) 885-7707. **$60-$90.** 246 Hwy P 65453. I-44, exit 208 (SR 19), just n, then just e. Ext corridors. **Pets:** Medium. $10 daily fee/pet. Designated rooms, service with restrictions, supervision. (SAVE) ⓧ 🔒 💻 🏊

▼▼ Super 8 **M**
(573) 885-2087. **$60-$115.** 28 Hwy P 65453. I-44, exit 208 (SR 19), just n, then just w. Ext/int corridors. **Pets:** Small. $10 one-time fee/pet. Designated rooms, service with restrictions, supervision. (ASK) ⓧ 🔒 💻

FESTUS

▼▼ Drury Inn-Festus **H**
(636) 933-2400. **$80-$134.** 1001 Veterans Blvd 63028. I-55, exit 175, just e. Int corridors. **Pets:** Other species. No service, supervision.
(ASK) ⓧ 🔒 💻 🏊

FULTON

▼▼▼ Loganberry Inn Bed & Breakfast **BB** 🐾
(573) 642-9229. **$99-$199, 14 day notice.** 310 W 7th St 65251. Jct US 54, exit CR F, 1 mi e, just n to Westminster, then just e. Int corridors. **Pets:** Dogs only. $10 daily fee/pet. Designated rooms, service with restrictions. (ASK) ⓧ 🔒 💻

HANNIBAL

AAA ▼▼▼▼ Quality Inn & Suites **H**
(573) 221-4001. **$60-$129.** 120 Lindsey Dr 63401. 2 mi w on US 36, exit Shinn Ln to south service road, then 0.6 mi e. Int corridors.
Pets: Medium. $10 daily fee/pet. Designated rooms, service with restrictions, supervision. (SAVE) ⓧ 🔒 💻 🏊 ⓧ

▼▼ Super 8 **M**
(573) 221-5863. **$55-$120.** 120 Huckleberry Heights Dr 63401. Jct US 36, 1.5 mi s on US 61. Int corridors. **Pets:** Small. $15 daily fee/pet. Designated rooms, service with restrictions, supervision.
(ASK) ⓧ 🔒 💻 🏊

HARRISONVILLE

AAA ▼▼▼ Harrisonville Inn & Suites **M**
(816) 884-3200. **$55-$98.** 2201 Rockhaven Rd 64701. Just n of jct US 71 and SR 291. Ext corridors. **Pets:** Medium, dogs only. $10 daily fee/pet. Designated rooms, no service, supervision.
(SAVE) ⓧ 🔒 💻 🏊

HAYTI

▼▼ Drury Inn & Suites-Hayti Caruthersville **H**
(573) 359-2702. **$80-$134.** 1317 Hwy 84 63851. I-55, exit 19 (US 412/SR 84), just w. Int corridors. **Pets:** Other species. No service, supervision. (ASK) ⓧ 🔒 💻 🏊

HIGGINSVILLE

▼▼ Super 8-Higginsville **H**
(660) 584-7781. **$62-$67.** 6471 Oakview Ln 64037. I-70, exit 49 (SR 13), just se. Int corridors. **Pets:** Accepted. (ASK) ⓧ 🔒 💻

JACKSON

▼▼▼ Comfort Suites **H**
(573) 204-0014. **$70-$150.** 2904 Old Orchard Rd 63755. I-55, exit 99, 0.5 mi e, then just n. Int corridors. **Pets:** Large. $25 daily fee/pet. Service with restrictions, supervision. (ASK) ⓧ 🔒M 🔒 💻 🏊

▼▼▼ Drury Inn & Suites-Jackson, MO **H**
(573) 243-9200. **$80-$149.** 225 Drury Ln 63755. I-55, exit 105 (SR 61), 0.3 mi w. Int corridors. **Pets:** Other species. No service, supervision.
(ASK) ⓧ 🔒M 🔒 💻 🏊

JANE

▼▼ Booneslick Lodge **H**
(417) 226-1888. **$64-$115.** 21140 US Hwy 71 64856. Just s on US 71. Int corridors. **Pets:** Accepted. (ASK) ⓧ 🔒 💻 🏊

JEFFERSON CITY

◆◆◆ **Capitol Plaza Hotel and Convention Center** [H]
(573) 635-1234. **$89-$139.** 415 W McCarty St 65101. On US 50 and 63 S, just e of jct US 54. Int corridors. **Pets:** Accepted.
[ASK] 🚭 ♿ ▤ 💻 🍴 🏊 🏋

◆◆ **Super 8 Jefferson City** [H]
(573) 636-5456. **$50-$90.** 1710 Jefferson St 65109. US 54, exit Ellis Blvd, 0.3 mi nw on frontage road. Int corridors. **Pets:** Accepted.
[ASK] 🚭 ▤ 💻

◆◆ **Truman Hotel & Conference Center** [H]
(573) 635-7171. **Call for rates.** 1510 Jefferson St 65109. US 54, exit Ellis Blvd, 0.5 mi nw. Ext/int corridors. **Pets:** Accepted.
🚭 ▤ 💻 🍴 🏊

JOPLIN

[AAA] ◆◆ **Best Western Oasis Inn & Suites** [H]
(417) 781-6776. **$79-$149.** 3508 S Range Line Rd 64804. I-44, exit 8B, just nw. Ext corridors. **Pets:** Medium. $10 one-time fee/pet. Service with restrictions, crate. [SAVE] 🚭 ▤ 💻 🏊

[AAA] ◆◆◆ **Candlewood Suites** [H]
(417) 623-9595. **$99-$129.** 3512 S Range Line Rd 64804. I-44, exit 8B, just nw. Int corridors. **Pets:** Other species. $75 one-time fee/room. Service with restrictions. [SAVE] 🚭 ♿ ▤ 💻

◆◆◆ **Drury Inn & Suites-Joplin** [H]
(417) 781-8000. **$85-$184.** 3601 S Range Line Rd 64804. I-44, exit 8B, just ne. Int corridors. **Pets:** Other species. No service, supervision.
[ASK] 🚭 ♿ ▤ 💻 🏊 🏋

◆◆◆ **La Quinta Inn** [H] 🐾
(417) 781-0500. **$65-$119.** 3320 S Range Line Rd 64804. I-44, exit 8B, just n. Int corridors. **Pets:** Medium, other species. Service with restrictions, supervision. [ASK] 🚭 ▤ 💻 🍴 🏊

[AAA] ◆◆◆ **Residence Inn by Marriott-Joplin** [H] 🐾
(417) 782-0908. **$119-$129.** 3128 E Hammons Blvd 64804. I-44, exit 8B, just ne. Int corridors. **Pets:** Medium. $75 one-time fee/room. Service with restrictions, crate. [SAVE] 🚭 ♿ ▤ 💻 🏊 🏋

[AAA] ◆◆ **Sleep Inn** [H]
(417) 782-1212. **Call for rates.** 4100 Hwy 43 S 64803. I-44, exit 4, just s. Int corridors. **Pets:** Accepted. [SAVE] 🚭 💻

◆◆◆ **TownePlace Suites By Marriott Joplin** [H]
(417) 659-8111. **$80-$98.** 4026 Arizona Ave 64804. I-44, exit 8A, just sw. Int corridors. **Pets:** Other species. $75 one-time fee/room. Service with restrictions, supervision. 🚭 ♿ ▤ 💻 🏊

KANSAS CITY METROPOLITAN AREA

BLUE SPRINGS

◆◆◆ **Hampton Inn Blue Springs** [H]
(816) 220-3844. **$79-$119.** 900 NW South Outer Rd 64015. I-70, exit 20 (SR 7), just s, then just w. Int corridors. **Pets:** Other species. Service with restrictions, crate. 🚭 ▤ 💻 🏊

INDEPENDENCE

[AAA] ◆◆ **Best Western Truman Inn** [M]
(816) 254-0100. **$50-$110.** 4048 S Lynn Court Dr 64055. I-70, exit 12, just n on Noland Rd, then just w. Ext corridors. **Pets:** Medium, other species. $50 deposit/room, $10 daily fee/pet. Supervision.
[SAVE] 🚭 ▤ 💻 🏊

[AAA] ◆◆◆ **Comfort Suites** [H] 🐾
(816) 373-9880. **$89-$139.** 19751 E Valley View Pkwy 64057. I-70, exit 17, just s on Little Blue Pkwy, then just w. Int corridors. **Pets:** Other species. $25 one-time fee/room. Service with restrictions, crate.
[SAVE] 🚭 ♿ ▤ 💻 🏊

[AAA] ◆◆◆ **Holiday Inn Express Hotel & Suites** [H]
(816) 795-8889. **Call for rates.** 19901 E Valley View Pkwy 64057. I-70, exit 17 (Little Blue Pkwy), just e, then w on E Valley View Pkwy (Eastland Business Park). Int corridors. **Pets:** Accepted.
[SAVE] 🚭 ♿ ▤ 💻 🏊

[AAA] ◆◆ **Super 8 Independence** [H]
(816) 833-1888. **$40-$120.** 4032 S Lynn Court Dr 64055. I-70, exit 12, just n on Noland Rd, then just w. Int corridors. **Pets:** Medium, other species. $50 deposit/room, $10 daily fee/pet. Supervision.
[SAVE] 🚭 ▤ 💻 🏊

KANSAS CITY

[AAA] ◆◆ **Best Western Country Inn-North** [M]
(816) 459-7222. **$50-$150.** 2633 NE 43rd St 64117. I-35, exit 8C (Antioch Rd), just s on SR 1, then just e. Ext corridors. **Pets:** Small, other species. $10 daily fee/pet. Service with restrictions, supervision.
[SAVE] 🚭 ▤ 💻 🏊

[AAA] ◆◆◆ **Best Western Seville Plaza Hotel** [H] 🐾
(816) 561-9600. **$83-$139.** 4309 Main St 64111. Jct 43rd St, just s. Int corridors. **Pets:** Large. $50 one-time fee/room. Designated rooms, service with restrictions. [SAVE] 🚭 ♿ ▤ 💻

[AAA] ◆◆◆ **Chase Suites by Woodfin** [H] 🐾
(816) 891-9009. **$99-$159.** 9900 NW Prairie View Rd 64153. I-29, exit 10, just w, then just n. Ext corridors. **Pets:** Other species. $10 daily fee/pet. Service with restrictions, crate. [SAVE] 🚭 ▤ 💻 🏊 🏋

[AAA] ◆◆◆ **Clarion Hotel Sports Complex** [H]
(816) 353-5300. **$79-$189.** 4011 Blue Ridge Cutoff 64133. I-70, exit 9 (Blue Ridge Cutoff), just se. Int corridors. **Pets:** Medium. $20 one-time fee/room. No service, supervision. [SAVE] 🚭 ♿ 💻 🍴 🏊 🏋

◆◆◆ **Drury Inn & Suites-Kansas City Airport** [H]
(816) 880-9700. **$85-$189.** 7900 NW Tiffany Springs Pkwy 64153-2310. I-29, exit 10, just w. Int corridors. **Pets:** Other species. No service, supervision. [ASK] 🚭 ♿ ▤ 💻 🏊

◆◆◆ **Drury Inn & Suites-Kansas City Stadium** [H]
(816) 923-3000. **$80-$169.** 3830 Blue Ridge Cutoff 64133. I-70, exit 9 (Blue Ridge Cutoff), just nw. Int corridors. **Pets:** Other species. No service, supervision. [ASK] 🚭 ♿ ▤ 💻 🏊

[AAA] ◆◆◆ **Embassy Suites Kansas City-International Airport** [H]
(816) 891-7788. **$119-$209.** 7640 NW Tiffany Springs Pkwy 64153. I-29, exit 10, just e. Int corridors. **Pets:** Small. $10 daily fee/pet. Designated rooms, service with restrictions, supervision.
[SAVE] 🚭 ♿ ▤ 💻 🍴 🏊 🏋

◆ **Extended StayAmerica-Kansas City Airport** [H]
(816) 270-7829. **$50-$110.** 11712 NW Plaza Cir 64153. I-29, exit 13, just e on CR D, just s on Ambassador Dr, then just w. Int corridors. **Pets:** Other species. $25 daily fee/room. Designated rooms, service with restrictions, crate. [ASK] 🚭 ▤ 💻

◆ **Extended StayAmerica-Kansas City South** [H]
(816) 943-1315. **$55-$120.** 550 E 105th St 64131. I-435, exit 74, just s on Holmes Rd, then just w. Int corridors. **Pets:** Other species. $25 daily fee/room. Designated rooms, service with restrictions, crate.
[ASK] 🚭 ▤ 💻

[AAA] ◆◆◆ **Hilton Kansas City Airport** [H]
(816) 891-8900. **$89-$189.** 8801 NW 112th St 64153. I-29, exit 12, just se. Int corridors. **Pets:** Accepted.
[SAVE] 🚭 ♿ ▤ 💻 🍴 🏊 🏋

Hilton President Kansas City H ❖
(816) 221-9490. **$119-$219.** 1329 Baltimore Ave 64105. Jct 14th St. Int corridors. **Pets:** Medium. $75 one-time fee/room. Service with restrictions.
[SAVE] [X] [🔒] [💻] [🍴]

Holiday Inn At The Plaza, Kansas City H ❖
(816) 753-7400. **$79-$129.** One E 45th St 64111. Jct Main St; in Country Club Plaza. Int corridors. **Pets:** Small. $25 one-time fee/pet. Designated rooms, service with restrictions, crate.
[ASK] [X] [🔒M] [🔒] [💻] [🍴] [🏊]

Holiday Inn Express Westport H
(816) 931-1000. **Call for rates.** 801 Westport Rd 64111. Jct Main St, 0.5 mi w; in Westport Plaza area. Int corridors. **Pets:** Accepted.
[X] [🔒M] [🔒] [💻]

Holiday Inn Kansas City Northeast H
(816) 455-1060. **$79-$99.** 7333 NE Parvin Rd 64117. I-435, exit 54, just w. Int corridors. **Pets:** Accepted.
[SAVE] [X] [🔒M] [🔒] [💻] [🍴] [🏊] [X]

Holiday Inn Kansas City SE–Water Park H
(816) 737-0200. **Call for rates.** 9103 E 39th St 64133. I-70, exit 9 (Blue Ridge Cutoff), just ne. Int corridors. **Pets:** Accepted.
[X] [🔒] [💻] [🍴] [🏊]

Holiday Inn KCI & Expo Center H ❖
(816) 801-8400. **$79-$139.** 11728 N Ambassador Dr 64153. I-29, exit 13, just e on CR D, then just s. Int corridors. **Pets:** Small. $30 one-time fee/room. Designated rooms, service with restrictions, supervision.
[SAVE] [X] [🔒M] [💻] [🍴] [🏊]

Homestead Studio Suites-Kansas City/Country Club Plaza H
(816) 531-2212. **$85-$170.** 4535 Main St 64111. Jct 45th St, just s; just ne of Country Club Plaza. Int corridors. **Pets:** Other species. $25 daily fee/room. Designated rooms, service with restrictions, crate.
[ASK] [X] [🔒M] [🔒] [💻]

Homewood Suites by Hilton H
(816) 880-9880. **$89-$169.** 7312 NW Polo Dr 64153. I-29, exit 10, just e. Int corridors. **Pets:** Other species. $100 one-time fee/room. Service with restrictions.
[X] [🔒] [💻] [🏊] [X]

Hotel Phillips H
(816) 221-7000. **Call for rates.** 106 W 12th St 64105. Jct Wyandotte St, just e. Int corridors. **Pets:** Accepted. [SAVE] [X] [💻] [🍴]

The InterContinental Kansas City at the Plaza H
(816) 756-1500. **$149-$449.** 401 Ward Pkwy 64112. Jct Wornall Rd; in Country Club Plaza. Int corridors. **Pets:** Small. $20 daily fee/pet. Service with restrictions, supervision. [SAVE] [X] [💻] [🍴] [🏊] [X]

La Quinta Inn & Suites–Northeast H ❖
(816) 483-7900. **$69-$109.** 1051 N Cambridge Ave 64120. I-435, exit 57, just w, then just s. Int corridors. **Pets:** Medium, other species. Service with restrictions, supervision. [ASK] [X] [🔒] [💻] [🏊] [X]

Microtel Inn & Suites H
(816) 270-1200. **$55-$65.** 11831 NW Plaza Cir 64153. I-29, exit 13, just e on CR D, then just s. Int corridors. **Pets:** Accepted.
[SAVE] [X] [🔒] [💻]

The Q Hotel & Spa H
(816) 931-0001. **Call for rates.** 560 Westport Rd 64111. Jct Main St, 0.4 mi w; in Westport Plaza area. Int corridors. **Pets:** Accepted.
[ECO] [SAVE] [X] [🔒] [💻]

Radisson Hotel Kansas City Airport H
(816) 464-2423. **$90-$110.** 11828 NW Plaza Cir 64153. I-29, exit 13, just e on CR D, just s on Ambassador Dr, then just w. Int corridors.
Pets: Accepted. [ASK] [X] [🔒M] [🔒] [💻] [🍴] [🏊]

Red Roof Inn-North-Worlds of Fun M
(816) 452-8585. **$43-$100.** 3636 NE Randolph Rd 64161. I-435, exit 55B northbound; exit 55 southbound, just e on SR 210, then just n. Ext corridors. **Pets:** Large. Service with restrictions, crate. [ASK] [X] [🔒M]

Residence Inn by Marriott Downtown/Union Hill H
(816) 561-3000. **$143-$175.** 2975 Main St 64108. Jct 31st St, just n. Ext corridors. **Pets:** Accepted. [ECO] [X] [🔒] [💻] [🏊]

Residence Inn by Marriott, Kansas City Airport H
(816) 741-2300. **$143-$175.** 10300 N Ambassador Dr 64153. I-29, exit 10, just ne, then 1.5 mi. Int corridors. **Pets:** Small, other species. $75 one-time fee/room. Service with restrictions, crate.
[X] [🔒M] [🔒] [💻] [🏊] [X]

Residence Inn by Marriott Kansas City Country Club Plaza H ❖
(816) 753-0033. **$159-$169.** 4601 Broadway Blvd 64112. Jct JC Nichols Pkwy, just w on 46th Terr; in Country Club Plaza. Int corridors.
Pets: Medium. $100 one-time fee/room. Designated rooms, service with restrictions, supervision. [X] [🔒] [💻] [🏊] [X]

Sheraton Suites Country Club Plaza H
(816) 931-4400. **Call for rates.** 770 W 47th St 64112. Jct Summit St; in Country Club Plaza. Int corridors. **Pets:** Accepted.
[SAVE] [X] [🔒M] [🔒] [💻] [🍴] [🏊]

Super 8–KCI H
(816) 464-2002. **Call for rates.** 11900 NW Plaza Cir 64153. I-29, exit 13, just e on CR D, then just s. Ext corridors. **Pets:** Small, dogs only. $25 one-time fee/pet. Service with restrictions, supervision.
[SAVE] [X] [🔒]

The Westin Crown Center H ❖
(816) 474-4400. **$129-$329, 3 day notice.** 1 E Pershing Rd 64108. 0.5 mi s. Int corridors. **Pets:** Dogs only. $50 one-time fee/room. Service with restrictions, supervision. [SAVE] [X] [🔒M] [🔒] [💻] [🍴] [🏊] [X]

KEARNEY

Kearney Lodging H
(816) 628-5000. **Call for rates.** 601 Centerville Ave 64060. I-35, exit 26, just w. Int corridors. **Pets:** Accepted. [X] [🔒] [💻] [🏊]

Kearney Super 8 H ❖
(816) 628-6800. **$50-$180.** 210 Platte Clay Way 64060. I-35, exit 26, just e on SR 92, then just n. Int corridors. **Pets:** Dogs only. $10 daily fee/pet. Designated rooms, service with restrictions, supervision.
[ASK] [X] [🔒] [💻]

LEE'S SUMMIT

Comfort Inn by Choice Hotels H
(816) 524-8181. **$58-$80.** 607 SE Oldham Pkwy 64081. Jct US 50 and SR 291 N. Int corridors. **Pets:** Medium. $25 one-time fee/pet. Service with restrictions, crate. [ASK] [X] [🔒M] [🔒] [💻] [🏊]

Lee's Summit Holiday Inn Express H
(816) 795-6400. **$74-$109.** 4825 NE Lakewood Way 64064. I-470, exit 14, just e on Bowlin Rd, then 0.4 mi s. Int corridors. **Pets:** Medium. $25 one-time fee/room. Designated rooms, service with restrictions, crate.
[SAVE] [X] [🔒M] [🔒] [💻] [🏊]

NORTH KANSAS CITY

La Quinta Inn Kansas City North H ❖
(816) 221-1200. **$45-$149.** 2214 Taney Rd 64116. I-29/35, exit 6A, just e on SR 210, then just n. Int corridors. **Pets:** Medium, other species. Service with restrictions, supervision. [ASK] [X] [🔒] [💻]

OAK GROVE (JACKSON COUNTY)

Econo Lodge M
(816) 690-3681. **Call for rates.** 410 SE 1st St 64075. I-70, exit 28, just s on Broadway St, just e on SE 4th St, then just n. Ext corridors.
Pets: Accepted. [X] [🔒]

PLATTE CITY

Best Western Airport Inn & Suites KCI North ⊞

(816) 858-0200. **$70-$95.** 2512 NW Prairie View Rd 64079. I-29, exit 18, just e, then just s. Int corridors. **Pets:** Small. $25 one-time fee/pet. Designated rooms. ⟦SAVE⟧ ⊠ ⟨ᴍ⟩ ⊟ ⊑ ⟿ ⟨⟩

END METROPOLITAN AREA

KIRKSVILLE

Super 8-Kirksville Ⓜ ❀

(660) 665-8826. **$56-$80.** 1101 Country Club Dr 63501. On US 63 and SR 6. Int corridors. **Pets:** $10 daily fee/pet. Designated rooms, service with restrictions, supervision. ⟦ASK⟧ ⊠ ⊟ ⊑

LAKE OZARK

The Resort at Port Arrowhead ⊞

(573) 365-2334. **Call for rates.** 3080 Bagnell Dam Blvd 65049. 2.6 mi s of Bagnell Dam. Ext/int corridors. **Pets:** Other species. $12 daily fee/pet. Service with restrictions. ⟦SAVE⟧ ⊠ ⟨ᴍ⟩ ⊟ ⊑ ⟨⟩ ⟿ ⟨⟩

LAMAR

Super 8-Lamar ⊞

(417) 682-6888. **$57-$80.** 45 SE 1st Ln 64759. Jct US 71 and 160. Int corridors. **Pets:** Accepted. ⟦ASK⟧ ⊠ ⊟ ⊑ ⟿

LEBANON

Best Western Wyota Inn ⊞

(417) 532-6171. **$77-$100.** 1221 Mill Creek Rd 65536. I-44, exit 130, just nw. Ext corridors. **Pets:** Medium. $15 daily fee/pet. Designated rooms, service with restrictions, crate. ⟦SAVE⟧ ⊠ ⊟ ⊑ ⟿

LICKING

Scenic Rivers Inn Ⓜ

(573) 674-4809. **$54-$60.** 209 S Hwy 63 65542. On US 63. Ext corridors. **Pets:** Medium. $10 daily fee/pet. Service with restrictions, supervision. ⟦ASK⟧ ⊠ ⊟ ⊑ ⟿

LINN

Settle Inn & Suites ⊞ ❀

(573) 897-9903. **$79-$99.** 1639 US Hwy 50 E 65051. 1 mi e of jct US 50 and SR 89. Int corridors. **Pets:** Small. $15 daily fee/pet. Designated rooms, service with restrictions, supervision. ⟦ASK⟧ ⊠ ⊟ ⊑

MACON

Super 8 ⊞

(660) 385-5788. **$64.** 203 E Briggs Dr 63552. Jct US 36 and 63. Int corridors. **Pets:** Accepted. ⟦ASK⟧ ⊠ ⊟ ⊑

MARSHFIELD

Holiday Inn Express ⊞

(417) 859-6000. **Call for rates.** 1301 Banning St 65706. I-44, exit 100 (SR 38), on southeast corner. Int corridors. **Pets:** Medium. $25 daily fee/pet. Service with restrictions, supervision. ⊠ ⟨ᴍ⟩ ⊟ ⊑ ⟿

MARYVILLE

Super 8 ⊞

(660) 582-8088. **$55-$61.** 222 Summit Dr 64468. On Business Rt US 71; just n of US 71 Bypass. Int corridors. **Pets:** Other species. $50 deposit/room. Service with restrictions, supervision. ⟦ASK⟧ ⊠ ⊟ ⊑

MINER

Best Western Coach House Inn ⊞

(573) 471-9700. **$75-$150.** 220 S Interstate Dr 63801. I-55, exit 67, just ne. Int corridors. **Pets:** Small. $25 one-time fee/room. Designated rooms, service with restrictions, supervision. ⟦SAVE⟧ ⊠ ⟨ᴍ⟩ ⊟ ⊑ ⟿

Drury Inn Suites–Sikeston ⊞

(573) 472-2299. **$90-$159.** 2608 E Malone Ave 63801. I-55, exit 67, just sw. Int corridors. **Pets:** Other species. No service, supervision. ⟦ASK⟧ ⊠ ⊟ ⊑ ⟿

Pear Tree Inn-Sikeston ⊞

(573) 471-4100. **$70-$134.** 2602 E Malone Ave 63801. I-55, exit 67, just sw. Int corridors. **Pets:** Other species. No service, supervision. ⟦ASK⟧ ⊠ ⟨ᴍ⟩ ⊟ ⊑ ⟿

MOUND CITY

Mound City Super 8 ⊞

(660) 442-4000. **Call for rates.** 109 W 8th St 64470. I-29, exit 84, just e. Int corridors. **Pets:** Medium. $20 daily fee/pet. Service with restrictions, supervision. ⟦SAVE⟧ ⊠ ⊟ ⊑ ⟿

NEOSHO

Best Western Big Spring Lodge ⊞

(417) 455-2300. **$70.** 1810 Southern View Dr 64850. 0.9 mi e of jct US 60 and 71. Int corridors. **Pets:** Small. $5 one-time fee/pet. Service with restrictions, supervision. ⟦SAVE⟧ ⊠ ⊟ ⊑ ⟿

NIXA

Super 8 ⊞

(417) 725-0880. **$54-$61.** 418 Massey Blvd 65714. 0.5 mi n of jct SR 14 and 160; US 65, 4.7 mi w on SR 14, then 0.4 mi n on SR 160. Int corridors. **Pets:** Accepted. ⟦ASK⟧ ⊠ ⟨ᴍ⟩ ⊟ ⊑ ⟿

OSAGE BEACH

Dogwood Hills Resort ⊞

(573) 348-1735. **$52-$114.** 1252 State Hwy KK 65065. 0.5 mi n, off US 54. Ext corridors. **Pets:** Accepted. ⟦ASK⟧ ⊠ ⊟ ⊑ ⟨⟩ ⟿

OZARK

Americas Best Value Inn ⊞

(417) 581-8800. **Call for rates.** 299 N 20th 65721. US 65, exit SR 14, just w to 20th St, then just s. Ext/int corridors. **Pets:** Accepted. ⊠ ⟿

PACIFIC

Comfort Inn ⊞

(636) 257-4600. **$79-$119.** 1320 Thornton St 63069. I-44, exit 257, just ne. Int corridors. **Pets:** Accepted. ⟦SAVE⟧ ⊠ ⊟ ⊑ ⟿ ⟨⟩

Quality Inn Near Six Flags ⊞

(636) 257-8400. **$69-$109.** 1400 W Osage St 63069. I-44, exit 257, just se. Ext/int corridors. **Pets:** Medium, other species. $15 daily fee/pet. Service with restrictions. ⟦SAVE⟧ ⊠ ⊟ ⊑ ⟿

PERRYVILLE

Americas Best Value Inn Ⓜ

(573) 547-1091. **$55-$76, 3 day notice.** 1500 Liberty St 63775. I-55, exit 129 (SR 51). Int corridors. **Pets:** Medium, dogs only. $10 daily fee/pet. Service with restrictions, supervision. ⟦SAVE⟧ ⊠ ⊟ ⊑

POPLAR BLUFF

Comfort Inn by Choice Hotels ⊞

(573) 686-5200. **$90-$110.** 2582 N Westwood Blvd 63901. 1.3 mi s from jct US 60 E. Int corridors. **Pets:** Other species. $20 one-time fee/room. Designated rooms, service with restrictions, supervision. ⟦SAVE⟧ ⊠ ⟨ᴍ⟩ ⊟ ⊑ ⟿

▼▼▼ Drury Inn-Poplar Bluff 🇭

(573) 686-2451. **$80-$119.** 2220 N Westwood Blvd 63901. On US 67, 1.4 mi s from jct US 60 E. Int corridors. **Pets:** Other species. No service, supervision. (ASK) ⊠ 🛢 🖵 ⇌

▼▼ Super 8 🇭

(573) 785-0176. **$60-$70.** 2831 N Westwood Blvd 63901. On US 67, 0.8 mi s from jct US 60 E. Int corridors. **Pets:** Other species. $50 one-time fee/room. Service with restrictions, supervision. (ASK) ⊠ 🛢 🖵

POTOSI

▼▼ Potosi Super 8 🇭

(573) 438-8888. **$60-$77.** 820 E High St 63664. Jct SR 8 and 21. Ext/int corridors. **Pets:** Other species. $10 one-time fee/pet. Service with restrictions, supervision. (ASK) ⊠ 🛢 🖵

REPUBLIC

▼▼ AmericInn Lodge & Suites of Republic 🇭 🐾

(417) 732-5335. **$85-$90.** 950 Austin Ln 65738. I-44, exit 67, 4.4 mi s to SR 174 (flashing red light/4-way stop), then 0.7 mi e to Highland Park Town Center; just nw of jct US 60, SR 413 and 174. Int corridors. **Pets:** Small. $10 daily fee/pet. Service with restrictions, crate. ⊠ 🛢 🖵 ⇌

ROLLA

▲▲▲ ▼▼▼ Baymont Inn & Suites 🇭

(573) 364-7000. **$76-$95.** 1801 Martin Springs Dr 65401. I-44, exit 184, just sw. Int corridors. **Pets:** Small. $10 one-time fee/pet. Service with restrictions, crate. (SAVE) ⊠ 🛢 🖵 ⇌

▲▲▲ ▼▼▼ Best Western Coachlight 🇲

(573) 341-2511. **$70-$155.** 1403 Martin Springs Dr 65401. Jct I-44 and Business Rt 44 S, exit 184. Ext corridors. **Pets:** Other species. $20 daily fee/pet. Designated rooms, service with restrictions, crate. (SAVE) ⊠ 🛢 🖵 ⇌

▼▼ Drury Inn-Rolla 🇭

(573) 364-4000. **$70-$114.** 2006 N Bishop Ave 65401. I-44, exit 186 (US 63), just ne. Int corridors. **Pets:** Other species. No service, supervision. (ASK) ⊠ 🛢 🖵 ⇌

▲▲▲ ▼▼▼ Super 8–Rolla–Mo Univ of Science & Technology 🇭

(573) 426-6688. **$60-$90.** 1641 Martin Springs Dr 65401. I-44, exit 184, just sw. Int corridors. **Pets:** Other species. $25 one-time fee/pet. Service with restrictions. (SAVE) ⊠ 🌢ᴹ 🛢 🖵 ⇌

ST. CLAIR

▲▲▲ ▼▼▼ Budget Lodging 🇲 🐾

(636) 629-1000. **$69-$79.** 866 S Outer Rd W 63077. I-44, exit 240, just w. Ext corridors. **Pets:** Other species. $10 daily fee/pet. Designated rooms, service with restrictions, crate. (SAVE) ⊠ 🛢 🖵 ⇌

ST. JOSEPH

▲▲▲ ▼▼▼ Best Western Classic Inn 🇲

(816) 232-2345. **$60-$80.** 4502 SE US 169 64507. I-29, exit 44, just e. Ext corridors. **Pets:** Accepted. (SAVE) ⊠ 🌢ᴹ 🛢 🖵 ⇌

▼▼▼ Drury Inn & Suites-St. Joseph 🇭

(816) 364-4700. **$75-$149.** 4213 Frederick Blvd 64506. I-29, exit 47, just e. Int corridors. **Pets:** Other species. No service, supervision. (ASK) ⊠ 🌢ᴹ 🛢 🖵 ⇌ ⊠

▼▼ Ramada and Monkey Cove Waterpark 🇭

(816) 233-6192. **$87-$149.** 4016 Frederick Ave 64506. I-29, exit 47, just w. Int corridors. **Pets:** Accepted. (ASK) ⊠ 🛢 🖵 🍽 ⇌ ⊠

▼▼ St. Joseph Holiday Inn-Riverfront 🇭 🐾

(816) 279-8000. **$85-$105.** 102 S Third St 64501. I-229, exit Edmond St northbound; exit Felix St southbound; downtown. Int corridors. **Pets:** Medium. $25 one-time fee/pet. Service with restrictions, supervision. (ASK) ⊠ 🌢ᴹ 🛢 🖵 🍽 ⇌ ⊠

ST. LOUIS METROPOLITAN AREA

BERKELEY

▲▲▲ ▼▼▼▼ Renaissance St. Louis Hotel Airport 🇭 🐾

(314) 429-1100. **$161-$197.** 9801 Natural Bridge Rd 63134. I-70, exit 237 (Natural Bridge Rd), just n; I-170, exit 6 (Natural Bridge Rd), just n. Int corridors. **Pets:** Dogs only. $50 one-time fee/room. No service, supervision. (SAVE) ⊠ 🛢 🖵 🍽 ⇌

BRIDGETON

▼▼ StudioPlus-St Louis-Earth City 🇭

(314) 209-1011. **$59-$74.** 3125 Rider Tr S 63045. I-70, exit 231B (Earth City Expwy), just n, then 0.7 mi e. Int corridors. **Pets:** Other species. $25 daily fee/room. Designated rooms, service with restrictions, crate. (ASK) ⊠ 🛢 🖵

CHESTERFIELD

▼▼▼ Drury Plaza Hotel-Chesterfield 🇭

(636) 532-3300. **$90-$299.** 355 Chesterfield Center E 63017. I-64/US 40, exit 19B (Clarkson Rd/Olive Blvd); jct I-64/US 40 and Clarkson Rd; southwest corner. Int corridors. **Pets:** Other species. No service, supervision. (ASK) ⊠ 🌢ᴹ 🛢 🖵 🍽 ⇌

▼▼▼ Homewood Suites by Hilton 🇭

(636) 530-0305. **$89-$149.** 840 N Chesterfield Pkwy W 63017. I-64, exit 20 (Chesterfield Pkwy), 1 mi n. Int corridors. **Pets:** Accepted. ⊠ 🛢 🖵 ⇌

CLAYTON

▲▲▲ ▼▼▼▼ Crowne Plaza St. Louis-Clayton 🇭 🐾

(314) 726-5400. **$99-$299.** 7750 Carondelet Ave 63105. I-64, exit 32B (Hanley Rd), 1.3 mi n, then just w. Int corridors. **Pets:** Designated rooms, service with restrictions, crate. (SAVE) ⊠ 🛢 🖵 🍽 ⇌ ⊠

▲▲▲ ▼▼▼▼ The Ritz-Carlton, St. Louis 🇭

(314) 863-6300. **$139-$525.** 100 Carondelet Plaza 63105. I-64, exit 32B (Hanley Rd), 1.2 mi n, then just e. Int corridors. **Pets:** Accepted. (SAVE) ⊠ 🖵 🍽 ⇌ ⊠

▲▲▲ ▼▼▼▼ Sheraton Clayton Plaza Hotel 🇭

(314) 863-0400. **Call for rates.** 7730 Bonhomme Ave 63105. I-64, exit 31 (Brentwood Blvd), 1.3 mi n, then 0.7 mi e. Int corridors. **Pets:** Accepted. (SAVE) ⊠ 🛢 🖵 🍽 ⇌

CREVE COEUR

▼▼▼ Drury Inn & Suites-Creve Coeur 🇭

(314) 989-1100. **$90-$174.** 11980 Olive Blvd 63141. I-270, exit 14 (Olive Blvd). Int corridors. **Pets:** Other species. No service, supervision. (ASK) ⊠ 🌢ᴹ 🛢 🖵 ⇌

EARTH CITY

▼▼▼▼ Residence Inn St. Louis Airport/Earth City 🇭 🐾

(314) 209-0995. **$144-$164.** 3290 Rider Tr S 63045. I-70, exit 231B (Earth City Expwy N), just n, then just e. Int corridors. **Pets:** Other species. $75 one-time fee/room. Service with restrictions, crate. ⊠ 🌢ᴹ 🛢 🖵 ⇌ ⊠

EDMUNDSON

▼▼▼▼ Drury Inn-St. Louis Airport 🅷

(314) 423-7700. **$80-$194.** 10490 Natural Bridge Rd 63134. I-70, exit 236 (Lambert Airport), just s, then just e. Int corridors. **Pets:** Other species. No service, supervision. (ASK) ⊠ 🕭ᴹ 🛇 💻 ⊅

EUREKA

▼▼▼▼ Holiday Inn at Six Flags 🅷

(636) 938-6661. **$99-$299.** 4901 Six Flags Rd 63025. I-44, exit 261 (Allenton Rd). Ext/int corridors. **Pets:** Accepted.

(ASK) ⊠ 🛇 💻 ❚❚ ⊅ ⊠

FENTON

▼▼▼▼ Drury Inn & Suites-Fenton 🅷

(636) 343-7822. **$80-$170.** 1088 S Highway Dr 63026. I-44, exit 274 (Bowles Ave), just se. Int corridors. **Pets:** Other species. No service, supervision. (ASK) ⊠ 🛇 💻 ⊅

▼▼ Pear Tree Inn by Drury-Fenton 🅷

(636) 343-8820. **$55-$119.** 1100 S Highway Dr 63026. I-44, exit 274 (Bowles Ave), just s. Int corridors. **Pets:** Other species. No service, supervision. (ASK) ⊠ 🛇 💻 ⊅

▼▼ TownePlace Suites by Marriott 🅷

(636) 305-7000. **$107-$131.** 1662 Fenton Business Park Ct 63026. I-44, exit 275 westbound; exit 274 eastbound to S Highway Dr, just s. Int corridors. **Pets:** Accepted. ⊠ 🕭ᴹ 🛇 💻 ⊅

FORISTELL

(AAA) ▼▼▼ Best Western West 70 Inn 🅷 🐾

(636) 673-2900. **$67-$72.** 12 Hwy W 63348. I-70, exit 203 (CR W), just n. Int corridors. **Pets:** Other species. $15 one-time fee/room. Service with restrictions, supervision. (SAVE) ⊠ 🛇 💻 ⊅

HAZELWOOD

▼▼▼ La Quinta Inn Hazelwood 🅷 🐾

(314) 731-4200. **Call for rates.** 318 Taylor Rd 63042. I-270, exit 25B (N Lindbergh Blvd), just s. Int corridors. **Pets:** Medium, other species. Service with restrictions, supervision. ⊠ 🛇 💻

▼▼▼ La Quinta Inn St. Louis (Airport) 🅷 🐾

(314) 731-3881. **Call for rates.** 5781 Campus Ct 63042. I-270, exit 23 (McDonnell Blvd), just s, just w on Campus Pkwy, then just n. Int corridors. **Pets:** Medium, other species. Service with restrictions, supervision. ⊠ 🛇 ⊅

KIRKWOOD

(AAA) ▼▼▼ Best Western Kirkwood Inn 🅷 🐾

(314) 821-3950. **$100-$120.** 1200 S Kirkwood Rd 63122. I-44, exit 277B (Lindbergh Blvd), just n. Int corridors. **Pets:** Other species. $10 daily fee/pet. Designated rooms, service with restrictions, supervision. (SAVE) ⊠ 🛇 💻 ❚❚ ⊅

MARYLAND HEIGHTS

(AAA) ▼▼▼▼ Doubletree Hotel St. Louis at Westport 🅷

(314) 434-0100. **$85-$189.** 1973 Craigshire Rd 63146. I-270, exit 16A (Page Ave), just e to Lackland Rd, then 0.4 mi sw on Lackland and Craigshire rds. Int corridors. **Pets:** Accepted.

(ECO) (SAVE) ⊠ 🕭ᴹ 🛇 💻 ❚❚ ⊅ ⊠

▼▼▼ Drury Inn & Suites-St. Louis-Westport 🅷

(314) 576-9966. **$75-$159.** 12220 Dorsett Rd 63043. I-270, exit 17 (Dorsett Rd), just e. Int corridors. **Pets:** Other species. No service, supervision. (ASK) ⊠ 🛇 💻 ⊅

▼▼▼▼ Residence Inn by Marriott–Westport 🅷

(314) 469-0060. **$152-$186.** 1881 Craigshire Rd 63146. I-270, exit 16A (Page Ave), 0.8 mi e, just w on Lackland Rd, just s on Craig Rd, then just w. Ext corridors. **Pets:** Accepted. ⊠ 🛇 💻 ⊅ ⊠

(AAA) ▼▼▼▼ Sheraton Westport Plaza Tower 🅷

(314) 878-1500. **Call for rates.** 900 Westport Plaza 63146. I-270, exit 16A (Page Ave), 0.8 mi e; exit Lackland Rd, just w, then just n. Int corridors. **Pets:** Accepted. (SAVE) ⊠ 🕭ᴹ 🛇 💻 ❚❚ ⊅ ⊠

▼▼▼▼ Staybridge Suites 🅷

(314) 878-1555. **$79-$189.** 1855 Craigshire Rd 63146. I-270, exit 16A (Page Ave), 0.8 mi e, exit Lackland Rd, 1 mi w, 0.4 mi s on Craig Rd, then just e. Ext/int corridors. **Pets:** Large. $150 one-time fee/room. Service with restrictions, crate. (ASK) ⊠ 🛇 💻 ⊅ ⊠

MEHLVILLE

▼▼▼▼ Holiday Inn St. Louis-South I-55 🅷

(314) 894-0700. **$84-$139.** 4234 Butler Hill Rd 63129. I-55, exit 195 (Butler Hill Rd), just e, then just s. Ext/int corridors. **Pets:** Accepted.

(ASK) ⊠ 🛇 💻 ❚❚ ⊅ ⊠

O'FALLON

▼▼▼▼ Hilton Garden Inn St. Louis/O'Fallon 🅷

(636) 625-2700. **$79-$169.** 2310 Technology Dr 63368. US 40/61, exit 6 (Wing Haven Blvd/CR DD), just ne; I-70, exit 216 (Bryan Rd), 4.2 mi s. Int corridors. **Pets:** Accepted. ⊠ 🕭ᴹ 🛇 💻 ❚❚ ⊅

▼▼▼▼ Staybridge Suites O'Fallon 🅷

(636) 300-0999. **$91-$137.** 1155 Technology Dr 63368. I-64/US 40, exit 9 (CR K), just nw. Int corridors. **Pets:** Medium, other species. $100 one-time fee/room. Service with restrictions, crate.

(ASK) ⊠ 🛇 💻 ⊅

RICHMOND HEIGHTS

▼▼▼▼ Residence Inn By Marriott-St. Louis Galleria 🅷 🐾

(314) 862-1900. **$139-$159.** 1100 McMorrow Ave 63117. I-170, exit 1C (Brentwood Blvd) northbound; exit 1D southbound, just s, just e on Galleria Pkwy, then just s. Ext corridors. **Pets:** Other species. $100 one-time fee/room. Service with restrictions. (ECO) ⊠ 🕭ᴹ 🛇 💻 ⊅ ⊠

ST. ANN

▼▼▼▼ Hampton Inn-St. Louis Airport 🅷

(314) 429-2000. **$79-$159.** 10820 Pear Tree Ln 63074. I-70, exit 236 (Airport Dr), just sw. Int corridors. **Pets:** Accepted. ⊠ 🛇 💻 ⊅

▼▼▼ Pear Tree Inn by Drury-St. Louis Airport 🅷

(314) 427-3400. **$70-$139.** 10810 Pear Tree Ln 63074. I-70, exit 236 (Airport Dr), just sw. Int corridors. **Pets:** Other species. No service, supervision. (ASK) ⊠ 🛇 💻 ⊅

ST. CHARLES

▼▼▼▼ Comfort Suites-St. Charles 🅷 🐾

(636) 949-0694. **Call for rates.** 1400 S 5th St 63301. I-70, exit 229 (5th St), just ne. Int corridors. **Pets:** Large. Service with restrictions, supervision. ⊠ 🛇 💻 ⊅

(AAA) ▼▼▼▼ Country Inn & Suites By Carlson 🅷

(636) 724-5555. **$120-$152.** 1190 S Main St 63301. I-70, exit 229A (5th St S) to S Main St, then 0.7 mi ne. Int corridors. **Pets:** Accepted. (SAVE) ⊠ 🛇 💻 ⊅ ⊠

▼▼ Red Roof Inn 🅷

(636) 947-7770. **$40-$77.** 2010 Zumbehl Rd 63303. I-70, exit 227 (Zumbehl Rd), just se. Ext corridors. **Pets:** Large. Service with restrictions, crate. (ASK) ⊠ 🕭ᴹ 🛇

▼▼▼ TownePlace Suites by Marriott 🅷 🐾

(636) 949-6800. **$80-$98.** 1800 Zumbehl Rd 63303. I-70, exit 227 (Zumbehl Rd), 0.6 mi s, just se. Int corridors. **Pets:** Other species. $75 one-time fee/room. Service with restrictions, supervision. ⊠ 🛇 💻 ⊅

ST. LOUIS

Best Western St. Louis Inn H
(314) 416-7639. **$55-$89.** 6224 Heimos Industrial Park Dr 63129. I-55, exit 193, just e on Meramec Bottom Rd, then just n. Int corridors. **Pets:** Large, other species. $10 daily fee/pet. Designated rooms, service with restrictions, supervision. SAVE ⊠ 🔒 💻 🐾

Drury Inn & Suites Near Forest Park H
(314) 646-0770. **$95-$229.** 2111 Sulphur Ave 63139. I-44, exit 286, just s. Int corridors. **Pets:** Other species. No service, supervision.
ASK ⊠ 🔥 🔒 💻 🍽 🐾

Drury Inn & Suites-St. Louis-Convention Center H
(314) 231-8100. **$90-$204.** 711 N Broadway 63102. I-70, exit 250B (Stadium/Memorial Dr), at convention center. Int corridors. **Pets:** Other species. No service, supervision. ASK ⊠ 🔒 💻 🍽 🐾 🐕

Drury Inn-St. Louis/Union Station H
(314) 231-3900. **$100-$189.** 201 S 20th St 63103. Just e of Jefferson Ave; between Market St and Clark Ave. Int corridors. **Pets:** Other species. No service, supervision. ASK ⊠ 🔒 💻 🍽 🐾

Drury Plaza Hotel-St. Louis At the Arch H
(314) 231-3003. **$105-$289.** 4th & Market Sts 63102. I-70, exit 250B (Stadium/Memorial Dr), just w on Pine St to Broadway, just s to Walnut St, just e to 4th St, then just n. Int corridors. **Pets:** Other species. No service, supervision. SAVE ⊠ 🔥 🔒 💻 🐾

Four Seasons Hotel St. Louis H
(314) 881-5800. **$195-$3000.** 999 N 2nd St 63102. I-70, exit 250A, just s, 1.1 mi e, then just s. Int corridors. **Pets:** Accepted.
SAVE ⊠ 🔥 💻 🍽 🐾 🐕

Hilton St. Louis at the Ballpark H
(314) 421-1776. **$109-$259.** 1 S Broadway 63102. Between Walnut and Market sts. Int corridors. **Pets:** Accepted.
SAVE ⊠ 🔥 🔒 💻 🍽 🐾 🐕

Hilton-St. Louis Downtown H 🐾
(314) 436-0002. **$99-$189.** 400 Olive St 63102. I-70, exit 249C/251C (6th St) to N Broadway to Olive St. Int corridors. **Pets:** Medium. $75 one-time fee/room. Service with restrictions, supervision.
⊠ 🔥 🔒 💻 🍽 🐕

Millennium Hotel St. Louis H 🐾
(314) 241-9500. **$99-$299.** 200 S 4th St 63102. Jct Market St, just s. Int corridors. **Pets:** Designated rooms, service with restrictions.
SAVE ⊠ 🔒 💻 🍽 🐾

Omni Majestic Hotel H
(314) 436-2355. **$159-$349.** 1019 Pine St 63101. Jct N Broadway, just w; at 10th St. Int corridors. **Pets:** Accepted. ASK ⊠ 💻 🍽

The Parkway Hotel H
(314) 256-7777. **$117-$269.** 4550 Forest Park Blvd 63108. I-64, exit 36 (Kingshighway Blvd), 0.6 mi n, then just e. Int corridors. **Pets:** Medium. $20 daily fee/pet. Designated rooms, service with restrictions.
SAVE ⊠ 🔥 🔒 💻 🍽

Pear Tree Inn–St. Louis/Union Station H
(314) 241-3200. **$85-$159.** 2211 Market St 63103. I-64/US 40, exit 39, just n on Jefferson Ave, then just e. Int corridors. **Pets:** Other species. No service, supervision. ASK ⊠ 🔒 💻 🍽 🐾

Sheraton St. Louis City Center Hotel & Suites H
(314) 231-5007. **$109-$429.** 400 S 14th St 63103. I-64, exit 39B (14th St) eastbound, just n; exit 40A westbound, just n, just w on Clark Ave, then just s. Int corridors. **Pets:** Accepted.
SAVE ⊠ 🔥 🔒 💻 🍽 🐾

The Westin St. Louis H 🐾
(314) 621-2000. **$119-$399.** 811 Spruce St 63102. I-64, exit 39C eastbound, just n on 8th St, then just e; exit 40A westbound, just n, just e on Clark Ave, just s on 8th St, then just w. Int corridors. **Pets:** Medium, dogs only. Service with restrictions, supervision.
SAVE ⊠ 🔥 💻 🍽

ST. PETERS

Drury Inn St. Peters H
(636) 397-9700. **$85-$169.** 170 Mid Rivers Mall Dr 63376. I-70, exit 222 (Mid Rivers Mall Dr), just se. Int corridors. **Pets:** Other species. No service, supervision. ASK ⊠ 🔥 🔒 💻 🐾

SUNSET HILLS

Holiday Inn-Southwest & Viking Conference Center H
(314) 821-6600. **$99-$139.** 10709 Watson Rd 63127. I-44, exit 277B, just s. Int corridors. **Pets:** Accepted. SAVE ⊠ 🔒 💻 🍽 🐾 🐕

VALLEY PARK

Drury Inn & Suites-St. Louis Southwest H
(636) 861-8300. **$80-$179.** 5 Lambert Drury Pl 63088. I-44, exit 272 (SR 141), just sw. Int corridors. **Pets:** Other species. No service, supervision.
ASK ⊠ 🔒 💻 🐾

Hampton Inn-St. Louis Southwest H
(636) 529-9020. **$94-$124.** 9 Lambert Drury Pl 63088. I-44, exit 272 (SR 141), just sw. Int corridors. **Pets:** Medium. Service with restrictions, supervision. ⊠ 🔒 💻 🐾

END METROPOLITAN AREA

ST. ROBERT

Baymont Inn & Suites Ft. Leonard Wood-St. Robert H
(573) 336-5050. **$80-$153.** 139 Carmel Valley Way 65584. I-44, exit 161, just nw. Int corridors. **Pets:** Small, other species. $50 deposit/pet, $10 daily fee/pet. Service with restrictions, supervision.
ASK ⊠ 🔒 💻 🐾

Best Western Montis Inn H
(573) 336-4299. **$75-$85.** 14086 Hwy Z 65584. I-44, exit 163, just s. Ext corridors. **Pets:** Accepted. SAVE ⊠ 🔒 💻 🐾

MainStay Suites H
(573) 451-2700. **$92-$160.** 227 St. Robert Blvd 65584. I-44, exit 159, 0.8 mi nw. Ext/int corridors. **Pets:** Other species. $15 daily fee/room. Service with restrictions, crate. ECO ASK ⊠ 🔒 💻 🐾

STE. GENEVIEVE

Microtel Inn & Suites H
(573) 883-8884. **$69-$84.** 21958 Hwy 32 63670. I-55, exit 150 (SR 32), 3.9 mi e. Int corridors. **Pets:** Large. $10 daily fee/room. Service with restrictions, crate. SAVE ⊠ 🔥 🔒 💻

SEDALIA

Best Western State Fair Inn H
(660) 826-6100. **$72-$149.** 3120 S Limit Ave 65301. Jct US 50, 1.5 mi s on US 65. Ext/int corridors. **Pets:** Medium. Designated rooms, service with restrictions, crate. SAVE ⊠ 🔒 💻 🍽 🐕

Hotel Bothwell, an Ascend Collection hotel H
(660) 826-5588. **Call for rates.** 103 E 4th St 65301. Corner of 4th and S Ohio sts; downtown. Int corridors. **Pets:** Accepted. ⊠ 💻 🍽

SPRINGFIELD

▼▼▼▼ Baymont Inn & Suites Airport Plaza 🅷 ❄
(417) 447-4466. **$75-$135.** 2445 N Airport Plaza Ave 65803. I-44, exit 77, just se. Int corridors. **Pets:** Medium, other species. $10 one-time fee/pet. Service with restrictions, supervision. 🅰🆂🅺 ⊠ 🛢 🖃 ⇌

◈ ▼▼ Best Western Deerfield Inn 🅷
(417) 887-2323. **$70-$80.** 3343 E Battlefield St 65804. US 65, exit Battlefield St, just w. Int corridors. **Pets:** Accepted. 🆂🅰🆅🅴 ⊠ 🛢 🖃 ⇌

◈ ▼▼▼ Candlewood Suites South 🅷
(417) 881-8500. **$99-$129.** 1035 E Republic Rd 65807. US 60, exit National Ave, just s. Int corridors. **Pets:** Accepted.
🆂🅰🆅🅴 ⊠ ♿ 🛢 🖃

◈ ▼▼▼ Candlewood Suites Springfield I-44 🅷
(417) 866-4242. **$99-$129.** 1920 E Kerr St 65803. I-44, exit 80A, just e to Evergreen St. Int corridors. **Pets:** Accepted. 🆂🅰🆅🅴 ⊠ ♿ 🛢 🖃

◈ ▼▼▼ Clarion Hotel & Conference Center 🅷
(417) 883-6550. **$80-$100.** 3333 S Glenstone Ave 65804. On US 60 (James River Expwy), 0.5 mi n. Int corridors. **Pets:** Accepted.
🆂🅰🆅🅴 ⊠ ♿ 🛢 🖃 🍽 ⇌

◈ ▼▼▼ Courtyard by Marriott Airport 🅷
(417) 869-6700. **$121-$147.** 3527 W Kearney 65803. I-44, exit 75 (US 160 W Bypass), just se to SR 744, then just w. Int corridors.
Pets: Accepted. 🆂🅰🆅🅴 ⊠ ♿ 🛢 🖃 ⇌

▼▼ ▼▼ Days Inn Battlefield 🅷 🐾
(417) 882-9484. **$66-$87.** 3260 E Montclair St 65804. US 65, exit Battlefield Rd, just w to Moulder Ave, then just sw. Int corridors. **Pets:** Other species. Service with restrictions, supervision.
🅰🆂🅺 ⊠ 🛢 🖃 ⇌

▼▼▼ Drury Inn & Suites-Springfield 🅷
(417) 863-8400. **$95-$184.** 2715 N Glenstone Ave 65803. I-44, exit 80A (Glenstone Ave), just s. Int corridors. **Pets:** Other species. No service, supervision. 🅰🆂🅺 ⊠ ♿ 🛢 🖃 ⇌

◈ ▼▼▼ Greenstay Hotel & Suites 🅷
(417) 863-1440. **$79-$112.** 222 N Ingram Mill Rd 65802. I-65, exit Chestnut Expwy, just sw. Ext/int corridors. **Pets:** Medium. $10 one-time fee/room. Designated rooms, service with restrictions, crate.
🆂🅰🆅🅴 ⊠ 🛢 🖃 ⇌

◈ ▼▼ La Quinta Inn-Springfield South 🅷 ❄
(417) 890-6060. **Call for rates.** 2535 S Campbell Ave 65807. Jct Battlefield Rd and Campbell Ave, 0.5 mi n. Int corridors. **Pets:** Medium, other species. Service with restrictions, supervision. 🆂🅰🆅🅴 ⊠ 🛢 🖃 ⇌

◈ ▼▼▼ Quality Inn & Suites 🅷
(417) 888-0898. **$85-$129.** 3930 S Overland Ave 65807. US 60 (James River Expwy), exit Kansas Expwy, just n to Chesterfield Blvd, then just w. Int corridors. **Pets:** Accepted. 🆂🅰🆅🅴 ⊠ ♿ 🛢 🖃 ⇌

◈ ▼▼▼ Quality Inn & Suites 🅷 ❄
(417) 869-0001. **$70-$120.** 2745 N Glenstone Ave 65803. I-44, exit 80A, just sw. Ext/int corridors. **Pets:** Other species. $10 daily fee/pet. Designated rooms, service with restrictions, crate. 🆂🅰🆅🅴 ⊠ 🛢 🖃 ⇌

▼▼ ▼▼ Sleep Inn of Springfield 🅷
(417) 886-2464. **$75-$90.** 233 El Camino Alto 65810. US 60 (James River Expwy), exit Campbell Ave, just se. Int corridors. **Pets:** Medium, other species. $20 one-time fee/room. Designated rooms, service with restrictions, supervision. 🅰🆂🅺 ⊠ 🛢 🖃 ⇌

◈ ▼▼▼▼ Springfield Doubletree 🅷 🐾
(417) 831-3131. **$89-$179.** 2431 N Glenstone Ave 65803. I-44, exit 80A, just s. Int corridors. **Pets:** Medium. $10 daily fee/room.
🆂🅰🆅🅴 ⊠ ♿ 🛢 🖃 🍽 ⇌

▼▼▼▼ University Plaza Hotel and Convention Center 🅷
(417) 864-7333. **$89-$189, 3 day notice.** 333 John Q Hammons Pkwy 65806. 0.5 mi e on St. Louis St. Int corridors. **Pets:** Accepted.
⊠ ♿ 🛢 🖃 🍽 ⇌

SULLIVAN

▼▼ Baymont Inn 🅷
(573) 860-3333. **$99.** 275 N Service Rd W 63080. I-44, exit 225. Int corridors. **Pets:** $10 one-time fee/pet. Service with restrictions, supervision.
🅰🆂🅺 ⊠ 🛢 🖃 ⇌

◈ ▼▼▼ Comfort Inn 🅷
(573) 468-7800. **Call for rates.** 736 S Service Rd W 63080. I-44, exit 225, just sw. Int corridors. **Pets:** Accepted. 🆂🅰🆅🅴 ⊠ 🛢 🖃 ⇌

TRENTON

▼▼ Trenton Knights Inn 🅷
(660) 359-2988. **$66-$79.** 1845A E 28th St 64683. US 65, 1 mi n of jct SR 6 and US 65. Int corridors. **Pets:** $50 daily fee/room. No service, supervision. 🅰🆂🅺 ⊠ 🛢

UNION

▼▼ Super 8 🅷
(636) 583-8808. **$78-$125.** 1015 E Main St 63084. I-44, exit 247 (US 50), 4.7 mi w; just w of jct SR 47. Int corridors. **Pets:** Small, dogs only. $10 daily fee/pet. Service with restrictions, supervision.
🅰🆂🅺 ⊠ ♿ 🛢 🖃 ⇌

WASHINGTON

▼▼ Sleep Inn & Suites 🅷
(636) 390-8877. **$90-$160.** 2621 E 5th St 63090. I-44, exit 251, 8.5 mi w on SR 100. Int corridors. **Pets:** Medium, dogs only. $25 daily fee/pet. Designated rooms, service with restrictions, crate.
🅰🆂🅺 ⊠ 🛢 🖃 ⊠

▼▼ Super 8 Washington 🅷
(636) 390-0088. **$77-$125.** 2081 Eckelkamp Ct 63090. I-44, exit 251, 10 mi w on SR 100, just s of SR 100 and 47. Int corridors. **Pets:** Small, dogs only. $25 deposit/pet, $10 daily fee/pet. Service with restrictions, supervision. 🅰🆂🅺 ⊠ 🛢 🖃

WEST PLAINS

▼▼ Super 8-West Plains 🅷
(417) 256-8088. **$55-$70.** 1210 Porter Wagoner Blvd 65775. On US 63B, 0.8 mi s of jct US 63. Int corridors. **Pets:** Accepted. 🅰🆂🅺 ⊠ 🛢 🖃

MONTANA

ALBERTON

▼▼▼ The Ghost Rails Inn B & B ⒝⒝
(406) 722-4990. $79-$99, 3 day notice. 702 Railroad Ave 59820.
Downtown. Int corridors. Pets: Accepted. (ASK) ⊠ 🕭 🕿

BELGRADE

▼▼▼ Gallatin River Lodge ⒞⒤
(406) 388-0148. $170-$450, 7 day notice. 9105 Thorpe Rd 59718. I-90, exit 298, 2.7 mi s on SR 85, 1 mi w on Valley Center Rd (gravel), then 0.5 mi s, follow sign. Int corridors. Pets: $20 daily fee/room. Designated rooms, service with restrictions, supervision. (ASK) ⊠ 🖳 ¶ ⊠

◈◈◈ ▼▼▼ Holiday Inn Express ⒣
(406) 388-0800. $69-$159. 6261 Jackrabbit Ln 59714. I-90, exit 298, just s on SR 85. Int corridors. Pets: Other species. $50 deposit/pet. Service with restrictions, supervision. (SAVE) ⊠ 🕭M 🕭 🖳 ¶

▼▼▼ La Quinta Inn & Suites Belgrade
(Bozeman/Belgrade) ⒣ ❁
(406) 388-1493. $109-$285, 7 day notice. 6445 Jackrabbit Ln 59714. I-90, exit 298, just s on SR 85. Int corridors. Pets: Medium, other species. Service with restrictions, supervision. ⊠ 🕭 🖳 ➷ ⊠

◈◈◈ ▼▼▼ Super 8-Belgrade/Bozeman Airport ⒣
(406) 388-1493. $65-$125. 6450 Jackrabbit Ln 59714. I-90, exit 298, just s on SR 85. Int corridors. Pets: Other species. $10 daily fee/pet. Designated rooms, supervision. (SAVE) ⊠ 🕭 🖳 ➷

BIGFORK

◈◈◈ ▼▼▼ Mountain Lake Lodge ⒣ ❁
(406) 837-3800. Call for rates, 7 day notice. 14735 Sylvan Dr 59911. On US 35, 5 mi s. Ext corridors. Pets: Other species. $15 daily fee/pet. Designated rooms, service with restrictions, supervision.
(SAVE) ⊠ 🕭M 🕭 🖳 ¶ ➷ ⊠

◈◈◈ ▼▼▼ Timbers Motel Ⓜ ❁
(406) 837-6200. $58-$124, 7 day notice. 8540 Hwy 35 59911. Just n on US 35 from jct SR 209. Ext corridors. Pets: $10 daily fee/pet. Designated rooms, service with restrictions, supervision.
(SAVE) ⊠ 🕭 🖳 ➷

BIG SKY

◈◈◈ ▼▼▼▼ Buck's T-4 Lodge ⒣
(406) 995-4111. $99-$159, 14 day notice. 46625 Gallatin Rd 59716. US 191, 1 mi s of Big Sky entrance. Ext/int corridors. Pets: Large, other species. $10 daily fee/pet. Service with restrictions, supervision.
(SAVE) ⊠ 🕭 🖳 ¶ ⊠

◈◈◈ ▼▼▼▼ Rainbow Ranch Lodge ⒣ ❁
(406) 995-4132. $215-$400. 42950 Gallatin Rd 59730. 5 mi s on US 191. Ext corridors. Pets: Large. $25 daily fee/pet. Designated rooms, service with restrictions, supervision.
(SAVE) ⊠ 🕭 🖳 ¶ ⊠ 🕭

BIG TIMBER

▼▼▼ Big Timber Super 8 ⒣
(406) 932-8888. $70-$140. 20A Big Timber Loop Rd 59011. I-90, exit 367. Int corridors. Pets: Medium, other species. $10 daily fee/pet. Designated rooms, service with restrictions, supervision.
(ASK) ⊠ 🕭M 🕭 🖳

▼▼▼ River Valley Inn ⒣
(406) 932-4943. $68-$90. 600 W 2nd St 59011. I-90, exit 367, just n, then 0.6 mi e. Int corridors. Pets: Small, other species. $20 one-time fee/room. Designated rooms, service with restrictions, supervision.
⊠ 🕭

BILLINGS

◈◈◈ ▼▼▼▼ Best Western Clocktower Inn ⒣ ❁
(406) 259-5511. $99-$119. 2511 1st Ave N 59101. On I-90 business loop; downtown. Ext/int corridors. Pets: Other species. $15 daily fee/pet. Service with restrictions, supervision. (SAVE) ⊠ 🕭 🖳 ¶ ➷

◈◈◈ ▼▼▼▼ Best Western Kelly Inn & Suites ⒣ ❁
(406) 256-9400. $95-$350. 4915 Southgate Dr 59101. I-90, exit 447, just w. Ext/int corridors. Pets: Large, other species. Designated rooms, service with restrictions, supervision. (SAVE) ⊠ 🕭M 🕭 🖳 ➷

▼▼▼▼ Billings Hotel and Convention Center ⒣
(406) 248-7151. $59-$139. 1223 Mullowney Ln 59101. I-90, exit 446, just s. Int corridors. Pets: Medium. $20 daily fee/room. Designated rooms, no service, supervision. (ASK) ⊠ 🕭 🖳 ¶ ➷ ⊠

◈◈◈ ▼▼▼ Billings Sleep Inn ⒣
(406) 254-0013. $60-$209. 4904 Southgate Dr 59101. I-90, exit 447, just w. Int corridors. Pets: Other species. $15 daily fee/pet. Service with restrictions, supervision. (SAVE) ⊠ 🕭M 🖳

▼▼▼ Billings Super 8 ⒣
(406) 248-8842. $35-$99. 5400 Southgate Dr 59102. I-90, exit 447, just n on S Billings Blvd, 0.8 mi w on King Ave, then just s on Parkway Ln. Int corridors. Pets: Small. $10 one-time fee/room. Designated rooms, service with restrictions, supervision. (ASK) ⊠ 🕭M 🕭 🖳

◈◈◈ ▼▼▼ Cherry Tree Inn ⒣
(406) 252-5603. $61. 823 N Broadway 59101. I-90, exit 450, 2 mi n on 27th St, then just w on 9th Ave. Int corridors. Pets: Accepted.
(SAVE) ⊠ 🕭 🖳

▼▼▼ Clubhouse Inn & Suites ⒣ ❁
(406) 248-9800. Call for rates. 5610 S Frontage Rd 59101. I-90, exit 446, just s. Ext/int corridors. Pets: Designated rooms, service with restrictions, supervision. ⊠ 🕭M 🕭 🖳 ➷

▼▼▼ Comfort Inn by Choice Hotels ⒣
(406) 652-5200. Call for rates. 2030 Overland Ave 59102. I-90, exit 446, 0.5 mi n, then just s. Int corridors. Pets: Accepted.
⊠ 🕭M 🕭 🖳 ➷

▼▼ Days Inn 🇭

(406) 252-4007. **$65-$98.** 843 Parkway Ln 59101. I-90, exit 447, just n on S Billings Blvd, 0.8 mi w on King Ave, then just s. Int corridors. **Pets:** Accepted. (ASK) ⊠ 🔋 🖥

▼▼ Extended StayAmerica-Billings-West End 🇭

(406) 245-3980. **$79-$85.** 4950 Southgate Dr 59101. I-90, exit 447, just w. Int corridors. **Pets:** Other species. $25 daily fee/room. Designated rooms, service with restrictions, crate. (ASK) ⊠ ⓜ 🔋 🖥

◈ ▼▼ Hilltop Inn 🇭

(406) 245-5000. **$70-$80.** 1116 N 28th St 59101. I-90, exit 450, 2 mi n on 27th St, just w on 11th Ave, then just n. Int corridors. **Pets:** Other species. $7 daily fee/pet. Designated rooms, service with restrictions, supervision. (SAVE) ⊠ ⓜ 🔋 🖥

◈ ▼▼▼ Holiday Inn Grand Montana Billings 🇭

(406) 248-7701. **$129-$159.** 5500 Midland Rd 59101. I-90, exit 446. Int corridors. **Pets:** Accepted. (SAVE) ⊠ ⓜ 🔋 🖥 🍴 🏊 🐾

◈ ▼▼ Kelly Inn 🇭

(406) 252-2700. **$69-$129.** 5425 Midland Rd 59101. I-90, exit 446, just se. Ext/int corridors. **Pets:** Accepted. (ASK) ⊠ 🔋 🖥 🏊

▼▼▼ La Quinta Inn & Suites 🇭 🐾

(406) 294-9090. **$79-$134.** 3040 King Ave W 59102. I-90, exit 446, 3 mi n. Int corridors. **Pets:** Medium, other species. Service with restrictions, supervision. ⊠ ⓜ 🔋 🖥 🏊

▼ Motel 6 #178 🅼

(406) 252-0093. **$49-$75.** 5400 Midland Rd 59101. I-90, exit 446, just se. Ext corridors. **Pets:** Other species. Service with restrictions, supervision. ⊠ ⓜ

▼▼▼ Quality Inn Homestead 🇭

(406) 652-1320. **Call for rates.** 2036 Overland Ave 59102. I-90, exit 446, 0.5 mi n, then just s. Int corridors. **Pets:** Other species. $5 daily fee/room. Service with restrictions, supervision. ⊠ 🔋 🖥 🏊 🐾

▼▼ Red Roof Inn #269 🇭

(406) 248-7551. **Call for rates.** 5353 Midland Rd 59102. I-90, exit 446, just se. Int corridors. **Pets:** Large. Service with restrictions, crate. ⊠ ⓜ 🔋 🏊

▼▼▼ Residence Inn by Marriott 🇭 🐾

(406) 656-3900. **$134-$164.** 956 S 25th St W 59102. I-90, exit 446, 1.5 mi w, just s on S 24th St, then just s; behind The Home Depot. Int corridors. **Pets:** Medium, other species. $75 one-time fee/room. Designated rooms, supervision. ⊠ ⓜ 🔋 🖥 🏊 🐾

◈ ▼▼ Riverstone Billings Inn 🇭

(406) 252-6800. **$70-$80.** 880 N 29th St 59101. I-90, exit 450, 2 mi n on 27th St, then just w on 9th Ave. Int corridors. **Pets:** Other species. $7 daily fee/pet. Designated rooms, service with restrictions, supervision. (SAVE) ⊠ 🔋 🖥

◈ ▼▼ Western Executive Inn 🇭

(406) 294-8888. **$60-$120.** 3121 King Ave W 59102. I-90, exit 446, 2.5 mi w. Int corridors. **Pets:** Medium. $10 daily fee/pet. Service with restrictions, supervision. (SAVE) ⊠ ⓜ 🔋 🖥

◈ ▼ Westwood's Rimview Inn 🅼

(406) 248-2622. **Call for rates.** 1025 N 27th St 59101. I-90, exit 450, 2 mi n. Ext/int corridors. **Pets:** Small, dogs only. $10 daily fee/pet. Service with restrictions, supervision. (SAVE) ⊠ 🔋 🖥

BOZEMAN

▼▼▼ AmericInn Lodge & Suites of Bozeman 🇭

(406) 522-8686. **$99-$189.** 1121 Reeves Rd W 59718. I-90, exit 305, just n. Int corridors. **Pets:** Dogs only. $20 daily fee/pet. Designated rooms, service with restrictions, supervision. (ASK) ⊠ ⓜ 🔋 🖥 🏊 🐾

◈ ▼▼▼ Best Western GranTree Inn 🇭

(406) 587-5261. **$89-$159.** 1325 N 7th Ave 59715. I-90, exit 306, just s. Int corridors. **Pets:** Service with restrictions, supervision. (SAVE) ⊠ 🔋 🖥 🍴 🏊 🐾

▼▼ Bozeman Days Inn & Suites 🇭 🐾

(406) 587-5251. **Call for rates.** 1321 N 7th Ave 59715. I-90, exit 306, just s. Int corridors. **Pets:** Other species. $5 daily fee/pet. Supervision. ⊠ 🔋 🖥 🏊 🐾

◈ ▼▼ Bozeman Inn 🅼

(406) 587-3176. **$48-$88.** 1235 N 7th Ave 59715. I-90, exit 306, just s. Ext corridors. **Pets:** Large. $5 one-time fee/room. Service with restrictions, supervision. (SAVE) ⊠ 🔋 🖥 🏊

▼▼ Bozeman's Western Heritage Inn 🇭 🐾

(406) 586-8534. **$58-$98.** 1200 E Main St 59715. I-90 business loop, exit 309, 0.5 mi w. Int corridors. **Pets:** Dogs only. $5 daily fee/pet. Service with restrictions, supervision. (ASK) ⊠ 🔋 🖥

▼▼ Holiday Inn Bozeman 🇭 🐾

(406) 587-4561. **$59-$159.** 5 E Baxter Ln 59715. I-90, exit 306, just s. Int corridors. **Pets:** Service with restrictions, supervision. (ASK) ⊠ 🔋 🖥 🍴 🏊 🐾

▼▼ Microtel Inn & Suites 🇭

(406) 586-3797. **Call for rates.** 612 Nikles Dr 59715. I-90, exit 306, just ne. Int corridors. **Pets:** Accepted. ⊠ 🔋 🖥 🏊

◈ ▼ Rainbow Motel 🅼

(406) 587-4201. **$50-$75.** 510 N 7th Ave 59715. I-90, exit 306, 0.8 mi s. Ext corridors. **Pets:** Accepted. (SAVE) ⊠ 🔋 🖥 🏊

◈ ▼▼▼ Ramada Limited 🇭

(406) 585-2626. **$65-$125, 3 day notice.** 2020 Wheat Dr 59715. I-90, exit 306, just n, then just w. Ext/int corridors. **Pets:** Accepted. (SAVE) ⊠ 🔋 🖥 🏊

▼▼ Rodeway Inn 🇭

(406) 585-7888. **Call for rates.** 817 Wheat Dr 59718. I-90, exit 306, just n. Int corridors. **Pets:** Other species. $15 daily fee/pet. Service with restrictions, supervision. ⊠ ⓜ 🔋 🖥

◈ ▼▼▼ Royal "7" Budget Inn 🅼 🐾

(406) 587-3103. **$52-$64.** 310 N 7th Ave 59715. I-90, exit 306, 0.8 mi s. Ext corridors. **Pets:** Other species. $3 one-time fee/pet. Designated rooms, supervision. (SAVE) ⊠ 🔋 🖥

◈ ▼ Super 8 🇭

(406) 586-1521. **$59-$109.** 800 Wheat Dr 59715. I-90, exit 306, just n, then just w. Int corridors. **Pets:** Dogs only. $10 one-time fee/room. Service with restrictions, supervision. (SAVE) ⊠ 🖥

BROWNING

◈ ▼ Western Motel LLC 🅼

(406) 338-7572. **$49-$160, 4 day notice.** 121 Central Ave E 59417. On US 2; center. Ext corridors. **Pets:** Accepted. (SAVE) ⊠ 🔋

BUTTE

◈ ▼▼▼ Best Western Butte Plaza Inn 🇭

(406) 494-3500. **$113-$160.** 2900 Harrison Ave 59701. I-90/15, exit 127 (Harrison Ave). Int corridors. **Pets:** Accepted. (SAVE) ⊠ 🔋 🖥 🍴 🏊 🐾

◈ ▼▼▼ Butte War Bonnet Hotel 🇭

(406) 494-7800. **$95-$189.** 2100 Cornell Ave 59701. I-90/15, exit 127B (Harrison Ave), just n, then just e. Int corridors. **Pets:** Small. $25 deposit/room, $10 one-time fee/room. Service with restrictions. (SAVE) ⊠ 🔋 🖥 🍴 🏊 🐾

Comfort Inn of Butte H ❀
(406) 494-8850. **$89-$155.** 2777 Harrison Ave 59701. I-90/15, exit 127 (Harrison Ave), just s. Int corridors. **Pets:** Other species. $10 daily fee/pet. Service with restrictions, supervision. SAVE ☒ 🖥 💻 ➳ ☒

Days Inn H
(406) 494-7000. **Call for rates.** 2700 Harrison Ave 59701. I-90/15, exit 127 (Harrison Ave), just n. Int corridors. **Pets:** Accepted.
☒ 🖥 🖥 💻 ➳

Rocker Inn M
(406) 723-5464. **$46-$57.** 122001 W Brown's Gulch Rd 59701. I-90/15, exit 122 (Rocker Rd). Int corridors. **Pets:** Medium. $7 daily fee/room. Designated rooms, service with restrictions, supervision. SAVE ☒ 🖥

Super 8 of Butte H
(406) 494-6000. **$75-$99.** 2929 Harrison Ave 59701. I-90/15, exit 127 (Harrison Ave), just s. Int corridors. **Pets:** Medium. $15 daily fee/pet. Designated rooms, service with restrictions, supervision. SAVE ☒ 🖥 💻

CHINOOK
Chinook Motor Inn M ❀
(406) 357-2248. **$69-$79.** 100 Indiana St 59523. On US 2. Int corridors. **Pets:** Other species. $5 daily fee/pet. Service with restrictions, supervision. SAVE ☒

COLUMBUS
Super 8 of Columbus H
(406) 322-4101. **$70-$140.** 602 8th Ave N 59019. I-90, exit 408, just s on SR 78. Int corridors. **Pets:** $10 daily fee/pet. Service with restrictions, supervision. SAVE ☒ 🖥 🖥 💻

CONRAD
Super 8 H
(406) 278-7676. **$70-$87.** 215 N Main St 59425. I-15, exit 339, just w. Int corridors. **Pets:** Other species. $10 daily fee/pet. Service with restrictions, crate. ASK ☒ 🖥 💻

COOKE CITY
Elk Horn Lodge M
(406) 838-2332. **$69-$119, 7 day notice.** 103 Main St 59020. Center. Ext corridors. **Pets:** $10 daily fee/pet. Designated rooms, crate.
☒ 🖥 💻 ☒ ☒

CUT BANK
Cut Bank Super 8 M
(406) 873-5662. **$68-$108, 7 day notice.** 609 W Main St 59427. On US 2, 0.3 mi w. Int corridors. **Pets:** Small, dogs only. $10 daily fee/pet. Designated rooms, service with restrictions, supervision.
SAVE ☒ 🖥 💻 ➳

DARBY
Rye Creek Lodge CA
(406) 821-3366. **$200-$250, 30 day notice.** 458 Rye Creek Rd 59829. US 93, 4.5 mi s, 1.5 mi e. Ext corridors. **Pets:** $10 daily fee/pet. Designated rooms, no service, supervision. ASK ☒ 🖥 💻 ☒

DEER LODGE
Rodeway Inn M
(406) 846-2370. **$60-$110.** 1150 N Main St 59722. I-90, exit 184, 0.3 mi s. Int corridors. **Pets:** Other species. $10 one-time fee/room. Service with restrictions, supervision. SAVE ☒ 🖥 💻

Western Big Sky Inn M
(406) 846-2590. **Call for rates.** 210 N Main St 59722. I-90, exit 184, 1 mi w. Ext corridors. **Pets:** Accepted. ☒ 🖥 💻

DILLON
Best Western Paradise Inn H ❀
(406) 683-4214. **$70-$120.** 650 N Montana St 59725. I-15, exit 63, 0.3 mi s on SR 41. Ext corridors. **Pets:** Other species. $10 daily fee/room. No service, supervision. SAVE ☒ 🖥 💻 🍽 ➳

Comfort Inn of Dillon H
(406) 683-6831. **$85-$105.** 450 N Interchange 59725. I-15, exit 63. Int corridors. **Pets:** Accepted. ASK ☒ 🖥 💻 ➳

GuestHouse International Inn & Suites H
(406) 683-3636. **$69-$199.** 580 Sinclair St 59725. I-15, exit 63. Int corridors. **Pets:** Accepted. ASK ☒ 🖥 🖥 💻 ☒

Super 8 H
(406) 683-4288. **$76-$85.** 550 N Montana St 59725. I-15, exit 63, just n on US 91. Int corridors. **Pets:** Dogs only. $15 daily fee/pet. Designated rooms, service with restrictions, crate. ☒ 🖥

EAST GLACIER PARK
Dancing Bears Inn LLC M
(406) 226-4402. **$49-$160, 4 day notice.** 40 Montana Ave 59434. Just off US 2, follow signs; center. Ext/int corridors. **Pets:** Accepted.
SAVE ☒ 🖥

EMIGRANT
Paradise Gateway Bed & Breakfast & Guest Cabin BB
(406) 333-4063. **$85-$350, 14 day notice.** Emigrant Mountain 59027. I-90, exit 333 (US 89), 4.5 mi s of Emigrant, between MM 26 and 27, then 0.3 mi e on gravel road, follow signs. Ext/int corridors.
Pets: Accepted. SAVE ☒ 🖥 💻

ENNIS
Riverside Motel & Outfitters M
(406) 682-4240. **$50-$145, 14 day notice.** 346 Main St 59729. US 287, east of town. Ext corridors. **Pets:** Accepted. ☒ 🖥 💻

FORSYTH
Magnuson Hotels Sundowner Inn M
(406) 346-2115. **$85-$120.** 1018 Front St 59327. I-94, exit 95, 0.5 mi nw on north frontage road. Ext corridors. **Pets:** Other species. $10 daily fee/pet. Service with restrictions, crate. SAVE ☒ 🖥 💻

Rails Inn Motel H
(406) 346-2242. **$67-$83, 3 day notice.** 290 Front St 59327. I-94, exit 93, just n, then 0.5 mi e on frontage road. Int corridors. **Pets:** Large, other species. $6 daily fee/pet. Service with restrictions, supervision.
SAVE ☒ 🖥 💻

Restwel Motel M
(406) 346-2771. **$61-$73.** 810 Front St 59327. I-94, exit 95, 0.8 mi nw on north frontage road. Ext corridors. **Pets:** Accepted. SAVE ☒ 🖥

Westwind Motor Inn M
(406) 346-2038. **$67-$83, 3 day notice.** 225 Westwind Ln 59327. I-94, exit 93, 0.3 mi n. Int corridors. **Pets:** Large, other species. $6 daily fee/pet. Service with restrictions, supervision. SAVE ☒ 🖥 💻

GARDINER
Best Western by Mammoth Hot Springs M
(406) 848-7311. **$99-$185, 3 day notice.** S Hwy 89 59030. 0.5 mi n. Ext/int corridors. **Pets:** Other species. $5 daily fee/pet. Designated rooms, service with restrictions, supervision.
SAVE ☒ 🖥 💻 🍽 ➳ ☒

Yellowstone River Motel M
(406) 848-7303. **$59-$105.** 14 E Park St 59030. Just e of US 89. Ext corridors. **Pets:** Accepted. SAVE ☒ 🖥 💻

Yellowstone Super 8-Gardiner H
(406) 848-7401. **$49-$149.** Hwy 89 S 59030. On US 89. Int corridors. **Pets:** Other species. $10 daily fee/pet. Designated rooms, supervision.
ASK ☒ 🖥 💻 ➳

GLASGOW

▼▼ ▼▼ Cottonwood Inn H

(406) 228-8213. **$78-$92.** 45 1st Ave NE 59230. 0.5 mi e on US 2. Int corridors. **Pets:** $5 daily fee/pet. Designated rooms, service with restrictions, supervision. ASK ✕ ⚁ ◻ ⑪ ⌕ ✕

GLENDIVE

⨀ ▼▼ ▼▼ Best Western Glendive Inn H

(406) 377-5555. **$64-$112.** 222 N Kendrick Ave 59330. I-94, exit 215; downtown. Ext/int corridors. **Pets:** Other species. $10 one-time fee/pet. Service with restrictions, supervision. SAVE ✕ ⚁ ◻ ⌕

▼▼ Super 8 Glendive M

(406) 365-5671. **$70-$95.** 1904 Merrill Ave 59330. I-94, exit 215, just n. Int corridors. **Pets:** Other species. $5 one-time fee/room. Service with restrictions, supervision. ASK ✕ ◻

GREAT FALLS

⨀ ▼▼▼ ▼▼ Best Western Heritage Inn H ❀

(406) 761-1900. **$109-$149.** 1700 Fox Farm Rd 59404. I-15, exit 278, 0.8 mi e on 10th Ave S and US 87/89 and SR 3/200. Int corridors. **Pets:** Small, other species. $10 one-time fee/room. Supervision.
SAVE ✕ ⚁ ◻ ⑪ ⌕ ✕

▼▼▼ ▼▼ Comfort Inn by Choice Hotels H

(406) 454-2727. **$70-$130.** 1120 9th St S 59405. I-15, exit 278, 3 mi e on 10th Ave S and US 87/89 and SR 3/200, then just s. Int corridors. **Pets:** Other species. $10 daily fee/room. No service.
ASK ✕ ⚁ ◻ ⌕

⨀ ▼▼▼▼ Crystal Inn H

(406) 727-7788. **$89-$129.** 3701 31st St SW 59404. I-15, exit 277, just e. Int corridors. **Pets:** Accepted. SAVE ✕ ⚁ ◻ ⌕

▼▼ ▼▼ Days Inn of Great Falls H

(406) 727-6565. **$68-$98.** 101 14th Ave NW 59404. I-15, exit 280 (Central Ave), 1.3 mi e on Central Ave/Business Rt I-15, 0.8 mi n on 3rd St NW, then just w. Int corridors. **Pets:** Dogs only. $5 daily fee/room. Designated rooms, service with restrictions, supervision. ASK ✕ ⚁ ◻

▼▼ ▼▼ Extended StayAmerica-Great Falls-Missouri River H

(406) 761-7524. **$68-$78.** 800 River Dr S 59405. I-15, exit 278, 1.7 mi e on 10th Ave S, then 0.7 mi n. Int corridors. **Pets:** Other species. $25 daily fee/room. Designated rooms, service with restrictions, crate.
ASK ✕ ⚁ ◻

⨀ ▼▼ ▼▼ The Great Falls Inn H

(406) 453-6000. **$75-$85.** 1400 28th St S 59405. I-15, exit 278, 5.3 mi e on 10th Ave S, 0.3 mi s on 26th St S, then just e on 15th Ave S. Int corridors. **Pets:** Other species. $7 daily fee/pet. Designated rooms, supervision. SAVE ✕ ⚁ ◻

⨀ ▼▼ ▼▼ Holiday Inn H ❀

(406) 727-7200. **$109-$179.** 400 10th Ave S 59405. I-15, exit 278, 2 mi e on 10th Ave S, then just s. Int corridors. **Pets:** Small, other species. $15 one-time fee/room. Service with restrictions, supervision.
SAVE ✕ ⚁ ◻ ⑪ ⌕

▼▼▼▼ La Quinta Inn & Suites Great Falls H ❀

(406) 761-2600. **$99-$229.** 600 River Dr S 59405. I-15, exit 278, 1.7 mi e on 10th Ave S, then 0.8 mi n. Int corridors. **Pets:** Medium, other species. Service with restrictions, supervision.
ASK ✕ ⚁ ◻ ⌕ ✕

⨀ ▼▼ Motel 6 #4238 M

(406) 453-1602. **$63-$95.** 2 Treasure State Dr 59404. I-15, exit 278, 0.8 mi e on 10th Ave S and US 87/89 and SR 3/200. Int corridors. **Pets:** Other species. Service with restrictions, supervision. SAVE ✕

▼▼ O'Haire Motor Inn M

(406) 454-2141. **$69-$110.** 17 7th St S 59403. Center of downtown. Ext/int corridors. **Pets:** Accepted. ASK ✕ ⚁ ◻ ⑪ ⌕

⨀ ▼▼ Quality Inn H

(406) 761-3410. **$60-$100.** 220 Central Ave 59401. Downtown. Ext/int corridors. **Pets:** Medium, dogs only. $10 daily fee/pet. Service with restrictions, supervision. SAVE ✕ ⚁ ◻ ⑪ ⌕

HAMILTON

⨀ ▼▼ ▼▼ Best Western Hamilton Inn M

(406) 363-2142. **$85-$105.** 409 S 1st St (US 93) 59840. On US 93, s of City Center. Ext corridors. **Pets:** Other species. $10 one-time fee/pet. Service with restrictions, supervision. SAVE ✕ ⚁ ◻

▼▼▼▼ Bitterroot River Inn & Conference Center H

(406) 375-2525. **$69-$139.** 139 Bitterroot Plaza Dr 59840. US 93, 1 mi n, then just w. Ext/int corridors. **Pets:** Designated rooms, service with restrictions, supervision. ASK ✕ ⚁ ◻ ⌕ ✕

▼▼ ▼▼ Town House Inns H

(406) 363-6600. **$60-$99.** 1113 N 1st St 59840. On US 93, n of City Center. Int corridors. **Pets:** Accepted. ASK ✕ ⚁ ◻

HARDIN

⨀ ▼▼ American Inn of Hardin H

(406) 665-1870. **Call for rates.** 1324 N Crawford Ave 59034. I-90, exit 495, just s on SR 47. Ext corridors. **Pets:** $10 one-time fee/pet. Designated rooms, service with restrictions, supervision.
SAVE ✕ ⚁ ◻ ⌕

▼▼ Western Motel M

(406) 665-2296. **$65-$95.** 830 W 3rd St 59034. I-90, exit 495 eastbound, 1.3 mi s on SR 47 and CR 313, then just e; exit 497 westbound, 0.3 mi w on I-90 business loop, continue straight on 3rd St for 0.7 mi. Ext corridors. **Pets:** $5 daily fee/pet. Service with restrictions, supervision.
✕ ⚁

HARLOWTON

▼▼ Countryside Inn M

(406) 632-4119. **$52-$60.** 309 3rd St NE 59036. US 12 E. Ext corridors. **Pets:** $5 daily fee/room. Designated rooms, service with restrictions, supervision. ✕ ⚁

HAVRE

▼▼ ▼▼ AmericInn Lodge & Suites of Havre H

(406) 395-5000. **$83-$148.** 2520 Hwy 2 W 59501. On US 2, west side of town. Int corridors. **Pets:** $20 daily fee/room. Designated rooms, service with restrictions, supervision. ✕ ⚁ ◻ ⌕

HELENA

▼▼▼▼ Barrister Bed & Breakfast BB ❀

(406) 443-7330. **$124-$139, 4 day notice.** 416 N Ewing St 59601. I-15, exit 192 (Prospect Ave), 1.5 mi sw via Prospect and Montana aves to 9th Ave, 0.8 mi w, then just s. Int corridors. **Pets:** Dogs only. ASK ✕ ✓

⨀ ▼▼▼▼ Best Western Helena Great Northern Hotel H

(406) 457-5500. **$149-$179.** 835 Great Northern Blvd 59601. I-15, exit 193 (Cedar St), 2 mi w, just w on Lyndale Ave, then just s on Getchell St; downtown. Int corridors. **Pets:** Medium, other species. $15 daily fee/pet. Designated rooms, service with restrictions, supervision.
SAVE ✕ ⚁ ⚁ ◻ ⑪ ⌕

▼▼ ▼▼ Days Inn Helena H

(406) 442-3280. **Call for rates.** 2001 Prospect Ave 59601. I-15, exit 192 (Prospect Ave), just w. Int corridors. **Pets:** $5 daily fee/pet. Service with restrictions, supervision. ✕ ⚁ ◻ ✕

⨀ ▼▼ ▼▼ Helena Super 8 H

(406) 443-2450. **$55-$95.** 2200 11th Ave 59601. I-15, exit 192 (Prospect Ave), just w, follow signs. Int corridors. **Pets:** Other species. $10 one-time fee/pet. Designated rooms, service with restrictions, supervision.
SAVE ✕ ⚁ ◻

Red Lion Colonial Hotel H
(406) 443-2100. **$115-$155.** 2301 Colonial Dr 59601. I-15, exit 192 (Prospect Ave), just w, follow signs. Int corridors. **Pets:** Other species. $20 one-time fee/room. Service with restrictions, supervision.
SAVE ☒ ⬛ ⬛ ⬤ ⬛ ≈

Wingate by Wyndham H
(406) 449-3000. **$130-$150.** 2007 N Oakes St 59601. I-15, exit 193 (Cedar St), just sw. Int corridors. **Pets:** Accepted.
ASK ☒ ⬛ ⬛ ⬤ ≈

HUNGRY HORSE

Mini Golden Inns Motel M
(406) 387-4313. **$86-$160, 30 day notice.** 8955 US 2 E 59919. East end of town. Ext corridors. **Pets:** Accepted. SAVE ☒ ⬛ ⬛ ⬤

KALISPELL

Aero Inn H
(406) 755-3798. **$49-$104.** 1830 US 93 S 59901. 1.3 mi s on US 93 from jct US 2. Int corridors. **Pets:** $20 deposit/room. Designated rooms, service with restrictions, supervision. SAVE ☒ ⬛ ≈

Airport area Super 8 Kalispell/Glacier Int'l H
(406) 755-1888. **Call for rates.** 1341 1st Ave E 59901. 1.2 mi s on US 93 from jct US 2. Int corridors. **Pets:** $10 one-time fee/room. Service with restrictions, supervision. ☒ ⬛ ⬛ ⬤

Americas Best Value Glacier Peaks Inn H
(406) 756-3222. **$75-$125.** 1550 Hwy 93 N 59901. 1.3 mi n on US 93 from jct US 2. Int corridors. **Pets:** $10 daily fee/pet. Supervision.
ASK ☒ ⬛ ⬛

Comfort Inn H
(406) 755-6700. **$80-$150.** 1330 Hwy 2 W 59901. 1 mi w on US 2 from jct US 93. Int corridors. **Pets:** Accepted. SAVE ☒ ⬛ ⬛ ⬤ ⬛ ≈

Holiday Inn Express & Suites H
(406) 755-7405. **Call for rates.** 275 Treeline Rd 59901. 3 mi n on US 93 from jct US 2, just w. Int corridors. **Pets:** Accepted.
☒ ⬛ ⬛ ⬤ ≈

Kalispell Grand Hotel H ❀
(406) 755-8100. **$85-$150.** 100 Main St 59901. On US 93; downtown. Int corridors. **Pets:** Other species. ASK ☒ ⬛

La Quinta Inn & Suites Kalispell H ❀
(406) 257-5255. **Call for rates.** 255 Montclair Dr 59901. Jct US 93 and 2, 1 mi e. Int corridors. **Pets:** Medium, other species. Service with restrictions, supervision. ☒ ⬛ ⬛ ⬤ ≈ ☒

Red Lion Hotel Kalispell H
(406) 751-5050. **Call for rates.** 20 N Main St 59901. Just s on US 93 from jct of US 2; connected to Kalispell Center Mall. Int corridors. **Pets:** Other species. $20 one-time fee/room. Service with restrictions, supervision. SAVE ☒ ⬛ ⬛ ⬤ ⬛ ≈ ☒

Travelodge H ❀
(406) 755-6123. **$50-$119.** 350 N Main St 59901. US 93, just n of jct US 2. Ext/int corridors. **Pets:** Other species. $10 daily fee/room.
SAVE ☒ ⬛ ⬤

LAUREL

Best Western Yellowstone Crossing H
(406) 628-6888. **$88-$109.** 205 SE 4th St 59044. I-90, exit 434, just n, then just e. Int corridors. **Pets:** Medium. $10 daily fee/pet. Designated rooms, service with restrictions, supervision.
SAVE ☒ ⬛ ⬛ ⬤ ≈

LEWISTOWN

B & B Motel M
(406) 535-5496. **$50-$90.** 520 E Main St 59457. Downtown. Ext corridors. **Pets:** Accepted. SAVE ☒ ⬛

LIBBY

Rodeway Inn H
(406) 293-2771. **$70-$100.** 448 US 2 W 59923. Just w on US 2 from jct SR 37. Int corridors. **Pets:** $15 one-time fee/room. Service with restrictions, supervision. SAVE ☒ ⬛ ⬤ ≈

Sandman Motel M
(406) 293-8831. **$55-$80.** 31901 US 2 59923. Just w on US 2 from jct SR 37. Ext corridors. **Pets:** Other species. $20 deposit/pet, $5 daily fee/pet. Designated rooms, service with restrictions, supervision.
ASK ☒ ⬛

LINCOLN

Leeper's Ponderosa Motel M
(406) 362-4333. **$64-$80.** Hwy 200 & 1st Ave 59639. On SR 200, just w. Ext corridors. **Pets:** Other species. $5 daily fee/room. Service with restrictions, supervision. SAVE ☒ ⬛ ⬤ ☒

LIVINGSTON

Best Western Yellowstone Inn & Conference Center H
(406) 222-6110. **$84-$129.** 1515 W Park St 59047. I-90, exit 333, just n. Int corridors. **Pets:** Accepted. SAVE ☒ ⬛ ⬤ ⬛ ≈

Livingston Rodeway Inn M
(406) 222-6320. **$59-$143.** 102 Rogers Ln 59047. I-90, exit 333, just n on US 89, then just w. Ext/int corridors. **Pets:** Other species. $10 daily fee/pet. Designated rooms, service with restrictions, supervision.
ASK ☒ ⬛ ⬤ ⬛ ≈

LOLO

Days Inn H
(406) 273-2121. **$80-$100, 3 day notice.** 11225 US 93 S 59847. North edge of town. Ext/int corridors. **Pets:** Accepted.
ASK ☒ ⬛ ⬛ ⬤

MALTA

Maltana Motel M
(406) 654-2610. **$69-$109.** 138 S 1st Ave W 59538. Just s of US 2 via US 191, just w; downtown. Ext corridors. **Pets:** Large, dogs only. $10 one-time fee/pet. Service with restrictions, supervision.
SAVE ☒ ⬛ ⬤

MILES CITY

Best Western War Bonnet Inn M ❀
(406) 234-4560. **$70-$200.** 1015 S Haynes Ave 59301. I-94, exit 138 (Broadus), 0.3 mi n. Ext corridors. **Pets:** Other species. $10 daily fee/pet. Service with restrictions, supervision. SAVE ☒ ⬛ ⬤ ≈ ☒

GuestHouse International Inn & Suites H ❀
(406) 232-3661. **$80.** 3111 Steel St 59301. I-94, exit 138 (Broadus), just s. Int corridors. **Pets:** $15 daily fee/pet. Designated rooms, service with restrictions, supervision. SAVE ☒ ⬛ ⬛ ⬤ ≈

MISSOULA

Best Western Grant Creek Inn H
(406) 543-0700. **$109-$199.** 5280 Grant Creek Rd 59808. I-90, exit 101 (Reserve St), just n. Int corridors. **Pets:** Small. $10 daily fee/room. Service with restrictions, supervision. SAVE ☒ ⬛ ⬛ ⬤ ≈ ☒

Broadway Inn Conference Center H
(406) 532-3300. **Call for rates.** 1609 W Broadway 59808. I-90, exit 104 (Orange St), 0.5 mi s, then 1 mi w. Int corridors. **Pets:** Accepted.
☒ ⬛ ⬤ ⬛ ≈

Campus Inn M
(406) 549-5134. **$70-$135.** 744 E Broadway 59802. I-90, exit 105 (Van Buren St), just s to Broadway, then just w. Ext/int corridors. **Pets:** Large. $6 daily fee/pet. Designated rooms, service with restrictions, supervision.
ASK ☒ ⬛ ⬤ ≈

🐾 Pet-Friendly Travel Notes 🐾

🐾 AAA PetBook Reader Questionnaire

We "paws-itively" want to hear from you! Your comments, opinions and suggestions are important to AAA. Please help us to improve the AAA PetBook® by taking a few minutes to complete this simple questionnaire.

> Please mail your completed questionnaire to: AAA PetBook, Mail Stop 64, 1000 AAA Drive, Heathrow, FL 32746-5063
>
> Or, email us your comments at PetBookFeedback@national.aaa.com

1. Where did you purchase the AAA PetBook®?
   - ☐ AAA Club _____ (club name)
   - ☐ Bookstore _____ (name of bookstore)
   - ☐ Online _____ (web site)

2. What specific pet-related information contained in the AAA PetBook is important to you when planning to travel with your pet? (Please check all that apply)
   - ☐ Lodgings
   - ☐ Campgrounds
   - ☐ National Public Lands
   - ☐ Attractions
   - ☐ Dog Parks
   - ☐ Emergency Animal Clinics
   - ☐ U.S. / Canada Border Crossing Procedures
   - ☐ Traveling by Car
   - ☐ Traveling by Air
   - ☐ Traveling with Disabilities

3. When traveling with your pet, what additional information would be helpful?
   _____

4. How well does the AAA PetBook® meet your expectations?
   - ☐ Exceeds
   - ☐ Meets all
   - ☐ Meets most
   - ☐ Falls below

5. Are you familiar with the annual photo contest at AAA.com/PetBook? ☐ Yes ☐ No
Additional feedback or comments about the AAA PetBook:
   _____
   _____

Which age group are you in? ☐ Under 25 ☐ 25-34 ☐ 35-44 ☐ 45-54 ☐ 55-64 ☐ 65+

On average, how many overnight leisure trips do you take a year?
   ☐ None ☐ One ☐ Two ☐ Three or more

How many trips/outings a year include traveling with your pet? _____

What is the average distance traveled? _____

In addition to the AAA PetBook, did you buy any other pet-travel or general travel guides for your trip? ☐ Yes ☐ No
If yes, which ones?
   _____
   _____

Optional:
Name (Mr/Mrs/Ms) _____
Address _____
City _____ State _____ Zip _____

Are you a AAA member? ☐ Yes ☐ No, If yes, name of AAA club: _____

Thank you for taking the time to complete this questionnaire. We appreciate your feedback.

All information including name and address is for AAA internal use only and will NOT be distributed outside the organization to any third parties.

12th edition

Save more.
Earn more.
Get more.

AAA/CAA Members Save up to 20% and earn 10% more points!

Join Best Western's free rewards program for AAA/CAA members, AAA/CAA Preferred[SM] Best Western Rewards®, and get the rewards card with the fastest earning potential around. As a AAA/CAA member, you can save up to 20% on your stay and get 10% bonus points*. Plus, the convenience of staying at over 4,000** Best Westerns worldwide – The World's Largest Hotel Chain®.

1.866.430.9022

bestwestern.com/AAA | bestwestern.com/CAA

Take the whole family on a vacation!

AAA PetBook® Photo Contest Entries

Each year, the winning entry in AAA's PetBook Photo Contest, sponsored by Best Western®, appears on a cover of *Traveling With Your Pet: The AAA PetBook®* and also receives other great prizes. You have already met the contest winners, but here are more great entries that we just had to make room for!

Check out AAA.com/PetBook for pictures, contest rules and an entry form.

"Siri & Ella"
Arthur Everly, Blackstone, MA

"Jake"
Katie Hardie, Denver, CO

"Buzz"
Suzanne Rider, Lutz, FL

"Nutmeg"
Sarah Pearcy, Long Beach, CA

"Truman"
Michael & Mary Kay Bowers, Kansas City, MO

"Duffy & Dory"
Dan & LaDonna Ishida, Grand Junction, CO

"Minnow"
Jillian Harrison, Winnipeg, MB

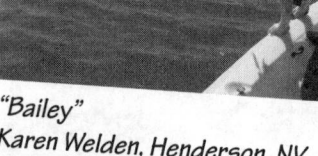

"Bailey"
Karen Welden, Henderson, NV

"Spot"
Lynne Pine, Chula Vista, CA

"Rusty"
Don & Debbie Callaway, Placerville, CA

"Maddie"
Charlene & Chris Chan, Irvine, CA

"Jonnie, Mattie & Sister Mary"
Corina Fernandez & Evelyn Egger, Pleasanton, CA

"Max"
Kevin Hamilton, Sardinia, OH

"Beau"
Beth Levine, Pleasanton, CA

"Mischief & Rusty"
Sheryl Clark, Las Vegas, NV

"Augustus"
Douglas & Dianemarie Collins, Reno, NV

"Kip & Tilda"
Allison Schwickerath, Longmont, CO

"Spike"
Evay Spurgeon, Beavercreek, OH

"Cha Cha"
Naomi Nakaoka, San Anselmo, CA

"Winnie the Poo & Tigger Too"
Linda Laine, Westerville, OH

"Biscuit"
Elizabeth Gratzek, Greensboro, NC

"Flynn"
Lauren Robbins, Leland, NC

"Osby"
Miranda Ruenroeng, Burlingame, CA

"Maxwell & Jackson"
Jean & John Jesensky, Bolton, MA

"Kooper-Dale"
Kimber Spencer, Santa Rosa, CA

"Silver"
Kay Boydston, Medford, OR

"Zion"
John Guertin, North Smithfield, RI

"Rosie"
Pamela Hoaglund, Plymouth, MA

"Sprocket"
Devin Holody, Sarasota, FL

"Ulysses"
Todd Schmidt, Moran, WY

"Kolu & Abednego"
David Culp, Troutman, NC

"Randy"
Anthony & Michelle Vinciguerra, Quincy, MA

"Kane"
Thomas Rickett, Jr., Providence, RI

"Avalanche"
Melanie Mattson, Golden, CO

"Dylan"
Karen Takahashi, Bandon, OR

"Buddy"
Nicole Roop, Littlestown, PA

A few more tail-wagging travelers

1) "Lucca & Posey," Mary McKinzie, San Diego, CA 2) "Zeke," Vallee Bordinaro, Rockport, MA
3) "Spencer," Valerie Jack, Niagara Falls, ON 4) "Ginger," Barbara Hanania, Lincoln, MA
5) "Cooper," Julia Pettee, Barre, MA 6) "Molly & Rumor," Laurie Roland, Bethpage, NY
7) "Miss Molly," Peggy King, Littleton, CO

Comfort Inn 🅷
(406) 542-0888. **$89-$129, 3 day notice.** 4545 N Reserve St 59808.
I-90, exit 101 (Reserve St), 0.5 mi s. Int corridors. **Pets:** Medium. $15
daily fee/room. Service with restrictions, supervision.

Days Inn/Missoula Airport 🅷 🐾
(406) 721-9776. **$80-$120.** 8600 Truck Stop Rd 59808. I-90, exit 96, just
n. Int corridors. **Pets:** Large, other species. $10 daily fee/pet. Designated
rooms, service with restrictions.

Days Inn University 🅷
(406) 543-7221. **$99-$129.** 201 E Main St 59802. I-90, exit 104 (Orange
St), 0.5 mi s to Broadway, 0.5 mi e to Washington, just s to Main St, then
just w. Ext corridors. **Pets:** Dogs only. $15 daily fee/pet. Designated
rooms, service with restrictions, supervision.

Doubletree Hotel Missoula/Edgewater 🅷
(406) 728-3100. **$109-$239.** 100 Madison St 59802. I-90, exit 105 (Van
Buren St), just s, then w on Front St. Int corridors. **Pets:** Accepted.

Econo Lodge 🅷
(406) 542-7550. **$75-$130.** 4953 N Reserve St 59808. I-90 W, exit 101
(Reserve St), just s. Int corridors. **Pets:** Medium, other species. $10 daily
fee/pet. Designated rooms.

Family Inn 🅼
(406) 543-7371. **Call for rates.** 1031 E Broadway 59802. I-90, exit 105
(Van Buren St), just s, then just e. Ext corridors. **Pets:** Medium. $10 one-
time fee/room.

Hampton Inn 🅷 🐾
(406) 549-1800. **Call for rates.** 4805 N Reserve St 59808. I-90, exit 101
(Reserve St), just s. Int corridors. **Pets:** Other species. $10 one-time fee/
room. Service with restrictions, supervision.

**Holiday Inn Missoula-Downtown at the
Park** 🅷 🐾
(406) 721-8550. **$103-$209.** 200 S Pattee St 59802. I-90, exit 104
(Orange St), 0.5 mi s to Broadway, just e to Pattee St, then just s. Int
corridors. **Pets:** Large, other species. $20 one-time fee/room. Designated
rooms, service with restrictions, supervision.

La Quinta Inn 🅷 🐾
(406) 549-9000. **Call for rates.** 5059 N Reserve St 59808. I-90, exit 101
(Reserve St), just s. Int corridors. **Pets:** Medium, other species. Service
with restrictions, supervision.

Quality Inn & Conference Center 🅷
(406) 251-2665. **$85-$150.** 3803 Brooks St 59804. I-90, exit 101
(Reserve St), 5 mi s to Brooks St, then just w. Int corridors.
Pets: Medium, other species. $10 daily fee/pet. Designated rooms.

Red Lion Inn 🅷
(406) 728-3300. **$99-$179.** 700 W Broadway 59802. I-90, exit 104
(Orange St), just s, then just w. Ext corridors. **Pets:** Other species. $20
one-time fee/room. Service with restrictions, supervision.

Ruby's Inn & Convention Center 🅷
(406) 721-0990. **$70-$125, 7 day notice.** 4825 N Reserve St 59808.
I-90, exit 101 (Reserve St), just s. Ext/int corridors. **Pets:** $10 one-time
fee/room. Service with restrictions, supervision.

Sleep Inn by Choice Hotels 🅷
(406) 543-5883. **Call for rates.** 3425 Dore Ln 59801. I-90, exit 101
(Reserve St), 5 mi s, then just e on Brooks St. Int corridors. **Pets:** $20
one-time fee/room. Designated rooms, supervision.

Southgate Inn 🅼
(406) 251-2250. **$60-$125.** 3530 Brooks St 59801. I-90, exit 101
(Reserve St), 5 mi s to Brooks St, then just e. Ext corridors.
Pets: Accepted.

Super 8-Brooks St 🅷
(406) 251-2255. **$55-$100.** 3901 Brooks St 59804. I-90, exit 101
(Reserve St), 5 mi s to Brooks St, then just w. Int corridors.
Pets: Accepted.

Thunderbird Motel 🅼
(406) 543-7251. **$65-$100.** 1009 E Broadway 59802. I-90, exit 105 (Van
Buren St), just s to Broadway, then just e. Ext/int corridors.
Pets: Accepted.

Travelers Inn Motel Inc 🅼
(406) 728-8330. **$65-$85.** 4850 N Reserve St 59808. I-90, exit 101
(Reserve St), just s. Ext corridors. **Pets:** Small, dogs only. $5 daily fee/
pet. Designated rooms, service with restrictions, supervision.

MONTANA CITY
Elkhorn Mountain Inn 🅷 🐾
(406) 442-6625. **$75-$90.** 1 Jackson Creek Rd 59634. I-15, exit 187
(Montana City), just w. Int corridors. **Pets:** Other species. $10 daily fee/
room. Service with restrictions, supervision.

POLSON
**Best Western KwaTaqNuk Resort &
Casino** 🅷 🐾
(406) 883-3636. **$80-$161, 3 day notice.** 49708 US Hwy 93 E 59860.
Just s of downtown. Int corridors. **Pets:** Medium. $25 daily fee/room. Des-
ignated rooms, service with restrictions, supervision.

RED LODGE
Comfort Inn of Red Lodge 🅷
(406) 446-4469. **$90-$170.** 612 N Broadway 59068. Jct US 212 and SR
78, north entrance. Int corridors. **Pets:** Other species. $15 one-time fee/
room. Designated rooms, supervision.

Lu Pine Inn 🅷
(406) 446-1321. **$69-$129.** 702 S Hauser Ave 59068. 0.4 mi s, just w of
US 212. Int corridors. **Pets:** Designated rooms, service with restrictions,
supervision.

Yodeler Motel 🅼
(406) 446-1435. **$69-$149.** 601 S Broadway Ave 59068. Just s on US
212. Ext corridors. **Pets:** Dogs only. $5 daily fee/pet. Designated rooms,
service with restrictions, supervision.

RONAN
Starlite Motel 🅼
(406) 676-7000. **$50-$74, 3 day notice.** 18 Main St SW 59864. Just w
of jct US 93 and Main St. Ext corridors. **Pets:** Dogs only. $10 daily fee/
pet. Designated rooms, service with restrictions, supervision.

ST. IGNATIUS
Sunset Motel 🅼
(406) 745-3900. **$60-$80.** 333 Mountain View 59865. Just s of downtown, exit US 93. Ext corridors. **Pets:** Dogs only. $5 daily fee/pet. Service
with restrictions, supervision.

ST. REGIS
Little River Motel 🅼
(406) 649-2713. **$45-$80.** 424 Little River Ln 59866. I-90, exit 33, just n
to flashing light, just w, then just sw. Ext corridors. **Pets:** $10 daily fee/pet.
Designated rooms, service with restrictions, supervision.

Super 8-St. Regis H
(406) 649-2422. **$75-$93.** 9 Old Hwy 10 E 59866. I-90, exit 33, just n. Ext/int corridors. **Pets:** $10 one-time fee/pet. Service with restrictions, supervision. SAVE ✕ 🖪 💻

SHELBY

Comfort Inn of Shelby H
(406) 434-2212. **$90-$115.** 455 McKinley Ave 59474. I-15, exit 363, just e, then just s. Int corridors. **Pets:** Accepted. ASK ✕ 🖪 💻 ✕

O'Haire Manor Motel M
(406) 434-5555. **$52-$80.** 204 2nd St S 59474. Just s of Main St via Maple St. Ext/int corridors. **Pets:** Large, dogs only. $5 daily fee/pet. Designated rooms, service with restrictions, supervision. SAVE ✕ 🖪 💻

SHERIDAN

Moriah Motel M
(406) 842-5491. **$62-$78.** 220 S Main St 59749. On SR 287; center. Ext corridors. **Pets:** $10 one-time fee/room. Service with restrictions, supervision. ASK ✕ 🖪

SIDNEY

Richland Motor Inn M
(406) 433-6400. **$99.** 1200 S Central Ave 59270. 1.5 mi n of jct SR 200 and 16. Int corridors. **Pets:** Other species. $10 daily fee/pet. Service with restrictions, crate. SAVE ✕ 🖪 💻

SUPERIOR

Budget Host Big Sky Motel M
(406) 822-4831. **$50-$85.** 103 4th Ave E 59872. I-90, exit 47, just n. Ext corridors. **Pets:** Accepted. SAVE ✕ 🖪

THREE FORKS

Broken Spur Motel M
(406) 285-3237. **$59-$119.** 124 W Elm (Hwy 2) 59752. I-90, exit 278 westbound, 1.3 mi sw; exit 274 eastbound, 1 mi s on SR 287 to jct SR 2, then 3 mi se. Ext corridors. **Pets:** $5 one-time fee/pet. Designated rooms, service with restrictions, supervision. SAVE ✕ 🖪

Fort Three Forks Motel & RV Park M
(406) 285-3233. **$56-$120.** 10776 Hwy 287 59752. I-90, exit 274. Ext corridors. **Pets:** Other species. $5 one-time fee/pet. Designated rooms, service with restrictions, supervision. ASK ✕ 🖪 💻

WEST YELLOWSTONE

Best Western Cross Winds Motor Inn M
(406) 646-9557. **$85-$180.** 201 Firehole Ave 59758. Just w of US 191 and 287, on US 20 at Dunraven St and Firehole Ave. Ext corridors. **Pets:** Designated rooms, service with restrictions, supervision. SAVE ✕ 🖪 💻 ⇒

Best Western Desert Inn H
(406) 646-7376. **$75-$200.** 133 Canyon Ave 59758. US 191 at US 20; corner of Canyon and Firehole aves. Int corridors. **Pets:** Designated rooms, service with restrictions, supervision. SAVE ✕ 🖪 💻 ⇒

Best Western Weston Inn M
(406) 646-7373. **$130-$160.** 108 Gibbon Ave 59758. US 191; jct Canyon Ave. Ext/int corridors. **Pets:** Accepted. SAVE ✕ 🖪 💻 ⇒

Brandin' Iron Inn M
(406) 646-9411. **$79-$134, 3 day notice.** 201 Canyon St 59758. Just w; just n of park entrance. Ext corridors. **Pets:** $15 one-time fee/room. Designated rooms, service with restrictions, crate. SAVE ✕ 🖪 💻

City Center Motel M
(406) 646-7337. **$59-$89, 3 day notice.** 214 Madison Ave 59758. W off US 191 at Madison Ave and Dunraven St; just nw of park entrance. Ext corridors. **Pets:** Dogs only. $15 one-time fee/room. Supervision. SAVE ✕ 💻 ⊘

ClubHouse Inn H
(406) 646-4892. **$100-$240.** 105 S Electric St 59758. Just sw of jct US 191, 187 and 20; just w of park entrance. Int corridors. **Pets:** Other species. Designated rooms, service with restrictions, supervision. ASK ✕ 🖎 🖪 💻 ⇒

Holiday Inn West Yellowstone H
(406) 646-7365. **$114-$279.** 315 Yellowstone Ave 59758. Just w of park entrance. Int corridors. **Pets:** Other species. $50 one-time fee/pet. Designated rooms, service with restrictions, supervision. SAVE ✕ 🖎 🖪 💻 🍴 ⇒ ✕

Kelly Inn H ✤
(406) 646-4544. **Call for rates.** 104 S Canyon Ave 59758. S of jct US 191, 287 and 20; just w of park entrance. Ext/int corridors. **Pets:** Other species. Service with restrictions, supervision. ✕ 🖪 💻 ⇒

Stage Coach Inn H
(406) 646-7381. **$59-$189.** 209 Madison Ave 59758. Corner of Dunraven St and Madison Ave, just w of park entrance. Ext/int corridors. **Pets:** Other species. Designated rooms, service with restrictions, supervision. SAVE ✕ 🖪 💻 ✕

The Three Bear Lodge M
(406) 646-7353. **$59-$179.** 217 Yellowstone Ave 59758. Just w of park entrance. Ext/int corridors. **Pets:** Accepted. SAVE ✕ 🖪 💻 🍴 ⇒ ✕

Yellowstone Lodge H
(406) 646-0020. **$69-$169.** 251 S Electric St 59758. Just w of park entrance. Int corridors. **Pets:** Designated rooms, service with restrictions, crate. SAVE ✕ 🖪 💻 ⇒

WHITEFISH

Best Western Rocky Mountain Lodge H ✤
(406) 862-2569. **$81-$199.** 6510 Hwy 93 S 59937. 1.3 mi s on US 93 from jct SR 487. Ext/int corridors. **Pets:** $20 one-time fee/room. Designated rooms, service with restrictions, crate. SAVE ✕ 🖎 🖪 💻 ⇒ ✕

Gaynor's Resort CA
(406) 862-3802. **Call for rates.** 1992 KM Ranch Rd 59937. Jct US 93 and SR 468, 4.6 mi w to Twin Bridges Rd, 0.6 mi s to KM Ranch Rd, then 1.8 mi e on gravel road. Ext corridors. **Pets:** Accepted. ✕ 🖪 💻

Hidden Moose Lodge BB
(406) 862-6516. **$99-$209, 30 day notice.** 1735 E Lakeshore Dr 59937. Jct US 93 and SR 487, 1.5 mi n on SR 487. Ext/int corridors. **Pets:** Accepted. ✕ 🖪 ✕

Kristianna Mountain Homes CO
(406) 862-2860. **$140-$1100, 30 day notice.** 331 Karrow Ave 59937. Jct US 93 and SR 487, 2.4 mi n on SR 487, at flashing light go 5.2 mi on Big Mountain Rd, just n on Gelande St, then just w on Kristianna Close. Ext/int corridors. **Pets:** Accepted. SAVE ✕ 🖪 💻 ✕ ⚿

North Forty Resort CA
(406) 862-7740. **$119-$259, 14 day notice.** 3765 Hwy 40 W 59912. 2.5 mi e on SR 40 from jct US 93. Ext corridors. **Pets:** Accepted. ✕ 🖪 💻 ✕ ⚿

Pine Lodge H
(406) 862-7600. **$79-$170.** 920 Spokane Ave 59937. 1 mi s on US 93 from jct SR 487. Int corridors. **Pets:** Other species. Service with restrictions, supervision. SAVE ✕ 🖎 🖪 💻 ⇒

WHITE SULPHUR SPRINGS

All Seasons Inn & Suites H ✤
(406) 547-8888. **$70-$140.** 808 3rd Ave SW 59645. On US 89/12, south end of town. Int corridors. **Pets:** $10 one-time fee/pet. Service with restrictions, supervision. SAVE ✕ 🖎 🖪

WIBAUX

Beaver Creek Inn & Suites M

(406) 796-2666. **$78-$125.** 400 W 2nd Ave N 59353. I-94, exit 241 westbound; exit 242 eastbound. Int corridors. **Pets:** Other species. $10 daily fee/pet. Designated rooms, service with restrictions, supervision.

NEBRASKA

AINSWORTH

Super 8 H
(402) 387-0700. **Call for rates.** 1025 E 4th St 69210. 0.5 mi e on US 20. Int corridors. **Pets:** Accepted.

ATKINSON

Sandhills Guest House Motel M
(402) 925-5600. **$65-$89.** 119 S Hyde St 68713. On US 20; east end of town. Int corridors. **Pets:** Very small, other species. $15 one-time fee/pet. No service, supervision.

BEATRICE

Holiday Inn Express Hotel & Suites H
(402) 228-7000. **$102-$132.** 4005 N 6th St 68310. 1 mi n on US 77. Int corridors. **Pets:** Other species. Supervision.

BELLEVUE

Best Western White House Inn H
(402) 293-1600. **$70-$130.** 305 Fort Crook Rd N 68005. US 75, 1.8 mi n of jct SR 370 and Fort Crook Rd N. Int corridors. **Pets:** Other species. $25 one-time fee/room. Designated rooms, service with restrictions, crate.

Hampton Inn H
(402) 292-1607. **$99-$219.** 3404 Samson Way 68123. US 75, 1 mi n on SR 370, just w on Golden, then 0.3 mi n. Int corridors. **Pets:** Accepted.

Settle Inn and Suites H ☙
(402) 292-1155. **$69-$175.** 2105 Pratt Ave 68123. US 75, exit Cornhusker Rd, just w. Int corridors. **Pets:** Dogs only. $15 daily fee/room. Designated rooms, service with restrictions, supervision.

BROKEN BOW

Americas Best Value Inn & Suites M
(308) 872-6428. **$70-$90.** 215 S E St 68822. SR 2/92, just e of town. Ext/int corridors. **Pets:** Medium, other species. $5 daily fee/pet. Designated rooms, service with restrictions, supervision.

The Arrow Hotel H
(308) 872-6662. **Call for rates.** 509 S 9th Ave 68822. On SR 2/92; downtown. Int corridors. **Pets:** Accepted.

CENTRAL CITY

Super 8 H ☙
(308) 946-5055. **$59-$65.** 1701 31st St 68826. SR 14, 1 mi s of jct US 30. Ext/int corridors. **Pets:** Medium, other species. $9 daily fee/pet. Designated rooms, service with restrictions, supervision.

CHADRON

Best Western West Hills Inn H
(308) 432-3305. **$72-$146.** 1100 W 10th St 69337. Just s of jct US 385 and 20. Ext/int corridors. **Pets:** Medium. $10 daily fee/pet. Service with restrictions, crate.

Grand Westerner Motel M
(308) 432-5595. **$55-$64.** 1050 W Hwy 20 69337. 0.8 mi w on US 20; just e of jct US 385. Ext corridors. **Pets:** Accepted.

Motel 6 of Chadron #4259 H
(308) 432-3000. **Call for rates.** 755 Microtel Dr 69337. Just s of jct US 385 and 20. Int corridors. **Pets:** Other species. Service with restrictions, supervision.

Westerner Motel M
(308) 432-5577. **$55-$64.** 300 Oak St 69337. On US 20, 0.5 mi e of jct US 385 and SR 87. Ext corridors. **Pets:** Dogs only. $5 one-time fee/room. No service, supervision.

COLUMBUS

Sleep Inn & Suites Hotel H
(402) 562-5200. **$72-$80.** 303 23rd St 68601. On US 30, 2 mi e of jct US 30 and 81; east side of town. Int corridors. **Pets:** Medium, other species. $25 daily fee/pet. Service with restrictions, crate.

Super 8-Columbus H
(402) 563-3456. **$50-$67.** 3324 20th St 68601. On US 30 and 81, just s. Int corridors. **Pets:** Accepted.

COZAD

Rodeway Inn H
(308) 784-4900. **Call for rates.** 809 S Meridian 69130. I-80, exit 222, just n. Int corridors. **Pets:** Medium, other species. Designated rooms, service with restrictions, supervision.

CRETE

Super 8 H
(402) 826-3600. **$55-$65.** 1880 W 12th St 68333. 1.3 mi sw at jct SR 33/103; west end of town. Int corridors. **Pets:** Other species. $10 daily fee/pet. Supervision.

FREMONT

Oak Tree Inn H
(402) 721-3700. **$79-$149.** 2700 N Diers Pkwy 68025. US 30, just s. Int corridors. **Pets:** Accepted.

GOTHENBURG

Gothenburg Super 8 H
(308) 537-2684. **$52-$72.** 401 Platte River Dr 69138. I-80, exit 211 (SR 47), just n. Int corridors. **Pets:** Accepted.

GRAND ISLAND

Holiday Inn-Interstate 80 H ☙
(308) 384-7770. **$69-$139.** 7838 S US Hwy 281 68803. I-80, exit 312 (US 281), just s. Int corridors. **Pets:** Medium, other species. $15 daily fee/room. Service with restrictions, supervision.

Travelodge H
(308) 382-5003. **$50-$101.** 1311 S Locust St 68801. I-80, exit 314, 5.2 mi n. Int corridors. **Pets:** Accepted.

HASTINGS

▼▼ Super 8 H

(402) 463-8888. **Call for rates.** 2200 N Kansas Ave 68901. Jct US 34 and 281, 2 mi n. Int corridors. **Pets:** Accepted. ☒ 🖥 💻

HOLDREGE

▼▼ Super 8 H

(308) 995-2793. **Call for rates.** 420 Broadway 68949. US 183, 0.5 mi w on US 6/34. Int corridors. **Pets:** Accepted. ☒ 🖥 💻 ➸

KEARNEY

⚛ ▼▼ AmericInn Lodge & Suites of Kearney H

(308) 234-7800. **$85-$155.** 215 W Talmadge Rd 68845. I-80, exit 272 (SR 44), just n. Int corridors. **Pets:** $10 one-time fee/pet. Designated rooms, service with restrictions, supervision.

[SAVE] ☒ 🖥 💻 ➸ ☒

⚛ ▼▼ Best Western Inn of Kearney H ❖

(308) 237-5185. **$79-$109.** 1010 3rd Ave 68845. I-80, exit 272 (SR 44), 1 mi n, then just w. Ext/int corridors. **Pets:** Other species. $15 one-time fee/room. Service with restrictions, supervision.

[SAVE] ☒ 🖥 💻 🍴 ➸ ☒

▼▼ Microtel Inn & Suites H

(308) 698-3003. **$55-$85.** 104 Talmadge Rd 68847. I-80, exit 272 (SR 44), just se. Int corridors. **Pets:** Accepted. [ASK] ☒ 🖥 💻

⚛ ▼▼ Quality Inn by Choice Hotels H

(308) 237-0838. **$70-$109.** 121 3rd Ave 68845. I-80, exit 272 (SR 44), 0.3 mi n. Int corridors. **Pets:** Accepted. [SAVE] ☒ 🖥 💻 ➸

⚛ ▼▼ Ramada Conference Center H

(308) 237-3141. **$79-$109.** 301 2nd Ave 68847. I-80, exit 272 (SR 44), 0.7 mi n. Int corridors. **Pets:** Large, other species. $10 daily fee/pet. Service with restrictions, supervision.

[SAVE] ☒ 🖥 💻 🍴 ➸ ☒

KIMBALL

▼▼ Days Inn-Kimball M

(308) 235-4671. **$70-$185.** 611 E 3rd St 69145. I-80, exit 20, 1.5 ne on SR 71, then 0.5 mi e on US 30. Ext corridors. **Pets:** Other species. $10 daily fee/pet. No service, supervision. [ASK] ☒ 🖥 💻 ➸

LEXINGTON

▼▼ Days Inn H

(308) 324-6440. **$70-$99.** 2506 Plum Creek Pkwy 68850. I-80, exit 237 (US 283), 0.6 mi n. Int corridors. **Pets:** Dogs only. $10 daily fee/pet. Designated rooms, no service, supervision. [ASK] ☒ 🖥 💻

⚛ ▼▼ Holiday Inn Express Hotel & Suites H ❖

(308) 324-9900. **$105-$149.** 2605 Plum Creek Pkwy 68850. I-80, exit 237 (US 283), 0.5 mi n. Int corridors. **Pets:** Other species. $20 daily fee/room. Designated rooms, service with restrictions, supervision.

[SAVE] ☒ 🖥 💻 ➸

▼▼ Lexington Comfort Inn H

(308) 324-3747. **$75-$135.** 2810 Plum Creek Pkwy 68850. I-80, exit 237 (US 283), 0.3 mi n. Ext/int corridors. **Pets:** Accepted.

[ASK] ☒ 🖥 💻 ➸

LINCOLN

⚛ ▼▼ Best Western Crown Inn H

(402) 438-4700. **$70-$130.** 6501 N 28th St 68504. I-80, exit 402 (27th St), 0.3 mi s via Wildcat Dr. Int corridors. **Pets:** Medium, dogs only. $125 deposit/room, $15 daily fee/pet. Designated rooms, service with restrictions, supervision. [SAVE] ☒ 🖥 💻 ➸

▼▼ Candlewood Suites H ❖

(402) 420-0330. **Call for rates.** 4100 Pioneer Woods Dr 68506. 4.6 mi e on SR 2, 2.2 mi n via 70th St, e on Pioneers Blvd, then just n. Int corridors. **Pets:** Medium. $75 one-time fee/pet. Service with restrictions, crate. ☒ 🖥 💻

▼▼ Chase Suites Hotel H

(402) 483-4900. **$89-$299.** 200 S 68th Pl 68510. On US 34, 4.3 mi e, then just s. Ext corridors. **Pets:** Accepted.

[SAVE] ☒ 🖥 💻 ➸ ☒

⚛ ▼▼ Comfort Suites H

(402) 325-8800. **$99-$109.** 331 N Cotner Blvd 68505. 3.3 mi e on US 6 city route, then 0.3 mi n. Int corridors. **Pets:** Accepted.

[SAVE] ☒ 🖥 💻 ➸

▼▼ Comfort Suites H

(402) 476-8080. **$80-$180.** 4231 Industrial Ave 68504. I-80, exit 403 (27th St), 2.3 mi s. Int corridors. **Pets:** Large. $10 daily fee/pet. Service with restrictions, supervision. [ASK] ☒ 🖥 💻 ➸

⚛ ▼▼ Country Inn & Suites By Carlson North H

(402) 476-5353. **Call for rates.** 5353 N 27th St 68521. I-80, exit 403 (27th St), 1.5 mi s. Int corridors. **Pets:** Medium. $15 daily fee/pet. Designated rooms, service with restrictions, supervision.

[SAVE] ☒ 🖥 💻 🍴 ➸ ☒

⚛ ▼▼ Countryside Suites H

(402) 742-7575. **Call for rates.** 6750 Wildcat Dr 68504. I-80, exit 403 (27th St), just s, then e. Int corridors. **Pets:** Accepted.

[SAVE] ☒ 🖥 💻 ➸

▼▼ Hampton Inn Lincoln Airport I-80 H

(402) 474-2080. **Call for rates.** 1301 W Bond Cir 68521. I-80, exit 399 (Airport), just e. Int corridors. **Pets:** Accepted. ☒ 🖥 💻 ➸

▼▼ Holiday Inn Express H ❖

(402) 435-0200. **Call for rates.** 1133 Belmont Ave 68521. I-80, exit 401; exit 401A; 2 mi s on I-180, exit 2 (Cornhusker Hwy E), then just n on 11th St. Int corridors. **Pets:** Other species.

☒ 🖥 💻 ➸ ☒

⚛ ▼▼ La Quinta Inn H ❖

(402) 476-2222. **Call for rates.** 4433 N 27th St 68501. I-80, exit 403 (27th St), 2.3 mi s. Int corridors. **Pets:** Medium, other species. Service with restrictions, supervision. [SAVE] ☒ 🖥 💻 ➸

▼▼ Microtel Inn & Suites H

(402) 476-2591. **Call for rates.** 2505 Fairfield St 68521. I-80, exit 403 (27th St), 2.7 mi s, then just w. Int corridors. **Pets:** $10 daily fee/pet. Service with restrictions, supervision. [SAVE] ☒ 🖥 💻 ➸

▼▼ New Victorian Suites H

(402) 464-4400. **$69-$149.** 216 N 48th St 68504. 2.5 mi e on US 6 and 34; just ne of jct O St; entrance off 48th St. Int corridors. **Pets:** Medium, dogs only. $10 daily fee/pet. Designated rooms, service with restrictions, supervision. [ASK] ☒ 🖥 💻

▼▼ Ramada Limited-South H

(402) 423-3131. **$75-$105.** 1511 Center Park Rd 68512. I-80, exit 397 (US 77), 5.7 mi s, then 1.7 mi ne on SR L55W. Int corridors. **Pets:** $5 daily fee/pet. Designated rooms, service with restrictions, supervision.

[ASK] ☒ 🖥 ➸

⚛ ▼▼ Residence Inn by Marriott–Lincoln South H ❖

(402) 423-1555. **$98-$120.** 5865 Boboli Ln 68516. 1 mi s of SR 2 (Nebraska Hwy) via 56th St, then just e on Pine Lake Rd (Southeast Lincoln). Int corridors. **Pets:** Medium, other species. $100 one-time fee/room. Designated rooms, service with restrictions, crate.

[SAVE] ☒ 🖥 💻 ☒

▼▼ Settle Inn & Suites H

(402) 435-8100. **$69-$109.** 7333 Husker Cir 68504. I-80, exit 403 (27th St), just s to Wildcat Dr, just e, then just n. Int corridors. **Pets:** Accepted. ☒ 🖥 💻 ➸

▼▼ Staybridge Suites Lincoln-I-80 H

(402) 438-7829. **$109-$296.** 2701 Fletcher Ave 68504. I-80, exit 403 (27th St), 0.4 mi s. Int corridors. **Pets:** Other species. $25 one-time fee/room. Service with restrictions. [ASK] ☒ 🖥 💻 ➸ ☒

▼▼▼ **Super 8-Lincoln/Cornhusker** 🅷
(402) 467-4488. **$49-$80.** 2545 Cornhusker Hwy 68521. I-80, exit 403
(27th St), 3 mi s. Int corridors. **Pets:** Accepted. (A$K) ⊠ 🐾🅜 🛏 🖵

▼▼▼ **Super 8-Lincoln/West "O" Street** 🅷
(402) 476-8887. **$55-$87.** 2635 West O St 68528. I-80, exit 396 eastbound, 0.5 mi e; exit 397 westbound, 0.5 mi w. Int corridors.
Pets: Accepted. (A$K) ⊠ 🐾🅜 🛏 🖵

MCCOOK
▼▼▼ **Days Inn-McCook** 🅷
(308) 345-7115. **$72-$84.** 901 N Hwy 83 69001. Jct US 6 and 34, 0.3 mi
n. Int corridors. **Pets:** Medium, dogs only. $15 daily fee/pet. Designated
rooms, service with restrictions, supervision.
(A$K) ⊠ 🐾🅜 🛏 🖵 🏊

◆▼▼ **Holiday Inn Express** 🅷
(308) 345-4505. **Call for rates.** 1 Holiday Bison Dr 69001. On US 83,
just n of jct US 6 and 34. Int corridors. **Pets:** Accepted.
⊠ 🐾🅜 🛏 🖵

MORRILL
◆▼▼ **Oak Tree Inn** 🅷
(308) 247-2111. **$59-$70.** 707 E Webster 69358. 0.5 mi e on US 26.
Ext/int corridors. **Pets:** Accepted. (A$K) ⊠ 🐾🅜 🛏 🖵 🍴

NORFOLK
🆎 ◆▼▼ **Norfolk Lodge & Suites, an Ascend Collection**
hotel 🅷
(402) 379-3833. **$85-$171.** 4200 W Norfolk Ave 68701. On US 275
Bypass, 3 mi w of jct US 81. Ext/int corridors. **Pets:** Small, dogs only.
$20 one-time fee/pet. Designated rooms, service with restrictions, crate.
(SAVE) ⊠ 🐾🅜 🛏 🖵 🍴 🏊 ⊠

▼▼▼ **Super 8-Norfolk** 🅷
(402) 379-2220. **$45-$69.** 1223 Omaha Ave 68701. Jct US 275 Bypass
and 81. Int corridors. **Pets:** Accepted. (A$K) ⊠ 🛏 🖵

NORTH PLATTE
🆎 ◆ **Americas Best Value Travelers Inn** Ⓜ
(308) 534-4020. **$40-$60.** 602 E 4th St 69101. I-80, exit 177 (US 83),
1.5 mi n, then 0.3 mi e. Ext corridors. **Pets:** Medium, other species. Service with restrictions, supervision. (SAVE) ⊠ 🛏 🏊

◆▼ **Comfort Inn** 🅷 🐾
(308) 532-6144. **$75-$165.** 2901 S Jeffers St 69101. I-80, exit 177 (US
83), just s. Int corridors. **Pets:** Medium. $15 daily fee/room. Service with
restrictions, supervision. (A$K) ⊠ 🐾🅜 🛏 🖵 🏊

◆▼▼ **Holiday Inn Express Hotel & Suites** 🅷
(308) 532-9500. **$99-$129.** 300 Holiday Frontage Rd 69101. I-80, exit
177 (US 83), just s. Int corridors. **Pets:** $20 one-time fee/room. Desig-
nated rooms, service with restrictions, supervision.
(A$K) ⊠ 🐾🅜 🛏 🖵 🏊 ⊠

🆎 ◆▼▼ **La Quinta Inn & Suites** 🅷 🐾
(308) 534-0700. **$89-$169.** 2600 Eagles Wings Pl 69101. I-80, exit 179,
just n, then just w. Int corridors. **Pets:** Medium, other species. Service
with restrictions, supervision. (SAVE) ⊠ 🐾🅜 🛏 🖵 🏊

🆎 ◆▼▼ **Rodeway Inn** Ⓜ
(308) 532-2313. **$49-$79.** 920 N Jeffers St 69101. I-80, exit 177 (US 83),
2 mi n on US 30 and 83. Ext corridors. **Pets:** Medium. $7 daily fee/pet.
Designated rooms, service with restrictions, supervision.
(SAVE) ⊠ 🐾🅜 🛏 🖵 🏊

OGALLALA
🆎 ◆▼▼ **Best Western Stagecoach Inn** 🅷 🐾
(308) 284-3656. **$60-$100.** 201 Stagecoach Tr 69153. I-80, exit 126 (US
26/SR 61), just n, then e on Frontage Rd. Ext corridors. **Pets:** Medium,
other species. $10 daily fee/pet. Designated rooms, service with restric-
tions, supervision. (SAVE) ⊠ 🐾🅜 🛏 🖵 🍴 🏊 ⊠

🆎 ◆▼▼ **Days Inn** Ⓜ 🐾
(308) 284-6365. **$59-$89.** 601 Stagecoach Tr 69153. I-80, exit 126 (US
26/SR 61), just n, then e on Frontage Rd. Int corridors. **Pets:** Dogs only.
$6 daily fee/room. Designated rooms, service with restrictions, supervision.
(SAVE) ⊠ 🐾🅜 🛏 🖵

▼▼▼ **Holiday Inn Express** 🅷
(308) 284-2266. **$94-$109, 10 day notice.** 501 Stagecoach Tr 69153.
I-80, exit 126 (US 26/SR 61), just n, then e on Frontage Rd. Ext/int corridors. **Pets:** Medium, other species. $20 one-time fee/pet. Designated
rooms, service with restrictions, supervision. ⊠ 🐾🅜 🛏 🖵

OMAHA
🆎 ◆▼▼ **Best Western Kelly Inn Omaha** 🅷 🐾
(402) 339-7400. **$79-$140.** 4706 S 108th St 68137. I-80, exit 445 (L St
E), 0.3 mi e, then just s. Int corridors. **Pets:** Other species. Service with
restrictions, supervision. (SAVE) ⊠ 🛏 🖵 🍴 🏊 ⊠

🆎 ◆▼▼ **Best Western Settle Inn** 🅷
(402) 431-1246. **$80-$140.** 650 N 109th Ct 68154. I-680, exit 3 (Dodge
St W), 0.7 mi w to 108th St and Old Mill Rd, then just w on Mill Valley
Rd. Int corridors. **Pets:** Small, dogs only. $15 daily fee/room. Designated
rooms, service with restrictions, supervision.
(SAVE) ⊠ 🐾🅜 🛏 🖵 🏊 ⊠

🆎 ◆▼▼ **Best Western Seville Plaza** 🅷 🐾
(402) 345-2222. **$69-$169.** 330 N 30th St 68131. I-480, exit 2B westbound; exit 2A northbound, just w on Dodge St, then just n on 30th St.
Int corridors. **Pets:** Other species. $10 daily fee/room. No service.
(SAVE) ⊠ 🐾🅜 🛏 🖵

◆▼ **Candlewood Suites** 🅷 🐾
(402) 758-2848. **$85-$86.** 360 S 108th Ave 68154. I-680, exit 3 (Dodge
St W), 0.7 mi to 108th St, then 0.8 mi s. Int corridors. **Pets:** Other species. $75 one-time fee/pet. Service with restrictions, crate.
(A$K) ⊠ 🐾🅜 🛏 🖵

◆▼ **Comfort Inn & Suites** 🅷 🐾
(402) 934-4900. **$79-$99.** 7007 Grover St 68106. I-80, exit 449 (72nd
St), just n, then e. Int corridors. **Pets:** Large. $10 daily fee/pet. Crate.
(A$K) ⊠ 🐾🅜 🛏 🖵 🍴 🏊

🆎 ◆▼▼ **Comfort Inn-Southwest** 🅷
(402) 593-2380. **$72-$90.** 10728 L St 68127. I-80, exit 445 (L St E), just
n on 108th St, then e. Int corridors. **Pets:** Accepted.
(SAVE) ⊠ 🐾🅜 🛏 🖵 🏊

🆎 ◆▼▼ **Countryside Suites** Ⓜ
(402) 884-2644. **$55-$75.** 9477 S 142nd St 68138. I-80, exit 440, just ne.
Ext corridors. **Pets:** Other species. $10 daily fee/pet. Service with restric-
tions, supervision. (SAVE) ⊠ 🐾🅜 🛏 🖵

◆▼▼ **Crowne Plaza Hotel** 🅷
(402) 496-0850. **$79-$189.** 655 N 108th Ave 68154. I-680, exit 3 (Dodge
St W), 0.7 mi to 108th St to 108th Ave and N Old Mill Rd exits, then just
n. Int corridors. **Pets:** Large. $100 deposit/room, $25 one-time fee/room.
Service with restrictions, crate. (A$K) ⊠ 🐾🅜 🛏 🖵 🍴 🏊 ⊠

🆎 ◆▼▼ **Doubletree Guest Suites Omaha** 🅷
(402) 397-5141. **$89-$249.** 7270 Cedar St 68124. I-80, exit 449 (72nd
St), 1.3 mi n. Int corridors. **Pets:** Accepted.
(SAVE) ⊠ 🐾🅜 🛏 🖵 🍴 🏊

◆▼▼ **Hawthorn Suites** 🅷
(402) 331-0101. **$119-$149.** 11025 M St 68137. I-80, exit 445 (L St E),
0.3 mi e, just s on 108th St, then just w. Ext corridors. **Pets:** Medium. $6
daily fee/room. Service with restrictions.
(A$K) ⊠ 🐾🅜 🛏 🖵 🏊 ⊠

◆▼▼ **Holiday Inn Express Hotel & Suites-West** 🅷 🐾
(402) 333-5566. **$109-$229.** 17677 Wright St 68130. I-80, exit 445 (L St
W), 5.5 mi w, then just s. Int corridors. **Pets:** Other species. $25 one-time
fee/room. Service with restrictions, supervision.
(A$K) ⊠ 🐾🅜 🛏 🖵 🏊 ⊠

▼▼▼▼ Homewood Suites 🅷
(402) 397-7500. **$159-$189.** 7010 Hascall St 68106. I-80, exit 449 (72nd St), just n, then just e. Ext/int corridors. **Pets:** Accepted.
❌ 🚹M 🔧 💻 🏊

▼▼▼ La Quinta Inn Omaha-Northwest 🅷 🐾
(402) 493-1900. **$52-$85.** 3330 N 104th Ave 68134-3764. I-680, exit 4 (Maple St), just w to 108th St, just n to Bedford, then just e. Int corridors. **Pets:** Medium, other species. Service with restrictions, supervision.
ASK ❌ 🚹M 🔧 💻 🏊

▼▼▼ La Quinta Inn Omaha Southwest 🅷 🐾
(402) 592-5200. **$52-$85.** 10760 M St 68127. I-80, exit 445 (L St E), 0.3 mi e, s on 108th St, then just e. Int corridors. **Pets:** Medium, other species. Service with restrictions, supervision. ASK ❌ 🚹M 🔧 💻

▲▲▲⟋ ▼▼▼ Ramada Omaha 🅷
(402) 391-8129. **$74.** 3301 S 72nd St 68124. I-80, exit 449 (72nd St), just n. Ext/int corridors. **Pets:** Medium, other species. $50 deposit/room, $10 daily fee/pet. Service with restrictions, crate.
SAVE ❌ 🚹M 🔧 💻

▲▲▲⟋ ▼▼▼ Relax Inn Motel & Suites 🅼 🐾
(402) 731-7300. **$50-$85.** 4578 S 60th St 68117. I-80, exit 450 (60th St), 0.8 mi s. Ext corridors. **Pets:** Small, dogs only. $20 deposit/room, $5 daily fee/pet. Service with restrictions, supervision. SAVE ❌ 🚹M 🔧 💻

▲▲▲⟋ ▼▼▼▼ Residence Inn by Marriott Omaha-Central 🅷
(402) 553-8898. **$161-$197.** 6990 Dodge St 68132. I-680, exit 3 (Dodge St E), 3 mi e. Ext corridors. **Pets:** Other species. $100 one-time fee/room. Service with restrictions, crate. SAVE ❌ 🚹M 🔧 💻 🏊 ❌

▲▲▲⟋ ▼▼▼ Satellite Motel 🅼
(402) 733-7373. **$45-$55.** 6006 L St 68117. I-80, exit 450 (60th St), 0.8 mi s; just n of US 275 and SR 92. Ext/int corridors. **Pets:** Accepted.
SAVE ❌ 🚹M 🔧 💻

▼▼▼ Sleep Inn & Suites 🅷
(402) 342-2525. **$77-$99.** 2525 Abbott Dr 68110. I-480 E, exit 14th St (Cuming St), 2 mi n, follow signs. Int corridors. **Pets:** Medium. $10 daily fee/pet. Service with restrictions, crate. ASK ❌ 🔧 💻

▼▼▼ Super 8-Omaha/Aksarben 🅷
(402) 390-0700. **$49-$85.** 7111 Spring St 68106. I-80, exit 449 (72nd St), 0.3 mi n. Int corridors. **Pets:** Accepted. ASK ❌ 🔧 💻

O'NEILL
▼▼ Elms Motel 🅼
(402) 336-3800. **Call for rates.** 414 E Hwy 20 68763. 1 mi se on US 20/275. Ext corridors. **Pets:** Accepted. ❌ 🔧 💻

▼▼▼ Super 8-O'Neill 🅷
(402) 336-3100. **$55-$106.** 106 E Hwy 20 68763. 0.5 mi e on US 20/275. Int corridors. **Pets:** Accepted. ASK ❌ 🚹M 🔧 💻

PAXTON
▼▼ Paxton Days Inn 🅼
(308) 239-4510. **Call for rates.** 851 Paxton Rd 69155. I-80, exit 145, just n. Ext corridors. **Pets:** Accepted. ❌ 🚹M 🔧 💻

ST. PAUL
▼ Bel-Air Motel & RV Park 🅼
(308) 754-4466. **$49-$60.** 1158 Highway 281 68873. On US 281, 1 mi s. Ext corridors. **Pets:** Accepted. ASK ❌ 🔧 💻

SCOTTSBLUFF
▼▼ Comfort Inn 🅷
(308) 632-7510. **$70-$90.** 1902 21st Ave 69361. 1.8 mi e on US 26, just n. Ext/int corridors. **Pets:** Other species. $10 deposit/pet. Service with restrictions, supervision. ASK ❌ 🚹M 🔧 💻 🏊

▼▼ Scottsbluff Super 8 🅷
(308) 635-1600. **Call for rates.** 2202 Delta Dr 69361. 1.8 mi e on US 26. Int corridors. **Pets:** Accepted. ❌ 🚹M 🔧 💻 🏊

SIDNEY
▲▲▲⟋ ▼▼▼ AmericInn Lodge & Suites of Sidney 🅷 🐾
(308) 254-0100. **$81-$155.** 645 Cabela Dr 69162. I-80, exit 59, just nw. Int corridors. **Pets:** Other species. $12 daily fee/pet. Service with restrictions, supervision. SAVE ❌ 🚹M 🔧 💻 🏊

▲▲▲⟋ ▼▼▼ Days Inn 🅷
(308) 254-2121. **$75-$150.** 3042 Silverberg Dr 69162. I-80, exit 59, just n. Int corridors. **Pets:** Medium. $10 daily fee/pet. Designated rooms, service with restrictions, supervision. SAVE ❌ 🚹M 🔧 💻 🏊

▼▼▼ Holiday Inn & Conference Center 🅷
(308) 254-2000. **$99-$309.** 664 Chase Blvd 69162. I-80, exit 59, just s. Int corridors. **Pets:** Accepted. ASK ❌ 🚹M 🔧 💻 🍴 🏊

SOUTH SIOUX CITY
▼▼ Americas Best Value Inn 🅷
(402) 494-4114. **$45-$80.** 4402 Dakota Ave 68776. US 20, exit 2, just s. Int corridors. **Pets:** Accepted. ASK ❌ 🚹M 🔧 💻

▼▼▼ Marina Inn Conference Center 🅷 🐾
(402) 494-4000. **Call for rates.** 4th St & B St 68776. I-29, exit 149 southbound; exit 148 northbound, e at traffic light by Nebraska side of bridge; on banks of Missouri River. Int corridors. **Pets:** Small, other species. $10 daily fee/pet. Designated rooms, service with restrictions, supervision. ❌ 🚹M 🔧 💻 🍴 🏊 ❌

SYRACUSE
▼▼▼ Sleep Inn & Suites 🅷
(402) 269-2700. **Call for rates.** 130 N 30th Rd 68446. Jct SR 2, 1 mi n on SR 50. Int corridors. **Pets:** Accepted. ❌ 🚹M 🔧 💻 🏊

THEDFORD
▲▲▲⟋ ▼▼▼ Roadside Inn 🅷
(308) 645-2284. **$66-$95.** 39357 E Hwy 2 69166. 1 mi e on SR 2, just w of US 83. Int corridors. **Pets:** Other species. $25 deposit/room, $8 daily fee/room. Designated rooms, service with restrictions, supervision.
SAVE ❌ 🚹M 🔧 💻

VALENTINE
▼▼ Dunes Lodge & Suites 🅼
(402) 376-3131. **$49-$139.** 340 E Hwys 20 & 83 69201. Jct US 20/83, 0.3 mi e. Ext corridors. **Pets:** Accepted. ASK ❌ 🔧 💻

▲▲▲⟋ ▼▼▼ Trade Winds Motel 🅼
(402) 376-1600. **$61-$89.** E Hwys 20 & 83 69201. Jct US 20/83, 1 mi se. Ext corridors. **Pets:** $10 daily fee/pet. Designated rooms, service with restrictions, supervision. SAVE ❌ 🔧 💻 🏊

WAHOO
▼▼ Wahoo Heritage Inn 🅷
(402) 443-1288. **$58-$74.** 950 N Chestnut 68066. On US 77 and SR 92, just nw of downtown. Ext/int corridors. **Pets:** Accepted.
ASK ❌ 🚹M 🔧 💻

WAYNE
▼ Super 8-Wayne 🅷
(402) 375-4898. **$52-$65.** 610 Tomar Dr 68787. SR 35, 0.6 mi e of jct SR 15. Int corridors. **Pets:** Accepted. ASK ❌ 🚹M 🔧 💻

YORK
▲▲▲⟋ ▼▼▼ Americas Best Value Inn-Palmer Inn 🅼 🐾
(402) 362-5585. **$45-$95.** 2426 S Lincoln Ave 68467. I-80, exit 353 (US 81), 1 mi n. Ext corridors. **Pets:** Other species. $10 daily fee/room. Designated rooms, service with restrictions, supervision.
SAVE ❌ 🚹M 🔧 💻 🏊

▼▼▼ Holiday Inn H

(402) 362-6661. **$105-$125, 7 day notice.** 4619 S Lincoln Ave 68467. I-80, exit 353 (US 81), just s. Int corridors. **Pets:** Other species. $25 one-time fee/room. Designated rooms, service with restrictions, supervision.

ASK ✕ &M 🖥 🖵 🍴 🏊

◇◇◇ ▼▼▼ Yorkshire Inn Motel M 🐾

(402) 362-6633. **$42-$79.** 3402 S Lincoln Ave 68467. I-80, exit 353 (US 81), 0.5 mi n. Ext/int corridors. **Pets:** Other species. $5 daily fee/pet. Service with restrictions, supervision. SAVE ✕ 🖥

NEVADA

BEATTY

⚥ ▼▼◆ Stagecoach Hotel Casino M ❖
(775) 553-2419. **$62-$77.** 900 E Hwy 95 N 89003. North end of town; west side of US 95. Ext/int corridors. **Pets:** Medium, other species. $10 deposit/pet. Designated rooms, service with restrictions, supervision.
[SAVE] [✕] [&M] [🖪] [¶] [⇌]

CARLIN

▼▼ Comfort Inn H
(775) 754-6110. **Call for rates.** 1018 Fir St 89822. I-80, exit 280, just s, just e, then just n. Int corridors. **Pets:** Accepted. [✕] [&M] [🖪] [💻]

CARSON CITY

⚥ ▼▼ Days Inn M
(775) 883-3343. **$50-$150.** 3103 N Carson St 89706. US 395 N, north end of town. Ext corridors. **Pets:** Medium. $10 daily fee/pet. Service with restrictions, supervision. [SAVE] [✕] [🖪] [💻]

▼▼▼ Holiday Inn Express & Suites H ❖
(775) 283-4055. **$100-$200.** 4055 N Carson St 89701. US 395, exit 43, 0.7 mi se. Int corridors. **Pets:** Medium. $20 one-time fee/room. Designated rooms, service with restrictions, crate.
[A$K] [✕] [&M] [🖪] [💻] [⇌]

⚥ ▼▼▼ The Plaza Hotel & Conference Center H
(775) 883-9500. **$49-$79.** 801 S Carson St 89701. South end of town. Ext/int corridors. **Pets:** Accepted. [SAVE] [✕] [🖪] [💻]

ELKO

⚥ ▼▼▼▼ Gold Country Inn & Casino H ❖
(775) 738-8421. **$79-$159.** 2050 Idaho St 89801. I-80, exit 303, just s. Ext corridors. **Pets:** Other species. $15 one-time fee/room. Designated rooms, service with restrictions, crate.
[SAVE] [✕] [&M] [🖪] [💻] [¶] [≋]

⚥ ▼▼ Oak Tree Inn H
(775) 777-2222. **$89-$109.** 95 Spruce Rd 89802. I-80, exit 301, just n. Int corridors. **Pets:** Other species. $10 daily fee/pet. Service with restrictions, supervision. [SAVE] [✕] [&M] [🖪] [💻]

⚥ ▼▼▼▼ Red Lion Hotel & Casino H
(775) 738-2111. **$99-$259.** 2065 Idaho St 89801. I-80, exit 303, just s. Int corridors. **Pets:** Other species. $20 one-time fee/room. Service with restrictions, supervision. [SAVE] [✕] [&M] [🖪] [💻] [¶] [⇌]

⚥ ▼ Rodeway Inn M
(775) 738-7152. **$49-$129, 7 day notice.** 736 Idaho St 89801. I-80, exit 301 or 303, 1 mi s. Ext corridors. **Pets:** Medium. $15 daily fee/pet. Designated rooms, service with restrictions, supervision. [SAVE] [✕] [🖪] [💻]

▼▼ Shilo Inn Suites–Elko H ❖
(775) 738-5522. **$95-$175.** 2401 Mountain City Hwy 89801. I-80, exit 301, just n. Int corridors. **Pets:** Dogs only. $25 one-time fee/room. Designated rooms, service with restrictions, supervision.
[A$K] [✕] [🖪] [💻] [⇌] [✕]

⚥ ▼ Thunderbird Motel M
(775) 738-7115. **$55-$100.** 345 Idaho St 89801. I-80, exit 301 or 303, 1 mi s. Ext corridors. **Pets:** Accepted. [SAVE] [✕] [🖪] [⇌]

ELY

⚥ ▼▼◆ Best Western Park Vue Motel M
(775) 289-4497. **$70-$90.** 930 Aultman St 89301. 0.8 mi w of jct US 50 and 93. Ext corridors. **Pets:** Accepted. [SAVE] [✕] [🖪] [💻]

⚥ ▼▼◆ Historic Hotel Nevada & Gambling Hall H ❖
(775) 289-6665. **$49-$69.** 501 Aultman St 89301. 1.1 mi w of jct US 50 and 93. Int corridors. **Pets:** Other species. $10 daily fee/pet. Designated rooms, service with restrictions. [SAVE] [✕] [🖪] [💻] [¶]

⚥ ▼▼◆ Prospector Hotel Gambling Hall H
(775) 289-8900. **$79-$110.** 1501 E Aultman St 89301. 0.8 mi e of jct US 50 and 93. Int corridors. **Pets:** Other species. $10 daily fee/pet. Designated rooms, supervision. [SAVE] [✕] [&M] [🖪] [💻] [¶] [⇌]

⚥ ▼▼◆ Ramada Inn-Copper Queen Casino H
(775) 289-4884. **$94-$199.** 805 Great Basin Blvd 89301. 0.3 mi s of jct US 6, 50 and 93. Ext/int corridors. **Pets:** Dogs only. Service with restrictions. [SAVE] [✕] [&M] [🖪] [💻] [¶] [⇌]

EUREKA

⚥ ▼▼◆ Best Western Eureka Inn H
(775) 237-5247. **$100-$105.** 251 N Main St 89316. On east side of Main St; center. Int corridors. **Pets:** $15 daily fee/pet. Designated rooms, service with restrictions, supervision. [SAVE] [✕] [&M] [🖪] [💻]

FALLON

⚥ ▼▼ Best Western Fallon Inn H
(775) 423-6005. **$90-$120.** 1035 W Williams Ave 89406. 0.4 mi w of jct US 50 and 95. Ext corridors. **Pets:** Dogs only. $15 daily fee/pet. Designated rooms, service with restrictions, supervision.
[SAVE] [✕] [🖪] [💻] [⇌]

▼▼▼ Holiday Inn Express H
(775) 428-2588. **$100-$250.** 55 Commercial Way 89406. At Williams Ave, 0.8 mi w of US 95. Int corridors. **Pets:** Other species. $25 daily fee/pet. Designated rooms, service with restrictions, supervision.
[A$K] [✕] [&M] [🖪] [💻] [⇌] [✕]

⚥ ▼ Motel 6 #4140 M
(775) 423-2277. **$48-$89.** 1705 S Taylor St 89406. 0.8 mi s of jct US 50. Ext corridors. **Pets:** Other species. Service with restrictions, supervision.
[SAVE] [✕] [🖪] [⇌]

FERNLEY

⚥ ▼▼◆ Best Western Fernley Inn M
(775) 575-6776. **$81-$105.** 1405 E Newlands Dr 89408. I-80, exit 48, just sw. Ext corridors. **Pets:** $10 daily fee/pet. Designated rooms, service with restrictions, crate. [SAVE] [✕] [&M] [🖪] [💻] [⇌]

GARDNERVILLE

⚥ ▼▼ Historian Inn M ❖
(775) 783-1175. **$69-$89.** 1427 Hwy 395 N 89410. Center. Ext corridors. **Pets:** Other species. $10 daily fee/pet. Service with restrictions, crate.
[SAVE] [✕] [&M] [🖪] [💻]

⚥ ▼▼ Super 8 Topaz Lodge H ❖
(775) 266-3338. **$59-$105, 3 day notice.** 1979 US 395 S 89410. US 395 S at Topaz Lake, 22 mi s. Ext corridors. **Pets:** Dogs only. $12 daily fee/room. No service. [SAVE] [✕] [💻] [¶] [⇌]

⚐ ▼ Westerner Motel M
(775) 782-3602. **$49-$99.** 1353 US 395 89410. On US 395, south end of town. Ext corridors. **Pets:** Small. Designated rooms, service with restrictions, supervision. [SAVE] [✕] [📶] [💻] [🔁]

HAWTHORNE

⚐ ▼▼ America's Best Inn & Suites M
(775) 945-2660. **$95-$110.** 1402 E 5th St 89415. US 95, 0.5 mi e. Ext corridors. **Pets:** Other species. $10 daily fee/room. Service with restrictions, crate. [SAVE] [✕] [📶] [💻] [🔁]

JACKPOT

▼▼ Horseshu Hotel & Casino H
(775) 755-7777. **$29-$109.** 1385 Hwy 93 89825. On US 93. Int corridors. **Pets:** $5 one-time fee/pet. Designated rooms, service with restrictions. [ASK] [✕] [💻] [🍴] [🔁]

LAKE TAHOE AREA

INCLINE VILLAGE

⚐ ▼▼ ▼▼ Hyatt Regency Lake Tahoe Resort, Spa & Casino H
(775) 832-1234. **$149-$479, 3 day notice.** 111 Country Club Dr 89450. 0.4 mi w of SR 28, toward lake via Country Club Dr; 2 mi s of Mt. Rose Hwy. Int corridors. **Pets:** Accepted.
[SAVE] [✕] [♿M] [📶] [💻] [🍴] [🔁] [✕]

STATELINE

▼▼ Lakeside Inn and Casino H
(775) 588-7777. **Call for rates.** 168 Hwy 50 89449. Just n of jct SR 207. Ext/int corridors. **Pets:** Accepted. [✕] [📶] [💻] [🍴] [🔁]

ZEPHYR COVE

⚐ ▼▼ ▼ Zephyr Cove Resort CA
(775) 589-4907. **Call for rates.** 760 Hwy 50 89449. 4 mi n of Stateline, NV. Ext/int corridors. **Pets:** Accepted. [SAVE] [✕] [📶] [💻] [🍴] [✕]

END AREA

LAS VEGAS METROPOLITAN AREA

BOULDER CITY

⚐ ▼▼ Best Western Lake Mead Inn M
(702) 293-6444. **$90-$110.** 110 Ville Dr 89005. Jct US 93. Ext corridors. **Pets:** $10 daily fee/pet. Designated rooms, service with restrictions. [SAVE] [✕] [📶] [💻] [🔁]

⚐ ▼▼ Boulder Inn & Suites M
(702) 369-1000. **$79-$229.** 704 Nevada Way 89005. On US 93. Ext corridors. **Pets:** Accepted. [SAVE] [✕] [📶] [💻] [🍴] [🔁]

⚐ ▼▼ El Rancho Boulder Motel M
(702) 293-1085. **$75-$120, 3 day notice.** 725 Nevada Way 89005. On US 93. Ext corridors. **Pets:** Dogs only. $10 daily fee/pet. Designated rooms, service with restrictions, supervision. [SAVE] [✕] [📶] [🔁]

⚐ ▼ Sands Motel M 🐾
(702) 293-2589. **$64-$99, 3 day notice.** 809 Nevada Way 89005. On US 93. Ext corridors. **Pets:** Medium, dogs only. $10 one-time fee/pet. Designated rooms, service with restrictions, supervision. [SAVE] [✕] [📶]

ECHO BAY

▼ Echo Bay Resort M
(702) 394-4000. **$70-$125, 3 day notice.** North Shore Rd 89040. 4 mi e of SR 167; on Lake Mead. Int corridors. **Pets:** $50 deposit/pet, $10 one-time fee/pet. Service with restrictions, supervision. [ASK] [✕] [♿M] [📶] [🍴] [✕]

HENDERSON

⚐ ▼▼ ▼▼ Green Valley Ranch Resort & Spa H
(702) 617-7777. **$85-$700.** 2300 S Paseo Verde Dr 89052. I-215, exit Green Valley Pkwy, just s. Int corridors. **Pets:** Accepted. [SAVE] [✕] [📶] [🍴] [🔁] [✕]

▼▼ Hawthorn Inn & Suites M
(702) 568-7800. **$69-$189.** 910 S Boulder Hwy 89015. S of Lake Mead Pkwy. Int corridors. **Pets:** Accepted. [ASK] [✕] [📶] [💻] [🔁]

⚐ ▼▼ ▼▼ Loews Lake Las Vegas Resort H 🐾
(702) 567-6000. **$129-$289.** 101 Montelago Blvd 89011. I-215, e to end, then n on Lake Las Vegas Pkwy. Int corridors. **Pets:** Other species. $25 one-time fee/room. Designated rooms, service with restrictions. [SAVE] [✕] [♿M] [📶] [💻] [🍴] [🔁] [✕]

▼▼ ▼ Residence Inn-Green Valley H
(702) 434-2700. **$109-$119.** 2190 Olympic Ave 89014. I-215, exit Green Valley Pkwy N, 3 mi n at Sunset Rd. Int corridors. **Pets:** Accepted. [✕] [♿M] [📶] [💻] [🔁] [✕]

▼▼ ▼▼ ▼ The Ritz-Carlton, Lake Las Vegas H 🐾
(702) 567-4700. **$119-$329.** 1610 Lake Las Vegas Pkwy 89011. I-515, exit Lake Mead Pkwy, 6.3 mi ne, then 0.5 mi n. Int corridors. **Pets:** Other species. $75 one-time fee/room. Service with restrictions. [ASK] [✕] [♿M] [📶] [💻] [🍴] [🔁] [✕]

LAS VEGAS

⚐ ▼▼ ▼ Alexis Park Resort Hotel H
(702) 796-3300. **$59-$289.** 375 E Harmon Ave 89109. Jct Las Vegas Blvd, just e. Ext corridors. **Pets:** Large. $50 one-time fee/pet. Designated rooms, service with restrictions, supervision. [SAVE] [✕] [♿M] [📶] [💻] [🍴] [🔁] [✕]

⚐ ▼▼ ▼ Best Western Main Street Inn M
(702) 382-3455. **$50-$150.** 1000 N Main St 89101. I-15, exit 43E northbound; exit 44E southbound. Ext corridors. **Pets:** Large, other species. $15 daily fee/pet. Service with restrictions, supervision. [SAVE] [✕] [📶] [💻] [🍴] [🔁]

⚐ ▼▼ ▼ Best Western Nellis Motor Inn M
(702) 643-6111. **$69-$89, 4 day notice.** 5330 E Craig Rd 89115. I-15, exit 48, 2.8 mi e; 0.3 mi from Nellis AFB. Ext corridors. **Pets:** Accepted. [SAVE] [✕] [📶] [💻] [🔁]

⚐ ▼▼ ▼ Best Western Parkview Inn M
(702) 385-1213. **$60-$200.** 921 Las Vegas Blvd N 89101. I-15, exit US 93/95, 0.3 mi n at Washington. Ext corridors. **Pets:** Large, other species. $8 daily fee/pet. Service with restrictions, supervision. [SAVE] [✕] [📶] [💻] [🔁]

▼▼ ▼▼ **Candlewood Suites** 🅷

(702) 836-3660. **$59-$169.** 4034 S Paradise Rd 89169. I-15, exit E Flamingo Rd to Paradise Rd, just ne. Int corridors. **Pets:** Accepted.

ⒶⓈⓀ ✕ ♿M 🛏 🖵 🏊

ⒶⒶⒶ ▼▼▼▼ **Element Hotel Las Vegas**
                  Summerlin 🅷 🐾

(702) 589-2000. **$89-$329.** 10555 Discovery Dr 89135. I-215, exit 23 (Town Center), just n. Int corridors. **Pets:** Medium, dogs only. $50 one-time fee/room. Service with restrictions, supervision.

ⓈⒶⓋⒺ ✕ ♿M 🛏 🖵 🏊

▼▼ ▼▼ **Emerald Suites** Ⓜ

(702) 948-9999. **$49-$199, 3 day notice.** 9145 Las Vegas Blvd S 89123. I-15, exit Silverado Ranch Blvd, just e, then 0.5 mi n. Ext corridors. **Pets:** Accepted. ⒶⓈⓀ ✕ 🛏 🖵 🏊

ⒶⒶⒶ ▼▼ **Highland Inn Motel** Ⓜ

(702) 896-4333. **$50-$130.** 8025 Dean Martin Dr 89139. I-15, exit W Blue Diamond Rd, just w. Ext corridors. **Pets:** Small. $50 deposit/room, $10 daily fee/pet. Service with restrictions, supervision.

ⓈⒶⓋⒺ ✕ 🛏 🖵

▼▼ ▼▼ **Homestead Studio Suites Hotel-Las**
              Vegas/Midtown Ⓜ

(702) 369-1414. **$70-$85.** 3045 S Maryland Pkwy 89109. I-15, exit Sahara Ave E, 1.7 mi e, then 0.6 mi s. Int corridors. **Pets:** Other species. $25 daily fee/room. Designated rooms, service with restrictions, crate.

ⒶⓈⓀ ✕ 🛏 🖵

▼▼▼▼ **La Quinta Inn & Suites Las Vegas**
          (Lakes/West) Ⓜ 🐾

(702) 243-0356. **$59-$225.** 9570 W Sahara Ave 89117. Just w of Fort Apache Rd. Int corridors. **Pets:** Medium, other species. Service with restrictions, supervision. ⒶⓈⓀ ✕ ♿M 🛏 🖵 🏊

▼▼▼▼ **La Quinta Inn & Suites Las Vegas (Summerlin Tech**
          Center) Ⓜ 🐾

(702) 360-1200. **$70-$140.** 7101 Cascade Valley Ct 89128-0455. US 95, exit W Cheyenne Ave. Int corridors. **Pets:** Medium, other species. Service with restrictions, supervision. ⒶⓈⓀ ✕ ♿M 🛏 🖵 🏊

ⒶⒶⒶ ▼▼▼▼ **La Quinta Inn Las Vegas (Nellis)** Ⓜ 🐾

(702) 632-0229. **$80-$190.** 4288 N Nellis Blvd 89115. I-15, exit Craig Rd, e to N Las Vegas Blvd. Int corridors. **Pets:** Medium, other species. Service with restrictions, supervision. ⓈⒶⓋⒺ ✕ ♿M 🛏 🖵 🏊

▼▼ ▼▼ **Microtel Inn & Suites** 🅷

(702) 273-2500. **$69-$199.** 55 E Robindale Rd 89123. I-15, exit Blue Diamond Rd, just e, then just n. Int corridors. **Pets:** Other species. $25 daily fee/room. Designated rooms, service with restrictions.

✕ 🛏 🖵 🏊

▼▼▼▼ **Residence Inn by Marriott Las Vegas South** 🅷

(702) 795-7378. **$139-$149.** 5875 Dean Martin Rd 89118. I-15, exit Russell Rd, just sw. Int corridors. **Pets:** Large. $100 one-time fee/room. Service with restrictions, crate. ✕ ♿M 🛏 🖵 🏊 ⌧

▼▼▼▼ **Residence Inn-Hughes Center** 🅷

(702) 650-0040. **$109-$119.** 370 Hughes Center Dr 89169. I-15, exit Paradise Rd. Int corridors. **Pets:** Accepted.

✕ ♿M 🛏 🖵 🏊 ⌧

▼▼▼▼ **Residence Inn Las Vegas Convention Center** 🅷

(702) 796-9300. **$104-$119.** 3225 Paradise Rd 89169. Opposite the convention center. Ext corridors. **Pets:** Accepted.

✕ ♿M 🛏 🖵 🏊 ⌧

▼▼▼▼ **Staybridge Suites Las Vegas** 🅷

(702) 259-2663. **Call for rates.** 5735 Dean Martin Dr 89118. I-15, exit Russell Rd, just w. Int corridors. **Pets:** Accepted.

✕ ♿M 🛏 🖵 🏊

ⒶⒶⒶ ▼▼▼▼ **Super 8** Ⓜ

(702) 794-0888. **$45-$175.** 4250 Koval Ln 89109. Jct Flamingo Rd and Koval Ln, just s. Int corridors. **Pets:** Large, other species. $15 daily fee/pet. Designated rooms, service with restrictions, supervision.

ⓈⒶⓋⒺ ✕ 🛏 🖵 🏊

ⒶⒶⒶ ▼▼▼▼ **Westgate Flamingo Bay** Ⓒ🅞

(702) 251-3435. **$89-$251, 3 day notice.** 5625 W Flamingo Rd 89103. I-15, exit E Flamingo Rd, just e of Jones Blvd. Ext corridors. **Pets:** Accepted. ⓈⒶⓋⒺ ✕ ♿M 🛏 🖵 🏊 ⌧

ⒶⒶⒶ ▼▼▼▼ **The Westin Casuarina Las Vegas Hotel,**
              Casino and Spa 🅷 🐾

(702) 836-5900. **Call for rates.** 160 E Flamingo Rd 89109. I-15, exit Flamingo Rd E, 1.1 mi. Int corridors. **Pets:** Large. $139 deposit/room, $35 one-time fee/room. Service with restrictions, supervision.

ⓈⒶⓋⒺ ✕ ♿M 🛏 🖵 🍽 🏊 ⌧

LAUGHLIN

ⒶⒶⒶ ▼▼▼▼ **Don Laughlin's Riverside Resort Hotel &**
              Casino 🅷

(702) 298-2535. **$45-$750.** 1650 S Casino Rd 89029. 2 mi s of Davis Dam. Int corridors. **Pets:** Accepted.

ⓈⒶⓋⒺ ✕ ♿M 🛏 🖵 🍽 🏊 ⌧

MESQUITE

ⒶⒶⒶ ▼▼▼▼ **Best Western Mesquite Inn** Ⓜ

(702) 346-7444. **$80-$120.** 390 N Sandhill Blvd 89027. I-15, exit 122. Ext corridors. **Pets:** Medium. $15 daily fee/pet. Designated rooms, service with restrictions, crate. ⓈⒶⓋⒺ ✕ 🛏 🖵 🏊

▼▼▼▼ **Falcon Ridge Hotel** 🅷

(702) 346-2200. **Call for rates.** 1030 W Pioneer Blvd 89027. I-15, exit 120, just w. Int corridors. **Pets:** Accepted. ✕ 🛏 🖵 🏊 ⌧

▼▼▼▼ **Virgin River Hotel Casino Bingo** Ⓜ

(702) 346-7777. **Call for rates.** 100 Pioneer Blvd 89027. I-15, exit 122, just w. Ext corridors. **Pets:** Accepted. ✕ ♿M 🛏 🍽 🏊

NORTH LAS VEGAS

▼▼▼▼ **Aliante Station Casino & Hotel** 🅷

(702) 692-7777. **$49-$299.** 7300 Aliante Pkwy 89084. I-215, exit Aliante Pkwy, just n. Int corridors. **Pets:** Small, dogs only. $100 one-time fee/pet. Service with restrictions, crate. ⒶⓈⓀ ✕ ♿M 🛏 🍽 🏊

OVERTON

ⒶⒶⒶ ▼▼▼▼ **Best Western North Shore Inn at Lake**
              Mead Ⓜ

(702) 397-6000. **$59-$99.** 520 N Moapa Valley Blvd 89040. I-15, exit 93, 10 mi ne on SR 169. Int corridors. **Pets:** Medium, dogs only. $10 daily fee/room. Designated rooms, service with restrictions, supervision.

ⓈⒶⓋⒺ ✕ 🛏 🖵 🏊

PAHRUMP

ⒶⒶⒶ ▼▼▼▼ **Best Western Pahrump Station** Ⓜ 🐾

(775) 727-5100. **$80-$130.** 1101 S Hwy 160 89048. Downtown. Ext/int corridors. **Pets:** Dogs only. $8 daily fee/pet. Designated rooms, service with restrictions, supervision. ⓈⒶⓋⒺ ✕ ♿M 🛏 🖵 🍽 🏊

▼▼ **Saddle West Hotel & Casino** Ⓜ

(775) 727-1111. **$75-$115.** 1220 S Hwy 160 89048. Downtown. Ext corridors. **Pets:** Medium, dogs only. $100 deposit/pet, $10 daily fee/pet. Designated rooms, no service, supervision.

(A$K) (✕) (♿) (🛏) (🖥) (🍴) (🏊)

END METROPOLITAN AREA

MINDEN

Ⓐ ▼▼▼ **Best Western Minden Inn** Ⓜ

(775) 782-7766. **$80-$95.** 1795 Ironwood Dr 89423. Just w of jct US 395. Ext corridors. **Pets:** Accepted. (SAVE) (✕) (♿) (🛏) (🖥) (🏊)

RENO

Ⓐ ▼▼▼▼ **Atlantis Casino Resort Spa Reno** Ⓗ

(775) 825-4700. **$69-$279.** 3800 S Virginia St 89502. 3 mi s on US 395, exit 63, just w. Ext/int corridors. **Pets:** Medium, other species. $25 one-time fee/room. Designated rooms, service with restrictions, crate.

(SAVE) (✕) (♿) (🛏) (🖥) (🍴) (🏊) (✕)

Ⓐ ▼▼▼▼ **Best Western Airport Plaza Hotel & Conference Center** Ⓗ 🐾

(775) 348-6370. **$79-$169.** 1981 Terminal Way 89502. US 395, exit 65A southbound (E Plumb Ln/Villanova Dr), just e on Villanova Dr; exit 65 northbound, just e on E Plumb Ln. Int corridors. **Pets:** Other species. $50 deposit/room, $10 daily fee/room. Service with restrictions, supervision.

(SAVE) (✕) (♿) (🛏) (🖥) (🍴) (🏊) (✕)

Ⓐ ▼▼▼ **Circus Circus Hotel & Casino-Reno** Ⓗ

(775) 329-0711. **Call for rates.** 500 N Sierra St 89503. I-80, exit Sierra St, just s, jct W 6th St. Int corridors. **Pets:** Accepted.

(SAVE) (✕) (♿) (🛏) (🖥) (🏊) (✕)

▼▼▼ **Extended StayAmerica-Reno-South Meadows** Ⓗ

(775) 852-5611. **$70-$85.** 9795 Gateway Dr 89521. US 395, exit 60 (S Meadows Pkwy), just e, then n. Int corridors. **Pets:** Other species. $25 daily fee/room. Designated rooms, service with restrictions, crate.

(A$K) (✕) (🛏) (🖥)

▼▼▼ **Grand Sierra Resort & Casino** Ⓗ 🐾

(775) 789-2000. **$69-$259.** 2500 E 2nd St 89595. 0.5 mi s of jct I-80 and US 395; US 395, exit 66 (Mill St). Int corridors. **Pets:** $30 daily fee/room. Designated rooms, service with restrictions, crate.

(A$K) (✕) (♿) (🛏) (🍴) (🏊) (✕)

▼▼▼ **Holiday Inn Express & Suites Reno Airport** Ⓗ

(775) 229-7070. **Call for rates.** 2375 Market St 89502. US 395, exit 66, just n. Int corridors. **Pets:** Medium. $50 deposit/room, $20 daily fee/pet. Designated rooms, service with restrictions, supervision.

(✕) (♿) (🛏) (🖥) (🏊)

▼▼▼ **Homewood Suites Reno** Ⓗ 🐾

(775) 853-7100. **$159-$199.** 5450 Kietzke Ln 89511. US 395, exit 62, just sw. Int corridors. **Pets:** Small. $75 one-time fee/room. Service with restrictions. (✕) (🛏) (🖥) (🏊) (✕)

▼▼▼ **La Quinta Inn Reno (Airport)** Ⓜ 🐾

(775) 348-6100. **$89-$249.** 4001 Market St 89502-3110. US 395, exit 65A southbound (E Plumb Ln/Villanova Dr), just w on Villanova Dr; exit 65 northbound, just n, then just w on Villanova Dr. Ext corridors. **Pets:** Medium, other species. Service with restrictions, supervision.

(A$K) (✕) (♿) (🛏) (🏊)

Ⓐ ▼▼▼ **Quality Inn South** Ⓗ

(775) 329-1001. **$60-$90.** 1885 S Virginia St 89502. US 395, exit Plumb Ln/Villanova Dr, 1 mi w. Ext/int corridors. **Pets:** Accepted.

(SAVE) (✕) (♿) (🛏) (🖥) (🍴) (🏊)

Ⓐ ▼▼▼▼ **Ramada Reno Hotel & Casino** Ⓗ

(775) 786-5151. **$69-$129.** 1000 E 6th St 89512. I-80, exit Wells Ave, 2 blks e. Int corridors. **Pets:** Accepted.

(SAVE) (✕) (♿) (🛏) (🖥) (🍴) (🏊)

▼▼▼ **Residence Inn by Marriott** Ⓗ

(775) 853-8800. **$166-$202.** 9845 Gateway Dr 89521. US 395, exit S Meadows Pkwy, just e. Int corridors. **Pets:** Accepted.

(✕) (♿) (🛏) (🖥) (🏊) (✕)

▼▼ **Sands Regency Casino Hotel** Ⓗ

(775) 348-2200. **$29-$169.** 345 N Arlington Ave 89501. At 4th St. Int corridors. **Pets:** Medium, dogs only. $15 daily fee/pet. Designated rooms, service with restrictions, crate. (A$K) (✕) (🍴) (🏊) (✕)

Ⓐ ▼▼ **Seasons Inn** Ⓜ 🐾

(775) 322-6000. **$59-$119, 3 day notice.** 495 West St 89503. Corner of West and 5th sts. Ext corridors. **Pets:** Large, other species. $10 daily fee/pet. Designated rooms, service with restrictions, supervision. (SAVE) (✕)

Ⓐ ▼▼▼ **Staybridge Suites Reno** Ⓗ

(775) 657-8999. **$129-$359.** 10559 Professional Cir 89511. US 395, exit 59 (Damonte Ranch Pkwy), just e, just n on Double R Blvd, then just w. Int corridors. **Pets:** Medium, dogs only. $75 one-time fee/room. Designated rooms, service with restrictions, crate. (✕) (🛏) (🖥) (🏊)

▼▼ **Super 8 at Meadow Wood Courtyard** Ⓗ

(775) 829-4600. **$49-$139.** 5851 S Virginia St 89502. Jct US 395 and S McCarran Blvd, 0.3 mi s. Ext corridors. **Pets:** Accepted.

(A$K) (✕) (♿) (🛏) (🖥) (🍴) (🏊)

SPARKS

Ⓐ ▼▼▼ **Holiday Inn Reno-Sparks** Ⓗ 🐾

(775) 358-6900. **$100-$190.** 55 E Nugget Ave 89431. I-80, exit 19 (McCarran Blvd), just se. Int corridors. **Pets:** $20 daily fee/pet. Designated rooms, service with restrictions, supervision.

(SAVE) (✕) (♿) (🛏) (🖥) (🍴) (🏊) (✕)

Ⓐ ▼▼▼ **Sparks Super 8** Ⓗ

(775) 358-8884. **$50-$250.** 1900 E Greg St 89431. I-80, exit 20, 0.6 mi n, then just e. Int corridors. **Pets:** Medium. $10 daily fee/pet. Service with restrictions, supervision. (SAVE) (✕) (🛏) (🖥) (🏊)

TONOPAH

Ⓐ ▼▼▼ **Best Western Hi-Desert Inn** Ⓜ 🐾

(775) 482-3511. **$79-$129.** 320 Main St 89049. On US 6 and 95. Int corridors. **Pets:** Dogs only. Designated rooms, supervision.

(SAVE) (✕) (♿) (🖥) (🏊)

Ⓐ ▼▼▼ **Ramada Inn-Tonopah Station** Ⓜ

(775) 482-9777. **$75-$125.** 1100 Main St 89049. On US 6 and 95. Int corridors. **Pets:** Accepted. (SAVE) (✕) (♿) (🖥) (🍴)

WINNEMUCCA

Ⓐ ▼▼▼ **Best Western Gold Country Inn** Ⓗ

(775) 623-6999. **$109-$179.** 921 W Winnemucca Blvd 89445. I-80, exit 176 or 178, just s. Int corridors. **Pets:** Other species. $20 one-time fee/room. Designated rooms, supervision. (SAVE) (✕) (🛏) (🖥) (🏊)

▼▼▼ Holiday Inn Express **H**
(775) 625-3100. **$99-$209.** 1987 W Winnemucca Blvd 89445. I-80, exit 176, just s. Int corridors. **Pets:** Medium. $50 deposit/pet, $20 daily fee/pet, $20 one-time fee/pet. Service with restrictions, supervision.

[ASK] [✕] [♿M] [🛏] [💻] [🍽] [🏊]

▼ Super 8 **H**
(775) 625-1818. **Call for rates.** 1157 W Winnemucca Blvd 89446. I-80, exit 176, 0.5 mi e. Int corridors. **Pets:** Accepted. [✕] [🛏] [💻]

◈◈▼ ▼▼ Town House Motel **M**
(775) 623-3620. **$78-$85.** 375 Monroe St 89445. I-80, exit 176 or 178, just s. Ext corridors. **Pets:** Small, dogs only. $10 one-time fee/pet. Designated rooms, service with restrictions, supervision.

[SAVE] [✕] [🛏] [💻] [🏊]

◈◈▼ ▼▼ Winnemucca Holiday Motel **M**
(775) 623-3684. **$79-$149.** 670 W Winnemucca Blvd 89445. I-80, exit 176 or 178, just s. Ext corridors. **Pets:** Other species. $25 deposit/room. Designated rooms, service with restrictions, supervision.

[SAVE] [✕] [🛏] [💻] [🏊]

◈◈▼ ▼▼ The Winnemucca Inn **H**
(775) 623-2565. **$89-$149.** 741 W Winnemucca Blvd 89445. I-80, exit 176 or 178, just s. Ext/int corridors. **Pets:** Accepted.

[SAVE] [✕] [🛏] [💻] [🍽] [🏊] [✕]

NEW HAMPSHIRE

ASHLAND

WWWW Glynn House Inn BB ❀

(603) 968-3775. **$159-$299, 21 day notice.** 59 Highland St 03217. I-93, exit 24 (SR 25 and US 3), 0.8 mi e to flag pole in center of town (Highland), then 0.3 mi nw. Ext/int corridors. **Pets:** Dogs only. $250 deposit/pet, $25 one-time fee/pet. Designated rooms, service with restrictions.
ECO ✕ ✆

BARTLETT

AAA WWW The Bartlett Inn BB

(603) 374-2353. **$109-$248, 14 day notice.** 1477 US Rt 302 03812. On US 302, 7 mi w of jct SR 16. Ext/int corridors. **Pets:** Dogs only. $15 one-time fee/pet. Designated rooms, service with restrictions, supervision.
SAVE ✕ ☎ ▥ ⤼ ✕ ✆

AAA WWW The Villager Motel M ❀

(603) 374-2742. **$49-$249, 7 day notice.** 1126 US 302 03812. 1 mi e on US 302; 1.3 mi w of Attitash Mountain. Ext corridors. **Pets:** Medium. $15 deposit/pet. Designated rooms, no service, supervision.
SAVE ✕ ☎ ▥ ⤼ ✕

BRETTON WOODS

WWW Omni Bretton Arms Inn CI

(603) 278-3000. **$195-$485, 3 day notice.** 310 Mount Washington Hotel Rd (US 302) 03575. Center. Int corridors. **Pets:** Accepted.
ASK ✕ ☎ ▥ ⤼ ✕

CAMPTON

WW Days Inn Campton/Plymouth H

(603) 536-3520. **$45-$149.** 1513 Daniel Webster Hwy 03223. I-93, exit 27, just e, then just n. Int corridors. **Pets:** Medium, other species. $20 daily fee/pet. Service with restrictions, supervision.
ASK ✕ ☎ ▥ ⤼ ✕

CHESTERFIELD

WWW Chesterfield Inn CI ❀

(603) 256-3211. **$175-$345, 5 day notice.** 20 Cross Rd 03466. I-91, exit 3, 2 mi e on SR 9. Ext/int corridors. **Pets:** Other species. Designated rooms, service with restrictions, crate. ECO ASK ✕ ☎ ▥ ✆

COLEBROOK

AAA W Northern Comfort Motel M

(603) 237-4440. **$69-$89, 3 day notice.** 1 Trooper Scott Phillips Hwy 03576. 1.5 mi s on US 3. Ext corridors. **Pets:** Accepted.
SAVE ✕ ☎ ⤼ ✕

CONCORD

AAA WWW Best Western Concord Inn & Suites H

(603) 228-4300. **$90-$280.** 97 Hall St 03301. I-93, exit 13, just n on Main St, then 0.5 mi w. Int corridors. **Pets:** Medium. $20 daily fee/pet. Designated rooms, service with restrictions, supervision.
SAVE ✕ ☎ ▥ ⤼

WW Concord Comfort Inn H

(603) 226-4100. **$89-$259.** 71 Hall St 03301. I-93, exit 13, just n on Main St, then 0.3 mi w. Int corridors. **Pets:** Dogs only. $15 daily fee/pet. Designated rooms, service with restrictions, supervision.
ASK ✕ ☾M ☎ ▥ ⤼ ✕

CONWAY

WW White Deer Motel M

(603) 447-5366. **Call for rates.** 379 White Mountain Hwy 03818. 2.1 mi s of jct US 302; 0.5 mi n of village center on SR 16. Ext/int corridors.
Pets: Accepted. ✕ ☎ ▥

DIXVILLE NOTCH

AAA WWWW The Balsams Grand Resort Hotel H

(603) 255-3400. **$278-$598, 7 day notice.** 1000 Cold Spring Rd 03576. Just off SR 26. Int corridors. **Pets:** Accepted.
ECO SAVE ✕ ☎ ▥ ⤼ ✕

DOVER

WW Days Inn M

(603) 742-0400. **$89-$179.** 481 Central Ave 03820. Spaulding Tpke, exit 7, 2 mi n on SR 108; downtown. Ext/int corridors. **Pets:** Other species. $50 deposit/room, $10 daily fee/pet. Service with restrictions, supervision.
ASK ✕ ☎ ▥ ⤼

WWW Homewood Suites Dover-UNH H ❀

(603) 516-0929. **$99-$269.** 21 Members Way 03820. SR 16, exit 9, 0.4 mi w. Int corridors. **Pets:** Medium, dogs only. $50 one-time fee/room. Designated rooms. ✕ ☾M ☎ ▥ ⤼

DURHAM

WW Hickory Pond Inn CI

(603) 659-2227. **Call for rates.** 1 Stagecoach Rd 03824. 2.8 mi s on SR 108. Int corridors. **Pets:** Accepted. ✕ ▥ ✕

FRANCONIA

AAA WWW Best Western White Mountain Resort H ❀

(603) 823-7422. **$90-$160, 3 day notice.** 87 Wallace Hill Rd 03580. I-93, exit 38, just e. Int corridors. **Pets:** Large. $14 daily fee/pet. Designated rooms, service with restrictions, supervision.
SAVE ✕ ☎ ▥ ▥ ⤼ ✕

WW Gale River Motel M ❀

(603) 823-5655. **$70-$200, 7 day notice.** 1 Main St 03580. I-93, exit 38, 0.8 mi n on SR 18. Ext corridors. **Pets:** Other species. $10 one-time fee/pet. Designated rooms, service with restrictions, supervision.
ECO ✕ ☎ ▥ ⤼ ✕

WWW Lovetts Inn by Lafayette Brook CI

(603) 823-7761. **Call for rates.** 1474 Profile Rd 03580. I-93, exit 38, just w on Wallace Hill Rd, then 2.1 mi s on SR 18. Ext/int corridors.
Pets: Accepted. ✕ ☎ ▥ ▥ ⤼ ✕ ✆

GILFORD

WW Fireside Resort Inn & Suites H

(603) 293-7526. **$100-$260.** 17 Harris Shore Rd 03249. Jct SR 11 and 11B, 2.5 mi e of jct US 3 N. Int corridors. **Pets:** Accepted.
ASK ✕ ☾M ☎ ▥ ⤼ ✕

▼▼▼▼ TownePlace Suites Gilford 🅷 ❀
(603) 524-5533. **$109-$139.** 14 Saw Mill Rd 03249. Just e of jct SR 3 and 11A. Int corridors. **Pets:** Large, other species. $100 one-time fee/room. Designated rooms, service with restrictions, supervision.
⊠ 🔊ᴹ 🔒 💻 ⇌

GLEN
▼▼ The Red Apple Inn 🅼
(603) 383-9680. **Call for rates.** 322 US 302 03838. On US 302, 1.5 mi w of jct SR 16. Ext/int corridors. **Pets:** Accepted. ⊠ 🔒 ⇌

GORHAM
▼▼▼ Moose Brook Motel 🅼
(603) 466-5400. **$59-$89, 7 day notice.** 65 Lancaster Rd 03581. Jct SR 16, 0.5 mi w on US 2. Ext corridors. **Pets:** $5 one-time fee/pet. Service with restrictions, crate. ⊠ 🔒 💻 ⇌

▼▼ Royalty Inn 🅷
(603) 466-3312. **$61-$161.** 130 Main St 03581. On US 2 and SR 16; center. Ext/int corridors. **Pets:** Other species. $5 daily fee/pet. Designated rooms, service with restrictions.
🅴🅲🅾 ⊠ 🔊ᴹ 🔒 💻 🍴 ⇌ ⊠

▲▲▲ ▼▼▼ Top Notch Inn 🅼 ❀
(603) 466-5496. **$49-$149.** 265 Main St 03581. On US 2 and SR 16; center. Ext/int corridors. **Pets:** Medium, dogs only. Designated rooms, service with restrictions, supervision. SAVE ⊠ 🔒 💻 ⇌

▼▼ Town & Country Motor Inn 🅷
(603) 466-3315. **$78-$148.** 20 SR 2 03581. 0.5 mi e of jct SR 16. Ext/int corridors. **Pets:** $10 daily fee/pet. Designated rooms, service with restrictions, crate. ⊠ 🔒 💻 🍴 ⇌ ⊠

HAMPTON
▲▲▲ ▼▼▼ Best Western The Inn at Hampton 🅷
(603) 926-6771. **$99-$195.** 815 Lafayette Rd, US 1 03842. 0.5 mi n on US 1. Int corridors. **Pets:** Medium, dogs only. $30 one-time fee/pet. Designated rooms, supervision. SAVE ⊠ 🔊ᴹ 🔒 💻 ⇌

▲▲▲ ▼▼▼ Lamie's Inn and The Old Salt 🅲🅸 ❀
(603) 926-0330. **$99-$160, 3 day notice.** 490 Lafayette Rd 03842. Jct SR 27 on US 1. Int corridors. **Pets:** Medium. $100 deposit/room. Designated rooms, service with restrictions, supervision. SAVE ⊠ 🔒 🍴

HAMPTON FALLS
▲▲▲ ▼▼ Hampton Falls Inn 🅼 ❀
(603) 926-9545. **Call for rates.** 11 Lafayette Rd 03844. I-95, exit 1, 0.5 mi e on SR 107, then 1 mi n on US 1. Int corridors. **Pets:** Medium, dogs only. $10 daily fee/pet. Service with restrictions, supervision.
SAVE ⊠ 🔒 ⇌

HANCOCK
▼▼▼ The Hancock Inn 🅲🅸
(603) 525-3318. **$105-$250, 15 day notice.** 33 Main St 03449. Jct SR 123 and 137; center. Int corridors. **Pets:** Accepted. ⊠ 🍴

HARTS LOCATION
▼▼▼ Notchland Inn 🅲🅸 ❀
(603) 374-6131. **Call for rates.** 2 Morey Rd 03812. On US 302, 6.4 mi w of town. Ext/int corridors. **Pets:** Dogs only. $15 daily fee/pet. Designated rooms, service with restrictions, crate.
🅴🅲🅾 ⊠ 🔒 💻 🍴 ⊠

HENNIKER
▼▼ Henniker Motel 🅼
(603) 428-3536. **$90-$149.** 61 Craney Pond Rd 03242. I-89, exit 5, 6.5 mi w on US 202 and SR 9 to jct SR 114, 3 mi s to Flanders Rd, then 0.5 mi w, follow signs; adjacent to Pat's Peak. Ext/int corridors. **Pets:** Large, other species. Designated rooms, service with restrictions, crate. ASK ⊠ 🔒 💻 ⇌

JACKSON
▼▼▼ Christmas Farm Inn & Spa 🅲🅸
(603) 383-4313. **$141-$327, 7 day notice.** 3 Blitzen Way (Rt 16B) 03846. Jct SR 16, 0.6 mi e on SR 16A (through covered bridge), then 0.4 mi. Ext/int corridors. **Pets:** Accepted.
ASK ⊠ 🔒 💻 🍴 ⇌ ⊠

▼▼▼▼ The Eagle Mountain House & Golf Club 🅷
(603) 383-9111. **Call for rates.** 179 Carter Notch Rd 03846. Jct SR 16B, from village center follow SR 16B across bridge to immediate right turn, 0.7 mi n. Int corridors. **Pets:** Medium. $35 daily fee/room. Designated rooms, service with restrictions, supervision.
🅴🅲🅾 ⊠ 🔒 🍴 ⇌ ⊠ 🅐🅒

▲▲▲ ▼▼▼ Nordic Village Resort 🅲🅾
(603) 383-9101. **$89-$869, 7 day notice.** Rt 16 03846. 1 mi n of jct US 302. Ext/int corridors. **Pets:** Other species. $25 daily fee/pet. Designated rooms, service with restrictions, supervision.
SAVE ⊠ 🔒 💻 ⇌ ⊠

▼▼▼ Snowflake Inn 🅱🅱
(603) 383-8259. **$169-$350, 14 day notice.** 95 Main St (SR 16A) 03846. On SR 16A; center. Int corridors. **Pets:** Accepted. ⊠ ⇌

JEFFERSON
▲▲▲ ▼▼▼ Jefferson Inn 🅱🅱
(603) 586-7998. **$95-$155, 14 day notice.** 6 Renaissance Ln 03583. US 2, 0.5 mi e of SR 116. Int corridors. **Pets:** Dogs only. Designated rooms, service with restrictions, crate. SAVE ⊠ 🔒 ⊠ 🅉

KEENE
▲▲▲ ▼▼▼ Best Western Sovereign Hotel 🅷
(603) 357-3038. **$80-$250.** 401 Winchester St 03431. SR 10, just s of jct SR 12 and 101. Int corridors. **Pets:** Other species. $25 one-time fee/pet. Service with restrictions, supervision. SAVE ⊠ 🔒 💻 🍴 ⇌

▲▲▲ ▼▼▼ Days Inn of Keene 🅷 ❀
(603) 352-9780. **$72-$249.** 3 Ashbrook Rd 03431. Jct SR 9 and 12, just w. Int corridors. **Pets:** $20 one-time fee/room. Service with restrictions, supervision. SAVE ⊠ 🔊ᴹ 🔒 💻

▼▼▼▼ Holiday Inn Express 🅷 ❀
(603) 352-7616. **$99-$349.** 175 Key Rd 03431. SR 101, just n, via Winchester St, 0.3 mi w. Int corridors. **Pets:** Medium, dogs only. $25 daily fee/pet. Designated rooms, no service, supervision.
ASK ⊠ 🔊ᴹ 🔒 💻 ⇌

LANCASTER
▲▲▲ ▼▼▼ Coos Motor Inn 🅷
(603) 788-3079. **$49-$100.** 209 Main St 03584. On US 2 and 3; center. Int corridors. **Pets:** Medium, dogs only. $10 daily fee/pet. Designated rooms, service with restrictions, supervision. SAVE ⊠ 🔒 💻

LEBANON
▲▲▲ ▼▼▼ Days Inn 🅼
(603) 448-5070. **Call for rates.** 135 SR 120 03766. I-89, exit 18, 0.8 mi n. Ext/int corridors. **Pets:** Accepted. SAVE ⊠ 🔒 💻

▼▼▼▼ Residence Inn Hanover Lebanon 🅷
(603) 643-4511. **$189-$209.** 32 Centerra Pkwy 03766. I-89, exit 18, 2.5 mi n on SR 120. Int corridors. **Pets:** Accepted.
⊠ 🔊ᴹ 🔒 💻 ⇌ ⊠

LINCOLN
▲▲▲ ▼▼▼ Comfort Inn & Suites 🅷
(603) 745-6700. **$89-$199, 3 day notice.** 21 Railroad St 03251. I-93, exit 32, just e on SR 112; at Hobo Railroad. Int corridors. **Pets:** Accepted.
SAVE ⊠ 🔊ᴹ 🔒 💻 ⇌ ⊠

▲▲▲ ▼▼▼ Econo Lodge Inn & Suites 🅼 ❀
(603) 745-3661. **$59-$299.** 381 US Rt 3 03251. I-93, exit 33 (US 3), 0.3 mi ne. Ext/int corridors. **Pets:** Medium, dogs only. $15 daily fee/pet. Designated rooms, service with restrictions, crate. SAVE ⊠ 🔒 ⇌ ⊠

(AAA) ▼▼▼ Parker's Motel M

(603) 745-8341. **$49-$89, 3 day notice.** 750 US Rt 3 03251. I-93, exit 33 (US 3), 2 mi ne. Ext corridors. **Pets:** Medium. $10 daily fee/pet. Designated rooms, no service, supervision. [SAVE] [X] [B] [▣] [▰] [X]

(AAA) ▼▼▼ Woodward's Resort M ☙

(603) 745-8141. **$89-$139, 7 day notice.** 527 US 3 03251. I-93, exit 33 (US 3), 1.4 mi ne. Ext/int corridors. **Pets:** Medium. Designated rooms, supervision. [SAVE] [X] [B] [▣] [¶] [▰] [X]

LITTLETON

(AAA) ▼▼▼ Eastgate Inn M

(603) 444-3971. **$69-$129.** 335 Cottage St 03561. I-93, exit 41, just e. Ext/int corridors. **Pets:** $10 daily fee/pet. Service with restrictions, supervision. [SAVE] [X] [B] [▣] [¶] [▰] [X]

▼▼ Thayers Inn H

(603) 444-6469. **Call for rates.** 111 Main St 03561. I-93, exit 42, 1.3 mi e on US 302 and SR 10; center. Int corridors. **Pets:** Accepted.
[X] [B] [▣] [¶]

LOUDON

(AAA) ▼▼▼ Red Roof Inn H

(603) 225-8399. **Call for rates.** 2 Staniels Rd 03307. I-393, exit 3, 1.5 mi n. Int corridors. **Pets:** Large. Service with restrictions, crate.
[SAVE] [X] [M] [B] [▰]

MANCHESTER

(AAA) ▼▼▼ Clarion Manchester Hotel H

(603) 669-2660. **$79-$159.** 21 Front St 03102. I-293, exit 6, just e. Int corridors. **Pets:** Accepted. [SAVE] [X] [M] [B] [▣] [¶] [▰]

(AAA) ▼▼ Comfort Inn H

(603) 668-2600. **$80-$189.** 298 Queen City Ave 03102. I-293, exit 4, just w. Int corridors. **Pets:** Medium. $50 one-time fee/pet. Designated rooms, service with restrictions, supervision. [SAVE] [X] [B] [▣] [▰]

▼▼▼ Holiday Inn Express Hotel & Suites–Manchester Airport H ☙

(603) 669-6800. **$99-$149.** 1298 S Porter St 03103. I-293, exit 1. Int corridors. **Pets:** Large, other species. $50 deposit/room. Service with restrictions, supervision. [ASK] [X] [M] [B] [▣] [▰]

▼▼▼ Homewood Suites by Hilton H

(603) 668-2200. **$139-$259.** 1000 Perimeter Rd 03103. I-293, exit 2, follow signs to Manchester-Boston Regional Airport. Int corridors.
Pets: Accepted. [X] [M] [B] [▣] [▰] [X]

▼▼▼ Radisson Hotel Manchester H

(603) 625-1000. **$99-$349.** 700 Elm St 03101. Jct Granite St; downtown. Int corridors. **Pets:** Accepted.
[ECO] [ASK] [X] [M] [B] [▣] [¶] [▰] [X]

▼▼ TownePlace Suites Manchester-Boston Regional Airport H

(603) 641-2288. **$139-$149.** 686 Huse Rd 03103. I-293, exit 1, 0.5 mi se on SR 28. Int corridors. **Pets:** Other species. $100 one-time fee/room. Service with restrictions, crate. [X] [M] [B] [▣] [▰]

MEREDITH

▼▼▼ Church Landing at Mill Falls H ☙

(603) 279-7006. **$239-$459, 3 day notice.** 281 Daniel Webster Hwy 03253. Jct US 3 and SR 104, 0.6 mi n. Ext/int corridors. **Pets:** Large. $350 deposit/room, $25 daily fee/pet. Designated rooms, service with restrictions, crate. [ASK] [X] [B] [▣] [¶] [▰] [X]

▼▼▼ The Inn at Mill Falls H ☙

(603) 279-7006. **$109-$289, 3 day notice.** 312 Daniel Webster Hwy 03253. Jct US 3 and SR 25; center. Int corridors. **Pets:** Large. $350 deposit/room, $25 daily fee/pet. Designated rooms, service with restrictions, crate. [ASK] [X] [B] [¶] [▰]

MERRIMACK

(AAA) ▼▼▼ Comfort Inn M

(603) 429-4600. **$60-$110.** 242 Daniel Webster Hwy 03054. Everett Tpke, exit 11, just e, then 0.7 mi s on US 3. Int corridors. **Pets:** Medium, other species. $25 daily fee/pet. No service, supervision.
[SAVE] [X] [M] [B] [▣]

▼▼▼ Residence Inn Nashua-Merrimack H

(603) 424-8100. **$139-$159.** 246 Daniel Webster Hwy 03054. Everett Tpke, exit 11, just e, then 0.6 mi s on US 3. Ext/int corridors.
Pets: Accepted. [ECO] [X] [M] [B] [▣] [▰] [X]

NASHUA

(AAA) ▼▼▼ Best Western's Granite Inn H

(603) 883-7700. **$69-$120.** 10 St. Laurent St 03060. US 3 (Everett Tpke), exit 7E, just e. Int corridors. **Pets:** Accepted.
[SAVE] [X] [B] [▣] [▰]

▼▼ Extended StayAmerica-Boston-Nashua H

(603) 577-9900. **$75-$95.** 2000 Southwood Dr 03063. US 3 (Everett Tpke), exit 8, just w. Int corridors. **Pets:** Other species. $25 daily fee/room. Designated rooms, service with restrictions, crate.
[ASK] [X] [M] [B] [▣]

(AAA) ▼▼▼ Hampton Inn Nashua H ☙

(603) 883-5333. **$79-$259.** 407 Amherst St 03063. US 3 (Everett Tpke), exit 8. Int corridors. **Pets:** Large, other species. $50 one-time fee/room. Designated rooms, service with restrictions, crate.
[ECO] [SAVE] [X] [M] [B] [▣] [▰]

▼▼▼ Holiday Inn Nashua H

(603) 888-1551. **Call for rates.** 9 Northeastern Blvd 03062. US 3 (Everett Tpke), exit 4, just w, then 0.3 mi n. Int corridors. **Pets:** Accepted.
[X] [M] [B] [▣] [¶] [▰]

▼▼▼ Motel 6 Nashua South M

(603) 888-1893. **Call for rates.** 77 Spitbrook Rd 03060. US 3 (Everett Tpke), exit 1, just e. Ext corridors. **Pets:** Other species. Service with restrictions, supervision. [X] [M] [B]

NEWBURY

(AAA) ▼▼▼ Best Western Sunapee Lake Lodge H

(603) 763-2010. **$120-$349, 14 day notice.** 1403 SR 103 03255. Jct SR 103B, just e. Int corridors. **Pets:** Accepted.
[SAVE] [X] [M] [B] [▣] [▰] [X]

NEW CASTLE

(AAA) ▼▼▼▼ Wentworth By The Sea Marriott Hotel & Spa H

(603) 422-7322. **$199-$339, 3 day notice.** 588 Wentworth Rd 03854. On SR 1B, 2 mi e of SR 1A. Ext/int corridors. **Pets:** Accepted.
[SAVE] [X] [B] [▣] [¶] [▰] [X]

NORTH CONWAY

(AAA) ▼▼▼ Green Granite Inn and Conference Center H ☙

(603) 356-6901. **$70-$280, 3 day notice.** 1515 White Mountain Hwy (Rt 16) 03860. 2.3 mi s on US 302/SR 16; village center. Ext/int corridors. **Pets:** Medium, dogs only. $100 deposit/pet. Designated rooms, service with restrictions, supervision. [SAVE] [X] [B] [▣] [▰] [X]

▼▼▼ North Conway Hampton Inn & Suites H ☙

(603) 356-7736. **$99-$289.** 1788 White Mountain Hwy 03860. Jct US 302/SR 16, 1 mi n. Int corridors. **Pets:** Medium. Designated rooms, service with restrictions, crate. [ECO] [X] [B] [▣] [X]

(AAA) ▼▼▼ North Conway Mountain Inn M

(603) 356-2803. **$79-$239, 3 day notice.** 2114 White Mountain Hwy 03860. 1 mi s on US 302/SR 16. Ext corridors. **Pets:** $20 daily fee/pet. Service with restrictions, crate. [SAVE] [X]

◇ ▽▽▽▽ Red Jacket Mountain View Resort and Indoor Waterpark H ❖

(603) 356-5411. **$109-$339.** 2251 White Mountain Hwy 03860. 1 mi s on US 302/SR 16. Ext/int corridors. **Pets:** $25 one-time fee/pet. Designated rooms, service with restrictions, supervision.

[SAVE] [✕] [&M] [🛏] [🖵] [🍴] [🏊] [✕]

▽ White Trellis Motel M

(603) 356-2492. **$49-$199, 3 day notice.** 3245 White Mountain Hwy 03860. 0.8 mi n on US 302/SR 16; village center. Ext corridors. **Pets:** Accepted. [ASK] [✕] [🛏] [🖵]

PITTSBURG

▽ The Glen CA

(603) 538-6500. **$220-$280 (no credit cards), 7 day notice.** 118 Glen Rd 03592. 9 mi n on US 3, from jct SR 145 to Varney Rd, then 0.3 mi s to Glen Rd, follow signs. Ext/int corridors. **Pets:** Accepted.

[✕] [🛏] [🖵] [🍴] [✕] [🎾] [W] [✓]

PORTSMOUTH

◇ ▽▽▽▽ Anchorage Inn & Suites H ❖

(603) 431-8111. **$79-$229.** 417 Woodbury Ave 03801. Jct US 1 and I-95; at Portsmouth Traffic Circle. Int corridors. **Pets:** Medium. $100 deposit/room, $20 daily fee/pet. Designated rooms, service with restrictions, supervision. [SAVE] [✕] [🛏] [🏊] [✕]

▽▽▽▽ Hampton Inn-Portsmouth H

(603) 431-6111. **Call for rates.** 99 Durgin Ln 03801. I-95, exit 7, 1 mi w via Market St and Woodbury Ave to Durgin Ln, then 0.3 mi s. Int corridors. **Pets:** Medium, other species. $50 one-time fee/room. Service with restrictions, supervision. [✕] [&M] [🛏] [🖵] [🏊] [✕]

▽▽▽▽ Hilton Garden Inn Portsmouth Downtown H

(603) 431-1499. **$129-$319.** 100 High St 03801. Downtown. Int corridors. **Pets:** Accepted. [✕] [&M] [🛏] [🖵] [🍴] [🏊]

▽▽▽▽ Homewood Suites by Hilton H

(603) 427-5400. **$179-$229.** 100 Portsmouth Blvd 03801. I-95, exit 7, 0.5 mi w, then 0.3 mi n. Int corridors. **Pets:** Accepted.

[✕] [&M] [🛏] [🖵] [🏊]

▽ Motel 6 Portsmouth #1424 M

(603) 334-6606. **$55-$75.** 3 Gosling Rd 03801. I-95, exit 4 to Spaulding Tpke (US 4 and SR 16), exit 1, then just e. Int corridors. **Pets:** Other species. Service with restrictions, supervision. [✕] [&M] [🛏] [🏊]

▽▽▽▽ Residence Inn Portsmouth H

(603) 436-8880. **$159-$229.** 1 International Dr 03801. SR 4/16, exit 1, just s. Int corridors. **Pets:** Other species. $75 one-time fee/room. Service with restrictions. [ECO] [✕] [&M] [🛏] [🖵] [🏊] [✕]

◇ ▽▽▽▽ Sheraton Portsmouth Harborside Hotel & Conference Center H ❖

(603) 431-2300. **$139-$309.** 250 Market St 03801. Downtown. Int corridors. **Pets:** Medium, dogs only. Designated rooms, service with restrictions, supervision. [ECO] [SAVE] [✕] [&M] [🛏] [🖵] [🍴] [🏊] [✕]

ROCHESTER

◇ ▽ Anchorage Inn M

(603) 332-3350. **$69-$149.** 13 Wadleigh Rd 03867. Jct Spaulding Tpke and SR 125, exit 12. Ext corridors. **Pets:** Medium. $50 deposit/room, $15 daily fee/room. Service with restrictions, supervision.

[SAVE] [✕] [🛏] [🏊]

▽▽▽▽ The Governor's Inn CI

(603) 332-0107. **Call for rates.** 78 Wakefield St 03867. On SR 125 and 108, just n of monument; center. Int corridors. **Pets:** Accepted.

[✕] [🛏] [🖵] [🍴]

◇ ▽▽▽▽ Holiday Inn Express Hotel & Suites Rochester H

(603) 994-1175. **$89-$159.** 77 Farmington Rd 03867. I-16, exit 15, 1 mi w on SR 11. Int corridors. **Pets:** Medium. $50 one-time fee/room. Designated rooms, service with restrictions, supervision.

[SAVE] [✕] [&M] [🛏] [🖵] [🏊]

SALEM

▽▽▽▽ La Quinta Inn & Suites H ❖

(603) 893-4722. **$49-$159.** 8 Keewaydin Dr 03079. I-93, exit 2, just sw. Int corridors. **Pets:** Medium, other species. Service with restrictions, supervision. [ASK] [✕] [&M] [🛏] [🖵] [🏊]

◇ ▽▽ Red Roof Inn #151 M

(603) 898-6422. **Call for rates.** 15 Red Roof Ln 03079. I-93, exit 2, just se. Ext corridors. **Pets:** Large. Service with restrictions, crate.

[SAVE] [✕] [&M] [🛏]

SUGAR HILL

▽▽▽▽ The Hilltop Inn BB ❖

(603) 823-5695. **$110-$195, 8 day notice.** 9 Norton Ln 03586. I-93, exit 38, 0.5 mi n on SR 18, then 2.8 mi w on SR 117. Int corridors. **Pets:** Dogs only. $10 daily fee/room. Supervision. [✕] [🛏] [🎾] [W]

▽▽▽▽ Sunset Hill House-A Grand Inn CI

(603) 823-5522. **$99-$499, 14 day notice.** 231 Sunset Hill Rd 03586. I-93, exit 38, 0.5 mi n on SR 18, 2.2 mi w on SR 117, then 0.5 mi s. Int corridors. **Pets:** Other species. $20 daily fee/room. Designated rooms, service with restrictions, supervision. [ECO] [✕] [🛏] [🍴] [🏊] [✕]

SUNAPEE

▽▽ Dexter's Inn CI ❖

(603) 763-5571. **$110-$185, 7 day notice.** 258 Stagecoach Rd 03782. Jct SR 103B and 11, 0.4 mi w on SR 11, 1.8 mi s (Winn Hill Rd). Ext/int corridors. **Pets:** Other species. $10 daily fee/pet. Designated rooms, service with restrictions. [ASK] [✕] [🛏] [🖵] [🍴] [🏊] [✕]

THORNTON

▽ Shamrock Motel M

(603) 726-3534. **$53-$85, 7 day notice.** 2913 US 3 03285. I-93, exit 29, 2.3 mi n. Ext corridors. **Pets:** Accepted.

[ECO] [ASK] [✕] [🛏] [🏊] [✕] [✓]

TILTON

▽▽▽▽ Black Swan Inn BB

(603) 286-4524. **$85-$170, 10 day notice.** 354 W Main St 03276. I-93, exit 20 southbound, 1.5 mi w on SR 3 and 11. Int corridors. **Pets:** Small. $100 deposit/pet. Designated rooms, service with restrictions, crate.

[ASK] [✕] [🛏] [🖵]

TROY

◇ ▽ ▽ The Inn at East Hill Farm CI

(603) 242-6495. **$84-$131, 21 day notice.** 460 Monadnock St 03465. Jct SR 12 and Monadnock St, 2 mi e. Ext/int corridors. **Pets:** Other species. $10 daily fee/pet. Designated rooms, service with restrictions.

[ECO] [SAVE] [✕] [🛏] [🍴] [🏊] [✕] [✓]

TWIN MOUNTAIN

◇ ▽ Shakespeare's Inn M

(603) 846-5562. **$60-$85, 7 day notice.** 675 Rt 3 03595. On US 3, 1.3 mi s of jct US 302. Ext/int corridors. **Pets:** Other species. $10 daily fee/room. Designated rooms, service with restrictions, supervision.

[SAVE] [✕] [🛏] [🍴] [🏊] [✕]

WATERVILLE VALLEY

◇ ▽▽▽ Best Western Silver Fox Inn H

(603) 236-3699. **$89-$139.** 70 Packards Rd 03215. I-93, exit 28, 11 mi e on SR 49, then just n. Int corridors. **Pets:** Small, other species. $20 one-time fee/room. Designated rooms, service with restrictions, supervision.

[SAVE] [✕] [🖵]

WEST LEBANON

◈◈◈ ▽▽ Baymont Inn Ⓜ ❀

(603) 298-8888. **$80-$150.** 45 Airport Rd 03784. I-89, exit 20 (SR 12A), just s, then just e. Int corridors. **Pets:** Other species. $10 one-time fee/pet. Service with restrictions, supervision. [SAVE] ⊠ [♿M] 🛏 💻 ⊃

▽▽▽ Fireside Inn and Suites Ⓗ

(603) 298-5900. **$120-$200.** 25 Airport Rd 03784. I-89, exit 20 (SR 12A), just s. Int corridors. **Pets:** Dogs only. $25 daily fee/pet. Designated rooms, service with restrictions, supervision.

[ASK] ⊠ 🛏 💻 🍴 ⊃ ⊠

WOLFEBORO

▽ The Lake Motel Ⓜ

(603) 569-1100. **$69-$199, 14 day notice.** 280 S Main St 03894. 0.5 mi se on SR 28. Ext/int corridors. **Pets:** Accepted. ⊠ 🛏 💻 ⊠

WOODSVILLE

◈◈◈ ▽ All Seasons Motel Ⓜ

(603) 747-2157. **$60-$105, 3 day notice.** 36 Smith St 03785. I-91, exit 17, 4.1 mi e on US 302, then just s. Ext corridors. **Pets:** Accepted.

[SAVE] ⊠ 🛏 💻 ⊃

◈◈◈ ▽▽ Nootka Lodge Ⓜ

(603) 747-2418. **$75-$235, 3 day notice.** 4982 Dartmouth College Hwy 03785. I-91, exit 17, 4.5 mi e on US 302. Ext corridors. **Pets:** Accepted.

[SAVE] ⊠ 🛏 ⊃ ⊠

NEW JERSEY

ATLANTIC CITY METROPOLITAN AREA

ABSECON

▼▼ Knights Inn-Atlantic City/ Absecon M

(609) 407-1919. **$19-$499.** 531 Absecon Blvd 08201. Garden State Pkwy, exit 40, 4.3 mi e on US 30 (White Horse Pike). Ext corridors. **Pets:** Dogs only. $40 daily fee/pet. Designated rooms, service with restrictions, supervision. (ASK) (X) (📶)

ATLANTIC CITY

◢◣◤ ▼▼▼ Sheraton Atlantic City Convention Center Hotel H

(609) 344-3535. **$99-$499, 3 day notice.** 2 Convention Blvd 08401. Garden State Expwy, exit 38 to Atlantic City Expwy to Arctic Ave, just e to Michigan Ave, then just n. Int corridors. **Pets:** Accepted.

(SAVE) (X) (📶) (💻) (🍽) (🏊)

BUENA

▼▼ Econo Lodge M

(856) 697-9000. **Call for rates.** 102 Tuckahoe Rd 08310. Corner of SR 40 and 54. Int corridors. **Pets:** Accepted. (X) (📶) (💻)

SOMERS POINT

▼▼◢◣▼ Residence Inn Atlantic City Somers Point H

(609) 927-6400. **$179-$219.** 900 Mays Landing Rd 08244. Garden State Pkwy, exit 30 southbound; exit 29 northbound, 1 mi e. Ext corridors. **Pets:** Accepted. (X) (📶) (💻) (🏊) (X)

WEST ATLANTIC CITY

▼▼ Quality Hotel Bayside Resort H

(609) 641-3546. **Call for rates.** 8029 Black Horse Pike 08232. Garden State Pkwy, exit 38 (Atlantic City Expwy), 2 mi e to exit 5, 0.5 mi s on US 9 to US 40/322, then 1.8 mi e. Int corridors. **Pets:** Accepted.

(X) (📶) (💻) (🍽) (🏊) (X)

◢◣◤ ▼▼▼ Ramada-West Atlantic City H

(609) 646-5220. **$45-$229.** 8037 Black Horse Pike 08232. Garden State Pkwy, exit 38 (Atlantic City Expwy), 2 mi e to exit 5, 0.5 mi s on US 9 to US 40/322, then 1.8 mi e. Ext/int corridors. **Pets:** Accepted.

(SAVE) (X) (📶) (💻) (🏊)

END METROPOLITAN AREA

BASKING RIDGE

▼▼◢◣▼ Hotel Indigo H

(908) 580-1300. **$99-$219.** 80 Allen Rd 07920. I-78, exit 33, 0.3 mi n on CR 525, then 0.3 mi w. Int corridors. **Pets:** Medium. $25 daily fee/room. Designated rooms, service with restrictions, crate.

(ASK) (X) (📶) (💻) (🍽)

BEACH HAVEN

◢◣◤ ▼▼▼ Engleside Inn H

(609) 492-1251. **Call for rates.** 30 Engleside Ave 08008. 6.9 mi s of SR 72 Cswy to Engleside Ave, then just e. Ext corridors. **Pets:** Accepted.

(SAVE) (X) (📶) (💻) (🍽) (🏊)

BRIDGEWATER

◢◣◤ ▼▼▼▼ Hyatt Summerfield Suites Bridgewater H

(908) 725-0800. **$89-$249.** 530 US 22 E 08807. I-287, exit 14B northbound; exit 17 southbound to US 22 W, then 0.8 mi. Ext corridors.
Pets: Accepted. (SAVE) (X) (♿) (📶) (💻) (🏊) (X)

BUDD LAKE

▼▼▼ Extended StayAmerica Mt. Olive-Budd Lake H

(973) 347-5522. **$84-$119.** 71 International Dr S 07828. I-80, exit 25, just n, follow signs for International Trade Center; just e of jct US 46. Int corridors. **Pets:** Other species. $25 daily fee/room. Designated rooms, service with restrictions, crate. (ASK) (X) (📶) (💻)

CAPE MAY

◢◣◤ ▼▼▼ Marquis de Lafayette Hotel H

(609) 884-3500. **$132-$545.** 501 Beach Ave 08204. Between Decatur and Ocean sts. Ext/int corridors. **Pets:** Other species. $100 deposit/room, $25 daily fee/pet. Designated rooms, service with restrictions, supervision.

(SAVE) (X) (📶) (💻) (🏊)

◢◣◤ ▼▼▼ Palace Hotel of Cape May H

(609) 898-8100. **$149-$329, 14 day notice.** 1101 Beach Ave 08204. Jct Beach and Philadelphia aves. Int corridors. **Pets:** Other species. $25 daily fee/pet. Designated rooms, service with restrictions, supervision.

(SAVE) (X) (📶) (💻) (🏊)

▼▼▼ White Dove Cottage BB

(609) 884-0613. **$150-$280, 21 day notice.** 619 Hughes St 08204. Between Franklin and Ocean sts. Ext/int corridors. **Pets:** Accepted.

(ASK) (X) (📶) (💻) (✂)

CAPE MAY COURT HOUSE

▼▼▼ The Doctors Inn BB

(609) 463-9330. **$100-$350, 14 day notice.** 2 N Main St 08210. At Main (US 9) and Mechanic sts; just s of Garden State Pkwy. Int corridors. **Pets:** Accepted. (ASK) (X) (📶) (✂)

CLINTON

▼▼▼ Hampton Inn H

(908) 713-4800. **Call for rates.** 16 Frontage Dr 08809. I-78, exit 15, 0.3 mi s on CR 513, then left at next light. Int corridors. **Pets:** Accepted.

(X) (♿) (📶) (💻) (🏊)

Holiday Inn-Clinton H
(908) 735-5111. **Call for rates.** 111 Rt 173 08809. I-78, exit 15, just nw. Int corridors. **Pets:** $25 one-time fee/pet. Designated rooms, service with restrictions, supervision. ⊠ 🖪 💻 🍽 ≈

CRANBURY

Courtyard by Marriott Cranbury/South Brunswick H
(609) 655-9950. **$189-$209.** 420 Forsgate Dr 08512. New Jersey Tpke, exit 8A to SR 32 W toward town, just w. Int corridors. **Pets:** Accepted.
⊠ ⛄ 🖪 💻 🍽 ≈

Residence Inn by Marriott/Cranbury-South Brunswick H
(609) 395-9447. **$161-$197.** 2662 US 130 08512. New Jersey Tpke, exit 8A to SR 32 W toward town, 2 mi w on S River Rd. Int corridors.
Pets: Accepted. ⊠ ⛄ 🖪 💻 ≈ ⊠

Staybridge Suites/Cranbury H
(609) 409-7181. **$99-$199.** 1272 S River Rd 08512. New Jersey Tpke, exit 8A to SR 32 toward town, 2 mi w. Int corridors. **Pets:** Accepted.
ASK ⊠ 🖪 💻 ≈

EAST BRUNSWICK

Motel 6, East Brunswick #1083 H
(732) 390-4545. **$59-$69.** 244 SR 18 N 08816. New Jersey Tpke, exit 9 (SR 18) to SR 18 S, 1 mi, exit Edgeboro Rd, w at U-turn, then just e. Ext/int corridors. **Pets:** Other species. Service with restrictions, supervision. ⊠ ⛄

Studio 6 East Brunswick #6020 H
(732) 238-3330. **$75-$85.** 246 Rt 18 at Edgeboro Rd 08816. New Jersey Tpke, exit 9 (SR 18) to SR 18 S, 1 mi, exit Edgeboro Rd, w at U-turn, then just e. Int corridors. **Pets:** Other species. $10 daily fee/room. Service with restrictions, supervision. ⊠ ⛄ 🖪 💻

EAST RUTHERFORD

Homestead Studio Suites Meadowlands/East Rutherford H
(201) 939-8866. **$105-$149.** 300 SR 3 E 07073. New Jersey Tpke, exit 16W (from western spur), sports complex right after toll. Int corridors. **Pets:** Other species. $25 daily fee/room. Designated rooms, service with restrictions, crate. ⊠ 🖪 💻

Residence Inn East Rutherford Meadowlands H
(201) 939-0020. **$219-$249.** 10 Murray Hill Pkwy 07073. New Jersey Tpke, exit 16W to SR 3 W to SR 17 N, 1.5 mi n to Paterson Plank Rd (SR 120), then just e. Int corridors. **Pets:** Accepted.
⊠ ⛄ 🖪 💻 ≈ ⊠

Sheraton Meadowlands Hotel & Conference Center H
(201) 896-0500. **$134-$800.** 2 Meadowlands Plaza 07073. New Jersey Tpke, exit 16W (from western spur), sports complex right after toll to Sheraton Plaza Dr. Int corridors. **Pets:** Accepted.
SAVE ⊠ ⛄ 🖪 💻 🍽 ≈ ⊠

EATONTOWN

Staybridge Suites Hotel Eatontown-Tinton Falls H 🐾
(732) 380-9300. **$89-$219.** 4 Industrial Way E 07724. Garden State Pkwy, exit 105, 0.7 mi e on SR 36, then 0.7 mi s on SR 35. Int corridors. **Pets:** Medium. $75 one-time fee/pet. Service with restrictions, crate. ASK ⊠ ⛄ 🖪 💻 ≈

EDISON

Courtyard by Marriott Edison/Woodbridge H
(732) 738-1991. **$179-$189.** 3105 Woodbridge Ave 08837. New Jersey Tpke, exit 10, 0.5 mi se on CR 514, then just e. Int corridors.
Pets: Accepted. ⊠ ⛄ 🖪 💻 ≈

Extended StayAmerica-Edison-Raritan Center H
(732) 346-9366. **$76-$129.** 1 Fieldcrest Ave 08837. I-287, exit SR 514 to King Georges Post Rd, then just w. Int corridors. **Pets:** Other species. $25 daily fee/room. Designated rooms, service with restrictions, crate.
ASK ⊠ ⛄ 🖪 💻

Red Roof Inn #7194 M
(732) 248-9300. **Call for rates.** 860 New Durham Rd 08817. I-287, exit 2A northbound, 0.3 mi w via Bridge St, then left; exit 3 southbound, just w. Ext corridors. **Pets:** Large. Service with restrictions, crate.
SAVE ⊠ ⛄ 🖪

Sheraton Edison Hotel Raritan Center H
(732) 225-8300. **$99-$289.** 125 Raritan Center Pkwy 08837. New Jersey Tpke, exit 10, 0.5 mi se on CR 514, keep right after tolls. Int corridors.
Pets: Accepted. SAVE ⊠ ⛄ 🖪 💻 🍽 ≈ ⊠

ELIZABETH

Extended StayAmerica Elizabeth-Newark Airport H
(908) 355-4300. **$79-$129.** 45 Glimcher Realty Way 07201. New Jersey Tpke, exit toll follow signs to Jersey Garden Blvd, 1 mi, left on Kapkowski Rd, then just e. Int corridors. **Pets:** Other species. $25 daily fee/room. Designated rooms, service with restrictions, crate.
ASK ⊠ ⛄ 🖪 💻

Hilton Newark Airport H
(908) 351-3900. **$99-$209.** 1170 Spring St 07201. New Jersey Tpke, exit 13A, on US 1 and 9 N, U-turn on McClellan St. Int corridors.
Pets: Accepted. SAVE ⊠ ⛄ 🖪 💻 ≈

Residence Inn Newark Elizabeth/Liberty International Airport H
(908) 352-4300. **$152-$186.** 83 Glimcher Realty Way 07201. New Jersey Tpke, exit 13A, after toll follow signs to Jersey Garden Blvd, 1 mi, left on Kapkowski Rd, then just e. Int corridors. **Pets:** Accepted.
⊠ ⛄ 🖪 💻 ≈

FAIRFIELD

La Quinta Inn & Suites Fairfield H 🐾
(973) 575-1742. **$59-$139.** 38 Two Bridges Rd 07004. I-80, exit 52 westbound; exit 47B (Caldwells) eastbound, 7 mi e on US 46, exit Passaic Ave. Int corridors. **Pets:** Medium, other species. Service with restrictions, supervision. ASK ⊠ ⛄ 🖪 💻 🍽 ≈

FLEMINGTON

Ramada M
(908) 782-7472. **$74-$134.** 250 US 202 & SR 31 08822. 0.5 mi s of the circle. Ext/int corridors. **Pets:** Accepted. ASK ⊠ 🖪 💻 🍽 ≈

HASBROUCK HEIGHTS

Hilton Hasbrouck Heights H
(201) 288-6100. **$109-$264.** 650 Terrace Ave 07604. I-80, exit 64B westbound; exit 64 eastbound, just s on SR 17 S. Int corridors.
Pets: Accepted. ⊠ 🖪 💻 🍽 ≈

HASKELL

Holiday Inn Express Haskell H
(973) 839-4405. **$89-$109.** 303 Union Ave 07420. I-287, exit 55, just s. Int corridors. **Pets:** $20 one-time fee/room. Designated rooms.
⊠ ⛄ 🖪 💻 ≈

HILLSBOROUGH

Days Inn H
(908) 685-9000. **$59-$130.** 118 Rt 206 S 08844. 2.6 mi s of jct SR 28, US 202 and 206, at circle. Int corridors. **Pets:** $20 daily fee/pet. Crate.
SAVE ⊠ ⛄ 🖪 💻 🍽 ≈

LAWRENCEVILLE

Red Roof Inn-Princeton #10111 M
(609) 896-3388. **Call for rates.** 3203 Brunswick Pike (US 1) 08648. I-295, exit 67A, just n. Ext corridors. **Pets:** Large. Service with restrictions, crate. ⊠ 🖪

LEDGEWOOD

▼▼ Quality Inn [H]

(973) 347-5100. **$79-$89.** 1691 US 46 W 07852. I-80, exit 27, 2 mi e via US 206 N and 183 N. Int corridors. **Pets:** Accepted.

(symbols)

LONG BRANCH

▼▼▼ Ocean Place Resort & Spa [H]

(732) 571-4000. **$125-$629, 7 day notice.** 1 Ocean Blvd 07740. 2.5 mi e of jct SR 71, 0.5 mi s. Int corridors. **Pets:** $100 one-time fee/room. Designated rooms, service with restrictions.

(symbols)

MAHWAH

▼▼▼ Homewood Suites by Hilton [H] ❖

(201) 760-9994. **$129-$209.** 375 Corporate Dr 07430. I-287, exit 66, 1.7 mi on SR 17 S to MacArthur Blvd, then 0.4 mi w. Int corridors. **Pets:** Other species. $150 one-time fee/pet. Service with restrictions, crate.

(symbols)

AAA ▼▼▼ Sheraton Mahwah Hotel [H]

(201) 529-1660. **Call for rates.** 1 International Blvd (Rt 17) 07495. I-287, exit 66; at SR 17 N. Int corridors. **Pets:** Accepted.

(symbols)

MIDDLETOWN

AAA ▼▼▼▼ Comfort Inn Middletown [H] ❖

(732) 671-3400. **$105-$179.** 750 Hwy 35 S 07748-3491. Garden State Pkwy, exit 114, 2 mi on Red Hill Rd, 1 mi s on King's Hwy to SR 35, then 0.3 mi s. Int corridors. **Pets:** Large. $25 daily fee/room. Service with restrictions, supervision.

(symbols)

MONMOUTH JUNCTION

▼▼ Extended StayAmerica Princeton/South Brunswick [H]

(732) 438-5010. **$77-$149.** 4230 US 1 S 08852. 0.5 mi s of jct US 1 and Raymond Rd. Int corridors. **Pets:** Other species. $25 daily fee/room. Designated rooms, service with restrictions, crate.

(symbols)

AAA ▼ Red Roof Inn/North Princeton #7198 [M]

(732) 821-8800. **Call for rates.** 208 New Rd 08852. On US 1 S. Ext corridors. **Pets:** Large. Service with restrictions, crate. (symbols)

▼▼▼ Residence Inn Princeton-South Brunswick [H]

(732) 329-9600. **$188-$230.** 4225 US 1 S 08543. 0.5 mi s of Raymond Rd. Int corridors. **Pets:** Accepted. (symbols)

MORRIS PLAINS

▼▼ Candlewood Suites Parsippany-Morris Plains [H]

(973) 984-9960. **Call for rates.** 100 Candlewood Dr 07950. I-287, exit 39 northbound; exit 39B southbound, 2 mi w on SR 10. Int corridors. **Pets:** Accepted. (symbols)

MORRISTOWN

AAA ▼▼▼▼ Hyatt Summerfield Suites Morristown [H]

(973) 971-0008. **$89-$299.** 194 Park Ave 07960. SR 24, exit 2A (Morristown), stay in far left lane. Int corridors. **Pets:** Accepted.

(symbols)

AAA ▼▼▼▼ The Westin Governor Morris [H] ❖

(973) 539-7300. **$119-$409.** 2 Whippany Rd 07960. I-287, exit 36 southbound, left lane to light, left to stop sign, then left 1 mi; exit 36A northbound thru Morris Ave, 0.8 mi, follow signs. Int corridors. **Pets:** Small, dogs only. $50 one-time fee/room. Service with restrictions, supervision.

(symbols)

MOUNT OLIVE

▼▼▼ Residence Inn Mt Olive at the International Trade Center [H]

(973) 691-1720. **$170-$190.** 271 Continental Dr 07828. I-80, exit 25, just n, follow signs for International Trade Center. Int corridors.
Pets: Accepted. (symbols)

NEPTUNE

▼▼▼ Residence Inn Neptune at Gateway Centre [H]

(732) 643-9350. **$179-$219.** 230 Jumping Brook Rd 07753. Garden State Pkwy, exit 100B, 0.5 mi e on SR 33, then 0.5 mi n. Int corridors. **Pets:** Other species. $100 one-time fee/room. Service with restrictions.

(symbols)

NEWARK

▼▼▼ Sheraton Newark Airport Hotel [H]

(973) 690-5500. **Call for rates.** 128 Frontage Rd 07114. New Jersey Tpke, exit 14 via Frontage Rd, 2nd right after toll booth. Int corridors. **Pets:** Accepted. (symbols)

▼▼▼ SpringHill Suites Newark Liberty International Airport [H] ❖

(973) 624-5300. **$130-$158.** 652 Rt 1 & 9 S 07114. I-95, exit 14, 1 mi sw via US 1 and 9 S. Int corridors. **Pets:** Medium. $100 one-time fee/pet. Service with restrictions. (symbols)

NORTH BERGEN

▼▼ Days Inn [H]

(201) 348-3600. **$129-$199.** 2750 Tonnelle Ave (US 1 & 9) 07047. Jct SR 3, 0.4 mi s. Int corridors. **Pets:** $50 deposit/room. Designated rooms, service with restrictions, crate. (symbols)

NORTH BRUNSWICK

▼▼▼ Holiday Inn Express Hotel & Suites [H]

(732) 297-7400. **Call for rates.** 2880 US 1 N 08902. Between Finnegans and Black Horse Lns. Int corridors. **Pets:** Accepted.

(symbols)

PARAMUS

▼▼ La Quinta Inn [H] ❖

(201) 265-4200. **$89-$135.** 393 Rt 17 S 07652. Garden State Pkwy, exit 163 northbound to SR 17 N, 0.6 mi to Midland Ave, then U-turn to SR 17 S; exit 165 southbound to Richwood Ave, 1 mi. Int corridors. **Pets:** Medium, other species. Service with restrictions, supervision.

(symbols)

PARSIPPANY

▼▼▼ Embassy Suites [H] ❖

(973) 334-1440. **$114-$269.** 909 Parsippany Blvd 07054. I-80, exit 42 to US 202 N; just ne of jct US 202 and 46 W. Int corridors. **Pets:** Medium. $20 daily fee/room. Designated rooms, service with restrictions, crate.

(symbols)

▼▼▼ Hilton Parsippany [H] ❖

(973) 267-7373. **$109-$329.** 1 Hilton Ct 07054. I-287, exit 39 northbound; exit 39B southbound, 1.3 mi w on SR 10; in Hilton Court. Int corridors. **Pets:** Medium. $25 one-time fee/room. Designated rooms, service with restrictions, supervision. (symbols)

AAA ▼▼ Red Roof Inn #7072 [M]

(973) 334-3737. **Call for rates.** 855 US 46 E 07054. I-80, exit 47 westbound; exit 45 eastbound, 0.5 mi e. Ext corridors. **Pets:** Large. Service with restrictions, crate. (symbols)

▼▼▼ Residence Inn by Marriott Parsippany [H] ❖

(973) 984-3313. **$188-$230.** 3 Gatehall Dr 07054. I-287, exit 39 northbound; exit 39B southbound, 2 mi w on SR 10. Int corridors. **Pets:** Large, other species. $100 one-time fee/room. Service with restrictions, supervision. (symbols)

AAA ▼▼▼ Sheraton Parsippany Hotel [H]

(973) 515-2000. **$109-$395.** 199 Smith Rd 07054. I-287, exit 41A northbound; exit 42 to US 46 E, 0.4 mi s. Int corridors. **Pets:** Accepted.

(symbols)

▼▼▼ Staybridge Suites Parsippany [H]

(973) 334-2907. **$75-$159.** 61 Interpace Pkwy 07054. I-80, exit 42, 0.3 mi s on Cherry Hill Rd, then just w. Int corridors. **Pets:** Accepted.

(symbols)

PHILADELPHIA METROPOLITAN AREA (NEARBY PENNSYLVANIA)

CARNEYS POINT

▼▼▼ Comfort Inn & Suites ⊞ ✿
(856) 299-8282. **$81-$150.** 634 Sodders Rd 08069. I-295, exit 2B, just e on Pennsville-Auburn Rd, then 0.3 mi s. Int corridors. **Pets:** Medium. $15 daily fee/pet. Service with restrictions, supervision.
[ASK] [✕] [🛏] [🍴] [🖵]

◇◇◇ ▼▼▼▼ Holiday Inn Express Hotel & Suites ⊞
(856) 351-9222. **$99-$150.** 506 Pennsville-Auburn Rd 08069. I-295, exit 2B, just e. Int corridors. **Pets:** Large, other species. $10 daily fee/pet. Service with restrictions, supervision. [SAVE] [✕] [🛏] [🖵]

CHERRY HILL

▼▼ Extended StayAmerica-Philadelphia-Cherry Hill ⊞
(856) 616-1200. **$79-$129.** 1653 E SR 70 (Marlton Pike) 08034. I-295, exit 34A, just e. Int corridors. **Pets:** Other species. $25 daily fee/room. Designated rooms, service with restrictions, crate. [ASK] [✕] [🛏] [🖵]

◇◇◇ ▼▼▼▼ Holiday Inn Philadelphia-Cherry Hill ⊞
(856) 663-5300. **$95-$169.** 2175 W Marlton Pike Rd 08002. I-295, exit 34B, 2.5 mi w. Int corridors. **Pets:** Medium. $75 deposit/room. Service with restrictions, supervision. [SAVE] [✕] [🛏] [🖵] [🍴] [🏊]

DEPTFORD

▼▼▼ Residence Inn Deptford ⊞
(856) 686-9188. **$150-$170.** 1154 Hurffville Rd 08096. SR 42, exit Deptford, Woodbury, Runnemede to CR 544, just e to CR 415. Int corridors. **Pets:** Accepted. [✕] [🛏] [🖵] [🏊] [🐾]

HADDONFIELD

▼▼▼ Haddonfield Inn 🅱🅱 ✿
(856) 428-2195. **$159-$369, 7 day notice.** 44 W End Ave 08033. I-295, exit 28, 0.7 mi n on SR 168, 2.6 mi e on Kings Hwy, then just n. Int corridors. **Pets:** Dogs only. $25 daily fee/pet. Designated rooms, service with restrictions, supervision. [✕] [🛏]

MOUNT LAUREL

▼▼ Candlewood Suites ⊞
(856) 642-7567. **$89-$109.** 4000 Crawford Pl 08054. New Jersey Tpke, exit 4, 1 mi s on SR 73 S. Int corridors. **Pets:** Accepted.
[ASK] [✕] [🛏] [🖵]

▼▼ Extended StayAmerica Philadelphia-Mt. Laurel ⊞
(856) 778-4100. **$74-$129.** 101 Diemer Dr 08054. New Jersey Tpke, exit 4, 1 mi se on SR 73, just n on Crawford Pl, then just e. Int corridors. **Pets:** Other species. $25 daily fee/room. Designated rooms, service with restrictions, crate. [ASK] [✕] [🛏] [🖵]

▼▼ Extended Stay Deluxe-Philadelphia-Mt. Laurel ⊞
(856) 608-9820. **$84-$129.** 500 Diemer Dr 08054. New Jersey Tpke, exit 4, 1 mi se on SR 73, just n on Crawford Pl, then just e. Int corridors. **Pets:** Other species. $25 daily fee/room. Designated rooms, service with restrictions, crate. [ASK] [✕] [🛏] [🖵]

◇◇◇ ▼▼▼▼ Hyatt Summerfield Suites Mt. Laurel ⊞
(856) 222-1313. **$109-$219.** 3000 Crawford Pl 08054. New Jersey Tpke, exit 4, 1 mi s on SR 73; I-295, exit 36A, 1.5 mi s on SR 73. Ext corridors. **Pets:** Accepted. [SAVE] [✕] [🛏] [🖵] [🏊] [🐾]

▼▼▼ Philadelphia/Mount Laurel Homewood Suites by Hilton ⊞
(856) 222-9001. **$99-$149.** 1422 Nixon Dr 08054. I-295, exit 36B, follow ramp to end, then just n. Int corridors. **Pets:** Accepted.
[✕] [🛏] [🖵] [🏊] [🐾]

◇◇◇ ▼▼▼ Red Roof Inn #7066 Ⓜ
(856) 234-5589. **Call for rates.** 603 Fellowship Rd 08054. New Jersey Tpke, exit 4, just nw on SR 73 to Fellowship Rd, then just s; I-295, exit 36A, just se on SR 73 to Fellowship Rd, then just s. Ext corridors. **Pets:** Large. Service with restrictions, crate. [SAVE] [✕] [🛏]

◇◇◇ ▼▼▼▼ Residence Inn by Marriott Mount Laurel at Bishop's Gate ⊞
(856) 234-1025. **$179-$219.** 1001 Sunburst Ln 08054. I-295, exit 40A. Int corridors. **Pets:** Other species. $100 one-time fee/room. Service with restrictions, supervision. [SAVE] [✕] [🛏] [🖵] [🏊] [🐾]

◇◇◇ ▼▼▼▼ Staybridge Suites ⊞
(856) 722-1900. **$89-$149.** 4115 Church Rd 08054. New Jersey Tpke, exit 4, 0.5 mi s on SR 73, then 0.5 mi w. Int corridors. **Pets:** Accepted.
[SAVE] [✕] [🛏] [🖵] [🏊] [🐾]

◇◇◇ ▼▼▼▼ Wyndham Mount Laurel ⊞
(856) 234-7000. **$108-$136.** 1111 SR 73 08054. New Jersey Tpke, exit 4; I-295, exit 36A, 0.5 mi se. Int corridors. **Pets:** Medium, other species. $100 deposit/room, $50 one-time fee/pet. Service with restrictions, supervision. [SAVE] [✕] [🛏] [🖵] [🍴] [🏊]

WESTAMPTON

◇◇◇ ▼▼ Best Western Burlington Inn ⊞
(609) 261-3800. **$90-$103.** 2020 Burlington/Mt Holly Rd 08060. New Jersey Tpke, exit 5, just n. Int corridors. **Pets:** Medium. $10 daily fee/pet. Service with restrictions, crate. [SAVE] [✕] [🛏] [🖵] [🏊]

END METROPOLITAN AREA

PISCATAWAY

▼▼▼ Embassy Suites Hotel ⊞
(732) 980-0500. **$99-$189.** 121 Centennial Ave 08854. I-287, exit 9 (Highland Park), just s to Centennial Ave. Int corridors. **Pets:** Accepted.
[✕] [🛏] [🖵] [🍴] [🏊]

▼▼ Extended Stay Deluxe Piscataway-Rutgers University ⊞
(732) 235-1000. **$84-$129.** 410 S Randolphville Rd 08854. I-287, exit 7, 0.4 mi s. Int corridors. **Pets:** Other species. $25 daily fee/room. Designated rooms, service with restrictions, crate.
[ASK] [✕] [🛏] [🖵] [🏊]

▼ Motel 6 Piscataway #1084 ⊞
(732) 981-9200. **$65-$75.** 1012 Stelton Rd 08854. I-287, exit 5, just e. Ext/int corridors. **Pets:** Other species. Service with restrictions, supervision.

▼▼▼ Radisson Hotel Piscataway ⊞
(732) 980-0400. **$110-$135.** 21 Kingsbridge Rd 08854. I-287, exit 9 (Highland Park) to Centennial Ave via River Rd S, then 0.4 mi s. Int corridors. **Pets:** Accepted. [ASK] [✕] [🛏] [🖵] [🍴] [🏊]

POMPTON PLAINS

◇◇◇ ▼▼▼▼ Best Western Regency House Hotel ⊞
(973) 696-0900. **$89-$119.** 140 SR 23 N 07444. 6 mi n of jct I-80, US 46 and SR 23. Int corridors. **Pets:** $20 daily fee/pet. Service with restrictions, supervision. [SAVE] [✕] [🛏] [🖵] [🍴] [🏊]

PRINCETON

▼▼▼ Clarion Hotel-The Palmer Inn ⊞
(609) 452-2500. **Call for rates.** 3499 US 1 S 08540. 2 mi s of jct CR 526 and 571. Ext/int corridors. **Pets:** Accepted. [✕] [🛏] [🖵] [🍴] [🏊]

▼▼▼ Courtyard by Marriott Princeton 🅷
(609) 716-9100. **$179-$219.** 3815 US 1 S 08540. 0.4 mi s of Scudders Mill Rd at Mapleton Rd. Int corridors. **Pets:** Medium. $100 one-time fee/room. No service, supervision. ⊠ 🔥M 🛗 🖵 🛩

⬥⬥⬥ ▼▼▼ Holiday Inn Princeton 🅷
(609) 520-1200. **$89-$155.** 100 Independence Way 08540. I-295, exit 67A (SR 1) northbound; exit 67 (SR 1) southbound, 7 mi n. Int corridors. **Pets:** Medium, other species. $50 one-time fee/room. Service with restrictions, supervision. 🆂🅰🆅🅴 ⊠ 🛗 🖵 🍴 🛩 🖾

⬥⬥⬥ ▼▼▼▼ Nassau Inn 🅷 🐾
(609) 921-7500. **$199-$245.** 10 Palmer Square E 08542. Center. Int corridors. **Pets:** Medium. $75 one-time fee/room. Designated rooms, service with restrictions, crate. 🆂🅰🆅🅴 ⊠ 🛗 🖵 🍴

▼▼▼▼ Residence Inn by Marriott-Princeton at Carnegie Center 🅷
(609) 799-0550. **$224-$274.** 3563 US 1 S 08540. 1.5 mi s of jct CR 527 and 571. Int corridors. **Pets:** Accepted. ⊠ 🔥M 🛗 🖵 🛩 🖾

▼▼▼▼ Staybridge Suites 🅷
(609) 951-0009. **Call for rates.** 4375 US 1 S 08543. Just past Ridge Rd. Ext corridors. **Pets:** Accepted. ⊠ 🛗 🖵 🛩 🖾

⬥⬥⬥ ▼▼▼▼ Westin Princeton at Forrestal Village 🅷 🐾
(609) 452-7900. **Call for rates.** 201 Village Blvd 08540. On US 1 southbound, 1.5 mi n of CR 571. Int corridors. **Pets:** Medium, dogs only. $50 one-time fee/room. Service with restrictions, crate.
🆂🅰🆅🅴 ⊠ 🔥M 🛗 🖵 🍴 🛩 🖾

RAHWAY

⬥⬥⬥ ▼▼▼▼ Hotel Indigo @ Skyview 🅷 🐾
(732) 340-0076. **$85-$155.** 1 Carriage City Plaza 07065. Center; across from train station. Int corridors. **Pets:** Small. $75 one-time fee/pet. Service with restrictions, supervision. 🆂🅰🆅🅴 ⊠ 🖵

RAMSEY

⬥⬥⬥ ▼▼▼ Best Western-The Inn at Ramsey 🅷
(201) 327-6700. **$79-$109.** 1315 Rt 17 S 07446. Jct I-287 and SR 17 S, 3 mi s. Int corridors. **Pets:** Dogs only. $10 daily fee/pet. Designated rooms, service with restrictions, supervision. 🆂🅰🆅🅴 ⊠ 🛗 🖵 🍴

▼▼▼ Extended StayAmerica Ramsey-Upper Saddle River 🅷
(201) 236-9996. **$99-$129.** 112 SR 17 N 07446. Just s of Lake St exit. Int corridors. **Pets:** Other species. $25 daily fee/room. Designated rooms, service with restrictions, crate. 🅰🆂🅺 ⊠ 🔥M 🛗 🖵

RED BANK

▼▼▼ Extended StayAmerica Red Bank-Middletown 🅷
(732) 450-8688. **$74-$149.** 329 Newman Springs Rd 07701. Garden State Pkwy, exit 109, just e. Int corridors. **Pets:** Other species. $25 daily fee/room. Designated rooms, service with restrictions, crate.
🅰🆂🅺 ⊠ 🔥M 🛗 🖵

RIDGEFIELD PARK

▼▼▼▼ Hilton Garden Inn Ridgefield Park 🅷
(201) 641-2024. **$129-$239.** 70 Challenger Rd 07660. I-95, exit 68, follow signs. Int corridors. **Pets:** Accepted. ⊠ 🔥M 🛗 🖵 🍴 🛩

ROCKAWAY

⬥⬥⬥ ▼▼▼ Best Western Rockaway Hotel 🅷
(973) 625-1200. **$129-$139.** 14 Green Pond Rd 07866. I-80, exit 37, just n. Int corridors. **Pets:** Accepted. 🆂🅰🆅🅴 ⊠ 🛗 🖵 🛩

RUTHERFORD

▼▼ ▼▼ Extended StayAmerica-Meadowlands-Rutherford 🅷
(201) 635-0266. **$94-$129.** 750 Edwin L Ward Sr Memorial Hwy 07070. I-95, exit 16W, 1.5 mi w on SR 3 to SR 17 N service road exit, then 0.5 mi e. Int corridors. **Pets:** Other species. $25 daily fee/room. Designated rooms, service with restrictions, crate. 🅰🆂🅺 ⊠ 🛗 🖵

SECAUCUS

▼▼ ▼▼ Extended StayAmerica-Secaucus-Meadowlands 🅷
(201) 617-1711. **$99-$149.** 1 Meadowlands Pkwy 07094. Between eastern and western spurs of New Jersey Tpke; exits 16E, 17, or 16W to SR 3, exit Meadowlands Pkwy, just n. Int corridors. **Pets:** Other species. $25 daily fee/room. Designated rooms, service with restrictions, crate.
🅰🆂🅺 ⊠ 🔥M 🖵

▼▼▼ Homestead Studio Suites Secaucus/Meadowlands 🅷
(201) 553-9700. **$130-$199.** 1 Plaza Dr 07094. New Jersey Tpke, exit 16E northbound; exit 17E southbound, 0.3 mi e. Int corridors. **Pets:** Other species. $25 daily fee/room. Designated rooms, service with restrictions, crate. 🅰🆂🅺 ⊠ 🔥M 🛗 🖵 🛩

▼▼▼▼ La Quinta Inn & Suites Secaucus 🅷 🐾
(201) 863-8700. **$119-$249.** 350 Lighting Way 07094. Between eastern and western spurs of New Jersey Tpke, exits 16E, 17 or 16W via SR 3 W and Harmon Meadow Blvd; in Mill Creek Mall. Int corridors. **Pets:** Medium, other species. Service with restrictions, supervision.
🅰🆂🅺 ⊠ 🛗 🖵 🍴 🛩

SHORT HILLS

⬥⬥⬥ ▼▼▼ ▼▼▼ Hilton Short Hills 🅷
(973) 379-0100. **$159-$329.** 41 John F Kennedy Pkwy 07078. I-78, exit 48 (SR 24), 2.5 mi to John F Kennedy Pkwy. Int corridors. **Pets:** Accepted. 🆂🅰🆅🅴 ⊠ 🔥M 🛗 🖵 🍴 🛩 🖾

SOMERSET

▼▼▼ Candlewood Suites 🅷
(732) 748-1400. **$72-$99.** 41 Worlds Fair Dr 08873. I-287, exit 10 (CR 527), left on Ramp (CR 527 S/Easton Ave), 0.3 mi, then 0.5 mi w. Int corridors. **Pets:** Accepted. 🅰🆂🅺 ⊠ 🛗 🖵

▼▼▼▼ Crowne Plaza Somerset/Bridgewater 🅷
(732) 560-0500. **$99-$169.** 110 Davidson Ave 08873. I-287, exit 10 (CR 527), just n (direction Bound Brook) to Davidson Ave, then just sw. Int corridors. **Pets:** Accepted. 🅰🆂🅺 ⊠ 🛗 🖵 🍴 🛩 🖾

▼▼▼ Extended StayAmerica-Somerset-Franklin 🅷
(732) 469-8080. **$79-$129.** 30 World Fair Dr 08873. I-287, exit 10 (CR 527), left on ramp (CR 527 S/Easton Ave), 0.3 mi, then 0.5 mi w. Int corridors. **Pets:** Other species. $25 daily fee/room. Designated rooms, service with restrictions, crate. 🅰🆂🅺 ⊠ 🛗 🖵

⬥⬥⬥ ▼▼▼ ▼▼▼ Holiday Inn-Somerset 🅷 🐾
(732) 356-1700. **$75-$129.** 195 Davidson Ave 08873. I-287, exit 10 (CR 527), just n (direction Bound Brook), then 0.5 mi sw. Int corridors. **Pets:** Other species. $15 daily fee/pet. Service with restrictions, crate.
🆂🅰🆅🅴 ⊠ 🔥M 🛗 🖵 🍴 🛩

▼▼▼▼ Homewood Suites by Hilton-Somerset 🅷
(732) 868-9155. **$89-$189.** 101 Pierce St 08873. I-287, exit 10 (CR 527), left on ramp (CR 527 S/Easton Ave), 0.3 mi, 0.7 mi w on World Fair Dr, then just s. Int corridors. **Pets:** Accepted. ⊠ 🛗 🖵 🛩 🖾

▼▼▼▼ Residence Inn by Marriott-Somerset 🅷
(732) 627-0881. **$170-$208.** 37 World Fair Dr 08873. I-287, exit 10 (CR 527), left on ramp (CR 527 S/Easton Ave) 0.3 mi, then 0.5 mi w. Int corridors. **Pets:** Accepted. ⊠ 🔥M 🛗 🖵 🛩 🖾

▼▼▼▼ Staybridge Suites Somerset 🅷
(732) 356-8000. **$119-$159.** 260 Davidson Ave 08873. I-287, exit 10 (CR 527), just n (direction Bound Brook) to Davidson Ave, then 0.8 mi sw. Ext corridors. **Pets:** Accepted. 🅰🆂🅺 ⊠ 🛗 🖵 🛩 🖾

SPRINGFIELD

▼▼▼ Holiday Inn Springfield H

(973) 376-9400. **$119-$129.** 304 US 22 W 07081. Garden State Pkwy, exit 140 northbound, 4 mi w; exit 140A southbound. Int corridors. **Pets:** Designated rooms, service with restrictions, crate.

(ASK) (X) ⊟ ⊑ (▯▯) ☞ (X)

TINTON FALLS

◈◈◈ ▼▼▼ Comfort Inn & Suites H

(732) 389-4800. **$119-$134.** 3 Centre Plaza 07724. Garden State Pkwy, exit 105, 1st right at Hope Rd after toll. Ext/int corridors. **Pets:** Medium. $50 one-time fee/pet. Designated rooms, service with restrictions, supervision. (SAVE) (X) ⊟ ⊑ ☞

◈◈◈ ▼ Red Roof Inn #7211 M

(732) 389-4646. **Call for rates.** 11 Centre Plaza 07724. Garden State Pkwy, exit 105, just right at 1st light after toll. Ext corridors. **Pets:** Large. Service with restrictions, crate. (SAVE) (X) (&M) ⊟

▼▼▼ Residence Inn Tinton Falls H

(732) 389-8100. **$169-$179.** 90 Park Rd 07724. Garden State Pkwy, exit 105, immediate left before Courtyard by Marriott, just n, then e. Ext corridors. **Pets:** Medium. $100 one-time fee/room. Service with restrictions. (X) ⊟ ⊑ ☞ (X)

TOMS RIVER

◈◈◈ ▼▼ Howard Johnson Hotel-Toms River H ❀

(732) 244-1000. **$99-$199.** 955 Hooper Ave 08753. Garden State Pkwy, exit 82, 1 mi e on SR 37. Int corridors. **Pets:** Other species. $50 one-time fee/pet. Designated rooms, no service.

(SAVE) (X) ⊟ ⊑ (▯▯) ☞

◈◈◈ ▼▼▼▼ Quality Inn H ❀

(732) 341-2400. **$85-$229.** 815 SR 37 W 08755. Garden State Pkwy, exit 82A, 1.5 mi w. Int corridors. **Pets:** Medium, dogs only. $39 daily fee/pet. Service with restrictions, supervision. (SAVE) (X) ⊟ ⊑ ☞

VERNON

◈◈◈ ▼▼▼ Appalachian Motel M

(973) 764-6070. **$55-$125, 3 day notice.** 367 Rt 94 N 07462. 1 mi n. Ext corridors. **Pets:** Small, other species. $25 daily fee/pet. Designated rooms, service with restrictions, supervision. (SAVE) (X) ⊟

WANTAGE

▼ High Point Country Inn M ❀

(973) 702-1860. **$89.** 1328 SR 23 N 07461. 1 mi n of Colesville Village Center. Ext corridors. **Pets:** Dogs only. $5 deposit/pet. Service with restrictions. (ASK) (X) ⊟ ☞ (▢)

WARREN

▼▼▼ Somerset Hills Hotel H

(908) 647-6700. **Call for rates.** 200 Liberty Corner Rd 07059. I-78, exit 33, just n on CR 525. Int corridors. **Pets:** Accepted.

(X) ⊟ ⊑ (▯▯) ☞

WAYNE

▼▼ La Quinta Inns & Suites H ❀

(973) 696-8050. **$67-$99.** 1850 SR 23 07470. I-80, exit 53 (Butler-Verona) westbound to SR 23 N, 3 mi to Ratzer Rd (service road), then just n; exit 54 eastbound to Minnisink Rd, U-turn for US 80 W, exit 53. Int corridors. **Pets:** Medium, other species. Service with restrictions, supervision. (ASK) (X) (&M) ⊟ ⊑ ☞

▼▼▼ Residence Inn by Marriott Wayne H

(973) 872-7100. **$188-$230.** 30 Nevins Rd 07470. Jct CR 640 (Riverview Dr) and 681 (Valley Rd), 3.5 mi n, just w on Barbour Pond Dr, then just n. Int corridors. **Pets:** Accepted. (X) (&M) ⊟ ⊑ ☞ (X)

WEEHAWKEN

◈◈◈ ▼▼▼ Sheraton Lincoln Harbor Hotel H

(201) 617-5600. **$159-$659.** 500 Harbor Blvd 07086. I-495 E toward Lincoln Tunnel, exit Weehawken/Hoboken, bear right at bottom of hill, then 0.4 mi e to Lincoln Harbor Complex; on 19th St. Int corridors. **Pets:** Accepted. (SAVE) (X) ⊑ (▯▯) ☞

WEST ORANGE

▼▼▼ Residence Inn by Marriott-West Orange H

(973) 669-4700. **$179-$199.** 107 Prospect Ave 07052. I-280, exit 8B, 1 mi n on CR 577 (Prospect Ave). Int corridors. **Pets:** Accepted.

(X) ⊟ ⊑ ☞

WHIPPANY

▼▼ Homestead Studio Suites Hanover/Parsippany H

(973) 463-1999. **$109-$149.** 125 Rt 10 E 07981. I-287, exit 39, 3.6 mi e. Int corridors. **Pets:** Other species. $25 daily fee/room. Designated rooms, service with restrictions, crate. (ASK) (X) (&M) ⊟ ⊑

◈◈◈ ▼▼▼ Hyatt Summerfield Suites Parsippany/Whippany H

(973) 605-1001. **$89-$289.** 1 Ridgedale Ave N 07981. I-287, exit 39, just nw. Int corridors. **Pets:** Accepted. (SAVE) (X) (&M) ⊟ ⊑ ☞

WOODBRIDGE

▼▼ Homestead Studio Suites Woodbridge-Edison H

(732) 442-8333. **$82-$119.** 1 Hoover Way 07095. New Jersey Tpke, exit 11, 1.4 mi to US 9 N, then just w on King Georges Post Rd. Int corridors. **Pets:** Other species. $25 daily fee/room. Designated rooms, service with restrictions, crate. (ASK) (X) (&M) ⊟ ⊑

ALAMOGORDO

▼▼▼ Quality Inn H

(575) 437-7100. **Call for rates.** 1401 S White Sands Blvd 88310. 1.6 mi s of jct US 82/70 and 54. Int corridors. **Pets:** $25 daily fee/pet. Service with restrictions. ✕ ⓜ 🛏 💻 🏊

▼▼▼ Super 8-Alamogordo H

(575) 434-4205. **Call for rates.** 3204 N White Sands Blvd 88310. Just s of jct US 54/70 and 82. Int corridors. **Pets:** Small. $10 daily fee/pet. Service with restrictions, supervision. ✕ 🛏 💻

ALBUQUERQUE

⨁ ▼▼▼▼ Albuquerque Sheraton Uptown Hotel H 🐾

(505) 881-0000. **$99-$219, 3 day notice.** 2600 Louisiana Blvd NE 87110. I-40, exit 162, 0.8 mi n. Int corridors. **Pets:** Medium. Service with restrictions, supervision. SAVE ✕ ⓜ 💻 🍴 🏊

⨁ ▼▼▼ Best Western Airport InnSuites Albuquerque Hotel & Suites H

(505) 242-7022. **$69-$169.** 2400 Yale Blvd SE 87106. I-25, exit 222 (Gibson Blvd) northbound; exit 222A southbound, 1 mi e, then just s. Int corridors. **Pets:** Other species. $25 one-time fee/pet. Designated rooms, service with restrictions, supervision. SAVE ✕ 🛏 💻 🏊

⨁ ▼▼▼▼ Best Western Rio Grande Inn H

(505) 843-9500. **$115-$135.** 1015 Rio Grande Blvd NW 87104. I-40, exit 157A (Rio Grande Blvd), just s. Int corridors. **Pets:** Medium. $25 one-time fee/room. Designated rooms, service with restrictions, supervision. SAVE ✕ 🛏 💻 🍴 🏊

⨁ ▼▼▼▼ Brittania & W E Mauger Estate Bed & Breakfast BB 🐾

(505) 242-8755. **$123-$204, 10 day notice.** 701 Roma Ave NW 87102. I-25, exit 225, 1 mi w, then just s on 7th Ave. Int corridors. **Pets:** Large, dogs only. $20 one-time fee/room. Designated rooms, service with restrictions. SAVE ✕ 🛏 💻

▼▼▼▼ Candlewood Suites H

(505) 888-3424. **$85-$190.** 3025 Menaul Blvd NE 87107. I-40, exit 160, just n to Menaul Blvd, then 0.5 mi w. Int corridors. **Pets:** Large, other species. $75 one-time fee/room. Service with restrictions. ASK ✕ ⓜ 💻

⨁ ▼▼▼▼ ClubHouse Inn & Suites H

(505) 345-0010. **$89-$129.** 1315 Menaul Blvd NE 87107. I-25, exit 227A southbound, 1.5 mi s to Menaul Blvd, then just w; exit 225 northbound, 1.8 mi, then just w. Int corridors. **Pets:** Medium, other species. $10 daily fee/pet. No service, supervision. SAVE ✕ ⓜ 🛏 💻 🏊

▼▼ Comfort Inn-Airport H

(505) 243-2244. **$62-$108.** 2300 Yale Blvd SE 87106. I-25, exit 222A southbound; exit 222 (Gibson Blvd) northbound, 1 mi n, then just s. Ext/int corridors. **Pets:** Small. $10 daily fee/pet. Designated rooms, service with restrictions, supervision. ASK ✕ ⓜ 🛏 💻 🏊

▼▼ Comfort Inn & Suites by Choice Hotels H 🐾

(505) 822-1090. **$60-$80.** 5811 Signal Ave NE 87113. I-25, exit 233, just e via Alameda. Int corridors. **Pets:** Medium, other species. $15 one-time fee/pet. Service with restrictions, crate. ASK ✕ ⓜ 🛏 💻 🏊

⨁ ▼▼▼ Comfort Inn East M

(505) 294-1800. **$50, 7 day notice.** 13031 Central Ave NE 87123. I-40, exit 167 (Central Ave), just w. Ext corridors. **Pets:** Medium, dogs only. $50 deposit/room, $15 daily fee/room. Service with restrictions, supervision. SAVE ✕ ⓜ 🛏 💻 🏊

▼▼▼ Country Inn & Suites By Carlson, Albuquerque Airport H

(505) 246-9600. **$69-$149.** 2601 Mulberry SE 87106. I-25, exit 222 (Gibson Blvd), just e. Int corridors. **Pets:** Accepted. ASK ✕ 🛏 💻 🏊

⨁ ▼▼▼ Days Inn-Hotel Circle H

(505) 275-3297. **$50-$60.** 10321 Hotel Ave NE 87123. I-40, exit 165 (Eubank Blvd), just n. Ext corridors. **Pets:** Accepted. SAVE ✕ 🛏 💻 🏊

▼▼▼◆ Drury Inn & Suites-Albuquerque H

(505) 341-3600. **$110-$169.** 4310 The 25 Way NE 87109. I-25, exit Jefferson St NE; northwest quadrant of exchange. Int corridors. **Pets:** Other species. No service, supervision. ASK ✕ ⓜ 🛏 💻 🏊

⨁ ▼▼▼ Econo Lodge Downtown/University M

(505) 243-1321. **$45-$125.** 817 Central Ave NE 87102. I-25, exit 224A northbound; exit 224B southbound, just w. Ext corridors. **Pets:** Medium. $25 deposit/pet, $5 daily fee/pet. Service with restrictions, supervision. SAVE ✕ 🛏 💻 🏊

⨁ ▼▼ Econo Lodge East H

(505) 292-7600. **$50-$119.** 13211 Central Ave NE 87123. I-40, exit 167 (Central Ave), just w. Ext corridors. **Pets:** Medium, other species. $7 daily fee/pet. Supervision. SAVE ✕ 🛏

⨁ ▼▼ Econo Lodge Midtown H

(505) 880-0080. **$55-$80.** 2412 Carlisle Blvd NE 87110. I-40, exit 160, just n. Ext corridors. **Pets:** Small. $15 one-time fee/pet. Service with restrictions, supervision. SAVE ✕ 🛏

⨁ ▼▼ Econo Lodge Old Town H

(505) 243-8475. **$55-$140.** 2321 Central Ave NW 87104. I-40, exit 157A, 0.6 mi s on Rio Grande Blvd, then 0.4 mi w. Ext corridors. **Pets:** Large, dogs only. $25 daily fee/pet. Service with restrictions, supervision. SAVE ✕ 🛏 💻 🏊

⨁ ▼▼ GuestHouse Inn & Suites H 🐾

(505) 271-8500. **$40-$99.** 10331 Hotel Ave NE 87123. I-40, exit 165 (Eubank Dr), just n. Int corridors. **Pets:** Very small, other species. $10 one-time fee/pet. Service with restrictions, supervision. SAVE ✕ 🛏 💻

⨁ ▼▼▼◆ Hacienda Antigua Inn BB 🐾

(505) 345-5399. **$139-$209, 10 day notice.** 6708 Tierra Dr NW 87107. I-25, exit 230 (Osuna Dr), 2 mi w, then just n. Ext/int corridors. **Pets:** Other species. $35 one-time fee/pet. Service with restrictions, supervision. SAVE ✕ 🛏 💻 🏊

⨁ ▼▼▼◆ Hampton Inn-North H

(505) 344-1555. **$79-$150.** 5101 Ellison NE 87109. I-25, exit 231 (San Antonio Dr), just w. Ext corridors. **Pets:** Other species. Service with restrictions, supervision. SAVE ✕ ⓜ 🛏 💻 🏊

AAA ▼▼▼▼ Hawthorn Inn & Suites H
(505) 242-1555. **$59-$89.** 1511 Gibson Blvd SE 87106. I-25, exit 222 (Gibson Blvd) northbound; exit 222A southbound, just e. Int corridors. **Pets:** $25 daily fee/room. Service with restrictions.
SAVE ✕ &M ⊟ ⬛ ⤳

▼▼▼▼ Hilton Albuquerque H
(505) 884-2500. **$119-$219.** 1901 University Blvd NE 87102. I-40, exit 160, just n to Menaul Blvd, then 1.1 mi w. Int corridors. **Pets:** Accepted.
✕ &M ⊟ ⬛ ⑪ ⤳

AAA ▼▼▼▼ Holiday Inn Express H
(505) 275-8900. **$95-$100.** 10330 Hotel Ave NE 87123. I-40, exit 165 (Eubank Blvd), just e. Ext corridors. **Pets:** Large, other species. $25 one-time fee/pet. Designated rooms, service with restrictions, supervision.
SAVE ✕ ⊟ ⬛ ⤳ ✕

▼▼ The Hotel Blue H
(505) 924-2400. **Call for rates.** 717 Central Ave NW 87102. 8th St and Central Ave; downtown. Ext corridors. **Pets:** Accepted.
✕ ⊟ ⬛ ⤳

AAA ▼▼▼ Howard Johnson Express Inn H
(505) 828-1600. **$65-$145.** 7630 Pan American Frwy NE 87109. I-25, exit 231 (San Antonio Dr), 0.8 mi n on frontage road. Int corridors. **Pets:** $10 one-time fee/pet. Designated rooms, service with restrictions, crate. SAVE ✕ ⊟ ⬛ ⤳

▼▼▼▼ La Quinta Inn Albuquerque (Airport) H ❀
(505) 243-5500. **$49-$99.** 2116 Yale Blvd SE 87106. I-25, exit 222 (Gibson Blvd) northbound; exit 222A southbound, 1 mi e. Int corridors. **Pets:** Medium, other species. Service with restrictions, supervision.
ASK ✕ &M ⊟ ⬛ ⤳

▼▼▼ La Quinta Inn Albuquerque (I-40 East) H ❀
(505) 884-3591. **$39-$89.** 2424 San Mateo Blvd NE 87110. I-40, exit 161 westbound; exit 161B eastbound, just n. Ext corridors. **Pets:** Medium, other species. Service with restrictions, supervision.
ASK ✕ ⊟ ⬛ ⤳

▼▼▼ La Quinta Inn Albuquerque (North) M ❀
(505) 821-9000. **$39-$82.** 5241 San Antonio Dr NE 87109. I-25, exit 231 (San Antonio Dr), just e. Ext corridors. **Pets:** Medium, other species. Service with restrictions, supervision. ASK ✕ &M ⊟ ⬛ ⤳

▼▼▼▼ La Quinta Inn & Suites Albuquerque (West) H ❀
(505) 839-1744. **$59-$99.** 6101 Iliff Rd NW 87121. I-40, exit 155, just sw. Int corridors. **Pets:** Medium, other species. Service with restrictions, supervision. ASK ✕ &M ⊟ ⬛ ⤳

▼▼▼▼ La Quinta Inn & Suites Northwest H ❀
(505) 345-7500. **$49-$95.** 7439 Pan American Frwy NE 87109. I-25, exit 231 (San Antonio Dr), just w. Int corridors. **Pets:** Medium, other species. Service with restrictions, supervision. ASK ✕ ⊟ ⬛ ⤳

▼▼▼▼ La Quinta Suites Midtown/University H ❀
(505) 761-5600. **$94-$159.** 2011 Menaul Blvd 87107. Jct University and Menaul blvds, just e. Int corridors. **Pets:** Medium, other species. Service with restrictions, supervision. ASK ✕ &M ⊟ ⬛ ⤳

▼▼▼ Nativo Lodge H
(505) 798-4300. **Call for rates.** 6000 Pan American Frwy NE 87109. I-25, exit 230, just e. Int corridors. **Pets:** Accepted.
✕ ⊟ ⬛ ⑪ ⤳ ✕

AAA ▼▼▼ Quality Inn & Suites Albuquerque Downtown H
(505) 242-5228. **$89-$159.** 411 McKnight Ave NW 87102. I-40, exit 159A, just s via 4th St S. Int corridors. **Pets:** Accepted.
SAVE ✕ ⊟ ⬛ ⤳

AAA ▼▼▼▼ Quality Suites H
(505) 797-0850. **$70-$115.** 5251 San Antonio Dr NE 87109. I-25, exit 231 (San Antonio Dr), just e. Int corridors. **Pets:** Medium, other species. $10 daily fee/pet. Designated rooms, service with restrictions, supervision.
SAVE ✕ ⊟ ⬛ ⤳

▼▼▼ Ramada Limited H
(505) 858-3297. **Call for rates.** 5601 Alameda Blvd NE 87113. I-25, exit 233, just w. Int corridors. **Pets:** Accepted. ✕ &M ⊟ ⬛ ⤳

▼▼▼▼ Residence Inn North by Marriott H
(505) 761-0200. **$143-$175.** 4331 The Lane at 25 NE 87109. I-25, exit 229 (Jefferson St), just w, just n to The Lane at 25 NE, then just e. Int corridors. **Pets:** Other species. $100 one-time fee/room. Service with restrictions, supervision. ✕ &M ⊟ ⬛ ⤳

AAA ▼▼▼ Sandia Peak Inn H
(505) 831-5036. **$50-$136.** 4614 Central Ave SW 87105. I-40, exit 157A (Rio Grande Blvd), just s, then 2 mi w. Ext corridors. **Pets:** Accepted.
SAVE ✕ ⊟ ⤳

AAA ▼▼▼▼ Sheraton Albuquerque Airport Hotel H
(505) 843-7000. **$99-$229.** 2910 Yale Blvd SE 87106. I-25, exit 225 northbound; exit 222A southbound, 1 mi n on Gibson Blvd, then 0.5 mi s. Int corridors. **Pets:** Medium. $250 deposit/room. Designated rooms, service with restrictions, supervision. SAVE ✕ ⊟ ⬛ ⑪ ⤳

AAA ▼▼▼ Sleep Inn Airport H
(505) 244-3325. **$65-$104.** 2300 International Ave SE 87106. I-25, exit 222 (Gibson Blvd) northbound; exit 222A southbound, 1 mi e to Yale Blvd, then just n. Int corridors. **Pets:** Accepted.
SAVE ✕ &M ⊟ ⬛ ⤳

AAA ▼▼▼▼ Staybridge Suites Albuquerque North H ❀
(505) 266-7829. **$89-$170.** 5817 Signal Ave NE 87113. I-25, exit 233 (Alameda), just e; jct Alameda Blvd and Signal Ave. Int corridors. **Pets:** Medium. $10 daily fee/room. Designated rooms, service with restrictions, supervision. SAVE ✕ ⊟ ⬛ ⤳ ✕

AAA ▼▼▼ Suburban Extended Stay Hotels M
(505) 883-8888. **$60.** 2401 Wellsley Dr NE 87107. I-40, exit 160, just n to Menaul Blvd, just w, then just s. Ext corridors. **Pets:** Medium. $25 one-time fee/room. Service with restrictions, supervision. SAVE ✕ ⊟ ⬛

▼▼▼ Super 8 East H
(505) 271-4807. **$54-$96.** 450 Paisano NE 87123. I-40, exit 166 (Juan Tabo Blvd), just n to Copper, then just s. Int corridors. **Pets:** Other species. $8 daily fee/pet. Service with restrictions, supervision.
ASK ✕ ⊟ ⬛

▼▼▼ Super 8 of Albuquerque H
(505) 888-4884. **$49-$79.** 2500 University Blvd NE 87107. I-25, exit 225 northbound, 1.9 mi n on frontage road to Menaul Blvd, then just e; exit 227 (Comanche Rd) southbound, 0.9 mi s to Menaul Blvd, then just e. Int corridors. **Pets:** Accepted. ASK ✕ ⊟ ⬛

▼▼▼ Super 8 West (Albuquerque) H
(505) 836-5560. **$51-$95.** 6030 Iliff Rd NW 87121. I-40, exit 155, 0.5 mi s. Int corridors. **Pets:** Accepted. ASK ✕ ⬛

AAA ▼▼▼▼ TownePlace Suites by Marriott H
(505) 232-5800. **$86-$105.** 2400 Centre Ave SE 87106. I-25, exit 222 (Gibson Blvd) northbound; exit 222A southbound, 1 mi e to Yale Blvd, at northeast jct of Gibson and Yale blvds, then just e. Int corridors. **Pets:** Accepted. SAVE ✕ &M ⊟ ⬛ ⤳

ALGODONES

▼▼▼▼ Hacienda Vargas Bed and Breakfast Inn BB ❀
(505) 867-9115. **$89-$169, 10 day notice.** 1431 SR 313 (El Camino Real) 87001. I-25, exit 248, 0.3 mi w, then 0.3 mi s. Int corridors. **Pets:** Other species. $10 one-time fee/room. Designated rooms.
ASK ✕ ⋈ ⌕

ARROYO SECO

▼▼◆◆ Adobe and Stars B & B BB
(575) 776-2776. **Call for rates.** 584 State Hwy 150 87571. 1.1 mi ne of Arroyo Seco village, at Valdez Rd. Ext/int corridors. **Pets:** Accepted.
⊠ 🖬 /ʌℂ/

▼▼◆◆ Cottonwood Inn Bed & Breakfast BB
(575) 776-5826. **$125-$275, 14 day notice.** 02 SR 230 87514. On SR 150 at SR 230. Ext/int corridors. **Pets:** Dogs only. $15 daily fee/pet. Designated rooms, service with restrictions, supervision.
ASK ⊠ 🖬 🖵 ⊠ /ʌℂ/ ☎

ARTESIA

◆◆◆ ▼▼ Artesia Inn M
(575) 746-9801. **$75-$110.** 1820 S 1st St 88210. 1.5 mi s on US 285. Ext corridors. **Pets:** Other species. $12 one-time fee/room. Service with restrictions. SAVE ⊠ 🖬 🖵 🏊

◆◆◆ ▼▼▼ Best Western Pecos Inn H
(575) 748-3324. **$95-$120.** 2209 W Main 88210. 1.5 mi w on US 82. Int corridors. **Pets:** $15 one-time fee/room. Service with restrictions, supervision. SAVE ⊠ 🖬 🖵 🍴 🏊 ⊠

BERNALILLO

◆◆◆ ▼▼▼ Days Inn Bernalillo H
(505) 771-7000. **$40-$140.** 107 N Camino del Pueblo 87004. I-25, exit 242, just w. Int corridors. **Pets:** Small. $30 deposit/pet. Service with restrictions, supervision. SAVE ⊠ 🖬 🖵 🏊

◆◆◆ ▼▼▼▼ Hyatt Regency Tamaya Resort and Spa H
(505) 867-1234. **$139-$359, 7 day notice.** 1300 Tuyuna Tr 87004. I-25, exit 242, 1 mi w on SR 44 to Tamaya Rd, then 1 mi n, follow signs. Int corridors. **Pets:** Accepted. SAVE ⊠ 🖬 🖳 🖵 🍴 🏊 ⊠

▼▼◆◆ La Hacienda Grande BB 🐾
(505) 867-1887. **$89-$129, 10 day notice.** 21 Barros Rd 87004. I-25, exit 242, 0.3 mi w to Camino del Pueblo, then 0.5 mi n. Ext/int corridors. **Pets:** Large, other species. Designated rooms, service with restrictions, supervision. ASK ⊠ ☎

◆◆◆ ▼▼ Quality Inn & Suites H
(505) 771-9500. **$55-$155.** 210 N Hill Rd 87004. I-25, exit 242, just w. Int corridors. **Pets:** Medium, other species. $10 daily fee/room. Service with restrictions, supervision. SAVE ⊠ 🖬 🖵

▼▼ Super 8 Bernalillo H
(505) 771-4700. **$49-$150.** 265 E Hwy 550 87004. I-25, exit 242, just w. Int corridors. **Pets:** Medium. $20 deposit/pet, $10 daily fee/pet. Designated rooms, service with restrictions, supervision. ASK ⊠ 🖬 🖵

BLOOMFIELD

▼▼ Super 8 M
(505) 632-8886. **$72-$98, 10 day notice.** 525 W Broadway Blvd 87413. Jct of US 64 and 550. Int corridors. **Pets:** Other species. $10 one-time fee/room. Service with restrictions, supervision. ASK ⊠ 🖵

CARLSBAD

◆◆◆ ▼▼ Best Western Stevens Inn H
(575) 887-2851. **$90.** 1829 S Canal St 88220. 1 mi s on US 62, 180 and 285. Ext corridors. **Pets:** Small. $20 daily fee/pet. Service with restrictions. SAVE ⊠ 🖬 🖵 🍴 🏊

◆◆◆ ▼▼ Continental Inn & Suites M
(575) 887-0341. **$49-$69.** 3820 National Parks Hwy 88220. 3.5 mi sw on US 62 and 180. Ext corridors. **Pets:** Other species. $10 one-time fee/room. Designated rooms, service with restrictions, supervision. SAVE ⊠ 🖬 🏊

◆◆◆ ▼▼ Days Inn of Carlsbad H
(575) 887-7800. **$89-$115.** 3910 National Parks Hwy 88220. 3.5 mi sw on US 62 and 180. Ext corridors. **Pets:** $10 daily fee/pet. Service with restrictions, supervision. SAVE ⊠ 🖳 🖬 🖵 🏊

CHIMAYO

▼▼ ◆◆ Casa Escondida Bed & Breakfast BB
(505) 351-4805. **$99-$159, 14 day notice.** 64 CR 0100 87522. Jct SR 76 and 98, just w on SR 76, then 0.5 mi ne on CR 100, follow signs. Ext/int corridors. **Pets:** Accepted. ⊠ 🖬 🖵 🏊 ☎

CIMARRON

◆◆◆ ▼▼ Cimarron Inn & RV Park M 🐾
(575) 376-2268. **$49-$60.** 212 10th St 87714. On US 64. Ext corridors. **Pets:** Other species. Crate. SAVE ⊠ 🖬 🖵

CLAYTON

◆◆◆ ▼▼◆◆ Best Western Kokopelli Lodge H 🐾
(575) 374-2589. **$110-$190.** 702 S 1st St 88415. US 87, 0.5 mi se of jct US 56 and 64. Ext corridors. **Pets:** $5 daily fee/pet. Service with restrictions, supervision. SAVE ⊠ 🖬 🖵 🍴 🏊

◆◆◆ ▼▼◆◆ Days Inn & Suites H
(575) 374-0133. **$89-$169.** 1120 S 1st St 88415. US 87, 1 mi s of jct US 56 and 64. Int corridors. **Pets:** Medium. $10 daily fee/pet. Service with restrictions, supervision. SAVE ⊠ 🖬 🖵 🏊

▼▼ Super 8–Clayton M
(575) 374-8127. **Call for rates.** 1425 S 1st St 88415. US 87, 1 mi se of jct US 56 and 64. Int corridors. **Pets:** Small. $10 daily fee/pet. Designated rooms, service with restrictions, supervision. ⊠ 🖬 🖵

CLOUDCROFT

◆◆◆ ▼▼◆◆ The Lodge Resort H
(575) 682-2566. **$130-$365, 14 day notice.** 601 Corona Pl 88317. US 82, 0.3 mi s on Curlew/Corona Pl. Int corridors. **Pets:** Large. $25 one-time fee/room. Designated rooms, service with restrictions, supervision. SAVE ⊠ 🖳 🖬 🖵 🍴 🏊 ⊠

CLOVIS

◆◆◆ ▼▼◆◆ Comfort Inn & Suites H
(575) 762-4536. **$86-$110.** 201 Schepps Blvd 88101. Jct US 60/70/84, and Schepps Blvd, just n. Int corridors. **Pets:** Small, dogs only. $10 daily fee/pet. Service with restrictions, crate. SAVE ⊠ 🖬 🖵 🏊

▼▼◆◆ Days Inn & Suites Hotel and Convention Center H
(575) 762-4491. **$69.** 2700 E Mabry Dr 88101. 1.5 mi e on US 60/70/84. Ext corridors. **Pets:** Accepted. ASK ⊠ 🖳 🖬 🖵 🏊 ⊠

▼▼◆◆ Econo Lodge M
(575) 763-3439. **$49-$99.** 1400 E Mabry Dr 88101. 0.5 mi e on US 60/70/84. Ext corridors. **Pets:** Accepted. ASK ⊠ 🖬 🖵 🏊

◆◆◆ ▼▼◆◆ La Quinta Inn & Suites Clovis H 🐾
(575) 763-8777. **$99-$139.** 4521 N Prince St 88101. Jct US 60/84 and Prince St, 3 mi n. Int corridors. **Pets:** Medium, other species. Service with restrictions, supervision. SAVE ⊠ 🖬 🖵 🏊

DEMING

◆◆◆ ▼▼◆◆ Best Western Mimbres Valley Inn H
(575) 546-4544. **$60-$121.** 1500 W Pine St 88030. I-10, exit 81, just e. Ext corridors. **Pets:** Accepted. SAVE ⊠ 🖬 🖵 🏊

▼▼◆◆ Comfort Inn & Suites H
(575) 544-3600. **Call for rates.** 1010 W Pine St 88030. I-10, exit 81, just e. Int corridors. **Pets:** Other species. $10 daily fee/pet. Designated rooms, service with restrictions, supervision. ⊠ 🖳 🖬 🖵 🏊

◆◆◆ ▼▼◆◆ Days Inn M
(575) 546-8813. **$57-$80.** 1601 E Pine St 88030. I-10, exit 85 westbound, 2 mi w on business loop; exit 81 eastbound, 1 mi e on business loop. Ext corridors. **Pets:** Small, other species. $5 daily fee/pet. Service with restrictions, supervision. SAVE ⊠ 🖬 🖵 🍴 🏊

AAA ◇◇◇ Grand Motor Inn 🅷 ❀
(575) 546-2632. **$50-$60.** 1721 E Pine St 88030. I-10, exit 85 westbound, 2 mi w on business loop; exit 82 eastbound, 1 mi e on business loop. Ext/int corridors. **Pets:** Medium, other species. $5 daily fee/pet. Designated rooms, service with restrictions, supervision.
[SAVE] [X] [🛏] [🍽] [🏊]

AAA ◇◇◇ Holiday Inn 🅷
(575) 546-2661. **$70-$90.** 4600 E Pine St 88030. I-10, exit 85, just w. Ext corridors. **Pets:** Service with restrictions, supervision.
[SAVE] [X] [🕭M] [🛏] [💻] [🍽] [🏊]

AAA ◇◇◇◇ La Quinta Inn & Suites 🅷 ❀
(575) 546-0600. **$69-$119.** 4300 E Pine St 88030. I-10, exit 85, just w. Int corridors. **Pets:** Medium, other species. Service with restrictions, supervision. [SAVE] [X] [🕭M] [🛏] [💻] [🏊]

◇◇ Super 8–Deming 🅷
(575) 546-0481. **$70-$120.** 1217 W Pine St 88030. I-10, exit 81, just e. Ext/int corridors. **Pets:** Large, other species. $10 daily fee/pet. Designated rooms, service with restrictions, supervision. [ASK] [X] [🛏] [💻] [🏊]

AAA ◇ Western Motel 🅼
(575) 544-8811. **$38-$49.** 1207 W Pine 88030. I-10, exit 81, just e. Ext corridors. **Pets:** Accepted. [SAVE] [X] [🛏] [💻]

DULCE

AAA ◇◇◇ Best Western Jicarilla Inn & Casino 🅷
(505) 759-3663. **$75-$115.** US Hwy 64 Jicarilla Blvd 87528. Center. Int corridors. **Pets:** Accepted. [SAVE] [X] [🛏] [💻] [🍽]

ELEPHANT BUTTE

AAA ◇◇◇ Elephant Butte Inn & Spa 🅷 ❀
(575) 744-5431. **$79-$149.** 401 Hwy 195 87935. I-25, exit 83, 4 mi e. Ext corridors. **Pets:** Large. $25 one-time fee/pet. Designated rooms, service with restrictions, supervision. [SAVE] [X] [🕭M] [🛏] [💻] [🍽] [🏊]

ESPANOLA

AAA ◇◇◇ Comfort Inn 🅷
(505) 753-2419. **$50-$160.** 604-B S Riverside Dr 87532. US 84 and 285, just s of jct SR 68. Int corridors. **Pets:** Large. $10 daily fee/pet. Service with restrictions, supervision. [SAVE] [X] [🛏] [💻] [🏊]

FARMINGTON

AAA ◇◇◇ Best Western Inn & Suites 🅷
(505) 327-5221. **$100-$120.** 700 Scott Ave 87401. 1 mi e on SR 516 (Main St), just s. Int corridors. **Pets:** Accepted.
[SAVE] [X] [🛏] [💻] [🍽] [🏊] [X]

AAA ◇◇◇ Comfort Inn 🅷
(505) 325-2626. **$80-$130.** 555 Scott Ave 87401. 1 mi e on SR 516 (Main St), just s. Int corridors. **Pets:** $20 daily fee/pet. Service with restrictions, supervision. [SAVE] [X] [🛏] [💻] [🏊]

◇◇◇ Holiday Inn Express 🅷 ❀
(505) 325-2545. **$89-$209.** 2110 Bloomfield Blvd 87401. 1.6 mi e on US 64 (Bloomfield Blvd); just past jct Broadway; on Frontage Rd. Int corridors. **Pets:** Medium, other species. $25 one-time fee/room. Service with restrictions, supervision. [ASK] [X] [🛏] [💻] [🏊]

◇◇ La Quinta Inn 🅷 ❀
(505) 327-4706. **$59-$109.** 675 Scott Ave 87401. 1 mi e on SR 516 (Main St), just s. Ext/int corridors. **Pets:** Medium, other species. Service with restrictions, supervision. [ASK] [X] [🛏] [💻] [🏊]

GALLUP

AAA ◇◇◇ Americas Best Value Inn & Suites 🅷
(505) 722-0757. **$52-$79, 3 day notice.** 2003 Hwy 66 W 87301. I-40, exit 20, 1 mi w. Ext/int corridors. **Pets:** Accepted.
[SAVE] [X] [🛏] [💻] [🍽]

AAA ◇◇◇ Best Western Inn & Suites 🅷 ❀
(505) 722-2221. **Call for rates.** 3009 US 66 W 87301. I-40, exit 16, 1 mi e. Int corridors. **Pets:** Other species. $10 one-time fee/pet. Service with restrictions, supervision. [SAVE] [X] [🛏] [💻] [🍽] [🏊]

AAA ◇◇◇ Best Western Red Rock Inn 🅷
(505) 722-7600. **$90-$110, 3 day notice.** 3010 US 66 E 87301. I-40, exit 26, 1 mi w. Int corridors. **Pets:** Other species. $15 daily fee/pet. Designated rooms, supervision. [SAVE] [X] [🛏] [💻] [🏊]

◇◇ Days Inn West 🅼
(505) 863-6889. **$56-$65.** 3201 W Hwy 66 87301. I-40, exit 16, 0.3 mi e. Ext corridors. **Pets:** Accepted. [ASK] [X] [🛏] [💻] [🏊]

◇◇◇ La Quinta Inn & Suites 🅷 ❀
(505) 722-2233. **$89-$159.** 3880 Hwy 66 E 87301. I-40, exit 26, just e. Int corridors. **Pets:** Medium, other species. Service with restrictions, supervision. [ASK] [X] [🛏] [💻] [🏊] [X]

AAA ◇◇◇ Quality Inn & Suites 🅷
(505) 726-1000. **$80-$90.** 1500 W Maloney Ave 87301. I-40, exit 20, just n on Munoz Dr, then just w. Ext/int corridors. **Pets:** Very small. $15 daily fee/pet. Service with restrictions, supervision. [SAVE] [X] [🛏] [💻] [🏊]

AAA ◇◇◇ Red Roof Inn 🅼
(505) 722-7765. **Call for rates.** 3304 W Hwy 66 87301. I-40, exit 16, just se. Ext corridors. **Pets:** Large. Service with restrictions, crate.
[SAVE] [X] [🛏] [💻] [🏊]

AAA ◇ Rodeway Inn 🅼
(505) 863-9301. **$42-$55.** 1709 W Historic US 66 87301. I-40, exit 20, s to US 66, then 0.5 mi w. Ext corridors. **Pets:** Accepted. [SAVE] [X] [🛏]

AAA ◇◇◇ Royal Holiday Motel 🅼
(505) 722-4900. **$55-$95.** 1903 W Hwy 66 87301. I-40, exit 20, 0.5 mi s to US 66, then 0.8 mi w. Int corridors. **Pets:** Accepted.
[SAVE] [X] [🛏] [💻] [🏊]

AAA ◇◇◇ Super 8 🅼
(505) 722-5300. **$50-$90.** 1715 W US Hwy 66 87301. I-40, exit 20, s to US 66, then 0.5 mi w. Int corridors. **Pets:** Medium. $10 daily fee/pet. Designated rooms, service with restrictions, supervision.
[SAVE] [X] [🛏] [💻] [🏊]

GRANTS

◇◇ Comfort Inn 🅷
(505) 287-8700. **$70-$100.** 1551 E Santa Fe Ave 87020. I-40, exit 85, 0.3 mi n. Int corridors. **Pets:** Medium. $20 one-time fee/room. Service with restrictions, supervision. [ASK] [X] [🛏] [💻] [🏊]

AAA ◇◇ Days Inn 🅼
(505) 287-8883. **$80, 4 day notice.** 1504 E Santa Fe Ave 87020. I-40, exit 85, 0.3 mi n. Ext corridors. **Pets:** Small. $20 daily fee/pet. Designated rooms, service with restrictions, supervision. [SAVE] [X] [🛏] [💻]

AAA ◇◇◇ Quality Inn & Suites 🅷
(505) 285-4676. **$100-$129, 7 day notice.** 1496 E Santa Fe Ave 87020. I-40, exit 85, 0.3 mi n. Int corridors. **Pets:** Small. $20 daily fee/pet. Designated rooms, no service, supervision. [SAVE] [X] [🛏] [💻] [🏊]

AAA ◇ Sands Motel 🅼
(505) 287-2996. **$31-$46.** 112 McArthur St 87020. I-40, exit 85, 1.5 mi w on Business Loop 40 (Santa Fe Ave). Ext corridors. **Pets:** Accepted.
[SAVE] [X] [🛏]

HOBBS

AAA ◇◇◇ Best Western Executive Inn 🅷
(575) 397-7171. **$70-$100.** 309 N Marland Blvd 88240. US 62, 180 and Snyder St. Ext corridors. **Pets:** Dogs only. $10 daily fee/pet. Service with restrictions, supervision. [SAVE] [X] [🛏] [💻] [🏊]

▼▼ **Days Inn** Ⓜ

(575) 397-6541. **Call for rates.** 211 N Marland Blvd 88240. 2 mi e on US 62 and 180. Ext corridors. **Pets:** Small. $10 daily fee/pet. Service with restrictions, supervision. ⊠ 🖬 💻 🏊

◈ ▼▼ **Econo Lodge** 🅷

(575) 397-3591. **$65-$80.** 619 N Marland Blvd 88240. 2.5 mi e on US 62 and 180. Ext corridors. **Pets:** Medium. $10 daily fee/pet. Designated rooms, service with restrictions, supervision. 🆂🅰🆅🅴 ⊠ 🖬 💻 🏊

◈ ▼▼ **Hobbs Family Inn** 🅷

(575) 397-3251. **$75-$125.** 501 N Marland Blvd 88240. 2.5 mi e on US 62 and 180. Ext/int corridors. **Pets:** Accepted.
🆂🅰🆅🅴 ⊠ 🖬 💻 🍴 🏊

◈ ▼▼▼ **La Quinta Inn & Suites** 🅷 ❀

(575) 397-1200. **$90-$120 (no credit cards).** 3312 N Lovington Hwy 88240. SR 18, just s of jct Joe Harvey Blvd. Int corridors. **Pets:** Medium, other species. Service with restrictions, supervision.
🆂🅰🆅🅴 ⊠ 🅰🅼 🖬 💻 🏊

◈ ▼▼▼ **Sleep Inn & Suites** 🅷 ❀

(575) 393-3355. **$90-$110.** 4630 Lovington Hwy 88240. Jct SR 18 N (Lovington Hwy) and W Millen Dr, 0.8 mi s. Int corridors. **Pets:** $20 daily fee/pet. Designated rooms, service with restrictions, supervision.
🆂🅰🆅🅴 ⊠ 🅰🅼 🖬 💻 🏊

LAS CRUCES

◈ ▼▼ **Best Western Mission Inn** 🅷 ❀

(575) 524-8591. **$85-$120.** 1765 S Main St 88005. I-10, exit 142, 1 mi n. Ext corridors. **Pets:** Large, other species. $10 daily fee/pet. Service with restrictions, supervision. 🆂🅰🆅🅴 ⊠ 🖬 💻 🍴 🏊

◈ ▼▼▼ **Comfort Inn & Suites de Mesilla** 🅷

(575) 527-1050. **$60-$100.** 1300 Avenida de Mesilla 88005. I-10, exit 140, just s. Int corridors. **Pets:** Accepted. 🆂🅰🆅🅴 ⊠ 🅰🅼 🖬 💻 🏊

◈ ▼▼▼ **Comfort Inn of Las Cruces** 🅷

(575) 527-2000. **$65-$105.** 2585 S Valley Dr 88005. I-10, exit 142, just n. Int corridors. **Pets:** Small, dogs only. $20 daily fee/pet. Designated rooms, service with restrictions, supervision. 🆂🅰🆅🅴 ⊠ 🖬 💻 🏊

▼▼▼ **Comfort Suites by Choice Hotels** 🅷

(575) 522-1300. **Call for rates.** 2101 S Triviz 88001. I-25, exit 1, just w on University Ave, then just n. Int corridors. **Pets:** Accepted.
⊠ 🅰🅼 🖬 💻 🏊

▼▼▼ **DreamCatcher Inn Bed & Breakfast de Las Cruces** 🅱🅱 ❀

(575) 522-3035. **$125-$150, 14 day notice.** 10201 Starfly Rd 88011. US 70 E to NASA/Baylor Canyon Rd, 0.5 mi s, then 0.5 mi w. Ext corridors. **Pets:** Other species. $25 one-time fee/room. ⊠ 🅰🅼

◈ ▼▼ **Hampton Inn** 🅷

(575) 526-8311. **$93-$103.** 755 Avenida de Mesilla 88005. I-10, exit 140, just e. Ext corridors. **Pets:** Accepted. 🆂🅰🆅🅴 ⊠ 🖬 💻 🏊

▼▼▼ **Hilltop Hacienda B & B** 🅱🅱

(575) 382-3556. **$95-$135, 14 day notice.** 2600 Westmoreland Ave 88012. I-25, exit 6 (US 70), just e to Del Rey Blvd, 3 mi n, then 1 mi e. Int corridors. **Pets:** Dogs only. Supervision. 🅰🆂🅺 ⊠ 📺

◈ ▼▼▼ **Hotel Encanto de Las Cruces** 🅷 ❀

(575) 522-4300. **$98-$159.** 705 S Telshor Blvd 88011. I-25, exit 3 (Lohman Ave), just e, then just s. Int corridors. **Pets:** Medium, dogs only. $15 daily fee/room. Designated rooms, service with restrictions, supervision.
🆂🅰🆅🅴 ⊠ 🖬 💻 🍴 🏊

▼▼▼ **La Quinta Inn & Suites Las Cruces** 🅷 ❀

(575) 523-0100. **$65-$109.** 1500 Hickory Dr 88005. I-10, exit 140, just se of jct I-25 and Avenida de Mesilla. Int corridors. **Pets:** Medium, other species. Service with restrictions, supervision.
🅰🆂🅺 ⊠ 🅰🅼 🖬 💻 🏊

▼▼ **La Quinta Inn Las Cruces** 🅷 ❀

(575) 524-0331. **$49-$109.** 790 Avenida de Mesilla 88005. I-10, exit 140, just e. Int corridors. **Pets:** Medium, other species. Service with restrictions, supervision. 🅰🆂🅺 ⊠ 🅰🅼 🖬 💻 🏊

▼▼ **Lundeen's Inn of the Arts** 🅱🅱

(575) 526-3326. **$79-$125, 3 day notice.** 618 S Alameda Blvd 88005. Jct Lohman Ave, just s; center. Int corridors. **Pets:** Accepted.
🅰🆂🅺 ⊠ 🖬 💻

▼▼ **Quality Inn & Suites** 🅷

(575) 524-4663. **Call for rates.** 2200 S Valley Dr 88005. I-10, exit 142, 2 blks w. Ext corridors. **Pets:** Other species. $15 daily fee/pet. Service with restrictions, supervision. ⊠ 🅰🅼 🖬 💻 🏊

▼▼ **Ramada Palms de Las Cruces** 🅷

(575) 526-4411. **$79-$249.** 201 E University Ave 88005. I-10, exit 142, just n. Int corridors. **Pets:** Accepted.
🅰🆂🅺 ⊠ 🅰🅼 🖬 💻 🍴 🏊 🐾

▼▼ **Sleep Inn by Choice Hotels** 🅷

(575) 522-1700. **$76-$84.** 2121 S Triviz 88001. I-25, exit 1, just w on University Ave, then just n. Int corridors. **Pets:** Accepted.
🅰🆂🅺 ⊠ 🅰🅼 🖬 💻 🏊

▼▼ **Staybridge Suites** 🅷

(575) 521-7999. **$99-$149.** 2651 Northrise Dr 88011. I-25, exit 6, just e. Int corridors. **Pets:** Accepted. 🅰🆂🅺 ⊠ 🅰🅼 🖬 💻 🏊 🐾

LAS VEGAS

◈ ▼▼▼ **Comfort Inn** 🅷

(505) 425-1100. **$89-$139.** 2500 N Grand Ave 87701. I-25, exit 347, just sw; US 85 and I-25 business route. Int corridors. **Pets:** Medium, other species. $15 daily fee/pet. Designated rooms, service with restrictions, supervision. 🆂🅰🆅🅴 ⊠ 🖬 💻 🏊

◈ ▼ **El Camino Motel** Ⓜ

(505) 425-5994. **$45-$65.** 1152 N Grand Ave 87701. I-25, exit 345, 0.3 mi w; US 85 and I-25 business route. Ext corridors. **Pets:** Accepted.
🆂🅰🆅🅴 ⊠ 🖬 💻 🍴

◈ ▼▼ **Plaza Hotel** 🅷 ❀

(505) 425-3591. **$79-$153.** 230 Plaza St 87701. I-25, exit 343 W, just w, follow signs to Old Town Plaza. Int corridors. **Pets:** Other species. $10 daily fee/pet. Designated rooms, service with restrictions.
🆂🅰🆅🅴 ⊠ 🖬 💻 🍴

▼▼ **Super 8-Las Vegas** Ⓜ

(505) 425-5288. **$66-$159.** 2029 N Grand Ave 87701. I-25, exit 347, 0.8 mi sw; US 85 and I-25 business route. Int corridors. **Pets:** Accepted.
🅰🆂🅺 ⊠ 🖬 💻

LORDSBURG

◈ ▼▼ **Days Inn & Suites** 🅷

(575) 542-3600. **$68-$95.** 1426 W Motel Dr 88045. I-10, exit 20, just n. Int corridors. **Pets:** Other species. $10 daily fee/pet. Service with restrictions, supervision. 🆂🅰🆅🅴 ⊠ 🖬 💻 🏊

▼▼ **Econo Lodge** 🅷

(575) 542-3666. **$80.** 1408 S Main St 88045. I-10, exit 22, just s. Ext corridors. **Pets:** Accepted. 🅰🆂🅺 ⊠ 🅰🅼 🖬 💻 🏊

LOS LUNAS

◈ ▼▼ **Western Skies Inn & Suites** 🅷

(505) 865-0001. **$65-$95.** 2258 Sun Ranch Village Loop 87031. I-25, exit 203, just w. Int corridors. **Pets:** Large, other species. $10 daily fee/pet. Service with restrictions, supervision. 🆂🅰🆅🅴 ⊠ 🅰🅼 🖬 💻 🏊

LOVINGTON

◈ ▼▼ **Lovington Inn** 🅷

(575) 396-5346. **$64-$70.** 1600 W Ave D 88260. Jct US 82 and SR 18, 1 mi w. Ext corridors. **Pets:** Accepted. 🆂🅰🆅🅴 ⊠ 🖬 💻 🍴

MORIARTY

▼▼▼ Comfort Inn H
(505) 832-6666. **$69-$109.** 119 Route 66 E 87035. I-40, exit 196, just s, then just e. Int corridors. **Pets:** Medium, other species. Service with restrictions, supervision. [ASK] [X] [&M] [■] [■] [≈]

◬ ▼▼▼ Days Inn H
(505) 832-4451. **$60-$70.** 1809 Route 66 W 87035. I-40, exit 194. Int corridors. **Pets:** Accepted. [SAVE] [X] [■] [■]

◬ ▼▼▼◈ Holiday Inn Express H
(505) 832-5000. **Call for rates.** 1507 Route 66 87035. I-40, exit 194, 0.4 mi e. Int corridors. **Pets:** Medium, other species. $10 one-time fee/room. Designated rooms, service with restrictions, supervision.
[SAVE] [X] [&M] [■] [■] [≈]

◬ ▼▼▼ Luxury Inn H
(505) 832-4457. **$52-$85.** 1316 Route 66 W 87035. I-40, exit 194, 0.5 mi se on US 66 and I-40 business loop. Int corridors. **Pets:** Medium, other species. $5 daily fee/pet. Service with restrictions, supervision.
[SAVE] [X] [■] [■]

◬ ▼▼▼ Super 8 H
(505) 832-6730. **$55-$89.** 1611 W Old Route 66 87035. I-40, exit 194, 0.5 mi e on Central Ave. Int corridors. **Pets:** Medium, other species. $5 daily fee/pet. Service with restrictions, supervision. [SAVE] [X] [■] [■]

PINOS ALTOS

▼▼ Bear Creek Motel & Cabins CA ❀
(575) 388-4501. **Call for rates.** 88 Main St 88053. 1 mi n of Pinos Altos on SR 15. Ext corridors. **Pets:** Other species. $10 daily fee/pet. Service with restrictions, crate. [■] [■] [X̶]

POJOAQUE PUEBLO

◬ ▼▼▼ Cities of Gold Hotel H
(505) 455-0515. **$79-$129.** 10A Cities of Gold Rd 87506. On US 84/265, just n. Int corridors. **Pets:** Accepted. [SAVE] [X] [&M] [■] [■] [¶¶]

RATON

◬ ▼▼▼ Americas Best Value Inn Sands Motel M
(575) 445-2737. **$66-$98, 7 day notice.** 300 Clayton Rd 87740. I-25, exit 451, just w. Ext/int corridors. **Pets:** Accepted.
[SAVE] [X] [■] [■] [¶¶] [≈]

◬ ▼▼ Budget Host Raton M
(575) 445-3655. **$50-$75.** 136 Canyon Dr 87740. I-25, exit 454, 0.8 mi s on I-25 business loop. Ext corridors. **Pets:** Medium. $5 daily fee/pet. Service with restrictions, supervision. [SAVE] [X] [&M] [■]

◬ ▼▼▼◈ Holiday Inn Express Hotel & Suites H
(575) 445-1500. **$109-$329.** 101 Card Ave 87740. I-25, exit 450, just w. Int corridors. **Pets:** Accepted. [SAVE] [X] [■] [■] [≈]

▼▼▼ Quality Inn H
(575) 445-4200. **$65-$110.** 533 Clayton Rd 87740. I-25, exit 451, just w of jct US 64 and 87. Int corridors. **Pets:** Small, other species. $50 deposit/room, $20 daily fee/pet. Service with restrictions, supervision.
[ASK] [X] [■] [■] [≈]

◈ Raton Microtel Inn H
(575) 445-9100. **$75-$95.** 1640 Cedar St 87740. I-25, exit 451, just w. Int corridors. **Pets:** Dogs only. $20 daily fee/pet. Designated rooms, no service, supervision. [ASK] [X] [■] [■]

◈ Raton Pass Inn M
(575) 445-3641. **$48-$64.** 308 Canyon Dr 87740. I-25, exit 454, 0.8 mi s. Ext corridors. **Pets:** Dogs only. $2 daily fee/pet. Service with restrictions, supervision. [ASK] [X] [■]

RED RIVER

◬ ▼▼▼ Best Western Rivers Edge Lodge H
(575) 754-1766. **Call for rates.** 301 W River St 87558. 1 blk s of W Main St (SR 38); center. Ext corridors. **Pets:** Accepted.
[SAVE] [X] [■] [■] [X̶]

RIO RANCHO

◬ ▼▼▼ Days Inn Rio Rancho H
(505) 892-8800. **$59-$129.** 4200 Crestview Dr 87124. I-25, exit 233 (Alameda Blvd), 8 mi w on SR 528; I-40, exit 155, 8 mi n on Coors Rd (SR 448). Ext corridors. **Pets:** Small, other species. $15 one-time fee/pet. Service with restrictions, supervision. [SAVE] [X] [■] [■] [≈]

▼▼▼◈ Extended StayAmerica Albuquerque-Rio Rancho M
(505) 792-1338. **$63-$73.** 2608 The American Rd NW 87124. Corner of SR 528 and Cottonwood, just n, then just w. Int corridors. **Pets:** Other species. $25 daily fee/room. Designated rooms, service with restrictions, crate. [ASK] [X] [■] [■]

◬ ▼▼▼ Inn at Rio Rancho H ❀
(505) 892-1700. **$79-$179.** 1465 Rio Rancho Blvd 87124. I-25, exit 233 (Alameda Blvd), 6.5 mi w; I-40, exit 155, 10 mi n on Coors Rd/Coors Bypass to SR 528, then 1 mi n. Ext corridors. **Pets:** Medium, other species. $25 daily fee/pet. Designated rooms, service with restrictions.
[SAVE] [X] [■] [■] [¶¶] [≈]

▼▼▼◈ Rio Rancho Super 8 H
(505) 896-8888. **$36-$120.** 4100 Barbara Loop SE 87124. I-25, exit 233 (Alameda Blvd), 0.5 mi w, 3.8 mi nw on SR 528, then just e. Int corridors. **Pets:** Other species. $10 daily fee/pet. Designated rooms, service with restrictions, crate. [ASK] [X] [■] [■]

ROSWELL

◬ ▼▼▼ Best Western El Rancho Palacio H
(575) 622-2721. **$70-$95.** 2205 N Main St 88201. 1.8 mi n on US 70 and 285. Ext corridors. **Pets:** Accepted. [SAVE] [X] [■] [■] [≈]

◬ ▼▼▼ Best Western Sally Port Inn & Suites H
(575) 622-6430. **$89-$119.** 2000 N Main St 88201. 1.5 mi n on US 70 and 285. Int corridors. **Pets:** Accepted.
[SAVE] [X] [■] [■] [¶¶] [≈] [X̶]

◬ ▼▼▼◈ Comfort Inn H
(575) 623-4567. **$99-$159.** 3595 N Main St 88201. 3 mi n on US 70 and 285. Int corridors. **Pets:** Accepted. [SAVE] [X] [&M] [■] [■] [≈]

◬ ▼▼▼ Days Inn H
(575) 623-4021. **$70-$90.** 1310 N Main St 88201. 0.8 mi n on US 70 and 285. Ext corridors. **Pets:** Other species. Service with restrictions, crate. [SAVE] [X] [■] [■] [≈]

◬ ▼▼▼◈ Holiday Inn Express H
(575) 627-9900. **$110-$170.** 2300 N Main St 88201. US 70. Int corridors. **Pets:** Medium. $10 daily fee/pet. Service with restrictions, supervision.
[SAVE] [X] [&M] [■] [■] [≈] [X̶]

◬ ▼▼▼◈ La Quinta Inn & Suites H ❀
(575) 622-8000. **$89-$169.** 200 E 19th St 88201. Jct N Main and 19th St, 2 blks e. Int corridors. **Pets:** Medium, other species. Service with restrictions, supervision. [SAVE] [X] [&M] [■] [■] [≈]

◈ Western Inn M
(575) 623-9425. **Call for rates.** 2331 N Main St 88201. Jct US 70/285/ 380, 2.2 mi n. Ext corridors. **Pets:** Accepted. [X] [■] [■] [≈]

RUIDOSO

▼▼▼ Dan Dee Cabins CA
(575) 257-2165. **$84-$199, 14 day notice.** 310 Main Rd 88345. 0.8 mi w on Upper Canyon Rd. Ext corridors. **Pets:** Other species. $10 one-time fee/pet. No service, crate. [ASK] [■] [■] [X̶]

(AAA) ▼▼▼▼ The Lodge at Sierra Blanca 🄷
(575) 258-5500. **$105-$193.** 107 Sierra Blanca Dr 88345. Jct Sudderth Dr. Int corridors. **Pets:** Accepted. [SAVE] [✕] 🔲🔲🔲🔲🔲

▼▼▼ Super 8–Ruidoso 🄷
(575) 378-8180. **Call for rates.** 100 Cliff Dr 88345. Just s of jct US 70 and Sudderth Dr. Int corridors. **Pets:** Accepted. [✕] 🔲🔲

(AAA) ▼▼▼ The Village Lodge 🄲🄾
(575) 258-5442. **$89-$159, 7 day notice.** 1000 Mechem Dr 88345. 2 mi n on SR 48. Ext corridors. **Pets:** Accepted. [SAVE] [✕] 🔲🔲

▼▼▼ Whispering Pine Cabins 🄲🄰 �
(575) 257-4311. **$99-$450, 14 day notice.** 422 Main Rd 88345. 0.9 mi w of jct SR 48 and Sudderth Dr. Ext corridors. **Pets:** Other species. $10 one-time fee/pet. No service. [✕] 🔲🔲🔲🔲

RUIDOSO DOWNS

(AAA) ▼▼ Best Western Pine Springs Inn 🄷
(575) 378-8100. **$79-$269, 7 day notice.** 1420 W Hwy 70 88346. Just e of jct US 70 and SR 48. Ext corridors. **Pets:** Large, other species. Designated rooms, service with restrictions, supervision.
[SAVE] [✕] 🔲🔲🔲

▼▼▼▼ La Quinta Inn & Suites 🄷 �
(575) 378-3333. **$90-$210.** 2115 W Hwy 70 88346. Just e of jct US 70 and SR 48. Int corridors. **Pets:** Medium, other species. Service with restrictions, supervision. [✕] 🔲🔲 🔲🔲🔲

SANTA FE

(AAA) ▼▼▼ Bishop's Lodge Ranch Resort & Spa 🄷
(505) 983-6377. **$159-$599, 3 day notice.** 1297 N Bishop's Lodge Rd 87501. 3.5 mi n of jct Paseo de Peralta. Ext/int corridors. **Pets:** Accepted.
[SAVE] [✕] 🔲🔲🔲🔲🔲

(AAA) ▼▼▼ Comfort Inn Santa Fe 🄷
(505) 474-7330. **$59-$89.** 4312 Cerrillos Rd 87507. I-25, exit 278, 1.6 mi n. Int corridors. **Pets:** Other species. $5 daily fee/pet. Service with restrictions, supervision. [SAVE] [✕] 🔲🔲🔲

(AAA) ▼▼▼ Econo Lodge 🄷
(505) 471-4000. **Call for rates.** 3470 Cerrillos Rd 87507. I-25, exit 278, 3 mi n. Int corridors. **Pets:** Other species. $10 daily fee/pet. Service with restrictions, supervision. [SAVE] [✕] 🔲🔲🔲🔲

(AAA) ▼▼▼▼ Eldorado Hotel & Spa 🄷 �
(505) 988-4455. **$139-$419, 3 day notice.** 309 W San Francisco St 87501. Just w of The Plaza; at Sandoval St. Int corridors. **Pets:** $50 one-time fee/room. [SAVE] [✕] 🔲🔲🔲🔲🔲

(AAA) ▼▼▼▼ El Paradero Bed & Breakfast 🄱🄱
(505) 988-1177. **$100-$185, 14 day notice.** 220 W Manhattan Ave 87501. 0.3 mi s on Cerrillos Rd, 1/2 blk e. Ext/int corridors. **Pets:** Dogs only. $20 daily fee/pet. Designated rooms, service with restrictions, crate. [SAVE] [✕] 🔲

(AAA) ▼▼▼▼▼ Encantado, An Auberge Resort 🄷 �
(505) 946-5700. **$275-$675, 14 day notice.** 198 SR 592 87506. US 285/84 N, exit 172, 0.5 mi e, then 2 mi n. Ext corridors. **Pets:** $100 one-time fee/room. Service with restrictions, supervision.
[SAVE] [✕] 🔲🔲🔲🔲

▼▼▼▼ Hacienda Nicholas 🄱🄱
(505) 986-1431. **$120-$240, 14 day notice.** 320 E Marcy St 87501. Just e of jct Paseo de Peralta; 4 blks e of historic plaza. Ext/int corridors. **Pets:** Accepted. [ASK] [✕]

▼▼▼▼ Hampton Inn Santa Fe 🄷
(505) 474-3900. **$89-$139.** 3625 Cerrillos Rd 87505. I-25, exit 278, 2.5 mi n. Int corridors. **Pets:** Small, dogs only. Designated rooms, service with restrictions, crate. [✕] 🔲🔲🔲🔲

(AAA) ▼▼▼▼ Hilton Santa Fe Golf Resort & Spa at Buffalo Thunder 🄷
(505) 455-5555. **$139-$249.** 20 Buffalo Thunder Tr 87506. N on US 285, exit Buffalo Thunder Rd, just e. Int corridors. **Pets:** Accepted.
[SAVE] [✕] 🔲🔲 🔲🔲🔲🔲

(AAA) ▼▼▼▼ Hilton Santa Fe Historic Plaza 🄷
(505) 988-2811. **$139-$259.** 100 Sandoval St 87501. Just sw of The Plaza; between San Francisco and W Alameda sts. Ext/int corridors.
Pets: Accepted. [SAVE] [✕] 🔲🔲 🔲🔲🔲

▼▼▼▼ Holiday Inn Express 🄷
(505) 474-7570. **$79-$199.** 3450 Cerrillos Rd 87507. I-25, exit 278, 3 mi n. Int corridors. **Pets:** Accepted. [ASK] [✕] 🔲🔲🔲🔲

(AAA) ▼▼▼▼ Holiday Inn Santa Fe 🄷
(505) 473-4646. **$79-$239.** 4048 Cerrillos Rd 87507. I-25, exit 278, 2.3 mi n; just n of Rodeo Dr. Int corridors. **Pets:** Accepted.
[SAVE] [✕] 🔲🔲 🔲🔲🔲🔲

▼▼▼▼ Hotel Plaza Real 🄷
(505) 988-4900. **Call for rates.** 125 Washington Ave 87501. Just ne of The Plaza; center. Ext/int corridors. **Pets:** Accepted. [✕] 🔲🔲🔲

▼▼▼▼ The Inn & Spa at Loretto 🄷 �
(505) 988-5531. **$189-$499, 3 day notice.** 211 Old Santa Fe Tr 87501. Just s of The Plaza. Int corridors. **Pets:** Medium. $20 daily fee/pet. Designated rooms, service with restrictions, crate.
[ASK] [✕] 🔲🔲 🔲🔲🔲

(AAA) ▼▼▼▼ Inn at Santa Fe 🄷
(505) 474-9500. **$89-$249.** 8376 Cerrillos Rd 87507. I-25, exit 278, 0.3 mi n. Int corridors. **Pets:** Other species. $25 one-time fee/pet. Service with restrictions, supervision. [SAVE] [✕] 🔲🔲🔲🔲

(AAA) ▼▼▼▼ Inn On The Alameda 🄷 �
(505) 984-2121. **$125-$390, 3 day notice.** 303 E Alameda St 87501. Just e of The Plaza; at jct Paseo de Peralta. Ext/int corridors.
Pets: Small, other species. $30 daily fee/pet. Designated rooms, service with restrictions, supervision. [SAVE] [✕] 🔲🔲🔲

(AAA) ▼▼▼▼ La Fonda Hotel 🄷 �
(505) 982-5511. **$219-$599.** 100 E San Francisco St 87501. On The Plaza. Int corridors. **Pets:** Medium, dogs only. Designated rooms, service with restrictions, supervision. [SAVE] [✕] 🔲🔲 🔲🔲🔲🔲

(AAA) ▼▼▼▼▼ La Posada de Santa Fe Resort & Spa 🄷 �
(505) 986-0000. **$232-$555, 3 day notice.** 330 E Palace Ave 87501. Jct Paseo de Peralta and E Palace Ave. Ext corridors. **Pets:** Other species. $75 one-time fee/pet. Service with restrictions, crate.
[SAVE] [✕] 🔲 🔲🔲🔲🔲

▼▼▼▼ La Quinta Inn Santa Fe 🄷 �
(505) 471-1142. **$49-$109.** 4298 Cerrillos Rd 87507. I-25, exit 278, 1.8 mi n. Ext/int corridors. **Pets:** Medium, other species. Service with restrictions, supervision. [ASK] [✕] 🔲🔲🔲

(AAA) ▼▼▼▼ Las Palomas 🄷
(505) 982-5560. **$99-$498.** 460 W San Francisco St 87501. Just w of jct Guadalupe St. Ext corridors. **Pets:** Accepted. [SAVE] [✕] 🔲🔲🔲

▼▼▼▼ The Lodge at Santa Fe 🄷
(505) 992-5800. **Call for rates.** 750 N St. Francis Dr 87501. Jct of Cerrillos Rd and St. Francis Dr (US 84/285), 1.1 mi nw to Alamo Dr, just w, then just n. Ext/int corridors. **Pets:** Accepted. [✕] 🔲🔲🔲

▼▼▼ Motel 6–150 🄼
(505) 473-1380. **$45-$95.** 3007 Cerrillos Rd 87507. I-25, exit 278, 3.8 mi n. Ext corridors. **Pets:** Other species. Service with restrictions, supervision. [✕] 🔲🔲

◈ ▼▼▼ The Old Santa Fe Inn M
(505) 995-0800. **$99-$390, 3 day notice.** 320 Galisteo St 87501. Just sw of The Plaza; center. Ext/int corridors. **Pets:** Medium. $20 daily fee/pet. Service with restrictions, supervision. SAVE ✕ 🛏 🖵

▼▼ Park Inn & Suites H
(505) 471-3000. **$69-$150, 3 day notice.** 2907 Cerrillos Rd 87507. I-25, exit 278, 7 mi n. Ext corridors. **Pets:** Medium. $10 one-time fee/pet. Service with restrictions, supervision. ASK ✕ 🛏 🖵 🏊

◈ ▼▼ Pecos Trail Inn M
(505) 982-1943. **$89-$155.** 2239 Old Pecos Tr 87505. I-25, exit 284, 0.8 mi n on CR 466 (Old Pecos Tr). Ext corridors. **Pets:** Accepted. SAVE ✕ 🛏 🖵 🍴 🏊

◈ ▼▼▼ Quality Inn H
(505) 471-1211. **$60-$85.** 3011 Cerrillos Rd 87507. I-25, exit 278B, 3.8 mi n. Int corridors. **Pets:** Accepted. SAVE ✕ 🛏 🖵 🏊

◈ ▼▼ Red Roof Inn H
(505) 438-8950. **$49-$149.** 4044 Cerrillos Rd 87507. I-25, exit 278, 1.5 mi n. Int corridors. **Pets:** Large. Service with restrictions, crate. SAVE ✕ 🛏 🏊

▼▼▼ Residence Inn by Marriott H
(505) 982-7300. **$149-$209.** 1698 Galisteo St 87505. I-25, exit 282, 1.7 mi n on St. Francis Dr to St. Michaels Dr, just e, then just n. Ext corridors. **Pets:** Accepted. ✕ 🛏 🖵 🏊

◈ ▼▼▼ ▼▼▼ Rosewood Inn of the Anasazi H ✿
(505) 988-3030. **$209-$1699, 3 day notice.** 113 Washington Ave 87501. Just ne of The Plaza. Int corridors. **Pets:** Medium, other species. $50 daily fee/pet. Service with restrictions, supervision. SAVE ✕ 🖵 🍴

◈ ▼▼ Santa Fe Motel & Inn M
(505) 982-1039. **$79-$199, 3 day notice.** 510 Cerrillos Rd 87501. 4 blks sw of The Plaza. Ext corridors. **Pets:** $15 daily fee/pet. Designated rooms, service with restrictions, crate. SAVE ✕ 🛏 🖵

◈ ▼▼ Santa Fe Plaza Travelodge H
(505) 982-3551. **$50-$200.** 646 Cerrillos Rd 87505. 0.8 mi sw of The Plaza. Ext/int corridors. **Pets:** Accepted. SAVE ✕ 🛏 🖵 🏊

◈ ▼▼ Santa Fe Sage Inn M
(505) 982-5952. **$45-$140.** 725 Cerrillos Rd 87505. 0.4 mi ne of St. Francis Dr (US 84). Ext corridors. **Pets:** Accepted. SAVE ✕ 🛏 🖵 🏊

◈ ▼▼▼ The Santa Fe Suites M ✿
(505) 989-3600. **$79-$99.** 3007 S St. Francis Dr 87505. 0.8 mi n on S St. Francis Dr, just e on Zia Rd via access drive. Ext corridors. **Pets:** Large, other species. $10 daily fee/room. Service with restrictions, crate. SAVE ✕ 🛏 🖵

SANTA ROSA

◈ ▼▼ Best Western Adobe Inn H
(575) 472-3446. **$46-$90.** 1501 Historic Route 66 88435. I-40, exit 275. Ext corridors. **Pets:** Medium. Service with restrictions, supervision. SAVE ✕ 🛏 🖵 🏊

◈ ▼▼ Best Western Santa Rosa Inn M
(575) 472-5877. **$50-$119.** 2491 Historic Route 66 88435. I-40, exit 277, 0.5 mi w. Ext corridors. **Pets:** Small, other species. $10 daily fee/pet. Designated rooms, no service, supervision. SAVE ✕ 🛏 🖵 🏊

◈ ▼▼ Days Inn of Santa Rosa H
(575) 472-5985. **Call for rates.** 1830 Historic Route 66 88435. I-40, exit 275. Ext corridors. **Pets:** $5 one-time fee/pet. Crate. SAVE ✕ 🛏 🖵

◈ ▼▼▼ Holiday Inn Express H
(575) 472-5411. **$79-$199.** 2516 Historic Route 66 88435. I-40, exit 277, 0.4 mi w. Int corridors. **Pets:** $25 one-time fee/pet. Designated rooms, service with restrictions, supervision. SAVE ✕ 🛏 🛏 🖵 🏊 🐾

▼▼▼ La Quinta Inn-Santa Rosa H ✿
(575) 472-4800. **$70-$110.** 2277 Historic Route 66 88435. I-40, exit 275, just e. Int corridors. **Pets:** Medium, other species. Service with restrictions, supervision. ASK ✕ 🛏 🖵 🏊

◈ ▼▼ Quality Inn H ✿
(575) 472-5570. **$70-$110.** 3343 E Historic Route 66 88435. I-40, exit 277, 0.3 mi w. Ext corridors. **Pets:** Medium. $15 one-time fee/pet. Service with restrictions, supervision. SAVE ✕ 🛏 🖵 🏊

▼▼ Super 8-Santa Rosa M
(575) 472-5388. **Call for rates.** 1201 Historic Route 66 88435. I-40, exit 275, just w. Int corridors. **Pets:** ✕ 🛏 🖵

SILVER CITY

◈ ▼▼ Comfort Inn H
(575) 534-1883. **$90-$110.** 1060 E Hwy 180 88061. Just e of jct SR 15. Int corridors. **Pets:** Accepted. SAVE ✕ 🛏 🖵

◈ ▼▼▼ Econo Lodge Silver City H
(575) 534-1111. **$55-$139.** 1120 Hwy 180 E 88061. 1.5 mi ne on US 180 and SR 90. Int corridors. **Pets:** Accepted. SAVE ✕ 🛏 🖵 🏊

◈ ▼▼▼ Holiday Inn Express H
(575) 538-2525. **$104-$115.** 1103 Superior St 88061. 3 mi ne on US 180 and SR 90. Int corridors. **Pets:** Other species. $35 deposit/room. Designated rooms, service with restrictions, supervision. SAVE ✕ 🛏 🖵

SOCORRO

◈ ▼▼ Best Western Socorro Hotel & Suites H
(575) 838-0556. **$105, 14 day notice.** 1100 California Ave NE 87801. Center. Ext/int corridors. **Pets:** Small. $10 one-time fee/room. Designated rooms, service with restrictions, crate. SAVE ✕ 🛏 🛏 🖵 🏊

▼▼ Comfort Inn & Suites H
(575) 838-4400. **$85-$125.** 1259 Frontage Rd NW 87801. I-25, exit 150, just w. Int corridors. **Pets:** Medium. $10 daily fee/pet. Service with restrictions, supervision. ASK ✕ 🛏 🖵 🏊

◈ ▼▼ Days Inn-Socorro H
(575) 835-0230. **$55-$95.** 507 N California St 87801. I-25, exit 147, 1.7 mi n; exit 150, just s. Ext corridors. **Pets:** Other species. $10 daily fee/pet. Service with restrictions, supervision. SAVE ✕ 🛏 🖵 🏊

TAOS

◈ ▼▼▼ American Artists Gallery House Bed & Breakfast BB
(575) 758-4446. **$95-$225, 14 day notice.** 132 Frontier Ln 87571. 1 mi s of jct US 64 and Taos Plaza, 0.3 mi e. Ext/int corridors. **Pets:** Dogs only. $25 one-time fee/pet. Designated rooms, service with restrictions, supervision. SAVE ✕ 🛏 🖵

◈ ▼▼▼ An Inn On The Rio BB
(575) 758-7199. **$100-$145, 14 day notice.** 910 Kit Carson Rd 87571. US 64, 1.5 mi e of jct SR 68 and Taos Plaza. Ext corridors. **Pets:** Dogs only. $25 daily fee/pet. Designated rooms, service with restrictions, supervision. SAVE ✕ 🛏 🏊

◈ ▼▼ Burch Street Casitas CA
(575) 737-9038. **$120-$150 (no credit cards), 21 day notice.** 310 Burch St 87571. US 64, just e of jct SR 68, then just s. Ext corridors. **Pets:** Medium, dogs only. $50 deposit/pet. No service, supervision. SAVE ✕ 🛏 🖵

AAA ◆◆◆ ◆◆◆ **El Monte Sagrado Living Resort and Spa** H

(575) 758-3502. **$229-$839, 14 day notice.** 317 Kit Carson Rd 87571. 0.5 mi e of jct US 64 and SR 68. Ext corridors. **Pets:** Accepted.

SAVE ✕ ▣ ¶¶ ☎ ✕

AAA ◆◆◆ ◆◆◆ **Inn on La Loma Plaza** BB ❀

(575) 758-1717. **$165-$450, 15 day notice.** 315 Ranchitos Rd 87571. 0.3 mi sw on Ranchitos Rd, just w of Taos Plaza; in La Loma Plaza Historic District. Ext/int corridors. **Pets:** Medium, dogs only. $25 one-time fee/pet. Designated rooms, service with restrictions, supervision.

SAVE ✕ ▪ ▣ ✕

AAA ◆◆◆◆ **La Posada de Taos** BB ❀

(575) 758-8164. **$129-$239.** 309 Juanita Ln 87571. From The Plaza, just w on Don Fernando St, just s on Manzanares St, then just w. Ext/int corridors. **Pets:** Medium, dogs only. $50 one-time fee/room. Supervision.

SAVE ✕ ▣ ☎

AAA ◆◆◆◆ **Orinda Bed & Breakfast** BB ❀

(575) 758-8581. **$104-$169, 14 day notice.** 461 Valverde St 87571. Just w from jct Don Fernando St and Camino de la Placita, then just s, follow signs. Ext/int corridors. **Pets:** Medium, dogs only. $7 deposit/pet. Service with restrictions, supervision. SAVE ✕ ▪ ▣ ☎

◆◆ **Quality Inn** H

(575) 758-2200. **$65-$109.** 1043 Paseo del Pueblo Sur 87571. SR 68, 2 mi sw of jct US 64 and Taos Plaza. Ext/int corridors. **Pets:** Accepted.

ASK ✕ ▪ ▣ ¶¶ ☎

◆◆ **Sagebrush Inn** H

(575) 758-2254. **$79-$219.** 1508 Paseo del Pueblo Sur 87571. SR 68, 3 mi sw of jct US 64 and Taos Plaza. Ext corridors. **Pets:** Other species. $7 daily fee/pet. Designated rooms, supervision.

ASK ✕ ▪ ▣ ¶¶ ☎

AAA ◆◆◆ ◆◆◆ **San Geronimo Lodge** BB

(575) 751-3776. **$99-$189, 15 day notice.** 1101 Witt Rd 87571. 1.3 mi e of jct SR 68 and Taos Plaza on US 64 (Kit Carson Rd), 0.6 mi s. Ext/int corridors. **Pets:** Large, dogs only. $15 one-time fee/pet. Designated rooms, service with restrictions, supervision. SAVE ✕ ☎ ⅋

THOREAU

◆◆ **Zuni Mountain Lodge** BB

(505) 862-7616. **$115 (no credit cards), 7 day notice.** 40 W Perch Dr 87323. I-40, exit 53, 13 mi s on SR 612, then w. Ext/int corridors. **Pets:** Other species. Service with restrictions, supervision.

ASK ✕ ⅋ 𝖕 ☎

TRUTH OR CONSEQUENCES

◆◆◆ **Comfort Inn & Suites** H

(575) 894-1660. **$65-$150.** 2250 N Date St 87901. I-25, exit 79, just e. Int corridors. **Pets:** Large. Designated rooms, service with restrictions, supervision. ASK ✕ ⅄ᴹ ▪ ▣ ☎

AAA ◆◆ **Hot Springs Inn** M

(575) 894-6665. **$60-$80.** 2270 N Date St 87901. I-25, exit 79. Ext corridors. **Pets:** Other species. Service with restrictions, supervision.

SAVE ✕ ▪ ▣ ☎

◆◆◆ **Sierra Grande Lodge & Spa** H

(575) 894-6976. **$99-$445.** 501 McAdoo St 87901. Just w of Foch St; center. Ext/int corridors. **Pets:** Small. $25 daily fee/pet. Designated rooms, supervision. ✕ ▪ ▣

TUCUMCARI

AAA ◆◆ **Americana Motel** M

(575) 461-0431. **$28-$34.** 406 E Tucumcari Blvd 88401. I-40, exit 332, 1.5 mi n on SR 18, then 0.5 mi e on Route 66. Ext corridors. **Pets:** Small. $5 daily fee/pet. Service with restrictions, supervision. SAVE ✕ ▪ ▣

AAA ◆◆◆ **Best Western Discovery Inn** H

(575) 461-4884. **$80-$125.** 200 E Estrella 88401. I-40, exit 332, just n. Ext corridors. **Pets:** Accepted. SAVE ✕ ▪ ▣ ☎

◆◆◆ **Comfort Inn** H

(575) 461-4094. **Call for rates.** 2800 E Tucumcari Blvd 88401. I-40, exit 335, 0.5 mi w. Ext corridors. **Pets:** $12 one-time fee/room. Service with restrictions, supervision. ✕ ▪ ▣ ☎

◆◆ **Days Inn** H

(575) 461-3158. **$50-$90.** 2623 S 1st St 88401. I-40, exit 332, just n. Ext/int corridors. **Pets:** $8 daily fee/pet. Service with restrictions, supervision. ASK ✕ ▪ ▣

AAA ◆◆ **Econo Lodge** H

(575) 461-4194. **Call for rates.** 3400 Route 66 Blvd 88401. I-40, exit 335, just n, then just w. Int corridors. **Pets:** $5 daily fee/pet. Designated rooms, service with restrictions, supervision. SAVE ✕ ▪

◆◆◆ **La Quinta Inn & Suites** H ❀

(575) 461-2233. **$85-$125 (no credit cards).** 2516 S Adams St 88401. I-40, exit 332, just n. Int corridors. **Pets:** Medium, other species. Service with restrictions, supervision. ✕ ▪ ▣ ☎

◆◆◆ **Microtel Inn-Tucumcari** H

(575) 461-0600. **Call for rates.** 2420 S 1st St 88401. I-40, exit 332, just n. Int corridors. **Pets:** Accepted. ✕ ▪ ▣ ☎

◆◆ **Super 8** M

(575) 461-4444. **$50-$72.** 4001 Old Route 66 88401. I-40, exit 335, just w. Int corridors. **Pets:** Accepted. ASK ✕ ▪ ▣ ☎

VAUGHN

◆◆ **Oak Tree Inn** H

(575) 584-8733. **$65-$75.** Hwy 54, 60 & 285 88353. On US 54, 60 and 285, 1.5 mi e. Ext/int corridors. **Pets:** Accepted.

ASK ✕ ⅄ᴹ ▪ ▣ ¶¶

NEW YORK

ALBANY

▼▼▼ CrestHill Suites Ⓗ
(518) 454-0007. **$99-$169.** 1415 Washington Ave 12206. I-90, exit 2 westbound, just s on Fuller Rd, then just e; exit eastbound, just e. Int corridors. **Pets:** Other species. $15 daily fee/pet. Designated rooms, service with restrictions. Ⓐ Ⓢ Ⓚ 🐾 ☒ ⬛ ⬛ 🛏

▼▼ Extended StayAmerica Albany-Capital Ⓗ
(518) 446-0680. **$85-$119.** 1395 Washington Ave 12206. I-90, exit 2 westbound, just s on Fuller Rd, then 0.5 mi e; exit eastbound, just e. Int corridors. **Pets:** Other species. $25 daily fee/room. Designated rooms, service with restrictions, crate. Ⓐ Ⓢ Ⓚ ☒ ⬛ ⬛

▼▼▼ TownePlace Suites Albany SUNY Ⓗ ❀
(518) 435-1900. **$140-$160.** 1379 Washington Ave 12206. I-90, exit 2 westbound, just s on Fuller Rd, then 0.6 mi e; exit eastbound, just e. Int corridors. **Pets:** Other species. $75 one-time fee/room. Service with restrictions. ☒ Ⓚ ⬛ ⬛ 🛏

ALEXANDRIA BAY

▼ The Ship Motel Ⓜ
(315) 482-4503. **$75-$125.** 6 Market St 13607. Center. Ext corridors. **Pets:** Medium. $10 one-time fee/room. Service with restrictions, supervision. Ⓐ Ⓢ Ⓚ ☒

ALLEGANY

▼▼ Microtel Inn & Suites-Olean/Allegany Ⓗ
(716) 373-5333. **Call for rates.** 3234 NYS Rt 417 14760. I-86, exit 24, 2.1 mi e on SR 417 (State St). Int corridors. **Pets:** Large, other species. $15 daily fee/pet. No service, supervision. ☒ Ⓚ ⬛ ⬛

AMSTERDAM

▼▼ Super 8 Ⓗ
(518) 843-5888. **$60-$110.** 5502 Rt 30 S 12010. I-90, exit 27 (SR 30 S). Int corridors. **Pets:** Accepted. Ⓐ Ⓢ Ⓚ ☒ ⬛ ⬛

ANGELICA

▼▼ Angelica Inn B & B ⒷⒷ
(585) 466-3063. **Call for rates.** 64 W Main St 14709. I-86, exit 31, 0.5 mi w. Ext/int corridors. **Pets:** Small. $10 daily fee/pet. Designated rooms, service with restrictions, supervision. ☒ ⬛ ⬛ Ⓜ ☕

APALACHIN

▼▼ Quality Inn Ⓗ
(607) 625-4441. **$84-$209.** 7666 SR 434 13732. SR 17, exit 66, just e. Int corridors. **Pets:** Accepted. Ⓐ Ⓢ Ⓚ ☒ ⬛ ⬛

AUBURN

ⒶⒶⒶ ▼▼▼▼ Holiday Inn-Auburn/Finger Lakes Ⓗ ❀
(315) 253-4531. **$79-$159.** 75 North St 13021. SR 34, just n of US 20/SR 5. Int corridors. **Pets:** Other species. $15 daily fee/room. Designated rooms, service with restrictions, crate. Ⓢ Ⓐ Ⓥ Ⓚ ☒ Ⓚ ⬛ ⬛ Ⓜ 🛏

▼▼ Inn at the Finger Lakes Ⓗ
(315) 253-5000. **$99-$179, 3 day notice.** 12 Seminary Ave 13021. Jct SR 34/38, just e on US 20/SR 5; center. Int corridors. **Pets:** $15 one-time fee/pet. Designated rooms, service with restrictions, supervision. Ⓐ Ⓢ Ⓚ ☒ Ⓚ ⬛ ⬛

BALDWINSVILLE

ⒶⒶⒶ ▼▼▼ Microtel Inn & Suites Ⓗ ❀
(315) 635-9556. **$60-$150, 7 day notice.** 131 Downer St 13027. SR 690, exit SR 31 W, 0.4 mi e. Int corridors. **Pets:** Medium, other species. $10 daily fee/pet. Service with restrictions, supervision. Ⓢ Ⓐ Ⓥ ☒ Ⓚ ⬛ ⬛

▼▼▼ The Red Mill Inn Ⓗ
(315) 635-4871. **$92-$299.** 4 Syracuse St 13027. Just w of jct SR 31 on SR 48; center. Int corridors. **Pets:** Medium, other species. $50 one-time fee/room. Designated rooms, service with restrictions, crate. Ⓐ Ⓢ Ⓚ ☒ ⬛ ⬛

BATAVIA

🅰🅰🅰 ▼ Budget Inn Ⓜ
(585) 343-7921. **$49-$129.** 301 Oak St 14020. I-90, exit 48, just n. Int corridors. **Pets:** Medium. $8 daily fee/pet. Designated rooms, service with restrictions, supervision. ⬛ ⬛ ⬛

🅰🅰🅰 ▼▼ Comfort Inn Ⓗ
(585) 344-9999. **$73-$189.** 4371 Federal Dr 14020. I-90, exit 48, just n on SR 98. Int corridors. **Pets:** Accepted. ⬛ ⬛ ⬛ ⬛ ⬛ ⬛

▼▼ Days Inn Ⓗ
(585) 343-6000. **$59-$139.** 200 Oak St 14020. I-90, exit 48, just s. Ext/int corridors. **Pets:** $10 daily fee/pet. Service with restrictions, supervision. ⬛ ⬛ ⬛ ⬛ ⬛ ⬛ ⬛

🅰🅰🅰 ▼▼▼ Holiday Inn-Darien Lake Ⓗ
(585) 344-2100. **$79-$159.** 8250 Park Rd 14020. I-90, exit 48, just w. Int corridors. **Pets:** $15 one-time fee/pet. Service with restrictions, supervision. ⬛ ⬛ ⬛ ⬛ ⬛ ⬛ ⬛

🅰🅰🅰 ▼▼▼ Quality Inn & Suites Ⓗ
(585) 344-7000. **$80-$160.** 8200 Park Rd 14020. I-90, exit 48, just w. Int corridors. **Pets:** Accepted. ⬛ ⬛ ⬛ ⬛ ⬛ ⬛

BATH

▼▼ Bath Super 8 Ⓗ
(607) 776-2187. **$56-$99, 3 day notice.** 333 W Morris St 14810. I-86, exit 38, just n. Int corridors. **Pets:** Medium. $10 one-time fee/pet. Service with restrictions, supervision. ⬛ ⬛ ⬛

▼▼ Microtel Inn & Suites Ⓗ
(607) 776-5333. **$49-$125.** 370 W Morris St 14810. I-86, exit 38. Int corridors. **Pets:** Other species. $15 daily fee/room. Service with restrictions, supervision. ⬛ ⬛ ⬛ ⬛ ⬛

BINGHAMTON

🅰🅰🅰 ▼▼ Comfort Inn of Binghamton Ⓗ
(607) 724-3297. **$108-$162.** 1000 Upper Front St 13905. I-81, exit 5, 1 mi n on US 11 (Front St). Int corridors. **Pets:** Large, other species. $5 daily fee/room. Designated rooms, supervision.
⬛ ⬛ ⬛ ⬛ ⬛ ⬛

▼▼ Grand Royale Hotel-A Clarion Collection Hotel Ⓗ
(607) 722-0000. **$79-$99.** 80 State St 13901. Just n of jct Hawley St; downtown. Int corridors. **Pets:** Accepted. ⬛ ⬛ ⬛ ⬛

▼ Motel 6–1222 Ⓗ
(607) 771-0400. **$45-$59.** 1012 Front St 13905. I-81, exit 6 southbound, 2 mi s on US 11 (Front St); exit 5 northbound, 1 mi n on US 11 (Front St). Int corridors. **Pets:** Other species. Service with restrictions, supervision. ⬛ ⬛

BOHEMIA

▼▼▼ La Quinta Inn & Suites-Islip Ⓗ ✿
(631) 881-7700. **$55-$169.** 10 Aero Rd 11716. I-495, exit 57, 5.1 mi se on SR 454, just s on Johnson Ave, then just e. Int corridors. **Pets:** Medium, other species. Service with restrictions, supervision. ⬛ ⬛ ⬛ ⬛ ⬛

BOONVILLE

🅰🅰🅰 ▼ Headwaters Motor Lodge Ⓜ
(315) 942-4493. **$68-$94, 3 day notice.** 13524 Rt 12 13309. Jct SR 12 and 120, 0.7 mi n. Int corridors. **Pets:** Medium. Service with restrictions, supervision. ⬛ ⬛ ⬛

BRIGHTON

🅰🅰🅰 ▼▼▼ La Quinta Inn & Suites Rochester South Ⓗ ✿
(585) 272-7800. **$99-$199.** 717 E Henrietta Rd 14623. I-390, exit 16B (Henrietta Rd) southbound; exit 16 (Henrietta Rd) northbound, just w. Int corridors. **Pets:** Medium, other species. Service with restrictions, supervision. ⬛ ⬛ ⬛ ⬛

BROCKPORT

▼▼▼ Holiday Inn Express Ⓗ
(585) 395-1000. **Call for rates.** 4908 Lake Rd S 14420. Just s of jct SR 31, on SR 19 S. Int corridors. **Pets:** Other species. $25 one-time fee/room. No service, supervision. ⬛ ⬛ ⬛ ⬛

BUFFALO METROPOLITAN AREA

AMHERST

🅰🅰🅰 ▼▼▼ Comfort Inn University Ⓗ ✿
(716) 688-0811. **$80-$150.** 1 Flint Rd 14226. I-290, exit 5B, just n on SR 263 (Millersport Hwy), then just w. Int corridors. **Pets:** Other species. $20 daily fee/pet. Designated rooms, service with restrictions.
⬛ ⬛ ⬛ ⬛ ⬛

▼▼▼ Homewood Suites Buffalo/Amherst Ⓗ
(716) 833-2277. **$119-$179.** 1138 Millersport Hwy 14226. I-290, exit 5A, just w. Int corridors. **Pets:** Accepted. ⬛ ⬛ ⬛ ⬛ ⬛ ⬛

▼▼▼ Hotel Indigo Buffalo-Amherst Ⓗ ✿
(716) 689-4414. **$109-$269.** 10 Flint Rd 14226. I-290, exit 5B, just n on SR 263 (Millersport Hwy). Int corridors. **Pets:** Large. $75 one-time fee/pet. Service with restrictions, crate. ⬛ ⬛ ⬛ ⬛ ⬛ ⬛ ⬛

🅰🅰🅰 ▼▼ Lord Amherst Hotel Ⓜ
(716) 839-2200. **$69-$135.** 5000 Main St 14226. I-290, exit 7A, just w on SR 5. Ext/int corridors. **Pets:** Designated rooms, service with restrictions, supervision. ⬛ ⬛ ⬛ ⬛ ⬛ ⬛

▼ Motel 6 Buffalo-Amherst #1298 Ⓜ
(716) 834-2231. **$45-$65.** 4400 Maple Rd 14226. I-290, exit 5B, just n to Maple Rd, then 0.7 mi w. Int corridors. **Pets:** Other species. Service with restrictions, supervision. ⬛ ⬛

🅰🅰🅰 ▼▼ Red Roof Inn #7104 Ⓜ
(716) 689-7474. **$50-$110.** 42 Flint Rd 14226. I-290, exit 5B, just n on SR 263 (Millersport Hwy). Ext corridors. **Pets:** Large. Service with restrictions, crate. ⬛ ⬛ ⬛ ⬛

BLASDELL

🅰🅰🅰 ▼▼ Econo Lodge South Ⓜ
(716) 825-7530. **$49-$110.** 4344 Milestrip Rd 14219. I-90, exit 56, just e on SR 179. Ext corridors. **Pets:** $10 daily fee/room. Designated rooms, service with restrictions, supervision. ⬛ ⬛ ⬛

🅰🅰🅰 ▼▼ McKinley's Hotel Ⓗ
(716) 648-5700. **$69-$169.** 3950 McKinley Pkwy 14219. I-90, exit 56, 0.4 mi e on SR 179, then 0.8 mi s. Int corridors. **Pets:** Accepted. ⬛ ⬛ ⬛ ⬛

BOWMANSVILLE

🅰🅰🅰 ▼▼ Red Roof Inn-Buffalo Airport #7137 Ⓜ
(716) 633-1100. **$60-$105.** 146 Maple Dr 14026. Just e of SR 78; just n of entrance to I-90 (New York State Thruway), exit 49. Ext corridors. **Pets:** Large. Service with restrictions, crate. ⬛ ⬛ ⬛

BUFFALO

🅰🅰🅰 ▼▼▼ Best Western Inn-On The Avenue Ⓗ
(716) 886-8333. **$125-$159.** 510 Delaware Ave 14202. Between Virginia and Allen sts; downtown. Int corridors. **Pets:** Medium, dogs only. Designated rooms, service with restrictions. ⬛ ⬛ ⬛ ⬛

CHEEKTOWAGA

AAA ▼▼▼▼ **Comfort Inn-Cheektowaga** H

(716) 896-2800. **$100-$250.** 475 Dingens St 14206. Just n of I-90, exit 53 (I-190); I-190, exit 1 (S Ogden St), just w. Int corridors. **Pets:** Medium, dogs only. $10 daily fee/pet. Service with restrictions, supervision.

SAVE ⊠ ⅃M ▌ 🖵 🐾

AAA ▼▼▼▼ **Comfort Suites-Buffalo Airport** H

(716) 633-6000. **$109-$169.** 901 Dick Rd 14225. SR 33, exit Dick Rd, just sw. Int corridors. **Pets:** Medium, dogs only. $15 daily fee/pet. No service, supervision. SAVE ⊠ ⅃M ▌ 🖵 🐾

▼▼▼▼ **Holiday Inn-Buffalo Airport** H

(716) 634-6969. **Call for rates.** 4600 Genesee St 14225. I-90, exit 51, 1 mi e on SR 33. Int corridors. **Pets:** Accepted.

⊠ ▌ 🖵 🍴 🐾 ⊠

▼▼▼▼ **Holiday Inn Express Hotel & Suites-Buffalo Airport** H

(716) 631-8700. **Call for rates.** 131 Buell Ave 14225. I-90, exit 51, just e on Genesee St (SR 33), then just s. Int corridors. **Pets:** Accepted.

⊠ ⅃M ▌ 🖵 🐾 ⊠

▼▼▼▼ **Homewood Suites by Hilton** H

(716) 685-0700. **$109-$169.** 760 Dick Rd 14225. SR 33, exit Dick Rd, 0.3 mi sw. Int corridors. **Pets:** Accepted. ⊠ ▌ 🖵 🐾

AAA ▼▼▼ **Oak Tree Inn** H

(716) 681-2600. **$69-$150.** 3475 Union Rd 14225. I-90, exit 52, 0.3 mi e on Walden Ave, just n on SR 277 (Union Rd). Int corridors. **Pets:** $5 daily fee/pet. Designated rooms, service with restrictions, supervision.

SAVE ⊠ ⅃M ▌ 🖵

▼▼▼▼ **Residence Inn Buffalo-Cheektowaga** H

(716) 892-5410. **$150-$180.** 107 Anderson Rd 14225. I-90, exit 52 westbound, stay to left off exit ramp. Int corridors. **Pets:** $100 one-time fee/ room. Service with restrictions. ⊠ ⅃M ▌ 🖵 🐾 ⊠

CLARENCE

AAA ▼▼▼▼ **Asa Ransom House** CI

(716) 759-2315. **$120-$190, 7 day notice.** 10529 Main St 14031. Jct SR 78 (Transit Rd), 5.3 mi e on SR 5 (Main St). Int corridors. **Pets:** Medium. Designated rooms, service with restrictions, crate.

ECO SAVE ⊠ ⅃M ▌ 🖵 🍴

▼▼▼▼ **Staybridge Suites-Buffalo Airport** H

(716) 810-7829. **$139-$239.** 8005 Sheridan Dr 14221. I-90, exit 49, 3 mi n on SR 78 (Transit Rd); jct SR 324. Int corridors. **Pets:** Other species. $100 one-time fee/pet. No service, supervision.

ASK ⊠ ⅃M ▌ 🖵 🐾 ⊠

GRAND ISLAND

AAA ▼▼▼▼ **Holiday Inn Grand Island Resort & Conference Center** H

(716) 773-1111. **$129-$199.** 100 Whitehaven Rd 14072. I-190, exit 19, 4 mi e. Int corridors. **Pets:** Large. $75 deposit/room, $25 one-time fee/room. Designated rooms, service with restrictions, supervision.

SAVE ⊠ ▌ 🖵 🍴 🐾 ⊠

HAMBURG

AAA ▼▼▼ **Comfort Inn & Suites** H

(716) 648-2922. **$70-$169.** 3615 Commerce Pl 14075. I-90, exit 57, just w. Int corridors. **Pets:** Other species. $20 daily fee/room. Service with restrictions, crate. SAVE ⊠ ⅃M ▌ 🖵 🐾

AAA ▼▼▼▼ **Quality Inn Hamburg** H 🐾

(716) 649-0500. **$110-$159.** 5440 Camp Rd 14075. I-90, exit 57, 0.3 mi se on SR 75 (Camp Rd). Int corridors. **Pets:** Medium. $15 one-time fee/ room. Service with restrictions. SAVE ⊠ ▌ 🖵 🍴 🐾

AAA ▼▼▼ **Red Roof Inn #7055** M

(716) 648-7222. **$50-$110.** 5370 Camp Rd 14075. I-90, exit 57, just se on SR 75 (Camp Rd). Ext corridors. **Pets:** Large. Service with restrictions, crate. SAVE ⊠ ▌ 🖵

KENMORE

▼▼▼ **Super 8-Buffalo/Niagara Falls** H

(716) 876-4020. **$59-$90.** 1288 Sheridan Dr 14217. I-190, exit 15, 1.5 mi e on SR 324 (Sheridan Dr). Int corridors. **Pets:** Medium. Service with restrictions, supervision. ⊠ ▌ 🖵

SPRINGVILLE

▼▼▼ **Microtel Inn & Suites** H

(716) 592-3141. **$69-$89.** 270 S Cascade Dr 14141. On US 219 S. Int corridors. **Pets:** Other species. $15 daily fee/room. Service with restrictions. ASK ⊠ ▌ 🖵

TONAWANDA

AAA ▼▼▼ **Econo Lodge** M

(716) 694-6696. **Call for rates.** 2000 Niagara Falls Blvd 14150. I-290, exit 3 (Niagara Falls Blvd), 0.5 mi n on US 62. Ext/int corridors. **Pets:** Accepted. SAVE ⊠ ▌ 🖵

WILLIAMSVILLE

▼▼▼ **La Quinta Inn–Buffalo Airport** H 🐾

(716) 633-1011. **$60-$160.** 6619 Transit Rd 14221. I-90, exit 49, just n. Int corridors. **Pets:** Medium, other species. Service with restrictions, supervision. ASK ⊠ ▌ 🖵

▼▼▼ **Microtel-Lancaster** H

(716) 633-6200. **$52-$139.** 50 Freeman Rd 14221. I-90, exit 49, 0.4 mi n on Transit Rd (SR 78), just e. Int corridors. **Pets:** Accepted.

ASK ⊠ ▌

▼▼▼ **Motel 6 #2013** H

(716) 626-1500. **$45-$59.** 52 Freeman Rd 14221. I-90, exit 49, 0.4 mi n on Transit Rd, then just e. Ext/int corridors. **Pets:** Other species. Service with restrictions, supervision. ⊠ ▌ 🐾

▼▼▼▼ **Residence Inn by Marriott Buffalo/Amherst** H

(716) 632-6622. **$139-$169.** 100 Maple Rd 14221. I-290, exit 5B, just n on Millersport Hwy, exit Maple Rd, then just e. Ext corridors. **Pets:** Accepted. ⊠ ⅃M ▌ 🖵 🐾 ⊠

END METROPOLITAN AREA

CALCIUM

▼▼▼ **Microtel Inn Watertown** H

(315) 629-5000. **$72-$76.** 8000 Virginia Smith Dr 13616. 4 mi e on SR 342; jct US 11. Int corridors. **Pets:** Medium. $10 daily fee/room. Designated rooms, service with restrictions, supervision. ASK ⊠ ▌

CANANDAIGUA

AAA ▼▼▼▼ **The Inn On The Lake** H

(585) 394-7800. **$119-$369.** 770 S Main St 14424. I-90, exit 44 (Canandaigua/SR 332), just s of jct US 20 and SR 5. Int corridors. **Pets:** Dogs only. $25 daily fee/pet. Designated rooms, supervision.

SAVE ⊠ ⅃M ▌ 🖵 🍴 🐾 ⊠

AAA ▼▼▼▼ **Red Carpet Inn** H

(585) 394-4140. **$45-$135.** 4232 Rt 5 & 20 14424. 1 mi e of jct SR 332. Ext/int corridors. **Pets:** $15 daily fee/pet. Service with restrictions, crate. SAVE ⊠ ▌

▼▼ Super 8 **H**

(585) 396-7224. **$72-$125.** 4450 Eastern Blvd 14424. Jct SR 332, 5 and US 20, 0.5 mi e. Int corridors. **Pets:** Large. $10 daily fee/pet. Service with restrictions, supervision. ⟨ASK⟩ ⓧ 🛏 💻

CANASTOTA
▼▼▼ Days Inn **H**

(315) 697-3309. **$60-$200.** 377 N Peterboro St 13032. I-90, exit 34 on SR 13. Int corridors. **Pets:** Other species. $15 daily fee/room. Service with restrictions, supervision. ⟨ASK⟩ ⓧ 🛏 💻

CHESTER
ⓐ ▼▼▼ Holiday Inn Express Hotel & Suites **H** ✿

(845) 469-3000. **$99-$153.** 2 Bryle Pl 10918. SR 17, exit 126, just n on SR 94, then just w on SR 17M (Brookside Ave). Int corridors. **Pets:** Other species. $30 one-time fee/room. Designated rooms, service with restrictions, crate. ⟨SAVE⟩ ⓧ 🖐ᴹ 🛏 💻 ≋ ⓧ

CLAY
▼▼▼▼ Hampton Inn-Syracuse/Clay **H**

(315) 622-3443. **$109-$199.** 3948 SR 31 13090. Jct SR 481, exit 12, just w. Int corridors. **Pets:** Accepted. ⓧ 🖐ᴹ 🛏 💻 ≋

CLAYTON
▼▼ Fair Wind Lodge **M**

(315) 686-5251. **Call for rates.** 38201 NYS Rt 12E 13624. 2.3 mi sw. Ext corridors. **Pets:** Accepted. ⓧ 🛏 💻 ≋ 🐾

CLINTON
▼▼▼ Amidst the Hedges **BB**

(315) 853-3031. **$95-$225, 7 day notice.** 180 Sanford Ave 13323. SR 412 (College St), 0.3 mi n on Elm St. Int corridors. **Pets:** Medium, dogs only. Designated rooms, no service, supervision. ⓧ 🛏 💻 ≋

COBLESKILL
ⓐ ▼▼▼ Best Western Inn of Cobleskill **H**

(518) 234-4321. **$84-$166.** 121 Burgin Dr 12043. I-88, exit 21 eastbound on SR 7, 0.8 mi e of jct SR 10; exit 22 westbound, 2.9 mi w on SR 7. Int corridors. **Pets:** Accepted. ⟨SAVE⟩ ⓧ 🖐ᴹ 🛏 💻 🍴 ≋

▼▼▼ Super 8 **H**

(518) 234-4888. **$69-$125.** 955 E Main St 12043. I-88, exit 22 westbound, 2.4 mi w on SR 7; exit 21 eastbound, 3.1 mi e on SR 7. Int corridors. **Pets:** Large, other species. $10 daily fee/room. No service, supervision. ⟨ASK⟩ ⓧ 🖐ᴹ 🛏 💻

COLONIE
ⓐ ▼▼▼ Best Western Albany Airport Inn **H** ✿

(518) 458-1000. **$79-$129.** 200 Wolf Rd 12205. I-87, exit se to Wolf Rd, then just sw. Int corridors. **Pets:** $20 daily fee/room. Designated rooms, service with restrictions, crate. ⟨SAVE⟩ ⓧ 🛏 💻 🍴 ≋

ⓐ ▼▼▼ Cocca's Inn & Suites, Wolf Rd **M**

(518) 459-2240. **$59-$149.** 2 Wolf Rd 12205. I-87, exit 2E, just e. Ext/int corridors. **Pets:** Other species. $10 daily fee/pet. Service with restrictions, supervision. ⟨SAVE⟩ ⓧ 🛏 💻

▼▼▼ Comfort Inn & Suites **H**

(518) 869-5327. **$100.** 1606 Central Ave 12205. I-87, exit 2, 0.8 mi w. Ext/int corridors. **Pets:** Small. $15 daily fee/pet. Designated rooms, service with restrictions, supervision. ⟨ASK⟩ ⓧ 🖐ᴹ 🛏 💻 ≋

▼▼▼ Holiday Inn Albany on Wolf Road **H**

(518) 458-7250. **$149-$230.** 205 Wolf Rd 12205. I-87, exit 4, 0.3 mi se. Int corridors. **Pets:** Large, other species. $35 daily fee/room. Service with restrictions, crate. ⓧ 🖐ᴹ 🛏 💻 🍴 ≋ ⓧ

ⓐ ▼▼▼ Red Roof Inn #7112 **M**

(518) 459-1971. **Call for rates.** 188 Wolf Rd 12205. I-87, exit 4, just se to Wolf Rd, then just sw. Ext corridors. **Pets:** Large. Service with restrictions, crate. ⟨SAVE⟩ ⓧ 🖐ᴹ 🛏

ⓐ ▼▼▼ Travelodge Inn & Suites, Albany Airport **H**

(518) 459-5670. **$65-$80.** 44 Wolf Rd 12205. I-87, exit 2E, just e, then just n. Int corridors. **Pets:** Small. $10 daily fee/pet. Service with restrictions, supervision. ⟨SAVE⟩ ⓧ 🛏 💻

CORNING
▼▼▼▼ Radisson Hotel Corning **H**

(607) 962-5000. **Call for rates.** 125 Denison Pkwy E 14830. Downtown. Int corridors. **Pets:** Accepted. ⟨ECO⟩ ⓧ 🛏 💻 🍴 ≋

▼▼▼ Staybridge Suites **H**

(607) 936-7800. **$131-$247.** 201 Townley Ave 14830. I-86/SR 17, exit 46, just s. Int corridors. **Pets:** Accepted. ⟨ASK⟩ ⓧ 🖐ᴹ 🛏 💻 ≋ ⓧ

CORTLAND
ⓐ ▼ Econo Lodge **M**

(607) 756-2856. **Call for rates.** 10 S Church St 13045. I-81, exit 11, 0.8 mi s on SR 13/41 and US 11. Ext corridors. **Pets:** Small. $20 daily fee/pet. Designated rooms, service with restrictions, supervision. ⟨SAVE⟩ ⓧ 🛏 💻

▼▼▼ Quality Inn Cortland **H**

(607) 756-5622. **$79-$199.** 188 Clinton Ave 13045. I-81, exit 11, just n. Int corridors. **Pets:** Accepted. ⟨ASK⟩ ⓧ 🛏 💻

ⓐ ▼▼▼ Ramada Cortland **H**

(607) 756-4431. **$69-$189.** 2 River St 13045. I-81, exit 11, just s on SR 13. Int corridors. **Pets:** $15 daily fee/room. Service with restrictions, supervision. ⟨SAVE⟩ ⓧ 🛏 💻 🍴 ≋

CUBA
ⓐ ▼▼▼ Cuba Econo Lodge **M**

(585) 968-1992. **$49-$149.** 1 N Branch Rd 14727. I-86, exit 28, just n to N Branch Rd, then e. Int corridors. **Pets:** Medium. $10 daily fee/pet. Service with restrictions, supervision. ⟨SAVE⟩ ⓧ 🛏

DELHI
ⓐ ▼ Buena Vista Inn **M**

(607) 746-2135. **$69-$110.** 18718 State Hwy 28 13753. Jct SR 10, 0.8 mi s. Ext corridors. **Pets:** Medium, dogs only. $15 daily fee/pet. Designated rooms, service with restrictions, supervision. ⟨SAVE⟩ ⓧ 🛏

DEWITT
ⓐ ▼▼▼ Econo Lodge **M**

(315) 446-3300. **$80-$170, 3 day notice.** 3400 Erie Blvd E 13214. I-481, exit 3, 1.2 mi w on SR 5; I-690, exit 17 S (Bridge St), just e on Erie Blvd (SR 5). Ext corridors. **Pets:** Medium. $10 daily fee/pet. Service with restrictions, supervision. ⟨SAVE⟩ ⓧ 🛏 💻

DIAMOND POINT
▼▼ Golden Sands Resort **M**

(518) 668-2203. **$75-$175, 30 day notice.** 3654 Lake Shore Dr 12845. I-87, exit 22, 3.3 mi n on SR 9N. Ext corridors. **Pets:** Medium, other species. $25 one-time fee/room. Designated rooms, service with restrictions, supervision. ⓧ 🛏 ⓧ

DUNKIRK
ⓐ ▼▼▼ Best Western Dunkirk/Fredonia **H**

(716) 366-7100. **$80-$250.** 3912 Vineyard Dr 14048. I-90, exit 59, just w. Int corridors. **Pets:** Large. $10 daily fee/pet. Service with restrictions, supervision. ⟨SAVE⟩ ⓧ 🛏 💻 ≋

ⓐ ▼▼▼ Comfort Inn **H**

(716) 672-4450. **Call for rates.** 3925 Vineyard Dr 14048. I-90, exit 59, just se on SR 75 (Camp Rd), then just w. Int corridors. **Pets:** Large. $10 daily fee/pet. Service with restrictions, supervision. ⟨SAVE⟩ ⓧ 🛏 💻

EAST GREENBUSH
▼▼▼▼ Residence Inn Albany East Greenbush/Tech Valley **H**

(518) 720-3600. **$159-$179.** 3 Tech Valley Dr 12061. I-90, exit 9, just e. Int corridors. **Pets:** Accepted. ⓧ 🖐ᴹ 🛏 💻 ≋ ⓧ

EAST SYRACUSE

▼▼▼ Candlewood Suites Syracuse 🅷
(315) 432-1684. **Call for rates.** 6550 Baptist Way 13057. I-90, exit 35 (Carrier Cir) to SR 298 E to Old Collamer Rd, just n. Int corridors. **Pets:** Accepted. ✖ 👍M 🛏 💻

▼▼ Comfort Inn-Carrier Circle 🅷 ✿
(315) 437-0222. **$75-$139.** 6491 Thompson Rd S 13206. I-90, exit 35 (Carrier Cir), just s. Ext/int corridors. **Pets:** Other species. $10 daily fee/room. Designated rooms, service with restrictions, supervision.
ASK ✖ 🛏 💻

▼▼ CrestHill Suites 🅷
(315) 432-5595. **$109-$249, 4 day notice.** 6410 New Venture Gear Dr 13057. I-90, exit 35 (Carrier Cir) to SR 298 E, 0.7 mi s, then just e. Int corridors. **Pets:** Other species. $50 one-time fee/room. Service with restrictions. ASK ✖ 🛏 💻

▼▼ Extended StayAmerica Hotels-Syracuse-DeWitt 🅷
(315) 463-1958. **$65-$110.** 6630 Old Collamer Rd S 13057. I-90, exit 35 (Carrier Cir) to SR 298 E, just n. Int corridors. **Pets:** Other species. $25 daily fee/room. Designated rooms, service with restrictions, crate.
ASK ✖ 🛏 💻

▼▼▼ Holiday Inn East-Carrier Circle 🅷
(315) 437-2761. **$109-$179.** 6555 Old Collamer Rd 13057. I-90, exit 35 (Carrier Cir) to SR 298 E, just n. Ext/int corridors. **Pets:** $25 one-time fee/room. Service with restrictions, supervision.
ASK ✖ 🛏 💻 ⑪ 🏊 ✖

▼▼ Quality Inn Syracuse 🅷
(315) 432-9333. **$69-$109.** 6611 Old Collamer Rd S 13057. I-90, exit 35 (Carrier Cir) to SR 298 E, just n. Ext/int corridors. **Pets:** $10 daily fee/room. Designated rooms, service with restrictions, supervision.
ASK ✖ 👍M 🛏 💻 🏊

AAA▼ ▼▼▼ Red Roof Inn #7157 Ⓜ
(315) 437-3309. **$50-$100.** 6614 N Thompson Rd 13206. I-90, exit 35 (Carrier Cir), just n. Ext corridors. **Pets:** Large. Service with restrictions, crate. SAVE ✖ 🛏

AAA▼ ▼▼▼▼ Residence Inn Syracuse 🅷
(315) 432-4488. **$169-$179.** 6420 Yorktown Cir 13057. I-90, exit 35 (Carrier Cir), SR 298 E to Old Collamer Rd, then just n. Ext/int corridors. **Pets:** Accepted. SAVE ✖ 👍M 🛏 💻 🏊 ✖

ELLICOTTVILLE

AAA▼ ▼▼▼▼ The Jefferson Inn of Ellicottville 🅱🅱 ✿
(716) 699-5869. **$89-$229, 30 day notice.** 3 Jefferson St 14731. Western jct US 219 and SR 242, just n; eastern jct, 0.8 mi w; downtown. Ext/int corridors. **Pets:** Other species. $15 daily fee/pet. Designated rooms, no service. SAVE ✖ 🛏

▼▼▼ Sugar Pine Lodge 🅱🅱
(716) 699-4855. **Call for rates.** 6158 Jefferson St, Rt 219 S 14731. Jct US 219 and SR 242, 0.5 mi s on US 219. Ext/int corridors.
Pets: Accepted. ✖ 🛏 💻 🏊

ELMIRA

AAA▼ ▼▼▼ Coachman Motor Lodge Ⓜ
(607) 733-5526. **$90-$120.** 908 Pennsylvania Ave 14904. SR 17, exit 56 (Church St), 0.7 mi w on SR 352, 0.5 mi s on Madison Ave (becomes Pennsylvania Ave), then 1.4 mi s. Ext corridors. **Pets:** Medium. $15 one-time fee/room. Service with restrictions, supervision. SAVE 🛏 💻

▼▼▼ Holiday Inn-Elmira Riverview 🅷
(607) 734-4211. **$99-$225.** 760 E Water St 14901. I-86, exit 56 (Water St), 0.5 mi s. Ext/int corridors. **Pets:** Other species. $25 one-time fee/room. Designated rooms, service with restrictions.
ASK ✖ 🛏 💻 ⑪ 🏊 ✖

FARMINGTON

AAA▼ ▼▼▼ Budget Inn Ⓜ
(585) 924-5020. **$49-$99, 3 day notice.** 6001 Rt 96 14425. I-90, exit 44, 1 mi s on SR 332, then just e. Ext corridors. **Pets:** Small, dogs only. $15 one-time fee/pet. Service with restrictions, supervision.
SAVE ✖ 🛏 💻

FAYETTEVILLE

AAA▼ ▼▼▼▼ Craftsman Inn and Conference Center 🅷
(315) 637-8000. **Call for rates.** 7300 E Genesee St (SR 5) 13066. Across from Fayetteville Towne Center. Int corridors. **Pets:** Medium, dogs only. Designated rooms, no service. SAVE ✖ 👍M 🛏 💻 ⑪

FISHKILL

▼▼▼ Extended StayAmerica-Fishkill-Poughkeepsie 🅷
(845) 896-0592. **$85-$159.** 55 W Merritt Blvd 12524. I-84, exit 13, just n. Int corridors. **Pets:** Other species. $25 daily fee/room. Designated rooms, service with restrictions, crate. ✖ 👍M 🛏 💻

▼▼▼ Fishkill Inn 🅷
(845) 896-4995. **$79-$169.** 20 Schuyler Blvd 12524. I-84, exit 13, just n. Int corridors. **Pets:** Accepted. SAVE ✖ 👍M 🛏 💻

▼▼▼ Homestead Studio
Suites-Fishkill-Poughkeepsie 🅷
(845) 897-2800. **$95-$159.** 25 Merritt Blvd 12524. I-84, exit 13, just n. Int corridors. **Pets:** Other species. $25 daily fee/room. Designated rooms, service with restrictions, crate. ASK ✖ 🛏 💻

AAA▼ ▼▼▼▼ Residence Inn Fishkill 🅷
(845) 896-5210. **$154-$239.** 14 Schuyler Blvd 12524. I-84, exit 13, just n. Ext corridors. **Pets:** Accepted. SAVE ✖ 👍M 🛏 💻 🏊 ✖

FREDONIA

AAA▼ ▼▼ Days Inn Dunkirk-Fredonia 🅷
(716) 673-1351. **$81-$143, 3 day notice.** 10455 Bennett Rd 14063. I-90, exit 59, just s on SR 60. Ext/int corridors. **Pets:** Other species. $10 one-time fee/pet. Service with restrictions, supervision.
SAVE ✖ 🛏 💻 ⑪ 🏊

FULTON

▼▼▼ Riverside Inn 🅷
(315) 593-2444. **Call for rates.** 930 S 1st St 13069. On SR 481. Int corridors. **Pets:** Accepted. ✖ 🛏 💻 ⑪ 🏊

GARDEN CITY

▼▼▼▼ La Quinta Garden City 🅷 ✿
(516) 705-9000. **$165-$299.** 821 Stewart Ave 11530. Meadowbrook Pkwy, exit 3, 0.5 mi w. Int corridors. **Pets:** Medium, other species. Service with restrictions, supervision. ASK ✖ 👍M 🛏 💻

GATES

▼▼▼▼ Holiday Inn-Rochester Airport 🅷
(585) 328-6000. **$99-$159.** 911 Brooks Ave 14624. I-390, exit 18A (SR 204), just e. Int corridors. **Pets:** Large. $50 deposit/room. Designated rooms, service with restrictions, supervision.
ASK ✖ 🛏 💻 ⑪ 🏊 ✖

AAA▼ ▼▼▼▼ Quality Inn-Rochester 🅷
(585) 464-8800. **$70-$150.** 1273 Chili Ave 14624. I-390, exit 19, just off exit on SR 33 W. Int corridors. **Pets:** Large, other species. $50 deposit/room. Designated rooms, service with restrictions, supervision.
SAVE ✖ 🛏 💻 ⑪ 🏊

GENESEO

▼▼▼ Quality Inn Geneseo 🅷
(585) 243-0500. **Call for rates.** 4242 Lakeville Rd 14454. I-390, exit 8, 3.4 mi w on SR 20A. Int corridors. **Pets:** Accepted. ✖ 🛏 💻 🏊

GENEVA

Cobtree Vacation Rental Homes 🏠 ❀
(315) 789-1144. **$125-$420, 90 day notice.** 440-450 Armstrong Rd 14456. 3 mi n on SR 14. Ext corridors. **Pets:** Large. $8 daily fee/pet. Designated rooms, no service, supervision. 🔲🔲🔲🔲🔲

Ramada Geneva Lakefront 🅷
(315) 789-0400. **$92-$170.** 41 Lakefront Dr 14456. Just e of SR 14, 5 and 20; downtown. Int corridors. **Pets:** Accepted.
🔲🔲🔲🔲🔲🔲🔲

GREAT NECK

The Andrew Hotel 🅷 ❀
(516) 482-2900. **$299-$309.** 75 N Station Plaza 11021. Jct SR 25A, 0.8 mi n on Middle Neck Rd, just e. Int corridors. **Pets:** Small. $25 daily fee/pet. Service with restrictions. 🔲🔲🔲🔲

Inn at Great Neck 🅷
(516) 773-2000. **$219-$279.** 30 Cutter Mill Rd 11021. Jct SR 25A, 0.8 mi n on Middle Neck Rd, just w. Int corridors. **Pets:** Accepted.
🔲🔲🔲🔲🔲🔲

GREECE

Comfort Inn West 🅷
(585) 621-5700. **$70-$90.** 1501 W Ridge Rd 14615. Jct I-390 and SR 104 (Ridge Rd), 0.5 mi e. Int corridors. **Pets:** Accepted.
🔲🔲🔲🔲

Extended StayAmerica-Rochester-Greece 🅷
(585) 663-5558. **$70-$95.** 600 Center Place Dr 14615. I-390, exit 24A, just e on SR 104 (Ridge Rd), just n on Buckman Rd, then just w. Int corridors. **Pets:** Other species. $25 daily fee/room. Designated rooms, service with restrictions, crate. 🔲🔲🔲🔲🔲

Hampton Inn-Rochester North 🅷
(585) 663-6070. **$119-$179.** 500 Center Place Dr 14615. I-390, exit 24A, just e on SR 104 (Ridge Rd), then just n on Buckman Rd. Int corridors. **Pets:** Accepted. 🔲🔲🔲🔲🔲🔲

Residence Inn Rochester West/Greece 🅷
(585) 865-2090. **$188-$230.** 500 Paddy Creek Cir 14615. I-390, exit 24A, just e on SR 104 (Ridge Rd), just s on Hoover Dr, then just w. Int corridors. **Pets:** Accepted. 🔲🔲🔲🔲🔲

GUILDERLAND

Best Western Sovereign Hotel Albany 🅷
(518) 489-2981. **$90-$130.** 1228 Western Ave 12203. I-90, exit 1 S, 1 mi e on US 20 (Western ave). Int corridors. **Pets:** Other species. $15 daily fee/pet. Designated rooms, service with restrictions.
🔲🔲🔲🔲🔲🔲

Days Inn-Albany/Sunny 🅷
(518) 489-4423. **$84-$115.** 1230 Western Ave 12203. I-90, exit 1 S, 0.7 mi e on US 20 (Western Ave). Int corridors. **Pets:** Large, dogs only. $20 one-time fee/room. No service, supervision. 🔲🔲🔲🔲🔲

HANCOCK

Smith's Colonial Motel 🅼
(607) 637-2989. **$65-$130.** 23085 State Hwy 97 13783. SR 17, exit 87, 2.7 mi s. Ext corridors. **Pets:** Accepted. 🔲🔲

HAUPPAUGE

Residence Inn Long Island-Hauppauge/Islandia 🅷
(631) 724-4188. **$139-$189.** 850 Veterans Memorial Hwy 11788. I-495, exit 57, 1.2 mi nw. Int corridors. **Pets:** Accepted.
🔲🔲🔲🔲🔲🔲

Sheraton Long Island Hotel 🅷 ❀
(631) 231-1100. **Call for rates.** 110 Vanderbilt Motor Pkwy 11788. I-495, exit 53 (Wicks Rd), just n, then 0.3 mi e. Int corridors. **Pets:** Medium, dogs only. Service with restrictions, supervision.
🔲🔲🔲🔲🔲🔲🔲

HENRIETTA

Comfort Suites by Choice Hotels of Rochester 🅷
(585) 334-6620. **$90-$140.** 2085 Hylan Dr 14623. I-390, exit 13, just e. Int corridors. **Pets:** Accepted. 🔲🔲🔲🔲🔲🔲

Homewood Suites by Hilton-Rochester 🅷
(585) 334-9150. **$109-$199.** 2095 Hylan Dr 14623. I-390, exit 13, just e. Int corridors. **Pets:** Accepted. 🔲🔲🔲🔲🔲

Microtel-Rochester 🅷
(585) 334-3400. **$65-$129.** 905 Lehigh Station Rd 14467. I-390, exit 12 northbound; exit 12A southbound, just w on SR 253. Int corridors. **Pets:** Accepted. 🔲🔲🔲

Radisson Rochester Airport 🅷
(585) 475-1910. **$109-$189, 3 day notice.** 175 Jefferson Rd 14623. I-390, exit 14A southbound; exit 14 northbound, 3 mi w on SR 252 (Jefferson Rd). Int corridors. **Pets:** Accepted.
🔲🔲🔲🔲🔲🔲🔲

Red Roof Inn-Henrietta #7042 🅼
(585) 359-1100. **Call for rates.** 4820 W Henrietta Rd 14467. I-390, exit 12 northbound; exit 12A southbound, 0.5 mi w on SR 253, then just s on SR 15 (Henrietta Rd). Ext corridors. **Pets:** Large. Service with restrictions, crate. 🔲🔲🔲

Residence Inn Rochester 🅷
(585) 272-8850. **$109-$199.** 1300 Jefferson Rd 14623. I-390, exit 14A southbound, 0.5 mi e on SR 252 (Jefferson Rd); exit 14 northbound, just n on SR 15A, then 0.5 mi e on SR 252 (Jefferson Rd). Ext/int corridors. **Pets:** Other species. $100 one-time fee/room. Service with restrictions, supervision. 🔲🔲🔲🔲🔲

R I T Inn & Conference Center 🅷
(585) 359-1800. **$109-$169.** 5257 W Henrietta Rd 14586. I-390, exit 12 northbound; exit 12A southbound, 0.5 mi w on SR 253, then 0.7 mi s. Int corridors. **Pets:** Small, other species. $50 one-time fee/room. Designated rooms, service with restrictions, crate. 🔲🔲🔲🔲🔲🔲🔲

HERKIMER

Herkimer Motel 🅼 ❀
(315) 866-0490. **$78-$98.** 100 Marginal Rd 13350. I-90, exit 30, just n on SR 28. Ext/int corridors. **Pets:** Large, other species. $10 one-time fee/room. Designated rooms, service with restrictions, supervision.
🔲🔲🔲🔲🔲

HIGHLAND

Super 8 🅼
(845) 691-6888. **$65-$120.** 3423 Rt 9W 12528. Just s of jct SR 299 and US 9W. Int corridors. **Pets:** Other species. $20 daily fee/pet. Service with restrictions, supervision. 🔲🔲🔲🔲🔲

HUNTINGTON STATION

Whitman Motor Lodge 🅼
(631) 271-2800. **$89-$170.** 295 E Jericho Tpke 11746. On SR 25 (Jericho Tpke), 0.6 mi e of SR 110. Ext/int corridors. **Pets:** Small. $20 daily fee/pet. Service with restrictions, crate. 🔲🔲🔲🔲

INLET

Marina Motel 🅼
(315) 357-3883. **$89-$189, 14 day notice.** 6 S Shore Rd 13360. Center. Ext corridors. **Pets:** Accepted. 🔲🔲🔲

IRONDEQUOIT

Holiday Inn Express 🅷
(585) 342-0430. **Call for rates.** 2200 Goodman St N 14609. SR 104, exit Goodman St, just n. Int corridors. **Pets:** Accepted.
🔲🔲🔲🔲

ITHACA

△△△ ▼▼▼▼ Best Western University Inn M

(607) 272-6100. **Call for rates.** 1020 Ellis Hollow Rd 14850. SR 79 E, 1 mi ne on Pine Tree Rd, just n; in East Hill Plaza. Int corridors. **Pets:** Small, other species. $10 daily fee/pet. Designated rooms, service with restrictions, supervision. ⟨SAVE⟩ ⤫ 🛡 💻 ⤳

△△△ ▼▼▼ Comfort Inn H ❖

(607) 272-0100. **Call for rates.** 356 Elmira Rd 14850. Jct SR 96, 89 and 79, 1.5 mi sw on SR 13. Int corridors. **Pets:** $25 one-time fee/pet. Service with restrictions, supervision. ⟨SAVE⟩ ⤫ ⟨&M⟩ 🛡 💻

▼▼▼ Country Inn & Suites By Carlson H ❖

(607) 256-1100. **$99-$359.** 1100 Danby Rd (SR 96B) 14850. 0.5 mi past entrance to Ithaca College at intersection with SR 96B. Int corridors. **Pets:** Other species. $25 daily fee/pet. Designated rooms, service with restrictions, supervision. ⟨ASK⟩ ⤫ ⟨&M⟩ 🛡 💻 ≋

△△△ ▼▼▼ Hampton Inn H

(607) 277-5500. **Call for rates.** 337 Elmira Rd 14850. On SR 13. Int corridors. **Pets:** Accepted. ⟨SAVE⟩ ⤫ ⟨&M⟩ 🛡 💻 ⤳

▼▼▼ Holiday Inn Ithaca Downtown H

(607) 272-1000. **$189-$239.** 222 S Cayuga St 14850. Just n of SR 96B. Int corridors. **Pets:** Accepted. ⟨ASK⟩ ⤫ 🛡 💻 ⑪ ⤳

▼▼▼ La Tourelle Resort and Spa CI ❖

(607) 273-2734. **$125-$700, 3 day notice.** 1150 Danby Rd 14850. 2.7 mi s on SR 96B. Int corridors. **Pets:** Other species. $50 deposit/room. Designated rooms, service with restrictions, supervision.
⟨ECO⟩ ⟨ASK⟩ ⤫ 🛡 💻 ⑪ ⤫

△△△ ▼▼▼ Meadow Court Inn M

(607) 273-3885. **$65-$225.** 529 S Meadow St 14850. 1.5 mi s on SR 13 and 96. Ext/int corridors. **Pets:** Accepted. ⟨SAVE⟩ ⤫ ⟨&M⟩ 🛡 💻 ⑪

△△△ ▼▼▼ Rodeway Inn & Suites M

(607) 272-5252. **$50-$170, 7 day notice.** 654 Elmira Rd 14850. On SR 13 S. Ext/int corridors. **Pets:** Small. $10 daily fee/pet. Designated rooms, service with restrictions. ⟨SAVE⟩ ⤫ 🛡 💻

JAMESTOWN

△△△ ▼▼▼ Best Western Downtown Jamestown H ❖

(716) 484-8400. **$80-$132, 3 day notice.** 200 W 3rd St 14701. I-86, exit 12, 2 mi s on SR 60 (Washington St). Int corridors. **Pets:** Medium, other species. $25 one-time fee/room. Designated rooms, service with restrictions, supervision. ⟨SAVE⟩ ⤫ ⟨&M⟩ 🛡 💻 ⤳

▼▼▼ Comfort Inn H ❖

(716) 664-5920. **$82-$159, 3 day notice.** 2800 N Main St 14701. I-86, exit 12, just s on SR 60. Int corridors. **Pets:** Other species. $25 one-time fee/pet. Service with restrictions, supervision. ⟨ASK⟩ ⤫ 🛡 💻

JOHNSON CITY

△△△ ▼▼▼ Best Western of Johnson City H

(607) 729-9194. **$90-$100, 21 day notice.** 569 Harry L Dr 13790. SR 17, exit 70N, 0.3 mi n. Int corridors. **Pets:** Other species. $10 one-time fee/room. Designated rooms, service with restrictions, supervision.
⟨SAVE⟩ ⤫ 🛡 💻

△△△ ▼▼▼ La Quinta Inn H ❖

(607) 770-9333. **$80-$160.** 581 Harry L Dr 13790. SR 17, exit 70N, 0.3 mi n. Int corridors. **Pets:** Medium, other species. Service with restrictions, supervision. ⟨SAVE⟩ ⤫ 🛡 💻

△△△ ▼▼▼ Red Roof Inn-Binghamton #7203 M

(607) 729-8940. **$56-$131.** 590 Fairview St 13790. SR 17, exit 70N, 0.3 mi n, then just n on Reynolds Rd. Ext corridors. **Pets:** Large. Service with restrictions, crate. ⟨SAVE⟩ ⤫ 🛡

JOHNSTOWN

▼▼▼ Holiday Inn H

(518) 762-4686. **$96-$160.** 308 N Comrie Ave 12095-1095. Jct SR 30A and 29 E, 1.3 mi n. Ext/int corridors. **Pets:** Accepted.
⟨ASK⟩ ⤫ ⟨&M⟩ 🛡 💻 ⑪ ⤳

KINGSTON

△△△ ▼▼▼ Holiday Inn H

(845) 338-0400. **$139-$189.** 503 Washington Ave 12401. I-87, exit 19, just e of traffic circle. Int corridors. **Pets:** $10 daily fee/room. Service with restrictions, supervision. ⟨SAVE⟩ ⤫ 🛡 💻 ⑪ ⤳ ⤫

LAKE GEORGE

▼ Green Haven Resort M

(518) 668-2489. **$64-$139, 10 day notice.** 3136 Lake Shore Dr 12845. I-87, exit 22, 0.8 mi n on SR 9N. Ext corridors. **Pets:** Medium, dogs only. $20 one-time fee/pet. Service with restrictions, supervision.
⟨ASK⟩ ⤫ 🛡 💻 ⤳ ⤫

▼▼ Lake George Inn M

(518) 668-2673. **$48-$139, 10 day notice.** 444 Canada St 12845. I-87, exit 22, 0.3 mi s on US 9. Ext corridors. **Pets:** Medium, other species. $15 daily fee/pet. Designated rooms, service with restrictions, crate.
⟨ASK⟩ ⤫ 🛡 💻 ⤳

▼▼ Lake Haven Motel M 🐾

(518) 668-2260. **$49-$132, 10 day notice.** 442 Canada St 12845. I-87, exit 22, 0.4 mi s on US 9. Ext corridors. **Pets:** Medium, dogs only. $10 daily fee/pet. Designated rooms, service with restrictions, crate.
⤫ 🛡 💻 ⤳

▼▼ Travelodge of Lake George M ❖

(518) 668-5421. **$69-$159.** 2011 SR 9 12845. I-87, exit 21, just s. Ext corridors. **Pets:** Medium, dogs only. $20 daily fee/pet. Service with restrictions, supervision. ⟨ASK⟩ ⤫ 🛡 💻 ⑪ ⤳

LAKE LUZERNE

△△△ ▼ Luzerne Court M 🐾

(518) 696-2734. **$75-$180, 14 day notice.** 508 Lake Ave 12846. I-87, exit 21, 8.7 mi s on SR 9N. Ext corridors. **Pets:** Dogs only. Supervision.
⟨SAVE⟩ ⤫ 🛡 ⑪ ⤳ ⤫

LAKE PLACID

△△△ ▼▼▼ Art Devlin's Olympic Motor Inn, Inc. M

(518) 523-3700. **$68-$248, 14 day notice.** 2764 Main St 12946. 0.5 mi e on SR 86. Ext corridors. **Pets:** Dogs only. $4 daily fee/pet. Designated rooms, supervision. ⟨SAVE⟩ ⤫ 🛡 ⤳

△△△ ▼▼▼ Comfort Inn on Lake Placid H

(518) 523-9555. **$100-$375.** 2125 Saranac Ave 12946. 0.5 mi w on SR 86. Ext/int corridors. **Pets:** Other species. Service with restrictions, supervision. ⟨SAVE⟩ ⤫ 🛡 💻 ⑪ ⤳ ⤫

△△△ ▼▼▼ Crowne Plaza Resort & Golf Club Lake Placid H

(518) 523-2556. **$119-$309, 7 day notice.** 101 Olympic Dr 12946. Downtown. Ext/int corridors. **Pets:** Large. $10 daily fee/pet. Service with restrictions, supervision. ⟨SAVE⟩ ⤫ 🛡 💻 ⑪ ⤳ ⤫

△△△ ▼▼▼ Golden Arrow Lakeside Resort H ❖

(518) 523-3353. **$99-$599, 7 day notice.** 2559 Main St 12946. On SR 86; center. Int corridors. **Pets:** Other species. $150 deposit/pet, $50 one-time fee/pet. Designated rooms, service with restrictions, supervision.
⟨ECO⟩ ⟨SAVE⟩ ⤫ 🛡 💻 ⑪ ⤳ ⤫

▼▼▼ High Peaks Resort H

(518) 523-4411. **$129-$349, 7 day notice.** 2384 Saranac Ave 12946. 0.3 mi w on SR 86. Int corridors. **Pets:** Accepted.
⟨ASK⟩ ⤫ ⟨&M⟩ 🛡 💻 ⑪ ⤳ ⤫

◬ ▼▼ Swiss Acres Inn ⊞
(518) 523-3040. **$59-$159, 7 day notice.** 1970 Saranac Ave 12946. 1 mi w on SR 86. Ext/int corridors. **Pets:** $15 daily fee/pet. Service with restrictions, supervision. [SAVE] [✕] [🛏] [💻] [🍴] [≈]

LANSING

▼▼▼ Homewood Suites by Hilton ⊞
(607) 266-0000. **$89-$409.** 36 Cinema Dr 14850. SR 13, exit Tripham-mer Rd, just e, then just n on Sheraton Dr (which becomes Cinema Dr). Int corridors. **Pets:** Other species. $100 one-time fee/room. Service with restrictions, supervision. [✕] [&M] [🛏] [💻] [≈] [✕]

▼▼ Ramada Inn Ithaca ⊞
(607) 257-3100. **$109-$339.** 2310 N Triphammer Rd 14850. SR 13, exit Triphammer Rd, just w; adjoins Triphammer Mall. Int corridors. **Pets:** Other species. $20 daily fee/room. Service with restrictions, crate. [ASK] [✕] [🛏] [🍴] [≈] [✕]

LATHAM

◬ ▼▼▼ The Century House, a Clarion Hotel ⊞
(518) 785-0931. **$130-$170.** 997 New Loudon Rd 12110. I-87, exit 7 (SR 7), just e, then 0.5 mi n on US 9. Int corridors. **Pets:** Accepted. [SAVE] [✕] [🛏] [💻] [🍴] [≈]

▼▼▼ Comfort Inn Albany Airport & Conference Center ⊞
(518) 783-1900. **$79-$99.** 20 Airport Park Blvd 12110. I-87, exit 4, 2.2 mi nw on Albany Shaker Rd. Int corridors. **Pets:** Accepted. [ASK] [✕] [🛏] [💻]

▼▼▼ Hotel Indigo ⊞
(518) 869-9100. **$99-$199.** 254 Old Wolf Rd 12110. I-87, exit 4, just w on Albany Shaker Rd. Int corridors. **Pets:** Accepted. [ASK] [✕] [&M] [🛏] [💻] [🍴]

◬ ▼▼▼ La Quinta Inn & Suites–Albany Airport ⊞ ❀
(518) 640-2200. **$90-$170.** 833 New Loudon Rd 12110. I-87, exit 7 (SR 7), just s on US 9 to Latham Cir, then just n on US 9. Int corridors. **Pets:** Medium, other species. Service with restrictions, supervision. [SAVE] [✕] [&M] [🛏] [💻] [≈]

◬ ▼▼▼ Microtel Inn, Albany Airport ⊞
(518) 782-9161. **$50-$169.** 7 Rensselaer Ave 12110. I-87, exit 6, just w. Int corridors. **Pets:** Medium. $10 daily fee/pet. Service with restrictions, supervision. [SAVE] [✕] [&M] [🛏] [💻]

◬ ▼▼▼ Quality Inn & Suites ⊞ ❀
(518) 785-5891. **$90-$150.** 611 Troy-Schenectady Rd 12110. I-87, exit 6, just w on SR 7. Ext/int corridors. **Pets:** Large, dogs only. $30 one-time fee/room. Designated rooms, service with restrictions, supervision. [SAVE] [✕] [🛏] [💻] [≈]

▼▼▼ Residence Inn by Marriott Albany Airport ⊞
(518) 783-0600. **$159-$209.** 1 Residence Inn Dr 12110. I-87, exit 6, 2 mi w on SR 7. Ext corridors. **Pets:** Other species. $75 one-time fee/room. Service with restrictions. [✕] [🛏] [💻] [≈] [✕]

◬ ▼▼▼ Travelodge Inn & Suites M
(518) 785-6626. **$69-$139.** 831 New Loudon Rd 12110. I-87, exit 6, just n of jct SR 2 and US 9. Ext corridors. **Pets:** Accepted. [SAVE] [✕] [🛏] [💻] [≈]

LITTLE FALLS

◬ ▼▼▼ Knights Inn of Little Falls ⊞
(315) 823-4954. **$75-$120, 3 day notice.** 20 Albany St 13365. On SR 5 and 167. Int corridors. **Pets:** Other species. $10 one-time fee/pet. Desig-nated rooms, service with restrictions, crate. [SAVE] [✕] [💻] [🍴]

LIVERPOOL

◬ ▼▼▼ Best Western Liverpool Grace Inn & Suites ⊞
(315) 701-4400. **$79-$210.** 136 Transistor Pkwy 13088. I-90, exit 37 (Electronics Pkwy), just n; I-81, exit 25 (7th North St), 1.3 mi w, just n on Electronics Pkwy, then just w. Int corridors. **Pets:** Small. $25 daily fee/pet. Service with restrictions, supervision. [SAVE] [✕] [🛏] [💻] [≈]

▼▼▼ Homewood Suites ⊞
(315) 451-3800. **$139-$199.** 275 Elwood Davis Rd 13088. I-81, exit 25 (7th North St), 1 mi w; I-90, exit 36. Int corridors. **Pets:** $100 one-time fee/room. Service with restrictions, crate. [✕] [&M] [🛏] [💻] [≈] [✕]

◬ ▼▼▼ Knights Inn M
(315) 453-6330. **$59-$189.** 430 Electronics Pkwy 13088. I-90, exit 37 (Electronics Pkwy), just w; I-81, exit 25 (7th North St), 1.3 mi nw, then just w. Ext corridors. **Pets:** Medium. $15 daily fee/pet. Designated rooms, service with restrictions, supervision. [SAVE] [✕]

◬ ▼▼▼ Super 8 Route 57 ⊞
(315) 451-8550. **$59-$119, 3 day notice.** 7360 Oswego Rd 13090. I-90, exit 38, 1 mi n on CR 57. Int corridors. **Pets:** Small, dogs only. $15 daily fee/pet. Service with restrictions, supervision. [SAVE] [✕] [💻]

MALONE

▼▼▼ Econo Lodge of Malone M
(518) 483-0500. **Call for rates.** 227 W Main St 12953. Just w of jct US 11 and SR 30. Ext/int corridors. **Pets:** Very small, dogs only. $10 daily fee/pet. Designated rooms, service with restrictions, supervision. [✕] [🛏]

◬ ▼▼▼ Four Seasons Motel M
(518) 483-3490. **$59-$99.** 206 W Main St 12953. 1 mi w on US 11. Ext corridors. **Pets:** Accepted. [SAVE] [✕] [🛏] [≈]

◬ ▼▼▼ Super 8 at Jons ⊞
(518) 483-8123. **$90-$150.** 42 Finney Blvd 12953. On SR 30, just s of jct US 11. Int corridors. **Pets:** Other species. Designated rooms, service with restrictions, supervision. [SAVE] [✕] [&M] [🛏] [💻]

MALTA

◬ ▼▼▼ Fairfield Inn & Suites Saratoga Malta ⊞
(518) 899-6900. **$109-$229.** 101 Saratoga Village Blvd 12020. I-87, exit 12, just e. Int corridors. **Pets:** Small, dogs only. $75 one-time fee/room. Service with restrictions, supervision. [SAVE] [✕] [&M] [🛏] [💻] [≈]

MANCHESTER

◬ ▼ Scottish Inns M
(585) 289-3811. **$49-$139.** 4078 Rt 96 14504. I-90, exit 43, just s, then just w. Ext/int corridors. **Pets:** Other species. $10 deposit/room, $10 one-time fee/pet. Service with restrictions. [SAVE] [✕] [🛏]

MASSENA

◬ ▼▼▼ Econo Lodge-Meadow View Motel ⊞
(315) 764-0246. **$65-$100.** 15054 SR 37 13662. On SR 37, 2.7 mi sw. Int corridors. **Pets:** $10 daily fee/pet. Service with restrictions, supervision. [SAVE] [✕] [🛏] [💻]

MCGRAW

◬ ▼▼▼ Cortland Days Inn ⊞
(607) 753-7594. **$54-$149.** 3775 US Rt 11 13101. I-81, exit 10 (McGraw/Cortland), just n. Int corridors. **Pets:** Accepted. [SAVE] [✕] [🛏] [💻]

MELVILLE

▼▼ Extended StayAmerica-Long Island-Melville ⊞
(631) 777-3999. **$105-$169.** 100 Spagnoli Rd 11747. I-495, exit 49S eastbound, 0.5 mi e on south service road, then 1.1 mi s on SR 110; exit westbound, 1.5 mi s on SR 110. Int corridors. **Pets:** Other species. $25 daily fee/room. Designated rooms, service with restrictions, crate. [ASK] [✕] [&M] [🛏] [💻]

▼▼▼ Hilton Long Island/Huntington ⬛ 🐾
(631) 845-1000. **$149-$379.** 598 Broad Hollow Rd (SR 110) 11747. I-495, exit 49, 1 mi s on SR 110. Int corridors. **Pets:** Medium, dogs only. $75 deposit/room. Service with restrictions, supervision.

⊠ 👟 🛏 💻 🍴 🏊 ⊠

MIDDLETOWN
▼▼ Microtel Inn & Suites ⬛
(845) 692-0098. **$59-$149.** 19 Crystal Run Crossing 10941. SR 17, exit 122, just nw. Int corridors. **Pets:** Accepted. 🅰️🆂🅺 ⊠ 👟 🛏 💻

MONTOUR FALLS
AAA ▼ Relax Inn Ⓜ
(607) 535-7183. **$45-$159, 4 day notice.** 100 Clawson Blvd 14865. Jct SR 14 and 224. Ext corridors. **Pets:** Small, dogs only. $10 daily fee/pet. Designated rooms, service with restrictions, supervision. 🆂🅰️🆅🅴 ⊠ 🛏

NEWARK
AAA ▼▼ Quality Inn Finger Lakes Region ⬛
(315) 331-9500. **$75-$130.** 125 N Main St 14513. Jct SR 31, just n on SR 88. Int corridors. **Pets:** Medium, other species. $25 deposit/room. Service with restrictions, crate. 🆂🅰️🆅🅴 ⊠ 🛏 💻 🍴 🏊

NEWBURGH
▼▼ Super 8 Ⓜ
(845) 564-5700. **$50-$150.** 1287 Rt 300 12550. I-87, exit 17, just w; I-84, exit 6, 2 mi e. Int corridors. **Pets:** Small, other species. $25 daily fee/pet. Designated rooms, service with restrictions, supervision.

🅰️🆂🅺 ⊠ 👟 🛏 💻

NEW HAMPTON
AAA ▼▼ Days Inn Ⓜ
(845) 374-2411. **$64-$130.** 4939 Rt 17M 10958. I-84, exit 3, 0.8 mi e on US 6 and SR 17M; SR 17, exit 123, 4 mi w. Ext/int corridors. **Pets:** Medium. $10 daily fee/pet. Service with restrictions, supervision.

🆂🅰️🆅🅴 ⊠ 🛏 💻 🏊

NEW HARTFORD
▼▼▼ Holiday Inn Utica ⬛
(315) 797-2131. **$89-$169.** 1777 Burrstone Rd 13413. I-90 (New York State Thruway), exit 31, 4.5 mi w on SR 5 W and 12 S, exit Burrstone Rd, then 1 mi nw. Int corridors. **Pets:** $35 one-time fee/room. Service with restrictions, supervision. 🄴🄲🄾 🅰️🆂🅺 ⊠ 👟 🛏 💻 🍴 🏊 ⊠

▼▼ Ramada ⬛
(315) 735-3392. **$89-$149.** 141 New Hartford St 13413. SR 8, 12 and 5, exit French Rd, just w, then just n. Int corridors. **Pets:** Medium. $20 daily fee/pet. Designated rooms, service with restrictions, supervision.

🅰️🆂🅺 ⊠ 🛏 💻 🍴 🏊

NEW PALTZ
▼▼ Rodeway Inn & Suites Ⓜ
(845) 883-7373. **$65-$200, 3 day notice.** 601 Main St (SR 299) 12561. I-87, exit 18, 0.5 mi e on SR 299. Ext/int corridors. **Pets:** Accepted.

🅰️🆂🅺 ⊠

NEW WINDSOR
▼▼▼ Homewood Suites by Hilton Newburgh-Stewart Airport ⬛
(845) 567-2700. **$119-$259.** 180 Breunig Rd 12553. 2.9 mi w on CR 69 (Union Ave), 1 mi w on Little Britain Rd (SR 207); at Stewart International Airport. Int corridors. **Pets:** Accepted. ⊠ 👟 🛏 💻 🏊 ⊠

NEW YORK METROPOLITAN AREA

ARMONK
▼▼▼ La Quinta Inn & Suites ⬛ 🐾
(914) 273-9090. **$79-$189.** 94 Business Park Dr 10504. I-684, exit 3S northbound; exit 3 southbound, 0.3 mi s on SR 22 to Business Park Dr. Int corridors. **Pets:** Medium, other species. Service with restrictions, supervision. 🅰️🆂🅺 ⊠ 🛏 💻 🍴

BROOKLYN
▼▼▼ Holiday Inn Express Brooklyn ⬛
(718) 797-1133. **$149-$319.** 625 Union St 11215. Between 3rd and 4th aves. Int corridors. **Pets:** Accepted. 🅰️🆂🅺 ⊠ 🛏 💻

▼▼▼ Holiday Inn Express Brooklyn Downtown ⬛
(718) 855-9600. **$149-$319.** 279 Butler St 11217. In Park Slope; between 3rd Ave and Nevins St. Int corridors. **Pets:** Accepted.

🅰️🆂🅺 ⊠ 🛏 💻

▼▼▼ Nu Hotel Brooklyn ⬛
(718) 852-8585. **$199-$399.** 85 Smith St 11201. Between Atlantic and State sts. Int corridors. **Pets:** Accepted. 🆂🅰️🆅🅴 ⊠ 🛏

CROTON-ON-HUDSON
▼▼▼ Alexander Hamilton House 🅱️🅱️
(914) 271-6737. **$125-$350, 7 day notice.** 49 Van Wyck St 10520. US 9, exit SR 129, e to light, n on Riverside, e on Grand, then n on Hamilton. Int corridors. **Pets:** Dogs only. $10 daily fee/pet. Designated rooms, service with restrictions, crate. ⊠ 🛏 🏊

EAST ELMHURST
AAA ▼▼▼ Courtyard by Marriott New York/La Guardia Airport ⬛
(718) 446-4800. **$269-$329.** 90-10 Grand Central Pkwy 11369. In East Elmhurst; Grand Central Pkwy, exit 6 (94th St) eastbound; exit 7 westbound, 0.5 mi s on 94th St to 23rd Ave, then just w to 90th St. Int corridors. **Pets:** Accepted. 🆂🅰️🆅🅴 ⊠ 👟 🛏 💻 🍴 🏊

ELMSFORD
▼▼▼ Extended StayAmerica-White Plains-Elmsford ⬛
(914) 347-8073. **$125-$169.** 118 Tarrytown Rd 10523. I-87, exit 8, just w. Int corridors. **Pets:** Other species. $25 daily fee/room. Designated rooms, service with restrictions, crate. 🅰️🆂🅺 ⊠ 👟 🛏 💻

FLUSHING
▼▼ Extended StayAmerica-NY City-La Guardia Airport ⬛
(718) 357-3661. **$135-$199.** 18-30 Whitestone 11357. In Flushing; I-678 (Van Wyck Expwy), exit 15, just w; in Whitestone. Int corridors. **Pets:** Other species. $25 daily fee/room. Designated rooms, service with restrictions, crate. 🅰️🆂🅺 ⊠ 🛏 💻

AAA ▼▼▼ Sheraton La Guardia East Hotel ⬛
(718) 460-6666. **Call for rates.** 135-20 39th Ave 11354. In Flushing; Grand Central Pkwy to Northern Blvd, 1 mi e to Main St, 0.3 mi s to 39th Ave, then just w. Int corridors. **Pets:** Accepted. 🆂🅰️🆅🅴 ⊠ 🛏 💻 🍴

JAMAICA

(AAA) ▼▼▼▼ Sheraton JFK Airport Hotel 🅷 ❀

(718) 322-7190. **Call for rates.** 132-26 S Conduit Ave 11430. In Jamaica; between S Conduit and 149th aves, off Nassau Expwy. Int corridors. **Pets:** Medium. Service with restrictions, crate.

[SAVE] [✕] [🛏] [▭] [🍴] [⊡]

MOUNT KISCO

▼▼▼ Holiday Inn 🅷

(914) 241-2600. **$119-$205.** 1 Holiday Inn Dr 10549. Saw Mill River Pkwy, exit 37, just e. Int corridors. **Pets:** Accepted.

[ASK] [✕] [🅼] [🛏] [▭] [🍴] [⊡]

NANUET

▼▼▼ Candlewood Suites 🅷

(845) 371-4445. **$115-$154.** 20 Overlook Blvd 10954. I-287/87 (New York State Thruway), exit 14 (SR 59 W) to New Clarkstown Rd. Int corridors. **Pets:** Accepted. [ASK] [✕] [🛏] [▭]

NEW YORK

(AAA) ▼▼▼▼ 70 Park Avenue Hotel 🅷

(212) 973-2400. **$299-$795.** 70 Park Ave 10016. At 38th St. Int corridors. **Pets:** Accepted. [SAVE] [✕] [🅼] [🍴]

(AAA) ▼▼▼▼ Affinia Dumont 🅷

(212) 481-7600. **$249-$689.** 150 E 34th St 10016. Between Lexington and 3rd aves. Int corridors. **Pets:** Accepted. [SAVE] [✕] [🛏] [▭] [🍴]

(AAA) ▼▼▼▼ Affinia 50 🅷

(212) 751-5710. **$189-$769.** 155 E 50th St 10022. Between 3rd and Lexington aves. Int corridors. **Pets:** Accepted. [SAVE] [✕] [🛏] [▭] [⊠]

(AAA) ▼▼▼▼ Affinia Gardens 🅷 ❀

(212) 355-1230. **$279-$769.** 215 E 64th St 10021. Between 2nd and 3rd aves. Int corridors. **Pets:** Other species. $25 one-time fee/room. Service with restrictions. [SAVE] [✕] [🛏] [▭] [⊠]

(AAA) ▼▼▼▼ Affinia Manhattan 🅷 ❀

(212) 563-1800. **$199-$519, 7 day notice.** 371 7th Ave 10001. At 31st St. Int corridors. **Pets:** Other species. $25 one-time fee/pet. Service with restrictions. [SAVE] [✕] [🛏] [▭] [🍴]

(AAA) ▼▼▼▼ Affinia Shelburne 🅷

(212) 689-5200. **$179-$669.** 303 Lexington Ave 10016. Between 37th and 38th sts. Int corridors. **Pets:** Accepted. [SAVE] [✕] [🛏] [▭] [🍴]

(AAA) ▼▼▼ The Alex 🅷

(212) 867-5100. **$350-$3700.** 205 E 45th St 10017. At 3rd Ave. Int corridors. **Pets:** Large. $250 deposit/room. Service with restrictions. [SAVE] [✕] [🛏] [🍴]

(AAA) ▼▼▼▼ Algonquin Hotel 🅷 🐾

(212) 840-6800. **$199-$950.** 59 W 44th St 10036. Between 5th and 6th (Ave of the Americas) aves. Int corridors. **Pets:** Medium, other species. Service with restrictions, supervision. [ECO] [SAVE] [✕] [🛏] [🍴]

▼▼▼ Beekman Tower Hotel 🅷

(212) 355-7300. **Call for rates.** 3 Mitchell Pl 10017. Jct 49th St and 1st Ave. Int corridors. **Pets:** Accepted. [ECO] [✕] [🛏] [▭] [🍴]

(AAA) ▼▼▼▼ The Benjamin Hotel 🅷

(212) 715-2500. **$239-$869.** 125 E 50th St 10022. Between Lexington and 3rd aves. Int corridors. **Pets:** Accepted.

[SAVE] [✕] [🛏] [▭] [🍴] [⊠]

(AAA) ▼▼▼ Best Western Seaport Inn Downtown 🅷

(212) 766-6600. **$199-$409.** 33 Peck Slip on Front St 10038. North end of South St Seaport. Int corridors. **Pets:** Accepted. [SAVE] [✕] [🛏] [▭]

▼▼▼▼ The Carlyle, a Rosewood Hotel 🅷

(212) 744-1600. **$450-$1050.** 35 E 76th St 10021. At Madison Ave. Int corridors. **Pets:** Accepted. [ASK] [✕] [🛏] [▭] [🍴] [⊠]

▼▼▼ Comfort Inn–Times Square 🅷

(212) 268-3040. **$189-$389.** 305 W 39th St 10018. At 8th Ave. Int corridors. **Pets:** Accepted. [ASK] [✕] [🛏] [▭]

▼▼▼▼ Doubletree Guest Suites Times Square-New York City 🅷

(212) 719-1600. **$199-$749.** 1568 Broadway 10036. 47th St and 7th Ave. Int corridors. **Pets:** Accepted. [✕] [🅼] [🛏] [▭] [🍴]

(AAA) ▼▼▼▼ Duane Street Hotel 🅷

(212) 964-4600. **Call for rates.** 130 Duane St 10013. Between Church and W Broadway. Int corridors. **Pets:** Accepted. [SAVE] [✕] [🍴]

(AAA) ▼▼▼▼ Eastgate Tower Hotel 🅷

(212) 687-8000. **$179-$559.** 222 E 39th St 10016. Between 2nd and 3rd aves. Int corridors. **Pets:** Accepted. [SAVE] [✕] [🅼] [🛏] [▭]

▼▼▼▼▼ Four Seasons Hotel New York 🅷

(212) 758-5700. **Call for rates.** 57 E 57th St 10022. Between Park and Madison aves. Int corridors. **Pets:** Accepted. [✕] [🅼] [🛏] [🍴] [⊠]

(AAA) ▼▼▼▼ The Franklin Hotel 🅷

(212) 369-1000. **$229-$469.** 164 E 87th St 10128. Between 3rd and Lexington aves. Int corridors. **Pets:** Accepted. [SAVE] [✕] [🛏]

(AAA) ▼▼▼▼ Hampton Inn-Madison Square Garden Area 🅷

(212) 947-9700. **Call for rates.** 116 W 31st St 10001. Between 6th (Ave of the Americas) and 7th aves. Int corridors. **Pets:** Small. $50 one-time fee/room. Service with restrictions, supervision. [SAVE] [✕] [🛏] [▭]

(AAA) ▼▼▼▼ Hampton Inn-Manhattan/Chelsea 🅷

(212) 414-1000. **Call for rates.** 108 W 24th St 10011. Between 6th (Ave of the Americas) and 7th aves. Int corridors. **Pets:** Accepted.

[SAVE] [✕] [🛏] [▭]

(AAA) ▼▼▼▼ Hampton Inn-Manhattan/Seaport/Financial District 🅷

(212) 571-4400. **Call for rates.** 320 Pearl St 10038. Between deck slip and Dover St. Int corridors. **Pets:** Accepted. [SAVE] [✕] [🛏] [▭]

(AAA) ▼▼▼▼ Hampton Inn Manhattan/Times Square South 🅷

(212) 967-2344. **$209-$509.** 337 W 39th St 10018. Between 8th and 9th aves. Int corridors. **Pets:** Accepted. [SAVE] [✕] [▭]

▼▼▼▼ Hilton Club New York 🅷

(646) 459-6500. **$459-$829.** 1335 Ave of the Americas, 37th Flr 10019. W 54th St; between 6th and 7th aves. Int corridors. **Pets:** Accepted.

[✕] [▭] [🍴] [⊠]

(AAA) ▼▼▼▼ Hilton Garden Inn New York City/Tribeca 🅷

(212) 966-4091. **$179-$499.** 6 York St 10013. Jct 6th Ave (Ave of the Americas). Int corridors. **Pets:** Accepted. [SAVE] [✕] [🛏] [▭] [🍴]

▼▼▼▼ Hilton New York 🅷

(212) 586-7000. **$219-$429.** 1335 Ave of the Americas 10019. Between 53rd and 54th sts. Int corridors. **Pets:** Accepted.

[✕] [🛏] [▭] [🍴] [⊠]

(AAA) ▼▼▼▼ Hilton Times Square 🅷 🐾

(212) 840-8222. **$229-$1499.** 234 W 42nd St 10036. Between 7th and 8th aves. Int corridors. **Pets:** Medium. $75 one-time fee/room. Service with restrictions, crate. [SAVE] [✕] [🅼] [🛏] [▭] [🍴]

▼▼▼▼ Holiday Inn Express Fifth Ave 🅷

(212) 302-9088. **Call for rates.** 15 W 45th St 10036. At 5th Ave. Int corridors. **Pets:** Accepted. [✕] [🛏] [▭]

▼▼▼ Holiday Inn Express Manhattan/Madison Square Garden 🅷
(212) 695-7200. **Call for rates.** 232 W 29th St 10001. Between 7th and 8th aves. Int corridors. **Pets:** Accepted. [SAVE] [✕] [▣]

⟳ ▼▼ Hotel 373 Fifth Avenue 🅷
(212) 213-3388. **$179-$399.** 373 Fifth Ave 10016. Jct 35th St. Int corridors. **Pets:** Accepted. [SAVE] [✕]

▼▼▼▼ Hotel Gansevoort 🅷
(212) 660-6700. **Call for rates.** 18 9th Ave 10014. At 13th St. Int corridors. **Pets:** Accepted. [✕] [⅄M] [🛏] [🍴] [⤴]

▼▼▼▼ Hotel Plaza Athenee 🅷 ❀
(212) 734-9100. **$875-$1250.** 37 E 64th St 10065. Between Madison and Park aves. Int corridors. **Pets:** Small, dogs only. $60 daily fee/room.
[✕] [🛏] [🍴] [✕]

⟳ ▼▼▼ Hotel Wales 🅷
(212) 876-6000. **$215-$595.** 1295 Madison Ave 10128. Between 92nd and 93rd sts E. Int corridors. **Pets:** $75 one-time fee/room. Service with restrictions, supervision. [SAVE] [✕] [🛏] [🍴] [✕]

⟳ ▼▼▼ Jolly Hotel Madison Towers 🅷
(212) 802-0600. **$188-$830.** 22 E 38th St 10016. Between Park and Madison aves. Int corridors. **Pets:** Small. Service with restrictions, supervision. [SAVE] [✕] [▣]

▼▼▼ Jumeirah-Essex House 🅷
(212) 247-0300. **Call for rates.** 160 Central Park S 10019. Between 6th (Ave of the Americas) and 7th aves. Int corridors. **Pets:** Accepted.
[✕] [⅄M] [🛏] [🍴] [✕]

⟳ ▼▼▼ La Quinta Inn Manhattan 🅷 ❀
(212) 736-1600. **$119-$510.** 17 W 32nd St 10001. Between 5th Ave and Broadway. Int corridors. **Pets:** Medium, other species. Service with restrictions, supervision. [SAVE] [✕] [▣]

▼▼▼ Le Parker Meridien New York 🅷
(212) 245-5000. **$289-$1129.** 118 W 57th St 10019. Between 6th (Ave of the Americas) and 7th aves; vehicle entrance on 56th St. Int corridors.
Pets: Accepted. [✕] [🛏] [🍴] [⤴] [✕]

⟳ ▼▼▼▼ Loews Regency Hotel 🅷 ❀
(212) 759-4100. **$489-$4500.** 540 Park Ave 10021. At 61st St. Int corridors. **Pets:** Other species. $25 one-time fee/room. Service with restrictions. [SAVE] [✕] [⅄M] [🛏] [▣] [🍴]

⟳ ▼▼▼▼ The London NYC 🅷
(212) 307-5000. **$299-$999, 3 day notice.** 151 W 54th St 10019. Between 6th (Ave of the Americas) and 7th aves. Int corridors.
Pets: Accepted. [SAVE] [✕] [🍴]

⟳ ▼▼▼ The Lowell Hotel 🅷 ❀
(212) 838-1400. **$625-$985, 3 day notice.** 28 E 63rd St 10021. Between Park and Madison aves. Int corridors. **Pets:** Medium. $125 one-time fee/room. Supervision. [SAVE] [✕] [🛏] [▣] [🍴] [✕]

⟳ ▼▼▼ Mandarin Oriental, New York 🅷
(212) 805-8800. **$955-$1435.** 80 Columbus Cir at 60th St 10023. At 60th St. Int corridors. **Pets:** Accepted. [SAVE] [✕] [🍴] [⤴]

⟳ ▼▼▼ The Mansfield 🅷
(212) 277-8700. **$199-$599.** 12 W 44th St 10036. Between 5th and 6th (Ave of the Americas) aves. Int corridors. **Pets:** Accepted.
[SAVE] [✕] [🛏] [🍴]

⟳ ▼▼▼▼ Millenium Hilton 🅷
(212) 693-2001. **$159-$419.** 55 Church St 10007. Between Dey and Fulton sts. Int corridors. **Pets:** Accepted.
[SAVE] [✕] [🛏] [▣] [🍴] [⤴] [✕]

▼▼▼ Millennium Broadway 🅷
(212) 768-4400. **$299-$999.** 145 W 44th St 10036. Between 6th (Ave of the Americas) and 7th aves; in Times Square. Int corridors.
Pets: Accepted. [ASK] [✕] [⅄M] [▣] [🍴] [✕]

⟳ ▼▼▼ The Muse Hotel 🅷
(212) 485-2400. **Call for rates.** 130 W 46th St 10036. Between 6th (Ave of the Americas) and 7th aves. Int corridors. **Pets:** Accepted.
[SAVE] [✕] [🍴] [✕]

⟳ ▼▼▼ The New York Helmsley Hotel 🅷
(212) 490-8900. **$250-$525.** 212 E 42nd St 10017. Between 2nd and 3rd aves. Int corridors. **Pets:** Accepted. [SAVE] [✕] [🛏] [🍴]

▼▼▼ New York Marriott Marquis 🅷
(212) 398-1900. **$299-$499.** 1535 Broadway 10036. Between 45th and 46th sts; motor entrance on 46th St. Int corridors. **Pets:** Accepted.
[✕] [🛏] [🍴]

⟳ ▼▼▼ The New York Palace 🅷
(212) 888-7000. **Call for rates.** 455 Madison Ave 10022. Between 50th and 51st sts. Int corridors. **Pets:** Accepted.
[SAVE] [✕] [⅄M] [🛏] [▣] [🍴] [✕]

⟳ ▼▼▼ Novotel New York 🅷
(212) 315-0100. **Call for rates.** 226 W 52nd St 10019. At Broadway. Int corridors. **Pets:** Accepted. [SAVE] [✕] [🛏] [🍴]

⟳ ▼▼▼ On The Ave Hotel 🅷
(212) 362-1100. **$129-$299.** 2178 Broadway 10024. At 77th St. Int corridors. **Pets:** Accepted. [SAVE] [✕] [🛏] [▣] [🍴]

▼▼▼ The Paramount Hotel New York 🅷
(212) 764-5500. **Call for rates.** 235 W 46th St 10036. Between Broadway and 8th Ave. Int corridors. **Pets:** Accepted. [✕] [🍴]

⟳ ▼▼▼ The Peninsula New York 🅷 ❀
(212) 956-2888. **$595-$975.** 700 5th Ave 10019. At 55th St. Int corridors. **Pets:** Other species. Service with restrictions, supervision.
[SAVE] [✕] [🛏] [🍴] [⤴] [✕]

⟳ ▼▼▼ The Pierre New York-A Taj Hotel 🅷 ❀
(212) 838-8000. **$695-$940.** 2 E 61st St 10065. At 5th Ave. Int corridors. **Pets:** Very small. Service with restrictions, crate.
[SAVE] [✕] [🛏] [🍴] [✕]

⟳ ▼▼▼ The Plaza Hotel 🅷 ❀
(212) 759-3000. **$595-$1150.** 5th Ave at Central Park S 10019. Corner of 5th Ave and Central Park S. Int corridors. **Pets:** Small. $200 deposit/room. Service with restrictions, crate. [SAVE] [✕] [⅄M] [🛏] [🍴]

⟳ ▼▼▼ Radisson Martinique on Broadway 🅷 ❀
(212) 736-3800. **$189-$499.** 49 W 32nd St 10001. Between Broadway and 5th Ave. Int corridors. **Pets:** Small, dogs only. $100 deposit/pet, $25 daily fee/pet. Service with restrictions, supervision.
[SAVE] [✕] [⅄M] [🛏] [▣]

⟳ ▼▼▼ Red Roof Inn Manhattan 🅷 ❀
(212) 643-7100. **$120-$510.** 6 W 32nd St 10001. Between Broadway and 5th Ave. Int corridors. **Pets:** Dogs only. $25 one-time fee/room. Designated rooms, service with restrictions, supervision. [SAVE] [✕] [🛏] [▣]

⟳ ▼▼▼ Renaissance New York Hotel Times Square 🅷
(212) 765-7676. **$299-$499.** 2 Times Square, 7th Ave at W 48th St 10036. Broadway and 7th Ave; auto access from 7th Ave, s of W 48th St. Int corridors. **Pets:** Medium, other species. $250 one-time fee/room. Service with restrictions, supervision. [SAVE] [✕] [▣] [🍴]

▼▼▼ **Residence Inn by Marriott New York Manhattan/Times Square** H
(212) 768-0007. **$279-$479.** 1033 6th Ave (Ave of the Americas) 10018. Between 38th and 39th sts. Int corridors. **Pets:** Other species. $100 one-time fee/room. Service with restrictions, crate. ⊠ ▤ ▭

ⒶⒶⒶ ▼▼▼ **The Ritz-Carlton New York, Battery Park** H
(212) 344-0800. **Call for rates.** Two West St 10004. Jct Battery Park. Int corridors. **Pets:** Accepted. SAVE ⊠ 𝕭ᴹ ▤ ⑪

ⒶⒶⒶ ▼▼▼ **The Ritz-Carlton New York, Central Park** H ☙
(212) 308-9100. **$565-$1905.** 50 Central Park S 10019. Jct 59th St (Central Park S) and 6th Ave (Ave of the Americas). Int corridors. **Pets:** Medium. $125 one-time fee/room. Service with restrictions.
SAVE ⊠ 𝕭ᴹ ▤ ⑪ ⊠

ⒶⒶⒶ ▼▼▼ **Sheraton Manhattan at Times Square** H
(212) 581-3300. **$199-$549.** 790 7th Ave 10019. Between 51st and 52nd sts. Int corridors. **Pets:** Accepted. SAVE ⊠ 𝕭ᴹ ▤ ▭ ⑪ ⊃

ⒶⒶⒶ ▼▼▼ **Sheraton New York Hotel & Towers** H ☙
(212) 581-1000. **$199-$549.** 811 7th Ave 10019. At 52nd St. Int corridors. **Pets:** Medium. Service with restrictions, crate.
SAVE ⊠ 𝕭ᴹ ▤ ▭ ⑪ ⊠

ⒶⒶⒶ ▼▼▼ **The Shoreham Hotel** H
(212) 247-6700. **$249-$499.** 33 W 55th St 10019. Between 5th and 6th (Ave of the Americas) aves. Int corridors. **Pets:** Accepted. SAVE ⊠ ⑪

▼▼▼ **Skyline Hotel** H ☙
(212) 586-3400. **$119-$450.** 725 10th Ave 10019. At 49th and 50th sts. Int corridors. **Pets:** $200 deposit/room. Service with restrictions, crate.
ASK ⊠ ⑪ ⊃

ⒶⒶⒶ ▼▼▼ ▼▼▼ **Sofitel Luxury Hotels New York** H
(212) 354-8844. **$395-$3000.** 45 W 44th St 10036. Between 5th and 6th (Ave of the Americas) aves. Int corridors. **Pets:** Accepted.
SAVE ⊠ ▤ ⑪ ⊠

▼▼▼ **The SoHo Grand Hotel** H
(212) 965-3000. **Call for rates.** 310 W Broadway 10013. In SoHo; jct Grand St. Int corridors. **Pets:** Accepted. ⊠ ⑪

▼▼▼ ▼▼▼ **Trump International Hotel & Tower** H ☙
(212) 299-1000. **$825-$875, 3 day notice.** 1 Central Park W 10023. Jct Central Park S; at Columbus Cir. Int corridors. **Pets:** Small, dogs only. $250 one-time fee/room. Service with restrictions.
⊠ ▤ ⑪ ⊠

ⒶⒶⒶ ▼▼▼ ▼▼▼ **The Westin New York at Times Square** H ☙
(212) 201-2700. **$249-$849, 3 day notice.** 270 W 43rd St 10036. Corner of 8th Ave. Int corridors. **Pets:** Small, dogs only. Designated rooms, service with restrictions, crate. ECO SAVE ⊠ 𝕭ᴹ ▤ ▭ ⑪ ⊠

ⒶⒶⒶ ▼▼▼ **W New York** H
(212) 755-1200. **$229-$729.** 541 Lexington Ave 10022. At 49th St. Int corridors. **Pets:** Accepted. SAVE ⊠ 𝕭ᴹ ▤ ⑪

ⒶⒶⒶ ▼▼▼ **W New York Times Square** H
(212) 930-7400. **$269-$869.** 1567 Broadway at 47th St 10036. Corner of 47th St. Int corridors. **Pets:** Accepted. SAVE ⊠ 𝕭ᴹ ▤ ⑪

ⒶⒶⒶ ▼▼▼ ▼▼▼ **W New York-Union Square** H
(212) 253-9119. **$329-$929.** 201 Park Ave S 10003. At 17th St. Int corridors. **Pets:** Accepted. SAVE ⊠ 𝕭ᴹ ▤ ⑪ ⊠

ⒶⒶⒶ ▼▼▼ **Wyndham Garden Hotel Times Square South** H
(212) 542-8990. **$159-$549.** 341 W 36th St 10018. Between 8th and 9th aves. Int corridors. **Pets:** Accepted. SAVE ⊠ ▤ ▭ ⑪

ORANGEBURG

ⒶⒶⒶ ▼▼▼ **Holiday Inn** H
(845) 359-7000. **$115-$175.** 329 Rt 303 10962. I-87/287, exit 12, 4 mi s on SR 303; 1 mi n of Palisades Interstate Pkwy, exit 5 northbound; 1 mi e of exit 6. Int corridors. **Pets:** Accepted. SAVE ⊠ ▤ ▭ ⑪ ⊃

PEARL RIVER

▼▼▼ **Hilton Pearl River** H ☙
(845) 735-9000. **$149-$279.** 500 Veterans Memorial Dr 10965. Palisades Interstate Pkwy, exit 6, 2.5 mi w on CR 20 (Veterans Memorial Dr). Int corridors. **Pets:** Large. $75 one-time fee/room. Service with restrictions.
⊠ 𝕭ᴹ ▤ ▭ ⑪ ⊃ ⊠

RYE BROOK

ⒶⒶⒶ ▼▼▼ **Hilton Rye Town** H
(914) 939-6300. **$119-$249.** 699 Westchester Ave 10573. I-287 (Cross Westchester Expwy), exit 10 eastbound, 0.6 mi ne on SR 120A; exit westbound, 0.3 mi n on Webb Ave, then 0.4 mi ne on SR 120A. Int corridors. **Pets:** Accepted. SAVE ⊠ 𝕭ᴹ ▤ ▭ ⑪ ⊃ ⊠

STATEN ISLAND

ⒶⒶⒶ ▼▼▼ **Hilton Garden Inn Staten Island** H ☙
(718) 477-2400. **$159-$199.** 1100 South Ave 10314. I-278, exit 6 (South Ave) westbound, just s; exit 5 eastbound to SR 440 S, exit South Ave, just s to South Ave, 1 mi n to Lois Ln, then just w. Int corridors. **Pets:** Medium, dogs only. $35 daily fee/pet. Service with restrictions, supervision. SAVE ⊠ ▤ ▭ ⑪ ⊃ ⊠

ⒶⒶⒶ ▼▼▼ **The Staten Island Hotel** H
(718) 698-5000. **$159-$208.** 1415 Richmond Ave 10314. I-278, exit Richmond Ave, 0.5 mi se. Int corridors. **Pets:** Accepted.
SAVE ⊠ ▤ ▭ ⑪

SUFFERN

ⒶⒶⒶ ▼▼▼ **Holiday Inn-Suffern** H
(845) 357-4800. **$99-$119.** 3 Executive Blvd 10901. I-87 (New York State Thruway), exit 14B, just n. Int corridors. **Pets:** Accepted.
SAVE ⊠ ▤ ▭ ⑪ ⊃ ⊠

TARRYTOWN

ⒶⒶⒶ ▼▼▼ **Sheraton Tarrytown Hotel** H ☙
(914) 332-7900. **Call for rates.** 600 White Plains Rd 10591. I-87, exit 9 northbound, 0.8 mi e on SR 119; exit southbound, just n on US 9, then 1 mi e on SR 119. Int corridors. **Pets:** Small, dogs only. $50 one-time fee/room. Service with restrictions, supervision.
SAVE ⊠ 𝕭ᴹ ▭ ⑪ ⊃

▼▼▼ **Westchester Marriott Hotel** H
(914) 631-2200. **$219-$249.** 670 White Plains Rd 10591. I-87 (New York State Thruway), exit 9 northbound, 0.8 mi e on SR 119; exit southbound, just n on US 9, then 1 mi e on SR 119. Int corridors. **Pets:** Accepted.
ECO ⊠ ▤ ▭ ⑪ ⊃ ⊠

WHITE PLAINS

ⒶⒶⒶ ▼▼▼ **Hyatt Summerfield Suites White Plains** H
(914) 251-9700. **$129-$329.** 101 Corporate Park Dr 10604. I-287 (Cross Westchester Expwy), exit 9A eastbound, 0.6 mi e on Westchester Ave, then 0.3 mi n; exit 9N-S westbound, 0.9 mi w on Westchester Ave. Int corridors. **Pets:** Large. $100 one-time fee/room. Service with restrictions.
SAVE ⊠ ▤ ▭ ⊃ ⊠

The Ritz-Carlton, Westchester H ❀
(914) 946-5500. **$199-$569.** 3 Renaissance Square 10601. Jct SR 22, just w on Main St, then just n. Int corridors. **Pets:** Medium. $125 one-time fee/room. Service with restrictions, supervision.

ECO SAVE ✕ &M 🖥 ¶¶ ⊇ ✕

END METROPOLITAN AREA

NIAGARA FALLS METROPOLITAN AREA

LOCKPORT
Comfort Inn H
(716) 434-4411. **$60-$160.** 551 S Transit St 14094. 1 mi s on SR 78. Int corridors. **Pets:** Medium. $10 daily fee/pet. Service with restrictions, supervision. SAVE ✕ &M 🖥 🖥

Holiday Inn Lockport H
(716) 434-6151. **$99-$159.** 515 S Transit St 14094. 1 mi s on SR 78. Int corridors. **Pets:** Other species. $10 daily fee/pet. Service with restrictions, supervision. SAVE ✕ &M 🖥 🖥 ¶¶ ⊇

NEWFANE
Lake Ontario Motel M
(716) 778-5004. **$59-$100.** 3330 Lockport-Olcott Rd 14108. 2.5 mi n of jct SR 104 on SR 78. Int corridors. **Pets:** Other species. $5 daily fee/room. Service with restrictions, supervision. ASK ✕ 🖥

NIAGARA FALLS
Holiday Inn Express Niagara Falls H
(716) 298-4500. **$80-$220.** 10111 Niagara Falls Blvd 14304. I-190, exit 22, 2.1 mi e on US 62. Int corridors. **Pets:** Small. $50 daily fee/pet. Designated rooms, service with restrictions, supervision.

SAVE ✕ 🖥 🖥 ⊇

Howard Johnson Inn Closest to the Falls H ❀
(716) 285-5261. **$59-$275.** 454 Main St 14301. I-190, exit 21 (Robert Moses Pkwy), eastbound to City Traffic exit, just n to Rainbow Blvd, then just w. Int corridors. **Pets:** Other species. $15 daily fee/pet. Service with restrictions, crate. SAVE ✕ &M 🖥 🖥 ⊇

Motel 6 M
(716) 205-8886. **$40-$200.** 9100 Niagara Falls 14304. I-190, exit 22, 1.8 mi e. Int corridors. **Pets:** Other species. Service with restrictions, supervision. ASK ✕ 🖥

Quality Hotel & Suites "At the Falls" H
(716) 282-1212. **Call for rates.** 240 First St 14303. I-190, exit 21 (Robert Moses Pkwy), eastbound to City Traffic exit, just w; downtown. Int corridors. **Pets:** Accepted. ✕ 🖥 🖥 ¶¶ ⊇

END METROPOLITAN AREA

NORTH HORNELL
Econo Lodge M
(607) 324-0800. **$50-$95.** 7462 Seneca Rd 14843. Jct I-86 and SR 36, exit 34, just s to SR 21, just e to Seneca Rd, then just s. Ext/int corridors. **Pets:** Other species. $10 daily fee/pet. Service with restrictions, supervision. SAVE ✕ 🖥 🖥 ¶¶

NORTH SYRACUSE
Budget Inn M
(315) 458-3510. **$49-$120, 7 day notice.** 901 S Bay Rd 13212. I-481, exit 10, just n. Ext corridors. **Pets:** Small, dogs only. $10 daily fee/pet. Service with restrictions, supervision. SAVE ✕ 🖥 🖥

Candlewood Suites Syracuse Airport H
(315) 454-8999. **$109-$134.** 5414 South Bay Rd 13212. I-90, exit 36; I-81, exit 26 (Mattydale Rd), follow South Bay Rd signs, just n. Int corridors. **Pets:** Accepted. ASK ✕ 🖥 🖥

Comfort Inn & Suites/Syracuse Airport H
(315) 457-4000. **$95-$134.** 6701 Buckley Rd 13212. I-81, exit 25 (7th North St), just w. Int corridors. **Pets:** Accepted.

ASK ✕ 🖥 🖥 ⊇ ✕

NORWICH
Super 8 of Norwich H
(607) 336-8880. **$60-$110.** 6067 State Hwy 12 13815. On SR 12, 0.9 mi n. Int corridors. **Pets:** Accepted. ASK ✕ 🖥 🖥

OGDENSBURG
Quality Inn Gran-View M
(315) 393-4550. **$78-$188.** 6765 State Hwy 37 13669. On SR 37, 3 mi sw. Ext/int corridors. **Pets:** Other species. $10 daily fee/room. Designated rooms, service with restrictions, crate.
SAVE ✕ 🖥 🖥 ¶¶ ⊇ ✕

The Stonefence Resort & Motel M
(315) 393-1545. **$69-$199.** 7191 SR 37 13669. Jct SR 68, 0.5 mi w. Ext/int corridors. **Pets:** Small. $15 one-time fee/room. Service with restrictions, supervision. SAVE ✕ 🖥 🖥 ⊇ ✕

Windjammer Lodge M
(315) 393-6300. **$80-$175.** 5843 SR 37 13669. On SR 37, 5 mi sw. Ext corridors. **Pets:** Other species. $10 daily fee/room. Service with restrictions, crate. SAVE ✕ 🖥 🖥 ⊇

OLD FORGE
Adirondack Lodge Old Forge M
(315) 369-6836. **$59-$299, 7 day notice.** 2752 SR 28 13420. 0.3 mi s. Ext/int corridors. **Pets:** Accepted. ASK ✕ 🖥 🖥 ⊇

ONEIDA
Super 8-Oneida H
(315) 363-5168. **$66-$110.** 215 Genesee St 13421. I-90, exit 33, 4 mi s on SR 365 to SR 5, then 0.5 mi w. Int corridors. **Pets:** Other species. $10 one-time fee/pet. Supervision. ASK ✕ 🖥 🖥

ONEONTA

AAA **WWWW** Holiday Inn Oneonta/Cooperstown Area **H**
(607) 433-2250. **$79-$259, 3 day notice.** 5206 State Hwy 23 13820-0634. I-88, exit 15 (SR 23 and 28), 1.5 mi e. Int corridors. **Pets:** Small. $25 one-time fee/room. Designated rooms, service with restrictions, supervision. [SAVE] [X] [&M] [H] [D] [TI] [A] [X]

WWW Super 8 **H**
(607) 432-9505. **$115-$200.** 4973 SR 23 13820. I-88, exit 15 (SR 23 and 28), 0.3 mi e. Int corridors. **Pets:** $10 daily fee/pet. Service with restrictions, supervision. [ASK] [X] [&M] [H] [D]

OWEGO

AAA **WW** Sunrise Motel **M**
(607) 687-5667. **$55-$65.** 3778 Waverly Rd 13827. SR 17, exit 64 (SR 96 N), across river, w to SR 17C, 2 mi w. Ext corridors. **Pets:** Accepted. [SAVE] [X]

PAINTED POST

AAA **WWW** Americas Best Value Inn Lodge on the Green **M** ❖
(607) 962-2456. **$76-$160.** 196 S Hamilton St 14870. SR 17, exit 44B eastbound; exit 44A westbound; US 15, exit 3, 1 mi n. Ext corridors. **Pets:** $10 one-time fee/room. Service with restrictions, supervision.
[SAVE] [X] [H] [D] [A]

WWW Econo Lodge **H**
(607) 962-4444. **$89-$139.** 200 Robert Dann Dr 14870. I-86, exit 44; US 15, exit 3 (Gang Mills), just n on Hamilton St, then just w. Int corridors. **Pets:** $10 daily fee/pet. Service with restrictions, supervision.
[ASK] [X] [&M] [H] [D]

AAA **WW** Erwin Motel **M** ❖
(607) 962-7411. **$29-$99.** 806 Addison Rd 14870. US 15, exit SR 417, just e. Ext corridors. **Pets:** Medium, dogs only. $10 daily fee. Designated rooms, service with restrictions, supervision. [SAVE] [X] [H] [A]

AAA **WWW** Ramada Inn **H**
(607) 962-5021. **$110-$260, 7 day notice.** 304 S Hamilton St 14870. I-86, exit 44, to US 15 S, exit 3, then just n. Int corridors. **Pets:** Accepted. [SAVE] [X] [&M] [H] [D] [TI] [A]

PEMBROKE

WWW Darien Lakes Econo Lodge **H**
(585) 599-4681. **$59-$159.** 8493 SR 77 14036. I-90, exit 48A, just s. Int corridors. **Pets:** Accepted. [ASK] [X] [H] [D]

PENN YAN

AAA **WWWW** Best Western Vineyard Inn & Suites **H**
(315) 536-8473. **$100-$170.** 142 Lake St 14527. I-90, exit 43, SR 14 S to SR 54 N; corner of SR 54 and 14A. Int corridors. **Pets:** $10 daily fee/pet. Service with restrictions, supervision. [SAVE] [X] [H] [D] [A]

PINE VALLEY

AAA **WWW** Best Western Marshall Manor **M**
(607) 739-3891. **$82-$114.** 3527 Watkins Rd 14845. I-86, exit 52B, 5 mi n on SR 14. Ext corridors. **Pets:** $15 daily fee/pet. Designated rooms, service with restrictions, supervision. [SAVE] [X] [H] [D] [A]

PLAINVIEW

AAA **WWWW** Homewood Suites Long Island Melville **H**
(516) 293-4663. **$129-$229.** 1585 Round Swamp Rd 11803. I-495, exit 48, just s. Int corridors. **Pets:** Large. $150 one-time fee/room. Service with restrictions, supervision. [SAVE] [X] [&M] [H] [D] [A] [X]

WWWW Residence Inn Plainview Long Island **H**
(516) 433-6200. **$195-$215.** 9 Gerhard Rd 11803. I-495, exit 44, 1.6 mi s on SR 135, exit 10, then just e on Old Country Rd. Int corridors.
Pets: Accepted. [X] [&M] [H] [D] [TI] [A] [X]

PLATTSBURGH

AAA **WWW** Best Western The Inn at Smithfield **H** ❖
(518) 561-7750. **$89-$139.** 446 Rt 3 12901. I-87, exit 37, just w. Int corridors. **Pets:** Other species. $25 one-time fee/room. Designated rooms, service with restrictions, supervision. [SAVE] [X] [H] [D] [TI] [A]

WWWW La Quinta Inn & Suites Plattsburgh **H** ❖
(518) 562-4000. **$62-$139.** 16 Plaza Blvd 12901. I-87, exit 37, just w. Int corridors. **Pets:** Medium, other species. Service with restrictions, supervision. [ASK] [X] [&M] [H] [D] [A]

WWW Microtel Inn & Suites **H**
(518) 324-3800. **$84-$139.** 554 SR 3 12901. I-87, exit 37, just w. Int corridors. **Pets:** Medium. $10 daily fee/room. Service with restrictions, supervision. [ASK] [X] [&M] [H] [D]

WW Super 8 **M**
(518) 562-8888. **$60-$99.** 7129 Rt 9 N 12901. I-87, exit 39, just e, then just n. Int corridors. **Pets:** Accepted. [ASK] [X] [&M] [H] [D] [A]

PORT JERVIS

AAA **WWW** Comfort Inn **H**
(845) 856-6611. **$59-$139.** 2247 Greenville Tpke 12771. I-84, exit 1, just se. Int corridors. **Pets:** Accepted. [SAVE] [X] [H] [D] [A]

POUGHKEEPSIE

AAA **WW** Days Inn **M**
(845) 454-1010. **$69-$249.** 536 Haight Ave 12603. 2 mi e of Mid-Hudson Bridge on US 44 and SR 55. Ext/int corridors. **Pets:** Medium, dogs only. $30 one-time fee/pet. Service with restrictions, supervision.
[SAVE] [X] [H] [D] [A]

AAA **WWWW** Mercury Grand Hotel **H**
(845) 462-4600. **$90-$210.** 2170 South Rd (Rt 9) 12601. I-84, exit 13N, 4.7 mi s of Mid-Hudson Bridge. Int corridors. **Pets:** Other species. $50 deposit/room. Designated rooms, service with restrictions, supervision. [SAVE] [X] [H] [D] [TI] [A]

WWW Poughkeepsie Inn **M**
(845) 452-6600. **$65-$130.** 2625 US 9 12601. I-84, exit 13N, 1.6 mi s of Mid-Hudson Bridge. Ext corridors. **Pets:** Medium. $50 deposit/pet, $25 one-time fee/pet. Service with restrictions, supervision.
[ASK] [X] [&M]

RHINEBECK

WWWW Beekman Arms & Delamater Inn and Conference Center **CI**
(845) 876-7077. **$120-$300, 14 day notice.** 6387 Mill St (Rt 9) 12572. Jct US 9 and SR 308; center of village. Ext/int corridors. **Pets:** Accepted.
[X] [H] [D] [TI]

RIVERHEAD

AAA **WWW** Best Western East End **H**
(631) 369-2200. **Call for rates.** 1830 SR 25 11901. I-495, exit 72 (SR 25 E). Int corridors. **Pets:** Accepted. [SAVE] [X] [H] [D] [TI] [A]

WWW Holiday Inn Express East End **H**
(631) 548-1000. **$129-$399, 3 day notice.** 1707 Old Country Rd (SR 58) 11901. I-495, exit 73, 0.5 mi e. Int corridors. **Pets:** Medium, dogs only. $50 one-time fee/room. Service with restrictions, crate.
[ASK] [X] [&M] [H] [D] [A]

ROCHESTER

AAA **WWWW** Hyatt Regency Rochester **H**
(585) 546-1234. **$89-$319.** 125 E Main St 14604. Jct South Ave; downtown. Int corridors. **Pets:** Accepted. [SAVE] [X] [&M] [H] [D] [TI] [A]

WW La Quinta Inn **H** ❖
(585) 254-1000. **$74-$139.** 1956 Lyell Ave 14606. I-390, exit 21 (SR 31), just e. Int corridors. **Pets:** Medium, other species. Service with restrictions, supervision. [ASK] [X] [H] [D]

▼▼▼▼ **Radisson Hotel Rochester Riverside** �H
(585) 546-6400. **$109-$199.** 120 E Main St 14604. Downtown. Int corridors. **Pets:** Accepted. 🔳 ⊠ 🔊 🛗 🖵 🍴 ⇔ ⊠

AAA▷ ▼▼▼▼ **Rochester Plaza Hotel & Conference Center** �H ✿
(585) 546-3450. **$99-$149.** 70 State St 14614. Jct Main St; downtown. Int corridors. **Pets:** Designated rooms, service with restrictions, supervision. 🔳 ⊠ 🛗 🖵 🍴 ⇔

▼▼▼▼ **Strathallan Hotel** �H
(585) 461-5010. **$117-$169.** 550 East Ave 14607. I-490, exit 17, 0.8 mi n on Goodman St, then just w. Int corridors. **Pets:** Accepted.
🔳 ⊠ 🔊 🛗 🖵 🍴

ROCKVILLE CENTRE

AAA▷ ▼▼▼▼ **Best Western Mill River Manor** �H
(516) 678-1300. **$110-$160.** 173 Sunrise Hwy 11570. On SR 27; between N Village and N Centre aves. Ext corridors. **Pets:** Accepted.
🔳 ⊠ 🛗 🖵 🍴 ⇔

ROME

▼▼ **Econo Lodge** 🅼
(315) 337-9400. **$60-$109.** 145 E Whitesboro St 13440. Just s of jct SR 26 (Turin Rd) and 46. Ext corridors. **Pets:** Medium. $25 daily fee/pet. Service with restrictions, crate. 🔳 ⊠ 🛗 🖵

AAA▷ ▼▼▼▼ **Inn at the Beeches** 🅼 ✿
(315) 336-1775. **$89-$295.** 7900 Turin Rd 13440. Jct SR 46, 2 mi n on SR 26 (Turin Rd). Ext corridors. **Pets:** Medium. Designated rooms, service with restrictions, crate. 🔳 ⊠ 🛗 🖵 🍴 ⇔

AAA▷ ▼▼▼ **Quality Inn of Rome** �H
(315) 336-4300. **$70-$200.** 200 S James St 13440. On SR 49; downtown. Ext/int corridors. **Pets:** $25 daily fee/pet. Designated rooms, service with restrictions. 🔳 ⊠ 🛗 🖵 🍴 ⇔

ROSCOE

AAA▷ ▼▼ **Roscoe Motel** 🅼
(607) 498-5220. **Call for rates.** 2054 Old Rt 17 12776. SR 17, exit 94, 0.5 mi n on SR 206, then just w. Ext corridors. **Pets:** Accepted.
🔳 ⊠ 🛗 🖵

ROTTERDAM

▼▼▼ **Super 8 Schenectady** �H
(518) 355-2190. **$75-$90.** 3083 Carman Rd 12303. I-890, exit 9 (Curry Rd), 0.4 mi w; I-90, exit 25. Int corridors. **Pets:** $10 daily fee/pet. Designated rooms, service with restrictions, supervision. ⊠ 🖵

SACKETS HARBOR

▼▼▼ **Ontario Place Hotel** �H ✿
(315) 646-8000. **$89-$370.** 103 General Smith Dr 13685. Center. Int corridors. **Pets:** Other species. $10 one-time fee/room. Designated rooms, service with restrictions. 🔳 ⊠ 🛗 🖵

SALAMANCA

▼▼▼▼ **Holiday Inn Express Hotel & Suites** �H ✿
(716) 945-7600. **$140-$229.** 779 Broad St 14779. I-86, exit 20, just n. Int corridors. **Pets:** Other species. $50 deposit/room, $25 one-time fee/room. Designated rooms, service with restrictions, supervision.
🔳 ⊠ 🔊 🛗 🖵 ⇔

SARANAC LAKE

AAA▷ ▼▼ **Adirondack Motel** 🅼
(518) 891-2116. **$75-$240.** 248 Lake Flower Ave 12983. 0.7 mi e on SR 86. Ext corridors. **Pets:** Dogs only. $10 daily fee/pet. Service with restrictions, supervision. 🔳 ⊠ 🛗 🖵 ⊠

AAA▷ ▼▼▼▼ **Best Western Mountain Lake Inn** �H
(518) 891-1970. **$89-$229.** 487 Lake Flower Ave 12983. 0.8 mi e on SR 86. Int corridors. **Pets:** Other species. $20 one-time fee/room. Designated rooms, service with restrictions, supervision.
🔳 ⊠ 🔊 🛗 🖵 🍴 ⇔

▼▼ **Lake Flower Inn** 🅼
(518) 891-2310. **$68-$138, 14 day notice.** 234 Lake Flower Ave 12983. 0.6 mi e on SR 86. Ext corridors. **Pets:** Dogs only. $10 daily fee/room. Designated rooms, supervision. ⊠ 🛗 ⇔ ⊠

▼▼ **Lake Side Motel** 🅼
(518) 891-4333. **$79-$159, 7 day notice.** 256 Lake Flower Ave 12983. 0.6 mi e on SR 86. Ext corridors. **Pets:** Dogs only. $20 one-time fee/pet. Designated rooms, service with restrictions, supervision.
⊠ 🛗 ⇔ ⊠

SARATOGA SPRINGS

AAA▷ ▼▼▼▼ **Best Western Park Inn** �H
(518) 584-2350. **$99-$339.** 3291 S Broadway 12866. I-87, exit 13N, 1.1 mi n on US 9. Int corridors. **Pets:** Accepted. 🔳 ⊠ 🔊 🛗 🖵

▼▼▼▼ **Holiday Inn** �H
(518) 584-4550. **Call for rates.** 232 Broadway 12866. On US 9, jct SR 50. Int corridors. **Pets:** Other species. Service with restrictions, supervision. ⊠ 🛗 🖵 🍴 ⇔

▼▼▼▼ **Residence Inn by Marriott-Saratoga Springs** �H
(518) 584-9600. **$129-$339.** 295 Excelsior Ave 12866. I-87, exit 15, just n, just s, then just e. Int corridors. **Pets:** Accepted.
⊠ 🔊 🛗 🖵 ⇔ ⊠

AAA▷ ▼▼▼▼ **The Saratoga Hilton** �H ✿
(518) 584-4000. **$89-$599.** 534 Broadway 12866. I-87, exit 15, on SR 50. Int corridors. **Pets:** Medium. $25 daily fee/pet. Service with restrictions, supervision. 🔳 ⊠ 🛗 🖵 🍴 ⇔

▼▼ **Saratoga Motel** 🅼
(518) 584-0920. **$79-$219, 14 day notice.** 440 Church St 12866. On SR 9N, 2.3 mi w of jct US 9/SR 50. Ext corridors. **Pets:** Accepted.
🔳 ⊠ 🛗 🖵

▼▼▼ **Union Gables Bed & Breakfast** 🅱🅱
(518) 584-1558. **Call for rates.** 55 Union Ave 12866. I-87, exit 14, 1.5 mi w. Int corridors. **Pets:** Accepted. ⊠ 🛗

SAUGERTIES

AAA▷ ▼▼▼ **Comfort Inn** �H
(845) 246-1565. **$89-$169.** 2790 SR 32 12477. I-87, exit 20, just n. Int corridors. **Pets:** Other species. $10 daily fee/room. Service with restrictions, supervision. 🔳 ⊠ 🛗 🖵

SCHENECTADY

▼▼▼ **Days Inn** �H
(518) 370-3297. **$59-$109.** 167 Nott Terr 12308. Jct State St (SR 5) and Nott Terr, 2 blks e; downtown. Int corridors. **Pets:** Accepted.
🔳 ⊠ 🛗 🖵

SCHOHARIE

▼▼▼ **Holiday Inn Express Hotel & Suites Schoharie** �H
(518) 295-6088. **$109-$199.** 160 Holiday Way 12157. I-88, exit 23, just e to Park Pl, then just s. Int corridors. **Pets:** Accepted.
🔳 ⊠ 🔊 🛗 🖵

SCHROON LAKE

AAA▷ ▼▼ **Blue Ridge Motel** 🅼
(518) 532-7521. **$80-$90, 3 day notice.** 2455 US Rt 9 12870. I-87, exit 28, 4 mi n. Ext/int corridors. **Pets:** $10 one-time fee/pet. Service with restrictions, supervision. 🔳 ⊠ 🛗 🖵 ⇔ 🆉

SKANEATELES
▼▼▼▼ Skaneateles Suites **M**

(315) 685-7568. **$99-$175.** 4114 W Genesee St Rd 13152. On US 20, 2 mi w. Ext corridors. **Pets:** Other species. $35 one-time fee/pet. Service with restrictions, crate. [ASK] [✕] 🔌 💻

SOLVAY
▼▼▼ Clarion Inn & Suites **H** ❧

(315) 457-8700. **$70-$100.** 100 Farrell Rd 13209. I-690, exit 4 (John Glenn Blvd). Int corridors. **Pets:** $25 one-time fee/room. Designated rooms, service with restrictions, supervision.

[ASK] [✕] 🔌 💻 [🍴] ⇋

SOUTHAMPTON
▲▲▲ ▼▼▼ Southampton Inn **H**

(631) 283-6500. **$159-$489.** 91 Hill St 11968. 0.3 mi n from corner of Main St and Jobs Ln. Ext corridors. **Pets:** Accepted.

[SAVE] [✕] 🔌M 🔌 [🍴] ⇋ [✕]

SYLVAN BEACH
▼▼ Cinderella's Cafe & Suites **M**

(315) 762-4280. **$59-$219, 15 day notice.** 1208 N Main St 13157. On SR 13; center. Ext corridors. **Pets:** Accepted. [ASK] [✕] 🔌 💻 [🍴]

SYRACUSE
▲▲▲ ▼▼▼▼ Renaissance Syracuse Hotel **H**

(315) 479-7000. **$206-$252.** 701 E Genesee St 13210. Jct Almond St; downtown. Int corridors. **Pets:** Accepted. [SAVE] [✕] 🔌M 🔌 💻 [🍴]

▲▲▲ ▼▼▼▼ Sheraton Syracuse University Hotel & Conference Center **H**

(315) 475-3000. **$139-$349.** 801 University Ave 13210. I-81, exit 18. Int corridors. **Pets:** Accepted. [ECO] [SAVE] [✕] 🔌 💻 [🍴] ⇋ [✕]

TICONDEROGA
▲▲▲ ▼▼▼▼ Best Western Ticonderoga Inn & Suites **H**

(518) 585-2378. **$95-$170, 3 day notice.** 260 Burgoyne Rd 12883. Jct SR 9 N and 74, just s on SR 74, then just w. Int corridors. **Pets:** Accepted. [SAVE] [✕] 🔌M 🔌 💻 [🍴] ⇋ [✕]

▲▲▲ ▼ Circle Court Motel **M**

(518) 585-7660. **$59-$92.** 6 Montcalm St 12883. SR 9N; at Liberty Monument traffic circle. Ext corridors. **Pets:** Large, dogs only. $10 daily fee/pet. Designated rooms, service with restrictions, supervision.

[SAVE] [✕] 💻

TROY
▲▲▲ ▼▼▼▼ Best Western Franklin Square Inn **H** ❧

(518) 274-8800. **$99-$199, 30 day notice.** One 4th St 12180. I-787, exit 8, just e on 23rd to Federal, just e to 4th St, then just s; downtown. Int corridors. **Pets:** Large, other species. $25 one-time fee/room. Service with restrictions. [SAVE] [✕] 🔌M 🔌 💻

TUPPER LAKE
▲▲▲ ▼ Red Top Inn **M**

(518) 359-9209. **$50-$90, 7 day notice.** 1562 SR 30 12986. 3 mi s. Ext/int corridors. **Pets:** Accepted. [SAVE] [✕] 🔌 💻

UTICA
▲▲▲ ▼▼▼ Red Roof Inn #7180 **M**

(315) 724-7128. **$49-$130.** 20 Weaver St 13502. I-90 (New York State Thruway), exit 31. Ext corridors. **Pets:** Large. Service with restrictions, crate. [SAVE] [✕] 🔌

▼▼▼▼ Rosemont Inn Bed & Breakfast **BB** ❧

(315) 797-9033. **$99-$179, 7 day notice.** 1423 Genesee St 13501. I-90 (New York State Thruway), exit 31, 2.5 mi s. Int corridors. **Pets:** $25 daily fee/room. Service with restrictions, crate. [ASK] [✕] [✎]

VALATIE
▲▲▲ ▼▼▼ Blue Spruce Inn & Suites **M** ❧

(518) 758-9711. **$75-$105, 3 day notice.** 3093 Rt 9 12184. I-90 (New York State Thruway), exit 12, 4 mi s on US 9 via New York State Thruway Extension, exit B1. Ext corridors. **Pets:** Medium. Service with restrictions, supervision. [SAVE] [✕] 🔌 ⇋

VESTAL
▲▲▲ ▼▼▼▼ Quality Inn & Suites at Binghamton University **H**

(607) 729-6371. **$81-$108.** 4105 Vestal Pkwy E 13850. SR 17, exit 70 westbound, 1 mi s on SR 201 S, 0.5 mi w on SR 434 W; exit 67 eastbound, just s on SR 26, 2.5 mi e on SR 434. Int corridors. **Pets:** Accepted. [SAVE] [✕] 🔌 💻 [🍴] ⇋

VICTOR
▲▲▲ ▼▼▼▼ Hampton Inn & Suites-Rochester/Victor **H**

(585) 924-4400. **$129-$199.** 7637 SR 96 14564. I-90 (New York State Thruway), exit 45, just n. Int corridors. **Pets:** Designated rooms, service with restrictions, supervision. [SAVE] [✕] 🔌 ⇋

▼▼ Microtel Inn Victor **H**

(585) 924-9240. **$55-$100.** 7498 Main St Fischer Rd 14564. I-90 (New York State Thruway), exit 45, just s on SR 96, then just e. Int corridors. **Pets:** Accepted. [ASK] [✕] 🔌 💻

WARRENSBURG
▼▼ Super 8 **M** ❧

(518) 623-2811. **$70-$125.** 3619 SR 9 12845. I-87, exit 23, just w. Int corridors. **Pets:** Other species. $15 one-time fee/room. Supervision. [ASK] [✕] 🔌

WATERLOO
▲▲▲ ▼▼▼ Holiday Inn Waterloo-Seneca Falls **H**

(315) 539-5011. **$75-$155.** 2468 SR 414 13165. I-90 (New York State Thruway), exit 41, 4 mi s; just n of jct SR 414/5 and US 20. Int corridors. **Pets:** Accepted. [SAVE] [✕] 🔌M 🔌 💻 [🍴] ⇋ [✕]

▲▲▲ ▼▼ Microtel Inn & Suites **H**

(315) 539-8438. **$56-$120.** 1966 Rt 5 & 20 13148. I-90 (New York State Thruway), exit 41, 4 mi s on SR 414, then just e. Int corridors. **Pets:** Other species. $15 daily fee/room. Service with restrictions, supervision. [SAVE] [✕] 🔌M 🔌 💻

WATERTOWN
▲▲▲ ▼▼ Best Western Carriage House Inn & Conference Center **H**

(315) 782-8000. **$110-$130, 5 day notice.** 300 Washington St 13601. Center. Int corridors. **Pets:** Other species. $15 daily fee/pet. Designated rooms, service with restrictions, supervision. [ECO] [SAVE] [✕] 🔌 💻 [🍴] ⇋

▲▲▲ ▼▼ Davidson's Motel **M**

(315) 782-3861. **$75-$110.** 26177 NYS Rt 3 13601. From Town Square, 3.5 mi e. Ext corridors. **Pets:** $5 daily fee/room. [SAVE] [✕] 🔌

▲▲▲ ▼▼ Ramada **H**

(315) 788-0700. **$104-$109, 7 day notice.** 21000 NYS Rt 3 13601. I-81, exit 45, just w. Int corridors. **Pets:** Accepted. [SAVE] [✕] 🔌 💻 [🍴] ⇋ [✕]

WATKINS GLEN
▲▲▲ ▼▼▼ Anchor Inn and Marina **M** ❧

(607) 535-4159. **$69-$169, 10 day notice.** 3425 Salt Point Rd 14891. Just n on SR 14, 0.8 mi n. Ext corridors. **Pets:** Medium, dogs only. $25 deposit/pet. Service with restrictions, supervision. [SAVE] [✕] 🔌 [✕]

▲▲▲ ▼▼▼ Chieftain Motel **M**

(607) 535-4759. **$69-$169, 10 day notice.** 3815 SR 14 14891. 3 mi n of town; on west side of SR 14. Ext corridors. **Pets:** Accepted. [SAVE] [✕] 🔌 💻

WELLSVILLE

◈ ▽ Long Vue Inn M
(585) 593-2450. **$54-$129.** 5081 Rt 417 W 14895. Jct SR 19, 3 mi w. Ext corridors. **Pets:** Accepted. 〔SAVE〕✕ 🛗 💻

▽ ▽ Microtel Inn & Suites H
(585) 593-3449. **Call for rates.** 30 W Dyke St 14895. Just n off SR 19 and 417. Int corridors. **Pets:** Accepted. ✕ 🛗 💻

WEST COXSACKIE

◈ ▽ ▽ Best Western New Baltimore Inn H
(518) 731-8100. **$90-$150.** 12600 Rt 9W 12192. I-87 (New York State Thruway), exit 21B, 0.5 mi s. Int corridors. **Pets:** Accepted.
〔SAVE〕✕ 🛗 💻 ⇝ ✕

WESTFIELD

▽ ▽ ▽ The William Seward Inn CI
(716) 326-4151. **$100-$235, 7 day notice.** 6645 S Portage Rd 14787. I-90 (New York State Thruway), exit 60, 4 mi se on SR 394. Int corridors. **Pets:** Accepted. 〔ASK〕 ✕ 〔¶〕 〔🐾〕

WESTMORELAND

◈ ▽ Carriage Motor Inn M
(315) 853-3561. **$35-$85, 5 day notice.** 5370 SR 233 13490. I-90 (New York State Thruway), exit 32, just n. Ext corridors. **Pets:** Medium, dogs only. $15 daily fee/pet. Service with restrictions, supervision.
〔SAVE〕✕ 🛗

WILMINGTON

▽ Green Mountain Lodge M
(518) 946-8232. **$69-$159, 7 day notice.** 5675 SR 86 12997. Jct SR 86 and 431 (Whiteface Mt Hwy). Ext corridors. **Pets:** $10 daily fee/pet. Service with restrictions, crate. ✕ 🛗 💻 ✕

◈ ▽ ▽ Hungry Trout Resort M
(518) 946-2217. **$79-$179, 7 day notice.** 5239 Rt 86 12997. On SR 86, 2 mi w. Ext corridors. **Pets:** Accepted.
〔SAVE〕✕ 🛗 💻 〔¶〕 ⇝ ✕

◈ ▽ ▽ ▽ Ledge Rock at Whiteface Mountain M
(518) 946-2379. **$79-$129, 10 day notice.** 5078 Rt 86 12997. On SR 86, 3 mi w. Ext corridors. **Pets:** $25 one-time fee/pet. Designated rooms, service with restrictions. 〔SAVE〕✕ 🛗 💻 ⇝ ✕

▽ ▽ Mountain Brook Lodge M 🐾
(518) 946-2262. **$74-$89, 7 day notice.** 5712 Rt 86 12997. Center. Ext corridors. **Pets:** $25 one-time fee/room. Service with restrictions, crate.
✕ 🛗 💻 ⇝

◈ ▽ ▽ North Pole Inn M
(518) 946-7733. **$65-$199, 7 day notice.** 5636 NYS Rt 86 12997. On SR 86, just w of jct CR 431. Ext corridors. **Pets:** Dogs only. $15 daily fee/room. Designated rooms, service with restrictions, supervision.
〔SAVE〕✕ 🛗 💻 ✕

◈ ▽ ▽ Willkommen Hof Bed & Breakfast BB 🐾
(518) 946-7669. **$70-$245, 14 day notice.** 5367 Rt 86 12997. On SR 86, 1.5 mi of jct CR 431. Int corridors. **Pets:** Other species. $50 deposit/pet, $10 daily fee/pet. Designated rooms, service with restrictions, crate.
〔SAVE〕✕ 🛗 💻 ✕ 〔Ⓩ〕

WOODBURY

◈ ▽ ▽ Best Western Woodbury Inn M
(516) 921-6900. **$125-$169.** 7940 Jericho Tpke (SR 25) 11797. Jct SR 25 and 135, 0.9 mi e. Ext/int corridors. **Pets:** Medium. $50 deposit/room, $50 one-time fee/room. Designated rooms, service with restrictions, crate.
〔SAVE〕✕ 🛗 💻 〔¶〕 ⇝

◈ ▽ ▽ Executive Inn at Woodbury M
(516) 921-8500. **$99-$209.** 8030 Jericho Tpke (SR 25) 11797. Jct SR 25 and 135, 1 mi e. Ext corridors. **Pets:** Accepted.
〔SAVE〕✕ 🛗 💻 ⇝

WURTSBORO

▽ ▽ Days Inn H
(845) 888-2727. **$79-$125.** 21 Perron Dr 12790. SR 17, exit 113, just n on SR 209. Ext/int corridors. **Pets:** Medium. Service with restrictions.
〔ASK〕✕ 🛗 💻 ⇝

CITY INDEX

ABERDEEN

◈ ◈◈◈ Hampton Inn & Suites H

(910) 693-4330. **Call for rates.** 200 Columbus Dr 28315. Jct US 1, just n on US 15/501, then just s. Int corridors. **Pets:** Accepted.

◈◈ Motel 6-1234 M

(910) 944-5633. **$43-$51.** 1408 Sandhills Blvd 28315. Jct US 15/501 N, just s on US 1. Ext corridors. **Pets:** Other species. Service with restrictions, supervision.

◈◈◈ Sandhills Value Inn M

(910) 944-2369. **$49-$129.** 1500 Sandhills Blvd 28315. Jct US 15/501 N, just s on US 1. Ext corridors. **Pets:** Accepted.

ALBEMARLE

◈◈ Executive Inn M

(704) 983-6990. **Call for rates.** 735 Hwy 24/27 Bypass E 28001. Jct US 52 S, 1.4 mi e. Ext corridors. **Pets:** Accepted.

ANDREWS

◈◈◈◈ Hawkesdene House Mountain Retreat CA

(828) 321-6027. **$179-$209, 7 day notice.** 381 Phillips Creek Rd 28901. From US 19 (Business) to Cherry St, 3.3 mi s, 0.5 mi s on Phillips Creek Rd,. Ext corridors. **Pets:** Accepted.

ARCHDALE

◈◈◈◈ Comfort Inn H

(336) 434-4797. **$62-$149.** 10123 N Main St 27263. I-85, exit 111, just n on US 311, then just sw on Balfour Dr. Int corridors. **Pets:** Small. $25 one-time fee/pet. No service, supervision.

◈◈◈◈ Hampton Inn-High Point H

(336) 434-5200. **$89-$199.** 10066 N Main St 27263. I-85, exit 111, just n on US 311. Int corridors. **Pets:** Small. Designated rooms, service with restrictions, crate.

◈◈◈◈ Holiday Inn Express Hotel & Suites H

(336) 861-3310. **Call for rates.** 10050 N Main St 27263. I-85, exit 111, just n on US 311. Int corridors. **Pets:** $25 one-time fee/room. Designated rooms, service with restrictions, supervision.

◈◈ Innkeeper High Point M

(336) 434-5151. **$52-$55, 3 day notice.** 10002 S Main St 27263. I-85, exit 111, just s on US 311. Ext/int corridors. **Pets:** Small. $10 one-time fee/room. Service with restrictions, supervision.

◈◈ Quality Inn–High Point H

(336) 861-3000. **Call for rates.** 1202 Liberty Rd 27263. I-85, exit 113, just s on SR 62. Int corridors. **Pets:** Accepted.

ARDEN

◈◈ Quality Inn & Suites Biltmore South H ❀

(828) 684-6688. **$64-$154.** 1 Skyline Inn Dr 28704. I-26, exit 37. Int corridors. **Pets:** Medium, other species. $25 one-time fee/room. Designated rooms, service with restrictions.

ASHEBORO

◈ ◈◈ Quality Inn H

(336) 626-3680. **Call for rates.** 242 Lakecrest Rd 27203. US 64, just nw on SR 42. Ext corridors. **Pets:** Medium, other species. $15 daily fee/pet. Service with restrictions, crate.

ASHEVILLE

◈◈◈◈ 1889 WhiteGate Inn & Cottage BB

(828) 253-2553. **$169-$369, 14 day notice.** 173 E Chestnut St 28801. I-240, exit 5B (Charlotte St), just n, then just w; in historic district. Ext/int corridors. **Pets:** Large, dogs only. $50 one-time fee/room. Designated rooms, service with restrictions, crate.

◈ ◈◈◈ ◈◈◈ 1900 Inn on Montford BB ❀

(828) 254-9569. **$145-$625, 14 day notice.** 296 Montford Ave 28801. I-240, exit 4C (Montford Ave/Haywood St), 0.7 mi n; in historic district. Ext/int corridors. **Pets:** Other species. Designated rooms, service with restrictions.

◈ ◈◈◈ Abbington Green Bed & Breakfast Inn BB

(828) 251-2454. **$150-$450, 30 day notice.** 46 Cumberland Cir 28801. I-240, exit 4C (Montford Ave/Haywood St), n to W Chestnut St, just e to Cumberland Ave, then 0.3 mi n; in historic district. Ext/int corridors. **Pets:** Dogs only. $15 daily fee/pet. Designated rooms, service with restrictions, crate.

◈ ◈◈◈ Applewood Manor Inn Bed & Breakfast BB

(828) 254-2244. **$160-$250, 7 day notice.** 62 Cumberland Cir 28801-1718. I-240, exit 4C (Montford Ave/Haywood St), n on Montford Ave, e on W Chestnut St, n on Cumberland Ave, then ne; in historic district. Ext/int corridors. **Pets:** Dogs only. $35 daily fee/pet. Designated rooms.

◈ ◈◈ Best Western of Asheville Biltmore East M

(828) 298-5562. **$55-$299.** 501 Tunnel Rd 28805. I-240, exit 7, 0.5 mi e on US 70 (Tunnel Rd). Ext corridors. **Pets:** Small, dogs only. $10 daily fee/pet. Service with restrictions, supervision.

Biltmore Village Inn BB ❖
(828) 274-8707. **$199-$335, 21 day notice.** 119 Dodge St 28803. I-40, exit 50/50B (US 25 N), 0.5 mi n, just e on Lula St, just n on Reed St, just e on Warren Ave, then just s. Ext/int corridors. **Pets:** Medium. $25 daily fee/pet. Designated rooms, service with restrictions, crate.
[SAVE] [X] [🛏] [📶]

Black Walnut Bed & Breakfast Inn BB ❖
(828) 254-3878. **$150-$320, 15 day notice.** 288 Montford Ave 28801. I-240, exit 4C (Montford Ave/Haywood St), 0.5 mi n; in historic district. Ext/int corridors. **Pets:** Other species. Designated rooms.
[SAVE] [X] [🛏] [📶] [☎]

Carolina Bed & Breakfast BB
(828) 254-3608. **$120-$225.** 177 Cumberland Ave 28801. I-240, exit 4C (Montford Ave/Haywood St), 0.5 mi n on Montford Ave, just e on Chestnut St, then just n. Ext/int corridors. **Pets:** Accepted.
[ASK] [X] [🛏] [📶] [☎]

Cedar Crest Inn BB
(828) 252-1389. **$129-$300, 30 day notice.** 674 Biltmore Ave 28803. I-40, exit 50, 1.1 mi n. Ext/int corridors. **Pets:** $50 one-time fee/room. Designated rooms, crate. [SAVE] [X] [🛏] [📶] [📺]

Comfort Suites-Biltmore Square Mall H
(828) 665-4000. **$75-$189.** 890 Brevard Rd 28806. I-26, exit 33, 0.3 mi w. Int corridors. **Pets:** $20 daily fee/room. Designated rooms, service with restrictions, crate. [X] [🛏] [📶] [📺] [☕]

Crowne Plaza Resort H
(828) 254-3211. **Call for rates.** 1 Resort Dr 28806. I-240, exit 3B (Resort Dr), just w. Int corridors. **Pets:** Large, other species. $25 daily fee/room. Service with restrictions, supervision.
[SAVE] [X] [🛏] [📶] [📺] [🍴] [🏊] [☒]

Days Inn-Asheville Mall M
(828) 252-4000. **$49-$249.** 201 Tunnel Rd 28805. I-240, exit 6, 0.5 mi e, on south side of road. Ext corridors. **Pets:** Accepted.
[SAVE] [X] [🛏] [📶] [🏊]

Days Inn-Biltmore East H
(828) 298-4000. **$49-$199.** 1435 Tunnel Rd 28805. I-40, exit 55, just n. Int corridors. **Pets:** Small, dogs only. $10 daily fee/pet. No service, supervision. [SAVE] [X] [🛏] [📶] [📺]

Extended StayAmerica Asheville-Tunnel Rd H
(828) 253-3483. **$67-$110.** 6 Kenilworth Knoll 28805. I-240, exit 6, 0.7 mi e on US 70 (Tunnel Rd), then just n. Int corridors. **Pets:** Other species. $25 daily fee/room. Designated rooms, service with restrictions, crate.
[ASK] [X] [🛏] [📶]

Four Points by Sheraton Asheville Downtown H
(828) 253-1851. **Call for rates.** 22 Woodfin St 28801. I-240, exit 5A (Merrimon Ave), just s, then just w. Int corridors. **Pets:** Medium. $75 one-time fee/room. Service with restrictions, supervision.
[SAVE] [X] [🛏] [📶] [📺] [🍴] [☕]

Grand Bohemian Hotel Asheville H ❖
(828) 505-2949. **$149-$399, 3 day notice.** 11 Boston Way 28803. I-40, exit 50/50B, 0.8 mi n on US 25, follow signs to Biltmore Estate Historic Biltmore Village. Int corridors. **Pets:** Dogs only. $75 one-time fee/pet. Designated rooms, service with restrictions, supervision.
[SAVE] [X] [🛏] [📺] [🍴]

Holiday Inn-Biltmore East at the Blue Ridge Parkway H
(828) 298-5611. **Call for rates.** 1450 Tunnel Rd 28805. I-40, exit 55, just n. Int corridors. **Pets:** Accepted. [X] [🛏] [📶] [📺] [🍴] [☕]

The Log Cabin Motor Court CA
(828) 645-6546. **$65-$120, 14 day notice.** 330 Weaverville Hwy 28804. US 19/23, exit 21 (New Stock Rd), 1 mi s on Weaverville Hwy. Ext corridors. **Pets:** Accepted. [SAVE] [X] [🛏] [📶] [📺] [🍴] [☎]

Quality Inn & Suites M
(828) 298-5519. **Call for rates.** 1430 Tunnel Rd 28805. I-40, exit 55, just n. Ext corridors. **Pets:** Other species. $20 daily fee/room. Designated rooms, no service. [SAVE] [X] [🛏] [📶] [📺] [☕]

Ramada H ❖
(828) 298-9141. **$74-$129, 7 day notice.** 800 Fairview Rd 28803. I-240, exit 8; jct I-40 and US 74. Int corridors. **Pets:** Large. $15 one-time fee/pet. Designated rooms, service with restrictions.
[SAVE] [X] [🛏] [📶] [☕] [☒]

Red Roof Inn-West M
(828) 667-9803. **Call for rates.** 16 Crowell Rd 28806. I-40, exit 44, just n on US 19 and 23, just w on Old Haywood Rd, then just s. Ext corridors. **Pets:** Large. Service with restrictions, crate. [SAVE] [X] [🛏] [📶]

Rodeway Inn Asheville M
(828) 667-8706. **$36-$119.** 8 Crowell Rd 28806. I-40, exit 44, just n on US 19 and 23. Int corridors. **Pets:** Medium, other species. $15 one-time fee/pet. Designated rooms, service with restrictions, supervision.
[X] [🛏] [📶]

Sleep Inn Biltmore H
(828) 277-1800. **$69-$179.** 117 Hendersonville Rd 28803. I-40, exit 50 eastbound; exit 50B westbound, just n on US 25. Int corridors.
Pets: Accepted. [X] [🛏] [📶] [📺] [☕]

BANNER ELK

The Banner Elk Inn B&B and Cottages BB
(828) 898-6223. **$90-$250, 30 day notice.** 407 Main St E 28604. Jct SR 184 and 194, 0.3 mi n on SR 194. Int corridors. **Pets:** Large, dogs only. Designated rooms, service with restrictions, supervision.
[X] [🛏] [📶]

Best Western Mountain Lodge at Banner Elk H ❖
(828) 898-4571. **$80-$210, 3 day notice.** 1615 Tynecastle Hwy 28604. Jct SR 194, 1.3 mi s on SR 184. Ext corridors. **Pets:** Other species. Designated rooms, service with restrictions.
[SAVE] [X] [🛏] [📶] [📺] [🍴] [☕]

BLACK MOUNTAIN

Inn On Mill Creek BB ❖
(828) 668-1115. **$149-$199, 30 day notice.** 3895 Mill Creek Rd 28711. I-40, exit 66, just n, 0.9 mi e on Yates Ave to white gate, then 1.5 mi n. Ext/int corridors. **Pets:** Other species. $10 daily fee/pet, $15 one-time fee/room. Designated rooms, service with restrictions, crate. [X] [🛏] [📺] [☒] [☎]

BLOWING ROCK

Alpine Village Inn M
(828) 295-7206. **$49-$129, 7 day notice.** 297 Sunset Dr 28605. Jct US 321, just w. Ext corridors. **Pets:** Dogs only. $15 daily fee/pet. Designated rooms, supervision. [X] [🛏] [📺]

Cliff Dwellers Inn M
(828) 295-3121. **Call for rates.** 116 Lakeview Terr 28605. Jct US 221/US 321 business route, just s on US 321, then just e. Ext corridors.
Pets: Accepted. [X] [🛏] [📺]

Hillwinds Inn M
(828) 295-7660. **$59-$299, 3 day notice.** 315 Sunset Dr 28605. Jct US 321, just w. Ext/int corridors. **Pets:** Accepted. [ASK] [X] [🛏] [📺]

Homestead Inn M ❖
(828) 295-9559. **$45-$99, 7 day notice.** 153 Morris St 28605. Jct US 321 business route (Main St), just e. Ext corridors. **Pets:** Other species. $10 daily fee/pet. Designated rooms. [ASK] [X] [🛏] [📺]

The Village Inn M
(828) 295-3380. **$65-$299, 3 day notice.** 7876 Valley Blvd 28605. Jct Sunset Dr, just s on US 321. Ext corridors. **Pets:** Accepted.
[ASK] [X] [🛏] [📶] [📺]

BOONE

▼▼▼▼ La Quinta Inn & Suites ⊞ ❀

(828) 262-1234. **$69-$219.** 165 Hwy 105 Ext 28607. US 321 NW, 1 mi n of jct US 321. Int corridors. **Pets:** Medium, other species. Service with restrictions, supervision. (ASK) ⊠ ⌂ᴹ ⊟ ⊡ ⊅

BREVARD

◢◣◥◤ ▼▼▼▼ Holiday Inn Express ⊞

(828) 862-8900. **$89-$159.** 2228 Asheville Hwy 28712. 3 mi e on US 64. Int corridors. **Pets:** Other species. $25 daily fee/room. Service with restrictions. (SAVE) ⊠ ⌂ᴹ ⊟ ⊡ ⊅

◢◣◥◤ ▼▼▼ The Inn at Brevard ⽥⽥

(828) 884-2105. **$125-$235, 14 day notice.** 315 E Main St 28712. I-26, exit Asheville Airport, just w on Broad St, then just e; center. Ext/int corridors. **Pets:** Accepted. (SAVE) ⊠ ⊡

BRYSON CITY

▼▼ Settlers Mountain ⽥⽥

(828) 488-8622. **$85-$225, 30 day notice.** 340 E Alarka Rd 28713. US 74, exit 64, 1.5 mi s on Alarka Rd, then 0.4 mi e. Ext corridors. **Pets:** Dogs only. $50 one-time fee/room. No service.

(ASK) ⊠ ⊅

BURLINGTON

▼▼▼ Comfort Inn ⊞

(336) 584-4447. **$78-$160.** 2701 Kirkpatrick Rd 27215. I-40/85, exit 141, just s, then just e on Longpine Rd. Int corridors. **Pets:** Other species. $25 one-time fee/pet. Service with restrictions. ⊠ ⊟ ⊡ ⊅

◢◣◥◤ ▼▼▼ Econo Lodge ⊞

(336) 227-1270. **$44-$51, 10 day notice.** 2133 W Hanford Rd 27215. I-40/85, exit 145, just s on SR 49, then just w. Int corridors. **Pets:** Accepted. (SAVE) ⊠ ⊅

▼▼ Motel 6–1257 Ⓜ

(336) 226-1325. **$39-$55.** 2155 Hanford Rd 27215. I-40/85, exit 145, just s on SR 49, then just w. Ext corridors. **Pets:** Other species. Service with restrictions, supervision. ⊠ ⊅

◢◣◥◤ ▼▼▼▼ Quality Inn ⊞

(336) 229-5203. **Call for rates.** 2444 Maple Ave 27215. I-40/85, exit 145, just n. Int corridors. **Pets:** Accepted. (SAVE) ⊠ ⌂ᴹ ⊟ ⊡ ⍔ ⊅

CANDLER

◢◣◥◤ ▼▼▼ Days Inn Asheville West #6116 Ⓜ

(828) 667-9321. **$50-$140.** 2551 Smoky Park Hwy 28715. I-40, exit 37, just w, then n. Ext corridors. **Pets:** Large. $10 daily fee/room. Designated rooms, service with restrictions, crate. (SAVE) ⊠ ⊟ ⊡ ⊅

CANTON

▼▼ Days Inn Ⓜ

(828) 648-0300. **Call for rates.** 1963 Champion Dr 28716. I-40, exit 31, just n. Ext corridors. **Pets:** Accepted. ⊠ ⊟ ⊡ ⊅

CARY

◢◣◥◤ ▼▼▼ Best Western Cary Inn & Extended Stay Suites ⊞

(919) 481-1200. **$75-$85.** 1722 Walnut St 27511. I-40, exit 293A, just s on US 1, exit 101A, then just e. Ext/int corridors. **Pets:** Accepted. (SAVE) ⊠ ⊟ ⊡ ⊅ ⊠

▼▼▼ Candlewood Suites-Raleigh/Cary ⊞

(919) 468-4222. **Call for rates.** 1020 Buck Jones Rd 27606. I-40, exit 293A, just s on US 1, exit 101B, 0.5 mi nw; in Buck Jones Village. Int corridors. **Pets:** Accepted. ⊠ ⊟ ⊡

▼▼▼▼ Comfort Suites Hotel ⊞

(919) 852-4318. **$79-$129.** 350 Ashville Ave 27518. US 1, exit 98A, 0.8 mi e on Tryon Rd, then just n. Int corridors. **Pets:** Medium. $50 one-time fee/pet. Designated rooms, service with restrictions, supervision.

⊠ ⌂ᴹ ⊟ ⊡ ⊅ ⊠

▼▼ Extended StayAmerica-Raleigh-Cary-Regency Pkwy ⊞

(919) 468-5828. **$55-$75.** 1500 Regency Pkwy 27511. US 1, exit 98A, 0.5 mi e on Tryon Rd, then just s. Int corridors. **Pets:** Other species. $25 daily fee/room. Designated rooms, service with restrictions, crate.

(ASK) ⊠ ⊟ ⊡

▼▼ Extended Stay Deluxe Raleigh-Cary-Regency Parkway ⊞

(919) 460-1161. **$64-$84.** 3100 Regency Pkwy 27511. US 1, exit 98A, 0.5 mi e on Tryon Rd, then just s. Int corridors. **Pets:** Other species. $25 daily fee/room. Designated rooms, service with restrictions, crate.

(ASK) ⊠ ⊟ ⊡ ⊅

▼▼▼ La Quinta Inn & Suites Raleigh (Cary) ⊞ ❀

(919) 851-2850. **$69-$115.** 191 Crescent Commons Dr 27511. US 1, exit 98A, 0.5 mi e on Tryon Rd, then just n. Int corridors. **Pets:** Medium, other species. Service with restrictions, supervision.

(ASK) ⊠ ⌂ᴹ ⊟ ⊡ ⊅ ⊠

▼▼▼ Residence Inn by Marriott ⊞

(919) 467-4080. **$161-$197.** 2900 Regency Pkwy 27518. US 1, exit 98A, 0.5 mi e on Tryon Rd, then just s. Int corridors. **Pets:** Large, other species. $100 one-time fee/room. Service with restrictions, crate.

(ECO) ⊠ ⌂ᴹ ⊟ ⊡ ⊅ ⊠

▼▼ StudioPLUS-Raleigh-Cary-Harrison Ave ⊞

(919) 677-9910. **$62-$81.** 600 Weston Pkwy 27513. I-40, exit 287, 0.5 mi s on Harrison Ave, then just w. Int corridors. **Pets:** Other species. $25 daily fee/room. Designated rooms, service with restrictions, crate.

(ASK) ⊠ ⊟ ⊡ ⊅

◢◣◥◤ ▼▼▼▼ TownePlace Suites by Marriott–Raleigh/Cary/ Weston Parkway ⊞

(919) 678-0005. **$152-$186.** 120 Sage Commons Way 27513. I-40, exit 287, 0.5 mi s on Harrison Ave, 2.3 w on Weston Pkwy, then just n. Int corridors. **Pets:** Medium, other species. $100 one-time fee/room. Designated rooms, service with restrictions. (SAVE) ⊠ ⌂ᴹ ⊟ ⊡ ⊅

◢◣◥◤ ▼▼▼▼▼ The Umstead Hotel & Spa ⊞ ❀

(919) 447-4000. **$199-$425.** 100 Woodland Pond Dr 27513. I-40, exit 287, just s on Harrison Ave, just e on SAS Campus Dr, then just n. Int corridors. **Pets:** $200 one-time fee/room. Service with restrictions, supervision. (SAVE) ⊠ ⌂ᴹ ⊟ ⍔ ⊅ ⊠

CASHIERS

◢◣◥◤ ▼▼▼▼ High Hampton Inn & Country Club ⊞ ❀

(828) 743-2411. **$264-$369.** 1525 Hwy 107 S 28717. Jct US 64, 1.5 mi s. Ext/int corridors. **Pets:** $50 deposit/room. Designated rooms, service with restrictions. (SAVE) ⊠ ⊟ ⊡ ⍔ ⊠ ⊗ ⌗ ⊘

▼▼ Laurelwood Mountain Inn Ⓜ

(828) 743-9939. **$79-$99, 3 day notice.** 58 Hwy 107 28717. Jct US 64, just n. Ext corridors. **Pets:** Medium, other species. Designated rooms, service with restrictions, supervision. (ASK) ⊠ ⌂ᴹ ⊟ ⊡

CHAPEL HILL

▼▼ Holiday Inn Ⓜ ❀

(919) 929-2171. **$90-$120.** 1301 N Fordham Blvd 27514. I-40, exit 270, 2 mi s on US 15/501. Ext corridors. **Pets:** Medium. $40 one-time fee/room. Service with restrictions. (ASK) ⊠ ⊟ ⊡ ⍔ ⊅

◢◣◥◤ ▼▼▼ Residence Inn by Marriott-Chapel Hill ⊞ ❀

(919) 933-4848. **$179-$219.** 101 Erwin Rd 27514. I-40, exit 270, 1.2 mi s on US 15/501, then just w. Int corridors. **Pets:** Large, other species. $100 one-time fee/room. Service with restrictions, crate.

(SAVE) ⊠ ⌂ᴹ ⊟ ⊡ ⊅ ⊠

⚑ ▽▽ ▽▽ The Siena Hotel 🅷 ☜

(919) 929-4000. **$119-$300.** 1505 E Franklin St 27514. I-40, exit 270, 2 mi s on US 15/501, then 0.5 mi w. Int corridors. **Pets:** Large, dogs only. $75 one-time fee/room. Designated rooms, service with restrictions.

[SAVE] [✕] [♿] [🛏] [🍴]

CHARLOTTE METROPOLITAN AREA

CHARLOTTE

⚑ ▽▽▽▽ aloft Charlotte Uptown @ the Epicentre 🅷 ☜

(704) 333-1999. **Call for rates.** 210 E Trade St 28202. Jct College and 4th sts. Int corridors. **Pets:** Small. Service with restrictions.

[SAVE] [✕] [♿] [🛏] [🏊] [🌊]

▽▽ Candlewood Suites–Charlotte University 🅷

(704) 598-9863. **$60-$75.** 8812 University East Dr 28213. I-85, exit 45A (W. T. Harris Blvd), 2.5 mi e on SR 24, then just s; in University East Business Park. Int corridors. **Pets:** Accepted. [ASK] [✕] [🛏] [🌊]

▽▽ Candlewood Suites-I77-South/Tyvola Rd 🅷 ☜

(704) 529-7500. **$70-$140.** 5840 Westpark Dr 28217. I-77, exit 5 (Tyvola Rd), just e, then 0.5 mi s. Int corridors. **Pets:** Medium, other species. $75 one-time fee/pet. Service with restrictions, crate.

[ASK] [✕] [♿] [🛏] [🌊]

⚑ ▽▽▽ Comfort Inn-Executive Park 🅷

(704) 525-2626. **$65-$125.** 5822 Westpark Dr 28217. I-77, exit 5 (Tyvola Rd), just e, then 0.5 mi s. Int corridors. **Pets:** Accepted.

[SAVE] [✕] [🛏] [🌊] [🌊]

▽▽▽▽ Comfort Suites-University 🅷

(704) 547-0049. **$89-$199.** 7735 University City Blvd 28213. I-85, exit 45A (W. T. Harris Blvd), 1 mi e on SR 24, then 0.5 mi s on SR 49. Int corridors. **Pets:** Medium. $25 one-time fee/pet. Designated rooms, service with restrictions, supervision. [✕] [♿] [🛏] [🌊] [🌊]

▽▽▽▽ Country Inn & Suites By Carlson, Charlotte-University Place 🅷

(704) 549-8770. **$89-$189.** 131 E McCullough Dr 28262. I-85, exit 45A, 0.5 mi e on SR 24, 0.4 mi s on US 29 (N Tryon St), then just e. Int corridors. **Pets:** Accepted. [ASK] [✕] [♿] [🛏] [🌊] [✕]

⚑ ▽▽▽▽ Crowne Plaza–Charlotte 🅷

(704) 372-7550. **$99-$229.** 201 S McDowell St 28204. I-277, exit 2A, just w on 4th St, then just s. Int corridors. **Pets:** Accepted.

[SAVE] [✕] [🛏] [🛏] [🍴] [🌊]

⚑ ▽▽▽▽ Doubletree Guest Suites-SouthPark 🅷

(704) 364-2400. **$80-$161.** 6300 Morrison Blvd 28211. I-77, exit 5 (Tyvola Rd), 3.3 mi e on Tyvola/Fairview rds, just n on Barclay Downs, then just e. Int corridors. **Pets:** Accepted. [SAVE] [✕] [🛏] [🛏] [🍴] [🌊]

⚑ ▽▽▽▽ DoubleTree Hotel Charlotte-Gateway Village 🅷

(704) 347-0070. **$99-$249.** 895 W Trade St 28202. I-77, exit 10 or 10B, just e. Int corridors. **Pets:** Accepted.

[SAVE] [✕] [♿] [🛏] [🛏] [🍴] [🌊]

▽▽▽▽ Drury Inn & Suites-Charlotte North 🅷

(704) 593-0700. **$95-$179.** 415 W W. T. Harris Blvd 28262. I-85, exit 45A, just e on SR 24. Int corridors. **Pets:** Other species. No service, supervision. [ASK] [✕] [♿] [🛏] [🛏] [🌊]

▽▽▽▽ Drury Inn & Suites-Charlotte Northlake 🅷

(704) 599-8882. **$85-$154.** 6920 Northlake Mall Dr 28216. I-77, exit 18 (W. T. Harris Blvd), just w on SR 24. Int corridors. **Pets:** Other species. No service, supervision. [ASK] [✕] [♿] [🛏] [🛏] [🌊]

▽▽ Extended StayAmerica-Charlotte-Pineville 🅷

(704) 341-0929. **$72-$81.** 10930 Park Rd 28226. I-485, exit 64A, just n on SR 51, then just e; behind Terraces at Park Place Shopping Center. Int corridors. **Pets:** Other species. $25 daily fee/room. Designated rooms, service with restrictions, crate. [ASK] [✕] [♿] [🛏] [🛏]

▽▽ Extended StayAmerica-Charlotte-University Place 🅷

(704) 510-1636. **$62-$72.** 8211 University Executive Park Dr 28262. I-85, exit 45A (W. T. Harris Blvd), 0.5 mi e on SR 24, then 0.5 mi s on US 29 (N Tryon St). Int corridors. **Pets:** Other species. $25 daily fee/room. Designated rooms, service with restrictions, crate. [ASK] [✕] [♿] [🛏] [🛏]

▽▽ Extended Stay Deluxe-Charlotte/Pineville 🅷

(704) 542-9521. **$81-$110.** 8405 Pineville-Matthews Rd 28226. I-485, exit 64A, 0.7 mi n on SR 51. Int corridors. **Pets:** Other species. $25 daily fee/room. Designated rooms, service with restrictions, crate.

[ASK] [✕] [🛏] [🌊]

⚑ ▽▽▽▽ Four Points by Sheraton-Charlotte 🅷

(704) 522-0852. **$75-$195.** 315 E Woodlawn Rd 28217. I-77, exit 6A, 0.5 mi e. Int corridors. **Pets:** Accepted. [SAVE] [✕] [🛏] [🛏] [🍴] [🌊]

⚑ ▽▽▽▽ Hilton Charlotte Center City 🅷 ☜

(704) 377-1500. **$109-$359.** 222 E 3rd St 28202. I-77, exit 10 or 10B, 0.8 mi e on Trade St, just s on Church St, then just e; jct S College St. Int corridors. **Pets:** Large. $75 one-time fee/room. Designated rooms, service with restrictions. [SAVE] [✕] [🛏] [🍴]

▽▽▽▽ Hilton Charlotte University Place 🅷

(704) 547-7444. **$99-$299.** 8629 J M Keynes Dr 28262. I-85, exit 45A (W. T. Harris Blvd), just e on SR 24, then just n. Int corridors. **Pets:** Accepted. [✕] [♿] [🛏] [🛏] [🍴] [🌊]

▽▽▽▽ Holiday Inn Airport 🅷

(704) 394-4301. **$99-$174.** 2707 Little Rock Rd 28214. I-85, exit 32, just e. Int corridors. **Pets:** Accepted. [ASK] [✕] [🛏] [🛏] [🍴] [🌊]

▽▽▽▽ Holiday Inn at University Executive Park 🅷

(704) 547-0999. **$94-$169.** 8520 University Executive Park Dr 28262. I-85, exit 45A (W. T. Harris Blvd), just e on SR 24, then just s. Int corridors. **Pets:** Medium, dogs only. $25 one-time fee/pet. Designated rooms, service with restrictions, supervision.

[ASK] [✕] [♿] [🛏] [🛏] [🍴] [🌊]

▽▽▽▽ Holiday Inn-Billy Graham Parkway 🅷

(704) 523-1400. **$79-$149.** 321 W Woodlawn Rd 28217. I-77, exit 6B northbound, just w; exit southbound, just s on S Tryon St. Int corridors. **Pets:** Accepted. [ASK] [✕] [♿] [🛏] [🛏] [🍴] [🌊] [✕]

▽▽ Homestead Studio Suites Hotel-Charlotte/Airport 🅼

(704) 676-0083. **$62-$72.** 710 Yorkmont Rd 28217. I-77, exit 6B northbound, just w, just s on S Tryon St, then just w; exit southbound, just s on S Tryon St, then just w. Ext corridors. **Pets:** Other species. $25 daily fee/room. Designated rooms, service with restrictions, crate.

[ASK] [✕] [🛏] [🛏]

▽▽▽▽ Homewood Suites by Hilton Airport 🅷

(704) 357-0500. **$169-$209.** 2770 Yorkmont Rd 28208. I-77, exit 6B, 2 mi nw on Billy Graham Pkwy, exit Coliseum/Tyvola Rd, just se on Tyvola Rd, then just w. Int corridors. **Pets:** Accepted. [✕] [♿] [🛏] [🛏] [🌊]

◈◈◈◈ ▼▼▼▼ Hyatt Summerfield Suites Charlotte Airport H
(704) 525-2600. **$69-$169.** 4920 S Tryon St 28217. I-77, exit 6B northbound, just w, then just s; exit southbound, just s. Int corridors. **Pets:** Medium. $5 daily fee/room, $150 one-time fee/room. Designated rooms, service with restrictions, crate.
[SAVE] [✕] [&M] [♿] [▦] [⊇] [✕]

▼▼▼ La Quinta Inn- Airport North H ✿
(704) 392-1600. **$59-$99.** 3127 Sloan Dr 28208. I-85, exit 33, just w, then just s. Int corridors. **Pets:** Medium, other species. Service with restrictions, supervision. [ASK] [✕] [♿] [▦]

▼▼▼ La Quinta Inn & Suites Charlotte Airport South H ✿
(704) 523-5599. **$59-$105.** 4900 S Tryon St 28217. I-77, exit 6B northbound, just w, then just s; exit southbound, just s. Int corridors. **Pets:** Medium, other species. Service with restrictions, supervision.
[ASK] [✕] [&M] [♿] [▦] [⊇]

▼▼▼ MainStay Suites H
(704) 521-3232. **$100-$170, 3 day notice.** 7926 Forest Pine Dr 28273. I-77, exit 3 southbound; exit 2 northbound, just e, then just s. Int corridors. **Pets:** Large. $35 daily fee/room. Service with restrictions, crate.
[✕] [&M] [♿] [▦] [⊇]

◈◈◈ ▼▼▼ ▼▼▼ Marriott-Charlotte SouthPark H
(704) 364-8220. **$161-$197.** 2200 Rexford Rd 28211. I-77, exit 5 (Tyvola Rd), 3.6 mi e on Tyvola/Fairview rds, just n on Sharon Rd, just w on Morrison Blvd, just n on Roxborough Rd, then just w. Int corridors.
Pets: Accepted. [SAVE] [✕] [&M] [♿] [▦] [⊓] [⊇] [✕]

◈◈◈ ▼▼▼ ▼▼▼ Omni Charlotte Hotel H
(704) 377-0400. **$149-$267.** 132 E Trade St 28202. I-77, exit 10 or 10B, 0.8 mi e; jct Tryon St. Int corridors. **Pets:** Accepted.
[SAVE] [✕] [♿] [▦] [⊓] [⊇] [✕]

▼▼▼▼ Quality Inn & Suites Airport H
(704) 393-5306. **$40-$159.** 3100 Queen City Dr 28208. I-85, exit 33, just w, then just n. Ext/int corridors. **Pets:** Accepted.
[✕] [&M] [♿] [▦]

▼▼▼ Ramada Airport North M
(704) 394-4111. **Call for rates.** 2625 Little Rock Rd 28214. I-85, exit 32, just w. Ext corridors. **Pets:** Accepted. [✕] [♿] [▦] [⊇]

▼▼▼ Ramada Conference Center "Airport South" H
(704) 525-8350. **Call for rates.** 212 W Woodlawn Rd 28217. I-77, exit 6A, just e. Int corridors. **Pets:** Accepted. [✕] [♿] [▦] [⊓] [⊇]

▼▼▼ Red Roof Inn-Airport M
(704) 392-2316. **$50-$129.** 3300 Queen City Dr 28208. I-85, exit 33, just w, then just s. Ext corridors. **Pets:** Large. Service with restrictions, crate.
[✕] [&M] [♿]

▼▼▼▼ Residence Inn by Marriott-Charlotte South H
(704) 527-8110. **$161-$197.** 5816 Westpark Dr 28217. I-77, exit 5 (Tyvola Rd), just e, then 0.4 mi s. Ext/int corridors. **Pets:** Accepted.
[✕] [&M] [♿] [▦] [✕]

◈◈◈ ▼▼▼▼ Residence Inn by Marriott-Charlotte Uptown H
(704) 340-4000. **$215-$263.** 404 S Mint St 28202. I-77, exit 10 or 10B, 0.6 mi e on Trade St, then just s. Int corridors. **Pets:** Large, other species. $100 one-time fee/room. Designated rooms, service with restrictions, crate. [SAVE] [✕] [&M] [♿] [▦] [⊓]

▼▼▼▼ Residence Inn by Marriott-Piper Glen H
(704) 319-3900. **$197-$241.** 5115 Piper Station Dr 28277. I-485, exit 59, just s on Rea Rd, then just e. Int corridors. **Pets:** Medium. $100 one-time fee/pet. Service with restrictions, crate. [✕] [&M] [♿] [▦] [⊇] [✕]

▼▼▼ Residence Inn by Marriott-University Research Park H
(704) 547-1122. **$170-$208.** 8503 N Tryon St 28262. I-85, exit 45A, 0.5 mi e on SR 24, then just s on US 29 (N Tryon St). Ext corridors.
Pets: Accepted. [✕] [&M] [♿] [▦] [⊇] [✕]

▼▼▼▼ Residence Inn Charlotte SouthPark H
(704) 554-7001. **$148-$180.** 6030 Piedmont Row Dr S 28287. I-77, exit 5 (Tyvola Rd), 3.2 mi e on Tyvola and Fairview rds, then just s. Int corridors. **Pets:** Large. $100 one-time fee/room. Service with restrictions, supervision. [✕] [&M] [♿] [▦] [⊇] [✕]

◈◈◈ ▼▼▼▼ Sheraton Charlotte Airport Hotel H
(704) 392-1200. **$89-$269.** 3315 Scott Futrell Dr 28208. I-85, exit 33, just e, then just s. Int corridors. **Pets:** Accepted.
[SAVE] [✕] [♿] [▦] [⊓] [⊇]

◈◈◈ ▼▼▼▼ Sleep Inn H ✿
(704) 549-4544. **$60-$160.** 8525 N Tryon St 28262. I-85, exit 45A (W. T. Harris Blvd), 0.5 mi e on SR 24, just s on US 29 (N Tryon St). Int corridors. **Pets:** Other species. $25 one-time fee/pet. Service with restrictions, supervision. [SAVE] [✕] [&M] [♿] [▦] [⊇]

▼▼▼ Sleep Inn–Billy Graham Parkway H
(704) 525-5005. **$50-$110.** 701 Yorkmont Rd 28217. I-77, exit 6B northbound, just w, just s on S Tryon St, then just w; exit southbound, just s on Tryon St, then just w. Int corridors. **Pets:** Small. $20 daily fee/pet. Designated rooms, service with restrictions, crate.
[✕] [&M] [♿] [▦] [⊇]

▼▼▼▼ Staybridge Suites-Arrowood H
(704) 527-6767. **$89-$149.** 7924 Forest Pine Dr 28273. I-77, exit 3 southbound; exit 2 northbound, just e, then just s. Int corridors. **Pets:** Medium, other species. $75 one-time fee/room. Designated rooms, service with restrictions. [ASK] [✕] [&M] [♿] [▦] [⊇]

▼▼▼▼ Staybridge Suites Charlotte-Ballantyne H ✿
(704) 248-5000. **$100-$150.** 15735 John J Delaney Dr 28277. I-485, exit 61 or 61B, just s. Int corridors. **Pets:** Large, other species. $150 one-time fee/room. Designated rooms, service with restrictions, supervision.
[ASK] [✕] [&M] [♿] [▦] [⊇] [✕]

▼▼▼ StudioPLUS-Charlotte-Tyvola Rd H
(704) 527-1960. **$60-$84.** 5830 Westpark Dr 28217. I-77, exit 5 (Tyvola Rd), just e, then 0.4 mi s. Int corridors. **Pets:** Other species. $25 daily fee/room. Designated rooms, service with restrictions, crate.
[ASK] [✕] [♿] [▦] [⊇]

▼▼▼ TownePlace Suites by Marriott-Arrowood H
(704) 227-2000. **$80-$98.** 7805 Forest Point Blvd 28217. I-77, exit 3 southbound; exit 2 northbound, just e. Int corridors. **Pets:** Other species. $50 one-time fee/room. Designated rooms, service with restrictions, supervision. [✕] [&M] [♿] [▦] [⊇]

◈◈◈ ▼▼▼ ▼▼▼ TownePlace Suites by Marriott–University H
(704) 548-0388. **$161-$197.** 8710 Research Dr 28262. I-85, exit 45B, just w on SR 24, then just n. Int corridors. **Pets:** Accepted.
[SAVE] [✕] [&M] [♿] [▦] [⊇]

◈◈◈ ▼▼▼ ▼▼▼ The Westin Charlotte H ✿
(704) 375-2600. **$119-$359.** 601 S College St 28202. I-277, exit College St, just n; jct E Stonewall St. Int corridors. **Pets:** Medium, dogs only. $50 deposit/room. Service with restrictions, supervision.
[SAVE] [✕] [&M] [♿] [▦] [⊓] [⊇] [✕]

CONCORD

▼▼▼ Americas Best Value Inn M
(704) 788-8550. **Call for rates.** 2451 Kannapolis Hwy 28025. I-85, exit 58, just s on US 29, then just w. Ext corridors. **Pets:** Accepted.
[✕] [♿] [▦]

♦♦♦ ▼▼▼ **Embassy Suites Charlotte-Concord Golf Resort & Spa** �H 🌸

(704) 455-8200. **$109-$189.** 5400 John Q Hammons Dr 28027. I-85, exit 49 (Speedway Blvd), 1 mi e, then just n. Int corridors. **Pets:** Small. $50 one-time fee/pet. Service with restrictions, supervision.

SAVE ✕ ♿M 🛇 💻 🍴 ➤ ✕

▼▼ **Sleep Inn** �H

(704) 788-2150. **$60-$100.** 1120 Copperfield Blvd 28025. I-85, exit 60, just e. Int corridors. **Pets:** Accepted. ✕ ♿M 🛇 💻 ➤

CORNELIUS

♦♦♦ ▼▼ **Clarion Inn–Lake Norman** �H

(704) 896-0660. **$75-$230, 14 day notice.** 19608 Liverpool Pkwy 28031. I-77, exit 28, just w, then s. Int corridors. **Pets:** Small, other species. $25 one-time fee/room. Designated rooms, service with restrictions, supervision. SAVE ✕ 🛇 💻 ➤

▼▼ **Econo Lodge Inn & Suites** Ⓜ

(704) 892-3500. **Call for rates.** 20740 Torrence Chapel Rd 28031. I-77, exit 28, just w, then just n. Ext corridors. **Pets:** Accepted.

✕ 🛇 💻 ➤

HUNTERSVILLE

▼▼▼ **Candlewood Suites** �H

(704) 895-3434. **Call for rates.** 16530 Northcross Dr 28078. I-77, exit 25, just w on SR 73, then just s. Int corridors. **Pets:** Accepted.

✕ 🛇 💻

▼▼ **Quality Inn** �H

(704) 892-6597. **$59-$126.** 16825 Caldwell Creek Dr 28078. I-77, exit 25, just e on SR 73, just n on US 21, then just w. Ext/int corridors. **Pets:** Medium. $25 one-time fee/room. Designated rooms, service with restrictions, crate. ✕ 🛇 💻

▼▼▼ **Residence Inn by Marriott-Lake Norman** �H

(704) 584-0000. **$193-$235.** 16830 Kenton Dr 28078. I-77, exit 25, 1 mi w on SR 73, then just n. Int corridors. **Pets:** Accepted.

✕ ♿M 🛇 💻 ➤ ✕

MATTHEWS

♦♦♦ ▼▼▼ **Country Inn & Suites By Carlson, Charlotte I-485 at Hwy 74E** �H 🌸

(704) 846-8000. **$99-$119.** 2001 Mount Harmony Church Rd 28104. I-485, exit 51B, 0.5 mi e on US 74, just n on Independence Commerce Dr, then just w. Int corridors. **Pets:** Other species. $15 daily fee/pet. Service with restrictions. SAVE ✕ ♿M 🛇 💻 ➤

END METROPOLITAN AREA

CHEROKEE

♦♦♦ ▼▼▼ **Best Western Great Smokies Inn** Ⓜ

(828) 497-2020. **$80-$160.** 1636 Acquoni Rd 28719. US 441 N, 2.5 mi n; downtown. Ext corridors. **Pets:** Accepted. SAVE ✕ 🛇 💻 🍴 ➤

▼▼▼ **Microtel Inn & Suites** �H 🌸

(828) 497-7800. **$50-$120.** 674 Casino Tr 28719. Jct US 441 and Business Rt US 441 S. Int corridors. **Pets:** Other species. $15 daily fee/room. Designated rooms, service with restrictions, supervision.

ASK ✕ ♿M 🛇 💻 ➤

♦♦♦ ▼ **Pioneer Motel** Ⓜ

(828) 497-2435. **$48-$80, 3 day notice.** 122 Tsalagi Rd 28719. 0.8 mi w on US 19 S. Ext corridors. **Pets:** Small, dogs only. $25 one-time fee/pet. Designated rooms, service with restrictions.

SAVE ✕ ♿M 🛇 💻 ➤ ✕

▼ **Two Rivers Lodge** Ⓜ

(828) 488-2284. **$35-$120, 3 day notice.** 5280 Ela Rd 28713. 5 mi e on US 19 S. Ext corridors. **Pets:** Dogs only. $15 one-time fee/room. Designated rooms, no service. ASK ✕ 🛇 💻 ➤

CHIMNEY ROCK

♦♦♦ ▼▼▼ **Mountain Village Chalets** Ⓒ🄰

(828) 625-9783. **$67-$336, 14 day notice.** 950 Main St 28720. 1 mi w on US 74A. Ext corridors. **Pets:** Other species. $50 one-time fee/pet. No service, supervision. SAVE ✕ 🛇 💻

CLAREMONT

♦♦♦ ▼▼▼ **Super 8** Ⓜ

(828) 459-7777. **$66-$99.** 3054 N Oxford St 28610. I-40, exit 135, just s. Ext/int corridors. **Pets:** Accepted. SAVE ✕ 🛇 💻 ➤

CLAYTON

▼▼ **Sleep Inn** �H

(919) 772-7771. **Call for rates.** 105 Commerce Pkwy 27529. I-40, exit 312, just w on SR 42, then just s. Int corridors. **Pets:** Accepted.

✕ ♿M 🛇 💻 ➤

♦♦♦ ▼▼▼ **Super 8** Ⓜ

(919) 661-1991. **$60-$70.** 101 Leone Ct 27529. I-40, exit 312, just e on SR 42, then just s. Ext corridors. **Pets:** Accepted.

SAVE ✕ 🛇 💻 ➤

CLEMMONS

▼▼ **Super 8** �H

(336) 778-0931. **$61-$116.** 6204 Ramada Dr 27012. I-40, exit 184, just s, then just e. Int corridors. **Pets:** Accepted. ASK ✕ ♿M 🛇

▼▼ **The Village Inn Golf & Conference Center** �H

(336) 766-9121. **$68-$79, 3 day notice.** 6205 Ramada Dr 27012. I-40, exit 184, just s, then just e. Int corridors. **Pets:** Medium. $50 one-time fee/room. Designated rooms, service with restrictions, crate.

ASK ✕ 🛇 💻 🍴 ➤

COLUMBUS

♦♦♦ ▼▼▼ **Days Inn** Ⓜ

(828) 894-3303. **Call for rates.** 626 W Mills St 28722. I-26, exit 67, just w on SR 108. Ext corridors. **Pets:** Medium. $25 one-time fee/room. Service with restrictions, supervision. SAVE ✕ 🛇 💻 ➤

DUNN

▼▼ **Jameson Inn** Ⓜ

(910) 891-5758. **$83-$90.** 901 Jackson Rd 28334. I-95, exit 73, just w, then just s. Ext corridors. **Pets:** Accepted.

ASK ✕ ♿M 🛇 💻 ➤

DURHAM

▼▼ **Candlewood Suites** �H

(919) 484-9922. **$70-$115.** 1818 E NC Hwy 54 27713. I-40, exit 278, just s, then just w. Int corridors. **Pets:** Accepted. ASK ✕ ♿M 🛇 💻

▼▼▼ **Comfort Inn Medical Park** �H

(919) 471-6100. **$75-$89.** 1816 Hillandale Rd 27705. I-85, exit 174, just w. Int corridors. **Pets:** Medium. $49 one-time fee/room. Designated rooms, service with restrictions, crate. ✕ 🛇 💻 ➤ ✕

◆◆ **Durham Skyland Inn, a Magnuson Hotel** Ⓜ
(919) 383-2508. **$59-$99.** 5400 US 70 W 27705. I-85, exit 170, 0.3 mi e on US 70, then just n. Ext corridors. **Pets:** Accepted.
ASK ✕ ⬛ ▢ ⇌

◆◆ **Extended Stay Deluxe-Durham-RTP-Miami Blvd North** Ⓗ
(919) 941-2878. **$76-$86.** 4610 S Miami Blvd 27703. I-40, exit 281, just n. Int corridors. **Pets:** Other species. $25 daily fee/room. Designated rooms, service with restrictions, crate. ASK ✕ ⬛ ▢ ⇌

◆◆◆ **Extended Stay Deluxe-RTP-Miami Blvd-South** Ⓗ
(919) 998-0400. **$76-$100.** 4919 S Miami Blvd 27703. I-40, exit 281, just s. Int corridors. **Pets:** Other species. $25 daily fee/room. Designated rooms, service with restrictions, crate. ASK ✕ ♿ ⬛ ▢ ⇌

Ⓐ **Four Points by Sheraton** Ⓗ
(919) 806-8200. **$79-$249.** 7807 Leonardo Dr 27713. I-40, exit 274, just s on SR 751. Int corridors. **Pets:** Large, other species. $50 one-time fee/room. Designated rooms, supervision. SAVE ✕ ⬛ ▢ 🍴 ⇌

Ⓐ **Hilton Durham near Duke University** Ⓗ 🐾
(919) 383-8033. **$119-$329.** 3800 Hillsborough Rd 27705. I-85, exit 173, just e and Cole Mill Rd, then 0.5 mi w on US 70 business route. Int corridors. **Pets:** Medium. $50 one-time fee/pet. Service with restrictions, crate.
SAVE ✕ ⬛ ▢ 🍴 ⇌

◆◆◆ **Holiday Inn Express** Ⓗ
(919) 313-3244. **$97.** 2516 Guess Rd 27705. I-85, exit 175, just e. Int corridors. **Pets:** Accepted. ASK ✕ ⬛ ▢ ⇌

◆◆◆ **Holiday Inn Express Hotel & Suites-RTP** Ⓗ
(919) 474-9800. **$108.** 4912 S Miami Blvd 27703. I-40, exit 281, just s. Int corridors. **Pets:** Accepted. ASK ✕ ♿ ⬛ ▢

◆◆◆ **Homestead Studio Suites Hotel-Durham/University** Ⓜ
(919) 402-1700. **$54-$74.** 1920 Ivy Creek Blvd 27707. I-40, exit 270, 2 mi n on US 15/501, exit 105B, just e on Martin Luther King Jr Pkwy then just s; in University Place. Ext corridors. **Pets:** Other species. $25 daily fee/room. Designated rooms, service with restrictions, crate.
ASK ✕ ⬛ ▢

◆◆◆ **La Quinta Inn & Suites Raleigh (Durham-Chapel Hill)** Ⓗ 🐾
(919) 401-9660. **$59-$119.** 4414 Durham Chapel Hill Blvd 27707. I-40, exit 270, 1.7 mi n on US 15/501. Int corridors. **Pets:** Medium, other species. Service with restrictions, supervision.
ASK ✕ ♿ ⬛ ▢ ⇌

◆◆◆ **La Quinta Inn & Suites Raleigh (Research Triangle Park)** Ⓗ 🐾
(919) 484-1422. **$65-$109.** 1910 W Park Dr 27713. I-40, exit 278, just n on SR 55, then just e. Int corridors. **Pets:** Medium, other species. Service with restrictions, supervision. ASK ✕ ♿ ⬛ ▢ ⇌

Ⓐ ◆◆◆ **Quality Inn & Suites** Ⓗ 🐾
(919) 382-3388. **$55-$170.** 3710 Hillsborough Rd 27705. I-85, exit 173, just e on Cole Mill Rd, then just w on US 70 business route. Ext/int corridors. **Pets:** Medium. $25 one-time fee/room. Service with restrictions, supervision. SAVE ✕ ⬛ ▢ ⇌

Ⓐ ◆◆◆ **Residence Inn by Marriott** Ⓗ
(919) 361-1266. **$170-$208.** 201 Residence Inn Blvd 27713. I-40, exit 278, just s, then just w. Ext/int corridors. **Pets:** Accepted.
SAVE ✕ ♿ ⬛ ▢ ✕

◆◆ **Sleep Inn-RDU/RTP** Ⓗ
(919) 993-3393. **$72-$149.** 5208 Page Rd 27703. I-40, exit 282, just s. Int corridors. **Pets:** Accepted. ✕ ♿ ⬛ ▢

◆◆◆ **Staybridge Suites of Durham** Ⓗ
(919) 401-9800. **$99-$129.** 3704 Mt. Moriah Rd 27707. I-40, exit 270, just n on US 15/501, then just e. Int corridors. **Pets:** Accepted.
ASK ✕ ♿ ⬛ ▢ ⇌

◆◆◆ **StudioPLUS-Research Triangle Park** Ⓗ
(919) 361-1853. **$59-$79.** 2504 NC Hwy 54 27713. I-40, exit 278, just s on SR 55, then just e. Int corridors. **Pets:** Other species. $25 daily fee/room. Designated rooms, service with restrictions, crate.
ASK ✕ ⬛ ▢ ⇌

Ⓐ ◆◆◆ **Washington Duke Inn & Golf Club** Ⓗ 🐾
(919) 490-0999. **$349-$379.** 3001 Cameron Blvd 27705. US 15/501 Bypass, exit 107, 0.8 mi s on SR 751. Int corridors. **Pets:** Dogs only. $50 one-time fee/room. Designated rooms, service with restrictions, supervision. SAVE ✕ ⬛ 🍴 ⇌ ✕

Ⓐ ◆◆◆ **Wyndham Raleigh Durham Research Triangle Park** Ⓗ 🐾
(919) 941-6066. **$80-$224.** 4620 S Miami Blvd 27703. I-40, exit 281, just n. Int corridors. **Pets:** Other species. $50 one-time fee/pet. Designated rooms, service with restrictions, crate. SAVE ✕ ⬛ ▢ 🍴 ⇌

EDEN

◆◆ **Econo Lodge** Ⓜ
(336) 627-5131. **$225-$250.** 110 E Arbor Ln 27288. Jct SR 700/770, 1.4 mi s on SR 87/14, then just e. Ext corridors. **Pets:** Small. $10 daily fee/pet. Service with restrictions, supervision. ✕ ⬛

◆◆ **Hampton Inn** Ⓗ
(336) 627-1111. **Call for rates.** 724 S Van Buren Rd 27288. Jct SR 700/770, 1.4 mi s on SR 87/14. Int corridors. **Pets:** Accepted.
✕ ⬛ ▢ ⇌

◆◆ **Jameson Inn** Ⓜ
(336) 627-0472. **$73-$78.** 716 Linden Dr 27288. Jct SR 700/770, 1.4 mi s on SR 87/14, then just e. Ext corridors. **Pets:** Accepted.
ASK ✕ ♿ ⬛ ▢

FAYETTEVILLE

◆◆ **Comfort Inn Cross Creek** Ⓗ
(910) 867-1777. **$80-$115.** 1922 Skibo Rd 28314. All American Frwy, exit US 401 Bypass, 0.8 mi s. Int corridors. **Pets:** Accepted.
✕ ⬛ ▢ ⇌

Ⓐ ◆◆ **Country Hearth Inn & Suites** Ⓜ
(910) 438-0748. **$60-$90.** 1902 Cedar Creek Rd 28312. I-95, exit 49, just w. Ext corridors. **Pets:** Other species. $10 daily fee/pet. Service with restrictions, crate. SAVE ✕ ♿ ⬛ ▢ ⇌

Ⓐ ◆◆ **Econo Lodge I-95** Ⓜ
(910) 433-2100. **$65-$100.** 1952 Cedar Creek Rd 28312. I-95, exit 49, just w. Ext corridors. **Pets:** Medium. $10 daily fee/pet. Service with restrictions, supervision. SAVE ✕ ⬛ ▢ ⇌

◆◆ **Extended StayAmerica Fayetteville-Owen Dr.** Ⓜ
(910) 485-2747. **$79-$99.** 408 Owen Dr 28304. Jct All American Frwy. Ext corridors. **Pets:** Other species. $25 daily fee/room. Designated rooms, service with restrictions, crate. ASK ✕ ⬛ ▢

◆◆ **Extended Stay Deluxe Fayetteville-Cross Creek Mall** Ⓗ
(910) 868-5662. **$89-$109.** 4105 Sycamore Dairy Rd 28303. All American Frwy, exit Morganton Rd, just e, then just n. Int corridors. **Pets:** Other species. $25 daily fee/room. Designated rooms, service with restrictions, crate. ASK ✕ ⬛ ▢ ⇌

◆◆ **Holiday Inn Bordeaux** Ⓗ 🐾
(910) 323-0111. **$90.** 1707 Owen Dr 28304. Jct I-95 business route/US 301 S, 2.3 mi w. Ext/int corridors. **Pets:** Small. $50 one-time fee/pet. Designated rooms, service with restrictions, supervision.
ASK ✕ ⬛ ▢ 🍴 ⇌

AAA   ▼▼▼▼ Holiday Inn I-95 H
(910) 323-1600. **Call for rates.** 1944 Cedar Creek Rd 28312. I-95, exit 49, just w. Ext/int corridors. **Pets:** Accepted.
[SAVE] [X] 🛡 💻 🍴 🏊

▼▼▼ Innkeeper-Cross Creek M
(910) 867-7659. **$72, 3 day notice.** 1720 Skibo Rd 28303. All American Frwy, exit US 401 Bypass, just s; enter thru Cross Creek Plaza entrance. Ext/int corridors. **Pets:** Accepted. [ASK] [X] 🛡 🏊

AAA ▼▼▼ Red Roof Inn H
(910) 321-1460. **$56-$85.** 1569 Jim Johnson Rd 28312. I-95, exit 49, just w on SR 53, then just n. Int corridors. **Pets:** Large. Service with restrictions, crate. [SAVE] [X] 🛡 💻 🏊

▼▼▼▼ Residence Inn by Marriott-Fayetteville-Cross Creek-Ft. Bragg H
(910) 868-9005. **$143-$175.** 1468 Skibo Rd 28303. Jct SR 24/87, just s on US 401 Bypass. Int corridors. **Pets:** Large, other species. $100 one-time fee/room. Service with restrictions, crate.
[X] 🛡 💻 🏊 [X]

FLAT ROCK

▼▼▼ Highland Lake Inn H
(828) 693-6812. **$79-$259, 7 day notice.** 86 Lily Pad Ln 28731. I-26, exit 53, 2.1 mi w. Ext/int corridors. **Pets:** Accepted.
[ASK] [X] 🛡 💻 🍴 🏊 [X]

▼▼▼ Mountain Lodge H
(828) 693-9910. **Call for rates.** 755 Upward Rd 28731. I-26, exit 53, just s. Int corridors. **Pets:** Accepted. [X] 🛡 💻 🏊

FLETCHER

AAA ▼▼▼▼ Chateau On The Mountain BB ❀
(828) 651-9810. **$185-$350, 7 day notice.** 1048 Sandy Flat Mountain Rd 28732. I-26, exit 44, 1.9 mi s on Hendersonville Rd to Old Airport Rd/Mills Gap Rd, then 1.2 mi e, follow signs. Ext/int corridors. **Pets:** $50 one-time fee/room. Designated rooms, service with restrictions.
[SAVE] [X] 🛡 💻 🏊

▼▼▼▼ Holiday Inn Asheville-Airport H
(828) 684-1213. **$100-$150, 3 day notice.** 550 Airport Rd 28732. I-26, exit 40, just e. Int corridors. **Pets:** Accepted.
[ASK] [X] 🛡 💻 🍴 🏊

FOREST CITY

▼▼▼ Jameson Inn M
(828) 287-8788. **$78-$85.** 164 Jameson Inn Dr 28043. US 74 Bypass, exit 181, 1.8 mi nw on US 74A. Ext corridors. **Pets:** $15 daily fee/room. No service, crate. [ASK] [X] 🛡 💻 🏊

▼▼▼ Quality Inn M
(828) 248-3400. **Call for rates.** 205 Commercial Dr 28043. US 74 Bypass, exit 181, 1.8 mi nw on US 74A. Ext corridors. **Pets:** Accepted.
[X] 🛡 💻 🏊

FRANKLIN

▼▼▼ The Franklin Motel M
(828) 524-4431. **Call for rates.** 17 W Palmer St 28734. Jct US 441 Bypass, 1 mi n on US 441 business route; downtown. Ext corridors. **Pets:** Accepted. [X] 🛡 💻 🏊

▼▼▼ Microtel Inn & Suites H
(828) 349-9000. **$60-$130.** 81 Allman Dr 28734. Jct US 441 Bypass, 0.4 mi s on US 441 and 23. Int corridors. **Pets:** Accepted.
[ASK] [X] 🛡 💻

GASTONIA

AAA ▼▼▼▼ Best Western Executive Inn Gastonia H
(704) 868-2000. **$70-$199.** 360 Best Western Ct 28054. I-85, exit 20, just n on SR 279, then just e. Ext/int corridors. **Pets:** Accepted.
[SAVE] [X] 🛡 💻 🏊

▼▼▼ Fairfield Inn by Marriott H
(704) 867-5073. **$80-$98.** 1860 Remount Rd 28054. I-85, exit 20, just n on SR 279, then just e. Int corridors. **Pets:** Accepted.
[X] 🛡 💻 🏊

AAA ▼▼▼ Hampton Inn H
(704) 866-9090. **Call for rates.** 1859 Remount Rd 28054. I-85, exit 20 (New Hope Rd), just n on SR 279, then just e. Int corridors.
Pets: Accepted. [SAVE] [X] 🛡 💻 🏊

GOLDSBORO

AAA ▼▼▼ Best Western Goldsboro Inn M
(919) 735-7911. **$60-$170.** 801 US 70 E Bypass 27534. US 70 E Bypass, exit Wayne Memorial Dr eastbound, just n, just w on Eleventh St, then 0.4 mi sw on service road; exit westbound, straight on Eleventh St, then 0.4 mi sw on service road. Ext corridors. **Pets:** Accepted.
[SAVE] [X] 🛡 💻 🏊

AAA ▼▼▼▼ Comfort Suites H ❀
(919) 759-0098. **Call for rates.** 2613 N Park Dr 27534. US 70 E Bypass, exit Spence Ave, just n, then just e. Int corridors. **Pets:** Other species. $25 one-time fee/room. Service with restrictions, supervision.
[SAVE] [X] 🛡 💻 🏊

▼▼▼▼ Country Inn & Suites By Carlson H
(919) 581-0503. **Call for rates.** 2302 Norwood Ave 27534. US 70 Bypass, exit Wayne Memorial Dr, just n, just w on Eleventh St, then just sw on Lincoln Mercury Dr. Int corridors. **Pets:** Accepted.
[X] 🛡 💻 🏊

AAA ▼▼▼▼ Hampton Inn H ❀
(919) 778-1800. **$99-$179.** 905 N Spence Ave 27534. US 70 E Bypass, exit Spence Ave, just s. Int corridors. **Pets:** Medium, other species. Service with restrictions, supervision. [SAVE] [X] 🛡 💻 🏊

▼▼▼▼ Holiday Inn Express Goldsboro H
(919) 751-1999. **$90-$150.** 909 N Spence Ave 27534. US 70 E Bypass, exit Spence Ave, just s. Int corridors. **Pets:** Accepted.
[ASK] [X] 🛡 💻 🏊

▼▼ Jameson Inn H
(919) 778-9759. **$83-$90.** 1408 Harding Dr 27530. US 70 E Bypass, exit Spence Ave, just n, then just e on North Park Dr. Int corridors.
Pets: Accepted. [X] 🛡 💻 🏊

GREENSBORO

AAA ▼▼▼ Baymont Inn & Suites H ❀
(336) 294-6220. **$68-$84, 7 day notice.** 2001 Veasley St 27407. I-40, exit 217, just s on High Point Rd, then just w. Int corridors. **Pets:** Other species. Service with restrictions, supervision. [SAVE] [X] 🛡 💻 🏊

AAA ▼▼▼▼ Best Western–Greensboro Airport H
(336) 454-0333. **$75-$95.** 7800 National Service Rd 27409. I-40, exit 210 (SR 68), just s, just w on Thorndike Rd, then just n. Int corridors.
Pets: Small. $25 one-time fee/room. Service with restrictions, supervision.
[SAVE] [X] 🛡 💻 🏊

▼▼▼ Candlewood Suites H
(336) 454-0078. **Call for rates.** 7623 Thorndike Rd 27409. I-40, exit 210 (SR 68), just s, then just w. Int corridors. **Pets:** Accepted.
[X] 🛡 💻

AAA ▼▼▼▼ Clarion Hotel-Airport H
(336) 299-7650. **$86-$159.** 415 Swing Rd 27409. I-40, exit 213, just n, then just w. Int corridors. **Pets:** Accepted. [SAVE] [X] 🛡 💻 🍴 🏊

▼▼▼ Comfort Suites Airport H
(336) 882-6666. **$93-$117.** 7619 Thorndike Rd 27409. I-40, exit 210 (SR 68), just s, then just w. Int corridors. **Pets:** Small. $20 one-time fee/room. Designated rooms, service with restrictions, crate.
[X] 🛡 💻 🏊

▼▼ **Crestwood Suites** �H
(336) 886-1250. **Call for rates.** 501 Americhase Dr 27409. I-40, exit 210 (SR 68), 0.5 mi s. Int corridors. **Pets:** Small. $15 daily fee/pet. Designated rooms, service with restrictions, crate. ⊠ 🖥 🖵

▼▼▼ **Drury Inn & Suites-Greensboro** �H
(336) 856-9696. **$80-$174.** 3220 High Point Rd 27407. I-40, exit 217, just s. Int corridors. **Pets:** Other species. No service, supervision.
🅰️🆂🅺 ⊠ 🖥 🖵 ⬳

▼▼ **Econo Lodge Inn & Suites** 🅼
(336) 275-9575. **$50-$100.** 120 Seneca Rd 27406. I-40/85 business route, exit 221, just s, then e. Ext/int corridors. **Pets:** Accepted.
⊠ 🖥 🖵 ⬳

▼▼ **Extended Stay Deluxe-Greensboro-Airport** �H
(336) 454-0080. **$81-$119.** 7617 Thorndike Rd 27409. I-40, exit 210 (SR 68), just s, then just w. Int corridors. **Pets:** Other species. $25 daily fee/room. Designated rooms, service with restrictions, crate.
🅰️🆂🅺 ⊠ 🖥 🖵 ⬳

▼▼ **Holiday Inn Express** �H
(336) 854-0090. **Call for rates.** 4305 Big Tree Way 27409. I-40, exit 214 or 214B, just ne on Wendover Ave, then just w. Int corridors.
Pets: Accepted. ⊠ 🅼 🖥 🖵 ⬳

▼▼▼ **Holiday Inn Express & Suites–Airport** �H
(336) 882-0004. **Call for rates.** 645 S Regional Rd 27409. I-40, exit 210 (SR 68), just s, then just e. Int corridors. **Pets:** Accepted.
⊠ 🖥 🖵 ⬳

▼▼ **Quality Inn & Suites** �H
(336) 697-4000. **$60-$100.** 3114 Cedar Park Rd 27405. I-40/85 business route, exit 224, just w on SR 6, then just n. Ext corridors. **Pets:** Accepted.
⊠ 🅼 🖥 🖵 ⬳

▼▼▼ **Quality Inn & Suites-Airpark East** �H
(336) 668-3638. **$65-$75.** 7067 Albert Pick Rd 27409. I-40, exit 210 (SR 68) westbound, just s, then just e; exit eastbound, just e. Int corridors. **Pets:** Small, other species. $25 one-time fee/room. Designated rooms, service with restrictions, supervision. ⊠ 🖥 🖵 ⬳

▲▲▲ ▼▼ **Red Roof Inn Airport** 🅼
(336) 271-2636. **$50-$106.** 615 Regional Rd S 27409. I-40, exit 210 (SR 68), just s, then just e. Ext corridors. **Pets:** Large. Service with restrictions, crate. 🆂🅰️🆅🅴 ⊠ 🅼 🖥

▼▼▼ **Residence Inn by Marriott-Greensboro Airport** �H
(336) 632-4666. **$130-$158.** 7616 Thorndike Rd 27409. I-40, exit 210 (SR 68), just s, then just w. Int corridors. **Pets:** Medium, other species. $100 one-time fee/room. Service with restrictions, supervision.
⊠ 🅼 🖥 🖵 ⬳ ⊠

▼▼▼ **Wyndham Garden Hotel–Greensboro Airport** �H
(336) 668-0421. **$105-$165.** 6426 Burnt Poplar Rd 27409. I-40, exit 211, just n on Gallimore Dairy Rd, then just w. Int corridors. **Pets:** Accepted.
🅰️🆂🅺 ⊠ 🖥 🖵 🍴 ⬳

GREENVILLE

▼▼ **Baymont Inn & Suites** 🅼
(252) 355-2521. **$69-$109.** 3439 S Memorial Dr 27834. Jct US 264 alternate route, just s on SR 11/903. Ext corridors. **Pets:** Accepted.
🅰️🆂🅺 ⊠ 🖥 🖵 ⬳

▼▼ **Home-Towne Suites** �H
(252) 752-3411. **$59-$130.** 2111 W Arlington Blvd 27834. Jct US 13/SR 11, 0.4 mi w on Stantonsburg Rd, then just s. Int corridors.
Pets: Medium. $25 daily fee/room. Service with restrictions, crate.
🅰️🆂🅺 ⊠ 🖥 🖵

▼▼ **Jameson Inn** 🅼
(252) 752-7382. **$73-$78.** 920 Crosswinds St 27834. Jct US 13/SR 11, then just w. Ext corridors. **Pets:** Small. $15 daily fee/pet. Service with restrictions, supervision.
🅰️🆂🅺 ⊠ 🅼 🖥 🖵 ⬳

HAVELOCK

▼▼▼ **Quality Inn** �H
(252) 444-1111. **Call for rates.** 400 Hwy 70 W 28532. Jct SR 101, 1.9 mi w. Int corridors. **Pets:** Medium. $25 daily fee/pet. Designated rooms, service with restrictions, supervision. ⊠ 🅼 🖥 🖵 ⬳

HAYESVILLE

▼▼ **Chatuge Mountain Inn** 🅼
(828) 389-9340. **$60-$90.** 4238 Hwy 64 E 28904. Jct SR 69, 4.2 mi e. Ext corridors. **Pets:** Accepted. 🅰️🆂🅺 ⊠ 🖥 🖵

▼▼ **Deerfield Inn** 🅼
(828) 389-8272. **$60-$100.** 40 Chatuge Ln 28904. 3 mi e on US 64. Ext corridors. **Pets:** Small. $10 daily fee/pet. Designated rooms, service with restrictions, supervision. 🅰️🆂🅺 ⊠ 🅼 🖥 🖵

HENDERSON

▼▼ **Econo Lodge** 🅼
(252) 438-8511. **$44-$60.** 112 Parham Rd 27536. I-85, exit 215, just e on US 158. Ext corridors. **Pets:** Medium, other species. $10 daily fee/pet. Service with restrictions, supervision. 🅰️🆂🅺 ⊠ 🖥 🖵 ⬳

▼▼ **Jameson Inn** �H
(252) 430-0247. **$78-$85.** 400 N Cooper Dr 27536. I-85, exit 212, just w on Ruin Creek Rd, then just n. Int corridors. **Pets:** Accepted.
🅰️🆂🅺 ⊠ 🅼 🖥 🖵 ⬳

▼▼ **Lamplight Inn B&B** 🅱️🅱️ 🐾
(252) 438-6311. **$90-$120, 7 day notice.** 1680 Flemingtown Rd 27537. I-85, exit 220, 1.5 mi nw. Int corridors. **Pets:** Small, other species. Designated rooms, service with restrictions, crate. ⊠ ☎

▲▲▲ ▼▼ **Sleep Inn** �H
(252) 433-9449. **$55-$85.** 18 Market St 27537. I-85, exit 212, just w on Ruin Creek Rd, then just se on Zeb Robinson Rd. Int corridors.
Pets: Small, other species. $15 daily fee/pet. Designated rooms, service with restrictions, supervision. 🆂🅰️🆅🅴 ⊠ 🖥 🖵

HENDERSONVILLE

▲▲▲ ▼▼ **Best Western Hendersonville Inn** 🅼
(828) 692-0521. **$50-$150.** 105 Sugarloaf Rd 28792. I-26, exit 49A, just e. Ext corridors. **Pets:** Medium. $10 daily fee/pet. Service with restrictions, crate. 🆂🅰️🆅🅴 ⊠ 🅼 🖥 🖵 🍴 ⬳

▲▲▲ ▼▼ **Comfort Inn** 🅼
(828) 693-8800. **Call for rates.** 206 Mitchell Dr 28792. I-26, exit 49B, just w. Ext corridors. **Pets:** Large, other species. $15 daily fee/pet. Service with restrictions, supervision. 🆂🅰️🆅🅴 ⊠ 🖥 🖵 ⬳

▲▲▲ ▼▼ **Days Inn** 🅼
(828) 697-5999. **$60-$120.** 102 Mitchell Dr 28772. I-26, exit 49B, just sw. Ext corridors. **Pets:** Medium. $15 daily fee/pet. No service, supervision.
🆂🅰️🆅🅴 ⊠ 🖥 🖵

▼▼▼ **Inn on Church Street** 🅲🅸
(828) 693-3258. **$109-$275, 7 day notice.** 201 3rd Ave W 28739. Jct of Church St; center. Int corridors. **Pets:** Dogs only. $30 one-time fee/room. Service with restrictions, supervision. ⊠ 🖥 🖵 🍴

▲▲▲ ▼▼▼ **Ramada Limited** �H
(828) 697-0006. **$48-$130.** 150 Sugarloaf Rd 28792. I-26, exit 49A, just e, then 1 mi s. Int corridors. **Pets:** Medium. $15 daily fee/pet. Designated rooms, service with restrictions, supervision. 🆂🅰️🆅🅴 ⊠ 🅼 🖥 🖵

HICKORY

▼▼ **Jameson Inn** 🅼
(828) 304-0410. **$78-$85.** 1120 13th Ave Dr SE 28602. I-40, exit 125, just s, then 0.4 mi w. Ext corridors. **Pets:** Accepted.
🅰️🆂🅺 ⊠ 🅼 🖥 🖵 ⬳

◈◈ ▼▼ Red Roof Inn Hickory Ⓜ

(828) 323-1500. **$50-$80, 14 day notice.** 1184 Lenoir Rhyne Blvd 28602. I-40, exit 125, just n. Int corridors. **Pets:** Large. Service with restrictions, crate. (SAVE) ⊠ ⬥M 🛗 🖥

HIGHLANDS

◈◈ ▼▼◈ Mountain High Lodge Ⓜ ❀

(828) 526-2790. **$49-$189, 7 day notice.** 200 Main St 28741. Just w on US 64; downtown. Ext corridors. **Pets:** Other species. Designated rooms, service with restrictions, supervision. (SAVE) ⊠ ⬥M 🛗 🖥

HILLSBOROUGH

◈◈ ▼▼◈▼ Holiday Inn Express Ⓗ

(919) 644-7997. **Call for rates.** 202 Cardinal Dr 27278. I-85, exit 164, just se, then just s; I-40, exit 261, 1.2 mi n, then just w. Int corridors. **Pets:** Medium. $25 daily fee/pet. Designated rooms, service with restrictions, supervision. (SAVE) ⊠ ⬥M 🛗 🖥 ⇆

JACKSONVILLE

▼▼▼▼ The Baymont Inn & Suites Jacksonville Ⓗ

(910) 347-6500. **$79-$129, 30 day notice.** 474 Western Blvd 28546. Jct US 17, just n. Ext corridors. **Pets:** Small. Service with restrictions, supervision. (ASK) ⊠ 🖥 ⇆

▼▼◈ Extended StayAmerica Jacksonville Camp Lejeune Ⓗ

(910) 347-7684. **$89-$109.** 20 McDaniel Dr 28546. Jct Western Blvd, just n on US 17, then just w. Int corridors. **Pets:** Other species. $25 daily fee/room. Designated rooms, service with restrictions, crate.

(ASK) ⊠ ⬥M 🛗 🖥

▼▼◈ Innkeeper Ⓗ

(910) 938-0800. **$72-$81, 3 day notice.** 2139 N Marine Blvd 28546. Jct Western Blvd, just n on US 17. Int corridors. **Pets:** Accepted.

(ASK) ⊠ ⬥M 🛗 🖥 ⇆

▼▼◈▼ TownePlace Suites by Marriott Ⓗ

(910) 478-9795. **$112-$136.** 400 Northwest Dr 28541. Jct US 17 (Marine Blvd), 2 mi w on Western Blvd, then just s. Int corridors. **Pets:** Accepted.

⊠ ⬥M 🛗 🖥 ⇆

JONESVILLE

◈◈ ▼▼ Comfort Inn Ⓜ ❀

(336) 835-9400. **Call for rates.** 1633 Winston Rd 28642. I-77, exit 82, just w on SR 67. Ext corridors. **Pets:** Medium, other species. $10 one-time fee/pet. Designated rooms, supervision.

(SAVE) ⊠ ⬥M 🛗 🖥 ⇆

◈◈ ▼▼▼ Days Inn Jonesville-Elkin Ⓜ

(336) 526-6777. **$69-$109.** 1540 NC 67 Hwy 28642. I-77, exit 82, 0.3 mi w. Ext corridors. **Pets:** Small. $10 daily fee/pet. Designated rooms, service with restrictions, supervision. (SAVE) ⊠ 🛗 🖥 ⇆

▼▼ Holiday Inn Express Ⓗ

(336) 835-6000. **$79-$99.** 1713 SR 67 28642. I-77, exit 82, just e. Int corridors. **Pets:** Small. $15 one-time fee/pet. Service with restrictions, supervision. (ASK) ⊠ ⬥M 🛗 🖥 ⇆

KENLY

▼▼ Super 8 Ⓜ

(919) 284-3800. **Call for rates.** 843 Johnston Pkwy 27542. I-95, exit 106, just w, then just s. Ext corridors. **Pets:** Accepted. ⊠ ⬥M ⇆

LAKE TOXAWAY

◈◈ ▼▼▼▼ Cabins at Seven Foxes Ⓒ❀

(828) 877-6333. **$150-$275, 30 day notice.** Seven Foxes Ln 28747. Jct US 64 and SR 281 N, 0.5 mi n to Slick Fisher Rd, then 1.4 mi w. Ext corridors. **Pets:** Dogs only. $50 one-time fee/pet. No service, supervision.

(SAVE) ⊠ 🛗 🖥 ⊠

LAURINBURG

▼▼▼ Jameson Inn Ⓜ

(910) 277-0080. **$73-$78.** 14 Jameson Inn Ct 28352. Jct US 74 Bypass, exit 183, just n on US 15/401 Bypass, just e. Ext corridors.
Pets: Accepted. (ASK) ⊠ 🛗 🖥 ⇆

LENOIR

◈◈ ▼▼▼ Days Inn Ⓜ

(828) 754-0731. **$51-$60.** 206 Blowing Rock Blvd 28645. Jct US 18, just n on US 321. Ext corridors. **Pets:** Very small, dogs only. $10 daily fee/pet. Service with restrictions, supervision. (SAVE) ⊠ 🛗 🖥

▼▼▼ Jameson Inn Ⓜ

(828) 758-1200. **$56-$71.** 350 Wilkesboro Blvd 28645. Jct US 321, 0.4 mi ne on SR 18. Ext corridors. **Pets:** Accepted.

⊠ ⬥M 🛗 🖥 ⇆

LEXINGTON

▼▼▼▼ Comfort Suites of Lexington Ⓗ

(336) 357-2333. **$87-$135.** 1620 Cotton Grove Rd 27292. I-85, exit 91, just s on SR 8, then just ne. Ext/int corridors. **Pets:** Small. $10 daily fee/room, $25 one-time fee/room. Designated rooms, no service, crate.

⊠ ⬥M 🛗 🖥 ⇆

LITTLE SWITZERLAND

◈◈ ▼▼▼▼ Switzerland Inn Ⓒ

(828) 765-2153. **$110-$220, 10 day notice.** 86 High Ridge Rd 28749. Jct SR 226A and Blue Ridge Pkwy, MM 334. Ext/int corridors.
Pets: Other species. $20 daily fee/room. Designated rooms, service with restrictions. (SAVE) ⊠ ⬥M 🛗 🖥 🍴 ⇆ ⊠

LUMBERTON

◈◈ ▼▼▼▼ Best Western Inn Ⓜ

(910) 618-9799. **$89-$139.** 201 Jackson Ct 28358. I-95, exit 22, just e, then just s. Ext corridors. **Pets:** Small, other species. $10 daily fee/pet. Service with restrictions, supervision. (SAVE) ⊠ 🛗 🖥 ⇆

MOCKSVILLE

◈◈ ▼▼▼▼ Comfort Inn & Suites Ⓗ

(336) 751-5966. **Call for rates.** 629 Madison Rd 27028. I-40, exit 170, just s on US 601, then just w. Int corridors. **Pets:** Accepted.

(SAVE) ⊠ ⬥M 🛗 🖥 ⇆

◈◈ ▼▼▼ Quality Inn Ⓜ ❀

(336) 751-7310. **Call for rates.** 1500 Yadkinville Rd 27028. I-40, exit 170, just s on US 601. Ext corridors. **Pets:** Large. $20 one-time fee/room. Service with restrictions, supervision. (SAVE) ⊠ 🛗 🖥 ⇆

MONROE

▼▼ Super 8 Ⓜ

(704) 289-1555. **$99-$419.** 608-E W Roosevelt Blvd 28110. Jct US 601, 1 mi e on US 74. Ext corridors. **Pets:** Other species. $10 daily fee/pet. Service with restrictions, crate. (ASK) ⊠ ⬥M 🛗 🖥 ⇆

MOREHEAD CITY

▼▼▼▼ Holiday Inn Express Hotel & Suites Ⓗ ❀

(252) 247-5001. **Call for rates.** 5063 Executive Dr 28557. Jct US 70 and SR 24. Int corridors. **Pets:** Large, other species. $25 one-time fee/room. Designated rooms, service with restrictions. ⊠ 🛗 🖥 ⇆

MORGANTON

◈◈ ▼▼▼▼ Comfort Inn & Suites Ⓗ

(828) 430-4000. **Call for rates.** 1273 Burkemont Ave 28655. I-40, exit 103, just s. Int corridors. **Pets:** Other species. $25 one-time fee/pet. Designated rooms, service with restrictions, supervision.

(SAVE) ⊠ ⬥M 🛗 🖥 ⇆

▼▼▼ Quality Inn Ⓗ

(828) 437-0171. **Call for rates.** 2400 S Sterling St 28655. I-40, exit 105 (SR 18), just s. Ext corridors. **Pets:** Accepted.

⊠ ⬥M 🛗 🖥 🍴 ⇆

▼▼ Sleep Inn H

(828) 433-9000. **$65-$130.** 2400A S Sterling St 28655. I-40, exit 105 (SR 18), just s. Int corridors. **Pets:** Accepted. ⊠ ⓖ 🛏 🖵

MORRISVILLE

▼▼ Extended StayAmerica-RDU Airport M

(919) 380-1499. **$67-$81.** 2700 Slater Rd 27560. I-40, exit 284 or 284A, 0.4 mi s on Airport Blvd, then just w. Ext corridors. **Pets:** Other species. $25 daily fee/room. Designated rooms, service with restrictions, crate.

ASK ⊠ 🛏 🖵

▼▼ Holiday Inn Express H

(919) 653-2260. **Call for rates.** 1014 Airport Blvd 27560. I-40, exit 284 or 284A, just s. Int corridors. **Pets:** Accepted. ⊠ ⓖ 🛏 🖵 ⊸

▼▼ Holiday Inn–Raleigh-Durham Airport H

(919) 465-1910. **Call for rates.** 930 Airport Blvd 27560. I-40, exit 284 or 284A, just s. Int corridors. **Pets:** Small. $10 daily fee/pet. Service with restrictions, supervision. ⊠ ⓖ 🛏 🖵 🍴 ⊸

◆◆◆ La Quinta Inn & Suites–Aerial Center Pkwy H ☙

(919) 481-3600. **$69-$99.** 1001 Aerial Center Pkwy 27560. I-40, exit 284 or 284A, just s, then just e; in Aerial Center Park. Int corridors. **Pets:** Medium, other species. Service with restrictions, supervision.

ASK ⊠ ⓖ 🛏 🖵 ⊸

◆◆◆ La Quinta Inn & Suites (Raleigh-Durham Int'l Airport) H ☙

(919) 461-1771. **$75-$109.** 1001 Hospitality Ct 27560. I-40, exit 284 or 284A, just s, just e on Aerial Center Pkwy, then just ne; in Aerial Center Park. Int corridors. **Pets:** Medium, other species. Service with restrictions, supervision. ASK ⊠ ⓖ 🛏 🖵 ⊸

▼▼▼ Residence Inn by Marriott-Raleigh/Durham Airport H

(919) 467-8689. **$184-$224.** 2020 Hospitality Ct 27560. I-40, exit 284 or 284A, just s on Airport Blvd, just e on Aerial Center Pkwy, then just ne. Int corridors. **Pets:** $75 one-time fee/room. Service with restrictions, supervision. ECO ⊠ ⓖ 🛏 🖵 ⊸ ⊠

▼▼▼ Staybridge Suites Raleigh Durham Airport H

(919) 468-0180. **Call for rates.** 1012 Airport Blvd 27560. I-40, exit 284 or 284A, just s; enter between Hampton Inn RDU and Holiday Inn Express. Int corridors. **Pets:** Accepted. ⊠ ⓖ 🛏 🖵 ⊠

MOUNT AIRY

▼▼ Quality Inn M

(336) 789-2000. **$69-$140.** 2136 Rockford St 27030. Jct US 52, 0.6 mi s on US 601. Ext corridors. **Pets:** Medium. $25 one-time fee/room. Designated rooms, service with restrictions, supervision. ⊠ 🛏 🖵 ⊸

MURPHY

AAA ▼▼ Best Western of Murphy H

(828) 837-3060. **$59-$79.** 1522 Andrews Rd 28906. US 74, 19 and 129, exit Andrews Rd. Ext corridors. **Pets:** Accepted.

SAVE ⊠ ⓖ 🛏 🖵 ⊸

AAA ▼▼ Days Inn M

(828) 837-8030. **$59-$99.** 754 Hwy 64 W 28906. US 64 W, 19 S, 74 W and 129 S. Ext corridors. **Pets:** Accepted. SAVE ⊠ 🛏 🖵 ⊸

ORIENTAL

▼▼ Oriental Marina & Inn CO ☙

(252) 249-1818. **$89-$174.** 103 Wall St 28571. Jct SR 55 (Broad St), just ne on Hodges St. Ext corridors. **Pets:** Other species. $50 one-time fee/room. Service with restrictions, supervision.

ASK ⊠ 🛏 🖵 🍴 ⊸

OUTER BANKS AREA

KILL DEVIL HILLS

▼▼▼ First Flight Retreat Condominiums CO

(252) 489-4747. **$145-$399.** 815 S Virginia Dare Tr 27948. SR 12, at MM 8.5. Int corridors. **Pets:** Accepted. ASK 🛏 🖵 ⊸ ⊠

▼▼ Quality Inn-John Yancey M

(252) 441-7141. **Call for rates.** 2009 S Virginia Dare Tr 27948. SR 12, at MM 10.3. Ext/int corridors. **Pets:** Other species. $20 daily fee/pet. Service with restrictions, crate. ⊠ 🛏 🖵 ⊸

AAA ▼▼▼ Ramada Plaza Nags Head Beach H ☙

(252) 441-2151. **$64-$259, 3 day notice.** 1701 S Virginia Dare Tr 27948. SR 12, at MM 9.5. Int corridors. **Pets:** $25 daily fee/pet. Designated rooms, service with restrictions.

SAVE ⊠ 🛏 🖵 🍴 ⊸ ⊠

AAA ▼▼▼ Travelodge-Nags Head Beach H ☙

(252) 441-0411. **$39-$189, 3 day notice.** 804 N Virginia Dare Tr 27948. SR 12, at MM 8.1. Ext/int corridors. **Pets:** Other species. Designated rooms, crate. SAVE ⊠ 🛏 🖵 ⊸

NAGS HEAD

▼▼▼ Comfort Inn Oceanfront South H ☙

(252) 441-6315. **$90-$190.** 8031 Old Oregon Inlet Rd 27959. SR 12, at MM 17. Int corridors. **Pets:** Other species. $20 daily fee/room. Designated rooms, service with restrictions, supervision. ⊠ 🛏 🖵 ⊸

OCRACOKE

AAA ▼▼▼ The Anchorage Inn M ☙

(252) 928-1101. **$99-$299, 7 day notice.** 205 Irvin Garrish Hwy (SR 12) 27960. From Cedar Island Ferry, just n. Ext corridors. **Pets:** Other species. $25 daily fee/room. Designated rooms, service with restrictions, supervision. SAVE ⊠ 🛏 🖵 ⊸ ⊠

END AREA

OXFORD

△△△▽ ▼▼▼▼ Comfort Inn & Suites
Oxford/Henderson **H**

(919) 692-1000. **Call for rates.** 1000 Linden Ave 27565. I-85, exit 204, just e. Int corridors. **Pets:** $10 daily fee/pet. Service with restrictions, supervision. [SAVE] [X] 🔒 💻 ➹

PILOT MOUNTAIN

▼▼▼ Quality Inn & Suites **M**

(336) 368-2237. **$60-$100.** 711 S Key St 27041. US 52, exit 134, just e on SR 268. Ext corridors. **Pets:** $25 one-time fee/pet. Service with restrictions, supervision. [X] 🔥M 🔒 💻 ➹

PINEHURST

△△△▽ ▼▼▼▼ Homewood Suites by Hilton **H**

(910) 255-0300. **$104-$199.** 250 Central Park Ave 28374. Jct SR 5 and 211; in Olmsted Village. Int corridors. **Pets:** $50 one-time fee/room. Service with restrictions, crate. [SAVE] [X] 🔥M 🔒 💻 ➹

▼▼▼▼ SpringHill Suites by Marriott **H**

(910) 695-0234. **$109-$119.** 10024 US 15/501 28374. Jct US 1, 2.3 mi n. Int corridors. **Pets:** Accepted. [X] 🔥M 🔒 💻 ➹

PLYMOUTH

▼▼▼ Holiday Inn Express **H**

(252) 793-4700. **Call for rates.** 840 US Hwy 64 W 27962. Jct SR 32 S, 1 mi w. Ext/int corridors. **Pets:** $25 one-time fee/room. Designated rooms, service with restrictions, supervision. [X] 🔥M 🔒 💻 ➹

△△△▽ ▼▼ Port-o Plymouth Inn **M**

(252) 793-5006. **$50-$100.** 510 Hwy 64 E 27962. On US 64. Ext corridors. **Pets:** Medium. $10 daily fee/pet. Designated rooms, service with restrictions, crate. [SAVE] [X] 🔒 ➹

RALEIGH

△△△▽ ▼▼▼ Best Western Raleigh North **H**

(919) 872-5000. **$75-$85.** 2715 Capital Blvd 27604. I-440, exit 11 or 11B, just n on US 1. Int corridors. **Pets:** Accepted. [SAVE] [X] 🔒 💻 ➹

▼▼▼ Candlewood Suites-Crabtree **H**

(919) 789-4840. **$89.** 4433 Lead Mine Rd 27612. I-440, exit 7 or 7B, just w, then just n. Int corridors. **Pets:** Accepted. [ASK] [X] 🔥M 🔒 💻

△△△▽ ▼▼▼▼ Comfort Suites **H**

(919) 876-2211. **$75-$138.** 4400 Capital Blvd 27604. I-440, exit 11 and 11B, 2.5 mi n on US 1. Int corridors. **Pets:** Medium, other species. $25 one-time fee/pet. Designated rooms, service with restrictions, crate.
[SAVE] [X] 🔥M 🔒 💻 ➹

▼▼▼ Days Inn **M**

(919) 878-9310. **$46-$69.** 3201 Wake Forest Rd 27609. I-440, exit 10 (Wake Forest Rd), just n, then just w. Ext corridors. **Pets:** $10 daily fee/room. Designated rooms, service with restrictions, crate.
[ASK] [X] 🔒 💻 ➹

▼▼▼ Extended StayAmerica-Raleigh-North Raleigh **H**

(919) 829-7271. **$49-$69.** 911 Wake Towne Dr 27609. I-440, exit 10 (Wake Forest Rd), just s, then w. Int corridors. **Pets:** Other species. $25 daily fee/room. Designated rooms, service with restrictions, crate.
[ASK] [X] 🔒 💻

△△△▽ ▼▼▼▼ Fairfield Inn & Suites by
Marriott-Crabtree **H**

(919) 881-9800. **$143-$175.** 2201 Summit Park Ln 27612. I-440, exit 7 or 7B, just w on US 70, just s on Blue Ridge Rd, then just e. Int corridors. **Pets:** Accepted. [SAVE] [X] 🔥M 🔒 💻 ➹

▼▼▼▼ Hilton North Raleigh **H** 🐾

(919) 872-2323. **$99-$219.** 3415 Wake Forest Rd 27609. I-440, exit 10 (Wake Forest Rd), 0.3 mi n. Int corridors. **Pets:** Medium. $75 one-time fee/pet. Designated rooms, service with restrictions, crate.
[X] 🔥M 🔒 💻 🍴 ➹

▼▼▼▼ Holiday Inn Crabtree Valley **H**

(919) 782-8600. **$79-$140.** 4100 Glenwood Ave 27612. I-440, exit 7 or 7B, just w on US 70. Int corridors. **Pets:** Medium, other species. $50 one-time fee/room. Service with restrictions, supervision.
[ASK] [X] 🔥M 🔒 💻 🍴 ➹ [X]

△△△▽ ▼▼▼▼ Holiday Inn Raleigh-North **H**

(919) 872-3500. **$69-$119, 3 day notice.** 2805 Highwoods Blvd 27604. I-440, exit 11 or 11B, just n on US 1, then just w. Int corridors.
Pets: Accepted. [SAVE] [X] 🔥M 🔒 💻 🍴 ➹ [X]

▼▼ Homestead Studio Suites Hotel-Raleigh/Crabtree
Valley **H**

(919) 510-8551. **$59-$79.** 4810 Bluestone Dr 27612. I-440, exit 7 or 7B, 1.6 mi w on US 70, then just s. Ext corridors. **Pets:** Other species. $25 daily fee/room. Designated rooms, service with restrictions, crate.
[ASK] [X] 🔒 ➹

▼▼▼ Homestead Studio Suites
Hotel-Raleigh/Northeast **H**

(919) 807-9970. **$59-$79.** 2601 Appliance Ct 27604. I-440, exit 11 or 11B, just n on US 1, then just e. Ext corridors. **Pets:** Other species. $25 daily fee/room. Designated rooms, service with restrictions, crate.
[ASK] [X] 🔒 💻 ➹

▼▼▼ Homestead Studio Suites Hotel-Raleigh/North
Raleigh **M**

(919) 981-7353. **$54-$74.** 3531 Wake Forest Rd 27609. I-440, exit 10 (Wake Forest Rd), 0.5 mi n. Ext corridors. **Pets:** Other species. $25 daily fee/room. Designated rooms, service with restrictions, crate.
[ASK] [X] 🔥M 🔒 💻

▼▼▼ La Quinta Inn & Suites Raleigh (Crabtree) **H** 🐾

(919) 785-0071. **$79-$119.** 2211 Summit Park Ln 27612. I-440, exit 7 or 7B, just w on US 70, just s on Blue Ridge Rd, then just e. Int corridors. **Pets:** Medium, other species. Service with restrictions, supervision.
[ASK] [X] 🔥M 🔒 💻 ➹

△△△▽ ▼▼▼ Red Roof Inn-South **H**

(919) 833-6005. **$60-$75.** 1813 S Saunders St 27603. I-40, exit 298B, just n. Int corridors. **Pets:** Large. Service with restrictions, crate.
[SAVE] [X] 🔥M 🔒

△△△▽ ▼▼▼▼ Residence Inn by Marriott Crabtree **H**

(919) 279-3000. **$179-$219.** 2200 Summit Park Ln 27612. I-440, exit 7 or 7B, just w on US 70, just s on Blue Ridge Rd, then just e. Int corridors. **Pets:** Accepted. [SAVE] [X] 🔥M 🔒 💻 [X]

△△△▽ ▼▼▼ Residence Inn by Marriott-North
Raleigh **H** 🐾

(919) 878-6100. **$157-$191.** 1000 Navaho Dr 27609. I-440, exit 10 (Wake Forest Rd), just n, then w. Ext corridors. **Pets:** Medium. $100 one-time fee/room. Designated rooms, service with restrictions.
[SAVE] [X] 🔥M 🔒 💻 ➹ [X]

REIDSVILLE

△△△▽ ▼▼▼ Comfort Inn **M**

(336) 634-1275. **Call for rates.** 2203 Barnes St 27320. US 29, exit 150 (Barnes St), just e. Ext corridors. **Pets:** Small. $15 daily fee/pet. Service with restrictions, supervision. [SAVE] [X] 🔥M 🔒 💻 ➹

RESEARCH TRIANGLE PARK

▼▼▼▼ Radisson Hotel in Research Triangle Park **H**

(919) 549-8631. **$199-$239.** 150 Park Dr 27709. I-40, exit 280, just s, then just w. Int corridors. **Pets:** Accepted.
[ASK] [X] 🔒 💻 🍴 ➹ [X]

ROANOKE RAPIDS

▼▼▼ Jameson Inn **M**

(252) 533-0022. **$83-$90.** 101 S Old Farm Rd 27870. I-95, exit 173, 0.5 mi w on US 158, then just s. Ext corridors. **Pets:** Accepted.
[ASK] [X] 🔒 💻 ➹

ROBBINSVILLE

▼▼ ▼▼ Microtel Inn & Suites 🅷
(828) 479-6772. **$59-$115.** 111 Rodney Orr Bypass (US 129) 28771.
Center of downtown. Int corridors. **Pets:** Accepted. A$K ⊠ 🛋 💻

ROCKY MOUNT

◈◈◈ ▼▼▼▼ Best Western Inn I-95 Gold Rock Ⓜ
(252) 985-1450. **$62-$82.** 7095 NC 4 27809. I-95, exit 145, just e. Ext
corridors. **Pets:** Other species. $20 daily fee/pet. Designated rooms, serv-
ice with restrictions, supervision. SAVE ⊠ 🛋 💻 ⊅

◈◈◈ ▼▼▼▼ Best Western–Rocky Mount Inn Ⓜ
(252) 442-8101. **$49-$79.** 1921 N Wesleyan Blvd 27804. US 64, exit
468A, 2.2 mi n on US 301 Bypass. Ext corridors. **Pets:** Other species.
$20 one-time fee/room. Service with restrictions.
SAVE ⊠ 🛋 💻 ⊅

◈◈◈ ▼▼▼▼ Comfort Inn 🅷
(252) 937-7765. **$76-$119.** 200 Gateway Blvd 27804. I-95, exit 138, 1 mi
e on US 64, exit Winstead Ave, then just s. Int corridors. **Pets:** Other
species. $25 one-time fee/room. Service with restrictions.
SAVE ⊠ 🛋 💻 ⊅

▼▼▼▼ Quality Inn Rocky Mount 🅷
(252) 972-9400. **$54-$75.** 1200 Benvenue Rd 27804. Jct US 64, exit
468A, 0.8 mi n on US 301 Bypass, then just nw on SR 43/48. Ext/int
corridors. **Pets:** Accepted. ⊠ ♿ 🛋 💻 ⊅

◈◈◈ ▼▼▼▼ Residence Inn by Marriott 🅷
(252) 451-5600. **$148-$180.** 230 Gateway Blvd 27804. I-95, exit 138, 1
mi e on US 64, exit Winstead Ave, just s, then just e. Int corridors.
Pets: Accepted. SAVE ⊠ ♿ 🛋 💻 ⊅ ⊠

ROXBORO

▼▼▼▼ Hampton Inn 🅷
(336) 599-8800. **$94-$99.** 920 Durham Rd 27573. Jct US 158, n on US
501. Int corridors. **Pets:** Accepted. ⊠ 🛋 💻 ⊅

SALISBURY

▼▼▼▼ Hampton Inn 🅷
(704) 637-8000. **Call for rates.** 1001 Klumac Rd 28144. I-85, exit 75,
just n on US 601, then just sw. Int corridors. **Pets:** Designated rooms,
service with restrictions, supervision. ⊠ 🛋 💻 ⊅

▼▼▼▼ Holiday Inn Hotel & Conference Center 🅷 ❖
(704) 637-3100. **$89-$139.** 530 Jake Alexander Blvd S 28147. I-85, exit
75, 0.5 mi n on US 601. Ext/int corridors. **Pets:** Small, dogs only. $15
daily fee/pet. Service with restrictions, supervision.
A$K ⊠ ♿ 🛋 💻 🍴 ⊅ ⊠

SALUDA

▼▼ ▼▼ The Oaks Bed & Breakfast 🅱🅱 ❖
(828) 749-2000. **$129-$209, 7 day notice.** 339 Greenville St 28773.
I-26, exit 59, 1.1 mi sw, 0.3 mi w on US 176, then cross railway tracks.
Ext/int corridors. **Pets:** Medium. $40 one-time fee/room. Designated
rooms, service with restrictions, supervision. A$K ⊠ 🛋 💻 ☎

SANFORD

▼▼▼▼ Holiday Inn Express Hotel & Suites 🅷
(919) 776-6600. **Call for rates.** 2110 Dalrymple St 27330. Jct US 1, exit
69A, 3.5 mi s on US 421 and SR 87, then just w. Int corridors.
Pets: Accepted. ⊠ ♿ 🛋 💻 ⊅

▼▼▼▼ Jameson Inn Ⓜ
(919) 708-7400. **$83-$90.** 2614 S Horner Blvd 27330. Jct US 1, exit 69A.
Ext corridors. **Pets:** Accepted. A$K ⊠ ♿ 🛋 💻 ⊅

SCOTLAND NECK

▼▼ ▼▼ Scotland Neck Inn Ⓜ
(252) 826-5141. **Call for rates.** 308 S Main St 27874. Jct SR 125 S,
just s on US 258. Int corridors. **Pets:** Other species. $25 daily fee/pet.
Designated rooms, service with restrictions, supervision.
⊠ 🛋 💻 ⊅

SELMA

▼▼▼▼ Holiday Inn Express 🅷
(919) 965-4000. **$76-$85.** 115 US 70A 27576. I-95, exit 97, just e, then
just n. Int corridors. **Pets:** $25 one-time fee/pet. Service with restrictions,
supervision. A$K ⊠ ♿ 🛋 💻 ⊅

▼▼ ▼▼ Quality Inn Ⓜ
(919) 965-5200. **Call for rates.** 1705 Industrial Park Dr 27576. I-95, exit
97, just w, then just s. Ext corridors. **Pets:** Other species. Service with
restrictions, crate. ⊠ 🛋 💻 ⊅

SMITHFIELD

▼▼ ▼▼ Jameson Inn Ⓜ
(919) 989-5901. **$78-$85.** 125 S Equity Dr 27577. I-95, exit 95, just w,
just n on Industrial Park Blvd, then just w. Ext corridors. **Pets:** Accepted.
A$K ⊠ ♿ 🛋 💻 ⊅

◈◈◈ ▼▼▼▼ Super 8 🅷
(919) 989-8988. **$75-$120.** 735 Industrial Park Dr 27577. I-95, exit 95,
just w, then just n. Int corridors. **Pets:** $15 daily fee/room. Designated
rooms, service with restrictions, supervision.
SAVE ⊠ ♿ 🛋 💻 ⊅

SOUTHERN PINES

◈◈◈ ▼▼▼▼ Best Western Pinehurst Inn 🅷
(910) 692-0640. **$70-$120.** 1675 US Hwy 1 S 28387. Jct US 15/501, 0.5
mi n on US 1. Ext corridors. **Pets:** Dogs only. $10 daily fee/pet. Service
with restrictions, supervision. SAVE ⊠ 🛋 💻 ⊅

▼▼ ▼▼ Econo Lodge Inn & Suites 🅷
(910) 692-2063. **Call for rates.** 408 W Morganton Rd 28387. US 1, exit
Morganton Rd, just w. Int corridors. **Pets:** Medium, other species. $20
daily fee/pet. Service with restrictions, supervision. ⊠ 🛋 💻

▼▼ ▼▼ Residence Inn by Marriott 🅷 ❖
(910) 693-3400. **$170-$208.** 105 Brucewood Rd 28387. Jct US 1, 1.2 mi
n on US 15/501, then just e. Int corridors. **Pets:** Large. $125 one-time
fee/room. Designated rooms. ⊠ 🛋 💻 ⊅ ⊠

SOUTHPORT

◈◈◈ ▼▼▼▼ Comfort Suites 🅷
(910) 454-7444. **$80-$150.** 4963 Southport Supply Rd (SR 211) 28461.
Jct SR 87, 1.8 mi n. Int corridors. **Pets:** Accepted.
SAVE ⊠ 🛋 💻

SPRING LAKE

▼▼ ▼▼ Super 8 🅷
(910) 436-8588. **Call for rates.** 256 S Main St 28390. Jct SR 210, just
se on SR 24/87, just s. Int corridors. **Pets:** Accepted. ⊠ 🛋 💻

SPRUCE PINE

◈◈◈ ▼▼▼▼ Richmond Inn 🅱🅱
(828) 765-6993. **Call for rates.** 51 Pine Ave 28777. Exit off US 19 E
and SR 226 to Oak Ave, just n on Walnut Ave, follow signs; center. Int
corridors. **Pets:** Accepted. SAVE ⊠ 🛋 💻 ☎

STATESVILLE

◈◈◈ ▼▼▼▼ Best Western Statesville Inn 🅷
(704) 881-0111. **$77-$165.** 1121 Morland Dr 28677. I-77, exit 49A, just e
on US 70 E. Ext corridors. **Pets:** Medium, other species. $15 daily fee/
pet. Designated rooms, service with restrictions, supervision.
SAVE ⊠ ♿ 🛋 💻 ⊅

◈◈◈ ▼▼▼▼ Courtyard by Marriott 🅷
(704) 768-2400. **$125-$153.** 1530 Cinema Dr 28625. I-77, exit 49B, just
e on Salisbury Rd, 0.6 mi n on Folger Dr, then just e. Int corridors.
Pets: Medium, other species. $75 daily fee/room. Service with restrictions,
supervision. SAVE ⊠ 🛋 💻 🍴 ⊅

▼▼ ▼▼ Econo Lodge Inn & Suites Ⓜ
(704) 872-4101. **Call for rates.** 740 Sullivan Rd 28677. I-40, exit 151,
just s. Ext corridors. **Pets:** Accepted. ⊠ ♿ 🛋 💻 ⊅

▼▼ **Quality Inn & Suites** 🅷

(704) 878-2721. **Call for rates.** 715 Sullivan Rd 28677. I-40, exit 151, just s. Ext corridors. **Pets:** $50 one-time fee/pet. Service with restrictions, supervision. ⊠ 🚫 📵 🖨 ⊠

SUNSET BEACH

⬙⬙⬙ ▼▼▼▼ **The Resort at Sea Trail** 🆑

(910) 287-1100. **$76-$176, 3 day notice.** 200 Royal Poste Rd 28468. US 17, 2.2 mi e on SR 904, then 1.5 mi s on SR 179. Ext corridors. **Pets:** $70 one-time fee/room. Designated rooms, service with restrictions, supervision. [SAVE] ⊠ 🚫 📵 🖨 ⊠ ⊠

THOMASVILLE

⬙⬙⬙ ▼▼▼ **Days Inn** 🅷

(336) 472-6600. **$50-$70.** 895 Lake Rd 27360. I-85, exit 102, just w, then just s. Int corridors. **Pets:** Medium, dogs only. $25 daily fee/pet. No service, supervision. [SAVE] ⊠ 🚫 📵 🖨 ⊠

▼▼ **Microtel Inn & Suites** 🅷

(336) 474-4515. **$60-$130.** 959 Lake Rd 27360. I-85, exit 102, just w, then just s. Int corridors. **Pets:** Accepted. (ASK) ⊠ 🦽 🚫 📵

TRYON

⬙⬙⬙ ▼▼▼▼ **1906 Pine Crest Inn & Restaurant** 🅲

(828) 859-9135. **$89-$249, 14 day notice.** 85 Pine Crest Ln 28782. I-26, exit 67, 4 mi w on SR 108, just s on New Market Rd, then just e. Ext/int corridors. **Pets:** Accepted. [SAVE] ⊠ 🚫 📵 🖨 ⊠

WASHINGTON

▼▼ **Comfort Inn** 🅷

(252) 946-4444. **Call for rates.** 1636 Carolina Ave 27889. Jct US 264, 1 mi n on US 17. Int corridors. **Pets:** Accepted. ⊠ 🚫 📵 🖨 ⊠

WAYNESVILLE

▼▼ **Days Inn-Waynesville** Ⓜ

(828) 452-9009. **Call for rates.** 232 Phillips Rd 28786. US 23/74, exit 102, just sw. Ext corridors. **Pets:** Accepted. ⊠ 🦽 🚫 📵 🖨 ⊠

WELDON

⬙⬙⬙ ▼▼▼ **Days Inn** Ⓜ

(252) 536-4867. **$55-$80.** 1611 Julian R Allsbrook Hwy 27890. I-95, exit 173, just e on US 158. Ext corridors. **Pets:** $8 daily fee/pet. Designated rooms, service with restrictions, crate. [SAVE] ⊠ 🚫 📵 🖨 ⊠

WEST JEFFERSON

▼▼ **Nation's Inn** Ⓜ

(336) 246-2080. **$72-$78.** 107 Beaver Creek School Rd 28694. Jct US 221, just n on SR 194, then just w. Ext corridors. **Pets:** Accepted. ⊠ 🦽 🚫 📵 🖨

WHITEVILLE

⬙⬙⬙ ▼▼▼ **Best Western Premiere Inn** Ⓜ

(910) 642-2378. **$75-$95.** 503 N J K Powell Blvd 28472-0396. Jct US 74/76, 1 mi s on US 701 Bypass. Ext corridors. **Pets:** Accepted. [SAVE] ⊠ 🚫 📵 🖨 ⊠

WILKESBORO

⬙⬙⬙ ▼▼▼ **Holiday Inn Express** 🅷

(336) 838-1800. **$74-$90.** 1700 Winkler St 28697. Jct SR 16 N, 2 mi nw on US 421/SR 16. Int corridors. **Pets:** Accepted. [SAVE] ⊠ 🦽 🚫 📵 🖨

WILLIAMSTON

⬙⬙⬙ ▼▼▼ **The Inn at Moratoc** 🅷

(252) 792-3184. **$69-$89.** 101 East Blvd 27892. US 64, exit 514, 1.5 mi n on US 17 business route. Ext/int corridors. **Pets:** Medium, other species. $25 one-time fee/pet. Service with restrictions, crate. [SAVE] ⊠ 🚫 📵 🖨 ⊠

WILMINGTON

▼▼ **Baymont Inn** Ⓜ

(910) 392-6767. **$63-$103, 14 day notice.** 306 S College Rd 28403. Jct US 17 business route, just s on SR 132. Ext/int corridors. **Pets:** Medium. $50 deposit/pet, $10 daily fee/pet. Designated rooms, service with restrictions, supervision. (ASK) ⊠ 🚫 📵 🖨 ⊠

⬙⬙⬙ ▼▼▼ **Comfort Inn Wilmington** 🅷

(910) 791-4841. **$70-$90.** 151 S College Rd 28403. Jct US 17 business route, just s on SR 132. Int corridors. **Pets:** Accepted. [SAVE] ⊠ 🚫 📵 🖨

▼▼ **Days Inn** Ⓜ

(910) 799-6300. **$42-$79.** 5040 Market St 28405. Jct SR 132, 0.6 mi s on US 17 business route. Ext corridors. **Pets:** Large, other species. $15 daily fee/room. Service with restrictions, crate. (ASK) ⊠ 🚫 📵 🖨 ⊠

▼▼ **Extended StayAmerica-Wilmington-New Centre Drive** 🅷

(910) 793-4508. **$49-$79.** 4929 New Centre Dr 28403. Jct SR 132, 0.4 mi s on US 17 business route, just e. Int corridors. **Pets:** Other species. $25 daily fee/room. Designated rooms, service with restrictions, crate. (ASK) ⊠ 🦽 🚫 📵

▼▼▼ **Hilton Wilmington Riverside** 🅷

(910) 763-5900. **$119-$229.** 301 N Water St 28401. Jct Market St, 0.4 mi n. Int corridors. **Pets:** Large. $75 one-time fee/room. Service with restrictions. ⊠ 🚫 📵 🖨 ⊠

▼▼ **Innkeeper** 🅷 🐾

(910) 799-4292. **$57-$67, 3 day notice.** 5345 W Market St 28405. Jct SR 132, just s on US 17 business route. Int corridors. **Pets:** Other species. $20 one-time fee/room. Service with restrictions, crate. (ASK) ⊠ 🚫 📵 🖨 ⊠

▼▼ **Jameson Inn** 🅷

(910) 452-5660. **$93-$102.** 5102 Dunlea Ct 28405. Jct SR 132, 0.5 mi s on US 17 business route, just w on New Centre Dr. Int corridors. **Pets:** Accepted. (ASK) ⊠ 🚫 📵 🖨 ⊠

▼▼ **MainStay Suites** 🅷

(910) 392-1741. **$72-$252.** 5229 Market St 28405. Jct SR 132, just s on US 17 business route. Int corridors. **Pets:** Accepted. ⊠ 🦽 🚫 📵

▼▼ **Quality Inn** Ⓜ 🐾

(910) 791-8850. **Call for rates.** 4926 Market St 28405. Jct SR 132, 0.9 mi s on US 17 business route. Ext corridors. **Pets:** Medium. $5 daily fee/pet, $25 one-time fee/pet. Designated rooms, service with restrictions, supervision. ⊠ 🚫 📵 🖨 ⊠

⬙⬙⬙ ▼▼▼▼ **Residence Inn by Marriott-Landfall** 🅷 🐾

(910) 256-0098. **$154-$209.** 1200 Culbreth Dr 28405. Jct US 17 business route, 2.4 mi e on US 74, 0.4 mi n on Military Cutoff Rd, then just e. Int corridors. **Pets:** Medium, dogs only. $100 one-time fee/room. Service with restrictions. [SAVE] ⊠ 🦽 🚫 📵 🖨 ⊠ ⊠

⬙⬙⬙ ▼▼▼▼ **TownPlace Suites by Marriott** 🅷 🐾

(910) 332-3326. **$139-$159.** 305 Eastwood Rd 28403. Jct US 17 business route, just e on US 74. Int corridors. **Pets:** Small. $75 one-time fee/room. Designated rooms, service with restrictions, supervision. [SAVE] ⊠ 🦽 🚫 📵 🖨 ⊠

WILSON

⬙⬙⬙ ▼▼▼ **Days Inn** Ⓜ

(252) 291-2323. **$64-$89.** 1801 S Tarboro St 27893. US 264, exit 40, 3.3 mi e on SR 42. Ext corridors. **Pets:** Accepted. [SAVE] ⊠ 🚫 📵 🖨 ⊠

▼▼▼ **Holiday Inn Express & Suites** 🅷

(252) 246-1588. **Call for rates.** 2308 Montgomery Dr 27893. US 264, exit 40, 3.2 mi e on SR 42 (Tarboro St), then just n. Int corridors. **Pets:** Accepted. ⊠ 🚫 📵 🖨 ⊠

▼▼▼▼ Whitehead Inn & Executive Suites BB

(252) 243-4447. **$90-$149.** 600 Nash St NE 27893-3045. Jct Tarboro Rd, 0.5 mi n; center. Int corridors. **Pets:** Accepted. ASK ✕

WINDSOR

▼▼▼▼ The Inn at Grays Landing BB

(252) 794-2255. **$70-$140.** 401 S King St 27983. US 17, just w on SR 308. Int corridors. **Pets:** Accepted. ASK ✕ ▤ ✑

WINSTON-SALEM

AAA ▼▼▼▼ Augustus T Zevely Inn BB

(336) 748-9299. **Call for rates.** 803 S Main St 27101. I-40 business route, exit 5D eastbound, 0.5 mi s on Liberty St to Old Salem Rd, just e on Academy St, then just s; exit 5C westbound, just n on Cherry St, just e on 2nd St, 1 mi s on Liberty St to Old Salem Rd, just e on Academy St, then just s. Ext/int corridors. **Pets:** Accepted. SAVE ✕

▼▼▼ Extended StayAmerica Winston-Salem-Hanes Mall Blvd M

(336) 768-0075. **$81-$86.** 1995 Hampton Inn Ct 27103. I-40, exit 189 (Stratford Rd), just s, just e on Hanes Mall Blvd, then just n. Ext corridors. **Pets:** Other species. $25 daily fee/room. Designated rooms, service with restrictions, crate. ASK ✕ ▤ ▣

▼▼▼▼ Fairfield Inn & Suites H

(336) 714-3000. **$89-$109.** 1680 Westbrook Plaza Dr 27103. I-40, exit 189 (Stratford Rd), 0.5 mi n, just w, then just s. Int corridors. **Pets:** Accepted. ✕ ☭M ▤ ▣ ➰

AAA ▼▼▼▼ The Hawthorne Inn & Conference Center H

(336) 777-3000. **$74-$159.** 420 High St 27101. I-40 business route, exit 5C (Cherry St) eastbound, just e; exit westbound, just w on 1st St, then just s on Marshall St. Int corridors. **Pets:** Accepted.

SAVE ✕ ☭M ▤ ▣ ❙❙ ➰

▼▼▼ Innkeeper M

(336) 721-0062. **$52-$60, 3 day notice.** 2115 Peters Creek Pkwy 27127. I-40, exit 192 (Peters Creek Pkwy), just e on SR 150. Ext/int corridors. **Pets:** Accepted. ASK ✕ ▤ ➰

▼▼▼▼ La Quinta Inns & Suites Winston-Salem H ✿

(336) 765-8777. **$59-$99.** 2020 Griffith Rd 27103. I-40, exit 189 (Stratford Rd), just s, just e on Hanes Mall Blvd, then just s. Int corridors. **Pets:** Medium, other species. Service with restrictions, supervision.

ASK ✕ ☭M ▤ ▣ ➰

AAA ▼▼▼▼ Quality Inn & Suites-Hanes Mall H

(336) 765-6670. **$65-$99.** 2008 S Hawthorne Rd 27103. I-40 business route, exit 2A, 0.5 mi s on Silas Creek Pkwy, then just e. Ext corridors. **Pets:** Medium, other species. $25 one-time fee/pet. Service with restrictions, crate. SAVE ✕ ☭M ▤ ▣ ❙❙ ➰

▼▼▼ Quality Inn-Coliseum H

(336) 767-8240. **$45-$80.** 531 Akron Dr 27105. US 52, exit 112, just e. Int corridors. **Pets:** Medium, other species. $15 daily fee/pet. Designated rooms, service with restrictions, supervision. ✕ ▤ ▣ ❙❙ ➰

AAA ▼▼▼▼ Quality Inn University H

(336) 767-9009. **Call for rates.** 5719 University Pkwy 27105. US 52, exit 115B, 0.4 mi w. Ext corridors. **Pets:** Other species. $25 one-time fee/ room. Service with restrictions, supervision. SAVE ✕ ▤ ▣ ➰

▼▼▼▼ Residence Inn by Marriott H

(336) 759-0777. **$170-$208.** 7835 North Point Blvd 27106. US 52 N, exit 115B, 2 mi s on University Pkwy, then just e. Ext corridors. **Pets:** Medium, other species. $75 one-time fee/room. Service with restrictions, crate. ✕ ▤ ▣ ➰ ✕

▼▼▼▼ Sundance Plaza Hotel and Spa H

(336) 723-2911. **$60-$180.** 3050 University Pkwy 27105. I-40 business route, exit 5C (Cherry St), 3 mi n. Int corridors. **Pets:** Accepted.

ASK ✕ ▤ ▣ ❙❙ ➰

YADKINVILLE

▼▼▼ Days Inn H

(336) 679-5000. **$60-$150.** 220 Sharon Dr 27055. US 421, exit 257, just s on US 601, then just e. Int corridors. **Pets:** Accepted.

ASK ✕ ☭M ▤ ▣ ➰

YANCEYVILLE

▼▼▼ Days Inn M

(336) 694-9494. **$65-$170.** 1858 NC Hwy 86 N 27379. Jct SR 62, 1.6 mi nw on US 158/SR 86. Ext corridors. **Pets:** Small. $10 daily fee/pet. Service with restrictions, supervision. ASK ✕ ▤ ➰

NORTH DAKOTA

BEULAH

AmericInn Lodge & Suites of Beulah H
(701) 873-2220. **Call for rates.** 2100 2nd Ave NW 58523. Jct SR 49/200, 1.2 mi s. Int corridors. **Pets:** Accepted.

BISMARCK

Best Western Doublewood Inn & Conference Center H
(701) 258-7000. **$90-$130.** 1400 E Interchange Ave 58501. I-94, exit 159 (US 83), just s. Int corridors. **Pets:** $10 one-time fee/room. Designated rooms, service with restrictions, supervision.

Best Western Ramkota Hotel H
(701) 258-7700. **$84-$109.** 800 S 3rd St 58504. Just s of jct I-94 business loop (Bismarck Expwy) and S 3rd St. Int corridors. **Pets:** Medium. $10 daily fee/pet. Designated rooms, service with restrictions, supervision.

Candlewood Suites H
(701) 751-8900. **$100-$176.** 4400 Skyline Crossings 58503. I-94, exit 159 (US 83), 1.7 mi n, then just e. Int corridors. **Pets:** Medium, dogs only. $50 one-time fee/pet. Designated rooms, service with restrictions, crate.

Comfort Inn H
(701) 223-1911. **Call for rates.** 1030 Interstate Ave 58503. I-94, exit 159 (US 83), 0.3 mi nw. Int corridors. **Pets:** Accepted.

Days Inn-Bismarck M
(701) 223-9151. **$59-$149.** 1300 E Capitol Ave 58501. I-94, exit 159 (US 83, just s. Int corridors. **Pets:** Accepted.

Expressway Inn H
(701) 222-2900. **$75-$100.** 200 Bismarck Expwy 58504. Jct I-94 business loop (Bismarck Expwy) and S 3rd St. Int corridors. **Pets:** Large. $10 daily fee/room. Designated rooms, service with restrictions, supervision.

Kelly Inn M
(701) 223-8001. **Call for rates.** 1800 N 12th St 58501. I-94, exit 159 (US 83), 0.3 mi s. Int corridors. **Pets:** Accepted.

Radisson Hotel Bismarck H
(701) 255-6000. **$96-$106.** 605 E Broadway Ave 58501. Jct 6th St; center. Int corridors. **Pets:** Other species. $25 one-time fee/room. Designated rooms, supervision.

Ramada Limited Bismarck H
(701) 221-3030. **$84-$105.** 3808 E Divide Ave 58501. I-94, exit 161, just s on E Bismarck Expwy. Int corridors. **Pets:** Other species. $10 one-time fee/room. Service with restrictions, crate.

Select Inn M
(701) 223-8060. **$56-$77.** 1505 Interchange Ave 58501. I-94, exit 159 (US 83), just se. Int corridors. **Pets:** Other species. $25 deposit/room, $5 daily fee/room. Designated rooms, service with restrictions, supervision.

BOTTINEAU

Super 8 of Bottineau H
(701) 228-2125. **Call for rates.** 1007 11th St E 58318. 0.5 mi e on SR 5. Int corridors. **Pets:** Accepted.

CARRINGTON

Carrington Inn & Suites M
(701) 652-3982. **$62-$90.** 101 4th Ave S 58421. Jct US 52 and 281, 0.5 mi e on US 52; just s of jct SR 200. Int corridors. **Pets:** Medium. $10 daily fee/pet. Designated rooms, service with restrictions, supervision.

Chieftain Conference Center M
(701) 652-3131. **$65-$110.** 60 4th Ave S 58421. Jct US 52 and 281, 0.5 mi e on US 52; just s of jct SR 200. Ext/int corridors. **Pets:** Large. $10 one-time fee/pet. Designated rooms, service with restrictions, crate.

CASSELTON

Governors' Inn and Conference Center H
(701) 347-4524. **$99-$159.** 2050 Governors Dr 58012. I-94, exit 331, just n on SR 18. Int corridors. **Pets:** Accepted.

DEVILS LAKE

Fireside Inn & Suites M
(701) 662-6760. **Call for rates.** 215 Hwy 2 E 58301. On US 2 at jct SR 20. Int corridors. **Pets:** Accepted.

DICKINSON

AmericInn Motel & Suites of Dickinson H
(701) 225-1400. **Call for rates.** 229 15th St W 58601. I-94, exit 61 (SR 22), just n, then e. Int corridors. **Pets:** Accepted.

Comfort Inn H
(701) 264-7300. **Call for rates.** 493 Elks Dr 58601. I-94, exit 61 (SR 22), just n, then w. Int corridors. **Pets:** $10 daily fee/room. Service with restrictions, supervision.

Hartfiel Inn BB
(701) 225-6710. **$99-$139.** 509 3rd Ave W 58601. I-94, exit 61 (SR 22), 0.8 mi s. Int corridors. **Pets:** Medium. Designated rooms.

Holiday Inn Express Hotel & Suites H
(701) 456-8000. **$114-$139.** 103 14th St W 58601. I-94, exit 61 (SR 22), just n, then just e. Int corridors. **Pets:** Large. $10 one-time fee/room. Service with restrictions, crate.

Quality Inn & Suites-Dickinson H
(701) 225-9510. **$90-$200.** 71 Museum Dr 58601. I-94, exit 61 (SR 22), just s, then e. Int corridors. **Pets:** Medium, other species. $10 daily fee/pet. Service with restrictions.

EDGELEY

Prairie Rose Inn M
(701) 493-2075. **$65-$85.** 111 Frontage Rd 58433. Jct US 281 and SR 13. Ext/int corridors. **Pets:** Accepted.

FARGO

AAA ▼▼▼ **AmericInn Lodge & Suites of Fargo** M
(701) 234-9946. **$78-$142.** 1423 35th St SW 58103. I-29, exit 64, just e on 13th Ave SW, just s on 34th St SW, then just w on 14th Ave SW. Int corridors. **Pets:** Small. $10 daily fee/pet. Designated rooms, service with restrictions, supervision. (SAVE) (X) (GM) (▤) (▦) (▰) (X)

AAA ▼▼▼ **Best Western Fargo Doublewood Inn & Conference Center** H
(701) 235-3333. **$95-$120.** 3333 13th Ave S 58103. I-29, exit 64, 0.3 mi e. Int corridors. **Pets:** Accepted.
(SAVE) (X) (GM) (▤) (▦) (▥) (▰) (X)

AAA ▼▼▼ **Best Western Kelly Inn & Suites** H ❀
(701) 282-2143. **$100-$135.** 1767 44th St S 58103. I-94, exit 348 (45th St SW), just n, then just e on 18th Ave. Ext/int corridors. **Pets:** Medium. Service with restrictions, supervision.
(SAVE) (X) (GM) (▤) (▦) (▰) (X)

▼▼▼ **Candlewood Suites** H
(701) 235-8200. **$104-$159.** 1831 NDSU Research Dr 58102. I-29, exit 67 (19th Ave), 1.6 mi e. Int corridors. **Pets:** Accepted.
(ASK) (X) (GM) (▤) (▦)

▼▼ **Comfort Inn Fargo East** H
(701) 280-9666. **Call for rates.** 1407 35th St SW 58103. I-29, exit 64, just e on 13th Ave SW, just s on 34th St SW, then just w on 14th Ave S. Int corridors. **Pets:** Medium, other species. $10 daily fee/room. Designated rooms, service with restrictions, supervision.
(X) (GM) (▤) (▦) (▰)

▼▼ **Comfort Suites** H
(701) 237-5911. **Call for rates.** 1415 35th St SW 58103. I-29, exit 64, just e on 13th Ave SW, just s on 34th St SW, then just w on 14th Ave S. Int corridors. **Pets:** $10 daily fee/room. Service with restrictions, supervision. (X) (GM) (▤) (▦) (▰)

▼▼▼▼ **Country Inn & Suites By Carlson** H
(701) 234-0565. **$89-$189.** 3316 13th Ave S 58103. I-29, exit 64 (13th Ave S), 0.3 mi e. Int corridors. **Pets:** Medium. $10 daily fee/pet. Service with restrictions, supervision. (ASK) (X) (GM) (▤) (▦) (▰) (X)

▼▼ **Econo Lodge** M ❀
(701) 232-3412. **Call for rates.** 1401 35th St SW 58103. I-29, exit 64, just e on 13th Ave SW, just s on 34th St SW, then just w on 14th Ave SW. Int corridors. **Pets:** Small, other species. $10 one-time fee/room. Service with restrictions. (X) (GM) (▤) (▦)

▼▼▼ **Holiday Inn of Fargo** H
(701) 282-2700. **$99-$179.** 3803 13th Ave S 58103. I-29, exit 64, just nw. Int corridors. **Pets:** $10 one-time fee/room. Supervision.
(ASK) (X) (GM) (▤) (▦) (▥) (▰) (X)

▼▼▼ **Kelly Inn** H
(701) 281-9700. **$79-$129.** 3800 Main Ave 58103. I-29, exit 65, just w on US 10. Ext/int corridors. **Pets:** Accepted.
(ASK) (X) (GM) (▤) (▦) (▥) (▰) (X)

▼▼▼ **Kelly Inn 13th Avenue** M
(701) 277-8821. **$87-$129.** 4207 13th Ave SW 58103. I-29, exit 64, 0.5 mi w. Ext/int corridors. **Pets:** Accepted. (ASK) (X) (GM) (▤) (▦) (▰)

▼▼▼▼ **La Quinta Inn & Suites** H ❀
(701) 499-2000. **Call for rates.** 2355 46th St S 58104. I-94, exit 348 (45th St SW), just s, then w. Int corridors. **Pets:** Medium, other species. Service with restrictions, supervision. (X) (GM) (▤) (▦)

AAA ▼▼▼ **MainStay Suites** H
(701) 277-4627. **$80-$160.** 1901 44th St SW 58103. I-94, exit 348 (45th St SW), just n, then just e. Int corridors. **Pets:** Accepted.
(SAVE) (X) (GM) (▤) (▦) (▰)

AAA ▼ **Select Inn** M
(701) 282-6300. **$54-$69.** 1025 38th St SW 58103. I-29, exit 64, just nw on 13th Ave S. Int corridors. **Pets:** Accepted. (SAVE) (X) (GM) (▤) (▦)

AAA ▼▼▼ **Sleep Inn** M
(701) 281-8240. **$55-$80.** 1921 44 St SW 58103. I-94, exit 348 (45th St SW), just n, then just e on 19th Ave S. Int corridors. **Pets:** Accepted.
(SAVE) (X) (GM) (▤) (▦) (▰) (X)

AAA ▼▼▼ **Staybridge Suites** H
(701) 281-4900. **$89-$249.** 4300 20th Ave S 58103. I-94, exit 348 (45th St SW), just n, then 0.4 mi e. Int corridors. **Pets:** Medium. $50 one-time fee/pet. Service with restrictions, supervision.
(SAVE) (X) (GM) (▤) (▦) (▰) (X)

GRAFTON

▼▼ **AmericInn Motel & Suites of Grafton** H
(701) 352-2788. **$72-$175.** 1015 12th St W 58237. SR 17, 1.2 mi w. Int corridors. **Pets:** Accepted. (ASK) (X) (GM) (▤) (▦) (▰) (X)

GRAND FORKS

AAA ▼ **Americas Best Value Inn of Grand Forks** M
(701) 775-0555. **$45-$110.** 1000 N 42nd St 58203. I-29, exit 141, just se on US 2 (Gateway Dr). Int corridors. **Pets:** $35 deposit/room, $10 daily fee/pet. Designated rooms, service with restrictions, crate. (SAVE) (X) (▤)

AAA ▼▼ **Days Inn–Grand Forks** M
(701) 775-0060. **$79-$149.** 3101 S 34th St 58201. I-29, exit 138, 0.5 mi e on 32nd Ave S, then just n. Int corridors. **Pets:** Very small. $20 daily fee/pet. Designated rooms, service with restrictions, supervision.
(SAVE) (X) (▤) (▦) (▰)

▼▼ **GuestHouse International Townhouse** M
(701) 746-5411. **$65-$115.** 710 1st Ave N Ave N 58203. I-29, exit 140, 3 mi e on DeMers Ave; downtown. Int corridors. **Pets:** $15 one-time fee/room. Designated rooms, service with restrictions, crate.
(ASK) (X) (▤) (▦) (▥) (▰) (X)

AAA ▼▼ **Ramada Inn** M
(701) 775-3951. **$62-$109.** 1205 N 43rd St 58203. I-29, exit 141, just se on US 2 (Gateway Dr). Int corridors. **Pets:** Small. Designated rooms, service with restrictions, supervision.
(SAVE) (X) (▤) (▦) (▥) (▰) (X)

▼▼ **Travelodge of Grand Forks** M
(701) 772-8151. **$64-$114, 14 day notice.** 2100 S Washington St 58201. I-29, exit 140, 2.5 mi e on Demers Ave, then 1.5 mi s. Int corridors. **Pets:** Accepted. (ASK) (X) (▤) (▦) (▰) (X)

JAMESTOWN

▼▼ **Comfort Inn Jamestown** M
(701) 252-7125. **$80-$110.** 811 20th St SW 58401. I-94, exit 258 (US 281), just nw. Int corridors. **Pets:** Accepted.
(ASK) (X) (GM) (▤) (▦) (▰)

KENMARE

▼▼ **Quilt Inn** H
(701) 385-4100. **$70-$81.** 1232 Central Ave N 58746. Just n on US 52. Int corridors. **Pets:** Accepted. (ASK) (X) (GM) (▤)

MANDAN

AAA ▼▼▼ **Best Western Seven Seas Hotel & Waterpark** H
(701) 663-7401. **$97-$108.** 2611 Old Red Tr 58554. I-94, exit 152, just n on Sunset Dr, then just w. Int corridors. **Pets:** Accepted.
(SAVE) (X) (GM) (▤) (▦) (▥) (▰) (X)

MEDORA

AAA ▼▼▼ **AmericInn Motel & Suites of Medora** H
(701) 623-4800. **$90-$250.** 75 E River Rd S 58645. I-94, exit 24, just se of downtown. Int corridors. **Pets:** Accepted.
(SAVE) (X) (GM) (▤) (▦) (▰) (X)

MINOT

AAA **WWW** Best Western Kelly Inn **M** ❀
(701) 852-4300. **$99-$139.** 1510 26th Ave SW 58701. US 2 and 52 Bypass, at 16th St SW. Ext/int corridors. **Pets:** Other species. Service with restrictions. (SAVE) ⊠ ᴹ⅃ 🖶 💻 ⇌ ⊠

WWW Days Inn Minot **M**
(701) 852-3646. **Call for rates.** 2100 4th St SW 58701. Jct US 2 and 52 Bypass, just n. Int corridors. **Pets:** Accepted. ⊠ 🖶 💻 ⇌

AAA **WWW** Fairfield Inn by Marriott **H**
(701) 838-2424. **$99-$121.** 900 24th Ave SW 58701. 0.5 mi e of jct US 2, 52 Bypass and 16th St SW. Int corridors. **Pets:** Accepted.
(SAVE) ⊠ ᴹ⅃ 🖶 💻 ⇌

WWWW Holiday Inn Riverside Minot **H**
(701) 852-2504. **$90-$134.** 2200 Burdick Expy E 58702. 1.3 mi e on US 2 business route (Burdick Expwy E). Int corridors. **Pets:** Small, dogs only. $15 daily fee/room. Designated rooms, service with restrictions, supervision. (ASK) ⊠ ᴹ⅃ 🖶 💻 ⊤⊤ ⊠

AAA **WWWW** Sleep Inn & Suites **H**
(701) 837-3100. **$90-$200.** 2400 10th St SW 58701. US 2 and 52 Bypass at 16th St SW. Int corridors. **Pets:** Accepted.
(SAVE) ⊠ ᴹ⅃ 🖶 💻 ⊤⊤ ⇌ ⊠

VALLEY CITY

WWWW AmericInn Lodge & Suites of Valley City **H**
(701) 845-5551. **$81-$140.** 280 Winter Show Rd SE 58072. I-94, exit 292, just ne. Int corridors. **Pets:** Accepted.
(ASK) ⊠ ᴹ⅃ 🖶 💻 ⇌ ⊠

WAHPETON

WWW Rodeway Inn **H**
(701) 642-1115. **Call for rates.** 209 13th St S 58075. SR 13, 0.3 mi e of jct SR 210 Bypass. Int corridors. **Pets:** Accepted.
⊠ ᴹ⅃ 🖶 💻 ⇌

WWW Wahpeton Super 8 **H**
(701) 642-8731. **Call for rates.** 995 21st Ave N 58075. 1.5 mi n on SR 210 Bypass. Int corridors. **Pets:** Accepted. ⊠ 🖶 💻 ⇌ ⊠

WATFORD CITY

AAA **WWW** McKenzie Inn **M**
(701) 444-3980. **$56-$110.** 132 SW 3rd St 58854. US 85, just w. Ext corridors. **Pets:** Small, dogs only. $5 daily fee/pet. No service, supervision. (SAVE) ⊠ 🖶

AAA **WWW** Roosevelt Inn & Suites **H**
(701) 842-3686. **$62-$143.** 600 2nd Ave SW 58854. US 85, 0.3 mi w. Int corridors. **Pets:** Other species. $10 daily fee/pet. Service with restrictions, supervision. (SAVE) ⊠ 🖶 💻 ⇌

WILLISTON

AAA **WWW** El Rancho Motor Hotel **H**
(701) 572-6321. **$69-$89.** 1623 2nd Ave W 58801. 1 mi n on US 2 and 85 N Bypass. Ext/int corridors. **Pets:** Accepted.
(SAVE) ⊠ ᴹ⅃ 🖶 💻 ⊤⊤

AAA **WWW** Marquis Plaza & Suites **H**
(701) 774-3250. **$90-$140.** 1525 9th Ave NW 58801. US 2 and 85, 4 mi e of jct US 85. Int corridors. **Pets:** Small. $10 daily fee/pet. Designated rooms, service with restrictions, supervision.
(SAVE) ⊠ ᴹ⅃ 🖶 💻 ⇌

AAA **WWW** Missouri Flats Inn **M**
(701) 572-4242. **$78.** 213 35th St W St W 58801. 1.3 mi n on US 2 and 85 Bypass. Int corridors. **Pets:** Small. $10 one-time fee/pet. Designated rooms, service with restrictions, supervision. (SAVE) ⊠ ᴹ⅃ 🖶 💻

OHIO

CITY INDEX

AKRON

◆ ▽▽▽ Red Roof Inn-Akron South #0207 M

(330) 644-7748. **$54-$80.** 2939 S Arlington Rd 44312. I-77, exit 120, just n. Ext corridors. **Pets:** Large. Service with restrictions, crate.

SAVE ✕ ☐

ALLIANCE

▽▽ Comfort Inn H

(330) 821-5555. **$72-$91.** 2500 W State St 44601. 2.5 mi w on US 62. Int corridors. **Pets:** $10 daily fee/pet. Designated rooms, service with restrictions, supervision. ASK ✕ ☐ ▣ ⇌

▽▽▽▽ Holiday Inn Express Hotel & Suites H

(330) 821-6700. **Call for rates.** 2341 W State St 44601. 2 mi w on US 62. Int corridors. **Pets:** Large. $10 one-time fee/pet. Designated rooms, service with restrictions, supervision. ✕ ⚲ ☐ ▣ ⇌

◆ ▽▽▽ Super 8 M

(330) 821-5688. **$56-$95.** 2330 W State St 44601. 2 mi w on US 62. Ext corridors. **Pets:** $5 daily fee/pet. Service with restrictions.

SAVE ✕ ☐ ⇌

AMHERST

▽▽ Days Inn M

(440) 985-1428. **$45-$75.** 934 N Leavitt Rd 44001. I-80, exit 140, 2.7 mi n on SR 58. Ext/int corridors. **Pets:** Medium. $10 daily fee/pet. Designated rooms, service with restrictions, supervision.

ASK ✕ ☐ ▣ ⇌

ASHLAND

▽▽ The Surrey Inn H

(419) 289-7700. **Call for rates.** 1065 Claremont Ave 44805. 1 mi s of town. Int corridors. **Pets:** Small, dogs only. No service, supervision.

✕ ☐ ▣

ASHTABULA

▽ Cedars Motel M

(440) 992-5406. **Call for rates.** 2015 W Prospect Rd 44004. Jct SR 11, 3 mi w on US 20. Ext corridors. **Pets:** Accepted. ✕ ☐

▽ Ho Hum Motel M

(440) 969-1136. **$55-$80.** 3801 N Ridge Rd W 44004. I-90, exit 223, 3 mi n on SR 45, then 1 mi e on SR 20. Ext corridors. **Pets:** Other species. $5 daily fee/pet. Service with restrictions, crate. ✕ ☐

ATHENS

▽▽▽ The Ohio University Inn & Conference Center H

(740) 593-6661. **Call for rates.** 331 Richland Ave 45701. 1 mi w on US 33 and 50. Int corridors. **Pets:** Accepted. ✕ ☐ ▣ ⍟ ⇌

AUSTINBURG

▽▽ Comfort Inn-Ashtabula H

(440) 275-2711. **$80-$164.** 1860 Austinburg Rd 44010. I-90, exit 223, just n. Int corridors. **Pets:** Accepted. ASK ✕ ☐ ▣ ⍟ ⇌

AUSTINTOWN

◆ ▽▽ Austintown Super 8 M

(330) 793-7788. **$54-$100.** 5280 76 Dr 44515. I-80, exit 223, just s on SR 46. Int corridors. **Pets:** $10 daily fee/pet. Service with restrictions, supervision. SAVE ✕ ☐ ▣

▽▽▽ Comfort Inn & Suites M ✿

(330) 792-9740. **Call for rates.** 5425 Clarkins Dr 44515. I-80, exit 223B, just n. Ext corridors. **Pets:** $15 daily fee/room. Service with restrictions.

✕ ☐ ▣ ⇌

BEAVERCREEK

▽▽▽ Residence Inn by Marriott Beavercreek H

(937) 427-3914. **$150-$155.** 2779 Fairfield Commons Blvd 45431. I-675, exit 17, just s on N Fairfield Rd, just w on Pentagon Rd, then s. Int corridors. **Pets:** Accepted. ✕ ⚲ ☐ ▣ ⇌ ✕

BELLEFONTAINE

▽▽▽ Comfort Inn Bellefontaine H

(937) 599-5555. **$72-$150.** 260 Northview Dr 43311. Jct US 33 and SR 68, just ne. Int corridors. **Pets:** Other species. $15 daily fee/room. Service with restrictions, supervision. ASK ✕ ☐ ▣ ⇌

BLUFFTON

▽▽▽ Comfort Inn H

(419) 358-6000. **$72-$90.** 117 Commerce Ln 45817. I-75, exit 142, just w on SR 103. Int corridors. **Pets:** Large, other species. $25 one-time fee/pet. Service with restrictions, supervision. ASK ✕ ☐ ▣ ⇌ ✕

BOARDMAN

▼▼ **Americas Best Value Inn & Suites** Ⓜ ❀

(330) 549-0157. **$49-$121.** 9988 Market St 44452. 0.5 mi n on SR 7. Int corridors. **Pets:** Medium, other species. $10 daily fee/pet. Service with restrictions, supervision. (ASK) ⊠ 🛠Ⓜ 🔓 💻

▼▼ **Days Inn Boardman Youngstown** Ⓜ

(330) 758-1816. **Call for rates.** 7393 South Ave 44512. Jct I-680 and US 224, 0.3 mi w. Int corridors. **Pets:** Accepted. ⊠ 🔓 💻

BOSTON HEIGHTS

ⒶⒶⒶ ▼▼▼ **Clarion Inn and Conference Center** Ⓗ ❀

(330) 653-9191. **$70-$90.** 240 E Hines Hill Rd 44236. I-80/90, exit 180, 0.3 mi n on SR 8. Int corridors. **Pets:** Large, other species. $10 daily fee/room. Service with restrictions, crate.
(SAVE) ⊠ 🛠Ⓜ 🔓 🔓 💻 ⑪ 🏊 🐾

ⒶⒶⒶ ▼▼▼ **Comfort Inn** Ⓜ ❀

(330) 650-2040. **$55-$79.** 6731 Industrial Pkwy 44236. I-80/90, exit 180, 0.3 mi n on SR 8. Int corridors. **Pets:** Medium, other species. $10 one-time fee/pet. Crate. (SAVE) ⊠ 🛠Ⓜ 🔓 🔓 💻 🏊

BOTKINS

▼ **Budget Host Inn** Ⓜ

(937) 693-6911. **$43-$75.** 505 E State St 45306. I-75, exit 104 (SR 219), just w. Ext corridors. **Pets:** Large. $40 deposit/room. Designated rooms, service with restrictions, supervision. (ASK) ⊠ 🔓 ⑪ 🏊

BOWLING GREEN

▼▼▼ **Holiday Inn Express** Ⓗ

(419) 353-5500. **$96.** 2150 E Wooster St 43402. I-75, exit 181, just e. Int corridors. **Pets:** $25 one-time fee/room. Service with restrictions, supervision. (ASK) ⊠ 🛠Ⓜ 🔓 💻 🏊

BROOKVILLE

ⒶⒶⒶ ▼▼▼ **Holiday Inn Express Hotel & Suites Dayton North (Brookville)** Ⓗ

(937) 833-9998. **$85-$150.** 95 N Parkview Dr 45309. I-70, exit 21, just s. Int corridors. **Pets:** Other species. $25 one-time fee/room. Designated rooms, service with restrictions, supervision.
(SAVE) ⊠ 🛠Ⓜ 🔓 💻 🏊

BRYAN

ⒶⒶⒶ ▼▼▼ **Colonial Manor Motel** Ⓜ

(419) 636-3123. **$67-$97.** 924 E High St 43506. US 127, 0.8 mi e on SR 2/34. Ext corridors. **Pets:** Medium. Designated rooms, service with restrictions, crate. (SAVE) ⊠ 🔓 💻 ⑪

ⒶⒶⒶ ▼ **Plaza Motel** Ⓜ

(419) 636-3159. **$65-$93.** 1604 S Main St 43506. 1.3 mi s on US 127 and SR 15. Ext corridors. **Pets:** Service with restrictions, supervision.
(SAVE) ⊠ 🔓 💻

CAMBRIDGE

▼▼ **Baymont Inn & Suites** Ⓜ

(740) 439-1505. **Call for rates.** 61595 Southgate Pkwy 43725. I-70, exit 178, just s on SR 209. Int corridors. **Pets:** Accepted.
⊠ 🛠Ⓜ 🔓 💻 🏊

▼▼ **Budget Inn** Ⓜ

(740) 432-2304. **$40-$60.** 6405 Glenn Hwy 43725. I-70, exit 176, just e on US 40. Ext/int corridors. **Pets:** Small. $10 daily fee/pet. Designated rooms, service with restrictions, supervision. (ASK) ⊠ 🔓 💻

ⒶⒶⒶ **Comfort Inn** Ⓗ

(740) 435-3200. **$90-$170.** 2327 Southgate Pkwy 43725. I-70, exit 178, just n on SR 209. Int corridors. **Pets:** Accepted.
(SAVE) ⊠ 🔓 💻 🏊

▼▼ **Days Inn-Cambridge** Ⓜ

(740) 432-5691. **$59-$89, 3 day notice.** 2328 Southgate Pkwy 43725. I-70, exit 178, just n on SR 209. Int corridors. **Pets:** $10 daily fee/pet. Service with restrictions, crate. (ASK) ⊠ 🔓 💻 🏊

CANTON

▼▼▼ **La Quinta Inn & Suites** Ⓗ 🐾

(330) 492-0151. **Call for rates.** 5335 Broadmoor Cir NW 44709. I-77, exit 109, 0.5 mi e on Everhard Rd. Int corridors. **Pets:** Medium, other species. Service with restrictions, supervision. ⊠ 🛠Ⓜ 🔓 💻

ⒶⒶⒶ ▼▼ **Red Roof Inn #7019** Ⓜ

(330) 499-1970. **$55-$65.** 5353 Inn Circle Ct NW 44720. I-77, exit 109, just w on Everhard Rd. Ext corridors. **Pets:** Large. Service with restrictions, crate. (SAVE) ⊠ 🔓

▼▼▼ **Residence Inn by Marriott** Ⓗ

(330) 493-0004. **$140-$150.** 5280 Broadmoor Cir NW 44709. I-77, exit 109, 0.5 mi e on Everhard Rd. Int corridors. **Pets:** Accepted.
⊠ 🛠Ⓜ 🔓 💻 🏊 🐾

CARROLLTON

▼▼ **Carrollton Days Inn** Ⓗ

(330) 627-9314. **$83-$140, 7 day notice.** 1111 Canton Rd 44615. On SR 43, 0.5 mi n of SR 39. Int corridors. **Pets:** Medium. $20 one-time fee/pet. Service with restrictions, supervision. (ASK) ⊠ 🔓 💻 🏊

CELINA

ⒶⒶⒶ ▼▼ **Americas Best Value Inn-Celina** Ⓜ

(419) 586-4656. **$56-$125.** 1421 SR 703 E 45822. Jct SR 29. Ext corridors. **Pets:** $10 daily fee/room. Designated rooms, service with restrictions, supervision. (SAVE) ⊠ 🔓 💻

CHILLICOTHE

ⒶⒶⒶ ▼▼ **Best Western Adena Inn** Ⓗ

(740) 775-7000. **$80-$180.** 1250 N Bridge St 45601. US 35, exit Bridge St, 0.8 mi n. Int corridors. **Pets:** Small. $15 daily fee/pet. Service with restrictions, supervision. (SAVE) ⊠ 🔓 💻 🏊

▼▼ **Christopher Inn & Suites** Ⓗ

(740) 774-6835. **Call for rates.** 30 N Plaza Blvd 45601. US 35, exit Bridge St, just n on US 23. Int corridors. **Pets:** Accepted.
⊠ 🔓 💻 🏊 🐾

CINCINNATI METROPOLITAN AREA

BATAVIA

▼▼ **Ameristay Inn & Suites** Ⓗ

(513) 735-4678. **$76-$139.** 2188 Winemiller Ln 45103. I-275, exit 63B (SR 32), 7.3 mi e. Int corridors. **Pets:** Accepted.
(ASK) 🔓 💻 🏊

▼▼▼ **Hampton Inn-Cincinnati Eastgate** Ⓗ

(513) 752-8584. **$89-$149.** 858 Eastgate North Dr 45245. I-275, exit 63B (SR 32), just e, just n on Glen.este Withamsville Rd, then just w; behind Longhorn Steakhouse. Int corridors. **Pets:** Accepted. ⊠ 🔓 💻 🏊

▼▼▼ **Holiday Inn Hotel & Suites** Ⓗ

(513) 752-4400. **Call for rates.** 4501 Eastgate Blvd 45245. I-275, exit 63B (SR 32), 0.5 mi e to Eastgate Mall exit, then 0.5 mi n. Int corridors. **Pets:** Accepted. ⊠ 🔓 💻 ⑪ 🏊 🐾

BLUE ASH

▼ Extended StayAmerica Cincinnati-Blue-Ash-North H

(513) 469-8900. $63-$99. 11145 Kenwood Rd 45242. I-71, exit 15, 0.5 mi w on Pfeiffer Rd, then 1.3 mi n. Int corridors. **Pets:** Other species. $25 daily fee/room. Designated rooms, service with restrictions, crate.

[ASK] [✕] [🛏] [💻]

▼ ▼ Extended StayAmerica-Cincinnati-Blue Ash-South H

(513) 793-6750. $58-$99. 4260 Hunt Rd 45242. I-71, exit 14, 1.3 mi w on Ronald Reagan Hwy, exit Hunt Rd, then just e. Int corridors. **Pets:** Other species. $25 daily fee/room. Designated rooms, service with restrictions, crate. [ASK] [✕] [🛏] [💻] [≈]

▼◆ ◆▼ Residence Inn by Marriott-Blue Ash H 🐾

(513) 530-5060. $125-$153. 11401 Reed-Hartman Hwy 45241. I-275, exit 47, 0.8 mi s. Ext/int corridors. **Pets:** Medium, other species. $100 one-time fee/room. Service with restrictions. [✕] [♿] [🛏] [💻] [≈]

▼◆ ◆▼ TownePlace Suites by Marriott Blue Ash H 🐾

(513) 469-8222. $107-$131. 4650 Cornell Rd 45241. I-275, exit 47, 0.9 mi s on Reed-Hartman Hwy, then just w. Int corridors. **Pets:** Other species. $100 one-time fee/room. Designated rooms, service with restrictions.

[✕] [🛏] [💻] [≈]

CHERRY GROVE

AAA ▼▼ Best Western Clermont M

(513) 528-7702. $65-$160. 4004 Williams Dr 45255. I-275, exit 65, just w, then just s. Ext corridors. **Pets:** Small. $25 one-time fee/pet. Service with restrictions, supervision. [SAVE] [✕] [🛏] [💻] [≈]

CINCINNATI

AAA ▼◆▼◆ Holiday Inn Express Cincinnati West H

(513) 574-6000. $99-$159. 5505 Rybolt Rd 45248. I-74, exit 11. Int corridors. **Pets:** Medium. $25 one-time fee/room. Designated rooms, service with restrictions, supervision. [SAVE] [✕] [♿] [🛏] [💻] [≈]

AAA ▼◆▼◆ Millennium Hotel Cincinnati H

(513) 352-2100. $79-$239. 150 W 5th St 45202. Between Elm and Race sts. Int corridors. **Pets:** Large, other species. $100 deposit/pet, $35 one-time fee/pet. Service with restrictions, crate.

[SAVE] [✕] [🛏] [💻] [🍽] [≈]

AAA ▼◆▼ ▼◆▼ The Westin Cincinnati H 🐾

(513) 621-7700. $99-$209. 21 E 5th St 45202. Between Vine and Walnut sts. Int corridors. **Pets:** Medium, dogs only. Designated rooms, service with restrictions, crate. [SAVE] [✕] [♿] [🛏] [💻] [🍽] [≈] [🐾]

HARRISON

▼◆▼ Comfort Inn H

(513) 367-9666. $60-$120. 391 Comfort Dr 45030. I-74, exit 1, just n on New Haven Rd, then just e on Biggs Blvd. Int corridors. **Pets:** Accepted.

[ASK] [✕] [♿] [🛏] [💻] [≈]

MASON

▼◆▼ La Quinta Inn & Suites H 🐾

(513) 459-1111. $49-$109. 9918 Escort Dr 45040. I-71, exit 19, just w, then just s. Int corridors. **Pets:** Medium, other species. Service with restrictions, supervision. [ASK] [✕] [🛏] [💻] [≈]

▼◆▼ Microtel Inn & Suites Kings Island H

(513) 754-1500. **Call for rates.** 5324 Beach Blvd 45040. I-71, exit 25, just nw. Int corridors. **Pets:** Accepted. [✕] [♿] [🛏] [💻]

▼◆▼ Ramada Limited Kings Island Area H

(513) 336-7911. **Call for rates.** 9665 Mason-Montgomery Rd 45040. I-71, exit 19, just w. Int corridors. **Pets:** Accepted.

[✕] [♿] [🛏] [💻] [≈]

▼◆▼ TownePlace Suites by Marriott H

(513) 774-0610. $107-$131. 9369 Waterstone Blvd 45249. I-71, exit 19, 0.5 mi e on Mason-Montgomery and Fields-Ertel rds, then 0.9 mi n. Int corridors. **Pets:** Accepted. [ECO] [✕] [♿] [🛏] [💻] [≈]

MIDDLETOWN

AAA ▼◆▼ Country Hearth Inn & Suites H

(513) 424-3551. $50-$110. 6475 Culbertson Rd 45005. I-75, exit 32. Int corridors. **Pets:** Accepted. [SAVE] [✕] [♿] [🛏] [💻] [🍽] [≈]

▼◆▼ Middletown Drury Inn & Suites H

(513) 425-6650. $85-$164. 3320 Village Dr 45005. I-75, exit 32, just w on SR 122. Int corridors. **Pets:** Other species. No service, supervision. [ASK] [✕] [♿] [🛏] [💻] [≈] [🐾]

▼◆ Super 8 Middletown H

(513) 422-4888. $59-$69. 3553 Commerce Dr 45005. I-75, exit 32, just e, then just n. Int corridors. **Pets:** Dogs only. $10 daily fee/pet. Service with restrictions, supervision. [ASK] [✕] [🛏] [💻]

MILFORD

▼◆▼ Homewood Suites by Hilton H

(513) 248-4663. $80-$150. 600 Chamber Dr 45150. I-275, exit 59 southbound; exit 59A northbound, 0.5 mi w on Milford Pkwy, then 0.5 mi s. Int corridors. **Pets:** Accepted. [✕] [♿] [🛏] [💻] [≈]

MOUNT ORAB

AAA ▼◆▼ Best Western Mount Orab Inn H

(937) 444-6666. $77-$85. 100 Leininger St 45154. Jct US 68 and SR 32, just n on US 68. Int corridors. **Pets:** Accepted. [SAVE] [✕] [🛏] [💻] [≈]

SHARONVILLE

AAA ▼◆▼◆ Crowne Plaza Cincinnati North-CoCo Key H

(513) 771-2080. $89-$219. 11320 Chester Rd 45246. I-75, exit 15, just w on Sharon Rd, then 0.5 mi n. Int corridors. **Pets:** Accepted.

[SAVE] [✕] [♿] [🛏] [💻] [🍽] [≈] [🐾]

▼◆▼ Drury Inn & Suites-Cincinnati North H

(513) 771-5601. $95-$204. 2265 E Sharon Rd 45241. I-75, exit 15, just e. Int corridors. **Pets:** Other species. No service, supervision. [ASK] [✕] [♿] [🛏] [💻] [≈] [🐾]

AAA ▼◆▼ Hawthorn Suites by Wyndham H 🐾

(513) 354-1000. $60-$130. 11180 Dowlin Dr 45241. I-75, exit 15, just e on Sharon Rd, then just n. Int corridors. **Pets:** Dogs only. $15 daily fee/room. Service with restrictions, crate. [SAVE] [✕] [🛏] [💻] [≈]

▼◆▼ Homewood Suites by Hilton-Cincinnati North H 🐾

(513) 772-8888. $109-$174. 2670 E Kemper Rd 45241. I-275, exit 44, jct Mosteller Rd. Int corridors. **Pets:** Other species. $25 daily fee/pet. Service with restrictions. [✕] [🛏] [💻] [≈] [🐾]

▼◆▼ La Quinta Inn & Suites H 🐾

(513) 771-0300. $69-$109. 11029 Dowlin Dr 45241. I-75, exit 15, just e. Int corridors. **Pets:** Medium, other species. Service with restrictions, supervision. [ASK] [✕] [♿] [🛏] [💻] [≈] [🐾]

▼◆▼ Residence Inn by Marriott H

(513) 771-2525. $116-$142. 11689 Chester Rd 45246. I-75, exit 15, just w on Sharon Rd, then 1 mi n. Ext corridors. **Pets:** Accepted.

[✕] [🛏] [💻] [≈] [🐾]

SPRINGDALE

▼◆▼ La Quinta Inn H 🐾

(513) 671-2300. $55-$89. 12150 Springfield Pike 45246. I-275, exit 41, just n on SR 4. Int corridors. **Pets:** Medium, other species. Service with restrictions, supervision. [ASK] [✕] [🛏] [💻]

WEST CHESTER

▼◆▼ Residence Inn by Marriott Cincinnati North/West Chester H

(513) 341-4040. $152-$186. 6240 Muhlhauser Rd 45069. I-75, exit 19, just w on Union Centre Blvd, then just n. Int corridors. **Pets:** Accepted.

[✕] [♿] [🛏] [💻] [≈] [🐾]

Staybridge Suites Cincinnati North ⓗ
(513) 874-1900. **$99-$250.** 8955 Lakota Dr W 45069. I-75, exit 19, just w on Union Centre Blvd, then 0.5 mi n. Int corridors. **Pets:** Other species. $75 one-time fee/room. Service with restrictions.
SAVE ✕ ⑤ⓜ 🛈 💻 ⇆ ✕

WILMINGTON
Baymont Inn ⓗ
(937) 383-3950. **Call for rates.** 201 Carrie Dr 45177. Jct US 22 and 68, 1.5 mi e on US 22. Int corridors. **Pets:** Accepted.
✕ 🛈 💻 ⇆ ✕

Holiday Inn Wilmington & Roberts Conference Centre ⓗ
(937) 283-3200. **$89-$149.** 123 Gano Rd 45177. I-71, exit 50, just w. Int corridors. **Pets:** Accepted. ASK ✕ ⑤ⓜ 🛈 💻 ¶ ⇆

END METROPOLITAN AREA

CLEVELAND METROPOLITAN AREA

BEACHWOOD
Embassy Suites ⓗ
(216) 765-8066. **$129-$249.** 3775 Park East Dr 44122. I-271, exit 29, just w on Chagrin Blvd. Int corridors. **Pets:** Small. $75 one-time fee/pet. Designated rooms, service with restrictions, supervision.
✕ 🛈 💻 ¶ ⇆ ✕

Extended StayAmerica-Cleveland-Beachwood ⓗ
(216) 595-9551. **$72-$99.** 3820 Orange Pl 44122. I-271, exit 29, 0.3 mi e on Chagrin Blvd, then 0.4 mi s. Int corridors. **Pets:** Other species. $25 daily fee/room. Designated rooms, service with restrictions, crate.
ASK ✕ 🛈 💻

Hilton Cleveland East/Beachwood ⓗ
(216) 464-5950. **$99-$189.** 3663 Park East Dr 44122. I-271, exit 29, just w on Chagrin Blvd, then just n. Int corridors. **Pets:** Accepted.
SAVE ✕ 🛈 💻 ¶ ⇆ ✕

Homestead Studio Suites Hotel-Cleveland/Beachwood ⓗ
(216) 896-5555. **$72-$99.** 3625 Orange Pl 44122. I-271, exit 29, 0.3 mi e on Chagrin Blvd, then 0.4 mi s. Int corridors. **Pets:** Other species. $25 daily fee/room. Designated rooms, service with restrictions, crate.
ASK ✕ 🛈 💻

Residence Inn by Marriott Cleveland-Beachwood ⓗ ❖
(216) 831-3030. **$99-$199.** 3628 Park East Dr 44122. I-271, exit 29, just w on Chagrin Blvd. Int corridors. **Pets:** Medium, other species. $100 one-time fee/room. Service with restrictions, crate.
✕ ⑤ⓜ 🛈 💻 ⇆ ✕

BROOKLYN
Extended StayAmerica Cleveland-Brooklyn ⓗ
(216) 267-7799. **$62-$99.** 10300 Cascade Crossing 44144. I-480, exit 13, just s. Int corridors. **Pets:** Other species. $25 daily fee/room. Designated rooms, service with restrictions, crate. ASK ✕ 🛈 💻

CLEVELAND
Comfort Inn Downtown Cleveland ⓗ
(216) 861-0001. **$80-$100.** 1800 Euclid Ave 44115. Corner of Euclid Ave and E 18th St. Int corridors. **Pets:** Medium. $100 one-time fee/room. Service with restrictions, supervision. ASK ✕ 🛈 💻

La Quinta Inn & Suites Cleveland Airport ⓗ ❖
(216) 251-8500. **$55-$89.** 4222 W 150th St 44135. I-71, exit 240, just n. Int corridors. **Pets:** Medium, other species. Service with restrictions, supervision. ASK ✕ 🛈 💻

Residence Inn by Marriott ⓗ
(216) 443-9043. **$99-$179.** 527 Prospect Ave 44115. Between E 9th St and Ontario. Int corridors. **Pets:** Accepted. ✕ 🛈 💻

The Ritz-Carlton Cleveland ⓗ ❖
(216) 623-1300. **$199-$399.** 1515 W 3rd St 44113. In Tower City Center (3rd St side). Int corridors. **Pets:** Other species. $75 one-time fee/room. Designated rooms. SAVE ✕ 🛈 💻 ¶ ⇆ ✕

Sheraton Cleveland Airport Hotel ⓗ
(216) 267-1500. **Call for rates.** 5300 Riverside Dr 44135. I-71, exit 237, just s of I-480 on SR 237, follow signs. Int corridors. **Pets:** Medium. $200 deposit/room. Service with restrictions, supervision.
SAVE ✕ ⑤ⓜ 💻 ¶ ⇆ ✕

Wyndham Cleveland at PlayhouseSquare ⓗ
(216) 615-7500. **$99-$209.** 1260 Euclid Ave 44115. Jct E 14th St. Int corridors. **Pets:** Accepted. ASK ✕ 🛈 💻 ¶ ⇆ ✕

INDEPENDENCE
La Quinta Inn ⓗ ❖
(216) 447-1133. **$59-$89.** 6161 Quarry Ln 44131. I-77, exit 155, just e on Rockside Rd, then just s. Int corridors. **Pets:** Medium, other species. Service with restrictions, supervision. ASK ✕ 🛈 💻

Red Roof Inn #0028 Ⓜ
(216) 447-0030. **$56-$86.** 6020 Quarry Ln 44131. I-77, exit 155, just e on Rockside Rd, then just s. Ext corridors. **Pets:** Large. Service with restrictions, crate. SAVE ✕ 🛈

Residence Inn by Marriott ⓗ
(216) 520-1450. **$89-$169.** 5101 W Creek Rd 44131. I-77, exit 155, just w on Rockside Rd, then just n. Ext corridors. **Pets:** Other species. $100 one-time fee/room. Service with restrictions, crate.
✕ 🛈 💻 ⇆ ✕

LAKEWOOD
Days Inn of Lakewood Ⓜ
(216) 226-4800. **$54-$79.** 12019 Lake Ave 44107. I-90, exit 166, 1.6 mi n on W 117th St, then just w. Int corridors. **Pets:** Accepted.
ASK ✕ 🛈 💻

Travelodge Ⓜ
(216) 221-9000. **Call for rates.** 11837 Edgewater Dr 44107. I-90, exit 166, 1.7 mi n on W 117th St, then just w. Int corridors. **Pets:** Accepted.
✕ 🛈 💻

MAYFIELD HEIGHTS
Baymont Inn & Suites-Cleveland (Mayfield Heights) ⓗ
(440) 442-8400. **$69-$129.** 1421 Golden Gate Blvd 44124. I-271, exit 34, 0.3 mi w on US 322, then just n. Int corridors. **Pets:** Other species. $10 daily fee/room. Service with restrictions. SAVE ✕ 🛈 💻

▼▼▼▼ Staybridge Suites Cleveland East 🅷
(440) 442-9200. **$99-$169.** 6103 Landerhaven Dr 44124. I-271, exit 32, just e on Cedar Rd, 0.7 mi n on Lander Dr, then just e. Int corridors. **Pets:** Medium. $75 one-time fee/pet. Service with restrictions, crate.
(ASK) ☒ ♿ ♨ 🖵 ⇨

MEDINA

▼▼▼ Executive Inn & Suites 🅷
(330) 723-4994. **$90-$100, 7 day notice.** 2850 Medina Rd 44256. I-71, exit 218, just e. Int corridors. **Pets:** Accepted. (ASK) ☒ ♨ 🖵 ⇨

▼▼ Motel 6 4112 🅷
(330) 723-3322. **$42-$65.** 3122 Eastpointe Dr 44256. I-71, exit 218, just w. Int corridors. **Pets:** Other species. Service with restrictions, supervision.
☒ ⇨

▼▼ Red Roof Inn Ⓜ
(330) 725-1395. **$51-$85.** 5021 Eastpointe Dr 44256. I-71, exit 218, just w. Ext corridors. **Pets:** Large. Service with restrictions, crate.
(ASK) ☒ ♨ ⇨

MIDDLEBURG HEIGHTS

▼▼▼▼ Comfort Inn-Cleveland Airport 🅷
(440) 234-3131. **$65-$99.** 17550 Rosbough Dr 44130. I-71, exit 235, 0.3 mi w to Engle Rd, then 0.3 mi n. Int corridors. **Pets:** Other species. $35 one-time fee/room. Service with restrictions, crate.
(ASK) ☒ ♿ ♨ 🖵 ⇨

(AAA) ▼▼▼▼▼ Days Inn Cleveland Airport South Ⓜ
(440) 243-2277. **$69-$149.** 7233 Engle Rd 44130. I-71, exit 235, just w. Ext corridors. **Pets:** Accepted. (SAVE) ☒ ♨ 🖵 ⇨

(AAA) ▼▼▼ Red Roof Inn-Middleburg Heights #7060 🅷
(440) 243-2441. **$45-$79.** 17555 Bagley Rd 44130. I-71, exit 235, just w, then just s. Ext/int corridors. **Pets:** Large. Service with restrictions, crate.
(SAVE) ☒ ♨

▼▼▼▼ Residence Inn by Marriott 🅷
(440) 234-6688. **$79-$169.** 17525 Rosbough Dr 44130. I-71, exit 235, just w on Bagley Rd, then just n on Engle Rd. Ext/int corridors. **Pets:** Other species. $100 one-time fee/room. Designated rooms, service with restrictions, crate. ☒ ♨ 🖵 ⇨ ⊗

▼▼▼▼ StudioPLUS-Cleveland-Middleburg Heights 🅷
(440) 243-7024. **$62-$99.** 17552 Rosbough Dr 44130. I-71, exit 235, 0.3 mi w to Engle Rd, then 0.3 mi n. Int corridors. **Pets:** Other species. $25 daily fee/room. Designated rooms, service with restrictions, crate.
(ASK) ☒ ♨ 🖵

▼▼▼▼ TownePlace Suites 🅷
(440) 816-9300. **$134-$164.** 7325 S Engle Rd 44130. I-71, exit 235, just w on Bagley Rd, then just s. Int corridors. **Pets:** Accepted.
(ECO) ☒ ♨ ⇨

NORTH OLMSTED

▼▼▼ Candlewood Suites Cleveland/North Olmsted 🅷
(440) 716-0584. **$89-$104.** 24741 Country Club Blvd 44070. I-480, exit 6B westbound; exit 6 eastbound, just n on SR 252. Int corridors.
Pets: Accepted. (ASK) ☒ ♨ 🖵

▼▼▼ Homestead Studio Suites Hotel-Cleveland/Airport/North Olmsted 🅷
(440) 777-8585. **$62-$99.** 24851 Country Club Blvd 44070. I-480, exit 6B westbound; exit 6 eastbound, just n on SR 252. Ext corridors.
Pets: Other species. $25 daily fee/room. Designated rooms, service with restrictions, crate. (ASK) ☒ ♿ ♨ 🖵

(AAA) ▼▼▼ La Quinta Inn & Suites North Olmsted 🅷 🐾
(440) 734-4477. **Call for rates.** 25105 Country Club Blvd 44070. I-480, exit 6B westbound; exit 6 eastbound, just n on SR 252. Int corridors.
Pets: Medium, other species. Service with restrictions, supervision.
(SAVE) ☒ ♿ ♨ 🖵

▼▼▼ Radisson Hotel Cleveland Airport West 🅷
(440) 734-5060. **$89-$199.** 25070 Country Club Blvd 44070. I-480, exit 6B westbound; exit 6 eastbound, just n on SR 252. Int corridors.
Pets: Other species. (ASK) ☒ ♿ ♨ 🖵 🍴 ⇨ ⊗

▼▼▼ StudioPLUS Cleveland-Airport-N Olmstead 🅷
(440) 716-2412. **$62-$99.** 25801 Country Club Blvd 44070. I-480, 6B westbound; exit 6 eastbound, just n on SR 252, then 0.3 mi w. Int corridors. **Pets:** Other species. $25 daily fee/room. Designated rooms, service with restrictions, crate. (ASK) ☒ ♨ 🖵 ⇨

RICHFIELD

▼▼▼ Quality Inn & Suites 🅷
(330) 659-6151. **$70-$90.** 4742 Brecksville Rd 44286. I-80, exit 173, just s; I-77, exit 145, 0.5 mi n. Int corridors. **Pets:** $25 one-time fee/room. Designated rooms, service with restrictions, supervision.
(ASK) ☒ ♨ 🖵 🍴 ⇨ ⊗

SOLON

▼▼▼ Hampton Inn 🅷 🐾
(440) 542-0400. **$92-$139.** 6035 Enterprise Pkwy 44139. US 422, exit Harper Rd, 0.6 mi s, then 0.4 mi e. Int corridors. **Pets:** Medium. $50 one-time fee/room. Service with restrictions, crate.
☒ ♿ ♨ 🖵 ⇨

TWINSBURG

(AAA) ▼▼▼ Comfort Suites-Twinsburg 🅷
(330) 963-5909. **$110-$199.** 2715 Creekside Dr 44087. I-480, exit 37 (SR 91), just n. Int corridors. **Pets:** Dogs only. $15 daily fee/room. Service with restrictions, crate. (SAVE) ☒ ♿ ♨ 🖵 ⇨

WESTLAKE

▼▼▼ Extended Stay Deluxe Cleveland-Westlake 🅷
(440) 899-4160. **$72-$99.** 30360 Clemens Rd 44145. I-90, exit 156, just n. Int corridors. **Pets:** Other species. $25 daily fee/room. Designated rooms, service with restrictions, crate. (ASK) ☒ ♨ 🖵

(AAA) ▼▼▼ Red Roof Inn-Westlake #7094 Ⓜ
(440) 892-7920. **$56-$89.** 29595 Clemens Rd 44145. I-90, exit 156, just n. Ext corridors. **Pets:** Large. Service with restrictions, crate.
(SAVE) ☒ ♨

▼▼▼ Residence Inn by Marriott 🅷
(440) 892-2254. **$89-$169.** 30100 Clemens Rd 44145. I-90, exit 156, just n. Ext corridors. **Pets:** Accepted. ☒ ♨ 🖵 ⇨ ⊗

(AAA) ▼▼ Super 8 Ⓜ
(440) 871-3993. **$54-$99.** 25200 Sperry Dr 44145. I-90, exit 159, just n. Ext corridors. **Pets:** Accepted. (SAVE) ☒ 🖵 ⇨

WILLOUGHBY

(AAA) ▼▼▼ Red Roof Inn-East #7053 Ⓜ
(440) 946-9872. **$50-$90.** 4166 SR 306 44094. I-90, exit 193, just s. Ext corridors. **Pets:** Large. Service with restrictions, crate. (SAVE) ☒ ♨

END METROPOLITAN AREA

CLYDE

▼▼ ▼▼ Red Roof Inn H
(419) 547-6660. **$59-$118.** 1363 W McPherson Hwy 43410. 1 mi w on SR 20. Int corridors. **Pets:** Large. Service with restrictions, crate.
[ASK] [X] [&M] [=] [≈]

COLUMBUS METROPOLITAN AREA

CIRCLEVILLE

▼▼▼▼ Holiday Inn Express Hotel & Suites H
(740) 420-7711. **Call for rates.** 23911 US 23 S 43113. Jct US 22, 1.2 mi s. Int corridors. **Pets:** Accepted. [X] [&M] [=] [≈] [≈]

COLUMBUS

▼▼ ▼▼ Baymont Inn & Suites Columbus at Rickenbacker H
(614) 491-4400. **Call for rates.** 2323 Rickenbacker Pkwy 43217. I-270, exit 49, 3.6 mi s, then just w. Int corridors. **Pets:** $25 one-time fee/room. Service with restrictions, crate. [X] [=] [≈] [≈]

AAA ▼▼▼▼ Best Western Columbus North H ❀
(614) 888-8230. **$90.** 888 E Dublin-Granville Rd 43229. I-71, exit 117, 0.5 mi w on SR 161. Int corridors. **Pets:** Medium, other species. $25 deposit/ room. No service, crate. [SAVE] [X] [=] [≈] [TI] [≈] [X]

▼▼▼▼ Candlewood Suites Polaris H
(614) 436-6600. **$79-$159.** 8515 Lyra Dr 43240. I-71, exit 121, 0.3 mi w on SR 750. Int corridors. **Pets:** Other species. $75 one-time fee/room. Service with restrictions, crate. [ASK] [X] [&M] [=] [≈] [≈] [X]

▼▼▼▼ Comfort Inn Polaris H ❀
(614) 791-9700. **$85-$170.** 8400 Lyra Dr 43240. I-71, exit 121, just w. Int corridors. **Pets:** Medium. $25 one-time fee/room. Designated rooms, service with restrictions. [ASK] [X] [&M] [=] [≈] [≈] [X]

▼▼▼▼ Doubletree Columbus/Worthington H
(614) 885-3334. **$89-$169.** 175 Hutchinson Ave 43235. I-270, exit 23, just n of jct US 23 N, just e on Dimension Dr, then just s on High Cross Blvd. Int corridors. **Pets:** Accepted. [X] [&M] [=] [≈] [TI] [≈]

▼▼▼▼ Doubletree Guest Suites H
(614) 228-4600. **$89-$275.** 50 S Front St 43215. Corner of Front and State sts, just n. Int corridors. **Pets:** Accepted. [X] [=] [≈] [TI]

▼▼▼▼ Drury Inn & Suites-Columbus Convention Center H
(614) 221-7008. **$100-$199.** 88 E Nationwide Blvd 43215. 0.3 mi n on US 23. Int corridors. **Pets:** Other species. No service, supervision.
[ASK] [X] [&M] [=] [≈] [≈] [X]

▼▼ ▼▼ Extended StayAmerica-Columbus-Easton H
(614) 428-6022. **$76-$99.** 4200 Stelzer Rd 43230. I-270, exit 32, just w on Morse Rd, then just n. Int corridors. **Pets:** Other species. $25 daily fee/room. Designated rooms, service with restrictions, crate.
[ASK] [X] [=] [≈]

▼▼ ▼▼ Extended StayAmerica-Columbus-North H
(614) 431-0033. **$46-$99.** 6255 Zumstein Dr 43229. I-71, exit 117, just w on SR 161, then 0.5 mi n. Int corridors. **Pets:** Other species. $25 daily fee/room. Designated rooms, service with restrictions.
[ASK] [X] [=] [≈]

▼▼ ▼▼ Extended StayAmerica-Columbus-Worthington H
(614) 785-1006. **$50-$99.** 7465 High Cross Blvd 43235. I-270, exit 23, just n on US 23, just e on Dimension Dr, then just s. Int corridors. **Pets:** Other species. $25 daily fee/room. Designated rooms, service with restrictions, crate. [ASK] [X] [=] [≈]

▼▼ ▼▼ Extended Stay Deluxe Columbus/Polaris H
(614) 431-5522. **$71-$99.** 8555 Lyra Dr 43240. I-71 N, exit 121, just w on Polaris Pkwy. Int corridors. **Pets:** Other species. $25 daily fee/room. Designated rooms, service with restrictions, crate.
[ASK] [X] [&M] [=] [≈] [≈]

▼▼▼▼ Harrison House Bed & Breakfast BB
(614) 421-2202. **$129-$169.** 313 W 5th Ave 43201. I-670, exit 3 (Neil Ave), 0.9 mi n, then just w. Int corridors. **Pets:** Accepted. [ASK] [X] [☎]

AAA ▼▼▼▼ Hawthorn Suites Airport Columbus East H ❀
(614) 864-8844. **$79-$279.** 2084 S Hamilton Rd 43232. I-70, exit 107, 0.5 mi s, then just e. Ext corridors. **Pets:** Small, dogs only. $25 daily fee/ pet. Service with restrictions. [SAVE] [X] [=] [≈] [≈]

AAA ▼▼▼▼ Hilton Columbus at Easton H ❀
(614) 414-5000. **$159-$309.** 3900 Chagrin Dr 43219. I-270, exit 33, 0.5 mi w; at Easton Town Center. Int corridors. **Pets:** Medium. $75 one-time fee/room. Service with restrictions, crate.
[SAVE] [X] [&M] [=] [≈] [TI] [≈] [X]

AAA ▼▼▼▼ Hilton Columbus/Polaris H ❀
(614) 885-1600. **$119-$219.** 8700 Lyra Dr 43240. I-71, exit 121, just w on Polaris Pkwy, then just n. Int corridors. **Pets:** Medium. $75 one-time fee/room. Service with restrictions.
[SAVE] [X] [&M] [=] [≈] [TI] [≈] [X]

AAA ▼▼▼▼ Holiday Inn Columbus Downtown Capitol Square H
(614) 221-3281. **$89-$149.** 175 E Town St 43215. I-70, exit 100B, 0.3 mi n on 4th St. Int corridors. **Pets:** $50 one-time fee/room. Service with restrictions, crate. [SAVE] [X] [=] [≈] [TI] [≈]

▼▼▼▼ La Quinta Inn & Suites H ❀
(614) 878-8844. **$89-$129.** 5510 Trabue Rd 43228. I-70, exit 91 eastbound; exit 91B westbound, just n on Renner Rd, then just e. Int corridors. **Pets:** Medium, other species. Service with restrictions, supervision.
[ASK] [X] [=] [≈] [≈]

▼▼ ▼▼ Ramada North Columbus H
(614) 890-8111. **$60-$129, 3 day notice.** 6767 Schrock Hill Ct 43229. I-270, exit 27, n off Cleveland Ave; enter off Schrock Rd. Int corridors. **Pets:** Medium, dogs only. $10 daily fee/pet. Service with restrictions, crate. [ASK] [X] [=] [≈]

AAA ▼▼▼▼ Red Roof Inn-Columbus Convention Center H
(614) 224-6539. **$80-$160.** 111 E Nationwide Blvd 43215. Jct 3rd St. Int corridors. **Pets:** Large. Service with restrictions, crate.
[SAVE] [X] [&M] [=]

▼▼ ▼▼ Red Roof Inn-OSU #7121 M
(614) 267-9941. **Call for rates.** 441 Ackerman Rd 43202. SR 315, exit Ackerman Rd, 0.6 mi e. Ext corridors. **Pets:** Large. Service with restrictions, crate. [X] [&M]

AAA ▼▼ ▼▼ Red Roof Inn-West #7009 M
(614) 878-9245. **Call for rates.** 5001 Renner Rd 43228. I-70, exit 91 eastbound; exit 91B westbound, just nw. Ext corridors. **Pets:** Large. Service with restrictions, crate. [SAVE] [X] [&M] [=]

▼▼▼▼ Residence Inn by Marriott H
(614) 885-0799. **$129-$139.** 7300 Huntington Park Dr 43235. I-270, exit 23, 0.4 mi n on US 23, 0.3 mi e on E Campus View Blvd, then 0.3 mi s. Int corridors. **Pets:** Accepted. [X] [&M] [=] [≈] [≈] [X]

▼▼▼▼ Residence Inn by Marriott H
(614) 222-2610. **$139-$159.** 36 E Gay St 43215. Between High and S 3rd sts. Int corridors. **Pets:** Accepted. [X] [&M] [=] [=]

◆◆◆◆ **Residence Inn by Marriott Easton** H
(614) 414-1000. **$170-$208.** 3999 Easton Loop W 43219. I-270, exit 33, 1 mi w, then just n. Int corridors. **Pets:** Accepted.
⊠ 🖪 💻 ⊠

◆◆◆ ◆◆◆ **Sheraton Suites Columbus** H ✿
(614) 436-0004. **$69-$189.** 201 Hutchinson Ave 43235. I-270, exit 23, 0.3 mi n on US 23, just e on Dimension Dr, then 0.4 mi se on Vantage Dr. Int corridors. **Pets:** Medium, other species. Service with restrictions, supervision. (SAVE) ⊠ 🖪 💻 ❙❙ ⇆

◆◆◆ ◆◆◆ **TownePlace Suites by Marriott** H
(614) 885-1557. **$98-$120.** 7272 Huntington Park Dr 43235. I-270, exit 23, 0.4 mi n, 0.3 mi e on E Campus View Blvd, then 0.3 mi s. Int corridors. **Pets:** Accepted. (ECO) ⊠ 🖪 💻 ⇆

◆◆◆ ◆◆◆ **Varsity Inn North** M
(614) 267-4646. **$69-$149.** 3246 Olentangy River Rd 43202. SR 315, exit N Broadway, 0.3 mi s. Ext corridors. **Pets:** Accepted.
(SAVE) ⊠ 🖪 💻 ⇆

◆◆◆ ◆◆◆◆ **The Westin Columbus** H ✿
(614) 228-3800. **Call for rates.** 310 S High St 43215. Corner of Main and High sts. Int corridors. **Pets:** Medium. Service with restrictions, supervision. (SAVE) ⊠ 🖪 💻 ❙❙

DUBLIN

◆◆◆ ◆◆◆ **Chase Suite Hotel** H
(614) 766-7762. **$99-$179.** 4130 Tuller Rd 43017. I-270, exit 20, 0.3 mi s on Sawmill Rd via Village Pkwy and Dublin Center Dr. Ext corridors. **Pets:** Accepted. (SAVE) ⊠ 🖪 💻 ⇆

◆◆◆◆ **Drury Inn & Suites-Columbus Northwest** H
(614) 798-8802. **$90-$159.** 6170 Parkcenter Cir 43017. I-270, exit 15 (Tuttle Crossing Blvd), 0.3 mi e, then just n on Blazer Pkwy. Int corridors. **Pets:** Other species. No service, supervision.
(ASK) ⊠ 🖪 🖪 💻 ⇆

◆◆◆◆ **Dublin Homewood Suites by Hilton** H
(614) 791-8675. **$79-$199.** 5300 Parkcenter Ave 43017. I-270, exit 15 (Tuttle Crossing Blvd), just e, just n on Blazer Blvd, then just e. Int corridors. **Pets:** Accepted. ⊠ 🖪 🖪 💻 ⇆ ⊠

◆◆◆ ◆◆◆ **Extended StayAmerica-Columbus-Dublin** H
(614) 760-0053. **$59-$99.** 450 Metro Pl N 43017. I-270, exit 17A, just e on SR 161, just s on Frantz Rd, then just n. Int corridors. **Pets:** Other species. $25 daily fee/room. Designated rooms, service with restrictions, crate. (ASK) ⊠ 🖪 💻

◆◆◆ ◆◆◆ **Extended StayAmerica Columbus-Sawmill** H
(614) 764-0159. **$57-$99.** 6601 Reflections Dr 43017. I-270, exit 20, 0.7 mi s on Sawmill Rd, just e on SR 161, just s on Martin, then just se. Int corridors. **Pets:** Other species. $25 daily fee/room. Designated rooms, service with restrictions, crate. (ASK) ⊠ 🖪 💻 ⇆

◆◆◆ ◆◆◆ **Extended Stay Deluxe (Columbus/Tuttle)** H
(614) 760-0245. **$67-$99.** 5530 Tuttle Crossing Blvd 43016. I-270, exit 15 (Tuttle Crossing Blvd), 0.5 mi w. Int corridors. **Pets:** Other species. $25 daily fee/room. Designated rooms, service with restrictions, crate.
(ASK) ⊠ 🖪 💻

◆◆◆ ◆◆◆ **La Quinta Inn** H ✿
(614) 792-8300. **$65-$99.** 6145 Parkcenter Cir 43017. I-270, exit 15 (Tuttle Crossing Blvd), just e, then just n on Blazer Pkwy. Int corridors. **Pets:** Medium, other species. Service with restrictions, supervision.
(ASK) ⊠ 🖪 🖪 💻 ⇆

◆◆◆ ◆◆◆ **Red Roof Inn-Dublin #127** M
(614) 764-3993. **$50-$80.** 5125 Post Rd 43017. I-270, exit 17A, just ne. Ext corridors. **Pets:** Large. Service with restrictions, crate.
(SAVE) ⊠ 🖪 🖪

◆◆◆ ◆◆◆ **Residence Inn by Marriott Dublin** H
(614) 791-0403. **$139-$149.** 435 Metro Pl S 43017. I-270, exit 17A, 0.5 mi e on SR 161, 0.5 mi s on Frantz Rd, then just w. Ext/int corridors.
Pets: Accepted. ⊠ 🖪 🖪 💻 ⇆ ⊠

◆◆◆ ◆◆◆ **Staybridge Suites** H
(614) 734-9882. **$99-$129.** 6095 Emerald Pkwy 43016. I-270, exit 15 (Tuttle Crossing Blvd), just w. Int corridors. **Pets:** Accepted.
(ASK) ⊠ 🖪 🖪 💻 ⇆ ⊠

GAHANNA

◆◆◆ ◆◆◆ **Candlewood Suites Columbus Airport** H ✿
(614) 863-4033. **$79-$129.** 590 Taylor Rd 43230. I-270, exit 37, just e, 0.6 mi s on Morrison Rd, then just e. Int corridors. **Pets:** Other species. $75 one-time fee/room. Designated rooms, service with restrictions, crate.
(ASK) ⊠ 🖪 💻

◆◆◆ ◆◆◆ **TownePlace Suites by Marriott Columbus Airport** H
(614) 861-1400. **$94-$114.** 695 Taylor Rd 43230. I-270, exit 37, just e, 0.6 mi s on Morrison Rd, then just e. Int corridors. **Pets:** Accepted.
(ECO) ⊠ 🖪 🖪 💻 ⇆

GROVE CITY

◆◆◆ ◆◆◆ **Best Western Executive Inn** M
(614) 875-7770. **$71-$109.** 4026 Jackpot Rd 43123. I-71, exit 100, just e. Ext corridors. **Pets:** Large, dogs only. $10 daily fee/pet. Designated rooms, service with restrictions, supervision. (SAVE) ⊠ 🖪 💻 ⇆

◆◆◆◆ **Drury Inn & Suites-Columbus South** H
(614) 875-7000. **$90-$199.** 4109 Parkway Centre Dr 43123. I-71, exit 100, just e. Int corridors. **Pets:** Other species. No service, supervision.
(ASK) ⊠ 🖪 🖪 💻 ⇆

◆◆◆ ◆◆◆ **La Quinta Inn South** H ✿
(614) 539-6200. **$49-$134.** 3962 Jackpot Rd 43123. I-71, exit 100, just e. Int corridors. **Pets:** Medium, other species. Service with restrictions, supervision. (SAVE) ⊠ 🖪 🖪 💻 ⇆ ⊠

◆◆◆ **Red Roof Inn Columbus/Grove City** M
(614) 871-9617. **$54-$76.** 4055 Jackpot Rd 43123. I-71, exit 100, just e. Ext corridors. **Pets:** Large. Service with restrictions, crate.
(ASK) ⊠ 🖪 🖪 💻 ⇆

HEBRON

◆◆◆ ◆◆◆ **Red Roof Inn** H
(740) 467-7663. **$53-$70.** 10668 Lancaster Rd SW 43025. I-70, exit 126, just s. Int corridors. **Pets:** Large. Service with restrictions, crate.
(ASK) ⊠ 🖪

HILLIARD

◆◆◆ ◆◆◆ **Comfort Suites by Choice Hotels-Columbus** H
(614) 529-8118. **$70-$120.** 3831 Park Mill Run Dr 43026. I-270, exit 13A northbound; exit 13 southbound, 0.3 mi e on Fishinger Blvd. Int corridors.
Pets: Accepted. (ASK) ⊠ 🖪 🖪 💻 ⇆

◆◆◆ ◆◆◆ **Homewood Suites by Hilton-Columbus** H
(614) 529-4100. **$89-$179.** 3841 Park Mill Run Dr 43026. I-270, exit 13 southbound; exit 13A northbound, 0.4 mi e on Fishinger Blvd. Int corridors. **Pets:** Accepted. ⊠ 🖪 🖪 💻 ⇆ ⊠

MARYSVILLE

◆◆◆ ◆◆◆ **Comfort Inn** H
(937) 644-0400. **$72-$76.** 16420 Allenby Dr 43040. Jct US 33 and 36. Int corridors. **Pets:** Accepted. (ASK) ⊠ 🖪 💻 ⇆

NEWARK

◆◆◆ ◆◆◆ **Cherry Valley Lodge** H ✿
(740) 788-1200. **$118-$189.** 2299 Cherry Valley Rd 43055. 4.6 mi w on SR 16, then 0.3 mi s. Int corridors. **Pets:** Other species. $150 deposit/room. Crate. (SAVE) ⊠ 🖪 🖪 💻 ❙❙ ⇆ ⊠

OBETZ

AAA ▼▼▼▼ **Comfort Inn Obetz Rickenbacker** 🅷
(614) 492-9000. **$59-$129.** 4870 Old Rathmell Ct 43207. I-270, exit 49, just e. Int corridors. **Pets:** Accepted. 🆂🅰🆅🅴 ⊗ 🔣 🛗 💻 🏊

REYNOLDSBURG

AAA ▼▼▼ **Days Inn & Suites Columbus East** 🅷
(614) 864-1280. **$53-$85.** 2100 Brice Rd 43068. I-70, exit 110 westbound; exit 110B eastbound, just n. Int corridors. **Pets:** Other species. $20 daily fee/room. Designated rooms, service with restrictions, supervision. 🆂🅰🆅🅴 ⊗ 🛗 💻 🍴 🏊

▼▼▼ **Extended StayAmerica-Columbus-East** 🅷
(614) 759-1451. **$52-$99.** 2200 Lake Club Dr 43232. I-70, exit 110 westbound; exit 110B eastbound, 0.5 mi n on Brice Rd, just w on Channingway, then just s. Int corridors. **Pets:** Other species. $25 daily fee/room. Designated rooms, service with restrictions, crate.
🅰🆂🅺 ⊗ 🛗 💻 🏊

▼▼▼▼ **The Fairfield Inn & Suites Columbus East** 🅷
(614) 864-4555. **$89-$109.** 2826 Taylor Rd SW 43068. I-70, exit 112B eastbound; exit 112 westbound, just n, then just e. Int corridors. **Pets:** $75 daily fee/pet. Service with restrictions, supervision.
⊗ 🔣 🛗 💻 🏊 ⊗

▼▼ **Super 8 Reynoldsburg** 🅼
(614) 864-3880. **$50-$90.** 2055 Brice Rd 43068. I-70, exit 110 westbound; exit 110B eastbound. Ext corridors. **Pets:** Accepted.
🅰🆂🅺 ⊗ 🛗 💻 🏊

WESTERVILLE

▼▼ **Baymont Inn & Suites North East** 🅼
(614) 890-1244. **Call for rates.** 909 S State St 43081. I-270, exit 29, 0.4 mi n on SR 3, just w on Heatherdown Dr, then just s. Ext corridors. **Pets:** Accepted. ⊗ 🛗 💻 🏊

END METROPOLITAN AREA

CONNEAUT

AAA ▼▼▼ **Days Inn of Conneaut** 🅷
(440) 593-6000. **$69-$129.** 600 Days Blvd 44030. I-90, exit 241, 0.3 mi n. Int corridors. **Pets:** Other species. $10 daily fee/pet. Designated rooms, service with restrictions, supervision. 🆂🅰🆅🅴 ⊗ 🛗 💻 🍴 🏊

CUYAHOGA FALLS

AAA ▼▼▼▼ **Sheraton Suites Akron-Cuyahoga Falls** 🅷
(330) 929-3000. **Call for rates.** 1989 Front St 44221. SR 8, exit Broad Blvd, just w. Int corridors. **Pets:** Accepted.
🆂🅰🆅🅴 ⊗ 🔣 🛗 💻 🍴 🏊 ⊗

DANVILLE

▼▼▼ **The White Oak Inn** 🅱🅱 🐾
(740) 599-6107. **Call for rates.** 29683 Walhonding Rd (SR 715) 43014. 3 mi s on US 62, 1.3 mi se on US 36, then 2.7 mi e on SR 715. Ext/int corridors. **Pets:** Other species. $25 daily fee/pet. Designated rooms, service with restrictions, crate. ⊗ 🛗 💻 🈯

DAYTON

▼▼ **Comfort Inn by Choice Hotels-North** 🅷
(937) 890-9995. **$68-$82.** 7125 Miller Ln 45414. I-75, exit 59 (Wyse Rd/Benchwood Rd), just w on Benchwood Rd, then 0.6 mi n. Int corridors. **Pets:** Accepted. 🅰🆂🅺 ⊗ 🔣 🛗 💻 🏊

AAA ▼▼▼▼ **Country Inn & Suites By Carlson South** 🅷
(937) 425-7400. **$89-$129.** 8277 Yankee St 45458. I-675, exit 2, just e on SR 725, then just s; southbound, just s on Yankee St. Int corridors. **Pets:** Small. $20 daily fee/pet. Designated rooms, service with restrictions, supervision. 🆂🅰🆅🅴 ⊗ 🔣 🛗 💻 🏊 ⊗

▼▼▼ **Dayton Marriott Hotel** 🅷
(937) 223-1000. **$143-$175.** 1414 S Patterson Blvd 45409. I-75, exit 51 (Edwin C Moses Blvd), 1.5 mi n, just e on Washington St, then 1 mi s. Int corridors. **Pets:** $75 one-time fee/room. Service with restrictions, supervision. ⊗ 🛗 💻 🍴 🏊 ⊗

▼▼▼ **Drury Inn & Suites-Dayton North** 🅷
(937) 454-5200. **$85-$229.** 6616 Miller Ln 45414. I-75, exit 59 (Wyse Rd/Benchwood Rd), just w on Benchwood Rd, then just n. Int corridors. **Pets:** Other species. No service, supervision.
🅰🆂🅺 ⊗ 🔣 🛗 💻 🏊

▼▼ **Extended StayAmerica Dayton South** 🅷
(937) 439-2022. **$49-$59.** 7851 Lois Cir 45459. I-75, exit 44, just e on SR 725; opposite mall. Int corridors. **Pets:** Other species. $25 daily fee/room. Designated rooms, service with restrictions, crate.
🅰🆂🅺 ⊗ 🛗 💻 🏊

▼▼ **Fairfield Inn by Marriott Dayton North** 🅷
(937) 898-1120. **$89-$109.** 6960 Miller Ln 45414. I-75, exit 59 (Wyse Rd/Benchwood Rd), just w on Benchwood Rd, then 0.5 mi n. Ext/int corridors. **Pets:** $30 one-time fee/room. Service with restrictions, supervision.
⊗ 🔣 🛗 💻 🏊

▼▼▼ **Hampton Inn-Dayton South** 🅷
(937) 436-3700. **$91-$99.** 8099 Old Yankee St 45458. I-675, exit 2, just e on SR 725, then just s; southbound, just s. Int corridors. **Pets:** Medium. Service with restrictions, supervision. ⊗ 🔣 🛗 💻 🏊

AAA ▼▼▼ **Red Roof Inn-North #7023** 🅼
(937) 898-1054. **$40-$90, 7 day notice.** 7370 Miller Ln 45414. I-75, exit 59 (Wyse Rd/Benchwood Rd), just w on Benchwood Rd, then 0.8 mi n. Ext corridors. **Pets:** Large. Service with restrictions, crate. 🆂🅰🆅🅴 ⊗ 🛗

▼▼▼▼ **TownePlace Suites by Marriott Dayton North** 🅷 🐾
(937) 898-5700. **$89-$109.** 3642 Maxton Rd 45414. I-75, exit 59 (Wyse Rd/Benchwood Rd), just w on Wyse Rd, 0.5 mi n on Miller Ln. Int corridors. **Pets:** Other species. $50 one-time fee/room. Designated rooms, service with restrictions, crate. ⊗ 🔣 🛗 💻

DELPHOS

▼▼ **Microtel Inn & Suites** 🅷
(567) 765-1500. **$64-$84.** 480 Moxie Ln 45833. US 30, just w on 5th St. Int corridors. **Pets:** Small. $20 one-time fee/room. Service with restrictions, crate. 🅰🆂🅺 ⊗ 🔣 🛗 💻

ELYRIA

AAA ▼▼▼ **Holiday Inn Cleveland Elyria Lorain** 🅷
(440) 324-5411. **$69-$119.** 1825 Lorain Blvd 44035. I-80, exit 145, just n on SR 57, exit Midway Blvd. Int corridors. **Pets:** Large. $25 one-time fee/room. Designated rooms, supervision.
🆂🅰🆅🅴 ⊗ 🔣 🛗 💻 🍴 🏊

AAA ▼▼▼▼ **Red Roof Inn & Suites** 🅷
(440) 324-4444. **$59-$99.** 621 Midway Blvd 44035. I-80, exit 145, just n on SR 57, exit Midway Blvd. Int corridors. **Pets:** Large. Service with restrictions, crate. 🆂🅰🆅🅴 ⊗ 🔣 🛗 💻 🏊

▼▼ **Super 8** 🅷
(440) 323-7488. **$50-$90.** 910 Lorain Blvd 44035. I-80, exit 145, 0.5 mi s on SR 57. Ext corridors. **Pets:** Accepted. 🅰🆂🅺 ⊗ 🛗 💻 🏊

ENGLEWOOD

AAA ▼▼▼▼ **Best Western Dayton/Northwest** 🅷
(937) 832-2222. **$62-$79.** 20 Rockridge Rd 45322. I-70, exit 29, just n. Int corridors. **Pets:** Medium. Service with restrictions, supervision.
🆂🅰🆅🅴 ⊗ 🛗 💻

▼▼▼▼ Comfort Inn & Suites-Dayton H

(937) 836-9400. **$54-$159.** 9305 N Main St 45415. I-70, exit 29, just s. Int corridors. **Pets:** Medium, other species. $25 daily fee/room. Service with restrictions, supervision. (SAVE) ✕ 🖥 🖵 ⚊

▼▼▼▼ Holiday Inn-Dayton Airport H

(937) 832-1234. **Call for rates.** 10 Rockridge Rd 45322. I-70, exit 29, just n. Int corridors. **Pets:** Accepted. ✕ 🖥 🖵 🍴 ⚊

▼▼ Motel 6 Dayton Englewood #1093 M

(937) 836-8339. **$35-$45.** 9325 N Main St 45415. I-70, exit 29, just s. Ext corridors. **Pets:** Other species. Service with restrictions, supervision. ✕ 🖥 ⚊

FAIRBORN

▼▼▼▼ Baymont Inn & Suites Dayton-Fairborn H

(937) 754-9109. **$69-$159.** 730 E Xenia Dr 45324. I-675, exit 22, 0.6 mi w. Int corridors. **Pets:** Accepted. (ASK) ✕ 🖥 🖵

▼▼▼▼ Holiday Inn Dayton/Fairborn/I-675 H

(937) 426-7800. **$99-$139.** 2800 Presidential Dr 45324. I-675, exit 17 (N Fairfield Rd), just w on N Fairfield Rd. Int corridors. **Pets:** Accepted. (ASK) ✕ 🕭M 🖥 🖵 🍴 ⚊

▼▼▼▼ Homewood Suites by Hilton-Fairborn/Dayton H ❀

(937) 429-0600. **$99-$149.** 2750 Presidential Dr 45324. I-675, exit 17 (N Fairfield Rd), just w. Ext/int corridors. **Pets:** Large, other species. $100 one-time fee/pet. Service with restrictions, crate.

✕ 🖥 🖵 ⚊ ⊠

(AAA) ▼▼▼▼ Ramada Limited & Suites-Fairborn Ohio H

(937) 490-2000. **$70-$100.** 2540 University Blvd 45324. I-675, exit 15 (Colonel Glenn Hwy), 1.5 mi e, then just s. Int corridors. **Pets:** $25 daily fee/pet. Service with restrictions, supervision. (SAVE) ✕ 🖥 🖵 ⚊

(AAA) ▼▼▼ Red Roof Inn-Fairborn #7205 H

(937) 426-6116. **$50-$70, 7 day notice.** 2580 Colonel Glenn Hwy 45324. I-675, exit 17 (N Fairfield Rd), just w. Ext corridors. **Pets:** Large. Service with restrictions, crate. (SAVE) ✕ 🖥

▼▼ StudioPLUS Dayton-Fairborn H

(937) 429-0140. **$64-$69.** 3131 Presidential Dr 45324. I-675, exit 15 (Colonel Glenn Hwy), 1.5 mi e, then just s. Int corridors. **Pets:** Other species. $25 daily fee/room. Designated rooms, service with restrictions, crate. (ASK) ✕ 🖥 🖵 ⚊

FAIRLAWN

▼▼ Americas Best Value Inn H

(330) 666-8887. **$42-$86.** 79 Rothrock Rd 44321. I-77, exit 137A, just e. Int corridors. **Pets:** Accepted. (ASK) ✕ 🖥 🖵

▼▼▼ Extended StayAmerica Akron-Copley H

(330) 668-9818. **$62-$99.** 185 W Montrose Ave 44321. I-77, exit 137B, just w on SR 18, then 0.6 mi s. Int corridors. **Pets:** Other species. $25 daily fee/room. Designated rooms, service with restrictions, crate.

(ASK) ✕ 🖥 🖵

(AAA) ▼▼▼▼ Hilton Akron/Fairlawn H

(330) 867-5000. **$99-$189.** 3180 W Market St 44333. I-77, exit 137A, 2 mi e on SR 18. Int corridors. **Pets:** Medium. $50 one-time fee/pet. Service with restrictions, supervision.

(SAVE) ✕ 🕭M 🖥 🖵 🍴 ⚊ ⊠

▼▼▼▼ The Residence Inn by Marriott H

(330) 666-4811. **$143-$175.** 120 Montrose West Ave 44321. I-77, exit 137B, 0.3 mi w on SR 18, then 0.5 mi s. Ext corridors. **Pets:** Accepted. ✕ 🖥 🖵 ⚊ ⊠

▼▼▼ StudioPLUS-Akron-Copley H

(330) 666-3177. **$67-$99.** 170 W Montrose Ave 44321. I-77, exit 137B, 0.3 mi w on SR 18, then 0.5 mi s. Int corridors. **Pets:** Other species. $25 daily fee/room. Designated rooms, service with restrictions, crate. (ASK) ✕ 🖥 🖵 ⚊

FINDLAY

▼▼▼ Country Inn & Suites By Carlson H

(419) 422-4200. **$94.** 903 Interstate Dr 45840. I-75, exit 159, just w. Int corridors. **Pets:** Small, dogs only. $25 one-time fee/room. Designated rooms, service with restrictions, supervision.

(ASK) ✕ 🕭M 🖥 🖵 ⚊

▼▼▼ Drury Inn & Suites H

(419) 422-9700. **$75-$149.** 820 Trenton Ave 45840. I-75, exit 159, just e. Int corridors. **Pets:** Other species. No service, supervision.

(ASK) ✕ 🕭M 🖥 🖵 ⚊ ⊠

▼▼▼ Extended Stay Deluxe Findlay-Tiffin Ave H

(419) 425-9696. **$71-$99.** 2355 Tiffin Ave 45840. 3 mi e on US 224. Int corridors. **Pets:** Other species. $25 daily fee/room. Designated rooms, service with restrictions, crate. (ASK) ✕ 🖥 🖵 ⚊ ⊠

▼▼▼ Holiday Inn Express Hotel & Suites H

(419) 420-1776. **$99-$109.** 941 Interstate Dr 45840. I-75, exit 159, just w. Int corridors. **Pets:** Other species. $25 one-time fee/room. Service with restrictions, supervision. (ASK) ✕ 🕭M 🖥 🖵 ⚊ ⊠

(AAA) ▼▼▼ Quality Inn M ❀

(419) 423-4303. **$58-$110.** 1020 Interstate Ct 45840. I-75, exit 159, just w. Ext corridors. **Pets:** Large. $15 daily fee/pet. Service with restrictions, crate. (SAVE) ✕ 🖥 🖵 ⚊

▼▼ Red Roof Inn M

(419) 424-0466. **$50-$60.** 1951 Broad Ave 45840. I-75, exit 159, 0.5 mi e. Ext corridors. **Pets:** Large. Service with restrictions, crate.

(ASK) ✕ 🖥 ⚊

▼▼▼ TownePlace Suites by Marriott Findlay H

(419) 425-9545. **$62-$76.** 2501 Tiffin Ave 45840. 2 mi e on US 224. Int corridors. **Pets:** Other species. $50 one-time fee/room. Service with restrictions. ✕ 🖥 🖵 ⚊

FOSTORIA

(AAA) ▼▼▼ Best Western Fostoria Inn & Suites H

(419) 436-3600. **$79-$99.** 1690 N County Line Rd 44830. SR 12, 2 mi n on SR 23. Int corridors. **Pets:** Accepted. (SAVE) ✕ 🕭M 🖥 🖵 ⚊

FREDERICKTOWN

▼▼▼ Heartland Country Resort (CA) ❀

(419) 768-9300. **$180-$240, 7 day notice.** 3020 Township Rd 190 43019. I-71, exit 151, 2 mi e on SR 95, 0.6 mi s on SR 314, then 1.3 mi e. Ext corridors. **Pets:** Other species. $15 daily fee/room.

(ASK) ✕ 🖥 🖵 ⊠

FREMONT

(AAA) ▼▼▼ Clarion Inn & Conference Center H

(419) 334-2682. **Call for rates.** 3422 Port Clinton Rd 43420. I-80/90, exit 91, just s. Int corridors. **Pets:** $25 one-time fee/pet. Service with restrictions, supervision. (SAVE) ✕ 🕭M 🖥 🖵 🍴 ⚊

▼▼▼ Comfort Inn & Suites H

(419) 355-9300. **$85-$129.** 840 Sean Dr 43420. I-80/90, exit 91, 2 mi s on SR 53. Int corridors. **Pets:** Large, other species. $25 one-time fee/pet. Service with restrictions, supervision. (ASK) ✕ 🖥 🖵 ⚊

▼▼ Days Inn H

(419) 334-9551. **$69-$129.** 3701 SR 53 N 43420. I-80/90, exit 91, just n. Int corridors. **Pets:** Small, dogs only. $50 deposit/pet. Designated rooms, service with restrictions, supervision. (ASK) ✕ 🖥 🖵 🍴 ⚊

GENEVA

(AAA) ▼▼ Motel 6 #4476 H

(440) 466-1168. **$60-$96.** 1715 SR 534 S 44041. I-90, exit 218, just n. Ext/int corridors. **Pets:** Other species. Service with restrictions, supervision. (SAVE) ✕ 🖥 🖵 ⚊

GENEVA-ON-THE-LAKE

△△△ **▽▽▽▽▽** The Lodge & Conference Center at
Geneva-on-the-Lake 🅗 ❀

(440) 466-7100. **$89-$279, 3 day notice.** 4888 N Broadway 44041.
I-90, exit 218, 6.1 mi n on SR 534. Ext corridors. **Pets:** Other species.
$25 one-time fee/room. Designated rooms, service with restrictions, crate.
SAVE ⊠ ⓖM 🗗 🖵 ⓣ ⊐ ⊠

GREEN

△△△ **▽▽▽** Super 8 🅗

(330) 899-9888. **$66-$160.** 1605 Corporate Woods Pkwy 44685. I-77,
exit 118, just w. Ext/int corridors. **Pets:** Medium. $10 daily fee/pet. Desig-
nated rooms, service with restrictions, supervision.
SAVE ⊠ 🗗 🖵 ⊐

GREENVILLE

△△△ **▽▽▽** Greenville Inn 🅗

(937) 548-3613. **$65-$115.** 851 E Martin 45331. Jct US 36 and 127, 0.3
mi w on SR 571. Int corridors. **Pets:** $10 daily fee/pet. Service with
restrictions, supervision. SAVE ⊠ 🗗 🖵 ⓣ

HILLSBORO

▽▽ Days Inn Hillsboro 🅗

(937) 393-0299. **$69-$109.** 103 Harry Sauner Rd 45133. 1.9 mi ne on
US 62. Int corridors. **Pets:** Dogs only. $20 deposit/room, $10 daily fee/pet.
Service with restrictions, supervision. ASK ⊠ 🗗 🖵 ⊐

HOLLAND

△△△ **▽▽▽** Econo Lodge 🅜

(419) 866-6565. **$40-$80.** 1201 E Mall Dr 43528. I-475, exit 8, just w on
SR 2. Ext corridors. **Pets:** Small, dogs only. $10 daily fee/pet. Designated
rooms, no service, crate. SAVE ⊠ 🗗 🖵 ⊐

▽▽ Extended StayAmerica Toledo-Holland 🅗

(419) 861-1133. **$57-$99.** 6155 Trust Dr 43528. I-475, exit 8, just e to
Holland-Sylvania Rd, then just n. Int corridors. **Pets:** Other species. $25
daily fee/room. Designated rooms, service with restrictions, crate.
ASK ⊠ 🗗 🖵

△△△ **▽▽▽** Quality Inn Toledo Airport 🅜

(419) 867-1144. **$60-$80.** 1401 E Mall Dr 43528. I-475, exit 8, just w on
SR 2. Ext/int corridors. **Pets:** Accepted. SAVE ⊠ 🗗 🖵 ⊐

HUBER HEIGHTS

▽▽ Baymont Inn & Suites 🅗

(937) 237-1888. **$69-$74.** 8110 Old Troy Pike 45424. I-70, exit 36, just n.
Int corridors. **Pets:** Accepted. ASK ⊠ 🗗 🖵 ⊐

▽▽▽ Holiday Inn Express Hotel & Suites 🅗

(937) 235-2000. **Call for rates.** 5612 Merily Way 45424. I-70, exit 36,
just se on SR 202. Int corridors. **Pets:** Medium. $25 one-time fee/room.
Service with restrictions, supervision. ⊠ ⓖM 🗗 🖵 ⊐

HURON

▽▽ Motel 6, Huron 🅗

(419) 433-7829. **$39-$139.** 601 Rye Beach Rd 44839. SR 2, exit Rye
Beach, 2.5 mi w on US 6. Int corridors. **Pets:** Accepted.
⊠ ⓖM 🗗 🖵 ⊐

△△△ **▽▽▽▽** River's Edge Inn 🅗

(419) 433-8000. **Call for rates.** 132 N Main St 44839. 3 blks
n on Williams St to South St, just e. Int corridors. **Pets:** Accepted.
SAVE ⊠ ⊐

JACKSON

△△△ **▽▽▽** Comfort Inn-Jackson 🅜

(740) 286-7581. **$80-$90, 30 day notice.** 605 E Main St 45640. Jct SR
32, 0.5 mi n on SR 93. Int corridors. **Pets:** Accepted.
SAVE ⊠ 🗗 🖵

▽▽ Red Roof Inn 🅜

(740) 288-1200. **Call for rates.** 1000 Acy Ave 45640. US 35, exit
McCarty Ln, just nw. Int corridors. **Pets:** Large. Service with restrictions,
crate. ⊠ 🗗

KENT

▽▽ Days Inn-Akron Kent 🅜

(330) 677-9400. **$55-$69.** 4422 Edson Rd 44240. I-76, exit 33. Ext corridors. **Pets:** Accepted. ASK ⊠ 🗗 🖵 ⊐

▽▽ Super 8 🅗

(330) 678-8817. **Call for rates.** 4380 Edson Rd 44240. I-76, exit 33. Int
corridors. **Pets:** Accepted. ⊠ 🗗

KINSMAN

▽▽▽▽ Dream Horse Guesthouse 🅑🅑

(330) 876-0428. **$75-$140, 14 day notice.** 9532 SR 7 44428. 0.5 mi n
on SR 7. Int corridors. **Pets:** Other species. $15 daily fee/pet. Service
with restrictions, supervision. ASK ⊠ 🗗 🖵

LOGAN

▽▽ Baymont Inn and Suites 🅗

(740) 385-1700. **$69-$199, 7 day notice.** 12819 SR 664 43138. Jct US
33, just n. Int corridors. **Pets:** Small, dogs only. $10 daily fee/pet. Desig-
nated rooms, service with restrictions, supervision.
ASK ⊠ ⓖM 🗗 🖵 ⊐

▽▽ The Cabins at Cedar Grove 🅒🅐

(740) 380-2209. **$139-$699, 30 day notice.** 19555 SR 664 S 43138.
US 33, exit SR 664 (Logan), 9.4 mi s. Ext corridors. **Pets:** Accepted.
ASK ⊠ 🗗 🖵

△△△ **▽▽▽▽** Holiday Inn Express Hocking Hills 🅗

(740) 385-7700. **$89-$160.** 12916 Grey St 43138. SR 664, just w to
Lake Logan Rd, then just n. Int corridors. **Pets:** Small, dogs only. Desig-
nated rooms, service with restrictions, supervision.
SAVE ⊠ ⓖM 🗗 🖵 ⊐

▽▽▽ The Inn & Spa At Cedar Falls 🅒🅘 ❀

(740) 385-7489. **$125-$289.** 21190 SR 374 43138. 9.5 mi s on SR 664,
1 mi e. Int corridors. **Pets:** Medium, dogs only. $45 one-time fee/room.
Designated rooms, service with restrictions, supervision.
ASK ⊠ 🗗 🖵 ⓣ ⊠ 🆆 ⊠

LOUDONVILLE

▽▽ Little Brown Inn 🅜

(419) 994-5525. **$49-$79.** 940 S Market St 44842. 1.3 mi s on SR 3.
Ext/int corridors. **Pets:** Accepted. ASK ⊠ 🗗

MANSFIELD

△△△ **▽▽** Best Western Richland Inn Mansfield 🅗

(419) 756-6670. **$59-$179.** 180 E Hanley Rd 44903. I-71, exit 169, jct
SR 13. Int corridors. **Pets:** $15 daily fee/room. Service with restrictions,
crate. SAVE ⊠ 🗗 🖵 ⊐

▽▽ La Quinta Inn Mansfield 🅗 ❀

(419) 774-0005. **$65-$89.** 120 Stander Ave 44903. I-71, exit 169. Int
corridors. **Pets:** Medium, other species. Service with restrictions, supervision. ASK ⊠ ⓖM 🗗 🖵 ⊐

△△△ **▽▽▽** Super 8 🅗

(419) 756-8875. **$60-$119.** 2425 Interstate Cir 44903. I-71, exit 169. Int
corridors. **Pets:** Other species. $50 deposit/room. No service, supervision.
SAVE ⊠ 🗗 🖵

△△△ **▽▽▽** Travelodge 🅜

(419) 756-7600. **$50-$100.** 90 W Hanley Rd 44903. I-71, exit 169, just s.
Ext corridors. **Pets:** Medium. $10 daily fee/pet. Service with restrictions,
supervision. SAVE ⊠ 🗗 🖵

MARIETTA

AAA ▼▼▼ **Best Western Marietta** Ⓜ
(740) 374-7211. **$66-$88.** 279 Muskingum Dr 45750. I-77, exit 6, 3.5 mi sw on SR 821, then 1 mi s on SR 60. Ext corridors. **Pets:** Accepted.
[SAVE] [✕] [🛗] [💻] [✕]

AAA ▼▼ **Comfort Inn Marietta** Ⓗ
(740) 374-8190. **$70-$150.** 700 Pike St 45750. I-77, exit 1, just e. Int corridors. **Pets:** Accepted. [SAVE] [✕] [🛗] [💻] [🍴] [🏊]

▼▼◈ **The Lafayette Hotel** Ⓗ
(740) 373-5522. **$65-$195.** 101 Front St 45750. Center. Int corridors. **Pets:** $50 deposit/room. Service with restrictions, crate.
[ASK] [✕] [🛗] [💻]

AAA ▼▼▼ **Super 8-Marietta** Ⓜ
(740) 374-8888. **$57-$62.** 46 Acme St 45750. I-77, exit 1, just w. Int corridors. **Pets:** Other species. $10 daily fee/pet. No service, supervision.
[SAVE] [✕] [🛗] [💻]

MARION

▼▼ **Comfort Inn by Choice Hotels** Ⓗ
(740) 389-5552. **$63-$68.** 256 Jamesway 43302. Jct US 23 and SR 95, just w. Int corridors. **Pets:** Large, other species. $10 daily fee/pet. Service with restrictions, crate. [ASK] [✕] [🛗] [💻] [🏊]

▼▼◈ **Super 8-Marion** Ⓗ
(740) 389-1998. **Call for rates.** 2117 Marion-Mt. Gilead Rd 43302. Jct US 23 and SR 95, just e. Int corridors. **Pets:** Accepted.
[✕] [🛗] [💻] [🏊]

MAUMEE

▼▼ **Baymont Inn & Suites** Ⓗ
(419) 865-9400. **Call for rates.** 6425 Kit Ln 43537. I-475, exit 6, just w. Int corridors. **Pets:** Accepted. [✕] [🛗] [💻] [🏊]

▼▼ **Comfort Inn West Toledo/Maumee** Ⓗ
(419) 893-2800. **$69-$105.** 1426 S Reynolds Rd 43537. I-80/90, exit 59, just s. Int corridors. **Pets:** Small. $10 daily fee/pet. Service with restrictions, supervision. [ASK] [✕] [🛗] [💻] [🏊]

▼▼◈ **Homewood Suites by Hilton-Toledo** Ⓗ
(419) 897-0980. **$119-$189.** 1410 Arrowhead Rd 43537. I-475, exit 6, just e. Int corridors. **Pets:** Accepted. [✕] [🄼] [🛗] [💻] [🏊] [✕]

AAA ▼ **Red Roof Inn-Maumee #7046** Ⓜ
(419) 893-0292. **$50-$80.** 1570 S Reynolds Rd 43537. I-80/90, exit 59, just s. Ext/int corridors. **Pets:** Large. Service with restrictions, crate.
[SAVE] [✕] [🛗]

AAA ▼▼▼ **Residence Inn by Marriott Maumee** Ⓗ
(419) 891-2233. **$125-$153.** 1370 Arrowhead Dr 43537. I-475, exit 6, just e. Int corridors. **Pets:** Accepted. [SAVE] [✕] [🛗] [💻] [🏊] [✕]

▼▼ **StudioPLUS-Toledo-Maumee** Ⓗ
(419) 891-1211. **$62-$99.** 542 W Dussel Dr 43537. I-475, exit 8, just e. Int corridors. **Pets:** Other species. $25 daily fee/room. Designated rooms, service with restrictions, crate. [ASK] [✕] [🛗] [💻]

AAA ▼▼▼ **Super 8-Maumee/Toledo** Ⓗ
(419) 897-3800. **$60-$90.** 1390 Arrowhead Rd 43537. I-475, exit 6, just e. Int corridors. **Pets:** $10 one-time fee/pet. Service with restrictions, supervision. [SAVE] [✕] [🛗] [💻]

MENTOR

AAA ▼▼▼ **Best Western Lawnfield Inn & Suites** Ⓗ
(440) 205-7378. **$82-$139.** 8434 Mentor Ave 44060. I-90, exit 195, 1.5 mi n to SR 20 (Mentor Ave), then just e. Int corridors. **Pets:** Accepted.
[SAVE] [✕] [🄼] [🛗] [💻] [🏊]

▼▼▼ **Residence Inn by Marriott** Ⓗ
(440) 392-0800. **$89-$159.** 5660 Emerald Ct 44060. Jct SR 2 and Heisley Rd, just s. Int corridors. **Pets:** Accepted. [✕] [🛗] [💻] [🏊] [✕]

▼▼ **Studio 6 #6019** Ⓜ
(440) 946-0749. **$43-$53.** 7677 Reynolds Rd 44060. Just s of SR 2 on SR 306. Ext corridors. **Pets:** Other species. $10 daily fee/room. Service with restrictions, supervision. [✕] [🛗] [💻]

AAA ▼▼▼ **Super 8** Ⓗ
(440) 951-8558. **$49-$110.** 7325 Palisades Pkwy 44060. On SR 306, just s of SR 2. Int corridors. **Pets:** $15 daily fee/pet. Service with restrictions, supervision. [SAVE] [✕] [🛗]

MIAMISBURG

AAA ▼▼◈ **Hawthorn Suites Dayton South** Ⓗ
(937) 434-7881. **Call for rates.** 155 Prestige Pl 45342. I-75, exit 44, just e on SR 725, just se on Prestige Plaza Dr, then just s. Ext corridors. **Pets:** Accepted. [SAVE] [✕] [🛗] [💻] [🏊] [✕]

▼▼▼ **Holiday Inn-Dayton Mall** Ⓗ
(937) 434-8030. **$85-$119.** 31 Prestige Dr 45342. I-75, exit 44, just e on SR 725, then just s. Int corridors. **Pets:** $30 one-time fee/room. Service with restrictions, supervision.
[ASK] [✕] [🄼] [🛗] [💻] [🍴] [🏊] [✕]

AAA ▼▼◈ **Homewood Suites by Hilton-Dayton South** Ⓗ 🐾
(937) 432-0000. **$89-$139.** 3100 Contemporary Ln 45342. I-75, exit 44, just e on SR 725, just se on Prestige Plaza Dr, then just s. Int corridors. **Pets:** Other species. $200 deposit/pet, $10 daily fee/room, $25 one-time fee/room. Designated rooms, service with restrictions, crate.
[SAVE] [✕] [🄼] [🛗] [💻] [🏊]

▼▼▼ **Quality Inn & Suites Dayton South** Ⓗ
(937) 865-0077. **Call for rates.** 250 Byers Rd 45342. I-75, exit 44, just w on SR 725. Int corridors. **Pets:** Other species. $10 daily fee/pet. Designated rooms, service with restrictions, crate. [✕] [🛗] [💻] [🏊]

AAA ▼▼▼ **Red Roof Inn-South #7006** Ⓜ
(937) 866-0705. **$50-$70, 7 day notice.** 222 Byers Rd 45342. I-75, exit 44, just w on SR 725. Ext corridors. **Pets:** Large. Service with restrictions, crate. [SAVE] [✕] [🛗]

▼▼ **Super 8 Miamisburg/South Dayton** Ⓗ
(937) 866-5500. **Call for rates.** 155 Monarch Ln 45342. I-75, exit 44, 0.5 mi w on SR 725. Int corridors. **Pets:** Accepted. [✕] [🛗] [💻]

MILAN

▼▼ **Motel 6-4016** Ⓗ
(419) 499-8001. **$39-$139, 3 day notice.** 11406 US 250 Milan Rd 44846. I-80/90, exit 118, 1.5 mi n. Int corridors. **Pets:** Other species. Service with restrictions, supervision. [ASK] [✕] [🏊]

▼▼ **Red Roof Inn** Ⓗ
(419) 499-4347. **$49-$159.** 11303 US 250 Milan Rd 44846. I-80/90, exit 118, 0.5 mi n. Int corridors. **Pets:** Large. Service with restrictions, crate.
[ASK] [✕] [🏊] [✕]

AAA ▼▼▼ **Super 8** Ⓗ
(419) 499-4671. **$44-$149.** 11313 US 250 Milan Rd 44846. I-80/90, exit 118, 0.5 mi n. Int corridors. **Pets:** Small, dogs only. $50 deposit/pet. Designated rooms, service with restrictions, supervision.
[SAVE] [✕] [🛗] [🍴] [🏊]

MILLERSBURG

▼▼▼ **Comfort Inn Millersburg** Ⓗ
(330) 674-7400. **Call for rates.** 1102 Glen Dr 44654. SR 39, 0.5 mi s on S Clay. Int corridors. **Pets:** Dogs only. $15 daily fee/pet. Designated rooms, service with restrictions, supervision. [✕] [🛗] [💻] [🏊] [✕]

▼▼ ▼▼ Hotel Millersburg ⊞
(330) 674-1457. **$70-$185, 3 day notice.** 35 W Jackson St 44654. Just w of jct SR 83; downtown. Int corridors. **Pets:** Small. $10 daily fee/room. Designated rooms, supervision. A$K ☒ 🖶 💻 🍽

MONTPELIER
▼▼▼▼ Holiday Inn Express Hotel & Suites Bryan/
　　　Montpelier ⊞
(419) 485-0008. **$96-$129.** 13399 SR 15 43543. I-80/90, exit 13, just s. Int corridors. **Pets:** Other species. $10 daily fee/pet. Service with restrictions, crate. A$K ☒ 🖶 💻 ⊷

▼▼ ▼▼ Ramada ⊞
(419) 485-5555. **$89-$129.** 13508 SR 15 43543. I-80/90, exit 13, just s. Int corridors. **Pets:** Large, other species. Service with restrictions, supervision. ☒ 🖶 💻 🍽 ⊷ ☒

MOUNT VERNON
▼▼ Comfort Inn ⊞
(740) 392-6886. **$70-$185, 14 day notice.** 150 Howard St 43050. Jct SR 13; south of downtown. Int corridors. **Pets:** Other species. $10 daily fee/pet. Service with restrictions, supervision. A$K ☒ 🖶 💻 ⊷

▼▼ ▼▼ Holiday Inn Express ⊞
(740) 392-1900. **$109-$139.** 11555 Upper Gilchrist Rd 43050. 2.6 mi e on US 36, then just s. Int corridors. **Pets:** Other species. Designated rooms, service with restrictions, supervision. A$K ☒ 🖶 💻 ⊷

▼▼ ▼▼ Super 8-Mt Vernon ⊞
(740) 397-8885. **$70-$150.** 1000 Coshocton Ave 43050. 1.8 mi e on US 36. Int corridors. **Pets:** Other species. $10 daily fee/pet. Service with restrictions. A$K ☒ 🔥M 🖶 💻 ⊷

NAPOLEON
◈◈◈ ▼▼▼▼ Best Western Napoleon Inn &
　　　　Suites ⊞ ☙
(419) 599-0850. **$75-$120.** 1290 Independence Dr 43545. US 6 and 24, just se. Int corridors. **Pets:** Other species. $15 daily fee/pet. Crate. SAVE ☒ 🖶 💻 ⊷ ☒

NEWCOMERSTOWN
▼▼▼▼ Hampton Inn ⊞ ☙
(740) 498-9800. **$79-$169.** 200 Morris Crossing 43832. I-77, exit 65, 0.8 mi w. Int corridors. **Pets:** Small, dogs only. Service with restrictions, supervision. ☒ 🔥M 🖶 💻 ⊷

NEWTON FALLS
◈◈◈ ▼▼▼▼ Econo Lodge 🅼
(330) 872-0988. **Call for rates.** 4248 SR 5 44444. I-80, exit 209, just w. Ext corridors. **Pets:** Other species. $15 daily fee/pet. Service with restrictions. SAVE ☒ 🖶 💻

NORTH LIMA
▼▼ ▼▼ Quality Inn & Suites 🅼 ☙
(330) 549-9190. **Call for rates.** 10076 Market St 44452. I-76, exit 232, 0.5 mi n. Ext corridors. **Pets:** Medium, other species. $10 daily fee/pet. Service with restrictions, crate. ☒ 🖶 💻

NORWALK
◈◈◈ ▼▼▼ All American Inn & Suites ⊞
(419) 663-1922. **$59-$249.** 415 Milan Ave 44857. 4 mi n on US 250; 5 mi s of I-80/90 (Ohio Tpke). Int corridors. **Pets:** Accepted. SAVE ☒ 🖶 💻 ⊷

◈◈◈ ▼▼▼ Best Western ⊞
(419) 663-3501. **$70-$270.** 351 Milan Ave 44857. 3.5 mi n on US 250; 5.5 mi s of I-80/90 (Ohio Tpke). Int corridors. **Pets:** Accepted. SAVE ☒ 🖶 💻 ⊷ ☒

◈◈◈ ▼▼▼ Econo Lodge 🅼
(419) 668-5656. **$44-$139.** 342 Milan Ave 44857. 3 mi n on US 250; 6 mi s of I-80/90 (Ohio Tpke). Ext corridors. **Pets:** Small, dogs only. $50 deposit/pet. Designated rooms, service with restrictions, supervision. SAVE ☒ 🖶 💻 ⊷

OBERLIN
▼▼▼ Oberlin Inn ⊞
(440) 775-1111. **$109-$189.** 7 N Main St 44074. On SR 58; jct College and Main sts; center. Int corridors. **Pets:** Accepted. A$K ☒ 🖶 💻 🍽

OREGON
▼▼ ▼▼ Comfort Inn East ⊞
(419) 691-8911. **$69-$87.** 2930 Navarre Ave 43616. I-280, exit 7, just n on access road, then 0.5 mi e on SR 2 (Navarre Ave). Int corridors. **Pets:** Accepted. A$K ☒ 🖶 💻 ⊷

▼▼ ▼▼ Sleep Inn & Suites ⊞
(419) 697-7800. **$72-$116.** 1761 Meijer Cir 43616. I-280, exit 6, just w. Int corridors. **Pets:** Accepted. A$K ☒ 🖶 💻 ⊷

PAINESVILLE
▼▼▼▼ Quail Hollow Resort ⊞
(440) 497-1100. **Call for rates.** 11080 Concord-Hambden Rd 44077-9557. I-90, exit 200, 0.3 mi s on SR 44, then just e on Auburn Rd. Int corridors. **Pets:** Medium. $200 deposit/pet, $50 one-time fee/pet. Service with restrictions, supervision. ☒ 🔥M 🖶 💻 🍽 ⊷ ☒

PERRYSBURG
▼▼ ▼▼ La Quinta Inn & Suites Toledo-Perrysburg ⊞ ☙
(419) 872-0000. **$59-$89.** 1154 Professional Dr 43551. I-75, exit 193, just w. Int corridors. **Pets:** Medium, other species. Service with restrictions, supervision. A$K ☒ 🖶 💻

◈◈◈ ▼▼▼ Super 8-Toledo/Perrysburg/Millbury 🅼
(419) 837-6409. **$39-$89.** 3491 Latcha Rd 43551. I-80/90, exit 71 to I-280, exit 1B, just n. Ext corridors. **Pets:** Accepted. SAVE ☒ 🖶

PIQUA
▼▼▼▼ Comfort Inn, Piqua, at Miami Valley Centre
　　　Mall ⊞
(937) 778-8100. **$64-$85.** 987 E Ash St 45356. I-75, exit 82, just w. Int corridors. **Pets:** Accepted. A$K ☒ 🖶 💻 ⊷ ☒

▼▼ ▼▼ La Quinta Inn Piqua ⊞ ☙
(937) 615-0140. **$55-$130.** 950 E Ash St 45356. I-75, exit 82, just w. Int corridors. **Pets:** Medium, other species. Service with restrictions, supervision. A$K ☒ 🖶 💻 ⊷

POLAND
▼▼ ▼▼ Red Roof Inn #7253 ⊞
(330) 758-1999. **$48-$99.** 1051 Tiffany S 44514. I-680, exit 11, just w. Int corridors. **Pets:** Large. Service with restrictions, crate. A$K ☒ 🖶 💻

▼▼▼▼ Residence Inn by Marriott-Youngstown ⊞
(330) 726-1747. **$135-$165.** 7396 Tiffany S 44514. I-680, exit 11, just w. Int corridors. **Pets:** Accepted. ☒ 🖶 💻 ⊷ ☒

PORT CLINTON
◈◈◈ ▼▼▼ Best Western Port Clinton ⊞
(419) 734-2274. **$49-$149.** 1734 E Perry St 43452. 1.7 mi e on SR 163, w of jct SR 2. Int corridors. **Pets:** Small, dogs only. $50 deposit/pet. Designated rooms, service with restrictions, supervision. SAVE ☒ 💻 ⊷

▼▼ ▼▼ Commodore Perry Inn & Suites ⊞
(419) 732-2645. **$60-$200, 3 day notice.** 255 W Lakeshore Dr 43452. Just n of bridge. Int corridors. **Pets:** Medium. $15 one-time fee/room. Service with restrictions, crate. ☒ 🖶 💻 🍽 ⊷

▼▼▼ Sleep Inn & Suites ⊞
(419) 732-7707. **$59-$239, 3 day notice.** 947 SR 53 N 43452. SR 2, exit SR 53, just n. Int corridors. **Pets:** Accepted.
[ASK] [✕] [⚙M] [🛏] [💻] [≈]

▼▼▼ Super 8 ⊞
(419) 734-4446. **$49-$149.** 1704 E Perry St 43452. 1.7 mi e on SR 163, w of jct SR 2. Int corridors. **Pets:** Small, dogs only. $50 deposit/pet. Designated rooms, service with restrictions, supervision. [ASK] [✕] [💻]

PORTSMOUTH
▼▼ Holiday Inn Express Ⓜ
(740) 353-3232. **Call for rates.** 5100 Old Scioto Tr 45662. 3.8 mi n of downtown. Int corridors. **Pets:** Accepted. [✕] [⚙M] [🛏] [💻] [≈]

ROSSFORD
△△△ ▼▼▼▼ Country Inn & Suites By Carlson, Toledo South ⊞
(419) 872-9900. **$89-$169.** 9790 Clark Dr 43460. I-75, exit 195, just e. Int corridors. **Pets:** Accepted. [SAVE] [✕] [⚙M] [🛏] [💻] [≈]

ST. CLAIRSVILLE
△△△ ▼ Americas Best Value Inn St. Clairsville/Wheeling Ⓜ
(740) 695-5038. **$59-$129.** 51260 National Rd 43950. I-70, exit 218, 0.5 mi ne on US 40. Ext corridors. **Pets:** Medium, other species. $10 one-time fee/room. Service with restrictions, supervision.
[SAVE] [✕] [🛏] [💻] [≈]

△△△ ▼ Red Roof Inn #7101 Ⓜ
(740) 695-4057. **$55-$85.** 68301 Red Roof Ln 43950. I-70, exit 218, just n. Ext corridors. **Pets:** Large. Service with restrictions, crate.
[SAVE] [✕] [🛏]

ST. MARYS
△△△ ▼▼ Americas Best Value Inn St Marys ⊞
(419) 394-2341. **$58-$128.** 1321 Celina Rd 45885. SR 66/29, 0.8 mi w on SR 703. Ext corridors. **Pets:** Accepted.
[SAVE] [✕] [🛏] [💻] [≈] [✕]

SALESVILLE
△△△ ▼▼▼▼ Pine Lakes Lodge Bed & Breakfast Cabins and Conference Center ⊞⊞
(740) 679-3617. **$150-$350.** 61680 Buskirk Ln 43778. I-70, exit 193, 6.6 mi s on SR 513, then 6 mi w on SR 265. Int corridors. **Pets:** Other species. Designated rooms, no service. [SAVE] [✕] [🛏] [💻] [✕] [🅟] [✍]

SANDUSKY
△△△ ▼▼ Best Budget Inn Ⓜ
(419) 626-3610. **$39-$129.** 2027 Cleveland Rd 44870. US 6, just e of Cedar Point Cswy. Ext/int corridors. **Pets:** Medium, dogs only. $50 deposit/pet. Designated rooms, service with restrictions, supervision.
[SAVE] [✕] [≈]

▼▼ Knights Inn Sandusky Ⓜ
(419) 621-9000. **$48-$139.** 2405 Cleveland Rd 44870. US 6, 2 mi e of Cedar Point Cswy. Int corridors. **Pets:** Small, dogs only. $25 deposit/room, $10 daily fee/pet. Designated rooms, service with restrictions, supervision. [ASK] [✕] [🛏] [💻] [≈]

▼▼▼ La Quinta Inn Ⓜ ❀
(419) 626-6766. **$59-$119.** 3304 Milan Rd 44870. US 250, 2 mi n of SR 2. Int corridors. **Pets:** Medium, other species. Service with restrictions, supervision. [ASK] [✕] [🛏] [💻] [≈]

△△△ ▼▼▼ Super 8 North Ⓜ
(419) 625-7070. **$49-$169, 3 day notice.** 5410 Milan Rd 44870. US 250, 0.3 mi n of SR 2. Ext corridors. **Pets:** Very small. $100 deposit/room. Service with restrictions, supervision. [SAVE] [✕] [🛏] [≈]

SEAMAN
▼▼ Comfort Inn Ⓜ
(937) 386-2511. **$60-$105.** 55 Stern Dr 45679. Jct SR 32 and 247. Int corridors. **Pets:** Accepted. [ASK] [✕] [🛏] [💻] [≈]

SEVILLE
△△△ ▼▼▼ Hawthorn Suites Ltd ⊞
(330) 769-5025. **$79-$129, 4 day notice.** 5025 Park Ave W 44273. I-76/US 224, exit 2, just n. Int corridors. **Pets:** Medium. $75 one-time fee/room. Designated rooms, service with restrictions, crate.
[SAVE] [✕] [🛏] [💻] [≈]

▼▼ Super 8-Seville ⊞
(330) 769-8880. **$59-$85.** 6116 Speedway Dr 44273. Jct US 224 and Lake Rd, just s. Int corridors. **Pets:** Accepted. [ASK] [✕] [⚙M] [🛏] [💻]

SIDNEY
▼▼ Comfort Inn ⊞
(937) 492-3001. **$85-$145.** 1959 W Michigan Ave 45365. I-75, exit 92, just sw of SR 47. Int corridors. **Pets:** Accepted.
[ASK] [✕] [🛏] [💻] [≈]

▼▼ Quality Inn Sidney ⊞
(937) 492-1131. **$49-$79.** 400 Folkerth Ave 45365. I-75, exit 92, just w. Int corridors. **Pets:** Other species. $50 deposit/room. Service with restrictions. [ASK] [✕] [🛏] [💻] [≈]

SPRINGFIELD
▼▼ Holiday Inn South Springfield Ohio ⊞
(937) 323-8631. **$78-$99.** 383 E Leffel Ln 45505. I-70, exit 54, just n, then e. Int corridors. **Pets:** Accepted.
[ASK] [✕] [🛏] [💻] [🍴] [≈] [✕]

▼▼ Ramada Limited ⊞
(937) 328-0123. **Call for rates.** 319 E Leffel Ln 45505. I-70, exit 54, just n, then e. Int corridors. **Pets:** Accepted. [✕] [🛏] [💻] [≈]

△△△ ▼▼▼ Red Roof Inn ⊞
(937) 325-5356. **Call for rates.** 155 W Leffel Ln 45506. I-70, exit 54, just n, then w. Int corridors. **Pets:** Large. Service with restrictions, crate.
[SAVE] [✕] [🛏] [💻] [≈]

STEUBENVILLE
△△△ ▼▼ University Inn Steubenville ⊞
(740) 282-0901. **$89-$99.** 1401 University Blvd 43952. Jct US 22 and SR 7, 1 mi sw. Ext/int corridors. **Pets:** Accepted.
[SAVE] [✕] [🛏] [💻] [🍴] [≈]

STRASBURG
△△△ ▼▼▼▼ Ramada Limited Dover/Strasburg ⊞
(330) 878-1400. **$70-$140.** 509 S Wooster Ave 44680. I-77, exit 87, 0.4 mi n on US 250 and SR 21. Int corridors. **Pets:** Dogs only. $15 daily fee/room. Service with restrictions, supervision.
[SAVE] [✕] [⚙M] [🛏] [≈]

STREETSBORO
△△△ ▼▼ Microtel Inn & Suites of Streetsboro ⊞
(330) 422-1234. **$54-$109.** 9371 SR 14 44241. I-80, exit 187, 1.2 mi s. Int corridors. **Pets:** Medium, other species. $15 daily fee/room. Designated rooms, service with restrictions, supervision.
[SAVE] [✕] [🛏] [💻] [≈]

▼▼ TownePlace Suites by Marriott ⊞ ❀
(330) 422-1855. **$134-$164.** 795 Mondial Pkwy 44241. I-80, exit 187, 0.8 mi s. Int corridors. **Pets:** Other species. $75 one-time fee/room. Service with restrictions, supervision. [✕] [🛏] [💻] [≈]

SWANTON
△△△ ▼▼ Days Inn ⊞
(419) 865-2002. **$49-$73.** 10753 Airport Hwy 43558. I-80/90, exit 52, just s, then e. Int corridors. **Pets:** Accepted. [SAVE] [✕] [🛏] [💻]

TIFFIN

▼▼▼ Holiday Inn Express H
(419) 443-5100. $69-$99. 78 Shaffer Park Dr 44883. Just w of Tiffin Mall. Int corridors. Pets: Medium, other species. $25 daily fee/room. Service with restrictions, supervision. (ASK) ✕ 🖪 💻 ➰

TIPP CITY

△△△ ▼▼▼ La Quinta Inn & Suites H ❀
(937) 667-1574. $69-$89. 19 Weller Dr 45371. I-75, exit 68, just w. Int corridors. Pets: Medium, other species. Service with restrictions, supervision. (SAVE) ✕ 🖪ᴹ 🖪 💻 ➰

TOLEDO

▼▼▼ Hilton Toledo and Dana Conference Center H
(419) 381-6800. $99-$189. 3100 Glendale Ave 43614. I-475, exit 8 (SR 2/Airport Hwy), 3.3 mi e on SR 2, 0.8 mi s on Byrne Rd, then 0.5 mi e. Int corridors. Pets: Large, other species. $75 one-time fee/room. Designated rooms, service with restrictions, supervision.

✕ 🖪 💻 ▢ ➰ ✕

△△△ ▼▼▼ Park Inn Hotel H
(419) 241-3000. $99-$139. 101 N Summit St 43604. Between Jefferson and Monroe sts; downtown. Int corridors. Pets: Other species. Designated rooms, service with restrictions, crate. (SAVE) ✕ 🖪 💻 ▢

△△△ ▼▼▼ Quality Inn & Suites H ❀
(419) 476-0170. $65-$110. 445 E Alexis Rd 43612. I-75, exit 210, 2 mi w on SR 184; just e of jct US 24 and SR 184. Int corridors. Pets: $15 daily fee/pet. Designated rooms, no service. (SAVE) ✕ 🖪 💻

▼ Red Roof Inn Toledo University #7196 M
(419) 536-0118. $44-$82, 3 day notice. 3530 Executive Pkwy 43606. I-475, exit 17, 0.5 mi s on Secor Rd, then just e. Ext corridors. Pets: Large. Service with restrictions, crate. (ASK) ✕ 🖪

TROY

▼▼▼▼ Holiday Inn Express Hotel & Suites H
(937) 332-1700. Call for rates. 60 Troy Town Dr 45373. I-75, exit 74, just w. Int corridors. Pets: Accepted. ✕ 🖪 💻 ➰

▼▼▼ Residence Inn By Marriott H
(937) 440-9303. $125-$153. 87 Troy Town Dr 45373. I-75, exit 74, just w. Int corridors. Pets: Accepted. ✕ 🖪 💻 ➰ ✕

UHRICHSVILLE

△△△ ▼▼▼ Best Western Country Inn M
(740) 922-0774. $65-$85. 111 W McCauley Dr 44683. US 250, exit McCauley Dr. Ext corridors. Pets: Large. $10 daily fee/pet. Service with restrictions, crate. (SAVE) ✕ 🖪 💻

UPPER SANDUSKY

▼▼▼ Upper Sandusky Inn H
(419) 294-3919. $49-$99. 1726 E Wyandot Ave 43351. Jct US 23 and 30, just e. Int corridors. Pets: Medium. $10 one-time fee/room. Service with restrictions, supervision. (ASK) ✕ 🖪 💻 ➰

VERMILION

▼▼▼ Holiday Inn Express H
(440) 967-8770. $89-$169. 2417 SR 60 44089. Jct SR 2 and 60. Int corridors. Pets: Medium. $15 one-time fee/pet. Service with restrictions, supervision. (ASK) ✕ 🖪 💻 ➰

WAPAKONETA

▼▼▼ Holiday Inn Express H
(419) 738-2050. $85-$140. 1008 Lunar Dr 45895. I-75, exit 111, just w. Int corridors. Pets: Accepted. (ASK) ✕ 🖪ᴹ 🖪 💻 ➰

WARREN

▼▼ Comfort Inn H
(330) 393-1200. $69-$109. 136 N Park Ave 44481. Downtown; east side of Courthouse Square. Int corridors. Pets: Accepted. (ASK) ✕ 🖪 💻

WAUSEON

△△△ ▼▼▼ Best Western Del Mar H
(419) 335-1565. $60-$126. 8319 SR 108 43567. I-80/90, exit 34, just s. Ext corridors. Pets: $17 one-time fee/room. (SAVE) ✕ 🖪 💻 ➰

WHEELERSBURG

△△△ ▼▼▼ Days Inn Wheelersburg M
(740) 574-8431. $59-$99. 8340 Ohio River Rd 45694. US 52, exit Wheelersburg. Ext corridors. Pets: Accepted. (SAVE) ✕ 🖪 💻 ➰

WOOSTER

△△△ ▼▼▼ Econo Lodge M
(330) 264-8883. $45-$99. 2137 E Lincoln Way 44691. US 30, 3 mi e. Ext corridors. Pets: Accepted. (SAVE) ✕ 🖪 ➰

YOUNGSTOWN

△△△ ▼▼▼ Days Inn & Suites M ❀
(330) 759-9820. $50-$130, 3 day notice. 1615 E Liberty St 44420. I-80, exit 229, just s. Int corridors. Pets: Medium. $25 daily fee/pet. Designated rooms, no service, supervision. (SAVE) ✕ 🖪 💻 ➰

ZANESVILLE

△△△ ▼▼▼ Baymont Inn & Suites Zanesville M
(740) 454-9332. $79-$129. 230 Scenic Crest Dr 43701. I-70, exit 155, just s. Int corridors. Pets: Accepted. (SAVE) ✕ 🖪 💻 ➰

△△△ ▼▼▼ Best Western–B.R. Guest H ❀
(740) 453-6300. $74-$134. 4929 E Pike 43701. I-70, exit 160, just s. Int corridors. Pets: Other species. $10 one-time fee/pet. Service with restrictions, supervision. (SAVE) ✕ 🖪ᴹ 🖪 💻 ➰

△△△ ▼▼▼ Comfort Inn H
(740) 454-4144. $69-$199. 500 Monroe St 43701. I-70, exit 155 westbound; exit 7th St eastbound, e on Elberon to light, just n on Underwood. Int corridors. Pets: Large, other species. $10 one-time fee/pet. Designated rooms, service with restrictions, supervision.
(SAVE) ✕ 🖪ᴹ 🖪 ➰

△△△ ▼▼▼ Super 8-Zanesville M
(740) 455-3124. $39-$99. 2440 National Rd 43701. I-70, exit 152, just n. Int corridors. Pets: Accepted. (SAVE) ✕ 🖪 💻

OKLAHOMA

ALTUS

Best Western Altus 🅷 ❀

(580) 482-9300. **$49-$99.** 2804 N Main St 73521. 2 mi n on US 283. Ext corridors. **Pets:** Other species. Service with restrictions, supervision.

Hampton Inn & Suites Altus 🅷 ❀

(580) 482-1273. **$99-$159.** 3601 N Main St 73521. 2.2 mi n on US 283. Int corridors. **Pets:** Service with restrictions, supervision.

ARDMORE

Best Western Inn 🅷

(580) 223-7525. **$70-$86.** 136 Holiday Dr 73401. I-35, exit 32, 0.5 mi se. Int corridors. **Pets:** Small. $10 daily fee/pet. Designated rooms, service with restrictions, supervision.

Holiday Inn 🅷

(580) 223-7130. **$99-$125.** 2705 W Broadway 73401. I-35, exit 31A, just e. Ext corridors. **Pets:** Small. $20 one-time fee/room. Designated rooms, service with restrictions, crate.

La Quinta Inn Ardmore 🅷 ❀

(580) 223-7976. **Call for rates.** 2432 Veterans Blvd 73401. I-35, exit 33, just e. Ext corridors. **Pets:** Medium, other species. Service with restrictions, supervision.

BARTLESVILLE

Microtel Inn & Suites of Bartlesville 🅷

(918) 333-2100. **$69-$99.** 2696 SE Washington Blvd 74006. 1.4 mi s of jct US 60 E. Int corridors. **Pets:** Accepted.

BIG CABIN

Super 8-Big Cabin 🅜

(918) 783-5888. **$60-$68.** 30954 S Hwy 69 74301. I-44, exit 283, just ne. Ext/int corridors. **Pets:** Accepted.

BLACKWELL

Best Western Blackwell Inn 🅷

(580) 363-1300. **$85-$93.** 4545 W White Ave 74631. I-35, exit 222, just ne. Int corridors. **Pets:** Small. $10 daily fee/pet. Designated rooms, service with restrictions, crate.

Comfort Inn 🅷

(580) 363-7000. **$75-$100.** 1201 N 44th St 74631. I-35, exit 222, just ne. Int corridors. **Pets:** Small, dogs only. $10 daily fee/pet. Designated rooms, service with restrictions, supervision.

CHICKASHA

Best Western Inn 🅷

(405) 224-4890. **$64-$85.** 2101 S 4th St 73018. I-44, exit 80, just nw. Ext/int corridors. **Pets:** Accepted.

DURANT

Comfort Inn & Suites 🅷

(580) 924-8881. **Call for rates.** 2112 W Main St 74701. Just e of jct US 75/69 and 70. Int corridors. **Pets:** Accepted.

ENID

Baymont Inn & Suites-Enid 🅷

(580) 234-6800. **Call for rates.** 3614 W Owen K Garriott Rd 73703. 2 mi w of jct US 81. Int corridors. **Pets:** Accepted.

GROVE

Best Western Timber Ridge Inn 🅷

(918) 786-6900. **$87.** 120 W 18th St 74344. Just w of jct US 59. Ext/int corridors. **Pets:** Medium, other species. $10 daily fee/pet. Designated rooms, service with restrictions, supervision.

GUYMON

Best Western Guymon Hotel & Suites 🅷

(580) 338-0800. **$64-$130.** 1102 NE 6th St (Hwy 54) 73942. Just s of jct US 64. Ext/int corridors. **Pets:** Other species. $10 one-time fee/pet. Designated rooms, service with restrictions, supervision.

Comfort Inn & Suites 🅷

(580) 338-0831. **$80-$90.** 501 5th St (Hwy 54 E) 73942. Just s of jct US 64. Int corridors. **Pets:** Medium. $15 daily fee/pet. Service with restrictions, crate.

Guymon Super 8 🅷

(580) 338-0507. **$70-$100.** 1201 Hwy 54 E 73942. Jct US 54 and 64. Int corridors. **Pets:** Medium, other species. $7 daily fee/pet. Service with restrictions, supervision.

HENRYETTA

Green Country Inn 🅜

(918) 652-9988. **$45-$58.** 2004 Old Hwy 75 W 74437. I-40, exit 237, just ne. Ext corridors. **Pets:** Small. $5 daily fee/pet. Designated rooms, service with restrictions, supervision.

IDABEL

Comfort Suites 🅷

(580) 286-9393. **$80-$100.** 400 SE Lincoln Rd 74745. Just s of jct US 70 and 259. Int corridors. **Pets:** Accepted.

LAWTON

Baymont Inn & Suites 🅷

(580) 353-5581. **Call for rates.** 1203 NW 40th St 73505. I-44, exit 39A, 3.7 mi w. Int corridors. **Pets:** Other species. $25 deposit/room. Service with restrictions, crate.

LOCUST GROVE

Best Western Locust Grove Inn & Suites 🅷

(918) 479-8082. **$72-$200.** 106 Holiday Ln 74352. Just nw of jct US 412 and SR 82. Int corridors. **Pets:** Small. $25 one-time fee/pet. Service with restrictions, crate.

MCALESTER

Best Western Inn of McAlester 🅷

(918) 426-0115. **$89-$129.** 1215 George Nigh Expwy 74502. 3 mi s on US 69. Ext corridors. **Pets:** Accepted.

▼▼▼▼ Comfort Suites 🄷

(918) 302-0001. **$108-$130.** 650 George Nigh Expwy 74501. 1.2 mi s on US 69. Int corridors. **Pets:** Accepted. [ASK] ✕ 📠 💻 ➹

MIAMI

🄰🄰🄰 ▼▼▼ Microtel Inn & Suites 🄷

(918) 540-3333. **$61-$105.** 2015 E Steve Owens Blvd 74355. I-44, exit 313, just w. Int corridors. **Pets:** Other species. $25 one-time fee/room. Service with restrictions, supervision. [SAVE] ✕ 📠 💻 ➹

MUSKOGEE

🄰🄰🄰 ▼▼▼▼ La Quinta Inn & Suites Muskogee 🄷 ❀

(918) 687-9000. **$69-$179.** 3031 Military Blvd 74401. Just se of jct US 62 and 69. Int corridors. **Pets:** Medium, other species. Service with restrictions, supervision. [SAVE] ✕ 📠 📶 💻 🍴 ➹

OKLAHOMA CITY METROPOLITAN AREA

DEL CITY

▼▼ La Quinta Inn Oklahoma City East (Del City) 🄷 ❀

(405) 672-0067. **$45-$95.** 5501 Tinker Diagonal Rd 73115-4613. I-40, exit 156A (Sooner Rd), just nw. Ext/int corridors. **Pets:** Medium, other species. Service with restrictions, supervision. [ASK] ✕ 📠 💻 ➹

EDMOND

🄰🄰🄰 ▼▼▼ Best Western Edmond Inn & Suites 🄷

(405) 216-0300. **$86-$91.** 2700 E 2nd St 73034. I-35, exit 141, 1.1 mi w. Int corridors. **Pets:** Accepted. [SAVE] ✕ 📠 💻 ➹

EL RENO

🄰🄰🄰 ▼▼▼ Best Western Hensley's 🄷

(405) 262-6490. **$80-$100.** 2701 S Country Club Rd 73036. I-40, exit 123, just s. Ext corridors. **Pets:** Medium. $25 deposit/pet, $5 daily fee/pet. Service with restrictions, supervision. [SAVE] ✕ 📠 💻 ➹

🄰🄰🄰 ▼ Motel 6 🄷

(405) 262-6060. **Call for rates.** 1506 Domino Dr 73036. I-40, exit 123, just ne. Int corridors. **Pets:** Other species. Service with restrictions, supervision. [SAVE] ✕ 📠 ➹

GUTHRIE

🄰🄰🄰 ▼▼▼ Best Western Territorial Inn 🄷

(405) 282-8831. **$84-$99.** 2323 Territorial Tr 73044. I-35, exit 157, just sw. Int corridors. **Pets:** Small, other species. Service with restrictions, supervision. [SAVE] ✕ 📠 ➹

MIDWEST CITY

▼▼▼▼ Hawthorn Suites 🄷

(405) 737-7777. **$105-$125, 3 day notice.** 5701 Tinker Diagonal Rd 73110. I-40, exit 156A (Sooner Rd), just n. Int corridors. **Pets:** Small. $10 daily fee/pet. Designated rooms, service with restrictions, crate. [ASK] ✕ 📶 📠 💻 ➹

🄰🄰🄰 ▼▼▼ Sheraton Midwest City Hotel at the Reed Conference Center 🄷 ❀

(405) 741-7333. **Call for rates.** 5750 Will Rogers Rd 73110. I-40, exit 156A (Sooner Rd), just ne. Int corridors. **Pets:** Medium, other species. Service with restrictions, supervision. [SAVE] ✕ 📠 💻 🍴 ➹ ✕

MOORE

🄰🄰🄰 ▼▼▼ Best Western Green Tree Inn & Suites 🄷

(405) 912-8882. **$85-$99.** 1811 N Moore Ave 73160. I-35, exit 118, just n on westbound frontage road. Int corridors. **Pets:** Small. $10 daily fee/pet. Service with restrictions, supervision. [SAVE] ✕ 📠 💻 ➹

NORMAN

🄰🄰🄰 ▼▼▼ Econo Lodge 🄜

(405) 364-5554. **$65-$90.** 100 SW 26th Dr 73069. I-35, exit 109 (Main St), just se. Ext corridors. **Pets:** $5 daily fee/pet. Service with restrictions, supervision. [SAVE] ✕ 💻

🄰🄰🄰 ▼▼▼ Embassy Suites Norman–Hotel & Conference Center

(405) 364-8040. **$109-$299.** 2501 Conference Dr 73069. 0.7 mi n of jct 24th Ave NW and Robinson. Int corridors. **Pets:** Medium. $25 daily fee/ room. Service with restrictions, crate. [SAVE] ✕ 📶 📠 💻 🍴 ➹

▼▼▼▼ La Quinta Inn & Suites Oklahoma City (Norman) 🄷 ❀

(405) 579-4000. **$79-$129.** 930 Ed Noble Dr 73072. I-35, exit 108B (Lindsey St), just nw. Int corridors. **Pets:** Medium, other species. Service with restrictions, supervision. [ASK] ✕ ♿ 📠 💻 ➹

▼▼▼▼ Residence Inn by Marriott 🄷

(405) 366-0900. **$134-$164.** 2681 Jefferson St 73072. I-35, exit 108A, just se. Ext corridors. **Pets:** Accepted. ✕ 📠 💻 ➹ ✕

OKLAHOMA CITY

▼▼ Baymont Inn 🄷

(405) 631-8661. **$39-$89.** 8315 I-35 S 73149. I-35, exit 121A (82nd St), just sw. Ext corridors. **Pets:** Other species. Service with restrictions, crate. ✕ 📠 💻 ➹

🄰🄰🄰 ▼▼▼▼ Best Western Broadway Inn & Suites 🄷 ❀

(405) 848-1919. **$90-$120.** 6101 N Santa Fe 73118. I-44, exit 127, just e on 63rd St, then just s. Int corridors. **Pets:** $25 one-time fee/pet. Service with restrictions, crate. [SAVE] ✕ 📠 💻 🍴 ➹

🄰🄰🄰 ▼▼▼▼ Best Western Memorial Inn & Suites 🄷

(405) 286-5199. **$85-$99.** 1301 W Memorial Rd 73114. John Kilpatrick Tpke, exit Western Ave, just nw. Int corridors. **Pets:** Medium. $10 daily fee/pet. Service with restrictions, supervision. [SAVE] ✕ 📶 📠 💻 ➹

🄰🄰🄰 ▼▼▼▼ Best Western Saddleback Inn & Conference Center 🄷

(405) 947-7000. **$89-$159.** 4300 SW 3rd St 73108. I-40, exit 145 (Meridian Ave), just ne. Ext/int corridors. **Pets:** Small. $50 deposit/pet. Supervision. [SAVE] ✕ 📠 💻 🍴 ➹ ✕

▼▼ Candlewood Suites Hotel 🄷

(405) 680-8770. **$104-$124.** 4400 River Park Dr 73108. I-40, exit 145 (Meridian Ave), 1.1 mi s. Int corridors. **Pets:** Accepted. [ASK] ✕ 📶 📠 💻

🄰🄰🄰 ▼▼▼ Comfort Inn 🄷

(405) 943-4400. **$74-$109.** 4240 W I-40 Service Rd 73108. I-40, exit 145 (Meridian Ave), just e on south frontage road. Ext/int corridors. **Pets:** Accepted. [SAVE] ✕ 📠 💻 ➹

🄰🄰🄰 ▼▼▼ Comfort Inn North 🄷

(405) 478-7282. **$70-$125.** 4625 NE 120th St 73131. I-35, exit 137 (122nd St), just sw. Int corridors. **Pets:** Dogs only. $20 daily fee/pet. Service with restrictions, crate. [SAVE] ✕ 📠 💻 ➹

▼▼▼ Country Inn & Suites By Carlson, Oklahoma City-NW Express H
(405) 843-2002. **$76-$107.** 3141 Northwest Expwy 73112. 0.4 mi e of jct SR 74 and 3. Int corridors. **Pets:** Accepted. [ASK] ⊠ 🛏 💻 🐾

🆑 ▼▼▼ Courtyard by Marriott-Downtown/Bricktown H ❀
(405) 232-2290. **$161-$197.** 2 W Reno Ave 73102. Gaylord and Reno aves; downtown. Int corridors. **Pets:** $100 one-time fee/room. Service with restrictions, supervision. [SAVE] ⊠ &M 🛏 💻 ⍾ 🐾

▼▼▼ Courtyard by Marriott-NW H
(405) 848-0808. **$107-$131.** 1515 Northwest Expy 73118. I-44, exit 125C westbound; exit 125B eastbound, just e. Int corridors. **Pets:** Accepted. ⊠ &M 🛏 💻 ⍾ 🐾 ⊠

▼▼ Econo Lodge H ❀
(405) 478-0400. **Call for rates.** 12001 N I-35 Service Rd 73131. I-35, exit 137, just sw. Ext corridors. **Pets:** Small, dogs only. $10 daily fee/pet. Designated rooms, service with restrictions, supervision. ⊠ 🛏 💻 🐾

🆑 ▼▼▼ Embassy Suites H
(405) 682-6000. **$109-$209.** 1815 S Meridian Ave 73108. I-40, exit 145 (Meridian Ave), 1 mi s. Int corridors. **Pets:** Other species. $50 one-time fee/room. Designated rooms, service with restrictions. [SAVE] ⊠ 🛏 💻 ⍾ 🐾 ⊠

🆑 ▼▼▼ Four Points by Sheraton Oklahoma City H
(405) 681-3500. **Call for rates.** 6300 Terminal Dr 73159. I-40, exit 145 (Meridian Ave), 4 mi s. Int corridors. **Pets:** Accepted. [SAVE] ⊠ 🛏 💻 ⍾ 🐾

▼▼▼ La Quinta Inn & Suites Oklahoma City (Northwest Expressway) H ❀
(405) 773-5575. **$49-$114.** 4829 Northwest Expwy 73132-5215. 1.9 mi w of jct SR 3 and 74. Int corridors. **Pets:** Medium, other species. Service with restrictions, supervision. [ASK] ⊠ 🛏 💻 🐾

▼▼▼ La Quinta Inn & Suites-Quail Springs H ❀
(405) 755-7000. **$89-$229.** 3003 W Memorial Rd 73134. John Kilpatrick Tpke, exit May Ave, just nw. Int corridors. **Pets:** Medium, other species. Service with restrictions, supervision. [ASK] ⊠ &M 🛏 💻 🐾 ⊠

▼▼▼ La Quinta Inn Oklahoma City (Airport) H ❀
(405) 942-0040. **$49-$125.** 800 S Meridian Ave 73108. I-40, exit 145 (Meridian Ave), just se. Ext/int corridors. **Pets:** Medium, other species. Service with restrictions, supervision. [ASK] ⊠ 🛏 💻 ⍾ 🐾

▼▼ Quality Inn H
(405) 632-6666. **$60-$90.** 7800 CA Henderson Blvd 73139. I-240, exit 2A, just s. Ext corridors. **Pets:** Small, dogs only. $20 one-time fee/room. Designated rooms, service with restrictions, supervision. [ASK] ⊠ 🛏 💻 🐾

🆑 ▼▼▼ Residence Inn by Marriott H ❀
(405) 601-1700. **$179-$219.** 400 E Reno Ave 73104. Just se of jct Joe Carter Ave; in Bricktown. Int corridors. **Pets:** $100 one-time fee/room. Service with restrictions, crate. [SAVE] ⊠ &M 🛏 💻 🐾

▼▼▼ Residence Inn by Marriott Oklahoma City South-Crossroads Mall H
(405) 634-9696. **$170-$208.** 1111 E I-240 Service Rd 73149. I-240, exit 4C eastbound, 0.4 mi nw; exit 5 westbound, 0.8 mi nw. Int corridors. **Pets:** Accepted. ⊠ 🛏 💻 🐾 ⊠

🆑 ▼▼▼ Residence Inn by Marriott-Oklahoma City West H
(405) 942-4500. **$161-$197.** 4361 W Reno Ave 73107. I-40, exit 145 (Meridian Ave), 0.3 mi n, then just e. Ext corridors. **Pets:** Accepted. [SAVE] ⊠ 🛏 💻 🐾

🆑 ▼▼▼ Sheraton Oklahoma City H ❀
(405) 235-2780. **Call for rates.** One N Broadway Ave 73102. Sheridan and Broadway aves; downtown. Int corridors. **Pets:** Medium, dogs only. No service, supervision. [SAVE] ⊠ 🛏 💻 ⍾ 🐾

🆑 ▼▼▼ Skirvin Hilton H ❀
(405) 272-3040. **$149-$269.** 1 Park Ave 73102. Just n of jct Robinson Ave; downtown. Int corridors. **Pets:** Medium. $75 one-time fee/room. Service with restrictions, supervision. [SAVE] ⊠ &M 🛏 💻 ⍾ 🐾

🆑 ▼▼▼ SpringHill Suites Oklahoma City Airport H
(405) 604-0200. **$134-$164.** 510 S MacArthur Blvd 73128. I-40, exit 144, just ne. Int corridors. **Pets:** Accepted. [SAVE] ⊠ &M 🛏 💻 🐾

▼▼ Super 8 Bricktown M
(405) 677-1000. **Call for rates.** 3030 S I-35 73129. I-35, exit 124B northbound; exit 125A southbound, just n on service road. Ext corridors. **Pets:** $10 daily fee/pet. Service with restrictions, supervision. ⊠ 💻

SHAWNEE

🆑 ▼▼▼ La Quinta Inn & Suites H ❀
(405) 275-7930. **$79-$155.** 5401 Enterprise Ct 74804. I-40, exit 186, just ne. Int corridors. **Pets:** Medium, other species. Service with restrictions, supervision. [SAVE] ⊠ &M 🛏 💻 🐾

YUKON

🆑 ▼▼▼ Best Western Inn & Suites Yukon H
(405) 265-2995. **$84-$144.** 11440 W I-40 Service Rd 73099. I-40, exit 138, just sw. Ext/int corridors. **Pets:** Medium, dogs only. $25 deposit/room, $5 daily fee/pet. Service with restrictions, supervision. [SAVE] ⊠ 🛏 💻 🐾

▼▼▼ Comfort Suites H
(405) 577-6500. **$86-$150.** 11424 NW 4th St 73099. I-40, exit 138, just nw. Int corridors. **Pets:** Small, other species. $50 deposit/room, $10 daily fee/pet. Designated rooms, service with restrictions, crate. [ASK] ⊠ 🛏 💻 🐾

▼▼▼ La Quinta Inn & Suites H ❀
(405) 494-7600. **Call for rates.** 11500 W I-40 73099. I-40, exit 138, just s. Int corridors. **Pets:** Medium, other species. Service with restrictions, supervision. ⊠ &M 🛏 💻 🐾

END METROPOLITAN AREA

OKMULGEE

🆑 ▼▼▼ Best Western Okmulgee H
(918) 756-9200. **$75-$89.** 3499 N Wood Dr 74447. Just n of jct US 75 and SR 56. Int corridors. **Pets:** Accepted. [SAVE] ⊠ 🛏 💻 🐾

PAULS VALLEY

▼▼▼ Comfort Inn & Suites H
(405) 207-9730. **$90-$100.** 103 S Humphrey Blvd 73075. I-35, exit 72, just e. Int corridors. **Pets:** Accepted. [ASK] ⊠ &M 🛏 💻 🐾

🆑 ▼▼ Days Inn H
(405) 238-7548. **$78.** 2606 W Grant Ave 73075. I-35, exit 72, just e. Int corridors. **Pets:** Accepted. [SAVE] ⊠ 🛏 💻

PONCA CITY

AAA **WWWW** **Comfort Inn & Suites** **H**
(580) 765-2322. **$81.** 3101 N 14th St 74604. I-35, exit 214, 3 mi n on US 77. Int corridors. **Pets:** Small. $10 daily fee/pet. Service with restrictions, crate. **SAVE** **X** **&M** **H** **P** **a**

SAVANNA

AAA **WWW** **Candlelight Inn & Suites** **H**
(918) 548-3676. **$75-$90, 3 day notice.** Hwy 69 74565. 1.5 mi sw of jct US 69 and Indian Creek Tpke. Int corridors. **Pets:** Medium, other species. Service with restrictions, supervision. **SAVE** **X** **H** **P**

SAYRE

WW **AmericInn Lodge & Suites of Sayre** **H**
(580) 928-2700. **Call for rates.** 2405 S El Camino Rd 73662. I-40, exit 20, just n. Int corridors. **Pets:** Accepted. **X** **&M** **H** **P** **a**

SEMINOLE

AAA **WWWW** **Best Western Seminole Inn & Suites** **H**
(405) 382-3139. **$87-$98.** 1525 N Milt Phillips Ave 74868. 0.5 mi s of jct US 377, SR 9 and 99. Int corridors. **Pets:** Accepted.
SAVE **X** **H** **P** **a**

THACKERVILLE

WWW **Winstar Microtel Inn & Suites** **H**
(580) 276-4487. **Call for rates.** Rt 1, Box 682 73459. I-35, exit 1, 1.2 mi n on E Service Rd. Int corridors. **Pets:** Accepted. **X** **H** **P** **a**

TULSA METROPOLITAN AREA

BROKEN ARROW

WWWW **Clarion Hotel** **H**
(918) 258-7085. **$80-$100.** 2600 N Aspen Ave 74012. Just s of jct SR 51. Int corridors. **Pets:** Accepted. **ASK** **X** **H** **P** **a**

WWWW **Homewood Suites by Hilton Tulsa South** **H**
(918) 392-7700. **$99-$159.** 4900 W Madison Pl 74012. Just ne of jct 71st St and Garnett Ave. Int corridors. **Pets:** Accepted.
X **&M** **H** **P** **a** **X**

CLAREMORE

AAA **WW** **Claremore Motor Inn** **M**
(918) 342-4545. **$44-$89.** 1709 N Lynn Riggs Blvd 74017. 1.2 mi n on SR 66. Ext/int corridors. **Pets:** Accepted. **SAVE** **X** **H**

WWW **Comfort Inn Claremore** **H**
(918) 343-3297. **$62-$95.** 1720 S Lynn Riggs Blvd 74017. 1.6 mi s on SR 66. Int corridors. **Pets:** Medium. $10 daily fee/pet. Service with restrictions, crate. **ASK** **X** **H** **P** **a**

WWW **Microtel Inn & Suites** **H**
(918) 343-2868. **$72-$79.** 10600 E Mallard Lake Rd 74017. 2.6 mi s on SR 66. Int corridors. **Pets:** Accepted. **ASK** **X** **H** **P** **a**

AAA **WWW** **Super 8** **H**
(918) 341-2323. **$59-$99.** 1100 E Will Rogers Blvd 74017. I-44, exit 255, just w. Ext/int corridors. **Pets:** Medium. $10 daily fee/pet. Designated rooms, service with restrictions, crate. **SAVE** **X** **H** **P**

GLENPOOL

AAA **WWW** **Best Western Glenpool/Tulsa** **H**
(918) 322-5201. **$85-$90.** 14831 S Casper St 74033. I-44, exit 224, 9.5 mi s on US 75. Ext corridors. **Pets:** Small. $5 daily fee/pet. Service with restrictions, supervision. **SAVE** **X** **H** **P** **a**

OWASSO

AAA **WWW** **Candlewood Suites** **H** ✿
(918) 272-4334. **$80-$100.** 11699 E 96th St N 74055. 0.4 mi nw of jct US 169. Int corridors. **Pets:** Other species. $75 one-time fee/pet. Service with restrictions, crate. **SAVE** **X** **&M** **H** **P**

TULSA

AAA **WWWW** **Ambassador Hotel** **H** ✿
(918) 587-8200. **$209-$339.** 1324 S Main St 74119. Jct 14th and Main sts. Int corridors. **Pets:** Other species. Service with restrictions, crate.
SAVE **X** **H** **P** **Y**

WWWW **Baymont Inn & Suites Tulsa** **H**
(918) 488-8777. **Call for rates.** 4530 E Skelly Dr 74135. I-44, exit 229 (Yale Ave/SR 66), just s, then w. Int corridors. **Pets:** Small. Service with restrictions, supervision. **X** **H** **P** **a**

AAA **WWW** **Best Western Airport** **H**
(918) 438-0780. **$70-$90.** 222 N Garnett Rd 74116. I-244, exit 14 (Garnett Rd), just s. Ext corridors. **Pets:** Other species. $25 one-time fee/room. Service with restrictions, crate. **SAVE** **X** **H** **P** **a**

WWW **Candlewood Suites** **H**
(918) 294-9000. **$89-$119.** 10008 E 73rd St S 74133. Just sw of jct 71st St and 101st E Ave. Int corridors. **Pets:** Accepted.
ASK **X** **&M** **H** **P**

AAA **WWWW** **Crowne Plaza Tulsa** **H**
(918) 582-9000. **$129-$169, 14 day notice.** 100 E 2nd St 74103. Jct 2nd St and Boston; downtown. Int corridors. **Pets:** Small, dogs only. $100 one-time fee/pet. Service with restrictions, supervision.
SAVE **X** **&M** **H** **P** **Y** **a**

WWWW **Doubletree Hotel At Warren Place** **H**
(918) 495-1000. **$89-$99.** 6110 S Yale Ave 74136. I-44, exit 229 (Yale Ave/SR 66), 1.3 mi s. Int corridors. **Pets:** Accepted.
X **&M** **H** **P** **Y** **a** **X**

WWWW **Doubletree Hotel Tulsa Downtown** **H**
(918) 587-8000. **$95-$209.** 616 W 7th St 74127. Jct 7th St and Houston. Int corridors. **Pets:** Other species. $50 one-time fee/room. Service with restrictions. **X** **H** **P** **Y** **a** **X**

WWWW **Embassy Suites Hotel** **H**
(918) 622-4000. **$119-$199.** 3332 S 79th E Ave 74145. I-44, exit 231 eastbound; exit 232 (Memorial Dr) westbound, just sw. Int corridors. **Pets:** Accepted. **X** **H** **P** **Y** **a**

WWWW **Hilton Tulsa Southern Hills** **H** ✿
(918) 492-5000. **$89-$199.** 7902 S Lewis Ave 74136. I-44, exit 227, 3 mi s. Int corridors. **Pets:** Large, other species. $75 one-time fee/room. Service with restrictions, supervision. **X** **H** **P** **Y** **a**

WWWW **La Quinta Inn & Suites Tulsa Central** **H** ✿
(918) 665-2630. **Call for rates.** 6030 E Skelly Dr 74135. I-44, exit 230, just s. Int corridors. **Pets:** Medium, other species. Service with restrictions, supervision. **X** **H** **P** **a**

WWWW **Radisson Tulsa** **H**
(918) 627-5000. **Call for rates.** 10918 E 41st St 74146. Just e of US 169. Int corridors. **Pets:** Small, dogs only. $75 one-time fee/room. No service, supervision. **X** **P** **Y** **a** **X**

WWW **Radisson Tulsa Airport** **H**
(918) 835-9911. **$109-$119.** 2201 N 77th E Ave 74115. SR 11, exit airport terminal. Int corridors. **Pets:** Accepted.
ASK **X** **H** **P** **Y** **a**

▼▼▼ Ramada Tulsa Airport East H ❀

(918) 437-7660. **Call for rates.** 1010 N Garnett Rd 74116. I-244, exit 14 (Garnett Rd), just n. Int corridors. **Pets:** Other species. $10 one-time fee/pet. Service with restrictions, supervision.

⊠ ⛿ 🖪 🖵 🍽 ⇝ ⊠

▼▼ Red Roof Inn M

(918) 622-6776. **$50-$100.** 4717 S Yale Ave 74135. I-44, exit 229 (Yale Ave), just s. Ext corridors. **Pets:** Large. Service with restrictions, crate.

(ASK) ⊠ 🖪 ⇝

⚠ ▼▼▼ Renaissance Tulsa Hotel & Convention Center H

(918) 307-2600. **$176-$215.** 6808 S 107th E Ave 74133. Just ne of jct US 169 and 71st St. Int corridors. **Pets:** Accepted.

(SAVE) ⊠ ⛿ 🖪 🖵 🍽 ⇝ ⊠

▼▼▼ Residence Inn by Marriott H

(918) 250-4850. **$134-$164.** 11025 E 73rd St 74133. US 169, exit 71st St, just e. Int corridors. **Pets:** Accepted. ⊠ 🖪 🖵 ⇝ ⊠

▼▼ Sleep Inn & Suites Tulsa Central H

(918) 663-2777. **$59-$89.** 8021 E 33rd St S 74145. I-44, exit 231 eastbound; exit 232 (Memorial Dr) westbound, just sw. Int corridors. **Pets:** Small, dogs only. $15 daily fee/pet. Service with restrictions, supervision. (ASK) ⊠ 🖪 🖵 ⇝ ⊠

▼▼▼ Staybridge Suites H

(918) 461-2100. **$139-$169.** 11111 E 73rd St 74133. Just se of jct US 169 and 71st St. Int corridors. **Pets:** Small, other species. $75 one-time fee/pet. Designated rooms, service with restrictions, supervision.

(ASK) ⊠ ⛿ 🖪 🖵 ⇝ ⊠

▼▼▼ Tulsa Marriott Southern Hills H

(918) 493-7000. **$188-$230.** 1902 E 71st St 74136. I-44, exit 227 (Lewis Ave), 2 mi s; jct 71st St and Lewis Ave. Int corridors. **Pets:** Accepted.

⊠ 🖪 🖵 🍽 ⇝ ⊠

▼▼▼ Tulsa Select Hotel H

(918) 622-7000. **$60-$129.** 5000 E Skelly Dr 74135. I-44, exit 229 (Yale Ave/SR 66); on south frontage road. Ext/int corridors. **Pets:** Accepted.

(ASK) ⊠ 🖪 🖵 🍽 ⇝

END METROPOLITAN AREA

WOODWARD

⚠ ▼▼▼ Northwest Inn H

(580) 256-7600. **$85-$119.** Hwy 270 S & 1st St 73802. 1.4 mi s of jct US 183 and 270, SR 3 and 34. Ext/int corridors. **Pets:** Accepted.

(SAVE) ⊠ 🖪 🖵 🍽 ⇝

OREGON

ALBANY

Comfort Suites–Linn County Fairgrounds and Expo H
(541) 928-2053. $75-$80. 100 Opal Ct NE 97322. I-5, exit 234A southbound; exit 234 northbound, just se. Int corridors. Pets: Medium, dogs only. $15 daily fee/pet. Service with restrictions, supervision.
SAVE X GM H 💻 ➤ X

Econo Lodge M
(541) 926-0170. $54-$66. 1212 SE Price Rd 97322. I-5, exit 233, just e on Santiam Hwy (US 20), then just n. Ext corridors. Pets: Small, dogs only. $10 daily fee/room. Service with restrictions, supervision.
SAVE X H

Holiday Inn Express Hotel & Suites H
(541) 928-8820. $99-$159. 105 Opal Ct NE 97322. I-5, exit 234A southbound; exit 234 northbound, just se. Int corridors. Pets: Medium, dogs only. $15 one-time fee/pet. Service with restrictions, supervision.
SAVE X GM H 💻 ➤ X

La Quinta Inn Albany H 🐾
(541) 928-0921. $64-$94. 251 Airport Rd SE 97322. I-5, exit 234B southbound; exit 234 northbound, just sw. Int corridors. Pets: Medium, other species. Service with restrictions, supervision.
ASK X H 💻 ➤ X

Motel 6 #4124 M
(541) 926-4233. $55-$75. 2735 E Pacific Blvd 97321. I-5, exit 234B southbound; exit 234 northbound, 0.5 mi w. Ext corridors. Pets: Other species. Service with restrictions, supervision. SAVE X H

Phoenix Inn Suites-Albany H
(541) 926-5696. $79-$139. 3410 Spicer Rd SE 97322. I-5, exit 233, just se. Int corridors. Pets: Accepted. SAVE X H 💻 ➤

Quality Inn H
(541) 928-5050. $59-$150. 1100 Price Rd SE 97322. I-5, exit 233, just e on Santiam Hwy (US 20), then just n. Int corridors. Pets: Small, dogs only. $10 daily fee/pet. Service with restrictions, supervision.
SAVE X GM H 💻 ➤

Super 8 H 🐾
(541) 926-6322. $65-$149. 315 Airport Rd SE 97322. I-5, exit 234B southbound; exit 234 northbound, just sw. Ext corridors. Pets: Large. $10 daily fee/pet. Service with restrictions. SAVE X H 💻 ➤

ASHLAND

Ashland Chanticleer Inn BB
(541) 482-1919. $135-$199, 31 day notice. 120 Gresham St 97520. Just se of downtown on Main St (SR 99), then just s. Int corridors. Pets: $10 daily fee/pet. Designated rooms, service with restrictions, crate.
X Z

Ashland Springs Hotel H
(541) 488-1700. $89-$259, 3 day notice. 212 E Main St 97520. Corner of 1st St; center. Int corridors. Pets: Other species. $30 one-time fee/room. Designated rooms, service with restrictions, crate.
SAVE X H T

Best Western Bard's Inn H
(541) 482-0049. $85-$225. 132 N Main St 97520. Just nw on SR 99 (N Main St) from Downtown Plaza. Ext/int corridors. Pets: $15 daily fee/pet. Designated rooms, service with restrictions, supervision.
SAVE X H 💻 ➤

Best Western Windsor Inn H
(541) 488-2330. $89-$175, 7 day notice. 2520 Ashland St 97520. I-5, exit 14, just se on Ashland St (SR 66). Ext corridors. Pets: Medium, other species. $15 daily fee/pet. Designated rooms, service with restrictions, supervision. SAVE X H 💻 ➤

Cedarwood Inn M
(541) 488-2000. $59-$119, 3 day notice. 1801 Siskiyou Blvd 97520. I-5, exit 11 northbound, 2.6 mi nw; exit 14 southbound, just w on Ashland St (SR 66), 0.6 mi s on Tolman Creek Rd, then 0.6 mi w. Ext corridors. Pets: Medium. $10 daily fee/pet. Designated rooms, service with restrictions, supervision. SAVE X H 💻 ➤

Flagship Inn of Ashland M
(541) 482-2641. $59-$119, 3 day notice. 1193 Siskiyou Blvd 97520. I-5, exit 14, 1.3 mi w on Ashland St (SR 66), then just n. Ext corridors. Pets: Medium. $10 daily fee/pet. Designated rooms, service with restrictions, supervision. SAVE X H 💻 ➤

Holiday Inn Express Hotel & Suites–Ashland H 🐾
(541) 201-0202. $119-$189. 565 Clover Ln 97520. I-5, exit 14, just e on Ashland St (SR 66), then s. Int corridors. Pets: Large. $15 daily fee/pet. Supervision. SAVE X GM H 💻 ➤

La Quinta Inn & Suites Ashland H 🐾
(541) 482-6932. $62-$182. 434 S Valley View Rd 97520. I-5, exit 19, just sw. Int corridors. Pets: Medium, other species. Service with restrictions, supervision. ASK X H 💻 ➤

Plaza Inn & Suites At Ashland Creek H 🐾
(541) 488-8900. $89-$289. 98 Central Ave 97520. From Downtown Plaza, just nw on N Main St (SR 99), just n on Water St, then just w. Int corridors. Pets: Medium. $25 daily fee/room. Designated rooms, service with restrictions, supervision. SAVE X H 💻

ᗯ ᗯᗯ Timbers Motel of Ashland M ❀
(541) 482-4242. **$47-$125, 3 day notice.** 1450 Ashland St 97520. I-5, exit 14, 1.2 mi w on Ashland St (SR 66). Ext corridors. **Pets:** Medium, other species. Designated rooms, service with restrictions.
[SAVE] [✕] [🛏] [📺] [🏊]

ᗯᗯ Village Suites at Ashland Hills H
(541) 482-8310. **$99-$149.** 2525 Ashland St 97520. I-5, exit 14, just ne on Ashland St (SR 66). Int corridors. **Pets:** Accepted.
[SAVE] [✕] [🛏] [📺] [✕]

ASTORIA
ᗯᗯᗯ Astoria Holiday Inn Express Hotel & Suites H ❀
(503) 325-6222. **$119-$339.** 204 W Marine Dr 97103. On US 30; west side of town. Int corridors. **Pets:** $15 daily fee/pet. Designated rooms, service with restrictions, supervision.
[ASK] [✕] [♿M] [🛏] [📺] [🏊] [✕]

ᗯᗯ Best Western Lincoln Inn H ❀
(503) 325-2205. **$89-$399.** 555 Hamburg Ave 97103. On US 101/30; at east end of Young's Bay Bridge. Int corridors. **Pets:** $15 daily fee/pet. Designated rooms, service with restrictions, supervision.
[SAVE] [✕] [🛏] [📺] [🏊] [✕]

ᗯᗯ Clementine's Bed & Breakfast BB ❀
(503) 325-2005. **$95-$165, 7 day notice.** 847 Exchange St 97103. At 8th and Exchange sts; in historic downtown. Int corridors. **Pets:** $15 one-time fee/room. Designated rooms, no service. [✕] [🛏] [📺] [🎬] [📷]

ᗯᗯ Crest Motel, P.C. M
(503) 325-3141. **$62-$137.** 5366 Leif Erickson Dr 97103. 4 mi e of Astoria Bridge on US 30. Ext corridors. **Pets:** Service with restrictions, supervision. [SAVE] [✕] [🛏] [📺] [🎬]

ᗯᗯ Red Lion Inn Astoria M
(503) 325-7373. **$99-$239.** 400 Industry St 97103. Just w of Astoria Bridge on US 30, just n on Basin St (caution: do not turn onto Astoria-Megler Bridge). Ext corridors. **Pets:** Other species. $20 one-time fee/room. Service with restrictions, supervision. [SAVE] [✕] [🛏] [📺] [🎬]

BAKER CITY
ᗯᗯ Best Western Sunridge Inn H
(541) 523-6444. **$89-$235, 3 day notice.** 1 Sunridge Ln 97814. I-84, exit 304, just w. Int corridors. **Pets:** Accepted.
[SAVE] [✕] [🛏] [📺] [🍴] [🏊]

ᗯᗯᗯ Geiser Grand Hotel H ❀
(541) 523-1889. **$89-$229, 3 day notice.** 1996 Main St 97814. I-84, exit 304, 0.9 mi w on Campbell St, then 0.3 mi s; downtown. Int corridors. **Pets:** Other species. $75 deposit/room, $15 daily fee/pet. Service with restrictions, crate. [ASK] [✕] [🍴]

ᗯᗯ Super 8 Baker City H
(541) 523-8282. **$65-$80.** 250 Campbell St 97814. I-84, exit 304, just e. Int corridors. **Pets:** Accepted. [SAVE] [✕] [♿M] [🛏] [📺] [🏊]

BANDON
ᗯᗯ Bandon Inn M ❀
(541) 347-4417. **$74-$139.** 355 US 101 97411. Center. Ext corridors. **Pets:** Medium. $15 daily fee/pet. Designated rooms, service with restrictions, supervision. [SAVE] [✕] [🛏] [📺] [🎬]

ᗯᗯ Best Western Inn at Face Rock H
(541) 347-9441. **$79-$289.** 3225 Beach Loop Dr 97411. 1 mi s on US 101, 0.8 mi w on Seabird Rd, then just s. Ext corridors. **Pets:** Accepted.
[SAVE] [✕] [🛏] [📺] [🍴] [🏊] [✕] [🎬]

BEND
ᗯᗯᗯ Bend Inn & Suites H
(541) 388-4114. **$79-$199.** 15 NE Butler Market Rd 97701. US 97, exit 136 (Butler Market Rd), just n. Ext corridors. **Pets:** Other species. $15 daily fee/pet. Designated rooms, supervision. [SAVE] [✕] [🛏] [📺] [🏊]

ᗯᗯ Bend Riverside Motel & Suites H
(541) 389-2363. **$68-$159.** 1565 NW Wall St 97701. US 97, exit 137 (Revere Ave), just s. Ext corridors. **Pets:** $10 daily fee/pet. Designated rooms, service with restrictions, supervision. [ASK] [✕] [🛏] [📺] [🏊]

ᗯᗯᗯ Best Western Inn & Suites of Bend H ❀
(541) 382-1515. **$89-$289.** 721 NE 3rd St 97701. Jct US 20 and Business Rt US 97 (NE 3rd St), just s. Ext corridors. **Pets:** $10 daily fee/pet. Designated rooms, service with restrictions, supervision.
[SAVE] [✕] [🛏] [📺] [🏊]

ᗯᗯᗯᗯ Cricketwood Country Bed & Breakfast BB ❀
(541) 330-0747. **$105-$145, 7 day notice.** 63520 Cricketwood Rd 97701. US 97, exit 136 (NE Butler Market Rd), 3.7 mi ne on Butler Market Rd (which becomes Hamehook Rd), 0.4 mi n on Hamehook Rd, 0.4 mi e on Repine Dr, then just n (0.7 mi of gravel road). Ext/int corridors. **Pets:** Dogs only. $10 daily fee/room. Designated rooms, no service.
[✕] [🛏] [📺]

ᗯᗯᗯ Days Inn H ❀
(541) 383-3776. **$59-$110.** 849 NE 3rd St 97701. Jct US 20 and Business Rt US 97 (NE 3rd St), just s. Ext corridors. **Pets:** Other species. Service with restrictions, supervision. [SAVE] [✕] [🛏] [📺] [🏊]

ᗯᗯ Dunes Motel M
(541) 382-6811. **$39-$125.** 1515 NE 3rd St 97701. Jct US 20 and Business Rt US 97 (NE 3rd St), just n. Ext corridors. **Pets:** Small. $6 one-time fee/pet. Service with restrictions, supervision. [SAVE] [✕] [🛏] [📺]

ᗯᗯᗯ Fairfield Inn & Suites by Marriott H
(541) 318-1747. **$99-$129.** 1626 NW Wall St 97701. US 97, exit 137 (Revere Ave), just s; downtown. Int corridors. **Pets:** Other species. $75 one-time fee/room. Service with restrictions.
[✕] [♿M] [🛏] [📺] [🏊] [✕]

ᗯᗯᗯ Holiday Inn Express Hotel & Suites H
(541) 317-8500. **$109-$169.** 20615 Grandview Dr 97701. On US 97; north end of town. Int corridors. **Pets:** $10 daily fee/pet. Service with restrictions, supervision. [SAVE] [✕] [♿M] [🛏] [📺] [🏊] [✕]

ᗯᗯᗯ La Quinta Inn Bend H ❀
(541) 388-2227. **$75-$219.** 61200 SE 3rd St (Business Rt US 97) 97702. From south of jct US 97 and Business Rt US 97 (NE 3rd St), just n. Int corridors. **Pets:** Medium, other species. Service with restrictions, supervision. [ASK] [✕] [🛏] [📺] [🏊]

ᗯᗯ Quality Inn H
(541) 318-0848. **$90-$140.** 20600 Grandview Dr 97701. On US 97; north end of town. Int corridors. **Pets:** Accepted.
[SAVE] [✕] [♿M] [🛏] [📺] [🏊]

ᗯᗯᗯ Red Lion Hotel Bend H
(541) 382-7011. **$95-$209.** 1415 NE 3rd St 97701. Jct US 20 and Business Rt US 97 (NE 3rd St), just n. Ext corridors. **Pets:** Other species. $20 one-time fee/room. Service with restrictions, supervision.
[SAVE] [✕] [♿M] [🛏] [📺] [🏊] [✕]

ᗯᗯᗯ The Riverhouse Hotel & Convention Center H ❀
(541) 389-3111. **$99-$219.** 3075 N Business 97 97701. US 97, exit 136 (Butler Market Rd) northbound, just n; exit 135B southbound. Ext/int corridors. **Pets:** Other species. Service with restrictions, supervision.
[SAVE] [✕] [🛏] [📺] [🍴] [🏊] [✕]

ᗯᗯᗯ Shilo Inn Suites Hotel–Bend H ❀
(541) 389-9600. **$112-$300.** 3105 OB Riley Rd 97701. US 97, exit 136 (Butler Market Rd) northbound, just n; exit 135B southbound. Ext corridors. **Pets:** Dogs only. $25 one-time fee/room. Designated rooms, service with restrictions, supervision. [SAVE] [✕] [🛏] [📺] [🍴] [🏊] [✕]

ᗯᗯ TownePlace Suites by Marriott H
(541) 382-5006. **$99-$149.** 755 SW 13th Pl 97702. US 97, exit 138 (Downtown/Mt Bachelor Dr); 1.7 mi sw on NW Colorado Ave. Int corridors. **Pets:** Accepted. [✕] [🛏] [📺] [🏊] [✕]

BOARDMAN

🔷 ▽▽▽ Rodeway Inn Ⓜ
(541) 481-2375. **$58-$129.** 105 SW Front St 97818. I-84, exit 164, just sw. Ext corridors. **Pets:** Other species. Service with restrictions, supervision. 🅢🅐🅥🅔 ⊠ 🔲 🖥 🏊

BROOKINGS

🔷 ▽▽▽ Best Western Beachfront Inn Ⓗ
(541) 469-7779. **$159-$295.** 16008 Boat Basin Rd 97415. US 101, 1.2 mi s of Chetco River Bridge, exit Benham Ln, then 0.6 mi w. Ext corridors. **Pets:** $5 daily fee/pet. Designated rooms, service with restrictions, supervision. 🅢🅐🅥🅔 ⊠ 🔅M 🔲 🖥 🏊 ℀

🔷 ▽▽▽ Spindrift Motel Ⓜ
(541) 469-5345. **$69-$89.** 1215 Chetco Ave (US 101) 97415. On US 101; north end of town. Ext corridors. **Pets:** Small, dogs only. $10 daily fee/pet. Designated rooms, service with restrictions, supervision.
🅢🅐🅥🅔 ⊠ 🔲 🖥 ℀

🔷 ▽▽▽ Westward Inn Ⓜ
(541) 469-7471. **$55-$99, 3 day notice.** 1026 Chetco Ave (US 101) 97415. On US 101; just n of downtown. Ext corridors. **Pets:** Accepted.
🅢🅐🅥🅔 ⊠ 🔲 🖥

🔷 ▽▽▽ Wild Rivers Motorlodge Ⓜ ✿
(541) 469-5361. **$69-$119.** 437 Chetco Ave (US 101) 97415. On US 101, just n of Chetco River Bridge. Ext corridors. **Pets:** Large. $20 one-time fee/room. Designated rooms, service with restrictions, supervision.
🅢🅐🅥🅔 ⊠ 🔲 🖥

BURNS

🔷 America's Best Inn Ⓜ
(541) 573-1700. **$60-$86.** 999 Oregon Ave (US 395/20) 97720. 1 mi w on US 395/20 from jct SR 78. Ext/int corridors. **Pets:** Dogs only. $50 deposit/room, $10 daily fee/pet. Designated rooms, service with restrictions, supervision. 🅢🅐🅥🅔 ⊠ 🔲 🖥 🏊

🔷 Silver Spur Motel Ⓜ
(541) 573-2077. **$44-$56.** 789 N Broadway 97720. US 395/20; at north edge of town center. Ext corridors. **Pets:** Accepted. 🅢🅐🅥🅔 ⊠ 🔲 🖥

CANNON BEACH

▽▽▽ Cannon Beach Ecola Creek Lodge Ⓜ
(503) 436-2776. **$59-$239, 3 day notice.** 208 5th St 97110. US 101, via north exit to Ecola State Park, then just w; north end of downtown. Ext corridors. **Pets:** Large, other species. $20 one-time fee/pet. Designated rooms, service with restrictions, supervision.
ⒶⓈⓀ ⊠ 🔅M 🔲 🖥 ℀

▽▽▽ Inn at Cannon Beach Ⓗ ✿
(503) 436-9085. **Call for rates.** 3215 S Hemlock St 97110. US 101, exit Tolovana Park, just w on Warren Way, then just n. Ext corridors. **Pets:** Dogs only. $10 daily fee/pet. Designated rooms, service with restrictions, supervision. ⊠ 🔲 🖥 ℀

▽▽▽ The Ocean Lodge Ⓗ
(503) 436-2241. **$199-$379, 7 day notice.** 2864 S Pacific St 97110. US 101, exit Tolovana Park, just w on Warren Way, just n on S Hemlock St, just w on W Chisana St, then just n. Ext/int corridors. **Pets:** Accepted.
⊠ 🔲 🖥

🔷 ▽▽▽ Surfsand Resort at Cannon Beach Ⓗ ✿
(503) 436-2274. **$179-$459, 7 day notice.** 148 W Gower St 97110. US 101, exit Cannon Beach (2nd exit); downtown. Ext corridors. **Pets:** $15 daily fee/pet. Designated rooms, service with restrictions, supervision.
🅢🅐🅥🅔 ⊠ 🔲 🖥 🍽 🏊 ℀

🔷 ▽▽▽ Tolovana Inn Ⓒ🅞 ✿
(503) 436-2211. **$69-$449, 3 day notice.** 3400 S Hemlock St 97145. US 101, exit Tolovana Park, just w on Warren Way, then just s. Ext corridors. **Pets:** $15 daily fee/pet. Designated rooms, service with restrictions, supervision. 🅢🅐🅥🅔 ⊠ 🔲 🖥 🏊 ℀ ℀

CANYONVILLE

🔷 ▽▽▽ Best Western Canyonville Inn & Suites Ⓗ
(541) 839-4200. **$80-$170.** 200 Creekside Dr 97417. I-5, exit 99, just w. Int corridors. **Pets:** Small. $10 daily fee/pet. Designated rooms, service with restrictions, supervision. 🅢🅐🅥🅔 ⊠ 🔲 🖥 🏊

▽▽▽ Seven Feathers Hotel & Casino Resort Ⓗ
(541) 839-1111. **Call for rates.** 146 Chief Miwaleta Ln 97417. I-5, exit 99, just e. Int corridors. **Pets:** Accepted.
⊠ 🔅M 🔲 🖥 🍽 🏊 ℀

CASCADE LOCKS

🔷 ▽▽▽▽ Best Western Columbia River Inn Ⓗ
(541) 374-8777. **$120-$190.** 735 WaNaPa St (US 30) 97014. I-84, exit 44 eastbound, 0.4 mi ne; exit westbound, 1.4 mi nw. Int corridors. **Pets:** Medium. $10 daily fee/pet. Designated rooms, service with restrictions, supervision. 🅢🅐🅥🅔 ⊠ 🔅M 🔲 🖥 🏊

CENTRAL POINT

▽▽▽ Holiday Inn Express Hotel & Suites Ⓗ ✿
(541) 423-1010. **$99-$139.** 285 Peninger St 97502. I-5, exit 33, just se. Int corridors. **Pets:** $25 daily fee/pet. Designated rooms, service with restrictions, supervision. ⒶⓈⓀ ⊠ 🔅M 🔲 🖥 🏊

▽▽▽ Super 8 Inn & Suites Ⓗ
(541) 664-5888. **Call for rates.** 4999 Biddle Rd 97502. I-5, exit 33, 0.5 mi e. Int corridors. **Pets:** Accepted. ⊠ 🔅M 🔲 🖥 🏊

CLATSKANIE

🔷 ▽▽▽ Clatskanie River Inn Ⓗ
(503) 728-9000. **$89-$149.** 600 E Columbia River Hwy (US 30) 97016. On US 30. Int corridors. **Pets:** Accepted. 🅢🅐🅥🅔 ⊠ 🔲 🖥 🏊

COOS BAY

🔷 ▽▽▽ Best Western Holiday Motel Ⓗ
(541) 269-5111. **$104-$199.** 411 N Bayshore Dr 97420. On US 101; just n of downtown. Ext/int corridors. **Pets:** Medium, dogs only. $15 daily fee/pet. Service with restrictions, supervision. 🅢🅐🅥🅔 ⊠ 🔲 🖥 🏊

🔷 ▽▽▽▽ Red Lion Hotel Coos Bay Ⓗ
(541) 267-4141. **$104-$156.** 1313 N Bayshore Dr 97420. On US 101; 0.5 mi n of downtown. Ext corridors. **Pets:** Other species. $20 one-time fee/room. Service with restrictions, supervision.
🅢🅐🅥🅔 ⊠ 🔅M 🔲 🖥 🍽 🏊

▽▽▽ Super 8 Coos Bay Ⓜ
(541) 808-0700. **$69-$199.** 1001 Bayshore Dr 97420. On US 101; just n of downtown. Ext corridors. **Pets:** Medium, other species. $20 daily fee/pet. Service with restrictions, supervision. ⒶⓈⓀ ⊠ 🔲 🖥 ℀

CORVALLIS

🔷 ▽▽▽ Best Western Grand Manor Inn & Suites Ⓗ ✿
(541) 758-8571. **$75-$200.** 925 NW Garfield Ave 97330. Jct SR 34 and US 20, just w on NW Harrison Blvd, 1.4 mi n on NW 9th St, then just w. Int corridors. **Pets:** Medium, dogs only. $10 daily fee/pet. Designated rooms, service with restrictions, supervision.
🅢🅐🅥🅔 ⊠ 🔅M 🔲 🖥 🏊

🔷 ▽▽▽ Days Inn Ⓗ
(541) 754-7474. **$59-$169.** 1113 NW 9th St 97330. Jct SR 34 and US 20, just w on NW Harrison Blvd, then 0.5 mi n. Int corridors.
Pets: Accepted. 🅢🅐🅥🅔 ⊠ 🔲 🖥 🏊

🔷 ▽▽▽ Holiday Inn Express On The River Ⓗ
(541) 752-0800. **$89-$199.** 781 NE 2nd St 97330. Jct SR 34 and US 20, 0.4 mi n. Int corridors. **Pets:** Accepted.
🅢🅐🅥🅔 ⊠ 🔅M 🔲 🖥 🏊 ℀

Motel 6 #4243 H

(541) 758-9125. **$65-$199.** 935 NW Garfield Ave 97330. Jct SR 34 and US 20, just w on NW Harrison Blvd, 1.4 mi n on NW 9th St, then just w. Int corridors. **Pets:** Other species. Service with restrictions, supervision.

SAVE ⊠ 🖥

Rodeway Inn Willamette River M

(541) 752-9601. **$45-$70.** 345 NW 2nd St 97330. Between NW Harrison Blvd and NW Van Buren St; downtown. Ext/int corridors. **Pets:** Dogs only. $10 daily fee/pet. Designated rooms, no service, supervision.

ASK ⊠ 🖥

Super 8 H

(541) 758-8088. **$56-$80, 3 day notice.** 407 NW 2nd St 97330. Jct SR 34 and US 20, just n; downtown. Int corridors. **Pets:** Accepted.

ASK ⊠ &M 🖥 ➸

COTTAGE GROVE

Comfort Inn H

(541) 942-9747. **$64-$150.** 845 Gateway Blvd 97424. I-5, exit 174, just sw. Ext/int corridors. **Pets:** $10 one-time fee/pet. Designated rooms, service with restrictions, supervision. SAVE ⊠ 🖥 🖵 ➸

Holiday Inn Express H

(541) 942-1000. **$89-$129.** 1601 Gateway Blvd 97424. I-5, exit 174, just sw. Int corridors. **Pets:** Medium, dogs only. $15 one-time fee/pet. Service with restrictions, supervision. SAVE ⊠ &M 🖥 🖵 ➸

CRESWELL

Super 8 Creswell Inn M 🐾

(541) 895-3341. **$55-$109.** 345 E Oregon Ave 97426. I-5, exit 182, just sw. Ext corridors. **Pets:** $15 one-time fee/pet. Designated rooms, service with restrictions, supervision. SAVE ⊠ 🖥 🖵 ➸

DALLAS

Best Western Dallas Inn & Suites H

(503) 623-6000. **$90-$100.** 250 Orchard Dr 97338. SR 223, just n. Int corridors. **Pets:** Accepted. SAVE ⊠ &M 🖥 🖵

DEPOE BAY

Crown Pacific Inn M

(541) 765-7773. **$75-$95.** 50 NE Bechill St 97341. Just n of downtown. Ext/int corridors. **Pets:** Medium, dogs only. $10 one-time fee/pet. Designated rooms, service with restrictions, supervision.

SAVE ⊠ 🖥 🖵 🅰C

Surfrider Resort H

(541) 764-2311. **$69-$199, 3 day notice.** 3115 NW US 101 97341. 2 mi n of Depoe Bay. Ext corridors. **Pets:** Accepted.

SAVE ⊠ 🖥 🖵 🍽 ➸ 🅧 🅰C

ENTERPRISE

Ponderosa Motel M

(541) 426-3186. **$56-$72.** 102 E Greenwood St 97828. Center. Ext corridors. **Pets:** Large, dogs only. $10 daily fee/pet. Service with restrictions, supervision. ASK ⊠ 🖥 🖵

The Wilderness Inn M

(541) 426-4535. **$51-$70.** 301 W North St 97828. Corner of NW 2nd St. Ext corridors. **Pets:** Dogs only. $10 daily fee/pet. Service with restrictions, supervision. ASK ⊠ 🖥 🖵

EUGENE

Americas Best Value Inn M

(541) 343-0730. **$49-$79.** 1140 W 6th Ave 97402. I-5, exit 194B, 3.5 mi w on I-105, then 0.3 mi w on SR 99 N (6th Ave). Ext corridors. **Pets:** Other species. $10 daily fee/pet. Service with restrictions, supervision. SAVE ⊠ 🖥

Best Western Greentree Inn H 🐾

(541) 485-2727. **$100-$114.** 1759 Franklin Blvd 97403. I-5, exit 194B southbound to I-105, exit University of Oregon, 0.9 mi e: exit 192 northbound, 1.2 mi w. Ext/int corridors. **Pets:** $50 deposit/pet. Designated rooms, service with restrictions, supervision. SAVE ⊠ 🖥 🖵 ➸

Best Western New Oregon Motel H 🐾

(541) 683-3669. **$100-$114.** 1655 Franklin Blvd 97403. I-5, exit 194B southbound to I-105, exit University of Oregon, 0.9 mi e; exit 192 northbound, then 1.2 mi w. Ext/int corridors. **Pets:** $50 deposit/pet. Service with restrictions, supervision. SAVE ⊠ 🖥 🖵 ➸ 🅧

Broadway Inn M

(541) 344-5233. **$60-$150.** 476 E Broadway St 97401. I-5, exit 194B southbound, 1.3 mi w on I-105, exit 2 (Coburg Rd), then 1.5 mi s, follow University of Oregon signs; exit 192 northbound, 2.2 mi w. Ext corridors. **Pets:** Accepted. SAVE ⊠ 🖥 🖵

Express Inn & Suites M

(541) 868-1520. **$54-$99, 3 day notice.** 990 W 6th Ave 97402. I-5, exit 194B, 3.5 mi w on I-105, then 0.3 mi w on SR 99 N (6th Ave). Ext corridors. **Pets:** Small, dogs only. $10 daily fee/pet. Designated rooms, service with restrictions, supervision. SAVE ⊠ 🖥

Hilton Eugene H

(541) 342-2000. **$129-$279.** 66 E 6th Ave 97401. At 6th Ave and Oak St; center. Int corridors. **Pets:** Accepted. ⊠ 🖥 🖵 🍽 ➸ 🅧

La Quinta Inn & Suites Waterfront H 🐾

(541) 344-8335. **$99-$199.** 155 Day Island Rd 97401. I-5, exit 194B, 1.3 mi w on I-105, exit 2 (Coburg Rd), straight through jct Coburg Rd to Southwood Ln, just w, then 0.5 mi se on Country Club Rd, follow signs for Autzen Stadium. Int corridors. **Pets:** Medium, other species. Service with restrictions, supervision. ASK ⊠ 🖥 🖵 ➸

Motel 6–#36 M

(541) 687-2395. **$49-$75.** 3690 Glenwood Dr 97403. I-5, exit 191, just sw. Ext corridors. **Pets:** Other species. Service with restrictions, supervision. ⊠ 🖥 ➸

Red Lion Hotel Eugene H

(541) 342-5201. **Call for rates.** 205 Coburg Rd 97401. I-5, exit 194B, 1.3 mi w on I-105, exit 2 (Coburg Rd), then just n. Int corridors. **Pets:** Other species. $20 one-time fee/room. Service with restrictions, supervision. SAVE ⊠ &M 🖥 🖵 🍽 ➸ 🅧

Residence Inn by Marriott Eugene Springfield H

(541) 342-7171. **$170-$208.** 25 Club Rd 97401. I-5, exit 194B, 1.3 mi w on I-105, exit 2 (Coburg Rd), straight through jct Coburg Rd to Southwood Ln, just w, then se on Country Club Rd; follow signs for Autzen Stadium. Int corridors. **Pets:** Accepted. ⊠ &M 🖥 🖵 ➸ 🅧

Valley River Inn H 🐾

(541) 743-1000. **$139-$249.** 1000 Valley River Way 97401. I-5, exit 194B, 2.5 mi w on I-105, exit 1, follow Valley River Center signs. Int corridors. **Pets:** Large, other species. Designated rooms, supervision.

ASK ⊠ 🖥 🖵 🍽 ➸ 🅧

FLORENCE

Best Western Pier Point Inn H

(541) 997-7191. **$124-$260.** 85625 US 101 S 97439. Jct SR 126, 1.1 mi s. Ext corridors. **Pets:** Accepted. SAVE ⊠ 🖥 🖵 ➸ 🅧 🅰C

Le Chateau Inn M

(541) 997-3481. **$54-$119.** 1084 US 101 N 97439. Jct SR 126, just n. Ext corridors. **Pets:** Accepted. SAVE ⊠ 🖥 🖵 ➸ 🅧 🅰C

Ocean Breeze Motel M

(541) 997-2642. **$59-$150.** 85165 US 101 S 97439. Jct SR 126, 2 mi s. Ext corridors. **Pets:** Large, dogs only. $10 daily fee/pet. Designated rooms, supervision. SAVE ⊠ 🖥 🖵 🅰C

Old Town Inn Ⓜ ✿
(541) 997-7131. **$65-$99.** 170 US 101 S 97439. Jct SR 126, 0.4 mi s. Ext corridors. **Pets:** $10 daily fee/pet. Designated rooms, service with restrictions, supervision. SAVE ⊠ 🛏 🖵 🐾

Park Motel Ⓜ ✿
(541) 997-2634. **$55-$150, 7 day notice.** 85034 US 101 S 97439. Jct SR 126, 2.2 mi s. Ext corridors. **Pets:** Large, other species. $10 daily fee/pet. Service with restrictions, supervision. SAVE ⊠ 🛏 🖵 🐾

FOREST GROVE

Best Western University Inn & Suites Ⓗ
(503) 992-8888. **$89-$199.** 3933 Pacific Ave 97116. East end of town on SR 8. Int corridors. **Pets:** Medium, dogs only. $15 daily fee/pet. Designated rooms, service with restrictions, crate.
SAVE ⊠ 🛗 🛏 🖵 🏊 ⊠

GARIBALDI

Comfort Inn Ⓗ
(503) 322-3338. **$89-$189.** 502 Garibaldi Ave 97118. On US 101 at jct 5th St; center. Int corridors. **Pets:** Accepted.
SAVE ⊠ 🛏 🖵 🏊 ⊠

GEARHART

Gearhart By The Sea ⒸⓄ
(503) 738-8331. **$126-$300, 3 day notice.** 1157 N Marion Ave 97138. US 101, exit City Center, 1 mi w. Ext corridors. **Pets:** $11 daily fee/pet. Designated rooms, service with restrictions, supervision.
SAVE ⊠ 🛏 🖵 🍴 🏊 🐾

GLIDE

Illahee Inn and Restaurant Ⓜ ✿
(541) 496-4870. **$75-$95.** 170 Wild Thyme Ln 97443. Just e on SR 138, then just s. Ext corridors. **Pets:** Medium. $10 daily fee/pet. Service with restrictions, supervision. SAVE ⊠ 🛏 🖵 🍴

GOLD BEACH

Gold Beach Inn Ⓜ
(541) 247-7091. **$79-$169.** 29346 Ellensburg Ave (US 101) 97444. On US 101; center. Ext corridors. **Pets:** Accepted. SAVE ⊠ 🛏 🖵 🐾

Gold Beach Resort and Condominiums Ⓗ
(541) 247-7066. **$79-$185.** 29232 Ellensburg Ave (US 101) 97444. On US 101; south end of town. Ext corridors. **Pets:** Accepted.
SAVE ⊠ 🛏 🖵 🏊

Inn of the Beachcomber Ⓜ
(541) 247-6691. **$79-$184.** 29266 Ellensburg Ave (US 101) 97444. On US 101; south end of town. Ext/int corridors. **Pets:** Accepted.
SAVE ⊠ 🛏 🖵 🏊

Jot's Resort Ⓜ
(541) 247-6676. **$65-$230, 3 day notice.** 94360 Wedderburn Loop 97491. Just w of US 101; north end of bridge. Ext corridors. **Pets:** Other species. $15 daily fee/pet. Designated rooms, service with restrictions, supervision. SAVE ⊠ 🛏 🖵 🍴 🏊 ⊠ 🐾

Motel 6–4047 Ⓜ
(541) 247-4533. **Call for rates.** 94433 Jerry's Flat Rd 97444. Just e of jct US 101; south end of bridge. Ext corridors. **Pets:** Other species. Service with restrictions, supervision. ⊠ 🛏 🖵 🐾

GOVERNMENT CAMP

Mt. Hood Inn Ⓗ
(503) 272-3205. **$99-$179.** 87450 E Government Camp Loop 97028. 0.5 mi w of center. Int corridors. **Pets:** Accepted. ASK ⊠ 🛏 🖵 🐾

GRANTS PASS

Bestway Inn Ⓜ
(541) 479-2952. **$55-$75.** 1253 NE 6th St 97526. I-5, exit 58, 0.9 mi s on SR 99. Ext corridors. **Pets:** Small, dogs only. $10 daily fee/pet. Service with restrictions, supervision. SAVE ⊠ 🛏 🖵

Best Western Grants Pass Inn Ⓗ
(541) 476-1117. **$89-$128.** 111 NE Agness Ave 97526. I-5, exit 55, just nw. Ext corridors. **Pets:** Other species. $10 daily fee/pet. Designated rooms, service with restrictions, supervision.
SAVE ⊠ 🛗 🛏 🖵 🏊

Best Western Inn at the Rogue Ⓗ ✿
(541) 582-2200. **$85-$110.** 8959 Rogue River Hwy 97527. I-5, exit 48, just nw. Int corridors. **Pets:** Other species. $20 daily fee/pet. Designated rooms, service with restrictions, supervision. SAVE ⊠ 🛏 🖵 🏊

Holiday Inn Express Grants Pass Ⓗ
(541) 471-6144. **$119-$149.** 105 NE Agness Ave 97526. I-5, exit 55, just nw. Int corridors. **Pets:** Large, other species. $10 daily fee/pet. Designated rooms, service with restrictions, supervision. SAVE ⊠ 🛏 🖵

Knights Inn Motel Ⓜ
(541) 479-5595. **$50-$85.** 104 SE 7th St 97526. I-5, exit 58, 1.7 mi s on SR 99, just e on G St, then just n. Ext corridors. **Pets:** Medium, dogs only. $10 one-time fee/pet. Service with restrictions, supervision.
SAVE ⊠

La Quinta Inn & Suites Grants Pass Ⓗ ✿
(541) 472-1808. **$65-$145.** 243 NE Morgan Ln 97526. I-5, exit 58, 0.4 mi s on SR 99, just e on Hillcrest Dr to SR 99 N, then just n. Int corridors. **Pets:** Medium, other species. Service with restrictions, supervision.
ASK ⊠ 🛗 🛏 🖵 🏊

Motel 6–#253 Ⓜ
(541) 474-1331. **$45-$65.** 1800 NE 7th St 97526. I-5, exit 58, 0.3 mi s on SR 99. Ext corridors. **Pets:** Other species. Service with restrictions, supervision. ⊠ 🛗 🛏 🏊

Redwood Motel Ⓗ ✿
(541) 476-0878. **$70-$352.** 815 NE 6th St 97526. I-5, exit 58, 1.2 mi s on SR 99. Ext corridors. **Pets:** Medium, dogs only. $200 deposit/room, $20 one-time fee/room. Designated rooms, service with restrictions, supervision. SAVE ⊠ 🛏 🖵 🏊

Riverside Inn Ⓗ
(541) 476-6873. **$125-$149, 3 day notice.** 986 SW 6th St 97526. I-5, exit 58, 2.5 mi s on SR 99. Ext corridors. **Pets:** Large, other species. $10 daily fee/pet. Designated rooms, service with restrictions, supervision.
SAVE ⊠ 🛏 🖵 🏊

Shilo Inn–Grants Pass Ⓗ ✿
(541) 479-8391. **$75-$159.** 1880 NW 6th St 97526. I-5, exit 58, 0.3 mi s on SR 99. Int corridors. **Pets:** Dogs only. $25 one-time fee/room. Designated rooms, service with restrictions, supervision.
SAVE ⊠ 🛗 🛏 🖵 🏊

Super 8–Grants Pass Ⓗ
(541) 474-0888. **$55-$108.** 1949 NE 7th St 97526. I-5, exit 58, 0.4 mi s on SR 99, just e on Hillcrest Dr to SR 99 N, then just n. Int corridors. **Pets:** Other species. $25 deposit/room. Service with restrictions, supervision. SAVE ⊠ 🛗 🛏 🖵 🏊

Sweet Breeze Inn Ⓜ
(541) 471-4434. **$60-$165.** 1627 NE 6th St 97526. I-5, exit 58, 0.5 mi s on SR 99. Ext/int corridors. **Pets:** Small. $50 deposit/room, $5 daily fee/pet. Designated rooms, service with restrictions, supervision.
SAVE ⊠ 🛏

Travelodge Ⓜ ✿
(541) 479-6611. **$59-$75.** 1950 NW Vine St 97526. I-5, exit 58, just s on SR 99. Ext corridors. **Pets:** Medium, other species. $10 one-time fee/pet. Designated rooms, service with restrictions, supervision.
SAVE ⊠ 🛏 🖵 🏊

HALSEY

Pioneer Villa Travelodge Ⓜ
(541) 369-2804. **$72-$85.** 33180 SR 228 97348. I-5, exit 216, just se. Ext corridors. **Pets:** Other species. $5 daily fee/pet. Service with restrictions, crate. ASK ⊠ 🛏 🖵 🍴 🏊

HERMISTON

▼▼◆ Comfort Inn & Suites Hermiston ⓗ
(541) 564-5911. **Call for rates.** 77514 SR 207 97838. I-84, exit 182, just nw. Int corridors. **Pets:** Accepted. ⊠ ⓖⱮ 🛏 🖵 ⇌

▼▼ Oak Tree Inn ⓗ
(541) 567-2330. **$69-$84.** 1110 SE 4th St 97838. 0.4 mi s on US 395, then just w. Int corridors. **Pets:** Small. $10 daily fee/pet. Service with restrictions, supervision. ⒶⓈⓀ ⊠ 🛏 🖵

▼▼ Oxford Suites ⓗ
(541) 564-8000. **$109-$119.** 1050 N 1st St 97838. 0.5 mi n on US 395. Int corridors. **Pets:** Small, dogs only. $25 one-time fee/pet. Designated rooms, service with restrictions, supervision.
ⒶⓈⓀ ⊠ ⓖⱮ 🛏 🖵 ⇌

HINES

◆◆ ▼▼▼ Best Western Rory & Ryan Inns ⓗ
(541) 573-5050. **$76-$91.** 534 US 20 N 97738. On US 20 (Central Oregon Hwy). Int corridors. **Pets:** Dogs only. $15 daily fee/pet. Designated rooms, service with restrictions, supervision.
ⓢⒶⓋⒺ ⊠ 🛏 🖵 ⇌

HOOD RIVER

◆◆ ▼▼▼▼ Best Western Hood River Inn ⓗ ❀
(541) 386-2200. **$95-$199.** 1108 E Marina Way 97031. I-84, exit 64, just ne. Int corridors. **Pets:** Dogs only. $12 daily fee/room. Designated rooms, service with restrictions, supervision.
ⓢⒶⓋⒺ ⊠ 🛏 🖵 ⓣ ⇌ ⊠

◆◆ ▼▼ Vagabond Lodge Ⓜ
(541) 386-2992. **$56-$109.** 4070 Westcliff Dr 97031. I-84, exit 62, 0.3 mi nw. Ext corridors. **Pets:** $5 daily fee/pet. Designated rooms.
ⓢⒶⓋⒺ ⊠ 🛏 🖵

JACKSONVILLE

◆◆ ▼▼▼ Jacksonville Inn Ⓒⓘ
(541) 899-1900. **$159-$465, 3 day notice.** 175 E California St 97530. On California St (SR 238); between 3rd and 4th sts; center. Ext/int corridors. **Pets:** Accepted. ⓢⒶⓋⒺ ⊠ 🛏 🖵 ⓣ

◆◆ ▼▼ Jacksonville's Magnolia Inn ⒷⒷ
(541) 899-0255. **$95-$165, 7 day notice.** 245 N 5th St 97530. At 5th (SR 238) and D sts. Int corridors. **Pets:** Accepted. ⓢⒶⓋⒺ ⊠ ⓖⱮ

▼▼ The Stage Lodge Ⓜ ❀
(541) 899-3953. **$110-$175, 7 day notice.** 830 N 5th St 97530. 0.5 mi ne of downtown. Ext corridors. **Pets:** Medium. $12 daily fee/pet. Designated rooms, service with restrictions, supervision. ⒶⓈⓀ ⊠ 🛏 🖵

JOHN DAY

◆◆ ▼▼▼ Best Western John Day Inn Ⓜ
(541) 575-1700. **$90-$100.** 315 W Main St 97845. Just w of jct US 26 and 395. Ext corridors. **Pets:** Accepted. ⓢⒶⓋⒺ ⊠ 🛏 🖵 ⇌

◆◆ ▼▼ Dreamers Lodge Ⓜ
(541) 575-0526. **$42-$99.** 144 N Canyon Blvd 97845. Just n of jct US 26 and 395. Ext corridors. **Pets:** Medium, dogs only. $5 daily fee/pet. Service with restrictions, supervision. ⓢⒶⓋⒺ ⊠ 🛏 🖵

KEIZER

◆◆ ▼▼▼ Keizer Renaissance Inn ⓗ
(503) 390-4733. **$79-$99.** 5188 Wittenberg Ln N 97303. I-5, exit 260B southbound; exit 260 northbound, 1.5 mi w via Chemawa Rd and Lockhaven Dr, just s on River Rd, just e on Claggett St NE, then just s. Int corridors. **Pets:** Dogs only. $100 deposit/room, $10 daily fee/pet. Service with restrictions, supervision. ⓢⒶⓋⒺ ⊠ ⓖⱮ 🛏 🖵 ⓣ ⇌ ⊠

KLAMATH FALLS

◆◆ ▼▼ Best Western Klamath Inn Ⓜ
(541) 882-1200. **$89-$139.** 4061 S 6th St 97603. Just w on 6th St (SR 140) from jct SR 140 E/39 S and SR 39 N/US 97 business route. Ext corridors. **Pets:** Other species. $10 daily fee/pet. Service with restrictions, supervision. ⓢⒶⓋⒺ ⊠ 🛏 🖵 ⇌

◆◆ ▼▼▼ Days Inn Klamath Falls Ⓜ
(541) 882-8864. **$69-$129.** 3612 S 6th St 97603. 0.3 mi w on 6th St (SR 140) from jct SR 140 E/39 S and SR 39 N/US 97 business route. Ext corridors. **Pets:** Accepted. ⓢⒶⓋⒺ ⊠ 🛏 🖵 ⇌ ⊠

◆◆ ▼ Econo Lodge Ⓜ ❀
(541) 884-7735. **$35-$110.** 75 Main St 97601. US 97, exit City Center Dr, 1.3 mi s. Ext corridors. **Pets:** Medium. $10 daily fee/pet. Designated rooms, service with restrictions, supervision. ⓢⒶⓋⒺ ⊠ 🛏 🖵

◆◆ ◆ Golden West Motel Ⓜ
(541) 882-1758. **$42-$68.** 6402 S 6th St 97603. On S 6th St (SR 140) at eastern edge of town. Ext corridors. **Pets:** Accepted. ⓢⒶⓋⒺ ⊠ 🛏

◆◆ ▼▼ Majestic Inn & Suites Ⓜ
(541) 883-7771. **$35-$105.** 5543 S 6th St 97603. 1 mi e on 6th St (SR 140) from jct SR 140 E/39 S and SR 39 N/US 97 business route. Ext corridors. **Pets:** Accepted. ⓢⒶⓋⒺ ⊠ 🛏

◆◆ ▼▼ Maverick Motel Ⓜ
(541) 882-6688. **$39-$109.** 1220 Main St 97601. US 97 N, exit City Center, 0.3 mi e. Ext corridors. **Pets:** $6 daily fee/pet. Designated rooms, service with restrictions, supervision. ⓢⒶⓋⒺ ⊠ 🛏

◆◆ ▼▼ Microtel Inn & Suites ⓗ
(541) 273-0206. **$69-$109.** 2716 Dakota Ct 97603. Jct US 97, 2.7 mi e on 6th St (SR 140), 1 mi n on Washburn Way, just e on Laverne Ave, then just s on Brooke Dr. Int corridors. **Pets:** Large, other species. $35 one-time fee/pet. Designated rooms, service with restrictions, crate.
ⓢⒶⓋⒺ ⊠ ⓖⱮ 🛏 🖵 ⇌

◆ Motel 6–226 Ⓜ
(541) 884-2110. **$45-$65.** 5136 S 6th St 97603. 0.5 mi e on 6th St E (SR 140) from jct SR 39/US 97 business route. Ext corridors. **Pets:** Other species. Service with restrictions, supervision. ⊠ ⓖⱮ 🛏 ⇌

◆◆ ▼▼ Oregon 8 Motel Ⓜ ❀
(541) 883-3431. **$35-$99.** 5225 Hwy 97 N 97601. Between MM 270 and 271; east side of highway. Ext corridors. **Pets:** Medium. $10 daily fee/pet. Designated rooms, service with restrictions, supervision.
ⓢⒶⓋⒺ ⊠ 🛏 🖵

◆◆ ▼▼ Quality Inn Ⓜ ❀
(541) 882-4666. **$65-$150.** 100 Main St 97601. Just e of US 97, exit City Center. Ext corridors. **Pets:** Medium. $10 daily fee/pet. Designated rooms, service with restrictions, supervision.
ⓢⒶⓋⒺ ⊠ ⓖⱮ 🛏 🖵 ⓣ ⇌

▼▼▼ The Running y Ranch ⓗ
(541) 850-5500. **Call for rates.** 5500 Running y Rd 97601. On 6th St (SR 140), 7.2 mi n from jct US 66 and SR 140. Int corridors.
Pets: Accepted. ⊠ ⓖⱮ 🛏 🖵 ⓣ ⇌ ⊠

◆◆ ▼▼▼ Shilo Inn Suites Hotel-Klamath Falls ⓗ ❀
(541) 885-7980. **$105-$210.** 2500 Almond St 97601-1119. North end of US 97. Int corridors. **Pets:** Dogs only. $25 one-time fee/room. Designated rooms, service with restrictions, supervision.
ⓢⒶⓋⒺ ⊠ ⓖⱮ 🛏 🖵 ⓣ ⇌ ⊠

◆ Super 8 ⓗ ❀
(541) 884-8880. **$74-$86.** 3805 Hwy 97 97601. On US 97, 2 mi n. Int corridors. **Pets:** Other species. $10 one-time fee/room. Service with restrictions, supervision. ⒶⓈⓀ ⊠ ⓖⱮ 🛏

LA GRANDE

AAA ▼▼ Americas Best Value Sandman Inn **H** ❖
(541) 963-3707. **$80-$85.** 2410 E R Ave 97850. I-84, exit 261, just s on Island Ave, then just n. Int corridors. **Pets:** Large. $25 one-time fee/room. Designated rooms, service with restrictions, supervision.

⛨ ✕ 🛏 ▣ ⇋

AAA ▼ Royal Motor Inn **M**
(541) 963-4154. **$40-$59.** 1510 Adams Ave 97850. I-84, exit 265 (US 30), exit La Grande; downtown. Ext corridors. **Pets:** Dogs only. $10 daily fee/pet. Designated rooms, service with restrictions, supervision.

⛨ ✕ 🛏

LAKEVIEW

AAA ▼▼▼ Best Western Skyline Motor Lodge **M**
(541) 947-2194. **$90-$150.** 414 N G St 97630. Jct US 395 and SR 140. Ext corridors. **Pets:** Accepted. ⛨ ✕ 🛏 ▣ ⇋

LA PINE

AAA ▼▼▼ Best Western Newberry Station **H**
(541) 536-5130. **$90-$150.** 16515 Reed Rd 97739. Just off US 97; north end of town. Int corridors. **Pets:** Small, dogs only. $10 one-time fee/room. Service with restrictions, supervision. ⛨ ✕ 🛏 ▣ ⇋

LINCOLN BEACH

AAA ▼▼▼ ▼▼▼ Salishan Spa & Golf Resort **H** ❖
(541) 764-2371. **$159-$309, 3 day notice.** 7760 US 101 N 97388. Just e of US 101; center. Ext corridors. **Pets:** Other species. $35 one-time fee/room. Designated rooms, service with restrictions, supervision.

⛨ ✕ 🛏 ▣ ⇋ 🍴 ⇋ ✕ ⛬

LINCOLN CITY

▼▼▼ Ashley Inn & Suites **H**
(541) 996-7500. **$69-$199.** 3430 NE US 101 97367. Just n of downtown. Int corridors. **Pets:** Medium, other species. $25 daily fee/pet. Designated rooms, service with restrictions. ⟨ASK⟩ ✕ 🛏 ▣ ⇋ ✕

AAA ▼▼▼▼ The Coho Oceanfront Lodge **H** ❖
(541) 994-3684. **$65-$290.** 1635 NW Harbor Ave 97367. US 101, exit N 17th St, just w. Ext corridors. **Pets:** Small, other species. $20 daily fee/pet. Designated rooms, service with restrictions, supervision.

⛨ ✕ 🛏 ▣ ⇋ ✕ ⛬

AAA ▼ Comfort Inn & Suites **H**
(541) 994-8155. **$89-$349.** 136 NE US 101 97367. Just n of D River. Int corridors. **Pets:** Accepted. ⛨ ✕ 🛏 ▣ ⇋

AAA ▼ Econo Lodge **H**
(541) 994-5281. **Call for rates.** 1713 NW 21st St 97367. US 101, exit NW 21st St, just w. Int corridors. **Pets:** Small, dogs only. $10 daily fee/pet. Designated rooms, service with restrictions, supervision.

⛨ ✕ 🛏 ▣ ⛬

▼▼ Looking Glass Inn **H** ❖
(541) 996-3996. **$79-$249, 3 day notice.** 861 SW 51st St 97367. US 101, exit 51st St; south end of town. Ext corridors. **Pets:** Dogs only. $10 daily fee/pet. Designated rooms, service with restrictions, crate.

⟨ASK⟩ ✕ 🛏 ▣ ⛬

▼ Motel 6–#4172 **H**
(541) 996-9900. **$46-$100.** 3517 NW US 101 97367. North end of downtown. Int corridors. **Pets:** Other species. Service with restrictions, supervision. ✕ ⌂M 🛏

AAA ▼▼▼▼ The O'dysius Hotel **H** ❖
(541) 994-4121. **$159-$365.** 120 NW Inlet Ave 97367. On US 101 at D River; center. Int corridors. **Pets:** Small, dogs only. $25 daily fee/pet. Service with restrictions, supervision. ⛨ ✕ 🛏 ▣ ⛬

AAA ▼▼▼ Palace Inn & Suites **H**
(541) 996-9466. **$69-$209.** 550 SE US 101 97367. Center. Int corridors. **Pets:** Small, dogs only. $25 one-time fee/pet. Designated rooms, service with restrictions, supervision. ⛨ ✕ 🛏 ▣ ✕

MADRAS

AAA ▼▼▼ Best Western Madras Inn **M**
(541) 475-6141. **$72-$120.** 12 SW 4th St 97741. On US 97/26 southbound, at B and 4th sts; downtown. Ext corridors. **Pets:** Medium, other species. $20 daily fee/pet. Designated rooms, service with restrictions, supervision. ⛨ ✕ ⌂M 🛏 ▣ ⇋

AAA ▼ Budget Inn **M**
(541) 475-3831. **$55-$99.** 133 NE 5th St 97741. On US 97/26 N; downtown. Ext corridors. **Pets:** Large, other species. $10 daily fee/pet. Service with restrictions, supervision. ⛨ ✕ 🛏

▼▼▼ Inn at Cross Keys Station **H**
(541) 475-5800. **$76-$146.** 66 NW Cedar St 97741. On US 26; north end of town. Int corridors. **Pets:** Accepted.

⟨ASK⟩ ✕ ⌂M 🛏 ▣ ⇋

MCMINNVILLE

AAA ▼ Americas Best Value Inn & Suites **M**
(503) 472-5187. **$70-$90.** 381 NE SR 99 W 97128. North end of SR 99 W. Ext corridors. **Pets:** Accepted. ⛨ ✕ 🛏 ▣

AAA ▼▼▼ Best Western Vineyard Inn **H**
(503) 472-4900. **$81-$141.** 2035 S SR 99 W 97128. Jct SR 99 W and 18. Int corridors. **Pets:** Accepted. ⛨ ✕ 🛏 ▣ ⇋

AAA ▼▼▼ Comfort Inn & Suites **H**
(503) 472-1700. **$95-$140.** 2520 SE Stratus Ave 97128. Jct SR 99 W, 3.6 mi e on SR 18. Int corridors. **Pets:** Accepted.

⛨ ✕ ⌂M 🛏 ▣ ⇋

AAA ▼▼▼ Red Lion Inn & Suites **H**
(503) 472-1500. **$84-$122.** 2535 NE Cumulus Ave 97128. Jct SR 99 W, 2.7 mi e on SR 18. Int corridors. **Pets:** Other species. $20 one-time fee/room. Service with restrictions, supervision.

⛨ ✕ ⌂M 🛏 ▣ ⇋ ✕

MEDFORD

AAA ▼▼▼ Best Western Horizon Inn **H**
(541) 779-5085. **$99-$109.** 1154 E Barnett Rd 97504. I-5, exit 27 (Barnett Rd), just ne. Ext corridors. **Pets:** Other species. $10 daily fee/pet. Designated rooms, service with restrictions, supervision.

⛨ ✕ 🛏 ▣ ⇋ ✕

AAA ▼▼▼ Candlewood Suites Medford Airport **H**
(541) 772-2800. **$109-$159.** 3548 Heathrow Way 97504. I-5, exit 33, 1.5 mi se via E Pine St and Biddle Rd, just w on O'Hare Pkwy, then just n. Int corridors. **Pets:** Other species. $10 daily fee/room. Service with restrictions. ⛨ ✕ ⌂M 🛏 ▣

▼▼▼ Homewood Suites by Hilton **H**
(541) 779-9800. **$79-$134.** 2010 Hospitality Way 97504. I-5, exit 27 (Barnett Rd), 0.4 mi e on Barnett Rd, just s on Ellendale Dr, then just w. Int corridors. **Pets:** Medium, other species. $75 one-time fee/room. Designated rooms, service with restrictions, supervision.

✕ ⌂M 🛏 ▣ ⇋ ✕

▼ Motel 6-Medford North–739 **M**
(541) 779-0550. **$53-$63.** 2400 Biddle Rd 97504. I-5, exit 30 southbound, just ne on Crater Lake Hwy, follow signs to Biddle Rd/Airport, then just n; exit northbound, follow signs to Biddle Rd/Airport, then just n. Ext corridors. **Pets:** Other species. Service with restrictions, supervision.

✕ ⌂M 🛏

▼ Motel 6-Medford South–#89 **M**
(541) 773-4290. **$45-$55.** 950 Alba Dr 97504. I-5, exit 27 (Barnett Rd), just w, then just n. Ext corridors. **Pets:** Other species. Service with restrictions, supervision. ✕ ⌂M 🛏 ⇋

AAA ▼▼ Quality Inn & Suites **H** ❖
(541) 779-0050. **$68-$160.** 1950 Biddle Rd 97504. I-5, exit 30 southbound, just ne on Crater Lake Hwy, follow signs to Biddle Rd/Airport, then just s; exit northbound, follow signs to Biddle Rd/Airport, then just s. Int corridors. **Pets:** Other species. $10 daily fee/pet. Designated rooms, service with restrictions, supervision. ⛨ ✕ ⌂M 🛏 ▣ ⇋ ✕

Red Lion Hotel Medford 🅗

(541) 779-5811. **$90-$129.** 200 N Riverside Ave 97501. I-5, exit 27 (City Center), 0.4 mi w on Garfield St, then 1.7 mi n on S Pacific Hwy. Ext corridors. **Pets:** Other species. $20 one-time fee/room. Service with restrictions, supervision. 🆂🅰🆅🅴 ✖ 👟ᴹ 🍴 💻 📶 🍴 🏊

Shilo Inn–Medford 🅗 🐾

(541) 770-5151. **$80-$160.** 2111 Biddle Rd 97504. I-5, exit 30 southbound, just ne on Crater Lake Hwy, follow signs to Biddle Rd/Airport, then just s; exit northbound, follow signs to Biddle Rd/Airport, then just s. Int corridors. **Pets:** Dogs only. $25 one-time fee/room. Designated rooms, service with restrictions, supervision. 🆂🅰🆅🅴 ✖ 🍴 💻 ✖

TownePlace Suites by Marriott 🅗

(541) 842-5757. **$134-$164.** 1395 Center Dr 97501. I-5, exit 27 (City Center), just w on Garfield St, then just n. Int corridors. **Pets:** Medium, dogs only. $25 daily fee/pet. Supervision. ✖ 👟ᴹ 🍴 💻 📶

MERLIN

Morrison's Rogue River Lodge 🅒🅐

(541) 476-3825. **$135-$535, 45 day notice.** 8500 Galice Rd 97532. I-5, exit 61, 12 mi w on Merlin-Galice Rd. Ext/int corridors. **Pets:** Medium. $10 daily fee/pet. Service with restrictions, crate.
✖ 🍴 💻 🍴 📶 ✖

MYRTLE POINT

Myrtle Trees Motel Ⓜ

(541) 572-5811. **$65-$75, 5 day notice.** 1010 8th St (SR 42) 97458. On SR 42, 0.5 mi e. Ext corridors. **Pets:** Accepted. 🆂🅰🆅🅴 ✖ 🍴 🅰🅲

NEWBERG

Shilo Inn Suites–Newberg 🅗 🐾

(503) 537-0303. **$80-$175.** 501 Sitka Ave 97132. Northeast of center on Portland Rd (SR 99 W). Int corridors. **Pets:** Dogs only. $25 one-time fee/room. Designated rooms, service with restrictions, supervision.
🆂🅰🆅🅴 ✖ 🍴 💻 📶 ✖

NEWPORT

The Best Western Agate Beach Inn 🅗 🐾

(541) 265-9411. **$100-$225.** 3019 N Coast Hwy 97365. Jct US 20, 1.5 mi n on US 101. Int corridors. **Pets:** $20 one-time fee/pet. Designated rooms, service with restrictions, supervision.
🆂🅰🆅🅴 ✖ 🍴 💻 🍴 📶 ✖ 🅰🅲

The Landing at Newport 🅒🅞 🐾

(541) 574-6777. **$109-$388.** 890 SE Bay Blvd 97365. Jct US 101, 0.5 mi e on US 20, then 0.3 mi s on John Moore Rd. Ext corridors. **Pets:** $75 deposit/room, $10 daily fee/room, $25 one-time fee/room. Designated rooms, service with restrictions, supervision. 🆂🅰🆅🅴 ✖ 🍴 💻 🅰🅲

La Quinta Inn & Suites Newport 🅗 🐾

(541) 867-7727. **$85-$139.** 45 SE 32nd St 97365. US 101, just s of Yaquina Bay Bridge. Int corridors. **Pets:** Medium, other species. Service with restrictions, supervision. 🅰🆂🅺 ✖ 👟ᴹ 🍴 💻 📶 ✖

Shilo Inn Suites Oceanfront Hotel–Newport 🅗 🐾

(541) 265-7701. **$105-$270.** 536 SW Elizabeth St 97365. Jct US 20, 0.5 mi s on US 101, then just w on SW Falls St. Ext/int corridors. **Pets:** Dogs only. $25 one-time fee/room. Designated rooms, service with restrictions, supervision. 🆂🅰🆅🅴 ✖ 🍴 💻 🍴 📶 🅰🅲

Waves of Newport Motel and Vacation Rentals 🅗

(541) 265-4661. **$68-$119, 3 day notice.** 820 NW Coast St 97365. Jct US 20, 0.5 mi n on US 101, just w on NW 11th St, then just s on Spring St. Ext corridors. **Pets:** Dogs only. $10 daily fee/room. Service with restrictions, supervision. ✖ 🍴 💻 📶 🅰🅲

The Whaler Motel Ⓜ 🐾

(541) 265-9261. **$109-$169.** 155 SW Elizabeth St 97365. Jct US 20, just s on US 101, then just w on SW 2nd St. Ext corridors. **Pets:** Dogs only. $10 daily fee/pet. Designated rooms, service with restrictions, supervision.
🆂🅰🆅🅴 ✖ 👟ᴹ 🍴 💻 📶 🅰🅲

NORTH BEND

Comfort Inn Coos Bay 🅗

(541) 756-3191. **$89-$180.** 1503 Virginia Ave 97459. 0.5 mi w of US 101. Ext/int corridors. **Pets:** Accepted. 🅰🆂🅺 ✖ 👟ᴹ 🍴 💻

The Mill Casino & Hotel 🅗 🐾

(541) 756-8800. **$108-$135.** 3201 Tremont Ave 97459. 0.7 mi n on US 101; on bayfront. Int corridors. **Pets:** Medium, dogs only. $25 one-time fee/room. Designated rooms, service with restrictions, crate.
🅰🆂🅺 ✖ 👟ᴹ 🍴 💻 🍴 📶

OAKLAND

Best Western Rice Hill Ⓜ

(541) 849-3335. **$77.** 621 John Long Rd 97462. I-5, exit 148, just e. Ext corridors. **Pets:** Other species. $10 daily fee/room. Supervision.
🆂🅰🆅🅴 ✖ 🍴 💻 📶 ✖

OAKRIDGE

Best Western Oakridge Inn Ⓜ

(541) 782-2212. **$86-$152.** 47433 SR 58 97463. West end of SR 58. Ext corridors. **Pets:** Medium. $10 daily fee/pet. Designated rooms, service with restrictions, supervision. 🆂🅰🆅🅴 ✖ 🍴 💻 📶

Cascade Motel Ⓜ

(541) 782-2489. **$56-$75.** 47487 SR 58 97463. Center. Ext corridors. **Pets:** Medium, dogs only. $10 one-time fee/room. Service with restrictions, supervision. 🆂🅰🆅🅴 ✖ 🍴

ONTARIO

Holiday Inn–Ontario 🅗

(541) 889-8621. **$79-$119.** 1249 Tapadera Ave 97914. I-84, exit 376B, just nw. Int corridors. **Pets:** Accepted. 🆂🅰🆅🅴 ✖ 🍴 💻 🍴 📶

Rodeway Inn Ⓜ 🐾

(541) 889-9188. **$58-$68.** 615 E Idaho Ave 97914. I-84, exit 376A, just sw. Ext corridors. **Pets:** Medium, other species. $5 daily fee/pet. Designated rooms, service with restrictions, supervision.
🆂🅰🆅🅴 ✖ 🍴 💻

Sleep Inn 🅗

(541) 881-0007. **$59-$129.** 1221 SE 1st Ave 97914. I-84, exit 376B, just ne. Int corridors. **Pets:** Dogs only. $10 daily fee/pet. Designated rooms, service with restrictions, supervision. 🆂🅰🆅🅴 ✖ 👟ᴹ 🍴 💻 📶

PACIFIC CITY

Inn at Cape Kiwanda 🅗 🐾

(503) 965-7001. **$129-$359.** 33105 Cape Kiwanda Dr 97135. Just w on Pacific Ave, 1 mi n. Ext corridors. **Pets:** $20 daily fee/pet. Designated rooms, service with restrictions, crate.
🆂🅰🆅🅴 ✖ 👟ᴹ 🍴 💻 🍴 🅰🅲

Pacific City Inn Ⓜ

(503) 965-6464. **$79-$99, 3 day notice.** 35280 Brooten Rd 97135. Center. Ext corridors. **Pets:** Dogs only. $16 daily fee/pet. Designated rooms, supervision. 🆂🅰🆅🅴 ✖ 🍴 💻 🍴 🅰🅲

PENDLETON

Americas Best Value Inn Ⓜ

(541) 276-1400. **$79-$99.** 201 SW Court Ave 97801. I-84, exit 210 (SR 11), 0.7 mi ne on SE 3rd St, then 0.6 mi w. Ext corridors. **Pets:** Dogs only. $15 one-time fee/room. Service with restrictions, crate.
🆂🅰🆅🅴 ✖ 🍴 💻 📶

Best Western Pendleton Inn 🅗

(541) 276-2135. **$95-$125.** 400 SE Nye Ave 97801. I-84, exit 210 (SR 11), just se. Int corridors. **Pets:** Small. $10 one-time fee/pet. Supervision.
🆂🅰🆅🅴 ✖ 👟ᴹ 🍴 💻 📶

Holiday Inn Express 🅗 🐾

(541) 966-6520. **$89-$129.** 600 SE Nye Ave 97801. I-84, exit 210 (SR 11), just se. Int corridors. **Pets:** Medium, dogs only. $25 one-time fee/pet. Designated rooms, service with restrictions, supervision.
🆂🅰🆅🅴 ✖ 🍴 💻 📶

▼ Motel 6–#349 [M]
(541) 276-3160. **$45-$55.** 325 SE Nye Ave 97801. I-84, exit 210 (SR 11), just se. Ext corridors. **Pets:** Other species. Service with restrictions, supervision. [X] [🐾] [➜]

▼▼▼▼ Oxford Suites [H] ✿
(541) 276-6000. **$109-$195.** 2400 SW Court Pl 97801. I-84, exit 209, just n on SW Emigrant Ave, just nw on SW 20th St, then just sw to SW Court Pl. Int corridors. **Pets:** Other species. $20 one-time fee/room. Designated rooms, service with restrictions, supervision.
[ASK] [X] [🐾M] [🛏] [💻] [➜] [X]

🌐 ▼▼▼▼ Red Lion Hotel Pendleton [H]
(541) 276-6111. **$109-$159.** 304 SE Nye Ave 97801. I-84, exit 210 (SR 11), just sw. Ext/int corridors. **Pets:** Other species. $20 one-time fee/room. Service with restrictions, supervision.
[SAVE] [X] [🛏] [💻] [🍴] [➜] [X]

▼▼ Rugged Country Lodge [H]
(541) 966-6800. **$72.** 1807 SE Court Ave 97801. I-84, exit 210 (SR 11), 0.7 mi ne on SE 3rd Dr, then 0.4 mi e. Ext/int corridors. **Pets:** Accepted.
[ASK] [X] [🛏] [💻]

▼▼ Super 8 [H]
(541) 276-8881. **Call for rates.** 601 SE Nye Ave 97801. I-84, exit 210 (SR 11), just se. Int corridors. **Pets:** Accepted. [X] [🛏] [💻] [➜]

🌐 ▼▼▼ Travelodge [M] ✿
(541) 276-7531. **$65-$80.** 411 SW Dorion Ave 97801. I-84, exit 209, 0.9 mi ne on SW Frazer Ave, then just nw on SW 4th St. Ext corridors. **Pets:** Large, dogs only. $10 daily fee/pet. Designated rooms, no service.
[SAVE] [X] [🛏] [💻]

PORTLAND METROPOLITAN AREA

BEAVERTON

▼▼▼ Comfort Inn & Suites [H]
(503) 643-9100. **$70-$160.** 13455 SW Tualatin Valley Hwy 97005. SR 217, exit 2A (Canyon Rd/SR 8), 1 mi w. Int corridors. **Pets:** Accepted.
[ASK] [X] [🛏] [💻] [➜]

▼▼▼▼ Homewood Suites By Hilton [H]
(503) 614-0900. **$129-$189.** 15525 NW Gateway Ct 97006. US 26, exit 65, just sw on NW Cornell Rd, just s on NW 158th Ave, just se on NW Waterhouse Ave, then just e. Int corridors. **Pets:** $15 daily fee/pet. Designated rooms, service with restrictions, supervision.
[X] [🐾M] [🛏] [💻] [➜]

🌐 ▼▼▼▼ Phoenix Inn Suites–Beaverton/Hillsboro [H]
(503) 614-8100. **$89-$149.** 15402 NW Cornell Rd 97006. US 26, exit 65, just ne. Int corridors. **Pets:** Accepted.
[SAVE] [X] [🐾M] [🛏] [💻] [➜] [X]

🌐 ▼▼▼ Shilo Inn Hotel &
Suites-Portland/Beaverton [H] ✿
(503) 297-2551. **$107-$187.** 9900 SW Canyon Rd 97225-2996. SR 217, exit 2A (Canyon Rd/SR 8), 0.7 mi e. Int corridors. **Pets:** Dogs only. $25 one-time fee/room. Designated rooms, service with restrictions, supervision. [SAVE] [X] [🛏] [💻] [🍴] [➜]

CLACKAMAS

▼▼▼ Comfort Suites [H]
(503) 723-3450. **$84-$129.** 15929 SE McKinley Ave 97015. I-205, exit 12 northbound; exit 12B southbound, just w. Int corridors. **Pets:** Large, other species. $30 one-time fee/room. Service with restrictions, supervision.
[ASK] [X] [🛏] [💻] [➜] [X]

🌐 ▼▼▼ Howard Johnson Clackamas Inn [H] ✿
(503) 652-1500. **$50-$109.** 12855 SE 97th Ave 97015. I-205, exit 14, follow signs for Sunnyside Rd E, just e, then just s. Ext corridors. **Pets:** Large, other species. $10 daily fee/room. Service with restrictions.
[SAVE] [X] [🛏] [💻] [➜]

GLADSTONE

▼▼▼ Oxford Suites [H]
(503) 722-7777. **$95-$125.** 75 82nd Dr 97027. I-205, exit 11, 0.3 mi sw. Int corridors. **Pets:** Accepted. [ASK] [X] [🛏] [💻] [➜] [X]

GRESHAM

🌐 ▼▼▼ Best Western Pony Soldier Inn [H]
(503) 665-1591. **$99-$169, 7 day notice.** 1060 NE Cleveland Ave 97030. I-84, exit 14 (Fairview Pkwy), 0.9 mi s, 0.4 mi e on NE Glisan St, 1.2 mi s on NE 223rd Ave, 0.7 mi e on Burnside Rd, then just s. Int corridors. **Pets:** Accepted. [SAVE] [X] [🛏] [💻] [➜] [X]

🌐 ▼▼▼ Days Inn & Suites [H]
(503) 465-1515. **$74-$114.** 24124 SE Stark St 97030. I-84, exit 16, 1.5 mi s on NE 238th Ave/NE 242nd Dr, then just w. Int corridors. **Pets:** Dogs only. $10 daily fee/pet. Designated rooms, service with restrictions, supervision. [SAVE] [X] [🛏] [💻] [➜]

▼▼ Days Inn-Portland East/Gresham [H]
(503) 618-8400. **$64-$100.** 2261 NE 181st Ave 97230. I-84, exit 13, just sw. Int corridors. **Pets:** Accepted. [ASK] [X] [🐾M] [🛏] [💻] [➜]

▼▼▼ Extended StayAmerica Portland/Gresham [H]
(503) 661-0226. **$69-$79.** 17777 NE Sacramento St 97230. I-84, exit 13, 0.3 mi s on NE 181st Ave, just s on NE San Rafael St, then just n on NE 178th Ave. Int corridors. **Pets:** Other species. $25 daily fee/room. Designated rooms, service with restrictions, crate.
[ASK] [X] [🐾M] [🛏] [💻]

▼▼▼ Holiday Inn Portland/Gresham [H]
(503) 907-1777. **$95-$195.** 2752 NE Hogan Dr 97030. I-84, exit 16, 1.8 mi s on NE 238th Ave/NE Hogan Dr. Int corridors. **Pets:** Small, dogs only. $35 daily fee/pet. Designated rooms, service with restrictions, supervision. [ASK] [X] [🐾M] [🛏] [💻] [🍴] [➜]

🌐 ▼▼▼ Howard Johnson Gresham [H]
(503) 666-9545. **$49-$179.** 1572 NE Burnside Rd 97030. I-84, exit 16, 2.7 mi s on NE 238th/NE 242nd drs, just w on Division St, then just se; I-205, exit 19, 5.5 mi e on Division St, then just se. Int corridors. **Pets:** Large. $20 daily fee/pet. Designated rooms, service with restrictions, crate. [SAVE] [X] [🛏] [💻] [➜]

🌐 ▼▼▼ Super 8 [H]
(503) 661-5100. **$64-$89.** 121 NE 181st Ave 97230. I-84, exit 13, 1 mi s. Int corridors. **Pets:** Medium, dogs only. $10 daily fee/pet. Designated rooms, service with restrictions, supervision. [SAVE] [X] [🛏] [💻]

HILLSBORO

▼▼ Extended StayAmerica-Portland-Beaverton [H]
(503) 439-1515. **$69-$79.** 18665 NW Elder Ct 97006. US 26, exit 64, 0.7 mi s on NW 185th Ave, then just w. Int corridors. **Pets:** Other species. $25 daily fee/room. Service with restrictions, crate.
[ASK] [X] [🛏] [💻]

▼▼ Extended Stay Deluxe-Portland-Hillsboro-NW Cornell
Rd [H]
(503) 439-0706. **$89.** 19311 NW Cornell Rd 97124. US 26, exit 64, 0.5 mi s on NW 185th Ave, then 0.4 mi w. Int corridors. **Pets:** Other species. $25 daily fee/room. Designated rooms, service with restrictions, crate.
[ASK] [X] [🛏] [💻] [➜]

🌐 ▼▼▼▼ Larkspur Landing Hillsboro/Portland [H]
(503) 681-2121. **$99-$184.** 3133 NE Shute Rd 97124. US 26, exit 61, 1.1 mi s. Int corridors. **Pets:** Accepted. [SAVE] [X] [🛏] [💻] [X]

▼▼▼ **Residence Inn by Marriott Portland West** 🅗
(503) 531-3200. **$179-$219.** 18855 NW Tanasbourne Dr 97124. US 26, exit 64, just s on NW 185th Ave, then just w. Ext/int corridors. **Pets:** Accepted. ✕ 🔊 🍴 📺 🏊 ✕

▼▼▼ **TownePlace Suites by Marriott-Portland Hillsboro** 🅗
(503) 268-6000. **$152-$186.** 6550 NE Brighton St 97124. US 26, exit 62A westbound; exit 62 eastbound, 1 mi s on Cornelius Pass Rd, 0.7 mi w on NE Cornell Rd, just n on NW 229th Ave, then just w. Ext/int corridors. **Pets:** Accepted. ✕ 🍴 📺 🏊 ✕

KING CITY

ⓐⓐⓐ ▼▼▼ **Best Western Northwind Inn & Suites** 🅗
(503) 431-2100. **$91-$179.** 16105 SW Pacific Hwy 97224. I-5, exit 292, just nw on SR 217, exit 6 (SR 99W), then 2.5 mi s. Int corridors. **Pets:** Medium. $20 daily fee/pet. Service with restrictions, supervision. SAVE ✕ 🔊 🍴 📺 🏊

LAKE OSWEGO

ⓐⓐⓐ ▼▼▼ **Crowne Plaza Hotel** 🅗 ❀
(503) 624-8400. **$79-$249.** 14811 Kruse Oaks Dr 97035. I-5, exit 292B northbound; exit 292 southbound, just e on Kruse Way, then just s. Int corridors. **Pets:** $25 one-time fee/room. Designated rooms, service with restrictions, supervision. SAVE ✕ 🔊 🍴 📺 🏊 ✕

ⓐⓐⓐ ▼▼▼ **Phoenix Inn Suites-Lake Oswego** 🅗 ❀
(503) 624-7400. **$84-$164.** 14905 SW Bangy Rd 97035. I-5, exit 292B northbound; exit 292 southbound, just s. Int corridors. **Pets:** Dogs only. $20 daily fee/room. Service with restrictions, crate.
SAVE ✕ 🔊 🍴 📺 🏊

▼▼▼ **Residence Inn by Marriott-Portland South** 🅗 ❀
(503) 684-2603. **$149-$174.** 15200 SW Bangy Rd 97035. I-5, exit 292B northbound; exit 292 southbound, 0.3 mi s. Ext corridors. **Pets:** Other species. $10 daily fee/room. ✕ 🔊 🍴 📺 🏊 ✕

MILWAUKIE

ⓐⓐⓐ ▼▼▼ **Econo Lodge Suites Inn** Ⓜ
(503) 654-2222. **$55-$79.** 17330 SE McLoughlin Blvd 97267. I-205, exit 9, 2.3 mi n on SR 99 E (McLoughlin Blvd). Ext corridors. **Pets:** Small, dogs only. $10 daily fee/pet. Designated rooms, service with restrictions, supervision. SAVE ✕ 🍴 🏊

OREGON CITY

ⓐⓐⓐ ▼▼▼ **Best Western Rivershore Hotel** 🅗 ❀
(503) 655-7141. **$95-$115.** 1900 Clackamette Dr 97045. I-205, exit 9, just n. Int corridors. **Pets:** Other species. $5 daily fee/pet. Service with restrictions, supervision.
SAVE ✕ 🔊 🍴 📺 🍴 🏊 ✕

PORTLAND

ⓐⓐⓐ ▼▼▼ **aloft Portland Airport at Cascade Station** 🅗 ❀
(503) 200-5678. **$79-$189.** 9920 NE Cascades Pkwy 97220. I-205, exit 24A northbound; exit 24 southbound, 0.5 mi w on Airport Way, 0.5 mi s on NE Mt Hood Ave, then just e. Int corridors. **Pets:** Medium. Designated rooms, service with restrictions, supervision.
SAVE ✕ 🔊 🍴 📺 🏊

ⓐⓐⓐ ▼▼ ▼▼ **The Benson Hotel, a Coast Hotel** 🅗
(503) 228-2000. **$129-$359.** 309 SW Broadway 97205. At SW Broadway and Oak St. Int corridors. **Pets:** Accepted. SAVE ✕ 🔊 📺 🍴

ⓐⓐⓐ ▼▼▼ **Best Western Inn At The Meadows** 🅗
(503) 286-9600. **$112-$151.** 1215 N Hayden Meadows Dr 97217. I-5, exit 306B, just e. Int corridors. **Pets:** Accepted. SAVE ✕ 🍴 📺

ⓐⓐⓐ ▼▼▼ **Best Western Pony Soldier Inn-Airport** 🅗 ❀
(503) 256-1504. **$125-$160.** 9901 NE Sandy Blvd 97220. I-205, exit 23A, just e. Int corridors. **Pets:** Small. $10 daily fee/pet. Designated rooms, service with restrictions, supervision.
SAVE ✕ 🔊 🍴 📺 🏊 ✕

ⓐⓐⓐ ▼▼▼ **Days Inn-Portland** 🅗
(503) 289-1800. **$72-$81.** 9930 N Whitaker Rd 97217. I-5, exit 306B, just e. Int corridors. **Pets:** Accepted. SAVE ✕ 🍴 📺

ⓐⓐⓐ ▼▼▼ **The Heathman Hotel** 🅗
(503) 241-4100. **$209-$895, 3 day notice.** 1001 SW Broadway 97205. At SW Broadway and Salmon St. Int corridors. **Pets:** $35 daily fee/room. Service with restrictions, supervision. SAVE ✕ 🔊 📺 🍴

ⓐⓐⓐ ▼▼▼ **Hilton Portland & Executive Tower** 🅗 ❀
(503) 226-1611. **$119-$229.** 921 SW 6th Ave 97204. I-405, exit 1B (6th Ave); at 6th Ave and Taylor St. Int corridors. **Pets:** Medium. $25 one-time fee/pet. Service with restrictions, supervision.
ECO SAVE ✕ 🍴 📺 🍴 🏊 ✕

▼▼▼ **Holiday Inn Express-I-205 Stark** 🅗
(503) 252-7400. **Call for rates.** 9707 SE Stark St 97216. I-205, exit 21A southbound; exit 20 northbound, just e on Washington St, just n on SE 99th Ave, then just w. Int corridors. **Pets:** Accepted. ✕ 🔊 🍴 📺

ⓐⓐⓐ ▼▼▼ **Holiday Inn Portland Airport Hotel & Convention Center** 🅗
(503) 256-5000. **$69-$149.** 8439 NE Columbia Blvd 97220. I-205, exit 23B, 0.5 mi w. Int corridors. **Pets:** Accepted.
SAVE ✕ 🍴 📺 🍴 🏊

ⓐⓐⓐ ▼▼▼ **Hospitality Inn** 🅗
(503) 244-6684. **$79-$129.** 10155 SW Capitol Hwy 97219. I-5, exit 295 southbound; exit 294 northbound, just e. Int corridors. **Pets:** Small, dogs only. $10 daily fee/pet. Designated rooms, service with restrictions, supervision. SAVE ✕ 🔊 🍴 📺

ⓐⓐⓐ ▼▼▼ **Hotel deLuxe** 🅗 ❀
(503) 219-2094. **$109-$299.** 729 SW 15th Ave 97205-1994. I-5 to I-405, exit Salmon St northbound, just n on 14th Ave, w on Morrison St, then s; exit Couch/Burnside St southbound; at SW 15th Ave and Yamhill St. Int corridors. **Pets:** Other species. $45 one-time fee/pet. Designated rooms, service with restrictions, supervision. SAVE ✕ 🔊 📺 🍴

ⓐⓐⓐ ▼▼▼ **Hotel Fifty** 🅗 ❀
(503) 221-0711. **Call for rates.** 50 SW Morrison St 97204. At Morrison St and Naito Pkwy (formerly Front Ave). Int corridors. **Pets:** Medium, dogs only. $50 one-time fee/room. Service with restrictions, supervision.
SAVE ✕ 🔊 🍴 📺 🍴

ⓐⓐⓐ ▼▼▼ **Hotel Lucia** 🅗 ❀
(503) 225-1717. **$119-$279.** 400 SW Broadway 97205. At SW Broadway and Stark St. Int corridors. **Pets:** $45 one-time fee/pet. Designated rooms, service with restrictions, crate. SAVE ✕ 🔊 🍴

ⓐⓐⓐ ▼▼ ▼▼ **Hotel Monaco Portland** 🅗 ❀
(503) 222-0001. **$149-$259.** 506 SW Washington St 97204. At SW 5th Ave and SW Washington St. Int corridors. **Pets:** Other species. Service with restrictions, supervision. ECO SAVE ✕ 🔊 📺 🍴 ✕

ⓐⓐⓐ ▼▼ ▼▼ **Hotel Vintage Plaza** 🅗
(503) 228-1212. **$129-$259.** 422 SW Broadway 97205. At Broadway and Washington St. Int corridors. **Pets:** Accepted. SAVE ✕ 📺 🍴

ⓐⓐⓐ ▼▼▼ **Howard Johnson Portland Airport** 🅗
(503) 256-4111. **$53-$120.** 8247 NE Sandy Blvd 97220. I-205, exit 23A southbound; exit 23B northbound (US 30 business route/Sandy Blvd W), 1 mi w. Ext/int corridors. **Pets:** Accepted. SAVE ✕ 🍴 📺 🏊

▼▼▼ **La Quinta Inn & Suites Portland Airport** �H ✿

(503) 382-3820. **$64-$149.** 11207 NE Holman St 97220. I-205, exit 24B northbound; exit 24 southbound, 0.4 mi e on Airport Way, then just sw. Int corridors. **Pets:** Medium, other species. Service with restrictions, supervision. 🄰🅂🄺 ☒ ♿ 🅟 🖥 🏊

▼▼ **La Quinta Inn Portland Lloyd Center/Convention Center** �H ✿

(503) 233-7933. **$79-$145.** 431 NE Multnomah St 97232. I-5, exit 302A, just e on NE Weidler St, just s on NE Martin Luther King Jr Blvd, then just e. Int corridors. **Pets:** Medium, other species. Service with restrictions, supervision. 🄰🅂🄺 ☒ 🅟 🖥 🏊

🆎 ▼▼▼ **The Mark Spencer Hotel** �H ✿

(503) 224-3293. **$99-$249.** 409 SW 11th Ave 97205. At SW Stark St and SW 11th Ave. Int corridors. **Pets:** Other species. $15 daily fee/pet. Designated rooms, service with restrictions, supervision.
🄴🄲🄾 🅂🄰🅅🄴 ☒ 🅟 🖥

🆎 ▼ **Motel 6 #4463** Ⓜ

(503) 234-4391. **$60-$110.** 518 NE Holladay St 97232. I-5, exit 302A, just e on NE Weidler St, just s on NE Martin Luther King Jr Blvd, then just e. Ext corridors. **Pets:** Other species. Service with restrictions, supervision. 🅂🄰🅅🄴 ☒ 🅟

▼ ▼ **Motel 6 North Portland #4198** �H

(503) 247-3700. **$53-$80.** 1125 N Schmeer Rd 97217. I-5, exit 306B, 0.4 mi s on N Whitaker Rd, then just e. Int corridors. **Pets:** Other species. Service with restrictions, supervision. ☒ 🅟

🆎 ▼▼▼▼ **The Nines** �H

(503) 222-9996. **Call for rates.** 525 SW Morrison St 97204. At SW Morrison St and SW 5th Ave. Int corridors. **Pets:** Accepted.
🄴🄲🄾 🅂🄰🅅🄴 ☒ ♿ 🍴

🆎 ▼ **Oxford Suites** �H

(503) 283-3030. **$139-$199.** 12226 N Jantzen Dr 97217. I-5, exit 308, just e on Hayden Island Dr. Int corridors. **Pets:** Large. $25 one-time fee/room. Service with restrictions, supervision.
🅂🄰🅅🄴 ☒ ♿ 🅟 🖥 🏊 🐾

🆎 ▼▼ **Park Lane Suites** Ⓜ

(503) 226-6288. **$99-$199.** 809 SW King Ave 97205. I-405, exit Couch/Burnside St southbound, 0.5 mi w on Burnside St, then just s; exit Everett St northbound, 0.3 mi w on Glisan St, just s on NW 21st Ave, just w on Burnside St, then just s. Ext corridors. **Pets:** Accepted.
🅂🄰🅅🄴 ☒ ♿ 🅟

🆎 ▼▼ **Ramada Portland** �H

(503) 255-6511. **$69-$199.** 6221 NE 82nd Ave 97220. I-205, exit 23B (Killingsworth St), just w on Columbia Blvd, then just n on 80th Ave. Int corridors. **Pets:** Accepted. 🅂🄰🅅🄴 ☒ ♿ 🅟 🖥 🍴 🏊 🐾

🆎 ▼▼▼ **Red Lion Hotel on the River Jantzen Beach-Portland** �H

(503) 283-4466. **$189.** 909 N Hayden Island Dr 97217. I-5, exit 308, just ne. Int corridors. **Pets:** Other species. $20 one-time fee/room. Service with restrictions, supervision. 🅂🄰🅅🄴 ☒ ♿ 🅟 🖥 🍴 🏊 🐾

▼▼▼▼ **Red Lion Hotel Portland Airport** �H

(503) 255-6722. **$89-$119.** 7101 NE 82nd Ave 97220. I-205, exit 24A northbound; exit 24 southbound, 1.3 mi w on NE Airport Way, then 0.5 mi s. Ext/int corridors. **Pets:** Other species. $20 one-time fee/room. Service with restrictions, supervision. 🄰🅂🄺 ☒ 🅟 🍴 🏊 🐾

🆎 ▼▼▼ **Red Lion Hotel Portland-Convention Center** �H

(503) 235-2100. **$129-$199.** 1021 NE Grand Ave 97232. I-5, exit 302A, just e on NE Weidler St, just s on NE Martin Luther King Jr Blvd, then just e. Int corridors. **Pets:** Other species. $20 one-time fee/room. Service with restrictions, supervision. 🅂🄰🅅🄴 ☒ 🅟 🖥 🍴

▼▼ ▼▼ **Residence Inn by Marriott Portland Airport at Cascade Station** �H

(503) 284-1800. **$139-$149.** 9301 NE Cascades Pkwy 97220. I-205, exit 24A northbound; exit 24 southbound, 0.5 mi w on Airport Way, 0.5 mi s on NE Mt Hood Ave, then just w. Int corridors. **Pets:** Accepted.
☒ ♿ 🅟 🖥 🏊 🐾

🆎 ▼▼▼ **Residence Inn by Marriott Portland Downtown/Lloyd Center** �H ✿

(503) 288-1400. **$159-$169.** 1710 NE Multnomah St 97232. I-5, exit 302A, 0.8 mi e on Weidler St, then just s on 15th Ave; I-84, exit 1 (Lloyd Center) westbound, just n on 13th St, then just e. Ext corridors. **Pets:** Other species. $75 one-time fee/room. Designated rooms, service with restrictions, crate. 🅂🄰🅅🄴 ☒ ♿ 🅟 🖥 🏊 🐾

▼▼▼ **Residence Inn by Marriott-Portland North Harbour** �H

(503) 285-9888. **$139-$159.** 1250 N Anchor Way 97217. I-5, exit 307, follow signs to Marine Dr E, then just n. Int corridors. **Pets:** Accepted.
☒ ♿ 🅟 🖥 🏊 🐾

🆎 ▼▼▼▼ **Residence Inn Portland Downtown at RiverPlace** �H

(503) 552-9500. **$229-$249.** 2115 SW River Pkwy 97201. At SW Moody Ave and SW River Pkwy; on the Willamette River Waterfront. Int corridors. **Pets:** Accepted. 🅂🄰🅅🄴 ☒ 🅟 🖥 🏊 🐾

🆎 ▼▼▼▼ **RiverPlace, a Larkspur Collection Hotel** �H

(503) 228-3233. **$159-$525.** 1510 SW Harbor Way 97201. At Naito Pkwy (formerly Front Ave) and SW Harbor Way. Int corridors. **Pets:** Accepted.
🅂🄰🅅🄴 ☒ ♿ 🅟 🖥 🏊 🐾

🆎 ▼▼▼▼ **Sheraton Portland Airport Hotel** �H ✿

(503) 281-2500. **$99-$249.** 8235 NE Airport Way 97220. I-205, exit 24A northbound; exit 24 southbound, 1.5 mi w. Int corridors. **Pets:** Medium. $25 one-time fee/room. Service with restrictions, supervision.
🅂🄰🅅🄴 ☒ ♿ 🖥 🍴 🐾

🆎 ▼▼▼ **Shilo Inn-Portland/Rose Garden** �H ✿

(503) 736-6300. **$92-$200.** 1506 NE 2nd Ave 97232. I-5, exit 302A, just e on NE Weidler St, then just s. Int corridors. **Pets:** Dogs only. $25 one-time fee/room. Designated rooms, service with restrictions, supervision.
🅂🄰🅅🄴 ☒ 🅟 🖥

🆎 ▼▼▼ **Shilo Inn Suites Hotel-Portland Airport** �H ✿

(503) 252-7500. **$120-$220.** 11707 NE Airport Way 97220. I-205, exit 24B northbound; exit 24 southbound, 0.5 mi e. Int corridors. **Pets:** Dogs only. $25 one-time fee/room. Designated rooms, service with restrictions, supervision. 🅂🄰🅅🄴 ☒ ♿ 🅟 🖥 🍴 🏊 🐾

▼▼▼ **Staybridge Suites Portland-Airport** �H ✿

(503) 262-8888. **$79-$159.** 11936 NE Glenn Widing Dr 97220. I-205, exit 24B northbound; exit 24 southbound, 0.7 mi e, then just nw. Int corridors. **Pets:** Medium. $75 one-time fee/room. Service with restrictions, supervision. 🄰🅂🄺 ☒ ♿ 🅟 🖥 🏊 🐾

▼▼ **University Place** �H

(503) 221-0140. **$109-$129.** 310 SW Lincoln St 97201. I-5 to I-405, exit 4th Ave, just n, then just e. Ext/int corridors. **Pets:** Medium. $75 one-time fee/room. Designated rooms, service with restrictions. 🄰🅂🄺 ☒ 🅟 🖥 🐾

🆎 ▼▼▼▼ **The Westin Portland** �H ✿

(503) 294-9000. **$129-$389, 3 day notice.** 750 SW Alder St 97205. At Park Ave and SW Alder St. Int corridors. **Pets:** Medium, dogs only. Service with restrictions. 🅂🄰🅅🄴 ☒ ♿ 🖥 🍴

TIGARD

AAA ▼▼▼▼ Embassy Suites Hotel-Portland Washington Square H
(503) 644-4000. **$99-$209.** 9000 SW Washington Square Rd 97223. SR 217, exit 4 (Progress/Scholls Ferry Rd), just ne on SW Scholls Ferry Rd, just e on SW Hall Blvd, then just s. Int corridors. **Pets:** Accepted.

SAVE ⊠ ⑤M 🖥 🖵 ❘❙ 🌊

▼▼▼ Homestead Studio Suites Hotel Portland-Tigard H
(503) 670-0555. **$64-$74.** 13009 SW 68th Pkwy 97223. I-5, exit 293 (Haines St) southbound, 0.5 mi s on SW 68th Ave; exit 293 northbound, just w on Atlanta Ave, then 0.7 mi s; SR 217, exit 7 (72nd Ave), just ne, just e on Hampton St, then just s. Ext corridors. **Pets:** Other species. $25 daily fee/room. Designated rooms, service with restrictions, crate.

A$K ⊠ 🖥 🖵

AAA ▼▼▼▼ Phoenix Inn Suites-Tigard H
(503) 624-9000. **$89-$149.** 9575 SW Locust St 97223. SR 217, exit 5 (Greenburg Rd), just ne on SW Greenburg Rd, then just e. Int corridors. **Pets:** Medium, other species. $25 one-time fee/pet. Designated rooms, service with restrictions, supervision.

SAVE ⊠ ⑤M 🖥 🖵 🌊 ⊠

AAA ▼▼▼ Quality Inn Tigard H
(503) 245-6421. **$89-$99.** 11460 SW Pacific Hwy 97223. I-5, exit 294, just w. Int corridors. **Pets:** Accepted. SAVE ⊠ 🖥 🖵 ⊠

AAA ▼▼▼ Shilo Inn-Tigard/Washington Square H ❄
(503) 620-4320. **Call for rates.** 10830 SW Greenburg Rd 97223-1409. SR 217, exit 5 (Greenburg Rd), just sw. Int corridors. **Pets:** Dogs only. $25 one-time fee/room. Designated rooms, service with restrictions, supervision. SAVE ⊠ 🖥 🖵 ⊠

TROUTDALE

AAA ▼▼▼ Comfort Inn & Suites, Columbia Gorge West H
(503) 669-6500. **$69-$159.** 477 NW Phoenix Dr 97060. I-84, exit 17, south side of interstate, just s off Frontage Rd. Int corridors. **Pets:** Medium, other species. $10 daily fee/pet. Designated rooms, service with restrictions, supervision. SAVE ⊠ 🖥 🖵 🌊

▼▼ Holiday Inn Express-Portland East H
(503) 492-2900. **$89-$109.** 1000 NW Graham Rd 97060. I-84, exit 17 eastbound, e on Frontage Rd, then just n; exit westbound, just n. Int corridors. **Pets:** Accepted. A$K ⊠ 🖥 🖵

▼▼▼ Motel 6-Portland Troutdale–407 M
(503) 665-2254. **$45-$65.** 1610 NW Frontage Rd 97060. I-84, exit 17 eastbound, just sw; exit westbound, just w on Frontage Rd, then just sw. Ext corridors. **Pets:** Other species. Service with restrictions, supervision.

⊠ ⑤M 🖥 🌊

TUALATIN

AAA ▼▼▼ Comfort Inn & Suites H
(503) 612-9952. **$99-$135.** 7640 SW Warm Springs St 97062. I-5, exit 289, just w on Nyberg St, just s on Martinazzi Ave, then just e; just behind Fred Meyer. Int corridors. **Pets:** Accepted.

SAVE ⊠ ⑤M 🖥 🖵 🌊

WILSONVILLE

AAA ▼▼▼ Best Western Willamette Inn H ❄
(503) 682-2288. **$86-$100.** 30800 SW Parkway Ave 97070. I-5, exit 283, just e on Wilsonville Rd, then 0.3 mi s. Int corridors. **Pets:** Medium. $10 daily fee/pet. Designated rooms, service with restrictions, supervision.

SAVE ⊠ 🖥 🖵 🌊

▼▼▼ Holiday Inn-Wilsonville H
(503) 682-2211. **$69-$149.** 25425 SW 95th Ave 97070. I-5, exit 286, just w on Boones Ferry Rd, then just se. Int corridors. **Pets:** Accepted.

A$K ⊠ 🖥 🖵 ❘❙ 🌊

AAA ▼▼▼ La Quinta Inn Wilsonville H ❄
(503) 682-3184. **$70-$119.** 8815 SW Sun Pl 97070. I-5, exit 286, just e on Elligsen Rd, just n on Parkway Ave, then just w. Int corridors. **Pets:** Medium, other species. Service with restrictions, supervision.

SAVE ⊠ ⑤M 🖥 🖵 🌊

AAA ▼▼▼ Wilsonville Inn & Suites H
(503) 570-9700. **$69-$159.** 29769 SW Boones Ferry Rd 97070. I-5, exit 283, just w on Wilsonville Rd, then just n. Int corridors. **Pets:** Small, other species. $15 daily fee/pet. Service with restrictions, supervision. SAVE ⊠ ⑤M 🖥 🖵 🌊 ⊠

END METROPOLITAN AREA

PORT ORFORD

AAA ▼▼ Castaway by the Sea M
(541) 332-4502. **$65-$160, 3 day notice.** 545 W 5th St 97465. Jct US 101, 1 blk w on Harbor Dr, then 1 blk n. Ext corridors. **Pets:** Accepted.

SAVE ⊠ 🖥 🖵 🏧

PRINEVILLE

AAA ▼▼▼ Best Western Prineville Inn H
(541) 447-8080. **$75-$100.** 1475 NE 3rd St 97754. 0.8 mi e on US 26. Int corridors. **Pets:** Small, dogs only. $15 daily fee/room. Designated rooms, service with restrictions, supervision.

SAVE ⊠ ⑤M 🖥 🖵 🌊

▼▼ Econo Lodge M
(541) 447-6231. **$45-$60.** 123 NE 3rd St 97754. Center; downtown. Int corridors. **Pets:** Dogs only. $10 one-time fee/pet. Service with restrictions, supervision. A$K ⊠ 🖥 🖵

▼▼▼▼ Stafford Inn H ❄
(541) 447-7100. **$82-$117.** 1773 NE 3rd St 97754. 1 mi e on US 26. Int corridors. **Pets:** Large. $20 one-time fee/room. Service with restrictions, supervision. A$K ⊠ ⑤M 🖥 🖵 🌊

PROSPECT

▼▼ Prospect Historic Hotel-Motel & Dinner House M ❄
(541) 560-3664. **$70-$205.** 391 Mill Creek Dr 97536. Jct SR 62, 0.3 mi s on 1st St (0.7 mi e of MM 43), just w. Ext/int corridors. **Pets:** Other species. $10 one-time fee/room. Designated rooms, service with restrictions, supervision. ⊠ 🖥 🖵 ❘❙ ⊠

REDMOND

▼▼▼ Comfort Suites-Redmond Airport H
(541) 504-8900. **$99-$174.** 2243 SW Yew Ave 97756. US 97, exit 124 (Yew Ave/Airport Way/Redmond Airport), just nw; 2 mi s of jct SR 126. Int corridors. **Pets:** Other species. $28 one-time fee/room. Service with restrictions, supervision. A$K ⊠ 🖥 🖵 🌊 ⊠

▼▼ Eagle Crest Resort H
(541) 923-2453. **Call for rates.** 1522 Cline Falls Rd 97756. 4.5 mi w on SR 126, 1 mi s. Int corridors. **Pets:** Accepted.

⊠ ⑤M 🖥 🖵 ❘❙ 🌊 ⊠

AAA ▼▼ Motel 6 Redmond-4076 H
(541) 923-2100. **$60-$100.** 2247 S US 97 97756. 1.1 mi s on US 97 from jct SR 126, just w. Int corridors. **Pets:** Other species. Service with restrictions, supervision. SAVE ⊠ ⑤M 🖥

ㅇㅇㅇ ▼▼▼ Redmond Inn M

(541) 548-1091. **$45-$125.** 1545 S US 97 97756. 0.7 mi s on US 97 from jct SR 126. Ext corridors. **Pets:** Medium. $5 daily fee/pet. Designated rooms, service with restrictions, supervision.

[SAVE] [X] [=] [=] [=]

ㅇㅇㅇ ▼▼▼▼ Sleep Inn & Suites-Redmond H

(541) 504-1500. **$65-$115.** 1847 N US 97 97756. US 97, exit 119, 0.6 mi s on Business Rt US 97; 1 mi n of downtown. Int corridors. **Pets:** Medium, other species. $10 daily fee/pet. Designated rooms, service with restrictions, supervision. [SAVE] [X] [&M] [=] [=] [=]

REEDSPORT

ㅇㅇㅇ ▼▼ Anchor Bay Inn M

(541) 271-2149. **$50-$80.** 1821 Winchester Ave (US 101) 97467. Jct SR 38, 0.8 mi s. Ext corridors. **Pets:** Dogs only. $7 daily fee/pet. Designated rooms, service with restrictions, supervision. [SAVE] [X] [=] [=] [AC]

ㅇㅇㅇ ▼▼▼▼ Best Western Salbasgeon Inn H

(541) 271-4831. **$111-$216.** 1400 US 101 S 97467. Jct SR 38, 0.4 mi s. Ext corridors. **Pets:** Medium, dogs only. $15 one-time fee/pet. Designated rooms, service with restrictions, supervision. [SAVE] [X] [=] [=] [=]

ㅇㅇㅇ ▼▼ Economy Inn M

(541) 271-3671. **Call for rates.** 1593 US 101 97467. Jct SR 38, 0.5 mi s. Ext corridors. **Pets:** Large, other species. $10 daily fee/pet. Designated rooms, service with restrictions, supervision. [SAVE] [X] [=] [=] [AC]

ㅇㅇㅇ ▼▼▼ Salbasgeon Inn of the Umpqua M

(541) 271-2025. **Call for rates.** 45209 SR 38 97467. Jct US 101, 7.5 mi e. Ext corridors. **Pets:** Large. $10 one-time fee/pet. Service with restrictions, supervision. [SAVE] [X] [=] [=] [X]

ROCKAWAY BEACH

ㅇㅇㅇ ▼▼▼ Tradewinds Motel M

(503) 355-2112. **$58-$169, 7 day notice.** 523 N Pacific St 97136. US 101, just w on NW 6th Ave, just s. Ext corridors. **Pets:** Large, dogs only. $15 daily fee/pet. Designated rooms, service with restrictions, supervision. [SAVE] [X] [=] [AC]

ROSEBURG

ㅇㅇㅇ ▼▼▼ Best Western Garden Villa Inn M

(541) 672-1601. **$70-$130.** 760 NW Garden Valley Blvd 97471. I-5, exit 125, just nw. Ext corridors. **Pets:** Accepted. [SAVE] [X] [=] [=] [=]

▼ Motel 6 #4108 H

(541) 464-8000. **$49-$72.** 3100 NW Aviation Dr 97470. I-5, exit 127, just se. Int corridors. **Pets:** Other species. Service with restrictions, supervision. [ASK] [X] [&M] [=]

ㅇㅇㅇ ▼▼ Quality Inn M

(541) 673-5561. **$65-$120.** 427 NW Garden Valley Blvd 97470. I-5, exit 125, just se. Ext corridors. **Pets:** Dogs only. $50 deposit/room, $10 daily fee/room. Designated rooms, service with restrictions, supervision. [SAVE] [X] [=] [=] [=]

ㅇㅇㅇ ▼▼ Roseburg Travelodge M

(541) 672-4836. **$75-$119.** 315 W Harvard Ave 97470. I-5, exit 124, just se. Ext corridors. **Pets:** Accepted. [SAVE] [X] [=] [=] [=]

ㅇㅇㅇ ▼▼ Shady Oaks Motel M

(541) 672-2608. **$45-$69.** 2954 Old Hwy 99 S 97471. I-5, exit 120, 0.5 mi n. Ext corridors. **Pets:** Dogs only. $8 daily fee/pet. Designated rooms, service with restrictions, supervision. [SAVE] [X] [=]

▼▼ Sleep Inn and Suites H

(541) 464-8338. **$70-$110.** 2855 NW Edenbower Blvd 97471. I-5, exit 127, just sw. Int corridors. **Pets:** $10 one-time fee/room. Service with restrictions, crate. [ASK] [X] [&M] [=] [=] [=]

▼▼ Super 8 H

(541) 672-8880. **$60-$75.** 3200 NW Aviation Dr 97470. I-5, exit 127, just ne. Int corridors. **Pets:** Other species. $15 daily fee/room. Service with restrictions, supervision. [ASK] [X] [&M] [=] [=] [=]

ㅇㅇㅇ ▼▼▼ Windmill Inn of Roseburg H ❖

(541) 673-0901. **Call for rates.** 1450 NW Mulholland Dr 97470. I-5, exit 125, just ne. Int corridors. **Pets:** Other species. Designated rooms, service with restrictions, supervision. [SAVE] [X] [=] [=] [=] [X]

ST. HELENS

ㅇㅇㅇ ▼▼▼ Best Western Oak Meadows Inn H

(503) 397-3000. **$96-$159.** 585 S Columbia River Hwy 97051. South end of town on US 30. Int corridors. **Pets:** Large. $10 one-time fee/pet. Service with restrictions, supervision. [SAVE] [X] [=] [=] [=]

SALEM

ㅇㅇㅇ ▼▼▼ Best Western Black Bear Inn M ❖

(503) 581-1559. **$69-$129, 7 day notice.** 1600 Motor Ct NE 97301. I-5, exit 256, just e on Market St NE, then just s. Ext corridors. **Pets:** Medium. $10 daily fee/room. Designated rooms, service with restrictions, supervision. [SAVE] [X] [=] [=] [X]

ㅇㅇㅇ ▼▼▼ Best Western Mill Creek Inn H

(503) 585-3332. **$101-$153.** 3125 Ryan Dr SE 97301. I-5, exit 253, just w on Mission St, just n on Hawthorn Ave, then just w. Int corridors. **Pets:** Medium, dogs only. $20 daily fee/pet. Designated rooms, service with restrictions, supervision. [SAVE] [X] [=] [=] [X]

ㅇㅇㅇ ▼▼▼ Best Western Pacific Hwy Inn M

(503) 390-3200. **$85-$93.** 4646 Portland Rd NE 97305. I-5, exit 258, 0.3 mi e. Ext corridors. **Pets:** Accepted. [SAVE] [X] [=] [=] [=]

▼▼▼ Comfort Suites Airport H

(503) 585-9705. **$109-$129.** 630 Hawthorne Ave SE 97301. I-5, exit 253, just w on Mission St, 0.4 mi n on Hawthorne Ave SE, then just e. Int corridors. **Pets:** Accepted. [ASK] [X] [&M] [=] [=] [=] [X]

▼ Crossland Studios Salem North M

(503) 363-7557. **$49-$59.** 3535 Fisher Rd NE 97305. I-5, exit 258, just e on Portland Rd NE, 0.3 mi s on Ward Dr, then 0.8 mi s. Ext corridors. **Pets:** Other species. $25 daily fee/room. Designated rooms, service with restrictions, crate. [ASK] [X] [=]

ㅇㅇㅇ ▼▼▼ Howard Johnson Inn H

(503) 375-7710. **$70-$110.** 2250 Mission St SE 97302. I-5, exit 253, 1.4 mi w. Int corridors. **Pets:** Medium, dogs only. $15 daily fee/pet. Designated rooms, service with restrictions, supervision. [SAVE] [X] [=] [=] [=]

ㅇㅇㅇ ▼▼▼ La Quinta Inn & Suites H ❖

(503) 391-7000. **$89-$149.** 890 Hawthorne Ave SE 97301. I-5, exit 253, just w on Mission St (SR 22), then just n. Int corridors. **Pets:** Medium, other species. Service with restrictions, supervision. [SAVE] [X] [&M] [=] [=] [=]

ㅇㅇㅇ ▼▼▼▼ Phoenix Inn Suites-North Salem H ❖

(503) 581-7004. **$79-$139.** 1590 Weston Ct NE 97301. I-5, exit 256, just w on Market St, then just s. Int corridors. **Pets:** Large, other species. $15 daily fee/pet. Service with restrictions, supervision. [SAVE] [X] [&M] [=] [=] [=]

ㅇㅇㅇ ▼▼▼▼ Phoenix Inn Suites-South Salem H ❖

(503) 588-9220. **$79-$139.** 4370 Commercial St SE 97302. I-5, exit 252, 1.5 mi w on Kuebler Rd, then 0.7 mi n. Int corridors. **Pets:** Medium. $20 daily fee/pet. Designated rooms, service with restrictions, supervision. [SAVE] [X] [&M] [=] [=] [=] [X]

ㅇㅇㅇ ▼▼▼▼ Red Lion Hotel Salem H

(503) 370-7888. **$124-$169.** 3301 Market St NE 97301. I-5, exit 256, just w. Int corridors. **Pets:** Other species. $20 one-time fee/room. Service with restrictions, supervision. [SAVE] [X] [&M] [=] [=] [¶] [=]

Residence Inn by Marriott H ❀

(503) 585-6500. **$171-$209.** 640 Hawthorne Ave SE 97301. I-5, exit 253, just w on Mission St, 0.4 mi n on Hawthorne Ave SE, then just e. Int corridors. **Pets:** Medium, other species. $100 one-time fee/room. Service with restrictions, supervision. ⊠ ⓜ 🔡 🖳 ⇀ ⊠

Shilo Inn Suites-Salem H ❀

(503) 581-4001. **$90-$180.** 3304 Market St NE 97301. I-5, exit 256, just w. Int corridors. **Pets:** Dogs only. $25 one-time fee/room. Designated rooms, service with restrictions, supervision.

SAVE ⊠ 🔡 🖳 ⇀ ⊠

Super 8 Salem H

(503) 370-8888. **$70-$90.** 1288 Hawthorne Ave NE 97301. I-5, exit 256, just w on Market St, then just s. Int corridors. **Pets:** Small. $10 daily fee/pet. Service with restrictions, supervision. ASK ⊠ 🔡 ⇀

Travelodge Salem Capital M

(503) 581-2466. **$57-$73.** 1555 State St 97301. I-5, exit 253, 1.8 mi w on Mission St, 0.4 mi n on 17th St SE, then just w. Ext corridors. **Pets:** Medium. $10 daily fee/pet. Designated rooms, supervision.

SAVE ⊠ 🔡 🖳 ⇀

SANDY

Best Western Sandy Inn H

(503) 668-7100. **$80-$126.** 37465 US 26 97055. West side of town. Int corridors. **Pets:** Medium, dogs only. $10 daily fee/pet. Service with restrictions, supervision. SAVE ⊠ ⓜ 🔡 🖳 ⇀

SEASIDE

Best Western Ocean View Resort H ❀

(503) 738-3334. **$60-$500, 3 day notice.** 414 N Prom 97138. US 101, exit 1st Ave, just w, just n on Necanicum Dr, then just w on 4th Ave. Ext/int corridors. **Pets:** Large, dogs only. $20 daily fee/pet. Designated rooms, service with restrictions, supervision.

SAVE ⊠ 🔡 🖳 ⇥ ⇀

Comfort Inn & Suites by Seaside Convention Center/Boardwalk H

(503) 738-3011. **$89-$399.** 545 Broadway 97138. US 101, just w on Ave A; downtown. Int corridors. **Pets:** Accepted.

SAVE ⊠ ⓜ 🔡 🖳 ⇀

Ebb-Tide Resort H

(503) 738-8371. **$60-$200, 3 day notice.** 300 N Prom 97138. US 101, exit 1st Ave, 0.4 mi w, just n on Columbia St, then just w on 2nd Ave. Ext/int corridors. **Pets:** Accepted. SAVE ⊠ 🔡 🖳 ⇀ ⊠ 🐾

Holiday Inn Express Hotel & Suites-Seaside Convention Center H

(503) 717-8000. **$89-$399.** 34 N Holladay Dr 97138. US 101, exit Broadway St, just w, then just n. Int corridors. **Pets:** Accepted.

SAVE ⊠ ⓜ 🔡 🖳 ⇀ ⊠

Inn at Seaside H

(503) 738-9581. **$65-$209, 3 day notice.** 441 2nd Ave 97138. US 101, exit 1st Ave, then just w. Ext/int corridors. **Pets:** Accepted.

SAVE ⊠ 🔡 🖳

Inn At The Shore M ❀

(503) 738-3113. **$69-$180, 3 day notice.** 2275 S Prom 97138. US 101, exit Ave U, just w. Ext corridors. **Pets:** $20 one-time fee/pet. Designated rooms, supervision. ASK ⊠ 🔡 🖳 🐾

Rivertide Suites H ❀

(503) 717-1100. **$95-$525, 3 day notice.** 102 N Holladay 97138. US 101, just w on Broadway St, then just n. Int corridors. **Pets:** Medium. $25 daily fee/pet. Designated rooms, service with restrictions, supervision.

SAVE ⊠ ⓜ 🔡 🖳 ⇀

Seashore Inn...on the Beach H ❀

(503) 738-6368. **$75-$249.** 60 N Prom 97138. US 101, exit 1st Ave, 0.4 mi w. Ext/int corridors. **Pets:** $20 daily fee/pet. Designated rooms, service with restrictions, supervision. SAVE ⊠ 🔡 🖳 ⇀ 🐾

The Seaside Oceanfront Inn H

(503) 738-6403. **Call for rates.** 581 S Prom 97138. US 101, exit Ave G, 0.6 mi w, then just n. Int corridors. **Pets:** Accepted. ⊠ 🔡 🍴

Shilo Inn Suites Oceanfront Hotel-Seaside H ❀

(503) 738-9571. **$100-$550.** 30 N Prom 97138. US 101, exit Broadway St, 0.4 mi w. Ext corridors. **Pets:** Dogs only. $25 one-time fee/room. Designated rooms, service with restrictions, supervision.

SAVE ⊠ 🔡 🖳 🍴 ⇀ ⊠ 🐾

SISTERS

Best Western Ponderosa Lodge M ❀

(541) 549-1234. **$100-$290.** 500 US 20 W 97759. Just w on US 20 from jct SR 242; at Barclay Dr; west end of town. Ext corridors. **Pets:** Other species. $15 daily fee/pet. Designated rooms, service with restrictions.

SAVE ⊠ 🔡 🖳 ⇀

FivePine Lodge & Spa Resort CA ❀

(541) 549-5900. **$149-$219, 7 day notice.** 1021 Desperado Tr 97759. Jct SR 126 and US 20, just e on US 20; east end of town. Int corridors. **Pets:** $25 daily fee/room. Designated rooms, service, with restrictions, supervision. ⊠ 🔡 🖳 🍴 ⇀ ⊠

Sisters Inn & Suites M ❀

(541) 549-7829. **$69-$150.** 1605 N Arrow Leaf Tr 97759. Just w on US 20 from jct SR 242; west end of town. Ext corridors. **Pets:** Medium. $15 daily fee/pet. Service with restrictions, supervision.

ASK ⊠ ⓜ 🔡 🖳

SPRINGFIELD

Best Western Grand Manor Inn H

(541) 726-4769. **$89-$149.** 971 Kruse Way 97477. I-5, exit 195A, just se. Int corridors. **Pets:** Dogs only. $100 deposit/room, $10 daily fee/pet. Designated rooms, service with restrictions, supervision.

SAVE ⊠ ⓜ 🔡 🖳 ⇀

Comfort Suites Eugene/Springfield H ❀

(541) 746-5359. **$90-$169.** 969 Kruse Way 97477. I-5, exit 195A, just se. Int corridors. **Pets:** Large, dogs only. $25 one-time fee/room. Designated rooms, service with restrictions, supervision. ASK ⊠ 🔡 🖳 ⇀

Holiday Inn Express Hotel & Suites H

(541) 746-8471. **$109-$149.** 3480 Hutton St 97477. I-5, exit 195A, just se. Int corridors. **Pets:** Medium. $20 daily fee/pet. Designated rooms, service with restrictions, supervision. ASK ⊠ 🔡 🖳 ⇀

Motel 6 #418 M

(541) 741-1105. **$51-$75.** 3752 International Ct 97477. I-5, exit 195A, just e on Beltline Rd, just nw on Gateway St, then just n. Ext corridors. **Pets:** Other species. Service with restrictions, supervision.

⊠ ⓜ 🔡 ⇀

Super 8 H

(541) 746-1314. **$65-$90.** 3315 Gateway St 97477. I-5, exit 195A, just e on Beltline Rd, then just s. Int corridors. **Pets:** Accepted.

SAVE ⊠ 🔡 🖳

Village Inn M

(541) 747-4546. **$84.** 1875 Mohawk Blvd 97477. I-5, exit 194A, 2.5 mi e on SR 126, exit Mohawk Blvd, then just n. Ext corridors. **Pets:** Small. Designated rooms, service with restrictions, crate.

SAVE ⊠ 🔡 🖳

SUNRIVER

Discover Sunriver Vacation Rentals VH

(541) 593-2482. **$90-$140, 60 day notice.** Sunriver Village Mall, Bldg #9 97707. US 97, exit 153 (S Century Dr), 2 mi w to Abbott Dr, then just n on Beaver Dr. Int corridors. **Pets:** Dogs only. $35 one-time fee/pet. Designated rooms, no service. SAVE ⊠ 🔡 🖳 ⇀ ⊠

Sunray Vacation Rentals VH
(541) 593-3225. **$100-$800, 60 day notice.** 56870 Venture Ln, #107 97707. US 97, exit 153 (S Century Dr), 2 mi w, follow signs to Mt Bachelor, just s on Century Dr, then just e;. Ext corridors. **Pets:** Other species. $100 deposit/room, $35 one-time fee/pet. Designated rooms, service with restrictions.

Sunriver Resort H
(541) 593-1000. **$149-$274, 21 day notice.** 17600 Center Dr 97707. US 97, exit 153 (S Century Dr), 1.5 mi w to Abbott Dr, then 0.6 mi w. Ext corridors. **Pets:** Accepted.

SUTHERLIN

Best Western Hartford Lodge H
(541) 459-1424. **$99-$139.** 150 Myrtle St 97479. I-5, exit 136, just ne. Ext corridors. **Pets:** Accepted.

Microtel Inn & Suites H
(541) 459-6800. **Call for rates.** 1400 Hospitality Pl 97479. I-5, exit 136, just se. Int corridors. **Pets:** Other species. $10 daily fee/room. Service with restrictions, supervision.

SWEET HOME

Sweet Home Inn M
(541) 367-5137. **$69-$99.** 805 Long St 97386. Just e of jct US 20 and SR 228; just s on 10th Ave, then just w. Ext corridors. **Pets:** Medium, dogs only. $15 one-time fee/pet. Service with restrictions, supervision.

THE DALLES

Comfort Inn Columbia Gorge H
(541) 298-2800. **$85-$174.** 351 Lone Pine Dr 97058. I-84, exit 87, just nw. Int corridors. **Pets:** Accepted.

Cousins Country Inn H ❖
(541) 298-5161. **$89-$189.** 2114 W 6th St 97058. I-84, exit 83 eastbound, just nw; exit 84 westbound, just nw on W 2nd St, just sw on Webber St, then just n. Ext corridors. **Pets:** Dogs only. $10 daily fee/pet. Designated rooms, service with restrictions, supervision.

The Dalles Inn H ❖
(541) 296-9107. **$84-$139.** 112 W 2nd St 97058. I-84, exit 84 eastbound, 0.6 mi se; exit 85 westbound, 0.8 mi nw; at Liberty and W 2nd sts; downtown. Ext/int corridors. **Pets:** $10 daily fee/pet. Designated rooms, service with restrictions, supervision.

Motel 6 #4268
(541) 296-1191. **Call for rates.** 2500 W 6th St 97058. I-84, exit 83 eastbound, just nw; exit 84 westbound, just nw on W 2nd St, just sw on Webber St, then just n. Int corridors. **Pets:** Other species. Service with restrictions, supervision.

Shilo Inn Suites Hotel-The Dalles H ❖
(541) 298-5502. **$85-$250.** 3223 Bret Clodfelter Way 97058-9718. I-84, exit 87, just ne. Int corridors. **Pets:** Dogs only. $25 one-time fee/room. Designated rooms, service with restrictions, supervision.

Super 8 H
(541) 296-6888. **Call for rates.** 609 Cherry Heights Rd 97058. I-84, exit 84 eastbound, just se on W 2nd St, then just sw; exit 84 westbound, just nw on W 2nd St, just sw on Webber St, then just se on W 8th St. Int corridors. **Pets:** Accepted.

TILLAMOOK

Best Western Inn & Suites H
(503) 842-7599. **$79-$185.** 1722 N Makinster Rd 97141. 1 mi n on US 101. Int corridors. **Pets:** Medium, other species. $11 one-time fee/pet. Designated rooms, service with restrictions, supervision.

Mar-Clair Inn M ❖
(503) 842-7571. **$86-$106.** 11 Main Ave 97141. US 101, just n of jct SR 6. Ext/int corridors. **Pets:** Small, dogs only. $10 one-time fee/pet. Service with restrictions, supervision.

Shilo Inn Suites Hotel-Tillamook H ❖
(503) 842-7971. **$95-$190.** 2515 N Main Ave 97141. 1 mi n on US 101. Int corridors. **Pets:** Dogs only. $25 one-time fee/room. Designated rooms, service with restrictions, supervision.

WARRENTON

Shilo Inn Suites
Hotel–Warrenton/Astoria H ❖
(503) 861-2181. **$125-$250.** 1609 E Harbor Dr 97146. On US 26/101; near west end of Young's Bay Bridge. Int corridors. **Pets:** Dogs only. $25 one-time fee/room. Designated rooms, service with restrictions, supervision.

WELCHES

The Resort at the Mountain H
(503) 622-3101. **Call for rates.** 68010 E Fairway Ave 97067. 0.8 mi s of US 26 on E Welches Rd. Ext corridors. **Pets:** Accepted.

WHITE CITY

La Quinta Inn and Suites–White City H ❖
(541) 826-0800. **$79-$109.** 2020 Leigh Way 97503. I-5, exit 30, 5.6 mi ne on Crater Lake Hwy (SR 62), then just w. Int corridors. **Pets:** Medium, other species. Service with restrictions, supervision.

WOODBURN

Best Western Woodburn Inn H
(503) 982-6515. **$99-$179.** 2887 Newberg Hwy 97071. I-5, exit 271, just ne. Int corridors. **Pets:** $10 daily fee/pet. Designated rooms, service with restrictions, supervision.

La Quinta Inn Woodburn H ❖
(503) 982-1727. **$69-$109.** 120 Arney Rd NE 97071. I-5, exit 271, just nw. Int corridors. **Pets:** Medium, other species. Service with restrictions, supervision.

Super 8–Woodburn H ❖
(503) 981-8881. **$60-$95.** 821 Evergreen Rd 97071. I-5, exit 271, just se. Int corridors. **Pets:** Medium, dogs only. $5 daily fee/room, $10 one-time fee/room. Service with restrictions, supervision.

YACHATS

The Adobe Resort H ❖
(541) 547-3141. **$75-$405.** 1555 US 101 97498. 0.5 mi n; just w of US 101. Int corridors. **Pets:** Other species. $10 daily fee/pet. Designated rooms, service with restrictions, supervision.

The Dublin House M
(541) 547-3703. **$49-$135.** 251 W 7th St 97498. US 101 at 7th St; downtown. Ext corridors. **Pets:** Dogs only. $10 daily fee/pet. Supervision.

Fireside Motel M ❖
(541) 547-3636. **$70-$160.** 1881 US 101 N 97498. 0.6 mi n; just w of US 101. Ext corridors. **Pets:** $10 daily fee/pet. Designated rooms, service with restrictions, supervision.

PENNSYLVANIA

ABBOTTSTOWN

AAA ▼▼▼ The Inn at the Altland House [CI]
(717) 259-9535. **$105-$175.** 35 Fleet St 17301. Jct SR 194. Int corridors.
Pets: Accepted. [SAVE] [✕] [✦] [⛉]

ALLENTOWN

AAA ▼▼▼ Allentown Howard Johnson Inn & Suites [H]
(610) 439-4000. **$38-$99.** 3220 Hamilton Blvd 18103. I-78, exit 54
(Hamilton Blvd), 0.8 mi n. Int corridors. **Pets:** Medium. $25 one-time fee/
pet. Service with restrictions, supervision. [SAVE] [✕] [&M] [✦] [🖻] [⛉]

▼▼▼ Comfort Inn Lehigh Valley-West [H]
(610) 391-0344. **$80-$119.** 7625 Imperial Way 18106. I-78, exit 49B (SR
100), just n. Int corridors. **Pets:** Medium, other species. $25 one-time
fee/room. Service with restrictions, crate. [ASK] [✕] [✦] [🖻]

AAA ▼▼▼ Four Points by Sheraton Hotel & Suites
Allentown Airport [H]
(610) 266-1000. **Call for rates.** 3400 Airport Rd 18109. On SR 987 N
(Airport Rd), 0.5 mi n of jct US 22. Int corridors. **Pets:** Medium. $25 daily
fee/room. Service with restrictions, supervision.
[SAVE] [✕] [&M] [✦] [🖻] [⛉] [⛉]

▼▼▼ Holiday Inn-Allentown Center City [H]
(610) 433-2221. **$109-$129.** 904 Hamilton Blvd 18101. 9th St and Hamilton Blvd; downtown. Int corridors. **Pets:** Accepted.
[✕] [✦] [🖻] [⛉] [⛉]

AAA ▼▼▼ Knights Inn [H]
(610) 266-9070. **$61-$130.** 1880 Steelstone Rd 18109. US 22, exit Airport Rd S. Int corridors. **Pets:** Medium. $25 one-time fee/pet. Service with
restrictions, supervision. [SAVE] [✕] [&M] [✦] [🖻]

AAA ▼▼▼ Quality Inn-Allentown [H]
(610) 435-7880. **$49-$299.** 1715 Plaza Ln 18104. US 22, exit 15th St,
just n. Int corridors. **Pets:** Accepted. [SAVE] [✕] [✦] [🖻]

AAA ▼▼▼ Staybridge Suites Allentown Airport Lehigh
Valley [H]
(610) 443-5000. **$89-$129.** 1787-A Airport Rd 18109. US 22, exit Airport
Rd S, 0.3 mi s. Int corridors. **Pets:** Large. $50 one-time fee/room. Service
with restrictions, crate. [SAVE] [✕] [&M] [✦] [🖻] [⛉]

ALTOONA

▼ Motel 6 #1415 [M]
(814) 946-7601. **$53-$63.** 1500 Sterling St 16602. I-99/US 220, exit 31
(Plank Rd), just w. Ext corridors. **Pets:** Other species. Service with restrictions, supervision. [✕] [&M] [⛉]

▼▼ Quality Inn of Altoona [H]
(814) 944-4581. **$70-$90.** 2915 Pleasant Valley Blvd 16602. I-99/US 220,
exit 32 (Frankstown Rd), 0.4 mi w, then 0.5 mi n. Ext corridors.
Pets: Accepted. [ASK] [✕] [✦] [🖻] [⛉] [⛉]

▼▼ Super 8 Altoona [M]
(814) 942-5350. **$59-$99.** 3535 Fairway Dr 16602. I-99/US 220, exit 32
(Frankstown Rd), just w. Ext corridors. **Pets:** Medium. $15 daily fee/pet.
Service with restrictions, supervision. [ASK] [✕] [&M] [✦] [🖻]

BARKEYVILLE

AAA ▼▼▼ Comfort Inn-Barkeyville [M]
(814) 786-7901. **$79-$140, 3 day notice.** 137 Gibb Rd 16038-3401.
I-80, exit 29, just n on SR 8. Ext corridors. **Pets:** Small. $10 one-time
fee/pet. Designated rooms, no service, supervision. [SAVE] [✕] [✦] [🖻]

AAA ▼▼▼ Motel 6-Barkeyville [M]
(814) 786-8375. **$60-$120.** 1010 Dholu Rd 16038. I-80, exit 29, just n on
SR 8. Int corridors. **Pets:** Other species. Service with restrictions, supervision. [SAVE] [✕] [✦]

BEDFORD

AAA ▼▼▼ Best Western Bedford Inn [H]
(814) 623-9006. **$76-$102.** 4517 Business Rt 220 15522. I-70/76 (Pennsylvania Tpke), exit 146, 0.3 mi n. Ext/int corridors. **Pets:** Medium, other
species. $50 deposit/room, $15 daily fee/room. Service with restrictions,
supervision. [SAVE] [✕] [✦] [🖻] [⛉] [⛉] [✕]

AAA ▼ Budget Host Inn [M] 🐾
(814) 623-8107. **$35-$90.** 4378 Business Rt 220 15522. I-70/76 (Pennsylvania Tpke), exit 146, just n. Ext corridors. **Pets:** Medium. $6 one-time
fee/pet. Designated rooms, no service, supervision. [SAVE] [✕] [✦] [⛉]

▼ M Star Hotel [M]
(814) 623-5880. **$60-$80.** 4498 Business Rt 220 15522. I-70/76 (Pennsylvania Tpke), exit 146, 0.3 mi n. Int corridors. **Pets:** $10 daily fee/room.
Service with restrictions. [ASK] [✕] [✦]

▼▼▼ ▼▼▼ Omni Bedford Springs Resort & Spa ◩

(814) 623-8100. **Call for rates.** 2138 Business Rt 220 15522. I-70-76 (Pennsylvania Tpke), exit 146, 3.9 mi s. Int corridors. **Pets:** Accepted.
⊠ 🛏 💻 🍴 ➳ 🐾

◈◈◈ ▼▼▼ Quality Inn Bedford ◩

(814) 623-5188. **$68-$145.** 4407 Business Rt 220 N 15522. I-70/76 (Pennsylvania Tpke), exit 146, just n. Ext/int corridors. **Pets:** Medium, other species. $15 one-time fee/room. Designated rooms, service with restrictions, supervision. 𝗦𝗔𝗩𝗘 ⊠ 🛏 💻 🍴 ➳

BELLEFONTE

▼▼▼ Reynolds Mansion Bed and Breakfast ◱◱

(814) 353-8407. **$135-$300, 14 day notice.** 101 W Linn St 16823. Corner of Allegheny and Linn sts; downtown. Int corridors. **Pets:** Medium. $50 deposit/pet, $15 daily fee/pet. Designated rooms, no service, crate.
⊠ ⓩ

BETHEL

◈◈◈ ▼▼▼ Comfort Inn-Bethel/Midway ◩

(717) 933-8888. **Call for rates.** 41 Diner Dr 19507. I-78, exit 16, just w. Int corridors. **Pets:** Other species. $10 daily fee/pet. Designated rooms, service with restrictions, crate. 𝗦𝗔𝗩𝗘 ⊠ ♿ 🛏 💻 ➳

BETHLEHEM

◈◈◈ ▼▼▼▼ Best Western Lehigh Valley Hotel & Conference Center ◩

(610) 866-5800. **Call for rates.** 300 Gateway Dr 18017. US 22, exit Center St and SR 512. Ext/int corridors. **Pets:** Accepted.
𝗦𝗔𝗩𝗘 ⊠ ♿ 🛏 💻 🍴 ➳

▼▼ ▼▼ Comfort Inn ◩ 🐾

(610) 865-6300. **$65-$90.** 3191 Highfield Dr 18020. US 22, exit SR 191, just s. Ext/int corridors. **Pets:** Other species. $10 daily fee/pet. Service with restrictions, supervision. 𝗔𝗦𝗞 ⊠ 🛏 💻

◈◈◈ ▼▼▼▼ Comfort Suites ◩

(610) 882-9700. **$99-$199.** 120 W 3rd St 18015. SR 378, exit 3rd St, at W 3rd and Brodhead sts; center. Int corridors. **Pets:** Medium. $10 daily fee/pet. Designated rooms, service with restrictions, supervision.
𝗦𝗔𝗩𝗘 ⊠ 🛏 💻 🍴

▼▼▼ Extended StayAmerica-Allentown/Bethlehem ◩

(610) 866-8480. **$59-$129.** 3050 Schoenersville Rd 18017. US 22, exit SR 378/Schoenersville Rd, follow signs for Schoenersville Rd, just n. Int corridors. **Pets:** Other species. $25 daily fee/room. Designated rooms, service with restrictions, crate. 𝗔𝗦𝗞 ⊠ 🛏 💻

◈◈◈ ▼▼▼ Historic Hotel Bethlehem ◩ 🐾

(610) 625-5000. **$169-$259.** 437 Main St 18018. SR 378 S, exit 3 (City Center), just n on 3rd Ave, 0.3 mi e on Union, then 0.3 mi s. Int corridors. **Pets:** Medium. $50 one-time fee/room. Designated rooms.
𝗦𝗔𝗩𝗘 ⊠ ♿ 🛏 💻

▼▼▼ Homewood Suites–Allentown/Bethlehem Airport ◩

(610) 264-7500. **$99-$169.** 2031 Avenue C 18017. US 22, exit SR 378/ Schoenersville Rd, follow signs for Schoenersville Rd, 0.7 mi n. Int corridors. **Pets:** Accepted. ⊠ ♿ 🛏 💻 ➳ 🐾

▼▼▼ Residence Inn Allentown Bethlehem/Route 22 ◩

(610) 317-2662. **$143-$175.** 2180 Motel Dr 18018. US 22, exit Airport Rd S, 0.8 mi se on Catasauqua Rd. Int corridors. **Pets:** Accepted.
⊠ 🛏 💻 ➳ 🐾

BLOOMSBURG

◈◈◈ ▼▼▼ Econo Lodge at Bloomsburg ◩ 🐾

(570) 387-0490. **$65-$139.** 189 Columbia Mall Dr 17815. I-80, exit 232, just n on SR 42. Int corridors. **Pets:** Medium. $10 daily fee/pet. Service with restrictions, crate. 𝗦𝗔𝗩𝗘 ⊠ 🛏 💻

▼▼▼ ▼▼▼ The Inn at Turkey Hill ◖◗ 🐾

(570) 387-1500. **$129-$239.** 991 Central Rd 17815. I-80, exit 236 eastbound; exit 236A westbound, just s. Ext/int corridors. **Pets:** Other species. $15 daily fee/room. Designated rooms, service with restrictions, supervision. 𝗔𝗦𝗞 ⊠ 🛏 💻 🍴

BLUE MOUNTAIN

◈◈◈ ▼▼▼ Kenmar Motel ⓜ

(717) 423-5915. **$60-$90.** 17788 Cumberland Hwy 17240. I-76, exit 201, just e on SR 997 N. Ext corridors. **Pets:** Dogs only. $10 daily fee/pet. Designated rooms, service with restrictions, supervision. 𝗦𝗔𝗩𝗘 ⊠ 🛏

BRADFORD

◈◈◈ ▼▼▼▼ Best Western Bradford Inn ◩

(814) 362-4501. **$105-$155.** 100 Davis St S 16701. US 219, exit Forman St southbound, just w to Davis St, then 0.3 mi s; exit Elm St northbound, just w. Ext/int corridors. **Pets:** Large. $10 daily fee/pet. Designated rooms, service with restrictions, crate. 𝗦𝗔𝗩𝗘 ⊠ 🛏 💻 🍴 ➳

▼▼▼ Comfort Inn-Bradford ◩ 🐾

(814) 368-6772. **Call for rates.** 76 Elm St 16701. US 219, exit Forman St southbound, just w to Davis St, then 0.3 mi s; exit Elm St northbound, just w. Int corridors. **Pets:** $10 daily fee/pet. Service with restrictions, supervision. ⊠ 🛏 💻 ➳

▼▼▼ ▼▼▼ Glendorn ◖◗ 🐾

(814) 362-6511. **Call for rates.** 1000 Glendorn Dr 16701. US 219, exit Forman St, just s on Mechanic St, then 4.3 mi w on W Corydon. Ext/int corridors. **Pets:** Other species. $75 daily fee/room. Designated rooms, service with restrictions, crate. ⊠ 🛏 💻 🍴 ➳ 🐾

BREEZEWOOD

◈◈◈ ▼▼▼ Best Western Plaza Inn ⓜ

(814) 735-4352. **$60-$85.** 16407 Lincoln Hwy 15533. I-76 (Pennsylvania Tpke), exit 161, just w on US 30; I-70, exit 147. Ext corridors.
Pets: Accepted. 𝗦𝗔𝗩𝗘 ⊠ 🛏 💻 ➳

◈◈◈ ▼▼▼ Howard Johnson of Breezewood ⓜ

(814) 735-2200. **$59-$89.** 16550 Lincoln Hwy 15533. I-76 (Pennsylvania Tpke), exit 161, just w on US 30; I-70, exit 147, just e on US 30. Int corridors. **Pets:** Medium, other species. $10 one-time fee/pet. Designated rooms, service with restrictions, supervision.
𝗦𝗔𝗩𝗘 ⊠ 🛏 💻 ➳ 🐾

▼▼▼ Wiltshire Motel ⓜ

(814) 735-4361. **$40-$49.** 140 S Breezewood Rd 15533. I-76 (Pennsylvania Tpke), exit 161, just w on US 30; I-70, exit 147. Ext corridors.
Pets: Medium, other species. Service with restrictions, supervision.
𝗔𝗦𝗞 ⊠ 💻

BROOKVILLE

◈◈◈ ▼▼ Budget Host Gold Eagle Inn ⓜ

(814) 849-7344. **$52-$85.** 250 W Main St 15825. I-80, exit 78, 0.5 mi s on SR 36. Ext corridors. **Pets:** Service with restrictions, crate.
𝗦𝗔𝗩𝗘 ⊠ 🛏 💻 🍴

◈◈◈ ▼▼▼ Quality Inn ⓜ

(814) 849-8381. **$70-$85.** 235 Allegheny Blvd 15825. I-80, exit 78, just s on SR 36. Int corridors. **Pets:** Other species. $15 one-time fee/pet. Service with restrictions, supervision. 𝗦𝗔𝗩𝗘 ⊠ 🛏 💻

◈◈◈ ▼▼▼ Super 8 ⓜ 🐾

(814) 849-8840. **$50-$65.** 251 Allegheny Blvd 15825. I-80, exit 78, just n on SR 36. Int corridors. **Pets:** Medium. $10 daily fee/pet. Supervision.
𝗦𝗔𝗩𝗘 ⊠ 🛏 💻

CAMBRIDGE SPRINGS

▼▼▼ The Riverside Inn ◖◗

(814) 398-4645. **$75-$180, 10 day notice.** 1 Fountain Ave 16403. Just ne of center. Int corridors. **Pets:** $25 one-time fee/room. Service with restrictions, crate. ⊠ 🛏 🍴 ➳ 🐾 ⓩ

CAMP HILL

▼▼▼▼ Radisson Penn Harris Hotel & Convention Center H

(717) 763-7117. **$109-$174.** 1150 Camp Hill Bypass 17011. Jct US 11, 15 and Erford Rd. Ext/int corridors. **Pets:** Accepted.

A$K ⊠ 🔥M 🔒 💻 ¶ ➿

CARLISLE

AAA ▼▼▼ America's Best Inn M

(717) 245-2242. **$58-$179, 3 day notice.** 1825 Harrisburg Pike 17013. I-81, exit 52 (US 11) southbound, 0.5 mi n; exit 52A northbound; I-76 (Pennsylvania Tpke), exit 226, 1.2 mi n on US 11. Int corridors. **Pets:** Accepted. SAVE ⊠ 💻

AAA ▼▼▼ Comfort Suites Hotel H

(717) 960-1000. **$119-$209.** 10 S Hanover St 17013. I-81, exit 47, 0.8 mi n on SR 34, just s of the square; downtown. Int corridors. **Pets:** Medium. $10 daily fee/pet. Designated rooms, service with restrictions.

SAVE ⊠ 🔥M 🔒 💻 ¶

AAA ▼▼▼ Days Inn Carlisle H

(717) 258-4147. **$79-$175, 14 day notice.** 101 Alexander Spring Rd 17013. I-81, exit 45, just sw. Int corridors. **Pets:** Accepted.

SAVE ⊠ 🔥M 🔒 💻 ➿

AAA ▼▼▼ Hampton Inn Carlisle H

(717) 240-0200. **$119-$144.** 1164 Harrisburg Pike 17013. I-76 (Pennsylvania Tpke), exit 226, just n; I-81, exit 52 (US 11) southbound; exit 52B northbound, 0.8 mi s. Int corridors. **Pets:** Accepted.

SAVE ⊠ 🔥M 🔒 💻 ➿

AAA ▼▼▼ Hotel Carlisle & Embers Convention Center H

(717) 243-1717. **$85-$175, 30 day notice.** 1700 Harrisburg Pike 17015. I-81, exit 52 (US 11) southbound; exit 52A northbound, 0.4 mi n; I-76 (Pennsylvania Tpke), exit 226, 1.2 mi n. Int corridors. **Pets:** Other species. $10 daily fee/room. Service with restrictions, supervision.

SAVE ⊠ 🔒 💻 ¶ ➿ ⊠

AAA ▼▼▼ Motel 6 Carlisle H

(717) 245-2400. **$40-$160, 7 day notice.** 1450 Harrisburg Pike 17015. I-81, exit 52 (US 11) southbound; exit 52A northbound, just se; I-76 (Pennsylvania Tpke), exit 226, 0.8 mi n. Int corridors. **Pets:** Other species. Service with restrictions, supervision.

SAVE ⊠ 🔒 💻 ¶ ➿

AAA ▼▼▼ Pheasant Field Bed & Breakfast BB ❀

(717) 258-0717. **$119-$239, 7 day notice.** 150 Hickorytown Rd 17015. I-76 (Pennsylvania Tpke), exit 226, 0.4 mi n on US 11, 2.3 mi se on S Middlesex Rd, 0.4 mi e on Ridge Dr, then just s. Ext/int corridors. **Pets:** Large, other species. $10 daily fee/room. Service with restrictions, crate. SAVE ⊠ 🔒

AAA ▼▼▼ Quality Inn Carlisle H

(717) 243-6000. **$64-$159.** 1255 Harrisburg Pike 17013. I-81, exit 52 (US 11) southbound; exit 52B northbound; I-76 (Pennsylvania Tpke), exit 226, 0.8 mi n. Int corridors. **Pets:** Medium, other species. $10 one-time fee/pet. Designated rooms, service with restrictions, supervision.

SAVE ⊠ 🔒 💻 ➿

AAA ▼▼▼ Ramada Limited H ❀

(717) 243-8585. **$50-$190.** 1252 Harrisburg Pike 17013. I-81, exit 52 (US 11) southbound; exit 52B northbound; I-76 (Pennsylvania Tpke), exit 226, 1 mi n on US 11. Ext/int corridors. **Pets:** Small, dogs only. Designated rooms, service with restrictions, supervision. SAVE ⊠ 🔒 💻

AAA ▼▼▼ Residence Inn by Marriott Harrisburg Carlisle H ❀

(717) 610-9050. **$129-$179.** 1164 Harrisburg Pike 17013. I-76 (Pennsylvania Tpke), exit 226, just n; I-81, exit 52 (US 11) southbound; exit 52B northbound, 0.8 mi s. Int corridors. **Pets:** Medium, other species. $75 one-time fee/room. Service with restrictions, crate.

SAVE ⊠ 🔥M 🔒 💻 ➿

AAA ▼▼▼ Super 8/Carlisle South M

(717) 245-9898. **$45-$140.** 100 Alexander Spring Rd 17015. I-81, exit 45, just se. Int corridors. **Pets:** Medium, other species. $10 daily fee/pet. Service with restrictions. SAVE ⊠ 🔥M 🔒 💻

CHAMBERSBURG

AAA ▼▼▼ Best Western Chambersburg H

(717) 262-4994. **$55-$129.** 211 Walker Rd 17201. I-81, exit 16, just w on US 30, then just n. Int corridors. **Pets:** Accepted.

SAVE ⊠ 🔒 💻 ➿

▼▼▼ Comfort Inn-Chambersburg H

(717) 263-6655. **$63-$150.** 3301 Black Gap Rd 17202. I-81, exit 20, just e, then just s on SR 997. Int corridors. **Pets:** Accepted.

A$K ⊠ 🔒 💻 ➿

▼▼▼ Country Inn & Suites By Carlson H

(717) 261-0900. **$80-$140.** 399 Bedington Blvd 17201. I-81, exit 17 (Walker Rd), 0.6 mi s, then just w. Int corridors. **Pets:** Small. $25 one-time fee/pet. Service with restrictions, crate.

A$K ⊠ 🔥M 🔒 💻 ➿

AAA ▼▼▼ Days Inn H

(717) 263-1288. **$60-$129.** 30 Falling Spring Rd 17202. I-81, exit 16, just e on US 30. Int corridors. **Pets:** Medium, other species. $10 daily fee/pet. Designated rooms, service with restrictions, supervision.

SAVE ⊠ 🔒 💻 ➿

▼▼ Econo Lodge M

(717) 264-8005. **$60-$90.** 1110 Sheller Ave 17201. I-81, exit 14, just w on SR 316. Int corridors. **Pets:** Small, other species. $10 daily fee/pet. Service with restrictions, supervision. A$K ⊠ 🔒 💻

▼▼ Red Carpet Inn M

(717) 267-2323. **Call for rates.** 1175 Wayne Ave 17201. I-81, exit 14, just e on SR 316. Ext corridors. **Pets:** Accepted. ⊠ 🔒 💻

CLARION

▼▼ Comfort Inn-Clarion H

(814) 226-5230. **Call for rates.** 129 Dolby St 16214. I-80, exit 62, 0.6 mi n on SR 68. Int corridors. **Pets:** Accepted. ⊠ 🔒 💻 ➿

▼▼▼ Holiday Inn Clarion H ❀

(814) 226-8850. **$99-$149.** 45 Holiday Inn Rd 16214. I-80, exit 62, 0.5 mi n on SR 68. Int corridors. **Pets:** $10 daily fee/pet. Service with restrictions, crate. A$K ⊠ 🔒 💻 ¶ ➿ ⊠

▼▼ Microtel Inn & Suites-Clarion H

(814) 227-2700. **Call for rates.** 151 Hotel Dr 16214. I-80, exit 62, just n on SR 68, then just e. Int corridors. **Pets:** Accepted. ⊠ 🔒 💻

AAA ▼▼▼ Quality Inn & Suites Clarion M

(814) 226-8682. **$45-$100.** 24 United Dr 16214. I-80, exit 62, just n on SR 68. Int corridors. **Pets:** Other species. $5 daily fee/pet. Service with restrictions, supervision. SAVE ⊠ 🔒 💻 ¶ ➿

CLARKS SUMMIT

AAA ▼▼▼ Comfort Inn-Clarks Summit/Scranton H

(570) 586-9100. **$76-$110.** 811 Northern Blvd 18411. I-81, exit 194, on US 6 and 11; I-476 (Pennsylvania Tpke), exit 131. Int corridors. **Pets:** Other species. $10 daily fee/pet. Service with restrictions, supervision. SAVE ⊠ 🔒

AAA ▼▼▼ Econo Lodge of Clarks Summit/Scranton North M ❀

(570) 586-1211. **$44-$149.** 649 Northern Blvd 18411. I-81, exit 194, on US 6 and 11 E; I-476 (Pennsylvania Tpke), exit 131, just e. Ext corridors. **Pets:** Medium, other species. $10 daily fee/pet. Service with restrictions, crate. SAVE ⊠ 🔒 💻

CLEARFIELD

AAA ▼▼ Budget Inn M ❖
(814) 765-2639. **$31-$75.** 6321 Clearfield/Woodland Hwy (US 322 E) 16830. I-80, exit 120, 1.5 mi sw on SR 879, then 1.2 mi e. Ext/int corridors. **Pets:** $10 daily fee/pet. Service with restrictions, supervision.
[SAVE] [X] [🍴]

▼▼ Super 8-Clearfield M
(814) 768-7580. **$68-$87.** 14597 Clearfield/Shawville Hwy (Rt 879) 16830. I-80, exit 120, just s. Int corridors. **Pets:** Other species. $5 daily fee/room. Service with restrictions, supervision. [ASK] [X] [♿] [🍴] [💻]

DANVILLE

AAA ▼▼▼ Best Western Danville Inn H ❖
(570) 275-5750. **$85-$169.** 79 Old Valley School Rd 17821. I-80, exit 224, just s. Int corridors. **Pets:** Medium, other species. $15 daily fee/room. Designated rooms, service with restrictions, crate.
[SAVE] [X] [🍴] [💻] [🏊]

AAA ▼▼▼ Danville Super 8 M ❖
(570) 275-4640. **$40-$170, 3 day notice.** 35 Sheraton Rd 17821. I-80, exit 224, just sw on SR 54. Ext corridors. **Pets:** Medium, other species. $15 one-time fee/room. Designated rooms, service with restrictions.
[SAVE] [X] [🍴]

AAA ▼▼▼ Quality Inn & Suites Danville M
(570) 275-5100. **$60-$190.** 15 Valley West Rd 17821. I-80, exit 224, just n on SR 54. Int corridors. **Pets:** Accepted.
[SAVE] [X] [🍴] [💻] [🍽] [🏊]

DICKSON CITY

▼▼ Days Inn Scranton H ❖
(570) 383-9979. **$54-$99.** 1946 Scranton-Carbondale Hwy 18508. I-81, exit 191A, 2 mi e on US 6; I-476 (Pennsylvania Tpke NE Ext), exit 131 (Clarks Summit), 4.5 mi e on US 6. Int corridors. **Pets:** Other species. $10 daily fee/pet. Service with restrictions, crate.
[ASK] [X] [🍴] [💻] [🏊] [X]

▼▼▼▼ Residence Inn by Marriott-Scranton H
(570) 343-5121. **$140-$170.** 947 Viewmont Dr 18519. I-81, exit 190, just e, follow signs to Viewmont Dr. Int corridors. **Pets:** Accepted.
[X] [🍴] [💻] [🏊] [X]

DU BOIS

AAA ▼▼▼ Best Western Inn & Conference Center H ❖
(814) 371-6200. **$79-$139.** 82 N Park Pl 15801. I-80, exit 97 eastbound, 2.5 mi e on DuBois Ave (US 219), then just s; exit 101 westbound, 2.7 mi w on DuBois Ave (SR 255), then just s on US 219. Int corridors. **Pets:** Other species. $12 daily fee/pet. Service with restrictions, crate.
[SAVE] [X] [🍴] [💻] [X]

DUNMORE

AAA ▼▼▼ Days Inn H
(570) 348-6101. **$59-$299.** 1226 O'Neill Hwy 18512. I-81, exit 188 (Throop), just e at SR 347 N. Int corridors. **Pets:** $10 daily fee/pet. Service with restrictions, supervision. [SAVE] [X] [🍴] [💻]

▼▼▼▼ Holiday Inn-Scranton East H
(570) 343-4771. **$79-$199.** 200 Tigue St 18512. I-84/380, exit 1 (Tigue St), 0.3 mi e of jct I-81. Int corridors. **Pets:** Large, other species. $15 daily fee/pet. Designated rooms, service with restrictions.
[ASK] [X] [🍴] [🍽] [🏊] [X]

AAA ▼▼▼ Sleep Inn & Suites H
(570) 961-1116. **$70-$100.** 102 Monahan Ave 18512. I-81, exit 188 (Throop), just e at SR 347 N (O'Neill Hwy), then just s. Int corridors. **Pets:** Large. $15 daily fee/pet. Designated rooms, service with restrictions, supervision. [SAVE] [X] [♿] [🍴] [💻] [🏊] [X]

EASTON

▼▼▼ Comfort Inn H
(610) 253-0546. **Call for rates.** 2555 Nazareth Rd 18042. US 22, exit 25th St, just e on N Service Rd. Int corridors. **Pets:** Medium. $20 daily fee/pet. Service with restrictions, crate. [X] [🍴] [💻]

▼▼▼▼ Grand Eastonian Suites Hotel H
(610) 258-6350. **$99-$239.** 140 N Northampton St 18042. US 22, exit 4th St (SR 611), just e to 3rd St, just s to downtown square, then just e toward river. Int corridors. **Pets:** Medium. $25 daily fee/room. Service with restrictions, crate. [ASK] [X] [🍴] [💻] [🏊]

▼▼▼ The Lafayette Inn BB ❖
(610) 253-4500. **$150-$250.** 525 W Monroe St 18042. US 22, exit 4th St (SR 611), just n on 3rd St, 0.3 mi ne on College Ave, then 0.3 mi n on Cattell St to jct Monroe St. Ext/int corridors. **Pets:** $20 daily fee/room. Designated rooms, service with restrictions, supervision. [X] [🍴] [💻]

EBENSBURG

▼▼▼ Comfort Inn H
(814) 472-6100. **$81-$90.** 111 Cook Rd 15931. Jct US 219, just e on US 22. Int corridors. **Pets:** Accepted. [ASK] [X] [♿] [🍴] [💻] [🏊]

ERIE

▼▼▼ Comfort Inn I-90 H
(814) 866-6666. **$59-$199.** 8051 Peach St 16509. I-90, exit 24, just s. Int corridors. **Pets:** Accepted. [ASK] [X] [🍴] [💻] [🏊]

AAA ▼▼▼ Glass House Inn M
(814) 833-7751. **$59-$116.** 3202 W 26th St 16506. I-79, exit 182, 1.4 mi w on US 20. Ext corridors. **Pets:** Dogs only. $20 one-time fee/pet. Service with restrictions, supervision. [SAVE] [X] [🍴] [💻] [🏊]

▼▼▼ Homewood Suites by Hilton H
(814) 866-8292. **$79-$179.** 2084 Interchange Rd 16565. I-79, exit 180, just e; in Pavillion Marketplace. Int corridors. **Pets:** Medium, other species. $75 one-time fee/room. Service with restrictions, supervision.
[X] [♿] [🍴] [💻] [🏊]

▼▼▼ La Quinta Inn & Suites H ❖
(814) 864-1812. **$59-$169.** 7820 Perry Hwy 16509. I-90, exit 27, just n. Int corridors. **Pets:** Medium, other species. Service with restrictions, supervision. [ASK] [X] [🍴] [💻] [🏊]

▼▼▼ Microtel Inn-Erie M
(814) 864-1010. **$70-$130.** 8100 Peach St 16509. I-90, exit 24, just s. Int corridors. **Pets:** Large. $10 daily fee/pet. Service with restrictions, crate.
[ASK] [X] [🍴] [💻]

AAA ▼▼▼ Red Roof Inn #7054 M
(814) 868-5246. **Call for rates.** 7865 Perry Hwy 16509. I-90, exit 27, just n on SR 97. Ext/int corridors. **Pets:** Large. Service with restrictions, crate. [SAVE] [X] [🍴]

AAA ▼▼▼▼ Sheraton Erie Bayfront Hotel H ❖
(814) 454-2005. **$109-$239, 3 day notice.** 55 West Bay Dr 16507. I-90, exit 22B to Bayfront Connector; I-79 to Bayfront Pkwy. Int corridors. **Pets:** Medium, dogs only. $50 one-time fee/room. Designated rooms, service with restrictions, supervision.
[SAVE] [X] [♿] [🍴] [💻] [🍽] [🏊] [X]

▼▼▼ TownePlace Suites Erie H ❖
(814) 866-7100. **$110-$130.** 2090 Interchange Rd 16565. I-79, exit 180, just e; in Pavillion Marketplace. Int corridors. **Pets:** Medium, other species. $50 one-time fee/room. [X] [🍴] [💻] [🏊]

▼▼▼ Wingate by Wyndham H
(814) 860-3050. **Call for rates.** 8060 Old Oliver Rd 16509. I-90, exit 24, just s on Peach St, just w, just n, then just e. Int corridors. **Pets:** Medium, dogs only. $50 one-time fee/pet. Service with restrictions, crate.
[X] [♿] [🍴] [💻] [🏊]

FOGELSVILLE

▼▼▼ **Glasbern** 🄲
(610) 285-4723. **$150-$485, 7 day notice.** 2141 Packhouse Rd 18051. I-78, exit 49B (SR 100), 0.3 mi n to 1st traffic light, 0.3 mi w on Main St, 0.6 mi n on Church St, then 0.8 mi ne. Ext/int corridors. **Pets:** Accepted.

Ⓐ𝔖Ⓚ ⊠ 🛏 💻 🍴 🏊 ⊠

▼▼▼ **Holiday Inn Conference Center** 🄷
(610) 391-1000. **Call for rates.** 7736 Adrienne Dr 18031. I-78, exit 49A, 0.3 mi s on SR 100. Int corridors. **Pets:** Accepted.

⊠ 🕭ᴹ 🛏 💻 🍴 🏊 ⊠

▼ ▼ **Sleep Inn** 🄷
(610) 395-6603. **$59-$159.** 327 Star Rd 18106. I-78, exit 49A, 0.3 mi s on SR 100, left at 1st traffic light, then immediate left on service road. Int corridors. **Pets:** Other species. $15 daily fee/pet. No service, supervision.

Ⓐ𝔖Ⓚ ⊠ 🕭ᴹ 🛏 💻

▼▼▼ **Staybridge Suites-Allentown West** 🄷
(610) 841-5100. **Call for rates.** 327 C Star Rd 18106. I-78, exit 49A, 0.3 mi s on SR 100, e at traffic light, then n on service road. Int corridors. **Pets:** Accepted. ⊠ 🛏 💻 🏊 ⊠

FRANKLIN

▼ ▼ **Franklin Super 8** 🄷
(814) 432-2101. **Call for rates.** 847 Allegheny Blvd 16323. 2 mi on SR 8 N. Int corridors. **Pets:** Small. $10 daily fee/pet. Service with restrictions, supervision. ⊠ 🛏 💻

GETTYSBURG

▼▼▼ **1863 Inn of Gettysburg** 🄷
(717) 334-6211. **$89-$200.** 516 Baltimore St 17325. Jct US 15 business route and SR 97. Ext/int corridors. **Pets:** Other species. $10 daily fee/room. Designated rooms, service with restrictions, supervision.

Ⓐ𝔖Ⓚ ⊠ 🛏 💻 🍴 🏊

𝔸𝔸𝔸 ▼ ▼ **Americas Best Value Inn** 🄼
(717) 334-1188. **$56-$155.** 301 Steinwehr Ave 17325. 1 mi s on US 15 business route, just s of jct SR 134. Ext/int corridors. **Pets:** Other species. Designated rooms, service with restrictions. 𝔖𝔄𝔙𝔈 ⊠ 🛏 💻 🏊

▼▼▼ **Battlefield Bed & Breakfast Inn** 🄱🄱 🐾
(717) 334-8804. **$175-$349, 7 day notice.** 2264 Emmitsburg Rd 17325. 4 mi s on Steinwehr Ave and Baltimore Pike. Int corridors. **Pets:** Large, dogs only. Service with restrictions. Ⓐ𝔖Ⓚ ⊠

▼ ▼ **Comfort Inn-Gettysburg** 🄼 🐾
(717) 337-2400. **$59-$139.** 871 York Rd 17325. 1 mi e on US 30. Int corridors. **Pets:** Other species. $10 daily fee/pet. Designated rooms, service with restrictions, crate. Ⓐ𝔖Ⓚ ⊠ 🛏 🏊

𝔸𝔸𝔸 ▼▼▼▼ **Country Inn & Suites By Carlson** 🄷
(717) 337-9518. **$69-$165.** 1857 Gettysburg Village Dr 17325. US 15, exit SR 97, just e. Int corridors. **Pets:** Accepted.

𝔖𝔄𝔙𝔈 ⊠ 🛏 💻 🏊

▼ ▼ **Gettysburg Travelodge** 🄼
(717) 334-9281. **$69-$159.** 613 Baltimore St 17325. On SR 97 at US 15 business route. Ext/int corridors. **Pets:** Large, other species. Service with restrictions, supervision. Ⓐ𝔖Ⓚ ⊠ 🛏 💻

𝔸𝔸𝔸 ▼▼▼ **Motel 6–President Inn** 🄷
(717) 334-4274. **$50-$159.** 606 York St 17325. 0.5 mi e on US 30 from square. Int corridors. **Pets:** Other species. Service with restrictions, supervision. 𝔖𝔄𝔙𝔈 ⊠ 🛏 🏊

𝔸𝔸𝔸 ▼ ▼ **Super 8** 🄷 🐾
(717) 337-1400. **$49-$169.** 869 York Rd 17325. 1 mi e on US 30. Int corridors. **Pets:** Medium. $10 daily fee/pet. Service with restrictions, supervision. 𝔖𝔄𝔙𝔈 ⊠ 🕭ᴹ 🛏 💻 🏊

𝔸𝔸𝔸 ▼▼▼ **Wyndham Gettysburg** 🄷
(717) 339-0020. **$89-$199.** 95 Presidential Cir 17325. US 15, exit York St, just e on US 30. Int corridors. **Pets:** Medium. $20 daily fee/pet. Designated rooms, service with restrictions, crate.

𝔖𝔄𝔙𝔈 ⊠ 🕭ᴹ 🛏 💻 🍴 🏊

GIRARD

▼ ▼ **The Green Roof Inn** 🄼
(814) 774-7072. **$56-$123.** 8790 Meadville Rd 16417. I-90, exit 9, 1.9 mi s. Ext corridors. **Pets:** Accepted. ⊠ 🛏 💻

GRANTVILLE

𝔸𝔸𝔸 ▼▼▼ **Days Inn Grantville-Hershey** 🄼
(717) 469-0631. **$89-$140.** 252 Bow Creek Rd 17028. I-81, exit 80. Ext corridors. **Pets:** Accepted. 𝔖𝔄𝔙𝔈 ⊠ 🛏 💻

𝔸𝔸𝔸 ▼▼▼▼ **Holiday Inn Harrisburg-Hershey Area,** I-81 🄷
(717) 469-0661. **$99-$199.** 604 Station Rd 17028. I-81, exit 80. Int corridors. **Pets:** $75 deposit/room, $25 one-time fee/room. No service, supervision. 𝔖𝔄𝔙𝔈 ⊠ 🕭ᴹ 🛏 💻 🍴 🏊 ⊠

GREENCASTLE

𝔸𝔸𝔸 ▼ ▼ **Comfort Inn** 🄷
(717) 597-8164. **$62-$100.** 50 Pine Dr 17225. I-81, exit 3, just s on US 11. Int corridors. **Pets:** Large. $15 daily fee/pet. Supervision.

𝔖𝔄𝔙𝔈 ⊠ 🛏 💻 🍴 ⊠

HAMBURG

▼ ▼ **Microtel Inn & Suites** 🄷
(610) 562-4234. **$74-$150.** 50 Industrial Dr 19526. I-78, exit 29B, 0.3 mi n on SR 61, then just e. Int corridors. **Pets:** Accepted.

Ⓐ𝔖Ⓚ ⊠ 🕭ᴹ 🛏 💻 🍴

HARRISBURG

𝔸𝔸𝔸 ▼▼▼ **Best Western Harrisburg/Hershey Hotel & Suites** 🄷
(717) 652-7180. **$90-$150.** 300 N Mountain Rd 17112. I-81, exit 72 southbound; exit 72B northbound. Int corridors. **Pets:** Other species. $25 daily fee/room. Service with restrictions. 𝔖𝔄𝔙𝔈 ⊠ 🛏 💻 🍴 🏊

𝔸𝔸𝔸 ▼▼▼ **Comfort Inn Harrisburg/Hershey** 🄷 🐾
(717) 540-8400. **$69-$169.** 7744 Linglestown Rd 17112. I-81, exit 77, 0.5 mi w. Int corridors. **Pets:** Other species. $10 daily fee/pet. Designated rooms, service with restrictions, crate. 𝔖𝔄𝔙𝔈 ⊠ 🛏 💻 🏊 ⊠

𝔸𝔸𝔸 ▼▼▼▼ **Comfort Inn Riverfront** 🄷 🐾
(717) 233-1611. **$90-$170.** 525 S Front St 17104. I-83, exit 43, 0.5 mi n. Int corridors. **Pets:** Small. $25 daily fee/pet. Designated rooms, service with restrictions, crate. 𝔖𝔄𝔙𝔈 ⊠ 🛏 💻 🍴 🏊

▼▼▼ **Crowne Plaza Harrisburg-Hershey** 🄷
(717) 234-5021. **$115-$199.** 23 S 2nd St 17101. Jct Chestnut St; downtown. Int corridors. **Pets:** Medium. $50 one-time fee/pet. Service with restrictions, supervision. Ⓐ𝔖Ⓚ ⊠ 🕭ᴹ 🛏 💻 🍴 🏊

𝔸𝔸𝔸 ▼▼▼ **Econo Lodge** 🄷
(717) 540-9100. **$54-$109.** 7930 Linglestown Rd 17112. I-81, exit 77. Int corridors. **Pets:** Small. $10 one-time fee/pet. Designated rooms, no service, supervision. 𝔖𝔄𝔙𝔈 ⊠ 🛏 💻

𝔸𝔸𝔸 ▼▼▼ **Hilton Harrisburg** 🄷 🐾
(717) 233-6000. **$109-$229.** One N 2nd St 17101. Center of downtown. Int corridors. **Pets:** Other species. $75 one-time fee/room. Designated rooms, service with restrictions, supervision.

𝔖𝔄𝔙𝔈 ⊠ 🕭ᴹ 🛏 💻 🍴 🏊 ⊠

𝔸𝔸𝔸 ▼▼▼ **Holiday Inn Express East** 🄷
(717) 561-8100. **$89-$179.** 4021 Union Deposit Rd 17109. I-83, exit 48, just w. Int corridors. **Pets:** Medium, dogs only. $15 daily fee/room. Service with restrictions, crate. 𝔖𝔄𝔙𝔈 ⊠ 🛏 💻

(AAA) ▼◆▼◆ Holiday Inn Express Hotel & Suites H
(717) 657-2200. **$89-$169.** 5680 Allentown Blvd 17112. I-81, exit 72, just
s on N Mountain Rd, then just w on US 22. Int corridors. **Pets:** Medium.
$25 daily fee/pet. Service with restrictions, crate.
[SAVE] [X] [&M] [🛏] [💻] [🏊]

(AAA) ▼◆▼◆▼ Holiday Inn Harrisburg East-Airport H
(717) 939-7841. **$89-$159.** 4751 Lindle Rd 17111. I-283, exit 2, just e. Int
corridors. **Pets:** Small, other species. $75 deposit/room, $25 one-time
fee/room. Service with restrictions, crate.
[SAVE] [X] [&M] [🛏] [💻] [🍴] [🏊] [X]

(AAA) ▼◆▼◆▼ Red Roof Inn- Harrisburg/Hershey #7027 M
(717) 939-1331. **Call for rates.** 950 Eisenhower Blvd 17111. I-283, exit
2, just e. Ext/int corridors. **Pets:** Large. Service with restrictions, crate.
[SAVE] [X] [🛏]

▼◆▼◆ Red Roof Inn-North #7037 M
(717) 657-1445. **Call for rates.** 400 Corporate Cir 17110. I-81, exit 69,
just n on Progress Ave. Ext/int corridors. **Pets:** Large. Service with restrictions, crate. [X] [🛏]

▼◆▼◆▼ Residence Inn by Marriott Harrisburg-Hershey H
(717) 561-1900. **$170-$208.** 4480 Lewis Rd 17111. US 322, exit Penhar
Dr, just e. Ext/int corridors. **Pets:** $100 one-time fee/room. Designated
rooms, service with restrictions. [X] [🛏] [💻] [🏊] [X]

▼◆▼◆ Sheraton Harrisburg Hershey H
(717) 564-5511. **$119-$325.** 4650 Lindle Rd 17111. I-283, exit 2, just e.
Int corridors. **Pets:** Accepted. [X] [&M] [🛏] [💻] [🍴] [🏊] [X]

(AAA) ▼◆▼◆▼ Staybridge Suites Harrisburg H
(717) 233-3304. **$109-$229.** 920 Wildwood Park Dr 17110. I-81, exit 67
A/B. Int corridors. **Pets:** Accepted. [SAVE] [X] [🛏] [💻] [🏊]

(AAA) ▼◆▼◆▼ TownePlace Suites Harrisburg Hershey H
(717) 558-0202. **$129-$159.** 450 Friendship Rd 17111. I-83, exit 45, 0.7
mi on Paxton St, then 0.3 mi. Int corridors. **Pets:** Other species. $100
one-time fee/pet. Service with restrictions, crate.
[SAVE] [X] [🛏] [💻] [🏊] [X]

HAZLETON

(AAA) ▼◆▼◆ Best Western Genetti Inn & Suites H
(570) 454-2494. **$81-$110, 3 day notice.** 1341 N Church St 18202.
I-80, exit 262, 6 mi s on SR 309; I-81, exit 145, 0.5 mi s on SR 93, 1 mi
e on Airport Rd, then 0.6 mi s. Ext/int corridors. **Pets:** Large, dogs only.
$10 daily fee/room. Service with restrictions, crate.
[SAVE] [X] [🛏] [🏊]

▼◆▼◆ Ramada Inn Hazleton H
(570) 455-2061. **Call for rates.** 1213 N Church St 18202. I-80, exit 262,
6 mi s on SR 309; I-81, exit 145, 0.5 mi s on SR 93, 1 mi e on Airport
Rd, then 0.7 mi s. Int corridors. **Pets:** Accepted.
[X] [🛏] [💻] [🍴] [🏊]

▼◆▼◆▼ Residence Inn Hazleton H ❀
(570) 455-9555. **$116-$142.** 1 Station Circle Dr 18202. I-81, exit 143, just
s on SR 924 S; at Humboldt Station, just e on Commerce Dr. Int corridors. **Pets:** Other species. $20 one-time fee/room. Service with restric-
tions. [X] [&M] [🛏] [💻] [🏊] [X]

HERSHEY

(AAA) ▼◆▼◆ Best Western Inn-Hershey H
(717) 533-5665. **$89-$239.** US 422 & Sipe Ave 17033. Jct US 322, just
e. Ext/int corridors. **Pets:** Small, dogs only. $25 daily fee/room. Desig-
nated rooms, service with restrictions, supervision.
[SAVE] [X] [🛏] [💻] [🏊] [X]

(AAA) ▼◆▼◆▼ Days Inn Hershey H ❀
(717) 534-2162. **$89-$269.** 350 W Chocolate Ave 17033. On US 422;
center. Int corridors. **Pets:** Medium, dogs only. $15 daily fee/pet. Desig-
nated rooms, service with restrictions, supervision.
[SAVE] [X] [&M] [🛏] [💻] [🏊] [X]

(AAA) ▼◆▼◆▼ Hampton Inn & Suites H
(717) 533-8400. **$99-$309.** 749 E Chocolate Ave 17033. 0.9 mi e on US
422. Int corridors. **Pets:** Small. Designated rooms, service with restrictions, crate. [SAVE] [X] [&M] [🛏] [💻] [🏊] [X]

HUNTINGDON

▼◆▼◆ Huntingdon Motor Inn M ❀
(814) 643-1133. **$51-$85.** 6920 Motor Inn Dr 16652. On US 22 at SR
26. Ext corridors. **Pets:** $10 daily fee/pet. No service, supervision.
[X] [🛏] [💻]

INDIANA

▼◆▼◆▼ Holiday Inn H
(724) 463-3561. **$99-$149.** 1395 Wayne Ave 15701. US 422, exit Wayne
Ave, 1 mi n. Ext/int corridors. **Pets:** Accepted.
[ASK] [X] [🛏] [💻] [🍴] [🏊]

JONESTOWN

▼◆▼◆ Days Inn Lebanon/Lickdale H
(717) 865-4064. **$50-$179.** 3 Everest Ln 17038. I-81, exit 90. Int corridors. **Pets:** Accepted. [ASK] [X] [🛏] [💻]

▼◆▼◆ Quality Inn Jonestown/Lebanon M
(717) 865-6600. **Call for rates.** 16 Marsanna Ln 17038. I-81, exit 90,
just w. Int corridors. **Pets:** Accepted. [X] [🛏] [💻] [🏊]

KITTANNING

▼◆▼◆ Quality Inn Royle H
(724) 543-1159. **$55-$99.** 405 Butler Rd 16201. SR 28, exit US 422 W
(Belmont). Ext/int corridors. **Pets:** Medium, other species. $20 daily fee/
pet. Designated rooms, service with restrictions, supervision.
[ASK] [X] [🛏] [💻] [🍴]

▼◆▼◆ Rodeway Inn Kittanning M
(724) 543-1100. **Call for rates.** 13607 US 422 16201. E of jct Business
Rt US 422, SR 66 and 28. Ext corridors. **Pets:** Dogs only. $5 one-time
fee/pet. [X] [🛏] [💻]

LAUREL HIGHLANDS AREA

CHALK HILL

(AAA) ▼◆▼◆ The Lodge at Chalk Hill M
(724) 438-8880. **$49-$110.** Rt 40 E 15421. Just w. Ext corridors.
Pets: Medium. $10 daily fee/pet. Designated rooms, service with restric-
tions, supervision. [SAVE] [X] [🛏] [💻] [X]

DONEGAL

▼◆▼◆ Lesley's Mountain View Country Inn CI
(724) 593-6349. **$160-$210, 7 day notice.** 327 Mountain View Rd
15628. I-70/76 (Pennsylvania Tpke), exit 91, 1 mi e, then 0.5 mi s. Ext/int
corridors. **Pets:** Medium. Designated rooms, service with restrictions,
supervision. [X] [🍴]

FARMINGTON

▼▼▼ Historic Summit Inn H
(724) 438-8594. **$139-$299, 3 day notice.** 101 Skyline Dr 15437. On US 40; center. Int corridors. **Pets:** Small, dogs only. $20 daily fee/pet. Designated rooms, service with restrictions, supervision.
ASK ✕ 🛏 🖵 🍴 ➰ ✕

⊕ ▼▼▼ Nemacolin Woodlands Resort H ✿
(724) 329-8555. **$239-$819, 14 day notice.** 1001 LaFayette Dr 15437. 1 mi e on US 40. Ext/int corridors. **Pets:** Small, dogs only. $150 one-time fee/room. Designated rooms, service with restrictions, supervision.
SAVE ✕ 🛏 🖵 🍴 ➰ ✕

GREENSBURG

⊕ ▼▼▼ Four Points by
Sheraton-Greensburg H ✿
(724) 836-6060. **$75-$175.** 100 Sheraton Dr 15601. I-76 (Pennsylvania Tpke), exit 75, 5.6 mi on US 119 N, 3 mi e on US 30, then just n. Int corridors. **Pets:** Medium, other species. $25 one-time fee/pet. Service with restrictions, supervision. SAVE ✕ 🛏 🖵 🍴 ➰

▼▼ Knights Inn-Greensburg H
(724) 836-7100. **$60-$125.** 1215 S Main St 15601. I-76 (Pennsylvania Tpke), exit 75, 4 mi s on US 119; just s of US 30. Ext corridors.
Pets: Accepted. ASK ✕ 🛏 🖵 ➰

JOHNSTOWN

▼▼▼ Comfort Inn & Suites H
(814) 266-3678. **$90-$100.** 455 Theatre Dr 15904. US 219, exit Elton (SR 756), just e. Int corridors. **Pets:** $15 daily fee/pet. Designated rooms, service with restrictions, supervision. ASK ✕ ♿M 🛏 🖵 ➰

▼▼ Econo Lodge M
(814) 536-1114. **Call for rates.** 430 Napoleon Pl 15901. Jct SR 271 and 403; downtown. Int corridors. **Pets:** Accepted. ✕ ♿M 🛏

▼▼▼ Holiday Inn Downtown H ✿
(814) 535-7777. **$117-$127.** 250 Market St 15901. Corner of Market and Vine sts; downtown. Int corridors. **Pets:** Medium. $25 one-time fee/pet. Service with restrictions, supervision.
ASK ✕ 🛏 🖵 🍴 ➰ ✕

▼▼ Holiday Inn Express Johnstown M
(814) 266-8789. **$104-$149.** 1440 Scalp Ave 15904. US 219, exit Windber (SR 56 E), just e. Int corridors. **Pets:** $25 one-time fee/pet. Service with restrictions, supervision. ASK ✕ ♿M 🛏 🖵

▼▼ Sleep Inn H
(814) 262-9292. **$76-$85.** 453 Theatre Dr 15904. US 219, exit Elton (SR 756), just e. Int corridors. **Pets:** $15 daily fee/pet. Designated rooms, service with restrictions, supervision. ASK ✕ ♿M 🛏 🖵

⊕ ▼▼▼ Super 8 Johnstown H ✿
(814) 535-5600. **$70-$90.** 627 Solomon Run Rd 15904. US 219, exit Galleria Dr, just w. Int corridors. **Pets:** $7 daily fee/pet. Supervision.
SAVE ✕ 🛏 🖵

NEW STANTON

⊕ ▼▼▼ Days Inn New Stanton H
(724) 925-3591. **$60-$95, 7 day notice.** 127 W Byers Ave, Box K 15672. I-76, exit 75, 0.5 mi sw; I-70, exit 57B westbound; exit 57 eastbound. Int corridors. **Pets:** Medium. $100 deposit/pet, $10 one-time fee/pet. Designated rooms, service with restrictions, supervision.
SAVE ✕ 🛏 🖵 🍴 ➰

⊕ ▼▼ Howard Johnson Inn M
(724) 925-3511. **$49-$119.** 112 W Byers Ave 15672. I-76, exit 75, 0.5 mi sw; I-70, exit 57B westbound; exit 57 eastbound. Ext/int corridors. **Pets:** Small. $7 daily fee/pet. Designated rooms, service with restrictions.
SAVE ✕ 🛏 🖵

⊕ ▼▼ Super 8-New Stanton M
(724) 925-8915. **$65-$85.** 103 Bair Blvd 15672. I-76, exit 75, 0.5 mi se; I-70, exit 57B westbound; exit 57 eastbound. Int corridors.
Pets: Accepted. SAVE ✕ 🛏 🖵

SOMERSET

▼▼ Budget Host Inn M
(814) 445-7988. **$45-$95, 3 day notice.** 799 N Center Ave 15501. I-70/76 (Pennsylvania Tpke), exit 110, 0.3 mi s. Ext corridors. **Pets:** Small. $7 daily fee/pet. No service, supervision. ASK ✕ 🛏

⊕ ▼▼▼ Comfort Inn H
(814) 445-9611. **$94-$149.** 202 Harmon St 15501. I-70/76 (Pennsylvania Tpke), exit 110, just s. Int corridors. **Pets:** Medium, other species. $35 one-time fee/room. Designated rooms, service with restrictions, supervision. SAVE ✕ 🖵 🍴 ➰

▼▼ Dollar Inn M
(814) 445-2977. **$40-$85.** 1146 N Center Ave 15501. I-70/76 (Pennsylvania Tpke), exit 110, 0.3 mi s, then just n on SR 601/N Central Ave; at top of hill. Ext corridors. **Pets:** Medium, other species. $7 daily fee/pet. Designated rooms, service with restrictions, supervision. ASK ✕ 🛏

▼▼ Glades Pike Inn BB
(814) 443-4978. **$65-$125, 3 day notice.** 2684 Glades Pike Rd 15501. I-70/76 (Pennsylvania Tpke), exit 110, 6 mi w on SR 31; exit 91, 13 mi e on SR 31. Int corridors. **Pets:** Other species. Service with restrictions, supervision. ASK ✕ 🇿

▼▼▼ The Inn at Georgian Place CI
(814) 443-1043. **$105-$195, 7 day notice.** 800 Georgian Place Dr 15501. I-70/76 (Pennsylvania Tpke), exit 110, 0.5 mi e, then 0.3 mi n on SR 601. Int corridors. **Pets:** No service, supervision. ASK ✕ 🍴

⊕ ▼▼▼ Quality Inn Somerset H
(814) 443-4646. **$69-$199.** 215 Ramada Rd 15501. I-70/76 (Pennsylvania Tpke), exit 110, just s. Int corridors. **Pets:** $25 one-time fee. Designated rooms, service with restrictions, supervision.
SAVE ✕ 🛏 🖵 ➰

▼▼ Super 8 M
(814) 445-8788. **$49-$125.** 125 Lewis Dr 15501. I-70/76 (Pennsylvania Tpke), exit 110, just s. Int corridors. **Pets:** Accepted. ASK ✕ 🛏 🖵

UNIONTOWN

▼▼▼ Uniontown Holiday Inn H
(724) 437-2816. **$99-$139.** 700 W Main St 15401. 1.8 mi w on US 40. Int corridors. **Pets:** Dogs only. $10 daily fee/pet, $50 one-time fee/pet. Designated rooms, service with restrictions, supervision.
ASK ✕ ♿M 🛏 🖵 🍴 ➰ ✕

END AREA

LEBANON

▼▼▼ Berry Patch Bed and Breakfast BB
(717) 865-7219. **$125-$229, 14 day notice.** 115 Moore Rd 17046. I-81, exit 90, 2.8 mi s on SR 72, 1 mi e on New Bunker Hill St, 0.8 mi s on S Lancaster St, just e, then follow signs. Ext/int corridors. **Pets:** Accepted.
ASK ✕ 🛏

LEWISBURG

▼▼ All Suites Inn M
(570) 523-8882. **$95-$225.** 4663 Westbranch Hwy (US 15) 17837. I-80, exit 210A, 7 mi s on US 15. Ext corridors. **Pets:** Dogs only. $100 deposit/room, $15 daily fee/pet. Designated rooms, service with restrictions, crate.
ASK ✕ ♿M 🛏 🖵 🍴

▼▼ ▼▼ Days Inn-Lewisburg 🄷
(570) 523-1171. **$81-$103.** 409 N Derr Dr 17837. 0.5 mi n of jct SR 45. Ext corridors. **Pets:** Other species. Service with restrictions, crate.
(ASK) 🆇 🛅 🖵 🏊

LINCOLN FALLS
▼▼ ▼▼ Morgan Century Farm 🄱🄱
(570) 924-4909. **$99-$145, 5 day notice.** 7043 Rt 154 18616. In village. Ext/int corridors. **Pets:** Medium. $10 deposit/pet. Designated rooms, service with restrictions, supervision. 🆇 🛅 🖵 🈯

LOCK HAVEN
◆◆◆ ▼▼ ▼▼ Best Western-Lock Haven 🄷 ❀
(570) 748-3297. **$87-$159.** 101 E Walnut St 17745. US 220, exit 111 (SR 120 W), just w. Int corridors. **Pets:** Other species. $12 daily fee/pet. Service with restrictions. (SAVE) 🆇 🛅 🖵

MANSFIELD
▼▼ ▼▼ Comfort Inn 🄷
(570) 662-3000. **$89-$149.** 300 Gateway Dr 16933. Jct US 6 and 15. Int corridors. **Pets:** Accepted. (ASK) 🆇 🛅 🖵 🏊

◆◆◆ ▼▼ Mansfield Inn 🄼
(570) 662-2136. **$55-$90, 3 day notice.** 26 S Main St 16933. SR 15, exit Mansfield, jct US 6, just s on Business Rt 15; downtown. Ext corridors. **Pets:** Dogs only. $8 daily fee/pet. No service, crate.
(SAVE) 🆇 🛅 🖵

MARIENVILLE
▼▼ The Forest Lodge & Campground 🄼
(814) 927-8790. **$40-$85, 14 day notice.** 44078 Rt 66 16239. 6 mi n of town. Ext/int corridors. **Pets:** Accepted. (ASK) 🆇 🛅 🖵

▼▼ ▼▼ Microtel Inn & Suites 🄷
(814) 927-8300. **Call for rates.** 252 Cherry St 16239. 0.6 mi sw of center, on SR 66. Int corridors. **Pets:** Accepted. 🆇 🛅 🖵

MEADVILLE
▼▼ ▼▼ Quality Inn 🄼 ❀
(814) 333-8883. **Call for rates.** 17259 Conneaut Lake Rd 16335. I-79, exit 147B, just w on US 322. Ext/int corridors. **Pets:** Dogs only. $10 daily fee/pet. Designated rooms, service with restrictions, supervision.
🆇 🛅 🖵

MECHANICSBURG
▼▼ ▼▼ Comfort Inn Capital City 🄷 ❀
(717) 766-3700. **$100-$140.** 1012 Wesley Dr 17055. I-76 (Pennsylvania Tpke), exit 236 (US 15), 1 mi n to Wesley Dr exit, then just w. Int corridors. **Pets:** Other species. $25 daily fee/pet. Service with restrictions, crate. (ASK) 🆇 🄼 🛅 🖵 🏊

◆◆◆ ▼▼ ▼▼ Comfort Inn West 🄷
(717) 790-0924. **$70, 3 day notice.** 6325 Carlisle Pike 17050. Jct Carlisle Pike and US 11, 1 mi w on US 11. Int corridors. **Pets:** Medium, other species. $25 deposit/room, $10 one-time fee/pet. Designated rooms, service with restrictions, supervision. (SAVE) 🆇 🛅 🖵

◆◆◆ ▼▼ ▼▼ Hampton Inn-Harrisburg West 🄷
(717) 691-1300. **$89-$169.** 4950 Ritter Rd 17055. I-76 (Pennsylvania Tpke), exit 236 (US 15), 1 mi n to Rossmoyne Rd exit. Int corridors. **Pets:** $15 one-time fee/pet. Designated rooms, service with restrictions, supervision. (SAVE) 🆇 🄼 🛅 🖵 🏊

▼▼ ▼▼ Holiday Inn Harrisburg-West 🄷
(717) 697-0321. **$99-$179.** 5401 Carlisle Pike 17050. Jct Carlisle Pike and US 11, just w. Ext/int corridors. **Pets:** Accepted.
(ASK) 🆇 🛅 🖵 🍴 🏊 🆇

MERCER
▼▼ Colonial Inn Motel 🄼
(724) 662-5600. **$35-$49.** 383 N Perry Hwy (US 19) 16137. I-80, exit 15, 3.5 mi n; I-79, exit 121, 4.5 mi s on SR 62, then 0.5 mi n on US 19. Ext/int corridors. **Pets:** Other species. $5 daily fee/pet. Service with restrictions, supervision. (ASK) 🆇 🛅 🖵

▼▼ ▼▼ Comfort Inn Mercer 🄷
(724) 748-3030. **$83-$91.** 835 Perry Hwy 16137. I-80, exit 15, just n on US 19. Int corridors. **Pets:** Other species. Service with restrictions, crate.
(ASK) 🆇 🛅 🖵 🍴 🏊 🆇

▼▼ ▼▼ Microtel Inn & Suites 🄷
(724) 748-9920. **Call for rates.** 2049 Leesburg Grove City Rd 16137. I-79, exit 113, 0.9 mi w on SR 208. Int corridors. **Pets:** Accepted.
🆇 🛅 🖵

MIFFLINVILLE
▼▼ ▼▼ Super 8 🄼
(570) 759-6778. **$55-$150.** 450 W 3rd St 18631. I-80, exit 242, just n on SR 339. Ext corridors. **Pets:** Medium, other species. $10 one-time fee/room. Service with restrictions, supervision. (ASK) 🆇 🛅 🖵

MILROY
◆◆◆ ▼▼ ▼▼ Best Western Nittany Inn 🄷
(717) 667-9595. **$90-$106.** 5 Commerce Dr 17063. US 322, exit Milroy, just e. Int corridors. **Pets:** Accepted. (SAVE) 🆇 🛅 🖵 🏊

MONTGOMERY
◆◆◆ ▼▼ White Deer Motel 🄼
(570) 547-1007. **Call for rates.** 6967 Rt 15 17752. Jct SR 54, 1.4 mi s. Ext corridors. **Pets:** Accepted. (SAVE) 🆇 🛅 🖵

MORGANTOWN
▼▼ ▼▼ Holiday Inn 🄷
(610) 286-3000. **$79-$129.** 6170 Morgantown Rd 19543. I-76, exit 298, just s on SR 10. Int corridors. **Pets:** Accepted.
(ASK) 🆇 🛅 🖵 🍴 🏊 🆇

MYERSTOWN
▼▼ ▼▼ Quality Inn & Suites at The Lantern Lodge 🄷 ❀
(717) 866-6536. **$79-$150, 3 day notice.** 411 N College St 17067. Just n of US 422 on SR 501. Ext/int corridors. **Pets:** $10 daily fee/pet. Designated rooms, service with restrictions, crate. (ASK) 🆇 🛅 🖵 🍴

NEW CASTLE
▼▼ ▼▼ Comfort Inn-New Castle 🄷
(724) 658-7700. **$70-$100.** 1740 New Butler Rd (US Business 422) 16101. Jct SR 65, 1 mi e on US 422, then 1 mi w on US 422 business route. Int corridors. **Pets:** Small, dogs only. $6 daily fee/pet. Service with restrictions, crate. (ASK) 🆇 🛅 🖵

NEW COLUMBIA
◆◆◆ ▼▼ ▼▼ Holiday Inn Express 🄷
(570) 568-1100. **$99-$189.** 160 Commerce Park Dr 17856. I-80, exit 210A (US 15/New Columbia), just s. Int corridors. **Pets:** Medium, other species. $25 one-time fee/room. Designated rooms, service with restrictions, supervision. (SAVE) 🆇 🄼 🛅 🖵 🏊

◆◆◆ ▼▼ ▼▼ New Columbia Comfort Inn 🄷
(570) 568-8000. **$75-$140.** 330 Commerce Park Dr 17856. I-80, exit 210A (US 15/New Columbia), just s. Int corridors. **Pets:** Other species.
(SAVE) 🆇 🄼 🛅 🖵 🍴 🏊

NEW CUMBERLAND
◆◆◆ ▼▼ ▼▼ Days Inn Harrisburg South 🄷
(717) 774-4156. **Call for rates.** 353 Lewisberry Rd 17070. I-83, exit 39A, just ne. Int corridors. **Pets:** Accepted. (SAVE) 🆇 🛅 🖵 🏊

🆎 ▼▼▼ Harrisburg Holiday Inn Hotel & Conference Center H

(717) 774-2721. **$99-$149.** 148 Sheraton Dr 17070. I-83, exit 40A, just se. Int corridors. **Pets:** Accepted. 🅂🅰🆅🅴 ⊠ 🈁 📟 🍴 ⌇

▼▼▼ Quality Inn Harrisburg West H

(717) 774-6200. **Call for rates.** 175 Beacon Hill Blvd 17070. I-83, exit 40A, just e, then just n. Ext/int corridors. **Pets:** Accepted.
⊠ 🈁 🈁 📟 ⌇

PENNSYLVANIA DUTCH COUNTRY AREA

AKRON

▼▼▼ Boxwood Inn BB ❀

(717) 859-3466. **$110-$235, 7 day notice.** 1320 Diamond St 17501. SR 272, 0.4 mi se on Main St to Diamond St, then 0.3 mi s. Ext/int corridors. **Pets:** Dogs only. Designated rooms, no service, crate.

A$K ⊠ 🈁 📟

DENVER

🆎 ▼▼▼ Black Horse Lodge and Suites H

(717) 336-7563. **$59-$199, 3 day notice.** 2180 N Reading Rd 17517. I-76 (Pennsylvania Tpke), exit 286, 1 mi w to SR 272, then 0.3 mi n. Ext/int corridors. **Pets:** Other species. Service with restrictions, supervision. 🅂🅰🆅🅴 ⊠ 🈁 📟 🍴 ⌇

🆎 ▼▼▼ Comfort Inn H

(717) 336-4649. **$80-$170, 3 day notice.** 2017 N Reading Rd 17517. I-76 (Pennsylvania Tpke), exit 286, 1 mi w to SR 272, then just s. Int corridors. **Pets:** Medium, dogs only. $20 one-time fee/room. Designated rooms, service with restrictions, supervision. 🅂🅰🆅🅴 ⊠ 🈁 📟

▼▼▼ Holiday Inn-Lancaster County H

(717) 336-7541. **$90-$160.** 1 Denver Rd 17517. I-76 (Pennsylvania Tpke), exit 286, 1 mi w to SR 272, then just s. Int corridors. **Pets:** Other species. $15 daily fee/pet. Service with restrictions, supervision.

A$K ⊠ 🈁 🈁 📟 🍴 ⌇

GORDONVILLE

🆎 ▼ Motel 6-Lancaster #4174 M

(717) 687-3880. **Call for rates.** 2959 Lincoln Hwy E 17529. On US 30; center. Int corridors. **Pets:** Other species. Service with restrictions, supervision. 🅂🅰🆅🅴 ⊠ 🈁 🈁

LANCASTER

🆎 ▼▼▼▼ Best Western Eden Resort & Suites H

(717) 569-6444. **$89-$235.** 222 Eden Rd 17601. Jct US 30 (Lincoln Hwy) and SR 272 (Oregon Pike). Ext/int corridors. **Pets:** Medium, other species. $15 daily fee/pet. Designated rooms, service with restrictions, supervision. 🅂🅰🆅🅴 ⊠ 🈁 🈁 🈁 📟 🍴 ⌇ 🈁

🆎 ▼▼▼ Days Inn & Suites H

(717) 293-8400. **$59-$129.** 1492 Lititz Pike 17601. US 30 (Lincoln Hwy), exit Lititz Pike (SR 501), just s. Ext corridors. **Pets:** Accepted.
🅂🅰🆅🅴 ⊠ 🈁 📟 ⌇

🆎 ▼▼▼ Hawthorn Suites by Wyndham H

(717) 290-7100. **$69-$159.** 2045 Lincoln Hwy 17602. Jct US 30 (Lincoln Hwy E). Int corridors. **Pets:** Medium, dogs only. $50 one-time fee/pet. Designated rooms, service with restrictions, supervision.

🅂🅰🆅🅴 ⊠ 🈁 📟

🆎 ▼▼▼▼ Lancaster Host Resort & Conference Center H

(717) 299-5500. **$109-$199.** 2300 Lincoln Hwy E 17602. On US 30 (Lincoln Hwy), 5 mi e. Int corridors. **Pets:** Medium, other species. $25 one-time fee/pet. Service with restrictions, crate.

🅂🅰🆅🅴 ⊠ 🈁 📟 🍴 ⌇ 🈁

🆎 ▼▼▼ Red Roof Inn of Lancaster M

(717) 299-9700. **$80-$98.** 2307 Lincoln Hwy E 17602. On US 30 (Lincoln Hwy), 5 mi e. Ext/int corridors. **Pets:** Large. Service with restrictions, crate. 🅂🅰🆅🅴 ⊠ 🈁 🈁 ⌇

LITITZ

🆎 ▼▼▼▼ Holiday Inn Express Hotel & Suites H

(717) 625-2366. **$119-$239.** 101 Crosswinds Dr 17543. 1.4 mi s on Lititz Pike/SR 501, then just w on Trolley Run Rd. Int corridors. **Pets:** Medium. $25 one-time fee/pet. Service with restrictions, supervision.

🅂🅰🆅🅴 ⊠ 🈁 🈁 📟 ⌇

MOUNTVILLE

🆎 ▼▼▼ MainStay Suites H

(717) 285-2500. **$99-$199.** 314 Primrose Ln 17554. US 30 (Lincoln Hwy), exit Mountville. Int corridors. **Pets:** Accepted.
🅂🅰🆅🅴 ⊠ 🈁 🈁 📟 ⌇

NEW HOLLAND

▼▼▼ Comfort Inn H

(717) 355-9900. **$110-$160.** 626 W Main St 17557. 0.5 mi w on SR 23. Int corridors. **Pets:** Medium. $20 daily fee/pet. Designated rooms, service with restrictions, supervision. A$K ⊠ 🈁 📟

STRASBURG

🆎 ▼▼▼ Carriage House Motor Inn M

(717) 687-7651. **$49-$109.** 144 E Main St 17579. 0.3 mi e on SR 896 and 741. Ext corridors. **Pets:** Accepted. 🅂🅰🆅🅴 ⊠ 🈁

END AREA

PHILADELPHIA METROPOLITAN AREA

AUDUBON

🆎 ▼▼▼▼ Homewood Suites by Hilton H

(610) 539-7300. **$119-$239.** 681 Shannondell Blvd 19403. I-422, exit Trooper Rd, 1.2 mi n. Int corridors. **Pets:** Large. $75 one-time fee/pet. Service with restrictions, supervision.

🅂🅰🆅🅴 ⊠ 🈁 🈁 📟 ⌇ 🈁

BENSALEM

▼▼▼ Extended StayAmerica-Philadelphia/Bensalem H

(215) 633-6900. **$94-$129.** 3216 Tillman Dr 19020. I-95, exit 37 (SR 132/Street Rd), 2.5 mi w, then just s; I-276, exit 351, 0.9 mi on US 1, 1.4 mi e, then just s. Int corridors. **Pets:** Other species. $25 daily fee/room. Designated rooms, service with restrictions, crate.

A$K ⊠ 🈁 🈁 📟

🆎 ▼▼▼▼ Holiday Inn-Philadelphia Northeast H

(215) 638-1500. **$119-$159.** 3499 Street Rd 19020. I-276 (Pennsylvania Tpke), exit 351, just s on US 1, then 0.3 mi e on SR 132. Ext/int corridors. **Pets:** Small, other species. $30 one-time fee/pet. Designated rooms, service with restrictions, crate. 🅂🅰🆅🅴 ⊠ 🈁 📟 🍴 ⌇

🆎 ▼▼▼▼ Sleep Inn & Suites-Bensalem H

(215) 244-2300. **$69-$159.** 3427 Street Rd 19020. I-276 (Pennsylvania Tpke), exit 351, just s on US 1, then 0.3 mi e on SR 132. Int corridors. **Pets:** Accepted. 🅂🅰🆅🅴 ⊠ 🈁 🈁 📟

BERWYN

▼▼▼▼ **Residence Inn Philadelphia-Valley Forge** H

(610) 640-9494. **$58-$70.** 600 W Swedesford Rd 19312. US 202, exit Paoli/SR 252, 1 mi n. Ext corridors. **Pets:** Accepted.

[X] [&M] [▯] [▭] [⇌] [X]

CHADDS FORD

◈◈◈ ▼▼▼▼ **Brandywine River Hotel** H

(610) 388-1200. **Call for rates.** 1609 Baltimore Pike 19317. Jct US 1 and SR 100, 2 mi w of US 202. Int corridors. **Pets:** Accepted.

[SAVE] [X] [▯] [▭]

CHESTER

◈◈◈ ▼▼▼▼ **Best Western Widener Hotel &**
Suites H ❧

(610) 872-8100. **$89-$169.** 1450 Providence Rd (SR 320) 19013. I-95, exit 6, just e to SR 320, follow signs. Int corridors. **Pets:** Medium. $40 one-time fee/pet. Service with restrictions, crate. [SAVE] [X] [▯] [▭]

CONSHOHOCKEN

▼▼▼▼ **Residence Inn by Marriott**
Philadelphia/Conshohocken H

(610) 828-8800. **$170-$208.** 191 Washington St 19428. I-76 (Schuylkill Expwy), exit 332 (SR 23); I-476, exit 16 (SR 23), 0.3 mi over Fayette Bridge to Elm St, then just se along the river. Int corridors.

Pets: Accepted. [X] [&M] [▯] [▭] [⇌] [X]

EAST NORRITON

◈◈◈ ▼▼▼▼ **Hyatt Summerfield Suites Philadelphia/**
Plymouth Meeting H

(610) 313-9990. **$89-$229.** 501 E Germantown Pike 19401. I-476, exit 20; I-276 (Pennsylvania Tpke), exit 333, 2.5 mi w. Int corridors.

Pets: Accepted. [SAVE] [X] [▯] [▭] [⇌]

ERWINNA

▼▼▼▼ **Golden Pheasant Inn** ◧ 🐾

(610) 294-9595. **$95-$225, 21 day notice.** 763 River Rd 18920. SR 32, 0.5 mi n of jct Dark Hollow Rd. Ext/int corridors. **Pets:** Medium, other species. $25 daily fee/pet. Designated rooms, service with restrictions, crate. [ASK] [X] [▯] [▭] [¶] [X]

ESSINGTON

◈◈◈ ▼ ▼ **Red Roof Inn-Airport #7119** M

(610) 521-5090. **Call for rates.** 49 Industrial Hwy 19029. I-95, exit 9A, 0.3 mi sw on SR 291. Ext corridors. **Pets:** Large. Service with restrictions, crate. [SAVE] [X] [&M] [▯]

FORT WASHINGTON

▼▼▼▼ **Hilton Garden Inn Philadelphia/Fort**
Washington H

(215) 646-4637. **$99-$199.** 530 Pennsylvania Ave 19034. I-276 (Pennsylvania Tpke), exit 339 (SR 309 S). Int corridors. **Pets:** Medium, dogs only. $100 deposit/room, $25 daily fee/pet. Service with restrictions, supervision.

[X] [&M] [▯] [▭] [¶] [⇌]

◈◈◈ ▼▼▼▼ **Holiday Inn Fort Washington Hotel &**
Conference Center H

(215) 643-3000. **$89-$139.** 432 W Pennsylvania Ave 19034. I-276 (Pennsylvania Tpke), exit 339 (SR 309 S), just w. Int corridors. **Pets:** Small. $45 one-time fee/pet. Designated rooms, service with restrictions, supervision. [SAVE] [X] [▯] [¶] [⇌]

GLEN MILLS

▼▼▼▼ **Sweetwater Farm Bed & Breakfast** BB

(610) 459-4711. **$150-$370, 14 day notice.** 50 Sweetwater Rd 19342. US 1, 2 mi w on Valley Rd, then 0.6 mi s. Int corridors. **Pets:** Accepted.

[X] [▯] [▭] [⇌] [X]

HORSHAM

▼▼▼▼ **Days Inn-Horsham/Willow Grove** H

(215) 674-2500. **$79-$129.** 245 Easton Rd 19044. I-276 (Pennsylvania Tpke), exit 343 (SR 611), 1 mi n. Int corridors. **Pets:** Accepted.

[ASK] [X] [▯] [▭]

▼▼▼▼ **Extended StayAmerica-Philadelphia/Horsham** H

(215) 784-9045. **$69-$99.** 114 Welsh Rd 19044. I-276, exit 343 (SR 611), s toward Jenkintown, 0.6 mi w on Maryland Rd, 0.5 mi sw on Computer Ave, then just n. Int corridors. **Pets:** Other species. $25 daily fee/room. Designated rooms, service with restrictions, crate.

[ASK] [X] [&M] [▯] [▭]

▼▼▼▼ **Residence Inn by Marriott-Willow Grove** H

(215) 443-7330. **$152-$186.** 3 Walnut Grove Dr 19044. I-276 (Pennsylvania Tpke), exit 343 (SR 611), 1 mi n on Easton Rd, then 1.3 mi w on Dresher Rd; inside Pennsylvania Business Campus. Ext corridors.

Pets: Accepted. [X] [&M] [▯] [▭] [⇌] [X]

KING OF PRUSSIA

◈◈◈ ▼▼▼▼ **Dolce Valley Forge Hotel & Conference**
Center H

(610) 337-1200. **$89-$206.** 301 W DeKalb Pike 19406. I-76 (Pennsylvania Tpke), exit 326 (Valley Forge), 1.4 mi ne on US 202 N. Int corridors. **Pets:** Small, dogs only. $50 daily fee/pet. Service with restrictions, crate.

[SAVE] [X] [▯] [▭] [¶] [⇌]

◈◈◈ ▼▼▼▼ **MainStay Suites** H

(484) 690-3000. **$69-$129.** 440 American Ave 19406. I-76 (Pennsylvania Tpke), exit 326 (Valley Forge); Schuylkill Expwy, exit 328A (Mall Blvd), 1.3 mi n on N Gulph Rd, 1 mi ne on 1st Ave, then just e. Int corridors.

Pets: Accepted. [SAVE] [X] [&M] [▯] [▭] [⇌]

KULPSVILLE

◈◈◈ ▼▼▼▼ **Best Western-The Inn at Towamencin** H

(215) 368-3800. **$105-$109.** 1750 Sumneytown Pike 19443. I-476, exit 31, just e. Int corridors. **Pets:** $10 daily fee/room. Designated rooms, service with restrictions, crate. [SAVE] [X] [▯] [▭] [¶] [⇌] [X]

LANGHORNE

◈◈◈ ▼▼▼▼ **Residence Inn Langhorne** H

(215) 946-6500. **$169-$259.** 15 E Cabot Blvd 19047. I-95, exit 46A (Oxford Valley Rd), just e off US 1 N; 0.5 mi n of Sesame Place. Int corridors. **Pets:** Accepted. [SAVE] [X] [&M] [▯] [▭] [⇌] [X]

◈◈◈ ▼▼▼▼ **Sheraton Bucks County Hotel** H ❧

(215) 547-4100. **$109-$249.** 400 Oxford Valley Rd 19047. I-95, exit 46A (Oxford Valley Rd), 0.8 mi e, exit off US 1 N. Int corridors. **Pets:** Medium, dogs only. Service with restrictions, supervision.

[SAVE] [X] [&M] [▯] [▭] [¶] [⇌] [X]

LIONVILLE

▼▼▼▼ **Extended StayAmerica-Philadelphia/Exton** H

(610) 524-7185. **$94-$129.** 877 N Pottstown Pike (Rt 100) 19353. I-76, exit 312, 1.8 mi s on SR 100. Int corridors. **Pets:** Other species. $25 daily fee/room. Designated rooms, service with restrictions, crate.

[ASK] [X] [▯] [▭]

▼▼▼▼ **Hampton Inn Exton** H ❧

(610) 363-5555. **$109-$179.** 4 N Pottstown Pike 19341. I-76 (Pennsylvania Tpke), exit 312, 0.5 mi s; jct SR 113 and 100. Int corridors. **Pets:** Large, other species. Service with restrictions.

[X] [&M] [▯] [▭]

▼▼▼▼ **Residence Inn Philadelphia Great Valley/Exton** H

(610) 594-9705. **$189-$199.** 10 N Pottstown Pike 19341. I-76 (Pennsylvania Tpke), exit 312, 1 mi s on SR 100. Int corridors. **Pets:** Other species. $100 one-time fee/room. Service with restrictions.

[X] [▯] [▭] [⇌] [X]

MALVERN

▼▼ Extended StayAmerica-Philadelphia/Malvern 🏠
(610) 240-0455. **$89-$129.** 300 Morehall Rd (US 29) 19355. US 202, exit SR 29 N. Int corridors. **Pets:** Other species. $25 daily fee/room. Designated rooms, service with restrictions, crate. (ASK) ⊠ &M 🖥 🖳 ⌁

▼▼◆▼ Homestead Studio Suites Philadelphia-Malvern 🏠
(610) 695-9200. **$95-$139.** 8 E Swedesford Rd 19355. Just w of US 202 and SR 29 N. Int corridors. **Pets:** Other species. $25 daily fee/room. Designated rooms, service with restrictions, crate. (ASK) ⊠ 🖥 🖳 ⌁

▼▼◆▼ Homewood Suites by Hilton 🏠 ❀
(610) 296-3500. **$129-$219.** 12 E Swedesford Rd 19355. US 202, exit SR 29, follow signs. Int corridors. **Pets:** Large. $50 one-time fee/pet. Service with restrictions, crate. ⊠ &M 🖥 🖳 ⌁

◈◈ ▼▼◆▼ Sheraton Great Valley Hotel 🏠 ❀
(610) 524-5500. **$139-$495.** 707 Lancaster Pike 19355. Jct US 202 and 30 E. Int corridors. **Pets:** Medium, dogs only. $50 one-time fee/room. Service with restrictions, supervision.
(SAVE) ⊠ &M 🖥 🖳 🍴 ⌁

▼▼◆▼ Staybridge Suites 🏠
(610) 296-4343. **$144-$219.** 20 Morehall Rd 19355. Jct US 30 and SR 29, just nw. Ext/int corridors. **Pets:** Accepted.
(ASK) ⊠ 🖥 🖳 ⌁ ⊠

MONTGOMERYVILLE

◈◈ ▼▼◆▼ Comfort Inn 🏠
(215) 361-3600. **$85-$153.** 678 Bethlehem Pike 18936. Jct SR 463 and US 202, 0.3 mi n on SR 309. Int corridors. **Pets:** Accepted.
(SAVE) ⊠ 🖥 🖳 🍴

▼▼◆▼ Quality Inn Conference Center 🏠
(215) 699-8800. **$85-$120.** 969 Bethlehem Pike 18936. I-276 (Pennsylvania Tpke), exit 339, 8 mi n on SR 309. Ext corridors. **Pets:** Large. $25 daily fee/room. Designated rooms, service with restrictions, supervision.
(ASK) ⊠ 🖥 🖳

▼▼◆▼ Residence Inn Philadelphia/Montgomeryville 🏠
(267) 468-0111. **$180-$220.** 1110 Bethlehem Pike 19454. I-276 (Pennsylvania Tpke), exit 339, 6.5 mi n on SR 309. Int corridors. **Pets:** Accepted.
⊠ 🖥 🖳 ⌁ ⊠

NEW HOPE

▼▼◆▼ 1870 Wedgwood Inn of New Hope 🅱🅱 ❀
(215) 862-2570. **$90-$295, 10 day notice.** 111 W Bridge St (SR 179) 18938. 0.5 mi w of SR 32; downtown. Ext/int corridors. **Pets:** Small, dogs only. $25 daily fee/pet. Service with restrictions, supervision.
⊠ 🖥 🖳

▼▼◆▼ Aaron Burr House Inn & Conference Center 🅱🅱
(215) 862-2520. **$95-$295, 10 day notice.** 80 W Bridge St (SR 179) 18938. 0.5 mi w of SR 32; at W Bridge and Chestnut sts. Int corridors. **Pets:** Medium, dogs only. $25 daily fee/pet. Designated rooms, service with restrictions, supervision. ⊠ 🖥

PHILADELPHIA

◈◈◈ ▼▼◆▼ aloft Philadelphia 🏠
(267) 298-1700. **$99-$279.** 4301 Island Ave 19153. Jct I-95 and SR 291, exit 13 northbound; exit 15 southbound. Int corridors. **Pets:** Accepted.
(SAVE) ⊠ &M 🖥 🖳 ⌁

▼▼◆▼ Extended StayAmerica-Philadelphia Airport 🏠
(215) 492-6766. **$79-$129.** 9000 Tinicum Blvd 19153. I-95, exit 12B (airport), just n on Essington Ave, then just w on Bartram Ave. Int corridors. **Pets:** Other species. $25 daily fee/room. Designated rooms, service with restrictions, crate. (ASK) ⊠ &M 🖥 🖳

◈◈◈ ▼▼◆▼ Four Points by Sheraton Philadelphia Airport 🏠
(215) 492-0400. **$100-$260.** 4101 Island Ave 19153. Jct I-95 and SR 291, exit 13 northbound; exit 15 southbound. Int corridors. **Pets:** Medium, dogs only. Designated rooms, service with restrictions, supervision.
(SAVE) ⊠ 🖥 🖳 🍴 ⌁

◈◈◈ ▼▼◆▼ Four Points by Sheraton Philadelphia Northeast 🏠
(215) 671-9600. **Call for rates.** 9461 Roosevelt Blvd 19114. I-276 (Pennsylvania Tpke), exit 351, 5 mi s on US 1. Int corridors. **Pets:** Accepted.
(SAVE) ⊠ 🖥 🖳 🍴 ⌁

◈◈◈ ▼▼◆▼▼ Four Seasons Hotel Philadelphia 🏠
(215) 963-1500. **$395-$505.** 1 Logan Square 19103. Corner of 18th St and Benjamin Franklin Pkwy. Int corridors. **Pets:** Accepted.
(SAVE) ⊠ &M 🖥 🖳 🍴 ⌁ ⊠

◈◈◈ ▼▼◆▼▼ Hyatt at The Bellevue 🏠
(215) 893-1234. **$85-$469, 3 day notice.** 200 S Broad St 19102. Between Walnut and Locust sts. Int corridors. **Pets:** Accepted.
(SAVE) ⊠ 🖥 🖳 🍴 ⌁

◈◈◈ ▼▼◆▼ Loews Philadelphia Hotel 🏠 ❀
(215) 627-1200. **$179-$299.** 1200 Market St 19107. Corner of 12th and Market sts. Int corridors. **Pets:** Designated rooms.
(SAVE) ⊠ 🖥 🖳 🍴 ⊠

▼▼◆▼ Philadelphia Airport Residence Inn by Marriott 🏠
(215) 492-1611. **$189-$219.** 4630 Island Ave 19153. I-95, exit 13 northbound; exit 15 southbound, 0.5 mi e; just e of SR 291. Ext/int corridors. **Pets:** Accepted. ⊠ &M 🖥 🖳 ⌁ ⊠

▼▼◆▼ Radisson Plaza-Warwick Hotel Philadelphia 🏠 ❀
(215) 735-6000. **$139-$389.** 1701 Locust St 19103-6179. Jct 17th and Locust sts. Int corridors. **Pets:** Large, dogs only. $10 daily fee/room, $50 one-time fee/room. Service with restrictions. (SAVE) ⊠ 🖥 🖳 🍴

▼▼◆▼ Residence Inn by Marriott Philadelphia City Center 🏠
(215) 557-0005. **$229-$249.** 1 E Penn Square 19107. Jct Market and Juniper sts. Int corridors. **Pets:** Accepted. ⊠ 🖥 🖳

◈◈◈ ▼▼◆▼ The Rittenhouse Hotel and Condominium Residences 🏠
(215) 546-9000. **$470-$540, 3 day notice.** 210 W Rittenhouse Square 19103. On Rittenhouse Square. Int corridors. **Pets:** Accepted.
(SAVE) ⊠ &M 🍴 ⌁ ⊠

▼▼◆▼▼ The Ritz-Carlton Philadelphia 🏠
(215) 523-8000. **$299-$499.** Ten Avenue of the Arts 19102. On Broad St; between Market and Chestnut sts. Int corridors. **Pets:** Accepted.
⊠ 🖳 🍴 ⊠

◈◈◈ ▼▼◆▼ Sheraton Philadelphia City Center Hotel 🏠
(215) 448-2000. **$100-$360.** 2 Franklin Plaza 19103. Jct 17th and Race sts. Int corridors. **Pets:** Accepted. (SAVE) ⊠ 🖥 🖳 🍴 ⌁

◈◈◈ ▼▼◆▼ Sheraton Philadelphia University City Hotel 🏠 ❀
(215) 387-8000. **$189-$379.** 36th & Chestnut Sts 19104. I-76 (Pennsylvania Tpke), exit 345, 0.5 mi w. Int corridors. **Pets:** Medium, dogs only. No service, crate. (SAVE) ⊠ &M 🖥 🖳 🍴 ⌁

◈◈◈ ▼▼◆▼ Sheraton Society Hill 🏠 ❀
(215) 238-6000. **$159-$419.** One Dock St 19106. Just s of jct 2nd and Walnut sts. Int corridors. **Pets:** Medium, dogs only. Service with restrictions, supervision. (SAVE) ⊠ 🖥 🖳 🍴 ⌁ ⊠

(AAA) ▼▼▼ Sheraton Suites Philadelphia Airport H
(215) 365-6600. **$109-$289.** 4101 Island Ave 19153. Jct I-95 and SR 291, exit 13 northbound; exit 15 southbound. Int corridors. **Pets:** Medium, dogs only. Designated rooms, service with restrictions, supervision.
SAVE ✕ 🔌 💻 ❙❙ ➔

(AAA)′ ▼▼▼ ▼▼▼ Sofitel Philadelphia H ❧
(215) 569-8300. **$159-$269.** 120 S 17th St 19103. Jct Sansom and 17th sts. Int corridors. **Pets:** $200 deposit/pet. Service with restrictions, supervision. SAVE ✕ &M ❙❙

(AAA)′ ▼▼▼ ▼▼▼ The Westin Philadelphia H
(215) 563-1600. **$139-$529.** 99 S 17th St at Liberty Pl 19103. Between Market and Chestnut sts. Int corridors. **Pets:** Accepted.
SAVE ✕ 💻 ❙❙ ✕

PLYMOUTH MEETING
▼▼ Extended StayAmerica-Philadelphia Plymouth Meeting H
(610) 260-0488. **$99-$129.** 437 Irwins Ln 19462. I-276, exit 333, follow signs for Plymouth Rd (Norristown), just w, then just n. Int corridors. **Pets:** Other species. $25 daily fee/room. Designated rooms, service with restrictions, crate. ASK ✕ &M 🔌 💻

POTTSTOWN
(AAA)′ ▼▼▼ Comfort Inn & Suites H
(610) 326-5000. **$89-$159.** 99 Robinson St 19464. SR 100, 1 mi n of jct US 422. Int corridors. **Pets:** Other species. $15 daily fee/room. Designated rooms, service with restrictions, crate.
SAVE ✕ &M 🔌 💻 ➔

QUAKERTOWN
(AAA)′ ▼▼▼▼ Comfort Inn & Suites H
(215) 538-3000. **$100-$150.** 1905 John Fries Hwy (SR 663) 18951. I-476 (Pennsylvania Tpke), exit 44, just e. Ext corridors. **Pets:** Accepted.
SAVE ✕ 🔌 💻

▼▼▼ Hampton Inn-Quakertown H
(215) 536-7779. **$109-$159.** 1915 John Fries Hwy (SR 663) 18951. I-476 (Pennsylvania Tpke), exit 44, just e. Int corridors. **Pets:** Small. $10 daily fee/pet. Service with restrictions, crate. ✕ &M 🔌 💻 ➔

TREVOSE
(AAA)′ ▼▼ ▼▼ Red Roof Inn #7185 M
(215) 244-9422. **Call for rates.** 3100 Lincoln Hwy 19053. I-276 (Pennsylvania Tpke), exit 351, 0.5 mi s on US 1 at US 132. Ext corridors. **Pets:** Large. Service with restrictions, crate. SAVE ✕ &M 🔌

UPPER BLACK EDDY
▼▼▼ The Bridgeton House on the Delaware BB
(610) 982-5856. **$169-$429.** 1525 River Rd 18972. On SR 32; center. Int corridors. **Pets:** Accepted. ✕ 🔌 💻

WEST CHESTER
(AAA)′ ▼▼ ▼▼ Microtel Inn & Suites H
(610) 738-9111. **$79-$129.** 500 Willowbrook Ln 19382. Just se of US 202, exit Matlack St. Int corridors. **Pets:** Medium, other species. $10 daily fee/pet. No service, supervision. SAVE ✕ &M 🔌

END METROPOLITAN AREA

PHILIPSBURG
▼▼ Main Liner Motel M
(814) 342-2004. **Call for rates.** One Mile W (US Hwy 322) 16866. 1 mi w of jct SR 53 N. Ext corridors. **Pets:** Accepted. ✕ 🔌

PINE GROVE
▼▼▼ Comfort Inn H
(570) 345-8031. **$79-$140.** 200 Swatara Dr 17963. I-81, exit 100, just e. Int corridors. **Pets:** Accepted. ASK ✕ &M 🔌 💻 ➔

▼▼▼ Hampton Inn Pine Grove H
(570) 345-4505. **$99-$219.** 481 Suedberg Rd 17963. I-81, exit 100. Int corridors. **Pets:** $15 daily fee/pet. Service with restrictions, supervision.
✕ &M 🔌 💻 ➔

PITTSBURGH METROPOLITAN AREA

BEAVER FALLS
▼▼▼▼ Holiday Inn H ❧
(724) 846-3700. **$89-$149.** 7195 Eastwood Rd 15010. I-76 (Pennsylvania Tpke), exit 13, just n. Int corridors. **Pets:** Medium. $35 daily fee/pet. Service with restrictions, supervision. ASK ✕ 🔌 💻 ❙❙ ➔ ✕

BETHEL PARK
(AAA)′ ▼▼▼▼ Crowne Plaza Pittsburgh South H
(412) 833-5300. **$84-$299.** 164 Ft Couch Rd 15241. 1 mi n on US 19. Int corridors. **Pets:** Medium. $25 one-time fee/room. Designated rooms, service with restrictions, crate. SAVE ✕ 🔌 💻 ❙❙ ➔

BUTLER
▼▼▼ Butler Days Inn Conference Center H
(724) 287-6761. **$79-$84.** 139 Pittsburgh Rd 16001. 2 mi s. Int corridors. **Pets:** Accepted. ASK ✕ 🔌 💻 ❙❙ ➔

▼▼ Locust Brook Lodge BB
(724) 283-8453. **$85-$150.** 179 Eagle Mill Rd 16001. 5 mi w on US 422 to jct Eagle Mill Rd, then 0.8 mi s; I-79, exit 99, 10 mi e on US 422 to jct Eagle Mill Rd, then 0.8 mi s. Ext/int corridors. **Pets:** Accepted. ASK ✕

▼▼ Super 8 M
(724) 287-8888. **$65-$69.** 138 Pittsburgh Rd 16001. 2 mi s. Int corridors. **Pets:** Medium. $15 daily fee/pet. Service with restrictions, supervision.
ASK ✕ 🔌 💻

CARNEGIE
▼▼ Extended StayAmerica-Pittsburgh-Carnegie H
(412) 278-4001. **$79-$129.** 520 N Bell Ave 15106. I-376 W, exit 64B (Rosslyn exit), just se. Int corridors. **Pets:** Other species. $25 daily fee/room. Designated rooms, service with restrictions, crate.
ASK ✕ &M 🔌 💻

CORAOPOLIS
▼▼ Americas Best Value Inn-Pittsburgh Airport M
(412) 604-2378. **Call for rates.** 8858 University Blvd 15108. 0.4 mi n of Business Rt SR 60. Ext corridors. **Pets:** Accepted. ✕ 🔌

(AAA)′ ▼▼▼▼ Embassy Suites-Pittsburgh International Airport H ❧
(412) 269-9070. **$99-$249.** 550 Cherrington Pkwy 15108. Business Rt SR 60, exit Thorn Run Rd. Int corridors. **Pets:** Medium. $50 one-time fee/room. Designated rooms, service with restrictions, crate.
SAVE ✕ &M 🔌 💻 ❙❙ ➔

▼▼▼ Hampton Inn Airport-Pittsburgh Ⓗ
(412) 264-0020. **$89-$169.** 8514 University Blvd 15108. Business Rt SR 60, 0.5 mi n. Int corridors. **Pets:** Accepted. ⊠ 🖥 💻

🅐🅐 ▼▼▼ Holiday Inn-Pittsburgh Airport Ⓗ
(412) 262-3600. **$89-$159.** 8256 University Blvd 15108. Business Rt SR 60, 1 mi n. Int corridors. **Pets:** Accepted.
(SAVE) ⊠ ⑤ᴹ 🖥 💻 🍴 ➔

🅐🅐 ▼▼▼ Hyatt Regency Pittsburgh International
Airport Ⓗ
(724) 899-1234. **$89-$339.** 1111 Airport Blvd 15231. SR 60, exit 6 (Airport Blvd). Int corridors. **Pets:** Accepted.
(SAVE) ⊠ 🖥 💻 🍴 ➔ 🐾

▼▼ La Quinta Inn Pittsburgh (Airport) Ⓗ ✿
(412) 269-0400. **$69-$119.** 8507 University Blvd 15108. 1 mi n of Business Rt SR 60. Int corridors. **Pets:** Medium, other species. Service with restrictions, supervision. (ASK) ⊠ ⑤ᴹ 🖥 💻

▼▼ Pittsburgh Airport Super 8 Ⓜ
(412) 264-7888. **$70-$100.** 8991 University Blvd 15108. 1 mi n of Business Rt SR 60. Int corridors. **Pets:** Accepted. (ASK) ⊠ 🖥 💻

CRANBERRY TOWNSHIP
▼▼▼ Holiday Inn Express Ⓗ
(724) 772-1000. **Call for rates.** 20003 Rt 19 16066. I-76 (Pennsylvania Tpke), exit 28, jct US 19 and I-76 (Pennsylvania Tpke); I-79, exit 76 northbound; exit 78 southbound, just s. Int corridors. **Pets:** Accepted.
⊠ 🖥 💻

▼▼▼ Pittsburgh Marriott North Ⓗ
(724) 772-3700. **$229-$299.** 100 Cranberry Woods Dr 16066. I-79, exit 78 (SR 228) to Cranberry Woods Dr. Int corridors. **Pets:** Small. $75 one-time fee/room. Designated rooms, service with restrictions, crate.
⊠ ⑤ᴹ 🖥 💻 🍴 ➔

▼▼ Red Roof Inn-Cranberry Township-Pittsburgh North
#7079 Ⓜ
(724) 776-5670. **Call for rates.** 20009 Rt 19 16066. I-76 (Pennsylvania Tpke), exit 28; I-79, exit 76 northbound; exit 78 southbound. Ext corridors. **Pets:** Large. Service with restrictions, crate. ⊠ 🖥

▼▼▼ Residence Inn Pittsburgh Cranberry Township Ⓗ
(724) 779-1000. **$152-$186.** 1308 Freedom Rd 16066. I-76 (Pennsylvania Tpke), exit 28, 0.5 mi n on US 19, then 0.3 mi w; I-79, exit 78 southbound, 0.5 mi w. Int corridors. **Pets:** Accepted. ⊠ 🖥 💻 ➔ 🐾

DELMONT
▼▼ Super 8 Ⓜ
(724) 468-4888. **Call for rates.** 180 Sheffield Dr 15626. SR 66, just s of US 22. Int corridors. **Pets:** Accepted. ⊠ ⑤ᴹ 🖥 💻

GIBSONIA
▼▼ Comfort Inn Gibsonia Ⓜ
(724) 444-8700. **$79-$149.** 5137 Rt 8 15044. I-76 (Pennsylvania Tpke), exit 39, just n. Ext corridors. **Pets:** Large, other species. $10 daily fee/pet. Service with restrictions, supervision. (ASK) ⊠ 🖥 💻

GREEN TREE
▼▼▼ Hampton Inn Hotel Green Tree Ⓗ
(412) 922-0100. **$119-$169.** 555 Trumbull Dr 15205. I-376 E, exit 65 (Old 3), jct US 22 and 30, 1 mi nw via Mansfield Ave. Int corridors.
Pets: Accepted. ⊠ 🖥 💻 ➔

🅐🅐 ▼▼▼ Radisson Hotel Pittsburgh/Green
Tree Ⓗ ✿
(412) 922-8400. **$99-$359.** 101 Radisson Dr 15205. I-376 E, exit 65 (Old 3) to jct US 22 and 30, 1.1 mi nw via Mansfield Ave. Int corridors. **Pets:** Medium, other species. $100 deposit/pet. Designated rooms, service with restrictions, supervision.
(SAVE) ⊠ ⑤ᴹ 🖥 💻 🍴 ➔ 🐾

MARS
▼▼ Comfort Inn Cranberry Township Ⓗ
(724) 772-2700. **$90-$140.** 924 Sheraton Dr 16046. I-76 (Pennsylvania Tpke), exit 28; I-79, exit 76 (US 19 N) northbound; exit 78 southbound, 0.5 mi s on US 19. Int corridors. **Pets:** Accepted. (ASK) ⊠ 🖥 💻

▼▼ Super 8-Cranberry Ⓗ
(724) 776-9700. **$75-$130.** 929 Sheraton Dr 16046. I-76 (Pennsylvania Tpke), exit 28; I-79, exit 76 (US 19 N) northbound; exit 78 southbound, 0.5 mi s on US 19. Int corridors. **Pets:** Accepted. (ASK) ⊠ 🖥 💻

MONACA
▼▼▼ Hampton Inn Beaver Valley/Pittsburgh Ⓗ
(724) 774-5580. **$117-$145.** 202 Fairview Dr 15061. SR 60, exit 12, just n. Int corridors. **Pets:** Medium, other species. Service with restrictions, crate. ⊠ ⑤ᴹ 🖥 💻 ➔

▼▼▼ Holiday Inn Express Hotel & Suites-Center
Township Ⓗ
(724) 728-5121. **$99-$159.** 105 Stone Quarry Rd 15061. SR 60, exit 12, just n. Int corridors. **Pets:** Small, dogs only. $20 daily fee/room. Service with restrictions, supervision. (ASK) ⊠ 🖥 💻 ➔

▼▼ The Inn Ⓗ
(724) 728-9270. **$79-$129.** 1525 Old Brodhead Rd 15061. SR 60, exit 12, 1 mi e. Int corridors. **Pets:** Medium. $20 daily fee/pet. Designated rooms, service with restrictions, supervision. (ASK) ⊠ 🖥 💻

MONROEVILLE
▼▼▼ Extended StayAmerica-Pittsburgh-Monroeville Ⓗ
(412) 856-8400. **$74-$129.** 3851 Northern Pike 15146. I-76 (Pennsylvania Tpke), exit 57, 1.2 mi w on Business Rt 22. Int corridors. **Pets:** Other species. $25 daily fee/room. Designated rooms, service with restrictions, crate. (ASK) ⊠ 🖥 💻

▼▼▼ Hampton Inn Monroeville/Pittsburgh Ⓗ
(412) 380-4000. **Call for rates.** 3000 Mosside Blvd 15146. I-76 (Pennsylvania Tpke), exit 57; I-376, exit 14A, 0.3 mi s on SR 48. Int corridors.
Pets: Accepted. ⊠ 💻 ➔

🅐🅐 ▼▼▼ Red Roof Inn-Monroeville #7174 Ⓜ
(412) 856-4738. **Call for rates.** 2729 Mosside Blvd 15146. I-76 (Pennsylvania Tpke), exit 57; I-376, exit 14A, 0.8 mi s on SR 48. Ext corridors.
Pets: Large. Service with restrictions, crate. (SAVE) ⊠ 🖥

▼▼ Super 8 Pittsburgh/Monroeville Ⓜ
(724) 733-8008. **$60-$200.** 1807 Golden Mile Hwy (Rt 286) Hwy 15239. I-76 (Pennsylvania Tpke), exit 57; I-376, exit 14A, 2 mi e on US 22 E, then 2 mi e. Int corridors. **Pets:** Accepted. (ASK) ⊠ 🖥 💻

MOON RUN
▼▼ Extended Stay Deluxe Pittsburgh Airport Ⓗ
(412) 490-0979. **$84-$129.** 200 Chauvet Dr 15275. SR 60, exit 1, just s. Int corridors. **Pets:** Other species. $25 daily fee/room. Designated rooms, service with restrictions, crate. (ASK) ⊠ 🖥 💻 ➔

🅐🅐 ▼▼▼ Four Points by Sheraton Pittsburgh
Airport Ⓗ ✿
(724) 695-0002. **Call for rates.** 1 Industry Ln 15275. SR 60, exit 2 (Montour Run Rd). Int corridors. **Pets:** $50 deposit/room. Designated rooms, service with restrictions, crate. (SAVE) ⊠ 🖥 💻 🍴 ➔

🅐🅐 ▼▼▼ Holiday Inn Express Pittsburgh Airport Ⓗ
(412) 788-8400. **Call for rates.** 5311 Campbells Run Rd 15205. US 22 and 30 W, exit SR 60 S (Crafton), just w. Int corridors. **Pets:** Accepted.
(SAVE) ⊠ 🖥 💻 ➔

▼▼ Motel 6 Pittsburgh #657 Ⓜ
(412) 922-9400. **$45-$55.** 211 Beecham Dr 15205. I-79, exit 60A, just s on Steubenville Pike (SR 60), then e. Ext corridors. **Pets:** Other species. Service with restrictions, supervision. ⊠ ⑤ᴹ

◈◈ ▼▼▼▼ Pittsburgh Airport Marriott 🅷

(412) 788-8800. **$99-$299.** 777 Aten Rd 15108. SR 60, exit 2 (Montour Run Rd). Int corridors. **Pets:** Medium. $50 one-time fee/pet. Service with restrictions, supervision. [SAVE] ⊠ 🖥 🖥 🍴 ⇌ ⊠

▼▼▼ Red Roof Inn South Airport #7030 Ⓜ

(412) 787-7870. **Call for rates.** 6404 Steubenville Pike 15205. I-79, exit 60A, 3.2 mi w on SR 60. Ext/int corridors. **Pets:** Large. Service with restrictions, crate. ⊠ 🖥

▼▼▼▼ Residence Inn Pittsburgh Airport Coraopolis 🅷

(412) 787-3300. **$143-$175.** 1500 Park Lane Dr 15275. SR 60, exit 2 (Montour Run Rd), just w on Cliff Mine Dr to Summit Park Dr, just s to Park Lane Dr, then just e. Int corridors. **Pets:** Accepted. ⊠ ⅖ 🖥 🖥 ⇌ ⊠

OAKDALE

◈◈ ▼▼▼ Comfort Inn-Pittsburgh Airport 🅷

(412) 787-2600. **$85-$135.** 7011 Old Steubenville Pike 15071. US 22 and 30, jct SR 60; 4 mi w of jct I-279 and 79. Ext/int corridors. **Pets:** Other species. $10 daily fee/pet. Designated rooms, service with restrictions, crate. [SAVE] ⊠ 🖥 🖥

PITTSBURGH

▼▼▼▼ Hilton Pittsburgh 🅷

(412) 391-4600. **$119-$409.** 600 Commonwealth Pl 15222. Jct I-279/376/SR 885; in Gateway Center. Int corridors. **Pets:** Accepted. ⊠ ⅖ 🖥 🍴

▼▼▼▼ Omni William Penn Hotel 🅷

(412) 281-7100. **$139-$499.** 530 William Penn Pl 15219. Jct 6th St and William Penn Pl. Int corridors. **Pets:** Accepted. [ASK] ⊠ 🖥 🖥 🍴 ⊠

◈◈ ▼▼▼▼ Residence Inn by Marriott Pittsburgh University/Medical Center 🅷

(412) 621-2200. **$175-$213.** 3896 Bigelow Blvd 15213. On SR 380. Int corridors. **Pets:** Medium. $100 one-time fee/room. Service with restrictions, supervision. [SAVE] ⊠ 🖥 🖥 ⇌ ⊠

◈◈ ▼▼▼ Sheraton Station Square Hotel 🅷

(412) 261-2000. **$129-$414.** 300 W Station Square St 15219. I-376, exit Grant St, south end of Smithfield St Bridge; across river. Int corridors. **Pets:** Accepted. [SAVE] ⊠ 🖥 🖥 🍴 ⇌ ⊠

◈◈ ▼▼▼▼ The Westin Convention Center Pittsburgh 🅷 ❀

(412) 281-3700. **$135-$485.** 1000 Penn Ave 15222. Jct 10th St; at Liberty Center. Int corridors. **Pets:** Medium, other species. Service with restrictions, supervision. [SAVE] ⊠ 🖥 🖥 🍴 ⇌ ⊠

WASHINGTON

◈◈ ▼▼▼ Ramada 🅷

(724) 225-9750. **$80-$125.** 1170 W Chestnut St 15301. I-70, exit 15, 0.5 mi e on US 40. Ext/int corridors. **Pets:** Small. $35 one-time fee/room. Designated rooms, service with restrictions, crate. [SAVE] ⊠ 🖥 🖥 🍴 ⇌

▼▼▼ Red Roof Inn #7048 Ⓜ

(724) 228-5750. **Call for rates.** 1399 W Chestnut St 15301. I-70, exit 15, just e on US 40. Ext/int corridors. **Pets:** Large. Service with restrictions, crate. ⊠ 🖥

WEST MIFFLIN

▼▼▼ Extended StayAmerica-Pittsburgh-West Mifflin 🅷

(412) 650-9096. **$74-$129.** 1303 Lebanon Church Rd 15122. 0.5 mi e of jct SR 51. Int corridors. **Pets:** Other species. $25 daily fee/room. Designated rooms, service with restrictions, crate. [ASK] ⊠ ⅖ 🖥 🖥

▼▼▼ Holiday Inn Express Hotel & Suites 🅷

(412) 469-1900. **$125-$175.** 3122 Lebanon Church Rd 15122. 1.5 mi e of jct SR 51. Int corridors. **Pets:** $10 one-time fee/room. Service with restrictions, supervision. [ASK] ⊠ 🖥 🖥

END METROPOLITAN AREA

POCONO MOUNTAINS AREA

BLAKESLEE

◈◈ ▼▼▼▼ Best Western Inn-Blakeslee/Pocono 🅷

(570) 646-6000. **$95-$175.** New Ventures Business Park 18610. I-80, exit 284, just n. Int corridors. **Pets:** $50 deposit/room. Service with restrictions, supervision. [SAVE] ⊠ ⅖ 🖥 🖥 ⇌

EAST STROUDSBURG

◈◈ ▼▼▼▼ Budget Inn & Suites 🅷 ❀

(570) 424-5451. **$67-$106, 3 day notice.** I-80, exit 308 18301. I-80, exit 308, just se on Greentree Rd. Ext/int corridors. **Pets:** Medium, other species. Designated rooms, service with restrictions, crate. [SAVE] ⊠ 🖥 🖥 🍴

▼▼▼ Super 8 Ⓜ

(570) 424-7411. **$58-$168.** 340 Greentree Dr 18301. I-80, exit 308, just se. Int corridors. **Pets:** Other species. $100 deposit/room, $10 daily fee/room. Designated rooms, service with restrictions, supervision. [ASK] ⊠ ⅖ 🖥

HAMLIN

◈◈ ▼▼▼ Comfort Inn 🅷

(570) 689-4148. **$70-$170.** 117 Twin Rocks Rd 18427. I-84, exit 17, just n on SR 191. Int corridors. **Pets:** Accepted. [SAVE] ⊠ 🖥 🖥

MARSHALLS CREEK

◈◈ ▼ Value Inn Ⓜ

(570) 588-1100. **$45-$129.** 5219 Milford Rd (Rt 209) 18335. I-80, exit 309, 7.9 mi n. Ext corridors. **Pets:** Accepted. [SAVE] ⊠ 🖥 ⇌ ⊠

MATAMORAS

◈◈ ▼▼▼▼ Best Western Inn at Hunt's Landing 🅷

(570) 491-2400. **$90-$170.** 120 Rt 6 & 209 18336. I-84, exit 53. Int corridors. **Pets:** Small. $10 daily fee/pet. Designated rooms, service with restrictions, supervision. [SAVE] ⊠ 🖥 🖥 🍴 ⇌ ⊠

MILFORD

▼▼▼▼ Hotel Fauchere 🅷

(570) 409-1212. **$175-$350, 14 day notice.** 401 Broad St 18337. Historic downtown. Int corridors. **Pets:** Accepted. ⊠ 🍴

◈◈ ▼▼▼ Milford Motel Ⓜ

(570) 296-6411. **$45-$110, 3 day notice.** 591 Rt 6 & 209 18337. US 6 and 209 N, 0.7 mi e. Ext corridors. **Pets:** Dogs only. Designated rooms, service with restrictions, supervision. [SAVE] ⊠ 🖥

◈◈ ▼▼▼ Red Carpet Inn-Milford Ⓜ

(570) 296-9444. **$55-$125, 7 day notice.** 240 Rt 6 18337. I-84, exit 46, just s. Ext corridors. **Pets:** Medium. $5 daily fee/pet. Designated rooms, no service, supervision. [SAVE] ⊠ 🖥

W W Scottish Inns **M**

(570) 491-4414. **$50-$110.** 274 Rt 6 & 209 18337. I-84, exit 53, 1 mi s. Ext corridors. **Pets:** Accepted. [SAVE] [X] [🛏] [💻]

STARLIGHT

W W The Inn at Starlight Lake **CI**

(570) 798-2519. **$115-$195, 14 day notice.** 289 Starlight Lake Rd 18461. Off SR 370, 1 mi n, follow signs. Ext/int corridors. **Pets:** Accepted.
[ASK] [X] [🍴] [X] [K] [W] [Z]

END AREA

PUNXSUTAWNEY

W W The Pantall Hotel **H**

(814) 938-6600. **$54-$99.** 135 E Mahoning St 15767. On US 119/SR 36; downtown. Int corridors. **Pets:** Accepted. [ASK] [X] [🛏] [🍴]

READING

W W Quality Inn Airport **H**

(610) 736-0400. **Call for rates.** 2017 Bernville Rd 19601. US 222, exit SR 183, 2 mi s. Int corridors. **Pets:** Small, other species. $20 daily fee/pet. Designated rooms, service with restrictions, supervision.
[X] [🛏] [💻]

ST. MARYS

W W Comfort Inn **H**

(814) 834-2030. **$106-$150, 3 day notice.** 195 Comfort Ln 15857. 1.8 mi s of center on SR 255, just w. Int corridors. **Pets:** Accepted.
[ASK] [X] [🛏] [💻] [🏊]

SAYRE

W W W Best Western Grand Victorian Inn **H**

(570) 888-7711. **$129-$229.** 255 Spring St 18840. SR 17, exit 61, just s. Int corridors. **Pets:** Accepted. [SAVE] [X] [🛏] [💻] [🍴] [🏊] [X]

SCRANTON

W W Clarion Hotel **H** ❀

(570) 344-9811. **$69-$109.** 300 Meadow Ave 18505. I-81, exit 184, just w. Int corridors. **Pets:** Other species. $25 daily fee/room. Designated rooms, service with restrictions, supervision.
[ASK] [X] [🛏] [💻] [🍴] [🏊] [X]

W W Hilton Scranton & Conference Center **H** ❀

(570) 343-3000. **$99-$269.** 100 Adams Ave 18503. I-81, exit 185, just w of jct Lackawanna Ave, Jefferson Ave and Spruce St; downtown. Int corridors. **Pets:** Medium, other species. $50 deposit/pet, $25 one-time fee/pet. Designated rooms, service with restrictions, supervision.
[ECO] [X] [&M] [🛏] [💻] [🍴] [🏊]

SHAMOKIN DAM

W W Econo Lodge Inn & Suites **H** ❀

(570) 743-1111. **$62-$90.** 3249 N Susquehanna Tr 17876. US 11 and 15, just n of jct SR 61. Ext corridors. **Pets:** Small, other species. $10 daily fee/pet. Service with restrictions, crate. [ASK] [X] [🛏] [💻] [🍴] [🏊]

W W Hampton Inn **H**

(570) 743-2223. **Call for rates.** 3 Stettler Ave 17876. US 11 and 15, 1 mi s of jct SR 61. Int corridors. **Pets:** Medium, other species. $25 one-time fee/room. Service with restrictions, supervision.
[SAVE] [X] [&M] [🛏] [💻] [🏊]

W W Phillips Motel **M**

(570) 743-3100. **$79-$159, 7 day notice.** 2943 N Susquehanna Tr 17876. 3 mi n of Selinsgrove. Ext corridors. **Pets:** Other species. $25 deposit/room. Designated rooms, service with restrictions, supervision.
[SAVE] [X] [🛏] [💻]

SHICKSHINNY

W W The Blue Heron Bed & Breakfast **BB**

(570) 864-3740. **Call for rates.** 1270 Bethel Hill Rd 18655. Jct US 11, 6.2 mi n on SR 239, then 2 mi n on CR 4016 (Harveyville/Bethel Hill Rd). Int corridors. **Pets:** Accepted. [X] [W] [Z]

SHILLINGTON

W W Best Western Reading Inn **H**

(610) 777-7888. **$65-$129.** 2299 Lancaster Pike 19607. US 422, exit Penn Ave, 1.5 mi e on SR 724, then 0.5 mi s on US 222; I-76 (Pennsylvania Tpke), exit 286, 9 mi n on US 222. Int corridors. **Pets:** Other species. $50 deposit/room, $20 daily fee/pet. Service with restrictions, crate.
[SAVE] [X] [🛏] [💻] [🏊]

SHIPPENSBURG

W W Best Western Shippensburg Hotel **H**

(717) 532-5200. **$55-$120.** 125 Walnut Bottom Rd 17257. I-81, exit 29, 0.5 mi w on SR 174. Int corridors. **Pets:** Medium. $10 daily fee/pet. Service with restrictions, supervision. [SAVE] [X] [🛏] [💻] [🏊] [X]

SOUTH WILLIAMSPORT

W W Ridgemont Motel **M** ❀

(570) 321-5300. **$49-$59.** 637 US Hwy 15 S 17702. 1.2 mi s on US 15. Ext corridors. **Pets:** Small, dogs only. $5 one-time fee/pet. Service with restrictions, supervision. [SAVE] [X] [🛏] [💻]

STATE COLLEGE

W W The Autoport Motel & Restaurant **H**

(814) 237-7666. **Call for rates.** 1405 S Atherton St 16801. US 322 business route, 1.4 mi e of jct SR 26. Ext/int corridors. **Pets:** Medium, dogs only. $10 daily fee/pet. Designated rooms, service with restrictions, crate.
[X] [🛏] [💻] [🍴] [🏊]

W W Days Inn Penn State **H**

(814) 238-8454. **$69-$129.** 240 S Pugh St 16801. Just e SR 26 northbound; 0.4 mi n jct US 322 business route; downtown. Int corridors. **Pets:** Other species. $10 daily fee/room. Designated rooms, service with restrictions, supervision. [SAVE] [X] [🛏] [💻] [🍴] [🏊]

W W Nittany Budget Motel **M**

(814) 238-0015. **$42-$195, 30 day notice.** 2070 Cato Ave 16801. SR 26, 2.6 mi s of jct US 322 business route. Ext corridors. **Pets:** Accepted. [SAVE] [X] [🛏]

W W Quality Inn Penn State **M** ❀

(814) 234-1600. **Call for rates.** 1274 N Atherton St 16803. US 322 business route, 1 mi w of jct SR 26. Int corridors. **Pets:** Medium, other species. $10 one-time fee/pet. Service with restrictions, supervision.
[SAVE] [X] [&M]

W W Residence Inn State College **H**

(814) 235-6960. **$119-$124.** 1555 University Dr 16801. US 322 business route, 1.5 mi e of jct SR 26. Int corridors. **Pets:** Large, other species. $75 one-time fee/room. Service with restrictions. [X] [🛏] [💻] [🏊] [X]

W W Super 8 State College **H**

(814) 237-8005. **$61-$99, 14 day notice.** 1663 S Atherton St 16801. US 322 business route, 1.6 mi e of jct SR 26. Int corridors. **Pets:** Accepted. [SAVE] [X] [🛏] [💻]

(AAA) ▼▼▼ Toftrees Golf Resort & Conference Center H

(814) 234-8000. **$69-$399.** One Country Club Ln 16803. US 322 business route, exit Toftrees/Woodycrest, 0.7 mi ne; 4 mi w of jct SR 26. Int corridors. **Pets:** Other species. $25 one-time fee/room. Designated rooms, service with restrictions, crate. (SAVE) ☒ 🖥 💻 ¶¶ ⌦ ☒

TOWN HILL

▼ Days Inn Breezewood H

(814) 735-3860. **Call for rates.** 9648 Old Rt 126 17267. I-70, exit 156, just n. Int corridors. **Pets:** Accepted. ☒ 🖥 💻 ¶¶

WARREN

(AAA) ▼▼▼ Holiday Inn of Warren H

(814) 726-3000. **$119-$139.** 210 Ludlow St 16365. Jct US 6, just n on Ludlow St (US 62 N). Int corridors. **Pets:** Other species. $10 deposit/room. (SAVE) ☒ 🖥 🖥 💻 ¶¶ ⌦

▼▼ Warren Super 8 H

(814) 723-8881. **$74-$82.** 204 Struthers St 16365. 1.5 mi w on US 6, exit Ludlow St, w on Allegheny, then s. Ext/int corridors. **Pets:** Accepted.

(ASK) ☒ 🖥 💻

WELLSBORO

(AAA) ▼▼▼ Penn Wells Lodge M

(570) 724-3463. **$60-$127.** 4 Main St 16901. Just n on US 6 and SR 287; downtown. Ext/int corridors. **Pets:** Accepted.

(SAVE) ☒ 🖥 💻 ⌦ ☒

WEST HAZLETON

(AAA) ▼▼▼ Comfort Inn Hazleton/West Hazleton H ❀

(570) 455-9300. **$79-$149.** 58 SR 93 18202. I-81, exit 145, 0.3 mi se; I-80, exit 256, 3.8 mi se. Int corridors. **Pets:** Other species. $15 one-time fee/room. Service with restrictions. (SAVE) ☒ 🖥 💻 ¶¶

WEST MIDDLESEX

▼▼ Super 8-West Middlesex/Sharon H

(724) 528-3888. **$65-$155.** 3369 New Castle Rd 16159. I-80, exit 4B (SR 60), just w to SR 18, then just s. Int corridors. **Pets:** Small, other species. $15 daily fee/pet. Service with restrictions, supervision.

(ASK) ☒ 🖥 💻

WHITE HAVEN

(AAA) ▼▼▼ Comfort Inn-Pocono Mountain H ❀

(570) 443-8461. **$70-$230.** Rt 940 18661. I-476, exit 95, just e; I-80, exit 277 (Lake Harmony). Int corridors. **Pets:** Large, other species. $15 daily fee/pet. Designated rooms, service with restrictions, supervision.

(SAVE) ☒ 🖥 💻 ⌦

WILKES-BARRE

(AAA) ▼▼ Best Western Genetti Hotel & Conference Center H ❀

(570) 823-6152. **$75-$115.** 77 E Market St 18701. Jct Washington St; downtown. Int corridors. **Pets:** $10 daily fee/room. Designated rooms, service with restrictions, crate. (SAVE) ☒ 🖥 💻 ¶¶ ⌦

(AAA) ▼▼ Days Inn H

(570) 826-0111. **$50-$175, 14 day notice.** 760 Kidder St 18702. I-81, exit 170B, to exit 1 (SR 309 S business route), just w; I-76 (Pennsylvania Tpke), exit 105 to exit 1 (SR 115 N). Int corridors. **Pets:** Small, dogs only. $10 daily fee/pet. Designated rooms, service with restrictions, supervision.

(SAVE) ☒ 🖥

(AAA) ▼▼ Econo Lodge Near The Arena H ❀

(570) 823-0600. **$65-$80.** 1075 Wilkes-Barre Township Blvd 18702. I-81, exit 165 southbound; exit 165B northbound, on SR 309 business route. Int corridors. **Pets:** Large, other species. $50 deposit/room, $10 daily fee/pet. Designated rooms, service with restrictions, supervision.

(SAVE) ☒ 🖥 💻

▼▼▼ Extended Stay Deluxe Wilkes-Barre Hwy 315 H

(570) 970-2500. **$90-$149.** 1067 Hwy 315 18702. I-81, exit 170B, to exit 1 (SR 309 S business route), 0.3 mi n. Int corridors. **Pets:** Other species. $25 daily fee/room. Designated rooms, service with restrictions, crate.

(ASK) ☒ 🖥 🖥 💻

▼▼▼ Host Inn All Suites Hotel H

(570) 270-4678. **Call for rates.** 860 Kidder St 18702. I-81, exit 170B to exit 1 (SR 309 S business route), then 0.5 mi w. Int corridors. **Pets:** Accepted. ☒ 🖥 🖥 💻 ⌦

(AAA) ▼▼▼ Red Roof Inn #7139 M

(570) 829-6422. **Call for rates.** 1035 Hwy 315 18702. I-81, exit 170B, to exit 1 (SR 309 S business route), just n. Ext corridors. **Pets:** Large. Service with restrictions, crate. (SAVE) ☒ 🖥

▼▼▼ The Woodlands Inn & Resort H

(570) 824-9831. **$119-$199.** 1073 Hwy 315 18702. I-81, exit 170B to exit 1 (SR 309 S business route), then 0.3 mi n. Int corridors. **Pets:** $50 one-time fee/room. Service with restrictions, supervision.

(ASK) ☒ 🖥 💻 ¶¶ ⌦ ☒

WILLIAMSPORT

(AAA) ▼▼▼ Best Western Williamsport Inn H

(570) 326-1981. **$75-$189.** 1840 E 3rd St 17701. I-180, exit 25 (Faxon St), just e; 1 mi w of W 3rd St. Ext corridors. **Pets:** Accepted.

(SAVE) ☒ 🖥 💻 ¶¶ ⌦

▼▼▼ Candlewood Suites H

(570) 601-9100. **$99-$139.** 1836 E 3rd St 17701. I-180, exit 25 (Faxon St), 0.5 mi e; 2.6 mi n of terminal. Int corridors. **Pets:** Accepted.

(ASK) ☒ 🖥 💻

(AAA) ▼▼▼ Genetti Hotel & Suites H ❀

(570) 326-6600. **$81-$296, 7 day notice.** 200 W 4th St 17701. Jct William St; downtown. Ext/int corridors. **Pets:** Dogs only. $15 daily fee/pet. Designated rooms, supervision. (SAVE) ☒ 🖥 💻 ¶¶ ⌦

WIND GAP

(AAA) ▼▼ Red Carpet Inn M

(610) 863-7782. **$50-$135.** 1395 Jacobsburg Rd 18091. SR 33, exit Wind Gap/Bath SR 512 S, just s on Jacobsburg Rd, follow signs. Ext/int corridors. **Pets:** Accepted. (SAVE) ☒ 🖥

WYOMISSING

▼▼▼ Crowne Plaza Reading Hotel H

(610) 376-3811. **$129-$189.** 1741 W Papermill Rd 19610. US 422, exit Papermill Rd. Int corridors. **Pets:** Accepted.

(ASK) ☒ 🖥 💻 ¶¶ ⌦ ☒

▼▼ Econo Lodge Inn & Suites H

(610) 378-5105. **$65-$109, 3 day notice.** 635 Spring St 19610. Just off US 422, exit Papermill Rd. Int corridors. **Pets:** Small. $10 daily fee/pet. Service with restrictions, supervision. (ASK) ☒ 🖥 💻

▼▼▼ Homewood Suites-Reading/Wyomissing H

(610) 736-3100. **$139-$219.** 2801 Papermill Rd 19610. US 422, exit Papermill Rd, 1.8 mi nw; US 222, exit Spring Ridge Rd. Int corridors. **Pets:** Medium. $75 daily fee/pet. Service with restrictions, supervision.

☒ 🖥 🖥 💻 ⌦

WYSOX

▼▼▼ Comfort Inn H

(570) 265-5691. **$115-$139.** US 6 18854. On US 6; center. Int corridors. **Pets:** Other species. $25 one-time fee/room. Supervision.

(ASK) ☒ 🖥 💻 ⌦

YORK

▼▼▼ Comfort Inn & Suites H

(717) 699-1919. **$90-$130.** 2250 N George St 17402. I-83, exit 22, just n. Int corridors. **Pets:** Accepted. (ASK) ☒ 🖥 🖥 💻

◆◆◆◆ **Holiday Inn Conference Center of York** 🅷

(717) 846-9500. **$109-$149.** 2000 Loucks Rd 17408. I-83, exit 21B northbound, 2.5 mi w on US 30, then just n; exit 22 southbound, 0.5 mi s on SR 181, 2.2 mi w on US 30, then just n. Int corridors. **Pets:** Accepted.

🆂🅺 ⊠ 🖥 💻 🍴 🏊 ⊗

◆◆◆ **Holiday Inn Express** 🅷 🐾

(717) 741-1000. **$100-$200.** 140 Leader Heights Rd 17403. I-83, exit 14, just w on SR 182. Int corridors. **Pets:** Medium, dogs only. $50 one-time fee/room. Designated rooms, service with restrictions, crate.

🆂🅺 ⊠ 🖥 💻

◆◆ **Red Roof Inn #315** 🅷

(717) 843-8181. **Call for rates.** 125 Arsenal Rd 17404. I-83, exit 21B northbound, 0.3 mi w on US 30; exit 21 southbound, 0.5 mi s on SR 181 to US 30. Int corridors. **Pets:** Large. Service with restrictions, crate.

⊠ 🖥

Ⓐ ◆◆◆ **The Yorktowne Hotel** 🅷

(717) 848-1111. **$109-$279.** 48 E Market St 17401. SR 462 eastbound and I-83 business route, just e of square, follow signs. Int corridors. **Pets:** Medium, other species. $25 daily fee/room. Service with restrictions.

🆂🅰🆅🅴 ⊠ 🖥 💻 🍴

RHODE ISLAND

EAST PROVIDENCE

▼▼ Extended StayAmerica Providence-East Providence 🅷

(401) 272-1661. **$75-$149.** 1000 Warren Ave 02914. I-195, exit 8 eastbound, just e; exit 6 westbound, 1.1 mi e via Warren Ave. Int corridors. **Pets:** Other species. $25 daily fee/room. Designated rooms, service with restrictions, crate. (A$K) ⊠ 🅼 🖪 🖵

MIDDLETOWN

▼▼ Econo Lodge Ⓜ

(401) 849-2718. **$45-$210.** 1359 W Main Rd 02842. On SR 114, just n of jct SR 214. Int corridors. **Pets:** Medium. $50 deposit/pet. Designated rooms, service with restrictions, supervision. (A$K) ⊠ 🖪 ⌁

⏿ ▼▼ Howard Johnson Inn-Newport 🅷 ❖

(401) 849-2000. **$49-$254.** 351 W Main Rd 02842. On SR 114, 0.3 mi s of jct SR 138. Int corridors. **Pets:** Large, other species. $10 daily fee/pet. Designated rooms, service with restrictions, supervision.

(SAVE) ⊠ 🅼 🖪 🖵 (¶) ⌁ 🗙

⏿ ▼▼ Residence Inn by Marriott-Newport/Middletown 🅷 ❖

(401) 845-2005. **$139-$275, 3 day notice.** 325 W Main Rd 02842. On SR 114, 0.3 mi s of jct SR 138. Int corridors. **Pets:** Other species. $75 one-time fee/room. Designated rooms, service with restrictions.

(SAVE) ⊠ 🖪 🖵 ⌁ 🗙

NEWPORT

⏿ ▼▼▼ Beech Tree Inn 🅱🅱 ❖

(401) 847-9794. **$99-$359, 14 day notice.** 34 Rhode Island Ave 02840. Just e of SR 114; 0.8 mi s of jct SR 138. Int corridors. **Pets:** Other species. $25 daily fee/pet. Service with restrictions. (SAVE) ⊠ 🖪

⏿ ▼▼▼ The Burbank Rose 🅱🅱

(401) 849-9457. **$89-$240, 7 day notice.** 111 Memorial Blvd W 02840. Just e on SR 138A. Int corridors. **Pets:** Small, other species. $15 daily fee/room. Designated rooms, service with restrictions, supervision.

(SAVE) ⊠ 🖪 🖵 ⌁

⏿ ▼▼▼ The Hotel Viking 🅷 ❖

(401) 847-3300. **$99-$499, 7 day notice.** 1 Bellevue Ave 02840. Corner of Kay and Church sts and Bellevue Ave. Int corridors. **Pets:** Large. $75 one-time fee/pet. Designated rooms, supervision.

(ECO) (SAVE) ⊠ 🖪 🖵 (¶) ⌁ 🗙

⏿ ▼▼▼ Hyatt Regency Newport Hotel & Spa 🅷 ❖

(401) 851-1234. **$109-$449, 3 day notice.** 1 Goat Island 02840. 0.8 mi w of America's Cup Ave, follow signs to Goat Island. Int corridors. **Pets:** Medium, dogs only. $75 one-time fee/pet. Designated rooms, service with restrictions, crate.

(ECO) (SAVE) ⊠ 🅼 🖪 🖵 (¶) ⌁ 🗙

NORTH KINGSTOWN

▼▼ Hamilton Village Inn Ⓜ

(401) 295-0700. **$79-$139, 7 day notice.** 642 Boston Neck Rd 02852. SR 1A, 1.3 mi s of jct SR 102. Ext corridors. **Pets:** Other species. Designated rooms, service with restrictions, supervision. ⊠ 🖪 🖵 (¶)

PROVIDENCE

▼▼▼ Hilton Providence 🅷

(401) 831-3900. **$129-$289.** 21 Atwells Ave 02903. I-95, exit 21. Int corridors. **Pets:** Accepted. (ECO) ⊠ 🖪 🖵 (¶) ⌁

⏿ ▼▼▼ The Hotel Providence 🅷

(401) 861-8000. **$149-$399.** 139 Mathewson St 02903. I-95, exit 22A, 0.5 mi se on Memorial Blvd, then 0.3 mi sw; entrance on Mathewson St. Int corridors. **Pets:** Accepted. (ECO) (SAVE) ⊠ 🖪 🖵 (¶)

⏿ ▼▼▼ Marriott Providence Downtown 🅷

(401) 272-2400. **$251-$307.** 1 Orms St 02904. I-95, exit 23 to state offices. Int corridors. **Pets:** Other species. $49 one-time fee/room. Designated rooms, service with restrictions, supervision.

(ECO) (SAVE) ⊠ 🅼 🖪 🖵 (¶) ⌁

▼▼▼ Providence Biltmore Hotel 🅷

(401) 421-0700. **$119-$299.** 11 Dorrance St 02903. I-95, exit 22A; downtown. Int corridors. **Pets:** Accepted. (ECO) (A$K) ⊠ 🅼 🖪 🖵 (¶)

⏿ ▼▼▼ The Westin Providence 🅷

(401) 598-8000. **$149-$419.** One W Exchange St 02903. I-95, exit 22A; downtown. Int corridors. **Pets:** Accepted.

(ECO) (SAVE) ⊠ 🅼 🖪 🖵 (¶) ⌁ 🗙

SMITHFIELD

⏿ ▼▼▼ Quality Inn Smithfield 🅷 ❖

(401) 232-2400. **$100-$280, 7 day notice.** 355 George Washington Hwy 02917. I-295, exit 8B, 0.3 mi n on SR 7, then 0.6 mi e on SR 116. Int corridors. **Pets:** Medium, dogs only. $25 daily fee/pet. Designated rooms, service with restrictions, supervision.

(SAVE) ⊠ 🅼 🖪 🖵 ⌁

WAKEFIELD

▼▼▼ The Kings' Rose Inn 🅱🅱

(401) 783-5222. **$110-$145.** 1747 Mooresfield Rd (SR 138) 02879. I-95, exit 3A, 11 mi e on SR 138; 3.3 mi w of US 1. Int corridors. **Pets:** No service, supervision. 🗙

WARWICK

⏿ ▼▼▼ Best Western Airport Inn 🅷

(401) 737-7400. **$85-$125.** 2138 Post Rd 02886. I-95, exit 13, e to US 1, then just ne. Int corridors. **Pets:** Small. $25 one-time fee/room. Designated rooms, service with restrictions, supervision. (SAVE) ⊠ 🖪 🖵

▼▼▼ Comfort Inn-Airport 🅷

(401) 732-0470. **$80-$149.** 1940 Post Rd 02886. I-95, exit 13, e to US 1, then 0.5 mi n. Int corridors. **Pets:** Medium, dogs only. $50 one-time fee/room. Service with restrictions, supervision. (A$K) ⊠ 🖪 🖵

▼▼ Crowne Plaza Hotel at the Crossings 🅷

(401) 732-6000. **$99-$149.** 801 Greenwich Ave 02886. I-95, exit 12A southbound; exit 12 northbound, 0.3 mi se on SR 5. Int corridors. **Pets:** Accepted. (ECO) (A$K) ⊠ 🅼 🖪 🖵 (¶) ⌁ 🗙

▼▼ Extended StayAmerica Providence-Airport-Warwick 🅷

(401) 732-2547. **$65-$149.** 245 W Natick Rd 02886. I-295, exit 2 northbound, just sw; exit 3A southbound, 1.1 mi e on SR 37, 2 mi s on SR 2, then just sw. Int corridors. **Pets:** Other species. $25 daily fee/room. Designated rooms, service with restrictions, crate. (A$K) ⊠ 🅼 🖪 🖵

⏿ ▼▼▼ Hampton Inn & Suites Providence-Warwick Airport 🅷

(401) 739-8888. **$89-$189.** 2100 Post Rd 02886. I-95, exit 13, e to US 1, then just n. Int corridors. **Pets:** Service with restrictions, supervision.

(SAVE) ⊠ 🅼 🖪 🖵 ⌁

▼▼▼ **Holiday Inn Express Hotel & Suites** 🄷

(401) 736-5000. **$79-$129.** 901 Jefferson Blvd 02886. I-95, exit 13, 0.4 mi on Airport Connector Rd, then exit Jefferson Blvd. Int corridors. **Pets:** Other species. Designated rooms, service with restrictions, supervision.

▼▼ **Homestead Studio Suites-Providence/Airport/Warwick** 🄷

(401) 732-6667. **$75-$149.** 268 Metro Center Blvd 02886. I-95, exit 12A, 0.4 mi e on SR 113, 0.4 mi n on SR 5, then 0.4 mi e. Int corridors. **Pets:** Other species. $25 daily fee/room. Designated rooms, service with restrictions, crate. 🄰🅂🄺 ⌧ ♿ⓜ 🔒 💻 ⊠

▼▼▼ **Homewood Suites by Hilton** 🄷

(401) 738-0008. **$85-$159.** 33 International Way 02886. I-95, exit 13, 0.4 mi n on Jefferson Blvd, 0.5 mi nw on Kilvert St, then 0.4 mi sw on Metro Center Blvd. Int corridors. **Pets:** Accepted.

⌧ ♿ⓜ 🔒 💻 ⇌ ⊠

▼▼ **La Quinta Inn & Suites** 🄷 🐾

(401) 941-6600. **$65-$159.** 36 Jefferson Blvd 02888. I-95, exit 15, just se. Int corridors. **Pets:** Medium, other species. Service with restrictions, supervision. 🄰🅂🄺 ⌧ 🔒 💻 ⇌

🅐🅐🅐 ▼▼▼▼ **NYLO Providence/Warwick** 🄷 🐾

(401) 734-4460. **$89-$229.** 400 Knight St 02886. Jct SR 5, just ne. Int corridors. **Pets:** Medium. $50 one-time fee/room. Designated rooms, service with restrictions, supervision. 🄴🄲🄾 🆂🅰🆅🅴 ⌧ ♿ⓜ 🔒 💻 🍴

▼▼▼▼ **Residence Inn Providence/Warwick** 🄷

(401) 737-7100. **$159-$169.** 500 Kilvert St 02886. I-95, exit 13 to Jefferson Blvd, 0.4 mi n, then 0.6 mi w. Ext corridors. **Pets:** Accepted.

⌧ ♿ⓜ 🔒 💻 ⇌ ⊠

🅐🅐🅐 ▼▼▼▼ **Sheraton Providence Airport Hotel** 🄷

(401) 738-4000. **$79-$209.** 1850 Post Rd 02886. I-95, exit 13, 0.6 mi n on US 1. Int corridors. **Pets:** Medium, dogs only. $50 one-time fee/room. Service with restrictions, supervision.

🆂🅰🆅🅴 ⌧ ♿ⓜ 🔒 💻 🍴 ⇌

WEST GREENWICH

▼▼▼ **Residence Inn by Marriott Providence / Coventry** 🄷

(401) 828-1170. **$117-$143.** 755 Center of New England Blvd 02817. I-95, exit 7, just ne; center of New England Plaza. Int corridors. **Pets:** Medium. $100 one-time fee/pet. Service with restrictions, crate.

⌧ ♿ⓜ 🔒 💻 ⇌ ⊠

WEST WARWICK

▼▼ **Extended StayAmerica Providence-Airport-West Warwick** 🄷

(401) 885-3161. **$69-$149.** 1235 Division Rd 02893. I-95, exit 8A northbound, just s on SR 2, then just w; exit 8 southbound, just s on SR 2, then just w. Int corridors. **Pets:** Other species. $25 daily fee/room. Designated rooms, service with restrictions, crate. 🄰🅂🄺 ⌧ ♿ⓜ 🔒 💻

WYOMING

🅐🅐🅐 ▼▼▼▼ **Stagecoach House Inn** 🄱🄱 🐾

(401) 539-9600. **$100-$199.** 1136 Main St (SR 138) 02898. I-95, exit 3B northbound, 0.7 mi nw; exit southbound, 0.4 mi nw. Ext/int corridors. **Pets:** Dogs only. $25 one-time fee/room. Designated rooms, service with restrictions, supervision. 🆂🅰🆅🅴 ⌧ 🔒 💻

SOUTH CAROLINA

AIKEN

▼▼▼▼ Holiday Inn Express Ⓜ ❖
(803) 648-0999. **$78-$275.** 155 Colony Pkwy/Whiskey Rd 29803. Jct US 1/78 and SR 19 (Whiskey Rd), 1.8 mi s on SR 19. Ext corridors. **Pets:** Other species. $45 one-time fee/room. Service with restrictions.
ⒶⓈⓀ ☒ 🛏 💻 🏊 ☒

ⓐⓐⓐ ▼▼▼ Quality Inn & Suites Ⓜ
(803) 641-1100. **$60-$275.** 3608 Richland Ave W 29801. Jct US 1/78 and SR 19 (Whiskey Rd), 2.9 mi w on US 1/78. Ext corridors. **Pets:** Large, other species. $10 daily fee/pet. Service with restrictions, supervision. ⓈⒶⓋⒺ ☒ 🛏 💻 🏊

▼▼▼ Super 8-Aiken Ⓗ
(803) 641-8800. **$72-$270, 3 day notice.** 2577 Whiskey Rd 29803. Jct US 1/78 and SR 19 (Whiskey Rd), 4.3 mi s on SR 19. Int corridors.
Pets: Accepted. ⒶⓈⓀ ☒ 🛏 💻 🏊

ANDERSON

▼▼▼▼ Country Inn & Suites By Carlson Ⓗ
(864) 622-2200. **$85-$215.** 116 Interstate Blvd 29621. I-85, exit 19B, just n, then just se. Int corridors. **Pets:** Accepted.
ⒶⓈⓀ ☒ 🛦 🛏 💻 🏊

▼▼▼ Days Inn Ⓜ
(864) 375-0375. **$63-$150.** 1007 Smith Mill Rd 29625. I-85, exit 19A, just se. Ext corridors. **Pets:** Dogs only. $5 daily fee/pet, $30 one-time fee/room. Service with restrictions, supervision.
ⒶⓈⓀ ☒ 🛦 🛏 💻 🏊

ⓐⓐⓐ ▼▼▼ Holiday Inn Express Ⓗ
(864) 231-0231. **Call for rates.** 410 Alliance Pkwy 29621. I-85, exit 27, just s on SR 81. Int corridors. **Pets:** Accepted.
ⓈⒶⓋⒺ ☒ 🛦 🛏 💻 🏊

▼▼▼ Home-Towne Suites Ⓗ
(864) 226-1112. **$69-$129.** 151 Civic Center Blvd 29625. I-85, exit 19A, 2.2 mi se on US 76, then 0.6 mi s. Int corridors. **Pets:** Accepted.
ⒶⓈⓀ ☒ 🛏 💻 🏊

▼▼ Jameson Inn Ⓜ
(864) 375-9800. **$78-$85.** 128 Interstate Blvd 29621. I-85, exit 19B, just n, then just se. Ext corridors. **Pets:** Accepted.
ⒶⓈⓀ ☒ 🛦 🛏 💻 🏊

▼▼▼ La Quinta Inn Anderson Ⓜ ❖
(864) 225-3721. **$49-$69.** 3430 Clemson Blvd 29621. I-85, exit 19A, 2.9 mi se on US 76/SR 28 (Clemson Blvd); exit 21 southbound, 2.6 mi s on US 178. Ext corridors. **Pets:** Medium, other species. Service with restrictions, supervision. ⒶⓈⓀ ☒ 🛏 💻 🏊

BENNETTSVILLE

ⓐⓐⓐ ▼▼▼ Best Western Bennettsville Ⓜ
(843) 479-1700. **$69-$149.** 213 US Hwy 15 & 401 Bypass E 29512. 0.6 mi s of center, just ne on US 15/401/SR 9. Ext corridors. **Pets:** Medium. $25 daily fee/pet. Service with restrictions, supervision.
ⓈⒶⓋⒺ ☒ 🛏 💻 🏊

BISHOPVILLE

▼▼ Econo Lodge Ⓜ
(803) 428-3200. **$52-$125.** 1135 Sumter Hwy 29010. I-20, exit 116, just sw. Ext corridors. **Pets:** Accepted. ☒ 🛏 💻

BLUFFTON

▼▼▼▼ Holiday Inn Express Hotel & Suites Ⓗ
(843) 757-2002. **$89-$139.** 35 Bluffton Rd 29910. Jct William Hilton Pkwy (US 278/Bluffton Rd US 46), just se. Int corridors. **Pets:** Accepted.
ⒶⓈⓀ ☒ 🛦 🛏 💻 🏊

ⓐⓐⓐ ▼▼▼ ▼▼▼ The Inn at Palmetto Bluff ⒸⒶ ❖
(843) 706-6500. **$475-$900, 16 day notice.** 476 Mount Pelia Rd 29910. Jct US 278/SR 170, 4.4 mi sw on SR 170, then 2.2 mi e on SR 46 to Palmetto Bluff Rd; check-in at gatehouse. Ext corridors. **Pets:** Medium. $25 daily fee/room. Designated rooms, service with restrictions, crate.
ⓈⒶⓋⒺ ☒ 🛏 💻 🍽 🏊 ☒

CAMDEN

ⓐⓐⓐ ▼▼▼ Colony Inn Ⓜ
(803) 432-5508. **$65-$75.** 2020 W DeKalb St 29020. Jct US 521/1/601, 1.6 mi w on US 1/601. Ext/int corridors. **Pets:** Medium. $10 one-time fee/room. Designated rooms, service with restrictions, supervision.
ⓈⒶⓋⒺ ☒ 🛏 💻 🍽 🏊

CAYCE

ⓐⓐⓐ ▼▼ Riverside Inn Ⓜ
(803) 939-4688. **$62.** 111 Knox Abbott Dr 29033. US 21, just w of Congaree River Bridge. Ext corridors. **Pets:** $20 one-time fee/room. Service with restrictions. ⓈⒶⓋⒺ ☒ 🛏 💻 🏊 ☒

CHARLESTON METROPOLITAN AREA

CHARLESTON

ⓐⓐⓐ ▼▼▼▼ Best Western

Charleston-Downtown Ⓗ ❖
(843) 722-4000. **$70-$205.** 146 Lockwood Dr/Blvd 29403. I-26, exit 221A (US 17 S), 1.2 mi sw; just e of Ashley River. Int corridors. **Pets:** $25 daily fee/room. Designated rooms, service with restrictions.
ⓈⒶⓋⒺ ☒ 🛏 💻 🍽 🏊

ⓐⓐⓐ ▼▼▼ Best Western Sweetgrass Inn Ⓗ
(843) 571-6100. **$49-$199.** 1540 Savannah Hwy 29407. US 17 S, 3.6 mi w of Ashley River Bridge; jct I-526 W to terminus and US 17 N, 1.7 mi e. Ext corridors. **Pets:** Medium, other species. $20 daily fee/room. Service with restrictions, supervision. ⓈⒶⓋⒺ ☒ 🛏 💻 🏊

▼▼▼ ◆ The Inn at Middleton Place ⒸⒾ ❖
(843) 556-0500. **$159-$250, 3 day notice.** 4290 Ashley River Rd 29414. I-526, exit 11B (Ashley River Rd/SR 61), then 10.3 mi on SR 61 N. Ext corridors. **Pets:** Medium, other species. $50 one-time fee/room. Service with restrictions, crate. ⒶⓈⓀ ☒ 🛏 💻 🍽 🏊 ☒

▼▼▼▼ **La Quinta Inn Riverview** 🅷 ❀

(843) 556-5200. **$79-$155.** 11 Ashley Point Dr 29407. US 17 S, just over Ashley River Bridge to Albermarle Rd, 0.4 mi s to Ashley Pointe Dr. Ext/int corridors. **Pets:** Medium, other species. Service with restrictions, supervision. A$K ⊠ 🛅 🖵 🐾

▼▼▼▼ **Residence Inn by Marriott Charleston Downtown/Riverview** 🅷

(843) 571-7979. **$139-$149.** 90 Ripley Point Dr 29407. US 17 S, just over Ashley River Bridge to Albermarle Rd, just s. Int corridors. **Pets:** Accepted. ⊠ ᴦᴹ 🛅 🖵 🐾 ⊠

▼▼▼▼ **Town & Country Inn & Conference Center** 🅼

(843) 571-1000. **$79-$159.** 2008 Savannah Hwy 29407. US 17 S, 3.5 mi nw of Ashley River Bridge; jct I-526 W to terminus and US 17 N, just se. Ext corridors. **Pets:** Large, other species. $100 deposit/room. Designated rooms, service with restrictions. A$K ⊠ 🛅 🖵 🍴 🐾 ⊠

🔵🔵🔵 ▼▼▼▼◆ **Vendue Inn** 🅲 ❀

(843) 577-7970. **$199-$459, 3 day notice.** 19 Vendue Range 29401. Off E Bay St, 1 blk from Waterfront Park; in historic district. Int corridors. **Pets:** $50 one-time fee/pet. Supervision. SAVE ⊠ 🛅 🍴

FOLLY BEACH

🔵🔵🔵 ▼▼▼▼◆ **Holiday Inn Folly Beach Oceanfront** 🅷

(843) 588-6464. **Call for rates.** 1 Center St 29439. Terminus of SR 171; center. Ext corridors. **Pets:** $75 one-time fee/room.

SAVE ⊠ 🛅 🖵 🍴 🐾

KIAWAH ISLAND

▼▼▼▼ **Kiawah Island Golf Resort–Courtside Villas** 🅒🅞

(843) 768-2121. **Call for rates.** 1401 Shipwatch Rd 29455. Just e of main gate to Kiawah Beach Dr, then just s; in West Beach Village area. Ext corridors. **Pets:** Accepted. ⊠ 🛅 🖵 🐾 ⊠

▼▼▼▼ **Kiawah Island Golf Resort–Fairway Oaks Villas** 🅒🅞

(843) 768-2121. **Call for rates.** 1301 Kiawah Beach Dr 29455. Just e of main gate, then just s; in West Beach Village area. Ext corridors. **Pets:** Accepted. ⊠ 🛅 🖵 🐾 ⊠

▼▼▼▼ **Kiawah Island Golf Resort–Mariners Watch Villas** 🅒🅞

(843) 768-2121. **Call for rates.** 4200 Sea Forest Dr 29455. 1.6 mi e of main gate, then just s; in East Beach Village area. Ext corridors. **Pets:** Accepted. ⊠ 🛅 🖵 🐾 ⊠

▼▼▼▼ **Kiawah Island Golf Resort–Parkside Villas** 🅒🅞

(843) 768-2121. **Call for rates.** 4501 Park Lake Dr 29455. 2 mi e of main gate, then just s; in East Beach Village area. Ext corridors. **Pets:** Accepted. ⊠ 🛅 🖵 🐾 ⊠

▼▼▼▼ **Kiawah Island Golf Resort–Seascape Villas** 🅒🅞

(843) 768-2121. **Call for rates.** 3510 Shipwatch Rd 29455. Just e of main gate, then just s; in West Beach Village area. Ext corridors. **Pets:** Accepted. ⊠ 🛅 🖵 🐾 ⊠

▼▼▼▼ **Kiawah Island Golf Resort–Shipwatch Villas** 🅒🅞

(843) 768-2121. **Call for rates.** 2200 Shipwatch Rd 29455. Just e of main gate, then just s; in West Beach Village area. Ext corridors. **Pets:** Accepted. ⊠ 🛅 🖵 🐾 ⊠

▼▼▼▼ **Kiawah Island Golf Resort–Tennis Club Villas** 🅒🅞

(843) 768-2121. **Call for rates.** 4659 Tennis Club Ln 29455. 2.2 mi e of main gate, then just s; at Roy Barth Tennis Center. Ext corridors. **Pets:** Accepted. ⊠ 🛅 🖵 🐾 ⊠

▼▼▼▼ **Kiawah Island Golf Resort–Turtle Cove Villas** 🅒🅞

(843) 768-2121. **Call for rates.** 5501 Green Dolphin Way 29455. 2.4 mi e of main gate, then just se; at Roy Barth Tennis Center. Ext corridors. **Pets:** Accepted. ⊠ 🛅 🖵 🐾 ⊠

▼▼▼▼ **Kiawah Island Golf Resort–Turtle Point Villas** 🅒🅞

(843) 768-2121. **Call for rates.** 4901 Green Dolphin Way 29455. 2.4 mi e of main gate, then just se; at Roy Barth Tennis Center and Turtle Point Golf Club. Ext corridors. **Pets:** Accepted. ⊠ 🛅 🖵 🐾 ⊠

▼▼▼▼ **Kiawah Island Golf Resort–Windswept Villas** 🅒🅞

(843) 768-2121. **Call for rates.** 4300 Sea Forest Dr 29455. 1.6 mi e of main gate, then just s; in East Beach Village area. Ext corridors. **Pets:** Accepted. ⊠ 🛅 🖵 🐾 ⊠

MOUNT PLEASANT

🔵🔵🔵 ▼▼▼ **Days Inn Patriots Point** 🅼

(843) 881-1800. **$69-$179, 3 day notice.** 261 Johnnie Dodds Blvd 29464. Just e of base of Cooper River Bridge on US 17. Ext corridors. **Pets:** Small, dogs only. $10 daily fee/pet. Designated rooms, service with restrictions, supervision. SAVE ⊠ 🛅 🖵 🍴 🐾

▼▼▼ **Extended StayAmerica-Charleston-Mount Pleasant** 🅷

(843) 884-4453. **$72-$110.** 304 Wingo Way 29464. Just e of Cooper River Bridge on US 17, then just n. Int corridors. **Pets:** Other species. $25 daily fee/room. Designated rooms, service with restrictions, crate. A$K ⊠ 🛅 🖵

▼▼▼▼ **Homewood Suites by Hilton** 🅷 ❀

(843) 881-6950. **$199-$259.** 1998 Riviera Dr 29464. I-526, exit 29 (Georgetown/US 17 N), 1.4 mi ne on US 17, 1 mi se on Isle of Palms connector (SR 517), then just sw. Int corridors. **Pets:** Large, other species. $75 one-time fee/room. Service with restrictions, crate. ⊠ ᴦᴹ 🛅 🖵 🐾 ⊠

🔵🔵🔵 ▼▼▼ **Red Roof Inn** 🅼

(843) 884-1411. **$56-$140.** 301 Johnnie Dodds Blvd 29464. Just e of base of Cooper River Bridge, on US 17 (Johnnie Dodds Blvd), then just s on McGrath-Darby Blvd. Ext corridors. **Pets:** Large. Service with restrictions, crate. SAVE ⊠ 🛅 🐾

▼▼▼▼ **Residence Inn by Marriott** 🅷

(843) 881-1599. **$139-$169.** 1116 Isle of Palms Connector 29464. I-526, exit 29 (Georgetown/US 17 N), 1.4 mi ne on US 17 to Isle of Palms Connector (SR 517), then just se. Int corridors. **Pets:** Accepted. ⊠ ᴦᴹ 🛅 🖵 🐾 ⊠

▼▼▼▼ **Rodeway Inn Charleston/Mt Pleasant** 🅼

(843) 884-5853. **Call for rates.** 310 Hwy 17 Bypass 29464. US 17, 0.7 mi n of Cooper River Bridge. Ext corridors. **Pets:** Medium, other species. $10 daily fee/room. Service with restrictions. ⊠ 🛅 🖵 🐾

🔵🔵🔵 ▼▼▼ **Sleep Inn Mt Pleasant** 🅷

(843) 856-5000. **$59-$149.** 299 Wingo Way 29464. Just e of base of Cooper River Bridge, then just n at McGrath-Darby Blvd. Int corridors. **Pets:** Accepted. SAVE ⊠ ᴦᴹ 🛅 🖵 🐾

NORTH CHARLESTON

🔵🔵🔵 ▼▼▼▼◆ **aloft Charleston Airport & Convention Center** 🅷 ❀

(843) 566-7300. **$109-$249.** 4875 Tanger Outlet Blvd 29405. I-526, exit 17 (International Blvd), just e; I-26, exit 213A eastbound; exit 213 westbound, follow signs to Tanger Outlet Mall, then just nw. Int corridors. **Pets:** Medium. Designated rooms, service with restrictions, supervision. SAVE ⊠ 🛅 🖵 🐾

▼▼▼▼ **Candlewood Suites** 🅷

(843) 797-3535. **$129-$169.** 2177 Northwoods Blvd 29406. I-26, exit 209 (Ashley Phosphate Rd), just e, then just n. Int corridors. **Pets:** Medium. $12 daily fee/pet, $150 one-time fee/pet. Service with restrictions, crate. A$K ⊠ 🛅 🖵

🔵🔵🔵 ▼▼▼▼ **Comfort Suites Charleston/N Charleston, SC** 🅷

(843) 725-5400. **$79-$149.** 2520 N Forest Dr 29420. I-26, exit 209 (Ashley Phosphate Rd), just w of Northside Dr. Int corridors. **Pets:** Dogs only. $10 one-time fee/pet. Service with restrictions, supervision. SAVE ⊠ ᴦᴹ 🛅 🖵 🐾

◆◆ Homestead Studio Suites

Hotel-Charleston/Airport 🅷

(843) 740-3440. **$76-$114.** 5045 N Arco Ln 29418. I-26, exit 213 westbound; exit 213A eastbound; enter through Tanger Outlet access roads. Int corridors. **Pets:** Other species. $25 daily fee/room. Designated rooms, service with restrictions, crate. 🅰🆂🅺 ⊠ 🔵 🔵 ⊠

◆◆ La Quinta Inn Charleston 🅼 ✿

(843) 797-8181. **$49-$109.** 2499 La Quinta Ln 29420. I-26, exit 209 (Ashley Phosphate Rd), just w. Ext/int corridors. **Pets:** Medium, other species. Service with restrictions, supervision. 🅰🆂🅺 ⊠ 🔵 🔵 ⊠

◆◆ Motel 6 #642 🅼

(843) 572-6590. **$39-$51.** 2551 Ashley Phosphate Rd 29418. I-26, exit 209 (Ashley Phosphate Rd), just w. Ext corridors. **Pets:** Other species. Service with restrictions, supervision. ⊠ ⊠

◆◆ Quality Inn-Charleston 🅷

(843) 572-6677. **$59-$109.** 7415 Northside Dr 29420. I-26, exit 209 (Ashley Phosphate Rd), just w. Ext corridors. **Pets:** Medium, other species. $50 deposit/room, $15 daily fee/room. Service with restrictions.

⊠ 🔵 🔵 ⊠

◉ ◆◆ Radisson Hotel Charleston Airport 🅷

(843) 744-2501. **$79-$239.** 5991 Rivers Ave 29406. I-26, exit 211B (Aviation Ave), just ne. Int corridors. **Pets:** Large, other species. $50 one-time fee/room. Service with restrictions, crate.

🆂🅰🆅🅴 ⊠ 🔵 🔵 🍽 ⊠ ⊠

◉ ◆◆ Red Roof Inn 🅼

(843) 572-9100. **$50-$95.** 7480 Northwoods Blvd 29406. I-26, exit 209 (Ashley Phosphate Rd), just e, then just n. Ext corridors. **Pets:** Large. Service with restrictions, crate. 🆂🅰🆅🅴 ⊠ 🔵

◆◆◆ Residence Inn by Marriott 🅷

(843) 572-5757. **$149-$182.** 7645 Northwoods Blvd 29406. I-26, exit 209 (Ashley Phosphate Rd), just e, then n. Ext corridors. **Pets:** Other species. $100 deposit/room. Service with restrictions, crate.

⊠ 🔵 🔵 ⊠ ⊠

◉ ◆◆◆ Residence Inn Charleston Airport 🅷 ✿

(843) 266-3434. **$179-$219.** 5035 International Blvd 29418. I-26, exit 213 westbound; exit 213A eastbound, just s; I-526, exit 16 (International Blvd), 0.7 mi e. Int corridors. **Pets:** Other species. $100 one-time fee/room. Service with restrictions, crate. 🆂🅰🆅🅴 ⊠ 🔵 🔵 🔵 ⊠ ⊠

◉ ◆◆◆ Sheraton Charleston Airport Hotel 🅷 ✿

(843) 747-1900. **Call for rates.** 4770 Goer Dr 29406. I-26, exit 213 westbound; exit 213B eastbound, just n. Int corridors. **Pets:** Medium, dogs only. $100 deposit/room, $40 one-time fee/room. Designated rooms, service with restrictions, supervision. 🆂🅰🆅🅴 ⊠ 🔵 🔵 🍽 ⊠

◉ ◆◆ Sleep Inn Charleston North 🅷

(843) 572-8400. **$59-$129.** 7435 Northside Dr 29420. I-26, exit 209 (Ashley Phosphate Rd), just w. Int corridors. **Pets:** Accepted.

🆂🅰🆅🅴 ⊠ 🔵 🔵

◆◆ StudioPlus Charleston-North Charleston 🅷

(843) 553-0036. **$67-$95.** 7641 Northwoods Blvd 29406. I-26, exit 209 (Ashley Phosphate Rd), just e, then just n. Int corridors. **Pets:** Other species. $25 daily fee/room. Designated rooms, service with restrictions, crate. 🅰🆂🅺 ⊠ 🔵 🔵 ⊠

SUMMERVILLE

◆◆◆ Country Inn & Suites By Carlson 🅷

(843) 285-9000. **$99-$109.** 220 Holiday Dr 29483. I-26, exit 199A, just w on US 17 alternate route to Holiday Dr, then just n. Int corridors. **Pets:** Medium. $10 daily fee/room. Service with restrictions, crate. 🅰🆂🅺 ⊠ 🔵 🔵 ⊠

◆◆◆ Holiday Inn

Express-Charleston/Summerville 🅷 ✿

(843) 875-3300. **$89-$99.** 120 Holiday Dr 29483. I-26, exit 199A, just w. Int corridors. **Pets:** Service with restrictions, supervision.

🅰🆂🅺 ⊠ 🔵 🔵 ⊠

◆ Summerville Econo Lodge 🅼

(843) 875-3022. **Call for rates.** 110 Holiday Dr 29483. I-26, exit 199A, just w on US 17A, then just n. Ext corridors. **Pets:** Small, other species. $10 daily fee/room. Service with restrictions, supervision. ⊠ 🔵 🔵

◉ ◆◆◆◆ Woodlands Inn 🅲 ✿

(843) 875-2600. **$295-$850, 7 day notice.** 125 Parsons Rd 29483. I-26, exit 199A, 2 mi sw on US 17 alternate route, to W Richardson Ave (SR 165), then 1.4 mi nw to Parsons Rd, then just s. Int corridors. **Pets:** $25 one-time fee/room. Service with restrictions, crate.

🆂🅰🆅🅴 ⊠ 🍽 ⊠ ⊠

END METROPOLITAN AREA

CHARLOTTE METROPOLITAN AREA (NEARBY NORTH CAROLINA)

FORT MILL

◉ ◆◆ Comfort Inn Carowinds 🅷

(803) 548-5200. **$79-$130.** 3725 Avenue of the Carolinas 29708. I-77, exit 90, just nw. Int corridors. **Pets:** Accepted. 🆂🅰🆅🅴 ⊠ 🔵 🔵 ⊠

ROCK HILL

◉ ◆◆ Baymont Inn & Suites 🅷

(803) 329-1330. **$74-$115.** 1106 N Anderson Rd 29730. I-77, exit 82B (US 21), 0.4 mi sw to US 21 Bypass, then just s. Int corridors. **Pets:** Medium. $10 daily fee/pet. Service with restrictions, supervision.

🆂🅰🆅🅴 ⊠ 🔵 🔵 ⊠

◆◆◆ The Book & the Spindle 🅱🅱 ✿

(803) 328-1913. **$90-$105, 10 day notice.** 626 Oakland Ave 29730. I-77, exit 82B (US 21), 3.1 mi s; before Aiken. Int corridors. **Pets:** Small, other species. $15 deposit/pet. Designated rooms, service with restrictions, supervision. 🅰🆂🅺 ⊠ 🔵 🔵

◆◆ Howard Johnson Inn 🅼

(803) 329-7900. **Call for rates.** 911 Riverview Rd 29730. I-77, exit 82B (US 21), just sw, then just s. Ext corridors. **Pets:** Accepted.

⊠ 🔵 🔵

▼▼▼ **Super 8** 🅷

(803) 980-0400. **$50-$70.** 888 Riverview Rd 29730. I-77, exit 82B (US 21), just sw, then just s. Int corridors. **Pets:** Medium. $10 daily fee/pet. Designated rooms, service with restrictions, supervision.

(ASK) (X) (&M) 🅱 (💻)

END METROPOLITAN AREA

CHERAW

▼▼ **Jameson Inn** 🅼

(843) 537-5625. **$83-$88.** 885 Chesterfield Hwy 29520. Jct US 1/52/SR 9, 1.6 mi w on SR 9. Ext corridors. **Pets:** Small. $15 daily fee/room. Service with restrictions, supervision. (ASK) (X) 🅱 (💻) (🔄)

CLEMSON

(AAA) ▼▼▼ **Comfort Inn-Clemson** 🅷

(864) 653-3600. **$85-$175.** 1305 Tiger Blvd 29631. Jct SR 133 (College Ave) and US 76/123, 0.5 mi e. Int corridors. **Pets:** Small, other species. $15 daily fee/pet. Designated rooms, service with restrictions.

(SAVE) (X) 🅱 (💻) (🔄)

CLINTON

(AAA) ▼▼▼ **Days Inn** 🅼

(864) 833-6600. **$54-$99.** 12374 Hwy 56 N 29325. I-26, exit 52, just s. Ext corridors. **Pets:** Medium, dogs only. $10 daily fee/room. Service with restrictions, supervision. (SAVE) (X) 🅱 (💻) (🔄)

(AAA) ▼▼▼ **Quality Inn** 🅼

(864) 833-5558. **Call for rates.** 105 Trade St 29325. I-26, exit 52, just n; behind truck stop. Ext corridors. **Pets:** $10 daily fee/room. Service with restrictions, supervision. (SAVE) (X) 🅱 (💻) (🔄)

COLUMBIA

▼▼▼▼ **Candlewood Suites Columbia-Fort Jackson** 🅷

(803) 727-1299. **$99-$108.** 921 Atlas Rd 29209. I-77, exit 9A (Garners Ferry Rd), 0.9 mi se to Atlas Rd, then just sw. Int corridors.
Pets: Accepted. (ASK) (X) (&M) 🅱 (💻) (🔄)

▼▼▼▼ **Chestnut Cottage Bed & Breakfast** (BB) 🐾

(803) 256-1718. **$159-$229, 15 day notice.** 1718 Hampton St 29201. SR 12 (Taylor St), just s; between Henderson and Barnwell sts; downtown. Int corridors. **Pets:** Other species. Supervision.

(ASK) (X) 🅱 (💻)

▼▼ **Comfort Inn Columbia** 🅷

(803) 798-5101. **$80-$200.** 911 Bush River Rd 29210. I-20, exit 108 (Bush River Rd), just e. Int corridors. **Pets:** Accepted.

(X) 🅱 (💻) (🔄)

▼▼ **Econo Lodge** 🅼

(803) 772-7275. **Call for rates.** 773 St Andrews Rd 29210. I-26, exit 106A westbound; exit 106 eastbound, just w. Ext corridors. **Pets:** Small. $10 daily fee/pet. Service with restrictions, supervision.

(X) 🅱 (💻) (🔄)

▼▼▼ **Extended StayAmerica Columbia-Fort Jackson** 🅼

(803) 782-2025. **$72-$86.** 5430 Forest Dr 29206. I-77, exit 12, just ne, then just s along service road; behind mall. Ext corridors. **Pets:** Other species. $25 daily fee/room. Designated rooms, service with restrictions, crate. (ASK) (X) 🅱 (💻) (🔄)

▼▼▼ **Extended StayAmerica-Columbia-West** 🅼

(803) 251-7878. **$57-$62.** 450 Gracern Rd 29210. I-126, exit Greystone Blvd, just n to Stoneridge Dr, just w to Gracern Rd, then s. Ext corridors. **Pets:** Other species. $25 daily fee/room. Designated rooms, service with restrictions, crate. (ASK) (X) 🅱 (💻) (🔄)

▼▼▼ **Jameson Suites** 🅷

(803) 736-6666. **$103-$113.** 7525 Two Notch Rd 29223. I-20, exit 74 (Two Notch Rd), just ne; I-77, exit 17 (Two Notch Rd), 0.5 mi sw. Int corridors. **Pets:** Large. $15 daily fee/room. Service with restrictions, supervision. (ASK) (X) 🅱 (💻) (🔄)

▼▼ **La Quinta Inn & Suites Columbia NE/Ft. Jackson Area** 🅷 🐾

(803) 736-6400. **$59-$95.** 1538 Horseshoe Dr 29223. I-20, exit 74 (Two Notch Rd), just n; I-77, exit 17 (Two Notch Rd), 0.5 mi s. Int corridors. **Pets:** Medium, other species. Service with restrictions, supervision.

(ASK) (X) 🅱 (💻) (🔄)

▼▼ **La Quinta Inn-Maingate Ft. Jackson** 🅷 🐾

(803) 783-5410. **$69-$139.** 7333 Garners Ferry Rd 29209. I-77, exit 9A (Garners Ferry Rd), just se. Int corridors. **Pets:** Medium, other species. Service with restrictions, supervision. (ASK) (X) 🅱 (💻) (🔄)

▼ **Motel 6 #1291** 🅷

(803) 736-3900. **$43-$55.** 7541 Nates Rd 29223. I-20, exit 74 (Two Notch Rd), just n, then just e; I-77, exit 17 (Two Notch Rd), 0.5 mi s, then e. Int corridors. **Pets:** Other species. Service with restrictions, supervision. (X) (&M) (🔄)

(AAA) ▼▼▼ **Quality Inn** 🅼

(803) 451-2400. **$60-$80.** 1335 Garner Ln 29210. I-20, exit 65, just s on US 176, then just ne. Ext corridors. **Pets:** Accepted. (SAVE) (X) (💻) (🔄)

(AAA) ▼▼▼ **Radisson Hotel Columbia & Conference Center** 🅷

(803) 731-0300. **$89-$199.** 2100 Bush River Rd 29210-5600. I-20, exit 63 (Bush River Rd), just e; I-26, exit 108 (Bush River Rd), 0.7 mi w. Int corridors. **Pets:** Accepted. (SAVE) (X) 🅱 (💻) (🍴) (🔄)

▼▼▼ **Residence Inn by Marriott** 🅷

(803) 788-8850. **$125-$153.** 2320 Legrand Rd 29223. I-77, exit 19 southbound, just ne on Farrow Rd to Rabon Rd, then just se; exit 18 northbound. Int corridors. **Pets:** Accepted. (X) 🅱 (💻) (🔄) (X)

▼▼▼ **Residence Inn by Marriott** 🅷

(803) 779-7000. **$152-$186.** 150 Stoneridge Dr 29210. I-126, exit Greystone Blvd, just n, then just e. Ext corridors. **Pets:** Accepted.

(X) 🅱 (💻) (🔄) (X)

(AAA) ▼▼▼▼ **Sheraton Columbia Downtown Hotel** 🅷 🐾

(803) 988-1400. **$109-$349.** 1400 Main St 29201. Jct Washington St; downtown; center. Int corridors. **Pets:** Medium, dogs only. Service with restrictions, supervision. (SAVE) (X) (💻) (🍴)

▼▼ **StudioPLUS Columbia-West** 🅷

(803) 771-0303. **$62-$91.** 180 Stoneridge Dr 29210. I-126, exit Greystone Blvd, just n, then just e. Int corridors. **Pets:** Other species. $25 daily fee/room. Designated rooms, service with restrictions, crate.

(ASK) (X) 🅱 (💻) (🔄)

▼ **Super 8** 🅼

(803) 735-0008. **Call for rates.** 5719 Fairfield Rd 29203. I-20, exit 70, just s. Ext corridors. **Pets:** Accepted. (X) 🅱 (💻)

▼▼▼▼ **TownePlace Suites by Marriott** 🅷

(803) 781-9391. **$103-$125.** 350 Columbiana Dr 29212. I-26, exit 103 (Harbison Blvd), just sw to Columbiana Dr, then 0.7 mi nw. Int corridors. **Pets:** Accepted. (X) (&M) 🅱 (💻) (🔄)

DUNCAN

▼▼ **Jameson Inn** 🅼

(864) 433-8405. **$78-$83.** 1546 E Main St 29334. I-85, exit 63, 0.4 mi se on SR 290. Ext corridors. **Pets:** Accepted. (ASK) (X) 🅱 (💻) (🔄)

EASLEY

(AAA) ▼▼▼ **Comfort Inn** M
(864) 859-7520. **Call for rates.** 5539 Calhoun Memorial Hwy 29640. Jct US 123 and SR 93, just e on US 123. Ext corridors. **Pets:** Small, dogs only. $25 daily fee/room. Designated rooms, service with restrictions, supervision. SAVE ✕ 🛢 💳 ⚮

▼▼ **Jameson Inn** M
(864) 306-9000. **$78-$85.** 211 Dayton School Rd 29642. Jct US 123 and SR 93, 0.6 mi e on US 123; jct US 123 and SR 153, 1.4 mi w. Ext corridors. **Pets:** Very small. $15 daily fee/pet. Service with restrictions, crate. ASK ✕ 🛢 💳 ⚮

FLORENCE

(AAA) ▼▼▼ **Econo Lodge** M
(843) 665-4558. **$59-$225, 60 day notice.** 1920 W Lucas St 29501. I-95, exit 164, just se. Ext/int corridors. **Pets:** Other species. $10 daily fee/pet. Designated rooms, service with restrictions, supervision. SAVE ✕ 🛢 💳 ⚮

(AAA) ▼▼▼ **Howard Johnson Express Inn & Suites** M ❖
(843) 664-9494. **$59-$95.** 3821 Bancroft Rd 29501. I-95, exit 157, just ne on US 76. Ext corridors. **Pets:** Medium, other species. $10 daily fee/pet. Service with restrictions, supervision. SAVE ✕ 🛢 💳 ⚮

▼▼ **Motel 6 #1250** M
(843) 667-6100. **$39-$49.** 1834 W Lucas St 29501. I-95, exit 164, just sw. Ext corridors. **Pets:** Other species. Service with restrictions, supervision. ✕ ⚮

(AAA) ▼▼▼ **Quality Inn & Suites** M ❖
(843) 664-2400. **$69-$130.** 150 Dunbarton Dr 29501. I-95, exit 160A, just e, then just n. Ext corridors. **Pets:** Other species. $20 one-time fee/pet. Designated rooms, service with restrictions, crate. SAVE ✕ 🛢 💳 ⚮

(AAA) ▼▼▼ **Ramada** M
(843) 665-4555. **$75-$120.** 1819 W Lucas St 29501. I-95, exit 164, just se. Ext corridors. **Pets:** Accepted. SAVE ✕ 🛢 🛢 💳 🍴 ⚮

(AAA) ▼▼▼ **Red Roof Inn** M
(843) 678-9000. **$45-$125.** 2690 David McLeod Blvd 29501. I-95, exit 160A, just e on service road. Ext corridors. **Pets:** Large. Service with restrictions, crate. SAVE ✕ 🛢 🛢

(AAA) ▼▼▼ **Super 8** M
(843) 661-7267. **$56-$180.** 1832 1/2 W Lucas St 29501. I-95, exit 164, just se. Ext corridors. **Pets:** Medium. $10 daily fee/pet. Service with restrictions, supervision. SAVE ✕ 🛢 💳 ⚮

GAFFNEY

▼▼ **Jameson Inn** M
(864) 489-0240. **$78-$85.** 101 Stuard St 29341. I-85, exit 92, 0.5 mi se on SR 11/W Floyd Baker Blvd. Ext corridors. **Pets:** Very small, other species. $15 daily fee/pet. Designated rooms, service with restrictions, supervision. ASK ✕ 🛢 💳 ⚮

(AAA) ▼▼▼ **Sleep Inn** H ❖
(864) 487-5337. **$80-$111.** 834 Windslow Ave 29341. I-85, exit 90, just se, then ne on frontage road. Int corridors. **Pets:** Large. $15 daily fee/pet. Service with restrictions, supervision. SAVE ✕ 🛢 🛢 💳 ⚮

(AAA) ▼▼▼ **Super 8** M
(864) 489-1699. **$54.** 100 Ellis Ferry Ave 29341. I-85, exit 92, 0.7 mi se on SR 11/W Floyd Baker Blvd. Int corridors. **Pets:** Medium. $10 one-time fee/room. Designated rooms, service with restrictions, supervision. SAVE ✕ 🛢 💳 ⚮

THE GRAND STRAND AREA

GEORGETOWN

▼▼ **Jameson Inn Georgetown** M
(843) 546-6090. **$78-$95.** 120 Church St 29440. Jct US 17/17 alternate route/701, 1.2 mi se on US 17; just w of ICW Bridge at Georgetown Landing. Ext corridors. **Pets:** Accepted. ASK ✕ 🛢 💳 ⚮

LITTLE RIVER

(AAA) ▼▼▼ **Holiday Inn Hotel & Suites-North Myrtle Beach** H
(843) 281-9400. **$49-$299.** 722 Hwy 17 29566. Jct SR 9/US 17, 1 mi e; at Coquina Harbor. Int corridors. **Pets:** Accepted. SAVE ✕ 🛢 💳 🍴 ⚮

MYRTLE BEACH

(AAA) ▼▼▼ **Hilton Myrtle Beach Resort and Royale Palms Condominiums** H
(843) 449-5000. **$99-$495.** 10000 Beach Club Dr 29572-5304. Jct SR 22, just n on US 17, 1.4 mi se on Kings Rd, then just e. Ext/int corridors. **Pets:** Accepted. SAVE ✕ 🛢 🛢 💳 🍴 ⚮ ✗

▼▼▼ **La Quinta Inn & Suites Myrtle Beach** H ❖
(843) 916-8801. **$49-$149.** 1561 21st Ave N 29577. Jct US 17 Bypass, just se. Int corridors. **Pets:** Medium, other species. Service with restrictions, supervision. ASK ✕ 🛢 🛢 💳 ⚮

▼▼▼ **La Quinta Inn Myrtle Beach** H ❖
(843) 449-5231. **$49-$149.** 4709 N Kings Hwy 29577. Jct 48th Ave N and US 17 business route. Int corridors. **Pets:** Medium, other species. Service with restrictions, supervision. ASK ✕ 🛢 💳 ⚮

▼▼ **Ocean Dunes Resort & Villas** CO
(843) 449-7441. **$59-$209, 4 day notice.** 201 75th Ave N 29578. Jct N Ocean Blvd, just se. Ext/int corridors. **Pets:** Accepted. ASK ✕ 🛢 💳 🍴 ⚮ ✗

(AAA) ▼▼▼ **Sea Mist Oceanfront Resort** H
(843) 448-1551. **$32-$199, 14 day notice.** 1200 S Ocean Blvd 29577. Jct 12th Ave S. Ext/int corridors. **Pets:** Accepted. SAVE ✕ 🛢 🍴 ⚮ ✗

(AAA) ▼▼▼ **Sheraton Myrtle Beach Convention Center Hotel** H ❖
(843) 918-5000. **$89-$259, 3 day notice.** 2101 N Oak St 29577. Jct 21st Ave N and US 17 business route, just nw on 21st Ave N. Int corridors. **Pets:** Dogs only. Designated rooms, service with restrictions, supervision. SAVE ✕ 🛢 🛢 💳 🍴 ⚮ ✗

▼▼▼ **Staybridge Suites At Hard Rock Park** H ❖
(843) 903-4000. **$65-$159.** 303 Hard Rock Pkwy 29579. Jct US 17 Bypass, 0.7 mi n on US 501, exit River Oaks Rd/George Bishop Pkwy, just w on River Oaks Rd, then 0.4 mi s. Int corridors. **Pets:** Medium. $20 daily fee/room. Service with restrictions. ASK ✕ 🛢 💳 ⚮ ✗

▼▼▼ **The Suites at the Market Common by ResortQuest** CO
(843) 238-1614. **$89-$220, 30 day notice.** 1232 Farrow Pkwy, Suite B 29577. Jct US 17 business route (S Kings Hwy), 1.4 mi nw; jct US 17, 1.9 mi se. Ext corridors. **Pets:** Accepted. ASK ✕ 🛢 💳 ✗

◇◇ ▽▽▽▽ **Westgate Myrtle Beach Oceanfront Resort** H

(843) 448-4481. **$49-$299, 3 day notice.** 415 S Ocean Blvd 29577. Jct 6th Ave S, just ne. Int corridors. **Pets:** Medium. $75 deposit/room, $80 one-time fee/room. Designated rooms, service with restrictions, crate.

[SAVE] ⊠ 🛢 🖵 🍴 ⇨ ⊠

PAWLEYS ISLAND

▽▽ **Signature Boutique Hotel** M

(843) 237-4261. **$49-$129.** 7903 Ocean Hwy 29585. 2.6 mi sw on US 17. Ext corridors. **Pets:** Accepted. [ASK] ⊠ 🛢 🖵 ⇨

SURFSIDE BEACH

◇◇ ▽▽▽▽ **Holiday Inn Oceanfront at Surfside Beach** H

(843) 238-5601. **$99-$199, 3 day notice.** 1601 N Ocean Blvd 29575. Jct 16th Ave N and N Ocean Blvd. Int corridors. **Pets:** Medium, other species. $100 one-time fee/room. Service with restrictions.

[SAVE] ⊠ 🛢 🖵 🍴 ⇨ ⊠

END AREA

GREENVILLE

◇◇ ▽▽▽ **Best Western Greenville Airport Inn** M

(864) 297-5353. **$53-$70.** 5009 Pelham Rd 29615. I-85, exit 54 (Pelham Rd), just se. Ext corridors. **Pets:** $10 daily fee/room. Designated rooms, service with restrictions, supervision. [SAVE] ⊠ 🛢 🖵 ⇨

◇◇ ▽▽▽▽ **Clarion Inn & Suites** M

(864) 254-6383. **$63-$100.** 50 Orchard Park Dr 29615. I-385, exit 39 (Haywood Rd), just n, just e on Orchard Park Rd, then just s. Ext corridors. **Pets:** Other species. $10 daily fee/room. Service with restrictions, supervision. [SAVE] ⊠ 🛢 🖵 ⇨

▽▽▽▽ **Drury Inn & Suites-Greenville** H

(864) 288-4401. **$90-$194.** 10 Carolina Point Pkwy 29607. I-85, exit 51A (Woodruff Rd), just se; I-385, exit 35 (Woodruff Rd), 0.6 mi nw. Int corridors. **Pets:** Other species. No service, supervision.

[ASK] ⊠ 🛢 🖵 ⇨

▽▽▽▽ **Extended StayAmerica-Greenville Airport** H

(864) 213-9698. **$68-$77.** 3715 Pelham Rd 29615. I-85, exit 54 (Pelham Rd), 0.5 mi w. Int corridors. **Pets:** Other species. $25 daily fee/room. Designated rooms, service with restrictions, crate. [ASK] ⊠ 🛢 🖵

▽▽▽▽ **Hawthorn Suites** H

(864) 297-0099. **Call for rates.** 48 McPrice Ct 29615. I-385, exit 39 (Haywood Rd), just n, just e on Orchard Park Rd, then just s. Ext corridors. **Pets:** Accepted. ⊠ 🛢 🖵 ⇨ ⊠

▽▽▽▽ **Holiday Inn Express Hotel & Suites Greenville Airport** H

(864) 213-9331. **$99-$140.** 2681 Dry Pocket Rd 29650. I-85, exit 54 (Pelham Rd), just w to The Parkway, just n to Parkway E, then just se. Int corridors. **Pets:** Medium. $25 daily fee/room. Designated rooms, service with restrictions, supervision. [ASK] ⊠ 🛢 🖵 ⇨ ⊠

▽▽▽▽ **Holiday Inn I-85 @ Augusta Rd** H ❖

(864) 277-8921. **Call for rates.** 4295 Augusta Rd 29605. I-85, exit 46A, just s. Int corridors. **Pets:** $30 one-time fee/room. Service with restrictions, crate. ⊠ 🔥 🛢 🖵 🍴 ⇨

◇◇ ▽▽▽▽ **Hyatt Regency Greenville** H

(864) 235-1234. **$79-$269.** 220 N Main St 29601. Just n; center. Int corridors. **Pets:** Accepted. [SAVE] ⊠ 🛢 🖵 🍴 ⇨

▽▽▽▽ **La Quinta Inn & Suites Greenville Haywood** H ❖

(864) 233-8018. **$59-$99.** 65 W Orchard Park Dr 29615. I-385, exit 39 (Haywood Rd), just n, then w. Int corridors. **Pets:** Medium, other species. Service with restrictions, supervision. [ASK] ⊠ 🛢 🖵 ⇨ ⊠

▽▽ **La Quinta Inn Greenville (Woodruff Rd)** M ❖

(864) 297-3500. **$49-$69.** 31 Old Country Rd 29607. I-85, exit 51A (Woodruff Rd), just nw on SR 146; I-385, exit 37, just sw on Roper Mountain Rd, then 0.9 mi se. Ext/int corridors. **Pets:** Medium, other species. Service with restrictions, supervision. [ASK] ⊠ 🛢 🖵 ⇨

▽▽▽ **MainStay Suites-Greenville** H

(864) 987-5566. **$66-$89.** 2671 Dry Pocket Rd 29650. I-85, exit 54 (Pelham Rd), just w to The Parkway, just n to Parkway E, then just se. Int corridors. **Pets:** Accepted. ⊠ 🛢 🖵 ⇨

▽▽▽ **Microtel Inn & Suites** H

(864) 297-3811. **$56-$79, 7 day notice.** 1024 Woodruff Rd 29607. I-85, exit 51A (Woodruff Rd), 0.5 mi nw; I-385, exit 37, just nw on Roper Mountain Rd, then just se. Int corridors. **Pets:** Large, other species. $35 one-time fee/room. Service with restrictions, supervision.

[ASK] ⊠ 🛢 🖵

▽▽▽▽ **The Phoenix Greenville's Inn** H

(864) 233-4651. **$89-$295, 3 day notice.** 246 N Pleasantburg Dr 29607. I-385, exit 40B, 0.6 mi s on SR 291. Ext corridors. **Pets:** Accepted. [ASK] ⊠ 🛢 🖵 🍴 ⇨

◇◇ ▽▽▽ **Red Roof Inn** M

(864) 297-4458. **$50-$100, 14 day notice.** 2801 Laurens Rd 29607. I-85, exit 48A, just se to frontage road, then just s to end. Ext corridors. **Pets:** Large. Service with restrictions, crate. [SAVE] ⊠ 🔥 M 🖵

▽▽▽▽ **Residence Inn by Marriott Greenville-Spartanburg Airport** H ❖

(864) 627-0001. **$116-$142.** 120 Milestone Way 29615. I-85, exit 54 (Pelham Rd), 0.6 mi w to Milestone Way, then just n. Int corridors. **Pets:** Other species. $25 daily fee/room, $100 one-time fee/room. Service with restrictions. ⊠ 🔥 M 🛢 🖵 ⇨

◇◇ ▽▽▽ **Sleep Inn Carolina First Center** H ❖

(864) 240-2006. **$50-$100.** 231 N Pleasantburg Dr 29607. I-385, exit 40B, 0.6 mi s on SR 291. Int corridors. **Pets:** Medium. $20 one-time fee/pet. No service, crate. [SAVE] ⊠ 🔥 M 🛢 🖵

▽▽▽▽ **Staybridge Suites Greenville/Spartanburg** H

(864) 288-4448. **$90-$160.** 31 Market Point Dr 29607. I-85, exit 51A (Woodruff Rd), 0.5 mi se to Miller Rd, 0.5 mi s to S Oak Forest Dr, then just nw; I-385, exit 35 (Woodruff Rd), nw to Miller Rd, 0.5 mi s to S Oak Forest Dr, then just nw. Int corridors. **Pets:** Accepted.

[ASK] ⊠ 🛢 🖵 ⇨

▽▽ **StudioPLUS-Greenville-Haywood Mall** H

(864) 288-4300. **$72-$95.** 530 Woods Lake Rd 29607. I-385, exit 39 (Haywood Rd), just s, then just w. Int corridors. **Pets:** Other species. $25 daily fee/room. Designated rooms, service with restrictions, crate.

[ASK] ⊠ 🛢 🖵 ⇨

▽▽▽▽ **TownePlace Suites Greenville By Marriott Greenville Haywood Mall** H

(864) 675-1670. **$116-$142.** 75 Mall Connector Rd 29607. I-385, exit 39 (Haywood Rd), just s to Woods Crossing Rd, just se to Mall Connector Rd, then just s. Int corridors. **Pets:** Accepted. ⊠ 🔥 M 🛢 🖵 ⇨

◇◇ ▽▽▽▽ **The Westin Poinsett** H

(864) 421-9700. **Call for rates.** 120 S Main St 29601. From center; just s. Int corridors. **Pets:** Accepted. [SAVE] ⊠ 🛢 🖵 🍴

GREENWOOD

▼▼▼ Econo Lodge M

(864) 229-5329. **$53-$65.** 719 Bypass 25 NE 29646. Jct US 25 Bypass NE/US 221, just se. Ext corridors. **Pets:** Medium. $10 daily fee/pet. Service with restrictions, supervision. ⊠ 🗋 🖵 🏊

AAA ▼▼▼▼ Inn on the Square, a Clarion Collection H

(864) 330-1010. **$70-$160.** 104 E Court Ave 29646. Jct Main St, just s of center; downtown. Int corridors. **Pets:** Accepted.
SAVE ⊠ 🗋 🖵 🍴 🏊

HARDEEVILLE

▼▼▼ Holiday Inn Express & Suites H ❖

(843) 784-2800. **$79-$159.** 145 Independence Blvd 29927. I-95, exit 8, just w. Int corridors. **Pets:** Medium. Designated rooms, service with restrictions. ASK ⊠ 🅜 🗋 🖵 🏊

AAA ▼▼▼ Sleep Inn Hardeeville H

(843) 784-7181. **$50-$130.** 16553 Whyte Hardee Blvd 29927. I-95, exit 5 (US 17), just se. Int corridors. **Pets:** Small. $10 one-time fee/pet. Service with restrictions, supervision. SAVE ⊠ 🅜 🗋 🖵 🏊

HILTON HEAD ISLAND

AAA ▼▼▼▼ Beachwalk Hotel & Condominiums H

(843) 842-8888. **Call for rates.** 40 Waterside Dr 29928. Sea Pines Cir, 0.7 mi se on Pope Rd, just e. Ext corridors. **Pets:** Accepted.
SAVE ⊠ 🗋 🖵 🏊

AAA ▼▼▼ Comfort Inn H

(843) 842-6662. **$59-$219.** 2 Tanglewood Dr 29928. Sea Pines Cir, 1.1 mi se on Pope Ave, just sw on Coligny Plaza. Int corridors.
Pets: Accepted. SAVE ⊠ 🗋 🖵 🏊

▼▼▼ ▼▼ Hilton Oceanfront Resort Hilton Head Island H

(843) 842-8000. **$149-$349.** 23 Ocean Ln 29928. Jct US 278 business route/Queens Folly Rd, 0.9 mi se to Ocean Ln, then just sw; in Palmetto Dunes Plantation. Ext/int corridors. **Pets:** Accepted.
⊠ 🅜 🗋 🖵 🍴 🏊 ⊠

AAA ▼▼▼▼ Park Lane Hotel & Suites H

(843) 686-5700. **Call for rates.** 12 Park Ln 29928. 10 mi of J Wilton Graves Bridge on US 278 business route. Int corridors. **Pets:** Accepted.
SAVE ⊠ 🗋 🖵 🏊 ⊠

▼▼▼ Quality Inn & Suites of Hilton Head Island M

(843) 681-3655. **Call for rates.** 200 Museum St 29926. 3.3 mi e of J Wilton Graves Bridge on US 278 business route. Ext corridors.
Pets: Accepted. ⊠ 🗋 🖵 🏊

AAA ▼▼▼ Red Roof Inn-Hilton Head M

(843) 686-6808. **Call for rates.** 5 Regency Pkwy 29928. 9 mi e of J Wilton Grave Bridge on US 278 business route; between Shipyard Plantation and Palmetto Dunes. Ext corridors. **Pets:** Large. Service with restrictions, crate. SAVE ⊠ 🗋 🏊

AAA ▼▼▼▼ Westin Hilton Head Island Resort & Spa H ❖

(843) 681-4000. **$89-$599, 5 day notice.** Two Grasslawn Ave 29928. 5.6 mi from J Wilton Graves Bridge on US 278 business route to Coggins Point Rd, then just e, follow signs. Int corridors. **Pets:** Small, dogs only. $150 one-time fee/room. Designated rooms, service with restrictions, supervision. SAVE ⊠ 🖵 🍴 🏊 ⊠

IRMO

▼▼▼▼ Extended Stay Deluxe (Columbia-Harbison) H

(803) 781-8590. **$81-$119.** 1170 Kinley Rd 29063. I-26, exit 102B, just e, then n. Int corridors. **Pets:** Other species. $25 daily fee/room. Designated rooms, service with restrictions, crate. ASK ⊠ 🅜 🗋 🖵 🏊

LANCASTER

▼▼ ▼▼ Jameson Inn M

(803) 283-1188. **$73-$78.** 114 Commerce Blvd 29720. Jct SR 9 Bypass and US 521, 1.3 mi w on SR 9 Bypass. Ext corridors. **Pets:** Accepted.
ASK ⊠ 🅜 🗋 🖵 🏊

LANDRUM

▼▼▼▼ The Red Horse Inn Cottages CA ❖

(864) 895-4968. **$210-$400, 30 day notice.** 45 Winstons Chase Ct 29356. Jct SR 14/414, 1.5 mi w on SR 414 to Campbell Rd, then 0.7 mi n. Ext corridors. **Pets:** Medium, other species. $25 one-time fee/pet. Designated rooms, no service. ASK ⊠ 🗋 🖵 ⊠

LUGOFF

▼▼ ▼▼ Ramada Limited M

(803) 438-1807. **$65.** 542 Hwy 601 S 29078. I-20, exit 92 (US 601), just n. Ext corridors. **Pets:** $25 daily fee/pet. Service with restrictions, supervision. ASK ⊠ 🗋 🖵 🏊

MANNING

AAA ▼▼▼ Best Western Palmetto Inn M

(803) 473-4021. **$63-$90.** 2825 Paxville Hwy 29102. I-95, exit 119 (SR 261), just se. Ext corridors. **Pets:** Accepted. SAVE ⊠ 🗋 🖵 🏊

AAA ▼▼▼ Ramada Inn M

(803) 473-5135. **$43-$89.** 2816 Paxville Hwy 29102. I-95, exit 119 (SR 261), just se. Ext corridors. **Pets:** Accepted. SAVE ⊠ 🗋 🖵 🏊

MAULDIN

AAA ▼▼▼ Super 8 H

(864) 751-0003. **$60-$70.** 310 W Butler Rd 29662. I-85, exit 46C, 3.8 mi s on Old Mauldin Rd (which becomes W Butler Rd). Int corridors.
Pets: Small, other species. $10 one-time fee/room. Designated rooms, service with restrictions, crate. SAVE ⊠ 🅜 🗋 🖵 🏊

NEWBERRY

AAA ▼▼▼ Americas Best Value Inn M

(803) 276-5850. **$65-$75.** 11701 Hwy 34 29108. I-26, exit 74 (SR 34), just ne. Ext corridors. **Pets:** Small. $10 daily fee/pet. Service with restrictions, supervision. SAVE ⊠ 🗋 🖵 🏊

ORANGEBURG

▼▼▼▼ Country Inn & Suites By Carlson H

(803) 928-5300. **$105-$190.** 731 Citadel Rd 29118. I-26, exit 145A (US 601), just s. Int corridors. **Pets:** $10 daily fee/room. Service with restrictions, supervision. ASK ⊠ 🅜 🗋 🖵 🏊

▼▼▼ Jameson Inn Orangeburg M

(803) 534-1611. **$78-$85.** 2350 Chestnut St NE 29115. I-26, exit 145A (US 601), 3.9 mi sw to jct US 601 and 21/178 Bypass, then 2 mi nw. Ext corridors. **Pets:** Accepted. ASK ⊠ 🗋 🖵 🏊

▼▼▼ Traveler's Inn M

(803) 531-2590. **$55-$150.** 3691 St Matthews Rd 29118. I-26, exit 145A (US 601), just sw. Ext corridors. **Pets:** Accepted.
ASK ⊠ 🗋 🖵 🏊

RICHBURG

AAA ▼▼▼ Super 8 M

(803) 789-7888. **$59-$89, 7 day notice.** 3085 Lancaster Hwy 29729. I-77, exit 65, just w on SR 9. Ext corridors. **Pets:** Other species. $10 one-time fee/pet. Service with restrictions, supervision.
SAVE ⊠ 🗋 🖵 🏊

RIDGELAND

AAA ▼▼▼ Comfort Inn H ❖

(843) 726-2121. **Call for rates.** Hwy 336 & I-95 29936. I-95, exit 21 (US 336), just nw. Ext/int corridors. **Pets:** Dogs only. $10 one-time fee/room. Service with restrictions, crate. SAVE ⊠ 🗋 🖵 🏊

ST. GEORGE

Comfort Inn M
(843) 563-4180. **$60-$90.** 139 Motel Dr 29477. I-95, exit 77 (US 78), just e. Ext corridors. **Pets:** Medium. $10 daily fee/pet. Designated rooms, service with restrictions, supervision.

Econo Lodge M
(843) 563-4195. **Call for rates.** 5971 W Jim Bilton Blvd 29477. I-95, exit 77 (US 78), just e. Ext corridors. **Pets:** Small. $5 daily fee/pet. Designated rooms, service with restrictions, supervision.

Quality Inn- St George M
(843) 563-4581. **Call for rates.** 6014 W Jim Bilton Blvd 29477. I-95, exit 77 (US 78), just e. Ext corridors. **Pets:** Other species. $10 daily fee/room. Service with restrictions, crate.

SANTEE

Holiday Inn Santee H
(803) 854-9800. **$115-$250.** 139 Bradford Blvd 29142. I-95, exit 98 (SR 6), just nw. Ext corridors. **Pets:** Small, other species. $20 daily fee/pet. Designated rooms, service with restrictions, supervision.

Howard Johnson Express Inn M
(803) 854-3870. **$58-$63.** 9112 Old Hwy 6 29142. I-95, exit 98 (SR 6), 0.4 mi se. Ext corridors. **Pets:** Large, other species. $10 daily fee/pet. Designated rooms, service with restrictions, crate.

Quality Inn & Suites Santee M
(803) 854-2121. **$77-$85.** 8929 Old Number 6 Hwy 29142. I-95, exit 98 (SR 6), just nw. Ext corridors. **Pets:** Medium, other species. $10 one-time fee/pet. Designated rooms, service with restrictions, supervision.

Super 8 M
(803) 854-3456. **$65-$75.** 9125 Old Hwy 6 29142. I-95, exit 98 (SR 6), 0.4 mi se. Ext corridors. **Pets:** $10 daily fee/pet. No service, supervision.

SENECA

Jameson Inn M
(864) 888-8300. **$83-$90.** 226 Hi-Tech Rd 29678. Jct SR 28 and US 76/123, 0.9 mi w on US 76/123, just se. Ext corridors. **Pets:** Medium. $15 daily fee/pet. No service, crate.

SIMPSONVILLE

Days Inn M
(864) 963-7701. **$60-$70.** 45 Ray E Talley Ct 29680. I-385, exit 27, just s, then just e. Ext corridors. **Pets:** Small. $15 daily fee/pet. No service, supervision.

Motel 6 #4266 H
(864) 962-8484. **$40-$90.** 3706 Grandview Dr 29680. I-385, exit 27, just s, then just w. Int corridors. **Pets:** Other species. Service with restrictions, supervision.

Quality Inn M
(864) 963-2777. **Call for rates.** 3755 Grandview Dr 29680. I-385, exit 27, just s. Ext corridors. **Pets:** Accepted.

SPARTANBURG

Extended StayAmerica-Spartanburg-Asheville Hwy M
(864) 573-5949. **$57-$72.** 130 Mobile Dr 29303. I-85 business route, exit 4/4B, just se, then just ne on service road. Ext corridors. **Pets:** Other species. $25 daily fee/room. Designated rooms, service with restrictions, crate.

Holiday Inn Express Hotel & Suites H
(864) 699-7777. **$109.** 895 Spartan Blvd 29301. I-26, exit 21B (US 29), just e to Blackstock Rd, then 0.7 mi n. Int corridors. **Pets:** Accepted.

SUMMERTON

Days Inn of Summerton M
(803) 485-2865. **$39-$72.** 400 Bluff Blvd 29148. I-95, exit 108, just n. Ext restrictions, supervision.

SUMTER

Econo Lodge M
(803) 775-2323. **Call for rates.** 226 N Washington St 29150. US 76 business route/521, just n. Int corridors. **Pets:** Accepted.

Travelers Inn & Suites M
(803) 469-9210. **$59-$89.** 1210 Camden Rd 29151. Jct US 521/US 76. Ext corridors. **Pets:** Medium. $9 daily fee/pet. Designated rooms, service with restrictions, supervision.

TRAVELERS REST

Sleep Inn H
(864) 834-7040. **Call for rates.** 110 Hawkins Rd 29690. Jct US 25, just e. Int corridors. **Pets:** $15 daily fee/room. Service with restrictions, supervision.

WALTERBORO

Best Western of Walterboro M
(843) 538-3600. **$69-$129.** 1428 Sniders Hwy 29488. I-95, exit 53 (SR 63), just e. Ext corridors. **Pets:** Small. $15 daily fee/pet. Designated rooms, service with restrictions, supervision.

Days Inn M
(843) 538-2933. **Call for rates.** 1787 Sniders Hwy 29488. I-95, exit 53 (SR 63), just w. Ext corridors. **Pets:** Accepted.

Econo Inn M
(843) 538-3830. **$46-$90.** 1145 Sniders Hwy 29488. I-95, exit 53 (SR 63), just e. Ext corridors. **Pets:** $10 one-time fee/pet. No service.

Microtel Inn and Suites H
(843) 539-5656. **$59-$69, 10 day notice.** 130 Cane Branch Rd 29488. I-95, exit 53 (SR 63), just w, then just s. Int corridors. **Pets:** Other species. $15 one-time fee/room. Service with restrictions, crate.

Quality Inn & Suites M
(843) 538-5473. **Call for rates.** 1286 Sniders Hwy 29488. I-95, exit 53 (SR 63), just e. Ext corridors. **Pets:** Accepted.

Ramada Inn of Walterboro M
(843) 538-5403. **$65.** 1245 Sniders Hwy 29488. I-95, exit 53 (SR 63), just e. Ext corridors. **Pets:** Very small. $10 daily fee/pet. Service with restrictions, supervision.

Rice Planters Inn M
(843) 538-8964. **$44.** 97 Ladson Ln 29488. I-95, exit 53 (SR 63), just e. Ext corridors. **Pets:** Small, other species. $5 daily fee/pet. Service with restrictions, supervision.

Sleep Inn of Walterboro H
(843) 539-1199. **Call for rates.** 3043 Hiers Corner Rd 29488. I-95, exit 57 (SR 64), just se. Int corridors. **Pets:** Accepted.

Super 8 M
(843) 538-5383. **$50-$65, 7 day notice.** 1972 Bells Hwy 29488. I-95, exit 57 (SR 64), just nw. Ext corridors. **Pets:** Accepted.

WINNSBORO

◆◆ Days Inn M
(803) 635-1447. **$57.** 1894 US Hwy 321 Bypass 29180. I-77, exit 34 (SR 34), 6.5 mi w; jct US 321/SR 34/213. Ext corridors. **Pets:** Small. $15 daily fee/pet. Designated rooms, service with restrictions, supervision.
ASK ✕ 🍴 💻 ⇋

◆◆◆ Fairfield Motel M
(803) 635-3458. **$50-$65.** 56 US 321 Bypass S 29180. Jct SR 213/US 321 Bypass S, 1.8 mi n. Ext corridors. **Pets:** Small. $10 daily fee/pet. Service with restrictions, supervision. SAVE ✕ 🍴 ⇋

YEMASSEE

◆◆◆ ◆◆ Best Western Point South M
(843) 726-8101. **$60-$85.** 3536 Point South Dr 29945. I-95, exit 33 (US17), just ne. Ext corridors. **Pets:** Accepted. SAVE ✕ 🍴 💻 ⇋

◆◆◆ Holiday Inn Express Point South/Yemassee H
(843) 726-9400. **$79-$99.** 138 Frampton Dr 29945. I-95, exit 33 (US 17), just ne. Int corridors. **Pets:** Small. $25 one-time fee/pet. Service with restrictions, supervision. ASK ✕ 🚹 🍴 💻 ⇋

SOUTH DAKOTA

ABERDEEN

▼▼ Aberdeen East Super 8 🅗
(605) 229-5005. **$65-$125.** 2405 6th Ave SE 57401. 1.8 mi e on US 12. Int corridors. **Pets:** Accepted. (ASK) ✕ (&M) 🔋 📺 🏊 ✕

▼▼ Aberdeen North Super 8 🅜
(605) 226-2288. **$59-$99.** 1023 8th Ave NW 57401. On US 281, 1.5 mi nw. Int corridors. **Pets:** Accepted. (ASK) ✕ (&M) 🔋 📺

▼▼ Aberdeen West Super 8 🅜
(605) 225-1711. **$59-$99.** 714 S Hwy 281 57401. Jct US 12 and 281. Int corridors. **Pets:** Accepted. (ASK) ✕ 🔋 📺

⨌ ▼▼▼ AmericInn Lodge & Suites of Aberdeen 🅗 🐾
(605) 225-4565. **$100-$250.** 310 Centennial St 57401. 2.2 mi e on US 12, just n. Int corridors. **Pets:** Medium, dogs only. $25 one-time fee/room. Service with restrictions, supervision.
(SAVE) ✕ (&M) 🔋 📺 🏊 ✕

⨌ ▼▼▼ Best Western Ramkota Hotel 🅗
(605) 229-4040. **$95-$125, 30 day notice.** 1400 8th Ave NW 57401. 1.5 mi nw on US 281. Ext/int corridors. **Pets:** Accepted.
(SAVE) ✕ (&M) 🔋 📺 ¶¶ 🏊 ✕

▼▼ Comfort Inn 🅗
(605) 226-0097. **$80-$140.** 2923 6th Ave SE 57401. 2 mi e on US 12. Int corridors. **Pets:** Accepted. (ASK) ✕ (&M) 🔋 📺 🏊 ✕

⨌ ▼▼▼▼ Holiday Inn Express Hotel & Suites 🅗 🐾
(605) 725-4000. **$110-$144.** 3310 7th Ave SE 57401. 2.1 mi e on US 12. Int corridors. **Pets:** Dogs only. $20 one-time fee/room. Designated rooms, service with restrictions, supervision.
(SAVE) ✕ (&M) 🔋 📺 ¶¶ 🏊 ✕

ARLINGTON

▼ Arlington Inn 🅜
(605) 983-4609. **$59-$98.** 402 S Hwy 81 57212. 1 mi s on US 81. Int corridors. **Pets:** Accepted. (ASK) ✕ (&M) 🔋

BLACK HILLS AREA

BELLE FOURCHE

▼ Ace Motel 🅜
(605) 892-2612. **$38-$78.** 109 6th Ave 57717. 0.5 mi n via US 85, just e; just s of US 212 Bypass. Ext corridors. **Pets:** Medium, dogs only. $8 one-time fee/pet. Designated rooms, service with restrictions, supervision.
✕ 🔋

CUSTER

⨌ ▼▼ Bavarian Inn Motel 🅗
(605) 673-2802. **$59-$119, 3 day notice.** 907 N 5th St 57730. 1 mi n on US 16 and 385. Ext/int corridors. **Pets:** Accepted.
(SAVE) ✕ (&M) 🔋 📺 ¶¶ 🏊 ✕

▼▼▼ Creekside Lodge 🅗
(605) 255-4541. **Call for rates.** 13389 US Hwy 16A 57730. On Alternate Rt US 16, 14 mi e. Int corridors. **Pets:** Accepted.
✕ (&M) 🔋 📺 ✕

⨌ ▼ Rock Crest Lodge and Cabins 🅒🅐
(605) 673-4323. **Call for rates.** 15 W Mt. Rushmore Rd 57730. US 16, 0.5 mi w. Ext/int corridors. **Pets:** Accepted.
(SAVE) ✕ 🔋 📺 🏊 ✕

⨌ ▼ Rocket Motel 🅜 🐾
(605) 673-4401. **$59-$99.** 211 Mt. Rushmore Rd 57730. On US 16; center. Ext corridors. **Pets:** Other species. $10 daily fee/pet. Designated rooms, service with restrictions, crate. (SAVE) ✕ 🔋 📺

▼▼ State Game Lodge 🅜
(605) 255-4541. **Call for rates.** 13389 US 16A 57730. On Alternate Rt US 16, 14 mi e. Ext/int corridors. **Pets:** Other species. $10 daily fee/pet. Designated rooms, service with restrictions, supervision.
✕ (&M) 📺 ¶¶ ✕

⨌ ▼▼ Super 8 Custer 🅗
(605) 673-2200. **$59-$199.** 535 W Mt. Rushmore Rd 57730. US 16, 0.8 mi w. Int corridors. **Pets:** Accepted. (SAVE) ✕ (&M) 🔋 📺 🏊

DEADWOOD

⨌ ▼▼▼ AmericInn Hotel & Suites of Deadwood 🅗
(605) 578-1500. **$49-$199.** 360 Main St 57732. 0.6 mi n on US 85. Int corridors. **Pets:** Large, dogs only. $25 daily fee/pet. Service with restrictions, supervision. (SAVE) ✕ (&M) 🔋 📺 ¶¶ 🏊 ✕

▼ Black Hills Inn & Suites 🅜
(605) 578-7791. **$43-$85, 3 day notice.** 206 Mountain Shadow Ln 57732. 0.3 mi s of jct US 385 and 85. Ext/int corridors. **Pets:** Accepted.
(ASK) ✕ 🔋 📺 🏊

⨌ ▼▼▼ Deadwood Gulch Gaming Resort 🅗
(605) 578-1294. **$77-$159.** 304 Cliff St 57732. 0.7 mi s on US 85 S. Ext/int corridors. **Pets:** Dogs only. $500 deposit/room, $20 one-time fee/pet. Designated rooms, service with restrictions.
(SAVE) ✕ (&M) 🔋 📺 ¶¶ ✕

⨌ ▼▼ First Gold Hotel & Gaming 🅗
(605) 578-9777. **$79-$299, 7 day notice.** 270 Main St 57732. 0.7 mi n on US 85. Int corridors. **Pets:** Medium. $25 one-time fee/room. Designated rooms, service with restrictions, supervision.
(SAVE) ✕ (&M) 📺 ¶¶

HILL CITY

Best Western Golden Spike Inn & Suites H
(605) 574-2577. **$85-$165.** 601 E Main St 57745. Just n on US 16 and 385. Ext/int corridors. **Pets:** Other species. $10 daily fee/pet. Designated rooms, service with restrictions, supervision.

Lantern Inn M
(605) 574-2582. **$64-$150, 3 day notice.** 580 E Main St 57745. on US 16 and 385; north side of town. Ext corridors. **Pets:** Very small. $10 daily fee/pet. Designated rooms, supervision.

The Lodge at Palmer Gulch H ❀
(605) 574-2525. **$50-$695, 10 day notice.** 12620 SR 244 57745. On SR 244, 5 mi w of Mt. Rushmore. Int corridors. **Pets:** Large, dogs only. $20 daily fee/pet. No service, supervision.

HOT SPRINGS

Americas Best Value Inn By The River M
(605) 745-4292. **$40-$90.** 602 W River St 57747. On US 385; downtown. Ext corridors. **Pets:** Accepted.

Best Western Sundowner Inn H
(605) 745-7378. **$60-$130.** 737 S 6th St 57747. 0.5 mi se off US 18 and 385. Int corridors. **Pets:** Other species. Service with restrictions, supervision.

Budget Host Hills Inn M
(605) 745-3130. **$49-$154.** 640 S 6th St 57747. 0.5 mi se off US 18 and 385. Ext corridors. **Pets:** Medium. Designated rooms, service with restrictions, supervision.

Holiday Inn Express Hotel & Suites H
(605) 745-4411. **Call for rates.** 1401 Hwy 18 57747. Jct US 18 and 385, 0.7 mi w on US 18 Bypass. Int corridors. **Pets:** Accepted.

Hot Springs Super 8 H
(605) 745-3888. **Call for rates.** 800 Mammoth St 57747. Jct US 18 and 385, 1 mi w on US 18 Bypass. Int corridors. **Pets:** Accepted.

KEYSTONE

Best Western Four Presidents Lodge H
(605) 666-4472. **$80-$280.** 24075 Hwy 16A 57751. On US 16A, 1 mi n. Int corridors. **Pets:** Accepted.

Econo Lodge of Mt. Rushmore H
(605) 666-4417. **$49-$179.** 908 Madill St 57751. SR 40, 1 mi e of jct US 16A. Int corridors. **Pets:** Accepted.

Holiday Inn Express Hotel & Suites-Mt. Rushmore H
(605) 666-4925. **$49-$269.** 321 Swanzey St 57751. Just e of jct US 16A and SR 40. Int corridors. **Pets:** Accepted.

Holy Smoke Resort CA ❀
(605) 666-4616. **$50-$145, 3 day notice.** 24105 Hwy 16A 57751. On US 16A, 1 mi n. Ext corridors. **Pets:** Dogs only. $10 daily fee/pet. Designated rooms, service with restrictions, crate.

Mt. Rushmore's Washington Inn H
(605) 666-5070. **$49-$99, 3 day notice.** 231 Winter St 57751. On US 16A; downtown. Ext/int corridors. **Pets:** Medium, other species. Designated rooms, service with restrictions, supervision.

Mt. Rushmore's White House Resort H
(605) 666-4917. **$49-$99, 3 day notice.** 115 Swanzey St 57751. Jct US 16A and SR 40. Ext/int corridors. **Pets:** Medium, other species. Designated rooms, service with restrictions, supervision.

Powder House Lodge CA
(605) 666-4646. **$70-$250, 3 day notice.** 24125 Hwy 16A 57751. On US 16A, 1.5 mi n. Ext corridors. **Pets:** Accepted.

RAPID CITY

Americas Best Value Inn H
(605) 343-5434. **$59-$259.** 620 Howard St 57701. I-90, exit 58, just nw of Haines Ave. Int corridors. **Pets:** Other species. $10 daily fee/pet. Service with restrictions, supervision.

AmericInn Lodge & Suites of Rapid City H
(605) 343-8424. **$59-$299.** 1632 Rapp St 57701. I-90, exit 59 (LaCrosse St), just se. Int corridors. **Pets:** Accepted.

Best Western Ramkota Hotel H ❀
(605) 343-8550. **Call for rates.** 2111 N LaCrosse St 57701. I-90, exit 59 (LaCrosse St), just n. Ext/int corridors. **Pets:** Large, other species. Designated rooms, service with restrictions, crate.

Best Western Town & Country Inn H ❀
(605) 343-5383. **$70-$240.** 2505 Mt. Rushmore Rd 57701. 1.3 mi s on US 16. Ext corridors. **Pets:** Dogs only. $250 deposit/room, $20 daily fee/pet. Designated rooms, service with restrictions, crate.

Big Sky Lodge M
(605) 348-3200. **$59-$129.** 4080 Tower Rd 57701. 3 mi s on US 16, 0.3 mi n on Skyline Dr, take service road off US 16. Ext corridors. **Pets:** Accepted.

Comfort Suites H
(605) 791-2345. **Call for rates.** 1333 N Elk Vale Rd 57703. I-90, exit 61, just s. Int corridors. **Pets:** Medium, dogs only. $10 daily fee/pet. Service with restrictions, supervision.

Country Inn & Suites By Carlson H
(605) 394-0017. **$59-$299.** 2321 N LaCrosse St 57701. I-90, exit 59 (LaCrosse St), 0.3 mi n. Int corridors. **Pets:** Accepted.

Days Inn I-90 H
(605) 348-8410. **$59-$299.** 1570 N LaCrosse St 57701. I-90, exit 59 (LaCrosse St), just s. Int corridors. **Pets:** Medium, dogs only. $10 daily fee/pet. Service with restrictions, supervision.

Fair Value Inn M
(605) 342-8118. **$45-$100.** 1607 LaCrosse St 57701. I-90, exit 59 (LaCrosse St), 0.3 mi s. Ext corridors. **Pets:** Dogs only. Designated rooms, service with restrictions, supervision.

Gold Star Motel M
(605) 341-7051. **$45-$78.** 801 E North St 57701. I-90, exit 60, 1.5 mi sw on I-90 business loop, 1.2 mi s, then just e, from exit 59 (LaCrosse St). Ext corridors. **Pets:** Medium. $5 daily fee/pet. Service with restrictions, supervision.

GrandStay Residential Suites Hotel H
(605) 341-5100. **$79-$299.** 660 Disk Dr 57701. I-90, exit 58C (Haines Ave), just n, then w. Int corridors. **Pets:** $10 daily fee/pet. Designated rooms, service with restrictions, supervision.

▼▼▼ **Holiday Inn Express Hotel & Suites, I-90** **H**

(605) 355-9090. **$99-$289.** 645 E Disk Dr 57701. I-90, exit 59 (LaCrosse St), just ne. Int corridors. **Pets:** Medium. $10 daily fee/pet. Designated rooms, service with restrictions, supervision.

[ASK] [X] [&M] [H] [■] [≈]

▼▼▼ **Holiday Inn-Rushmore Plaza** **H**

(605) 348-4000. **$79-$199.** 505 N 5th St 57701. I-90, exit 58, 1.3 mi s on Haines. Int corridors. **Pets:** Accepted.

[ASK] [X] [&M] [H] [■] [¶] [≈] [X]

AAA ▼▼▼ **La Quinta Inn & Suites** **H** ❀

(605) 718-7000. **$49-$149.** 1416 N Elk Vale Rd 57703. I-90, exit 61 (Elk Vale Rd), just s, then just e. Int corridors. **Pets:** Medium, other species. Service with restrictions, supervision.

[SAVE] [X] [H] [■] [¶] [≈] [X]

AAA ▼ **Lazy U Motel** **M**

(605) 343-4242. **$42-$72.** 2215 Mt. Rushmore Rd 57701. 1 mi s on US 16. Ext corridors. **Pets:** Medium, dogs only. $5 daily fee/pet. Service with restrictions, crate. [SAVE] [X] [H]

AAA ▼▼▼ **Microtel Inn & Suites** **H**

(605) 348-2523. **$57-$369.** 1740 Rapp St 57701. I-90, exit 59 (LaCrosse St), just se. Int corridors. **Pets:** $25 one-time fee/room. Designated rooms, service with restrictions. [SAVE] [X] [&M] [H] [■] [≈]

AAA ▼▼▼ **Quality Inn** **H** ❀

(605) 342-3322. **Call for rates.** 1902 N LaCrosse St 57701. I-90, exit 59 (LaCrosse St), just s. Ext/int corridors. **Pets:** Other species. $10 daily fee/pet. Service with restrictions, supervision.

[SAVE] [X] [&M] [H] [■] [¶] [≈] [X]

▼▼▼ **Sleep Inn & Suites** **H**

(605) 791-5678. **Call for rates.** 4031 Cheyenne Blvd 57703. I-90, exit 61, just s. Int corridors. **Pets:** Accepted. [X] [&M] [H] [■] [≈]

AAA ▼▼▼ **Super 8 LaCrosse St** **H**

(605) 348-8070. **$44-$195.** 2124 LaCrosse St 57701. I-90, exit 59 (LaCrosse St), just n. Int corridors. **Pets:** Medium, other species. $10 daily fee/pet. Service with restrictions, crate. [SAVE] [X] [&M] [H] [■]

AAA ▼▼▼ **Super 8 Mt. Rushmore Rd** **H**

(605) 342-4911. **$35-$250.** 2520 Tower Rd 57701. 1.4 mi s on US 16, then just e. Int corridors. **Pets:** Accepted. [SAVE] [X] [H] [■]

SPEARFISH

▼▼▼ **Bell's Motor Lodge Motel** **M**

(605) 642-3812. **$38-$190.** 230 N Main St 57783. 0.5 mi s of center. Ext corridors. **Pets:** Small, dogs only. Supervision. [ASK] [X] [H] [■] [≈]

AAA ▼▼▼ **Best Western Black Hills Lodge** **H** ❀

(605) 642-7795. **$59-$129.** 540 E Jackson Blvd 57783. I-90, exit 12, just s. Ext/int corridors. **Pets:** Dogs only. $20 daily fee/pet. Designated rooms, service with restrictions, supervision. [SAVE] [X] [&M] [H] [■] [≈]

▼▼ **Days Inn** **H** 🐾

(605) 642-7101. **$65-$300.** 240 Ryan Rd 57783. I-90, exit 10, 1.2 mi s. Ext/int corridors. **Pets:** Other species. $10 daily fee/room. Designated rooms, service with restrictions, supervision. [ASK] [X] [&M] [H] [■]

AAA ▼▼▼ **Holiday Inn Hotel & Convention Center** **H** ❀

(605) 642-4683. **$79-$159.** 305 N 27th St 57783. I-90, exit 14 (Spearfish Canyon), just n. Ext/int corridors. **Pets:** $100 deposit/room, $25 one-time fee/pet. Designated rooms, service with restrictions, supervision.

[SAVE] [X] [&M] [H] [■] [¶] [≈] [X]

▼▼ **Howard Johnson Express Inn** **H**

(605) 642-8105. **$55-$120.** 323 S 27th St 57783. I-90, exit 14 (Spearfish Canyon), just s. Int corridors. **Pets:** Other species. $10 daily fee/pet. Service with restrictions, supervision.

[ASK] [X] [&M] [H] [■] [¶] [≈]

AAA ▼▼▼ **Spearfish Canyon Lodge** **H** ❀

(605) 584-3435. **$89-$172, 5 day notice.** 10619 Roughlock Falls Rd 57754. I-90, exit 14 (Spearfish Canyon), 13 mi s. Int corridors. **Pets:** $25 daily fee/pet. Service with restrictions, supervision.

[SAVE] [X] [&M] [H] [■] [¶] [X]

▼▼ **Spearfish Super 8** **H**

(605) 642-4721. **$54-$225.** 440 Heritage Dr 57783. I-90, exit 14 (Spearfish Canyon), just s, then e, then s. Int corridors. **Pets:** Other species. $10 daily fee/pet. Service with restrictions, supervision.

[ASK] [X] [&M] [H] [■] [≈]

STURGIS

AAA ▼▼▼ **Best Western of Sturgis** **H**

(605) 347-3604. **$49-$120.** 2431 S Junction Ave 57785. I-90, exit 32. Ext/int corridors. **Pets:** Other species. Designated rooms, service with restrictions, crate. [SAVE] [X] [&M] [H] [■] [¶] [≈]

▼▼▼ **Holiday Inn Express & Suites–Sturgis** **H**

(605) 347-4140. **$80-$500.** 2721 Lazelle St 57785. I-90, exit 30 (US 14A), just s. Int corridors. **Pets:** Accepted.

[ASK] [X] [&M] [H] [■] [≈] [X]

AAA ▼ **Star Lite Motel** **M**

(605) 347-2506. **$35-$80.** 2426 Junction Ave 57785. I-90, exit 32, just n. Ext corridors. **Pets:** Small, dogs only. $10 daily fee/pet. Designated rooms, no service, supervision. [SAVE] [X] [H] [■]

END AREA

BRANDON

▼▼ **Comfort Inn** **H**

(605) 582-5777. **$89-$169.** 1105 N Splitrock Blvd 57005. I-90, exit 406, just s. Int corridors. **Pets:** $15 one-time fee/room. No service, supervision.

[ASK] [X] [&M] [H] [■] [≈] [X]

BROOKINGS

▼▼ **Brookings Super 8** **H**

(605) 692-6920. **$66-$89.** 3034 Lefevre Dr 57006. I-29, exit 132, just e. Int corridors. **Pets:** $10 daily fee/pet. Service with restrictions, supervision.

[ASK] [X] [&M] [H] [≈]

AAA ▼▼▼ **Fairfield Inn & Suites** **H**

(605) 692-3500. **$94-$114.** 3000 Lefevre Dr 57006. I-29, exit 132, just e. Int corridors. **Pets:** Accepted. [SAVE] [X] [&M] [H] [■] [≈] [X]

▼▼▼ **Holiday Inn Express Hotel & Suites** **H**

(605) 692-9060. **$109-$159.** 3020 Lefevre Dr 57006. I-29, exit 132, just se. Int corridors. **Pets:** Other species. $10 daily fee/room. Service with restrictions, crate. [ASK] [X] [&M] [H] [■] [≈] [X]

BUFFALO

▼ **Tipperary Lodge** **M**

(605) 375-3721. **$52-$54.** 604 1st St W 57720. 0.5 mi n on US 85, turn at sign. Int corridors. **Pets:** Other species. Designated rooms, service with restrictions, supervision. [ASK] [X] [H]

CHAMBERLAIN

▼▼▼ AmericInn Lodge & Suites of Chamberlain H
(605) 734-0985. **$60-$150.** 1981 E King St 57325. I-90, exit 265, just e. Int corridors. **Pets:** $10 daily fee/room. Service with restrictions, supervision. ASK ✕ ⟨⟩M ⎙ ▭ ⟿ ⟨✕⟩

▼▼ Bel Aire Motel M
(605) 734-5595. **Call for rates.** 312 E King St 57325. On US 16 and I-90 business loop; downtown. Ext/int corridors. **Pets:** Accepted. ⟨SAVE⟩ ✕ ⎙

▼▼▼ Best Western Lee's Motor Inn H
(605) 734-5575. **$60-$95.** 220 W King St 57325. US 16 and I-90 business loop; downtown. Ext/int corridors. **Pets:** Small, other species. Service with restrictions, supervision. ⟨SAVE⟩ ✕ ⟨⟩M ▭ ⟿ ⟨✕⟩

▼▼▼▼ Cedar Shore Resort H ✿
(605) 734-6376. **$90-$200.** 1500 Shoreline Dr 57365. I-90, exit 260, 2.5 mi e on Business Rt I-90, then 1 mi ne on Mickelson county road, follow signs. Int corridors. **Pets:** $20 daily fee/room. Service with restrictions, supervision. ⟨SAVE⟩ ✕ ⟨⟩M ▭ ⎙ ⟦⟧ ⟿ ⟨✕⟩

▼▼ Holiday Inn Express H
(605) 734-5593. **$90-$180.** 100 W Hwy 16 57365. I-90, exit 260, just n. Int corridors. **Pets:** Accepted. ASK ✕ ⟨⟩M ▭

▼▼▼ Oasis Inn H
(605) 734-6061. **Call for rates.** 1100 E Hwy 16 57365. I-90, exit 260, 0.4 mi e on US 16 and I-90 business loop. Ext/int corridors. **Pets:** Designated rooms, no service, supervision. ⟨SAVE⟩ ✕ ⟨⟩M ⎙ ▭ ⟿

DELL RAPIDS

▼▼▼ Bilmar Inn & Suites H
(605) 428-4288. **Call for rates.** 510 N Hwy 77 57022. I-29, exit 98 (SR 115), 3 mi e, then just n. Int corridors. **Pets:** Accepted. ⟨SAVE⟩ ✕ ⎙

DE SMET

▼▼ De Smet Super Deluxe Inn & Suites H
(605) 854-9388. **$65-$140.** 288 Hwy 14 E 57231. US 14, just e. Int corridors. **Pets:** Accepted. ASK ✕ ⎙ ▭ ⟿

FAITH

▼▼ Prairie Vista Inn H
(605) 967-2343. **$70-$86.** Hwy 212 & E 1st St 57626. On US 212; east end of town. Int corridors. **Pets:** Other species. $15 daily fee/pet. Designated rooms, service with restrictions, supervision. ⟨SAVE⟩ ✕ ⟨⟩M ⎙ ▭ ⟨✕⟩

FLANDREAU

▼▼ Royal River Casino & Hotel H
(605) 997-3746. **$71-$205.** 607 S Veterans St 57028. I-29, exit 114, 7 mi e, follow signs. Int corridors. **Pets:** Medium, dogs only. $50 deposit/pet. Designated rooms, service with restrictions, supervision. ⟨SAVE⟩ ✕ ⟨⟩M ⎙ ▭ ⟦⟧ ⟿ ⟨✕⟩

FORT PIERRE

▼▼▼ AmericInn Lodge & Suites of Fort Pierre H
(605) 223-2358. **$90-$180.** 312 Island Dr 57532. Jct US 14 and SR 34, just w of Missouri River Bridge, then just s. Int corridors. **Pets:** Accepted. ASK ✕ ⟨⟩M ⎙ ▭ ⟿

▼▼ Fort Pierre Motel M
(605) 223-3111. **$58-$78, 3 day notice.** 211 S 1st St 57532. On US 83, 1.2 mi s of jct US 14. Ext corridors. **Pets:** Other species. Supervision. ✕ ⟨⟩M ⎙

FREEMAN

▼▼ Freeman Country Inn H
(605) 925-4888. **$70-$75.** 1019 S Hwy 81 57029. On US 81, just s. Int corridors. **Pets:** Other species. $20 daily fee/pet. Designated rooms, service with restrictions, supervision. ✕ ⟨⟩M ⎙

HURON

▼▼▼ Best Western of Huron H ✿
(605) 352-2000. **$86-$92.** 2000 Dakota Ave 57350. 1.3 mi s on SR 37. Ext/int corridors. **Pets:** Medium, dogs only. $10 daily fee/room. Service with restrictions, supervision. ⟨SAVE⟩ ✕ ⟨⟩M ⎙ ▭ ⟨✕⟩

INTERIOR

▼▼ Badlands Budget Host Inn M
(605) 433-5335. **$59-$69.** 900 SD Hwy 377 57750. Jct SR 44 and 377, 2 mi s of Badlands National Park. Ext corridors. **Pets:** Other species. $5 daily fee/room. Service with restrictions, supervision. ⟨SAVE⟩ ▭ ⟿ ⟨W⟩ ⟨Z⟩

KADOKA

▼▼ Budget Host Sundowner Motor Inn M
(605) 837-2296. **$50-$145.** 510 SD Hwy 73 57543. I-90, exit 150, just s. Ext corridors. **Pets:** Medium. $10 one-time fee/pet. Designated rooms, service with restrictions, supervision. ⟨SAVE⟩ ✕ ⟨⟩M ⎙ ⟿

▼▼▼ Rodeway Inn M
(605) 837-2287. **$59-$109.** 915 Hwy 248 57543. 1.5 mi w on I-90 business route from exit 152, 1.3 mi e from exit 150. Ext corridors. **Pets:** Medium, other species. Designated rooms, service with restrictions. ⟨SAVE⟩ ✕ ⟨⟩M ▭ ⟦⟧ ⟿

MADISON

▼▼ AmericInn Lodge & Suites of Madison H ✿
(605) 256-3076. **Call for rates.** 504 10th St SE 57042. SR 34, 0.5 mi se; south side of town. Int corridors. **Pets:** Dogs only. $10 daily fee/room. Service with restrictions, supervision. ✕ ⟨⟩M ⎙ ▭ ⟿

MITCHELL

▼▼ AmericInn Lodge & Suites of Mitchell H
(605) 996-9700. **Call for rates.** 1421 S Burr St 57301. I-90, exit 332, just n. Int corridors. **Pets:** Accepted. ✕ ⟨⟩M ⎙ ▭ ⟿

▼▼ Best Western Motor Inn M
(605) 996-5536. **$49-$89.** 1001 S Burr St 57301. I-90, exit 332, 0.6 mi n. Ext corridors. **Pets:** $25 deposit/pet. Service with restrictions, supervision. ⟨SAVE⟩ ✕ ⟨⟩M ⎙ ▭ ⟿

▼▼ Days Inn Mitchell H
(605) 996-6208. **$69-$109.** 1506 S Burr St 57301. I-90, exit 332, just n. Int corridors. **Pets:** Accepted. ASK ✕ ⟨⟩M ⎙ ▭ ⟿ ⟨✕⟩

▼▼▼▼ Hampton Inn H ✿
(605) 995-1575. **$79-$139.** 1920 Highland Way 57301. I-90, exit 332, just se. Int corridors. **Pets:** Dogs only. $20 one-time fee/room. Service with restrictions. ⟨SAVE⟩ ✕ ⟨⟩M ⎙ ▭ ⟿ ⟨✕⟩

▼▼▼▼ Kelly Inn & Suites H
(605) 995-0500. **$69-$130.** 1010 Cabela Dr 57301. I-90, exit 332, just sw. Ext/int corridors. **Pets:** Other species. Service with restrictions, supervision. ⟨SAVE⟩ ✕ ⟨⟩M ⎙ ▭ ⟿ ⟨✕⟩

▼▼▼▼ Ramada Inn & Suites Conference Center H
(605) 996-6501. **$85-$140, 14 day notice.** 1525 W Havens St 57301. I-90, exit 330, 0.5 mi n. Ext/int corridors. **Pets:** Accepted. ⟨SAVE⟩ ✕ ⟨⟩M ⎙ ▭ ⟦⟧ ⟿ ⟨✕⟩

MOBRIDGE

▼▼ Wrangler Inn H
(605) 845-3641. **$66-$149.** 820 W Grand Crossing 57601. 0.5 mi w on US 12. Ext/int corridors. **Pets:** Dogs only. Designated rooms, service with restrictions, supervision. ASK ✕ ⟨⟩M ⎙ ▭ ⟦⟧ ⟿ ⟨✕⟩

MURDO

AAA ◈◈◈ **Best Western Graham's** Ⓜ
(605) 669-2441. **$49-$139, 7 day notice.** 301 W 5th 57559. On I-90 business loop, 0.5 mi w of jct US 83; I-90, exit 191 or 192. Ext corridors. **Pets:** Other species. $10 one-time fee/room. Designated rooms, supervision. ⓢⒶⓥⒺ ☒ ⓖⓂ ⊟ ⬜ ⇌

AAA ◈◈◈ **Days Inn Range Country** Ⓗ
(605) 669-2425. **$63-$150.** 302 W 5th 57559. I-90 business loop, 0.5 mi w of jct US 83, exit 192 or 191. Ext/int corridors. **Pets:** Other species. No service, supervision. ⓢⒶⓥⒺ ☒ ⓖⓂ ⬜ ⇌

NORTH SIOUX CITY

◈◈◈ **Hampton Inn** Ⓗ
(605) 232-9739. **$79-$199.** 101 S Sodrac Dr 57049. I-29, exit 2, just w. Int corridors. **Pets:** Accepted. ☒ ⓖⓂ ⊟ ⬜ ⇌ ☒

PICKSTOWN

◈◈ **Fort Randall Inn** Ⓜ
(605) 487-7801. **$65-$80.** 116 US Hwy 18 57367. On US 18/281; just e of dam. Ext corridors. **Pets:** Dogs only. $10 daily fee/room. Service with restrictions, crate. ⒶⓈⓀ ☒ ⊟

PIERRE

AAA ◈◈◈ **Best Western Ramkota Hotel** Ⓗ
(605) 224-6877. **$109-$112.** 920 W Sioux Ave 57501. 1 mi w on US 14/83. Ext/int corridors. **Pets:** Other species. Service with restrictions, supervision. ⓢⒶⓥⒺ ☒ ⓖⓂ ⊟ ⬜ �𝄖 ⇌

◈◈ **Comfort Inn of Pierre** Ⓗ
(605) 224-0377. **$65-$120.** 410 W Sioux Ave 57501. 0.3 mi w on US 14/83 and SR 34. Int corridors. **Pets:** Dogs only. $10 daily fee/pet. Service with restrictions, supervision. ⒶⓈⓀ ☒ ⓖⓂ ⊟ ⬜ ⇌

AAA ◈◈◈ **Governor's Inn** Ⓗ
(605) 224-4200. **$75-$140.** 700 W Sioux Ave 57501. 0.8 mi w on US 14/83 and SR 34. Ext/int corridors. **Pets:** Small. $25 one-time fee/room. Designated rooms, service with restrictions, supervision.
ⓢⒶⓥⒺ ☒ ⓖⓂ ⊟ ⬜ ⇌

◈◈ **River Lodge** Ⓗ
(605) 224-4140. **$62-$79.** 713 W Sioux Ave 57501. 0.8 mi w on US 14/83. Int corridors. **Pets:** Large. $8 daily fee/room. Service with restrictions, supervision. ⓢⒶⓥⒺ ☒ ⓖⓂ ⊟ ⬜

PINE RIDGE

◈◈◈ **Prairie Winds Casino & Hotel** Ⓗ
(605) 867-2683. **$46-$106.** HC 49 Box 10 57770. On US 18, 13 mi e of US 385 on Pine Ridge Indian Reservation. Int corridors. **Pets:** Accepted.
ⒶⓈⓀ ☒ ⓖⓂ ⊟ ⬜ �𝄖 ⇌ ☒

PLANKINTON

◈◈ **Smart Choice Inn & Suites** Ⓗ
(605) 942-7722. **$40-$80.** 801 S Main St 57368. I-90, exit 308, just n. Int corridors. **Pets:** Other species. $9 daily fee/pet. Supervision.
ⒶⓈⓀ ☒ ⊟

SIOUX FALLS

◈◈ **Baymont Inn** Ⓗ
(605) 362-0835. **$69-$145.** 3200 Meadow Ave 57106. I-29, exit 77 (41st St), just w, then just n. Int corridors. **Pets:** Other species. $15 one-time fee/room. Service with restrictions, supervision.
ⒶⓈⓀ ☒ ⓖⓂ ⊟ ⬜ ⇌

AAA ◈◈◈ **Best Western Empire Towers** Ⓗ ☙
(605) 361-3118. **$80-$140.** 4100 W Shirley Pl 57106. I-29, exit 77 (41st St), just ne. Int corridors. **Pets:** Other species. $15 one-time fee/pet. Designated rooms, service with restrictions, crate.
ⓢⒶⓥⒺ ☒ ⓖⓂ ⊟ ⬜ ⇌

AAA ◈◈◈ **Best Western Ramkota Hotel & Conference Center** Ⓗ ☙
(605) 336-0650. **$90-$170.** 3200 W Maple St 57107. I-29, exit 81 (Airport/Russell St), just e. Ext/int corridors. **Pets:** Service with restrictions, supervision. ⓢⒶⓥⒺ ☒ ⓖⓂ ⊟ ⬜ �𝄖 ⇌ ☒

AAA ◈◈◈ **ClubHouse Hotel & Suites** Ⓗ ☙
(605) 361-8700. **Call for rates.** 2320 S Louise Ave 57106. I-29, exit 78 (26th St), just e. Ext/int corridors. **Pets:** Other species. Service with restrictions, supervision. ⓢⒶⓥⒺ ☒ ⓖⓂ ⊟ ⬜ ⇌ ☒

◈◈ **Comfort Inn by Choice Hotels South** Ⓗ
(605) 361-2822. **$69-$199.** 3216 S Carolyn Ave 57106. I-29, exit 77 (41st St), just e, then n. Int corridors. **Pets:** Accepted.
ⒶⓈⓀ ☒ ⓖⓂ ⊟ ⬜ ⇌

◈◈ **Comfort Suites by Choice Hotels** Ⓗ
(605) 362-9711. **$70-$115.** 3208 S Carolyn Ave 57106. I-29, exit 77 (41st St), just e, then n. Int corridors. **Pets:** Large, other species. $10 daily fee/room. Designated rooms, service with restrictions, supervision.
ⒶⓈⓀ ☒ ⓖⓂ ⊟ ⬜ ⇌

AAA ◈◈◈ **Country Inn & Suites By Carlson** Ⓗ
(605) 373-0153. **$84-$159.** 200 E 8th St 57103. Just e of Phillips Ave; downtown. Int corridors. **Pets:** Accepted.
ⓢⒶⓥⒺ ☒ ⓖⓂ ⊟ ⬜ �𝄖 ⇌

◈ **Days Inn Airport** Ⓗ ☙
(605) 331-5959. **$59-$139.** 5001 N Cliff Ave 57104. I-90, exit 399 (Cliff Ave), just s. Int corridors. **Pets:** Other species. $10 daily fee/room. Service with restrictions, supervision. ⒶⓈⓀ ☒ ⓖⓂ ⊟ ⬜

◈ **Days Inn-Empire** Ⓗ
(605) 361-9240. **$59-$139.** 3401 Gateway Blvd 57106. I-29, exit 77 (41st St), just w. Int corridors. **Pets:** Dogs only. $10 daily fee/pet. Designated rooms, service with restrictions, supervision. ☒ ⓖⓂ ⊟ ⬜

AAA ◈◈◈ **Homewood Suites By Hilton** Ⓗ ☙
(605) 338-8585. **$69-$139.** 3620 W Avera Dr 57108. I-229, exit 1C (Louise Ave), just s. Int corridors. **Pets:** Other species. $5 daily fee/room, $20 one-time fee/room. Service with restrictions, crate.
ⓢⒶⓥⒺ ☒ ⓖⓂ ⊟ ⬜ ⇌ ☒

AAA ◈◈◈ **Kelly Inn** Ⓗ
(605) 338-6242. **$59-$109.** 3101 W Russell St 57107. I-29, exit 81 (Airport/Russell St), 0.3 mi e. Ext/int corridors. **Pets:** Service with restrictions, crate. ⓢⒶⓥⒺ ☒ ⓖⓂ ⊟ ⬜ ⇌

AAA ◈◈◈ **Quality Inn & Suites** Ⓗ ☙
(605) 336-1900. **$70-$160.** 5410 N Granite Ln 57107. I-29, exit 83 (SR 38), just e, then 0.3 mi n. Int corridors. **Pets:** Large, other species. $10 daily fee/pet. Designated rooms, service with restrictions, supervision.
ⓢⒶⓥⒺ ☒ ⓖⓂ ⊟ ⬜ ⇌

◈◈ **Red Roof Inn** Ⓗ
(605) 361-1864. **$43-$80, 7 day notice.** 3500 S Gateway Blvd 57106. I-29, exit 77 (41st St), just w. Int corridors. **Pets:** Large. Service with restrictions, crate. ⒶⓈⓀ ☒ ⓖⓂ ⊟

◈◈◈ **Residence Inn by Marriott** Ⓗ
(605) 361-2202. **$100-$125.** 4509 W Empire Pl 57106. I-29, exit 77 (41st St), 0.5 mi se. Int corridors. **Pets:** Accepted.
☒ ⓖⓂ ⊟ ⬜ ⇌ ☒

AAA ◈◈◈ **Sheraton Sioux Falls** Ⓗ
(605) 331-0100. **$79, 24 day notice.** 1211 N West Ave 57104. I-29, exit 81 (Airport/Russell St), 1.3 mi e. Int corridors. **Pets:** Medium, dogs only. Service with restrictions, supervision.
ⓢⒶⓥⒺ ☒ ⓖⓂ ⊟ ⬜ ⟦⟧ ⇌ ☒

◈◈◈ **Staybridge Suites** Ⓗ ☙
(605) 361-2298. **Call for rates.** 2505 S Carolyn Ave 57106. I-29, exit 78 (26th St), just se. Int corridors. **Pets:** Medium, other species. $25 daily fee/pet. Designated rooms, service with restrictions, supervision.
☒ ⓖⓂ ⊟ ⬜ ⇌ ☒

♦♦ **Super 8-East** [H]
(605) 338-8881. **$80-$149.** 2616 E 10th St 57103. I-229, exit 6, just e. Int corridors. **Pets:** Accepted. ASK ⊠ ♿ ▣ ▭ 🏊

(AAA) ♦♦ **Super 8/I-90/Airport East** [H]
(605) 339-9212. **$50-$125, 3 day notice.** 4808 N Cliff Ave 57104. I-90, exit 399 (Cliff Ave), 0.3 mi s. Int corridors. **Pets:** Large. $10 daily fee/pet. Designated rooms, service with restrictions, supervision.
SAVE ⊠ ▣ ▭

(AAA) ♦♦♦ **TownePlace Suites by Marriott** [H]
(605) 361-2626. **$99-$109.** 4545 W Homefield Dr 57106. I-29, exit 78 (26th St), just w. Int corridors. **Pets:** Medium. $75 one-time fee/room. Service with restrictions, supervision.
SAVE ⊠ ♿ ▣ ▭ 🏊 🏋

SUMMERSET

♦♦ **Ramada** [H]
(605) 787-4844. **Call for rates.** 7900 Stagestop Rd 57718. I-90, exit 48, just s. Int corridors. **Pets:** Accepted. ⊠ ♿ ▣ ▭ 🏊

VERMILLION

(AAA) ♦♦ **Comfort Inn** [H]
(605) 624-8333. **$79-$109.** 701 W Cherry St 57069. I-29, exit 26 (SR 50), 7.5 mi w on Business Rt SR 50. Int corridors. **Pets:** Medium. $10 daily fee/pet. Service with restrictions, supervision.
SAVE ⊠ ♿ ▣ ▭ 🏊 🏋

WALL

(AAA) ♦♦♦ **Best Western Plains Motel** [M]
(605) 279-2145. **$60-$180.** 712 Glenn St 57790. I-90, exit 110, just n. Ext corridors. **Pets:** Other species. $10 one-time fee/pet. Service with restrictions, supervision. SAVE ⊠ ♿ ▣ ▭ 🏊 🏋

(AAA) ♦ **Sunshine Inn** [M]
(605) 279-2178. **$49-$69.** 608 Main St 57790. Downtown. Ext corridors. **Pets:** Other species. $5 one-time fee/room. Service with restrictions.
SAVE ⊠

WATERTOWN

(AAA) ♦♦♦ **Best Western Ramkota Hotel** [H] 🐾
(605) 886-8011. **$95-$180.** 1901 9th Ave SW 57201. I-29, exit 177 (US 212), 4 mi w. Int corridors. **Pets:** Dogs only. Designated rooms, service with restrictions, supervision. SAVE ⊠ ♿ ▣ ▭ 🍴 🏊 🏋

(AAA) ♦♦ **Country Inn & Suites By Carlson** [H] 🐾
(605) 886-8900. **$96-$140.** 3400 8th Ave SE 57201. I-29, exit 177 (US 212), just w. Int corridors. **Pets:** $10 one-time fee/room. Designated rooms, service with restrictions, supervision.
SAVE ⊠ ♿ ▣ ▭ 🏊

(AAA) ♦♦ **Days Inn** [H]
(605) 886-3500. **$75-$150.** 2900 9th Ave SE 57201. I-29, exit 177 (US 212), 0.5 mi w. Ext/int corridors. **Pets:** $15 one-time fee/room. Service with restrictions, supervision. SAVE ⊠ ♿ ▣ ▭ 🏊

(AAA) ♦♦♦ **Holiday Inn Express Hotel & Suites** [H]
(605) 882-3636. **Call for rates.** 3901 9th Ave SE Ave SE 57201. I-29, exit 177 (US 212), just e. Int corridors. **Pets:** $10 one-time fee/room. Service with restrictions, supervision.
SAVE ⊠ ♿ ▣ ▭ 🏊 🏋

(AAA) ♦♦♦ **Quality Inn & Suites** [H]
(605) 886-3010. **$80-$150.** 800 35th St Cir 57201. I-29, exit 177 (US 212), just w. Ext/int corridors. **Pets:** Other species. $15 one-time fee/room. Designated rooms, service with restrictions, supervision.
SAVE ⊠ ♿ ▣ ▭ 🏊

♦ **Super 8-Watertown** [H]
(605) 882-1900. **$56-$73.** 503 14th Ave SE 57201. On US 81, 0.3 mi s of jct US 212. Int corridors. **Pets:** Accepted.
ASK ⊠ ♿ ▣ ▭ 🏊

(AAA) ♦♦ **Travelers Inn Motel** [H]
(605) 882-2243. **$55-$75.** 920 14th St SE 57201. I-29, exit 177 (US 212), 1.5 mi w, then just s. Int corridors. **Pets:** Other species. $6 daily fee/pet. Designated rooms, service with restrictions, supervision.
SAVE ⊠ ▣ ▭

(AAA) ♦ **Travel Host Motel** [M]
(605) 886-6120. **$45-$69.** 1714 9th Ave SW 57201. I-29, exit 177 (US 212), 4 mi w. Int corridors. **Pets:** $5 daily fee/room. Service with restrictions, crate. SAVE ⊠ ▣

WINNER

♦♦♦ **Holiday Inn Express Hotel & Suites** [H]
(605) 842-2255. **$89-$204.** 1360 E Hwy 44 57580. Just ne of jct US 18 and 183. Int corridors. **Pets:** Accepted. ASK ⊠ ♿ ▣ ▭ 🏊

YANKTON

(AAA) ♦♦ **Best Western Kelly Inn-Yankton** [H]
(605) 665-2906. **$80-$117.** 1607 Hwy 50 E 57078. On US 50, 1.8 mi e. Ext/int corridors. **Pets:** Large, other species. Designated rooms, service with restrictions, supervision. SAVE ⊠ ♿ ▣ ▭ 🍴 🏊 🏋

(AAA) ♦♦ **Days Inn** [H]
(605) 665-8717. **$65-$110.** 2410 Broadway St 57078. US 81, 1.7 mi n. Int corridors. **Pets:** Large, other species. $10 daily fee/pet. Service with restrictions, supervision. SAVE ⊠ ♿ ▣ ▭

♦♦ **Lewis & Clark Resort** [M]
(605) 665-2680. **$70-$125, 30 day notice.** 43496 Shore Dr 57078. 4 mi w on SR 52; in Lewis and Clark State Park, turn into park, just w of marina. Ext corridors. **Pets:** Dogs only. $5 daily fee/pet. Service with restrictions, supervision. ⊠ ♿ ▣ ▭ 🏊 🏋 ⊘

ALCOA

▼▼ Family Inns of America M

(865) 970-2006. **$49-$59.** 2450 Airport Hwy 37701. US 129, just e. Ext corridors. **Pets:** Small, other species. Designated rooms, service with restrictions, supervision. SAVE ✕ 🛗 ➿

▼▼▼▼ Jameson Inn Alcoa H ❀

(865) 984-6800. **$93-$100.** 206 Corporate Pl 37701. US 129, just s. Int corridors. **Pets:** Other species. $15 daily fee/room. Designated rooms, service with restrictions, crate. ASK ✕ 🛗 🖵 ➿ ✕

▼▼▼ MainStay Suites H ❀

(865) 379-7799. **$69-$149.** 361 Fountain View Cir 37701. US 129, just n on SR 35, just se on Associates Blvd, then just w. Int corridors. **Pets:** Other species. $25 one-time fee/room. Service with restrictions, crate. SAVE ✕ 🛗 🖵 ➿

ATHENS

▼▼ Days Inn-Athens M

(423) 745-5800. **Call for rates.** 2541 Decatur Pike 37303. I-75, exit 49, 0.3 mi e. Ext corridors. **Pets:** Medium. $10 daily fee/pet. Service with restrictions, crate. ✕ 🛗 🖵 ➿

BRENTWOOD

▼▼▼ Baymont Inn & Suites H

(615) 376-4666. **$90-$111.** 111 Penn Warren Dr 37027. I-65, exit 74B, 1.5 mi w, then just s on West Park. Int corridors. **Pets:** Accepted. SAVE ✕ 🛗 🖵 ➿

▼▼ Candlewood Suites H

(615) 309-0600. **$70.** 5129 Virginia Way 37027. I-65, exit 74B, 0.5 mi w, 0.5 mi s on Franklin Rd (US 31), 1.2 mi w on Maryland Way, just s on Ward Cir, then just s. Int corridors. **Pets:** Accepted. ASK ✕ 🛗 🖵

▼▼▼▼ Hilton Brentwood H ❀

(615) 370-0111. **$109-$209.** 9000 Overlook Blvd 37027. I-65, exit 74B, 0.5 mi s on US 31, then e on Church St. Int corridors. **Pets:** Medium. $75 one-time fee/room. Designated rooms, service with restrictions, supervision. ✕ 🛗 🖵 🍴 ➿

▼▼ MainStay Suites-Brentwood H ❀

(615) 371-8477. **$65-$80.** 107 Brentwood Blvd 37027. I-65, exit 74B, 1 mi w. Int corridors. **Pets:** Other species. $10 one-time fee/pet. Service with restrictions. ✕ 🛗 🖵 ➿

▼▼▼▼ Residence Inn Brentwood H ❀

(615) 371-0100. **$175-$213.** 206 Ward Cir 37027. I-65, exit 74B, 0.3 mi s on Franklin Pike Cir (US 31 S), then 0.5 mi w on Maryland Way. Ext/int corridors. **Pets:** Large, other species. $100 one-time fee/room. Service with restrictions, supervision. SAVE ✕ 🛗 🖵 ➿ ✕

▼▼ Sleep Inn H

(615) 376-2122. **Call for rates.** 1611 Galleria Blvd 37027. I-65, exit 69, 0.4 mi w, then just n. Int corridors. **Pets:** Accepted. ✕ 🛗 🖵 ➿

BULLS GAP

▼▼▼ Best Western Executive Inn H ❀

(423) 235-9111. **$59-$189.** 50 Speedway Ln 37711. I-81, exit 23. Int corridors. **Pets:** Large, other species. $20 daily fee/pet. Designated rooms, supervision. SAVE ✕ 🛗 🖵 ➿

BUTLER

▼▼▼▼ Iron Mountain Inn B&B and Creekside Chalet BB

(423) 768-2446. **$125-$350, 14 day notice.** 138 Moreland Dr 37640. 1.6 mi w on Pine Orchard Rd from SR 67 at Stout Store, follow signs; 13 mi w on SR 67 from US 421 in Mountain City, follow sign at Stout Store area; 15.1 mi from Shell Station in Hampton to Pine Orchard Rd, 1.6 mi to Moreland Dr. Ext/int corridors. **Pets:** $50 one-time fee/pet. Designated rooms, no service, supervision. ASK ✕ 🛗 🖵 ✕

CARYVILLE

▼▼ Budget Host Inn M

(423) 562-9595. **Call for rates.** 115 Woods Ave 37714. I-75, exit 134, just w. Ext corridors. **Pets:** Accepted. ✕ 🛗

CHATTANOOGA

▼▼▼ America's Best Inn-Hamilton Mall Area M

(423) 894-5454. **Call for rates.** 7717 Lee Hwy 37421. I-75, exit 7B northbound; exit 7 southbound. Ext corridors. **Pets:** Accepted. ✕ 🛗 🖵 ➿

▼▼▼▼ Baymont Inn & Suites-Chattanooga H

(423) 821-1090. **$60-$130.** 3540 Cummings Hwy 37419. I-24, exit 174, 0.4 mi s. Int corridors. **Pets:** Medium. $10 daily fee/pet. Designated rooms, service with restrictions, supervision. SAVE ✕ 🛗 🖵 ➿

▼▼▼ Best Western Heritage Inn H

(423) 899-3311. **$69-$99.** 7641 Lee Hwy 37421. I-75, exit 7, just w. Ext corridors. **Pets:** Small, other species. $10 daily fee/pet. No service, supervision. SAVE ✕ 🛗 🖵 🍴 ➿

▼▼▼▼ Best Western Royal Inn H

(423) 821-6840. **$80-$100.** 3644 Cummings Hwy 37419. I-24, exit 174, 0.4 mi s. Ext corridors. **Pets:** Small. $10 daily fee/pet. Service with restrictions, supervision. SAVE ✕ 🛗 🖵 ➿

▼▼▼▼ Chattanooga Choo-Choo H

(423) 266-5000. **$109-$229.** 1400 Market St 37402. I-24, exit 178 (Broad St) eastbound, then E Main St; exit 178 (Market St) westbound, 0.5 mi n. Ext/int corridors. **Pets:** Accepted. SAVE ✕ 🛗 🖵 🍴 ➿ ✕

(AAA) ▼▼▼ Comfort Inn H
(423) 499-1993. **Call for rates.** 7620 Hamilton Park Dr 37421. I-75, exit 7B northbound; exit 7 southbound, just w to Lee Hwy, just s, then just e. Int corridors. **Pets:** Accepted. [SAVE] [🅿] [🖥] [⛱]

(AAA) ▼▼▼ Country Inn & Suites By Carlson, Chattanooga I-24 West H ✿
(423) 825-6100. **$99-$108.** 3725 Modern Industries Blvd 37419. I-24, exit 174, just s. Int corridors. **Pets:** Small, dogs only. $25 one-time fee/room. Designated rooms, service with restrictions.
[SAVE] [✕] [Ⓜ] [🅿] [🖥] [⛱]

(AAA) ▼▼ Days Inn-Lookout Mountain/Tiftonia H
(423) 821-6044. **$49-$89.** 3801 Cummings Hwy 37419-2201. I-24, exit 174, just n. Ext corridors. **Pets:** $10 daily fee/pet. Service with restrictions, supervision. [SAVE] [✕] [Ⓜ] [🅿] [🖥] [⛱]

▼▼ Extended StayAmerica-Chattanooga-Airport H
(423) 892-1315. **$57-$67.** 6240 Airpark Dr 37421. SR 153, exit 1 (Lee Hwy), 0.3 mi s to Vance Rd, then just w to cul de sac. Ext corridors. **Pets:** Other species. $25 daily fee/room. Designated rooms, service with restrictions, crate. [ASK] [✕] [Ⓜ] [🅿] [🖥]

▼▼ GuestHouse International Inn H
(423) 510-0800. **$40-$65.** 2201 Park Dr 37421. I-75, exit 5 (Shallowford Rd), 0.5 mi w. Ext corridors. **Pets:** $10 daily fee/pet. Service with restrictions, supervision. [ASK] [✕] [🅿] [🖥]

▼▼ La Quinta Inn–Chattanooga H ✿
(423) 855-0011. **$45-$89.** 7015 Shallowford Rd 37421. I-75, exit 5 (Shallowford Rd), just w. Ext corridors. **Pets:** Medium, other species. Service with restrictions, supervision. [ASK] [✕] [Ⓜ] [🅿] [🖥] [⛱]

(AAA) ▼▼▼ La Quinta Inn-Downtown H ✿
(423) 265-3151. **$59-$139.** 100 W 21st St 37408. I-24, exit 178, US 11 to Lookout Mountain, w to 20th St, w to Williams St, then w. Int corridors. **Pets:** Medium, other species. Service with restrictions, supervision.
[SAVE] [✕] [Ⓜ] [🅿] [🖥] [⛱]

▼▼▼ MainStay Suites-Chattanooga H
(423) 485-9424. **$60-$105.** 7030 Amin Dr 37421. I-75, exit 5 (Shallowford Rd), just w, then s. Int corridors. **Pets:** Medium, dogs only. $15 daily fee/pet. Designated rooms, service with restrictions, crate.
[✕] [Ⓜ] [🅿] [🖥]

▼▼ Microtel Inn-Chattanooga H
(423) 510-0761. **Call for rates.** 7014 McCutcheon Rd 37421. I-75, exit 5 (Shallowford Rd), just w, 0.3 mi n on Shallowford Village Dr, then just w. Int corridors. **Pets:** Medium, other species. $10 one-time fee/room. Service with restrictions, supervision. [✕] [Ⓜ] [🅿]

▼▼ Motel 6 Downtown #4145 H
(423) 265-7300. **$40-$100.** 2440 Williams St 37408. I-24, exit 178 (Market St). Int corridors. **Pets:** Other species. Service with restrictions, supervision. [✕] [🅿]

(AAA) ▼▼ Quality Inn H
(423) 821-1499. **Call for rates.** 3109 Parker Ln 37419. I-24, exit 175, just s. Ext corridors. **Pets:** $15 daily fee/pet. Service with restrictions, supervision. [SAVE] [✕] [🅿] [🖥] [⛱]

(AAA) ▼▼▼ Quality Suites H ✿
(423) 892-1500. **$69-$89.** 7324 Shallowford Rd 37421. I-75, exit 5 (Shallowford Rd), just e. Ext corridors. **Pets:** Small. $10 daily fee/pet. Service with restrictions, supervision. [SAVE] [✕] [🅿] [🖥] [⛱]

▼▼ Ramada Limited-Lookout Mountain West H
(423) 821-7162. **$40-$80.** 30 Birmingham Hwy 37419. I-24, exit 174, just s. Ext/int corridors. **Pets:** Accepted. [ASK] [✕] [🅿] [🖥] [⛱]

(AAA) ▼▼▼ Red Roof Inn-Chattanooga M
(423) 899-0143. **$40-$70, 14 day notice.** 7014 Shallowford Rd 37421. I-75, exit 5 (Shallowford Rd), just w. Ext corridors. **Pets:** Large. Service with restrictions, crate. [SAVE] [✕] [Ⓜ]

▼▼▼ Residence Inn by Marriott H
(423) 266-0600. **$164-$189.** 215 Chestnut St 37402. US 27, exit 1C (4th St), just n. Int corridors. **Pets:** Accepted. [✕] [Ⓜ] [🅿] [🖥] [⛱]

(AAA) ▼▼▼▼ The Sheraton Read House Hotel H ❀
(423) 266-4121. **Call for rates.** 827 Broad St 37402. US 27, exit 1A, just e. Int corridors. **Pets:** Medium, dogs only. $50 one-time fee/pet. Designated rooms, service with restrictions, crate.
[SAVE] [✕] [Ⓜ] [🅿] [🖥] [🍽] [⛱]

▼▼▼ Staybridge Suites H
(423) 267-0900. **$129-$159.** 1300 Carter St 37402. US 27 N, exit 1A (Martin Luther King Blvd), just e to Carter St, then 0.3 mi s. Int corridors. **Pets:** Other species. $25 one-time fee/room. Service with restrictions.
[ASK] [✕] [Ⓜ] [🅿] [🖥] [⛱]

▼▼▼ Staybridge Suites-Hamilton Place H
(423) 826-2700. **Call for rates.** 7015 Shallowford Rd 37421. I-75, exit 5 (Shallowford Rd), just w. Int corridors. **Pets:** Accepted.
[✕] [Ⓜ] [🅿] [🖥] [⛱]

▼▼ Super 8 H
(423) 490-8560. **Call for rates.** 7024 McCutcheon Rd 37421. I-75, exit 5 (Shallowford Rd), just w, then 0.3 mi n on Shallowford Village Dr. Int corridors. **Pets:** Accepted. [✕] [Ⓜ] [🅿] [🖥] [⛱]

▼▼ Super 8/Lookout Mountain H
(423) 821-8880. **$46-$121.** 20 Birmingham Hwy 37419. I-24, exit 174. Int corridors. **Pets:** $15 daily fee/pet. Designated rooms, service with restrictions, supervision. [ASK] [✕] [🅿] [🖥] [⛱]

CLARKSVILLE

▼▼▼ Candlewood Suites H
(931) 906-0900. **Call for rates.** 3050 Clay Lewis Rd 37040. I-24, exit 4, 0.3 mi s. Int corridors. **Pets:** Medium. $50 one-time fee/room. Service with restrictions, crate. [✕] [Ⓜ] [🅿] [🖥]

▼▼▼ Days Inn North H
(931) 552-1155. **Call for rates.** 130 Westfield Ct 37040. I-24, exit 4, just s. Ext corridors. **Pets:** Accepted. [✕] [Ⓜ] [🅿] [🖥] [⛱]

(AAA) ▼▼▼ Econo Lodge Inn & Suites M
(931) 647-2002. **Call for rates.** 3065 Wilma Rudolph Blvd 37040. I-24, exit 4, 0.3 mi w. Ext corridors. **Pets:** Accepted. [SAVE] [✕] [🅿] [🖥] [⛱]

▼▼▼ MainStay Suites H
(931) 648-3400. **$100-$130.** 115 Fairbrook Pl 37043. I-24, exit 4, 0.3 mi s on Wilma Rudolph Blvd, then just w. Int corridors. **Pets:** Medium. $50 one-time fee/room. Service with restrictions, crate.
[ASK] [✕] [Ⓜ] [🅿] [🖥] [⛱]

(AAA) ▼▼▼ Quality Inn-Exit 4 H ✿
(931) 648-4848. **$72-$81.** 3095 Wilma Rudolph Blvd 37040. I-24, exit 4, just e. Ext corridors. **Pets:** Medium, other species. $15 daily fee/room. Designated rooms, service with restrictions, crate.
[SAVE] [✕] [🅿] [🖥] [🍽] [⛱] [✗]

▼▼ Red Roof Inn M
(931) 905-1555. **$41-$79.** 197 Holiday Dr 37040. I-24, exit 4, just se. Ext corridors. **Pets:** Large. Service with restrictions, crate.
[ASK] [✕] [🅿] [⛱]

CLEVELAND

(AAA) ▼▼ America's Best Inn & Suites M
(423) 472-3281. **$40-$70.** 2655 Westside Dr NW 37312. I-75, exit 25, just e. Ext corridors. **Pets:** $10 daily fee/pet. Designated rooms, service with restrictions. [SAVE] [✕] [🅿] [🖥] [⛱]

▼▼ Colonial Inn M
(423) 472-6845. **$35-$45, 7 day notice.** 1555 25th St 37311. I-75, exit 25, 0.3 mi e. Ext corridors. **Pets:** Very small, dogs only. $10 daily fee/pet. Designated rooms, service with restrictions, supervision.
[✕] [🅿] [🖥] [⛱]

Comfort Inn & Suites-Cleveland H

(423) 339-1000. **Call for rates.** 107 Interstate Dr NW Dr NW 37312. I-75, exit 25, just w. Int corridors. **Pets:** Accepted.

Douglas Inn & Suites H

(423) 559-5579. **$55-$115.** 2600 Westside Dr NW 37312. I-75, exit 25, just e. Ext/int corridors. **Pets:** Medium, other species. $10 daily fee/pet. Service with restrictions, crate.

Fairfield Inn & Suites by Marriott Cleveland H

(423) 664-2501. **$109-$119.** 2815 Westside Dr NW 37312. I-75, exit 25, just e, then just n. Int corridors. **Pets:** Accepted.

Holiday Inn Mountain View H

(423) 472-1500. **Call for rates.** 2400 Executive Park Dr 37312. I-75, exit 25, just w. Ext/int corridors. **Pets:** Accepted.

Howard Johnson Chalet H

(423) 476-8511. **$65-$85.** 2595 Georgetown Rd 37311. I-75, exit 25, just e. Ext corridors. **Pets:** Other species. $10 daily fee/pet. Designated rooms, service with restrictions, supervision.

Jameson Inn H

(423) 614-5583. **$83-$90.** 360 Paul Huff Pkwy 37312. I-75, exit 27, 1 mi e. Ext corridors. **Pets:** Accepted.

Quality Inn H

(423) 478-5265. **Call for rates.** 153 James Asbury Dr 37312. I-75, exit 27, just w. Ext/int corridors. **Pets:** Accepted.

Ramada Limited H

(423) 472-5566. **Call for rates.** 156 James Asbury Dr 37312. I-75, exit 27, just w. Ext corridors. **Pets:** Small. $10 one-time fee/pet. Designated rooms, service with restrictions, supervision.

Super 8 M

(423) 476-5555. **Call for rates.** 163 Bernham Dr 37312. I-75, exit 27, just w. Ext/int corridors. **Pets:** Medium. $10 daily fee/pet. Designated rooms, no service, supervision.

CLINTON

Red Roof Inn & Suites H

(865) 457-9070. **$59-$99, 3 day notice.** 141 Buffalo Rd 37716. I-75, exit 122, just w. Ext corridors. **Pets:** Large. Service with restrictions, crate.

Super 8 M

(865) 457-2311. **Call for rates.** 720 Park Pl 37716. I-75, exit 122, just w. Ext corridors. **Pets:** Accepted.

COLUMBIA

Americas Best Value Inn M

(931) 381-1410. **$60-$70.** 1548 Bear Creek Pike 38401. I-65, exit 46, just w. Ext corridors. **Pets:** $6 daily fee/pet. Service with restrictions, supervision.

Jameson Inn H

(931) 388-3326. **$93-$100.** 715 James M Campbell Blvd 38402. 0.9 mi w of jct SR 50 and US 31. Int corridors. **Pets:** Accepted.

COOKEVILLE

Alpine Lodge & Suites H

(931) 526-3333. **$44-$68.** 2021 E Spring St 38506. I-40, exit 290, just s. Int corridors. **Pets:** Medium, other species. $5 one-time fee/pet. Designated rooms, service with restrictions, supervision.

Baymont Inn & Suites Cookeville H

(931) 525-6668. **$79-$110.** 1151 S Jefferson Ave 38506. I-40, exit 287, just s. Int corridors. **Pets:** Medium. $10 daily fee/pet. Designated rooms, service with restrictions, crate.

Best Western Thunderbird Motel H

(931) 526-7115. **$63-$120.** 900 S Jefferson Ave 38501. I-40, exit 287, just n. Ext corridors. **Pets:** $15 daily fee/pet. Designated rooms, service with restrictions.

Clarion Inn H

(931) 526-7125. **$60-$90.** 970 S Jefferson Ave 38501. I-40, exit 287, just n. Ext/int corridors. **Pets:** Small. $10 daily fee/pet. Designated rooms, service with restrictions, supervision.

Days Inn M

(931) 528-1511. **$55-$120.** 1296 S Walnut Ave 38501. I-40, exit 287. Ext corridors. **Pets:** Small, dogs only. $10 one-time fee/pet. Service with restrictions, supervision.

CORNERSVILLE

Econo Lodge M

(931) 293-2111. **Call for rates.** 3731 Pulaski Hwy 37047. I-65, exit 22 at US 31A. Ext corridors. **Pets:** Accepted.

CROSSVILLE

La Quinta Inn-Crossville H 🐾

(931) 456-9338. **$65-$185.** 4038 Hwy 127 N 38571. I-40, exit 317 (US 127), just n. Int corridors. **Pets:** Medium, other species. Service with restrictions, supervision.

DANDRIDGE

Holiday Inn Express H

(865) 397-1910. **Call for rates.** 119 Sharon Dr 37725. I-40, exit 417, just s. Int corridors. **Pets:** Medium, dogs only. $25 one-time fee/room. Designated rooms, service with restrictions.

Jefferson Inn H

(865) 940-5042. **$50-$60.** 127 Sharon Dr 37725. I-40, exit 417, just s. Int corridors. **Pets:** Accepted.

Super 8 H

(865) 397-1200. **$50-$150.** 125 Sharon Dr 37725. I-40, exit 417, just s. Int corridors. **Pets:** Accepted.

DAYTON

Best Western Dayton H

(423) 775-6560. **$72-$90.** 7835 Rhea County Hwy 37321. 1 mi n on US 27. Ext corridors. **Pets:** Small. $10 one-time fee/pet. Service with restrictions, supervision.

DECHERD

Jameson Inn H

(931) 962-0130. **$78-$83.** 1838 Decherd Blvd 37324. Jct Main St and SR 41A, just s. Ext corridors. **Pets:** Small, other species. $15 daily fee/room. Designated rooms, service with restrictions, crate.

DICKSON

Best Western Executive Inn H

(615) 446-0541. **$55-$80.** 2338 Hwy 46 37055. I-40, exit 172, just n. Ext corridors. **Pets:** Medium, dogs only. $10 daily fee/pet. Designated rooms, service with restrictions, supervision.

Comfort Inn H

(615) 740-1000. **$55-$85.** 1085 E Christi Dr 37055. I-40, exit 172, just n of SR 46, then just e. Int corridors. **Pets:** Accepted.

AAA WW Econo Lodge Inn & Suites H
(615) 441-5252. **Call for rates.** 1025 E Christi Rd 37055. I-40, exit 172, just s. Int corridors. **Pets:** Small, dogs only. $10 daily fee/pet. Designated rooms, service with restrictions, supervision. (SAVE) [X] [phone] [ ] [ ] [~]

AAA WWW Holiday Inn Express H
(615) 446-2781. **$89-$119.** 100 Barzani Blvd 37055. I-40, exit 172, just n. Int corridors. **Pets:** Small. $20 daily fee/pet. Service with restrictions, supervision. (SAVE) [X] [&M] [ ] [ ] [~]

AAA WW Super 8 H
(615) 446-1923. **$50-$70, 3 day notice.** 150 Suzanne Dr 37055. I-40, exit 172, just n on SR 46, then just e. Int corridors. **Pets:** Large. $10 daily fee/pet. Service with restrictions, supervision.
(SAVE) [X] [ ] [ ] [~]

DYERSBURG

AAA WWW Best Western Dyersburg Inn H
(731) 285-8601. **$69-$79.** 770 Hwy 51 Bypass W 38024. I-155, exit 13, 0.5 mi s; jct US 51 Bypass and SR 78. Ext corridors. **Pets:** Medium, other species. $20 daily fee/pet. Service with restrictions, supervision.
(SAVE) [X] [ ] [ ] [Y1] [~]

WW Days Inn H
(731) 287-0888. **$63-$79.** 2600 Lake Rd 38024. I-155, exit 13, just s. Int corridors. **Pets:** Accepted. (ASK) [X] [&M] [ ] [ ]

WW Executive Inn & Suites H
(731) 287-0044. **Call for rates.** 2331 Lake Rd 38024. I-155, exit 13, 0.5 mi s. Ext corridors. **Pets:** Large, other species. $5 daily fee/pet. Service with restrictions, supervision. [X] [ ]

WWW Hampton Inn H
(731) 285-4778. **Call for rates.** 2750 Mall Loop Rd 38024. I-155, exit 13, just s. Int corridors. **Pets:** Medium, other species. Service with restrictions, supervision. [X] [&M] [ ] [~]

WWWW Holiday Inn Express & Suites H
(731) 286-1021. **Call for rates.** 822 Reelfoot Dr 38024. I-155, exit 13, just s. Int corridors. **Pets:** Very small. $10 daily fee/pet. Service with restrictions, crate. [X] [&M] [ ] [ ] [~]

FAIRVIEW

AAA WWW Deerfield Inn & Suites H
(615) 799-4700. **$60-$80.** 1407 Hwy 96 N 37062. I-40, exit 182. Ext corridors. **Pets:** Medium. $10 one-time fee/pet. Designated rooms, service with restrictions, supervision. (SAVE) [X] [ ] [ ]

FARRAGUT

WW Super 8-West M ☙
(865) 675-5566. **$49-$99.** 11748 Snyder Rd 37934. I-40/75, exit 373 (Campbell Station Rd), just ne. Ext corridors. **Pets:** Medium. $10 daily fee/pet. Designated rooms, service with restrictions, crate.
(ASK) [X] [&M] [ ] [ ] [~]

FAYETTEVILLE

AAA WWW Best Western-Fayetteville Inn H
(931) 433-0100. **$85-$105.** 3021 Thornton Taylor Pkwy 37334. 0.7 mi e of US 431, on US 64 and 231 Bypass. Ext corridors. **Pets:** Small. $10 daily fee/pet. Service with restrictions, supervision.
(SAVE) [X] [ ] [ ] [Y1] [~]

FRANKLIN

AAA WWWW aloft Nashville-Cool Springs H ☙
(615) 435-8700. **$89-$199.** 7109 S Springs Dr 37067. I-65, exit 68B, just w, 0.3 mi n on Mallory Ln, then just e. Int corridors. **Pets:** Medium, dogs only. Service with restrictions, supervision.
(SAVE) [X] [&M] [ ] [ ] [~]

AAA WWW Best Western Franklin Inn H
(615) 790-0570. **$40-$70, 7 day notice.** 1308 Murfreesboro Rd 37064. I-65, exit 65, just w. Ext corridors. **Pets:** $10 one-time fee/pet. Service with restrictions, supervision. (SAVE) [X] [ ] [ ] [~]

AAA WW Days Inn H
(615) 790-1140. **$69-$99.** 4217 S Carothers Rd 37064. I-65, exit 65, just e. Ext corridors. **Pets:** $10 daily fee/pet. Service with restrictions, supervision. (SAVE) [X] [ ] [ ] [~]

WWW Homestead Studio Suites Hotel-Nashville/Franklin-Cool Springs H
(615) 771-7600. **$57-$86.** 680 Bakers Bridge Ave 37067. I-65, exit 69 (Galleria Blvd), 0.3 mi e on Moore's Ln to Carothers Pkwy, 0.5 mi s, then 0.3 mi w. Ext corridors. **Pets:** Other species. $25 daily fee/room. Designated rooms, service with restrictions, crate. (ASK) [X] [ ] [ ]

WWWW La Quinta Inn & Suites Nashville-Franklin M ☙
(615) 791-7700. **$59-$109.** 4207 Franklin Commons Ct 37067. I-65, exit 65, just e. Int corridors. **Pets:** Medium, other species. Service with restrictions, supervision. (ASK) [X] [ ] [ ] [~]

AAA WWW Ramada Inn & Suites H
(615) 791-4004. **$75-$150.** 6210 Hospitality Dr 37064. I-65, exit 65, 0.5 mi e on US 96. Int corridors. **Pets:** Small, other species. $15 daily fee/pet. Service with restrictions, supervision. (SAVE) [X] [&M] [ ] [ ] [~]

GALLATIN

WW Jameson Inn M
(615) 451-4494. **$93-$100.** 1001 Village Green Crossing 37066. 2 mi s on US 31. Ext corridors. **Pets:** Small. $15 daily fee/pet. Service with restrictions, supervision. (ASK) [X] [&M] [ ] [ ] [~]

GATLINBURG

AAA WWW Cobbly Nob Rentals Inc CA
(865) 436-5298. **$100-$155, 30 day notice.** 3722 E Parkway 37738. On US 321, 10.3 mi n of jct US 441. Ext corridors. **Pets:** Large, dogs only. $15 daily fee/pet. Designated rooms, service with restrictions, crate.
(SAVE) [X] [ ] [ ] [~] [X]

WWW Garden Plaza Hotel M ☙
(865) 436-9201. **$59-$129.** 520 Historic Nature Tr 37738. 0.4 mi e of US 441 at traffic light 8. Ext/int corridors. **Pets:** Other species. $15 one-time fee/pet. Designated rooms, service with restrictions, crate.
(ASK) [X] [&M] [ ] [ ] [Y1] [~] [X]

AAA WWWW Greenbrier Valley Resorts at Cobbly Nob CA ☙
(865) 436-2015. **$75-$1000, 30 day notice.** 3629 E Parkway 37738. On US 321, 10.1 mi n of jct US 441. Ext corridors. **Pets:** Other species. $100 deposit/pet. Designated rooms, service with restrictions.
(SAVE) [X] [ ] [ ] [~]

AAA WWW Microtel Gatlinburg H
(865) 436-0107. **$45-$159, 3 day notice.** 211 Historic Nature Tr 37738. Just e of US 441 at traffic light 8. Int corridors. **Pets:** Small. $10 daily fee/pet. Service with restrictions, supervision.
(SAVE) [X] [&M] [ ] [ ]

WWWW Outback Resort Rentals & Sales VH
(865) 430-9385. **$120-$799, 30 day notice.** 902 Street of Dreams Way 37738. SR 441 S, 2 mi e on Wiley Oakley Dr, 2 mi e on N Woodland Dr. Ext corridors. **Pets:** Accepted. (ASK) [X] [ ] [ ] [~]

WWW The Park Vista Hotel & Convention Center H ☙
(865) 436-9211. **$70-$169, 3 day notice.** 705 Cherokee Orchard Rd 37738. 0.6 mi e of jct US 441 at traffic light 8. Int corridors. **Pets:** Medium. $25 daily fee/pet. Designated rooms, service with restrictions, supervision. (ASK) [X] [&M] [ ] [ ] [Y1] [~] [X]

GREENEVILLE

AAA WWWW Comfort Inn of Greeneville H ☙
(423) 639-4185. **$70-$200.** 1790 E Andrew Johnson Hwy 37745. US 11 E, 2.9 mi ne. Ext/int corridors. **Pets:** Other species. $10 one-time fee/room. Service with restrictions, supervision. (SAVE) [X] [ ] [ ] [~]

◆◆ **Days Inn** **M**
(423) 639-2156. **Call for rates.** 935 E Andrew Johnson Hwy 37745. US 11 E, 2 mi ne. Ext corridors. **Pets:** Large. $10 daily fee/room. Service with restrictions, supervision. ⊠ 🖥 💻 🐾

◆◆◆ **Jameson Inn** **H**
(423) 638-7511. **$83-$90.** 3160 E Andrew Johnson Hwy 37745. US 11 E Bypass, 3.6 mi ne. Int corridors. **Pets:** Very small, other species. $15 daily fee/pet. Designated rooms, service with restrictions, supervision.
 (ASK) ⊠ 🕭ᴹ 🖥 💻 🐾

HARRIMAN

(AAA) ◆◆◆ **Best Western Harriman Inn** **M**
(865) 882-6200. **$65-$99.** 120 Childs Rd 37748. I-40, exit 347, just n. Ext corridors. **Pets:** Medium. $10 daily fee/pet. Service with restrictions.
(SAVE) ⊠ 🕭ᴹ 🖥 💻

◆◆ **Quality Inn by Choice Hotels** **M**
(865) 882-5340. **Call for rates.** 1845A S Roane St 37748. I-40, exit 347, just s on US 27/SR 61. Ext corridors. **Pets:** Accepted.
⊠ 🕭ᴹ 🖥 💻 🐾

◆◆ **Rodeway Inn Harriman** **M**
(865) 882-5400. **Call for rates.** 1845B S Roane St 37748. I-40, exit 347, just s on US 27/SR 61. Int corridors. **Pets:** Accepted. ⊠ 🖥 💻

HIXSON

◆◆ **Home Away Extended Stay Studios** **H**
(423) 643-4663. **$58-$64.** 1949 North Point Blvd 37343. Jct SR 153 and Hixson Pike, just w. Ext corridors. **Pets:** $10 daily fee/pet. Service with restrictions, supervision. (ASK) ⊠ 🖥 💻 🐾

HURRICANE MILLS

(AAA) ◆◆◆ **Best Western of Hurricane Mills** **M** 🐾
(931) 296-4251. **$75-$110.** 15542 Hwy 13 S 37078. I-40, exit 143, just n. Ext corridors. **Pets:** Other species. $10 daily fee/pet. Designated rooms, service with restrictions, crate. (SAVE) ⊠ 🖥 💻 🐾

JACKSON

(AAA) ◆◆◆ **Best Western Inn & Suites Carriage House** **H**
(731) 664-3030. **$80-$100.** 1936 Hwy 45 Bypass 38305. I-40, exit 80A, just s. Ext corridors. **Pets:** Accepted. (SAVE) ⊠ 🖥 💻 🐾

◆◆◆◆ **Jackson Hampton Inn & Suites** **H**
(731) 427-6100. **$119-$159.** 150 Campbell Oaks Dr 38305. I-40, exit 83. Int corridors. **Pets:** Medium, other species. Service with restrictions, crate.
⊠ 🕭ᴹ 🖥 💻 🐾

◆◆◆◆ **Jameson Inn** **H**
(731) 660-8651. **$90-$120.** 1292 Vann Dr 38305. I-40, exit 80B, 0.6 mi w. Int corridors. **Pets:** Small, other species. $15 daily fee/pet. Designated rooms, service with restrictions, supervision. (ASK) ⊠ 🖥 💻 🐾

◆◆◆◆ **La Quinta Inn of Jackson** **H** 🐾
(731) 664-1800. **$55-$99.** 2370 N Highland Ave 38305. I-40, exit 82A. Int corridors. **Pets:** Medium, other species. Service with restrictions, supervision. (ASK) ⊠ 🖥 💻 🐾

◆◆ **Quality Inn** **H** 🐾
(731) 668-1400. **$72-$77.** 535 Wiley Parker Rd 38305. I-40, exit 80A, just s, then e on Carriage House Dr. Ext/int corridors. **Pets:** Small. $15 one-time fee/pet. Designated rooms, service with restrictions, supervision.
⊠ 🖥 💻 🐾

JELLICO

(AAA) ◆ **Americas Best Value Inn** **M**
(423) 784-7241. **$55.** 133 Holiday Ln 37762. I-75, exit 160, just w. Ext corridors. **Pets:** Other species. $5 daily fee/pet. Service with restrictions, crate. (SAVE) ⊠ 🕭ᴹ 🖥 💻 🐾

JOHNSON CITY

◆◆ **Comfort Inn of Johnson City** **H**
(423) 928-9600. **Call for rates.** 1900 S Roan St 37604. I-26, exit 24, just w on US 321. Ext corridors. **Pets:** Other species. $15 daily fee/pet. No service. ⊠ 🖥 💻 🐾

◆◆◆ **DoubleTree Hotel** **H**
(423) 929-2000. **$99-$199.** 211 Mockingbird Ln 37604. I-26, exit 35 eastbound; exit 35B westbound, 0.6 mi e on N Roan St. Int corridors.
Pets: Accepted. ⊠ 🕭ᴹ 🖥 💻 🍴 🐾

◆◆◆ **Holiday Inn-Johnson City** **H** 🐾
(423) 282-4611. **$94.** 101 W Springbrook Dr 37604. I-26, exit 20A westbound; exit 20 eastbound, just e on N Roan St, then just n. Int corridors. **Pets:** Large. $25 one-time fee/room. Designated rooms, service with restrictions, crate. (ASK) ⊠ 🕭ᴹ 🖥 💻 🍴 🐾

◆◆ **Jameson Inn** **H**
(423) 282-0488. **$84-$91.** 119 Pinnacle Dr 37615. I-26, exit 17, just w on CR 354, then just s. Ext corridors. **Pets:** Accepted.
(ASK) ⊠ 🕭ᴹ 🖥 💻 🐾

(AAA) ◆◆ **Red Roof Inn-Johnson City** **M**
(423) 282-3040. **$50-$80, 14 day notice.** 210 Broyles Dr 37601. I-26, exit 20A westbound; exit 20 eastbound, just w on N Roan St. Ext corridors. **Pets:** Large. Service with restrictions, crate. (SAVE) ⊠ 🕭ᴹ 🖥

◆◆ **Sleep Inn & Suites** **H**
(423) 915-0081. **Call for rates.** 2020 Franklin Terrace Ct 37604. I-26, exit 19, just w, then just n, follow signs; entrance on Oakland Ave at light. Int corridors. **Pets:** Accepted. ⊠ 🕭ᴹ 🖥 💻

KIMBALL

(AAA) ◆ **Super 8–Kimball** **M**
(423) 837-7185. **$45-$90, 5 day notice.** 395 Main St 37347. I-24, exit 152, 0.5 mi n. Ext corridors. **Pets:** Accepted. (SAVE) ⊠ 🖥 💻 🐾

KINGSPORT

(AAA) ◆◆ **Best Western Colonial Inn** **M**
(423) 239-3400. **$50-$80.** 4234 Fort Henry Dr 37663. I-81, exit 59, 0.7 mi n on SR 36. Ext corridors. **Pets:** Accepted. (SAVE) ⊠ 🕭ᴹ 🖥 💻

◆◆◆ **Jameson Inn** **H**
(423) 230-0534. **$83-$90.** 3004 Bay Meadow Pl 37664. I-26, exit 4, just n. Int corridors. **Pets:** Accepted. (ASK) ⊠ 🕭ᴹ 🖥 💻 🐾

◆◆◆ **La Quinta Inn Kingsport** **H** 🐾
(423) 323-0500. **$59-$119.** 10150 Airport Pkwy 37663. I-81, exit 63, just e. Int corridors. **Pets:** Medium, other species. Service with restrictions, supervision. (ASK) ⊠ 🕭ᴹ 🖥 💻 🐾

◆◆ **Quality Inn & Conference Center** **H** 🐾
(423) 245-0271. **$62-$100.** 1900 American Way 37660. On US 11 W at SR 93. Ext corridors. **Pets:** Small. $25 one-time fee/pet. Service with restrictions, crate. ⊠ 🖥 💻 🍴 🐾

◆◆ **Sleep Inn** **H**
(423) 279-1811. **Call for rates.** 200 Hospitality Pl 37663. I-81, exit 63, just s. Int corridors. **Pets:** Accepted. ⊠ 🖥 💻

KINGSTON

◆◆ **Motel 6 #4403** **M**
(865) 376-2069. **$43-$90.** 495 Gallaher Rd 37763. I-40, exit 356, just n. Ext corridors. **Pets:** Other species. Service with restrictions, supervision.
(ASK) ⊠ 🖥 🐾

(AAA) ◆◆◆ **Super 8** **M**
(865) 376-4965. **$90-$100.** 905 N Kentucky St 37763. I-40, exit 352, 0.3 mi s. Ext corridors. **Pets:** Medium, other species. $10 daily fee/pet. Service with restrictions, supervision. (SAVE) ⊠ 🖥 💻

KINGSTON SPRINGS

Best Western Harpeth Inn H

(615) 952-3961. **$50-$100.** 116 Luyben Hills Rd 37082. I-40, exit 188, just n. Ext corridors. **Pets:** Large, other species. $10 daily fee/pet. Service with restrictions, supervision. [SAVE] [X] [🔲] [🔲] [≈]

KNOXVILLE

Baymont Inn & Suites East Knoxville H

(865) 246-3600. **$60-$130.** 814 Brakebill Rd 37914. I-40, exit 398 (Strawberry Plains), just n, then w. Ext corridors. **Pets:** Small. $10 daily fee/pet. Service with restrictions, crate. [ASK] [X] [🔲] [🔲] [🔲] [≈]

Best Western Knoxville Suites H

(865) 687-9922. **$65-$139.** 5317 Pratt Rd 37912. I-75, exit 108 (Merchants Dr), just e, then n. Int corridors. **Pets:** Accepted.
[SAVE] [X] [🔲] [🔲] [🔲] [≈]

Candlewood Suites-Knoxville H

(865) 777-0400. **$108-$115.** 10206 Parkside Dr 37922. I-40/75, exit 374 (Lovell Rd), 0.5 mi s, then 1 mi e. Int corridors. **Pets:** Medium. $75 one-time fee/room. Service with restrictions, crate. [ASK] [X] [🔲] [🔲] [🔲]

The Clarion Inn H

(865) 687-8989. **$69-$99.** 5634 Merchants Center Blvd 37912. I-75, exit 108 (Merchants Dr), just w, then just n. Int corridors. **Pets:** Small. $20 daily fee/pet. Service with restrictions, supervision.
[SAVE] [X] [🔲] [🔲] [🔲] [≈]

Crowne Plaza Knoxville H ✿

(865) 522-2600. **$129-$139.** 401 W Summit Hill Dr 37902. Corner of Walnut St; downtown. Int corridors. **Pets:** Large, other species. $25 one-time fee/room. Service with restrictions.
[ASK] [X] [🔲] [🔲] [🔲] [🍴] [≈]

Econo Lodge Inn & Suites–East Knoxville M

(865) 932-1217. **$49-$129.** 7424 Strawberry Plains Pike 37924. I-40, exit 398 (Strawberry Plains Pike), just n. Ext corridors. **Pets:** Medium, other species. $10 daily fee/room. Service with restrictions, supervision.
[SAVE] [X] [🔲] [🔲] [≈]

Econo Lodge-North M

(865) 687-5680. **$41-$60.** 5505 Merchants Center Blvd 37912. I-75, exit 108 (Merchants Dr), just w, then just n. Ext corridors. **Pets:** Small. $10 one-time fee/pet. Supervision. [SAVE] [X] [🔲]

Extended StayAmerica Knoxville-Cedar Bluff M

(865) 769-0822. **$57-$67.** 214 Langley Pl 37922. I-40/75, exit 378 (Cedar Bluff Rd), just s, then 1 mi w on N Peters Rd. Ext corridors. **Pets:** Other species. $25 daily fee/room. Designated rooms, service with restrictions, crate. [ASK] [X] [🔲] [🔲] [🔲]

Extended StayAmerica Knoxville-West Hills H

(865) 694-4178. **$62-$90.** 1700 Winston Rd 37909. I-40/75, exit 380 (West Hills), just w on Kingston Pike, then just s. Int corridors. **Pets:** Other species. $25 daily fee/room. Designated rooms, service with restrictions, crate. [ASK] [X] [🔲] [🔲] [🔲] [≈]

Hilton Knoxville Downtown H ✿

(865) 523-2300. **$100-$330.** 501 W Church Ave 37902. Between Locust and Walnut sts; downtown. Int corridors. **Pets:** $35 one-time fee/room. Designated rooms, service with restrictions.
[X] [🔲] [🔲] [🔲] [🍴] [≈]

Holiday Inn Cedar Bluff H ✿

(865) 693-1011. **$99-$186.** 304 Cedar Bluff Rd 37923. I-40/75, exit 378 (Cedar Bluff Rd) eastbound; exit 378B westbound, just n to Executive Park Dr. Int corridors. **Pets:** $50 one-time fee/room. Designated rooms, service with restrictions, supervision.
[ASK] [X] [🔲] [🔲] [🔲] [🍴] [≈] [X]

Holiday Inn Express Knoxville-East H

(865) 525-5100. **Call for rates.** 730 Rufus Graham Rd 37924. I-40, exit 398 (Strawberry Plains Pike), just n. Int corridors. **Pets:** Accepted.
[X] [🔲] [🔲] [🔲] [≈]

Homewood Suites by Hilton H

(865) 777-0375. **$169-$179.** 10935 Turkey Dr 37922. I-40/75, exit 374 (Lovell Rd), just s to Parkside Dr, then 0.5 mi n on Snow Goose. Int corridors. **Pets:** Large. $100 one-time fee/room. Service with restrictions.
[X] [🔲] [🔲] [🔲] [≈] [X]

La Quinta Inn & Suites East H ✿

(865) 633-5100. **$69-$149.** 7210 Saddle Rack St 37914. I-40, exit 398 (Strawberry Plains Pike), just s, just e on Region Ln, then just se on Shumard Ave. Int corridors. **Pets:** Medium, other species. Service with restrictions, supervision. [ASK] [X] [🔲] [🔲] [🔲] [≈]

La Quinta Inn Knoxville (West) M ✿

(865) 690-9777. **$49-$105.** 258 N Peters Rd 37923. I-40/75, exit 378 (Cedar Bluff Rd), just s, then just e. Ext corridors. **Pets:** Medium, other species. Service with restrictions, supervision.
[ASK] [X] [🔲] [🔲] [🔲] [≈]

Motel 6–1252 M

(865) 675-7200. **$39-$51.** 402 Lovell Rd 37922. I-40/75, exit 374 (Lovell Rd), just s. Ext corridors. **Pets:** Other species. Service with restrictions, supervision. [X] [🔲] [≈]

Quality Inn Merchants Dr M

(865) 342-3701. **$51-$56.** 117 Cedar Ln 37912. I-75, exit 108 (Merchants Dr), just e. Ext corridors. **Pets:** Medium. $20 one-time fee/pet. Designated rooms, service with restrictions. [X] [🔲] [🔲] [🔲] [≈]

Red Roof Inn M

(865) 688-1010. **$65-$99, 3 day notice.** 5334 Central Ave Pike 37912. I-75, exit 108 (Merchants Dr), just e. Ext corridors. **Pets:** Large. Service with restrictions, crate. [ASK] [X] [🔲] [≈]

Red Roof Inn-West M

(865) 691-1664. **$50-$100, 14 day notice.** 209 Advantage Pl 37922. I-40/75, exit 378 (Cedar Bluff Rd), just s to N Peters Rd, then w. Ext corridors. **Pets:** Large. Service with restrictions, crate.
[SAVE] [X] [🔲] [🔲]

Residence Inn Knoxville Cedar Bluff H ✿

(865) 539-5339. **$152-$186.** 215 Langley Pl 37922. I-40, exit 378 (Cedar Bluff Rd), just s, then 1 mi w on N Peters Blvd. Int corridors. **Pets:** Other species. $75 one-time fee/room. Service with restrictions, supervision.
[X] [🔲] [🔲] [🔲] [≈] [X]

KODAK

Big Bear Extended Stay Suites H

(865) 225-1719. **Call for rates.** 2162 Parkway 37764. I-40, exit 407, just s on SR 66, then w. Ext corridors. **Pets:** Medium, other species. $10 daily fee/room. Service with restrictions. [X] [🔲] [🔲]

Quality Inn Interstate M

(865) 933-1719. **$55-$149.** 155 W Dumplin Valley Rd 37764. I-40, exit 407, just s on SR 66, then just w. Ext corridors. **Pets:** Medium, other species. $10 daily fee/room. Service with restrictions.
[SAVE] [X] [🔲] [🔲] [🔲] [≈]

LAKE CITY

Days Inn M

(865) 426-2816. **$77-$98, 3 day notice.** 221 Colonial Ln 37769. I-75, exit 129, just w. Ext corridors. **Pets:** Accepted. [ASK] [X] [🔲] [🔲] [🔲] [≈]

LAWRENCEBURG

Best Western Villa Inn H

(931) 762-4448. **Call for rates.** 2126 N Locust Ave 38464. On US 43, 2.2 mi n of jct US 64. Ext corridors. **Pets:** Small. $10 daily fee/pet. Designated rooms, service with restrictions, supervision.
[SAVE] [X] [🔲] [🔲] [≈]

LEBANON

Americas Best Value Inn & Suites M

(615) 449-5781. **$30-$100.** 822 S Cumberland St 37087. I-40, exit 238, just n. Ext corridors. **Pets:** Very small. $12 daily fee/pet. Designated rooms, service with restrictions, supervision. [SAVE] [X] [🔲] [🔲] [≈]

▼▼ **Econo Lodge** Ⓜ
(615) 444-1001. **$45-$70.** 829 S Cumberland St 37087. I-40, exit 238, just n. Ext corridors. **Pets:** Accepted. ⊠ 📱 🖥 ⤖

▼▼▼ **Ramada Inn & Suites Lebanon** Ⓜ
(615) 444-7400. **$69.** 704 S Cumberland St 37087. I-40, exit 238, just n. Ext corridors. **Pets:** Other species. Service with restrictions, supervision.
⊠ Ꭾᴹ 📱 🖥 ⤖

ᗩᗩᗩ ▼▼▼ **Sleep Inn &**
         Suites-Lebanon/Nashville 🄷 ❀
(615) 449-7005. **$69-$130, 3 day notice.** 150 S Eastgate Ct 37090. I-40, exit 232. Int corridors. **Pets:** Medium, other species. $25 one-time fee/room. Service with restrictions, supervision.
(SAVE) ⊠ Ꭾᴹ 📱 🖥 ⤖

LENOIR CITY

ᗩᗩᗩ ▼▼▼ **Days Inn** 🄷
(865) 986-2011. **$70-$90.** 1110 Hwy 321 N 37771. I-75, exit 81, just e. Ext corridors. **Pets:** Small. $10 daily fee/pet. Service with restrictions, supervision. (SAVE) ⊠ 📱 🖥 ⤖

ᗩᗩᗩ ▼▼▼ **Econo Lodge** 🄷
(865) 986-0295. **$46-$90.** 1211 Hwy 321 N 37771. I-75, exit 81, just w. Ext corridors. **Pets:** Medium. $10 daily fee/pet. Service with restrictions, supervision. (SAVE) ⊠ 📱 ⤖

LEWISBURG

▼▼ **A Richland Inn Hotel** 🄷
(931) 359-1800. **$50-$70.** 723 E Commerce St 37091. Jct US 431 and 31A, just w; just e of town. Ext corridors. **Pets:** Accepted. (ASK) ⊠ 📱

LOUDON

ᗩᗩᗩ ▼▼ **Americas Best Value Inn** Ⓜ
(865) 458-5855. **$55-$69.** 15100 Hwy 72 37774. I-75, exit 72, just w. Ext corridors. **Pets:** $7 daily fee/pet. Service with restrictions, supervision.
(SAVE) ⊠ 📱 ⤖

MANCHESTER

▼▼▼ **Ambassador Inn** 🄷
(931) 728-2200. **$59-$89.** 925 Interstate Dr 37355. I-24, exit 110, just n. Ext/int corridors. **Pets:** Accepted. (ASK) ⊠ 📱 🖥 ⤖

▼▼▼ **Country Inn & Suites By Carlson** 🄷
(931) 728-7551. **Call for rates.** 126 Expressway Dr 37355. I-24, exit 114, just w. Int corridors. **Pets:** Accepted. ⊠ Ꭾᴹ 📱 🖥 ⤖

ᗩᗩᗩ ▼▼▼ **Ramada Limited** 🄷
(931) 728-0800. **$69-$99.** 2314 Hillsboro Blvd 37355. I-24, exit 114, just n. Ext corridors. **Pets:** Medium, other species. $10 daily fee/pet. Designated rooms, no service, supervision. (SAVE) ⊠ 📱 🖥 ⤖

MARTIN

▼▼ **Days Inn** 🄷
(731) 587-9577. **$63-$199.** 800 University St 38237. Jct US 431 and 43 Bypass. Ext corridors. **Pets:** Medium. $10 daily fee/pet. Service with restrictions, supervision. (ASK) ⊠ 📱 🖥 ⤖

MARYVILLE

▼▼ **LuxBury Inn & Suites** Ⓜ ❀
(865) 983-9839. **$69-$99.** 805 Foothills Mall Dr 37801. Jct US 321. Ext corridors. **Pets:** Small, dogs only. $25 one-time fee/pet. Designated rooms, service with restrictions, supervision. (ASK) ⊠ Ꭾᴹ 📱 🖥

MCKENZIE

ᗩᗩᗩ ▼▼▼ **Best Western Inn McKenzie** 🄷
(731) 352-1083. **$64-$68, 3 day notice.** 16180 N Highland Ave 38201. Jct US 79 and SR 22, just s. Ext corridors. **Pets:** Small, other species. $10 daily fee/pet. Designated rooms, service with restrictions, supervision.
(SAVE) ⊠ 📱 🖥 ⤖

MCMINNVILLE

ᗩᗩᗩ ▼▼▼ **Best Western Tree City Inn** 🄷
(931) 473-2159. **$67-$70.** 809 Sparta Hwy 37110. Jct US 70 S Bypass and Red Rd, 1 mi s, follow signs. Ext corridors. **Pets:** Medium, dogs only. $10 daily fee/pet. Designated rooms, service with restrictions, supervision.
(SAVE) ⊠ 📱 🖥 ⤖

MEMPHIS METROPOLITAN AREA

COLLIERVILLE

▼▼▼ **Hampton Inn Collierville** 🄷
(901) 854-9400. **$99-$139.** 1280 W Poplar Ave 38017. 0.9 mi w of jct CR 175 on US 72. Int corridors. **Pets:** Accepted. ⊠ Ꭾᴹ 🖥 ⤖

CORDOVA

▼▼ **Quality Suites-Cordova** 🄷
(901) 386-4600. **$79-$159.** 8166 Varnavas Dr 38018. I-40, exit 16, 0.3 mi s on Germantown Pkwy, then e. Int corridors. **Pets:** Accepted.
⊠ 📱 🖥 ⤖

▼▼ **StudioPLUS-Memphis-Cordova** 🄷
(901) 754-4030. **$62-$100.** 8110 Cordova Centre Dr 38016. I-40, exit 16, 0.8 mi s. Int corridors. **Pets:** Other species. $25 daily fee/room. Designated rooms, service with restrictions, crate.
(ASK) ⊠ 📱 🖥 ⤖

GERMANTOWN

ᗩᗩᗩ ▼▼▼ **Comfort Inn & Suites-Germantown** 🄷
(901) 757-7800. **Call for rates.** 7787 Wolf River Blvd 38138. I-40, exit 16, 5 mi s on Germantown Pkwy to Wolf River Blvd, then just w. Int corridors. **Pets:** $25 one-time fee/room. Service with restrictions, crate.
(SAVE) ⊠ Ꭾᴹ 📱 🖥 ⤖

▼▼▼ **Homewood Suites by Hilton-Germantown** 🄷
(901) 751-2500. **$129-$149.** 7855 Wolf River Blvd 38138. I-40, exit 16, 5.7 mi s on Germantown Pkwy, then just e. Int corridors. **Pets:** Large. $50 one-time fee/room. Service with restrictions, crate.
⊠ 📱 🖥 ⤖

▼▼▼ **Residence Inn by Marriott** 🄷
(901) 752-0900. **$125-$153.** 9314 Poplar Pike 38138. I-240, exit 15 (Poplar Ave), 7 mi e. Int corridors. **Pets:** Other species. $100 one-time fee/room. Service with restrictions, supervision.
⊠ Ꭾᴹ 📱 🖥 ⤖ ⊠

MEMPHIS

▼▼▼▼ **Baymont Inn & Suites Memphis East** 🄷
(901) 377-2233. **Call for rates.** 6020 Shelby Oaks Dr 38134. I-40, exit 12, just n. Int corridors. **Pets:** Accepted. ⊠ 📱 🖥 ⤖

ᗩᗩᗩ ▼▼▼ **Best Western Executive Inn** 🄷
(901) 312-7000. **$59-$85.** 3105 Millbranch Rd 38116. I-240, exit 24, just s. Ext corridors. **Pets:** Accepted. (SAVE) ⊠ 📱 🖥 ⤖

ᗩᗩᗩ ▼▼▼ **Best Western Travelers Inn** 🄷
(901) 363-8430. **$66-$86.** 5024 US Hwy 78 38118. I-240, exit 21 (US 78), 6 mi s. Ext corridors. **Pets:** Medium, other species. $15 daily fee/pet. Designated rooms, service with restrictions. (SAVE) ⊠ 📱 🖥 ⤖

▼▼▼▼ **Drury Inn & Suites-Memphis Northeast** 🅷
(901) 373-8200. **$80-$159.** 1556 Sycamore View 38134. I-40, exit 12, just n. Int corridors. **Pets:** Other species. No service, supervision.
🅰🆂🅺 ⊠ 🔒 💻 ⇒

▼▼▼ **Extended StayAmerica-Memphis-Poplar Ave.** 🅷
(901) 685-7575. **$62-$81.** 6325 Quail Hollow 38120. I-240, exit 15 (Poplar Ave), 0.4 mi e, then just n on Briarcrest. Int corridors. **Pets:** Other species. $25 daily fee/room. Designated rooms, service with restrictions, crate. 🅰🆂🅺 ⊠ 🕭 🔒 💻

▼▼▼ **Hilton Memphis** 🅷
(901) 684-6664. **$109-$239.** 939 Ridge Lake Blvd 38120. I-240, exit 15 (Poplar Ave), just e, then n under overpass. Int corridors. **Pets:** Accepted.
⊠ 🕭 🔒 💻 🍽 ⇒

▼▼ **Homestead Studio Suites Hotel-Memphis/Poplar Ave** 🅷
(901) 767-5522. **$67-$76.** 6500 Poplar Ave 38119. I-240, exit 15 (Poplar Ave), 1 mi e. Int corridors. **Pets:** Other species. $25 daily fee/room. Designated rooms, service with restrictions, crate. 🅰🆂🅺 ⊠ 🕭 🔒 💻

▼▼▼▼ **Homewood Suites by Hilton–Hacks Cross** 🅷
(901) 758-5018. **$119-$139.** 3583 Hacks Cross Rd 38125. I-240, exit 16, 4 mi e on SR 385, then 1 mi n. Int corridors. **Pets:** Accepted.
⊠ 🕭 🔒 💻 ⇒

▼▼▼ **Homewood Suites by Hilton–Poplar** 🅷
(901) 763-0500. **$139-$159.** 5811 Poplar Ave 38119. I-240, exit 15 (Poplar Ave). Ext/int corridors. **Pets:** Accepted. ⊠ 🔒 💻 ⇒

🅰🅰🅰 ▼▼▼ **La Quinta Inn & Suites Memphis (Primacy Parkway)** 🅷 ☀
(901) 374-0330. **$65-$129.** 1236 Primacy Pkwy 38119. I-240, exit 15 (Poplar Ave), just e, s on Ridgeway, just w, then just s. Int corridors. **Pets:** Medium, other species. Service with restrictions, supervision.
🅰🆂🅺 ⊠ 🕭 🔒 💻 ⇒

🅰🅰🅰 ▼▼▼▼ **La Quinta Inn & Suites Sycamore View-Memphis** 🅷 ☀
(901) 381-0044. **$80-$180.** 6069 Macon Cove 38134. I-40, exit 12, just s. Int corridors. **Pets:** Medium, other species. Service with restrictions, supervision. 🆂🅰🆅🅴 ⊠ 🕭 🔒 💻 ⇒

▼▼ **Quality Inn** 🅷
(901) 382-2323. **$70-$170.** 6068 Macon Cove Rd 38134. I-40, exit 12, just s. Ext/int corridors. **Pets:** Accepted. ⊠ 🕭 🔒 💻 ⇒

🅰🅰🅰 ▼▼▼ **Quality Inn Airport/Graceland** 🅷
(901) 345-3344. **$55-$100, 5 day notice.** 1581 E Brooks Rd 38116. I-55, exit 5A (Brooks Rd), 0.3 mi n. Ext corridors. **Pets:** Other species. $25 daily fee/pet. Service with restrictions, supervision.
🆂🅰🆅🅴 ⊠ 🔒 💻 ⇒

▼▼▼▼ **Residence Inn by Marriott Memphis Downtown** 🅷
(901) 578-3700. **$188-$230.** 110 Monroe Ave 38103. I-40, exit 1; I-55, exit Riverside Dr, 0.6 mi s, then just e. Int corridors. **Pets:** Accepted.
⊠ 🕭 🔒 💻 🐾

🅰🅰🅰 ▼▼▼▼ **Residence Inn by Marriott Memphis East** 🅷
(901) 685-9595. **$116-$142.** 6141 Poplar Pike 38119. I-240, exit 15 (Poplar Ave), 0.5 mi e. Int corridors. **Pets:** Accepted.
🆂🅰🆅🅴 ⊠ 🕭 🔒 💻 ⇒

▼▼▼ **Sleep Inn** 🅷
(901) 312-7777. **$66-$100.** 2855 Old Austin Peay Hwy 38128. I-40, exit 8. Int corridors. **Pets:** Accepted. ⊠ 🕭 🔒 💻 ⇒

▼▼▼ **Staybridge Suites** 🅷
(901) 682-1722. **$79-$89.** 1070 Ridge Lake Blvd 38120. I-240, exit 15 (Poplar Ave), just e, then n under overpass. Int corridors. **Pets:** Accepted.
🅰🆂🅺 ⊠ 🕭 🔒 💻 ⇒

🅰🅰🅰 ▼▼▼▼ **The Westin Memphis Beale Street** 🅷 ☀
(901) 334-5900. **Call for rates.** 170 Lt. George W. Lee Ave 38103. Jct S 3rd St and Lt. George W. Lee Ave. Int corridors. **Pets:** Medium, dogs only. Service with restrictions, supervision. 🆂🅰🆅🅴 ⊠ 🕭 💻 🍽

END METROPOLITAN AREA

MONTEAGLE

🅰🅰🅰 ▼▼▼ **Best Western Smoke House Lodge** 🅷
(931) 924-2091. **$60-$136.** 850 W Main St 37356. I-24, exit 134, just s. Ext corridors. **Pets:** Accepted. 🆂🅰🆅🅴 ⊠ 🔒 💻 🍽 ⇒ ⊠

▼▼▼ **Edgeworth Inn** 🅱🅱
(931) 924-4000. **$150-$200.** 19 Wilkins Ave 37356. I-24, exit 134, 0.4 mi e on US 41A, 2nd left through assembly gates, follow signs. Ext/int corridors. **Pets:** Accepted. 🅰🆂🅺 ⊠ 🔒 💻 🄯

MORRISTOWN

🅰🅰🅰 ▼▼▼ **Days Inn** 🅼
(423) 587-2200. **$42-$149, 7 day notice.** 2512 E Andrew Johnson Hwy 37814. I-81, exit 8, 6 mi n on US 25 E to exit 2B (Greenville-Morristown), then just w. Ext corridors. **Pets:** Small. $10 daily fee/pet. Service with restrictions, supervision. 🆂🅰🆅🅴 ⊠ 🕭 🔒 💻 ⇒

🅰🅰🅰 ▼▼▼▼ **Holiday Inn Morristown Conference Center** 🅷
(423) 587-2400. **$105-$199.** 5435 S Davy Crockett Pkwy 37813. I-81, exit 8, just n. Int corridors. **Pets:** Accepted.
🆂🅰🆅🅴 ⊠ 🕭 🔒 💻 🍽 ⇒

▼▼▼ **Ramada Morristown** 🅷
(423) 581-8700. **$69-$200.** 3304 W Andrew Johnson Hwy 37814. 2.5 mi w on US 11 E. Ext corridors. **Pets:** Large, other species. $5 daily fee/pet. Service with restrictions. 🅰🆂🅺 ⊠ 🕭 🔒 💻 ⇒

▼▼ **Super 8** 🅼
(423) 318-8888. **$40-$60.** 5400 S Davy Crockett Pkwy 37813. I-81, exit 8, just n. Int corridors. **Pets:** Large, other species. $9 one-time fee/pet. Designated rooms, service with restrictions, supervision.
🅰🆂🅺 ⊠ 🔒 💻

MOUNT JULIET

🅰🅰🅰 ▼▼▼ **Quality Inn & Suites** 🅷
(615) 773-3600. **Call for rates.** 1000 Hershel Dr 37122. I-40, exit 226, just s. Int corridors. **Pets:** Small, other species. $25 one-time fee/room. Service with restrictions. 🆂🅰🆅🅴 ⊠ 🔒 💻 ⇒

MURFREESBORO

▼▼▼ **Baymont Inn & Suites** 🅼 ☀
(615) 896-1172. **$80-$140.** 2230 Armory Dr 37129. I-24, exit 78B, just n. Ext corridors. **Pets:** Large. $15 daily fee/room. Designated rooms, service with restrictions, crate. 🅰🆂🅺 ⊠ 🕭 🔒 💻 ⇒

Best Western Chaffin Inn M
(615) 895-3818. **$66-$131.** 168 Chaffin Pl 37129. I-24, exit 78B. Ext corridors. **Pets:** Medium. $15 daily fee/pet. Service with restrictions, crate.

DoubleTree Hotel Murfreesboro H
(615) 895-5555. **$99-$159.** 1850 Old Fort Pkwy 37129. I-24, exit 78B. Int corridors. **Pets:** $50 one-time fee/room. Designated rooms, service with restrictions, crate.

Hampton Inn & Suites H
(615) 890-2424. **Call for rates.** 325 N Thompson Ln 37129. I-24, exit 78B, just n. Int corridors. **Pets:** Large, other species. $25 daily fee/room. Service with restrictions, crate.

Quality Inn Murfreesboro H
(615) 890-1006. **Call for rates.** 2135 S Church St 37130. I-24, exit 81 westbound; exit 81B eastbound. Int corridors. **Pets:** Other species. $10 one-time fee/room. Service with restrictions, crate.

Vista Inn and Suites H
(615) 848-9030. **$55-$200, 3 day notice.** 118 Westgate Blvd 37128. I-24, exit 81A eastbound; exit 81 westbound. Int corridors. **Pets:** Medium, other species. $10 daily fee/pet. Service with restrictions, supervision.

NASHVILLE METROPOLITAN AREA

ANTIOCH

Holiday Inn-The Crossings H
(615) 731-2361. **$94.** 201 Crossings Pl 37013. I-24, exit 60, 0.5 mi e. Int corridors. **Pets:** Other species. $25 one-time fee/room. Service with restrictions, supervision.

GOODLETTSVILLE

Best Western Fairwinds Inn H
(615) 851-1067. **Call for rates.** 100 Northcreek Blvd 37072. I-65, exit 97 (Long Hollow Pike), 0.5 mi e. Ext corridors. **Pets:** Medium. $10 daily fee/pet. Service with restrictions, crate.

Holiday Inn Express Hotel & Suites H
(615) 851-1891. **$100-$105.** 120 Cartwright St 37072. I-65, exit 97 (Long Hollow Pike), just w. Int corridors. **Pets:** Accepted.

Quality Inn H
(615) 859-5400. **Call for rates.** 925 Conference Dr 37072. I-65, exit 97 (Long Hollow Pike), 0.6 mi e. Ext corridors. **Pets:** Accepted.

Rodeway Inn M
(615) 859-1416. **Call for rates.** 650 Wade Cir 37072. I-65, exit 96, just ne. Ext corridors. **Pets:** Accepted.

NASHVILLE

Airport Super 8 Nashville H
(615) 889-8887. **$69-$92.** 720 Royal Pkwy 37214. I-40, exit 216C (Donelson Pike N), 0.5 mi n, then just e. Int corridors. **Pets:** Accepted.

Baymont Inn & Suites Nashville-West H
(615) 353-0700. **$80-$100, 15 day notice.** 5612 Lenox Ave 37209. I-40, exit 204. Int corridors. **Pets:** Accepted.

Best Western Music City Inn H
(615) 641-7721. **$49-$85, 5 day notice.** 13010 Old Hickory Blvd 37013. I-24, exit 62, just n. Ext corridors. **Pets:** Small. $25 one-time fee/room. Designated rooms, supervision.

Best Western Music Row H
(615) 242-1631. **$79-$299.** 1407 Division St 37203. I-40, exit 209B (Broadway), just w around circle, then just e. Int corridors. **Pets:** Small, other species. $10 daily fee/pet. Service with restrictions.

Comfort Inn Opryland H
(615) 889-0086. **$65-$110.** 2516 Music Valley Dr 37214. I-40, exit 215 (Briley Pkwy), 4 mi n; I-65, exit 90, exit McGavock Pike off Briley Pkwy. Int corridors. **Pets:** Small. $25 one-time fee/room. Designated rooms, service with restrictions.

Crossland Studios-Nashville-Airport-Briley Pkwy H
(615) 366-0559. **$53-$62.** 1210 Murfreesboro Rd 37217. I-40, exit 215 (Briley Pkwy), 2 mi s to exit 4, then 0.8 mi n. Ext corridors. **Pets:** Other species. $25 daily fee/room. Designated rooms, service with restrictions, crate.

Days Inn H
(615) 889-0090. **$60-$105.** 2460 Music Valley Dr 37214. I-40, exit 215B (Briley Pkwy), 4 mi n to exit 11 (McGavock Pike). Int corridors. **Pets:** Accepted.

Drury Inn & Suites-Nashville Airport H
(615) 902-0400. **$95-$164.** 555 Donelson Pike 37214. I-40, exit 216 (Donelson Pike). Int corridors. **Pets:** Other species. No service, supervision.

Extended StayAmerica-Nashville-Vanderbilt H
(615) 383-7490. **$81-$91.** 3311 West End Ave 37203. I-440, exit 1A, then just e. Int corridors. **Pets:** Other species. $25 daily fee/room. Designated rooms, service with restrictions, crate.

GuestHouse International Inn & Suites H
(615) 885-4030. **$109-$169.** 2420 Music Valley Dr 37214. Briley Pkwy, exit 12, 0.3 mi n, then 0.3 mi n. Int corridors. **Pets:** Other species. $25 one-time fee/room. Designated rooms, service with restrictions, crate.

Hampton Inn & Suites Vanderbilt Elliston Place H
(615) 320-6060. **Call for rates.** 2330 Elliston Pl 37203. I-40, exit 209A (Church St), 3.5 mi w. Int corridors. **Pets:** Accepted.

Hampton Inn Vanderbilt H
(615) 329-1144. **Call for rates.** 1919 West End Ave 37203. I-40, exit 209B (Broadway), 0.3 mi w. Int corridors. **Pets:** Medium, other species.

The Hermitage Hotel H
(615) 244-3121. **Call for rates.** 231 6th Ave N 37219. Corner of Union St; center. Int corridors. **Pets:** Accepted.

Hilton Nashville Downtown H
(615) 620-1000. **$179-$399.** 121 4th Ave S 37201. Center. Int corridors. **Pets:** Medium, other species. $75 one-time fee/room. Designated rooms, service with restrictions, crate.

Homestead Studio Suites Hotel-Nashville/Airport H
(615) 316-9020. **$57-$76.** 727 McGavock Pike 37214. I-40, exit 215B (Briley Pkwy), 1 mi n to exit 7 (Elm Hill Pike), then just e. Ext corridors. **Pets:** Other species. $25 daily fee/room. Designated rooms, service with restrictions, crate.

Homewood Suites by Hilton H
(615) 884-8111. **$119-$139.** 2640 Elm Hill Pike 37214. I-40, exit 216C (Donelson Pike). Int corridors. **Pets:** Accepted.

▼▼▼◆ **Homewood Suites Nashville Downtown** ⛔
(615) 742-5550. **$149-$189.** 706 Church St 37203. Jct 7th Ave N and Church St. Int corridors. **Pets:** Accepted. ⊠ 🚫 ❚ 🖳

▼▼▼▼ **Hotel Indigo-Nashville West End** ⛔
(615) 329-4200. **$109-$399.** 1719 West End Ave 37203. I-40/65, exit 209B (Broadway), 0.4 mi w. Int corridors. **Pets:** Accepted.
ⒶⓈⓀ ⊠ 🚫 ❚ 🖳 🍽

ⒶⒶⒶ ▼▼▼▼ **Hotel Preston** ⛔
(615) 361-5900. **$109-$219, 3 day notice.** 733 Briley Pkwy 37217. I-40, exit 215 (Briley Pkwy), just s. Int corridors. **Pets:** Small. $49 one-time fee/room. Designated rooms, service with restrictions, supervision.
ⓈⒶⓋⒺ ⊠ ❚ 🖳 🍽 🏊

▼▼ **La Quinta Inn & Suites Nashville-Airport** ⛔ ❀
(615) 885-3100. **$59-$119.** 531 Donelson Pike 37214. I-40, exit 216C (Donelson Pike), 0.3 mi n. Int corridors. **Pets:** Medium, other species. Service with restrictions, supervision. ⒶⓈⓀ ⊠ ❚ 🖳 🏊

ⒶⒶⒶ ▼▼▼ ▼▼▼ **Loews Vanderbilt Hotel Nashville** ⛔
(615) 320-1700. **$169-$459.** 2100 West End Ave 37203. I-40, exit 209B (Broadway), 1.3 mi w. Int corridors. **Pets:** Accepted.
ⓈⒶⓋⒺ ⊠ ❚ 🖳 🍽 🏊

ⒶⒶⒶ ▼▼▼ **Microtel Inn & Suites** ⛔
(615) 662-0004. **$63-$94.** 100 Coley Davis Ct 37221. I-40, exit 196. Int corridors. **Pets:** Medium. $15 daily fee/pet. Service with restrictions, supervision. ⓈⒶⓋⒺ ⊠ ❚ 🖳 🏊

ⒶⒶⒶ ▼▼▼▼ **Radisson Hotel Nashville Airport** ⛔
(615) 889-9090. **$179.** 1112 Airport Center Dr 37214. I-40, exit 216C (Donelson Pike N), 0.5 mi n, then just e. Int corridors. **Pets:** Accepted.
ⓈⒶⓋⒺ ⊠ 🚫 ❚ 🖳 🍽 🏊

ⒶⒶⒶ ▼▼▼▼ **Radisson Hotel Opryland** ⛔
(615) 889-0800. **$109-$119.** 2401 Music Valley Dr 37214. Briley Pkwy, exit 12B. Ext/int corridors. **Pets:** Accepted.
ⓈⒶⓋⒺ ⊠ 🚫 ❚ 🖳 🍽 🏊

ⒶⒶⒶ ▼▼▼ **Red Roof Inn Airport** Ⓜ
(615) 872-0735. **$50-$90, 14 day notice.** 510 Claridge Dr 37214. I-40, exit 216C (Donelson Pike), 0.3 mi n. Ext corridors. **Pets:** Large. Service with restrictions, crate. ⓈⒶⓋⒺ ⊠ ❚

ⒶⒶⒶ ▼▼▼▼ **Residence Inn** ⛔
(615) 889-8600. **$149-$182.** 2300 Elm Hill Pike 37214. I-40, exit 215B (Briley Pkwy), 1.5 mi n. Ext corridors. **Pets:** Accepted.
ⓈⒶⓋⒺ ⊠ ❚ 🖳 🏊

ⒶⒶⒶ ▼▼▼▼ **Sheraton Music City Hotel** ⛔ ❀
(615) 885-2200. **Call for rates.** 777 McGavock Pike 37214. I-40, exit 215B (Briley Pkwy), 1 mi n to exit 7 (Elm Hill Pike), 0.5 mi e, then s. Int corridors. **Pets:** Large, dogs only. Service with restrictions, supervision.
ⓈⒶⓋⒺ ⊠ 🚫 ❚ 🖳 🍽 🏊 🏊

ⒶⒶⒶ ▼▼▼ **Sheraton Nashville Downtown Hotel** ⛔ ❀
(615) 259-2000. **$109-$289.** 623 Union St 37219. I-40, exit 209, just s of State Capitol. Int corridors. **Pets:** Medium, dogs only. Service with restrictions, supervision. ⓈⒶⓋⒺ ⊠ 🚫 ❚ 🖳 🍽 🏊 🏊

ⒶⒶⒶ ▼▼ **Sleep Inn** ⛔
(615) 227-8686. **Call for rates.** 3200 Dickerson Pike 37207. I-65, exit 90A, just s. Int corridors. **Pets:** Accepted. ⓈⒶⓋⒺ ⊠ 🚫 ❚ 🖳

ⒶⒶⒶ ▼▼▼ **Super 8-West** ⛔
(615) 356-6005. **$60-$180.** 6924 Charlotte Pike 37209. I-40, exit 201, just w. Ext corridors. **Pets:** Medium. $10 daily fee/pet. Service with restrictions, supervision. ⓈⒶⓋⒺ ⊠ ❚ 🖳

END METROPOLITAN AREA

NEWPORT

ⒶⒶⒶ ▼▼▼ **Best Western Newport Inn** Ⓜ
(423) 623-8713. **$50-$170, 7 day notice.** 1015 Cosby Hwy 37821. I-40, exit 435, just w. Ext corridors. **Pets:** Accepted.
ⓈⒶⓋⒺ ⊠ 🚫 ❚ 🖳

ⒶⒶⒶ ▼▼▼ **Comfort Inn** ⛔
(423) 623-5355. **$54-$160.** 1149 Smokey Mountain Ln 37821. I-40, exit 432B. Int corridors. **Pets:** Other species. $10 daily fee/pet. Designated rooms, service with restrictions, supervision.
ⓈⒶⓋⒺ ⊠ 🚫 ❚ 🖳 🏊

ⒶⒶⒶ ▼▼▼ **Motel 6-4090** Ⓜ
(423) 623-1850. **$35-$60.** 255 Heritage Blvd 37822. I-40, exit 435. Int corridors. **Pets:** Other species. Service with restrictions, supervision.
ⓈⒶⓋⒺ ⊠ 🚫 ❚ 🖳 🏊

OAK RIDGE

▼▼▼▼ **DoubleTree Oak Ridge** ⛔ ❀
(865) 481-2468. **$99-$189.** 215 S Illinois Ave 37830. 0.3 mi se of SR 95 on SR 62. Int corridors. **Pets:** Medium, other species. $50 one-time fee/room. Service with restrictions, supervision.
⊠ 🚫 ❚ 🖳 🍽 🏊

▼▼▼▼ **Jameson Inn** ⛔
(865) 483-6809. **$89-$94.** 216 S Rutgers Ave 37830. Jct SR 95 and 62, 0.9 mi se on SR 62 to Rutgers Ave, then 0.7 mi n. Int corridors. **Pets:** Small. $15 daily fee/room. Designated rooms, no service, supervision. ⒶⓈⓀ ⊠ 🚫 ❚ 🖳 🏊

OOLTEWAH

▼▼▼ **Super 8** Ⓜ
(423) 238-5951. **$45-$65.** 5111 Hunter Rd 37363. I-75, exit 11, just w. Ext corridors. **Pets:** Accepted. ⒶⓈⓀ ⊠ ❚ 🖳

PICKWICK DAM

▼▼▼ **Pickwick Landing State Resort Park Inn** ⛔
(731) 689-3135. **$68-$82.** 220 Playground Loop 38365. Jct US 57 and SR 128; in State Park. Ext/int corridors. **Pets:** Accepted.
ⒶⓈⓀ ⊠ 🚫 ❚ 🖳 🍽 🏊 🏊

PIGEON FORGE

▼▼▼ **Blackberry Ridge-Accommodations by Sunset Cottage** 🅒🅐
(865) 429-8478. **Call for rates.** 3630 S River Rd 37863. Just e of jct US 441 at traffic light 8, then just n. Ext corridors. **Pets:** $50 one-time fee/pet. Designated rooms, no service, crate. ⊠ ❚ 🖳

▼▼▼ **Briarstone Inn** Ⓜ
(865) 453-4225. **Call for rates.** 3626 Parkway 37868. On US 441; between traffic lights 7 and 8. Ext corridors. **Pets:** Accepted.
⊠ ❚ 🖳 🏊

ⒶⒶⒶ ▼▼▼▼ **Eden Crest Vacation Rentals** 🅒🅐 ❀
(865) 774-0059. **$110-$395.** 652 Wears Valley Rd 37863. US 321 to light 3, just w. Ext corridors. **Pets:** Dogs only. $100 one-time fee/pet. Designated rooms, service with restrictions, crate. ⓈⒶⓋⒺ ⊠ ❚ 🖳 🏊

◇◇◇ ▼▼▼ **Grand Resort Hotel & Convention Center** H
(865) 453-1000. **$49-$149, 3 day notice.** 3171 Parkway 37863-0010. On US 441 at traffic light 6. Ext/int corridors. **Pets:** Accepted.
[SAVE] [X] [&M] [🛏] [💻] [🍴] [⇨]

▼▼▼ **Hampton Inn & Suites** H ❄
(865) 428-1600. **$64-$229.** 2025 Parkway 37863. On US 441 at traffic light 0. Int corridors. **Pets:** Large. $20 daily fee/room. Designated rooms, service with restrictions, crate. [X] [&M] [🛏] [💻] [⇨]

▼▼◇ **La Quinta Inn** H ❄
(865) 429-3010. **$55-$135.** 219 Emert St 37863. Just w of jct US 441; between traffic lights 7 and 8. Int corridors. **Pets:** Medium, other species. Service with restrictions, supervision. [ASK] [X] [&M] [🛏] [💻] [⇨]

▼▼ **Microtel Suites at Music Road** H
(865) 453-1116. **$35-$115.** 2045 Parkway 37863. On US 441, just s of traffic light 0. Int corridors. **Pets:** Accepted.
[ASK] [X] [&M] [🛏] [💻] [⇨]

◇◇◇ ▼ **Motel 6 #4021** M
(865) 908-1244. **$29-$99.** 336 Henderson Chapel Rd 37863. Jct US 441, just w at traffic light 1. Int corridors. **Pets:** Other species. Service with restrictions, supervision. [SAVE] [X] [&M] [⇨]

▼▼ **National Parks Resort Lodge** H
(865) 453-4106. **Call for rates.** 2385 Parkway 37863. On US 441 at traffic light 1. Int corridors. **Pets:** Accepted. [X] [🛏] [💻] [⇨]

◇◇◇ ▼▼▼ **Ramada Inn** M
(865) 453-1823. **$35-$149.** 4010 Parkway 37863. On US 441; between traffic lights 8 and 10. Ext corridors. **Pets:** Small. $10 daily fee/room. Designated rooms, service with restrictions, crate. [SAVE] [X] [🛏] [💻] [⇨]

◇◇◇ ▼▼▼▼ **Red Roof Inn Pigeon Forge** H ❄
(865) 908-6633. **Call for rates.** 2510 Parkway 37863. Jct US 441, just w on Community Center Dr at traffic light 2B. Int corridors. **Pets:** Dogs only. $25 one-time fee/room. Designated rooms, service with restrictions, supervision. [SAVE] [X] [&M] [🛏] [💻] [⇨]

◇◇◇ ▼▼◇ **Smoky Shadows Motel, Tower & Conference Center** H
(865) 453-7155. **$39-$119, 3 day notice.** 4215 Parkway 37863. On US 441, just n of traffic light 10. Ext/int corridors. **Pets:** Accepted.
[SAVE] [X] [&M] [🛏] [💻] [⇨]

▼▼◇▼ **Starr Crest Resort Cabin Rentals** CA
(865) 429-0156. **$99-$1269, 30 day notice.** 1431 Upper Middle Creek Rd 37876. I-40, US 441, e at traffic light 8, 1.5 mi on Dollywood Ln. Ext corridors. **Pets:** Accepted. [ASK] [X] [🛏] [💻] [⇨]

POWELL
◇◇◇ ▼▼◇ **Super 8 of Powell** M
(865) 938-5501. **$60-$130.** 323 E Emory Rd 37849. I-75, exit 112. Ext corridors. **Pets:** Very small, dogs only. $10 daily fee/pet. Designated rooms, service with restrictions, supervision. [SAVE] [X] [🛏] [💻] [⇨]

PULASKI
▼▼ **Richland Inn** H
(931) 363-0006. **Call for rates.** 1020 W College St 38478. On US 64, 1 mi w of jct US 31. Ext corridors. **Pets:** Accepted. [X] [🛏] [💻]

▼▼ **Super 8** H
(931) 363-4501. **Call for rates.** I-65 & Hwy 64, Exit 14 East 38478. I-65, exit 14, just e. Ext corridors. **Pets:** Accepted. [X] [🛏] [💻] [⇨]

ROGERSVILLE
▼▼◇▼ **Comfort Inn & Suites** H
(423) 272-8700. **Call for rates.** 128 James Richardson Ln 37857. US 11 W. Int corridors. **Pets:** Accepted. [X] [&M] [🛏] [💻] [⇨]

▼◇ **Quality Inn** H
(423) 272-1842. **$80-$100, 14 day notice.** 7139 Hwy 11 W 37857. Jct SR 66 and US 11, 0.5 mi sw. Int corridors. **Pets:** Accepted.
[X] [&M] [🛏] [💻] [⇨]

SELMER
▼▼ **America's Best Inn** H
(731) 645-8880. **$50-$65.** 644 Mulberry Ave 38375. Jct SR 64 and 45, just s on SR 45. Ext corridors. **Pets:** Dogs only. $10 daily fee/pet. Designated rooms, service with restrictions, supervision.
[ASK] [X] [🛏] [💻] [⇨]

SEVIERVILLE
▼▼▼ **Baymont Inn & Suites** H
(865) 933-9448. **$60-$130.** 2863 Winfield Dunn Pkwy 37764. I-40, exit 407, 2.3 mi s on SR 66. Int corridors. **Pets:** Large. $10 daily fee/pet. Service with restrictions. [ASK] [X] [&M] [🛏] [💻] [⇨]

▼▼▼▼ **La Quinta Sevierville** H ❄
(865) 933-3339. **$50-$110.** 2428 Winfield Dunn Pkwy 37764. I-40, exit 407, 3.2 mi on SR 66. Int corridors. **Pets:** Medium, other species. Service with restrictions, supervision. [ASK] [X] [&M] [🛏] [💻] [⇨]

◇◇◇ ▼▼◇ **Sleep Inn** H
(865) 429-0484. **$44-$96.** 1020 Parkway 37862. On US 441, 1.2 mi s of jct US 411. Int corridors. **Pets:** Large, other species. $10 daily fee/room. Service with restrictions, crate. [SAVE] [X] [&M] [🛏] [💻] [⇨]

SHELBYVILLE
◇◇◇ ▼▼◇▼ **Best Western Celebration Inn & Suites** H
(931) 684-2378. **$70-$199.** 724 Madison St 37160. Jct SR 231 and US 41. Ext corridors. **Pets:** Medium. $15 daily fee/pet. Service with restrictions, crate. [SAVE] [X] [🛏] [💻] [⇨]

SWEETWATER
◇◇◇ ▼▼◇ **Comfort Inn West** H ❄
(423) 337-3353. **Call for rates.** 249 Hwy 68 37874. I-75, exit 60, just e. Ext/int corridors. **Pets:** Small. $10 daily fee/pet. Designated rooms, service with restrictions, supervision. [SAVE] [X] [🛏] [💻] [⇨]

◇◇◇ ▼▼◇ **Econo Lodge** M ❄
(423) 337-6646. **Call for rates.** 731 S Main St 37874. On US 11, jct SR 68. Ext/int corridors. **Pets:** Small. $10 daily fee/pet. Designated rooms, service with restrictions, supervision. [SAVE] [X] [🛏] [💻] [⇨]

▼▼◇ **Magnuson Hotel** H
(423) 337-3541. **$69-$99.** 1421 Murray's Chapel Rd 37874. I-75, exit 60, just w. Ext/int corridors. **Pets:** Small. $15 one-time fee/room. Designated rooms, service with restrictions, supervision.
[ASK] [X] [🛏] [💻] [🍴] [⇨]

◇◇◇ ▼▼◇ **Quality Inn & Suites** H ❄
(423) 337-4900. **Call for rates.** 1116 Hwy 68 37874. I-75, exit 60, just w. Int corridors. **Pets:** Other species. $20 one-time fee/pet. Service with restrictions. [SAVE] [X] [&M] [🛏] [💻] [⇨]

TOWNSEND
▼▼ **Econo Lodge** M
(865) 448-9000. **$50-$160.** 7824 E Lamar Alexander Pkwy 37882. On US 321, 0.7 mi s of jct SR 73. Ext corridors. **Pets:** Accepted.
[X] [&M] [🛏] [💻] [⇨]

▼▼◇ **Valley View Lodge** M
(865) 448-2237. **$45-$100, 3 day notice.** 7726 E Lamar Alexander Pkwy 37882. On US 321, 1.1 mi s of jct SR 73. Ext corridors.
Pets: Accepted. [ASK] [X] [&M] [🛏] [💻] [⇨] [X]

TULLAHOMA
▼▼ **Jameson Inn** H
(931) 455-7891. **$83-$90.** 2113 N Jackson St 37388. 3 mi n on SR 41A (N Jackson St). Ext corridors. **Pets:** Small, dogs only. $15 daily fee/pet. Service with restrictions. [ASK] [X] [🛏] [💻] [⇨]

VONORE

▼▼▼ **Grand Vista Hotel & Suites** ⓗ

(423) 884-6200. **$79-$149.** 117 Grand Vista Dr 37885. I-75, exit 172, 14 mi e. Int corridors. **Pets:** $10 daily fee/pet. Designated rooms, service with restrictions, supervision. [A$K] [✕] [&M] [❚] [▣] [➾]

WHITE HOUSE

◈◈ ▼▼▼ **Holiday Inn Express** ⓗ

(615) 672-7200. **$89-$109.** 206 Knight Cir 37188. I-65, exit 108, just e. Int corridors. **Pets:** Medium. $25 one-time fee/room. Service with restrictions, crate. [SAVE] [✕] [&M] [❚] [▣] [➾]

Quality Inn ⓗ

▼▼ **Quality Inn** ⓗ

(615) 672-7000. **$57-$69.** 354 Hester Dr 37188. I-65, exit 108, just e. Ext corridors. **Pets:** Medium. $5 one-time fee/pet. Designated rooms, service with restrictions, crate. [SAVE] [✕] [&M] [❚] [▣] [➾]

WHITEVILLE

▼▼ **Super 8** ⓗ

(731) 254-8884. **$50-$60.** 2040 Hwy 64 38075. US 64 and SR 179. Ext corridors. **Pets:** $5 daily fee/pet. Service with restrictions, supervision. [A$K] [✕] [&M] [❚] [▣]

CITY INDEX

ABILENE

Americas Best Value Inn **H**
(325) 673-5424. **$47-$60.** 1633 W Stamford St 79601. I-20, exit 285, 1 mi e on S Frontage Rd. Ext corridors. **Pets:** Accepted.
SAVE ⊠ 🛏 📺

Best Western Mall South **H**
(325) 695-1262. **$96-$100, 7 day notice.** 3950 Ridgemont Dr 79606. US 83/84, exit Buffalo Gap Rd to Ridgemont Dr, just w. Ext corridors. **Pets:** Medium. $30 daily fee/pet. Designated rooms, service with restrictions, crate. SAVE ⊠ 🛏 📺 ⇄

Comfort Suites University **H**
(325) 672-0338. **Call for rates.** 1902 E Overland Tr 79601. I-20, exit 288, on N Frontage Rd. Int corridors. **Pets:** Small. $30 one-time fee/ room. Designated rooms, service with restrictions, supervision.
SAVE ⊠ ⓜ 🛏 📺 ⇄

Frontier Inn **M**
(325) 677-2683. **$60-$100.** 3210 Pine St 79601. Jct I-20 and US 83 business route, exit 286A. Ext/int corridors. **Pets:** Accepted.
ASK ⊠ 🛏 📺 ⇄

Holiday Inn Express Mall South **H**
(325) 695-0500. **$99-$139.** 3112 S Clack 79606. US 83/277 and Southwest Dr, just e to Catclaw Dr, then just n. Int corridors. **Pets:** Medium, other species. $30 one-time fee/room. Designated rooms, service with restrictions, crate. SAVE ⊠ ⓜ 🛏 📺 ⇄

Knights Inn Civic Plaza **H**
(325) 676-0222. **$50-$80.** 505 Pine St 79601. Downtown. Ext corridors. **Pets:** $25 one-time fee/pet. No service, supervision.
SAVE ⊠ 🛏 📺 🍴 ⇄

La Quinta Inn Abilene **H** 🐾
(325) 676-1676. **$59-$129.** 3501 W Lake Rd 79601-1909. I-20, exit 286C. Ext corridors. **Pets:** Medium, other species. Service with restrictions, supervision. ASK ⊠ 🛏 📺 ⇄

Motel 6 Abilene #79 **M**
(325) 672-8462. **$45-$56.** 4951 W Stamford St 79603. I-20, exit 282, on eastbound frontage road. Ext corridors. **Pets:** Other species. Service with restrictions, supervision. ⊠ 🛏 ⇄

Quality Inn **H** 🐾
(325) 676-0203. **Call for rates.** 1758 E I-20 79601. I-20, exit 288, on N Frontage Rd. Ext corridors. **Pets:** Medium, other species. $20 one-time fee/pet. Service with restrictions, supervision. ⊠ 🛏 ⇄

Residence Inn by Marriott **H** 🐾
(325) 677-8700. **$143-$175.** 1641 Musgrave Blvd 79601. I-20, exit 288, on N Frontage Rd. Int corridors. **Pets:** Other species. $75 one-time fee/ room. Service with restrictions, crate. ⊠ ⓜ 🛏 📺 ⇄ ⊠

Super 8 **H** 🐾
(325) 701-4779. **$79-$109.** 4397 Sayles Blvd 79605. US 83/84 southbound, exit Buffalo Gap Rd, just e to Industrial Blvd, 0.5 mi e to Sayles, then just s; northbound, exit Buffalo Gap Rd, just e. Int corridors. **Pets:** Other species. $20 daily fee/pet. Designated rooms, service with restrictions, supervision. SAVE ⊠ 🛏 📺 ⇄

▼▼▼ Super 8 Abilene North **M**
(325) 673-5251. **$60-$95.** 1525 E I-20 79601. I-20, exit 288. Ext corridors. **Pets:** Accepted. [SAVE] [X] [🛏] [📺] [≈]

ALAMO

▼▼▼ La Quinta Inn & Suites **H** ❀
(956) 783-6955. **$69-$139.** 909 E Frontage Rd 78516. US 83, exit Alamo Rd. Int corridors. **Pets:** Medium, other species. Service with restrictions, supervision. [ASK] [X] [&M] [🛏] [📺] [≈]

▼▼▼ Super 8 **M**
(956) 787-9444. **Call for rates.** 714 N Alamo Rd 78516. US 83, exit FM 907, just n. Ext corridors. **Pets:** Accepted. [X] [🛏] [≈]

ALICE

▼ Days Inn **H**
(361) 664-6616. **$75-$120.** 555 N Johnson St 78332. On US 281 business route, n of Johnson St. Int corridors. **Pets:** Accepted.
[ASK] [X] [🛏] [📺] [≈]

▼▼▼ La Quinta Inn & Suites **H** ❀
(361) 661-1777. **$79-$139.** 2400 E Main 78332. 0.8 mi e of downtown. Int corridors. **Pets:** Medium, other species. Service with restrictions, supervision. [X] [&M] [🛏] [📺] [≈]

ALPINE

▲▲▲ ▼▼▼ Oak Tree Inn **H**
(432) 837-5711. **$59-$79.** 2407 E Holland (Hwy 90/67) 79830. US 90, 2 mi e. Int corridors. **Pets:** Other species. $10 daily fee/room. Service with restrictions. [SAVE] [X] [&M] [🛏] [📺]

ALVARADO

▼▼▼ Super 8 **H**
(817) 790-7378. **Call for rates.** 5445 S I-35W 76009. I-35W, exit 27A (US 67), just e to 1st traffic light on US 67, then 0.4 mi n on access road. Int corridors. **Pets:** Medium. $50 deposit/room, $10 daily fee/pet. Designated rooms, no service, supervision. [X] [&M] [🛏] [📺] [≈]

ALVIN

▼▼▼ Americas Best Value Inn & Suites **M**
(281) 331-0335. **$60-$70.** 1588 S Hwy 35 Loop 77511. Jct SR 35 and 6, 0.5 mi sw. Ext corridors. **Pets:** Medium. $15 daily fee/pet. Service with restrictions, crate. [ASK] [X] [🛏] [📺] [≈]

AMARILLO

▲▲▲ ▼▼▼▼ Ambassador Hotel **H** ❀
(806) 358-6161. **$99-$169.** 3100 I-40 W 79102. I-40, exit 68, just w on north frontage road. Int corridors. **Pets:** Large, other species. $50 one-time fee/pet. No service, crate. [SAVE] [X] [🛏] [📺] [🍴] [≈] [X]

▲▲▲ ▼▼▼ Baymont Inn & Suites **H**
(806) 356-6800. **$69-$179.** 3411 I-40 W 79109. I-40, exit 67, 0.3 mi e on south frontage road. Int corridors. **Pets:** Medium, other species. $15 daily fee/pet. Service with restrictions, crate. [SAVE] [X] [🛏] [📺] [≈]

▲▲▲ ▼▼▼ Best Western Amarillo Inn **H**
(806) 358-7861. **$80-$130.** 1610 Coulter Dr 79106. I-40, exit 65 (Coulter Dr), 0.6 mi n. Ext/int corridors. **Pets:** Accepted. [SAVE] [X] [🛏] [📺] [≈]

▲▲▲ ▼▼▼ Best Western Santa Fe **H**
(806) 372-1885. **$83-$96.** 4600 I-40 E 79103. I-40, exit 73 (Eastern St) eastbound; exit 73 (Bolton St) westbound, U-turn on south frontage road. Int corridors. **Pets:** Accepted. [SAVE] [X] [🛏] [📺] [≈]

▲▲▲ ▼▼▼ Big Texan Motel **M**
(806) 372-5000. **$59-$90, 14 day notice.** 7701 I-40 E 79118. I-40, exit 75 (Lakeside Dr), 0.3 mi w on north frontage road. Ext corridors.
Pets: Accepted. [SAVE] [X] [🛏] [📺] [🍴] [≈]

▼▼▼ Country Inn & Suites By Carlson, I-40 West **H**
(806) 356-9977. **$79-$229.** 2000 Soncy Rd 79121. I-40, exit 64, just n. Int corridors. **Pets:** $20 one-time fee/room. Service with restrictions, supervision. [ASK] [X] [🛏] [📺] [≈]

▲▲▲ ▼▼▼ Days Inn East Amarillo **H**
(806) 379-6255. **$50-$89.** 1701 I-40 E 79102. I-40, exit 71 (Ross-Osage), just w on north frontage road. Int corridors. **Pets:** Other species. $10 one-time fee/pet. Designated rooms, service with restrictions, supervision. [SAVE] [X] [🛏] [📺] [≈]

▼▼▼ Days Inn South **H**
(806) 468-7100. **Call for rates.** 8601 Canyon Dr 79110. I-27, exit 116, just n on east service road. Int corridors. **Pets:** Accepted. [X] [🛏] [≈]

▼▼▼ Drury Inn & Suites-Amarillo **H**
(806) 351-1111. **$95-$164.** 8540 W I-40 79121. I-40, exit 64. Int corridors. **Pets:** Other species. No service, supervision.
[ASK] [X] [&M] [🛏] [📺] [≈]

▼▼ Extended StayAmerica Amarillo West **H**
(806) 351-0117. **$65-$80.** 2100 Cinema Dr 79124. I-40, exit 64, just n. Int corridors. **Pets:** Other species. $25 daily fee/room. Designated rooms, service with restrictions, crate. [ASK] [X] [🛏] [📺]

▲▲▲ ▼▼▼▼ Hampton Inn **H**
(806) 372-1425. **$79-$119.** 1700 I-40 E 79103. I-40, exit 71 (Ross-Osage), just e on south frontage road. Int corridors. **Pets:** Large, other species. Service with restrictions, supervision. [SAVE] [X] [🛏] [📺] [≈]

▲▲▲ ▼▼▼▼ Holiday Inn-I-40 **H**
(806) 372-8741. **Call for rates.** 1911 I-40 at Ross-Osage 79102. I-40, exit 71 (Ross-Osage), on north frontage road. Int corridors. **Pets:** $25 one-time fee/room. Designated rooms, service with restrictions, supervision. [SAVE] [X] [🛏] [📺] [🍴] [≈]

▼▼▼▼ La Quinta Inn Amarillo (East/Airport Area) **H** ❀
(806) 373-7486. **Call for rates.** 1708 I-40 E 79103-2114. I-40, exit 71 (Ross-Osage), just e on south frontage road. Ext corridors. **Pets:** Medium, other species. Service with restrictions, supervision. [X] [🛏] [📺] [≈]

▼▼▼ La Quinta Inn Amarillo (West/Medical Center) **H** ❀
(806) 352-6311. **Call for rates.** 2108 S Coulter Dr 79106. I-40, exit 65 (Coulter Dr), just n. Ext corridors. **Pets:** Medium, other species. Service with restrictions, supervision. [X] [&M] [🛏] [📺] [≈]

▲▲▲ ▼▼▼ Magnuson Hotel **H** ❀
(806) 374-2020. **Call for rates.** 1620 I-40 E 79103. I-40, exit 71 (Ross-Osage), just e on south frontage road. Ext corridors. **Pets:** Small. $10 daily fee/pet. Designated rooms, no service, supervision.
[SAVE] [X] [🛏] [📺] [≈]

▲▲▲ ▼▼▼ Microtel Inn & Suites **H**
(806) 372-8373. **$59-$119.** 1501 S Ross St 79102. I-40, exit 71 (Ross-Osage), just n. Int corridors. **Pets:** $20 one-time fee/pet. Designated rooms, service with restrictions, supervision.
[SAVE] [X] [&M] [🛏] [📺] [≈]

▲▲▲ ▼▼▼▼ Quality Inn & Suites West **H**
(806) 358-7943. **Call for rates.** 6800 I-40 W 79106. I-40, exit 66 (Bell St), 0.5 mi w on north frontage road. Ext corridors. **Pets:** Medium, other species. $20 one-time fee/pet. Designated rooms, service with restrictions, crate. [SAVE] [X] [🛏] [📺]

▲▲▲ ▼▼▼ Quality Inn-East **H** ❀
(806) 376-9993. **$60-$80.** 1515 I-40 E 79102. I-40, exit 71 (Ross-Osage), just w on north frontage road. Ext corridors. **Pets:** Other species. $10 daily fee/pet. Designated rooms, service with restrictions, crate.
[SAVE] [X] [🛏] [📺] [≈]

▼▼▼ Residence Inn by Marriott **H**
(806) 354-2978. **$117-$143.** 6700 I-40 W 79106. I-40, exit 66 (Bell St), 0.5 mi w on north frontage road. Int corridors. **Pets:** Accepted.
[X] [&M] [🛏] [📺] [≈] [X]

♦♦ ▼▼▼ Travelodge West 🄷

(806) 353-3541. **$55-$59.** 2035 Paramount Blvd 79109. I-40, exit 68A (Paramount Blvd), just s. Ext corridors. **Pets:** Medium, other species. $5 daily fee/pet. Service with restrictions, crate. ⓢⒶⓥⒺ ✕ 🄷 🄿 ⇆

ANGLETON

♦♦ ▼▼▼ Best Western Angleton Inn 🄷

(979) 849-5822. **$80-$100.** 1809 N Velasco St 77515. Jct SR 35 and Business Rt SR 288, 1 mi n. Ext corridors. **Pets:** Small. $25 one-time fee/pet. Service with restrictions, supervision. ⓢⒶⓥⒺ ✕ 🄷 🄿 ⇆

ANTHONY

♦♦ ▼▼▼▼ Best Western Oasis of the Sun 🄷

(915) 886-3333. **$86-$99.** 9401 S Desert Blvd 79821. I-10, exit 0, just s. Ext corridors. **Pets:** Small. $20 daily fee/pet. Designated rooms, service with restrictions, supervision. ⓢⒶⓥⒺ ✕ 🄼 🄷 🄿 ⇆ ✕

ARLINGTON

▼▼▼ Arlington TownePlace Suites by Marriott 🄷

(817) 861-8728. **$143-$175.** 1709 E Lamar Blvd 76006. 2 mi w of SR 360. Int corridors. **Pets:** Accepted. ✕ 🄼 🄷 🄿 ✕

♦♦ ▼▼▼ Baymont Inn & Suites @ Six Flags Dr 🄷

(817) 633-2400. **Call for rates.** 2401 Diplomacy Dr 76011. I-30, exit 30 (SR 360), 0.5 mi s; off SR 360, exit Six Flags Dr northbound; exit Ave H/Lamar Blvd southbound, on southbound service road. Int corridors. **Pets:** Very small. $10 daily fee/pet. Service with restrictions, crate.

ⓢⒶⓥⒺ ✕ 🄼 🄷 🄿 ⇆

♦♦ ▼▼▼ Best Western Cooper Inn & Suites Ⓜ

(817) 784-9490. **Call for rates.** 4024 Melear Dr 76015. I-20, exit 449B (Cooper St), just n to Melear Dr, then just w. Ext corridors. **Pets:** Accepted. ⓢⒶⓥⒺ ✕ 🄷 🄿 ⇆

▼▼▼ Comfort Suites Six Flags in Arlington 🄷

(817) 460-8700. **$79-$129.** 411 W Road To Six Flags St 76011. I-30, exit 27 (Cooper St) eastbound; exit 28 (Cooper St) westbound, just s. Int corridors. **Pets:** Accepted. ⒶⓈⓀ ✕ 🄼 🄷 🄿 ⇆

♦♦ ▼▼▼ Days Inn Six Flags/Ballpark/Cowboys Stadium 🄷

(817) 261-8444. **$57-$250, 3 day notice.** 910 N Collins St 76011. I-30, exit 28 (Collins St/FM 157), 1 mi s. Int corridors. **Pets:** Accepted.

ⓢⒶⓥⒺ ✕ 🄷 🄿 ⇆

▼▼ Econo Lodge Inn & Suites 🄷

(817) 261-8900. **$60-$130.** 1075 Wet N Wild Way 76011. I-30, exit 28 (Collins St/FM 157), just e. Ext corridors. **Pets:** Accepted.

ⒶⓈⓀ ✕ 🄷 🄿 ⇆ ✕

▼▼ Hawthorn Suites 🄷

(817) 640-1188. **$79-$299.** 2401 Brookhollow Plaza Dr 76006. I-30, exit 30 (SR 360), just n to Lamar Blvd, just w to Brookhollow Plaza Dr, then just n. Ext corridors. **Pets:** Medium. $50 one-time fee/pet. Service with restrictions, crate. ⒶⓈⓀ ✕ 🄷 🄿 ⇆ ✕

▼▼ Howard Johnson Express Inn 🄷

(817) 461-1122. **$70-$299.** 2001 E Copeland Rd 76011. I-30, exit 30 (SR 360) westbound, just s to Six Flags Dr, just w to Copeland Rd, then 0.9 mi w; exit 29 (Ball Pkwy) eastbound. Int corridors. **Pets:** Medium. $25 daily fee/pet. Service with restrictions, crate. ⒶⓈⓀ ✕ 🄷 🄿 ⇆

▼▼▼ La Quinta Inn & Suites Dallas/Arlington North 🄷 🐾

(817) 640-4142. **$79-$149.** 825 N Watson Rd 76011. I-30, exit 30 (SR 360), exit Six Flags Dr northbound; exit Ave H/Lamar Blvd southbound. Int corridors. **Pets:** Medium, other species. Service with restrictions, supervision. ⒶⓈⓀ ✕ 🄷 🄿 ⇆

▼▼▼▼ La Quinta Inn & Suites Dallas/Arlington South 🄷 🐾

(817) 467-7756. **$69-$129.** 4001 Scott's Legacy Dr 76015. I-20, exit 450 (Matlock Rd), on westbound service road. Int corridors. **Pets:** Medium, other species. Service with restrictions, supervision.

ⒶⓈⓀ ✕ 🄼 🄷 🄿 ⇆

♦♦♦ ▼▼▼▼ Sheraton Arlington Hotel 🄷 🐾

(817) 261-8200. **$119-$329.** 1500 Convention Center Dr 76011. I-30, exit 29 (Ballpark Way) westbound; exit 28B (Nolan Ryan Expwy) eastbound, 0.4 mi e on Copeland Rd to Convention Center Dr, then just s. Int corridors. **Pets:** Large, dogs only. $50 one-time fee/pet. Service with restrictions, supervision. ⓢⒶⓥⒺ ✕ 🄼 🄷 🄿 🍴 ⇆

▼▼ Sleep Inn Main Gate-Six Flags 🄷

(817) 649-1010. **$50-$140.** 750 Six Flags Dr 76011. I-30, exit 30 (SR 360), 0.5 mi s. Int corridors. **Pets:** Medium, other species. $35 daily fee/pet. Service with restrictions, supervision. ⒶⓈⓀ ✕ 🄷 🄿 ⇆

▼▼ Studio 6-South Arlington #6036 🄷

(817) 465-8500. **$53-$63.** 1980 W Pleasant Ridge Rd 76015. I-20, exit 449 (Cooper St), 0.3 mi n, then just w. Ext corridors. **Pets:** Other species. $10 daily fee/room. Service with restrictions, supervision. ✕ 🄷 🄿

▼▼ StudioPLUS Dallas-Arlington 🄷

(817) 649-0021. **$60-$80.** 2420 E Lamar Blvd 76006. I-30, exit 30 (SR 360), just n to Lamar Blvd; just w of SR 360. Int corridors. **Pets:** Other species. $25 daily fee/room. Designated rooms, service with restrictions, crate. ⒶⓈⓀ ✕ 🄷 🄿 ⇆

AUSTIN

▼▼▼ Baymont Inn Highland Mall 🄷

(512) 452-9401. **Call for rates.** 7100 I-35 N 78752. I-35, exit 239, on west frontage road. Ext corridors. **Pets:** Accepted. ✕ 🄷 🄿 ⇆

♦♦♦ ▼▼▼ Best Western Atrium North 🄷

(512) 339-7311. **$99-$139.** 7928 Gessner Dr 78753. I-35, exit 240A, 0.4 mi w on Anderson Ln. Int corridors. **Pets:** Accepted.

ⓢⒶⓥⒺ ✕ 🄷 🄿 ⇆

▼▼▼▼ Candlewood Suites Austin Northwest 🄷 🐾

(512) 338-1611. **$109-$135.** 9701 Stonelake Blvd 78759. Jct SR 360 (Capital of Texas Hwy) and Stonelake Blvd, just s. Int corridors. **Pets:** Small. $75 one-time fee/pet. Service with restrictions, supervision.

ⒶⓈⓀ ✕ 🄼 🄷 🄿

▼▼▼▼ Candlewood Suites-South 🄷 🐾

(512) 444-8882. **$109-$159.** 4320 S I-35 78745. I-35, exit 230 northbound; exit 230B southbound, on southbound frontage road. Int corridors. **Pets:** Medium, other species. $75 one-time fee/room. Service with restrictions. ⒶⓈⓀ ✕ 🄼 🄷 🄿

♦♦♦ ▼▼▼▼ Clarion Inn & Suites Conference Center 🄷

(512) 444-0561. **$99-$159.** 2200 S I-35 78704. I-35, exit 232A (Oltorf Blvd), on west side access road. Ext/int corridors. **Pets:** Other species. $20 one-time fee/room. Service with restrictions, supervision.

ⓢⒶⓥⒺ ✕ 🄷 🄿 🍴 ⇆

▼▼▼ Comfort Suites Airport 🄷

(512) 386-6000. **$89-$109.** 7501 E Ben White Blvd 78741. I-35, exit 230B (Ben White Blvd/SR 71), 3.6 mi e. Int corridors. **Pets:** Small. $30 one-time fee/pet. Service with restrictions, supervision.

ⒶⓈⓀ ✕ 🄼 🄷 🄿

▼▼▼ Crossland Studios Austin West 🄷

(512) 331-4747. **$49-$54.** 12621 Hymeadow Rd 78729. US 183 N, exit Lake Creek, just n, then just e. Ext corridors. **Pets:** Other species. $25 daily fee/room. Designated rooms, service with restrictions, crate.

ⒶⓈⓀ ✕ 🄷 🄿

▼▼▼ Doubletree Guest Suites-Austin 🄷

(512) 478-7000. **$179-$329.** 303 W 15th St 78701. Just nw of state capitol building. Int corridors. **Pets:** Small, other species. $50 one-time fee/room. Designated rooms, service with restrictions, supervision.

✕ 🄷 🄿 🍴 ⇆

(AAA) ▼▼▼ ▼▼▼ The Driskill 🏨 ❀
(512) 474-5911. **$199-$509.** 604 Brazos St 78701. Jct 6th St. Int corridors. **Pets:** Medium, other species. $50 one-time fee/pet. Designated rooms, service with restrictions, supervision. (SAVE) ⊠ 📶 ⊗

▼▼▼▼ Drury Inn & Suites-Austin North 🏨
(512) 467-9500. **$95-$164.** 6711 I-35 N 78752. I-35, exit 238A, on east frontage road. Int corridors. **Pets:** Other species. No service, supervision.
(ASK) ⊠ 📶 📟 ⊃

▼▼ Econo Lodge 🏨
(512) 835-7070. **Call for rates.** 9102 Burnet Rd 78758. US 183 and Burnet Rd; on northeast corner. Ext corridors. **Pets:** Small. $35 one-time fee/pet. Designated rooms, no service, supervision. ⊠ 📶 📟

▼▼▼▼ Embassy Suites Austin Arboretum 🏨
(512) 372-8771. **$129-$249.** 9505 Stonelake Blvd 78759. Jct Capital of Texas Hwy (SR 360) and Stonelake Blvd, 0.5 mi s. Int corridors.
Pets: Accepted. ⊠ 📶 📟 ⫶¶ ⊃

▼▼▼▼ Embassy Suites Austin North 🏨
(512) 454-8004. **$129-$209.** 5901 I-35 N 78723. I-35, exit 238A, on east frontage road. Int corridors. **Pets:** Accepted. ⊠ 📶 📟 ⫶¶ ⊃

▼▼▼▼ Embassy Suites Hotel-Downtown 🏨
(512) 469-9000. **$169-$289.** 300 S Congress Ave 78704. Just s of Congress Ave Bridge. Int corridors. **Pets:** Accepted.
⊠ 📶 📟 ⫶¶ ⊃

▼▼ ▼▼ Extended StayAmerica Austin Arboretum 🏨
(512) 231-1520. **$79-$85.** 10100 Capital of Texas Hwy 78759. Jct Loop 1 (Mo-Pac Expwy) and Capital of Texas Hwy (SR 360), just w. Int corridors. **Pets:** Other species. $25 daily fee/room. Designated rooms, service with restrictions, crate. (ASK) ⊠ 📶 📟

▼▼ ▼▼ Extended StayAmerica Austin Downtown-6th St 🏨
(512) 457-9994. **$114-$134.** 600 Guadalupe St 78701. Jct 6th and Guadalupe sts; on northwest corner. Int corridors. **Pets:** Other species. $25 daily fee/room. Designated rooms, service with restrictions, crate.
(ASK) ⊠ 📶 📶 📟

▼▼ ▼▼ Extended StayAmerica Austin Northwest Lakeline Mall 🏨
(512) 258-3365. **$69-$74.** 13858 US Hwy 183 N 78750. Jct US 183 and SR 620; on southwest corner. Int corridors. **Pets:** Other species. $25 daily fee/room. Designated rooms, service with restrictions, crate.
(ASK) ⊠ 📶 📶 📟

▼▼ ▼▼ Extended StayAmerica Austin Southwest 🏨
(512) 892-4272. **$59-$64.** 5100 US Hwy 290 W 78735. I-35, exit 230, US 290 W to Brodie Ln exit, then 1 mi w. Int corridors. **Pets:** Other species. $25 daily fee/room. Designated rooms, service with restrictions, crate. (ASK) ⊠ 📶 📶 📟

▼▼ ▼▼ ▼▼ Extended StayAmerica Deluxe Austin-North Central 🏨
(512) 339-6005. **$69-$79.** 8221 N I-35 78753. I-35, exit 241, on east frontage road. Int corridors. **Pets:** Other species. $25 daily fee/room. Designated rooms, service with restrictions, crate. (ASK) ⊠ 📶 📟 ⊃

▼▼ ▼▼ ▼▼ Extended Stay Deluxe Austin-Arboretum-North 🏨
(512) 833-0898. **$84-$87.** 2700 Gracy Farms Ln 78758. 2 mi n of US 183 on Loop 1 (Mo-Pac Expwy), exit Burnet Rd (FM 1325). Int corridors. **Pets:** Other species. $25 daily fee/room. Designated rooms, service with restrictions, crate. (ASK) ⊠ 📶 📟 ⊃

▼▼ ▼▼ ▼▼ Extended Stay Deluxe Austin Metro 🏨
(512) 452-0880. **$62-$69.** 6300 US Hwy 290 E 78723. Jct I-35 and US 290 E. Int corridors. **Pets:** Other species. $25 daily fee/room. Designated rooms, service with restrictions, crate. (ASK) ⊠ 📶 📟 ⊃

▼▼ ▼▼ ▼▼ Extended Stay Deluxe (Austin/Northwest/Research Park) 🏨
(512) 219-6500. **$69-$74.** 12424 Research Blvd 78759. US 183, exit Oak Knoll, on eastbound frontage road. Int corridors. **Pets:** Other species. $25 daily fee/room. Designated rooms, service with restrictions, crate.
(ASK) ⊠ 📶 📶 📟 ⊃

▼▼ ▼▼▼ Fairfield Inn & Suites Austin NW 🏨
(512) 527-0734. **$125-$153.** 11201 N Mo-Pac Blvd 78759. US 183 N, 1.5 mi n on Loop 1 (Mo-Pac Expwy) to Braker Ln exit, on east frontage road. Int corridors. **Pets:** Accepted. ⊠ 📶 📶 📟 ⊃ ⊗

▼▼ ▼▼▼ Four Seasons Hotel 🏨 ❀
(512) 478-4500. **$440-$2500.** 98 San Jacinto Blvd 78701. Bordering Town Lake. Int corridors. **Pets:** Very small. Designated rooms, service with restrictions, supervision. ⊠ 📶 📟 ⫶¶ ⊃ ⊗

▼▼ ▼▼▼ Hampton Inn Northwest 🏨
(512) 349-9898. **$99-$149.** 3908 W Braker Ln 78759. 1 mi n of US 183 on Loop 1 (Mo-Pac Expwy) to Braker Ln exit. Int corridors.
Pets: Accepted. ⊠ 📶 📟 ⊃

(AAA) ▼▼ ▼▼ ▼▼ Hilton Austin 🏨 🐾
(512) 482-8000. **$209-$384.** 500 E 4th St 78701. Jct 4th St and Neches. Int corridors. **Pets:** Medium. $75 one-time fee/room. Service with restrictions, crate. (SAVE) ⊠ 📶 📟 ⫶¶ ⊃ ⊗

▼▼ ▼▼ Holiday Inn Express 🏨
(512) 386-7600. **$139-$149.** 7601 E Ben White Blvd 78741. I-35, exit 230B (Ben White Blvd), 3.2 mi e. Int corridors. **Pets:** Small. $50 one-time fee/pet. Designated rooms, service with restrictions, supervision.
(ASK) ⊠ 📶 📶 📟

▼▼ ▼▼ Holiday Inn Express Hotel & Suites 🏨
(512) 251-9110. **$99-$119.** 14620 N I-35 78728. I-35, exit 247, on west frontage road. Int corridors. **Pets:** Accepted.
(ASK) ⊠ 📶 📶 📟

▼▼ ▼▼ Homestead Studio Suites Hotel-Austin/Arboretum-South 🏨
(512) 837-6672. **$59-$69.** 9100 Waterford Centre Blvd 78758. US 183, exit Burnet Rd, on westbound frontage road. Ext corridors. **Pets:** Other species. $25 daily fee/room. Designated rooms, service with restrictions, crate. (ASK) ⊠ 📶 📟

▼▼ ▼▼▼ Homestead Studio Suites Hotel-Austin/Downtown/Town Lake 🏨
(512) 476-1818. **$104-$129.** 507 S 1st St 78704. I-35, exit 234B southbound; exit 234A northbound, 1.8 mi w on Cesar Chavez/E 1st St, then 0.5 mi s. Int corridors. **Pets:** Other species. $25 daily fee/room. Designated rooms, service with restrictions, crate. (ASK) ⊠ 📶 📟

▼▼ ▼▼ Homewood Suites-Austin South 🏨
(512) 445-5050. **$159-$189.** 4143 Governor's Row 78744. I-35, exit 231 (Ben White Blvd/SR 71) southbound; exit 229 northbound, at Ben White Blvd. Int corridors. **Pets:** Small, other species. $150 one-time fee/pet. Service with restrictions, crate. ⊠ 📶 📶 📟 ⊃

▼▼ ▼▼ ▼▼ Homewood Suites by Hilton Arboretum NW 🏨
(512) 349-9966. **$124-$219.** 10925 Stonelake Blvd 78759. US 183 N to Loop 1 (Mo-Pac Expwy), 1.5 mi n to Braker Ln; on northwest corner. Int corridors. **Pets:** Accepted. ⊠ 📶 📶 📟 ⊃ ⊗

▼▼ ▼▼▼ Hotel Saint Cecelia 🏨
(512) 852-2400. **Call for rates.** 112 Academy Dr 78704. Jct S Congress and Riverside, 2 blks s. Ext corridors. **Pets:** Accepted. ⊠ 📶 ⊃

▼▼ ▼▼ Howard Johnson 🏨
(512) 462-9201. **Call for rates.** 2711 I-35 S 78741. I-35, exit 231 (Woodward Ave) southbound; exit 232A (Oltorf St) northbound, on northbound frontage road; just n of jct I-35 and US 290/SR 71. Int corridors.
Pets: Accepted. ⊠ 📶 📟 ⊃

Hyatt Regency Austin 🏨

(512) 477-1234. **$129-$399.** 208 Barton Springs Rd 78704. At south end of Congress Ave Bridge; on south bank of Town Lake. Int corridors. **Pets:** Accepted.

Hyatt Regency Lost Pines Resort and Spa 🏨 🐾

(512) 308-1234. **$149-$599, 3 day notice.** 575 Hyatt Lost Pines Rd 78612. SR 71, 13 mi e of Austin-Bergstrom International Airport; 9 mi w of Bastrop. Int corridors. **Pets:** Other species. $35 one-time fee/room. Designated rooms, service with restrictions, supervision.

InterContinental Stephen F. Austin Hotel 🏨

(512) 457-8800. **$159-$349.** 701 Congress Ave 78701. Northeast corner of 7th St and Congress Ave. Int corridors. **Pets:** Accepted.

La Quinta Inn & Suites 🏨 🐾

(512) 246-2800. **$59-$99.** 150 Parker Dr 78728. I-35, exit 250, on west frontage road. Int corridors. **Pets:** Medium, other species. Service with restrictions, supervision.

La Quinta Inn & Suites Austin (Airport) 🏨 🐾

(512) 386-6800. **$59-$119.** 7625 E Ben White Blvd 78741. I-35, exit 230B (Ben White Blvd/SR 71), 3.8 mi e. Int corridors. **Pets:** Medium, other species. Service with restrictions, supervision.

La Quinta Inn & Suites Austin (Mopac North) 🏨 🐾

(512) 832-2121. **$59-$129.** 11901 N Mo-Pac Expwy 78759. US 183, 2 mi n on Loop 1 (Mo-Pac Expwy) to Duval exit. Int corridors. **Pets:** Medium, other species. Service with restrictions, supervision.

La Quinta Inn & Suites Austin (Southwest at Mopac) 🏨 🐾

(512) 899-3000. **$59-$139.** 4424 S Loop 1 (Mo-Pac Expwy) 78735. Jct Loop 1 (Mo-Pac Expwy), US 290 and SR 71 E, on southbound frontage road. Int corridors. **Pets:** Medium, other species. Service with restrictions, supervision.

La Quinta Inn Austin (Capitol) 🏨 🐾

(512) 476-1166. **$59-$129.** 300 E 11 St 78701. Just e of state capitol building. Ext/int corridors. **Pets:** Medium, other species. Service with restrictions, supervision.

La Quinta Inn Austin (Highland Mall) 🏨 🐾

(512) 459-4381. **$59-$99.** 5812 I-35 N 78751. I-35, exit 238A, on west frontage road. Ext corridors. **Pets:** Medium, other species. Service with restrictions, supervision.

La Quinta Inn Austin (I-35 South/Ben White) 🏨 🐾

(512) 443-1774. **$59-$109.** 4200 I-35 S 78745-1202. I-35, exit 231 (St. Edwards/Woodward Ave) southbound; exit 230 northbound, just s of jct I-35, US 290 and SR 71, on frontage road. Ext corridors. **Pets:** Medium, other species. Service with restrictions, supervision.

La Quinta Inn Austin (Oltorf) 🏨 🐾

(512) 447-6661. **$59-$109.** 1603 E Oltorf Blvd 78741. I-35, exit 232A (Oltorf Blvd), just s. Ext/int corridors. **Pets:** Medium, other species. Service with restrictions, supervision.

La Quinta Inn North 🏨 🐾

(512) 467-1701. **$74-$199.** 7622 N I-35 & 183 78752. I-35, exit 240A, on west frontage road. Int corridors. **Pets:** Medium, other species. Service with restrictions, supervision.

Mansion at Judges' Hill 🏨 🐾

(512) 495-1800. **$139-$399, 3 day notice.** 1900 Rio Grande 78705. Jct Rio Grande and Martin Luther King Jr Blvd. Int corridors. **Pets:** Other species. $50 one-time fee/room. Service with restrictions, crate.

Northcross Suites 🏨

(512) 452-9391. **Call for rates.** 7685 Northcross Dr 78757. Loop 1 (Mo-Pac Expwy), exit Anderson Rd, just e to Northcross Dr, then just s. Ext corridors. **Pets:** Accepted.

Omni Austin Hotel & Suites 🏨

(512) 476-3700. **$119-$379.** 700 San Jacinto Blvd 78701. 8th St and San Jacinto Blvd. Int corridors. **Pets:** Accepted.

Omni Austin Hotel Southpark 🏨 🐾

(512) 448-2222. **$109-$279.** 4140 Governor's Row 78744. I-35, exit 230B southbound; exit 230 northbound, on east frontage road. Int corridors. **Pets:** Small. $50 one-time fee/room. Service with restrictions, supervision.

Ramada Austin Central 🏨

(512) 454-1144. **$79-$109.** 919 E Koenig Ln 78751. I-35, exit 238A, on west frontage road. Int corridors. **Pets:** Other species. $10 daily fee/pet. Service with restrictions, supervision.

Red Roof Inn-Austin South 🏨

(512) 448-0091. **$55-$100.** 4701 I-35 S 78744. I-35, exit 230B (Ben White Blvd/SR 71) southbound; exit 229 (Stassney Rd) northbound, on northbound frontage road. Int corridors. **Pets:** Large. Service with restrictions, crate.

Renaissance Austin Hotel 🏨 🐾

(512) 343-2626. **$197-$241.** 9721 Arboretum Blvd 78759. Jct US 183 and Capital of Texas Hwy (SR 360); southwest corner. Int corridors. **Pets:** $75 one-time fee/room. Service with restrictions.

Residence Inn by Marriott Austin Airport/South 🏨

(512) 912-1100. **$134-$164.** 4537 S I-35 78744. I-35, exit 229 (Stassney Rd) southbound; exit 230 (Ben White Blvd/SR 71) northbound, on northbound frontage road. Int corridors. **Pets:** Accepted.

Residence Inn by Marriott Austin/Downtown/ Convention Center 🏨

(512) 472-5553. **$189-$269.** 300 E 4th St 78701. Between Trinity St and San Jacinto Blvd. Int corridors. **Pets:** Large, other species. $100 one-time fee/room. Designated rooms, service with restrictions.

Residence Inn by Marriott-Austin North/Parmer Lane 🏨

(512) 977-0544. **$143-$175.** 12401 N Lamar Blvd 78753. I-35, exit 245, just w. Int corridors. **Pets:** Accepted.

Staybridge Suites Austin Arboretum 🏨

(512) 349-0888. **$169-$189.** 10201 Stonelake Blvd 78759. Jct Capital of Texas Hwy (SR 360) and Stonelake Blvd, 1 blk n. Int corridors. **Pets:** Medium. $25 daily fee/pet. Service with restrictions, crate.

Staybridge Suites Austin Northwest 🏨

(512) 336-7829. **Call for rates.** 13087 Hwy 183 N, Lot 3 78750. US 183 N, exit Anderson Mill, just n of exit on east frontage road and s of Anderson Mill. Int corridors. **Pets:** Accepted.

Studio 6-Northwest #6032 Ⓜ

(512) 258-3556. **$63-$73.** 11901 Pavilion Blvd 78759. US 183, exit Oak Knoll westbound; exit Duval/Balcones Woods eastbound, on eastbound frontage road. Ext corridors. **Pets:** Other species. $10 daily fee/room. Service with restrictions, supervision.

▼▼ Super 8 Austin North 🅷
(512) 339-1300. **Call for rates.** 8128 N I-35 78753. I-35, exit 241, on west frontage road. Int corridors. **Pets:** Accepted. ⊗ 🅸 💻 ⤴

🔺 ▼▼ Super 8 University Austin 🅷
(512) 451-7001. **$50-$100.** 5526 I-35 N 78751. I-35, exit 238B southbound; exit 238B northbound, on southbound frontage road. Ext corridors. **Pets:** Accepted. (SAVE) ⊗ 🅸 💻 ⤴

▼▼▼ Wyndham Garden Hotel 🅷 ❀
(512) 448-2444. **$99-$189.** 3401 I-35 S 78741. I-35, exit 231 (Woodward St) southbound; exit 230 (Ben White Blvd/SR 71) northbound; on northbound frontage road. Ext/int corridors. **Pets:** $35 one-time fee/room. Designated rooms, service with restrictions.
(ASK) ⊗ 🅜 🅸 💻 🍴 ⤴ ⊗

BASTROP
▼▼ Comfort Inn 🅷
(512) 321-3303. **$90.** 106 Hasler Blvd 78602. Jct SR 71 and Hasler Blvd. Int corridors. **Pets:** Accepted. (ASK) ⊗ 🅜 🅸 💻 ⤴

🔺 ▼▼ Days Inn Bastrop 🅷
(512) 321-1157. **$75-$110.** 4102 Hwy 71 E 78602. On SR 71, 2 mi e of river at Loop 150 E. Ext corridors. **Pets:** Small. $25 daily fee/pet. Service with restrictions, supervision. (SAVE) ⊗ 🅸 💻 ⤴

BAY CITY
🔺 ▼▼▼ Best Western Matagorda Hotel & Conference Center 🅷
(979) 244-5400. **$99-$150.** 407 7th St 77414. SR 35 (7th St), 1 mi s of jct SR 35 and 60. Ext corridors. **Pets:** Small. $20 one-time fee/pet. Service with restrictions, supervision. (SAVE) ⊗ 🅸 💻 ⤴

BEAUMONT
🔺 ▼▼ Best Western Jefferson Inn 🅷
(409) 842-0037. **$89-$109.** 1610 I-10 S 77707. I-10, exit 851 (College St), westbound service road; 0.5 mi s of jct US 90. Ext corridors. **Pets:** Other species. Service with restrictions, crate.
(SAVE) ⊗ 🅸 💻 ⤴

🔺 ▼▼▼ Holiday Inn Beaumont Plaza 🅷
(409) 842-5995. **$80-$139.** 3950 I-10 S 77705. I-10, exit 848 (Walden Rd), just n. Int corridors. **Pets:** Small. $25 daily fee/room. Service with restrictions, supervision. (SAVE) ⊗ 🅸 💻 🍴 ⤴

▼▼▼ La Quinta Inn & Suites 🅷 ❀
(409) 842-0002. **$79-$159.** 5820 Walden Rd 77707. I-10, exit 848 (Walden Rd), just n. Int corridors. **Pets:** Medium, other species. Service with restrictions, supervision. (ASK) ⊗ 🅜 🅸 💻 ⤴

▼▼▼ Midtown Plaza 🅷
(409) 892-2222. **Call for rates.** 2095 N 11th St 77703. I-10, exit 853B (11th St), just n. Int corridors. **Pets:** Accepted.
⊗ 🅜 🅸 💻 🍴 ⤴

BEDFORD
🔺 ▼▼▼ Baymont Inn DFW West 🅷
(817) 267-5200. **Call for rates.** 1450 W Airport Frwy 76022. SR 121/183, 0.3 mi e of jct Bedford Rd/Forest Ridge Dr. Ext corridors.
Pets: Accepted. (SAVE) ⊗ 🅸 💻 ⤴

▼▼ Extended Stay Deluxe Dallas-Bedford 🅷
(817) 354-5210. **$70-$81.** 1908 Forest Ridge Dr 76021. SR 183, exit Forest Ridge Dr, just n. Int corridors. **Pets:** Other species. $25 daily fee/room. Designated rooms, service with restrictions, crate.
(ASK) ⊗ 🅸 💻 ⤴

BEEVILLE
🔺 ▼▼▼ Best Western Texan Inn 🅷
(361) 358-9999. **$90-$100.** 2001 Hwy 59 78102. US 181 at US 59, just e. Ext/int corridors. **Pets:** Accepted. (SAVE) ⊗ 🅸 💻 ⤴

▼▼ Motel 6 🅷
(361) 358-4000. **$42-$110.** 400 S US 181 Bypass 78102. 0.3 mi s of jct US 59 and 181. Ext corridors. **Pets:** Other species. Service with restrictions, supervision. (ASK) ⊗ 🅸 ⤴

BELTON
🔺 ▼▼ Budget Host Inn 🅷 🐾
(254) 939-0744. **$49-$75.** 1520 S I-35 76513. I-35, exit 292 southbound; exit 293A northbound. Ext corridors. **Pets:** Small. $10 one-time fee/pet. Service with restrictions, supervision. (SAVE) ⊗ 🅸 💻 ⤴

▼▼▼ La Quinta Inn & Suites 🅷 ❀
(254) 939-2772. **$74-$204.** 229 W Loop 121 76513. I-35, exit 292, just w. Int corridors. **Pets:** Medium, other species. Service with restrictions, supervision. (ASK) ⊗ 🅸 💻 ⤴

BENBROOK
🔺 ▼▼▼ Best Western Winscott Inn & Suites 🅷
(817) 249-0076. **$90-$160.** 590 Winscott Rd 76126. I-20, exit 429B. Int corridors. **Pets:** Accepted. (SAVE) ⊗ 🅸 💻 ⤴

▼ Motel 6-4051 🅷
(817) 249-8885. **$62-$74.** 8601 Benbrook Blvd (Hwy 377 S) 76126. I-20, exit 429A, 0.7 mi s. Int corridors. **Pets:** Other species. Service with restrictions, supervision. (ASK) ⊗ 🅜 🅸 ⤴

BIG SPRING
🔺 ▼▼ Comfort Inn 🅷
(432) 267-4553. **Call for rates.** 2900 E I-20 79720. I-20, exit 179. Ext corridors. **Pets:** Accepted. (SAVE) ⊗ 🅸 💻 ⤴

🔺 ▼▼ Quality Inn & Suites 🅷
(432) 264-7086. **Call for rates.** 300 Tulane Ave 79720. I-20, exit 179, just s. Ext corridors. **Pets:** Small, other species. $20 daily fee/pet. Service with restrictions, crate. (SAVE) ⊗ 🅜 🅸 💻 ⤴

BOERNE
🔺 ▼▼ Americas Best Value Inn Ⓜ
(830) 249-9791. **$89-$112.** 35150 I-10 W 78006. I-10, exit 540 (SR 46), westbound access road. Ext corridors. **Pets:** Medium. $20 one-time fee/pet. Service with restrictions, crate. (SAVE) ⊗ 🅸 💻 ⤴

▼▼▼ Holiday Inn Express Hotel & Suites-Six Flags West Boerne 🅷
(830) 249-6800. **Call for rates.** 35000 I-10 W 78006. I-10, exit 540 (SR 46), just e to Norris Ln, then just s. Int corridors. **Pets:** $50 one-time fee/room. Supervision. ⊗ 🅸 💻 ⤴

▼▼▼ La Quinta Boerne 🅷 🐾
(830) 249-1212. **$99-$199.** 36756 IH-10 W 78006. I-10, exit 539 (Johns Rd), eastbound exit 540 (Bandera) and u-turn back. Int corridors. **Pets:** Medium, other species. Service with restrictions, supervision.
⊗ 🅜 🅸 💻 ⤴

BONHAM
🔺 ▼ Americas Best Value Inn Ⓜ
(903) 583-3121. **$57-$67.** 1515 Old Ector Rd 75418. Jct SR 56 W and 121 S. Ext corridors. **Pets:** Medium. $25 deposit/room. Designated rooms, service with restrictions, supervision. (SAVE) ⊗ 🅸 💻 ⤴

BORGER
🔺 ▼▼▼ Best Western Borger Inn 🅷
(806) 274-7050. **$69-$130.** 206 S Cedar St 79007. Jct SR 136 and 207, just n. Int corridors. **Pets:** Other species. $10 one-time fee/pet. Designated rooms, service with restrictions, supervision.
(SAVE) ⊗ 🅸 💻 ⤴

BOWIE
▼▼ Americas Best Value Inn 🅷
(940) 872-5426. **Call for rates.** 2436 S US 287 76230. Jct SR 59. Ext corridors. **Pets:** Accepted. ⊗ 🅸 💻 ⤴

Park's Inn M

(940) 872-1111. **$60-$70.** 708 W Wise St 76230. 0.5 mi n of jct SR 59; downtown. Ext corridors. **Pets:** Accepted. [SAVE] [X] [🔲] [➰]

BRADY

Best Western Brady Inn H

(325) 597-3997. **$80-$90.** 2200 S Bridge St 76825. 1.1 mi s on US 87/377. Ext corridors. **Pets:** Small. $10 daily fee/pet. Designated rooms, service with restrictions, supervision. [SAVE] [X] [🔲] [➰]

Days Inn M

(325) 597-0789. **$59-$74.** 2108 S Bridge St 76825. 1 mi s on US 87/377 at US 190. Ext corridors. **Pets:** Accepted. [SAVE] [X] [🔲] [➰]

BRENHAM

Best Western Inn of Brenham H

(979) 251-7791. **$90-$130.** 1503 Hwy 290 E 77833. Eastbound, 0.7 mi w of jct US 290 E and SR 577; westbound, 1.3 mi e of jct SR 36 and US 290. Ext corridors. **Pets:** Small. $10 daily fee/pet. Service with restrictions, supervision. [SAVE] [X] [🔲] [🍴] [➰]

Comfort Suites H

(979) 421-8100. **$110-$180.** 2350 S Day St 77833. US 290, exit SR 36 S, just n on Business Rt SR 36. Int corridors. **Pets:** Small. $20 daily fee/pet. Service with restrictions, supervision. [SAVE] [X] [🔲] [➰]

La Quinta Inn & Suites H ✿

(979) 836-5551. **$89-$179.** 2950 Woodridge Blvd 77833. Jct US 290 and SR 36, just s. Int corridors. **Pets:** Medium, other species. Service with restrictions, supervision. [ASK] [X] [♿] [🔲] [➰]

BROWNFIELD

Best Western Caprock Inn H

(806) 637-9471. **$95-$105.** 321 Lubbock Rd 79316. Jct US 385 and 82, 2 blks n. Ext corridors. **Pets:** Accepted. [SAVE] [X] [🔲] [➰]

BROWNSVILLE

Homewood Suites by Hilton H

(956) 574-6900. **$119-$129.** 3759 N Expwy 78520. US 77, exit Ruben Torres Blvd; on southbound access road. Int corridors. **Pets:** Accepted. [X] [🔲] [➰] [X]

La Quinta Inn & Suites H ✿

(956) 350-2118. **$79-$139.** 5051 N Expwy US 77 78520. US 77, exit Alton Gloor Rd southbound; exit Stillman northbound U-turn; on southbound access road. Int corridors. **Pets:** Medium, other species. Service with restrictions, supervision. [ASK] [X] [🔲] [➰]

Residence Inn by Marriott Brownsville H

(956) 350-8100. **$125-$153.** 3975 N Expwy 77 78520. US 77 and 83, exit Ruben Torres Blvd. Int corridors. **Pets:** Accepted. [X] [♿] [🔲] [➰] [X]

Staybridge Suites H

(956) 504-9500. **$99-$159.** 2900 Pablo Kisel Blvd 78526. US 77 and 83 exit Ruben Torres Sr Blvd (FM 802), 0.8 mi n on access road to Pablo Kisel Blvd, then 0.5 mi e. Int corridors. **Pets:** Large, other species. $75 one-time fee/room. Service with restrictions, supervision.

[ASK] [X] [♿] [🔲] [➰] [X]

BUFFALO

Best Western Craig's Inn H

(903) 322-5831. **$70-$95.** IH-45 & US 79 75831. I-45, exit 178, just n on NW Frontage Rd. Ext/int corridors. **Pets:** Small, other species. $10 daily fee/pet. Service with restrictions, supervision. [SAVE] [X] [🔲] [➰]

BURKBURNETT

Burkburnett Hampton Inn H

(940) 569-8109. **$59-$149.** 1008 Sheppard Rd 76354. I-44, exit 12, just e. Int corridors. **Pets:** Accepted. [X] [♿] [🔲] [➰]

BURLESON

Best Western Burleson Inn and Suites H

(817) 744-7747. **$90-$110.** 516 Memorial Plaza 76028. I-35 W, exit 36 northbound; exit 35 southbound, on northbound access road. Int corridors. **Pets:** Small. $15 daily fee/pet. Service with restrictions, supervision.

[SAVE] [X] [🔲] [🔲] [➰]

Comfort Suites H

(817) 426-6666. **$70-$100.** 321 S Burleson Blvd 76028. I-35W, exit 34 southbound, 2 mi s to crossover, U-turn; exit 36 northbound, on northbound access road. Int corridors. **Pets:** Accepted.

[SAVE] [X] [♿] [🔲] [🔲] [➰]

BURNET

Best Western Post Oak Inn M

(512) 756-4747. **$50-$115.** 908 Buchanan Dr 78611. Jct US 281 and FM 29, 1 mi w. Ext corridors. **Pets:** Small. $15 daily fee/pet. Service with restrictions, supervision. [SAVE] [X] [🔲] [🔲] [➰]

Log Country Cove VH

(512) 756-9132. **Call for rates.** 617 Log Country Cove 78611. Jct FM 1431 and 2342, 2 mi n; Park Rd 4 and FM 2342, 3 mi s. Ext corridors. **Pets:** Medium, dogs only. Supervision. [X] [🔲] [🔲] [X]

CAMERON

Budget Host Inn & Suites H

(254) 605-0610. **$89-$200.** 102 Lafferty Ave 76520. US 77/190, 0.5 mi s. Int corridors. **Pets:** Medium. $25 daily fee/pet. Designated rooms, service with restrictions, supervision. [SAVE] [X] [🔲] [🔲] [➰]

CANTON

Best Western Canton Inn H

(903) 567-6591. **$80-$170, 3 day notice.** 2251 N Trade Days Blvd 75103. Jct I-20 and SR 19, exit 527. Ext corridors. **Pets:** Medium. $5 daily fee/pet. Service with restrictions, supervision.

[SAVE] [X] [🔲] [🔲] [➰]

Comfort Inn & Suites H

(903) 567-0909. **Call for rates.** 2406 N Trade Days Blvd 75103. I-20, exit 527. Ext corridors. **Pets:** Accepted. [X] [♿] [🔲] [🔲] [➰]

Super 8 H

(903) 567-6567. **Call for rates.** 17350 I-20 75103. I-20, exit 527. Ext corridors. **Pets:** Accepted. [X] [🔲] [🔲] [➰]

CANYON

Best Western Palo Duro Canyon H

(806) 655-1818. **$60-$170.** 2801 4th Ave 79015. I-27, exit 106, 1 mi w. Int corridors. **Pets:** Accepted. [SAVE] [X] [♿] [🔲] [🔲] [➰]

Holiday Inn Express Hotel & Suites H

(806) 655-4445. **$99-$144.** 2901 4th Ave 79015. I-27, exit 106, 2 mi w. Int corridors. **Pets:** Medium. $25 one-time fee/room. Service with restrictions, supervision. [SAVE] [X] [♿] [🔲] [🔲] [➰]

CEDAR PARK

Comfort Inn H

(512) 259-1810. **$88-$120.** 300 E Whitestone Blvd 78613. Jct US 183 and CR 1431, just e. Int corridors. **Pets:** Other species. $10 daily fee/pet. Service with restrictions, supervision. [SAVE] [X] [♿] [🔲] [🔲] [➰]

CHILDRESS

Best Western Childress H

(940) 937-6353. **$90.** 1801 Ave F NW (Hwy 287) 79201. On US 287, just s of jct US 62/83. Ext corridors. **Pets:** Other species. $10 daily fee/pet. No service, supervision. [SAVE] [X] [🔲] [🔲] [➰]

Comfort Inn H

(940) 937-6363. **$95-$159.** 1804 Ave F NW (Hwy 287) 79201. On US 287, just s of jct US 62/83. Ext corridors. **Pets:** Accepted.

[SAVE] [X] [♿] [🔲] [🔲] [➰]

▼▼ **Rodeway Inn** 🅷
(940) 937-3695. **Call for rates.** 1612 Ave F NW 79201. On US 287, just s of jct US 62/83. Ext corridors. **Pets:** Accepted. ⊠ 🖥 💻

🔊 ▼▼▼ **Super 8 Childress** Ⓜ
(940) 937-8825. **$50-$150.** 411 Ave F NE (Hwy 287 S) 79201. Jct US 83/287, 1.5 mi e. Ext corridors. **Pets:** $13 daily fee/pet. Service with restrictions. 🆂🅰🆅🅴 ⊠ 🖥 💻 ⇌

CISCO

▼▼▼ **Americas Best Value Inn** Ⓜ
(254) 442-3735. **Call for rates.** 1898 Hwy 206 W 76437. I-20, exit 330. Ext corridors. **Pets:** Accepted. ⊠ 🖥 💻 ⇌

CLARENDON

🔊 ▼▼▼ **Best Western Red River Inn** 🅷
(806) 874-0160. **$89-$109.** 902 W 2nd St 79226. Jct US 287 and SR 70. Int corridors. **Pets:** Accepted. 🆂🅰🆅🅴 ⊠ 🅲🅼 🖥 💻 ⇌

🔊 ▼▼▼ **Western Skies Motel** Ⓜ
(806) 874-3501. **$45-$99.** 800 W 2nd St 79226. 0.5 mi nw on US 287 and SR 70. Ext corridors. **Pets:** $5 one-time fee/pet. Service with restrictions, supervision. 🆂🅰🆅🅴 ⊠ 🖥 ⇌

CLAUDE

🔊 ▼ **L a Motel** Ⓜ
(806) 226-4981. **$35-$65, 5 day notice.** Hwy 287/200 E 1st St 79019. 0.3 mi s. Ext corridors. **Pets:** Small. $5 one-time fee/pet. No service, supervision. 🆂🅰🆅🅴 ⊠ 🖥 💻

CLEAR LAKE CITY

▼▼▼▼ **Candlewood Suites-Houston-Clear Lake** 🅷
(281) 461-3060. **$90-$139.** 2737 Bay Area Blvd 77058. I-45, exit 26 (Bay Area Blvd), 3.7 mi e. Int corridors. **Pets:** Accepted. 🅰🆂🅺 ⊠ 🖥 💻

▼▼▼▼ **Residence Inn-Houston Clear Lake** 🅷 ❀
(281) 486-2424. **$170-$208.** 525 Bay Area Blvd 77598. I-45 S, exit 26 (Bay Area Blvd), 1.2 mi e. Ext/int corridors. **Pets:** Medium. $100 one-time fee/room. ⊠ 🖥 💻 ⇌ ⊠

CLEBURNE

▼▼▼ **Budget Host Inn-Sagamar Inn** Ⓜ
(817) 556-3631. **$65-$80.** 2107 N Main St 76033. US 67, exit SR 174, just e. Ext corridors. **Pets:** Small, dogs only. $15 daily fee/pet. Designated rooms, no service, supervision. 🅰🆂🅺 ⊠ 🖥 💻

▼▼▼▼ **Comfort Inn** 🅷
(817) 641-4702. **$79-$149.** 2117 N Main St 76033. On SR 174, just s of jct US 67. Int corridors. **Pets:** Other species. $10 daily fee/room. Designated rooms, service with restrictions, supervision.
🅰🆂🅺 ⊠ 🅲🅼 🖥 💻

🔊 ▼▼▼▼ **La Quinta Inn & Suites** 🅷 ❀
(817) 641-4455. **$90-$220.** 107 E Kilpatrick Rd 76033. Just n of jct SR 171/174 and FM 4. Int corridors. **Pets:** Medium, other species. Service with restrictions, supervision. 🆂🅰🆅🅴 ⊠ 🅲🅼 🖥 💻 ⇌

CLIFTON

🔊 ▼▼▼ **Best Western Velkommen** 🅷
(254) 675-8999. **$90, 7 day notice.** 1215 N Avenue G 76634. SR 6, 1.5 mi n. Int corridors. **Pets:** Accepted. 🆂🅰🆅🅴 ⊠ 🖥 💻 ⇌

CLUTE

▼▼ **La Quinta Inn Clute/Lake Jackson** Ⓜ ❀
(979) 265-7461. **$49-$99.** 1126 Hwy 332 W 77531-5399. On SR 288/332, just w of jct Business Rt SR 288. Ext corridors. **Pets:** Medium, other species. Service with restrictions, supervision. 🅰🆂🅺 ⊠ 🖥 💻 ⇌

🔊 ▼▼▼ **Mainstay Suites Clute/Lake Jackson** 🅷
(979) 388-9300. **Call for rates.** 1003 W Hwy 332 77531. Just w of jct SR 288. Int corridors. **Pets:** Small. $75 one-time fee/room. Service with restrictions, supervision. 🆂🅰🆅🅴 ⊠ 🖥 💻 ⇌

COLLEGE STATION

▼▼▼▼ **Hawthorn Suites** 🅷
(979) 695-9500. **Call for rates.** 1010 University Dr E 77840. SR 6, exit University Dr, 0.5 mi w. Int corridors. **Pets:** Accepted.
⊠ 🅲🅼 🖥 💻 ⇌

▼▼▼▼ **Hilton College Station & Conference Center** 🅷 ❀
(979) 693-7500. **$109-$299.** 801 University Dr E 77840. SR 6, exit University Dr, 1.1 mi w. Int corridors. **Pets:** Medium, other species. Service with restrictions. ⊠ 🖥 💻 🍴 ⇌

▼▼▼▼ **Holiday Inn Express Hotel & Suites** 🅷
(979) 846-8700. **Call for rates.** 1203 University Dr E 77840. SR 6, exit University Dr, 1 mi w. Int corridors. **Pets:** Accepted.
⊠ 🅲🅼 🖥 💻 ⇌

▼▼▼▼ **Homewood Suites-College Station** 🅷
(979) 846-0400. **$139-$259.** 950 University Dr E 77840. Jct SR 6 and 60 (Texas Ave), 1.5 mi e. Int corridors. **Pets:** Accepted.
⊠ 🅲🅼 🖥 💻 ⇌ ⊠

🔊 ▼▼▼ **Howard Johnson** 🅷
(979) 693-6810. **$55-$150.** 3702 Hwy 6 S 77845. SR 6 S, exit Rock Prairie Rd. Ext corridors. **Pets:** Medium, dogs only. $15 daily fee/pet. Service with restrictions, crate. 🆂🅰🆅🅴 ⊠ 🖥 💻 ⇌

▼▼▼ **La Quinta Inn College Station** 🅷 ❀
(979) 696-7777. **$59-$119.** 607 Texas Ave 77840. Just s on jct SR 60 and 6 business route to Live Oak St, then just e. Ext corridors. **Pets:** Medium, other species. Service with restrictions, supervision.
🅰🆂🅺 ⊠ 🖥 💻 ⇌

▼▼▼ **Manor Inn College Station** 🅷 ❀
(979) 764-9540. **$49-$145, 4 day notice.** 2504 Texas Ave S 77840. 2.4 mi s of jct SR 60. Ext corridors. **Pets:** $40 one-time fee/pet. Designated rooms, service with restrictions, supervision. 🅰🆂🅺 ⊠ 🖥 💻 ⇌

▼▼▼▼ **Residence Inn by Marriott College Station** 🅷
(979) 268-2200. **$125-$153.** 720 University Dr E 77840. Jct Texas Ave, 0.5 mi e. Int corridors. **Pets:** Medium, other species. $100 one-time fee/room. Service with restrictions. ⊠ 🅲🅼 🖥 💻 ⇌ ⊠

▼▼▼▼ **TownePlace Suites By Marriott** 🅷
(979) 260-8500. **$125-$153.** 1300 E University Dr 77840. SR 6, exit University Dr, 1 mi w. Ext corridors. **Pets:** Other species. $106 one-time fee/room. ⊠ 🖥 💻 ⇌

COLUMBUS

🔊 ▼▼▼▼ **Holiday Inn Express Hotel & Suites** 🅷
(979) 733-9300. **$110-$130.** 4321 I-10 78934. I-10, exit 696 (SR 71), just w on westbound service road. Int corridors. **Pets:** Accepted.
🆂🅰🆅🅴 ⊠ 🖥 💻 ⇌

CONWAY

▼▼▼ **Budget Host S & S Motel** Ⓜ
(806) 537-5111. **Call for rates.** I-40 & SR 207 79068. I-40, exit 96 (SR 207), 0.3 mi w on southbound access road. Ext corridors.
Pets: Accepted. ⊠ 🖥 🍴

CORPUS CHRISTI

🔊 ▼▼▼ **Best Western Garden Inn** 🅷
(361) 241-6675. **$89-$129.** 11217 I-37 78410. I-37, exit 11B (Violet Rd); on southbound access road. Ext corridors. **Pets:** $15 daily fee/pet. Service with restrictions, supervision. 🆂🅰🆅🅴 ⊠ 🅲🅼 🖥 💻 ⇌

Best Western Marina Grand Hotel H ❀
(361) 883-5111. **$109-$160.** 300 N Shoreline Blvd 78401. Center of downtown. Int corridors. **Pets:** Small, dogs only. $25 daily fee/room. Service with restrictions, supervision. SAVE ✕ 🖥 💻 ➿

Best Western on the Island H
(361) 949-2300. **Call for rates.** 14050 S Padre Island Dr 78418. On Park Rd 22. Ext corridors. **Pets:** Accepted. SAVE ✕ 🖥 💻 ➿

Budget Inn & Suites M
(361) 884-2485. **$60-$150.** 801 S Shoreline Blvd 78401. I-37, exit Shoreline; between Park and Furnan aves. Ext corridors. **Pets:** Accepted.
ASK ✕ 🖥 💻 ➿

Christy Estate Suites CO
(361) 854-1091. **Call for rates.** 3942 Holly Rd 78415. SR 358, exit Weber Rd, 0.5 mi s. Ext/int corridors. **Pets:** Accepted.
✕ 🖥 💻 ➿

Days Inn Corpus Christi South H
(361) 854-0005. **Call for rates.** 2838 S Padre Island Dr 78415. On SR 358 westbound access road, 0.4 mi w, exit Kostoryz Rd. Ext corridors. **Pets:** Accepted. ✕ 🖥 💻 ➿

Extended Stay Deluxe–Corpus Christi-Staples H
(361) 991-1967. **$73-$103.** 6218 S Staples St 78413. SR 358 southbound, exit S Staples St, 0.3 mi, then 1.5 mi s. Int corridors. **Pets:** Other species. $25 daily fee/room. Designated rooms, service with restrictions, crate. ASK ✕ 🖥 💻 ➿

Holiday Inn-Airport and Conference Center H
(361) 289-5100. **$109-$179.** 5549 Leopard St 78408. Jct SR 358 and Leopard St, 5.5 mi w. Int corridors. **Pets:** Accepted.
SAVE ✕ 🖥 💻 🍴 ➿

Holiday Inn-Emerald Beach H
(361) 883-5731. **$125-$199.** 1102 S Shoreline Blvd 78401. 1.5 mi s on bay from downtown marina. Ext/int corridors. **Pets:** Accepted.
ASK ✕ 🆖 🖥 💻 🍴 ➿ ✕

Homewood Suites by Hilton H
(361) 854-1331. **$114-$129.** 5201 Crosstown Expwy (SR 286) 78417. I-37, exit SR 358 E (Greenwood Dr), 0.6 mi e on eastbound access road. Int corridors. **Pets:** Medium. $100 one-time fee/room. Service with restrictions, crate. ✕ 🖥 💻 ➿

La Quinta Inn & Suites H ❀
(361) 299-2600. **$79-$139.** 546 S Padre Island Dr 78405. SR 358, exit Old Brownsville Rd, on access road. Int corridors. **Pets:** Medium, other species. Service with restrictions, supervision. ✕ 🆖 🖥 💻 ➿

La Quinta Inn Corpus Christi (North) M ❀
(361) 888-5721. **$59-$129.** 5155 I-37 N 78408-2614. I-37, exit 3A (Navigation Blvd), on southbound access road. Ext corridors. **Pets:** Medium, other species. Service with restrictions, supervision.
ASK ✕ 🖥 💻 ➿

La Quinta Inn Corpus Christi (South) H ❀
(361) 991-5730. **$59-$149.** 6225 S Padre Island Dr 78412-4011. SR 358, exit Airline Rd. Ext corridors. **Pets:** Medium, other species. Service with restrictions, supervision. ASK ✕ 🖥 💻 ➿

Motel 6 #231 M
(361) 289-9397. **$43-$53.** 845 Lantana St 78408. I-37, exit 4B (Lantana St), on southbound access road. Ext corridors. **Pets:** Other species. Service with restrictions, supervision. ✕ 🖥 💻 ➿

Omni Corpus Christi Hotel-Bayfront Tower H
(361) 887-1600. **$179.** 900 N Shoreline Blvd 78401. In town across from bay; downtown; in marina district. Int corridors. **Pets:** Accepted.
SAVE ✕ 🆖 🖥 💻 🍴 ➿ ✕

Omni Corpus Christi Hotel-Marina Tower H
(361) 887-1600. **$179.** 707 N Shoreline Blvd 78401. Just n across from bay. Int corridors. **Pets:** Accepted. ASK ✕ 🖥 💻 🍴 ➿ ✕

Plaza Inn Corpus Christi H
(361) 289-8200. **$70-$113.** 2021 N Padre Island Dr 78408. I-37, exit SR 358, just se at Leopard St. Int corridors. **Pets:** Accepted.
ASK ✕ 🖥 💻 ➿

Quality Inn & Suites Sandy Shores H
(361) 883-7456. **$75-$295, 3 day notice.** 3202 Surfside Blvd 78402. 1 mi n on US 181; at north end of Harbor Bridge, exit Bridge St. Ext/int corridors. **Pets:** Small. $20 daily fee/pet. Service with restrictions, supervision. SAVE ✕ 🖥 💻 ➿

Red Roof Inn H
(361) 992-9222. **$45-$75.** 6805 S Padre Island Dr 78412. SR 358, exit Nile Dr. Ext corridors. **Pets:** Large. Service with restrictions, crate.
SAVE ✕ 🖥 💻 ➿

Surfside Condominiums CO
(361) 949-8128. **$140-$215, 3 day notice.** 15005 Windward Dr 78418. Park Rd 22 on N Padre Island Dr, jct Whitecap Blvd, 0.6 mi n to Windward Dr, then 0.8 mi w. Ext corridors. **Pets:** Medium. $18 daily fee/pet. Designated rooms, service with restrictions. SAVE ✕ 🖥 💻 ➿

CORSICANA

Comfort Inn H
(903) 875-0616. **Call for rates.** 1946 E Hwy 31 75110. I-45, exit 231, just w. Int corridors. **Pets:** Accepted. ✕ 🖥 💻 ➿

La Quinta Inn & Suites H ❀
(903) 874-6292. **$75-$149.** 2020 Regal Dr 75109. I-45, exit 231, just e. Int corridors. **Pets:** Medium, other species. Service with restrictions, supervision. ✕ 🖥 💻 ➿

DALHART

Best Western Nursanickel Motel H ❀
(806) 244-5637. **$69-$99.** 102 Scott Ave (Hwy 87 S) 79022. Just s of jct US 54 and 87. Ext corridors. **Pets:** Large. $10 daily fee/pet. Service with restrictions, supervision. SAVE ✕ 🖥 💻 ➿

Budget Inn M
(806) 244-4557. **$45-$55.** 415 Liberal St (Hwy 54) 79022. On US 54, just e of US 87 and 385. Ext corridors. **Pets:** Small, other species. Service with restrictions, supervision. SAVE ✕ 🖥

Days Inn H
(806) 244-5246. **$70-$130.** 701 Liberal St (Hwy 54) 79022. On US 54, 0.5 mi e. Int corridors. **Pets:** Accepted. SAVE ✕ 🖥 💻 ➿

Rodeway Inn M
(806) 249-8585. **Call for rates.** 1110 Liberal St (Hwy 54 E) 79022. 0.5 mi e of jct US 54 and 87. Ext corridors. **Pets:** Accepted.
SAVE ✕ 🖥 💻 ➿

Sands Motel M
(806) 244-4568. **$30-$60.** 301 Liberal St (Hwy 54) 79022. On US 54, just e of US 87 and 385. Ext corridors. **Pets:** Service with restrictions.
SAVE ✕ 🖥

Super 8 M
(806) 249-8526. **$65-$95.** 403 Tanglewood Rd (Hwy 54 E) 79022. Jct US 87 and 54, 0.5 mi e. Int corridors. **Pets:** Small. $25 deposit/pet. Designated rooms, service with restrictions, supervision. SAVE ✕ 🖥

DALLAS METROPOLITAN AREA

ADDISON

▼▼▼ Homewood Suites by Hilton 🄷

(972) 788-1342. **$149-$159.** 4451 Belt Line Rd 75001. Just e of jct Belt Line and Midway rds. Ext/int corridors. **Pets:** Small, other species. $75 one-time fee/pet. Service with restrictions, supervision.

ⓧ 🄼 🄷 🖵 ⇌ ⊠

ⒶⒶⒶ ▼▼▼ Hyatt Summerfield Suites Dallas/Addison 🄷

(972) 661-3113. **$89-$209.** 4900 Edwin Lewis Dr 75001. Just n of jct Belt Line Rd and Quorum Dr to Edwin Lewis Dr, then just w. Ext/int corridors. **Pets:** Large. $150 one-time fee/room. Service with restrictions, crate.

SAVE ⓧ 🄼 🄷 🖵 ⇌

▼▼▼ La Quinta Inn & Suites Dallas (Addison-Galleria Area) 🄷 ❀

(972) 404-0004. **$59-$99.** 14925 Landmark Blvd 75254. Jct Belt Line Rd and Landmark Blvd, just s. Int corridors. **Pets:** Medium, other species. Service with restrictions, supervision. ASK ⓧ 🄼 🄷 🖵 ⇌

▼▼▼ Quality Inn & Suites 🄷

(972) 991-8888. **$55-$149.** 4103 Belt Line Rd 75001. Between Midway Rd and Marsh Ln. Ext corridors. **Pets:** Accepted.

ASK ⓧ 🄷 🖵 ⇌

▼▼▼ Residence Inn by Marriott-Addison 🄷

(972) 866-9933. **$152-$186.** 14975 Quorum Dr 75001. Just s of jct Belt Line Rd and Quorum Dr. Int corridors. **Pets:** Accepted.

ⓧ 🄷 🖵 ⇌ ⊠

ALLEN

▼▼ Pyramids Hotel 🄷 ❀

(972) 396-9494. **$89-$149.** 407 Central Expwy S 75013. US 75, exit 33 (Bethany Dr). Int corridors. **Pets:** Medium, other species. $30 one-time fee/room. Service with restrictions, supervision.

ASK ⓧ 🄷 🖵 ⇌ ⊠

ATHENS

▼▼ Quality Inn & Suites 🄷

(903) 675-9214. **Call for rates.** 2050 Hwy 31 E 75751. 2.6 mi e of jct SR 19 and 31 (city square). Ext corridors. **Pets:** Very small, dogs only. $50 deposit/room, $10 daily fee/pet. Service with restrictions, supervision.

ⓧ 🄷 🖵 ⑪ ⇌

BALCH SPRINGS

▼▼ La Quinta Inn 🄷 ❀

(972) 286-1010. **$55-$129.** 12875 Seagoville Rd 75180. I-20, exit 481 (Seagoville Rd), just n. Int corridors. **Pets:** Medium, other species. Service with restrictions, supervision. ASK ⓧ 🄷 🖵 ⇌

CARROLLTON

▼▼ Rodeway Inn 🄷

(972) 245-9900. **Call for rates.** 1832 N I-35E 75006. I-35E, exit 443C (Northside Dr) northbound; exit 443B southbound (Belt Line Rd), U-turn 1 mi n. Int corridors. **Pets:** Small. $10 daily fee/pet. Service with restrictions, supervision. ⓧ 🄷

COMMERCE

ⒶⒶⒶ ▼▼▼ Holiday Inn Express Hotel & Suites 🄷

(903) 886-4777. **$89-$159.** 2207 Culver St 75428. 0.9 mi e of jct SR 224, 24 and 50. Int corridors. **Pets:** Accepted.

SAVE ⓧ 🄼 🄷 🖵 ⇌

DALLAS

▼▼▼ Baymont Inn & Suites 🄷

(214) 350-5577. **Call for rates.** 2370 W Northwest Hwy 75220. I-35E, exit 436 Northwest Hwy (Loop 12), 0.8 mi e. Int corridors. **Pets:** Accepted. ⓧ 🄷 🖵 ⇌

ⒶⒶⒶ ▼▼▼ Best Western Executive Inn 🄷

(972) 613-5000. **$70-$75.** 12670 E Northwest Hwy 75228. I-635, exit 11B, just s. Ext corridors. **Pets:** Other species. $10 daily fee/pet, $10 one-time fee/pet. Service with restrictions, supervision.

SAVE ⓧ 🄷 🖵 ⇌

ⒶⒶⒶ ▼▼▼ Candlewood Dallas Market Center 🄷

(214) 631-3333. **$89-$109.** 7930 N Stemmons Frwy 75247. I-35, exit 433B (Mockingbird Ln), on northbound frontage road. Int corridors. **Pets:** Medium. $75 one-time fee/pet. Service with restrictions, supervision.

SAVE ⓧ 🄷 🖵 ⇌

▼▼▼▼ Candlewood Suites-Dallas by the Galleria 🄷

(972) 233-6888. **$105-$125.** 13939 Noel Rd 75240. Jct Dallas Pkwy and Spring Valley, just e to Noel Rd, then just s. Int corridors. **Pets:** Medium, other species. $75 one-time fee/pet. Service with restrictions, crate.

ASK ⓧ 🄼 🄷 🖵

▼▼▼ Candlewood Suites Dallas North/Richardson 🄷

(972) 669-9606. **Call for rates.** 12525 Greenville Ave 75243. I-635, exit 18A (Greenville Ave), just n. Int corridors. **Pets:** Accepted.

ⓧ 🄼 🖵 ⇌

ⒶⒶⒶ ▼▼▼ Comfort Inn & Suites Market Center 🄷

(214) 461-2677. **$59-$70.** 7138 N Stemmons Frwy 75247. I-35E, exit 433B (Mockingbird Ln) northbound; exit 432B (Commonwealth Dr) southbound, turn under freeway, 0.7 mi on north access road. Int corridors. **Pets:** Other species. $25 one-time fee/room. Service with restrictions, supervision. SAVE ⓧ 🄷 🖵

▼▼▼ Country Inn & Suites By Carlson, Dallas-Park Central 🄷

(972) 907-9500. **Call for rates.** 13185 N Central Expwy 75243. US 75 N, exit 22 (Midpark Rd). Int corridors. **Pets:** Small. $10 daily fee/pet, $25 one-time fee/pet. Designated rooms, service with restrictions, supervision.

ⓧ 🄷 🖵 ⇌

ⒶⒶⒶ ▼▼▼▼ Crowne Plaza Suites Hotel Dallas Park Central 🄷

(972) 233-7600. **$169-$219.** 7800 Alpha Rd 75240. I-635, exit 19C (Coit Rd) eastbound; exit 19B (Coit Rd) westbound, 0.3 mi nw of jct US 75. Int corridors. **Pets:** Accepted. SAVE ⓧ 🄷 🖵 ⑪ ⇌

▼▼ Extended StayAmerica Dallas-Richardson 🄷

(972) 238-1133. **$60-$74.** 12270 Greenville Ave 75243. I-635, exit 18A (Greenville Ave), just s. Int corridors. **Pets:** Other species. $25 daily fee/room. Designated rooms, service with restrictions, crate.

ASK ⓧ 🄷 🖵

▼▼ Extended Stay Deluxe Dallas-Market Center 🄷

(214) 630-0154. **$70-$80.** 2979 N Stemmons Frwy 75247. I-35E, exit 432B, on eastbound access road. Int corridors. **Pets:** Other species. $25 daily fee/room. Designated rooms, service with restrictions, crate.

ASK ⓧ 🄷 🖵 ⇌

▼▼ Extended Stay Deluxe Dallas-North-Park Central 🄷

(972) 671-7722. **$60-$74.** 9019 Vantage Point Rd 75243. I-635, exit 18A (Greenville Ave), just sw. Ext corridors. **Pets:** Other species. $25 daily fee/room. Designated rooms, service with restrictions, crate.

ASK ⓧ 🄷 🖵

▼▼▼ Fairfield Inn by Marriott-Park Central 🄷 ❀

(972) 437-9905. **$95-$116.** 9230 LBJ Frwy 75243. I-635, exit 18A (Greenville Ave S), just s, then just e. Int corridors. **Pets:** Medium, other species. $75 one-time fee/room. Service with restrictions.

ⓧ 🄷 🖵 ⇌

ⒶⒶⒶ ▼▼▼▼ The Fairmont Dallas 🄷 ❀

(214) 720-2020. **$129-$329.** 1717 N Akard St 75201. Corner of Ross Ave and N Akard St. Int corridors. **Pets:** Other species. $25 daily fee/room. Designated rooms, service with restrictions, supervision.

SAVE ⓧ 🄼 🄷 🖵 ⑪ ⇌

Hilton Anatole Dallas 🏨
(214) 748-1200. **$139-$394.** 2201 Stemmons Frwy 75207. I-35E, exit 430B (Market Center Blvd), just nw. Int corridors. **Pets:** Other species. $75 one-time fee/room. Service with restrictions, supervision.

SAVE ✕ ⑤M 🛇 💻 ¶¶ 🌊 ✕

Hilton Dallas Lincoln Centre 🏨
(972) 934-8400. **$99-$319.** 5410 LBJ Frwy 75240. N at jct I-635 and North Dallas Tollway/Dallas Pkwy, exit 22C (Montfort Dr) eastbound; exit 22B (Dallas Pkwy/Inwood Rd) westbound. Int corridors. **Pets:** Medium. $75 one-time fee/room. Designated rooms, service with restrictions.

SAVE ✕ 🛇 💻 ¶¶ 🌊

Hilton Dallas Park Cities 🏨 🐾
(214) 368-0400. **$129-$309.** 5954 Luther Ln 75225. North Dallas Tollway, exit Northwest Hwy (Loop 12), just e to Douglas Ave, then just s. Int corridors. **Pets:** Medium. $75 one-time fee/room. Service with restrictions, supervision. SAVE ✕ 🛇 💻 ¶¶ 🌊

Homestead Studio Suites Hotel-Dallas/Plano 🏨
(972) 248-2233. **$75-$92.** 18470 N Dallas Pkwy 75287. North Dallas Tollway, exit Frankford, just ne. Int corridors. **Pets:** Other species. $25 daily fee/room. Designated rooms, service with restrictions, crate.

ASK ✕ ⑤M 💻 🌊

Homewood Suites by Hilton 🏨
(214) 819-9700. **$139-$159.** 2747 N Stemmons Frwy 75207. I-35E, exit 432A (Inwood Rd), just s. Int corridors. **Pets:** Accepted.

✕ ⑤M 💻 🌊

Homewood Suites by Hilton–I-635 🏨
(972) 437-6966. **$139-$159.** 9169 Markville Dr 75243. I-635, exit 18A (Greenville Ave S), just s, then just e. Int corridors. **Pets:** Accepted.

✕ 🛇 💻 ✕

Hotel Indigo Dallas Downtown 🏨
(214) 741-7700. **$99-$159.** 1933 Main St 75201. Main and Harwood sts; northwest corner. Int corridors. **Pets:** Accepted. ASK ✕ 🛇 💻 ¶¶

Hotel Lawrence 🏨
(214) 761-9090. **Call for rates.** 302 S Houston St 75202. I-35E, exit 428A (Commerce St), 0.8 mi to Griffin, just s to Jackson St, then just w. Int corridors. **Pets:** Accepted. SAVE ✕ 💻 ¶¶

Hotel Palomar 🏨
(214) 520-7969. **$159-$359.** 5300 E Mockingbird Ln 75206. US 75, exit 3 (Mockingbird Ln), on southeast corner. Int corridors. **Pets:** Accepted.
SAVE ✕ ⑤M ¶¶ 🌊 ✕

Hotel St. Germain 🏨 🐾
(214) 871-2516. **$305-$700, 7 day notice.** 2516 Maple Ave 75201. I-35, exit 430A (Oak Lawn Ave), 0.5 mi e, then 1 mi s. Int corridors.
Pets: Small, dogs only. $50 daily fee/pet. Designated rooms, service with restrictions, supervision. SAVE ✕ ¶¶

Hotel ZaZa 🏨 🐾
(214) 468-8399. **$275-$375.** 2332 Leonard St 75201. Jct Maple Ave/ Routh St and McKinney sts, southeast corner. Int corridors.
Pets: Medium. $50 one-time fee/room.
SAVE ✕ ⑤M 🛇 💻 ¶¶ 🌊 ✕

Hyatt Summerfield Suites Dallas/Lincoln Park 🏨
(214) 696-1555. **$89-$229.** 8221 N Central Expwy 75225. US 75, exit 5A southbound; exit 4B northbound, just w on Caruth Haven to Lincoln Pl, then just n. Int corridors. **Pets:** Accepted. SAVE ✕ ⑤M 🛇 💻 🌊

Knights Inn Ⓜ
(214) 638-5151. **$45-$66.** 1550 Empire Central Dr 75235. I-35E, exit 434A (Empire Central Dr), 0.3 mi e. Ext corridors. **Pets:** Accepted. ✕

La Quinta Inn & Suites Dallas (North Central) 🏨 🐾
(214) 361-8200. **$59-$129.** 10001 N Central Expwy 75231-4193. US 75, exit 6 (Walnut Hill Ln/Meadow Rd) northbound, 0.5 mi n to Meadow Rd, then U-turn under highway; exit 7 (Royal St/Meadow Rd) southbound, 1 mi s on feeder. Int corridors. **Pets:** Medium, other species. Service with restrictions, supervision. ASK ✕ ⑤M 🛇 💻

La Quinta Inn & Suites Dallas Northwest 🏨 🐾
(214) 904-9955. **$69-$199.** 2380 W Northwest Hwy 75220. I-35, exit 436 Northwest Hwy (Loop 12), 0.8 mi e. Int corridors. **Pets:** Medium, other species. Service with restrictions, supervision. ASK ✕ 🛇 💻 🌊

La Quinta Inn Dallas (East) 🏨 🐾
(214) 324-3731. **$39-$89.** 8303 E RL Thornton Frwy 75228-7105. I-30, exit 52A (Jim Miller Rd). Ext corridors. **Pets:** Medium, other species. Service with restrictions, supervision. ASK ✕ ⑤M 🛇 💻 🌊

La Quinta Inn Dallas Uptown 🏨 🐾
(214) 821-4220. **$69-$109.** 4440 N Central Expwy 75206-6525. N off US 75, exit 2 (Henderson-Knox) northbound; exit 1B (Haskell/Blackburn) southbound. Ext corridors. **Pets:** Medium, other species. Service with restrictions, supervision. ASK ✕ 🛇 💻 🌊

McM Elegante Hotel & Suites 🏨
(214) 351-4477. **$89-$139.** 2330 W Northwest Hwy 75220. I-35E, exit 436; e of I-35E and US 77 at Northwest Hwy (Loop 12). Ext/int corridors. **Pets:** Small. $25 one-time fee/room. Service with restrictions, supervision.

ASK ✕ 🛇 💻 ¶¶ 🌊

Motel 6 Forest Lane-South #1119 🏨
(972) 484-9111. **$45-$57.** 2660 Forest Ln 75234. I-635, exit 26 (Josey Ln) eastbound, 0.5 mi s to Forest Ln, then just w; exit 25 (Josey Ln) westbound, just s to Forest Ln, then just w. Ext corridors. **Pets:** Other species. Service with restrictions, supervision. ✕ 🌊

Quality Inn & Suites-North Dallas 🏨
(972) 484-3330. **Call for rates.** 2421 Walnut Hill Ln 75229. I-35E, exit 438 (Walnut Hill Ln). Int corridors. **Pets:** Accepted. ✕ 🛇 💻 🌊

Radisson Hotel & Suites Dallas Love Field 🏨
(214) 630-7000. **$104-$129.** 1241 W Mockingbird Ln 75247. I-35E, exit 433B, just ne of jct I-35E and W Mockingbird Ln. Int corridors.
Pets: Accepted. SAVE ✕ 🛇 💻 ¶¶ 🌊

Radisson Hotel Central/Dallas 🏨
(214) 750-6060. **$109-$199.** 6060 N Central Expwy 75206. US 75, exit 3 (Mockingbird Ln), on northbound frontage road. Int corridors.
Pets: Accepted. SAVE ✕ 🛇 💻 🌊

Red Roof Inn Dallas (Richardson) #0673 🏨
(972) 234-1016. **Call for rates.** 13685 N Central Expwy 75243-1001. US 75 N, exit 22 (Midpark Rd). Ext/int corridors. **Pets:** Large. Service with restrictions, crate. SAVE ✕ 🛇 🌊

Residence Inn by Marriott at Dallas Central 🏨
(214) 750-8220. **$179-$199.** 10333 N Central Expwy 75231. US 75, exit 6 (Walnut Hill Ln/Meadow Rd) northbound, 0.5 mi n to Meadow Rd, U-turn under highway; exit 7 (Royal St/Meadow Rd) southbound, 1 mi s on access road. Ext corridors. **Pets:** Accepted. ✕ 🛇 💻 🌊 ✕

Residence Inn by Marriott-Dallas Market Center 🏨
(214) 631-2472. **$152-$186.** 6950 N Stemmons Frwy 75247. I-35E, exit 432B (Commonwealth Ln), 0.6 mi n on northbound frontage road. Ext/int corridors. **Pets:** Accepted. ✕ 🛇 💻 🌊

Residence Inn by Marriott-Dallas Park Central 🏨
(972) 503-1333. **$80-$129.** 7642 LBJ Frwy 75251. I-635, exit 20 (Hillcrest Ave), just e, on eastbound access road. Int corridors. **Pets:** Other species. $100 one-time fee/room. Service with restrictions, supervision.

✕ ⑤M 🛇 💻 🌊 ✕

▼▼▼▼ The Ritz-Carlton, Dallas H

(214) 922-0200. **$199-$569.** 2121 McKinney Ave 75201. SR 366 (Woodall Rodgers Frwy), exit Pearl St, just sw to Olive St, then just nw. Int corridors. **Pets:** Accepted. ⊠ 🖾 🗐 🗏 🍴 ➷

▼▼▼▼ Rosewood Crescent Hotel H ❀

(214) 871-3200. **Call for rates.** 400 Crescent Ct 75201. Corner of Crescent Ct and McKinney Ave; uptown. Int corridors. **Pets:** Medium. $100 one-time fee/pet. Service with restrictions, supervision.

⊠ 🗐 🗏 🍴 ➷ ⊠

⚫ ▼▼▼▼ Rosewood Mansion On Turtle Creek H

(214) 559-2100. **$595-$2400.** 2821 Turtle Creek Blvd 75219. 2 mi nw, entrance on Gillespie St, just e of jct Gillespie St and Oak Lawn Ave. Int corridors. **Pets:** Accepted. SAVE ⊠ 🗐 🗏 🍴 ➷ ⊠

⚫ ▼▼▼ Sheraton Dallas Hotel H

(214) 922-8000. **Call for rates.** 400 N Olive St 75201. Live Oak and Olive sts, just w off Central Expwy. Int corridors. **Pets:** Accepted.

SAVE ⊠ 🗐 🗏 🍴 ➷

⚫ ▼▼▼ Sheraton Suites Market Center-Dallas H

(214) 747-3000. **Call for rates.** 2101 N Stemmons Frwy 75207. Nw off I-35 E and US 77, exit 430B (Market Center Blvd). Int corridors.
Pets: Accepted. SAVE ⊠ 🗐 🗏 🍴 ➷

▼▼▼ Staybridge Suites Dallas Near The Galleria H ❀

(972) 391-0000. **$109-$179.** 7880 Alpha Rd 75240. I-635, exit 19B (Coit Rd), 0.3 mi n, then just w. Int corridors. **Pets:** Medium, other species. $150 one-time fee/pet. Service with restrictions, crate.

ASK ⊠ 🗐 🗏 ➷

▼▼▼ Staybridge Suites North Dallas H

(972) 726-9990. **$89-$199.** 16060 N Dallas Pkwy 75248. North Dallas Tollway, exit Keller Springs northbound, just n on north access road; exit Keller Springs southbound, just e to Noel Tr, then just s. Int corridors. **Pets:** Medium. $75 one-time fee/pet. Service with restrictions.

ASK ⊠ 🖾 🗐 🗏 ➷

⚫ ▼▼▼ The Stoneleigh Hotel & Spa H ❀

(214) 871-7111. **Call for rates.** 2927 Maple Ave 75201. I-35E, exit 430A (Oak Lawn Ave), 0.5 mi e, then 1.2 mi s. Int corridors. **Pets:** Medium. $50 one-time fee/pet. Service with restrictions, supervision.

SAVE ⊠ 🖾 🍴

▼▼▼ Super 8 H

(972) 572-1030. **Call for rates.** 8541 S Hampton Rd 75232. I-20, exit 465, 0.3 mi e to S Hampton Rd, then just s. Ext corridors.
Pets: Accepted. ⊠ 🗐 🗏 ➷

⚫ ▼▼▼▼ Warwick Melrose Hotel H ❀

(214) 521-5151. **$129-$499.** 3015 Oak Lawn Ave 75219. I-35E, exit 430 (Oak Lawn Ave), 0.8 mi n; entrance off Cedar Springs, just n. Int corridors. **Pets:** Large. $50 one-time fee/room. Designated rooms, service with restrictions, crate. SAVE ⊠ 🗐 🗏 🍴

⚫ ▼▼▼▼ W Dallas–Victory H

(214) 397-4100. **$199-$529.** 2440 Victory Park Ln 75219. Southwest corner of Olive and N Houston sts; uptown Dallas; across from American Airlines Center. Int corridors. **Pets:** Accepted. SAVE ⊠ 🍴 ➷

⚫ ▼▼▼ The Westin City Center, Dallas H

(214) 979-9000. **$139-$399.** 650 N Pearl St 75201. Between San Jacinto and Bryan sts, 0.3 mi w of US 75 Central Expwy. Int corridors.
Pets: Accepted. SAVE ⊠ 🗐 🗏 🍴

⚫ ▼▼▼▼ The Westin Galleria, Dallas H

(972) 934-9494. **$149-$409.** 13340 Dallas Pkwy 75240. Just n of jct I-635 and N Dallas Pkwy. Int corridors. **Pets:** Accepted.

SAVE ⊠ 🖾 🗏 🍴 ➷

⚫ ▼▼▼ Westin Park Central H ❀

(972) 385-3000. **Call for rates.** 12720 Merit Dr 75251. I-635, exit 19C (Coit Rd) eastbound; exit 19B (US 75/Coit Rd) westbound; 0.3 mi w of jct US 75. Int corridors. **Pets:** Medium, other species. Service with restrictions. SAVE ⊠ 🗐 🗏 ➷

DENTON

▼▼▼ La Quinta Inn Denton H ❀

(940) 387-5840. **$69-$129.** 700 Fort Worth Dr 76201. I-35E, exit 465B (Fort Worth Dr), just n. Ext corridors. **Pets:** Medium, other species. Service with restrictions, supervision. ASK ⊠ 🖾 🗐 🗏 ➷

▼ Motel 6 Denton #97 M

(940) 566-4798. **$45-$57.** 4125 I-35 N 76207. I-35, exit 469. Ext corridors. **Pets:** Other species. Service with restrictions, supervision. ⊠ ➷

▼▼▼ Quality Inn & Suites Denton H

(940) 387-3511. **$60-$110.** 1500 Dallas Dr 76205. 2 mi se of jct I-35E and US 77 business route, exit 464 westbound; exit 465A (Teasley Ln) eastbound, 0.4 mi n to Dallas Dr, then 0.5 mi e. Ext corridors.
Pets: Accepted. ASK ⊠ 🗐 🗏 ➷

⚫ ▼▼▼ Super 8-Denton H

(940) 380-8888. **$69-$75.** 620 S I-35E 76205. I-35, exit 465A (Teasley Ln). Int corridors. **Pets:** Other species. $25 daily fee/pet. Service with restrictions, supervision. SAVE ⊠ 🗐 🗏 ➷

▼▼ Travelodge H ❀

(940) 383-1471. **$69-$79.** 4211 I-35 N 76207. Jct US 380 and I-35, exit 469, just n. Int corridors. **Pets:** Other species. $25 deposit/room. Service with restrictions, crate. ASK ⊠ 🗐 🗏 ➷

DESOTO

⚫ ▼▼▼ McM Grande Hotel H

(972) 224-9100. **$79-$119.** 1515 N I-35E 75115. I-35E, exit 416 (Wintergreen Rd), just s. Ext/int corridors. **Pets:** Designated rooms, service with restrictions, supervision. SAVE ⊠ 🗐 🗏 🍴 ➷

⚫ ▼ Red Roof Inn Dallas/DeSoto H

(972) 224-7100. **$36-$90.** 1401 N I-35E 75115. I-35E, exit 416 (Wintergreen Rd), just s. Ext/int corridors. **Pets:** Large. Service with restrictions, crate. SAVE ⊠ 🗐

DUNCANVILLE

▼ Motel 6–#1130 H

(972) 296-0345. **$43-$55.** 202 Jellison Blvd 75116. I-20, exit 462A (Duncanville Rd) eastbound; exit 462B (Main St) westbound, just s to Camp Wisdom, just w to Duncanville Rd, just n to Jellison Blvd, then just w. Ext/int corridors. **Pets:** Other species. Service with restrictions, supervision. ⊠ 🗐 ➷

ENNIS

▼▼▼ Comfort Suites H

(972) 872-9898. **$70-$90.** 400 S I-45 75119. I-45, exit 251A, 0.7 mi n on N Frontage Rd to Dolfie Ln, then just e. Int corridors. **Pets:** Accepted. ASK ⊠ 🖾 ➷

FARMERS BRANCH

▼▼▼▼ Fairfield Inn & Suites by Marriott Dallas North H

(972) 661-9800. **$98-$120.** 13900 Parkside Center Blvd 75244. I-635, exit 23, 0.9 mi n to Spring Valley, just w, then just s. Int corridors.
Pets: $75 one-time fee/room. Service with restrictions, crate.

⊠ 🗐 🗏 ➷

▼▼▼▼ Holiday Inn North Dallas H

(972) 243-3363. **$89-$129.** 2645 LBJ Frwy 75234. I-635, exit 26 (Josey Ln) eastbound, just n; exit 25 westbound, 0.4 mi w. Int corridors.
Pets: Dogs only. $50 one-time fee/room. Service with restrictions, supervision. ASK ⊠ 🗐 🗏 🍴 ➷

▼▼ **La Quinta Inn Dallas (NW-Farmers Branch)** ⊞ ❀
(972) 620-7333. **$39-$89.** 13235 Stemmons Frwy N 75234-5757. I-35E, exit 441 (Valley View Ln), on southbound frontage road. Ext corridors. **Pets:** Medium, other species. Service with restrictions, supervision.
[ASK] [✕] [🛏] [💻] [🏊]

▼▼ ▼▼ **Omni Dallas Hotel Park West** ⊞
(972) 869-4300. **$90-$207.** 1590 LBJ Frwy 75234. Nw off I-635, 1.5 mi w of jct I-35E, exit 29 (Luna Rd). Int corridors. **Pets:** Accepted.
[ASK] [✕] [🛏] [💻] [🍴] [🏊] [✕]

▼▼ ▼▼ **Sheraton Dallas North by the Galleria** ⊞
(972) 661-3600. **$89-$249.** 4801 LBJ Frwy 75244. I-635, exit 22C (Inwood Rd) eastbound, then n; exit 22B (Dallas Pkwy) westbound. Int corridors. **Pets:** Accepted. [✕] [♿M] [🛏] [💻] [🍴] [🏊]

▼▼ ▼▼ **StudioPLUS Hotel Dallas-Farmers Branch** ⊞
(972) 385-6006. **$70-$86.** 4022 Parkside Center Blvd 75244. I-635, exit 23 (Midway Rd), 0.9 mi n to Parkside Center Blvd. Int corridors. **Pets:** Other species. $25 daily fee/room. Designated rooms, service with restrictions, crate. [ASK] [✕] [🛏] [💻] [🏊]

▼▼ ▼▼ **Super 8** ⊞
(972) 406-3030. **$49-$99.** 14040 Stemmons Frwy 75234. I-35E, exit 442 (Valwood Pkwy). Int corridors. **Pets:** Small, other species. $10 daily fee/pet. Service with restrictions, supervision. [ASK] [✕] [🛏] [💻] [🏊]

FRISCO

▼▼ ▼▼ **aloft Frisco** ⊞
(972) 668-6011. **Call for rates.** 3202 Parkwood Blvd 75034. North Dallas Tollway, exit Warren Pkwy, 0.5 mi e to Parkwood Blvd, then just s. Int corridors. **Pets:** Accepted. [SAVE] [✕] [♿M] [🛏] [💻] [🏊]

▼▼ ▼▼ **Hilton Garden Inn Frisco** ⊞
(469) 362-8485. **$69-$169.** 7550 Gaylord Pkwy 75034. North Dallas Tollway, exit Gaylord Parkway, just e. Int corridors. **Pets:** Accepted.
[✕] [♿M] [🛏] [💻] [🍴] [🏊]

▼▼ ▼▼ **Sheraton Stonebriar Hotel** ⊞
(972) 668-8700. **$99-$309.** 5444 State Hwy 121 75034. SR 121, exit Legacy Dr; northwest corner. Int corridors. **Pets:** Accepted.
[SAVE] [✕] [♿M] [🛏] [💻] [🍴]

▼▼ ▼▼ ▼▼ **The Westin Stonebriar Resort** ⊞
(972) 668-8000. **$119-$389.** 1549 Legacy Dr 75034. 0.3 mi n of jct SR 121. Int corridors. **Pets:** Accepted.
[SAVE] [✕] [♿M] [🛏] [💻] [🍴] [🏊] [✕]

GARLAND

▼▼ ▼▼ **Best Western Lakeview Inn** ⊞
(972) 303-1601. **$69-$119.** 1635 E I-30 at Bass Pro Rd 75043. I-30, exit 62 (Chaha Rd). Ext corridors. **Pets:** Accepted. [SAVE] [✕] [🛏] [💻] [🏊]

▼▼ ▼▼ **La Quinta Inn Dallas (Garland)** ⊞ ❀
(972) 271-7581. **$39-$89.** 12721 I-635 75041. I-635, exit 11B, just nw. Ext/int corridors. **Pets:** Medium, other species. Service with restrictions, supervision. [ASK] [✕] [🛏] [💻] [🏊]

▼▼ **Motel 6–0620** ⊞
(972) 226-7140. **$43-$57.** 436 W I-30 75043. I-30, exit 59 (Belt Line Rd). Ext corridors. **Pets:** Other species. Service with restrictions, supervision.
[✕] [🏊]

▼▼ ▼▼ **Radisson Hotel Dallas East** ⊞
(214) 341-5400. **$79-$99, 3 day notice.** 11350 LBJ Frwy 75238. I-635, exit 13 (Jupiter/Kingsley rds), just sw. Int corridors. **Pets:** Accepted.
[ASK] [✕] [🛏] [💻] [🍴] [🏊]

GRAND PRAIRIE

▼▼ ▼▼ **La Quinta Inn Dallas (Grand Prairie)** ⊞ ❀
(972) 641-3021. **$39-$89.** 1410 NW 19th St 75050-2802. I-30, exit 32, just e. Ext corridors. **Pets:** Medium, other species. Service with restrictions, supervision. [ASK] [✕] [♿M] [🛏] [💻] [🏊]

GREENVILLE

△△△ ▼▼ ▼▼ **Best Western Monica Royale Inn & Suites** ⊞
(903) 454-3700. **$79-$99.** 3001 Mustang Crossing 75402. I-30, exit 93A. Int corridors. **Pets:** Small, other species. $50 deposit/room. Service with restrictions, supervision. [SAVE] [✕] [♿M] [🛏] [💻] [🏊]

▼▼ ▼▼ **Holiday Inn Express Hotel & Suites** ⊞
(903) 454-8680. **$99-$109.** 2901 Mustang Crossing 75402. I-30, exit 93A. Int corridors. **Pets:** Accepted. [ASK] [✕] [♿M] [🛏] [💻] [🏊]

▼▼ ▼▼ **Quality Inn** ⊞
(903) 454-7000. **$55.** 1215 E I-30 75402. I-30, exit 94B, just e of jct I-30 and US 69. Int corridors. **Pets:** Small. $25 one-time fee/room. Service with restrictions, supervision. [ASK] [✕] [🛏] [💻] [🍴] [🏊]

IRVING

△△△ ▼▼ ▼▼ **aloft Las Colinas** ⊞ ❀
(972) 717-6100. **Call for rates.** 122 E John Carpenter Frwy 75062. SR 114, exit O'Connor Rd, just s. Int corridors. **Pets:** Medium, other species. Service with restrictions, supervision. [SAVE] [✕] [♿M] [🛏] [💻] [🏊]

▼▼ ▼▼ **Candlewood Dallas/Las Colinas** ⊞
(972) 714-9990. **$81-$126.** 5300 Green Park Dr 75038. SR 114, exit Walnut Hill Ln, just s. Int corridors. **Pets:** Accepted.
[ASK] [✕] [♿M] [🛏] [💻]

▼▼ ▼▼ **Days Inn DFW North** ⊞
(972) 621-8277. **$55.** 4325 W Hwy 114 75063. SR 114, exit Belt Line Rd, on westbound service road. Ext corridors. **Pets:** Medium, other species. $25 one-time fee/room. Service with restrictions, crate.
[ASK] [✕] [🛏] [💻] [🍴] [🏊]

▼▼ ▼▼ **Drury Inn & Suites-DFW Airport** ⊞
(972) 986-1200. **$80-$139.** 4210 W Airport Frwy 75062. SR 183, exit Esters Rd, on southbound access road. Int corridors. **Pets:** Other species. No service, supervision. [ASK] [✕] [🛏] [💻] [🏊]

▼▼ ▼▼ **Extended Stay Deluxe (Dallas-Las Colinas-Green Park Dr)** ⊞
(972) 751-0808. **$70-$80.** 5401 Green Park Dr 75038. SR 114, exit Walnut Hill Ln, just s. Int corridors. **Pets:** Other species. $25 daily fee/room. Designated rooms, service with restrictions, crate.
[ASK] [✕] [♿M] [🛏] [💻] [🏊]

△△△ ▼▼ ▼▼ ▼▼ **Four Seasons Resort and Club** ⊞
(972) 717-0700. **$275-$3000.** 4150 N MacArthur Blvd 75038. SR 114, exit MacArthur Blvd, 1.5 mi s. Int corridors. **Pets:** Accepted.
[SAVE] [✕] [♿M] [🛏] [💻] [🍴] [🏊] [✕]

▼▼ ▼▼ **Homestead Studio Suites Hotel-Dallas/DFW Airport North** ⊞
(972) 929-3333. **$65-$80.** 7825 Heathrow Dr 75063. SR 114, exit Freeport Pkwy; on eastbound service road, just w. Int corridors. **Pets:** Other species. $25 daily fee/room. Designated rooms, service with restrictions, crate. [ASK] [✕] [🛏] [💻]

▼▼ ▼▼ **Homewood Suites by Hilton Las Colinas** ⊞
(972) 556-0665. **$179-$199.** 4300 Wingren Dr 75039. Ne off SR 114, exit O'Connor Rd/Wingren Dr eastbound, just n to Las Colinas Blvd, 0.4 mi e to Rochelle Rd, then just s; exit Rochelle Rd westbound. Ext/int corridors. **Pets:** Accepted. [✕] [♿M] [🛏] [💻] [🏊] [✕]

△△△ ▼▼ ▼▼ **Hyatt Summerfield Suites Dallas/Las Colinas** ⊞
(972) 831-0909. **$79-$189.** 5901 N MacArthur Blvd 75039. SR 114, exit MacArthur Blvd, northwest corner. Ext/int corridors. **Pets:** Accepted.
[SAVE] [✕] [♿M] [🛏] [💻] [🏊] [✕]

WWW La Quinta Inn & Suites Dallas (DFW-Airport North) H ❀
(972) 915-4022. **$69-$129.** 4850 W John Carpenter Frwy 75063. SR 114, exit Freeport Pkwy, on eastbound service road. Int corridors. **Pets:** Medium, other species. Service with restrictions, supervision.
(ASK) ⊠ (&M) ⊟ ▣ ⟶

WWW La Quinta Inn & Suites Dallas DFW Airport South (Irving) H ❀
(972) 252-6546. **$59-$129.** 4105 W Airport Frwy 75062-5997. 3 mi nw off SR 183, exit Esters Rd; on northbound access road. Int corridors. **Pets:** Medium, other species. Service with restrictions, supervision.
(ASK) ⊠ ⊟ ▣ ⟶

WWW La Quinta Inn & Suites-Las Colinas H ❀
(972) 261-4900. **$59-$179 (no credit cards).** 4225 N MacArthur Blvd 75038. Se off SR 114; 1.4 mi s of exit MacArthur Blvd. Int corridors. **Pets:** Medium, other species. Service with restrictions, supervision.
⊠ ⊟ ▣ ⟶

WWW Motel 6 #1274 DFW North M
(972) 915-3993. **$51-$61.** 7800 Heathrow Dr 75063. SR 114, exit Freeport Pkwy, just se. Int corridors. **Pets:** Other species. Service with restrictions, supervision. ⊠ ⊟ ⟶

WWW WWW Omni Mandalay Hotel at Las Colinas H
(972) 556-0800. **$129-$499.** 221 E Las Colinas Blvd 75039. Nw off SR 114, exit O'Connor Rd. Int corridors. **Pets:** Accepted.
(ASK) ⊠ ⊟ ▣ (¶¶) ⟶ ⊠

AAA WWW Red Roof Inn/DFW Airport North M
(972) 929-0020. **$48-$70.** 8150 Esters Blvd 75063. SR 114, exit Esters Blvd, just n. Ext corridors. **Pets:** Large. Service with restrictions, crate.
(SAVE) ⊠ ⊟

WWW WWW Residence Inn by Marriott at Las Colinas H ❀
(972) 580-7773. **$125-$153.** 950 W Walnut Hill Ln 75038. SR 114, exit MacArthur Blvd, 0.5 mi s, then just e. Ext corridors. **Pets:** Other species. $100 one-time fee/room. Service with restrictions, crate.
⊠ (&M) ⊟ ▣ ⟶ ⊠

WWW WWW Residence Inn by Marriott-DFW/Irving H
(972) 871-1331. **$80-$169.** 8600 Esters Blvd 75063. SR 114, exit Esters Blvd, 0.9 mi n. Int corridors. **Pets:** Accepted.
⊠ (&M) ⊟ ▣ ⟶ ⊠

WWW WWW Sheraton Grand Hotel H ❀
(972) 929-8400. **$79-$219.** 4440 W John Carpenter Frwy 75063. SR 114, exit Esters Blvd, just s. Int corridors. **Pets:** Medium, dogs only. $35 one-time fee/pet. (ASK) ⊠ ⊟ ▣ (¶¶) ⟶

AAA WWW WWW Staybridge Suites Dallas-Las Colinas H
(972) 465-9400. **Call for rates.** 1201 Executive Cir 75038. SR 114, exit MacArthur Blvd, just s to W Walnut Hill Ln, then just w. Int corridors.
Pets: Accepted. (SAVE) ⊠ ⊟ ▣ ⟶

AAA WWW WWW The Westin Dallas Fort Worth Airport H
(972) 929-4500. **Call for rates.** 4545 W John Carpenter Frwy 75063. Nw off SR 114, exit Esters Blvd. Int corridors. **Pets:** Accepted.
(SAVE) ⊠ ⊟ ▣ (¶¶) ⟶

WWW WWW Wyndham-Las Colinas H
(972) 650-1600. **$79-$199.** 110 W John Carpenter Frwy 75039. Sw off SR 114, exit O'Connor Rd. Int corridors. **Pets:** Accepted.
(ASK) ⊠ ⊟ ▣ (¶¶) ⟶

KAUFMAN

AAA WWW WWW Best Western La Hacienda Inn M
(972) 962-6272. **$65-$150.** 200 E Hwy 175 75142. Just e of jct US 175 and SR 34. Ext corridors. **Pets:** Very small. $10 one-time fee/pet. Service with restrictions, supervision. (SAVE) ⊠ ⊟ ▣ ⟶

LAKE DALLAS

AAA WWW WWW Best Western Lake Dallas Inn & Suites H
(940) 497-1007. **$90-$110.** 305 Swisher Rd 75065. I-35E, exit 458 (Swisher Rd), 0.6 mi on N Frontage Rd. Int corridors. **Pets:** Accepted.
(SAVE) ⊠ ⊟ ▣ ⟶

LEWISVILLE

WWW Comfort Suites by Choice Hotels H
(972) 315-6464. **$80-$120.** 755A Vista Ridge Mall Dr 75067. I-35E, exit 448A (Round Grove Rd) southbound, 0.5 mi s of jct I-35 and Round Grove Rd on southbound service road to Vista Ridge Mall Dr, then just w; exit 447B northbound, just w on SR 121 Bypass. Int corridors.
Pets: Accepted. (ASK) ⊠ ⊟ ▣ ⟶

WWW WWW Country Inn & Suites By Carlson H
(972) 315-6565. **$75-$115.** 755B Vista Ridge Mall Dr 75067. I-35E, exit 448A (Round Grove Rd) southbound, 0.5 mi s on service road to Vista Ridge Mall Dr, then just w; exit 447B northbound, just w on SR 121 Bypass. Int corridors. **Pets:** Accepted. (ASK) ⊠ ⊟ ▣ ⟶

WWW WWW Extended StayAmerica Dallas-Lewisville H
(972) 315-7455. **$65-$80.** 1900 Lakepointe Dr 75057. I-35E, exit 449 (Corporate Dr), just e to Lakepointe Dr, then just s. Int corridors. **Pets:** Other species. $25 daily fee/room. Designated rooms, service with restrictions, crate. (ASK) ⊠ ⊟ ▣ ⟶

WWW WWW La Quinta Inn Dallas (Lewisville) H ❀
(972) 221-7525. **$39-$89.** 1657 S Stemmons Frwy 75067-6401. I-35E, exit 449 (Corporate Dr), just w. Ext corridors. **Pets:** Medium, other species. Service with restrictions, supervision.
(ASK) ⊠ (&M) ⊟ ▣ ⟶

WWW Motel 6–1288 H
(972) 436-5008. **$43-$55.** 1705 Lakepointe Dr 75057. I-35E, exit 449 (Corporate Dr), just n on access road. Int corridors. **Pets:** Other species. Service with restrictions, supervision. ⊠ ⊟ ⟶

WWW WWW Residence Inn by Marriott Dallas H
(972) 315-3777. **$140-$150.** 755C Vista Ridge Mall Dr 75067. I-35E, exit 448A (Round Grove Rd), 0.5 mi s on service road; jct I-35 and Round Grove Rd to Vista Ridge Mall Dr, just w; exit 447B northbound, just w. Int corridors. **Pets:** Accepted. ⊠ (&M) ⊟ ▣ ⟶ ⊠

WWW WWW Rodeway Inn H
(972) 221-2121. **Call for rates.** 1102 Texas St 75057. I-35E, exit 450 (SR 121), just e. Ext corridors. **Pets:** Medium, other species. Service with restrictions, supervision. ⊠ ⊟ ▣ ⟶

MCKINNEY

WWW WWW Days Inn McKinney H
(972) 548-8888. **$60.** 2104 N Central Expwy 75070. US 75, exit 41 0.5 mi n of jct US 380. Ext corridors. **Pets:** Accepted.
(ASK) ⊠ ⊟ ▣ ⟶

WWW WWW Super 8-McKinney H
(972) 548-8880. **$60-$75.** 910 N Central Expwy 75070. US 75, exit 40A (Virginia St/Louisiana St), 0.5 mi n on northbound service road. Int corridors. **Pets:** Small. $10 daily fee/pet. No service, supervision.
(ASK) ⊠ ⊟ ⟶

MESQUITE

WWW WWW Comfort Inn H ❀
(972) 285-6300. **Call for rates.** 923 Windbell Cir 75149. I-635, exit 5, just e. Int corridors. **Pets:** Other species. $10 one-time fee/room. Service with restrictions, supervision. ⊠ (&M) ⊟ ▣ ⟶

AAA WWW WWW La Quinta Inn & Suites H ❀
(972) 216-7460. **$59-$155.** 118 E Hwy 80 75149. US 80 E, exit Belt Line Rd. Int corridors. **Pets:** Medium, other species. Service with restrictions, supervision. (SAVE) ⊠ (&M) ⊟ ▣ ⟶

WWW WWW Super 8 H
(972) 289-5481. **$57-$62.** 121 Grand Junction Blvd 75149. I-635, exit 4 (Military Pkwy). Ext corridors. **Pets:** Other species. $5 daily fee/room. Service with restrictions, supervision. (ASK) ⊠ ⊟ ▣ ⟶

MIDLOTHIAN

Americas Best Value Inn & Suites 🔷
(972) 775-1891. **$79-$110.** 220 N Hwy 67 76065. On US 67, just n of jct US 287. Ext corridors. **Pets:** Medium, other species. $10 daily fee/pet. Service with restrictions, crate.

PLANO

aloft Plano 🔷 🐾
(214) 474-2520. **Call for rates.** 6853 N Dallas Pkwy 75024. North Dallas Tollway, exit Spring Creek Pkwy/Tennyson Pkwy, on south access road. Int corridors. **Pets:** Medium, dogs only. Designated rooms, service with restrictions, supervision.

Best Western Park Suites Hotel 🔷
(972) 578-2243. **$85-$90.** 640 Park Blvd E 75074. US 75, exit 29A northbound, just e; exit 29 southbound, 0.5 mi s on access road, just e on 15th St, then 0.5 mi n on access road. Int corridors. **Pets:** Accepted.

Candlewood Suites-Plano 🔷
(972) 618-5446. **$62-$132.** 4701 Legacy Dr 75024. Jct SR 289 (Preston Rd) and Legacy Dr, just e. Int corridors. **Pets:** Medium. $75 one-time fee/pet. Service with restrictions.

Extended Stay Deluxe (Dallas/Plano) 🔷
(972) 378-9978. **$95-$109.** 2900 Dallas Pkwy 75093. Dallas Pkwy, exit Park Blvd northbound; exit Parker Rd southbound, on northbound service road. Int corridors. **Pets:** Other species. $25 daily fee/room. Designated rooms, service with restrictions, crate.

Extended Stay Deluxe Dallas-Plano-Plano Parkway 🔷
(972) 398-0135. **$80-$97.** 4636 W Plano Pkwy 75093. Jct SR 289 (Preston Rd) and W Plano Pkwy, 0.4 mi e. Int corridors. **Pets:** Other species. $25 daily fee/room. Designated rooms, service with restrictions, crate.

Holiday Inn Express Hotel & Suites Plano East 🔷
(972) 881-1881. **$99-$109.** 700 Central Pkwy E 75074. Just e of US 75; 0.3 mi ne of jct FM 544, exit 29A northbound; exit 29 southbound, 0.5 mi s on access road, just e on 15th St, then 0.5 mi n on access road. Int corridors. **Pets:** Small. $50 one-time fee/room. Service with restrictions, supervision.

Homestead Studio Suites Hotel-Dallas/Plano Parkway 🔷
(972) 596-9966. **$65-$80.** 4709 W Plano Pkwy 75093. Just n of jct Plano Pkwy and SR 289 (Preston Rd), then just e. Int corridors. **Pets:** Other species. $25 daily fee/room. Designated rooms, service with restrictions, crate.

Homewood Suites by Hilton 🔷
(972) 758-8800. **$169-$179.** 4705 Old Shepherd Pl 75093. Jct Plano Pkwy and SR 289 (Preston Rd), 0.4 mi n, then just e. Int corridors. **Pets:** Accepted.

La Quinta Inn & Suites Dallas (West Plano) 🔷 🐾
(972) 599-0700. **$59-$129.** 4800 W Plano Pkwy 75093. Just n of jct SR 289 (Preston Rd), then just e. Int corridors. **Pets:** Medium, other species. Service with restrictions, supervision.

La Quinta Inn Dallas (Plano) 🔷 🐾
(972) 423-1300. **$39-$89.** 1820 N Central Expwy 75074-5606. US 75, exit 29A (Park Blvd), northbound, just ne; exit 29 southbound, 0.5 mi s on access road, just e on 15th St, then just n on northbound access road. Ext corridors. **Pets:** Medium, other species. Service with restrictions, supervision.

Nylo Plano at Legacy 🔷 🐾
(972) 624-6990. **$109-$189.** 8201 Preston Rd 75024. Just s of jct SR 121 and Preston Rd. Int corridors. **Pets:** Large. $50 daily fee/room. Service with restrictions, supervision.

Red Roof Inn Dallas-Plano 🔷
(972) 881-8191. **Call for rates.** 301 Ruisseau Dr 75023. US 75, exit 30 (Parker Rd), 0.5 mi w to Premier, then just n. Ext/int corridors. **Pets:** Large. Service with restrictions, crate.

Southfork Hotel 🔷
(972) 578-8555. **$89-$99.** 1600 N Central Expwy 75074. US 75, exit 29A northbound; exit 29 southbound, on northbound access road. Int corridors. **Pets:** Accepted.

Super 8-Plano 🔷
(972) 423-8300. **$60-$70.** 1704 N Central Expwy 75074. US 75, exit 29A (Park Blvd) northbound, just e; exit 29 southbound, 0.5 mi s on access road, just e on 15th St, then just n on access road. Int corridors. **Pets:** Accepted.

TownePlace Suites by Marriott 🔷
(972) 943-8200. **$134-$164.** 5005 Whitestone Ln 75024. North Dallas Tollway, exit Spring Creek Pkwy, 1.9 mi e, just n on SR 289 (Preston Rd), to Whitestone Ln, then just w. Int corridors. **Pets:** Accepted.

RICHARDSON

Doubletree Dallas/Richardson 🔷
(972) 644-4000. **$89-$249.** 1981 N Central Expwy 75080. US 75, exit 26 (Campbell Rd), 1.8 mi n; jct SR 5. Int corridors. **Pets:** Accepted.

Homestead Studio Suites Hotel-Dallas/Richardson 🔷
(972) 479-0500. **$69-$88.** 901 E Campbell Rd 75081. US 75, exit 26 (Campbell Rd), just e. Int corridors. **Pets:** Other species. $25 daily fee/room. Designated rooms, service with restrictions, crate.

Hyatt Summerfield Suites Dallas/Richardson 🔷
(972) 671-8080. **$79-$189.** 2301 N Central Expwy 75080. US 75, exit 26 (Campbell Rd), 0.5 mi w to Collins Blvd, then 0.6 mi n. Int corridors. **Pets:** Accepted.

Renaissance Dallas-Richardson Hotel 🔷
(972) 367-2000. **$170-$208.** 900 E Lookout Dr 75082. US 75, exit 27A (Gallatin Pkwy/Renner Rd) northbound; exit 26 (Gallatin Pkwy/Campbell Rd) southbound, just e. Int corridors. **Pets:** Accepted.

Residence Inn by Marriott Richardson 🔷
(972) 669-5888. **$97-$119.** 1040 Waterwood Dr 75082. US 75, exit 26 (Campbell Rd), just e to Greenville Ave, 0.4 mi n to Glenville Rd, then just w. Int corridors. **Pets:** Accepted.

ROANOKE

Comfort Suites Roanoke 🔷
(817) 490-1455. **$90-$100.** 801 Byron Nelson Blvd 76262. I-35, exit 70 (SR 114), 3.4 mi e, exit Rufe/Snow, then just se. Int corridors. **Pets:** Accepted.

Speedway Sleep Inn & Suites 🔷
(817) 491-3120. **$70-$109.** 13471 Raceway Dr 76262. I-35, exit 70 (SR 114), just e, then just s. Int corridors. **Pets:** Medium, other species. $30 deposit/room. Service with restrictions, supervision.

ROCKWALL

Hilton Bella Harbor on Lake Ray Hubbard 🔷 🐾
(214) 771-3700. **$99-$409.** 2055 Summer Lee Dr 75032. I-30 E, exit 67A (Horizon Rd) eastbound; exit 67B (Horizon Rd) westbound, just s to Summer Lee Dr, then 0.5 mi s. Int corridors. **Pets:** Medium. $75 one-time fee/room. Designated rooms, service with restrictions.

▼▼▼▼ La Quinta Inn & Suites 🄷 ❀
(972) 771-1685. **$79-$339.** 689 E I-30 75087. I-30, exit 67 westbound; exit 67B eastbound. Int corridors. **Pets:** Medium, other species. Service with restrictions, supervision. (A$K) [✕] [&M] 🛏 🖵 ⇄

ROWLETT
▼▼▼ Comfort Suites Lake Ray Hubbard 🄷
(972) 463-9595. **$90.** 8701 E I-30 75088. I-30, exit 64 (Dalrock Rd). Int corridors. **Pets:** Accepted. (A$K) [✕] [&M] 🛏 🖵 ⇄

TERRELL
🔷🔷🔷 ▼▼▼ Best Western Country Inn 🄷
(972) 563-1521. **$60-$70.** 1604 Hwy 34 S 75160. I-20, exit 501 (SR 34), just n. Ext corridors. **Pets:** Accepted. (SAVE) [✕] 🛏 🖵 ⇄

UNIVERSITY PARK
🔷🔷🔷 ▼▼▼▼ Hotel Lumen 🄷
(214) 219-2400. **$149-$399.** 6101 Hillcrest Ave 75205. Just n of jct Mockingbird Ln and Hillcrest Ave. Int corridors. **Pets:** Accepted.
(SAVE) [✕] 🛏 🍽

END METROPOLITAN AREA

DECATUR
🔷🔷🔷 ▼▼▼ Best Western Decatur Inn 🄼
(940) 627-5982. **$59-$125.** 1801 S Hwy 287 76234. 0.6 mi s of jct Business Rt US 380. Ext corridors. **Pets:** Accepted.
(SAVE) [✕] 🛏 🖵 ⇄

▼▼▼▼ Holiday Inn Express Hotel & Suites 🄷
(940) 627-0776. **$107-$117.** 1051 N Hwy 287 76234. US 380, exit US 287 N, just n. Int corridors. **Pets:** Small. $50 one-time fee/pet. Service with restrictions, supervision. (A$K) [✕] 🛏 🖵 ⇄

DEL RIO
🔷🔷🔷 ▼▼▼ Best Western Inn of Del Rio 🄼
(830) 775-7511. **$65-$75.** 810 Veterans Blvd 78840. Between E 6th and E 7th sts. Ext corridors. **Pets:** Small. $10 daily fee/pet. Service with restrictions, supervision. (SAVE) [✕] 🛏 🖵 ⇄

🔷🔷🔷 ▼▼▼ Comfort Inn & Suites 🄷
(830) 775-2933. **$65-$99.** 3616 Veterans Blvd 78840. 3.2 mi nw on US 90. Ext/int corridors. **Pets:** Medium. $10 daily fee/pet. Service with restrictions, supervision. (SAVE) [✕] 🛏 🖵 ⇄

▼▼▼ La Quinta Inn Del Rio 🄷 ❀
(830) 775-7591. **$45-$89.** 2005 Veterans Blvd 78840. 1.8 mi nw on US 90, 277 and 377. Ext/int corridors. **Pets:** Medium, other species. Service with restrictions, supervision. (A$K) [✕] 🛏 🖵 ⇄

▼ Motel 6 Del Rio #323 🄷
(830) 774-2115. **$39-$51.** 2115 Veterans Blvd 78840. Jct US 90/277 and Garner Dr. Ext corridors. **Pets:** Other species. Service with restrictions, supervision. [✕] ⇄

🔷🔷🔷 ▼▼▼▼ Ramada Inn 🄷
(830) 775-1511. **$84-$114.** 2101 Veterans Blvd 78840. 1.8 mi nw on US 90, 277 and 377. Ext/int corridors. **Pets:** Accepted.
(SAVE) [✕] 🛏 🖵 🍽 ⇄ [✕]

DONNA
▼▼▼ Super 8 🄼
(956) 461-2226. **Call for rates.** 2005 E Expwy 83 78537. US 83, exit CR 493. Ext corridors. **Pets:** Accepted. [✕] 🛏 🖵 ⇄

▼▼▼ Victoria Palms Inn & Suites 🄷
(956) 464-7801. **Call for rates.** 602 N Victoria Rd 78537. US 83, exit Victoria Rd. Ext corridors. **Pets:** Accepted.
[✕] 🛏 🖵 🍽 ⇄ [✕]

DUMAS
🔷🔷🔷 ▼▼▼ Best Western Windsor Inn 🄷
(806) 935-9644. **$69-$109.** 1701 S Dumas Ave 79029. US 287, 2 mi s of US 87 and SR 152. Ext corridors. **Pets:** Dogs only. $20 deposit/room, $10 daily fee/pet. Service with restrictions, supervision.
(SAVE) [✕] 🛏 🖵 ⇄ [✕]

🔷🔷🔷 ▼▼▼ Econo Lodge 🄷
(806) 935-9098. **$63-$90.** 1719 S Dumas Ave 79029. US 287, 2 mi s of US 87 and SR 152. Int corridors. **Pets:** Accepted. (SAVE) [✕] 🛏

▼▼▼ Quality Inn 🄷
(806) 935-4000. **Call for rates.** 1525 S Dumas Ave 79029. US 287, 1.1 mi s of US 87 and SR 152. Int corridors. **Pets:** Accepted.
[✕] 🛏 🖵 ⇄

▼▼ Super 8 🄼
(806) 935-6222. **$89-$119.** 119 W 17th St 79029. US 287, 2 mi s of jct US 87 and SR 152. Ext corridors. **Pets:** Accepted. (A$K) [✕] 🛏 🖵

EAGLE PASS
🔷🔷🔷 ▼▼▼ Americas Best Value Inn 🄷
(830) 773-9531. **$61-$68.** 2150 N US Hwy 277 78852. On US 277, 4 mi n. Ext corridors. **Pets:** Very small. Designated rooms, service with restrictions, supervision. (SAVE) [✕] 🛏 🖵 ⇄

▼▼▼▼ La Quinta Inn Eagle Pass 🄼 ❀
(830) 773-7000. **$59-$99.** 2525 E Main St 78852-4498. US 57 and 277 at Loop 431. Ext corridors. **Pets:** Medium, other species. Service with restrictions, supervision. (A$K) [✕] 🛏 🖵 ⇄

EASTLAND
▼▼ Super 8 & RV Park 🄼
(254) 629-3336. **$59-$64.** 3900 I-20 E 76448. I-20, exit 343, on north service road. Ext corridors. **Pets:** Accepted. (A$K) [✕] 🛏 🖵 ⇄

EDINBURG
🔷🔷🔷 ▼▼▼ Best Western Edinburg 🄷
(956) 318-0442. **$79-$129.** 2708 S Bus Hwy 281 78539. US 281, exit Canton Ave, 1 mi w to Bus Hwy 281. Ext corridors. **Pets:** Very small, dogs only. $15 daily fee/pet. Designated rooms, service with restrictions, supervision. (SAVE) [✕] [&M] 🛏 🖵 ⇄

🔷🔷🔷 ▼▼▼▼ Comfort Inn Edinburg 🄼
(956) 318-1117. **$65-$125.** 4001 S US Hwy 281 78539. US 281, exit Trenton Rd, just w, then just n on Business Rt US 281. Int corridors. **Pets:** Accepted. (SAVE) [✕] 🛏 🖵 ⇄

EL PASO
🔷🔷🔷 ▼▼▼▼ Chase Suites by Woodfin 🄷
(915) 772-8000. **$150-$299.** 6791 Montana Ave 79925. I-10, exit 25 (Airway Blvd), 1 mi n, then just e. Ext corridors. **Pets:** Accepted.
(SAVE) [✕] 🛏 🖵 ⇄

🔷🔷🔷 ▼▼▼ Comfort Inn Airport East 🄷 ❀
(915) 594-9111. **$68-$85.** 900 Yarbrough Dr 79915. I-10, exit 28B. Ext corridors. **Pets:** Medium. $20 one-time fee/room. Service with restrictions.
(SAVE) [✕] 🛏 🖵 ⇄

▼▼ **Days Inn Hotel East** Ⓜ ❖
(915) 595-1913. **$49-$70.** 10635 Gateway Blvd W 79935. I-10, exit 28B westbound; exit 29 (Lomaland Dr) eastbound, U-turn under freeway, 1 mi w on frontage road. Ext corridors. **Pets:** $10 one-time fee/pet. Designated rooms, supervision. (ASK) ✕ 🔲 🖵 ⤸

▼▼ **Extended StayAmerica-El Paso-Airport** Ⓗ
(915) 772-5754. **$75-$92.** 6580 Montana Ave 79925. I-10, exit 24 (Geronimo Dr), westbound, exit 24B (Geronimo Dr) eastbound, 0.5 mi n, then 0.5 mi e. Ext corridors. **Pets:** Other species. $25 daily fee/room. Designated rooms, service with restrictions, crate. (ASK) ✕ 🔲 🖵

▼▼▼ **GuestHouse International Suites** Ⓗ
(915) 772-0395. **$95-$165.** 1940 Airway Blvd 79925. I-10, exit 25 (Airway Blvd), 1.2 mi n. Int corridors. **Pets:** Medium, other species. $100 deposit/room. Designated rooms, service with restrictions, supervision.
(ASK) ✕ (&M) 🔲 🖵 ⤸

🅰🅰🅰 ▼▼▼ **Holiday Inn-Airport** Ⓗ
(915) 778-6411. **$89-$209.** 6655 Gateway Blvd W 79925. I-10, exit 25 (Airway Blvd). Ext/int corridors. **Pets:** Medium, other species. $49 one-time fee/room. Service with restrictions, crate.
(SAVE) ✕ 🔲 🖵 (🍴) ⤸

🅰🅰🅰 ▼▼▼ **Holiday Inn El Paso Sunland Park** Ⓗ ❖
(915) 833-2900. **$99-$179.** 900 Sunland Park Dr 79922. I-10, exit 13, just s. Ext corridors. **Pets:** Other species. $25 one-time fee/room. Supervision. (SAVE) ✕ 🔲 🖵 ⤸

▼▼ **La Quinta Inn Airport East** Ⓗ ❖
(915) 593-8400. **$45-$89.** 9125 Gateway Blvd W 79925. I-10, exit 28B westbound; exit 27 eastbound. Ext corridors. **Pets:** Medium, other species. Service with restrictions, supervision. (ASK) ✕ 🔲 🖵 ⤸

▼▼ **La Quinta Inn & Suites El Paso East** Ⓗ ❖
(915) 591-3300. **$49-$99.** 7944 Gateway Blvd E 79915. I-10, exit 28B. Int corridors. **Pets:** Medium, other species. Service with restrictions, supervision. (ASK) ✕ (&M) 🔲 🖵 ⤸

▼▼ **La Quinta Inn & Suites El Paso West** Ⓗ ❖
(915) 585-2999. **$49-$99.** 7620 N Mesa St 79912. I-10, exit 11 (Mesa St), just ne. Int corridors. **Pets:** Medium, other species. Service with restrictions, supervision. (ASK) ✕ 🔲 🖵 ⤸

▼▼ **La Quinta Inn El Paso (Airport)** Ⓜ ❖
(915) 778-9321. **$59-$109.** 6140 Gateway Blvd E 79905-2004. I-10, exit 24B (Geronimo Dr) eastbound; exit 24 westbound. Ext corridors. **Pets:** Medium, other species. Service with restrictions, supervision.
(ASK) ✕ 🔲 🖵 ⤸

▼▼ **La Quinta Inn El Paso (Lomaland)** Ⓗ ❖
(915) 591-2244. **$59-$99.** 11033 Gateway Blvd W 79935-5003. I-10, exit 29 eastbound; exit 30 westbound, 1 mi w. Ext corridors. **Pets:** Medium, other species. Service with restrictions, supervision.
(ASK) ✕ (&M) 🔲 🖵 ⤸

▼▼ **La Quinta Inn El Paso (West)** Ⓜ ❖
(915) 833-2522. **$45-$89.** 7550 Remcon Cir 79912-3513. I-10, exit 11 (Mesa St). Ext corridors. **Pets:** Medium, other species. Service with restrictions, supervision. (ASK) ✕ 🔲 🖵 ⤸

▼▼ **Microtel Inn & Suites** Ⓗ
(915) 772-3650. **$78-$96.** 2001 Airway Blvd 79925. I-10, exit 25 (Airway Blvd), 1.3 mi n. Int corridors. **Pets:** Small, other species. $100 deposit/pet. Service with restrictions, crate. (ASK) ✕ (&M) 🔲 🖵

▼▼ **Microtel Inn & Suites El Paso East** Ⓗ
(915) 858-1600. **$53-$71.** 12211 Gateway Blvd W 79936. I-10, exit 34 (Joe Battle), on westbound frontage road. Int corridors. **Pets:** Accepted. (ASK) ✕ (&M) 🔲 🖵 ⤸

▼▼ **Microtel Inn & Suites West** Ⓜ
(915) 584-2026. **$68-$86.** 6185 S Desert Blvd 79932. I-10, exit 8 (Artcraft Rd/Paseo del Norte), on eastbound frontage road. Int corridors.
Pets: Accepted. (ASK) ✕ (♿) 🔲 🖵 ⤸

▼▼ **Motel 6 El Paso-Airport-Fort Bliss #4487** Ⓜ
(915) 778-3311. **Call for rates.** 6363 Montana Ave 79925. I-10, exit 24 (Geronimo Dr) westbound; exit 24B eastbound, 0.5 mi n on Geronimo Dr, 0.5 mi e. Ext corridors. **Pets:** Other species. Service with restrictions, supervision. ✕ 🔲 🖵 ⤸

▼▼▼ **Quality Inn & Suites** Ⓗ
(915) 772-3300. **Call for rates.** 6099 Montana Ave 79925. I-10, exit 24 (Geronimo Dr) westbound; exit 24B (Geronimo Dr) eastbound, 0.5 mi n. Ext corridors. **Pets:** Accepted. ✕ 🔲 🖵 (🍴) ⤸

▼▼▼ **Residence Inn by Marriott El Paso** Ⓗ
(915) 771-0504. **$162-$198.** 6355 Gateway Blvd W 79925. I-10, exit 24B (Geronimo Dr) eastbound, n to Edgemere, then just e; exit 25 (Airway Blvd) westbound, on westbound frontage road. Int corridors.
Pets: Accepted. ✕ 🔲 🖵 ⤸ (✕)

▼▼ **Sleep Inn by Choice Hotels** Ⓗ
(915) 585-7577. **Call for rates.** 953 Sunland Park Dr 79922. I-10, exit 13. Int corridors. **Pets:** Other species. $20 one-time fee/pet. Service with restrictions, crate. ✕ 🔲 🖵 ⤸

▼▼ **Super 8** Ⓗ
(915) 584-4030. **Call for rates.** 7840 N Mesa St 79932. I-10, exit 11 (N Mesa), just s. Ext corridors. **Pets:** Medium. $10 one-time fee/pet. Service with restrictions, supervision. ✕ 🔲 🖵 ⤸

▼▼ **Wingate by Wyndham** Ⓗ
(915) 772-4088. **$119-$139.** 6351 Gateway Blvd W 79925. I-10, exit 24B (Geronimo Dr) westbound; exit 25 (Airport Blvd) eastbound, U-turn, 0.5 mi. Int corridors. **Pets:** Large, other species. $150 deposit/room. Service with restrictions, supervision. (ASK) ✕ (&M) 🔲 🖵 ⤸

▼▼ **Wyndham El Paso Airport** Ⓗ
(915) 778-4241. **$129-$172, 6 day notice.** 2027 Airway Blvd 79925. I-10, exit 25 (Airway Blvd), 1.3 mi n. Int corridors. **Pets:** Small. $150 deposit/room. Service with restrictions, supervision.
(ASK) ✕ 🔲 🖵 (🍴) ⤸ (✕)

EULESS

▼▼ **Microtel Inn and Suites** Ⓗ
(817) 545-1111. **$54-$99.** 901 W Airport Frwy 76040. SR 183, exit Industrial Blvd (FM 157), just e. Int corridors. **Pets:** Medium, dogs only. $25 one-time fee/room. Service with restrictions, supervision.
(ASK) ✕ (&M) 🔲 🖵 ⤸

▼ **Motel 6-Euless #1345** Ⓗ
(817) 545-0141. **$42-$55.** 110 Airport Frwy 76039. SR 183, exit Euless/Main St, on westbound access road. Ext corridors. **Pets:** Other species. Service with restrictions, supervision. ✕ ⤸

▼▼ **Quality Inn Euless** Ⓗ
(817) 540-0233. **$49-$109.** 1001 W Airport Frwy 76040-4299. SR 183, exit Industrial Blvd (FM 157). Ext corridors. **Pets:** $25 one-time fee/pet. Service with restrictions, supervision. (ASK) ✕ 🔲 🖵

FORT DAVIS

▼ **Historical Prude Guest Ranch** 🆁🅰
(432) 426-3202. **$61-$150, 3 day notice.** 6 mi n Hwy 118 79734. 4.5 mi n of jct SR 118 and 17. Ext corridors. **Pets:** Other species. $10 one-time fee/room. Designated rooms, service with restrictions, crate.
(ASK) ✕ 🔲 (🍴) ⤸ (✕) (🐾) (🗲)

FORT STOCKTON

🅰🅰🅰 ▼▼ **Best Western Swiss Clock Inn** Ⓗ
(432) 336-8521. **$90-$110.** 3201 W Dickinson Blvd 79735. I-10, exit 256, 0.5 mi e. Ext corridors. **Pets:** Accepted. (SAVE) ✕ 🔲 🖵 (🍴) ⤸

🅰🅰🅰 ▼▼ **Days Inn** Ⓗ
(432) 336-7500. **$79-$140.** 1408 N US Hwy 285 79735. I-10, exit 257, just s. Ext corridors. **Pets:** Medium. $10 daily fee/pet. Designated rooms, service with restrictions, supervision. (SAVE) ✕ 🔲 🖵 ⤸

▼▼▼ ◆ La Quinta Inn Fort Stockton ⓗ ❀
(432) 336-9781. **$49-$109.** 1537 N US Hwy 285 79735. I-10, exit 257. Ext corridors. **Pets:** Medium, other species. Service with restrictions, supervision. (ASK) ⊠ 🛢 💻 ➡

◆◆◆ ▼▼▼▼ Quality Inn ⓗ
(432) 336-5955. **$79-$119.** 1308 N US Hwy 285 79735. I-10, exit 257, just s. Ext corridors. **Pets:** Small, other species. Service with restrictions, supervision. (SAVE) ⊠ 🛢 💻 ➡

◆◆◆ ▼▼▼ Sleep Inn & Suites ⓗ
(432) 336-8338. **$90-$135.** 3401 W Dickinson Blvd 79735. I-10, exit 256, just e. Int corridors. **Pets:** Medium. $35 daily fee/pet. Designated rooms, service with restrictions, supervision. (SAVE) ⊠ 🔧M 🛢 💻 ➡

FORT WORTH

◆◆◆ ▼▼▼ ▼▼▼ The Ashton Hotel ⓗ ❀
(817) 332-0100. **$199-$795.** 610 Main St 76102. Jct 6th and Main sts; center. Int corridors. **Pets:** Medium, dogs only. $150 deposit/pet. Service with restrictions, supervision. (SAVE) ⊠ 💻 ⑪

▼▼▼▼ Candlewood Suites ⓗ
(817) 838-8229. **$99-$114.** 5201 Endicott Ave 76137. I-820, exit 17B (Beach St), just s. Int corridors. **Pets:** Accepted. (ASK) ⊠ 🛢 💻

▼▼▼▼ Comfort Suites Hotel ⓗ
(817) 731-9600. **$79-$92.** 6851 West Frwy 76116. I-30, exit 7B, 0.8 mi e to Green Oaks Rd. Int corridors. **Pets:** Accepted.
(ASK) ⊠ 🔧M 🛢 💻 ➡

◆◆◆ ▼▼▼▼ Country Inn & Suites By Carlson ⓗ
(817) 831-9200. **$109-$219.** 2200 Mercado Dr 76106. I-35W, exit 53, just w. Int corridors. **Pets:** Medium, other species. $25 one-time fee/pet. Service with restrictions. (SAVE) ⊠ 🔧M 🛢 💻 ➡

▼▼ Crossland Economy Studios Fort Worth-Fossil Creek ⓗ
(817) 838-3500. **$45-$63.** 3804 Tanacross Dr 76137. I-820, exit 17B (Beach St), just s. Ext corridors. **Pets:** Other species. $25 daily fee/room. Designated rooms, service with restrictions, crate. (ASK) ⊠ 🛢 💻

▼▼ Extended StayAmerica Fort Worth-City View ⓗ
(817) 263-9006. **$80-$97.** 5831 Overton Ridge Blvd 76132. I-20, exit 431 (Bryant Irvin Rd), 0.5 mi s to Overton Ridge Blvd. Int corridors. **Pets:** Other species. $25 daily fee/room. Designated rooms, service with restrictions, crate. (ASK) ⊠ 🛢 💻

▼▼ Extended Stay Deluxe Fort Worth-City View ⓗ
(817) 263-8700. **$90-$114.** 4701 City Lake Blvd W 76132. I-20, exit 431 (Bryant Irvin Rd), just e. Int corridors. **Pets:** Other species. $25 daily fee/room. Designated rooms, service with restrictions, crate.
(ASK) ⊠ 🛢 💻 ➡

▼▼ Extended Stay Deluxe Hotel Fort Worth-Fossil Creek ⓗ
(817) 232-1622. **$80-$92.** 3261 NE Loop 820 76137. I-820, exit 17B (N Beach St), 0.5 mi w. Int corridors. **Pets:** Other species. $25 daily fee/room. Designated rooms, service with restrictions, crate.
(ASK) ⊠ 🛢 💻 ➡

▼▼▼▼ Historic Hilton Fort Worth ⓗ ❀
(817) 870-2100. **$159-$289.** 815 Main St 76102. Northeast corner of Main and 8th sts; center. Int corridors. **Pets:** Medium, other species. $50 one-time fee/room. Service with restrictions, crate.
⊠ 🔧M 🛢 💻 ⑪

▼▼▼▼ Holiday Inn Express Hotel & Suites ⓗ
(817) 744-7755. **$108-$124.** 3541 NW Loop 820 76106. I-820, exit 10A eastbound; exit 10B westbound. Int corridors. **Pets:** Accepted.
(ASK) ⊠ 🔧M 🛢 💻 ➡

◆◆◆ ▼▼▼▼ Holiday Inn Express Hotel & Suites Fort Worth Downtown ⓗ
(817) 698-9595. **$89-$179.** 1111 W Lancaster Ave 76102. I-30, exit 13B (Henderson St), just n. Int corridors. **Pets:** Accepted.
(SAVE) ⊠ 🔧M 🛢 💻 ➡

▼▼▼▼ Holiday Inn Express Hotel & Suites-Fort Worth West ⓗ
(817) 560-4200. **$117-$149.** 2730 Cherry Ln 76116. I-30, exit 7A. Int corridors. **Pets:** Accepted. (ASK) ⊠ 🛢 💻 ➡

▼▼▼▼ Homewood Suites by Hilton ⓗ
(817) 834-7400. **$169-$209.** 3701 Tanacross Dr 76137. I-820, exit 17B (Beach St), just s. Int corridors. **Pets:** Accepted.
⊠ 🔧M 🛢 💻 ➡

▼▼▼ Howard Johnson ⓗ
(817) 834-8001. **Call for rates.** 4850 North Frwy 76137. I-35W, exit 56A. Int corridors. **Pets:** Accepted. ⊠ 🛢 💻 ➡

▼▼▼▼ La Quinta Inn & Suites Fort Worth (North) ⓗ ❀
(817) 222-2888. **$59-$129.** 4700 North Frwy 76137. I-35W, exit 56A, just n. Int corridors. **Pets:** Medium, other species. Service with restrictions, supervision. (ASK) ⊠ 🛢 💻 ➡

▼▼▼▼ La Quinta Inn & Suites Fort Worth (Southwest) ⓗ ❀
(817) 370-2700. **$59-$99.** 4900 Bryant Irvin Rd 76132. I-20, exit 431 (Bryant Irvin Rd). Int corridors. **Pets:** Medium, other species. Service with restrictions, supervision. (ASK) ⊠ 🔧M 🛢 💻 ➡

▼▼ La Quinta Inn Fort Worth (West/Medical Center) ⓗ ❀
(817) 246-5511. **$59-$99.** 7888 I-30 W (W Freeway) 76108. I-30, exit 7A. Ext/int corridors. **Pets:** Medium, other species. Service with restrictions, supervision. (ASK) ⊠ 🛢 💻 ➡

▼▼▼ Microtel Inn & Suites ⓗ
(817) 222-3740. **Call for rates.** 3740 Tanacross Dr 76137. I-820, exit 17B (Beach St), just s. Int corridors. **Pets:** Accepted. ⊠ 🛢 💻

▼▼▼▼ Omni Hotel ⓗ
(817) 535-6664. **Call for rates.** 1300 Houston St 76102. Between 12th and 14th sts; downtown. Int corridors. **Pets:** Accepted.
⊠ 🔧M 💻 ⑪ ➡ ⊗

▼▼▼▼ Quality Inn & Suites ⓗ
(817) 560-4180. **$67-$97.** 2700 Cherry Ln 76116. I-30, exit 7A, just s. Ext corridors. **Pets:** Accepted. (ASK) ⊠ 🛢 💻 ➡

◆◆◆ ▼▼▼ ▼▼▼ The Renaissance Worthington Hotel ⓗ ❀
(817) 870-1000. **$233-$285.** 200 Main St 76102. Northwest corner of 2nd and Main sts. Int corridors. **Pets:** Other species. $200 deposit/room. Service with restrictions, crate. (SAVE) ⊠ 🛢 💻 ⑪ ➡ ⊗

▼▼▼▼ Residence Inn-Alliance Airport ⓗ
(817) 750-7000. **$170-$208.** 13400 North Frwy 76177. I-35W, exit 66. Int corridors. **Pets:** $75 one-time fee/room. Service with restrictions.
⊠ 🛢 💻 ➡ ⊗

▼▼▼▼ Residence Inn by Marriott Fort Worth Cultural District ⓗ
(817) 885-8250. **$188-$230.** 2500 Museum Way 76107. I-30, exit 13B (Henderson St), 0.4 mi n to 7th St, 0.8 mi w to Stayton St, then just s. Int corridors. **Pets:** Accepted. ⊠ 🔧M 🛢 💻 ➡ ⊗

▼▼▼▼ Residence Inn by Marriott-Fossil Creek ⓗ
(817) 439-1300. **$161-$197.** 5801 Sandshell Dr 76137. I-35W, exit 58 (Western Center Blvd) northbound to Sandshell, 0.7 mi s; exit southbound, first road to right through strip center, just s to Sandshell, then 0.7 mi s. Int corridors. **Pets:** Accepted. ⊠ 🔧M 🛢 💻 ➡ ⊗

▼▼▼▼ Residence Inn University by Marriott 🅗
(817) 870-1011. **$179-$219.** 1701 S University Dr 76107. I-30, exit 12 (University Dr), 0.4 mi s. Ext corridors. **Pets:** Accepted.
🗙 Ġ📶 🛢 🎦 🎦 🗙

▼▼ TownePlace Suites by Marriott-Fort Worth 🅗
(817) 732-2224. **$152-$186.** 4200 International Plaza Dr 76109. I-820, exit 433. Int corridors. **Pets:** Accepted. 🗙 🛢 🎦 🎦

FREDERICKSBURG

🅐🅐🅐 ▼▼▼▼ Best Western Fredericksburg 🅗
(830) 992-2929. **$85-$179.** 314 E Highway St 78624. Jct US 87 and 290, 6 blks s. Int corridors. **Pets:** Small. $15 daily fee/pet. Service with restrictions, supervision. 🆂🅰🆅🅴 🗙 🛢 🎦 🎦

🅐🅐🅐 ▼▼▼▼ Comfort Inn & Suites 🅗
(830) 990-2552. **$70-$180.** 723 S Washington St 78624. W on Main St, then s. Int corridors. **Pets:** Small. $40 daily fee/pet. Designated rooms, supervision. 🆂🅰🆅🅴 🗙 🛢 🎦 🎦

🅐🅐 ▼▼▼ Dietzel Motel 🅜 🐾
(830) 997-3330. **$52-$99.** 1141 W US 290 78624. 1 mi w on US 290 at US 87. Ext corridors. **Pets:** Other species. $10 daily fee/pet. Designated rooms, service with restrictions. 🆂🅰🆅🅴 🗙 🛢 🎦

🅐🅐🅐 ▼▼▼ Fredericksburg Econo Lodge 🅜 🐾
(830) 997-3437. **$49-$79.** 810 S Adams St 78624. Jct US 290 and SR 16 S, 1 mi s. Ext corridors. **Pets:** Other species. $10 daily fee/pet. No service, supervision. 🆂🅰🆅🅴 🗙 🛢 🎦 🎦

▼▼▼ Fredericksburg Inn & Suites 🅗 🐾
(830) 997-0202. **$79-$229.** 201 S Washington St 78624. US 290 and 87, 3 blks s. Ext corridors. **Pets:** Small, dogs only. $35 one-time fee/room. Designated rooms, service with restrictions, crate. 🗙 🛢 🎦 🎦

▼▼▼ Holiday Inn Express 🅗
(830) 990-4200. **$99-$149.** 1220 N Hwy 87 78624. 1 mi w on US 290 at US 87. Int corridors. **Pets:** Small, dogs only. $50 one-time fee/pet. Service with restrictions, crate. 🅐🆂🅺 🗙 Ġ📶 🛢 🎦 🎦

▼▼▼ La Quinta Inn & Suites 🅗 🐾
(830) 990-2899. **$79-$159.** 1465 E Main St 78624. 1 mi e of downtown. Int corridors. **Pets:** Medium, other species. Service with restrictions, supervision. 🅐🆂🅺 🗙 Ġ📶 🛢 🎦 🎦

▼▼ Quality Inn 🅗
(830) 997-9811. **$80-$116.** 908 S Adams St 78624. 0.8 mi sw on SR 16; 0.8 mi sw of jct US 87 and 290. Ext corridors. **Pets:** Medium. $20 daily fee/pet. Service with restrictions, crate. 🅐🆂🅺 🗙 🛢 🎦 🎦

▼▼ Sunday House Inn & Suites 🅗
(830) 997-4484. **$99-$229.** 501 E Main St 78624. 0.4 mi e on US 290. Ext corridors. **Pets:** Small. $25 daily fee/pet. Designated rooms, service with restrictions, supervision. 🅐🆂🅺 🗙 🛢 🎦 🎦

🅐🅐 ▼▼▼ Sunset Inn 🅜
(830) 997-9581. **$59-$75.** 900 S Adams St 78624. 0.8 mi sw of jct US 290 and SR 16. Ext corridors. **Pets:** Accepted. 🆂🅰🆅🅴 🗙 🛢 🎦 🎦 🍽

🅐🅐 ▼▼▼ Super 8 Fredericksburg 🅜
(830) 997-6568. **$63-$99.** 514 E Main St 78642. US 290, just e of jct US 87. Ext corridors. **Pets:** Medium. $10 daily fee/pet. Service with restrictions, supervision. 🆂🅰🆅🅴 🗙 🛢 🎦 🎦

FREER

🅐🅐🅐 ▼▼▼▼ Best Western Windwood Inn & Suites 🅜
(361) 394-6200. **$90-$100.** 1172 E Riley St 78357. On US 59 and SR 44 E. Ext corridors. **Pets:** Medium. $25 one-time fee/room. Designated rooms, service with restrictions, supervision.
🆂🅰🆅🅴 🗙 Ġ📶 🛢 🎦 🎦

FULTON

🅐🅐 ▼▼▼ Best Western Inn by the Bay 🅜
(361) 729-8351. **$70-$140.** 3902 N Hwy 35 78358. SR 35, 0.5 mi n of jct Business Rt SR 35 and FM 3063. Ext corridors. **Pets:** Accepted.
🆂🅰🆅🅴 🗙 Ġ📶 🛢 🎦

GAINESVILLE

🅐🅐 ▼▼ Budget Host Inn 🅜
(940) 665-2856. **$38-$48.** 1900 N I-35 76240. I-35, exit 499 northbound; exit 498B southbound. Ext corridors. **Pets:** Accepted.
🆂🅰🆅🅴 🗙 🛢 🎦

▼▼▼▼ Holiday Inn Express Hotel & Suites 🅗
(940) 665-0505. **$100-$130.** 320 N I-35 76240. I-35, exit 496B (California St). Int corridors. **Pets:** Accepted. 🅐🆂🅺 🗙 🛢 🎦 🎦

▼▼▼▼ La Quinta Inn & Suites 🅗 🐾
(940) 665-5700. **$79-$209.** 4201 N I-35 76240. I-35, exit 501, just w on FM 1202, then just s on access road. Int corridors. **Pets:** Medium, other species. Service with restrictions, supervision.
🅐🆂🅺 🗙 Ġ📶 🛢 🎦 🎦

🅐🅐 ▼▼▼ Rodeway Inn 🅜
(940) 665-7737. **$55-$99.** 2103 N I-35 76240. I-35, exit 499 northbound, 1.4 mi n on access road to S Frontage Rd; exit 498B southbound. Ext corridors. **Pets:** Small. $10 daily fee/pet. Service with restrictions, supervision. 🆂🅰🆅🅴 🗙 🛢 🎦 🎦

🅐🅐 ▼▼▼ Super 8 🅗
(940) 665-5599. **$55-$65.** 1936 I-35 N 76240. I-35, exit 499 northbound; exit 498A southbound. Int corridors. **Pets:** Medium. $50 deposit/room, $10 daily fee/pet. Designated rooms, service with restrictions, supervision.
🆂🅰🆅🅴 🗙 🛢 🎦 🎦

GALVESTON

🅐🅐 ▼▼▼▼▼ Hilton Galveston Island Resort 🅗 🐾
(409) 744-5000. **$159-$399.** 5400 Seawall Blvd 77551. Seawall Blvd at 54th St. Int corridors. **Pets:** Small, dogs only. $75 one-time fee/pet. Designated rooms, service with restrictions.
🆂🅰🆅🅴 🗙 Ġ📶 🛢 🎦 🍽 🎦 🗙

🅐🅐🅐 ▼▼▼▼ Holiday Inn Resort on the Beach 🅗
(409) 740-3581. **$79-$309, 3 day notice.** 5002 Seawall Blvd 77551. Just e of jct Seawall Blvd and 53rd St. Ext corridors. **Pets:** Accepted.
🆂🅰🆅🅴 🗙 🛢 🍽 🎦

▼▼▼▼ La Quinta Inn & Suites 🅗 🐾
(409) 740-9100. **$79-$249.** 8710 Seawall Blvd 77554. Jct Seawall Blvd and 87th St, just w. Int corridors. **Pets:** Medium, other species. Service with restrictions, supervision. 🅐🆂🅺 🗙 Ġ📶 🛢 🎦 🎦

GATESVILLE

🅐🅐🅐 ▼▼▼ Best Western Chateau Ville Motor Inn 🅗
(254) 865-2281. **$76-$86, 14 day notice.** 2501 E Main St 76528. Jct US 84 and SR 36, 0.5 mi w. Ext corridors. **Pets:** Small. Service with restrictions, supervision. 🆂🅰🆅🅴 🗙 🛢 🎦 🎦

GEORGETOWN

▼▼▼ La Quinta Inn Georgetown 🅗 🐾
(512) 869-2541. **$59-$109.** 333 I-35 N 78628. I-35, exit 264 northbound; exit 262 southbound; on west frontage road. Ext corridors. **Pets:** Medium, other species. Service with restrictions, supervision.
🅐🆂🅺 🗙 🛢 🎦 🎦

GEORGE WEST

🅐🅐🅐 ▼▼▼ Best Western George West Executive Inn 🅜
(361) 449-3300. **$90-$120.** 208 N Nueces St 78022. Just n of US 59 on SR 281. Ext corridors. **Pets:** Medium. $25 one-time fee/room. Service with restrictions. 🆂🅰🆅🅴 🗙 🛢 🎦 🎦

GIDDINGS

᪲᪲ ᪲᪲᪲ Executive Inn M
(979) 542-5791. **$59-$104, 3 day notice.** 3556 E Austin St 78942. 2 mi e on US 290. Ext corridors. **Pets:** Medium. $10 daily fee/pet. Service with restrictions, supervision. ⌂ ⊠ 🛏 💻 ≋

GLEN ROSE

᪲᪲ ᪲᪲᪲ Best Western Dinosaur Valley Inn & Suites H ❀
(254) 897-4818. **$101-$114.** 1311 NE Big Bend Tr 76043. On US 67. Int corridors. **Pets:** Medium. $5 daily fee/pet, $25 one-time fee/pet. Service with restrictions, crate. ⌂ ⊠ 🛏 💻 ≋ ⊠

GRAHAM

᪲᪲ ᪲᪲᪲ Wildcatter Ranch H ❀
(940) 549-3500. **$119-$369, 3 day notice.** 6062 Hwy 16 S 76450. SR 16, 7 mi s. Ext/int corridors. **Pets:** Medium. $50 daily fee/pet. Service with restrictions, crate. ⌂ ⊠ ⊾M 🛏 💻 ¶¶ ≋ ⊠

GRANBURY

᪲᪲ ᪲᪲᪲ Americas Best Value Inn H
(817) 573-4411. **$69-$129.** 800 Harbor Lakes Dr 76048. Jct SR 144 and US 377 Bypass, 1.9 mi n on US 377 Bypass. Int corridors.
Pets: Accepted. ⌂ ⊠ ⊾M 🛏 💻 ≋

᪲᪲ ᪲᪲᪲ Best Western Granbury Inn & Suites H ❀
(817) 573-4239. **$69-$199.** 1517 N Plaza Dr 76048. On US 377 Bypass, 2.2 mi n of jct SR 144 and US 377 Bypass. Int corridors. **Pets:** Large, other species. $25 one-time fee/room. Service with restrictions, crate.
⌂ ⊠ ⊾M 🛏 💻 ≋

᪲᪲ Days Inn Granbury H
(817) 573-2611. **Call for rates.** 1201 Plaza Dr N 76048. 1.5 mi n of jct SR 144 and US 377 Bypass, on US 377 Bypass. Ext corridors.
Pets: Medium, other species. $15 daily fee/pet. Service with restrictions, crate. ⊠ 🛏 💻 ≋

᪲᪲ ᪲᪲᪲ Plantation Inn on the Lake H
(817) 573-8846. **$75-$100.** 1451 E Pearl St 76048. 0.3 mi w of Business Rt US 377 at US 377 Bypass. Ext/int corridors. **Pets:** Medium, dogs only. $10 daily fee/pet. Service with restrictions, supervision.
⌂ ⊠ 🛏 💻 ≋

GRAPEVINE

᪲᪲ ᪲᪲᪲ ᪲᪲᪲ Embassy Suites Outdoor World H
(972) 724-2600. **$149-$299.** 2401 Bass Pro Dr 76051. SR 121, exit Bass Pro Dr. Int corridors. **Pets:** Small. $25 one-time fee/room. Service with restrictions, supervision. ⌂ ⊠ ⊾M 🛏 💻 ¶¶ ≋ ⊠

᪲᪲ ᪲᪲᪲ ᪲᪲᪲ Hilton DFW Lakes H ❀
(817) 481-8444. **$99-$309.** 1800 Hwy 26 E 76051. SR 26A, 0.3 mi sw of jct SR 121; 0.5 mi nw of I-635, exit SR 121 N. Int corridors. **Pets:** Large. $75 one-time fee/room. Designated rooms, service with restrictions.
⌂ ⊠ ⊾M 🛏 💻 ¶¶ ≋ ⊠

᪲᪲᪲ ᪲᪲᪲ Homewood Suites by Hilton H
(972) 691-2427. **$169-$199.** 2214 Grapevine Mills Cir W 76051. SR 121 N, exit Bass Pro Dr. Int corridors. **Pets:** Accepted.
⊠ ⊾M 🛏 💻 ≋ ⊠

᪲᪲ ᪲᪲᪲ ᪲᪲᪲ Hyatt Regency DFW H
(972) 453-1234. **$99-$399.** 2334 N International Pkwy 75261. In Dallas-Fort Worth International Airport Terminal C area. Int corridors.
Pets: Accepted. ⌂ ⊠ ⊾M 🛏 💻 ¶¶ ≋

᪲᪲᪲ Super 8-Grapevine H
(817) 329-7222. **$84-$104.** 250 E Hwy 114 76051. SR 114, exit Main St. Int corridors. **Pets:** $10 daily fee/pet. No service, crate.
⌂⌂ ⊠ ⊾M 🛏 💻 ≋

GROOM

᪲᪲ ᪲᪲᪲ Chalet Inn M
(806) 248-7524. **$39-$60.** I-40 FM 2300 79039. I-40, exit 113, just s. Ext corridors. **Pets:** Accepted. ⌂ ⊠ ⊾M

HALLETTSVILLE

᪲᪲ ᪲᪲᪲ Best Western Executive Inn H
(361) 798-9200. **$100-$130, 3 day notice.** 207 US Hwy 77 S 77964. Jct US 77 S and Alternate US 90. Ext corridors. **Pets:** Small. $10 daily fee/pet. Service with restrictions, supervision. ⌂ ⊠ 🛏 💻 ≋

HARLINGEN

᪲᪲᪲ La Quinta Inn Harlingen H ❀
(956) 428-6888. **$39-$109.** 1002 S Expwy 83 78552. US 83 and 77, exit M St. Ext corridors. **Pets:** Medium, other species. Service with restrictions, supervision. ⌂⌂ ⊠ ⊾M 🛏 💻 ≋

HEARNE

᪲᪲᪲ Oak Tree Inn H
(979) 279-5599. **$89-$120, 3 day notice.** 1051 N Market St 77859. 0.6 mi n of jct US 79 and SR 6. Ext/int corridors. **Pets:** Accepted.
⌂⌂ ⊠ 🛏 💻 ¶¶

HENDERSON

᪲᪲ ᪲᪲᪲ Best Western Inn of Henderson H
(903) 657-9561. **$70-$100.** 1500 Hwy 259 S 75654. 2 mi s on US 259, 0.7 mi s of jct US 79 and 259 S. Ext/int corridors. **Pets:** Accepted.
⌂ ⊠ 🛏 💻 ≋

HEREFORD

᪲᪲ ᪲᪲᪲ Best Western Red Carpet Inn H
(806) 364-0540. **$70-$80.** 830 W 1st St 79045. Just w of jct US 385 and 60. Ext corridors. **Pets:** Service with restrictions, supervision.
⌂ ⊠ 🛏 💻 ≋

᪲᪲᪲ Holiday Inn Express H
(806) 364-3322. **Call for rates.** 1400 W 1st St 79045. Jct US 385 and 60, just w. Int corridors. **Pets:** Medium. $20 daily fee/pet. Service with restrictions, supervision. ⊠ ⊾M 🛏 💻 ≋

HILLSBORO

᪲᪲ ᪲᪲᪲ Best Western Hillsboro Inn H
(254) 582-8465. **$65-$129.** 307 I-35 76645. I-35, exit 368A northbound; exit 368B southbound, just w. Ext corridors. **Pets:** Other species. $12 daily fee/room. Service with restrictions. ⌂ ⊠ 🛏 💻 ≋

᪲᪲᪲ Comfort Inn of Hillsboro H
(254) 582-3333. **$50-$160.** 1515 Old Brandon Rd 76645. I-35, exit 368A northbound; exit 368B southbound, just w. Ext corridors. **Pets:** Accepted.
⌂⌂ ⊠ ⊾M 🛏 💻 ≋

᪲᪲᪲ Motel 6–4136 H
(254) 580-9000. **Call for rates.** 1506 Hillview Dr 76645. I-35, exit 368 southbound; exit 368A northbound. Int corridors. **Pets:** Other species. Service with restrictions, supervision. ⊠ ⊾M 🛏 ≋

᪲᪲᪲ Super 8 H
(254) 580-0404. **Call for rates.** 1512 Hillview Dr 76645. I-35, exit 368A northbound; 368 southbound, just e. Int corridors. **Pets:** Accepted.
⊠ 🛏 💻 ≋

HONDO

᪲᪲ ᪲᪲᪲ Americas Best Value Inn M
(830) 426-3031. **$50-$60.** 401 Hwy 90 E 78861. Jct SR 173. Ext corridors. **Pets:** Accepted. ⌂ ⊠ 🛏 ≋

᪲᪲ ᪲᪲᪲ Hondo Executive Inn M
(830) 426-2535. **$45-$95.** 102 E 19th St 78861. On US 90 W. Ext corridors. **Pets:** $15 one-time fee/pet. Service with restrictions, supervision.
⌂ ⊠ 🛏 💻 ≋

HORSESHOE BAY

Horseshoe Bay Resort Marriott Hotel 🅷

(830) 598-8600. **$200-$286, 3 day notice.** 200 Hi Cir N 78657. Jct US 281 and SR 2147, 6.6 mi w. Ext/int corridors. **Pets:** $75 one-time fee/room. Designated rooms, supervision.

[SAVE] [X] [&M] [🛏] [💻] [🍴] [🎣] [X]

HOUSTON METROPOLITAN AREA

BAYTOWN

La Quinta Inn Baytown East 🅷 ❀

(281) 421-5566. **$59-$119.** 5215 I-10 E 77521. I-10, exit 792 (Garth Rd). Int corridors. **Pets:** Medium, other species. Service with restrictions, supervision. [ASK] [X] [&M] [🛏] [💻] [🎣]

CLEVELAND

Super 8 🅷

(281) 432-8800. **$100-$119, 3 day notice.** 427 W Southline 77327. US 59, exit SR 105, just e to W Southline, then just s. Int corridors. **Pets:** Accepted. [ASK] [X] [🛏] [💻]

CONROE

Baymont Inn and Suites-Conroe/Woodlands 🅷

(936) 539-5100. **$69-$120.** 1506 I-45 S 77304. I-45, exit 85 (Gladstell St) northbound; exit 84 (Frazier St) southbound. Int corridors. **Pets:** Medium, dogs only. $10 daily fee/pet. Designated rooms, service with restrictions, supervision. [SAVE] [X] [🛏] [💻] [🎣]

La Quinta Inn & Suites 🅷 ❀

(936) 228-0790. **$89-$139.** 4006 Sprayberry Ln 77303. I-45, exit 91 (League Line Rd), just e. Int corridors. **Pets:** Medium, other species. Service with restrictions, supervision. [ASK] [X] [&M] [🛏] [💻] [🎣]

DEER PARK

La Quinta Inn & Suites 🅷 ❀

(281) 476-5300. **$79-$149.** 1400 East Blvd 77536. Jct SR 225 and East Blvd, 0.8 mi s. Int corridors. **Pets:** Medium, other species. Service with restrictions, supervision. [X] [&M] [🛏] [💻] [🎣]

HOUSTON

Best Western Westchase Mini Suites 🅷

(713) 782-1515. **$69-$129.** 2950 W Sam Houston Pkwy S 77042. Just w of Sam Houston Pkwy (Beltway 8) and Westheimer Rd, on southbound frontage road. Int corridors. **Pets:** Small. Service with restrictions, crate. [SAVE] [X] [🛏] [💻] [🎣]

Candlewood Suites Houston by the Galleria 🅷

(713) 839-9411. **$79-$86.** 4900 Loop Central Dr 77081. I-610, exit 7 (Furnace Rd) southbound; exit 7 (Westpark) northbound, on northbound frontage road. Int corridors. **Pets:** Accepted. [ASK] [X] [🛏] [💻]

Candlewood Suites-Town & Country 🅷

(713) 464-2677. **$110-$130.** 10503 Town & Country Way 77024. I-10, exit 755 eastbound, 1.1 mi on frontage road to Town & Country Blvd, then 0.4 mi s; exit 756A westbound, U-turn under I-10, just e to Town & Country Blvd, then 0.4 mi s. Int corridors. **Pets:** Accepted.

[ASK] [X] [&M] [🛏] [💻]

Candlewood Suites-Westchase 🅷 ❀

(713) 780-7881. **$75-$129.** 4033 W Sam Houston Pkwy S 77042. Sam Houston Pkwy (Beltway 8), exit Westpark, southeast corner of Westpark and Sam Houston Pkwy (Beltway 8) on northbound frontage road. Int corridors. **Pets:** Small. $75 one-time fee/pet. Service with restrictions, crate. [ASK] [X] [&M] [🛏] [💻]

Comfort Suites Galleria 🅷

(713) 787-0004. **$100-$110.** 6221 Richmond Ave 77057. US 59, exit Hillcroft St, 1 mi n to Richmond Ave, then 0.6 mi e. Int corridors. **Pets:** Other species. $50 one-time fee/room. Service with restrictions, supervision. [SAVE] [X] [🛏] [💻] [🎣]

Crossland Economy Studios Houston-Northwest 🅷

(713) 934-7600. **$55-$69.** 5959 Guhn Rd 77040. US 290, exit Fairbanks, just e on eastbound frontage road, then just s. Ext corridors. **Pets:** Other species. $25 daily fee/room. Designated rooms, service with restrictions, crate. [ASK] [X] [&M] [🛏] [💻]

Crowne Plaza Northwest Hotel 🅷

(713) 462-9977. **$80-$179.** 12801 Northwest Frwy 77040. Nw on US 290, exit Hollister Rd, 0.7 mi e on south service road. Ext/int corridors. **Pets:** Medium, other species. $25 one-time fee/pet. Designated rooms, service with restrictions, supervision.

[ASK] [X] [🛏] [💻] [🍴] [🎣] [X]

Crowne Plaza Suites–Houston–Sugar Land Southwest 🅷 ❀

(713) 995-0123. **$79-$179.** 9090 Southwest Frwy 77074. US 59, exit Beechnut/Gessner; on southbound frontage road. Int corridors. **Pets:** Small, other species. $25 one-time fee/room. Designated rooms. [SAVE] [X] [🛏] [💻] [🍴] [🎣]

Doubletree Guest Suites Houston by the Galleria 🅷 ❀

(713) 961-9000. **$149-$369.** 5353 Westheimer Rd 77056. I-610, exit 8C (Westheimer Rd) northbound; exit 9A (San Felipe Rd/Westheimer Rd) southbound, 0.8 mi w. Int corridors. **Pets:** Medium, other species. $50 one-time fee/pet. Service with restrictions, supervision.

[X] [🛏] [💻] [🍴] [🎣] [X]

Doubletree Houston Downtown 🅷

(713) 759-0202. **$109-$299.** 400 Dallas St 77002. At Dallas and Bagby sts. Int corridors. **Pets:** Medium. $75 deposit/room, $25 one-time fee/room. Service with restrictions. [X] [🛏] [💻] [🍴]

Drury Inn & Suites-Houston Hobby 🅷

(713) 941-4300. **$75-$179.** 7902 Mosley Rd 77061. I-45, exit 36 (Airport Blvd/College Rd) northbound, just w on Airport Blvd, then just n; exit southbound, follow frontage road to Mosley Rd. Int corridors. **Pets:** Other species. No service, supervision. [ASK] [X] [&M] [🛏] [💻] [🎣]

Drury Inn & Suites-Houston Near the Galleria 🅷

(713) 963-0700. **$95-$234.** 1615 W Loop S 77027. I-610, exit 9 (San Felipe Rd) northbound; exit 9A (San Felipe Rd/Westheimer Rd) southbound, on east service road. Int corridors. **Pets:** Other species. No service, supervision. [ASK] [X] [&M] [🛏] [💻] [🎣]

Drury Inn & Suites-Houston West 🅷

(281) 558-7007. **$90-$184.** 1000 N Hwy 6 77079. I-10, exit 751 (Addicks Rd/SR 6), just n on SR 6. Int corridors. **Pets:** Other species. No service, supervision. [ASK] [X] [🛏] [💻] [🎣]

Element Houston Vintage Park 🅷 ❀

(281) 379-7300. **$89-$299.** 14555 Vintage Preserve Pkwy 77070. US 290, exit Louetta, just e to Chasewood Park, then just s. Int corridors. **Pets:** Medium. Designated rooms, service with restrictions, crate. [SAVE] [X] [🛏] [💻] [🎣]

Extended StayAmerica Houston-Greenway Plaza 🅷

(713) 521-0060. **$90-$109.** 2330 Southwest Frwy 77098. US 59, exit Greenbriar/Shepherd; on southbound frontage road. Int corridors. **Pets:** Other species. $25 daily fee/room. Designated rooms, service with restrictions, crate. [ASK] [X] [🛏] [💻]

▼▼▼ Extended Stay Deluxe Houston-Northwest 🅗
(713) 895-0965. **$90-$115.** 5454 Hollister St 77040. US 290, exit Tidwell/
Hollister, just s. Int corridors. **Pets:** Other species. $25 daily fee/room.
Designated rooms, service with restrictions, crate.
🆎🅧📇📟➿

⨁⨁ ▼▼▼ Four Seasons Hotel Houston 🅗 ❖
(713) 650-1300. **$350-$850.** 1300 Lamar St 77010-3098. Jct Lamar and
Austin sts. Int corridors. **Pets:** Small. Service with restrictions, crate.
🆂🅧📇📟🍽➿🅧

⨁⨁▷ ▼▼▼ ▼▼▼ Hilton Americas-Houston 🅗
(713) 739-8000. **$174-$454.** 1600 Lamar St 77010. At George R Brown
Convention Center; between Crawford and Avenida De Las Americas. Int
corridors. **Pets:** Accepted.
🌿 🆂🅧🆖📇📟🍽➿🅧

⨁⨁▷ ▼▼▼▼ Hilton Garden Inn Energy Corridor 🅗
(281) 531-0220. **$79-$269.** 12245 Katy Frwy 77079. I-10, exit 753B
(Dairy Ashford), on eastbound frontage road. Int corridors.
Pets: Accepted. 🆂🅧🆖📇📟🍽➿

▼▼▼▼ Hilton Houston North 🅗
(281) 875-2222. **$99-$349.** 12400 Greenspoint Dr 77060. I-45, exit 61
(Greens Rd), 0.5 mi e. Int corridors. **Pets:** Medium. $75 deposit/room.
Service with restrictions. 🅧📇📟🍽➿

⨁⨁▷ ▼▼▼ ▼▼▼ Hilton Houston Post Oak 🅗 ❖
(713) 961-9300. **$139-$359.** 2001 Post Oak Blvd 77056. I-610, exit 8C
(Westheimer Rd) northbound, just w; exit 9A (San Felipe Rd/Westheimer
Rd) southbound; between San Felipe and Westheimer rds. Int corridors.
Pets: $75 one-time fee/room. Service with restrictions, supervision.
🆂🅧📇📟🍽➿

▼▼▼▼ Hilton Houston Southwest 🅗
(713) 977-7911. **$89-$239.** 6780 Southwest Frwy 77074. US 59, exit
Hillcroft St, on southbound frontage road. Int corridors. **Pets:** Accepted.
🅧📇📟🍽➿

⨁⨁▷ ▼▼▼ Holiday Inn Express Hotel &
Suites-Intercontinental 🅗
(281) 372-1000. **$99-$139.** 1330 N Sam Houston Pkwy E 77032. Off
Sam Houston Pkwy (Beltway 8), exit Aldine Westfield eastbound, 0.8 mi e
on service road; exit Hardy Toll Rd westbound, U-turn, then 1 mi e on
service road. Int corridors. **Pets:** Accepted. 🆂🅧📇📟➿

⨁⨁▷ ▼▼▼ Holiday Inn Express Hotel & Suites Memorial
Area 🅗
(713) 688-2800. **$128-$171.** 7625 Katy Frwy 77024. I-10, exit 762 (Silber
Rd), on eastbound frontage road. Int corridors. **Pets:** Accepted.
🆂🅧🆖📇📟➿

⨁⨁▷ ▼▼▼ Holiday Inn Houston Hobby Airport 🅗
(713) 946-8900. **$129-$169, 3 day notice.** 8611 Airport Blvd 77061.
I-45, exit 36 (Airport Blvd), 1.3 mi w. Int corridors. **Pets:** Medium, dogs
only. $50 one-time fee/pet. Service with restrictions, supervision.
🆂🅧📇📟🍽➿

⨁⨁▷ ▼▼▼ Holiday Inn Houston Intercontinental
Airport 🅗
(281) 449-2311. **$99-$209.** 15222 John F Kennedy Blvd 77032. Jct N
Sam Houston Pkwy (Beltway 8) E and John F Kennedy Blvd. Int corridors. **Pets:** Accepted. 🆂🅧📟🍽➿🅧

▼▼ ▼▼ Homestead Studio Suites Hotel-Houston/Galleria
Area 🅗
(713) 960-9660. **$85-$120.** 2300 W Loop S 77027. I-610, exit 9A (San
Felipe Rd) southbound, exit 9 (San Felipe Rd) northbound, on southbound frontage road. Int corridors. **Pets:** Other species. $25 daily fee/
room. Designated rooms, service with restrictions, crate.
🆎🅧📇📟

⨁⨁▷ ▼▼▼ Homewood Suites by Hilton
Intercontinental 🅗
(281) 219-9100. **$89-$159.** 1340 N Sam Houston Pkwy E 77032. Sam
Houston Pkwy (Beltway 8), exit Aldine Westfield eastbound, 0.8 mi e on
frontage road; exit Hardy Toll Rd westbound, U-turn, then 1 mi e on frontage road. Int corridors. **Pets:** Accepted.
🆂🅧🆖📇📟➿🅧

▼▼▼▼ Homewood Suites by Hilton-Westchase 🅗
(713) 334-2424. **$209-$249.** 2424 Rogerdale Rd 77042. Sam Houston
Pkwy (Beltway 8), exit Westheimer Rd, just w to Rogerdale Rd, then just
n. Int corridors. **Pets:** Medium, other species. $175 one-time fee/pet. Des-
ignated rooms, service with restrictions, crate.
🅧🆖📇📟➿🅧

▼▼▼▼ Homewood Suites by Hilton-Willowbrook 🅗
(281) 955-5200. **$169-$299.** 7655 W FM 1960 77070. Just e of jct SR
249 and FM 1960. Int corridors. **Pets:** Other species. $100 one-time fee/
room. Service with restrictions, crate. 🅧🆖📇📟➿🅧

⨁⨁▷ ▼▼▼ ▼▼▼ Hotel Icon 🅗
(713) 224-4266. **$109-$509.** 220 Main St 77002. Between Travis and
Main sts; entrance on Congress St. Int corridors. **Pets:** Small. Service
with restrictions, crate. 🆂🅧📇📟🍽

⨁⨁▷ ▼▼▼ ▼▼▼ Hotel Za Za Houston Museum
District 🅗 ❖
(713) 526-1991. **$199-$2500.** 5701 Main St 77005. US 59, exit Main St
northbound, 0.5 mi s; exit Fannin southbound, 0.5 mi s to Ewing, then
just w. Int corridors. **Pets:** $50 one-time fee/pet.
🆂🅧🆖📇🍽➿🅧

▼▼▼ ▼▼▼ Houston Marriott at the Texas Medical Center 🅗
(713) 796-0080. **$242-$296.** 6580 Fannin St 77030. I-610, exit 2 (Main
St), 2.5 mi ne to Holcombe St, 0.3 mi e, then just n. Int corridors.
Pets: Accepted. 🅧🆖📇📟➿🅧

⨁⨁▷ ▼▼▼ Hyatt Summerfield Suites
Houston/Galleria 🅗
(713) 629-9711. **$89-$207.** 3440 Sage Rd 77056. I-610, exit 9A (San
Felipe Rd/Westheimer Rd) southbound; exit 8C (Westheimer Rd) northbound, just w to Sage Rd, then 0.8 mi s. Int corridors. **Pets:** Small, dogs
only. $200 one-time fee/pet. Service with restrictions, supervision.
🆂🅧📇📟➿

⨁⨁▷ ▼▼▼ Hyatt Summerfield Suites Houston-West/
Energy Corridor 🅗
(281) 646-9990. **$99-$199.** 15405 Katy Frwy (I-10) 77094. I-10, exit 751
(SR 6), just s to Grisby Rd, then just w. Int corridors. **Pets:** Small. $200
one-time fee/room. Service with restrictions, supervision.
🆂🅧📇📟➿

▼▼▼ La Quinta Inn & Suites 🅗 ❖
(713) 680-8282. **$49-$129.** 11130 Northwest Frwy 77092. US 290 W, exit
W 34th St, on southeast corner. Int corridors. **Pets:** Medium, other species. Service with restrictions, supervision. 🆎🅧📇📟➿

⨁⨁▷ ▼▼▼ La Quinta Inn & Suites 🅗 ❖
(281) 784-1112. **$89-$159 (no credit cards).** 415 FM 1960 77073. I-45,
exit 66 (FM 1960), just e. Int corridors. **Pets:** Medium, other species.
Service with restrictions, supervision. 🆂🅧📇📟➿

▼▼▼ La Quinta Inn & Suites at Normandy 🅗 ❖
(713) 451-0009. **$79-$139.** 930 Normandy St 77015. I-10, exit 778, just
n. Int corridors. **Pets:** Medium, other species. Service with restrictions,
supervision. 🅧📇📟➿

▼▼▼ La Quinta Inn & Suites Houston (Bush
Intercontinental Airport) 🅗 ❖
(281) 219-2000. **$59-$159.** 15510 John F Kennedy Blvd 77032. Sam
Houston Pkwy (Beltway 8), exit John F Kennedy Blvd/Vickery, just n. Int
corridors. **Pets:** Medium, other species. Service with restrictions, supervision. 🆎🅧🆖📇📟➿

▽▽▽ La Quinta Inn & Suites Houston (Galleria Area) H ❀

(713) 355-3440. **$59-$179.** 1625 W Loop S 77027. I-610, exit 9 (San Felipe Rd) northbound; exit 9A (San Felipe Rd/Westheimer Rd) southbound, on northbound service road. Int corridors. **Pets:** Medium, other species. Service with restrictions, supervision.

ASK ✕ ᏜM 🛏 🖥 ⟲

▽▽▽ La Quinta Inn & Suites Houston Hobby Airport H ❀

(713) 490-1008. **$89-$159.** 8776 Airport Blvd 77061. I-45, exit 36 (Airport /College), 1.3 mi w. Int corridors. **Pets:** Medium, other species. Service with restrictions, supervision. ASK ✕ 🛏 🖥 ⟲

▽▽▽ La Quinta Inn & Suites Houston (Park 10) H ❀

(281) 646-9200. **$59-$149.** 15225 Katy Frwy 77094. I-10, exit 748 (Barker Cypress Rd) eastbound, 2.6 mi on eastbound service road; exit 751 (SR 6) westbound, just s to Grisby Rd, then 0.5 mi w. Int corridors. **Pets:** Medium, other species. Service with restrictions, supervision.

ASK ✕ 🛏 🖥 ⟲

▽▽▽ La Quinta Inn & Suites Westchase H ❀

(281) 495-7700. **$89-$179.** 10850 Harwin Dr 77072. Sam Houston Pkwy (Beltway 8), exit Bellaire/Harwin northbound; exit Westpark/Harwin southbound. Int corridors. **Pets:** Medium, other species. Service with restrictions, supervision. ASK ✕ 🛏 🖥 ⟲

▽▽▽ La Quinta Inn & Suites–Willowbrook H ❀

(281) 897-8868. **$89-$189.** 18828 State Hwy 249 (Tomball Pkwy) 77070. SR 249, exit Grant/Schroeder; on northbound frontage road. Int corridors. **Pets:** Medium, other species. Service with restrictions, supervision.

ASK ✕ ᏜM 🛏 🖥 ⟲

▽▽ La Quinta Inn Houston (Cyfair) H ❀

(281) 469-4018. **$49-$109.** 13290 FM 1960 W 77065-4005. Just w of jct US 290 and FM 1960. Ext corridors. **Pets:** Medium, other species. Service with restrictions, supervision. ASK ✕ 🛏 🖥 ⟲

▽▽ La Quinta Inn Houston (Wilcrest) H ❀

(713) 932-0808. **$79-$139.** 11113 Katy Frwy 77079-2102. I-10, exit 754 (Kirkwood Dr) westbound; exit 755 (Wilcrest Rd) eastbound, on eastbound service road. Ext corridors. **Pets:** Medium, other species. Service with restrictions, supervision. ASK ✕ 🛏 🖥 ⟲

◈◈◈ ▽▽▽ Marriott Houston Hobby Airport H ❀

(713) 943-7979. **$170-$208.** 9100 Gulf Frwy 77017. I-45, exit 36 (Airport Blvd/College Rd) southbound; exit 38 (Monroe) northbound, on southbound frontage road. Int corridors. **Pets:** Small. $50 one-time fee/room. Service with restrictions, crate. SAVE ✕ 🛏 🖥 🍴 ⟲

▽▽ ▽▽ Omni Houston Hotel H

(713) 871-8181. **$289-$459, 7 day notice.** Four Riverway 77056-1999. I-610, exit 10 (Woodway Dr), 0.3 mi w. Int corridors. **Pets:** Accepted.

ASK ✕ 🛏 🖥 🍴 ⟲ ⊠

◈◈◈ ▽▽ ▽▽ Omni Houston Hotel Westside H

(281) 558-8338. **$119-$339.** 13210 Katy Frwy 77079. I-10, exit 753A (Eldridge St), just n. Int corridors. **Pets:** Small. $50 deposit/room. Service with restrictions, crate. SAVE ✕ 🛏 🖥 🍴 ⟲

◈◈◈ ▽▽ ▽▽ Quality Inn & Suites Houston West/Energy Corridor M ❀

(281) 493-0444. **$69-$179.** 715 Hwy 6 S 77079. I-10, exit 751 (Addicks/SR 6), 0.4 mi s. Ext corridors. **Pets:** Medium. $15 daily fee/pet. Service with restrictions, crate. SAVE ✕ 🛏 🖥 ⟲

◈◈◈ ▽▽▽ Quality Suites H

(281) 442-4444. **$70-$130.** 15321 Vantage Pkwy E 77032. Sam Houston Pkwy (Beltway 8), exit Aldine Westfield, just w on frontage road. Int corridors. **Pets:** Small. $25 daily fee/room. Service with restrictions, supervision. SAVE ✕ 🛏 🖥 ⟲

▽▽ Red Roof Inns H

(713) 785-9909. **$55-$75.** 2960 W Sam Houston Pkwy S 77042. Sam Houston Pkwy (Beltway 8), exit Westheimer Rd, on southbound frontage road. Ext/int corridors. **Pets:** Large. Service with restrictions, crate.

ASK ✕ 🛏 ⟲

◈◈◈ ▽▽ ▽▽ Renaissance Houston Hotel Greenway Plaza H

(713) 629-1200. **$242-$296.** 6 Greenway Plaza E 77046. US 59 (Southwest Frwy), exit Buffalo Speedway. Int corridors. **Pets:** Small. Service with restrictions, supervision. SAVE ✕ 🛏 🖥 🍴 ⟲ ⊠

▽▽ ▽▽ Residence Inn by Marriott H

(832) 366-1000. **$224-$274.** 904 Dallas St 77002. At Main St. Int corridors. **Pets:** Accepted. ✕ ᏜM 🛏 🖥 ⟲

▽▽ ▽▽ Residence Inn by Marriott Houston by the Galleria H ❀

(713) 840-9757. **$180-$220.** 2500 McCue Rd 77056. I-610, exit 8C (Westheimer Rd) northbound; exit 9A (San Felipe Rd/Westheimer Rd) southbound, just w to McCue, then just n. Ext/int corridors. **Pets:** Other species. $100 one-time fee/room. Service with restrictions, crate.

✕ 🛏 🖥 ⟲

▽▽▽ Residence Inn by Marriott-Medical Center/Reliant Park H

(713) 660-7993. **$161-$197.** 7710 Main St 77030. I-610, exit 2 (S Main St/Buffalo Speedway), 1.5 mi n. Ext corridors. **Pets:** Accepted.

✕ 🛏 🖥 ⟲ ⊠

▽▽ Residence Inn by Marriott-West University H

(713) 661-4660. **$94-$199.** 2939 Westpark Dr 77005. US 59, exit Kirby Dr, just s, then just w. Int corridors. **Pets:** Accepted.

✕ ᏜM 🛏 🖥 ⟲ ⊠

▽▽▽ Residence Inn by Marriott Willowbrook H

(832) 237-2002. **$162-$198.** 7311 W Greens Rd 77064. SR 249, exit Greens Rd, just e. Int corridors. **Pets:** Other species. $100 one-time fee/room. Service with restrictions, crate. ✕ 🛏 🖥 ⟲ ⊠

◈◈◈ ▽▽ ▽▽ The St. Regis Houston H

(713) 840-7600. **$199-$650.** 1919 Briar Oaks Ln 77027. I-610, exit 9A (San Felipe Rd/Westheimer Rd), 0.3 mi e. Int corridors. **Pets:** Accepted. SAVE ✕ 🛏 🖥 🍴 ⟲ ⊠

◈◈◈ ▽▽▽ Sheraton Houston Brookhollow H

(713) 688-0100. **$89-$259, 3 day notice.** 3000 N Loop W 77092. I-610, exit 13C (TC Jester Blvd), on southbound frontage road. Int corridors. **Pets:** Accepted. SAVE ✕ ᏜM 🛏 🖥 🍴 ⟲ ⊠

◈◈◈ ▽▽▽ Sheraton North Houston Hotel H

(281) 442-5100. **Call for rates.** 15700 John F Kennedy Blvd 77032. Sam Houston Pkwy (Beltway 8), exit John F Kennedy Blvd, just n. Int corridors. **Pets:** Accepted. SAVE ✕ ᏜM 🛏 🖥 ⟲ ⊠

◈◈◈ ▽▽▽ Sheraton Suites Houston Near The Galleria H

(713) 586-2444. **Call for rates.** 2400 W Loop S 77027. I-610, exit 9 (San Felipe Rd) northbound; exit 9A (San Felipe Rd/Westheimer Rd) southbound. Int corridors. **Pets:** Accepted. SAVE ✕ 🛏 🖥 🍴 ⟲

▽▽▽ Staybridge Suites Houston-Near The Galleria H

(713) 355-8888. **$159-$195.** 5190 Hidalgo St 77056. I-610, exit 9A (San Felipe Rd/Westheimer Rd) southbound; exit 8C (Westheimer Rd) northbound, 0.4 mi w to Sage Rd, then just s. Int corridors. **Pets:** Medium. $150 one-time fee/room. Designated rooms, service with restrictions, crate. ASK ✕ ᏜM 🛏 🖥 ⟲

▽▽▽ Staybridge Suites Houston West Energy Corridor H

(281) 759-7829. **$135-$159.** 1225 Eldridge Pkwy 77077. I-10, exit 753A (Eldridge Pkwy), 1.8 mi s. Int corridors. **Pets:** Accepted.

ASK ✕ 🛏 🖥 ⟲

▼▼ ▼▼ TownePlace Suites by Marriott-Central H
(713) 690-4035. **$139-$169.** 12820 Northwest Frwy (US 290) 77040. US 290, exit Bingle/43rd St eastbound; exit Bingle/Pinemont/43rd St westbound, on westbound feeder. Int corridors. **Pets:** Accepted.

⊠ ⓢM ▤ 🖃 ⊠

▼▼ ▼▼ TownePlace Suites by Marriott-West H
(281) 646-0058. **$122-$149.** 15155 Katy Frwy 77094. I-10, exit 751, just s on SR 6 to Grisby Rd, then w. Int corridors. **Pets:** Accepted.

⊠ ▤ 🖃 ⌒

◇◇◇ ▼▼▼▼ The Westin Galleria, Houston H
(713) 960-8100. **$189-$429.** 5060 W Alabama St 77056. I-610, exit 8C (Westheimer Rd) northbound; exit 9A (San Felipe Rd/Westheimer Rd) southbound, 0.5 mi w on Westheimer Rd to Sage, just s, then just e. Int corridors. **Pets:** Accepted. SAVE ⊠ ⓢM 🖃 🍴 ⌒

KATY

◇◇◇ ▼▼▼▼ Best Western Katy Inn and Suites H
(281) 395-6200. **$120-$140.** 2006 Katy Mills Blvd 77494. I-10, exit 741, on S Frontage Rd. Int corridors. **Pets:** Accepted.

SAVE ⊠ ⓢM ▤ 🖃 ⌒

◇◇◇ ▼▼▼▼ La Quinta Inn & Suites Katy H ❀
(281) 392-9800. **$89-$179.** 22455 Katy Frwy (I-10) 77450. I-10, exit 743 (Grand Pkwy), on eastbound service road. Int corridors. **Pets:** Medium, other species. Service with restrictions, supervision.

SAVE ⊠ ⓢM ▤ 🖃 ⌒

KINGWOOD

▼▼▼▼ Homewood Suites by Hilton at Kingwood Parc H
(281) 358-5566. **$169-$189.** 23320 Hwy 59 N 77339. US 59, exit Kingwood Dr, 1.4 mi n on northbound access road. Int corridors.
Pets: Accepted. ⊠ ⓢM ▤ 🖃 ⌒ ⊠

MONTGOMERY

◇◇◇ ▼▼▼ Best Western Lake Conroe H
(936) 588-3030. **$85-$90.** 14643 Hwy 105 W 77356. I-45, exit 87 (SR 105), 8.1 mi w. Ext corridors. **Pets:** Accepted. SAVE ⊠ ▤ 🖃 ⌒

◇◇◇ ▼▼▼▼ La Torretta Del Lago Resort & Spa H
(936) 448-4400. **$159-$499, 3 day notice.** 600 Del Lago Blvd 77356. SR 105, 2.5 mi n on Walden Rd to La Torretta Blvd. Ext/int corridors.
Pets: Accepted. SAVE ⊠ ▤ 🖃 🍴 ⌒ ⊠

NASSAU BAY

▼▼▼▼ Hilton Houston NASA Clear Lake H
(281) 333-9300. **$99-$229.** 3000 NASA Pkwy 77058. I-45, exit 25 (NASA Rd One), 3.8 mi e. Int corridors. **Pets:** Accepted.

⊠ ▤ 🖃 🍴 ⌒ ⊠

ROSENBERG

▼▼▼▼ La Quinta Inn & Suites H ❀
(832) 595-6111. **$79-$149.** 28332 Southwest Frwy 77471. Jct US 59 and SR 36; on southbound Frontage Rd. Int corridors. **Pets:** Medium, other species. Service with restrictions, supervision. ASK ⊠ ▤ 🖃 ⌒

SEABROOK

▼▼▼▼ La Quinta Inn & Suites #618 H ❀
(281) 326-7300. **$89-$159.** 3636 NASA Pkwy 77586. I-45, exit 25 (NASA Rd One), 6 mi e; SR 146, 2 mi w. Int corridors. **Pets:** Medium, other species. Service with restrictions, supervision. ASK ⊠ ▤ 🖃 ⌒

SHENANDOAH

▼▼▼ TownePlace Suites by Marriott The Woodlands H
(936) 273-7772. **$152-$186.** 107 Vision Park Blvd 77384. I-45, exit 79 (College Park/Needham Rd), 1 mi s, on southbound frontage road. Int corridors. **Pets:** Accepted. ⊠ ⓢM ▤ 🖃 ⌒

STAFFORD

▼▼ ▼▼ La Quinta Inn Houston (Stafford/Sugarland) H ❀
(281) 240-2300. **$49-$109.** 12727 Southwest Frwy 77477. US 59 eastbound service road, exit Corporate Dr southbound; exit Airport Blvd/Kirkwood Rd northbound. Int corridors. **Pets:** Medium, other species. Service with restrictions, supervision. ASK ⊠ ▤ 🖃 ⌒

▼▼▼▼ Residence Inn by Marriott Houston/Sugar Land H
(281) 277-0770. **$153-$187.** 12703 Southwest Frwy 77477. US 59, exit 90 (Corporate Dr) southbound; exit Airport Blvd/Kirkwood Rd northbound; on northbound service road. Int corridors. **Pets:** Accepted.

⊠ ▤ 🖃 ⌒ ⊠

SUGAR LAND

▼▼▼ Drury Inn & Suites-Houston/Sugar Land H
(281) 277-9700. **$100-$184.** 13770 Southwest Frwy 77478. Sw on US 59, exit Dairy Ashford/Sugar Creek southbound; exit Dairy Ashford/Sugar Creek northbound, left under US 59. Int corridors. **Pets:** Other species. No service, supervision. ASK ⊠ ▤ 🖃 ⌒

THE WOODLANDS

◇◇◇ ▼▼▼▼ Best Western The Woodlands H
(936) 271-2378. **$85-$119.** 17081 I-45 S 77385. I-45, exit 79 (SR 242) College Park/Needham Rd, northeast corner of SR 242 and I-45; on N Frontage Rd. Int corridors. **Pets:** Accepted. SAVE ⊠ ▤ 🖃 ⌒

▼▼▼▼ Drury Inn & Suites-Houston/The Woodlands H
(281) 362-7222. **$95-$179.** 28099 I-45 N 77380. I-45, exit 77, on southbound frontage road. Int corridors. **Pets:** Other species. No service, supervision. ASK ⊠ ⓢM ▤ 🖃 ⌒

▼▼▼▼ Holiday Inn Express Hotel & Suites H
(281) 681-8088. **$109.** 24888 I-45 N 77386. I-45, exit 73 (Rayford/Sawdust Rd), on northbound access road. Int corridors. **Pets:** Accepted.

ASK ⊠ ▤ 🖃 ⌒ ⊠

▼▼▼▼ Residence Inn by Marriott H
(281) 292-3252. **$158-$193.** 1040 Lake Front Cir 77380. I-45, exit 78 southbound; exit 79 (SR 242) northbound, 0.8 mi s of jct I-45 and Research Forest Dr, just w. Int corridors. **Pets:** Other species. $100 one-time fee/room. Service with restrictions, supervision.

⊠ ▤ 🖃 ⌒ ⊠

WEBSTER

◇◇◇ ▼▼▼ Comfort Suites H 🐾
(281) 554-5400. **$110-$150.** 16931 N Texas Ave 77598. I-45, exit 26 (Bay Area Blvd), 0.5 mi e to Texas Ave, then just s. Int corridors.
Pets: Medium. $50 one-time fee/room. SAVE ⊠ ⓢM ▤ 🖃 ⌒

◇◇◇ ▼▼ ▼▼ Econo Lodge-NASA H
(281) 333-3737. **$55-$85.** 904 E NASA Rd 1 77598. I-45, exit 25 (NASA Rd 1/Alvin), 1.5 mi e. Ext corridors. **Pets:** Accepted.

SAVE ⊠ ▤ 🖃 ⌒

▼▼ ▼▼ Extended Stay Deluxe Houston NASA-Bay Area Blvd H
(281) 338-7711. **$95-$126.** 720 W Bay Area Blvd 77598. I-45, exit 26 (Bay Area Blvd), just e. Int corridors. **Pets:** Other species. $25 daily fee/room. Designated rooms, service with restrictions, crate.

ASK ⊠ ▤ 🖃 ⌒

▼▼ ▼▼ La Quinta Inn & Suites Webster H ❀
(281) 554-5290. **$89-$159.** 520 W Bay Area Blvd 77598. I-45, exit 26 (Bay Area Blvd), just e. Int corridors. **Pets:** Medium, other species. Service with restrictions, supervision. ASK ⊠ ⓢM ▤ 🖃 ⌒

◇◇◇ ▼▼ ▼▼ Super 8-Houston-Webster-NASA M
(281) 333-5385. **$65-$150, 3 day notice.** 18103 Kingsrow Rd 77058. I-45, exit 25 (NASA Rd One), 1.5 mi e. Ext corridors. **Pets:** Accepted.

SAVE ⊠ ▤ 🖃 ⌒

WINNIE

▼▼▼▼ Comfort Inn & Suites H
(409) 296-6200. **Call for rates.** 338 Spur 5 77665. I-10, exit 829, just s.
Int corridors. **Pets:** Accepted. ☒ 🛢 💻 ⤳

▼▼▼ Days Inn & Suites H
(409) 296-2866. **$59-$149.** 14932 FM 1663 77665. I-10, exit 829, just n.
Ext corridors. **Pets:** Small. $20 daily fee/pet. Service with restrictions,
supervision. A$K ☒ 🛢 💻 ⤳

▼▼▼▼ Winnie Inn & Suites H
(409) 296-2947. **$50-$90.** 205 Spur 5, Hwy 124 77665. I-10, exit 829,
just s. Ext corridors. **Pets:** Accepted. A$K ☒ 🛢 💻 ⤳

END METROPOLITAN AREA

HUNTSVILLE

▼▼▼ GuestHouse Inn Huntsville H
(936) 293-8800. **Call for rates.** 201 W Hill Park Cir 77320. I-45, exit
116, just w on US 190. Ext corridors. **Pets:** Accepted.
☒ &M 🛢 💻 ⤳

▼▼▼ La Quinta Inn Huntsville H 🐾
(936) 295-6454. **$59-$119.** 124 I-45 N 77340. I-45, exit 116, on northbound frontage road. Ext corridors. **Pets:** Medium, other species. Service
with restrictions, supervision. A$K ☒ 🛢 💻 ⤳

INGLESIDE

AAA▷ ▼▼▼ Best Western Naval Station Inn H
(361) 776-2767. **$70-$150.** 2025 State Hwy 361 78362. 1 mi e of jct SR
1069. Ext corridors. **Pets:** Medium. $10 daily fee/pet. Service with restric-
tions, supervision. SAVE ☒ 🛢 💻 ⤳

JACKSONVILLE

▼▼▼▼ Holiday Inn Express H
(903) 589-8500. **$84-$89.** 1848 S Jackson St 75766. On US 69, 2 mi s
of jct US 69 and 79. Int corridors. **Pets:** Accepted.
A$K ☒ &M 🛢 💻 ⤳

JASPER

▼▼▼ Econo Lodge M
(409) 384-2511. **$70.** 612 W Gibson St 75951. US 190 and SR 63, 1.2
mi w of jct US 96. Ext corridors. **Pets:** Accepted. A$K ☒ 🛢 ⤳

▼▼▼▼ Super 8 H
(409) 384-8600. **$79-$99.** 2100 N Wheeler 75951. US 96, 1.8 mi n of jct
US 190. Ext corridors. **Pets:** Accepted. A$K ☒ 🛢 💻 ⤳

JUNCTION

AAA▷ ▼▼▼ Days Inn H
(325) 446-3730. **$70-$100.** 111 S Martinez St 76849. I-10, exit 457, 0.3
mi s. Ext corridors. **Pets:** Other species. $10 one-time fee/pet. Service
with restrictions. SAVE ☒ 🛢 💻 ⤳

AAA▷ ▼▼▼ Econo Lodge H
(325) 446-2475. **$44-$79.** 311 S Segovia Access Rd 76849. I-10, exit
465, on S Frontage Rd. Ext corridors. **Pets:** Accepted.
SAVE ☒ 🛢 💻 ⤳

▼▼▼ The Hills Motel M
(325) 446-2567. **$32-$42.** 1520 Main St 76849. I-10, exit 456, 1.3 mi s
on US 377. Ext corridors. **Pets:** Accepted. ☒ 🛢 ⤳

AAA▷ ▼▼▼ Motel 6 H
(325) 446-3572. **$65-$149.** 200 I-10 W 76849. I-10, exit 456. Ext corridors. **Pets:** Other species. Service with restrictions, supervision.
SAVE ☒ 🛢 ⤳

▼▼▼ Rodeway Inn H
(325) 446-4588. **$55-$69.** 2343 N Main St 76849. I-10, exit 456, just s
on US 377. Ext corridors. **Pets:** Small, other species. $10 one-time fee/
room. Service with restrictions, supervision. A$K ☒ 🛢 💻 ⤳

▼▼▼ Sun Valley Motel M
(325) 446-2505. **Call for rates.** 1611 Main St 76849. I-10, exit 456 eastbound, 1 mi s on US 377; exit 460 westbound, 3 mi w on Loop 481 to
jct US 377, then just n. Ext corridors. **Pets:** Accepted. ☒ 🛢 ⤳

KERRVILLE

AAA▷ ▼▼▼ Best Western Sunday House Inn H
(830) 896-1313. **$85-$95.** 2124 Sidney Baker St 78028. I-10, exit 508
(SR 16), just s. Ext corridors. **Pets:** Small. $10 daily fee/pet. Designated
rooms, service with restrictions, crate. SAVE ☒ 🛢 💻 ⫦ ⤳

▼▼▼ Days Inn of Kerrville M
(830) 896-1000. **$79-$149.** 2000 Sidney Baker St 78028. I-10, exit 508
(SR 16), 0.5 mi s. Ext/int corridors. **Pets:** Medium, dogs only. $10 daily
fee/pet. Designated rooms, service with restrictions, supervision.
A$K ☒ 🛢 ⤳

**AAA▷ ▼▼▼▼ Y. O. Ranch Resort Hotel & Conference
Center** H
(830) 257-4440. **$79-$129.** 2033 Sidney Baker St 78028. I-10, exit 508
(SR 16), 0.3 mi s. Ext/int corridors. **Pets:** Other species. Service with
restrictions, supervision. SAVE ☒ 🛢 💻 ⫦ ⤳ ⊠

KILGORE

AAA▷ ▼▼▼ Best Western Inn of Kilgore H
(903) 986-1195. **$85-$120.** 1411 N Hwy 259 75662. I-20, exit 589, 3.9 mi
s. Ext corridors. **Pets:** Dogs only. $20 one-time fee/pet. Service with
restrictions, supervision. SAVE ☒ 🛢 💻 ⤳

KILLEEN

AAA▷ ▼▼▼ Holiday Inn Express H 🐾
(254) 554-2727. **$70-$99.** 1602 E Central Texas Expy 76541. US 190,
exit Trimmier Rd. Ext corridors. **Pets:** Medium, other species. Service with
restrictions, crate. SAVE ☒ 🛢 💻

▼▼▼ La Quinta Inn Killeen H 🐾
(254) 526-8331. **$39-$89.** 1112 S Fort Hood St 76541-7493. US 190, exit
Fort Hood St, on westbound access road. Ext corridors. **Pets:** Medium,
other species. Service with restrictions, supervision.
A$K ☒ 🛢 💻 ⤳

▼▼▼▼ Residence Inn by Marriott H
(254) 634-1020. **$125-$153.** 400 E Central Texas Expwy 76541. US 190,
exit Fort Hood/Jasper (SR 195) on S Frontage Rd. Int corridors.
Pets: Accepted. ☒ &M 🛢 💻 ⤳ ⊠

AAA▷ ▼▼▼▼ Shilo Inn Suites Hotel–Killeen H 🐾
(254) 699-0999. **$125-$215.** 3701 S W S Young Dr 76542. US 190, exit
W S Young Dr, 1 mi s. Int corridors. **Pets:** Dogs only. $25 one-time fee/
room. Designated rooms, service with restrictions, supervision.
SAVE ☒ &M 🛢 💻 ⫦ ⤳ ⊠

▼▼▼▼ TownePlace Suites by Marriott H
(254) 554-8899. **$89-$109.** 2401 Florence Rd 76542. US 190, exit Trimmier Rd to Jasper, on south access road go 1 blk e to Florence Rd, then
just s. Int corridors. **Pets:** Accepted. ☒ &M 🛢 💻 ⤳

KINGSLAND

▼▼ Rio Vista Resort 🅒🅞
(325) 388-6331. **$100-$880, 30 day notice.** 234 Rio Vista Dr 78639. Colorado River Bridge, 0.5 mi nw on FM 1431, 0.5 mi s on Reynolds St. Ext corridors. **Pets:** Other species. Designated rooms, service with restrictions, supervision. 🅐🅢🅚 ✖ 🛑 💻 ⊅ ⊠

KINGSVILLE

🏵 ▼▼ Quality Inn 🅗
(361) 592-5251. **$69-$89, 4 day notice.** 221 S Hwy 77 Bypass 78363. On US 77, just s of jct SR 141. Ext corridors. **Pets:** Small. $150 deposit/room, $10 daily fee/pet. Designated rooms, service with restrictions, crate. 🆂🅰🆅🅴 ✖ 🛑 💻 ⊅

🏵 ▼▼ Rodeway Inn 🅜
(361) 595-5753. **$71-$76.** 3430 Hwy 77 78363. 4.5 mi s on US 77. Ext corridors. **Pets:** Accepted. 🆂🅰🆅🅴 ✖ 🛑 💻 ⊅

🏵 ▼▼ Super 8 🅜
(361) 592-6471. **$55-$90.** 105 S US Hwy 77 Bypass 78363. 0.8 mi e on US 77. Ext corridors. **Pets:** $20 one-time fee/pet. No service, supervision. 🆂🅰🆅🅴 ✖ 🛑 💻 ⊅

LA GRANGE

🏵 ▼▼ Best Western La Grange Inn and
Suites 🅗
(979) 968-6800. **$89-$200.** 600 E State Hwy 71 Bypass 78945. Jct US 77 and SR 71, just e on N Frontage Rd. Int corridors. **Pets:** Accepted. 🆂🅰🆅🅴 ✖ 🛑 💻 ⊅

LAJITAS

🏵 ▼▼ Lajitas Golf Resort and Spa 🅗
(432) 424-5000. **$179-$750.** 1 Main St 79852. Center. Ext/int corridors. **Pets:** $50 one-time fee/room. Designated rooms, service with restrictions, crate. 🆂🅰🆅🅴 ✖ 🛑 💻 🍴 ⊅ ⊠

LAKE JACKSON

▼▼▼ Cherotel Brazosport Hotel & Conference
Center 🅗
(979) 297-1161. **$50-$100.** 925 Hwy 332 77566. On SR 228/332, just w of jct Business Rt SR 288. Int corridors. **Pets:** Accepted. 🅐🅢🅚 ✖ 🛑 💻 🍴 ⊅

LAMESA

🏵 ▼▼ Shiloh Inn 🅜
(806) 872-6721. **$53-$71, 3 day notice.** 1707 Lubbock Hwy 79331. Jct US 87 and 180, 1 mi n. Ext corridors. **Pets:** Medium, other species. $10 one-time fee/room. Service with restrictions, supervision. 🆂🅰🆅🅴 ✖ 🛑 💻 🍴 ⊅

LAREDO

▼▼ Americas Best Value Inn 🅜
(956) 723-1510. **$50-$110.** 5240 San Bernardo Ave 78041. I-35, exit 3B (Mann Rd), on southbound access road. Ext corridors. **Pets:** Other species. $10 daily fee/pet. Service with restrictions. 🅐🅢🅚 ✖ ⊅

▼▼ Days Inn & Suites 🅗
(956) 724-8221. **$40-$159.** 7060 N San Bernardo Ave 78041. I-35, exit 4 (San Bernardo Ave), just s on southbound access road. Ext/int corridors. **Pets:** Accepted. 🅐🅢🅚 ✖ 🛑 💻 🍴 ⊅

▼▼▼ Extended StayAmerica Laredo-Del Mar 🅗
(956) 724-1920. **$55-$69.** 106 W Village 78040. I-35, exit 3B (Mann Rd), just n on northbound access road to W Village, then just e. Int corridors. **Pets:** Other species. $25 daily fee/room. Designated rooms, service with restrictions, crate. 🅐🅢🅚 ✖ 🛑 💻

▼▼▼ La Posada Hotel & Suites 🅗
(956) 722-1701. **Call for rates.** 1000 Zaragoza St 78040. I-35, exit downtown; just e of International Bridge I. Ext/int corridors. **Pets:** Accepted. ✖ ♿🅼 🛑 💻 🍴 ⊅

▼▼▼ La Quinta Inn & Suites 🅗 🐾
(956) 724-7222. **$79-$139.** 7220 Bob Bullock Loop 78041. Jct US 59, 2.5 mi n on Loop 20 N. Int corridors. **Pets:** Medium, other species. Service with restrictions, supervision. ✖ ♿🅼 🛑 💻 ⊅

▼▼ La Quinta Inn Laredo (I-35) 🅜 🐾
(956) 722-0511. **$39-$89.** 3610 Santa Ursula Ave 78041-4453. I-35, exit 2 (US 59). Ext corridors. **Pets:** Medium, other species. Service with restrictions, supervision. 🅐🅢🅚 ✖ 🛑 💻 ⊅

▼▼ Motel 6 South-142 🅜
(956) 725-8187. **$48-$59.** 5310 San Bernardo Ave 78041. I-35, exit 3B (Mann Rd). Ext corridors. **Pets:** Other species. Service with restrictions, supervision. ✖ ♿🅼 ⊅

🏵 ▼▼ Red Roof Inn Laredo 🅜
(956) 712-0733. **$57-$80.** 1006 W Calton Rd 78041. I-35, exit 3A, 0.3 mi w. Ext/int corridors. **Pets:** Large. Service with restrictions, crate. 🆂🅰🆅🅴 ✖ 🛑 ⊅

▼▼▼ Residence Inn Laredo Del Mar 🅗
(956) 753-9700. **$116-$142.** 310 Lost Oaks Blvd 78041. From airport, Loop 20 S to US 59 W to I-35 N, exit 3B, then right. Int corridors. **Pets:** Medium, other species. $100 one-time fee/room. Service with restrictions, supervision. ✖ ♿🅼 🛑 💻 ⊅

▼▼▼ Staybridge Suites-Laredo 🅗
(956) 722-0444. **$83-$88.** 7010 Bob Bullock Loop 78041. US 83, exit onto Loop 20 (Bob Bullock Loop); hotel is on west side. Int corridors. **Pets:** Accepted. 🅐🅢🅚 ✖ 🛑 💻 ⊅

LITTLEFIELD

🏵 ▼▼ Best Western Littlefield Inn & Suites 🅗
(806) 385-3400. **$110-$120.** 2600 Hall Ave 79339. Jct US 84 and 385, just s. Int corridors. **Pets:** Other species. $10 daily fee/pet. Designated rooms, service with restrictions, supervision. 🆂🅰🆅🅴 ✖ ♿🅼 🛑 💻 ⊅

LIVINGSTON

🏵 ▼▼ Best Western Livingston Inn & Suites 🅗
(936) 327-8500. **$85-$105.** 335 Hwy 59 Loop S 77351. Just s of jct US 59 and 190, on southbound frontage road. Int corridors. **Pets:** Small. $100 deposit/room. Designated rooms, service with restrictions, supervision. 🆂🅰🆅🅴 ✖ 🛑 💻 ⊅

LLANO

🏵 ▼▼ Best Western Llano 🅗
(325) 247-4101. **$70-$100.** 901 W Young St 78643. 1 mi w on SR 71 and 29. Ext corridors. **Pets:** Accepted. 🆂🅰🆅🅴 ✖ 🛑 💻 ⊅

LONGVIEW

▼▼ Baymont Inn 🅗
(903) 757-3663. **$69-$99.** 502 S Access Rd 75602-4202. I-20, exit 595. Ext corridors. **Pets:** Medium, other species. Service with restrictions, supervision. 🅐🅢🅚 ✖ 🛑 💻 ⊅

▼▼ Motel 6–158 🅜
(903) 758-5256. **$45-$58.** 110 S Access Rd 75603. I-20, exit 595A. Ext corridors. **Pets:** Other species. Service with restrictions, supervision. ✖ ⊅

LUBBOCK

🏵 ▼▼ Americas Best Value Inn–Lubbock 🅜
(806) 745-2515. **$50-$150.** 150 Slaton Rd 79404. I-27, exit 1B, just e on US 84. Ext corridors. **Pets:** Small. $100 deposit/room, $10 one-time fee/pet. Designated rooms, no service, supervision. 🆂🅰🆅🅴 ✖ 🛑 ⊅

🏵 ▼▼ Arbor Inn & Suites 🅗
(806) 722-2726. **$89-$179.** 5310 Englewood Ave 79424. Loop 289, exit 50th St, just w. Int corridors. **Pets:** Large, dogs only. Service with restrictions, supervision. 🆂🅰🆅🅴 ✖ ♿🅼 🛑 💻 ⊅

Best Western Lubbock Windsor Inn 🅷
(806) 762-8400. **$70-$180.** 5410 I-27 79404. 3.5 mi s on I-27, exit 1B southbound; U-turn at exit 1A (50th St) northbound. Int corridors. **Pets:** Large, other species. $15 daily fee/pet. Service with restrictions, supervision. SAVE ✕ 🅱 💻 ➰

Extended StayAmerica Lubbock Southwest 🅷
(806) 785-9881. **$70-$97.** 4802 S Loop 289 79414. S Loop 289, exit Slide Rd, on north access road. Int corridors. **Pets:** Other species. $25 daily fee/room. Designated rooms, service with restrictions, crate.
A$K ✕ 🅱 💻

Hawthorn Suites 🅷
(806) 792-3600. **$110-$270.** 4435 Marsha Sharp Frwy 79407. W Loop 289, exit US 62/82, then 2.7 mi e. Int corridors. **Pets:** Accepted.
SAVE ✕ 🅱M 🅱 💻 ➰

La Quinta Inn & Suites 🅷 🐾
(806) 749-1600. **$90-$180.** 5006 Auburn St 79416. Jct Loop 289 W and Quaker Ave, 1 mi s on W Frontage Rd. Int corridors. **Pets:** Medium, other species. Service with restrictions, supervision.
SAVE ✕ 🅱 💻 ➰

La Quinta Inn & Suites Lubbock (West/Medical Center) 🅷 🐾
(806) 792-0065. **Call for rates.** 4115 Marsha Sharp Frwy 79407. 3.3 mi sw; 2.5 mi ne of Loop 289 on US 62 and 82. Ext/int corridors. **Pets:** Medium, other species. Service with restrictions, supervision.
✕ 🅱 💻 ➰

La Quinta Inn Lubbock 🅷 🐾
(806) 763-9441. **$39-$89.** 601 Ave Q 79401-2613. 0.8 mi nw on US 84 (Ave Q). Ext corridors. **Pets:** Medium, other species. Service with restrictions, supervision. A$K ✕ 🅱 💻 ➰

Lubbock Super 8 Ⓜ
(806) 762-8726. **$40-$129, 3 day notice.** 501 Ave Q 79401. 1 mi nw on US 84. Ext corridors. **Pets:** $10 daily fee/pet. No service.
A$K ✕ 🅱

Residence Inn by Marriott 🅷
(806) 745-1963. **$129-$134.** 2551 S Loop 289 79423. Loop 289, exit University Ave, 3 mi s, on south frontage road. Ext corridors.
Pets: Accepted. ✕ 🅱 💻 ➰ ✕

Staybridge Suites 🅷
(806) 765-8900. **$110-$260.** 2515 19th St 79410. Jct University Ave and 19th St; on southwest corner. Int corridors. **Pets:** Large. $75 one-time fee/room. Service with restrictions, supervision. A$K ✕ 🅱 💻 ➰

TownePlace Suites by Marriott 🅷
(806) 799-6226. **$108-$132.** 5310 W Loop 289 79424. W Loop 289, exit US 62/82 (Brownfield Rd), 0.5 mi s on west frontage road. Int corridors. **Pets:** Medium, other species. $100 one-time fee/room. Service with restrictions, supervision. SAVE ✕ 🅱M 🅱 💻 ➰

LUFKIN

Best Western Crown Colony Inn & Suites 🅷
(936) 634-3481. **$99-$129.** 3211 S 1st St 75901. 2 mi s of jct US 59 and Loop 287. Int corridors. **Pets:** Large. $25 one-time fee/room. Service with restrictions. SAVE ✕ 🅱 💻 ➰

La Quinta Inn Lufkin 🅷 🐾
(936) 634-3351. **$69-$119.** 2119 S 1st St 75901-5902. US 59, exit Carriageway northbound, 0.3 mi s of jct S Loop 287 and US 59 business route. Ext corridors. **Pets:** Medium, other species. Service with restrictions, supervision. A$K ✕ 🅱 💻 ➰

Quality Inn & Suites 🅷 🐾
(936) 639-3333. **Call for rates.** 4306 S 1st St 75901. 2.2 mi s of jct US 59 and E Loop 287. Ext corridors. **Pets:** Medium, other species. $10 one-time fee/pet. Service with restrictions, crate.
✕ 🅱 💻 🍴 ➰

MADISONVILLE

Best Western Executive Inn & Suites 🅷
(936) 349-1700. **$99-$109.** 3307 E Main St 77864. I-45, exit 142, just e. Int corridors. **Pets:** Accepted. SAVE ✕ 🅱M 🅱 💻 ➰

MANSFIELD

Best Western Mansfield Inn & Suites 🅷
(817) 539-0707. **$89-$94.** 775 N Hwy 287 76063. US 287, exit Walnut Creek Rd, just s west side on frontage road. Int corridors. **Pets:** Medium. $15 daily fee/pet. Service with restrictions, supervision.
SAVE ✕ 🅱M 🅱 💻 ➰

Comfort Inn 🅷
(817) 453-8848. **Call for rates.** 175 N Hwy 287 76063. US 287 S, exit E Broad St. Int corridors. **Pets:** Accepted. ✕ 🅱M 🅱 💻 ➰

La Quinta Inn & Suites 🅷 🐾
(817) 453-5040. **$79-$169.** 1503 Breckenridge Rd 76063. US 287, exit Walnut Creek Rd/Debbie Ln, 1.2 mi n to Debbie Ln, then just e to Breckenridge Rd. Int corridors. **Pets:** Medium, other species. Service with restrictions, supervision. A$K ✕ 🅱M 🅱 💻 ➰

MARBLE FALLS

Best Western Marble Falls Inn 🅷
(830) 693-5122. **$69-$129.** 1403 US Hwy 281 78654. 0.4 mi n of jct SR 281 and FM 1431. Ext/int corridors. **Pets:** Medium. $10 daily fee/pet. Designated rooms, service with restrictions, supervision.
SAVE ✕ 🅱 💻 ➰

La Quinta Inn & Suites 🅷 🐾
(830) 798-2020. **$79-$199.** 501 Hwy 2147 W 78654. Jct US 281 and SR 2147, just w. Int corridors. **Pets:** Medium, other species. Service with restrictions, supervision. SAVE ✕ 🅱M 🅱 💻 ➰

Quality Inn-Marble Falls 🅷
(830) 693-7531. **$65-$120.** 1206 Hwy 281 N 78654. 0.3 mi n of jct US 281 and FM 1431. Ext corridors. **Pets:** Medium. $10 one-time fee/pet. Service with restrictions, supervision. SAVE ✕ 🅱 💻 ➰

MARSHALL

Best Western Executive Inn 🅷
(903) 935-0707. **$79-$149.** 5201 E End Blvd S 75672. I-20, exit 617, 0.4 mi n on US 59. Ext corridors. **Pets:** Medium. $25 daily fee/pet. Service with restrictions, supervision. SAVE ✕ 🅱 💻 ➰

La Quinta Inn & East Texas Conference Center 🅷 🐾
(903) 927-0009. **$69-$269.** 5301 E End Blvd S 75672. I-20, exit 617, just n on US 59. Int corridors. **Pets:** Medium, other species. Service with restrictions, supervision. A$K ✕ 🅱 💻 ➰

Motel 6 Marshall #422 Ⓜ
(903) 935-4393. **$41-$55.** 300 I-20 E 75670. I-20, exit 617, just e on access road. Ext corridors. **Pets:** Other species. Service with restrictions, supervision. ✕ 🅱 ➰

MCALLEN

Drury Inn-McAllen 🅷
(956) 687-5100. **$85-$149.** 612 W Expwy 83 78501. US 83, exit 2nd St, on northwest frontage road. Int corridors. **Pets:** Other species. No service, supervision. A$K ✕ 🅱 💻 ➰

Drury Suites-McAllen 🅷
(956) 682-3222. **$99-$229.** 228 W Expwy 83 78501. At US 83 and 6th St. Int corridors. **Pets:** Other species. No service, supervision.
A$K ✕ 🅱 💻 ➰

La Quinta Inn McAllen 🅷 🐾
(956) 687-1101. **$59-$129.** 1100 S 10th St 78501. Just n of US 83. Ext corridors. **Pets:** Medium, other species. Service with restrictions, supervision. A$K ✕ 🅱 💻 ➰

▼▼ Motel 6 McAllen #212 **M**
(956) 687-3700. **$47-$59.** 700 W Expwy 83 78501. US 83, exit 2nd St, on northwest frontage road. Ext corridors. **Pets:** Other species. Service with restrictions, supervision. ⊠ ≈

▼▼▼▼ Pear Tree Inn by Drury **H**
(956) 682-4900. **$80-$115.** 300 W Expwy 83 78501. US 83, exit 2nd St, on northwest frontage road. Int corridors. **Pets:** Other species. No service, supervision. ASK ⊠ 🛗 💻 ≈

▼▼▼ Posada Ana Inn **H**
(956) 631-6700. **$62-$100.** 620 W Expwy 83 78501. US 83, exit 2nd St, on northwest frontage road. Int corridors. **Pets:** Other species. No service, supervision. ASK ⊠ 💻

▼▼▼ Residence Inn by Marriott **H**
(956) 994-8626. **$116-$142.** 220 W Expwy 83 78501. US 83, exit 2nd St, just w, then just n on 2nd St. Int corridors. **Pets:** Medium, other species. $75 one-time fee/room. Service with restrictions, supervision.
⊠ 🛗 💻 ≈ ⊠

▼▼ Super 8 **M** ❀
(956) 688-6666. **$55-$89.** 6420 S 23rd St 78503. US 83, exit 23rd St, 3 mi s; jct W Military Hwy 1016. Ext corridors. **Pets:** Very small, dogs only. $10 one-time fee/pet. Designated rooms, service with restrictions, supervision. ASK ⊠ 🛗 💻 ≈

MIDLAND

▲▲▲ ▼▼▼ Best Western Airport Plaza Inn **H**
(432) 561-8000. **$80-$90, 14 day notice.** 3312 S CR 1276 79706. I-20, exit 126, 0.8 mi n on I-20 business loop to W CR 117, then 0.4 mi e. Int corridors. **Pets:** Small, other species. $35 one-time fee/room. Service with restrictions, supervision. SAVE ⊠ 🛗 💻 🍴 ≈

▲▲▲ ▼▼▼ Clarion Hotel & Conference Center **H**
(432) 697-3181. **$85-$109.** 4300 W Wall St 79703. I-20, exit 134 (Midkiff Rd), 1 mi n to I-20 business loop, then 0.7 mi w. Ext/int corridors.
Pets: Accepted. SAVE ⊠ 🛗 💻 🍴 ≈ ⊠

▲▲▲ ▼▼▼ Comfort Suites **H**
(432) 620-9191. **Call for rates.** 4706 N Garfield St 79705. Loop 250, exit Garfield St, just n. Int corridors. **Pets:** Accepted.
SAVE ⊠ 🛗 💻 ≈

▼▼▼ Hilton Midland Plaza **H** ❀
(432) 683-6131. **$129-$389.** 117 W Wall St 79701. Jct Wall and Loraine sts; downtown. Int corridors. **Pets:** Other species. $50 one-time fee/room. Designated rooms, service with restrictions.
⊠ 🔊 🛗 💻 🍴 ≈ ⊠

▼▼▼ La Quinta Inn & Suites **H** ❀
(432) 697-9900. **$100-$200.** 2606 N Loop 250 W 79707. Loop 250 W, exit SR 158/191, 0.5 mi n on E Frontage Rd. Int corridors. **Pets:** Medium, other species. Service with restrictions, supervision.
⊠ 🔊 🛗 💻 ≈

▼▼▼ La Quinta Inn Midland **H** ❀
(432) 697-9900. **$49-$109.** 4130 W Wall St 79703-7718. I-20, exit 131, 0.9 mi n on Loop 250 to exit 1A; 1.2 mi e on I-20 business route. Ext corridors. **Pets:** Medium, other species. Service with restrictions, supervision. ASK ⊠ 🛗 💻 ≈

▼▼▼ Residence Inn Midland **H**
(432) 689-3511. **$170-$208.** 5509 Deauville Blvd 79706. Loop 250 W, exit SR 158/191 to S Frontage Rd. Int corridors. **Pets:** Small, other species. $100 one-time fee/room. Service with restrictions, crate.
⊠ 🔊 🛗 💻 ≈

MINERAL WELLS

▲▲▲ ▼▼▼ Best Western Clubhouse Inn & Suites **H**
(940) 325-2270. **$80-$130.** 4410 Hwy 180 E 76067. Jct US 180 and SR 1195; in East Mineral Wells. Int corridors. **Pets:** Large, other species. $10 one-time fee/pet. Service with restrictions, supervision.
SAVE ⊠ 🔊 🛗 💻 ≈

MISSION

▼▼▼▼ El Rocio Retreat **BB**
(956) 584-7432. **$75-$315.** 2519 S Inspiration Rd 78572. Jct US 83 at Inspiration Rd, 2 mi s. Ext/int corridors. **Pets:** Accepted. ASK ⊠

▼▼▼▼ Hawthorn Suites **H**
(956) 519-9696. **$99-$119.** 3700 Plantation Grove Blvd 78572. US 83, exit Shary Rd, 2.1 mi s. Ext corridors. **Pets:** Accepted.
ASK ⊠ 🛗 💻 ≈

MONAHANS

▼▼▼ Americas Best Value Colonial Inn **M**
(432) 943-4345. **$100-$140.** 702 W I-20 79756. I-20, exit 80, just s. Ext/int corridors. **Pets:** Accepted. ASK ⊠ 🛗 💻 ≈

MOUNT PLEASANT

▲▲▲ ▼▼▼ Best Western Mt. Pleasant Inn **M**
(903) 572-5051. **$72-$80.** 102 E Burton Rd 75455. I-30, exit 162, just e. Ext corridors. **Pets:** Small. $10 daily fee/pet. Service with restrictions, supervision. SAVE ⊠ 🛗 💻 ≈

▲▲▲ ▼▼▼ Comfort Inn **H**
(903) 577-7553. **$72-$100.** 2515 W Ferguson Rd 75455. I-30, exit 160. Ext corridors. **Pets:** Other species. $20 one-time fee/room. Service with restrictions. SAVE ⊠ 🛗 💻 ≈

▼▼▼▼ Holiday Inn Express Hotel & Suites **H**
(903) 577-3800. **$99-$139.** 2306 Greenhill Rd 75455. I-30, exit 162, just n. Int corridors. **Pets:** Accepted. ASK ⊠ 🔊 🛗 💻 ≈

MOUNT VERNON

▲▲▲ ▼▼▼ Super 8 of Mount Vernon **H**
(903) 588-2882. **$60-$70.** 401 W I-30 75457. I-30, exit 146 (SR 37). Ext corridors. **Pets:** Very small. $10 daily fee/pet. Service with restrictions, supervision. SAVE ⊠ 🛗 💻

NACOGDOCHES

▲▲▲ ▼▼▼ Best Western Northpark Inn **H**
(936) 560-1906. **$60-$120.** 4809 NW Stallings Dr 75964. Jct US 59 N and Loop 224, exit Westward Dr. Ext corridors. **Pets:** $20 one-time fee/pet. Service with restrictions, crate. SAVE ⊠ 🛗 💻 ≈

▼▼▼ Days Inn & Suites **H**
(936) 715-0005. **$60-$139.** 2724 North St 75965. On US 59 business route (North St), 0.6 mi n of Stephen F. Austin University's main entrance (Griffith Blvd). Ext corridors. **Pets:** Accepted. ASK ⊠ 🛗 💻 ≈

▼▼▼ La Quinta Inn Nacogdoches **H** ❀
(936) 560-5453. **$59-$119.** 3215 South St 75961-7212. US 59, jct Loop 224 and US 59 business route, south of town. Ext corridors.
Pets: Medium, other species. Service with restrictions, supervision.
ASK ⊠ 🛗 💻 ≈

NEW BOSTON

▲▲▲ ▼▼▼ Americas Best Value Inn–New Boston **H**
(903) 628-6999. **$69-$90.** 1024 N Center St 75570. I-30, exit 201, on westbound access road. Ext corridors. **Pets:** Accepted.
SAVE ⊠ 🛗 💻 ≈

NORTH RICHLAND HILLS

▲▲▲ ▼▼▼ Best Western NE Mall Inn & Suites **H**
(817) 656-8881. **$80-$140.** 8709 Airport Frwy 76180. SR 121 and 183, 0.5 mi sw of FM 3029, exit Precinct Line Rd, 0.5 mi e of I-820. Ext corridors. **Pets:** Small. $15 daily fee/pet. Designated rooms, service with restrictions, supervision. SAVE ⊠ 🛗 💻 ≈

▼▼▼ Studio 6 #6034 **H**
(817) 788-6000. **$43-$53.** 7450 NE Loop 820 76180. I-820, exit 21 (Holiday Ln), 0.4 mi e on south access road. Ext corridors. **Pets:** Other species. $10 daily fee/room. Service with restrictions, supervision.
⊠ 🛗 💻

ODEM

ΔΔΔ △▽▽ Budget Inn-Odem M

(361) 368-2166. **$55-$120, 3 day notice.** 1505 Voss Ave (US 77) 78370. US 77, 1 mi s of jct SR 631. Ext corridors. **Pets:** Accepted.

[SAVE] [✕] [📞] [💻] [🏊]

ODESSA

ΔΔΔ △▽▽ Best Western Garden Oasis H

(432) 337-3006. **$90-$150.** 110 W I-20 79761-6838. Jct I-20 and US 385, exit 116, just w. Ext/int corridors. **Pets:** Accepted.

[SAVE] [✕] [📞] [💻] [🍴] [🏊] [✕]

△▽▽ La Quinta Inn Odessa H 🐾

(432) 333-2820. **$49-$109.** 5001 E Business Loop I-20 79761-3510. I-20, exit 121, 0.8 mi n on Loop 338, then just w. Ext corridors. **Pets:** Medium, other species. Service with restrictions, supervision.

[ASK] [✕] [📞] [💻] [🏊]

△▽ McM Grande Hotel H

(432) 362-2311. **$80-$95.** 6201 E Business Loop I-20 79762. I-20, exit 121, 0.8 mi n on Loop 338, then 1 mi e. Ext/int corridors. **Pets:** Large, other species. $50 deposit/room. Service with restrictions, supervision.

[ASK] [✕] [📞] [💻] [🍴] [🏊] [✕]

△▽ Motel 6 Odessa #439 M

(432) 333-4025. **$40-$50.** 200 E I-20 Service Rd 79766. I-20, exit 116, on eastbound frontage road. Ext corridors. **Pets:** Other species. Service with restrictions, supervision. [✕] [🏊]

ΔΔΔ △▽▽ Quality Inn & Suites H

(432) 333-3931. **$85-$300.** 3001 E Business Loop I-20 79761. I-20, exit 121, 0.7 mi n on Loop 338, then 0.5 mi w. Ext/int corridors. **Pets:** Medium. $25 one-time fee/pet. Service with restrictions, supervision.

[SAVE] [✕] [📞] [💻] [🏊] [✕]

△▽▽▽ TownePlace Suites by Marriott H

(432) 362-1077. **$143-$175.** 4412 Tanglewood Ln 79762. Jct JBS Pkwy and 42nd St, 2 blks w to Tanglewood Ln, then just n. Int corridors. **Pets:** Accepted. [✕] [♿] [📞] [💻] [🏊]

OLMITO

△▽▽ La Quinta Inn H 🐾

(956) 350-8855. **$59-$99.** 8280 North Expwy 78575. US 77/83, exit SR 511, just e. Int corridors. **Pets:** Medium, other species. Service with restrictions, supervision. [ASK] [✕] [📞] [💻] [🏊]

OZONA

ΔΔΔ △▽▽ Travelodge M

(325) 392-2656. **$65-$95.** 8 11th St 76943. I-10, exit 368 westbound, 2 mi w; exit 365 eastbound to Loop 466, 1 mi e. Ext corridors. **Pets:** Other species. $10 one-time fee/pet. Service with restrictions, supervision.

[SAVE] [✕] [📞] [🏊]

PALESTINE

ΔΔΔ △▽▽ Best Western Palestine Inn H

(903) 723-4655. **$79-$129.** 1601 W Palestine Ave 75801. Jct US 287/SR 19, 0.7 mi sw on US 79. Ext corridors. **Pets:** Small. $10 daily fee/pet. Designated rooms, service with restrictions, supervision.

[SAVE] [✕] [📞] [💻] [🍴] [🏊]

ΔΔΔ △▽▽ La Quinta Inn & Suites-Palestine H 🐾

(903) 723-1387. **$79-$129.** 3000 S Loop 256 75801. 1.8 mi e of jct US 79 and Loop 256. Int corridors. **Pets:** Medium, other species. Service with restrictions, supervision. [SAVE] [✕] [📞] [💻] [🏊]

PAMPA

ΔΔΔ △▽▽▽ AmericInn Lodge & Suites of Pampa H

(806) 665-4404. **$90-$120, 30 day notice.** 1101 N Hobart St 79065. SR 70, Hobart and Somerville sts. Int corridors. **Pets:** Accepted.

[SAVE] [✕] [♿] [📞] [💻] [🏊]

PARIS

ΔΔΔ △▽▽ Best Western Inn of Paris H

(903) 785-5566. **$59-$79.** 3755 NE Loop 286 75460. Jct US 82 and E Loop 286, just n. Ext corridors. **Pets:** Accepted.

[SAVE] [✕] [📞] [💻] [🏊]

ΔΔΔ △▽▽ Days Inn H

(903) 784-8164. **$85-$100.** 2650 N Main St 75460. NE Loop 286, exit US 271, just n. Ext corridors. **Pets:** Accepted. [SAVE] [✕] [📞] [💻] [🏊]

ΔΔΔ △▽▽▽ Holiday Inn H

(903) 785-5545. **$71-$81.** 3560 NE Loop 286 75460. E Loop 286, 0.3 mi n of jct US 82. Ext corridors. **Pets:** Very small. $100 one-time fee/pet. Service with restrictions, supervision. [SAVE] [✕] [📞] [💻] [🍴] [🏊]

PEARLAND

ΔΔΔ △▽▽ Best Western Pearland Inn H

(281) 997-2000. **$100-$110.** 1855 N Main St 77581. Jct Loop 8 S and SR 35, 1.5 mi s. Ext corridors. **Pets:** Accepted.

[SAVE] [✕] [📞] [💻] [🏊]

ΔΔΔ △▽▽▽ La Quinta Inn & Suites H 🐾

(281) 412-5454. **$89-$179.** 9002 Broadway St 77584. Jct SR 288 and 518, 1.6 mi e. Int corridors. **Pets:** Medium, other species. Service with restrictions, supervision. [SAVE] [✕] [♿] [📞] [💻] [🏊]

PEARSALL

ΔΔΔ △▽▽▽ Best Western Pearsall Inn H 🐾

(830) 334-4900. **$90-$160.** 1808 W Comal 78061. I-35, exit 101 (Pearsall), just e. Ext/int corridors. **Pets:** Small. $10 daily fee/pet. Designated rooms, service with restrictions, crate. [SAVE] [✕] [♿] [📞] [💻] [🏊]

△▽▽ Executive Inn M

(830) 334-3693. **$59-$99.** 613 N Oak 78061. I-35, exit 104, 3 mi e; jct Arnold St. Ext corridors. **Pets:** Small. $15 daily fee/pet. Service with restrictions, supervision. [ASK] [✕] [📞] [💻]

PECOS

ΔΔΔ △▽▽ Knights Inn Laura Lodge Motel & Suites M

(432) 445-4924. **$59-$99.** 1000 E Business I-20 79772. I-20, exit 42 (US 285), 1 mi nw to Business Rt I-20, then 0.5 mi e. Ext corridors. **Pets:** Small. $10 daily fee/pet. Designated rooms, service with restrictions, supervision. [SAVE] [✕] [📞] [💻] [🏊]

ΔΔΔ △▽▽ Oak Tree Inn H

(432) 447-0180. **$59-$79.** 22 N Frontage Rd 79772. I-20, exit 42 (US 285), just w on north access road. Int corridors. **Pets:** Other species. $10 daily fee/room. Service with restrictions. [SAVE] [✕] [📞] [💻]

PERRYTON

ΔΔΔ △▽▽▽ Best Western Perryton Inn H

(806) 434-2850. **$69-$130.** 3505 S Main St (US 83) 79070. US 83, just s of town. Int corridors. **Pets:** Other species. $10 one-time fee/pet. Designated rooms, service with restrictions, supervision.

[SAVE] [✕] [📞] [💻] [🍴] [🏊]

PHARR

△▽▽▽ La Quinta Inn & Suites H 🐾

(956) 787-2900. **$79-$139.** 4603 N Cage 78577. US 281 northbound, exit Nolana Loop, just w. Int corridors. **Pets:** Medium, other species. Service with restrictions, supervision. [ASK] [✕] [♿] [📞] [💻] [🏊]

PLAINVIEW

ΔΔΔ △▽▽ Best Western Conestoga Inn H

(806) 293-9454. **Call for rates.** 600 N I-27 79072. I-27, exit 49, just s of US 70, on eastbound access road. Ext corridors. **Pets:** Medium. $15 daily fee/pet. No service, supervision. [SAVE] [✕] [📞] [💻] [🏊]

△▽▽ Holiday Inn Express Hotel & Suites H

(806) 296-9900. **$100.** 4213 W 13th St 79072. I-27, exit 49 northbound, just w to Mesa, then just n; exit 50 southbound, just s to 13th St, then just w. Int corridors. **Pets:** Accepted. [ASK] [✕] [♿] [📞] [💻] [🏊]

PORT ARANSAS

AAA **WW** **Alister Square Inn** **M** ✿
(361) 749-3000. **$59-$268.** 122 S Alister St 78373. Just n of Ave C. Ext corridors. **Pets:** Other species. $35 one-time fee/room. Designated rooms, service with restrictions. (SAVE) (✕) 🛏 💻 🗪

WW **Beachgate CondoSuites & Motel** (CO)
(361) 749-5900. **$40-$610, 30 day notice.** 2000 On the Beach Dr 78373. Between markers 8 and 9; street access on Anchor Rd off 11th St. Ext/int corridors. **Pets:** Accepted. (ASK) (✕) 🛏 💻 🗪 (✕)

AAA **WW** **Best Western Ocean Villa** H
(361) 749-3010. **$59-$199.** 400 E Ave G 78373. Just se of S Alister St (SR 361). Int corridors. **Pets:** Other species. $25 one-time fee/pet. Designated rooms, service with restrictions, supervision.
(SAVE) (✕) (&M) 🛏 💻 🗪

WW **Mariner Inn & Suites** M
(361) 749-8200. **$59-$259, 3 day notice.** 2607 State Hwy 361 78373. 0.6 mi n of Gulf Beach Rd. Ext corridors. **Pets:** Accepted.
(ASK) (✕) 🛏 💻 🗪

AAA **WWW** **Plantation Suites & Conference Center** M
(361) 749-3866. **Call for rates.** 1909 Hwy 361 78373. On SR 361, 0.4 mi s. Ext corridors. **Pets:** Large, other species. $57 one-time fee/room. Service with restrictions, crate. (SAVE) (✕) 🛏 💻 🗪

PORT LAVACA

AAA **WW** **Best Western Port Lavaca Inn** H
(361) 553-6800. **$81-$90.** 2202 N Hwy 35 77979. 1 mi e. Int corridors. **Pets:** Small. $25 one-time fee/pet. Service with restrictions, supervision.
(SAVE) (✕) 🛏 💻 🗪

POST

AAA **WWW** **Best Western Post Inn** H
(806) 495-9933. **$87-$137.** 1011 N Broadway 79356. 1 mi n on US 84. Int corridors. **Pets:** Small. $15 daily fee/pet. Designated rooms, service with restrictions, supervision. (SAVE) (✕) 🛏 💻 🗪

RAYMONDVILLE

AAA **WW** **Best Western Executive Inn Raymondville** M
(956) 689-4141. **$59-$69, 7 day notice.** 118 N Expwy 77 78580. US 77, jct FM 186 on southbound access road. Ext corridors. **Pets:** Small. $10 one-time fee/pet. Designated rooms, service with restrictions, supervision. (SAVE) (✕) 🛏 💻 🗪

WWW **La Quinta Inn & Suites** H ✿
(956) 689-4000. **$79-$139.** 128 N Expwy 77 78580. US 77, jct FM 186 on southbound access road. Int corridors. **Pets:** Medium, other species. Service with restrictions, supervision. (✕) (&M) 🛏 💻 🗪

ROBSTOWN

WWW **Days Inn** M
(361) 387-8600. **$80-$100.** 650 Hwy 77 S 78380. Just n of jct CR 892 and US 77. Ext corridors. **Pets:** Medium. $10 daily fee/pet. Service with restrictions, supervision. (ASK) (✕) 🛏 💻 🗪

AAA **WW** **Executive Inn** M
(361) 387-9416. **$56-$89.** 620 Hwy 77 S 78380. On US 77, 1 mi s. Ext corridors. **Pets:** Accepted. (SAVE) (✕) 🛏 🗪

ROCKPORT

WW **Days Inn** M
(361) 729-6379. **$59-$200.** 1212 Laurel St 78382. Jct Laurel St and Business Rt SR 35; center. Ext corridors. **Pets:** Small, dogs only. $15 daily fee/pet. Service with restrictions, supervision.
(ASK) (✕) 🛏 💻 🗪

WWW **Laguna Reef Hotel** (CO)
(361) 729-1742. **Call for rates.** 1021 Water St 78382. 0.5 mi s, just e of Business Rt SR 35; entrance on S Austin St. Ext corridors.
Pets: Accepted. (✕) (&M) 🛏 💻 🗪 (✕)

ROUND ROCK

AAA **WWW** **Best Western Executive Inn** H
(512) 255-3222. **$79-$119.** 1851 N I-35 78664. I-35, exit 253 northbound; exit 253A (U-turn) southbound. Ext corridors. **Pets:** Accepted.
(SAVE) (✕) (&M) 🛏 💻 🗪

WWW **Candlewood Suites** H ✿
(512) 828-0899. **$59-$89.** 521 S I-35 78664. I-35, exit 252A, just n on northbound frontage road. Int corridors. **Pets:** $75 one-time fee/room. Service with restrictions, crate. (ASK) (✕) 🛏 💻

WWW **Extended Stay America Austin-Round Rock-N** H
(512) 671-7872. **$49-$54.** 555 S I-35 City Centre Business Park 78664. I-35, exit 252A, on northbound frontage road. Int corridors. **Pets:** Other species. $25 daily fee/room. Designated rooms, service with restrictions, crate. (ASK) (✕) 🛏 💻

WWW **La Quinta Inn & Suites North** H ✿
(512) 255-6666. **$55-$115.** 2004 I-35 N 78681. I-35, exit 254, on west frontage road. Int corridors. **Pets:** Medium, other species. Service with restrictions, supervision. (ASK) (✕) 🛏 💻 🗪

WWW **Residence Inn by Marriott Austin Round Rock** H ✿
(512) 733-2400. **$143-$175.** 2505 S I-35 78664. I-35, exit 250 southbound; exit 251 northbound, on east frontage road. Int corridors. **Pets:** Medium, other species. $100 one-time fee/room. Designated rooms, service with restrictions, crate. (✕) (&M) 🛏 💻 🗪 (✕)

WWW **SpringHill Suites** H
(512) 733-6700. **$116-$142.** 2960 Hoppe Tr 78681. I-35, exit 256 southbound; exit 254 northbound on west frontage road. Int corridors.
Pets: Accepted. (✕) (&M) 🛏 💻 🗪 (✕)

WWW **Staybridge Suites Austin-Round Rock** H
(512) 733-0942. **Call for rates.** 520 I-35 S 78681. I-35, exit 252B northbound; exit 252AB southbound, on west frontage road. Int corridors.
Pets: Accepted. (✕) (&M) 🛏 💻 🗪

SALADO

WWW **Holiday Inn Express Salado** H
(254) 947-4004. **$99-$139.** 1991 N Stagecoach Rd 76571. I-35, exit 286. Int corridors. **Pets:** Accepted. (ASK) (✕) (&M) 🛏 💻 🗪

SAN ANGELO

AAA **WW** **Best Western San Angelo** H
(325) 223-1273. **$79-$90.** 3017 W Loop 306 76904. Loop 306, exit College Hills Blvd, just s. Ext corridors. **Pets:** Accepted.
(SAVE) (✕) 🛏 💻 🗪

WW **Days Inn San Angelo** H
(325) 658-6594. **Call for rates.** 4613 S Jackson St 76903. Jct US 87 and Jackson St. Ext corridors. **Pets:** Accepted. (✕) 🛏 💻 🍴 🗪

AAA **WW** **Howard Johnson San Angelo** H
(325) 653-2995. **$68-$86.** 415 W Beauregard Ave 76903. Just w on US 67 business route at US 87 southbound. Ext/int corridors. **Pets:** Small. Service with restrictions. (SAVE) (✕) 🛏 💻 🍴 🗪

WW **La Quinta Inn San Angelo (Conference Center)** H ✿
(325) 949-0515. **$59-$99.** 2307 Loop 306 76904-6663. Loop 306, exit Knickerbocker Rd, just s. Ext corridors. **Pets:** Medium, other species. Service with restrictions, supervision. (ASK) (✕) 🛏 💻 🗪

WW **Rodeway Inn** H
(325) 944-2578. **Call for rates.** 2502 Loop 306 76904. Loop 306, exit Knickerbocker Rd. Ext corridors. **Pets:** Accepted. (✕) 🛏 💻 🗪

WWW **Staybridge Suites** H
(325) 653-1500. **$144-$153.** 1355 Knickerbocker Rd 76904. US 87 S, 1 mi w. Int corridors. **Pets:** Accepted. (ASK) (✕) 🛏 💻 🗪

SAN ANTONIO METROPOLITAN AREA

ELMENDORF

GuestHouse International Inn & Suites Braunig Lake M
(210) 633-1833. **$65-$110.** 13800 I-37 S 78112. I-37, exit 130 (Donop/Southton rds), on northbound access lane. Ext corridors. **Pets:** Medium. $7 daily fee/pet. Service with restrictions, supervision.

FLORESVILLE

Best Western Floresville Inn M
(830) 393-0443. **$90-$130.** 1720 S 10th St 78114. US 181, just s of downtown. Ext corridors. **Pets:** Small. $10 daily fee/pet. Service with restrictions, supervision.

LIVE OAK

La Quinta Inn San Antonio (I-35 North at Toepperwein)
(210) 657-5500. **$49-$99.** 12822 I-35 N 78233. I-35, exit 170B (Toepperwein), on northbound access road. Ext/int corridors. **Pets:** Medium, other species. Service with restrictions, supervision.

NEW BRAUNFELS

Executive Inn & Suites M
(830) 625-3932. **$49-$199.** 808 Hwy 46 S 78130. I-35, exit 189, 0.4 mi e. Ext corridors. **Pets:** Small, dogs only. $25 daily fee/pet. Designated rooms, service with restrictions, supervision.

Holiday Inn
(830) 625-8017. **Call for rates.** 1051 I-35 E 78130. I-35, exit 189, on southbound access road. Ext corridors. **Pets:** Accepted.

La Quinta Inn & Suites
(830) 627-3333. **$100-$170.** 365 Hwy 46 S 78130. I-35, exit 189, just s on SR 46. Int corridors. **Pets:** Medium, other species. Service with restrictions, supervision.

Quality Inn & Suites
(830) 643-9300. **$59-$400.** 1533 IH-35 N 78130. I-35, exit 190, on southbound access road. Int corridors. **Pets:** Accepted.

Rodeway Inn
(830) 629-6991. **Call for rates.** 1209 I-35 N 78130. I-35, exit 189, on southbound access road. Ext corridors. **Pets:** Small. $40 one-time fee/pet. Service with restrictions, supervision.

Super 8-New Braunfels M
(830) 629-1155. **$59-$199.** 510 Hwy 46 S 78130. I-35, exit 189 (SR 46), just e. Ext corridors. **Pets:** Medium. $25 daily fee/pet. Service with restrictions, supervision.

SAN ANTONIO

Alamo Inn M
(210) 227-2203. **$55-$130.** 2203 E Commerce St 78203. I-37, exit 141A, at Commerce St and New Braunfels Ave. Ext corridors. **Pets:** Small, other species. $10 one-time fee/pet. Designated rooms, service with restrictions, crate.

Aloft San Antonio Airport
(210) 541-8881. **Call for rates.** 838 NW Loop 410 78216. I-410, exit Blanco Rd, just s. Int corridors. **Pets:** Accepted.

Arbor House Suites Bed & Breakfast BB
(210) 472-2005. **$129-$207, 14 day notice.** 109 Arciniega St 78205. Just s of E Nueva; between S Presa and S St. Marys sts; near La Villita Historic District. Ext/int corridors. **Pets:** Medium. Supervision.

Baymont Inn & Suites
(210) 593-0338. **Call for rates.** 9542 I-10 W 78230. I-10, exit Wurzbach Rd, just e on eastbound access road. Ext corridors. **Pets:** Accepted.

Best Western Casa Linda San Antonio Airport
(210) 366-1800. **$60-$89.** 8818 Jones Maltsberger Rd 78216. I-410, exit 21B (Jones Maltsberger Rd), on westbound access road. Int corridors. **Pets:** Accepted.

Best Western-Garden Inn M
(210) 599-0999. **$80-$230.** 11939 N I-35 78236. I-35, exit 170, on southbound access road, 0.5 mi s to Judson Rd exit. Ext corridors. **Pets:** Very small. $25 daily fee/pet. Service with restrictions, crate.

Best Western Posada Ana Inn-Medical Center
(210) 561-9300. **$105-$135.** 9411 Wurzbach Rd 78240. I-10, exit 561 (Wurzbach Rd), on eastbound access road. Int corridors. **Pets:** Medium. Designated rooms, service with restrictions, crate.

Best Western Posada Ana Inn-San Antonio Airport
(210) 342-1400. **Call for rates.** 8600 Jones Maltsberger Rd 78216. I-410, exit 21A (Jones Maltsberger Rd), 0.5 mi s. Int corridors. **Pets:** Accepted.

Brackenridge House B & B BB
(210) 271-3442. **$125-$300, 14 day notice.** 230 Madison St 78204. Just s of S St. Marys St at Durango St. Ext/int corridors. **Pets:** Small. Designated rooms, service with restrictions, crate.

Candlewood Suites Hotel
(210) 615-0550. **$69-$129.** 9350 I-10 W 78230. I-10 W, exit 561 (Wurzbach Rd), eastbound access road; between Wurzbach Rd and Callaghan. Int corridors. **Pets:** Accepted.

Clarion Inn & Suites
(210) 226-4361. **$79-$149.** 3855 I-35 N 78219. I-35, exit 162 (Binz-Engleman Rd) southbound; exit 161 northbound, on southbound access road. Ext corridors. **Pets:** Small. $10 one-time fee/room. Service with restrictions, supervision.

Comfort Inn & Suites
(210) 733-8080. **$60-$150.** 6039 IH 10 W 78201. I-10, exit Vance Jackson Rd, on westbound access road. Int corridors. **Pets:** Small. $35 one-time fee/pet. Designated rooms, service with restrictions, crate.

Comfort Inn & Suites Airport
(210) 249-2000. **$69-$159.** 8640 Crownhill Blvd 78209. I-410, exit Airport Blvd, just off I-410 eastbound access road; just e of Broadway Ave. Int corridors. **Pets:** Accepted.

Comfort Inn-Fiesta M
(210) 696-4766. **$79-$109.** 6755 N Loop 1604 W 78249. I-10, exit CR 1604 W, 0.5 mi w of La Cantera Blvd. Int corridors. **Pets:** Small, other species. $25 one-time fee/room. Service with restrictions, supervision.

▼▼◆ Continental Inn H
(210) 569-6791. **Call for rates.** 9735 I-35 N 78233-6648. I-35, exit 167 (Starlight Terr) northbound; exit 167A (Randolph Blvd) southbound; just n of Loop 410 NE; on southbound access road. Ext corridors.
Pets: Accepted. ⊠ 🖐M 🍴 📺 🛬

◆◆◆ ▼▼◆ ▼▼◆ Crowne Plaza San Antonio Riverwalk H
(210) 354-2800. **$149-$239.** 111 Pecan St E 78205. Corner of Pecan and Soledad sts. Int corridors. **Pets:** Medium. $50 one-time fee/pet. No service, crate. (SAVE) ⊠ 🖐 📺 🍴 🛬 ⊠

▼▼◆ Drury Inn & Suites Northeast H
(210) 657-1107. **$95-$154.** 4900 Crestwind Dr 78239. I-35, exit 165 (Walzem Rd), on northbound access road. Int corridors. **Pets:** Other species. No service, supervision. (ASK) ⊠ 🖐M 🖐 📺 🛬

▼▼◆ Drury Inn & Suites-San Antonio Airport H
(210) 308-8100. **$105-$209.** 95 NE Loop 410 78216. I-410, exit 21A (Jones Maltsberger Rd), 1.8 mi w of airport. Int corridors. **Pets:** Other species. No service, supervision. (ASK) ⊠ 🖐M 🖐 📺 🛬

▼▼◆ Drury Inn & Suites-San Antonio North H
(210) 404-1600. **$105-$219.** 801 N Loop 1604 E 78232. On FM 1604, 0.4 mi w on US 281. Int corridors. **Pets:** Other species. No service, supervision. (ASK) ⊠ 🖐 📺 🛬

▼▼◆ Drury Inn & Suites-San Antonio Northwest H
(210) 561-2510. **$100-$319.** 9806 I-10 W 78230. I-10, exit 561 (Wurzbach Rd), on southeast corner. Int corridors. **Pets:** Other species. No service, supervision. (ASK) ⊠ 🖐 📺 🛬

▼▼◆ Drury Inn & Suites-San Antonio Riverwalk H
(210) 212-5200. **$125-$274.** 201 N St. Mary's St 78205. Just s of College St. Int corridors. **Pets:** Other species. No service, supervision. (ASK) ⊠ 🖐M 🖐 📺 🍴 🛬

▼▼◆ Drury Plaza Hotel-San Antonio Riverwalk H
(210) 270-7799. **$135-$349.** 105 S St. Mary's St 78205. Commerce, St. Mary's and Market sts. Int corridors. **Pets:** Other species. No service, supervision. (ASK) ⊠ 🖐M 🖐 📺 🛬

◆◆◆ ▼▼◆ Econo Lodge Inn & Suites Fiesta Park M ☼
(210) 690-5500. **$60-$160.** 13575 I-10 W 78249. I-10, exit 557, westbound access road. Ext corridors. **Pets:** Medium, dogs only. $10 one-time fee/pet. Service with restrictions, supervision. (SAVE) ⊠ 🖐 📺 🛬

◆◆◆ ▼▼◆ ▼▼◆ Emily Morgan Hotel H
(210) 225-8486. **$149-$429, 3 day notice.** 705 E Houston St 78205. Just n of Bonham St. Int corridors. **Pets:** $75 one-time fee/room. Service with restrictions, supervision. (SAVE) ⊠ 🖐M 📺 🍴 🛬 ⊠

▼▼◆ The Fairmount Hotel H
(210) 224-8800. **Call for rates.** 401 S Alamo St 78205. Opposite convention center and Hemisfair Plaza. Ext/int corridors. **Pets:** Dogs only. $75 one-time fee/room. Service with restrictions, crate. ⊠ 🖐 📺 🍴 ⊠

◆◆◆ ▼▼◆ ▼▼◆ Grand Hyatt San Antonio H
(210) 224-1234. **$149-$499.** 600 E Market St 78205. I-37, exit 141A (Market St); between S Alamo St and I-37. Int corridors. **Pets:** Accepted. (SAVE) ⊠ 🖐M 🖐 📺 🍴 🛬

▼▼◆ Hampton Inn Six Flags Area H
(210) 561-9058. **$77-$115.** 11010 I-10 W 78230. I-10, exit 560 westbound; exit 559 (Huebner Rd) eastbound. Int corridors. **Pets:** Accepted. ⊠ 🖐 📺 🛬

◆◆◆ ▼▼◆ ▼▼◆ Hilton Palacio del Rio H
(210) 222-1400. **$149-$425.** 200 S Alamo St 78205. Adjacent to convention center. Int corridors. **Pets:** Accepted. (SAVE) ⊠ 🖐M 🖐 📺 🍴 🛬

▼▼◆ ▼▼◆ Hilton San Antonio Airport H
(210) 340-6060. **$104-$264.** 611 NW Loop 410 78216. I-410, exit San Pedro Ave, on westbound access road. Int corridors. **Pets:** Medium. $75 one-time fee/room. Service with restrictions. ⊠ 🖐 📺 🍴 🛬 ⊠

▼▼◆ ▼▼◆ Holiday Inn Express-San Antonio Airport H ☼
(210) 308-6700. **$119-$149.** 91 NE Loop 410 78216. I-410, exit 21A (Jones Maltsberger Rd) eastbound; exit 20B westbound, on westbound access road; between San Pedro Ave and Jones Maltsberger Rd. Int corridors. **Pets:** Small. $25 deposit/pet. Designated rooms, service with restrictions, supervision. (ASK) ⊠ 🖐M 🖐 📺 🛬

◆◆◆ ▼▼◆ ▼▼◆ Holiday Inn San Antonio International Airport H ☼
(210) 349-9900. **$109-$209.** 77 NE Loop 410 78216. I-410, exit 20B (McCullough St), on westbound access road. Int corridors. **Pets:** Medium. $100 deposit/room, $25 one-time fee/room. Service with restrictions, supervision. (SAVE) ⊠ 🖐M 🖐 📺 🍴 🛬

▼▼◆ HomeGate Studios & Suites H
(210) 342-4800. **$49-$99.** 11221 San Pedro Ave 78216. I-410, exit US 281 (San Pedro Ave), 2.3 mi n, then exit Nakoma, on west frontage road. Ext corridors. **Pets:** Medium. $50 one-time fee/pet. Service with restrictions, supervision. (ASK) ⊠ 🖐 📺 🛬

▼▼◆ Homestead Studio Suites Hotel-San Antonio-Airport M
(210) 491-9009. **$59-$69.** 1015 Central Pkwy S 78232. I-410, exit US 281 (San Pedro Ave), just n of Bitters Rd; on northbound access road. Ext corridors. **Pets:** Other species. $25 daily fee/room. Designated rooms, service with restrictions, crate. (ASK) ⊠ 🖐 📺

◆◆◆ ▼▼◆ ▼▼◆ Hotel Contessa H
(210) 229-9222. **$179-$399.** 306 W Market St 78205. Market St at St. Mary's St. Int corridors. **Pets:** Accepted. (SAVE) ⊠ 📺 🍴 🛬 ⊠

◆◆◆ ▼▼◆ ▼▼◆ Howard Johnson Lackland Inn & Suites H ☼
(210) 675-9690. **$69-$95.** 6815 Hwy 90 W 78227. I-410, exit US 90 to Military Dr, 0.5 mi e on westbound access road. Ext corridors. **Pets:** Other species. $25 one-time fee/room. Service with restrictions, crate. (SAVE) ⊠ 🖐 📺

▼▼◆ ▼▼◆ Inn on the Riverwalk BB
(210) 225-6333. **$99-$309, 7 day notice.** 129 Woodward Pl 78204. Just n of W Durango Blvd. Ext/int corridors. **Pets:** Accepted. (ASK) ⊠ 🖐 📺

▼▼◆ ▼▼◆ Knights Inn Northwest Fiesta H
(210) 558-9070. **$50-$149.** 9447 I-10 W 78230. I-10, exit 561 (Wurzbach Rd) westbound; exit Callaghan Rd, circle back eastbound. Ext corridors. **Pets:** Accepted. (ASK) ⊠ 🖐 📺

▼▼◆ ▼▼◆ La Quinta Inn H ☼
(210) 661-4545. **$70-$140.** 6075 IH 10 E 78219. I-10, exit 583 (Foster Rd), on westbound access road. Int corridors. **Pets:** Medium, other species. Service with restrictions, supervision. (ASK) ⊠ 🖐M 🖐 📺 🛬

▼▼◆ ▼▼◆ La Quinta Inn Alamo Dome South H 🐾
(210) 337-7171. **$79-$139.** 3180 Goliad Rd 78223. I-37, exit 135 (Brooks City Base/SE Military Dr), just w of interstate. Int corridors. **Pets:** Medium, other species. Service with restrictions, supervision. (ASK) ⊠ 🖐 📺 🛬

▼▼◆ ▼▼◆ La Quinta Inn & Suites Medical Center H 🐾
(210) 525-8090. **$89-$169.** 4431 Horizon Hill Blvd 78229. I-10, exit 562, on eastbound access road; between Callaghan and Wurzbach rds. Int corridors. **Pets:** Medium, other species. Service with restrictions, supervision. ⊠ 🖐M 🖐 📺 🛬

▼▼▼▼ La Quinta Inn & Suites San Antonio Airport 🅷 ❀
(210) 342-3738. **$59-$99.** 850 Halm Blvd 78216. I-410, exit US 281 S, southwest corner. Int corridors. **Pets:** Medium, other species. Service with restrictions, supervision. (ASK) (✕) (&M) (🛏) (💻) (🐾)

▼▼▼▼ La Quinta Inn & Suites San Antonio (Convention Center) 🅷 ❀
(210) 222-9181. **$59-$119.** 303 Blum St 78202. 0.5 mi ne. Ext/int corridors. **Pets:** Medium, other species. Service with restrictions, supervision.
(ASK) (✕) (&M) (🛏) (💻) (🐾)

▼▼▼▼ La Quinta Inn & Suites San Antonio-Downtown 🅷 ❀
(210) 212-5400. **$69-$189.** 100 W Durango Blvd 78204. I-35, exit 155B (Durango Blvd), 3 blks e of jct E Flores St. Int corridors. **Pets:** Medium, other species. Service with restrictions, supervision.
(ASK) (✕) (&M) (🛏) (💻) (🐾)

(AAA) ▼▼▼▼ La Quinta Inn & Suites Stoneoak 🅷 ❀
(210) 497-0506. **Call for rates.** 18502 Hardy Oak Blvd 78258. exit US 281, US 281, Loop 1604, on west bound access road. Int corridors. **Pets:** Medium, other species. Service with restrictions, supervision.
(SAVE) (✕) (&M) (🛏) (💻) (🐾)

▼▼ La Quinta Inn San Antonio (I-35 North @ Windsor Park Mall) 🅷 ❀
(210) 653-6619. **$49-$99.** 6410 I-35 N 78218-4405. I-35, exit 163B northbound, on I-35 northbound access road; between Rittiman and Eisenhauer rds; exit 164A (Rittiman Rd) southbound. Ext corridors. **Pets:** Medium, other species. Service with restrictions, supervision.
(ASK) (✕) (🛏) (💻) (🐾)

▼▼ La Quinta Inn San Antonio (Lackland) 🅷 ❀
(210) 674-3200. **$59-$109.** 6511 Military Dr W 78227-3615. Sw of jct US 90 and Military Dr W. Ext corridors. **Pets:** Medium, other species. Service with restrictions, supervision. (ASK) (✕) (🛏) (💻) (🐾)

▼▼ La Quinta Inn San Antonio (Market Square) 🅷 ❀
(210) 271-0001. **$59-$129.** 900 Dolorosa St 78207-4540. I-10/35, exit Durango Blvd, just n on Santa Rosa St, then just w on Nueva St. Ext corridors. **Pets:** Medium, other species. Service with restrictions, supervision. (ASK) (✕) (&M) (🛏) (💻) (🐾)

▼▼▼▼ La Quinta Inn San Antonio (SeaWorld/Ingram Park) 🅷 ❀
(210) 680-8883. **$59-$129.** 7134 NW Loop 410 78238-4116. I-410, exit 10 (Culebra Rd), on eastbound access road. Ext corridors. **Pets:** Medium, other species. Service with restrictions, supervision.
(ASK) (✕) (🛏) (💻) (🐾)

▼▼▼▼ La Quinta Inn San Antonio (South Park) 🅷 ❀
(210) 922-2111. **$49-$99.** 7202 S Pan American Expwy 78224-1415. I-35, exit 150A (Military Dr) northbound; exit 150B southbound, se of jct I-35 and Military Dr SW. Ext corridors. **Pets:** Medium, other species. Service with restrictions, supervision. (ASK) (✕) (&M) (🛏) (💻) (🐾)

▼▼ La Quinta Inn San Antonio (Vance Jackson) 🅷 ❀
(210) 734-7931. **$39-$89.** 5922 I-10 W 78201-2814. I-10, exit 565B eastbound; exit 565C (Vance Jackson Rd) westbound, on eastbound access road. Ext corridors. **Pets:** Medium, other species. Service with restrictions, supervision. (ASK) (✕) (🛏) (💻) (🐾)

▼▼▼▼ Marriott Plaza San Antonio 🅷
(210) 229-1000. **$179-$219.** 555 S Alamo St 78205. Opposite convention center and Hemisfair Plaza. Int corridors. **Pets:** Accepted.
(✕) (&M) (💻) (🍽) (🐾) (✕)

▼▼ Microtel Inn & Suites 🅷
(210) 404-1900. **Call for rates.** 15314 Hwy 281 N 78232. US 281 N, exit Brook Hollow. Int corridors. **Pets:** Accepted.
(✕) (&M) (🛏) (💻) (🐾)

▼▼ Motel 6 🅼
(210) 447-9000. **$40-$66.** 126 Kenley Pl 78232. US 281, exit Brookhollow, just n on northbound access road. Int corridors. **Pets:** Other species. Service with restrictions, supervision. (ASK) (✕) (&M) (🛏) (🐾) (✕)

▼▼ Motel 6–1122 🅼
(210) 225-1111. **$55-$85.** 211 N Pecos St 78207. I-10/35, exit 155B (Pecos St), on I-10 E/35 S access road. Ext corridors. **Pets:** Other species. Service with restrictions, supervision. (✕) (🛏) (🐾)

▼▼ Motel 6–134 🅼
(210) 650-4419. **$41-$55.** 9503 I-35 N 78233. I-35, exit 167A (Randolf Blvd) southbound; exit 167 (Starlight Terr) northbound. Ext corridors. **Pets:** Other species. Service with restrictions, supervision. (✕) (🐾)

▼▼ Motel 6–651 🅼
(210) 673-9020. **$43-$61.** 2185 SW Loop 410 78227. I-410, exit 7 (Marbach Rd), 0.7 mi w; on westbound access road. Ext corridors. **Pets:** Other species. Service with restrictions, supervision. (✕) (🛏) (🐾)

▼▼ Motel 6 East #183 🅷
(210) 333-1850. **$41-$53.** 138 N WW White Rd 78219. I-10, exit 580 (WW White Rd), just off westbound access road. Ext corridors. **Pets:** Other species. Service with restrictions, supervision. (✕) (🐾)

▼▼ Motel 6 Fort Sam Houston #1350 🅼
(210) 661-8791. **$41-$55.** 5522 N Pan Am Expwy 78218. I-35/410, exit 164 (Rittiman Rd), just s on northbound access road; just off Goldfield St. Ext corridors. **Pets:** Other species. Service with restrictions, supervision. (✕) (🐾)

▼▼ Motel 6–Medical Center South 🅷
(210) 616-0030. **$69-$175, 7 day notice.** 7500 Louis Pasteur Dr 78229. I-410, exit 14C (Babcock Rd), 1 mi nw on Babcock Rd, then 0.5 mi n on Louis Pasteur Dr. Int corridors. **Pets:** Other species. Service with restrictions, supervision. (ASK) (✕) (&M) (🛏) (💻)

(AAA) ▼▼▼▼ Omni La Mansión del Rio 🅷
(210) 518-1000. **$169-$309, 3 day notice.** 112 College St 78205. Just s on the Riverwalk. Ext/int corridors. **Pets:** Small. $25 one-time fee/room. Designated rooms, service with restrictions, supervision.
(SAVE) (✕) (🛏) (💻) (🍽) (🐾)

(AAA) ▼▼▼▼ Omni San Antonio Hotel 🅷
(210) 691-8888. **$109-$299.** 9821 Colonnade Blvd 78230. I-10, exit Wurzbach Rd, 12 mi nw on westbound access road. Int corridors. **Pets:** Medium. $50 one-time fee/pet. Supervision.
(SAVE) (✕) (💻) (🍽) (🐾) (✕)

▼▼ Pear Tree Inn by Drury-San Antonio Northeast 🅷
(210) 654-1144. **$75-$134.** 8300 I-35 N 78239. I-35, exit 165 (Walzem Rd), northbound access road. Ext/int corridors. **Pets:** Other species. No service, supervision. (ASK) (✕) (&M) (🛏) (💻) (🐾)

▼▼ Pear Tree Inn San Antonio Airport 🅷
(210) 366-9300. **$90-$129.** 143 NE Loop 410 78216. Loop 410 W, exit 21 (Jones Maltsberger Rd), on westbound access road; between Airport Blvd and Jones Maltsberger Rd. Int corridors. **Pets:** Other species. No service, supervision. (ASK) (✕) (🛏) (💻) (🐾)

(AAA) ▼▼▼▼ Quality Inn & Suites 🅷
(210) 359-7200. **$60-$130.** 222 S WW White Rd 78219. I-10, exit 580 (WW White Rd), 0.4 mi s. Ext corridors. **Pets:** Very small. $10 daily fee/pet. Service with restrictions, supervision. (SAVE) (✕) (🛏) (💻) (🐾)

(AAA) ▼▼▼▼ Quality Inn & Suites North Airport 🅷
(210) 545-5400. **$70-$130.** 1505 Bexar Crossing 78232. US 281, Loop 1604 (Anderson Loop), 0.5 mi s on southbound access road. Int corridors. **Pets:** Small. $25 one-time fee/pet. Designated rooms, service with restrictions, supervision. (SAVE) (✕) (&M) (🛏) (💻) (🐾)

(AAA) ▼▼▼▼ Quality Inn Medical 🅷
(210) 684-8606. **$69-$159.** 4 Piano Pl 78228. I-410, exit Evers Rd westbound, U-turn; exit 14 (Callaghan/Babcock Rd) eastbound. Ext corridors. **Pets:** Small. $25 daily fee/pet. Designated rooms, no service, supervision. (SAVE) (✕) (🛏) (💻) (🐾)

⚑ ▼▼▼ Radisson Downtown Market Square 🅗

(210) 224-7155. **$99-$199.** 502 W Durango St 78207. I-35, exit Durango St, 1 blk e. Int corridors. **Pets:** Accepted. (SAVE) ⊠ 🖥 💻 🍽 ⊷

⚑ ▼▼▼ Red Roof Inn 🅗

(210) 333-9430. **Call for rates.** 4403 I-10 E 78219. I-10, exit 580 (WW White Rd), on westbound access road. Ext corridors. **Pets:** Large. Service with restrictions, crate. (SAVE) ⊠ 🖥 💻 🍽 ⊷

⚑ ▼▼▼ Red Roof Inn Lackland 🅗

(210) 675-4120. **$60-$140.** 6861 Hwy 90 W 78227. Ne jct of US 90 and Military Dr W; access via Renwick St, off Military Dr, just n of jct US 90. Ext corridors. **Pets:** Large. Service with restrictions, crate. (SAVE) ⊠ 🖥 💻 ⊷

⚑ ▼▼▼ Red Roof Inn-San Antonio Airport 🅗

(210) 340-4055. **$50-$100.** 333 Wolfe Rd 78216. On southbound access road, just s of US 281 at Isom Rd. Ext/int corridors. **Pets:** Large. Service with restrictions, crate. (SAVE) ⊠ ♿ 🖥

⚑ ▼▼▼ Red Roof Inn San Antonio (Downtown) 🅗

(210) 229-9973. **$70-$200.** 1011 E Houston St 78205. I-37, exit 141 northbound; exit 141B southbound. Int corridors. **Pets:** Large. Service with restrictions, crate. (SAVE) ⊠ 🖥 ⊷

⚑ ▼▼▼ Red Roof Inn San Antonio (NW-SeaWorld) 🅗

(210) 509-3434. **Call for rates.** 6880 NW Loop 410 78238. I-410, exit 11 (Alamo Downs Pkwy), on eastbound access road. Ext/int corridors. **Pets:** Large. Service with restrictions, crate. (SAVE) ⊠ ♿ 🖥 ⊷

▼▼▼ Residence Inn Alamo Plaza 🅗

(210) 212-5555. **$215-$263.** 425 Bonham St 78205. I-37/281, exit Commerce St, just w to Bowie St, then 4 blks n. Int corridors. **Pets:** Accepted. ⊠ 🖥 💻 ⊷

▼▼▼ Residence Inn by Marriott San Antonio Downtown/ Market Square 🅗

(210) 231-6000. **$144-$176.** 628 S Santa Rosa Blvd 78204. I-10/35, exit Durango St, 0.5 mi e. Int corridors. **Pets:** Accepted. ⊠ 🖥 💻 ⊷ ⊠

▼▼▼ Residence Inn North San Antonio 🅗

(210) 490-1333. **$148-$180.** 1115 N SR 1604 E 78258. Loop 1604, just w of US 281 on westbound access road. Int corridors. **Pets:** $75 one-time fee/room. Service with restrictions. ⊠ ♿ 🖥 💻 ⊷

▼▼▼ Residence Inn NW/Six Flags 🅗

(210) 561-9660. **$134-$164.** 4041 Bluemel Rd 78240. I-10, exit 561 (Wurzbach Rd), 0.3 mi w on eastbound access road. Ext corridors. **Pets:** Accepted. ⊠ 💻 ⊷ ⊠

▼▼▼ Residence Inn San Antonio-Airport 🅗 🐾

(210) 805-8118. **$170-$208.** 1014 NE Loop 410 78209-0000. Loop 410, exit Broadway St, 0.4 mi e on eastbound access road. Ext corridors. **Pets:** Large. $100 one-time fee/room. Service with restrictions, crate. ⊠ 💻 ⊷ ⊠

⚑ ▼▼▼ ▼▼▼ Sheraton Gunter 🅗 🐾

(210) 227-3241. **$99-$329.** 205 E Houston St 78205. Center. Int corridors. **Pets:** Medium, dogs only. Designated rooms, no service, supervision. (SAVE) ⊠ 💻 🍽 ⊷

▼▼▼ Staybridge Suites San Antonio-Airport 🅗

(210) 341-3220. **$129-$149.** 66 NE Loop 410 78216. I-410, exit 20B (McCullough St), on eastbound access road; next to Texas Land & Cattle Restaurant. Int corridors. **Pets:** Accepted. (ASK) ⊠ ♿ 🖥 💻 ⊷

▼▼▼ Staybridge Suites San Antonio NW-Colonnade 🅗

(210) 558-9009. **Call for rates.** 4320 Spectrum One 78230. I-10 W, exit 561 (Wurzbach Rd), follow westbound access road through light, then just n. Int corridors. **Pets:** Large. $150 one-time fee/room. Service with restrictions. ⊠ 🖥 💻 ⊷

▼▼▼ Staybridge Suites Sunset Station 🅗

(210) 444-2700. **$129-$229.** 123 Hoefgen 78205. In historic downtown Sunset Station. Int corridors. **Pets:** Accepted. (ASK) ⊠ ♿ 🖥 💻 ⊷

▼▼▼ Studio 6 #6046 Ⓜ

(210) 691-0121. **$53-$73.** 11802 I-10 W 78230. I-10, exit 558 (De Zavala Rd), 0.7 mi e on eastbound access road. Ext corridors. **Pets:** Other species. $10 daily fee/room. Service with restrictions, supervision. ⊠ 💻

▼▼▼ Super 8 on Roland 🅗

(210) 798-5500. **Call for rates.** 302 Roland Ave 78210. I-10, exit 577 (Roland Ave) eastbound. Ext corridors. **Pets:** Other species. $10 daily fee/pet. Service with restrictions. ⊠ 🖥 💻 ⊷

▼▼▼ Super 8-Six Flags Fiesta 🅗

(210) 696-6916. **Call for rates.** 5319 Casa Bella 78249. I-10, exit 557 westbound; exit 558 eastbound, on westbound access road. Int corridors. **Pets:** Accepted. ⊠ 🖥 💻 ⊷

▼▼▼ Towne Place Suites by Marriott San Antonio Northwest 🅗

(210) 694-5100. **$139-$149.** 5014 Prue Rd 78240. I-10, exit Huebner Rd, 1 blk se to Fredericksburg Rd, then just n. Int corridors. **Pets:** Accepted. ⊠ ♿ ⊷

⚑ ▼▼▼▼ Watermark Hotel & Spa 🅗

(210) 396-5800. **$209-$459, 3 day notice.** 212 W Crockett 78205. Between St. Mary's and Navarro sts; on the Riverwalk. Int corridors. **Pets:** Accepted. (SAVE) ⊠ ♿ 💻 🍽 ⊷ ⊠

⚑ ▼▼▼▼ The Westin Riverwalk 🅗

(210) 224-6500. **$159-$309, 3 day notice.** 420 W Market St 78205. 2 blks w of Navarro St. Int corridors. **Pets:** Accepted. (SAVE) ⊠ ♿ 💻 🍽 ⊷ ⊠

SEGUIN

▼▼▼ La Quinta Inn & Suites 🅗 🐾

(830) 372-0567. **$80-$160.** 1501 Hwy 46 N 78155. I-10, exit 607 (SR 46). Int corridors. **Pets:** Medium, other species. Service with restrictions, supervision. (ASK) ⊠ ♿ 🖥 💻 ⊷

▼▼ Quality Inn–Seguin Ⓜ

(830) 372-0860. **$75-$99.** 2950 N 123 Bypass 78155. I-10, exit 610 (SR 123). Ext corridors. **Pets:** Small. $25 one-time fee/pet. Service with restrictions, supervision. (ASK) ⊠ 🖥 💻 ⊷

▼▼ Super 8 of Seguin 🅗

(830) 379-6888. **$59-$179.** 1525 N Hwy 46 78155. I-10, exit 607 (SR 46), on eastbound access road. Int corridors. **Pets:** Medium, other species. $10 daily fee/pet. Designated rooms, service with restrictions, supervision. (ASK) ⊠ 🖥 💻

UNIVERSAL CITY

▼▼ ▼▼ Hawthorn Suites-San Antonio Northeast 🄷

(210) 655-9491. **$89-$149, 3 day notice.** 13101 E Loop, 1604 N 78233. Loop 1604 at Pat Booker Rd; 0.8 mi e of I-35. Ext corridors. **Pets:** Medium. $10 daily fee/room. Designated rooms, service with restrictions, supervision. (ASK) ⊠ 🄷 🖵 ⇌

END METROPOLITAN AREA

SAN MARCOS

(AAA) ▼▼▼ Days Inn 🄷

(512) 353-5050. **$49-$135.** 1005 I-35 N 78666. I-35, exit 205 northbound; exit 204B southbound, on southbound frontage road, jct SR 80. Ext corridors. **Pets:** Accepted. (SAVE) ⊠ 🄷 🖵 ⇌

(AAA) ▼▼▼ Econo Lodge 🄷

(512) 353-5300. **$45-$130.** 811 S Guadalupe St 78666. I-35, exit 204 northbound; exit 204A southbound, on west frontage road. Ext corridors. **Pets:** Medium, other species. $15 one-time fee/room. Service with restrictions, supervision. (SAVE) ⊠ 🄷 🖵 ⇌

(AAA) ▼▼▼ Embassy Suites-San Marcos Hotel, Spa and Conference Center 🄷

(512) 392-6450. **$119-$239.** 1001 E McCarty Ln 78666. I-35, exit 201, on east frontage road. Int corridors. **Pets:** Small, dogs only. $50 one-time fee/room. Designated rooms, service with restrictions, crate. (SAVE) ⊠ (&M) 🄷 🖵 (Y) ⇌ (⊠)

▼▼▼ La Quinta Inn San Marcos 🄷 🐾

(512) 392-8800. **$55-$139.** 1619 I-35 N 78666. I-35, exit 206 southbound, 0.5 mi s, on west frontage road; exit northbound, 1 mi n to turnaround to west frontage road, then 1.5 mi s. Ext/int corridors. **Pets:** Medium, other species. Service with restrictions, supervision. (ASK) ⊠ (&M) 🄷 🖵 ⇌

(AAA) ▼▼▼ Ramada Limited 🄷

(512) 395-8000. **$50-$175.** 1701 I-35 N 78666. I-35, exit 206 southbound, 0.4 mi s on west frontage road; exit northbound, 1 mi n to turnaround to west frontage road, then 1.4 mi s. Ext corridors. **Pets:** Very small, dogs only. $10 daily fee/pet. Service with restrictions, supervision. (SAVE) ⊠ 🄷 🖵 ⇌

▼▼ ▼▼ Rodeway Inn 🄷

(512) 353-8011. **Call for rates.** 1635 Aquarena Springs Dr 78666. I-35, exit 206, 0.5 mi s. Ext corridors. **Pets:** Medium. $10 daily fee/room. Designated rooms, service with restrictions, supervision. ⊠ 🄷 ⇌

SCHULENBURG

(AAA) ▼▼▼ Best Western Schulenburg Inn & Suites 🄷

(979) 743-2030. **$90-$142.** 101 Huser Blvd 78956. I-10, exit 674, just s. Int corridors. **Pets:** Accepted. (SAVE) ⊠ 🄷 🖵 ⇌

SEALY

▼▼ ▼▼ Super 8 🄷

(979) 885-2121. **$69-$109.** 267 Gebhardt Rd 77474. I-10, exit 720. Ext corridors. **Pets:** Small. $5 daily fee/pet. Designated rooms, service with restrictions, supervision. ⊠ (&M) 🄷 🖵 ⇌

SEMINOLE

(AAA) ▼▼▼ Seminole Inn M

(432) 758-9881. **$69-$84.** 2200 Hobbs Hwy 79360. 1.5 mi w on US 62 and 180. Ext corridors. **Pets:** Accepted. (SAVE) ⊠ 🄷 🖵

SHAMROCK

(AAA) ▼▼▼▼ Best Western Shamrock Inn & Suites 🄷

(806) 256-1001. **$90-$120.** 1802 N Main St 79079. I-40, exit 163, just n. Int corridors. **Pets:** Other species. $10 daily fee/pet. Designated rooms, service with restrictions, supervision. (SAVE) ⊠ (&M) 🄷 🖵 ⇌

(AAA) ▼▼ Western Motel M

(806) 256-3244. **$59-$99.** 104 E 12th St 79079. Business Rt I-40 and US 83. Ext corridors. **Pets:** Medium. $5 daily fee/pet. Service with restrictions, supervision. (SAVE) ⊠ 🄷 (Y)

SHERMAN

▼▼▼ Comfort Suites of Sherman 🄷

(903) 893-0499. **Call for rates.** 2900 US Hwy 75 N 75090. US 75, exit 63, 0.3 mi s of jct US 82. Int corridors. **Pets:** Medium, other species. $20 one-time fee/room. Service with restrictions, crate. ⊠ 🄷 🖵 ⇌

▼▼▼ La Quinta Inn & Suites Sherman/Denison 🄷 🐾

(903) 870-1122. **Call for rates.** 2912 US 75 N 75090. US 75, exit 63, just sw of jct US 82. Int corridors. **Pets:** Medium, other species. Service with restrictions, supervision. ⊠ 🄷 🖵 ⇌

SINTON

(AAA) ▼▼▼ Best Western Sinton M

(361) 364-2882. **$80-$89.** 8108 US Hwy 77 78387. US 77 at CR 36A. Ext corridors. **Pets:** Accepted. (SAVE) ⊠ 🄷 🖵 ⇌

SMITHVILLE

▼▼ ▼▼ Americas Best Value Inn & Suites 🄷

(512) 237-2040. **$75-$85.** 1503 Dorothy Nichol Ln 78957. Jct SR 71 and Dorothy Nichol Ln. Ext corridors. **Pets:** Accepted. (ASK) ⊠ 🄷 🖵 ⇌

SNYDER

(AAA) ▼▼▼ Purple Sage Motel M

(325) 573-5491. **$55-$75.** 1501 E Coliseum Dr 79549. 1 mi w on US 180 from jct US 84. Ext corridors. **Pets:** Accepted. (SAVE) ⊠ 🄷 🖵 ⇌

SONORA

(AAA) ▼▼ Holiday Host Motel M

(325) 387-2532. **$45-$55.** 127 Loop 467 (Hwy 290) 76950. Loop 467, exit 404 westbound, 3 mi w; exit 399 eastbound, 3 mi e. Ext corridors. **Pets:** $5 deposit/pet. No service, supervision. (SAVE) ⊠ 🄷 🖵 ⇌

▼▼ Twin Oaks Inn M

(325) 387-2551. **Call for rates.** 1009 N Crockett Ave 76950. I-10, exit 400 westbound; exit 399 eastbound, 0.5 mi e, then 0.3 mi s on US 277. Ext corridors. **Pets:** Accepted. ⊠ 🄷

SOUTH PADRE ISLAND

(AAA) ▼▼▼▼ Best Western La Copa Inn & Suites Beach Resort 🄷

(956) 761-6000. **$60-$250.** 350 Padre Blvd 78597. Just s of Queen Isabella Cswy. Int corridors. **Pets:** Accepted. (SAVE) ⊠ 🄷 🖵 ⇌

▼▼ ▼▼ Howard Johnson Inn 🄷

(956) 761-5658. **$69-$299.** 1709 Padre Blvd 78597. SR 100, 0.9 mi n at corner of W Palm St. Int corridors. **Pets:** Accepted. (ASK) ⊠ (&M) 🄷 🖵 ⇌

▼▼ ▼▼ Inverness at South Padre (CO)

(956) 761-7919. **Call for rates.** 5600 Gulf Blvd 78597. 2.7 mi n on SR 100 from Queen Isabella Cswy. Ext corridors. **Pets:** Accepted. ⊠ 🄷 🖵 ⇌

▼▼▼▼ **La Quinta Inn & Suites South Padre Island** 🅷 ❖

(956) 772-7000. **$79-$279.** 7000 Padre Blvd 78597. I-77, exit SR 100, over Queen Isabella Cswy, then 3 mi n. Int corridors. **Pets:** Medium, other species. Service with restrictions, supervision.
[ASK] [✕] [&M] [🛏] [💻] [🍴] [🏊] [✕]

▼ **Motel 6 South Padre Island #1237** 🅼

(956) 761-7911. **$51-$95.** 4013 Padre Blvd 78597. 2 mi n of Queen Isabella Cswy. Ext corridors. **Pets:** Other species. Service with restrictions, supervision. [✕] [🏊]

🅐🅐🅐 ▼▼▼ **Ramada Limited** 🅷

(956) 761-4097. **$66-$309, 3 day notice.** 4109 Padre Blvd 78597. 2 mi n of Queen Isabella Cswy. Ext corridors. **Pets:** Medium. $10 daily fee/pet. Service with restrictions, supervision. [SAVE] [✕] [🛏] [💻] [🏊]

▼▼ **Super 8** 🅷

(956) 761-6300. **$99-$249.** 4205 Padre Blvd 78597. 2.7 mi n of Queen Isabella Cswy. Ext corridors. **Pets:** Small, dogs only. $25 daily fee/pet. Designated rooms, service with restrictions, supervision.
[ASK] [✕] [🛏] [💻] [🏊]

▼▼ **Travelodge** 🅷

(956) 761-4744. **$59-$249.** 6200 Padre Blvd 78597. 3 mi n of Queen Isabella Cswy. Ext corridors. **Pets:** Medium, other species. $10 daily fee/room. Service with restrictions, crate. [ASK] [✕] [&M] [🛏] [💻] [🏊]

STEPHENVILLE

🅐🅐🅐 ▼▼▼ **Best Western Cross Timbers** 🅷

(254) 968-2114. **$69-$79.** 1625 W South Loop (US 377) 76401. 1.8 mi sw on US 377 Bypass and 67. Ext corridors. **Pets:** Medium. $20 daily fee/pet. Service with restrictions, crate. [SAVE] [✕] [🛏] [💻] [🏊]

▼▼▼ **La Quinta Inn & Suites** 🅷 ❖

(254) 918-2444. **$80-$135.** 105 Christy Plaza 76401. US 67/377 S, 5 mi s of jct US 281. Int corridors. **Pets:** Medium, other species. Service with restrictions, supervision. [✕] [&M] [🛏] [💻] [🏊]

▼▼▼▼ **Quality Inn Near Tarleton State University** 🅷

(254) 968-5256. **Call for rates.** 2865 W Washington St 76401. 1.5 mi s on US 377/167. Ext corridors. **Pets:** Accepted. [✕] [🛏] [💻] [🍴] [🏊]

▼▼▼▼ **Stephenville Hampton Inn & Suites** 🅷

(254) 918-5400. **$123-$179.** 910 S Harbin Dr 76401. US 67/377 S, 3 mi s of jct US 281. Int corridors. **Pets:** Large. $25 daily fee/pet. Service with restrictions, supervision. [✕] [&M] [🛏] [💻] [🏊]

SULPHUR SPRINGS

🅐🅐🅐 ▼▼▼ **Best Western Trail Dust Inn & Suites** 🅷 ❖

(903) 885-7515. **$79-$99.** 1521 Shannon Rd 75482. Jct I-30 and Loop 301, exit 127. Ext/int corridors. **Pets:** Small, other species. $10 daily fee/pet. Designated rooms, service with restrictions, supervision.
[SAVE] [✕] [🛏] [💻] [🏊]

▼▼▼▼ **Comfort Suites** 🅷

(903) 438-0918. **$80-$98.** 1521 E Industrial Dr 75482-0789. I-30, exit 127, just n. Int corridors. **Pets:** Accepted. [ASK] [✕] [&M] [🛏] [💻] [🏊]

SWEETWATER

🅐🅐🅐 ▼▼▼ **Days Inn** 🅷

(325) 235-4853. **$70-$110.** 701 SW Georgia Ave 79556. I-20, exit 244, just w on south frontage road. Ext corridors. **Pets:** Accepted.
[SAVE] [✕] [🛏] [💻] [🍴] [🏊]

▼▼▼▼ **La Quinta Inn** 🅷 ❖

(325) 236-6887. **$59-$109.** 500 NW Georgia Ave 79556. I-20, exit 244, just w of jct SR 70 on north access road. Ext/int corridors. **Pets:** Medium, other species. Service with restrictions, supervision.
[ASK] [✕] [🛏] [💻] [🏊]

🅐🅐🅐 ▼▼▼ **Ranch House Motel & Restaurant** 🅷

(325) 236-6341. **$59-$89.** 301 SW Georgia Ave 79556. I-20, exit 244, just w of jct SR 70 on south access road. Ext/int corridors. **Pets:** Medium, other species. Designated rooms, service with restrictions, supervision.
[SAVE] [✕] [🛏] [💻] [🍴] [🏊]

TEMPLE

▼▼▼ **La Quinta Inn Temple** 🅷 ❖

(254) 771-2980. **$39-$89.** 1604 W Barton Ave 76504. SR 53, just e; jct I-35 and US 81, exit 301. Ext/int corridors. **Pets:** Medium, other species. Service with restrictions, supervision. [ASK] [✕] [🛏] [💻] [🏊]

▼▼▼▼ **Residence Inn by Marriott** 🅷

(254) 773-8400. **$125-$153.** 4301 S General Bruce Dr 76502. I-35, exit 298, on E Frontage Rd. Int corridors. **Pets:** Accepted.
[✕] [&M] [🛏] [💻] [🏊] [✕]

TERLINGUA

🅐🅐🅐 ▼▼▼▼ **Big Bend Resort & Adventures** 🅼

(432) 371-2218. **$90-$150, 3 day notice.** Hwy 118/170 79852. SR 118, 2 mi from entrance of Big Bend National Park. Ext corridors. **Pets:** Dogs only. $20 daily fee/pet. Designated rooms, service with restrictions, supervision. [SAVE] [✕]

TEXARKANA

▼▼▼ **La Quinta Inn** 🅷 ❖

(903) 794-1900. **$65-$109.** 5201 State Line Ave 75503. I-30, exit 223A, sw of jct US 59 and 71. Ext corridors. **Pets:** Medium, other species. Service with restrictions, supervision. [ASK] [✕] [🛏] [💻] [🏊]

▼▼▼ **Ramada Inn** 🅷

(903) 792-3366. **Call for rates.** 5401 N State Line Ave 75503. I-30, exit 223B, 0.3 mi n on US 71. Int corridors. **Pets:** Accepted.
[✕] [🛏] [💻] [🏊]

🅐🅐🅐 ▼▼▼ **Rodeway Inn** 🅷

(903) 792-6688. **$63-$73.** 5105 N State Line Ave 75503. I-30, exit 223A, just sw. Ext corridors. **Pets:** Accepted. [SAVE] [✕] [🛏] [💻] [🏊]

THREE RIVERS

▼▼▼ **Econo Lodge** 🅼

(361) 786-3563. **$60-$100.** 1401 N Harborth Ave 78071. I-37, exit 72 (US 281), 3.8 mi s. Ext corridors. **Pets:** Accepted.
[ASK] [✕] [🛏] [💻] [🏊]

TULIA

▼▼▼ **Select Inn of Tulia** 🅼

(806) 995-3248. **$50-$90.** 1591 I-27 79088. I-27, exit 74. Ext corridors. **Pets:** Accepted. [ASK] [✕] [&M] [🛏]

TYLER

🅐🅐🅐 ▼▼▼▼ **Candlewood Suites** 🅷

(903) 509-4131. **$89-$129.** 315 E Rieck Rd 75703. 1.1 mi s of jct Loop 323 and US 69 (S Broadway) to Rieck Rd, just e. Int corridors. **Pets:** Accepted. [SAVE] [✕] [&M] [🛏] [💻] [🏊]

▼▼▼ **Holiday Inn South Broadway** 🅷 🐾

(903) 561-5800. **$109-$149.** 5701 S Broadway Ave 75703. 1.1 mi s of jct Loop 323 and US 69 (S Broadway). Int corridors. **Pets:** $50 one-time fee/room. Service with restrictions, supervision.
[ASK] [✕] [🛏] [💻] [🍴] [🏊]

▼▼▼ **La Quinta Inn Tyler** 🅷 🐾

(903) 561-2223. **$59-$104.** 1601 W SW Loop 323 75701-8533. 1 mi w of S US 69. Ext corridors. **Pets:** Medium, other species. Service with restrictions, supervision. [ASK] [✕] [🛏] [💻] [🏊]

▼▼▼▼ **Residence Inn by Marriott** 🅷

(903) 595-5188. **$134-$164.** 3303 Troup Hwy 75701. 0.3 mi n of jct E Loop 323 and SR 110. Ext corridors. **Pets:** Other species. $100 one-time fee/room. Designated rooms, service with restrictions, crate.
[✕] [🛏] [💻] [🏊] [✕]

UVALDE

◆◆◆ Quality Inn of Uvalde 🅷
(830) 278-4511. **$79-$120.** 920 E Main St 78801. 0.5 mi e on US 90. Ext corridors. **Pets:** Large, other species. $25 one-time fee/room. Service with restrictions. (ASK) 🖪 💻 🍴 🏊

VAN HORN

◆◆◆ ◆◆◆ Americas Best Value Inn Ⓜ
(432) 283-2410. **$50-$120.** 1705 W Broadway St 79855. I-10, exit 138, 0.3 mi e, then 1 mi w on US 80. Ext corridors. **Pets:** Accepted.
(SAVE) ✕ 🖪 💻 🏊

◆◆◆ ◆◆ Budget Inn Ⓜ
(432) 283-2019. **$36-$40.** 1303 W Broadway St 79855. I-10, exit 138, 0.7 mi e. Ext corridors. **Pets:** Accepted. (SAVE) ✕ 🖪

◆◆◆ Days Inn Ⓜ
(432) 283-1007. **$65-$105.** 600 E Broadway St 79855. I-10, exit 140B, just w. Ext corridors. **Pets:** $10 daily fee/pet. Service with restrictions, supervision. (SAVE) ✕ 🖪 💻 🏊

◆◆◆ ◆◆ Econo Lodge 🅷
(432) 283-2211. **$60-$95.** 1601 W Broadway St 79855. I-10, exit 138, 0.5 mi e on Business Rt I-10. Ext corridors. **Pets:** Medium. $10 daily fee/pet. Designated rooms, service with restrictions, supervision.
(SAVE) ✕ 🖪 💻 🏊

◆◆◆ ◆◆ Economy Inn Ⓜ
(432) 283-2754. **$38-$42.** 1500 W Broadway St 79855. I-10, exit 138, 0.5 mi e on US 80. Ext corridors. **Pets:** Medium. $3 daily fee/pet. Service with restrictions, supervision. (SAVE) 🖪

◆◆◆◆ Hampton Inn 🅷
(432) 283-0088. **Call for rates.** 1921 SW Frontage Rd 79855. I-10, exit 138, just w on S Frontage Rd. Int corridors. **Pets:** Accepted.
✕ 🖪Ⓜ 🖪 💻 🏊

◆◆◆◆ ◆◆ Motel 6–4024 Ⓜ
(432) 283-2992. **$46-$56.** 1805 W Broadway St 79855. I-10, exit 138. Ext corridors. **Pets:** Other species. Service with restrictions, supervision.
(SAVE) ✕ 🖪 🏊

◆◆◆ ◆◆◆ Ramada Inn 🅷
(432) 283-2780. **Call for rates.** 200 Golf Course Dr 79855. I-10, exit 138. Ext/int corridors. **Pets:** Accepted. (SAVE) ✕ 🖪 💻 🏊

◆◆◆ ◆◆◆ Van Horn Super 8 Ⓜ
(432) 283-2282. **$65-$105.** 1807 E Service Rd 79855. I-10, exit 138. Ext corridors. **Pets:** $10 daily fee/pet. Service with restrictions, supervision.
(SAVE) ✕ 🖪 💻

VEGA

◆◆◆ ◆◆◆ Best Western Country Inn Ⓜ ☀
(806) 267-2131. **$69-$89.** 1800 W Vega Blvd 79092. 0.5 mi w on US 40 business loop. Ext corridors. **Pets:** Medium. $10 daily fee/pet. Designated rooms, service with restrictions, supervision. (SAVE) ✕ 🖪 💻 🏊

◆◆◆◆ Comfort Inn 🅷
(806) 267-0126. **Call for rates.** 1005 S Main St 79092. I-40, exit 36. Int corridors. **Pets:** Accepted. ✕ 🖪 💻 🏊

VERNON

◆◆◆ ◆◆◆ Best Western Village Inn 🅷
(940) 552-5417. **$65-$90.** 1615 US Hwy 287 E 76384. US 287, exit Main St, just w. Ext/int corridors. **Pets:** Accepted.
(SAVE) ✕ 🖪 💻 🍴 🏊

◆◆◆◆ Holiday Inn Express Hotel & Suites 🅷 ☀
(940) 552-0200. **$99-$109.** 700 Hillcrest Dr 76384. Jct US 287 and 70. Int corridors. **Pets:** Very small. $25 one-time fee/room. Service with restrictions, supervision. (ASK) ✕ 🖪Ⓜ 🖪 💻 🏊

VICTORIA

◆◆◆ ◆◆◆ Best Western Victoria Inn & Suites 🅷 ☀
(361) 485-2300. **$90-$176.** 8106 NE Zac Lenz Pkwy 77904. Jct Zac Lenz Pkwy and Invitational Dr. Int corridors. **Pets:** Small. $20 daily fee/pet. Designated rooms, service with restrictions, crate.
(SAVE) ✕ 🖪 💻 🏊

◆◆◆◆ Howard Johnson 🅷
(361) 575-0251. **Call for rates.** 2705 E Houston Hwy (Business Rt 59) 77901. On Business Rt US 59, 2.5 mi ne. Ext/int corridors.
Pets: Accepted. ✕ 🖪 💻 🍴 🏊 ✕

◆◆◆◆ La Quinta Inn Victoria 🅷 ☀
(361) 572-3585. **$59-$119.** 7603 N Navarro St (US 77 N) 77904. 4 mi n; at Loop 463. Ext corridors. **Pets:** Medium, other species. Service with restrictions, supervision. (ASK) ✕ 🖪 💻 🏊

◆◆◆ ◆◆◆ Lone Star Inn & Suites 🅷
(361) 579-0225. **$65-$150.** 1907 US 59 N 77905. US 59, exit Bloomington (US 185); on northeast corner. Ext corridors. **Pets:** Medium. $25 deposit/pet, $25 daily fee/pet. Service with restrictions, supervision.
(SAVE) ✕ 🖪 💻 🏊

◆◆◆ Motel 6 Victoria #225 Ⓜ
(361) 573-1273. **$49-$62.** 3716 Houston Hwy 77901. On Business Rt US 59. Ext corridors. **Pets:** Other species. Service with restrictions, supervision. ✕ 🖪 🏊

◆◆◆◆ Quality Inn-Victoria 🅷
(361) 578-2030. **$71.** 3112 E Houston Hwy (Business Rt 59) 77901. On Business Rt US 59, 2 mi ne. Ext corridors. **Pets:** Small. $25 one-time fee/pet. Designated rooms, service with restrictions, supervision.
(ASK) ✕ 🖪 💻 🏊

VIDOR

◆◆◆◆ La Quinta Inn of Vidor 🅷 ☀
(409) 783-2600. **$69-$119.** 165 E Courtland St 77662. I-10, exit 861A, just s. Int corridors. **Pets:** Medium, other species. Service with restrictions, supervision. (ASK) ✕ 🖪 💻 🏊

WACO

◆◆◆ ◆◆◆ Best Western Old Main Lodge 🅷
(254) 753-0316. **$86-$120.** I-35 & 4th St 76706. I-35 and US 81, exit 335A (4th-5th sts). Ext corridors. **Pets:** Small. Service with restrictions, supervision. (SAVE) ✕ 🖪 💻 🏊

◆◆◆ ◆◆◆ Clarion Hotel 🅷
(254) 757-2000. **$69-$129.** 801 S 4th St 76706. I-35, exit 335A. Ext/int corridors. **Pets:** Accepted. (SAVE) ✕ 🖪 💻 🍴 🏊

◆◆◆ ◆◆◆ Days Inn 🅷
(254) 799-8585. **$60-$125.** 1504 I-35 N 76705. I-35, exit 338B (Behrens Cir), just n. Ext corridors. **Pets:** Accepted. (SAVE) ✕ 🖪 💻 🏊

◆◆◆◆ Hilton-Waco 🅷 ☀
(254) 754-8484. **$89-$254.** 113 S University Parks Dr 76701. I-35, exit 335B, 0.5 mi w. Int corridors. **Pets:** Medium. $25 one-time fee/room. Service with restrictions. ✕ 🖪 💻 🍴 🏊

◆◆◆◆ La Quinta Inn Waco (University) 🅷 ☀
(254) 752-9741. **$49-$109.** 1110 S 9th St 76706-2399. I-35, exit 334 (17th St) southbound; exit 334A (18th St) northbound. Ext corridors. **Pets:** Medium, other species. Service with restrictions, supervision.
(ASK) ✕ 🖪 💻 🏊

◆◆◆◆ Residence Inn by Marriott 🅷
(254) 714-1386. **$126-$154.** 501 S University Parks Dr 76706. I-35, exit 335B, 0.3 mi w. Int corridors. **Pets:** Accepted. ✕ 🖪 💻 🏊 ✕

◆◆◆ Super 8-Waco 🅷
(254) 754-1023. **Call for rates.** 1320 S Jack Kultgen Frwy 76706. I-35, exit 334, just e. Int corridors. **Pets:** Accepted. ✕ 🖪 💻

AAA ▼▼ Super 8 Waco Mall **H**
(254) 776-3194. **$60-$110, 3 day notice.** 6624 Woodway Dr (Hwy 84 W) 76712. Jct US 84 and SR 6, just w. Ext corridors. **Pets:** Medium. $10 daily fee/pet. Service with restrictions, supervision.
[SAVE] [X] [i] [▣] [≈]

WAXAHACHIE
▼▼ Super 8 **H**
(972) 938-9088. **$67-$99, 7 day notice.** 400 N I-35E 75165. I-35E, exit 401B. Int corridors. **Pets:** Small. $15 daily fee/pet. No service, supervision. [ASK] [X] [i] [▣] [≈]

WEATHERFORD
AAA ▼▼ Best Western Santa Fe Inn **H**
(817) 594-7401. **$89-$99, 5 day notice.** 1927 Santa Fe Dr 76086. I-20, exit 409 (Clear Lake Rd/FM 2552), 0.3 mi nw. Ext corridors.
Pets: Accepted. [SAVE] [X] [i] [▣] [≈]

▼▼▼ Express Inn & Suites **H**
(817) 599-3700. **$65-$200.** 2500 S Main St 76087. I-20, exit 408. Ext/int corridors. **Pets:** Small. $10 daily fee/pet. Service with restrictions, supervision. [ASK] [X] [&M] [i] [▣] [≈]

▼▼▼ Hampton Inn **H**
(817) 599-4800. **Call for rates.** 2524 S Main St 76087. I-20, exit 408. Int corridors. **Pets:** Small. $15 daily fee/pet. Service with restrictions, supervision. [X] [i] [▣] [≈]

▼▼▼ La Quinta Inn & Suites **H** ❀
(817) 594-4481. **$79-$239.** 1915 Wall St 76086. I-20, exit 408, just se. Int corridors. **Pets:** Medium, other species. Service with restrictions, supervision. [ASK] [X] [&M] [i] [▣] [≈]

▼▼▼ Weatherford Comfort Suites **H**
(817) 599-3300. **$95.** 210 Alford Dr 76086. I-20, exit 408, just s on SR 171, then just w. Int corridors. **Pets:** Accepted.
[ASK] [X] [&M] [i] [▣] [≈]

WEIMAR
AAA ▼▼ Days Inn **H**
(979) 725-9700. **$61-$71.** 102 Townsend Dr 78962. I-10, exit 682, just w on north access road. Int corridors. **Pets:** Accepted.
[SAVE] [X] [i] [▣] [≈]

WELLINGTON
▼ Cherokee Inn & Restaurant **M**
(806) 447-2508. **Call for rates.** 1105 Houston St 79095. US 83, just n of jct FM 338. Ext corridors. **Pets:** Accepted. [X] [¶]

WESLACO
AAA ▼▼▼ Best Western Palm Aire Hotel & Suites **H**
(956) 969-2411. **$65-$70.** 415 S International Blvd 78596. US 83, exit International Blvd, just s. Ext corridors. **Pets:** Small. $3 daily fee/room. Service with restrictions, crate. [SAVE] [X] [i] [▣] [¶] [≈] [X]

▼▼ Super 8 **H**
(956) 969-9920. **$40-$90.** 1702 E Expwy 83 78596. US 83, exit Airport Dr. Ext corridors. **Pets:** Accepted. [ASK] [X] [i] [▣] [≈]

WICHITA FALLS
AAA ▼▼▼ Best Western Northtown Inn **H**
(940) 766-3300. **Call for rates.** 1317 Kenley Ave 76306. I-44, exit 2, just w. Int corridors. **Pets:** Accepted. [SAVE] [X] [i] [▣] [≈]

AAA ▼▼▼ Best Western University Inn & Suites **H**
(940) 687-2025. **Call for rates.** 4540 Maplewood Ave 76308. Jct Southwest Pkwy (CR 369). Int corridors. **Pets:** Accepted.
[SAVE] [X] [&M] [i] [▣] [≈]

AAA ▼▼ Best Western Wichita Falls Inn **H**
(940) 766-6881. **$62-$89.** 1032 Central Frwy 76306. I-44, exit 2, just w. Ext corridors. **Pets:** Medium. $10 daily fee/pet. Service with restrictions, supervision. [SAVE] [X] [i] [▣] [≈]

▼▼▼ Hawthorn Suites Limited **H** ❀
(940) 692-7900. **$90-$153.** 1917 Elmwood Ave N 76308. US 281 S, exit Southwest Pkwy (CR 369), 2.3 mi w to Kemp Blvd, 2 blks n to Elmwood Ave, then just e. Int corridors. **Pets:** Medium. $15 daily fee/pet. Designated rooms, service with restrictions, supervision.
[ASK] [X] [&M] [i] [▣] [≈]

▼▼▼ Holiday Inn **H**
(940) 761-6000. **$79-$109.** 100 Central Frwy 76306. I-287, exit 1C, on west side access road. Int corridors. **Pets:** Accepted.
[ASK] [X] [&M] [i] [▣] [¶] [≈]

▼▼▼ La Quinta Inn Wichita Falls **H** 🐾
(940) 322-6971. **$49-$109.** 1128 Central Frwy N 76306. I-44, exit 2 (Maurine St), just w. Ext corridors. **Pets:** Medium, other species. Service with restrictions, supervision. [ASK] [X] [i] [▣] [≈]

▼▼ Motel 6 #130 **M**
(940) 322-8817. **$45-$55.** 1812 Maurine St 76306. I-44, exit 2, just e. Ext corridors. **Pets:** Other species. Service with restrictions, supervision.
[X] [≈]

AAA ▼▼▼ Ramada Limited **H**
(940) 855-0085. **$67-$74.** 3209 Northwest Frwy 76305. US 287, exit Beverly (CR 11), just w. Ext corridors. **Pets:** Accepted.
[SAVE] [X] [i] [▣] [≈]

WOODWAY
▼▼ Extended StayAmerica Waco-Woodway **H**
(254) 399-8836. **$85-$103.** 5903 Woodway Dr 76712. I-35, exit 330 (SR 6), 5 mi sw; Loop 340, exit 330 to jct SR 84. Int corridors. **Pets:** Other species. $25 daily fee/room. Designated rooms, service with restrictions, crate. [ASK] [X] [i] [▣]

AAA ▼▼ Travelodge Waco **H**
(254) 751-7400. **$75-$110, 14 day notice.** 7007 Woodway Dr 76712. I-35, exit 330 (SR 6 N), 2.4 mi w to exit US 84, then 1.1 mi s. Int corridors. **Pets:** $25 one-time fee/pet. Service with restrictions, supervision.
[SAVE] [X] [i] [▣] [≈]

ZAPATA
AAA ▼▼ Best Western Inn by the Lake **H**
(956) 765-8403. **$85-$90.** 1896 S US Hwy 83 78076. On US 83, 0.5 mi se. Ext corridors. **Pets:** Accepted. [SAVE] [X] [i] [▣] [≈] [X]

BEAVER

⚫⚫⚫/ ▼▼/▼▼ Best Western Butch Cassidy Inn M ❀
(435) 438-2438. **$64-$80.** 161 S Main St 84713. I-15, exit 112, 1.8 mi e. Ext corridors. **Pets:** Other species. $7 daily fee/pet.
[SAVE] [X] 🛇 💷 ⊃

⚫⚫⚫/ ▼▼/▼▼ Best Western Paradise Inn H
(435) 438-2455. **$83-$106.** 314 W 1425 N 84713. I-15, exit 112, just e. Ext corridors. **Pets:** Medium. $9 one-time fee/room. Service with restrictions, crate. [SAVE] [X] 🛇 ❘❘ ⊃

▼▼ ▼▼ Quality Inn M
(435) 438-5426. **$65-$95.** 781 W 1800 S 84713. I-15, exit 109, just w. Int corridors. **Pets:** Accepted. [ASK] [X] 🛇 💷 ⊃

▼▼ ▼▼ Rodeway Inn M
(435) 438-1666. **Call for rates.** 1345 N 400 W 84713. I-15, exit 112, just e, then just s. Int corridors. **Pets:** Medium. $10 daily fee/pet. Designated rooms, service with restrictions, supervision. [X] 🛇 ⊃

BICKNELL

⚫⚫⚫/ ▼▼ ▼▼ Aquarius Motel and Restaurant M
(435) 425-3835. **$52-$64.** 240 W Main St 84715. SR 24, 9 mi w of Capitol Reef National Park; downtown. Ext/int corridors. **Pets:** Other species. $25 deposit/room, $5 daily fee/room. Service with restrictions, crate.
[SAVE] [X] 🛇 💷 ❘❘ ⊃ [X]

BLANDING

⚫⚫⚫/ ▼▼ ▼▼ Gateway Inn M
(435) 678-2278. **$55-$85.** 88 E Center St 84511. East side on US 191. Ext corridors. **Pets:** Accepted. [SAVE] [X] 🛇 💷 ⊃

BLUFF

⚫⚫⚫/ ▼▼ Kokopelli Inn M
(435) 672-2322. **$59-$69.** 160 E Main St 84512. On US 191. Int corridors. **Pets:** Small. $11 daily fee/pet. Service with restrictions, supervision.
[SAVE] [X]

⚫⚫⚫/ ▼▼ Recapture Lodge M
(435) 672-2281. **$65-$68.** 220 E Main St 84512. On US 191. Ext corridors. **Pets:** Other species. Service with restrictions, supervision.
[SAVE] [X] 🛇 💷 ⊃ [X] [✆]

BOULDER

▼▼/▼▼/▼▼ Boulder Mountain Lodge H ❀
(435) 335-7460. **$75-$190, 30 day notice.** 20 N Hwy 12 84716. Between MM 73 and 74. Ext/int corridors. **Pets:** $15 daily fee/pet. Designated rooms, service with restrictions, supervision.
[X] 🛇 💷 ❘❘ [X]

BRIGHAM CITY

⚫⚫⚫/ ▼▼ ▼▼ Crystal Inn H
(435) 723-0440. **$85-$129.** 480 Westland Dr 84302. I-15, exit 362, 1 mi e. Int corridors. **Pets:** Accepted. [SAVE] [X] 🛇 💷 ⊃

BRYCE CANYON CITY

⚫⚫⚫/ ▼▼/▼▼ Best Western Ruby's Inn H
(435) 834-5341. **$59-$179.** 1000 S Hwy 63 84764. On SR 63, 1 mi s of SR 12. Ext/int corridors. **Pets:** Other species. $15 one-time fee/pet. Designated rooms, service with restrictions, supervision.
[SAVE] [X] [&M] 🛇 💷 ❘❘ ⊃ [X]

⚫⚫⚫/ ▼▼/▼▼ Bryce View Lodge M
(435) 834-5180. **$60-$110.** 991 S SR 63 84764. On SR 63, 1 mi s of SR 12; 1 mi n of Bryce Canyon National Park entrance. Ext corridors. **Pets:** Other species. $15 one-time fee/pet. Service with restrictions, supervision. [SAVE] [X] 🛇 💷 [X]

CEDAR CITY

⚫⚫⚫/ ▼▼/▼▼ Comfort Inn & Suites H
(435) 865-0003. **$70-$130.** 1288 S Main St 84720. I-15, exit 57, just e, then just n. Int corridors. **Pets:** Small, other species. $15 daily fee/pet. Designated rooms, service with restrictions, supervision.
[SAVE] [X] [&M] 🛇 💷 ⊃ [X]

⚫⚫⚫/ ▼▼ ▼▼ Crystal Inn Cedar City H
(435) 586-8888. **$69-$119.** 1575 W 200 N 84720. I-15, exit 59, just w. Ext/int corridors. **Pets:** Other species. $15 one-time fee/room. Designated rooms, service with restrictions, crate.
[SAVE] [X] 🛇 💷 ❘❘ ⊃ [X]

⚫⚫⚫/ ▼▼ ▼▼ Days Inn M
(435) 867-8877. **$64-$149.** 1204 S Main St 84720. I-15, exit 57, 0.4 mi ne. Ext corridors. **Pets:** Small, other species. $10 daily fee/pet. Designated rooms, service with restrictions, supervision.
[SAVE] [X] 🛇 💷 ⊃

▼▼/▼▼/▼▼ Holiday Inn Express Hotel & Suites M
(435) 865-7799. **$89-$139.** 1555 S Old Hwy 91 84720. I-15, exit 57, just e, then s. Int corridors. **Pets:** Accepted. [ASK] [X] [&M] 🛇 💷 ⊃

▼▼/▼▼/▼▼ Motel 6 of Cedar City–4041 M
(435) 586-9200. **Call for rates.** 1620 W 200 N 84720. I-15, exit 59, just w. Int corridors. **Pets:** Other species. Service with restrictions, supervision.
[X] [&M]

▼▼ ▼▼ Quality Inn M
(435) 586-2082. **$59-$129.** 250 N 1100 W 84720. I-15, exit 59, just e. Ext corridors. **Pets:** Medium, other species. $10 daily fee/pet. Designated rooms, service with restrictions, supervision. [ASK] [X] 🛇 💷 ⊃

▼▼ ▼▼ Super 8 M
(435) 586-8880. **Call for rates.** 145 N 1550 W 84720. I-15, exit 59, just w. Int corridors. **Pets:** Accepted. [X] [&M] 🛇 💷

COALVILLE

⚫⚫⚫/ ▼▼/▼▼ Best Western Holiday Hills H
(435) 336-4444. **$72-$110.** 200 S 500 W 84017. I-80, exit 162, just w. Int corridors. **Pets:** Other species. $15 daily fee/pet. Designated rooms, supervision. [SAVE] [X] 🛇 💷 ⊃ [X]

DELTA

▼▼ Days Inn M
(435) 864-3882. **Call for rates.** 527 E Topaz Blvd 84624. US 6, at US 50. Ext corridors. **Pets:** Other species. $15 one-time fee/pet. Designated rooms, service with restrictions, supervision. ✕ 🖶 🖥 ⇆

ESCALANTE

▼▼ Rainbow Country Bed & Breakfast 📖
(435) 826-4567. **$69-$99, 3 day notice.** 585 E 300 S 84726. Just off SR 12; east end of town. Int corridors. **Pets:** $10 one-time fee/pet. Service with restrictions, supervision. A$K ✕ 🏴 ☎

FILLMORE

🏵 ▼▼ Best Western Paradise Resort M
(435) 743-6895. **$80-$99.** 905 N Main St 84631. I-15, exit 167, just e. Ext corridors. **Pets:** Accepted. SAVE ✕ 🖶 🖥 🍴 ⇆

🏵 ▼▼ Comfort Inn & Suites M
(435) 743-4334. **$70-$120.** 940 S Hwy 99 84631. I-15, exit 163, just e. Int corridors. **Pets:** Medium. $6 one-time fee/pet. Designated rooms, service with restrictions, supervision. SAVE ✕ 🖶 🖥 ⇆

GLENDALE

▼▼ Historic Smith Hotel Bed & Breakfast 📖 ❀
(435) 648-2156. **$60-$98.** 295 N Main St 84729. US 89; north end of town. Int corridors. **Pets:** Other species. $5 one-time fee/pet. Designated rooms, service with restrictions, supervision. A$K ✕ ☎

GREEN RIVER

▼▼▼ Holiday Inn Express H ❀
(435) 564-4439. **$79-$139.** 1845 E Main St 84525. I-70, exit 160, 2.6 mi ne. Int corridors. **Pets:** $10 one-time fee/pet. Service with restrictions, supervision. A$K ✕ 🖶 🖥 ⇆

▼▼ Ramada Limited M
(435) 564-8441. **$50-$150.** 2125 E Main St 84525. I-70, exit 164, 1 mi nw. Ext/int corridors. **Pets:** Accepted. A$K ✕ 🖶 🖥 ⇆

🏵 ▼▼ Super 8 M
(435) 564-8888. **$50-$90.** 1248 E Main St 84525. I-70, exit 160, 3.1 mi ne. Int corridors. **Pets:** Large, other species. $5 daily fee/pet. Designated rooms, service with restrictions, supervision. SAVE ✕ 🖶 🖥 ⇆

HEBER CITY

🏵 ▼▼ Swiss Alps Inn M
(435) 654-0722. **$60-$110.** 167 S Main St 84032. I-80, exit 146 (US 40), 15 mi s. Ext corridors. **Pets:** Service with restrictions, supervision.
SAVE ✕ 🖶 🖥 🍴 ⇆ ✕

HUNTSVILLE

▼▼ Jackson Fork Inn M
(801) 745-0051. **$80-$140, 3 day notice.** 7345 E 900 S 84317. I-15, exit 344 (12th St), 12 mi e on SR 39. Int corridors. **Pets:** Medium. $20 one-time fee/room. Designated rooms, service with restrictions, supervision. A$K ✕ 🍴 ☎

HURRICANE

▼▼ Super 8 M
(435) 635-0808. **$49-$115.** 65 S 700 W 84737. Just s of SR 9. Ext corridors. **Pets:** Accepted. A$K ✕ 🖶 🖥 ⇆

KANAB

🏵 ▼▼ Best Western Red Hills M
(435) 644-2675. **$50-$130.** 125 W Center St 84741. Center. Ext/int corridors. **Pets:** Other species. $10 one-time fee/room. Service with restrictions. SAVE ✕ 🖶 🖥 ⇆

🏵 ▼ Bob-Bon Inn M
(435) 644-5094. **$49-$85, 3 day notice.** 236 Hwy 89 N 84741. On US 89. Ext corridors. **Pets:** $10 daily fee/pet. Designated rooms, service with restrictions, supervision. SAVE ✕ 🖶 ⇆

▼▼ Comfort Inn Kanab M
(435) 644-8888. **$70-$180.** 815 E Hwy 89 84741. On US 89, just e. Int corridors. **Pets:** Accepted. A$K ✕ 🖶&M 🖶 🖥 ⇆

🏵 ▼▼▼ Holiday Inn Express Hotel & Suites H
(435) 644-3100. **$89-$149.** 217 S 100 E 84741. On US 89; jct 200 S. Int corridors. **Pets:** Medium. $20 daily fee/room. Designated rooms, supervision. SAVE ✕ 🖶 🖥 ⇆

▼ Parry Lodge M
(435) 644-2601. **$49-$102.** 89 E Center St 84741. On US 89; corner of 100 E; center. Ext/int corridors. **Pets:** Accepted.
A$K ✕ 🖶 🖥 🍴 ⇆

🏵 ▼▼ Quail Park Lodge M ❀
(435) 644-8700. **$69-$139.** 125 N 300 W (Hwy 89) 84741. On US 89. Ext corridors. **Pets:** Large, dogs only. Designated rooms, service with restrictions, supervision. SAVE ✕ 🖶 ⇆

▼▼ Rodeway Inn M
(435) 644-5500. **$50-$150.** 70 S 200 W 84741. Just s of US 89. Ext corridors. **Pets:** Large, other species. $6 daily fee/room. Designated rooms, service with restrictions. A$K ✕ 🖶 🖥 ⇆

🏵 ▼▼ Shilo Inn Suites-Kanab H ❀
(435) 644-2562. **$80-$196.** 296 W 100 N 84741. On US 89; n of downtown. Int corridors. **Pets:** Dogs only. $25 one-time fee/room. Designated rooms, service with restrictions, supervision. SAVE ✕ 🖶 🖥 ⇆

▼▼▼ Victorian Charm Inn-Clarion Collection M
(435) 644-8660. **$69-$159.** 190 N Hwy 89 84741. North end of town. Int corridors. **Pets:** Accepted. A$K ✕

LAKE POWELL

🏵 ▼▼ Defiance House Lodge H
(435) 684-3032. **Call for rates.** Hwy 276 84533. 1 mi from entrance; at Bullfrog sign. Int corridors. **Pets:** Accepted. SAVE ✕ 🖶 🖥

LAYTON

▼▼▼ Hampton Inn H
(801) 775-8800. **$89-$139.** 1700 Woodland Park Dr 84041. I-15, exit 332 (Antelope Dr), 0.3 mi se. Int corridors. **Pets:** Service with restrictions, crate. ✕ 🖶 🖥 ⇆

▼▼▼ Holiday Inn Express H
(801) 773-3773. **$99-$129.** 1695 Woodland Park Dr 84041. I-15, exit 332 (Antelope Dr), 0.3 mi se. Int corridors. **Pets:** Small. $25 one-time fee/room. Designated rooms, service with restrictions, supervision.
A$K ✕ 🖶 🖥 ⇆

▼▼▼ La Quinta Inn H 🐾
(801) 776-6700. **$52-$109.** 1965 N 1200 W 84041. I-15, exit 332 (Antelope Dr), just e. Int corridors. **Pets:** Medium, other species. Service with restrictions, supervision. A$K ✕ 🖶 🖥 ⇆

▼▼ TownePlace Suites by Marriott H
(801) 779-2422. **$116-$142.** 1743 Woodland Park Dr 84041. I-15, exit 332 (Antelope Dr), 0.3 mi se. Int corridors. **Pets:** Accepted. ✕ 🖶 🖥 ⇆

LEHI

🏵 ▼▼▼ Best Western Timpanogos Inn H
(801) 768-1400. **$89-$129.** 195 S 850 E 84043. I-15, exit 279, just w, then just s. Int corridors. **Pets:** Accepted. SAVE ✕ 🖶 🖥 ⇆

▼▼ Super 8 M
(801) 766-8800. **Call for rates.** 125 S 850 E 84043. I-15, exit 279, just w, then just s. Int corridors. **Pets:** Accepted. ✕ 🖶 🖥 ⇆

LOGAN

Best Western Baugh Motel **M**
(435) 752-5220. **$85-$165.** 153 S Main St 84321. 0.3 mi s of Center St. Ext corridors. **Pets:** Accepted. [SAVE] [X] [H] [IMG] [≈]

Best Western Weston Inn **H** ✿
(435) 752-5700. **$80-$110.** 250 N Main St 84321. 0.3 mi n of Center St. Ext corridors. **Pets:** $15 daily fee/room. Designated rooms, service with restrictions, supervision. [SAVE] [X] [H] [IMG] [≈] [X]

Holiday Inn Express & Suites **H**
(435) 752-3444. **Call for rates.** 2235 N Main St 84341. 2.8 mi n of Center St. Int corridors. **Pets:** Medium. $25 one-time fee/room. Service with restrictions, crate. [X] [H] [IMG] [≈]

Super 8 **M**
(435) 753-8883. **$45-$86.** 865 S Hwy 89/91 84321. 2 mi s of Center St. Int corridors. **Pets:** $10 daily fee/pet. Service with restrictions, supervision. [ASK] [X] [H] [≈]

MANTI

Manti Country Village Motel **M**
(435) 835-9300. **$72-$99.** 145 N Main St 84642. On US 89. Ext corridors. **Pets:** Accepted. [ASK] [X] [H] [¶]

MEXICAN HAT

San Juan Inn & Trading Post **M**
(435) 683-2220. **$64-$85.** Hwy 163 & San Juan River 84531. Center. Ext corridors. **Pets:** Dogs only. $10 daily fee/pet. Designated rooms, service with restrictions, supervision. [SAVE] [X] [H] [¶]

MOAB

Bowen Motel **M**
(435) 259-7132. **$50-$111.** 169 N Main St 84532. Just n of center. Ext corridors. **Pets:** Small. $10 daily fee/pet. Designated rooms, service with restrictions, supervision. [SAVE] [X] [H] [≈]

The Gonzo Inn **H**
(435) 259-2515. **$98-$330.** 100 W 200 S 84532. Just s of center, then w. Ext/int corridors. **Pets:** Accepted. [SAVE] [X] [H] [IMG] [≈]

La Quinta Inn **H** ✿
(435) 259-8700. **$53-$232.** 815 S Main St 84532. South end of town. Int corridors. **Pets:** Medium, other species. Service with restrictions, supervision. [ASK] [X] [H] [IMG] [≈]

Moab Valley Inn **H**
(435) 259-4419. **$69-$169.** 711 S Main St 84532. 1 mi s on US 191. Int corridors. **Pets:** Other species. $10 daily fee/room. Designated rooms, service with restrictions, supervision. [ASK] [X] [H] [IMG] [≈] [X]

Motel 6 Moab #4119 **M**
(435) 259-6686. **$59-$199.** 1089 N Main St 84532. North end of town. Int corridors. **Pets:** Other species. Service with restrictions, supervision. [ASK] [X] [≈]

Red Cliffs Adventure Lodge **H**
(435) 259-2002. **$99-$320, 30 day notice.** Milepost 14 Hwy 128 84532. On SR 128, 14.5 mi e of jct US 191, MM 14. Ext corridors. **Pets:** Accepted. [SAVE] [X] [H] [IMG] [¶] [≈] [X]

Red Stone Inn **M** ✿
(435) 259-3500. **$39-$110.** 535 S Main St 84532. South end of town. Ext/int corridors. **Pets:** Medium. $5 daily fee/room. Service with restrictions. [SAVE] [X] [H]

River Canyon Lodge, An Extended Stay Inn & Suites **M** ✿
(435) 259-8838. **$59-$290.** 71 W 200 N 84532. Jct 200 N and Main St, just w. Int corridors. **Pets:** Medium. $20 one-time fee/pet. Designated rooms, no service, supervision. [SAVE] [X] [H] [IMG] [≈]

Silver Sage Inn **M**
(435) 259-4420. **$45-$95.** 840 S Main St 84532. On US 191; south end of town. Int corridors. **Pets:** Accepted. [SAVE] [X] [H] [IMG]

Sleep Inn **H**
(435) 259-4655. **$59-$189.** 1051 S Main St 84532. On US 191; south end of town. Int corridors. **Pets:** Other species. $50 deposit/room. Designated rooms, service with restrictions, supervision. [ASK] [X] [H] [IMG] [≈]

Sorrel River Ranch Resort & Spa **H** ✿
(435) 259-4642. **$329-$699, 45 day notice.** Hwy 128 at MM 17 84532. On SR 128, 17 mi e of jct US 191; at MM 17. Ext/int corridors. **Pets:** Medium, dogs only. $50 daily fee/pet. Service with restrictions, crate. [SAVE] [X] [H] [IMG] [¶] [≈] [X]

Super 8 **M**
(435) 259-8868. **$59-$189.** 889 N Main St 84532. 1 mi n of center. Int corridors. **Pets:** Medium. $20 one-time fee/pet. Designated rooms, no service, supervision. [SAVE] [X] [H] [IMG] [≈]

MONTICELLO

Best Western Wayside Inn **M**
(435) 587-2261. **$60-$103, 7 day notice.** 197 E Central St 84535. On US 491, just e of US 191. Ext corridors. **Pets:** Medium. $10 one-time fee/pet. Designated rooms, service with restrictions, supervision. [SAVE] [X] [H] [IMG] [≈]

Rodeway Inn & Suites **M**
(435) 587-2489. **$70-$130.** 649 N Main St 84535. On US 191; north end of town. Int corridors. **Pets:** Medium. $10 daily fee/pet. Designated rooms, service with restrictions, supervision. [SAVE] [X] [H] [IMG] [≈]

MONUMENT VALLEY

Goulding's Trading Post & Lodge **H**
(435) 727-3231. **$80-$189, 3 day notice.** 1000 Main St 84536. 2 mi w of US 163; just n of Arizona border. Ext corridors. **Pets:** Accepted. [SAVE] [X] [H] [IMG] [¶] [≈]

NEPHI

Best Western Paradise Inn **M**
(435) 623-0624. **$78-$90.** 1025 S Main St 84648. I-15, exit 222, 0.5 mi n. Ext corridors. **Pets:** Accepted. [SAVE] [X] [H] [IMG] [≈]

OGDEN

Best Rest Inn **H** ✿
(801) 393-8644. **$55-$105.** 1206 W 2100 S 84401. I-15, exit 343 (21st St), just e. Ext corridors. **Pets:** Large, other species. $20 deposit/room. Service with restrictions, supervision. [SAVE] [X] [H] [IMG] [¶] [≈]

Best Western Canyon Pines **H**
(801) 675-5534. **$99-$129.** 6650 S Hwy 89 84405. I-84, exit 87 (US 89/S Ogden), 0.6 mi. Int corridors. **Pets:** Accepted. [SAVE] [X] [H] [IMG] [≈]

Best Western High Country Inn **H**
(801) 394-9474. **$59-$130.** 1335 W 12th St 84404. I-15, exit 344 (12th St), just e. Ext/int corridors. **Pets:** Accepted. [SAVE] [X] [H] [IMG] [¶] [≈]

Comfort Suites of Ogden **H** ✿
(801) 621-2545. **$80-$150.** 2250 S 1200 W 84401. I-15, exit 343 (21st St), just e. Int corridors. **Pets:** Other species. $25 one-time fee/room. Designated rooms, service with restrictions, supervision. [ASK] [X] [H] [IMG] [¶] [≈] [X]

Holiday Inn Express Hotel & Suites **H** ✿
(801) 392-5000. **$105-$130.** 2245 S 1200 W 84401. I-15, exit 343 (21st St), 0.3 mi e. Int corridors. **Pets:** Other species. $25 one-time fee/room. Designated rooms, service with restrictions, supervision. [ASK] [X] [H] [IMG] [≈]

▼▼ ▼▼ Motel 6 #1082 M

(801) 627-2880. **$45-$65.** 1500 W Riverdale Rd 84405. I-15 N, exit 339 (Riverdale Rd); I-15 S, exit 340. Ext/int corridors. **Pets:** Other species. Service with restrictions, supervision. ✖ 🔌 ⤴

▼▼ Sleep Inn M

(801) 731-6500. **Call for rates.** 1155 S 1700 W 84404. I-15, exit 344 (12th St), just w. Int corridors. **Pets:** Accepted. ✖ 🔌 💻

AAA ▼▼ Super 8 M ❖

(801) 731-7100. **$60-$100.** 1508 W 2100 S 84401. I-15, exit 343 (21st St), just w. Int corridors. **Pets:** Other species. $10 daily fee/pet. Designated rooms, service with restrictions, supervision. SAVE ✖ 🔌 💻

OREM

▼▼▼ La Quinta Inn & Suites University Pkwy H ❖

(801) 226-0440. **$49-$129.** 521 W University Pkwy 84058. I-15, exit 269 (University Pkwy), 0.4 mi e. Int corridors. **Pets:** Medium, other species. Service with restrictions, supervision. ASK ✖ 🔌 💻 ⤴

AAA ▼▼ La Quinta Inn Orem H ❖

(801) 235-9555. **$59-$109.** 1100 W 780 N 84057. I-15, exit 272 (800 N), 0.3 mi e. Int corridors. **Pets:** Medium, other species. Service with restrictions, supervision. SAVE ✖ 🔌 💻 ⤴

PANGUITCH

AAA ▼▼ Color Country Motel M

(435) 676-2386. **$34-$82.** 526 N Main St 84759. 0.3 mi n of center. Ext corridors. **Pets:** Small, other species. $10 one-time fee/pet. Designated rooms, service with restrictions, supervision. SAVE ✖

▼▼ Harold's Place Cabins CA

(435) 676-2350. **$85-$95.** 3066 Hwy 12 84759. Jct US 89 and SR 12, 0.5 mi e. Ext corridors. **Pets:** Medium. $20 deposit/room. Designated rooms, service with restrictions. ASK ✖ 💻 🍴 ✉

▼▼ Harold's Place Inn M

(435) 676-2350. **$75-$95.** 3090 Hwy 12 84759. Jct US 89 and SR 12, 0.5 mi e. Int corridors. **Pets:** Medium. $20 deposit/room. Designated rooms, service with restrictions. ASK ✖ 🍴 ✉

▼▼ Horizon Motel M

(435) 676-2651. **Call for rates.** 730 N Main St 84759. 0.4 mi n of center. Ext corridors. **Pets:** Accepted. ✖ 🔌 💻 ✉

PARK CITY

AAA ▼▼▼ Best Western Landmark Inn H

(435) 649-7300. **$69-$399.** 6560 N Landmark Dr 84098. I-80, exit 145 (Kimball Jct), 0.3 mi s, then 0.3 mi nw. Int corridors. **Pets:** Medium, other species. $10 daily fee/room. Designated rooms, service with restrictions, supervision. SAVE ✖ 🔌 💻 ⤴ ✖

▼▼▼ Holiday Inn Express H

(435) 658-1600. **$89-$199.** 1501 W Ute Blvd 84098. I-80, exit 145 (Kimball Jct), just s, then 0.3 mi e. Int corridors. **Pets:** Medium, other species. $20 daily fee/room. Service with restrictions, supervision. ASK ✖ 🔌 💻 ⤴ ✖

PRICE

AAA ▼▼▼ Legacy Inn M

(435) 637-2424. **$54-$125.** 145 N Carbonville Rd 84501. US 6, exit 240 Business Loop; 0.6 mi e, then ne at W 600 St. Ext corridors. **Pets:** Accepted. SAVE ✖ 🔌 💻

PROVO

AAA ▼▼▼ Days Inn M

(801) 375-8600. **$59-$89.** 1675 N 200 W 84604. I-15, exit 269 (University Pkwy), 3.7 mi e. Ext corridors. **Pets:** Other species. $25 one-time fee/room. Service with restrictions, supervision. SAVE ✖ 🔌 💻 ⤴

▼▼ ▼▼ Econo Lodge M ❖

(801) 373-0099. **$69-$89.** 1625 W Center St 84601. I-15, exit 265 (Center St) southbound; exit 265B northbound, just w. Ext corridors. **Pets:** Large, other species. $12 daily fee/pet. Service with restrictions, supervision. ASK ✖ 🔌 💻

▼▼▼ La Quinta Inn Provo Town Centre H ❖

(801) 374-9750. **$65-$189.** 1460 S University Ave 84601. I-15, exit 263 (University Ave), 0.4 me e. Int corridors. **Pets:** Medium, other species. Service with restrictions, supervision. ASK ✖ 🔌 💻 🍴 ⤴

▼▼ ▼▼ Residence Inn by Marriott H

(801) 374-1000. **$125-$153.** 252 W 2230 N 84604. I-15, exit 269 (University Pkwy), 3.1 mi e. Int corridors. **Pets:** $100 one-time fee/room. Service with restrictions. ✖ 🔌 💻 ⤴ ✖

▼▼ ▼▼ Sleep Inn M

(801) 377-6597. **$55-$229.** 1505 S 40 E 84606. I-15, exit 263 (University Ave), just e. Int corridors. **Pets:** Medium. $10 daily fee/pet. Service with restrictions, supervision. ASK ✖ 🔌 💻 ⤴

AAA ▼▼▼ Super 8 M

(801) 374-6020. **$59-$200.** 1555 N Canyon Rd 84604. I-15, exit 269 (University Pkwy), 4.2 mi e. Ext/int corridors. **Pets:** Small. $20 daily fee/pet. Service with restrictions, supervision. SAVE ✖ 🔌 💻 ⤴

RICHFIELD

AAA ▼▼▼ Best Western Richfield Inn M

(435) 893-0100. **$80-$110.** 1275 N Main St 84701. I-70, exit 40, just s. Int corridors. **Pets:** Small. $15 daily fee/pet. Designated rooms, service with restrictions, supervision. SAVE ✖ 🔌 💻 ⤴

AAA ▼▼▼ Days Inn M

(435) 896-6476. **Call for rates.** 333 N Main St 84701. I-70, exit 40, 1 mi s on US 89. Int corridors. **Pets:** Other species. $10 one-time fee/pet. Designated rooms, service with restrictions, supervision. SAVE ✖ 🔌 💻 🍴 ⤴

▼▼▼ Holiday Inn Express & Suites H ❖

(435) 896-8552. **$89-$139.** 20 W 1400 N 84701. I-70, exit 40, 0.3 mi s. Int corridors. **Pets:** Other species. $15 daily fee/pet. Supervision. ASK ✖ 🔌 💻 ⤴

▼▼ ▼▼ Richfield Travelodge M

(435) 896-9271. **Call for rates.** 647 S Main St 84701. I-70, exit 37; south end of town. Int corridors. **Pets:** Other species. $10 one-time fee/room. Designated rooms, service with restrictions, supervision. ✖ 🔌 💻 🍴 ⤴

▼▼ ▼▼ Super 8 M

(435) 896-9204. **$50-$55, 7 day notice.** 1377 N Main St 84701. I-70, exit 40, just s. Ext/int corridors. **Pets:** Medium. $20 daily fee/pet. Service with restrictions, supervision. ASK ✖ 🔌 💻

ROOSEVELT

AAA ▼▼ Frontier Motel M

(435) 722-2201. **$94-$114.** 75 S 200 E 84066. Jct US 40 and SR 191, 0.3 mi s. Ext corridors. **Pets:** Designated rooms. SAVE ✖ 🔌 🍴 ⤴

ST. GEORGE

▼▼ ▼▼ America's Best Inn & Suites M

(435) 652-3030. **$54-$145.** 245 N Red Cliffs Dr 84790. I-15, exit 8, just e. Ext corridors. **Pets:** Accepted. ASK ✖ 🔌 💻 ⤴

AAA ▼▼ ▼▼ Americas Best Value Inn M

(435) 688-8383. **$44-$89.** 915 S Bluff St 84770. I-15, exit 6 (Bluff St), just w. Int corridors. **Pets:** Accepted. SAVE ✖ 🔌 💻 ⤴

AAA ▼▼ ▼▼ Budget Inn & Suites H

(435) 673-6661. **Call for rates.** 1221 S Main St 84770. I-15, exit 6 (Bluff St), just w. Ext corridors. **Pets:** Medium. $15 daily fee/room. Designated rooms, service with restrictions, supervision. SAVE ✖ 🔌 💻 ⤴ ✖

▼▼▼▼ Comfort Inn 🅷

(435) 628-8544. **Call for rates.** 138 E Riverside Dr 84790. I-15, exit 6 (Bluff St), just e. Int corridors. **Pets:** Medium, dogs only. $10 daily fee/room. Service with restrictions, supervision. 🅇 🍴 💻 🏊

Ⓐ▼▼▼ Crystal Inn St. George 🅷

(435) 688-7477. **$82-$149.** 1450 S Hilton Dr 84770. I-15, exit 6 (Bluff St), just w. Int corridors. **Pets:** Small, dogs only. $25 one-time fee/room. Designated rooms, service with restrictions, supervision.

[SAVE] 🅇 🍴 💻 🍴 🏊 🅇

Ⓐ▼▼▼▼ The Green Valley Spa & Resort 🅷 🐾

(435) 628-8060. **$149-$650, 30 day notice.** 1871 W Canyon View Dr 84770. Bluff and S Main sts, 4 mi sw via Hilton Dr to Dixie Dr, then to Canyon View Dr. Ext corridors. **Pets:** Medium. $25 daily fee/room. Service with restrictions, crate. [SAVE] 🅇 🅖M 🍴 💻 🍴 🏊 🅇

▼▼▼ Holiday Inn 🅷

(435) 628-4235. **$69-$159.** 850 S Bluff St 84770. I-15, exit 6 (Bluff St), just w. Ext/int corridors. **Pets:** Accepted.

[ASK] 🅇 🍴 💻 🍴 🏊 🅇

Ⓐ▼▼▼ Howard Johnson Inn 🅼

(435) 628-8000. **$49-$139.** 1040 S Main St 84770. I-15, exit 6 (Bluff St), just w, then just e. Ext corridors. **Pets:** $10 daily fee/pet. Designated rooms, service with restrictions, supervision. [SAVE] 🅇 🍴 💻 🏊

▼▼▼▼ La Quinta Inn & Suites–St. George 🅷 🐾

(435) 674-2664. **$72-$129.** 91 E 2680 S 84790. I-15, exit 4, just e on Brigham Rd. Int corridors. **Pets:** Medium, other species. Service with restrictions, supervision. [ASK] 🅇 🅖M 🍴 💻 🏊

Ⓐ▼▼◆ Red Cliffs Inn & Suites 🅷

(435) 673-3537. **Call for rates.** 912 Red Cliffs Dr 84780. I-15, exit 10, just e. Ext/int corridors. **Pets:** Accepted.

[SAVE] 🅇 🅖M 🍴 💻 🍴 🏊

Ⓐ▼▼▼ TownPlace Suites by Marriott 🅷

(435) 986-9955. **$98-$120.** 251 S 1470 E 84790. I-15, exit 8, just e. Int corridors. **Pets:** Accepted. [SAVE] 🅇 🅖M 🍴 💻 🏊

SALINA

Ⓐ▼ ▼▼ Econo Lodge 🅼

(435) 529-7455. **Call for rates.** 1225 S State St 84654. I-70, exit 56, just n. Ext corridors. **Pets:** Accepted. [SAVE] 🅇 💻 🏊

Ⓐ▼ ▼▼ Scenic Hills Super 8 🅼

(435) 529-7483. **Call for rates.** 75 E 1500 S 84654. I-70, exit 56, just n. Ext corridors. **Pets:** Accepted. [SAVE] 🅇 🍴 💻 🏊

SALT LAKE CITY METROPOLITAN AREA

COTTONWOOD HEIGHTS

▼▼ Candlewood Suites Cottonwood 🅷

(801) 567-0111. **$45-$55.** 6990 S Park Centre Dr 84121. I-15, exit 297 (7200 S), 2.8 mi e via 7200 S, then just s. Int corridors. **Pets:** Accepted.

[ASK] 🅇 🍴 💻

DRAPER

▼▼▼▼ Comfort Inn 🅷

(801) 571-2511. **$69-$120, 14 day notice.** 12033 S Factory Outlet Dr 84020. I-15, exit 291, just e, then just n. Int corridors. **Pets:** Accepted.

[ASK] 🅇 🍴 💻 🏊

Ⓐ▼ ▼▼ Ramada Limited 🅼

(801) 571-1122. **$65-$90.** 12605 S Minuteman Dr 84020. I-15, exit 291, just e, then 0.5 mi s on frontage road. Int corridors. **Pets:** Accepted.

[SAVE] 🅇 🍴 💻

MIDVALE

Ⓐ▼ ▼▼ Best Western Executive Inn 🅷

(801) 566-4141. **$70-$100, 14 day notice.** 280 W 7200 S 84047. I-15, exit 297 (7200 S), just e. Int corridors. **Pets:** Accepted.

[SAVE] 🅇 🍴 💻 🏊

◆ ▼ Extended StayAmerica-Salt Lake City-Union Park 🅼

(801) 567-0404. **$65-$80.** 7555 S Union Park Ave 84047. I-215, exit 9 (Union Park Ave), 0.3 mi s. Int corridors. **Pets:** Other species. $25 daily fee/room. Designated rooms, service with restrictions, crate.

[ASK] 🅇 🍴 💻

▼▼ La Quinta Inn 🅷 🐾

(801) 566-3291. **$45-$95.** 7231 S Catalpa St 84047. I-15, exit 297 (7200 S), just e. Int corridors. **Pets:** Medium, other species. Service with restrictions, supervision. [ASK] 🅇 🍴 💻 🏊

▼ Motel 6 #476 🅼

(801) 561-0058. **$45-$65.** 7263 S Catalpa St 84047. I-15, exit 297 (7200 S), just e, then just s. Ext corridors. **Pets:** Other species. Service with restrictions, supervision. 🅇 🍴 🏊

Ⓐ▼ ▼▼ Super 8 🅼

(801) 255-5559. **$59-$89.** 7048 S 900 E 84047. I-15, exit 297 (7200 S), 1.5 mi e, then just n. Int corridors. **Pets:** Other species. $100 deposit/room. Service with restrictions, supervision. [SAVE] 🅇 🍴 💻

MURRAY

▼▼▼ Holiday Inn Express 🅷 🐾

(801) 268-2533. **$113-$125.** 4465 S Century Dr 84123. I-15, exit 301 (4500 S), just w, then just n. Int corridors. **Pets:** $25 daily fee/pet. Designated rooms, service with restrictions, supervision.

[ASK] 🅇 🍴 💻 🏊

▼▼ Pavilion Inn 🅷

(801) 506-8000. **Call for rates.** 5335 S College Dr 84123. I-15, exit 300 (5300 S), 0.3 mi w. Int corridors. **Pets:** Accepted. 🅇 🍴 🏊

NORTH SALT LAKE

Ⓐ▼ ▼◆ Best Western CottonTree Inn 🅷

(801) 292-7666. **$89-$129.** 1030 N 400 E 84054. I-15, exit 315 (Woods Cross), just e, then just s. Int corridors. **Pets:** Medium. $25 deposit/pet, $25 one-time fee/room. Designated rooms, service with restrictions, supervision. [SAVE] 🅇 🍴 💻 🏊

SALT LAKE CITY

▼▼ Airport Inn 🅼

(801) 539-5005. **$90, 30 day notice.** 315 N Admiral Byrd Rd 84116. I-80, exit 113 (5600 W), 0.6 mi n, then just e. Int corridors. **Pets:** Accepted. [ASK] 🅇 🍴 💻 🏊

Ⓐ▼ ▼▼ Best Western City Center 🅷

(801) 325-5300. **$99-$119.** 171 W 500 S 84101. I-15, exit 306 (600 S/Temple Square), just n to W Temple, just n, then just w; 0.7 mi s of Temple Square. Ext/int corridors. **Pets:** Accepted. [SAVE] 🅇 🍴 💻

▼▼ Candlewood Suites 🅷

(801) 359-7500. **$45-$59.** 2170 W N Temple 84116. 3 mi w of Temple Square. Int corridors. **Pets:** Accepted. [ASK] 🅇 🍴 💻

City Creek Inn M
(801) 533-9100. **$62-$76.** 230 W N Temple St 84103. Cross street 200 W; just w of Temple Square. Ext corridors. **Pets:** Small, dogs only. $100 deposit/pet. Designated rooms, service with restrictions, supervision.
[SAVE] [X]

Comfort Inn Airport H
(801) 746-5200. **Call for rates.** 200 N Admiral Byrd Rd 84116. I-80, exit 113 (5600 W), 0.6 mi n, just e, then just s. Int corridors. **Pets:** Other species. $20 daily fee/room. Designated rooms, service with restrictions, supervision. [SAVE] [X] [🛏] [💻] [🍴] [🏊]

Days Inn H
(801) 539-8538. **$63-$165.** 1900 W N Temple 84116. 2.6 mi w of Temple Square. Int corridors. **Pets:** Accepted. [ASK] [X] [🛏] [💻] [🏊]

Econo Lodge M
(801) 363-0062. **$62-$129.** 715 W N Temple 84116. 0.8 mi w of Temple Square. Ext corridors. **Pets:** Accepted. [ASK] [X] [🛏] [💻] [🏊]

Hilton Salt Lake City Airport H ❀
(801) 539-1515. **$69-$229.** 5151 Wiley Post Way 84116. I-80, exit 114 westbound, 0.4 mi nw via Wright Brothers Dr and Wiley Post; exit 113 eastbound, 1.3 mi n via 5600 W, Amelia Earhart Dr, then just s on Charles Lindbergh Dr. Int corridors. **Pets:** Large, other species. $50 one-time fee/room. Designated rooms, service with restrictions, crate.
[SAVE] [X] [🛏] [💻] [🍴] [🏊] [X]

Hilton Salt Lake City Center H
(801) 328-2000. **$119-$329.** 255 S W Temple 84101. Just s of Temple Square. Int corridors. **Pets:** Accepted.
[SAVE] [X] [🛏] [💻] [🍴] [🏊] [X]

Holiday Inn Express Airport East H
(801) 741-1500. **$89-$209.** 200 N 2100 W 84116. I-80, exit 118 (Redwood Rd) westbound; exit 115 (N Temple) eastbound, 3.1 mi w of Temple Square. Int corridors. **Pets:** Accepted. [ASK] [X] [🛏] [💻] [🏊]

Holiday Inn Hotel & Suites Airport West H
(801) 741-1800. **$89-$149.** 5001 W Wiley Post Way 84116. I-80, exit 114 (Wright Brothers Dr) westbound, just n, then 0.3 mi w; exit 113 (56th W) eastbound, 0.6 mi n on 5600 W, just e on Amelia Earhart Dr, just s on Jimmy Doolittle Rd, then 0.5 mi e. Int corridors. **Pets:** Accepted.
[ASK] [X] [🛏] [💻] [🍴] [🏊]

Homestead Studio Suites Salt Lake City-Sugar House M
(801) 474-0771. **$95-$110.** 1220 E 2100 S 84106. I-80, exit 126 (1300 E), 0.5 mi n, then just w. Ext corridors. **Pets:** Other species. $25 daily fee/room. Designated rooms, service with restrictions, crate.
[ASK] [X] [🛏] [💻]

Hotel Monaco H
(801) 595-0000. **$119-$299.** 15 W 200 S 84101. Cross streets 200 S and Main St. Int corridors. **Pets:** Accepted. [SAVE] [X] [🍴]

Howard Johnson Express Inn M
(801) 521-3450. **$79-$99.** 121 N 300 W 84103. 0.3 mi w of Temple Square. Ext/int corridors. **Pets:** $25 one-time fee/room. Designated rooms, service with restrictions, supervision. [SAVE] [X] [🛏] [💻] [🏊]

Metropolitan Inn M
(801) 531-7100. **Call for rates.** 524 SW Temple 84101. Cross street 500 S. Ext corridors. **Pets:** Accepted. [X] [🛏] [💻] [🏊]

Peery Hotel H
(801) 521-4300. **$129-$300.** 110 W Broadway 84101. W Temple and 300 S. Int corridors. **Pets:** Accepted. [SAVE] [X] [💻] [🍴]

Radisson Hotel Salt Lake City (Downtown) H
(801) 531-7500. **$89-$229.** 215 W S Temple 84101. Opposite Energy Solutions Arena. Int corridors. **Pets:** Accepted.
[SAVE] [X] [🛏] [💻] [🍴] [🏊] [X]

Red Lion Hotel Salt Lake Downtown H
(801) 521-7373. **$80-$170.** 161 W 600 S 84101. At W Temple and 600 S. Int corridors. **Pets:** Other species. $20 one-time fee/room. Service with restrictions, supervision. [ASK] [X] [🛏] [💻] [🏊]

Residence Inn by Marriott H
(801) 532-4101. **$169-$179.** 4883 W Douglas Corrigan Way 84116. I-80, exit 113 eastbound, 2.6 mi ne via 5600 W, Amelia Earhart and Wright Brothers drs; exit 114 westbound, just nw off ramp. Int corridors.
Pets: Accepted. [X] [🛏] [🛏] [💻] [🏊] [X]

Residence Inn by Marriott City Center H 🐾
(801) 355-3300. **$161-$197.** 285 W Broadway (300 S) 84101. Cross streets 300 W and 300 S. Int corridors. **Pets:** Medium. $100 one-time fee/room. Service with restrictions, crate. [X] [🛏] [💻] [🏊] [X]

Sheraton City Centre H
(801) 401-2000. **Call for rates.** 150 W 500 S 84101. At 200 W and 500 S. Int corridors. **Pets:** Accepted. [SAVE] [X] [💻] [🍴] [🏊] [X]

Shilo Inn Suites Hotel H ❀
(801) 521-9500. **$100-$296.** 206 S W Temple 84101-1994. Cross streets 200 S and W Temple. Int corridors. **Pets:** Dogs only. $25 one-time fee/room. Designated rooms, service with restrictions, supervision.
[SAVE] [X] [🛏] [💻] [🍴] [🏊] [X]

Super 8 M
(801) 533-8878. **$60-$180.** 223 N Jimmy Doolittle Rd 84116. I-80, exit 113 eastbound, 0.6 mi n, then e, then just s; exit 114 westbound, just n, 0.7 mi w, then just s. Int corridors. **Pets:** Accepted.
[ASK] [X] [🛏] [💻] [🏊]

SANDY

Best Western CottonTree Inn H
(801) 523-8484. **$85-$120.** 10695 S Auto Mall Dr 84070. I-15, exit 293 (10600 S), 0.3 mi e. Int corridors. **Pets:** Other species. $10 one-time fee/room. Service with restrictions, supervision. [SAVE] [X] [🛏] [💻] [🏊]

Comfort Inn M
(801) 255-4919. **$60-$160.** 8955 S 255 W 84070. I-15, exit 295 (9000 S), just e, then just n. Int corridors. **Pets:** Accepted.
[ASK] [X] [🛏] [💻] [🏊]

Holiday Inn Express H
(801) 495-1317. **Call for rates.** 10680 S Auto Mall Dr 84070. I-15, exit 293 (10600 S), 0.3 mi e, then just s. Int corridors. **Pets:** $10 daily fee/room. Designated rooms, no service. [X] [🛏] [💻] [🏊]

Residence Inn by Marriott H
(801) 561-5005. **$143-$175.** 270 W 10000 S 84070. I-15, exit 293 (10600 S), just e. Int corridors. **Pets:** Medium. $100 one-time fee/room. Designated rooms, service with restrictions. [X] [🛏] [💻] [🏊] [X]

SOUTH JORDAN

Sleep Inn M
(801) 572-2020. **$50-$110.** 10676 S 300 W 84095. I-15, exit 293 (10600 S), just w. Int corridors. **Pets:** Other species. $6 daily fee/pet.
[ASK] [X] [🛏] [💻] [🏊]

Super 8 M
(801) 553-8888. **Call for rates.** 10722 S 300 W 84095. I-15, exit 293 (10600 S), just w. Int corridors. **Pets:** Accepted. [X] [🛏] [💻] [🏊]

TAYLORSVILLE

Homestead Studio Suites Salt Lake City-Mid Valley M
(801) 269-9292. **$65-$80.** 5683 S Redwood Rd 84123. I-215, exit 13, just n. Ext corridors. **Pets:** Other species. $25 daily fee/room. Designated rooms, service with restrictions, crate. [ASK] [X] [🛏] [💻]

WEST VALLEY CITY

▼▼ Baymont Inn & Suites 🅷

(801) 886-1300. **$59-$119.** 2229 W City Center Ct 84119. I-215, exit 18 (3500 S), just e, then just w. Int corridors. **Pets:** Accepted.

🅰🅢🅚 ☒ 🔒 🖵 ⊃

▼▼ Country Inn & Suites By Carlson 🅷

(801) 908-0311. **$89-$129.** 3422 S Decker Lake Dr 84119. I-215, exit 18 (3500 S), just e, then just n. Int corridors. **Pets:** Large, other species. $10 daily fee/room. Designated rooms, service with restrictions, crate.

🅰🅢🅚 ☒ 🔒 🖵 ⊃

⨈ ▼▼▼ Holiday Inn Express Waterpark 🅷

(801) 517-4000. **$90-$150.** 3036 S Decker Lake Dr 84119. I-215, exit 18A (3500 S), just e, 0.5 mi n, then just w. Int corridors. **Pets:** Other species. $15 daily fee/room. Supervision. ⟨SAVE⟩ ☒ 🔒 🖵 ⊃ ☒

▼▼ La Quinta Inn 🅷 🐾

(801) 954-9292. **$69-$93.** 3540 S 2200 W 84119. I-215, exit 18 (3500 S), just e. Int corridors. **Pets:** Medium, other species. Service with restrictions, supervision. 🅰🅢🅚 ☒ 🔒 🖵 ⊃

▼▼ Sleep Inn 🅜

(801) 975-1888. **$50-$85.** 3440 S 2200 W 84119. I-215, exit 18 (3500 S), just e, then just n. Int corridors. **Pets:** Small, other species. Service with restrictions, supervision. 🅰🅢🅚 ☒ 🔒 🖵

▼▼ Staybridge Suites Hotel 🅷

(801) 746-8400. **$129-$199.** 3038 S Decker Lake Dr 84119. I-215, exit 18A, just e, 0.5 mi n, then just w. Int corridors. **Pets:** Accepted.

🅰🅢🅚 ☒ 🔒 🖵 ⊃ ☒

WOODS CROSS

▼▼▼ Hampton Inn 🅷

(801) 296-1211. **$99-$199.** 2393 S 800 W 84087. I-15, exit 315, just w, then just n. Int corridors. **Pets:** Small. Designated rooms, service with restrictions, supervision. ☒ 🔒 🖵 ⊃

END METROPOLITAN AREA

SPANISH FORK

⨈ ▼▼ Western Inn 🅜

(801) 798-9400. **$50-$80.** 632 Kirby Ln 84660. I-15, exit 258 southbound, 0.5 mi e; exit 257 northbound, 1 mi ne. Int corridors. **Pets:** Dogs only. $50 deposit/room, $12 daily fee/pet. Designated rooms, supervision.

⟨SAVE⟩ ☒ 🔒

SPRINGDALE

⨈ ▼▼▼ Best Western Zion Park Inn 🅜

(435) 772-3200. **$70-$123.** 1215 Zion Park Blvd 84767. 2 mi s of park entrance. Int corridors. **Pets:** Medium. $25 one-time fee/room. Designated rooms, service with restrictions, supervision.

⟨SAVE⟩ ☒ 🔒 🖵 🍴 ⊃ ☒

▼▼ Canyon Ranch Motel 🅜

(435) 772-3357. **Call for rates.** 668 Zion Park Blvd 84767. SR 9, just s of south gate to Zion National Park. Ext corridors. **Pets:** Medium, dogs only. $24 daily fee/pet. Designated rooms, supervision.

☒ 🔒 🖵 ⊃

SPRINGVILLE

⨈ ▼▼ Best Western Mountain View Inn 🅷

(801) 489-3641. **$65-$105.** 1455 N 1750 W 84663. I-15, exit 261, just e. Int corridors. **Pets:** Accepted. ⟨SAVE⟩ ☒ 🔒 🖵 ⊃

TOOELE

▼▼▼ Holiday Inn Express Hotel & Suites 🅷

(435) 833-0500. **$99-$149.** 1531 N Main St 84074. I-80, exit 99, 11 mi s. Int corridors. **Pets:** Accepted. 🅰🅢🅚 ☒ 🔒 🖵 ⊃

TORREY

⨈ ▼▼ Affordable Inns @ Capitol Reef 🅜

(435) 425-3688. **$59-$89.** 600 E Hwy 24 84775. 0.3 mi w of SR 12; 3.3 mi w of Capitol Reef National Park entrance. Int corridors. **Pets:** Accepted. ⟨SAVE⟩ ☒ 🔒 ⊃

⨈ ▼▼ Best Western Capitol Reef Resort 🅷

(435) 425-3761. **$51-$148.** 2600 E Hwy 24 84775. 2 mi e of jct SR 12 and 24, 1.5 mi w of Capitol Reef National Park entrance. Ext corridors. **Pets:** Small. $10 daily fee/room. Designated rooms, service with restrictions, supervision. ⟨SAVE⟩ ☒ 🔒 🖵 🍴 ⊃ ☒

▼▼ Howard Johnson 🅷

(435) 425-3866. **$50-$100.** 877 N SR 24 84775. On SR 24, 1.5 mi e of jct SR 12; east end of town. Ext corridors. **Pets:** Accepted.

🅰🅢🅚 ☒ 🔒 🖵

⨈ ▼▼ Rim Rock Inn 🅜 🐾

(435) 425-3398. **$59-$79.** 2523 E Hwy 24 84775. 2.5 mi e of town; 3 mi w of Capitol Reef National Park entrance. Ext corridors. **Pets:** Other species. $10 one-time fee/pet. Service with restrictions. ⟨SAVE⟩ ☒ 🍴

⨈ ▼▼▼ Sandstone Inn & Restaurant 🅷

(435) 425-3775. **$64-$125.** 955 E SR 24 84775. Jct SR 12 and 24; 3 mi w of Capitol Reef National Park entrance. Ext corridors. **Pets:** Medium. $10 daily fee/pet. Designated rooms, service with restrictions.

⟨SAVE⟩ ☒ 🔒 🍴 ⊃

TREMONTON

▼▼▼ Hampton Inn 🅷

(435) 257-6000. **$109-$119.** 2145 W Main St 84337. I-84, exit 40, 0.4 mi e. Int corridors. **Pets:** Small. $25 one-time fee/room. Designated rooms, service with restrictions, crate. ☒ 🔒 🖵 ⊃

VERNAL

▼ Sage Motel 🅜

(435) 789-1442. **$55-$95.** 54 W Main St 84078. On US 40; center. Ext corridors. **Pets:** Medium, other species. $50 deposit/pet. Designated rooms, service with restrictions, supervision. 🅰🅢🅚 ☒ 🔒 🍴

WASHINGTON

▼▼▼ Holiday Inn Express & Suites 🅷

(435) 986-1313. **$99-$149.** 2450 N Town Center Dr 84780. I-15, exit 16, just e. Int corridors. **Pets:** Medium. $35 one-time fee/room. Service with restrictions, supervision. 🅰🅢🅚 ☒ 🔒 🖵 ⊃

WELLSVILLE

▼▼ Sherwood Hills Resort Conference Center & Spa 🅷

(435) 245-5054. **$99-$399.** 7877 S Hwy 89 & 91 84339. I-15, exit 362 (Logan), 2.5 mi s on US 89 and 91. Int corridors. **Pets:** Accepted.

🅰🅢🅚 ☒ 🔒 🖵 ⊃ ☒

VERMONT

ALBURG

▼▼ **Ransom Bay Inn & Restaurant** BB

(802) 796-3399. **$95-$120.** 4 Center Bay Rd 05440. Jct SR 78, 0.5 mi s on US 2, then just e. Int corridors. **Pets:** Medium. $10 one-time fee/pet. Designated rooms, service with restrictions, supervision.

⊠ ⑪ �PⱮ ⓩ

ARLINGTON

AAA ▼ **Candlelight Motel** M

(802) 375-6647. **$59-$115, 14 day notice.** 4893 SR 7A 05250. Historic SR 7A, 1 mi n. Ext corridors. **Pets:** Accepted. SAVE ⊠ 🖶 ➔

BARRE

AAA ▼ **Pierre Motel** M

(802) 476-3188. **$62-$95, 7 day notice.** 362 N Main St 05641. I-89, exit 7, 4 mi e on SR 62; jct US 302. Ext corridors. **Pets:** Medium, dogs only. $5 daily fee/pet. Service with restrictions, supervision.

SAVE ⊠ 🖶 ➔

BENNINGTON

AAA ▼▼ **Bennington Motor Inn** M

(802) 442-5479. **$65-$169, 3 day notice.** 143 W Main St 05201. Jct US 7, 0.4 mi w on SR 9. Ext corridors. **Pets:** Accepted. SAVE ⊠ 🖶 P

AAA ▼ **Harwood Hill Motel** M

(802) 442-6278. **$63-$95, 3 day notice.** 864 Harwood Hill Rd (SR 7A) 05201. Jct SR 9, 1.2 mi n on US 7, then 1.7 mi n on Historic SR 7A. Ext corridors. **Pets:** Accepted. SAVE ⊠ 🖶 P

AAA ▼ **Knotty Pine Motel** M 🐾

(802) 442-5487. **$79-$98.** 130 Northside Dr (SR 7A) 05201. Jct SR 9, 1.2 mi n on US 7, then just n on Historic SR 7A. Ext corridors. **Pets:** Other species. Service with restrictions, supervision.

⊠ 🖶 P ➔

BERLIN

▼▼ **HillTop Inn** H

(802) 229-5766. **$69-$149.** 3472 Airport Rd 05641. I-89, exit 7 (SR 62), 1.3 mi e. Int corridors. **Pets:** Accepted. ASK ⊠ 🖶 ➔

BOLTON VALLEY

▼▼▼▼ **Black Bear Inn** CI 🐾

(802) 434-2126. **$89-$355, 21 day notice.** 4010 Bolton Access Rd 05477. I-89, exit 10 northbound, 6.2 mi w on US 2, then 4 mi n; exit 11 southbound, 8.4 mi e on US 2, then 4 mi n. Ext/int corridors. **Pets:** Other species. $20 daily fee/room. Designated rooms, service with restrictions.

ECO ⊠ 🖶 P ⑪ ➔

BRANDON

AAA ▼▼ **Brandon Motor Lodge** M 🐾

(802) 247-9594. **$75-$145.** 2095 Franklin St 05733. 2 mi s on US 7. Ext corridors. **Pets:** Large. $10 one-time fee/room. Service with restrictions, supervision. ECO SAVE ⊠ 🖶 ➔ ⊠

◆◆▼▼ **The Lilac Inn** CI 🐾

(802) 247-5463. **$135-$345, 30 day notice.** 53 Park St 05733. Just e on SR 73. Int corridors. **Pets:** Dogs only. $35 one-time fee/pet. Service with restrictions, crate. ECO ASK ⊠ ⑪ ⓩ

BRATTLEBORO

▼▼ **Colonial Motel & Spa** H

(802) 257-7733. **$79-$145.** 889 Putney Rd 05301. I-91, exit 3, just e on SR 9, then 0.5 mi s on US 5. Ext corridors. **Pets:** Dogs only. $15 daily fee/room. Service with restrictions, supervision.

ASK ⊠ 🖶 P ➔ ⊠

AAA ▼▼ **Econo Lodge** M

(802) 254-2360. **$45-$175.** 515 Canal St 05301. I-91, exit 1, 0.3 mi n on US 5. Ext/int corridors. **Pets:** Accepted. SAVE ⊠ 🖶 P ➔

AAA ▼▼ **Super 8** M

(802) 254-8889. **$50-$195.** 1043 Putney Rd 05301. I-91, exit 3, just e on SR 9, then just s on US 5. Int corridors. **Pets:** Other species. $20 one-time fee/room. Service with restrictions, supervision.

SAVE ⊠ 🖶ᴹ 🖶 P ➔

CAVENDISH

▼▼▼ **The Pointe at Castle Hill Resort & Spa** H

(802) 226-7688. **$89-$449, 14 day notice.** 2940 SR 103 05142. On SR 103, just n of jct SR 131. Int corridors. **Pets:** $20 one-time fee/pet. Service with restrictions, crate. ASK ⊠ 🖶 P ⑪ ➔ ⊠

COLCHESTER

▼▼ **Days Inn** H

(802) 655-0900. **$50-$135.** 124 College Pkwy 05446. I-89, exit 15 northbound, just e on SR 15; exit 16 southbound, 1.1 mi s on US 7, then 1 mi e on SR 15. Int corridors. **Pets:** Dogs only. $10 daily fee/pet. Designated rooms, service with restrictions. ASK ⊠ 🖶ᴹ 🖶 ➔

▼▼▼ **Hampton Inn & Conference Center** H 🐾

(802) 655-6177. **$99-$450.** 42 Lower Mountain View Dr 05446. I-89, exit 16, just n on US 7. Int corridors. **Pets:** Other species. Designated rooms, service with restrictions, supervision. ECO ⊠ 🖶ᴹ 🖶 P ➔

▼▼ **Motel 6 #1407** H

(802) 654-6860. **$45-$65.** 74 S Park Dr 05446. I-89, exit 16, just s on US 7. Int corridors. **Pets:** Other species. Service with restrictions, supervision. ⊠ 🖶 ➔

ESSEX JUNCTION

AAA ▼▼ ▼▼ **The Essex Resort & Spa** H 🐾

(802) 878-1100. **$169-$349, 7 day notice.** 70 Essex Way 05452. SR 289, exit 10, 0.3 mi s. Int corridors. **Pets:** $300 deposit/room, $25 daily fee/pet. Designated rooms, service with restrictions, crate. ECO SAVE ⊠ 🖶ᴹ 🖶 P ⑪ ➔ ⊠

▼▼▼ **Handy Suites-Essex** H 🐾

(802) 872-5200. **$74-$249.** 27 Susie Wilson Rd 05452. I-89, exit 15 northbound, 2 mi e, then just n. Int corridors. **Pets:** Medium, dogs only. $50 deposit/room. Designated rooms, service with restrictions. ASK ⊠ 🖶ᴹ 🖶 P ➔

FAIRLEE

AAA ▼▼▼ **Silver Maple Lodge & Cottages** BB

(802) 333-4326. **$76-$119, 14 day notice.** 520 US 5 S 05045. I-91, exit 15, 0.5 mi s. Ext/int corridors. **Pets:** Other species. Designated rooms. SAVE ⊠ 🖶 P ⓩ

FLETCHER

◆◆◆◆ The Inn at Buck Hollow Farm BB ❀
(802) 849-2400. **$93-$105, 14 day notice.** 2150 Buck Hollow Rd 05454.
From Fairfax, 6 mi n of jct SR 104 via Buck Hollow Rd. Int corridors.
Pets: $20 daily fee/pet. Service with restrictions, crate.
[ASK] [X] [≈] [X] [Z]

JAMAICA

◆◆◆ ◆◆◆◆ Three Mountain Inn CI
(802) 874-4140. **$165-$370, 21 day notice.** 3732 Main St 05343. On
SR 30; center. Ext/int corridors. **Pets:** Accepted.
[SAVE] [X] [▼] [≈] [X]

KILLINGTON

◆◆◆ ◆◆◆◆ The Cascades Lodge H
(802) 422-3731. **$94-$299, 21 day notice.** 58 Old Mill Rd 05751. 3.6 mi
s on Killington Rd, from jct SR 100/US 4, then just e. Int corridors.
Pets: $50 daily fee/pet. Designated rooms, crate.
[SAVE] [X] [✱] [▬] [▼] [≈] [X]

LONDONDERRY

◆◆◆◆ Snowdon Motel M
(802) 824-6047. **$65-$125, 7 day notice.** 4071 VT Rt 11 05148. Jct SR
100, 2 mi e. Ext corridors. **Pets:** Accepted. [ASK] [X] [✱] [Z]

LUDLOW

◆◆◆ ◆◆◆◆ All Seasons Motel M
(802) 228-8100. **$70-$250, 14 day notice.** 112 Main St 05149. On SR
103; center. Ext/int corridors. **Pets:** Accepted. [SAVE] [X] [✱] [▬] [≈]

◆◆◆◆ The Andrie Rose Inn BB ❀
(802) 228-4846. **$110-$364, 20 day notice.** 13 Pleasant St 05149. Corner of Depot St; center. Int corridors. **Pets:** Other species. $25 daily fee/
room. Designated rooms, service with restrictions. [X] [✱] [▼] [Z]

◆◆◆ ◆◆◆◆ Timber Inn Motel M
(802) 228-8666. **$69-$249, 14 day notice.** 112 Rt 103 S 05149. On SR
103 S, 1 mi e. Ext corridors. **Pets:** Dogs only. $15 daily fee/pet. Desig-
nated rooms, service with restrictions, crate.
[SAVE] [X] [✱] [▬] [≈] [X]

MANCHESTER CENTER

◆◆◆◆ Casablanca Motel CA ❀
(802) 362-2145. **$62-$125, 14 day notice.** 5927 Main St (Rt 7A) 05255.
Jct SR 11/30 N, 1 mi n on Historic SR 7A. Ext corridors. **Pets:** Other
species. $15 daily fee/pet. Designated rooms, service with restrictions.
[ECO] [ASK] [X] [▬] [▼]

◆◆◆ ◆◆◆◆ Stamford Motel M
(802) 362-2342. **$60-$110, 14 day notice.** 6458 Main St (SR 7A N)
05255. Jct SR 11/30, 1.5 mi n on Historic SR 7A. Ext/int corridors.
Pets: Medium, dogs only. $50 one-time fee/room. Designated rooms,
service with restrictions, supervision. [SAVE] [X] [✱] [▬] [≈]

MANCHESTER VILLAGE

◆◆◆ ◆◆◆◆ ◆ The Equinox, a Luxury Collection Golf
Resort & Spa H
(802) 362-4700. **Call for rates.** 3567 Main St 05254. 1.3 mi s on Historic SR 7A, from jct SR 11/30. Int corridors. **Pets:** Accepted.
[ECO] [SAVE] [X] [ﾑ] [✱] [▬] [▼] [▼] [≈] [X]

MENDON

◆◆◆ ◆◆◆◆ Econo Lodge-Killington Area H
(802) 773-6644. **Call for rates.** 51 US 4 05701. Jct US 7, 5.3 mi e. Int
corridors. **Pets:** Accepted. [ECO] [SAVE] [X] [✱] [▬] [≈]

◆◆◆ ◆◆◆◆ Mendon Mountainview Lodge H
(802) 773-4311. **$69-$259, 7 day notice.** 78 US 4 05751. On US 4, 6
mi e of jct US 7. Int corridors. **Pets:** Accepted. [ASK] [X] [✱] [▬] [≈] [X]

MIDDLEBURY

◆◆◆ ◆◆◆◆ The Middlebury Inn H ❀
(802) 388-4961. **$119-$299, 3 day notice.** 14 Court Square 05753. On
US 7; center. Ext/int corridors. **Pets:** Other species. $25 one-time fee/
room. Designated rooms, service with restrictions, crate.
[SAVE] [X] [✱] [▬] [▼] [▼]

◆◆◆◆ Swift House Inn CI
(802) 388-9925. **$120-$285, 14 day notice.** 25 Stewart Ln 05753. 0.3
mi n on US 7 from jct SR 125 W. Ext/int corridors. **Pets:** Accepted.
[ECO] [ASK] [X] [▬] [▼] [▼] [X]

MONTGOMERY CENTER

◆◆◆ ◆◆◆◆ Phineas Swann Bed & Breakfast Inn BB
(802) 326-4306. **$99-$395, 30 day notice.** 195 Main St 05471. Center.
Ext/int corridors. **Pets:** Accepted. [SAVE] [X] [✱] [▬] [▼] [X]

MORRISVILLE

◆◆◆ ◆◆◆◆ Sunset Motor Inn M
(802) 888-4956. **$83-$182, 7 day notice.** 160 SR 15 05661. Jct SR
100, just w on SR 15. Ext/int corridors. **Pets:** $50 deposit/room. Desig-
nated rooms, service with restrictions, supervision.
[SAVE] [X] [ﾑ] [✱] [≈]

◆◆◆◆ Village Victorian Bed & Breakfast BB
(802) 888-8850. **$90-$140, 15 day notice.** 107 Union St 05661. Just e
on Congress St, then just n. Int corridors. **Pets:** Small, dogs only. $10
daily fee/pet. Designated rooms, service with restrictions, supervision.
[ECO] [ASK] [X] [Z]

NORTH HERO

◆◆◆ ◆◆◆◆ Shore Acres Inn H
(802) 372-8722. **$95-$250, 21 day notice.** 237 Shore Acres Dr 05474.
0.5 mi s on US 2. Ext/int corridors. **Pets:** Dogs only. $5 daily fee/pet, $20
one-time fee/pet. Crate. [SAVE] [X] [✱] [▼] [X] [Z]

PERU

◆◆◆ ◆◆◆◆ Bromley Sun Lodge H
(802) 824-6941. **$85-$299, 3 day notice.** 4216 Rt 11/30 05152. On SR
11/30. Int corridors. **Pets:** Medium, dogs only. $75 deposit/pet. Designated
rooms, service with restrictions, supervision.
[SAVE] [X] [✱] [▬] [▼] [≈]

PUTNEY

◆◆◆◆ The Putney Inn H
(802) 387-5517. **$98-$198.** 57 Putney Landing Rd 05346. I-91, exit 4,
just e. Ext corridors. **Pets:** Accepted. [X] [✱] [▬] [▼]

RANDOLPH

◆◆◆ ◆◆◆◆ Three Stallion Inn CI
(802) 728-5575. **$125-$250.** 665 Stock Farm Rd 05060. I-89, exit 4, 2 mi
w on SR 66; jct SR 12, just e on SR 66, then just s. Ext/int corridors.
Pets: Dogs only. $400 deposit/room, $25 daily fee/pet. Designated rooms,
crate. [SAVE] [X] [▼] [≈] [X]

RUTLAND

◆◆◆◆ Comfort Inn at Trolley Square H
(802) 775-2200. **$100-$220.** 19 Allen St 05701. On US 7, 1 mi s from jct
US 4 W; 1.5 mi n from US 4 E. Int corridors. **Pets:** Accepted.
[ASK] [X] [ﾑ] [✱] [▬] [≈]

◆◆◆◆ Holiday Inn Rutland/Killington H
(802) 775-1911. **$119-$249.** 476 US Rt 7 S 05701. 2.4 mi s on US 7,
from US 4 W; 0.4 mi n, US 7 from US 4 E. Int corridors. **Pets:** $27 daily
fee/room. Service with restrictions, supervision.
[ASK] [X] [ﾑ] [✱] [▬] [▼] [≈] [X]

◆◆◆◆ Ramada Limited of Rutland H
(802) 773-3361. **$59-$159.** 253 S Main St, US 7 05701. 1.3 mi s on US
7, from US 4 W; 1.5 mi n on US 7, from US 4 E. Int corridors.
Pets: Accepted. [ASK] [X] [✱] [▬] [▼] [≈]

AAA ▼▼▼▼ **Red Roof Inn Rutland-Killington** H

(802) 775-4303. **Call for rates.** 401 US Hwy 7 S 05701. On US 7/4. Int corridors. **Pets:** Large. Service with restrictions, crate.

[SAVE] [X] [📶] [🖵] [≈]

AAA ▼ **Rodeway Inn** M

(802) 775-2575. **$49-$169, 5 day notice.** 138 N Main St 05701. 0.5 mi n of jct US 4 E. Ext corridors. **Pets:** Accepted. [SAVE] [X] [📶] [🖵] [≈]

AAA ▼ **Rodeway Inn** M

(802) 773-9176. **$49-$169, 5 day notice.** 115 Woodstock Ave 05701. Jct US 7, 0.5 mi e on US 4. Ext/int corridors. **Pets:** Accepted.

[SAVE] [X] [📶] [🖵] [≈]

ST. ALBANS

AAA ▼▼▼ **Econo Lodge** M

(802) 524-5956. **Call for rates.** 287 S Main St (US 7) 05478. I-89, exit 19, 1 mi w on Interstate Access Rd, then 0.5 mi s. Ext/int corridors. **Pets:** Accepted. [SAVE] [X] [📶] [🖵]

ST. JOHNSBURY

▼▼ **Fairbanks Inn** M

(802) 748-5666. **Call for rates.** 401 Western Ave 05819. I-91, exit 21, 0.8 mi e on US 2. Ext corridors. **Pets:** Accepted. [X] [📶] [≈]

SHAFTSBURY

▼ **Governor's Rock Motel** M

(802) 442-4734. **$55-$105.** 4325 Rt 7A 05262. 3.3 mi n on Historic SR 7A, from jct SR 67. Ext corridors. **Pets:** Other species. $5 daily fee/room. Designated rooms, service with restrictions, supervision. [X] [📶] [🖵]

▼ **Hillbrook Motel** M

(802) 447-7201. **$65-$90, 3 day notice.** 2629 Rt 7A 05262. SR 7, exit 2, 2 mi n. Ext corridors. **Pets:** Accepted. [X] [📶] [🖵] [≈]

▼ **Serenity Motel** CA

(802) 442-6490. **$65-$85.** 4379 Rt 7A 05262. 3.3 mi n on Historic SR 7A, from jct SR 67. Ext corridors. **Pets:** Other species. Designated rooms, service with restrictions, supervision. [X] [📶] [🖵]

SOUTH BURLINGTON

AAA ▼▼▼ **Best Western Windjammer Inn & Conference Center** H ❀

(802) 863-1125. **$100-$160.** 1076 Williston Rd 05403. I-89, exit 14E, 0.3 mi e on US 2. Int corridors. **Pets:** $10 daily fee/pet. Designated rooms, service with restrictions, supervision.

[SAVE] [X] [♿M] [📶] [🖵] [🍴] [≈] [X̄]

AAA ▼▼▼▼ **Doubletree Hotel Burlington** H

(802) 658-0250. **$89-$239.** 1117 Williston Rd 05403. I-89, exit 14E, just e on US 2. Int corridors. **Pets:** Large. $75 deposit/room. Service with restrictions, supervision. [ECO] [SAVE] [X] [♿M] [📶] [🖵] [🍴] [≈]

▼▼▼ **Green Mountain Suites Hotel** H ❀

(802) 860-1212. **$149-$399, 3 day notice.** 401 Dorset St 05403. I-89, exit 14E, just e on US 2, then 0.8 mi s. Int corridors. **Pets:** Other species. $25 daily fee/room. Designated rooms.

[ECO] [ASK] [X] [♿M] [📶] [🖵] [≈]

▼▼▼ **La Quinta Inn & Suites** H ❀

(802) 865-3400. **$55-$159.** 1285 Williston Rd 05403. I-89, exit 14E, 0.5 mi e on US 2. Int corridors. **Pets:** Medium, other species. Service with restrictions, supervision. [ASK] [X] [♿M] [📶] [🖵] [≈]

AAA ▼▼▼ **Sheraton Burlington Hotel & Conference Center** H ❀

(802) 865-6600. **$129-$349.** 870 Williston Rd 05403. I-89, exit 14W, just w on US 2. Int corridors. **Pets:** Medium. $25 deposit/room. Supervision.

[ECO] [SAVE] [X] [📶] [🖵] [🍴] [≈]

AAA ▼▼▼ **Smart Suites** H

(802) 860-9900. **$99-$179.** 1700 Shelburne Rd 05403. I-89, exit 13 to US 7, then 1.5 mi s. Int corridors. **Pets:** Small. $25 one-time fee/room. Designated rooms, service with restrictions. [SAVE] [X] [📶] [🖵]

SOUTH WOODSTOCK

▼▼▼ **Kedron Valley Inn** CI

(802) 457-1473. **$135-$350, 14 day notice.** 10671 South Rd 05071. Jct US 4, 5 mi s. Ext/int corridors. **Pets:** Accepted.

[ASK] [X] [📶] [🍴] [🏊]

SPRINGFIELD

▼▼▼ **Holiday Inn Express** H ❀

(802) 885-4516. **$109-$189.** 818 Charlestown Rd 05156. I-91, exit 7. Int corridors. **Pets:** Large, other species. $25 one-time fee/pet. Service with restrictions, supervision. [ASK] [X] [♿M] [📶] [🖵] [≈]

STOWE

▼▼▼ **1066 Ye Olde England Inne** CI ❀

(802) 253-7558. **$109-$189, 15 day notice.** 433 Mountain Rd 05672. 0.4 mi w on SR 108, from jct SR 100. Ext/int corridors. **Pets:** Other species. $20 daily fee/pet. Designated rooms, service with restrictions.

[ECO] [ASK] [X] [📶] [🖵] [🍴] [≈] [X̄]

AAA ▼▼▼ **Commodores Inn** H

(802) 253-7131. **$98-$198.** 823 S Main St 05672. Jct SR 108, 0.8 mi s on SR 100. Int corridors. **Pets:** Other species. $10 daily fee/room.

[SAVE] [X] [📶] [🍴] [≈] [X̄]

▼▼▼ **Edson Hill Manor** CI

(802) 253-7371. **$179-$239, 15 day notice.** 1500 Edson Hill Rd 05672. Jct SR 100, 3.4 mi w on SR 108, 1.3 mi n. Ext/int corridors. **Pets:** Designated rooms, service with restrictions, supervision. [X] [🍴] [≈] [X̄]

AAA ▼▼▼ **Golden Eagle Resort** M ❀

(802) 253-4811. **$99-$389, 7 day notice.** 511 Mountain Rd 05672. 0.5 mi w on SR 108, from jct SR 100. Ext corridors. **Pets:** $25 one-time fee/room. Designated rooms, service with restrictions, crate.

[ECO] [SAVE] [X] [📶] [🖵] [🍴] [≈] [X̄]

▼▼▼ **Hob Knob Inn & Restaurant** M

(802) 253-8549. **$95-$300, 14 day notice.** 2364 Mountain Rd 05672. Jct SR 100, 2.5 mi w on SR 108. Ext/int corridors. **Pets:** $20 daily fee/pet. Designated rooms. [ECO] [ASK] [X] [📶] [🖵] [🍴] [≈]

AAA ▼▼▼ **Honeywood Country Lodge** M

(802) 253-4124. **$99-$149, 15 day notice.** 4527 Mountain Rd 05672. Jct SR 100, 4.7 mi w on SR 108. Ext corridors. **Pets:** Accepted.

[SAVE] [X] [📶] [🖵] [≈] [X̄]

AAA ▼▼▼ **Innsbruck Inn at Stowe** M ❀

(802) 253-8582. **$79-$199, 15 day notice.** 4361 Mountain Rd 05672. 4.5 mi w on SR 108, from jct SR 100. Ext/int corridors. **Pets:** Large, dogs only. $10 daily fee/pet. Designated rooms, service with restrictions, crate. [ECO] [SAVE] [X] [📶] [🖵] [X̄]

▼▼▼ **The Mountain Road Resort at Stowe** M

(802) 253-4566. **$79-$159.** 1007 Mountain Rd 05672. 1 mi w on SR 108, from jct SR 100. Ext corridors. **Pets:** Other species. $15 daily fee/pet. Service with restrictions. [ASK] [X] [📶] [🖵] [≈] [X̄]

▼▼▼ **The Snowdrift Motel** M

(802) 253-7305. **$78-$150, 15 day notice.** 2135 Mountain Rd 05672. Jct SR 100, 2.1 mi w on SR 108. Ext/int corridors. **Pets:** Dogs only. $10 daily fee/pet. Designated rooms, service with restrictions, crate.

[ASK] [X] [📶] [🖵] [≈] [X̄]

AAA ▼▼▼ ▼▼▼ **Topnotch Resort and Spa** H

(802) 253-8585. **$195-$1600, 14 day notice.** 4000 Mountain Rd 05672. Jct SR 100, 4.2 mi w on SR 108. Ext/int corridors. **Pets:** Accepted.

[SAVE] [X] [📶] [🖵] [🍴] [≈] [X̄]

SUNDERLAND

▼▼ ▼▼ Arcady at the Sunderland Ⓜ ❖
(802) 362-1176. **$75-$185, 3 day notice.** 6249 Rt 7A 05250. On Historic SR 7A, 6.3 mi s of jct SR 11. Ext corridors. **Pets:** $18 daily fee/pet. Designated rooms, service with restrictions, crate. ☒ 🖶 🖵 🏊

WARREN

▼▼▼ ▼▼▼ The Pitcher Inn Ⓒ
(802) 496-6350. **Call for rates.** 275 Main St 05674. Center. Ext/int corridors. **Pets:** Medium, dogs only. $75 daily fee/room. Designated rooms, service with restrictions, supervision. ☒ 🖶 🖵 🍽 🏊

WEST BRATTLEBORO

▼▼ Molly Stark Motel Ⓜ
(802) 254-2440. **$45-$95.** 829 Marlboro Rd 05301. I-91, exit 2, 3.3 mi w on SR 9. Ext corridors. **Pets:** Large, dogs only. $5 one-time fee/pet. ☒ 🖶 🖵

WEST DOVER

▼▼ ▼▼ The Gray Ghost Inn Ⓗ
(802) 464-2474. **$95-$174, 14 day notice.** 290 Rt 100 N 05356. 7.8 mi n on SR 100, from jct SR 9. Int corridors. **Pets:** Dogs only. Service with restrictions, supervision. ☒ 🏊 🏊

▼▼ ▼▼ Red Oak Inn Ⓒ
(802) 464-8817. **$79-$149, 7 day notice.** 45 Rt 100 05356. 5 mi n. Int corridors. **Pets:** Accepted. ☒ 🖶 🖵 🏊 🏊

WESTMORE

⨁ ▼▼▼ ▼▼▼ WilloughVale Inn on Lake Willoughby Ⓒ
(802) 525-4123. **$115-$280, 14 day notice.** 793 SR 5A 05860. Jct SR 16 and SR 5A, just s. Ext/int corridors. **Pets:** Medium, dogs only. $20 daily fee/pet. Designated rooms, service with restrictions, supervision. 🆂🅰🆅🅴 ☒ 🖶 🖵 🍽 🏊

WHITE RIVER JUNCTION

▼▼ Comfort Inn Ⓗ
(802) 295-3051. **$89-$209.** 56 Ralph Lehman Dr 05001. I-91, exit 11, just e. Int corridors. **Pets:** Service with restrictions, supervision. 🅰🆂🅺 ☒ 🅶🅼 🖶 🖵 🏊

⨁ ▼▼▼ ▼▼▼ Econo Lodge Ⓗ
(802) 295-3015. **$80-$204.** 91 Ballardvale Dr 05001. I-91, exit 11, just s on US 5. Int corridors. **Pets:** Accepted. 🆂🅰🆅🅴 ☒ 🖶 🖵 🏊

▼▼ Super 8-White River Junction Ⓗ
(802) 295-7577. **$67-$129.** 442 N Hartland Rd 05001. US 5, just w of jct I-89 and 91. Ext corridors. **Pets:** Other species. Service with restrictions, supervision. 🅰🆂🅺 ☒ 🖵 🏊

WILLISTON

⨁ ▼▼▼ ▼▼▼ Residence Inn Burlington Williston Ⓗ
(802) 878-2001. **$149-$199.** 35 Hurricane Ln 05495. I-89, exit 12, just s on SR 2A, then just e. Ext corridors. **Pets:** Accepted. 🆂🅰🆅🅴 ☒ 🖶 🖵 🏊 🏊

▼▼▼ ▼▼▼ TownePlace Suites Burlington Williston Ⓗ ❖
(802) 872-5900. **$119-$139.** 66 Zephyr Rd 05495. I-89, exit 12, 1.1 mi n on SR 2A. Int corridors. **Pets:** Other species. $10 daily fee/room. ☒ 🅶🅼 🖶 🖵 🏊

WILMINGTON

⨁ ▼▼ ▼▼ Nordic Hills Lodge Ⓗ
(802) 464-5130. **$105-$219, 3 day notice.** 34 Look Rd 05363. 2.5 mi s on SR 100, from jct SR 9, then 0.6 mi w on Colbrook Rd. Int corridors. **Pets:** Other species. $25 one-time fee/pet. Designated rooms, service with restrictions, supervision. 🆂🅰🆅🅴 ☒ 🍽 🏊 🏊 🏊

WINDSOR

▼▼▼ ▼▼▼ Juniper Hill Inn Ⓒ
(802) 674-5273. **Call for rates.** 153 Pembroke Rd 05089. I-91, exit 9, 2.9 mi s on US 5 to Juniper Hill Rd, then 0.5 mi w. Int corridors. **Pets:** Accepted. ☒ 🍽 🏊 🏊

WOODSTOCK

▼▼ Ottauquechee Motor Lodge Ⓜ
(802) 672-3404. **Call for rates.** 529 US Rt 4 05091. US 4, 4.5 mi w. Ext/int corridors. **Pets:** Accepted. ☒ 🖶

VIRGINIA

ABINGDON

Holiday Inn Express
(276) 676-2829. **$89-$179.** 940 E Main St 24210. I-81, exit 19 (US 11), just w. Int corridors. **Pets:** Accepted.

Super 8 of Abingdon
(276) 676-3329. **Call for rates.** 298 Towne Centre Dr 24210. I-81, exit 17, just ne. Int corridors. **Pets:** Accepted.

ALTAVISTA

Comfort Inn
(434) 369-4000. **Call for rates.** 1558 Main St 24517. US 29 business route, at jct US 29. Int corridors. **Pets:** Other species. $10 daily fee/pet. Designated rooms, service with restrictions, supervision.

BIG STONE GAP

Country Inn Motel
(276) 523-0374. **$46-$57.** 627 Gilley Ave 24219. US 23, 1 mi w on US 23 business route and 58A. Ext corridors. **Pets:** $3 daily fee/pet. Service with restrictions, supervision.

BLACKSBURG

Comfort Inn
(540) 951-1500. **$85-$159.** 3705 S Main St 24060. 3.5 mi s on US 460, jct US 460 Bypass. Int corridors. **Pets:** Other species. Service with restrictions.

Days Inn Blacksburg
(540) 951-1330. **$69-$99.** 3503 Holiday Ln 24060. 3.8 mi s on US 460; jct US 460 Bypass. Ext corridors. **Pets:** Accepted.

BRISTOL

Holiday Inn Hotel & Suites
(276) 466-4100. **Call for rates.** 3005 Linden Dr 24202. I-81, exit 7, just w. Int corridors. **Pets:** $25 one-time fee/pet. Designated rooms, service with restrictions, crate.

La Quinta Inn Bristol
(276) 669-9353. **Call for rates.** 1014 Old Airport Rd 24201. I-81, exit 7, just e. Ext corridors. **Pets:** Medium, other species. Service with restrictions, supervision.

Motel 6 #4125
(276) 466-6060. **$58-$200.** 21561 Clear Creek Rd 24202. I-81, exit 7, 0.3 mi w. Int corridors. **Pets:** Other species. Service with restrictions, supervision.

Super 8
(276) 466-8800. **$45-$280.** 2139 Lee Hwy 24201. I-81, exit 5, just s. Int corridors. **Pets:** Other species. $10 daily fee/pet. Service with restrictions, supervision.

BUCHANAN

Wattstull Inn
(540) 254-1551. **$58-$75, 7 day notice.** 130 Arcadia Rd 24066. I-81, exit 168, just e on SR 614. Ext corridors. **Pets:** Medium. $10 daily fee/pet. Designated rooms, service with restrictions, supervision.

BURKEVILLE

Comfort Inn Burkeville
(434) 767-3750. **$90-$140, 3 day notice.** 419 N Agnew St 23922. On US 460, just e of jct US 360. Int corridors. **Pets:** Medium. $25 daily fee/pet. No service, supervision.

CHARLOTTESVILLE

The Cavalier Inn at the University
(434) 296-8111. **$79-$175.** 105 N Emmet St 22903. Jct US 29 and 250 Bypass, 1.3 mi s on US 29 business route. Ext/int corridors. **Pets:** Accepted.

Comfort Inn University
(434) 293-6188. **$79-$129.** 1807 Emmet St 22901. Jct US 250 Bypass, just n on US 29. Int corridors. **Pets:** Accepted.

Doubletree Hotel Charlottesville
(434) 973-2121. **$89-$239.** 990 Hilton Heights Rd 22901. I-64, exit 118B (US 29), 4 mi n of jct US 250 Bypass. Int corridors. **Pets:** Medium. $25 one-time fee/pet. Designated rooms, service with restrictions, crate.

Fairfield Inn by Marriott
(434) 964-9411. **$89-$109.** 577 Branchlands Blvd 22901. US 29 (Emmet St), 1.3 mi n of US 250 Bypass. Int corridors. **Pets:** Accepted.

Holiday Inn-Monticello/Charlottesville
(434) 977-5100. **$100-$301.** 1200 5th St SW 22902. I-64, exit 120, just n on SR 631. Int corridors. **Pets:** Accepted.

Omni Charlottesville Hotel
(434) 971-5500. **$115-$219.** 235 W Main St 22902. I-64, exit 120, 2.3 mi n on SR 631; downtown. Int corridors. **Pets:** Small. $50 one-time fee/room. Service with restrictions.

▼▼ **Quality Inn-University Area** H

(434) 971-3746. **Call for rates.** 1600 Emmet St 22901. US 29 (Emmet St), just n of jct US 250 Bypass, then just e on Holiday Dr. Ext corridors. **Pets:** Accepted. ✕ ⊟ ▣

▲▲▲ ▼▼ **Red Roof Inn of Charlottesville** H

(434) 295-4333. **$80-$176.** 1309 W Main St 22903. US 29 (Emmet St), 1 mi e on US 250 (University Ave). Int corridors. **Pets:** Large. Service with restrictions, crate. SAVE ✕ ⊟

▲▲▲ ▼▼▼ **Residence Inn by Marriott** H ❀

(434) 923-0300. **$139-$169.** 1111 Millmont St 22903. I-64, exit 118B (US 29), 2.5 mi n on US 29/250 E, just s on Barracks Rd, then just se. Int corridors. **Pets:** Other species. $100 one-time fee/room. Service with restrictions, crate. ECO SAVE ✕ ⊟ ▣ ➜ ✕

▲▲▲ ▼▼▼ **Sleep Inn & Suites Monticello** H

(434) 244-9969. **$89-$213, 3 day notice.** 1185 5th St 22902. I-64, exit 120, just n. Int corridors. **Pets:** Accepted. SAVE ✕ ⊟ ▣ ➜

CHINCOTEAGUE

▲▲▲ ▼▼▼ **Americas Best Value Inn & Suites** M

(757) 336-6562. **$60-$199, 10 day notice.** 6151 Maddox Blvd 23336. Just e on Maddox Blvd. Ext corridors. **Pets:** Medium, dogs only. $10 daily fee/pet. Designated rooms, service with restrictions, crate.

SAVE ✕ ⊟ ▣ ➜

▼▼ **Quality Inn** H

(757) 336-6565. **$35-$280.** 6273 Maddox Blvd 23336. Just e on Maddox Blvd. Ext corridors. **Pets:** Accepted. ASK ✕ ⊟ ▣ ➜ ✕

CHRISTIANSBURG

▲▲▲ ▼▼ **Econo Lodge** M

(540) 382-6161. **$49-$189.** 2430 Roanoke St 24073. I-81, exit 118, just w on US 11/460. Ext corridors. **Pets:** Accepted.

SAVE ✕ ⚑ ⊟ ▣ ➜

▲▲▲ ▼▼▼ **Quality Inn** M

(540) 382-2055. **$75-$85.** 50 Hampton Blvd 24073. I-81, exit 118C, just e. Ext corridors. **Pets:** Other species. $10 daily fee/room. Service with restrictions, crate. SAVE ✕ ⊟ ▣ ➜

▲▲▲ ▼▼▼ **Super 8-Christiansburg East** M

(540) 382-7421. **$50-$169, 3 day notice.** 2780 Roanoke Rd 24073. I-81, exit 118C, just e. Ext corridors. **Pets:** Accepted.

SAVE ✕ ⊟ ▣ ➜

▼▼ **Super 8-Christiansburg West** M

(540) 382-5813. **$58-$63.** 55 Laurel St NE 24073. I-81, exit 118, 1 mi w on US 11/460, then 3.5 mi nw on US 460 Bypass; jct SR 114. Int corridors. **Pets:** Medium. $10 daily fee/pet. Designated rooms, service with restrictions, supervision. ASK ✕ ⊟

CLARKSVILLE

▲▲▲ ▼▼▼ **Best Western On The Lake** H

(434) 374-5023. **$85-$110, 3 day notice.** 103 Second St 23927. Just n of US 58 business route; downtown. Int corridors. **Pets:** $100 deposit/pet, $20 daily fee/pet. Designated rooms, service with restrictions, supervision.

SAVE ✕ ⚑ ⊟ ▣ ➜

COLLINSVILLE

▲▲▲ ▼▼ **Knights Inn** M

(276) 647-3716. **$55-$70.** 2357 Virginia Ave 24078. Jct US 58, 3 mi n on US 220 business route. Ext corridors. **Pets:** Medium. $5 one-time fee/pet. Service with restrictions, supervision. SAVE ✕ ⊟ ➜

▼▼▼ **Quality Inn-Dutch Inn Hotel and Convention Center** H

(276) 647-3721. **$80-$300.** 2360 Virginia Ave 24078. Jct US 58, 3 mi n on US 220 business route. Ext corridors. **Pets:** $10 daily fee/pet. Service with restrictions, crate. ASK ✕ ⊟ ▣ ▯▯ ➜

COVINGTON

▲▲▲ ▼▼ **Best Western Mountain View** H

(540) 962-4951. **$99-$115.** 820 E Madison St 24426. I-64, exit 16, just n. Ext corridors. **Pets:** Other species. $12 one-time fee/room. Service with restrictions, supervision. SAVE ✕ ⊟ ▣ ▯▯ ➜

CULPEPER

▼▼ **Comfort Inn-Culpeper** M

(540) 825-4900. **Call for rates.** 890 Willis Ln 22701. 2 mi s on US 29 business route; jct US 29, then just e. Ext corridors. **Pets:** Accepted. ✕ ⊟ ➜

DALEVILLE

▲▲▲ ▼▼▼ **Howard Johnson Inn** M

(540) 992-1234. **$45-$79.** 437 Roanoke Rd 24083. I-81, exit 150B, just nw on US 220. Ext corridors. **Pets:** Accepted.

SAVE ✕ ⊟ ▣ ➜ ✕

DANVILLE

▼▼▼ **Comfort Inn & Suites** H

(434) 793-2000. **$79-$139, 14 day notice.** 100 Tower Dr 24540. US 58, just w of jct US 29 business route. Int corridors. **Pets:** Accepted.

ASK ✕ ⊟ ▣ ▯▯ ➜

▼▼▼ **Courtyard by Marriott** H

(434) 791-2661. **$98-$120.** 2136 Riverside Dr 24540. On US 58, just w of jct US 29 business route. Int corridors. **Pets:** Medium. $10 one-time fee/pet. Supervision. ✕ ⚑ ⊟ ▣ ➜

▼▼▼ **Holiday Inn Express Danville** H

(434) 793-4000. **Call for rates.** 2121 Riverside Dr 24541. US 58, 0.5 mi e of jct US 86 and 29. Ext/int corridors. **Pets:** Accepted.

✕ ⊟ ▣ ➜

▼▼▼ **Innkeeper Danville North** M

(434) 836-1700. **$52-$67, 3 day notice.** 1030 Piney Forest Rd 24540. US 29 N business route, 0.5 mi n of US 58. Ext corridors. **Pets:** Accepted. ASK ✕ ⊟ ➜

▼▼▼ **Innkeeper Danville West** H

(434) 799-1202. **$52-$67, 3 day notice.** 3020 Riverside Dr 24541. US 58 W, just w of jct US 29. Ext/int corridors. **Pets:** Accepted.

ASK ✕ ⊟ ➜

▼▼ **Super 8** M

(434) 799-5845. **$63-$150, 3 day notice.** 2385 Riverside Dr 24541. On US 58, just e of jct US 29 business route. Int corridors. **Pets:** $10 daily fee/pet. Service with restrictions, supervision. ASK ✕ ⊟ ▣

DISTRICT OF COLUMBIA METROPOLITAN AREA

ALEXANDRIA

◈ ▼▼▼ Comfort Inn Alexandria ℍ
(703) 922-9200. **$79-$119.** 5716 S Van Dorn St 22310. I-95/495, exit 173, 2 mi e of jct I-395 and 495. Int corridors. **Pets:** Small. $25 one-time fee/pet. Designated rooms, service with restrictions, supervision.
🆂🅰🆅🅴 ⊠ 🅱 🛢 📟 🍴 ⤳

▼▼ Extended StayAmerica-Washington, DC-Alexandria ℳ
(703) 941-9440. **$104-$204.** 205 N Breckinridge Pl 22312. I-395, exit 3B, 0.3 mi w on SR 236, 0.4 mi ne on Beauregard St, just e on Gloucester Rd, then just s. Int corridors. **Pets:** Other species. $25 daily fee/room. Designated rooms, service with restrictions, crate.
🅰🆂🅺 ⊠ 🅼 🛢 📟

▼▼▼ Hawthorn Suites Alexandria ℍ
(703) 370-1000. **$104-$200.** 420 N Van Dorn St 22304. I-395, exit 3A, 0.3 mi e on SR 236 to S Van Dorn St, then 0.5 mi n. Int corridors.
Pets: Accepted. ⊠ 🛢 📟 ⤳

▼▼▼ Hilton Alexandria Old Town ℍ
(703) 837-0440. **$119-$349.** 1767 King St 22314. I-95/495, exit 176B, 0.5 mi n on SR 241, 0.5 mi e on SR 236, then just ne on Diagonal Rd. Int corridors. **Pets:** Accepted. ⊠ 🛢 📟 🍴 ⤳ ⊠

◈ ▼▼▼▼ Holiday Inn Hotel & Suites-Historic District Alexandria ℍ
(703) 548-6300. **$69-$249.** 625 First St 22314. George Washington Memorial Pkwy, just e of jct 1st and Washington sts. Int corridors.
Pets: Accepted. 🆂🅰🆅🅴 ⊠ 🛢 📟 🍴 ⤳ ⊠

▼▼ Homestead Studio Suites Hotel-Washington DC-Alexandria ℍ
(703) 329-3399. **$94-$194.** 200 Bluestone Rd 22304. I-95/495, exit 174 (Eisenhower Ave Connector), just n to Eisenhower Ave, then 1.2 mi e. Int corridors. **Pets:** Other species. $25 daily fee/room. Designated rooms, service with restrictions, crate. 🅰🆂🅺 ⊠ 🅼 🛢 📟

◈ ▼▼▼ Hotel Monaco Alexandria ℍ ❀
(703) 549-6080. **Call for rates.** 480 King St 22314. On SR 7; between S Pitt and S Royal sts; just sw of City Hall. Int corridors. **Pets:** Other species. Service with restrictions, supervision. 🆂🅰🆅🅴 ⊠ 🍴 ⤳ ⊠

◈ ▼▼▼ ▼▼ Morrison House-A Kimpton Hotel ℍ
(703) 838-8000. **Call for rates.** 116 S Alfred St 22314. Jct King and S Alfred sts, just s. Int corridors. **Pets:** Accepted. 🅴🅲🅾 🆂🅰🆅🅴 ⊠ 🍴

◈ ▼▼ ▼▼ Red Roof Inn-Alexandria ℳ
(703) 960-5200. **$83-$121.** 5975 Richmond Hwy 22303. I-95/495, exit 177A, 0.5 mi s on US 1. Ext corridors. **Pets:** Large. Service with restrictions, crate. 🆂🅰🆅🅴 ⊠ 🅼 🛢

▼▼▼ Residence Inn by Marriott Alexandria at Carlyle ℍ
(703) 549-1155. **$260-$318.** 2345 Mill Rd 22314. I-95/495, exit 176B, just n on Telegraph Rd (SR 241N), just e on Pershing Ave and Stovall St, then just n; in Carlyle area. Int corridors. **Pets:** Accepted.
⊠ 🅼 🛢 📟

▼▼▼ Residence Inn by Marriott Alexandria-Old Town ℍ
(703) 548-5474. **$260-$318.** 1456 Duke St 22314. I-95/495, exit 176, 0.5 mi n on SR 241, then 0.7 mi e on SR 236. Int corridors. **Pets:** Accepted.
⊠ 🅼 🛢 📟 ⤳

◈ ▼▼▼ Sheraton Suites Old Town Alexandria ℍ ❀
(703) 836-4700. **Call for rates.** 801 N St Asaph St 22314. Just e of Washington St. Int corridors. **Pets:** Medium, dogs only. $25 one-time fee/pet. Designated rooms, service with restrictions, supervision.
🆂🅰🆅🅴 ⊠ 🛢 📟 🍴 ⤳ ⊠

◈ ▼▼▼ Washington Suites-Alexandria ℍ
(703) 370-9600. **$159-$409.** 100 S Reynolds St 22304. I-395, exit 3A, 0.8 mi e on SR 236 E (Duke St), then just s. Int corridors. **Pets:** Medium, other species. $20 daily fee/pet. Designated rooms, service with restrictions. 🆂🅰🆅🅴 ⊠ 🅼 🛢 📟 🍴 ⤳ ⊠

◈ ▼▼▼▼ The Westin Alexandria ℍ ❀
(703) 253-8600. **$129-$399.** 400 Courthouse Square 22314. I-95/495, exit 176B, just n on Telegraph Rd (SR 241 N), 0.4 mi e on SR 236, then just s on Dulaney St; opposite US Courthouse; in Carlyle area. Int corridors. **Pets:** Medium, dogs only. Service with restrictions, supervision.
🆂🅰🆅🅴 ⊠ 🅼 🛢 📟 🍴 ⤳ ⊠

ARLINGTON

▼▼▼ Arlington Court Suites Hotel, a Clarion Collection ℍ
(703) 524-4000. **$119-$499.** 1200 N Courthouse Rd 22201. 1.5 mi sw of Theodore Roosevelt Bridge on US 50. Int corridors. **Pets:** Medium. $10 daily fee/pet, $75 one-time fee/room. Designated rooms, service with restrictions, crate. 🅰🆂🅺 ⊠ 🛢 📟

◈ ▼▼▼ Hilton Arlington ℍ ❀
(703) 528-6000. **$86-$409.** 950 N Stafford St 22203. I-66, exit 71 (Glebe Rd/SR 120), 0.3 mi e of jct SR 120 and 237 (Glebe Rd and Fairfax Dr). Int corridors. **Pets:** Large, other species. $75 one-time fee/room. Service with restrictions, supervision. 🆂🅰🆅🅴 ⊠ 🛢 📟

◈ ▼▼▼ Hotel Palomar Arlington at Waterview ℍ
(703) 351-9170. **$129-$399.** 1121 N 19th St 22209. I-66, exit 73, just sw of Key Bridge; in Rosslyn area. Int corridors. **Pets:** Accepted.
🆂🅰🆅🅴 ⊠ 🅼 🍴

▼▼▼ Residence Inn by Marriott Arlington At Rosslyn ℍ
(703) 812-8400. **$209-$279.** 1651 N Oak St 22209. I-66, exit 73, 0.3 mi s on Fort Myer Dr, 0.3 mi w on Wilson Blvd to N Pierce St, then 2 blks e on Clarendon Blvd; 2 blks from Rosslyn Metro Station. Int corridors. **Pets:** Medium, other species. $100 one-time fee/room. Service with restrictions, supervision. ⊠ 🛢 📟

▼▼▼ Residence Inn by Marriott-Pentagon City ℍ
(703) 413-6630. **$296-$362.** 550 Army Navy Dr 22202. I-395, exit 8C, just 1 mi s of 14th St Bridge. Int corridors. **Pets:** Accepted.
🅴🅲🅾 ⊠ 🅼 🛢 📟 ⤳ ⊠

▼▼▼ ▼▼ The Ritz-Carlton, Pentagon City ℍ ❀
(703) 415-5000. **Call for rates.** 1250 S Hayes St 22202. 1 mi s of 14th St Bridge. Int corridors. **Pets:** Large. $125 one-time fee/pet. Designated rooms. ⊠ 🅼 🛢 📟 ⤳ ⊠

◈ ▼▼▼ Sheraton Crystal City Hotel ℍ ❀
(703) 486-1111. **Call for rates.** 1800 Jefferson Davis Hwy 22202. I-395, exit 8C, 1.4 mi s of 14th St Bridge on US 1; hotel entrance, corner of Eads St. Int corridors. **Pets:** Medium, dogs only. Service with restrictions, supervision. 🆂🅰🆅🅴 ⊠ 🛢 📟 🍴 ⤳ ⊠

◈ ▼▼▼ Sheraton National Hotel ℍ
(703) 521-1900. **Call for rates.** 900 S Orme St 22204. I-395, exit 8A, at SR 27 and 244; 1.3 mi s of 14th St Bridge. Int corridors. **Pets:** Accepted. 🆂🅰🆅🅴 ⊠ 🛢 📟 🍴 ⤳

▼▼▼ Virginian Suites, Arlington ℍ
(703) 522-9600. **Call for rates.** 1500 Arlington Blvd 22209. 1 mi w of Theodore Roosevelt Bridge on US 50. Int corridors. **Pets:** Accepted.
⊠ 🛢 📟 ⤳ ⊠

◈ ▼▼▼ The Westin Arlington Gateway ℍ ❀
(703) 717-6200. **$139-$459.** 801 N Glebe Rd 22203. I-66, exit 71, just e on Fairfax Dr to Vermont Ave; just n of jct SR 120 and Wilson Blvd; 2 blks from metro station. Int corridors. **Pets:** Service with restrictions.
🅴🅲🅾 🆂🅰🆅🅴 ⊠ 🅼 🛢 📟 🍴 ⤳ ⊠

ASHBURN

aloft Dulles North 🏨 ❖

(703) 723-6969. **$89-$259.** 22390 Flagstaff Plaza 20148. On Loudoun County Pkwy (CR 607), just s of jct SR 267 (Toll Rd). Int corridors. **Pets:** Medium, dogs only. Designated rooms, service with restrictions, supervision. ⊞ ⊞ ⊠ ⌖ ⊟ ⊡ ⇌

Homewood Suites by Hilton/Dulles North 🏨

(703) 723-7500. **$149-$299.** 44620 Waxpool Rd 20147. 1.7 mi w of jct SR 28 and Waxpool Rd (SR 625); SR 7, 3.4 mi s on Loudoun County Pkwy (CR 607), 0.3 mi w. Int corridors. **Pets:** Accepted.

⊠ ⌖ ⊟ ⊡ ⇌

CENTREVILLE

Extended StayAmerica-Washington DC-Centreville 🏨

(703) 988-9955. **$99-$169.** 5920 Fort Dr 20121. I-66, exit 53, 0.9 mi s on SR 28; off SR 28, 0.3 mi s of jct US 29. Int corridors. **Pets:** Other species. $25 daily fee/room. Designated rooms, service with restrictions, crate. ⊞ ⊠ ⊟ ⊡

CHANTILLY

Extended Stay Deluxe Washington DC-Chantilly 🏨

(703) 263-7200. **$109-$199.** 4506 Brookfield Corporate Dr 20151. I-66, exit 53, 3 mi n on SR 28; 1 mi s of jct SR 28 and US 50. Int corridors. **Pets:** Other species. $25 daily fee/room. Designated rooms, service with restrictions, crate. ⊞ ⊠ ⌖ ⊟ ⊡ ⇌ ⊠

Holiday Inn Chantilly-Dulles Expo Center 🏨

(703) 815-6060. **$179-$249.** 4335 Chantilly Shopping Center 20151. I-66, exit 53, 3 mi n on SR 28; 1 mi s of jct US 50 and SR 28. Int corridors. **Pets:** Accepted. ⊞ ⊠ ⌖ ⊟ ⊡ ⌴ ⇌ ⊠

Residence Inn by Marriott Chantilly Dulles South 🏨

(703) 263-7900. **$233-$285.** 14440 Chantilly Crossing Ln 20151. I-66, exit 57B, on US 50, just w of jct SR 28. Int corridors. **Pets:** Large, other species. $100 one-time fee/room. Service with restrictions.

⊞ ⊠ ⌖ ⊟ ⊡ ⇌ ⊠

Staybridge Suites Hotel Chantilly/Dulles International Airport 🏨 ❖

(703) 435-8090. **$99-$299.** 3860 Centerview Dr 20151. Jct SR 28, just e on US 50. Int corridors. **Pets:** Medium. $75 one-time fee/room. Designated rooms, service with restrictions, crate.

⊞ ⊞ ⊠ ⌖ ⊟ ⊡ ⇌

TownePlace Suites by Marriott-Chantilly 🏨

(703) 709-0453. **$179-$219.** 14036 Thunderbolt Pl 20151. Jct SR 28, just e on US 50. Int corridors. **Pets:** Other species. $75 one-time fee/room. Service with restrictions. ⊠ ⊟ ⊡ ⇌ ⊠

Wingate by Wyndham Dulles Airport-Chantilly 🏨

(571) 203-0999. **$145-$269.** 3940 Centerview Dr 20151. Jct SR 28, just e on US 50. Int corridors. **Pets:** Medium. $75 one-time fee/room. Service with restrictions, supervision. ⊞ ⊠ ⌖ ⊟ ⊡ ⇌ ⊠

FAIRFAX

Candlewood Suites Fairfax-Washington, D.C. 🏨

(703) 359-4490. **$69-$159.** 11400 Random Hills Rd 22030. I-66, exit 57A, 0.5 mi e on US 50, just s on Waples Mill Rd, then 0.4 mi w. Int corridors. **Pets:** Medium. $75 one-time fee/pet. Service with restrictions, supervision.

⊠ ⌖ ⊟ ⊡

Comfort Inn University Center 🏨 ❖

(703) 591-5900. **$70-$189, 3 day notice.** 11180 Fairfax Blvd 22030. I-66, exit 57A, 0.8 mi se on US 50, then 0.5 mi nw of jct US 29. Int corridors. **Pets:** Medium, other species. $25 daily fee/room. Designated rooms, service with restrictions, crate. ⊞ ⊠ ⊟ ⊡ ⌴ ⇌ ⊠

Extended Stay Deluxe Washington DC-Fairfax 🏨

(703) 359-5000. **$89-$199.** 3997 Fair Ridge Dr 22033. I-66, exit 57B, 1.2 mi w on US 50. Int corridors. **Pets:** Other species. $25 daily fee/room. Designated rooms, service with restrictions, crate.

⊞ ⊠ ⌖ ⊟ ⊡ ⇌

Homestead Studio Suites Hotel-Washington DC-Fairfax-Fair Oaks 🅼

(703) 273-3444. **$74-$179.** 12104 Monument Dr 22033. I-66, exit 57B, 0.8 mi w on US 50, 0.3 mi s on SR 620 (West Ox Rd), then just se. Ext corridors. **Pets:** Other species. $25 daily fee/room. Designated rooms, service with restrictions, crate. ⊞ ⊠ ⌖ ⊟ ⊡

Homestead Studio Suites Washington DC-Falls Church-Merrifield 🏨

(703) 204-0088. **$94-$194.** 8281 Willow Oaks Corporate Dr 22031. I-495, exit 50A, just w on US 50 to Gallows Rd, then just s. Ext corridors. **Pets:** Other species. $25 daily fee/room. Designated rooms, service with restrictions, crate. ⊞ ⊠ ⌖ ⊟ ⊡

Residence Inn by Marriott-Fair Lakes 🏨

(703) 266-4900. **$206-$252.** 12815 Fair Lakes Pkwy 22033. I-66, exit 55 (Fairfax County Pkwy N), just w. Int corridors. **Pets:** Medium. $150 one-time fee/room. Service with restrictions. ⊠ ⌖ ⊟ ⊡ ⇌ ⊠

FALLS CHURCH

Homewood Suites by Hilton-Falls Church 🏨

(703) 560-6644. **$159-$269.** 8130 Porter Rd 22042. I-495, exit 50A, just w to SR 650; 0.4 mi n of SR 650. Int corridors. **Pets:** Medium, dogs only. $100 one-time fee/room. Service with restrictions, crate.

⊠ ⌖ ⊟ ⊡ ⇌ ⊠

Residence Inn by Marriott Fairfax-Merrifield 🏨 ❖

(703) 573-5200. **$242-$296.** 8125 Gatehouse Rd 22042. I-495, exit 50A, just w to SR 640 N. Int corridors. **Pets:** Other species. $100 one-time fee/room. ⊠ ⌖ ⊟ ⊡ ⇌ ⊠

TownePlace Suites by Marriott-Falls Church 🏨 ❖

(703) 237-6172. **$206-$252.** 205 Hillwood Ave 22046. I-495, exit 50B, 2.5 mi e on US 50, 0.6 mi n on Annandale Rd (CR 649), then e; just s of US 29. Int corridors. **Pets:** Other species. $100 one-time fee/room. Service with restrictions, crate. ⊠ ⌖ ⊟ ⊡ ⇌ ⊠

The Westin Tysons Corner 🏨 ❖

(703) 893-1340. **$89-$299.** 7801 Leesburg Pike 22043. I-495, exit 47B, just e on SR 7. Int corridors. **Pets:** Medium, dogs only.

⊞ ⊠ ⊟ ⊡ ⌴ ⇌ ⊠

HERNDON

Candlewood Suites Washington-Dulles Herndon 🏨 ❖

(703) 793-7100. **$59-$159.** 13845 Sunrise Valley Dr 20171. SR 28, 0.4 mi e on Frying Pan Rd, 0.7 mi nw. Int corridors. **Pets:** Large. $150 one-time fee/room. Service with restrictions, crate. ⊞ ⊠ ⌖ ⊟ ⊡

Comfort Inn Dulles International Airport 🏨

(703) 437-7555. **$79-$169.** 200 Elden St 20170. Just w on CR 606 from jct CR 7100 (Fairfax County Pkwy). Int corridors. **Pets:** Small, other species. $25 daily fee/room. Designated rooms, service with restrictions, supervision. ⊞ ⊠ ⊟ ⊡

Extended StayAmerica-Washington DC-Herndon 🅼

(703) 481-5363. **$99-$189.** 1021 Elden St 20170. 0.8 mi n on SR 657 of jct SR 267 (Dulles Toll Rd), exit 10. Int corridors. **Pets:** Other species. $25 daily fee/room. Designated rooms, service with restrictions, crate.

⊠ ⌖ ⊟ ⊡

Hilton Washington Dulles Airport 🏨

(703) 478-2900. **$89-$299.** 13869 Park Center Rd 20171. SR 267 (Dulles Toll Rd), exit 9, 3 mi s on SR 28; at McLearen Blvd (SR 668). Int corridors. **Pets:** Accepted.

⊞ ⊞ ⊠ ⌖ ⊟ ⊡ ⌴ ⇌ ⊠

Hyatt Summerfield Suites Herndon 🏨

(703) 437-5000. **$195-$225.** 467 Herndon Pkwy 20170. SR 267 (Dulles Toll Rd), exit 11 CR 7100 (Fairfax County Pkwy), just n to Spring St exit, just s to Herndon Pkwy (CR 606), just w on CR 606. Int corridors. **Pets:** Medium. $25 daily fee/pet. Designated rooms, service with restrictions, supervision. ⊞ ⊠ ⊟ ⊡ ⇌ ⊠

▼▼◆◆ Residence Inn by
Marriott-Herndon/Reston **H** ❀
(703) 435-0044. **$242-$296.** 315 Elden St 20170. 0.4 mi w on CR 606 from jct CR 7100 (Fairfax County Pkwy). Int corridors. **Pets:** Other species. $75 one-time fee/room. Service with restrictions, crate.
⊠ 🗄 💻 ➦ ⊠

▼▼◆◆ Staybridge Suites Herndon Dulles **H**
(703) 713-6800. **$79-$199.** 13700 Coppermine Rd 20171. SR 267 (Dulles Toll Rd), exit 10, 0.7 mi s on Centreville Rd (SR 657), then 0.4 mi w. Ext corridors. **Pets:** Medium. $75 one-time fee/room. Service with restrictions, crate. 🅰🆂🅺 ⊠ 🗄 💻 ➦ ⊠

LEESBURG

◆◆◆ ▼◆◆◆ Best Western Leesburg Hotel & Conference
Center **H** ❀
(703) 777-9400. **$99-$149.** 726 E Market St 20176. 0.5 mi e on SR 7 business route. Int corridors. **Pets:** Medium. $10 daily fee/room. Service with restrictions, crate. 🆂🅰🆅🅴 ⊠ 🗄 💻 ➦

▼◆▼◆ Holiday Inn Leesburg at Historic Carradoc Hall **H**
(703) 771-9200. **Call for rates.** 1500 E Market St 20176. 2 mi e on SR 7. Int corridors. **Pets:** Accepted. ⊠ 🗄ᴹ 🗄 💻 ❚❙ ➦

◆◆◆ ▼◆◆◆ ▼◆◆◆ Lansdowne Resort **H**
(703) 729-8400. **$139-$1200, 3 day notice.** 44050 Woodridge Pkwy 20176. SR 7, 3.6 mi w of jct SR 28; 4.4 mi e of jct US 15. Int corridors. **Pets:** Small, dogs only. $125 one-time fee/room. Designated rooms, service with restrictions, supervision.
🆂🅰🆅🅴 ⊠ 🗄ᴹ 🗄 💻 ❚❙ ➦ ⊠

LORTON

▼◆◆◆ Comfort Inn Gunston Corner **H**
(703) 643-3100. **$129-$159.** 8180 Silverbrook Rd 22079. I-95, exit 163, just w. Int corridors. **Pets:** Other species. $25 one-time fee/pet. Designated rooms, service with restrictions, supervision.
🅰🆂🅺 ⊠ 🗄 💻 ➦ ⊠

MANASSAS

◆◆◆ ▼◆◆◆ Best Western Battlefield Inn **H**
(703) 361-8000. **$89-$175.** 10820 Balls Ford Rd 20109. I-66, exit 47A westbound; exit 47 eastbound, just s on SR 234 business route. Ext corridors. **Pets:** Dogs only. $10 daily fee/pet. Service with restrictions, crate.
🆂🅰🆅🅴 ⊠ 🗄 💻 ❚❙ ➦

▼◆◆◆ Comfort Suites Manassas **H**
(703) 686-1100. **$99-$129.** 7350 Williamson Blvd 20109. I-66, exit 47A westbound; exit 47 eastbound, 0.5 mi s on SR 234 business route, then just e. Int corridors. **Pets:** Accepted. 🅰🆂🅺 ⊠ 🗄 💻 ➦ ⊠

◆◆◆ ▼◆◆ Red Roof Inn-Manassas **M**
(703) 335-9333. **Call for rates.** 10610 Automotive Dr 20109. I-66, exit 47 eastbound; exit 47A westbound, just s on SR 234 business route, then just e on Balls Ford Rd. Ext corridors. **Pets:** Large. Service with restrictions, crate. 🆂🅰🆅🅴 ⊠ 🗄ᴹ 🗄

▼◆◆◆ Residence Inn by Marriott Manassas Battlefield **H**
(703) 330-8808. **$144-$176.** 7345 Williamson Blvd 20109. I-66, exit 47A westbound; exit 47 eastbound, 0.5 mi s on SR 234 business route, then just e. Int corridors. **Pets:** Medium, other species. $100 one-time fee/ room. Designated rooms, service with restrictions, crate.
⊠ 🗄ᴹ 🗄 💻 ➦ ⊠

MCLEAN

◆◆◆ ▼◆◆◆ Best Western Tysons Westpark Hotel **H**
(703) 734-2800. **$90-$200.** 8401 Westpark Dr 22102. I-495, exit 47A, 1.3 mi w on SR 7. Int corridors. **Pets:** $10 daily fee/room. Service with restrictions, crate. 🆂🅰🆅🅴 ⊠ 🗄ᴹ 🗄 💻 ❚❙ ➦

◆◆◆ ▼◆◆◆ Crowne Plaza Tysons Corner **H**
(703) 893-2100. **$99-$259.** 1960 Chain Bridge Rd 22102. I-495, exit 46A, 0.5 mi s on SR 123, just nw on International Dr, then just sw on Greens-boro Dr. Int corridors. **Pets:** Accepted.
🄴🄲🄾 🆂🅰🆅🅴 ⊠ 🗄ᴹ 🗄 💻 ❚❙ ➦ ⊠

▼◆◆◆ Hilton McLean Tysons Corner **H**
(703) 847-5000. **$79-$319.** 7920 Jones Branch Dr 22102. I-495, exit 46A, 0.3 mi sw on SR 123, just nw on Tysons Blvd, 0.4 mi ne on Galleria/Westpark Dr, then just s. Int corridors. **Pets:** Accepted.
⊠ 🗄ᴹ 🗄 💻 ❚❙ ➦

▼◆◆◆ ▼◆◆◆ The Ritz-Carlton, Tysons Corner **H**
(703) 506-4300. **$159-$349.** 1700 Tysons Blvd 22102. I-495, exit 46A, 0.3 mi sw on SR 123, then just nw. Int corridors. **Pets:** Accepted.
🄴🄲🄾 ⊠ 🗄ᴹ 🗄 💻 ❚❙ ➦ ⊠

◆◆◆ ▼◆◆◆ Staybridge Suites-McLean/Tysons
Corner **H**
(703) 448-5400. **$129-$349.** 6845 Old Dominion Dr 22101. I-495, exit 46B, 2 mi n on SR 123, then 0.3 mi e on SR 309. Int corridors.
Pets: Accepted. 🆂🅰🆅🅴 ⊠ 🗄ᴹ 🗄 💻 ➦ ⊠

RESTON

▼◆▼◆ Homestead Studio Suites Washington
DC-Reston **M**
(703) 707-9700. **$119-$229.** 12190 Sunset Hills Rd 20190. SR 267 (Dulles Toll Rd), exit 12 (Reston Pkwy), just n, then just w. Ext corridors. **Pets:** Other species. $25 daily fee/room. Designated rooms, service with restrictions, crate. 🅰🆂🅺 ⊠ 🗄 💻

◆◆◆ ▼◆◆◆ Sheraton Reston Hotel **H**
(703) 620-9000. **Call for rates.** 11810 Sunrise Valley Dr 20191. SR 267 (Dulles Toll Rd), exit 12 (Reston Pkwy), just s. Int corridors.
Pets: Accepted. 🆂🅰🆅🅴 ⊠ 🗄ᴹ 🗄 💻 ❚❙ ➦

◆◆◆ ▼◆◆◆ The Westin Reston Heights **H** ❀
(703) 391-9000. **Call for rates.** 11750 Sunrise Valley Dr 20191. SR 267 (Dulles Toll Rd), exit 12 (Reston Pkwy), just s. Int corridors.
Pets: Medium, dogs only. Designated rooms, service with restrictions, supervision. 🆂🅰🆅🅴 ⊠ 🗄ᴹ 💻 ❚❙ ➦ ⊠

SPRINGFIELD

▼◆▼◆ Comfort Inn Washington DC/Springfield **H**
(703) 922-9000. **$80-$139.** 6560 Loisdale Ct 22150. I-95, exit 169A, just e on SR 644 E; jct I-395 and 495, 0.8 mi s. Int corridors. **Pets:** Large, other species. Service with restrictions, crate. 🅰🆂🅺 ⊠ 🗄 💻

▼◆▼◆ Extended StayAmerica-Washington,
DC-Springfield **H**
(703) 822-0992. **$104-$204.** 6800 Metropolitan Center Dr 22150. I-95, exit 169A, just e on SR 644, 0.6 mi s on Loisdale Rd, then just e. Int corridors. **Pets:** Other species. $25 daily fee/room. Designated rooms, service with restrictions, crate. 🅰🆂🅺 ⊠ 🗄ᴹ 🗄 💻 ➦

▼◆▼◆ Hampton Inn Washington DC/Springfield **H**
(703) 924-9444. **Call for rates.** 6550 Loisdale Ct 22150. I-95, exit 169A, just e on SR 644 E; jct I-395 and 495, 0.8 mi s. Int corridors.
Pets: Accepted. ⊠ 🗄ᴹ 🗄 💻 ➦

◆◆◆ ▼◆▼◆ Hilton Springfield **H** ❀
(703) 971-8900. **$109-$339.** 6550 Loisdale Rd 22150. I-95, exit 169A, just e on SR 644 E; jct I-395 and 495, 0.7 mi s. Int corridors.
Pets: Medium. $75 one-time fee/pet. Service with restrictions, supervision.
🆂🅰🆅🅴 ⊠ 🗄ᴹ 🗄 💻 ❚❙ ➦ ⊠

▼◆▼◆ Motel 6 Washington DC SW-Springfield **H**
(703) 644-5311. **Call for rates.** 6868 Springfield Blvd 22150. I-95, exit 169B, just sw of SR 644; jct I-395 and 495, 0.8 mi s. Int corridors.
Pets: Other species. Service with restrictions, supervision. ⊠ 🗄ᴹ 🗄

▼◆▼◆ TownePlace Suites by Marriott Springfield **H**
(703) 569-8060. **$220-$230.** 6245 Brandon Ave 22150. I-95, exit 169B, just nw of SR 644; jct I-395 and 495, 0.8 mi s. Int corridors. **Pets:** Other species. $75 one-time fee/room. Service with restrictions, supervision.
⊠ 🗄ᴹ 🗄 💻 ➦

STERLING

Best Western Dulles Airport Inn M
(703) 471-8300. **$69-$120.** 45440 Holiday Dr 20166. 1.7 mi n on SR 28 from jct SR 267 (Dulles Toll Rd), just e on CR 846, then just s on Shaw Rd. Ext corridors. **Pets:** Accepted.

Candlewood Suites Washington Dulles/Sterling H
(703) 674-2288. **Call for rates.** 45520 E Severn Way 20166. 1.6 mi s on SR 28 from jct SR 7, 0.3 mi e. Int corridors. **Pets:** Accepted.

Extended StayAmerica-Washington DC-Sterling M
(703) 444-7240. **$99-$169.** 46001 Waterview Plaza 20166. 1.3 mi e on SR 7 from jct SR 28. Int corridors. **Pets:** Other species. $25 daily fee/room. Designated rooms, service with restrictions, crate.

Hampton Inn-Dulles/Cascades H
(703) 450-9595. **Call for rates.** 46331 McClellan Way 20165. 1.7 mi e on SR 7, from jct SR 28, 0.5 mi n on CR 1794 (Cascades Pkwy) to Palisade Pkwy, just e, then 0.4 mi s on Whitfield Pl. Int corridors. **Pets:** Service with restrictions, crate.

Holiday Inn Washington Dulles International Airport H
(703) 471-7411. **$89-$209.** 45425 Holiday Dr 20166. 1.7 mi n on SR 28 from jct SR 267 (Dulles Toll Rd), just e on CR 846, then just s on Shaw Rd. Int corridors. **Pets:** Accepted.

Residence Inn by Marriott Dulles Airport @ Dulles 28 Center H
(703) 421-2000. **$233-$285.** 45250 Monterey Pl 20166. SR 28, exit CR 625 (Waxpool Rd), just w, just n on Pacific Blvd, then just e on Commercial Dr. Int corridors. **Pets:** Large. $150 one-time fee/room. Service with restrictions.

Suburban Extended Stay Hotel Washington-Dulles/Sterling H
(703) 674-2299. **$99-$999.** 45510 Severn Way 20166. 1.6 mi s on SR 28 from jct SR 7, 0.3 mi e. Int corridors. **Pets:** Accepted.

TownePlace Suites by Marriott at Dulles Airport H
(703) 707-2017. **$152-$186.** 22744 Holiday Park Dr 20166. 1.7 mi n on SR 28 from jct SR 267 (Dulles Toll Rd), just e on CR 846, then just s on Shaw Rd. Int corridors. **Pets:** Accepted.

TownePlace Suites by Marriott Sterling H
(703) 421-1090. **$116-$142.** 21123 Whitfield Pl 20165. 1.7 mi e on SR 7 from jct SR 28, 0.5 mi n on SR 1794 (Cascades Pkwy) to Palisades Pkwy, just e, then just s. Int corridors. **Pets:** Large, other species. $100 one-time fee/room. Service with restrictions.

VIENNA

Comfort Inn Tysons Corner M
(703) 448-8020. **$70-$230.** 1587 Spring Hill Rd 22182. I-495, exit 47A, 1.8 mi w on SR 7, then just s; just e of jct SR 267 (Dulles Toll Rd). Ext corridors. **Pets:** Accepted.

Homestead Studio Suites Hotel-Washington DC-Tysons Corner H
(703) 356-6300. **$104-$214.** 8201 Old Courthouse Rd 22182. I-495, exit 47A, 0.6 mi w on SR 7, then just s on Gallows Rd. Int corridors. **Pets:** Other species. $25 daily fee/room. Designated rooms, service with restrictions, crate.

Residence Inn by Marriott-Tysons Corner H ❀
(703) 893-0120. **$224-$274.** 8616 Westwood Center Dr 22182. I-495, exit 47A, 1.9 mi w on SR 7, then just s. Ext corridors. **Pets:** Medium, other species. $100 one-time fee/room. Service with restrictions, crate.

Residence Inn by Marriott Tysons Corner Mall H
(703) 917-0800. **$215-$263.** 8400 Old Courthouse Rd 22182. I-495, exit 46A, 1.1 mi s on SR 123; 0.3 mi s of jct SR 7 and 123. Int corridors. **Pets:** Large, other species. $75 one-time fee/room. Designated rooms, service with restrictions.

Sheraton Premiere At Tysons Corner H ❀
(703) 448-1234. **$69-$349.** 8661 Leesburg Pike 22182. SR 7, just e of jct SR 267 (Dulles Toll Rd). Int corridors. **Pets:** Medium. $50 deposit/room. Designated rooms, supervision.

WOODBRIDGE

Residence Inn by Marriott Potomac Mills H
(703) 490-4020. **$159-$199.** 14301 Crossing Pl 22192. I-95, exit 158B (Prince William Pkwy), 0.5 mi sw. Int corridors. **Pets:** Medium, other species. $100 one-time fee/room. Service with restrictions.

END METROPOLITAN AREA

EMPORIA

Best Western Emporia H
(434) 634-3200. **$65-$85.** 1100 W Atlantic St 23847. I-95, exit 11B, just w on US 58. Ext corridors. **Pets:** Other species. $10 daily fee/pet. Service with restrictions, crate.

Country Inn & Suites By Carlson H
(434) 336-0001. **$79-$149.** 107 Sadler Ln 23847. I-95, exit 11A, just e. Int corridors. **Pets:** Medium. $15 daily fee/pet. Designated rooms, service with restrictions, supervision.

Days Inn-Emporia H
(434) 634-9481. **$59-$80.** 921 W Atlantic St 23847. I-95, exit 11B, just w on US 58. Ext corridors. **Pets:** Other species. $10 daily fee/pet. Service with restrictions, supervision.

Hampton Inn H
(434) 634-9200. **$99-$120.** 898 Wiggins Rd 23847. I-95, exit 11B, just w. Int corridors. **Pets:** Other species. Designated rooms, service with restrictions, supervision.

Quality Inn H
(434) 348-8888. **Call for rates.** 1207 W Atlantic St 23847. I-95, exit 11B, just w on US 58. Ext corridors. **Pets:** Accepted.

Sleep Inn H
(434) 348-3900. **$69-$119.** 899 Wiggins Rd 23847. I-95, exit 11B, just e on US 58, then just s. Int corridors. **Pets:** Other species. $10 one-time fee/pet. Designated rooms, service with restrictions, supervision.

EXMORE

Best Western Eastern Shore Inn H
(757) 442-7378. **$70-$150.** 2543 Lankford Hwy 23350. US 13, just n of SR 178. Ext/int corridors. **Pets:** $15 daily fee/room. Service with restrictions, supervision.

Holiday Inn Express & Suites H
(757) 442-5522. **Call for rates.** 3446 Lankford Hwy 23350. On US 13. Int corridors. **Pets:** Medium, other species. $25 daily fee/room. Service with restrictions, supervision.

FANCY GAP

▼▼ Days Inn **M**

(276) 728-5101. **$50-$75.** 142 Kelly Rd 24328. I-77, exit 8, 0.3 mi w; on top of the hill. Ext/int corridors. **Pets:** Accepted. 🆎 ☒ 📳 💻

▼▼ Doe Run Lodging at Groundhog Mountain **CO**

(276) 398-4099. **$99-$500, 3 day notice.** 27 Buck Hollar Rd 24328. MM 189.2 on Blue Ridge Parkway; 10 mi n from US 52. Ext corridors. **Pets:** Accepted. 🆎 ☒ 📳 💻

FRANKLIN

▼ Super 8 **M**

(757) 562-2888. **Call for rates.** 1599 Armory Dr 23851. Jct US 58 Bypass and SR 671. Int corridors. **Pets:** Accepted. ☒ 📳 💻

FREDERICKSBURG

◈◈◈ ▼▼▼ Best Western Central Plaza **M**

(540) 786-7404. **$78-$99.** 3000 Plank Rd 22401. I-95, exit 130B on SR 3. Ext corridors. **Pets:** Large, other species. $10 daily fee/pet. Service with restrictions, supervision. [SAVE] ☒ 🔥 📳 💻

◈◈◈ ▼▼▼ Best Western Fredericksburg **H** ❀

(540) 371-5050. **$69-$109.** 2205 Plank Rd 22401. I-95, exit 130A, 0.3 mi e on SR 3. Ext corridors. **Pets:** $10 daily fee/pet. Designated rooms, service with restrictions, supervision. [SAVE] ☒ 🔥 📳 💻 🐾

◈◈◈ ▼▼▼ Clarion Hotel-Fredericksburg **H**

(540) 371-5550. **Call for rates.** 564 Warrenton Rd 22405. I-95, exit 133, just nw on US 17. Ext corridors. **Pets:** Medium. Service with restrictions, supervision. [SAVE] ☒ 📳 💻 🍴 🐾 ☒

◈◈◈ ▼▼▼ Comfort Inn Fredericksburg Southpoint **H**

(540) 898-5550. **$79-$109.** 5422 Jefferson Davis Hwy 22407. I-95, exit 126, just s on US 1; exit 126B northbound; in Southpoint. Int corridors. **Pets:** Accepted. [SAVE] ☒ 📳 💻 🐾 ☒

◈◈◈ ▼▼▼ Country Inn & Suites By Carlson, South **H** ❀

(540) 898-1800. **$98-$108.** 5327 Jefferson Davis Hwy 22408. I-95, exit 126 southbound; exit 126A northbound; just n on US 1. Int corridors. **Pets:** Medium. $10 daily fee/pet. Designated rooms, service with restrictions, crate. [SAVE] ☒ 📳 💻 🐾

◈◈◈ ▼▼▼ Fredericksburg Hospitality House Hotel & Conference Center **H**

(540) 786-8321. **$79-$169.** 2801 Plank Rd 22401. I-95, exit 130B (SR 3). Int corridors. **Pets:** Accepted. [SAVE] ☒ 🔥 📳 💻 🍴 🐾

▼▼ Quality Inn Fredericksburg **M** ❀

(540) 373-0000. **$59-$99.** 543 Warrenton Rd 22406. I-95, exit 133, just n on US 17. Ext corridors. **Pets:** Other species. $15 daily fee/pet. Service with restrictions. 🆎 ☒ 💻

◈◈◈ ▼▼ Quality Inn near Central Park **H**

(540) 371-0330. **Call for rates.** 2310 Plank Rd 22401. I-95, exit 130A on SR 3 E. Ext corridors. **Pets:** Accepted. [ECO] [SAVE] ☒ 📳 💻 🐾

▼▼▼ Residence Inn by Marriott **H**

(540) 786-9222. **$110-$140.** 60 Town Centre Blvd 22407. I-95, exit 130B (SR 3), just w to Spotsylvania Towne Centre (Mall Dr), then just s. Int corridors. **Pets:** Accepted. ☒ 🔥 📳 💻 🐾 ☒

▼▼▼ TownePlace Suites by Marriott **H**

(540) 891-0775. **$89-$109.** 4700 Market St 22408. I-95, exit 126 southbound; exit 126A northbound, just n on US 1, then just e. Int corridors. **Pets:** Accepted. ☒ 📳 💻 🐾

FRONT ROYAL

◈◈◈ ▼ Budget Inn **M**

(540) 635-2196. **$45-$65.** 1122 N Royal Ave 22630. I-66, exit 6, 2.2 mi s on US 340/522 and SR 55. Ext corridors. **Pets:** Medium. $10 daily fee/pet. Designated rooms, service with restrictions, crate. [SAVE] ☒ 📳

◈◈◈ ▼ Relax Inn **M** ❀

(540) 635-4101. **$45-$65.** 1801 Shenandoah Ave 22630. I-66, exit 6, 1.5 mi s on US 340/522. Ext corridors. **Pets:** Medium. $10 daily fee/pet. Service with restrictions, supervision. [SAVE] ☒ 📳 💻 🐾

GLADE SPRING

▼ Swiss Inn Motel & Suites **M**

(276) 429-5191. **Call for rates.** 33361 Lee Hwy 24340. I-81, exit 29, just e. Ext corridors. **Pets:** Accepted. ☒ 📳

GORDONSVILLE

◈◈◈ ▼▼▼ Best Western Crossroads Inn & Suites **H**

(540) 832-1700. **$105-$160.** 135 Wood Ridge Terr 22942. I-64, exit 136, just n. Int corridors. **Pets:** Other species. $15 daily fee/pet. Service with restrictions, crate. [SAVE] ☒ 📳 💻 🐾

GREENVILLE

◈◈◈ ▼ Budget Host-Historic Hessian House **M**

(540) 337-1231. **$45-$75, 3 day notice.** 3554 Lee Jackson Hwy 24401. I-81, exit 213, 0.3 mi e. Ext corridors. **Pets:** $7 daily fee/pet. Designated rooms, service with restrictions, crate. [SAVE] ☒ 📳

GRETNA

▼▼▼ Smith Mountain Lake Hampton Inn **H** ❀

(434) 656-9000. **$89-$159.** 200 McBride Ln 24557. On SR 40; jct US 29. Int corridors. **Pets:** Small, dogs only. Service with restrictions, supervision. ☒ 🔥 📳 💻 🐾

GRUNDY

▼▼▼ Comfort Inn **H**

(276) 935-5050. **Call for rates.** 22006 Riverside Dr 24614. On US 460, 0.5 mi e. Int corridors. **Pets:** Accepted. ☒ 🔥 📳 💻

HAMPTON ROADS AREA

CHESAPEAKE

▼▼▼ Candlewood Suites **H**

(757) 405-3030. **$75-$119.** 4809 Market Pl 23321. I-664, exit 11A (E Portsmouth Blvd/SR 337). Int corridors. **Pets:** Accepted. [ECO] 🆎 ☒ 🔥 📳 💻

▼▼ Extended StayAmerica Chesapeake-Greenbrier Circle **H**

(757) 523-7377. **$65-$115.** 809 Greenbrier Cir 23320. I-64, exit 289A (Greenbrier Pkwy), just n. Int corridors. **Pets:** Other species. $25 daily fee/room. Designated rooms, service with restrictions, crate. 🆎 ☒ 🔥 📳 💻

▼▼ Extended StayAmerica Hotel Chesapeake-Churchland Blvd **H**

(757) 483-9200. **$45-$90.** 3214 Churchland Blvd 23321. I-664, exit 9B northbound; exit 8B southbound, 1 mi s on US 17. Int corridors. **Pets:** Other species. $25 daily fee/room. Designated rooms, service with restrictions, crate. 🆎 ☒ 📳 💻

▼▼▼ Residence Inn by Marriott, Chesapeake-Greenbrier **H**

(757) 502-7300. **$179-$189.** 1500 Crossways Blvd 23320. I-64, exit 289B (Greenbrier Pkwy), just s to Jarman Rd (at Crossways Center) to Crossways Blvd, then 0.6 mi n. Int corridors. **Pets:** Accepted.

⊠ 🛢 💻 ⊰ ⊠

▼▼ Sleep Inn & Suites **H**

(757) 638-5000. **$70-$83.** 3280 Western Branch Blvd 23321. I-664, exit 9B, 1 mi s on SR 17. Int corridors. **Pets:** Accepted.

ECO ASK ⊠ 🖑 🛢 💻 ⊰

▼▼▼ Staybridge Suites Greenbrier **H**

(757) 420-2525. **$99-$159.** 709 Woodlake Dr 23320. I-64, exit 289A (Greenbrier Pkwy), just n. Int corridors. **Pets:** Accepted.

ASK ⊠ 🖑 🛢 💻 ⊰

▼ Super 8 **M** 🐾

(757) 686-8888. **$59-$102.** 3216 Churchland Blvd 23321. I-664, exit 9B, 1 mi s on SR 17. Int corridors. **Pets:** Other species. $10 daily fee/room. Designated rooms, service with restrictions, crate. ASK ⊠ 🛢 💻

▼▼ TownePlace Suites By Marriott **H**

(757) 523-5004. **$129-$139.** 2000 Old Greenbrier Rd 23320. I-64, exit 289A (Greenbrier Pkwy), just n. Int corridors. **Pets:** Other species. $75 one-time fee/room. Service with restrictions, supervision.

⊠ 🖑 🛢 💻 ⊰

GLOUCESTER

▼▼▼ Comfort Inn Gloucester **H**

(804) 695-1900. **$77-$90.** 6639 Forest Hill Ave 23061. US 17, just s. Int corridors. **Pets:** Accepted. ASK ⊠ 🛢 💻 ⊰

HAMPTON

⟨AAA⟩ ▼▼▼ Best Western Coliseum Inn & Suites **H**

(757) 838-5011. **$80-$110, 3 day notice.** 1809 W Mercury Blvd 23666. I-64, exit 263B (Mercury Blvd), jct SR 58. Int corridors. **Pets:** Medium. $25 one-time fee/room. Designated rooms, service with restrictions, supervision. SAVE ⊠ 🖑 🛢 💻 ⧯ ⊰

▼▼ Candlewood Suites **H**

(757) 766-8976. **$84-$144.** 401 Butler Farm Rd 23666. I-64, exit 261B (Hampton Roads Center Pkwy) eastbound; exit 262B (Magruder Blvd) westbound, then n. Int corridors. **Pets:** Accepted.

ASK ⊠ 🖑 🛢 💻

▼▼ Extended StayAmerica-Hampton Coliseum **M**

(757) 896-3600. **$50-$90.** 1915 Commerce Dr 23666. I-64, exit 263 (Mercury Blvd), just n, then just e. Int corridors. **Pets:** Other species. $25 daily fee/room. Designated rooms, service with restrictions, crate.

ASK ⊠ 🖑 🛢 💻

⟨AAA⟩ ▼▼▼ Holiday Inn Hampton Hotel & Conference Center **H**

(757) 838-0200. **$79-$229.** 1815 W Mercury Blvd 23666. I-64, exit 263B (Mercury Blvd) westbound; exit 263 eastbound. Ext/int corridors. **Pets:** Accepted. SAVE ⊠ 🖑 🛢 💻 ⧯ ⊰ ⊠

▼▼ Ramada Hampton Coliseum & Convention Center **H**

(757) 827-7400. **$49-$149, 15 day notice.** 1905 Coliseum Dr 23666. I-64, exit 263 (Mercury Blvd) eastbound, just n, then just e towards Hampton Coliseum; exit 263B westbound. Ext/int corridors. **Pets:** Small, dogs only. $10 daily fee/pet. Service with restrictions, supervision.

ASK ⊠ 🛢 💻 ⊰

▼ Super 8 **M**

(757) 723-2888. **Call for rates.** 1330 Thomas St 23669. I-64, exit 265B westbound; exit 265C eastbound. Int corridors. **Pets:** Accepted.

⊠ 🛢 💻

NEWPORT NEWS

▼▼▼ Comfort Inn **H**

(757) 249-0200. **$79-$135, 5 day notice.** 12330 Jefferson Ave 23602. I-64, exit 255A, just s on Claire Ln (mall parking lot). Int corridors. **Pets:** Accepted. ASK ⊠ 🖑 🛢 💻 ⊰

▼▼ Crestwood Suites **M**

(757) 951-1017. **Call for rates.** 11 Old Oyster Point Rd 23602. I-64, exit 256A, just s on Oyster Point Rd to Canon Blvd, just e, then just n. Int corridors. **Pets:** Accepted. ⊠ 🛢 💻

⟨AAA⟩ ▼▼▼ Days Inn-Oyster Point at City Center **H**

(757) 873-6700. **$89-$119.** 11829 Fishing Point Dr 23606. I-64, exit 255A, 2.5 mi s to Thimble Shoals Dr E, then 1 blk. Int corridors. **Pets:** $25 daily fee/room. Service with restrictions.

SAVE ⊠ 🛢 💻 ⊰

▼▼ Extended StayAmerica Newport News-Oyster Point **H**

(757) 873-2266. **$45-$100.** 11708 Jefferson Ave 23606. I-64, exit 258A (US 17), 1 mi s. Ext corridors. **Pets:** Other species. $25 daily fee/room. Designated rooms, service with restrictions, crate. ASK ⊠ 🛢 💻

⟨AAA⟩ ▼▼▼ Mulberry Inn **H** 🐾

(757) 887-3000. **$79-$139.** 16890 Warwick Blvd 23603. I-64, exit 250A (SR 105/Ft Eustis Blvd S), s to US 60, then 0.3 mi w. Ext/int corridors. **Pets:** Medium. $10 daily fee/pet, $50 one-time fee/pet. Designated rooms, service with restrictions, supervision. SAVE ⊠ 🛢 💻 ⊰

▼▼▼ Omni Newport News Hotel **H**

(757) 873-6664. **$144-$164, 7 day notice.** 1000 Omni Blvd 23606. I-64, exit 258A (US 17), just s to Oyster Point Rd. Int corridors. **Pets:** Small. $50 one-time fee/room. Designated rooms, service with restrictions, crate.

ASK ⊠ 🖑 🛢 💻 ⧯ ⊰

⟨AAA⟩ ▼▼▼ Point Plaza-Suites at City Center **H** 🐾

(757) 599-4460. **$69-$159.** 950 J Clyde Morris Blvd 23601. I-64, exit 258B (US 17), just n. Ext/int corridors. **Pets:** $50 one-time fee/room. Designated rooms, service with restrictions, crate.

SAVE ⊠ 🛢 💻 ⧯ ⊰

▼▼▼ Residence Inn by Marriott Newport News Airport **H**

(757) 842-6214. **$134-$164.** 531 St Johns Rd 23602. I-64, exit 255A, just s on Jefferson Ave to Freedom Way, then just nw. Int corridors. **Pets:** Accepted. ⊠ 🖑 🛢 💻 ⊰

▼▼▼ StudioPLUS-Newport News–I-64–Jefferson Ave **H**

(757) 882-8847. **$63-$115.** 12359 Hornsby Ln 23602. I-64, exit 255A, just s on Jefferson Ave. Int corridors. **Pets:** Other species. $25 daily fee/room. Designated rooms, service with restrictions, crate.

ASK ⊠ 🛢 💻

NORFOLK

⟨AAA⟩ ▼▼▼ Hilton Norfolk Airport **H**

(757) 466-8000. **$99-$209.** 1500 N Military Hwy 23502. I-64, exit 281 (Military Hwy), just s at jct US 13 and SR 165. Int corridors. **Pets:** Medium, other species. $75 one-time fee/room. Designated rooms, service with restrictions, supervision.

ECO SAVE ⊠ 🖑 💻 ⧯ ⊰

⟨AAA⟩ ▼▼▼ La Quinta Inn & Suites Norfolk Airport **H** 🐾

(757) 466-7001. **$59-$134 (no credit cards).** 1387 N Military Hwy 23502. I-64, exit 281 (Military Hwy), just s. Int corridors. **Pets:** Medium, other species. Service with restrictions, supervision.

SAVE ⊠ 🛢 💻 ⊰

⟨AAA⟩ ▼▼▼ Page House Inn Bed & Breakfast **BB** 🐾

(757) 625-5033. **$145-$230, 7 day notice.** 323 Fairfax Ave 23507. I-264, exit 9, 1.4 mi n on Waterside Dr to Olney Rd, just w to Mowbray Arch, then just s; in Ghent historic district. Int corridors. **Pets:** Small, other species. $25 daily fee/pet. Service with restrictions, crate.

SAVE ⊠ 🛢 ⊠

▲▲▲⟢ ▼▼▼▼ **Quality Suites Lake Wright** 🅷 ❖
(757) 461-6251. **$109-$169.** 6280 Northampton Blvd 23502. I-64, exit 282, just w on US 13. Int corridors. **Pets:** $35 one-time fee/room. Service with restrictions, supervision. 🌱 [SAVE] ⊠ 🖥 📷 💻 ⦿ 🍴 ⨼

▼▼▼▼ **Residence Inn by Marriott Downtown** 🅷 ❖
(757) 842-6216. **$169-$189.** 227 W Brambleton Ave 23510. Jct Duke St; downtown. Int corridors. **Pets:** $100 one-time fee/room. Service with restrictions, crate. ⊠ 🖥 📷 💻 ⨼

▲▲▲⟢ ▼▼▼▼ **Residence Inn by Marriott Norfolk Airport** 🅷
(757) 333-3000. **$149-$169.** 1590 N Military Hwy 23502. I-64, exit 281B (Military Hwy). Int corridors. **Pets:** Other species. $75 one-time fee/room. Service with restrictions. 🌱 [SAVE] ⊠ 🖥 📷 💻 ⨼ ⨂

▲▲▲⟢ ▼▼▼▼ **Sheraton Norfolk Waterside Hotel** 🅷
(757) 622-6664. **Call for rates.** 777 Waterside Dr 23510. I-264, exit 9 (Waterside Dr); downtown. Int corridors. **Pets:** Accepted.
[SAVE] ⊠ 🖥 📷 💻 ⨼

▲▲▲⟢ ▼▼▼▼ **Sleep Inn Lake Wright** 🅷 ❖
(757) 461-1133. **$79-$139.** 6280 Northampton Blvd 23502. I-64, exit 282, just w on US 13. Int corridors. **Pets:** $25 one-time fee/room. Service with restrictions, supervision. 🌱 [SAVE] ⊠ 🖥 📷 💻 ⨼

▲▲▲⟢ ▼▼▼▼ **Tazewell Hotel and Suites** 🅷
(757) 623-6200. **Call for rates.** 245 Granby St 23510. Jct Tazewell St; downtown. Int corridors. **Pets:** Accepted. [SAVE] ⊠ 🖥 📷 🍴

SMITHFIELD

▼▼▼ **Smithfield Station** 🅷
(757) 357-7700. **$99-$299.** 415 S Church St 23430. 0.5 mi s on SR 10. Ext/int corridors. **Pets:** Small, other species. $75 deposit/room, $15 daily fee/pet. Designated rooms, service with restrictions, crate.
🌱 [ASK] ⊠ 🖥 💻 🍴 ⨼

SUFFOLK

▼▼▼ **TownePlace Suites by Marriott** 🅷
(757) 483-5177. **$119-$139.** 8050 Harbour View Blvd 23435. I-664, exit 8A (College Dr), just n. Int corridors. **Pets:** Medium, other species. $100 one-time fee/room. Designated rooms, service with restrictions, supervision. 🌱 ⊠ 📷 🖥 💻 ⨼

VIRGINIA BEACH

▼▼▼ **Candlewood Suites** 🅷
(757) 213-1500. **$99-$159, 3 day notice.** 4437 Bonney Rd 23462. I-264, exit 17B (Independence Blvd/Pembroke Area), just n to Bonney Rd, then just e. Int corridors. **Pets:** Accepted. 🌱 [ASK] ⊠ 🖥 💻

▲▲▲⟢ ▼▼▼▼ **Crowne Plaza Virginia Beach** 🅷
(757) 473-1700. **$110-$165.** 4453 Bonney Rd 23462. I-264, exit 17B (Independence Blvd/Pembroke Area), 0.5 mi se. Int corridors.
Pets: Accepted. [SAVE] ⊠ 🖥 💻 🍴 ⨼ ⨂

▲▲▲⟢ ▼▼▼▼ **Doubletree Hotel Virginia Beach** 🅷
(757) 422-8900. **$59-$259.** 1900 Pavilion Dr 23451. I-264, exit 22 (Birdneck Rd), just e. Int corridors. **Pets:** Accepted.
🌱 [SAVE] ⊠ 🖥 💻 🍴 ⨼

▼▼ **Extended StayAmerica-Virginia Beach-Independence Blvd** Ⓜ
(757) 473-9200. **$45-$125.** 4548 Bonney Rd 23462. I-264, exit 17B (Independence Blvd/Pembroke Area), just n to Bonney Rd, then just e. Ext corridors. **Pets:** Other species. $25 daily fee/room. Designated rooms, service with restrictions, crate. [ASK] ⊠ 🖥 ⨼

▼▼▼ **Holiday Inn-Executive Center** 🅷
(757) 499-4400. **$89-$179.** 5655 Greenwich Rd 23462. I-64, exit 284B (Newtown Rd); jct I-64 and 264. Int corridors. **Pets:** Accepted.
[ASK] ⊠ 📷 🖥 💻 🍴 ⨼ ⨂

▼▼▼ **Holiday Inn SunSpree Resort** 🅷
(757) 428-1711. **$84-$299, 3 day notice.** 3900 Atlantic Ave 23451. I-264, 2 mi n from terminus; at 39th St. Int corridors. **Pets:** Accepted.
🌱 [ASK] ⊠ 📷 🖥 💻 🍴 ⨼ ⨂

▼▼▼ **La Quinta Inn & Suites** 🅷 ❖
(757) 428-2203. **$49-$279.** 2800 Pacific Ave 23451. I-264, 0.5 mi n of terminus. Int corridors. **Pets:** Medium, other species. Service with restrictions, supervision. [ASK] ⊠ 📷 🖥 💻 ⨼ ⨂

▲▲▲⟢ ▼▼▼ **Red Roof Inn VA Beach (Norfolk Airport)** Ⓜ
(757) 460-6700. **$56-$190.** 5745 Northampton Blvd 23455. I-64, exit 282, 1 mi n on US 13 (Northampton Blvd). Ext corridors. **Pets:** Large. Service with restrictions, crate. [SAVE] ⊠ 🖥 ⨼

▼▼▼ **Residence Inn Virginia Beach Oceanfront** 🅷
(757) 425-1141. **$178-$305.** 3217 Atlantic Ave 23451. I-264, 1.5 mi n of terminus; jct 33rd St. Int corridors. **Pets:** Accepted.
🌱 ⊠ 📷 🖥 💻 ⨼

▲▲▲⟢ ▼▼▼▼ **Sheraton Virginia Beach Oceanfront Hotel** 🅷
(757) 425-9000. **$79-$329, 3 day notice.** 3501 Atlantic Ave 23451. I-264, 1 mi n of terminus; jct 36th St. Int corridors. **Pets:** Accepted.
🌱 [SAVE] ⊠ 🖥 💻 🍴 ⨼ ⨂

▲▲▲⟢ ▼▼▼▼ **TownePlace Suites By Marriott** 🅷
(757) 490-9367. **$129-$139.** 5757 Cleveland St 23462. I-64, exit 284B to I-264 (Virginia Beach-Norfolk Expwy), exit Newtown Rd N. Int corridors.
Pets: Accepted. 🌱 [SAVE] ⊠ 📷 🖥 💻

▲▲▲⟢ ▼▼▼▼ **The Westin Virginia Beach Town Center** 🅷
(757) 557-0550. **$109-$229.** 4535 Commerce St 23462. I-264, exit 17B (Independence Blvd), just n, then just e. Int corridors. **Pets:** Accepted.
🌱 [SAVE] ⊠ 🖥 💻 🍴 ⨼

END AREA

HARRISONBURG

▼▼▼ **Candlewood Suites Harrisonburg** 🅷 ❖
(540) 437-1400. **$69-$299.** 1560 Country Club Rd 22802. I-81, exit 247, just e. Int corridors. **Pets:** Medium. $50 one-time fee/room. Designated rooms, service with restrictions, supervision. [ASK] ⊠ 🖥 💻

▼▼▼ **Comfort Inn** 🅷
(540) 433-6066. **$79-$130.** 1440 E Market St 22801. I-81, exit 247A, just e. Int corridors. **Pets:** Medium, other species. $15 daily fee/room. Service with restrictions, supervision. [ASK] ⊠ 🖥 💻 ⨼

▲▲▲⟢ ▼▼▼ **Days Inn Harrisonburg** Ⓜ
(540) 433-9353. **Call for rates.** 1131 Forest Hill Rd 22801. I-81, exit 245, just e. Int corridors. **Pets:** Medium, dogs only. $10 one-time fee/pet. Service with restrictions, supervision. [SAVE] ⊠ 🖥 💻 ⨼

▲▲▲⟢ ▼▼▼ **Harrisonburg Econo Lodge** Ⓜ
(540) 433-2576. **Call for rates.** 1703 E Market St 22801. I-81, exit 247A, 0.5 mi e on US 33. Ext/int corridors. **Pets:** Accepted.
[SAVE] ⊠ 🖥 💻 ⨼

▼▼▼ **Jameson Inn** 🅷
(540) 442-1515. **$80-$85.** 1881 Evelyn Byrd Ave 22801. I-81, exit 247A, just e. Int corridors. **Pets:** Small, other species. $15 daily fee/pet. Designated rooms, service with restrictions, supervision.
[ASK] ⊠ 🖥 💻 ⨼

▼▼ Ramada Inn H
(540) 434-9981. **$49-$99.** 1 Pleasant Valley Rd 22801. I-81, exit 243, just w, then just n on US 11. Ext corridors. **Pets:** Accepted.
[ASK] [✕] [🛏] [➔]

▼▼ Sleep Inn & Suites H
(540) 433-7100. **$85-$120.** 1891 Evelyn Byrd Ave 22801. I-81, exit 247A, 0.5 mi e on US 33 to University Blvd, 0.3 mi s to Evelyn Byrd Ave, then just w. Int corridors. **Pets:** Accepted. [ASK] [✕] [🛏] [💻]

◇◇ ▼▼ Super 8 M
(540) 433-8888. **$45-$89, 3 day notice.** 3330 S Main St 22801. I-81, exit 243, just e, then just s on US 11. Int corridors. **Pets:** Small. $10 one-time fee/pet. Designated rooms, no service, supervision.
[SAVE] [✕] [🛏] [💻]

◇◇ ▼▼▼ The Village Inn H
(540) 434-7355. **$75-$82.** 4979 S Valley Pike 22801. I-81, exit 240 southbound, 0.6 mi w on SR 257, then 1.5 mi n on US 11; exit 243 northbound, just w to US 11, then 1.7 mi s. Ext corridors. **Pets:** Other species. $10 daily fee/pet. Service with restrictions, crate.
[ECO] [SAVE] [✕] [🛏] [💻] [🍴] [➔] [✕]

HILLSVILLE

◇◇ ▼▼ Best Western Four Seasons South M
(276) 728-4136. **$71-$91, 3 day notice.** 57 Airport Rd 24343. I-77, exit 14, just w on US 58 and 221. Ext corridors. **Pets:** Accepted.
[SAVE] [✕] [🛏] [💻] [➔]

◇◇ ▼▼▼ Quality Inn H
(276) 728-2120. **$70-$165.** 85 Airport Rd 24343. I-77, exit 14, just w on US 58 and 221. Ext corridors. **Pets:** Medium. $10 daily fee/pet. Designated rooms, service with restrictions, supervision.
[SAVE] [✕] [&M] [🛏] [💻] [➔]

◇◇ ▼▼ Super 8 of Hillsville M
(276) 728-4125. **$59-$150.** 99 Farmers Market Dr 24343. I-77, exit 14, just w on US 58 and 221. Ext/int corridors. **Pets:** Accepted.
[SAVE] [✕] [🛏] [💻]

HOPEWELL

◇◇ ▼▼ Candlewood Suites H
(804) 541-0200. **Call for rates.** 5113 Plaza Dr 23860. I-295, exit 9B (SR 36), just w; adjacent to Oak Lawn Plaza. Int corridors. **Pets:** Large. $75 one-time fee/pet. Service with restrictions. [SAVE] [✕] [&M] [🛏] [💻]

▼▼▼ Fairfield Inn & Suites by Marriott H
(804) 458-2600. **$98-$120.** 3952 Courthouse Rd 23860. I-295, exit 9A (SR 36), just e. Int corridors. **Pets:** Accepted. [✕] [🛏] [💻] [➔]

HOT SPRINGS

◇◇ ▼▼ ▼▼ The Homestead H
(540) 839-1766. **$185-$400, 7 day notice.** 1766 Homestead Dr 24445. Center. Int corridors. **Pets:** Accepted. [SAVE] [✕] [🍴] [➔] [✕]

HUDDLESTON

▼▼▼ Mariners Landing CO
(540) 297-4900. **$80-$260, 7 day notice.** 1217 Graves Harbor Tr 24104. On SR 626; on Smith Mountain Lake. Ext/int corridors.
Pets: Accepted. [ASK] [✕] [&M] [🛏] [💻] [🍴] [➔] [✕]

IRVINGTON

◇◇ ▼▼▼ ▼▼ The Tides Inn H ❀
(804) 438-5000. **$210-$395, 7 day notice.** 480 King Carter Dr 22480. 0.3 mi w of SR 200. Ext/int corridors. **Pets:** Dogs only. $25 daily fee/pet. Designated rooms. [ECO] [SAVE] [✕] [&M] [🛏] [💻] [🍴] [➔] [✕]

KESWICK

◇◇ ▼▼▼ ▼▼▼ Keswick Hall at Monticello H ❀
(434) 979-3440. **$225-$725, 7 day notice.** 701 Club Dr 22947. I-64, exit 129, just n. Int corridors. **Pets:** Large. $75 one-time fee/room. Designated rooms, service with restrictions, crate.
[SAVE] [✕] [&M] [🛏] [🍴] [➔] [✕]

LAWRENCEVILLE

▼▼▼ Brunswick Mineral Springs B & B Circa 1785 BB
(434) 848-4010. **Call for rates.** 14910 Western Mill Rd 23868. 5 mi e on US 58, 1 mi s on SR 712, then just e. Int corridors. **Pets:** Accepted.
[✕] [🛏] [💻] [➔]

LEBANON

▼▼ Lebanon Super 8 M
(276) 889-1800. **$66-$150.** 71 Townview Dr 24266. Just e on SR 654 from US 19 Bypass. Int corridors. **Pets:** Medium. $10 daily fee/pet. Service with restrictions. [ASK] [✕] [&M] [🛏] [💻]

LEXINGTON

◇◇ ▼▼▼ Best Western Inn at Hunt Ridge H
(540) 464-1500. **$95-$125.** 25 Willow Spring Rd 24450. I-64, exit 55, just n on US 11 to SR 39; I-81, exit 191, 0.6 mi w. Int corridors.
Pets: Accepted. [SAVE] [✕] [&M] [🛏] [💻] [🍴] [➔]

◇◇ ▼▼▼ Best Western Lexington Inn M
(540) 458-3020. **$63-$110.** 850 N Lee Hwy 24450. I-64, exit 55, just s on US 11; I-81, exit 191, 1.6 mi w. Ext corridors. **Pets:** Accepted.
[SAVE] [✕] [🛏] [💻]

◇◇ ▼▼▼ Comfort Inn-Virginia Horse Center H
(540) 463-7311. **Call for rates.** 62 Comfort Way 24450. I-64, exit 55, just s on US 11; I-81, exit 191, 0.6 mi w. Int corridors. **Pets:** Medium. $25 one-time fee/room. Designated rooms, service with restrictions, supervision. [SAVE] [✕] [🛏] [💻] [➔]

◇◇ ▼▼▼ Days Inn H
(540) 463-9131. **$60-$190.** 2809 N Lee Hwy 24450. I-81, exit 195, just sw on US 11. Ext corridors. **Pets:** Small. $10 daily fee/pet. Service with restrictions, supervision. [SAVE] [✕] [🛏] [💻] [🍴] [➔]

▼▼ Economy Inn M
(540) 463-7371. **Call for rates.** 65 Econo Ln 24450. I-81, exit 191, just s on US 11. Ext corridors. **Pets:** Accepted. [✕] [🛏] [💻]

◇◇ ▼▼▼▼ Holiday Inn Express H
(540) 463-7351. **$109-$189.** 880 N Lee Hwy 24450. I-64, exit 55, just s on US 11; I-81, exit 191, 1 mi w. Int corridors. **Pets:** Large, other species. $25 one-time fee/room. Service with restrictions, supervision.
[SAVE] [✕] [🛏] [💻]

◇◇ ▼▼▼ Howard Johnson Inn H ❀
(540) 463-9181. **$44-$200.** 2836 N Lee Hwy 24450. I-81, exit 195, just s on US 11. Int corridors. **Pets:** $12 daily fee/pet. Service with restrictions, supervision. [SAVE] [✕] [🛏] [💻] [➔]

▼▼ Super 8 M
(540) 463-7858. **Call for rates.** 1139 N Lee Hwy 24450. I-64, exit 55, just n. Int corridors. **Pets:** Accepted. [✕] [🛏] [💻]

LURAY

▼▼ Days Inn-Luray M
(540) 743-4521. **$49-$159.** 138 Whispering Hill Rd 22835. US 211 Bypass, 1.7 mi e of jct US 340. Ext/int corridors. **Pets:** Accepted.
[ASK] [✕] [🛏] [💻] [➔] [✕]

◇◇ ▼▼▼ The Mimslyn Inn H
(540) 743-5105. **$89-$329.** 401 W Main St 22835. 0.3 mi w on US 211 business route. Int corridors. **Pets:** Accepted.
[ECO] [SAVE] [✕] [🛏] [💻] [🍴] [➔] [✕]

LYNCHBURG

▼▼ Extended StayAmerica–Lynchburg–University Blvd M
(434) 239-8863. **$60-$95.** 1910 University Blvd 24502. US 460, exit Candlers Mountain Rd/University Blvd. Int corridors. **Pets:** Other species. $25 daily fee/room. Designated rooms, service with restrictions, crate.
[ASK] [✕] [&M] [🛏] [💻]

▼▼ Hampton Inn 🅷
(434) 237-2704. **Call for rates.** 5604 Seminole Ave 24502. US 460, exit Candlers Mountain Rd, 0.3 mi w; US 29, exit Candlers Mountain Rd. Ext/int corridors. **Pets:** Accepted. 🐾 &M 🔒 💻

▼▼▼ Holiday Inn 🅷
(434) 528-2500. **Call for rates.** 601 Main St 24504. US 29 business route, exit 1 (Main St), just w; downtown. Int corridors. **Pets:** Accepted.
🐾 🔒 💻 🍴 ➿

▼▼ Holiday Inn Express 🅷
(434) 237-7771. **$95-$129.** 5600 Seminole Ave 24502. US 460, exit Candlers Mountain Rd, 0.3 mi w; US 29 business route, exit Candlers Mountain Rd. Int corridors. **Pets:** Medium. $25 one-time fee/pet. Service with restrictions, crate. ASK 🐾 🔒 💻 ➿

◮◮◮ ▼▼▼ Kirkley Hotel & Conference Center 🅷
(434) 237-6333. **$89-$199.** 2900 Candlers Mountain Rd 24502. US 29 business route, exit 8A, just w. Int corridors. **Pets:** Accepted.
SAVE 🐾 🔒 💻 🍴 ➿ ☒

▼▼ Lynchburg Super 8 🅷
(434) 846-1668. **Call for rates.** 3736 Candlers Mountain Rd 24502. US 29, exit 8B, just e. Int corridors. **Pets:** Accepted. 🐾 &M 🔒 💻

◮◮◮ ▼▼▼ Quality Inn 🅷
(434) 847-9041. **$60-$130, 3 day notice.** 3125 Albert Lankford Dr 24501. US 29 business route, exit 7, just s. Int corridors. **Pets:** Medium, other species. $25 one-time fee/pet. Designated rooms, service with restrictions, supervision. SAVE 🐾 🔒 💻 ➿

MARION
▼▼ Magnuson Hotel Marion 🅼
(276) 783-3193. **Call for rates.** 1424 N Main St 24354. I-81, exit 47, 0.3 mi s on US 11. Ext corridors. **Pets:** Accepted. 🐾 🔒 💻 🍴 ➿

MARTINSVILLE
▼ Best Lodge 🅼
(276) 647-3941. **$48-$68.** 1985 Virginia Ave 24112. Jct US 58, 2.5 mi n on US 220 business route. Ext corridors. **Pets:** Accepted.
ASK 🐾 🔒 💻

▼▼ Econo Lodge Inn & Suites 🅷
(276) 632-5611. **Call for rates.** US 220 Business Rt S 24112. Jct US 58, 2.3 mi n. Ext corridors. **Pets:** Accepted. 🐾 🔒 💻 🍴 ➿

▼▼▼ Hampton Inn 🅷
(276) 647-4700. **Call for rates.** 50 Hampton Dr 24112. Jct US 58, 2.5 mi n on US 220 business route. Int corridors. **Pets:** Accepted.
🐾 🔒 💻 ➿

▼▼▼ Holiday Inn Express 🅷
(276) 666-6835. **$89-$94.** 1895 Virginia Ave 24112. Jct US 58, 2.4 mi n on US 220 business route. Int corridors. **Pets:** Accepted.
ASK 🐾 🔒 💻 ➿

MAX MEADOWS
▼▼ Super 8 🅼
(276) 637-4141. **Call for rates.** 194 Ft Chiswell Rd 24360. I-77/81, exit 80, just e. Ext corridors. **Pets:** Accepted. 🐾 🔒 💻

MIDDLETOWN
◮◮◮ ▼▼▼ Super 8 🅷
(540) 868-1800. **$49-$250.** 91 Reliance Rd 22645. I-81, exit 302. Int corridors. **Pets:** Accepted. SAVE 🐾 🔒 💻 ➿

MINT SPRING
▼▼ Days Inn-Staunton 🅼
(540) 337-3031. **$65-$175.** 372 White Hill Rd 24401. I-81, exit 217, just e on SR 654. Ext corridors. **Pets:** Accepted. ASK 🐾 🔒 💻 ➿

MOUNT JACKSON
◮◮◮ ▼▼▼ Super 8–Mt. Jackson 🅼
(540) 477-2911. **Call for rates.** 250 Conicville Blvd 22842. I-81, exit 273, just e. Ext corridors. **Pets:** Medium. $10 daily fee/pet. Designated rooms, service with restrictions, crate. SAVE 🔒 💻 ➿

▼▼▼ The Widow Kip's BB ❀
(540) 477-2400. **$110-$135, 5 day notice.** 355 Orchard Dr 22842-9753. I-81, exit 273, 1.5 mi s on US 11, just w on SR 263, then just sw on SR 698. Int corridors. **Pets:** Other species. $20 daily fee/pet. Designated rooms, service with restrictions. ECO ASK 🐾 🔒 💻 ➿

NEW CHURCH
▼▼▼ The Garden & The Sea Inn BB ❀
(757) 824-0672. **$95-$225, 10 day notice.** 4188 Nelson Rd 23415. US 13, 0.3 mi n, just w on CR 710 (Nelson Rd). Int corridors. **Pets:** Other species. ECO ASK 🐾 🔒 💻 ➿ ☒

NEW MARKET
◮◮◮ ▼ Budget Inn 🅼
(540) 740-3105. **$29-$69, 3 day notice.** 2192 Old Valley Pike 22844. I-81, exit 264, 1 mi n on US 11. Ext corridors. **Pets:** Small. $8 one-time fee/pet. No service, supervision. SAVE 🐾 🔒

▼▼ Days Inn 🅷
(540) 740-4100. **$41-$116, 3 day notice.** 9360 George Collins Pkwy 22844. I-81, exit 264, just w on US 211. Ext corridors. **Pets:** Medium. $10 daily fee/pet. Designated rooms, service with restrictions, supervision.
ASK 🐾 🔒 💻 ➿

NORTON
▼▼ Days Inn 🅼
(276) 679-5340. **Call for rates.** 375 Wharton Ln 24273. Jct US 58 and 23. Int corridors. **Pets:** Accepted. 🐾 🔒 💻

▼ Super 8-Norton 🅼
(276) 679-0893. **$57-$108.** 425 Wharton Ln 24273. Jct US 58 and 23. Int corridors. **Pets:** Accepted. ASK 🐾 🔒 💻

ONANCOCK
◮◮◮ ▼▼▼ 1890 Spinning Wheel Bed & Breakfast BB ❀
(757) 787-7311. **$85-$125, 3 day notice.** 31 North St 23417. Just n of jct Market (SR 179) and North sts. Int corridors. **Pets:** Large, other species. $10 daily fee/pet. Designated rooms, service with restrictions, supervision. ECO SAVE 🐾 📺 ☒

ORANGE
▼▼▼ Mayhurst Inn BB
(540) 672-5597. **$165-$245, 10 day notice.** 12460 Mayhurst Ln 22960. On US 15, 0.5 mi s of town from SR 20 at the divided highway. Int corridors. **Pets:** Medium. $25 one-time fee/room. Designated rooms.
ECO ASK 🐾 🔒 💻 ☒

PETERSBURG
▼▼ Howard Johnson Inn-Steven Kent 🅷
(804) 733-0600. **$60-$66.** 12205 S Crater Rd 23805. I-95, exit 45, jct US 301. Ext/int corridors. **Pets:** Other species. $10 daily fee/pet. Service with restrictions, crate. ASK 🐾 🔒 💻 🍴 ➿

POUNDING MILL
▼▼▼ Claypool Hill Holiday Inn Express Hotel & Suites 🅷
(276) 596-9880. **$90-$145.** 180 Clay Dr 24637. 0.5 mi e of US 19/460. Int corridors. **Pets:** Medium. $25 daily fee/pet. Service with restrictions, supervision. ASK 🐾 🔒 💻

▼ Claypool Hill Super 8 🅼
(276) 964-9888. **Call for rates.** 12367 Governor GC Peery Hwy 24637. 0.3 mi w on US 19/460. Int corridors. **Pets:** Accepted. 🐾 🔒 💻

RADFORD

△△△ ▽▽▽▽ Best Western Radford Inn Ⓗ
(540) 639-3000. **$75-$119.** 1501 Tyler Ave 24141. I-81, exit 109, 2.7 mi nw on SR 177. Int corridors. **Pets:** Accepted.
⟨SAVE⟩ ⟨X⟩ ⟨◧⟩ ⟨▣⟩ ⟨¶⟩ ⟨⇀⟩ ⟨⊠⟩

▽▽▽▽ La Quinta Inn Ⓜ ❖
(540) 633-6800. **$59-$99.** 1450 Tyler Ave 24141. I-81, exit 109, 2.6 mi w on SR 177. Int corridors. **Pets:** Medium, other species. Service with restrictions, supervision. ⟨X⟩ ⟨◧⟩ ⟨▣⟩ ⟨¶⟩

▽▽▽ Super 8-Radford Ⓜ
(540) 731-9355. **Call for rates.** 1600 Tyler Ave 24141. I-81, exit 109, just w. Int corridors. **Pets:** Accepted. ⟨X⟩ ⟨◧⟩ ⟨▣⟩

RAPHINE

△△△ ▽▽▽ Days Inn-Shenandoah Valley Ⓜ
(540) 377-2604. **$65-$190.** 584 Oakland Cir 24472. I-81, exit 205, just sw. Int corridors. **Pets:** Small. $10 daily fee/pet. Service with restrictions, supervision. ⟨SAVE⟩ ⟨X⟩ ⟨◧⟩ ⟨▣⟩ ⟨⇀⟩

RICHMOND METROPOLITAN AREA

CHESTERFIELD

△△△▽ ▽▽▽ La Quinta Inn Ⓗ ❖
(804) 743-0770. **$59-$109.** 9040 Pams Ave 23237. I-95, exit 64, just w. Int corridors. **Pets:** Medium, other species. Service with restrictions, supervision. ⟨SAVE⟩ ⟨X⟩ ⟨&M⟩ ⟨◧⟩ ⟨▣⟩

COLONIAL HEIGHTS

▽▽▽ Candlewood Suites Ⓗ
(804) 526-0111. **$99-$119.** 15820 Woods Edge Rd 23834. I-95, exit 58 northbound; exit 58B southbound, just w. Int corridors. **Pets:** Medium. $75 one-time fee/pet. Service with restrictions, supervision.
⟨ASK⟩ ⟨X⟩ ⟨&M⟩ ⟨◧⟩ ⟨▣⟩

DOSWELL

△△△▽ ▽▽ Best Western-Kings Quarters Ⓗ
(804) 876-3321. **$70-$200, 3 day notice.** 16102 Theme Park Way 23047. I-95, exit 98, just e on SR 30; entrance to theme park. Ext corridors. **Pets:** Medium, other species. $25 deposit/room. Service with restrictions, supervision. ⟨SAVE⟩ ⟨X⟩ ⟨◧⟩ ⟨▣⟩ ⟨¶⟩ ⟨⇀⟩ ⟨⊠⟩

GLEN ALLEN

△△△▽ ▽▽▽▽ Candlewood Suites Ⓗ
(804) 262-2240. **$80-$309.** 10609 Telegraph Rd 23059. I-295, exit 43C, 1.7 mi n to JEB Stuart Pkwy, just w to Telegraph Rd; I-95, exit 86B (SR 656-Elmont) just w, 1 mi s. Int corridors. **Pets:** Other species. $25 one-time fee/pet. Service with restrictions, supervision.
⟨SAVE⟩ ⟨X⟩ ⟨&M⟩ ⟨◧⟩ ⟨▣⟩

▽▽▽▽ Candlewood Suites Richmond-West Ⓗ
(804) 364-2000. **Call for rates.** 4120 Brookriver Dr 23060. I-64, exit 178, just w on W Broad St. Int corridors. **Pets:** Accepted. ⟨X⟩ ⟨&M⟩ ⟨◧⟩ ⟨▣⟩

▽▽▽ Holiday Inn Express Ⓗ
(804) 934-9300. **Call for rates.** 9933 Mayland Dr 23233. I-64, exit 180B, just n to Mayland Dr, then just w. Int corridors. **Pets:** Accepted.
⟨X⟩ ⟨&M⟩ ⟨◧⟩ ⟨▣⟩ ⟨⇀⟩

▽▽▽▽ Homewood Suites by Hilton Richmond West End-Innsbrook Ⓗ
(804) 217-8000. **$99-$159.** 4100 Innslake Dr 23060. I-64, exit 178B, just e on W Broad St to Cox Rd, then just n. Int corridors. **Pets:** Large, other species. $100 one-time fee/room. Service with restrictions, crate.
⟨X⟩ ⟨&M⟩ ⟨◧⟩ ⟨▣⟩ ⟨⇀⟩

△△△▽ ▽▽▽▽ Hotel Sierra Richmond West Ⓗ
(804) 360-7021. **$109-$229.** 11800 W Broad St, Suite 1098 23233. I-64, exit 178, 1.3 mi w; in Short Pump Town Center. Int corridors. **Pets:** Accepted. ⟨SAVE⟩ ⟨X⟩ ⟨◧⟩ ⟨▣⟩ ⟨⇀⟩ ⟨⊠⟩

▽▽▽ Residence Inn by Marriott Ⓗ
(804) 762-9852. **$134-$164.** 3940 Westerre Pkwy 23233. I-64, exit 180, n on Gaskins Rd to W Broad St. Int corridors. **Pets:** Accepted.
⟨X⟩ ⟨&M⟩ ⟨◧⟩ ⟨▣⟩ ⟨⇀⟩ ⟨⊠⟩

RICHMOND

▽▽ Candlewood Suites Ⓗ
(804) 271-0016. **$99-$149.** 4301 Commerce Rd 23234. I-95, exit 69, just n. Int corridors. **Pets:** Accepted. ⟨ASK⟩ ⟨X⟩ ⟨&M⟩ ⟨◧⟩ ⟨▣⟩

△△△▽ ▽▽▽▽ Comfort Inn Midlothian Turnpike Ⓗ
(804) 320-8900. **$79-$119.** 8710 Midlothian Tpke 23235. Jct Powhite Pkwy (US 76) and Midlothian Tpke (US 60), just e. Int corridors. **Pets:** Small. $20 daily fee/pet. Designated rooms, service with restrictions, crate. ⟨SAVE⟩ ⟨X⟩ ⟨◧⟩ ⟨▣⟩

△△△▽ ▽▽▽▽ Commonwealth Park Suites Ⓗ ❖
(804) 343-7300. **Call for rates.** 901 Bank St 23219. Jct 9th and Bank sts. Int corridors. **Pets:** $50 daily fee/room. Service with restrictions.
⟨SAVE⟩ ⟨X⟩ ⟨◧⟩ ⟨▣⟩ ⟨¶⟩ ⟨⊠⟩

▽▽▽ Extended Stay Deluxe Richmond- I-64–W Broad St Ⓗ
(804) 285-7050. **$60-$115.** 6807 Paragon Pl 23230. I-64, exit 183C (W Broad St), just w to Glenside Dr, just n. Int corridors. **Pets:** Other species. $25 daily fee/room. Designated rooms, service with restrictions, crate.
⟨ASK⟩ ⟨X⟩ ⟨◧⟩ ⟨▣⟩ ⟨⇀⟩

▽▽▽ Homestead Studio Suites Hotel-Richmond/Midlothian Ⓗ
(804) 272-1800. **$60-$109.** 241 Arboretum Pl 23236. Jct Powhite Pkwy (US 76) and Midlothian Tpke (US 60), just w. Int corridors. **Pets:** Other species. $25 daily fee/room. Designated rooms, service with restrictions, crate. ⟨ASK⟩ ⟨X⟩ ⟨&M⟩ ⟨◧⟩ ⟨▣⟩

△△△▽ ▽▽▽▽▽ The Jefferson Hotel Ⓗ ❖
(804) 788-8000. **$265-$395.** 101 W Franklin St 23220. Franklin and Adams sts; center. Int corridors. **Pets:** Dogs only. $50 daily fee/pet. Service with restrictions. ⟨ECO⟩ ⟨SAVE⟩ ⟨X⟩ ⟨◧⟩ ⟨¶⟩ ⟨⇀⟩ ⟨⊠⟩

▽▽▽▽ Omni Richmond Hotel Ⓗ ❖
(804) 344-7000. **$139-$309.** 100 S 12th St 23219. I-95, exit 74A; I-195, exit Canal St; in James Center. Int corridors. **Pets:** Medium, other species. $50 one-time fee/room. Crate. ⟨ASK⟩ ⟨X⟩ ⟨&M⟩ ⟨◧⟩ ⟨▣⟩ ⟨¶⟩ ⟨⇀⟩

▽▽▽ Red Roof Inn-Richmond South Ⓜ
(804) 271-7240. **$50-$120.** 4350 Commerce Rd 23234. I-95, exit 69. Ext corridors. **Pets:** Large. Service with restrictions, crate. ⟨X⟩ ⟨◧⟩

△△△▽ ▽▽▽▽ Sheraton Park South Hotel Ⓗ ❖
(804) 323-1144. **$79-$309.** 9901 Midlothian Tpke 23235. US 60, 1 mi w of Powhite Pkwy (US 76). Int corridors. **Pets:** Large, dogs only. Designated rooms, service with restrictions, supervision.
⟨SAVE⟩ ⟨X⟩ ⟨&M⟩ ⟨◧⟩ ⟨▣⟩ ⟨¶⟩ ⟨⇀⟩ ⟨⊠⟩

△△△▽ ▽▽▽▽ Sheraton Richmond West Ⓗ
(804) 285-2000. **$99-$239.** 6624 W Broad St 23230. I-64, exit 183 eastbound; exit 183B westbound. Int corridors. **Pets:** Accepted.
⟨SAVE⟩ ⟨X⟩ ⟨&M⟩ ⟨◧⟩ ⟨▣⟩ ⟨¶⟩ ⟨⇀⟩

▽▽ Super 8 Ⓜ
(804) 262-8880. **Call for rates.** 5615 Chamberlayne Rd 23227. I-95, exit 82. Int corridors. **Pets:** Accepted. ⟨X⟩ ⟨◧⟩ ⟨▣⟩

△△△▽ ▽▽▽▽ The Westin Richmond Ⓗ ❖
(804) 282-8444. **$129-$329.** 6631 W Broad St 23230. I-64, exit 183 eastbound; exit 183B westbound; in Reynolds Crossing. Int corridors. **Pets:** Medium, dogs only. Service with restrictions, crate.
⟨SAVE⟩ ⟨X⟩ ⟨&M⟩ ⟨◧⟩ ⟨▣⟩ ⟨¶⟩ ⟨⇀⟩ ⟨⊠⟩

SANDSTON

▼▼▼▼ Candlewood Suites Richmond Airport 🅗
(804) 652-1888. **Call for rates.** 5400 Audubon Dr 23231. I-64, exit 197A
(Richmond International Airport), 1 mi w. Int corridors. **Pets:** Accepted.
☒ ⚙ 🖥 🖥

ⒶⒶⒶ ▼▼▼ Red Roof Inn 🅜
(804) 440-5770. **Call for rates.** 5209 Williamsburg Rd 23150. I-64, exit
195, 1.5 mi s to Williamsburg Rd, then just e. Ext corridors. **Pets:** Large.
Service with restrictions, crate. 𝗦𝗔𝗩𝗘 ☒ 🖥

END METROPOLITAN AREA

ROANOKE

ⒶⒶⒶ ▼▼▼▼ Best Western Inn at Valley View 🅗
(540) 362-2400. **$69-$129.** 5050 Valley View Blvd 24012. I-581, exit 3E,
just e, then just s via shopping center exit. Int corridors. **Pets:** Medium,
dogs only. $25 one-time fee/room. Designated rooms, service with restric-
tions, crate. 𝗦𝗔𝗩𝗘 ☒ 🖥 🖥 ⤳

ⒶⒶⒶ ▼▼▼▼ Comfort Inn Airport 🅗
(540) 527-2020. **$80-$140.** 5070 Valley View Blvd 24012. I-81, exit 143
to I-581, exit 3, e to Hershberger Rd. Int corridors. **Pets:** Accepted.
𝗦𝗔𝗩𝗘 ☒ 🖥 🖥

ⒶⒶⒶ ▼▼ Days Inn 🅜
(540) 366-0341. **$60-$100.** 8118 Plantation Rd 24019. I-81, exit 146, just
e on SR 115. Ext/int corridors. **Pets:** Other species. $15 one-time fee/
room. Service with restrictions, supervision. 𝗦𝗔𝗩𝗘 ☒ 🖥 🖥 ⤳

▼ Extended StayAmerica Roanoke-Airport 🅗
(540) 366-3216. **$55-$100.** 2705 W Frontage Rd NW 24017. I-581, exit
3W, just w to Ordway Dr, then 0.4 mi n via service frontage road. Ext
corridors. **Pets:** Other species. $25 daily fee/room. Designated rooms,
service with restrictions, crate. 𝗔𝗦𝗞 ☒ 🖥 🖥

ⒶⒶⒶ ▼▼▼ Holiday Inn Hotel Tanglewood 🅗
(540) 774-4400. **$104-$149.** 4468 Starkey Rd 24018. I-581, exit Franklin
Rd/Salem, 0.8 mi n on SR 419. Int corridors. **Pets:** Medium. $35 one-
time fee/room. Designated rooms, service with restrictions, supervision.
𝗦𝗔𝗩𝗘 ☒ 🖥 🖥 🍽 ⤳

▼▼▼▼ Holiday Inn Roanoke 🅗
(540) 362-4500. **$95-$139.** 3315 Ordway Dr 24017. I-581, exit 3W, just w
to Ordway Dr, then 0.6 mi n via service road. Int corridors. **Pets:** Large.
$25 one-time fee/room. Service with restrictions, crate.
𝗔𝗦𝗞 ☒ 🖥 🖥 🍽 ⤳ ⊠

ⒶⒶⒶ ▼▼▼▼ MainStay Suites Roanoke Airport 🅗
(540) 527-3030. **$99-$175.** 5080 Valley View Blvd 24012. I-581, exit 3E,
just n. Int corridors. **Pets:** Accepted. 𝗦𝗔𝗩𝗘 ☒ 🖥 🖥

▼▼ Quality Inn Airport 🅗
(540) 366-8861. **$59-$149.** 6626 Thirlane Rd 24019. I-581, exit 2 southbound, just s on SR 117 (Peters Creek Rd), then just w. Ext corridors.
Pets: Accepted. 𝗔𝗦𝗞 ☒ 🖥 🖥 🍽 ⤳ ⊠

ⒶⒶⒶ ▼▼◆ Quality Inn/Tanglewood 🅜
(540) 989-4000. **$60-$85.** 3816 Franklin Rd SW 24014. I-581, exit US
220 (Franklin Rd/Salem), just n on US 220 business route, then w on
Frontage Rd. Ext corridors. **Pets:** Accepted. 𝗦𝗔𝗩𝗘 ☒ 🖥 🖥

▼▼▼ Residence Inn Roanoke Airport 🅗
(540) 265-1119. **$161-$197.** 3305 Ordway Dr NW 24017. I-581, exit 3W,
just s. Int corridors. **Pets:** Accepted. ☒ ⚙ 🖥 🖥 ⤳ ⊠

ⒶⒶⒶ ▼▼▼ Sleep Inn Tanglewood 🅗
(540) 772-1500. **$90-$130.** 4045 Electric Rd 24018. I-581/US 220, exit
Franklin Rd/Salem, 0.7 mi n on SR 419. Int corridors. **Pets:** Small, other
species. $25 daily fee/pet. Supervision. 𝗦𝗔𝗩𝗘 ☒ 🖥 🖥

◆ Super 8 🅜
(540) 563-8888. **$68-$110, 7 day notice.** 6616 Thirlane Rd 24019.
I-581, exit 25, s on SR 117 (Peters Creek Rd), then just w. Int corridors.
Pets: Accepted. 𝗔𝗦𝗞 ☒ 🖥

ROCKY MOUNT

▼▼ Comfort Inn-Rocky Mount 🅗
(540) 489-4000. **Call for rates.** 1730 N Main St 24151. 1.5 mi n on US
220 business route. Int corridors. **Pets:** Dogs only. $25 one-time fee/pet.
Service with restrictions, supervision. ☒ 🖥 🖥 ⤳

**◆▼▼◆ Rocky Mount Holiday Inn Express Hotel &
Suites** 🅗
(540) 489-5001. **Call for rates.** 395 Old Franklin Tpke 24151. US 220 S
and SR 40, 0.3 mi e. Int corridors. **Pets:** Accepted. ☒ 🖥 🖥 ⤳

RUTHER GLEN

▼▼ Super 8-Ruther Glen 🅜
(804) 448-2608. **$70-$140.** 24011 Ruther Glen Rd 22546. I-95, exit 104
(SR 207), just e on Rogers Clark Blvd. Ext corridors. **Pets:** Accepted.
☒ 🖥 ⤳

SALEM

▼▼▼▼ Comfort Suites Inn at Ridgewood Farm 🅗
(540) 375-4800. **$79-$110.** 2898 Keagy Rd 24153. I-81, exit 141, 4.7 mi
s on SR 419, then just w. Int corridors. **Pets:** Dogs only. $25 daily fee/
pet. Designated rooms, service with restrictions, supervision.
𝗔𝗦𝗞 ☒ 🖥 🖥

ⒶⒶⒶ ▼▼◆ Days Inn 🅜
(540) 986-1000. **$60-$100.** 1535 E Main St 24153. I-81, exit 141, 2 mi s
on SR 419, then just w on US 460. Ext/int corridors. **Pets:** $15 one-time
fee/room. Supervision. 𝗦𝗔𝗩𝗘 ☒ 🖥 🖥

ⒶⒶⒶ ▼▼ ◆ Econo Lodge-Roanoke/Salem 🅜
(540) 389-0280. **$34-$99.** 301 Wildwood Rd 24153. I-81, exit 137, just e
on SR 112. Ext corridors. **Pets:** Accepted. 𝗦𝗔𝗩𝗘 ☒ 🖥 🖥

▼▼◆▼ La Quinta Inn 🅗 ❀
(540) 562-2717. **$69-$149.** 140 Sheraton Dr 24153. I-81, exit 141, 0.5 mi
se on SR 419. Int corridors. **Pets:** Medium, other species. Service with
restrictions, supervision. 𝗔𝗦𝗞 ☒ 🖥 🖥 ⤳

ⒶⒶⒶ ▼▼▼▼ Quality Inn 🅜 🐾
(540) 387-1600. **$70-$89.** 151 Wildwood Rd 24153. I-81, exit 137, 0.3 mi
e on SR 112. Ext corridors. **Pets:** Dogs only. $25 one-time fee/room.
Service with restrictions, supervision. 𝗦𝗔𝗩𝗘 ☒ 🖥 🖥 ⤳

SOUTH BOSTON

▼▼▼ Holiday Inn-Express 🅗
(434) 575-4000. **Call for rates.** 1074 Bill Tuck Hwy 24592. Just e on US
58, from jct US 501. Int corridors. **Pets:** Accepted.
☒ ⚙ 🖥 🖥 ⤳

◇ Super 8 **M**

(434) 572-8868. **$55-$99, 3 day notice.** 1040 Bill Tuck Hwy 24592. Just e on US 58, from jct US 501. Int corridors. **Pets:** Medium. $10 daily fee/pet. Designated rooms, service with restrictions, supervision.

ASK ⊠ 🛏 💻 🏊

SOUTH HILL

◇◇◇◇ Fairfield Inn & Suites by Marriott **H**

(434) 447-6800. **$76-$92.** 150 Arnold Dr 23970. I-85, exit 12A, just e on US 58. Int corridors. **Pets:** Accepted. ⊠ &M 🛏 💻 🏊

AAA ◇◇◇ Quality Inn **H**

(434) 447-2600. **Call for rates.** 918 E Atlantic St 23970. I-85, exit 12B, just w. Ext corridors. **Pets:** Other species. $10 daily fee/pet. Service with restrictions, supervision. SAVE ⊠ 🛏 💻

◇◇ Super 8 **H**

(434) 447-2313. **Call for rates.** 250 Thompson St 23950. I-85, exit 12A, just n. Int corridors. **Pets:** Accepted. ⊠ &M 🛏

STAFFORD

AAA ◇◇◇◇ Best Western Aquia/Quantico Inn **H**

(540) 659-0022. **$90-$110.** 2868 Jefferson Davis Hwy 22554. I-95, exit 143A, jct US 1 and SR 610. Ext corridors. **Pets:** Medium, other species. $10 daily fee/pet. Designated rooms, crate. SAVE ⊠ 🛏 💻 🏊

◇◇◇◇ Holiday Inn Express **H** ❀

(540) 657-5566. **$99-$149.** 28 Greenspring Dr 22554. I-95, exit 143B, just w on Garrisonville Rd. Int corridors. **Pets:** Medium. $20 daily fee/pet. Service with restrictions, crate. ASK ⊠ 🛏 💻

AAA ◇◇◇◇ TownePlace Suites by Marriott **H** ❀

(540) 657-1990. **$89-$109.** 2772 Jefferson Davis Hwy 22554. I-95, exit 143A, just s on US 1. Int corridors. **Pets:** Other species. $10 daily fee/pet. Designated rooms, service with restrictions, crate.

SAVE ⊠ &M 🛏 💻 🏊

STAUNTON

AAA ◇◇◇ Best Western Staunton Inn **H** ❀

(540) 885-1112. **$85-$120.** 92 Rowe Rd 24401. I-81, exit 222, just e on US 250. Int corridors. **Pets:** Service with restrictions, supervision.

SAVE ⊠ 🛏 💻 🏊

AAA ◇◇◇ Comfort Inn **H** ❀

(540) 886-5000. **$72-$135.** 1302 Richmond Ave 24401. I-81, exit 222, just w on US 250. Int corridors. **Pets:** Other species. $10 daily fee/pet. Designated rooms, service with restrictions, crate.

SAVE ⊠ 🛏 💻 🏊

AAA ◇◇◇ Econo Lodge Staunton **H**

(540) 885-5158. **$45-$109, 3 day notice.** 1031 Richmond Ave 24401. I-81, exit 222, 0.7 mi w on US 250. Ext/int corridors. **Pets:** Medium. $10 daily fee/pet. Service with restrictions, supervision. SAVE ⊠ 🛏 💻

AAA ◇◇◇◇ Holiday Inn Golf & Conference Center **H**

(540) 248-6020. **$99-$199.** 152 Fairway Ln 24401. I-81, exit 225, 0.3 mi w on SR 275 (Woodrow Wilson Pkwy). Int corridors. **Pets:** $25 one-time fee/pet. Designated rooms, service with restrictions, supervision.

SAVE ⊠ 🛏 💻 ⫴ 🏊

◇◇ Red Roof Inn #706 **M**

(540) 885-3117. **$50-$110.** 42 Sangers Ln 24401. I-81, exit 222, just e on US 250. Ext corridors. **Pets:** Large. Service with restrictions, crate.

ASK ⊠ 🛏 💻

AAA ◇◇◇ Sleep Inn **H** ❀

(540) 887-6500. **Call for rates.** 222 Jefferson Hwy 24401. I-81, exit 222, just e on US 250. Int corridors. **Pets:** Service with restrictions, supervision. SAVE ⊠ 🛏 💻

AAA ◇◇◇◇ Stonewall Jackson Hotel & Conference Center **H** ❀

(540) 885-4848. **$112-$199.** 24 S Market St 24401. Between Beverly and Johnson sts; downtown. Int corridors. **Pets:** $25 daily fee/room. Service with restrictions, crate. ECO SAVE ⊠ 💻 ⫴ 🏊 ⊠

STEPHENS CITY

AAA ◇◇◇ Comfort Inn-Stephens City **H**

(540) 869-6500. **Call for rates.** 167 Town Run Ln 22655. I-81, exit 307, just se. Int corridors. **Pets:** Medium, other species. $10 one-time fee/pet. Service with restrictions, supervision. SAVE ⊠ 🛏 💻 🏊

STONY CREEK

AAA ◇◇◇◇ Hampton Inn-Stony Creek **H**

(434) 246-5500. **$79-$149.** 10476 Blue Star Hwy 23882. I-95, exit 33, 0.3 mi s on SR 301. Int corridors. **Pets:** Medium, other species. $15 daily fee/pet. Service with restrictions, supervision.

SAVE ⊠ &M 🛏 💻 🏊

AAA ◇◇◇◇ Sleep Inn & Suites **H**

(434) 246-5100. **$60-$140.** 11019 Blue Star Hwy 23882. I-95, exit 33, 0.3 mi s on SR 301. Int corridors. **Pets:** Medium, other species. $15 daily fee/pet. Designated rooms, service with restrictions, supervision.

SAVE ⊠ 🛏 💻 🏊

STRASBURG

◇◇◇ Hotel Strasburg **CI**

(540) 465-9191. **$89-$190.** 213 S Holliday St 22657. I-81, exit 298, 2.2 mi s on US 11, then just s. Int corridors. **Pets:** Accepted. ASK ⊠ ⫴

AAA ◇◇◇ Ramada **H**

(540) 465-2444. **$65-$99.** 21 Signal Knob Dr 22657. I-81, exit 298, just e. Int corridors. **Pets:** Accepted. ASK ⊠ 🛏 💻 ⫴ 🏊 ⊠

TAPPAHANNOCK

◇◇◇ The Essex Inn **BB**

(804) 443-9900. **$165-$205, 7 day notice.** 203 Duke St 22560. 0.3 mi s on US 17, then just e. Ext/int corridors. **Pets:** Medium, other species. $30 daily fee/pet. Designated rooms. ECO ASK ⊠ 🛏 💻

◇◇ Super 8 **M**

(804) 443-3888. **$72-$90.** 1800 Tappahannock Blvd 22560. US 17 and 360. Int corridors. **Pets:** $10 daily fee/room. Designated rooms, service with restrictions, supervision. ASK ⊠ 🛏 💻

WARRENTON

AAA ◇◇◇ Comfort Inn **M**

(540) 349-8900. **$90-$108.** 7379 Comfort Inn Dr 20187. 1.5 mi n on US 15/29, on service road. Ext/int corridors. **Pets:** Medium. $10 daily fee/pet. Supervision. SAVE ⊠ 🛏 💻 🏊

◇◇◇ Holiday Inn Express Hotel & Suites **H**

(540) 341-3461. **Call for rates.** 410 Holiday Ct 20186. US 15/29 and 17, exit Meetze Rd (SR 643), just w, then 0.8 mi n on Walker Rd. Int corridors. **Pets:** Accepted. ⊠ &M 🛏 💻 🏊

WARSAW

AAA ◇◇◇ Best Western Warsaw **H**

(804) 333-1700. **$84-$100.** 4522 Richmond Rd 22572. US 360, just w of town. Int corridors. **Pets:** Small. $10 daily fee/pet. Service with restrictions, supervision. SAVE ⊠ 🛏 💻 🏊

WASHINGTON

AAA ◇◇◇◇ Middleton Inn **BB**

(540) 675-2020. **$245-$595, 14 day notice.** 176 Main St 22747. 0.5 mi w on US 211 business route. Ext/int corridors. **Pets:** Accepted.

SAVE ⊠ 🛏 💻

WAYNESBORO

Best Western Waynesboro Inn & Suites Conference Center H

(540) 942-1100. **$95-$160.** 109 Apple Tree Ln 22980. I-64, exit 94, just n. Int corridors. **Pets:** Other species. $10 daily fee/room. Service with restrictions, supervision. SAVE ⊠ ⊟ ⊑ ⇶

Days Inn Waynesboro H ❀

(540) 943-1101. **$55-$120.** 2060 Rosser Ave 22980. I-64, exit 94, 0.5 mi n on US 340. Ext corridors. **Pets:** $10 daily fee/room. Service with restrictions, supervision. SAVE ⊠ ⊟ ⊑ ⇶

Quality Inn Waynesboro H

(540) 942-1171. **$61-$136.** 640 W Broad St 22980. I-64, exit 96, 3 mi w on SR 624; jct US 250 and 340. Ext/int corridors. **Pets:** $10 daily fee/pet. Service with restrictions. SAVE ⊠ ⊟ ⊑ ⇶

Residence Inn by Marriott Waynesboro H ❀

(540) 943-7426. **$107-$131.** 44 Windi Grove Dr 22980. I-64, exit 94, 0.5 mi n on US 340, then just e. Int corridors. **Pets:** Medium. $100 one-time fee/room. Designated rooms, service with restrictions, crate. ⊠ ⊟ ⊑ ⇶ ⊠

Super 8 H

(540) 943-3888. **$54-$110.** 2045 Rosser Ave 22980. I-64, exit 94, n on US 340 to Lew DeWitt Blvd, then just w to Apple Tree Ln. Int corridors. **Pets:** $5 daily fee/pet. Service with restrictions, supervision. SAVE ⊠ ⊟ ⊑

WILLIAMSBURG, JAMESTOWN & YORKTOWN AREA

WILLIAMSBURG

Americas Best Value Inn H

(757) 253-1663. **$49-$129.** 119 Bypass Rd 23185. US 60 Bypass Rd, 0.3 mi e of Richmond Rd. Ext corridors. **Pets:** Other species. $30 one-time fee/pet. Service with restrictions. SAVE ⊠ ⊟ ⊑ ⇶

Clarion Hotel Historic District H

(757) 229-4100. **$69-$169, 3 day notice.** 351 York St 23185. US 60 E, 0.3 mi se of jct SR 5 and 31. Ext/int corridors. **Pets:** Medium. $25 daily fee/pet. Designated rooms, service with restrictions, crate.
SAVE ⊠ ⊟ ⊑ ⇶ ⊠

Crowne Plaza Williamsburg at Fort Magruder H

(757) 220-2250. **$79-$189.** 6945 Pocahontas Tr 23185. US 60, 0.8 mi e of jct SR 5 and 31. Int corridors. **Pets:** Medium, other species. $45 one-time fee/pet. Service with restrictions, crate.
ECO ASK ⊠ ⊟ ⊑ ⇶ ⊠

Patrick Henry Inn & Suites H

(757) 229-9540. **$59-$89.** 249 York St 23185. E on US 60 (Richmond Rd) of jct SR 5 and 31; 1 blk from Colonial Williamsburg. Int corridors. **Pets:** Accepted. ECO SAVE ⊠ ⊟ ⊑ ⇶ ⊠

Residence Inn by Marriott Williamsburg H ❀

(757) 941-2000. **$97-$329.** 1648 Richmond Rd 23185. US 60, just w of jct Bypass Rd. Int corridors. **Pets:** $75 one-time fee/room. Service with restrictions, crate. SAVE ⊠ ⊟ ⊑ ⇶ ⊠

Super 8 Motel-Historic M

(757) 229-0500. **$30-$85.** 304 2nd St 23185. I-642, exit 242 (SR 199 W), 0.6 mi w to SR 143, 1.6 mi w to SR 162, then just w. Ext corridors. **Pets:** Medium. $10 daily fee/pet. Service with restrictions, crate.
SAVE ⊠ ⊟ ⊑ ⇶

Williamsburg Inn H

(757) 220-7978. **$319-$619, 3 day notice.** 136 E Francis St 23185. In Colonial Williamsburg restored area. Int corridors. **Pets:** Accepted.
ASK ⊠ ⊟ ⊟ ⇶ ⊠

YORKTOWN

Candlewood Suites-Yorktown H

(757) 952-1120. **Call for rates.** 329 Commonwealth Dr 23693. I-64, exit 256B, just n, then just e. Int corridors. **Pets:** Accepted.
⊠ ⊟ ⊟ ⊑ ⇶

Days Inn H

(757) 283-1111. **$70-$100.** 4531 George Washington Memorial Hwy 23692. I-64, exit 256B, 0.8 mi ne on Victory Blvd (SR 171), then 2.4 mi n on US 17. Int corridors. **Pets:** Accepted. ASK ⊠ ⊟ ⊑ ⇶

Staybridge Suites H

(757) 251-6644. **$99-$199.** 401 Commonwealth Dr 23693. I-64, exit 256B, just n, then just e. Int corridors. **Pets:** Accepted.
⊠ ⊟ ⊟ ⊑ ⇶

TownePlace Suites by Marriott H

(757) 874-8884. **$109-$119.** 200 Cybernetics Way 23693. I-64, exit 256B, e to Kiln Creek Pkwy. Int corridors. **Pets:** Other species. $100 one-time fee/room. Service with restrictions. SAVE ⊠ ⊟ ⊟ ⊑ ⇶

END AREA

WINCHESTER

Best Western Lee-Jackson Inn & Conference Center H

(540) 662-4154. **$63-$73.** 711 Millwood Ave 22601. I-81, exit 313B, just nw on US 50/522/17. Ext corridors. **Pets:** $5 daily fee/room. Service with restrictions, supervision. SAVE ⊠ ⊟ ⊑ ⊟ ⇶

Candlewood Suites H

(540) 667-8323. **$65-$139.** 1135 Millwood Pike 22602. I-81, exit 313 northbound; exit 313A southbound, just se. Int corridors. **Pets:** Accepted.
ASK ⊠ ⊟ ⊑

Days Inn M

(540) 667-1200. **$58-$85.** 2951 Valley Ave 22601. I-81, exit 310, just w, then 1.8 mi n on US 11. Ext/int corridors. **Pets:** Other species. $5 daily fee/pet. Designated rooms. SAVE ⊠ ⊟ ⊑

Quality Inn of Winchester H

(540) 545-8121. **$59-$75.** 1017 Millwood Pike 22602. I-81, exit 313 northbound; exit 313A southbound, just se on US 50/17, at US 522. Ext/int corridors. **Pets:** Accepted. SAVE ⊠ ⊟ ⊑ ⊟ ⇶

Red Roof Inn M

(540) 667-5000. **$58-$73.** 991 Millwood Pike 22602. I-81, exit 313 northbound; exit 313A southbound, just se on US 50/17. Ext corridors. **Pets:** Large. Service with restrictions, crate. SAVE ⊠ ⊟

Super 8 M

(540) 665-4450. **$49-$100.** 1077 Millwood Pike 22602. I-81, exit 313 northbound; exit 313A southbound, 0.3 mi se on US 50/17. Int corridors. **Pets:** Small. $10 daily fee/pet. Service with restrictions, supervision.
[SAVE] [X] [♨] [▭]

Travelodge of Winchester H

(540) 665-0685. **$60-$90, 7 day notice.** 160 Front Royal Pike 22602. I-81, exit 313 northbound; exit 313A southbound, just s on US 522. Int corridors. **Pets:** Other species. $10 one-time fee/pet. Service with restrictions, supervision. [SAVE] [X] [♨] [▭] [≈]

WOODSTOCK

Comfort Inn H ❀

(540) 459-7600. **$72-$119.** 1011 Motel Dr 22664. I-81, exit 283, just e. Int corridors. **Pets:** Large. $10 daily fee/pet. Service with restrictions, supervision. [SAVE] [X] [♨] [▭] [≈]

WYTHEVILLE

Best Western Wytheville Inn H

(276) 228-7300. **$62-$160, 7 day notice.** 355 Nye Rd 24382. I-77, exit 41, just e. Int corridors. **Pets:** $10 daily fee/pet. Designated rooms, service with restrictions, supervision. [SAVE] [X] [♨] [▭] [≈]

Budget Host Inn/Interstate Inn M

(276) 228-8618. **$45-$145.** 705 Chapman Rd 24382. I-77/81, exit 73, just w. Ext corridors. **Pets:** Small. $12 daily fee/pet. Service with restrictions, supervision. [ASK] [X] [♨]

Comfort Inn H

(276) 637-4281. **Call for rates.** 2594 E Lee Hwy 24382. I-77/81, exit 80, just w. Int corridors. **Pets:** Accepted. [X] [♨M] [♨] [▭] [≈]

Days Inn M ❀

(276) 228-5500. **$55-$85.** 150 Malin Dr 24382. I-77/81, exit 73, just w. Ext corridors. **Pets:** Medium. $10 daily fee/room. Service with restrictions, supervision. [ASK] [X] [♨] [▭]

Econo Lodge M

(276) 228-5525. **$45-$90, 7 day notice.** 280 Lithia Rd 24382. I-77/81, exit 73, just w. Ext corridors. **Pets:** Large, other species. $10 daily fee/pet. Service with restrictions, supervision. [SAVE] [X]

La Quinta Inn H ❀

(276) 228-7400. **$59-$109.** 1800 E Main 24382. I-77/81, exit 73, just w. Int corridors. **Pets:** Medium, other species. Service with restrictions, supervision. [SAVE] [X] [♨] [▭] [≈]

Ramada M

(276) 228-6000. **Call for rates.** 955 Peppers Ferry Rd 24382. I-77, exit 41, just e. Ext corridors. **Pets:** Accepted. [X] [♨] [▭] [¶] [≈]

Red Roof Inn & Suites M

(276) 223-1700. **Call for rates.** 1900 E Main St 24382. I-77/81, exit 73, just w. Ext corridors. **Pets:** Large. Service with restrictions, crate. [SAVE] [X] [♨] [▭] [≈]

Super 8 M

(276) 228-6620. **$59-$79.** 130 Nye Cir 24382. I-77, exit 41, just e. Ext corridors. **Pets:** Other species. $10 one-time fee/room. Service with restrictions, crate. [ASK] [X] [♨] [▭]

WASHINGTON

ABERDEEN

▼▼▼ GuestHouse International Inn & Suites ⊞

(360) 537-7460. **Call for rates.** 701 E Heron St 98520. Just e on US 12, cross street to Kansas St; downtown. Int corridors. **Pets:** Accepted.
✕ 🔲 🖵 🐾

AIRWAY HEIGHTS

AAA ▼▼▼ Days Inn & Suites ⊞ ❖

(509) 244-0222. **$65-$140.** 1215 S Garfield Rd 99001. I-90/US 2, exit 277 to SR 2, 4 mi w. Int corridors. **Pets:** Small, dogs only. $10 daily fee/ pet. Service with restrictions, supervision. SAVE ✕ 🔲 🖵

▼▼▼ Stratford Suites ⊞

(509) 321-1600. **Call for rates.** 11808 W Center Ln 99001. I-90/US 2, exit 277, 4 mi w on SR 2. Ext corridors. **Pets:** Large, other species. $15 daily fee/room. Service with restrictions, crate. ✕ ♿ 🔲 🖵

ANACORTES

AAA ▼▼▼ Anacortes Inn 🅼

(360) 293-3153. **$72-$128.** 3006 Commercial Ave 98221. Just s of down-town. Ext corridors. **Pets:** Dogs only. $10 daily fee/pet. Service with restrictions, supervision. SAVE ✕ 🔲 🖵 🐾

▼▼▼ Anacortes Ship Harbor Inn 🅼 ❖

(360) 293-5177. **$79-$179, 3 day notice.** 5316 Ferry Terminal Rd 98221. 0.3 mi s of ferry landing. Ext corridors. **Pets:** Medium, other spe-cies. $30 daily fee/pet. Service with restrictions, supervision.
ASK ✕ 🔲 🖵 🐾

AAA ▼▼ Cap Sante Inn 🅼 ❖

(360) 293-0602. **$71-$140.** 906 9th St 98221. On 9th St, just e. Ext corri-dors. **Pets:** Dogs only. $10 daily fee/pet. Designated rooms, service with restrictions, supervision. SAVE ✕ 🔲 🐾

AAA ▼▼▼▼ Fidalgo Country Inn & Suites ⊞ ❖

(360) 293-3494. **Call for rates.** 7645 SR 20 98221. Jct Fidalgo Bay Rd. Ext/int corridors. **Pets:** Medium, other species. $20 daily fee/pet. Desig-nated rooms, service with restrictions, crate.
SAVE ✕ ♿ 🔲 🖵 🐾

▼▼ Islands Inn 🅼

(360) 293-4644. **Call for rates.** 3401 Commercial Ave 98221. Just s of downtown. Ext corridors. **Pets:** Accepted. ✕ 🔲 🖵 🍴 🐾

▼▼▼▼ Majestic Inn & Spa ⊞

(360) 299-1400. **$159-$394.** 419 Commercial Ave 98221. Downtown. Int corridors. **Pets:** Small, dogs only. $50 one-time fee/pet. Service with restrictions, supervision. ASK ✕ 🔲 🖵 🍴 🐾

ASHFORD

▼▼ ▼▼ Mountain Meadows Inn Bed & Breakfast 🅑🅑

(360) 569-2788. **$99-$165, 14 day notice.** 28912 SR 706 E 98304. West end of town. Ext/int corridors. **Pets:** Medium, other species. $10 daily fee/pet. Designated rooms, supervision.
✕ 🔲 🖵 🐾 🐾 🐾

BELLINGHAM

▼▼ ▼▼ Bellingham GuestHouse Inn ⊞

(360) 671-9600. **$79-$130.** 805 Lakeway Dr 98229. I-5, exit 253 (Lake-way Dr), just ne. Int corridors. **Pets:** Medium, dogs only. $10 daily fee/ room. Designated rooms, service with restrictions, supervision.
ASK ✕ 🔲 🖵

AAA ▼▼▼▼ Best Western Heritage Inn ⊞ ❖

(360) 647-1912. **$99-$159, 14 day notice.** 151 E McLeod Rd 98226. I-5, exit 256A, just e. Int corridors. **Pets:** $20 daily fee/pet. Service with restrictions, supervision. SAVE ✕ 🔲 🖵 🐾 ✕

AAA ▼▼▼▼ Best Western Lakeway Inn & Conference Center ⊞ ❖

(360) 671-1011. **$89-$189.** 714 Lakeway Dr 98229. I-5, exit 253 (Lake-way Dr), just se. Int corridors. **Pets:** Small. $25 daily fee/room. Desig-nated rooms, service with restrictions, supervision.
SAVE ✕ 🔲 🖵 🍴 🐾 ✕

AAA ▼▼▼ Econo Lodge Inn & Suites ⊞

(360) 671-4600. **$59-$109.** 3750 Meridian St 98225. I-5, exit 256A, just w. Ext corridors. **Pets:** Very small, dogs only. $10 one-time fee/pet. Desig-nated rooms, service with restrictions, supervision.
SAVE ✕ 🔲 🖵 🐾

AAA ▼▼▼ Holiday Inn Express-Bellingham ⊞ ❖

(360) 671-4800. **$98-$168.** 4160 Meridian St 98226. I-5, exit 256A, 0.7 mi e. Int corridors. **Pets:** $15 one-time fee/room. Service with restrictions, supervision. SAVE ✕ ♿ 🔲 🖵 🐾

AAA ▼▼▼ Hotel Bellwether ⊞

(360) 392-3100. **$161-$589, 3 day notice.** One Bellwether Way 98225. I-5, exit 253 (Lakeway Dr), 0.9 mi nw via Lakeway Dr and E Holly St, just w on Bay St, 0.6 mi n via W Chestnut St and Roeder Ave, then just w. Int corridors. **Pets:** Accepted. SAVE ✕ 🔲 🖵 🍴 ✕

La Quinta Inn Bellingham H ❄
(360) 671-6200. **$69-$119.** 125 E Kellogg Rd 98226. I-5, exit 256A, 1 mi ne via Meridian St. Int corridors. **Pets:** Medium, other species. Service with restrictions, supervision.

Motel 6-44 M
(360) 671-4494. **$55-$75.** 3701 Byron Ave 98225. I-5, exit 252, just nw. Ext corridors. **Pets:** Other species. Service with restrictions, supervision.

Quality Inn Baron Suites H ❄
(360) 647-8000. **$90-$190.** 100 E Kellogg Rd 98226. I-5, exit 256A, 1 mi ne via Meridian St. Ext/int corridors. **Pets:** Medium, other species. $10 daily fee/pet. Designated rooms, service with restrictions, supervision.

BLAINE

Semiahmoo Resort H ❄
(360) 318-2000. **$119-$439, 3 day notice.** 9565 Semiahmoo Pkwy 98230. I-5, exit 270, 9.5 mi nw on Semiahmoo Spit. Int corridors. **Pets:** Medium, dogs only. $50 one-time fee/room. Designated rooms, service with restrictions.

BURLINGTON

Cocusa Motel H
(360) 757-6044. **$63-$135.** 370 W Rio Vista 98233. I-5, exit 230, just e. Ext corridors. **Pets:** $20 one-time fee/room. Designated rooms, service with restrictions, supervision.

CASHMERE

Village Inn Motel M
(509) 782-3522. **$59-$94, 7 day notice.** 229 Cottage Ave 98815. On Business Rt US 2 and 97; downtown. Ext corridors. **Pets:** Small, dogs only. $10 daily fee/pet. Designated rooms, no service, supervision.

CASTLE ROCK

Blue Heron Inn B&B BB
(360) 274-9595. **Call for rates.** 2846 Spirit Lake Hwy 98611. I-5, exit 49, 5 mi e on US 504. Int corridors. **Pets:** Accepted.

Timberland Inn & Suites M
(360) 274-6002. **$60-$200.** 1271 Mount St. Helens Way 98611. I-5, exit 49, just ne. Ext corridors. **Pets:** Small, dogs only. $15 daily fee/pet. Service with restrictions, supervision.

CENTRALIA

Motel 6-394 M
(360) 330-2057. **$41-$65.** 1310 Belmont Ave 98531. I-5, exit 82, just w on Harrison Ave, then just n. Ext corridors. **Pets:** Other species. Service with restrictions, supervision.

CHEHALIS

Best Western Park Place Inn & Suites H ❄
(360) 748-4040. **$90-$109.** 201 SW Interstate Ave 98532. I-5, exit 76, just se. Int corridors. **Pets:** Small, dogs only. $10 daily fee/pet. Designated rooms, service with restrictions, supervision.

CHELAN

Best Western Lakeside Lodge & Suites H
(509) 682-4396. **$89-$329.** 2312 W Woodin Ave 98816. West end of town. Ext corridors. **Pets:** Medium, dogs only. $15 daily fee/pet. Designated rooms, service with restrictions, supervision.

CHEWELAH

Nordlig Motel M
(509) 935-6704. **$58-$63.** W 101 Grant Ave 99109. North edge of town on US 395. Ext corridors. **Pets:** Medium, dogs only. $5 one-time fee/pet. Service with restrictions, supervision.

CLARKSTON

Best Western Rivertree Inn H ❄
(509) 758-9551. **$99-$149.** 1257 Bridge St 99403. 0.9 mi w of Snake River Bridge on US 12. Ext corridors. **Pets:** Large. $20 one-time fee/room. Designated rooms, service with restrictions, supervision.

Motel 6 M
(509) 758-1631. **$56-$70, 7 day notice.** 222 Bridge St 99403. Just w of Snake River Bridge. Ext corridors. **Pets:** Other species. Service with restrictions, supervision.

Quality Inn & Suites Conference Center H
(509) 758-9500. **$90-$113.** 700 Port Dr 99403. Just w of Snake River Bridge on US 12, just n on 5th St. Int corridors. **Pets:** $10 daily fee/pet. Designated rooms, service with restrictions, supervision.

CLE ELUM

Cascade Mountain Inn M
(509) 674-2380. **$54-$119.** 906 E 1st St 98922. I-90, exit 85, 1 mi nw. Int corridors. **Pets:** Small, dogs only. $20 daily fee/pet. Designated rooms, service with restrictions, supervision.

Cle Elum Travelers Inn M
(509) 674-5535. **$60-$85.** 1001 E 1st St 98922. I-90, exit 85, 1 mi w on SR 903. Ext/int corridors. **Pets:** Accepted.

Lodge at Suncadia H
(509) 649-6460. **$99-$399, 7 day notice.** 3600 Suncadia Tr 98922. I-90, exit 80, 2 mi n, then 0.3 mi w. Int corridors. **Pets:** Accepted.

Stewart Lodge M
(509) 674-4548. **$74-$97.** 805 W 1st St 98922. I-90, exit 84 eastbound, just n; exit westbound, 0.6 mi w. Ext corridors. **Pets:** Medium. $10 daily fee/pet. Designated rooms, service with restrictions, supervision.

Timber Lodge Inn M
(509) 674-5966. **$70-$90.** 301 W 1st St 98922. I-90, exit 84 eastbound, 1 mi ne; exit westbound, just w; downtown. Ext/int corridors. **Pets:** Medium, other species. $16 one-time fee/pet. Designated rooms, service with restrictions, supervision.

COLFAX

Best Western Wheatland Inn H
(509) 397-0397. **$95-$175.** 701 N Main 99111. Downtown. Int corridors. **Pets:** Accepted.

CONCRETE

Ovenell's Heritage Inn B&B and Log Cabins CA
(360) 853-8494. **$110-$160, 3 day notice.** 46276 Concrete Sauk Valley Rd 98237. 0.5 mi w of downtown on SR 20, 3 mi se. Ext/int corridors. **Pets:** Dogs only. $20 daily fee/pet. Designated rooms, service with restrictions, supervision.

COULEE DAM

Coulee House Inn & Suites M
(509) 633-1101. **$99-$199, 7 day notice.** 110 Roosevelt Way 99116. Just e of river bridge. Ext corridors. **Pets:** Accepted.

COUPEVILLE

The Coupeville Inn H
(360) 678-6668. **Call for rates.** 200 Coveland St 98239. Just s of Front St; w of Main St; downtown. Int corridors. **Pets:** Accepted.

DAYTON

▼▼▼▼ The Weinhard Hotel 🅷

(509) 382-4032. **$125-$180, 7 day notice.** 235 E Main St 99328. Downtown. Int corridors. **Pets:** Dogs only. $20 one-time fee/pet. Supervision. ⒶⓈⓀ ☒ 🔛

EAST WENATCHEE

▼▼ Cedars Inn, East Wenatchee 🅷

(509) 886-8000. **Call for rates.** 80 Ninth St NE 98802. Just e of SR 28. Int corridors. **Pets:** Accepted. ☒ 🔛 🔋 🖥 ⤳

EATONVILLE

Ⓐ Ⓐ Ⓐ ▼▼ Mill Village Motel 🅜

(360) 832-3200. **$80-$100.** 210 Center St E 98328. Just e of jct SR 161; center. Ext corridors. **Pets:** Small, other species. $10 one-time fee/room. Service with restrictions, supervision. ⓈⒶⓋⒺ ☒ 🔋 🖥

ELLENSBURG

Ⓐ Ⓐ Ⓐ ▼▼▼▼ Best Western Lincoln Inn & Suites 🅷 🐾

(509) 925-4244. **$100-$300.** 211 W Umptanum Rd 98926. I-90, exit 109, just n, then just w. Int corridors. **Pets:** Medium, dogs only. $15 daily fee/pet. Designated rooms, service with restrictions, supervision.

ⓈⒶⓋⒺ ☒ 🔋 🖥 ⤳

▼▼▼▼ Ellensburg Comfort Inn 🅷

(509) 925-7037. **Call for rates.** 1722 Canyon Rd 98926. I-90, exit 109. Int corridors. **Pets:** Medium. $10 daily fee/pet. Service with restrictions, supervision. ☒ 🔋 🖥 ⤳

Ⓐ Ⓐ Ⓐ ▼▼▼▼ Holiday Inn Express 🅷 🐾

(509) 962-9400. **$99-$159.** 1620 Canyon Rd 98926. I-90, exit 109, just n. Int corridors. **Pets:** Other species. $10 daily fee/room. Designated rooms, service with restrictions, supervision. ⓈⒶⓋⒺ ☒ 🔋 🖥 ⤳

Ⓐ Ⓐ Ⓐ ▼▼▼▼ I-90 Inn Motel 🅜

(509) 925-9844. **$64-$84.** 1390 N Dollarway Rd 98926. I-90, exit 106, just n. Ext corridors. **Pets:** Accepted. ⓈⒶⓋⒺ ☒ 🔋

▼▼ Quality Inn & Conference Center 🅷

(509) 925-9800. **Call for rates.** 1700 Canyon Rd 98926. I-90, exit 109, just n. Int corridors. **Pets:** Accepted. ☒ 🔋 🖥 🍽 ⤳

ELMA

▼▼ Microtel Inn & Suites-Elma 🅷

(360) 482-6868. **Call for rates.** 800 E Main St 98541. Just ne of jct US 12 and SR 8. Int corridors. **Pets:** Accepted. ☒ 🔋 🖥

EPHRATA

Ⓐ Ⓐ Ⓐ ▼▼▼▼ Best Western Rama Inn 🅷 🐾

(509) 754-7111. **$110-$170.** 1818 Basin St SW 98823. On SR 28; west end of town. Int corridors. **Pets:** Other species. $25 one-time fee/room. Service with restrictions, supervision. ⓈⒶⓋⒺ ☒ 🔛 🔋 🖥 ⤳

FERNDALE

▼▼ Ferndale Super 8 🅷

(360) 384-8881. **$70-$185.** 5788 Barrett Rd 98248. I-5, exit 262, just ne. Int corridors. **Pets:** Large. $15 one-time fee/room. Designated rooms, service with restrictions, supervision. ⒶⓈⓀ ☒ 🔛 🔋 🖥 ⤳

Ⓐ Ⓐ Ⓐ ▼▼▼▼ Silver Reef Hotel Casino & Spa 🅷

(360) 383-0777. **$116-$269.** 4876 Haxton Way 98248. I-5, exit 260, 3.6 mi w. Int corridors. **Pets:** Accepted. ⓈⒶⓋⒺ ☒ 🔋 🖥 🍽 ⤳ ☒

FORKS

Ⓐ Ⓐ Ⓐ ▼▼▼▼ Forks Motel 🅜

(360) 374-6243. **$58-$150.** 351 US 101 98331. On US 101 (S Forks Ave) just s of Division St. Ext corridors. **Pets:** Accepted.

ⓈⒶⓋⒺ ☒ 🔋 🖥 ⤳

▼▼ Manitou Lodge 🅱🅱 ✿

(360) 374-6295. **$99-$179, 14 day notice.** 813 Kilmer Rd 98331. 7.7 mi sw on SR 110 (LaPush Rd), 0.7 mi w on Mora Rd, then 0.8 mi n. Ext/int corridors. **Pets:** Large, other species. $10 daily fee/room. Designated rooms, supervision. ☒ 🔋 🖥 🐾 📺 🗙

▼▼ Miller Tree Inn Bed & Breakfast 🅱🅱

(360) 374-6806. **$105-$205, 7 day notice.** 654 E Division St 98331. 0.3 mi e of US 101 (S Forks Ave). Ext/int corridors. **Pets:** Other species. $10 daily fee/room. Designated rooms, service with restrictions.

☒ 🔋 🖥 🐾 🗙

Ⓐ Ⓐ Ⓐ ▼▼▼▼ Olympic Suites Inn 🅜

(360) 374-5400. **$49-$129.** 800 Olympic Dr 98331. North end of town; just ne off US 101 (S Forks Ave). Ext corridors. **Pets:** Dogs only. $10 one-time fee/pet. Designated rooms, service with restrictions, supervision.

ⓈⒶⓋⒺ ☒ 🔋 🖥 🐾

GOLDENDALE

Ⓐ Ⓐ Ⓐ ▼▼▼▼ Quality Inn & Suites 🅷

(509) 773-5881. **$89-$179.** 808 E Simcoe Dr 98620. US 97, exit Simcoe Dr, just sw. Ext corridors. **Pets:** Accepted.

ⓈⒶⓋⒺ ☒ 🔋 🖥 🍽 ⤳

ILWACO

Ⓐ Ⓐ Ⓐ ▼▼ Heidi's Inn 🅜

(360) 642-2387. **$59-$89.** 126 E Spruce St 98624. Downtown. Ext corridors. **Pets:** Small, dogs only. $6 one-time fee/pet. Designated rooms, service with restrictions, supervision. ⓈⒶⓋⒺ ☒ 🔋 🖥 🐾

KALALOCH

Ⓐ Ⓐ Ⓐ ▼▼▼▼ Kalaloch Lodge 🅲🅰

(360) 962-2271. **Call for rates.** 157151 Hwy 101 98331. In Kalaloch; at MM 157. Ext/int corridors. **Pets:** Accepted.

🅴🅲🅾 ⓈⒶⓋⒺ ☒ 🔋 🖥 🍽 🐾 🗙

KALAMA

Ⓐ Ⓐ Ⓐ ▼▼ Kalama River Inn 🅜

(360) 673-2855. **$53-$70.** 602 NE Frontage Rd 98625. I-5, exit 30 northbound, 0.4 mi n; exit southbound, 0.4 mi s. Ext corridors. **Pets:** Small, dogs only. $500 daily fee/pet. Service with restrictions, supervision.

ⓈⒶⓋⒺ ☒ 🔋

KELSO

Ⓐ Ⓐ Ⓐ ▼▼▼▼ Best Western Aladdin 🅷

(360) 425-9660. **$81-$99.** 310 Long Ave 98626. I-5, exit 39, 1.1 mi w via Allen and W Main sts, then just n on 5th Ave NW. Int corridors. **Pets:** Accepted. ⓈⒶⓋⒺ ☒ 🔋 🖥 ⤳

▼▼▼▼ GuestHouse Inn & Suites 🅷

(360) 414-5953. **Call for rates.** 501 Three Rivers Dr 98626. I-5, exit 39, 0.3 mi w on Allen St, then 0.3 mi s. Int corridors. **Pets:** Accepted.

☒ 🔋 🖥 ⤳

▼▼▼▼ Motel 6–43 🅜

(360) 425-3229. **$55-$65.** 106 Minor Rd 98626. I-5, exit 39, 0.3 mi ne. Ext corridors. **Pets:** Other species. Service with restrictions, supervision.

☒ 🔋 ⤳

▼▼▼▼ Red Lion Hotel & Conference Center Kelso/Longview 🅷

(360) 636-4400. **$153-$265.** 510 Kelso Dr 98626. I-5, exit 39, 0.3 mi se. Int corridors. **Pets:** Other species. $20 one-time fee/room. Service with restrictions, supervision. ⒶⓈⓀ ☒ 🔋 🖥 🍽 ⤳

▼▼ Super 8 🅷

(360) 423-8880. **$60-$108.** 250 Kelso Dr 98626. I-5, exit 39, just se. Int corridors. **Pets:** Other species. $10 daily fee/room. Service with restrictions, supervision. ⒶⓈⓀ ☒ 🔛 🔋 🖥 ⤳

KENNEWICK

▼▼▼ Best Western Kennewick Inn ⊞
(509) 586-1332. **$89-$170.** 4001 W 27th Ave 99337. I-82, exit 113 (US 395), 0.8 mi n. Int corridors. **Pets:** Medium. $10 one-time fee/room. Service with restrictions, supervision. [SAVE] [✕] [&M] [🛏] [💻] [🏊] [✕]

▼▼ Clover Island Inn ⊞ ❀
(509) 586-0541. **$89-$349.** 435 Clover Island Dr 99336. US 395, exit Port of Kennewick, 1 mi e on Columbia Dr, then 0.7 mi n. Int corridors. **Pets:** $10 one-time fee/pet. Service with restrictions, supervision.
[ASK] [✕] [💻] [🏊] [✕]

▼▼ Comfort Inn Ⓜ
(509) 783-8396. **$65-$140.** 7801 W Quinault Ave 99336. 0.5 mi s on Columbia Center Blvd from SR 240. Int corridors. **Pets:** Medium, dogs only. $10 daily fee/pet. Designated rooms, service with restrictions, supervision. [ASK] [✕] [&M] [🛏] [💻] [🏊]

▼▼ Days Inn Kennewick ⊞
(509) 735-9511. **$63-$150.** 2811 W 2nd Ave 99336. Jct US 395 and Clearwater Ave, just s, just w. Ext/int corridors. **Pets:** Accepted.
[SAVE] [✕] [🛏] [💻] [🏊]

▼▼ Fairfield Inn by Marriott ⊞
(509) 783-2164. **$130-$158.** 7809 W Quinault Ave 99336. 0.5 mi s on Columbia Center Blvd from SR 240. Int corridors. **Pets:** Medium. $15 daily fee/pet. Service with restrictions, supervision.
[✕] [&M] [🛏] [💻] [🏊]

▼▼ Guesthouse International Suites ⊞
(509) 735-2242. **$72-$82.** 5616 W Clearwater Ave 99336. US 395, 1.9 mi w. Int corridors. **Pets:** Small, dogs only. $20 one-time fee/pet. Designated rooms, service with restrictions, supervision.
[SAVE] [✕] [&M] [🛏] [💻]

▼▼ Kennewick Super 8 ⊞
(509) 736-6888. **$71-$91, 10 day notice.** 626 N Columbia Center Blvd 99336. 1.1 mi s of SR 240. Int corridors. **Pets:** Other species. $10 daily fee/room. Service with restrictions, supervision.
[SAVE] [✕] [&M] [🛏] [💻] [🏊]

▼▼ Quality Inn & Suites ⊞
(509) 736-3326. **$69-$119.** 4220 W 27th Pl 99338. I-82, exit 113 (US 395), 0.8 mi n. Int corridors. **Pets:** Accepted.
[ASK] [✕] [&M] [🛏] [💻] [🏊] [✕]

▼▼ Quality Inn Kennewick ⊞
(509) 735-6100. **Call for rates.** 7901 W Quinault Ave 99336. 0.5 mi s on Columbia Center Blvd from SR 240. Int corridors. **Pets:** Accepted.
[✕] [&M] [🛏] [💻] [🏊]

▼▼▼ Red Lion Hotel Columbia Center-Kennewick ⊞
(509) 783-0611. **Call for rates.** 1101 N Columbia Center Blvd 99336. SR 240, 0.5 mi s. Int corridors. **Pets:** Other species. $20 one-time fee/room. Service with restrictions, supervision.
[SAVE] [✕] [&M] [🛏] [💻] [🍴] [🏊]

LACEY

▼▼▼ Candlewood Suites Olympia/Lacey ⊞ ❀
(360) 491-1698. **$140-$186.** 4440 3rd Ave SE 98503. I-5, exit 108 northbound, just n; exit 109 southbound, just s on Martin Ave E, just e on College Way, then just s. Int corridors. **Pets:** Medium, other species. $75 one-time fee/room. Service with restrictions, supervision.
[ASK] [✕] [🛏] [💻]

▼▼ La Quinta Inn ⊞ ❀
(360) 412-1200. **$79-$119.** 4704 Park Center Ave NE 98516. I-5, exit 109, just sw. Int corridors. **Pets:** Medium, other species. Service with restrictions, supervision. [ASK] [✕] [🛏] [💻] [🏊]

▼▼ Quality Inn & Suites ⊞ ❀
(360) 493-1991. **$70-$130.** 120 College Site SE 98503. I-5, exit 109, just sw. Int corridors. **Pets:** Medium. $15 daily fee/pet. Service with restrictions, supervision. [ASK] [✕] [🛏] [💻] [✕]

LA CONNER

▼▼▼ La Conner Country Inn ⊞ ❀
(360) 466-3101. **$129-$239.** 107 S 2nd St 98257. 2nd and Morris sts; downtown. Ext/int corridors. **Pets:** Dogs only. $50 one-time fee/room. Designated rooms, service with restrictions, supervision.
[SAVE] [✕] [🛏] [💻] [🍴]

LANGLEY

▼▼▼ Boat Yard Inn ⊞
(360) 221-5120. **$140-$250, 10 day notice.** 200 Wharf St 98260. East end of town on the waterfront. Ext corridors. **Pets:** Small, dogs only. $50 one-time fee/pet. Designated rooms, supervision.
[ASK] [✕] [&M] [🛏] [💻] [AC]

▼▼▼ The Inn at Langley ⊞
(360) 221-3033. **Call for rates.** 400 1st St 98260. Center. Ext corridors. **Pets:** Accepted. [✕] [🛏] [💻] [AC]

LEAVENWORTH

▼▼▼ Bavarian Ritz Hotel ⊞
(509) 548-5455. **$89-$269, 3 day notice.** 633 Front St 98826. Center. Ext/int corridors. **Pets:** Dogs only. $10 daily fee/room. Service with restrictions, supervision. [SAVE] [✕] [🛏] [💻]

▼▼▼ Best Western Icicle Inn Resort ⊞
(509) 548-7000. **$140-$190.** 505 W US 2 98826. West side of town. Int corridors. **Pets:** Small. $25 one-time fee/pet. Designated rooms, service with restrictions, supervision. [SAVE] [✕] [🛏] [💻] [🍴] [🏊] [✕]

▼▼▼ Der Ritterhof Motor Inn ⊞ ❀
(509) 548-5845. **$70-$107, 3 day notice.** 190 US 2 98826. 0.3 mi w. Ext corridors. **Pets:** Large, dogs only. $15 daily fee/pet. No service, supervision. [SAVE] [✕] [&M] [🛏] [💻] [🏊]

▼ The Evergreen Inn Ⓜ ❀
(509) 548-5515. **Call for rates.** 1117 Front St 98826. US 2, just s. Ext corridors. **Pets:** $10 daily fee/pet. Designated rooms, service with restrictions, supervision. [✕] [🛏] [💻]

▼▼▼ Howard Johnson Ⓜ
(509) 548-4326. **$80-$296.** 405 US 2 98826. West end of town. Ext corridors. **Pets:** Accepted. [ASK] [✕] [&M] [🛏] [💻] [🏊]

▼▼ Obertal Inn Ⓜ
(509) 548-5204. **$79-$179.** 922 Commercial St 98826. Off US 2; center. Ext corridors. **Pets:** Accepted. [SAVE] [✕] [🛏] [💻]

▼▼ Quality Inn & Suites ⊞
(509) 548-7992. **$70-$296.** 185 US 2 98826. 0.3 mi w. Ext corridors. **Pets:** Accepted. [✕] [&M] [🛏] [💻] [🏊]

▼▼ River's Edge Lodge Ⓜ
(509) 548-7612. **$99-$299, 7 day notice.** 8401 US 2 98826. 3.5 mi e. Ext corridors. **Pets:** Accepted. [✕] [🛏] [💻] [🏊]

LIBERTY LAKE

▼▼▼ Best Western Peppertree Liberty Lake Inn ⊞
(509) 755-1111. **$70-$299.** 1816 N Pepper Ln 99019. I-90, exit 296 (Liberty Lake), just n. Int corridors. **Pets:** Accepted.
[SAVE] [✕] [&M] [🛏] [💻] [🏊] [✕]

▼▼▼ Cedars Inn Spokane at Liberty Lake ⊞
(509) 340-3333. **$69-$110.** 2327 N Madson Rd 99019. I-90, exit 296 (Liberty Lake), 1 mi e on Appleway Ave, then just n. Int corridors. **Pets:** Large, other species. $15 daily fee/pet. Service with restrictions, supervision. [SAVE] [✕] [&M] [🛏] [💻] [🏊]

LONG BEACH

▼▼◆ Anchorage Cottages 🅲🄰 ☘

(360) 642-2351. **$70-$128, 30 day notice.** 2209 Boulevard N 98631. Just w of SR 103. Ext corridors. **Pets:** Other species. $10 daily fee/pet. Designated rooms, supervision. 🅧 ⊟ 💻 🅰 🛈

▲▲▲ ▼▼◆ The Breakers 🄲🄾

(360) 642-4414. **$68-$298, 20 day notice.** 210 26th St NW 98631. North end of downtown. Ext corridors. **Pets:** Dogs only. $15 daily fee/room. Designated rooms, service with restrictions, supervision. 🆂🅰🆅🅴 🅧 ⊟ 💻 🅰 🅧 🅰

▼▼ Our Place at the Beach 🄷

(360) 642-3793. **Call for rates.** 1309 South Blvd 98631. Just w of SR 103; south end of town. Ext corridors. **Pets:** Accepted.
🅧 ⊟ 💻 🅧 🅰

▼▼◆ Rodeway Inn & Suites 🄷 ☘

(360) 642-3714. **Call for rates.** 115 3rd St SW 98631. Downtown. Ext corridors. **Pets:** Other species. $7 daily fee/pet. Service with restrictions, supervision. 🅧 ⊟ 💻 🅰 🅰

▲▲▲ ▼▼▼ Super 8 🄷

(360) 642-8988. **$79-$199.** 500 Ocean Beach Blvd 98631. On SR 103; downtown. Int corridors. **Pets:** Accepted. 🆂🅰🆅🅴 🅧 🄼 ⊟ 💻 🅰

LONGVIEW

▲▲▲ ▼▼▼ Hudson Manor Inn & Suites 🄼

(360) 425-1100. **$65-$90.** 1616 Hudson St 98632. Downtown. Ext corridors. **Pets:** Accepted. 🆂🅰🆅🅴 🅧 ⊟ 💻

▲▲▲ ▼▼▼ Longview Travelodge 🄼

(360) 423-6460. **$55-$95.** 838 15th Ave 98632. Downtown; opposite Medical Center. Ext corridors. **Pets:** Other species. $15 daily fee/pet. Designated rooms, service with restrictions, supervision. 🆂🅰🆅🅴 🅧 ⊟ 💻

▼▼▼ Quality Inn & Suites 🄷

(360) 414-1000. **$70-$100.** 723 7th Ave 98632. I-5, exit 36, 3 mi w on SR 432. Int corridors. **Pets:** Medium, other species. $20 daily fee/pet. Designated rooms, service with restrictions, supervision. 🄰🆂🅺 🅧 🄼 ⊟ 💻 🅰

▲▲▲ ▼ The Townhouse Motel 🄼

(360) 423-7200. **$55-$95, 3 day notice.** 744 Washington Way 98632. Downtown. Ext corridors. **Pets:** Large, other species. $10 one-time fee/pet. Supervision. 🆂🅰🆅🅴 🅧 ⊟ 💻 🅰

MOCLIPS

▲▲▲ ▼▼▼ Ocean Crest Resort 🄷

(360) 276-4465. **$79-$209, 7 day notice.** 4651 SR 109 98562. South edge of town. Ext corridors. **Pets:** Other species. $18 daily fee/pet. Designated rooms, service with restrictions, supervision.
🆂🅰🆅🅴 🅧 ⊟ 💻 🍴 🅰 🅧 🅰

MORTON

▲▲▲ ▼▼▼ The Seasons Motel 🄼

(360) 496-6835. **$80-$100.** 200 Westlake Ave 98356. On US 12; jct SR 7. Ext corridors. **Pets:** Small, other species. $10 one-time fee/room. Service with restrictions, supervision. 🆂🅰🆅🅴 🅧 ⊟ 💻

MOSES LAKE

▼▼▼ AmeriStay Inn & Suites 🄷

(509) 764-7500. **$89-$259.** 1157 N Stratford Rd 98837. I-90, exit 179, 1 mi n to SR 17, 2.8 mi nw, exit Stratford Rd, just n, then just e. Int corridors. **Pets:** Accepted. 🄰🆂🅺 🅧 🄼 ⊟ 💻 🅰

▲▲▲ ▼▼▼▼ Best Western Lake Front Hotel 🄷 ☘

(509) 765-9211. **$119-$139.** 3000 Marina Dr 98837. I-90, exit 176, just nw. Int corridors. **Pets:** Large, other species. $20 one-time fee/room. Designated rooms, service with restrictions, supervision.
🆂🅰🆅🅴 🅧 🄼 ⊟ 💻 🍴 🅰 🅧

▲▲▲ ▼▼▼▼ Comfort Suites Moses Lake 🄷

(509) 765-3731. **$99-$299.** 1700 E Kittleson Rd 98837. I-90, exit 179, just nw. Int corridors. **Pets:** Small, dogs only. $15 daily fee/pet. Designated rooms, service with restrictions, supervision.
🆂🅰🆅🅴 🅧 🄼 ⊟ 💻 🅰

▼▼▼ Inn at Moses Lake 🄷

(509) 766-7000. **$79-$139.** 1741 E Kittleson Rd 98837. I-90, exit 179, just n. Int corridors. **Pets:** $10 one-time fee/room. Designated rooms, service with restrictions, supervision. 🄰🆂🅺 🅧 ⊟ 💻 🅰

▲▲▲ ▼▼▼ Moses Lake Super 8 🄷

(509) 765-8886. **$80-$140.** 449 Melva Ln 98837. I-90, exit 176, just n. Int corridors. **Pets:** Large, other species. $10 daily fee/pet. Service with restrictions, supervision. 🆂🅰🆅🅴 🅧 ⊟ 💻 🅰

▲▲▲ ▼▼▼ Shilo Inn Suites-Moses Lake 🄷 ☘

(509) 765-9317. **$80-$175.** 1819 E Kittleson Rd 98837-9719. I-90, exit 179, just n. Int corridors. **Pets:** Dogs only. $25 one-time fee/room. Designated rooms, service with restrictions, supervision.
🆂🅰🆅🅴 🅧 ⊟ 💻 🅰 🅧

MOUNT RAINIER NATIONAL PARK

▲▲▲ ▼▼▼▼▼ Alta Crystal Resort at Mt Rainier 🄷 ☘

(360) 663-2500. **$139-$269, 30 day notice.** 68317 SR 410 E 98022. 2 mi outside northeast entrance. Ext corridors. **Pets:** Dogs only. $50 one-time fee/pet. Designated rooms, service with restrictions.
🆂🅰🆅🅴 🅧 ⊟ 💻 🅰 🅧 🅰

MOUNT VERNON

▲▲▲ ▼▼▼ Best Western College Way Inn 🄷

(360) 424-4287. **$95-$166.** 300 W College Way 98273. I-5, exit 227, just w. Ext corridors. **Pets:** $20 daily fee/pet. Designated rooms, service with restrictions, supervision. 🆂🅰🆅🅴 🅧 ⊟ 💻 🅰

▲▲▲ ▼▼▼ Best Western CottonTree Inn & Convention Center 🄷 ☘

(360) 428-5678. **$99-$180.** 2300 Market St 98273. I-5, exit 227, 0.3 mi e on College Way, then 0.5 mi n on Riverside Dr. Int corridors. **Pets:** Dogs only. $25 deposit/room. Designated rooms, service with restrictions, supervision. 🆂🅰🆅🅴 🅧 🄼 ⊟ 💻 🅰

▲▲▲ ▼▼▼ Quality Inn-Mount Vernon 🄷

(360) 428-7020. **Call for rates.** 1910 Freeway Dr 98273. I-5, exit 227, just w on College Way, then just n. Ext corridors. **Pets:** $10 daily fee/pet. Designated rooms, service with restrictions, supervision.
🆂🅰🆅🅴 🅧 ⊟ 💻

▲▲▲ ▼▼ Tulip Inn 🄼

(360) 428-5969. **$65-$109.** 2200 Freeway Dr 98273. I-5, exit 227, just w on College Way, then just n. Ext corridors. **Pets:** Accepted.
🆂🅰🆅🅴 🅧 ⊟ 💻

OAK HARBOR

▲▲▲ ▼▼▼ Acorn Motor Inn 🄷

(360) 675-6646. **$46-$119.** 31530 SR 20 98277. On SR 20 at 300th Ave W (SE Barrington Dr). Int corridors. **Pets:** Other species. $10 daily fee/room. Designated rooms, service with restrictions, supervision.
🆂🅰🆅🅴 🅧 ⊟

▲▲▲ ▼▼▼ Candlewood Suites 🄷

(360) 279-2222. **$99-$169.** 33221 SR 20 98277. Just n of town. Int corridors. **Pets:** Medium. $10 daily fee/pet. Service with restrictions, supervision. 🆂🅰🆅🅴 🅧 🄼 ⊟ 💻

▲▲▲ ▼▼▼ Coachman Inn 🄷

(360) 675-0727. **$84-$209.** 32959 SR 20 98277. Jct Goldie Rd and Midway Blvd. Ext corridors. **Pets:** Medium. $8 daily fee/pet. Designated rooms, service with restrictions, supervision.
🆂🅰🆅🅴 🅧 ⊟ 💻 🅰 🅧

OCEAN PARK

◇ Ocean Park Resort Ⓜ

(360) 665-4585. **$65-$168, 10 day notice.** 25904 R St 98640. Just e of SR 103; downtown. Ext corridors. **Pets:** Accepted.

Ⓐ$Ⓚ ⊠ 🛏 💻 🏊 ✕ 𝒦 ☎

OCEAN SHORES

◇◇ ◇◇◇◇ Canterbury Inn Ⓒⓞ

(360) 289-3317. **$82-$198.** 643 Ocean Shores Blvd NW 98569. 0.3 mi s of Chance a La Mer Blvd. Int corridors. **Pets:** Large, dogs only. $150 deposit/room, $15 daily fee/pet. Designated rooms, no service, supervision. SAVE ⊠ 🛏 💻 🏊 𝒦

◇◇ ◇◇◇◇ The Polynesian Condominium Resort Ⓒⓞ

(360) 289-3361. **Call for rates.** 615 Ocean Shores Blvd NW 98569. 0.3 mi s of Chance a La Mer Blvd. Ext/int corridors. **Pets:** $15 daily fee/pet. Designated rooms, service with restrictions, supervision.

SAVE ⊠ 🛏 💻 ❙❙ 🏊 ✕ 𝒦

◇◇ ◇◇◇◇ Shilo Inn Suites Hotel–Ocean Shores Ⓗ ❀

(360) 289-4600. **$140-$330.** 707 Ocean Shores Blvd NW 98569-9593. Northwest corner of Chance a La Mer and Ocean Shores blvds NW. Int corridors. **Pets:** Dogs only. $25 one-time fee/room. Designated rooms, service with restrictions, supervision.

SAVE ⊠ 🔥 🛏 💻 ❙❙ 🏊 ✕

OLYMPIA

◇◇ ◇◇◇◇ Red Lion Hotel Olympia Ⓗ

(360) 943-4000. **$179.** 2300 Evergreen Park Dr SW 98502. I-5, exit 104, 0.7 mi w on US 101, just n on Cooper Point Rd N, 0.7 mi e on S Evergreen Park Dr SW, then just n on Lakeridge Way SW. Int corridors. **Pets:** Other species. $20 one-time fee/room. Service with restrictions, supervision. SAVE ⊠ 🔥 🛏 💻 ❙❙ 🏊

OLYMPIC NATIONAL PARK

◇◇ ◇◇◇ Lake Crescent Lodge Ⓗ

(360) 928-3211. **$107-$241, 7 day notice.** 416 Lake Crescent Rd 98363. 22 mi w of Port Angeles on US 101. Ext/int corridors.
Pets: Accepted. SAVE ⊠ 🛏 💻 ❙❙ ✕ 𝒦 𝒲 ☎

◇ Log Cabin Resort ⒸⒶ

(360) 928-3325. **Call for rates.** 3183 E Beach Rd 98363. 3.3 mi nw of US 101 (MM 232). Ext corridors. **Pets:** Other species. $17 daily fee/pet. Designated rooms, service with restrictions, supervision.

⊠ 🛏 💻 ❙❙ ✕ 𝒦 𝒲 ☎

OMAK

◇◇ ◇◇◇◇ Best Western Peppertree Inn at Omak Ⓗ

(509) 422-2088. **$70-$250.** 820 Koala Dr 98841. US 97, just n of Riverside Dr. Int corridors. **Pets:** Accepted. SAVE ⊠ 🔥 🛏 💻 🏊

◇◇ ◇◇◇ Omak Inn LLC Ⓗ

(509) 826-3822. **$75-$90.** 912 Koala Dr 98841. On US 97, just n of Riverside Dr. Int corridors. **Pets:** $25 one-time fee/room. Designated rooms, service with restrictions, supervision. SAVE ⊠ 🛏 💻 🏊

OTHELLO

◇◇ ◇◇◇◇ Best Western Othello Inn Ⓗ ❀

(509) 488-5671. **$105-$125.** 1020 E Cedar St 99344. Just off Main St; jct 10th St. Int corridors. **Pets:** Other species. $20 one-time fee/room. Service with restrictions, supervision. SAVE ⊠ 🛏 💻 🏊

PACIFIC BEACH

◇ Sandpiper Beach Resort Ⓒⓞ

(360) 276-4580. **Call for rates.** 4159 SR 109 98571. 1.8 mi s. Ext corridors. **Pets:** Accepted. ⊠ 🛏 💻 𝒦 𝒲 ☎

PACKWOOD

◇◇ Cowlitz River Lodge Ⓜ

(360) 494-4444. **$65-$95, 7 day notice.** 13069 US 12 98361. East end of town. Ext corridors. **Pets:** Medium, other species. $20 daily fee/pet. Designated rooms, service with restrictions, supervision. ⊠ 🛏

◇◇ ◇◇◇ Crest Trail Lodge Ⓗ

(360) 494-4944. **$70-$100.** 12729 US 12 98361. Just w of town. Int corridors. **Pets:** Small, dogs only. $10 one-time fee/room. Designated rooms, supervision. SAVE ⊠ 🛏 💻

◇ Packwood Inn Ⓜ

(360) 494-5500. **Call for rates.** 13032 US 12 98361. Center. Ext corridors. **Pets:** Accepted. ⊠ 🛏 💻 🏊

PASCO

◇◇ ◇◇◇◇ Best Western Pasco Inn & Suites Ⓗ

(509) 543-7722. **$100-$170.** 2811 N 20th Ave 99301. I-182, exit 12B, just n. Int corridors. **Pets:** Medium. $10 one-time fee/room. Service with restrictions, supervision. SAVE ⊠ 🔥 🛏 💻 🏊

◇◇◇◇ Holiday Inn Express Pasco at TRAC Ⓗ

(509) 543-7000. **$109-$189.** 4525 Convention Pl 99301. I-182, exit 9 (Rd 68), just n, then just e. Int corridors. **Pets:** Small, dogs only. $10 daily fee/pet. Service with restrictions, supervision.

Ⓐ$Ⓚ ⊠ 🔥 🛏 💻 🏊

◇ Motel 6-Pasco Ⓜ

(509) 546-2010. **Call for rates.** 1520 N Oregon St 99301. I-182, exit 14A (SR 395 S). Ext corridors. **Pets:** Other species. Service with restrictions, supervision. ⊠ 🛏 🏊

◇◇ ◇◇◇◇ Red Lion Hotel Pasco Ⓗ

(509) 547-0701. **Call for rates.** 2525 N 20th Ave 99301. I-182, exit 12B, just n. Int corridors. **Pets:** Other species. $20 one-time fee/room. Service with restrictions, supervision. SAVE ⊠ 🔥 🛏 💻 ❙❙ 🏊

◇◇ ◇◇◇ Sleep Inn Ⓗ ❀

(509) 545-9554. **$81-$115.** 9930 Bedford St 99301. I-182, exit 7, just ne. Int corridors. **Pets:** $10 daily fee/room. Designated rooms, service with restrictions, supervision. SAVE ⊠ 🔥 🛏 💻 🏊

PORT ANGELES

◇◇ ◇◇◇ Days Inn Ⓗ

(360) 452-4015. **$59-$180.** 1510 E Front St 98362. Front St at Alder St; on east side. Ext corridors. **Pets:** Small. $5 daily fee/pet. Designated rooms, service with restrictions, crate. SAVE ⊠ 🛏 💻 🏊

◇◇ ◇◇◇ Quality Inn-Uptown Ⓜ ❀

(360) 457-9434. **$80-$300.** 101 E 2nd St 98362. At Laurel St, just w of US 101; on the bluff. Ext corridors. **Pets:** Small, dogs only. $10 daily fee/pet. Designated rooms, service with restrictions, supervision.

SAVE ⊠ 🛏 💻 𝒦

◇◇ ◇◇◇◇ Red Lion Hotel Port Angeles Ⓗ

(360) 452-9215. **$119-$299.** 221 N Lincoln St 98362. On US 101 westbound; at ferry landing. Ext/int corridors. **Pets:** Other species. $20 one-time fee/room. Service with restrictions, supervision.

SAVE ⊠ 🛏 💻 ❙❙ 🏊 ✕

◇◇ ◇◇◇ Riviera Inn Ⓜ

(360) 417-3955. **$69-$159.** 535 E Front St 98362. On US 101 W; downtown. Ext corridors. **Pets:** Small. $15 daily fee/pet. Designated rooms, service with restrictions, supervision. SAVE ⊠ 🛏 💻 𝒦

◇ Super 8 Ⓜ

(360) 452-8401. **Call for rates.** 2104 E 1st St 98362. 1.8 mi e of downtown, just s of US 101. Int corridors. **Pets:** Accepted.

⊠ 🔥 🛏 💻

PORTLAND METROPOLITAN AREA (NEARBY OREGON)

VANCOUVER

▼▼ Comfort Suites H
(360) 253-3100. **$90-$160.** 4714 NE 94th Ave 98662. I-205, exit 30 (SR 500 W), 0.6 mi w to Thurston Way, just n to Vancouver Mall Dr, then 0.5 mi e; southeast edge of Westfield Shopping Center. Int corridors. **Pets:** Medium, other species. $20 one-time fee/room. Service with restrictions, supervision. (A$K) ⊠ 🖪 🖃 ➾

▼▼ Days Inn H
(360) 574-6000. **$79-$149.** 13207 NE 20th Ave 98686. I-5, exit 7, just e; I-205, exit 36, just w. Int corridors. **Pets:** Accepted.
(A$K) ⊠ 🖪 🖃 ➾

▼▼ Days Inn & Suites H
(360) 253-5000. **$60-$100.** 9107 NE Vancouver Mall Dr 98662. I-205, exit 30 (SR 500 W), 0.6 mi w to Thurston Way, just n to Vancouver Mall Dr, then 0.5 mi e; southeast edge of Westfield Shopping Center. Int corridors. **Pets:** Medium, other species. $15 one-time fee/pet. Service with restrictions, supervision. (A$K) ⊠ 🖪 🖃 ➾

▼▼ Extended StayAmerica-Portland-Vancouver H
(360) 604-8530. **$80-$90.** 300 NE 115th Ave 98684. I-205, exit 28 (Mill Plain Blvd E), just ne. Int corridors. **Pets:** Other species. $25 daily fee/room. Designated rooms, service with restrictions, crate.
(A$K) ⊠ 🖪 🖃

◆ ▼◆▼ Hilton Vancouver Washington and Vancouver Convention Center H
(360) 993-4500. **$99-$219.** 301 W 6th St 98660. I-5, exit 1C (Mill Plain Blvd) southbound, 0.3 mi w, then 0.3 mi s on W Columbia St; exit 1B northbound, 0.5 mi, follow signs to City Center/6th St. Int corridors. **Pets:** Accepted. (ECO) (SAVE) ⊠ 🖾 🖪 🖃 🍴 ➾ 🐾

▼◆▼ Homewood Suites by Hilton H
(360) 750-1100. **$109-$169.** 701 SE Columbia Shores Blvd 98661. SR 14, exit 1, just s. Ext/int corridors. **Pets:** Other species. $10 daily fee/pet, $25 one-time fee/pet. Supervision. ⊠ 🖪 🖃 ➾ 🐾

▼◆▼ La Quinta Inn & Suites H ❀
(360) 566-1100. **$61-$129.** 1500 NE 134th St 98685. I-5, exit 7, just w; I-205, exit 36, 0.5 mi w. Int corridors. **Pets:** Medium, other species. Service with restrictions, supervision. (A$K) ⊠ 🖾 🖪 🖃 ➾

◆ ▼◆▼ Phoenix Inn Suites-Vancouver H
(360) 891-9777. **$79-$149.** 12712 SE 2nd Cir 98684. I-205, exit 28 (Mill Plain Blvd E), 0.8 mi e, then just n on SE 126th Ave. Int corridors. **Pets:** Medium. $15 daily fee/pet. Designated rooms, service with restrictions, supervision. (SAVE) ⊠ 🖪 🖃 ➾

◆ ▼◆▼ Quality Inn & Suites H
(360) 696-0516. **$63-$85.** 7001 NE Hwy 99 98665. I-5, exit 4, 0.5 mi se. Int corridors. **Pets:** Other species. $10 daily fee/room. Service with restrictions, supervision. (SAVE) ⊠ 🖪 🖃 ➾

▼◆▼ Red Lion Hotel Vancouver @ the Quay H
(360) 694-8341. **$99-$179.** 100 Columbia St 98660. 0.5 mi s on dock at foot of Columbia St. Int corridors. **Pets:** Other species. $20 one-time fee/room. Service with restrictions, supervision.
(A$K) ⊠ 🖾 🖪 🖃 🍴 ➾ 🐾

▼◆▼ Residence Inn Vancouver H
(360) 253-4800. **$139-$149.** 8005 NE Parkway Dr 98662. I-205, exit 30 (SR 500 W), 0.5 mi w to Thurston Way, just n to NE Parkway Dr, then just w. Ext corridors. **Pets:** Other species. $75 one-time fee/room. Service with restrictions. ⊠ 🖾 🖪 🖃 ➾ 🐾

◆ ▼◆▼ Rodeway Inn & Suites H
(360) 254-0900. **$55-$99.** 9201 NE Vancouver Mall Dr 98662. I-205, exit 30 (SR 500 W), 0.6 mi w to Thurston Way, just n to Vancouver Mall Dr, then 0.5 mi e; southeast edge of Westfield Shopping Center. Int corridors. **Pets:** Accepted. (SAVE) ⊠ 🖾 🖪 🖃 ➾

◆ ▼◆▼ Shilo Inn & Suites-Salmon Creek H ❀
(360) 573-0511. **$82-$190.** 13206 Hwy 99 98686. I-5, exit 7, just e; I-205, exit 36, just w. Int corridors. **Pets:** Dogs only. $25 one-time fee/room. Designated rooms, service with restrictions, supervision.
(SAVE) ⊠ 🖪 🖃 ➾ 🐾

▼◆▼ Staybridge Suites Vancouver-Portland H
(360) 891-8282. **Call for rates.** 7301 NE 41st St 98662. I-205, exit 30 (SR 500 W), 1.5 mi w to NE Andresen Rd, just n to NE 40th St, just e to NE 72nd St, just n to NE 41st St, then just e. Int corridors.
Pets: Accepted. ⊠ 🖾 🖪 🖃 ➾ 🐾

END METROPOLITAN AREA

PORT LUDLOW

▼◆▼ The Resort at Port Ludlow H ❀
(360) 437-7000. **$89-$699, 3 day notice.** 1 Heron Rd 98365. 8 mi n of Hood Canal Floating Bridge; in town. Int corridors. **Pets:** $30 one-time fee/room. Supervision. ⊠ 🖪 🖃 🍴 🐾 🃏

PORT TOWNSEND

◆ ▼◆▼ Bishop Victorian Hotel H
(360) 385-6122. **$110-$245, 3 day notice.** 714 Washington St 98368. Corner of Washington and Quincy sts. Int corridors. **Pets:** Accepted.
(SAVE) ⊠ 🖪 🖃 🃏

◆ ▼◆▼ Palace Hotel H ❀
(360) 385-0773. **$59-$289.** 1004 Water St 98368. Downtown. Int corridors. **Pets:** Large. $10 daily fee/pet. Supervision.
(SAVE) ⊠ 🖪 🖃 🃏

◆ ▼◆▼ The Swan Hotel M
(360) 385-1718. **$90-$510, 3 day notice.** 216 Monroe St 98368. Downtown. Ext corridors. **Pets:** Accepted. (SAVE) ⊠ 🖪 🖃 🃏

PROSSER

◆ ▼◆▼ Best Western The Inn at Horse Heaven H
(509) 786-7977. **$99-$149.** 259 Merlot Dr 99350. I-82, exit 80, just s. Int corridors. **Pets:** Accepted. (SAVE) ⊠ 🖾 🖪 🖃 ➾

PULLMAN

◆ ▼◆▼ Hilltop Inn H
(509) 332-0928. **$70-$249, 3 day notice.** 928 NW Olsen St 99163. 1.6 mi e on SR 270 from US 195. Int corridors. **Pets:** Large. $15 daily fee/pet. Designated rooms, service with restrictions, supervision.
(SAVE) ⊠ 🖾 🖪 🖃 ➾ 🐾

▼◆▼ Holiday Inn Express Hotel & Suites H ❀
(509) 334-4437. **$99-$179.** SE 1190 Bishop Blvd 99163. Jct US 195 business route, 0.5 mi s, 1 mi e on SR 270. Int corridors. **Pets:** Medium, dogs only. $20 daily fee/pet. Designated rooms, service with restrictions, supervision. (A$K) ⊠ 🖾 🖪 🖃 ➾

◆ ▼◆▼ Quality Inn Paradise Creek H
(509) 332-0500. **$85-$160, 3 day notice.** 1400 SE Bishop Blvd 99163. Jct US 195 business route, just s, 1 mi e on SR 270. Int corridors.
Pets: Accepted. (SAVE) ⊠ 🖪 🖃 🐾

QUINAULT

AAA WWW Lake Quinault Lodge **H** ❀
(360) 288-2900. **$99-$284, 3 day notice.** 345 S Shore Rd 98575. 2 mi off US 101. Ext/int corridors. **Pets:** $25 one-time fee/room. Designated rooms, service with restrictions, supervision.
ECO **SAVE** ✕ 🖥 💻 ⑪ 🚬 ✕ 🐾 ✆

QUINCY

AAA WWW Traditional Inns **M**
(509) 787-3525. **$85-$149.** 500 F St SW 98848. West end of town on SR 28. Ext corridors. **Pets:** Accepted. **SAVE** ✕ 🖥 💻

REPUBLIC

AAA WWW Prospector Inn **H**
(509) 775-3361. **$51-$175.** 979 S Clark Ave 99166. Downtown. Int corridors. **Pets:** Other species. $12 daily fee/pet. Designated rooms, service with restrictions, supervision. **SAVE** ✕ 🖥 💻 ✕

RICHLAND

WWW Clarion Hotel & Conference Center **H**
(509) 946-4121. **Call for rates.** 1515 George Washington Way 99352. I-182, exit 5B, 2.5 mi n. Int corridors. **Pets:** Accepted.
✕ 🖥 💻 ⑪ 🚬 ✕

AAA WWW Days Inn **M**
(509) 943-4611. **$67-$79.** 615 Jadwin Ave 99352. I-182, exit 5B, 0.9 mi n; just w of SR 240 business route; downtown. Ext corridors. **Pets:** Accepted. **SAVE** ✕ 🖥 💻 🚬

WWW Holiday Inn Express Hotel & Suites **H**
(509) 737-8000. **Call for rates.** 1970 Center Pkwy 99352. Just s on Columbia Center Blvd from SR 240, just w. Int corridors. **Pets:** Accepted.
✕ 🖥 🖥 💻 🚬

RICHLAND (continued)

AAA WWWW Red Lion Hotel Richland Hanford House **H**
(509) 946-7611. **$139.** 802 George Washington Way 99352. I-182, exit 5B, 1.3 mi n on SR 240 business route. Ext/int corridors. **Pets:** Other species. $20 one-time fee/room. Service with restrictions, supervision.
SAVE ✕ 🖥 🖥 💻 ⑪ 🚬 ✕

AAA WWWW Shilo Inn Suites Hotel–Richland **H** ❀
(509) 946-4661. **$102-$185.** 50 Comstock St 99352. I-182, exit 5B, 0.5 mi n. Ext corridors. **Pets:** Dogs only. $25 one-time fee/room. Designated rooms, service with restrictions, supervision.
SAVE ✕ 🖥 💻 ⑪ 🚬 ✕

RITZVILLE

AAA WWW Americas Best Value Inn- Colwell **M**
(509) 659-1620. **$52-$85.** 501 W 1st Ave 99169. I-90, exit 220, 0.9 mi n; downtown. Ext corridors. **Pets:** Medium. $10 daily fee/pet. Designated rooms, service with restrictions. **SAVE** ✕ 🖥 💻 🚬

AAA WWW Best Western Bronco Inn **H**
(509) 659-5000. **$70-$200.** 105 W Galbreath Way 99169. I-90, exit 221, cross overpass, then second left. Int corridors. **Pets:** Accepted.
SAVE ✕ 🖥 💻 🚬

WWW La Quinta Inn Ritzville **H** ❀
(509) 659-1007. **$59-$129.** 1513 Smitty's Blvd 99169. I-90, exit 221, just n. Int corridors. **Pets:** Medium, other species. Service with restrictions, supervision. **ASK** ✕ 🖥 🖥 💻 🚬 ✕

WWW Top Hat Motel **M**
(509) 659-1100. **$42-$64.** 210 E 1st Ave 99169. I-90, exit 221, 1 mi ne via Division St. Ext corridors. **Pets:** Accepted. **ASK** 🖥

SAN JUAN ISLANDS AREA

DEER HARBOR

WW Deer Harbor Inn **CI** ❀
(360) 376-4110. **Call for rates.** 33 Inn Ln 98243. In Deer Harbor; 7 mi sw of ferry landing; 3.5 mi sw of Westsound. Ext/int corridors. **Pets:** $25 daily fee/pet. Designated rooms, service with restrictions, supervision.
✕ 🖥 💻 ⑪ ✕ ✆

FRIDAY HARBOR

WW Argyle House Bed & Breakfast **BB**
(360) 378-4084. **$100-$250, 14 day notice.** 685 Argyle Ave 98250. In Friday Harbor; 0.3 mi e of jct Spring St. Ext/int corridors. **Pets:** Dogs only. Supervision. ✕ 🖥 💻 ✕ ✆

WW Earthbox Motel & Spa **H**
(360) 378-4000. **$147-$407, 10 day notice.** 410 Spring St 98250. In Friday Harbor; 0.5 mi w of ferry dock. Ext corridors. **Pets:** $15 daily fee/pet. Designated rooms, service with restrictions, supervision.
✕ 🖥 💻 🚬 ✕

WWW Friday Harbor House **H**
(360) 378-8455. **Call for rates.** 130 West St 98250. In Friday Harbor; just w of Spring St; at the waterfront. Ext/int corridors. **Pets:** Accepted.
✕ 🖥 💻 ⑪

AAA WWW Lakedale Resort **H**
(360) 378-2350. **Call for rates.** 4313 Roche Harbor Rd 98250. 4 mi n of Friday Harbor via Tucker Ave. Ext/int corridors. **Pets:** Dogs only. $35 one-time fee/pet. Designated rooms, no service, supervision.
SAVE ✕ 🖥 💻 ✕ ✆

AAA WWW Trumpeter Inn Bed & Breakfast **BB**
(360) 378-3884. **$125-$195, 7 day notice.** 318 Trumpeter Way 98250. 1.5 mi w of Friday Harbor via Spring St and San Juan Valley Rd. Int corridors. **Pets:** Accepted. **SAVE** ✕ ✆ 🐾 ✆

END AREA

SEATTLE METROPOLITAN AREA

AUBURN

▼▼▼ Auburn GuestHouse Inn 🅗

(253) 735-9600. **$89-$99.** 9 14th St NW 98001. SR 167, exit 15th St NW, 0.8 mi e, just s on a St NE, then just w. Int corridors. **Pets:** Dogs only. $10 daily fee/pet. Service with restrictions, supervision.

🅐🆂🅺 ⊠ 🔧 🖵

ⓐⓐ▼ ▼▼▼▼ Best Western Peppertree Auburn Inn 🅗

(253) 887-7600. **$80-$299.** 401 8th St SW 98001. SR 18, exit C St, just s, then just w. Int corridors. **Pets:** Small, dogs only. $10 daily fee/pet. Service with restrictions, supervision. 🆂🅰🆅🅴 ⊠ 🔧 🖵 ⋙ ⊠

ⓐⓐ▼ ▼ Cedars Inn Auburn 🅗

(253) 833-8007. **$55-$109.** 102 15th St NE 98002. SR 167, exit 15th St NW, 0.8 mi e. Int corridors. **Pets:** Accepted. 🆂🅰🆅🅴 ⊠ 🔧

▼▼ Travelodge Inn & Suites 🅗 🐾

(253) 833-7171. **$69-$129.** 9 16th St NW 98001. SR 167, exit 15th St NW, 0.8 mi e, then just n on a St NE. Int corridors. **Pets:** Large, other species. $10 daily fee/pet. Service with restrictions, supervision.

🅐🆂🅺 ⊠ 🅶🅼 🔧 🖵

BAINBRIDGE ISLAND

ⓐⓐ▼ ▼▼▼▼ Best Western Bainbridge Island Suites 🅗

(206) 855-9666. **$129-$169.** 350 NE High School Rd 98110. 0.8 mi n of ferry dock on SR 305, then just w. Int corridors. **Pets:** Medium. $50 one-time fee/room. Designated rooms, service with restrictions, supervision.

🆂🅰🆅🅴 ⊠ 🔧 🖵

BELLEVUE

ⓐⓐ▼ ▼▼▼▼ ▼▼▼▼ Bellevue Club Hotel 🅗 🐾

(425) 454-4424. **$285-$655.** 11200 SE 6th St 98004. I-405, exit 12, 0.4 mi nw. Int corridors. **Pets:** Medium, dogs only. $50 daily fee/pet. Service with restrictions, supervision. 🆂🅰🆅🅴 ⊠ 🅶🅼 🔧 🖵 🍴 ⋙ ⊠

ⓐⓐ▼ ▼▼ Days Inn Bellevue 🅗

(425) 643-6644. **$75-$120.** 3241 156th Ave SE 98007. I-90, exit 11 westbound; exit 11A (156th Ave SE) eastbound, just ne. Ext corridors. **Pets:** Medium. $25 one-time fee/pet. Supervision. 🆂🅰🆅🅴 ⊠ 🔧 🖵

▼▼▼ Extended StayAmerica-Seattle-Bellevue 🅗

(425) 453-8186. **$110-$120.** 11400 Main St 98004. I-405, exit 13A, just se. Int corridors. **Pets:** Other species. $25 daily fee/room. Designated rooms, service with restrictions, crate. 🅐🆂🅺 ⊠ 🔧 🖵

▼▼▼ Hilton Bellevue 🅗 🐾

(425) 455-1300. **$129-$269.** 300 112th Ave SE 98004. I-405, exit 12, just nw. Int corridors. **Pets:** Large. $75 one-time fee/pet. Designated rooms, service with restrictions, supervision. ⊠ 🔧 🖵 🍴 ⋙

ⓐⓐ▼ ▼▼ ▼ La Residence Suite Hotel 🅗

(425) 455-1475. **$125-$199.** 475 100th Ave NE 98004. I-405, exit 13B, 0.9 mi w on NE 8th St, then just s. Int corridors. **Pets:** Other species. $10 daily fee/pet. Service with restrictions, crate. 🆂🅰🆅🅴 ⊠ 🔧 🖵

ⓐⓐ▼ ▼▼▼▼ Larkspur Landing Bellevue/Seattle 🅗

(425) 373-1212. **$169-$219.** 15805 SE 37th St 98006. I-90, exit 11 westbound; exit 11A (156th Ave SE) eastbound, 0.9 mi se on south frontage road. Int corridors. **Pets:** Accepted. 🆂🅰🆅🅴 ⊠ 🔧 🖵

ⓐⓐ▼ ▼▼ Red Lion Hotel Bellevue 🅗

(425) 455-5240. **$69-$189.** 11211 Main St 98004. I-405, exit 12, 0.4 mi n on 114th St. Int corridors. **Pets:** Other species. $20 one-time fee/room. Service with restrictions, supervision. 🆂🅰🆅🅴 ⊠ 🔧 🖵 🍴 ⋙

▼▼▼ Residence Inn by Marriott, Bellevue-Redmond 🅗

(425) 882-1222. **$197-$241.** 14455 NE 29th Pl 98007. I-405, exit 14 (SR 520), 2.3 mi e to 148th Ave NE (north exit), then just nw. Ext corridors. **Pets:** Medium, other species. $75 one-time fee/room. Service with restrictions, supervision. ⊠ 🔧 🖵 ⋙ ⊠

▼▼▼ Residence Inn by Marriott Seattle-Bellevue/Downtown 🅗

(425) 637-8500. **$161-$197.** 605 114th Ave SE 98004. I-405, exit 12, just sw. Int corridors. **Pets:** Accepted. ⊠ 🅶🅼 🔧 🖵 ⋙

ⓐⓐ▼ ▼▼▼▼ Sheraton Bellevue Hotel 🅗 🐾

(425) 455-3330. **$89-$359.** 100 112th Ave NE 98004. I-405, exit 12 northbound; exit 13 southbound, just s. Int corridors. **Pets:** Medium, dogs only. Service with restrictions, crate. 🆂🅰🆅🅴 ⊠ 🅶🅼 🔧 🖵 🍴

ⓐⓐ▼ ▼▼▼▼ ▼▼▼▼ The Westin Bellevue 🅗

(425) 638-1000. **$149-$429.** 600 Bellevue Way NE 98004. I-405, exit 13B, 1.5 mi w on NE 8th St. Int corridors. **Pets:** Accepted.

🆂🅰🆅🅴 ⊠ 🖵 🍴 ⋙

BOTHELL

▼▼▼ Extended StayAmerica-Seattle-Bothell 🅗

(425) 402-4252. **$90-$100.** 923 228th St SE 98021. I-405, exit 26, just sw. Int corridors. **Pets:** Other species. $25 daily fee/room. Designated rooms, service with restrictions, crate. 🅐🆂🅺 ⊠ 🔧 🖵

▼▼▼ Residence Inn by Marriott Seattle NE 🅗

(425) 485-3030. **$188-$230.** 11920 NE 195th St 98011. I-405, exit 24, 0.4 mi ne. Ext corridors. **Pets:** Accepted. ⊠ 🔧 🖵 ⋙ ⊠

BREMERTON

ⓐⓐ▼ ▼▼▼ Flagship Inn 🅗

(360) 479-6566. **$75-$115.** 4320 Kitsap Way 98312. 3.5 mi w of ferry terminal; SR 3, exit Kitsap Way, 0.5 mi e. Int corridors. **Pets:** Small, dogs only. $6 daily fee/pet. Supervision. 🆂🅰🆅🅴 ⊠ 🔧 🖵 ⋙

▼▼ Midway Inn 🅗

(360) 479-2909. **$84-$160.** 2909 Wheaton Way 98310. SR 303, 2 mi n. Int corridors. **Pets:** Dogs only. $25 one-time fee/room. Designated rooms, service with restrictions, crate. 🅐🆂🅺 ⊠ 🔧 🖵

▼▼ Oyster Bay Inn 🅗

(360) 377-5510. **$84-$99.** 4412 Kitsap Way 98312. 3.8 mi w of ferry terminal; SR 3, exit Kitsap Way, 0.5 mi e. Int corridors. **Pets:** $20 daily fee/pet. Supervision. 🅐🆂🅺 ⊠ 🔧 🖵 🍴

ⓐⓐ▼ ▼▼▼ Quality Inn & Suites 🅗 🐾

(360) 405-1111. **$83-$170.** 4303 Kitsap Way 98312. 3.5 mi w of ferry terminal; SR 3, exit Kitsap Way, 0.5 mi e. Ext corridors. **Pets:** Medium. $50 deposit/pet, $10 daily fee/pet. Designated rooms, service with restrictions, supervision. 🆂🅰🆅🅴 ⊠ 🔧 🖵

▼▼ Super 8 🅗

(360) 377-8881. **Call for rates.** 5068 Kitsap Way 98312. 4.2 mi w of ferry terminal; SR 3, exit Kitsap Way, just ne. Int corridors. **Pets:** Accepted. ⊠ 🅶🅼 🔧 🖵

DUPONT

▼▼▼ GuestHouse Inn & Suites 🅗

(253) 912-8900. **$125-$180.** 1609 McNeil St 98327. I-5, exit 118, just nw on Center Dr, then just w. Int corridors. **Pets:** Accepted.

🅐🆂🅺 ⊠ 🅶🅼 🔧 🖵 ⋙ ⊠

EDMONDS

ⓐⓐ▼ ▼▼▼▼ Best Western Edmonds Harbor Inn 🅗 🐾

(425) 771-5021. **$119-$159.** 130 W Dayton St 98020. Just s at Port of Edmonds. Ext/int corridors. **Pets:** Large. $20 daily fee/pet. Designated rooms, service with restrictions, supervision.

🆂🅰🆅🅴 ⊠ 🔧 🖵 ⋙ ⊠

△△△ ▽ K & E Motor Inn **M**
(425) 778-2181. **$50-$70, 3 day notice.** 23921 Hwy 99 98026. I-5, exit 177, 1 mi w on SR 104, exit SR 99 (Aurora Ave), then just n. Ext corridors. **Pets:** Small, dogs only. $20 one-time fee/pet. Designated rooms, no service, supervision. [SAVE] [✕] [🐾]

EVERETT

▽▽ Days Inn Seattle/Everett **H**
(425) 355-1570. **$80-$121.** 1602 SE Everett Mall Way 98208. I-5, exit 189 northbound, 0.5 mi w on SR 527, then 0.5 mi s; exit southbound, 0.7 mi s. Ext corridors. **Pets:** Accepted. [ASK] [✕] [🐾] [▣] [≈]

▽▽ Extended StayAmerica-Seattle-Everett **H**
(425) 355-1923. **$80-$90.** 8410 Broadway 98208. I-5, exit 189, follow signs to Broadway, just nw. Int corridors. **Pets:** Other species. $25 daily fee/room. Designated rooms, service with restrictions, crate.
[ASK] [✕] [🐾] [▣]

▽▽ Extended Stay Deluxe-Seattle-Everett **H**
(425) 337-1341. **$110-$115.** 1431 112th St SE 98208. I-5, exit 189, 1.5 mi se on 19th Ave SE, then 0.3 mi w. Int corridors. **Pets:** Other species. $25 daily fee/room. Designated rooms, service with restrictions, crate.
[ASK] [✕] [🐾] [▣]

▽▽ Holiday Inn Downtown Everett **H**
(425) 339-2000. **$99-$149.** 3105 Pine St 98201. I-5, exit 193 northbound; exit 194 southbound, just sw. Int corridors. **Pets:** Accepted.
[ASK] [✕] [🐾] [▣] [¶] [≈]

△△△ ▽▽▽ Inn at Port Gardner **H**
(425) 252-6779. **$109-$249.** 1700 W Marine View Dr 98201. I-5, exit 193 northbound, 1.2 mi w on Pacific Ave, then 1.2 mi n; exit 194 southbound, 1.2 mi w on Everett Ave, then 1 mi n; in Everett Marina Village. Int corridors. **Pets:** Medium, other species. $15 one-time fee/room. Service with restrictions, supervision. [SAVE] [✕] [🐾] [▣]

△△△ ▽▽▽ La Quinta Inn Everett **H** ❀
(425) 347-9099. **$69-$129.** 12619 4th Ave W 98204. I-5, exit 186, just w. Int corridors. **Pets:** Medium, other species. Service with restrictions, supervision. [SAVE] [✕] [🐾] [▣] [≈]

FEDERAL WAY

△△△ ▽▽▽ Clarion Hotel Federal Way **H**
(253) 941-6000. **$89-$159.** 31611 20th Ave S 98003. I-5, exit 143, 0.5 mi w on 320th St, then just n. Int corridors. **Pets:** Small, dogs only. $25 one-time fee/room. Service with restrictions, supervision.
[SAVE] [✕] [🐾] [▣] [≈]

△△△ ▽▽ Days Inn Federal Way **H**
(253) 838-3164. **Call for rates.** 34827 Pacific Hwy S 98003. I-5, exit 142B, 0.6 mi w. Ext corridors. **Pets:** Accepted. [SAVE] [✕] [🐾] [▣]

▽▽ Extended StayAmerica-Seattle-Federal Way **H**
(253) 946-0553. **$72-$82.** 1400 S 320th St 98003. I-5, exit 143, 0.6 mi w. Int corridors. **Pets:** Other species. $25 daily fee/room. Designated rooms, service with restrictions, crate. [ASK] [✕] [🐾] [▣]

▽▽ Quality Inn & Suites **H**
(253) 835-4141. **$90-$140.** 1400 S 348th St 98003. I-5, exit 142B, 0.5 mi w. Int corridors. **Pets:** $20 one-time fee/pet. Supervision.
[ASK] [✕] [♿] [🐾] [▣] [≈]

FIFE

▽▽ Baymont Inn & Suites–Fife **H**
(253) 922-2500. **$89-$119.** 5805 Pacific Hwy E 98424. I-5, exit 137, just ne. Ext corridors. **Pets:** Accepted. [ASK] [✕] [🐾] [▣] [✕]

△△△ ▽▽▽ Emerald Queen Hotel & Casino **H**
(253) 922-2000. **$89-$119.** 5700 Pacific Hwy E 98424. I-5, exit 137, just ne. Int corridors. **Pets:** Accepted. [SAVE] [✕] [♿] [🐾] [▣] [¶]

▽▽ Extended StayAmerica-Tacoma-Fife **H**
(253) 926-6316. **$84-$94.** 2820 Pacific Hwy E 98424. I-5, exit 136B northbound; exit 136 southbound, just nw. Int corridors. **Pets:** Other species. $25 daily fee/room. Designated rooms, service with restrictions, crate. [ASK] [✕] [🐾] [▣]

GIG HARBOR

△△△ ▽▽▽▽ Best Western Wesley Inn **H** ❀
(253) 858-9690. **$160-$300, 3 day notice.** 6575 Kimball Dr 98335. SR 16, exit City Center, just e on Pioneer Way, then 0.3 mi s. Int corridors. **Pets:** Other species. $10 daily fee/pet. Designated rooms, service with restrictions, crate. [SAVE] [✕] [♿] [🐾] [▣] [≈]

△△△ ▽▽▽▽ The Inn at Gig Harbor **H** ❀
(253) 858-1111. **$164-$232, 3 day notice.** 3211 56th St NW 98335. SR 16, exit Olympic Dr, just w, then 0.4 mi n. Int corridors. **Pets:** Medium. $10 daily fee/pet, $25 one-time fee/room. Designated rooms, service with restrictions, supervision. [SAVE] [✕] [♿] [🐾] [▣] [¶] [✕]

KENT

▽▽▽ Hawthorn Suites **H**
(253) 395-3800. **$129-$199.** 6329 S 212th St 98032. I-5, exit 152, 2.6 mi se via Orilla Rd and 212th St. Ext corridors. **Pets:** Accepted.
[ASK] [✕] [🐾] [▣] [≈] [✕]

△△△ ▽▽▽ Howard Johnson Inn **H** 🐾
(253) 852-7224. **$50-$129.** 1233 N Central 98032. SR 167, exit 84th Ave S, just s. Ext corridors. **Pets:** Medium, dogs only. $10 daily fee/pet. Service with restrictions, supervision. [SAVE] [✕] [🐾] [▣] [≈] [✕]

▽▽▽ TownePlace Suites by Marriott-Seattle
        Southcenter **H**
(253) 796-6000. **$170-$208.** 18123 72nd Ave S 98032. I-405, exit 1 (SR 181), 1.6 mi s on W Valley Hwy, just e on S 180th St, then just s. Ext corridors. **Pets:** Accepted. [✕] [♿] [🐾] [▣] [≈] [✕]

KIRKLAND

△△△ ▽▽▽▽ The Heathman Hotel **H** ❀
(425) 284-5800. **$149-$399.** 220 Kirkland Ave 98033. I-405, exit 18 (NE 85th St), 1 mi w, then just s on 3rd St. Int corridors. **Pets:** Other species. Service with restrictions, supervision. [SAVE] [✕] [♿] [▣] [¶]

▽▽▽ La Quinta Inn & Suites Seattle
        (Bellevue/Kirkland) **H** ❀
(425) 828-6585. **$69-$149.** 10530 NE Northup Way 98033. I-405, exit 14 (SR 520) via 108th Ave exit, n on 108th Ave, then just w. Int corridors. **Pets:** Medium, other species. Service with restrictions, supervision. [ASK] [✕] [🐾] [▣] [≈]

▽▽▽ Motel 6–687 **M**
(425) 821-5618. **$59-$81.** 12010 120th Pl NE 98034. I-405, exit 20B northbound; exit 20 southbound, just se. Ext corridors. **Pets:** Other species. Service with restrictions, supervision. [✕] [≈]

△△△ ▽▽▽ ▽▽▽ Woodmark Hotel, Yacht Club &
        Spa **H** ❀
(425) 822-3700. **$279-$1800.** 1200 Carillon Point 98033. On Lake Washington Blvd, 1 mi n of SR 520. Int corridors. **Pets:** Medium, other species. Service with restrictions, supervision. [SAVE] [✕] [▣] [¶] [✕]

LAKEWOOD

▽▽▽ La Quinta–Lakewood Inn & Suites **H** ❀
(253) 582-7000. **$125.** 11751 Pacific Hwy SW 98499. I-5, exit 125, just nw. Int corridors. **Pets:** Medium, other species. Service with restrictions, supervision. [✕] [🐾] [▣] [≈]

△△△ ▽▽▽ Western Inn **H**
(253) 588-5241. **$59-$78.** 9920 S Tacoma Way 98499. I-5, exit 127 (S Tacoma Way), just w on SR 512, then just n. Ext corridors.
Pets: Accepted. [SAVE] [✕] [🐾] [▣]

LYNNWOOD

AAA ▽▽▽▽ **Best Western Alderwood** H ❀
(425) 775-7600. **$99-$109.** 19332 36th Ave W 98036. I-5, exit 181B northbound, just n on Poplar Way, just w on 196th St SW, then just n; exit 181 (SR 524 W) southbound, just nw. Int corridors. **Pets:** Small, dogs only. $25 one-time fee/pet. Designated rooms, service with restrictions.
SAVE ✕ 🛎 💻 ➿

AAA ▽▽▽▽ **La Quinta Inn Lynnwood** H ❀
(425) 775-7447. **$69-$119.** 4300 Alderwood Mall Blvd 98036. I-5, exit 181A northbound, just w; exit 181 (SR 524 W) southbound, 0.5 mi w on 196th St SW, just s on 44th Ave SW, then just e. Int corridors. **Pets:** Medium, other species. Service with restrictions, supervision.
SAVE ✕ 🛎 💻

▽▽▽▽ **Residence Inn by Marriott-Seattle North/Lynnwood** H
(425) 771-1100. **$179-$219.** 18200 Alderwood Mall Pkwy 98037. I-5, exit 183 southbound, just w on 164th St SW, then 1.5 mi se on 28th St W; exit 182 northbound on SR 525, exit 1, then just s; just n of Alderwood Mall Shopping Center. Ext corridors. **Pets:** Large, other species. $15 daily fee/room, $75 one-time fee/room. Service with restrictions, supervision.
✕ 🛎 💻 ➿ ✕

MONROE

AAA ▽▽▽▽ **Best Western Sky Valley Inn** H
(360) 794-3111. **$104-$230.** 19233 US 2 98272. West end of town. Int corridors. **Pets:** Large, other species. $10 daily fee/pet. Service with restrictions, supervision. SAVE ✕ 🛎 💻 ➿

AAA ▽▽▽▽ **GuestHouse International Inn & Suites** H
(360) 863-1900. **$114-$144.** 19103 US 2 98272. West end of town. Int corridors. **Pets:** Large, other species. $20 daily fee/room. Service with restrictions, crate. SAVE ✕ 🛎 💻 ➿

MUKILTEO

▽▽ **Extended StayAmerica-Seattle-Mukilteo** M
(425) 493-1561. **$100-$110.** 3917 Harbour Pointe Blvd SW 98275. Jct SR 526 and 525 (Mukilteo Speedway), 1.5 mi s, then just w. Int corridors. **Pets:** Other species. $25 daily fee/room. Designated rooms, service with restrictions, crate. ASK ✕ 🛎 💻

▽▽▽▽ **TownePlace Suites by Marriott-Mukilteo** H
(425) 551-5900. **$134-$164.** 8521 Mukilteo Speedway 98275. Just se of jct 84th St SW and SR 525 (Mukilteo Speedway). Ext corridors. **Pets:** Other species. $10 daily fee/pet. Service with restrictions, crate.
✕ 🔥M 🛎 💻 ➿ ✕

PORT ORCHARD

AAA ▽▽▽ **Comfort Inn Port Orchard** M
(360) 895-2666. **$77-$104.** 1121 Bay St 98366. SR 16, exit Tremont St, 0.9 mi e to Sidney Ave, 1.2 mi n to Bay St, then just e. Ext corridors. **Pets:** Large. $15 daily fee/room. Service with restrictions.
SAVE ✕ 🛎 💻

▽▽▽ **Days Inn Port Orchard** H
(360) 895-7818. **$89-$149.** 220 Bravo Terr 98366. SR 16, exit 160 E (Sedgewick Rd), just se. Int corridors. **Pets:** Small. $10 daily fee/room. Designated rooms, service with restrictions, supervision.
ASK ✕ 🛎 💻 ➿

POULSBO

▽▽▽▽ **Holiday Inn Express** H ❀
(360) 697-4400. **$83-$179.** 19801 7th Ave NE 98370. On SR 305. Int corridors. **Pets:** Small. $30 daily fee/pet. Service with restrictions, supervision. ASK ✕ 🔥M 🛎 💻

AAA ▽▽▽▽ **Poulsbo Inn & Suites** H
(360) 779-3921. **$99-$130, 7 day notice.** 18680 SR 305 98370. SR 3, 2.3 mi e. Ext corridors. **Pets:** Medium. $15 daily fee/pet. Designated rooms, service with restrictions, supervision.
SAVE ✕ 🔥M 🛎 💻 ➿ ✕

PUYALLUP

AAA ▽▽▽▽ **Best Western Park Plaza** H ❀
(253) 848-1500. **$149-$189.** 620 S Hill Park Dr 98373. SR 512, exit S Hill Park Dr southbound, just w; exit 9th St SW northbound, just w. Int corridors. **Pets:** Dogs only. $25 one-time fee/room. Service with restrictions, supervision. SAVE ✕ 🔥M 🛎 💻 ➿

▽▽ **Crossland Economy Suites-Tacoma-Puyallup** M
(253) 445-5945. **$54-$64.** 2101 N Meridian 98371. SR 512, exit Milton/Tacoma, just w on SR 167, then just n. Ext corridors. **Pets:** Other species. $25 daily fee/room. Designated rooms, service with restrictions, crate. ASK ✕ 🔥M 🛎 💻

▽▽▽▽ **Holiday Inn Express Hotel & Suites Puyallup** H ❀
(253) 848-4900. **$159-$199.** 812 S Hill Park Dr 98373. SR 512, exit S Hill Park Dr southbound, just w; exit 9th St SW northbound, just w. Int corridors. **Pets:** Dogs only. $25 one-time fee/room. Service with restrictions, supervision. ASK ✕ 🛎 💻 ➿

REDMOND

▽▽▽ **Residence Inn by Marriott Redmond Town Center** H
(425) 497-9226. **$179-$219.** 7575 164th Ave NE 98052. I-405, exit 14 (SR 520), 4.5 mi e to W Lake Sammamish Pkwy, just n to Leary Way, just e to Bear Creek Pkwy, just s to NE 74th Ave, just w to 164th Ave NE, then just n; center. Int corridors. **Pets:** Accepted.
✕ 🛎 💻 ➿

RENTON

▽▽ **Extended Stay Deluxe-Seattle-Renton** H
(425) 228-2454. **$100-$105.** 1150 Oakesdale Ave SW 98055. I-405, exit 1 southbound, just s; exit Renton northbound, just n on Interurban Ave, 0.6 mi e on SW Grady Way, then just n. Int corridors. **Pets:** Other species. $25 daily fee/room. Designated rooms, service with restrictions, crate. ASK ✕ 🛎 💻 ➿

▽▽ **Guest House Inn & Suites** M
(425) 228-2858. **Call for rates.** 4710 Lake Washington Blvd NE 98056. I-405, exit 7, just ne. Ext corridors. **Pets:** Medium, other species. $10 daily fee/pet. Service with restrictions, supervision. ✕ 🛎 💻

▽▽ **Holiday Inn-Renton** H
(425) 226-7700. **$79-$169.** One S Grady Way 98057. I-405, exit 2 (SR 167/Rainier Ave), jct SR 167 N. Int corridors. **Pets:** Accepted.
ASK ✕ 🛎 💻 🍴 ➿

AAA ▽▽▽▽ **Larkspur Landing Renton/Seattle** H
(425) 235-1212. **$159-$179.** 1701 E Valley Rd 98057. SR 167, exit E Valley Rd, 1 mi nw. Int corridors. **Pets:** Accepted. SAVE ✕ 🛎 💻

▽▽▽ **Quality Inn Renton** H
(425) 226-7600. **$99-$119.** 1850 Maple Valley Hwy 98057. I-405, exit 4 (Bronson Way) northbound, follow Maple Valley Hwy; exit southbound, 0.6 mi s to 2nd light, then just e. Int corridors. **Pets:** Accepted.
ASK ✕ 🛎 💻

▽▽▽ **TownePlace Suites Seattle South/Renton** H
(425) 917-2000. **$112-$136.** 300 SW 19th St 98057. SR 167, exit E Valley Rd, 1 mi nw, then just w. Int corridors. **Pets:** Other species. $100 one-time fee/room. Service with restrictions. ✕ 🔥M 🛎 💻 ➿

SEATAC

▽▽ **Clarion Hotel** H
(206) 242-0200. **$85-$150.** 3000 S 176th St 98188. Just e of SR 99. Int corridors. **Pets:** Medium, other species. $20 daily fee/pet. Service with restrictions, supervision. ASK ✕ 🔥M 🛎 💻 🍴 ➿

▽▽▽ **Doubletree Hotel Seattle Airport** H
(206) 246-8600. **$119-$279.** 18740 International Blvd 98188. On SR 99. Int corridors. **Pets:** Accepted. ✕ 🛎 💻 🍴 ➿

▼▼▼ **Hilton Seattle Airport & Conference Center** 🅷 ❀

(206) 244-4800. **$129-$309.** 17620 International Blvd 98188. On SR 99. Int corridors. **Pets:** Medium. $75 daily fee/room. Service with restrictions.

[⊠] [▣] [🍽] [🏊]

▼▼▼ **Holiday Inn Express Hotel & Suites-Seattle Sea-Tac Airport** 🅷

(206) 824-3200. **Call for rates.** 19621 International Blvd 98188. On SR 99. Int corridors. **Pets:** Other species. $75 deposit/room, $50 one-time fee/room. Service with restrictions, crate. [⊠] [🖥] [▣]

(AAA) ▼▼▼ **Holiday Inn Seattle SeaTac International Airport** 🅷

(206) 248-1000. **$89-$159.** 17338 International Blvd 98188. On SR 99. Int corridors. **Pets:** Small. $20 daily fee/room. Service with restrictions, supervision. [SAVE] [⊠] [🖥] [🖥] [▣] [🍽] [🏊]

▼ **Motel 6–1332** 🅼

(206) 246-4101. **$55-$69.** 16500 International Blvd 98188. On SR 99. Ext corridors. **Pets:** Other species. Service with restrictions, supervision. [⊠]

▼ **Motel 6–736** 🅼

(206) 824-9902. **$49-$65.** 20651 Military Rd 98198. I-5, exit 151, just se. Ext corridors. **Pets:** Other species. Service with restrictions, supervision. [⊠] [🖥] [🏊]

▼▼▼ **Red Lion Hotel Seattle Airport** 🅷

(206) 246-5535. **$99-$279.** 18220 International Blvd 98188. On SR 99. Int corridors. **Pets:** Other species. $20 one-time fee/room. Service with restrictions, supervision. [ASK] [⊠] [🖥] [▣] [🍽] [🏊]

▼▼ **Super 8 Sea-Tac** 🅷 ❀

(206) 433-8188. **$72-$97.** 3100 S 192nd St 98188. Just e of SR 99. Int corridors. **Pets:** Other species. $10 daily fee/room. Service with restrictions, supervision. [ASK] [⊠] [▣]

SEATTLE

(AAA) ▼▼▼ **Alexis Hotel** 🅷

(206) 624-4844. **$139-$349.** 1007 1st Ave 98104. Corner of Madison St and 1st Ave. Int corridors. **Pets:** Accepted. [SAVE] [⊠] [🖥] [🍽] [⊠]

(AAA) ▼▼▼ **Comfort Inn & Suites Seattle** 🅷

(206) 361-3700. **$85-$139.** 13700 Aurora Ave N 98133. I-5, exit 175, 1.1 mi w on NE 145th St, then 0.3 mi s. Int corridors. **Pets:** Accepted. [SAVE] [⊠] [🖥] [▣] [⊠]

(AAA) ▼▼▼ **Crowne Plaza Seattle-Downtown** 🅷

(206) 464-1980. **$99-$259.** 1113 6th Ave 98101. Corner of 6th Ave and Seneca St. Int corridors. **Pets:** Medium. $50 one-time fee/room. Designated rooms, service with restrictions, supervision.

[SAVE] [⊠] [🖥] [▣] [🍽]

(AAA) ▼▼▼ **Doubletree Arctic Club Hotel-Seattle Downtown** 🅷

(206) 340-0340. **$109-$249.** 700 3rd Ave 98104. Corner of 3rd Ave and Cherry St. Int corridors. **Pets:** Accepted. [SAVE] [⊠] [🖥] [▣] [🍽]

(AAA) ▼▼▼ **The Edgewater** 🅷

(206) 728-7000. **$209-$729.** 2411 Alaskan Way, Pier 67 98121. On waterfront at Pier 67; at base of Wall St. Int corridors. **Pets:** Other species. Service with restrictions, supervision. [SAVE] [⊠] [🖥] [▣] [🍽]

▼▼ **Executive Hotel Pacific** 🅷

(206) 623-3900. **$129-$249.** 400 Spring St 98104. Between 4th and 5th aves. Int corridors. **Pets:** Accepted. [ASK] [⊠] [▣]

(AAA) ▼▼▼▼ **The Fairmont Olympic Hotel** 🅷 ❀

(206) 621-1700. **Call for rates.** 411 University St 98101. Corner of 4th Ave and University St. Int corridors. **Pets:** Small. $40 one-time fee/room. Service with restrictions, supervision.

[SAVE] [⊠] [🖥] [▣] [🍽] [🏊] [⊠]

(AAA) ▼▼▼ ▼▼ **Four Seasons Hotel Seattle** 🅷 ❀

(206) 749-7000. **$365-$525.** 99 Union St 98101. Southwest corner of 1st Ave and Union St. Int corridors. **Pets:** Small, other species. Service with restrictions, supervision. [SAVE] [⊠] [🍽] [🏊] [⊠]

▼▼▼▼ **Homewood Suites by Hilton-Seattle Downtown** 🅷

(206) 281-9393. **$169-$279.** 206 Western Ave W 98119. I-5, exit 167 (Mercer St), 0.3 mi w, 0.5 mi s on Fairview Ave, 1.2 mi w on Denny Way, then just n. Int corridors. **Pets:** Medium, other species. $20 daily fee/pet. [⊠] [🖥] [▣]

▼▼▼ **Hotel 1000** 🅷

(206) 957-1000. **$235-$439.** 1000 1st Ave 98104. Northeast corner of 1st Ave and Madison St. Int corridors. **Pets:** Accepted. [ASK] [⊠] [▣] [🍽]

(AAA) ▼▼▼ **Hotel Max** 🅷

(206) 728-6299. **$119-$269.** 620 Stewart St 98101. Corner of 7th Ave and Stewart St. Int corridors. **Pets:** Accepted.

[SAVE] [⊠] [🖥] [🖥] [▣] [🍽]

(AAA) ▼▼▼ ▼▼ **Hotel Monaco** 🅷

(206) 621-1770. **$139-$349.** 1101 4th Ave 98101. Corner of 4th Ave and Spring St. Int corridors. **Pets:** Accepted. [SAVE] [⊠] [▣] [🍽] [⊠]

(AAA) ▼▼▼ **Hotel Nexus Seattle** 🅷

(206) 365-0700. **$99-$159.** 2140 N Northgate Way 98133. I-5, exit 173, just nw. Ext corridors. **Pets:** Accepted. [SAVE] [⊠] [🖥] [▣] [🍽] [🏊]

(AAA) ▼▼▼ **Hotel Vintage Park** 🅷

(206) 624-8000. **$139-$309.** 1100 5th Ave 98101. Corner of Spring St and 5th Ave. Int corridors. **Pets:** Accepted. [SAVE] [⊠] [🍽] [⊠]

▼▼▼▼ **La Quinta Inn & Suites Seattle Downtown** 🅷 ❀

(206) 624-6820. **$89-$159.** 2224 8th Ave 98121. Corner of 8th Ave and Blanchard St. Int corridors. **Pets:** Medium, other species. Service with restrictions, supervision. [ASK] [⊠] [🖥] [▣]

(AAA) ▼▼▼▼ **Pan Pacific Hotel Seattle** 🅷

(206) 264-8111. **$149-$425.** 2125 Terry Ave 98121. Just s of jct E Denny Way. Int corridors. **Pets:** Accepted. [SAVE] [⊠] [🖥] [▣] [🍽] [⊠]

(AAA) ▼▼▼▼ **Red Lion Hotel on Fifth Avenue-Seattle** 🅷

(206) 971-8000. **Call for rates.** 1415 5th Ave 98101. Between Pike and Union sts. Int corridors. **Pets:** Other species. $20 one-time fee/room. Service with restrictions, supervision. [SAVE] [⊠] [▣] [🍽]

(AAA) ▼▼▼▼ **Residence Inn Marriott Seattle Downtown/ Lake Union** 🅷 ❀

(206) 624-6000. **$269-$289.** 800 Fairview Ave N 98109. I-5, exit 167 (Mercer St); south end of Lake Union. Int corridors. **Pets:** Other species. $10 daily fee/pet. Service with restrictions.

[SAVE] [⊠] [🖥] [▣] [🏊] [⊠]

(AAA) ▼▼▼ **The Roosevelt, a Coast Hotel** 🅷 ❀

(206) 621-1200. **$159-$279.** 1531 7th Ave 98101. Corner of 7th Ave and Pine St. Int corridors. **Pets:** Medium. $50 one-time fee/pet. Designated rooms, service with restrictions, crate. [SAVE] [⊠] [🖥] [▣] [🍽]

(AAA) ▼▼▼▼ **Sheraton Seattle Hotel** 🅷

(206) 621-9000. **$169-$459.** 1400 6th Ave 98101. Corner of 6th Ave and Pike St. Int corridors. **Pets:** Accepted. [SAVE] [⊠] [▣] [🍽] [🏊]

(AAA) ▼▼▼ ▼▼ **Sorrento Hotel** 🅷 ❀

(206) 622-6400. **$179-$439.** 900 Madison St 98104. I-5, exit Madison St, just e; at 9th Ave and Madison St. Int corridors. **Pets:** $60 one-time fee/ room. Service with restrictions, crate. [SAVE] [⊠] [▣] [🍽] [⊠]

▼▼▼ **University Inn** 🅷

(206) 632-5055. **$145-$185.** 4140 Roosevelt Way NE 98105. I-5, exit 169, 0.5 mi e, then just s. Int corridors. **Pets:** Large, dogs only. $20 daily fee/room. Designated rooms, service with restrictions, supervision.

[ASK] [⊠] [🖥] [▣] [🍽] [🏊]

AAA ▼▼ ▼▼ **The Westin Seattle** **H** ❀
(206) 728-1000. **$170-$399.** 1900 5th Ave 98101. Corner of 5th Ave and Stewart St. Int corridors. **Pets:** Medium. Service with restrictions, supervision. [SAVE] [✕] [&M] [🛏] [📺] [🍴] [🏊]

AAA ▼▼ ▼▼ **W Seattle** **H** ❀
(206) 264-6000. **$229-$509.** 1112 4th Ave 98101. Corner of 4th Ave and Seneca St. Int corridors. **Pets:** Large. $25 daily fee/room, $100 one-time fee/room. Service with restrictions, supervision. [SAVE] [✕] [🍴]

SILVERDALE

▼▼ ▼▼ **Oxford Inn** **H**
(360) 692-7777. **$79-$119.** 9734 NW Silverdale Way 98383. SR 3, exit Newberry Hill Rd, just e, then 1.2 mi n. Int corridors. **Pets:** Small. $20 one-time fee/room. Designated rooms, service with restrictions, crate.
[ASK] [✕] [🛏] [📺]

AAA ▼▼ ▼▼ **Silverdale Beach Hotel** **H**
(360) 698-1000. **$115-$160.** 3073 NW Bucklin Hill Rd 98383. SR 3, exit Newberry Hill Rd, just e, 1 mi n on Silverdale Way, then just e. Int corridors. **Pets:** Medium. $25 daily fee/pet. Service with restrictions, crate.
[SAVE] [✕] [🛏] [📺] [🍴] [🏊] [🏊]

SNOQUALMIE

AAA ▼▼ ▼▼ ▼▼ **Salish Lodge & Spa** **H** ❀
(425) 888-2556. **$259-$529, 7 day notice.** 6501 Railroad Ave SE 98065. I-90, exit 27 eastbound, 5 mi ne via North Bend Way, Meadowbrook Way and SR 202; exit 31 westbound, 7 mi nw via SR 202. Int corridors. **Pets:** Dogs only. $50 one-time fee/room. Service with restrictions. [SAVE] [✕] [📺] [🍴] [🏊]

SUQUAMISH

▼▼ ▼▼ ▼▼ **Suquamish Clearwater Casino Resort** **H** ❀
(360) 598-8700. **$79-$459, 3 day notice.** 15347 Suquamish Way 98392. SR 3, exit SR 305, 6.2 mi se. Ext/int corridors. **Pets:** $200 deposit/room, $20 daily fee/room. Crate.
[ASK] [✕] [🛏] [📺] [🍴] [🏊] [🏊]

TACOMA

▼▼ **Crossland Studios-Tacoma-Hosmer** **M**
(253) 538-9448. **$59-$69.** 8801 S Hosmer St 98444. I-5, exit 128 northbound, just se; exit 129 southbound, just e on 72nd St, then 1.0 mi s. Ext corridors. **Pets:** Other species. $25 daily fee/room. Designated rooms, service with restrictions, crate. [ASK] [✕] [🛏] [📺]

AAA ▼▼ ▼▼ **Hotel Murano** **H**
(253) 238-8000. **$189-$469.** 1320 Broadway Plaza 98402. I-5, exit 133 (City Center) to I-705 N, exit a St, just w on 11th St, then just s; downtown. Int corridors. **Pets:** Accepted. [SAVE] [✕] [🛏] [📺] [🍴] [🏊]

▼▼ ▼▼ ▼▼ **La Quinta Inn & Suites Conference Center, Restaurant and Lounge** **H** ❀
(253) 383-0146. **$69-$149.** 1425 E 27th St 98421. I-5, exit 135 southbound; exit 134 northbound, just n. Int corridors. **Pets:** Medium, other species. Service with restrictions, supervision.
[ASK] [✕] [🛏] [📺] [🍴] [🏊]

AAA ▼▼ ▼▼ **Red Lion Hotel Tacoma** **H**
(253) 548-1212. **$109-$149.** 8402 S Hosmer St 98444. I-5, exit 128 northbound, just ne; exit 129 southbound, just e on 72nd St, then 1 mi s. Int corridors. **Pets:** Other species. $20 one-time fee/room. Service with restrictions, supervision. [SAVE] [✕] [🛏] [📺] [🏊]

AAA ▼▼ ▼▼ **Shilo Inn & Suites -Tacoma** **H** ❀
(253) 475-4020. **$112-$200.** 7414 S Hosmer St 98408. I-5, exit 129, just se. Int corridors. **Pets:** Dogs only. $25 one-time fee/room. Designated rooms, service with restrictions, supervision.
[SAVE] [✕] [🛏] [📺] [🏊] [🏊]

TUKWILA

▼▼ ▼▼ **Extended StayAmerica-Seattle-Tukwila** **H**
(206) 244-2537. **$80-$90.** 15451 53rd Ave S 98188. I-5, exit 153 northbound, just n on Southcenter Pkwy, just n on 61st St, just w on Southcenter Blvd, then just sw; exit 154B (Southcenter Mall) southbound, just sw. Ext corridors. **Pets:** Other species. $25 daily fee/room. Designated rooms, service with restrictions, crate. [ASK] [✕] [🛏] [📺]

▼▼ ▼▼ **Homewood Suites by Hilton** **H**
(206) 433-8000. **$119-$189.** 6955 Fort Dent Way 98188. I-405, exit 1 (SR 181), just ne. Ext/int corridors. **Pets:** $20 daily fee/pet.
[✕] [🛏] [📺] [🏊] [🏊]

▼▼ ▼▼ **Ramada Limited Sea-Tac Airport** **H**
(206) 244-8800. **$60-$90.** 13900 Tukwila International Blvd 98168. I-5, exit 158 southbound, 2 mi s; exit 154A (SR 518 W) northbound, 1 mi n on SR 99. Int corridors. **Pets:** Medium. $25 daily fee/room. Designated rooms, service with restrictions, supervision. [ASK] [✕] [🛏] [📺]

▼▼ ▼▼ **Residence Inn by Marriott-Seattle South** **H**
(425) 226-5500. **$170-$208.** 16201 W Valley Hwy 98188. I-405, exit 1 (SR 181), just s. Ext corridors. **Pets:** Accepted.
[✕] [&M] [🛏] [📺] [🏊] [🏊]

VASHON

▼▼ **The Swallow's Nest Guest Cottages** **CA** ❀
(206) 463-2646. **$90-$280.** 6030 SW 248th St 98070. North end Ferry Landing, 7.8 mi s on Vashon Hwy; south end (Tahlequah) Ferry Landing, 5.8 mi n on Vashon Hwy, 1.4 mi e on Quartermaster Dr, 1.5 mi s on Dockton Rd, 0.4 mi s on 75th Ave, then 1 mi e. Ext corridors. **Pets:** Other species. $15 daily fee/pet. Designated rooms, service with restrictions, crate. [ASK] [✕] [🛏] [📺] [🎿]

END METROPOLITAN AREA

SEDRO-WOOLLEY

▼▼ ▼▼ **South Bay Bed and Breakfast @ Lake Whatcom** **BB**
(360) 595-2086. **Call for rates.** 4095 S Bay Dr 98284. I-5, exit 240, 5.5 mi ne via Lake Samish and Cain Lake rds, then 3.2 mi e. Int corridors.
Pets: Accepted. [✕] [🎿] [W] [🏊]

SEQUIM

▼▼ ▼▼ ▼▼ **Juan de Fuca Cottages** **CA** ❀
(360) 683-4433. **$110-$325, 14 day notice.** 182 Marine Dr 98382. 7 mi n via Sequim Ave and E Anderson Rd; downtown. Ext corridors.
Pets: Medium, dogs only. $20 daily fee/pet. Designated rooms, supervision. [✕] [🛏] [📺] [🎿] [🏊]

AAA ▼▼ ▼▼ **Quality Inn & Suites–Sequim** **H** ❀
(360) 683-2800. **$100-$186.** 134 River Rd 98382. US 101, exit River Rd, just nw. Int corridors. **Pets:** Dogs only. $20 daily fee/pet. Designated rooms, service with restrictions, supervision.
[ECO] [SAVE] [✕] [🛏] [📺] [🏊]

AAA ▼▼ ▼▼ **Sequim West Inn** **M**
(360) 683-4144. **$54-$125, 3 day notice.** 740 W Washington St 98382. US 101, exit River Rd, 0.9 mi ne via River Rd and W Washington St. Ext corridors. **Pets:** Small. $10 daily fee/pet. Service with restrictions, supervision. [SAVE] [✕] [🛏] [📺]

SHELTON

(AAA) ▼▼▼▼ **Little Creek Casino Resort** 🅷 ❀
(360) 427-7711. **$89-$439.** W 91 SR 108 98584. Jct US 101 and SR 108. Int corridors. **Pets:** Other species. $30 one-time fee/pet. Designated rooms, service with restrictions, supervision.
[SAVE] [✕] [&M] [🛏] [💻] [🍴] [≈]

▼▼ **Super 8 of Shelton** 🅷
(360) 426-1654. **Call for rates.** 2943 Northview Cir 98584. US 101, exit Wallace-Kneeland Blvd, just se. Int corridors. **Pets:** Accepted.
[✕] [🛏] [💻]

SNOQUALMIE PASS

▼▼ **Howard Johnson Summit Inn** 🅷
(425) 434-6300. **$119-$279, 3 day notice.** 603 SR 906 98068. I-90, exit 52 eastbound, 0.3 mi e; exit 53 westbound, 0.3 mi w. Int corridors. **Pets:** Other species. $25 one-time fee/pet. Designated rooms, service with restrictions, crate. [ASK] [✕] [🛏] [💻] [🍴] [≈] [✕]

SOAP LAKE

▼▼ **Notaras Lodge** Ⓜ
(509) 246-0462. **$75-$135.** 236 E Main Ave 98851. Just w of SR 17. Ext corridors. **Pets:** Accepted. [✕] [🛏] [💻]

SPOKANE

(AAA) ▼▼▼ **Apple Tree Inn** Ⓜ
(509) 466-3020. **$49-$69.** 9508 N Division St 99218. Jct US 2 and 395, just n. Ext/int corridors. **Pets:** Small, dogs only. $10 daily fee/pet. Designated rooms, service with restrictions, supervision. [SAVE] [✕] [🛏] [≈]

(AAA) ▼▼▼▼ **Best Western Peppertree Airport Inn** 🅷
(509) 624-4655. **$70-$250.** 3711 S Geiger Blvd 99224. I-90, exit 276 (Geiger Field), just n. Int corridors. **Pets:** Accepted.
[SAVE] [✕] [&M] [🛏] [💻] [≈] [✕]

▼▼ **Comfort Inn North** 🅷
(509) 467-7111. **$59-$119.** 7111 N Division St 99208. I-90, exit 281 (Division St), 4.6 mi n. Int corridors. **Pets:** Medium, other species. $10 daily fee/pet. Service with restrictions, supervision.
[ASK] [✕] [🛏] [💻] [≈] [✕]

(AAA) ▼▼▼ **Comfort Inn University District/Downtown** 🅷 ❀
(509) 535-9000. **$71-$139.** 923 E 3rd Ave 99202. I-90, exit 281 (Division St), just n to E 3rd Ave, then 0.7 mi e. Int corridors. **Pets:** Medium. $10 daily fee/pet. Service with restrictions, supervision.
[SAVE] [✕] [&M] [🛏] [💻] [≈]

(AAA) ▼▼▼▼ **The Davenport Hotel and Tower** 🅷
(509) 455-8888. **$169-$319.** 10 S Post St 99201. Downtown. Int corridors. **Pets:** Accepted. [SAVE] [✕] [&M] [🛏] [🍴] [≈] [✕]

(AAA) ▼▼▼ **Doubletree Hotel Spokane City Center** 🅷 ❀
(509) 455-9600. **$124-$279.** 322 N Spokane Falls Ct 99201. I-90, exit 281 (Division St), just n; downtown. Int corridors. **Pets:** $50 one-time fee/room. Service with restrictions, supervision.
[SAVE] [✕] [🛏] [💻] [🍴] [≈] [✕]

▼▼ **Fairbridge Inn Express** 🅷
(509) 838-6630. **$80.** 211 S Division St 99202. I-90, exit 281 (Division St), just n. Int corridors. **Pets:** Accepted. [ASK] [✕] [🛏] [💻]

▼▼▼ **Holiday Inn Express-Downtown** 🅷
(509) 328-8505. **$105-$199.** 801 N Division St 99202. I-90, exit 281 (Division St), 0.8 mi n. Ext/int corridors. **Pets:** Medium, dogs only. $50 deposit/room. Designated rooms, service with restrictions, supervision.
[ASK] [✕] [&M] [🛏] [💻]

▼▼▼ **Holiday Inn Spokane Airport** 🅷 ❀
(509) 838-1170. **$89-$149.** 1616 S Windsor Dr 99224. I-90, exit 277 westbound; exit 277B eastbound, just w on US 2, then just s. Int corridors. **Pets:** Medium. $50 deposit/room. Service with restrictions, crate.
[ASK] [✕] [&M] [🛏] [💻] [🍴] [≈]

(AAA) ▼▼▼ **The Madison Inn** 🅷
(509) 474-4200. **$75-$90.** 15 W Rockwood Blvd 99204. I-90, exit 281 (Division St) eastbound, just e to Cowley St, 0.4 mi s, then just w; exit westbound, just n to 2nd Ave, just w to Browne St, 0.5 mi s to 9th Ave, then just e. Int corridors. **Pets:** Accepted. [SAVE] [✕] [&M] [🛏] [💻]

▼▼▼ **Oxford Suites-Downtown Spokane** 🅷
(509) 353-9000. **$139-$199.** 115 W North River Dr 99201. I-90, exit 281 (Division St), 1 mi n, then just n. Int corridors. **Pets:** Small, dogs only. $25 one-time fee/room. Designated rooms, service with restrictions, supervision. [ASK] [✕] [🛏] [💻] [≈]

▼▼▼ **Ramada Limited Suites** 🅷
(509) 468-4201. **$80-$150, 7 day notice.** 9601 N Newport Hwy 99218. US 2 and 395, just n on US 2 (Newport Hwy). Int corridors.
Pets: Accepted. [ASK] [✕] [&M] [🛏] [💻] [≈]

▼▼▼ **Ramada Spokane Airport & Indoor Waterpark** 🅷
(509) 838-5211. **$120-$129.** 8909 Airport Dr 99224. I-90, exit 277B eastbound; exit 277 westbound, 3.4 mi n. Int corridors. **Pets:** Medium. $10 one-time fee/room. Designated rooms, service with restrictions, supervision. [ASK] [✕] [🛏] [💻] [🍴] [≈] [✕]

(AAA) ▼▼▼▼ **Red Lion Hotel at the Park-Spokane** 🅷
(509) 326-8000. **$99-$249.** 303 W North River Dr 99201. I-90, exit 281 (Division St), 1.5 mi n on US 195, then just w. Int corridors. **Pets:** Other species. $20 one-time fee/room. Service with restrictions, supervision.
[SAVE] [✕] [🛏] [💻] [🍴] [≈] [✕]

▼▼▼ **Red Lion River Inn-Spokane** 🅷
(509) 326-5577. **$109-$199.** 700 N Division St 99202. I-90, exit 281 (Division St), 0.8 mi n; downtown. Int corridors. **Pets:** Other species. $20 one-time fee/room. Service with restrictions, supervision.
[✕] [&M] [🛏] [💻] [🍴] [≈] [✕]

(AAA) ▼▼▼ **Super 8 Airport West** Ⓜ
(509) 838-8800. **$60-$150.** 11102 W Westbow Blvd 99224. I-90, exit 272 (Medical Lake Rd), just s. Int corridors. **Pets:** Other species. $15 one-time fee/room. Service with restrictions, supervision.
[SAVE] [✕] [&M] [🛏] [💻] [≈]

▼▼ **Travelodge** 🅷 ❀
(509) 623-9727. **$89-$149.** W 33 Spokane Falls Blvd 99201. I-90, exit 281 (Division St), 0.5 mi n, then just w. Int corridors. **Pets:** Dogs only. $13 daily fee/pet. Supervision. [ASK] [✕] [&M] [🛏] [💻]

▼▼▼ **Wingate by Wyndham Spokane Airport** 🅷
(509) 838-3226. **$108.** 2726 S Flint Rd 99201. I-90, exit 277B eastbound; exit 277 westbound, 3 mi w, then just s. Int corridors. **Pets:** Other species. $150 deposit/room. Service with restrictions.
[ASK] [✕] [&M] [🛏] [💻] [≈]

SPOKANE VALLEY

▼▼▼ **Crossland Studios-Spokane Valley** 🅷
(509) 928-5948. **$55-$65.** 12803 E Sprague Ave 99216. I-90, exit 289, 1.1 mi s, then just e. Ext corridors. **Pets:** Other species. $25 daily fee/room. Designated rooms, service with restrictions, crate.
[ASK] [✕] [🛏] [💻]

▼▼▼ **Holiday Inn Express-Valley** 🅷
(509) 927-7100. **$119-$229.** 9220 E Mission Ave 99206. I-90, exit 287, just s. Ext/int corridors. **Pets:** Other species. Designated rooms, service with restrictions, supervision. [ASK] [✕] [&M] [🛏] [💻] [≈]

▼▼▼ **La Quinta Inn & Suites Spokane** 🅷 ❀
(509) 893-0955. **$89-$159.** 3808 N Sullivan Rd 99216. I-90, exit 291B, 1.3 mi n. Int corridors. **Pets:** Medium, other species. Service with restrictions, supervision. [ASK] [✕] [&M] [🛏] [💻] [≈]

AAA ▽▽▽ **Mirabeau Park Hotel and Convention Center** H
(509) 924-9000. **$99-$169.** 1100 N Sullivan Rd 99037. I-90, exit 291B, just s. Int corridors. **Pets:** Accepted. SAVE ✕ 🛏 🖥 🍴 🐾 ✕

AAA ▽▽▽ **Oxford Suites Spokane Valley** H ❀
(509) 847-1000. **$115-$199.** 15015 E Indiana Ave 99216. I-90, exit 291A eastbound; exit 291B westbound, just nw. Int corridors. **Pets:** Small, dogs only. $25 one-time fee/room. Designated rooms, service with restrictions, supervision. SAVE ✕ ᴳᴹ 🛏 🖥 🐾 ✕

AAA ▽▽▽ **Pheasant Hill Inn & Suites** H ❀
(509) 926-7432. **$80-$190.** 12415 E Mission Ave 99216. I-90, exit 289, just se. Int corridors. **Pets:** $15 daily fee/pet. Designated rooms, service with restrictions, supervision. SAVE ✕ ᴳᴹ 🛏 🖥 🐾 ✕

▽▽▽ **Quality Inn Valley Suites** H
(509) 928-5218. **$90-$140.** 8923 E Mission Ave 99212. I-90, exit 287. Int corridors. **Pets:** Medium, dogs only. $50 deposit/room. Service with restrictions, supervision. ASK ✕ ᴳᴹ 🛏 🖥 🐾 ✕

▽▽▽ **Residence Inn by Marriott** H
(509) 892-9300. **$139-$149.** 15915 E Indiana Ave 99216. I-90, exit 291 westbound, just e; exit 291B eastbound, just n, then just e. Int corridors. **Pets:** Accepted. ✕ ᴳᴹ 🛏 🖥 🐾 ✕

AAA ▽▽◇ **Rodeway Inn & Suites** H
(509) 535-7185. **$49-$99, 7 day notice.** 6309 E Broadway 99212. I-90, exit 286, just w. Ext/int corridors. **Pets:** Medium. $10 daily fee/pet. Designated rooms, service with restrictions, supervision.
SAVE ✕ 🛏 🖥 🐾

AAA ▽▽◇ **Super 8** M
(509) 928-4888. **$57-$132.** 2020 N Argonne Rd 99212. I-90, exit 287, just n. Int corridors. **Pets:** Other species. $25 deposit/room, $15 one-time fee/room. Designated rooms, service with restrictions, supervision.
SAVE ✕ 🛏 🖥 🐾 ✕

STEVENSON

AAA ▽▽▽ **Skamania Lodge** H ❀
(509) 427-7700. **$129-$289, 5 day notice.** 1131 SW Skamania Lodge Way 98648. 1 mi w on SR 14, just n on Rock Creek Dr, then just w. Int corridors. **Pets:** $50 one-time fee/room. Designated rooms, service with restrictions, supervision. SAVE ✕ 🛏 🖥 🍴 🐾 ✕

SULTAN

AAA ▽ **Dutch Cup Motel** M
(360) 793-2215. **$80-$97, 3 day notice.** 819 Main St 98294. Jct US 2 and Main St. Ext corridors. **Pets:** Small, other species. $10 daily fee/pet. Designated rooms, service with restrictions, supervision.
SAVE ✕ 🛏 🖥

SUNNYSIDE

AAA ▽▽▽ **Best Western Grapevine Inn** H
(509) 839-6070. **$100-$110.** 1849 Quail Ln 98944. I-82, exit 69, just n, then just w. Int corridors. **Pets:** Small, dogs only. $25 one-time fee/room. Designated rooms, supervision. SAVE ✕ ᴳᴹ 🛏 🖥 🐾

AAA ▽▽◇ **Country Inn & Suites Sunnyside** M ❀
(509) 837-7878. **$49-$79.** 408 Yakima Valley Hwy 98944. Downtown. Ext corridors. **Pets:** Medium. $10 daily fee/room. Designated rooms, service with restrictions, supervision. SAVE ✕ 🛏 🖥 🐾

TOPPENISH

AAA ▽▽▽ **Quality Inn & Suites** H
(509) 865-5800. **$80-$90.** 511 S Elm St 98948. I-82, exit 50, 3.2 mi e. Int corridors. **Pets:** Accepted. SAVE ✕ ᴳᴹ 🛏 🖥

TUMWATER

AAA ▽▽▽ **Best Western Tumwater Inn** H
(360) 956-1235. **$95-$115.** 5188 Capitol Blvd 98501. I-5, exit 102, just e. Int corridors. **Pets:** Accepted. SAVE ✕ 🛏 🖥 ✕

▽▽▽ **Comfort Inn and Conference Center** H ❀
(360) 352-0691. **$80-$120.** 1620 74th Ave SW 98501. I-5, exit 101, just se. Int corridors. **Pets:** Small. $10 daily fee/pet. Service with restrictions, supervision. ASK ✕ 🛏 🖥 🐾

▽▽ **Extended StayAmerica-Olympia-Tumwater** H
(360) 754-6063. **$89-$99.** 1675 Mottman Rd SW 98512. I-5, exit 104, 0.4 mi nw on US 101, just s on Crosby Blvd, then just se. Int corridors. **Pets:** Other species. $25 daily fee/room. Designated rooms, service with restrictions, crate. ASK ✕ 🛏 🖥

▽▽▽ **GuestHouse Inn & Suites** H ❀
(360) 943-5040. **$89-$120.** 1600 74th Ave SW 98501. I-5, exit 101, just se. Int corridors. **Pets:** Small. $10 daily fee/pet. Designated rooms, service with restrictions, supervision. ASK ✕ ᴳᴹ 🛏 🖥 🐾

UNION

▽▽▽ **Alderbrook Resort & Spa** H
(360) 898-2200. **Call for rates.** 7101 E SR 106 98592. Just e of town. Ext/int corridors. **Pets:** Accepted. ✕ 🛏 🖥 🍴 🐾 ✕

UNION GAP

AAA ▽▽▽ **Best Western Ahtanum Inn** H
(509) 248-9700. **$80-$179.** 2408 Rudkin Rd 98903. I-82, exit 36, just n. Int corridors. **Pets:** Accepted. SAVE ✕ ᴳᴹ 🛏 🖥 🐾 ✕

AAA ▽▽▽ **Quality Inn-Yakima Valley** M
(509) 248-6924. **$69-$169.** 12 E Valley Mall Blvd 98903. I-82, exit 36, just s. Ext corridors. **Pets:** Medium. $10 daily fee/pet. Service with restrictions, crate. SAVE ✕ ᴳᴹ 🛏 🖥 🐾

▽▽ **Super 8 Yakima** H
(509) 248-8880. **$76-$120.** 2605 Rudkin Rd 98903. I-82, exit 36, just s. Int corridors. **Pets:** Other species. $10 daily fee/room. Service with restrictions, supervision. ASK ✕ ᴳᴹ 🛏 🖥 🐾

WALLA WALLA

AAA ▽▽▽ **Best Western Walla Walla Suites Inn** H
(509) 525-4700. **$89-$159.** 7 E Oak St 99362. US 12, exit 2nd Ave, just s. Int corridors. **Pets:** Dogs only. $10 daily fee/pet. Service with restrictions, crate. SAVE ✕ ᴳᴹ 🛏 🖥 🐾

▽▽▽ **Comfort Inn & Suites** H ❀
(509) 522-3500. **$99-$179.** 1419 W Pine St 99362. US 12, exit Pendleton/Prescott. Int corridors. **Pets:** Medium, dogs only. $15 daily fee/pet. Designated rooms, service with restrictions, supervision.
ASK ✕ 🛏 🖥 🐾

▽▽▽ **Holiday Inn Express** H ❀
(509) 525-6200. **$99-$199.** 1433 W Pine St 99362. US 12, exit Pendleton/Prescott. Int corridors. **Pets:** Other species. $20 daily fee/pet. Designated rooms, service with restrictions, supervision.
ASK ✕ 🛏 🖥 🐾 ✕

▽▽▽ **La Quinta Inn Walla Walla** H ❀
(509) 525-2522. **Call for rates.** 520 N 2nd Ave 99362. US 12, exit 2nd Ave, just s. Int corridors. **Pets:** Medium, other species. Service with restrictions, supervision. ✕ 🛏 🖥 🐾 ✕

AAA ▽▽▽ **Marcus Whitman Hotel & Conference Center** H
(509) 525-2200. **$119-$349.** 6 W Rose St 99362. Downtown. Int corridors. **Pets:** Large, dogs only. $25 daily fee/room. Designated rooms, service with restrictions, crate. SAVE ✕ 🛏 🖥 🍴

▽▽▽ **Walla Walla Super 8** H ❀
(509) 525-8800. **$77-$110.** 2315 Eastgate St N 99362. US 12, exit Wilbur Ave, just se. Int corridors. **Pets:** Large. $10 daily fee/room. Service with restrictions, supervision. ASK ✕ ᴳᴹ 🛏 🐾

(AAA) ▼▼◆ **Walla Walla Travelodge** **M** ❀
(509) 529-4940. **$55-$150.** 421 E Main St 99362. US 12, exit 2nd Ave, 0.5 mi s, then just e. Ext/int corridors. **Pets:** Medium. $7 daily fee/pet. Designated rooms, service with restrictions, supervision.
[SAVE] [✕] [☐] [☐] [➰]

WENATCHEE

(AAA) ▼▼ **Avenue Motel** **M**
(509) 663-7161. **$50-$76.** 720 N Wenatchee Ave 98801. On US 2 business loop; just nw of downtown. Ext/int corridors. **Pets:** Accepted.
[SAVE] [✕] [☐] [☐] [➰]

(AAA) ▼▼◆ **Coast Wenatchee Center Hotel** **H**
(509) 662-1234. **$79-$165.** 201 N Wenatchee Ave 98801. Jct 2nd St; downtown. Int corridors. **Pets:** $10 one-time fee/room. Service with restrictions, supervision. [SAVE] [✕] [☐] [☐] [❑] [➰]

(AAA) ▼▼▼ **Comfort Inn** **H** ❀
(509) 662-1700. **$60-$190.** 815 N Wenatchee Ave 98801. Downtown. Int corridors. **Pets:** Medium, other species. $25 one-time fee/room. Service with restrictions, supervision. [SAVE] [✕] [☐] [☐] [➰]

(AAA) ▼▼ **Econo Lodge** **M**
(509) 663-7121. **$55-$120.** 232 N Wenatchee Ave 98801. Downtown. Ext corridors. **Pets:** Small, dogs only. $10 daily fee/pet. Service with restrictions, supervision. [SAVE] [✕] [☐] [☐] [➰]

▼▼▼ **Holiday Inn Express** **H** ❀
(509) 663-6355. **Call for rates.** 1921 N Wenatchee Ave 98801. Northwest side of town. Int corridors. **Pets:** Medium, other species. Service with restrictions, supervision. [✕] [♿M] [☐] [☐] [➰]

▼▼▼ **La Quinta Inn & Suites Wenatchee** **H** ❀
(509) 664-6565. **Call for rates.** 1905 N Wenatchee Ave 98801. Northwest side of town. Int corridors. **Pets:** Medium, other species. Service with restrictions, supervision. [✕] [♿M] [☐] [☐] [➰] [✕]

(AAA) ▼▼▼ **Red Lion Hotel Wenatchee** **H**
(509) 663-0711. **$99-$199.** 1225 N Wenatchee Ave 98801. Just nw of downtown. Int corridors. **Pets:** Other species. $20 one-time fee/room. Service with restrictions, supervision. [SAVE] [✕] [☐] [☐] [❑] [➰]

(AAA) ▼▼▼ **Super 8** **H** ❀
(509) 662-3443. **$59-$129.** 1401 N Miller St 98801. 1.5 mi n on US 2. Int corridors. **Pets:** Medium. $50 deposit/room, $10 daily fee/pet. Service with restrictions, supervision. [SAVE] [✕] [☐] [☐] [➰]

(AAA) ▼▼▼ **Travelodge-Wenatchee** **M**
(509) 662-8165. **$55-$140.** 1004 N Wenatchee Ave 98801. Downtown. Ext corridors. **Pets:** Accepted. [SAVE] [✕] [♿M] [☐] [☐] [➰]

WESTPORT

(AAA) ▼▼▼ **Chateau Westport** **H**
(360) 268-9101. **$89-$388.** 710 W Hancock St 98595. Just w of SR 105 Spur N; 1.5 mi n of Twin Harbors State Park. Int corridors.
Pets: Accepted. [SAVE] [✕] [♿M] [☐] [☐] [➰] [✕] [🐾]

▼▼ **Windjammer Motel** **M**
(360) 268-9351. **Call for rates.** 461 E Pacific Ave 98595. Downtown. Ext corridors. **Pets:** Other species. $10 daily fee/pet. Service with restrictions, supervision. [✕] [☐] [☐] [🐾] [✉]

WINTHROP

(AAA) ▼▼▼ **Americas Best Value Cascade Inn** **M**
(509) 996-3100. **$70-$150, 3 day notice.** 1006 SR 20 98862. 1 mi e. Ext corridors. **Pets:** Medium, dogs only. $10 daily fee/pet. Designated rooms, service with restrictions, supervision. [SAVE] [✕] [☐] [☐] [➰]

(AAA) ▼▼▼ **River Run Inn** **M** ❀
(509) 996-2173. **$75-$150, 10 day notice.** 27 Rader Rd 98862. 0.5 mi w on SR 20. Ext corridors. **Pets:** Small, dogs only. $15 daily fee/pet. Designated rooms, service with restrictions, supervision.
[SAVE] [✕] [☐] [☐] [➰] [✕]

(AAA) ▼▼▼ **Winthrop Inn** **M**
(509) 996-2217. **$70-$135, 7 day notice.** 960 SR 20 98862. 0.9 mi e. Int corridors. **Pets:** Medium, dogs only. $10 daily fee/pet. Service with restrictions, supervision. [SAVE] [✕] [☐] [➰] [✕]

(AAA) ▼▼▼ **Winthrop Mtn View Chalets** **CA**
(509) 996-3113. **$75-$140, 7 day notice.** 1120 Hwy 20 98862. South end of town. Ext corridors. **Pets:** Dogs only. $30 daily fee/room. Designated rooms, service with restrictions, supervision.
[SAVE] [✕] [☐] [☐] [✉]

WOODLAND

(AAA) ▼▼◆ **Lewis River Inn** **M**
(360) 225-6257. **$64-$110.** 1100 Lewis River Rd 98674. I-5, exit 21, just e. Ext corridors. **Pets:** Large, other species. $10 daily fee/pet. Designated rooms, service with restrictions, supervision. [SAVE] [✕] [☐] [☐]

YAKIMA

(AAA) ▼▼▼ **Best Western Lincoln Inn** **H**
(509) 453-8898. **$80-$200, 7 day notice.** 1614 N 1st St 98901. I-82, exit 31, just s. Int corridors. **Pets:** Medium, dogs only. $20 daily fee/pet. Designated rooms, service with restrictions, supervision.
[SAVE] [✕] [♿M] [☐] [☐] [➰]

▼▼▼▼ **Birchfield Manor Country Inn** **CI**
(509) 452-1960. **$119-$219, 14 day notice.** 2018 Birchfield Rd 98901. I-82, exit 34, 2 mi e to Birchfield Rd, then just s. Int corridors.
Pets: Accepted. [ASK] [✕] [♿M] [☐] [☐] [❑] [➰] [✉]

(AAA) ▼▼◆ **Cedars Suites Yakima Downtown** **M**
(509) 452-8101. **$69-$129.** 1010 E a St 98901. I-82, exit 33B eastbound; exit 33 westbound, just w to 9th St, just n to a St, then just e. Ext corridors. **Pets:** Small. $10 daily fee/pet. Designated rooms, service with restrictions, supervision. [SAVE] [✕] [☐]

▼▼ **Clarion Hotel & Conference Center** **H**
(509) 248-7850. **$79-$139.** 1507 N 1st St 98901. I-82, exit 31, 0.5 mi s. Int corridors. **Pets:** Medium. $10 daily fee/pet. Service with restrictions, crate. [ASK] [✕] [♿M] [☐] [☐] [❑] [➰] [✕]

(AAA) ▼▼◆ **Comfort Suites** **H**
(509) 249-1900. **$99-$300.** 3702 Fruitvale Blvd 98902. US 12, exit 40th Ave, just s. Int corridors. **Pets:** Accepted. [SAVE] [✕] [♿M] [☐] [☐] [➰]

▼▼ **Days Inn Yakima** **H**
(509) 248-3393. **$70-$130.** 1504 N 1st St 98901. I-82, exit 31, 0.6 mi s. Int corridors. **Pets:** $15 daily fee/pet. Service with restrictions, supervision.
[ASK] [✕] [♿M] [☐] [☐] [➰]

▼▼▼ **Fairfield Inn & Suites by Marriott** **H**
(509) 452-3100. **$89-$109.** 137 N Fair Ave 98901. I-82, exit 33A eastbound, just s; exit 33 westbound, just w to 9th St, just n to B St, then just e. Int corridors. **Pets:** Medium. $25 daily fee/room. Designated rooms, service with restrictions, supervision. [✕] [♿M] [☐] [☐] [➰]

(AAA) ▼▼▼▼ **Holiday Inn Express Yakima** **H**
(509) 249-1000. **$94-$153.** 1001 E a St 98901. I-82, exit 33B eastbound; exit 33 westbound, just w to 9th St, just n to a St, then just e. Int corridors. **Pets:** Accepted. [SAVE] [✕] [♿M] [☐] [☐] [➰]

(AAA) ▼▼▼▼ **Howard Johnson Plaza Yakima** **H**
(509) 452-6511. **$72-$129.** 9 N 9th St 98901. I-82, exit 33 westbound; exit 33B eastbound, just s. Int corridors. **Pets:** $15 daily fee/pet. Designated rooms, service with restrictions, crate.
[SAVE] [✕] [♿M] [☐] [☐] [❑] [➰]

▼▼▼ **Knights Inn Yakima** **M**
(509) 453-0391. **Call for rates.** 818 N 1st St 98901. I-82, exit 31, 1.2 mi s. Ext corridors. **Pets:** Accepted. [✕] [♿M] [☐] [☐] [➰]

▼▼▼ **Oxford Inn** 🅗

(509) 457-4444. **$79-$99.** 1603 E Yakima Ave 98901. I-82, exit 33 westbound, just e; exit 33B eastbound. Int corridors. **Pets:** Small, dogs only. $25 one-time fee/room. Service with restrictions, crate.

A$K ⊠ ⅋M 📶 💻 🏊 ⊠

▼▼▼ **Oxford Suites** 🅗

(509) 457-9000. **$105-$165.** 1701 E Yakima Ave 98901. I-82, exit 33 westbound; exit 33B eastbound. Int corridors. **Pets:** Medium. $25 one-time fee/room. Designated rooms, service with restrictions, supervision.

A$K ⊠ ⅋M 📶 💻 🏊 ⊠

ⒶⒶⒶ ▼▼▼ **Red Lion Hotel Yakima Center** 🅗

(509) 248-5900. **Call for rates.** 607 E Yakima Ave 98901. I-82, exit 33 westbound; exit 33B eastbound, 0.8 mi w. Ext/int corridors. **Pets:** Other species. $20 one-time fee/room. Service with restrictions, supervision.

SAVE ⊠ 📶 💻 ⅋ 🏊

▼▼ **Sun Country Inn** Ⓜ

(509) 248-5650. **$58-$70, 3 day notice.** 1700 N 1st St 98901. I-82, exit 31, just s. Ext corridors. **Pets:** Large, other species. $8 daily fee/pet. Designated rooms, service with restrictions, supervision.

A$K ⊠ ⅋M 📶 💻 🏊

ZILLAH

▼▼ **Comfort Inn** 🅗

(509) 829-3399. **$104-$160.** 911 Vintage Valley Pkwy 98953. I-82, exit 52, just n. Int corridors. **Pets:** Other species. $10 daily fee/pet.

A$K ⊠ ⅋M 📶 💻 🏊

WEST VIRGINIA

BARBOURSVILLE

Best Western Huntington Mall Inn M
(304) 736-9772. **$79-$99.** 3441 US 60 E 25504. I-64, exit 20A eastbound; exit 20 westbound, 0.3 mi s. Int corridors. **Pets:** Other species. $15 one-time fee/room. Service with restrictions, supervision.

Comfort Inn by Choice Hotels H
(304) 733-2122. **$80-$100.** 249 Mall Rd 25504. I-64, exit 20, 0.4 mi n. Int corridors. **Pets:** Accepted.

BECKLEY

Americas Best Value Inn M
(304) 252-0671. **$67-$110.** 1939 Harper Rd 25801. I-64/77, exit 44, just e on SR 3. Ext/int corridors. **Pets:** Other species. $7 daily fee/pet. Service with restrictions, supervision.

Country Inn & Suites By Carlson H
(304) 252-5100. **$99-$199.** 2120 Harper Rd 25801. I-64/77, exit 44, just w on SR 3. Int corridors. **Pets:** Accepted.

Econo Lodge M ❄
(304) 255-2161. **$50-$125.** 1909 Harper Rd 25801. I-64/77, exit 44, 0.3 mi e on SR 3. Ext/int corridors. **Pets:** Other species. Service with restrictions, crate.

Fairfield Inn H
(304) 252-8661. **$85-$103.** 125 Hylton Ln 25801. I-64/77, exit 44, just e. Int corridors. **Pets:** Accepted.

Howard Johnson Express Inn M
(304) 255-5900. **$49-$125.** 1907 Harper Rd 25801. I-64/77, exit 44, 0.4 mi e on SR 3. Int corridors. **Pets:** $15 one-time fee/pet. Designated rooms, service with restrictions, supervision.

Microtel Inn M
(304) 256-2000. **$55-$129, 3 day notice.** 2130 Harper Rd 25801. I-64/77, exit 44, just w. Int corridors. **Pets:** Medium. $10 daily fee/pet. Service with restrictions, supervision.

Park Inn & Suites H
(304) 255-9091. **$59-$109.** 134 Harper Park Dr 25801. I-64/77, exit 44, just w on SR 3. Int corridors. **Pets:** Medium. $10 one-time fee/pet. Service with restrictions, supervision.

Super 8 M
(304) 253-0802. **$59-$109.** 2014 Harper Rd 25801. I-64/77, exit 44, just e. Int corridors. **Pets:** Medium. $10 daily fee/pet. Service with restrictions, supervision.

BLUEFIELD

Holiday Inn Bluefield-On The Hill H
(304) 325-6170. **Call for rates.** 3350 Big Laurel Hwy 24701. I-77, exit 1, 3.8 mi nw via US 52/460. Int corridors. **Pets:** Accepted.

BRIDGEPORT

Holiday Inn Clarksburg-Bridgeport H
(304) 842-5411. **$95-$110.** 100 Lodgeville Rd 26330. I-79, exit 119, just e on US 50. Int corridors. **Pets:** Accepted.

Sleep Inn M
(304) 842-1919. **$76-$81.** 115 Tolley Dr 26330. I-79, exit 119, just e on US 50. Int corridors. **Pets:** Service with restrictions, supervision.

Super 8–Bridgeport M
(304) 842-7381. **$54-$100.** 168 Barnett Run Rd 26330. I-79, exit 121, just w. Ext corridors. **Pets:** Medium. $10 daily fee/pet. Service with restrictions, crate.

BRUCETON MILLS

Microtel Inn and Suites M ❄
(304) 379-7900. **$69-$95.** 886 Casteel Rd 26525. I-68, exit 29 (Hazelton), just n. Int corridors. **Pets:** Other species. $10 daily fee/pet. Designated rooms, service with restrictions, crate.

CHARLESTON

Charleston Comfort Suites H ❄
(304) 925-1171. **Call for rates.** 107 Alex Ln 25304. I-77, exit 95, just s on SR 61. Int corridors. **Pets:** Medium. $25 daily fee/pet. Designated rooms, service with restrictions, crate.

Charleston Residence Inn by Marriott H
(304) 345-4200. **$139-$149.** 200 Hotel Cir 25311. I-64/77, exit 99, just e. Int corridors. **Pets:** Accepted.

Country Inn & Suites By Carlson South H ❄
(304) 925-4300. **$110-$130.** 105 Alex Ln 25304. I-77, exit 95, just s on SR 61. Int corridors. **Pets:** Medium. Designated rooms, service with restrictions, crate.

Days Inn Charleston East M
(304) 925-1010. **$55-$105.** 6400 MacCorkle Ave SE 25304. I-77, exit 95, just s on SR 61. Int corridors. **Pets:** Accepted.

Knights Inn-Charleston East M
(304) 925-0451. **$50-$70.** 6401 MacCorkle Ave SE 25304. I-77, exit 95, just s on SR 61. Ext corridors. **Pets:** Accepted.

Red Roof Inn-Kanawha City M
(304) 925-6953. **$48-$76.** 6305 SE MacCorkle Ave 25304. I-77, exit 95, just s on SR 61. Ext corridors. **Pets:** Large. Service with restrictions, crate.

CROSS LANES

Comfort Inn West Charleston M
(304) 776-8070. **$90-$134.** 102 Racer Dr 25313. I-64, exit 47, just s. Int corridors. **Pets:** Large. $25 daily fee/room. Designated rooms, service with restrictions, supervision.

DANIELS

AAA **WWWW** The Resort at Glade Springs **H**
(304) 763-2000. **$152-$442, 7 day notice.** 255 Resort Dr 25832. I-64, exit 125, 1.5 mi w on SR 307, then 2.8 mi w on US 19. Ext/int corridors. **Pets:** Large, dogs only. $20 daily fee/pet. Designated rooms, service with restrictions, crate. (SAVE) [X] [fridge] [TV] [pool] [exercise]

DAVIS

WWWW Black Bear Resort **CA**
(304) 866-4391. **$90-$510.** Cortland Rd, Canaan Valley 26260. 4.5 mi s on SR 32. Ext corridors. **Pets:** Dogs only. $50 one-time fee/pet. Designated rooms, no service. (ASK) [X] [fridge] [TV] [pool] [exercise]

DUNBAR

WWW Dunbar Super 8 **M**
(304) 768-6888. **$64-$100.** 911 Dunbar Ave 25064. I-64, exit 53, just w. Int corridors. **Pets:** $10 daily fee/pet. Service with restrictions, supervision.
(ASK) [X] [fridge] [TV]

EDRAY

AAA **WWW** Marlinton Motor Inn **M** ✿
(304) 799-4711. **$65-$129, 3 day notice.** US 219 N 24954. Center. Ext corridors. **Pets:** Medium, dogs only. $12 daily fee/pet. Designated rooms, service with restrictions, supervision. (SAVE) [X] [fridge] [TV] [TV] [pool]

ELKINS

AAA **WWWW** Cheat River Lodge **CA** ✿
(304) 636-2301. **$73-$88.** Rt 1, Box 115 26241. 4.8 mi e on US 33, then 1.5 mi ne. Ext corridors. **Pets:** Dogs only. $10 daily fee/pet. Supervision.
(SAVE) [X] [fridge] [TV] [TV] [exercise]

WWW Econo Lodge **M**
(304) 636-5311. **Call for rates.** US 33 E 26241. 1 mi e. Ext/int corridors.
Pets: Accepted. [X] [fridge] [TV] [pool]

WWW Elkins Super 8 **M**
(304) 636-6500. **Call for rates.** 350 Beverly Pike 26241. 0.8 mi s on SR 219. Int corridors. **Pets:** Accepted. [X] [fridge] [TV]

FAIRMONT

AAA **WWWW** Holiday Inn Fairmont **H**
(304) 366-5500. **$84-$189.** 930 E Grafton Rd 26554. I-79, exit 137, just e. Int corridors. **Pets:** Other species. $25 one-time fee/room. Service with restrictions, crate. (SAVE) [X] [fridge/M] [fridge] [TV] [TV] [pool]

WWW Super 8 **M**
(304) 363-1488. **$57-$106.** 2208 Pleasant Valley Rd 26554. I-79, exit 133, just e. Int corridors. **Pets:** Medium. $10 daily fee/pet. Service with restrictions, crate. (ASK) [X] [fridge] [TV]

FALLING WATERS

WWWW Holiday Inn Express Martinsburg North **H**
(304) 274-6100. **Call for rates.** 1220 TJ Jackson Dr 25419. I-81, exit 20, just w. Int corridors. **Pets:** Accepted. [X] [fridge] [TV] [pool]

FROST

WWWW The Inn at Mountain Quest **CI**
(304) 799-7267. **$130-$150.** Rt 92 Frost 24954. On SR 92, 0.4 mi n. Ext corridors. **Pets:** $10 daily fee/pet. Designated rooms, no service, supervision. (ASK) [X] [TV] [exercise]

HARPERS FERRY

AAA **WWWW** Quality Hotel Conference Center **H** ✿
(304) 535-6302. **Call for rates.** 4328 William L Wilson Frwy 25425. Just w on US 340. Int corridors. **Pets:** Dogs only. $50 one-time fee/room. Designated rooms, service with restrictions, crate.
(SAVE) [X] [fridge] [TV] [TV] [pool]

HUNTINGTON

AAA **WWW** Red Roof Inn **H**
(304) 733-3737. **$50-$79.** 5190 US Rt 60 E 25705. I-64, exit 15, just s. Ext corridors. **Pets:** Large. Service with restrictions, crate. (SAVE) [X] [fridge]

JANE LEW

WWW Plantation Inn & Suites **M**
(304) 884-7806. **$65-$100.** 1322 Hackers Creek Rd 26378. I-79, exit 105, just e. Ext corridors. **Pets:** Accepted. (ASK) [X] [fridge] [TV]

KEYSER

AAA **WWW** Keyser Inn **M**
(304) 788-0913. **$58-$72.** 51 Josie Dr 26726. On US 220, 2.3 mi s. Int corridors. **Pets:** Small. $25 one-time fee/room. Designated rooms, service with restrictions, supervision. (SAVE) [X] [fridge] [TV]

LEWISBURG

WWWW Lewisburg Holiday Inn Express Hotel & Suites **H**
(304) 645-5750. **Call for rates.** 222 Hunter Ln 24901. I-64, exit 169, just s. Int corridors. **Pets:** Accepted. [X] [fridge] [TV] [pool]

AAA **WWWW** Quality Inn–Lewisburg **H**
(304) 645-7722. **Call for rates.** 540 N Jefferson St 24901. I-64, exit 169, just s on US 219. Ext corridors. **Pets:** Small. $50 daily fee/pet. Designated rooms, service with restrictions, supervision.
(SAVE) [X] [fridge] [TV] [TV] [pool]

WWW Super 8 **M**
(304) 647-3188. **Call for rates.** 550 N Jefferson St 24901. I-64, exit 169, just s on US 219. Int corridors. **Pets:** $10 daily fee/pet. Service with restrictions, supervision. [X] [fridge] [TV]

LOGAN

WWW Super 8-Logan **M**
(304) 752-8787. **Call for rates.** 316 Riverview Ave 25601. 1.8 mi e on SR 73. Int corridors. **Pets:** Accepted. [X] [fridge] [TV]

MARTINSBURG

WWW Days Inn Martinsburg **M**
(304) 263-1800. **$61-$71.** 209 Viking Way 25404. I-81, exit 13, just e on W King St (CR 15). Ext/int corridors. **Pets:** Small, other species. $10 daily fee/pet. No service, supervision. (ASK) [X] [fridge] [TV]

WWW Econo Lodge **M**
(304) 274-2181. **$60-$64.** 5595 Hammonds Mill Rd 25404. I-81, exit 20, just e. Ext/int corridors. **Pets:** Accepted. (ASK) [X] [TV]

WWWW Holiday Inn Martinsburg **H**
(304) 267-5500. **$109-$149.** 301 Foxcroft Ave 25401. I-81, exit 13, just e on W King St (CR 15). Int corridors. **Pets:** Other species. $25 one-time fee/room. Designated rooms, service with restrictions, supervision.
(ASK) [X] [fridge] [TV] [TV] [pool]

WWW Knights Inn-Martinsburg **M**
(304) 267-2211. **Call for rates.** 1997 Edwin Miller Blvd 25404. I-81, exit 16E, 0.4 mi e on SR 9. Ext corridors. **Pets:** Accepted. [X] [fridge]

WWW Super 8-Martinsburg **M**
(304) 263-0801. **Call for rates.** 2048 Edwin Miller Blvd 25404. I-81, exit 16E, just e on SR 9. Int corridors. **Pets:** Accepted. [X] [fridge] [TV]

MORGANTOWN

WWW Comfort Inn-Morgantown **M**
(304) 296-9364. **$81-$162.** 225 Comfort Inn Dr 26508. I-68, exit 1, 0.3 mi n on US 119. Int corridors. **Pets:** Medium, other species. $10 one-time fee/pet. Designated rooms, service with restrictions, supervision.
(ASK) [X] [fridge] [TV] [TV] [pool]

W Friends Inn **M**

(304) 599-4850. **$50-$175, 14 day notice.** 452 Country Club Rd 26505. I-79, exit 155, s on US 19 to SR 705, then e on University Ave. Ext corridors. **Pets:** Very small. $5 daily fee/pet. Designated rooms, service with restrictions, crate. (SAVE) [X] [=]

WWWW Ramada Conference Center **H**

(304) 296-3431. **$95-$150.** 20 Scott Ave 26508. I-68, exit 1, 0.3 mi n. Int corridors. **Pets:** Other species. Service with restrictions, supervision. (SAVE) [X] [=] [=] [¶] [≈]

WWWW Residence Inn by Marriott Morgantown **H** ❀

(304) 599-0237. **$134-$164.** 1046 Willowdale Rd 26505. I-79, exit 155, 2 mi s on US 19, then 0.9 mi e on SR 705. Int corridors. **Pets:** Large, other species. $75 one-time fee/pet. Designated rooms, crate. [X] [♨] [=] [=] [≈] [✕]

PARKERSBURG

WWWW The Blennerhassett **H** ❀

(304) 422-3131. **$119-$269.** 320 Market St 26101. Between 4th and 5th sts; downtown. Int corridors. **Pets:** Cats only. $50 one-time fee/pet. Designated rooms. (ASK) [X] [=] [¶]

W Knights Inn **M**

(304) 420-2420. **$42-$61.** 3604 1/2 7th St 26104. I-77, exit 176, just w. Ext corridors. **Pets:** Medium, other species. $5 daily fee/pet. Service with restrictions, supervision. (ASK) [X] [=]

WW Red Carpet Inn **M**

(304) 485-1851. **$45-$65.** 6333 Emerson Ave 26101. I-77, exit 179, 0.4 mi sw on SR 68. Ext corridors. **Pets:** Accepted. (SAVE) [X] [=] [=]

WW Red Roof Inn **M**

(304) 485-1741. **$49-$72.** 3714 E 7th St 26104. I-77, exit 176, just w on US 50. Ext corridors. **Pets:** Large. Service with restrictions, crate. (ASK) [X] [=] [=]

W Travelodge Parkersburg **M**

(304) 424-5100. **$41-$66.** 3604 E 7th St 26104. I-77, exit 176, just w. Ext corridors. **Pets:** Medium, other species. $5 daily fee/pet. Service with restrictions, supervision. (ASK) [X] [=] [=] [≈]

PHILIPPI

WW Budget Inn Philippi **M**

(304) 457-5888. **$49-$85.** Rt 4, Box 155 26416. 2.5 mi s on US 250. Int corridors. **Pets:** Medium, dogs only. $10 one-time fee/pet. Service with restrictions, supervision. (SAVE) [X] [♨] [=]

PRINCETON

WW Comfort Inn-Princeton **M**

(304) 487-6101. **Call for rates.** 136 Ambrose Ln 24740. I-77, exit 9, 0.3 mi w on US 460. Int corridors. **Pets:** Accepted. [X] [=] [=]

WW Days Inn **M**

(304) 425-8100. **$63-$88, 3 day notice.** 347 Meadowfield Ln 24740. I-77, exit 9, 0.3 mi w on US 460, just s on Ambrose Ln, then just e. Ext corridors. **Pets:** Accepted. (SAVE) [X] [=] [≈]

WWW Holiday Inn Express Princeton **H**

(304) 425-8156. **$85-$150.** 805 Oakvale Rd 24740. I-77, exit 9, just w. Int corridors. **Pets:** Accepted. (SAVE) [X] [=] [=] [≈]

WW Sleep Inn & Suites **H**

(304) 431-2800. **$65-$120.** 1015 Oakvale Rd 24740. I-77, exit 9, just w on US 460, then just n via service road. Int corridors. **Pets:** Accepted. (ASK) [X] [=] [=] [≈]

RIPLEY

WWW McCoys Inn & Conference Center **H** ❀

(304) 372-9122. **$80-$99.** 701 W Main St 25271. I-77, exit 138, just e. Ext/int corridors. **Pets:** Medium. $15 daily fee/room. Designated rooms, service with restrictions, crate. (SAVE) [X] [=] [¶] [≈] [✕]

WWWW Quality Inn **H**

(304) 372-5000. **$89.** 1 Hospitality Dr 25271. I-77, exit 138, just w on US 33, then 0.3 mi n. Ext/int corridors. **Pets:** Accepted. (SAVE) [X] [=] [=]

W Ripley Super 8 **M**

(304) 372-8880. **$65-$110.** 102 Duke Dr 25271. I-77, exit 138, just e on US 33. Int corridors. **Pets:** Accepted. (ASK) [X] [=] [=]

ROANOKE

WWWW WWW Stonewall Resort **H**

(304) 269-7400. **$99-$219, 3 day notice.** 940 Resort Dr 26447. I-79, exit 91, just e. Ext/int corridors. **Pets:** Small. Service with restrictions, supervision. (SAVE) [X] [=] [=] [¶] [≈] [✕]

SHEPHERDSTOWN

WW Comfort Inn Shepherdstown **M**

(304) 876-3160. **Call for rates.** 70 Maddex Square Dr 25443. Just w on SR 45; center. Int corridors. **Pets:** Accepted. [X] [=] [=]

SNOWSHOE

WW Inn at Snowshoe **H**

(304) 572-6520. **Call for rates.** SR 66 26209. Jct US 219, 0.5 mi e, follow signs. Int corridors. **Pets:** Accepted. [X] [=] [=] [¶] [≈] [✕]

SOUTH CHARLESTON

WWWW Ramada **H** ❀

(304) 744-4641. **$89-$139.** 400 2nd Ave 25303. I-64, exit 56, just nw. Int corridors. **Pets:** Medium. $25 daily fee/pet. Designated rooms, service with restrictions, supervision. (SAVE) [X] [=] [=] [¶] [≈]

STAR CITY

W Econo Lodge-Coliseum **M**

(304) 599-8181. **$64-$75.** 3506 Monongahela Blvd 26505. I-79, exit 155, 1.4 mi s on US 119/SR 7. Ext corridors. **Pets:** Medium. $10 daily fee/room. Service with restrictions, supervision. (ASK) [X] [=] [=]

SUMMERSVILLE

WW Best Western Summersville Lake Motor Lodge **H**

(304) 872-6900. **$56-$89.** 1203 S Broad St 26651. US 19 and Broad St; 0.6 mi s of jct SR 39. Ext corridors. **Pets:** Other species. $10 daily fee/pet. Crate. (SAVE) [X] [=] [=]

WWW Comfort Inn **M**

(304) 872-6500. **$75-$180, 30 day notice.** 903 Industrial Dr N 26651. US 19, 1.9 mi n of jct SR 39. Int corridors. **Pets:** Small. $10 daily fee/pet. Designated rooms, service with restrictions, supervision. (SAVE) [X] [=] [=] [✕]

WWW Country Inn & Suites By Carlson **H**

(304) 872-0555. **$89-$150.** 106 Merchants Walk 26651. US 19, just w. Int corridors. **Pets:** Small. $20 one-time fee/room. Designated rooms, service with restrictions, supervision. (SAVE) [X] [=] [=] [≈]

WWW Hampton Inn **H**

(304) 872-7100. **Call for rates.** 5400 Webster Rd 26651. Just s on SR 41 from US 19. Int corridors. **Pets:** Accepted. [X] [♨] [=] [≈] [✕]

WW Sleep Inn of Summersville **M**

(304) 872-4500. **$65-$155, 30 day notice.** 701 Professional Park Dr 26651. US 19, 1.7 mi n of jct SR 39. Int corridors. **Pets:** Small. $10 daily fee/pet. Designated rooms, service with restrictions, supervision. (SAVE) [X] [=] [=] [≈]

W Super 8-Summersville **M**

(304) 872-4888. **Call for rates.** 306 Merchants Walk 26651. US 19, just n. Int corridors. **Pets:** Accepted. [X] [=]

TRIADELPHIA

▼▼▼ **Comfort Inn-Wheeling** M

(304) 547-0610. **$62-$149.** 675 Fort Henry Rd 26059. I-70, exit 11, just n. Int corridors. **Pets:** $10 daily fee/pet. Service with restrictions, supervision. (ASK) ⊠ 🖬 🖵 🛋

▼▼▼ **Holiday Inn Express Wheeling East** M

(304) 547-1380. **Call for rates.** 87 Jenkins Ln 26059. I-70, exit 11. Int corridors. **Pets:** Accepted. ⊠ 🖬 🖵 🛋

WEIRTON

▼▼▼ **Holiday Inn** H

(304) 723-5522. **$99-$149.** 350 Three Springs Dr 26062. 4.5 mi e on US 22, exit Three Springs Dr. Int corridors. **Pets:** $25 one-time fee/room. Service with restrictions, supervision.

(ASK) ⊠ 🖬 🖵 🍽 🛋 ⊠

WESTON

AAA ▼▼▼ **Comfort Inn** H

(304) 269-7000. **$65-$130.** 2906 US Hwy 33 E 26452. I-79, exit 99, just e. Ext corridors. **Pets:** Medium. $10 daily fee/room. Designated rooms, service with restrictions, supervision. (SAVE) ⊠ 🖬 🖵 🛋

▼▼▼ **Holiday Inn Express Hotel & Suites** H

(304) 269-3550. **$90-$140.** 215 Staunton Dr 26452. I-79, exit 99, just e. Int corridors. **Pets:** Accepted. (ASK) ⊠ 🖬 🖵 🛋

▼▼ **Weston Super 8** M

(304) 269-1086. **$64-$69.** 100 Market Place Mall, Suite 12 26452. I-79, exit 99, just e. Int corridors. **Pets:** Accepted. (ASK) ⊠ 🖬 🖵

WHEELING

▼▼ **Wheeling Super 8** M

(304) 243-9400. **$67-$110.** 2400 National Rd 26003. I-70, exit 5, just e. Int corridors. **Pets:** Accepted. (ASK) ⊠ 🖬 🖵

WHITE SULPHUR SPRINGS

AAA ▼▼▼▼ **The Greenbrier** H

(304) 536-1110. **$299-$650, 15 day notice.** 300 W Main St 24986. I-64, exit 181 westbound, 1.8 mi w on US 60; exit 175 eastbound, just n, then 3.2 mi e on US 60. Ext/int corridors. **Pets:** Accepted.

(SAVE) ⊠ 🚹 🖬 🖵 🍽 🛋 ⊠

ABBOTSFORD

▼▼▼ Sleep Inn 🅗
(715) 223-3337. **$63-$70.** 300 E Elderberry Rd 54405. SR 29, exit 132 (SR 13), just se. Int corridors. **Pets:** Medium, other species. $100 deposit/ pet, $10 one-time fee/pet. Designated rooms, service with restrictions.

(A$K) (✕) (க்M) (🛏) (🖵) (🏊)

ALGOMA

🛰 ▼ Algoma Beach Motel 🅜
(920) 487-2828. **$79-$159, 3 day notice.** 1500 Lake St 54201. Jct SR 54, 0.4 mi s on SR 42. Ext/int corridors. **Pets:** Dogs only. $15 daily fee/ pet. Designated rooms, service with restrictions, supervision.

(SAVE) (✕) (க்M) (🛏)

▼ Scenic Shore Inn 🅜
(920) 487-3214. **$50-$68, 3 day notice.** 2221 Lake St 54201. Jct SR 54, 0.8 mi s on SR 42. Ext corridors. **Pets:** Dogs only. $20 deposit/room. Designated rooms, service with restrictions, supervision. (✕) (🛏) (🖵)

ANTIGO

▼▼ Days Inn 🅗
(715) 623-0506. **Call for rates.** 525 Memory Ln 54409. 0.4 mi n of jct SR 64 E and US 45, then just w. Int corridors. **Pets:** Accepted.

(✕) (🛏) (🖵) (🏊)

▼▼ Super 8-Antigo 🅗 🐾
(715) 623-4188. **$59-$112.** 535 Century Ave 54409. On US 45 at SR 64 E. Int corridors. **Pets:** $15 daily fee/pet. Designated rooms, service with restrictions, supervision. (A$K) (✕) (க்M) (🛏) (🖵) (🏊)

APPLETON

🛰 ▼▼ Best Western Midway Hotel 🅗
(920) 731-4141. **$100-$120.** 3033 W College Ave 54914. US 41, exit 137 (SR 125), 0.5 mi e. Int corridors. **Pets:** Medium, other species. $10 daily fee/pet. Designated rooms, service with restrictions, crate.

(SAVE) (✕) (🛏) (🖵) (🍴) (🏊) (🝮)

▼▼ Candlewood Suites 🅗
(920) 739-8000. **$79-$179.** 4525 W College Ave 54914. Just w of US 41. Int corridors. **Pets:** Other species. $75 one-time fee/pet. Service with restrictions, supervision. (A$K) (✕) (க்M) (🛏) (🖵)

▼▼▼ Comfort Suites Appleton Airport 🅗
(920) 730-3800. **$79-$175.** 3809 W Wisconsin Ave 54914. US 41, exit 138 (Wisconsin Ave), just e. Int corridors. **Pets:** Service with restrictions, supervision. (ECO) (A$K) (✕) (க்M) (🛏) (🖵) (🏊) (🝮)

▼▼▼ Country Inn & Suites By Carlson 🅗
(920) 830-3240. **$99-$130.** 355 Fox River Dr 54913. US 41, exit 137 (SR 125), just nw. Int corridors. **Pets:** Accepted.

(A$K) (✕) (🛏) (🖵) (🏊) (🝮)

▼ Days Inn 🅜
(920) 733-5551. **Call for rates.** 210 Westhill Blvd 54914. US 41, exit 137 (SR 125), just e. Int corridors. **Pets:** Accepted. (✕) (🛏) (🖵)

▼▼ Extended StayAmerica-Appleton-Fox Cities 🅗
(920) 830-9596. **$40-$75.** 4141 Boardwalk Ct 54915. US 41, exit 137 (SR 125), just w on College Ave, then just s on Nicolet Rd. Int corridors. **Pets:** Other species. $25 daily fee/room. Designated rooms, service with restrictions, crate. (A$K) (✕) (க்M) (🛏) (🖵)

▼▼ Fairfield Inn by Marriott 🅗 🐾
(920) 954-0202. **$95-$116.** 132 Mall Dr 54913. US 41, exit 137 (SR 125), just nw. Int corridors. **Pets:** Other species. $20 one-time fee/room. Designated rooms, service with restrictions, supervision.

(✕) (🛏) (🖵) (🏊)

▼▼▼ La Quinta Inn & Suites College Ave 🅗 🐾
(920) 734-7777. **$69-$109.** 3730 W College Ave 54914. US 41, exit 137 (SR 125), just e. Int corridors. **Pets:** Medium, other species. Service with restrictions, supervision. (A$K) (✕) (க்M) (🛏) (🖵) (🏊) (🝮)

▼▼ La Quinta Inn Appleton Fox River Mall Area 🅜 🐾
(920) 734-6070. **$45-$99.** 3920 W College Ave 54914. US 41, exit 137 (SR 125), just e. Ext/int corridors. **Pets:** Medium, other species. Service with restrictions, supervision. (A$K) (✕) (🛏) (🖵) (🏊)

▼▼ Microtel Inn & Suites 🅗
(920) 997-3121. **Call for rates.** 321 Metro Dr 54913. US 41, exit 137 (SR 125), just nw. Int corridors. **Pets:** Accepted. (✕) (🛏) (🖵)

▼▼▼ Residence Inn by Marriott 🅗
(920) 954-0570. **$150-$160.** 310 Metro Dr 54913. US 41, exit 137 (SR 125), just nw on Mall Dr. Int corridors. **Pets:** Accepted.

(✕) (🛏) (🖵) (🏊) (🝮)

ARKDALE

▼▼▼ Northern Bay Golf Resort & Marina (CO)
(608) 339-2090. **Call for rates.** 1844 20th Ave 54613. 2.9 mi nw on SR 21, 4 mi s on CR Z, then 1.5 nw via Dakota Ave and 20th Ave. Int corridors. **Pets:** Accepted. (✕) (🛏) (🖵) (🍴) (🝮) (🏊)

ASHLAND

AmericInn of Ashland H
(715) 682-9950. **$79-$199.** 3009 Lake Shore Dr E 54806. On US 2, 2.1 mi e of jct SR 13 S. Int corridors. **Pets:** Accepted.
[SAVE] [X] [&M] [🛏] [💭] [🏊] [X]

Ashland Motel M
(715) 682-5503. **Call for rates.** 2300 W Lake Shore Dr 54806. 1.8 mi w on US 2. Ext corridors. **Pets:** Accepted. [X] [🛏] [💭]

Best Western Lake Superior Lodge H
(715) 682-5235. **$130-$150, 7 day notice.** 30600 US Hwy 2 54806. 2.5 mi w. Ext/int corridors. **Pets:** Other species. $15 daily fee/room. Designated rooms, service with restrictions. [SAVE] [X] [&M] [💭] [🍴] [🏊]

BALDWIN

AmericInn Lodge & Suites of Baldwin H 🐾
(715) 684-5888. **$70-$185.** 500 Baldwin Plaza Dr 54002. I-94, exit 19 (US 63), just ne. Int corridors. **Pets:** Medium, dogs only. $10 daily fee/room. Designated rooms, service with restrictions, crate.
[X] [&M] [🛏] [💭] [🏊]

Super 8 H
(715) 684-2700. **$64-$149.** 2110 10th Ave 54002. I-94, exit 19 (US 63), just se. Int corridors. **Pets:** Accepted. [X] [🛏] [💭] [🏊]

BARABOO

Clarion Hotel H
(608) 356-6422. **$69-$145.** 626 W Pine St 53913. On US 12, 0.3 mi n of SR 33. Int corridors. **Pets:** Small. $50 daily fee/room. Designated rooms, service with restrictions, supervision.
[ASK] [X] [&M] [🛏] [💭] [🍴] [🏊] [X]

BEAVER DAM

Super 8 H
(920) 887-8880. **$68-$90.** 711 Park Ave 53916. US 151, exit 132 (SR 33), just w. Int corridors. **Pets:** Accepted. [ASK] [X] [🛏] [💭]

BELMONT

Baymont Inn & Suites H
(608) 762-6900. **$63-$77.** 103 W Moundview Ave 53510. US 151, exit 26, just w. Int corridors. **Pets:** Other species. $25 one-time fee/room. Service with restrictions. [ASK] [X] [&M] [🛏] [💭] [🏊] [X]

BELOIT

Beloit Inn H 🐾
(608) 362-5500. **$89-$209.** 500 Pleasant St 53511. Downtown. Int corridors. **Pets:** $100 deposit/pet, $10 daily fee/pet. Service with restrictions, supervision. [SAVE] [X] [🛏] [💭] [🍴]

Comfort Inn of Beloit H
(608) 362-2666. **Call for rates.** 2786 Milwaukee Rd 53511. I-90, exit 185A, just w at I-43 and SR 81. Int corridors. **Pets:** Medium. $10 daily fee/pet. Service with restrictions, supervision. [SAVE] [X] [🛏] [💭] [🏊]

Econo Lodge H
(608) 365-8680. **Call for rates.** 3002 Milwaukee Rd 53511. I-90, exit 185A, just sw at I-43 and SR 81. Int corridors. **Pets:** Small. $15 one-time fee/pet. Service with restrictions, supervision. [X] [&M] [🛏] [💭]

Fairfield Inn & Suites H
(608) 365-2200. **$104-$119.** 2784 Milwaukee Rd 53511. I-90, exit 185A, just sw, at I-43 and SR 81. Int corridors. **Pets:** Accepted.
[X] [&M] [🛏] [💭] [🏊]

Rodeway Inn M
(608) 364-4000. **$53-$80.** 2956 Milwaukee Rd 53511. I-90, exit 185A, 0.3 mi w. Ext/int corridors. **Pets:** Medium. $10 daily fee/pet. Service with restrictions. [SAVE] [X] [&M] [🛏] [💭] [🍴]

BERLIN

Countryside Lodge M
(920) 361-4411. **$74-$125.** 227 Ripon Rd 54923. On SR 49, at CR F. Int corridors. **Pets:** Accepted. [ASK] [X] [🛏] [💭]

BLACK RIVER FALLS

Best Western-Arrowhead Lodge & Suites H
(715) 284-9471. **$60-$190.** 600 Oasis Rd 54615. I-94, exit 116, jct SR 54. Int corridors. **Pets:** Medium. $50 deposit/room, $15 daily fee/room. Designated rooms, service with restrictions, supervision.
[SAVE] [X] [&M] [🛏] [💭] [🍴] [🏊] [X]

Days Inn H 🐾
(715) 284-4333. **$89-$110.** 919 Hwy 54 E 54615. I-94, exit 116, just w. Int corridors. **Pets:** Large, other species. $15 daily fee/pet. Designated rooms, service with restrictions, supervision.
[ASK] [X] [&M] [🛏] [💭] [🏊] [X]

BURLINGTON

AmericInn Lodge & Suites of Burlington H
(262) 534-2125. **$82-$112.** 2709 Browns Lake Dr 53105. 3 mi n on SR 36 and 83, jct CR W. Int corridors. **Pets:** Medium, dogs only. $25 daily fee/pet. Designated rooms, service with restrictions, supervision.
[ASK] [X] [&M] [🛏] [💭] [🏊] [X]

CADOTT

Countryside Motel M
(715) 289-4000. **$50-$100.** 545 Lavorata Rd 54727. SR 29, exit 91 (SR 27), just s. Int corridors. **Pets:** Small, dogs only. $5 daily fee/pet. Designated rooms, service with restrictions, supervision. [X]

CHILTON

Best Western Stanton Inn H
(920) 849-3600. **$69-$106.** 1101 E Chestnut St 53014. Jct US 151 and SR 32/57. Int corridors. **Pets:** Accepted.
[SAVE] [X] [&M] [💭] [🏊] [X]

CHIPPEWA FALLS

AmericInn Motel & Suites of Chippewa Falls H
(715) 723-5711. **$85-$146.** 11 W South Ave 54729. 2 mi s on SR 124, access via CR J. Int corridors. **Pets:** Accepted.
[ASK] [X] [&M] [🛏] [💭] [🏊] [X]

Avalon Hotel & Conference Center H
(715) 723-2281. **$80-$125.** 1009 W Park Ave 54729. Jct SR 124 and CR J. Ext/int corridors. **Pets:** Medium, dogs only. $10 daily fee/pet. Designated rooms, service with restrictions.
[ASK] [X] [🛏] [💭] [🍴] [🏊] [X]

CLINTONVILLE

Cobblestone Inn & Suites H
(715) 823-2000. **$80-$110.** 175 Waupaca St 54929. Jct US 45 and CR C. Int corridors. **Pets:** Accepted. [ASK] [X] [&M] [🛏] [💭]

COLUMBUS

Super 8-Columbus H
(920) 623-8800. **$70-$118.** 219 Industrial Dr 53925. US 151, exit 118 (SR 16/60), just ne. Int corridors. **Pets:** Medium. $10 one-time fee/room. Designated rooms, service with restrictions, supervision.
[ASK] [X] [&M] [🛏] [💭] [🏊]

CRANDON

Four Seasons Motel M
(715) 478-3377. **$55-$80.** 304 W Glen St 54520. 0.5 mi w on US 8. Ext/int corridors. **Pets:** Medium. $20 deposit/room. Service with restrictions, supervision. [X] [🛏] [💭]

DE FOREST

Comfort Inn & Suites H 🐾
(608) 846-9100. **$80-$130.** 5025 County Hwy V 53532. I-90/94, exit 126 (CR V), just w. Int corridors. **Pets:** Other species. $20 one-time fee/room. Service with restrictions, crate. [ASK] [X] [&M] [🛏] [💭] [🏊] [X]

▼▼▼ **Holiday Inn Express** H
(608) 846-8686. **$95-$109.** 7184 Morrisonville Rd 53532. I-90/94, exit 126 (CR V), just e. Int corridors. **Pets:** Medium, other species. $20 one-time fee/room. Designated rooms, service with restrictions, supervision.

ASK ✕ ᴹ 🛏 💻 ➿

DELAVAN

▼▼ **Sky Lodge Inn & Suites** H
(262) 728-9399. **$59-$199.** 5560 SR 50 53115. On SR 50, just se of jct CR F. Int corridors. **Pets:** Accepted. ASK ✕ ᴹ 🛏 💻 ➿

▼▼ **Super 8-Delavan** H
(262) 728-1700. **Call for rates.** 518 Borg Rd 53115. I-43, exit 21 (SR 50), just w. Int corridors. **Pets:** Accepted. ✕ ᴹ 🛏 💻

DE PERE

▼▼▼ **Kress Inn, an Ascend Collection hotel** H
(920) 403-5100. **$80-$109.** 300 Grant St 54115. US 41, exit 163 (Main Ave), 1 mi e, then just s on 3rd St. Int corridors. **Pets:** Accepted.

ASK ✕ ᴹ 🛏 💻

DODGEVILLE

AAA ▼▼▼ **Best Western Quiet House & Suites** H
(608) 935-7739. **Call for rates.** 1130 N Johns St 53533. On US 18, just e of jct SR 23. Int corridors. **Pets:** Other species. $15 daily fee/pet. Designated rooms, supervision. SAVE ✕ 🛏 💻 ➿

AAA ▼ **Pine Ridge Motel** M ❀
(608) 935-3386. **$30-$79, 3 day notice.** 405 CR YZ 53533. 0.5 mi e of jct SR 23. Ext corridors. **Pets:** Very small, dogs only. $25 deposit/pet. Designated rooms, service with restrictions, crate. SAVE ✕ 🛏 💻

AAA ▼▼ **Super 8 of Dodgeville** H
(608) 935-3888. **$60-$156, 14 day notice.** 1308 Johns St 53533. Just n of US 18. Int corridors. **Pets:** $30 deposit/pet, $10 one-time fee/pet. Supervision. ECO SAVE ✕ ᴹ 🛏 💻

DOOR COUNTY AREA

EGG HARBOR

AAA ▼▼▼ **The Shallows** M
(920) 868-3458. **$75-$410, 30 day notice.** 7353 Horseshoe Bay Rd, Hwy G 54209. On CR G, 2.5 mi s. Ext corridors. **Pets:** Medium, dogs only. $20 daily fee/pet. Service with restrictions, supervision.

SAVE ✕ 🛏 💻 ➿ ✕

FISH CREEK

▼ **Julie's Park Cafe & Motel** M
(920) 868-2999. **Call for rates.** 4020 Hwy 42 54212. On SR 42, 0.3 mi n. Ext corridors. **Pets:** $15 daily fee/pet. Designated rooms, supervision.

✕ 🛏 🍽

GILLS ROCK

▼▼ **Harbor House Inn** BB ❀
(920) 854-5196. **$129-$159, 21 day notice.** 12666 SR 42 54210. Center. Ext/int corridors. **Pets:** Medium, dogs only. $10 daily fee/pet. Designated rooms, service with restrictions, supervision. ✕ 🛏 ✕ 🐾

▼ **Maple Grove Motel** M
(920) 854-2587. **Call for rates.** 809 SR 42 54210. On SR 42, 0.3 mi e; 1.5 mi w of car ferry. Ext corridors. **Pets:** Accepted. ✕ 🛏 💻 🐾

STURGEON BAY

AAA ▼▼ **Best Western Maritime Inn** H
(920) 743-7231. **$61-$150.** 1001 N 14th Ave 54235. 1 mi n on Business Rt SR 42/57. Int corridors. **Pets:** Accepted.

SAVE ✕ ᴹ 🛏 💻 ➿

END AREA

EAGLE RIVER

AAA ▼▼▼ **Best Western Derby Inn** H
(715) 479-1600. **$71-$200.** 1800 Hwy 45 N 54521. On US 45, 1 mi n. Int corridors. **Pets:** Medium. Designated rooms, service with restrictions, supervision. SAVE ✕ ᴹ 🛏 💻 ➿ ✕

▼▼ **Days Inn** H
(715) 479-5151. **$79-$104.** 844 Railroad St N 54521. 0.5 mi n on US 45. Int corridors. **Pets:** Medium, other species. $5 daily fee/room. Designated rooms, service with restrictions, supervision.

ASK ✕ 🛏 💻 ➿ ✕

▼▼ **Super 8** M
(715) 477-0888. **$59-$155.** 200 W Pine St 54521. On SR 70; center. Int corridors. **Pets:** Accepted. ASK ✕ ᴹ 🛏 💻 ➿ ✕

EAST TROY

▼▼▼ **Country Inn & Suites By Carlson** H ❀
(262) 642-2100. **Call for rates.** 2921 O'Leary Ln 53120. I-43, exit 36, at jct SR 120. Int corridors. **Pets:** Large, dogs only. $25 one-time fee/room. Designated rooms, service with restrictions, supervision.

✕ ᴹ 🛏 💻 ➿

EAU CLAIRE

AAA ▼▼▼ **AmericInn Motel & Suites of Eau Claire** H ❀
(715) 874-4900. **$75-$175.** 6200 Texaco Dr 54703. I-94, exit 59, jct US 12. Int corridors. **Pets:** Dogs only. $10 daily fee/pet. Service with restrictions, supervision. SAVE ✕ ᴹ 🛏 💻 ➿

AAA ▼▼▼ **Best Western Trail Lodge Hotel & Suites** H
(715) 838-9989. **$80-$90.** 3340 Mondovi Rd 54701. I-94, exit 65, just n. Int corridors. **Pets:** Accepted. SAVE ✕ ᴹ 🛏 💻 ➿ ✕

▼ **Days Inn** H
(715) 834-3193. **Call for rates.** 2305 Craig Rd 54701. I-94, exit 65, 1.3 mi n on SR 37; just w of jct US 12. Int corridors. **Pets:** Accepted.

✕ ᴹ 🛏 💻

▼▼ **Econo Lodge** H
(715) 833-8818. **Call for rates.** 4608 Royal Dr 54701. I-94, exit 68, just n on SR 93, just w on Golf Rd, then just s. Int corridors. **Pets:** Accepted.

✕ ᴹ 🛏 💻

AAA ▽▽▽ **Grandstay Residential Suites** ⊞
(715) 834-1700. **$100-$169.** 5310 Prill Rd 54701. I-94, exit 70, 0.8 mi n on US 53. Int corridors. **Pets:** Medium. $10 daily fee/pet. Designated rooms, service with restrictions, crate.
[SAVE] [✕] [&M] [📶] [🖥] [➰] [✕]

▽▽▽ **Holiday Inn Campus Area** ⊞
(715) 835-2211. **$70-$139.** 2703 Craig Rd 54701. I-94, exit 65, 1.3 mi n on SR 37; just w of jct US 12. Int corridors. **Pets:** Medium. $15 daily fee/room. Designated rooms, no service, supervision.
[ASK] [✕] [&M] [📶] [🖥] [¶] [➰] [✕]

▽▽▽ **The Plaza Hotel & Suites** ⊞
(715) 834-3181. **$70-$199.** 1202 W Clairemont Ave 54701. I-94, exit 65, 1.3 mi n on SR 37; just w of jct US 12. Int corridors. **Pets:** Medium. $15 one-time fee/room. Service with restrictions, crate.
[ASK] [✕] [&M] [📶] [🖥] [¶] [➰] [✕]

▽▽ **Ramada Convention Center** ⊞
(715) 835-6121. **Call for rates.** 205 S Barstow St 54701. Jct S Barstow and Gibson sts; downtown. Int corridors. **Pets:** Accepted.
[✕] [&M] [📶] [¶] [➰]

▽▽ **Rodeway Inn & Suites** Ⓜ
(715) 835-3600. **Call for rates.** 1828 S Hastings Way 54701. I-94, exit 70 (US 53), 2 mi n. Int corridors. **Pets:** Other species. $10 one-time fee/room. Designated rooms, service with restrictions, supervision.
[✕] [&M] [📶] [🖥] [➰] [✕]

▽▽▽ **Sleep Inn & Suites Conference Center** ⊞ ❖
(715) 874-2900. **$50-$100.** 5872 N 33rd Ave 54703. I-94, exit 69 (Hwy T), just s. Int corridors. **Pets:** Other species. $10 one-time fee/pet. Service with restrictions, crate. [ASK] [✕] [&M] [📶] [🖥] [¶] [➰] [✕]

EDGERTON
▽▽▽ **Comfort Inn** ⊞
(608) 884-2118. **$77-$135.** 11102 N Goede Rd 53534. I-90, exit 163, just e. Int corridors. **Pets:** Accepted. [ASK] [✕] [&M] [📶] [🖥] [➰]

ELKHORN
▽▽ **AmericInn Lodge & Suites of Elkhorn** ⊞
(262) 723-7799. **$82-$112.** 210 E Commerce Ct 53121. I-43, exit 25, just s. Int corridors. **Pets:** Medium, dogs only. $25 daily fee/pet. Designated rooms, service with restrictions, supervision.
[ASK] [✕] [&M] [📶] [🖥] [➰] [✕]

FITCHBURG
▽▽▽ **Candlewood Suites** ⊞
(608) 271-3400. **Call for rates.** 5421 Caddis Bend 53711. US 12/18, exit 260 (Fish Hatchery/CR D), 1.5 mi s. Int corridors. **Pets:** Accepted.
[✕] [&M] [📶] [🖥]

▽▽▽ **Quality Inn & Suites** ⊞
(608) 274-7200. **$70-$100.** 2969 Cahill Main 53711. US 12/18, exit 260 (Fish Hatchery/CR D), 1.5 mi s at CR PD (McKee Rd). Int corridors.
Pets: Accepted. [ASK] [✕] [&M] [📶] [🖥] [¶] [➰] [✕]

FOND DU LAC
▽▽ **Comfort Inn Fond du Lac** ⊞
(920) 921-4000. **Call for rates.** 77 Holiday Ln 54937. Sw of jct US 41 and Military Rd. Int corridors. **Pets:** Accepted.
[✕] [&M] [📶] [🖥] [➰] [✕]

▽▽▽ **Executive Lodge of Fond du Lac** ⊞
(920) 923-2020. **$53-$89.** 649 W Johnson St 54935. On SR 23, 0.3 mi e of jct US 41. Int corridors. **Pets:** Other species. $5 daily fee/pet. Designated rooms, service with restrictions, supervision.
[ASK] [✕] [📶] [🖥] [➰]

▽▽▽ **Holiday Inn** ⊞ ❖
(920) 923-1440. **$109-$319.** 625 W Rolling Meadows Dr 54937. On US 151, just sw of jct Military Rd. Int corridors. **Pets:** Other species. $200 deposit/room. Service with restrictions, supervision.
[ASK] [✕] [&M] [📶] [🖥] [¶] [➰] [✕]

▽▽ **Microtel Inn & Suites** ⊞
(920) 929-4000. **$59-$80.** 920 S Military Rd 54935. Jct US 41 and Military Rd. Int corridors. **Pets:** Medium. $10 daily fee/room. Service with restrictions, supervision. [ASK] [✕] [&M] [📶] [🖥]

▽▽▽ **Ramada Plaza Hotel** ⊞
(920) 923-3000. **$69-$299.** 1 N Main St 54935. Downtown. Int corridors.
Pets: Small, dogs only. $20 one-time fee/pet. Designated rooms, service with restrictions, crate. [ASK] [✕] [&M] [📶] [🖥] [¶] [➰] [✕]

GRANTSBURG
AAA ▽ **Wood River Motel** Ⓜ
(715) 463-2541. **$68-$115, 3 day notice.** 703 W SR 70 54840. 1 mi w on SR 70. Ext corridors. **Pets:** $10 one-time fee/pet. Designated rooms, service with restrictions, supervision. [SAVE] [✕] [&M] [📶]

GREEN BAY
▽▽ **AmericInn Green Bay East** ⊞
(920) 964-0177. **Call for rates.** 2628 Manitowoc Rd 54311. I-43, exit 181, just w. Int corridors. **Pets:** Dogs only. $20 daily fee/room. Designated rooms, service with restrictions, supervision.
[✕] [&M] [📶] [🖥] [➰] [✕]

AAA ▽▽◆ **AmericInn Lodge & Suites of Green Bay West** ⊞ ❖
(920) 434-9790. **$85-$150, 30 day notice.** 2032 Velp Ave 54303. US 41, exit 170, 0.3 mi w. Int corridors. **Pets:** Medium. $15 daily fee/pet. Designated rooms, service with restrictions, supervision.
[SAVE] [✕] [📶] [🖥] [➰]

▽▽ **Baymont Inn-Green Bay** ⊞
(920) 494-7887. **$74-$159.** 2840 S Oneida St 54304. US 41, exit 164 (Oneida St), just e. Int corridors. **Pets:** Accepted. [ASK] [✕] [📶] [🖥]

AAA ◆ **Bay Motel** Ⓜ
(920) 494-3441. **$49-$79.** 1301 S Military Ave 54304. US 41, exit 167 (Lombardi Ave), 0.4 mi e to Marlee Ln, then 0.6 mi n. Ext corridors.
Pets: Accepted. [SAVE] [✕] [📶] [🖥] [¶]

AAA ▽▽▽ **Best Western Midway Hotel** ⊞ ❖
(920) 499-3161. **$69-$320.** 780 Armed Forces Dr 54304. US 41, exit 167 (Lombardi Ave), 1.4 mi w to Holmgren Way, then just s. Int corridors.
Pets: Medium, dogs only. $35 one-time fee/room. Designated rooms, service with restrictions, supervision.
[SAVE] [✕] [📶] [🖥] [¶] [➰] [✕]

▽▽ **Candlewood Suites** ⊞
(920) 430-7040. **Call for rates.** 1125 E Mason St 54301. US 41, exit 168 (Mason St), 4 mi e. Int corridors. **Pets:** Accepted.
[✕] [&M] [📶] [🖥]

▽▽ **Country Inn & Suites By Carlson** ⊞
(920) 336-6600. **$99-$140.** 2945 Allied St 54304. US 41, exit 164 (Oneida St), just nw. Int corridors. **Pets:** Medium, other species. $15 daily fee/room. Service with restrictions, supervision.
[ASK] [✕] [📶] [🖥] [➰] [✕]

▽▽ **Days Inn-Lambeau Field** ⊞
(920) 498-8088. **$59-$94.** 1978 Holmgren Way 54304. US 41, exit 167 (Lombardi Ave), 1.4 mi e, then just s. Int corridors. **Pets:** Accepted.
[ASK] [✕] [📶] [🖥] [➰]

▽▽ **Holiday Inn City Centre** ⊞
(920) 437-5900. **Call for rates.** 200 Main St 54301. Downtown. Int corridors. **Pets:** Other species. $35 one-time fee/room. Designated rooms, no service, supervision. [✕] [&M] [📶] [¶] [➰] [✕]

▽▽ **Quality Inn & Suites** ⊞ ❖
(920) 437-8771. **$60-$100.** 321 S Washington St 54301-4214. On east side of Fox River, just s of Walnut St (SR 29); downtown. Int corridors.
Pets: Large. $10 one-time fee/room. Designated rooms, service with restrictions, supervision. [ASK] [✕] [📶] [🖥] [➰] [✕]

 ▼▼▼ **Ramada Plaza Hotel** H
(920) 499-0631. **$79-$309.** 2750 Ramada Way 54304. US 41, exit 164 (Oneida St), just e. Int corridors. **Pets:** Other species. $20 daily fee/pet. Designated rooms, service with restrictions, crate.
[SAVE] [X] [&M] [■] [▣] [†‡] [≈] [X]

▼▼▼ **Residence Inn by Marriott** H
(920) 435-2222. **$116-$142.** 335 W St. Joseph St 54301. SR 172, exit Riverside Dr, 1.1 mi n on SR 57, then just e. Ext corridors. **Pets:** Other species. $100 one-time fee/room. Service with restrictions, crate.
[X] [■] [▣] [≈] [X]

▼▼ **Super 8** H ❀
(920) 494-2042. **$75-$92.** 2868 S Oneida St 54304. US 41, exit 164 (Oneida St), just e. Int corridors. **Pets:** $15 one-time fee/room. Service with restrictions, supervision. [ASK] [X] [■] [▣] [X]

▼▼ **Travelodge Green Bay/Lambeau** H
(920) 499-3599. **$52-$79.** 2870 Ramada Way 54304. US 41, exit 164 (Oneida St), just e. Int corridors. **Pets:** Accepted. [ASK] [X] [■] [▣]

HAYWARD

▼▼ **AmericInn of Hayward** H
(715) 634-2700. **$85-$195.** 15601 US Hwy 63 54843. Just n of jct SR 77. Int corridors. **Pets:** Medium. $10 daily fee/pet. Designated rooms, service with restrictions, supervision. [ASK] [X] [&M] [■] [▣] [≈]

▼▼▼ **Comfort Suites** H
(715) 634-0700. **Call for rates.** 15586 CR B 54843. 0.5 mi s of jct SR 27. Int corridors. **Pets:** Accepted. [X] [&M] [■] [▣] [≈] [X]

▼▼ **Edelweiss Motel** M
(715) 634-4679. **$39-$105.** Hwy 27 S & Park Rd 54843. On SR 27, 1.8 mi s of jct US 63. Ext corridors. **Pets:** Accepted. [ASK] [X] [■] [▣]

◆◆◆ ▼▼▼ **The Flat Creek Inn & Suites** H
(715) 634-4100. **$77-$165.** 10290 Hwy 27 S 54843. On SR 27 S, 0.7 mi s of jct US 63. Int corridors. **Pets:** Small, dogs only. $15 daily fee/pet. Designated rooms, no service, supervision.
[SAVE] [X] [&M] [■] [▣] [†‡] [≈] [X]

▼▼▼ **Ross' Teal Lake Lodge and Teal Wing Golf Club** CA ❀
(715) 462-3631. **$170-$350, 21 day notice.** 12425 N Ross Rd 54843. On SR 77, 20 mi ne of jct US 63. Ext corridors. **Pets:** Other species. $10 daily fee/pet. Service with restrictions, supervision.
[ASK] [X] [■] [▣] [†‡] [≈] [X] [Z]

▼▼ **Super 8** H
(715) 634-2646. **$65-$120.** 10444 N SR 27 54843. On SR 27, 0.3 mi s of jct US 63. Ext/int corridors. **Pets:** Dogs only. Service with restrictions, supervision. [ASK] [X] [&M] [■] [▣] [≈]

HILLSBORO

◆◆◆ ▼▼ **Hotel Hillsboro** H
(608) 489-3000. **$70-$125.** 1235 Water Ave (Hwy 33) 54634. SR 33 and 80/82, just w. Int corridors. **Pets:** $10 one-time fee/room. Designated rooms, service with restrictions, supervision.
[SAVE] [X] [&M] [■] [▣] [†‡] [≈] [X]

HUDSON

▼▼ **Quality Inn Hudson** H
(715) 386-6355. **Call for rates.** 811 Dominion Dr 54016. I-94, exit 2 (CR F), 1 mi w on south frontage road (Crestview Dr). Int corridors. **Pets:** Medium, dogs only. $10 daily fee/pet. Service with restrictions, supervision. [X] [■] [▣] [≈]

◆◆◆ ▼▼ **Super 8 of Hudson** H
(715) 386-8800. **$70-$110.** 808 Dominion Dr 54016. I-94, exit 2 (CR F), 1 mi w on south frontage road (Crestview Dr). Int corridors. **Pets:** Medium. $15 daily fee/pet. Designated rooms, service with restrictions, supervision. [SAVE] [X] [■] [▣] [≈]

HURLEY

▼▼ **Days Inn of Hurley** H
(715) 561-3500. **$84-$110.** 13355 N US Hwy 51 54534. Jct US 2 and 51, 0.4 mi s on US 51. Int corridors. **Pets:** Large, other species. $15 daily fee/room. Designated rooms, service with restrictions, supervision.
[ASK] [X] [■] [▣] [X]

JANESVILLE

◆◆◆ ▼▼▼ **Best Western Janesville** H
(608) 756-4511. **$75-$189.** 3900 Milton Ave 53546. I-90, exit 171A (SR 26), just e. Int corridors. **Pets:** Accepted.
[SAVE] [X] [&M] [■] [▣] [†‡] [≈] [X]

◆◆◆ ▼▼ **Econo Lodge-Janesville** H
(608) 754-0251. **Call for rates.** 3520 Milton Ave 53545. I-90/39, exit 171A, just sw via Frontage Rd. Int corridors. **Pets:** Other species. $8 daily fee/room. Supervision. [SAVE] [X] [■] [▣]

▼▼ **Microtel Inn** H ❀
(608) 752-3121. **$56-$80.** 3121 Wellington Pl 53546. I-90, exit 171C (US 14), just se. Int corridors. **Pets:** Other species. $10 one-time fee/pet. Service with restrictions, supervision. [ASK] [X] [&M] [■]

JEFFERSON

▼▼ **Rodeway Inn** M
(920) 674-4404. **$65-$85.** 1456 S Ryan Ave 53549. On SR 26, 1.2 mi s of jct US 18. Int corridors. **Pets:** Small. $12 daily fee/pet. Designated rooms, service with restrictions, supervision.
[ASK] [X] [&M] [■] [▣] [≈]

JOHNSON CREEK

▼▼ **Days Inn-Johnson Creek** H
(920) 699-8000. **Call for rates.** W4545 Linmar Ln 53038. I-94, exit 267 (SR 26), just ne. Int corridors. **Pets:** Accepted. [X] [■] [▣] [≈] [X]

KENOSHA

◆◆◆ ▼▼▼ **Best Western Harborside Inn & Kenosha Convention Center** H
(262) 658-3281. **$89-$159.** 5125 6th Ave 53140. Just ne of jct SR 32 and 158; downtown. Int corridors. **Pets:** Small, other species. $25 one-time fee/pet. Designated rooms, service with restrictions, supervision.
[SAVE] [X] [&M] [■] [▣] [≈] [X]

◆◆◆ ▼▼▼ **Candlewood Suites** H
(262) 842-5000. **Call for rates.** 10200 74th St 53142. SR 50, exit 104th Ave, just n. Int corridors. **Pets:** Accepted. [SAVE] [X] [&M] [■] [▣]

▼▼ **Country Inn & Suites By Carlson** H
(262) 857-3680. **$99-$140.** 7011 122nd Ave 53142. I-94, exit 344 (SR 50), just nw. Int corridors. **Pets:** Small. $15 daily fee/pet. Designated rooms, service with restrictions, supervision.
[ASK] [X] [&M] [■] [▣] [X]

KOHLER

◆◆◆ ▼▼▼▼ **Inn On Woodlake** H ❀
(920) 452-7800. **Call for rates.** 705 Woodlake Rd 53044. I-43, exit 126, 0.5 mi w on SR 23, 0.5 mi s on CR y and Highland Dr; in Woodlake Shopping Center. Int corridors. **Pets:** Large, dogs only. $75 one-time fee/room. Designated rooms, service with restrictions, crate.
[SAVE] [X] [■] [▣] [X]

LA CROSSE

◆◆◆ ▼▼ **Americas Best Value Inn** H
(608) 781-3070. **$48-$110.** 2622 Rose St 54603. I-90, exit 3, just s. Int corridors. **Pets:** Small. $50 deposit/room, $7 daily fee/pet. Designated rooms, service with restrictions, supervision. [SAVE] [X] [■] [▣]

◆◆◆ ▼▼▼ **Best Western-Midway Hotel Riverfront Resort** H ❀
(608) 781-7000. **$100-$115, 3 day notice.** 1835 Rose St 54603. I-90, exit 3, 1 mi s on US 53. Int corridors. **Pets:** Dogs only. $15 daily fee/pet. Designated rooms, service with restrictions, supervision.
[SAVE] [X] [&M] [■] [▣] [†‡] [≈] [X]

▼▼ Days Hotel & Conference Center [H]

(608) 783-1000. **$49-$119.** 101 Sky Harbour Dr 54603. I-90, exit 2, just sw; on French Island. Int corridors. **Pets:** Accepted.

[ASK] [✕] [&M] [🛏] [💻] [🍴] [🏊] [✕]

⬦⬦⬦ ▼▼ Econo Lodge [H]

(608) 781-0200. **Call for rates.** 1906 Rose St 54603. I-90, exit 3, 0.9 mi s on US 53. Int corridors. **Pets:** Small, other species. $50 deposit/pet, $10 daily fee/pet. Designated rooms, service with restrictions, supervision.

[SAVE] [✕] [&M] [🛏] [💻] [🏊]

⬦⬦⬦ ▼▼▼ Grandstay Residential Suites of La Crosse [H]

(608) 796-1615. **$85-$179.** 525 Front St N 54601. I-90, exit 3; downtown. Int corridors. **Pets:** Other species. $200 deposit/room, $10 daily fee/pet. Designated rooms, service with restrictions.

[SAVE] [✕] [&M] [🛏] [💻] [🏊]

▼▼▼ Holiday Inn Hotel & Suites [H]

(608) 784-4444. **Call for rates.** 200 Pearl St 54601. Downtown. Int corridors. **Pets:** Accepted. [✕] [&M] [🛏] [💻] [🍴] [🏊] [✕]

▼▼ Howard Johnson Hotel La Crosse [H]

(608) 781-0400. **$49-$79.** 2150 Rose St 54603. I-90, exit 3, 0.8 mi s on US 53. Int corridors. **Pets:** Accepted. [ASK] [✕] [&M] [🛏] [💻]

▼▼ Settle Inn [H]

(608) 781-5100. **$60-$120.** 2110 Rose St 54603. I-90, exit 3, 0.9 mi s on US 53. Int corridors. **Pets:** Small, dogs only. $15 daily fee/pet. Designated rooms, service with restrictions, supervision.

[ASK] [✕] [&M] [🛏] [💻] [🏊]

⬦⬦⬦ ▼▼ Super 8-La Crosse [H]

(608) 781-8880. **$49-$200.** 1625 Rose St 54603. I-90, exit 3, 1.2 mi s on US 53. Int corridors. **Pets:** Other species. $25 one-time fee/room. Service with restrictions, crate. [SAVE] [✕] [&M] [🛏] [💻] [🏊]

LADYSMITH

⬦⬦⬦ ▼▼▼ AmericInn Motel & Suites of Ladysmith [H]

(715) 532-6650. **$72-$144, 3 day notice.** 800 W College Ave 54848. On SR 27, 0.5 mi s of US 8. Int corridors. **Pets:** $15 daily fee/pet. Designated rooms, service with restrictions, supervision.

[SAVE] [✕] [&M] [🛏] [💻] [🏊]

LAKE GENEVA

⬦⬦⬦ ▼▼▼ Budget Host Diplomat Motel [M]

(262) 248-1809. **$58-$106, 7 day notice.** 1060 Wells St 53147. 1 mi s of SR 50. Ext corridors. **Pets:** Accepted. [SAVE] [✕] [🛏] [💻] [🏊]

LAKE MILLS

▼▼▼ Americas Best Value Inn [H]

(920) 648-3800. **Call for rates.** W 7614 Oasis Ln 53551. I-94, exit 259 (SR 89), just n. Int corridors. **Pets:** Medium. $15 one-time fee/pet. Designated rooms, service with restrictions, crate. [✕] [&M] [🛏] [💻] [🏊]

LAND O'LAKES

▼▼ Sunrise Lodge [CA]

(715) 547-3684. **$85-$210, 21 day notice.** 5894 W Shore Dr 54540. 2 mi s on US 45, 2.8 mi e on CR E, then 1 mi n. Ext corridors. **Pets:** Other species. Crate. [ASK] [🛏] [💻] [🍴] [✕] [🏊]

LODI

⬦⬦⬦ ▼▼▼ Best Western Countryside Inn [H]

(608) 592-1450. **$80-$140.** W 9250 Prospect Dr 53555. I-90/94, exit 119, just w. Int corridors. **Pets:** $15 one-time fee/pet. Designated rooms, service with restrictions, supervision. [SAVE] [✕] [&M] [🛏] [💻] [🏊] [✕]

▼▼ Lodi Valley Suites [H]

(608) 592-7331. **Call for rates.** 1440 N Hwy 113 53555. 1.5 mi n of jct SR 60. Int corridors. **Pets:** Accepted. [✕] [🛏] [🏊]

LUCK

⬦⬦⬦ ▼▼▼ Luck Country Inn [H]

(715) 472-2000. **$70-$155.** 10 Robertson Rd 54853. Jct SR 35 and 48. Int corridors. **Pets:** Large. $10 daily fee/pet. Designated rooms, service with restrictions, supervision. [SAVE] [✕] [🛏] [💻] [🍴] [🏊]

MADISON

▼▼ Baymont Inn & Suites [H]

(608) 241-3861. **Call for rates.** 4202 E Towne Blvd 53704. I-90/94, exit 135A (US 151), 0.5 mi w. Int corridors. **Pets:** Other species. $10 daily fee/pet. Service with restrictions, crate. [✕] [🛏] [💻]

⬦⬦⬦ ▼▼▼ Best Western East Towne Suites [H]

(608) 244-2020. **$79-$189.** 4801 Annamark Dr 53704. I-90/94, exit 135A southbound; exit 135C northbound, just sw on US 151. Int corridors. **Pets:** Other species. $25 daily fee/pet. Designated rooms, service with restrictions, supervision. [SAVE] [✕] [🛏] [💻] [🏊]

⬦⬦⬦ ▼▼▼ Best Western West Towne Suites [H] 🐾

(608) 833-4200. **$80-$160.** 650 Grand Canyon Dr 53719. US 12 and 14, exit 255 (Gammon Rd), just e on Odana Rd, then just sw. Int corridors. **Pets:** Large. $25 deposit/room, $15 daily fee/room. Designated rooms, service with restrictions, supervision. [SAVE] [✕] [🛏] [💻]

⬦⬦⬦ ▼▼▼ Clarion Suites Madison-Central [H] 🐾

(608) 284-1234. **$80-$260.** 2110 Rimrock Rd 53713. US 12 and 18, exit 262 (Rimrock Rd), just nw. Int corridors. **Pets:** Large. $25 daily fee/pet. Designated rooms, service with restrictions, supervision.

[SAVE] [✕] [🛏] [💻] [🏊]

▼▼▼ Comfort Suites-Madison [H] 🐾

(608) 836-3033. **$70-$112.** 1253 John Q Hammons Dr 53717. US 12 and 14, exit 252 (Greenway Blvd), just sw. Int corridors. **Pets:** $10 one-time fee/pet. Service with restrictions, supervision.

[ASK] [✕] [🛏] [💻] [🏊] [✕]

⬦⬦⬦ ▼▼▼ Crowne Plaza Hotel Madison-East Towne [H] 🐾

(608) 244-4703. **$139-$209.** 4402 E Washington Ave 53704. I-90/94, exit 135A (US 151), 0.4 mi w. Int corridors. **Pets:** Other species. $25 one-time fee/room. Designated rooms, service with restrictions.

[ECO] [SAVE] [✕] [&M] [🛏] [💻] [🍴] [🏊] [✕]

⬦⬦⬦ ▼▼▼ Days Inn of Madison [H]

(608) 223-1800. **$75-$165.** 4402 E Broadway Service Rd 53716. US 12 and 18, exit 266 (US 51), just ne. Int corridors. **Pets:** Medium. $10 fee/pet. Service with restrictions, supervision.

[ECO] [SAVE] [✕] [🛏] [💻] [🏊]

⬦⬦⬦ ▼▼ Econo Lodge of Madison [H]

(608) 241-4171. **$55-$99.** 4726 E Washington Ave 53704. I-90/94, exit 135A (US 151), just w. Int corridors. **Pets:** Medium. $10 one-time fee/pet. Service with restrictions, supervision. [SAVE] [✕] [🛏] [💻]

▼▼▼ Extended Stay Deluxe Madison West [H]

(608) 833-2121. **$55-$100.** 45 Junction Ct 53717. US 12, exit 253 (Old Sauk Rd), just w. Int corridors. **Pets:** Other species. $25 daily fee/room. Designated rooms, service with restrictions, crate.

[ASK] [✕] [&M] [🛏] [💻]

▼▼▼ Fairfield Inn & Suites Madison East [H]

(608) 661-2700. **$107-$131.** 2702 Crossroads Dr 53718. I-90/94, exit 135C (US 151/High Crossing Blvd). Int corridors. **Pets:** Accepted.

[✕] [&M] [🛏] [💻] [🏊]

⬦⬦⬦ ▼▼▼ GrandStay Residential Suites [H]

(608) 241-2500. **$69-$169.** 5317 High Crossing Blvd 53718. I-90/94, exit 135C (US 151/High Crossing Blvd), 0.5 mi e. Int corridors. **Pets:** Accepted. [SAVE] [✕] [&M] [🛏] [💻] [🏊] [✕]

⬦⬦⬦ ▼▼▼ Hilton Madison Monona Terrace [H] 🐾

(608) 255-5100. **$129-$509.** 9 E Wilson St 53703. 2 blks e of Capitol Square; downtown. Int corridors. **Pets:** Medium. $50 one-time fee/room. Service with restrictions, supervision.

[SAVE] [✕] [&M] [🛏] [💻] [🍴] [🏊]

♦♦♦ **Howard Johnson Plaza** [H] 🐾
(608) 244-2481. **$59-$149.** 3841 E Washington Ave 53704. I-90/94, exit 135A (US 151), 1 mi w. Int corridors. **Pets:** Other species. $15 one-time fee/room. Service with restrictions, supervision.
[A$K] ☒ ♿ ▣ ☕ 🍴 🏊 🏋

♦♦♦ **La Quinta Inn & Suites** [H] 🐾
(608) 245-0123. **$75-$139.** 5217 E Terrace Dr 53718. US 151, exit 98B (American Pkwy), just sw. Int corridors. **Pets:** Medium, other species. Service with restrictions, supervision. [A$K] ☒ ♿ ▣ ☕ 🏊

[AAA] ♦♦♦ **Magnuson Grand Hotel Madison** [H]
(608) 224-1500. **$79-$199.** 3510 Mill Pond Rd 53718. I-90, exit 142B, just e on US 12 and 18, then w on south frontage road. Int corridors. **Pets:** $20 daily fee/pet. Service with restrictions, supervision.
[SAVE] ☒ ♿ ▣ ☕ 🏊

[AAA] ♦♦ **Microtel Inn & Suites** [H]
(608) 242-9000. **$59-$89.** 2139 E Springs Dr 53704. I-90/94, exit 135A (US 151), just s, then 0.5 mi e. Int corridors. **Pets:** Small. $10 daily fee/pet. Designated rooms, service with restrictions, supervision.
[SAVE] ☒ ♿ ▣ ☕

[AAA] ♦♦ **Red Roof Inn-Madison #7052** [M]
(608) 241-1787. **$52-$90.** 4830 Hayes Rd 53704. I-90/94, exit 135A (US 151), just sw. Ext corridors. **Pets:** Large. Service with restrictions, crate.
[SAVE] ☒ ♿ ▣

♦♦♦ **Residence Inn by Marriott** [H]
(608) 244-5047. **$140-$150.** 4862 Hayes Rd 53704. I-90/94, exit 135A (US 151), just sw to Hayes Rd, then just ne. Int corridors. **Pets:** Other species. $100 one-time fee/room. Service with restrictions, supervision.
☒ ♿ ▣ ☕ 🏊 🏋

[AAA] ♦♦ **Select Inn** [H]
(608) 249-1815. **$50-$105.** 4845 Hayes Rd 53704. I-90/94, exit 135A (US 151), just sw. Int corridors. **Pets:** $25 deposit/pet, $10 daily fee/pet. Designated rooms, service with restrictions, supervision.
[SAVE] ☒ ▣ ☕ 🏋

[AAA] ♦♦♦ **Sheraton Madison Hotel** [H]
(608) 251-2300. **Call for rates.** 706 John Nolen Dr 53713. US 12/18, exit 263 (John Nolen Dr), just n. Int corridors. **Pets:** Accepted.
[SAVE] ☒ ♿ ▣ ☕ 🍴 🏊 🏋

[AAA] ♦♦♦ **Sleep Inn & Suites** [H]
(608) 221-8100. **$79-$119.** 4802 Tradewinds Pkwy 53718. US 12/14/18/151, exit 266, 0.5 mi se, then 0.6 mi on Dutch Mill Rd. Int corridors. **Pets:** Other species. Service with restrictions, supervision.
[SAVE] ☒ ♿ ▣ ☕ 🏊 🏋

♦♦♦ **Staybridge Suites** [H]
(608) 241-2300. **Call for rates.** 3301 City View Dr 53718. I-90/94, exit 135C (US 151/High Crossing Blvd), just e. Int corridors. **Pets:** Accepted.
☒ ♿ ▣ ☕ 🏊 🏋

♦♦ **Super 8-Madison** [H]
(608) 258-8882. **$60-$140.** 1602 W Beltline Hwy 53713. US 12 and 18, exit 260B (CR D), just w on N Frontage Rd. Int corridors. **Pets:** Medium, other species. Designated rooms, service with restrictions, crate.
[A$K] ☒ ▣ ☕ 🏊

♦♦ **Super 8-Madison East** [H]
(608) 249-5300. **$54-$149, 7 day notice.** 4765 Hayes Rd 53704. I-90/94, exit 135A (US 151), just sw to Hayes Rd, then 0.5 mi ne. Ext/int corridors. **Pets:** Accepted. [A$K] ☒ ♿ ▣ ☕ 🏊

MANITOWOC

[AAA] ♦♦ **Best Western Lakefront Hotel** [H] 🐾
(920) 682-7000. **$110-$130.** 101 Maritime Dr 54220. I-43, exit 152, 4.2 mi e on SR 42 N, then 1 mi s. Int corridors. **Pets:** $25 one-time fee/room. Service with restrictions, crate.
[SAVE] ☒ ▣ ☕ 🍴 🏊 🏋

♦♦ **Comfort Inn by Choice Hotels** [H]
(920) 683-0220. **$70-$90.** 2200 S 44th St 54220. I-43, exit 149, just e. Int corridors. **Pets:** Dogs only. $25 one-time fee/room. Supervision.
[A$K] ☒ ♿ ▣ ☕

♦♦♦ **Holiday Inn Manitowoc** [H]
(920) 682-6000. **$119-$159.** 4601 Calumet Ave 54220. I-43, exit 149, just e. Int corridors. **Pets:** Other species. $100 deposit/room. Service with restrictions. [A$K] ☒ ♿ ▣ ☕ 🍴 🏊 🏋

MARSHFIELD

♦♦ **Baymont Inn & Suites-Marshfield** [H]
(715) 384-5240. **$79-$99.** 2107 N Central Ave 54449. On SR 97; 1.6 mi n of SR 13. Int corridors. **Pets:** $10 daily fee/pet. Designated rooms, service with restrictions, crate. ☒ ♿ ▣ ☕ 🏊 🏋

♦♦ **Comfort Inn** [H]
(715) 387-8691. **$85-$110.** 114 E Upham St 54449. On SR 97; 0.8 mi n of jct SR 13. Int corridors. **Pets:** Dogs only. $40 deposit/room, $15 one-time fee/room. Designated rooms, service with restrictions, supervision.
[A$K] ☒ ♿ ▣ ☕ 🏊

[AAA] ♦♦♦ **Holiday Inn & Conference Center** [H]
(715) 486-1500. **$104-$134.** 750 S Central Ave 54449. Jct SR 13 and 97, 0.5 mi s on Business Rt 13. Int corridors. **Pets:** Accepted.
[SAVE] ☒ ♿ ▣ ☕ 🍴 🏊 🏋

MAUSTON

[AAA] ♦♦ **Best Western Park Oasis Inn** [H]
(608) 847-6255. **$80-$160.** W5641 Hwy 82 E 53948. I-90/94, exit 69, just se. Int corridors. **Pets:** Medium, other species. $50 deposit/pet, $5 daily fee/pet. Designated rooms, service with restrictions, supervision.
[SAVE] ☒ ▣ ☕ 🏊 🏋

♦♦ **Country Inn & Suites By Carlson** [H]
(608) 847-5959. **Call for rates.** 1001 SR 82 53948. I-90/94, exit 69, just ne. Int corridors. **Pets:** $10 one-time fee/pet. Designated rooms, service with restrictions. ☒ ▣ ☕ 🏊

♦♦ **Super 8** [M]
(608) 847-2300. **$63-$170.** 1001A Hwy 82 E 53948. I-90/94, exit 69, just ne. Int corridors. **Pets:** Medium, other species. $10 one-time fee/pet. Service with restrictions, crate. [A$K] ☒ ▣ ☕ 🏊

MEDFORD

♦♦ **AmericInn Motel of Medford** [H]
(715) 748-2330. **$74-$89.** 435 S 8th St 54451. On SR 13, 0.5 mi s of jct SR 64. Int corridors. **Pets:** Small. $25 deposit/room. Designated rooms, service with restrictions, supervision. ☒ ♿ ▣ ☕ 🏊 🏋

♦ **Woodlands Inn & Suites** [M]
(715) 748-3995. **$75-$124.** 854 N 8th St 54451. On SR 13, 0.6 mi n of jct SR 64. Int corridors. **Pets:** $25 one-time fee/room. Designated rooms, supervision. ☒ ▣ ☕ 🏊

MENOMONIE

♦ **Menomonie Motel 6 #4109** [H]
(715) 235-6901. **$40-$63.** 2100 Stout St 54751. I-94, exit 41 (SR 25), just se. Int corridors. **Pets:** Other species. Service with restrictions, supervision. [A$K] ☒ ▣

[AAA] ♦♦ **Quality Inn & Suites** [H] 🐾
(715) 233-1500. **$60-$65.** 1721 Plaza Dr NE 54751. I-94, exit 45 (CR B), just sw. Int corridors. **Pets:** Other species. $15 one-time fee/pet. Service with restrictions, supervision. [SAVE] ☒ ♿ ▣ ☕ 🏊

♦♦ **Super 8-Menomonie** [H]
(715) 235-8889. **$60-$100.** 1622 N Broadway 54751. I-94, exit 41 (SR 25), just s. Int corridors. **Pets:** $10 daily fee/room. Service with restrictions, supervision. [A$K] ☒ ▣ ☕ 🏊

MERRILL

AmericInn Lodge & Suites of Merrill **H**
(715) 536-7979. **$89-$149.** 3300 E Main St 54452. US 51, exit 208, 0.5 mi w on SR 64. Int corridors. **Pets:** Large. $10 daily fee/pet. Service with restrictions, supervision. (ASK) (X) (&M) 🛏 💻 ➰ (X)

Super 8 **H**
(715) 536-6880. **$69-$80.** 3209 E Main St 54452. US 51, exit 208, 0.5 mi w on SR 64. Int corridors. **Pets:** Other species. $10 daily fee/pet. Service with restrictions, supervision.
(ASK) (X) (&M) 🛏 💻 ➰ (X)

MIDDLETON

Country Inn & Suites By Carlson, Madison West **H** 🌼
(608) 831-6970. **$114-$169.** 2212 Deming Way 53562. US 12/14, exit 251A, 0.3 mi w on University Ave, then just n. Int corridors. **Pets:** Medium. $25 daily fee/pet. Designated rooms, service with restrictions, supervision. (SAVE) (X) (&M) 🛏 💻 ➰

Marriott Madison West **H**
(608) 831-2000. **$152-$186.** 1313 John Q Hammons Dr 53562. US 12/14, exit 252 (Greenway Blvd), just w. Int corridors. **Pets:** Other species. $50 one-time fee/room. Supervision.
(SAVE) (X) (&M) 🛏 💻 (T) ➰

Residence Inn by Marriott-Madison West/Middleton **H**
(608) 662-1100. **$152-$186.** 8400 Market St 53562. US 12/14, exit 252 (Greenway Blvd), just w, then just n; in Greenway Station. Int corridors. **Pets:** Accepted. (X) (&M) 🛏 💻 ➰ (X)

Staybridge Suites **H**
(608) 664-5888. **Call for rates.** 7790 Elmwood Ave 53562. US 12/14, exit 251 (University Ave), just nw. Int corridors. **Pets:** Medium, other species. $75 one-time fee/room. (X) (&M) 🛏 💻 ➰

MILWAUKEE METROPOLITAN AREA

BROOKFIELD

Best Western Midway Hotel **H**
(262) 786-9540. **$89-$149.** 1005 S Moorland Rd 53005. I-94, exit 301A (Moorland Rd), just s. Int corridors. **Pets:** Accepted.
(SAVE) (X) 🛏 💻 (T) ➰ (X)

Country Inn & Suites By Carlson, Milwaukee-West **H**
(262) 782-1400. **$99-$269.** 1250 S Moorland Rd 53005. I-94, exit 301A (Moorland Rd), just se. Int corridors. **Pets:** Accepted.
(SAVE) (X) 🛏 💻 (T) ➰ (X)

Homestead Studio Suites Hotel-Milwaukee/Brookfield **H**
(262) 782-9300. **$45-$85.** 325 N Brookfield Rd 53045. I-94, exit 297, 1.1 mi e on US 18, then just e. Int corridors. **Pets:** Other species. $25 daily fee/room. Designated rooms, service with restrictions, crate.
(ASK) (X) (&M) 🛏 💻

La Quinta Inn **H** 🌼
(262) 782-9100. **$59-$95.** 20391 W Bluemound Rd 53045. I-94, exit 297, just e on US 18. Int corridors. **Pets:** Medium, other species. Service with restrictions, supervision. (ASK) (X) (&M) 🛏 💻

Sheraton Milwaukee Brookfield **H** 🌼
(262) 786-1100. **$109-$269.** 375 S Moorland Rd 53005. I-94, exit 301B (Moorland Rd), just n. Int corridors. **Pets:** Medium, dogs only. Designated rooms, service with restrictions, supervision.
(SAVE) (X) (&M) 🛏 💻 (T) ➰

TownePlace Suites by Marriott **H**
(262) 784-8450. **$144-$159.** 600 N Calhoun Rd 53005. I-94, exit 297 eastbound, 2.1 mi e on US 18; exit 301B (Moorland Rd) westbound, 1.5 mi n, then 0.4 mi w on US 18. Int corridors. **Pets:** Accepted.
(X) 🛏 💻 ➰

BROWN DEER

Candlewood Suites **H**
(414) 355-3939. **$95-$144.** 4483 W Schroeder Dr 53223. Just nw of SR 100 and 57. Int corridors. **Pets:** Accepted. (ASK) (X) (&M) 🛏 💻

DELAFIELD

La Quinta Inn & Suites Milwaukee-Delafield **H** 🌼
(262) 646-8500. **$62-$129.** 2801 Hillside Dr 53018. I-94, exit 287, just s on SR 83, then just e. Int corridors. **Pets:** Medium, other species. Service with restrictions, supervision. (ASK) (X) (&M) 🛏 💻 ➰

FRANKLIN

Staybridge Suites Milwaukee Airport South **H**
(414) 761-3800. **$99-$159.** 9575 S 27th St 53132. I-94, exit Ryan Rd; corner of 27th St and Rowland Rd. Int corridors. **Pets:** Accepted.
(ECO) (SAVE) (X) (&M) 🛏 💻 ➰ (X)

GERMANTOWN

AmericInn Lodge & Suites of Germantown **H**
(262) 502-9750. **$80-$100.** W190 N10862 Commerce Cir 53022. US 41 and 45, exit Lannon/Mequon rds, just e on SR 167 to Maple Rd. Int corridors. **Pets:** Medium, dogs only. $30 one-time fee/room. Designated rooms, service with restrictions, crate. (ASK) (X) 🛏 💻 ➰

Holiday Inn Express Milwaukee NW-Germantown **H**
(262) 255-1100. **Call for rates.** W 177 N9675 Riversbend Ln 53022. US 41 and 45, exit CR Q (County Line Rd), just w. Int corridors.
Pets: Accepted. (X) (&M) 🛏 💻 ➰ (X)

Super 8-Germantown/Milwaukee **H** 🌼
(262) 255-0880. **$70-$159.** N96 W17490 County Line Rd 53022. US 41 and 45, exit CR Q (County Line Rd), just w. Int corridors. **Pets:** Other species. $10 daily fee/pet. Service with restrictions, supervision.
(SAVE) (X) 🛏 ➰ (X)

GLENDALE

Baymont Inn & Suites Glendale/Milwaukee Northeast **H**
(414) 961-7272. **Call for rates.** 5485 N Port Washington Rd 53217. I-43, exit 78A (Silver Spring Dr), just se. Int corridors. **Pets:** Accepted.
(X) 🛏 💻

Hilton Milwaukee River **H**
(414) 962-6040. **$91-$119.** 4700 N Port Washington Rd 53212. I-43, exit 77A northbound, just e on Hampton Ave; exit 78A (Silver Springs Dr) southbound, just e, then just s. Int corridors. **Pets:** Accepted.
(SAVE) (X) (&M) 🛏 💻 (T) ➰

La Quinta Inn & Suites-Bayshore Town Center **H** 🌼
(414) 962-6767. **$79-$129.** 5423 N Port Washington Rd 53217. I-43, exit 78A (Silver Spring Dr), just se. Int corridors. **Pets:** Medium, other species. Service with restrictions, supervision. (ASK) (X) 🛏 💻 ➰ (X)

La Quinta Inn Milwaukee-Glendale **H** 🌼
(414) 964-8484. **$59-$99.** 5110 N Port Washington Rd 53217. I-43, exit 78A (Silver Spring Dr), 0.4 mi se. Int corridors. **Pets:** Medium, other species. Service with restrictions, supervision. (ASK) (X) (&M) 🛏 💻

▼▼▼ **Residence Inn by Marriott** 🅷
(414) 352-0070. **$130-$150.** 7275 N Port Washington Rd 53217. I-43, exit 80 (Good Hope Rd), just e. Ext corridors. **Pets:** Large, other species. $100 one-time fee/room. Service with restrictions, crate.

GRAFTON

▼▼ **Baymont Inn & Suites Milwaukee-Grafton** 🅷 ❀
(262) 387-1180. **$70-$130.** 1415 Port Washington Rd 53024. I-43, exit 92 (SR 60), just w, then just s. Int corridors. **Pets:** Medium. $10 one-time fee/pet. Designated rooms, supervision.

JACKSON

▼▼ **Comfort Inn & Suites of Jackson** 🅷
(262) 677-1133. **$80-$140.** W227 N 16890 Tillie Lake Ct 53037. Northwest of jct US 45 and SR 60. Int corridors. **Pets:** Medium. $30 one-time fee/pet. Service with restrictions, supervision.

MEQUON

◆◆◆ ▼▼ **Best Western Quiet House & Suites** 🅷
(262) 241-3677. **$91-$245.** 10330 N Port Washington Rd 53092. I-43, exit 85 (Mequon Rd), just w on SR 167, then 1 mi s. Int corridors.
Pets: Accepted.

▼▼ **The Chalet Motel of Mequon** Ⓜ ❀
(262) 241-4510. **$62-$159.** 10401 N Port Washington Rd 53092. I-43, exit 85 (Mequon Rd), just w on SR 167, then 1 mi s. Ext corridors.
Pets: Other species. $10 daily fee/room. Designated rooms, service with restrictions, crate.

MILWAUKEE

◆◆◆ ▼▼ **Best Western Inn Towne Hotel** 🅷
(414) 224-8400. **$59-$109.** 710 N Old World 3rd St 53203. Corner of Wisconsin Ave and N Old World 3rd St. Int corridors. **Pets:** Accepted.

▼▼ **Comfort Suites at Park Place** 🅷
(414) 979-0250. **$90-$200.** 10831 W Park Pl 53224. US 41/45, exit 47B (Good Hope Rd), then right. Int corridors. **Pets:** Small, other species. $15 daily fee/pet. Designated rooms, service with restrictions, supervision.

◆◆ ▼▼ **Country Inn & Suites By Carlson, Milwaukee Airport** 🅷
(414) 762-6018. **$99-$140.** 6200 S 13th St 53221. I-94, exit 319, just e on College Ave (CR ZZ). Int corridors. **Pets:** Small. $15 daily fee/pet. Designated rooms, service with restrictions, supervision.

▼▼ **Holiday Inn Express Hotel & Suites Milwaukee Airport** 🅷
(414) 563-4000. **$90-$130.** 1400 W Zellman Ct 53221. I-94, exit 319, 0.4 mi e on College Ave (CR ZZ) to S 13th St, then just s. Int corridors.
Pets: Accepted.

◆◆ ▼▼ **Holiday Inn Hotel & Suites Milwaukee Airport** 🅷 ❀
(414) 482-4444. **Call for rates.** 545 W Layton Ave 53207. I-94, exit 317, 1.3 mi e. Int corridors. **Pets:** Medium. $30 one-time fee/pet. Designated rooms, service with restrictions, supervision.

▼▼ **Hotel Metro-Milwaukee** 🅷
(414) 272-1937. **$179-$359.** 411 E Mason St 53202. Corner of Mason and Milwaukee sts. Int corridors. **Pets:** Accepted.

◆◆◆ ▼▼ **The Iron Horse Hotel** 🅷 ❀
(414) 831-4601. **$149-$329.** 500 W Florida St 53204. 6 mi to 6th St, just e. Int corridors. **Pets:** $50 one-time fee/room. Designated rooms, service with restrictions, supervision.

◆◆ ▼▼ **The Pfister Hotel** 🅷
(414) 273-8222. **$145-$2000.** 424 E Wisconsin Ave 53202. Corner of E Wisconsin Ave and Jefferson St. Int corridors. **Pets:** $100 one-time fee/room. Service with restrictions.

NEW BERLIN

▼▼ **La Quinta Inn & Suites** 🅷 ❀
(262) 717-0900. **$69-$139.** 15300 W Rock Ridge Rd 53151. I-43, exit 57 (Moorland Rd), just se. Int corridors. **Pets:** Medium, other species. Service with restrictions, supervision.

OAK CREEK

▼▼ **Comfort Suites Milwaukee Airport** 🅷
(414) 570-1111. **$130-$150.** 6362 S 13th St 53154. I-94, exit 319 (College Ave), just e on CR 22, then just s. Int corridors. **Pets:** Medium, other species. $20 one-time fee/pet. Service with restrictions, crate.

▼▼ **Days Inn of Milwaukee South** 🅷
(414) 764-1776. **Call for rates.** 1201 W College Ave 53154. I-94, exit 319 (College Ave), just e. Int corridors. **Pets:** Medium, other species. $75 deposit/room. Service with restrictions, crate.

▼▼ **La Quinta Inn & Suites Milwaukee-Airport** 🅷 ❀
(414) 762-2266. **$52-$99.** 7141 S 13th St 53154. I-94, exit 320 (Rawson Ave), just se. Int corridors. **Pets:** Medium, other species. Service with restrictions, supervision.

▼▼ **MainStay Suites Oak Creek** 🅷
(414) 571-8800. **Call for rates.** 1001 W College Ave 53154. I-94, exit 319 (College Ave), just e. Int corridors. **Pets:** Accepted.

▼▼ **Red Roof Inn-Milwaukee #7031** Ⓜ
(414) 764-3500. **$67-$82.** 6360 S 13th St 53154. I-94, exit 319 (College Ave), just e. Ext corridors. **Pets:** Large. Service with restrictions, crate.

OCONOMOWOC

◆◆◆ ▼▼ **Olympia Resort, Spa & Conference Center** 🅷
(262) 369-4999. **$149.** 1350 Royale Mile Rd 53066. I-94, exit 282 (SR 67), 1 mi n. Int corridors. **Pets:** Other species. $10 one-time fee/room. Service with restrictions, supervision.

◆◆◆ ▼▼ **Staybridge Suites Milwaukee West** 🅷
(262) 200-2900. **$99-$169.** 1141 Blue Ribbon Dr 53066. I-94, exit 282 (SR 67), just s. Int corridors. **Pets:** Medium. $75 one-time fee/pet. Service with restrictions, crate.

PORT WASHINGTON

◆◆◆ ▼▼ **Holiday Inn Harborview** 🅷 ❀
(262) 284-9461. **$89-$299.** 135 E Grand Ave 53074. On SR 33; waterfront of Lake Michigan; downtown. Int corridors. **Pets:** Medium. $25 one-time fee/room. Designated rooms, service with restrictions, crate.

SAUKVILLE

◆◆◆ ▼▼ **Saukville Super 8** 🅷
(262) 284-9399. **$60-$125.** 180 Foster Rd 53080. I-43, exit 96, just s. Int corridors. **Pets:** Other species. $15 daily fee/pet. Designated rooms, supervision.

WAUKESHA

◆◆◆ ▼▼ **Best Western Waukesha Grand** 🅷
(262) 524-9300. **$75-$200.** 2840 N Grandview Blvd 53072. I-94, exit 293, just s on CR T. Int corridors. **Pets:** Accepted.

▼▼ **Extended StayAmerica-Milwaukee-Waukesha** H

(262) 798-0217. **$40-$80.** 2520 Plaza Ct 53186. I-94, exit 297, just e on SR 18, then just s. Int corridors. **Pets:** Other species. $25 daily fee/room. Designated rooms, service with restrictions, crate.

(ASK) ✕ ᴹ ⊟ 🖵

◈◈◈ ▼▼ **Super 8–Waukesha** H

(262) 786-6015. **$50-$170.** 2510 Plaza Ct 53186. I-94, exit 297, just w on CR JJ (Bluemound Rd). Int corridors. **Pets:** Medium. $10 daily fee/pet. Designated rooms, service with restrictions, supervision.

(SAVE) ✕ ᴹ ⊟ 🖵

WAUWATOSA

▼▼ **Extended StayAmerica-Milwaukee-Wauwatosa** H

(414) 443-1909. **$45-$90.** 11121 W North Ave 53226. US 45, exit 42A, just n. Int corridors. **Pets:** Other species. $25 daily fee/room. Designated rooms, service with restrictions, crate. (ASK) ✕ ᴹ ⊟ 🖵

▼▼ **Holiday Inn Express-Medical Center** H

(414) 778-0333. **$109-$139.** 11111 W North Ave 53226. US 45, exit 42A, just n on SR 100, then just w. Int corridors. **Pets:** Accepted.

(ASK) ✕ ᴹ ⊟ 🖵

▼▼ **Super 8 of Milwaukee West** H

(414) 257-0140. **Call for rates.** 115 N Mayfair Rd 53226. I-94, exit 304B, just n on SR 100. Int corridors. **Pets:** Accepted. ✕ ᴹ ⊟ 🖵

END METROPOLITAN AREA

MINERAL POINT

▼▼ **Quality Inn** H

(608) 987-4747. **$68-$108.** 1345 Business Park Rd 53565. On US 151; 0.6 mi n of jct SR 23 and 39. Int corridors. **Pets:** Medium. $10 daily fee/ pet. Service with restrictions, supervision. (ASK) ✕ ᴹ ⊟ 🖵 🏊

MINOCQUA

◈◈ ▼▼ **AmericInn of Minocqua** H

(715) 356-3730. **$64-$129.** 700 Hwy 51 54548. On US 51; downtown. Int corridors. **Pets:** Accepted. (ECO) (ASK) ✕ ᴹ ⊟ 🖵 🏊 ✕

◈◈◈ ▼▼ **Best Western Concord Inn** H

(715) 356-1800. **$79-$145.** 320 Front St 54548. On US 51; downtown. Int corridors. **Pets:** Medium, dogs only. $10 daily fee/pet. Designated rooms, service with restrictions, supervision.

(SAVE) ✕ ᴹ ⊟ 🖵 🏊 ✕

▼▼ **Comfort Inn-Minocqua** H

(715) 358-2588. **$55-$200.** 8729 Hwy 51 54548. On US 51 at SR 70 W. Int corridors. **Pets:** Other species. $10 daily fee/room. Service with restrictions, crate. (ASK) ✕ ⊟ 🖵 🏊

▼ **Northwoods Inn & Suites** M

(715) 356-9541. **Call for rates.** 8730 Hwy 51 N 54548. On US 51 at SR 70 W. Ext/int corridors. **Pets:** Accepted. ✕

▼▼ **The Waters of Minocqua** H ❀

(715) 358-4000. **$69-$225.** 8116 Hwy 51 S 54548. On US 51, 1 mi s. Int corridors. **Pets:** $10 daily fee/pet. Designated rooms, service with restrictions, crate. (ECO) (ASK) ✕ ᴹ ⊟ 🖵 🍴 🏊 ✕

MONONA

◈◈◈ ▼▼ **AmericInn of Madison South/Monona** H ❀

(608) 222-8601. **$99-$179.** 101 W Broadway 53716-3901. US 12/18, exit 265 (Monona Dr), just nw. Int corridors. **Pets:** Large, other species. $5 daily fee/room. Service with restrictions.

(SAVE) ✕ ᴹ ⊟ 🖵 🏊 ✕

▼▼▼ **Country Inn & Suites By Carlson, Madison** H

(608) 221-0055. **$99-$140.** 400 River Pl 53716. US 12/18, exit 265 (Monona Dr), just nw. Int corridors. **Pets:** Medium. $20 daily fee/room. Designated rooms, service with restrictions, crate.

(ASK) ✕ ᴹ ⊟ 🖵 🏊 ✕

MONROE

◈◈◈ ▼▼ **Gasthaus Motel** M ❀

(608) 328-8395. **$59-$99.** 685 30th St 53566. 1.5 mi s on SR 69. Ext corridors. **Pets:** Other species. $10 daily fee/pet. Service with restrictions, crate. (SAVE) ✕ ᴹ ⊟ 🖵

▼▼ **Super 8 of Monroe** H

(608) 325-1500. **$59-$89.** 500 6th St 53566. On SR 69 S, 0.5 mi s of jct SR 81/11. Int corridors. **Pets:** Accepted. (ECO) (ASK) ✕ ⊟ 🖵 🏊

NEILLSVILLE

▼▼ **Super 8-Neillsville** H

(715) 743-8080. **Call for rates.** 1000 E Division St 54456. US 10, jct Boon and Division St. Int corridors. **Pets:** Accepted.

✕ ᴹ ⊟ 🖵 🏊

NEW GLARUS

◈◈◈ ▼▼▼ **Chalet Landhaus Inn** H

(608) 527-5234. **$85-$225.** 801 Hwy 69 53574. On SR 69. Int corridors. **Pets:** Accepted. (SAVE) ✕ ᴹ ⊟ 🖵 🍴 🏊 ✕

◈◈◈ ▼▼ **Swiss Aire Motel** H

(608) 527-2138. **$59-$99.** 1200 Hwy 69 53574. Just s of jct SR 39/69. Ext/int corridors. **Pets:** Other species. $10 daily fee/room. Designated rooms, supervision. (SAVE) ✕ ⊟ 🖵

NEW LISBON

◈◈◈ ▼▼ **Travelers Inn of New Lisbon** H

(608) 562-5141. **$58-$159.** 1700 E Bridge St 53950. I-90/94, exit 61 (SR 80), just ne. Int corridors. **Pets:** Accepted.

(SAVE) ✕ ᴹ ⊟ 🖵 🏊

NEW LONDON

▼▼ **AmericInn Lodge & Suites of New London** H

(920) 982-5700. **$59-$189.** 1404 N Shawano St 54961. US 45, exit US 54, just n. Int corridors. **Pets:** Medium, other species. $10 one-time fee/ pet. Service with restrictions, supervision. (ASK) ✕ ᴹ ⊟ 🖵 🏊

NEW RICHMOND

▼▼ **AmericInn Motel & Suites of New Richmond** H

(715) 246-3993. **$69-$95.** 1020 S Knowles Ave 54017. Just s on SR 65. Int corridors. **Pets:** Other species. $15 one-time fee/room. Service with restrictions, supervision. (ASK) ✕ ⊟ 🖵 🏊

▼▼ **Super 8** H

(715) 246-7829. **Call for rates.** 1561 Dorset Ln 54017. Just s on SR 65. Int corridors. **Pets:** Accepted. ✕ ⊟ 🖵

ONALASKA

▼▼ **Baymont Inn & Suites LaCrosse-Onalaska** H

(608) 783-7191. **$55-$189.** 3300 Kinney Coulee Rd N 54650. I-90, exit 5, just ne. Int corridors. **Pets:** Accepted. (ASK) ✕ ᴹ ⊟ 🖵 🏊

▼▼ **Comfort Inn by Choice Hotels** H ❀

(608) 781-7500. **$60-$90.** 1223 Crossing Meadows Dr 54650. I-90, exit 4, just e on SR 157, then w on CR SS. Int corridors. **Pets:** Large. Service with restrictions, crate. (ASK) ✕ ᴹ ⊟ 🖵 🏊

▼▼▼▼ **Holiday Inn Express** 🅷
(608) 783-6555. **$99-$159.** 9409 Hwy 16 54650. I-90, exit 5, 1 mi e. Int corridors. **Pets:** Service with restrictions, supervision.
(A$K) (X) (&M) 🛏 🖥 (≈)

▼▼▼ **Microtel Inn** 🅷 🐾
(608) 783-0833. **$60-$90.** 3240 N Kinney Coulee Rd 54650. I-90, exit 5, just ne. Int corridors. **Pets:** Dogs only. $10 daily fee/pet. Service with restrictions. (A$K) (X) 🛏 🖥

OSCEOLA
🅐🅐🅐 ▼▼▼ **River Valley Inn & Suites** 🅷
(715) 294-4060. **$75-$135.** 1030 Cascade St 54020. Just n on SR 35. Int corridors. **Pets:** Small, dogs only. $10 daily fee/pet. Designated rooms, no service, supervision. (SAVE) (X) 🛏 🖥 (≈)

OSHKOSH
▼▼▼ **Comfort Suites** 🅷
(920) 230-7378. **$90-$270.** 400 S Koeller St 54902. US 41, exit 117 (9th Ave), just e. Int corridors. **Pets:** Dogs only. $15 daily fee/room. Designated rooms, service with restrictions, crate.
(A$K) (X) (&M) 🛏 🖥 (≈) (X)

▼▼▼ **Fairfield Inn by Marriott** 🅷
(920) 233-8504. **$68-$83.** 1800 S Koeller St 54902. US 41, exit 117 (9th Ave), 0.8 mi s on east frontage road. Int corridors. **Pets:** $10 daily fee/pet. Service with restrictions, supervision. (X) (&M) 🛏 🖥 (≈)

▼▼▼ **Hawthorn Inn & Suites** 🅷
(920) 303-1133. **$109-$449.** 3105 S Washburn St 54904. US 41, exit 116 (SR 44), just w, then just s. Int corridors. **Pets:** Accepted.
(A$K) (X) (&M) 🛏 🖥 (🍴) (≈) (X)

▼▼▼ **Holiday Inn Express Hotel & Suites** 🅷
(920) 303-1300. **$99-$189.** 2251 Westowne Ave 54904. US 41, exit 119, 0.4 mi w of jct SR 21. Int corridors. **Pets:** Accepted.
(A$K) (X) (&M) 🛏 🖥 (≈) (X)

▼▼ **La Quinta Inn Oshkosh** 🅷 🐾
(920) 233-4190. **$49-$95.** 1950 Omro Rd 54902. US 41, exit 119, jct SR 21. Int corridors. **Pets:** Medium, other species. Service with restrictions, supervision. (A$K) (X) (&M) 🛏 🖥

PLATTEVILLE
▼▼ **Governor Dodge Hotel & Conference Center** 🅷
(608) 348-2301. **$76-$92.** 300 Business Hwy 151 53818. Jct US 151 and SR 80, just w. Int corridors. **Pets:** Other species. $50 deposit/room, $10 daily fee/pet. Designated rooms, no service.
(A$K) (X) (&M) 🛏 🖥 (🍴) (≈)

▼▼▼ **Mound View Inn** 🅷
(608) 348-9518. **Call for rates.** 1755 E Business Hwy 151 53818. On US 151, exit 21, just w. Int corridors. **Pets:** Accepted. (X) 🛏 (X)

🅐🅐🅐 ▼▼▼ **Super 8** 🅷
(608) 348-8800. **$65-$154.** 100 Hwy 80/81 S 53818. Jct US 151 and SR 80. Int corridors. **Pets:** Other species. $10 daily fee/pet. Service with restrictions, crate. (SAVE) (X) (&M) 🛏 🖥 (X)

PLEASANT PRAIRIE
▼▼▼ **La Quinta Inn-Pleasant Prairie** 🅷 🐾
(262) 857-7911. **$49-$119.** 7540 118th Ave 53158. I-94, exit 344 (SR 50), just e. Int corridors. **Pets:** Medium, other species. Service with restrictions, supervision. (A$K) (X) (&M) 🛏 🖥

PLOVER
🅐🅐🅐 ▼▼▼ **AmericInn of Plover** 🅷
(715) 342-1244. **$69-$109.** 1501 American Dr 54467. I-39, exit 153 (CR B), just nw. Int corridors. **Pets:** Dogs only. $15 one-time fee/room. Service with restrictions, supervision. (SAVE) (X) (&M) 🛏 🖥 (≈) (X)

▼▼▼ **Comfort Inn** 🅷
(715) 342-0400. **$74-$99.** 1560 American Dr 54467. I-39, exit 153 (CR B), just w. Int corridors. **Pets:** Accepted. (A$K) (X) (&M) 🛏 🖥 (≈)

PORTAGE
🅐🅐🅐 ▼▼▼ **Days Inn** 🅼
(608) 742-1554. **$49-$150.** N5781 Kinney Rd 53901. I-90/94, exit 108A (SR 78), just s. Int corridors. **Pets:** Accepted.
(SAVE) (X) (&M) 🛏 🖥 (≈)

▼▼▼ **Super 8-Portage** 🅷
(608) 742-8330. **$55-$85.** 3000 New Pinery Rd 53901. I-39, exit 92, just s. Int corridors. **Pets:** Accepted. (A$K) (X) 🛏 🖥

PRAIRIE DU CHIEN
🅐🅐🅐 ▼▼▼ **Best Western Bluffview Inn & Suites** 🅷
(608) 326-4777. **$86-$180.** 37268 US Hwy 18 S 53821. On US 18, 1.9 mi e of jct SR 27 N. Ext/int corridors. **Pets:** Accepted.
(SAVE) (X) (&M) 🛏 🖥 (≈)

🅐🅐🅐 ▼▼ **Brisbois Motor Inn** 🅼
(608) 326-8404. **$49-$109.** 533 N Marquette Rd 53821. On SR 35 N, 0.5 mi n of jct US 18/SR 35 S and 27 N. Ext/int corridors.
Pets: Accepted. (SAVE) (X) 🛏 🖥 (≈)

▼▼▼ **Country Inn & Suites By Carlson** 🅷
(608) 326-5700. **$80-$149.** 1801 Cabela's Dr 53821. On SR 35, 2 mi n of jct US 18/SR 35 S and 27 N. Int corridors. **Pets:** Large, other species. $20 daily fee/room. Service with restrictions, supervision.
(A$K) (X) (&M) 🛏 🖥 (🍴) (≈) (X)

▼ **Holiday Motel** 🅼
(608) 326-2448. **Call for rates.** 1010 S Marquette Rd 53821. On US 18, 1 mi e of jct SR 27 N. Ext corridors. **Pets:** Small. $10 one-time fee/pet. Service with restrictions, supervision. (X) 🛏

▼▼▼ **Super 8-Prairie Du Chien** 🅷
(608) 326-8777. **$60-$100.** 1930 S Marquette Rd 53821. On US 18, 1.9 mi e of jct SR 27 N. Ext/int corridors. **Pets:** Small. $15 daily fee/pet. Designated rooms, service with restrictions, supervision. (X) (&M) 🛏 🖥

RACINE
🅐🅐🅐 ▼▼▼ **Comfort Inn Racine** 🅷
(262) 886-6055. **$69-$149.** 1154 Prairie Dr 53406. I-94, exit 333, 4.1 mi e on SR 20. Int corridors. **Pets:** Accepted. (SAVE) (X) (&M) 🛏 🖥

▼▼▼ **Racine Marriott Hotel** 🅷
(262) 886-6100. **$125-$153.** 7111 Washington Ave 53406. I-94, exit 333, 4 mi e on SR 20. Int corridors. **Pets:** Accepted.
(X) (&M) 🛏 🖥 (🍴) (≈)

REEDSBURG
▼▼ **Quality Inn** 🅷 🐾
(608) 524-8535. **Call for rates.** 2115 E Main St 53959. 1.5 mi e on SR 23 and 33. Int corridors. **Pets:** Other species. $10 daily fee/pet. Service with restrictions. (X) 🛏 🖥 (X)

RHINELANDER
▼ **Americas Best Value Inn** 🅼
(715) 369-5880. **$70-$75.** 667 W Kemp St 54501. On Business Rt US 8, just e of jct SR 47. Int corridors. **Pets:** Other species. $10 one-time fee/room. Service with restrictions, crate. (A$K) (X) (&M) 🛏 🖥

🅐🅐🅐 ▼▼▼ **Best Western Claridge Motor Inn** 🅷
(715) 362-7100. **$89-$160.** 70 N Stevens St 54501. Between Davenport and Rives sts; downtown. Int corridors. **Pets:** Medium, other species. $25 deposit/room, $10 daily fee/pet. Designated rooms, service with restrictions, supervision. (SAVE) (X) (&M) 🖥 (🍴) (≈) (X)

◆◆◆ **Comfort Inn** M

(715) 369-1100. **$79-$135.** 1490 Lincoln St 54501. On Business Rt US 8, 2.6 mi e of jct SR 47. Int corridors. **Pets:** Large. $25 one-time fee/room. Service with restrictions, supervision.

(ASK) (X) (&M) (🔌) (💻) (🏊) (✕)

◆◆◆ **Quality Inn** H

(715) 369-3600. **$70-$80.** 668 W Kemp St 54501. On Business Rt US 8, just e of jct SR 47. Int corridors. **Pets:** Accepted.

(SAVE) (X) (&M) (🔌) (💻) (🏊) (✕)

RICE LAKE

◆◆◆ **Microtel Inn & Suites** H

(715) 736-2010. **$50-$99.** 2771 Decker Dr 54868. US 53, exit 140 (CR O), just ne. Int corridors. **Pets:** $15 one-time fee/room. Service with restrictions, supervision. (ASK) (X) (🔌) (💻)

RICHLAND CENTER

◆◆◆ **The Center Lodge** H

(608) 647-8988. **$70-$90, 10 day notice.** 100 Foundry Dr 53581. 0.9 mi e on US 14. Int corridors. **Pets:** Accepted.

(ASK) (X) (&M) (🔌) (💻) (🏊)

RIPON

◆◆◆ **AmericInn Lodge & Suites of Ripon** H

(920) 748-7578. **$69-$185.** 1219 W Fond du Lac St 54971. 1.8 mi w on SR 23. Int corridors. **Pets:** $10 daily fee/room. Service with restrictions, supervision. (ASK) (X) (&M) (🔌) (💻) (🏊) (✕)

◆◆◆◆ **Comfort Suites at Royal Ridges** H

(920) 748-5500. **$69-$179.** 2 Westgate Dr 54971. 2 mi w on SR 23. Int corridors. **Pets:** Medium. $15 daily fee/room. Designated rooms, service with restrictions, supervision. (ASK) (X) (&M) (🔌) (💻) (🏊) (✕)

RIVER FALLS

◆◆◆ ◆◆◆◆ **Best Western River Falls** H

(715) 425-1045. **$80-$160.** 100 Spring St 54022. Downtown. Int corridors. **Pets:** Large. $10 one-time fee/pet. Designated rooms, service with restrictions, supervision. (SAVE) (X) (&M) (🔌) (💻) (🍴) (🏊)

ROTHSCHILD

◆◆◆ **Candlewood Suites–Wausau** H 🐾

(715) 355-8900. **$79-$149.** 803 Industrial Park Dr 54474. I-39, exit 185 (Business Rt US 51), just se. Int corridors. **Pets:** Medium. $25 one-time fee/pet. Designated rooms, service with restrictions, supervision.

(ASK) (X) (&M) (🔌) (💻)

◆◆◆ **Comfort Inn** H 🐾

(715) 355-4449. **$56-$120.** 1510 County Hwy XX 54474. I-39, exit 185 (Business Rt US 51), just se. Int corridors. **Pets:** Large, dogs only. $10 daily fee/pet. Designated rooms, service with restrictions, supervision.

(ASK) (X) (🔌) (💻) (🏊)

◆◆◆ **Motel 6 Rothschild** H

(715) 355-3030. **Call for rates.** 904 Industrial Park Ave 54474. I-39, exit 185 (Business Rt US 51), just se. Int corridors. **Pets:** Other species. Service with restrictions, supervision. (X) (🔌) (💻) (🏊) (✕)

SHAWANO

◆◆◆ **Super 8-Shawano** M

(715) 526-6688. **$46-$90.** 211 Waukechon St 54166. 1.2 mi e on SR 29 business route; SR 29, exit 227, 1.8 mi n. then 1.1 mi w. Int corridors. **Pets:** Accepted. (ASK) (X) (🔌) (💻)

SHEBOYGAN

◆◆◆ ◆ **Americas Best Value Inn-Sheboygan** H 🐾

(920) 458-8080. **$60-$99.** 3402 Wilgus Rd 53081. I-43, exit 126, just ne. Int corridors. **Pets:** Dogs only. $15 one-time fee/room. Service with restrictions, supervision. (SAVE) (X) (🔌) (💻)

◆◆◆ **Comfort Inn-Sheboygan** H

(920) 457-7724. **$70-$190.** 4332 N 40th St 53083. I-43, exit 128, 0.3 mi e on Business Rt SR 42. Int corridors. **Pets:** Other species. $10 daily fee/pet. Designated rooms, service with restrictions, supervision.

(ASK) (X) (&M) (🔌) (💻) (🏊)

◆◆◆ ◆◆◆◆ **Grandstay Residential Suites Hotel** H

(920) 208-8000. **$90-$170.** 708 Niagara Ave 53081. Downtown. Int corridors. **Pets:** Small. $10 daily fee/room. Designated rooms, service with restrictions. (SAVE) (X) (&M) (🔌) (💻) (🏊) (✕)

◆◆◆ **La Quinta Inn Sheboygan** H 🐾

(920) 457-2321. **$59-$105.** 2932 Kohler Memorial Dr 53081. I-43, exit 126, 1 mi e on SR 23. Int corridors. **Pets:** Medium, other species. Service with restrictions, supervision. (ASK) (X) (&M) (🔌) (💻)

◆◆◆◆ **Sleep Inn & Suites** H

(920) 694-0099. **Call for rates.** 3912 Motel Rd 53081. I-43, exit 120, just e. Int corridors. **Pets:** Accepted. (X) (&M) (🔌) (💻) (🏊) (✕)

SHEBOYGAN FALLS

◆◆◆ **Days Inn & Suites** H

(920) 467-4314. **Call for rates.** 600 Hwy 32 N 53085. SR 23, exit 32 (Sheboygan Falls/Howards Grove), just w. Int corridors. **Pets:** Accepted.

(X) (&M) (🔌) (💻) (🏊) (✕)

SHELL LAKE

◆◆◆ **AmericInn Lodge & Suites of Shell Lake** H

(715) 468-4494. **$69-$189.** 315 Hwy 63 S 54871. On SR 63, just s. Int corridors. **Pets:** Accepted. (ASK) (X) (🔌) (💻) (🏊) (✕)

SIREN

◆◆◆ ◆◆◆◆ **The Lodge at Crooked Lake** H

(715) 349-2500. **$89-$265.** 24271 SR 35 N 54872. On SR 35, 0.5 mi n of jct SR 70. Int corridors. **Pets:** Dogs only. $10 one-time fee/pet. Service with restrictions. (SAVE) (X) (🔌) (💻) (🍴) (🏊) (✕)

◆◆◆ **Pine Wood Motel** M

(715) 349-5225. **$35-$65.** 23862 Hwy 35 S 54872. On SR 35, 0.3 mi s of jct SR 70 W and CR B E. Ext corridors. **Pets:** Medium, dogs only. No service, supervision. (ASK) (X) (🔌) (💻)

SPARTA

◆◆◆ ◆ **Best Nights Inn** M

(608) 269-3066. **$35-$119.** 303 W Wisconsin St 54656. I-90, exit 25 (SR 27), 0.5 mi n; exit 28 (SR 16), 1 mi w. Ext corridors. **Pets:** $7 one-time fee/pet. Designated rooms, service with restrictions, supervision.

(SAVE) (X) (🔌) (💻) (🏊)

◆◆◆ ◆◆◆◆ **Best Western Sparta Trail Lodge** H

(608) 269-2664. **$89-$129.** 4445 Theatre Rd 54656. I-90, exit 28 (SR 16), just w. Int corridors. **Pets:** Accepted. (SAVE) (X) (&M) (🔌) (💻) (🍴) (🏊) (✕)

◆◆◆ ◆◆◆◆ **Country Inn & Suites By Carlson** H 🐾

(608) 269-3110. **$87-$148.** 737 Avon Rd 54656. I-90, exit 25 (SR 27), just n. Int corridors. **Pets:** Dogs only. $10 one-time fee/pet. Service with restrictions, supervision. (ASK) (X) (&M) (🔌) (💻) (🏊)

◆◆◆ **Super 8 Sparta** H

(608) 269-8489. **$70-$175.** 716 Avon Rd 54656. I-90, exit 25 (SR 27), just n. Int corridors. **Pets:** Other species. $10 daily fee/pet. Service with restrictions, crate. (ASK) (X) (🔌) (💻) (🏊)

SPOONER

◆◆◆ ◆◆◆◆ **Best Western American Heritage Inn** H 🐾

(715) 635-9770. **$90-$170.** 101 W Maple St 54801. On SR 70, just e of US 63, 1 mi w of US 53. Int corridors. **Pets:** Small, other species. $15 daily fee/pet. Designated rooms, service with restrictions, supervision.

(SAVE) (X) (🔌) (💻) (🏊) (✕)

⬗ ▼▼ Country House Motel & RV Park M
(715) 635-8721. **$55-$109.** 717 S River St 54801-9692. On US 63, 0.5 mi s of jct SR 70. Ext/int corridors. **Pets:** $10 one-time fee/pet. Designated rooms, service with restrictions, supervision.
[SAVE] [✕] [♿M] [🛏] [💻] [🏊]

▼ Inn Town Motel M
(715) 635-3529. **$40-$71, 3 day notice.** 801 River St 54801. 0.8 mi n of jct US 63 and SR 70. Ext corridors. **Pets:** Other species. $10 daily fee/pet. Designated rooms, service with restrictions, supervision. [✕] [🛏]

STEVENS POINT

⬗ ▼ Americas Best Value Inn H ❀
(715) 341-8888. **$50-$80.** 247 N Division St 54481. I-39, exit 161 (US 51 business route), 0.6 mi s. Int corridors. **Pets:** Dogs only. $15 one-time fee/room. Service with restrictions, supervision. [SAVE] [✕] [🛏] [💻]

▼▼▼ Country Inn & Suites By Carlson H
(715) 345-7000. **$81-$144.** 301 Division St N 54481. I-39, exit 161 (US 51 business route), 0.6 mi s. Int corridors. **Pets:** Other species. $25 one-time fee/room. No service, supervision. [ASK] [✕] [♿M] [🛏] [💻] [🏊]

▼▼ Fairfield Inn by Marriott H
(715) 342-9300. **$90-$110.** 5317 Hwy 10 E 54481. I-39, exit 158A (US 10), just se. Int corridors. **Pets:** Other species. $50 one-time fee/room. Service with restrictions, crate. [✕] [🛏] [💻] [🏊]

▼▼▼ Holiday Inn Express H
(715) 344-0000. **$79-$139.** 1100 Amber Ave 54481. I-39, exit 158 (US 10), 1 mi e, then just n. Int corridors. **Pets:** Other species. $25 daily fee/room. Service with restrictions, supervision.
[ASK] [✕] [♿M] [🛏] [💻] [🏊]

▼▼ La Quinta Inn & Suites Stevens Point H ❀
(715) 344-1900. **$59-$99.** 4917 Main St 54481. I-39, exit 158B (US 10), just sw. Int corridors. **Pets:** Medium, other species. Service with restrictions, supervision. [ASK] [✕] [🛏] [💻] [🏊]

▼ Point Motel M
(715) 344-8312. **$35-$80.** 209 Division St 54481. I-39, exit 161 (US 51 business route), 0.7 mi s. Ext corridors. **Pets:** Accepted.
[ASK] [✕] [🛏]

⬗ ▼▼ Stay Inn & Suites H
(715) 341-9090. **Call for rates.** 159 Division St N 54481. I-39, exit 161 (US 51 business route), 0.6 mi s. Int corridors. **Pets:** Accepted.
[ECO] [SAVE] [✕] [🛏]

SUN PRAIRIE

⬗ ▼ McGovern's Motel & Suites M
(608) 837-7321. **$61-$92.** 820 W Main St 53590. On US 151, exit 101, 1.2 mi ne. Ext/int corridors. **Pets:** Dogs only. $10 daily fee/pet. Designated rooms, service with restrictions, supervision.
[SAVE] [✕] [♿M] [🛏] [💻] [🍴]

⬗ ▼▼ Quality Inn & Suites-Sun Prairie H
(608) 834-9889. **$74-$149.** 105 Business Park Dr 53590. US 151, exit 103 (CR N), just n. Int corridors. **Pets:** Medium, dogs only. $10 daily fee/pet. Service with restrictions, supervision. [SAVE] [✕] [♿M] [🛏] [💻] [🏊]

SUPERIOR

⬗ ▼▼ Barkers Island Inn H
(715) 392-7152. **$89-$189.** 300 Marina Dr 54880. Just ne of US 2/53; on Barkers Island. Int corridors. **Pets:** Large, other species. $10 daily fee/room. Service with restrictions, supervision.
[SAVE] [✕] [♿M] [🛏] [💻] [🍴] [🏊] [✕]

⬗ ▼▼▼ Best Western Bay Walk Inn H
(715) 392-7600. **$60-$170.** 1405 Susquehanna Ave 54880. Just e of US 2 on Belknap St. Int corridors. **Pets:** Accepted.
[SAVE] [✕] [♿M] [🛏] [💻] [🏊] [✕]

⬗ ▼▼ Best Western Bridgeview Motor Inn H
(715) 392-8174. **$59-$169.** 415 Hammond Ave 54880. 0.8 mi n at south end of Blatnik Bridge. Int corridors. **Pets:** Accepted.
[SAVE] [✕] [♿M] [🛏] [💻] [🏊] [✕]

⬗ ▼▼ Superior Inn H
(715) 394-7706. **$45-$165.** 525 Hammond Ave 54880. 0.8 mi n; south end of Blatnik Bridge. Int corridors. **Pets:** Accepted.
[SAVE] [✕] [♿M] [🛏] [💻] [🏊]

THORP

▼▼ AmericInn Lodge & Suites of Thorp H
(715) 669-5959. **Call for rates.** 203 1/2 W Hill St 54771. US 29, exit 108 (SR 73), just nw. Int corridors. **Pets:** Accepted.
[✕] [♿M] [🛏] [💻] [🏊]

TOMAH

▼▼ AmericInn Lodge & Suites of Tomah H ❀
(608) 372-4100. **$79-$159.** 750 Vandervort St 54660. I-94, exit 143 (SR 21), just e. Int corridors. **Pets:** Medium. $10 daily fee/pet. Designated rooms, service with restrictions, supervision.
[ASK] [✕] [♿M] [🛏] [💻] [🏊]

▼▼ Comfort Inn by Choice Hotels H ❀
(608) 372-6600. **$77-$180.** 305 Wittig Rd 54660. I-94, exit 143 (SR 21), just w. Int corridors. **Pets:** Medium. $10 one-time fee/room. Service with restrictions, supervision. [ASK] [✕] [🛏] [💻] [🏊]

▼▼▼ Cranberry Country Lodge Convention Center and Water Park H
(608) 374-2801. **Call for rates.** 319 Wittig Rd 54660. I-94, exit 143 (SR 21), just w. Int corridors. **Pets:** Dogs only. $10 daily fee/room. Designated rooms. [✕] [🛏] [💻] [🏊] [✕]

▼▼ Econo Lodge H
(608) 372-9100. **Call for rates.** 2005 N Superior Ave 54660. I-94, exit 143 (SR 21), just w. Ext/int corridors. **Pets:** $10 one-time fee/pet. Service with restrictions, supervision. [✕] [🛏] [💻] [🏊]

▼▼ Holiday Inn H
(608) 372-3211. **$85-$135.** 1017 E McCoy Blvd 54660. I-94, exit 143 (SR 21), just e. Int corridors. **Pets:** Accepted.
[ASK] [✕] [🛏] [💻] [🍴] [🏊] [✕]

⬗ ▼▼ Lark Inn M ❀
(608) 372-5981. **$62-$128.** 229 N Superior Ave 54660. I-94, exit 143 (SR 21), 1.5 mi s on US 12; I-90, exit 41, 2 mi n on US 12. Ext/int corridors. **Pets:** Small, dogs only. $7 daily fee/pet. Service with restrictions, supervision. [SAVE] [✕] [♿M] [🛏] [💻]

▼▼ Super 8-Tomah H ❀
(608) 372-3901. **$50-$120.** 1008 E McCoy Blvd 54660. I-94, exit 143 (SR 21), just e. Int corridors. **Pets:** Medium, other species. $10 one-time fee/pet. Service with restrictions, supervision. [ASK] [✕] [🛏] [💻]

TOMAHAWK

▼▼▼ Rodeway Inn & Suites H
(715) 453-8900. **$70-$130.** 1738 E Comfort Dr 54487. US 51, exit 229, just nw. Int corridors. **Pets:** Other species. $25 one-time fee/room. Service with restrictions, crate. [ASK] [✕] [♿M] [🛏] [💻] [🏊] [✕]

▼▼ Super 8-Tomahawk H ❀
(715) 453-5210. **$65-$125.** 108 W Mohawk Dr 54487. On US 51 business route, 0.6 mi n of downtown. Int corridors. **Pets:** Other species. $10 daily fee/pet. Designated rooms, service with restrictions, supervision.
[ASK] [✕] [♿M] [🛏] [💻] [✕]

TWO RIVERS

⬗ ▼▼▼ Lighthouse Inn on Lake Michigan H ❀
(920) 793-4524. **$79-$151.** 1515 Memorial Dr 54241. 0.3 mi s on SR 42. Int corridors. **Pets:** Small, dogs only. $50 deposit/pet. Designated rooms, supervision. [SAVE] [✕] [♿M] [🛏] [💻] [🍴] [🏊] [✕]

VERONA

▼▼▼▼ **Holiday Inn Express Hotel & Suites Madison-Verona** H

(608) 497-4500. **$119-$189.** 515 W Verona Ave 53593. On US 51 business route, exit 81, 1.8 mi w. Int corridors. **Pets:** $13 daily fee/pet. Designated rooms, service with restrictions, supervision.

ASK ✕ 🔥M 🔌 💻 🏊

VIROQUA

▼ **Hickory Hill Motel** M

(608) 637-3104. **$54-$75.** US 14 S 3955 54665. On US 14 and SR 27 and 82, 1.8 mi se. Ext corridors. **Pets:** Small. Designated rooms, service with restrictions, supervision. ASK ✕ 🔌 🏊

WATERFORD

▼▼▼▼ **Baymont Inn & Suites-Waterford** H

(262) 534-4100. **$84-$199.** 750 Fox Ln 53185. On SR 36, 1 mi s of jct SR 164. Int corridors. **Pets:** Accepted. ASK ✕ 🔥M 🔌 💻 🏊

WATERTOWN

▼▼ **Super 8** H

(920) 261-1188. **$69-$89.** 1730 S Church St 53094. On SR 26, 1.5 mi s of jct SR 19. Int corridors. **Pets:** Accepted.

ASK ✕ 🔥M 🔌 💻 🏊

WAUPACA

🆔 ▼▼▼▼ **Best Western Grand Seasons Hotel** H

(715) 258-9212. **$79-$139.** 110 Grand Seasons Dr 54981. Jct US 10 and SR 54 W. Int corridors. **Pets:** $50 deposit/pet. Designated rooms, supervision. SAVE ✕ 🔥M 🔌 💻 🏊 🐾

WAUPUN

▼ **Inn Town Motel** M

(920) 324-4211. **$49-$94.** 27 S State St 53963. US 151, exit 146 (SR 49), 1 mi w on Main St, then just s. Ext corridors. **Pets:** $10 daily fee/pet. Service with restrictions, crate. ASK ✕ 🔥M 🔌 💻

WAUSAU

🆔 ▼▼▼ **Best Western Midway Hotel** H

(715) 842-1616. **$79-$119.** 2901 Hummingbird Rd 54401. I-39, exit 190 (CR NN), just sw. Int corridors. **Pets:** Medium. $20 one-time fee/room. Designated rooms, service with restrictions, supervision.

SAVE ✕ 🔥M 🔌 💻 🍴 🐾

▼▼ **Days Inn** M

(715) 842-0641. **$51-$71.** 116 S 17th Ave 54401. I-39, exit 192, just ne. Int corridors. **Pets:** $10 daily fee/room. Designated rooms, service with restrictions, supervision. ASK ✕ 🔌 💻

🆔 ▼▼▼▼ **Jefferson Street Inn** H ✿

(715) 845-6500. **$109-$299, 3 day notice.** 201 Jefferson St 54403. Just w of jct 6th St; center. Int corridors. **Pets:** $30 daily fee/pet. Service with restrictions, crate. SAVE ✕ 🔥M 🔌 💻 🏊 🐾

▼▼ **La Quinta Inn-Wausau** H ✿

(715) 842-0421. **$49-$85.** 1910 Stewart Ave 54401. I-39, exit 192, just se. Int corridors. **Pets:** Medium, other species. Service with restrictions, supervision. ASK ✕ 🔌 💻 🏊

▼▼ **Rib Mountain Inn** H

(715) 848-2802. **Call for rates.** 2900 Rib Mountain Way 54401. I-39, exit 190 (CR NN), 1 mi w on N Mountain Rd (CR NN), then just s. Ext/int corridors. **Pets:** Accepted. 🔌 💻 🐾

▼▼▼▼ **Stewart Inn Bed and Breakfast** BB ✿

(715) 849-5858. **$150-$215, 10 day notice.** 521 Grant St 54403. Just n on 6th St (SR 52), then just w. Int corridors. **Pets:** Other species. Crate. ECO ✕

🆔 ▼▼▼ **Super 8 Wausau** H

(715) 848-2888. **$62-$80.** 2006 Stewart Ave W 54401. I-39, exit 192, just se. Int corridors. **Pets:** Dogs only. $10 daily fee/pet. Designated rooms, service with restrictions, supervision. SAVE ✕ 🔌 💻 🏊

WAUTOMA

▼▼ **AmericInn Lodge & Suites of Wautoma** H

(920) 787-5050. **$78-$169.** W7696 SR 21/73 54982. On SR 21 and 73, 1.2 mi e. Int corridors. **Pets:** Accepted. ASK ✕ 🔥M 🔌 💻 🏊

▼▼ **Super 8-Wautoma** H

(920) 787-4811. **$70-$95.** W7607 SR 21/73 54982. On SR 21 and 73, 1.5 mi e. Int corridors. **Pets:** Large, other species. $10 one-time fee/pet. Designated rooms, service with restrictions, supervision.

ASK ✕ 🔥M 🔌 💻 🏊

WEST SALEM

▼▼ **AmericInn Motel & Suites of West Salem** H

(608) 786-3340. **$83-$153.** 125 Buol Rd 54669. I-90, exit 12, just sw on CR C. Int corridors. **Pets:** Accepted.

ASK ✕ 🔥M 🔌 💻 🏊 🐾

WINDSOR

▼▼ **Days Inn** H

(608) 846-7473. **$62-$110.** 6311 Rostad Cir 53598. I-90/94, exit 131 (SR 19). Int corridors. **Pets:** Medium, dogs only. $10 daily fee/pet. Designated rooms, service with restrictions, supervision.

ASK ✕ 🔥M 🔌 💻 🏊 🐾

WISCONSIN DELLS

🆔 ▼ **Americas Best Value Day's End Motel** M

(608) 254-8171. **$34-$152, 3 day notice.** N 604 Hwy 12-16 53965. I-90/94, exit 85 (US 12), 0.8 mi nw. Ext corridors. **Pets:** $10 daily fee/pet. Designated rooms, service with restrictions, crate.

SAVE ✕ 🔌 💻 🏊

🆔 ▼ **Black Hawk Motel** M

(608) 254-7770. **$36-$255, 3 day notice.** 720 Race St 53965. I-90/94, exit 87 (SR 13), 2 mi e on SR 13, 16 and 23. Ext corridors.
Pets: Accepted. SAVE ✕ 🔌 💻 🏊 🐾

▼ **Bridge View Motel** M

(608) 254-6114. **$49-$118, 3 day notice.** 1020 River Rd 53965. Just n of SR 13; center. Ext corridors. **Pets:** Medium. $10 daily fee/pet. Designated rooms, service with restrictions, crate. ASK ✕ 🔌 💻 🏊

🆔 ▼▼▼ **Days Inn of Wisconsin Dells** H

(608) 254-6444. **$48-$159, 3 day notice.** 944 Hwy 12 N 53965. I-90/94, exit 87 (SR 13), 1 mi n at jct US 12 and SR 16. Int corridors. **Pets:** Medium, dogs only. $50 deposit/pet, $10 daily fee/pet. Service with restrictions, supervision. SAVE ✕ 🔌 💻 🏊

▼▼ **Super 8-Wisconsin Dells** H

(608) 254-6464. **$39-$200.** 800 CR H 53965. I-90/94, exit 87 (SR 13), just e. Int corridors. **Pets:** Medium, dogs only. $10 daily fee/pet. Designated rooms, service with restrictions, supervision.

✕ 🔌 💻 🏊 🐾

WISCONSIN RAPIDS

🆔 ▼▼▼ **Americas Best Value Inn** H ✿

(715) 423-8080. **$50-$80.** 3410 8th St S 54494. 1.9 mi s on SR 13 of jct SR 54 W. Int corridors. **Pets:** Dogs only. $15 one-time fee/room. Service with restrictions, supervision. SAVE ✕ 🔌 💻

🆔 ▼▼▼▼ **Hotel Mead** H

(715) 423-1500. **$89-$250.** 451 E Grand Ave 54494. Just e of downtown. Int corridors. **Pets:** Medium, other species. $15 daily fee/pet. Designated rooms, service with restrictions, crate.

SAVE ✕ 🔥M 🔌 💻 🍴 🏊 🐾

▼▼ **Quality Inn** H

(715) 423-5506. **$70-$85.** 3120 8th St S 54494. 1.5 mi s on SR 13. Int corridors. **Pets:** Medium, dogs only. $5 daily fee/pet. Service with restrictions, supervision. ASK ✕ 🔌 💻 🏊

▼▼▼ Sleep Inn & Suites ⊞

(715) 424-6800. **$90-$155.** 4221 8th St S 54494. I-39, exit 136 (SR 73), 16.6 mi w; 3.5 mi n on SR 13. Int corridors. **Pets:** Medium, dogs only. $15 daily fee/pet. Service with restrictions, supervision.

(A$K) (✗) (&M) (🖥) (💻) (➰)

WITTENBERG

◇◇◇ ▼▼▼ Best Western Red Oak Inn ⊞

(715) 253-3755. **$80-$120.** W17267 Red Oak Ln 54499. US 29, exit 198, just se. Int corridors. **Pets:** Accepted.

(SAVE) (✗) (&M) (🖥) (💻) (➰) (✗)

WYOMING

AFTON

◬ ▼ Lazy B Motel M

(307) 885-3187. **$65-$95.** 219 Washington St (US 89) 83110. On US 89; center. Ext corridors. **Pets:** Dogs only. Service with restrictions, supervision. ⬛ ✕ 🔲 💻 🏊

BUFFALO

◬ ▼◈▼ Best Western Crossroads Inn H ❀

(307) 684-2256. **Call for rates.** 75 N Bypass Rd 82834. I-25, exit 299 (US 16), just w. Ext/int corridors. **Pets:** Other species. $10 one-time fee/ pet. Designated rooms, service with restrictions. ⬛ ✕ 🔲 💻 🍴 🏊

▼▼ Comfort Inn H

(307) 684-9564. **$66-$165.** 65 US Highway 16 E 82834. I-25, exit 299 (US 16 E), just e; I-90, exit 58, 1.3 mi w. Ext/int corridors. **Pets:** Medium, other species. $10 daily fee/pet. Designated rooms, service with restrictions, crate. ⬛ ✕ 📶 🔲 💻 🏊

◬ ▼◈▼ The Occidental Hotel H ❀

(307) 684-0451. **$75-$210, 14 day notice.** 10 N Main St 82834. Center. Int corridors. **Pets:** Other species. $10 daily fee/room. ⬛ ✕ 🔲 🍴 ☎

◬ ▼ Super 8 of Buffalo H

(307) 684-2531. **$60-$140.** 655 E Hart St 82834. I-25, exit 299 (US 16), just w; I-90, exit 58, 1.3 mi w. Int corridors. **Pets:** Other species. $50 deposit/room, $11 one-time fee/pet. Designated rooms, service with restrictions, supervision. ⬛ ✕ 🔲 💻

◬ ▼ WYO Motel M

(307) 684-5505. **$49-$169.** 610 E Hart St 82834. I-25, exit 299 (US 16), just w; I-90, exit 58, 1.3 mi w. Ext corridors. **Pets:** Accepted. ⬛ ✕ 🔲 💻 🏊

CASPER

◬ ▼◈▼ Best Western Ramkota H

(307) 266-6000. **$79-$129.** 800 N Poplar St 82601. I-25, exit 188B, just e. Int corridors. **Pets:** Other species. $50 deposit/room. Designated rooms, supervision. ⬛ ✕ 📶 🔲 💻 🍴 🏊 🐾

▼▼ Days Inn Casper H

(307) 234-1159. **$94-$114, 7 day notice.** 301 E 'E' St 82601. I-25, exit 188A, just s. Int corridors. **Pets:** Accepted. 🅰🆂🅺 ✕ 🔲 💻 🏊

▼▼ La Quinta Inn H ❀

(307) 265-1200. **$89-$159, 30 day notice.** 400 W 'F' St 82601. I-25, exit 188A, just e. Int corridors. **Pets:** Medium, other species. Service with restrictions, supervision. ✕ 📶 🔲 💻 🏊

◬ ▼◈▼ Parkway Plaza Hotel & Convention Centre H

(307) 235-1777. **$90-$129.** 123 W 'E' St 82601. I-25, exit 188A, just w. Ext/int corridors. **Pets:** Large. $25 deposit/room. Service with restrictions, crate. ⬛ ✕ 🔲 💻 🍴 🏊 🐾

◬ ▼◈▼ Quality Inn & Suites H ❀

(307) 266-2400. **$86-$91.** 821 N Poplar St 82601. I-25, exit 188B, just e. Int corridors. **Pets:** Large, dogs only. $10 daily fee/room. Designated rooms, service with restrictions, supervision. ⬛ ✕ 🔲 💻

◬ ▼◈▼ Ramada Plaza H

(307) 235-2531. **$90-$129.** 300 W 'F' St 82601. I-25, exit 188A, just e. Int corridors. **Pets:** Accepted. ⬛ ✕ 📶 🔲 💻 🍴 🏊 🐾

◬ ▼ The Royal Inn M

(307) 234-3501. **$55-$70.** 440 E a St 82601. I-25, exit 188A, just s to a St, then just e. Ext corridors. **Pets:** $25 one-time fee/pet. Service with restrictions, supervision. ⬛ ✕ 🔲

◬ ▼ Skyler Inn H

(307) 232-5100. **$79-$125.** 111 S Wilson St 82601. I-25, exit 186, 0.5 mi s to Yellowstone Hwy, then 1 mi w, jct 1st St. Int corridors. **Pets:** Small, dogs only. $25 one-time fee/pet. Service with restrictions, supervision. ⬛ ✕ 🔲 💻

▼▼ Super 8 M

(307) 266-3480. **$99-$109.** 3838 CY Ave 82604. I-25, exit 188B, 1.7 mi w on S Poplar St (SR 220), then 1.8 mi n. Int corridors. **Pets:** Accepted. 🅰🆂🅺 ✕ 🔲

CHEYENNE

▼▼ Cheyenne Super 8 M

(307) 635-8741. **$75-$99.** 1900 W Lincolnway 82001. I-25, exit 9, 0.7 mi e. Int corridors. **Pets:** Other species. $11 daily fee/pet. Service with restrictions, crate. 🅰🆂🅺 ✕ 📶 🔲 💻

▼◈▼ Days Inn Cheyenne H

(307) 778-8877. **Call for rates.** 2360 W Lincolnway 82001. I-25, exit 9, just e. Int corridors. **Pets:** Accepted. ✕ 🔲 💻 🏊 🐾

◬ ▼◈▼ Historic Plains Hotel H

(307) 638-3311. **$109-$359.** 1600 Central Ave 82001. I-80, exit 362, 1 mi n on I-180/I-25 business loop/US 85/87 business route, then just w on I-80 business loop/US 30; downtown. Int corridors. **Pets:** Accepted. ⬛ ✕ 🔲 💻 🍴

▼◈▼ La Quinta Inn Cheyenne H ❀

(307) 632-7117. **$55-$119.** 2410 W Lincolnway 82009. I-25, exit 9, just e. Int corridors. **Pets:** Medium, other species. Service with restrictions, supervision. 🅰🆂🅺 ✕ 📶 🔲 💻 🏊

◬ ▼◈▼ Nagle Warren Mansion B & B BB ❀

(307) 637-3333. **$158-$192, 3 day notice.** 222 E 17th St 82001. I-80, exit 362, 1.2 mi n on I-25 business loop/US 85/87 business route, then just e; jct House St; downtown. Int corridors. **Pets:** Large, other species. $25 daily fee/pet. Designated rooms, service with restrictions, supervision. ⬛ ✕ 🐾

▼ Oak Tree Inn H

(307) 778-6620. **Call for rates.** 1625 Stillwater Ave 82009. 1.2 mi e of jct Dell Range Blvd and Yellowstone Rd, 0.4 mi s. Ext/int corridors. **Pets:** Accepted. ✕ 🔲 💻 🍴

▼▼ Porch Swing Bed & Breakfast BB ❀

(307) 778-7182. **$75-$95.** 502 E 24th St 82001. I-80, exit 362, 1.8 mi n on I-25 business loop/US 85/87 business route, then just e; downtown. Int corridors. **Pets:** Service with restrictions, supervision. ✕ 🄰🄲

▼▼▼ Windy Hills Guest House 🅱🅱 ❀
(307) 632-6423. **$139-$310, 3 day notice.** 393 Happy Jack Rd 82007. I-25, exit 10B, 22 mi w on SR 210 (Happy Jack Rd), then 1 mi s on private gravel road. Ext corridors. **Pets:** Other species. $12 daily fee/pet. Designated rooms, service with restrictions, supervision.
🅰🆂🅺 ☒ 🔒 💻 ➿ ☒ 🅰🅲

CODY

ⓐⓐⓐ ▼▼▼ Best Western Sunset Motor Inn Ⓜ
(307) 587-4265. **$69-$209.** 1601 8th St 82414. 0.8 mi w on US 14/16/20. Ext corridors. **Pets:** Small, dogs only. $25 one-time fee/pet. Designated rooms, service with restrictions, supervision.
🆂🅰🆅🅴 ☒ 🔒 💻 🍴 ➿ ☒

ⓐⓐⓐ ▼ Big Bear Motel Ⓜ ❀
(307) 587-3117. **$49-$109.** 139 W Yellowstone Ave 82414. 2 mi w on US 14/16/20, from city center. Ext corridors. **Pets:** Other species. $10 daily fee/pet. Designated rooms, supervision. 🆂🅰🆅🅴 ☒ 🔒 💻 ➿ 🅰🅵

ⓐⓐⓐ ▼▼▼ The Cody Ⓗ ❀
(307) 587-5915. **$99-$259.** 232 W Yellowstone Ave 82414. 2 mi w on US 14/16/20. Int corridors. **Pets:** Dogs only. $10 daily fee/pet. Designated rooms, service with restrictions, supervision.
🆂🅰🆅🅴 ☒ 🅶🅼 🔒 💻 ➿ 🅰🅵

ⓐⓐⓐ ▼ Cody Motor Lodge Ⓜ ❀
(307) 527-6291. **$75-$125.** 1455 Sheridan Ave 82414. Just w on US 14/16/20 and SR 120. Int corridors. **Pets:** Other species. Designated rooms, service with restrictions, supervision. 🆂🅰🆅🅴 ☒ 🔒 💻

▼▼ Green Gables Inn Ⓜ
(307) 587-6886. **$69-$129.** 1636 Central Ave 82414. Just e on US 14/16/20 and SR 120. Ext corridors. **Pets:** Small, dogs only. Designated rooms, service with restrictions, supervision. 🅰🆂🅺 ☒ 🔒 💻

ⓐⓐⓐ ▼▼ Sunrise Motor Inn Ⓜ
(307) 587-5566. **$49-$169.** 1407 8th St 82414. 0.8 mi w on US 14/16/20. Ext corridors. **Pets:** Large, other species. $10 daily fee/pet. Designated rooms, service with restrictions, crate. 🆂🅰🆅🅴 ☒ 🔒 💻 ➿

DOUGLAS

ⓐⓐⓐ ▼▼ Best Western Douglas Inn & Conference Center Ⓗ ❀
(307) 358-9790. **$90-$100.** 1450 Riverbend Dr 82633. I-25, exit 140, 0.8 mi e. Int corridors. **Pets:** Medium. $10 daily fee/room. Service with restrictions, supervision. 🆂🅰🆅🅴 ☒ 🅶🅼 🔒 💻 🍴 ➿ ☒

ⓐⓐⓐ ▼▼▼ Holiday Inn Express Hotel & Suites Ⓗ ❀
(307) 358-4500. **$115-$175.** 900 W Yellowstone Ave 82633. I-25, exit 140, 0.5 mi e. Int corridors. **Pets:** Other species. Designated rooms, service with restrictions, supervision. 🆂🅰🆅🅴 ☒ 🅶🅼 🔒 💻 ➿

▼▼ ▼ Sleep Inn & Suites Ⓗ ❀
(307) 358-2777. **$99-$124.** 508 Cortez Dr 82633. I-25, exit 140, 0.5 mi e. Int corridors. **Pets:** Other species. Designated rooms, service with restrictions, supervision. 🅰🆂🅺 ☒ 🅶🅼 🔒 💻 ➿

DUBOIS

ⓐⓐⓐ ▼▼▼ Longhorn RV & Motel Ⓜ
(307) 455-2337. **Call for rates.** 5810 US Hwy 26 82513. 3 mi e on US 26 and 287. Ext corridors. **Pets:** Accepted.
🆂🅰🆅🅴 ☒ 🔒 💻 🍴 ☒

▼ Rocky Mountain Lodge Ⓜ ❀
(307) 455-2844. **$60-$95, 3 day notice.** 1349 W Ramshorn St 82513. 1.6 mi w on US 26 and 287. Ext corridors. **Pets:** Dogs only. $5 daily fee/pet. Designated rooms, service with restrictions, supervision.
☒ 🔒 💻 🅰🅵

ⓐⓐⓐ ▼▼ Stagecoach Motor Inn Ⓜ ❀
(307) 455-2303. **$58-$98.** 103 Ramshorn St 82513. On US 26 and 287; center. Ext corridors. **Pets:** Small, dogs only. $25 daily fee/pet. Designated rooms, service with restrictions, supervision.
🆂🅰🆅🅴 ☒ 🔒 💻 ➿ ☒ 🅰🅲

EVANSTON

▼▼ Comfort Inn Ⓗ
(307) 789-7799. **$75-$135.** 1931 Harrison Dr 82930. I-80, exit 3 (Harrison Dr), just n. Int corridors. **Pets:** Accepted. 🅰🆂🅺 ☒ 🔒 💻 ➿

ⓐⓐⓐ ▼▼ Days Inn Ⓗ
(307) 789-0783. **$69-$109.** 1983 Harrison Dr 82930. I-80, exit 3 (Harrison Dr), just n. Int corridors. **Pets:** Medium. $10 daily fee/pet. Designated rooms, service with restrictions, supervision. 🆂🅰🆅🅴 ☒ 🔒 💻 ➿

ⓐⓐⓐ ▼▼ Prairie Inn Ⓜ
(307) 789-2920. **$65-$90.** 264 Bear River Dr 82930. I-80, exit 6, 0.3 mi n. Ext/int corridors. **Pets:** Accepted. 🆂🅰🆅🅴 ☒ 🔒

EVANSVILLE

▼▼ Comfort Inn by Choice Hotels-Casper Ⓗ
(307) 235-3038. **$95-$104.** 480 Lathrop Rd 82636. I-25, exit 185, just e. Int corridors. **Pets:** $10 daily fee/pet. Service with restrictions.
🅰🆂🅺 ☒ 🅶🅼 🔒 💻 ➿

▼▼▼ Sleep Inn & Suites Ⓗ
(307) 235-3100. **Call for rates.** 6733 Bonanza 82636. I-25, exit 182, n on Hat Six Rd, then w. Int corridors. **Pets:** Accepted.
☒ 🔒 💻 ➿

▼▼▼ Super 8 East Casper Ⓗ ❀
(307) 237-8100. **$99-$119.** 269 Miracle Dr 82636. I-25, exit 185, just e. Int corridors. **Pets:** Medium, other species. $10 daily fee/room. Service with restrictions, supervision. 🅰🆂🅺 ☒ 🅶🅼 🔒 💻 ➿

GILLETTE

ⓐⓐⓐ ▼▼▼ Best Western Tower West Lodge Ⓗ
(307) 686-2210. **$90-$170.** 109 N US Hwy 14-16 82716. I-90, exit 124, just n. Int corridors. **Pets:** Other species. $15 one-time fee/pet. Service with restrictions, supervision. 🆂🅰🆅🅴 ☒ 🅶🅼 🔒 💻 🍴 ➿ ☒

ⓐⓐⓐ ▼ Budget Inn Express Ⓗ
(307) 686-1989. **$69-$199.** 2011 Rodgers Dr 82716. I-90, exit 124, just n. Int corridors. **Pets:** $10 daily fee/pet. Designated rooms, service with restrictions, supervision. 🆂🅰🆅🅴 ☒ 🔒 ➿

▼▼▼ Comfort Inn & Suites of Gillette Ⓗ
(307) 685-2223. **$90-$240.** 1607 W 2nd Ave 82716. I-90, exit 124, just ne. Int corridors. **Pets:** Accepted. 🅰🆂🅺 ☒ 🅶🅼 🔒 💻 ➿

▼▼▼ Holiday Inn Express Hotel & Suites Ⓗ ❀
(307) 686-9576. **$149-$189.** 1908 Cliff Davis Dr 82718. I-90, exit 126, just s, then e. Int corridors. **Pets:** Designated rooms, service with restrictions, supervision. 🅰🆂🅺 ☒ 🅶🅼 🔒 💻 ➿

GREEN RIVER

▼▼▼ Green River Hampton Inn & Suites Ⓗ
(307) 875-5300. **$89-$250.** 1055 Wild Horse Canyon Rd 82935. I-80, exit 89, 0.5 mi s, then 0.8 mi w. Int corridors. **Pets:** Accepted.
☒ 🅶🅼 🔒 💻 ➿

ⓐⓐⓐ ▼▼▼ Oak Tree Inn Ⓗ ❀
(307) 875-3500. **$80-$95.** 1170 W Flaming Gorge Way 82935. I-80, exit 89, just s. Ext/int corridors. **Pets:** Other species. $6 daily fee/pet. Designated rooms, service with restrictions, supervision.
🆂🅰🆅🅴 ☒ 🅶🅼 🔒 💻 🍴

GUERNSEY

ⓐⓐⓐ ▼ The Bunkhouse Motel Ⓜ
(307) 836-2356. **$65-$139.** 350 W Whalen St 82214. On US 26; center. Ext corridors. **Pets:** Accepted. 🆂🅰🆅🅴 ☒ 🔒 💻

HULETT

(AAA) ▼▼▼ Best Western Devil's Tower Inn 🅷
(307) 467-5747. **$70-$170.** 229 Hwy 24 82720. Center. Int corridors. **Pets:** Dogs only. $25 one-time fee/room. Designated rooms, service with restrictions, supervision. [SAVE] [✕] [&M] [🛏] [📺] [🐾]

(AAA) ▼▼ Hulett Motel Ⓜ 🐾
(307) 467-5220. **$65-$85.** 202 Main St 82720. SR 24; at north end of town. Ext corridors. **Pets:** Dogs only. $20 one-time fee/pet. Designated rooms, service with restrictions, supervision. [SAVE] [✕]

JACKSON HOLE AREA

ALPINE

(AAA) ▼▼ Alpen Haus Hotel Resort 🅷
(307) 654-7545. **$55-$150.** 50 W Hwy 26 83128. Jct US 26 and 89. Int corridors. **Pets:** Small, dogs only. $10 daily fee/pet. Designated rooms, service with restrictions, supervision. [SAVE] [✕] [🛏] [🍽]

GRAND TETON NATIONAL PARK

(AAA) ▼▼▼ Flagg Ranch Resort 🅷
(307) 543-2861. **$180-$200, 6 day notice.** Hwy 89 83013. US 89 and 191; 2 mi s of Yellowstone National Park south entrance; 5 mi n of Grand Teton National Park north entrance. Ext corridors. **Pets:** Accepted.
[SAVE] [✕] [&M] [📺] [🍽] [🐕] [🅰] [🐾]

▼▼▼ Jackson Lake Lodge 🅷
(307) 543-2811. **Call for rates.** US Hwy 89 83013. 5 mi nw of Moran. Ext/int corridors. **Pets:** Accepted.
[ECO] [✕] [&M] [🛏] [📺] [🍽] [🛎] [🅰] [🐾]

(AAA) ▼▼▼ Signal Mountain Lodge 🅷 🐾
(307) 543-2831. **$135-$315, 7 day notice.** 1 Inner Park Rd 83013. Teton Park Rd, 2 mi s of US 89, 191 and 287. Ext corridors. **Pets:** Other species. $15 daily fee/room. Designated rooms, service with restrictions, supervision. [ECO] [SAVE] [✕] [🛏] [📺] [🍽] [🐕] [🅰] [🐾]

▼▼ Togwotee Mountain Lodge 🅲🅰
(307) 543-2847. **$89-$259, 7 day notice.** 27655 Hwy US 26 & 287 83013. 16.5 mi e of Moran at jct US 26 and 287. Ext/int corridors. **Pets:** Accepted. [ASK] [✕] [🛏] [📺] [🍽] [🐕]

JACKSON

(AAA) ▼▼▼ 49'er Inn and Suites (Quality Inn and Suites) 🅷
(307) 733-7550. **$79-$179, 14 day notice.** 330 W Pearl St 83001. Just w; just s of town square. Ext/int corridors. **Pets:** Service with restrictions, supervision. [SAVE] [✕] [🛏] [📺] [🐕]

(AAA) ▼▼▼ Antler Inn 🅷
(307) 733-2535. **$72-$275, 4 day notice.** 43 W Pearl St 83001. Just s of town square. Ext/int corridors. **Pets:** Dogs only. Designated rooms, service with restrictions, supervision. [SAVE] [✕] [🛏] [📺] [🐕]

(AAA) ▼▼◆ Cowboy Village Resort 🅲🅰 🐾
(307) 733-3121. **$86-$258.** 120 S Flat Creek Dr 83002. 0.3 mi w on Broadway to Flat Creek Dr, just s; downtown. Ext corridors. **Pets:** Dogs only. Supervision. [SAVE] [✕] [🛏] [📺] [🛎] [🐕]

(AAA) ▼▼◆ Elk Country Inn Ⓜ 🐾
(307) 733-2364. **$76-$220, 14 day notice.** 480 W Pearl St 83001. Just w, then just s of town square. Ext/int corridors. **Pets:** Other species. Designated rooms, service with restrictions, supervision.
[SAVE] [✕] [🛏] [📺] [🐕]

▼▼◆ Homewood Suites by Hilton 🅷
(307) 739-0808. **$299-$359.** 260 N Millward St 83001. Just nw of town square, n on Millward St or w on Mercil Ave, from US 26/89/191. Int corridors. **Pets:** Accepted. [✕] [&M] [🛏] [📺] [🐕]

(AAA) ▼▼◆ Jackson Hole Lodge 🅷
(307) 733-2992. **$89-$329, 15 day notice.** 420 W Broadway 83001. 0.3 mi w on US 26/89/191. Ext corridors. **Pets:** Medium. $15 daily fee/pet. Designated rooms, service with restrictions, supervision. [SAVE] [✕] [🛏] [📺] [🛎] [🐕]

(AAA) ▼▼◆◆ Snow King Resort 🅷
(307) 733-5200. **$150-$760, 3 day notice.** 400 E Snow King Ave 83001. Just se of town square. Ext/int corridors. **Pets:** Accepted. [SAVE] [✕] [🛏] [📺] [🍽] [🛎] [🐕]

TETON VILLAGE

(AAA) ▼▼◆◆◆ Four Seasons Resort Jackson Hole 🅷
(307) 732-5000. **$375-$6750, 30 day notice.** 7680 Granite Loop Rd 83025. At base of Jackson Hole Mountain Resort. Int corridors. **Pets:** Very small, dogs only. Designated rooms, service with restrictions, supervision. [SAVE] [✕] [&M] [🛏] [📺] [🍽] [🛎] [🐕]

▼▼◆ Inn at Jackson Hole 🅷
(307) 733-2311. **$69-$549, 7 day notice.** 3345 W Village Dr 83025. Center. Ext corridors. **Pets:** Accepted.
[ASK] [✕] [🛏] [📺] [🍽] [🛎] [🐕]

END AREA

KEMMERER

(AAA) ▼▼◆ Best Western Fossil Country Inn & Suites 🅷
(307) 877-3388. **$95-$140.** 760 Hwy 189/30 83101. Jct US 30 and 189. Int corridors. **Pets:** Medium, other species. $25 one-time fee/room. Designated rooms, service with restrictions, supervision.
[SAVE] [✕] [&M] [🛏] [🛎]

LANDER

(AAA) ▼▼ Holiday Lodge Ⓜ
(307) 332-2511. **$65-$75.** 210 McFarlane Dr 82520. Just e of jct US 287 and SR 789. Ext corridors. **Pets:** $10 daily fee/pet. Designated rooms, service with restrictions, supervision. [SAVE] [✕] [🛏]

LARAMIE

(AAA) ▼▼▼ Best Western Laramie Inn & Suites 🅷
(307) 745-5700. **$89-$109.** 1767 N Banner Rd 82072. I-80, exit 310, just n. Int corridors. **Pets:** $20 daily fee/pet. Designated rooms, service with restrictions, supervision. [SAVE] [✕] [&M] [🛏] [📺] [🛎]

▼▼ Days Inn 🅷
(307) 745-5678. **$99-$130.** 1368 McCue St 82072. I-80, exit 310 (Curtis St), just n, then just e. Int corridors. **Pets:** Accepted.
[ASK] [✕] [&M] [🛏] [📺] [🛎]

(AAA) ▼▼ Gas Lite Motel Ⓜ
(307) 742-6616. **$56-$68.** 960 N 3rd St 82072. I-80, exit 313, 1.6 mi n on US 287; downtown. Ext corridors. **Pets:** Other species. $5 daily fee/room. Service with restrictions, supervision. [SAVE] [✕] [🛏] [🛎]

▼▼▼ Holiday Inn-Laramie 🅷
(307) 721-9000. **$139-$179.** 204 S 30th St 82070. I-80, exit 316 (Grand Ave), 2.5 mi w; jct 30th St. Int corridors. **Pets:** Accepted.
[ASK] [✕] [&M] [🛏] [📺] [🍽] [🛎]

(AAA) ▼▼ **Travelodge Downtown** M
(307) 742-6671. **$65-$170.** 165 N 3rd St 82072. I-80, exit 313, 1 mi n on US 287; downtown. Ext corridors. **Pets:** Other species. $50 deposit/pet. Designated rooms, service with restrictions, supervision.
[SAVE] [X] [fridge] [icon]

LITTLE AMERICA

(AAA) ▼▼▼ **Little America Hotel & Travel Center** M
(307) 875-2400. **$89-$109.** I-80, exit 68 82929. I-80, exit 68. Ext/int corridors. **Pets:** Other species. $20 daily fee/pet. Designated rooms, service with restrictions, supervision. [SAVE] [X] [&M] [fridge] [icon] [restaurant] [pool]

LUSK

(AAA) ▼▼ **Americas Best Value Inn Covered Wagon** M
(307) 334-2836. **$72-$155.** 730 S Main St 82225. Just n of jct US 20/85. Ext/int corridors. **Pets:** Accepted. [SAVE] [X] [&M] [fridge] [icon] [pool] [X]

(AAA) ▼▼ **Best Western Pioneer** M
(307) 334-2640. **$90-$190.** 731 S Main St 82225. Just n of jct US 20/85. Ext corridors. **Pets:** $20 one-time fee/room. Designated rooms, supervision. [SAVE] [X] [fridge] [icon] [pool]

NEWCASTLE

(AAA) ▼▼ **Auto Inn Motel** M
(307) 746-2734. **$59-$175.** 2503 W Main St 82701. West end of town on US 16. Ext corridors. **Pets:** Other species. $6 daily fee/pet. Designated rooms, no service, supervision. [SAVE] [X] [fridge] [icon]

(AAA) ▼▼ **Sage Motel** M
(307) 746-2724. **$75-$110, 3 day notice.** 1227 S Summit Ave 82701. 0.3 mi s of jct US 16 on US 85, just w. Ext corridors. **Pets:** Small, dogs only. $10 daily fee/pet. Designated rooms, service with restrictions, supervision. [SAVE] [X] [fridge] [icon]

PAINTER

▼ **Hunter Peak Ranch** RA
(307) 587-3711. **$150-$220.** 4027 Crandall Rd 82414. SR 296, 5 mi s of US 212; 40 mi n of SR 120. Ext corridors. **Pets:** Dogs only. $15 daily fee/pet. Designated rooms, no service, supervision.
[X] [fridge] [icon] [restaurant] [X] [X] [X] [X]

PINEDALE

▼▼ **Baymont Inn & Suites** H
(307) 367-8300. **Call for rates.** 1624 W Pine St 82941. 1 mi n on US 191. Int corridors. **Pets:** Accepted. [X] [&M] [fridge] [icon] [pool]

(AAA) ▼▼ **Best Western Pinedale Inn** H
(307) 367-6869. **$100-$170.** 850 W Pine St 82941. 0.5 mi n on US 191. Int corridors. **Pets:** Designated rooms, service with restrictions, supervision. [SAVE] [X] [fridge] [icon] [pool]

(AAA) ▼▼ **The Lodge at Pinedale** H
(307) 367-8800. **$80-$139.** 1054 W Pine St 82941. 0.7 mi n on US 191. Int corridors. **Pets:** Medium, dogs only. $10 daily fee/room. Designated rooms, service with restrictions, supervision. [SAVE] [X] [fridge] [icon] [pool]

▼ **Sun Dance Motel** M
(307) 367-4336. **Call for rates.** 148 E Pine St 82941. US 191; city center. Ext corridors. **Pets:** Accepted. [X] [fridge] [icon]

POWELL

▼▼▼ **Americas Best Value Inn** M
(307) 754-5117. **Call for rates.** 777 E 2nd St 82435. 0.3 mi e on US 14A. Ext corridors. **Pets:** Accepted. [X] [fridge] [icon] [pool]

RAWLINS

(AAA) ▼▼▼ **Best Western CottonTree Inn** H
(307) 324-2737. **$114-$140.** 2221 W Spruce St 82301. I-80, exit 211, just n. Ext/int corridors. **Pets:** Accepted. [SAVE] [X] [fridge] [icon] [pool] [X]

▼▼ **Days Inn Rawlins** H
(307) 324-6615. **Call for rates.** 2222 E Cedar St 82301. I-80, exit 215 (Cedar St), just n. Int corridors. **Pets:** Accepted. [X] [fridge] [icon] [pool]

▼▼▼ **Hampton Inn** H
(307) 324-2320. **Call for rates.** 406 Airport Rd 82301. I-80, exit 215 (Cedar St), just n. Int corridors. **Pets:** Accepted.
[X] [&M] [fridge] [icon] [pool]

▼▼ **Holiday Inn Express** H
(307) 324-3760. **$99-$169.** 201 Airport Rd 82301. I-80, exit 215 (Cedar St), just n. Int corridors. **Pets:** Accepted. [ASK] [X] [&M] [fridge] [icon] [pool]

▼▼ **Microtel Inn & Suites** H
(307) 324-5588. **$90-$119.** 812 Locust St 82301. I-80, exit 214, just n. Int corridors. **Pets:** Medium. $15 daily fee/pet. Designated rooms, no service, supervision. [ASK] [X] [&M] [fridge] [icon]

(AAA) ▼▼▼ **Oak Tree Inn** H
(307) 324-4700. **$69-$129.** 2005 E Daley St 82301. I-80, exit 215 (Cedar St), 0.5 mi w, then just n on US 287. Int corridors. **Pets:** Other species. Service with restrictions, supervision. [SAVE] [X] [&M] [fridge] [icon] [restaurant]

RIVERTON

▼▼▼ **Comfort Inn & Suites** H
(307) 856-8900. **$89-$139.** 2020 N Federal Blvd 82501. 1.5 mi ne on US 26/SR 789. Int corridors. **Pets:** Large, other species. $15 daily fee/pet. Designated rooms, service with restrictions, supervision.
[ASK] [X] [&M] [fridge] [icon] [pool]

▼▼ **Days Inn** M
(307) 856-9677. **$70-$150.** 909 W Main St 82501. 0.5 mi nw on US 26. Ext corridors. **Pets:** Small. $25 daily fee/pet. Service with restrictions, supervision. [ASK] [X] [fridge] [icon]

▼ **Super 8** M
(307) 857-2400. **$59-$120, 7 day notice.** 1040 N Federal Blvd 82501. 1 mi ne on US 26/SR 789. Int corridors. **Pets:** Small. $10 daily fee/pet. Service with restrictions, supervision. [ASK] [X] [fridge] [icon]

ROCK SPRINGS

▼▼▼ **Hampton Inn** H
(307) 382-9222. **Call for rates.** 1901 Dewar Dr 82901. I-80, exit 102 (Dewar Dr), 1 mi s. Int corridors. **Pets:** Medium, other species. Service with restrictions, supervision. [X] [&M] [fridge] [icon] [pool]

▼▼▼ **Holiday Inn** H ❀
(307) 382-9200. **$109-$135.** 1675 Sunset Dr 82901. I-80, exit 102 (Dewar Dr), 0.3 mi sw. Ext/int corridors. **Pets:** Other species. $10 daily fee/room. Designated rooms, service with restrictions, supervision.
[ASK] [X] [fridge] [icon] [restaurant] [pool]

▼▼ **La Quinta Inn** H ❀
(307) 362-1770. **$94-$149.** 2717 Dewar Dr 82901. I-80, exit 102 (Dewar Dr), just n. Int corridors. **Pets:** Medium, other species. Service with restrictions, supervision. [ASK] [X] [fridge] [icon] [pool]

▼ **Motel 6–#395** M
(307) 362-1850. **$51-$65.** 2615 Commercial Way 82901. I-80, exit 102 (Dewar Dr), n to Foothills Blvd, then just e. Ext corridors. **Pets:** Other species. Service with restrictions, supervision. [X] [fridge] [icon]

▼▼ **Quality Inn** M
(307) 382-9490. **$90.** 1670 Sunset Dr 82901. I-80, exit 102 (Dewar Dr), 0.3 mi s, then just w. Ext corridors. **Pets:** Accepted.
[ASK] [X] [fridge] [icon] [pool] [X]

▼▼▼ **Rock Springs Homewood Suites** H
(307) 382-0764. **Call for rates.** 60 Winston Dr 82901. I-80, exit 102 (Dewar Dr), 1 mi s. Int corridors. **Pets:** Accepted.
[X] [&M] [fridge] [icon] [pool] [X]

SARATOGA

◈ Hacienda Motel Ⓜ

(307) 326-5751. **$79-$89, 7 day notice.** 1500 S First St 82331. 0.5 mi s on SR 130. Int corridors. **Pets:** $10 daily fee/pet. Designated rooms, service with restrictions, supervision. ⒜ⓈⓀ ✕ 🛏

SHERIDAN

AAA ◈ Americas Best Value Inn Ⓜ ☙

(307) 672-9757. **$59-$99.** 580 E 5th St 82801. I-90, exit 23 (5th St), 0.4 mi w. Ext corridors. **Pets:** Other species. Designated rooms, service with restrictions, supervision. SAVE ✕ 🛏 ▣

AAA ◈◈◈ Best Western Sheridan Center 🄷

(307) 674-7421. **$80-$140.** 612 N Main St 82801. I-90, exit 23 (5th St), 1 mi w, then just s. Ext/int corridors. **Pets:** Other species. $25 one-time fee/room. Designated rooms, service with restrictions, supervision.
SAVE ✕ 🛏 ▣ 🍴 ⌇

◈ Budget Host Inn Ⓜ ☙

(307) 674-7496. **$70-$129.** 2007 N Main St 82801. I-90, exit 20, 0.7 mi s. Ext corridors. **Pets:** Other species. $10 daily fee/pet. Designated rooms, service with restrictions, supervision. ⒜ⓈⓀ ✕ 🛏 ▣

◈ Candlewood Suites 🄷

(307) 675-2100. **$119-$139.** 1709 Sugarland Dr 82801. I-90, exit 25, just w, then just n. Int corridors. **Pets:** Accepted. ⒜ⓈⓀ ✕ 🖳 🛏 ▣

AAA ◈◈◈ Holiday Inn Atrium & Convention Center 🄷

(307) 672-8931. **$108-$126.** 1809 Sugarland Dr 82801. I-90, exit 25, 0.3 mi nw. Int corridors. **Pets:** Accepted.
SAVE ✕ 🛏 ▣ 🍴 ⌇ ✕

AAA ◈◈◈ Mill Inn Ⓜ ☙

(307) 672-6401. **$65-$130.** 2161 Coffeen Ave 82801. I-90, exit 25, 0.3 mi w. Ext/int corridors. **Pets:** $15 daily fee/pet. Service with restrictions, supervision. SAVE ✕ 🛏 ▣

SUNDANCE

AAA ◈◈◈ Best Western Inn at Sundance 🄷

(307) 283-2800. **$65-$225.** 2719 E Cleveland Ave 82729. I-90, exit 189, just n, then just w on I-90 business loop. Int corridors. **Pets:** Accepted. SAVE ✕ 🖳 ▣ ⌇

AAA ◈ Budget Host Arrowhead Motel Ⓜ

(307) 283-3307. **$49-$79.** 214 Cleveland Ave 82729. I-90 business loop and US 14. Ext corridors. **Pets:** Dogs only. Service with restrictions, supervision. SAVE ✕ 🛏

THERMOPOLIS

◈◈ Days Inn 🄷

(307) 864-3131. **$93-$149.** 115 E Park St 82443. In Hot Springs State Park. Ext/int corridors. **Pets:** Other species. $15 daily fee/pet. Service with restrictions, supervision. ⒜ⓈⓀ ✕ ▣ 🍴 ⌇ ✕

◈◈ Hot Springs Super 8 🄷

(307) 864-5515. **$80-$160.** Lane 5, Hwy 20 S 82443. On US 20, just se. Int corridors. **Pets:** Accepted. ✕ 🖳 🛏 ▣ ⌇

TORRINGTON

◈◈◈ Holiday Inn Express Hotel & Suites 🄷

(307) 532-7600. **Call for rates.** 1700 E Valley Rd 82240. US 85, e on US 26. Int corridors. **Pets:** Dogs only. $15 daily fee/pet. Designated rooms, service with restrictions, supervision. ✕ 🖳 🛏 ▣ ⌇

UCROSS

AAA ◈◈◈ The Ranch at Ucross 🅁🄰

(307) 737-2281. **$229-$300, 3 day notice.** 2673 US Hwy 14 E 82835. Jct US 14/16, 0.5 mi w. Ext/int corridors. **Pets:** Small, dogs only. $100 deposit/pet. Designated rooms, no service, crate.
SAVE ✕ 🍴 ⌇ ✕ 🅦

WAPITI

AAA ◈ Green Creek Inn Ⓜ ☙

(307) 587-5004. **$65-$180, 5 day notice.** 2908 Northfork Hwy 82414. 2.8 mi w on US 14/16/20; between Cody and Yellowstone National Park. Ext corridors. **Pets:** $10 daily fee/pet. Supervision. SAVE ✕ 🛏 🅩

◈ Yellowstone Valley Inn Ⓜ

(307) 587-3961. **$59-$169, 21 day notice.** 3324 Yellowstone Park Hwy 82450. 3.3 mi w on US 14/16/20; halfway between Cody and Yellowstone National Park. Ext corridors. **Pets:** Accepted.
⒜ⓈⓀ ✕ 🛏 ▣ 🍴 ⌇ ✕ 🅩

WHEATLAND

AAA ◈◈◈ Best Western Torchlite Motor Inn 🄷

(307) 322-4070. **$100-$150.** 1809 N 16th St 82201. I-25, exit 78, just e; 1.5 mi n on US 87/I-25 business loop (16th St). Ext corridors. **Pets:** Other species. $10 daily fee/pet. Service with restrictions, supervision. SAVE ✕ 🛏 ▣ ⌇

YELLOWSTONE NATIONAL PARK

AAA ◈◈◈ Elephant Head Lodge 🄲🄰

(307) 587-3980. **$150-$350, 30 day notice.** 1170 Yellowstone Hwy 82190. 11.7 mi e of Yellowstone National Park east gate on US 14/16/20. Ext corridors. **Pets:** $20 one-time fee/pet. Crate.
SAVE ✕ 🛏 ▣ 🍴 ✕ 🄰🄲 🅦 🅩

◈◈ Shoshone Lodge 🄲🄰

(307) 587-4044. **$100-$325, 30 day notice.** 349 Yellowstone Hwy 82190. 3.5 mi e of Yellowstone National Park East Gate on US 14/16/20. Ext corridors. **Pets:** Accepted. ✕ 🛏 ▣ 🍴 ✕ 🄰🄲 🅩

Canadian Lodgings

ALBERTA

BANFF

▼▼▼ Banff Rocky Mountain Resort CO
(403) 762-5531. **$170-$385, 3 day notice.** 1029 Banff Ave T1L 1A2. Banff Ave and Tunnel Mountain Rd; just s of Trans-Canada Hwy 1. Ext corridors. **Pets:** Small. $20 daily fee/pet. Designated rooms, service with restrictions, supervision. ⊠ ⊟ ▣ ⓣ ➤ ⊠ ⓐ

CAA ▼▼▼▼ Best Western Siding 29 Lodge H
(403) 762-5575. **$100-$400.** 453 Marten St T1L 1B3. 0.6 mi (1 km) ne, just off Banff Ave. Int corridors. **Pets:** Accepted.
⊠ ⊠ ⊟ ▣ ➤

▼▼▼ Castle Mountain Chalets CA
(403) 762-3868. **$150-$345, 14 day notice.** Bow Valley Pkwy (Hwy 1A) T1L 1B5. 20 mi (32 km) w on Trans-Canada Hwy 1, jct Castle, 0.6 mi (1 km) ne on Hwy 1A (Bow Valley Pkwy). Ext corridors. **Pets:** Accepted.
⊠ ⊠ ⊟ ▣ ⊠ ⓐ ⓩ

CAA ▼▼▼▼ Douglas Fir Resort & Chalets CO
(403) 762-5591. **$117-$459.** 525 Tunnel Mountain Rd T1L 1B2. Jct Banff Ave and Wolf St, 1 mi (1.6 km) ne. Ext/int corridors. **Pets:** Accepted.
⊠ ⊠ ⊟ ▣ ➤ ⊠

CAA ▼▼▼▼ The Fairmont Banff Springs H
(403) 762-2211. **Call for rates.** 405 Spray Ave T1L 1J4. Just s on Banff Ave over the bridge, 0.3 mi (0.5 km) e. Int corridors. **Pets:** Accepted.
ⓔ ⊠ ⊠ ⊟ ▣ ⓣ ➤ ⊠

▼▼▼ Hidden Ridge Resort CO
(403) 762-3544. **Call for rates.** 901 Hidden Ridge Way T1L 1B7. 1.5 mi (2.4 km) ne at Tunnel Mountain Rd. Ext corridors. **Pets:** Accepted.
⊠ ⊟ ▣

CAA ▼▼ Irwin's Mountain Inn H
(403) 762-4566. **$79-$165.** 429 Banff Ave T1L 1B2. N of Rabbit St. Int corridors. **Pets:** Medium. $10 daily fee/pet. Designated rooms, no service, supervision. ⊠ ⊠ ⊟ ▣ ⓣ ⊠

CAA ▼▼▼ Johnston Canyon Resort CA
(403) 762-2971. **$119-$314, 3 day notice.** Hwy 1A T1L 1A9. 15 mi (24 km) nw on Hwy 1A (Bow Valley Pkwy). Ext corridors. **Pets:** Accepted.
ⓔ ⊠ ⊠ ⊟ ▣ ⓣ ⓐ ⓩ

▼▼▼ The Juniper H
(403) 762-2281. **$119-$339, 3 day notice.** 1 Juniper Way T1L 1E1. Trans-Canada Hwy 1, exit Mt. Norquay Rd, just n. Int corridors. **Pets:** Accepted. ⓔ ⊠ ⊠ ⊟ ▣ ⓣ

CAA ▼▼▼ Red Carpet Inn H
(403) 762-4184. **$79-$159.** 425 Banff Ave T1L 1B6. Between Beaver and Rabbit sts. Ext/int corridors. **Pets:** $10 daily fee/pet. Designated rooms, service with restrictions, supervision. ⊠ ⊠ ⊟ ▣

BROOKS

CAA ▼▼▼▼ Brooks Super 8 H
(403) 363-0080. **$120-$125, 5 day notice.** 115 Fifteenth Ave W T1R 1C4. Just s off Trans-Canada Hwy 1. Ext/int corridors. **Pets:** Accepted.
ⓔ ⊠ ⊠ ⊟ ▣ ⓣ ➤ ⊠

▼▼▼ Heritage Inn H
(403) 362-6666. **$105-$169.** 1217 2nd St W T1R 1P7. Trans-Canada Hwy 1, exit Hwy 873, 0.5 mi (0.8 km) s. Int corridors. **Pets:** $20 daily fee/room. Service with restrictions, supervision. ⊠ ⊠ ⊟ ▣ ⓣ

CAA ▼▼▼▼ Lakeview Inns & Suites H
(403) 362-7440. **$119-$179.** 1307 2nd St W T1R 1P7. Trans-Canada Hwy 1, exit Hwy 873, 0.5 mi (0.8 km) s. Int corridors. **Pets:** Accepted.
⊠ ⊠ ⊟ ▣ ➤ ⊠

CALGARY METROPOLITAN AREA

AIRDRIE

CAA ▼▼▼▼ Ramada Inn & Suites H
(403) 945-1288. **Call for rates.** 191 E Lake Crescent T4A 2H7. Hwy 2, exit E Airdrie. Int corridors. **Pets:** Accepted.
ⓔ ⊠ ⊠ ⓜ ⊟ ▣ ⓣ ➤ ⊠

▼▼ Super 8 Airdrie H
(403) 948-4188. **$109-$155.** 815 E Lake Blvd T4A 2G4. Hwy 2, exit E Airdrie, 0.5 mi (0.8 km) e on Hwy 587 E. Int corridors. **Pets:** Accepted.
⊠ ⊠ ⊟ ▣

CALGARY

▼▼ 5 Calgary Downtown Suites H
(403) 263-0520. **$89-$269.** 618 5th Ave SW T2P 0M7. Corner of 5th Ave SW and 5th St SW. Int corridors. **Pets:** Accepted.
ⓔ ⊠ ⊠ ⊟ ▣ ⓣ ➤ ⊠

CAA ▼▼▼ Best Western Port O'Call Hotel H
(403) 291-4600. **$129-$199.** 1935 McKnight Blvd NE T2E 6V4. 1.6 mi (2.5 km) ne of jct Hwy 2 (Deerfoot Tr); at 19th St NE. Int corridors. **Pets:** Large. $10 daily fee/pet. Designated rooms, service with restrictions. ⊠ ⊠ ⓜ ⊟ ▣ ⓣ ➤ ⊠

▼▼▼ Blackfoot Inn H
(403) 252-2253. **$169-$335.** 5940 Blackfoot Tr SE T2H 2B5. At 58th Ave SE; access to property from 58th Ave only. Int corridors. **Pets:** Other species. $30 daily fee/room. Service with restrictions, crate.
⊠ ⊠ ⓜ ⊟ ▣ ⓣ ➤ ⊠

CAA ▼▼▼ Calgary Marriott Hotel H
(403) 266-7331. **$209-$249.** 110 9th Ave SE T2G 5A6. Jct 9th Ave and Centre St; adjacent to Telus Convention Centre. Int corridors. **Pets:** Other species. Service with restrictions, crate.
ⓔ ⊠ ⊠ ⊟ ▣ ⓣ ➤

Calgary Westways Guest House 🅱🅱 ❖
(403) 229-1758. **$99-$180, 4 day notice.** 216 25th Ave SW T2S 0L1.
1.1 mi (1.7 km) s on Hwy 2A (MacLeod Tr S), then just w. Int corridors.
Pets: Other species. $8 daily fee/pet. ⓢⒶⓋⒺ ☒

Carriage House Inn 🅷
(403) 253-1101. **$149-$229.** 9030 MacLeod Tr S T2H 0M4. On Hwy 2A
(MacLeod Tr); corner of 90th Ave SW. Int corridors. **Pets:** Accepted.
ⓔⓒⓞ ⓢⒶⓋⒺ ☒ 📶 💻 🍴 ➿ ☒

Coast Plaza Hotel & Conference Centre 🅷
(403) 248-8888. **$129-$334.** 1316 33rd St NE T2A 6B6. Just s of jct 16th
Ave (Trans-Canada Hwy 1) and 36th St NE, just w on 12th Ave NE. Int
corridors. **Pets:** Small, other species. $200 deposit/room, $20 one-time
fee/pet. Designated rooms, service with restrictions, crate.
ⓔⓒⓞ ⒶⓈⓀ ☒ 📶 💻 🍴 ➿ ☒

Delta Bow Valley 🅷
(403) 266-1980. **$119-$399.** 209 4th Ave SE T2G 0C6. 1st St SE and
4th Ave SE. Int corridors. **Pets:** Small. $35 one-time fee/room. Designated
rooms, service with restrictions, supervision.
ⓔⓒⓞ ⓢⒶⓋⒺ ☒ 📶 📶 💻 🍴 ➿ ☒

Delta Calgary Airport 🅷
(403) 291-2600. **$149-$329.** 2001 Airport Rd NE T2E 6Z8. At Calgary
International Airport. Int corridors. **Pets:** Large, other species. $35 daily
fee/room. Service with restrictions, crate.
ⓔⓒⓞ ⒶⓈⓀ ☒ 📶 📶 💻 🍴 ➿

Delta Calgary South 🅷
(403) 278-5050. **$89-$369.** 135 Southland Dr SE T2J 5X5. On Hwy 2A
(MacLeod Tr); corner of Southland Dr. Int corridors. **Pets:** Other species.
$35 one-time fee/room. Designated rooms, service with restrictions, crate.
ⓔⓒⓞ ⒶⓈⓀ ☒ 📶 💻 🍴 ➿ ☒

Econo Lodge South 🅼
(403) 252-4401. **$89-$129.** 7505 MacLeod Tr SW T2H 0L8. Corner of
Hwy 2A (MacLeod Tr) and 75th Ave. Ext/int corridors. **Pets:** Accepted.
ⓢⒶⓋⒺ ☒ 📶 💻 ➿

Executive Royal Inn North Calgary 🅷
(403) 291-2003. **$130-$325.** 2828 23rd St NE T2E 8T4. Barlow Tr NE,
just w; at 27th Ave NE. Int corridors. **Pets:** Accepted.
ⓔⓒⓞ ⒶⓈⓀ ☒ 📶 💻 🍴 ☒

The Fairmont Palliser 🅷
(403) 262-1234. **$149-$449.** 133 9th Ave SW T2P 2M3. 9th Ave SW and
1st St SW. Int corridors. **Pets:** Accepted.
ⓔⓒⓞ ⒶⓈⓀ ☒ 📶 💻 🍴 ➿ ☒

Holiday Inn Calgary-MacLeod Trail South 🅷
(403) 287-2700. **$129-$159.** 4206 MacLeod Tr S T2G 2R7. Corner of
42nd Ave SW and MacLeod Tr S. Int corridors. **Pets:** $20 one-time fee/
pet. Designated rooms, service with restrictions, supervision.
ⓔⓒⓞ ⓢⒶⓋⒺ ☒ 📶 💻 🍴 ➿

**Holiday Inn Express Hotel & Suites Calgary
Downtown** 🅷
(403) 269-8262. **Call for rates.** 1020 8th Ave SW T2P 1J2. At 10th St
SW. Int corridors. **Pets:** Accepted. ☒ 📶 💻

**Holiday Inn Express Hotel & Suites
Calgary-South** 🅷
(403) 225-3000. **$129-$259, 3 day notice.** 12025 Lake Fraser Dr SE
(MacLeod Tr S) T2J 7G5. Hwy 2 (Deerfoot Tr), exit Anderson Rd W, just
s on MacLeod Tr, just e on Lake Fraser Gate, then 0.4 mi (0.7 km) n. Int
corridors. **Pets:** Medium. $3 daily fee/pet. Designated rooms, service with
restrictions, crate. ⒶⓈⓀ ☒ 📶 💻 ➿

Hotel Arts 🅷
(403) 266-4611. **$139-$319.** 119 12th Ave SW T2R 0G8. At 1st St SW;
centre. Int corridors. **Pets:** Accepted.
ⓢⒶⓋⒺ ☒ 📶 📶 💻 🍴 ➿

Lakeview Signature Inn 🅷
(403) 735-3306. **$139-$309.** 2622 39th Ave NE T1Y 7J9. Barlow Tr NE,
just e. Int corridors. **Pets:** Small, other species. $100 one-time fee/room.
Designated rooms, service with restrictions, crate.
ⓔⓒⓞ ⓢⒶⓋⒺ ☒ 📶 📶 💻 ➿ ☒

Radisson Hotel Calgary Airport 🅷
(403) 291-4666. **Call for rates.** 2120 16th Ave NE T2E 1L4. Just e of jct
16th Ave NE (Trans-Canada Hwy 1) and Hwy 2 (Deerfoot Tr). Int corridors. **Pets:** Accepted. ⓔⓒⓞ ☒ 📶 📶 💻 🍴 ➿

Sandman Hotel Downtown Calgary 🅷
(403) 237-8626. **$149-$218.** 888 7th Ave SW T2P 3J3. Corner of 7th
Ave SW and 8th St SW. Int corridors. **Pets:** Medium. $10 daily fee/room.
Designated rooms, service with restrictions, crate.
ⓔⓒⓞ ⒶⓈⓀ ☒ 📶 💻 🍴 ➿

Sandman Hotel Suites & Spa Calgary Airport 🅷
(403) 219-2475. **$129-$199.** 25 Hopewell Way NE T3J 4V7. Just n of jct
Barlow Tr and McKnight Blvd. Int corridors. **Pets:** $10 daily fee/room.
Service with restrictions, crate. ⓔⓒⓞ ⒶⓈⓀ ☒ 📶 📶 💻 🍴 ➿

Service Plus Inn & Suites Calgary 🅷
(403) 256-5352. **$159.** 3503 114th Ave SE T2Z 3X2. South end of Bar-
low Tr, just w. Int corridors. **Pets:** Medium. Designated rooms, service
with restrictions, supervision. ⓢⒶⓋⒺ ☒ 📶 💻 ➿ ☒

Sheraton Cavalier Hotel 🅷 ❖
(403) 291-0107. **Call for rates.** 2620 32nd Ave NE T1Y 6B8. Barlow Tr
at 32nd Ave NE. Int corridors. **Pets:** Service with restrictions, supervision.
ⓔⓒⓞ ⓢⒶⓋⒺ ☒ 💻 ➿ ☒

**Sheraton Suites Calgary Eau
Claire** 🅷 ❖
(403) 266-7200. **Call for rates.** 255 Barclay Parade SW T2P 5C2. At
3rd St SW and 2nd Ave SW. Int corridors. **Pets:** Medium, dogs only. Designated rooms, service with restrictions, supervision.
ⓔⓒⓞ ⓢⒶⓋⒺ ☒ 📶 💻 🍴 ➿ ☒

Travelodge Calgary MacLeod Trail 🅷 ❖
(403) 253-7070. **$119-$179.** 9206 MacLeod Tr S T2J 0P5. On MacLeod
Tr; just s of 90th Ave SW. Int corridors. **Pets:** Other species. $25 one-
time fee/room. Service with restrictions, supervision.
ⓔⓒⓞ ⓢⒶⓋⒺ ☒ 📶 💻 🍴 ➿

Travelodge Calgary University 🅷
(403) 289-6600. **$98-$199.** 2227 Banff Tr NW T2M 4L2. 16th Ave NW
(Trans-Canada Hwy 1) and Banff Tr NW. Int corridors. **Pets:** Other species. $10 daily fee/pet, $10 one-time fee/pet. Designated rooms, service
with restrictions, supervision. ⓔⓒⓞ ⓢⒶⓋⒺ ☒ 📶 📶 💻 ➿

Travelodge Hotel Calgary Airport 🅷
(403) 291-1260. **$119-$179.** 2750 Sunridge Blvd NE T1Y 3C2. Just se of
jct 32nd Ave NE and Barlow Tr NE. Int corridors. **Pets:** Accepted.
ⓔⓒⓞ ⓢⒶⓋⒺ ☒ 📶 💻 🍴 ➿

The Westin Calgary 🅷 🐾
(403) 266-1611. **$139-$489.** 320 4th Ave SW T2P 2S6. Corner of 4th
Ave SW and 3rd St. Int corridors. **Pets:** Service with restrictions, supervision. ⓢⒶⓋⒺ ☒ 📶 💻 🍴 ➿ ☒

Wingate by Wyndham Calgary 🅷 ❖
(403) 514-0099. **$149-$259, 4 day notice.** 400 Midpark Way SE T2X
3S4. Hwy 2A (MacLeod Tr), 0.3 mi (0.5 km) e on Sun Valley Blvd SE,
just n on Midpark Blvd SE, then just s. Int corridors. **Pets:** Large. $25
daily fee/room. Service with restrictions, supervision.
ⓔⓒⓞ ⒶⓈⓀ ☒ 📶 📶 💻 ➿ ☒

COCHRANE

Best Western Harvest Country Inn 🅷
(403) 932-1410. **$90-$160.** 11 West Side Dr T4C 1M1. Jct Hwy 1A, 0.3
mi (0.5 km) s on Hwy 22; just e on Quigley Dr, then just s. Ext/int corridors. **Pets:** Accepted. ⓢⒶⓋⒺ ☒ 📶 💻

◆◆ **Days Inn & Suites Cochrane** ⛨

(403) 932-5588. **$99-$169.** 5 West Side Dr T4C 1M1. Jct Hwy 1A, 0.3 mi (0.5 km) s on Hwy 22, just e on Quigley Dr, then just s. Int corridors. **Pets:** Accepted. 🔲 🔲 🔲 🔲 🔲 🔲

◆◆◆ **Super 8-Cochrane** ⛨

(403) 932-6355. **$143-$181.** 10 West Side Dr T4C 1M1. Jct Hwy 1A, 0.3 mi (0.5 km) s on Hwy 22, just e on Quigley Dr, then just s. Int corridors. **Pets:** Medium. $15 daily fee/pet. Designated rooms, service with restrictions, supervision. 🔲 🔲 🔲 🔲 🔲 🔲

OKOTOKS

◉◉ ◆◆◆ **Lakeview Inns & Suites** ⛨ ❖

(403) 938-7400. **$129-$149, 14 day notice.** 22 Southridge Dr T1S 1N1. Hwy 2, exit 2A, 2.5 mi (4 km) s to Southridge Dr. Int corridors. **Pets:** Other species. $10 daily fee/pet. Designated rooms, service with restrictions, supervision. 🔲 🔲 🔲 🔲 🔲

STRATHMORE

◉◉ ◆◆◆ **Best Western Strathmore Inn** ⛨

(403) 934-5777. **$110-$131.** 550 Hwy 1 T1P 1M6. Trans-Canada Hwy 1, jct SR 817; centre. Int corridors. **Pets:** Medium. $10 one-time fee/room. Designated rooms, service with restrictions. 🔲 🔲 🔲 🔲 🔲

◆◆◆ **Holiday Inn Express Hotel & Suites** ⛨ ❖

(403) 934-1134. **$135-$150.** 400 Ranch Market T1P 0B2. Trans-Canada Hwy 1, just n at Lakeside Blvd (Centre St). Int corridors. **Pets:** $15 one-time fee/pet. Designated rooms, service with restrictions, crate. 🔲 🔲 🔲 🔲 🔲 🔲 🔲

◆◆◆ **Travelodge Strathmore** ⛨ ❖

(403) 901-0000. **$119-$144.** 350 Ridge Rd T1P 1B5. Just n of Trans-Canada Hwy 1 at Ridge Rd. Int corridors. **Pets:** Medium, other species. $15 daily fee/room. Designated rooms, service with restrictions, crate. 🔲 🔲 🔲 🔲 🔲 🔲

END METROPOLITAN AREA

CAMROSE

◆◆ **Norsemen Inn** ⛨

(780) 672-9171. **$99-$129.** 6505 48th Ave T4V 3K3. Hwy 13 (48th Ave) at 65th St; west end of town. Int corridors. **Pets:** Accepted. 🔲 🔲 🔲 🔲 🔲

CANMORE

◉◉ ◆◆◆ **Banff Boundary Lodge** 🏢

(403) 678-9555. **$89-$239, 3 day notice.** 1000 Harvie Heights Rd T1W 2W2. Trans-Canada Hwy 1, exit 86, just n. Ext corridors. **Pets:** Other species. $15 daily fee/pet. No service. 🔲 🔲 🔲 🔲 🔲

◉◉ ◆◆◆◆ **Best Western Pocaterra Inn** ⛨ ❖

(403) 678-4334. **$120-$210.** 1725 Mountain Ave T1W 2W1. Trans-Canada Hwy 1, exit 86, 1.3 mi (2.1 km) e. Int corridors. **Pets:** $15 one-time fee/room. Designated rooms, service with restrictions, supervision. 🔲 🔲 🔲 🔲 🔲 🔲 🔲

◉◉ ◆◆◆ **Canadian Rockies Chalets** 🏢

(403) 678-3799. **$79-$275, 3 day notice.** 1206 Bow Valley Tr T1W 1N6. Trans-Canada Hwy 1, exit 89, 0.9 mi (1.5 km) se. Ext corridors. **Pets:** Other species. $15 daily fee/pet. No service. 🔲 🔲 🔲 🔲 🔲

◆◆◆ **Canmore Inn & Suites** ⛨

(403) 609-4656. **$79-$262.** 1402 Bow Valley Tr T1W 1N5. Trans-Canada Hwy 1, exit 89, 1 mi (1.7 km) se. Int corridors. **Pets:** Other species. $15 daily fee/pet. Designated rooms, service with restrictions. 🔲 🔲 🔲 🔲 🔲 🔲

◉◉ ◆◆◆ **Econo Lodge Canmore** ⛨

(403) 678-5488. **$90-$150.** 1602 2nd Ave T1W 1M8. Trans-Canada Hwy 1, exit 89, 1.3 mi (2.1 km) e. Int corridors. **Pets:** Accepted. 🔲 🔲 🔲 🔲 🔲

◆◆ **The Lodges at Canmore** 🏢 ❖

(403) 678-9350. **$132-$385.** 107 Montane Rd T1W 3J2. Trans-Canada Hwy 1, exit 86, 0.5 mi (0.8 km) s. Int corridors. **Pets:** Medium, other species. $20 daily fee/pet. Designated rooms, service with restrictions, crate. 🔲 🔲 🔲 🔲 🔲

◆◆◆◆ **Mystic Springs Chalets & Hot Pools** 🏢 ❖

(403) 609-0333. **$180-$380.** 140 Kananaskis Way T1W 2X2. Trans-Canada Hwy 1, exit 89, 1.1 mi (1.8 km) s. Ext corridors. **Pets:** Medium. $20 daily fee/room. Designated rooms, service with restrictions, crate. 🔲 🔲 🔲 🔲 🔲 🔲

◉◉ ◆◆◆ **Radisson Hotel & Conference Centre** ⛨ ❖

(403) 678-3625. **Call for rates.** 511 Bow Valley Tr T1W 1N7. Trans-Canada Hwy 1, exit 89, 1.4 mi (0.8 km) s. Ext/int corridors. **Pets:** $50 one-time fee/room. Designated rooms, service with restrictions, supervision. 🔲 🔲 🔲 🔲 🔲 🔲 🔲 🔲 🔲

◉◉ ◆◆◆ **Rocky Mountain Ski Lodge** 🏢

(403) 678-5445. **$119-$209.** 1711 Bow Valley Tr T1W 2T8. Trans-Canada Hwy 1, exit 86, 0.5 mi (0.8 km) s. Ext corridors. **Pets:** $10 daily fee/room. Designated rooms, service with restrictions, supervision. 🔲 🔲 🔲 🔲 🔲

◉◉ ◆◆◆ **Rundle Mountain Lodge** 🏢 ❖

(403) 678-5322. **$75-$210, 7 day notice.** 1723 Bow Valley Tr T1W 1L7. Trans-Canada Hwy 1, exit 86, 0.5 mi (0.8 km) s. Ext corridors. **Pets:** Other species. $20 daily fee/pet. Designated rooms, service with restrictions, supervision. 🔲 🔲 🔲 🔲 🔲

◆◆◆ **Windtower Lodge & Suites** 🏢 ❖

(403) 609-6600. **$149-$429, 3 day notice.** 160 Kananaskis Way T1W 3E2. Trans-Canada Hwy 1, exit 89, 1.1 mi (1.8 km) s. Int corridors. **Pets:** $25 daily fee/pet. Designated rooms, service with restrictions, supervision. 🔲 🔲 🔲 🔲 🔲 🔲

CLAIRMONT

◉◉ ◆◆◆◆ **Ramada Inn & Suites** ⛨

(780) 814-7448. **$149-$349.** 7201 99th St T0H 0W0. Jct Hwy 43 and 2, 0.7 mi (0.4 km) n, then just e, 0.7 mi (0.4 km) s. Int corridors. **Pets:** Accepted. 🔲 🔲 🔲 🔲 🔲

CLARESHOLM

◆◆ **Bluebird Motel** 🏢

(403) 625-3395. **$84-$94.** 5505 1st St W T0L 0T0. 0.3 mi (0.5 km) n on Hwy 2. Ext corridors. **Pets:** Other species. $10 daily fee/room. Designated rooms, service with restrictions, supervision. 🔲 🔲 🔲

◆◆ **Motel 6 Claresholm** ⛨

(403) 625-4646. **Call for rates.** 11 Alberta Rd (Hwy 2) T0L 0T0. North end of town. Int corridors. **Pets:** Other species. Service with restrictions, supervision. 🔲 🔲 🔲

DRAYTON VALLEY

◆◆◆ **Drayton Valley Ramada Inn** ⛨

(780) 514-7861. **$124-$133.** 2051 50th St T7A 1S5. Just n on Hwy 39; south end of town. Ext/int corridors. **Pets:** Accepted. 🔲 🔲 🔲 🔲 🔲 🔲

(CAA) ▼▼▼ **Lakeview Inns & Suites** H

(780) 542-3200. **$113-$150.** 4302 50th St T7A 1M4. Hwy 22, exit Drayton Valley, 1.5 mi (2.4 km) n; east end of town. Int corridors. **Pets:** Accepted. [SAVE] [X] [🦽] [🛏] [🍴] [X]

DRUMHELLER

(CAA) ▼▼▼ **Best Western Jurassic Inn** H

(403) 823-7700. **$126-$180.** 1103 Hwy 9 S T0J 0Y0. Hwy 9, southeast access to town. Ext/int corridors. **Pets:** Accepted.

[ECO] [SAVE] [X] [🦽] [🛏] [🍴] [X]

(CAA) ▼▼▼ **Inn and Spa at Heartwood** H

(403) 823-6495. **$99-$280, 3 day notice.** 320 N Railway Ave E T0J 0Y4. Downtown. Ext/int corridors. **Pets:** Other species. $25 one-time fee/pet. Designated rooms, service with restrictions, supervision.

[SAVE] [X] [🦽] [🛏]

EDMONTON METROPOLITAN AREA

EDMONTON

(CAA) ▼▼▼ **Best Western Cedar Park Inn** H

(780) 434-7411. **$99-$189.** 5116 Gateway Blvd T6H 2H4. Hwy 2 (Gateway Blvd) at 51st Ave. Int corridors. **Pets:** Accepted.

[SAVE] [X] [&M] [🦽] [🛏] [🍴] [🏊]

(CAA) ▼▼▼ **Best Western Westwood Inn** H

(780) 483-7770. **$109-$189.** 18035 Stony Plain Rd T5S 1B2. Hwy 16A (Stony Plain Rd) at 180th St. Int corridors. **Pets:** Small. $15 daily fee/pet. Designated rooms, service with restrictions, crate.

[SAVE] [X] [🦽] [🛏] [🍴] [🏊]

▼▼▼ **Coast Edmonton House** [CO] ❖

(780) 420-4000. **Call for rates.** 10205 100th Ave T5J 4B5. Just se of jct 102nd St and 100th Ave. Int corridors. **Pets:** Other species. $10 daily fee/pet. Designated rooms, service with crate.

[ECO] [X] [🦽] [🛏] [🍴] [🏊]

(CAA) ▼▼▼ **Comfort Inn West** H

(780) 484-4415. **$99-$159.** 17610 100th Ave T5S 1S9. At 176th St. Int corridors. **Pets:** Medium. $10 daily fee/pet. Service with restrictions, supervision. [ECO] [SAVE] [X] [&M] [🦽] [🛏] [🍴]

(CAA) ▼▼▼ **Continental Inn** H

(780) 484-7751. **$110-$145, 6 day notice.** 16625 Stony Plain Rd T5P 4A8. On Hwy 16A (Stony Plain Rd) at 166th St. Int corridors. **Pets:** Small. $20 deposit/room. Designated rooms, supervision.

[SAVE] [X] [🦽] [🛏] [🍴]

▼▼▼ **Courtyard by Marriott Edmonton** H

(780) 423-9999. **$206-$252.** 1 Thornton Ct T5J 2E7. Just off Jasper Ave; between 99th and 97th sts. Int corridors. **Pets:** Accepted.

[X] [&M] [🦽] [🛏]

▼▼▼ **Delta Edmonton Centre Suite Hotel** H

(780) 429-3900. **$99-$379.** 10222 102nd St T5J 4C5. At 102nd St at 103rd Ave. Int corridors. **Pets:** Medium. $35 one-time fee/room. Crate.

[ECO] [ASK] [X] [&M] [🦽] [🛏] [🍴] [X]

▼▼▼ **Delta Edmonton South Hotel and Conference Centre** H ❖

(780) 434-6415. **Call for rates.** 4404 Gateway Blvd T6H 5C2. Jct Calgary Tr (Hwy 2) and Whitemud Dr. Int corridors. **Pets:** Other species. $35 one-time fee/room. Supervision. [ECO] [X] [🦽] [🛏] [🍴] [🏊]

▼▼▼ **Executive Royal Inn West Edmonton** H

(780) 484-6000. **$120.** 10010 178th St T5S 1T3. Corner of 178th St and 100th Ave. Int corridors. **Pets:** $25 daily fee/room. Designated rooms, service with restrictions, supervision. [ECO] [ASK] [X] [🦽] [🛏] [🍴]

(CAA) ▼▼▼▼ **The Fairmont Hotel Macdonald** H

(780) 424-5181. **Call for rates.** 10065 100th St T5J 0N6. Just s of Jasper Ave. Int corridors. **Pets:** Accepted.

[ECO] [SAVE] [X] [🦽] [🛏] [🍴] [🏊] [X]

▼▼▼ **Ramada Inn & Suites** H

(403) 823-2028. **Call for rates.** 680 2nd St SE T0J 0Y0. Off Hwy 9. Ext/int corridors. **Pets:** Accepted. [ECO] [X] [🦽] [🛏] [🏊] [X]

▼▼ **Super 8** H

(403) 823-8887. **$139-$250.** 600-680 2nd St SE T0J 0Y0. Off Hwy 9. Ext/int corridors. **Pets:** Accepted. [ECO] [ASK] [X] [🦽] [🛏] [🏊] [X]

(CAA) ▼▼▼ **Four Points by Sheraton Edmonton South** H

(780) 465-7931. **Call for rates.** 7230 Argyll Rd T6C 4A6. Hwy 2 (Gateway Blvd), 2.3 mi (3.7 km) e at 63rd Ave (which becomes Argyll Rd); at 75th St. Int corridors. **Pets:** Small. $10 daily fee/pet. Designated rooms, service with restrictions, supervision.

[SAVE] [X] [&M] [🦽] [🛏] [🍴] [🏊]

(CAA) ▼▼▼ **Holiday Inn Express Edmonton-Downtown** H

(780) 423-2450. **$149-$189.** 10010 104th St T5J 0Z1. Corner of 100th Ave; centre. Int corridors. **Pets:** Small. $25 one-time fee/pet. Designated rooms, service with restrictions, supervision.

[ECO] [SAVE] [X] [&M] [🦽] [🛏] [🏊] [X]

(CAA) ▼▼▼ **Mayfield Inn & Suites at West Edmonton** H

(780) 484-0821. **$150-$225.** 16615 109th Ave T5P 4K8. 1 mi (1.6 km) n of jct Hwy 2 (170th St) and 16A (Stony Plain Rd). Int corridors. **Pets:** Accepted. [ECO] [SAVE] [X] [🦽] [🛏] [🏊] [X]

▼▼ **Metterra Hotel on Whyte** H

(780) 465-8150. **Call for rates.** 10454 82nd Ave (Whyte Ave) T6E 4Z7. Just e of 105th St. Int corridors. **Pets:** Accepted.

[ECO] [X] [&M] [🦽] [🛏]

▼▼ **Quality Inn West Harvest** H ❖

(780) 484-8000. **$105-$199.** 17803 Stony Plain Rd NW T5S 1B4. Hwy 16A (Stony Plain Rd) at 178th St. Int corridors. **Pets:** Medium. $250 deposit/room, $15 daily fee/pet. Designated rooms, service with restrictions, supervision. [ASK] [X] [🦽] [🛏] [🍴]

(CAA) ▼▼▼ **Radisson Hotel Edmonton South** H

(780) 437-6010. **$165-$200.** 4440 Gateway Blvd NW T6H 5C2. Between Whitemud Dr and 45th Ave. Int corridors. **Pets:** Medium, other species. $35 daily fee/room. Designated rooms, service with restrictions, crate.

[ECO] [SAVE] [X] [🦽] [🛏] [🍴] [X]

▼▼ **Rosslyn Inn & Suites** H ❖

(780) 476-6241. **$117-$159.** 13620 97th St T5E 4E2. Hwy 16 (Yellowhead Tr), exit 97th St, 1 mi (1.6 km) n. Int corridors. **Pets:** Medium. $10 one-time fee/pet. Service with restrictions, supervision.

[ECO] [ASK] [X] [🦽] [🛏] [🍴]

(CAA) ▼▼▼ **Sawridge Inn Edmonton South** H

(780) 438-1222. **$129-$159, 14 day notice.** 4235 Gateway Blvd T6J 5H2. Just s of Whitemud Dr. Int corridors. **Pets:** Accepted.

[SAVE] [X] [🦽] [🛏] [🍴] [X]

▼▼ **Super 8 Edmonton South** H

(780) 433-8688. **Call for rates.** 3610 Gateway Blvd T6J 7H8. Jct 36th Ave. Int corridors. **Pets:** Accepted. [X] [&M] [🦽] [🛏] [🏊]

▼▼▼▼ The Sutton Place Hotel Edmonton 🅷
(780) 428-7111. **$235-$395.** 10235 101st St T5J 3E9. 102nd Ave at
101st St. Int corridors. **Pets:** Small. $150 deposit/room, $35 one-time
fee/room. Service with restrictions, supervision.

🄴🄲🄾 🄰🅂🄺 ✖ 🎒 💻 🍴 ⊇ 🐾

🄒🄐 ▼▼▼ Travelodge Edmonton East 🅷
(780) 474-0456. **$89-$139.** 3414 118th Ave T5W 0Z4. 5 mi (8 km) e of
Capilano Dr, 0.6 mi (1 km) s from W Hwy 16 (Yellowhead Tr), exit Victoria Tr. Int corridors. **Pets:** Medium, dogs only. $100 deposit/room, $25
one-time fee/room. Designated rooms, service with restrictions, supervision. 🅂🄰🅅🄴 ✖ 🎒 💻 🍴

▼▼▼ Travelodge Edmonton South 🅷
(780) 436-9770. **$109-$159.** 10320 45th Ave S T6H 5K3. Jct Calgary Tr
(Hwy 2) and 45th Ave, just n of Whitemud Dr. Int corridors.
Pets: Accepted. 🄴🄲🄾 🄰🅂🄺 ✖ 🎒 💻 ⊇

🄒🄐 ▼▼▼ Travelodge Edmonton West 🅷 🐾
(780) 483-6031. **$109-$159.** 18320 Stony Plain Rd T5S 1A7. Hwy 16A
(Stony Plain Rd) at 184th St. Int corridors. **Pets:** $50 deposit/room. Desig-
nated rooms, service with restrictions, supervision.

🄴🄲🄾 🅂🄰🅅🄴 ✖ 🎒 💻 🍴 ⊇ 🐾

▼▼▼▼ Varscona Hotel on Whyte 🅷 🐾
(780) 434-6111. **$160-$350.** 8208 106th St T6E 6R9. Corner of 82nd Ave
(Whyte Ave) and 106th St. Int corridors. **Pets:** Medium, dogs only. $20
daily fee/room. Designated rooms, service with restrictions, supervision.

🄴🄲🄾 🄰🅂🄺 ✖ 🎒 💻 🍴

▼▼▼ West Edmonton Mall Inn 🅷
(780) 444-9378. **$149.** 17504 90th Ave T5T 6L6. Whitemud Dr, exit 170th
St N, just w. Int corridors. **Pets:** Accepted. 🄰🅂🄺 ✖ 🄼 🎒 💻

🄒🄐 ▼▼▼▼ The Westin Edmonton 🅷 🐾
(780) 426-3636. **$119-$499.** 10135 100th St T5J 0N7. 101st Ave at
100th St. Int corridors. **Pets:** Large. Service with restrictions, supervision.

🄴🄲🄾 🅂🄰🅅🄴 ✖ 💻 🍴 ⊇ 🐾

▼▼▼▼ Wingate Inn Edmonton West 🅷
(780) 443-1000. **$139-$160.** 18220 100th Ave T5S 2V2. From Anthony
Henday Dr, 0.9 mi (1.5 km) e at 182nd St. Int corridors. **Pets:** Accepted.

🄰🅂🄺 ✖ 🎒 💻 ⊇ 🐾

FORT SASKATCHEWAN

🄒🄐 ▼▼▼ Lakeview Inns & Suites 🅷
(780) 998-7888. **$125-$179.** 10115 88th Ave T8L 2T1. Just w of Hwy
15/21 and 101st St. Int corridors. **Pets:** Accepted.

🄴🄲🄾 🅂🄰🅅🄴 ✖ 🎒 💻 🍴

SHERWOOD PARK

🄒🄐 ▼▼▼ Franklin's Inn 🅷
(780) 467-1234. **$129-$169, 3 day notice.** 2016 Sherwood Dr T8A 3X3.
At Granada Blvd. Int corridors. **Pets:** Large, other species. $10 daily fee/
room. Designated rooms, service with restrictions, supervision.

🅂🄰🅅🄴 ✖ 🎒 💻 🍴

▼▼▼ Ramada Limited-Edmonton East/Sherwood Park 🅷
(780) 467-6727. **Call for rates.** 30 Broadway Blvd T8H 2A2. Hwy 16,
exit Broadmoor Blvd, 1.2 mi (2 km) s. Int corridors. **Pets:** Accepted.

✖ 🎒 💻

▼▼▼ Roadking Inns 🅷
(780) 464-1000. **Call for rates.** 26 Strathmoor Dr T8H 2B6. Hwy 16, exit
Broadmoor Blvd, just sw. Int corridors. **Pets:** Accepted.

✖ 🎒 💻 🍴

STONY PLAIN

▼▼ Motel 6 Stony Plain 🅷
(780) 968-5123. **$75-$91.** 66 Boulder Blvd T7Z 1V7. Just off Hwy 16A
(Township Rd 530). Int corridors. **Pets:** Other species. Service with
restrictions, supervision. 🄰🅂🄺 ✖ 🎒

▼▼ Ramada Inn & Suites 🅷
(780) 963-0222. **$90-$180.** 3301 43rd Ave T7Z 1L1. Hwy 16A (Township
Rd 530), just s on S Park Dr, then just e. Ext/int corridors.
Pets: Accepted. 🄰🅂🄺 ✖ 🎒 💻 🍴 ⊇

END METROPOLITAN AREA

EDSON

🄒🄐 ▼▼▼▼ Best Western High Road Inn 🅷
(780) 712-2378. **$109-$129.** 300 52nd St T7E 1V8. On 2nd Ave; centre.
Int corridors. **Pets:** Accepted. 🅂🄰🅅🄴 ✖ 🎒 💻 🍴 ⊇ 🐾

🄒🄐 ▼▼▼ Guest House Inn & Suites 🄼
(780) 723-4486. **$101-$124.** 4411 4th Ave T7E 1B8. 0.6 mi (1 km) e on
Hwy 16. Ext/int corridors. **Pets:** Medium. Service with restrictions, supervision. 🅂🄰🅅🄴 ✖ 🎒 💻 🍴 🐾

🄒🄐 ▼▼▼ Lakeview Inns & Suites 🅷
(780) 723-2500. **$120.** 4300 2nd Ave T7E 1B8. 0.6 mi (1.1 km) e on
Hwy 16. Int corridors. **Pets:** Accepted. 🅂🄰🅅🄴 ✖ 🎒 💻

FORT MACLEOD

🄒🄐 ▼▼ Sunset Motel 🄼
(403) 553-4448. **$72-$80.** 104 Hwy 3 W T0L 0Z0. 0.6 mi (1 km) w on
Hwy 2 and 3. Ext corridors. **Pets:** Other species. Service with restrictions,
supervision. 🅂🄰🅅🄴 ✖ 🎒

FORT MCMURRAY

▼▼▼▼ Clearwater Suite Hotel 🅷
(780) 799-7676. **Call for rates.** 4 Haineault St T9H 1L6. Hwy 63 (Saki-
tawaw Tr), just n on Hardin St, just e on Franklin Ave, then just s. Int
corridors. **Pets:** Accepted. ✖ 🎒 💻 🐾

GRANDE CACHE

🄒🄐 ▼▼▼▼ Best Western Grande Mountain Getaways &
Hotel 🅷
(780) 827-3303. **$140-$190.** 9901 100th St T0E 0Y0. Hwy 40 (100th St);
south end of town. Int corridors. **Pets:** Small, dogs only. $10 daily fee/pet.
Designated rooms, service with restrictions, supervision.

🅂🄰🅅🄴 ✖ 🄼 🎒 💻 🍴 🐾

GRANDE PRAIRIE

🄒🄐 ▼▼▼▼ Best Western Grande Prairie Hotel &
Suites 🅷 🐾
(780) 402-2378. **$130-$160.** 10745 117th Ave T8V 7N6. Corner of Hwy
43 (100th Ave) and 117th Ave. Int corridors. **Pets:** $25 one-time fee/room.
Service with restrictions, supervision.

🄴🄲🄾 🅂🄰🅅🄴 ✖ 🎒 💻 🍴 ⊇

▼▼ Motel 6 Grande Prairie 🅷
(780) 830-7744. **Call for rates.** 15402 101st St T8V 0P7. Jct Hwy 2 and
43 (100th Ave), just s. Int corridors. **Pets:** Other species. Service with
restrictions, supervision. ✖ 🄼 🎒 💻

▼▼▼ Podollan Inn & Spa 🅷
(780) 830-2000. **$149-$199.** 10612 99th Ave T8V 8E8. Jct Hwy 43
(100th Ave) and 40 (108th St), just e. Int corridors. **Pets:** Accepted.

✖ 🎒 💻 🍴

ⒸⒶ ▼▼▼ **Pomeroy Inn & Suites, Grande Prairie** 🄷
(780) 831-2999. **$150-$160.** 11710 102nd St T8V 7S7. 102nd St at
117th Ave. Int corridors. **Pets:** Accepted. 🆂🅰🆅🅴 ⊠ 🛅 🖵 🛏 🔁 ⊠

ⒸⒶ ▼▼▼ **Quality Hotel & Conference Centre Grande**
Prairie 🄷
(780) 539-6000. **$90-$135.** 11201 100th Ave T8V 5M6. 1.8 mi (2.9 km) w
on Hwy 2. Int corridors. **Pets:** Accepted. 🄴🄲🄾 🆂🅰🆅🅴 ⊠ 🛅 🖵 🍴

▼▼▼ **Service Plus Inns and Suites** 🄷 🐾
(780) 538-3900. **$159-$300.** 10810 107A Ave T8V 7A9. 1.4 mi (2.2 km)
w on Hwy 2, just n. Int corridors. **Pets:** Medium. $10 one-time fee/pet.
Designated rooms, no service, supervision. ⊠ 🛅 🖵 🔁 ⊠

▼▼ **Stanford Inn** 🄷 🐾
(780) 539-5678. **$99-$120.** 11401 100th Ave T8V 5M6. 1.8 mi (2.8 km) w
on Hwy 2. Ext/int corridors. **Pets:** Other species. $8 daily fee/pet. No
service, crate. 🄰🅂🄺 ⊠ 🛅 🖵 🍴

▼▼ **Stonebridge Hotel** 🄷
(780) 539-5561. **Call for rates.** 12102 100th St T8V 5P1. 100th St at
121st Ave. Int corridors. **Pets:** Accepted. ⊠ 🛅 🖵 🍴

▼▼ **Super 8** 🄷
(780) 532-8288. **Call for rates.** 10050 116th Ave T8V 4K5. 102nd St at
117th Ave. Int corridors. **Pets:** Accepted. 🄴🄲🄾 ⊠ 🛅 🖵 🔁 ⊠

GRIMSHAW
▼▼▼ **Pomeroy Inn & Suites** 🄷
(780) 332-2000. **Call for rates.** 4311 51st St T0H 1W0. Hwy 2, south
end of town. Int corridors. **Pets:** Accepted. ⊠ 🛅 🖵 🔁 ⊠

HANNA
▼▼ **Super 8 Hanna** 🄷
(403) 854-2400. **$130-$140.** 113 Palliser Tr T0J 1P0. Hwy 9, just n. Ext/
int corridors. **Pets:** Accepted. 🄴🄲🄾 🄰🅂🄺 ⊠ 🛅 🖵 🔁

HIGH LEVEL
▼▼ **Super 8 High Level** 🄷
(780) 841-3448. **Call for rates.** 9502 114th Ave T0H 1Z0. Hwy 35, just
se, south end of town. Ext/int corridors. **Pets:** Accepted.
⊠ 🗒 🛅 🖵 🔁 ⊠

HIGH PRAIRIE
▼▼▼ **Pomeroy Inn & Suites High Prairie** 🄷 🐾
(780) 523-2398. **$149-$169.** 3905 51st Ave T0G 1E0. Hwy 2, just n; east
end of town. Ext/int corridors. **Pets:** $25 daily fee/room. Service with
restrictions, supervision. 🄰🅂🄺 ⊠ 🛅 🖵 🍴 🔁 ⊠

HIGH RIVER
▼▼ **Heritage Inn** 🄷
(403) 652-3834. **$124-$249.** 1104 11th Ave SE T1V 1M4. Trans-Canada
Hwy 2, exit 23, 0.5 mi (0.8 km) w of Hwy 2. Int corridors. **Pets:** Accepted.
🄰🅂🄺 ⊠ 🛅 🖵 🍴 🔁

▼▼▼ **Super 8** 🄷
(403) 652-4448. **Call for rates.** 1601 13th Ave SE T1V 2B1. Trans-
Canada Hwy 2, exit High River, just w. Int corridors. **Pets:** $15 daily fee/
pet. Designated rooms, service with restrictions, supervision.
⊠ 🛅 🖵 🔁 ⊠

HINTON
ⒸⒶ ▼▼▼ **Best Western White Wolf Inn** 🄷
(780) 865-7777. **Call for rates.** 828 Carmichael Ln T7V 1T1. At west
end of town; just off Hwy 16. Ext corridors. **Pets:** Accepted.
🆂🅰🆅🅴 ⊠ 🛅 🖵

ⒸⒶ ▼▼▼ **Lakeview Inns & Suites** 🄷 🐾
(780) 865-2575. **$120-$140.** 500 Smith St T7V 2A1. 1.1 mi (1.7 km) e
on Hwy 16. Ext/int corridors. **Pets:** $25 daily fee/room. Service with
restrictions, crate. 🄴🄲🄾 🆂🅰🆅🅴 ⊠ 🛅 🖵

▼▼ **Super 8** 🄷
(780) 817-2228. **Call for rates.** 284 Smith St T7V 2A1. 1 mi (1.6 km) e
on Hwy 16. Int corridors. **Pets:** Accepted. ⊠ 🛅 🖵 🔁

JASPER
ⒸⒶ ▼▼▼ **Amethyst Lodge** 🄷 🐾
(780) 852-3394. **$85-$285.** 200 Connaught Dr T0E 1E0. 0.3 mi (0.5 km)
e. Ext/int corridors. **Pets:** Other species. $10 daily fee/room. Designated
rooms, service with restrictions, crate. 🄴🄲🄾 🆂🅰🆅🅴 ⊠ 🛅 🖵 🍴

ⒸⒶ ▼▼▼▼ **Best Western Jasper Inn & Suites** 🄷
(780) 852-4461. **$110-$246, 3 day notice.** 98 Geikie St T0E 1E0. Corner of Geikie and Bonhomme sts. Ext/int corridors. **Pets:** Accepted.
🆂🅰🆅🅴 ⊠ 🛅 🖵 🍴 🔁 ⊠ 🄰🄺

ⒸⒶ ▼▼▼▼ **The Coast Pyramid Lake Resort** 🄷
(780) 852-4900. **$161-$368, 3 day notice.** Pyramid Lake Rd T0E 1E0.
Jct Connaught Dr and Cedar St, 3.8 mi (6 km) nw via Pyramid Lake Rd.
Ext corridors. **Pets:** $25 one-time fee/pet. Service with restrictions, crate.
🄴🄲🄾 🆂🅰🆅🅴 ⊠ 🛅 🖵 🍴 ⊠ 🄰🄺

ⒸⒶ ▼▼▼▼ **The Fairmont Jasper Park Lodge** 🄷
(780) 852-3301. **$229-$499, 3 day notice.** Lodge Rd T0E 1E0. 3 mi
(4.8 km) ne via Hwy 16; 2 mi (3.2 km) se off highway via Maligne Rd,
follow signs. Ext corridors. **Pets:** Accepted.
🄴🄲🄾 🆂🅰🆅🅴 ⊠ 🗒 🛅 🖵 🍴 🔁 ⊠ 🄰🄺

ⒸⒶ ▼▼▼▼ **Lobstick Lodge** 🄷 🐾
(780) 852-4431. **$99-$255.** 94 Geikie St T0E 1E0. Corner of Geikie and
Juniper sts. Int corridors. **Pets:** Other species. $10 daily fee/room. Desig-
nated rooms, service with restrictions, supervision.
🄴🄲🄾 🆂🅰🆅🅴 ⊠ 🛅 🖵 🍴 🔁 🄰🄺

▼▼ **Maligne Lodge** Ⓜ
(780) 852-3143. **$99-$400, 3 day notice.** 900 Connaught Dr T0E 1E0.
0.6 mi (1 km) sw. Ext/int corridors. **Pets:** Accepted.
⊠ 🛅 🖵 🍴 🔁 ⊠

ⒸⒶ ▼▼▼ **Marmot Lodge** Ⓜ 🐾
(780) 852-4471. **$89-$255.** 86 Connaught Dr T0E 1E0. 1 mi (1.6 km) ne.
Ext corridors. **Pets:** Other species. $10 daily fee/room. Designated rooms,
service with restrictions, crate. 🄴🄲🄾 🆂🅰🆅🅴 ⊠ 🗒 🛅 🖵 🍴 🔁

▼▼ **Patricia Lake Bungalows** ⒸⒶ
(780) 852-3560. **$87-$325, 7 day notice.** Pyramid Lake Rd T0E 1E0. 3
mi (4.8 km) nw via Pyramid Lake Rd. Ext corridors. **Pets:** Medium, dogs
only. $10 daily fee/pet. Designated rooms, service with restrictions, super-
vision. ⊠ 🛅 🖵 ⊠ 🄯

ⒸⒶ ▼▼▼▼ **The Sawridge Inn and Conference Centre** 🄷
(780) 852-5111. **$112-$282, 3 day notice.** 82 Connaught Dr T0E 1E0.
1.1 mi (1.7 km) e. Int corridors. **Pets:** Small, other species. $20 one-time
fee/room. Designated rooms, service with restrictions, supervision.
🄴🄲🄾 🆂🅰🆅🅴 ⊠ 🗒 🛅 🖵 🔁 ⊠

ⒸⒶ ▼▼▼ **Sunwapta Falls Resort** ⒸⒶ
(780) 852-4852. **$89-$395, 7 day notice.** Hwy 93 T0E 1E0. 34.7 mi (55
km) s on Icefields Pkwy (Hwy 93). Ext corridors. **Pets:** $25 daily fee/pet.
No service. 🆂🅰🆅🅴 ⊠ 🛅 🖵 🍴 ⊠ 🄰🄺 🄯

▼▼ **Tonquin Inn** Ⓜ
(780) 852-4987. **$135-$400, 3 day notice.** 100 Juniper St T0E 1E0.
Corner of Juniper and Geikie sts. Ext/int corridors. **Pets:** Accepted.
🄰🅂🄺 ⊠ 🛅 🖵 🍴 🔁 ⊠

KANANASKIS
▼▼▼ **Delta Lodge at Kananaskis** 🄷
(403) 591-7711. **$139-$309, 3 day notice.** Kananaskis Village T0L 2H0.
Trans-Canada Hwy 1, 14.7 mi (23.5 km) s on Hwy 40 (Kananaskis Tr),
then 1.8 mi (3 km) on Kananaskis Village access road, follow signs. Int
corridors. **Pets:** Accepted. 🄴🄲🄾 🄰🅂🄺 ⊠ 🛅 🖵 🍴 🔁 ⊠

LAKE LOUISE

▽▽▽▽ ▽▽▽▽ The Fairmont Chateau Lake Louise H
(403) 522-3511. **$279-$2123, 3 day notice.** 111 Lake Louise Dr T0L 1E0. 1.8 mi (3 km) up the hill from the village. Int corridors.
Pets: Accepted. ECO SAVE ⊠ 🛏 💻 �10 ⌁ ⊠

▽▽ ▽▽ Lake Louise Inn H
(403) 522-3791. **$98-$431, 7 day notice.** 210 Village Rd T0L 1E0. Just w of 4-way stop. Ext/int corridors. **Pets:** Medium. $50 daily fee/pet. Designated rooms, service with restrictions, supervision.
ASK ⊠ 🛏 💻 �10 ⌁ ⊠

LETHBRIDGE

▽▽ ▽▽ Comfort Inn H
(403) 320-8874. **Call for rates.** 3226 Fairway Plaza Rd S T1K 7T5. Hwy 3 (Crowsnest Tr), exit Mayor Magrath Dr S, 1.8 mi (3 km) s, then just e on 24th Ave. Int corridors. **Pets:** Accepted. ⊠ 🛏 💻 ⌁

▽▽ ▽▽ Days Inn Lethbridge H
(403) 327-6000. **$105-$185.** 100 3rd Ave S T1J 4L2. Corner of 3rd Ave and Scenic Dr; centre. Ext/int corridors. **Pets:** Other species. $10 daily fee/pet. Designated rooms, service with restrictions, supervision.
ASK ⊠ 🛏 💻 ⌁

ⒸⒶ ▽▽▽▽ Holiday Inn Express Hotel & Suites Lethbridge H
(403) 394-9292. **Call for rates.** 120 Stafford Dr S T1J 4W4. Hwy 3 (Crowsnest Tr), exit Stafford Dr, just s; downtown. Int corridors. **Pets:** Other species. $40 one-time fee/room. Designated rooms, service with restrictions, crate. SAVE ⊠ 🛏 💻 ⌁ ⊠

ⒸⒶ ▽▽▽▽ Lethbridge Lodge Hotel and Conference Centre H
(403) 328-1123. **$119-$199.** 320 Scenic Dr T1J 4B4. Scenic Dr at 4th Ave S; centre. Int corridors. **Pets:** Accepted.
ECO SAVE ⊠ 🛏 💻 �10 ⌁

ⒸⒶ ▽▽▽▽ Quality Inn & Suites H
(403) 331-6440. **$99-$115.** 4040 2nd Ave S T1J 3Z2. Hwy 3 (Crowsnest Tr), just s on WT Hill Blvd, then just e. Int corridors. **Pets:** Dogs only. Designated rooms, service with restrictions, supervision.
SAVE ⊠ ⼚ 🛏 💻 ⌁ ⊠

▽▽▽▽ Ramada Lethbridge H
(403) 380-5050. **$140-$160.** 2375 Mayor Magrath Dr S T1K 7M1. Hwy 3 (Crowsnest Tr), exit Mayor Magrath Dr S, 1.8 mi (3 km) s, then just e on 22nd St. Int corridors. **Pets:** Accepted.
ECO ASK ⊠ 🛏 💻 �10 ⌁ ⊠

▽▽▽▽ Sandman Hotel Lethbridge H
(403) 328-1111. **$109-$159.** 421 Mayor Magrath Dr S T1J 3L8. Hwy 3 (Crowsnest Tr), exit Mayor Magrath Dr, just s. Int corridors.
Pets: Accepted. ECO ASK ⊠ 🛏 💻 �10 ⌁

MEDICINE HAT

ⒸⒶ ▽▽▽▽ Best Western Inn H
(403) 527-3700. **$105-$250.** 722 Redcliff Dr T1A 5E3. On Trans-Canada Hwy 1, 0.3 mi (0.4 km) w of jct Hwy 3, access 7th St SW. Ext/int corridors. **Pets:** Small. $10 one-time fee/pet. Designated rooms, service with restrictions, supervision. ECO SAVE ⊠ ⼚ 🛏 💻 ⌁ ⊠

▽▽▽▽▽ Holiday Inn Express Hotel & Suites H
(403) 504-5151. **$145-$309.** 9 Strachan Bay SE T1B 4Y2. Trans-Canada Hwy 1, just s on Dunmore Rd, then just e; east end of city. Int corridors.
Pets: Accepted. ECO ASK ⊠ ⼚ 🛏 💻 ⌁ ⊠

▽▽▽▽▽ Medicine Hat Lodge Resort, Casino & Spa H
(403) 529-2222. **$139-$174.** 1051 Ross Glen Dr SE T1B 3T8. Trans-Canada Hwy 1, just n on Dunmore Rd. Int corridors. **Pets:** Other species. $10 daily fee/room. Designated rooms, service with restrictions, crate.
ASK ⊠ ⼚ 🛏 💻 �10 ⌁ ⊠

▽▽ Motel 6-Medicine Hat #5700 H
(403) 527-1749. **$85-$95.** 20 Strachan Ct SE T1B 4R7. Trans-Canada Hwy 1, just s on Dunmore Rd, then just w; southeast end of city. Int corridors. **Pets:** Other species. Service with restrictions, supervision.
ECO ASK ⊠ ⼚ 🛏

▽▽ Super 8 H
(403) 528-8888. **$87-$149.** 1280 Trans-Canada Way SE T1B 1J5. Trans-Canada Hwy 1 at 13th Ave SE; just n off Trans-Canada Hwy 1. Ext/int corridors. **Pets:** Large, other species. $10 daily fee/pet. Designated rooms, service with restrictions, supervision. ASK ⊠ 🛏 💻 ⌁

PINCHER CREEK

▽▽ ▽▽ Heritage Inn H
(403) 627-5000. **$120-$289.** 919 Waterton Ave (Hwy 6) T0K 1W0. Hwy 3 (Crowsnest Tr), 1.3 mi (2.1 km) s, follow Hwy 6 (Waterton Ave) e, then 1.6 mi (2.6 km) s. Int corridors. **Pets:** Other species. $20 daily fee/pet. Designated rooms, service with restrictions, supervision.
ASK ⊠ 🛏 💻 �10 ⌁ ⊠

▽▽▽▽ Ramada Inn & Suites H
(403) 627-3777. **$150-$250.** 1132 Table Mountain St T0K 1W0. Hwy 3 (Crowsnest Tr), 1.3 mi (2.1 km) s on Hwy 6. Ext/int corridors.
Pets: Accepted. ECO ⊠ 🛏 💻 ⌁ ⊠

RED DEER

ⒸⒶ ▽▽▽▽ Best Western Red Deer Inn & Suites H
(403) 346-3555. **$105-$150.** 6839 66th St T4P 3T5. Hwy 2, exit 67th St, just e. Int corridors. **Pets:** Accepted.
ECO SAVE ⊠ ⼚ 🛏 💻 ⌁

ⒸⒶ ▽▽▽▽ Comfort Inn & Suites H 🐾
(403) 348-0025. **$105-$159.** 6846 66th St T4P 3T5. Hwy 2, exit 67th St, just e. Int corridors. **Pets:** Small. $20 one-time fee/pet. Designated rooms, service with restrictions. SAVE ⊠ 🛏 💻 ⌁ ⊠

▽▽ Motel 6-Red Deer H
(403) 340-1749. **$65-$85.** 900-5001 19th St T4R 3R1. Hwy 2, exit 394 (Gaetz Ave), just w; in Southpointe Common Shopping District. Int corridors. **Pets:** Other species. Service with restrictions, supervision.
ASK ⊠ 🛏

▽▽▽▽ Sandman Hotel Red Deer H
(403) 343-7400. **$119-$214.** 2818 Gaetz Ave T4R 1M4. Hwy 2, exit 394 (Gaetz Ave), 1.6 mi (2.6 km) n. Int corridors. **Pets:** Accepted.
ECO ASK ⊠ ⼚ 🛏 💻 �10 ⌁

ROCKY MOUNTAIN HOUSE

ⒸⒶ ▽▽▽▽ Best Western Rocky Mountain House H 🐾
(403) 844-3100. **$135-$145.** 4407 41st Ave T4T 1A5. Hwy 11 and 22, just w on 42nd Ave, then just s; east end of town. Int corridors. **Pets:** $10 daily fee/pet. Service with restrictions, supervision.
ECO SAVE ⊠ 🛏 💻 ⌁ ⊠

▽▽ Chinook Inn M
(403) 845-2833. **Call for rates.** 5321 59th Ave T4T 1J4. 0.8 mi (1.3 km) w on Hwy 11, then s. Int corridors. **Pets:** Accepted. ⊠ 🛏 💻

ⒸⒶ ▽▽▽ Holiday Inn Express Rocky Mountain House H
(403) 845-2871. **$99-$119.** 4715 45th St T4T 1B1. Hwy 11 and 22, just e on 47th Ave, then just n. Int corridors. **Pets:** Accepted.
ECO SAVE ⊠ ⼚ 🛏 💻 ⌁ ⊠

▽▽▽▽ Super 8 H
(403) 846-0088. **Call for rates.** 4406 41st Ave T4T 1J6. Hwy 11 and 22, just w on 42nd Ave, then just s; east end of town. Ext/int corridors.
Pets: Accepted. ECO ⊠ ⼚ 🛏 💻 ⌁ ⊠

SLAVE LAKE

CAA ◆◆◆◆ Lakeview Inns & Suites ⊞
(780) 849-9500. **Call for rates.** 1550 Holmes Tr SE T0G 2A3. Hwy 2, just n, east end of town. Int corridors. **Pets:** Accepted.
⬛ECO⬛ ⬛SAVE⬛ ⊠ 🖬 🖵

STETTLER

CAA ◆◆◆◆ Best Western Crusader Inn ⊞
(403) 742-3371. **$119-$129.** 6020 50th Ave T0C 2L2. Hwy 12 (50th Ave); at 61st St. Ext/int corridors. **Pets:** Accepted.
⬛ECO⬛ ⬛SAVE⬛ ⊠ ⬛&M⬛ 🖬 🖵 🍽 ➥ ⊠

TABER

◆◆ Heritage Inn Taber ⊞
(403) 223-4424. **$100-$165.** 4830 46th Ave T1G 2A4. Just s of jct Hwy 3 and 36 S, on Hwy 3. Int corridors. **Pets:** Accepted.
⬛A$K⬛ ⊠ 🖬 🖵 🍽 ⊠

◆◆ Super 8, Taber ⊞
(403) 223-8181. **$89.** 5700 46th Ave T1G 2B1. Hwy 3; west end of town. Ext/int corridors. **Pets:** Accepted. ⊠ 🖬 🖵

THREE HILLS

CAA ◆◆◆◆ Best Western Diamond Inn ⊞
(403) 443-7889. **$110-$125.** 351 7th Ave N T0M 2A0. Hwy 21 and 27, 1.1 mi (1.9 km) w. Int corridors. **Pets:** Accepted.
⬛SAVE⬛ ⊠ 🖬 🖵 🍽

VALLEYVIEW

CAA ◆◆◆ Western Valley Inn Ⓜ
(780) 524-4000. **$89-$149.** 5402 Highway St T0H 3N0. Just w of jct Hwy 43 and 49. Ext corridors. **Pets:** Accepted. ⬛SAVE⬛ ⊠ 🖬 🖵

WATERTON PARK

CAA ◆◆◆ Bayshore Inn Ⓜ
(403) 859-2211. **$119-$249, 3 day notice.** 111 Waterton Ave T0K 2M0. Centre. Ext/int corridors. **Pets:** Accepted. ⬛SAVE⬛ ⊠ ⬛&M⬛ 🖬 🖵 🍽

CAA ◆◆◆◆ Waterton Lakes Resort ⊞
(403) 859-2150. **$125-$255, 3 day notice.** 101 Clematis Ave T0K 2M0. Centre. Ext/int corridors. **Pets:** Accepted.
⬛SAVE⬛ ⊠ 🖬 🖵 🍽 ➥ ⊠

WESTEROSE

◆◆ Village Creek Country Inn ⊞
(780) 586-0006. **Call for rates.** 15 Village Dr, RR2 T0C 2V0. Hwy 2, exit 482, 17.5 mi (28 km) w on Hwy 13; in Village at Pigeon Lake. Ext/int corridors. **Pets:** Small. $10 daily fee/pet. Designated rooms, no service, supervision. ⊠ 🖬 🖵

WETASKIWIN

CAA ◆◆◆ Best Western Wayside Inn ⊞
(780) 312-7300. **$125-$145.** 4103 56th St T9A 1V2. On Hwy 2A, just n of jct Hwy 13 W. Int corridors. **Pets:** Other species. $200 deposit/room. Designated rooms. ⬛SAVE⬛ ⊠ 🖬 🖵 🍽

WHITECOURT

CAA ◆◆◆ Super 8 ⊞
(780) 778-8908. **$129-$139.** 4121 Kepler St T7S 0A3. On Hwy 43, just e of Hwy 32. Int corridors. **Pets:** Accepted. ⬛ECO⬛ ⬛SAVE⬛ ⊠ 🖬 🖵

BRITISH COLUMBIA

CITY INDEX

100 MILE HOUSE

▼▼ 100 Mile House Super 8 ℳ

(250) 395-8888. **$100-$150, 7 day notice.** 989 Alder Ave V0K 2E0. 0.6 mi (1 km) s on Hwy 97. Ext corridors. **Pets:** Accepted.

🄰🅂🄺 ✕ &ᴹ 🅑 🅒

▼▼ Ramada Limited ℳ

(250) 395-2777. **$90-$179.** 917 Alder Ave V0K 2E0. 0.6 mi (1 km) s on Hwy 97. Int corridors. **Pets:** Accepted. 🄰🅂🄺 ✕ &ᴹ 🅑 🅒

108 MILE HOUSE

🄰🄰 ▼▼ 108 Resort & Conference Centre 🄷

(250) 791-5211. **$95-$135, 30 day notice.** 4816 Telqua Dr V0K 2Z0. Hwy 97, 1 mi (1.6 km) nw on access road, follow signs. Ext corridors. **Pets:** Accepted. 🅂🄰🅅🄴 ✕ &ᴹ 🅑 🅒 🍽 🀢 ✕

ABBOTSFORD

🄰🄰 ▼▼ Best Western Bakerview Inn ℳ ❀

(604) 859-1341. **$116-$146.** 1821 Sumas Way V2S 4L5. Trans-Canada Hwy 1, exit 92 (Town Centre), just n on Hwy 11. Ext corridors. **Pets:** Other species. Service with restrictions, crate.

🄴🄲🄾 🅂🄰🅅🄴 ✕ 🅑 🅒 🍽 🀢

▼▼▼ Coast Abbotsford Hotel & Suites 🄷

(604) 853-1880. **Call for rates.** 2020 Sumas Way V2S 2C7. Trans-Canada Hwy 1, exit 92 (Town Centre), just n on Hwy 11. Int corridors. **Pets:** Accepted. 🄴🄲🄾 ✕ &ᴹ 🅑 🅒 🍽 🀢

🄰🄰 ▼▼ Super 8 Abbotsford 🄷

(604) 853-1141. **$99-$399.** 1881 Sumas Way V2S 4L5. Trans-Canada Hwy 1, exit 92 (Town Centre), just n on Hwy 11. Ext/int corridors. **Pets:** Accepted. 🅂🄰🅅🄴 ✕ &ᴹ 🅑 🅒 🀢 ✕

BLUE RIVER

▼▼ Glacier Mountain Lodge ℳ ❀

(250) 673-2393. **$99-$209.** 869 Shell Rd V0E 1J0. On Hwy 5 (Yellowhead Hwy); at Shell Rd, follow signs. Int corridors. **Pets:** $15 one-time fee/room. Designated rooms, service with restrictions, supervision.

🄰🅂🄺 ✕ 🅑

BOWEN ISLAND

▼▼ Wildwood Lane Cottages 🄲🄰 ❀

(604) 947-2253. **Call for rates.** 1321 Adams Rd V0N 1G0. From ferry terminal, 3.5 mi (5.6 km) w on Grafton Rd, then 0.6 mi (1 km) n. Ext corridors. **Pets:** Dogs only. No service, supervision. ✕ 🅑 🅒 🀢

CACHE CREEK

🄰🄰 ▼▼ Bonaparte Motel ℳ

(250) 457-9693. **$49-$129.** 1395 Hwy 97 N V0K 1H0. Just n of jct Trans-Canada Hwy 1. Ext corridors. **Pets:** Small, dogs only. $10 daily fee/pet. Designated rooms, service with restrictions, supervision.

🅂🄰🅅🄴 ✕ 🅑 🀢

CAMPBELL RIVER

▼▼ Anchor Inn & Suites 🄷 ❀

(250) 286-1131. **Call for rates.** 261 Island Hwy V9W 2B3. On Island Hwy 19A, 1.3 mi (2 km) s. Int corridors. **Pets:** Medium, other species. $10 daily fee/pet. Designated rooms, service with restrictions, supervision.

✕ &ᴹ 🅑 🅒 🍽 🀢 🀢

🄰🄰 ▼▼▼ Best Western Austrian Chalet ℳ

(250) 923-4231. **$124-$175.** 462 S Island Hwy V9W 1A5. 2 mi (3.2 km) s on Island Hwy 19A. Ext/int corridors. **Pets:** Small, other species. $25 daily fee/room. Designated rooms, service with restrictions, supervision.

🅂🄰🅅🄴 ✕ &ᴹ 🅑 🅒 🀢 ✕ 🀢

🄰🄰 ▼▼ Campbell River Lodge Fishing & Adventure
       Resort ℳ ❀

(250) 287-7446. **$74-$129, 3 day notice.** 1760 N Island Hwy V9W 2E7. On Island Hwy 19A, 1.3 mi (2 km) nw of downtown; just e from Hwy 19 and 28. Ext/int corridors. **Pets:** $10 one-time fee/pet. Service with restrictions, supervision. 🅂🄰🅅🄴 ✕ 🅑 🅒 🍽 🀢

▼▼ Ocean Resort ℳ ❀

(250) 923-4281. **Call for rates.** 4834 S Island Hwy V9H 1E8. 11 mi (18 km) s on Island Hwy 19A. Int corridors. **Pets:** Medium. $20 daily fee/pet. Service with restrictions, supervision. ✕ 🅑 🍽 🀢

▼▼ Town Centre Inn ℳ

(250) 287-8866. **$74-$99.** 1500 Dogwood St V9W 3A6. Follow Island Hwy 19A through town, watch for signs, just e on Dogwood St; corner of 16th Ave. Ext corridors. **Pets:** Small. $5 daily fee/pet. No service, crate.

🄰🅂🄺 ✕ 🅑 🀢

▼▼ Travelodge Campbell River ℳ

(250) 286-6622. **$85-$125.** 340 S Island Hwy V9W 1A5. 1.9 mi (3 km) s on Island Hwy 19A. Int corridors. **Pets:** Accepted.

🄴🄲🄾 🄰🅂🄺 ✕ &ᴹ 🅑 🅒 🀢

CASTLEGAR

▼▼ Quality Inn Castlegar 🄷

(250) 365-2177. **$90-$160.** 1935 Columbia Ave V1N 2W8. Jct Hwy 3A and 3B, just s. Ext/int corridors. **Pets:** Medium. $10 daily fee/pet. Designated rooms, service with restrictions, supervision.

🄰🅂🄺 ✕ 🅑 🅒 🍽

▼▼▼ Super 8-Castlegar 🅷
(250) 365-2700. **$125-$329.** 651 18th St V1N 2N1. Hwy 3, exit city centre. Int corridors. **Pets:** Other species. $10 daily fee/pet. Designated rooms, no service. 🔲 🔲 ⊠ 🔲 🔲 🔲 🔲

CHASE

▼▼▼ Chase Country Inn Motel 🅼
(250) 679-3333. **$69-$99.** 576 Coburn St V0E 1M0. Trans-Canada Hwy 1 and Coburn St. Ext corridors. **Pets:** Small, dogs only. $5 daily fee/pet. Designated rooms, service with restrictions, supervision.
🔲 ⊠ 🔲 🔲 🔲

▼▼▼ Talking Rock Resort and Quaaout Lodge 🅷
(250) 679-3090. **$100-$250.** 1663 Little Shuswap Lake Rd W V0E 1M0. Trans-Canada Hwy 1, exit Squilax Bridge, 1.5 mi (2.5 km) w. Int corridors.
Pets: Accepted. 🔲 ⊠ 🔲 🔲 🔲 🔲 🔲 🔲

CHEMAINUS

🅐 ▼▼▼ Best Western Chemainus Festival
Inn 🅷 🐾
(250) 246-4181. **$132-$160.** 9573 Chemainus Rd V0R 1K5. Trans-Canada Hwy 1, exit Henry Rd, 0.9 mi (1.4 km) e. Int corridors.
Pets: Other species. $15 one-time fee/room. Designated rooms, service with restrictions. 🔲 🔲 ⊠ 🔲 🔲 🔲 🔲

CHETWYND

🅐 ▼▼▼ Lakeview Inns & Suites 🅷
(250) 788-3000. **$129.** 4820 N Access Rd V0C 1J0. Hwy 29 and 97, just n on 48th St, then just e. Int corridors. **Pets:** Accepted.
🔲 🔲 ⊠ 🔲 🔲

▼▼▼ Pomeroy Inn & Suites 🅷 🐾
(250) 788-4800. **Call for rates.** 5200 N Access Rd V0C 1J0. Hwy 29 and 97, just n on 52nd St. Int corridors. **Pets:** Other species. $25 one-time fee/room. ⊠ 🔲 🔲 🔲 🔲

CHILLIWACK

🅐 ▼▼▼ Best Western Rainbow Country Inn 🅷
(604) 795-3828. **$120-$270.** 43971 Industrial Way V2R 3A4. Trans-Canada Hwy 1, exit 116 (Lickman Rd). Int corridors. **Pets:** Accepted.
🔲 ⊠ 🔲 🔲 🔲 🔲 🔲

🅐 ▼▼▼ Chilliwack Travelodge 🅷
(604) 792-4240. **$91-$225, 7 day notice.** 45466 Yale Rd W V2R 3Z8. Trans-Canada Hwy 1, exit 119, just n. Int corridors. **Pets:** Accepted.
🔲 🔲 ⊠ 🔲 🔲 🔲 🔲 🔲

▼▼▼ Comfort Inn 🅼
(604) 858-0636. **$95-$155.** 45405 Luckakuck Way V2R 3C7. Trans-Canada Hwy 1, exit 119, s on Vedder Rd, then 0.6 mi (1 km) w. Int corridors. **Pets:** Medium. $5 daily fee/pet. Designated rooms, service with restrictions, supervision. 🔲 🔲 ⊠ 🔲 🔲

CLEARWATER

🅐 ▼▼ Clearwater Valley Resort & KOA
Kampground 🆑
(250) 674-3909. **$92-$152.** 373 Clearwater Valley Rd V0E 1N0. Jct Hwy 5 (Yellowhead Hwy) and Clearwater Valley Rd. Ext corridors.
Pets: Accepted. 🔲 ⊠ 🔲 🔲 🔲 🔲 🔲

COMOX

🅐 ▼▼▼ Port Augusta Inn & Suites 🅼
(250) 339-2277. **$85-$165, 3 day notice.** 2082 Comox Ave V9M 1P8. Hwy 19A (Cliffe Ave), follow signs to Comox Ave, then 2.5 mi (4 km) e. Ext/int corridors. **Pets:** Other species. $10 daily fee/pet. Designated rooms, service with restrictions, supervision.
🔲 ⊠ 🔲 🔲 🔲 🔲 🔲

COURTENAY

🅐 ▼▼▼ Best Western The Westerly Hotel 🅷
(250) 338-7741. **$144-$209.** 1590 Cliffe Ave V9N 2K4. Corner of Cliffe Ave and Island Hwy 19A N. Int corridors. **Pets:** Large. $10 daily fee/pet. Designated rooms, service with restrictions, supervision.
🔲 🔲 ⊠ 🔲 🔲 🔲 🔲 🔲 🔲

▼▼▼▼ Kingfisher Oceanside Resort & Spa 🅷
(250) 338-1323. **Call for rates.** 4330 S Island Hwy V9N 9R9. 3.8 mi (6 km) s on Island Hwy 19A S, watch for signs. Ext corridors.
Pets: Accepted. ⊠ 🔲 🔲 🔲 🔲 🔲 🔲 🔲

▼▼ Travelodge Courtenay 🅼
(250) 334-4491. **$93-$118.** 2605 Cliffe Ave V9N 2L8. 0.8 mi (1.2 km) s on Island Hwy 19A S. Ext corridors. **Pets:** $10 daily fee/pet. Service with restrictions, supervision. 🔲 🔲 ⊠ 🔲 🔲 🔲

CRANBROOK

🅐 ▼▼▼ Best Western Cranbrook Hotel 🅷
(250) 417-4002. **$139-$199.** 1019 Cranbrook St N V1C 3S4. Hwy 3 and 95; centre. Int corridors. **Pets:** Accepted.
🔲 ⊠ 🔲 🔲 🔲 🔲 🔲

▼▼▼ Days Inn Cranbrook 🅷
(250) 426-6683. **$119-$154.** 600 Cranbrook St N V1C 3R7. Corner of 6th St and Cranbrook St N. Int corridors. **Pets:** Accepted.
🔲 🔲 ⊠ 🔲 🔲 🔲 🔲

▼▼▼ Heritage Inn Cranbrook 🅷
(250) 489-4301. **$135-$210.** 803 Cranbrook St N V1C 3S2. Hwy 3 and 95; centre. Int corridors. **Pets:** Accepted.
🔲 ⊠ 🔲 🔲 🔲 🔲 🔲

🅐 ▼▼▼▼ St. Eugene Golf Resort & Casino 🅷 🐾
(250) 420-2000. **$132-$190.** 7731 Mission Rd V1C 7E5. Hwy 3, exit Kimberley/Airport (Hwy 95A) to Mission Rd, 2.8 mi (4.5 km) n. Int corridors. **Pets:** Small. $25 daily fee/pet. Designated rooms, service with restrictions, supervision. 🔲 ⊠ 🔲 🔲 🔲 🔲 🔲

▼▼ Super 8 🅷
(250) 489-8028. **$90-$115.** 2370 Cranbrook St N V1C 3T2. Just w of jct Hwy 93 and 95. Int corridors. **Pets:** Accepted. 🔲 🔲 ⊠ 🔲 🔲

CRESTON

🅐 ▼ Downtowner Motor Inn 🅼
(250) 428-2238. **$55-$80.** 1218 Canyon St V0B 1G0. Corner of 12th Ave N; centre. Int corridors. **Pets:** Medium, other species. $5 daily fee/pet. Service with restrictions, crate. 🔲 ⊠ 🔲

🅐 ▼▼▼ Skimmerhorn Inn 🅼 🐾
(250) 428-4009. **$87-$157.** 2711 Hwy 3 V0B 1G0. On Hwy 3, 0.8 mi (1.3 km) e. Ext corridors. **Pets:** Medium, dogs only. $10 daily fee/pet. Designated rooms, service with restrictions, crate. 🔲 ⊠ 🔲 🔲 🔲

🅐 ▼▼▼ Sunset Motel 🅼
(250) 428-2229. **$79-$109.** 2705 Canyon St (Hwy 3 E) V0B 1G0. On Hwy 3, 0.8 mi (1.3 km) e. Ext corridors. **Pets:** Accepted.
🔲 ⊠ 🔲 🔲 🔲

DAWSON CREEK

🅐 ▼▼▼▼ Best Western Dawson Creek Hotel &
Suites 🅷
(250) 782-6226. **$179.** 500 Hwy 2 V1G 0A4. 1.8 mi (3 km) e of center. Int corridors. **Pets:** Accepted. 🔲 ⊠ 🔲 🔲 🔲 🔲 🔲

🅐 ▼▼▼ Dawson Creek Super 8 🅷
(250) 782-8899. **$135-$220.** 1440 Alaska Ave V1G 1Z5. Just s of jct Hwy 97 S (Hart Hwy) and 97 N (Alaska Hwy). Int corridors.
Pets: Accepted. 🔲 ⊠ 🔲 🔲 🔲

▼▼▼ **Pomeroy Inn & Suites** 🅗 ❖

(250) 782-3700. **$189-$329.** 540 Hwy #2 V1G 0A4. 1.8 mi (3 km) e of centre. Int corridors. **Pets:** Other species. $25 one-time fee/room. Service with restrictions, supervision. (A$K) ⊠ 🛢 🖃 ➷ ⊠

DUNCAN

Ⓐ ▼▼▼ **Best Western Cowichan Valley Inn** 🅗

(250) 748-2722. **$124-$161.** 6474 Trans-Canada Hwy 1 V9L 6C6. 1.8 mi (3 km) n. Int corridors. **Pets:** Accepted. (SAVE) ⊠ 🛢 🖃 🍴 ➷

▼▼▼ **Travelodge Silver Bridge Inn Duncan** 🅗

(250) 748-4311. **$109-$249.** 140 Trans-Canada Hwy 1 V9L 3P7. Just n of Silver Bridge. Ext corridors. **Pets:** Accepted.

(ECO) (A$K) ⊠ 🛢 🖃 🍴

FERNIE

Ⓐ ▼▼▼▼ **Best Western Fernie Mountain Lodge** 🅗

(250) 423-5500. **$136-$176.** 1622 7th Ave V0B 1M0. Jct Hwy 3 and 7th Ave; east end of town. Int corridors. **Pets:** Small. $20 one-time fee/room. Designated rooms, service with restrictions, supervision.

(ECO) (SAVE) ⊠ 🛢 🖃 🍴 ➷

Ⓐ ▼▼▼▼ **Park Place Lodge** 🅗

(250) 423-6871. **$129-$298.** 742 Hwy 3 V0B 1M0. At 7th St. Int corridors. **Pets:** Accepted. (SAVE) ⊠ 🛢 🖃 🍴 ➷ ⊠

▼▼ **Stanford Hotels & Resorts** ⓒ

(250) 423-5000. **Call for rates.** 100 Riverside Way V0B 1M1. 1.2 mi (2 km) on Hwy 3. Ext/int corridors. **Pets:** Medium, dogs only. $10 daily fee/room. Designated rooms, service with restrictions, supervision.

⊠ 🛢 🖃 🍴 ➷ ⊠

▼▼ **Super 8-Fernie** 🅗 ❖

(250) 423-6788. **$85-$119.** 2021 Hwy 3 V0B 1M1. On Hwy 3; west end of town. Int corridors. **Pets:** Medium, other species. $10 daily fee/pet. Designated rooms, service with restrictions, supervision. ⊠ 🛢 🖃

FORT NELSON

Ⓐ ▼▼▼ **Lakeview Inns & Suites** 🅗

(250) 233-5001. **$137-$149.** 4507-50th Ave S V0C 1R0. Just off Hwy 97 (Alaska Hwy); at 44th St. Int corridors. **Pets:** Accepted.

(ECO) (SAVE) ⊠ 🛢 🖃 ⊠

FORT ST. JOHN

Ⓐ ▼▼▼ **Coachman Inn** 🅗 ❖

(250) 787-0651. **$150.** 8540 Alaska Rd V1J 5L6. 1.2 mi (2 km) s on Hwy 97 (Alaska Hwy). Int corridors. **Pets:** Other species. $15 daily fee/pet. Designated rooms, service with restrictions, supervision.

(SAVE) ⊠ 🛢 🍴 ⊠

Ⓐ ▼▼▼ **Lakeview Inns & Suites** 🅗

(250) 787-0779. **$109-$129.** 10103 98th Ave V1J 1P8. Corner of 100th Ave; centre of downtown. Int corridors. **Pets:** Medium. $25 daily fee/pet. Designated rooms, service with restrictions, supervision.

(ECO) (SAVE) ⊠ 🛢 🖃

Ⓐ ▼▼▼▼ **Pomeroy Hotel** 🅗

(250) 262-3233. **$169-$249.** 11308 Alaska Rd V1J 5T5. Just w on Hwy 97 (Alaska Hwy). Int corridors. **Pets:** Accepted.

(SAVE) ⊠ (&M) 🛢 🖃 🍴 ➷ ⊠

Ⓐ ▼▼ **Pomeroy Inn & Suites** 🅗 ❖

(250) 262-3030. **$149-$169.** 9304 Alaska Rd V1J 6Z5. Just s on Hwy 97 (Alaska Hwy). Int corridors. **Pets:** $25 one-time fee/room. Designated rooms, service with restrictions, crate. (A$K) ⊠ 🛢 🖃

▼▼▼ **Quality Inn Northern Grand** 🅗

(250) 787-0521. **$129-$174.** 9830 100th Ave V1J 1Y5. Centre. Int corridors. **Pets:** Accepted. (ECO) (A$K) ⊠ 🛢 🖃 🍴 ➷ ⊠

Ⓐ ▼▼▼ **Super 8-Fort St. John** 🅗 ❖

(250) 785-7588. **$150-$160.** 9500 Alaska Hwy V1J 6S7. Just s on Hwy 97 (Alaska Hwy). Int corridors. **Pets:** Medium. $25 daily fee/pet. Designated rooms, service with restrictions, supervision.

(ECO) (SAVE) ⊠ (&M) 🛢 🖃 🍴 ➷ ⊠

FORT STEELE

▼▼ **Bull River Guest Ranch** 🅗

(250) 429-3760. **Call for rates.** 2975 Bull River Rd V1C 4H7. Hwy 95, 12.9 mi (21.4 km) se of town on Ft Steele-Wardner Rd, 7.2 mi (12 km) ne on gravel road; Hwy 3 W, 24.6 mi (41 km) e of Cranbrook, 5 mi (8.2 km) n on Ft Steele-Wardner Rd, 7.2 mi (12 km) ne on gravel road. Ext corridors. **Pets:** Accepted. ⊠ 🛢 🖃 ⊠ 🐾 🅿 🐾

GIBSONS

▼▼▼ **Bonniebrook Lodge Oceanfront Inn** ⓒ

(604) 886-2887. **$129-$299, 7 day notice.** 1532 Ocean Beach Esplanade V0N 1V5. Hwy 101, 3.8 mi (6 km) s on Veterans Rd to Fichett St, just sw to King St, 0.6 mi (1 km) sw to Chaster, then 5 mi (8 km) sw to Gowers Pt Rd, follow signs. Ext/int corridors. **Pets:** Accepted.

(A$K) ⊠ 🛢 🖃 🍴 🐾

Ⓐ ▼▼▼ **Cedars Inn Hotel & Convention Centre** 🅜 ❖

(604) 886-3008. **$94-$156.** 895 Gibsons Way V0N 1V0. Hwy 101 and Shaw Rd; 3.8 mi (6 km) n from ferry terminal. Ext/int corridors. **Pets:** Medium, other species. $15 daily fee/pet. Designated rooms, service with restrictions, supervision. (SAVE) ⊠ 🛢 🖃 🍴 ➷ ⊠

GOLD BRIDGE

▼▼▼ **Morrow Chalets** 🅒🅐

(250) 238-2462. **$275-$375, 30 day notice.** 2440 Gun Creek Rd V0K 1P0. 5 mi (8 km) n from the Tyaughton Lake turnoff, follow signs. Ext corridors. **Pets:** Accepted. ⊠ 🛢 🖃 🐾

▼▼ **Tyax Mountain Lake Resort** 🅗

(250) 238-2221. **$169-$203, 60 day notice.** Tyaughton Lake Rd V0K 1P0. 5 mi (8 km) n from the Tyaughton Lake turnoff, follow signs. Int corridors. **Pets:** Accepted. ⊠ 🛢 🍴 ⊠ 🐾

GOLDEN

Ⓐ ▼▼▼ **Best Western Mountain View Inn** 🅗

(250) 344-2333. **$129-$189.** 1024 11th St N V0A 1H2. Just w of jct Hwy 95 and Trans-Canada Hwy 1; on S Service Rd. Int corridors. **Pets:** Accepted. (SAVE) ⊠ 🛢 🖃 ➷

▼▼ **Golden Rim Motor Inn** 🅜

(250) 344-2216. **$79-$185.** 1416 Golden View Rd V0A 1H1. On Trans-Canada Hwy 1, 1 mi (1.6 km) e of jct Hwy 95. Ext corridors. **Pets:** Medium. $6 daily fee/pet. Service with restrictions, supervision.

(A$K) ⊠ 🛢 🖃 🍴 ➷ ⊠

Ⓐ ▼▼▼ **Hillside Lodge & Chalets** 🅒🅐 ❖

(250) 344-7281. **$138-$260, 5 day notice.** 1740 Seward Frontage Rd V0A 1H0. 9.4 mi (15 km) w on Hwy 1, follow signs n off highway. Ext corridors. **Pets:** $15 one-time fee/room. Designated rooms, service with restrictions, supervision. (SAVE) ⊠ 🛢 🖃 ⊠ 🐾 🐾

GRAND FORKS

▼▼ **Ramada Limited** 🅜

(250) 442-2127. **Call for rates.** 2729 Central Ave V0H 1H2. West end of town on Hwy 3. Ext corridors. **Pets:** Accepted. ⊠ 🛢 🖃 🍴 ➷

Ⓐ ▼▼▼ **Western Traveller Motel** 🅜

(250) 442-5566. **$64-$139.** 1591 Central Ave V0H 1H0. West end of town on Hwy 3. Ext corridors. **Pets:** Small, dogs only. $7 daily fee/pet. Designated rooms, no service, supervision. (SAVE) ⊠ 🛢 🖃

GULF ISLANDS NATIONAL PARK RESERVE AREA

GALIANO ISLAND

▼▼▼ **Galiano Oceanfront Inn & Spa** 🅷

(250) 539-3388. **$199-$425, 7 day notice.** 134 Madrona Dr V0N 1P0. From Sturdies Bay ferry terminal, just ne on Sturdies Bay Rd. Ext/int corridors. **Pets:** Accepted. ⒶⓈⓀ ☒ &M 🖿 💻 🍴 🐾

PENDER ISLAND

🅐🅐 ▼▼▼ **Poets Cove Resort & Spa** 🅷 🐾

(250) 629-2100. **$189-$299, 3 day notice.** 9801 Spalding Rd, South Pender Island V0N 2M3. From Otter Bay Ferry Terminal, follow signs to South Pender Island, then 10 mi (16 km) s; Otter Bay Rd to Bidwell Harbour Rd to Canal Rd. Ext/int corridors. **Pets:** Large. $50 one-time fee/pet. Designated rooms, service with restrictions.

SAVE ☒ 🖿 💻 🍴 🏊 ☒ 🐾

QUADRA ISLAND

▼▼ **Taku Resort & Marina** 🅼

(250) 285-3031. **$89-$305, 30 day notice.** 616 Taku Rd V0P 1H0. From Campbell River ferry terminal, 4.1 mi (6.6 km) n on West Rd, then just e on Heriot Bay Rd, follow signs to Heriot Bay. Ext corridors. **Pets:** $15 daily fee/pet. Designated rooms, service with restrictions, supervision. ☒ 🖿 💻 ☒ 🐾 📶

SALT SPRING ISLAND

▼▼▼ **Harbour House Hotel** 🅷

(250) 537-5571. **$79-$199.** 121 Upper Ganges Rd V8K 2S2. 0.6 mi (1 km) n on Lower Ganges Rd, then just e, towards Long Harbour ferry terminal. Ext/int corridors. **Pets:** Accepted.

ⒶⓈⓀ ☒ &M 🖿 💻 🍴

▼▼▼ **Seabreeze Inne** 🅼

(250) 537-4145. **Call for rates.** 101 Bittancourt Rd V8K 2K2. From Ganges Township, 0.6 mi (1 km) s on Fulford-Ganges Rd. Ext corridors. **Pets:** Accepted. ☒ 🖿 💻

END AREA

HARRISON HOT SPRINGS

🅐🅐 ▼▼▼ **Harrison Beach Hotel** 🅷

(604) 796-1111. **$99-$249.** 160 Esplanade Ave V0M 1K0. Just w; on lakefront. Int corridors. **Pets:** Accepted.

ECO SAVE ☒ &M 🖿 💻 🍴 🏊

🅐🅐 ▼▼▼ **Harrison Hot Springs Resort & Spa** 🅷

(604) 796-2244. **$139-$249, 3 day notice.** 100 Esplanade Ave V0M 1K0. Just w; on lakefront. Int corridors. **Pets:** Accepted.

SAVE ☒ &M 🖿 💻 🍴 🏊 ☒

HOPE

🅐🅐 ▼▼ **Alpine Motel** 🅼

(604) 869-9931. **$78-$115.** 505 Old Hope-Princeton Way V0X 1L0. Trans-Canada Hwy 1, exit 173 westbound; exit 170 eastbound, just n from lights. Ext corridors. **Pets:** Small. $50 deposit/room, $10 daily fee/room. No service, supervision. SAVE ☒ 🖿 💻

🅐🅐 ▼▼ **Best Continental Motel** 🅼

(604) 869-9726. **$69-$125.** 860 Fraser Ave V0X 1L0. Trans-Canada Hwy 1, exit 170 to downtown; at Fort St. Ext corridors. **Pets:** Small, dogs only. $6 daily fee/pet. No service, supervision. SAVE ☒ 🖿 💻

🅐🅐 ▼▼ **Heritage Inn** 🅼

(604) 869-7166. **$89-$116.** 570 Old Hope-Princeton Way V0X 1L0. Trans-Canada Hwy 1, exit 173 westbound; exit 170 eastbound, just n from lights. Ext corridors. **Pets:** Small, dogs only. $10 one-time fee/pet. No service, supervision. SAVE ☒ &M 🖿 💻

🅐🅐 ▼▼ **Quality Inn** 🅼

(604) 869-9951. **$80-$145.** 350 Old Hope-Princeton Way V0X 1L0. Trans-Canada Hwy 1, exit 173 westbound; exit 170 eastbound, just n from lights. Int corridors. **Pets:** Medium. Service with restrictions, supervision. SAVE ☒ &M 🖿 💻 🏊

INVERMERE

🅐🅐 ▼▼▼ **Best Western Invermere Inn** 🅷

(250) 342-9246. **$120-$210.** 1310 7th Ave V0A 1K0. Hwy 93 and 95, exit Invermere, 1.8 mi (3 km) w; centre. Int corridors. **Pets:** Accepted.

SAVE ☒ 🖿 💻 🍴

KAMLOOPS

🅐🅐 ▼▼▼ **Accent Inns** 🅼 🐾

(250) 374-8877. **$99-$179.** 1325 Columbia St W V2C 6P4. Trans-Canada Hwy 1, exit 369 (Columbia St) eastbound, at Notre Dame Dr; exit 370 (Summit Dr) westbound. Ext corridors. **Pets:** Small. $15 daily fee/pet. Designated rooms, service with restrictions, supervision.

ECO SAVE ☒ &M 🖿 💻 🏊 ☒

🅐🅐 ▼▼▼ **Econo Lodge Inn & Suites** 🅼

(250) 372-8533. **$59-$129.** 1773 Trans-Canada Hwy E V2C 3Z6. 1.5 mi (2.4 km) e on Trans-Canada Hwy 1, south side of service access road. Ext corridors. **Pets:** $10 daily fee/pet. Designated rooms, service with restrictions, supervision. SAVE ☒ 🖿 💻 🏊

🅐🅐 ▼▼▼ **Hampton Inn by Hilton** 🅷 🐾

(250) 571-7897. **Call for rates.** 1245 Rogers Way V1S 1R9. Trans-Canada Hwy 1, exit 368 (Hillside Ave), just s via Hillside Way. Int corridors. **Pets:** Large, dogs only. $20 daily fee/pet. Designated rooms, service with restrictions, supervision. ECO SAVE ☒ &M 🖿 💻 🏊 ☒

▼▼▼ **Holiday Inn Express Kamloops** 🅷

(250) 372-3474. **Call for rates.** 1550 Versatile Dr V1S 1X4. Trans-Canada Hwy 1, exit 367 (Pacific Way), just w. Int corridors. **Pets:** Accepted. ECO ☒ &M 🖿 💻 🏊

▼▼▼ **Kamloops Super 8** 🅼

(250) 374-8688. **$119-$149.** 1521 Hugh Allan Dr V1S 1P4. Trans-Canada Hwy 1, exit 367 (Pacific Way). Int corridors. **Pets:** Accepted.

☒ &M 🖿 💻

🅐🅐 ▼▼▼ **Kamloops TowneLodge** 🅷

(250) 828-6660. **$140-$185.** 1250 Rogers Way V1S 1N5. Trans-Canada Hwy 1, exit 368 (Hillside Ave), just s. Int corridors. **Pets:** Medium, other species. $20 daily fee/room. Designated rooms, service with restrictions, supervision. ECO SAVE ☒ &M 🖿 💻 🍴 🏊 ☒

🅐🅐 ▼▼ **Quality Inn** 🅼

(250) 851-0111. **$70-$180.** 1860 Rogers Pl V1S 1T7. Trans-Canada Hwy 1, exit 368 (Hillside Ave). Int corridors. **Pets:** Small. $15 daily fee/pet. Designated rooms, service with restrictions, supervision.

SAVE ☒ &M 🖿 💻 🏊 ☒

▼▼ Ranchland Motel **M**

(250) 828-8787. **$69-$110.** 2357 Trans-Canada Hwy E V2C 4A8. 2.8 mi (4.5 km) e on Trans-Canada Hwy 1, exit River Rd, then just w along service access road. Ext corridors. **Pets:** Medium, dogs only. $20 daily fee/pet. Designated rooms, service with restrictions, supervision.

A$K ☒ 🛏 🖭

Ⓐ ▼▼▼ Scott's Inn & Restaurant **M**

(250) 372-8221. **$80-$120.** 551 11th Ave V2C 3Y1. Trans-Canada Hwy 1, exit 369 (Columbia St) eastbound, 3.1 mi (5 km) n; exit City Centre westbound, 1 mi (1.6 km) s on Columbia St. Ext corridors. **Pets:** Medium. $10 daily fee/pet. Designated rooms, service with restrictions, supervision.

SAVE ☒ 🛏 🖭 🍽 🌫

KIMBERLEY

Ⓐ ▼▼▼ Trickle Creek Lodge **H** ❀

(250) 427-5175. **$163-$272, 14 day notice.** 500 Stemwinder Dr V1A 2Y6. From Gerry Sorensen Way, follow signs. Int corridors. **Pets:** Other species. $75 one-time fee/room. Designated rooms, service with restrictions, crate. SAVE ☒ 🛏 🖭 🍽 🌫 ☒

MADEIRA PARK

▼▼▼ Sunshine Coast Resort & Marina Ⓒ ❀

(604) 883-9177. **$95-$495, 21 day notice.** 12695 Sunshine Coast Hwy V0N 2H0. Just n of Madeira Park Rd, follow signs. Ext/int corridors. **Pets:** Other species. $10 daily fee/pet. Supervision.

☒ 🖢 🛏 🖭 ☒

MCBRIDE

Ⓐ ▼▼▼ North Country Lodge **M**

(250) 569-0001. **$85-$100, 3 day notice.** 868 Frontage Rd N V0J 2E0. Just w of village main exit, on Hwy 16 north service road. Ext corridors. **Pets:** $10 daily fee/room. Designated rooms, service with restrictions, supervision. SAVE ☒ 🛏 🖭 🍽

MERRITT

▼▼ Super 8 Merritt **M**

(250) 378-9422. **$95-$130.** 3561 Voght St V1K 1C5. Hwy 5, exit 290, just w. Ext corridors. **Pets:** Accepted.

A$K ☒ 🖢 🛏 🖭 🍽 🌫

NAKUSP

Ⓐ ▼▼▼ The Selkirk Inn **M**

(250) 265-3666. **$59-$95.** 210 W 6th Ave V0G 1R0. Centre. Int corridors. **Pets:** Small. $20 deposit/room, $10 daily fee/pet. Designated rooms, service with restrictions, supervision. SAVE ☒ 🖢 🛏 🖭

NANAIMO

Ⓐ ▼▼▼ Best Western Dorchester Hotel **H** ❀

(250) 754-6835. **$135-$200.** 70 Church St V9R 5H4. Hwy 19A (Island Hwy) to Comox Rd; downtown. Int corridors. **Pets:** Medium, dogs only. $15 daily fee/pet. Designated rooms, service with restrictions, supervision.

ECO SAVE ☒ 🛏 🖭 🍽

Ⓐ ▼▼▼ Best Western Northgate Inn **H** ❀

(250) 390-2222. **$94-$142.** 6450 Metral Dr V9T 2L8. Hwy 19A (Island Hwy), just w on Aulds Rd, then just s. Int corridors. **Pets:** Other species. $20 daily fee/room. Designated rooms, service with restrictions, supervision. SAVE ☒ 🛏 🖭 🍽 ☒

▼▼▼ Days Inn Nanaimo Harbourview **H**

(250) 754-8171. **$89-$129.** 809 Island Hwy S V9R 5K1. On Island Hwy 1, 1.3 mi (2 km) s. Int corridors. **Pets:** $10 one-time fee/room. Designated rooms, service with restrictions. ECO A$K ☒ 🛏 🖭 🍽 🌫

▼▼▼▼ The Grand Hotel Nanaimo **H** ❀

(250) 758-3000. **$129-$350.** 4898 Rutherford Rd V9T 4Z4. 3.8 mi (6 km) n on Hwy 19A (Island Hwy) from Departure Bay ferry terminal, then just e. Int corridors. **Pets:** $30 daily fee/pet. Designated rooms, service with restrictions. A$K ☒ 🖢 🛏 🖭 🍽 🌫

Ⓐ ▼▼▼▼ Inn on Long Lake **H** ❀

(250) 758-1144. **$109-$299.** 4700 Island Hwy N V9T 1W6. 3.1 mi (5 km) n on Hwy 19A (Island Hwy) from Departure Bay ferry terminal. Ext corridors. **Pets:** Other species. $20 one-time fee/pet. Designated rooms, service with restrictions, supervision. ECO SAVE ☒ 🖢 🛏 🖭 ☒

Ⓐ ▼▼ ▼▼ Travelodge Nanaimo **H**

(250) 754-6355. **$105-$139.** 96 Terminal Ave N V9S 4J2. Jct Terminal Ave and Hwy 19A (Island Hwy). Int corridors. **Pets:** Accepted.

ECO SAVE ☒ 🛏 🖭

NELSON

Ⓐ ▼▼▼▼ Best Western Baker Street Inn & Convention Centre **H**

(250) 352-3525. **$109-$149.** 153 Baker St V1L 4H1. Jct Hwy 6 and 3A. Int corridors. **Pets:** Accepted. SAVE ☒ 🖢 🛏 🖭 🍽

▼▼ North Shore Inn **M** ❀

(250) 352-6606. **$62-$85.** 687 Hwy 3A V1L 5P7. 1.9 mi (3 km) n on Hwy 3A via Nelson Bridge. Int corridors. **Pets:** Large, dogs only. $10 daily fee/pet. Designated rooms, service with restrictions, supervision.

A$K ☒ 🛏

NEW DENVER

▼▼ ▼▼ Sweet Dreams Guesthouse **BB**

(250) 358-2415. **$65-$95, 14 day notice.** 702 Eldorado St V0G 1S0. Just w of Hwy 6 on Slocan Ave. Int corridors. **Pets:** Accepted.

A$K ☒ 🐾 📺 ☒

OKANAGAN VALLEY AREA

ENDERBY

Ⓐ ▼▼ ▼ Howard Johnson Inn Fortunes Landing **H**

(250) 838-6825. **$69-$109.** 1510 George St V0E 1V0. 0.6 mi (1 km) n on Hwy 974. Ext corridors. **Pets:** Accepted.

SAVE ☒ 🛏 🖭 🍽 🌫

KELOWNA

Ⓐ ▼▼▼ Accent Inns **H** ❀

(250) 862-8888. **$99-$189.** 1140 Harvey Ave V1Y 6E7. Corner of Hwy 97 N (Harvey Ave) and Gordon Dr. Ext corridors. **Pets:** $15 daily fee/room. Designated rooms, service with restrictions, supervision.

ECO SAVE ☒ 🖢 🛏 🖭 🍽 🌫 ☒

Ⓐ ▼▼▼ Best Western Inn-Kelowna **H** ❀

(250) 860-1212. **$150-$289.** 2402 Hwy 97 N V1X 4J1. 0.6 mi (1 km) s of jct Hwy 33 and 97 N (Harvey Ave); corner of Leckie Rd. Ext/int corridors. **Pets:** Medium. $20 daily fee/room. Designated rooms, service with restrictions, crate. ECO SAVE ☒ 🖢 🛏 🖭 🍽 🌫 ☒

Ⓐ ▼▼▼ Comfort Inn Kelowna-Westside **H** ❀

(250) 769-2355. **$89-$229.** 1655 Westgate Rd V1Z 3P1. Jct Hwy 97 (Harvey Ave) and Bartley Rd, s to Ross Rd. Int corridors. **Pets:** Large. $10 daily fee/room. Designated rooms, service with restrictions, crate.

SAVE ☒ 🛏 🖭 🍽 🌫

Ⓐ ▼▼ ▼ Days Inn **M**

(250) 868-3297. **$99-$179.** 2649 Hwy 97 N V1X 4J6. Jct Hwy 97 (Harvey Ave) and 33, just n. Ext/int corridors. **Pets:** Medium. $10 one-time fee/room. Designated rooms, service with restrictions, supervision.

ECO SAVE ☒ 🛏 🖭 🌫

▼▼▼ Delta Grand Okanagan Resort & Conference Centre 🅷 ❀

(250) 763-4500. **Call for rates.** 1310 Water St V1Y 9P3. Hwy 97 (Harvey Ave), 0.6 mi (1 km) w along Water St. Int corridors. **Pets:** Medium. $35 one-time fee/room. Designated rooms, service with restrictions, supervision. 🌱 ⊠ ♿ 🛏 💻 🍴 🏊 ⊠

Ⓐ ▼▼▼ Econo Lodge 🅼

(250) 762-3221. **$86-$234.** 1780 Gordon Dr V1Y 3H2. Hwy 97 N (Harvey Ave), just e. Ext corridors. **Pets:** Accepted. 🆂🅰🆅🅴 ⊠ 🛏 💻 🏊

▼▼▼ Fairfield Inn & Suites by Marriott Kelowna 🅷 ❀

(250) 763-2800. **$135-$215.** 1655 Powick Rd V1X 4L1. Just s of Jct Hwy 97 N (Harvey Ave) and 33 W. Int corridors. **Pets:** Other species. $15 daily fee/room. Designated rooms, service with restrictions. 🌱 ⊠ ♿ 🛏 🏊 ⊠

Ⓐ ▼▼▼ Recreation Inn & Suites 🅼 ❀

(250) 860-3982. **$92-$242.** 1891 Parkinson Way V1Y 7V6. Hwy 97 N (Harvey Ave), just w on Spall Rd. Ext corridors. **Pets:** Small. $10 daily fee/pet. Service with restrictions, supervision. 🆂🅰🆅🅴 ⊠ 🛏 💻 🏊

Ⓐ ▼▼▼ The Royal Anne Hotel 🅷 ❀

(250) 763-2277. **$89-$189.** 348 Bernard Ave V1Y 6N5. Corner of Pandosy St and Bernard Ave; downtown. Int corridors. **Pets:** Medium. $20 daily fee/pet. Service with restrictions, supervision. 🆂🅰🆅🅴 ⊠ 🛏 💻

▼▼ Vineyard Inn 🅼

(250) 860-5703. **$94-$189, 3 day notice.** 2486 Hwy 97 N V1X 4J3. Southwest corner of jct Hwy 97 (Harvey Ave) and 33. Ext corridors. **Pets:** Very small, dogs only. $10 daily fee/pet. Designated rooms, service with restrictions, supervision. 🅰🆂🅺 ⊠ 🛏 💻 🏊 ⊠

NARAMATA

▼▼ The Village Motel 🅼

(250) 496-5535. **$90-$145, 14 day notice.** 244 Robinson Dr V0H 1N0. 8.8 mi (14 km) n on Naramata Rd from Penticton. Ext corridors. **Pets:** Accepted. ⊠ 🛏 💻 🐾 ⊠

OSOYOOS

Ⓐ ▼▼▼ Best Western Sunrise Inn 🅷 ❀

(250) 495-4000. **$99-$255, 7 day notice.** 5506 Main St V0H 1V0. Jct Hwy 97, 1.9 mi (3 km) on Hwy 3 (Main St). Int corridors. **Pets:** Small. $20 daily fee/pet. Designated rooms, service with restrictions, supervision. 🆂🅰🆅🅴 ⊠ ♿ 🛏 💻 🍴 🏊

▼▼▼ Spirit Ridge Vineyard Resort & Spa 🅲🅾

(250) 495-5445. **Call for rates.** 1200 Rancher Creek Rd V0H 1V6. Hwy 97 S, e on Hwy 3 (Main St), cross bridge, left on 45th St, 0.9 mi (1.5 km) e. Ext/int corridors. **Pets:** Accepted. ⊠ ♿ 🛏 💻 🍴 🏊 ⊠

PENTICTON

Ⓐ ▼▼▼ Best Western Inn at Penticton 🅷 ❀

(250) 493-0311. **$99-$199.** 3180 Skaha Lake Rd V2A 6G4. 2.5 mi (4 km) s. Ext corridors. **Pets:** Small, dogs only. $10 daily fee/pet. Designated rooms, service with restrictions, supervision. 🌱 🆂🅰🆅🅴 ⊠ 🛏 💻 🍴 🏊

Ⓐ ▼▼▼ Days Inn & Conference Centre Penticton 🅷

(250) 493-6616. **$99-$299.** 152 Riverside Dr V2A 5Y4. Hwy 97, just n. Int corridors. **Pets:** Accepted. 🌱 🆂🅰🆅🅴 ⊠ ♿ 🛏 💻 🍴 🏊 ⊠

Ⓐ ▼▼▼ Penticton Lakeside Resort, Convention Centre & Casino 🅷 ❀

(250) 493-8221. **$165-$235, 7 day notice.** 21 Lakeshore Dr W V2A 7M5. Main St at Lakeshore Dr W. Int corridors. **Pets:** Other species. $15 daily fee/room. Designated rooms, service with restrictions, supervision. 🌱 🆂🅰🆅🅴 ⊠ 🛏 💻 🍴 🏊 ⊠

Ⓐ ▼▼▼ Ramada Inn & Suites 🅷

(250) 492-8926. **$89-$269.** 1050 Eckhardt Ave W V2A 2C3. 0.8 mi (1.2 km) w on Hwy 97. Ext/int corridors. **Pets:** Accepted. 🌱 🆂🅰🆅🅴 ⊠ 🛏 💻 🍴 🏊 ⊠

Ⓐ ▼▼ Spanish Villa Resort 🅼

(250) 492-2922. **$68-$350, 14 day notice.** 890 Lakeshore Dr W V2A 1C1. Corner of Power St and Lakeshore Dr W. Ext corridors. **Pets:** Medium, dogs only. $10 daily fee/pet. Designated rooms, service with restrictions, supervision. 🆂🅰🆅🅴 ⊠ 🛏 💻 🏊

▼▼ Super 8 Penticton 🅼

(250) 492-3829. **Call for rates.** 1706 Main St V2A 5G8. Jct Main St and Industrial Ave. Ext/int corridors. **Pets:** Accepted. ⊠ ♿ 🛏 💻 🏊

SUMMERLAND

Ⓐ ▼▼▼ Summerland Motel 🅼

(250) 494-4444. **$80-$150, 10 day notice.** 2107 Tait St V0H 1Z4. 3.1 mi (5 km) s on Hwy 97. Ext corridors. **Pets:** $10 daily fee/room. Designated rooms, service with restrictions, crate. 🆂🅰🆅🅴 ⊠ 🛏 💻 🏊

VERNON

Ⓐ ▼▼▼ Best Western Vernon Lodge & Conference Centre 🅷 ❀

(250) 545-3385. **$111-$159.** 3914 32nd St V1T 5P1. 1 mi (1.5 km) n on Hwy 97 (32nd St). Int corridors. **Pets:** $15 daily fee/room. Designated rooms, service with restrictions, supervision. 🆂🅰🆅🅴 ⊠ ♿ 🛏 💻 🍴 🏊

Ⓐ ▼▼▼ Best Western Villager Motor Inn 🅼 ❀

(250) 549-2224. **$96-$141.** 5121 26th St V1T 8G4. 1.5 mi (2.5 km) n on 27th St. Ext corridors. **Pets:** Medium. $15 daily fee/pet. Designated rooms, supervision. 🆂🅰🆅🅴 ⊠ 🛏 💻 🏊

Ⓐ ▼▼▼ Holiday Inn Express Hotel & Suites Vernon 🅷

(250) 550-7777. **$109-$189.** 4716 34th St V1T 5Y9. Hwy 97 (32nd St) northbound at 48th Ave. Int corridors. **Pets:** Medium. $20 one-time fee/pet. Designated rooms, service with restrictions, supervision. 🆂🅰🆅🅴 ⊠ 🛏 💻 🏊

▼▼ Vernon Travelodge 🅼

(250) 545-2161. **$85-$159.** 3000 28th Ave V1T 1W1. Hwy 97 (32nd St), just e on 28th Ave. Ext corridors. **Pets:** Medium, dogs only. $10 daily fee/pet. Designated rooms, service with restrictions, supervision. 🌱 🅰🆂🅺 ⊠ 🛏 💻 🏊

WEST KELOWNA

▼▼▼ The Cove Lakeside Resort 🅷

(250) 707-1800. **$149-$889, 3 day notice.** 4205 Gellatly Rd V4T 2K2. Hwy 97 (Dobbin Rd), 1 mi (1.6 km) s, follow signs. Int corridors. **Pets:** Medium. $20 daily fee/pet. Service with restrictions, supervision. 🌱 🅰🆂🅺 ⊠ ♿ 🛏 💻 🍴 🏊 ⊠

END AREA

PARKSVILLE

▼▼ Arbutus Grove Motel 🅼

(250) 248-6422. **Call for rates.** 1182 E Island Hwy V9P 1W3. Island Hwy 19, exit 46 (Parksville), 1 mi (1.6 km) n on Hwy 19A. Ext corridors. **Pets:** Accepted. ⊠ 🛏 💻

▼▼▼ Oceanside Village Resort 🅲🅰

(250) 248-8961. **Call for rates.** 1080 Resort Dr V9P 2E3. Island Hwy 19, exit 46 (Parksville), 1.8 mi (2.5 km) n on Hwy 19A. Ext corridors. **Pets:** $15 daily fee/pet. Designated rooms, service with restrictions, supervision. ⊠ 🛏 💻 🏊 🐾

ⒸⒶⒶ ▼▼▼ **Quality Resort Bayside** Ⓗ

(250) 248-8333. **$119-$179.** 240 Dogwood St V9P 2H5. Island Hwy 19, exit 51 (Parksville/Coombs), 1.3 mi (2 km), then 0.6 mi (1 km) n on Hwy 19A. Int corridors. **Pets:** Accepted. 🅂🄰🅅🄴 ⊠ 🄶M ▣ 🍴 🏊

▼ **Skylite Motel** Ⓜ

(250) 248-4271. **$89-$139.** 459 E Island Hwy V9P 2G5. Island Hwy 19, exit 46 (Parksville), 2.2 mi (3.5 km) n on Hwy 19A. Ext corridors. **Pets:** Other species. $10 daily fee/pet. Service with restrictions, supervision. 🄰🅂🄺 ⊠ 🄗 ▣

▼▼▼ **Tigh-Na-Mara Seaside Spa Resort & Conference Center** Ⓗ 🐾

(250) 248-2072. **$119-$359, 5 day notice.** 1155 Resort Dr V9P 2E5. Island Hwy 19, exit 46 (Parksville), 1.3 mi (2 km) n on Hwy 19A. Ext corridors. **Pets:** Medium, dogs only. $30 one-time fee/room. Designated rooms, service with restrictions, crate.

🄰🅂🄺 ⊠ 🄗 ▣ 🍴 🏊 ⊠ 🄐🄲

▼▼ **Travelodge Parksville** Ⓗ

(250) 248-2232. **$99-$239.** 424 W Island Hwy V9P 1K8. Island Hwy 19, exit 51 (Parksville/Coombs), 1.3 mi (2 km) e, then just n on Hwy 19A. Int corridors. **Pets:** Medium. $10 daily fee/pet. Designated rooms, no service, supervision. 🄰🅂🄺 ⊠ 🄶M 🏊

ⒸⒶⒶ ▼▼ **V.I.P. Motel** Ⓜ

(250) 248-3244. **$69-$169.** 414 W Island Hwy V9P 1K8. Island Hwy 19, exit 51 (Parksville/Coombs), 1.3 mi (2 km) e, then just n on Hwy 19A. Ext corridors. **Pets:** Large. $10 daily fee/pet. Service with restrictions, supervision. 🅂🄰🅅🄴 ⊠ 🄗 ▣

PARSON

▼▼ **Alexa Chalets-Timber Inn & Restaurant** Ⓗ

(250) 348-2228. **Call for rates.** 3483 Hwy 95 V0A 1L0. Just off Hwy 95; 21.3 mi (34 km) s of Golden. Ext/int corridors. **Pets:** Accepted.

⊠ 🄗 ▣ 🍴 ⊠ 🄐🄲 🐾 ⊠

PEMBERTON

▼▼▼ **Pemberton Valley Lodge** Ⓗ 🐾

(604) 894-2000. **$139-$409.** 1490 Portage Rd V0N 2L1. Just e on Hwy 99 from Pioneer Junction. Int corridors. **Pets:** Medium, dogs only. $45 one-time fee/pet. Designated rooms, supervision.

🄴🄲🄾 🄰🅂🄺 ⊠ 🄶M 🄗 ▣ 🏊

PORT ALBERNI

ⒸⒶⒶ ▼▼▼ **Best Western Barclay Hotel** Ⓗ

(250) 724-7171. **$109-$159.** 4277 Stamp Ave V9Y 7X8. Johnston Rd (Hwy 4), just s on Gertrude St. Int corridors. **Pets:** Accepted.

🅂🄰🅅🄴 ⊠ 🄗 ▣ 🍴 🏊 ⊠

▼▼▼ **The Hospitality Inn** Ⓗ

(250) 723-8111. **$129-$155.** 3835 Redford St V9Y 3S2. 2 mi (3.2 km) sw of jct Hwy 4 via City Centre/Port Alberni South Route. Int corridors. **Pets:** Other species. $10 daily fee/pet. Designated rooms, crate.

🄴🄲🄾 🄰🅂🄺 ⊠ ▣ 🍴 🏊

ⒸⒶⒶ ▼ **Riverside Motel** Ⓜ

(250) 724-9916. **$69-$139.** 5065 Roger St V9Y 3Y9. Johnston Rd (Hwy 4), just s on Gertrude St, then just w. Ext corridors. **Pets:** Accepted.

🅂🄰🅅🄴 ⊠ 🄗 ▣

▼▼ **Somass Motel** Ⓜ

(250) 724-3236. **$60-$130.** 5279 River Rd V9Y 6Z3. 2 mi (3.2 km) on River Rd (Hwy 4) from Johnston Rd. Ext corridors. **Pets:** Small. $10 daily fee/pet. Designated rooms, service with restrictions, supervision.

⊠ 🄗 ▣ 🏊

PORT HARDY

▼▼ **Glen Lyon Inn** Ⓗ

(250) 949-7115. **$105-$180, 3 day notice.** 6435 Hardy Bay Rd V0N 2P0. Hwy 19, 0.9 mi (1.5 km) n, follow signs. Ext corridors. **Pets:** Accepted. 🄰🅂🄺 ⊠ 🄗 ▣ 🍴 🄐🄲

POWELL RIVER

▼▼ **Powell River Town Centre Hotel** Ⓗ

(604) 485-3000. **$99-$200.** 4660 Joyce Ave V8A 3B6. 0.5 mi (0.8 km) e on Duncan St (BC ferry terminal), then 0.6 mi (1 km) n. Int corridors. **Pets:** Accepted. 🄰🅂🄺 ⊠ 🄗 ▣ 🍴

PRINCE GEORGE

ⒸⒶⒶ ▼▼▼ **Best Western City Centre** Ⓜ 🐾

(250) 563-1267. **$110-$140.** 910 Victoria St V2L 2K8. Just n of Victoria St (Hwy 16) and Patricia Blvd; downtown. Ext corridors. **Pets:** Other species. $25 daily fee/pet. Designated rooms, service with restrictions, supervision. 🅂🄰🅅🄴 ⊠ 🄗 ▣ 🍴 🏊

ⒸⒶⒶ ▼▼▼▼ **Four Points by Sheraton Prince George** Ⓗ

(250) 564-7100. **Call for rates.** 1790 Hwy 97 S V2L 5L3. Hwy 97, exit Spruce northbound; exit city centre via Queensway southbound. Int corridors. **Pets:** Accepted. 🅂🄰🅅🄴 ⊠ 🄶M 🄗 ▣ 🍴 🏊

PRINCE RUPERT

ⒸⒶⒶ ▼ **Aleeda Motel** Ⓜ

(250) 627-1367. **$50-$105.** 900 3rd Ave W V8J 1M8. Corner of 3rd Ave W and 8th St. Int corridors. **Pets:** Other species. $5 one-time fee/pet. Designated rooms, service with restrictions. 🅂🄰🅅🄴 ⊠ 🄗 ▣ 🄐🄲

▼▼ **The Coast Prince Rupert Hotel** Ⓗ 🐾

(250) 624-6711. **$116-$197.** 118 6th St V8J 3L7. Between 1st and 2nd aves W. Int corridors. **Pets:** Medium, other species. $15 daily fee/pet. Service with restrictions, crate. 🄴🄲🄾 🄰🅂🄺 ⊠ 🄶M ▣ 🍴

▼▼ **Inn on the Harbour** Ⓜ

(250) 624-9107. **$85-$145.** 720 1st Ave W V8J 3V6. Corner of 6th St. Int corridors. **Pets:** Accepted. 🄰🅂🄺 ⊠ 🄶M 🄗 ▣ 🄐🄲

ⒸⒶⒶ ▼▼ **Totem Lodge Motel** Ⓜ

(250) 624-6761. **$69-$99, 7 day notice.** 1335 Park Ave V8J 1K3. 1 mi (1.6 km) w on Hwy 16 (2nd Ave W) from downtown. Int corridors. **Pets:** Small, dogs only. $10 daily fee/pet. Designated rooms, service with restrictions, supervision. 🅂🄰🅅🄴 ⊠ 🄗 ▣ 🄐🄲

PRINCETON

ⒸⒶⒶ ▼▼▼ **Canadas Best Value Princeton Inn & Suites** Ⓜ

(250) 295-3537. **$99-$139.** 169 Hwy 3 V0X 1W0. On Hwy 3. Ext corridors. **Pets:** Small. $10 one-time fee/pet. Designated rooms, service with restrictions, supervision. 🅂🄰🅅🄴 ⊠ 🄶M 🄗 ▣ 🏊

ⒸⒶⒶ ▼ **Villager Inn** Ⓜ

(250) 295-6996. **$69-$95.** 244 4th St V0X 1W0. Just off Hwy 3. Ext corridors. **Pets:** Medium. $10 daily fee/pet. Designated rooms, service with restrictions, crate. 🅂🄰🅅🄴 ⊠ 🄗 ▣

QUALICUM BEACH

▼▼ **Old Dutch Inn (By The Sea)** Ⓗ

(250) 752-6914. **$80-$140.** 2690 Island Hwy W V9K 1G8. Hwy 19, exit 60 (Qualicum Beach/Port Alberni), 2.5 mi (4 km) on Memorial Ave at jct Hwy 19A. Int corridors. **Pets:** Accepted.

🄰🅂🄺 ⊠ 🄗 ▣ 🍴 🏊 🄐🄲

QUESNEL

ⒸⒶⒶ ▼▼ **Talisman Inn** Ⓜ

(250) 992-7247. **$69-$149.** 753 Front St V2J 2L2. Hwy 97, 0.6 mi (1 km) n of Carson Ave. Int corridors. **Pets:** Small. $10 daily fee/pet. Designated rooms, service with restrictions, supervision. 🅂🄰🅅🄴 ⊠ 🄶M 🄗 ▣

RADIUM HOT SPRINGS

ⒸⒶⒶ ▼▼▼ **Chalet Europe** Ⓜ

(250) 347-9305. **$89-$189, 7 day notice.** 5063 Madsen Rd V0A 1M0. Hwy 95, just w on Hwy 93, then 0.4 mi (0.7 km) s, up the hill. Ext corridors. **Pets:** Accepted. 🅂🄰🅅🄴 🄗 ▣ ⊠

Lido Motel M
(250) 347-9533. **$65-$95, 7 day notice.** 4876 McKay St V0A 1M0. Jct Hwy 93 and 95, just e, just e, just s along Main St, then just e. Ext corridors. **Pets:** Other species. $10 daily fee/pet. Crate. ⊠ 🛄 🖥 🐾

Prestige Radium Hot Springs H
(250) 347-2300. **$129-$209.** 7493 Main St W V0A 1M0. Jct Hwy 93 and 95. Int corridors. **Pets:** Small, dogs only. $20 daily fee/pet. Designated rooms, service with restrictions, supervision.
SAVE ⊠ 🛄 🖥 🍽 🏊 ⊠

REVELSTOKE

The Coast Hillcrest Resort Hotel H ❀
(250) 837-3322. **$159-$239.** 2100 Oak Dr V0E 2S0. 2.7 mi (4.3 km) e on Trans-Canada Hwy 1, 0.6 mi (0.9 km) sw. Int corridors. **Pets:** $15 daily fee/room. Designated rooms, service with restrictions, crate.
ECO SAVE ⊠ 🛄 🖥 🍽 ⊠

Days Inn & Suites Revelstoke H
(250) 837-2191. **$89-$199.** 301 Wright St V0E 2S0. South side of Trans-Canada Hwy 1, just e of Columbia River Bridge at Victoria Rd, then just se. Ext/int corridors. **Pets:** Accepted.
ECO SAVE ⊠ 🛄 🖥 ⊠

Monashee Lodge M
(250) 837-6778. **Call for rates.** 1601 3rd St W V0E 2S0. South side of Trans-Canada Hwy 1, just e of Columbia River Bridge at Victoria Rd, then just se on Wright St. Ext corridors. **Pets:** Accepted. ⊠ 🛄 🖥

Sandman Hotel H
(250) 837-5271. **Call for rates.** 1901 LaForme Blvd V0E 2S0. North side of Trans-Canada Hwy 1, at intersection nearest east end of Columbia River Bridge. Ext/int corridors. **Pets:** Accepted.
SAVE ⊠ 🛄 🖥 🍽 🏊

Swiss Chalet Motel M
(250) 837-4650. **$89-$155.** 1101 Victoria Rd V0E 2S0. 0.6 mi (1 km) s from Trans-Canada Hwy 1. Ext corridors. **Pets:** Accepted.
SAVE ⊠ 🛄 🖥

SALMON ARM

Best Western Salmon Arm Inn M
(250) 832-9793. **$99-$149.** 61 10th St SW V1E 1E4. 0.7 mi (1.1 km) w on Trans-Canada Hwy 1. Ext corridors. **Pets:** Small. $15 daily fee/pet. Designated rooms, service with restrictions, supervision.
SAVE ⊠ 🛄 🖥 🏊

SICAMOUS

Sicamous Super 8 M
(250) 836-4988. **$70-$170.** 1120 Riverside Ave V0E 2V0. Trans-Canada Hwy 1, s on Hwy 97A, just w on Main St to traffic circle, then just s. Ext corridors. **Pets:** Accepted. ⊠ 🛄 🖥

SILVERTON

William Hunter Cabins CA
(250) 358-2844. **$88-$128, 14 day notice.** 303 Lake Ave V0G 2B0. Centre. Ext corridors. **Pets:** Accepted. ASK ⊠ 🛄 🖥 🐾 🐾

SMITHERS

Aspen Inn & Suites M
(250) 847-4551. **Call for rates.** 4628 Yellowhead Hwy V0J 2N0. 0.9 mi (1.5 km) w on Hwy 16 (Yellowhead Hwy). Ext corridors. **Pets:** Accepted.
⊠ 🛄 🖥 🍽 ⊠

SQUAMISH

Executive Suites Garibaldi Springs Golf Resort H
(604) 815-0048. **$119-$389.** 40900 Tantalus Rd V8B 0R3. Hwy 99, just e on Garibaldi Way, then 0.6 mi (1 km) n. Int corridors. **Pets:** Accepted.
SAVE ⊠ 🛄 🖥 🖥 🍽 🏊 ⊠

Mountain Retreat Hotel & Suites H
(604) 815-0883. **$125-$140.** 38922 Progress Way V8B 0K5. 0.9 mi (1.5 km) n on Hwy 99 at Industrial Way. Int corridors. **Pets:** Other species. $25 daily fee/room. Designated rooms, service with restrictions, supervision. SAVE ⊠ 🛄 🖥 🖥 🍽 🏊 ⊠

SUN PEAKS

Delta Sun Peaks Resort H
(250) 578-6000. **$99-$399.** 3240 Village Way V0E 5N0. Hwy 5, 19.4 mi (31 km) ne on Todd Mountain Rd, follow signs to village. Int corridors. **Pets:** Accepted. ECO ASK ⊠ 🛄 🖥 🖥 🍽 🏊 ⊠

TERRACE

Best Western Terrace Inn H
(250) 635-0083. **$139-$248.** 4553 Greig Ave V8G 1M7. Hwy 16, just e on Greig Ave, follow city centre signs. Int corridors. **Pets:** Medium. $10 daily fee/room. Designated rooms, service with restrictions.
ECO SAVE ⊠ 🛄 🖥 🍽

Coast Inn of the West H
(250) 638-8141. **$109-$229.** 4620 Lakelse Ave V8G 1R1. Hwy 16 to city centre; between Emerson and Kalum sts; downtown. Int corridors. **Pets:** Large, other species. $25 one-time fee/room. Designated rooms, service with restrictions, supervision. ECO ASK 🛄 🖥 🍽

TOFINO

Best Western Tin Wis Resort H
(250) 725-4445. **$165-$395.** 1119 Pacific Rim Hwy V0R 2Z0. 1.8 mi (3.5 km) s on Hwy 4. Ext corridors. **Pets:** Accepted.
SAVE ⊠ 🛄 🖥 🖥 🍽 🏊 ⊠

Long Beach Lodge Resort H
(250) 725-2442. **Call for rates.** 1441 Pacific Rim Hwy V0R 2Z0. 4.7 mi (7.5 km) s on Hwy 4. Ext/int corridors. **Pets:** Accepted.
⊠ 🛄 🖥 🖥 🍽 ⊠

Pacific Sands Beach Resort H
(250) 725-3322. **$185-$600.** 1421 Pacific Rim Hwy V0R 2Z0. 4.7 mi (7.5 km) s on Hwy 4. Ext corridors. **Pets:** Accepted.
SAVE ⊠ 🛄 🖥 🖥 ⊠

Wickaninnish Inn H
(250) 725-3100. **$300-$560, 14 day notice.** 500 Osprey Ln at Chesterman Beach V0R 2Z0. 2.7 mi (4.3 km) e on Hwy 4. Int corridors. **Pets:** Other species. $40 daily fee/pet. Designated rooms, service with restrictions, crate. ECO SAVE ⊠ 🛄 🖥 🍽 ⊠ ⊠

UCLUELET

Black Rock Oceanfront Resort H
(250) 726-4800. **Call for rates.** 596 Marine Dr V0R 3A0. 1 mi (1.6 km) e on Peninsula Rd, just s on Materson Rd, then just w. Ext/int corridors. **Pets:** Accepted. ⊠ 🛄 🖥 🖥 🍽 ⊠ ⊠

VALEMOUNT

Best Western Valemount Inn & Suites H
(250) 566-0086. **$107-$193.** 1950 Hwy 5 S V0E 2Z0. 0.9 mi (1.5 km) s on Hwy 5 (Yellowhead Hwy). Int corridors. **Pets:** Accepted.
SAVE ⊠ 🛄 🖥 🍽 🏊 ⊠

Chalet Continental Motel H
(250) 566-9787. **$79-$149.** 1450 5th Ave V0E 2Z0. Off Hwy 5 (Yellowhead Hwy), just e. Int corridors. **Pets:** Accepted.
SAVE ⊠ 🛄 🖥 🖥 🏊 ⊠

VANCOUVER METROPOLITAN AREA

ALDERGROVE

ⓐ ▼▼▼ Best Western Country Meadows ⊞ ❀
(604) 856-9880. **$90-$225.** 3070 264th St V4W 3E1. Trans-Canada Hwy 1, exit 73 (264th St/Aldergrove), 3.1 mi (5 km) s on 264th St (Hwy 13). Int corridors. **Pets:** Small. $15 daily fee/room. Designated rooms, service with restrictions, supervision. ⚐ ⊠ ⚑ ⊞ ⬛ ⏁ ⚐

BURNABY

ⓐ ▼▼ Accent Inns ⊞ ❀
(604) 473-5000. **$119-$179.** 3777 Henning Dr V5C 6N5. Trans-Canada Hwy 1, exit 28 (Grandview Hwy), just n on Boundary Rd. Ext corridors. **Pets:** Medium. $20 daily fee/pet. Designated rooms, service with restrictions, supervision. ⒺⒸⓄ ⚐ ⊠ ⚑ ⊞ ⬛ ⏁ ⚐

ⓐ ▼▼▼▼ Best Western Kings Inn and Conference Centre ⊞
(604) 438-1383. **$119-$169.** 5411 Kingsway V5H 2G1. Trans-Canada Hwy 1, exit 29 (Willingdon Ave), 1.9 mi (3 km) s to Kingsway, then 1.2 mi (2 km) e. Ext corridors. **Pets:** Small. $15 daily fee/room. Designated rooms, service with restrictions, crate. ⚐ ⊠ ⚑ ⬛ ⏁ ⚐

ⓐ ▼▼▼▼ Delta Burnaby Hotel and Conference Centre ⊞
(604) 453-0750. **$139-$279.** 4331 Dominion St V5G 1B2. Trans-Canada Hwy 1, exit 29 (Willingdon Ave S), just w on Canada Way, then n on Sumner St. Int corridors. **Pets:** Accepted.
⚐ ⊠ ⚑ ⊞ ⬛ ⏁ ⚐

ⓐ ▼▼▼▼ Hilton Vancouver Metrotown ⊞ ❀
(604) 438-1200. **$119-$799.** 6083 McKay Ave V5H 2W7. Trans-Canada Hwy 1, exit 29 (Willingdon Ave), 1.8 mi (3 km) s to Kingsway, then just e. Int corridors. **Pets:** $29 one-time fee/pet. Designated rooms, supervision.
ⒺⒸⓄ ⚐ ⊠ ⚑ ⊞ ⬛ ⏁ ⚐

▼▼▼ Holiday Inn Express Metrotown ⊞
(604) 438-1881. **$99-$199.** 4405 Central Blvd V5H 4M3. Trans-Canada Hwy 1, exit 29 (Willingdon Ave), 3.1 mi (5 km) s to Central Blvd, then just e. Int corridors. **Pets:** Small. $25 one-time fee/room. Designated rooms, service with restrictions, crate. ⒺⒸⓄ Ⓐ$Ⓚ ⊠ ⚑ ⊞ ⬛ ⚐

ⓐ ▼▼ Lake City Inn & Suites Ⓜ
(604) 294-5331. **$89-$109.** 5415 Lougheed Hwy V5B 2Z7. Trans-Canada Hwy 1, exit 29 (Willingdon Ave), just n, 0.6 mi (1 km) e on Lougheed Hwy, just n on Springer Ave, then just e on Broadway. Ext corridors.
Pets: Accepted. ⚐ ⊠ ⚑ ⬛ ⚐

COQUITLAM

▼▼ Ramada Coquitlam ⊞
(604) 931-4433. **$90-$150.** 631 Lougheed Hwy V3K 3S5. Trans-Canada Hwy 1, exit 44 (Coquitlam), 1.9 mi (3 km) w on Lougheed Hwy (Hwy 7). Ext/int corridors. **Pets:** Accepted. Ⓐ$Ⓚ ⊠ ⚑ ⬛ ⏁ ⚐

DELTA

ⓐ ▼▼▼ The Coast Tsawwassen Inn ⊞ ❀
(604) 943-8221. **$111-$128.** 1665 56th St V4L 2B2. Hwy 99, exit 28 (Tsawwassen Ferries), 5 mi (8 km) w on Hwy 17; 3.1 mi (5 km) from the BC ferry terminal. Int corridors. **Pets:** Medium. $10 daily fee/pet. Service with restrictions, supervision.
ⒺⒸⓄ ⚐ ⊠ ⚑ ⊞ ⬛ ⏁ ⚐ ⚐

▼▼▼ River Run Cottages ⒷⒷ
(604) 946-7778. **$149-$225, 21 day notice.** 4551 River Rd W V4K 1R9. Hwy 17, 1.6 mi (2.5 km) n on Ladner Trunk Rd (which becomes 47A St, then becomes River Rd W). Ext corridors. **Pets:** Accepted.
Ⓐ$Ⓚ ⊠ ⚑ ⬛ ⅏ ⚐ ⚐

LANGLEY

ⓐ ▼ Best Value Westward Inn Ⓜ
(604) 534-9238. **$89-$99.** 19650 Fraser Hwy V3A 4C7. Trans-Canada Hwy 1, exit 58 (200th St/Langley City), 3.1 mi (5 km) s on 200th St, 0.6 mi (1 km) w on Hwy 10, then just w. Ext corridors. **Pets:** Large. $4 daily fee/room. Service with restrictions, supervision. ⚐ ⊠ ⚑ ⬛

ⓐ ▼▼▼ Best Western Langley Inn ⊞
(604) 530-9311. **$110-$231.** 5978 Glover Rd V3A 4H9. Trans-Canada Hwy 1, exit 66 (232nd St), 6 km s, follow signs. Int corridors.
Pets: Accepted. ⚐ ⊠ ⚑ ⊞ ⬛ ⏁ ⚐

ⓐ ▼▼▼▼ Coast Hotel & Convention Centre ⊞
(604) 530-1500. **$125-$175.** 20393 Fraser Hwy V3A 7N2. Trans-Canada Hwy 1, exit 58 (200th St/Langley City), 3.9 mi (6.3 km) s on 200th St, then just e. Int corridors. **Pets:** Medium. $15 daily fee/room. Designated rooms, service with restrictions. ⚐ ⊠ ⚑ ⬛ ⏁

ⓐ ▼▼▼▼ Holiday Inn Express Hotel & Suites Langley ⊞
(604) 882-2000. **$115-$199.** 8750 204th St V1M 2Y5. Trans-Canada Hwy 1, exit 58 (200th St/Langley City), just e on 88th Ave. Int corridors.
Pets: Accepted. ⒺⒸⓄ ⚐ ⊠ ⚑ ⊞ ⬛ ⏁ ⚐ ⚐

▼▼ Sandman Hotel Langley ⊞
(604) 888-7263. **$119-$169.** 8855 202nd St V1M 2N9. Trans-Canada Hwy 1, exit 58 (200th St/Langley City), just e on 88th Ave. Int corridors.
Pets: Accepted. ⒺⒸⓄ Ⓐ$Ⓚ ⊠ ⚑ ⊞ ⬛ ⏁

▼▼ Super 8 Langley/Aldergrove Ⓜ
(604) 856-8288. **$109-$169.** 26574 Gloucester Way V4W 4A8. Trans-Canada Hwy 1, exit 73 (264th St/Aldergrove), just e on 56th Ave. Int corridors. **Pets:** Accepted. ⒺⒸⓄ Ⓐ$Ⓚ ⊠ ⚑ ⊞ ⬛ ⚐ ⚐

MAPLE RIDGE

ⓐ ▼▼▼ Maple Ridge Inn & Suites ⊞
(604) 463-5111. **$89-$129.** 21735 Lougheed Hwy V2X 2S2. 1.2 mi (2 km) w on Lougheed Hwy (Hwy 7). Ext corridors. **Pets:** Small, other species. $15 one-time fee/room. Designated rooms, service with restrictions, supervision. ⚐ ⊠ ⚑ ⊞ ⬛ ⏁

ⓐ ▼▼▼ Travelodge Maple Ridge Ⓜ ❀
(604) 467-1511. **$89-$169.** 21650 Lougheed Hwy V2X 2S1. 1.2 mi (2 km) w on Lougheed Hwy (Hwy 7). Int corridors. **Pets:** Large. $35 one-time fee/room. Service with restrictions, supervision.
⚐ ⊠ ⚑ ⊞ ⬛

MISSION

ⓐ ▼▼▼ Best Western Mission City Lodge ⊞ ❀
(604) 820-5500. **$95-$249.** 32281 Lougheed Hwy V2V 1A3. Just w of Hwy 11; corner of Lougheed Hwy (Hwy 7) and Hurd St. Int corridors.
Pets: Small. $15 daily fee/pet. Designated rooms, service with restrictions, supervision. ⚐ ⊠ ⚑ ⊞ ⬛ ⏁ ⚐ ⚐

NORTH VANCOUVER

ⓐ ▼▼▼ Holiday Inn Hotel & Suites North Vancouver ⊞ ❀
(604) 985-3111. **$199-$350.** 700 Old Lillooet Rd V7J 2H5. Trans-Canada Hwy 1, exit 22 (Mt Seymour Pkwy), follow signs. Int corridors.
Pets: Medium, dogs only. $25 daily fee/pet. Designated rooms, service with restrictions, supervision.
ⒺⒸⓄ ⚐ ⊠ ⚑ ⊞ ⬛ ⏁ ⚐ ⚐

▼▼▼ Lionsgate Travelodge Ⓜ
(604) 985-5311. **$59-$149.** 2060 Marine Dr V7P 1V7. Trans-Canada Hwy 1, exit 14 (Capilano Rd), 0.9 mi (1.5 km) s, then just w; from north end of Lions Gate Bridge, just e. Ext corridors. **Pets:** Medium, other species. Designated rooms. Ⓐ$Ⓚ ⊠ ⚑ ⬛ ⚐

⁜ ▼▼ North Vancouver Hotel Ⓜ

(604) 987-4461. **$79-$169.** 1800 Capilano Rd V7P 3B6. Trans-Canada Hwy 1, exit 14 (Capilano Rd), 0.9 mi (1.5 km) s; from north end of Lions Gate Bridge, 0.6 mi (1 km) e on Marine Dr, then just n. Ext corridors. **Pets:** Medium. $20 daily fee/room. Designated rooms, service with restrictions, supervision. SAVE ⨯ ⅏M 🛏 💻 🍽 ⊇

RICHMOND

⁜ ▼▼ Accent Inns Ⓗ ❀

(604) 273-3311. **$89-$179.** 10551 St Edwards Dr V6X 3L8. Hwy 99, exit 39 (Bridgeport Rd/Airport) northbound to St Edwards Dr; exit 39A (Richmond/Airport) southbound to St Edwards Dr. Ext corridors. **Pets:** Large. $20 daily fee/room. Designated rooms, service with restrictions. ECO SAVE ⨯ ⅏M 🛏 💻 ⊇

⁜ ▼▼ Best Western Abercorn Inn Ⓗ

(604) 270-7576. **$125-$160.** 9260 Bridgeport Rd V6X 1S1. Hwy 99, exit 39 (Bridgeport Rd/Airport) northbound; exit 39A (Richmond/Airport) southbound. Int corridors. **Pets:** Accepted.
ECO SAVE ⨯ ⅏M 🛏 💻 🍽

⁜ ▼▼▼ Delta Vancouver Airport Ⓗ

(604) 278-1241. **$159-$329.** 3500 Cessna Dr V7B 1C7. Corner of Russ Baker Way and Cessna Dr; near Moray Bridge. Int corridors. **Pets:** $35 one-time fee/pet. Service with restrictions, crate.
ECO SAVE ⨯ ⅏M 💻 🍽 ⊇

⁜ ▼▼▼▼ The Fairmont Vancouver Airport Ⓗ

(604) 207-5200. **$319-$429.** 3111 Grant McConachie Way V7B 1X9. In Vancouver International Airport. Int corridors. **Pets:** Accepted.
ECO SAVE ⨯ ⅏M 💻 🍽 ⊇ ⊠

⁜ ▼▼▼▼ Hilton Vancouver Airport Ⓗ ❀

(604) 273-6336. **$159-$799.** 5911 Minoru Blvd V6X 4C7. Corner of Minoru Blvd and Westminster Hwy. Int corridors. **Pets:** Medium. $35 one-time fee/room. Designated rooms, service with restrictions, crate.
ECO SAVE ⨯ ⅏M 🛏 💻 🍽 ⊇ ⊠

⁜ ▼▼▼ Holiday Inn Express Vancouver-Airport Ⓗ

(604) 273-8080. **$129-$179.** 9351 Bridgeport Rd V6X 1S3. Hwy 99, exit 39 (Bridgeport Rd/Airport) northbound; exit 39A (Richmond/Airport) southbound. Int corridors. **Pets:** $25 daily fee/pet. Designated rooms, service with restrictions, supervision. ECO SAVE ⨯ ⅏M 🛏 💻

⁜ ▼▼▼ Holiday Inn International Vancouver Airport Ⓗ

(604) 821-1818. **$115-$189.** 10720 Cambie Rd V6X 1K8. Hwy 99, exit 39A (Bridgeport Rd/Airport) northbound to St. Edwards Dr, then 0.6 mi (1 km) n; exit 39B (No 4 Rd) southbound, just e. Int corridors. **Pets:** $25 daily fee/pet. Designated rooms, service with restrictions, supervision.
ECO SAVE ⨯ ⅏M 🛏 💻 🍽

⁜ ▼▼▼▼ River Rock Casino Resort Ⓗ

(604) 247-8900. **Call for rates.** 8811 River Rd V6X 3P8. Hwy 99, exit 39 (Bridgeport Rd/Airport) northbound; exit 39A (Richmond/Airport) southbound, just w on Bridgeport Rd, then just w on Great Canadian Way. Int corridors. **Pets:** Other species. $25 daily fee/room. Service with restrictions. SAVE ⨯ ⅏M 🛏 💻 🍽 ⊇ ⊠

▼▼ Sandman Hotel Vancouver Airport Ⓗ

(604) 303-8888. **$99-$159.** 3233 St Edwards Dr V6X 3K4. Hwy 99, exit 39 (Bridgeport Rd/Airport) northbound to St Edwards Dr; exit 39A (Richmond/Airport) southbound. Int corridors. **Pets:** Accepted.
ECO ASK ⨯ ⅏M 🛏 💻 🍽 ⊇

⁜ ▼▼▼ Sheraton Vancouver Airport Ⓗ ❀

(604) 273-7878. **$139-$349.** 7551 Westminster Hwy V6X 1A3. Corner of Minoru Blvd and Westminster Hwy. Int corridors. **Pets:** $20 one-time fee/room. Service with restrictions, supervision.
ECO SAVE ⨯ ⅏M 🛏 💻 🍽 ⊇

⁜ ▼▼ Travelodge Hotel Vancouver Airport Ⓗ

(604) 278-5155. **$99-$399.** 3071 St Edwards Dr V6X 3K4. Hwy 99, exit 39 (Bridgeport Rd/Airport) northbound to St Edwards Dr; exit 39A (Richmond/Airport) southbound. Int corridors. **Pets:** Accepted.
ECO SAVE ⨯ ⅏M 🛏 💻 🍽 ⊇

⁜ ▼▼▼ Vancouver Airport Marriott Ⓗ

(604) 276-2112. **$259-$289.** 7571 Westminster Hwy V6X 1A3. Corner of Minoru Blvd and Westminster Hwy. Int corridors. **Pets:** Accepted.
ECO SAVE ⨯ ⅏M 🛏 💻 🍽 ⊇

SURREY

⁜ ▼▼ Compass Point Inn Ⓗ

(604) 588-9511. **$99-$129.** 9850 King George Hwy V3T 4Y3. Jct Fraser Hwy (Hwy 1A) and Hwy 99A (King George Hwy). Int corridors. **Pets:** Medium. $20 daily fee/pet. Designated rooms, service with restrictions, supervision. ECO SAVE ⨯ ⅏M 🛏 💻 🍽 ⊇

▼▼ Ramada Hotel & Suites Surrey/Guildford Ⓗ

(604) 930-4700. **$89-$159.** 10410 158th St V4N 5C2. Trans-Canada Hwy 1, exit 50 (160th St), just w on 104th Ave. Int corridors. **Pets:** Small. $10 daily fee/pet. Designated rooms, service with restrictions, supervision.
ASK ⨯ ⅏M 🛏 💻 🍽 ⊇

⁜ ▼▼▼ Ramada Langley-Surrey Ⓗ

(604) 576-8388. **$119-$169.** 19225 Hwy 10 V3S 8V9. Trans-Canada Hwy 1, exit 58 (200th St/Langley City), 3.1 mi (5 km) s on 200th St, then 1.2 mi (2 km) w on Rt 10; corner of 192nd St and Rt 10. Int corridors. **Pets:** Accepted. SAVE ⨯ ⅏M 🛏 💻 🍽 ⊇

⁜ ▼▼▼ Sheraton Vancouver Guildford Hotel Ⓗ

(604) 582-9288. **Call for rates.** 15269 104th Ave V3R 1N5. Trans-Canada Hwy 1, exit 50 eastbound, 0.6 mi (1 km) s on 152nd St, then just e; exit 50 westbound, then just w. Int corridors. **Pets:** Accepted.
ECO SAVE ⨯ ⅏M 🛏 💻 🍽 ⊇

VANCOUVER

⁜ ▼ 2400 Motel Ⓜ

(604) 434-2464. **$81-$199.** 2400 Kingsway V5R 5G9. 4.5 mi (7.2 km) se on Hwy 1A and 99A (Kingsway and 33rd Ave). Ext corridors.
Pets: Accepted. SAVE ⨯ 🛏 💻 🐾

⁜ ▼▼▼ Best Western Downtown Vancouver Ⓗ

(604) 669-9888. **$99-$199.** 718 Drake St V6Z 2W6. Corner of Drake and Granville sts. Int corridors. **Pets:** Accepted.
ECO SAVE ⨯ ⅏M 🛏 💻 🍽 ⊠

⁜ ▼▼▼ Best Western Sands by the Sea Ⓗ ❀

(604) 682-1831. **$99-$259.** 1755 Davie St V6G 1W5. Between Bidwell and Denman sts. Int corridors. **Pets:** Large, other species. $16 daily fee/room. Designated rooms, service with restrictions, supervision.
ECO SAVE ⨯ ⅏M 🛏 💻 🍽

⁜ ▼▼▼ Cascadia Hotel & Suites Ⓗ

(604) 688-1234. **$189-$289.** 1234 Hornby St V6Z 1W2. Between Drake and Davie sts. Int corridors. **Pets:** $75 one-time fee/pet. Service with restrictions. ECO SAVE ⨯ ⅏M 🛏 💻 🍽 ⊇

⁜ ▼▼▼ Delta Vancouver Suites Ⓗ

(604) 689-8188. **$159-$299.** 550 W Hastings St V6B 1L6. Between Seymour and Richards sts; entrance in alley way. Int corridors.
Pets: Accepted. ECO SAVE ⨯ ⅏M 💻 🍽

⁜ ▼▼▼▼ The Fairmont Hotel Vancouver Ⓗ

(604) 684-3131. **Call for rates.** 900 W Georgia St V6C 2W6. Corner of Burrard at W Georgia St; enter from Hornby St. Int corridors.
Pets: Accepted. ECO SAVE ⨯ ⅏M 🛏 💻 🍽 ⊇ ⊠

⁜ ▼▼▼▼ The Fairmont Waterfront Ⓗ ❀

(604) 691-1991. **Call for rates.** 900 Canada Place Way V6C 3L5. Howe St at Cordova St. Int corridors. **Pets:** $35 one-time fee/room. Service with restrictions, supervision. ECO SAVE ⨯ ⅏M 💻 🍽 ⊇ ⊠

⁜ ▼▼▼▼ Four Seasons Hotel Vancouver Ⓗ

(604) 689-9333. **$245-$820.** 791 W Georgia St V6C 2T4. Between Howe and Granville sts. Int corridors. **Pets:** Accepted.
SAVE ⨯ ⅏M 🍽 ⊇ ⊠

(CAA) ▼▼▼▼ **The Georgian Court Hotel** H
(604) 682-5555. **$179-$419.** 773 Beatty St V6B 2M4. Between Georgia and Robson sts. Int corridors. **Pets:** Accepted.
[SAVE] [X] [&M] [■] [¶] [⊠]

(CAA) ▼▼▼▼ **Granville Island Hotel** H
(604) 683-7373. **$189-$550.** 1253 Johnston St V6H 3R9. Granville Island; below the bridge, follow signs. Int corridors. **Pets:** Other species. $25 daily fee/room. Designated rooms. [SAVE] [X] [&M] [■] [¶] [⊠]

(CAA) ▼▼▼▼ **Holiday Inn Express Vancouver** H ❀
(604) 254-1000. **$119-$309.** 2889 E Hastings St V5K 2A1. Between Renfrew and Kaslo sts. Int corridors. **Pets:** Small, other species. $15 daily fee/pet. Designated rooms, service with restrictions, crate.
[ECO] [SAVE] [X] [&M] [■] [■]

(CAA) ▼▼▼▼ **Hotel Le Soleil** H ❀
(604) 632-3000. **$375-$475.** 567 Hornby St V6C 2E8. Between Dunsmuir and Pender sts. Int corridors. **Pets:** Medium. $75 one-time fee/pet. Designated rooms, supervision. [ECO] [SAVE] [X] [&M] [■] [¶]

(CAA) ▼▼▼ **Howard Johnson Hotel Downtown Vancouver** H
(604) 688-8701. **$79-$279.** 1176 Granville St V6Z 1L8. Between Davie and Helmcken sts. Int corridors. **Pets:** Accepted.
[ECO] [SAVE] [X] [■] [■] [¶]

(CAA) ▼▼▼▼ **Hyatt Regency Vancouver** H
(604) 683-1234. **$159-$439.** 655 Burrard St V6C 2R7. Between W Georgia and Melville sts. Int corridors. **Pets:** Medium, other species. $50 one-time fee/room. Service with restrictions, crate.
[ECO] [SAVE] [X] [&M] [■] [¶] [■]

(CAA) ▼▼▼▼ **L'Hermitage Hotel** H
(778) 327-4100. **Call for rates.** 788 Richards St V6B 3A4. Between Robson and W Georgia sts. Int corridors. **Pets:** Accepted.
[SAVE] [X] [■] [■] [■] [■] [⊠]

(CAA) ▼▼▼▼ **Pan Pacific Vancouver** H ❀
(604) 662-8111. **$179-$449.** 300-999 Canada Pl V6C 3B5. Motor entrance off Burrard St. Int corridors. **Pets:** Small. $30 one-time fee/room. Service with restrictions, supervision.
[ECO] [SAVE] [X] [&M] [■] [■] [¶] [■] [⊠]

▼▼ **Quality Hotel Downtown-The Inn at False Creek** H
(604) 682-0229. **$80-$259.** 1335 Howe St V6Z 1R7. Between Drake and Pacific sts. Int corridors. **Pets:** Medium, other species. $15 daily fee/pet.
[ECO] [ASK] [X] [&M] [■] [■] [¶] [■]

(CAA) ▼▼▼ **Ramada Inn & Suites Downtown Vancouver** H
(604) 685-1111. **$89-$279.** 1221 Granville St V6Z 1M6. Between Davie and Drake sts. Int corridors. **Pets:** Other species. $20 daily fee/pet. Service with restrictions, supervision. [ECO] [SAVE] [X] [■] [■] [¶]

(CAA) ▼▼▼▼ **Renaissance Vancouver Hotel Harbourside** H
(604) 689-9211. **$219-$299.** 1133 W Hastings St V6E 3T3. Between Bute and Thurlow sts. Int corridors. **Pets:** Accepted.
[ECO] [SAVE] [X] [&M] [■] [■] [¶] [■]

▼▼▼ **Sandman Hotel Vancouver City Center** H
(604) 681-2211. **$109-$209.** 180 W Georgia St V6B 4P4. Between Cambie and Beatty sts. Int corridors. **Pets:** Medium. $15 one-time fee/pet. Designated rooms, service with restrictions, supervision.
[ECO] [X] [&M] [■] [¶] [■]

(CAA) ▼▼▼▼ **Sheraton Vancouver Wall Centre Hotel** H ❀
(604) 331-1000. **Call for rates.** 1088 Burrard St V6Z 2R9. Between Helmcken and Nelson sts. Int corridors. **Pets:** Dogs only. $60 one-time fee/room. Service with restrictions.
[ECO] [SAVE] [X] [&M] [■] [■] [¶] [■] [⊠]

(CAA) ▼▼▼▼ **The Sutton Place Hotel** H ❀
(604) 682-5511. **$169-$599.** 845 Burrard St V6Z 2K6. Between Smithe and Robson sts. Int corridors. **Pets:** Other species. $150 one-time fee/room. [ECO] [SAVE] [X] [&M] [■] [¶] [■] [⊠]

(CAA) ▼▼▼▼ **Vancouver Marriott Pinnacle Downtown** H
(604) 684-1128. **$219-$299.** 1128 W Hastings St V6E 4R5. Between Thurlow and Bute sts. Int corridors. **Pets:** Accepted.
[ECO] [SAVE] [X] [&M] [■] [■] [¶] [■] [⊠]

(CAA) ▼▼▼▼ **The Westin Bayshore Vancouver** H
(604) 682-3377. **$195-$580.** 1601 Bayshore Dr V6G 2V4. W Georgia and Cardero sts. Int corridors. **Pets:** Accepted.
[ECO] [SAVE] [X] [&M] [■] [¶] [■] [⊠]

(CAA) ▼▼▼▼ **The Westin Grand, Vancouver** H ❀
(604) 602-1999. **$169-$679.** 433 Robson St V6B 6L9. Between Homer and Richards sts. Int corridors. **Pets:** Dogs only. $50 one-time fee/room. Designated rooms. [ECO] [SAVE] [X] [&M] [■] [¶] [■] [⊠]

WHITE ROCK

(CAA) ▼▼▼▼ **Ocean Promenade Hotel** H
(604) 542-0102. **$129-$469.** 15611 Marine Dr V4B 1E1. Hwy 99, exit 2B southbound; exit 2 (White Rock/8th Ave) northbound, 1.3 mi (2 km) w. Ext/int corridors. **Pets:** Small, dogs only. $50 one-time fee/pet. Designated rooms, service with restrictions, supervision. [SAVE] [X] [&M] [■] [■]

END METROPOLITAN AREA

VICTORIA METROPOLITAN AREA

MALAHAT

▼▼ **Malahat Bungalows Motel** M
(250) 478-3011. **$62-$165, 3 day notice.** 300 Trans-Canada Hwy V0R 2L0. Trans-Canada Hwy 1, 16.3 mi (26 km) n of Victoria, follow signs. Ext corridors. **Pets:** Medium, other species. $10 daily fee/pet. Service with restrictions, supervision. [X] [■] [◎] [⊠]

SAANICH

▼▼▼▼ **Howard Johnson Hotel & Suites** H
(250) 704-4656. **$117-$153.** 4670 Elk Lake Dr V8Z 5M2. Blanshard St (Hwy 17), just w on Royal Oak Dr, then just n. Ext/int corridors.
Pets: Accepted. [ECO] [ASK] [X] [&M] [■] [■] [¶] [■]

SAANICHTON

(CAA) ▼▼▼ **Quality Inn Waddling Dog** H ❀
(250) 652-1146. **$109-$145.** 2476 Mt Newton Crossroad V8M 2B8. Corner of Blanshard St (Hwy 17) and Mt Newton Crossroad. Int corridors. **Pets:** Dogs only. $15 daily fee/pet. Service with restrictions, supervision.
[SAVE] [X] [■] [■]

(CAA) ▼▼▼ **Victoria Airport Super 8** H
(250) 652-6888. **Call for rates.** 2477 Mt Newton Crossroad V8M 2B7. Just e of Blanshard St (Hwy 17). Int corridors. **Pets:** Accepted.
[SAVE] [X] [&M] [■]

SIDNEY

[CAA] ◆◆◆ **Best Western Emerald Isle Motor Inn** [H] 🐾
(250) 656-4441. **$109-$349.** 2306 Beacon Ave V8L 1X2. Hwy 17, exit Sidney, just e. Int corridors. **Pets:** Medium, other species. $15 daily fee/pet. Designated rooms, service with restrictions, supervision.
[ECO] [SAVE] 🚭 ♿ 🧊 ☕ 🍴 🏋

[CAA] ◆◆◆ **The Cedarwood Inn & Suites** [H]
(250) 656-5551. **$95-$255, 3 day notice.** 9522 Lochside Dr V8L 1N8. Hwy 17, just e on McTavish Rd, then 0.8 mi (1.4 km) n. Ext corridors. **Pets:** Large, other species. $15 daily fee/pet. Designated rooms, service with restrictions, supervision. [SAVE] 🚭 🧊 ☕ [AC]

◆◆◆ **Miraloma on the Cove** [H]
(250) 656-6622. **$159-$449.** 2326 Harbour Rd V8L 2P8. Beacon Ave, 1.3 mi (2 km) n on Resthaven Dr, then 0.6 mi (1 km) e. Int corridors. **Pets:** Accepted. [A$K] 🚭 ♿ 🧊 ☕ 🍴 🏋 [AC]

[CAA] ◆◆◆ **The Sidney Pier Hotel & Spa** [H] 🐾
(250) 655-9445. **$119-$649.** 9805 Seaport Pl V8L 4X3. Hwy 17, 0.6 mi (1 km) e on Beacon Ave. Int corridors. **Pets:** Small, dogs only. $30 one-time fee/pet. Designated rooms, service with restrictions.
[ECO] [SAVE] 🚭 ♿ 🧊 ☕ 🍴 🏋

[CAA] ◆◆ **Victoria Airport Travelodge Sidney** [H]
(250) 656-1176. **$99-$199.** 2280 Beacon Ave V8L 1X1. Hwy 17, exit Sidney, just e. Int corridors. **Pets:** Large, other species. $15 daily fee/room. Designated rooms, service with restrictions, supervision.
[SAVE] 🚭 ♿ 🧊 ☕ 🏊

SOOKE

◆◆ **Ocean Wilderness Inn** [BB]
(250) 646-2116. **$130-$220, 7 day notice.** 9171 W Coast Rd V9Z 1G3. 8.6 mi (14 km) w on Hwy 14. Ext/int corridors. **Pets:** Accepted.
[A$K] 🚭 🧊 [AC] [PV] ☎

[CAA] ◆◆◆ **Sooke Harbour House** [CI] 🐾
(250) 642-3421. **$315-$675, 7 day notice.** 1528 Whiffen Spit Rd V9Z 0T4. 1.2 mi (2 km) w on Hwy 14. Ext/int corridors. **Pets:** Large, other species. $40 daily fee/pet. Service with restrictions, crate.
[SAVE] 🚭 ♿ 🧊 ☕ 🍴 [AC] [PV]

VICTORIA

◆◆◆ **Abbeymoore Manor Bed & Breakfast Inn** [BB] 🐾
(250) 370-1470. **$109-$249, 14 day notice.** 1470 Rockland Ave V8S 1W2. Blanshard St (Hwy 17), 1.2 mi (2 km) e on Fort St, just s on St Charles St, then just w. Ext/int corridors. **Pets:** Dogs only. $15 daily fee/pet. Designated rooms. 🚭 🧊 ☕ [AC]

[CAA] ◆◆◆ **Abigail's Hotel** [H]
(250) 388-5363. **$189-$480, 14 day notice.** 906 McClure St V8V 3E7. Blanshard St (Hwy 17), just e on Fairfield Rd, then just n on Vancouver St. Int corridors. **Pets:** Accepted. [SAVE] 🚭 🧊 ☕

[CAA] ◆◆ **Accent Inns** [H] 🐾
(250) 475-7500. **$99-$189.** 3233 Maple St V8X 4Y9. 1.9 mi (3 km) n on Blanshard St (Hwy 17); corner of Blanshard St and Cloverdale Ave. Ext corridors. **Pets:** $20 daily fee/room. Designated rooms, service with restrictions, supervision. [ECO] [SAVE] 🚭 ♿ 🧊 ☕ 🍴

[CAA] ◆◆ **Admiral Inn** [M] 🐾
(250) 388-6267. **$99-$269, 15 day notice.** 257 Belleville St V8V 1X1. Corner of Belleville and Quebec sts. Ext corridors. **Pets:** Large, other species. $15 one-time fee/pet. Designated rooms, service with restrictions, supervision. [SAVE] 🚭 🧊 ☕

[CAA] ◆◆◆ **Best Western Carlton Plaza Hotel** [H] 🐾
(250) 388-5513. **$114-$199.** 642 Johnson St V8W 1M6. Between Douglas and Broad sts. Int corridors. **Pets:** Other species. $10 daily fee/room. Designated rooms, service with restrictions, supervision.
[ECO] [SAVE] 🚭 ♿ 🧊 ☕ 🍴

[CAA] ◆◆ **Blue Ridge Inns** [M]
(250) 388-4345. **$69-$129.** 3110 Douglas St V8Z 3K4. Between Finlayson St and Speed Ave. Ext corridors. **Pets:** Accepted.
[ECO] [SAVE] 🚭 🧊 ☕ 🍴 🏊 [AC]

◆◆◆ **Chateau Victoria Hotel and Suites** [H] 🐾
(250) 382-4221. **$95-$229.** 740 Burdett Ave V8W 1B2. Between Douglas and Blanshard (Hwy 17) sts. Int corridors. **Pets:** Dogs only. $15 deposit/pet. Designated rooms, service with restrictions, crate.
[ECO] [A$K] 🚭 🧊 ☕ 🍴 🏊

[CAA] ◆◆ **Comfort Inn & Suites** [M] 🐾
(250) 388-7861. **$119-$299.** 101 Island Hwy V9B 1E8. Douglas St, 3.1 mi (5 km) w on Gorge Rd, then just s on Admirals Rd. Ext/int corridors. **Pets:** Dogs only. $15 daily fee/pet. Designated rooms, service with restrictions, supervision. [SAVE] 🚭 🧊 ☕ 🏊

[CAA] ◆◆ **Days Inn Victoria on the Harbour** [H] 🐾
(250) 386-3451. **$79-$213.** 427 Belleville St V8V 1X3. Between Oswego and Menzies sts. Int corridors. **Pets:** $10 daily fee/room. Designated rooms, service with restrictions.
[ECO] [SAVE] 🚭 🧊 ☕ 🍴 🏊 [AC]

[CAA] ◆◆◆◆ **Delta Victoria Ocean Pointe Resort and Spa** [H] 🐾
(250) 360-2999. **$129-$328.** 45 Songhees Rd V9A 6T3. Just w of Johnson St Bridge, Esquimalt at Tyee Rd. Int corridors. **Pets:** Medium. $35 one-time fee/pet. Designated rooms, service with restrictions, supervision. [ECO] [SAVE] 🚭 ♿ 🧊 ☕ 🍴 🏊 🏋

[CAA] ◆◆ **Executive House Hotel** [H]
(250) 388-5111. **$99-$215.** 777 Douglas St V8W 2B5. Between Blanshard (Hwy 17) and Douglas sts; downtown. Int corridors. **Pets:** $15 daily fee/pet. Service with restrictions, supervision.
[SAVE] 🚭 🧊 ☕ 🍴 🏋 [AC]

◆◆◆◆ **The Fairmont Empress** [H]
(250) 384-8111. **Call for rates.** 721 Government St V8W 1W5. Between Belleville and Humboldt sts. Int corridors. **Pets:** Small, dogs only. $25 one-time fee/room. Designated rooms, service with restrictions, supervision. [ECO] 🚭 ♿ 🧊 ☕ 🍴 🏊 🏋 [AC]

[CAA] ◆◆◆ **Harbour Towers Hotel & Suites** [H]
(250) 385-2405. **$94-$450.** 345 Quebec St V8V 1W4. Between Oswego and Pendray sts. Int corridors. **Pets:** Accepted.
[ECO] [SAVE] 🚭 ♿ 🧊 ☕ 🍴 🏊 🏋 [AC]

[CAA] ◆◆◆◆ **Hotel Grand Pacific** [H]
(250) 386-0450. **$149-$329.** 463 Belleville St V8V 1X3. Between Oswego and Menzies sts. Int corridors. **Pets:** Accepted.
[ECO] [SAVE] 🚭 ♿ ☕ 🍴 🏊 🏋

[CAA] ◆◆ **Howard Johnson Hotel-City of Victoria** [H]
(250) 382-2151. **$59-$159.** 310 Gorge Rd E V8T 2W2. From Douglas St, 0.6 mi (1.4 km) w; between Jutland St and Washington Ave. Int corridors. **Pets:** Medium, dogs only. $25 one-time fee/room. Designated rooms, service with restrictions, supervision.
[ECO] [SAVE] 🚭 ♿ 🧊 ☕ 🍴 🏊

[CAA] ◆◆ **Huntingdon Hotel & Suites** [H]
(250) 381-3456. **$99-$389.** 330 Quebec St V8V 1W3. Between Oswego and Pendray sts. Int corridors. **Pets:** Accepted. [SAVE] 🚭 🧊 ☕ 🍴

[CAA] ◆◆◆◆ **The Magnolia Hotel & Spa** [H] 🐾
(250) 381-0999. **$149-$349.** 623 Courtney St V8W 1B8. Corner of Courtney and Gordon sts. Int corridors. **Pets:** Dogs only. $60 one-time fee/room. Designated rooms, service with restrictions, supervision.
[SAVE] 🚭 ♿ ☕ 🍴 🏋

[CAA] ◆◆◆◆ **Marriott Victoria Inner Harbour** [H] 🐾
(250) 480-3800. **$209-$339.** 728 Humboldt St V8W 3Z5. Between Blanshard (Hwy 17) and Douglas sts. Int corridors. **Pets:** Small. $50 one-time fee/pet. Designated rooms, service with restrictions, crate.
[ECO] [SAVE] 🚭 ♿ 🧊 ☕ 🍴 🏊 🏋

(CAA) ▼▼▼ The Oswego Hotel ⊞

(250) 294-7500. **$139-$599.** 500 Oswego St V8V 5C1. Between Kingston and Quebec sts. Int corridors. **Pets:** Accepted.

ECO SAVE ⊠ &M ⊟ 🖵 ⊤⊤ 𝓐𝓒

(CAA) ▼▼▼▼ Prior House B&B Inn BB ❖

(250) 592-8847. **$159-$259, 14 day notice.** 620 St. Charles St V8S 3N7. Blanshard St (Hwy 17), 1.2 mi (2 km) e on Fort St, then just s. Int corridors. **Pets:** Medium, dogs only. $15 one-time fee/room. Designated rooms, service with restrictions, supervision. SAVE ⊠ ⊟ 🖵 𝓐𝓒

▼▼▼ Quality Inn Downtown ⊞

(250) 385-6787. **$69-$169.** 850 Blanshard St V8W 2H2. Between Courtney St and Burnett Ave; downtown. Int corridors. **Pets:** Small. $20 daily fee/pet. Designated rooms, service with restrictions, supervision.

ECO A$K ⊠ ⊟ 🖵 ⊤⊤ 🏊 𝓐𝓒

▼▼▼ Ramada Victoria ⊞

(250) 386-1422. **$59-$185.** 123 Gorge Rd E V9A 1L1. From Douglas St, 1.2 mi (2.4 km) w. Int corridors. **Pets:** Accepted.

ECO A$K ⊠ ⊟ 🖵 ⊤⊤ 🏊

(CAA) ▼▼▼ Robin Hood Motel M

(250) 388-4302. **$66-$109.** 136 Gorge Rd E V9A 1L4. Douglas St, 1.2 mi (2.4 km) w. Ext corridors. **Pets:** Dogs only. $5 daily fee/pet. Designated rooms, service with restrictions, supervision. SAVE ⊠ ⊟ 🖵

(CAA) ▼▼▼ Royal Scot Hotel & Suites ⊞

(250) 388-5463. **$145-$265.** 425 Quebec St V8V 1W7. Between Menzies and Oswego sts. Int corridors. **Pets:** Large, dogs only. $15 daily fee/pet. Designated rooms, supervision.

ECO SAVE ⊠ ⊟ 🖵 ⊤⊤ 🏊 ⊠ 𝓐𝓒

(CAA) ▼▼▼ Travelodge Victoria ⊞

(250) 388-6611. **$79-$189.** 229 Gorge Rd E V9A 1L1. From Douglas St, 1.2 mi (2 km) w on Gorge Rd E; at Washington Ave. Ext corridors. **Pets:** Medium. $10 daily fee/pet. Designated rooms, service with restrictions. ECO SAVE ⊠ ⊟ 🖵 ⊤⊤

▼▼▼ Union Club of British Columbia ⊞

(250) 384-1151. **$179-$409.** 805 Gordon St V8W 1Z6. Between Courtney and Humboldt sts. Int corridors. **Pets:** Accepted. A$K ⊠ ⊤⊤ 𝓐𝓒

(CAA) ▼▼▼▼ The Westin Bear Mountain Golf Resort & Spa ⊞ ❖

(250) 391-7160. **Call for rates.** 1999 Country Club Way V9B 6R3. Trans-Canada Hwy 1, exit 14 (Highlands), 1.1 mi (1.7 km) n on Millstream Rd, then 1.9 mi (3 km) ne on Bear Mountain Pkwy, follow signs. Int corridors. **Pets:** Medium, dogs only. $20 one-time fee/room. Designated rooms, service with restrictions, supervision.

ECO SAVE ⊠ &M ⊟ 🖵 ⊤⊤ 🏊 ⊠

END METROPOLITAN AREA

WHISTLER

(CAA) ▼▼▼ Best Western Listel Whistler Hotel ⊞

(604) 932-1133. **$89-$349.** 4121 Village Green V0N 1B4. Hwy 99, just e on Village Gate Blvd, then follow Whistler Way. Int corridors. **Pets:** Accepted. SAVE ⊠ ⊟ 🖵 ⊤⊤ 🏊

(CAA) ▼▼▼▼ Crystal Lodge & Suites ⊞

(604) 932-2221. **$99-$339, 3 day notice.** 4154 Village Green V0N 1B4. Hwy 99, just e on Village Gate Blvd, then follow road to Whistler Way. Int corridors. **Pets:** Accepted.

ECO SAVE ⊠ ⊟ 🖵 ⊤⊤ 🏊 ⊠

(CAA) ▼▼▼▼ Delta Whistler Village Suites ⊞

(604) 905-3987. **$99-$409, 30 day notice.** 4308 Main St V0N 1B4. Hwy 99, just e on Village Gate Blvd, just n on Northlands Blvd, then just e. Int corridors. **Pets:** Accepted.

ECO SAVE ⊠ &M ⊟ 🖵 ⊤⊤ 🏊 ⊠

(CAA) ▼▼▼ Edgewater Lodge ⊞

(604) 932-0688. **$124-$225, 14 day notice.** 8020 Alpine Way V0N 1B0. 2.5 mi (4 km) n of Whistler Village via Hwy 99, then just e. Ext corridors. **Pets:** Accepted. SAVE ⊠ ⊤⊤ 𝓐𝓒

(CAA) ▼▼▼▼ The Fairmont Chateau Whistler ⊞

(604) 938-8000. **$179-$900, 3 day notice.** 4599 Chateau Blvd V0N 1B4. Hwy 99, 0.6 mi (1 km) e on Lorimer Rd (Upper Village), just w on Blackcomb Way. Int corridors. **Pets:** Accepted.

ECO SAVE ⊠ &M 🖵 ⊤⊤ 🏊 ⊠

(CAA) ▼▼▼▼ Four Seasons Resort Whistler ⊞ ❖

(604) 935-3400. **$265-$920, 30 day notice.** 4591 Blackcomb Way V0N 1B4. Hwy 99, 0.6 mi (1 km) e on Lorimer Rd (Upper Village). Int corridors. **Pets:** Service with restrictions, supervision.

SAVE ⊠ &M ⊟ 🖵 ⊤⊤ 🏊 ⊠

(CAA) ▼▼▼▼ Hilton Whistler Resort & Spa ⊞

(604) 932-1982. **$185-$799.** 4050 Whistler Way V0N 1B4. Hwy 99, just e on Village Gate Blvd, then follow Whistler Way. Int corridors. **Pets:** Accepted. ECO SAVE ⊠ &M ⊟ 🖵 ⊤⊤ 🏊 ⊠

(CAA) ▼▼▼ Nita Lake Lodge ⊞ ❖

(604) 966-5700. **$159-$799, 30 day notice.** 2131 Lake Placid Rd V0N 1B2. 1.8 mi (3 km) s on Hwy 99, just w. Int corridors. **Pets:** $25 daily fee/room. Designated rooms, service with restrictions, supervision.

ECO SAVE ⊠ &M ⊟ 🖵 ⊤⊤ ⊠

▼▼▼ Pan Pacific Whistler Village Centre ⊞ ❖

(604) 966-5500. **Call for rates.** 4299 Blackcomb Way V0N 1B4. Hwy 99, just e on Village Gate Blvd. Int corridors. **Pets:** Other species. $25 daily fee/pet. Service with restrictions, supervision.

ECO ⊠ &M ⊟ 🖵 🏊 ⊠

(CAA) ▼▼▼ Residence Inn by Marriott CO

(604) 905-3400. **$449-$549, 60 day notice.** 4899 Painted Cliff Rd V0N 1B4. Hwy 99, 0.6 mi (1 km) e on Lorimer Rd (Upper Village), just se on Blackcomb Way, then just w, follow road all the way to the end. Int corridors. **Pets:** Accepted. ECO SAVE ⊠ &M ⊟ 🖵 🏊 𝓐𝓒

▼▼▼ Tantalus Resort Lodge CO

(604) 932-4146. **Call for rates.** 4200 Whistler Way V0N 1B4. Hwy 99, just e on Village Gate Blvd, then follow Whistler Way to the end. Int corridors. **Pets:** Accepted. ⊠ ⊟ 🖵 🏊 ⊠ 𝓐𝓒

(CAA) ▼▼▼▼ The Westin Resort & Spa ⊞

(604) 905-5000. **Call for rates.** 4090 Whistler Way V0N 1B4. Hwy 99, just e on Village Gate Blvd, then s. Int corridors. **Pets:** Accepted.

ECO SAVE ⊠ &M ⊟ 🖵 ⊤⊤ 🏊 ⊠

WILLIAMS LAKE

▼▼▼ Drummond Lodge Motel M

(250) 392-5334. **$72-$140.** 1405 Cariboo Hwy V2G 2W3. 0.6 mi (1 km) s on Hwy 97. Ext corridors. **Pets:** Accepted. ⊠ ⊟ 🖵

(CAA) ▼▼▼ Williams Lake Super 8 M

(250) 398-8884. **$82-$120.** 1712 Broadway Ave S V2G 2W4. 1.2 mi (2 km) s on Hwy 97. Int corridors. **Pets:** Small. $10 daily fee/pet. Designated rooms, supervision. SAVE ⊠ &M ⊟ 🖵

MANITOBA

BEAUSEJOUR

▼▼▼ Superior Inn H ❀

(204) 268-9050. **$94-$99.** 1055 Park Ave R0E 0C0. On Hwy 215; jct Hwy 12/44/302. Int corridors. **Pets:** Other species. $10 daily fee/pet. Designated rooms, service with restrictions, crate.

ASK ✕ 🖬 🖵 ⌦ ✕

BRANDON

CAA ▼▼▼▼ Canad Inns-Destination Centre Brandon H

(204) 727-1422. **$105-$230.** 1125 18th St R7A 7C5. On Hwy 10 (18th St); jct Brandon Ave. Int corridors. **Pets:** Accepted.

ECO SAVE ✕ 🖬 🖵 ⛽ ⌦

▼▼ Comfort Inn H

(204) 727-6232. **$97-$147.** 925 Middleton Ave R7C 1A8. Trans-Canada Hwy 1; between Hwy 10 (18th St) N and Hwy 10 S; on northside of service road. Int corridors. **Pets:** $10 daily fee/room. Service with restrictions, supervision. ECO ASK ✕ ⅏M 🖬 🖵

▼▼ Days Inn Brandon H

(204) 727-3600. **$104-$139.** 2130 Currie Blvd R7B 4E7. Jct Trans-Canada Hwy 1, 4.9 mi (7.9 km) s on Hwy 10 (18th St). Int corridors. **Pets:** $10 daily fee/pet. Designated rooms, service with restrictions, supervision. ASK ✕ 🖬 🖵 ⌦

▼▼ Royal Oak Inn & Suites H

(204) 728-5775. **$120-$125.** 3130 Victoria Ave R7B 0N2. 3.1 mi (5 km) s on Hwy 10 (18th St) from jct Trans-Canada Hwy 1, then 1.1 mi (1.8 km) w. Int corridors. **Pets:** Accepted. ASK ✕ 🖬 🖵 ⛽ ⌦ ✕

▼▼ Super 8 Brandon H

(204) 729-8024. **$115-$160.** 1570 Highland Ave R7C 1A7. Jct Trans-Canada Hwy 1, just s on Hwy 10 (18th St), then just e. Int corridors. **Pets:** Accepted. ECO ✕ ⅏M 🖬 🖵 ⌦

▼▼ Victoria Inn H

(204) 725-1532. **$103-$199.** 3550 Victoria Ave R7B 2R4. Jct Trans-Canada Hwy 1, 3.1 mi (5 km) s on Hwy 10 (18th St), then 0.9 mi (1.4 km) w. Int corridors. **Pets:** Accepted.

ECO ASK ✕ 🖬 🖵 ⛽ ⌦

CHURCHILL

▼▼ Polar Inn & Suites M

(204) 675-8878. **$119-$245.** 153 Kelsey Blvd R0B 0E0. Centre. Int corridors. **Pets:** Accepted. ASK ✕ 🖬 🖵 ✗

▼▼ The Tundra Inn H

(204) 675-8831. **$111-$220, 30 day notice.** 34 Franklin St R0B 0E0. Centre. Int corridors. **Pets:** Accepted. ECO ✕ 🖬 🖵 ⛽ ✗

FLIN FLON

▼▼ Victoria Inn North H

(204) 687-7555. **Call for rates.** 160 Hwy 10A N R8A 0C6. Jct Hwy 10 and 10A, 0.6 mi (1 km) nw (eastern approach to city). Int corridors. **Pets:** Accepted. ✕ 🖬 🖵 ⛽ ⌦

HECLA

▼▼▼ Radisson Hecla Oasis Resort H ❀

(204) 279-2041. **$149-$242, 7 day notice.** Hwy 8 R0C 2R0. Hwy 8, n of Hecla Village. Int corridors. **Pets:** $35 daily fee/room. Designated rooms. ECO ASK ✕ 🖬 🖵 ⛽ ⌦ ✕

NEEPAWA

▼▼ Bay Hill Inns & Suites H

(204) 476-8888. **Call for rates.** 160 Main St W R0J 1H0. On Hwy 16, just w of jct Rt 5. Int corridors. **Pets:** Accepted.

✕ 🖬 🖵 ⛽ ⌦

PORTAGE LA PRAIRIE

▼▼ Super 8 H

(204) 857-8883. **$90-$101.** 2668 Hwy 1A W R1N 3B2. On Hwy 1A, 0.9 mi (1.5 km) w. Int corridors. **Pets:** $5 daily fee/room. Designated rooms, service with restrictions, supervision. ✕ 🖬 🖵 ⌦

▼▼ Westgate Inn Motel M

(204) 239-5200. **$60-$89.** 1010 Saskatchewan Ave E R1N 0K1. 0.6 mi (1 km) e on Hwy 1A. Ext corridors. **Pets:** Small. Service with restrictions, supervision. ASK ✕ 🖬 🖵

RUSSELL

▼▼ The Russell Inn Hotel & Conference Centre H ❀

(204) 773-2186. **$98-$196, 14 day notice.** Hwy 16 R0J 1W0. 0.8 mi (1.2 km) se on Hwy 16 and 83. Int corridors. **Pets:** Very small. Service with restrictions, crate. ASK ✕ 🖬 🖵 ⌦ ✕

STEINBACH

▼▼ Days Inn H

(204) 320-9200. **Call for rates.** 75 Hwy 12 N R5G 1T3. 0.5 mi (0.8 km) n of jct Hwy 52. Int corridors. **Pets:** Accepted. ✕ 🖬 🖵 ⌦ ✕

THE PAS

▼▼ Kikiwak Inn H

(204) 623-1800. **Call for rates.** Hwy 10 N R0B 2J0. On Hwy 10, 0.4 mi (0.6 km) n. Int corridors. **Pets:** Accepted. ✕ ⅏M 🖬 🖵 ⛽ ⌦

▼▼ Super 8 H

(204) 623-1888. **$115.** 1717 Gordon Ave R9A 1K3. At southern approach to town. Int corridors. **Pets:** Medium. Designated rooms, service with restrictions, supervision. ✕ 🖬 🖵 ⌦

THOMPSON

▼▼ Country Inn & Suites By Carlson H

(204) 778-8879. **Call for rates.** 70 Thompson Dr N R8N 1Y8. Just w of Hwy 6. Int corridors. **Pets:** Accepted. ECO ✕ 🖬 🖵

WINNIPEG METROPOLITAN AREA

WINNIPEG

CAA ▼▼▼ Best Western Pembina Inn & Suites H ❀

(204) 269-8888. **$122-$126.** 1714 Pembina Hwy R3T 2G2. 0.6 mi (1 km) n of jct Bishop Grandin Blvd. Int corridors. **Pets:** $10 daily fee/pet. Service with restrictions, crate. SAVE ✕ 🖬 🖵 ⌦ ✕

CAA ▼▼▼ Best Western Viscount Gort Hotel H

(204) 775-0451. **$110-$200.** 1670 Portage Ave R3J 0C9. Jct Rt 90. Int corridors. **Pets:** Accepted. SAVE ✕ 🖬 🖵 ⛽ ⌦ ✕

Canad Inns Destination Centre Polo Park H
(204) 775-8791. **$104-$279.** 1405 St. Matthews Ave R3G 0K5. Just e of St. James St. Int corridors. **Pets:** Accepted.
[ECO] [SAVE] [X] [B] [P] [TI] [Z] [X]

Clarion Hotel & Suites H
(204) 774-5110. **$149-$209.** 1445 Portage Ave R3G 3P4. Jct Empress St. Int corridors. **Pets:** Accepted.
[ECO] [ASK] [X] [B] [P] [TI] [Z] [X]

Comfort Inn Airport H
(204) 783-5627. **$108-$122.** 1770 Sargent Ave R3H 0C8. At King Edward St. Int corridors. **Pets:** Accepted. [ECO] [ASK] [X] [M] [B] [P]

Comfort Inn South H
(204) 269-7390. **$113-$175.** 3109 Pembina Hwy R3T 4R6. Just n of jct Perimeter Hwy 100 and 75. Int corridors. **Pets:** Small. $10 daily fee/room. Designated rooms, service with restrictions, supervision.
[ECO] [SAVE] [X] [B] [P]

Country Inn & Suites By Carlson H
(204) 783-6900. **$105-$135, 4 day notice.** 730 King Edward St R3H 1B4. Just s of Wellington Ave. Int corridors. **Pets:** Accepted.
[ASK] [X] [M] [B] [P]

Days Inn Winnipeg H
(204) 586-8525. **Call for rates.** 550 McPhillips St R2X 2H2. Just n of Logan Ave. Int corridors. **Pets:** Accepted. [X] [B] [P] [TI] [Z]

Delta Winnipeg H ✿
(204) 942-0551. **$89-$399.** 350 St. Mary Ave R3C 3J2. At Hargrave St. Int corridors. **Pets:** Medium. Service with restrictions, crate.
[ECO] [SAVE] [X] [M] [B] [P] [TI] [Z] [X]

The Fairmont Winnipeg H ✿
(204) 957-1350. **Call for rates.** 2 Lombard Pl R3B 0Y3. Just e of Portage Ave and Main St. Int corridors. **Pets:** Other species. $25 daily fee/room. Service with restrictions, supervision.
[ECO] [X] [B] [P] [TI] [Z] [X]

The Fort Garry H
(204) 942-8251. **Call for rates.** 222 Broadway Ave R3C 0R3. Just w of Main St. Int corridors. **Pets:** Accepted. [X] [B] [TI] [Z] [X]

Greenwood Inn & Suites H
(204) 775-9889. **Call for rates.** 1715 Wellington Ave R3H 0G1. At Century St. Int corridors. **Pets:** Accepted. [X] [B] [P] [TI] [Z] [X]

Hilton Suites Winnipeg Airport H ✿
(204) 783-1700. **$139-$229.** 1800 Wellington Ave R3H 1B2. At Berry St. Int corridors. **Pets:** Large, other species. $75 deposit/room. Service with restrictions, supervision. [ECO] [SAVE] [X] [M] [B] [P] [TI] [Z] [X]

Holiday Inn Winnipeg South H
(204) 452-4747. **Call for rates.** 1330 Pembina Hwy R3T 2B4. At McGillivray Blvd. Int corridors. **Pets:** Accepted.
[ECO] [X] [B] [P] [TI] [Z]

Place Louis Riel Suite Hotel H
(204) 947-6961. **$125-$400.** 190 Smith St R3C 1J8. At St. Mary Ave. Int corridors. **Pets:** Accepted. [ECO] [ASK] [X] [M] [B] [P] [TI] [X]

Quality Inn & Suites H
(204) 453-8247. **$90-$270.** 635 Pembina Hwy R3M 2L4. Jct s of Grant Ave. Int corridors. **Pets:** Accepted. [SAVE] [X] [B] [P] [TI]

Radisson Hotel Winnipeg Downtown H
(204) 956-0410. **$120-$182.** 288 Portage Ave R3C 0B8. At Smith St. Int corridors. **Pets:** Accepted. [ECO] [SAVE] [X] [B] [P] [TI] [Z] [X]

Travelodge Winnipeg H ✿
(204) 255-6000. **$82-$159.** 20 Alpine Ave R2M 0Y5. Just e of jct Fermor Ave and St. Anne's Rd. Int corridors. **Pets:** Large, other species. $10 daily fee/pet. Service with restrictions, supervision.
[ECO] [SAVE] [X] [B] [P] [TI] [Z] [X]

Victoria Inn Hotel & Convention Centre H
(204) 786-4801. **$129-$174.** 1808 Wellington Ave R3H 0G3. At Berry St. Int corridors. **Pets:** Accepted. [ECO] [SAVE] [X] [B] [P] [TI] [Z] [X]

END METROPOLITAN AREA

NEW BRUNSWICK

BATHURST

▼▼ ▼▼ Atlantic Host Hotel [H]

(506) 548-3335. **$105-$120.** 1450 Vanier Blvd E2A 4H7. Rt 11, exit 310 (Vanier Blvd). Int corridors. **Pets:** Small. $25 one-time fee/pet. No service, supervision. ⊠ 🖵 ℌ ⇌ ⊠

▼▼ ▼▼ Comfort Inn [H]

(506) 547-8000. **$81-$99.** 1170 St Peter's Ave E2A 2Z9. 2.1 mi (3.4 km) n on Rt 134 (St Peter's Ave). Int corridors. **Pets:** Accepted. (A$K) ⊠ ▊ 🖵

▼▼ ▼▼ Danny's Inn & Conference Centre [H]

(506) 546-6621. **$86-$149.** Rt 134 E2A 3Z2. Rt 11, exit 310 (Vanier Blvd) northbound to Rt 134 (St Peter's Ave), 2.5 mi (4 km) n; exit 318 southbound to Rt 134 (St Peter's Ave), 2.3 mi (3.8 km) s. Ext/int corridors. **Pets:** Accepted. (A$K) ⊠ ▊ 🖵 ℌ ⇌ ⊠

(CAA) ▼▼ ▼▼ Lakeview Inns & Suites [H]

(506) 548-4949. **$100-$190.** 777 St Peter's Ave E2A 2Y9. 1.8 mi (3 km) n on Rt 134 (St Peter's Ave). Int corridors. **Pets:** Medium, dogs only. $25 daily fee/pet. Designated rooms, service with restrictions, supervision. (ECO) (SAVE) ⊠ (&M)

BOUCTOUCHE

▼▼ ▼▼ Auberge Bouctouche Inn & Suites [H]

(506) 743-5003. **$79-$159.** 50 Industrielle St E4S 3H9. Rt 11, exit 32A/B. Int corridors. **Pets:** Accepted. ⊠ (&M) ▊ 🖵

CAMPBELLTON

▼▼ ▼▼ Comfort Inn [H]

(506) 753-4121. **$100-$130.** 111 Val D'Amour Rd E3N 5B9. Hwy 11, exit 415, 0.6 mi (1 km) e on Sugarloaf St W. Ext/int corridors. **Pets:** Accepted. (ECO) (A$K) ⊠ ▊ 🖵

(CAA) ▼▼ ▼▼ Howard Johnson [H]

(506) 753-4133. **$119-$139.** 157 Water St E3N 3H2. Hwy 134; in City Centre Complex. Int corridors. **Pets:** Accepted. (SAVE) ⊠ ▊ 🖵 ℌ

▼▼ ▼▼ Super 8-Campbellton [H] ❀

(506) 753-8080. **$69-$279.** 26 Duke St E3N 2K3. Just s of Roseberry St; jct George and Duke sts; downtown. Ext/int corridors. **Pets:** $20 daily fee/room. Designated rooms, service with restrictions, supervision. (ECO) (A$K) ⊠ (&M) ▊ 🖵 ⇌ ⊠

CARAQUET

▼▼ ▼▼ Super 8 [H]

(506) 727-0888. **Call for rates.** 9 Carrefour Ave E1W 1B6. Just e of jct Rt 11 and St Pierre Blvd E. Int corridors. **Pets:** Accepted. ⊠ (&M) ▊ 🖵 ⇌ ⊠

COCAGNE

▼▼ ▼▼ Cocagne Motel [M]

(506) 576-6657. **Call for rates.** 1718 Rt 535 E4R 1N6. Rt 11, exit 15, 0.6 mi (1 km) n. Ext corridors. **Pets:** Accepted. ⊠ ▊

DALHOUSIE

(CAA) ▼▼ ▼▼ ▼▼ Best Western Manoir Adelaide [H]

(506) 684-5681. **$110-$120.** 385 Adelaide St E8C 1B4. Centre. Int corridors. **Pets:** Very small, dogs only. $10 one-time fee/room. Designated rooms, service with restrictions, supervision. (SAVE) ⊠ ▊ 🖵 ℌ

DOAKTOWN

▼▼ ▼▼ The Ledges Inn [CI]

(506) 365-1820. **$100-$150.** 30 Ledges Inn Ln E9C 1A7. On Rt 8; centre. Int corridors. **Pets:** Accepted. (A$K) ⊠ ℌ

EDMUNDSTON

▼▼ ▼▼ Auberge Les Jardins Inn [H]

(506) 739-5514. **$119-$189.** 60 Principale St E7B 1V7. Trans-Canada Hwy 2, exit 8. Ext/int corridors. **Pets:** Accepted. (A$K) ⊠ ▊ 🖵 ℌ ⇌

(CAA) ▼▼ ▼▼ ▼▼ Clarion Hotel & Conference Center [H]

(506) 739-7321. **$110-$160.** 100 rue Rice E3V 1T4. Trans-Canada Hwy 2, exit 18 (Hebert Blvd), 1 mi (1.6 km) sw, then just w on Church Rd. Int corridors. **Pets:** Accepted. (SAVE) ⊠ ▊ 🖵 ℌ ⇌

(CAA) ▼▼ ▼▼ Comfort Inn [H]

(506) 739-8361. **$79-$190.** 5 Bateman Ave E3V 3L1. Trans-Canada Hwy 2, exit 18 (Hebert Blvd). Int corridors. **Pets:** Other species. Service with restrictions, crate. (ECO) (SAVE) ⊠ ▊ 🖵

▼▼ ▼▼ ▼▼ Days Inn Edmundston [H]

(506) 263-0000. **$139-$159.** 10 rue Mathieu E7C 3E1. Trans-Canada Hwy 2, exit 26. Int corridors. **Pets:** $10 daily fee/pet. Service with restrictions, supervision. (A$K) ⊠ ▊ 🖵

▼▼ ▼▼ ▼▼ Quality Inn [H]

(506) 735-5525. **$80-$160.** 919 Canada Rd E3V 3X2. Trans-Canada Hwy 2, exit 13B eastbound; exit 13BA westbound. Ext/int corridors. **Pets:** Accepted. (A$K) ⊠ (&M) ▊ 🖵 ℌ ⇌ ⊠

FREDERICTON

(CAA) ▼▼ ▼▼ ▼▼ Best Western Fredericton [H]

(506) 455-8448. **$150-$170.** 333 Bishop Dr E3C 2M6. Rt 8, exit 6A eastbound; exit 6B westbound, just w of Regent Mall. Int corridors. **Pets:** Accepted. (SAVE) ⊠ (&M) ▊ 🖵 ⇌

▼▼ ▼▼ City Motel [H]

(506) 450-9900. **Call for rates.** 1216 Regent St E3B 3Z4. Trans-Canada Hwy 2, exit 285A and B eastbound; exit 285B westbound, 2 mi (3.3 km) n on Rt 101 (Regent St). Int corridors. **Pets:** Accepted. ⊠ 🖵 ℌ

(CAA) ▼▼ ▼▼ Comfort Inn [H] ❀

(506) 453-0800. **$112-$199.** 797 Prospect St E3B 5Y4. Trans-Canada Hwy 2, exit 281, 2.5 mi (4 km) ne on Rt 640 (Hanwell Rd). Int corridors. **Pets:** Other species. Designated rooms, service with restrictions. (ECO) (SAVE) ⊠ ▊ 🖵

(CAA) ▼▼ ▼▼ ▼▼ Crowne Plaza Fredericton Lord Beaverbrook [H] ❀

(506) 455-3371. **$119-$159.** 659 Queen St E3B 5A6. Corner of Regent St. Int corridors. **Pets:** Other species. Service with restrictions. (ECO) (SAVE) ⊠ ▊ 🖵 ℌ ⇌ ⊠

(CAA) ▼▼ ▼▼ ▼▼ Delta Fredericton [H]

(506) 457-7000. **$129-$210.** 225 Woodstock Rd E3B 2H8. 1 mi (1.6 km) n on Rt 102; downtown. Int corridors. **Pets:** Accepted. (ECO) (SAVE) ⊠ (&M) ▊ 🖵 ℌ ⇌ ⊠

▼▼ **Howard Johnson Plaza Hotel Fredericton** 🅷

(506) 462-4444. **$90-$120.** 958 Prospect St E3B 2T8. Rt 8, exit 3 (Hanwell Rd) eastbound; exit 5 (Smythe St) westbound. Ext/int corridors. **Pets:** Accepted. (A$K) ⊠ 🛢 💻 🍴 ⊇ ⊠

(CAA) ▼▼▼ **Lakeview Inns & Suites-Fredericton** 🅷

(506) 459-0035. **$107-$140.** 665 Prospect St E3B 6B8. Rt 8, exit 3 (Hanwell Rd) eastbound; exit 5 (Smythe St) westbound. Int corridors. **Pets:** Accepted. (ECO) (SAVE) ⊠ 🛢 💻

(CAA) ▼▼▼ **Ramada Hotel Fredericton** 🅷

(506) 460-5500. **$119-$179.** 480 Riverside Dr E3A 8C2. On Rt 105 at the north end of Princess Margaret Bridge. Int corridors. **Pets:** Accepted. (ECO) (SAVE) ⊠ 🛢 💻 ⊇ ⊠

GRAND FALLS

(CAA) ▼▼▼ **Best Western Grand Sault Hotel & Suites** 🅷

(506) 473-6200. **$140-$170.** 187 Ouellette St E3Z 3E8. Trans-Canada Hwy 2, exit 79. Int corridors. **Pets:** Other species. $25 daily fee/pet. Designated rooms, service with restrictions. (SAVE) ⊠ 🅖M 🛢 💻 ⊇

▼▼ **Quality Inn Grand Falls** 🅷

(506) 473-1300. **$120-$190.** 10039 Rt 144 E3Y 3H5. Trans-Canada Hwy 2, exit 75, just w. Ext/int corridors. **Pets:** Small. $15 one-time fee/room. Designated rooms, service with restrictions, supervision.

(A$K) ⊠ 🅖M 🛢 💻 🍴 ⊇ ⊠

MIRAMICHI

(CAA) ▼▼▼ **Canadas Best Value Inn & Suites** 🅷

(506) 622-1215. **$79-$129.** 201 Edward St E1V 2Y7. 0.6 mi (1 km) w on Rt 8. Int corridors. **Pets:** Accepted. (ECO) (SAVE) ⊠ 🛢 💻

(CAA) ▼▼▼ **Lakeview Inns & Suites** 🅷

(506) 627-1999. **$84-$114, 7 day notice.** 333 King George Hwy E1V 1L2. 1.1 mi (1.8 km) w on Rt 8. Int corridors. **Pets:** Small. $50 deposit/pet. Designated rooms, service with restrictions, supervision. (ECO) (SAVE) ⊠ 🛢 💻

(CAA) ▼▼▼ **Park Inn & Suites on the River** 🅷

(506) 622-0302. **$99-$139, 3 day notice.** 1 Jane St E1V 2S6. Just s off King George Hwy on Bridge St. Int corridors. **Pets:** Accepted. (SAVE) ⊠ 🛢 💻 🍴

(CAA) ▼▼▼▼ **Rodd Miramichi River-A Rodd Signature Hotel** 🅷

(506) 773-3111. **$118-$182.** 1809 Water St E1N 1B2. Hwy 11, exit 120, 0.4 mi (0.6 km) e. Int corridors. **Pets:** Other species. $10 one-time fee/room. Service with restrictions, supervision.

(ECO) (SAVE) ⊠ 🅖M 🛢 💻 🍴 ⊇ ⊠

MONCTON

▼▼ **Beacon Light Motel** 🅼

(506) 384-1734. **$75-$125.** 1062 Mountain Rd E1C 2T1. Trans-Canada Hwy 2, exit 454 (Mapleton Rd), 1.7 mi (2.8 km) n on Rt 126 (Mountain Rd), then just s. Ext/int corridors. **Pets:** Medium. $10 daily fee/pet. Service with restrictions, supervision. (A$K) ⊠ 🛢 💻 ⊇

(CAA) ▼▼▼ **Coastal Inn Champlain** 🅷

(506) 857-9686. **$119-$154.** 502 Kennedy St E1A 5Y7. At Paul St; opposite Champlain Place Shopping Centre. Ext/int corridors. **Pets:** Accepted. (ECO) (SAVE) ⊠ 🛢 💻 🍴 ⊇

▼▼ **Colonial Inns** 🅷

(506) 382-3395. **$89-$178.** 42 Highfield St E1C 8T6. 1 blk n of Main St; centre. Ext/int corridors. **Pets:** Accepted. (A$K) ⊠ 🛢 💻 🍴 ⊇

(CAA) ▼▼▼ **Comfort Inn** 🅷 🐾

(506) 859-6868. **$99-$349.** 20 Maplewood Dr E1A 6P9. Trans-Canada Hwy 2, exit 459A on Hwy 115 S, left on Rt 134 E (Lewisville Rd). Int corridors. **Pets:** Service with restrictions, crate. (ECO) (SAVE) ⊠ 🛢 💻

▼▼ **Comfort Inn** 🅷

(506) 384-3175. **$89-$325.** 2495 Mountain Rd E1G 2W4. Trans-Canada Hwy 2, exit 450. Int corridors. **Pets:** Accepted. (ECO) (A$K) ⊠ 🛢 💻

▼▼ **Country Inn & Suites By Carlson** 🅷 🐾

(506) 852-7000. **$89-$249.** 2475 Mountain Rd E1G 2J5. Trans-Canada Hwy 2, exit 450. Int corridors. **Pets:** $25 one-time fee/room. Service with restrictions, crate. (ECO) (A$K) ⊠ 🛢 💻

(CAA) ▼▼▼ **Crowne Plaza Moncton Downtown** 🅷

(506) 854-6340. **$129-$159.** 1005 Main St E1C 1G9. Highfield and Main sts; downtown. Int corridors. **Pets:** Accepted.
(ECO) (SAVE) ⊠ 🛢 💻 🍴 ⊇ ⊠

▼▼▼ **Delta Beausejour** 🅷

(506) 854-4344. **$209-$329.** 750 Main St E1C 1E6. Main and Bacon sts; downtown. Int corridors. **Pets:** Accepted.
(ECO) (A$K) ⊠ 🛢 💻 ⊇ ⊠

▼▼▼ **Future Inns Moncton Hotel & Conference Centre** 🅷

(506) 852-9600. **$129-$189.** 40 Lady Ada Blvd E1G 0E3. Trans-Canada Hwy 2, exit 454. Int corridors. **Pets:** Accepted. (A$K) ⊠ 🅖M 💻 🍴

(CAA) ▼▼▼ **Hampton Inn & Suites Moncton** 🅷 🐾

(506) 855-4819. **Call for rates.** 700 Mapleton Rd E1G 0L7. Trans-Canada Hwy 2, exit 454. Int corridors. **Pets:** Other species. Service with restrictions, supervision. (SAVE) ⊠ 🅖M 🛢 💻 ⊇

(CAA) ▼▼▼ **Holiday Inn Express Hotel & Suites Moncton** 🅷 🐾

(506) 384-1050. **$119-$219.** 2515 Mountain Rd E1G 2W4. Trans-Canada Hwy 2, exit 450. Ext/int corridors. **Pets:** Medium. $20 one-time fee/room. Designated rooms, service with restrictions, supervision.
(ECO) (SAVE) ⊠ 🅖M 🛢 💻 ⊇ ⊠

(CAA) ▼▼▼ **Residence Inn by Marriott Moncton** 🅷

(506) 854-7100. **$152-$186.** 600 Main St E1C 0M6. At Assomption Blvd. Int corridors. **Pets:** Large, other species. $75 one-time fee/room. Supervision. (SAVE) ⊠ 🅖M 🛢 💻 🍴 ⊇

▼▼ **Rodd Park House Inn** 🅷

(506) 382-1664. **$123-$159.** 434 Main St E1C 1B9. On Rt 106 (Main St) at King St. Ext/int corridors. **Pets:** Accepted.
(ECO) (A$K) ⊠ 💻 🍴 ⊇

▼▼▼ **Super 8 Moncton/Dieppe** 🅷

(506) 858-8880. **Call for rates.** 370 Dieppe Blvd E1A 8H4. Hwy 15, exit 16, 0.6 mi (1 km) s. Int corridors. **Pets:** Accepted.
(ECO) ⊠ 🅖M 🛢 💻 ⊇ ⊠

OROMOCTO

(CAA) ▼▼▼ **Days Inn Oromocto** 🅷

(506) 357-5657. **$108-$130.** 60 Brayson Blvd E2V 4T9. Trans-Canada Hwy 2, exit 301 eastbound; exit 303 westbound, just s to Pioneer Ave, then 1 mi (1.6 km) w. Int corridors. **Pets:** Medium, other species. $15 daily fee/pet. Designated rooms, service with restrictions, supervision.
(ECO) (SAVE) ⊠ 🅖M 🛢 💻 ⊇

PERTH-ANDOVER

(CAA) ▼▼▼ **The Castle Inn** 🅲🅸

(506) 273-9495. **$99-$179.** 21 Brentwood Dr E7H 1P1. Trans-Canada Hwy 2, exit 115, follow signs over St. John River. Int corridors. **Pets:** Accepted. (SAVE) ⊠ 💻 🍴 ⊠

ROTHESAY

▼▼▼ **Shadow Lawn Inn** 🅲🅸

(506) 847-7539. **$119-$195, 3 day notice.** 3180 Rothesay Rd E2E 5V7. Hwy 1, exit 137B eastbound; exit 137A westbound, follow signs for Rothesay Rd and Rt 100, 1 mi (1.6 km) left on Old Hampton Rd (Rt 100), then left on Rt 100. Int corridors. **Pets:** $10 daily fee/pet. Service with restrictions, supervision. (A$K) ⊠ 🛢 💻 🍴

SACKVILLE

▼▼ ▼▼ Coastal Inn Sackville ℍ
(506) 536-0000. **$115-$135.** 15 Wright St E4L 4P8. Trans-Canada Hwy 2, exit 504. Int corridors. **Pets:** Accepted. ⒺⒸⓄ Ⓐ$Ⓚ ⊠ 🗋

ⒸⒶⒶ ▼▼▼▼ Marshlands Inn ℂℐ
(506) 536-0170. **$95-$205.** 55 Bridge St E4L 3N8. On Hwy 106; centre. Int corridors. **Pets:** Accepted. ⓈⒶⓋⒺ ⊠ 🍴

ST. ANDREWS

ⒸⒶⒶ ▼▼▼▼ The Fairmont Algonquin ℍ ❀
(506) 529-8823. **$119-$569, 3 day notice.** 184 Adolphus St E5B 1T7. Off Hwy 127. Int corridors. **Pets:** Other species. $25 daily fee/room. Supervision. ⒺⒸⓄ ⓈⒶⓋⒺ ⊠ 🗋 💻 🍴 🏊 ⊠

SAINT JOHN

ⒸⒶⒶ ▼▼▼▼ Best Western Saint John Hotel & Suites ℍ
(506) 657-9966. **$110-$220.** 55 Majors Brook Dr E2J 0B2. Hwy 1, exit 129, 1 mi (1.6 km) e on Rothesay Ave to McAllister Dr, then just s. Int corridors. **Pets:** Accepted. ⓈⒶⓋⒺ ⊠ 🖭ℳ 🗋 💻 🏊

ⒸⒶⒶ ▼▼ Colonial Inn Saint John ℍ
(506) 652-3000. **$95-$118.** 175 City Rd E2L 3T5. Hwy 1, exit 123. Ext/int corridors. **Pets:** $10 daily fee/pet. Service with restrictions, supervision. ⓈⒶⓋⒺ ⊠ 🗋 🍴 🏊 ⊠

▼▼ ▼▼ Comfort Inn ℍ
(506) 674-1873. **$107-$147.** 1155 Fairville Blvd E2M 5T9. Hwy 1, exit 117 westbound; exit 119 eastbound, turn left. Int corridors. **Pets:** Accepted. ⒺⒸⓄ Ⓐ$Ⓚ ⊠ 🗋 💻

▼▼▼▼ Country Inn & Suites By Carlson ℍ
(506) 635-0400. **$99-$154.** 1011 Fairville Blvd E2M 5T9. Hwy 1, exit 119B eastbound, left on Catherwood Dr, left at lights; exit 119A westbound. Int corridors. **Pets:** Accepted. ⒺⒸⓄ Ⓐ$Ⓚ ⊠ 🗋 💻

▼▼▼▼ Delta Brunswick ℍ
(506) 648-1981. **$99-$199.** 39 King St E2L 4W3. Centre of downtown; in Brunswick Square Mall. Int corridors. **Pets:** Accepted. Ⓐ$Ⓚ ⊠ 🖭ℳ 🗋 💻 🍴 🏊 ⊠

ⒸⒶⒶ ▼▼ ▼▼ Fort Howe Hotel and Convention Centre ℍ
(506) 657-7320. **$109-$149, 30 day notice.** 10 Portland St E2K 4H8. Hwy 1, exit 121 eastbound off Harbour Bridge; exit 123 westbound. Int corridors. **Pets:** Accepted. ⒺⒸⓄ ⓈⒶⓋⒺ ⊠ 🗋 💻 🍴 ⊠

ⒸⒶⒶ ▼▼▼▼ Hampton Inn & Suites ℍ ❀
(506) 657-4600. **$109-$165.** 51 Fashion Dr E2J 0A7. Hwy 1, exit 129, 1 mi (1.6 km) e on Rothesay Ave to Retail Dr; behind Home Depot. Int corridors. **Pets:** Medium. Designated rooms, service with restrictions, supervision. ⓈⒶⓋⒺ ⊠ 🖭ℳ 🗋 💻 🏊 ⊠

ⒸⒶⒶ ▼▼▼▼ Hilton Saint John ℍ
(506) 693-8484. **$99-$239.** 1 Market Square E2L 4Z6. Hwy 1, exit 122, at Market Square. Int corridors. **Pets:** Accepted. ⒺⒸⓄ ⓈⒶⓋⒺ ⊠ 💻 🍴 🏊 ⊠

ⒸⒶⒶ ▼▼▼▼ Holiday Inn Express & Suites ℍ
(506) 642-2622. **$109-$189.** 400 Main St/Chesley Dr E2K 4N5. 0.6 mi (1 km) w on Hwy 1; north end of Chesley Dr, exit 121; off Harbour Bridge. Int corridors. **Pets:** Accepted. ⒺⒸⓄ ⓈⒶⓋⒺ ⊠ 🗋 💻 🏊

▼▼ ▼▼ Hotel Courtenay Bay ℍ
(506) 657-3610. **Call for rates.** 350 Haymarket Square E2L 3P1. At Crown and Waterloo sts; downtown. Int corridors. **Pets:** Accepted. ⊠ 🗋 💻 🍴 🏊

ⒸⒶⒶ ▼▼▼▼ Inn on the Cove and Spa ℂℐ
(506) 672-7799. **Call for rates.** 1371 Sand Cove Rd E2M 4Z9. Hwy 1, exit 119A, just s on Bleury St to Sand Cove Rd, then 3.2 mi (2 km) w. Int corridors. **Pets:** Medium. $35 one-time fee/room. Designated rooms, service with restrictions, supervision. ⓈⒶⓋⒺ ⊠ 🖭ℳ 💻 🍴

ST-LEONARD

ⒸⒶⒶ ▼▼ ▼▼ Daigle's Motel ℍ
(506) 423-6351. **$78-$99.** 68 rue DuPont E7E 1Y1. Hwy 17, 0.6 mi (1 km) s of Trans-Canada Hwy 2, exit 58. Ext corridors. **Pets:** Accepted. ⓈⒶⓋⒺ ⊠ 🍴 🏊

ST. STEPHEN

▼▼ St. Stephen Inn ℳ
(506) 466-1814. **$55-$130.** 99 King St E3L 2C6. On Hwy 1; centre. Ext/int corridors. **Pets:** Accepted. Ⓐ$Ⓚ ⊠ 🗋

SHEDIAC

▼▼ ▼▼ Gaudet Chalets & Motel ℳ
(506) 533-8877. **$55-$119, 30 day notice.** 14 Bellevue Heights E4P 1H2. On Rt 133, 1.4 mi (2.4 km) w of Rt 15, exit 37. Ext corridors. **Pets:** Accepted. ⊠ 🗋 💻

ⒸⒶⒶ ▼▼ ▼▼ Seely's Motel ℳ
(506) 532-6193. **$69-$159, 3 day notice.** 21 Bellevue Heights E4P 1G9. On Rt 133, 1.5 mi (2.4 km) w of Rt 15, exit 37. Ext corridors. **Pets:** Small, dogs only. $15 daily fee/pet. Designated rooms, service with restrictions, supervision. ⓈⒶⓋⒺ ⊠ 🗋 💻 🏊

SUSSEX

▼▼ All Seasons Inn ℳ
(506) 433-2220. **$95-$125.** 1015 Main St E4E 2M6. Hwy 1, exit 192 eastbound; exit 198 westbound, left towards Sussex Corner; centre. Ext corridors. **Pets:** Accepted. Ⓐ$Ⓚ ⊠ 🍴

▼▼ ▼▼ Fairway Inn ℍ
(506) 433-3470. **$100-$175.** 216 Roachville Rd E4E 5L6. Hwy 1, exit 193. Ext/int corridors. **Pets:** Medium. $10 daily fee/pet. Designated rooms, service with restrictions, supervision. Ⓐ$Ⓚ ⊠ 🗋 🍴 🏊

▼▼ Pine Cone Motel ℳ
(506) 433-3958. **$55-$75.** 12808 Rt 114 E4E 5L9. Hwy 1, exit 198, 1.2 mi (2 km) e on Rt 114 towards Penobsquis. Ext corridors. **Pets:** Accepted. Ⓐ$Ⓚ ⊠ 🗋

WOODSTOCK

▼▼ ▼▼ Econo Lodge ℍ
(506) 328-8876. **$90-$140.** 168 Rt 555 E7M 6B5. Trans-Canada Hwy 2, exit 188 (Houlton Rd). Ext/int corridors. **Pets:** Accepted. Ⓐ$Ⓚ ⊠ 💻 🍴 🏊

▼▼ ▼▼ Howard Johnson Inn ℍ
(506) 328-3315. **$90-$150.** 159 Rt 555, exit 188 TCH E7M 6B5. Trans-Canada Hwy 2, exit 188 (Houlton Rd). Ext/int corridors. **Pets:** Accepted. Ⓐ$Ⓚ ⊠ 💻 🍴 🏊

YOUNGS COVE

▼▼ McCready's Motel ℳ
(506) 362-2916. **Call for rates.** 10995 Rt 10 E4C 2G5. Trans-Canada Hwy 2, exit 365, just w. Ext corridors. **Pets:** Accepted. ⊠ 🍴 ✂ 🐾

NEWFOUNDLAND AND LABRADOR

CHANNEL-PORT-AUX-BASQUES

▼▼ Hotel Port Aux Basques 🏨

(709) 695-2171. **$110-$120.** 1 Grand Bay Rd A0M 1C0. Jct Trans-Canada Hwy 1. Int corridors. **Pets:** Other species. $10 one-time fee/pet. Service with restrictions, supervision. (ASK) ⊠ 🛏 💻 🍴

▼▼ St. Christopher's Hotel 🏨

(709) 695-7034. **Call for rates.** 146 Caribou Rd A0M 1C0. Trans-Canada Hwy 1, exit Port Aux Basques (downtown), follow signs 1.2 mi (2 km). Int corridors. **Pets:** Accepted. ⊠ 🛏 💻 🍴

CLARENVILLE

▼ Restland Motel 🏨

(709) 466-7636. **Call for rates.** 262 Memorial Dr A5A 1N9. Centre. Ext/int corridors. **Pets:** Accepted. ⊠ 🛏 🍴 (AC)

▼▼ St. Jude Hotel 🏨

(709) 466-1717. **$99-$130.** 247 Trans-Canada Hwy A5A 1Y4. On Trans-Canada Hwy 1; centre. Int corridors. **Pets:** Accepted.
(ASK) ⊠ 🛏 💻 🍴

CORNER BROOK

▼▼ Comfort Inn 🏨 🐾

(709) 639-1980. **$110-$150.** 41 Maple Valley Rd A2H 6T2. Trans-Canada Hwy 1, exit 5 eastbound; exit 6 westbound, via Confederation Ave. Int corridors. **Pets:** Other species. Designated rooms, service with restrictions, supervision. (ECO) (ASK) ⊠ 🛏 💻 🍴

▼▼▼ Glynmill Inn 🏨

(709) 634-5181. **$121-$205.** 1B Cobb Ln A2H 6E6. Centre. Int corridors. **Pets:** Accepted. ⊠ 🛏 💻 🍴

▼▼▼ Greenwood Inn & Suites-Corner Brook 🏨

(709) 634-5381. **Call for rates.** 48 West St A2H 2Z2. At Chestnut St; centre. Int corridors. **Pets:** Accepted. (ECO) ⊠ 🛏 💻 🍴 🏊

▼▼ Mamateek Inn 🏨

(709) 639-8901. **Call for rates.** 64 Maple Valley Rd A2H 6G7. Trans-Canada Hwy 1, exit 5 eastbound; exit 6 westbound, via Confederation Ave. Int corridors. **Pets:** Accepted. ⊠ 💻 🍴

COW HEAD

▼▼ Shallow Bay Motel & Cabins 🏨

(709) 243-2471. **$95-$125.** Rt 430, The Viking Tr A0K 2A0. Hwy 430, 2.5 mi (4 km) w towards the ocean, follow signs. Ext/int corridors. **Pets:** Other species. $10 one-time fee/pet. Designated rooms, service with restrictions, supervision. ⊠ 🛏 💻 🍴 🏊 🐾

GANDER

▼▼ Albatross Hotel 🏨

(709) 256-3956. **Call for rates.** Trans-Canada Hwy A1V 1W8. On Trans-Canada Hwy 1. Ext/int corridors. **Pets:** Other species. $100 deposit/room. Service with restrictions, supervision. ⊠ 💻 🍴

▼▼ Comfort Inn 🏨

(709) 256-3535. **Call for rates.** 112 Trans-Canada Hwy 1 A1V 1P8. Centre. Ext/int corridors. **Pets:** Accepted. ⊠ 🛏 💻 🍴

▼▼ Sinbad's Hotel & Suites 🏨

(709) 651-2678. **$98-$255.** Bennett Dr A1V 1W8. Centre; opposite Gander Mall. Ext corridors. **Pets:** Other species. $100 deposit/room. Service with restrictions, supervision. (ASK) ⊠ 🛏 💻 🍴

GRAND FALLS-WINDSOR

▼▼ Mount Peyton Hotel 🏨

(709) 489-2251. **Call for rates.** 214 Lincoln Rd A2A 1P8. 0.6 mi (1 km) ne on Trans-Canada Hwy 1. Ext/int corridors. **Pets:** Accepted.
(ECO) ⊠ 🛏 💻 🍴

HAPPY VALLEY-GOOSE BAY

▼▼ Goose River Lodges (CA)

(709) 896-2600. **Call for rates.** NW River Rd A0P 1C0. From jct Rt 500, 10.6 mi (17 km) nw on Rt 520. Ext corridors. **Pets:** Accepted.
⊠ 🛏 💻 🐾 🐾

LABRADOR CITY

▼▼ Carol Inn 🏨

(709) 944-7736. **Call for rates.** 215 Drake Ave A2V 2B6. Centre. Int corridors. **Pets:** Accepted. ⊠ 🛏 💻 🍴

L'ANSE AU CLAIR

▼▼ Northern Light Inn 🏨

(709) 931-2332. **$115, 31 day notice.** Rt 510 A0K 3K0. Centre. Int corridors. **Pets:** Accepted. (ASK) ⊠ 🛏 🍴

ST. JOHN'S

▼ The Battery Hotel & Conference Centre 🏨

(709) 576-0040. **$99-$159.** 100 Signal Hill Rd A1A 1B3. 1 mi (1.6 km) e; on historic Signal Hill. Int corridors. **Pets:** Accepted.
(ASK) ⊠ 🛏 💻 🍴 (AC)

▼▼▼ Capital Hotel 🏨

(709) 738-4480. **$126-$139.** 208 Kenmount Rd A1B 3P9. Trans-Canada Hwy 1, exit 45, 4 mi (6.4 km) s on Team Gushue Hwy to Kenmount Rd. Int corridors. **Pets:** Accepted. (ASK) ⊠ 🛏 💻 🍴

(CAA) ▼▼▼ Comfort Inn Airport 🏨

(709) 753-3500. **$119.** 106 Airport Rd A1A 4Y3. Trans-Canada Hwy 1, exit 47A, 0.6 mi (1 km) n on Rt 40 (Portugal Cove Rd). Int corridors. **Pets:** Accepted. (SAVE) ⊠ 🛏 💻 🍴

▼▼▼▼ Delta St. John's Hotel and Conference Centre 🏨

(709) 739-6404. **Call for rates.** 120 New Gower St A1C 6K4. At Barter's Hill Rd; centre. Int corridors. **Pets:** Accepted.
(ECO) ⊠ (&M) 🛏 💻 🍴 🏊 🐾

▼▼▼ Extended Stay Deluxe St. John's–Downtown 🏨

(709) 754-7888. **$99-$124.** 222 LeMarchant Rd A1C 2H9. Corner of Pleasant St. Int corridors. **Pets:** Other species. $25 daily fee/room. Designated rooms, service with restrictions, crate. (ASK) ⊠ (&M) 🛏 💻

▼▼▼ The Guv'nor Inn 🏨

(709) 726-0092. **$100-$200.** 389 Elizabeth Ave A1B 1V1. 2 blks n of Freshwater Rd. Ext/int corridors. **Pets:** Accepted. ⊠ 🛏 💻 🍴

▼▼▼ Holiday Inn St. John's-Govt Centre 🏨 🐾

(709) 722-0506. **$139-$169.** 180 Portugal Cove Rd A1B 2N2. Trans-Canada Hwy 1, exit 47A, 0.9 mi (1.4 km) s. Ext/int corridors. **Pets:** Designated rooms, service with restrictions, supervision.
(ECO) (ASK) ⊠ (&M) 🛏 💻 🍴 🐾

(CAA) ▼▼▼▼ Sheraton Hotel Newfoundland 🏨

(709) 726-4980. **Call for rates.** 115 Cavendish Square A1C 3K2. At Duckworth and Ordnance sts. Int corridors. **Pets:** Accepted.
(SAVE) ⊠ 🛏 💻 🍴 🏊 🐾

▼▼▼ Super 8 **H** ❀

(709) 739-8888. **$119-$179.** 175 Higgins Line A1B 4N4. Trans-Canada Hwy 1, exit 47A, just s on Rt 40 (Portugal Cove Rd). Int corridors. **Pets:** Designated rooms, service with restrictions, supervision.

ECO ASK ✕ &M ⬛ 🖥 🏊

CAA ▼▼▼ Travellers Inn St. John's **H**

(709) 722-5540. **$99-$139.** 199 Kenmount Rd A1B 3P9. Trans-Canada Hwy 1, exit 45, 1 mi (1.6 km) s on Team Gushue Hwy to Kenmount Rd. Ext/int corridors. **Pets:** Accepted. ECO SAVE ✕ ⬛ 🖥 🍴 🏊

STEPHENVILLE

▼▼ Holiday Inn Stephenville **H** ❀

(709) 643-6666. **$121-$128.** 44 Queen St A2N 2M5. Centre. Int corridors. **Pets:** Service with restrictions, crate. ECO ASK ✕ ⬛ 🖥 🍴

NORTHWEST TERRITORIES

YELLOWKNIFE

(AAA) ◆◆◆ Chateau Nova Hotel & Suites H
(867) 873-9700. **$149-$199.** 4401 50th Ave X1A 2N2. Downtown. Int corridors. **Pets:** Dogs only. $50 one-time fee/pet. Designated rooms, service with restrictions, supervision. [SAVE] [✕] [🛏] [💻] [🍴] [✕]

◆◆◆ Coast Fraser Tower H
(867) 873-8700. **Call for rates.** 5303 52nd St X1A 1V1. Corner of 52nd St and 53rd Ave. Int corridors. **Pets:** Accepted. [ECO] [✕] [🛏] [💻] [AC]

◆◆◆ The Explorer Hotel H
(867) 873-3531. **$185-$205.** 4825 49th Ave X1A 2R3. Downtown. Int corridors. **Pets:** $20 daily fee/room. Designated rooms, service with restrictions, supervision. [ASK] [✕] [🛏] [💻] [🍴]

◆◆ Yellowknife Super 8 M
(867) 669-8888. **$169-$199.** 308 Old Airport Rd X1A 3G3. 1.2 mi (2 km) s on Franklin Ave, 0.6 mi (1 km) w; in Wal-Mart Plaza. Int corridors. **Pets:** Accepted. [ECO] [ASK] [✕] [🛏] [💻]

NOVA SCOTIA

AMHERST

▼▼▼ Amherst Wandlyn Inn ⊞
(902) 667-3331. **$105-$135.** 1539 Southhampton Rd B4H 3Z2. Trans-Canada Hwy 104, exit 3, 0.6 mi (1 km) w. Ext/int corridors. **Pets:** Accepted. (ASK) ⊠ 📶 🖵 🍽 🏊

▼▼ Comfort Inn ⊞
(902) 667-0404. **$119-$153.** 143 Albion St S B4H 2X2. Trans-Canada Hwy 104, exit 4, 1 mi (1.6 km) n on Rt 2. Int corridors. **Pets:** Accepted. (ECO) (ASK) ⊠ 📶 🖵

▼▼▼ Super 8 ⊞ 🐾
(902) 660-8888. **$89-$249.** 40 Lord Amherst Dr B4H 4W6. Trans-Canada Hwy 104, exit 4. Int corridors. **Pets:** Medium. $10 daily fee/pet. Service with restrictions, supervision. (ECO) (ASK) ⊠ 📶 🖵 🏊

ANNAPOLIS ROYAL

▼▼▼ Annapolis Royal Inn Ⓜ
(902) 532-2323. **$89-$150, 30 day notice.** 3924 Hwy 1 B0S 1A0. 0.6 mi (1 km) w. Ext corridors. **Pets:** Accepted. (ASK) ⊠ 🖵

▼▼ Champlain Motel Ⓜ
(902) 532-5473. **$100-$207, 30 day notice.** RR 2 B0S 1A0. 2.5 mi (4.2 km) w on Rt 1. Ext corridors. **Pets:** Accepted. (ASK) ⊠ 📶 🖵 🏊

ⒸⒶⒶ ▼▼▼ Hillsdale House Inn (BB) 🐾
(902) 532-2345. **$82-$152.** 519 St George St B0S 1A0. Just e of Rt 1; centre. Int corridors. **Pets:** Other species. $25 one-time fee/room. Designated rooms, service with restrictions. (SAVE) ⊠

▼▼▼ The King George Inn (BB) 🐾
(902) 532-5286. **$80-$160.** 548 Upper St George St B0S 1A0. Jct Rt 1 and 8, just e on Rt 8. Int corridors. **Pets:** Crate. (ASK) ⊠ 🖵

ANTIGONISH

ⒸⒶⒶ ▼▼▼ Maritime Inn Antigonish ⊞
(902) 863-4001. **$115-$180.** 158 Main St B2G 2B7. Between St. Mary's and Court sts; centre. Ext/int corridors. **Pets:** Accepted. (SAVE) ⊠ 📶 🖵 🍽

AULD'S COVE

ⒸⒶⒶ ▼▼▼ Cove Motel & Restaurant/Gift Shop Ⓜ
(902) 747-2700. **$105-$130.** 227 Auld's Cove Rd B0H 1P0. 0.6 mi (1 km) n off Trans-Canada Hwy 104; 1.9 mi (3 km) w of Canso Cswy. Ext corridors. **Pets:** Designated rooms, service with restrictions, supervision. (SAVE) ⊠ 📶 🖵 🍽

BADDECK

ⒸⒶⒶ ▼▼▼ Hunter's Mountain Chalets ⒸⒶ
(902) 295-3392. **$78-$138, 4 day notice.** 562 Cabot Tr B0E 1B0. Trans-Canada Hwy 105, exit 7, 1.6 mi (2.6 km) n. Ext corridors. **Pets:** Dogs only. $5 daily fee/pet. No service, supervision. (SAVE) ⊠ 📶 🐕 🔒

ⒸⒶⒶ ▼▼▼ Inverary Resort ⊞
(902) 295-3500. **$109-$189, 3 day notice.** 368 Shore Rd B0E 1B0. Trans-Canada Hwy 105, exit 8, 1 mi (1.6 km) e on Rt 205 (Shore Rd). Ext/int corridors. **Pets:** Accepted. (SAVE) ⊠ 🔥 📶 🖵 🍽 🏊 🐾

▼▼ McIntyre's Housekeeping Cottages ⒸⒶ
(902) 295-1133. **$75-$350, 4 day notice.** 8908 Hwy 105 B0E 1B0. Trans-Canada Hwy 105, 3 mi (5 km) w. Ext corridors. **Pets:** Large, other species. $8 daily fee/pet. Designated rooms, service with restrictions. ⊠ 🔥 📶 🖵

ⒸⒶⒶ ▼▼▼ Silver Dart Lodge & MacNeil House ⊞
(902) 295-2340. **$99-$206.** 257 Shore Rd B0E 1B0. Trans-Canada Hwy 105, exit 8, 0.6 mi (1 km) e on Rt 205 (Shore Rd). Ext/int corridors. **Pets:** Designated rooms, service with restrictions, supervision. (SAVE) ⊠ 🔥 📶 🖵 🍽 🏊 🐾

BAYFIELD

▼▼ Sea'Scape Cottages ⒸⒶ
(902) 386-2825. **$110-$140, 30 day notice.** 6 Sea Scape Cottage Lane B0H 1R0. Trans-Canada Hwy 104, exit 36, 3.2 mi (5.3 km) n on Sunrise Tr, then 1.1 mi (1.8 km) w on Ferry Rd. Ext corridors. **Pets:** Medium, dogs only. $20 deposit/pet. No service, supervision. (ASK) ⊠ 📶 🖵 🐾 🔒 🐕

BRIDGETOWN

▼▼ Bridgetown Motor Inn ⊞
(902) 665-4403. **$75-$87.** 396 Granville St B0S 1C0. Hwy 101, exit 20, 0.6 mi (1 km) w on Rt 1. Ext corridors. **Pets:** Accepted. (ASK) ⊠ 📶 🏊

BRIDGEWATER

▼▼ The Bridgewater Hotel ⊞
(902) 543-8171. **Call for rates.** 35 High St B4V 1V8. Hwy 103, exit 13, just e. Int corridors. **Pets:** Accepted. ⊠ 🖵 🍽 🏊

▼▼ Comfort Inn ⊞
(902) 543-1498. **$100-$134.** 49 North St B4V 2V7. Hwy 103, exit 12, 1.1 mi (1.7 km) s on Rt 10. Int corridors. **Pets:** Accepted. (ECO) (ASK) ⊠ 🔥 📶 🖵

▼▼ Days Inn & Conference Centre Bridgewater ⊞
(902) 543-7131. **Call for rates.** 50 North St B4V 2V6. Hwy 103, exit 12, 1.1 mi (1.7 km) s on Rt 10. Int corridors. **Pets:** Accepted. ⊠ 📶 🖵 🍽 🏊

CHARLOS COVE

▼▼▼▼ Seawind Landing Country Inn ⒸⒾ
(902) 525-2108. **$85-$169.** 159 Wharf Rd B0H 1T0. Rt 316, 0.5 mi (0.8 km) se on gravel road. Ext/int corridors. **Pets:** Accepted. (ASK) ⊠ 🔥 🍽 🐕

CHESTER

▼▼ Windjammer Motel Ⓜ 🐾
(902) 275-3567. **$65-$85.** 4070 Rt 3 B0J 1J0. 0.6 mi (1 km) w. Ext corridors. **Pets:** Medium, other species. Designated rooms, service with restrictions, supervision. (ASK) ⊠ 📶

CHETICAMP

▼▼ ▼▼ Cabot Trail Sea & Golf Chalets 🅲🅰

(902) 224-1777. **$129-$169, 7 day notice.** 71 Fraser Doucet Ln B0E 1H0. Centre. Ext corridors. **Pets:** $15 daily fee/pet. Service with restrictions, supervision. 🅰🆂🅺 ⊠ ⅃ ⅃ ⊟ ⊡ ⊠ 🅺 ⊿

🅒🅐 ▼▼ ▼▼ Laurie's Motor Inn 🅷

(902) 224-2400. **$85-$169, 3 day notice.** 15456 Laurie Rd B0E 1H0. Centre. Ext/int corridors. **Pets:** Large. Service with restrictions, crate. ⟨SAVE⟩ ⊠ ⅃

CHURCH POINT

▼▼ ▼▼ Le Manoir Samson 🅼

(902) 769-2526. **$80-$110.** 1768 Rt 1 B0W 1M0. On Hwy 1; centre. Ext corridors. **Pets:** Accepted. ⊠ ⅃ 🅺

DARTMOUTH

🅒🅐 ▼▼ ▼▼ Comfort Inn 🅷 ❀

(902) 463-9900. **$105-$195.** 456 Windmill Rd B3A 1J7. Hwy 111, exit Shannon Park. Int corridors. **Pets:** Service with restrictions, supervision. ⟨ECO⟩ ⟨SAVE⟩ ⊠ ⅃ ⊡

▼▼ ▼▼ Country Inn & Suites By Carlson 🅷 ❀

(902) 465-4000. **$105-$200.** 101 Yorkshire Ave Ext B2Y 3Y2. Hwy 111, exit Princess Margaret Blvd; at toll booths for A. Murray Mackay Bridge. Int corridors. **Pets:** Medium. $150 deposit/room, $25 one-time fee/pet. Designated rooms, service with restrictions, supervision. ⟨ECO⟩ 🅰🆂🅺 ⊠ ⅃ ⊡

🅒🅐 ▼▼ ▼▼ Days Inn 🅷 ❀

(902) 465-6555. **$99-$109.** 20 Highfield Park Dr B3A 4S8. From A. Murray Mackay Bridge, 0.8 mi (1.2 km) n on Hwy 111, exit 3 (Burnside Dr). Ext/int corridors. **Pets:** Other species. Designated rooms, service with restrictions. ⟨ECO⟩ ⟨SAVE⟩ ⊠ ⅃ ⊡

🅒🅐 ▼▼ ▼▼ ▼ Holiday Inn Halifax-Harbourview 🅷 ❀

(902) 463-1100. **$119-$224.** 101 Wyse Rd B3A 1L9. Adjacent to Angus L MacDonald Bridge. Int corridors. **Pets:** Small, other species. $25 one-time fee/room. Designated rooms, service with restrictions, supervision. ⟨ECO⟩ ⟨SAVE⟩ ⊠ ⅃ ⅃ ⊟ ⊡ ⅃⅃ ⊿ ⊠

🅒🅐 ▼▼ ▼▼ ▼ Park Place Hotel & Conference Centre Ramada Plaza 🅷 ❀

(902) 468-8888. **$149-$169.** 240 Brownlow Ave B3B 1X6. From A. Murray Mackay Bridge, 0.7 mi (1.2 km) n on Hwy 111, exit 3 (Burnside Dr). Int corridors. **Pets:** Small. $75 deposit/pet, $35 one-time fee/pet. Designated rooms, service with restrictions, supervision. ⟨ECO⟩ ⟨SAVE⟩ ⊠ ⅃⅃ ⅃ ⊡ ⅃⅃ ⊿ ⊠

▼▼ ▼▼ Quality Inn Halifax/Dartmouth 🅷

(902) 469-5850. **$70-$130.** 313 Prince Albert Rd B2Y 1N3. Hwy 111, exit 6A, 1 blk s. Int corridors. **Pets:** Accepted. 🅰🆂🅺 ⊠ ⅃ ⊡ ⅃⅃

▼▼ ▼▼ Super 8 Hotel-Dartmouth 🅷

(902) 463-9520. **$89-$139.** 65 King St B2Y 4C2. Corner of King and Queen sts; centre of downtown. Int corridors. **Pets:** Accepted. ⟨ECO⟩ 🅰🆂🅺 ⊠ ⅃

DIGBY

🅒🅐 ▼▼ ▼▼ Admiral Digby Inn & Cottages 🅷 ❀

(902) 245-2531. **$75-$129.** 441 Shore Rd B0V 1A0. Hwy 101, exit 26, 1.5 mi (2.5 km) n, follow St John Ferry signs, 3 mi (5 km) w on Victoria Rd, just e of ferry terminal. Ext corridors. **Pets:** Designated rooms, service with restrictions, crate. ⟨SAVE⟩ ⊠ ⅃ ⊡ ⅃⅃ ⊿

▼▼ ▼▼ Dockside Suites 🅷

(902) 245-4950. **$89-$159.** 34 Water St B0V 1A0. Centre; in Fundy Complex. Ext/int corridors. **Pets:** Accepted. 🅰🆂🅺 ⊠ ⅃ ⊡ ⅃⅃

▼▼ ▼▼ Thistle Down Country Inn 🅒🅘

(902) 245-4490. **Call for rates.** 98 Montague Row B0V 1A0. Centre. Ext/int corridors. **Pets:** Accepted. ⊠ ⅃ ⊡ ⅃⅃

ECONOMY

▼▼ ▼▼ ▼ Four Seasons Retreat 🅲🅰

(902) 647-2628. **$109, 5 day notice.** 320 Cove Rd B0M 1J0. 3 mi (5 km) e on Rt 2. Ext corridors. **Pets:** Accepted. ⊠ ⅃ ⊡ ⊿ ⊠ 🅺 ⊿

HALIFAX

🅒🅐 ▼▼ ▼▼ ▼ Atlantica Hotel Halifax 🅷 ❀

(902) 423-1161. **$130-$230.** 1980 Robie St B3H 3G5. Jct Quinpool St. Int corridors. **Pets:** Medium. Service with restrictions, supervision. ⟨ECO⟩ ⟨SAVE⟩ ⊠ ⅃ ⊡ ⅃⅃ ⊿ ⊠

🅒🅐 ▼▼ ▼▼ ▼ Best Western Chocolate Lake Hotel 🅷 ❀

(902) 477-5611. **$89-$219.** 20 St. Margaret's Bay Rd B3N 1J4. 0.4 mi (0.7 km) e of Armdale Rotary. Ext/int corridors. **Pets:** Other species. Designated rooms, supervision. ⟨ECO⟩ ⟨SAVE⟩ ⊠ ⅃ ⊡ ⅃⅃ ⊿ ⊠

🅒🅐 ▼▼ ▼▼ ▼ Cambridge Suites Hotel 🅷 ❀

(902) 420-0555. **$135-$155.** 1583 Brunswick St B3J 3P5. Corner of Brunswick and Sackville sts. Int corridors. **Pets:** Large, other species. Designated rooms, service with restrictions, supervision. ⟨ECO⟩ ⟨SAVE⟩ ⊠ ⅃ ⅃ ⊡ ⅃⅃ ⊠

▼▼ Chebucto Inn 🅷

(902) 453-4330. **$85-$145.** 6151 Lady Hammond Rd B3K 2R9. Jct Hwy 111 and Rt 2 (Bedford Hwy), 0.4 mi (0.7 km) e. Ext corridors. **Pets:** Accepted. 🅰🆂🅺 ⊠ ⅃⅃

🅒🅐 ▼▼ ▼▼ ▼ Citadel Halifax Hotel 🅷

(902) 422-1391. **$99-$311.** 1960 Brunswick St B3J 2G7. Between Cogswell and Duke sts. Int corridors. **Pets:** Medium, other species. $50 deposit/room. Designated rooms, service with restrictions, supervision. ⟨ECO⟩ ⟨SAVE⟩ ⊠ ⅃ ⊡ ⅃⅃ ⊿ ⊠

🅒🅐 ▼▼ ▼▼ Comfort Inn Halifax 🅷 ❀

(902) 443-0303. **$79-$169.** 560 Bedford Hwy B3M 2L8. On Rt 2 (Bedford Hwy), 6 mi (9.6 km) w. Int corridors. **Pets:** $10 one-time fee/pet. Service with restrictions, supervision. ⟨SAVE⟩ ⊠ ⅃⅃ ⅃ ⊡ ⊿

🅒🅐 ▼▼ ▼▼ ▼ Delta Barrington 🅷

(902) 429-7410. **$209-$259.** 1875 Barrington St B3J 3L6. Between Cogswell and Duke sts. Int corridors. **Pets:** Other species. $35 one-time fee/room. Service with restrictions, supervision. ⟨ECO⟩ ⟨SAVE⟩ ⊠ ⅃ ⊡ ⅃⅃ ⊿ ⊠

🅒🅐 ▼▼ ▼▼ Delta Halifax 🅷 ❀

(902) 425-6700. **$115-$209.** 1990 Barrington St B3J 1P2. Corner of Cogswell and Barrington sts. Int corridors. **Pets:** Medium, other species. $35 one-time fee/room. Service with restrictions, supervision. ⟨ECO⟩ ⟨SAVE⟩ ⊠ ⅃⅃ ⅃ ⊡ ⅃⅃ ⊿ ⊠

🅒🅐 ▼▼ Esquire Motel 🅼 ❀

(902) 835-3367. **$69-$145.** 771 Bedford Hwy B4A 1A1. Hwy 102, exit 4A, 3.3 mi (5.3 km) e on Rt 2 (Bedford Hwy). Ext corridors. **Pets:** Other species. $10 one-time fee/pet. Designated rooms, service with restrictions, supervision. ⟨SAVE⟩ ⊠ ⅃ ⊡ ⊿ 🅺

▼▼ ▼▼ Future Inns Halifax 🅷

(902) 443-4333. **$119-$179.** 30 Fairfax Dr B3S 1P1. Hwy 102, exit 2A. Int corridors. **Pets:** Accepted. ⊠ ⅃⅃ ⅃ ⊡ ⅃⅃

🅒🅐 ▼▼ ▼▼ ▼ Halifax Marriott Harbourfront 🅷 ❀

(902) 421-1700. **$189-$239.** 1919 Upper Water St B3J 3J5. Adjacent to historic properties and Casino Nova Scotia. Int corridors. **Pets:** $50 one-time fee/room. Service with restrictions, supervision. ⟨ECO⟩ ⟨SAVE⟩ ⊠ ⅃⅃ ⅃ ⊡ ⅃⅃ ⊿ ⊠

▼▼ ▼▼ Holiday Inn Express Halifax Airport 🅷 ❀

(902) 576-7600. **$129-$159.** 180 Pratt & Whitney Dr B2T 0A2. Hwy 102, exit 5A, 0.8 mi (1.2 km) e, then just n. Int corridors. **Pets:** Medium, other species. Service with restrictions. 🅰🆂🅺 ⊠ ⅃⅃ ⅃ ⊡ ⊿

(CAA) ▼▼▼▼ **Holiday Inn Express Halifax/Bedford** **H**
(902) 445-1100. **Call for rates.** 133 Kearney Lake Rd B3M 4P3. Hwy 102, exit 2. Int corridors. **Pets:** Accepted.
[ECO] [SAVE] [✕] [⅚M] [🛏] [📺] [➿]

(CAA) ▼▼▼ **Lakeview Inns & Suites** **H** ❖
(902) 450-3020. **$139-$299.** 98 Chain Lake Dr B3S 1A2. Hwy 102, exit 2A eastbound; Hwy 103, exit 2. Int corridors. **Pets:** Medium. $150 deposit/room, $20 daily fee/pet. Service with restrictions, supervision.
[ECO] [SAVE] [✕] [⅚M] [🛏] [📺] [➿]

(CAA) ▼▼▼▼ **The Lord Nelson Hotel & Suites** **H**
(902) 423-6331. **$125-$155.** 1515 S Park St B3J 2L2. Corner of Park St and Spring Garden Rd. Int corridors. **Pets:** Accepted.
[ECO] [SAVE] [✕] [⅚M] [🛏] [📺] [🍴]

(CAA) ▼▼▼▼ **The Prince George Hotel** **H** ❖
(902) 425-1986. **$149-$279.** 1725 Market St B3J 3N9. Between Prince and Carmichael sts. Int corridors. **Pets:** Large, other species. $20 one-time fee/pet. Service with restrictions, supervision.
[ECO] [SAVE] [✕] [⅚M] [🛏] [📺] [🍴] [➿] [✕]

▼▼▼ **Quality Inn & Suites Halifax** **H** ❖
(902) 444-6700. **$119-$169.** 980 Parkland Dr B3M 4Y7. Hwy 102, exit 2. Int corridors. **Pets:** Service with restrictions, supervision.
[ECO] [ASK] [✕] [⅚M] [🛏] [📺] [➿] [✕]

▼▼▼ **Quality Inn Halifax Airport** **H**
(902) 873-3000. **$136-$186.** 60 Sky Blvd B2T 1K3. Hwy 102, exit 6. Int corridors. **Pets:** Accepted. [ECO] [ASK] [✕] [🛏] [📺] [🍴] [➿] [✕]

(CAA) ▼▼▼ **Residence Inn Halifax Downtown** **H**
(902) 422-0493. **$179-$209.** 1599 Grafton St B3J 2C3. Corner of Sackville St. Int corridors. **Pets:** $100 one-time fee/room. Service with restrictions, crate. [ECO] [SAVE] [✕] [⅚M] [🛏] [📺]

(CAA) ▼▼▼▼ **The Westin Nova Scotian** **H** ❖
(902) 421-1000. **$109-$399.** 1181 Hollis St B3H 2P6. Between Barrington and Lower Water sts. Int corridors. **Pets:** Designated rooms, service with restrictions, supervision. [ECO] [SAVE] [✕] [⅚M] [📺] [🍴] [➿] [✕]

INGONISH BEACH

(CAA) ▼▼▼▼ **Keltic Lodge Resort & Spa** **H**
(902) 285-2880. **$175-$335, 3 day notice.** Middle Head Peninsula B0C 1L0. In Cape Breton Highlands National Park; off Cabot Tr. Ext/int corridors. **Pets:** Accepted. [SAVE] [✕] [⅚M] [🛏] [📺] [🍴] [➿] [✕]

KEMPTVILLE

▼▼▼ **Trout Point Lodge** **CI**
(902) 482-8360. **$205-$400, 21 day notice.** 189 Trout Point Rd B0W 1Y0. 6.6 mi (11 km) e on Rt 203, 2.1 mi (3.5 km) n on gravel entry road. Ext corridors. **Pets:** Accepted. [ECO] [ASK] [✕] [🍴] [✕] [🐾] [📶]

KENTVILLE

▼▼▼ **Sun Valley Motel** **M**
(902) 678-7368. **Call for rates.** 843 Park St B4N 3V7. Hwy 101, exit 14, 0.5 mi (0.8 km) e on Rt 1. Ext corridors. **Pets:** Accepted.
[✕] [🛏] [📺] [🐾] [🖼]

KINGSTON

(CAA) ▼▼▼ **Best Western Aurora Inn** **H**
(902) 765-3306. **$121-$130.** 831 Main St B0P 1R0. Hwy 101, exit 17 to Rt 1, follow signs. Ext corridors. **Pets:** $10 one-time fee/pet. Service with restrictions, supervision. [SAVE] [✕] [🛏] [📺] [🍴]

LISCOMB

(CAA) ▼▼▼▼ **Liscombe Lodge Resort & Conference Centre** **H**
(902) 779-2307. **$157-$177, 3 day notice.** 2884 Hwy 7 (RR 1) B0J 2A0. On Hwy 7. Ext/int corridors. **Pets:** Large. Designated rooms, service with restrictions, crate. [SAVE] [✕] [⅚M] [🛏] [📺] [🍴] [➿] [✕]

LIVERPOOL

(CAA) ▼▼▼▼ **Best Western Liverpool Hotel & Conference Centre** **H** ❖
(902) 354-2377. **$140-$150.** 63 Queens Place Dr B0T 1K0. Hwy 103, exit 19, just e. Int corridors. **Pets:** Medium, other species. $25 one-time fee/room. Designated rooms, service with restrictions, supervision.
[SAVE] [✕] [⅚M] [🛏] [📺] [➿]

(CAA) ▼▼▼▼ **Lane's Privateer Inn** **H**
(902) 354-3456. **$95-$142, 7 day notice.** 27 Bristol Ave B0T 1K0. Hwy 103, exit 19, 1.2 mi (2 km) se on Rt 8 and 3. Ext/int corridors.
Pets: Accepted. [SAVE] [✕] [🍴]

LOWER ARGYLE

(CAA) ▼▼▼▼ **Ye Olde Argyler Lodge** **CI**
(902) 643-2500. **$100-$215, 14 day notice.** Rt 3 B0W 1W0. Hwy 103, exit 32, 4.5 mi (7.5 km) e. Int corridors. **Pets:** Accepted. [SAVE] [✕] [🍴]

LUNENBURG

▼▼▼ **The Homeport Motel** **M**
(902) 634-8234. **$85-$180.** 167 Victoria Rd B0J 2C0. 0.6 mi (1 km) w on Rt 3. Ext corridors. **Pets:** Accepted. [ASK] [✕] [🛏] [📺]

▼▼▼ **Lunenburg Arms Hotel & Spa** **H**
(902) 640-4040. **$109-$239.** 94 Pelham St B0J 2C0. Corner of Pelham and Duke sts; centre. Int corridors. **Pets:** $25 one-time fee/room. Service with restrictions, supervision. [✕] [⅚M] [🛏] [📺] [🍴]

MAHONE BAY

▼▼▼ **Bayview Pines Country Inn** **BB** ❖
(902) 624-9970. **$90-$165, 5 day notice.** 678 Oakland Rd B0J 2E0. Hwy 103, exit 10, 1.2 mi (2 km) w on Rt 3 to Kedy's Landing, 3.6 mi (6 km) e of Mahone Bay. Ext/int corridors. **Pets:** Medium, dogs only. Designated rooms, service with restrictions, supervision.
[✕] [🛏] [📺] [🖼] [🖌]

MAVILLETTE

▼▼▼ **Cape View Motel & Cottages** **M**
(902) 645-2258. **$80-$100.** 124 John Doucette Rd B0W 2Y0. Rt 1, 19.2 mi (32 km) ne of Yarmouth; centre. Ext corridors. **Pets:** Accepted.
[✕] [🛏] [📺] [🖼] [🖌]

MIDDLETON

▼▼▼ **Mid-Valley Motel** **M**
(902) 825-3433. **Call for rates.** 121 Main St B0S 1P0. Hwy 101, exit 18, 0.6 mi (1 km) w on Rt 1. Ext corridors. **Pets:** Accepted.
[✕] [🛏] [🍴] [➿]

MUSQUODOBOIT HARBOUR

(CAA) ▼▼▼▼ **Elephant's Nest Bed & Breakfast** **BB** ❖
(902) 827-3891. **$95-$145, 3 day notice.** 127 Pleasant Dr B0J 1N0. Jct Hwy 107 and 7, 1.8 mi (3 km) w, follow signs. Int corridors. **Pets:** Dogs only. Designated rooms, service with restrictions, supervision.
[SAVE] [✕] [✕] [🖌]

NEW GLASGOW

▼▼▼ **Comfort Inn** **H**
(902) 755-6450. **$120-$170.** 740 Westville Rd B2H 2J8. On Hwy 289, just e of jct Trans-Canada Hwy 104, exit 23. Int corridors. **Pets:** Service with restrictions, supervision. [ECO] [ASK] [✕] [🛏] [📺]

▼▼▼ **Country Inn & Suites By Carlson** **H** ❖
(902) 928-1333. **$124-$137.** 700 Westville Rd B2H 2J8. On Hwy 289, just e of jct Trans-Canada Hwy 104, exit 23. Int corridors. **Pets:** Large. Service with restrictions, crate. [ECO] [ASK] [✕] [🛏] [📺]

NEW HARBOUR

▼▼▼▼ **Lonely Rock Seaside Bungalows** **CA**
(902) 387-2668. **$90-$230, 14 day notice.** 150 New Harbour Rd B0H 1T0. Rt 316, 0.4 mi (0.7 km) s. Ext corridors. **Pets:** Dogs only. $10 daily fee/pet. No service, supervision. [✕] [⅚M] [🛏] [✕] [🖌]

NORTH SYDNEY

Clansman Motel
(902) 794-7226. **$89-$125.** 9 Baird St B2A 3M3. Hwy 125, exit 2, just e on King St. Ext/int corridors. **Pets:** Designated rooms, service with restrictions, supervision.

PARRSBORO

Gillespie House Inn
(902) 254-3196. **$95-$129.** 358 Main St B0M 1S0. On Rt 2; centre. Int corridors. **Pets:** Dogs only. $25 one-time fee/room. Designated rooms, service with restrictions, supervision.

The Sunshine Inn
(902) 254-3135. **$82-$150.** Rt 2 B0M 1S0. 2 mi (3.2 km) n. Ext corridors. **Pets:** Accepted.

PICTOU

Pictou Lodge Beachfront Resort
(902) 485-4322. **$89-$499, 3 day notice.** 172 Lodge Rd B0K 1H0. 4.3 mi (7 km) nw on Braeshore Rd; midway between Pictou and PEI ferry terminal at Caribou. Ext corridors. **Pets:** Accepted.

Willow House Inn
(902) 485-5740. **$60-$120.** 11 Willow St B0K 1H0. Corner of Willow and Church sts; centre. **Pets:** Accepted.

PORT DUFFERIN

Marquis of Dufferin Seaside Inn
(902) 654-2696. **$94.** 25658 Hwy 7, RR 1 B0J 2R0. On Hwy 7. Ext corridors. **Pets:** Other species. Designated rooms, service with restrictions.

PORT HASTINGS

Cape Breton Causeway Inn
(902) 625-0460. **Call for rates.** 21 Old Victoria Rd B9A 1L2. E of Canso Cswy on Trans-Canada Hwy 105 rotary; entrance through north side of church. Ext/int corridors. **Pets:** Accepted.

Econo Lodge MacPuffin
(902) 625-0621. **$81-$119.** 373 Hwy 4 B9A 1M8. 1 mi (1.6 km) n on Hwy 4; 1 mi (1.6 km) s of Canso Cswy. Ext corridors. **Pets:** Large, other species. Designated rooms, service with restrictions, crate.

PORT HAWKESBURY

Maritime Inn Port Hawkesbury
(902) 625-0320. **$117-$199.** 717 Reeves St B9A 2S2. 4.2 mi (6.4 km) e of Canso Cswy on Hwy 4. Ext/int corridors. **Pets:** Accepted.

SCOTSBURN

Stonehame Lodge & Chalets
(902) 485-3468. **$85-$235, 14 day notice.** 310 Fitzpatrick Mountain Rd B0K 1R0. Rt 256, 7.5 mi (12 km) w of Pictou via Rt 376, last 1.2 mi (2 km) on gravel entry road. Ext corridors. **Pets:** Accepted.

SMITHS COVE

Harbourview Inn
(902) 245-5686. **$94-$149, 7 day notice.** 25 Harbourview Rd B0S 1S0. Hwy 101, exit 25 eastbound; exit 24 westbound. Ext/int corridors. **Pets:** Medium, dogs only. Service with restrictions, supervision.

Hedley House Inn By The Sea
(902) 245-2500. **$75-$169.** RR 1 B0S 1S0. Hwy 101, exit 25 eastbound; exit 24 westbound. Ext corridors. **Pets:** Accepted.

Mountain Gap Inn
(902) 245-5841. **Call for rates.** 217 Hwy 1, Smiths Cove B0S 1S0. Hwy 101, exit 25 eastbound; exit 24 westbound. Ext corridors. **Pets:** Accepted.

STELLARTON

Holiday Inn Express Stellarton-New Glasgow
(902) 755-1020. **$125-$143.** 86 Lawrence Blvd B0K 1S0. Hwy 104, exit 24, just s, then 0.6 mi (1 km) w. Int corridors. **Pets:** Accepted.

SYDNEY

Cambridge Suites Hotel
(902) 562-6500. **$119-$145, 30 day notice.** 380 Esplanade B1P 1B1. Hwy 4, 3.1 mi (5 km) e of jct Hwy 125, exit 6E; downtown. Int corridors. **Pets:** Accepted.

Comfort Inn
(902) 562-0200. **$70-$150.** 368 Kings Rd B1S 1A8. Hwy 4, 2.1 mi (3.5 km) e of jct Hwy 125, exit 6E. Int corridors. **Pets:** Accepted.

Days Inn Sydney
(902) 539-6750. **$89-$119.** 480 Kings Rd B1S 1A8. Hwy 4, 1.7 mi (2.8 km) e of jct Hwy 125, exit 6E. Int corridors. **Pets:** Designated rooms, service with restrictions, supervision.

Delta Sydney
(902) 562-7500. **Call for rates.** 300 Esplanade B1P 1A7. At Prince St; centre. Int corridors. **Pets:** Other species. $35 one-time fee/room. Crate.

Quality Inn Sydney
(902) 539-8101. **$65-$120.** 560 Kings Rd B1S 1B8. Hwy 4, 2 mi (3.3 km) e of jct Hwy 125. Int corridors. **Pets:** Accepted.

SYDNEY MINES

Gowrie House Country Inn
(902) 544-1050. **Call for rates.** 840 Shore Rd B1V 1A6. Hwy 105, exit 21E, 1.9 mi (3 km) n on Rt 305. Ext/int corridors. **Pets:** Accepted.

TRURO

Comfort Inn
(902) 893-0330. **$100-$199.** 12 Meadow Dr B2N 5V4. Hwy 102, exit 14. Int corridors. **Pets:** Service with restrictions, supervision.

Holiday Inn Truro Hotel & Convention Centre
(902) 895-1651. **Call for rates.** 437 Prince St B2N 1E6. Centre. Int corridors. **Pets:** Accepted.

Super 8
(902) 895-8884. **$120-$150.** 85 Treaty Tr B2N 5A9. Hwy 102, exit 13A. Int corridors. **Pets:** Accepted.

WESTERN SHORE

Oak Island Resort
(902) 627-2600. **$114-$169.** 36 Treasure Dr B0J 3M0. Hwy 103, exit 9 or 10, follow signs on Rt 3; 6 mi (10 km) e of Mahone Bay. Int corridors. **Pets:** Accepted.

WHITE POINT

White Point Beach Resort
(902) 354-2711. **$100-$190, 3 day notice.** 75 White Point Rd 2 B0T 1G0. Hwy 103, exit 20A westbound, 5 mi (8 km) w on Rt 3; exit 20 eastbound, 6 mi (10 km) e on Rt 3. Ext/int corridors. **Pets:** Other species. Designated rooms.

WHYCOCOMAGH

◆◆◆ **Keltic Quay Bayfront Lodge & Cottages** 🅒🅐
(902) 756-1122. **$149-$299, 3 day notice.** 90 Main St B0E 3M0. Just se off Trans-Canada Hwy 105; centre. Ext corridors. **Pets:** Accepted.
🅐🆂🅺 ⊠ 🅼 📵 📼 ⊠ 🅰🅲

WINDSOR

◆◆◆ **Super 8** 🄷
(902) 792-8888. **$99-$117.** 63 Cole Dr B0N 2T0. Hwy 101, exit 5A, just s. Int corridors. **Pets:** Accepted.
🄴🄲🄾 🅐🆂🅺 ⊠ 🅼 📵 📼 ⊇ ⊠

YARMOUTH

◆◆ **Best Western Mermaid** 🄼
(902) 742-7821. **$89-$170.** 545 Main St B5A 1J6. Corner of Main St and Starrs Rd. Ext corridors. **Pets:** Accepted. 🆂🄰🆅🄴 ⊠ 📵 📼 ⊇ 🅰🅲

◆◆ **Comfort Inn** 🄷
(902) 742-1119. **$95-$195.** 96 Starrs Rd B5A 2T5. Jct Hwy 101 E and 3. Int corridors. **Pets:** Accepted. 🄴🄲🄾 🅐🆂🅺 ⊠ 📵 📼

◆ **Lakelawn Motel** 🄼
(902) 742-3588. **$59-$99.** 641 Main St B5A 1K2. 0.6 mi (1 km) n on Hwy 1. Ext/int corridors. **Pets:** Accepted. 🅐🆂🅺 ⊠ 🅰🅲 ☎

◆◆ **Rodd Colony Harbour Inn** 🄷
(902) 742-9194. **$98-$145.** 6 Forest St B5A 3K8. At ferry terminal. Int corridors. **Pets:** Accepted. 🅐🆂🅺 ⊠ 📵 📼 🍽 🅰🅲

Ⓐ ◆◆◆ **Rodd Grand Yarmouth-A Rodd Signature Hotel** 🄷
(902) 742-2446. **$133-$185.** 417 Main St B5A 4B2. Near centre of downtown. Int corridors. **Pets:** Accepted.
🄴🄲🄾 🆂🄰🆅🄴 ⊠ 📵 📼 🍽 ⊇ ⊠

◆◆ **Voyageur Motel** 🄼
(902) 742-7157. **$79-$189, 3 day notice.** RR 1 B5A 4A5. 3 mi (4.8 km) ne on Hwy 1. Ext corridors. **Pets:** Accepted. 🅐🆂🅺 ⊠ 📵 🅰🅲

AJAX

▼▼ ▼▼ Super 8-Ajax 🄷

(905) 428-6884. **Call for rates.** 210 Westney Rd S L1S 7P9. Hwy 401, exit Westney Rd, 0.6 mi (1 km) s, jct Bayly St. Int corridors.
Pets: Accepted. ⊠ 🛢 💻 ⌇

ALGONQUIN PROVINCIAL PARK

▼▼ ▼▼ Killarney Lodge 🄲🄰

(705) 633-5551. **$318-$658, 3 day notice.** Hwy 60-Lake of Two Rivers-Algonquin P1H 2G9. 21 mi (33 km) into park from west gate; 14 mi (23 km) from east gate. Ext corridors. **Pets:** Large. $25 daily fee/pet. Designated rooms, service with restrictions, supervision.

⊠ 🍴 ⊠ 🄰🄵 🄦 🖉

ALLISTON

▼▼ ▼▼ Red Pine Inn and Conference Center 🄼

(705) 435-4381. **$129-$149.** 497 Victoria St E L9R 1T9. 1.8 mi (3 km) e of King St. Ext/int corridors. **Pets:** Accepted.

🄰🄢🄚 ⊠ 🛢 💻 🍴 ⌇

ARNPRIOR

🄲🄰🄰 ▼▼ Country Squire Motel 🄼

(613) 623-6556. **$59-$120, 3 day notice.** 111 Staye Court Dr K7S 3G8. Hwy 17, exit White Lake Rd, just n to Staye Court Dr, then just w. Ext corridors. **Pets:** Small, dogs only. $15 daily fee/pet. Service with restrictions, supervision. 🅂🄰🅅🄴 ⊠ 🛢 💻

🄲🄰🄰 ▼▼ Quality Inn 🄷

(613) 623-7991. **$125-$145.** 70 Madawaska Blvd K7S 1S5. Hwy 17, exit 180, 0.4 mi (0.7 km) n on CR 29, then 1.4 mi (2.3 km) w. Int corridors. **Pets:** $10 daily fee/room. Service with restrictions, crate.

🅂🄰🅅🄴 ⊠ 🛢 💻 🍴

BANCROFT

🄲🄰🄰 ▼▼ Best Western Sword Motor Inn 🄼

(613) 332-2474. **$119-$199.** 146 Hastings St K0L 1C0. On Hwy 62 N; centre. Ext/int corridors. **Pets:** Accepted.

🅂🄰🅅🄴 ⊠ 🛢 💻 🍴 ⌇ ⊠

BARRIE

🄲🄰🄰 ▼▼ ▼▼ Comfort Inn 🄷 ✿

(705) 722-3600. **$89-$140.** 75 Hart Dr L4N 5M3. Hwy 400, exit 96A E (Dunlop St). Int corridors. **Pets:** $6 daily fee/room. Designated rooms, service with restrictions, supervision. 🄴🄲🄾 🅂🄰🅅🄴 ⊠ 🛢 💻

🄲🄰🄰 ▼▼ ▼▼ Comfort Inn & Suites 🄷 ✿

(705) 721-1122. **$70-$130.** 210 Essa Rd L4N 3L1. Hwy 400, exit 94 (Essa Rd), just e. Int corridors. **Pets:** Designated rooms, service with restrictions, supervision. 🄴🄲🄾 🅂🄰🅅🄴 ⊠ 🛢 💻

▼▼ ▼▼ Days Inn Barrie 🄷 ✿

(705) 733-8989. **$99-$160.** 60 Bryne Dr L4N 9Y4. Hwy 400, exit 94 (Essa Rd), just s, then just e. Int corridors. **Pets:** Other species. $10 daily fee/pet. Designated rooms, service with restrictions, supervision.

🄴🄲🄾 🄰🅂🄚 ⊠ 🛢 💻 ⌇

🄲🄰🄰 ▼▼ ▼▼ ▼▼ Holiday Inn Barrie-Hotel & Conference Centre 🄷

(705) 728-6191. **$125-$138.** 20 Fairview Rd L4N 4P3. Hwy 400, exit 94 (Essa Rd), just e. Int corridors. **Pets:** Medium, other species. Designated rooms, service with restrictions.

🄴🄲🄾 🅂🄰🅅🄴 ⊠ 🛢.🄼 🛢 💻 🍴 ⌇ ⊠

🄲🄰🄰 ▼▼ ▼▼ ▼▼ Holiday Inn Express Hotel & Suites Barrie 🄷

(705) 725-1002. **$112-$189.** 506 Bryne Dr L4N 9P6. Hwy 400, exit 90 (Mapleview Dr), just sw. Int corridors. **Pets:** Medium. $15 one-time fee/room. Service with restrictions, supervision. 🅂🄰🅅🄴 ⊠ 🛢 💻 ⌇

🄲🄰🄰 ▼▼ ▼▼ ▼▼ Horseshoe Resort 🄷 ✿

(705) 835-2790. **$109-$329, 7 day notice.** 1101 Horseshoe Valley Rd W L4M 4Y8. Hwy 400, exit 117 (Horseshoe Valley Rd), 3.8 mi (6 km) e. Int corridors. **Pets:** Medium. $25 daily fee/room, $25 one-time fee/room. Service with restrictions, supervision.

🅂🄰🅅🄴 ⊠ 🛢 💻 🍴 ⌇ ⊠

🄲🄰🄰 ▼▼ ▼▼ Super 8 🄷 ✿

(705) 814-8888. **$110-$170.** 441 Bryne Dr L4N 6C8. Hwy 400, exit 90 (Mapleview Dr), just nw. Int corridors. **Pets:** Large. $15 one-time fee/pet. Designated rooms, service with restrictions, supervision.

🄴🄲🄾 🅂🄰🅅🄴 ⊠ 🛢 💻 ⌇

🄲🄰🄰 ▼▼ ▼▼ Travelodge Barrie 🄷 ✿

(705) 734-9500. **$90-$120, 14 day notice.** 55 Hart Dr L4N 5M3. Hwy 400, exit 96A E (Dunlop St). Int corridors. **Pets:** Medium. $50 deposit/room. Designated rooms, service with restrictions, crate.

🄴🄲🄾 🅂🄰🅅🄴 ⊠ 🛢 💻 🍴 ⌇

BARRY'S BAY

▼▼ Mountain View Motel 🄼

(613) 756-2757. **$75-$190, 7 day notice.** 18508 Hwy 60 E K0J 1B0. 2.5 mi (4 km) e of town. Ext corridors. **Pets:** Accepted. ⊠ 🛢 💻

BAYFIELD

🄲🄰🄰 ▼▼ ▼▼ ▼▼ The Little Inn of Bayfield 🄲🄸 ✿

(519) 565-2611. **$192-$275, 4 day notice.** 26 Main St N0M 1G0. Hwy 21, exit Main St, jct Catherine St. Int corridors. **Pets:** $50 one-time fee/pet. Designated rooms, service with restrictions, supervision.

🅂🄰🅅🄴 ⊠ 💻 🍴

▼▼ **The Martha Ritz House** 🄲
(519) 565-2325. **$125, 4 day notice.** 27 Main St N0M 1G0. Hwy 21, exit Main St, jct Catherine St. Int corridors. **Pets:** Accepted.
[ASK] [⛌] [☎]

BELLEVILLE

▥▼▼▼ **Best Western Belleville** 🄷
(613) 969-1112. **$110-$220.** 387 N Front St K8P 3C8. Hwy 401, exit 543A, 0.3 mi (0.5 km) s on Hwy 62. Int corridors. **Pets:** Accepted.
[ECO] [SAVE] [✕] [🛏] [▣] [≈]

▼▼▼ **Clarion Inn & Suites** 🄷
(613) 962-4531. **$90-$120.** 211 Pinnacle St K8N 3A7. Hwy 401, exit 543A, 1.8 mi (3 km) s on Hwy 62; corner of Bridge St; downtown. Int corridors. **Pets:** Small. $15 daily fee/room. Service with restrictions, supervision. [ECO] [ASK] [✕] [🛏] [▣] [⛌]

▥▼▼▼ **Comfort Inn** 🄷
(613) 966-7703. **$112-$130.** 200 N Park St K8P 2Y9. Hwy 401, exit 543A, 0.6 mi (1 km) s on Hwy 62. Int corridors. **Pets:** Accepted.
[SAVE] [✕] [🛏] [▣]

▥▼▼▼ **Ramada Hotel, Resort and Conference Centre** 🄷 ❀
(613) 968-3411. **$120-$169.** 11 Bay Bridge Rd K8P 3P6. 0.3 mi (0.5 km) s of Hwy 2 (Dundas St). Int corridors. **Pets:** $10 daily fee/room. Designated rooms, service with restrictions, supervision.
[ECO] [SAVE] [✕] [🛏] [▣] [⛌] [≈] [⊠]

BLIND RIVER

▼▼ **Lakeview Inn** 🄼
(705) 356-0800. **$99-$114, 3 day notice.** 143 Causley St P0R 1B0. On Hwy 17, just e of Hwy 557. Ext corridors. **Pets:** Small. $10 daily fee/pet. Designated rooms, service with restrictions, supervision. [✕] [🛏] [⛌]

BRACEBRIDGE

▥▼▼▼ **Travelodge Bracebridge** 🄼
(705) 645-2235. **$80-$159.** 320 Taylor Rd P1L 1K1. Hwy 11, exit 189 (Hwy 42/Taylor Rd), 0.6 mi (1 km) w. Ext corridors. **Pets:** Accepted.
[SAVE] [✕] [🛏] [▣] [≈]

BRAMPTON

▼▼▼ **Motel 6 Brampton #1902** 🄷
(905) 451-3313. **$75-$81.** 160 Steelwell Rd L6T 5T3. Hwy 410, exit Steeles Ave E, s on Tomken Rd, then just w. Int corridors. **Pets:** Other species. Service with restrictions, supervision. [ECO] [✕] [🛏]

BRANTFORD

▥▼▼▼ **Comfort Inn** 🄷
(519) 753-3100. **$95-$117.** 58 King George Rd N3R 5K4. Just s of jct Hwy 403 and 24. Int corridors. **Pets:** Other species. $10 one-time fee/ room. Designated rooms, service with restrictions, supervision.
[SAVE] [✕] [🛏] [▣] [⛌]

▼▼▼ **Days Inn** 🄷 ❀
(519) 759-2700. **$86-$140.** 460 Fairview Dr N3R 7A9. Hwy 403, exit Wayne Gretzky Pkwy, 0.5 mi (0.8 km) n. Int corridors. **Pets:** Dogs only. $15 one-time fee/room. Designated rooms, service with restrictions, supervision. [ECO] [ASK] [✕] [🛏] [▣] [⛌]

▥▼▼▼▼ **Quality Inn & Suites** 🄷
(519) 758-9999. **$77-$120.** 664 Colborne St N3S 3P8. Hwy 403, exit Wayne Gretzky Pkwy, 1.3 mi (2 km) s to Colborne St, then just w. Int corridors. **Pets:** Accepted. [SAVE] [✕] [🛏] [▣] [⛌] [≈]

BROCKVILLE

▥▼▼▼ **Comfort Inn** 🄷
(613) 345-0042. **$144-$229.** 7777 Kent Blvd K6V 6N7. Hwy 401, exit 696, just nw. Int corridors. **Pets:** Accepted. [SAVE] [✕] [🛏] [▣]

BURLINGTON

▥▼▼▼ **Comfort Inn** 🄷
(905) 639-1700. **$90-$140.** 3290 S Service Rd L7N 3M6. QEW, exit Walker's Line Rd westbound, just s to Harvester Rd, then just w; exit Guelph Line Rd eastbound, just s to Harvester Rd, then just e. Int corridors. **Pets:** Accepted. [ECO] [SAVE] [✕] [🛏] [▣]

▥▼▼▼▼ **Homewood Suites by Hilton** 🄷
(905) 631-8300. **$99-$189.** 975 Syscon Rd L7L 5S3. QEW, exit Burloak Dr S, w on Harvester Rd. Int corridors. **Pets:** Accepted.
[SAVE] [✕] [🛏] [▣] [≈]

▼▼▼ **Motel 6 Burlington #1900** 🄷
(905) 331-1955. **$75-$85.** 4345 N Service Rd L7L 4X7. QEW, exit Walker's Line Rd N to N Service Rd, then 0.9 mi (1.4 km) e. Int corridors. **Pets:** Other species. Service with restrictions, supervision. [ECO] [✕] [🛏]

▼▼▼ **Travelodge Hotel Burlington on the Lake** 🄷
(905) 681-0762. **Call for rates.** 2020 Lakeshore Rd L7R 4G8. Corner of Brant St; downtown. Int corridors. **Pets:** Accepted.
[ECO] [✕] [🛏] [▣] [⛌]

CAMBRIDGE

▥▼▼▼▼ **Best Western Cambridge Hotel and Conference Centre** 🄷
(519) 623-4600. **$99-$159.** 730 Hespeler Rd N3H 5L8. Hwy 401, exit 282, just s. Ext/int corridors. **Pets:** Accepted.
[SAVE] [✕] [🛏] [▣] [≈] [⛌]

▥▼▼▼ **Cambridge Hotel Conference Centre** 🄷
(519) 622-1505. **$124-$369.** 700 Hespeler Rd N3H 5L8. Hwy 401, exit 282, just s. Int corridors. **Pets:** $50 one-time fee/room. Service with restrictions, supervision. [SAVE] [✕] [🛏] [▣] [⛌]

▥▼▼▼ **Comfort Inn** 🄷 ❀
(519) 658-1100. **$105-$127.** 220 Holiday Inn Dr N3C 1Z4. Hwy 401, exit 282, just n to Groh Ave. Int corridors. **Pets:** Other species. Service with restrictions, supervision. [ECO] [SAVE] [✕] [🛏] [▣] [⛌]

▥▼▼▼▼ **Homewood Suites by Hilton Cambridge/Waterloo** 🄷
(519) 651-2888. **$134-$204.** 800 Jamieson Pkwy N3C 4N6. Hwy 401, exit 286 (Townline Rd), just n. Int corridors. **Pets:** Small, other species. $100 one-time fee/room. Service with restrictions, supervision.
[SAVE] [✕] [⬤M] [🛏] [▣] [≈] [⛌]

▥▼▼▼▼ **Langdon Hall Country House Hotel & Spa** 🄲
(519) 740-2100. **$229-$629, 3 day notice.** 1 Langdon Dr N3H 4R8. Hwy 401, exit 275, 0.8 mi (1.3 km) se on Fountain St, then 0.6 mi (1 km) s on Blair Rd, follow signs. Ext/int corridors. **Pets:** Accepted.
[SAVE] [✕] [🛏] [▣] [⛌] [≈] [⛌]

CHATHAM

▼▼▼ **Comfort Inn** 🄷
(519) 352-5500. **$87-$95.** 1100 Richmond St N7M 5J5. Hwy 401, exit 81 (Bloomfield Rd), 3.1 mi (5 km) n. Int corridors. **Pets:** Other species. Service with restrictions, crate. [ECO] [ASK] [✕] [🛏] [▣]

▥▼▼▼ **Super 8 Chatham** 🄼
(519) 354-3366. **$63-$100.** 25 Michener Rd N7L 4B8. 3.1 mi (5 km) e on Hwy 2. Int corridors. **Pets:** Accepted. [SAVE] [✕] [🛏] [▣] [≈]

CHATSWORTH

▼▼ **Key Motel** 🄼
(519) 794-2350. **$60-$85.** 317051 Hwy 6/10 N0H 1G0. On Hwy 6 and 10. Ext/int corridors. **Pets:** Accepted. [✕] [🛏] [≈] [⛌]

COBOURG

Ⓐ ▼▼▼ **Best Western Cobourg Inn and Convention Centre** 🏠 ❀

(905) 372-2105. **$160.** 930 Burnham St K9A 2X9. Hwy 401, exit 472 (Burnham St S). Int corridors. **Pets:** Service with restrictions, supervision.

[SAVE] ⊠ 🛏 💻 🍴 ⌣

▼▼▼ **Comfort Inn** 🏠

(905) 372-7007. **$95-$121.** 121 Densmore Rd K9A 4J9. Hwy 401, exit 474, just se. Int corridors. **Pets:** Accepted. [ECO] [ASK] ⊠ 🛏 💻

▼▼▼ **The Woodlawn Inn** 🅲🅸

(905) 372-2235. **$109-$299.** 420 Division St K9A 3R9. Hwy 401, exit 474, 1 mi (2.4 km) s. Int corridors. **Pets:** Accepted.

⊠ 🛏 💻 🍴

COLLINGWOOD

Ⓐ ▼▼▼ ▼▼▼ **The Westin Trillium House Blue Mountain** 🏠 ❀

(705) 443-8080. **Call for rates.** 220 Mountain Dr L9Y 3Z2. Jct Hwy 26 and Mountain Rd, 6.3 mi (10 km) w on Mountain Rd, just w on Jozo Weider Blvd, then just w. Int corridors. **Pets:** Medium, dogs only. Designated rooms, service with restrictions, supervision.

[SAVE] ⊠ 🛏 💻 🍴 ⌣

CORNWALL

Ⓐ ▼▼▼▼ **Best Western Parkway Inn & Conference Centre** 🏠

(613) 932-0451. **$139-$239.** 1515 Vincent Massey Dr K6H 5R6. Hwy 401, exit 789 (Brookdale Ave), 1.8 mi (2.8 km) s, then just w. Int corridors. **Pets:** $10 daily fee/room. Designated rooms, service with restrictions, supervision. [ECO] [SAVE] ⊠ 🛏 💻 🍴 ⌣

▼▼▼ **Comfort Inn-Cornwall** 🏠

(613) 937-0111. **$79-$125.** 1625 Vincent Massey Dr K6H 5R6. Hwy 401, exit 789 (Brookdale Ave), 1.8 mi (2.8 km) s, then 0.4 mi (0.7 km) w. Int corridors. **Pets:** Accepted. [ASK] ⊠ 🛏 💻 ⌣

Ⓐ ▼ **Econo Lodge** 🏠

(613) 936-1996. **$59-$110.** 1142 Brookdale Ave K6J 4P4. Hwy 401, exit 789 (Brookdale Ave), 1.9 mi (3 km) s. Int corridors. **Pets:** Accepted.

[SAVE] ⊠ 🛏

DRYDEN

Ⓐ ▼▼▼▼ **Best Western Motor Inn** 🏠

(807) 223-3201. **$125-$150.** 349 Government St P8N 2P4. On Hwy 17. Int corridors. **Pets:** Designated rooms, service with restrictions, crate.

[ECO] [SAVE] ⊠ 🛏 💻 🍴 ⌣ ⊠

▼▼▼ **Comfort Inn** 🅼

(807) 223-3893. **$117-$127.** 522 Government St P8N 2P7. On Hwy 17. Int corridors. **Pets:** Accepted. [ECO] [ASK] ⊠ 🛏 💻

FONTHILL

▼ **Hipwell's Motel** 🅼

(905) 892-3588. **$45-$75.** 299 Reg Rd 20 W L0S 1E0. 1 mi (1.6 km) w; centre. Ext corridors. **Pets:** $5 daily fee/pet. Service with restrictions, supervision. [ASK] ⊠ 🛏 ⌣

FORT FRANCES

▼▼ **Super 8** 🏠 ❀

(807) 274-4945. **$106.** 810 Kings Hwy P9A 2X4. On Hwy 11. Int corridors. **Pets:** $10 one-time fee/pet. Designated rooms, service with restrictions, crate. [ASK] ⊠ 🛏 💻 ⌣ ⊠

FRENCH RIVER

Ⓐ ▼ **French River Trading Post Motel** 🅼

(705) 857-2115. **$77-$90.** 20112 Hwy 69 P0M 1A0. Trans-Canada Hwy 69, 0.6 mi (1 km) n of French River Bridge. Ext corridors. **Pets:** $10 daily fee/pet. Designated rooms, service with restrictions, supervision.

[SAVE] ⊠ 🛏 💻 🍴 🐾 ⊠

GANANOQUE

Ⓐ ▼▼▼ **Best Western Country Squire Resort** 🏠

(613) 382-3511. **$90-$250.** 715 King St E K7G 1H4. Hwy 401, exit 647 eastbound; exit 648 westbound, 0.6 mi (1 km) w on Hwy 2 (King St). Ext/int corridors. **Pets:** Accepted. [SAVE] ⊠ 🛏 💻 🍴 ⌣ ⊠

Ⓐ ▼▼▼ **Clarion Inn & Conference Centre 1000 Islands** 🏠

(613) 382-7272. **$69-$249.** 50 Main St K7G 2L7. Corner of Hwy 2 (King St); centre. Int corridors. **Pets:** $15 daily fee/pet. Designated rooms, service with restrictions, supervision. [SAVE] ⊠ 🛏 💻 🍴 ⌣

Ⓐ ▼▼▼ **Comfort Inn 1000 Islands** 🅼

(613) 382-4728. **$59-$249.** 785 King St E K7G 1H4. Hwy 401, exit 647 eastbound; exit 648 westbound, 0.3 mi (0.5 km) w on Hwy 2 (King St). Ext/int corridors. **Pets:** $15 daily fee/pet. Designated rooms, service with restrictions, supervision. [SAVE] ⊠ 🛏 💻 ⌣

Ⓐ ▼▼▼▼ **Holiday Inn Express & Suites 1000 Islands** 🏠

(613) 382-8338. **$99-$249.** 777 King St E K7G 1H4. Just w of jct Hwy 2 (King St), 401 and 1000 Islands Pkwy. Int corridors. **Pets:** $15 daily fee/pet. Designated rooms, service with restrictions, supervision.

[ECO] [SAVE] ⊠ 🛏 💻 ⌣

Ⓐ ▼▼▼ **Quality Inn & Suites 1000 Islands** 🅼

(613) 382-1453. **$69-$249.** 650 King St E K7G 1H3. Hwy 401, exit 647 eastbound; exit 648 westbound, 0.6 mi (1 km) w on Hwy 2 (King St). Ext corridors. **Pets:** $15 daily fee/pet. Designated rooms, service with restrictions, supervision. [SAVE] ⊠ 🛏 💻 🍴 ⌣

▼▼▼ **Ramada Provincial Inn** 🅼

(613) 382-2038. **$89-$239.** 846 King St E K7G 1H3. Hwy 401, exit 647 eastbound; exit 648 westbound, 0.3 mi (0.5 km) w on Hwy 2 (King St). Ext corridors. **Pets:** Accepted. [ASK] ⊠ 🛏 💻 ⌣

▼▼▼ **Trinity House Inn** 🅲🅸

(613) 382-8383. **$99-$250, 7 day notice.** 90 Stone St S K7G 1Z8. Corner of Pine St; centre. Int corridors. **Pets:** Designated rooms, service with restrictions, crate. ⊠ 🛏 💻 🍴 🐾

GRIMSBY

Ⓐ ▼▼▼ **Super 8-Grimsby** 🏠

(905) 309-8800. **$99-$169.** 11 Windward Dr L3M 4E9. QEW, exit 74 (Casablanca N). Int corridors. **Pets:** Other species. $10 daily fee/pet. Service with restrictions, crate. [SAVE] ⊠ 🛏 💻 ⌣

GUELPH

Ⓐ ▼▼▼ **Best Western Royal Brock Hotel & Conference Centre** 🏠

(519) 836-1240. **$92-$112.** 716 Gordon St N1G 1Y6. Jct Stone Rd; 5 mi (8 km) n of Hwy 401 via Brock Rd. Int corridors. **Pets:** Medium. $12 one-time fee/room. Designated rooms, service with restrictions, crate.

[SAVE] ⊠ 🛏 💻 🍴 ⌣

Ⓐ ▼▼▼ **Comfort Inn Guelph** 🏠 ❀

(519) 763-1900. **$95-$130.** 480 Silvercreek Pkwy N1H 7R5. Jct Hwy 6 and 7. Int corridors. **Pets:** Designated rooms, service with restrictions.

[ECO] [SAVE] ⊠ 🛏 💻

Ⓐ ▼▼▼ **Days Inn-Guelph** 🏠

(519) 822-9112. **$110-$138.** 785 Gordon St N1G 1Y8. Hwy 401, exit 299 (Brock Rd), 7 mi (11.5 km) n. Int corridors. **Pets:** Medium. Service with restrictions, supervision. [ECO] [SAVE] ⊠ 🛏 💻

▼▼▼ **Delta Guelph Hotel and Conference Centre** 🏠 ❀

(519) 780-3700. **$129-$219.** 50 Stone Rd W N1G 0A9. Jct Gordon St. Int corridors. **Pets:** $35 one-time fee/pet. Service with restrictions.

[ASK] ⊠ ⌂M 🛏 💻 🍴

ⒶⒶ ▼▼▼ **Hampton Inn & Suites by Hilton Guelph** Ⓗ

(519) 821-2144. **$109-$149.** 725 Imperial Rd N N1K 1X4. Hwy 401, exit 295 (Hwy 6 N) to Woodlawn Rd, w to Imperial Rd, then n. Int corridors. **Pets:** Accepted. ⓈⒶⓋⒺ ⓧ 🛆 📺 ⌫

ⒶⒶ ▼▼▼▼ **Holiday Inn Guelph Hotel and Conference Centre** Ⓗ ✿

(519) 836-0231. **Call for rates.** 601 Scottsdale Dr N1G 3E7. Jct Hwy 6 N and Stone Rd E; 5 mi (8 km) n of jct Hwy 401. Int corridors. **Pets:** Other species. $35 one-time fee/room. Service with restrictions, supervision. ⒺⒸⓄ ⓈⒶⓋⒺ ⓧ 🛆 📺 🍴 ⌫ ⓧ

ⒶⒶ ▼▼▼ **Staybridge Suites** Ⓗ

(519) 767-3300. **$119-$199.** 11 Corporate Ct N1G 5G5. Jct Hwy 6 and Laird St, just e. Int corridors. **Pets:** Accepted.

ⒺⒸⓄ ⓈⒶⓋⒺ ⓧ Ⓜ 🛆 📺 ⌫

ⒶⒶ ▼▼▼ **Super 8-Guelph** Ⓜ

(519) 836-5850. **$84-$199.** 281 Woodlawn Rd W N1H 7K7. Jct Hwy 6 and 7. Ext/int corridors. **Pets:** Accepted. ⓈⒶⓋⒺ ⓧ 🛆 📺 🍴

HALIBURTON

▼▼▼ **Lakeview Motel** Ⓜ

(705) 457-1027. **$105-$235, 5 day notice.** 4951 CR 21 K0M 1S0. Jct Hwy 118, 1.6 mi (2.5 km) w. Ext corridors. **Pets:** Accepted.

ⓧ 🛆 📺 🍴 ⌫

HAMILTON

ⒶⒶ ▼▼▼ **Sheraton Hamilton** Ⓗ

(905) 529-5515. **Call for rates.** 116 King St W L8P 4V3. Between Bay and James sts; downtown. Int corridors. **Pets:** Medium. Designated rooms, service with restrictions, crate.

ⓈⒶⓋⒺ ⓧ Ⓜ 🛆 📺 🍴 ⌫

▼▼▼▼ **Staybridge Suites** Ⓗ

(905) 577-9000. **$135-$145.** 118 Market St L8R 3P9. Hwy 403, exit King St, then e; jct Caroline St; across from Jackson Square. Int corridors. **Pets:** Medium. $95 one-time fee/room. Service with restrictions, supervision. ⒶⓈⓀ ⓧ 🛆 📺 ⌫

▼▼▼ **Super 8-Hamilton Airport/Mount Hope** Ⓗ

(905) 679-3355. **$100-$120.** 2975 Homestead Dr L0R 1W0. Jct Hwy 6 S (Upper James St) and Homestead Dr. Int corridors. **Pets:** Medium. $10 daily fee/pet. Service with restrictions, supervision. ⒶⓈⓀ ⓧ 📺

HUNTSVILLE

▼▼▼ **Comfort Inn** Ⓗ ✿

(705) 789-1701. **$79-$320.** 86 King William St P1H 1E4. Jct Hwy 60. Int corridors. **Pets:** Other species. Designated rooms, service with restrictions, supervision. ⒺⒸⓄ ⒶⓈⓀ ⓧ 🛆 📺

▼▼▼ **Holiday Inn Express Hotel & Suites** Ⓗ

(705) 788-9500. **$99-$159.** 100 Howland Dr P1H 2P9. Jct Hwy 11 and 60, just se. Int corridors. **Pets:** Accepted. ⓧ 🛆 📺 ⌫

ⒶⒶ ▼▼▼ **HV Hidden Valley Resort** Ⓗ ✿

(705) 789-2301. **$89-$239, 5 day notice.** 1755 Valley Rd P1H 1Z8. Jct Hwy 11, 4 mi (6.5 km) e on Hwy 60 to Canal, follow signs. Int corridors. **Pets:** Medium. Designated rooms, service with restrictions, supervision.

ⓈⒶⓋⒺ ⓧ 🛆 📺 🍴 ⌫ ⓧ

▼▼ **King William Inn** Ⓜ

(705) 789-9661. **$69-$129.** 23 King William St P1H 1G4. Hwy 60, 0.6 mi (1 km) s. Ext corridors. **Pets:** Accepted. ⒶⓈⓀ ⓧ 🛆 📺

▼▼ **Motel 6-Huntsville** Ⓗ

(705) 787-0118. **$65-$150.** 70 Howland Dr P1H 2P9. Jct Hwy 11 and 60, just se. Int corridors. **Pets:** Other species. Service with restrictions, supervision. ⒺⒸⓄ ⒶⓈⓀ ⓧ 🛆 ⌫

▼▼ **Travelodge** Ⓗ

(705) 789-5504. **$80-$100.** 225 Main St W P1H 1Y1. Hwy 11, exit 219 (Muskoka Rd 3), just e. Int corridors. **Pets:** Accepted.

ⒶⓈⓀ ⓧ 🛆 📺

▼▼ **Tulip Inn** Ⓜ

(705) 789-4001. **$60-$130, 3 day notice.** 211 Arrowhead Park Rd P1H 2J4. Hwy 11, exit 226 (Muskoka Rd 3), follow signs for Arrowhead Park. Ext corridors. **Pets:** Accepted. ⒶⓈⓀ ⓧ 🛆 📺

INGERSOLL

▼▼▼ **Comfort Inn & Suites** Ⓗ

(519) 425-1100. **$80-$125.** 20 Samnah Cres N5C 3J7. Hwy 401, exit 216 (Culloden Rd). Int corridors. **Pets:** Accepted.

ⒶⓈⓀ ⓧ 🛆 📺 ⌫

ⒶⒶ ▼▼▼▼ **Elm Hurst Inn and Country Spa** Ⓒ

(519) 485-5321. **$185, 3 day notice.** 415 Harris St N5C 3J8. Jct Hwy 401 and 19 N. Int corridors. **Pets:** Small. No service, supervision.

ⓈⒶⓋⒺ ⓧ 🛆 📺 🍴 ⓧ

KANATA

ⒶⒶ ▼▼▼ **Comfort Inn Ottawa West Kanata** Ⓗ ✿

(613) 592-2200. **$109-$135.** 30 Edgewater St K2L 1V8. Hwy 417, exit 138 (Eagleson Rd), 0.4 mi (0.6 km) s, just w on Katimavik Rd, then 0.5 mi (0.8 km) n. Int corridors. **Pets:** Other species. Designated rooms, service with restrictions, supervision. ⒺⒸⓄ ⓈⒶⓋⒺ ⓧ 🛆 📺

KAPUSKASING

▼▼▼ **Comfort Inn** Ⓗ

(705) 335-8583. **$95-$124.** 172 Government Rd E P5N 2W9. Hwy 11; corner of Brunelle Rd. Int corridors. **Pets:** Accepted.

ⒺⒸⓄ ⒶⓈⓀ ⓧ 🛆 📺

KENORA

ⒶⒶ ▼▼▼ **Best Western Lakeside Inn & Conference Centre** Ⓗ ✿

(807) 468-5521. **$117-$144.** 470 First Ave S P9N 1W5. Just s on 4th Ave S from Jct Hwy 17. Int corridors. **Pets:** Medium, other species. Service with restrictions, supervision. ⒺⒸⓄ ⓈⒶⓋⒺ ⓧ 🛆 📺 🍴 ⌫

▼▼▼ **Comfort Inn** Ⓜ

(807) 468-8845. **$88-$117.** 1230 Hwy 17 E P9N 1L9. 0.9 mi (1.5 km) e. Int corridors. **Pets:** Accepted. ⒶⓈⓀ ⓧ 🛆 📺

ⒶⒶ ▼▼▼ **Kenora Travelodge** Ⓗ

(807) 468-3155. **$95-$160.** 800 Hwy 17 E P9N 1L9. 0.6 mi (1 km) e. Int corridors. **Pets:** $15 daily fee/pet. Designated rooms, service with restrictions, supervision. ⓈⒶⓋⒺ ⓧ 🛆 📺 🍴 ⌫ ⓧ

KILLALOE

▼▼▼ **Annie's Inn Bed & Breakfast** ⒷⒷ

(613) 757-0950. **$70-$200 (no credit cards), 7 day notice.** 67 Roche St K0J 2A0. Hwy 60, exit Maple St, 1 blk to Roche St, then w; driveway entrance is at the end of the street. Int corridors. **Pets:** Accepted.

ⒶⓈⓀ ⓧ 🛆 📺 ⓩ

KINGSTON

ⒶⒶ ▼▼▼ **Comfort Inn Hwy 401** Ⓗ

(613) 546-9500. **$95-$200.** 55 Warne Cres K7K 6Z5. Hwy 401, exit 617 (Division St), just s to Dalton Ave. Int corridors. **Pets:** Other species. Service with restrictions. ⒺⒸⓄ ⓈⒶⓋⒺ ⓧ 🛆 📺

▼▼ **Comfort Inn Midtown** Ⓗ ✿

(613) 549-5550. **$100-$180.** 1454 Princess St K7M 3E5. Hwy 401, exit 613 (Sydenham Rd), 2.5 mi (4 km) se. Int corridors. **Pets:** Large, other species. Service with restrictions, supervision. ⒺⒸⓄ ⒶⓈⓀ ⓧ 🛆 📺

▼▼ **Confederation Place Hotel** Ⓗ ✿

(613) 549-6300. **$89-$209.** 237 Ontario St K7L 2Z4. Centre of downtown. Int corridors. **Pets:** Medium. $15 daily fee/pet. Designated rooms, service with restrictions. ⒶⓈⓀ ⓧ 🛆 📺 🍴 ⌫

(CAA) ▼▼ **Days Inn Conference Centre Kingston** H

(613) 546-3661. **$99-$159.** 33 Benson St K7K 5W2. Hwy 401, exit 617 (Division St), south side. Int corridors. **Pets:** $200 deposit/room. Designated rooms, service with restrictions, supervision.

ECO SAVE ✕ 🛗 💻 🍽 🏊

(CAA) ▼▼▼ **The Executive Inn & Suites** M

(613) 549-1620. **$99-$149, 3 day notice.** 794 Hwy 2 E K7L 4V1. Hwy 401, exit 623, 5 mi (8 km) s, then 1.3 mi (2 km) e. Ext corridors. **Pets:** Medium, dogs only. $10 daily fee/pet. Designated rooms, service with restrictions, supervision. SAVE ✕ 🛗 💻 🏊

(CAA) ▼▼▼ **Holiday Inn Kingston-Waterfront** H

(613) 549-8400. **Call for rates.** 2 Princess St K7L 1A2. Corner of Ontario St; centre of downtown. Int corridors. **Pets:** Accepted.

ECO SAVE ✕ 🛗 💻 🍽 🏊 🐾

KIRKLAND LAKE

▼▼ **Comfort Inn** H

(705) 567-4909. **$120-$250.** 455 Government Rd W P0K 1A0. On Rt 66. Int corridors. **Pets:** Other species. Service with restrictions.

ECO ASK ✕ 🛗 💻

KITCHENER

(CAA) ▼▼▼ **Delta Kitchener-Waterloo** H

(519) 744-4141. **$119-$169.** 105 King St E N2G 2K8. Corner of King and Benton sts; downtown. Int corridors. **Pets:** Accepted.

ECO SAVE ✕ 🛗 💻 🍽 🏊 🐾

(CAA) ▼▼▼ **Radisson Hotel Kitchener-Waterloo** H ❧

(519) 894-9500. **$129-$189.** 2960 King St E N2A 1A9. Hwy 401, exit 278, 3.8 mi (6 km) w on Hwy 8, exit Weber St. Int corridors. **Pets:** Medium, other species. Designated rooms, service with restrictions, crate. ECO SAVE ✕ 🛗 💻 🍽 🏊

(CAA) ▼▼▼ **Walper Terrace Hotel** H

(519) 745-4321. **$89-$179.** 1 King St W N2G 1A1. Corner of King and Queen sts; downtown. Int corridors. **Pets:** $200 deposit/room, $35 one-time fee/room. Supervision. SAVE ✕ 🛗 💻 🍽

LEAMINGTON

▼▼ **Comfort Inn** H ❧

(519) 326-9071. **$80-$150.** 279 Erie St S N8H 3C4. 0.6 mi (1 km) s of jct Talbot and Erie sts; on direct route to Point Pelee National Park. Int corridors. **Pets:** Medium. $10 daily fee/room. Designated rooms, service with restrictions, supervision. ECO ASK ✕ 🛗 💻

(CAA) ▼▼▼ **Howard Johnson Inn Leamington** H

(519) 325-0260. **$100-$300, 3 day notice.** 201 Erie St N N8H 3A5. 0.6 mi (1 km) n of Talbot St. Int corridors. **Pets:** Small, other species. $150 deposit/room, $15 daily fee/pet. Designated rooms, service with restrictions, supervision. ECO SAVE ✕ 🛗 💻 🏊 🐾

LONDON

▼▼ **Airport Inn & Suites** H

(519) 457-1200. **$99, 7 day notice.** 2230 Dundas St E N5V 1R5. Hwy 401, exit Veteran's Memorial Pkwy, 4.8 mi (7.7 km) n; corner of Airport Rd and Dundas St E. Int corridors. **Pets:** Medium. $15 daily fee/pet. Designated rooms, service with restrictions, supervision. ASK ✕ 🛗 💻

(CAA) ▼▼▼ **Best Western Lamplighter Inn & Conference Centre** H

(519) 681-7151. **$109-$179.** 591 Wellington Rd S N6C 4R3. 2.3 mi (3.7 km) n off Hwy 401, exit 186 (Wellington Rd). Int corridors. **Pets:** Accepted. SAVE ✕ 🛗 💻 🏊 🐾

(CAA) ▼▼ **Comfort Inn** H

(519) 685-9300. **$75-$120.** 1156 Wellington Rd N6E 1M3. Hwy 401, exit 186B (Wellington Rd), just n. Int corridors. **Pets:** Accepted.

ECO SAVE ✕ 🛗 💻

(CAA) ▼▼▼ **Days Inn London** H

(519) 681-1240. **$65-$129.** 1100 Wellington Rd S N6E 1M2. Hwy 401, exit 186B (Wellington Rd), 0.9 mi (1.5 km) n. Int corridors. **Pets:** Medium. Designated rooms, service with restrictions, supervision.

ECO SAVE ✕ 🛗 💻 🍽 🏊

(CAA) ▼▼▼▼ **Delta London Armouries** H

(519) 679-6111. **$119-$239.** 325 Dundas St N6B 1T9. Between Wellington and Waterloo sts. Int corridors. **Pets:** Other species. $35 one-time fee/room. Service with restrictions, crate.

ECO SAVE ✕ 🛗 💻 🍽 🏊 🐾

(CAA) ▼▼▼▼ **Hilton London Ontario** H ❧

(519) 439-1661. **$119-$229.** 300 King St N6B 1S2. Jct King St and Wellington Rd. Int corridors. **Pets:** Large, other species. $65 one-time fee/room. Designated rooms.

ECO SAVE ✕ 🛗 💻 🍽 🏊 🐾

(CAA) ▼▼▼▼ **Holiday Inn Hotel & Suites-London** H

(519) 680-0077. **$99-$144.** 864 Exeter Rd N6E 1L5. Hwy 401, exit 186 (Wellington Rd) westbound; exit 186B eastbound. Int corridors. **Pets:** Accepted. SAVE ✕ 🛗 💻 🍽 🏊

(CAA) ▼▼▼▼ **Homewood Suites by Hilton London** H

(519) 686-7700. **$119-$169.** 45 Bessemer Rd N6E 0A2. Hwy 401, exit 186 (Wellington Rd). Int corridors. **Pets:** Accepted.

SAVE ✕ 🛗 🛗 💻

▼▼ **Motel 6** H

(519) 680-0900. **Call for rates.** 810 Exeter Rd N6E 1L5. Hwy 401, exit 186 (Wellington Rd), just n. Int corridors. **Pets:** Other species. Service with restrictions, supervision. ✕ 🛗 🛗 💻 🏊

(CAA) ▼▼▼▼ **Quality Suites** H

(519) 680-1024. **$79-$124.** 1120 Dearness Dr N6E 1N9. Hwy 401, exit 186B (Wellington Rd), 1 mi (1.6 km) n. Int corridors. **Pets:** Large. Service with restrictions, supervision. ECO SAVE ✕ 🛗 💻

(CAA) ▼▼▼▼ **Radisson Hotel and Suites London** H

(519) 668-7900. **$99-$169.** 855 Wellington Rd S N6E 3N5. Jct Wellington and Southdale rds. Int corridors. **Pets:** $35 one-time fee/room. Service with restrictions. ECO SAVE ✕ 🛗 💻 🍽 🏊

▼▼▼▼ **Residence Inn London** H ❧

(519) 433-7222. **$157-$191.** 383 Colborne St N6B 3P5. Jct King St. Int corridors. **Pets:** Other species. $75 one-time fee/room. Service with restrictions, supervision. ECO ✕ 🛗 💻

(CAA) ▼▼▼▼ **StationPark All Suite Hotel** H

(519) 642-4444. **$129-$204.** 242 Pall Mall St N6A 5P6. Hwy 401, exit 186B (Wellington Rd), 5.6 mi (9 km) n. Int corridors. **Pets:** Accepted. SAVE ✕ 🛗 💻 🍽 🏊

(CAA) ▼▼▼▼ **Staybridge Suites** H

(519) 649-4500. **$99-$159.** 824 Exeter Rd N6E 1L5. Hwy 401, exit 186 (Wellington Rd). Int corridors. **Pets:** $35 one-time fee/room. Service with restrictions, supervision. ECO SAVE ✕ 🛗 🛗 💻 🏊

MARATHON

(CAA) ▼▼ **Peninsula Inn** M

(807) 229-0651. **$88-$99, 6 day notice.** Hwy 17 P0T 2E0. 1.5 mi (2.4 km) w of jct Hwy 626. Ext corridors. **Pets:** Medium. $10 one-time fee/pet. Designated rooms, service with restrictions, supervision.

SAVE ✕ 🛗 🍽

▼▼ **Travelodge Marathon** H

(807) 229-1213. **$105-$195.** Hwy 17 & Peninsula Rd P0T 2E0. On Hwy 17, jct Peninsula Rd. Int corridors. **Pets:** Accepted.

ASK ✕ 🛗 💻 🍽

MASSEY

(CAA) ▼▼ **Mohawk Motel Canada** M

(705) 865-2722. **$78-$155.** 335 Sable St P0P 1P0. Centre. Ext/int corridors. **Pets:** Accepted. SAVE ✕ 🛗 💻

MIDLAND

Comfort Inn 🏨 🐾

(705) 526-2090. **$94-$140.** 980 King St L4R 4K3. Jct Hwy 12 and King St. Int corridors. **Pets:** $10 daily fee/room. Designated rooms, service with restrictions, crate. 🖼️ 🅰️🅺 ✖️ 📶 💻

Super 8 Motel Midland 🏨 🐾

(705) 526-8288. **$98-$141.** 1144 Hugel Ave L4R 0B1. At jct Hwy 93 N. Int corridors. **Pets:** Large, other species. $8 daily fee/room. Designated rooms, service with restrictions, crate. 🖼️ 🖼️ ✖️ 📶 💻 🏊

MILTON

Best Western Milton Inn 🏨

(905) 875-3818. **$120-$160.** 161 Chisholm Dr L9T 4A6. Jct Hwy 401 and 25 S. Int corridors. **Pets:** Accepted. 🖼️ ✖️ 📶 💻 🍴 🏊

MINDEMOYA

Mindemoya Motel 🅼

(705) 377-4779. **$82-$129, 3 day notice.** 6375 Hwy 542 P0P 1S0. In Mindemoya; 0.6 mi (1 km) w of jct Hwy 551 and 542. Ext corridors. **Pets:** Medium, dogs only. $50 deposit/room. Designated rooms, service with restrictions, crate. 🅰️🅺 ✖️ 📶 💻

MISSISSAUGA

Comfort Inn Airport West 🏨

(905) 624-6900. **$80-$109.** 1500 Matheson Blvd L4W 3Z4. Hwy 401, exit Dixie Rd, then s. Int corridors. **Pets:** Other species. $10 daily fee/room. Designated rooms, service with restrictions, supervision. 🖼️ 🅰️🅺 ✖️ 📶 💻 🍴

Comfort Inn Toronto Airport 🏨

(905) 677-7331. **$95-$109.** 6355 Airport Rd L4V 1E4. 1.3 mi (2 km) s of Derry Rd. Int corridors. **Pets:** Other species. $10 daily fee/pet. Service with restrictions, crate. 🖼️ ✖️ 📶 💻 🍴

Delta Meadowvale Resort and Conference Centre 🏨

(905) 821-1981. **$99-$229.** 6750 Mississauga Rd L5N 2L3. Hwy 401 W, exit 336 (Mississauga Rd), just s. Int corridors. **Pets:** Medium. $40 one-time fee/pet. Service with restrictions, crate. 🖼️ 🖼️ ✖️ 🗺️ 📶 💻 🍴 🏊 ✖️

Delta Toronto Airport West 🏨 🐾

(905) 624-1144. **$99-$219.** 5444 Dixie Rd L4W 2L2. 0.6 mi (1 km) s of jct Hwy 401 and Dixie Rd. Int corridors. **Pets:** $35 one-time fee/room. Service with restrictions, supervision. 🖼️ 🖼️ ✖️ 📶 💻 🍴 🏊 ✖️

Four Points by Sheraton Mississauga Meadowvale 🏨

(905) 858-2424. **$90-$220.** 2501 Argentia Rd L5N 4G8. Hwy 401 exit 336, just s on Erin Mills Pkwy, then 1 mi (1.6 km) w. Int corridors. **Pets:** Accepted. 🖼️ 🖼️ ✖️ 🗺️ 📶 💻 🍴 🏊

Hilton Toronto Airport Hotel & Suites 🏨

(905) 677-9900. **$119-$299.** 5875 Airport Rd L4V 1N1. Hwy 401, exit Dixon Rd, 2.2 mi (3.5 km) w. Int corridors. **Pets:** Accepted. 🖼️ 🖼️ ✖️ 🗺️ 💻 🍴 🏊

Holiday Inn Express Hotel & Suites, Mississauga 🏨

(905) 795-1011. **$119-$189.** 40 Admiral Blvd L5T 2W1. Hwy 401, exit Hwy 10 (Hurontario St), 0.9 mi (1.5 km) n; just s of Derry Rd. Int corridors. **Pets:** Accepted. 🅰️🅺 ✖️ 📶 💻 🏊

Holiday Inn Toronto-Mississauga 🏨

(905) 855-2000. **$89-$159.** 2125 N Sheridan Way L5K 1A3. QEW, exit Erin Mills Pkwy. Int corridors. **Pets:** Accepted. 🅰️🅺 ✖️ 🗺️ 📶 💻 🍴 🏊

Motel 6 Mississauga #1910 🏨

(905) 814-1664. **$65-$75.** 2935 Argentia Rd L5N 8G6. Hwy 401, exit 333 (Winston Churchill Blvd), just s. Int corridors. **Pets:** Other species. Service with restrictions, supervision. 🖼️ ✖️ 🗺️ 📶

Novotel Toronto Mississauga Centre 🏨 🐾

(905) 896-1000. **$299.** 3670 Hurontario St L5B 1P3. Hwy 403, exit 344, 0.8 mi s (1.2 km) on Hwy 10 (Hurontario St); at Burnhamthorpe Rd. Int corridors. **Pets:** $35 one-time fee/room. Service with restrictions, supervision. 🖼️ 🖼️ ✖️ 📶 💻 🍴 🏊 ✖️

Residence Inn by Marriott Mississauga Airport Corporate Centre West 🏨

(905) 602-7777. **$170-$208.** 5070 Creekbank Rd L4W 5R2. Hwy 401 W, exit Dixie Rd S, 0.9 mi (1.5 km) to Eglinton Ave, then 0.6 mi (1 km). Int corridors. **Pets:** Accepted. ✖️ 📶 💻 🏊 ✖️

Residence Inn Toronto-Mississauga/Meadowvale 🏨

(905) 567-2577. **$170-$208.** 7005 Century Ave L5N 7K2. Hwy 401, exit Erin Mills Pkwy/Mississauga Rd, s to Argentia Rd. Int corridors. **Pets:** Medium, other species. $100 one-time fee/room. Service with restrictions, supervision. ✖️ 🗺️ 📶 💻 🏊 ✖️

Sandalwood Suites Hotel Toronto Airport 🏨

(905) 238-9600. **$69-$159.** 5050 Orbitor Dr L4W 4X2. Jct Eglinton Ave and Renforth Dr, 1.4 mi (2.3 km) w on Eglinton Ave. Int corridors. **Pets:** Medium. $35 one-time fee/room. Designated rooms, service with restrictions, supervision. 🖼️ 🖼️ ✖️ 📶 💻

Sheraton Gateway Hotel in Toronto International Airport 🏨 🐾

(905) 672-7000. **$119-$349.** Terminal 3, Toronto AMF L5P 1C4. In Toronto Pearson International Airport. Int corridors. **Pets:** Small. Designated rooms, service with restrictions, supervision. 🖼️ 🖼️ ✖️ 🗺️ 📶 💻 🍴 🏊 ✖️

Staybridge Suites Mississauga 🏨

(905) 564-6892. **Call for rates.** 6791 Hurontario St L5T 2W1. Hwy 401 W, exit Hwy 10 (Hurontario St), 0.9 mi (1.5 km) n; just s of Derry Rd. Int corridors. **Pets:** Accepted. ✖️ 📶 💻 🏊

Studio 6 Mississauga #1908 🅼

(905) 502-8897. **$73-$83.** 60 Britannia Rd E L4Z 2T2. Hwy 401, exit Hwy 10 (Hurontario St). Int corridors. **Pets:** Other species. $10 daily fee/room. Service with restrictions, supervision. 🖼️ ✖️ 📶 💻

MONETVILLE

Memquisit Lodge 🅲🅰

(705) 898-2355. **Call for rates.** 506 Memquisit Rd P0M 2K0. 13 mi (20.8 km) ne on west arm of Lake Nipissing, on Hwy 64 and Memquisit Lodge Rd; 23 mi (36.8 km) sw off Hwy 17, on Hwy 64. Ext corridors. **Pets:** Accepted. 📶 💻 🍴 ✖️ 🎿 🚲

MORRISBURG

The McIntosh Country Inn & Conference Centre 🏨

(613) 543-3788. **$69-$129.** 12495 Hwy 2 E K0C 1X0. Hwy 401, exit 750, 1.2 mi (2 km) s on Rt 31, then 0.6 mi (1 km) e. Int corridors. **Pets:** Medium. $10 one-time fee/pet. Service with restrictions, crate. 🖼️ ✖️ 📶 💻 🍴 🏊 ✖️

NEWMARKET

Comfort Inn 🏨 🐾

(905) 895-3355. **$91-$117.** 1230 Journey's End Cir L3Y 8Z6. Hwy 404, exit 51 (Davis Dr), just w, then just n on Harry Walker Pkwy. Int corridors. **Pets:** Other species. $5 daily fee/room. Designated rooms, service with restrictions, supervision. 🖼️ 🅰️🅺 ✖️ 📶 💻

NIAGARA FALLS METROPOLITAN AREA

FORT ERIE

Ⓐ ▽▽▽▽ **Holiday Inn Fort Erie/Niagara-Convention Centre** 🄷

(905) 871-8333. **$129-$349, 14 day notice.** 1485 Garrison Rd L2A 1P8. QEW, exit Gilmore Rd. Int corridors. **Pets:** $30 daily fee/pet. Designated rooms, service with restrictions, supervision.

ⒺⒸⓄ ⓢⒶⓋⒺ ⊠ 🛢 🖵 🍴 ⇌ ⊠

LINCOLN

Ⓐ ▽▽▽ **Best Western Beacon Harbourside Inn & Suites Conference Centre** 🄷

(905) 562-4155. **$80-$210.** 2793 Beacon Blvd L0R 1S0. QEW, exit 55. Int corridors. **Pets:** Other species. $10 daily fee/room. Designated rooms, service with restrictions. ⓢⒶⓋⒺ ⊠ 🛢 🖵 🍴 ⇌ ⊠

NIAGARA FALLS

Ⓐ ▽▽▽ **Best Western Fallsview** 🄷 ❀

(905) 356-0551. **$75-$300, 3 day notice.** 6289 Fallsview Blvd L2G 3V7. Jct Niagara River Pkwy, just n on Murray St. Ext/int corridors. **Pets:** Other species. $25 daily fee/pet. Supervision. ⓢⒶⓋⒺ ⊠ 🖵 🍴 ⇌

Ⓐ ▽▽▽ **Falls Manor Motel & Restaurant** Ⓜ

(905) 358-3211. **$49-$149.** 7104 Lundy's Ln L2G 1W2. On Hwy 20, 2.1 mi (3.4 km) w. Ext corridors. **Pets:** Accepted. ⓢⒶⓋⒺ ⊠ 🛢 🍴 ⇌

Ⓐ ▽▽▽ **Howard Johnson Express Inn** Ⓜ

(905) 358-9777. **$40-$200, 30 day notice.** 8100 Lundy's Ln L2H 1H1. QEW, exit Hwy 20, 3.1 mi (5 km) w. Ext corridors. **Pets:** Other species. $15 daily fee/pet. Designated rooms, service with restrictions.

ⓢⒶⓋⒺ ⊠ 🛢 🖵 ⇌

Ⓐ ▽▽▽ **Howard Johnson Hotel by the Falls** 🄷 ❀

(905) 357-4040. **$59-$349.** 5905 Victoria Ave L2G 3L8. On Hwy 20; 0.4 mi (0.6 km) from the falls. Int corridors. **Pets:** Small. $20 daily fee/pet. Designated rooms, service with restrictions, crate.

ⒺⒸⓄ ⓢⒶⓋⒺ ⊠ 🛢 🖵 🍴 ⇌ ⊠

Ⓐ ▽▽▽ **Knights Inn** Ⓜ

(905) 354-6939. **Call for rates.** 7034 Lundy's Ln L2G 1V9. On Hwy 20, 2.1 mi (3.4 km) w. Ext corridors. **Pets:** Accepted. ⓢⒶⓋⒺ ⊠ 🛢 ⇌

Ⓐ ▽▽▽ **Motel 6 Niagara Falls** 🄷

(905) 356-6696. **$50-$150.** 5700 Stanley Ave L2G 3X5. Just n of Hwy 20, just s of Hwy 420. Int corridors. **Pets:** Other species. Service with restrictions, supervision. ⒺⒸⓄ ⓢⒶⓋⒺ ⊠ ⓖⓜ 🛢 ⇌

Ⓐ ▽▽ **Niagara Parkway Court Motel** Ⓜ

(905) 295-3331. **$39-$149.** 3708 Main St (Niagara Pkwy S) L2G 6B1. 1.6 mi (2.5 km) s of the falls. Ext corridors. **Pets:** $10 daily fee/pet. Designated rooms, service with restrictions, supervision. ⓢⒶⓋⒺ ⊠ 🛢 🖵

Ⓐ ▽▽▽ **Peninsula Inn & Resort** 🄷

(905) 354-8812. **$59-$339.** 7373 Niagara Square Dr L2E 6S5. QEW, exit McLeod Rd, just w. Int corridors. **Pets:** Small. $10 daily fee/pet. Designated rooms, service with restrictions, crate.

ⓢⒶⓋⒺ ⊠ ⓖⓜ 🛢 🖵 🍴 ⇌ ⊠

Ⓐ ▽▽▽▽ **Sheraton on the Falls** 🄷

(905) 374-4445. **$99-$1199.** 5875 Falls Ave L2E 6W7. Entrance to Rainbow Bridge on Hwy 20. Int corridors. **Pets:** Accepted.

ⓢⒶⓋⒺ ⊠ 🛢 🖵 🍴 ⇌ ⊠

Ⓐ ▽▽▽ **Stanley Motor Inn** Ⓜ

(905) 358-9238. **$55-$125, 4 day notice.** 6220 Stanley Ave L2G 3Y4. 2 blks from the falls; w of Skylon Tower. Ext/int corridors. **Pets:** Medium, dogs only. $10 one-time fee/pet. Service with restrictions, crate.

ⓢⒶⓋⒺ ⊠ 🛢 ⇌ ⓩ

Ⓐ ▽▽▽ **Super 8–North of the Falls** Ⓜ

(905) 356-0131. **$49-$300.** 4009 River Rd L2E 3E5. 1.9 mi (3 km) n of Rainbow Bridge. Ext corridors. **Pets:** Accepted.

ⓢⒶⓋⒺ ⊠ 🛢 🖵 🍴 ⇌

NIAGARA-ON-THE-LAKE

▽▽▽▽ **Harbour House Hotel** 🄷

(905) 468-4683. **$199-$475, 10 day notice.** 85 Melville St L0S 1J0. Jct Ricardo St. Int corridors. **Pets:** Accepted. ⒶⓈⓀ ⊠ 🖵

Ⓐ ▽▽▽ ▽▽▽ **The Oban Inn and OSpa** 🄷

(905) 468-2165. **$150-$410, 7 day notice.** 160 Front St L0S 1J0. Jct Gate St. Ext/int corridors. **Pets:** Accepted.

ⓢⒶⓋⒺ ⊠ 🖵 🍴 ⇌ ⊠

▽▽▽▽ **Old Bank House** Ⓑ Ⓑ

(905) 468-7136. **$149-$249, 28 day notice.** 10 Front St L0S 1J0. Corner of King and Front sts; centre. Int corridors. **Pets:** Accepted.

ⒶⓈⓀ ⊠ ⓩ

Ⓐ ▽▽▽ ▽▽▽ **The Pillar and Post Hotel** Ⓒ Ⓘ

(905) 468-2123. **$150-$550.** 48 John St L0S 1J0. Just n on Hwy 55 (Mississauga St), just e; 13 mi from QEW. Ext/int corridors. **Pets:** Accepted. ⓢⒶⓋⒺ ⊠ 🛢 🖵 🍴 ⇌ ⊠

Ⓐ ▽▽▽ ▽▽▽ **Prince of Wales Hotel** 🄷

(905) 468-3246. **$150-$420.** 6 Picton St L0S 1J0. Jct Picton and King sts; 9 mi (14.4 km) e of jct QEW and Hwy 55, via Hwy 55. Ext/int corridors. **Pets:** Small. $35 daily fee/pet. Designated rooms, service with restrictions, supervision. ⓢⒶⓋⒺ ⊠ 🛢 🖵 🍴 ⇌ ⊠

Ⓐ ▽▽▽ ▽▽▽ **Queen's Landing Hotel** 🄷

(905) 468-2195. **$150-$550.** 155 Byron St L0S 1J0. Just n on King St, just e. Int corridors. **Pets:** Small, dogs only. $35 one-time fee/pet. Designated rooms, supervision. ⓢⒶⓋⒺ ⊠ 🛢 🖵 🍴 ⇌ ⊠

▽▽▽ ▽▽▽ **Shaw Club Hotel and Spa** 🄷 ❀

(905) 468-5711. **$99-$510, 10 day notice.** 92 Picton St L0S 1J0. Jct Wellington St. Int corridors. **Pets:** Dogs only. $25 daily fee/room. Designated rooms, service with restrictions, supervision.

ⒶⓈⓀ ⊠ 🛢 🖵 🍴 ⊠

ST. CATHARINES

Ⓐ ▽▽▽ **Best Western St. Catharines Conference Center** 🄷

(905) 934-8000. **$129-$210.** 2 N Service Rd L2N 4G9. QEW, exit 46 (Lake St), just e. Int corridors. **Pets:** Accepted.

ⒺⒸⓄ ⓢⒶⓋⒺ ⊠ 🛢 🖵 🍴 ⇌ ⊠

Ⓐ ▽▽▽ **Comfort Inn** 🄷

(905) 687-8890. **$89-$150.** 2 Dunlop Dr L2R 1A2. QEW, exit 46 (Lake St); between Lake and Geneva sts. Int corridors. **Pets:** Designated rooms, service with restrictions, supervision.

ⒺⒸⓄ ⓢⒶⓋⒺ ⊠ ⓖⓜ 🛢 🖵

Ⓐ ▽▽▽ **Days Inn St. Catharines Niagara** 🄷

(905) 934-5400. **$89-$289.** 89 Meadowvale Dr L2N 3Z8. QEW, exit 46 (Lake St). Int corridors. **Pets:** Other species. $10 daily fee/pet. Designated rooms, service with restrictions, supervision.

ⓢⒶⓋⒺ ⊠ 🛢 🖵 🍴 ⇌ ⊠

Ⓐ ▽▽▽ **Holiday Inn & Suites Convention Centre** 🄷

(905) 688-2324. **$95-$299.** 327 Ontario St L2R 5L3. QEW, exit 47 (Ontario St), 0.5 mi (0.8 km) s. Int corridors. **Pets:** $10 one-time fee/room. Designated rooms, service with restrictions, crate.

ⓢⒶⓋⒺ ⊠ 🛢 🖵 🍴 ⇌ ⊠

THOROLD

(CAA) ▼▼▼ **Four Points by Sheraton St. Catharines Niagara Suites** H

(905) 984-8484. **Call for rates.** 3530 Schmon Pkwy L2V 4Y6. Hwy 406, exit St. David's Rd W; just s of Brock University. Int corridors. **Pets:** $10 daily fee/room. Designated rooms, service with restrictions, supervision.

[SAVE] [X] [■] [■] [¶] [≈] [X]

END METROPOLITAN AREA

NORTH BAY

(CAA) ▼▼▼ **Best Western North Bay Hotel and Conference Centre** H ✿

(705) 474-5800. **$100-$260.** 700 Lakeshore Dr P1A 2G4. Hwy 11, exit 338, 2.5 mi (4 km) w. Int corridors. **Pets:** Large, other species. Service with restrictions, crate. [ECO] [SAVE] [X] [■] [■] [≈] [X]

(CAA) ▼▼▼▼ **Clarion Resort Pinewood Park** H

(705) 472-0810. **$109-$179.** 201 Pinewood Park Dr P1B 8Z4. Hwy 11, exit 338, just w on Lakeshore Dr, then 0.4 mi (0.7 km) s. Int corridors. **Pets:** Designated rooms, service with restrictions, supervision.

[SAVE] [X] [■] [■] [¶] [≈] [X]

(CAA) ▼▼▼ **Comfort Inn-Airport** H

(705) 476-5400. **$99-$165.** 1200 O'Brien St P1B 9B3. On Hwy 11/17; jct O'Brien St. Int corridors. **Pets:** Medium. Designated rooms, service with restrictions, supervision. [SAVE] [X] [■] [■]

(CAA) ▼▼▼ **Holiday Inn Express Hotel & Suites** H ✿

(705) 476-7700. **$135-$165.** 1325 Seymour St P1B 9V6. Jct Hwy 11/17. Int corridors. **Pets:** Small. Designated rooms, supervision.

[ECO] [SAVE] [X] [■] [■] [≈]

▼▼ **Super 8 North Bay** H

(705) 495-4551. **$100-$140.** 570 Lakeshore Dr P1A 2E6. Hwy 11, exit 338, 2.8 mi (4.5 km) w. Int corridors. **Pets:** Accepted.

[ASK] [X] [■] [■]

(CAA) ▼▼▼ **Travelodge Airport North Bay** H

(705) 495-1133. **$109-$189.** 1525 Seymour St P1B 8G4. Jct Hwy 11/17. Int corridors. **Pets:** Accepted. [ECO] [SAVE] [X] [■] [≈]

(CAA) ▼▼ **Travelodge Lakeshore** H

(705) 472-7171. **$85-$105.** 718 Lakeshore Dr P1A 2G4. Hwy 11, exit 338, 2.5 mi (4 km) w. Int corridors. **Pets:** Other species. Designated rooms, service with restrictions, supervision. [ECO] [SAVE] [X] [■] [■]

OAKVILLE

(CAA) ▼▼▼▼ **Holiday Inn Oakville Centre** H

(905) 842-5000. **$89-$129.** 590 Argus Rd L6J 3J3. QEW, exit 118 (Trafalgar Rd), just s. Int corridors. **Pets:** Accepted.

[ECO] [SAVE] [X] [♿] [■] [■] [¶] [≈] [X]

(CAA) ▼▼▼▼ **Staybridge Suites Oakville Burlington** H ✿

(905) 847-2600. **$135-$252.** 2511 Wyecroft Rd L6L 6P8. QEW, exit 111 (Bronte Rd/Hwy 25), 0.3 mi (0.5 km) s, then just e. Int corridors. **Pets:** Medium. $50 one-time fee/room. Designated rooms, service with restrictions, supervision. [SAVE] [X] [♿] [■] [■] [≈]

ORILLIA

(CAA) ▼▼▼ **Comfort Inn** H

(705) 327-7744. **$108-$122.** 75 Progress Dr L3V 6H1. Hwy 11 N, exit Hwy 12, s on Memorial Ave; corner of Progress Dr and Memorial Ave. Int corridors. **Pets:** Medium. $10 daily fee/room. Designated rooms, service with restrictions, supervision. [ECO] [SAVE] [X] [■] [■]

(CAA) ▼▼▼ **Highwayman Inn & Conference Centre** H

(705) 326-7343. **$79-$129.** 201 Woodside Dr L3V 6T4. Hwy 11, exit Hwy 12 (Coldwater Rd), just e, then just s. Int corridors. **Pets:** Dogs only. Service with restrictions, supervision.

[ECO] [SAVE] [X] [■] [¶] [≈] [X]

OSHAWA

▼▼ **Comfort Inn** H

(905) 434-5000. **$99-$149.** 605 Bloor St W L1J 5Y6. Hwy 401, exit 416 (Park Rd), s to Bloor St, then 0.5 mi (0.8 km) w. Int corridors. **Pets:** Accepted. [ECO] [ASK] [X] [■] [■]

(CAA) ▼▼▼▼ **Holiday Inn Oshawa Whitby Conference Centre** H

(905) 576-5101. **$119-$149.** 1011 Bloor St E L1H 7K6. Hwy 401, exit 419 (Harmony Rd). Int corridors. **Pets:** Large, other species. $25 daily fee/pet. Designated rooms, service with restrictions, crate.

[SAVE] [X] [■] [■] [¶] [≈] [X]

▼▼ **Oshawa Travelodge** H

(905) 436-9500. **Call for rates.** 940 Champlain Ave L1J 7A6. Hwy 401, exit 412 (Thickson Rd N). Int corridors. **Pets:** Accepted.

[ECO] [X] [■] [■] [≈]

OTTAWA METROPOLITAN AREA

OTTAWA

(CAA) ▼▼▼▼ **Albert House Inn** BB

(613) 236-4479. **$125-$180, 3 day notice.** 478 Albert St K1R 5B5. Between Bay St and Bronson Ave; at west end. Int corridors. **Pets:** Accepted. [SAVE] [X]

(CAA) ▼▼▼ **Best Western Barons Hotel & Conference Centre** H

(613) 828-2741. **$140-$163.** 3700 Richmond Rd K2H 5B8. Hwy 417, exit 130, 1.8 mi (2.9 km) s. Int corridors. **Pets:** Small, other species. $20 daily fee/room. Designated rooms, service with restrictions, supervision.

[SAVE] [X] [■] [■] [¶] [≈] [X]

▼▼▼ **Bostonian Executive Suites** H

(613) 594-5757. **$135-$199.** 341 MacLaren St K2P 2E2. Between Bank and O'Connor sts. Int corridors. **Pets:** Accepted. [ASK] [X] [■] [■]

(CAA) ▼▼ ▼▼ **Brookstreet** H

(613) 271-1800. **$149-$499.** 525 Legget Dr K2K 2W2. Hwy 417, exit 138 (March Rd), 2.3 mi (3.7 km) n, just e on Solandt Dr to Legget Dr, then just n. Int corridors. **Pets:** Small. $25 daily fee/pet. Designated rooms, service with restrictions, supervision.

[ECO] [SAVE] [X] [■] [¶] [≈] [X]

(CAA) ▼▼▼ **Cartier Place Suite Hotel** 🅷 ❀
(613) 236-5000. **$149-$239.** 180 Cooper St K2P 2L5. Between Elgin and Cartier sts. Int corridors. **Pets:** Large, other species. $25 daily fee/room. Service with restrictions, crate. (SAVE) ⊠ 🖥 💻 🍴 ➤ ⊠

(CAA) ▼▼ **Comfort Inn** 🅷
(613) 744-2900. **$95-$121.** 1252 Michael St K1J 7T1. Hwy 417, exit 115 (St. Laurent Blvd), just ne. Int corridors. **Pets:** Medium. Service with restrictions, supervision. (ECO) (SAVE) ⊠ 🖥 💻

(CAA) ▼▼▼ **Crowne Plaza Ottawa** 🅷
(613) 237-3600. **$119-$189.** 101 Lyon St K1R 5T9. Entrance at corner of Albert St. Int corridors. **Pets:** Accepted.
(ECO) (SAVE) ⊠ 🖥 💻 🍴 ➤ ⊠

(CAA) ▼▼▼ **Days Inn-Downtown Ottawa** 🅷
(613) 789-5555. **$115-$169.** 319 Rideau St K1N 5Y4. Between Nelson St and King Edward Ave. Ext/int corridors. **Pets:** Accepted.
(ECO) (SAVE) ⊠ 🖥 💻 🍴

(CAA) ▼▼▼ **The Days Inn Ottawa West** 🅷
(613) 726-1717. **$130-$210.** 350 Moodie Dr K2H 8G3. Hwy 417, exit 134, 0.9 mi (1.5 km) s. Int corridors. **Pets:** Accepted.
(ECO) (SAVE) ⊠ 🖥 💻 🍴

(CAA) ▼▼▼ **Delta Ottawa Hotel and Suites** 🅷
(613) 238-6000. **$149-$350.** 361 Queen St K1R 7S9. Corner of Lyon St. Int corridors. **Pets:** Medium, other species. $35 one-time fee/room. Service with restrictions, supervision.
(ECO) (SAVE) ⊠ 🖥 💻 🍴 ➤ ⊠

▼▼ ▼▼ **Extended Stay Deluxe Ottawa Downtown** 🅷
(613) 236-7500. **$129-$149.** 141 Cooper St K2P 0E8. Between Elgin and Cartier sts. Int corridors. **Pets:** Other species. $25 daily fee/room. Designated rooms, service with restrictions, crate.
(ASK) ⊠ 🖥 💻 🍴 ⊠

(CAA) ▼▼▼ ▼▼ **Fairmont Chateau Laurier** 🅷
(613) 241-1414. **$179-$369.** 1 Rideau St K1N 8S7. Just e of Parliament buildings. Int corridors. **Pets:** Accepted.
(ECO) (SAVE) ⊠ 🔊M 🖥 💻 🍴 ➤ ⊠

▼▼▼▼ **Holiday Inn & Suites Ottawa Downtown** 🅷
(613) 238-1331. **$146-$201.** 111 Cooper St K2P 2E3. Corner of Cartier St. Int corridors. **Pets:** Other species. Service with restrictions.
(ECO) (ASK) ⊠ 🖥 💻 🍴

▼▼▼▼ **Hotel Indigo Ottawa** 🅷
(613) 231-6555. **$149-$269.** 123 Metcalfe St K1P 5L9. Corner of Laurier Ave W. Int corridors. **Pets:** Accepted.
(ECO) (ASK) ⊠ 🖥 💻 🍴 ➤ ⊠

(CAA) ▼▼▼ **Les Suites Hotel Ottawa** 🅷
(613) 232-2000. **$149-$259.** 130 Besserer St K1N 9M9. Between Nicholas and Waller sts. Int corridors. **Pets:** $35 daily fee/pet. Designated rooms, service with restrictions, supervision.
(ECO) (SAVE) ⊠ 🔊M 🖥 💻 🍴 ➤ ⊠

▼▼▼▼ **Lord Elgin Hotel** 🅷
(613) 235-3333. **$129-$289.** 100 Elgin St K1P 5K8. Between Laurier Ave and Slater St. Int corridors. **Pets:** Accepted.
(ECO) (ASK) ⊠ 🖥 💻 🍴 ➤ ⊠

(CAA) ▼▼▼ ▼▼ **Marriott Ottawa Hotel** 🅷
(613) 238-1122. **$229-$269.** 100 Kent St K1P 5R7. Corner of Queen St. Int corridors. **Pets:** Service with restrictions, supervision.
(ECO) (SAVE) ⊠ 🖥 💻 🍴 ➤ ⊠

(CAA) ▼▼▼ **Monterey Inn Resort & Conference Centre** 🅷
(613) 288-3500. **$109-$139.** 2259 Prince of Wales Dr K2E 6Z8. 0.5 mi (0.8 km) s of Hunt Club Rd. Ext corridors. **Pets:** $10 daily fee/room. Designated rooms, service with restrictions, crate.
(ECO) (SAVE) ⊠ 🖥 💻 🍴 ➤ ⊠

(CAA) ▼▼▼ **Novotel Ottawa Hotel** 🅷 ❀
(613) 230-3033. **$159-$259.** 33 Nicholas St K1N 9M7. Corner of Daly Ave. Int corridors. **Pets:** Service with restrictions, crate.
(ECO) (SAVE) ⊠ 🖥 💻 🍴 ➤ ⊠

(CAA) ▼▼▼ **Quality Hotel Ottawa, Downtown** 🅷
(613) 789-7511. **$122-$169.** 290 Rideau St K1N 5Y3. Corner of King Edward Ave. Int corridors. **Pets:** Other species. Service with restrictions, crate. (ECO) (SAVE) ⊠ 🖥 💻 🍴

(CAA) ▼▼▼ **Radisson Hotel Ottawa Parliament Hill** 🅷
(613) 236-1133. **$129-$179.** 402 Queen St K1R 5A7. Corner of Bay and Queen sts. Int corridors. **Pets:** Accepted. (SAVE) ⊠ 🖥 💻 🍴

▼▼▼▼ **Residence Inn Ottawa** 🅷
(613) 231-2020. **$197-$241.** 161 Laurier Ave W K1P 5J2. Corner of Elgin St. Int corridors. **Pets:** Accepted. (ECO) ⊠ 🖥 💻 ➤ ⊠

(CAA) ▼▼▼ **Rideau Heights Motor Inn** Ⓜ 🐾
(613) 226-4152. **$99-$129.** 72 Rideau Heights Dr K2E 7A6. Hwy 16 (Prince of Wales Dr), 0.3 mi (0.5 km) n of Hunt Club Rd. Ext corridors. **Pets:** Small. $10 daily fee/room. Designated rooms, service with restrictions, supervision. (SAVE) ⊠ 🖥 💻

(CAA) ▼▼▼▼ **Sheraton Ottawa Hotel** 🅷
(613) 238-1500. **$119-$480.** 150 Albert St K1P 5G2. Corner of O'Connor St. Int corridors. **Pets:** Accepted. (ECO) (SAVE) ⊠ 🖥 💻 🍴 ➤

(CAA) ▼▼▼▼ **Southway Inn of Ottawa** 🅷
(613) 737-0811. **$155-$170.** 2431 Bank St K1V 8R9. On Hwy 31; jct Hunt Club Rd. Int corridors. **Pets:** Accepted.
(SAVE) ⊠ 🖥 💻 🍴 ➤ ⊠

▼▼▼▼ **Travelodge Ottawa Downtown Doral** 🅷
(613) 230-8055. **$125-$175.** 486 Albert St K1R 5B5. Between Bay St and Bronson Ave. Int corridors. **Pets:** Accepted.
(ECO) (ASK) ⊠ 🖥 💻

(CAA) ▼▼▼ **Travelodge Ottawa East** 🅷
(613) 745-1133. **$109-$149.** 1486 Innes Rd K1B 3V5. Hwy 417, exit 112 (Innes Rd), just e. Int corridors. **Pets:** Accepted.
(ECO) (SAVE) ⊠ 🖥 💻 🍴 ➤

(CAA) ▼▼▼ **Travelodge Ottawa Hotel & Conference Centre** 🅷
(613) 722-7600. **$129-$149.** 1376 Carling Ave K1Z 7L5. Hwy 417, exit 124, just s. Int corridors. **Pets:** Designated rooms, service with restrictions, supervision. (ECO) (SAVE) ⊠ 🖥 💻 🍴 ⊠

(CAA) ▼▼▼ **Webb's Motel** Ⓜ
(613) 728-1881. **$85-$125.** 1705 Carling Ave K2A 1C8. Hwy 417, exit 126, 0.3 mi (0.5 km) n on Maitland Ave, then 0.3 mi (0.5 km) e. Ext/int corridors. **Pets:** Service with restrictions, crate. (SAVE) ⊠ 🖥 💻

▼▼ ▼▼ **WelcomINNS** 🅷 ❀
(613) 748-7800. **$110-$130.** 1220 Michael St K1J 7T1. Hwy 417, exit 115 (St. Laurent Blvd), just ne. Int corridors. **Pets:** Small, dogs only. $15 daily fee/pet. Designated rooms, service with restrictions, crate.
(ECO) (ASK) ⊠ 🖥 💻

(CAA) ▼▼ ▼▼ The Westin Ottawa **H**
(613) 560-7000. **$189-$429.** 11 Colonel By Dr K1N 9H4. Corner of Rideau St. Int corridors. **Pets:** Accepted.
ECO SAVE X H 💻 ¶ ≈ 🚫

END METROPOLITAN AREA

OWEN SOUND
▼▼ ▼▼ Comfort Inn **H** ❀
(519) 371-5500. **$81-$180.** 955 9th Ave E N4K 6N4. Jct Hwy 6, 10, 21 and 26. Int corridors. **Pets:** Other species. $10 one-time fee/room. Service with restrictions, supervision. ECO ASK X H 💻

(CAA) ▼▼ ▼▼ Days Inn and Conference Centre **H**
(519) 376-1551. **$109-$149, 7 day notice.** 950 6th St E N4K 1H1. Jct Hwy 6 and 10. Int corridors. **Pets:** Other species. $20 one-time fee/room. Service with restrictions, crate. ECO SAVE X H 💻 ¶ ≈ 🚫

▼▼ ▼▼ Owen Sound Inn **H**
(519) 371-3011. **Call for rates.** 485 9th Ave E N4K 3E2. Jct Hwy 6, 10, 26 and 21; follow Hwy 6 and 10, 0.6 mi (1 km) s. Int corridors. **Pets:** Accepted. X H 💻

PARRY SOUND
▼▼ ▼▼ Comfort Inn **H**
(705) 746-6221. **$105-$160.** 120 Bowes St P2A 2L7. Hwy 69, exit 224 (Bowes St), just w. Int corridors. **Pets:** Accepted.
ECO ASK X H 💻

▼▼ ▼▼ Microtel Inn & Suites **H**
(705) 746-2700. **$99-$169.** 292 Louisa St P2A 0A1. Hwy 69, exit 224 (Bowes St), just w. Int corridors. **Pets:** Accepted. ASK X H 💻

PEMBROKE
▼▼ Colonial Fireside Inn **M**
(613) 732-3623. **$59-$120.** 1350 Pembroke St W K8A 7A3. 2.7 mi (4.3 km) n on Forest Lea Rd (CR 42) from jct Hwy 17, just e. Ext corridors. **Pets:** Accepted. ASK X H 💻 ≈

▼▼ ▼▼ Comfort Inn **H** ❀
(613) 735-1057. **$137-$164.** 959 Pembroke St E K8A 3M3. 1 mi (1.6 km) e of town centre. Int corridors. **Pets:** Other species. Designated rooms, service with restrictions, supervision. ECO ASK X H 💻

PETAWAWA
(CAA) ▼▼ ▼▼ Petawawa River Inn & Suites **H** ❀
(613) 687-4686. **$110-$200.** 3520 Petawawa Blvd K8H 1W9. Hwy 17, exit Paquette Rd, 1.5 mi (2.4 km) e, then just s. Int corridors. **Pets:** $10 daily fee/pet. Designated rooms, service with restrictions, supervision.
ECO SAVE X H 💻 ¶

PETERBOROUGH
▼▼ ▼▼ King Bethune House, Guest House & Spa **BB**
(705) 743-4101. **$115-$399, 14 day notice.** 270 King St K9J 2S2. From Charlotte and George sts (clock tower), 1 blk s on George St to King St, then just w. Int corridors. **Pets:** Other species. $10 daily fee/pet. No service, supervision. X H 💻

▼▼ ▼▼ Motel 6–Peterborough **H**
(705) 748-0550. **$69-$109.** 133 Landsdowne St E K9J 7P7. 1.6 mi (2.6 km) e of The Parkway. Int corridors. **Pets:** Other species. Service with restrictions, supervision. ECO ASK X H

(CAA) ▼▼ ▼▼ Quality Inn **H** ❀
(705) 748-6801. **$70, 3 day notice.** 1074 Landsdowne St W K9J 1Z9. 1.9 mi (3 km) from jct Hwy 115. Int corridors. **Pets:** Other species. Service with restrictions. ECO SAVE X H 💻

(CAA) ▼▼ ▼▼ Super 8 Peterborough **H** ❀
(705) 876-8898. **$90-$125.** 1257 Lansdowne St W K9J 7M2. 0.3 mi (0.5 km) from jct Hwy 28. Int corridors. **Pets:** Other species. $25 one-time fee/room. Designated rooms, service with restrictions.
ECO SAVE X H 💻 ≈

PICKERING
▼▼ ▼▼ Comfort Inn **H**
(905) 831-6200. **$89-$135.** 533 Kingston Rd L1V 3N7. Hwy 401, exit 394 N (White's Rd) to Hwy 2, 0.3 mi (0.5 km) w. Int corridors.
Pets: Accepted. ECO ASK X H 💻

PLANTAGENET
▼▼ ▼▼ Motel de Champlain **M**
(613) 673-5220. **$64-$110.** 5999 Hwy 17 K0B 1L0. Jct CR 9. Ext/int corridors. **Pets:** Other species. $20 daily fee/pet. No service, supervision.
ASK X H ¶

PORT CARLING
▼▼ ▼▼ Delta Sherwood Inn **H**
(705) 765-3131. **Call for rates.** 1090 Sherwood Rd P0B 1J0. Hwy 169, just n of jct Hwy 118; on Lake Joseph. Ext/int corridors. **Pets:** Accepted.
ECO X H 💻 ¶ 🚫

PORT HOPE
▼▼ ▼▼ Comfort Inn **H**
(905) 885-7000. **$90-$170.** Hwy 401 & 28 L1A 3Z3. Hwy 401, exit 464, just n. Int corridors. **Pets:** Accepted. ASK X H 💻

PROVIDENCE BAY
(CAA) ▼▼ Huron Sands Motel **M**
(705) 377-4616. **$80-$150, 3 day notice.** 5216 Hwy 551 P0P 1T0. In Providence Bay; on Hwy 551; centre. Ext corridors. **Pets:** Other species. $10 daily fee/room. Service with restrictions, supervision.
SAVE X H 🗂

RENFREW
(CAA) ▼▼ ▼▼ Best Western Renfrew Inn & Conference Centre **H**
(613) 432-8109. **$120-$190.** 760 Gibbons Rd K7V 4A2. Hwy 17, exit O'Brien Rd, just s to Wrangler Rd, then just w. Int corridors. **Pets:** $15 daily fee/pet. Service with restrictions, supervision.
SAVE X H 💻 ¶ ≈

▼▼ The Rocky Mountain Lodge **M**
(613) 432-5801. **Call for rates.** 409 Stewart St N K7V 1Y4. Hwy 17, exit Bruce St, 1.9 mi (3.1 km) s. Ext corridors. **Pets:** Accepted.
X H 💻 ¶

ROSSPORT
▼▼ ▼▼ The Willows Inn Bed & Breakfast **BB**
(807) 824-3389. **$100-$110, 10 day notice.** 116 Main St P0T 2R0. Centre. Int corridors. **Pets:** Dogs only. $15 one-time fee/room. Designated rooms, supervision. X 🎯 🗂

ST. THOMAS
(CAA) ▼▼ ▼▼ Comfort Inn **H**
(519) 633-4082. **$90-$140, 7 day notice.** 100 Centennial Ave N5R 5B2. On Hwy 3, 4.1 mi (6.5 km) e. Int corridors. **Pets:** Medium, other species. $20 one-time fee/room. Service with restrictions, supervision.
SAVE X H 💻

SARNIA

▼▼▼▼ Comfort Inn 🅷

(519) 383-6767. **$90-$170.** 815 Mara St N7V 1X4. Jct Church St. Int corridors. **Pets:** Accepted. (A$K) (✕) 🍴 💻 📺

▼▼▼▼ Holiday Inn Sarnia-Point Edward Hotel & Conference Centre 🅷

(519) 336-4130. **$115-$230.** 1498 Venetian Blvd N7T 7W6. East of Bluewater Bridge. Int corridors. **Pets:** Other species. $25 daily fee/room. Designated rooms, service with restrictions, supervision.
🅴🅲🅾 (A$K) (✕) 🍴 💻 📺 🍴 🏊 (✕)

▼▼▼ Super 8-Sarnia 🅷

(519) 337-3767. **$95-$105.** 420 Christina St N N7T 5W1. Between Exmouth and London rds. Ext/int corridors. **Pets:** Accepted.
(A$K) (✕) ♿M 🍴 💻 🍴

SAULT STE. MARIE

▼ Adams Motel Ⓜ

(705) 254-4345. **$69-$99.** 647 Great Northern Rd P6B 5A1. 2.8 mi (4.4 km) n on Hwy 17B. Ext corridors. **Pets:** Accepted. (A$K) (✕) 🍴 💻

ⒸⒶⒶ ▼▼▼▼ Algoma's Water Tower Inn 🅷

(705) 949-8111. **$125-$195, 7 day notice.** 360 Great Northern Rd P6B 4Z7. Jct Hwy 17 and Second Line. Int corridors. **Pets:** Accepted.
🅴🅲🅾 (SAVE) (✕) 🍴 💻 🍴 🏊 (✕)

▼▼▼ Ambassador Motel Ⓜ

(705) 759-6199. **$59-$89.** 1275 Great Northern Rd P6A 5K7. 4 mi (6.4 km) n on Hwy 17. Ext corridors. **Pets:** Accepted.
(✕) 🍴 💻 🏊 (✕)

ⒸⒶⒶ ▼ Bel-Air Motel Ⓜ

(705) 945-7950. **$55-$99.** 398 Pim St P6B 2V1. 1.3 mi (2 km) n on Hwy 17B. Ext corridors. **Pets:** $5 daily fee/pet, $5 one-time fee/pet. No service.
(SAVE) (✕) 🍴 💻

ⒸⒶⒶ ▼ Catalina Motel Ⓜ

(705) 945-9260. **$95-$132.** 259 Great Northern Rd P6B 4Z2. 2 mi (3.2 km) n on Hwy 17B. Ext corridors. **Pets:** No service, crate.
(SAVE) (✕) 🍴 💻

ⒸⒶⒶ ▼▼▼ City Centre Travelodge 🅷

(705) 759-1400. **$99-$139.** 332 Bay St P6A 1X1. Between Elgin and Bruce sts; downtown; opposite Station Mall. Int corridors. **Pets:** Medium. Designated rooms, service with restrictions, supervision.
🅴🅲🅾 (SAVE) (✕) 🍴 💻 🍴

ⒸⒶⒶ ▼▼▼ Comfort Inn 🅷

(705) 759-8000. **$110-$159.** 333 Great Northern Rd P6B 4Z8. 2.3 mi (3.6 km) n on Hwy 17B. Int corridors. **Pets:** Medium. $10 daily fee/pet. Designated rooms, service with restrictions, supervision.
🅴🅲🅾 (SAVE) (✕) 🍴 💻

▼▼▼ Glenview Cottages 🅲🅰 🐾

(705) 759-3436. **$109-$160.** 2611 Great Northern Rd P6A 5K7. 6 mi (9.6 km) n on Hwy 17. Ext corridors. **Pets:** $10 daily fee/room. Designated rooms, service with restrictions, crate. (A$K) (✕) 🍴 💻 🏊 (✕)

▼▼ Holiday Motel Ⓜ

(705) 759-8608. **$55-$75.** 435 Trunk Rd P6A 3T1. On Hwy 17, just e of jct Hwy 17B. Ext corridors. **Pets:** Other species. Service with restrictions, supervision. (✕) 🍴 💻

ⒸⒶⒶ ▼ Northlander Motel Ⓜ

(705) 254-6452. **$55-$80.** 243 Great Northern Rd P6B 4Z2. 1.9 mi (3 km) n on Hwy 17B. Ext corridors. **Pets:** Other species. Service with restrictions, supervision. (SAVE) (✕) 🍴 💻

▼ Satelite Motel Ⓜ

(705) 759-2897. **$55-$95, 5 day notice.** 248 Great Northern Rd P6B 4Z6. 1.9 mi (3 km) n on Hwy 17B. Ext corridors. **Pets:** Accepted.
(A$K) (✕) 🍴 💻

ⒸⒶⒶ ▼ Skyline Motel Ⓜ

(705) 942-1240. **$65-$85, 5 day notice.** 232 Great Northern Rd P6B 4Z5. 1.9 mi (3 km) n on Hwy 17B. Ext corridors. **Pets:** Accepted.
(SAVE) (✕) 🍴 💻

▼▼▼ Sleep Inn 🅷

(705) 253-7533. **$77-$108.** 727 Bay St P6A 6Y3. Between East and Church sts; downtown. Int corridors. **Pets:** Accepted.
(A$K) (✕) 🍴 💻 (✕)

ⒸⒶⒶ ▼▼▼ Super 8 🅷

(705) 254-6441. **$75-$135.** 184 Great Northern Rd P6B 4Z3. 1.3 mi (2 km) n on Hwy 17B. Int corridors. **Pets:** Other species. $15 one-time fee/room. Designated rooms, service with restrictions, supervision.
(SAVE) (✕) 🍴 💻

▼ Villa Inn Motel Ⓜ

(705) 942-2424. **Call for rates.** 724 Great Northern Rd P6B 5A3. 2.9 mi (4.6 km) n on Hwy 17B. Ext corridors. **Pets:** Accepted. (✕) 🍴 💻

SIMCOE

ⒸⒶⒶ ▼▼▼ Best Western Little River Inn 🅷

(519) 426-2125. **$100-$110.** 203 Queensway W N3Y 2M9. Jct Hwy 24, just w on Hwy 3. Int corridors. **Pets:** Large. Service with restrictions, supervision. (SAVE) (✕) 🍴 💻 🍴 🏊

▼▼▼ Comfort Inn 🅷

(519) 426-2611. **$96-$136.** 85 Queensway E N3Y 4M5. 0.3 mi (0.5 km) e on Hwy 3. Int corridors. **Pets:** Medium, other species. Designated rooms, service with restrictions, supervision. 🅴🅲🅾 (A$K) (✕) 🍴 💻

SOUTH BAYMOUTH

ⒸⒶⒶ ▼ Huron Motor Lodge Ⓜ

(705) 859-3131. **$99-$155.** 24 Water St N P0P 1Z0. In South Baymouth; centre. Ext corridors. **Pets:** Medium. $10 daily fee/pet. Designated rooms, service with restrictions, supervision. (SAVE) (✕) 🍴 🏊 🅰🅲 🇿

STRATFORD

▼▼▼▼ Arden Park Hotel 🅷

(519) 275-2936. **$139-$199.** 552 Ontario St (Hwy 7 & 8) N5A 3J3. Jct Romeo St. Int corridors. **Pets:** Accepted. (✕) ♿M 🍴 💻 🍴 🏊

▼▼▼▼ The River Garden Inn 🅷

(519) 271-4650. **$95-$213.** 10 Romeo St N N5A 5M7. Just n of Ontario St. Ext/int corridors. **Pets:** Accepted. (✕) 🍴 💻 🏊

STURGEON FALLS

▼▼▼ Comfort Inn 🅷

(705) 753-5665. **$80-$130.** 11 Front St P2B 3L3. On Hwy 17 at western approach to town. Int corridors. **Pets:** Small. Designated rooms, service with restrictions, supervision. (A$K) (✕) 🍴 💻 🏊

SUDBURY

ⒸⒶⒶ ▼▼▼ Best Western Downtown Sudbury Centre-Ville 🅷

(705) 673-7801. **$110-$115, 7 day notice.** 151 Larch St P3E 1C3. Just w of Paris St; centre. Int corridors. **Pets:** Accepted.
(SAVE) (✕) 🍴 💻 🍴

ⒸⒶⒶ ▼▼▼ Comfort Inn 🅷

(705) 522-1101. **$118-$134.** 2171 Regent St P3E 5V3. Trans-Canada Hwy 17, exit Hwy 69/RR 46, 1.8 mi (2.8 km) n. Int corridors.
Pets: Accepted. 🅴🅲🅾 (SAVE) (✕) 🍴 💻

ⒸⒶⒶ ▼▼▼ Comfort Inn East 🅷 🐾

(705) 560-4502. **$70-$155.** 440 Second Ave N P3B 4A4. Just s of Kingsway Rd. Int corridors. **Pets:** Medium, other species. $18 daily fee/pet. Service with restrictions, supervision. 🅴🅲🅾 (SAVE) (✕) ♿M 🍴 💻

▼▼ Days Inn-Sudbury 🅷 ❄

(705) 674-7517. **$115-$150.** 117 Elm St P3C 1T3. Corner of Lorne St; downtown. Int corridors. **Pets:** Medium. $20 one-time fee/pet. Designated rooms, service with restrictions, supervision.

ECO ASK ⊠ 🛏 📺 ⑪ 🌊 ⊠

▼▼▼▼ Holiday Inn Hotel Sudbury 🅷

(705) 522-3000. **$124-$154.** 1696 Regent St P3E 3Z8. Trans-Canada Hwy 17, exit Hwy 69/RR 46, 2.4 mi (3.9 km) n. Int corridors. **Pets:** Medium. Designated rooms, service with restrictions.

SAVE ⊠ 🛏 📺 ⑪ 🌊 ⊠

▼▼▼▼ Homewood Suites by Hilton Sudbury 🅷

(705) 523-8100. **$119-$169.** 2270 Regent St P3E 0B4. Trans-Canada Hwy 17, exit Hwy 69/RR 46, 1.6 mi (2.5 km) n. Int corridors. **Pets:** Accepted. ⊠ &M 🛏 📺 ⊠

▼▼▼ Quality Inn & Conference Centre 🅷 ❄

(705) 675-1273. **$89-$149.** 390 Elgin St S P3B 1B1. 0.6 mi (0.9 km) s on Paris St from jct Kingsway Rd and Elm St. Int corridors. **Pets:** Medium. $15 one-time fee/room. Designated rooms, service with restrictions, supervision. ECO SAVE ⊠ 🛏 📺 ⑪ 🌊

▼▼▼▼ Radisson Hotel Sudbury Downtown 🅷

(705) 675-1123. **$135-$175.** 85 Ste. Anne Rd P3E 4S4. Jct Notre Dame Ave; downtown. Int corridors. **Pets:** Medium. $30 one-time fee/room. Designated rooms, service with restrictions, supervision.

SAVE ⊠ 🛏 📺 ⑪ 🌊

▼▼▼▼ Travelodge Hotel Sudbury 🅷 ❄

(705) 522-1100. **$109-$189.** 1401 Paris St P3E 3B6. Trans-Canada Hwy 17, exit Hwy 69/RR 46, 2 mi (3.2 km) n on Regent St, then 0.9 mi (1.5 km) e. Int corridors. **Pets:** Other species. Designated rooms, service with restrictions, crate. ECO SAVE ⊠ 🛏 📺 ⑪ 🌊

THESSALON

▼ Carolyn Beach Motor Inn 🅼

(705) 842-3330. **$92-$135.** 1 Lakeside Dr P0R 1L0. On Hwy 17B, just s of jct Hwy 17. Ext corridors. **Pets:** $12 daily fee/pet. Service with restrictions, supervision. SAVE ⊠ 🛏 📺 ⑪ ⊠

THUNDER BAY

▼▼▼ Best Western Crossroads Motor Inn 🅷

(807) 577-4241. **$130.** 655 W Arthur St P7E 5R6. Just e of jct Hwy 61. Int corridors. **Pets:** Accepted. SAVE ⊠ 🛏 📺

▼▼▼ Best Western Nor'Wester Resort Hotel 🅷 ❄

(807) 473-9123. **$115-$160, 3 day notice.** 2080 Hwy 61 P7J 1B8. On Hwy 61 at Loch Lomond Rd. Int corridors. **Pets:** $20 one-time fee/room. Designated rooms, service with restrictions, crate.

SAVE ⊠ 🛏 📺 ⑪ 🌊 ⊠

▼▼ Comfort Inn 🅼 ❄

(807) 475-3155. **$80-$135.** 660 W Arthur St P7E 5R8. Just e of jct Hwy 61. Int corridors. **Pets:** Other species. Service with restrictions, supervision. ECO SAVE ⊠ 🛏 📺

▼▼ Super 8 🅷

(807) 344-2612. **$80-$125.** 439 Memorial Ave P7B 3Y6. Jct Hwy 11, 17 and Harbour Expwy, 1.9 mi (3 km) e on Harbour Expwy, 1.3 mi (2 km) n. Int corridors. **Pets:** Accepted. SAVE ⊠ 🛏 📺

▼▼▼ Victoria Inn Hotel & Convention Centre 🅷

(807) 577-8481. **$118-$142.** 555 W Arthur St P7E 5R5. 0.5 mi (0.8 km) e of jct Hwy 11B, 17B and 61 (western access to town). Int corridors. **Pets:** Accepted. ASK ⊠ 🛏 📺 ⑪ 🌊 ⊠

TILLSONBURG

▼▼ Howard Johnson/Tillsonburg 🅷

(519) 842-7366. **$110-$140.** 92 Simcoe St N4G 2J1. Hwy 19, just e. Int corridors. **Pets:** $10 daily fee/pet. Supervision.

ECO ASK ⊠ 🛏 📺 ⑪

TIMMINS

▼▼ Comfort Inn 🅷

(705) 264-9474. **$92-$102.** 939 Algonquin Blvd E P4N 7J5. Hwy 101, 0.3 mi (0.5 km) e of Hwy 655. Int corridors. **Pets:** Accepted.

ECO ASK ⊠ 🛏 📺

▼▼ Travelodge 🅷

(705) 360-1122. **Call for rates.** 1136 Riverside Dr P4R 1A2. Hwy 101, 2.8 mi (4.4 km) w on Hwy 655. Int corridors. **Pets:** Accepted.

ECO ⊠ 🛏 📺

TOBERMORY

▼▼ Coach House Inn 🅼

(519) 596-2361. **$59-$120.** 7189 Hwy 6 N0H 2R0. Hwy 6, 1.2 mi (2 km) s of ferry docks. Ext corridors. **Pets:** Accepted. ⊠ 🛏 🌊 ⊠ ⊠

TORONTO METROPOLITAN AREA

MARKHAM

▼▼▼ Comfort Inn 🅷

(905) 477-6077. **$89-$129.** 8330 Woodbine Ave L3R 2N8. Hwy 401, exit 375, 5.6 mi (9 km) n; Hwy 404, exit Hwy 7, just e, then s. Int corridors. **Pets:** Accepted. ASK ⊠ 🛏 📺 🌊 ⊠

▼▼▼ Delta Markham 🅷 ❄

(905) 477-2010. **$99-$199.** 50 E Valhalla Dr L3R 0A3. Hwy 404, exit Hwy 7, then e. Int corridors. **Pets:** Medium, other species. $35 one-time fee/room. Service with restrictions, crate.

ECO ASK ⊠ 🛏 📺 ⑪ 🌊 ⊠

▼▼▼▼ Hilton Suites Toronto/Markham Conference Centre & Spa 🅷 ❄

(905) 470-8500. **$119-$239.** 8500 Warden Ave L6G 1A5. Hwy 404, exit Hwy 7, 2 mi (3.2 km) e. Int corridors. **Pets:** Medium. $75 one-time fee/room. Service with restrictions.

ECO SAVE ⊠ 🛏 📺 ⑪ 🌊 ⊠

▼▼▼ Homewood Suites by Hilton Toronto/Markham 🅷

(905) 477-4663. **$109-$159.** 50 Bodrington Ct L6G 0A9. Hwy 407, exit 84 (Woodbine Ave), just ne. Int corridors. **Pets:** Accepted.

⊠ &M 🛏 📺 🌊

▼▼▼ Howard Johnson Hotel Toronto-Markham 🅷

(905) 479-5000. **$99-$169.** 555 Cochrane Dr L3R 8E3. Hwy 404 N, exit Hwy 7 E to E Valhalla Dr. Int corridors. **Pets:** Accepted.

ECO SAVE ⊠ 🛏 📺 ⑪ 🌊 ⊠

▼▼▼ Residence Inn by Marriott Toronto-Markham 🅷

(905) 707-7933. **$143-$175.** 55 Minthorn Blvd L3T 7N5. Hwy 404, exit Hwy 7, 0.7 mi (1.1 km) w. Int corridors. **Pets:** Other species. $100 one-time fee/pet. Service with restrictions, supervision.

⊠ 🛏 📺 🌊 ⊠

▼▼▼ Staybridge Suites Toronto-Markham 🅷

(905) 771-9333. **$124-$239.** 355 S Park Rd L3T 7W2. Hwy 404, exit Hwy 7, 0.9 mi (1.4 km) w, 0.3 mi (0.5 km) s on Commerce Valley Dr W, then just e. Int corridors. **Pets:** Other species. $75 one-time fee/pet. Service with restrictions. ASK ⊠ 🛏 📺 🌊

RICHMOND HILL

▼▼▼ Holiday Inn Express & Suites Toronto-Markham 🅷

(905) 695-5990. **$98-$143.** 10 E Pearce St L4B 0A8. Just n of jct Leslie and Hwy 7. Int corridors. **Pets:** Medium. $50 one-time fee/room. Designated rooms, service with restrictions, supervision.

ECO SAVE ⊠ &M 🛏 📺 🌊

(CAA) ▼▼▼ ▼▼▼ **Sheraton Parkway Toronto North Hotel, Suites & Conference Centre** 🄷
(905) 881-2121. **Call for rates.** 600 Hwy 7 E L4B 1B2. Hwy 404, exit 27, 0.6 mi (1 km) w. Int corridors. **Pets:** Accepted.
ⒺⒸⓄ ⓈⒶⓋⒺ ☒ 🛏 🖵 🍴 🏊 ☒

TORONTO

(CAA) ▼▼▼ ▼▼▼ **Best Western Roehampton Hotel & Suites** 🄷
(416) 487-5101. **$110-$160.** 808 Mt. Pleasant Rd M4P 2L2. Just n of Eglinton Ave. Int corridors. **Pets:** Small. $50 one-time fee/room. Service with restrictions, supervision. ⓈⒶⓋⒺ ☒ 🛏 🖵 🍴 🏊

▼▼ ▼▼ **Carlingview Airport Inn** 🄷
(416) 675-3303. **$95.** 221 Carlingview Dr M9W 5E8. QEW, exit Hwy 427 N to Dixon Rd E, 0.6 mi (1 km) to Carlingview Dr, then just s. Ext/int corridors. **Pets:** Medium. $30 one-time fee/room. Designated rooms, service with restrictions, supervision. ⒺⒸⓄ ⒶⓈⓀ ☒ 🛏 🖵 🍴

(CAA) ▼▼ **Comfort Inn** 🄷
(416) 736-4700. **$90-$109.** 66 Norfinch Dr M3N 1X1. Hwy 400, exit Finch Ave E, just n. Int corridors. **Pets:** Accepted.
ⒺⒸⓄ ⓈⒶⓋⒺ ☒ 🛏 🖵

(CAA) ▼▼▼ **Cosmopolitan Toronto Hotel & Spa** 🄷
(416) 350-2000. **$179-$460.** 8 Colborne St M5E 1E1. Between King and Wellington sts. Int corridors. **Pets:** Accepted.
ⒺⒸⓄ ⓈⒶⓋⒺ ☒ 🛏 🖵 🍴

(CAA) ▼▼▼ **Crowne Plaza Toronto Airport** 🄷
(416) 675-1234. **$99-$189.** 33 Carlson Ct M9W 6H5. Just w of jct Hwy 27, n of Dixon Rd. Int corridors. **Pets:** Accepted.
ⒺⒸⓄ ⓈⒶⓋⒺ ☒ 🛏 🖵 🍴 🏊 ☒

(CAA) ▼▼▼ **Delta Chelsea Hotel** 🄷
(416) 595-1975. **$119-$199.** 33 Gerrard St W M5G 1Z4. Just w of Yonge St; just s of College St. Int corridors. **Pets:** Accepted.
ⒺⒸⓄ ⓈⒶⓋⒺ ☒ 🛏 🖵 🍴 🏊 ☒

▼▼▼▼ **Delta Toronto East** 🄷
(416) 299-1500. **$119-$299.** 2035 Kennedy Rd M1T 3G2. Just ne of jct Hwy 401 and Kennedy Rd, exit 379. Int corridors. **Pets:** Medium. $30 one-time fee/room. Designated rooms, service with restrictions, supervision. ⒺⒸⓄ ⒶⓈⓀ ☒ 🛏 🖵 🍴 🏊 ☒

(CAA) ▼▼▼ ▼▼▼ **Doubletree by Hilton Toronto Airport** 🄷
(416) 244-1711. **$89-$219.** 655 Dixon Rd M9W 1J3. Jct Hwy 27 N, just w of jct Hwy 401. Int corridors. **Pets:** Accepted.
ⓈⒶⓋⒺ ☒ ⒻⓂ 🛏 🖵 🍴 🏊 ☒

(CAA) ▼▼▼ ▼▼▼ **The Fairmont Royal York** 🄷
(416) 368-2511. **$189-$389.** 100 Front St W M5J 1E3. QEW/Gardiner Expwy, exit n on York or Bay sts; entrance on Wellington St. Int corridors. **Pets:** $25 daily fee/pet. Service with restrictions, supervision.
ⒺⒸⓄ ⓈⒶⓋⒺ ☒ ⒻⓂ 🛏 🖵 🍴 🏊 ☒

(CAA) ▼▼ ▼▼▼ **Four Seasons Hotel** 🄷
(416) 964-0411. **$365-$3900.** 21 Avenue Rd M5R 2G1. Corner of Avenue Rd and Cumberland Ave. Int corridors. **Pets:** Accepted.
ⓈⒶⓋⒺ ☒ 🛏 🖵 🍴 🏊 ☒

▼▼ ▼▼ **Gloucester Square Inns of Toronto** 🄱🄱
(416) 966-0013. **Call for rates.** 512-514 Jarvis St M4Y 2H6. Jct Gloucester St. Int corridors. **Pets:** Accepted. ☒

(CAA) ▼▼ ▼▼ **Hilton Toronto** 🄷
(416) 869-3456. **$209-$319.** 145 Richmond St W M5H 2L2. Jct University Ave. Int corridors. **Pets:** Accepted.
ⒺⒸⓄ ⓈⒶⓋⒺ ☒ 🛏 🖵 🍴 🏊 ☒

(CAA) ▼▼ ▼▼ **Holiday Inn Express Toronto Downtown** 🄷
(416) 367-5555. **$119-$189.** 111 Lombard St M5C 2T9. Gardiner Expwy, exit Jarvis St, 0.6 mi (1 km) n, then just w; between Adelaide and Richmond sts; Int corridors. **Pets:** Medium. Service with restrictions, supervision. ⒺⒸⓄ ⓈⒶⓋⒺ ☒ 🛏 🖵

(CAA) ▼▼ ▼▼ **Holiday Inn Express Toronto-North York** 🄷
(416) 665-3500. **$99-$139.** 30 Norfinch Dr M3N 1X1. Hwy 400, exit Finch Ave E. Int corridors. **Pets:** $25 daily fee/room. Service with restrictions, supervision. ⒺⒸⓄ ⓈⒶⓋⒺ ☒ ⒻⓂ 🛏 🖵

(CAA) ▼▼ ▼▼ **Hotel Indigo** 🄷
(416) 637-7000. **$99-$169.** 135 Carlingview Dr M9W 5E7. Just n of Dixon Rd. Int corridors. **Pets:** Accepted.
ⓈⒶⓋⒺ ☒ 🛏 🖵 🍴 🏊 ☒

▼▼ ▼▼ **Hotel Le Germain Toronto** 🄷 🐾
(416) 345-9500. **$235-$2500.** 30 Mercer St M5V 1H3. Between John St and Blue Jays Way. Int corridors. **Pets:** Other species. $35 daily fee/room. Service with restrictions, crate. ☒ ⒻⓂ 🖵 🍴

(CAA) ▼▼ ▼▼ **InterContinental Toronto Centre** 🄷 🐾
(416) 597-1400. **$229-$279.** 225 Front St W M5V 2X3. Between Spadina and University aves. Int corridors. **Pets:** Medium. $50 one-time fee/room. Service with restrictions, crate. ⒺⒸⓄ ⓈⒶⓋⒺ ☒ 🛏 🖵 🍴 🏊 ☒

(CAA) ▼▼ ▼▼ **InterContinental Toronto Yorkville** 🄷 🐾
(416) 960-5200. **$195-$605.** 220 Bloor St W M5S 1T8. Just w of Avenue Rd. Int corridors. **Pets:** $25 daily fee/room, $50 one-time fee/room. Designated rooms, supervision. ⒺⒸⓄ ⓈⒶⓋⒺ ☒ 🛏 🖵 🍴 🏊 ☒

(CAA) ▼▼ ▼▼ **Le Meridien King Edward Hotel** 🄷
(416) 863-9700. **$199-$425.** 37 King St E M5C 1E9. Just e of Yonge St. Int corridors. **Pets:** Accepted. ⓈⒶⓋⒺ ☒ 🛏 🍴

(CAA) ▼▼ ▼▼ **Metropolitan Hotel** 🄷
(416) 977-5000. **$125-$285.** 108 Chestnut St M5G 1R3. Just s of Dundas St. Int corridors. **Pets:** Accepted.
ⓈⒶⓋⒺ ☒ 🛏 🖵 🍴 🏊 ☒

▼▼ ▼▼ **Montecassino Hotel & Event Venue** 🄷
(416) 630-8100. **$105-$145.** 3710 Chesswood Dr M3J 2W4. Jct Sheppard Ave. Int corridors. **Pets:** Accepted. ⒶⓈⓀ ☒ 🛏 🖵

(CAA) ▼▼ ▼▼ **Novotel Toronto Centre** 🄷 🐾
(416) 367-8900. **$125-$145.** 45 The Esplanade M5E 1W2. Just ne of Gardiner Expwy via Yonge St. Int corridors. **Pets:** Medium. Service with restrictions, supervision. ⒺⒸⓄ ⓈⒶⓋⒺ ☒ 🛏 🖵 🍴 🏊 ☒

(CAA) ▼▼ ▼▼ **Novotel Toronto North York** 🄷
(416) 733-2929. **$145-$335.** 3 Park Home Ave M2N 6L3. Hwy 401, exit Yonge St, 1.1 mi (1.7 km) n, then just w. Int corridors. **Pets:** Small, other species. Service with restrictions, supervision.
ⒺⒸⓄ ⓈⒶⓋⒺ ☒ 🛏 🖵 🍴

(CAA) ▼▼ ▼▼ **Pantages Hotel Toronto Centre** 🄷
(416) 362-1777. **$179-$440.** 200 Victoria St M5B 1V8. Jct Shuter St. Int corridors. **Pets:** Accepted. ⒺⒸⓄ ⓈⒶⓋⒺ ☒ 🛏 🖵 🍴

(CAA) ▼▼ ▼▼ **Park Inn Toronto** 🄷
(416) 743-9997. **$89-$99.** 30 Vice Regent Blvd M9W 7A4. Hwy 27, just s of Rexdale Blvd. Int corridors. **Pets:** Accepted. ⓈⒶⓋⒺ ☒ 🛏 🖵

(CAA) ▼▼ ▼▼ **Quality Hotel & Suites Toronto Airport East** 🄷
(416) 240-9090. **$85-$224.** 2180 Islington Ave M9P 3P1. Hwy 401, exit 356, just s. Int corridors. **Pets:** Medium, other species. $150 deposit/room, $10 daily fee/room. Designated rooms, service with restrictions, supervision. ⒺⒸⓄ ⓈⒶⓋⒺ ☒ 🛏 🖵

(CAA) ▼▼ ▼▼ **Quality Suites Toronto Airport** 🄷
(416) 674-8442. **$85-$126.** 262 Carlingview Dr M9W 5G1. 0.6 mi (1 km) w of jct Hwy 27 N and Dixon Rd. Int corridors. **Pets:** Designated rooms, service with restrictions, supervision. ⒺⒸⓄ ⓈⒶⓋⒺ ☒ 🛏 🖵 🍴

(CAA) ▼▼ ▼▼ **Radisson Hotel Toronto East** 🄷
(416) 493-7000. **$119-$275.** 55 Hallcrown Pl M2J 4R1. Hwy 401, exit Victoria Park N to Consumers Rd, then w. Int corridors. **Pets:** Accepted.
ⒺⒸⓄ ⓈⒶⓋⒺ ☒ ⒻⓂ 🛏 🖵 🍴 🏊

(AA) ▼▼▼▼ **Radisson Suite Hotel Toronto Airport** H
(416) 242-7400. **$129-$189.** 640 Dixon Rd M9W 1J1. Just e of jct Hwy 27; just w of jct Hwy 401. Int corridors. **Pets:** Small. $30 one-time fee/room. Designated rooms, service with restrictions, crate.
ECO SAVE ⊠ 🛏 💻 🍴

(AA) ▼▼▼▼ **Renaissance Toronto Hotel Downtown** H
(416) 341-7100. **$269-$329.** 1 Blue Jays Way M5V 1J4. Jct Front St. Int corridors. **Pets:** Accepted. ECO SAVE ⊠ 🛏 💻 🍴 ⊃ ⊠

(AA) ▼▼▼▼ **Residence Inn by Marriott Downtown Toronto/ Entertainment District** H
(416) 581-1800. **$224-$274.** 255 Wellington St W M5V 3P6. Jct Blue Jays Way. Int corridors. **Pets:** Accepted. ECO SAVE ⊠ 🛏 💻 ⊃

▼▼▼▼ **Residence Inn by Marriott Toronto Airport** H
(416) 798-2900. **$170-$208.** 17 Reading Ct M9W 7K7. Just w of jct Hwy 27 and Dixon Rd. Int corridors. **Pets:** Medium. $100 one-time fee/room. Designated rooms, service with restrictions, supervision.
ECO ⊠ ＆M 🛏 💻 ⊃ ⊠

(AA) ▼▼▼▼ **Sheraton Centre Toronto Hotel** H ❀
(416) 361-1000. **$199-$429.** 123 Queen St W M5H 2M9. Opposite Toronto Civic Centre and City Hall. Int corridors. **Pets:** Medium, dogs only. Service with restrictions, supervision.
ECO SAVE ⊠ ＆M 🛏 💻 🍴 ⊃ ⊠

(AA) ▼▼▼▼ **Sheraton Toronto Airport Hotel & Conference Centre** H
(416) 675-6100. **Call for rates.** 801 Dixon Rd M9W 1J5. Jct Hwy 27 N and Dixon Rd. Int corridors. **Pets:** Accepted.
ECO SAVE ⊠ 🛏 💻 🍴 ⊃

(AA) ▼▼▼▼ **SoHo Metropolitan Hotel** H
(416) 599-8800. **$250-$895.** 318 Wellington St W M5V 3T4. Jct Blue Jays Way. Int corridors. **Pets:** Accepted.
SAVE ⊠ 🛏 💻 🍴 ⊃ ⊠

(AA) ▼▼ **Super 8 Downtown Toronto** H
(647) 426-8118. **$120-$240.** 222 Spadina Ave M5T 2C2. At Dundas St; at Chinatown Center. Int corridors. **Pets:** Accepted.
ECO SAVE ⊠ 🛏 💻

(AA) ▼▼▼▼ **The Sutton Place Hotel** H
(416) 924-9221. **$145-$550.** 955 Bay St M5S 2A2. Jct Wellesley St. Int corridors. **Pets:** Other species. $150 deposit/room, $50 one-time fee/room. Service with restrictions, supervision.
ECO SAVE ⊠ 🛏 💻 🍴 ⊃ ⊠

(AA) ▼▼▼▼ **Toronto Airport Marriott Hotel** H
(416) 674-9400. **$197-$241.** 901 Dixon Rd M9W 1J5. Corner of Carling-view Dr. Int corridors. **Pets:** $30 one-time fee/room. Service with restrictions. ECO SAVE ⊠ ＆M 🛏 💻 🍴 ⊃ ⊠

(AA) ▼▼▼▼ **Toronto Don Valley Hotel & Suites** H
(416) 449-4111. **$99-$149.** 1250 Eglinton Ave E M3C 1J3. Don Valley Pkwy, exit 375 (Wynford Dr); jct Don Valley Pkwy and Eglinton Ave E. Int corridors. **Pets:** Accepted. ECO SAVE ⊠ 🛏 💻 ⊃ ⊠

(AA) ▼▼▼▼ **Toronto Marriott Bloor Yorkville** H
(416) 961-8000. **$259-$309.** 90 Bloor St E M4W 1A7. Just e of Yonge St. Int corridors. **Pets:** Medium. $50 one-time fee/room. Service with restrictions, supervision. ECO SAVE ⊠ ＆M 🛏 💻 🍴

(AA) ▼▼▼▼ **Travelodge Toronto Airport (Dixon Road)** H
(416) 674-2222. **$109-$189.** 925 Dixon Rd M9W 1J8. Corner of Carling-view Dr. Int corridors. **Pets:** Accepted.
ECO SAVE ⊠ 🛏 💻 🍴 ⊃

▼▼ **Travelodge Toronto East** H
(416) 299-9500. **Call for rates.** 20 Milner Business Ct M1B 3C6. Jct Hwy 401 and Markham Rd, just n on Markham Rd. Int corridors.
Pets: Accepted. ECO ⊠ 🛏 💻 🍴 ⊃

▼▼ **Travelodge Toronto North (North York)** H ❀
(416) 663-9500. **$109-$169.** 50 Norfinch Dr M3N 1X1. Hwy 400, exit 25 (Finch Ave E). Int corridors. **Pets:** Other species. Service with restrictions.
ECO ASK ⊠ 🛏 💻 🍴 ⊃

(AA) ▼▼▼▼ **The Westin Bristol Place Toronto Airport** H ❀
(416) 675-9444. **$99-$370.** 950 Dixon Rd M9W 5N4. 1.6 mi (2.6 km) w of jct Hwy 401. Int corridors. **Pets:** Medium, dogs only. Service with restrictions, supervision. SAVE ⊠ 💻 🍴 ⊃

(AA) ▼▼▼▼ **The Westin Harbour Castle** H
(416) 869-1600. **$189-$409.** One Harbour Sq M5J 1A6. At the foot of Bay St; on shore of Lake Ontario. Int corridors. **Pets:** Accepted.
ECO SAVE ⊠ 🛏 💻 🍴 ⊃ ⊠

(AA) ▼▼▼▼ **The Westin Prince Toronto** H
(416) 444-2511. **$129-$359.** 900 York Mills Rd M3B 3H2. Just s of Hwy 401 via Leslie St exit to York Mills Rd E. Int corridors. **Pets:** Accepted.
SAVE ⊠ ＆M 💻 🍴 ⊃ ⊠

(AA) ▼▼▼▼ **Windsor Arms Hotel** H
(416) 971-9666. **$295-$2000.** 18 St. Thomas St M5S 3E7. Just s of Bloor St. Int corridors. **Pets:** Accepted. SAVE ⊠ 🍴 ⊃ ⊠

▼▼▼▼ **The Yorkland Hotel** H
(416) 493-9000. **$89-$139.** 185 Yorkland Blvd M2J 4R2. Just s of Sheppard Ave. Int corridors. **Pets:** Accepted.
ECO ASK ⊠ 🛏 💻 🍴 ⊃

VAUGHAN

▼▼▼▼ **Holiday Inn Express Hotel & Suites Vaughan-Southwest** H
(905) 851-1510. **$139-$159.** 6100 Hwy 7 L4H 0R2. Jct Hwy 27. Int corridors. **Pets:** Other species. $75 one-time fee/room. Service with restrictions, supervision. ECO ASK ⊠ 🛏 💻 ⊃

▼▼▼▼ **Residence Inn by Marriott Toronto/Vaughan** H
(905) 695-4002. **$161-$197.** 11 Interchange Way L4K 5W3. Hwy 400, exit 29 (Hwy 7), 0.6 mi (1 km) e. Int corridors. **Pets:** Accepted.
⊠ ＆M 🛏 💻 ⊃ ⊠

END METROPOLITAN AREA

TRENTON

▼▼ **Comfort Inn** H ❀
(613) 965-6660. **$85-$120.** 68 Monogram Pl K8V 6S3. Hwy 401, exit 526 (Glen Miller Rd), just s, then just e. Int corridors. **Pets:** Other species. Designated rooms, service with restrictions, crate.
ECO ASK ⊠ ＆M 🛏 💻

(AA) ▼▼▼▼ **Holiday Inn Trenton** H
(613) 394-4855. **$109-$119.** 99 Glen Miller Rd K8V 5P8. Hwy 401, exit 526 (Glen Miller Rd), just s. Int corridors. **Pets:** Accepted.
ECO SAVE ⊠ 🛏 💻 ⊃

(AA) ▼▼ **Travelodge** H
(613) 965-6789. **$90-$150.** 598 Old Hwy 2 K8V 5P5. Hwy 401, exit 538, 1.3 mi (2 km) s to Old Hwy 2, then 3.8 mi (6 km) w; 3.1 mi (4.9 km) e of jct Hwy 33. Int corridors. **Pets:** Accepted. ECO SAVE ⊠ 🛏 💻

TWEED

▼▼ Park Place Motel Ⓜ

(613) 478-3134. **$85-$110, 4 day notice.** 43 Victoria St K0K 3J0. Hwy 37, 0.3 mi (0.5 km) s of centre. Ext corridors. **Pets:** Accepted.

(A$K) (✕) (🛏)

WALLACEBURG

ⒸⒶ ▼▼▼ Days Inn Wallaceburg Ⓗ

(519) 627-0781. **Call for rates.** 76 McNaughton Ave N8A 1R9. On Hwy 40 (McNaughton Ave), south side of town. Int corridors. **Pets:** Accepted.

(SAVE) (✕) (🛏) (🖥)

WATERLOO

ⒸⒶ ▼▼▼ Comfort Inn Ⓗ

(519) 747-9400. **$107-$161.** 190 Weber St N N2J 3H4. Jct University Ave, just s. Int corridors. **Pets:** Other species. Service with restrictions, supervision. (ECO) (SAVE) (✕) (🛏) (🖥) (🍴)

▼▼▼▼ The Waterloo Inn Conference Hotel Ⓗ

(519) 884-0220. **$149-$209.** 475 King St N N2J 2Z5. 1.9 mi (3 km) n on King St, jct Hwy 85. Int corridors. **Pets:** Large. $15 one-time fee/pet. Designated rooms, service with restrictions, supervision.

(✕) (&M) (🛏) (🖥) (🍴) (🏊) (✕)

WAWA

ⒸⒶ ▼▼ Best Northern Motel & Restaurant Ⓜ

(705) 856-7302. **$89-$135.** 150 Hwy 17 S P0S 1K0. On Hwy 17, 3.3 mi (5.3 km) s of jct Hwy 101. Ext corridors. **Pets:** Accepted.

(SAVE) (✕) (🛏) (🍴) (✕) (🐾)

ⒸⒶ ▼▼ Northern Lights Motel & Breakfast Ⓜ ❖

(705) 856-1900. **$79-$109.** 1014 Hwy 17 P0S 1K0. On Hwy 17, 5 mi (8 km) n of jct Hwy 101. Ext corridors. **Pets:** Other species. Designated rooms, service with restrictions, supervision. (SAVE) (✕) (🛏) (🖥) (🐾)

ⒸⒶ ▼▼▼ Parkway Motel Ⓜ

(705) 856-7020. **$89-$109.** 232 Hwy 17 S P0S 1K0. On Hwy 17, 2.5 mi (4 km) s of jct Hwy 101. Ext corridors. **Pets:** Other species. $10 daily fee/pet. Designated rooms, service with restrictions, supervision.

(SAVE) (✕) (🛏) (🖥) (✕) (🐾)

▼▼ Sportsman's Motel Ⓜ

(705) 856-2272. **$85.** 171 Mission Rd P0S 1K0. On Hwy 101, 1.5 mi (2.4 km) e of jct Hwy 17 101, 1.5 mi (2.4 km) e of jct Hwy 17. Ext corridors. **Pets:** Other species. $5 daily fee/pet. (✕) (🛏) (🖥)

WHITBY

▼▼ Canadiana Inn Ⓜ

(905) 668-3686. **$75-$120.** 732 Dundas St E (Hwy 2) L1N 2J7. Hwy 401, exit 410 (Brock St/Hwy 12), 1 mi (1.6 km) n to Dundas St, then 0.6 mi (1 km) e. Ext corridors. **Pets:** Dogs only. Service with restrictions, supervision. (✕) (🛏) (🖥) (🏊)

▼▼ Motel 6 Whitby #1907 Ⓗ

(905) 665-8883. **$71-$85.** 165 Consumers Dr L1N 1C4. Hwy 401, exit 410 (Brock St/Hwy 12), just ne. Int corridors. **Pets:** Other species. Service with restrictions, supervision. (ECO) (✕) (🛏)

ⒸⒶ ▼▼▼ Quality Suites Ⓗ

(905) 432-8800. **$119-$179.** 1700 Champlain Ave L1N 6A7. Hwy 401, exit 412 (Thickson Rd), 0.3 mi (0.5 km) n to Champlain Ave, then 0.6 mi (1 km) e. Int corridors. **Pets:** Accepted. (ECO) (SAVE) (✕) (🛏) (🖥)

ⒸⒶ ▼▼▼ Residence Inn Whitby Ⓗ

(905) 444-9756. **$143-$175.** 160 Consumers Dr L1N 9S3. Hwy 401, exit 410 (Brock St/Hwy 12). Int corridors. **Pets:** Large, other species. $75 one-time fee/room. Service with restrictions.

(SAVE) (✕) (&M) (🛏) (🖥) (🏊)

WIARTON

ⒸⒶ ▼▼▼ Glen Miller Motel Ⓜ

(519) 534-0175. **Call for rates.** 143 Hwy 6 N0H 2T0. 1.6 mi (2.5 km) n of town; centre. Ext corridors. **Pets:** Accepted. (SAVE) (✕) (🛏) (🖥) (✕)

WINDSOR

▼▼▼ Cadillac Motel Ⓜ

(519) 969-9340. **$79-$109, 7 day notice.** 2498 Dougall Ave N8X 1T2. 2.5 mi (4 km) s on Hwy 3B from Detroit-Windsor Tunnel, just w on Eugenie St, then just n. Ext corridors. **Pets:** Accepted. (A$K) (✕) (🛏) (🏊)

▼▼ Comfort Inn Ⓗ

(519) 972-1331. **$80-$159, 7 day notice.** 2765 Huron Church Rd N9E 3Y7. West side of Huron Church Rd; 0.5 mi (0.8 km) s of EC Row Expwy. Int corridors. **Pets:** Medium. $10 daily fee/room. Service with restrictions, supervision. (ECO) (A$K) (✕) (🛏) (🖥) (🍴)

▼▼ Comfort Inn Ⓗ ❖

(519) 966-7800. **$90-$150.** 2955 Dougall Ave N9E 1S1. 3.3 mi (5.3 km) s on Hwy 3B, off Hwy 401 via Detroit-Windsor Tunnel exit. Int corridors. **Pets:** Other species. Designated rooms, service with restrictions, supervision. (ECO) (A$K) (✕) (🛏) (🖥)

▼▼▼▼ Hampton Inn & Suites by Hilton Ⓗ

(519) 972-0770. **Call for rates.** 1840 Huron Church Rd N9C 2L5. 0.9 mi (1.5 km) n of EC Row Expwy. Int corridors. **Pets:** Accepted.

(✕) (&M) (🛏) (🖥) (🏊)

ⒸⒶ ▼▼▼ Hilton Windsor Ⓗ 🐾

(519) 973-5555. **$129-$249.** 277 Riverside Dr W N9A 5K4. 0.6 mi (1 km) w of Detroit-Windsor Tunnel; 0.6 mi (1 km) e of Ambassador Bridge; downtown. Int corridors. **Pets:** Small, other species. $50 one-time fee/room. No service, crate. (SAVE) (✕) (🖥) (🍴) (🏊) (✕)

ⒸⒶ ▼▼▼ Holiday Inn Downtown Windsor Ⓗ

(519) 256-4656. **$119-$299.** 430 Ouellette Ave N9A 1B2. 0.3 mi (0.5 km) s of Riverside Dr at Park St W. Int corridors. **Pets:** Accepted.

(SAVE) (✕) (&M) (🛏) (🖥) (🍴) (🏊)

ⒸⒶ ▼▼▼ Holiday Inn Select Windsor (Ambassador Bridge) Ⓗ 🐾

(519) 966-1200. **$99-$189.** 1855 Huron Church Rd N9C 2L6. Jct Huron Church and Malden rds; 0.9 mi (1.5 km) n of EC Row Expwy. Int corridors. **Pets:** Medium. Service with restrictions, crate.

(ECO) (SAVE) (✕) (🛏) (🖥) (🍴) (🏊) (✕)

ⒸⒶ ▼▼▼ Ivy Rose Motor Inn Ⓜ

(519) 966-1700. **$74-$99.** 2885 Howard Ave N8X 3Y4. 3 mi (4.8 km) s of downtown; just n of Devonshire Shopping Mall. Ext corridors. **Pets:** Accepted. (SAVE) (✕) (🛏) (🍴) (🏊)

▼▼▼▼ Quality Suites Windsor Ⓗ 🐾

(519) 977-9707. **$103-$175.** 250 Dougall Ave N9A 7C6. Jct Chatham St; downtown. Int corridors. **Pets:** Small, other species. $100 deposit/room. Service with restrictions, supervision. (ECO) (A$K) (✕) (&M) (🛏) (🖥)

ⒸⒶ ▼▼▼▼ Radisson Riverfront Hotel Ⓗ 🐾

(519) 977-9777. **$139-$199.** 333 Riverside Dr W N9A 5K4. 0.6 mi (1 km) w of Detroit-Windsor Tunnel; 0.6 mi (1 km) e of Ambassador Bridge; downtown. Int corridors. **Pets:** Small. Service with restrictions, supervision.

(SAVE) (✕) (🛏) (🖥) (🍴) (🏊) (✕)

▼▼▼ Towne and Country Motel Ⓜ

(519) 969-9120. **Call for rates.** 2883 Howard Ave N8X 3Y4. Just n of Devonshire Mall and EC Row Expwy. Ext/int corridors. **Pets:** $10 daily fee/room. Service with restrictions, supervision. (✕) (🛏) (🍴) (🏊)

ⒸⒶ ▼▼▼▼ Travelodge Hotel Downtown Windsor Ⓗ

(519) 258-7774. **$99-$139.** 33 Riverside Dr E N9A 2S4. Jct Ouellette Ave; downtown. Int corridors. **Pets:** Medium. Service with restrictions, supervision. (SAVE) (✕) (🛏) (🖥)

ⒸⒶ ▼▼▼ Travelodge Windsor Ambassador Bridge Ⓗ

(519) 972-1100. **$92-$125.** 2330 Huron Church Rd N9E 3S6. N of EC Row Expwy. Int corridors. **Pets:** Accepted.

(ECO) (SAVE) (✕) (🛏) (🖥) (🏊)

WOODSTOCK

(AA) ◆◆◆ Quality Hotel and Suites **H** 🐾

(519) 537-5586. **$89-$299.** 580 Bruin Blvd N4V 1E5. Hwy 401, exit 232, just n; w of Hwy 59. Int corridors. **Pets:** $50 deposit/room. Service with restrictions, supervision. [ECO] [SAVE] ⊠ ▣ ▣ 🍴 ⊠ ⊠

◆◆ Super 8 **H**

(519) 421-4588. **$90-$125.** 560 Norwich Ave N4V 1C6. Jct Hwy 401 and 59, exit 232, just n. Int corridors. **Pets:** Large, other species. $10 one-time fee/room. Service with restrictions, supervision. [ASK] ⊠ ▣ ▣

PRINCE EDWARD ISLAND

ALBERTON

▼▼▼ Briarwood Inn, Cottages & Lodge **M**
(902) 853-2518. **$60-$125.** 253 Matthews Ln C0B 1B0. 1.9 mi (3 km) e on Rt 12. Ext/int corridors. **Pets:** Accepted. ⒶⓈⓀ ⊠ ⊟ ⬛ ⤳ ㋐

CAVENDISH

▼▼▼ Bay Vista Motel **M**
(902) 963-2225. **$59-$129.** 9517 Cavendish Rd C0A 1E0. Jct Rt 13, 2.8 mi (4.8 km) w on Rt 6. Ext corridors. **Pets:** Accepted. ⊠ ⊟ ⤳

▼▼▼ Cavendish Bosom Buddies Cottages & Suites **CA**
(902) 963-3449. **$85-$295, 14 day notice.** RR 1 C0A 1N0. Jct Rt 6 and 13, 0.4 mi (0.7 km) e on Rt 6. Ext corridors. **Pets:** Dogs only. $10 daily fee/pet. Service with restrictions, supervision. ⊠ ⊟ ⬛ ㋐ ㊟

Ⓐ ▼▼▼▼ Cavendish Maples Cottages **CA**
(902) 963-2818. **$75-$309, 30 day notice.** 73 Avonlea Blvd C0A 1M0. Jct Rt 6 and 13, 1.5 mi (2.5 km) w on Rt 6. Ext corridors.
Pets: Accepted. ⓈⒶⓋⒺ ⊠ ⊟ ⬛ ⤳ ⊠

Ⓐ ▼▼▼▼ Sundance Cottages **CA**
(902) 963-2149. **$85-$300, 14 day notice.** 34 Mac Coubrey Ln C0A 1N0. Jct Rt 13, 0.4 mi (0.6 km) e on Rt 6. Ext corridors. **Pets:** Other species. $10 daily fee/pet. Service with restrictions, crate.
ⓈⒶⓋⒺ ⊠ ⊟ ⤳ ⊠

CHARLOTTETOWN

Ⓐ ▼▼▼ Best Western Charlottetown **H**
(902) 892-2461. **$129-$199.** 238 Grafton St C1A 1L5. Centre. Int corridors. **Pets:** Accepted. ⒺⒸⓄ ⓈⒶⓋⒺ ⊠ ♿Ⓜ ⊟ ⬛ ⍥ ⤳ ⊠

▼▼▼ Comfort Inn **H** ❀
(902) 566-4424. **$101-$148.** 112 Trans-Canada Hwy 1 C1E 1E7. Trans-Canada Hwy 1, 2.8 mi (4.5 km) w. Int corridors. **Pets:** Large. Service with restrictions, supervision. ⒺⒸⓄ ⒶⓈⓀ ⊠ ⊟ ⬛

Ⓐ ▼▼▼▼ Delta Prince Edward **H** ❀
(902) 566-2222. **$115-$318.** 18 Queen St C1A 8B9. At Water and Queen sts. Int corridors. **Pets:** Medium. $35 one-time fee/room. Service with restrictions, supervision. ⒺⒸⓄ ⓈⒶⓋⒺ ⊠ ⊟ ⬛ ⍥ ⤳ ⊠

▼▼▼ Econo Lodge **M**
(902) 368-1110. **$79-$149.** 20 Lower Malpeque Rd C1A 7J9. Jct Trans-Canada Hwy 1 and Lower Malpeque Rd, 2.8 mi (4.5 km) w. Ext/int corridors. **Pets:** Accepted. ⒶⓈⓀ ⊠ ⊟ ⬛ ⤳

Ⓐ ▼▼▼ Holiday Inn Express Hotel & Suites
Charlottetown **H** ❀
(902) 892-1201. **$99-$319.** 200 Capital Dr C1E 2E8. On Trans-Canada Hwy 1, 3 mi (5 km) w. Int corridors. **Pets:** Other species. Service with restrictions, crate. ⒺⒸⓄ ⓈⒶⓋⒺ ⊠ ♿Ⓜ ⊟ ⬛ ⤳

▼▼▼ Quality Inn on the Hill **H**
(902) 894-8572. **$99-$319.** 150 Euston St C1A 1W5. Just e of University Ave. Int corridors. **Pets:** Accepted. ⒶⓈⓀ ⊠ ⊟ ⬛ ⍥

Ⓐ ▼▼▼▼ Rodd Charlottetown-A Rodd Signature
Hotel **H**
(902) 894-7371. **$119-$234.** 75 Kent St C1A 7K4. Corner of Kent and Pownal sts. Int corridors. **Pets:** Accepted.
ⒺⒸⓄ ⓈⒶⓋⒺ ⊠ ⊟ ⬛ ⍥ ⤳ ⊠

▼▼▼ Rodd Royalty **H**
(902) 894-8566. **$109-$187.** Intersection Hwy 1 & 2 C1A 8C2. 2.5 mi (4 km) w on Trans-Canada Hwy 1. Ext/int corridors. **Pets:** Accepted.
ⒺⒸⓄ ⒶⓈⓀ ⊠ ⊟ ⬛ ⍥ ⤳

CORNWALL

▼▼▼ Howard Johnson Hotel **H**
(902) 566-2211. **$89-$170.** 100 Trans-Canada Hwy C0A 1H0. On Hwy 1, 4.3 mi (7 km) w of Charlottetown. Ext/int corridors. **Pets:** $10 one-time fee/pet. Supervision. ⒺⒸⓄ ⒶⓈⓀ ⊠ ⊟ ⬛ ⍥ ⤳

▼▼▼ Sunny King Motel **M**
(902) 566-2209. **$54-$116, 3 day notice.** Trans-Canada Hwy C0A 1H0. On Hwy 1; centre. Ext corridors. **Pets:** Accepted.
⊠ ⊟ ⬛ ⤳ ㋐

Ⓐ ▼▼▼ Super 8 **H**
(902) 892-7900. **$89-$160.** 15 York Point Rd C0A 1H0. On Hwy 1, 3.7 mi (6 km) w of Charlottetown. Int corridors. **Pets:** Accepted.
ⓈⒶⓋⒺ ⊠ ⊟ ⬛ ⤳

FRENCH RIVER

▼▼▼ The Beach House Inn **BB** ❀
(902) 886-2145. **$79-$179, 14 day notice.** Cape Rd C0B 1M0. Just off Rt 20; centre. Ext/int corridors. **Pets:** Medium, dogs only. $10 daily fee/pet. Designated rooms, service with restrictions, crate.
⊠ ⊟ ⬛ ㋐

MAYFIELD

▼▼▼ Cavendish Gateway Resort by Clarion Collection **M**
(902) 963-2213. **$99-$199.** 6596 Rt 13 C0A 1N0. On Rt 13, 3.6 mi (6 km) w of Cavendish; centre. Ext/int corridors. **Pets:** Medium. $200 deposit/room. Designated rooms, service with restrictions, supervision.
ⒶⓈⓀ ⊠ ⊟ ⬛ ⤳

RICHMOND

Ⓐ ▼▼▼▼ Caernarvon Cottages & Gardens **CA**
(902) 854-3418. **$80-$135, 10 day notice.** 4697 Hwy 12, RR 1 C0B 1Y0. Jct Hwy 2 and Rt 131, 6 mi (10 km) e. Ext/int corridors. **Pets:** No service, supervision. ⓈⒶⓋⒺ ⊟ ⬛ ㋐

ROSENEATH

Ⓐ ▼▼▼▼ Rodd Brudenell River-A Rodd Signature
Resort **H**
(902) 652-2332. **$142-$251, 3 day notice.** Rt 3 C0A 1L0. Jct Rt 4, 3.3 mi (5.5 km) e. Ext/int corridors. **Pets:** Other species. $10 one-time fee/room. Service with restrictions, supervision.
ⓈⒶⓋⒺ ⊠ ⊟ ⬛ ⍥ ⤳ ⊠

ST. PETERS

Ⓐ ▼▼▼ The Inn at St. Peters **CI** ❀
(902) 961-2135. **$220-$315, 7 day notice.** 1668 Greenwich Rd C0A 2A0. Jct Rt 16 and 313, 0.6 mi (1 km) w on Rt 313. Ext corridors.
Pets: Large. Service with restrictions. ⓈⒶⓋⒺ ⊠ ♿Ⓜ ⊟ ⬛ ⍥

SUMMERSIDE

▼▼▼ Econo Lodge **H**
(902) 436-9100. **$90-$155.** 80 All Weather Hwy C1N 4P3. Jct Hwy 1A and 2, 3.1 mi (5 km) w on Hwy 2. Int corridors. **Pets:** Medium, dogs only. Designated rooms, service with restrictions, supervision.
ⒶⓈⓀ ⊠ ⊟ ⬛ ⍥ ⤳

(CAA) ▼▼ **Quality Inn & Suites** 🄷

(902) 436-2295. **$86-$270.** 618 Water St C1N 2V5. 1 mi (1.6 km) e on Hwy 11. Ext/int corridors. **Pets:** $10 one-time fee/room. Service with restrictions, supervision. [SAVE] [✕] [🖥] [🖵] [⚓] [✕]

(CAA) ▼▼ **Slemon Park Hotel & Conference Centre** 🄷

(902) 432-1780. **$102-$125.** 12 Redwood Ave C0B 1T0. On Rt 2, 3 mi (5 km) w at Summerside Airport. Int corridors. **Pets:** Small. $100 deposit/ pet. Designated rooms, service with restrictions, supervision.
[SAVE] [✕] [🔽M] [🖥] [🖵] [🍴]

WOODSTOCK

(CAA) ▼▼◆ **Rodd Mill River–A Rodd Signature Resort** 🄷

(902) 859-3555. **$105-$166, 3 day notice.** Rt 136 C0B 1V0. On Rt 136, just e of jct Rt 2. Int corridors. **Pets:** $10 daily fee/room. Service with restrictions. [SAVE] [✕] [🖥] [🖵] [🍴] [⚓] [✕]

QUEBEC

CITY INDEX

ALMA

◈◈◈ Comfort Inn H

(418) 668-9221. **$96-$122.** 870 ave du Pont S G8B 2V8. On Hwy 169; centre. Int corridors. **Pets:** Accepted. ECO ASK ⊠ 🛏 📶 💻

AMOS

◉◈◈◈ Amosphere Complexe Hotelier H

(819) 732-7777. **$89-$115.** 1031 Rt 111 est J9T 1N2. On Rt 111; centre. Ext/int corridors. **Pets:** Other species. Service with restrictions, supervision. SAVE ⊠ 🛏 📶 ⊠

BAIE-COMEAU

◈◈ Comfort Inn H

(418) 589-8252. **$115-$150.** 745 boul Lafleche G5C 1C6. On Rt 138. Int corridors. **Pets:** Medium. $25 one-time fee/room. Service with restrictions, supervision. ECO ASK ⊠ 🛏 💻

◈◈ Econo Lodge Baie-Comeau M

(418) 589-7835. **$71-$180.** 1060 boul Lafleche G5C 2W9. On Rt 138; centre. Ext corridors. **Pets:** Accepted. ⊠ 🛏 💻

◈◈◈ Hotel Le Manoir H ❀

(418) 296-3391. **$109-$119.** 8 ave Cabot G4Z 1L8. Rt 138, 2.6 mi (4.4 km) e, follow signs. Int corridors. **Pets:** No service, supervision.
ASK ⊠ 💻 🛏 ⊠

BAIE-ST-PAUL

◉◈◈◈ Hotel Baie-Saint-Paul H

(418) 435-3683. **$69-$129, 7 day notice.** 911 boul Mgr-de-Laval G3Z 1A1. On Rt 138, 0.3 mi (0.5 km) e of Rt 362. Int corridors.
Pets: Accepted. SAVE ⊠ 🛏 💻 📶 ⊠

BERTHIERVILLE

◈◈ Days Inn Berthierville H ❀

(450) 836-1621. **$75-$165, 7 day notice.** 760 rue Gadoury J0K 1A0. Hwy 40, exit 144. Ext/int corridors. **Pets:** $10 daily fee/pet. Designated rooms, service with restrictions, supervision. ECO ASK ⊠ 🛏 💻

BROMONT

◈◈ Hotel Le Menhir H

(450) 534-3790. **$98-$198.** 125 boul Bromont J2L 2K7. Hwy 10, exit 78, 1.6 mi (2.7 km) s. Ext/int corridors. **Pets:** Accepted.
ASK ⊠ 🛏 💻 📶

◉◈◈◈ Le St-Martin Bromont Hotel & Suites H

(450) 534-0044. **$159-$349.** 111 boul du Carrefour J2L 3L1. Hwy 10, exit 78. Int corridors. **Pets:** Medium, dogs only. $30 daily fee/pet. Designated rooms, service with restrictions, supervision. SAVE ⊠ 🛏 💻 📶

CHICOUTIMI

◉ ◈◈◈◈ Centre de Congres et Hotel La Sagueneenne H

(418) 545-8326. **$123-$172.** 250 des Sagueneens G7H 3A4. Just w of jct Rt 175 (boul Talbot); in Saguenay sector. Int corridors. **Pets:** Medium. $25 one-time fee/room. Designated rooms, service with restrictions, supervision. SAVE ⊠ 📶 🛏 💻 📶 ❘❙ 📶 ⊠

COWANSVILLE

◈◈◈ Auberge des Carrefours H

(450) 263-7331. **$99-$160.** 111 Place Jean-Jacques Bertrand J2K 3R5. Hwy 10, exit 68, 9.9 mi (15.9 km) s on Rt 139. Int corridors.
Pets: Accepted. ASK ⊠ 🛏 💻 ❘❙

DRUMMONDVILLE

◉ ◈◈◈ Best Western Hotel Universel H

(819) 478-4971. **$99-$399.** 915 rue Hains J2C 3A1. Hwy 20, exit 177, just s on boul St-Joseph, then just e. Int corridors. **Pets:** Accepted.
SAVE ⊠ 🛏 💻 ❘❙ 📶

◈◈ Comfort Inn H

(819) 477-4000. **$79-$149.** 1055 rue Hains J2C 6G6. Hwy 20, exit 177, 0.3 mi (0.5 km) s on boul St-Joseph, then just w. Int corridors.
Pets: Other species. $25 one-time fee/pet. Designated rooms, service with restrictions, supervision. ECO ASK ⊠ 🛏 💻

◈◈◈ Quality Suites H

(819) 472-2700. **$90-$180.** 2125 rue Canadien J2C 7V8. Hwy 20, exit 175, just s. Int corridors. **Pets:** Other species. $25 one-time fee/room. Designated rooms, service with restrictions, supervision.
ECO ASK ⊠ 🛏 💻 📶

FORESTVILLE

◈◈ Econo Lodge M

(418) 587-2278. **$89-$109.** 5 Rt 138 est G0T 1E0. On Rt 138; centre. Ext/int corridors. **Pets:** Accepted. ASK ⊠ 🛏 💻 ❘❙

GATINEAU

◉ ◈◈◈ Comfort Inn Gatineau H

(819) 243-6010. **$115-$158.** 630 boul La Gappe J8T 7S8. Hwy 50, exit 140, 1.1 mi (1.9 km) e. Int corridors. **Pets:** Accepted.
ECO SAVE ⊠ 🛏 💻

◉ ◈◈◈◈ Four Points by Sheraton Hotel & Conference Centre Gatineau-Ottawa H

(819) 778-6111. **$95-$240.** 35 rue Laurier J8X 4E9. Corner of rue Victoria, across from Canadian Museum of Civilization; in Hull sector. Int corridors. **Pets:** Service with restrictions, crate.
ECO SAVE ⊠ 🛏 💻 ❘❙ 📶

◉ ◈◈◈◈ Hilton Lac Leamy H

(819) 790-6444. **$199-$339.** 3 boul du Casino J8Y 6X4. In Casino du Lac Leamy; in Hull sector. Int corridors. **Pets:** Accepted.
ECO SAVE ⊠ 📶 🛏 💻 ❘❙ 📶 ⊠

Ⓐ ▼▼▼▼ **Holiday Inn Plaza La Chaudiere**
Gatineau-Ottawa 🄷

(819) 778-3880. **$95-$189.** 2 rue Montcalm J8X 4B4. 0.5 mi (0.8 km) w of Portage Bridge at Rt 148 and rue Montcalm; in Hull sector. Int corridors. **Pets:** Large. $35 one-time fee/room. Designated rooms, service with restrictions, supervision. 🆂🅰🆅🅴 ⊠ 🗐 ▣ ⑪ ⤳ ⊠

GRENVILLE-SUR-LA-ROUGE

Ⓐ ▼▼▼▼ **Hôtel du Lac Carling** 🄷

(450) 533-9211. **Call for rates.** 2255 Rt 327 nord J0V 1B0. 3.1 mi (5 km) n. Int corridors. **Pets:** Accepted.
🆂🅰🆅🅴 ⊠ 🗐 ▣ ⑪ ⤳ ⊠

LAC-BROME (KNOWLTON)

▼▼▼▼ **Auberge Knowlton** 🄲🄸

(450) 242-6886. **$130-$160.** 286 chemin Knowlton J0E 1V0. Corner of Hwy 104 and Rt 243; centre. Int corridors. **Pets:** Accepted. ⊠ ⑪

Ⓐ ▼▼▼▼ **Auberge Quilliams Inn** 🄲🄸

(450) 243-0404. **$159-$350, 3 day notice.** 572 chemin Lakeside J0E 1R0. Hwy 10, exit 90, 3.1 mi (4.9 km) s on Rt 243. Int corridors. **Pets:** $10 daily fee/room. Service with restrictions, supervision.
🆂🅰🆅🅴 ⊠ 🗐 ▣ ⑪ ⤳ ⊠

LA MALBAIE

Ⓐ ▼▼▼▼ **Fairmont Le Manoir Richelieu** 🄷 🐾

(418) 665-3703. **$139-$269.** 181 rue Richelieu G5A 1X7. On Rt 362, 2.6 mi (4.1 km) w of jct Rt 138. Int corridors. **Pets:** Dogs only. $25 daily fee/room. Supervision. 🄴🄲🄾 🆂🅰🆅🅴 ⊠ 🗐 ▣ ⑪ ⤳ ⊠

▼▼▼▼ **La Pinsonnière** 🄲🄸

(418) 665-4431. **$295-$495, 15 day notice.** 124 rue St-Raphael G5A 1X9. Just off Rt 138, follow signs; in Cap-a-L'Aigle sector. Int corridors. **Pets:** Dogs only. $25 daily fee/pet. Designated rooms, service with restrictions, supervision. ⊠ ▣ ⑪ ⤳ ⊠

LOUISEVILLE

▼▼▼ **Gite du Carrefour et Maison historique J.L.L.**
Hamelin 🄱🄱

(819) 228-4932. **$65-$95 (no credit cards), 15 day notice.** 11 ave St-Laurent ouest J5V 1J3. On Rt 138; Hwy 40, exit 174 westbound; exit 166 eastbound; centre. Int corridors. **Pets:** Small. No service, supervision.
⊠ 🄰🄿 🅿🅦 🅿

MONTEBELLO

Ⓐ ▼▼▼▼ **Fairmont Le Château Montebello** 🄷

(819) 423-6341. **$179-$389, 3 day notice.** 392 rue Notre-Dame J0V 1L0. On Rt 148. Int corridors. **Pets:** Accepted.
🄴🄲🄾 🆂🅰🆅🅴 ⊠ 🗐 ▣ ⑪ ⤳ ⊠

MONT-LAURIER

Ⓐ ▼▼▼▼ **Best Western Hotel Dynastie** 🄷

(819) 623-5252. **Call for rates.** 1231 boul A-Paquette J9L 1M6. On Rt 117; centre. Ext/int corridors. **Pets:** Accepted. 🆂🅰🆅🅴 ⊠ 🗐 ▣ ⤳

Ⓐ ▼▼▼▼ **Quality Inn Mont-Laurier** 🄷

(819) 623-3555. **$110-$130.** 111 boul A-Paquette J9L 1J2. On Rt 117; centre. Ext/int corridors. **Pets:** Small, dogs only. $10 daily fee/room. Supervision. 🆂🅰🆅🅴 ⊠ 🗐 ▣ ⑪ ⤳ ⊠

MONTMAGNY

▼▼▼ **Manoir des Erables** 🄲🄸

(418) 248-0100. **Call for rates.** 220 boul Tache est (Rt 132) G5V 1G5. Hwy 20, exit 376, 1.4 mi (2.2 km) e on Rt 228, 0.9 mi (1.5 km) e. Ext/int corridors. **Pets:** $35 one-time fee/pet. Designated rooms, service with restrictions, supervision. ⊠ ▣ ⑪ ⤳ ⊠

MONTREAL METROPOLITAN AREA

BROSSARD

▼▼▼ **Alt Hotel Quartier Dix 30** 🄷

(450) 443-1030. **Call for rates.** 6500 boul de Rome J4Y 0B6. Jct Hwy 10 and 30, just w on Hwy 30, exit boul de Rome; in Quartier Dix 30 Mall. Int corridors. **Pets:** Accepted. 🄴🄲🄾 ⊠ 🗐 ▣

▼▼ **Comfort Inn** 🄷

(450) 678-9350. **$95-$115.** 7863 boul Taschereau J4Y 1A4. Rt 134, 0.9 mi (1.5 km) w of Hwy 10, exit boul Taschereau ouest. Int corridors. **Pets:** $25 one-time fee/pet. Designated rooms, service with restrictions, supervision. 🄴🄲🄾 🄰🆂🅺 ⊠ 🗐 ▣

▼▼ **Econo Lodge Montreal–Brossard** 🄼

(450) 466-2186. **$85-$200.** 8350 boul Taschereau J4X 1C2. Rt 134, 1.4 mi (2.3 km) w of Hwy 10, exit boul Taschereau ouest. Ext/int corridors. **Pets:** Small, dogs only. $10 daily fee/pet. Service with restrictions, supervision. 🄰🆂🅺 ⊠ 🗐 ▣

DORVAL

Ⓐ ▼▼▼▼ **aloft Montreal Airport** 🄷 🐾

(514) 633-0900. **$99-$229.** 500 boul McMillan H9P 0A2. Just n of Hwy 520 on north side service road at airport entrance. Int corridors. **Pets:** Medium. Service with restrictions, supervision.
🆂🅰🆅🅴 ⊠ 🅶🄼 🗐 ▣ ⤳

Ⓐ ▼▼ **Comfort Inn Dorval** 🄷

(514) 636-3391. **$70-$250.** 340 ave Michel-Jasmin H9P 1C1. Hwy 520, exit 2 eastbound; exit 1 westbound, just e along service road to ave Marshall, follow to ave Michel-Jasmin. Int corridors. **Pets:** Very small. $25 daily fee/pet. Designated rooms, no service, supervision.
🄴🄲🄾 🆂🅰🆅🅴 ⊠ 🗐 ▣

Ⓐ ▼▼▼▼ **Hampton Inn & Suites by Hilton Montreal** 🄷

(514) 633-8243. **$99-$180.** 1900 Rt Transcanadienne (Hwy 40) H9P 2N4. Hwy 40, exit 55, 0.5 mi (0.8 km) e of boul des Sources on south side service road. Int corridors. **Pets:** Accepted.
🆂🅰🆅🅴 ⊠ 🅶🄼 🗐 ▣ ⤳

Ⓐ ▼▼ ▼ **Travelodge Aeroport Montreal-Trudeau Airport** 🄷

(514) 631-4537. **$89-$129.** 1010 chemin Herron H9S 1B3. Hwy 20, exit 54 westbound, just s on boul Fenelon to ave Dumont, follow to chemin Herron; exit 56 eastbound, 1.1 mi (1.7 km) along service road. Int corridors. **Pets:** Small. $40 one-time fee/room. Designated rooms, service with restrictions, supervision. 🄴🄲🄾 🆂🅰🆅🅴 ⊠ 🗐 ▣ ⊠

Ⓐ ▼▼▼▼ **Wyndham Montreal Aeroport** 🄷

(514) 631-2411. **$129-$189.** 12505 boul Cote-de-Liesse H9P 1B7. Just n of Hwy 520 on northside service road at airport entrance. Int corridors. **Pets:** Accepted. 🄴🄲🄾 🆂🅰🆅🅴 ⊠ 🅶🄼 🗐 ▣ ⑪ ⤳ ⊠

LAVAL

▼▼ **Comfort Inn** 🄷

(450) 686-0600. **$99-$129.** 2055 Autoroute des Laurentides H7S 1Z6. Hwy 15, exit 8 (boul St-Martin) eastbound, 0.4 mi (0.7 km) n on boul Le Corbusier, then w on boul Tessier. Int corridors. **Pets:** Medium. $10 daily fee/pet. Designated rooms, service with restrictions, supervision.
🄴🄲🄾 🄰🆂🅺 ⊠ 🗐 ▣ ⑪

▼▼ **Econo Lodge** 🄷

(450) 681-6411. **$79-$124.** 1981 boul Cure-Labelle H7T 1L4. Hwy 15, exit 8 (boul St-Martin) northbound; exit 10 southbound, 1.3 mi (2 km) w on boul St-Martin ouest, then 0.3 mi (0.5 km) n. Ext/int corridors. **Pets:** Designated rooms, service with restrictions, supervision.
🄰🆂🅺 ⊠ 🗐 ▣ ⤳

Ⓐ ▼▼▼ **Hampton Inn & Suites-Laval** 🅷
(450) 687-0010. **Call for rates.** 1961 boul Cure-Labelle H7T 1L4. Hwy 15, exit 8 (boul St-Martin) northbound; exit 10 southbound, 1.4 mi (2.3 km) w on boul St-Martin ouest, then just n. Int corridors. **Pets:** Accepted. 𝖲𝖠𝖵𝖤 ⊠ 🖥 💻 🏊

Ⓐ ▼▼ **Hotel Chateauneuf Laval** 🅷
(450) 681-9000. **$100-$199.** 3655 Autoroute des Laurentides H7L 3H7. Hwy 15, exit 10, just n on east side service road. Int corridors. **Pets:** Service with restrictions, supervision. 𝖲𝖠𝖵𝖤 ⊠ 🖥 💻 🏊

Ⓐ ▼▼ **Quality Suites Laval** 🅷
(450) 686-6777. **$113-$144.** 2035 Autoroute des Laurentides H7S 1Z6. Hwy 15, exit 8 (boul St-Martin), 0.4 mi (0.7 km) n on boul Le Corbusier, w on boul Tessier. Int corridors. **Pets:** Medium. $10 daily fee/pet. Designated rooms, service with restrictions, supervision.
𝖤𝖢𝖮 𝖲𝖠𝖵𝖤 ⊠ 🖥 💻

Ⓐ ▼▼▼ **Sheraton Laval Hotel** 🅷 ❀
(450) 687-2440. **Call for rates.** 2440 Autoroute des Laurentides H7T 1X5. Hwy 15, exit 10. Int corridors. **Pets:** Large, dogs only. Designated rooms, service with restrictions, supervision.
𝖲𝖠𝖵𝖤 ⊠ 🖥 💻 🍴 🏊 ⊠

MONTREAL

Ⓐ ▼▼▼ **Candlewood Suites** 🅷 ❀
(514) 667-5002. **$99-$169.** 191 boul Rene-Levesque est H2X 3Z9. Corner of rue Hotel-de-ville. Int corridors. **Pets:** Medium. $50 one-time fee/room. Service with restrictions, supervision. 𝖤𝖢𝖮 𝖲𝖠𝖵𝖤 ⊠ 🖥 💻

Ⓐ ▼▼▼ **Chateau Versailles Hotel** 🅷 ❀
(514) 933-3611. **$155-$399.** 1659 rue Sherbrooke ouest H3H 1E3. Corner rue St-Mathieu. Int corridors. **Pets:** $15 daily fee/pet. Designated rooms, service with restrictions, crate. 𝖲𝖠𝖵𝖤 ⊠ 🖥 💻

Ⓐ ▼▼▼ **Crowne Plaza Montreal Airport** 🅷
(514) 344-1999. **$119-$250.** 6600 Cote-de-Liesse H4T 1E3. Hwy 520, exit 5 eastbound on south side service road; exit westbound to rue Ness, follow signs for rue Hickmore and Hwy 520 E; in St-Laurent sector. Int corridors. **Pets:** Small. $35 one-time fee/room. Designated rooms, service with restrictions, supervision. 𝖲𝖠𝖵𝖤 ⊠ 🖥 💻 🍴 🏊 ⊠

Ⓐ ▼▼▼ **Days Hotel Montreal** 🅷
(514) 938-4611. **$109-$179.** 1005 rue Guy H3H 2K4. Just s of boul Rene-Levesque. Int corridors. **Pets:** Accepted.
𝖲𝖠𝖵𝖤 ⊠ 🖥 💻 🍴 🏊 ⊠

Ⓐ ▼▼▼ **Delta Montreal** 🅷
(514) 286-1986. **$145-$322.** 475 ave President-Kennedy H3A 1J7. Corner of rue City Councillors. Int corridors. **Pets:** $35 one-time fee/room. Service with restrictions, supervision.
𝖤𝖢𝖮 𝖲𝖠𝖵𝖤 ⊠ 🖥 💻 🍴 🏊 ⊠

Ⓐ ▼▼▼ **Embassy Suites Montreal par/by Hilton** 🅷 ❀
(514) 288-8886. **$189-$699.** 208 rue St-Antoine ouest H2Y 0A6. Corner of rue St-Francois-Xavier. Int corridors. **Pets:** Small, dogs only. $35 one-time fee/room. Service with restrictions. 𝖤𝖢𝖮 𝖲𝖠𝖵𝖤 ⊠ 🖥 💻 🍴

Ⓐ ▼▼▼ **Fairmont The Queen Elizabeth** 🅷 ❀
(514) 861-3511. **$149-$599.** 900 boul Rene-Levesque ouest H3B 4A5. Between rue University and Mansfield. Int corridors. **Pets:** $25 daily fee/room. Service with restrictions, supervision.
𝖤𝖢𝖮 𝖲𝖠𝖵𝖤 ⊠ 🔓 🖥 💻 🍴 🏊 ⊠

Ⓐ ▼▼▼ **Grand Plaza Montreal Centre-Ville** 🅷
(514) 842-8581. **$109-$329.** 505 rue Sherbrooke est H2L 4N3. Between rue Berri and St-Hubert. Int corridors. **Pets:** $30 one-time fee/pet. Designated rooms, service with restrictions, crate.
𝖤𝖢𝖮 𝖲𝖠𝖵𝖤 ⊠ 💻 🍴 🏊

Ⓐ ▼▼▼ **Hilton Montréal Bonaventure** 🅷
(514) 878-2332. **$190-$350.** 900 rue de la Gauchetiere ouest H5A 1E4. Corner of Mansfield and de la Gauchetiere. Int corridors. **Pets:** Accepted.
𝖤𝖢𝖮 𝖲𝖠𝖵𝖤 ⊠ 🔓 🖥 💻 🍴 🏊

Ⓐ ▼▼▼ **Holiday Inn Express Hotel & Suites Montreal Centre-Ville** 🅷 ❀
(514) 448-7100. **$107-$179.** 155 rue Rene-Levesque est H2X 3Z8. Corner de Bullion. Int corridors. **Pets:** Medium. $50 one-time fee/room. Service with restrictions, supervision. 𝖤𝖢𝖮 𝖲𝖠𝖵𝖤 ⊠ 🖥 💻

Ⓐ ▼▼▼ **Holiday Inn Montreal-Airport** 🅷
(514) 739-3391. **$95-$175.** 6500 Cote-de-Liesse H4T 1E3. Hwy 520, exit 5 eastbound on south side service road; exit westbound to rue Ness, follow signs for rue Hickmore and Hwy 520 E; in St-Laurent sector. Ext/int corridors. **Pets:** Medium. $35 one-time fee/pet. Designated rooms, service with restrictions, supervision. 𝖲𝖠𝖵𝖤 ⊠ 🔓 🖥 💻 🍴 🏊 ⊠

Ⓐ ▼▼▼ **Holiday Inn Montreal-Midtown** 🅷
(514) 842-6111. **$109-$149.** 420 rue Sherbrooke ouest H3A 1B4. Between rue de Bleury and Aylmer. Int corridors. **Pets:** Medium. $35 one-time fee/room. Service with restrictions, supervision.
𝖤𝖢𝖮 𝖲𝖠𝖵𝖤 ⊠ 🖥 💻 🍴 🏊 ⊠

▼▼▼ **Hotel Gault** 🅷
(514) 904-1616. **$199-$589.** 449 rue Ste-Helene H2Y 2K9. Just s of rue Notre-Dame. Int corridors. **Pets:** Accepted. ⊠ 🖥 💻 🍴

Ⓐ ▼▼ **Hotel La Tour Centre-Ville** 🅲🅾
(514) 866-8861. **$90-$350.** 400 boul Rene-Levesque ouest H2Z 1V5. Corner of rue de Bleury. Int corridors. **Pets:** Medium. $15 daily fee/pet. Designated rooms, service with restrictions.
𝖲𝖠𝖵𝖤 ⊠ 🖥 💻 🍴 🏊

Ⓐ ▼▼▼ **Hôtel Le Crystal** 🅷 ❀
(514) 861-5550. **$249-$1999.** 1100 rue de la Montagne H3G 0A1. Corner of boul Rene-Levesque. Int corridors. **Pets:** Small. $75 one-time fee/room. Service with restrictions, supervision.
𝖤𝖢𝖮 𝖲𝖠𝖵𝖤 ⊠ 🔓 🖥 💻 🍴 🏊 ⊠

▼▼▼ **Hôtel Le Germain** 🅷 ❀
(514) 849-2050. **$230-$305.** 2050 rue Mansfield H3A 1Y9. Corner of ave President-Kennedy. Int corridors. **Pets:** $30 daily fee/room. Service with restrictions, supervision. ⊠ 🖥 💻 🍴

Ⓐ ▼▼▼ **Hôtel Le St-James** 🅷 ❀
(514) 841-3111. **$320-$625.** 355 rue St-Jacques ouest H2Y 1N9. Corner of rue St-Pierre. Int corridors. **Pets:** $125 one-time fee/pet. Service with restrictions, crate. 𝖲𝖠𝖵𝖤 ⊠ 💻 🍴 ⊠

Ⓐ ▼▼▼ **Hôtel Omni Mont-Royal** 🅷 ❀
(514) 284-1110. **$139-$279.** 1050 rue Sherbrooke ouest H3A 2R6. Corner of rue Peel. Int corridors. **Pets:** Medium, dogs only. $50 one-time fee/room. Designated rooms, service with restrictions, supervision.
𝖲𝖠𝖵𝖤 ⊠ 🖥 💻 🍴 🏊 ⊠

▼▼ **Hotel St-Paul** 🅷
(514) 380-2222. **$189-$279.** 355 rue McGill H2Y 2E8. Corner of rue St-Paul. Int corridors. **Pets:** Accepted. 𝖠𝖲𝖪 ⊠ 💻 🍴

▼▼ **Hotel Terrasse Royale** 🅷
(514) 739-6391. **Call for rates.** 5225 chemin Cote-des-Neiges H3T 1Y1. Just n of chemin Queen Mary. Int corridors. **Pets:** Accepted.
⊠ 🖥 💻

Ⓐ ▼▼ **Hotel Travelodge Montreal Centre** 🅷
(514) 874-9090. **$89-$260.** 50 boul Rene-Levesque ouest H2Z 1A2. Between rue Clark and St-Urbain. Int corridors. **Pets:** Small. $10 daily fee/pet. Designated rooms, service with restrictions, supervision.
𝖤𝖢𝖮 𝖲𝖠𝖵𝖤 ⊠ 🖥 💻 🍴

Ⓐ ▼▼▼ **InterContinental Montréal** 🅷
(514) 987-9900. **$169-$575.** 360 rue St-Antoine ouest H2Y 3X4. Corner of rue St-Pierre. Int corridors. **Pets:** Small. $35 one-time fee/room. Service with restrictions, crate. 𝖲𝖠𝖵𝖤 ⊠ 🖥 💻 🍴 🏊 ⊠

◎ ▽▽▽ L'Appartement Hotel ⊂O
(514) 284-3634. **$115-$245.** 455 rue Sherbrooke ouest H3A 1B7. Corner of rue Durocher. Int corridors. **Pets:** Designated rooms, service with restrictions, crate. 🔲 🔲 ✕ 🔲 🔲 🔲

▽▽▽▽ La Presidence Hotel and Suites ⊂O
(514) 842-9988. **Call for rates.** 505 rue Sherbrooke est H2L 4N3. Between rue Berri and St-Hubert. Int corridors. **Pets:** $30 one-time fee/pet. Designated rooms, service with restrictions, crate.
✕ 🔲 🔲 🔲 🔲

◎ ▽▽▽▽ Le Centre Sheraton 🅗 ❧
(514) 878-2000. **$169-$319.** 1201 boul Rene-Levesque Ouest H3B 2L7. Between rue Drummond and rue Stanley. Int corridors. **Pets:** Medium. Service with restrictions, supervision.
🔲 🔲 ✕ 🔲 🔲 🔲 🔲 🔲

◎ ▽▽▽▽ Le Meridien Versailles-Montreal 🅗 ❧
(514) 933-8111. **$149-$419.** 1808 rue Sherbrooke ouest H3H 1E5. Corner of rue St-Mathieu. Int corridors. **Pets:** Other species. $15 daily fee/pet. Designated rooms, service with restrictions, crate.
🔲 ✕ 🔲 🔲 🔲

◎ ▽▽▽▽▽ Le Saint-Sulpice Hôtel Montréal 🅗 ❧
(514) 288-1000. **$189-$539.** 414 rue St-Sulpice H2Y 2V5. Just n of rue St-Paul. Int corridors. **Pets:** Small. $50 one-time fee/room. Service with restrictions, supervision. 🔲 ✕ 🔲 🔲 🔲 🔲

◎ ▽▽▽▽ Le Square Phillips Hotel & Suites 🅗
(514) 393-1193. **$141-$323.** 1193 Place Phillips H3B 3C9. Between rue Ste-Catherine and boul Rene-Levesque. Int corridors. **Pets:** Accepted.
🔲 🔲 ✕ 🔲 🔲 🔲 🔲

◎ ▽▽▽▽ Loews Hôtel Vogue 🅗 ❧
(514) 285-5555. **$152-$764.** 1425 de la Montagne H3G 1Z3. Between rue Ste-Catherine and boul de Maisonneuve. Int corridors. **Pets:** Large, other species. $25 one-time fee/pet. Supervision.
🔲 ✕ 🔲 🔲 🔲 🔲

▽▽▽ Novotel Montreal Aeroport 🅗
(514) 337-3222. **$119-$329.** 2599 boul Alfred-Nobel H4S 2G1. Hwy 40, exit 60 (boul Alfred-Nobel); in St-Laurent Technoparc, just s of south side service road; in St-Laurent sector. Int corridors. **Pets:** Accepted.
🔲 🔲 ✕ 🔲 🔲 🔲 🔲

▽▽▽ Novotel Montreal Centre 🅗 ❧
(514) 861-6000. **$127-$499.** 1180 rue de la Montagne H3G 1Z1. Between rue Ste-Catherine and boul Rene-Levesque. Int corridors. **Pets:** Other species. $20 one-time fee/room. Service with restrictions, supervision. 🔲 🔲 ✕ 🔲 🔲

◎ ▽▽▽▽ Opus Hotel Montreal 🅗 ❧
(514) 843-6000. **$269-$349.** 10 rue Sherbrooke ouest H2X 4C9. Corner of boul St-Laurent. Int corridors. **Pets:** $30 one-time fee/pet. Supervision.
🔲 ✕ 🔲 🔲 🔲

▽▽▽ Quality Hotel Dorval 🅗
(514) 731-7821. **Call for rates.** 7700 Cote-de-Liesse H4T 1E7. Hwy 520, exit 4 eastbound, on south side service road; exit 4 (Montee-de-Liesse) westbound; in St-Laurent sector. Int corridors. **Pets:** Accepted.
✕ 🔲 🔲 🔲 🔲 🔲

◎ ▽▽▽ Quality Hotel Downtown Montreal 🅗
(514) 849-1413. **$108-$189.** 3440 ave du Parc H2X 2H5. Between rue Sherbrooke and Milton. Int corridors. **Pets:** Accepted.
🔲 🔲 ✕ 🔲 🔲 🔲

◎ ▽▽▽ Quality Hotel East 🅗
(514) 493-6363. **$80-$250.** 8100 ave Neuville H1J 2T2. Hwy 40, exit 78, just n on boul Langelier, 0.4 mi (0.7 km) e on rue Jarry, then s; in Anjou sector. Int corridors. **Pets:** Accepted. 🔲 🔲 ✕ 🔲 🔲 🔲

◎ ▽▽▽▽ Residence Inn by Marriott Montreal Westmount 🅗
(514) 935-9224. **$139-$159.** 2170 ave Lincoln H3H 2N5. Just e of rue Atwater. Int corridors. **Pets:** Accepted.
🔲 🔲 ✕ 🔲 🔲 🔲 🔲

▽▽▽ Residence Inn Montreal Airport 🅗
(514) 336-9333. **$179-$219.** 6500 Place Robert-Joncas H4M 2Z5. Hwy 40, exit 65 (boul Cavendish), 0.3 mi (0.5 km) w on north side service road, then just n on rue Beaulac. Int corridors. **Pets:** Accepted.
🔲 ✕ 🔲 🔲 🔲 🔲 🔲

◎ ▽▽▽ Residence Inn Montreal-Downtown 🅗 ❧
(514) 982-6064. **$169-$219.** 2045 rue Peel H3A 1T6. Between rue Sherbrooke and boul de Maisonneuve. Int corridors. **Pets:** Medium. $100 one-time fee/room. Service with restrictions, crate. 🔲 🔲 ✕ 🔲 🔲 🔲

▽▽▽ Sofitel Montréal Le Carré Doré 🅗 ❧
(514) 285-9000. **$400-$800, 3 day notice.** 1155 rue Sherbrooke ouest H3A 2N3. Corner of rue Stanley. Int corridors. **Pets:** Medium, other species. Service with restrictions, supervision.
🔲 🔲 ✕ 🔲 🔲 🔲

◎ ▽▽▽ ▽▽▽ W Montréal 🅗 ❧
(514) 395-3100. **$199-$729.** 901 Square Victoria H2Z 1R1. Corner of rue St-Antoine. Int corridors. **Pets:** Medium, other species. $25 daily fee/room, $100 one-time fee/room. Designated rooms, service with restrictions, supervision. 🔲 ✕ 🔲 🔲 🔲

◎ ▽▽▽ ▽▽▽ XIXe siecle Hotel Montreal 🅗
(514) 985-0019. **$150-$325.** 262 rue St-Jacques ouest H2Y 1N1. Between rue St-Jean and St-Pierre. Int corridors. **Pets:** Accepted.
🔲 ✕ 🔲 🔲

POINTE-CLAIRE

◎ ▽▽▽ Comfort Inn 🅗
(514) 697-6210. **$70-$160.** 700 boul St-Jean H9R 3K2. Hwy 40, exit 52, just s. Int corridors. **Pets:** Service with restrictions, supervision.
🔲 🔲 ✕ 🔲 🔲

◎ ▽▽▽▽ Quality Suites Montreal Aeroport, Pointe-Claire 🅗
(514) 426-5060. **$104-$160.** 6300 Rt Transcanadienne H9R 1B9. Hwy 40, exit 52 eastbound, south side service road; westbound, follow signs for boul St-Jean sud and Hwy 40 est to access south side service road. Int corridors. **Pets:** Accepted. 🔲 🔲 ✕ 🔲 🔲 🔲 🔲

ROSEMERE

▽▽▽ Hotel Le Rivage 🅗
(450) 437-2171. **Call for rates.** 125 boul Cure-Labelle J7A 2G9. Hwy 15, exit 14, 2.4 mi (4 km) e. Int corridors. **Pets:** Accepted.
✕ 🔲 🔲 🔲 🔲

ST-JEROME

◎ ▽▽▽▽ Super 8 St-Jerome 🅗 ❧
(450) 438-4388. **$109-$139.** 3 boul J. F. Kennedy J7Y 4B4. Hwy 15, exit 41 southbound, just n; on west side of autoroute. Int corridors. **Pets:** Medium. $15 daily fee/pet. Designated rooms, service with restrictions, supervision. 🔲 ✕ 🔲 🔲 🔲 🔲 🔲

ST-LAURENT

◎ ▽▽▽ Park Inn Montreal 🅗
(514) 733-8818. **$125-$198.** 7300 Cote-de-Liesse H4T 1E7. Hwy 520, exit 4 eastbound on southside service road; exit 4 (Montee-de-Liesse) westbound; in St-Laurent sector. Int corridors. **Pets:** Accepted.
🔲 ✕ 🔲 🔲 🔲 🔲

TERREBONNE

◎ ▽▽▽▽ Super 8 Hotel Lachenaie Terrebonne 🅗 ❧
(450) 582-8288. **$89-$149.** 1155 ave Yves-Blais J6V 0A9. Hwy 640, exit 50, just s on Montee des Pionniers, then just e; in Lachenaie sector. Int corridors. **Pets:** Small. $15 daily fee/room. Service with restrictions, supervision. 🔲 🔲 ✕ 🔲 🔲 🔲 🔲 🔲

VAUDREUIL-DORION

(CAA) ▼▼▼▼ **Château Vaudreuil Suites Hôtel** H

(450) 455-0955. **$160-$185.** 21700 Trans-Canada Hwy 40 J7V 8P3. Hwy 40, exit 36 westbound; exit 35 eastbound. Int corridors. **Pets:** Large. Service with restrictions, supervision.

ECO SAVE ✕ 🛏 💻 🍴 🏊 ✕

▼▼▼ **Super 8** H

(450) 424-8898. **Call for rates.** 3200 boul de la Gare J7V 8W5. Hwy 40, exit 35, just s on ave St-Charles, 0.3 mi (0.4 km) w on boul de la Cite-des-Jeunes, then just w. Int corridors. **Pets:** Accepted.

ECO ✕ 🛏 💻 🏊

END METROPOLITAN AREA

MONT-TREMBLANT

(CAA) ▼▼▼▼ **Chateau Beauvallon** CO

(819) 681-6611. **Call for rates.** 6385 Montee-Ryan J8E 1S5. Hwy 117, exit 119, 4 mi (6.4 km) e. Int corridors. **Pets:** Small. $25 one-time fee/room. Service with restrictions, supervision.

SAVE ✕ 🛏 💻 🍴 🏊 ✕

(CAA) ▼▼▼▼▼ **Fairmont Tremblant** H ❀

(819) 681-7000. **$139-$609, 7 day notice.** 3045 chemin de la Chapelle J8E 1E1. In Mont-Tremblant Resort centre. Int corridors. **Pets:** Small. $25 daily fee/room. Supervision. ECO SAVE ✕ 🛁M 💻 🍴 🏊 ✕

▼▼▼ **Le Grand Lodge Mont-Tremblant** H

(819) 425-2734. **$119-$299, 8 day notice.** 2396 rue Labelle J8E 1T8. On Rt 327, 0.3 mi (0.4 km) s of Montee Ryan. Int corridors. **Pets:** Small. $35 daily fee/pet. Designated rooms, service with restrictions, supervision.

ASK ✕ 🛏 💻 🍴 🏊 ✕

(CAA) ▼▼▼ ▼▼▼ **Le Westin Resort & Spa, Tremblant** H

(819) 681-8000. **Call for rates.** 100 chemin Kandahar J8E 1E2. Hwy 117 N, exit 119 (Montee Ryan), 6 mi (10 km) e, follow signs; in Mont-Tremblant Resort centre. Int corridors. **Pets:** Accepted.

SAVE ✕ 🛏 💻 🍴 🏊 ✕

PERCE

▼▼▼ **Au Pic de l'Aurore** CA

(418) 782-2151. **$72-$240, 15 day notice.** 1 Rt 132 G0C 2L0. 1.2 mi (2 km) e from village. Ext corridors. **Pets:** Medium. $25 one-time fee/pet. Designated rooms, service with restrictions, supervision. ✕ 🛏 💻

▼▼▼ **Hotel La Normandie** H

(418) 782-2112. **$79-$259.** 221 Rt 132 ouest G0C 2L0. Centre. Int corridors. **Pets:** Medium. $30 one-time fee/room. Designated rooms, service with restrictions, crate. ✕ 🛏 💻 🍴 🎜

▼▼▼ **Hotel/Motel Le Mirage** M

(418) 782-5151. **$74-$198.** 288 Rt 132 ouest G0C 2L0. On Rt 132. Ext corridors. **Pets:** Very small, dogs only. ✕ 🛏 🍴 🏊

▼▼ **Hotel Motel Manoir de Perce** H

(418) 782-2022. **$66-$168.** 212 Rt 132 G0C 2L0. Centre. Ext/int corridors. **Pets:** $25 one-time fee/room. Service with restrictions, supervision.

✕ 🛏 🍴

QUEBEC METROPOLITAN AREA

BEAUPRE

(CAA) ▼▼▼▼ **Chateau Mont Sainte-Anne** H

(418) 827-5211. **$99-$499, 14 day notice.** 500 boul du Beau-Pre G0A 1E0. Hwy 360, 2.3 mi (3.7 km) ne from jct Hwy 138. Int corridors. **Pets:** Accepted. ECO SAVE ✕ 🛏 🍴 🏊 ✕

(CAA) ▼▼▼ **Hotel Val des Neiges** H

(418) 827-5711. **$92-$249.** 201 rue Val-des-Neiges G0A 1E0. Just off Hwy 360. Int corridors. **Pets:** $10 deposit/pet. Designated rooms, service with restrictions, supervision. SAVE ✕ 🛏 💻 🍴 🏊 ✕

BOISCHATEL

(CAA) ▼▼ **Econo Lodge Montmorency** H

(418) 822-4777. **$75-$145.** 5490 boul Ste-Anne G0A 1H0. On Hwy 138. Int corridors. **Pets:** Accepted. SAVE ✕ 🛏 💻

L'ANCIENNE-LORETTE

▼▼ **Comfort Inn** H

(418) 872-5900. **$120-$175.** 1255 boul Duplessis G2G 2B4. Jct boul Duplessis and Wilfrid-Hamel (Hwy 138). Int corridors. **Pets:** Medium. $25 one-time fee/room. Service with restrictions, crate.

ECO ASK ✕ 🛏 💻

LEVIS

▼▼ **Comfort Inn** H

(418) 835-5605. **$95-$185.** 10 du Vallon est G6V 9J3. Hwy 20, exit 325S eastbound; exit 325 westbound. Int corridors. **Pets:** Accepted.

ECO ASK ✕ 🛏 💻

(CAA) ▼▼▼ **Comfort Inn & Suites Rive-Sud Quebec** H

(418) 836-3336. **$119-$169.** 495 Rte-du-Pont G7A 2N9. Hwy 20, exit 311, just ne on Rt 116; in St-Nicolas sector. Int corridors. **Pets:** Small. $25 one-time fee/pet. Service with restrictions, supervision.

SAVE ✕ 🛁M 🛏 💻 🏊

▼▼ **Hotel Kennedy** H

(418) 837-0233. **Call for rates.** 129 Rte du President-Kennedy G6V 6C8. Hwy 20, exit 325N, just n. Ext/int corridors. **Pets:** Accepted.

✕ 🛏 💻

▼▼▼ **Quality Inn & Suites Levis** H

(418) 833-1212. **$109-$199.** 5800 rue des Arpents G6V 0B5. Hwy 20, exit 325, just ne. Int corridors. **Pets:** Accepted. ASK ✕ 🛏 💻 🏊

QUEBEC

▼▼▼ **ALT Hotel-Quebec** H

(418) 658-1224. **Call for rates.** 1200 ave Germain-des-Pres G1V 3M7. Just n of boul Laurier; in Ste-Foy sector. Int corridors. **Pets:** Accepted.

✕ 🍴

▼▼▼ **Appartements La Pergola** CO

(418) 681-1428. **Call for rates.** 405 boul Rene-Levesque ouest G1S 1S2. Between aves Moncton and des Erables. Int corridors. **Pets:** Accepted. ✕ 🛏 💻

(CAA) ▼▼▼▼ **Auberge Saint-Antoine** H ❀

(418) 692-2211. **$159-$1299.** 8 rue St-Antoine G1K 4C9. Corner of rue Dalhousie. Int corridors. **Pets:** Other species. $150 one-time fee/room. Service with restrictions, supervision. SAVE ✕ 🛏 💻 🍴 ✕

(CAA) ▼▼▼ ▼▼▼ **Best Western City Centre/Centre-Ville** H

(418) 649-1919. **$110-$400.** 330 rue de la Couronne G1K 6E6. Corner of rue du Roi. Int corridors. **Pets:** Medium. $30 one-time fee/room. Designated rooms, service with restrictions, supervision.

SAVE ✕ 🛏 💻 🍴 🏊

(CAA) ▼▼▼ ▼▼▼ **Château Bonne Entente** H ❀

(418) 653-5221. **$169-$499.** 3400 chemin Ste-Foy G1X 1S6. Hwy 540 (Autoroute Duplessis), exit chemin Ste-Foy, just w; in Ste-Foy sector. Int corridors. **Pets:** Other species. $60 one-time fee/room. Service with restrictions, supervision. SAVE ✕ 🛁M 💻 🍴 🏊 ✕

▼▼ **Comfort Inn** H

(418) 666-1226. **$90-$199.** 240 boul Ste-Anne G1E 3L7. Hwy 440, exit Francois-de-Laval. Int corridors. **Pets:** Other species. $15 one-time fee/room. Supervision. (ASK) ⊠ 🛏 💻

(CAA) ▼▼ **Comfort Inn de l'Aeroport-Hamel** H

(418) 872-5038. **$90-$135.** 7320 boul Wilfrid-Hamel G2G 1C1. Hwy 138, 0.9 mi (1.5 km) w of boul Duplessis. Int corridors. **Pets:** Medium, other species. $25 one-time fee/pet. Service with restrictions, supervision. (ECO) (SAVE) ⊠ 🛏 💻

(CAA) ▼▼▼ **Delta Quebec** H ❖

(418) 647-1717. **$100-$270.** 690 boul Rene-Levesque est G1R 5A8. Just w of boul Honore-Mercier. Int corridors. **Pets:** Medium, other species. $35 one-time fee/room. Designated rooms, no service, supervision. (ECO) (SAVE) ⊠ 🛏 💻 🍴 🐾

(CAA) ▼▼ ▼▼ **Fairmont Le Château Frontenac** H ❖

(418) 692-3861. **$161-$499.** 1 rue des Carrieres G1R 4P5. In Old Quebec. Int corridors. **Pets:** Dogs only. $25 daily fee/pet. Service with restrictions, supervision. (ECO) (SAVE) ⊠ 🛏 💻 🍴 🐾 ⊠

▼▼ **Gite du Vieux-Bourg** BB

(418) 661-0116. **Call for rates.** 492 ave Royale G1E 1Y1. Hwy 440, exit Francois-de-Laval, just n, then 0.3 mi (0.5 km) e; in Beauport sector. Int corridors. **Pets:** Accepted. ⊠ 🛏 💻 🐾 ❖

(CAA) ▼▼ ▼▼ **Hilton Québec** H ❖

(418) 647-2411. **$109-$349.** 1100 boul Rene-Levesque est G1R 4P3. Corner of ave Honore-Mercier. Int corridors. **Pets:** Other species. $25 one-time fee/room. Service with restrictions, supervision. (ECO) (SAVE) ⊠ 🛏 💻 🍴 🐾 ⊠

▼▼ ▼▼ **Hotel Clarion Quebec** H

(418) 653-4901. **$90-$199.** 3125 boul Hochelaga G1V 4A8. Hwy 73, exit 136 (Hochelaga ouest); in Ste-Foy sector. Int corridors. **Pets:** Designated rooms, service with restrictions, supervision. (SAVE) ⊠ 🛏 💻 🍴 🐾 ⊠

▼▼▼▼ **Hotel Gouverneur Quebec-Sainte-Foy** H

(418) 651-3030. **$72-$153.** 3030 boul Laurier G1V 2M5. Corner of rue Lavigerie; in Ste-Foy sector. Ext/int corridors. **Pets:** Accepted. (ECO) (ASK) ⊠ 🛏 💻 🍴 🐾

▼▼▼▼ **Hotel Le Germain Dominion** H 🐾

(418) 692-2224. **$169-$385.** 126 rue St-Pierre G1K 4A8. Corner rue St-Paul. Int corridors. **Pets:** Dogs only. $30 daily fee/room. Designated rooms, supervision. ⊠ 💻

(CAA) ▼▼▼▼ **Hotel Pur** H

(418) 647-2611. **$109-$500.** 395 rue de la Couronne G1K 7X4. Corner of rue St-Joseph est. Int corridors. **Pets:** Accepted. (SAVE) ⊠ 🛏 💻 🍴 🐾 ⊠

(CAA) ▼▼▼ **Hotel Quality Suites Quebec** H ❖

(418) 622-4244. **$99-$185.** 1600 rue Bouvier G2K 1N8. Hwy 40, exit 312N (Pierre-Bertrand nord), 1.3 mi (2 km) w of jct Rt 358. Int corridors. **Pets:** Other species. $25 one-time fee/room. Designated rooms, service with restrictions, crate. (ECO) (SAVE) ⊠ 🛏 💻

(CAA) ▼▼▼▼ **Hotel Quartier** H ❖

(418) 650-1616. **$100-$350.** 2955 boul Laurier G1V 2M2. Just e of Hwy 73; in Ste-Foy sector. Int corridors. **Pets:** Large. $30 daily fee/pet. Service with restrictions, supervision. (SAVE) ⊠ 🛏 💻 🍴 🐾

(CAA) ▼▼▼ **Hotel Super 8 Quebec Ste-Foy** H ❖

(418) 877-6888. **$81-$200.** 7286 boul Wilfred Hamel G2G 1C1. Hwy 138, 0.7 mi (1.1 km) w of boul Duplessis; in Ste-Foy sector. Int corridors. **Pets:** Small. $100 deposit/room, $20 daily fee/pet. Designated rooms, service with restrictions, supervision. (ECO) (SAVE) ⊠ 🛏 💻 🐾 ⊠

(CAA) ▼▼ ▼▼ **L'Hotel du Vieux Quebec** H

(418) 692-1850. **$104-$328.** 1190 rue St-Jean G1R 1S6. Corner of rue de l'Hotel-Dieu. Int corridors. **Pets:** $25 daily fee/pet. Designated rooms, service with restrictions, supervision. (ECO) (SAVE) ⊠ 🛏 💻 🍴

(CAA) ▼▼ ▼▼ **Loews Le Concorde** H

(418) 647-2222. **$119-$359.** 1225 Cours du General-de-Montcalm G1R 4W6. Corner of Grande Allee est. Int corridors. **Pets:** Accepted. (ECO) (SAVE) ⊠ 🛏 💻 🍴 🐾 ⊠

ST-FERREOL-LES-NEIGES

▼▼ **Chalets Montmorency Condominiums**
Mont-Sainte-Anne Quebec CO

(418) 826-2600. **$99-$159, 30 day notice.** 1768 ave Royale G0A 3R0. On Hwy 360. Ext corridors. **Pets:** Dogs only. $25 daily fee/pet. Designated rooms, no service, crate. (ASK) ⊠ 🛏 💻 🐾 ⊠

▼▼ **Chalets-Village Mont-Sainte-Anne** CA

(418) 826-3331. **$200-$3000, 60 day notice.** 1815 boul Les Neiges G0A 3R0. On north side of Hwy 360; village centre. Ext corridors. **Pets:** Other species. $100 one-time fee/room. No service, supervision. (ECO) ⊠ 🛏 ⊠

STE-ANNE-DE-BEAUPRE

▼▼ **Hotel Confort Sainte-Anne** H

(418) 827-1570. **Call for rates.** 9800 boul Ste-Anne G0A 3C0. On Hwy 138. Int corridors. **Pets:** Accepted. ⊠ 🛏 💻

(CAA) ▼▼ **Manoir Ste-Anne** M

(418) 827-8383. **$65-$125.** 9776 boul Ste-Anne G0A 3C0. On Hwy 138. Ext corridors. **Pets:** Service with restrictions, supervision. (SAVE) ⊠ 🛏 💻

END METROPOLITAN AREA

RIGAUD

▼▼ **Howard Johnson** H ❖

(450) 458-7779. **$69-$139.** 93 Montee Lavigne J0P 1P0. Hwy 40, exit 17, just ne. Int corridors. **Pets:** $25 daily fee/pet. Designated rooms, service with restrictions, supervision. (ASK) ⊠ 🛏 💻

RIMOUSKI

▼▼ **Comfort Inn** H

(418) 724-2500. **$119-$149.** 455 boul St-Germain ouest G5L 3P2. On Rt 132. Int corridors. **Pets:** Other species. Supervision. (ECO) (ASK) ⊠ 🛏 💻

▼▼▼▼ **Hotel Rimouski** H

(418) 725-5000. **$119-$149, 15 day notice.** 225 boul Rene-Lepage est G5L 1P2. On Rt 132, corner of rue Julien-Rehel. Int corridors. **Pets:** Small. Service with restrictions, supervision. (ASK) ⊠ (GM) 🛏 💻 🍴 🐾 ⊠

RIVIERA-DU-LOUP

▼▼ **Comfort Inn** H

(418) 867-4162. **$100-$190.** 85 boul Cartier G5R 4X4. Hwy 20, exit 507, just se; Hwy 85, exit 96 (Fraserville); follow signs. Int corridors. **Pets:** Accepted. (ECO) (ASK) ⊠ 🛏 💻

(CAA) ▼▼▼▼ **Days Inn Riviere-du-Loup** H

(418) 862-6354. **$94-$159.** 182 rue Fraser G5R 1C8. Hwy 20, exit 503, 0.6 mi (1 km) e on Rt 132. Ext corridors. **Pets:** $10 daily fee/pet. Service with restrictions, supervision. (ECO) (SAVE) ⊠ 🛏 💻 🐾

ROUYN-NORANDA

(CAA) ▼▼▼ **Best Western Albert Centre-Ville** H

(819) 762-3545. **$106-$111.** 84 Principale Ave J9X 4P2. Centre. Int corridors. **Pets:** Accepted. (SAVE) ⊠ 🛏 💻 🍴

▼▼ Comfort Inn H

(819) 797-1313. **$99-$122.** 1295 rue Lariviere J9X 6M6. On Rt 117, 2.5 mi (4 km) s from town centre. Int corridors. **Pets:** Accepted.

ECO ASK ⊠ 🖬 ▣

ST-ANTOINE-DE-TILLY

▼▼▼ Manoir De Tilly CI

(418) 886-2407. **$105-$995, 3 day notice.** 3854 chemin de Tilly G0S 2C0. Jct Hwy 20, exit 291, 5.3 mi (8.5 km) n on Rt 273; centre. Int corridors. **Pets:** Small, dogs only. $50 daily fee/room. Supervision. ⊠ 🍴

ST-FAUSTIN-LAC-CARRE

▼▼ Motel Tremblant sur la Colline M

(819) 688-2102. **$79-$129, 7 day notice.** 357 Rt 117 J0T 1J2. On Rt 117, 2.5 mi (4 km) n of exit for city. Ext/int corridors. **Pets:** Accepted.

ASK ⊠ 🖬 ▣ ⌘

ST-HYACINTHE

▼▼▼ Hotel des Seigneurs Saint-Hyacinthe H 🐾

(450) 774-3810. **$188-$240.** 1200 rue Johnson J2S 7K7. Hwy 20, exit 130S, just e on rue Gauvin from boul Laframboise. Int corridors. **Pets:** Medium. $25 one-time fee/room. Service with restrictions, crate.

ECO ASK ⊠ ⓺ᴹ 🖬 ▣ 🍴 ⌘ ⊠

ST-JEAN-PORT-JOLI

▼▼ Auberge Du Faubourg M

(418) 598-6455. **Call for rates.** 280 ave de Gaspe ouest (Rt 132) G0R 3G0. 1.4 mi (2.4 km) w on Rt 132 from jct Rt 204; Hwy 20, exit 414. Ext corridors. **Pets:** Other species. $35 daily fee/pet. Service with restrictions, supervision. ⊠ 🖬 ▣ 🍴 ⌘ 🐾

ST-JEAN-SUR-RICHELIEU

▼▼▼ Holiday Inn Express H

(450) 359-4466. **$119-$179.** 700 rue Gadbois J3A 1V1. Hwy 35, exit 9, e on rue Pierre-Caisse. Int corridors. **Pets:** Accepted.

ASK ⊠ ⓺ᴹ 🖬 ▣ ⌘

STE-AGATHE-DES-MONTS

▼▼▼ Chalets Domaine Ste-Agathe CA

(819) 326-5836. **$100-$320, 7 day notice.** 650 rue du Domaine J8C 3C9. Hwy 15, exit 86, 0.3 mi (0.5 km) s on Rt 117. Ext corridors. **Pets:** Medium. $10 deposit/pet. Service with restrictions, supervision.

ASK ⊠ ⌘ ⊠

CAA ▼▼▼ Super 8 H 🐾

(819) 324-8880. **$88-$149.** 500 rue Leonard J8C 0A3. Hwy 15, exit 86, just w on Rt 117 to rue Leonard, then 0.3 mi (0.5 km) s. Int corridors. **Pets:** Medium. $15 daily fee/pet. Designated rooms, service with restrictions, supervision. ECO SAVE ⊠ 🖬 ▣ ⌘ ⊠

STE-MARTHE

▼▼▼ Auberge des Gallant CI

(450) 459-4241. **$160-$250, 7 day notice.** 1171 chemin St-Henri J0P 1W0. 5.3 mi (8.5 km) w on chemin St-Henri from Hwy 201. Int corridors. **Pets:** Accepted. ⊠ ▣ 🍴 ⌘ ⊠

SHAWINIGAN

▼▼ Auberge Escapade Inn H

(819) 539-6911. **$97-$179.** 3383 rue Garnier G9N 6R4. Hwy 55, exit 217, 0.3 mi (0.5 km) n on Rt 351. Ext/int corridors. **Pets:** Medium. $15 daily fee/pet. Service with restrictions, supervision. ASK ⊠ 🖬 🍴

CAA ▼▼▼ Auberge Gouverneur & Centre de Congres Shawinigan H

(819) 537-6000. **$103-$148.** 1100 Promenade-du-St-Maurice G9N 1L8. Hwy 55 N, exit 211, 2.8 mi (4.4 km) n on Hwy 153, follow signs. Int corridors. **Pets:** Accepted. SAVE ⊠ 🖬 ▣ 🍴 ⌘ ⊠

▼▼ Comfort Inn & Suites H

(819) 536-2000. **$81-$101.** 500 boul du Capitaine G9P 5J6. Hwy 55 N, exit 211, 2.8 mi (4.4 km) n on Hwy 153, then 1.3 mi (2 km) s on Rt 157. Int corridors. **Pets:** Accepted. ASK ⊠ 🖬 ▣

SHERBROOKE

▼▼ Comfort Inn H

(819) 564-4400. **$108-$114.** 4295 boul Bourque J1N 1S4. Hwy 410, exit 4W, 0.9 mi (1.5 km) w on Rt 112. Ext/int corridors. **Pets:** Small. $25 one-time fee/pet. Designated rooms, service with restrictions, supervision.

ECO ASK ⊠ 🖬 ▣

▼▼▼▼ Delta Sherbrooke Hotel and Conference Centre H

(819) 822-1989. **$104-$279.** 2685 rue King ouest J1L 1C1. Hwy 410, exit 4W, 0.6 mi (1 km) e on Rt 112. Int corridors. **Pets:** Accepted.

ECO ASK ⊠ 🖬 ▣ 🍴 ⌘ ⊠

THETFORD MINES

▼▼ Comfort Inn H

(418) 338-0171. **$107-$124.** 123 boul Frontenac ouest G6G 7S7. On Rt 112. Int corridors. **Pets:** Other species. Service with restrictions, crate.

ECO ASK ⊠ 🖬 ▣

TROIS-RIVIERES

▼▼ Comfort Inn H

(819) 371-3566. **$105-$110.** 6255 rue Corbeil G8Z 4P9. Hwy 55, exit 183 (boul Jean XXIII); 1.3 mi (2 km) n of Centennial Bridge, then 0.3 mi (0.5 km) e. Int corridors. **Pets:** Accepted. ECO ASK ⊠ 🖬 ▣

CAA ▼▼ Days Inn H

(819) 377-4444. **$80-$170.** 3155 boul St-Jean G9B 2M4. Hwy 55, exit 183 (boul Jean XXIII), 0.3 mi (0.5 km) w, then 0.3 mi (0.4 km) n. Int corridors. **Pets:** Medium, other species. $20 daily fee/room. Designated rooms, service with restrictions, crate. ECO SAVE ⊠ 🖬 ▣

CAA ▼▼▼ Delta Trois-Rivieres Hotel and Conference Center H 🐾

(819) 376-1991. **$107-$260.** 1620 rue Notre-Dame Centre G9A 6E5. Corner of rue St-Roch; centre. Int corridors. **Pets:** Large. $35 one-time fee/room. Service with restrictions, supervision.

ECO SAVE ⊠ 🖬 ▣ 🍴 ⌘ ⊠

CAA ▼▼▼ Super 8 Hotel Trois-Rivieres H

(819) 377-5881. **$115-$290.** 3185 boul St-Jean G9B 2M4. Hwy 55, exit 183 (boul Jean XXIII), just nw. Int corridors. **Pets:** Medium, other species. $20 daily fee/pet. Designated rooms, service with restrictions, supervision. ECO SAVE ⊠ 🖬 ▣ ⌘ ⊠

VAL-D'OR

▼▼ Comfort Inn H

(819) 825-9360. **$114-$123.** 1665 3ieme Ave J9P 1V9. In town centre. Int corridors. **Pets:** Accepted. ECO ASK ⊠ 🖬 ▣

▼▼▼ Motel L'Escale Hotel Suite H

(819) 824-2711. **$105-$135.** 1100 rue L'Escale J9P 4G8. In town centre. Ext/int corridors. **Pets:** Accepted. ⊠ 🖬 ▣ 🍴

SASKATCHEWAN

CARONPORT

▼▼ The Pilgrim Inn 🏠
(306) 756-5002. **Call for rates.** Hwy 1 W S0H 0S0. On Trans-Canada Hwy 1. Int corridors. **Pets:** Other species. Designated rooms, service with restrictions. ⊠ 🛢 🖵

ESTEVAN

🅐 ▼▼ Perfect Inns & Suites 🏠
(306) 634-8585. **$100-$130.** 134 2nd Ave S4A 2W6. Just n of jct Hwy 39. Int corridors. **Pets:** Accepted. 🆂🅰🆅🅴 ⊠ 🛢 🖵

KINDERSLEY

▼▼ Nova Inn 🏠
(306) 463-4687. **Call for rates.** 100 12th Ave NW S0L 1S0. Jct of Hwy 7 and 21. Ext/int corridors. **Pets:** Accepted. ⊠ 🛢 🖵 🍴

MOOSE JAW

▼▼ Comfort Inn 🏠
(306) 692-2100. **$120-$170.** 155 Thatcher Dr W S6J 1M1. 0.8 mi (1.2 km) s on Hwy 2 from jct Trans-Canada Hwy 1, then just w. Int corridors. **Pets:** Medium. $15 one-time fee/pet. Designated rooms, service with restrictions, supervision. 🅰🆂🅺 ⊠ 🛢 🖵

▼▼ Heritage Inn Moose Jaw 🏠
(306) 693-7550. **$112-$210.** 1590 Main St N S6J 1L3. On Hwy 2, 0.9 mi (1.4 km) s of jct Trans-Canada Hwy 1. Int corridors. **Pets:** Accepted.
🅰🆂🅺 ⊠ 🛢 🖵 🍴 ⇨

▼ Prairie Oasis Motel Ⓜ
(306) 692-4894. **$86-$96.** 955 Thatcher Dr E S6H 4N9. Just s of jct Trans-Canada Hwy 1. Ext corridors. **Pets:** Medium, dogs only. Designated rooms, service with restrictions, crate. ⊠ 🛢 🖵 ⇨ ⊠

▼▼ Super 8-Moose Jaw 🏠
(306) 692-8888. **Call for rates.** 1706 Main St N S6J 1L4. On Hwy 2, 0.7 mi (1.1 km) s of jct Trans-Canada Hwy 1. Int corridors. **Pets:** Other species. $15 daily fee/room. Designated rooms, service with restrictions, supervision. 🄴🄲🄾 ⊠ 🆄🅼 🛢 🖵

NORTH BATTLEFORD

▼ Super 8 🏠
(306) 446-8888. **$95-$125.** 1006 Hwy 16 Bypass S9A 3W2. 0.3 mi (0.5 km) nw of jct Hwy 16. Int corridors. **Pets:** Small. $25 one-time fee/room. Designated rooms, service with restrictions, supervision. 🅰🆂🅺 ⊠ 🛢

▼▼ Tropical Inn 🏠
(306) 446-4700. **$90-$94.** 1001 Hwy 16 Bypass S9A 3W2. Corner of Battleford Rd. Int corridors. **Pets:** Accepted.
⊠ 🛢 🖵 🍴 ⇨ ⊠

PRINCE ALBERT

🅐 ▼▼ Best Western Marquis Inn & Suites 🏠
(306) 922-9595. **$110-$150.** 602 36th St E S6V 7P2. Jct Hwy 3 (6th Ave E) and Marquis Rd. Int corridors. **Pets:** Other species. Designated rooms, supervision. 🆂🅰🆅🅴 ⊠ 🛢 🖵 🍴

▼▼ Comfort Inn 🏠
(306) 763-4466. **$98-$125.** 3863 2nd Ave W S6W 1A1. 1.6 mi (2.6 km) s on Hwy 2. Int corridors. **Pets:** Accepted. 🄴🄲🄾 🅰🆂🅺 ⊠ 🛢 🖵

🅐 ▼▼ Ramada Prince Albert 🏠
(306) 922-1333. **$105.** 3245 2nd Ave W S6V 5G1. 1.2 mi (2 km) s on Hwy 2. Int corridors. **Pets:** Dogs only. $10 daily fee/pet. Designated rooms. 🆂🅰🆅🅴 ⊠ 🛢 🖵 🍴

▼▼ Super 8 🏠
(306) 953-0088. **$114-$129.** 4444 2nd Ave W S6V 5R7. 1.7 mi (2.7 km) s on Hwy 2. Int corridors. **Pets:** Small. $10 daily fee/room. Designated rooms, service with restrictions, supervision. 🅰🆂🅺 ⊠ 🛢 🖵

▼▼ Travelodge Prince Albert 🏠
(306) 764-6441. **$110-$175.** 3551 2nd Ave W S6V 5G1. 1.4 mi (2.2 km) s on Hwy 2. Int corridors. **Pets:** Other species. Service with restrictions, crate. 🄴🄲🄾 🅰🆂🅺 ⊠ 🛢 🖵 🍴

REGINA

🅐 ▼▼▼ Best Western Seven Oaks Inn 🏠
(306) 757-0121. **$135.** 777 Albert St S4R 2P6. On Hwy 6; jct 2nd Ave. Int corridors. **Pets:** $10 daily fee/room. Service with restrictions, supervision. 🆂🅰🆅🅴 ⊠ 🛢 🖵 🍴 ⇨ ⊠

🅐 ▼▼ Comfort Inn 🏠
(306) 789-5522. **$119-$125.** 3221 E Eastgate Dr S4Z 1A4. Trans-Canada Hwy 1, 1.3 mi (2 km) e of Ring Rd; at eastern approach to city. Int corridors. **Pets:** Accepted. 🄴🄲🄾 🆂🅰🆅🅴 ⊠ 🛢 🖵

▼▼ Country Inn & Suites By Carlson 🏠 🐾
(306) 789-9117. **$120-$155, 3 day notice.** 3321 Eastgate Bay S4Z 1A4. Trans-Canada Hwy 1, 1.3 mi (2 km) e of Ring Rd; at eastern approach to city. Int corridors. **Pets:** Other species. $100 deposit/room, $25 one-time fee/room. Designated rooms, service with restrictions, crate.
🄴🄲🄾 🅰🆂🅺 ⊠ 🆄🅼 🛢 🖵

▼▼▼ Delta Regina 🏠
(306) 525-5255. **$165-$230.** 1919 Saskatchewan Dr S4P 4H2. At Rose St; centre. Int corridors. **Pets:** Accepted.
🄴🄲🄾 🅰🆂🅺 ⊠ 🛢 🖵 🍴 ⇨ ⊠

▼▼▼ Holiday Inn Express Hotel & Suites Regina 🏠
(306) 569-4600. **$145-$195.** 1907 11th Ave S4P 0J2. Corner of Rose St; centre. Int corridors. **Pets:** Medium. $15 daily fee/room. Designated rooms, service with restrictions, supervision. 🅰🆂🅺 ⊠ 🛢 🖵

▼▼▼ Holiday Inn Hotel & Suites 🏠 🐾
(306) 789-3883. **$159-$224.** 1800 Prince of Wales Dr S4Z 1A4. 1.2 mi (1.9 km) e on Trans-Canada Hwy 1, jct Ring Rd, then just n; at eastern approach to city. Int corridors. **Pets:** $20 daily fee/pet. Designated rooms, service with restrictions, supervision.
🄴🄲🄾 🅰🆂🅺 ⊠ 🛢 🖵 🍴 ⇨ ⊠

🅐 ▼▼ Howard Johnson Inn 🏠
(306) 565-0455. **$100-$110.** 1110 Victoria Ave E S4N 7A9. On Trans-Canada Hwy 1, just w of Ring Rd; at eastern approach to city. Int corridors. **Pets:** Accepted. 🆂🅰🆅🅴 ⊠ 🛢 🖵 ⇨

🅐 ▼▼▼ Quality Hotel 🏠
(306) 569-4656. **$99-$169.** 1717 Victoria Ave S4P 0P9. Just e of Broad St; downtown. Int corridors. **Pets:** Accepted. 🆂🅰🆅🅴 ⊠ 🛢 🖵 🍴

🅐 ▼▼▼ Radisson Plaza Hotel Saskatchewan 🏠
(306) 522-7691. **$173-$280.** 2125 Victoria Ave S4P 0S3. At Scarth St; centre. Int corridors. **Pets:** Other species. $35 one-time fee/room. Crate.
🄴🄲🄾 🆂🅰🆅🅴 ⊠ 🆄🅼 🖵 🍴 ⊠

▼▼ Ramada Hotel & Convention Centre 🏠
(306) 569-1666. **$134-$194.** 1818 Victoria Ave S4P 0R1. At Broad St; centre. Int corridors. **Pets:** Accepted.
🄴🄲🄾 🅰🆂🅺 ⊠ 🛢 🖵 🍴 ⇨ ⊠

ⒶⒶ ▼▼▼▼ Regina Inn Hotel & Conference Centre 🅷

(306) 525-6767. **$129-$210.** 1975 Broad St S4P 1Y2. Jct Victoria Ave; centre. Int corridors. **Pets:** Medium. $45 one-time fee/room. Service with restrictions, crate. ⒺⒸⓄ ⓈⒶⓋⒺ ☒ 🔔 💻 🍴

▼▼▼▼ Sandman Hotel Suites & Spa 🅷

(306) 757-2444. **Call for rates.** 1800 Victoria Ave E S4N 7K3. On Trans-Canada Hwy 1, just e of Ring Rd; at eastern approach to city. Int corridors. **Pets:** Accepted. ⒺⒸⓄ ☒ 🔔 💻 🍴 ⇆

▼ Super 8 Regina 🅷

(306) 789-8833. **$104-$135.** 2730 Victoria Ave E S4N 6M5. On Trans-Canada Hwy 1, 1 mi (1.6 km) e of Ring Rd; at eastern approach to city. Int corridors. **Pets:** Medium. $10 daily fee/pet. Service with restrictions, crate. ⒶⓈⓀ ☒ 🔔 💻

▼ ▼ West Harvest Inn 🅷

(306) 586-6755. **Call for rates.** 4025 Albert St S S4S 3R6. On Hwy 6, 1.3 mi (2 km) n of jct Trans-Canada Hwy 1. Int corridors. **Pets:** Accepted. ☒ 🔔 🍴

ⒶⒶ ▼▼▼▼ Wingate by Wyndham 🅷 🐾

(306) 584-7400. **$162-$200.** 1700 Broad St S4P 1X4. Corner of Saskatchewan Dr; centre. Int corridors. **Pets:** Medium. $25 daily fee/room. Service with restrictions, crate. ⒺⒸⓄ ⓈⒶⓋⒺ ☒ ♿ 🔔 💻

SASKATOON

ⒶⒶ ▼▼▼ Best Western Harvest Inn 🅷 🐾

(306) 244-5552. **$127-$230.** 1715 Idylwyld Dr N S7L 1B4. On Hwy 11 (Idylwyld Dr), 0.4 mi (0.7 km) s of jct Circle Dr. Int corridors. **Pets:** Medium, dogs only. $25 one-time fee/room. Designated rooms, service with restrictions, supervision. ⓈⒶⓋⒺ ☒ 🔔 💻 🍴

ⒶⒶ ▼▼▼ Colonial Square Inn & Suites 🅷

(306) 343-1676. **$99-$139, 7 day notice.** 1301 8th St E S7H 0S7. 1.5 mi (2.4 km) e of jct Hwy 11 (Idylwyld Dr); 1.4 mi (2.3 km) w of jct Circle Dr. Int corridors. **Pets:** $10 one-time fee/pet. Designated rooms, service with restrictions, supervision. ⓈⒶⓋⒺ ☒ 🔔 💻

ⒶⒶ ▼▼▼ Comfort Inn 🅷

(306) 934-1122. **$124-$128.** 2155 Northridge Dr S7L 6X6. Just ne of jct Hwy 11 (Idylwyld Dr) and Circle Dr. Int corridors. **Pets:** Accepted. ⒺⒸⓄ ⓈⒶⓋⒺ ☒ ♿ 🔔 💻

▼▼▼ Country Inn & Suites By Carlson 🅷

(306) 934-3900. **$112-$140.** 617 Cynthia St S7L 6B7. Just w on Circle Dr from jct Hwy 11 (Idylwyld Dr), then just n on Ave CN. Int corridors. **Pets:** $25 one-time fee/room. Service with restrictions, crate. ⒺⒸⓄ ⒶⓈⓀ ☒ ♿ 🔔 💻

▼▼▼▼ Delta Bessborough 🅷

(306) 244-5521. **$122-$340.** 601 Spadina Crescent E S7K 3G8. At 21st St E; centre. Int corridors. **Pets:** Accepted. ⒺⒸⓄ ⒶⓈⓀ ☒ 🔔 💻 🍴 ⇆ ☒

▼▼▼▼ Holiday Inn Express Hotel & Suites 🅷

(306) 384-8844. **$144-$189.** 315 Idylwyld Dr N S7L 0Z1. On Hwy 11 (Idylwyld Dr), just n of 23rd St. Int corridors. **Pets:** Accepted. ⒺⒸⓄ ⒶⓈⓀ ☒ ♿ 🔔 💻 ⇆

▼▼▼ Motel 6 Saskatoon 🅷

(306) 665-6688. **$102-$142.** 231 Marquis Dr S7R 1B7. E of jct Trans-Canada Hwy 16; 0.4 mi (0.7 km) w of Hwy 11 (Idylwyld Dr). Int corridors. **Pets:** Other species. Service with restrictions, supervision. ⒶⓈⓀ ☒ ♿ 🔔 💻 ⇆

▼▼ Sandman Hotel 🅷

(306) 477-4844. **Call for rates.** 310 Circle Dr W S7L 2Y5. Just w of Hwy 11 (Idylwyld Dr). Int corridors. **Pets:** Accepted. ⒺⒸⓄ ☒ 🔔 💻 🍴 ⇆

ⒶⒶ ▼▼▼ Sheraton Cavalier Saskatoon Hotel 🅷

(306) 652-6770. **Call for rates.** 612 Spadina Crescent E S7K 3G9. At 21st St E; centre. Int corridors. **Pets:** Accepted. ⒺⒸⓄ ⓈⒶⓋⒺ ☒ 🔔 🍴 ⇆ ☒

▼▼ Super 8 🅷

(306) 384-8989. **$110-$122.** 706 Circle Dr E S7K 3T7. 1.3 mi (2 km) e of jct Hwy 11 (Idylwyld Dr). Int corridors. **Pets:** $5 one-time fee/room. Service with restrictions, crate. ⒶⓈⓀ ☒ 🔔 💻

▼▼▼ Travelodge Hotel Saskatoon 🅷

(306) 242-8881. **$129-$189.** 106 Circle Dr W S7L 4L6. Just w of jct Hwy 11 (Idylwyld Dr). Int corridors. **Pets:** Accepted. ⒺⒸⓄ ⒶⓈⓀ ☒ 🔔 💻 🍴 ⇆ ☒

SHAUNAVON

▼ Hidden Hilten Motel Ⓜ

(306) 297-4166. **$68-$86.** 352 5th St W S0N 2M0. 0.3 mi (0.5 km) e of jct Hwy 37, then just n. Ext corridors. **Pets:** Accepted. ⒶⓈⓀ ☒ 🔔 💻

SWIFT CURRENT

▼▼ Comfort Inn 🅷

(306) 778-3994. **$95-$105, 7 day notice.** 1510 S Service Rd E S9H 3X6. On south side service road of Trans-Canada Hwy 1, just w of 22nd Ave NE. Int corridors. **Pets:** Accepted. ⒺⒸⓄ ⒶⓈⓀ ☒ 🔔 💻

ⒶⒶ ▼▼ Safari Inn Motel Ⓜ

(306) 773-4608. **$68-$77.** 810 S Service Rd E S9H 3T9. On south side service road of Trans-Canada Hwy 1, just e of Central Ave. Ext corridors. **Pets:** Accepted. ⓈⒶⓋⒺ ☒ 🔔 💻

▼▼ Super 8 🅷

(306) 778-6088. **$121-$191.** 405 N Service Rd E S9H 3X6. Trans-Canada Hwy 1, just e of Central Ave N; on north side of Service Rd. Int corridors. **Pets:** Accepted. ⒺⒸⓄ ⒶⓈⓀ ☒ 🔔 💻 ⇆

WEYBURN

ⒶⒶ ▼▼▼ Perfect Inns & Suites Ⓜ

(306) 842-2691. **$74-$170.** 238 Sims Ave S4H 2J8. 0.3 mi (0.5 km) w of jct Hwy 35 and 39. Ext/int corridors. **Pets:** Accepted. ⓈⒶⓋⒺ ☒ 🔔 💻

YORKTON

▼▼ Comfort Inn & Suites 🅷

(306) 783-0333. **$120-$200.** 22 Dracup Ave S3N 3W1. Just w of jct Hwy 9, 10 and 16 (Yellowhead Hwy). Int corridors. **Pets:** Accepted. ⒶⓈⓀ ☒ 🔔 💻 ⇆

▼▼ Days Inn 🅷

(306) 783-3297. **$120-$190.** 2 Kelsey Bay S3N 3Z4. Just e of jct Hwy 9, 10 and 16 (Yellowhead Hwy). Int corridors. **Pets:** Accepted. ⒺⒸⓄ ⒶⓈⓀ ☒ ♿ 🔔 💻 ⇆ ☒

ⒶⒶ ▼▼▼ Ramada 🅷

(306) 783-9781. **$119-$149.** 100 Broadway St E S3N 0K9. On Hwy 9, 10, and 16 (Yellowhead Hwy); downtown. Int corridors. **Pets:** $20 one-time fee/pet. Designated rooms, service with restrictions. ⓈⒶⓋⒺ ☒ 🔔 💻 🍴 ⇆ ☒

YUKON TERRITORY

DAWSON CITY

◆ Bonanza Gold Motel M
(867) 993-6789. **$89-$189.** Bonanza Creek Rd Y0B 1G0. 1.5 mi (2.4 km) s on Hwy 2. Ext corridors. **Pets:** Other species. $20 one-time fee/room. Designated rooms, service with restrictions, supervision.
⊠ 🛏 🖵 🍴

◆◆ Klondike Kate's Cabins CA ❀
(867) 993-6527. **$100-$160.** 1103 3rd Ave & King St Y0B 1G0. Corner of 3rd Ave and King St. Ext corridors. **Pets:** $20 one-time fee/room. Service with restrictions. ⊠ 🛏 🖵 🍴 🐾

ⒶⒶ ◆◆ Westmark Inn Dawson City M
(867) 993-5542. **$129-$169.** 5th Ave & Harper Y0B 1G0. At 5th Ave and Harper St; downtown. Ext/int corridors. **Pets:** Accepted.
SAVE ⊠ 🖵 🍴

HAINES JUNCTION

◆◆ Alcan Motor Inn M
(867) 634-2371. **$110-$176, 3 day notice.** Alaska & Haines Hwys Y0B 1L0. Jct Hwy 1 (Alaska Hwy) and 3 (Haines Hwy). Ext corridors. **Pets:** Medium, other species. $10 daily fee/pet. Designated rooms, service with restrictions, supervision. ⊠ 🛏 🖵 🍴

WHITEHORSE

ⒶⒶ ◆◆◆ Best Western Gold Rush Inn H
(867) 668-4500. **$115-$205.** 411 Main St Y1A 2B6. Centre. Int corridors. **Pets:** Accepted. SAVE ⊠ 🛏 🖵 🍴

ⒶⒶ ◆◆ High Country Inn H
(867) 667-4471. **$129-$259, 3 day notice.** 4051 4th Ave Y1A 1H1. 0.4 mi (0.6 km) e of Main St. Int corridors. **Pets:** Accepted.
SAVE ⊠ 🛏 🖵 🍴

ⒶⒶ ◆◆◆ Westmark Whitehorse Hotel & Conference Centre H
(867) 393-9700. **$159-$179.** 201 Wood St Y1A 2E4. At 2nd Ave; centre. Int corridors. **Pets:** Designated rooms, no service, supervision.
SAVE ⊠ 🛅M 🛏 🖵 🍴 🐾

Pet-Friendly Campgrounds

United States
Canada

United States

Alabama

CHILDERSBURG — DESOTO CAVERNS PARK CAMP-GROUND. (256) 378-7252. **$29-$32.** 5181 DeSoto Caverns Pkwy 35044. On SR 76, 5 mi e. 🏕️

PELHAM — BIRMINGHAM SOUTH CAMPGROUND. (205) 664-8832. **2P $37-$43, XP: $2.** 222 Hwy 33 35124. I-65, exit 242, 0.5 mi w on CR 52, then 0.3 mi n. 🚐 🏕️ 🅜

Arizona

AMADO — DE ANZA TRAILS RV RESORT. (520) 398-8628. **2P $32.** 2869 E Frontage Rd 85645. I-19, exit 48, just e, then 1.6 mi s. (HC 65, Box 381, TUMACACORI 85640). 🏕️ 🏕️

ANTHEM — PIONEER RV PARK. (623) 465-7465. **2P $34, XP: $3.** 36408 N Black Canyon Hwy 85086. I-17, exit 225, 0.3 mi w, follow signs. 🏕️ 🚐 🏕️

APACHE JUNCTION — SUPERSTITION SUNRISE LUXURY RV RESORT. (480) 986-4524. **2P $30-$50, XP: $5-$75. (no credit cards).** 702 S Meridian Rd 85220. US 60, exit 193 (Signal Butte Rd), 0.4 mi n to Southern, 1 mi e, then 0.5 mi n. 🏕️ 🚐 🏕️

BENSON — BUTTERFIELD RV RESORT. (520) 586-4400. **2P $29-$38, XP: $2.** 251 S Ocotillo Ave 85602. I-10, exit 304 (Ocotillo Ave), 0.6 mi s. 🏕️ 🚐 🏕️

BENSON — COCHISE TERRACE RV RESORT. (520) 586-0600. **2P $23-$35, XP: $3.** 1030 S Barrel Cactus Ridge 85602. I-10, exit 302, 1 mi s on SR 90, then just w. 🏕️ 🚐 🏕️

BENSON — PATO BLANCO LAKES RV RESORT. (520) 586-8966. **$38-$43.** 635 E Pearl St 85602. I-10, exit 306, just s, 0.7 mi w on Frontage Rd, then 0.4 mi n on County Rd. 🏕️ 🚐 🏕️

BENSON — SAN PEDRO RESORT COMMUNITY. (520) 586-9546. **2P $30, XP: $2.** 1110 S Hwy 80, Box 1 85602. I-10, exit 304 (Ocotillo Ave), 0.5 mi s, 1 mi e on 4th St, then 1.3 mi se. 🏕️ 🚐 🏕️

CAMP VERDE — DISTANT DRUMS RV RESORT. (928) 554-8000. **2P $33-$39, XP: $3.** 583 W Middle Verde Rd 86322. I-17, exit 289, just sw. 🏕️ 🚐 🏕️

CASA GRANDE — FIESTA GRANDE-RV RESORT. (520) 836-7222. **Call for rates.** 1511 E Florence Blvd 85222. I-10, exit 194, 2 mi w. 🏕️ 🚐 🏕️

CASA GRANDE — PALM CREEK GOLF AND RV RESORT. (520) 421-7000. **4P $30-$49.** 1110 N Henness Rd 85222. I-10, exit 194, 1 mi w, then just n. 🏕️ 🚐 🏕️

ELOY — DESERT VALLEY RV RESORT. (520) 466-4500. **2P $32, XP: $3.** 4555 W Tonto Rd 85231. I-10, exit 203 (Toltec Rd), 0.5 mi n, then 0.5 mi w. 🏕️ 🚐 🏕️

FORT MCDOWELL — EAGLE VIEW RV RESORT AT FT MCDOWELL. 🔺 (480) 789-5310. **4P $42-$47, XP: $10.** 9605 N Ft McDowell Rd 85264. Jct Shea Blvd, 2 mi ne on SR 87, 0.5 mi se. 🏕️ 🚐 🏕️

GOLD CANYON — CANYON VISTAS RV RESORT. (480) 288-8844. **2P $20-$39, XP: $3.** 6601 E US Hwy 60 85218. 1.2 mi w of Kings Ranch Rd; between MM 202 and 201. 🅢 🏕️ 🚐 🏕️

HUACHUCA CITY — TOMBSTONE TERRITORIES RV PARK. 🔺 (520) 457-2584. **2P $30-$34, XP: $1.** 2111 E Hwy 82 85616. Jct SR 90, 7.7 mi e; between MM 59 and 60. 🏕️ 🚐 🏕️

LAKE HAVASU CITY — CRAZY HORSE CAMPGROUNDS. (928) 855-4033. **Call for rates. (no credit cards).** 1534 Beachcomber Blvd 86403. 0.7 mi w of London Bridge/US 95 on McCulloch Blvd, just w. 🚐 🏕️

LAKE HAVASU CITY — HAVASU RV RESORT. (928) 764-2020. **Call for rates.** 1905 Victoria Farms Rd 86404. From London Bridge, 5.3 mi n on SR 95, just e on Chenoweth Dr, then 0.4 mi n. 🏕️ 🚐 🏕️

LAKE HAVASU CITY — ISLANDER RV RESORT. (928) 680-2000. **Call for rates.** 751 Beachcomber Blvd 86403. Jct Lake Havasu Blvd, 1.7 mi sw on McCulloch Blvd. 🏕️ 🚐 🏕️

LAKE HAVASU CITY — PROSPECTOR'S RV RESORT. (928) 764-2000. **$25-$34.** 4750 London Bridge Rd N 86404. 7.6 mi n of London Bridge; 1.5 mi sw of jct SR 95. 🏕️ 🚐 🏕️

MESA — APACHE WELLS RV RESORT. (480) 832-4324. **2P $22-$44, XP: $3.** 2656 N 56th St 85215. Jct N Higley Rd, 0.4 mi e on E McDowell Rd, just s. 🏕️ 🚐 🏕️

MESA — GOOD LIFE RV RESORT. 🔺 (480) 832-4990. **2P $30-$40, XP: $3.** 3403 E Main St 85213. US 60, exit 184 (Val Vista Dr), 2 mi n, then just w. 🏕️ 🚐 🏕️

MESA — MESA REGAL RV RESORT. (480) 830-2821. **Call for rates. (no credit cards).** 4700 E Main St 85205. Just e of Greenfield Rd. 🏕️ 🚐 🏕️

MESA — MESA SPIRIT RV RESORT. 🔺 (480) 832-1770. **2P $30-$53, XP: $4.** 3020 E Main St 85213. US 60, exit 184 (Val Vista Dr), 2 mi n to Main St, then 0.8 mi w. 🏕️ 🚐 🏕️

MESA — MONTE VISTA VILLAGE RESORT. (480) 833-2223. **2P $51, XP: $2.** 8865 E Baseline Rd 85209. US 60, exit 191 (Ellsworth Rd), 0.6 mi s, then just w. 🏕️ 🚐 🏕️

MESA — SUN LIFE VACATION RESORT. (480) 981-9500. **Call for rates. (no credit cards).** 5055 E University Dr 85205. Just w of Higley Rd. 🅢 🏕️ 🚐 🏕️

MESA — TOWERPOINT RV RESORT. 🔺 (480) 832-4996. **2P $30-$40, XP: $3.** 4860 E Main St 85205. US 60, exit 186 (Higley Rd), 2 mi n, then just w. 🏕️ 🚐 🏕️

MESA — VAL VISTA VILLAGE. (480) 832-2547. **2P $20-$65, XP:** $3. 233 N Val Vista Dr 85213. US 60, exit 184 (Val Vista Dr), 2.2 mi n. 🛡️📶 🐾 ⊃ ⊠

MESA — VALLE DEL ORO RV RESORT. (480) 984-1146. **Call for rates.** 1452 S Ellsworth Rd 85209. US 60, exit 191 (Ellsworth Rd), just n. 🐾 ⊃ ⊠

MESA — VIEWPOINT RV & GOLF RESORT. (480) 373-8700. $30-$59. 8700 E University Dr 85207. 2.4 mi e of Power Rd. 🐾 ⊃ ⊠

PHOENIX — DESERT SHADOWS RV RESORT. ⨀ (623) 869-8178. **2P $34, XP:** $3. 19203 N 29th Ave 85027. I-17, exit 214A (Union Hills) northbound, 0.3 mi w, then 0.4 mi n; exit 214 A&B southbound, 0.5 mi s, 0.3 mi w on Union Hills, then 0.4 mi n. 🐾 ⊃ ⊠

PICACHO — PICACHO PEAK RV RESORT. (520) 466-7841. **2P** $30-$35, XP: $2. 17065 E Peak Ln 85241. I-10, exit 219, 0.7 mi s on frontage road. (PO Box 300). 🐾 ⊃ ⊠

SUN CITY — PARADISE RV RESORT. ⨀ (623) 977-0344. **2P** $30-$48, XP: $2. 10950 W Union Hills Dr 85373. Loop 101, exit 15 (Union Hills Dr), 3.8 mi w. 🛡️📶 🐾 ⊃ ⊠

TONOPAH — SADDLE MOUNTAIN RV PARK. (623) 386-3892. **2P $28, XP:** $2. 3607 N 411th Ave 85354. I-10, exit 94, 0.6 mi s. 🐾 ⊃ ⊠

TUCSON — BEAUDRY RV RESORT. (520) 239-1300. **2P $25-$50.** 5151 S Country Club Rd 85706. I-10, exit 264B (Palo Verde and Irvington), just n to Irvington, 0.5 mi w, then just s. 🐾 ⊃ ⊠

TUCSON — VOYAGER RV RESORT. ⨀ (520) 574-5000. **4P** $25-$54, XP: $5. 8701 S Kolb Rd 85706. I-10, exit 270, 0.7 mi s. 🐾 ⊃ ⊠

YUMA — ARABY ACRES RV RESORT. (928) 344-8666. **Call for rates.** 6649 E 32nd St 85365. I-8, exit 7 (Araby Rd), just s, then just e. 🐾 ⊃ ⊠

YUMA — BONITA MESA RV RESORT. (928) 342-2999. **2P $35,** XP: $5. 9400 N Frontage Rd 85365. I-8, exit 12 (Fortuna Rd), just n, then 1.6 mi w. 🐾 ⊃ ⊠

YUMA — COCOPAH RV & GOLF RESORT. (928) 343-9300. **2P** $43-$46, XP: $2. 6800 Strand Ave 85364. I-8, exit Winterhaven/4th Ave eastbound, 0.5 mi s on 4th Ave, 2.4 mi w on 1st St, just s on Ave C, 1.4 mi w on Riverside, then 0.9 mi nw. 🐾 ⊃ ⊠

YUMA — DEL PUEBLO RV PARK & TENNIS RESORT. (928) 341-2100. **Call for rates. (no credit cards).** 14794 Ave 3 E 85365. I-8, exit 3 (Ave 3 E/SR 280 S), 5.3 mi s. 🐾 ⊃ ⊠

YUMA — HIDDEN SHORES RV VILLAGE. (928) 539-6700. **6P** $54-$74. 10300 Imperial Dam Rd 85365. I-8, exit 12 (Fortuna Rd), 1.9 mi n, 10.4 mi n on US 95, then 6.5 mi w; Yuma Proving Ground Base. 🐾 ⊃ ⊠

YUMA — LAS QUINTAS OASIS RESORT. (928) 305-9005. **2P** $38, XP: $2. 10442 E Frontage Rd 85365. I-8, exit 12 (Fortuna Rd), just n, then 0.6 mi w; north side of interstate. 🐾 ⊃ ⊠

YUMA — SUN VISTA RV RESORT. ⨀ (928) 726-8920. **2P** $46, XP: $3. 7201 E 32nd St (Business 8) 85365. I-8, exit 7 (Araby Rd), just s, then 0.5 mi e. 🐾 ⊃ ⊠

YUMA — WESTWIND RV & GOLF RESORT. ⨀ (928) 342-2992. **2P $40-$50, XP:** $3. 9797 E 32nd St (S Frontage Rd) 85365. I-8, exit 12 (Fortuna Rd) on south side, 1 mi w. 🐾 ⊃ ⊠ ♿

California

AGUANGA — OUTDOOR RESORTS RANCHO CALIFORNIA. (951) 767-0848. **4P $65, XP:** $2. 45525 Hwy 79 S 92536. I-15, exit 58 (SR 79 S), 14 mi e; just e of SR 371. 🐾 ⊃ ⊠

BIG BEAR LAKE — BIG BEAR SHORES RV RESORT & YACHT CLUB. (909) 866-4151. **$66-$150.** 40751 North Shore Ln 92315. SR 18, 5 mi e of the dam on SR 38 (North Shore Dr), 1.2 mi se. (PO Box 1572). 🐾 ⊃ ⊠

BUELLTON — FLYING FLAGS RV PARK & CAMPGROUND. ⨀ (805) 688-3716. **2P $22-$88, XP:** $3. 180 Ave of the Flags 93427. Just w of US 101, exit 140A (SR 246). ⊃ ⊠

CASTAIC — VALENCIA TRAVEL VILLAGE. ⨀ (661) 257-3333. **2P $40-$59, XP:** $2. 27946 Henry Mayo Rd 91384. I-5, exit SR 126, 1.3 mi w. 🛡️📶 🐾 ⊃ ⊠

CATHEDRAL CITY — OUTDOOR RESORTS/PALM SPRINGS. (760) 324-4005. **6P $45-$77.** 69-411 Ramon Rd 92234. I-10, exit 126 (Date Palm Dr), 2.2 mi s, then 0.5 mi e. ⊃ ⊠

CHULA VISTA — CHULA VISTA RV RESORT. (619) 422-0111. **4P $47-$77, XP:** $3. 460 Sandpiper Way 91910. I-5, exit 7B (J St/Marina Pkwy), 4 mi w, then 0.5 mi n. 🛡️📶 🐾 ⊃ ⊠

CHULA VISTA — SAN DIEGO METRO KOA. (619) 427-3601. **4P $47-$86, XP:** $4. 111 N 2nd Ave 91910. I-5, exit 8B (E St), 1 mi e to 2nd Ave, then 1 mi n; I-805, exit E St, 1 mi w, then just n. ⊃ ⊠

COLOMA — COLOMA RESORT. (530) 621-2267. **Call for rates. (no credit cards).** 6921 Mt. Murphy Rd 95613. E off SR 49 on Mt. Murphy Rd; on south fork of American River. (PO Box 516). ⊃ ⊠

DEL LOMA — DEL LOMA RV PARK & CAMPGROUND. (530) 623-2834. **2P $25, XP:** $2. 21720 SR 299 96010. On SR 299; in southwest Del Loma. ⊃ ⊠

DESERT HOT SPRINGS — SKY VALLEY RESORT. (760) 329-2909. **2P $36-$44, XP:** $5. 74-711 Dillon Rd 92241. I-10, exit 123 (Palm Dr/Gene Autry Tr), 3.3 mi n, then 8.5 mi e. 🐾 ⊃ ⊠

EL CENTRO — DESERT TRAILS RV PARK. (760) 352-7275. **2P** $23-$41, XP: $3. 225 Wake Ave 92243. I-8, exit 115 (4th St/SR 86), just s, then just e. ⊃ ⊠

EL CENTRO — SUNBEAM LAKE RV RESORT. (760) 352-7154. **Call for rates.** 1716 W Sunbeam Lake Dr 92243. I-8, exit 107 (Drew Rd), 0.6 mi n. ⊃ ⊠

FORTUNA — RIVERWALK RV PARK & CAMPGROUND. (707) 725-3359. **2P $42, XP: $5.** 2189 Riverwalk Dr 95540. W of US 101, exit Kenmar Rd. 🆂 ➥ ✕

GARBERVILLE — BENBOW VALLEY RV RESORT & GOLF COURSE. **AAA** (707) 923-2777. **2P $30-$85, XP: $6.** 7000 Benbow Dr 95542. US 101, exit Benbow Dr, 2 mi s. 🅰 ➥ ✕

HEMET — GOLDEN VILLAGE PALMS RV RESORT. **AAA** (951) 925-4123. **2P $42-$61, XP: $10.** 3600 W Florida Ave 92545. SR 79 N (San Jacinto St), 3 mi w. ➥ ✕

INDIO — INDIAN WELLS RV PARK. (760) 347-0895. **2P $49-$63, XP: $5.** 47-340 Jefferson St 92201. I-10, exit 139 (Jefferson St/Indio Blvd), 2.8 mi s. 🅰 ➥ ✕

INDIO — OUTDOOR RESORTS INDIO-THE ULTIMATE MOTOR-COACH RESORT. (760) 775-7255. **Call for rates.** 80-394 48th Ave 92201. I-10, exit 139 (Jefferson St/Indio Blvd), 3.1 mi s, then 0.3 mi e. ➥ ✕

JACKSON — JACKSON RANCHERIA RV PARK. (209) 223-8358. **$30-$55.** 12222 New York Ranch Rd 95642. 2.5 mi e from jct SR 49 and 88, then just 1 mi n. 🅰 ➥ ✕ 🅼

JULIAN — PINEZANITA TRAILER RANCH & CAMPGROUND. (760) 765-0429. **2P $25-$32, XP: $3.** 4446 SR 79 92036. On SR 79, 3.6 mi s of SR 78. (PO Box 2380).

LODI — FLAG CITY RV RESORT. **AAA** (209) 339-8300. **6P $44, XP: $2.** 6120 W Banner St 95242. I-5, exit SR 12 E, s on Star St, then just e. 🆂 🅰 ➥ 🅼

NEWPORT BEACH — NEWPORT DUNES WATERFRONT RV RESORT. (949) 729-3863. **6P $60-$350.** 1131 Back Bay Dr 92660. SR 73, exit 15 (Jamboree Rd) southbound, 3 mi s, then just n on SR 1; exit 13 (Bison Ave) northbound, just w to MacArthur Blvd, 2.5 mi s to SR 1, then 1.5 mi n. ➥ ✕

NILAND — FOUNTAIN OF YOUTH SPA. (760) 354-1340. **2P $21-$46, XP: $2.** 1500 Spa Rd 92257. 14 mi nw on SR 111, 1.6 mi ne on Hot Mineral Spa Rd, then 1.2 mi sw. ➥ ✕

ORANGE — ORANGELAND RECREATION VEHICLE PARK. **AAA** (714) 633-0414. **$60-$80.** 1600 W Struck Ave 92867. SR 57, exit 2 (Katella Ave), 0.5 mi e, then just s. 🅰 ➥ ✕

OROVILLE — FEATHER FALLS CASINO KOA. (530) 533-9020. **Call for rates. (no credit cards).** #1 Feather Falls Blvd 95966. SR 70, exit Ophir Rd, 3 mi e. 🅰 ➥ ✕ 🅼

PALM DESERT — EMERALD DESERT RV RESORT. (760) 345-4770. **Call for rates. (no credit cards).** 76000 Frank Sinatra Dr 92211. I-10, exit 134 (Cook St), 1 mi s, then 1 mi e. 🅰 ➥ ✕

PASO ROBLES — WINE COUNTRY RV RESORT. (805) 238-4560. **2P $43-$70, XP: $4.** 2500 Airport Rd 93446. US 101, exit 231B (SR 46/Fresno/Bakersfield), 2 mi e, then just n. 🅰 ➥

PETALUMA — SAN FRANCISCO NORTH/PETALUMA CAMP-GROUNDS. **AAA** (707) 763-1492. **2P $30-$80, XP: $5-$7.** 20 Rainsville Rd 94952. US 101, exit Penngrove, just w to Stony Point Rd, then 0.5 mi n. ➥ ✕

PISMO BEACH — PACIFIC DUNES RANCH RV PARK. (805) 489-7787. **6P $45-$59.** 1205 Silver Spur Pl 93445. In Oceano; SR 1, exit 22nd St, 0.3 mi s, then 0.4 mi w. 🅰 ✕

PISMO BEACH — PISMO COAST VILLAGE RV RESORT. (805) 773-1811. **6P $38-$56, XP: $2.** 165 S Dolliver St 93449. 0.5 mi s on SR 1. 🅰 ➥ ✕

PLYMOUTH — FAR HORIZONS 49'ER VILLAGE. **AAA** (209) 245-6981. **4P $37-$74, XP: $5.** 18265 Hwy 49 95669. On SR 49, 0.3 mi s. 🅰 ➥ ✕ 🅼

RED BLUFF — DURANGO RV RESORT. (530) 527-5300. **2P $41-$55, XP: $3.** 100 Lake Ave 96080. I-5, exit 649 (SR 36/Antelope Rd), just w, just ne on Belle Mill Rd, n on East Ave, then just ne. 🅰 ➥ ✕ 🅼

REDDING — PREMIER RV RESORTS. (530) 246-0101. **2P $35-$45, XP: $3.** 280 N Boulder Dr 96003. I-5, exit 680 (SR 299/Burney-Alturas/Lake Blvd), just w on Lake Blvd, then just n. ➥ ✕

SAN DIEGO — CAMPLAND ON THE BAY. (858) 581-4260. **Call for rates.** 2211 Pacific Beach Dr 92109. I-5, exit 23A (Grand Ave) northbound, 1 mi w to Olney, then 0.3 mi s; exit 23 (Balboa/Garnet) southbound, s on Mission Bay Dr to Grand Ave, then 1 mi w to Olney. 🆂 ➥ ✕

SAN DIMAS — EAST SHORE RV PARK. **AAA** (909) 599-8355. **2P $46-$49, XP: $3.** 1440 Camper View Rd 91773. I-10, exit 44 (Fairplex Dr), 0.6 mi n, 0.6 mi w on Via Verde, then 0.6 mi n; in Frank G Bonelli Regional Park. 🆂 ➥ ✕

SAN JUAN BAUTISTA — BETABEL RV RESORT. **AAA** (831) 623-2202. **2P $35-$38, XP: $3.** 9664 Betabel Rd 95045. US 101, exit Betabel Rd, just w. 🅰 ➥

SANTA BARBARA — OCEAN MESA AT EL CAPITAN. (805) 879-5751. **4P $40-$90, XP: $10.** 101 El Capitan Terrace Ln 93117. US 101, exit 117 (El Capitan State Beach), just n to Ocean Mesa RV Resort sign, then e. ➥ ✕

SHAVER LAKE — CAMP EDISON. (559) 841-3134. **Call for rates.** 42696 Tollhouse Rd 93664. Just ne of Huntington Lake Rd; e of Deer Creek Ln. (PO Box 600). 🆂 ✕

TEMECULA — PECHANGA RV RESORT. **AAA** (951) 770-2658. **$42-$52.** 45000 Pechanga Pkwy 92592. I-15, exit 58 (SR 79 S), 1 mi e, then 2 mi s. 🅰 ➥ ✕

TEMECULA — VAIL LAKE RESORT. (951) 303-0173. **Call for rates.** 38000 Hwy 79 S 92592. I-15, exit 58 (SR 79 S), 9 mi se. 🆂 ➥ ✕

TRINIDAD — EMERALD FOREST OF TRINIDAD. **AAA** (707) 677-3554. **2P $26-$42, XP: $3.** 753 Patrick's Point Dr 95570. US 101, exit Patrick's Point Dr W. (PO Box 870). ✕

WEAVERVILLE — TRINITY LAKE RESORTS AT PINEWOOD COVE RV PARK & CAMPGROUND. (530) 286-2201. **$15-$40, XP: $4.** 45110 State Hwy 3 96091. 14 mi ne of town. ➥ ✕

WILLITS — WILLITS-UKIAH KOA. (707) 459-6179. **Call for rates.** 1600 Hwy 20 95490. 1.5 mi w on SR 20, from jct US 101. (PO Box 946). 🛶 ⊠

WINTERHAVEN — RIVER'S EDGE RV RESORT. (760) 572-5105. **2P $28-$30, XP: $2.** 2299 Winterhaven Dr 92283. I-8, exit 170 (Winterhaven Dr), 0.5 mi e. 🏕 🛶 ⊠

Colorado

BRECKENRIDGE — TIGER RUN RESORT. (970) 453-9690. **$39-$74.** 85 Tiger Run Rd 80424. I-70, exit 203, 6 mi s on SR 9, then just e on Revette Dr. 🏕 🛶 ⊠

FORT COLLINS — FORT COLLINS LAKESIDE KOA. (970) 484-9880. **2P $34-$110, XP: $3-$8.** 1910 N Taft Hill Rd 80524. I-25, exit 269B, 6 mi w to Taft Hill Rd, then 2.2 mi n. 🛶 ⊠

GOLDEN — DAKOTA RIDGE RV PARK. (303) 279-1625. **2P $40-$49, XP: $5.** 17800 W Colfax Ave 80401. I-70, exit 262 (W Colfax Ave), 1.8 mi w on US 40. 🏕 🛶 ⊠

GRAND LAKE — WINDING RIVER RESORT INC. ⨁ (970) 627-3215. **2P $29-$40, XP: $4.** 1447 CR 491 80447. 1.5 mi ne on US 34 to CR 491, then 1.5 mi w. (PO Box 629). ⊠

LOVELAND — JOHNSON'S CORNER RV RETREAT. (970) 669-8400. **$38, XP: $3.** 3618 SE Frontage Rd 80537. I-25, exit 254, 0.3 mi se; adjacent to Great Colorado Marketplace. 🛡 🏕 🛶 ⊠

Florida

ARCADIA — LITTLE WILLIES RV RESORT. (863) 494-2717. **Call for rates. (no credit cards).** 5905 NE Cubitus Ave 34266. 3.8 mi n on US 17, just w on NE McKay St, then 1.4 mi n. 🏕 🛶 ⊠ &M

ARCADIA — TOBY'S RV RESORT. (863) 494-1744. **2P $28-$51.** 3550 NE Hwy 70 34266. On SR 70, 2.7 mi e. 🏕 🛶 ⊠

BRADENTON — HORSESHOE COVE RV RESORT. (941) 758-5335. **Call for rates.** 5100 60th St E 34203. I-75, exit 217 southbound; exit 217B northbound, 1.7 mi w on SR 70, then just n on Caruso Rd. 🏕 🛶 ⊠

BRADENTON — MANATEE ENCORE RV RESORT. (941) 745-2600. **6P $27-$67.** 800 Kay Rd NE 34212. I-75, exit 220 southbound; exit 220B northbound, 0.6 mi w on SR 64, then 0.8 mi n on Cypress Creek Blvd (merges to Kay Rd NE). 🛡 🛶 ⊠

CHOKOLOSKEE — OUTDOOR RESORTS OF AMERICA OF CHOKOLOSKEE. (239) 695-2881. **Call for rates.** 100 CR 29 S 34138. On CR 29; center. (PO Box 39). 🏕 🛶 ⊠

CLERMONT — CLERBROOK RESORT. (352) 394-5513. **Call for rates. (no credit cards).** 20005 US 27 34711. Florida Tpke, exit 285, 1.2 mi s. 🛶 ⊠

CRYSTAL RIVER — CRYSTAL ISLES RV RESORT. (352) 795-3774. **6P $38-$60, XP: $5.** 11419 W Fort Island Tr 34429. Jct US 19, 4.5 mi w on SR 44 W. 🛶 ⊠

CRYSTAL RIVER — ELITE RESORTS AT CRYSTAL RIVER. (352) 685-1900. **$32-$40.** 275 S Rock Crusher Rd 34429. 1.5 mi s of SR 44. 🏕 🛶 ⊠

DAVENPORT — DEER CREEK RV RESORT. (863) 424-2839. **4P $45-$65.** 42749 Hwy 27 33837. I-4, exit 55, 1 mi se. 🛡 🛶 ⊠

DAVENPORT — ORLANDO SW/FORT SUMMIT KOA. ⨁ (863) 424-1880. **2P $35-$70, XP: $2-$5.** 2525 Frontage Rd 33837. I-4, exit 55; jct US 27. 🛶 ⊠

DEBARY — HIGH BANKS MARINA & CAMP RESORT. (386) 668-4491. **$45-$65, XP: $5-$10.** 488 W Highbanks Rd 32713. 2.7 mi w of US 17-92. 🛶 ⊠

DESTIN — DESTIN RV BEACH RESORT. (850) 837-3529. **Call for rates.** 362 Miramar Beach Dr 32550. 4.1 mi e of SR 293 (Mid-Bay Bridge), just s. 🏕 🛶

FORT MYERS — SIESTA BAY RV RESORT. ⨁ (239) 466-8988. **$32-$49.** 19333 Summerlin Rd 33908. 1.6 mi sw of jct US 41 on Gladiolus Dr (CR 865), 4.8 mi s on CR 869. 🏕 🛶 ⊠

FORT MYERS BEACH — GULF WATERS RV RESORT. ⨁ (239) 437-5888. **Call for rates.** 11301 Summerlin Square Rd 33931. 2.6 mi nw of jct Matanzas Pass Bridge, 0.4 mi e on Summerlin Rd, just s on Pine Ridge Rd, then just w. 🏕 🛶 ⊠ &M

JACKSONVILLE — FLAMINGO LAKE RV RESORT. ⨁ (904) 766-0672. **2P $42-$65, XP: $3.** 3640 Newcomb Rd 32218. I-295, exit 32, just nw on SR 115. 🏕 🛶 ⊠

JENNINGS — JENNINGS OUTDOOR RESORT CAMP-GROUND. (386) 938-3321. **2P $27-$32, XP: $2.** 2039 Hamilton Ave 32053. I-75, exit 467, just w on SR 143. 🛡 🛶 ⊠

JENSEN BEACH — NETTLES ISLAND. ⨁ (772) 229-1300. **4P $37-$64.** 9803 S Ocean Dr 34957. On SR A1A, 2.3 mi n of jct SR 732 (Jensen Beach Cswy); on S Hutchinson Island. 🏕 🛶 ⊠

KISSIMMEE — OUTDOOR RESORTS AT ORLANDO. (863) 424-1407. **$30.** 9000 W US 192 34714. On US 192, 1 mi e of jct US 27; I-4, exit 64B, 6.3 mi w. 🛶 ⊠

KISSIMMEE — TROPICAL PALMS RV RESORT. ⨁ (407) 396-4595. **$25-$79.** 2650 Holiday Tr 34746. I-4, exit 64, 1.5 mi e on US 192, then 0.8 mi s. 🛶 ⊠

LA BELLE — WHISPER CREEK RV RESORT. ⨁ (863) 675-6888. **2P $35. (no credit cards).** 3745 N SR 29 SW 33935. On SR 29, 1.8 mi n of jct SR 80. 🏕 🛶 ⊠

LAKE BUENA VISTA — DISNEY'S FORT WILDERNESS RESORT & CAMPGROUND. ⨁ (407) 824-2900. **10P $59-$121.** 4510 N Fort Wilderness Tr 32830. In Walt Disney World. (PO Box 10000). 🛶 ⊠

LAKELAND — LAKELAND CAREFREE RV RESORT. (863) 687-6146. **Call for rates.** 900 Old Combee Rd 33805. I-4, exit 33 eastbound, 1 mi ne on SR 33, then just w; exit 38 westbound, 5 mi sw on SR 33, then just nw. [symbols]

LAKELAND — SANLAN RV PARK. ⚫ (863) 665-1726. **2P $18-$47, XP: $3.** 3929 US 98 S 33812. I-4, exit 32, 8.7 mi s; just s of SR 570 (exit 10). [symbols]

LEESBURG — HOLIDAY TRAVEL RESORT. ⚫ (352) 787-5151. **2P $39, XP: $5.** 28229 CR 33 34748. 3.5 mi s via US 27, 0.5 mi w. [symbols]

MELBOURNE BEACH — OUTDOOR RESORTS MELBOURNE BEACH LUXURY RV RESORT. (321) 724-2600. **4P $37-$72, XP: $3.** 214 Horizon Ln 32951. 2.5 mi s. [symbols]

MIMS — SEASONS IN THE SUN MOTOR COACH RESORT. (321) 385-0440. **2P $28-$38, XP: $3.** 2400 Seasons In The Sun Blvd 32754. I-95, exit 223, 0.5 mi w on SR 46. [symbols]

NAPLES — NEAPOLITAN COVE RV RESORT. (239) 793-0091. **2P $35-$65.** 3729 Neapolitan Cir 34112. On US 41; 1.1 mi n of jct CR 864 (Rattlesnake Hammock Rd). [symbols]

NOKOMIS — ENCORE ROYAL COACHMEN RESORT ON DONA BAY. (941) 488-9674. **4P $40-$62, XP: $5.** 1070 Laurel Rd E 34275. I-75, exit 195, 1.9 mi w (CR 762). [symbols]

OCALA — OCALA RV CAMP RESORT. (352) 237-2138. **4P $29-$46, XP: $2-$4.** 3200 SW 38th Ave 34474. I-75, exit 350, just w on SR 200, just n on SW 38th Ct, then 0.5 mi e. [symbols]

OKEECHOBEE — OKEECHOBEE KOA RESORT & GOLF COURSE. (863) 763-0231. **Call for rates.** 4276 Hwy US 441 S 34974. On US 98 and 441, 3 mi s of jct SR 70; 0.3 mi n of Lake Okeechobee and jct SR 78. [symbols]

OLD TOWN — YELLOW JACKET CAMPGROUND RESORT. (352) 542-8365. **2P $32-$49, XP: $6.** 55 SE 503 Ave 32680. 10.7 mi s on SR 349, then 1.2 mi on dirt road. [symbols]

ORMOND BEACH — ENCORE SUNSHINE HOLIDAY DAYTONA. (386) 672-3045. **Call for rates. (no credit cards).** 1701 N US 1 32174. I-95, exit 273, 0.5 mi nw. [symbols]

PANAMA CITY BEACH — EMERALD COAST RV BEACH RESORT. ⚫ (850) 235-0924. **2P $53-$70, XP: $3-$4.** 1957 Allison Ave 32407. US 98/98A and Allison Ave, 1.5 mi w of Hathaway Bridge. [symbols]

PORT CHARLOTTE — ENCORE HARBOR LAKES RV RESORT. (941) 624-4511. **6P $33-$61, XP: $5.** 3737 El Jobean Rd 33953. On SR 776, 4.6 mi w of jct US 41. [symbols]

PORT CHARLOTTE — RIVERSIDE RV RESORT & CAMPGROUND. ⚫ (863) 993-2111. **4P $39-$55, XP: $2-$3.** 9770 SW CR 769 34269. I-75, exit 170, 4.5 mi ne on Kings Hwy. [symbols]

REDDICK — OCALA NORTH RV PARK. (352) 591-1723. **$22-$36.** 16905 NW CR 225 32686. I-75, exit 368, just w on CR 318, then 0.8 mi s. [symbols]

RIVER RANCH — RIVER RANCH RV RESORT. (863) 692-1116. **8P $50-$85, XP: $2.** 3400 River Ranch Blvd 33867. 3.5 mi s of SR 60; 25 mi e of US 27; 23 mi w of Florida Tpke and US 441; just w of the Kissimmee River. (30529 River Ranch Blvd). [symbols]

ROCKLEDGE — SPACE COAST RV RESORT. (321) 636-2873. **2P $50-$55, XP: $3.** 820 Barnes Blvd 32955. I-95, exit 195 (Fiske Blvd), just e, then just s on CR 502. [symbols]

SARASOTA — SUN-N-FUN RV RESORT. ⚫ (941) 371-2505. **Call for rates.** 7125 Fruitville Rd 34240. I-75, exit 210, 1.2 mi e on SR 780. [symbols]

SEBASTIAN — ENCORE RV PARK-VERO BEACH. (772) 589-7828. **2P $31-$52, XP: $5.** 9455 108th Ave 32978. I-95, exit 156, just e on CR 512. [symbols]

SEBRING — BUTTONWOOD BAY RV RESORT. ⚫ (863) 655-1122. **2P $29-$40, XP: $5.** 10001 US 27 S 33876. 1.5 mi s of SR 98. [symbols]

SILVER SPRINGS — THE SPRINGS RV RESORT. (352) 236-5250. **2P $30, XP: $3.** 2950 NE 52nd Ct 34488. On SR 40, 0.5 mi w of Silver Springs attraction, 0.5 mi n. [symbols]

SILVER SPRINGS — WILDERNESS RV PARK ESTATES. (352) 625-1122. **2P $37-$40, XP: $3.** 10313 E Hwy 40 34488. On SR 40, 4.5 mi e of Silver Springs attraction. [symbols]

ST. PETERSBURG — ST. PETERSBURG-MADEIRA BEACH RESORT KOA. (727) 392-2233. **Call for rates.** 5400 95th St N 33708. Jct 38th Ave N, 1.4 mi n on Tyrone/Bay Pines Blvd (Alternate Rt US 19), 0.5 mi e. [symbols]

SUMTERVILLE — SHADY BROOK GOLF & RV RESORT. (352) 568-2244. **Call for rates.** 178 N US 301 33585. I-75, exit 321, 2.5 mi e on CR 470, then 0.7 mi n. (PO Box 130). [symbols]

TAMPA — BAY BAYOU RV RESORT. ⚫ (813) 855-1000. **2P $39-$56.** 12622 Old Memorial Hwy 33635. Jct SR 580 (Hillsborough Ave W), 0.4 mi n on Countryway Blvd, then 0.8 mi w. [symbols]

TITUSVILLE — THE GREAT OUTDOORS RV & GOLF RESORT. (321) 269-5004. **2P $40-$65, XP: $3.** 125 Plantation Dr 32780. I-95, exit 215, 0.5 mi w on SR 50, 1.8 mi s on paved entrance road. [symbols]

UMATILLA — OLDE MILL STREAM RV RESORT. ⚫ (352) 669-3141. **2P $37-$48, XP: $3.** 1000 N Central Ave 32784. 0.8 mi n on SR 19. [symbols]

Georgia

PINE MOUNTAIN — PINE MOUNTAIN RV RESORT. (706) 663-4329. **Call for rates.** 8804 Hamilton Rd 31822. I-185, exit 42, 8 mi s on US 27. [symbols]

STONE MOUNTAIN — STONE MOUNTAIN PARK CAMPGROUND. (770) 498-5710. **Call for rates.** 1900 Stonewall Jackson Dr 30086. On east side of Stone Mountain; in Stone Mountain Memorial Park. (PO Box 778). [symbols]

Idaho

CASCADE — ARROWHEAD R.V. PARK ON THE RIVER. ⒶⒶⒶ (208) 382-4534. **2P $27-$32, XP: $1-$4.** 955 S Hwy 55 83611. South end of town. (PO Box 337). ⊠

COEUR D'ALENE — BLACKWELL ISLAND RV RESORT. (208) 665-1300. **2P $39-$53, XP: $5.** 800 S Marina Dr 83814. I-90, exit 12, 1.5 mi s on US 95. ⊠

KAMIAH — LEWIS-CLARK RESORT RV PARK. (208) 935-2556. **Call for rates.** 4243 Hwy 12 83536. On US 12, 1.5 mi e. ⊶ ⊠

WHITE BIRD — SWIFTWATER RV PARK. ⒶⒶⒶ (208) 839-2700. **2P $25-$28, XP: $5.** 3154 Salmon River Ct 83554. Just n of Milepost 222, exit Hammer Creek Recreational area, 0.8 mi nw. (PO Box 150). ⊠

Illinois

LEE CENTER — MHC O'CONNELL'S YOGI BEAR JELLYSTONE PARK. ⒶⒶⒶ (815) 857-3860. **2P $42-$65, XP: $10-$20.** 970 Greenwing Rd 61310. I-39, exit 87 (US 30), 12.8 mi w to CR 1955 E, then 3.3 mi se, follow signs. (PO Box 200, AMBOY). ⊶ ⊠

MILLBROOK — YOGI BEAR'S JELLYSTONE PARK CAMP RESORT. ⒶⒶⒶ (630) 553-5172. **2P $45-$57, XP: $10-$15.** 8574 Millbrook Rd 60536. 1.5 mi n of jct SR 71. (PO Box 306). ⊶ ⊠

Indiana

CRAWFORDSVILLE — CRAWFORDSVILLE KOA. (765) 362-4190. **Call for rates.** 1600 Lafayette Rd 47933. I-74, exit 34, 2 mi s on US 231. ⊶ ⊠

FREMONT — YOGI BEAR'S JELLYSTONE PARK CAMP RESORT. ⒶⒶⒶ (260) 833-1114. **5P $21-$60, XP: $10.** 140 Ln, 201 Barton Lake 46737-9652. I-69, exit 157 southbound; exit 154 northbound, 3 mi w on SR 120, then 0.5 mi n on CR 300 W; Toll Rd, exit 144 to SR 120. ⊶ ⊠

GRANGER — SOUTH BEND EAST KOA. (574) 277-1335. **2P $27-$53, XP: $3-$4.** 50707 Princess Way 46530. I-80/90, exit 83, just w on SR 331, 2 mi n on SR 23 (Adams Rd), then just w. ⊶ ⊠

MONTICELLO — INDIANA BEACH CAMPGROUND. (574) 583-8306. **Call for rates.** 5224 E Indiana Beach Rd 47960. 0.5 mi w on US 24, 3.5 mi n on W Shafer Dr (6th St). ⊠

MONTICELLO — YOGI BEAR'S JELLYSTONE PARK AT INDIANA BEACH. (574) 583-8646. **Call for rates. (no credit cards).** 2882 NW Shafer Dr 47960. 0.5 mi w on US 24, then 3.5 mi n. ⊶ ⊠

PIERCETON — YOGI BEAR'S JELLYSTONE PARK CAMP-RESORT. (574) 594-2124. **5P $38-$60, XP: $6-$10.** 1916 N 850 E 46562. US 30, 4.3 mi n on SR 13, 1.3 mi e on CR 200. ⊶ ⊠

SANTA CLAUS — LAKE RUDOLPH CAMPGROUND & RV RESORT. (812) 937-4458. **8P $25-$52.** 78 N Holiday Blvd 47579. I-64, exit 63, 7.9 mi s on SR 162. (PO Box 98). ⊶ ⊠

Louisiana

CARENCRO — BAYOU WILDERNESS RV RESORT. (337) 896-0598. **4P $43-$46, XP: $2-$5.** 201 St Clair Rd 70520. I-49, exit 2, 2.5 mi e on SR 98, then 1 mi n on Wilderness Tr. ⊠ ⊶ ⊠

HAMMOND — CALLOWAY RV & CAMPGROUND. (985) 542-8094. **2P $30-$33, XP: $2-$3.** 14154 Club De Luxe Rd 70403. I-12 to I-55 S, exit 28, 1 blk n, then 0.7 mi w. ⓈⒹ ⊶ ⊠

KINDER — COUSHATTA CASINO RV RESORT. (337) 738-1200. **$19-$24.** 777 Pow Wow Pkwy 70648. N of jct US 190 and 165, 4.5 mi on US 165. (PO Box 1240). ⊠ ⊶ ⊠ ⓁⓂ

ROBERT — YOGI BEAR'S JELLYSTONE CAMP-RESORT. (985) 542-1507. **5P $30-$60, XP: $20.** 46049 Hwy 445 N 70455. I-12, exit 47, 3 mi n. (PO Box 519). ⊶ ⊠

SCOTT — KOA KAMPGROUND OF LAFAYETTE. (337) 235-2739. **4P $39-$51, XP: $5-$6.** 537 Apollo Rd 70583. I-10, exit 97, 0.5 mi s. ⊶ ⊠

VIDALIA — RIVER VIEW RV PARK. ⒶⒶⒶ (318) 336-1400. **2P $30-$35, XP: $2.** 100 River View Pkwy 71373. Jct US 65/84, 0.8 mi s on SR 131. ⊶ ⊠

Maine

CASCO — POINT SEBAGO RESORT. (207) 655-3821. **4P $35-$90, XP: $5-$35.** 261 Point Sebago Rd 04015. Jct SR 121, 3.7 mi n on US 302, then 1 mi w, follow signs. ⊠

DAMARISCOTTA — LAKE PEMAQUID CAMPGROUND. ⒶⒶⒶ (207) 563-5202. **4P $24-$44, XP: $5-$10.** 100 Twin Cove Ln 04543. 0.8 mi n on US 1 business route, 2 mi e on Biscay Rd, then 0.3 mi n on Egypt Rd. (PO Box 967). ⊶ ⊠

NORTH WATERFORD — PAPOOSE POND RESORT & CAMPGROUND. (207) 583-4470. **2P $24-$75, XP: $5-$10.** 700 Norway Rd 04088. 1.9 mi w on SR 118 from jct SR 37; from Norway, 10 mi w on SR 118. ⊶ ⊠

OLD ORCHARD BEACH — POWDER HORN FAMILY CAMPING RESORT. (207) 934-4733. **2P $40-$65, XP: $4-$8.** 48 Cascade Rd (SR 98) 04064. 1 mi nw on SR 98; jct US 1, 1.8 mi se on SR 98. (PO Box 366). ⊶ ⊠ ⓁⓂ

ORLAND — SHADY OAKS CAMPGROUND & CABINS. (207) 469-7739. **2P $30-$32, XP: $3.** 32 Leaches Pt 04472. Jct US 1 and SR 175, sharp right, then 0.3 mi. ⊶ ⊠

SCARBOROUGH — BAYLEY'S CAMPING RESORT. ⒶⒶⒶ (207) 883-6043. **2P $29-$86, XP: $5-$8.** 275 Pine Point Rd 04074. Jct US 1, 2 mi e via SR 9 (Pine Point Rd), watch for sign. ⊶ ⊠

WELLS — WELLS BEACH RESORT CAMPGROUND. (AAA) (207) 646-7570. **2P $38-$75, XP: $8.** 1000 Post Rd (US 1) 04090. Jct SR 109/9, 1.3 mi s. 🛥️ 🗙

PORT SANILAC — LAKE HURON CAMPGROUND. (810) 622-0110. **Call for rates.** 2353 N Lakeshore Rd (M25) 48469. Jct SR 25 and 46, 5 mi n. 🛥️ 🗙

Maryland

BERLIN — FRONTIER TOWN CAMPGROUND. (410) 641-0880. **2P $27-$88, XP: $6-$12.** 8428 Stephen Decatur Hwy 21811. Jct SR 50, 4 mi s on SR 611. (PO Box 691, OCEAN CITY 21843). 🛥️ 🗙

COLLEGE PARK — CHERRY HILL PARK. (AAA) (301) 937-7116. **2P $57-$67, XP: $5.** 9800 Cherry Hill Rd 20740. I-95, exit 29B, 1 mi w on SR 212 (Powder Mill Rd), then 1 mi s; I-495, exit 25, just s to Cherry Hill Rd, then 1 mi nw. 🛥️ 🗙

FLINTSTONE — HIDDEN SPRINGS CAMPGROUND. (814) 767-9676. **4P $29-$33, XP: $2.** I-68, exit 50 to Rocky Gap State Park, 3.5 mi n on Pleasant Valley Rd. (PO Box 190 21530). 🛥️ 🗙

FREELAND — MORRIS MEADOWS RECREATION FARM. (AAA) (410) 329-6636. **2P $29-$56, XP: $5-$10.** 1523 Freeland Rd 21053. I-83, exit 36 (SR 439), w to jct SR 45, 1 mi n, then 3 mi w, follow signs. 🛥️ 🗙

WILLIAMSPORT — YOGI BEAR'S JELLYSTONE PARK CAMP RESORT HAGERSTOWN. (301) 223-7117. **$36-$62, XP: $3-$8.** 16519 Lappans Rd 21795. I-81, exit 1, 1.2 mi e on SR 68. 🏊 🛥️ 🗙

Massachusetts

BRIMFIELD — QUINEBAUG COVE CAMPGROUND. (413) 245-9525. **Call for rates.** 49 E Brimfield-Holland Rd 01010. I-84, exit 3B, 3.8 mi w on US 20, then 0.3 mi s. 🛥️ 🗙

FOXBORO — NORMANDY FARMS CAMPGROUND. (508) 543-7600. **2P $28-$72, XP: $5-$10.** 72 West St 02035. I-495, exit 14A, 1 mi n on US 1, then 1.3 mi e on Thurston and West sts. 🛥️ 🗙

OAKHAM — PINE ACRES FAMILY CAMPING RESORT. (508) 882-9509. **2P $35-$75, XP: $8-$15.** 203 Bechan Rd 01068. Jct SR 122, 2 mi sw on SR 148, just s via Spencer Rd. 🛥️ 🗙

SAVOY — SHADY PINES CAMPGROUND. (413) 743-2694. **Call for rates.** 547 Loop Rd 01256. On SR 8A and 116, 3.1 mi se. 🛥️ 🗙

Michigan

BAY VIEW — PETOSKEY KOA RV & CABIN RESORT. (231) 347-0005. **Call for rates.** 1800 N US 31 49770. US 31, 1 mi n of SR 119. 🛥️ 🗙

PORT HURON — PORT HURON KOA KAMPGROUND. (810) 987-4070. **$30-$80, XP: $3-$5.** 5111 Lapeer Rd 48074. I-94, exit 262, 8 mi n on Wadhams Rd, then 0.3 mi e; I-69, exit 196, 0.4 mi n on Wadhams Rd, then 0.3 mi e. 🛥️ 🗙

Minnesota

AUSTIN — BEAVER TRAILS JELLYSTONE PARK & CAMP RESORT. (AAA) (507) 584-6611. **$30-$60, XP: $3-$5.** 21943 630th Ave 55912. I-90, exit 187 (SR 20), just sw. 🛥️ 🗙

CALEDONIA — DUNROMIN' PARK. (507) 724-2514. **Call for rates.** 12757 Dunromin Dr 55921. Jct SR 44, 2.8 mi s on SR 76 S, 0.5 mi e. 🏊 🛥️ 🗙

CASS LAKE — STONY POINT RESORT, TRAILER PARK CAMPGROUNDS. (AAA) (218) 335-6311. **2P $28-$35, XP: $3.** 5510 US 2 NW 56633. On US 2, 2 mi e of jct SR 371. (PO Box 518). 🗙

COKATO — COKATO LAKE CAMPING & RV RESORT. (320) 286-5779. **Call for rates.** 2945 CR 4 SW 55321. 2.8 mi n of jct SR 12. 🛥️ 🗙

HINCKLEY — GRAND CASINO HINCKLEY RV RESORT & CHALETS. (AAA) (320) 384-4886. **$15-$28.** 1326 Fire Monument Rd 55037. I-35, exit 183, 1 mi e on SR 48. 🏊 🏕️ 🛥️ 🗙 ♿M

PARK RAPIDS — BREEZE CAMPING & RV RESORT ON EAGLE LAKE. (218) 732-5888. **Call for rates.** 25824 CR 89 56470. 9 mi n on US 71 from jct SR 34. 🛥️ 🗙

PARK RAPIDS — VAGABOND VILLAGE CAMPGROUND. (218) 732-5234. **Call for rates. (no credit cards).** 23801 Green Pines Rd 56470. 2 mi e on SR 34, 5.7 mi n on CR 4, just w on CR 40, then 0.5 mi w via signs. 🛥️ 🗙

PRIOR LAKE — DAKOTAH MEADOWS RV PARK. (AAA) (952) 445-8800. **$21-$30.** 2341 Park Pl 55372. Just w of CR 83. 🏕️ ♿M

RICHMOND — EL RANCHO MANANA CAMPGROUND & RIDING STABLE. (AAA) (320) 597-2740. **4P $25-$50, XP: $3.** 27302 Ranch Rd 56368. Jct SR 23 and 24, 4 mi n on CR 9, 2 mi ne on Manana and Ranch rds; 9 mi s of jct I-94, exit 153, via CR 9. 🗙

WALKER — SHORES OF LEECH LAKE CAMPGROUND & MARINA. (218) 547-1819. **2P $45, XP: $8.** 6166 Morriss Point Rd 56484. 2.8 mi nw on SR 371 and 200 from jct SR 34, 0.5 mi e, follow signs. 🗙

Mississippi

BILOXI — MAJESTIC OAKS RV RESORT. (228) 436-4200. **2P $39-$44.** 1750 Pass Rd 39531. I-110, exit 46A, 3.1 mi w on US 90, 0.6 mi n on Rodenberg Ave, then just w. 🏕️ 🛥️

OCEAN SPRINGS — CAMP JOURNEY'S END. (228) 875-2100. **2P $32-$38, XP: $5.** 7501 Hwy 57 39565. I-10, exit 57, 0.5 mi n. 🛥️ 🗙

PELAHATCHIE — YOGI ON THE LAKE. (AAA) (601) 854-6859. **Call for rates.** 143 Campground Rd 39145. I-20, exit 68, 2 mi n on SR 43, 0.5 mi w on Lake Rd, then just n. 🛥️ 🗙 ♿M

PICAYUNE — SUN ROAMERS RV RESORT. ⬥ (601) 798-5818. **Call for rates.** 41 Mississippi Pines Blvd 39466. I-59, exit 4, 0.8 mi e on SR 43 S, then 0.5 mi s on Stafford Rd. 🅺 ⬛ ⬛

TOOMSUBA — MERIDIAN EAST/TOOMSUBA KOA. (601) 632-1684. **Call for rates.** 3953 KOA Campground Rd 39364. I-20/59, exit 165, 1.5 mi s, follow signs. ⬛ ⬛ ⬛

TUNICA — HARRAH'S MID-SOUTH RV PARK. (662) 363-2788. **Call for rates.** 111 Resort Village Rd 38664. US 61, just w to Grand Casino Pkwy S. ⬛ 🅺 ⬛ ⬛ ⬛

VICKSBURG — MAGNOLIA RV PARK RESORT. ⬥ (601) 631-0388. **4P $26-$29, XP: $3.** 211 Miller St 39180. I-20, exit 1B, 1.1 mi s on US 61, just w. 🅺 ⬛ ⬛ ⬛

Missouri

BRANSON — THE WILDERNESS AT SILVER DOLLAR CITY LOG CABINS AND RV'S. (417) 338-8189. **2P $30-$37, XP: $3.** 5125 Hwy 265 65616. 0.5 mi s of jct SR 76. ⬛ ⬛

EUREKA — YOGI BEAR'S JELLYSTONE PARK CAMP-RESORT. (636) 938-5925. **2P $26-$53, XP: $4-$5.** 5300 Fox Creek Rd 63069. I-44, exit 261, 0.5 mi w. (PO Box 626 63025). ⬛ ⬛

KANSAS CITY — WORLDS OF FUN VILLAGE. (816) 453-7280. **Call for rates.** 8000 Parvin Rd 64161. I-435, exit 54, just se. (4545 Worlds of Fun Ave). ⬛ ⬛

MONROE CITY — MARK TWAIN LANDING RV RESORT. (573) 735-9422. **Call for rates.** 42819 Landing Ln 63456. Jct US 36 and SR J, 8.2 mi s. ⬛ ⬛

PLATTE CITY — BASSWOOD RESORT. (816) 858-5556. **2P $26-$49, XP: $5.** 15880 Interurban Rd 64079. I-29, exit 18, just e, 3.5 mi e on SR 92 to Winan Rd, then 1.9 mi n, follow signs. ⬛ ⬛ ⬛

Montana

MISSOULA — JELLYSTONE RV RESORT. (406) 543-9400. **2P $32-$36, XP: $3-$4.** 9900 Jellystone Ave 59808. I-90, exit 96 (west side entry), 0.9 mi n. ⬛ ⬛

POLSON — POLSON MOTOR COACH & RV RESORT/KOA. (406) 883-2151. **2P $41-$65, XP: $3-$5.** 200 Irvine Flats Rd 59860. 1 mi n on US 93, 0.3 mi w. ⬛ ⬛

WEST GLACIER — WEST GLACIER KOA. (406) 387-5341. **2P $30-$50, XP: $5-$6.** 355 Halfmoon Flats Rd 59936. 2.5 mi w on US 2, 1 mi s. (PO Box 215). ⬛ ⬛

Nebraska

NORTH PLATTE — HOLIDAY RV PARK & CAMPGROUND. ⬥ (308) 534-2265. **2P $20-$34, XP: $2.** 601 E Halligan Dr 69101. I-80, exit 177, just n on US 83, just right on frontage road (Halligan Dr), then 0.5 mi e. ⬛ ⬛ ⬛

Nevada

BOULDER CITY — BOULDER OAKS RV RESORT. (702) 294-4425. **4P $40-$45, XP: $3.** 1010 Industrial Rd 89005. Jct US 93, just w. (PO Box 62364 89006). 🅺 ⬛ ⬛

CARSON CITY — COMSTOCK COUNTRY RV RESORT. ⬥ (775) 882-2445. **$28-$45, XP: $2.** 5400 S Carson St (US 395) 89701. Just s of jct US 50 W. ⬛ ⬛

LAS VEGAS — OASIS LAS VEGAS RV RESORT. ⬥ (702) 260-2020. **4P $40-$62, XP: $2.** 2711 W Windmill Ln 89123. I-15, exit 33 (Blue Diamond Rd), 0.5 mi e. 🅺 ⬛ ⬛

MESQUITE — DESERT SKIES RV RESORT. (928) 347-6000. **Call for rates.** 350 E Hwy 91 89024. I-15, exit 122, 1.5 mi ne via Hillside Dr. (PO Box 3780). 🅺 ⬛ ⬛

MINDEN — CARSON VALLEY RV RESORT & CASINO. (775) 782-9711. **4P $22-$35.** 1639 US 395 N 89423. Center. 🅺 ⬛ ⬛

MINDEN — SILVER CITY RV RESORT. ⬥ (775) 267-3359. **2P $35.** 3165 US 395 89423. 6 mi s of Carson City; 3 mi s of jct US 50 W. ⬛ ⬛ ⬛

PAHRUMP — NEVADA TREASURE LUXURY RV RESORT. ⬥ (775) 751-1174. **2P $28-$55, XP: $5.** 301 W Leslie St 89060. 10 mi n of SR 160 and 372, jct SR 160. 🅺 ⬛ ⬛

PAHRUMP — TERRIBLE'S LAKESIDE CASINO & RV RESORT. (775) 751-7770. **6P $27-$39.** 5870 S Homestead Rd 89048. SR 160, 3.5 mi s. ⬛ 🅺 ⬛ ⬛

New Hampshire

BARRINGTON — AYERS LAKE FARM CAMPGROUND. ⬥ (603) 335-1110. **4P $32-$47, XP: $5-$7. (no credit cards).** 557 US 202 03825. Spaulding Tpke, exit 13, 4.5 mi w. ⬛ ⬛

BARRINGTON — BARRINGTON SHORES CAMPGROUND. ⬥ (603) 664-9333. **2P $36-$49, XP: $3-$12.** 7 Barrington Shores Dr 03825. Jct SR 125 and US 4, 2.5 mi w on US 4, then 3 mi n. ⬛

CHICHESTER — HILLCREST CAMPGROUND. (603) 798-5124. **Call for rates.** 78 Dover Rd 03234. I-93, exit 15, 8 mi e on SR 4; jct SR 28 and 4, 2 mi w on SR 4. ⬛ ⬛

FREEDOM — DANFORTH BAY CAMPING & RV RESORT. ⬥ (603) 539-2069. **2P $30-$71, XP: $8-$10.** 196 Shawtown Rd 03836. Jct SR 25/153, 1 mi n on SR 153, then 3 mi w on Ossipee Lake Rd. ⬛ ⬛

HAMPTON FALLS — WAKEDA CAMPGROUND LLC. (603) 772-5274. **5P $36-$80, XP: $10.** 294 Exeter Rd (SR 88) 03844. SR 88, 3.8 mi w of jct US 1. ⬛

LACONIA — PAUGUS BAY CAMPGROUND. (603) 366-4757. **Call for rates. (no credit cards).** 96 Hilliard Rd 03246. Jct US 3 and SR 11B, 0.5 mi n on US 3, then w. ⬛

MEREDITH — CLEARWATER CAMPGROUND. (603) 279-7761. **Call for rates.** 26 Campground Rd (SR 104) 03253. I-93, exit 23, 3 mi e. 🗙

MEREDITH — MEREDITH WOODS 4 SEASON CAMPING AREA. (603) 279-5449. **Call for rates.** 551 SR 104 03253. I-93, exit 23, 3 mi e. 🛶 🗙

MILTON — MI-TE-JO LAKESIDE FAMILY CAMPGROUND. ⒶⒶⒶ (603) 652-9022. **2P $40-$46, XP: $5-$8.** 111 Mi-Te Jo Rd 03851. SR 16, exit 17 northbound, 0.8 mi e on SR 75, 3.3 mi n on SR 125, then 1 mi e on Townhouse Rd; exit southbound, 3.3 mi on SR 125, then 1 mi e on Townhouse Rd. (PO Box 830). 🗙

NEW HAMPTON — TWIN TAMARACK FAMILY CAMPING & RV RESORT. ⒶⒶⒶ (603) 279-4387. **4P $33, XP: $1-$8.** 41 Twin Tamarack Rd 03256. I-93, exit 23, 2.5 mi e on SR 104. 🛶 🗙

SOUTH WEARE — COLD SPRINGS CAMP RESORT. (603) 529-2528. **2P $48-$52, XP: $7.** 62 Barnard Hill Rd 03281. Jct SR 77/149, 1.5 mi se, 0.3 mi n on sign posted road; jct SR 114/101, 10 mi nw. (22 Wildlife Dr). 🛶 🗙

TAMWORTH — CHOCORUA CAMPING VILLAGE KOA. ⒶⒶⒶ (603) 323-8536. **2P $30-$64, XP: $6-$8.** 893 White Mountain Hwy 03817. SR 16, 2.5 mi n of jct SR 25. (PO Box 484, CHOCORUA). 🛶 🗙

TWIN MOUNTAIN — TWIN MOUNTAIN KOA KAMP-GROUND. ⒶⒶⒶ (603) 846-5559. **2P $31-$149, XP: $4-$10.** 372 SR 115 03595. Jct US 302, 2.1 mi n on US 3, then 0.8 mi ne. (PO Box 148). 🛶 🗙

WOODSTOCK — WOODSTOCK/BROKEN BRANCH KOA. (603) 745-8008. **2P $29-$80, XP: $5-$10.** 1000 Eastside Rd (SR 175) 03293. I-93, exit 31, 2 mi s, follow signs. (PO Box 6). 🛶 🗙

New Jersey

CAPE MAY — BEACHCOMBER CAMPING RESORT. (609) 886-6035. **4P $22-$66, XP: $5-$8.** 462 Seashore Rd 08204. Garden State Pkwy, exit 4A (SR 47 N), w to 3rd traffic light, then 1 mi s; Railroad Ave and Seashore Rd. 🛶 🗙

CAPE MAY — HOLLY SHORES CAMPGROUND. ⒶⒶⒶ (609) 886-1234. **2P $22-$59, XP: $5-$8.** 491 US 9 08204. Garden State Pkwy, exit 4A (SR 47 N) to 2nd traffic light, then 1 mi s. 🛶 🗙

CAPE MAY — SEASHORE CAMPSITES. ⒶⒶⒶ (609) 884-4010. **4P $20-$60, XP: $3-$5.** 720 Seashore Rd 08204. Garden State Pkwy, exit 4A (SR 47 N), 1 mi n to CR 626, then 2.7 mi s. 🛶 🗙

CAPE MAY COURT HOUSE — BIG TIMBER LAKE CAMP-ING RESORT. ⒶⒶⒶ (609) 465-4456. **2P $43-$69, XP: $3-$10.** 116 Swainton Goshen Rd 08210. Garden State Pkwy, exit 13 southbound, 0.5 mi w on paved road, 1 mi s on US 9, then 1 mi w (CR 646). (PO Box 366). 🛶 🗙

OCEAN VIEW — OCEAN VIEW RESORT CAMPGROUND. ⒶⒶⒶ (609) 624-1675. **4P $39-$77, XP: $7.** 2555 Rt 9 08230. US 9, 0.8 mi nw of Garden State Pkwy, exit 17 southbound; exit northbound, use service area turnaround. (PO Box 607). 🛶 🗙 🚹M

New Mexico

ALBUQUERQUE — ALBUQUERQUE CENTRAL KOA. (505) 296-2729. **Call for rates.** 12400 Skyline Rd NE 87123. I-40, exit 166, just s, then 0.4 mi e. 🛶 🗙

ALBUQUERQUE — AMERICAN RV PARK OF ALBUQUER-QUE. ⒶⒶⒶ (505) 831-3545. **4P $38-$65, XP: $5.** 13500 Central Ave SW 87121. I-40, exit 149, just s, then w. 🏍 🛶 🗙

BERNALILLO — ALBUQUERQUE NORTH/BERNALILLO KOA. (505) 867-5227. **$21-$38, XP: $3.** 555 S Hill Rd 87004. I-25, exit 240. (PO Box 758). 🛶 🗙

CARLSBAD — CARLSBAD KOA. (575) 457-2000. **2P $39-$54, XP: $3-$4.** 2 Manthei Rd 88220. US 285, 16 mi n; between MM 51 and 52. 🛶 🗙

DEMING — LITTLE VINEYARD RV PARK. ⒶⒶⒶ (575) 546-3560. **2P $25, XP: $5.** 2901 E Pine St 88030. I-10, exit 85, 1 mi w. 🅂 🏍 🛶 🗙

GALLUP — USA RV PARK. ⒶⒶⒶ (505) 863-5021. **2P $20-$30, XP: $2.** 2925 W Hwy 66 87301. I-40, exit 16, 1 mi e. 🛶 🗙

LAS CRUCES — HACIENDA RV RESORT. ⒶⒶⒶ (575) 528-5800. **2P $45-$59, XP: $2.** 740 Stern Dr 88005. I-10, exit 140, just e. 🅂 🏍 🗙

SILVER CITY — SILVER CITY KOA. (575) 388-3351. **4P $22-$41, XP: $3-$4.** 11824 E Hwy 180 88022. 4.9 mi e on US 180 and SR 90. 🛶 🗙

New York

BATH — HICKORY HILL CAMPING RESORT. (607) 776-4345. **2P $42-$55, XP: $5.** 7531 CR 13 14810. SR 17, exit 38, 1 mi n on SR 54, then at fork, 2 mi n on Haverling St (CR 13). 🛶 🗙 🚹M

DEWITTVILLE — CHAUTAUQUA HEIGHTS CAMPING RESORT CAMPGROUND. (716) 386-3804. **4P $25-$42, XP: $4-$8.** 5652 Thumb Rd 14728. I-86, exit 10 westbound, 5 mi on CR 430 W; I-90, exit 60 to Mayville, 2.4 mi on CR 430 E, then just e. 🛶 🗙

FARMINGTON — CANANDAIGUA/ROCHESTER KOA CAMP-GROUND. (585) 398-3582. **Call for rates.** 5374 Farmington Townline Rd 14425. I-90, exit 44, 3.2 mi s on SR 332, then 1 mi e. 🛶 🗙

GARDINER — YOGI BEAR'S JELLYSTONE PARK CAMP-RESORTS AT LAZY RIVER. (845) 255-5193. **4P $45-$65, XP: $4-$10.** 50 Bevier Rd 12525. 2.5 mi w on US 44 and SR 55, just s on Albany Post, then just e. 🛶 🗙

GARRATTSVILLE — YOGI BEAR'S JELLYSTONE PARK AT CRYSTAL LAKE. (607) 965-8265. **Call for rates.** 111 E Turtle Lake Rd 13342. Jct SR 80, 6.2 mi s on CR 16, 0.7 mi n on CR 51, then 1.1 mi w on CR 17. 🛶 🗙

GREENFIELD PARK — SKYWAY CAMPING RESORT. (845) 647-5747. **2P $54-$65, XP: $10.** 99 Mountaindale Rd 12435. Jct US 209 and SR 52, 5.2 mi w on SR 52, then 1.1 mi sw. 🛶 🗙

GREENFIELD PARK — YOGI BEAR'S JELLYSTONE PARK CAMP-RESORT AT BIRCHWOOD ACRES. (845) 434-4743. **4P $39-$67, XP: $7-$14.** 85 Martinfeld Rd 12435. Jct US 209 and SR 52, 8 mi w on SR 52, then 0.5 mi s. (PO Box 482, WOODRIDGE 12789).

LAKE GEORGE — LAKE GEORGE ESCAPE. (518) 623-3207. **2P $32-$71, XP: $6.** 175 E Schroon River Rd 12845. I-87, exit 23, 0.4 mi e on Diamond Point Rd, then 0.8 mi n. (PO Box 431).

LAKE GEORGE — LAKE GEORGE RV PARK. (518) 792-3775. **2P $48-$72, XP: $8.** 74 SR 149 12845. I-87, exit 20, 0.5 mi n on US 9, then 0.4 mi e.

NORTH JAVA — YOGI BEAR'S JELLYSTONE PARK OF WNY. (585) 457-9644. **Call for rates.** 5204 Youngers Rd 14113. 3 mi s on SR 98, 1.3 mi e on Pee-Dee Rd, then 0.8 mi s.

OLD FORGE — OLD FORGE CAMPING RESORT. (315) 369-6011. **2P $25-$170, XP: $4-$6.** 3347 SR 28 13420. 1 mi n of town. (PO Box 51).

PLATTEKILL — NEWBURGH/NEW YORK CITY NORTH KOA. (845) 564-2836. **2P $37-$64, XP: $5-$7.** 119 Freetown Hwy 12568. 1.5 mi n on SR 32, 3 mi s of jct US 44 and SR 55, then 0.5 mi e, follow signs.

PULASKI — BRENNAN BEACH RV RESORT. (315) 298-2242. **Call for rates.** 80 Brennan Beach 13142. I-81, exit 36, 4 mi w on SR 13, 1 mi n on SR 3.

VERONA — THE VILLAGES AT TURNING STONE. (315) 361-7275. **4P $40-$55.** 5065 SR 365 13478. I-90, exit 33, 1.3 mi w. (PO Box 126).

WATKINS GLEN — WATKINS GLEN-CORNING KOA KAMP-GROUND. (607) 535-7404. **Call for rates.** 1710 SR 414 S 14891. SR 414 (Franklin St), 4.5 mi s of jct SR 14. (PO Box 228).

North Carolina

BOONE — KOA-BOONE. (828) 264-7250. **2P $35-$38, XP: $5-$6.** 123 Harmony Mountain Ln 28607. Jct US 221 and 421, 3 mi n on SR 194, then 1 mi w on Ray Brown Rd.

CANDLER — KOA ASHEVILLE WEST. (828) 665-7015. **2P $25-$40, XP: $3-$5.** 309 Wiggins Rd 28715. I-40, exit 37, just s, 0.5 mi w on US 19/23, then 0.3 mi n.

CEDAR MOUNTAIN — BLACK FOREST CAMPING RESORT. (828) 884-2267. **2P $25-$36, XP: $3-$5.** 100 Summer Rd 28718. On US 276, 12.6 mi s of Brevard. (PO Box 709).

North Dakota

BISMARCK — BISMARCK KOA. (701) 222-2662. **2P $24-$65, XP: $3.** 3720 Centennial Rd 58503. I-94, exit 161, 1 mi n.

Ohio

BROOKVILLE — DAYTON TALL TIMBERS RESORT KOA. (937) 833-3888. **2P $35-$58, XP: $2-$15.** 7796 Wellbaum Rd 45309. I-70, exit 24, 0.3 mi n on SR 49, 0.5 mi w on Pleasant Plain Rd, then 0.3 mi s.

LATHAM — LONG'S RETREAT FAMILY RESORT. (937) 588-3725. **$24-$35, XP: $2-$5.** 50 Bell Hollow Rd 45646. 4.3 mi e on SR 124 from jct SR 41.

SHELBY — SHELBY/MANSFIELD KOA. (419) 347-1392. **2P $32-$75, XP: $5-$10.** 6787 Baker 47 44875. 4 mi nw on SR 39, then 4.5 mi n, follow signs.

Oklahoma

GORE — MARVAL RESORT. (918) 489-2295. **4P $34-$51, XP: $5.** Rt 3, Box 60 Gore 74435. I-40, exit 287, 6 mi n on SR 100, then just e.

Oregon

BEND — CROWN VILLA RV RESORT. (541) 388-1131. **4P $34-$85, XP: $3.** 60801 Brosterhous Rd 97702. South end of jct US 97 and Business Rt US 97, just n on SE 3rd St (Business Rt US 97), 1 mi e on Murphy Rd, then just s.

CANNON BEACH — RV RESORT AT CANNON BEACH. (503) 436-2231. **2P $30-$41, XP: $3.** 340 Elk Creek Rd 97110. US 101, exit Sunset Blvd, just ne. (PO Box 1037).

CANYONVILLE — SEVEN FEATHERS RV RESORT. (541) 839-3599. **6P $36-$44.** 325 Creekside Dr 97417. I-5, exit 99 southbound, just w; exit northbound, just nw.

COBURG — PREMIER RV RESORT OF EUGENE. (541) 686-3152. **2P $35-$45, XP: $3.** 33022 Van Duyn Rd 97408. I-5, exit 199, just e on Van Duyn Rd, then just s.

HAMMOND — ASTORIA/WARRENTON/SEASIDE KOA. (503) 861-2606. **2P $25-$68, XP: $7.** 1100 NW Ridge Rd 97121. 4.6 mi nw of jct US 101, follow signs to Fort Stevens State Park.

LEBANON — MALLARD CREEK GOLF & RV RESORT. (541) 259-0070. **$37.** 31958 Bellinger Scale Rd 97355. 4.6 mi se on US 20, 1.4 mi ne on Waterloo Rd, just e on Berlin Rd, then 0.7 mi n.

NETARTS — NETARTS BAY RV PARK & MARINA. (503) 842-7774. **4P $24-$35, XP: $5.** 2260 Bilyeu 97143. Just w. (PO Box 218).

NEWPORT — OUTDOOR RESORTS PACIFIC SHORES MOTORCOACH RESORT. (541) 265-3750. **6P $50-$90, XP: $5.** 6225 N Coast Hwy 101 97365. Jct US 20, 3.4 mi n on US 101, then just w.

PORTLAND — COLUMBIA RIVER RV PARK. (503) 285-1515. **2P $30, XP: $3.** 10649 NE 13th Ave 97211. I-5, exit 307, follow signs for Marine Dr E, 1.5 mi e, then just s.

SALEM — PHOENIX RV PARK. ◉ (503) 581-2497. **2P $29-$32, XP: $2.** 4130 Silverton Rd NE 97305. I-5, exit 256, 0.3 mi e on Market, 1.3 mi n on Lancaster, then just e. 🏕 ⊠

SALEM — SALEM PREMIER RV RESORT. (503) 364-7714. **$35-$45, XP: $3.** 4700 Salem-Dallas Hwy 22 97304. I-5, exit 260A (Salem Pkwy), follow signs to city center; 3 mi sw to Commercial St NE, then 1 mi s to Marion St; 4.7 mi sw from Marion St Bridge via SR 22; 4.3 mi e of jct SR 22 and 99 W. ⊶ ⊠

SISTERS — SISTERS/BEND KOA. (541) 549-3021. **2P $38-$78, XP: $4-$10.** 67667 US 20 W 97701. On US 20, 3.5 mi e. 🏕 ⊶ ⊠

WARM SPRINGS — KAHNEETA HIGH DESERT RESORT & CASINO RV PARK. (541) 553-1112. **2P $25-$49.** 6823 Hwy 8 97761. 11 mi ne off US 26; on Warm Springs Indian Reservation. (PO Box 1240). 🏕 ⊶ ⊠

WELCHES — MT. HOOD VILLAGE VACATION COTTAGES & RV RESORT. ◉ (503) 622-4011. **6P $28-$48.** 65000 E US 26 97067. On US 26, 2 mi w. ⊶ ⊠

WILSONVILLE — PHEASANT RIDGE RV RESORT. ◉ (503) 682-7829. **2P $40-$46, XP: $1.** 8275 SW Elligsen Rd 97070. I-5, exit 286, just e. 🏕 ⊶ ⊠

Pennsylvania

BEDFORD — FRIENDSHIP VILLAGE CAMPGROUND. ◉ (814) 623-1677. **4P $22-$35, XP: $3.** 348 Friendship Village Rd 15522. 1.3 mi w on US 30 from jct US 220, 0.5 mi n via signs. ⊶ ⊠

BELLEFONTE — BELLEFONTE/STATE COLLEGE KOA. ◉ (814) 355-7912. **2P $22-$55, XP: $3-$6.** 2481 Jacksonville Rd 16823. I-80, exit 161, 2 mi ne on SR 26. ⊶ ⊠

BOWMANSVILLE — LAKE IN WOOD CAMPGROUND. (717) 445-5525. **2P $30-$59, XP: $6.** 576 Yellow Hill Rd 17555. SR 23, 4.5 mi n on SR 625, 1 mi ne on Oaklyn Dr, then 1.5 mi e, follow signs. ⊶ ⊠

BOWMANSVILLE — OAK CREEK CAMPGROUND. ◉ (717) 445-6161. **Call for rates.** 400 E Maple Grove Rd 17507. SR 625, 1.5 mi e. (PO Box 128). ⊶ ⊠

BOWMANSVILLE — SUN VALLEY CAMPGROUND. (717) 445-6262. **Call for rates.** 451 E Maple Grove Rd 17507. SR 625, 1.9 mi e. (PO Box 129). ⊶ ⊠

CLAY — STARLITE CAMPING RESORT. (717) 733-9655. **2P $37-$39, XP: $2-$5.** 1500 Furnace Hill Rd 17578. US 322, 1.1 mi n on Clay Rd, 2.4 mi ne, follow signs. ⊶ ⊠

COOKSBURG — KALYUMET CAMPING & CABINS. (814) 744-9622. **4P $28-$45, XP: $5-$10.** 8630 Miola Rd 16235. I-80, exit 62, 2 mi e on SR 68 E to light at Clarion Courthouse, then continue 9.5 mi. ⊶ ⊠

FARMINGTON — BENNER'S MEADOW RUN CAMPING & CABINS. (724) 329-4097. **4P $41-$165, XP: $7-$10.** 315 Nelson Rd 15437. 2.5 mi n of US 40, follow signs. 🔳 ⊶ ⊠

GARDNERS — MOUNTAIN CREEK CAMPGROUND. (717) 486-7681. **Call for rates.** 349 Pine Grove Rd 17324. 2 mi w of SR 34, follow signs. ⊶ ⊠

GETTYSBURG — GETTYSBURG CAMPGROUND. ◉ (717) 334-3304. **4P $30-$52, XP: $2-$4.** 2030 Fairfield Rd 17325. 3 mi w on SR 116 W. ⊶ ⊠

GETTYSBURG — GETTYSBURG KOA KAMPGROUND. ◉ (717) 642-5713. **2P $20-$65, XP: $3-$6.** 20 Knox Rd 17325. 3 mi w on US 30, 3 mi s on Knoxlyn Rd, follow signs. ⊶ ⊠

GETTYSBURG — GRANITE HILL CAMPING RESORT. ◉ (717) 642-8749. **2P $30-$50, XP: $2-$8.** 3340 Fairfield Rd 17325. 5.8 mi w on SR 116. ⊶ ⊠

GETTYSBURG — ROUND TOP CAMPGROUND. (717) 334-9565. **4P $25-$65, XP: $3-$6.** 180 Knight Rd 17325. 3 mi s on SR 134 at US 15. ⊶ ⊠

HARRISVILLE — KOZY REST KAMPGROUND. ◉ (724) 735-2417. **4P $25-$38, XP: $2-$5.** 449 Campground Rd 16038. Jct SR 8 and 58, 0.5 mi e on SR 58 to Campground Rd, then 1.9 mi ne. ⊶ ⊠

HERSHEY — HERSHEY HIGHMEADOW CAMPGROUND. ◉ (717) 534-8999. **4P $33-$51, XP: $5.** 1200 Matlack Rd 17036. 0.5 mi n on SR 39 W from jct US 322 and 422. (PO Box 866 17033). ⊶ ⊠

HOLTWOOD — MUDDY RUN RECREATION PARK. (717) 284-5850. **6P $23, XP: $3.** 172 Bethesda Church Rd W 17532. 1.8 mi ne on SR 372. ⊠

JONESTOWN — JONESTOWN KOA. (717) 865-2526. **Call for rates.** 145 Old Rt 22 17038. 2 mi e on US 22 from jct SR 72, 0.5 mi s; I-81, exit 90, 5 mi se; I-78, exit 6, 5 mi w, follow signs. (PO Box 867). ⊶ ⊠

KNOX — WOLFS CAMPING RESORT. ◉ (814) 797-1103. **2P $28-$41, XP: $3-$5.** 308 Timberwolf Run 16232. I-80, exit 53. ⊶ ⊠

LANCASTER — OLD MILL STREAM CAMPGROUND. (717) 299-2314. **4P $33-$43, XP: $3.** 2249 Lincoln Hwy E 17602. 5 mi e on US 30. ⊠

LENHARTSVILLE — ROBIN HILL CAMPING RESORT. (610) 756-6117. **2P $33-$52, XP: $5-$6.** 149 Robin Hill Rd 19534. I-78, exit 40 (Krumsville) or exit 35 (Lenhartsville) for 3 mi, follow signs. ⊶ ⊠

LICKDALE — LICKDALE CAMPGROUND. (717) 865-6411. **4P $29-$37, XP: $4.** 11 Lickdale Rd 17038. I-81, exit 90, just e. ⊠

LIVERPOOL — FERRY BOAT CAMPSITES. ◉ (717) 444-3200. **4P $38-$43, XP: $3.** 32 Ferry Ln 17045. 2 mi s on US 11/15. ⊠

MANHEIM — PINCH POND FAMILY CAMPGROUND & RV PARK. ⟨AAA⟩ (717) 665-7640. **Call for rates.** 3075 Pinch Rd 17545. I-76 (Pennsylvania Tpke), exit 266, 1 mi s on SR 72, 0.5 mi w on Cider Press Rd, then 1 mi n. ⟨⟩ ⟨⟩

MANSFIELD — BUCKTAIL CAMPING RESORT. (570) 662-2923. **$19-$53, XP: $8-$11.** 130 Bucktail Rd 16933. US 15, exit US 6, just e, 1.5 mi n on Lambs Creek Rd, then 1 mi w. ⟨⟩ ⟨⟩

MARSHALLS CREEK — OTTER LAKE CAMP RESORT. ⟨AAA⟩ (570) 223-0123. **2P $36-$59, XP: $4-$8.** 4805 Marshalls Creek Rd 18335. I-80, exit 309, 3 mi n on US 209, just n on SR 402, then 7 mi w. (PO Box 850). ⟨⟩ ⟨⟩

MCKEAN — ERIE KOA KAMPGROUNDS. (814) 476-7706. **2P $30-$70, XP: $3-$7.** 6624 West Rd 16426. I-90, exit 18, 1.3 mi s on SR 832, then 0.8 mi e; I-79, exit 174, 1.5 mi w. (6645 West Rd). ⟨⟩ ⟨⟩

MEADVILLE — BROOKDALE FAMILY CAMPGROUND. (814) 789-3251. **4P $29-$46, XP: $4-$6.** 25164 State Hwy 27 16335. On SR 27, 8 mi e. ⟨⟩ ⟨⟩

MERCER — MERCER-GROVE CITY KOA. (724) 748-3160. **2P $35-$70, XP: $5-$10.** 1337 Butler Pike 16137. I-79, exit 113, 3 mi n on SR 258, follow signs. ⟨⟩ ⟨⟩

MERCER — ROCKY SPRINGS CAMPGROUND. (724) 662-4415. **Call for rates. (no credit cards).** 84 Rocky Spring Rd, Rt 318 16137. I-80, exit 15 westbound, 2 mi n on US 19 to Butler St (SR 318), then 4.5 mi w; exit eastbound, jct I-80 and exit 4A (SR 318), 6.5 mi ne. ⟨⟩ ⟨⟩

MERCERSBURG — SAUNDEROSA PARK INC. (717) 328-2216. **4P $26-$30, XP: $1-$2.** 5909 Little Cove Rd 17236. 4.8 mi w on SR 16, 2.5 mi s on SR 456. ⟨⟩ ⟨⟩

MEXICO — BUTTONWOOD CAMPGROUND. (717) 436-8334. **4P $27-$44, XP: $6.** River Rd 17056. US 322, exit 24 (Port Royal), 0.6 mi s on SR 75 S, 0.8 mi se on Old US 322, then 0.4 mi s. (PO Box 223). ⟨⟩ ⟨⟩ ⟨⟩

MILL RUN — YOGI BEAR'S JELLYSTONE PARK CAMP RESORT. (724) 455-2929. **4P $18-$60, XP: $4-$10.** 839 Mill Run Rd 15464. Just s on SR 381. (PO Box 91). ⟨⟩ ⟨⟩

MOUNT BETHEL — DRIFTSTONE ON THE DELAWARE. ⟨AAA⟩ (570) 897-6859. **2P $37-$46, XP: $5-$8.** 2731 River Rd 18343. SR 611, exit Portland, 4 mi s on River Rd, slight left at split. ⟨⟩ ⟨⟩

NEW COLUMBIA — WILLIAMSPORT SOUTH/NITTANY MOUNTAIN KOA KAMPGROUND. (570) 568-5541. **2P $32-$52, XP: $3-$5.** 2751 Millers Bottom Rd 17856. I-80, exit 210A, 0.5 mi s on US 15, 4.5 mi w on New Columbia Rd, then 0.4 mi nw. ⟨⟩ ⟨⟩

NEW HOLLAND — SPRING GULCH RESORT. (717) 354-3100. **Call for rates.** 475 Lynch Rd 17557. Jct SR 23 and 897, 4 mi s on SR 897. ⟨⟩ ⟨⟩

NORTHUMBERLAND — SPLASH MAGIC CAMPGROUND & RV RESORT. (570) 473-8021. **Call for rates.** 213 Yogi Blvd 17857. I-80, exit 224, 2 mi e on SR 54, 8 mi s on US 11; 2.5 mi n on US 11. ⟨⟩ ⟨⟩

PINE GROVE — PINE GROVE KOA AT TWIN GROVE PARK. ⟨AAA⟩ (717) 865-4602. **4P $34-$150, XP: $8.** 1445 Suedburg Rd 17963. I-81, exit 100, 5 mi w on SR 443. ⟨⟩ ⟨⟩

PORTERSVILLE — BEAR RUN CAMPGROUND. ⟨AAA⟩ (724) 368-3564. **2P $27-$50, XP: $4-$10.** 184 Badger Hill Rd 16051. I-79, exit 96, 0.8 mi n on SR 488. ⟨⟩ ⟨⟩

QUARRYVILLE — YOGI BEAR'S JELLYSTONE PARK. (717) 786-3458. **4P $60-$100, XP: $14-$25.** 340 Blackburn Rd 17566. 2.7 mi s on US 222, 1.5 mi se, follow signs. ⟨⟩ ⟨⟩

ROBESONIA — ADVENTURE BOUND CAMPING RESORT AT EAGLES PEAK. (610) 589-4800. **Call for rates.** 397 Eagles Peak Rd 19551. 1.6 mi s on SR 419 from jct US 422, just s on Main St, 0.5 mi w Memorial Blvd, then 1.1 mi s on Sheridan Rd, follow signs for Eagles Peak. ⟨⟩ ⟨⟩

ROSE POINT — COOPER'S LAKE. (724) 368-8710. **$15-$20, XP: $8-$12.** 205 Currie Rd 16057. I-79, exit 99, 0.8 mi w on US 422, then 1 mi n. ⟨⟩

SANDY LAKE — GODDARD PARK VACATION LAND CAMP-GROUND. (724) 253-4645. **2P $24-$35, XP: $1-$3.** 867 Georgetown Rd 16145. I-79, exit 130, 0.3 mi w on SR 358, then 3.5 mi n, follow signs. ⟨⟩ ⟨⟩

SHARTLESVILLE — MOUNTAIN SPRINGS CAMPING RESORT. (610) 488-6859. **4P $30-$43, XP: $5-$8.** 3450 Mountain Rd 19554. I-78, exit 23, 1 mi n. (PO Box 365). ⟨⟩ ⟨⟩

SIGEL — CAMPERS PARADISE CAMPGROUNDS & CABINS. (814) 752-2393. **2P $28-$38, XP: $3-$5.** 37 Steele Dr 15860. On SR 949 N, 3 mi n of SR 36. ⟨⟩ ⟨⟩

SOMERSET — PIONEER PARK CAMPGROUND. (814) 445-6348. **2P $25-$38, XP: $3-$12.** 273 Trent Rd 15501. Just e on SR 31, 0.5 mi s, follow signs. ⟨⟩ ⟨⟩

STRASBURG — WHITE OAK CAMPGROUND. ⟨AAA⟩ (717) 687-6207. **2P $26-$33, XP: $3.** 3156 White Oak Rd 17566. 3.7 mi s of Centre Square on S Decatur St/May Post Office Rd, 0.3 mi e. (PO Box 90 17579). ⟨⟩

UPPER BLACK EDDY — COLONIAL WOODS FAMILY CAMPING RESORT. (610) 847-5808. **Call for rates.** 545 Lonely Cottage Dr 18972. 1.5 mi e on Marienstein Rd from jct SR 611, then 1 mi n, follow signs. ⟨⟩ ⟨⟩

WATERFORD — SPARROW POND FAMILY CAMPGROUND AND RECREATION FACILITY. ⟨AAA⟩ (814) 796-6777. **4P $28-$50, XP: $3-$5.** 11103 Route 19 N 16441. I-90, exit 24, 10 mi s on US 19 (Peach St). ⟨⟩ ⟨⟩

South Carolina

HILTON HEAD ISLAND — HILTON HEAD HARBOR RV RESORT & MARINA. (843) 681-3256. **4P $45-$59, XP: $3.** 43A Jenkins Rd 29926. 0.9 mi se of Intracoastal Waterway Bridge off US 278, 0.4 mi n, follow signs. (PO Box 21585 29925). ⟨⟩ ⟨⟩ ⟨⟩

HILTON HEAD ISLAND — HILTON HEAD ISLAND MOTORCOACH RESORT. (AAA) (843) 785-7699. **$55-$65.** 133 Arrow Rd 29928. 5.6 mi e on Cross Island Pkwy (US 278 toll), then just w. (PO Box 6037 29938). 🛒 ✕ 👤M

MYRTLE BEACH — APACHE FAMILY CAMPGROUND AND OCEANFRONT PIER. (843) 449-7323. **8P $27-$58, XP: $4.** 9700 Kings Rd 29572. Jct SR 22, 1.3 mi sw on US 17, then 0.8 mi e on Lake Arrowhead Rd. 🛒 ✕ 👤M

MYRTLE BEACH — LAKEWOOD CAMPING RESORT. (AAA) (843) 238-5161. **Call for rates.** 5901 S Kings Hwy 29575. Jct SR 544, 0.5 mi ne on US 17 business route. 🅂🄳 🛒 ✕ 👤M

MYRTLE BEACH — MYRTLE BEACH TRAVEL PARK. (843) 449-3714. **4P $36-$65, XP: $4.** 10108 Kings Rd 29572. Jct US 17 business route/SR 22, 1.3 mi s. 🛒 ✕ 👤M

MYRTLE BEACH — OCEAN LAKES FAMILY CAMP-GROUND. (AAA) (843) 238-5636. **$29-$67.** 6001 S Kings Hwy 29575. Jct SR 544 and US 17 business route. 🛒 ✕ 👤M

MYRTLE BEACH — PIRATELAND FAMILY CAMPING RESORT. (843) 238-5155. **4P $27-$67, XP: $3.** 5401 S Kings Hwy 29575. Jct SR 544, 1.2 mi ne on US 17 business route. 🛒 ✕ 👤M

South Dakota

CHAMBERLAIN — CEDAR SHORE CAMPGROUND. (AAA) (605) 734-5273. **$20-$35.** 1400 Shoreline Dr 57365. I-90, exit 260, 2.5 mi e on US 16 and I-90 business loop, then 1 mi ne on Mickelson country road, follow signs. (PO Box 308 57325). 🛒 ✕ 👤M

DEADWOOD — WHISTLER GULCH CAMPGROUND & RV PARK. (605) 578-2092. **$22-$36.** 235 Cliff St 57732. 0.7 mi s on US 85. 🛒 ✕ 👤M

HILL CITY — RAFTER J BAR RANCH CAMPGROUND. (AAA) (605) 574-2527. **Call for rates.** 12325 Rafter J Rd 57745. 3.3 mi s on US 16 and 385 at SR 87/244. (PO Box 128). 🛒 ✕ 👤M

INTERIOR — BADLANDS WHITE RIVER KOA. (AAA) (605) 433-5337. **2P $19-$70, XP: $3-$4.** 20720 SD Hwy 44 57750. 4 mi e of jct SR 377. 🛒 ✕

MITCHELL — MITCHELL KOA. (605) 996-1131. **2P $22-$39, XP: $3.** 41255 SD Hwy 38 57301. I-90, exit 335, 0.5 mi n, then 0.3 mi w. 🛒 ✕ 👤M

NORTH SIOUX CITY — SIOUX CITY NORTH KOA. (605) 232-4519. **2P $24-$42, XP: $2-$4.** 675 Streeter Dr 57049. I-29, exit 2 northbound, 1 mi n on west service road; exit 4 southbound, 1 mi w on west service road. 🛒 ✕ 👤M

SIOUX FALLS — YOGI BEAR CAMP RESORT. (605) 332-2233. **Call for rates.** 26014 478th Ave 57005. I-90, exit 402, just n. 🛒 ✕ 👤M

SPEARFISH — ELKHORN RIDGE RV RESORT. (AAA) (605) 722-1800. **$29-$145.** 20189 US 85 57783. I-90, exit 17 (US 85), 0.5 mi s. 🛒 ✕ 👤M

Tennessee

EAST RIDGE — HOLIDAY TRAV-L-PARK/CHATTANOOGA. (706) 891-9766. **2P $29-$39, XP: $3.** 1709 Mack Smith Rd 37412. I-75, exit 1 southbound; exit 1B northbound, 0.3 mi w, then 1 mi s. 🛒 ✕

GATLINBURG — OUTDOOR RESORTS OF GATLINBURG. (865) 436-5861. **Call for rates.** 4229 Parkway E 37738. 11.5 mi e on US 321 N. 🛒 ✕

PIGEON FORGE — RIVEREDGE RV PARK. (865) 453-5813. **2P $29-$39, XP: $4.** 4220 Huskey St 37863. Just off US 441 at traffic light 10. 🏕 🛒 ✕

Texas

ABILENE — KOA-ABILENE. (325) 672-3681. **2P $20-$60, XP: $3.** 4851 W Stamford St 79603. I-20, exit 282 (Shirley Rd), 0.5 mi w of US 83-277, follow signs. 🛒

AMARILLO — AMARILLO RV RANCH. (AAA) (806) 373-4962. **2P $33, XP: $2.** 1414 Sunrise Dr 79104. I-40, exit 74 (Whitaker Rd), 0.3 mi w on north frontage road. 🏕 🛒 ✕

AMARILLO — FORT AMARILLO RV RESORT. (806) 331-1700. **2P $33, XP: $2.** 10101 Amarillo Blvd W 79124. I-40, exit 64 westbound, 0.3 mi n on Soncy Rd to Amarillo Blvd, then 1 mi w; exit 62B eastbound, 0.7 mi e. 🏕 🛒 ✕

AUSTIN — AUSTIN LONE STAR CAREFREE RV RESORT. (512) 444-6322. **2P $28-$50.** 7009 S I-35 78744. I-35, exit 226B/227 (Slaughter Ave/S Congress Ave) southbound; exit 228/229 (Wm Cannon Dr) northbound, on N Frontage Rd. 🅂🄳 🛒 ✕

BEAUMONT — GULF COAST RV RESORT. (409) 842-2285. **2P $35, XP: $4-$6.** 5175 Brooks Rd 77705. I-10, exit 846 westbound; exit 845 eastbound, follow signs. 🏕 🛒 ✕

BOERNE — ALAMO FIESTA RV RESORT. (AAA) (830) 249-4700. **Call for rates.** 33000 IH-10 W 78006. I-10, exit 543, 1 mi w on westbound access road. 🏕 🛒 ✕

DONNA — VICTORIA PALMS RESORT. (956) 464-7801. **Call for rates.** 602 N Victoria Rd 78537. Just s of jct US 83. 🏕 🛒 ✕

GALVESTON — JAMAICA BEACH RV PARK. (409) 632-0200. **2P $44-$56, XP: $2-$3.** 17200 FM 3005 77554. Jct 61st St and Seawall Blvd, 11 mi w. 🛒 ✕ 👤M

GOODLETT — OLE TOWNE COTTON GIN RV PARK. (940) 674-2477. **Call for rates.** 230 Market St 79252. US 287, 1 blk e; in town. 🛒 ✕

HARLINGEN — PARADISE PARK. (956) 425-6881. **2P $31-$34, XP: $2.** 1201 N Expwy 77 78552. US 77 Expwy N, exit Wilson Rd, 0.5 mi s on W Frontage Rd. 🏕 🛒 ✕

KERRVILLE — GUADALUPE RIVER RV RESORT. (830) 367-5676. **$34-$44, XP: $5-$8.** 2605 Junction Hwy 78028. I-10, exit 505 (Harper Rd), 2.5 mi s, then 2.5 mi w on SR 27. 🏕 🛒 ✕

KERRVILLE — KERRVILLE KOA. (830) 895-1665. **Call for rates.** 2400 Goat Creek Rd 78028. I-10, exit 501, 1.5 mi s on FM 1338. 🛶 ⊠

LUBBOCK — LUBBOCK KOA. (806) 762-8653. **Call for rates.** 5502 CR 6300 79416. 2.5 mi nw of Loop 289 on US 84. 🛶 ⊠

LUBBOCK — LUBBOCK RV PARK. ⏺ (806) 747-2366. **2P $28-$30, XP: $2.** 4811 N I-27 79403. I-27, exit 9, 2 mi n of Loop 289. (PO Box 597). Ⓢ🛶 ⊠

MERCEDES — LLANO GRANDE LAKE PARK RESORT AND COUNTRY CLUB. (956) 565-2638. **Call for rates.** 489 Yolanda St 78570. On Mile 2 W Rd, 1.8 mi s of jct US 83. 🎿 🛶 ⊠

MERCEDES — PARADISE SOUTH R.V. RESORT. (956) 565-2044. **2P $34, XP: $2.** 9099 N Mile 2 Rd W 78570. On Mile 2 W Rd, just n of US 83. 🎿 🛶 ⊠

SAN ANTONIO — ADMIRALTY RV RESORT. (210) 647-7878. **6P $36-$45.** 1485 N Ellison Dr 78251. Jct Loop 1604 and SR 151, 1.3 mi nw on SR 151 to Military Dr, just w to Ellison Dr, then 0.7 mi n. 🎿 🛶 ⊠ 🖟M

SAN ANTONIO — BLAZING STAR RV RESORT. ⏺ (210) 680-7827. **2P $40-$65, XP: $3-$4.** 1120 W Loop 1604 N 78251. Just s of Military Dr. Ⓢ🛶 ⊠ 🖟M

SAN ANTONIO — SAN ANTONIO KOA KAMPGROUND. (210) 224-9296. **2P $39-$43, XP: $3.** 602 Gembler Rd 78219. I-35, exit AT&T Center Pkwy, 0.5 mi s, then 0.8 mi e; I-10, exit WW White Rd, 0.3 mi n, then 1 mi w. 🛶 ⊠

SAN BENITO — FUN-N-SUN RV RESORT. (956) 399-5125. **Call for rates.** 1400 Zillock Rd 78586. 4 mi nw from US 83 and 77, exit Paso Real Rd, 0.4 mi s. 🎿 🛶 ⊠

SOUTH PADRE ISLAND — LONG ISLAND VILLAGE. (956) 943-6449. **4P $46-$135, XP: $5.** 900 S Garcia St 78597. On SR 100, turn right before crossing causeway. (PO Box 695 78578). 🎿 🛶 ⊠

UVALDE — QUAIL SPRINGS RV PARK. (830) 278-8182. **Call for rates.** 2727 E Main St 78801. 2.2 mi e on US 90. 🎿

WICHITA FALLS — WICHITA FALLS RV PARK. ⏺ (940) 723-1532. **2P $25-$28, XP: $3.** 2944 Seymour Hwy (Business 277 S) 76301. I-44, exit 1A, 1.2 mi s. 🎿 🛶

Utah

BRYCE CANYON CITY — RUBY'S INN RV PARK & CAMP-GROUND. ⏺ (435) 834-5301. **2P $35-$45, XP: $2.** 300 S Main St 84764. On SR 63, 1 mi n of Bryce Canyon National Park entrance. (PO Box 640022). 🛶 ⊠

CANNONVILLE — CANNONVILLE-BRYCE VALLEY KOA. (435) 679-8988. **2P $24-$42, XP: $3-$4.** Hwy 12 at Redrock Rd 84718. On SR 12; north end of town; 12 mi e of Bryce Canyon National Park. (PO Box 50). 🛶 ⊠

FRUIT HEIGHTS — CHERRY HILL CAMPING RESORT. ⏺ (801) 451-5379. **2P $25-$38, XP: $2.** 1325 S Main St 84037. I-15, exit 324 (US 89) northbound, then exit 397 off US 89; exit 328 (Kaysville) southbound, 0.3 mi e to S Main St, then 2 mi s. 🛶 ⊠ 🖟M

MOAB — MOAB VALLEY RV RESORT. (435) 259-4469. **$20-$42, XP: $5.** 1773 N Hwy 191 84532. From center of town, 2.3 mi n. 🛶 ⊠

ST. GEORGE — MCARTHUR'S TEMPLE VIEW RV RESORT. ⏺ (435) 673-6400. **2P $37-$43, XP: $3.** 975 S Main St 84770. I-15, exit 6 (Bluff St), 0.5 mi w, then just n. 🛶 ⊠

VIRGIN — ZION RIVER RESORT RV PARK & CAMPGROUND. ⏺ (435) 635-8594. **4P $48-$56, XP: $3.** 551 E Hwy 9 84779. I-15, exit 16 northbound, 22 mi ne; exit 27 southbound, 12 mi ne. (PO Box 790219). 🛶 ⊠

Virginia

CHARLOTTESVILLE — CHARLOTTESVILLE KOA. (434) 296-9881. **2P $29-$40, XP: $3-$5.** 3825 Red Hill Rd 22903. US 29 (s of I-64), 4.2 mi e on CR 708; SR 20, 1.4 mi w on CR 708. 🛶 ⊠

CHERITON — CHERRYSTONE FAMILY CAMPING RESORT. ⏺ (757) 331-3063. **2P $17-$70, XP: $5-$15.** 1511 Townfields Dr 23316. 1.5 mi w on SR 680 from jct US 13. (PO Box 545). 🛶 ⊠

FRONT ROYAL — FRONT ROYAL RV CAMPGROUND. ⏺ (540) 635-2741. **2P $30-$65, XP: $2-$5.** 585 KOA Dr 22630. I-66, exit 6 or 13, 2 mi s on US 340 S. (PO Box 274). 🛶 ⊠

LURAY — LURAY RV RESORT COUNTRY WAYE. (540) 743-7222. **2P $35-$45.** 3402 Kimball Rd 22835. Jct US 211, 2 mi n on US 340, then 0.3 mi e on SR 658. 🛶 ⊠

LURAY — YOGI BEAR'S JELLYSTONE PARK. (540) 743-4002. **2P $37-$64, XP: $5-$10.** 2250 Hwy 211 E 22835. On US 211, 3 mi e. (PO Box 191). Ⓢ🛶 ⊠

MADISON — SHENANDOAH HILLS CAMPGROUND. ⏺ (540) 948-4186. **Call for rates.** 110 Campground Ln 22727. 2 mi s on US 29. 🛶 ⊠

MINT SPRING — STAUNTON/WALNUT HILLS KOA. (540) 337-3920. **2P $28-$39, XP: $4.** 484 Walnut Hills Rd 24463. I-81, exit 217, 0.7 mi w to US 11, 1.5 mi s, then 1.2 mi e on SR 655. 🛶 ⊠

NAOLA — WILDWOOD CAMPGROUND. (434) 299-5228. **2P $22-$32, XP: $3-$5.** SR 130, 1.3 mi e from jct Blue Ridge Pkwy, 14 mi w of SR 29. (6252 Elon Rd, MONROE 24574). 🛶 ⊠

NATURAL BRIDGE — NATURAL BRIDGE KOA KAMP-GROUND. ⏺ (540) 291-2770. **2P $24-$129, XP: $3-$5.** 214 Kildeer Ln 24578. I-81, exit 180 northbound; exit 180B southbound, just nw on US 11. (PO Box 148). 🛶 ⊠

TOPPING — GREY'S POINT CAMP. (804) 758-2485. **Call for rates.** 3601 Grey's Point Rd 23169. On US 3; just s of Rappahannock River Bridge. (PO Box 8). 🎿 🛶 ⊠

URBANNA — BETHPAGE CAMP RESORT. (804) 758-4349. **4P $40-$73.** 679 Brown's Ln 23175. 1 mi n of town on CR 602. (PO Box 178). 🅰 🚱 🖾

VIRGINIA BEACH — HOLIDAY TRAV-L-PARK. 🆎 (757) 425-0249. **2P $24-$76, XP: $6.** 1075 General Booth Blvd 23451. I-264 terminus to Pacific Ave, 2.5 mi s. 🚱 🖾

VIRGINIA BEACH — OUTDOOR RESORTS/VIRGINIA BEACH. (757) 721-2020. **4P $50-$75, XP: $5.** 3665 S Sandpiper Rd 23456. I-264 terminus to Pacific Ave, 2 mi s to Rudee Inlet Bridge/ General Booth Blvd, 5.6 mi s to Princess Anne Rd, 0.8 mi e to Sand- bridge Rd, 5.5 mi e to Sandpiper Rd, then 3.5 mi s. 🚱 🖾

Washington

BURLINGTON — BURLINGTON KOA. (360) 724-5511. **2P $26- $45, XP: $3-$4.** 6397 N Green Rd 98233. I-5, exit 232, 3.5 mi n on Old US 99. 🆂 🚱 🖾

CHENEY — PONDEROSA FALLS RV RESORT. (509) 747-9415. **Call for rates.** 7520 S Thomas Mallen Rd 99004. I-90, exit 272, 1.4 mi s. 🚱 🖾

CLARKSTON — GRANITE LAKE PREMIER RV RESORT. 🆎 (509) 751-1635. **2P $31-$39, XP: $3.** 306 Granite Lake Dr 99403. Just w of Snake River Bridge on US 12, just n on 5th St. 🖾

COULEE CITY — SUN LAKES PARK RESORT. (509) 632-5291. **Call for rates.** 34228 Park Lake Rd NE 99115. US 2, 4 mi s on SR 17. 🚱 🖾

EPHRATA — STARS AND STRIPES RV PARK & DRIVING RANGE. (509) 787-1062. **Call for rates.** 5707 SR 28 W 98823. On SR 28, 5 mi w. 🚱 🖾

LYNDEN — LYNDEN KOA. (360) 354-4772. **2P $28-$41, XP: $5.** 8717 Line Rd 98264. 1.7 mi n of downtown on SR 539 (Guide Merid- ian Rd), 3 mi e on SR 546 (E Badger Rd), then 0.5 mi s. 🚱 🖾

MOSSYROCK — HARMONY LAKESIDE RV PARK. 🆎 (360) 983-3804. **2P $32-$38, XP: $5.** 563 SR 122 98585. I-5, exit 68, 21 mi e on US 12, then 5.7 mi n. 🅰 🖾

OAK HARBOR — NORTH WHIDBEY RV PARK. (360) 675- 9597. **2P $30, XP: $3.** 565 W Cornet Bay Rd 98277. On SR 20, 1 mi s of Deception Pass Bridge; 8 mi n of town. 🖾

PORT ANGELES — PORT ANGELES/SEQUIM KOA. (360) 457-5916. **2P $22-$81, XP: $3-$6.** 80 O'Brien Rd & US 101 E 98362. 7 mi e on US 101; 8 mi w of Sequim on US 101; just e of US 101, MM 255. 🚱 🖾

SPOKANE — ALDERWOOD RV RESORT. (509) 467-5320. **2P $27-$37, XP: $3.** 14007 N Newport Hwy 99021. I-90, exit 287, 8 mi n to SR 206, then 1.5 mi w. 🚱

SPOKANE VALLEY — SPOKANE KOA. (509) 924-4722. **Call for rates.** 3025 N Barker Rd 99027. I-90, exit 293, 1.5 mi n. 🚱 🖾

West Virginia

HARPERS FERRY — HARPERS FERRY/CIVIL WAR BATTLE- FIELDS KOA. 🆎 (304) 535-6895. **2P $25-$90, XP: $4-$6.** 343 Campground Rd 25425. 1 mi sw on US 340 from Shenandoah River Bridge, 0.3 mi s, follow signs. 🚱 🖾

MILTON — HUNTINGTON/FOX FIRE KOA. (304) 743-5622. **4P $31-$50, XP: $3-$5.** 290 Fox Fire Rd 25541. I-64, exit 28, 0.3 mi s on US 60, then 2.7 mi w. 🚱 🖾

Wisconsin

BAGLEY — YOGI BEAR'S JELLYSTONE PARK CAMP RESORT. (608) 996-2201. **5P $22-$49, XP: $6.** 11354 Hwy X 53801. 1.3 mi n. 🚱 🖾

ELKHART LAKE — PLYMOUTH ROCK CAMPING RESORT. (920) 892-4252. **Call for rates.** N7271 Lando St 53073. 3 mi s on SR 67, 4 mi n of Plymouth. (PO Box 445 53020). 🚱 🖾

FORT ATKINSON — JELLYSTONE PARK OF FORT ATKIN- SON. (920) 568-4100. **4P $28-$40, XP: $5-$9.** N 551 Wishing Well Dr 53538. 5 mi s on SR 26 from jct US 12, 0.8 mi w on Koshkonong Lake Rd, then just s. 🚱 🖾

FREMONT — YOGI BEAR'S JELLYSTONE PARK CAMP RESORT. (920) 446-3420. **Call for rates.** E 6506 Hwy 110 54940. On SR 110 S, 1.5 mi w. (PO Box 497). 🚱 🖾

WISCONSIN DELLS — CHRISTMAS MOUNTAIN CAMP- GROUND. (608) 253-1000. **Call for rates. (no credit cards).** 944 S Christmas Mountain Rd 53913. I-90/94, exit 87 (SR 13), 0.4 mi ne to CR H, 4 mi sw, then just s. 🚱 🖾

WISCONSIN DELLS — YOGI BEAR'S JELLYSTONE PARK CAMP-RESORT. 🆎 (608) 254-2568. **4P $19-$109, XP: $5-$10.** S 1915 Ishnala Rd 53965. I-90/94, exit 89 eastbound; exit 92 (US 12) westbound, follow signs. (PO Box 510). 🚱 🖾

Canada

Alberta

EDMONTON — GLOWING EMBERS TRAVEL CENTRE & RV PARK. 🆎 (780) 962-8100. **4P $38-$45.** 26309 Hwy 16A T7X 5A6. Hwy 60 S, exit 16A, 1.1 mi (1.8 km) w, follow signs; 1.9 mi (3 km) w of city limits. 🖾 🅜

HINTON — HINTON/JASPER KOA. 🆎 (780) 865-5062. **$27- $42, XP: $3-$5.** 50409B Hwy 16 T7V 1X3. On Hwy 16, 2.5 mi (4 km) w. (4720 Vegas Rd NW, CALGARY T3A 1W3). 🖾 🅜

PINE LAKE — LEISURE CAMPGROUNDS. (403) 886-4705. **Call for rates.** On Hwy 42, 14.7 mi (24.6 km) e of Hwy 2. (PO Box 68 T0M 1S0). 🖾 🅜

SUNDRE — TALL TIMBER LEISURE PARK. (403) 638-3555. **Call for rates.** 0.6 mi (1 km) e of Centre St on Main Ave E (Hwy 27 E). (PO Box 210 T0M 1X0). 🏕️ 🛶 ⊠

British Columbia

BURNABY — BURNABY CARIBOO R.V. PARK. 🆎 (604) 420-1722. **2P $54-$57, XP: $3-$5.** 8765 Cariboo Pl V3N 4T2. Trans-Canada Hwy 1, exit 37 (Gaglardi Way), follow signs. 🛶 ⊠

CAMPBELL RIVER — RIPPLE ROCK RV PARK. (250) 287-7108. **Call for rates.** 15011 Browns Bay Rd V9H 1N9. Jct Hwy 19A, 28 and 19, 12 mi (19 km) n on Hwy 19, then 2.8 mi (4.5 km) e. ⊠ 💧

FAIRMONT HOT SPRINGS — FAIRMONT HOT SPRINGS RV PARK. (250) 345-6033. **$20-$55.** 5225 Fairmont Resort Rd V0B 1L1. 1 mi (1.6 km) e off Hwy 93 and 95; adjacent to Fairmont Hot Springs Resort. 🏕️ ⊠

MALAHAT — VICTORIA WEST KOA. (250) 478-3332. **$34-$39, XP: $4-$6.** 230 Trans-Canada Hwy V0R 2L0. On Trans-Canada Hwy 1 (Malahat Dr), 15.9 mi (25.6 km) n of Victoria. (PO Box 103). 🛶 ⊠ 💧

OLIVER — DESERT GEM RV AND RESORT. 🆎 (250) 498-5544. **2P $27-$40, XP: $5.** 34037 Hwy 97 V0H 1T0. Just s of 340th Ave. (PO Box 1920). 🏕️ 💧

SURREY — PEACE ARCH RV PARK. (604) 594-7009. **$40-$46, XP: $2.** 14601 40th Ave V3S 0L2. Hwy 99, exit 10, follow signs. 🛶

WHISTLER — RIVERSIDE RV RESORT AND CAMPGROUND. (604) 905-5533. **2P $40-$57, XP: $5.** 8018 Mons Rd V0N 1B8. Hwy 99, from Upper Village, 0.9 mi (1.5 km) n, exit Blackcomb Way, follow signs. ⊠ 💧

New Brunswick

WOODSTOCK — YOGI BEAR'S JELLYSTONE PARK AT KOZY ACRES. (506) 328-6287. **$36-$41, XP: $8.** 174 Hemlock St E7M 6B5. Trans-Canada Hwy 2, exit 191 (Beardsley Rd). (PO Box 9004). 🛶 ⊠

Ontario

BRADFORD — YOGI BEAR'S JELLYSTONE PARK & CAMP-RESORT. 🆎 (905) 775-1377. **2P $40-$50, XP: $6-$8.** 3666 Simcoe Rd 88 L3Z 2A4. Hwy 400, exit 64B; jct Hwy 400 and Simcoe Rd 88. (PO Box 290, BOND HEAD L0G 1B0). 🆂 🛶 ⊠

FOREST — OUR PONDEROSA RV RESORT & GOLF RESORT. (519) 786-2031. **Call for rates.** 9338 W Ipperwash Rd N0N 1J0. Jct CR 7, 1.9 mi (3 km) n. (RR 2). 🛶 ⊠

KINCARDINE — FISHERMAN'S COVE TENT & TRAILER PARK LTD. (519) 395-2757. **2P $44-$54, XP: $3.** 13 Southline Ave N2Z 2X5. Jct Hwy 21 and 9, 10.6 mi (17.7 km) e to Kinloss, then 1.9 mi (3 km) s, follow signs. (RR 4). 🛶 ⊠

KITCHENER — BINGEMANS. (519) 744-1002. **$35-$55.** 425 Bingemans Centre Dr N2B 3X7. 3.5 mi (5.6 km) on Hwy 7; 1 mi (1.6 km) e of jct Hwy 7 and Conestoga Pkwy (Hwy 86). 🛶 ⊠

NIAGARA FALLS — CAMPARK RESORTS. 🆎 (905) 358-3873. **2P $38-$58, XP: $3-$5.** 9387 Lundy's Ln L2E 6S4. 3.9 mi (6.3 km) w of Falls on Hwy 20. 🛶 ⊠

NIAGARA FALLS — NIAGARA FALLS KOA KAMPGROUND. (905) 356-2267. **2P $50-$85, XP: $7-$12.** 8625 Lundy's Ln L2H 1H5. 3.5 mi (5.6 km) w on Hwy 20. 🛶 ⊠

NIAGARA FALLS — YOGI BEAR'S JELLYSTONE PARK CAMP-RESORT. 🆎 (905) 354-1432. **2P $36-$42, XP: $4-$6.** 8676 Oakwood Dr L2E 6S5. QEW, exit 27 (McLeod Rd), 1.5 mi (2.4 km) se. 🛶 ⊠

SAUBLE BEACH — CARSON'S CAMP LTD. (519) 422-1143. **2P $27-$43, XP: $3-$12. (no credit cards).** 110 Southampton Pkwy N0H 2G0. 0.6 mi (1 km) s on CR 13. (Rt 1). 🛶 ⊠

SAUBLE BEACH — WOODLAND PARK. (519) 422-1161. **2P $32-$50, XP: $2-$25.** 47 Sauble Falls, RR 1 Pkwy N0H 2G0. 0.6 mi (1 km) n on CR 13. 🛶 ⊠

Quebec

FRELIGHSBURG — LE CAMPING DES CHUTES HUNTER. (450) 298-5005. **Call for rates.** 18 chemin des Chutes J0J 1C0. Jct Rt 237, just w on chemin du Moulin a Scie. 🛶 ⊠

LEVIS — KOA-QUEBEC CITY. 🆎 (418) 831-1813. **2P $20-$65, XP: $3-$5.** 684 chemin Olivier G7A 2N6. Hwy 20, exit 311, 0.9 mi (1.5 km) w, northside service road; in St-Nicolas sector. 🛶 ⊠

ST-MATHIEU-DE-BELOEIL — CAMPING ALOUETTE. 🆎 (450) 464-1661. **2P $35-$43, XP: $3.** 3449 de l'Industrie J3G 4S5. Hwy 20, exit 105, follow signs. 🛶 ⊠

STE-SABINE — CAMPING CARAVELLE. (450) 293-7637. **Call for rates. (no credit cards).** 180 Rang de la Gare J0J 2B0. Jct Rt 104, 2.9 mi (4.7 km) s on Rt 235, then 0.5 mi (0.8 km) w; 3.6 mi (6 km) s of Farnham. 🛶 ⊠